2025 DIR National Minority and Women-Owned Business Directory
Fifty-Sixth Edition

HISTORY

Diversity Information Resources was founded in Minneapolis in 1968 by H. Peter Meyerhoff, a Honeywell aeronautics engineer, who sought to advance race relations by improving economic conditions for Blacks after the assassination of Dr. Martin Luther King, Jr. Meyerhoff and his wife were European Jews who managed to escape Hitler at the outset of World War II. Themselves victims of discrimination, they were motivated by Dr. King's death to launch the "Buy Black" directory, a 10-page directory of black-owned businesses.

In 2001 DIR partnered with an IT firm and developed an online Supplier Diversity Database Management Portal. The dynamic portal allows corporations online access to certified minority and women-owned businesses, veteran, service-disabled veteran, LGBTQ, Disabled and HUBZone businesses, supplier registration, certification validation, and data enrichment. Please contact Diversity Information Resources at (612) 781-6819 or www.diversityinforesources.com for more information. A Board of Directors, representative of major U.S. corporations set policy and direction for Diversity Information Resources.

MISSION

To develop, maintain, and provide information resources that enhance supplier diversity initiatives and support the development and economic growth of diverse businesses.

INCLUSION CRITERIA AND LISTING PROCESS

In identifying minority-owned businesses, fifty-one percent of the business must be owned, operated and controlled by minority group members who are U.S. citizens, capable of national and/or regional sales and physically located in the United States or its trust territories. In identifying woman-owned businesses, at least fifty-one percent or more is owned by a woman (or women), who is a U.S. citizen, and who controls the firm by exercising the power to make policy decisions and operates the business by being actively involved in day-to-day management.

CERTIFICATION

Information on certification(s). The following certifications are:
- State   State Agencies
- City   City Agencies
- WBENC   Women's Business Enterprise National Council
- NWBOC   National Women Business Owners Corporation
- NMSDC   National Minority Supplier Development Council
- CPUC   California Public Utilities Commission (M/WBE Clearinghouse)
- SDB   Small Business Administration's Self-Certified Small Disadvantaged Business
- 8(a)   SBA's 8(a) Business Development Program

ETHNICITY CLASSIFICATION

The following code indicates the ethnicity type:
- AA   African American
- Hisp   Hispanic American
- Nat Ame   Native American
- As-Pac   Asian Pacific American
- As-Ind   Asian Indian American

USING THE DIRECTORY

Directory Format:

- The Table of Classifications on the next page gives the section numbers for each category and the range of numbers in that category. The Table of NAIC codes list the two-digit NAIC code for each category.
- Firms are listed by state, in alphabetical order, in each category.
- An alphabetical listing of companies (page ii-1) appears at the back of the directory.
- See codes to identify certification and ownership type on the first printed page: "2025 DIR National Minority and Women-Owned Business Directory Fifty-Sixth Edition."

An Example:

If you are looking for a supplier to print a company brochure, go to the "Printing and Engraving" section, you will find suppliers listed alphabetically, according to the state in which they reside. A typical entry might appear as follows:

7600   ABC Printing Company
1234 XYZ Avenue NE
New York, NY 10001
Contact: R. Smith, Pres.
Tel: (212) 555-1234
Email: Rsmith@www.net
Web Site: www.print.com
4-5 color offset presses. In-house 4-color, bindery, die cutting, mounting & finishing. (AA, est. 1965, empl 45, sales $4,000,000, cert: State, NMSDC, SDB)

LIABILITY DISCLAIMER

Although the information listed herein has been compiled with the utmost care and is believed by the publisher to be reliable, its accuracy or completeness cannot be guaranteed. The publishers and sponsors assume no responsibility for transactions resulting from the use of information herein and do not guarantee the quality or reliability of products or services listed. The content of the advertising copy contained in this Directory is the sole responsibility of those firms which submitted it. Diversity Information Resources assumes no responsibility for its accuracy.

For further information on any of the above resources, please contact DIR at (612) 781-6819 or visit www.diversityinforesources.com

TABLE OF CLASSIFICATIONS

Sec.	Category	INDEX#
1	ADVERTISING	1000-1299
2	ADVERTISING SPECIALTIES	1300-1602
3	ALARM SYSTEMS	1603-1664
4	APPAREL	1665-1727
5	ARCHITECTS	1728-1824
6	AUTOMOBILES	1825-1846
7	AUTOMOTIVE PARTS & ACCESSORIES	1847-1889
8	CHEMICALS	1890-2075
9	CLEANING PRODUCTS & SUPPLIES	2076-2273
10	CONSTRUCTION: General Contractors	2274-2574
11	COSMETICS	2575-2598
12	DETECTIVE & SECURITY AGENCIES	2599-2704
13	EDUCATIONAL MATERIALS	2705-2725
14	ELECTRONIC ASSEMBLY	2726-2783
15	ELECTRONICS & ELECTRICAL Dist.	2784-2922
16	ELECTRONICS & ELECTRICAL MFG.	2923-3042
17	ENGINEERING SERVICES	3043-3340
18	ENVIRONMENTAL SERVICES	3341-3548
19	FOOD PRODUCTS & SERVICES	3549-3735
20	FURNISHINGS	3736-3851
21	GIFTWARES, ARTS & CRAFTS	3852-3875
22	HARDWARE & TOOLS DIST.	3876-3945
23	HARDWARE & TOOLS MFG.	3946-3986
24	HYDRAULIC & COMPRESSED AIR EQUIPMENT	3987-4037
25	INDUSTRIAL EQUIPMENT & SUPPLIES	4038-4202
26	INDUSTRIAL MACHINES	4203-4236
27	INFORMATION TECHNOLOGY: Services	4237-5827
28	INFORMATION TECHNOLOGY: Supplies	5828-5951
29	INFORMATION TECHNOLOGY: Systems/Machines	5952-5985
30	INSURANCE COMPANIES	5986-6018
31	LABORATORY/SCIENTIFIC SUPPLIES & SERVICES	6019-6069
32	LEGAL SERVICES	6070-6254
33	MATERIAL HANDLING EQUIPMENT	6255-6301
34	MEASURING INSTRUMENTS	6302-6330
35	MEDICAL SUPPLIES & SERVICES	6331-6544
36	METAL CASTING	6545-6553
37	METAL COATING	6554-6574
38	METAL FABRICATION	6575-6711
39	METAL STAMPING	6712-6761
40	METAL, GENERAL MACHINING	6762-6928
41	METAL, RAW STOCK	6929-6957
42	METAL, WIRE PRODUCTS	6958-6971
43	OFFICE SUPPLIES	6972-7086
44	PACKAGING & PACKING SERVICES & SUPPLIES	7087-7299
45	PHOTOGRAPHY, MOTION & STILL	7300-7317
46	PLASTIC PRODUCTS	7318-7450
47	PRINTING & ENGRAVING	7451-7713
48	PROFESSIONAL SERVICES: Financial	7714-7872
49	PROFESSIONAL SERVICES: Human Resources	7873-7978
50	PROFESSIONAL SERVICES: Management Consulting	7979-8317
51	PROFESSIONAL SERVICES: Public Relations/Marketing	8318-8869
52	PROFESSIONAL SERVICES: Staffing Services	8870-9542
53	PROFESSIONAL SERVICES: Technical	9543-9562
54	RECORDING & VIDEO PRODUCTION	9563-9633
55	TELECOMMUNICATIONS	9634-9796
56	TEXTILES	9797-9819
57	TRANSPORTATION	9820-10196
58	TRAVEL ARRANGEMENTS	10197-10226
59	WOOD PRODUCTS	10227-10253

TABLE OF NAICS

Sec.	Category	NAICS
1	ADVERTISING	54
2	ADVERTISING SPECIALTIES	42
3	ALARM SYSTEMS	33
4	APPAREL	42
5	ARCHITECTS	54
6	AUTOMOBILES	44
7	AUTOMOTIVE PARTS & ACCESSORIES	42
8	CHEMICALS	32
9	CLEANING PRODUCTS & SUPPLIES	32
10	CONSTRUCTION: General Contractors	23
11	COSMETICS	32
12	DETECTIVE & SECURITY AGENCIES	54
13	EDUCATIONAL MATERIALS	42
14	ELECTRONIC ASSEMBLY	33
15	ELECTRONICS & ELECTRICAL Dist.	42
16	ELECTRONICS & ELECTRICAL MFG.	33
17	ENGINEERING SERVICES	54
18	ENVIRONMENTAL SERVICES	54
19	FOOD PRODUCTS & SERVICES	31
20	FURNISHINGS	42
21	GIFTWARES, ARTS & CRAFTS	42
22	HARDWARE & TOOLS DIST.	42
23	HARDWARE & TOOLS MFG.	33
24	HYDRAULIC & COMPRESSED AIR EQUIPMENT	33
25	INDUSTRIAL EQUIPMENT & SUPPLIES	42
26	INDUSTRIAL MACHINES	42
27	INFORMATION TECHNOLOGY: Services	54
28	INFORMATION TECHNOLOGY: Supplies	42
29	INFORMATION TECHNOLOGY: Systems/Machines	33
30	INSURANCE COMPANIES	52
31	LABORATORY/SCIENTIFIC SUPPLIES & SERVICES	33
32	LEGAL SERVICES	54
33	MATERIAL HANDLING EQUIPMENT	42
34	MEASURING INSTRUMENTS	42
35	MEDICAL SUPPLIES & SERVICES	32
36	METAL CASTING	33
37	METAL COATING	33
38	METAL FABRICATION	33
39	METAL STAMPING	33
40	METAL, GENERAL MACHINING	33
41	METAL, RAW STOCK	33
42	METAL, WIRE PRODUCTS	33
43	OFFICE SUPPLIES	42
44	PACKAGING & PACKING SERVICES & SUPPLIES	32
45	PHOTOGRAPHY, MOTION & STILL	54
46	PLASTIC PRODUCTS	42
47	PRINTING & ENGRAVING	32
48	PROFESSIONAL SERVICES: Financial	54
49	PROFESSIONAL SERVICES: Human Resources	54
50	PROFESSIONAL SERVICES: Management Consulting	54
51	PROFESSIONAL SERVICES: Public Relations/Marketing	54
52	PROFESSIONAL SERVICES: Staffing Services	54
53	PROFESSIONAL SERVICES: Technical	54
54	RECORDING & VIDEO PRODUCTION	51
55	TELECOMMUNICATIONS	51
56	TEXTILES	31
57	TRANSPORTATION	48
58	TRAVEL ARRANGEMENTS	48
59	WOOD PRODUCTS	32

> **ADVERTISING**
> Advertising agencies which provide clients with full service from conception to completion. Other services listed in this category include graphic arts, direct mail & list maintenance, sign manufacturing and engraving. (See also PROFESSIONAL SERVICES: Public Relations/Marketing). NAICS Code 54

Alabama

1000 GASmith Enterprises, Inc.
      464 Cahaba Park Cir
      Birmingham, AL 35242
      Contact: George A. Smith President
      Tel: (205) 981-5391
      Email: info@signarama-bham.com
      Website: www.signarama-bham.com
Full service sign center. (AA, estab 2010, empl 6, sales $3,000,000, cert: State, NMSDC)

Arizona

1001 Creative Merchandise Displays Inc.
      1839 W 1st Ave
      Mesa, AZ 85202
      Contact: Debra Mendoza COO
      Tel: (480) 668-7225
      Email: deb@cmdracks.com
      Website: www.cmdracks.com
Mfr point-of-purchase display racks, point-of-purchase display design, engineering, manufacturing, finishing, assembly & packaging. (Woman, estab 2008, empl 12, sales $686,921, cert: City, WBENC, SDB)

1002 Double T. Signs Inc.
      1835 S Alvernon Ste 214
      Tucson, AZ 85711
      Contact: David Torres President
      Tel: (520) 750-0189
      Email: dave@doubletsigns.com
      Website: www.doubletsigns.com
Mfr & install signs. (Hisp, estab 1993, empl 6, sales $601,161, cert: State, City)

1003 Language Concepts Consulting LLC
      8502 E Princess Dr, Ste 230
      Scottsdale, AZ 85255
      Contact: Katherine Paredes Managing Dir
      Tel: (480) 626-2926
      Email: kathy.paredes@languageconceptsllc.com
      Website: www.languageconceptsllc.com
Translation services, Document Translation, Linguistic Validation. (Minority, Woman, estab 2009, empl 1, sales $112,000, cert: NMSDC)

California

1004 1-Stop Translation
      3700 Wilshire Blvd, Ste 630
      Los Angeles, CA 90010
      Contact: Diana Chi Mktg Mgr
      Tel: (213) 480-0011
      Email: diana@1stoptr.com
      Website: www.1stoptr.com
Translation and interpretation services with a specialty in Asian languages, including typesetting, desktop publishing, web localization, software testing, budding & subtitling services. (As-Pac, estab 2001, empl 8, sales , cert: CPUC)

1005 Aahs Entertainment, Inc.
      10707 Camarillo St, Ste 312
      Toluca Lake, CA 91602
      Contact: Gwenn Smith President
      Tel: (818) 279-2416
      Email: gwenn@aahsentertainment.com
      Website: www.aahsentertainment.com
Video Production Services, Media Production, Media Services, Advertising, Marketing, Content Creation, Branded Content, Brand Marketing, DVD Extras, DVD Special Features, Marketing, Advertising, EPKs. (Woman/AA, estab 2011, empl 1, sales , cert: WBENC)

1006 AL & CM Broadcasting Network, Inc.
      517 S Main St
      Salinas, CA 93901
      Contact: Tim Luce Managing Dir
      Tel: (702) 218-6670
      Email: tim@alcmbroadcasting.com
      Website: www.alexelgeniolucas.com
Spanish-language radio networks. (Hisp, estab 2009, empl 14, sales $1,900,000, cert: NMSDC)

1007 American Language Services
      1849 Sawtelle BLVD. Ste 600
      Los Angeles, CA 90025
      Contact: Jay Herzog Sr Acct Rep
      Tel: (310) 829-0741
      Email: jay@alsglobal.net
      Website: www.alsglobal.net
Translations, transcriptions & verbal interpreting. (Woman, estab , empl , sales $3,000,000, cert: WBENC)

1008 Artisan Creative Inc.
      1830 Stoner Ave Ste 6
      Los Angeles, CA 90025
      Contact: Katty Douraghy President
      Tel: (310) 312-2062
      Email: kattyd@artisancreative.com
      Website: www.artisancreative.com
Design & development solutions: marketing, advertising, communications & production teams in the digital, broadcast, mobile & print space. (Woman, estab 1996, empl 15, sales $3,000,000, cert: WBENC)

1009 Canela Media
      2715 Palomino Circle
      La Jolla, CA 92037
      Contact: Annette Salinas Dir
      Tel: (858) 699-6640
      Email: annette@canelamedia.com
      Website: www.canelamedia.com
Create multimedia programs for brand and/or co-opt efforts. (Hisp, estab 2019, empl 12, sales $1,000,000, cert: NMSDC)

1010 Carmazzi of Florida, Inc.
      8926 Beckington Dr
      Elk Grove, CA 95624
      Contact: Angela Carmazzi President
      Tel: (888) 452-6543
      Email: sales@carmazzi.com
      Website: www.carmazzi.com/
Translations, interpretations & transcriptions. (Minority, Woman, estab 1998, empl 8, sales $1,900,000, cert: CPUC)

1011 Coast Sign Inc.
1500 W Embassy St.
Anaheim, CA 92802
Contact: Charlie President
Tel: (714) 999-1900
Email: charlie.alemi@coastsign.com
Website: www.coastsign.com
Mfr electrical signage, ATM surrounds & kiosks, project management, design, engineering, lighting, installation, service & maintenance. (Woman, estab 1964, empl 220, sales $80,535,032, cert: WBENC)

1012 Competitive Edge Media Management
3261 S Higuera St Ste 110
San Luis Obispo, CA 93401
Contact: Suzy da Silva President
Tel: (805) 788-0966
Email: suzy@cemm.com
Website: www.cemm.com
Media buying, brand promotion plans, product launch, direct-to-consumer sales strategy, hybrid campaigns. (Woman, estab 2007, empl 8, sales $6,874,176, cert: WBENC)

1013 CR&A Custom, Inc.
312 W Pico Blvd
Los Angeles, CA 90015
Contact: Carmen Rad Acct Exec
Tel: (213) 749-4440
Email: carmen@cracustom.com
Website: www.cracustom.com
Large format digital printing, embroidery, promotional products, custom designs, carwraps, banners, billboards, tents, POP displays. (Minority, Woman, estab 1993, empl 31, sales $5,900,000, cert: NMSDC, CPUC, 8(a))

1014 Direct Results Radio, Inc.
815 Hamton Dr, Ste 2
Venice, CA 90291
Contact: Sheri White Business Dev Dir
Tel: (310) 441-9100
Email: sheriwhite@directresults.com
Website: www.directresults.com
Advertising agency, audio & radio. (Woman, estab 2007, empl 20, sales , cert: NWBOC)

1015 Everfield Consulting, LLC
2075 W 235th Pl
Torrance, CA 90501
Contact: Delbara Dorsey Partner
Tel: (310) 251-7165
Email: deldorsey@everfieldconsulting.com
Website: www.everfieldconsulting.com
Marketing Consulting Services, Administrative & Management, Display Advertising, Advertising, Public Relations, Media Buying, Direct Mail Advertising, Advertising Material Distribution Services. (Woman/AA, As- Pac, estab 2011, empl 2, sales , cert: State, City, CPUC)

1016 Exponential Interactive, Inc.
5858 Horton St, Ste 300
Emeryville, CA 94608
Contact: Catherine Avenido Sr Mgr, Intl Ops
Tel: (510) 250-5500
Email: mbe@exponential.com
Website: www.exponential.com/
Advertising intelligence & digital media solutions. (As-Ind, estab 2000, empl 690, sales $219,740,000, cert: NMSDC, CPUC)

1017 Fraser/White, Inc.
1631 Pontius Ave
Los Angeles, CA 90025
Contact: Renee Fraser CEO
Tel: (310) 319-3737
Email: rfraser@frasercommunications.com
Website: www.frasercommunications.com
Advertising, marketing, market research, display advertising, media planning, media buying, qualitative research, quantitative research, strategic planning, outdoor advertising. (Woman, estab 1998, empl 25, sales $40,000,000, cert: WBENC)

1018 Frisson, Inc.
12 Geary St, Ste 607
San Francisco, CA 94108
Contact: Deboran N Loeb President
Tel: (415) 922-1482
Email: purchasing@brainchildcreative.com
Website: www.brainchildcreative.com
Advertising ; marketing-branding vonsulting services; commercial production services. (Woman, estab 2001, empl 7, sales $16,700,000, cert: CPUC, WBENC)

1019 Global Language Solutions
19800 MacArthur Blvd Ste 750
Irvine, CA 92612
Contact: Inna Kassatkina President
Tel: (949) 798-1400
Email: info@globallanguages.com
Website: www.globallanguages.com
Translation svcs: document & web site translations, conference interpretation, multimedia production & graphic design services. (Woman, estab 1994, empl 50, sales $16,300,000,000, cert: WBENC)

1020 I. Studio, Inc.
51 E Colorado Blvd
Pasadena, CA 91105
Contact: Gabriel Avalos Principal
Tel: (626) 683-3101
Email: g.avalos@interiorstudioinc.com
Website: www.interiorstudioinc.com
Interior Planning & Design Firm: programming, schematic design, design development, contract documents, construction administration. (Hisp, estab 2006, empl 3, sales , cert: State, NMSDC)

1021 IW Group, Inc.
6300 Wilshire Blvd. Ste 2150
Los Angeles, CA 90048
Contact: Nita Song President
Tel: (310) 289-5500
Email: nita.song@iwgroupinc.com
Website: www.iwgroupinc.com/
Advertising & PR, creative development, research, media planning, media buying, production, events, cultural training. (As-Pac, estab 1990, empl 50, sales $10,506,000, cert: NMSDC, CPUC)

1022 Kaplan Interpreting Services
2432 S Halm Ave
Los Angeles, CA 90034
Contact: Alexandra Kaplan
Tel: (310) 498-3089
Email: info@kaplaninterpreting.com
Website: www.kaplaninterpreting.com
Interpreting Services. (Hisp, estab 2017, empl 8, sales $1,057,000, cert: NMSDC)

1023 Kramer Translation
      893 Massasso St
      Merced, CA 95341
      Contact: Keith Ensminger Principal
      Tel: (209) 385-0425
      Email: keith@kramertranslations.com
      Website: www.kramertranslations.com
Translation svcs: personal, business & government documents. (Minority, Woman, estab 1995, empl 3, sales $701,672, cert: State, NMSDC, CPUC)

1024 Limelight Media LLC, Inc.
      15619 Gaymont Dr
      La Mirada, CA 90638
      Contact: Christina Roach President
      Tel: (818) 501-4043
      Email: christina@limelightmedia.net
      Website: www.limelightmedia.net
Advertising and PR campaigns. (Woman, estab 2004, empl 1, sales $2,000,000, cert: WBENC)

1025 Local Concept
      1510 Front St, Ste 200
      San Diego, CA 92101
      Contact: Localization Solutions Specialist
      Tel: (619) 295-2682
      Email: info@localconcept.com
      Website: www.localconcept.com
Localization, translation, foreign language typesetting & multimedia for all languages. (Hisp, estab 1985, empl 25, sales $1,435,306, cert: NMSDC)

1026 Motivate, Inc.
      4141 Jutland Dr Ste 300
      San Diego, CA 92117
      Contact: SVP Finance
      Tel: (866) 664-4432
      Email: hello@motivateroi.com
      Website: www.MotivateROI.com
Media representation, consumer event marketing services. (Woman, estab 1977, empl 25, sales $40,690,000, cert: WBENC)

1027 Muse Communications, Inc.
      5358 Melrose Ave West Bldg, Ground Fl
      Hollywood, CA 90038
      Contact: Norma Keffer
      Tel: (323) 960-4080
      Email: norma@museusa.com
      Website: www.musecordero.com
Advertising, marketing, promotions & public relations programs. (AA, estab 1985, empl 35, sales $5,975,000, cert: CPUC)

1028 Nonpareil Ventures LLC
      710 C St, Ste 206
      San Rafael, CA 94901
      Contact: Nicolas Campos Mgr
      Tel: (415) 404-7409
      Email: drcampos2002@yahoo.com
      Website: www.instalogistics.biz
Advertising services, sign manufacturing, repair & maintenance. (As-Ind, estab 2011, empl 5, sales $250,000, cert: State)

1029 Paragon Language Services, Inc.
      5055 Wilshire Blvd Ste 835
      Los Angeles, CA 90036
      Contact: Marina Mintz President
      Tel: (323) 966-4655
      Email: marina@paragonls.com
      Website: www.paragonls.com
Foreign language translation, adaptation, interpreting, typesetting/desktop publishing, internationalization, globalization, localization, cultural and linguistic consulting, dialog/dialect coaching, captioning, subtitling, narrations. (Woman, estab 1991, empl 10, sales $2,600,000, cert: City, CPUC, WBENC)

1030 Quigley-Simpson & Heppelwhite, Inc.
      11601 Wilshire Blvd 7th Fl
      Los Angeles, CA 90025
      Contact: Gerald Bagg Co-Chairman
      Tel: (310) 996-5820
      Email: geraldb@quigleysimpson.com
      Website: www.quigleysimpson.com
Direct response advertising agency. (Woman, estab 2002, empl 180, sales , cert: WBENC)

1031 RBG Marketing, Inc. dba Crescendo
      5000 Executive Pkwy Ste 350
      San Ramon, CA 94583
      Contact: A.K. Ahuja Managing Dir
      Tel: (925) 939-1800
      Email: aka@crescendoagency.com
      Website: www.crescendoagency.com
Marketing & advertising, creative, media planning & media buying in-house. (As-Ind, estab 2003, empl 30, sales $9,000,000, cert: State, NMSDC, CPUC)

1032 RP & Associates, Inc.
      2205 Pacific Coast Hwy
      Hermosa Beach, CA 90254
      Contact: Lisa Pola CEO
      Tel: (310) 372-9709
      Email: lpola@mac.com
      Website: www.rpandassociates.com
Marketing solutions, branded products & programs, custom packaging, premiums & promotional items. (Minority, Woman, estab 1988, empl 34, sales $2,306,595,900, cert: NMSDC)

1033 Sensis Inc.
      1651 South Central Ave, Ste A
      Glendale, CA 91204
      Contact: Dreux Dougall
      Tel: (213) 341-0171
      Email: ddougall@sensisagency.com
      Website: www.sensisagency.com
Advertising, digital marketing & communications services, online media & marketing, web design & development, online creative strategy, analytics & planning. (Hisp, estab 1998, empl 90, sales $24,000,000, cert: NMSDC)

1034 Simply Displays
      12200 Los Nietos Rd
      Santa Fe Springs, CA 90670
      Contact: Mila Thompson President
      Tel: (888) 767-0676
      Email: mthompson@simplydisplays.com
      Website: www.simplydisplays.com
Mfr Point of Purchase Displays & Store Fixtures, Sign Holders, Hospitality & Retail Signage (Woman, estab 2002, empl 16, sales $36,000,000, cert: WBENC)

ADVERTISING

1035 Think Ink
927 Mariner St
Brea, CA 92821
Contact: Mary Sanchez Dir of Sales
Tel: (714) 672-0017
Email: info@thinkinkinfo.com
Website: www.thinkinkinfo.com
Creative marketing, graphic design, print & promotions. (Hisp, estab 2002, empl 5, sales $1,105,519, cert: NMSDC, CPUC)

1036 Tylie Jones & Associates, Inc.
58 E Santa Anita Ave
Burbank, CA 91502
Contact: Sheri Lawrence President
Tel: (818) 955-7600
Email: slawrence@tylie.com
Website: www.tylie.com
Broadcast advertising services: spot duplication & digital distribution; post production, closed captioning, tagging, encoding; production element vaulting/storage. (Woman, estab 1971, empl 35, sales , cert: WBENC)

1037 Unique Image, Inc.
19365 Business Center Dr. Bldg. 1
Northridge, CA 91324
Contact: Wafa Kanan President
Tel: (818) 727-7785
Email: kelly@uniqueimageinc.com
Website: www.uniqueimageinc.com
Printing & marketing svcs: strategic campaigns, print media, design & direct mail. (Woman, estab 1992, empl 10, sales $1,200,000, cert: CPUC, WBENC)

1038 Weldon Works, Inc.
1650 Mabury Rd
San Jose, CA 95133
Contact: Jennifer Easom CEO
Tel: (408) 251-1161
Email: jenn@weldonworks.com
Website: www.weldonworks.com
Plastic Fabrication & Signage, Interior & Exterior Signs, ADA Signage, Lobby Signs, Window Graphics & Lettering, Menu Boards, Isle Signage, Banner, Stencils, Reflective Road Work/ Parking Signs, Full Color Digital Printing. (Woman, estab 1982, empl 3, sales $100,000, cert: State)

1039 Zeesman Communications, Inc.
6255 Sunset Blvd. Ste 1040
Los Angeles, CA 90028
Contact: Bonnie Nijst President
Tel: (323) 658-8000
Email: bonnie@zeesman.com
Website: www.zeesman.com
Marketing, advertising & design: branding programs, logos, corporate identity, collateral, direct mail, print advertising & web design. (Minority, Woman, estab 1990, empl 4, sales $570,000, cert: NMSDC, CPUC, WBENC)

Connecticut

1040 Andrew Associates, Inc.
6 Pearson Way
Enfield, CT 06082
Contact: Dir Marketing & Business Dev
Tel: (860) 918-5041
Email:
Website: www.andrewdm.com
Data management, digital printing, bulk mailing services, labeling, inserting, stamping, sorting & literature fulfillment services. (Woman, estab 1985, empl 60, sales $7,600,000, cert: WBENC)

1041 Crew Design Inc.
PO Box 400
Kent, CT 06757
Contact: Gil Aviles CEO
Tel: (860) 927-5001
Email: gil@crewdesign.com
Website: www.crewdesign.com
Custom in store display & merchandising equipment: signage, merchandising fixtures, point of purchase displays. (Hisp, estab 1998, empl 25, sales $11,000,000, cert: NMSDC)

1042 Desai Communication
34 Oakwood Ave Ste 102
Norwalk, CT 06850
Contact: Amanda Desai Acct Exec
Tel: (203) 324-6000
Email: amanda@desaicomm.com
Website: www.desaicomm.com
Web design & hosting, promotions, premiums, fulfillment, graphic design, computer graphics, digital retouching, power point pesentations, pint avertising & promotional material, trade show displays, B/W & color printing. (Minority, Woman, estab 1979, empl 11, sales $1,500,000, cert: State, NMSDC)

1043 Point View Displays, LLC
200 Morgan Ave
East Haven, CT 06512
Contact: Cynthia Sedlmeyer Owner
Tel: (203) 468-0887
Email: cindy@pointviewdisplays.com
Website: www.pointviewdisplays.com
Press conference backdrops, displays, indoor/outdoor banner stands & graphics. (Woman, estab 2001, empl 4, sales $400,000, cert: WBENC)

1044 Tanen Directed Advertising
12 South Main St
South Norwalk, CT 06854
Contact: President
Tel: (203) 855-5855
Email: ilene@tanendirected.com
Website: www.tanendirected.com
Advertising, direct marketing, integrated marketing, online marketing, direct mail, email, print ads, collateral, sales presentations, human resources communications, benefits communications materials, employee communications. (Woman, estab 1985, empl 10, sales $1,865,652, cert: WBENC)

District of Columbia

1045 APCO Worldwide LLC
1299 Pennsylvania ave NW
Washington, DC 20005
Contact: Jim Moorhead
Tel: (202) 778-1000
Email: jmoorhead@apcoworldwide.com
Website: www.wwwapcoworldwide.com
Global communication consulting: advertising, antitrust & competition, branding, broadcast film, video & multimedia production, business diplomacy, coalition building, corporate restructuring communication. (Woman, estab 1984, empl 638, sales $172,200,000, cert: WBENC)

1046 SRB Communications, LLC
      1020 16th St, NW Ste 400
      Washington, DC 20036
      Contact: Sheila Brooks CEO
      Tel: (202) 775-7721
      Email: sbrooks@srbcommunications.com
      Website: www.srbcommunications.com
Media & communications: video production, advertising, lay-out & design, copywriting services, media placement & webcasting. (Woman/AA, estab 1990, empl 7, sales , cert: State, City, NMSDC)

Delaware

1047 Keen Branding
      17601 Coastal Hwy., Ste. 11-416
      Nassau, DE 19969
      Contact: Alicia Stack Principal
      Tel: (302) 644-6885
      Email: astack@keenbranding.com
      Website: www.keenbranding.com
Identity creation & design: logos, packaging, look & feel programs, identity mgmt. (Woman, estab 2000, empl 14, sales , cert: WBENC)

1048 Meetings by Design, Inc.
      312 Nonantum Dr
      Newark, DE 19711
      Contact: Jan White President
      Tel: (302) 738-8318
      Email: info@MeetingsbyDesign.net
      Website: www.meetingsbydesign.net
Business meetings & special events production. (Woman, estab , empl , sales $200,000, cert: State, WBENC)

Florida

1049 Adventures in Advertising dba Resource Marketing
      2520 Illinois St
      Orlando, FL 32803
      Contact: Christyl Seymour President
      Tel: (407) 228-0881
      Email: cseymour@advinadv.com
      Website: www.resourcemarketinginc.net
Graphic design/art services, product research support, custom design, online store solution, fulfillment svcs, direct import, promotional svcs, website searchable database, promotion design & implementation. (Woman, estab 2002, empl 1, sales $3,175,125, cert: WBENC)

1050 Avanza Advertising
      5465 NW 36 St Ste 100
      Miami Springs, FL 33166
      Contact: Alejandro Perez-Eguren CEO
      Tel: (786) 565-7601
      Email: alejandro@avanzaad.com
      Website: www.avanzaad.com
Advertising, design, digital media & video. (Hisp, estab 2013, empl 6, sales $500,000, cert: NMSDC, CPUC, 8(a))

1051 Baron Sign Manufacturing
      900 W 13th St
      Riviera Beach, FL 33404
      Contact: Jerry Foland CEO
      Tel: (800) 531-9558
      Email: jerry@baronsign.com
      Website: www.baronsign.com
Interior & exterior signage, awards, plaques. (Woman, estab , empl , sales , cert: State, City)

1052 Black Dog Inc.
      4803 George Rd Ste 370
      Tampa, FL 33634
      Contact: Dorothy Johnson President
      Tel: (813) 249-6398
      Email: djohnson@nextdaysignstampa.com
      Website: www.nextdaysignstampa.com
Vinyl signs, banners, digital printing, vehicle & boat graphics & lettering. (Woman, estab 2003, empl 3, sales $429,460, cert: State)

1053 BroadBased Communications, Inc.
      1301 Riverplace Blvd, Ste 1830
      Jacksonville, FL 32207
      Contact: Jan Hirabayashi CEO
      Tel: (904) 398-7279
      Email: jan@bbased.com
      Website: www.bbased.com
Marketing plans, branding, direct mail, publication design, exhibit design, annual reports, web sites, fleet graphics, copywriting, art direction. (Woman, estab 1996, empl 7, sales $1,381,791, cert: WBENC)

1054 Catalyst Advertizing
      737 W Colonial Dr
      Orlando, FL 32804
      Contact: Edward Rees Agent
      Tel: (407) 425-5646
      Email: edrees@catalystholdingsco.com
      Website: www.catalystadvertizing.com
Advertising & Marketing: creative writing, art, graphics, market analysis, planning, buying, media relations, full design, production and coordination services. (Hisp, estab 1989, empl 8, sales $750,000, cert: 8(a))

1055 CCOM Group, Inc
      6380 NE 4th Ave
      Miami, FL 33138
      Contact: Ray De Leon Managing Dir
      Tel: (305) 447-4015
      Email: ray@ccomgroupinc.com
      Website: www.ccomgroupinc.com
Multicultural advertising agency. (Hisp, estab 2001, empl 75, sales $53,711,969, cert: NMSDC)

1056 Certified Translations LLC
      11663 Vicolo Loop
      Windermere, FL 34786
      Contact: Mara Cawthorn Managing Dir
      Tel: (407) 205-9494
      Email: certifiedtranslationsllc@gmail.com
      Website: www.certifiedtranslationsllc.com
Language Translation & Interpreting Services: Legal, Technical, Mechanical, Medical, & Business / Finance. Spanish, Portuguese, Creole, Mandarin, Cantonese, French, Italian, German, etc. (Minority, Woman, estab 2013, empl 2, sales , cert: NMSDC)

1057 Doubletake Studios, Inc.
      105 S Fielding Ave, Ste A & B
      Tampa, FL 33606
      Contact: Terri Hall President
      Tel: (813) 251-6308
      Email: Info@doubletakeFL.com
      Website: www.doubletakestudios.com
Advertising agency & creative marketing, creative coaching, branding, web site design & development & print advertising. (Woman, estab 1999, empl 7, sales $725,000, cert: WBENC)

1058 Eco Graphics Media
      7034 NW 50th St
      Miami, FL 33166
      Contact: Jose Contreras Project Mgr
      Tel: (305) 640-9600
      Email: info@ecogm.com
      Website: www.ecogm.com/index.html
Corporate Image & Concept, Product & trade Mark Campaigns, billboards, Trade shows and displays, Banners - Posters, Gran Format prints, Signs & Graphics, vehicle wraps, Trade Shows, Custom Displays, Store Fixtures. (Hisp, estab 2005, empl 11, sales $820,000, cert: NMSDC)

1059 Kreative Kontent Co.
      3019 Ravenswood Road Ste 110
      Fort Lauderdale, FL 33312
      Contact: Debbie Margolis-Horwitz Exec Producer
      Tel: (954) 312-3660
      Email: debbie@kreativekontent.com
      Website: www.kreativekontent.com
Content creation, broadcast, web based, theatrical & marketing fulfillment programs, broadcast commercials, corporate video communications, product placement, branded content, promotional products. (Woman, estab 2010, empl 4, sales $2,000,000, cert: State, WBENC)

1060 KVJINC Consulting
      7016 San Ramon Pl Ste. 202
      Tampa, FL 33617
      Contact: Kimberly Jackson Owner
      Tel: (813) 987-9083
      Email: kvjinc@yahoo.com
      Website: www.kvjincpr.com
Public, media relations, strategic, crisis communications, press conferences, kits, event planning, image consulting, sponsorship procurement & market research. (Woman/AA, estab 1999, empl 3, sales $100,000, cert: State, City)

1061 LanguageSpeak, Inc.
      5975 Sunset Dr Ste 803
      Miami, FL 33143
      Contact: Annette Taddeo CEO
      Tel: (305) 668-9797
      Email: acct@languagespeak.com
      Website: www.languagespeak.com
Language svcs: document translation, language instruction, conference interpretation, software localization, website translation, cross cultural training. (Minority, Woman, estab 1995, empl 5, sales , cert: NMSDC, WBENC)

1062 MarkMaster, Inc.
      11111 N 46th St
      Tampa, FL 33617
      Contact: Deborah Jordan Sales Rep
      Tel: (813) 988-6000
      Email: sales@markmasterinc.com
      Website: www.markmasterinc.com
Mfr rubber stamps, engraved & screened signage & badges; industrial marking equip. (Hisp, estab 1933, empl 65, sales $8,700,993, cert: NMSDC)

1063 Multi Image Group, Inc.
      1701 Clint Moore Rd
      Boca Raton, FL 33487
      Contact: Jim Ballentine President
      Tel: (917) 319-8127
      Email: ballentine@mig.cc
      Website: www.mig.cc
Meeting production & staging, video & audio production, graphic design, signage printing, web & teleconferencing services, trade show exhibits, lighting rentals. (Woman, estab 1979, empl 106, sales $28,400,000, cert: NWBOC)

1064 Retail Solution Center
      475 N Cleary Road
      West Palm Beach, FL 33413
      Contact: Deborah Leo CEO
      Tel: (561) 567-9000
      Email: debleo@rsc-ny.com
      Website: www.rsc-ny.com
Point of purchase displays, merchandising systems, mfr & design. (Woman, estab 2003, empl 49, sales $8,110,000, cert: WBENC)

1065 Sunlure, Inc.
      3700 NW 124 Ave Unit 140
      Coral Springs, FL 33065
      Contact: Craig Sage Mgr
      Tel: (754) 484-7929
      Email: craig.sage@sunlure.com
      Website: www.sunlure.com
Promotional Products, Apparel Products Custom imprinted apparel, Writing Products, Candy. (Minority, Woman, estab 2003, empl 7, sales $900,000, cert: State, NMSDC)

1066 T Wynne Art & Design Inc.
      1401 Manatee Ave W, Ste 1005
      Bradenton, FL 34205
      Contact: Tanya Wynne Williams President
      Tel: (941) 906-7124
      Email: tanya@twynne.com
      Website: www.twynne.com
Package graphic design & and point of sale (POS) design. (Woman, estab 1991, empl 8, sales $2,430,822, cert: WBENC)

1067 The Best Direct Marketing Group LLC
      250 N Orange Ave Ste 990
      Orlando, FL 32801
      Contact: Latif Qadri
      Tel: (407) 730-6569
      Email: latif@bestdirectgroup.com
      Website: www.bestdirectgroup.com
Direct mail & staffed event, print & ad creative design. (As-Ind, estab 2012, empl 4, sales $112,000, cert: NMSDC)

1068 Thomas Sign and Awning Company, Inc.
      4590 118th Ave N 33762
      Clearwater, FL 33762
      Contact: Aimee Pavlovich Marketing Mgr
      Tel: (727) 573-7757
      Email: aimee.pavlovich@thomassign.com
      Website: www.thomassign.com
Design, mfr, install & service illuminated electrical signs. LED, neon, vinyl graphics, permit acquisition, variance applications, turnkey project mgmt. (Woman, estab 1969, empl 156, sales $21,000,000, cert: WBENC)

Georgia

1069 AEE Productions
      1650 Westfork Dr, Ste 110
      Lithia Springs, GA 30122
      Contact: Yergan Jones President
      Tel: (404) 352-2201
      Email: yerganjones@aeeproductions.com
      Website: www.aeeproductions.com
Audio visual services. (AA, estab 1990, empl 6, sales $975,000, cert: NMSDC)

1070 American Systems, Inc. dba Simon Sign Systems
      2158 Sylvan Rd
      Atlanta, GA 30344
      Contact: Simon Robinson President
      Tel: (404) 766-5208
      Email: gen-info@simonsignsystems.com
      Website: www.simonsignsystems.com
Mfr signs: interior & exterior, banners, digital & screen printing, posters, corporate apparel & promotional items. (AA, estab 1989, empl 5, sales $300,670, cert: NMSDC)

1071 Basiqa, LLC
      1555 Oakbrook Dr Ste 135
      Norcross, GA 30093
      Contact: Winston Dzose VP Digital Marketing
      Tel: (678) 824-6460
      Email: winston@basiqa.com
      Website: www.basiqa.com
Direct mail, advertising, material preparation services for mailing or other direct distribution, digital printing. (AA, estab 2009, empl 16, sales $3,000,000, cert: NMSDC)

1072 CK&M Direct Mail Advertising, Inc.
      1250 Northmeadow Pkwy Ste 116
      Roswell, GA 30076
      Contact: Gary Kern General Mgr
      Tel: (770) 442-2166
      Email: gkern@ckmdirect.com
      Website: www.ckmdirectmail.com
Lettershop services, fulfillment, distribution, warehousing, list broker. (Hisp, estab 1992, empl 7, sales $1,992,000, cert: NMSDC)

1073 Cloud Track, LLC
      36111 Indigo Creek Trail NW
      Kennesaw, GA 30144
      Contact: Samir Mullick CEO
      Tel: (404) 934-7408
      Email: Samir.Mullick@cloudtrackusa.com
      Website: www.cloudtrackusa.com
Digital Branding, Lead Generation. (As-Ind, estab 2014, empl 2, sales , cert: NMSDC)

1074 Display America
      195 Andrew Dr
      Stockbridge, GA 30281
      Contact: Carlos Quinones CEO
      Tel: (770) 416-7047
      Email: carlos@displayamerica.com
      Website: www.displayamerica.com
Dist exhibit marketing products & turnkey services: image & identity, rent exhibits, high impact graphics, trade shows, conventions, expositions, hospitality & retail environments. (Hisp, estab 2003, empl 15, sales $1,400,000, cert: NMSDC)

1075 Dove Direct
      5601 Fulton Industrial Blvd SW
      Atlanta, GA 30336
      Contact: Travis L Benjamin Business Dev Exec
      Tel: (404) 629-0122
      Email: tbenjamin@dovedirect.com
      Website: www.dovedirect.com
First class barcoding, third class mail, lettershop svcs, personalization, list, data mgmt, fulfillment svcs, design analysis, etc. (Woman/AA, estab 1987, empl 59, sales $24,000,000, cert: NMSDC)

1076 Exhibits South
      1000 Satellite Blvd Ste 120
      Suwanee, GA 30024
      Contact: Nichole Holliday VP
      Tel: (678) 225-5200
      Email: nholliday@exhibitssouth.com
      Website: www.exhibitssouth.com
Dist & rent portable, modular & custom displays, graphic production & design department, tradeshow services, logistics & exhibit storage. (Woman, estab 1983, empl 35, sales $10,750,000, cert: WBENC)

1077 Jones Worley Design, Inc.
      723 Piedmont Ave
      Atlanta, GA 30308
      Contact: Cynthia Jones Parks President
      Tel: (404) 876-9272
      Email: cjonesparks@jonesworley.com
      Website: www.jonesworley.com
Graphic design svcs: print graphics & signage, design, planning & implementation. (Woman/AA, estab 1990, empl 15, sales $939,838, cert: WBENC)

1078 Mail Centers Plus LLC
      17 Executive Park Dr Ste 230
      Atlanta, GA 30329
      Contact: John Smithson Business Devel Analyst
      Tel: (404) 321-1010
      Email: jsmithson@mailcentersplus.com
      Website: www.mailcentersplus.com
Document distribution & mail center solutions. (AA, estab 2000, empl 140, sales $5,500,000, cert: NMSDC)

1079 PM Publicidad
      1776 Peachtree St
      Atlanta, GA 30309
      Contact: Philip Polk EVP General Mgr
      Tel: (404) 844-5757
      Email: info@pm3.agency
      Website: www.pm3.agency
Multicultural advertising solutions in the Hispanic market, account services, broadcast production, media planning & buying, sports marketing, market research, strategic account planning, experiential & event marketing. (Hisp, estab 2004, empl 35, sales $23,307,370, cert: NMSDC)

1080 Profitmaster Displays Inc.
      6190 Powers Ferry Rd Ste 510
      Atlanta, GA 30339
      Contact: President
      Tel: (800) 633-5454
      Email: sales@ProfitmasterDisplays.com
      Website: www.profitmasterdisplays.com
Point of purchase displays & racks: wire, sheet metal, wood, plastic & corrugated paperboard. (Woman, estab 1984, empl 18, sales $20,000,000, cert: WBENC)

1081 Shared Vision LLC
      225 Ottley Dr NE Ste 140
      Atlanta, GA 30324
      Contact: Doug Jackson Principal
      Tel: (678) 694-1965
      Email: djackson@shared-vision.net
      Website: www.shared-vision.net
Marketing & advertising, strategic & creative services. (Woman/AA, estab 2006, empl 20, sales $1,700,000, cert: NMSDC)

ADVERTISING

1082 TDEFERIAMEDIA, Inc.
      9795 Talisman Dr
      Johns Creek, GA 30022
      Contact: Antenor Tony President
      Tel: (404) 630-0639
      Email: contact@tdeferiamedia.com
      Website: www.tdeferiamedia.com
Marketing, branding consulting & creative production, ethnic market study & plans, media buying, translation & interpretation in Spanish, digital & social media expertise. (Hisp, estab 2007, empl 1, sales $140,000, cert: NMSDC)

1083 The Symmetry Group, LLC
      600 W Peachtree St Ste 510
      Atlanta, GA 30308
      Contact: Scott Robinson President
      Tel: (404) 237-2378
      Email: scott@tsgatl.com
      Website: www.tsgatl.com
Graphic design, radio/TV production, print/outdoor advertising production, event development, management & production, promotion development & execution. (AA, estab 2001, empl 6, sales $1,200,000, cert: NMSDC)

1084 Viswam Bala Enterprises
      440 Barrett Pkwy, Ste 33
      Kennesaw, GA 30144
      Contact: Giridhar Iyer President
      Tel: (770) 421-8110
      Email: giri.iyer@fastsigns.com
      Website: www.fastsigns.com/201
Marketing strategy creation, brand /product identity creation, graphic design services, production/printing & installation services, static signs, banners, posters, decals, vehicle art/wraps, cutting-edge digital signs & visual magnetic solutions. (As-Ind, estab 1994, empl 6, sales $1,047,000, cert: City, NMSDC)

1085 Yellobee Studio
      750 Hammond Dr Ste 350 Bldg 15
      Atlanta, GA 30328
      Contact: Alison Scheel Creative Dir
      Tel: (404) 249-6407
      Email: ascheel@yellobee.com
      Website: www.yellobee.com
Bilingual design & marketing, promotional communications, brand identity & packaging, direct mail design, brochures, newsletters, web design, banner & poster art, tradeshow displays, court graphics, typography, illustration,photography. (Woman, estab 1998, empl 4, sales $850,000, cert: WBENC)

Iowa

1086 Hawthorne Direct LLC
      2280 W Tyler Ave, Ste 200
      Fairfield, IA 52556
      Contact: Karla Crawford Kerr VP Marketing
      Tel: (310) 844-0606
      Email: diversity@hawthornedirect.com
      Website: www.hawthornedirect.com/
Advertising, strategic planning, creative development, production, media planning, buying, analytics & campaign management. (Woman, estab 1986, empl 61, sales $11,500,000, cert: WBENC)

Illinois

1087 1st Metropolitan Translation Services, Inc.
      875 North Michigan Ave Ste 3100
      Chicago, IL 60611
      Contact: Shannon Ewasiuk President
      Tel: (312) 621-1500
      Email: firstmetro@sbcglobal.net
      Website: www.1stmetropolitan.info
Foreign language interpreters & translations. (Woman, estab 2000, empl 1, sales $222,810, cert: State, WBENC)

1088 2.718 Marketing
      54 W Hubbard St, Ste LLE
      Chicago, IL 60654
      Contact: Liz Brohan President
      Tel: (312) 661-1050
      Email: lbrohan@2718marketing.com
      Website: www.2718marketing.com
B2B & B2C advertising, marketing, creative development & design, internet & email marketing & consulting. (Woman, estab 1988, empl 20, sales $2,500,000, cert: WBENC)

1089 Angel Flight Marketing Services, Inc.
      1006 S. Michigan Ave Ste 606
      Chicago, IL 60605
      Contact: Gabriel Mitchell President
      Tel: (312) 933-1878
      Email: gmitchell@angelfly.com
      Website: www.angelfly.com
Direct mail, graphic design, call center, market research. (AA, estab 1992, empl 10, sales $1,220,000, cert: City, NMSDC)

1090 Bluedog Design, LLC
      403 N Carpenter
      Chicago, IL 60642
      Contact: Michelle Hayward President
      Tel: (312) 243-1101
      Email: michelle@bluedogdesign.com
      Website: www.bluedogdesign.com
Brand strategy & package design: brand positioning, identity development & revitalization, innovation, nomenclature, consumer research &bstrategic graphic design. (Woman, estab 1999, empl , sales $4,334,286, cert: WBENC)

1091 commonground
      600 W Fluton Fl 4
      Chicago, IL 60661
      Contact: Sherman Wright Managing Partner
      Tel: (312) 384-1906
      Email: alicepollard@discovercg.com
      Website: www.discovercg.com
Marketing, advertising, cultural consulting, brand strategy, promotions. (AA, estab 2003, empl 75, sales $24,367,000, cert: NMSDC)

1092 Cor Creative, Inc.
      1412 W Jarvis
      Chicago, IL 60626
      Contact: Linda Tuke-Larkin President
      Tel: (773) 381-3811
      Email: linda@corcreate.com
      Website: www.corcreate.com
Design, advertising, production, web site design & programming, strategy, branding, social media, marketing, creative, media placement. (Woman, estab 2006, empl 1, sales $100,000, cert: City)

ADVERTISING

1093 J.C. Schultz Enterprises, Inc./FlagSource
      951 Swanson Dr
      Batavia, IL 60510
      Contact: Joseph Smurawski Controller
      Tel: (800) 323-9127
      Email: jsmurawski@flagsource.com
      Website: www.flagsource.com
Mfr flags & banners: screen printing, appique, dye sub, 4 color process, table banners, vinyl & polyethylene POP banners, flag poles. (Woman/As-Ind, estab 1920, empl 65, sales $8,500,000, cert: WBENC)

1094 Jayne Agency, LLC
      1231 Eastwood Ave
      Highland Park, IL 60035
      Contact: Brooke Foley CEO
      Tel: (312) 464-8100
      Email: brooke@jayneagency.com
      Website: www.jayneagency.com
Creative, Strategy, Media, Digital Strategy & Technology. (Woman, estab 2009, empl 4, sales $484,000, cert: WBENC)

1095 Linguanational Translations, Inc.
      401 N Michigan Ave Ste 1200
      Chicago, IL 60611
      Contact: Janie Markos President
      Tel: (312) 833-1399
      Email: jmarkos@linguanational.com
      Website: www.linguanational.com
Translation services: interpretation, typesetting, transcription & desktop publishing. (Woman, estab 2009, empl 3, sales , cert: WBENC)

1096 Mail Everything, Inc.
      325 N Fourth St
      Libertyville, IL 60048
      Contact: Mary Trifunovich President
      Tel: (847) 573-9999
      Email: mary@maileverything.com
      Website: www.maileverything.com
Direct mail & fulfillment services: printing, warehousing, dist literature, product & promotional items, kitting & assembly. (Woman, estab 2002, empl 16, sales $3,000,000, cert: WBENC)

1097 Medius & Associates, Inc.
      13175 Cold Springs Dr
      Huntley, IL 60142
      Contact: Karen Holmes President
      Tel: (847) 609-8165
      Email: kholmes@mediusinc.com
      Website: www.mediusinc.com
Graphic design, illustration, photography & printing: brochures, catalogs, ads, point of purchase, tradeshow graphics & web design. (Woman, estab 1993, empl 2, sales , cert: WBENC)

1098 NorthStar Strategies, Inc.
      448 Greenwood Ave
      Glencoe, IL 60022
      Contact: Dinny Cosyns Sr Partner
      Tel: (847) 242-9107
      Email: dinny@northstarstrategies.biz
      Website: www.northstarstrategies.biz
Marketing & advertising agency. (Woman, estab 2004, empl 3, sales $240,000, cert: State, WBENC)

1099 Suncraft Technologies, Inc.
      1301 Frontenac Road
      Naperville, IL 60563
      Contact: Holly Winters Diversity Lead
      Tel: (630) 369-7900
      Email: hwinters@suncraft-tech.com
      Website: www.suncraft-tech.com
Inline & conventional direct mail, digital storefront, signage, inventory mgmt, creative format design, graphic design, fulfillment, kitting & mailing services. (Woman, estab 1993, empl 100, sales $30,000,000, cert: WBENC)

Indiana

1100 Deborah Wood Associates, Inc.
      630 W Carmel Dr Ste 200
      Carmel, IN 46032
      Contact: Dana Walker Strategic Acct Dir
      Tel: (317) 208-3600
      Email: dana_walker@avanthcm.com
      Website: www.dwahcg.com
Comprehensive launch & mature-product strategy, promotional programming strategy design & implementation, scientific content development, thought leader & emerging leader identification, advisory board identification, recruitment. (Woman, estab 1994, empl 150, sales $23,000,000, cert: WBENC)

1101 L & D Mail Masters Inc.
      110 Security Pkwy
      New Albany, IN 47150
      Contact: Jill Peden Business Devel Mgr
      Tel: (812) 981-7161
      Email: jpeden@ldmailmasters.com
      Website: www.ldmailmasters.com
Direct mail processing. (Woman, estab 1986, empl 110, sales $25,000,000, cert: WBENC)

1102 RLR Associates, Inc.
      1302 N Illinois St
      Indianapolis, IN 46202
      Contact: Ryan Scott President
      Tel: (317) 632-1300
      Email: ryan@rlr.biz
      Website: www.rlr.biz
Professional design services: corporate identity & branding, signage, wayfinding programs, interiors & interpretive spaces. (AA, estab 1994, empl 6, sales $710,000, cert: State, City)

Kansas

1103 Callahan Creek, Inc.
      805 New Hampshire
      Lawrence, KS 66044
      Contact: Sarah Etzel VP Mktg Svcs
      Tel: (785) 838-4774
      Email: cmaude@callahancreek.com
      Website: www.callahancreek.com
Advertising & marketing, graphic design, qualitative, quantitative & competitive intelligence research, interactive, brand development, media planning & placement. (Woman, estab 1982, empl 35, sales $6,000,000, cert: WBENC)

Kentucky

1104 John F. Ruggles, Inc.
93 Industry Dr
Versailles, KY 40383
Contact: Tim Cambron President
Tel: (859) 879-1199
Email: tim@rugglessign.com
Website: www.rugglessign.com
Mfr & install signage. (Woman, estab 1946, empl 95, sales $16,000,000, cert: WBENC)

1105 Life's Eyes Media, LLC
1717 Dixie Hwy, Ste 150
Fort Wright, KY 41011
Contact: Kristan Getsy CEO
Tel: (859) 363-3916
Email: kgetsy@lifeseyesmedia.com
Website: www.lifeseyesmedia.com
Corporate Video, Commercial Video Production, Motion Graphics, After Effects, DSLR Production, DSLR, Creative, Creative Agency, Agency, Non-Profit Video, Scriptwriting, Scripting, Web Video, Social Media Video. (Woman, estab 2005, empl 3, sales $263,704, cert: WBENC)

1106 Madison Design Group
515 Madison Ave, Ste 201
Covington, KY 41011
Contact: Julie Courtney Partner
Tel: (859) 655-9900
Email:
Website: www.madison-design.com
Design services: editorial layout, collateral, point-of-sale, fundraising mailings, newsletter design & layout, annual reports, website design, brand identity creation. (Woman, estab 1998, empl 7, sales $159,498,680, cert: WBENC)

1107 New West LLC
9630 Ormsby Station Rd
Louisville, KY 40223
Contact: Melvin Graham Managing Dir
Tel: (888) 867-7811
Email: mgraham@newwestagency.com
Website: www.newwestagency.com
Advertising, Public Relations, Brand Strategy, Website & Mobile App Development, Social Media, Multicultural Marketing, SEO/SEM/PPC, Event Planning & Video Production. (AA, estab 2002, empl 28, sales $5,500,000, cert: NMSDC)

1108 Vest Marketing Design, LLC
3007 Sprowl Rd
Louisville, KY 40299
Contact: Keith Searles Healthcare Marketing Dir
Tel: (502) 267-5335
Email: bizdev@urbangis.com
Website: www.vestadvertising.com
Digital, video, print & comprehensive media strategy & implementation. (Woman, estab 1991, empl 40, sales $8,500,000, cert: WBENC)

Massachusetts

1109 Buyer Advertising & Talent Solutions
189 Wells Ave Ste 201A
Newton, MA 02459
Contact: Charles Buyer President
Tel: (617) 404-0860
Email: cbuyer@buyerads.com
Website: www.buyerads.com
Search Engine Optimization (SEO), Mobile marketing, Social Networking, Facebook Advertising, Facebook Applications, Employer Brand Development, market Research & Analysis. (Woman, estab 1966, empl 32, sales $15,877,337, cert: State)

1110 Carroll Communications Group
PO Box 401
Milton, MA 02186
Contact: Marc Carroll Principal
Tel: (781) 248-2125
Email: mcarroll@carrollcommunications.net
Website: www.carrollcommunications.net
Advertising agency: web design, graphic design, branding strategies, social media strategies, on-line marketing, media planning & media buying. (AA, estab 2008, empl 3, sales $100,000, cert: State)

1111 Color Media Group, LLC
4 Copley Pl, Ste 120
Boston, MA 02116
Contact: Josefina Bonilla President
Tel: (617) 266-6961
Email: josefina@colorboston.com
Website: www.colormagazineusa.com
Web advertising, signature events, event management, strategic marketing initiatives, new markets, media buying services, public relations. (Minority, Woman, estab 2007, empl 3, sales $289,000, cert: State)

1112 National Electric Corporation
57 Providence Hwy
Norwood, MA 02062
Contact: Rhonda Rothberg Sr Acct Mgr
Tel: (888) 344-4632
Email: rrothberg@natlelec.com
Website: www.natlelec.com
Provide electrical and sign services for retail stores nationwide plus Canada and Puerto Rico. (Woman, estab 1999, empl 10, sales $1,500,000, cert: WBENC)

1113 Rapport International, LLC
93 Moore Rd
Sudbury, MA 01776
Contact: Owner, Exec Dir
Tel: (978) 443-2540
Email: rapport@rapportintl.com
Website: www.rapporttranslations.com
Translation & interpretation services in over 100 languages. (Woman, estab 1987, empl 5, sales $1,200,000, cert: WBENC)

1114 Spectrum Broadcasting Corporation
114 Wrentham St
Boston, MA 02124
Contact: Tessil Collins CEO
Tel: (617) 287-8770
Email: thewiz@spectrumbroadcasting.com
Website: www.spectrumbroadcasting.com
Media streaming & production, advertising creative services, training & mgmt, internet, television, radio, graphic & web design, product & artist mgmt, training, facilitation & consultation services. (AA, estab 1998, empl 5, sales , cert: State, City)

1115 TSM Design, Inc.
      293 Bridge St
      Springfield, MA 01103
      Contact: Nancy Urbschat Principal
      Tel: (413) 731-7600
      Email: nancy@tsmdesign.com
      Website: www.tsmdesign.com
Integrated branding, multi-channel marketing & standout graphic design services. (Woman, estab 2005, empl 7, sales $900,000, cert: State)

Maryland

1116 21st Century Expo Group, Inc.
      3321 75th Ave, Ste P
      Landover, MD 20785
      Contact: Leslie McFarland President
      Tel: (301) 386-9771
      Email: lmcfarland@21stceg.com
      Website: www.21stceg.com
Exhibit mgmt, marketing, dist displays & decorating svcs. (Woman/AA, estab 1991, empl 9, sales , cert: NMSDC, WBENC)

1117 A. Bright Idea
      210 Archer St
      Bel Air, MD 21014
      Contact: CEO
      Tel: (410) 836-7180
      Email:
      Website: www.abrightideaonline.com
Advertising, public relations & graphic design support. (Woman, estab 1996, empl 35, sales $2,100,000, cert: WBENC)

1118 American International Mailing, Inc.
      3916 Vero Rd Ste K
      Baltimore, MD 21227
      Contact: Tom Parry VP
      Tel: (410) 247-4900
      Email: tomp@aimmailing.com
      Website: www.aimmailing.com
International mailing & distribution svcs: letter mail, direct mail, catalogs, publications, parcels & freight. (Woman, estab 2004, empl 25, sales $8,000,000, cert: WBENC)

1119 ArachnidWorks, Inc.
      5104 Pegasus Court Ste B
      Frederick, MD 21704
      Contact: Monica Kolbay CEO
      Tel: (240) 285-9844
      Email: monica@arachnidworks.com
      Website: www.arachnidworks.com
Advertising, internet marketing, logo design, print media, ad creation & copywriting, web design & development. (Woman, estab 2008, empl 3, sales $158,335, cert: State)

1120 Barb Clapp Advertising and Marketing, LLC
      6115 Falls Rd
      Baltimore, MD 21209
      Contact: Barb Clapp President
      Tel: (410) 561-8886
      Email: lisa@barbclapp.com
      Website: www.clappcommunications.com
Advertising, marketing & public relations. (Woman, estab 2000, empl 6, sales $354,737, cert: State)

1121 Catalpha Advertising & Design
      6801 Loch Raven Blvd
      Towson, MD 21286
      Contact: Karen Kerski Principal
      Tel: (410) 337-0066
      Email:
      Website: www.catalpha.com
Design & produce product & event promotional signs & materials: banners, fact tags, headers, danglers, hang tags, counter cards. (Woman, estab 1986, empl 6, sales $720,000, cert: State)

1122 Harvey & Daughters, Inc.
      952 Ridgebrook Rd, Ste 1000
      Sparks, MD 21152
      Contact: Jade Reider Office Mgr
      Tel: (410) 771-5566
      Email: jreider@harveyagency.com
      Website: www.harveyagency.com
Brand activation, purchasing strategy, package design, logo development & graphic design. (Woman, estab 1986, empl 35, sales $6,000,000, cert: WBENC)

1123 Herrmann Advertising|Branding|Technology
      30 West St
      Annapolis, MD 21401
      Contact: Jane Farrell Sr Acct. Exec.
      Tel: (410) 267-6522
      Email: jane@herrmann.com
      Website: www.herrmann.com
Advertising agency: market research, creative design, media management, print management, photography, copy writing & technology. (Woman, estab 1979, empl 14, sales $3,663,968, cert: State, City, WBENC)

1124 Media Works, Ltd.
      1425 Clarkview Rd Ste 500
      Baltimore, MD 21209
      Contact: Michele Selby President
      Tel: (443) 470-4400
      Email: mselby@medialtd.com
      Website: www.medialtd.com
Advertising agency, research, plan & place media. (Woman, estab 1989, empl 34, sales $887,604, cert: City)

1125 Pure Advertising, LLC
      137 National Plaza Ste 300
      Oxon Hill, MD 20745
      Contact: Rick Tyner Managing Partner
      Tel: (301) 646-4392
      Email: rick.tyner@prosum.com
      Website: www.pureadsww.com
Outdoor advertising & graphic design, taxi advertising, transit, airport advertising & billboards. (AA, estab 2010, empl 2, sales $200,000, cert: State, NMSDC)

Michigan

1126 BlueWater Technologies Group Inc.
      24050 Northwestern Hwy
      Southfield, MI 48075
      Contact: Suzanne Schoeneberger President
      Tel: (248) 356-4399
      Email: sue@bluewatertech.com
      Website: www.bluewatertech.com
Retail POP and POS displays, complete turn key merchandising solutions, Literature displays, Audio Visual Systems. (Woman, estab 1985, empl 187, sales $148,000,000, cert: WBENC)

ADVERTISING

1127 Graphicolor Systems, Inc.
      12788 Currie Court
      Livonia, MI 48150
      Contact: Anita Mitzel President
      Tel: (248) 347-0271
      Email: anita@graphicolor.com
      Website: www.graphicolor.com
Design trade show displays & corporate signage. (Woman, estab 1984, empl 8, sales $1,002,000, cert: WBENC)

1128 Immersion Graphics Inc.
      1020 Metro Dr
      Commerce, MI 48390
      Contact: Pat Hernandez President
      Tel: (248) 624-6520
      Email: pat@immersion-graphics.com
      Website: www.immersion-graphics.com
Engineering & audio visual systems solutions. (Hisp, estab 1998, empl 10, sales $3,439,000, cert: NMSDC)

1129 LA Exhibits, Inc.
      1091 Centre Rd Ste 130
      Auburn Hills, MI 48326
      Contact: Della Dotson President
      Tel: (248) 340-1144
      Email: della@laexhibits.com
      Website: www.laexhibits.com
Design, build & support tradeshow displays & events, portable, modular & custom displays, design & production, warehousing. (Woman, estab 1991, empl 3, sales , cert: WBENC)

1130 Languages International Inc.
      4665 - 44th St SE Ste A1101
      Grand Rapids, MI 49512
      Contact: Beverly Wall Owner
      Tel: (616) 285-0005
      Email: beverly@lang-int.com
      Website: www.lang-int.com
Foreign language translation & interpreting services. (Woman, estab 1988, empl 7, sales $400,000, cert: WBENC)

1131 Marketing Displays, Inc.
      38271 W Twelve Mile Rd
      Farmington, MI 48331
      Contact: Lisa Sarkisian President
      Tel: (248) 553-1900
      Email: lisa.sarkisian@mdiworldwide.com
      Website: www.mdiworldwide.com
Custom & stock retail display products & Traffic Control Products for temporary traffic control devices. (Woman, estab , empl , sales $30,639,000, cert: WBENC)

1132 PALS International
      900 Wilshire Dr, Ste 105
      Troy, MI 48084
      Contact: David Schroeder VP Business Dev
      Tel: (248) 362-2060
      Email: dschroeder@palsintl.com
      Website: www.palsintl.com
Translations & interpretations; language instruction; cross-cultural programs; accent reduction; global relocation; videovoice-overs. (Minority, Woman, estab 1983, empl 80, sales $1,509,900, cert: NMSDC, WBENC)

1133 STS Marketing Services, LLC
      22840 Woodward Ave
      Ferndale, MI 48220
      Contact: Theresa Bland Business Mgr
      Tel: (248) 548-1011
      Email: tbland@stsmktg.com
      Website: www.stsmktg.com
Editorial boutique editing, internal/external corporate communications packages, production services. (AA, estab 1994, empl 1, sales , cert: NMSDC)

1134 The Ajamu Group, LLC.
      29155 Northwestern Hwy, Ste 687
      Southfield, MI 48034
      Contact: Cheryl D Parks Ajamu CEO
      Tel: (248) 223-0904
      Email: cheryl.ajamu@ajamugroup.com
      Website: www.ajamugroup.com
The Ajamu Group, LLC. secures print, digital and mobile advertising for national media companies, and also provides Event Management services for local and national companies. (Woman/AA, estab 2004, empl 1, sales , cert: NMSDC, WBENC)

1135 Tiger Studio Co.
      418 E 8th St
      Holland, MI 49423
      Contact: Luciano Hernandez Owner
      Tel: (616) 748-7532
      Email: luciano@tigerstudiodesign.com
      Website: www.tigerstudiodesign.com
Product, Interaction, Brand, and Strategy. (Hisp, estab 2000, empl 4, sales , cert: NMSDC)

1136 Trent Design LLC
      114 E Second St
      Rochester, MI 48307
      Contact: Marilyn Trent Principal
      Tel: (248) 652-8307
      Email: marilyn@trentcreative.com
      Website: www.trentcreative.com
Graphic design, digital media, web design & development, advertising, social media marketing. (Woman, estab 1991, empl 5, sales $600,000, cert: WBENC)

1137 Wensco of Michigan Corporation
      5760 Safety Dr NE
      Belmont, MI 49306
      Contact: Yolanda Cain Inside Sales Support
      Tel: (800) 253-1569
      Email: ycain@wensco.com
      Website: www.wensco.com
Dist signs: digital inkjet media & laminates, cut vinyls, banners, neon, l.e.d.'s, ballasts, plywood, metal & plastic substrates, aluminum, polycarbonate, acrylic, plexiglass, aluminum composite panels. (Woman, estab 1937, empl 50, sales , cert: WBENC)

Minnesota

1138 Bella Creative LLC
      16860 Judicial Rd
      Lakeville, MN 55044
      Contact: Stacy A Parizek Owner
      Tel: (952) 232-6411
      Email: stacy@bella-creative.net
      Website: www.bellaexhibts.com
Mfr trade show exhibits, off-the-shelf displays to custom booths. (Woman, estab 2008, empl 1, sales $108,353, cert: WBENC)

1139 Betmar Languages, Inc.
      6260 Hwy 65 NE, Ste 308
      Minneapolis, MN 55432
      Contact: President
      Tel: (763) 572-9711
      Email:
      Website: www.betmar.com
Translation svcs: on site interpreters; voice-overs for audio, video & interactive projects; typesetting; document translation; cultural diversity training. (Woman, estab 1985, empl 4, sales $949,266, cert: WBENC)

1140 cmnd+m LLC
      867 Pierce Butler Route
      St. Paul, MN 55104
      Contact: Krista O'Malley
      Tel: (612) 867-6273
      Email: accounting@cmndm.com
      Website: www.cmndm.com
Design, production, engineering, retail, advertising, project management, construction, and training. (Minority, Woman, estab 2011, empl 11, sales $700,000, cert: NMSDC, WBENC)

1141 Deep Well, Inc.
      123 N 3rd St Ste 700
      Minneapolis, MN 55401
      Contact: Phil Nelson
      Tel: (612) 338-7947
      Email: phil@crash-sues.com
      Website: www.crash-sues.com
Advertising, marketing, production, video editing, animation, 3D, traditional animation, stop motion, graphics, effects, color, media, web apps, strategy, creative, branding, brand development, ideation, web development, post-production. (Woman, estab 2008, empl 12, sales $1,600,000, cert: WBENC)

1142 Designer Sign Systems
      9975 Flanders Ct NE
      Blaine, MN 55449
      Contact: Karen Fisher CEO
      Tel: (763) 784-5858
      Email: customerservice@designersign.com
      Website: www.designersign.com
Mfr & design architectural interior & exterior signage. (Woman, estab 1984, empl 30, sales $5,246,000, cert: WBENC)

1143 Dudak Production, Inc.
      582 Bavaria Lane
      Chaska, MN 55318
      Contact: Shirley Dudak President
      Tel: (952) 443-0097
      Email: shirley.dudak@dudakproductioninc.com
      Website: www.dudakproductioninc.com
Advertising, Graphic Design Services, Marketing, Commercial Gravure Printing, Commercial Screen Printing, Packing & Crating, Print Advertising, Marketing & Distribution, Printing, Brand Marketing. (Woman, estab 1996, empl 3, sales $1,675,000, cert: WBENC)

1144 IN Food Mktg & Design, Inc.
      600 N Washington Ave Ste C101
      Minneapolis, MN 55401
      Contact: Anita M Nelson President
      Tel: (612) 353-3410
      Email: anita@infoodmktg.com
      Website: www.infoodmktg.com
Marketing & communications: brand building & product promotions. (Woman, estab 1995, empl 12, sales $1,215,000, cert: WBENC)

1145 Intercross Design, Inc.
      2238 Edgewood Ave S
      Minneapolis, MN 55426
      Contact: Lori Fuller VP
      Tel: (952) 935-2080
      Email: lori.fuller@intercross.com
      Website: www.intercross.com
Advertising agency: branding, videos, websites, collateral & advertising. (Woman, estab 1997, empl 17, sales $3,876,000, cert: WBENC)

1146 JPG & Associates, Inc.
      8991 33rd St N
      Lake Elmo, MN 55042
      Contact: Jerry Grohovsky President
      Tel: (651) 779-1072
      Email: jerry@jpgassoc.com
      Website: www.jpgassoc.com
Technical publications, temporary staffing & off-site production, technical writing, instructional design, marketing writing, graphic design, desktop publishing, web site development, web-based help development. (Woman, estab 1993, empl 30, sales $2,000,000, cert: WBENC)

1147 KJ International Resources, Ltd.
      800 Washington Ave N Ste 905
      Minneapolis, MN 55401
      Contact: Kristen Giovanis
      Tel: (612) 288-9494
      Email: kgiovanis@kjinternational.com
      Website: www.kjinternational.com
Language translation & validation, web translation & localization, voice-overs, etc. (Woman, estab 1994, empl 30, sales $6,400,000, cert: WBENC)

1148 KNOCK, inc.
      1307 Glenwood Ave
      Minneapolis, MN 55405
      Contact: Tom Newton VP Business Dev
      Tel: (612) 333-6511
      Email: tom.newton@KNOCKinc.com
      Website: www.KNOCKinc.com
Graphic design, branding, marketing, advertising, packaging, illustration, photo art direction. (Minority, Woman, estab 2001, empl 102, sales $24,145,000, cert: NMSDC, WBENC)

1149 Latitude Prime LLC
      80 S 8th St Ste 900
      Minneapolis, MN 55402
      Contact: Nat LeBrun
      Tel: (888) 341-9080
      Email: email@latitudeprime.com
      Website: www.latitudeprime.com
Multilingual translation services, media & document translation, interpretation, localization, transcription, proofreading/editing & DTP services. (Woman/As-Ind, estab 2009, empl 15, sales , cert: State, City, NMSDC, WBENC, 8(a))

1150 Media Bridge, Inc.
      212 3rd Ave N
      Minneapolis, MN 55401
      Contact: Shannon Knoepke SVP Marketing
      Tel: (612) 353-6077
      Email: Procurement@mediabridgeadvertising.com
      Website: www.mediabridgeadvertising.com
Ad agency. Media buying, strategy, branding, creative services, social media and video production. (Woman, estab 2010, empl 26, sales $24,420,385, cert: WBENC)

1151 Northcott Banners, Inc.
2645 - 26th Ave S, Ste 400
Minneapolis, MN 55406
Contact: Millie Northcott Owner
Tel: (612) 722-1733
Email: millie@northcottbanner.com
Website: www.northcottbanner.com

Mfr banners: fabric, vinyl, interior & exterior applications. (Woman, estab 1984, empl 9, sales $712,698, cert: WBENC)

1152 Oceandrum LLC dba Zydeco Design
231 2nd St
Excelsior, MN 55331
Contact: Nathalie Wilson President
Tel: (612) 202-7421
Email: nathaliew@zydecodesign.com
Website: www.zydecodesign.com

Brand & design, branding strategy, brand experience strategy, brand architecture, naming, identity, image system, packaging, annual reports, corporate social responsibility & sustainable development. (Woman, estab 2009, empl 2, sales $300,000, cert: State, WBENC)

1153 Peggy Lauritsen Design Group, Inc.
125 SE Main St Ste 340
Minneapolis, MN 55414
Contact: Linda Gosslin Sr Acct Dir
Tel: (612) 623-4200
Email: lgosslin@pldg.com
Website: www.pldg.com

Corporate & brand identity, graphic & communications sesign, marketing communications, website design, event communications, print or electronic media. (Woman, estab 1979, empl 9, sales , cert: WBENC)

1154 Portage Marketing
2401 Sheridan Ave S
Minneapolis, MN 55405
Contact: Laureen Carlson President
Tel: (612) 381-0621
Email: lcarlson@portagemarketing.com
Website: www.portagemarketing.com

Advertising agency & media placement. (Woman, estab 2000, empl 1, sales $5,000,000, cert: WBENC)

1155 Tembua Inc (fka Precision Language Services)
17595 Kenwood Trail Ste 120
Lakeville, MN 55044
Contact: Paula Town Exec Admin Assist
Tel: (952) 435-8178
Email: office@tembua.com
Website: www.tembua.com

Document translation: bilingual, bicultural translations. (Woman, estab 1993, empl 36, sales $700,000, cert: WBENC)

1156 Wrap City Graphics
62 6th Ave S
Hopkins, MN 55343
Contact: President
Tel: (952) 920-4664
Email: sales@wrapcitygraphics.com
Website: www.WrapCityGraphics.com

Commercial signage & digitally printed wide-format adhesive backed vinyl graphics , vehicle graphics/wraps, window/wall graphics, dimensional letters/logos & architectural products. (Woman, estab 2005, empl 7, sales $745,000, cert: WBENC)

Missouri

1157 Brighton Agency, Inc.
7711 Bonhomme Ave Ste 100
Saint Louis, MO 63105
Contact: Tina VonderHaar CEO
Tel: (314) 726-0700
Email: accounting@brightonagency.com
Website: www.brightonagency.com

Strategic planning, brand develop, digital marketing & production, marketing consulting, PR, advertising, promotions, media planning, audio & video production, event marketing. (Woman, estab 1989, empl 71, sales $9,030,143, cert: State, WBENC)

1158 Language Solutions Inc.
230 South Bemiston Ave. Ste 610
St. Louis, MO 63105
Contact: Melissa Wurst President
Tel: (314) 725-3711
Email: melissa@langsolinc.com
Website: www.langsolinc.com

Written translation & multilingual typesetting. (Woman, estab 1998, empl 2, sales $677,610, cert: WBENC)

1159 Schisla Design, LLC dba Enrich
12 N Sarah St
St. Louis, MO 63108
Contact: Suzanne Duvald'Adrian Marketing & Social Media
Tel: (314) 553-9500
Email: suzanne@enrichcreative.com
Website: www.enrichcreative.com

Branding programs: audits & research, Strategy and Development, Naming, Logo Design, Strategic Messaging, Positioning, Brand Guides & Product, Service and Event Branding. (Woman, estab 2002, empl 4, sales $438,502, cert: WBENC)

North Carolina

1160 Crutchfield & Associates Inc.
515 College Rd, Ste 14
Greensboro, NC 27410
Contact: Bernadette Trinidad President
Tel: (336) 297-1222
Email: bernadette@ca-ideas.com
Website: www.ca-ideas.com

Advertising agency, integrated, strategic & innovative marketing & communications solutions. (Minority, Woman, estab 1985, empl 3, sales $121,707, cert: NMSDC)

1161 Fly My Photo, LLC
560 Davidson Gateway Dr Ste 101
Davidson, NC 28036
Contact: Susan Boaz President
Tel: (855) 347-4922
Email: susan@flagology.com
Website: www.flagology.com

Mfr decorative flags, printed & appliqued, photo flags, monogram flags, signage, flag poles & brackets, door mats, monograms & personalized flags. (Woman, estab 2013, empl 1, sales , cert: WBENC)

1162 Jervay Agency, LLC
338 S Sharon Amity, Ste 302
Charlotte, NC 28211
Contact: Adria Jervay Media Acct Rep
Tel: (704) 780-7004
Email: adria@thejervayagency.com
Website: www.TheJervayAgency.com
Advertising & marketing materials. (Woman/AA, estab 2012, empl 3, sales , cert: City)

1163 Language Resource Center Inc.
PO Box 18066
Charlotte, NC 28218
Contact: Abdullahi Sheikh CEO
Tel: (704) 464-0016
Email: abdullah.sheikh@languagerc.com
Website: www.languagerc.com
Interpretation & translation service providers. (Woman/AA, estab , empl , sales $1,428,268, cert: State, City)

1164 Main Street Mobile Billboards
2610 Tuckaseegee Rd
Charlotte, NC 28208
Contact: Brendon Henderson CEO
Tel: (888) 788-7492
Email: brendon@mainstreetmobilebillboards.com
Website: www.mainstreetmobilebillboards.com
Mobile truck billboard & walking billboards advertising. (AA, estab 2013, empl 2, sales , cert: State, City, NMSDC)

1165 Moving Ideas, Inc.
7519 Royal Bliss Ct, Ste 205
Denver, NC 28037
Contact: Jennifer Moates President
Tel: (704) 655-2870
Email: jmoates@movingideasinc.com
Website: www.movingideasinc.com
Advertising, Branding & Identity, Copywriting & Content, Creative Campaigns, Direct Mail, Infographics, Email Marketing, Graphic Design, Strategic Marketing Plans, Naming, Social Media, Tradeshow, Video, Websites. (Woman, estab 2005, empl 5, sales $500,000, cert: WBENC)

New Hampshire

1166 Kelley Solution, Inc.
210 West Rd Unit 3
Portsmouth, NH 03801
Contact: Lisa Finneral President
Tel: (603) 431-3881
Email: lfinneral@kelleysolutions.com
Website: www.kelleysolutions.com
E-business solutions & svcs: online fulfillment, graphic design, strategic sourcing, warehousing, distribution, integrated marketing campaigns & direct mail management. (Woman, estab 1972, empl 6, sales $2,200,000, cert: WBENC)

1167 Polaris Direct
300 Technology Dr
Hooksett, NH 03106
Contact: Judith Maloy Dir & CEO
Tel: (603) 626-5800
Email: diversity@polarisdirect.net
Website: www.polarisdirect.net
Direct mail, data processing, ink jet & laser personalization, mailing services, bindery & print management. (Woman, estab 2003, empl 78, sales $25,546,966, cert: WBENC)

New Jersey

1168 Clark Media Corp.
655 Jersey Ave
Jersey City, NJ 07302
Contact: Ken Clark COO
Tel: (800) 872-6752
Email: kclark@resptrans.com
Website: www.responsivetranslation.com
Translation & interpretation services: machine translation, translation memory, content management systems & multi-platform publishing in 157 languages. (Minority, Woman, estab 1990, empl 2, sales $1,628,455, cert: WBENC)

1169 CQ fluency, Inc.
2 University Plaza, STE 406
Hackensack, NJ 07601
Contact: Elisabete Miranda President
Tel: (201) 487-8007
Email: info@cqfluency.com
Website: www.cqfluency.com
Translation services: 180 languages, web localization, cultural consulting, desktop publishing, phone interpretation, multimedia production, tape transcription. (Minority, Woman, estab 2000, empl 82, sales $3,844,722, cert: State, NMSDC, WBENC)

1170 Digital Outdoor Advertising
788 Shrewsbury Ave
Tinton Falls, NJ 07724
Contact: Christine Lanziano President
Tel: (732) 491-8726
Email: christine@digitaloutdooradvertising.com
Website: www.digitaloutdooradvertising.com
Digital & static outdoor billboards, mall kiosks & bus advertising. (Woman, estab 2012, empl 7, sales $6,000,000, cert: WBENC)

1171 Eclipse Marketing Services Inc.
490 Headquarters Plaza North Tower, 10th Fl
Morristown, NJ 07960
Contact: Margaret Boller President
Tel: (800) 837-4648
Email: mboller@eclipse2.com
Website: www.eclipsemarketingservices.com
Advertising Services: campaigns; Hispanic Marketing Consulting; Graphic Design; Website design; Marketing programs; Promotional printing; Magazine advertising and publishing; Coop Marketing & promotion; Digital & social media. (Woman, estab 1992, empl 39, sales $10,980,994, cert: WBENC)

1172 Encore Events, ltd. dba Encore Design
31 Industrial Ave., Ste 7
Mahwah, NJ 07430
Contact: Kathleen Orbe Principal
Tel: (973) 890-0088
Email: encoredesign@mac.com
Website: www.encoredesign.com
Design services: strategic identity & branding. (Woman, estab 1994, empl 5, sales $425,000, cert: WBENC)

ADVERTISING

1173 Expect Advertising, Inc.
1033 Route 46
Clifton, NJ 07013
Contact: Ravi Sachdev President
Tel: (973) 777-8886
Email: ravi.sachdev@expectad.com
Website: www.expectad.com
Medical marketing & communications: advertising, branding, web design, web marketing, sales incentive programs, premiums, trade shows, public relations, media planning, market research. (As-Ind, estab 1996, empl 16, sales $2,000,000, cert: NMSDC)

1174 Graphic Matter, Inc.
601 Route 206, Ste 26-405
Hillsborough, NJ 08844
Contact: Beverly Thomas President
Tel: (908) 359-8760
Email: wbe@graphicmatter.com
Website: www.graphicmatter.com
Creative services: print & web. (Woman, estab 2002, empl 6, sales $297,570, cert: State, WBENC)

1175 Iris Communications LLC
11 Belaire Dr
Roseland, NJ 07068
Contact: Barbara Bochese Managing Dir
Tel: (973) 902-7027
Email: bbochese@iriscommunications.org
Website: www.iriscommunications.org
Marketing services, corporate communications & branding, presentations, branding, educational/training, video production & animation, website design & development, media planning & buying. (Woman, estab 2011, empl 12, sales , cert: State, NWBOC)

1176 Jouard Wozniak LLC dba JWDesign
165 Passaic Ave Ste 410
Fairfield, NJ 07004
Contact: Faith Wozniak President
Tel: (973) 244-9191
Email: faith@jwadv.com
Website: www.jwadv.com
Advertising & design, creative, design & marketing services, web & print, trade show graphics, promotional events, video & audio production, photography & retouching. (Woman, estab 1989, empl 4, sales $178,000, cert: WBENC)

1177 Newtype, Inc.
447 Route 10 East
Randolph, NJ 07869
Contact: Jo Ann Porto CEO
Tel: (973) 361-6000
Email: accounting@newtypeinc.com
Website: www.newtypeinc.com
Translations & publishing svcs in over 130 languages. (Woman, estab 1966, empl 12, sales , cert: WBENC)

1178 Para-Plus Translations, Inc.
2 Coleman Ave
Cherry Hill, NJ 08034
Contact: Carlos Santiago VP
Tel: (856) 547-3695
Email: csantiago@para-plus.com
Website: www.para-plus.com
Translation & interpretation svcs: technical & medical reports, legal documents, oral & written depositions, audio tapes, video tapes, patents, manuscripts, manuals, product literature, web sites. (Minority, Woman, estab 1980, empl 15, sales $3,028,000, cert: State)

1179 Personal Mail International, Inc.
5 Cold Hill Rd S, Ste 28
Mendham, NJ 07945
Contact: Debra Seyler President
Tel: (973) 543-6001
Email: dseyler@pmipmi.com
Website: www.pmipmi.com
International & domestic mail & package forwarding services. (Woman, estab 1987, empl 11, sales $950,000, cert: WBENC)

1180 Seliger-Braun Inc. dba Keylingo Translations
116 Village Blvd, Ste 200
Princeton, NJ 08540
Contact: Managing Dir
Tel: (609) 423-1077
Email:
Website: www.keylingo.com/
Translations services: localization, transcreation, interpretation & tele-interpretation. (Woman, estab 2011, empl 2, sales $106,775, cert: State, WBENC)

1181 Sign Up Inc.
255 Route 3 E
Secaucus, NJ 07094
Contact: President
Tel: (201) 902-8640
Email: 153@fastsigns.com
Website: www.fastsigns.com/153
Signs: vinyl, wood, windows, walls or vehicles, channel letters, window graphics, exhibits & displays, flags & banners, banner stands, vehicle graphics, vinyl lettering, posters, murals. (Woman, estab 1992, empl 8, sales $87,542,162, cert: State)

1182 Sunset Printing and Engraving Corp
10 Kice Ave
Wharton, NJ 07885
Contact: Deron Wainer
Tel: (732) 335-2165
Email: dwainer@sunsetcorpid.com
Website: www.sunsetcorpid.com
Corporate identity campaigns: printing, engraving, embossing & foil stamping. (Hisp, estab 1945, empl 28, sales $3,820,000, cert: NMSDC)

1183 The S3 Agency
716 Main St
Boonton, NJ 07005
Contact: Denise Blasevick CEO
Tel: (973) 257-5533
Email: dblasevick@thes3agency.com
Website: www.theS3agency.com
Advertising & marketing: print, tv, radio, outdoor, online, public relations, collateral, direct mail & direct marketing, e-marketing, websites, product launches, POP, business-to-business & consumer marketing, internal communications. (Woman, estab 2001, empl 25, sales $3,800,000, cert: WBENC)

1184 TriStar Fulfillment Services, Inc.
520 Pedricktown Rd
Bridgeport, NJ 08014
Contact: Susan Harker Owner
Tel: (972) 355-6256
Email: sharker@tristarfulfillment.com
Website: www.tristarfulfillment.com
Rebates, gift cards, merchandise, sweepstake offers, online order entry, reporting, tracking, billing, data processing, telemarketing, ondemand printing, sampling, direct mail, warehousing & distribution. (Woman, estab 1976, empl 135, sales $30,000,000, cert: WBENC)

Nevada

1185 El Mundo, Ltd.
      760 N Eastern Ave, Ste 110
      Las Vegas, NV 89101
      Contact: Hilda Escobedo CEO
      Tel: (702) 649-8553
      Email: hescobedo@elmundo.net
      Website: www.elmundo.net
Advertising, display advertising, graphic design, Spanish publication, Spanish readers, advertising in Spanish, display ads in Spanish, Spanish, newspaper, (Minority, Woman, estab 1980, empl 9, sales $1,347,788, cert: State)

1186 The Design Factory, LLC
      4318 W Cheyenne Ave
      North Las Vegas, NV 89032
      Contact: Mgr
      Tel: (702) 656-0555
      Email:
      Website: www.dflv.com
Exhibit design & sales, exhibit rental, graphic design, graphic printing, vinyl production, event services, furniture rental, floral rental, carpet rental, custom exhibit production, convention labor, sales of signs & banners. (Woman, estab 1999, empl 12, sales $2,081,369, cert: WBENC)

New York

1187 ADDO, LLC
      155 W 118th St, Ste 1
      New York, NY 10026
      Contact: S Courtney Booker, CEO
      Tel: (212) 933-0670
      Email: courtney@theaddo.com
      Website: www.theaddo.com
Brand marketing. (AA, estab 2006, empl 1, sales , cert: City, NMSDC)

1188 Adventium Marketing & Design
      320 E 35th St, Ste 5B
      New York, NY 10016
      Contact: Penny Chuang President
      Tel: (212) 481-9576
      Email: penny@adventium.net
      Website: www.adventium.net
Marketing collateral, graphic design, advertising, direct mail, corp communications, catalogs, videos, invitations, logo design, media kits, signage, trade show exhibits, web design, web banners. (Minority, Woman, estab 1992, empl 3, sales $370,000, cert: State, City)

1189 Aether NY LLC
      138 Wooster St 5th Fl
      New York, NY 10012
      Contact: Evan Hunerberg New Business Dir
      Tel: (347) 217-4842
      Email: evan@aetherny.com
      Website: www.aetherny.com
Brand Strategy, Graphic Design, Industrial Design, Product Visualization. (As-Pac, estab 2017, empl 7, sales , cert: NMSDC)

1190 Baseline Design, Inc
      236 W. 30th St 5th Fl
      New York, NY 10001
      Contact: Flanders Founder
      Tel: (212) 925-1656
      Email: darcy@baselinedesign.com
      Website: www.baselinegroupny.com/
Design solutions, printing, logo design & corporate identity programs, fund rollouts, conference support materials, brochures, catalogs, newsletters, direct mail pieces, advertising & annual reports. (Woman, estab 1997, empl 8, sales , cert: State, WBENC)

1191 Big Apple Visual Group Inc.
      3 Oval Dr
      Islandia, NY 11749
      Contact: Mobin Shroff Sr Sales Exec
      Tel: (631) 342-0303
      Email: mobin@bigapplegroup.com
      Website: www.bigapplegroup.com
Design & mfr interior & exterior architectural signs: subsurface graphics, cut out letters & logos, directional & informational signs, fabricated letters, POP displays, engraved signs, etc. (As-Pac, estab 1979, empl 82, sales $19,000,000, cert: NMSDC)

1192 Brand Cool Marketing, Inc.
      2300 East Ave
      Rochester, NY 14610
      Contact: Sue Kochan CEO
      Tel: (585) 381-3350
      Email: doorsopen@brandcoolmarketing.com
      Website: www.brandcool.com
Advertising services. (Woman, estab 1997, empl 20, sales $4,360,000, cert: WBENC)

1193 Butler/Till Media Services, Inc.
      260 E Broad St
      Rochester, NY 14604
      Contact: Andria DiFelice Group Acct Dir
      Tel: (585) 274-5108
      Email: adifelice@butlertill.com
      Website: www.butlertill.com
Advertising agency: research analysis, media planning & placement, post-buy analysis & reconciliation, results measurement & analysis, & independent media audit services. (Woman, estab , empl , sales , cert: WBENC)

1194 Crown Sign Systems
      7 Odell Plaza
      Yonkers, NY 10701
      Contact: Michelle Strum President
      Tel: (914) 375-2118
      Email: mstrum@crownsigns.com
      Website: www.crownsigns.com
Mfr interior & exterior architectural signage. (Woman, estab 1994, empl 14, sales $22,000,000, cert: State)

1195 DePirro/GarroneLLC
      25 W 13th St Ste 6NN
      New York, NY 10011
      Contact: Lisa Garrone CEO
      Tel: (212) 206-6967
      Email: lgarrone@depirrogarrone.com
      Website: www.depirrogarrone.com
Creative advertising, size or media channel, traditional or digital, online or offline. Flexible & scalable. (Woman, estab 2008, empl 8, sales $1,000,000, cert: City, WBENC)

ADVERTISING

1196 Eriksen Translations Inc.
360 Court St, #37
Brooklyn, NY 11231
Contact: Vigdis Eriksen President
Tel: (718) 802-9010
Email: vigdis.eriksen@eriksen.com
Website: www.eriksen.com
Multilingual services, translation, interpreting, typesetting, project management, web localization & cultural consulting in over 75 languages. (Woman, estab 1986, empl 35, sales $8,040,294, cert: State, City, WBENC)

1197 Fusia Communications, Inc.
45 Main St, Ste 212
Brooklyn, NY 11201
Contact: Elizabeth Kay President
Tel: (718) 643-0311
Email: ekay@fusia.net
Website: www.fusia.net
Marketing, strategic consulting, media planning & buying, media tracking, design/production, copywriting, translations. (Minority, Woman, estab 2002, empl 4, sales $514,627, cert: City, WBENC)

1198 Harquin Graphics, Inc.
80 Surrey Dr
New Rochelle, NY 10804
Contact: Sherry Bruck President
Tel: (914) 738-9620
Email: sbruck@harquin.com
Website: www.harquin.com
Graphic design, printing & web design. (Woman, estab 1992, empl 9, sales $450,000, cert: State, City)

1199 JUICE Pharma Worldwide
322 8th Ave, 10th Fl
New York, NY 10001
Contact: Howard Nagelberg CFO
Tel: (212) 647-1595
Email: hnagelberg@juicepharma.com
Website: www.juicepharma.com
Professional, patient, and consumer promotion and advertising. (Woman, estab 2002, empl 169, sales $45,000,000, cert: WBENC)

1200 Keeper of the Brand
894 Otsego Rd
West Hempstead, NY 11552
Contact: Donyshia Boston-Hill CEO
Tel: (917) 697-1699
Email: db@keeperofthebrand.com
Website: www.keeperofthebrand.com/
Marketing Plans & Strategies, Media Buying, TV, Radio, Print & Digital Solutions, Broadcast Media Distribution, Brand Development, Consumer Insight, Copyright, Transactional Engagement, Programming & Campaign Mgmt, Graphic Design, Creative Services. (Woman/AA, estab 2013, empl 6, sales , cert: State, NMSDC, WBENC)

1201 MAD Studio LLC
1123 Broadway, Ste 707
New York, NY 10010
Contact: FirstName LastName Principal
Tel: (212) 982-4613
Email: smatiz@mad-nyc.com
Website: www.mad-nyc.com
Brand marketing & design: positioning, logo development, stationery, brochures, email campaigns, websites, exhibits, packaging, promotional items, advertising. (Woman, estab 2011, empl 3, sales , cert: City, WBENC)

1202 Millennium Signs & Display, Inc.
90 W Graham Ave
Hempstead, NY 11550
Contact: Saj Khalfan President
Tel: (516) 292-8000
Email: saj@msdny.com
Website: www.msdny.com
Signs and Graphics; Point of Purchase Displays; Large Format Digital Printing; Wayfinding Signage; 3-Dimensional Letters and Logos; Lenticular Graphics; Laser & Waterjet Cutting; Architectural Signage. (Minority, estab 2008, empl 28, sales $5,255,000, cert: City, NMSDC)

1203 Mix On Digital, LLC
1867 Amsterdam Ave Ste 3F
New York, NY 10034
Contact: Christina Mixon Managing Dir
Tel: (917) 383-8121
Email: christina@mixondigital.com
Website: www.mixondigital.com
Digital media design & consulting, social, mobile & digital platforms. (Woman/AA, As- Pac, estab 2012, empl 2, sales $385,000, cert: City)

1204 Signs & Decal Corp.
410 Morgan Ave
Brooklyn, NY 11211
Contact: Hasnain Khalfan VP Sales & Marketing
Tel: (718) 486-6400
Email: salesadmin@signsanddecal.com
Website: www.signsanddecal.com
Mfr & install signage, signs. (Minority, estab 1972, empl 30, sales $7,204,781, cert: City)

1205 SpikeDDB, LLC
437 Madison Ave 20 FL
New York, NY 11201
Contact: Sterling Green
Tel: (718) 596-5400
Email: joel@spikeddb.com
Website: www.spikeddb.com
Advertising agency. (AA, estab 1997, empl 30, sales $6,000,000, cert: NMSDC)

1206 Squeaky
55 Broadway 3th Fl
New York, NY 10006
Contact: Mailet Lopez Managing Dir
Tel: (212) 994-5270
Email: mailet@squeaky.com
Website: www.squeaky.com
Design interface, web design, flash animation, e-commerce, database. (Hisp, estab 2001, empl 30, sales $1,754,683, cert: State, NMSDC)

1207 The Language Shop
114-26 146th St
Jamaica, NY 11436
Contact: Deborah Lockhart Dir of Operations
Tel: (646) 245-4129
Email: deborah.lockhart@thelanguageshop.org
Website: www.languageshop.org
Translation & interpreting legal, medical, financial, corporate, commercial, marketing, online games, website translation & localization. (Minority, Woman, estab 2007, empl 1, sales $122,000, cert: City)

1208   TITANIUM Worldwide LLC
        350 7th Ave Ste 1403
        New York, NY 10001
        Contact: Streisand Chief Financial Operations Officer
        Tel: (646) 952-8440
        Email: accounting@titaniumww.com
        Website: www.titaniumww.com
Media, marketing, communications & consulting: Branding/Creative/Strategy, Content/Messaging, Digital/Social/Mobile, Film/Video Production, Event Marketing, Business Intelligence, Data Warehousing, Development/Deployment. (Woman, estab 2014, empl 4, sales , cert: WBENC)

1209   Uniworld Group Inc.
        One Metro Tech Center North 11th Fl
        Brooklyn, NY 11201
        Contact: Ronald Hughes Group Acct Dir
        Tel: (212) 219-1600
        Email: ronald.hughes@uwgatl.com
        Website: www.uwginc.com
Multicultural advertising agency. (AA, estab 1969, empl 138, sales $18,717,000, cert: NMSDC)

1210   Visual Citi Inc.
        110-30 Dunkirk St
        St. Albans, NY 11412
        Contact: Mirza Kermani Acct Exec
        Tel: (718) 479-5500
        Email: mirza@visualciti.com
        Website: www.visualciti.com
Digitally Printed Signs & Graphics, Banners, POP Displays, Window Signs & Graphics, Cutout logos & letters, Silk Screen printing, ADA Signs, Etched Signs & Custom Fabrication. (As-Ind, estab 2004, empl 25, sales , cert: City, NMSDC)

1211   Weinrib & Connor Associates, Inc.
        297 Knollwood Rd
        White Plains, NY 10607
        Contact: President
        Tel: (914) 686-3900
        Email:
        Website: www.weinconn.com
Advertising agency. (Woman, estab 1993, empl 7, sales $1,300,000, cert: WBENC)

1212   Womenkind, LLC
        114 E 25th St, Ste 710
        New York, NY 10010
        Contact: Sandy Sabean Partner
        Tel: (212) 660-0400
        Email: sandy@womenkind.net
        Website: www.womenkind.net
Advertising & marketing communications. (Woman, estab 2007, empl 2, sales $1,800,000, cert: WBENC)

Ohio

1213   Baker Creative Ltd.
        386 Main St
        Groveport, OH 43125
        Contact: Michele Cuthbert Principal
        Tel: (614) 836-3845
        Email: mbaker@baker-creative.com
        Website: www.baker-creative.com
Graphic Design, Marketing Consulting, Advertising, Public Relations, Display Advertising. (Minority, Woman, estab 2003, empl 10, sales , cert: State, WBENC, SDB)

1214   Blink Marketing LLC dba Blink Signs; BlinkSwag
        1925 St. Clair Ave NE
        Cleveland, OH 44114
        Contact: Todd Davis Natl Sales
        Tel: (216) 503-2568
        Email: t.davis@blinksigns.com
        Website: www.blinksigns.com
Manufacture all types of illuminated or non-illuminated interior signage (including ADA) and exterior signage including awnings, sign service and maintenance. (Minority, Woman, estab 2007, empl 65, sales $9,069,699, cert: State, City)

1215   Bright Future Partners, Inc. dba RED212
        5509 Fair Lane
        Cincinnati, OH 45227
        Contact: Donna Zaring Dir Business Devel
        Tel: (513) 772-1020
        Email: donnazaring@red212.com
        Website: www.red212.com
Marketing communications, production & post production services. (Woman, estab 2001, empl 18, sales $3,971,726, cert: WBENC)

1216   Commercial Cutting & Graphics, LLC
        208 Central Ave
        Mansfield, OH 44905
        Contact: Natl Sales Exec
        Tel: (714) 493-4714
        Email: custservice@commercialcutting.com
        Website: www.commercialcutting.com
Design & mfr temporary point of purchase displays. (Woman, estab 1986, empl 42, sales $6,800,001, cert: WBENC)

1217   Dayton Mailing Services, Inc.
        888 Dayton St
        Yellow Springs, OH 45387
        Contact: Barbara Deer Sales Exec
        Tel: (937) 222-5056
        Email: barbara.deer@dmsink.us
        Website: www.daytonmailing.com
Digital printing, variable printing, direct mail, inserting, inkjetting, product fulfillment, collation, labeling, tipping, folding/glue. (Minority, Woman, estab , empl , sales $8,625,000, cert: State, WBENC)

1218   INNERSOURCE Inc.
        755 Wick Ave
        Youngstown, OH 44505
        Contact: Gloria Byce Principal
        Tel: (330) 799-7619
        Email: gbyce@innersourceinc.com
        Website: www.innersourceinc.com
Interior & Exterior Signage, ADA Signage, Room Identification Signage. (Woman, estab 1996, empl 7, sales , cert: WBENC)

1219   Modern Technique, LLC
        1050 Lear Industrial Pkwy
        Avon, OH 44011
        Contact: Kristi Blosser President
        Tel: (440) 497-8547
        Email: kristi@whatsyourtechnique.com
        Website: www.whatsyourtechnique.com
Advertising, digital & mobile media development, website design, SEO & email marketing, broadcast & social media planning & devel, mobile app devel & mobile marketing. (Woman, estab 2012, empl 4, sales $250,000, cert: WBENC)

1220 MRA Advertising/Production Support Services, Inc.
    3979 Erie Ave
    Cincinnati, OH 45208
    Contact: Stacey St. John Dir Business Dev
    Tel: (513) 561-5610
    Email: diversity@mraservices.com
    Website: www.mraservices.com
Advertising production management & cost control. (Minority, Woman, estab 1980, empl 25, sales $4,900,000, cert: WBENC)

1221 Skyline Exhibits of Central Ohio, LLC
    2801 Charter St
    Columbus, OH 43228
    Contact: Mark Armbrust President
    Tel: (614) 684-2050
    Email: mark@skylineohio.com
    Website: www.skylineohio.com
Exhibits, displays, kiosks, graphics, accessories & services for trade shows & events, pop ups, banner stands, portable displays, custom modular exhibits, hanging signs & structures. (Woman, estab 2001, empl 12, sales $3,108,655, cert: WBENC)

1222 Swath Design, LLC
    30 Garfield Place Ste 1020
    Cincinnati, OH 45202
    Contact: CEO
    Tel: (513) 421-1773
    Email: people@swathdesign.com
    Website: www.swathdesign.com
Environmental graphic design, wayfinding, signage, interior design, architectural design, branding, marketing & print communications & interactive media. (Woman, estab 1991, empl 6, sales , cert: State, WBENC, SDB)

1223 Vocalink, Inc.
    405 W First St
    Dayton, OH 45402
    Contact: Jill A. Mead Compliance Counsel
    Tel: (877) 492-7754
    Email: rfp@vocalinkglobal.com
    Website: www.vocalinkglobal.com/
Translation & web localization services: documentation & online content, multimedia
Linguistic asset mgmt, terminology mgmt, web content & e-commerce sites, server side scripting. (Minority, Woman, estab 1995, empl 450, sales , cert: State, NMSDC, WBENC)

1224 Xela Group, LLC dba Grupo Xela
    1775 Mentor Ave, Ste 404
    Cincinnati, OH 45212
    Contact: Jose D. Cuesta Managing Partner
    Tel: (513) 351-2200
    Email: info@grupoxela.com
    Website: www.grupoxela.com
Hispanic marketing research: questionnaire dev, focus groups, bilingual moderators, surveys, data collection & tabulation, interpreting, corporate identity, collateral design, media buying, web dev, translation svcs. (Hisp, estab 2002, empl 10, sales , cert: State)

Oregon

1225 Hanlon Brown Design
    2130 NW 29th Ave
    Portland, OR 97210
    Contact: Noma Hanlon Sr Acct Exec
    Tel: (503) 944-1000
    Email: matthew@hbdesign.com
    Website: www.hbdesign.com
Design services: print, web, interactive & catalog, graphic design, programming, software engineering, quality assurance & project management. (Woman, estab 1978, empl 25, sales $5,500,000, cert: State, WBENC)

Pennsylvania

1226 Anderson Advertising dba The Anderson Group
    879 Fritztown Rd
    Sinking Spring, PA 19608
    Contact: Julie LaSalle
    Tel: (610) 678-1506
    Email: jlasalle@theandersongrp.com
    Website: www.theandersongrp.com
Brand development & continuity programs: strategic planning, corporate identity, advertising & creative services, interactive services, media placement & public relations. (Woman, estab 1987, empl 18, sales $2,961,323, cert: State, WBENC)

1227 Communications Media, Inc.
    2200 Renaissance Blvd Ste 160
    King of Prussia, PA 19406
    Contact: Theresa Heintz Exec Dir
    Tel: (484) 322-0880
    Email: theintz@cmicompas.com
    Website: www.cmimedia.com
Media planning specializing in Healthcare media. (Minority, estab 1989, empl 40, sales $6,000,000, cert: NMSDC)

1228 ConnectedSign, LLC
    120A W Airport Rd
    Lititz, PA 17543
    Contact: Loren Bucklin President
    Tel: (866) 833-2723
    Email: lbucklin@connectedsign.com
    Website: www.connectedsign.com
Digital Signage Software, Navori Tycoon Software, Digital Signage Hardware, Digital Signage Content, Website Development and Content, Kiosks Software, Kiosks Hardware, Kiosks Content. (Woman, estab 2003, empl 12, sales $1,000,000, cert: WBENC)

1229 DMC Design
    120 Ave A
    Pittsburgh, PA 15221
    Contact: Dorothy Clark Owner
    Tel: (412) 824-7844
    Email: dmcdesign@verizon.net
    Website: www.dmcdesign.com
Design tradeshow exhibits, graphic design, print, promotional items, embroidered or silkscreened apparel. (Woman, estab 1991, empl 1, sales , cert: WBENC)

ADVERTISING

1230 Domus Inc.
Two Bala Plaza, Ste 300
Bala Cynwyd, PA 19004
Contact: Lisa Samara President
Tel: (215) 772-2800
Email: lsamara@domusinc.com
Website: www.domusinc.com/
Traditional advertising, public relations, soical media, online advertising, internal/corporate communications. (Woman, estab 1993, empl 13, sales $6,659,848, cert: WBENC)

1231 Harmelin Media
525 Righters Ferry Rd
Bala Cynwyd, PA 19004
Contact: Mary Meder President
Tel: (610) 668-7900
Email: mmeder@harmelin.com
Website: www.harmelin.com
Media planning & buying company. (Woman, estab 1982, empl 204, sales $25,000,000, cert: WBENC)

1232 Hoffmann Murtaugh Advertising, Inc.
355 Chestnut St
Sewickley, PA 15143
Contact: Adele Lawhead Controller
Tel: (412) 741-8618
Email: shea@hoffmannmurtaugh.com
Website: www.hoffmannmurtaugh.com
Media Immersion & Discovery, Discovery Worksheets, Custom Exercises, Data Mining, Competitive/Challenge Identification, Goal Setting, Brainstorming/ideation, Media Research & Insights, 1st Party Data Analysis, Nielsen Ratings, MRI. (Woman, estab 2004, empl 17, sales $2,145,000, cert: WBENC)

1233 Ideamart Inc.
232 Conestoga Rd
Wayne, PA 19087
Contact: Tom King Owner
Tel: (610) 971-2000
Email: tom@23k.com
Website: www.23k.com
Advertising, direct marketing, interactive, social media, branding/identity, packaging & retail POS. (As-Pac, estab 1991, empl 15, sales $2,185,947, cert: NMSDC)

1234 Language Services Associates
455 Business Center Dr Ste 100
Horsham, PA 19044
Contact: Jerry Lotierzo Strategic Sales Mgr
Tel: (215) 259-7000
Email: jlotierzo@lsaweb.com
Website: www.lsaweb.com
Foreign language translation & interpretation: 175 languages, sign language. (Minority, Woman, estab 1991, empl 200, sales $45,000,000, cert: NMSDC, WBENC)

1235 Media Advantage, Inc.
78 Second St Pike
Southampton, PA 18966
Contact: Adraiane Thomson President
Tel: (800) 985-5596
Email: athomson@mediaadvantage.com
Website: www.mediaadvantage.com
Sign and graphic design. (Woman, estab 2009, empl 8, sales $675,000, cert: State)

1236 Mendoza Group Inc.
3813 West Chester Pike
Newtown Square, PA 19073
Contact: Mia Mendoza CEO
Tel: (484) 445-4017
Email: mmendoza@mendozagroup.com
Website: www.mendozagroup.com
Translation, marketing & advertising agency. (Minority, Woman, estab 1995, empl 7, sales $1,984,611, cert: State, NMSDC, WBENC)

1237 MTM LinguaSoft
705 S 50th St, 2nd Fl
Philadelphia, PA 19143
Contact: Myriam Siftar President
Tel: (215) 729-6765
Email: siftar@mtmlinguasoft.com
Website: www.mtmlinguasoft.com
Translation & localization svcs: websites, software & online applications, e-learning modules, document translation & multilingual publishing services. (Woman, estab 2003, empl 5, sales $496,685, cert: WBENC)

1238 Munroe Creative Partners
121 S. Broad St. Ste 1900
Philadelphia, PA 19107
Contact:
Tel: (215) 563-8080
Email:
Website: www.munroe.com
Corporate identity launches, brochures, print and online advertising, direct mail campaigns, and web site creation. (Woman, estab 1989, empl 20, sales $2,019,757, cert: State, WBENC)

1239 NetPlus Marketing, Inc.
625 Ridge Pike, Blg E, Ste 300
Conshohocken, PA 19428
Contact: Robin Neifield CEO
Tel: (610) 897-2380
Email: rn@netplusmarketing.com
Website: www.netplusmarketing.com
Online advertising: branding & direct response objectives, sponsorships, email marketing & search engine marketing. (Woman, estab 1996, empl 18, sales , cert: WBENC)

1240 PMG, Inc.
583 Skippack Pike, Ste 200
Blue Bell, PA 19422
Contact: Peg Fitzpatrick
Tel: (215) 628-4737
Email: p.fitzpatrick@pmginc.net
Website: www.pmginc.net
Marketing & creative development, print mgmt, web development. (Woman, estab 1990, empl 8, sales $1,500,000, cert: WBENC)

1241 SSKJ Enterprises Inc. dba Vital Signs
2812 Idlewood Rd
Carnegie, PA 15106
Contact: Sandy Burkett President
Tel: (412) 494-3308
Email: sandy@vitalsignspgh.com
Website: www.VitalSignsLLC.net
Mfr interior & exterior signage, large digital format printing, promotional items, ADA signage, architectural, banners, bar code labels, business graphics, buttons, channel letters, commercial awnings, corporate identification, custom displays. (Minority, Woman, estab 2005, empl 4, sales $342,350, cert: NMSDC)

Puerto Rico

1242 Arteaga & Arteaga Advertising
PO Box 70336
San Juan, PR 00926
Contact: Juan Arteaga VP Strategy & New Business
Tel: (787) 620-1600
Email: jat@arteaga.com
Website: www.arteaga.com
Advertising, marketing, public relations, media, creative, interactive, packaging design, event planning, strategic planning, youth marketing. (Hisp, estab 1984, empl 40, sales $21,000,000, cert: NMSDC)

Rhode Island

1243 MoonRock Enterprises LLC
225 Dyer St 2nd Fl
Providence, RI 02903
Contact: Maria Prescod CEO
Tel: (401) 644-8783
Email: mariap@moonrockri.com
Website: www.moonrockri.com
Language Skills: Spanish, Portuguese and Creole (AA, estab 2020, empl 2, sales $1,200,000, cert: State)

Tennessee

1244 FlagCenter.com, LLC
4550 Summer Ave
Memphis, TN 38122
Contact: Maureen Criscuolo Owner
Tel: (901) 762-0044
Email: maureen@flagcenter.com
Website: www.flagcenter.com
Mfr custom nylon & vinyl signs, street banners, banners, flags, table covers & banners. (Woman, estab 2006, empl 6, sales $550,000, cert: State, City)

1245 nomADic genius, LLC
5049 Trousdale Dr
Nashville, TN 37220
Contact: Regis Dir of Operations
Tel: (615) 336-6678
Email: regis@nomadicgenius.com
Website: www.nomadicgenius.com
Non traditional advertising company specializing in mobile billboards and street teams. (Woman, estab 2009, empl 4, sales $400,000, cert: State, WBENC)

1246 Three Point Graphics, Inc.
750 Eaton St
Memphis, TN 38120
Contact: Sabrina Owner
Tel: (901) 537-0537
Email: sabrina@threepointgraphics.com
Website: www.3ptgraphics.com
Mission critical & complex graphic & signage products. (Woman, estab 2004, empl 1, sales $100,000,000, cert: State, City)

Texas

1247 Asher Media, Inc.
15303 Dallas Pkwy Ste 1300
Addison, TX 75001
Contact: Kalyn Asher President
Tel: (972) 732-6464
Email: kalyn@ashermedia.com
Website: www.ashermedia.com
Strategic planning & buying solutions. (Woman, estab 1999, empl 27, sales , cert: State, WBENC)

1248 B2B Enterprises Inc. dba Prism Sign Group
3645 Dallas Pkwy, Ste 535
Plano, TX 75093
Contact: Bill Brooks CEO
Tel: (972) 403-7770
Email: bbrooks@prismsigngroup.com
Website: www.prismsigngroup.com
Mfr signs: banners, vehicle wraps, advertising specialties, business cards, awards/recognition. (AA, estab 2007, empl 4, sales , cert: State, NMSDC)

1249 Blue Sun LLC
4650 Lockheed Lane, Unit 104
Denton, TX 76207
Contact: Gulnara Balic Owner
Tel: (800) 238-6064
Email: gulnara@dallasdigitalsigns.com
Website: www.dallasdigitalsigns.com
Mfr, install & repair Interior & exterior electrical signs, graphic design. (Minority, Woman, estab 2012, empl 6, sales $360,000, cert: State)

1250 Brown Graphics Inc.
11404 Chairman Dr
Dallas, TX 75243
Contact: Melanie Brown President
Tel: (214) 553-9988
Email: melanie@browngraphics.com
Website: www.browngraphics.com
Designs & mfr architectural signs: monuments, wayfinding, suite signs, cubicle, reception area, garage, directories, crown & building signage. (Woman, estab 1989, empl 8, sales $765,816, cert: State)

1251 Cartel Creativo, Inc.
5835 Callaghan Rd Ste 600
San Antonio, TX 78228
Contact: Sean Salas CEO
Tel: (210) 602-8880
Email: ssalas@thecartel.com
Website: www.thecartel.com
Advertising agency: research & planning, creative development, production & in-house audio. (Hisp, estab 1994, empl 10, sales $4,400,000, cert: NMSDC)

1252 Castle Business Solutions, LLC
2777 North Stemmons Frwy Ste 1242
Dallas, TX 75207
Contact: Sharon King CEO
Tel: (214) 599-2880
Email: sharon@castlebusinesssolutions.net
Website: www.castlebusinesssolutions.com/
Directory & mailing list publishing, direct mail advertising, packaging & labeling services, warehousing & storage. (Woman/AA, estab 2010, empl 3, sales $615,880, cert: State, NMSDC)

1253 Desert Star Enterprises, Inc
8409 Sterling St Ste B
Irving, TX 75063
Contact: Myra Brown President
Tel: (972) 915-6970
Email: myra@highvaluesigns.com
Website: www.highvaluesigns.com
Create & install signs: wayfinding signs, banners, car wraps & monument signs. (Woman, estab 2014, empl 3, sales $300,000, cert: State, WBENC)

ADVERTISING

1254 Digital Thrive, LLC
1910 Anita Dr
Austin, TX 78704
Contact: Kevin Co-Founder, CMO
Tel: (512) 900-7699
Email: kevin@digthrive.com
Website: www.digthrive.com
Graphic design & media: website design, mobile application design & development, animation & video production, print collateral & promotional materials. (Woman, estab 2010, empl 10, sales , cert: State, WBENC)

1255 DMN3
2190 North Loop W, Ste 200
Houston, TX 77018
Contact: Pamela Lockard President
Tel: (713) 868-3000
Email: accounting@dmn3.com
Website: www.dmn3.com
Direct mail & print advertising, e-marketing, multicultural marketing, event promotions, radio & TV placement, data processing & mgt, interactive & promotional mktg, outdoor media, print colateral. (Woman, estab 1985, empl 9, sales $4,267,600, cert: State, City, WBENC)

1256 Duncan/Day Advertising, LP
6513 Preston Rd Ste 200
Plano, TX 75024
Contact: Leslie Duncan COO
Tel: (469) 429-1974
Email: duncan@duncanday.com
Website: www.duncanday.com
Advertising, brand develop, copywriting, corporate identity, corporate communications, design, direct marketing, email marketing, event planning, interactive marketing, logo design & devel. (Woman, estab 1986, empl 7, sales $1,470,755, cert: WBENC)

1257 Enigma, LLC
100 Crescent Ct. Ste 700
Dallas, TX 75201
Contact: Sherilyn K Smith-Rudolph President
Tel: (214) 459-8208
Email: sherilyn@enigmallc.com
Website: www.enigmallc.com
Advertising & marketing agency. (Woman/AA, estab 2003, empl 4, sales , cert: NMSDC, 8(a))

1258 Excalibur Exhibits
7120 Brittmoore Rd, Ste 430
Houston, TX 77041
Contact: Peggy Swords President
Tel: (713) 856-8853
Email: pswords@excaliburexhibits.com
Website: www.excaliburexhibits.com
Design & build custom, portable, modular & system solutions. (Woman, estab 1997, empl 26, sales $5,628,500, cert: WBENC)

1259 Gilbreath Communications, Inc.
15995 N Barkers Landing, Ste 100 Ste 100
Houston, TX 77079
Contact: Debra Johnson VP
Tel: (281) 649-9595
Email: debra@gilbcomm.com
Website: www.gilbcomm.com
Ad campaigns, promotional materials, media relations, PR, press relations, community relations, employee communications, press conferences, press releases, press kits, speeches & scripts, graphic design, etc. (Woman/AA, estab 1990, empl 11, sales , cert: State, City, WBENC)

1260 J.O. Agency
440 S Main St
Fort Worth, TX 76104
Contact: Business Dev Mgr
Tel: (817) 335-0100
Email:
Website: www.joagency.com
Full service marketing, public relations and advertising: branding, public relations, graphic design, market research, marketing campaigns, digital marketing, etc. (Woman, estab 1998, empl 10, sales $950,825, cert: WBENC)

1261 Latinworks
410 Baylor St
Austin, TX 78703
Contact: Marly Ramstad CEO
Tel: (512) 479-6200
Email: m.ramstad@latinworks.com
Website: www.latinworks.com
Advertising agency. (Hisp, estab 1998, empl 174, sales , cert: State, NMSDC)

1262 Limb Design LLC
1702 Houston Ave
Houston, TX 77007
Contact: Partner
Tel: (713) 529-1117
Email:
Website: www.limbdesign.com
Marketing, graphic design & web site design. (Woman, estab 1983, empl 14, sales $1,600,000, cert: WBENC)

1263 LiveWell Insurance Products, Inc.
2425 Holly Hall, Ste H 106
Houston, TX 77054
Contact: Glen Reaux President
Tel: (281) 827-7909
Email: g.reaux@thenewfaceofhealthcare.com
Website: www.thenewfaceofhealthcare.com
Marketing & advertising services. (AA, estab 2013, empl 4, sales , cert: State, NMSDC)

1264 Lopez Marketing Group, Inc.
11169 La Quinta Pl
El Paso, TX 79936
Contact: Jose Luis Lopez President
Tel: (915) 772-8018
Email: jllopez1@lopezgroup.com
Website: www.lopezgroup.com
Advertising, Hispanic marketing, public relations. (Hisp, estab 1989, empl 16, sales $4,500,000, cert: State, NMSDC)

1265 Lopez Negrete Communications, Inc.
3336 Richmond Ave Ste 200
Houston, TX 77098
Contact: Alex Lopez Negrete President
Tel: (713) 877-8777
Email: alex@lopeznegrete.com
Website: www.lopeznegrete.com
Brand Leadership, Media Planning & Buying, Creative, Production, Social Media, Public Relations. (Hisp, estab 1985, empl 100, sales $14,265,000, cert: State, NMSDC, CPUC)

1266 MasterWord Services, Inc.
      303 Stafford St
      Houston, TX 77079
      Contact: Ludmila Golovine President
      Tel: (281) 589-0810
      Email: hr@masterword.com
      Website: www.masterword.com
Translation, interpretation, language training & assessments, cultural intelligence training & language compliance consulting. (Woman, estab 1993, empl 96, sales $14,620,522, cert: WBENC)

1267 Metromarketing Services Inc
      8707 Katy Freeway, Ste 100
      Houston, TX 77024
      Contact: Becky Dunn Grider
      Tel: (713) 973-7900
      Email: becky.dunn@metromkt.com
      Website: www.metromkt.com
Graphic design, promotional products & fine printing, catalogs & e-store programs. (Woman, estab 1975, empl 13, sales , cert: WBENC)

1268 One Pytchblack, LLC DBA PytchBlack
      1612 Summit Ave Ste 415
      Fort Worth, TX 76102
      Contact: Andre Yanez Owner/Managing Partner
      Tel: (817) 570-0915
      Email: aryanez@pytchblack.com
      Website: www.pytchblack.com
Advertising agency, website design, trademark and identity design, product design, media buying & graphic design. (Hisp, estab 2013, empl 2, sales $115,000, cert: State, NMSDC)

1269 Preferred Translations, Inc.
      PO Box 42065
      Houston, TX 77242
      Contact: Gina Guerrero Managing Dir
      Tel: (281) 882-3080
      Email: projects@preferredtranslationsinc.com
      Website: www.preferredTranslationsInc.com
Language Translation, Interpretation, Multilingual Desktop Publishing, Transcription, Voiceover, and subtitling. (Minority, Woman, estab 2012, empl 1, sales , cert: State)

1270 Reach Media Inc.
      13760 Noel Rd Ste 750
      Dallas, TX 75240
      Contact: Reggie Denson VP Sales
      Tel: (972) 789-1058
      Email: reggie.denson@reachmediainc.com
      Website: www.reachmediainc.com
African-American advertising for the Tom Joyner Morning Show. (AA, estab 2001, empl 92, sales $53,000,000, cert: State, NMSDC)

1271 St. Julien Communications Group, LLC
      PO Box 3724
      Houston, TX 77253
      Contact: Jaa St. Julien CEO
      Tel: (713) 965-7084
      Email: jaa@stjuliencg.com
      Website: www.stjuliencg.com
Advertising, public relations, marketing, media placement, strategy development, graphic & web design, web development, mobile app development, photography, videography consulting, community outreach. (Minority, estab 2007, empl 1, sales $196,000, cert: State, NMSDC)

1272 SuperLatina Inc.
      4200 South Frwy Ste 2370
      Fort Worth, TX 76115
      Contact: Andres Suarez CEO
      Tel: (214) 431-5783
      Email: andres@aganarmedia.com
      Website: www.aganarmedia.com
Multicultural marketing services, video & interactive campaigns for television & digital (Minority, Woman, estab 2007, empl 8, sales $787,000, cert: NMSDC)

1273 Techstyle Group LLC
      PO Box 692347
      Houston, TX 77269
      Contact: Laurel Prokop CEO
      Tel: (281) 251-2436
      Email: lp.info@techstyle.com
      Website: www.techstylegroup.com
Document, presentation & written-content production. (Woman, estab 1986, empl 5, sales , cert: City)

1274 Universal Display & Fixtures
      726 E Hwy 121
      Lewisville, TX 75057
      Contact: Michele Skene Dir Marketing
      Tel: (972) 829-2402
      Email: barbara.stoddard@udfc.com
      Website: www.udfc.com
Design & mfr displays & fixtures, components, project management, EDI, fulfillment. (Nat Ame, estab 1961, empl 200, sales $56,000,000, cert: State, NMSDC)

1275 Web-Hed Technologies, Inc. dba Webhead
      1710 N Main Ave
      San Antonio, TX 78212
      Contact: Juanita I. Gonzalez CEO
      Tel: (210) 354-1661
      Email: contracts@webheadtech.com
      Website: www.webheadtech.com
Hispanic interactive marketing svcs: media & animated graphics, online & interactive games & sweepstakes. (Minority, Woman, estab 1995, empl 15, sales , cert: State)

1276 What's the Big Idea?
      5603 Kingston Court
      Richardson, TX 75082
      Contact: Tracy Cink President
      Tel: (972) 509-0081
      Email: tracy_cink@wtbi.com
      Website: www.wtbi.com
Advertising & graphic design. (Woman, estab , empl 5, sales , cert: WBENC)

Utah

1277 Infinite Scale Design Group
      16 Exchange Place
      Salt Lake City, UT 84111
      Contact: Molly Mazzolini Managing Member
      Tel: (801) 363-1881
      Email: molly@infinitescale.com
      Website: www.infinitescale.com
Brand strategy, logo design, creative briefs, identity systems, collateral, website design, environmental graphics, master plan, interpretive design, wayfinding signage, recognition & donor, signage, uniform systems, vehicle graphics. (Woman, estab , empl , sales , cert: State)

ADVERTISING

1278 U.S. Translation Company
      320 W 200 S
      Salt Lake City, UT 84101
      Contact: Kathy Sprouse Dir of Operations
      Tel: (801) 393-5300
      Email: kathy@ustranslation.com
      Website: www.ustranslation.com
Language services, document formatting, interpreting services. (Hisp, estab 1995, empl 15, sales $2,987,864, cert: NMSDC)

Virginia

1279 AAA Ventures LLC
      2811 Tipton St
      Colonial Heights, VA 23834
      Contact: Anthony Mijares Owner
      Tel: (804) 586-4513
      Email: rvablueprint@gmail.com
      Website: www.blueprintrva.com
Digital prints, Social media marketing, Custom Signs, Car Decals, Store Front Decals, Channel lettering, Sign Lighting install and maintenance, Screen printing, Embroiderer, Signage, Decals, Paper Prints, Vehicle Wraps, Promotion Products. (Hisp, estab 2013, empl 5, sales , cert: State)

1280 AB Design, Inc.
      10005 Stonemill Rd
      Richmond, VA 23233
      Contact: Gladys Brenner President
      Tel: (804) 346-4771
      Email: gbrenner@abdesignonline.com
      Website: www.abdesignonline.com
Environmental graphic design: interior & exterior signage, dev wayfinding systems & architectural graphics, site analysis/evaluation, master planning & comprehensive wayfinding systems. (Woman/Hisp, estab 1991, empl 3, sales $182,000, cert: State)

1281 Advanta Pacific International
      9336 Braymore Circle
      Fairfax Station, VA 22039
      Contact: Adam Tran Managing Dir
      Tel: (703) 226-9605
      Email: contact@vernacularlanguage.com
      Website: www.vernacularlanguage.com
Translation & interpretation services in over 200 languages and dialects, including sign language. (Woman/As-Pac, estab 2009, empl 4, sales $150,000, cert: State)

1282 Capital Exhibits
      8245-B Backlick Rd
      Lorton, VA 22079
      Contact: Jennifer Warren Sales
      Tel: (540) 219-9372
      Email: jennifer@capitalexhibits.com
      Website: www.capitalexhibits.com
Indoor & outdoor signage, tradeshow displays, banners & banner stands, channel lettering, wayfinding & directional signage, temporary signage, hard or thick signage, custom flirting titles, fabric & vinyl signs. (As-Ind, estab 1994, empl 6, sales , cert: State)

1283 Eighth Day Design
      7653 Leesburg Pike
      Falls Church, VA 22043
      Contact: Carol Muszynski President
      Tel: (703) 562-3636
      Email: info@eighthday.com
      Website: www.eighthday.com
Productivity & image solutions, architecture & design, programming, space planning, design dev, sustainable design, exhibit design, construction documents, construction administration, move coordination & facilities maintenance support. (Woman, estab 1989, empl 25, sales $3,800,000, cert: WBENC)

1284 Hybrid Studios LLC
      1940 Duke St Ste 200
      Alexandria, VA 22314
      Contact: Susan Yates Mgr
      Tel: (703) 671-6975
      Email: susan@hybrid-studios.com
      Website: www.hybriddc.com
Communications solutions: print, interactive development, advertising, corporate identity, direct marketing & social media marketing services. (Woman, estab 2002, empl 2, sales $532,000, cert: State)

1285 Mail Call Direct LLC
      5616 Eastport Blvd
      Henrico, VA 23231
      Contact: Lisa Jacoby Co-Owner
      Tel: (804) 222-0608
      Email: lisa@mailcalldirect.com
      Website: www.MailCallDirect.com
Direct mail services, digital lasering, inkjet & insert, data processing, mailing lists, barcode printing, variable data, stamping, metering, permits, hand fulfillment, parcel fulfillment, folding bindery services, glue dotting, poly bagging. (Woman, estab 2014, empl 8, sales , cert: State)

1286 Nvision Media Group, LLC
      114 W Hicks St
      Lawrenceville, VA 23868
      Contact: David Fant Owner
      Tel: (866) 848-8822
      Email: david.fant@nvisn.net
      Website: www.nvisn.net
Indoor advertising. (Woman/AA, estab 2006, empl 6, sales $100,000, cert: State)

1287 Tandem By Design LLC
      306 N 26th St, Ste 227
      Richmond, VA 23223
      Contact: Bev Gray President
      Tel: (804) 239-2539
      Email: bev@tandembydesign.com
      Website: www.tandembydesign.com
Marketing & advertising solutions, one-to-one marketing, B2B sales collateral, B2C POP/POS, packaging design, corporate communications, corporate & brand videos, grassroots campaigns, social media. (Woman, estab 2012, empl 1, sales , cert: State)

1288 Trusted Translations, Inc.
      108 N Virginia Ave
      Falls Church, VA 22046
      Contact: Diversity Manager Acct Mgr
      Tel: (877) 255-0717
      Email: mbe@trustedtranslations.com
      Website: www.trustedtranslations.com
English to Spanish translation agency. (Hisp, estab 2003, empl 10, sales $2,400,000, cert: City)

1289 West Cary Group
      5 W Cary St
      Richmond, VA 23220
      Contact: Moses Foster CEO
      Tel: (804) 343-2029
      Email: mfoster@westcarygroup.com
      Website: www.westcarygroup.com
Marketing communications & advertising. (AA, estab 2007, empl 20, sales $2,586,876, cert: State, NMSDC)

Washington

1290 Dynamic Language
      15215 52nd Ave S, Ste 100
      Seattle, WA 98188
      Contact: Rick Antezana Partner
      Tel: (206) 244-6709
      Email: rick@dynamiclanguage.com
      Website: www.dynamiclanguage.com
Foreign language translation, desktop publishing services, narration, language & ASL interpreting services. (Minority, Woman, estab 1985, empl 50, sales $10,155,200, cert: NMSDC)

1291 TDW+Co
      92 Lenora St #888
      Seattle, WA 98121
      Contact: Tim Wang Principal
      Tel: (206) 623-6888
      Email: biz@tdwandco.com
      Website: www.tdwandco.com
Marketing communications & advertising agency. (As-Pac, estab 2004, empl 25, sales $10,015,295, cert: State, NMSDC, CPUC)

1292 The Garrigan Lyman Group
      1524 Fifth Ave
      Seattle, WA 98101
      Contact: Jean Zartman Mgr Business Devel
      Tel: (206) 223-5548
      Email: jean.zartman@glg.com
      Website: www.glg.com
Brand & interactive strategic insight, creative vision & technology-forward solutions. (Woman, estab 1993, empl 65, sales , cert: WBENC)

1293 Thinking Cap Communications & Design
      9 S Washington Ste 201
      Spokane, WA 99201
      Contact: Marvin Reguindin President
      Tel: (509) 747-4930
      Email: marvo@tcapdesign.com
      Website: www.tcapdesign.com
Advertising & graphic design, creative & account services, websites, radio & TV/video spots. (As-Pac, estab 1995, empl 3, sales $124,753, cert: State, NMSDC)

1294 Translation Solutions Corp.
      1201 Pacific Ave Corp Ste 600
      Tacoma, WA 98402
      Contact: Rosa Capdevielle Project Management
      Tel: (808) 404-1270
      Email: rosa@translationsolutions.org
      Website: www.translationsolutions.org
Translations & interpretation services. (Minority, Woman, estab 1994, empl 5, sales , cert: State, NMSDC)

1295 Trio Northwest Business Solutions, Inc.
      239 SW 41st St
      Renton, WA 98057
      Contact: Jeffrey Quint EVP Sales & Mktg
      Tel: (206) 728-8181
      Email: info@triogroupnw.com
      Website: www.triogroupnw.com/
Brand management, advertising, marketing, strategy, campaign development, project management, marcom strategy, web development, mobile app development, media buying, social media strategy & deployment. (Nat Ame, estab 2000, empl 6, sales $1,300,000, cert: NMSDC)

1296 Worktank Enterprises, LLC
      400 E Pine St, Ste 301
      Seattle, WA 98122
      Contact: Leslie Rugaber CEO
      Tel: (206) 658-2555
      Email: leslie@worktankseattle.com
      Website: www.worktankseattle.com
Media strategy & production: integrated media & marketing campaigns, video & film production, CD, DVD & web content production, software & product demos, webcast management & production staffing services. (Woman, estab 2001, empl 10, sales , cert: WBENC)

1297 Everbrite, LLC
      4949 S 110th St
      Greenfield, WI 53228
      Contact: Nicki LaFrance Sales Admin
      Tel: (414) 529-3500
      Email: supplierdiversity@everbrite.com
      Website: www.everbrite.com
Outdoor illuminated identification signage. (Woman, estab 1927, empl 850, sales , cert: WBENC)

1298 Revelation, LLC
      222 N Midvale Blvd Ste 18
      Madison, WI 53705
      Contact: Brian Lee President
      Tel: (608) 622-7767
      Email: brian@experiencerevelation.com
      Website: www.experiencerevelation.com
Public relations, media buying, ad buying, advertising, social media consulting, internet marketing, web marketing & speaking engagements. (As-Pac, estab 2010, empl 3, sales $170,000, cert: NMSDC)

1299 The Geo Group
      6 Odana Court
      Madison, WI 53719
      Contact: Georgia Roeming President
      Tel: (608) 230-1000
      Email: georgia.roeming@thegeogroup.com
      Website: www.thegeogroup.com
Translation of radio, TV, website & print advertising. (Woman, estab 1991, empl 20, sales , cert: WBENC)

> **ADVERTISING SPECIALTIES**
> Supply advertising specialties, premium and promotional products, or travel incentives. Includes frims which do silkscreening and embroidery on various products. NAICS Code 42

Alabama

1300 Concepts & Associates
105 19th St S
Birmingham, AL 35210
Contact: Tim Hennessy President
Tel: 205-870-1111
Email: tim@conceptsusa.com
Website: www.conceptsusa.com
Corporate gifts & promotional products, embroidery & fulfillment center. (Woman, estab 1983, empl 15, sales , cert: State, WBENC)

1301 LogoBranders Inc.
1161 Lagoon Business Loop
Montgomery, AL 36117
Contact: Dean Flynn Branding Specialist
Tel: 334-277-1144
Email: dean@logobranders.com
Website: www.logobranders.biz/
Promotional items, executive gifts, embroidery, screen print, hardline, health and safety, computer and electronic products, wearables, bags, writing instruments, drinkwear, desk/office business accessories, calenders, person products, etc. (Woman, estab 1993, empl 34, sales $6,000,000, cert: WBENC)

Arizona

1302 Everyone Loves Buttons Inc.
24825 N 16th Ave Ste 100
Phoenix, AZ 85085
Contact: Maura Statman President
Tel: 623-445-9975
Email: maura@elbusa.com
Website: www.custombuttons.com
Promotional products, buttons. (Woman, estab 1997, empl 12, sales $1,350,000, cert: WBENC)

1303 Six Twenty Six, LLC.
12751 N 89th St
Scottsdale, AZ 85260
Contact: Michele Cochran Owner
Tel: 615-499-4228
Email: michele@sixtwentysix.net
Website: www.sixtwentysix.net
Promotional products & branding solutions. (Woman, estab 2005, empl 1, sales $506,489, cert: CPUC, WBENC)

California

1304 American Casuals
19827 Hamilton Ave.
Torrance, CA 90502
Contact: Peter Newhouse President
Tel: 714-630-2002
Email: petern@american-casuals.com
Website: www.american-casual.com
Mfr & dist promotional merchandise, head wear, apparel & hard goods. (Woman/As-Pac, estab 2004, empl 10, sales $5,000,000, cert: NMSDC, WBENC)

1305 Apropos Promotions
1401 N Broadway Ste 280
Walnut Creek, CA 94596
Contact: Ann Auelmann President
Tel: 925-274-5700
Email: ann@apropospromotions.com
Website: www.apropospromotions.com
Promotional merchandise: tradeshow giveaways, staff appreciation, gifts, special events, etc. (Woman, estab 2002, empl 4, sales , cert: WBENC)

1306 Avid Promotions
499 Nibus St Unit C
Brea, CA 92821
Contact: Dena Gibbs CEO
Tel: 949-387-9890
Email: dena@avidpromotions.com
Website: www.AvidPromotions.com
Promotional products, marketing materials, and apparel/corporate uniforms. (Hisp, estab 2009, empl 4, sales $540,000, cert: NMSDC, CPUC)

1307 Beyond Zebra Inc.
1443 E Washington Blvd, Ste 641
Pasadena, CA 91104
Contact: CFO
Tel: 818-435-8202
Email: info@beyondzebra.net
Website: www.beyondzebra.net
Promotional products: bags, desk accessories, apparel, hats, memo pads, housewares, sales incentive & corporate gift programs. (Minority, Woman, estab 2000, empl 4, sales $1,043,151, cert: WBENC)

1308 Caden Concepts
13412 Ventura Blvd #300
Sherman Oaks, CA 91423
Contact: Katie Llanos Acct Dir
Tel: 707-486-6017
Email: annie@cadenconcepts.com
Website: www.cadenconcepts.com
Dist advertising specialties: logoed corporate wearables, giveaways, incentives, employee awards & tradeshow projects, embroidery silk screen & pad printing. (Woman, estab 1998, empl 10, sales $12,000,000, cert: CPUC, WBENC)

1309 Elementi Designs
1655 22nd Ave
San Francisco, CA 94122
Contact: Ken Lou President
Tel: 415-887-3889
Email: elementidesigns@gmail.com
Website: www.elementidesigns.com
Corporate promotional items, apparel & printing, fashion jewelry & accessories, wedding party supplies, gift items, home decor products & car assortments. (Minority, Woman, estab 2004, empl 5, sales $194,902, cert: CPUC)

1310 Ellen's Silkscreening, Inc.
1500 Mission St
South Pasadena, CA 91030
Contact: Ellen Daigle President
Tel: 626-441-4415
Email: info@ellenssilkscreening.com
Website: www.ellenssilkscreening.com
Screen printed & embroidered goods & promotional products. (Woman, estab 1978, empl 15, sales $2,087,125, cert: WBENC)

ADVERTISING SPECIALTIES

1311 Gorilla Marketing
 4100 Flat Rock Dr, Ste A
 Riverside, CA 92505
 Contact: Chris Arranga CEO
 Tel: 951-353-8133
 Email: chris@gorillamarketing.net
 Website: www.gorillamarketing.net
Imprinted promotional products, advertising specialties. (Hisp, estab 1985, empl 10, sales $1,700,000, cert: NMSDC)

1312 Infocus Specialties, Inc.
 1655 Hauser Circle
 Thousand Oaks, CA 91362
 Contact: Steve Leo Co-Owner
 Tel: 805-379-9192
 Email: steve@infocusspecialties.com
 Website: www.infocusspecialties.com
Promotional and advertising impressions. (Woman, estab 2013, empl 2, sales $720,000, cert: WBENC)

1313 Intention Advertising
 2995 Bonnie Lane
 Pleasant Hill, CA 94523
 Contact: Mara Villa Owner
 Tel: 925-274-1774
 Email: mara@intentionadvertising.com
 Website: www.intentionadvertising.com
Promotional products, t-shirts to pens, etc. (Woman, estab 2011, empl 1, sales $400,000, cert: State)

1314 Janco & Winnex Inc
 3018 Durfee Ave, Ste E
 El Monte, CA 91732
 Contact: Jennifer Renshaw President
 Tel: 626-454-4882
 Email: jenniferjan@yahoo.com
 Website: www.jancoline.com
Dist folding chairs, promotional stationery & bags. (Minority, Woman, estab 1996, empl 9, sales , cert: State, 8(a))

1315 JLT Promotions Inc.
 24238 Hawthorne Blvd
 Torrance, CA 90505
 Contact: John Tulchin CFO
 Tel: 310-791-7006
 Email: jtulchin@thepromotionsdept.com
 Website: www.instadiumpromotions.com
Sports & team promotional items & stadium giveaways. (Woman, estab 1990, empl 10, sales $5,700,000, cert: State, CPUC)

1316 J-n-K Services, Inc.
 9350 Oso Ave
 Chatsworth, CA 91311
 Contact: Jave Tripp CEO
 Tel: 818-505-8155
 Email: jave@jnkservices.com
 Website: www.jnkservices.com
Promotional Items (Pens, Mugs, Lanyards) Wearables (Shirts/Hats/Polos) Banners Backdrops. (Hisp, estab 1988, empl 5, sales $1,202,156, cert: NMSDC)

1317 KV & Associates, LLC
 5694 Mission Center Rd, Ste 357
 San Diego, CA 92108
 Contact: Kathy Valadez President
 Tel: 858-277-7036
 Email: info@kvapromotions.com
 Website: www.KVAPromotions.com
Promotional & merchandise. (Minority, Woman, estab 2000, empl 1, sales $640,500, cert: NMSDC, WBENC, SDB)

1318 Laughing Willow, Inc.
 1110 Quintana Rd
 Morro Bay, CA 93442
 Contact: Elizabeth Espy CEO
 Tel: 805-772-4770
 Email: liz@doghousepromotions.com
 Website: www.doghousepromotions.com
Advertising specialty, apparel, awards, bags, banners, brand names, conventions, corporate gifts, custom merchandise, drink ware, eco-friendly, embroidery, gift baskets, headwear, hospitality, incentive programs. (Woman, estab 1998, empl 4, sales $2,029,491, cert: WBENC)

1319 Lexicon Promo
 1281 Ninth Ave, Unit 2004
 San Diego, CA 92101
 Contact: Brandon Christopher CEO
 Tel: 760-681-8248
 Email: jbsc@trylexicon.com
 Website: www.trylexicon.com
Carbon neutral, full-service print and promo (swag) agency with capabilities of fulfilling orders of any size from 100 quantity to 100,000 quantity. (AA, estab 2019, empl 1, sales $315,000, cert: NMSDC)

1320 Macro Industries, Inc
 5595 Daniels St Ste F
 Chino, CA 91710
 Contact: Cynthia Phillips Marketing Mgr
 Tel: 909-364-8100
 Email: sales106@goldensundirect.com
 Website: www.3cfactory.com
Dist safety vests, safety t-shirts, safety jackets, ANSI/ISEA 107-2004 Class 2, Class 3, gloves, caps, hats, uniforms, bags, backpacks, tote bags, custom-made orders, imprint, embroidery. (As-Pac, estab 2001, empl 7, sales $1,020,000, cert: CPUC)

1321 Matel Manufacturing Inc.
 13205 Estrella Ave Unit A
 Gardena, CA 90248
 Contact: Nagendra Bolla President
 Tel: 310-217-9111
 Email: bobbolla@matelinc.com
 Website: www.matelinc.com
Leather & Metal desk accessories, letter trays, form holders, business cards, desk pads, pen sets, bill holders, book ends, memo boxes, coasters & conference pads. (As-Ind, estab 1985, empl 7, sales $720,000, cert: CPUC)

1322 O2 Marketing & Design, Inc.
 367 Civic Dr Ste 15
 Pleasant Hill, CA 94523
 Contact: Sabina Rica Treasurer
 Tel: 510-553-0202
 Email: sabina@o2marketing.com
 Website: www.O2MARKETING.COM
promotional products: tradeshow giveaways, corporate branding, employee incentive programs, awards. (Woman/As-Ind, estab 2000, empl 8, sales , cert: CPUC, WBENC)

1323 PMP Products Inc.
      1210 W Jon St, Ste B
      Torrance, CA 90502
      Contact: Peter Newhouse President
      Tel: 310-547-8064
      Email: petern@american-casuals.com
      Website: www.american-casuals.com
Promotional products, apparel (soft goods) headwear, hard goods. (Minority, Woman, estab 2003, empl 10, sales , cert: NMSDC, WBENC)

1324 Premium Resource
      5460B Lincoln Way
      Felton, CA 09018
      Contact: Andrea Casella CEO
      Tel: 408-777-0711
      Email: andrea@premiumresource.com
      Website: www.premiumresource.com
Full-service advertising specialties & promotional items. (Minority, Woman, estab 2001, empl 2, sales , cert: CPUC)

1325 Red Cloud LLC
      1600 Sawtelle Blvd, Ste 108
      Los Angeles, CA 90025
      Contact: Denise Lyons Controller
      Tel: 310-444-5583
      Email: denise@redcloudllc.com
      Website: www.redcloudpromotions.com
Promotional products, advertising specialties. (Woman, estab 2005, empl 10, sales , cert: WBENC)

1326 Seba International
      1210 W Jon St
      Torrance, CA 90502
      Contact: Mariah M. Qian CEO
      Tel: 310-549-5122
      Email: seba@globalxlr.com
      Website: www.sebaintl.com
Promotional items: sports Jerseys, shirts, jackets, sweatshirts, caps & hats. (Minority, Woman, estab 2013, empl 8, sales $5,171,671, cert: NMSDC)

1327 Sun Coast Merchandise Corporation
      6315 Bandini Blvd
      Los Angeles, CA 90040
      Contact: Dilip Bhavnani President
      Tel: 800-432-4274
      Email: dilip@sunscopeusa.com
      Website: www.sunscopeusa.com
Promotional products. (As-Pac, estab 1943, empl 48, sales $108,000,000, cert: NMSDC)

1328 The Corporate Gift Service, Inc.
      4120 W Burbank Blvd
      Burbank, CA 91505
      Contact: Lydia Eltringham Accounting Dept
      Tel: 818-845-9500
      Email: accounting@corpgiftservice.com
      Website: www.thecorporategiftservice.com
Handmade Custom Gift Baskets, Embroidered Corporate Apparel, High End Corporate Gifts, Branded Promotional Products & Advertising Specialties. (Woman, estab 1990, empl 7, sales $1,600,000, cert: WBENC)

1329 TSG Direct LLC
      20992 Avenida Amapola
      Lake Forest, CA 92630
      Contact: Gregg Moschides Dir of Sales
      Tel: 650-224-9146
      Email: gmoschides@tsgdirectllc.com
      Website: www.tsgdirectllc.com
Print, direct mail & fulfillment services, promotional products, branded apparel, uniforms & office supplies. (Woman, estab 2014, empl 5, sales , cert: State, CPUC)

1330 Wearable Imaging, Inc.
      26741 Portola Pkwy Ste 1E, 608
      Foothill Ranch, CA 92610
      Contact: Robin Richter President
      Tel: 949-888-7837
      Email: robin@wearableimaging.com
      Website: www.wearableimaging.com
Screenprinting & embroidered apparel: t-shirts, polo's, hats & caps, pens, travel mugs, etc. (Minority, Woman, estab 1992, empl 5, sales $941,828, cert: CPUC, WBENC)

Colorado

1331 AC Flag & Banner, Inc.
      11616 Shaffer Pl Unit S-103
      Littleton, CO 80127
      Contact: Wendy Willson President
      Tel: 303-948-9774
      Email: wendy@acflag.com
      Website: www.acflagandbanner.com
Custom logo flags & banners. (Woman, estab 2004, empl 4, sales $225,000, cert: WBENC)

1332 Artistic Promotions
      2168 S Birch St
      Denver, CO 80222
      Contact: Radhika Hess Sales Assoc
      Tel: 303-759-5559
      Email: sharon@artisticpromo.com
      Website: www.artisticpromo.com
Advertising specialties: marketing programs, promotional products, logo apparel, incentive & safety programs, events items, trade shows, corporate awards. (Woman, estab 1991, empl 4, sales , cert: WBENC)

Connecticut

1333 Church Hill Classics
      594 Pepper St
      Monroe, CT 06468
      Contact: Sales & Marketing Rep
      Tel: 800-477-9005
      Email: info@diplomaframe.com
      Website: www.diplomaframe.com
Corporate frames & gifts: custom designed insignias awards, recognition certificates & events. (Woman, estab 1991, empl 73, sales , cert: WBENC)

1334 GBG The Corporate Gift Source, Inc.
      204 Spring Hill Rd
      Trumbull, CT 06611
      Contact: Charlotte O'Banion President
      Tel: 203-459-4424
      Email: charlotte@gbginc.com
      Website: www.gbginc.com
Promotional products, logo apparel, warehousing, fulfillment svcs, employee award redemption programs, premiums & sales incentives. (Minority, Woman, estab 1987, empl 6, sales $3,700,000, cert: NMSDC)

1335 John Michael Associates, Inc.
      94 Holmes Rd
      Newington, CT 06111
      Contact: Paul Sposito Exec VP
      Tel: 860-666-1414
      Email: paul@jmalogos.com
      Website: www.jmalogos.com
Logo apparel & merchandise, corporate online stores, awards, recognition & loyalty programs, fulfillment, event, incentive & sales marketing, importing, trade shows & fundraisers, kitting, collating & custom packaging, creative services. (Woman, estab 1980, empl 27, sales $12,000,000, cert: State, WBENC)

1336 Preferred Promotions, LLC
      1801 Berlin Turnpike
      Berlin, CT 06037
      Contact: Dottie Nelson Owner
      Tel: 860-829-1317
      Email: dnelson@preferredpromo.com
      Website: www.preferredpromos.com
Promotional products: imprinted wearables, engraved awards.. (Minority, Woman, estab 2003, empl 5, sales $725,000, cert: State)

1337 Stay Visible, LLC
      1 Pinewood Dr
      New Fairfield, CT 06812
      Contact: Theresa Gonzalez President
      Tel: 203-746-2111
      Email: theresa@stayvisible.com
      Website: www.stayvisible.com
Promotional products, Direct mail and fulfillment services; Design and print services; Custom packaging. (Woman, estab 2000, empl 1, sales , cert: State, WBENC)

District of Columbia

1338 The Hamilton Group
      4406 Gault Place NE
      Washington, DC 20019
      Contact: Kaari Hamilton President
      Tel: 202-689-4304
      Email: kayhhpbp@verizon.net
      Website: www.thehamiltongroupllc.net
Dist office supplies, advertisement & promotional products, office equipment & clothing wearables. (Woman/AA, estab 2007, empl 1, sales $731,000, cert: City, NMSDC, WBENC)

Delaware

1339 Promo Victory, Inc.
      4142 Ogletown-Stanton Rd, Ste 238
      Newark, DE 19713
      Contact: Vicki Lam President
      Tel: 800-385-7573
      Email: vlam@promovictory.com
      Website: www.promovictory.com
Promotional products. (Minority, Woman, estab 2008, empl 1, sales , cert: State, WBENC)

Florida

1340 Ad Specs of Delaware,LLC d/b/a Levy Recognition
      2415 N Albany Ave, Unit 1
      Tampa, FL 33607
      Contact: Michele Adams President
      Tel: 813-868-3923
      Email: michele.adams@levyrecognition.com
      Website: www.levyrecognition.com
Mfr medals, medallions & emblematic jewelry, custom design awards, promotional products, branded apparell & business gifts. (Woman, estab 1960, empl 38, sales $4,000,000, cert: WBENC)

1341 Ad Specs of Florida, LLC
      2415 N Albany Ave Unit 1
      Tampa, FL 33607
      Contact: Michele Adams President
      Tel: 716-553-1655
      Email: michele.adams@proforma.com
      Website: www.proformaglobalsourcing.com
Print & promotional products. (Woman, estab 2005, empl 5, sales $17,334,000, cert: WBENC)

1342 American Traders Enterprises, Inc.
      2900 Glades Circle, Ste 1250
      Weston, FL 33327
      Contact: Josie Musch President
      Tel: 954-888-9206
      Email: josie@americantraders.com
      Website: www.americantraders.com
Promotional products. (Woman/Hisp, estab 1996, empl 6, sales , cert: NMSDC)

1343 American Trading International Co, LLC
      13866 SW 256 Terr
      Homestead, FL 33032
      Contact: Juan Penso Owner
      Tel: 813-810-1610
      Email: sales@atipromotions.com
      Website: www.atipromotions.com
Promotional products, gifts, awards, souvenirs, business cards, advertising specialties. (Hisp, estab 2007, empl 1, sales , cert: State, NMSDC)

1344 Bilmor with Advertising Specialties Inc.
      16155 SW 117th Ave, Unit B-19
      Miami, FL 33177
      Contact: Andrew Headley Dir
      Tel: 305-232-3323
      Email: support@bilmoradv.com
      Website: www.bilmoradv.com
Dist promotional items: custom embroidery, heat transfers, pad printing, hot stamping, awards & recognition gifts. (AA, estab 1985, empl 4, sales $614,000, cert: State)

1345 CottonImages.com, Inc.
      10481 NW 28th St
      Miami, FL 33172
      Contact: Scott Hertzbach CEO
      Tel: 305-251-2560
      Email: scott@cottonimages.com
      Website: www.cottonimages.com
Embroidered garments, imprinted mugs, umbrellas & promotional products. (Woman, estab 1989, empl 85, sales $6,700,000, cert: WBENC)

1346 Design & Promotions Corp.
      12333 SW 132nd Ct
      Miami, FL 33186
      Contact: Vicente Buraglia President
      Tel: 305-232-8119
      Email: service@design-promotions.com
      Website: www.design-promotions.com
Custom promotional products, custom packaging, custom displays, P.O.P. material, graphic design. (Hisp, estab 1990, empl 4, sales , cert: NMSDC)

1347 Entertainment Retail Enterprises, LLC
      2437 E LandSt Rd
      Orlando, FL 32824
      Contact: Melinda Wenderlein Dir of Finance
      Tel: 407-649-6552
      Email: melinda@ere-sri.com
      Website: www.ere-sri.com
CAT workwear, menswear, thermos, lunch bags, mugs (Woman, estab 2008, empl 102, sales $45,000,000, cert: WBENC)

1348 Gossett Marketing
      3701 Poinciana Ave
      Coconut Grove, FL 33133
      Contact: President
      Tel: 305-443-1332
      Email: danette@gossettmktg.com
      Website: www.gossettmktg.com
Promotional products, awards, corporate apparel, banners, trade show booths, POP, creative design, direct mail, advertising. (Woman, estab 1992, empl 4, sales , cert: WBENC)

1349 I Love Promos, Inc.
      6627 NW 25th Way Ste 100
      Boca Raton, FL 33496
      Contact: Mary Turel SVP
      Tel: 866-546-7001
      Email: mary@ilovepromos.com
      Website: www.ilovepromos.com
Promotional products, apparel, writing instruments, eco-friendly items. (Minority, Woman, estab 2013, empl 2, sales $3,200,000, cert: WBENC)

1350 Ingage, LLC
      1395 Black Willow Trail
      Altamonte, FL 32714
      Contact: Lisa Marcheskie CEO
      Tel: 407-521-7777
      Email: info@ingageincentives.com
      Website: www.ingageincentives.com
Recognition Incentives and Promotional Products. (Woman, estab 2012, empl 25, sales $15,000,000, cert: State, WBENC)

1351 Jamapchi LLC
      13885 SW 151ST Ln
      Miami, FL 33186
      Contact: Pamela Chin Managing Dir
      Tel: 786-708-9623
      Email: pam@jamapchi.com
      Website: www.her-mine.com
Corporate gifting items for retirement, appreciation, on-boarding and women self-care gift boxes for personal care and well being. We also supply school items and toys for children ages 4 through 12. (AA, estab 2015, empl 5, sales $193,000, cert: State, City)

1352 JT Promotions
      4378 LB Mcleod Rd
      orlando, FL 32811
      Contact: James Stillwell Owner
      Tel: 407-730-7990
      Email: info@aclipsemarketing.net
      Website: www.aclipsemarketing.net
Embroidery, silk screening, promotional & novelty items, event planning & execution. (AA, estab 2003, empl 4, sales $250,000, cert: NMSDC)

1353 Merchandise Partners
      11111 N 46th St
      Tampa, FL 33617
      Contact: Wendy Knapp
      Tel: 404-460-7190
      Email: wendy@merchandisepartners.com
      Website: www.merchandisepartners.com
Corporate promotions, merchandising solutions, retail programs, sponsorship promotions, sales promotions, dealer networks, web stores. (Hisp, estab 2006, empl 6, sales $35,000,000, cert: NMSDC)

1354 MH Specialties LLC
      9896 White Sands Place
      Bonita Springs, FL 34135
      Contact: Tondalaya (Mike) Herbert CEO
      Tel: 313-268-5907
      Email: mike@mhspecialties.com
      Website: www.mhspecialties.com
Rewards & Recognition, wall/desk custom designed plaques, recognition jewelry, awards rings & promotional jewelry, premium incentives gifts for Safety Programs & Training, employees recognition awards, corporate awards/gifts. (Woman, estab 2002, empl 1, sales $300,000, cert: WBENC)

1355 Rimco Marketing Products, Inc.
      6344 All American Blvd
      Orlando, FL 32810
      Contact: Connie Jones President
      Tel: 407-290-0883
      Email: connie@rimcoinc.com
      Website: www.rimcoinc.com
Custom packaging: binders, tabs, boxes, folding cartons, bags, totes, mailers, portfolios & bound books, briefcases, menus, guest service directories, gifts, incentives & promotional products, fulfillment, warehousing & shipping. (Woman, estab 1984, empl 8, sales $4,600,000, cert: WBENC)

1356 SpringboardPC
      4517 W. Dale Ave
      Tampa, FL 33609
      Contact: Wendy Pepe President
      Tel: 813-918-0371
      Email: wendy@springboardpc.com
      Website: www.springboardpc.com
Advertising promotional products. (Woman, estab 1992, empl 5, sales $2,400,000, cert: State, City, WBENC)

1357 Tampa T-Shirts
      5112 N 22nd St
      Tampa, FL 33610
      Contact: Juan Davis Mgr
      Tel: 813-879-3298
      Email: juan@fastlaneclothing.com
      Website: www.fastlaneclothing.com
Apparel, logo shirts, lab coats, promotional items. (Minority, Woman, estab 1985, empl 19, sales $1,480,000, cert: State, City)

1358 The Olab Group, LLC
      501 E Las Olas Blvd Ste 300
      Fort Lauderdale, FL 33301
      Contact: Keel Russell CEO
      Tel: 866-606-1110
      Email: info@orangelmg.com
      Website: www.orangelabmedia.com
Branded merchandise fulfillment services, promotional products, branded apparel, corporate gifts & awards, employee incentive programs, and global sourcing & logistics. (AA, estab 2015, empl 10, sales $1,575,432, cert: NMSDC)

1359 Think Tank Studio
      626 Lakeview Rd, Ste A
      Clearwater, FL 33756
      Contact: Marlies Schoenau President
      Tel: 727-441-4488
      Email: mus@thinktankstudio.com
      Website: www.thinktankstudio.com
Promotional marketing services, logo apparel, hats, drink ware, office items, pens, bags, awards, signage, trade-show hand-outs. (Woman, estab 1998, empl 7, sales $1,487,596, cert: WBENC)

1360 Underground Graphics Inc.
      13355 Belcher Rd S Unit H
      Largo, FL 33773
      Contact: Grace Newcomer President
      Tel: 727-535-9582
      Email: grace@undergroundgraphics.us
      Website: www.undergroundgraphics.us
Promotional products: pens, mugs, keychains etc. (Woman, estab 1993, empl 4, sales $165,000, cert: State)

1361 Wendt Productions Inc.
      17301 Solie Rd
      Odessa, FL 33556
      Contact: Susan Wendt President
      Tel: 813-920-5000
      Email: swendt@wendtpro.com
      Website: www.wendtpro.com
Advertising, marketing & promotional products. (Woman, estab 1986, empl 9, sales $1,450,000, cert: State, City)

1362 Y-Not Design & Mfg. Inc.
      1041 E 24th St
      Hialeah, FL 33013
      Contact: Angelina Garcia CEO
      Tel: 855-843-1422
      Email: contactus@y-not.com
      Website: www.y-not.com/
Promotional & gifts products. (Minority, Woman, estab 2005, empl 61, sales $86,000,000, cert: NMSDC, WBENC)

Georgia

1363 Accolades, Inc.
      3081 Holcomb Bridge Rd, Ste C-1
      Norcross, GA 30071
      Contact: Daryll Griffin President
      Tel: 770-449-8568
      Email: dgriffin@accolades-inc.com
      Website: www.accolades-inc.com
Reward & Recognition Programs, Premiums, Incentives, Awards, Promotional Products, Corporate Gifts. (Woman/AA, estab 1990, empl 6, sales $800,000, cert: NMSDC, WBENC)

1364 Atlanta Brand Central LLC
      880 Glenwood Ave se unit 1317
      Atlanta, GA 30316
      Contact: Darryl Armstrong Owner
      Tel: 404-312-8777
      Email: darryl@abcatl.com
      Website: www.abcatl.com
Promotional products & sourcing. (AA, estab 2008, empl 4, sales $170,000, cert: NMSDC)

1365 Atlanta Promotional Products
      911 High Green Court
      Marietta, GA 30068
      Contact: Glynis Holihan Managing Partner
      Tel: 770-310-9860
      Email: glynis@atlpromo.com
      Website: www.atlpromo.com
Advertising specialty, logoed merchandise, corporate gifts & apparel. (Woman, estab 2004, empl 3, sales $1,196,294, cert: CPUC)

1366 Barazzo, LLC
      2221 Peachtree Rd NE Ste D357
      Atlanta, GA 30309
      Contact: Quiana Lloyd Member
      Tel: 888-716-5785
      Email: quiana@barazzo.com
      Website: www.barazzo.com
Custom gift & accessory solutions, corporate brand identity & marketing solutions. (Woman/AA, estab 2009, empl , sales , cert: State, NMSDC, SDB)

1367 Blue Rose Promotions, LLC
      2660 Holcomb Bridge Road Ste 200
      Alpharetta, GA 30022
      Contact: Jennifer Pines VP Sales
      Tel: 770-695-7673
      Email: jennifer@bluerosepromotions.com
      Website: www.bluerosepromotions.com
Promotional marketing with access to over 700,000 products. (Woman, estab 2013, empl 4, sales $4,165,561, cert: WBENC)

1368 Brand Spirit Inc.
      245 N Highland Ave NE Ste 230-272
      Atlanta, GA 30307
      Contact: Jenna Banks President
      Tel: 877-804-7906
      Email: jenna@gobrandspirit.com
      Website: www.gobrandspirit.com
Branded gifts, promotional items, printed materials, business forms, logo apparel, badges, awards, uniforms, lanyards, brochures & business cards. (Woman, estab 2012, empl 1, sales $430,400, cert: NWBOC)

1369 Capital Ideas, Inc.
      990 Hammond Dr Ste 620
      Atlanta, GA 30328
      Contact: Gina Sealey Acct Mgr
      Tel: 678-320-1630
      Email: gsealey@capitalideas.net
      Website: www.capitalideas.net
Promotional products. (Woman, estab 1987, empl 8, sales $4,162,000, cert: WBENC)

ADVERTISING SPECIALTIES

1370 Choice Premiums
      560 Arlington Pl
      Macon, GA 31201
      Contact: President
      Tel: 478-741-8888
      Email: request@choicepremiums.com
      Website: www.choicepremiums.com
Promotional products & marketing. (Woman, estab 1996, empl 4, sales $402,067, cert: WBENC)

1371 CKSports and Associates LLC
      3655 Altama Ave
      Brunswick, GA 31520
      Contact: Charles Loving CEO
      Tel: 912-547-7504
      Email: charles@cksportsandassociates.com
      Website: www.cksportsandassociates.com
Football Helmet Shaped Cooler on Wheels, Baseball Cap & Player Head Cooler on Wheels, Football Helmet Grill, Baseball Helmet Grill, Racecar Grill. (AA, estab 2016, empl 6, sales , cert: NMSDC)

1372 Creative Corporate Ideas Inc
      1010 Huntcliff Ste.1350
      Atlanta, GA 30350
      Contact: Creative Corporate Ideas Inc Owner
      Tel: 404-252-2588
      Email: cwalina@bellsouth.net
      Website: www.creativecorporateideas.com
Promotional items, logo merchandise & wearables. (Woman, estab 1993, empl 2, sales $500,000, cert: WBENC)

1373 Creative Innovators, Inc.
      1797 Spring Rd, Ste 6
      Smyrna, GA 30080
      Contact: Omar Horton Mgr
      Tel: 770-435-7552
      Email: sales@creativeinnovators.net
      Website: www.creativeinnovators.net
Embroidery, screen printing, signs, banners, advertising specialty & promotional items. (AA, estab 1999, empl 3, sales $150,000, cert: State, City)

1374 FireSign Inc. Promotional Products & Print
      4480-H S Cobb Dr, Ste 540
      Smyrna, GA 30080
      Contact: Jen Lyles Lead Ignitor
      Tel: 678-574-2461
      Email: jlyles@firesigninc.com
      Website: www.firesigninc.com
Promotional product & print services, (Woman/AA, estab 2003, empl 5, sales $1,295,000, cert: NMSDC)

1375 Henry-Aaron Inc.
      754 Woodson St
      Atlanta, GA 30315
      Contact: Aaron Turpeau President
      Tel: 404-622-4308
      Email: info@aarongroup.us
      Website: www.henry-aaroninc.logomall.com/
Premium & promotional items. (AA, estab 1991, empl 3, sales $2,189,931, cert: State, NMSDC)

1376 Jansen Advertising
      5565 Glenrich Court
      Atlanta, GA 30338
      Contact: Paige Jansen-Nichols VP Sales
      Tel: 770-452-0252
      Email: paige@jansenadvertising.com
      Website: www.jansenadvertising.com
Custom promotional, incentive & recognition merchandise. (Woman, estab 1993, empl 9, sales , cert: WBENC)

1377 NorthStar Print, LLC
      6050 Peachtree Pkwy Ste 240359
      Norcross, GA 30092
      Contact: Jacki Suckow President
      Tel: 770-490-6251
      Email: jacki@northstarprint.net
      Website: www.northstarprint.net
Print & promotional products, marketing materials, traditional business forms, POP items, promotional items & just-in-time digital printing, distribution & kitting services. (Woman, estab 1991, empl 8, sales $3,000,000, cert: NWBOC)

1378 The Corporate Shop, Inc.
      11455 Lakefield Dr Ste 200
      Johns Creek, GA 30097
      Contact: Wendy Neubauer CEO
      Tel: 770-242-0090
      Email: wendy@thecorporateshop.com
      Website: www.thecorporateshop.com
Corporate promotional products & logoed apparel. (Woman, estab , empl , sales $3,000,000, cert: WBENC)

1379 Universal Graphics, Inc.
      2931 Lewis St, Ste 301
      Kennesaw, GA 30144
      Contact: Celia Reed Sales
      Tel: 678-581-1221
      Email: ccmem@aol.com
      Website: www.ugiinc.biz
Silk screening, embroidery, promotional items, corporate apparel, printing. (AA, estab , empl , sales , cert: NMSDC)

Iowa

1380 World of Colors - Break The Cycle LLC
      1624 7th Ave SE, Ste 7000
      Cedar Rapids, IA 52403
      Contact: Rick Rodriguez Owner
      Tel: 319-447-7282
      Email: rrodri7855@aol.com
      Website: www.worldofcolors.us
Design, print & dist screen printed bags, shirts, hats & specialty items. (Hisp, estab 2012, empl 5, sales , cert: NMSDC)

Illinois

1381 Action Bag Company
      1001 Entry Dr.
      Bensenville, IL 60640
      Contact: Martha Quintero
      Tel: 866-349-8853
      Email: mquintero@actionbag.com
      Website: www.actionhealth.com
Printed bags, bags, retail packaging products, printed promotional products, promotional items, packaging supplies, labels, tissue paper, gift cards, specialty packaging, custom bags, custom printed items, rush orders, in-stock products. (Woman, estab , empl , sales , cert: City, WBENC)

ADVERTISING SPECIALTIES

1382 B. Gunther & Company, Inc.
      4742 Main St
      Lisle, IL 60532
      Contact: Jeanne Brommer President
      Tel: 630-969-5595
      Email: jeanne@bgunther.com
      Website: www.bgunther.com
Promotional products, business gifts, imprinted pens to the leather portfolio or high end wearables. (Woman, estab 1985, empl 9, sales $1,220,000, cert: WBENC)

1383 Bridgeforth Wolf & Associates, Inc.
      47 W Division St Ste 223
      Chicago, IL 60610
      Contact: Donna Bridgeforth
      Tel: 312-663-5171
      Email: donna@bridgeforthwolf.com
      Website: www.bridgeforthwolf.com
Advertising specialties, corporate gifts & awards. (Woman/AA, estab 1987, empl 6, sales $2,500,000, cert: NMSDC, WBENC)

1384 Brilliant Gifts LLC
      1605 S Waukegan Rd
      Waukegan, IL 60085
      Contact: Nick Phillips Dir of Business Dev
      Tel: 773-885-3532
      Email: nick@brilliantmade.com
      Website: www.brilliantmade.com
Curate and produce memorable gifts, branded merchandise and custom products, while providing our clients with a suite of tools to enable distribution, analytics, and ROI measurement. (Woman, estab 2015, empl 100, sales $25,000,000, cert: WBENC)

1385 Corporate Identity, Inc.
      223 W Main St
      Barrington, IL 60010
      Contact: Debbie Story Sales Mgr
      Tel: 847-304-8550
      Email: msparks@Corpid.com
      Website: www.corpid.com
Promotional products, awards, logo apparel, trade show giveaways, corporate gifts, notepads, golf balls, banners, table throws, business forms, labels, folders, nameplates, tags. (Woman, estab 1976, empl 9, sales , cert: WBENC)

1386 eLead Resources, Inc. DBA eLead Promo
      125 S Clark St 17th Fl
      Chicago, IL 60603
      Contact: Michael Wheeler VP
      Tel: 888-420-1788
      Email: mike@eleadresources.com
      Website: www.eleadresources.com
Promotional marketing products & brand consulting. (AA, estab , empl , sales $4,328,835, cert: NMSDC)

1387 Essential Creations Chicago, Inc.
      2112 W 95th St
      Chicago, IL 60643
      Contact: Sandtricia Andrews-Strickland' President
      Tel: 773-238-1700
      Email: sandtricia@ecreations2000.com
      Website: www.ecreations2000.com
Custom Embroidery, Patches, Screen Printing and Sublimation. We also do promotional Products. (AA, estab 2000, empl 3, sales $222,000, cert: State, WBENC)

1388 Excel Screen Printing & Embroidery, Inc.
      10507 Delta Pkwy
      Schiller Park, IL 60176
      Contact: Leon Johnson President
      Tel: 847-801-5200
      Email: leon@excelscreenprinting.com
      Website: www.excelscreenprinting.com
Screen printed & embroidered apparel, imprinted glassware, premiums, etc. (AA, estab 2005, empl 63, sales $4,500,000, cert: State)

1389 Fancy That
      3712 N Broadway, Ste 336
      Chicago, IL 60613
      Contact: Deborah Epstein Owner
      Tel: 888-369-8428
      Email: fancythatpromos@cs.com
      Website: www.fancythatpromos.com
Promotional items, corporate giftware, awards & trophies. (Woman, estab 1991, empl 1, sales , cert: WBENC)

1390 Global Sourcing Connection, Ltd.
      2610 Lake Cook Road Ste 190
      Riverwoods, IL 60015
      Contact: Jennifer Arenson CEO
      Tel: 847-317-9000
      Email: jarenson@gloso.com
      Website: www.gloso.com
Mfr & import headwear, apparel & promotional items. (Woman, estab 2001, empl 24, sales $9,200,000, cert: WBENC)

1391 Graphic Source Group, Inc.
      1119 W Algonquin Rd Ste B
      Lake in the Hills, IL 60156
      Contact: Sharon Meyer President
      Tel: 847-854-2670
      Email: sharon@graphicsourcegroup.com
      Website: www.graphicsourcegroup.com
Promotional products, screen printing, embroidery. (Woman, estab 1993, empl 6, sales $2,050,000, cert: WBENC)

1392 Konik and Company, Inc.
      7535 North Lincoln Ave
      Skokie, IL 60076
      Contact: Amy Lederer Owner
      Tel: 847-933-1805
      Email: amy@konik.com
      Website: www.konik.com
Premium & promotional products: apparel, drinkware, dental sampling bags, bag, plush toys, technology items, brand name products, desk accessories, conference items, awards/recognition gifts, etc. (Woman, estab 1991, empl 18, sales $11,000,000, cert: WBENC)

1393 L and N Promotions, Inc.
      99 Oak Leaf Lane #203
      Vernon Hills, IL 60061
      Contact: Kristi Marquardt President
      Tel: 847-612-9215
      Email: lnpromotionsinc@aol.com
      Website: www.companycasuals.com/lnpromotions
Promotional, incentive & speciatly premium items. (Woman, estab 1996, empl 2, sales $585,000, cert: WBENC)

ADVERTISING SPECIALTIES

1394 LinJen Promotions, Inc.
      15519 Harbor Town Dr
      Orland Park, IL 60462
      Contact: Linda Heyse-Highland President
      Tel: 708-478-8222
      Email: sales@linjen.com
      Website: www.linjen.com
Promotional solutions ideas & products. (Woman, estab 2000, empl 6, sales $1,250,000, cert: WBENC)

1395 M.R. Nyren Company
      600 Academy Dr Ste 110
      Northbrook, IL 60062
      Contact: Kim Nyren Acct Exec
      Tel: 800-323-8066
      Email: kim@nyren-tms.com
      Website: www.companycasuals.com/nyrencompany
Textile & promotional products: apparel, bags, hats, towels, blanets, golf accessories, etc. (Woman, estab 1963, empl 7, sales $4,880,454, cert: WBENC)

1396 Overture, LLC
      800 S Northpoint
      Waukegan, IL 60085
      Contact: Brian Lisinski VP Client Services
      Tel: 847-573-6080
      Email: brianl@overturepromo.com
      Website: www.overturepromotions.com
Promotional products, awards, incentive & recognition programs, giveaways, logo merchandise, ad specialties, apparel, t-shirts, fulfillment. (Woman, estab 2001, empl 135, sales $47,091,020, cert: WBENC)

1397 Premium Surge Promotions, L.L.C.
      640 N. LaSalle Ste 540
      Chicago, IL 60654
      Contact: Pam Crain EVP Marketing/Client Service
      Tel: 312-951-2303
      Email: pcrain@surge-innovations.com
      Website: www.surge-creates.com/
Marketing, creative & promotional product design and manufacturing. (Minority, estab 2001, empl 15, sales $33,000,000, cert: NMSDC)

1398 Pro Biz Products LLC
      350 N Orleans St Ste 9000N
      Chicago, IL 60654
      Contact: Richard Smith President
      Tel: 312-961-4513
      Email: r.smith@probizproducts.com
      Website: www.probizproducts.com
Screen printing or embroidery, office supplies, furniture, janitorial products & promotional items. (AA, estab 2014, empl 6, sales $15,000,000, cert: State, NMSDC)

1399 Silk Screen Express, Inc.
      7611 W 185TH ST
      TINLEY PARK, IL 60477
      Contact: Dawn Coleman President
      Tel: 708-845-5600
      Email: dcoleman@silkscreenx.com
      Website: www.silkscreenx.com
Silk screened & embroidered apparel, promotional items, uniforms & safety programs. (Woman, estab , empl , sales $3,000,000, cert: WBENC)

1400 Stitch Me LLC
      329 W 18th St, Unit 308
      Chicago, IL 60616
      Contact: Brenda Nelson Owner
      Tel: 312-933-2608
      Email: brenda@stitchmeapparel.com
      Website: www.stitchmeapparel.com
Embroidered Sportswear, Hats, Caps, Jackets, T-Shirts, Fleece, Sweaters, Tote Bags, Cut Goods, Finished Goods, Polo Shirts, Women's Wear, Promotional Products Screen Printed Apparel - T-shirts, Jackets, Hats, Team Uniforms, Sports (Woman/AA, estab 2011, empl 3, sales , cert: City, NMSDC, WBENC, 8(a))

1401 TBK Promotions, Inc.
      3055 W 111th St 2 South
      Chicago, IL 60655
      Contact: Kevin Flynn Dir of Sales
      Tel: 773-239-2222
      Email: k@tbkpromotions.com
      Website: www.tbkpromotions.com
Promotional products, advertising specialties & branded wearable items. (Woman, estab 1990, empl 5, sales $502,500, cert: State, WBENC)

1402 The Certif-a-gift Company Inc.
      1625 E Alqonqion Rd
      Arlington Heights, IL 60005
      Contact: Trish Duh President
      Tel: 847-718-0300
      Email: tduh@certif-a-gift.com
      Website: www.certif-a-gift.com
Incentive programs. (Woman, estab 1954, empl 50, sales $15,600,000, cert: WBENC)

1403 Windy City Silkscreening, Inc.
      2715 S Archer
      Chicago, IL 60608
      Contact: Jessica Trojanowski Cstmr Service
      Tel: 312-842-0030
      Email: jessicat@wcstshirts.com
      Website: www.wcsshirts.com
Custom screen printed apparel: t-shirts, sweats, hats, jackets, towels, hot-market printing, rally towels, promotional products. (Woman, estab 1978, empl 36, sales $1,380,000, cert: WBENC)

1404 World Of Promotions
      1310 Louis Ave
      Elk Grove Village, IL 60007
      Contact: Layla Rosenfeld President
      Tel: 847-439-7930
      Email: rosenfeldlayla@yahoo.com
      Website: www.aworldofpromotions.com
Promotional products: pens, mugs, hats, clothing, bags. (Woman, estab 2003, empl 8, sales $1,120,000, cert: State)

Indiana

1405 Awards Unlimited, Inc.
      3031 Union St
      Lafayette, IN 47904
      Contact: Stacey Shirar President
      Tel: 765-447-9413
      Email: sjs@awardsunlimitedinc.net
      Website: www.awardsunlimitedinc.net
Advertising specialties. (Woman, estab 1978, empl 12, sales $500,000, cert: WBENC)

ADVERTISING SPECIALTIES

1406 Bardach Awards, Inc.
      4222 W 86th St
      Indianapolis, IN 46268
      Contact: Diane Bardach Beck CEO
      Tel: 317-872-7444
      Email: dbardach@bardachawards.com
      Website: www.bardachawards.com
Custom corporate awards: plaques, trophies, crystal, acrylic, plates, marble, glass, leather items such as portfolios, name badges, medals, ribbons, bronze castings, donor recognition, signage, jewelry, executive gifts. (Woman, estab 1969, empl 36, sales $2,960,000, cert: State)

1407 Karm Corporation
      2017 N Bedford Ave
      Evansville, IN 47711
      Contact: Kena Campbell President
      Tel: 812-426-1323
      Email: kcampbell@promarkin.com
      Website: www.promarkin.com
Screen printing, embroidery, labels, stickers, decals, promotional products, t-shirts, uniforms. (Woman, estab 1976, empl 24, sales $2,900,000, cert: State, WBENC)

1408 Linz and Company
      8231 Hohman Ave Ste 200
      Munster, IN 46321
      Contact: Heather Koetteritz Sales/Import Mgr
      Tel: 708-757-7800
      Email: heather@linzco.com
      Website: www.linzco.com
Promotional products: apparel, housewares, novelties, personal care items, etc. (Woman, estab 2000, empl 4, sales $3,007,000, cert: WBENC)

1409 M. Nelson and Associates
      4011 Vincennes Rd
      Indianapolis, IN 46268
      Contact: Carolina Pimental-Nelson President
      Tel: 317-228-1422
      Email: carolina@mnelson.com
      Website: www.mnelson.com
Promotional products, printing services, graphic design & screen-print/embroidery of apparel. (Minority, Woman, estab 1991, empl 4, sales , cert: State, 8(a))

1410 Metro Printed Products, Inc.
      1001 Commerce Pkwy South Dr Ste H
      Greenwood, IN 46143
      Contact: Gloria James Marketing
      Tel: 317-885-0077
      Email: gloria.james@proforma.com
      Website: www.metroprintedproducts.com
Advertising specialties and promotional products. (Woman, estab 1989, empl 6, sales $2,361,600, cert: WBENC)

1411 OmniSource Marketing Group, Inc.
      8945 N Meridian St Ste 150
      Indianapolis, IN 46260
      Contact: Janet Calderon Goldberg President
      Tel: 317-575-3318
      Email: jgoldberg@omnisourcemarketing.com
      Website: www.omnisourcemarketing.com
Custom promotional products & packaging, embroidery, fulfillment, graphic services & design, screen printing. (Woman, estab 1988, empl 30, sales $10,400,000, cert: WBENC)

1412 PlaqueMakerPlus, Inc.
      5713 Park Plaza Ct
      Indianapolis, IN 46220
      Contact: Edson Pereira President
      Tel: 317-594-5556
      Email: edson@plaquemakerplus.com
      Website: www.plaquemakerplus.com
Mfr awards, plaques, name badges, name plates & signs. (Woman, estab 1995, empl 6, sales $640,000, cert: State)

1413 Pro-Am Team Sports
      1650 US Hwy 41 Ste E
      Schererville, IN 46375
      Contact: Mary Dolan Owner
      Tel: 219-515-6900
      Email: mary@pro-amteamsports.com
      Website: www.pro-amteamsports.com
Branded, customized name-brand apparel & equipment. (Woman, estab 2014, empl 60, sales $4,200,000, cert: WBENC)

1414 Smiling Cross Inc.
      700 S College Ave, Ste A
      Bloomington, IN 47403
      Contact: Rula Hanania President
      Tel: 812-323-9290
      Email: rhanania@smilepromotions.com
      Website: www.smilepromotions.com
Promotional products. (Minority, Woman, estab 2003, empl 10, sales $2,400,000, cert: State, NMSDC)

1415 Table Thyme Designs
      217 W 10th St Ste 125
      Indianapolis, IN 46202
      Contact: Laurie Rice Owner
      Tel: 317-634-0281
      Email: coloredthreads@sbcglobal.net
      Website: www.colored-threads.com
Promotional products & embroidered apparel & accessories, screen printing. (Woman, estab 2002, empl 2, sales , cert: State, City)

1416 Thomas E. Slade, Inc.
      6220 Vogel Road
      Evansville, IN 47715
      Contact: Lisa Slade President
      Tel: 812-437-5233
      Email: tom@sladeprint.com
      Website: www.sladeprint.com
Printing, graphic design, website design, wide format posters & banners, mailing, promotional products, letterhead, envelopes, business cards, labels, tags, inserts, marketing services, augmented reality, QR codes for tracking, signs. (Woman, estab 1993, empl 17, sales $2,500,000, cert: State)

1417 Wolf Run Marketing
      6020 N Emerson Ave
      Indianapolis, IN 46220
      Contact: Susan Fryer Owner
      Tel: 317-445-5180
      Email: susan@wolfrunmarketing.com
      Website: www.wolfrunmarketing.com
Promotional products, logoed apparel, service & safety awards, employee & customer recognition awards, tradeshow handouts, conference materials, incentives, safety apparel, graphic design, logo devel. (Woman, estab 2009, empl 2, sales $200,000, cert: City)

ADVERTISING SPECIALTIES

Kansas

1418 Grapevine Designs, LLC
      8406 Melrose Dr
      Lenexa, KS 66214
      Contact: Bob Offord VP Business Dev
      Tel: 913-307-0225
      Email: bob.offord@abrandcompany.com
      Website: www.grapevinedesigns.com/
Promotional marketing, promotional products, creative design, corporate giveaways, tradeshow giveaways, corporate branding, branded merchandise. (Woman, estab 2000, empl 72, sales $8,000,000, cert: WBENC)

1419 Promo Depot Inc.
      2266 N Ridge Rd
      Wichita, KS 67205
      Contact: Rick McKay President
      Tel: 316-722-2500
      Email: rick@4mypromo.com
      Website: www.4mypromo.com
Promotional products: logo wearables & printed ad specialty products, embroidery & screeen printing, wards & recognition products. (Hisp, estab 1997, empl 15, sales $2,600,000, cert: NMSDC)

Kentucky

1420 Ad-Venture Promotions
      2625 Regency Rd
      Lexington, KY 40503
      Contact: Cathy Stafford Owner
      Tel: 859-263-4299
      Email: cathy@ad-venturepromotions.com
      Website: www.ad-venturepromotions.com
Advertising specialties & promotional products. (Woman, estab 2004, empl 6, sales , cert: WBENC)

1421 Presence Inc.
      2311 Mohican Hill Ct
      Louisville, KY 40207
      Contact: Gail Iwaniak President
      Tel: 502-365-4616
      Email: gail@stuffology.com
      Website: www.stuffology.com
Promotional marketing & products. (Woman, estab 1989, empl 2, sales $350,000, cert: City)

1422 The Logo Warehouse
      1963 Meadowcreek Dr
      Louisville, KY 40218
      Contact: Leah Scott Owner
      Tel: 502-451-5421
      Email: lscott@thelogowarehouse.com
      Website: www.thelogowarehouse.com
Promotional products & apparel. (Woman/AA, estab 2008, empl 1, sales , cert: City, WBENC)

1423 Walker Flags, Inc.
      8134 New LaGrange Rd, Ste 200
      Louisville, KY 40222
      Contact: Donna Walker Mancini Owner
      Tel: 502-394-1474
      Email: customercare@walkerflags.com
      Website: www.walkerflags.com
Flags, Banners, Flagpoles, Flag & Flagpole Accessories. (Woman, estab 1960, empl 3, sales , cert: State)

Louisiana

1424 Augie Leopold Advertising Specialties, Inc.
      3214 Roman St
      Metairie, LA 70001
      Contact: Leeanne Leopold CEO
      Tel: 504-836-0525
      Email: leeanne@augieleopold.com
      Website: www.augieleopold.com
Advertising specialties, promotional items, premium gifts, casino monthly giveaways, safety programs. (Woman, estab 0, empl , sales , cert: WBENC)

1425 Impress Marketing Studios, LLC
      PO Box 38845
      Shreveport, LA 71133
      Contact: Janelle Marks Owner
      Tel: 888-773-0183
      Email: jmarks@impressmarketingstudios.com
      Website: www.ImpressMarketingStudios.com
Marketing & promotional, premiums, advertising specialties, apparel & signage. (Woman/AA, estab 2014, empl 2, sales $127,000, cert: NMSDC)

1426 The Creative Touch, Inc.
      7725 Jefferson Hwy
      Baton Rouge, LA 70809
      Contact: Maureen Kahl President
      Tel: 225-925-0022
      Email: maureen@creativetouchembroidery.com
      Website: www.createyourtouch.com
Embroidery, silk screening, promotional products, (Woman, estab 1982, empl 7, sales $489,000, cert: WBENC)

1427 Wilkin Enterprises, Inc.
      2323 Bainbridge St, Bldg B, Ste 13
      Kenner, LA 70062
      Contact: Kathleen Wilkin President
      Tel: 504-464-2520
      Email: kwilkin@gosafeguard.com
      Website: www.safeguardprints.com
Full color printing, promotional items & embroidered apparel. (Woman, estab 1993, empl 7, sales $1,458,066, cert: WBENC)

Massachusetts

1428 AMDA dba New England Promotional Marketing
      15 Main St
      Wilbraham, MA 01095
      Contact: Nealy Martin
      Tel: 413-596-4800
      Email: nealy.martin55@gmail.com
      Website: www.nepm.com
Custom imprinted promotiopnal products & advertising specialties. (Woman, estab 1989, empl 18, sales , cert: State, WBENC)

1429 Ellco Promotions, Inc.
      113 Smoke Hill Ridge Road
      Marshfield, MA 02050
      Contact: Max Cohen VP
      Tel: 508-641-6274
      Email: max@ellcopromotions.com
      Website: www.ellcopromotions.com
Promotional/premium product & apparel agency. (Woman, estab 2010, empl 2, sales $150,000, cert: State)

1430 GAP Promotions LLC
1 Washington St
Gloucester, MA 01930
Contact: Gayle Piraino President
Tel: 978-281-0083
Email: gayle.piraino@gappromo.com
Website: www.gappromo.com/
Promotional programs and products. (Woman, estab 2006, empl 10, sales $5,602,133, cert: WBENC)

1431 Infinart, Inc.
44 Mechanic St
Newton, MA 02464
Contact: Felicity Green President
Tel: 617-964-3279
Email: felicityinfinart@gmail.com
Website: www.infinart.com
Custom branding, logo embroidery, silk screening, imprinted promotional products, awards, corporate gifts incentives, signage, banners. (Woman, estab 1980, empl 5, sales , cert: State)

1432 Jazzy Sportswear Promotional Co.
90 Munroe
Lynn, MA 01903
Contact: Vincent Williams President
Tel: 781-593-7197
Email: jazzypc@jazzysportswear.com
Website: www.jazzysportswear.com
Screen printing, embroidery, and a wide array of promotional items, banners, awards. (AA, estab 1997, empl 1, sales $189,000, cert: State, NMSDC)

Maryland

1433 APISource, Inc.
7850 Walker Dr Ste 400
Greenbelt, MD 20770
Contact: Julie Pierce CEO
Tel: 301-731-6100
Email: julie.pierce@apisource.com
Website: www.apisource.com
Promotional products: t-shirts, collared shirts, polo shirts, hats, jackets, bags, computer accessories, pens, note pads, mugs, novelties, giveaways, awards, premiums, incentives, fulfillment services. (Woman, estab 1965, empl 150, sales $50,000,000, cert: WBENC)

1434 Debbie Lynn, Inc.
952 Ridgebrook Rd Ste 1100
Sparks, MD 21152
Contact: Stephanie Bloom Operations Mgr
Tel: 443-595-8178
Email: stephanie@debbielynn.net
Website: www.debbielynn.net
Writing instruments, office accessories, Back to School & novelty products. (Woman, estab 1998, empl 5, sales $10,200,000, cert: WBENC)

1435 Lord & Mitchell, Inc.
9205 Locksley Rd
Fort Washington, MD 20744
Contact: Toya Mitchell President
Tel: 800-491-8026
Email: toya@lord-mitchell.com
Website: www.lord-mitchell.com
Promotional products distributors and wholesale trade agents/brokers. (Woman/AA, estab 1991, empl 3, sales $1,475,910, cert: NMSDC, WBENC)

1436 Products 2 Brand, LLC
8217 Cloverleaf Dr
Millersville, MD 21108
Contact: Macgill Antor President
Tel: 301-787-0077
Email: macgill@products2brand.com
Website: www.products2brand.com
Promotional products, tradeshow registration bags, totes, briefcases, luggage, lanyards, name badges. (Woman, estab 2007, empl 22, sales , cert: City)

1437 Williams Solutions Group, LLC
20140 Scholar Dr, Ste 315
Hagerstown, MD 21742
Contact: Peter E. Perini, Sr. VP
Tel: 301-739-7532
Email: peter.perini@williamssolutionsgroup.com
Website: www.WilliamsSolutionsGroup.com
Promotional items, marketing items, tchotchkies, giveaway items, logo branded items. (AA, estab 2009, empl 2, sales $100,000, cert: State)

Michigan

1438 Alfie Logo Gear
2425 Switch Dr
Traverse City, MI 49684
Contact: Bonnie Alfonso President
Tel: 800-507-0040
Email: bonnie@goalfie.com
Website: www.GoAlfie.com
Logowear, embroidery, screen printing & promotional products, uniforms, rewards & incentives, trade show giveaways. (Woman, estab 1990, empl 18, sales $2,863,520, cert: WBENC)

1439 Antina Promotions, LLC
84 Leslie Lane
Waterford, MI 48328
Contact: Christina Concord Managing Partner
Tel: 248-254-3845
Email: christina@antinapromo.com
Website: www.antinapromo.com
Promotional Products, Exhibit Displays, Corporate Gifts, Awards, Signage, Branded Apparel, Company Stores, Custom Packaging, Marketing Materials. (Woman, estab 2010, empl 2, sales , cert: WBENC, SDB)

1440 CE Competitive Edge LLC
5924 Red Arrow Hwy
Stevensville, MI 49127
Contact: Mary Tomasini CEO
Tel: 269-429-0404
Email: mjtomasini@competitive-edge.net
Website: www.competitive-edge.net
Incentive & promotional products, ideas & services. (Woman, estab 1993, empl 15, sales , cert: WBENC)

1441 CompleteSource Inc.
4455 44th St SE
Grand Rapids, MI 49512
Contact: VP Sales
Tel: 800-868-7018
Email: customerservice@completesource.com
Website: www.completesource.com
Commercial printing, promotional products, awards & incentives, embroidery & silk screened apparel & uniforms, saftey awards & incentives, banners & signs. (Woman, estab 1989, empl 11, sales $2,000,000, cert: WBENC)

ADVERTISING SPECIALTIES

1442 Graphix 2 Go
7200 Tower Rd
Battle Creek, MI 49014
Contact: Amy Howard Sales Mgr
Tel: 269-969-7321
Email: amy@graphix2goinc.com
Website: www.graphix2goinc.com
Promotional products. (Woman, estab 1997, empl 8, sales $2,500,000, cert: WBENC)

1443 InmartGroup, Ltd.
37570 Hills Tech Dr
Farmington Hills, MI 48331
Contact: Stephanie Master Acct Exec
Tel: 248-489-0344
Email: stephanie@inmartgroup.com
Website: www.inmartgroup.com
Custom imprinted promotional & premium items, branded merchandise, warehouse, distribution & on-line payment. (Woman, estab 1989, empl 6, sales , cert: WBENC)

1444 Krystal Marketing, Inc.
1120 E Long Lake Rd, Ste 200
Troy, MI 48085
Contact: Carolyn Boccia Mktg Mgr
Tel: 248-619-9000
Email: carolyn@krystalmarketing.com
Website: www.krystalmarketing.com
Promotional products, awards & incentives. (Woman, estab 1987, empl 10, sales , cert: WBENC)

1445 Mendoza Enterprises LLC
1847 N Main St
Royal Oak, MI 48073
Contact: Sue Johnson President
Tel: 248-588-0335
Email: sue@mendozaenterprises.us
Website: www.mendozaenterprises.us
Printing and promotional products. (Hisp, estab 0, empl , sales , cert: NMSDC)

1446 Mercury P&F
35610 Mound Rd
Sterling Heights, MI 48310
Contact: Betsy Canova Business Dev Mgr
Tel: 586-825-9300
Email: canovab@mercuryfs.com
Website: www.mercuryfs.com
Branded merchandise & premiums. (Woman/AA, estab 1996, empl 70, sales $25,000,000, cert: NMSDC, WBENC)

1447 Mixed Promotions, LLC
3759 S Baldwin Rd, Ste 222
Lake Orion, MI 48359
Contact: Lona Carson CEO
Tel: 248-783-4099
Email: lcarson@mixedpromotions.com
Website: www.mixedpromotions.com
Promotional products. (Minority, Woman, estab 2000, empl 1, sales $462,000, cert: NMSDC, WBENC)

1448 Promotion Concepts Inc.
414 S Burdick St
Kalamazoo, MI 49007
Contact: Lauren A. Powers President
Tel: 269-488-2987
Email: laurene.powers@promotionconcepts.com
Website: www.promotionconcepts.com
Incentive marketing svcs, promotional products, premium incentives programs, awards, recognition, brand-building. (Woman, estab 1982, empl 18, sales , cert: WBENC)

1449 Promotional Solutions LLC
48530 Van Dyke Ave
Shelby Township, MI 48317
Contact: Kathy Ferguson Member
Tel: 586-739-1132
Email: promotionalsolutions@onemain.com
Website: www.promotionalsolutionsonline.com
Advertising specialty goods & services. Logowear embroidered or screen print, awards & trophys, special event gifts, employee appreciation items. (Woman, estab 2001, empl 8, sales $622,000, cert: WBENC)

1450 The Bradley Company, Inc.
26777 Central Park Blvd Ste 180
Southfield, MI 48076
Contact: Marci Taran CEO
Tel: 248-538-1909
Email: marcit@thebradco.com
Website: www.thebradco.com
Advertising specialties, Assembly, Awards, Branded merchandise, Branding, Commemorative items, Corporate apparel, Corporate gifts, Corporate identity, Corporate webstores, Custom packaging, etc. (Woman, estab 2004, empl 11, sales $5,000,000, cert: WBENC)

1451 Tier One Marketing
3160 Belle Terre
Commerce Township, MI 48382
Contact: Jeanne Snyder President
Tel: 313-274-1179
Email: jeannesnyder@sbcglobal.net
Website: www.tierone.biz
Ad specialties: coffee cups, pens, portfolios, golf items, technology driven give-a-ways, coolers, tote bags, flashlights, key chains, awards, custom pieces, collectables. (Woman, estab 2003, empl 2, sales $250,000, cert: WBENC)

1452 Unique Expressions, LLC
22050 Woodward Ave
Ferndale, MI 48220
Contact: Beverly Bantom CEO
Tel: 248-547-9300
Email: info@uniquex.net
Website: www.UniqueX.net
Dist promotional products. (AA, estab 1999, empl 6, sales $1,000,000, cert: NMSDC)

1453 Wellard, Inc.
10377 Mesic Dr
West Olive, MI 49460
Contact: Ann Wellard CEO
Tel: 312-752-0155
Email: ann@logodance.com
Website: www.logodance.com
Custom promotional branded items. (Woman, estab 2016, empl 4, sales $1,725,000, cert: WBENC)

Minnesota

1454 2020 Brand Solutions
135 Grand Ave East
South St. Paul, MN 55075
Contact: Dan Livengood VP Sales & Mktg
Tel: 651-451-3850
Email: dan.livengood@2020brands.com
Website: www.2020collection.com
Corporate Apparel & Uniform Programs, Branded Merchandise, Incentives & Recognition, Print Management & Specialty Fulfillment. (Nat Ame, estab 2014, empl 62, sales $20,000,000, cert: NMSDC)

ADVERTISING SPECIALTIES

1455 A.K. Rose Inc.
3701 Shoreline Dr Ste 200B
Wayzata, MN 55391
Contact: Barb DeRonde Cstmr Service
Tel: 952-474-3050
Email: barb@akrose.com
Website: www.akrose.com
Promotional merchandise. (Woman, estab 1985, empl 4, sales $1,200,000, cert: WBENC)

1456 Altobelli Advantage, Inc.
19760 Pembrook Cir
Rogers, MN 55374
Contact: Michelle Altobelli CEO
Tel: 763-428-7521
Email: michelle@altobelliadvantage.com
Website: www.AltobelliAdvantage.com
Bags, awards, crystal, pens, shirts, t-shirts, hats, blankets, buttons, pins, gifts, recognition, safety, planners, binders, portfolios, folders, marketing solutions, etc. (Woman, estab 2004, empl 2, sales $733,000, cert: WBENC)

1457 Corporate Advertising & Incentives
6289 Niagara Lane N
Maple Grove, MN 55311
Contact: Loni Spence Promotional Consultant
Tel: 763-559-8388
Email: lspence@corpadvertising.net
Website: www.corpadvertising.net
Promorional products. (Woman, estab 2003, empl 3, sales $150,000, cert: WBENC)

1458 Creality Promo+Retail, inc.
3201 West County Rd. 42 Ste 105
Burnsville, MN 55306
Contact: Tony Pesante President
Tel: 952-854-9202
Email: tonyp@crealitypromo.com
Website: www.crealitypromo.com
Promotional products, logo merchandise, custom apparel, gift store merchandise, give-away items, premiums, awards. (Minority, Woman, estab 1999, empl 19, sales $6,850,000, cert: NMSDC)

1459 Creative Resources Agency
1208 5th St South
Minneapolis, MN 55343
Contact: Caren Schweitzer CEO
Tel: 952-988-9407
Email: caren@acreativeresource.com
Website: www.acreativeresource.com
Promotional products, direct mail, trade show give-aways, corporate holiday gifts, lead generators & client thank-you gifts. (Woman, estab 1995, empl 24, sales $5,700,000, cert: WBENC, 8(a))

1460 High Five, LLC
750 2nd St NE Ste 122
Hopkins, MN 55343
Contact: Co-President
Tel: 952-746-0355
Email: info@highfiveonline.com
Website: www.highfiveonline.com
Promotional products & advertising specialties. (Woman, estab 2003, empl 4, sales $455,000, cert: WBENC)

1461 Ithaca Promotions
PO Box 220
Wahkon, MN 56386
Contact: Katrina Chang President
Tel: 612-669-7833
Email: katrina@ithacapromotions.com
Website: www.ithacapromotions.com
Promotional, incentive, corporate gifts, gift certificates, gift checks, American Express Gift Cheques, banners, etc. (Minority, Woman, estab 1991, empl 1, sales $631,227, cert: State, NMSDC)

1462 J Michael Industries
1086 W 7th St
St. Paul, MN 55102
Contact: Jamie Flynn Owner
Tel: 651-698-3333
Email: jamiemm@extendedexposure.com
Website: www.extendedexposure.com
Design, create & source give-away mementos, memorable keepsakes & corporate gifts. (Woman, estab 1999, empl 7, sales $1,200,000, cert: WBENC)

1463 M Plus Embroidery & Promotions
5 Viking Dr W
Little Canada, MN 55117
Contact: Beth Mulcahy Owner
Tel: 651-777-3624
Email: beth@mplus-embroidery.com
Website: www.mplus-embroidery.com
Embroidery, silk screening, direct to garment, polo's, t-shirts, sweatshirts/pants, caps, hats, bags, etc. (Woman, estab 1984, empl 7, sales $324,800, cert: WBENC)

1464 Personal Touch Marketing & Manufacturing, Inc.
2600 24th Ave S
Moorhead, MN 56560
Contact: Benjamin Syltie Creative Dir
Tel: 701-403-3417
Email: bsyltie@ptmark.com
Website: www.ptmark.com
Custom apparel, promotional products & accessories. (Woman, estab 1990, empl 30, sales $4,041,278, cert: WBENC)

1465 Rutabaga Rags, Inc.
8700 West 36th St Ste 3E
St. Louis Park, MN 55426
Contact: Julie Miller Owner
Tel: 952-938-4841
Email: julie@rutabagarags.com
Website: www.rutabagaragsshop.com
Promotional products & stadium giveaways: baseball caps, jerseys, bats, gloves, toys, banks, bracelets, lip balm, magnets, pens, schedules, memo pads, padfolios, portfolios, duffles, bags, backpacks, cinch sacks, mugs, coffee tumblers, stuffed animals. (Woman, estab 1993, empl 3, sales $600,000, cert: WBENC)

1466 Spartan Promotional Group, Inc.
711 Hale Ave N
Oakdale, MN 55128
Contact: Dan Perdue Sales Assoc
Tel: 309-827-2215
Email: phyllisohenwald@spartanpromo.com
Website: www.spartanpromo.com/index.html
Advertising specialties: keychains, magnets, pens, distribution services, promotional marketing programs. (Woman, estab 1966, empl 80, sales , cert: WBENC)

ADVERTISING SPECIALTIES

Missouri

1467 Accent Group Solutions
      1154 Reco Ave
      St. Louis, MO 63126
      Contact: Erica Hughes CEO
      Tel: 314-965-5388
      Email: ehughes@accentgroupsolutions.com
      Website: www.AccentGroupSolutions.com
Warehousing, Distribution Services, Pick Pack & Ship, Custom Fulfillment, Publisher Services, Logo Apparel & Promotional Products, Printing, Converting Printed Materials, Literature Fulfillment, Container Management. (Woman, estab 2003, empl 26, sales $6,621,042, cert: WBENC)

1468 Blue Sky Apparel & Promotions, LLC
      12732 Pennridge Dr
      Bridgeton, MO 63044
      Contact: Kathy Gralike Owner
      Tel: 314-739-4531
      Email: kgralike@aol.com
      Website: www.blueskypromotion.com/
Promotional products: pens, coffee mugs, apparel & caps. (Woman, estab 2002, empl 5, sales $1,369,654, cert: State)

Mississippi

1469 Zebra Marketing Corporation
      289 Commerce Park Dr, Ste E
      Ridgeland, MS 39157
      Contact: Sharon Thompson Sales Exec
      Tel: 251-438-2422
      Email: sharon.thompson@zebrapromos.com
      Website: www.zebrapromos.com
Advertising specialties, service awards, clothing-jackets, t-shirts, sport shirts, trade show give aways. (Woman, estab 2000, empl 14, sales $7,000,000, cert: WBENC)

North Carolina

1470 Adsource Media, Inc.
      8313-101 Six Forks Rd
      Raleigh, NC 27615
      Contact: Darlene Brand Acct Exec
      Tel: 919-871-9990
      Email: darlene@am3adsource.com
      Website: www.am3adsource.com
Branded merchandise, decorated apparel, medical educational material, dimensional packaging, imported product, trade show supplies, direct mailing, signage, training board games. (Woman, estab 1999, empl 4, sales $675,000, cert: WBENC)

1471 Austin Business Forms Inc.
      PO Box 1905
      Matthews, NC 28016
      Contact: Acct Exec
      Tel: 704-821-6165
      Email: sales@printwithaustin.com
      Website: www.printwithaustin.com
Printing, graphic design, screen printing & embroidery, promotional products. (Woman, estab 1991, empl 6, sales $1,514,990, cert: WBENC)

1472 Blue Dove Promotions LLC
      5539 Alma Dr
      Winston-Salem, NC 27105
      Contact: Joyce Williams Owner
      Tel: 336-624-5223
      Email: jwilliams@bluedovepromotions.com
      Website: www.bluedovepromotions.com
Pomotional items. (Woman/AA, estab 2012, empl 1, sales $161,000, cert: NMSDC)

1473 Bob Williams Specialty Co.
      5539 Monroe Rd
      Charlotte, NC 28212
      Contact: Janet VP Sales
      Tel: 704-568-3411
      Email: janet@bobwilliamsspecialty.com
      Website: www.bobwilliamsspecialty.com
Imprinted promotional products. (Woman, estab 1961, empl 5, sales $800,000, cert: City)

1474 BrandRPM, LLC
      4910 Starcrest Dr
      Monroe, NC 28110
      Contact: Keith Brent VP Strategic Sales
      Tel: 704-225-1800
      Email: keithb@brandrpm.com
      Website: www.brandrpm.com
Corporate apparel & branded merchandise. (Minority, Woman, estab 2008, empl , sales $5,000,000, cert: State, NMSDC)

1475 Crown Trophy Winston-Salem
      2871 Reynolda Rd
      Winston-Salem, NC 27106
      Contact: Michael Robinson President
      Tel: 336-723-7400
      Email: crowntrophy419@bellsouth.net
      Website: www.crowntrophy.com
Awards & recogniton: badges, signage, corporate awards, plaques, trophies, ribbons, medallians, promotional items, cast bronze, etc. (Woman/AA, estab , empl , sales , cert: State, City)

1476 Daybreak Marketing Services, LLC
      14460 Falls of Neuse Rd Ste 149-326
      Raleigh, NC 27614
      Contact: Dawn Nakash COO
      Tel: 919-926-1452
      Email: dawn@daybreakmarketing.com
      Website: www.DaybreakMarketing.com
Promotional Products, Advertising Specialties, Silk Screening, Embroidery, Debossing, Embossing Imprinted, Pens, mugs, t-shirts, magnets, pins, buttons, uniforms, awards, bags, desk and auto accessories, flash drives, power banks. (Woman, estab 1998, empl 1, sales $150,000, cert: State)

1477 G. ALAN Inc.
      5317 Highgate Dr Ste 212
      Durham, NC 27713
      Contact: Gregory Harris
      Tel: 919-544-0055
      Email: gregory@imwithg.com
      Website: www.imwithg.com
Embroidery, screenprinting & promotional products. (AA, estab 1994, empl 2, sales $422,500, cert: State, NMSDC)

1478 PIA International LLC
PO Box 481232
Charlotte, NC 28269
Contact: Donna Daniels Owner
Tel: 704-593-1256
Email: donna@piapromo.com
Website: www.piapromo.com
Promotional products, ad specialties, t-shirts, sports uniforms & equipment, safety wear, etc. (Woman/AA, estab 2003, empl 1, sales , cert: State, NMSDC)

1479 PROMOQUEST Inc.
1308 Ballyclare Ct
Raleigh, NC 27614
Contact: Pam Williams President
Tel: 919-845-3448
Email: pam@promoquest.com
Website: www.promoquest.com
Imprinted promotional products: screenprinting, embroidery, lithography, digital printing, emboss, deboss, laser, t-shirts, jackets, fleece, athletic apparel, pants, bumper stickers, signs, buttons, pens note pads. (Woman/AA, estab 1994, empl 1, sales , cert: State)

New Jersey

1480 3D Promoplastic, Inc.
31 Summer Rd
Flemington, NJ 08822
Contact: Sibel Toy Owner
Tel: 469-955-6282
Email: mail@3dpromoplastic.com
Website: www.3d-promo.com
Promotional products, plastic promotional products, custom mold clip pens, promotional give aways, ballpoint pens, pen holders & eco friendly products. (Woman, estab 2002, empl 50, sales $500,000, cert: State)

1481 Aberson Narotzky & White
945 Lincoln Ave E
Cranford, NJ 07016
Contact: Shelly Aberson President
Tel: 908-789-2700
Email: shelly@anwinc.com
Website: www.anwinc.com
Advertising specialties, promotional products. (Woman, estab 1989, empl 7, sales $3,100,000, cert: WBENC)

1482 Action Calendar & Specialty Co., Inc.
5 Underwood Ct
Delran, NJ 08075
Contact: Lora Dunnigan President
Tel: 856-764-4000
Email: lora.dunnigan@renpromo.com
Website: www.wellnesseducationkits.com
Dist promotional products, on-site distribution center, graphic arts, web dev, customer care call center, on-line company stores. (Woman, estab 1975, empl 10, sales $6,121,000, cert: WBENC)

1483 Balady Promotions, Inc.
1719 Route 10 Ste 103
Parsippany, NJ 07054
Contact: Balady CEO
Tel: 973-682-8440
Email: jbalady@balady.com
Website: www.balady.com
Promotional product & decorated apparel programs, trade show exhibits, signage & giveaways, business gifts/premiums & award programs for employee achievement, sales rewards & years of service. (Woman, estab 1989, empl 7, sales $2,951,425, cert: WBENC)

1484 Blank2Branded powered by Axis
160 Main Rd
Montville, NJ 07045
Contact: Marcia Tarnoff President
Tel: 973-917-3100
Email: marcia@blank2branded.com
Website: www.blank2branded.com
Promotional solutions. (Woman, estab 2013, empl 5, sales $1,900,000, cert: WBENC)

1485 Compas, Inc.
4300 Haddonfield Rd Ste 200
Pennsauken, NJ 08109
Contact: Robert Kadar SVP
Tel: 856-667-8577
Email: rkadar@cmicompas.com
Website: www.compasonline.com
Media & promotional svcs. (AA, estab , empl , sales $250,000,000, cert: NMSDC)

1486 Cotapaxi Custom Design & Manufacturing, LLC
338 Hackensack St
Carlstadt, NJ 07072
Contact: Vincent Sposito Sr Vice President
Tel: 201-507-5111
Email: vsposito@cotapaxi.com
Website: www.cotapaxi.com
Create, develop, and deliver effective, high value, low cost exclusive promotional products. (Minority, Woman, estab , empl , sales $87,000,000, cert: NMSDC)

1487 Focus Merchandising
127 E Ridgewood Ave
Ridgewood, NJ 07450
Contact: Allison Rao President
Tel: 201-445-5858
Email: allisonr@focusmc.com
Website: www.focusmerchandising.com
Promotional marketing & premium items. (Woman, estab 2003, empl 8, sales $8,000,000, cert: WBENC)

1488 Glazer Design, LLC
330 Franklin Turnpike
Mahwah, NJ 07430
Contact: Trish Glazer Office Mgr
Tel: 201-684-1132
Email: trish@glazerpromos.com
Website: www.glazerpromos.com
Promotional products. (Woman, estab 2002, empl 7, sales $669,828, cert: City, WBENC)

1489 Graphics Solutions
473 Chapel Heights Rd
Sewell, NJ 08080
Contact: Steven Riggs Owner
Tel: 877-931-1636
Email: support@graphics-solution.com
Website: www.graphics-solution.com
Marketing communications products, print products, promotional products, customized apparel, signage, graphic design, web design, marketing consulting, audio/video production. (AA, estab 2008, empl 5, sales $423,000, cert: NMSDC)

1490 Ideas to Impress, LLC
      35 Longman St
      Toms River, NJ 08753
      Contact: Debbie Dennerlein President
      Tel: 201-750-0222
      Email: debbie@ideastoimpress.com
      Website: www.ideastoimpress.com
Dist promotional products, company brand / logo, customized printed, embroidered & laser etched products: t-shirts, polo shirts, sweatshirts & uniforms, pens, desk accessories, to signs, and table covers, executive gift & give-aways. (Woman, estab 2006, empl 1, sales $103,211, cert: WBENC)

1491 Impact Dimensions, LLC and Affiliate
      725 Hylton Rd
      Pennsauken, NJ 08110
      Contact: Norbert McGettigan COO
      Tel: 856-382-4501
      Email: norbertm@impactdimensions.com
      Website: www.impactdimensions.com
Embroidery & apparel, advertising specialties, and corporate gifts. (Hisp, estab 2002, empl , sales $12,368,000, cert: NMSDC, SDB)

1492 Imprint Source LLC
      15 Charles St
      Westwood, NJ 07675
      Contact: Karen Adler Acct Exec
      Tel: 201-358-1010
      Email: karen@theimprintsource.com
      Website: www.TheImprintSource.com
Imprinted promotional products. (Woman, estab 1994, empl 6, sales , cert: WBENC)

1493 LeRoe Corporate Gifts, Inc.
      43 Haytown Rd
      Lebanon, NJ 08833
      Contact: Rochelle Moneta Owner
      Tel: 908-236-8754
      Email: rmoneta@leroe.com
      Website: www.LeRoe.com
Promotional, incentive & business gifts, employee recognition & gifts. (Woman, estab 1999, empl 2, sales $250,000, cert: WBENC)

1494 Marissa L. Promotions
      1020 Campus Dr W
      Morganville, NJ 07751
      Contact: Marissa Harkavay Partner
      Tel: 732-689-2299
      Email: hello@creativesolutions.net
      Website: www.creativesolutions.net
Promotional & advertising specialties: trade show give-aways, corporate gifts, screen printing, graphic design. (Woman, estab 1990, empl 20, sales , cert: WBENC)

1495 Nygala Corp.
      115 Moonachie Ave
      Moonachie, NJ 07074
      Contact: Giancarlo Carrillo Key Accounts Mgr
      Tel: 201-288-6400
      Email: Giancarlo@flomousa.com
      Website: www.flomoglobal.com
Dist school supplies, gift bags & accessories. (Minority, Woman, estab 1992, empl 18, sales , cert: NMSDC, WBENC)

1496 Progressive Promotions Inc.
      145 Cedar Lane
      Englewood, NJ 07631
      Contact: Julie Levi President
      Tel: 201-945-0500
      Email: julie@progressivepromotions.com
      Website: www.progressivepromotions.com
Promotional products: corporate apparel, gifts, awards, uniforms, web stores, fulfillment, packaging & assembly. (Woman, estab 1987, empl 30, sales , cert: WBENC)

1497 Sabella Gabino Inc. dba Bella Marketing Inc.
      5 Deer Path
      Holmdel, NJ 07733
      Contact: Isabella Petruzzelli Founder/CEO
      Tel: 917-951-3025
      Email: isabella@bellamarketinginc.com
      Website: www.bellamarketinginc.com
Custom designed, promotional branded products specializing in the medical & pharmaceutical industry. (Minority, Woman, estab 2001, empl 1, sales , cert: NMSDC, WBENC)

1498 Significant Printz
      663-665 Elizabeth Ave
      Newark, NJ 07112
      Contact: TIffany Ryan Owner
      Tel: 862-755-8658
      Email: significantprintz@gmail.com
      Website: www.significantprintz.com
In-house graphic tshirt, hoodies and other apparel printing & production capabilities. (AA, estab 2020, empl 1, sales , cert: State)

1499 Stackable Sensations
      2200 Rt. 10 West, Ste 206
      Parsippany, NJ 07054
      Contact: Shari Verrone President
      Tel: 973-442-2831
      Email: Shariv@stackablesensations.com
      Website: www.stackablesensations.com/
Promotional marketing solution, online stores, fulfillment, global unique promotional items. (Woman, estab 2003, empl 14, sales $2,802,447, cert: WBENC)

1500 Thomas Direct Sales, Inc.
      30 Plymouth St
      Fairfield, NJ 07004
      Contact: Guy DAndrea COO
      Tel: 973-614-2307
      Email: mmarinzulich@thomasdirect.com
      Website: www.thomasdirect.com
Promotional products, premium & incentive programs, importing, on-site design & illustration, graphic arts, technology & website development. (Woman, estab 1986, empl 12, sales $1,000,000, cert: WBENC)

1501 Wisco Promo Uniform, INC.
      160 US Hwy 46
      Saddle Brook, NJ 07663
      Contact: Linda Briscoe President
      Tel: 973-767-2022
      Email: briscoe_linda@yahoo.com
      Website: www.wiscopnu.com
Mfr apparel, uniforms & aprons, silk screen & embroidery, promotional products, corporate identity & promotion. (Minority, Woman, estab 1999, empl 10, sales , cert: NMSDC)

Nevada

1502 Eagle Promotions
4575 W Post Rd Ste 100
Las Vegas, NV 89118
Contact: Mario Stadtlander President
Tel: 702-388-7100
Email: mario@eaglepromotions.com
Website: www.eaglepromotions.com
Advertising specialties: apparel, awards, catalog, company store fulfillment programs. (As-Pac, estab 2001, empl 203, sales $36,400,000, cert: NMSDC)

New York

1503 AIA New Dimensions in Marketing, Inc.
124 S Central Ave
Elmsford, NY 10523
Contact: Maria Perex President
Tel: 914-348-4872
Email: perez@effectivepromos.com
Website: www.effectivepromos.com
Promotional & specialty advertising items. (Minority, Woman, estab 1999, empl 3, sales $355,000, cert: State, WBENC)

1504 Dakota Print and Premiums LLC
150 Barton Road
White Plains, NY 10605
Contact: Stuart Standard President
Tel: 914-831-9101
Email: stuart@fuseprinting.com
Website: www.fuseprinting.com
Promotional products, commercial printing, wide format & transit advertising, vehicle wraps, transit & marketing tools provider, screen printing, banners, posters, postcards, journals, award items, etc. (Woman/AA, estab 2004, empl 3, sales $606,000, cert: State, City, NMSDC)

1505 Don Jagoda Associates, Inc
100 Marcus Dr
Melville, NY 11747
Contact: Rich Fascianella Acct Dir
Tel: 631-454-1800
Email: rfascianella@dja.com
Website: www.dja.com
Full-service promotion marketing, sweepstakes, contests, instant win games, and consumer incentive, reward, and loyalty programs. (Woman, estab 1962, empl 55, sales $11,107,000, cert: WBENC)

1506 Freestyle Marketing, LLC
362 Fifth Ave Ste 1003
New York, NY 10001
Contact: Caryn Stoll President
Tel: 212-599-5995
Email: info@freestylemktg.com
Website: www.freestylemktg.com
Promotional marketing materials & premiums. (Woman, estab 2001, empl 40, sales $7,000,000, cert: WBENC)

1507 Innovative Premiums Inc.
3571 Hargale Rd
Oceanside, NY 11572
Contact: VP
Tel: 516-766-3800
Email: contactus@innovativepremiums.com
Website: www.innovativepremiums.com
Custom & standard promotional merchandise. (Woman, estab 1980, empl 14, sales $9,000,000, cert: WBENC)

1508 inQueue Designs LLC
25 Central Park W
New York, NY 10023
Contact: Alison Schneiderman Co-Owner
Tel: 917-699-8259
Email: alison@inqueuedesigns.com
Website: www.inQueuedesigns.com
Custom branded, designed products, stationery goods, seasonal promotions, corporate gifts, journal books, log books, die-cut folders & boxes, ipad book case, (Woman, estab 2010, empl 2, sales , cert: WBENC)

1509 KarSun Enterprises, Inc.
1133 Broadway, Ste 1311
New York, NY 10010
Contact: Sung Park President
Tel: 212-420-6688
Email: sung@customdirectpromo.com
Website: www.karsunenterprises.com
Promotional & merchandise bags, backpacks & duffels. (Minority, Woman, estab 1996, empl 10, sales $3,500,000, cert: NMSDC)

1510 Multi Media Promotions
33 Southwick Court S
Plainview, NY 11803
Contact: FirstName LastName Managing Partner
Tel: 516-935-0553
Email: beth@mmpromos.com
Website: www.mmpromos.com
Promotional advertising & premium incentives, logos, graphic design, printing, imprinting, embroidery, embossing & engraving. (Woman, estab 2004, empl 3, sales $1,200,000, cert: State, City, WBENC)

1511 National Gifts Ltd.
6 Poole St
Oceanside, NY 11572
Contact: Elaine Goodman CEO
Tel: 516-763-9000
Email: elaine@nationalgifts.com
Website: www.nationalgifts.com
Advertising specialities, premiums, gifts, awards, trophies, wearables, promotional items, etc. (Woman, estab 1983, empl 6, sales $12,250,000, cert: WBENC)

1512 Print & Mail Partners, Inc.
2152 Ralph Ave Ste 317
Brooklyn, NY 11234
Contact: Rose Mazzone President
Tel: 646-771-4245
Email: rose.mazzone@theperfectpromo.com
Website: www.theperfectpromo.com
Custom imprinted T-shirts, advertising specialties, promotional items, buttons, badges, premiums, corporate merchandise & giveaways. (Woman, estab 1997, empl 3, sales , cert: State, City)

1513 Sauerbach Associates
1745 Merrick Ave Ste 27
Merrick, NY 11566
Contact: Janet Silver President
Tel: 516-868-9650
Email: customerservice@sauerbach.com
Website: www.sauerbach.com
Sales incentive programs, promotional products programs, company stores, trade show marketing, new product launches, road shows, sales training meetings. (Woman, estab 1954, empl 6, sales $1,600,000, cert: WBENC)

1514 Sentec Promotions, Inc
      4367 Harlem Rd
      Amherst, NY 14226
      Contact: Susan Cataudella President
      Tel: 716-839-2294
      Email: susiespec@aol.com
      Website: www.susiespecialties.com
Promotional products.
(Woman, estab 1994, empl 3, sales $1,090,404, cert: WBENC)

1515 United Print Group, Inc.
      36-36 33rd St
      Long Island City, NY 11106
      Contact: Bob Sanchez President
      Tel: 718-392-4242
      Email: rsanchez@unitedpg.com
      Website: www.unitedpg.com
Promotional products, commerical printing, signage & table skirts. (Hisp, estab , empl , sales $6,000,000, cert: NMSDC)

1516 Von Pok & Chang
      60 E 42 St, Ste 666
      New York, NY 10165
      Contact: Peter Sebastian Sales
      Tel: 212-599-0556
      Email: peter.sebastian@vonpok.com
      Website: www.vonpok.com
Contract mfr & import promotional products. (As-Pac, estab 1981, empl 8, sales , cert: NMSDC)

Ohio

1517 Airmate Company
      16280 County Rd D
      Bryan, OH 43506
      Contact: Carol Czech President
      Tel: 419-636-3184
      Email: carol@airmatecompany.com
      Website: www.airmatecompany.com
Safety signs, promotional products, custom fabrication, custom printing. (Woman, estab 1946, empl 35, sales $4,200,000, cert: WBENC)

1518 Arrasmith Promotions LLC
      6115 Wiehe Rd
      Cincinnati, OH 45237
      Contact: Jerry Arrasmith Jr. President
      Tel: 513-681-9400
      Email: sales@arrasmithpromotions.com
      Website: www.arrasmithpromotions.com
Advertising specialties & promotional items. (Woman, estab 2003, empl 6, sales $2,100,000, cert: WBENC)

1519 Bouzounis LLC dba Artina Promotional Products
      50 S Liberty St Ste 250
      Powell, OH 43065
      Contact: Lesley Jennings Sr Acct Exec
      Tel: 614-635-8865
      Email: ljennings@artina.com
      Website: www.artina.com
Promotional products. (Woman, estab 1967, empl 22, sales $4,353,500, cert: WBENC)

1520 Eat It Read It Placemats
      45 W Main St
      McConnelsville, OH 43756
      Contact: Heather Hill CEO
      Tel: 740-962-6899
      Email: hbhill@ergraphics.com
      Website: www.ergraphics.com
Advertising specialties, apparel, uniforms, signs, website design, printing. (Woman/AA, estab 2001, empl 3, sales $175,000, cert: State)

1521 EB ART EB ADS LLC
      9045 Spooky Ridge Ln
      Cincinnati, OH 45242
      Contact: Eileen Bloustein CEO
      Tel: 513-405-6469
      Email: sales@ebartebads.com
      Website: www.ebartebads.com
Dist promotional products: corporate awards, portraits, limited editions giclee, digital art & sculpture. (Woman, estab 1999, empl 1, sales , cert: WBENC)

1522 Global Promotions & Incentives, LLC
      3375 Gilchrist Rd
      Mogadore, OH 44260
      Contact: Jonathan Thornton Reg Dir, Key Accounts Exec
      Tel: 330-798-5175
      Email: jdthornton@aswglobal.com
      Website: www.shopglobalpai.com/
Promotional & incentive products, programs & event planning. (AA, estab 2002, empl 31, sales $5,500,000, cert: NMSDC)

1523 Ketterer Company
      12110 Ellington Ct
      Cincinnati, OH 45249
      Contact: Kimberly W. Ketterer CEO
      Tel: 513-247-0100
      Email: kim_ketterer@kettererco.com
      Website: www.getLOGOstuff.com
Promotional advertising: logo design, graphic art, warehousing, distribution & fulfillment services, company stores & online rewards programs. (Woman, estab 1955, empl 6, sales $3,609,077, cert: WBENC)

1524 Leader Promotions, Inc.
      790 E Johnstown Rd
      Columbus, OH 43230
      Contact: Stephanie Leader CEO
      Tel: 614-416-6565
      Email: supplierdiversity@leaderpromos.com
      Website: www.leaderpromos.com
Fulfillment programs, corporate apparel, promotional products & uniforms. (Woman, estab 1995, empl 105, sales $50,000,000, cert: WBENC)

1525 LIZard Apparel & Promotions
      775 Congress Park Dr
      Dayton, OH 45459
      Contact: Kelly Davis VP Sales
      Tel: 937-848-7100
      Email: kelly@lizardap.com
      Website: www.lizardap.com
Promotional, recognition & rewards programs, uniform fittings, Shoe programs, Uniform accessories, name badges, stethoscopes, scissors, arm sleeves. (Woman, estab 2013, empl 10, sales $1,231,824, cert: WBENC)

ADVERTISING SPECIALTIES

1526 Outreach Promotional Solutions
111 Liberty St Ste 101
Columbus, OH 43215
Contact: Nevin Bansal President
Tel: 216-452-5319
Email: bansal@outreachpromos.com
Website: www.outreachpromos.com
Provides creative promotional product solutions. (As-Ind, estab 2012, empl 12, sales $1,000,000, cert: State)

1527 Palmer Promotions
5245 Indian Run
Cincinnati, OH 45243
Contact: Steven Palmer Owner
Tel: 800-697-0053
Email: steve@palmerpromotions.com
Website: www.palmerpromotions.com
Promotional products, awards, business gifts & decorated apparel. (As-Pac, estab 1983, empl 2, sales $578,066, cert: NMSDC)

1528 Park Place Services
8800 E Pleasant Valley Rd
Cleveland, OH 44131
Contact: Bill Byrne President
Tel: 216-520-8400
Email: bbyrne@proforma.com
Website: www.proforma.com/parkplace
Printing, Promotional products, Corporate Apparel, Marketing literature, Packaging, Trade Show Supplies & giveaways, Business Forms, labels, envelopes. (Woman, estab 1996, empl 700, sales $500,000,000, cert: NWBOC)

1529 Proforma Albrecht & Co.
1040 Technecenter Dr
Milford, OH 45150
Contact: Suzette Albrecht
Tel: 202-237-2828
Email: suzette@albrechtco.com
Website: www.albrechtco.com
Promotional products, tees & clothing, custom logos & designs, decorated corporate gifts. (Woman, estab 1999, empl 150, sales $2,200,000, cert: WBENC)

1530 Proforma Joe Thomas Group
13500 Pearl Rd, Ste 139-107
Cleveland, OH 44136
Contact: Joe Thomas President
Tel: 440-268-0881
Email: joe@proformajoethomasgroup.com
Website: www.proformajoethomasgroup.com
Advertising specialties. (As-Ind, estab 1999, empl 2, sales $1,123,000, cert: NMSDC)

1531 PromoHits! Ltd.
141B N Main St
Bluffton, OH 45817
Contact: Melinda Bowden Owner
Tel: 419-358-0700
Email: mbowden@wcoil.com
Website: www.promohitsltd.com
Promotional items: gift & specialty baskets, jackets, shirts, sweatshirts, pants, hats, windshirts, mousepads, pencil holders, pens, paperclips, USB drives, flash drives/memory drives. (Woman, estab 2000, empl 4, sales $382,780, cert: WBENC)

1532 Promotions Etc., LLC
5000 Acme Dr. Unit A
Fairfield, OH 45014
Contact: Julie Holderbach CEO
Tel: 513-795-7021
Email: julie@mypromotionsetc.com
Website: www.mypromotionsetc.com
Promotional products: apparel & uniforms, corporate gifts, give-a-ways, awards, engraved items, decals, labels, trade show give-a-ways, booth display & signage. (Woman, estab 2012, empl 2, sales $125,000, cert: State)

1533 Race Ahead
7100 Euclid Ave Ste 175
Cleveland, OH 44103
Contact: Beth Eaton President
Tel: 440-554-7018
Email: beth@raceaheadcle.com
Website: www.raceaheadcle.com
Customized apparel & branded accessories. (Woman, estab 2016, empl 1, sales $260,000, cert: City)

1534 RJ Manray - Promotional Products
9500 Springfield Rd, Unit 5
Poland, OH 44514
Contact: Rowena Henderson CEO
Tel: 234-201-0160
Email: rrlimos18@gmail.com
Website: www.rjmanray.com/
Dist personalized and custom logo tote bags. (Woman, estab 1986, empl 11, sales $640,000, cert: WBENC)

1535 Schaffer Partners, Inc.
6545 Carnegie Ave
Cleveland, OH 44103
Contact: Susan Mayrant VP Business Dev
Tel: 863-299-6392
Email: susan.mayrant@spihq.com
Website: www.pfi-awards.com
Incentive merchandise fulfillment & program administration resources, design & manage online & paper based solutions, brand name merchandise awards, travel rewards & event tickets. (Woman, estab 1968, empl 40, sales $10,017,858, cert: WBENC)

1536 Ten 10 Design LLC
119 Main St
Chardon, OH 44024
Contact: Casey Zulandt Owner
Tel: 440-286-4367
Email: casey@ten10design.com
Website: www.ten10design.com
Printing (offset and digital), promotional items, ad specialties, mailing services, labels & decals, graphic design, web design. (Woman/AA, estab 2009, empl 5, sales $3,093,663, cert: State, NMSDC, WBENC)

1537 The AG Group, Inc. dba AG PrintPromo Solutions
960 Graham Rd, Ste 1
Cuyahoga Falls, OH 44221
Contact: Anup Gupta President
Tel: 330-315-9600
Email: agupta@theaggroup.com
Website: www.theaggroup.com
Dist promotional products, gifts, corporate apparel, embroidered & screen printed. (Minority, Woman, estab 1996, empl 5, sales $3,300,000, cert: State)

1538 The Callard Company
811 Green Crest Dr Ste 300
Westerville, OH 43081
Contact: Robin Welch Acct Exec
Tel: 614-933-0303
Email: rwelch@callard.com
Website: www.callard.com
Promotional products & creative marketing: awards, trade show giveaways, team rewards, client gifts, recruitment incentives & golf outing supplies. (Woman, estab 1987, empl 24, sales , cert: WBENC)

1539 The John K. Howe Company, Inc.
7188 Main St
Cincinnati, OH 45244
Contact: CEO
Tel: 513-651-1888
Email: salesinfo@ehowe.com
Website: www.ehowe.com
Branded apparel, promotional products & business recognition. (Woman, estab 1972, empl 10, sales $2,232,110, cert: WBENC)

1540 Vorce & Associates
1335 Dublin Rd Ste 216C
Columbus, OH 43215
Contact: Donna Vorce Owner
Tel: 614-488-5450
Email: donna@firstimpressionsohio.com
Website: www.firstimpressionsohio.com
Promotional & imprinted apparel. (Woman, estab 1983, empl 2, sales $810,000, cert: State)

Oregon

1541 Enthusias Media Group
1631 NE Broadway, Ste 614
Portland, OR 97232
Contact: Marcy Hall Reg acct Mgr
Tel: 503-376-6839
Email: info@enthusiastmediagroup.com
Website: www.enthusiastmediagroup.com
Promotional & print items. (Woman, estab 2005, empl 7, sales $2,000,000, cert: State)

Pennsylvania

1542 As You Wish Promotions
3801 Germantown Pike Ste 202
Collegeville, PA 19426
Contact: Alyssa Heininger Client Relationship Coord
Tel: 484-973-6565
Email: aheininger@wishpromo.com
Website: www.wishpromo.com
Promotional products, graphic arts capabilities, marketing, service, client support & customer relations, trade show give-aways, corporate gifts, promotional apparel & employee awards. (Woman, estab 1992, empl 5, sales $1,913,640, cert: WBENC)

1543 BDJ Ventures, LLC
3024 Bainbridge Dr
Lansdale, PA 19446
Contact: Bernard Wright Principal
Tel: 215-266-2062
Email: bwright@bdjventuresllc.com
Website: www.bdjventuresllc.com
Premiums & promotional products. (AA, estab 2009, empl 3, sales , cert: State, NMSDC)

1544 Bry-Lex Promotional LLC
19 Nelson Dr
Southampton, PA 18966
Contact: Bev Kaytes CEO
Tel: 800-251-9101
Email: bev@brylex.com
Website: www.bry-lex.com
Promotional items, imprinted logos, blank logos, embroidery/silkscreen. (Woman, estab 1996, empl 11, sales $550,000, cert: State, WBENC)

1545 Carol Philp Inc
336 1st St
Pittsburgh, PA 15215
Contact: Carol Philp President
Tel: 412-782-2675
Email: info@cpicreative.com
Website: www.cpicreative.com
Design & fulfil custom programs: service awards, safety, sales incentives, fundraising, trade shows, education, product introduction, ad specialties. (Woman, estab 1994, empl 5, sales $3,370,160, cert: WBENC)

1546 Diversified Business Consultants, Inc.
1009 Sage Rd
West Chester, PA 19382
Contact: President
Tel: 610-692-3600
Email: jerry@DiversifiedCorp.com
Website: www.diversifiedcorp.com
Promotional products & printing services. (Woman/As-Ind, estab 2000, empl 4, sales , cert: WBENC)

1547 Signature Promotions
715 Twining Road Ste 107
Dresher, PA 19025
Contact: Maureen Coffey Owner
Tel: 215-641-1168
Email: sigpro@comcast.net
Website: www.sigpromo.com
Promotional advertising products, grahic design, product development & fulfillment capabilities. (Woman, estab 1992, empl 1, sales , cert: WBENC)

1548 The Jay Group
700 Indian Springs Dr
Lancaster, PA 17601
Contact: Nicole Sensenig Administrative Asst
Tel: 717-285-6200
Email: nicole.sensenig@jaygroup.com
Website: www.jaygroup.com
Product, literature & catalog fulfillment services, inbound call center, customer service support, co-packing, promotional processing, information technology, sampling services, promotional products, e-business solutions. (Woman, estab 1965, empl 300, sales $25,887,011, cert: WBENC)

Rhode Island

1549 Ahlers Designs, Inc.
999 Main St, Unit 707
Pawtucket, RI 02860
Contact: Gail Ahlers CEO
Tel: 401-365-1010
Email: operations@ahlersdesigns.com
Website: www.ahlersdesigns.com
Designs & mfr custom corporate gifts & awards, engraving, custom cards or packaging. (Woman, estab 1989, empl 3, sales $132,751, cert: State, WBENC

South Carolina

1550 2 Oceans Promotions, LLC
       6175 Caravelle Court
       Awendaw, SC 29429
       Contact: Michele Johnson Owner
       Tel: 843-971-8499
       Email: michele@2oceanspromotions.com
       Website: www.2oceanspromotions.com
Promotional marketing & products. (Woman, estab 2001, empl 6, sales , cert: WBENC)

1551 Promotions Unlimited, LLC
       327 Miller Rd, Ste E
       Mauldin, SC 29662
       Contact: Jo Dir of Sales
       Tel: 864-527-1193
       Email: jo@promoultd.com
       Website: www.promoultd.com
Promotional Items, Uniform Programs (Woman, estab 2005, empl 9, sales $2,254,086, cert: State, WBENC)

1552 Pueri Elmental LLC dba Bonk Fit
       412 Hwy 90 E
       Little River, SC 29566
       Contact: Donna Brin Managing Member
       Tel: 866-639-1430
       Email: donna@bfive40.com
       Website: www.bfive40.com
Digital printer and full-service sew and embroidery operation, offering sustainable solutions for apparel, uniforms and printed signage, especially designed to minimize environmental impact, with a mission of net zero waste. (Woman, estab 2014, empl 14, sales $1,250,000, cert: WBENC)

1553 Red Iron Brand Solutions, LLC
       104 Saluda Run Dr
       Piedmont, SC 29673
       Contact: Vishnu Jampala Owner
       Tel: 800-325-3824
       Email: vishnujam@rwts.net
       Website: www.redironbrand.com
Mfr & import event display items: Tablecovers & runners in stretch fabric, polyester, polyvalue, plastic (cut table covers and imprinted banquet rolls), and 400 denier. (Woman, estab 2016, empl 10, sales , cert: State, WBENC)

Tennessee

1554 Imagination Specialties, Inc.
       623 Old Hickory Blvd.
       Old Hickory, TN 37138
       Contact: Lori Armes Controller
       Tel: 615-255-5688
       Email: loria@imaginationbranding.com
       Website: www.imaginationbranding.com
Ad specialty & promotional products, corporate gifts, baskets, event planning, event room drops, custom printing, invitations, mail outs, online company stores, warehousing, distribution & fulfillment services. (Woman, estab 1989, empl 39, sales $11,275,000, cert: WBENC)

1555 Signet, Inc.
       1801 N Shelby Oaks Dr, Ste 12
       Memphis, TN 38134
       Contact: Elizabeth Tate CEO
       Tel: 901-387-5555
       Email: etate@gosignet.com
       Website: www.gosignet.com
Promotional products, branding, kitting, warehousing, event management. (Woman, estab 0, empl , sales $11,000,000, cert: WBENC)

1556 The Barr Group, Inc.
       230 Great Circle Road, Ste 234
       Nashville, TN 37228
       Contact: Jim Barr Dir of Sales
       Tel: 615-612-0444
       Email: jim@barrgroupinc.com
       Website: www.barrgroupinc.com
Promotional products, printing, indoor & outdoor signage, corrugated packagin, MRO items, transportation brokerage & hauling. (Minority, Woman, estab 1999, empl 6, sales $2,505,000, cert: WBENC)

Texas

1557 Ad-Image Creative Promotions Co.
       851 Lakeview Dr
       Coppell, TX 75019
       Contact: Terri Finazzo President
       Tel: 972-462-0919
       Email: adimagedallas@aol.com
       Website: www.adimagedallas.com
Advertising specialties & promotional products. (Woman, estab 1999, empl 2, sales , cert: State, WBENC)

1558 Artist Touch Design Firm
       8300 Montana Ave
       El Paso, TX 79925
       Contact: Sales
       Tel: 915-778-5515
       Email: contact@artisttouch.com
       Website: www.artisttouch.com
Package graphics to support graphics to Ad Specialties. (Woman/Hisp, estab 1979, empl 4, sales $990,000, cert: State)

1559 Austin Ad Group
       5960 W Parker Rd, Ste 278
       Plano, TX 75093
       Contact: Rhonda Aicklen President
       Tel: 972-307-7100
       Email: orders@austinadgroup.com
       Website: www.AustinAdGroup.com
Promotional logo/branded items: apparel, pens, bags, hats, cups, trinkets, coolers, armbands, badges, balloons, bandana, buttons, flashlights, floor mats, jewelry, tattoos, stuffed animals, awards, grills, etc. (Woman, estab 1993, empl 7, sales , cert: State)

1560 Aztec Promotional Group, LP
       2815 Manor Rd
       Austin, TX 78722
       Contact: Patti Winstanley President
       Tel: 512-744-0195
       Email: patti@aztecworld.com
       Website: www.aztecworld.com
Sscreen printed & embroidered textiles, advertising specialty items & design. (Woman/AA, estab 1995, empl 25, sales $1,350,000, cert: State, WBENC)

1561 Beehive Specialty Co.
      8701 Wall St, Ste 900
      Austin, TX 78754
      Contact: Kelli Dillon Mgr/new business dept
      Tel: 512-912-7940
      Email: kelli@specialbee.com
      Website: www.beehivespecialty.com
Promotional products, custom product fabrication, on-line programs, high impact mail, packaging, fulfillment & integrated project management. (Woman, estab 1998, empl 12, sales $8,000,000, cert: WBENC)

1562 Cadena Specialty Advertising
      PO Box 150655
      Arlington, TX 76015
      Contact: Olga Quiroz Owner
      Tel: 817-459-4474
      Email: olga_cadenaspecialty@yahoo.com
      Website: www.cadenausa.com
Dist promotional marketing products: pens, cups, key tags, calendards, silkscreened & embroidered caps & apparel, employee recognition & safety awards & gifts. (Minority, Woman, estab 1993, empl 1, sales $155,000, cert: State, City)

1563 CFJ Manufacturing
      701 Eight Twenty Blvd. Ste 145
      Fort Worth, TX 76106
      Contact: Sharon Evans CEO
      Tel: 817-625-9559
      Email: marketing@cfjmfg.com
      Website: www.cfjmfg.com
Promotional marketing & employee recognition solutions. (Woman, estab 1983, empl 201, sales $50,000,000, cert: WBENC)

1564 Creative Menus & Folders, LLC dba Texas Covers
      409 Old Hwy 80
      Olden, TX 76466
      Contact: Renee Ferguson Asst Production Mgr
      Tel: 254-653-2775
      Email: reneeferguson@texascovers.com
      Website: www.texascovers.com
Presentation/Executive Binders, folders, business cards, printing (screen, digital, offset, foil stamp, deboss, specialty color cast printing, plastic ID badge holders, ID badges, name tags, souvenir printing, banners, signage, laminating, caps. (As-Pac, estab 2015, empl 19, sales , cert: NMSDC)

1565 Davis & Stanton, Inc.
      4002 W Miller Rd, Ste 140
      Garland, TX 75041
      Contact: Charlee Castillo Owner
      Tel: 214-340-1321
      Email: charlee@davstan.com
      Website: www.davstan.com
Advertising specialties, promotional products, plaques & awards & police commendation bars. (Minority, Woman, estab 1949, empl 26, sales $5,000,000, cert: State, WBENC)

1566 DBS Marketing & Promotions LLC
      24466 Pipestem Dr
      Magnolia, TX 77355
      Contact: Sue Becknell President
      Tel: 281-356-2386
      Email: sue@dbspromo.com
      Website: www.dbspromo.com
Logo branded promotional products, corporate apparel, awards, pens, notepads, shirts, caps, jackets, screen printing, laser engraving, embroidery, pad folios, backpacks, duffel bags, tote bags, tee shirts, golf items, flyers, etc. (Woman, estab 2005, empl 3, sales $1,230,000, cert: WBENC)

1567 Distinctive Marketing Ideas
      3415 Custer Rd, Ste 133
      Plano, TX 75023
      Contact: Bonnie Shackelford Owner
      Tel: 972-612-0050
      Email: bonnie.shack@dmipromotions.com
      Website: www.dmipromotions.com
Promotional products/premiums, warehouse & fulfillment. (Woman, estab 1992, empl 4, sales $1,750,000, cert: State, WBENC)

1568 Fuel7 Inc.
      11910 Greenville Ave, Ste 275
      Dallas, TX 75243
      Contact: Steven Pratt
      Tel: 888-669-4009
      Email: steven@fuel7.com
      Website: www.fuel7.com
Fuel7 provides embedded development services, both hardware and software, specializing in new embedded Linux projects. From design and architecture through development and board bringup (Hisp, estab 2004, empl 12, sales $2,200,000, cert: NMSDC)

1569 Graves Group Promotions
      3851 Camp Bowie Blvd Ste 300
      Fort Worth, TX 76107
      Contact: President
      Tel: 817-738-8446
      Email: info@gravesgroup.com
      Website: www.gravesgroup.com
Custom promotional products: apparel, awards, novelty, golf, computer, sports & leisure items. (Woman, estab 1997, empl 4, sales , cert: WBENC)

1570 Henya Direct LLC
      5555 W University Blvd
      Dallas, TX 75209
      Contact: Terence Johnson Natl Accts Mgr
      Tel: 214-701-0671
      Email: tjohnson@henyadirect.com
      Website: www.henyadirect.com
Promotional merchandise: uniforms, hats, cups, stress balls, pens, bags, watches, etc. (Woman, estab 2007, empl 3, sales $1,500,000, cert: WBENC)

1571 Holden Custom Products
      7920 Beltline Rd Ste 960
      Dallas, TX 75254
      Contact: Marnie Holden Dir Major Accounts
      Tel: 214-543-1133
      Email: holdenll@flash.net
      Website: www.holdenbrand.com
Corporate packaging, promotional products, imports & wearables. (Woman, estab 1978, empl 16, sales $9,500,000, cert: State)

ADVERTISING SPECIALTIES

1572 I Chispa, LLC
      129 Thunderbird
      El Paso, TX 79912
      Contact: Horacio Arras VP Sales & Mktg
      Tel: 915-239-7430
      Email: horacio@ichispa.us
      Website: www.ichispa.us
Promotional & sports items. (Minority, Woman, estab 2010, empl 5, sales , cert: State, NMSDC)

1573 IncentiveAmerica, Inc.
      18208 Preston Rd Ste D924
      Dallas, TX 75252
      Contact: Elizabeth Montgomery President
      Tel: 972-380-9990
      Email: elizabethm@incentiveamerica.com
      Website: www.incentiveamerica.com
Pre-paid MasterCard gift cards & dining gift cards, personalized, premium note card & gold-embossed greeting card. (Woman/AA, estab , empl , sales $968,290, cert: State, NMSDC, 8(a))

1574 Insignia Marketing
      32731 Egypt Lane Ste 301
      Magnolia, TX 77354
      Contact: Christine McAtee President
      Tel: 281-465-0040
      Email: orders@visicare.com
      Website: www.VisiCare.com
Promotional advertising: corporate brand identity, creativity, pens, coffee mugs, t-shirts & awards. (Woman, estab 2002, empl 3, sales $2,000,000, cert: State, WBENC)

1575 Network Embroidery Inc.
      10600 Shadow Wood Dr Ste 201
      Houston, TX 77043
      Contact: Lily Clark President
      Tel: 713-865-8032
      Email: micael.shea@networkinterstateco.com
      Website: www.networkinterstateco.com
Mfr & dist promotional products, catalog programs, awards, trophies, graphics, warehousing & fulfillment. (Woman, estab 0, empl , sales , cert: WBENC)

1576 Potenza Promotions, LLC
      810 Genoa
      Argyle, TX 76226
      Contact: Laura Hulke President
      Tel: 940-595-9555
      Email: lhulke@potenzapromotions.com
      Website: www.potenzapromotions.com
Promotional products: mugs, pens, stress balls, awards, office items, USB pens, etc. (Woman, estab 2006, empl 6, sales $147,000, cert: State)

1577 Power Of Two Productions, LLC
      9901 Brodie Ln, Ste 160-279
      Austin, TX 78748
      Contact: LeeAnn Wick CEO
      Tel: 512-872-5000
      Email: leeann@ptwopromo.com
      Website: www.PTwoPromo.com
Promotional products, business gifts, trade show giveaways, wellness programs, incentives, awards, safety, screen printing, embroidery, apparel, employee retention, sustainable, eco friendly, tote bags, promotions. (Minority, Woman, estab 2007, empl 3, sales $419,000, cert: State, NMSDC, WBENC)

1578 Radia Enterprises Inc.
      3800 Juniper St
      Houston, TX 77087
      Contact: Rupendra Radia CEO
      Tel: 713-645-6383
      Email: rradia56@gmail.com
      Website: www.spectrumuniforms.com
Uniforms and promotional products. (As-Ind, estab 1992, empl 20, sales $3,500,000, cert: NMSDC)

1579 RG Apparel Co.
      2912 N MacArthur, Ste 103
      Irving, TX 75062
      Contact: Joe Temple COO
      Tel: 972-793-0583
      Email: jt@rgapparel.com
      Website: www.rgapparel.com
Mfr textiles: uniforms, work shirts, polos, tees, woven button up shirts & headwear, promotional marketing items & gifts. (AA, estab 2006, empl 6, sales $3,200,000, cert: State, NMSDC)

1580 SWAG247 Branded Solutions
      5 Cowboys Way Ste #300
      Frisco, TX 75034
      Contact: Reginald Hilliard CEO
      Tel: 469-826-2277
      Email: swag247@swag247.biz
      Website: www.swag247.world
Premium Promotional Products & Imprinted Advertising Specialty Items. (AA, estab 1989, empl 4, sales $875,000, cert: City)

1581 The Donna Bender Company
      6860 North Dallas Pkwy Ste 200
      Plano, TX 75024
      Contact: Donna Bender President
      Tel: 214-520-8577
      Email: donna@donnaco.com
      Website: www.donnaco.com
Promotional products; specialty advertising; business gifts; service, achievement & recognition awards; incentive & awareness programs. (Woman, estab 2007, empl 3, sales , cert: State, WBENC)

1582 TLC Adcentives LLC
      21101 Kingsland Blvd. Ste. 1113
      Katy, TX 77450
      Contact: Terri Hornsby President
      Tel: 281-828-2270
      Email: terri@tlcadcentives.com
      Website: www.tlcadcentives.com
Advertising promotional incentives, awards & trophies, cups & mugs, apparel & headgear, desk accessories, writing instruments, portfolios, briefcases. (Woman/AA, estab 1995, empl 4, sales $175,000, cert: State, NMSDC, WBENC)

1583 Trademarks Promotional Products
      11333 Todd St
      Houston, TX 77055
      Contact: Kelli Cochran Acct Mgr
      Tel: 713-680-3000
      Email: tpp@tmarks.com
      Website: www.trademarkspromos.com
Promotional products, screenprinting, embroidery, direct digital garment printing, graphic design, award engraving, ad specialty items. (Woman, estab 1979, empl 60, sales $7,100,001, cert: State, WBENC)

1584 Trinity Enterprise Group LLC
 400 S Zang Blvd, Ste 240
 Dallas, TX 75208
 Contact: Casey Gonzales COO
 Tel: 214-785-6741
 Email: casey@tegroup.biz
 Website: www.tegroup.biz
Advertising items, Apparel, Uniforms, Hats, Gifts, Trophies, Awards, Nameplates, PPE, Sports Bags, Pens, Business Supplies, Technology items, Signage, and Custom ordered goods. (Hisp, estab 2020, empl 5, sales , cert: NMSDC)

1585 W. M. Martin Advertising
 PO Box 795818
 Dallas, TX 75379
 Contact: Wendy Fahle Owner
 Tel: 972-732-8040
 Email: cs@wmmadv.com
 Website: www.wmmadv.com
Advertising specialties: pens, shirts, caps, calendars, golf items. (Woman, estab 1983, empl 4, sales $850,000, cert: State, WBENC)

Virginia

1586 E&R Sales Inc.
 4800 Market Square Lane
 Midlothian, VA 23112
 Contact: Elissa Mast President
 Tel: 804-744-8000
 Email: headcoach@ersales.com
 Website: www.ersales.com
Balloons, pens and novelty trend items. (Minority, Woman, estab , empl , sales , cert: WBENC)

1587 Fishnet, LLC
 PO Box 7311
 Charlottesville, VA 22906
 Contact: David Goloversic Sr Acct Exec
 Tel: 434-409-6177
 Email: contactus@fishnetllc.com
 Website: www.fishnetllc.com
Printing & promotional products: writing instruments, office accessories, food and drink ware, doormats, banners, flags, tents, table covers, displays, retractors, bags, health and safety items, coloring books, business cards. (Minority, Woman, estab 2006, empl 2, sales , cert: State)

1588 Global Partner's of Virginia, LLC
 3005 E Boundary Terr, Ste G
 Midlothian, VA 23112
 Contact: Norm Falkner VP
 Tel: 804-744-8112
 Email: logos@globalpromosonline.com
 Website: www.globalpromosonline.com
Logo wear, embroidery, silk screen, screen printing, direct to garment ink jet printing, heat transfer. Corporate apparel, mens, ladies, kids, uniforms. Promotional Products, pens, magnets, calendars, Bags, towels, luggage, sportwear, team uniforms. (Woman, estab 2001, empl 4, sales $350,000, cert: State)

1589 It's A Breeze Specialties, LLC
 8221 Little Florida Rd
 Mechanicsville, VA 23111
 Contact: Shirley Husz President
 Tel: 804-779-0183
 Email: shirley@itsabreez.com
 Website: www.itsabreez.com
Promotional products, corporate apparel, screen printed & embroidered, awards, incentives & award programs. (Woman, estab 2002, empl 2, sales $140,000, cert: State)

1590 Rivanna Natural Designs, Inc.
 3009 Lincoln Ave
 Richmond, VA 23228
 Contact: Crystal Mario President
 Tel: 434-244-3447
 Email: cmario@rivannadesigns.com
 Website: www.rivannadesigns.com
Environmentally responsible gifts, plaques & awards. (Woman, estab , empl , sales , cert: State)

1591 The Advertising Specialist, L.C.
 PO Box 5325
 Midlothian, VA 23112
 Contact: Jeanette Mayo President
 Tel: 804-744-0044
 Email: advertisingspecialist@verizon.net
 Website: www.advertisingspecialist.com
Promotional products, banners, sport uniforms, T-Shirts, Website Design, Screen Printing & Embroidery. (Woman/AA, estab 1997, empl 3, sales , cert: State)

1592 WKG Global Enterprises, Inc.
 100 Stafford Ct
 Williamsburg, VA 23185
 Contact: Regina Kenerley General Mgr
 Tel: 757-220-9259
 Email: rkenerley@kernergroup.com
 Website: www.alogoforyou.com
Custom embroidery, screen printing, laser engraving, promotional products, trophies, awards, corporate gifts, monogramming, webstores. (Woman, estab 2011, empl 10, sales $1,500,000, cert: State)

Washington

1593 Brand|Pride
 6523 California Ave SW, Ste 329
 Seattle, WA 98136
 Contact: Elise Lindborg CEO
 Tel: 206-938-8828
 Email: glittertheunicorn@brand-pride.com
 Website: www.brand-pride.com
Promotional products. (Woman, estab 2000, empl 3, sales $1,100,000, cert: CPUC, WBENC)

1594 Bravo! Promotional Products
 569 Occidental Ave S
 Seattle, WA 98104
 Contact: Peggie Dickens President
 Tel: 206-682-3953
 Email: peggie@bravobranding.com
 Website: www.bravobranding.com
Offshore sourcing, fulfillment services, creative art services, event fulfillment. (Woman, estab 1995, empl 12, sales $5,969,545, cert: WBENC)

ADVERTISING SPECIALTIES

1595 Gifts by Design, Inc.
66 S Hanford St Ste 100
Seattle, WA 98134
Contact: Andy Sroufe Acct Exec
Tel: 206-286-6688
Email: andy@giftsbydesign.net
Website: www.giftsbydesign.net

Dist art objects, wearables, logo items, awards, baskets, etc. (Woman, estab 1988, empl 11, sales $2,950,000, cert: WBENC)

1596 Unique Experience Custom Embroidery & Screen-Print
234 First St
Bremerton, WA 98337
Contact: Ronald Flemister Mgr
Tel: 360-373-2076
Email: un234@silverlink.net
Website: www.companycasuals.com/uniqueexperience

Custom embroidery, screen printing & promotional products. (Woman/AA, estab 1990, empl 3, sales $250,000, cert: State)

Wisconsin

1597 A Branovan Company, LLC.
6505 W Calumet Rd
Milwaukee, WI 53223
Contact: Marie Branovan CEO
Tel: 414-352-5000
Email: marie@abcgifts.com
Website: www.abcgifts.com

Advertising specilties: custom embroidery & screen printing apparel. (Woman, estab 1996, empl 12, sales $3,712,200, cert: WBENC)

1598 Actualink Designs LLC
N65W12525 Sycamore Ln
Menomonee Falls, WI 53051
Contact: Anthony Martin Owner
Tel: 414-349-4367
Email: info@actualinkdesigns.com
Website: www.actualinkdesigns.com

Embroidery, screen printing & digital printing, polo shirts, caps, graphic design studio. (AA, estab 2012, empl 3, sales , cert: NMSDC)

1599 Madison Avenue Worldwide, LLC
5515 Catfish Court
Westport, WI 53597
Contact: Donna Smith Business Mgr
Tel: 608-850-9663
Email: donna.smith@madisonavenueworldwide.com
Website: www.madisonavenueworldwide.com

Promotional & marketing agency. (Woman, estab 2008, empl 8, sales $2,100,000, cert: WBENC)

1600 on3 Promotional Partners, LLC
1543 Sheridan Rd
Kenosha, WI 53140
Contact: Lora Lehmann Owner
Tel: 262-551-8715
Email: llehmann@on3promopartners.com
Website: www.on3promopartners.com

Promotional products, incentive & loyalty programs, fulfillment, packaging & collateral print needs. (Woman, estab 2005, empl 6, sales $1,850,000, cert: State, WBENC)

1601 Promolux Inc.
6027 W Vliet St
Milwaukee, WI 53213
Contact: CEO
Tel: 414-771-1831
Email: sales@epromolux.com
Website: www.epromolux.com

Dist promotional products: screen printed & embroidered apparel, employee uniforms, trade show giveaways, customer loyalty programs, custom souvenirs & gifts, sales incentives, corporate identity programs, marketing premiums, etc. (Woman, estab 2003, empl 6, sales , cert: WBENC)

1602 Royal Recognition, Inc.
S83 W19105 Saturn Dr
Muskego, WI 53150
Contact: Joseph Cull VP
Tel: 262-679-6050
Email: jcull@royalrec.com
Website: www.royalrec.com

Employee service awads, corporate apparel, recognition/sales awards & promotional items. (Woman, estab 1983, empl 52, sales , cert: State)

**Advocacy.
Support.
Expertise.
Industry Resources.
Seminars & Trainings.
Good to know.**

DIR drives supplier diversity success by providing diverse-supplier data management, education and publications to corporations and diverse-owned suppliers.

Get to know what we know about supplier diversity. Visit www.DiversityInfoResources.com to learn more.

DIR
DIVERSITY
INFORMATION
RESOURCES

VALIDATION
data management
EVALUATE
engage strategy
BEST PRACTICES
reporting
data scrubs
SOURCING
SUPPORT

DIVERSITY recognizes differences, respects individuality & encourages dialog. **INFORMATION** educates & encourages intelligent decisions. **RESOURCES** provide alternatives to create informed solutions. **Work it.**

www.DiversityInfoResources.com

> **ALARM SYSTEMS**
> Manufacturers or wholesalers of fire, security, intercom, CCTV, or other alarm components or systems. NAICS Code 33

Arizona

1603 American Fire Equipment
   3107 W Virginia Ave
   Phoenix, AZ 85009
   Contact: Rose Koppy Admin
   Tel: 602-433-2484
   Email: info@americanfire.com
   Website: www.americanfire.com
Sells, designs, installs, services & repairs all types of fire protection systems, special hazards fire protection, building fire alarm, mass notification, fire sprinkler, kitchen fire suppression. (Woman, estab 1992, empl 125, sales $12,331,853, cert: WBENC)

California

1604 Aponi Products and Services
   3805 Florin Rd Ste 1228
   Sacramento, CA 95823
   Contact: Lisa M Davis lacy Owner
   Tel: 916-392-6571
   Email: lisad@aponitelecommunication.com
   Website: www.aponitelecom.com
Telecommunication Equipment, Installation, Voice, Data, Cabling, Maintenance, Repair, Security System, DVR, Security Cameras. (Woman/Nat-Ame, estab 2007, empl 7, sales $360,000, cert: State, 8(a))

1605 EARL Security, Inc.
   745 E Valley Blvd, Ste 518
   San Gabriel, CA 91776
   Contact: Lynn Chen CEO
   Tel: 626-285-9178
   Email: lynn.chen@earl-security.com
   Website: www.earl-security.com
Install & maintain burglar/intrusion alarms, fire alarms, intercoms, access control closed circuit TV surveillance, metal detectors, electrical. (Minority, Woman, estab 1988, empl 6, sales $596,987, cert: CPUC)

1606 L Tech network Services, Inc.
   9926 Pioneer Blvd, Ste 101
   Santa Fe Springs, CA 90670
   Contact: David McMonigle Dir of Mktg
   Tel: 562-222-1121
   Email: dmcmonigle@ltechnet.com
   Website: www.ltechnet.com
Design, install, integrate, telecommunication networks, fiber optic or wireless, voice, data, security, CCTV. (Hisp, estab 1996, empl 85, sales $4,300,000, cert: NMSDC)

1607 Ramtec Controls Corporation
   9420 Reseda blvd
   Northridge, CA 91324
   Contact: John Finamore GM
   Tel: 818-867-7070
   Email: jfinamore@ramtec.org
   Website: www.ramtec.org
Design, install & service security & fire alarm systems: Access Control, Intrusion Alarms, Video Surveillance, Sound Systems, Fire Alarm. (Woman, estab 1991, empl 8, sales $550,000, cert: State)

District of Columbia

1608 MJS Communications LLC
   1343 First St NW
   Washington, DC 20001
   Contact: Marlon Boykin President
   Tel: 888-829-1658
   Email: mboykin@mjscommunications.biz
   Website: www.mjscommunications.biz
Information technology, telecommunications services, structure cabling system, voice/data cabling, CCTV cabling, POS & wireless, CCTV, digital video recorders, Interior/exterior cameras, monitors, perimeter security. (AA, estab 2009, empl 2, sales $110,000, cert: State, City)

Florida

1609 Aegis Fire and Integrated Services, LLC
   156 Industrial Loop S
   Orange Park, FL 32073
   Contact: Shelli Schmid Reg Sales
   Tel: 904-215-9669
   Email: sschmid@afps.com
   Website: www.aegisfis.com
Fire sprinkler, extinguishers & alarm systems. (As-Pac, estab 2004, empl 42, sales , cert: State, NMSDC)

1610 Audio Video Systems, Inc.
   1860 Old Okeechobee Rd, Ste 104
   West Palm Beach, FL 33409
   Contact: Angela Barnard President
   Tel: 561-686-4473
   Email: angela@cctvrepair.com
   Website: www.cctvrepair.com
Commercial audio, video & electronic security projects, sales, service, installation & integration: burglar alarm, access control, CCTV/video surveillance, commercial audio, commercial video, business class projectors & displays. (Woman, estab 1981, empl 6, sales $800,000, cert: State, City)

1611 AVI Integrators Inc. dba Security 101
   1520 N Powerline Rd
   Pompano Beach, FL 33069
   Contact: Stacy Bjork Controller
   Tel: 954-984-4282
   Email: sbjork@security101.com
   Website: www.Security101.com
Card access, Badging, CCTV, Intercom, Alarms, IP video, Wireless mesh systems. (Hisp, estab 2005, empl 37, sales $7,296,000, cert: State)

1612 Blue Wave Communications, Inc.
   8399 NW 30th Terrace
   Doral, FL 33122
   Contact: Michelle Fernandez Sales Coord
   Tel: 305-436-8886
   Email: mfernandez@bluewavemiami.com
   Website: www.bluewavemiami.com
Low Voltage Cabling, Audio Visual, CCTV/ IP Surveillance Systems, Access Control, Sound Masking/ White Noise, Wireless Installations, Nurse Call Systems (Hisp, estab , empl , sales , cert: State)

1613 Carter Brothers Security Services LLC
      1 Portofino Dr
      Pensacola Beach, FL 32561
      Contact: John F. Carter CEO
      Tel: 770-954-7010
      Email: cbregistrations@carterbrothers.com
      Website: www.carterbrothers.com
Project & program management, fire safety & security systems. (AA, estab 2019, empl 4, sales $350,000, cert: State, NMSDC)

1614 Mainstream IP Solutions, Inc.
      6905 El Dorado Dr
      Tampa, FL 33615
      Contact: Arnie Solomon Acct Mgr
      Tel: 813-549-7768
      Email: asolomon@mcsoftampa.com
      Website: www.mainstreamipsolutions.com
Electrical, structured cabling, audio-visual, security & fire alarm systems. (AA, estab 2010, empl 5, sales $250,000, cert: State, NMSDC, 8(a), SDB)

Georgia

1615 AAA Fire Protection Resources, Inc.
      PO Box 1122
      Lawrenceville, GA 30046
      Contact: President
      Tel: 770-963-0887
      Email:
      Website: www.aaafirepro.com
Fire Extinguisher Sales & Service, Recharging & Inspections, Emergency Exit Lighting. (Woman, estab 1982, empl 4, sales $977,756, cert: WBENC)

1616 Alliance Fire Protection Services, Inc.
      PO Box 1798
      Loganville, GA 30052
      Contact: Angie Jordan Office Mgr
      Tel: 770-554-5004
      Email: acjordan@alliancefire.com
      Website: www.alliancefire.com
Life Safety Inspections & Service, Fire Alarm, Fire Sprinkler, Extinguishers, Hydrants, Backflows & Fire Pumps. (Woman, estab 1999, empl 75, sales $7,768,000, cert: City, WBENC)

1617 DH Security Solutions
      303 Perimeter Center N Ste 300
      Atlanta, GA 30346
      Contact: Tina Dungy President
      Tel: 678-341-9451
      Email: tdungy@dhsecuritysolutions.com
      Website: www.dhsecuritysolutions.com
Locksmith, access control, card readers, door hardware, door closers, electronic gates, safes, vaults, CCTV, door repair, high security solutions. (Woman/AA, estab 2011, empl 12, sales $510,000, cert: NWBOC)

1618 Strickland Security & Safety Solutions
      541 Tenth St NW, Ste 135
      Atlanta, GA 30318
      Contact: Robert Strickland Owner
      Tel: 800-422-9075
      Email: rob@stricklandsecurity.com
      Website: www.stricklandsecurity.com
Service & equipment replacement: CCTV & alarm systems components. (AA, estab 2007, empl 12, sales $2,150,000, cert: NMSDC)

Illinois

1619 A. Ashland Lock Company
      2510 N Ashland Ave
      Chicago, IL 60614
      Contact: Anne Gruber President
      Tel: 773-348-5106
      Email: anne@ashlandlock.com
      Website: www.ashlandlock.com
Door Locks, Locking Hardware, Access Controls, CCTV, Door Closers, Panic Hardware, Fire Rated Door Hardware, Levers, Knobs, Deadbolts, Hollow Metal Doors, Wood Doors, Aluminum Doors & Storefronts. (Woman, estab 1963, empl 12, sales $778,500, cert: WBENC)

1620 Applied Controls & Contracting Services, Inc.
      537 W Taft Dr
      South Holland, IL 60473
      Contact: George Kinnison President
      Tel: 708-596-7400
      Email: gkinnison@accshome.com
      Website: www.accshome.com
Engineering design, project management & estimations, technical analysis, emergency dispatch services installation, design security ad alarm systems, fire detection systems, closed circuit tv system & card access. (AA, estab 1990, empl 11, sales $1,090,522, cert: State, NMSDC)

Indiana

1621 Geyer Fire Protection, LLC
      700 N High School Rd
      Indianapolis, IN 46214
      Contact: Rosemily Geyer
      Tel: 317-490-9357
      Email: rosemily@geyerfire.com
      Website: www.geyerfire.com
Design, install, serve & maintain fire sprinkler systems, fire extinguishers & alarms. (Minority, Woman, estab 2011, empl 12, sales $686,733, cert: State, City, NMSDC)

Kansas

1622 American Fire Sprinkler Corp.
      6750 W 47th Terr
      Mission, KS 66203
      Contact: Tara Beeler Office Mgr
      Tel: 216-361-5730
      Email: tbeeler@americanfiresprinkler.com
      Website: www.americanfiresprinkler.com
Installation, inspection, repair, and maintenance of fire sprinkler systems. (Woman, estab 1968, empl 75, sales $16,209,460, cert: City)

Louisiana

1623 Fire Boss of Louisiana, Inc.
      7905 Hwy 90 W
      New Iberia, LA 70560
      Contact: Debra Denais Romero President
      Tel: 337-365-6729
      Email: debbie@fireboss.com
      Website: www.fireboss.com
Fire & safety protection services, DBI/SALA authorized distributor/repair center, fire & gas detection/suppression system design, engineering & installation, commercial inspection of portable fire extinguishing systems, foam & water systems. (Woman, estab 1975, empl , sales , cert: WBENC)

1624 Fire Tech Systems, Inc.
      721 N Ashley Ridge Loop
      Shreveport, LA 71106
      Contact: Linda Biernacki President
      Tel: 318-688-8800
      Email: lbiernacki@firetechsystems.com
      Website: www.firetechsystems.com
Design, install & service fire sprinkler systems, fire suppression systems, fire extinguishers. (Woman, estab 1990, empl 85, sales , cert: WBENC)

Maryland

1625 Digital Video Solutions, Inc.
      7526 Connelley Dr Ste A
      Hanover, MD 21076
      Contact: John Webster President
      Tel: 240-547-0143
      Email: jwebster@remoteeyes.com
      Website: www.digitalvideosolutions.biz
Designs & integrate physical security systems: CCTV, access control, alarm, public address & intercom systems. (AA, estab 2008, empl 3, sales $302,000, cert: State, NMSDC)

1626 Truth Technology Inc.
      5201 Maries Retreat Dr
      Bowie, MD 20720
      Contact: April Brown President
      Tel: 240-472-9833
      Email: atb@trutechi.com
      Website: www.trutechi.com
CCTV, Key Card Access System, & Biometric devices. (Woman/AA, estab 2006, empl 2, sales $475,000, cert: 8(a))

Michigan

1627 Edgewood Electrical, LLC
      3633 Michigan Ave Ste 100
      Detroit, MI 48216
      Contact: Robert Bell Sr Project Mgr
      Tel: 313-263-0440
      Email: robertb@edgewoodelectric.com
      Website: www.edgewoodelectric.com
Electrical Installations, Design/Build, Design/Assist, Fire Alarm & Low Voltage Systems. (AA, estab 2008, empl 45, sales $12,000,000, cert: NMSDC)

Minnesota

1628 Castle Cop Inc.
      17003 E Lake Netta Dr
      Ham Lake, MN 55304
      Contact: Barb Underdahl CEO
      Tel: 763-438-2761
      Email: castlecopinc@earthlink.net
      Website: www.castlecop.com
Dist stainless steel doorjamb reinforcing device. (Woman, estab 2003, empl 1, sales , cert: State)

1629 Lloyd Security Incorporated
      5051 Hwy 7 Ste 270
      Minneapolis, MN 55416
      Contact: Me'Lea Connelly GM
      Tel: 612-874-9295
      Email: info@lloydsecurity.com
      Website: www.lloydsecurity.com
Installation, repair, service & monitoring of security systems, access control, surveillance and video, perimeter detection, safe rooms, CCTV & ballistic solutions. (Woman, estab 2001, empl 14, sales , cert: State, City)

Missouri

1630 Alternatives In Engineering, Inc.
      1314 Highway DD
      Defiance, MO 63341
      Contact: Jim Wright Business Development Mgr
      Tel: 503-840-2926
      Email: info@aiefirestl.com
      Website: www.aiefirestl.com
Test, inspect & repair fire protection systems: fire sprinklers, pumps, tanks, hydrants, backflow preventers, fire alarms, fire extinguishers, cooking hood suppression sytems. (Woman, estab 1983, empl 37, sales $18,677,400, cert: WBENC)

1631 Mark One
      909 Troost
      Kansas City, MO 64106
      Contact: Rosana Privitera Biondo President
      Tel: 816-842-7023
      Email: rosana.priviterabiondo@markone.com
      Website: www.markone.com
General Electrical Construction, Fire Alarm, Security, CCTV, Utilities, Lighting, Electrical Engineering, Specialty Electrical Construction. (Woman, estab 1974, empl 250, sales $40,000,000, cert: State, WBENC)

Mississippi

1632 HC Services Fire Protection
      1455 West Dr
      Laurel, MS 39440
      Contact: Sue Bridges President
      Tel: 601-399-4800
      Email: sue@hcservicesinc.com
      Website: www.hcservicesinc.com
Dist, service & install fire protection products: extinguishers, fire systems, detection, fire alarms, access control, sprinklers, Fm-200, inergen, halon & speciality hazards. (Woman, estab 1991, empl 13, sales $13,000,000, cert: State, City, WBENC)

North Carolina

1633 SAF Technologies, Inc.
      2032 Independence Commerce Dr Ste B
      Matthews, NC 28105
      Contact: Alan Weeks President
      Tel: 704-844-0955
      Email: alan.weeks@saftechnologies.com
      Website: www.saftechnologies.com
Install, program & maintain security Systems, fire alarm, CCTV, surveillance & access control. (Woman, estab 2004, empl 40, sales , cert: WBENC)

1634 Video & Security Specialists
      2313 Wedgewood Dr
      Matthews, NC 28104
      Contact: Erika Gordon Partner
      Tel: 704-821-9396
      Email: egordon@carolina.rr.com
      Website: www.videoandsecurityspecialists.com
Dist electrical & security products: alarm/security systems, fire alarm systems, structured wiring, access control, security cameras, networking, phone system, intercom & gates. (Woman, estab 1975, empl 7, sales $220,866, cert: State)

New Jersey

1635 DGX, LLC
      840 Bergen Ave
      Jersey City, NJ 07306
      Contact: Sal Austin Sr VP
      Tel: 201-370-4761
      Email: Sal@dgxsecurity.com
      Website: www.dgxsecurity.com
Electronic security: dist, install & miantain video surveillance camera systems, alarm systems, access control systems, card access readers & intercom systems. (AA, estab 2003, empl 20, sales $15,030,000, cert: State)

New York

1636 American Fire Control
      2388 Adam Clayton Powell Blvd
      New York, NY 10030
      Contact: Londel Davis CEO
      Tel: 212-234-1025
      Email: ldavis@americanfirecontrol.com
      Website: www.americanfirecontrol.com
Fire extinguisher maintenance, service, repair, inspection, installation & sales. (AA, estab 2007, empl 8, sales $325,000, cert: State, City, NMSDC)

1637 ASM Security Inc.
      8003 Myrtle Ave
      Glendale, NY 11385
      Contact: Simon Ruderman President
      Tel: 718-839-6000
      Email: sruderman@asmintegrators.com
      Website: www.asmintegrators.com
Design, engineering, filing & expediting fire alarm & security systems. (Minority, Woman, estab 2006, empl 28, sales $2,000,000, cert: State, City)

1638 Care Security Systems Inc
      9 Hemion Road
      Montebello, NY 10952
      Contact: Eli Ribowsky Acct Mgr
      Tel: 845-282-1245
      Email: eribowsky@care-inc.com
      Website: www.caresecuritysystems.com
Design, assembly, testing, installation, maintenance, and management of high-level integrated security systems. (Woman, estab 1987, empl 30, sales , cert: City, WBENC)

1639 Foos Fire, Inc.
      909 Marconi Ave
      Ronkonkoma, NY 11779
      Contact: Kristie Johnson President
      Tel: 631-689-6869
      Email: bids@foosfire.com
      Website: www.foosfire.com
Fire Sprinkler System Installation, Service & Inspections; Fire Protection, Fire Suppression, Wet Systems, Dry Systems, Standpipe Systems & Fire Pumps. (Woman, estab 2008, empl 70, sales $13,000,000, cert: State, WBENC)

Ohio

1640 ABEL Building Systems
      1185 Prairie
      Cincinnati, OH 45215
      Contact: Mgr
      Tel: 513-772-0401
      Email:
      Website: www.abelbuildingsystems.com
Test, maintain, service & install fire alarm, security systems, surveillance cameras, card readers, intercom systems. (Woman/AA, estab 2000, empl 20, sales $2,000,000, cert: WBENC)

1641 Advance Federated Protection
      2000 lee road #202
      Cleveland Heights, OH 44118
      Contact: Alan Lewis Managing General Partner
      Tel: 216-321-1369
      Email: afp044@aol.com
      Website: www.afpsecurity.net
Low Votage Technolgy Burglar Alarm system, Surveillance Cameras-CCTV Fire System, Access Control Medal Detectors (Walk Thru), Guards/ Consulting. (AA, estab 1984, empl 9, sales $184,622, cert: State, City)

1642 American Fire & Sprinkler LLC
      1285 E 49th St
      Cleveland, OH 44114
      Contact: Sharon Lunato President
      Tel: 913-722-6900
      Email: slunato@afsllc.biz
      Website: www.afsllc.biz
Fire protection services: new installation & repairs (Woman, estab , empl , sales $2,457,459, cert: State, City)

1643 Gene Ptacek & Son Fire Equipment Co, Inc.
      7310 Associate Ave
      Brooklyn, OH 44144
      Contact: Gene Ptacek VP
      Tel: 216-651-8300
      Email: gene@gpsfire.com
      Website: www.gpsfire.com
Fire extinguishers, fire suppression systems, Fire alarm & fire sprinkler systems, Inspections, fire extinguisher training, dist fire hose, brass adapters & nozzles. (Woman, estab 1975, empl 52, sales , cert: City)

1644 Rika Group Corporation
      13701 Enterprise Ave
      Cleveland, OH 44135
      Contact: Ryan Temple Dir of Operations
      Tel: 216-325-1006
      Email: ryan@pcsurveillance.net
      Website: www.pcsurveillance.net
Design, dist & install surveillance equipment & systems. (Woman, estab 2001, empl 20, sales $1,600,000, cert: City)

1645 TaiParker Consulting LLC
 4020 Sara Dr
 Uniontown, OH 44685
 Contact: Tai Parker Owner
 Tel: 330-472-2115
 Email: tai@taiparkerconsulting.com
 Website: www.taiparkerconsulting.com
Video Systems Installation / Monitoring / Service, Real Time Remote Video Monitoring, Remote Video Storage, Cellular Only Video Camera Solutions, WiFi / IP Video Camera Solutions, Alarm Systems Installation / Monitoring / Service. (AA, estab 2010, empl 1, sales , cert: State, NMSDC)

Oklahoma

1646 Data Video Systems
 2007 W Shawnee
 Muskogee, OK 74402
 Contact: Gary Wilson CEO
 Tel: 918-681-3282
 Email: info@datavideosystems.com
 Website: www.datavideosystems.com
Design & install CCTV systems, Access Control Systems, Perimeter Detection Systems, turnkey fiber optic networks, computer cabling, LAN/WAN. (Nat-Ame, estab 1993, empl 15, sales , cert: 8(a))

Pennsylvania

1647 Arora Systems Group, LLC
 61 Wilmington-West Chester Pike Ste 100
 Chadds Ford, PA 19317
 Contact: Adam Oliver GM
 Tel: 610-500-0714
 Email: aoliver@arorasystemsgroup.com
 Website: www.arorasystemsgroup.com
Facility Maintenance, testing, management, and code consulting, Fire Alarm testing, maintenance & repair, Fire Suppression, sprinkler system testing maintenance & repair, Hydrant, Standpipe & Fire extinguisher testing. (As-Ind, estab 2004, empl 17, sales $2,885,827, cert: City, NMSDC)

1648 Fire Fighter Sales & Service Company
 791 Commonwealth Dr
 Warrendale, PA 15086
 Contact: Richard Malady VP
 Tel: 724-720-6000
 Email: rmalady@all-lines-tech.com
 Website: www.firefighter-pgh.com
Alarms, sprinkler systems & fire protection. (Woman, estab 1946, empl 125, sales $12,500,000, cert: WBENC)

1649 Gabba LLC
 630 W Germantown Pike Ste 120
 Plymouth Meeting, PA 19462
 Contact: Finance & Office Ops
 Tel: 877-933-2288
 Email: support@isgprotect.com
 Website: www.invisionsecuritygroup.com
Security system installation. (Woman, estab 2010, empl 15, sales $3,500,000, cert: State, WBENC)

Puerto Rico

1650 Guardmax Corporation
 N 20, Ste B, Fagot Ave
 Ponce, PR 00716
 Contact: Manuel Santana CEO
 Tel: 787-806-5525
 Email: manuelsantana@guardmaxpr.com
 Website: www.guardmaxpr.com
Security services, security technology integration, service & maintenance, access control, asset conservation, automatic door repair & service, burglar alarms, CCTV, analog & Matrix Systems, IP Systems, Wireless IP. (Hisp, estab 2014, empl 16, sales , cert: NMSDC)

1651 One Corps, Inc
 PO Box 79767
 Carolina, PR 00984
 Contact: Sonia Fuentes
 Tel: 787-776-0062
 Email: sfuentes@one-corps.com
 Website: www.one-corps.com
Armed & Unarmed Security Guards, IP Monitoring Station with Patrol Response Service, Sales, Installation & Maintenance of Cameras, Access Control, Fire Watch. (Hisp, estab 2007, empl 134, sales $2,641,716, cert: NMSDC)

1652 Puerto Rico Alarm Systems, Inc.
 PO Box 488
 Dorado, PR 00646
 Contact: Jose Sanchez President
 Tel: 787-883-4587
 Email: jsanchez@pralarms.com
 Website: www.pralarms.com
Dist, install & service commercial fire, access control, burglar, page, close circuit tv, nurse call, interlock & infant protection systems, security alarm monitoring service & conduits. (Hisp, estab 1997, empl 20, sales $1,823,161, cert: NMSDC)

1653 The Security Group Corp.
 Urb. Villa Blanca 42 Aquamarina
 Caguas, PR 00725
 Contact: Luis Benet President
 Tel: 787-743-3299
 Email: info@securitygroupcorp.com
 Website: www.securitygroupcorp.com
Electronic security & automation: design, sale, installation, programming, service & maintenance of electronic security & automation systems. (Hisp, estab 1988, empl 18, sales $901,822, cert: NMSDC)

South Carolina

1654 Quintech Security Consultants, Inc.
 102 Sangaree Park Court Ste 4
 Summerville, SC 29483
 Contact: Harold Gillens President
 Tel: 843-695-0170
 Email: hgillens@quintechengineering.com
 Website: www.quintechengineering.com
Security risk assessments, emergency response planning, security site surveys, surveillance system design, alarm system design, access control systems, AV/ intercom systems. (AA, estab 1997, empl 11, sales $5,227,488, cert: NMSDC)

Texas

1655 Action Fire Alarm and Action Automatic Sprinkler
200 Sharron Dr
Woodway, TX 76712
Contact: Patricia Green Sales Coord
Tel: 254-235-8300
Email: pbreen@actionfirepros.com
Website: www.actionfirepros.com
Inspect, service & install fire extinguishers, fire alarms, fire sprinkler & backflows. (Woman, estab 1993, empl 73, sales $9,005,218, cert: State, WBENC)

1656 Asez Inc.
1716 S San Marcos, Ste 120
San Antonio, TX 78207
Contact: Robert Lozano CEO
Tel: 210-736-6200
Email: corporate@asezinc.com
Website: www.asezinc.com
Armed & unarmed security officers, security systems services, security alarm systems, fire alarm systems, access control, closed circuit television, alarm monitoring, intergraded system. (Hisp, estab 2000, empl 75, sales $2,575,000, cert: State, 8(a))

1657 Champion Life Safety Solutions
2701 W. Plano Pkwy Ste 500
Plano, TX 75075
Contact: Chuck Henderson President
Tel: 972-663-5000
Email: charles.henderson@championfiresecurity.com
Website: www.championfiresecurity.com
Design, install, inspect & monitor fire sprinkler & other suppression systems, fire alarm systems & security systems for new construction, retrofit to existing facilities. (AA, estab 2001, empl 112, sales $14,200,000, cert: State, NMSDC)

1658 CLS Technology, Inc.
5206 E 3rd St
Katy, TX 77493
Contact: Amber Wolfe Accounting Clerk
Tel: 281-347-7973
Email: monitoring@clstechnology.net
Website: www.clstechnology.net
Fire alarm and sound systems, annual inspections, installations, sound, shooter detection, temperature taking devices, access control systems and install. (Woman, estab 2006, empl 50, sales $8,000,000, cert: WBENC)

1659 Laredo Technical Services, Inc.
22011 Roan Bluff
San Antonio, TX 78259
Contact: Joseph Lukowski President
Tel: 210-705-2904
Email: joseph@laredotechnical.com
Website: www.laredotechnical.com/
Dist SpiderTech Security perimeter detection systems. (Hisp, estab 2007, empl 23, sales $6,210,000, cert: State, NMSDC, 8(a))

1660 Nationwide Investigations & Security, Inc.
2425 West Loop South, Ste 200
Houston, TX 77027
Contact: Allen G Hollimon CEO
Tel: 713-297-8830
Email: ahollimon@ntwinvestigations.com
Website: www.ntwinvestigations.com
Security guard services, investigations, dignitary protection, communications cabling, CCTV/CATV, alarms, automated controls, networking, home theaters. (AA, estab 1999, empl 123, sales , cert: State, NMSDC)

1661 TotalCom Management Inc
PO Box 460230
San Antonio, TX 78246
Contact: Moe Oroian President
Tel: 210-366-1116
Email: moe@totalcom-inc.com
Website: www.totalcom-inc.com
Dist, install & service voice & data cabling, fire systems, security systems, access control systems, CCTV/CATV, cameras & DVR recording systems, alarm monitoring, telephone systems, blown fiber. (As-Ind, estab 1994, empl 19, sales $1,755,237, cert: State)

Virginia

1662 Quality CCTV Systems, Inc.
3513 Gregory Pond Rd
Richmond, VA 23236
Contact: Dianne Rust President
Tel: 804-276-7300
Email: dianne@qualitycctv.net
Website: www.qualitycctv.net
Install & maintain security systems to include: video surveillance, CCTV, access control systems, burglar & fire systems, etc. (Woman, estab 1989, empl 14, sales $1,240,000, cert: State)

Washington

1663 Sybis LLC
9925 NE 134th Ct Ste 100
Kirkland, WA 98034
Contact: Jonathan Djajadi Partner
Tel: 206-686-8463
Email: jon@sybissolution.com
Website: www.sybissolution.com
Converts existing mechanical locks into an access control system. (As-Pac, estab 2012, empl 3, sales $198,621, cert: State, NMSDC)

Wisconsin

1664 Hurt Electric Inc.
N57 W14502 Shawn Circle
Menomonee Falls, WI 53051
Contact: Henry Hurt President
Tel: 262-252-0500
Email: hurtelectric@hotmail.com
Website: www.hurtelectric.com
Fire alarm systems, lighting systems & controls, motor control. (AA, estab 1996, empl 27, sales $4,500,000, cert: State)

APPAREL

Manufacturers or wholesalers of men's and women's clothing, accessories and notions. Many firms listed are contract sewing houses. NAICS Code 54

Alabama

1665 At Work Sales Corporation
PO Box 40
Orange Beach, AL 36561
Contact: CEO
Tel: 251-981-6701
Email: online@atworkuniforms.com
Website: www.atworkuniforms.com
Mfr & dist uniform & career apparel, embroidery & screen-printing. (Woman, estab 1991, empl 58, sales $10,000,000, cert: WBENC)

California

1666 Abell Marketing Group, Inc.
15057 Avenida De Las Flores
Chino Hills, CA 91709
Contact: James Lohan Project Mgr
Tel: 909-456-8905
Email: james@abellmarketinggroup.com
Website: www.abellmarketinggroup.com
Protective clothing & medical/industrial nitrile, vinyl & latex gloves. (Woman, estab 1998, empl 2, sales $375,000, cert: WBENC)

1667 Alpha Athletics Sports LLC
220 11th St
Redlands, CA 92374
Contact: Juan Ramirez Owner
Tel: 909-747-7707
Email: Owner@AgloveAbove.com
Website: www.alphaathletics.net
Design, mfr & dist AAA high performanace sport gloves & apparel for men, women and youth. (Hisp, estab 2019, empl 1, sales , cert: State)

1668 Blubandoo Inc.
27128-B Paseo Espada Ste 602
San Juan Capistrano, CA 92675
Contact: Cindy Benedict President
Tel: 949-240-2617
Email: cindy@blubandoo.com
Website: www.blubandoo.com
Cooling headwear: caps/hats, fashionable visors, neckbands, cool ties, headbands & doorags. (Woman, estab 1993, empl 2, sales $5,500,000, cert: CPUC)

1669 Clipper Corporation
21124 Figueroa St
Carson, CA 90745
Contact: Deena Conner VP Business Units
Tel: 310-533-8585
Email: deena.conner@clippercorp.com
Website: www.clippercorp.com
Mfr & dist uniforms & smallwares. (Minority, Woman, estab , empl 45, sales $30,000,000, cert: NMSDC, WBENC)

1670 ECO Trend Cases, LLC
14242 Ventura Blvd Ste 203
Sherman Oaks, CA 91423
Contact: Sandy Rouse CEO
Tel: 310-770-6422
Email: srouse@ecostylecases.com
Website: www.ecostylecases.com
Mfr laptop, netbook & iPad cases: topload shoulder case, backpack, messenger case, rolling case & sleeves. (Woman, estab 2009, empl 4, sales $150,000, cert: WBENC)

1671 Kool Breeze Solar Hats, Inc.
827 E Princeton
Fresno, CA 93704
Contact: Tommie Nellon Owner
Tel: 559-456-8510
Email: tnellon@koolbreezesolarhat.com
Website: www.koolbreezesolarhat.com
Mfr solar cooling hats, Kool Breeze Solar Hats. (Woman/AA, estab 2012, empl 11, sales , cert: City)

1672 L.A. Rag Maker, LLC
8939 S Sepulveda, Ste 102
Los Angeles, CA 90045
Contact: George Arrington Owner
Tel: 213-407-4508
Email: g@laragmaker.com
Website: www.barbecuewhizz.com
Mfr & dist grilling aprons. (AA, estab 2021, empl 1, sales , cert: NMSDC)

1673 The Green Garmento, LLC
20109 Nordhoff St
Chatsworth, CA 91311
Contact: Jennie Nigrosh CEO
Tel: 323-512-2600
Email: jennie@thegreengarmento.com
Website: www.thegreengarmeno.com
A reusable dry-cleaning bag, eco-friendly all-in-one laundry, reusable hanging garment bag, carrying & duffel bag, hanger hamper, "green" drycleaning bag. (Woman, estab 2008, empl 6, sales $ 0, cert: WBENC)

Connecticut

1674 PrintabiliTees, LLC
180 Turn Of River Rd Ste 13D
Stamford, CT 06905
Contact: Jere Eaton President
Tel: 203-322-3390
Email: jere@printabilitees.com
Website: www.printabilitees.com
Custom apparel: screen printing, embroidery, document printing & promotional products. (Woman/AA, estab 2004, empl 1, sales $180,000, cert: State, NMSDC)

Florida

1675 Global Trading, Inc.
7500 NW 25 St, Unit 12
Miami, FL 33122
Contact: Viraj Wikramanayake President
Tel: 305-471-4455
Email: accounting@gtim.com
Website: www.gtim.com
Provide safety footwear. (As-Ind, estab 1991, empl 20, sales $ 0, cert: State)

1676 Supreme Discount Uniforms, LLC
7410 SW 15th St
Plantation, FL 33317
Contact: Victor Albo Dir Sales/Marketing
Tel: 877-535-2540
Email: victor@supremediscountuniforms.com
Website: www.discountuniformsonline.com

Uniforms, embroidered lab coats, maintenance uniforms, housekeeping uniforms & embroidered polo t-shirts. (Hisp, estab 2009, empl 2, sales $168,000, cert: State)

1677 Tampa T-Shirts
5112 N 22nd St
Tampa, FL 33610
Contact: Juan Davis Mgr
Tel: 813-879-3298
Email: juan@fastlaneclothing.com
Website: www.fastlaneclothing.com

Apparel, logo shirts, lab coats, promotional items. (Minority, Woman, estab 1985, empl 19, sales $1,480,000, cert: State, City)

1678 Tavarez Sporting Goods
1840 22nd St
Miami, FL 33145
Contact: Manuel Tavarez Managing Partner
Tel: 347-441-9690
Email: tavarezsports@gmail.com
Website: www.tavarezsports.com

Sporting goods & fitness apparel, baseballs, softballs, baseball bats, gloves, batting gloves, catcher's equipment, helmets, volleyballs, soccer balls, basketballs, boxing equipment, martial arts equipment, sports bags to sports apparel. (Hisp, estab 2014, empl 5, sales , cert: NMSDC)

Georgia

1679 ERB Industries, Inc.
1 Safety Way
Woodstock, GA 30188
Contact: Jackie Barker EVP
Tel: 770-926-7944
Email: jbarker@e-erb.com
Website: www.e-erb.com

Mfr & dist personal protective equipment & uniform apparel: head, eye, face, body & hand protection, hard hats, safety glasses, high visibility apparel, aprons, smocks, lab coats. (Woman, estab 1956, empl 100, sales $ 0, cert: WBENC)

1680 O.G.I.H. Enterprises, Inc.
201 17th St NW, Ste 30303
Atlanta, GA 30363
Contact: Benny Nesbitt, Jr. CEO
Tel: 404-478-7852
Email: b.nesbitt@ogih-enterprises.com
Website: www.invisibleigloves.com

Dist work safety gloves, protective clothing. (AA, estab 2012, empl 4, sales , cert: State)

1681 Staffwear 2
155 Westridge Pkwy, Ste 307
McDonough, GA 30253
Contact: Towanda Scott President
Tel: 800-727-9289
Email: t.scott@staffwear2.com
Website: www.staffwear2.com

Corporate branded apparel & national uniform programs. (Woman/AA, estab 2008, empl 10, sales $502,438, cert: NMSDC)

Hawaii

1682 Coradorables,LLC
1707 Mahani Loop
Honolulu, HI 96819
Contact: Cora Spearman CEO
Tel: 808-782-4267
Email: coraspearman@hotmail.com
Website: www.coradorables.com

Men , women, children's hats and clothing, specializing in men's button down s/s shirts, boys button down s/s shirts, girls dresses. (Woman, estab 2010, empl 20, sales , cert: WBENC)

Illinois

1683 JERO Medical Equipment & Supplies, Inc.
4108 W Division St
Chicago, IL 60651
Contact: President
Tel: 312-829-5376
Email:
Website: www.jeromedical.com

Mfr disposbable wearing apparels, kit assembler, 1st aid, disaster, admission. (AA, estab 1987, empl 24, sales $4,000,000, cert: City)

1684 McKlein Company, LLC
4447 W. Cortland St
Chicago, IL 60639
Contact: Parinda Saetia CEO
Tel: 773-235-0600
Email: psaetia@mckleincompany.com
Website: www.mckleincompany.com

Mfr briefcases, computer cases, luggage, travel bags. (Minority, Woman, estab 1997, empl 7, sales $7,507,695, cert: WBENC)

Indiana

1685 RiverCity Workwear LLC
4020 Earnings Way
New Albany, IN 47150
Contact: Tina Dotson
Tel: 812-948-9020
Email: tina@rivercityworkwear.com
Website: www.rivercityworkwear.com

Dist safety glasses, hard hats, safety vest, shirts, rainwear, steel & non steel toe boots, tshirts, polos, jackets. (Woman, estab 2004, empl 3, sales , cert: State)

Louisiana

1686 Abform, Inc.
167 Industrial Pkwy
Lafayette, LA 70508
Contact: Kim Leblanc Comptroller
Tel: 337-837-9675
Email: kim@abform.com
Website: www.abform.com

Dist uniforms & work wear. (Woman, estab 1981, empl 20, sales $ 0, cert: WBENC)

1687 Company Apparel Safety Items, Inc.
802 N Range Ave
Denham Springs, LA 70726
Contact: Nancy David President
Tel: 225-664-2713
Email: nancyestilldavid@gmail.com
Website: www.companyapparelsafetyitems.com
Mfr disposable garments: medical scrubs, lab jackets, lab coats & multi-purpose coveralls. (Woman, estab 1994, empl 22, sales , cert: WBENC)

1688 Denison Consulting Group LLC
6221 S Claiborne Ave Ste 450
New Orleans, LA 70125
Contact: Dianne Denison CEO
Tel: 504-982-6110
Email: sales@denisonconsultinggroup.com
Website: www.denisonconsultinggroup.com/
Dist corporate work wear, uniforms, apparel, protective work wear, industrial clothing, flame retardant (FR) clothing, FR shirts, FR pants, FR coveralls, FR coats, FR jackets, FR jeans, rainwear, raingear. (Woman, estab 2015, empl 6, sales , cert: WBENC)

Maryland

1689 janlitlfeather
3813 Terka Circle
Randallstown, MD 21133
Contact: Stephanie Gladden CEO
Tel: 410-830-9244
Email: janlitlfeather@aol.com
Website: www.janlitlfeather.com
Signature feathered ponytail holder, key chains, car mirror hangs, bow ties, earrings, neck ties, hat clips & hair accessories. (Woman/AA, estab 2010, empl 1, sales , cert: NMSDC)

1690 Unitec Distribution Systems
289 E Green St
Westminster, MD 21157
Contact: Elise Elfman CEO
Tel: 410-876-6227
Email: eelfman@unitec-corp.com
Website: www.unitec-corp.com
Provide uniforms & Total Uniform Management Solution (TUMS). (Woman, estab 1927, empl 22, sales $5,000,000, cert: State, WBENC)

Michigan

1691 BluCase
6026 Kalamazoo Ave. Ste. 237
Grand Rapids, MI 49508
Contact: Bill McCurdy CEO
Tel: 708-263-9522
Email: bmccurdy@blucase.com
Website: www.blucase.com
Mfr innovative cellphone accessory products. (AA, estab 2014, empl 5, sales $12,000,000, cert: NMSDC)

1692 POSHnFIT
17910 Van Dyke
Detroit, MI 48234
Contact: Tyanieka Jackson Owner
Tel: 313-282-6008
Email: admin@poshnfit.com
Website: www.poshnfit.com
Creates fitness accessories for women. (Woman/AA, estab 2017, empl 1, sales , cert: NMSDC, WBENC)

1693 Stars Clothing Manufacturing Company
300 River Place, Ste 5350
Detroit, MI 48226
Contact: Darrell Washington President
Tel: 734-476-6709
Email: dw@starsactivewear.com
Website: www.starsactivewear.com
Mfr men and women apparel. (AA, estab 2017, empl 3, sales , cert: NMSDC)

1694 StarSource Management Services, Inc.
39080 Webb Dr
Westland, MI 48185
Contact: Melvin Brown CEO
Tel: 734-721-8540
Email: sales@starsourceinc.com
Website: www.starsourceinc.com
Dist uniforms, protective clothing, cutting tools, fasteners, janitorial chemical supplies, cleaning equipment, paper towels, plastic liners, welding supplies, automotive cleaning supplies, cooling tower chemicals, laundry services. (AA, estab , empl , sales $6,000,000, cert: NMSDC)

Minnesota

1695 Amaril Uniform Company
8020 University Ave NE
Fridley, MN 55432
Contact: CEO
Tel: 763-717-2037
Email: cartsales@amaril.com
Website: www.amaril.com
Dist uniforms, fire resistant clothing, actionwear, tailoring,e mbroidering, logos, stocking caps, neckwarmers, hardhat linner, rain gear. (Woman, estab 2000, empl 10, sales $1,257,080, cert: WBENC)

1696 TLB Holdings, Inc.
20110 Auger Ave
Corcoran, MN 55340
Contact: Tammy Boyd
Tel: 763-478-5010
Email: dstattman@tlbholdings.com
Website: www.tlbholdings.com
Domestic & international apparel production. (Woman, estab 2003, empl 7, sales $8,700,000, cert: State, WBENC)

Missouri

1697 Cherry
1712 Main St, Ste 232
Kansas City, MO 64108
Contact: Thalia Cherry President
Tel: 816-377-1832
Email: info@cherrysportsgear.com
Website: www.cherrysportsgear.com
Sporting goods, corporate apparel, tee shirts, athletic equipment & uniforms. (AA, estab 2011, empl 3, sales , cert: NMSDC)

North Carolina

1698 Century Hosiery, Inc.
PO Box 1410
Denton, NC 27239
Contact: Kathy Martin President
Tel: 336-859-3806
Email: kmartin@centuryhosiery.com
Website: www.centuryhosiery.com
Mfr hosiery products. (Woman, estab 1989, empl 120, sales $6,000,000, cert: State, WBENC)

1699 Darlyng & Co.
1585 Yanceyville St
Greensboro, NC 27405
Contact: Tara Darnley Co-Founder
Tel: 929-376-8584
Email: info@darlyngandco.com
Website: www.darlyngandco.com
Fun and innovative line of baby products and apparel. (AA, estab 2014, empl 4, sales $350,000, cert: City)

1700 Transportation Safety Apparel
11 Conrad Industrial Dr
Weaverville, NC 28787
Contact: Rob DeLoach Natl Sales Dir
Tel: 828-767-9632
Email: rob.deloach@tsasafety.com
Website: www.tsasafety.com
Dist OCEA approved ANSI safety apparel, safety vests, tshirts, sweat shirts raingear, hardhats, gloves, uniforms, custom workshirts. (Woman, estab 2003, empl 15, sales $5,100,000, cert: WBENC)

New Jersey

1701 Design Alternatives NY LLC
169 Boyd Ave
Jersey City, NJ 07304
Contact: Cenia Peredes President
Tel: 973-583-9553
Email: cenia@ceniany.com
Website: www.goo.gl/3f8E3Q
Women's Apparel (Minority, estab , empl 2, sales $ 0, cert: NMSDC)

1702 Shani International Corporation
8 Conifer Dr
Warren, NJ 07059
Contact: Arti Mohin VP
Tel: 908-484-7070
Email: arti@shaniintl.com
Website: www.shaniintl.com
Mfr & import uniforms (knit & woven tops & bottoms), lab & chef coats, aprons, non-woven bags & basic fashion items. (Woman/As-Ind, estab 2005, empl 4, sales , cert: NMSDC)

1703 Tronex International Inc
300 International Dr
Mount Olive, NJ 07828
Contact: Edmund Tai VP Healthcare Division
Tel: 973-355-2888
Email: etai@tronexcompany.com
Website: www.tronexcompany.com
Dist disposable gloves & apparel products. (As-Pac, estab 1989, empl 75, sales , cert: NMSDC)

1704 Wisco Promo Uniform, INC.
160 US Hwy 46
Saddle Brook, NJ 07663
Contact: Linda Briscoe President
Tel: 973-767-2022
Email: briscoe_linda@yahoo.com
Website: www.wiscopnu.com
Mfr apparel, uniforms & aprons, silk screen & embroidery, promotional products, corporate identity & promotion. (Minority, Woman, estab 1999, empl 10, sales $ 0, cert: NMSDC)

Nevada

1705 Dellrone Services LLC
8550 W Charleston Blvd, Ste 228
Las Vegas, NV 89117
Contact: Willie Endsley President
Tel: 702-457-7855
Email: admin@dellroneservices.com
Website: www.dellroneservices.com
Dist safety clothing & equipment: fire safety jacket & pants, helmets, construction safety clothing: helmets, jackets, parkas, rain coats, safety vest, goggles & shoes. (Woman/AA, estab 2010, empl 4, sales , cert: NMSDC)

New York

1706 American Fashion Network, LLC
5852 Heritage Landing Dr
East Syracuse, NY 13057
Contact: Alina Kirnie Sales Team Support
Tel: 315-560-3652
Email: akirnie@americanfashionnetwork.com
Website: www.americanfashionnetwork.com
Knit and woven apparel and a supplier of knit and woven apparel to American and Multi-National Corporations. Our apparel categories include corporate, event, swag, uniforms, workwear, lab coats, masks, and PPE. (Woman, estab 2005, empl 35, sales $15,666,015, cert: CPUC, WBENC)

1707 Hamburger Woolen Company
23 Denton Ave
New Hyde Park, NY 11040
Contact: Ilene Rosen President
Tel: 516-352-7400
Email: irosen@hwcny.com
Website: www.hwcny.com
Dist uniform fabrics, law enforcement & public safety equipment: duty belts, flashlights, raincoats, reflective vests, protective eyewear & earwear. (Woman, estab 1940, empl 12, sales $6,105,831, cert: State, City)

1708 PKP Industries, Inc.
1407 Broadway Ste 3412
New York, NY 10018
Contact: Puneet Pasricha
Tel: 646-586-3044
Email: puneet@pkpindustries.com
Website: www.pkpindustries.com
Wholesale apparel, clothing, women's tops, bottoms, skirts, dresses, pants. (Woman/As-Ind, estab 2014, empl 1, sales , cert: NMSDC)

1709 S & H Uniform Corp.
      1 Aqueduct Rd
      White Plains, NY 10606
      Contact: Rosa Greco VP
      Tel: 914-937-6800
      Email: info@sandhuniforms.com
      Website: www.sandhuniforms.com
Workwear & footwear, outerwear/jackets, coveralls, hats, shirts, polos, t-shirts, pants, shorts, vests, flame resistant wear, Hi visibility, boots & shoes, medical uniforms, aprons, chef's apparel. (Woman, estab 1969, empl 40, sales $8,500,000, cert: City)

1710 Salsa-The Designer Solution LLC.
      1441 Broadway 3 Fl, Ste 3021
      New York, NY 10018
      Contact: Gigi De Jesus-Frerichs President
      Tel: 212-575-6565
      Email: gigi@gicleeapparel.com
      Website: www.SalsaProfessionalApparel.com
Mfr uniforms, sports apparel, collegiate apparel, varsity-wear, tees, tanks, polo shirts, sweatshirts, shorts, pants, lounge-wear & pajamas. (Minority, Woman, estab 2000, empl 6, sales $10,000,000, cert: State, City, NMSDC, WBENC)

Ohio

1711 Liniform Service
      1050 Northview Ave
      Barberton, OH 44203
      Contact: Jennifer Peroli VP
      Tel: 330-825-6911
      Email: jenniferperoli@liniform.com
      Website: www.liniform.com
Uniforms: lab coats, scrubs, jackets, warm-up jackets, maintenance uniforms, chef coats & cook apparel. Linens: patient gowns, mammo capes, sheets, pillowcases, blankets, towels & washcloths, tablecloths, skirting, napkins. (Woman, estab 1924, empl 60, sales $4,700,000, cert: WBENC)

1712 MASCOT Workwear
      320 Springfield Dr, Ste 150
      Fairlawn, OH 44333
      Contact: Michael Allio Sales
      Tel: 330-618-3997
      Email: michael@maworkwear.com
      Website: www.mascotworkwear.com
Dist MASCOT Workwear in North America. (Woman, estab 2013, empl 7, sales $1,000,000, cert: WBENC)

1713 RJ Manray - Promotional Products
      9500 Springfield Rd, Unit 5
      Poland, OH 44514
      Contact: Rowena Henderson CEO
      Tel: 234-201-0160
      Email: rrlimos18@gmail.com
      Website: www.rjmanray.com/
Dist personalized and custom logo tote bags. (Woman, estab 1986, empl 11, sales $640,000, cert: WBENC)

1714 VDP Safety & Uniforms Ltd.
      11811 Shaker Blvd Ste 416
      Cleveland, OH 44120
      Contact: Phoebe Lee President
      Tel: 216-352-1026
      Email: info@vdpsafety.com
      Website: www.vdpsafety.com
Uniform apparel & safety supplies/equipment: high visibility shirts, safety vests, hard hats, traffic cones, jackets, hospital uniforms. (Woman/AA, estab 2013, empl 1, sales , cert: State)

Pennsylvania

1715 Tyndale Company
      5050 Applebutter Rd
      Pipersville, PA 18947
      Contact: Barbara Fitzgeorge Marketing Specialist
      Tel: 215-766-5660
      Email: Marketing@TyndaleUSA.com
      Website: www.tyndaleusa.com
Mfr & dist flame resistant clothing. (Woman, estab 1982, empl 120, sales $40,000,000, cert: WBENC)

Texas

1716 Career Uniforms
      3800 Juniper
      Houston, TX 77087
      Contact: President
      Tel: 713-645-3600
      Email: sales@careeruniforms.com
      Website: www.careeruniforms.com
Mfr uniforms: medical, governmental & restaurant. (As-Ind, estab 1980, empl 25, sales $ 0, cert: NMSDC)

1717 Fresh Comfort, Inc.
      3200 Rifle Gap Rd, Ste 1470
      Frisco, TX 75034
      Contact: Maria E. Valencia President
      Tel: 214-705-0408
      Email: maria.valencia@freshcomfortinc.com
      Website: www.freshcomfortinc.com
Adaptive intimate apparel (bras, panties, boxers), front Velcro & zipper closure bras for easy dressing & undressing, seamless bra & underwear. (Minority, Woman, estab 2012, empl 1, sales , cert: State)

1718 Radia Enterprises Inc.
      3800 Juniper St
      Houston, TX 77087
      Contact: Rupendra Radia CEO
      Tel: 713-645-6383
      Email: rradia56@gmail.com
      Website: www.spectrumuniforms.com
Uniforms and promotional products. (As-Ind, estab 1992, empl 20, sales $3,500,000, cert: NMSDC)

1719 RG Apparel Co.
      2912 N MacArthur, Ste 103
      Irving, TX 75062
      Contact: Joe Temple COO
      Tel: 972-793-0583
      Email: jt@rgapparel.com
      Website: www.rgapparel.com
Mfr textiles: uniforms, work shirts, polos, tees, woven button up shirts & headwear, promotional marketing items & gifts. (AA, estab 2006, empl 6, sales $3,200,000, cert: State, NMSDC)

1720 Santex
 4211 W Illinois, Ste 100
 Dallas, TX 75211
 Contact: Jose Lopez Owner
 Tel: 214-256-2169
 Email: karla.leal@santexallsports.com
 Website: www.santexallsports.com
Manufacturing business uniforms. (Hisp, estab 2013, empl 4, sales $160,000, cert: State)

1721 Wholesale T-shirts Depot, Inc.
 11311 Harry Hines Blvd, Ste 201
 Dallas, TX 75229
 Contact: Joe Turner Exec VP
 Tel: 972-243-4785
 Email: info@wtdapparel.com
 Website: www.wtdapparel.com
Licensed military branded apparel & accessories. (As-Pac, estab 2006, empl 18, sales $2,500,000, cert: NMSDC)

Virginia

1722 First Due Gear
 2111 Apperson Dr
 Salem, VA 24153
 Contact: Sarah Fuhrman Owner
 Tel: 540-725-8850
 Email: firstduegear@yahoo.com
 Website: www.firstduegear.com
Dist Fire, EMS, swiftwater & technical rescue gear, apparel & equipment. (Woman, estab 2006, empl 1, sales , cert: State)

1723 Global Partner's of Virginia, LLC
 3005 E Boundary Terr, Ste G
 Midlothian, VA 23112
 Contact: Norm Falkner VP
 Tel: 804-744-8112
 Email: logos@globalpromosonline.com
 Website: www.globalpromosonline.com
Logo wear, embroidery, silk screen, screen printing, direct to garment ink jet printing, heat transfer. Corporate apparel, mens, ladies, kids, uniforms. Promotional Products, pens, magnets, calendars, Bags, towels, luggage, sportwear, team uniforms. (Woman, estab 2001, empl 4, sales $350,000, cert: State)

1724 Sayre Enterprises Inc.
 45 Natural Bridge School Rd
 Natural Bridge Station, VA 24579
 Contact: Danielle Ayres Commerical Rep
 Tel: 800-552-6064
 Email: dayres@sayreinc.com
 Website: www.sayreinc.com
Reflective products: vests, belts, headbands, wrist & arm bands. (Woman, estab 1987, empl 104, sales $9,092,000, cert: State)

1725 The Uniform Store, LLC
 10 Weems Lane
 Winchester, VA 22601
 Contact: Lisa B Beggs President
 Tel: 540-678-8711
 Email: lisa@uniformstoreonline.com
 Website: www.uniformstoreonline.com
Dist ChefWorks, Edwards Garments & Uncommon Threads for men & women in chef coats (executive chef & basic), kitchen shirts, pants, aprons, headwear, neckwear, front of the house (shirts, blouses, pants, vests, ties). (Woman, estab 2009, empl 5, sales $455,781, cert: State, WBENC)

Washington

1726 Bootie Shoe Cover Inc
 5616 NE 55 Circle
 Vancouver, WA 98661
 Contact: Marla Gillette President
 Tel: 360-903-0992
 Email: info@bootieshoecover.com
 Website: www.bootieshoecover.com
Dist reusable shoe covers. (Woman, estab 2009, empl 3, sales , cert: WBENC)

Wisconsin

1727 Straight-Up, Inc.
 1190 Richards Rd
 Hartland, WI 53029
 Contact: Craig Zirbel Mktg Exec
 Tel: 608-335-3676
 Email: zirbs@straightupinc.com
 Website: www.straightupinc.com
Embroidery svcs: up to 14 color screen print presses. (Woman, estab 1994, empl 84, sales $22,200,000, cert: WBENC)

ARCHITECTS

Most firms have agreements with other state architects permitting them to work anywhere in the nation. Nearly all are members of the American Institute of Architects (AIA). (See ENGINEERING & SURVEYING SERVICES for civil, structural, electrical and mechanical engineers).   NAICS Code 54

Arizona

1728 Fore Dimensions LLC
3337 E. Sells Dr
Phoenix, AZ 85018
Contact: Lisa Foreman Principal
Tel: 602-748-4664
Email: lisa@foredimensions.com
Website: www.foredimensions.com
Architectural consulting, remodel, tenant improvements & new construction for transportation facilities, wet & dry labs, clean rooms, testing buildings, office & training centers. (Woman, estab 2001, empl 2, sales $500,000, cert: State, City, WBENC)

California

1729 A2 Studios Inc.
3788 Park Blvd Studio 6
San Diego, CA 92103
Contact: Vincent Stroop Partner
Tel: 619-688-2606
Email: asquared@asquaredstudios.com
Website: www.asquaredstudios.com
Architecture & design services, interior design services, drafting, lighting design services. (Woman/Hisp, estab 2004, empl 3, sales $510,000, cert: State)

1730 Aetypic, Inc.
7 Freelon St
San Francisco, CA 94107
Contact: Dennis Wong
Tel: 415-762-8388
Email: dennis.wong@aetypic.com
Website: www.aetypic.com
Architecture & engineering services: structural engineering, civil engineering, construction engineering & inspection, technology integration, & sustainable design. (As-Pac, estab 2011, empl 25, sales , cert: State, NMSDC)

1731 ArchaeoPaleo Resource Management, Inc.
1531 Pontius Ave, Ste 200
Los Angeles, CA 90025
Contact: Robin Turner President
Tel: 424-248-3316
Email: rturner@archaeopaleo.com
Website: www.archaeopaleo.com
Provide public & private entities with archaeological (prehistoric and historic), cultural, ethnographic, historic building assessments, and paleontological technical document services, third party reviews, Construction Management services. (Woman, estab 2004, empl 7, sales $500,000, cert: State, City, CPUC)

1732 Blackbird Associates, Inc.
2320 J St
Sacramento, CA 95816
Contact: Franc Blackbird President
Tel:
Email: franc@blackbirdassoc.com
Website: www.blackbirdassoc.com
Architecture and Project Management. (Minority, Woman, estab 1994, empl 7, sales $1,311,000, cert: NMSDC, WBENC)

1733 CDS Architects, Inc.
12220 El Camino Real Ste 200
San Diego, CA 92130
Contact: Dir Business Dev
Tel: 858-793-4777
Email: info@sca-sd.com
Website: www.sca-sd.com
Architectural & drafting services, interior space planning, project management & consulting services, LEED AP. (Woman, estab 1988, empl 18, sales $5,898,423, cert: WBENC)

1734 Development One, Inc.
2020 E. 1st St, Ste 525
Santa Ana, CA 92705
Contact: Geoff Chapluk Dir Marketing & Operations
Tel: 714-689-0298
Email: gchapluk@developmentone.net
Website: www.developmentone.net
Architecture/engineering, CADD, environmental. (Hisp, estab 1987, empl 25, sales , cert: State, NMSDC)

1735 H. Hendy Associates
4770 Campus Dr Ste 100
Newport Beach, CA 92660
Contact: Heidi Hendy Principal
Tel: 949-851-3080
Email: hhendy@hhendy.com
Website: www.hhendy.com
Interior architecture firm. (Woman, estab 1979, empl 30, sales $4,800,000, cert: CPUC, WBENC)

1736 Line2Line Architectural Design Group, LLP
2413 Webb Ave Ste D
Alameda, CA 94501
Contact: Angelus Cheng Principal
Tel: 510-995-8278
Email: info@line2lineadg.com
Website: www.line2lineadg.com
Architectural & design, Feasibility Studies, ADA Consultation, Sustainability, Programming, Urban/Site Planning, Entitlement, Due Diligence, Project Mgmt, Site & Building Evaluations, Interior Design, Design presentations. (Minority, Woman, estab 2012, empl 4, sales $354,156, cert: NMSDC)

1737 M+M Design Construction Project Management
1503 Bainum Dr
Topanga, CA 90290
Contact: Mohan Joshi President
Tel: 310-455-0064
Email: mjoshi@mpji.net
Website: www.mpji.net
Architecture, interior design, planning & advisory services. (As-Ind, estab 2002, empl 1, sales , cert: NMSDC, 8(a))

ARCHITECTS

1738 Quezada Architecture, Inc.
      639 Front St 1st Fl
      San Francisco, CA 94111
      Contact: Kate Albee Marketing Dir
      Tel: 415-331-5133
      Email: kate@qa-us.com
      Website: www.qa-us.com
Architectural svcs: architecture, planning, interior architecture, design. (Minority, Woman, estab 1994, empl 10, sales , cert: NMSDC, WBENC)

1739 Source West
      1631 Aspen Grove Lane
      Diamond Bar, CA 91765
      Contact: Roberto Manzini Dir Business Dev
      Tel: 909-872-0010
      Email: r.manzini@greencubicles.com
      Website: www.greencubicles.com
Commercial architecture & interior design. (Woman, estab 1988, empl 25, sales $2,500,000, cert: State)

1740 Torres Architects, Inc.
      400 Crenshaw Blvd Ste 200
      Torrance, CA 90503
      Contact: Denise Torres Managing Principal
      Tel: 310-320-6285
      Email: denise@tarci.com
      Website: www.tarci.com
Architect, Interior Design, Computer Aided Drafting, Design, Mechanical Engineering, Electrical Engineering, Plumbing Engineering. (Hisp, estab 1991, empl 5, sales $1,127,237, cert: NMSDC)

1741 TSAO Design Group
      160 Pine St, Ste 650
      San Francisco, CA 94111
      Contact: Jonathan Tsao Principal
      Tel: 415-398-5500
      Email: jtsao@tsaodesign.com
      Website: www.tsaodesign.com
Architectural & interior design. (As-Pac, estab 1981, empl 12, sales $1,750,000, cert: CPUC)

Colorado

1742 Coover-Clark & Associates, Inc.
      1936 Market St
      Denver, CO 80202
      Contact: Carol Coover-Clark President
      Tel: 303-783-0040
      Email: marketing@cooverclark.com
      Website: www.cooverclark.com
Architectural planning & design services, commercial & military aviation facilities. (Woman, estab 1987, empl 22, sales $2,800,000, cert: WBENC)

Connecticut

1743 Bavier Design, LLC
      277 Rowayton Ave
      Rowayton, CT 06853
      Contact: Anne Bavier Principal
      Tel: 203-388-1818
      Email: abavier@bavierdesign.com
      Website: www.bavierdesign.com
Architectural & interior design. (Woman, estab 2004, empl 8, sales $1,255,000, cert: WBENC)

District of Columbia

1744 Systems Design, Inc.
      1420 9th St NW
      Washington, DC 20001
      Contact: Darlene Mathis CEO
      Tel: 202-232-5631
      Email: meka_mathis@msn.com
      Website: www.systemsdesignbuild.com
Interior design, space planning, architectural design svcs. (Woman/AA, estab 2002, empl 6, sales $700,000, cert: 8(a))

Florida

1745 Architechnical, Inc.
      2908 Clubhouse Dr
      Plant City, FL 33566
      Contact: Erick Gulke President
      Tel: 813-312-2455
      Email: egulke@architechnical.biz
      Website: www.architechnical.biz
Architectural design solutions & environments. (Hisp, estab 2008, empl 3, sales , cert: City)

1746 Architectural Design Collaborative
      235 Alcazar Ave
      Coral Gables, FL 33134
      Contact: Raymundo Feito President
      Tel: 305-442-1188
      Email: rfeito@adcinternational.net
      Website: www.adcinternational.net
Architectural, planning & interior design. (Hisp, estab 1984, empl 25, sales $7,600,000, cert: NMSDC)

1747 MGE Architects, Inc.
      3081 Salzedo St, 3rd Fl
      Coral Gables, FL 33134
      Contact: Jose Estevez President
      Tel: 305-444-0413
      Email: jestevez@mgearchitects.com
      Website: www.mgearchitects.com
Architectural services: private health systems, major government hospitals, teaching facilities & small community hospitals. (Hisp, estab 1982, empl 23, sales $7,937,182, cert: State)

1748 Rhodes+Brito Architects
      605 E Robinson St, Ste 750
      Orlando, FL 32801
      Contact: Ruffin Rhodes Principal
      Tel: 407-648-7288
      Email: info@rbarchitects.com
      Website: www.rbarchitects.com
Architectural Services. (AA, estab 1996, empl 19, sales $3,024,653, cert: State, City, 8(a))

Georgia

1749 Arseal Technologies, LLC
      5900 Windward Pkwy, Ste 475
      Alpharetta, GA 30005
      Contact: Edith Lakip CEO
      Tel: 678-387-1200
      Email: edith.lakip@arseal.com
      Website: www.arseal.com
Architectural & engineering design-build, electrical, mechanical & civil, CADD design services, project management & procurement. (Minority, Woman, estab 1999, empl 18, sales $1,500,000, cert: State, NMSDC)

ARCHITECTS

1750 GSB Architects & Interiors, Inc.
3500 Lenox Rd. Ste 1500
Atlanta, GA 30326
Contact: Jennifer Mercier Interior Designer
Tel: 404-233-6450
Email: jennifer@gsbarchitects.com
Website: www.gsbarchitects.com
Architectural services, interior design, construction mgmt, project mgmt, space planning, move mgmt. (Minority, Woman, estab 1998, empl 5, sales $1,414,000, cert: NMSDC, WBENC)

1751 SpaceCraft International
195 14th St, NE Ste 2908
Atlanta, GA 30309
Contact: Managing Dir
Tel: 404-348-4732
Email: info@spacecraftintl.com
Website: www.spacecraftintl.com
Architectural & interior design svcs. (Woman, estab 2003, empl 10, sales , cert: WBENC)

1752 Utilicon Services, Inc.
13275 Hwy 231
Davisboro, GA 31018
Contact: Tom Glover COO
Tel: 478-348-3233
Email: tom.glover@utilicon.net
Website: www.utilicon.net
Architecture Services. (Woman/Nat Ame, estab 1998, empl 140, sales $12,800,000, cert: WBENC)

Illinois

1753 Bailey Edward Design, Inc.
35 E Wacker Dr Ste 2800
Chicago, IL 60601
Contact: Ellen B. Dickson President
Tel: 312-440-2300
Email: edickson@baileyedward.com
Website: www.baileyedward.com
Architectural services, Interior design services, Drafting services, Building inspection services
Engineering Services, Historical Preservation, Cost Estimating (Woman, estab 1991, empl 39, sales $2,973,760, cert: State, City, WBENC, NWBOC)

1754 Bauer Latoza Studio, Ltd.
2241 S Wabash
Chicago, IL 60616
Contact: Edward Torrez President
Tel: 312-567-1000
Email: etorrez@bauerlatozastudio.com
Website: www.bauerlatozastudio.com
Architectural design, evaluation & renovation services. (Hisp, estab 1990, empl 12, sales $2,195,986, cert: State)

1755 Brook Architecture
2325 S Michigan Ave Ste 300
Chicago, IL 60616
Contact: Jeanne Franks Dir of Marketing
Tel: 312-528-0890
Email: jfranks@brookarchitecture.com
Website: www.brookarchitecture.com
Design, urban planning, consulting, project management & services, new construction & renovation of institutional, residential, office & retail spaces. (Woman/AA, estab 1995, empl 6, sales $1,495,915, cert: State, City, NMSDC, 8(a))

1756 EC Purdy & Associates
53 W Jackson Blvd Ste 1631
Chicago, IL 60604
Contact: Elizabeth Purdy Architect
Tel: 312-408-1631
Email: ecpurdy@ecpurdy.com
Website: www.ecpurdy.com
Architectural, interior design planning services. (Minority, Woman, estab 1994, empl 1, sales $563,878, cert: State)

1757 Muller & Muller Ltd.
700 N Sangamon
Chicago, IL 60642
Contact: Mark Stromberg Principal
Tel: 312-432-4180
Email: mstromberg@muller2.com
Website: www.muller2.com
Architectural services: Feasibility Studies; Building Analysis; Schematic Design; Design Development; Construction Documents; LEED; ADA Review; Presentations; Renderings; 3D Animations; Specifications; Cost Estimating. (Woman, estab 1984, empl 20, sales $2,000,000, cert: State, City)

1758 Studio AH LLC dba HPZS
213 West Institute Place Ste 502
Chicago, IL 60610
Contact: April Hughes Owner
Tel: 312-944-9600
Email: ahughes@hpzs.com
Website: www.hpzs.com
Architectural design, Interior Design, Historic Preservation, Facade Maintenance & Sustainable Design, green renovation & design services. (Woman, estab 2015, empl 4, sales $133,310, cert: State, WBENC)

1759 Sumac Inc.
3701 N Ravenswood Ave Ste 202
Chicago, IL 60613
Contact: Liliana Gonzalez VP
Tel: 773-857-7906
Email: lgonzalez@sumacinc.com
Website: www.sumacinc.com
Architecture & construction management: architectural design, sustainable design, project scheduling, cost estimating, construction procurement, construction management services & general contracting. (Hisp, estab 2008, empl 10, sales $2,000,000, cert: NMSDC)

1760 Tigerman McCurry Architects
444 N Wells St Ste 206
Chicago, IL 60654
Contact: Margaret McCurry President
Tel: 312-644-5880
Email: tma@tigerman-mccurry.com
Website: www.Tigerman-McCurry.com
Architectural & interior design services. (Woman, estab 1967, empl 10, sales $1,200,000, cert: City)

ARCHITECTS

Indiana

1761 Brenner Design Incorporated
      620 N Delaware St
      Indianapolis, IN 46204
      Contact: Diana Brenner President
      Tel: 317-262-1220
      Email: dbrenner@brennerdesign.com
      Website: www.brennerdesign.com
Architecture; Interior Architecture; Historic Preservation; Interior Design; Furniture Mgmt Services; Owner's Rep Services; Space Planning; Project Mgmt. (Woman, estab 1992, empl 10, sales , cert: State, City, WBENC)

1762 Jung Design, Inc.
      8910 Purdue Rd Ste 680
      Indianapolis, IN 46268
      Contact: Connie Jung President
      Tel: 317-471-1221
      Email: cjung@jungdes.com
      Website: www.jungdes.com
Architectural & interior design services, master planning, signage, programming, space planning. (Woman, estab 2004, empl 3, sales $200,000, cert: State)

1763 Rowland Design, Inc.
      702 N Capitol Ave
      Indianapolis, IN 46204
      Contact: Sarah Schwartzkopf CEO
      Tel: 317-636-3980
      Email: smschwartzkopf@rowlanddesign.com
      Website: www.rowlanddesign.com
Architecture, interior design & graphic design. (Woman, estab 1968, empl 32, sales $4,050,000, cert: State)

1764 Studio 3 Design, Inc.
      8604 Allisonville Rd Ste 330
      Indianapolis, IN 46250
      Contact: Heather Leslie President
      Tel: 317-595-1000
      Email: hleslie@studio3design.net
      Website: www.studio3design.net
Architectural & interior design services. (Woman, estab 2002, empl 7, sales , cert: State)

1765 WDi Architecture, Inc.
      15 W 28th St
      Indianapolis, IN 46208
      Contact: Williams-Dotson Daryl CEO
      Tel: 317-251-6172
      Email: daryl_wd@wdiarchitecture.com
      Website: www.wdiarchitecture.com
Architectural design, space planning & programming, feasibility studies, facilities evaluation, project managment & existing conditions documentation. (Woman/AA, estab 1995, empl 5, sales $400,000, cert: State, City, WBENC)

Kentucky

1766 First World Architects Studio, PSC
      15 E 9th St
      Covington, KY 41011
      Contact: B. Charles Alexander President
      Tel: 859-431-1999
      Email: alexcama@fuse.net
      Website: www.1stworldarchitectsstudio.com
Architectural & engineering services: master planning & project mgmt, construction mgmt, design/build, facility assessments. (AA, estab 1982, empl 6, sales $415,000, cert: State, 8(a))

Louisiana

1767 Marrero Couvillon & Associates, LLC
      4354 S Sherwood Forest Blvd, Ste D200
      Baton Rouge, LA 70816
      Contact: Stacey Vincent Producation Mgr
      Tel: 225-408-8249
      Email: svincent@mca-llc.com
      Website: www.mca-llc.com
Mechanical, Electrical, Plumbing, Fire Protection Engineering Services, Architectural Services and Construction Management (Hisp, estab 1968, empl 17, sales $2,800,000, cert: State, NMSDC, 8(a), SDB)

Maryland

1768 K. Dixon Architecture, PLLC
      137 National Plaza, Ste 300
      National Harbor, MD 20745
      Contact: K. Dixon Principal
      Tel: 301-364-5053
      Email:
      Website: www.kdixonarchitecture.com
Architectural design & planning services: commercial, education, government, residential, and institutional. (Woman/AA, estab 2003, empl 1, sales $100,000, cert: State, City, WBENC)

1769 Mimar Architects & Engineers, Inc.
      7004 Security Blvd Ste 210
      Baltimore, MD 21244
      Contact: Maria Khalid Marketing Coord
      Tel: 410-944-4900
      Email: mkhalid@mimarch.net
      Website: www.mimarch.net
Architectural-engineering, architectural/planning, interior/graphic design, engineering & construction management services. (Minority, estab 1995, empl 25, sales $3,991,379, cert: State)

1770 NFD, Inc.
      124 Lakefront Dr
      Hunt Valley, MD 21030
      Contact: Laura Schlicht Business Dev Dir
      Tel: 410-785-7795
      Email: lschlicht@nfd.com
      Website: www.nfd.com
Commercial interior design & planning: programming & budgeting; schematic design; furniture/equipment inventorying; space planning; 3D modeling; furniture & finish specs; project coordination. (Woman, estab 1978, empl 9, sales $973,000, cert: State, City, WBENC)

1771 Sugar Associates, LLC
      2909 Old Court Rd
      Baltimore, MD 21208
      Contact: Karen Sugar President
      Tel: 410-602-2909
      Email: karen@sugarassociates.com
      Website: www.sugarassociates.com
Interior design & planning, space programming, 24-hour-turn-around space planning & facility planning services. (Woman, estab , empl , sales $212,000, cert: State, City)

Michigan

1772 Gala & Associates Inc.
      31455 Southfield Rd
      Beverly Hills, MI 48025
      Contact: Chuni Gala President
      Tel: 248-642-8610
      Email: cgala@galaandassociates.com
      Website: www.galaandassociates.com
Electrical, mechanical, structural, civil & architectural engineering svcs, CAD services. (As-Ind, estab 1987, empl 50, sales $6,000,000, cert: NMSDC)

Minnesota

1773 Studio Hive Inc.
      901 N Third St, Ste 228
      Minneapolis, MN 55401
      Contact: Shari Bjork Principal
      Tel: 612-279-0430
      Email: sbjork@studiohive.com
      Website: www.studiohive.com
Architectural & interior design. (Woman, estab 2003, empl 8, sales $1,098,036, cert: State)

Missouri

1774 Arcturis, Inc.
      720 Olive St Ste 200
      St. Louis, MO 63101
      Contact: Julie Keil Principal
      Tel: 314-206-7100
      Email: jkeil@arcturis.com
      Website: www.arcturis.com
Architecture, interior design, landscape architecture, urban planning, graphic design, workplace optimization, master planning, site planning & building evaluation services. (Woman, estab 1977, empl 50, sales $8,500,000, cert: State, WBENC)

1775 Bozoian Group Architects, LLC
      2201 S Brentwood Blvd Ste 105
      St. Louis, MO 63144
      Contact: Katherine Bozoian President
      Tel: 314-962-4100
      Email: information@bozoiangroup.com
      Website: www.bozoiangroup.com
Architectural svcs: master planning, facility & needs assessment, new building design, renovation, interior design, adaptive re-use, re-purpose, sustainable design, owners representation, construction administration. (Woman, estab 1996, empl 6, sales $958,000, cert: State, WBENC)

1776 CORE10 Architecture
      4501 Lindell Blvd Ste 1a
      St. Louis, MO 63108
      Contact: Michael Byrd
      Tel: 314-726-4858
      Email: mbyrd@core10architecture.com
      Website: www.core10architecture.com
Architecture, Interior Design, Master Planning, Sustainable Design, LEED, Residential, Mixed Use, Multi-Family, Commercial, Office, Industrial. (Minority, estab 2007, empl 6, sales $881,934, cert: State, City)

1777 Gray Design Group, Inc.
      Nine Sunnen Dr, Ste 110
      Saint Louis, MO 63143
      Contact: Lorrie Kramer
      Tel: 314-646-0400
      Email: lkramer@graydesigngroup.com
      Website: www.graydesigngroup.com
Commercial architecture & interior design. (Woman, estab , empl , sales $2,397,779, cert: State, City)

1778 Kennedy Associates/Architects, Inc.
      2060 Craigshire Rd
      St. Louis, MO 63146
      Contact: Michael B. Kennedy, Jr. President
      Tel: 314-241-8188
      Email: kaibuild@kai-db.com
      Website: www.kai-db.com
Architecture, planning & interior design, mechanical engineering, electrical, plumbing. (AA, estab 1980, empl 110, sales $26,000,000, cert: State, City, NMSDC)

1779 Oculus Inc.
      1 S Memorial Dr, Ste 1500
      St. Louis, MO 63102
      Contact: Shevaun McNaughton Marketing Dir
      Tel: 314-367-6100
      Email: shevaunm@oculusinc.com
      Website: www.oculusinc.com
Architecture, strategic planning, interior design & move management. (Woman, estab 1994, empl , sales $6,338,825, cert: State, WBENC)

1780 Pendulum Studio LLC
      1512 Holmes St
      Kansas City, MO 64108
      Contact: Jonathan Cole Owner
      Tel: 816-399-5251
      Email: jonathan@pendulumkc.com
      Website: www.pendulumkc.com
Architectural svcs: master planning, new facility design, green building strategy, accessibility consulting, existing facility renovation, strategic expansion planning, facility assessment. (AA, estab 2007, empl 9, sales $1,120,578, cert: State, City, NMSDC

North Carolina

1781 Arcons Design Studio Professional Corporation
      10550 Independence Point Pkwy Ste 300
      Matthews, NC 28105
      Contact: Rajeev Bhave President
      Tel: 704-542-5252
      Email: rbhave@arconsds.com
      Website: www.arconsds.com
Architectural services, retail, commercial, institutional and mixed use projects. (As-Ind, estab 2004, empl 7, sales $1,400,000, cert: State)

1782 CSBO Architecture P.C.
      1589 Skeet Club Rd Ste 102-172
      High Point, NC 27265
      Contact: Carlos Sanchez President
      Tel: 336-617-3079
      Email: carlos.sanchez@csboinc.com
      Website: www.csboinc.com
Architectural design services. (Hisp, estab 2002, empl 2, sales , cert: State)

1783 Espinosa Architecture + Consulting, PC
937 Bryansplace Rd
Winston-Salem, NC 27104
Contact: Carlos V Espinosa President
Tel: 336-407-8419
Email: arlos@espinosaarchitecture.com
Website: www.espinosaarchitecture.com
Architecture services, architectural design, space planning, needs evaluation & programming, evaluation of existing structures, cost analysis, interior design. (Hisp, estab 2014, empl 3, sales , cert: State)

1784 McCulloch England Associates Architects, Inc.
100 Queens Rd, Ste 200
Charlotte, NC 28204
Contact: Grace Murray COO
Tel: 704-372-2740
Email: gmurray@mceaa.com
Website: www.mccullochengland.com
Architecture services, design services, healthcare architecture, interior design services, planning, programming, schematic design, design development, construction documents, bidding documents, construction administration. (Hisp, estab 1971, empl 24, sales , cert: State, NMSDC)

1785 Neighboring Concepts, PLLC
1230 W Morehead St Ste 204
Charlotte, NC 28208
Contact: Robin Holloway Dir of Mktg/Business Dev
Tel: 704-374-0916
Email: robin@neighboringconcepts.com
Website: www.neighboringconcepts.com
Architectural design: concept, construction, post-construction services, urban planning, development & revitalization. (Minority, estab 1996, empl 17, sales $1,903,763, cert: State)

New Jersey

1786 Gramieri Design Services
353 Georges Rd, Ste C
Dayton, NJ 08810
Contact: Frank Gramieri President
Tel: 732-274-9540
Email: fgramieri@gdsinc.net
Website: www.gdsinc.net
Interior architectural & engineering services: site analysis, design development, project budgeting & programming, space planning, schematics design, 3D rendering & modeling, architectural & engineering contract documents. (Minority, estab 1992, empl 7, sales $638,903, cert: City, NMSDC)

1787 Kamlesh Shah Designs Inc.
18 Lovell Dr
Plainsboro, NJ 08536
Contact: Kamlesh Shah Principal
Tel: 609-655-9908
Email: kshah@ksdarchitects.com
Website: www.ksdarchitects.com
Architectural, Interior Space Planning, Programing, Lab Design, Process Manufacuring Design, Mechanical, Electrical, Plumbing, Engineering Services. (As-Pac, estab 1998, empl 6, sales $2,115,234, cert: State)

1788 O&S Associates, Inc.
145 Main St
Hackensack, NJ 07601
Contact: Kelly O'Leary Dir Business Devel
Tel: 201-488-7144
Email: kaoleary@oandsassociates.com
Website: www.oandsassociates.com
Planning, Design and Restoration of full building envelope, inclusive of roof, windows, facade. Specializing in parking planning, design & restoration. Engineers and Architects. (Minority, estab 1996, empl 40, sales $6,500,000, cert: NMSDC)

1789 KME Architects LLC
231 W Charleston Blvd
Las Vegas, NV 89102
Contact: Melvin Green Principal
Tel: - - -1902
Email: melvin@kmearchitects.com
Website: www.kmearchitects.com/
Architectural services, interior design, landscape design, sustainable design, Historic preservation, tenant improvements, fire code violations, master planning, laser scanning. (AA, Hisp, estab 2009, empl 9, sales , cert: NMSDC)

New York

1790 Avinash K. Malhotra Architects (AKM)
148 W 24th St
New York, NY 10706
Contact: Richard Saunderson Associate
Tel: 212-808-0000
Email: rsaunderson@akmarch.com
Website: www.akmarch.com
Architectural solutions: high-rise buildings, large scale conversions, historical preservation & landmarks re-use, renovations & architectural interiors. (As-Ind, estab 1982, empl 10, sales $1,900,000, cert: State, City, NMSDC)

1791 AWA Lighting Designers Inc.
61 Greenpoint Ave
Brooklyn, NY 11222
Contact: Abhay Wadhwa CEO
Tel: 212-473-9797
Email: abhay@awalightingdesigners.com
Website: www.awalightingdesigners.com
Architectural lighting design, design & implement lighting solutions for commercial, civic, cultural & residential projects. (As-Ind, estab 2011, empl 27, sales , cert: State)

1792 Foit-Albert Associates, Architecture, Engineering and Surveying, P.C.
215 W 94th St, Ste 517
New York, NY 10025
Contact: Gregory Carballada President
Tel: 716-856-3933
Email: cstoebe@foit-albert.com
Website: www.foit-albert.com
Architecture, Engineering, Environmental & Land Surveying Consulting. (Hisp, estab 1977, empl 70, sales $10,000,000, cert: State, City)

1793 Kahn Architecture & Design, PC
      2 West 45th St Ste 501
      New York, NY 10036
      Contact: Heidi Kahn President
      Tel: 646-253-9864
      Email: hwiley@kahnarchitecture.com
      Website: www.kahnarchitecture.com
Architecture, interior design & planning solution services to commercial and retail clients. (Woman, estab 2005, empl 17, sales $2,200,000, cert: State, City, WBENC)

1794 Kenne Shepherd Interior Design Architecture PLLC
      54 W 21st St, Ste 1208
      New York, NY 10010
      Contact: Kenne Shepherd Principal
      Tel: 212-206-6336
      Email: kshepherd@kenneshepherd.com
      Website: www.kenneshepherd.com
Multi-disciplinary interior architectural, workspace, retail store or residence, strategic planning, site evaluation, code/zoning analysis, lease/workletter review, architectural design, sustainable design, construction documents, construction observation (Woman, estab 1993, empl 3, sales , cert: WBENC)

1795 Lewandowska Architect PLLC
      14 Wall St, 20th Floor
      New York, NY 10005
      Contact: Barbara Lewandowska Principal
      Tel: 212-787-4558
      Email: barbara@lewandowskaarchitect.com
      Website: www.LewandowskaArchitect.com
Architectural, interior design & space planning services. (Woman, estab 2002, empl 3, sales $200,000, cert: State, City)

1796 SWITZER Architecture, P.C.
      255 W 36th St Ste 1101
      New York, NY 10018
      Contact: Gregory T Switzer Principal
      Tel: 212-391-1519
      Email: gswitzer@switzerarchitecture.com
      Website: www.switzerpc.com
Architectural design & holistic management. (AA, estab 2003, empl 6, sales $750,000, cert: NMSDC)

1797 The Switzer Group
      3 E 54th St
      New York, NY 10022
      Contact: Wendy Hall Principal, Client Devel
      Tel: 212-922-1313
      Email: whall@theswitzergroup.com
      Website: www.theswitzergroup.com
Interior design. (AA, estab 1975, empl 70, sales $13,500,000, cert: City, NMSDC)

1798 ZELJKA ONE Management LLC dba: Green Way Pavement
      PO Box 2927
      Binghamton, NY 13902
      Contact: Robert V Gerard Co-Owner
      Tel: 607-724-2438
      Email: robertgerard@me.com
      Website: www.greenwaypavements.com
LEED architects & construction services. (Woman, estab 2011, empl 2, sales $11,000,000, cert: State)

Ohio

1799 Brockman Designs LLC
      27600 Chagrin Blvd Ste 260
      Cleveland, OH 44122
      Contact: Sharon Brockman Principal
      Tel: 216-504-4040
      Email: sbrockman@brockmandesigns.com
      Website: www.brockmandesigns.com
Interior design, healthcare spaces & facilities, higher education & corporate offices, interior space planning, interior finish selections & specifications, furniture planning & specifications, project coordination. (Woman, estab 2001, empl 2, sales , cert: State, City)

1800 DNK Architects, Inc.
      2616 Central Pkwy
      Cincinnati, OH 45214
      Contact: Guinette Kirk VP
      Tel: 513-948-4146
      Email: gkirk@dnkarchitects.com
      Website: www.dnkarchitects.com
Interior design & space planning services, Cadd drafting. (AA, estab 1986, empl 20, sales $2,000,000, cert: State, NMSDC)

1801 Quinn Engineering & Employment Network LLC
      125 W Market St, Ste 221
      Warren, OH 44481
      Contact: Candys Mayo Owner
      Tel: 330-423-1923
      Email: info@queen-ohio.com
      Website: www.queen-ohio.com
Computer Aided Drafting and Engineering/Architecture support, Naval Architecture and Aerospace. (AA, estab 2015, empl 2, sales , cert: State)

1802 Robert P Madison International, Inc
      1215 Superior Ave E Ste 110
      Cleveland, OH 44114
      Contact: R. Kevin Madison, AIA President
      Tel: 216-861-8195
      Email: rklann@rpmadison.com
      Website: www.rpmadison.com
Architectural svcs; civil, structural, electrical & mechanical engineering. (Woman/AA, estab 1954, empl 13, sales $1,692,000, cert: State, City)

1803 Ubiquitous Design, Ltd.
      3443 Lee Rd
      Shaker Heights, OH 44120
      Contact: W. Daniel Bickerstaff, II Founder & Principal Architect
      Tel: 216-752-4444
      Email: arcatek@udltd.com
      Website: www.udltd.com
Architectural design services, conceptual design/feasibility analysis, construction administration. (AA, estab 2001, empl 2, sales $200,000, cert: City)

1804 WA, Inc. (dba WA Architects, Inc.)
      807 Broadway St 2nd Fl
      Cincinnati, OH 45202
      Contact: Wade Price Principal
      Tel: 513-641-0111
      Email: wprice@wa-inc.biz
      Website: www.wa-architectsinc.com
Healthcare Design & Planning. (AA, estab 1971, empl 16, sales $1,750,000, cert: State, NMSDC)

ARCHITECTS 1805-1815

1805 Wanix Architects, LLC
4208 Prospect Ave
Cleveland, OH 44103
Contact: Xin Wan Owner
Tel: 440-570-9829
Email: xinwan@wanixarchitects.com
Website: www.wanixarchitects.com
Architectural design, site planning, interior space planning & 3D. (Minority, Woman, estab 2008, empl 2, sales , cert: City)

Pennsylvania

1806 Alexander Perry Inc.
2929 Arch St, Ste 1700
Philadelphia, PA 19104
Contact: Patricia Sanford CEO
Tel: 215-948-8148
Email: psanford@alexanderperryinc.com
Website: www.alexanderperryinc.com
Interior design, project management, construction management, flooring & window treatments, furniture, signage. (Woman/AA, estab 1992, empl 13, sales , cert: State, City, NMSDC, WBENC)

1807 DJDC Inc.
12300 Perry Hwy, Ste 204
Wexford, PA 15090
Contact: Marcia Guth Principal
Tel: 412-996-6771
Email: mguth@djdc.com
Website: www.djdc.com
Interior architecture design, space planning & facilities planning svcs. (Woman, estab 1972, empl 6, sales $243,000, cert: WBENC)

1808 Genesis Architects Inc.
1850 N Gravers Rd
Plymouth Meeting, PA 19462
Contact: Meryl Towarnicki President
Tel: 610-592-0280
Email: mtowarnicki@geiarc.com
Website: www.geiarc.com
Architecture, Engineering, Commissioning & Construction Management. (Woman, estab 2017, empl 50, sales $60,480,129, cert: WBENC)

1809 MKSD. LLC
1209 Hausman Rd, Ste A
Allentown, PA 18104
Contact: President
Tel: 610-366-2081
Email:
Website: www.mksdarchitects.com
Architecture, planning, design & construction for new buildings, additions & renovations. (Woman, estab 2005, empl 16, sales $3,103,884, cert: State, WBENC)

1810 SMC Consulting, LLC d/b/a/ Studio SMC
379 Insurance St
Beaver, PA 15009
Contact: Sam McWilliams Managing Partner
Tel: 724-728-8625
Email: sam@studio-smc.com
Website: www.studio-smc.com
Interior Design, Space Planning, Furniture Planning, Furniture Specification, Move Management, Project Management, Construction Administration. (Woman, estab 1999, empl 5, sales $213,544, cert: State)

1811 Styer & Associates, Inc.
412 Dekalb St
Norristown, PA 19401
Contact: Amy Styer Tahtabrounian Principal
Tel: 610-275-6000
Email: amy@styergroup.com
Website: www.styergroup.com
Architecture, engineering, interior design, construction, project management, purchase management. (Woman, estab 1985, empl 9, sales $190,000,000, cert: WBENC)

Puerto Rico

1812 CMA Architects & Engineers LLC
1509 Ave FD Roosevelt
Guaynabo, PR 00968
Contact: Jorge A. Tirado, PE Managing Member
Tel: 787-792-1509
Email: jtirado@cmapr.com
Website: www.cmapr.com
Architectural design services, preparation of construction documents, field & construction management, environmental & permitting, electrical, mechanical, structural, transportation & infrastructure engineering. (Hisp, estab 1959, empl 90, sales $8,300,000, cert: NMSDC, SDB)

1813 UNIPRO Architects Engineers LLP
PO Box 10914
San Juan, PR 00922
Contact: Jose R. Gonzalez Dir planning/Projects
Tel: 787-793-3950
Email: jgonzalez@uniproaep.net
Website: www.uniproaep.com
Architecture, civil engineering, structural engineering, mechanical engineering, electrical engineering, environmental engineering, construction management. (Hisp, estab 1980, empl 30, sales $3,200,000, cert: NMSDC)

Texas

1814 Architect for Life - A Professional Corporation
2450 Louisiana St, Ste 400-233
Houston, TX 77006
Contact: Lolalisa King
Tel: 888-986-7771
Email: lking@architectforlife.com
Website: www.architectforlife.com
Green consulting professional services, develop & manage energy efficient strategies, programs, & projects, retrofit strategies, benchmarking building energy performance, long-term energy management & water saving goals assessment. (Woman/AA, estab 1995, empl 12, sales , cert: City)

1815 BSA Design Group Inc.
8750 N Central Expressway, Ste 1725
Dallas, TX 75231
Contact: Vanessa Witliff President
Tel: 214-818-0563
Email: vwittliff@bsa-designgroup.com
Website: www.bsa-designgroup.com
Architectural, interior design, design build, project management, programming and scheduling, studies and analyses, specifications, furnishing procurement. (Woman, estab 1989, empl 13, sales $5,000,000, cert: WBENC)

1816 Interprise/Southwest Interior & Space Planning
5080 Spectrum Dr Ste 115E
Addison, TX 75001
Contact: Lesley Leahy VP Business Dev
Tel: 972-385-3991
Email: lleahy@interprisedesign.com
Website: www.interprisedesign.com
Commerical interior design & space planning. (Woman, estab 1981, empl 36, sales $4,500,000, cert: WBENC)

1817 R & T Architects, Inc.
3300 S Gessner, Ste 119
Houston, TX 77063
Contact: Spencer Tsui Principal
Tel: 713-974-2008
Email: rtarch@swbell.net
Website: www.rtarch.net
Architectural services: design & built. (As-Pac, estab 1982, empl 4, sales $110,000, cert: State, City)

1818 STOA International Architects, Inc.
6001 Savoy Dr, Ste 100
Houston, TX 77036
Contact: Alice Hu
Tel: 713-995-8784
Email: stoaintl@globalxlr.com
Website: www.stoaintl.com
Architectural design, interior design, planning, construction management, architectural rendering. (As-Pac, estab 1995, empl 10, sales $750,000, cert: State, City, NMSDC)

1819 VAI Architects Inc.
16000 N Dallas Pkwy, Ste 200
Dallas, TX 75248
Contact: William Vidaud Principal
Tel: 972-934-8888
Email: wvidaud@vaiarchitects.com
Website: www.vaiarchitects.com
Architecture, master planning, feasibility analysis, interior planning & design, building condition assessments, CADD, renovation, alteration & expansion, demolition specifications, roofing assessments/corrective design. (Hisp, estab 1985, empl 28, sales $4,945,000, cert: State)

Virginia

1820 nbj Architecture
11537-B Nuckols Rd
Glen Allen, VA 23059
Contact: Neil Bhatt President
Tel: 804-273-9811
Email: nbhatt@nbjarch.com
Website: www.nbjarch.com
Architectural, space planning, interior design, construction administration, feasibility studies & value engineering. (Minority, estab 2000, empl 12, sales $2,000,000, cert: State)

1821 SandHurst-AEC
1069 W Broad St, Ste 777
Falls church, VA 22046
Contact: Kwafo Djan Principal
Tel: 703-533-1413
Email: kdjan@sandhurstaec.com
Website: www.sandhurstaec.com
Architecture & Urban Planning, Program Management, Site Analysis, Feasibility Studies, Architectural Design, Construction, Documentation, Interior Design Services, Space Planning, Project Management. (AA, estab 2013, empl 3, sales , cert: State, 8(a))

Washington

1822 Ato Apiafi Architects PLLC
10940 NE 33rd Place Ste 208
Bellevue, WA 98004
Contact: Jeff Thompson
Tel: 425-202-7760
Email: jeff.t@atoapiafi.com
Website: www.atoapiafi.com
Full service architectural firm. (AA, estab 2004, empl 2, sales , cert: State, NMSDC)

1823 Magellan Architects
8383 158th Ave NE, Ste 280
Redmond, WA 98052
Contact: Principal
Tel: 425-885-4300
Email: office@magellanarchitects.com
Website: www.magellanarchitects.com
Architectural design services & construction administration. (Hisp, estab 2000, empl 30, sales $1,928,209, cert: NMSDC)

Wisconsin

1824 Continuum Architects + Planners, S.C.
228 S First
Milwaukee, WI 53204
Contact: Ursula Twombly Principal
Tel: 414-220-9649
Email: ursula.twombly@continuumarchitects.com
Website: www.continuumarchitects.com
Master planning site selection site planning, pre-design studies. (Woman, estab 1996, empl 13, sales $1,700,000, cert: City)

AUTOMOBILES

New and used car dealerships. Distributors of single cars, trucks and fleet sales. Provide rental and leasing services. NAICS Code 44

California

1825 Premiere Solutions, LLC
11501 Dublin Blvd Ste 200
Dublin, CA 94568
Contact: Holly Michael
Tel: 925-467-1000
Email: holly@premieresolutionsllc.com
Website: www.premieresolutionsllc.com

Fleet management services: vehicle acquisition (lease, purchase or rental), vehicle disposal, fuel card, preventative maintenance, accident management, roadside assistance, transportation, licensing & registration. (AA, estab 2005, empl 7, sales $15,950,000, cert: NMSDC, CPUC)

1826 Rotolo Chevrolet, Inc.
16666 S Highland Ave
Fontana, CA 92336
Contact: Jamie Harshman Dir Fleet Sales
Tel: 909-822-1111
Email: jamie@rotolo.com
Website: www.rotolochevy.com

Sell & service Chevrolet light duty cars & trucks. (Woman, estab 1971, empl 104, sales $82,651,283, cert: CPUC)

Colorado

1827 Burt Fleet Services, Inc.
5210 S Broadway
Englewood, CO 80113
Contact: Lloyd Chavez CEO
Tel: 303-789-6701
Email: lgchavezjr@burt.com
Website: www.burt.com

National fleet vehicle sales & leasing. (Minority, Woman, estab 2009, empl 6, sales $600,001, cert: NMSDC)

Florida

1828 NM1, LLC
16725 NW 57th Ave
Miami Gardens, FL 33055
Contact: Rogelio (Roger) Tovar President
Tel: 888-423-7756
Email: rogeliotovar@gmail.com
Website: www.palmetto57nissan.com

Sell new & used cars, parts & service. (Hisp, estab 2012, empl 110, sales $74,200,851, cert: NMSDC)

1829 Sun State International Trucks, LLC
6020 Adamo Dr
Tampa, FL 33619
Contact: Dave Metcalf VP, Dir of Sales
Tel: 813-769-2541
Email: dave.metcalf@sunstateintl.com
Website: www.sunstateintl.com

Medium & heavy duty commercial truck dealership. (AA, estab 1982, empl 163, sales $115,000,000, cert: NMSDC)

Illinois

1830 Advantage Chevrolet
9510 W. Joliet Rd
Hodgkins, IL 60525
Contact: Rick Zureick GM
Tel: 847-561-5281
Email: rzureick@advantagechev.com
Website: www.advantagechev.com

Automotive & commercial truck sales. (AA, estab 2000, empl 122, sales $91,265,959, cert: NMSDC)

1831 Sutton Ford, Inc.
21315 Central
Matteson, IL 60443
Contact: Michael Miller Fleet Mgr
Tel: 708-720-8034
Email: mmiller@suttonford.com
Website: www.suttonford.com

Ford cars, trucks, sales, service & parts. (AA, estab 1989, empl 80, sales , cert: State, NMSDC, CPUC)

Indiana

1832 Truck City of Gary, Inc.
PO Box 64800
Gary, IN 46401
Contact: Gerri Davis-Parker CEO
Tel: 219-949-8595
Email: wbe@mytruckcity.com
Website: www.mytruckcity.com

Heavy Duty Trucks: Agricultural, Landscaping, Bucket, Vacuum, Fuel, Aerial, Welding, Digger Derrick, Pole, Straight, Box, Flat-bed, Bucket, Service, Platform, Dump, Runway Snow Plow, Railway, Refuse, Logging, Mounted Cranes, etc. (Woman, estab 1946, empl 58, sales $45,799,499, cert: State, WBENC)

Massachusetts

1833 Minuteman Trucks, Inc.
2181 Providence Hwy
Walpole, MA 02081
Contact: William L Witcher COO
Tel: 508-668-3112
Email: bwitcher@minutemantrucks.com
Website: www.minutemantrucks.com

Medium & Heavy Duty Truck Support Center. (Minority, estab 1990, empl 87, sales $47,359,662, cert: State, NMSDC)

Maryland

1834 K. Neal International Trucks, Inc.
5000 Tuxedo Rd
Hyattsville, MD 20781
Contact: Sharon Calomese CEO
Tel: 301-772-5100
Email: scalomese@knealinternational.com
Website: www.knealinternational.com

Commercial truck dealership: International, Hino, Mitsubishi Fuso trucks & IC Bus. Sales, service, parts & body shop services, leasing & rental services. (AA, estab 1982, empl 90, sales $110,000,000, cert: State, City, NMSDC)

Michigan

1835 Hall Whitener Investments, Inc.
13475 Portage Rd
Vicksburg, MI 49097
Contact: Laura Awe Customer Relations Dir
Tel: 269-649-2000
Email: laura.awe@vicksburgchrysler.com
Website: www.vicksburgchryslerdodgejeepram.com
Sale & service Chrysler, Dodge, Jeep, Ram vehicles. (AA, estab 2013, empl 32, sales , cert: NMSDC)

1836 Vicksburg Chrysler Dodge Jeep
13475 Portage Rd
Vicksburg, MI 49097
Contact: Monti Long President
Tel: 269-649-2000
Email: mlong007@comcast.net
Website: www.VicksburgChryslerDodge.com
New & used cars, Chrysler, Dodge, Jeep retail, lease & fleet services. (AA, estab 1989, empl 46, sales $22,521,322, cert: NMSDC)

Minnesota

1837 Holt Motors, Inc
245 Cokato St W
Cokato, MN 55321
Contact: Kate Keith GM
Tel: 320-286-2176
Email:
Website: www.holtmotors.com
Ford Vehicles, Commercial Ford Fleet Program. (Woman, estab 1951, empl 48, sales , cert: WBENC)

Nevada

1838 SVI. Inc.
440 Mark Leany Dr
Henderson, NV 89011
Contact: Nancy Munoz Sales Mgr
Tel: 702-567-5256
Email: nancy.munoz@specialtyvehicles.com
Website: www.specialtyvehicles.com
Dist people mover products, Buses, Trams, Trolleys, Golf Carts, Ground Maintence Vehicles and vehicle parts. (Minority, Woman, estab 2003, empl 13, sales $14,036,900, cert: State, WBENC)

New York

1839 Fleet Maintenance, Inc.
67 Ransier Dr
West Seneca, NY 14224
Contact: Deborah Gawron President
Tel: 716-675-9220
Email: debg@fmibuffalo.com
Website: www.fmifreightliner.com
Truck dealership, Daimler Truck NA (Woman, estab 1979, empl 40, sales $70,000,000, cert: State, WBENC)

Ohio

1840 Auld Technologies, LLC
2030 Dividend Dr
Columbus, OH 43228
Contact: Project Coord
Tel: 614-755-2853
Email: info@auldtech.com
Website: www.auldtech.com
Dist decorative emblems, trim, labels, overlays & coating solutions. (Woman, estab 2009, empl 26, sales $3,500,000, cert: WBENC)

1841 Bob Ross Auto Group
85 Loop Rd
Centerville, OH 45459
Contact: Fleet FSP Mgr
Tel: 937-433-0990
Email: fleet@bobrossauto.com
Website: www.bobrossauto.com
New Vehicle Dealer, automobiles & light/medium duty trucks: Buick, GMC Light Duty Trucks, Vans and SUVs; Fiat Automobiles; Alfa Romeo Automobiles & Specialized Equipped Fleet & Commercial Vehicles. (Woman/AA, estab 1974, empl 92, sales $66,226,386, cert: State, WBENC)

Pennsylvania

1842 Buick GMC of Moosic Inc.
4230 Birney Ave
Moosic, PA 18507
Contact: Lori Guitson President
Tel: 570-414-1000
Email: lori@sunbpg.com
Website: www.sunbuickgmc.com
New Buick GMC's, economical cars to vehicles for executives. (Woman, estab 2004, empl 18, sales $14,000,000, cert: WBENC)

Texas

1843 Ancira
10807 W IH 10
San Antonio, TX 78230
Contact: Betty Ferguson Mgr
Tel: 210-558-1500
Email: ljust@ancira.com
Website: www.ancira.com
Automobile dealership. (Hisp, estab 1985, empl 25, sales , cert: State)

1844 Kahlig Enterprises, Inc
351 IH 35 South
New Braunfels, TX 78130
Contact: Larry Brown Exec Dir Fleet Sales
Tel: 210-426-3295
Email: lbrown@kahligauto.com
Website: www.kahligauto.com
New Ford, Lincoln & Jeep automobiles, light trucks & SUVs. (Hisp, estab 1984, empl 212, sales $343,000,000, cert: NMSDC)

1845 Metro Golf Cars, Inc.
4063 South Frwy
Fort Worth, TX 76110
Contact: Ben King GM
Tel: 817-921-5491
Email: ben@metrogolfcars.com
Website: www.metrogolfcars.com
Golf cars, utility, off road, sales, service, parts & rental. (Woman/As-Ind, estab 1974, empl 48, sales , cert: State)

1846 Rio Motor
4350 E Hwy 83
Rio Grande City, TX 78582
Contact: O.C. Canales President
Tel: 956-487-2596
Email: riomotorco@aol.com
Website: www.riomotors.com
Sell Chevrolet cars, trucks, van parts & servicing. (Hisp, estab 1953, empl 29, sales , cert: State)

> **AUTOMOTIVE PARTS & ACCESSORIES**
> Manufacturers of batteries, cables, recapping of tires, remanufacturing of auto parts, etc. Also lists wholesale distributors of automotive supplies & equipment. NAICS Code 42

Alabama

1847 Alignment Simple Solutions, LLC
 106 David Green Rd Ste E
 Birmingham, AL 35244
 Contact: Tess Winningham CEO
 Tel: 205-475-2419
 Email: tess@quicktrickalignment.com
 Website: www.alignmentsimplesolutions.com
Mfr portable, compact & cost efficient QuickTrick wheel alignment measurement systems. (Woman, estab , empl 5, sales $406,500, cert: WBENC)

California

1848 Concours Direct, Inc.
 3212 El Camino Real
 Atascadero, CA 93422
 Contact: William M Vega
 Tel: 805-466-4040
 Email: wvega@concoursdirect.com
 Website: www.concoursdirect.com
Dist Automotive & Truck Performance Parts, Ford Performance Racing Parts, Edelbrock, MSD, Airaid, Readylift, MBRP, Moroso, Diablosport, Bullydog, Performance Automatic, Centerforce, Tremec, Powermaster, Holly, etc. (Hisp, estab 2005, empl 2, sales $2,412,993, cert: NMSDC, CPUC)

1849 Prime Wheel Corp.
 17705 S Main St
 Gardena, CA 90248
 Contact: Albert Huang
 Tel: 310-516-9126
 Email: ahuang@primewheel.com
 Website: www.primewheel.com
Motor Vehicle Parts Manufacturing. (As-Pac, estab 1989, empl 800, sales $185,000,000, cert: NMSDC)

1850 VIAIR Corporation
 15 Edelman
 Irvine, CA 92618
 Contact: Alan Basham Dir of Operations
 Tel: 949-585-0011
 Email: alanb@viaircorp.com
 Website: www.viaircorp.com
Dist Air Compressor, Air Tank, LED Light, Air accessories for automotive industry. (As-Pac, estab 1998, empl 32, sales $22,000,000, cert: NMSDC)

Florida

1851 Astra/CFX Holdings, LLC
 11971 NW37th St
 Coral Springs, FL 33065
 Contact: Sharon McTurk President
 Tel: 954-494-3948
 Email: smcturk@astraservices.com
 Website: www.astraservices.com
3PL Tire and Wheel Assembly, heavy Sub Assembly for all major vehicle modules. (Minority, Woman, estab 1989, empl 217, sales $8,950,000, cert: NMSDC, WBENC)

1852 Indus Solutions LLC
 4260 NW 1st Ave
 Boca Raton, FL 33433
 Contact: Sandeep Vijay
 Tel: 248-875-8010
 Email: sv@indus-sol.com
 Website: www.indus-sol.com
Mfr automotive parts & components, sub assemblies & assemblies of door, hood & tailgate systems, exhaust, steering & suspension, gaskets, rubber mounts, engine, electrical & electronics parts, wire harness & integrated products & prototyping. (As-Ind, estab 2015, empl 15, sales , cert: NMSDC)

1853 NM1, LLC
 16725 NW 57th Ave
 Miami Gardens, FL 33055
 Contact: Rogelio (Roger) Tovar President
 Tel: 888-423-7756
 Email: rogeliotovar@gmail.com
 Website: www.palmetto57nissan.com
Sell new & used cars, parts & service. (Hisp, estab 2012, empl 110, sales $74,101,851, cert: NMSDC)

1854 Vehicle Maintenance Program, Inc.
 3595 N Dixie Hwy, Bay 7
 Boca Raton, FL 33431
 Contact: Penny Brooks CEO
 Tel: 561-362-6080
 Email: accounting@vmpparts.com
 Website: www.vmpparts.com
Dist vehicle repair parts: filters, wiper blades, lenses, lamps, bulbs, mirrors, batteries, seals, bearings, brake drums. (Woman, estab 1988, empl 15, sales $23,443,700, cert: State, WBENC)

Georgia

1855 Battle and Battle Distributors, Inc
 2410 Park Central Blvd.
 Decatur, GA 30035
 Contact: Sylvia Battle VP
 Tel: 770-987-8147
 Email: sylvia@battleandbattle.net
 Website: www.battleandbattle.net
Dist industrial batteries, automotive, batteries & battery equip. (AA, estab , empl , sales , cert: NMSDC)

Illinois

1856 Bearings & Industrial Supply
 431 Imen Ave
 Addison, IL 60101
 Contact: Sejal Khandwala Acct Exec
 Tel: 630-628-1966
 Email: Sejal@BearingsNow.Com
 Website: www.bearingsnow.com
Dist bearings & power transmission products; pump & pump repair parts, HVAC & electrical parts. (As-Pac, estab , empl , sales $ 0, cert: NMSDC)

1857 Chicago Parts & Sound, LLC
 1150 Lively Blvd
 Elk Grove Village, IL 60007
 Contact: Dennis Hoffberg Sales Mgr
 Tel: 630-350-1500
 Email: sales@clickoncps.com
 Website: www.clickoncps.com/
Dist automotive parts. (Minority, Woman, estab 1978, empl 80, sales , cert: City)

1858 J&J's Creative Colors, Inc.
19015 S Jodi Rd - Ste E Ste E
Mokena, IL 60448
Contact: Terri Sniegolski
Tel: 708-478-1437
Email: terri@creativecolorsintl.com
Website: www.WeCanFixThat.com
On-site repair for leather, vinyl, fabric and plastics to the auto industry. (Woman, estab 1980, empl 21, sales $18,384,759, cert: WBENC)

1859 Reliance Distributing
3609 Pebble Beach Rd
Northbrook, IL 60062
Contact: Anne Chessick CEO
Tel: 847-372-6125
Email: annieparts@aol.com
Website: www.reliancedistributing.com
Automotive & truck lighting, flashers, wiper blades, fuses, hose clamps, halogen headlight sockets, permatex products (Woman, estab 2012, empl 1, sales , cert: WBENC)

Indiana

1860 Wingard Wheel Works, LLC
1521 Kepner Dr
Lafayette, IN 47905
Contact: David Oliver GM
Tel: 765-449-3509
Email: doliver@wingard.biz
Website: www.wingardllc.com
Wingard Wheel Works specializes in Tire and Wheel Assembly as well as offering services in logistics management and procurement of material. (AA, estab 2007, empl 20, sales $51,432,000, cert: NMSDC)

Kentucky

1861 HJI Supply Chain Solutions
13200 Complete Court
Louisville, KY 40223
Contact: Lynn Moore VP Finance & Admin
Tel: 502-638-8064
Email: lmoore@hjisolutions.com
Website: www.hjisolutions.com
Automotive parts: door panel/trim, switch bezels, running boards, driveshafts, shocks, corner pillars, floor mats & hub caps. (Woman, estab , empl , sales $ 0, cert: NMSDC)

1862 LB Manufacturing
360 Industry Dr
Springfield, KY 40069
Contact: Keith Hamilton CEO
Tel: 859-336-0090
Email: hamiltonk@leanbmfg.com
Website: www.leanbmfg.com
Automotive stamping, welding & mfg assemblies, mig & resistance, robotic, window glass & exhaust system assemblies. (AA, estab 1998, empl 40, sales $17,000,000, cert: NMSDC)

Michigan

1863 Advanced Assembly Products, Inc.
1300 East Nine Mile Road
Hazel Park, MI 48030
Contact: Ron Waring IT Systems Mgr
Tel: 248-543-2427
Email: rwaring@aapincorp.com
Website: www.aapincorp.com
Body hardware, door hinges, door checks, strikers, hood hinges, deck lid hinges, stampings, welded assemblies, mechanical assemblies. (As-Ind, estab 1993, empl 140, sales $20,000,000, cert: NMSDC)

1864 BBW Holdings Inc.
318 John R Rd
Troy, MI 48083
Contact: Barry Williams President
Tel: 248-935-6161
Email: barry@bbwholdings.com
Website: www.bbwholdings.com
Vehicle manage solutions, vehicle inspection, processing tracking storage. (AA, estab 2009, empl 37, sales $ 0, cert: NMSDC)

1865 CAMACO, LLC
40000 Grand River Ste 110
Novi, MI 48375
Contact: Pamela Cooper Admin Coord
Tel: 248-442-6800
Email: pcooper@camacollc.com
Website: www.camacollc.com
Mfr auto components & assemblies. (As-Ind, estab 1987, empl 68, sales, cert: NMSDC)

1866 Capsonic Automotive & Aersopace
3121 University Dr, Ste 120
Auburn Hills, MI 48326
Contact: George E. Albrecht
Tel: 248-754-1100
Email: georgea@capsonic.com
Website: www.capsonic.com
Automotive assemblies. (AA, estab 1996, empl 449, sales $18,000,000, cert: NMSDC)

1867 Concept Industries, Inc.
4950 Kraft Ave SE
Grand Rapids, MI 49512
Contact: David Foote, Troy Caswell CFO
Tel: 616-554-9000
Email: dfoote@conceptind.com, troyc@conceptind.com
Website: www.conceptind.com
Thermoforming, interior acoustical applications, engine side noise absorbers, dash insulators, package trays, load floors, undercarpet absorbers, headliners, trunk liners, needle punch, laminating, plastic vacuum forming, die cut. (Minority, Woman, estab 1984, empl 150, sales $20,000,000, cert: NMSDC)

1868 Dawson Mfg Co. - Benton Harbor Division
1042 N Crystal Ave
Benton Harbor, MI 49022
Contact: Neil Trivedi VP
Tel: 269-925-0100
Email: neil.trivedi@vibracoustic.com.com
Website: www.dawsonmfg.com
Mfr body mounts, engine mounts, strut mounts, link assemblies & bushings, dist anti-vibration components, rubber injection molding. (As-Pac, estab 1988, empl 90, sales $36,000,000, cert: NMSDC)

1869 Detroit Chassis LLC
      6501 Lynch Rd
      Detroit, MI 48234
      Contact: Darin Burns VP Business Dev
      Tel: 313-571-2100
      Email: dburns@detroitchassis.com
      Website: www.detroitchassis.com
Niche vehicle, motor home chassis & commercial truck assembly; complex sub-assemblies & sub-assemblies. (AA, estab 1998, empl 150, sales $7,615,052, cert: NMSDC)

1870 Diversitech, Inc.
      16620 Industrial St
      Roseville, MI 48066
      Contact: Roger Olle President
      Tel: 586-445-7600
      Email: rho@div-techusa.com
      Website: www.div-techusa.com
Design & build automation assembly machines, leak test, special machines for powertrain & body & assembly, parts feeding & handling systems. (As-Ind, estab 2009, empl 4, sales $1,500,000, cert: NMSDC)

1871 Firstronic LLC
      1655 Michigan St NE
      Grand Rapids, MI 49503
      Contact: Tony Bellitto Quality Dir
      Tel: 616-808-3878
      Email: tbellitto@firstronic.com
      Website: www.firstronic.com
Dist automotive components: lighting controls, various sensors & control modules. (Woman, estab 1995, empl 50, sales $20,000,000, cert: WBENC)

1872 Global Enterprises
      26909 Woodward Ave
      Huntington Woods, MI 48070
      Contact: Pat Vizcarra Business Dev
      Tel: 248-542-2000
      Email: pvizcarra@globalent.org
      Website: www.globalent.org
Extrusion, die-cutting, compression molding, laminating & glueing interior trim components & assemblies. (Minority, Woman, estab 1998, empl 280, sales $ 0, cert: WBENC)

1873 H.R. Technologies, Inc.
      32500 N. Avis Dr
      Madison Heights, MI 48071
      Contact: Tushar Patel President
      Tel: 248-284-1170
      Email: tpatel@hrtechinc.com
      Website: www.hrtechinc.com
Laminate fabrics & vinyl, carpet, die cutting, headliner glass fiber reinforcements, headliner glass polypropylene substrate materials. (As-Ind, estab 1996, empl 48, sales $11,000,000, cert: NMSDC)

1874 Integrated Manufacturing and Assembly, LLC
      5200 Auto Club Dr
      Dearborn, MI 48126
      Contact: Leslie Thumm Financial Anyalyst
      Tel: 313-593-9246
      Email: lthumm@lear.com
      Website: www.comerholdings.com/about.htm
Interior Systems; seat assemblies, foam & trim assemblies & injection molded & painted interior components - Exterior Systems; Exterior mirror assemblies, inection molded & painted interiors. (AA, estab 1996, empl 700, sales $ 0, cert: NMSDC)

1875 Intex Technologies LLC
      3133 Highland Dr
      Hudsonville, MI 49426
      Contact: Randi Sniegowski Sales
      Tel: 616-662-0276
      Email: randi.sniegowski@intextech.net
      Website: www.intextech.net
Mfr integral skin flexible foam automotive interior parts: arm rests, center console, console door, sun visor, steering wheel, soft-touch points on door handles, cup holders, seals, jounce bumpers & insulation components. (Hisp, estab 2008, empl 50, sales $14,800,000, cert: NMSDC)

1876 La Solucion Corp.
      19930 Conner
      Detroit, MI 48234
      Contact: Patricia Leon CEO
      Tel: 313-893-9760
      Email: patleon@la-solucion.com
      Website: www.la-solucion.com
Mfr & dist liquid & air filtration systems. (Minority, Woman, estab 1999, empl 4, sales $ 0, cert: NMSDC, WBENC)

1877 Marimba Auto, LLC
      41133 Van Born Rd Ste 200
      Belleville, MI 48111
      Contact: Venkat Chigulla VP Admin
      Tel: 734-398-9000
      Email: vchigulla@marimbaauto.com
      Website: www.marimbaauto.com
Import tubing, tube processing, global supply mgmt, in-house engineering, warehousing. (As-Pac, estab 2003, empl 35, sales $17,000,000, cert: NMSDC)

1878 McKechnie Vehicle Components
      27087 Gratiot Ave, 2 Fl
      Roseville, MI 48066
      Contact: Linda Torakis President
      Tel: 586-491-2622
      Email: ltorakis@mvcusa.com
      Website: www.mvcusa.com
Mfr decorative trim products: nickel chrome plating on plastic & stainless surfaces, plastic injection molding, metal stamping, base & clear coat painting & assembly. (Woman, estab , empl , sales $ 0, cert: WBENC)

1879 Need a Part Now, LLC
      1157 Manufacturers Dr
      Westland, MI 48186
      Contact: Erin Brazill VP
      Tel: 888-201-9061
      Email: erina@needapartnow.com
      Website: www.needapartnow.com
Mfr parts from AutoCad, blueprints, drawings, sketches, or reverse engineer. (Woman, estab 2006, empl 20, sales , cert: WBENC)

1880 NYX Inc.
       30111 Schoolcraft Rd
       Livonia, MI 48150
       Contact: Dan DePalma VP Sales
       Tel: 734-462-2385
       Email: sales@nyxinc.com
       Website: www.nyxinc.com
Automotive interior solutions: Door Panels, Center Consoles, Overhead Consoles, Glove Box Systems, Knee Bolster Assemblies, Interior Garnish, Seating Components, Rear Shelf package Trays, Design and Engineering. (As-Pac, estab 1985, empl 2100, sales $ 0, cert: NMSDC)

1881 Piston Automotive
       12723 Telegraph Rd
       Redford, MI 48239
       Contact: James Edwards Sales Mgr
       Tel: 313-541-8674
       Email: jedwards@pistongroup.com
       Website: www.pistongroup.com
Manufacturing, module assembly & sequencing, & logistics management. (AA, estab 1995, empl 750, sales $ 0, cert: NMSDC)

1882 Sigma International
       36800 Plymouth Rd
       Livonia, MI 48150
       Contact: Alessandra Konopczyk Operations Mgr
       Tel: 248-230-9681
       Email: akonopczyk@sigmaintl.com
       Website: www.sigmaintl.com
Mfr labels, decals, badges, chrome abs parts, wheel center caps, dimensional graphics, stone chip protection film. (AA, estab 2003, empl 10, sales $ 0, cert: NMSDC)

1883 Sino Brite (USA), Inc.
       30600 Telegraph Rd, Ste 1131
       Bingham Farms, MI 48025
       Contact: Julinda Kong President
       Tel: 659-819-7871
       Email: sales@sinobrite-sg.com
       Website: www.sinobrite-sg.com
Motor Vehicle Supplies & New Parts Merchant Wholesalers. (As-Pac, estab 2003, empl 5, sales , cert: NMSDC)

1884 Ventura Manufacturing
       471 E Roosevelt
       Zeeland, MI 49464
       Contact: Ana Figueroa Finance
       Tel: 616-772-7405
       Email: ana.figueroa@venturamfg.com
       Website: www.venturamfg.com
Mfr automotive dimming rearview mirror components, wire processing components, overhead grabhandles. (Woman/Hisp, estab 1997, empl 140, sales $26,000,000, cert: NMSDC)

Minnesota

1885 DV Roland Enterprises, Inc.
       15171 Freeland Ave N
       Hugo, MN 55038
       Contact: Kenny Scamp General Mgr
       Tel: 651-429-9012
       Email: ken@jtservicesinc.com
       Website: www.jtservicesinc.com
Dist & service industrial diesel engines & diesel engine parts. (AA, estab 2004, empl 6, sales $1,433,333, cert: City, NMSDC)

Missouri

1886 JCM Machine, Inc.
       5655 Old Hwy 21
       House Springs, MO 63051
       Contact: Laura Borrini Owner
       Tel: 636-942-4567
       Email: lborrini@jcmmachineandcoatings.com
       Website: www.jcmmachineandcoatings.com
Automotive machine shop, cylinder head & engine rebuilding, certified ceramic coatings applicators & dry film lubricants. (Woman, estab 1976, empl 4, sales $223,000, cert: State)

New Jersey

1887 Suburban Auto Seat Co., Inc.
       35 Industrial Rd
       Lodi, NJ 07644
       Contact: Amy Winfield President
       Tel: 973-778-9227
       Email: amyw@suburbanseats.com
       Website: www.suburbanseats.com
Dist aftermarket truck seats, delivery truck seats, truck parts, material handling equipment seats, truck & cab accessories, safety equipment. (Woman, estab 1947, empl 10, sales $7,002,253, cert: WBENC)

1888 Wexco Industries
       3 Barnet Rd
       Pine Brook, NJ 07058
       Contact: Paula Lombard President
       Tel: 973-244-5777
       Email: plombard@wexcoind.com
       Website: www.wexcoind.com
Dist complete windshield wiper systems. (Woman, estab 1991, empl 30, sales $18,367,600, cert: WBENC)

Tennessee

1889 Wingard Quality Supply, LLC
       5901 Shallowford Rd Ste 20
       Chattanooga, TN 37421
       Contact: James Wingard President
       Tel: 423-521-4600
       Email: james@wingard.biz
       Website: www.wingardll.com
Automotive assembly: tire & wheel. (AA, estab 2002, empl 25, sales $60,000,000, cert: NMSDC)

CHEMICALS

Manufacturers and distributors of organic and inorganic chemicals, fertilizers, blasting materials, radioactive, cosmetic & industrial chemicals, paints, glues, drilling mud, oil derivatives, pharmaceutical preservatives, blowing agents, coatings, lubricants and solvents. Also chemical and custom packaging.
NAICS Code 42

Alabama

1890　EALI Logistics Solutions LLC
　　　123 N 7th St
　　　Gadsden, AL 35901
　　　Contact: JT Johnson President
　　　Tel:　785-213-5493
　　　Email: jt@ealilogistics.com
　　　Website: www.EaliLogistics.com
100% biodegradable cleaner/degreaser. (AA, estab 2014, empl 6, sales , cert: NMSDC)

1891　Stutton Corporation
　　　1256 McCaig Rd
　　　Lincoln, AL 35096
　　　Contact: Lorraine Studin President
　　　Tel:　205-763-2000
　　　Email: info@stuttoncorp.com
　　　Website: www.stuttoncorp.com
Mfr & dist chemicals: lubricants, greases, degreasers, cleaners, sealers, epoxy strippers, paint strippers, citrus solvents, deodorizers, corrosion barriers, rust penetrants, spray insulation, sealers, adhesives. (Woman, estab 1977, empl 12, sales $1,900,000, cert: State)

Arizona

1892　Chemical Distribution Solutions, LLC
　　　1125 Oak St Ste 303
　　　Conway, AR 72032
　　　Contact: Anthony Wilmington President
　　　Tel:　501-978-1111
　　　Email: admin@chemicalds.com
　　　Website: www.chemicalds.com
Custom Blending, Valued Products, Chemical Distribution (AA, estab 2011, empl 4, sales $7,198,033, cert: NMSDC)

Arkansas

1893　Welsco, Inc.
　　　9006 Crystal Hill Rd
　　　North Little Rock, AR 72113
　　　Contact: Chris Layton President
　　　Tel:　501-771-1204
　　　Email: chris.layton@welsco.com
　　　Website: www.Welsco.com
Welding gases & Supplies, industrial supplies, Spec gases. (Woman, estab 1941, empl 127, sales $40,000,000, cert: NWBOC)

California

1894　Anahau Energy, LLC
　　　2041 Rosecrans Ave, Ste 322
　　　El Segundo, CA 90245
　　　Contact: Suyen Pell CEO
　　　Tel:　310-414-2300
　　　Email: proposals@anahauenergy.com
　　　Website: www.anahauenergy.com
Electric power, natural gas, and renewable products. (As-Pac, estab 2005, empl 10, sales , cert: NMSDC)

1895　Apac Chemical Corp.
　　　150 N. Santa Anita Ave, Ste 850
　　　Arcadia, CA 91006
　　　Contact: Tom Kusaka
　　　Tel:　626-203-0066
　　　Email: sales@apacchemical.com
　　　Website: www.apacchemical.com
Mfr Sorbic acid & Potassium sorbate. (As-Pac, estab 1999, empl 7, sales $19,000,000, cert: NMSDC)

1896　Cervantes Distribution Companies, Inc.
　　　471 W Lambert Rd, Ste 100
　　　Brea, CA 92821
　　　Contact: Rick Gross President
　　　Tel:　714-990-3940
　　　Email: rsg@cervantes-delgado.com
　　　Website: www.cervantesdistribution.com
Marketing and distributing dry urea and urea solutions for SCR and SNCR NOx systems. (Hisp, estab 2001, empl 3, sales , cert: CPUC)

1897　Ensunet Consulting Corporation
　　　10679 Westview Pkwy, 2nd Fl
　　　San Diego, CA 92126
　　　Contact: Paul Robinson President
　　　Tel:　858-348-4690
　　　Email: paul.robinson@ensucorp.com
　　　Website: www.ensunet.com
Dist lubricants, fuel additives & safety fluids. (AA, estab 2008, empl 8, sales , cert: NMSDC)

1898　Ferco Color
　　　2315 Baker Ave
　　　Ontario, CA 91761
　　　Contact: Jennifer Thaw President
　　　Tel:　909-930-0773
　　　Email: info@fercocolor.com
　　　Website: www.fercocolor.com/
Mfr color & additives for plastics, bottles, closures. (Woman, estab 1994, empl 48, sales $16,000,000, cert: WBENC)

1899　Genard, inc. dba Lennova
　　　1717 Boyd St
　　　Santa Ana, CA 92705
　　　Contact: Tony Genova VP Sales & Mktg
　　　Tel:　562-860-3213
　　　Email: tony@lennova.net
　　　Website: www.lennova.net
Install epoxy & urethane protective floor & wall coatings. (Hisp, estab 2000, empl 15, sales $2,387,000, cert: CPUC)

CHEMICALS

1900 Impact Absorbents, Inc.
      5255 Traffic Way
      Atascadero, CA 93422
      Contact: Tammy Rayner Dir of Corporate Sales
      Tel: 800-339-7672
      Email: trayner@spillhero.com
      Website: www.spillhero.com
Mfr & dist granular absorbents, sorbent pads, sorbents socks, spill clean up programs and products, non-hazardous, earth friendly, cost effective. XSORB, FiberDuck, FiberLink, Spill Station, Spill Caddy, Spill Rack, Biohazard Kit. (Woman, estab 1992, empl 30, sales $5,300,000, cert: State)

1901 LMC Enterprises, dba Chemco Products Company
      6401 Alondra Blvd
      Paramount, CA 90723
      Contact: Erica Utz Wochna VP Human Resources
      Tel: 866-243-6261
      Email: erica@chemcoprod.com
      Website: www.chemcoprod.com
Chemical commodities: sodium hydroxide, potassium hydroxide, sulfuric acid, phosphoric acid, citric acid, sodium hypochlorite. (Woman, estab 1976, empl 125, sales $43,324,790, cert: WBENC)

1902 Merrimac Energy Group
      1240 E Wardlow Rd
      Long Beach, CA 90807
      Contact: Mary Hazelrigg President
      Tel: 562-427-6565
      Email: mhazelrigg@merrimacenergy.net
      Website: www.merrimacenergy.net
Transportation and generator fuels. (Woman, estab 1988, empl 5, sales $30,000,000, cert: CPUC)

1903 Pinnacle Petroleum, Inc.
      16651 Gemini Lane
      Huntington Beach, CA 92647
      Contact: Liz McKinley President
      Tel: 714-841-8877
      Email: lmckinley@pinnaclepetroleum.com
      Website: www.pinnaclepetroleum.com
Dist petroleum & lubricants, fuel management services. (Woman, estab 1995, empl 25, sales $176,000,000, cert: WBENC)

1904 Pynergy, LLC
      4495 S Santa Fe Dr
      Englewood, CA 80110
      Contact: Darrell Jackson President
      Tel: 303-292-5005
      Email: djackson@pynergy.com
      Website: www.pynergy.com
Dist Diesel, On-Site Refueling, Gasoline, Wet Hose Refueling, High Octane Fuels, Diesel Generator Fuel Delivery, Ethanol, Diesel Fuel Treatment Program, Biodiesel Kerosene, Lubricant/Fuel Management, Aviation Fuel & Lubricants. (Woman/AA, estab 1999, empl 44, sales $31,103,590, cert: City)

1905 Ramos Oil Company, Inc.
      1515 S River Rd
      West Sacramento, CA 95691
      Contact: Sarah Russell
      Tel: 916-371-2570
      Email: sarahr@ramosoil.com
      Website: www.ramosoil.com
Dist fuel & oils. (Hisp, estab 1951, empl 185, sales , cert: CPUC)

1906 RCI Technologies, Inc.
      462 Borrego Ct, Ste D
      San Dimas, CA 91773
      Contact: Gabriel Gutierrez President
      Tel: 909-305-1241
      Email: gabeg@rcitechnologies.com
      Website: www.rcitechnologies.com
Dist diesel fuel purification products, universal fuel purifiers, portable tank cleaning units & automatic fuel recirculating systems. (Minority, Woman, estab 1994, empl 5, sales $2,042,449, cert: WBENC)

1907 STARDUST Spill Products, LLC
      45 Mirador
      Irvine, CA 92612
      Contact: Timothy McDuffie CEO
      Tel: 714-550-4999
      Email: tim@stardustspillproducts.com
      Website: www.stardustspillproducts.com
Mfr STARDUST Super Absorbent™: absorbs animal, vegetable, mineral, petroleum & chemical liquids. (AA, estab 2018, empl 4, sales $1,017,723, cert: NMSDC)

1908 Western States Distributing
      1790 S 10 St
      San Jose, CA 95112
      Contact: Louis Burford Admin
      Tel: 482-292-1041
      Email: slopes@lubeoil.com
      Website: www.lubeoil.com
Dist petroleum. (Hisp, estab 1956, empl 44, sales , cert: CPUC)

Colorado

1909 Birko Corporation
      9152 Yosemite St
      Henderson, CO 80640
      Contact: Kelly Green President
      Tel: 303-289-1090
      Email: kgreen@birkocorp.com
      Website: www.birkocorp.com
Mfr & dist chemicals, industrial hygiene, hand soaps & sanitizers, surface sanitizers, specialty white-oil based lubricants, chemical dispensing equip, chemical allocation tracking equip, steam/water temp control valves. (Woman, estab 1952, empl 59, sales , cert: WBENC)

Connecticut

1910 Hartford Technologies, Inc.
      1022 Elm St, Ste 201
      Rocky Hill, CT 06067
      Contact: Vickie Brown Dir Natl Sales
      Tel: 860-571-3602
      Email: vbrown@hartfordtechnologies.com
      Website: www.hartfordtechnologies.com
Dist adhesives & coatings. (Woman, estab 1930, empl 129, sales , cert: WBENC)

1911 Prochimie International, Inc.
      2 Waterside Crossing
      Windsor, CT 06095
      Contact: Anna Malz VP
      Tel: - -
      Email: amalz@prochimieinternational.com
      Website: www.prochimieinternational.com
Chemical products: Automotive/Tire, Agrochemical, Oil field, Water Treatment, Pharmaceutical, Photographic and Specialty chemicals. (Woman, estab 1975, empl 10, sales $6,000,000, cert: WBENC)

1912 U.S. Chemicals, LLC
22 Thorndal Circle
Darien, CT 06820
Contact: Carol Piccaro President
Tel: 203-202-2808
Email: cpiccaro@uschemicals-wob.com
Website: www.uschemicals-wob.com
Dist chemicals. (Woman, estab 0, empl 15, sales $90,000,000, cert: WBENC)

Delaware

1913 KRETETEK Industries, LLC
1000 N West St
Wilmington, DE 19801
Contact: Joshua Moore Owner
Tel: 855-573-8383
Email: support@kretetek.com
Website: www.ghostshield.com
Mfr concrete sealing products designed to provide long-lasting protection for their concrete projects. (Hisp, estab 2013, empl 10, sales , cert: NMSDC)

Florida

1914 Algon Corporation
12000 SW 132 Court
Miami, FL 33186
Contact: Eduardo Suarez-Troconis Dir
Tel: 305-253-6901
Email: edal@algon.com
Website: www.algon.com
Chemical raw materials, laboratory supplies & machine parts. (Woman/Hispanic, estab 1989, empl 24, sales $20,570,883, cert: NMSDC)

1915 Bell Performance
1340 Bennett Dr
Longwood, FL 32750
Contact: Deb Moon Dir of Sales
Tel: 407-831-5021
Email: dmoon@bellperformance.net
Website: www.bellperformance.com
Mfr commercial grade treatments for diesel, ethanol, gasoline, fuel oil & power plant fuels. (Woman, estab , empl 16, sales $1,543,035, cert: WBENC)

1916 Burck Oil Co., Inc.
1401 53rd St
West Palm Beach, FL 33407
Contact: Jefffrey Burck President
Tel: 561-842-3600
Email: jeffburck@burckoil.com
Website: www.burckoil.com
Dist oil, grease & lubricants; food grade lubricants. (Woman, estab 1996, empl 4, sales $3,600,000, cert: State)

1917 Chemical Systems
PO Box 810
Zellwood, FL 32798
Contact: Corky Thein President
Tel: 407-886-2329
Email: corky.thein@chemicalsystems.com
Website: www.chemicalsystems.com
Mfr sanitation & specialty chemicals. (Hisp, estab 1979, empl 23, sales $20,000,000, cert: State, NMSDC)

1918 Graham Trading Company, LLC
3001 N. Rocky Point Dr. East, Ste 200
Tampa, FL 33607
Contact: Darrell Graham CEO
Tel: 855-256-8237
Email: info@gratraco.com
Website: www.gratraco.com
Dist diesel, gasoline, jet fuel & lubricants. (AA, estab 2014, empl 2, sales $250,000, cert: State, NMSDC)

1919 Osceola Supply, Inc.
915 Commerce Blvd
Midway, FL 32343
Contact: Doro Hittinger President
Tel: 850-580-9800
Email: dhittinger@osceolasupply.com
Website: www.osceolasupply.com
Dist chemicals. (Woman, estab 1991, empl 46, sales $13,000,000, cert: State)

1920 Petruj Chemical Corporation
8055 NW 98th St
Hialeah Gardens, FL 33016
Contact: Adrian Garcia Sales Dir
Tel: 305-556-1271
Email: adrian@formula88.com
Website: www.formula88.com
Dist chemicals. (Minority, Woman, estab 1976, empl 12, sales $2,552,032, cert: NMSDC)

1921 Stone Environmental Services
6151 Lake Osprey Dr
Sarasota, FL 33946
Contact: Anna Milantoni Owner
Tel: 941-628-5693
Email: amilantoni@stoneenvironmentalservices.com
Website: www.stoneenvironmentalservices.com
Dist metal/plastic cleaning chemistry, refrigerants, disposal of non-hazardous & hazardous waste disposal, cleaning equipment. (Woman, estab 2001, empl 1, sales $446,000, cert: WBENC)

Georgia

1922 ABC Eco Solutions LLC
1740 Hudson Bridge Rd
Stockbridge, GA 30281
Contact: VP
Tel: 404-819-7933
Email:
Website: www.abcecosol.com
Dist eco friendly, hospital grade sanitizing & decontamination products. (Woman/AA, estab 2015, empl 10, sales $976,000, cert: WBENC)

1923 DES Wholesale, LLC
601 West Crossville Road
Roswell, GA 30075
Contact: Allison Sheffield de Aguero President
Tel: 404-671-9593
Email: info@diversified.energy
Website: www.diversifiedenergy.com/
Dist natural gas, electric power & fleet fuel. (Woman/Hisp, estab 2011, empl 20, sales $149,224,828, cert: CPUC, WBENC)

CHEMICALS

1924   DJG Chemical, Inc.
       4761 Hugh Howell Rd D
       Tucker, GA 30084
       Contact: Carla Doleman CEO
       Tel: 404-244-4606
       Email: cdoleman@djgchem.com
       Website: www.djgchemical.com
Mfr & dist chemical products: adhesives, janitorial, lubricants, raw materials, water treatment chemicals, foam soaps, herbicides, cosmetic chemicals, etc. (AA, estab 2003, empl 8, sales , cert: NMSDC)

1925   PS Energy Group, Inc.
       4480 North Shallowford Rd Ste 100
       Dunwoody, GA 30338
       Contact: Allison Laudano Sales & Marketing Assistant
       Tel: 800-334-7548
       Email: allison.laudano@psenergy.com
       Website: www.psenergy.com
Dist natural gas, vehicle fleet fuel mgmt, diesel fuel, gasoline, jet fuel, propane, etc. (Minority, Woman, estab , empl , sales $165,000,000, cert: NMSDC, WBENC)

1926   Simcol Group, LLC
       3455 Peachtree Rd NE, 5th Fl
       Atlanta, GA 30326
       Contact: Simon Guobadia CEO
       Tel: 404-995-7037
       Email: simon@simcolgroup.com
       Website: www.simcolgroup.com
Fuel, gasoline, jet fuel, aviation fuel, diesel fuel, lubricants, wax. (AA, estab 2009, empl 10, sales , cert: NMSDC)

1927   Supreme Resources, Inc.
       285 E Smoketree Terr
       Alpharetta, GA 30005
       Contact: Victor Tan Business Dir
       Tel: 770-475-4638
       Email: victortan@supremeresources.com
       Website: www.supremeresources.com
Dist chemicals, resins, adhesives & raw materials. (As-Pac, estab 1988, empl 10, sales , cert: NMSDC)

1928   TDMC Enterprises Inc.
       370 Great Southwest Pkwy
       Atlanta, GA 30336
       Contact: Chuck Smith President
       Tel: 404-699-5404
       Email: cesmith@chemstationatlanta.com
       Website: www.chemstation.com
Mfr industrial chemicals: cleaners, degreasers, vehicle & airplane cleaners, food processing, odor control, parts washing, scrubber soaps, asphalt release products, strippers, etc. (AA, estab 1991, empl 14, sales $870,000, cert: NMSDC)

Iowa

1929   Searle Petroleum Co.
       PO Box A
       Council Bluffs, IA 51502
       Contact: David Bills VP
       Tel: 712-323-2441
       Email: davidb@redgiantoil.com
       Website: www.redgiantoil.com
Dist engine oils, hydraulic, compressor, journal, grease. (Woman, estab , empl 88, sales $53,500,000, cert: WBENC)

Illinois

1930   Blackdog Corporation
       2305 Enterprise Dr
       Westchester, IL 60154
       Contact: Marc Whitaker Chief Marketing Officer
       Tel: 877-617-4104
       Email: marc@blackdogcorp.com
       Website: www.blackdogcorp.com
Dist fuel, oil & lubricants. (As-Pac, estab 2006, empl 46, sales $23,500,000, cert: City, NMSDC)

1931   Budnick Converting Inc.
       200 Admiral Weinel Blvd
       Columbia, IL 62236
       Contact: Lori Baltz Acct Mgr
       Tel: 800-282-0090
       Email: samwi@budnickconverting.com
       Website: www.budnickconverting.com
Convert & dist adhesive tapes & foams, cutting, slitting, laminating, printing & spooling. (Woman, estab 1952, empl 85, sales $20,000,000, cert: WBENC)

1932   Cedar Concepts Corporation
       4342 S Wolcott Ave
       Chicago, IL 60609
       Contact: Roxanne Hubbard Marketing Mgr
       Tel: 773-890-5790
       Email: roxanne@cedarconcepts.net
       Website: www.cedarconcepts.net
Mfr surfactants & chemical intermediates. (Woman/AA, estab 1991, empl 41, sales $15,000,000, cert: WBENC)

1933   Celta Chemical, Inc.
       1301 W First St, Ste 1A
       Granite City, IL 62040
       Contact: Patrick Riordan VP
       Tel: 314-440-6194
       Email: pat@celtachem.com
       Website: www.celtachem.com
Chemical & food ingredient toll manufacturer and supplier. (Woman, estab 2014, empl 8, sales $15,000,000, cert: WBENC)

1934   Essential Water Technologies LLC
       6625 N. Avondale Ave
       Chicago, IL 60631
       Contact: Lori Hilson Cioromski President
       Tel: 630-344-6770
       Email: lori@essentialwatertech.com
       Website: www.essentialwatertech.com
Water treatment chemicals & services. (Woman, estab 2011, empl 8, sales $902,221, cert: WBENC)

1935   Petrochem, Inc.
       6N999 Whispering Trail Rd
       St. Charles, IL 60175
       Contact: Jill Dohner VP
       Tel: 630-513-6350
       Email: jdohner@petrochem1.com
       Website: www.petrochem1.com
Dist synthetic lubricants: proofer chains, food grade lubricants for cooler chains, gears & hydraulics. (Woman, estab 1998, empl 2, sales $1,000,000, cert: WBENC)

1936 Quimex, Inc.
      14702 S Hamlin
      Midlothian, IL 60445
      Contact: Felipe Estrada Acct Mgr
      Tel: 708-597-6201
      Email: quimex@quimexinc.com
      Website: www.quimexinc.com
Dist industrial chemicals, oils, lubricants, solvents & coatings. (Hisp, estab 1975, empl 14, sales $6,309,695, cert: City)

1937 West Fuels Inc.
      82 S La Grange Road Ste 201
      La Grange, IL 60525
      Contact: Deborah Stange President
      Tel: 708-588-1900
      Email: dstange@westfuels.com
      Website: www.westfuels.com
Dist petroleum products. (Woman, estab 1991, empl 9, sales $10,600,000, cert: State, City, WBENC)

Indiana

1938 Advance Energy LLC
      3580 N Hobart Rd, Ste C
      Hobart, IN 46342
      Contact: Vance Kenney Managing Partner
      Tel: 219-794-1277
      Email: vance.kenney@advanceegy.com
      Website: www.advanceegy.com
Petroleum related products & services: gas, diesel & oil related products. (AA, estab 2012, empl 10, sales , cert: NMSDC)

1939 Harris and Ford, LLC
      9307 E 56th St
      Indianapolis, IN 46216
      Contact: Tim Harris II Business Devel
      Tel: 317-591-0000
      Email: tth@harrisandford.com
      Website: www.harrisandford.com
Dist chemicals & ingredients. (AA, estab 1994, empl 50, sales $220,000,000, cert: NMSDC)

1940 J2 Systems and Supply, LLC
      803 E 38th St
      Indianapolis, IN 46205
      Contact: James Leonard Owner
      Tel: 317-602-3940
      Email: jleonard@j2ssllc.com
      Website: www.j2systemsandsupply.com
Dist chemicals: water treatment, waste-water treatment, metal surface cleaning & coating, food ingredients & additives, industrial floor & general purpose cleaners. (AA, estab 2007, empl 5, sales $245,949, cert: State, NMSDC)

1941 Lemak, LLC dba Lemak Lubricants
      PO Box 1381
      Noblesville, IN 46061
      Contact: Elizabeth Reynolds President
      Tel: 260-906-6433
      Email: beth@lemakllc.com
      Website: www.lemakllc.com/
Dist petroleum & chemicals: Industrial & Automotive Lubricants, Propane, Fuels, Coolants and Cutting Fluids, Antifreeze, Specialty & Commodity Chemicals. (Woman, estab 2008, empl 2, sales $3,289,096, cert: State, WBENC)

1942 Mays Chemical Company
      5611 E 71st St
      Indianapolis, IN 46220
      Contact: Julie Brown Inventory Planning Admin
      Tel: 317-558-2045
      Email: julieb@mayschem.com
      Website: www.mayschem.com
Dist process chemicals: bags, drums & totes, technical, reagent & USP/FCC grades. Electronic grade chemicals, antifreeze, caustic soda, etc. (Hisp, estab 1980, empl 70, sales $95,000,000, cert: NMSDC)

1943 Supreme Oil Company
      1319 Vincennes St
      New Albany, IN 47150
      Contact: Matt Sexton VP
      Tel: 812-945-5266
      Email: msexton@heritageoil.com
      Website: www.supremelubricants.com
Mobil & Chevron oils, lubricants & greases, hydraulic oil, motor oil, gear oil, synthetic oil, biodegradeable oil, antifreeze, coolants & cleaners. (Woman, estab 1937, empl 7, sales $15,359,000, cert: NWBOC)

1944 VTI Contracting, Inc.
      831 Elston Dr
      Shelbyville, IN 46176
      Contact: Judy Montgomery President
      Tel: 317-398-7911
      Email: jm@vtitotalsolutions.com
      Website: www.vtitotalsolutions.com
Concrete coatings, sealants, epoxy and resinous coatings, polishing, repair, staining, traffic coatings, striping, caulking, expansion joints, joint filler, fire proof caulking, air barriers, waterproofing. (Woman, estab 1985, empl 30, sales $3,000,010,000, cert: State, City)

Kentucky

1945 Hexagon Technologies, Inc.
      PO Box 23163
      Louisville, KY 40223
      Contact: Mr. Kiran Shah President
      Tel: 502-429-8990
      Email: hexafloc@bellsouth.net
      Website: www.hexagontech.net
Water & wastewater treatment chemicals & services. (As-Ind, estab 1982, empl 6, sales , cert: NMSDC)

Louisiana

1946 Golden Leaf Energy, Inc.
      PO Box 3605
      Harvey, LA 70059
      Contact: Troy Clark CEO
      Tel: 504-252-4838
      Email: troyclark@goldenleafenergy.com
      Website: www.goldenleafenergy.com
Mfr biodiesel for use as a solvent as well as bio-based lubricants & other products. (AA, estab 2011, empl 9, sales , cert: State)

1947 Rig-Chem Inc.
      132 Thompson Rd
      Houma, LA 70363
      Contact: Lori Davis President
      Tel: 985-873-7208
      Email: ldavis@rigchem.com
      Website: www.rigchem.com
Mfr & dist specialty chemicals. (Woman, estab 1980, empl 11, sales , cert: WBENC)

Massachusetts

1948 Grimes Oil Co., Inc.
      PO Box 276
      West Tisbury, MA 02575
      Contact: Calvin Grimes, Jr. President
      Tel: 617-825-1200
      Email: sales@grimesoil.com
      Website: www.grimesoil.com
Dist distillate & risidual heating oils, diesel fuels & gasoline. (AA, estab 1940, empl 4, sales $3,925,000, cert: State, City, NMSDC)

Maryland

1949 HIC Energy, LLC
      5937 Belair Rd
      Baltimore, MD 21206
      Contact: Troy Holland Mgr
      Tel: 410-914-7161
      Email: th@hicenergy.com
      Website: www.hicenergy.com
Dist natural gas. (AA, estab 2015, empl 5, sales , cert: NMSDC)

1950 Maryland Chemical Company, Inc.
      1551 Russell St
      Baltimore, MD 21230
      Contact: Sandra Dove inside Sales
      Tel: 410-752-1800
      Email: sandradove@mdchem.com
      Website: www.marylandchemical.com
Dist chemicals: alums, ammonia, hydrogen peroxide, ice-melt products, ketones, mineral spirits, potassium, sodium silicates, soil amendments, solvating agents. (Woman, estab 1955, empl 18, sales , cert: WBENC)

Michigan

1951 2V Industries, Inc.
      48553 West Rd
      Wixom, MI 48393
      Contact: Sharron Craig
      Tel: 248-624-7943
      Email: scraig@2vindustries.com
      Website: www.2vindustries.com
Dist metalworking compounds, coolants, RPS, cleaners, etc. (As-Ind, estab 1968, empl 20, sales , cert: NMSDC)

1952 Adhesive Systems, Inc.
      14410 Woodrow Wilson
      Detroit, MI 48238
      Contact: Randall Jaymes Tech Sales Acct Mgr
      Tel: 313-530-6654
      Email: randallj@dchem.com
      Website: www.dchem.com
Mfr hot melt, water base & pressure sensitive adhesives. (AA, estab 1985, empl 28, sales $60,000,000, cert: NMSDC)

1953 Adhezion, Inc.
      7730 Childsdale Ave
      Rockford, MI 49341
      Contact: Chris Telman Reg Acct Mgr
      Tel: 616-726-1775
      Email: ctelman@adhezioninc.com
      Website: www.adhezioninc.com
Adhesives & coatings. (Woman, estab 2010, empl 7, sales , cert: WBENC)

1954 Americhem Sales Corporation
      340 North St
      Mason, MI 48854
      Contact: Matthew Bueche Govt Business Devel
      Tel: 517-676-7718
      Email: buechem@americhemsales.com
      Website: www.americhemsales.com
Dist solvents, chemicals & lubricants, custom oil blends. (Minority, estab 1997, empl 25, sales $22,300,000, cert: NMSDC)

1955 C.J. Chemicals, LLC
      47635 Old US 23
      Brighton, MI 48114
      Contact: Eric Earl Reg Mgr
      Tel: 269-788-2317
      Email: eric@cjchemicals.net
      Website: www.cjchemicals.net
Dist Chemicals, Solvents & Oils used for water & wastewater treatment, cleaning, painting, metal finishing & other industrial & commercial applications. (Woman, estab 2011, empl 10, sales , cert: WBENC)

1956 Chemico Systems, Inc.
      50725 Richard W. Blvd.
      Chesterfield, MI 48051
      Contact: Paul Duff Natl Accts mgr
      Tel: 248-723-3263
      Email: pduff@chemicosystems.com
      Website: www.chemicosystems.com
Mfr & dist chemicals: building maintenance, janitorial, paint shop & process cleaners; coating removal svcs, chemical mgmt svcs. (AA, estab 1989, empl 90, sales $20,000,000, cert: NMSDC)

1957 ChemicoMays, LLC
      25200 Telegraph Rd
      Southfield, MI 48034
      Contact: Dave Macleod VP Bus Dev
      Tel: 248-723-3263
      Email: dmacleod@chemicomays.com
      Website: www.chemicomays.com
Chemical management, purchasing, distribution & logistics. (AA, estab 2005, empl 250, sales $86,000,000, cert: NMSDC)

1958 Chrysan Industries, Inc.
      14707 Keel St
      Plymouth, MI 48170
      Contact: Suk-Kyu Koh CEO
      Tel: 734-451-5411
      Email: skoh@chrysanindustries.com
      Website: www.chrysanindustries.com
Mfr industrial lubricants, cleaners, rust-preventatives, cutting fluids, stamping compounds, specialty chemicals, chemical mgmt. (As-Pac, estab 1977, empl 21, sales $10,300,000, cert: NMSDC)

1959 Diversified Chemical Technologies, Inc.
      15477 Woodrow Wilson
      Detroit, MI 48238
      Contact: Michael Joseff Dir of Sales
      Tel: 313-530-6630
      Email: mjoseff@dchem.com
      Website: www.dchem.com
Dist chemicals. (AA, estab 1971, empl 185, sales $80,000,000, cert: NMSDC)

1960 Infiniti Energy & Environmental, Inc.
24755 W Five Mile Rd Ste 100
Redford, MI 48239
Contact: Sherman Larkins President
Tel: 313-538-0172
Email: sl@infinitigroup.us
Website: www.infinitigroup.us
Dist natural gas, oil, lubricant & petroleum products, waste recycling, consulting & industrial cleaning, waste hauling. (AA, estab 1997, empl 5, sales $2,300,000, cert: NMSDC)

1961 Infiniti Energy & Environmental, Inc. dba Infiniti
15930 19 Mile Rd, Ste 150
Clinton Township, MI 48038
Contact: Mark Coaster Marketing Mgr
Tel: 616-583-9292
Email: coaster@lakeshoreenergy.com
Website: www.lakeshoreenergy.com
Natural gas brokering & supply management. (AA, estab 1997, empl 8, sales $3,000,000, cert: NMSDC)

1962 Ipax Cleanogel, Inc.
8301 Lyndon
Detroit, MI 48238
Contact: Veronika Maltsev CEO
Tel: 313-933-4211
Email: vmaltsev@ipax.com
Website: www.ipax.com
Mfr & dist quality cleaning & maintenance products. (Woman, estab 1988, empl 12, sales $1,680,000, cert: WBENC)

1963 MCEM LLC
31153 Plymouth Rd
Livonia, MI 48150
Contact: BK Masti President
Tel: 517-881-1226
Email: bkm@mcem.co
Website: www.mcem.co
Lubricants, valves, conduit fittings. (As-Pac, estab 2011, empl 5, sales , cert: NMSDC)

1964 Parson Adhesives Inc.
3345 Auburn Rd, Ste 107
Rochester Hills, MI 48309
Contact: Hammie Dogan NA Acct Mgr
Tel: 248-299-5585
Email: hammie@parsonadhesives.com
Website: www.parsonadhesives.com
Industrial adhesives in small and large packing sizes, (As-Pac, estab 2002, empl 45, sales , cert: NMSDC)

1965 RKA Petroleum Company, Inc.
28340 Wick Rd
Romulus, MI 48174
Contact: Timothy Dluzynski Natl Acct Exec
Tel: 734-946-2202
Email: tdluzynski@rkapetroleum.com
Website: www.rkapetroleum.com
Dist refined & renewable fuel products and fuel management solutions. (Woman, estab 1969, empl 49, sales $675,365,826, cert: WBENC)

1966 Roy Smith Company
14650 Dequindre
Detroit, MI 48212
Contact: Peter Wong Owner
Tel: 313-883-6969
Email: angela.summers@rscmain.com
Website: www.rscmain.com
Industrial gases & welding, dist industrial bulk gas systems, packaged & cylinder specialty gases, welding equipment & consumables. (As-Pac, estab 1924, empl 20, sales $24,000,000, cert: NMSDC)

Minnesota

1967 LKT Laboratories, Inc.
545 Phalen Blvd
Saint Paul, MN 55130
Contact: Luke Lam President
Tel: 651-644-8424
Email: llam@lktlabs.com
Website: www.lktlabs.com/
Mfr biochemicals for life science research, inhibitors, activators, modulators, and many other high purity small molecules, phytochemical isolation and analysis. (As-Pac, estab 1990, empl 11, sales $1,300,000, cert: NMSDC)

Missouri

1968 The Kiesel Company
4801 Fyler Ave
St. Louis, MO 63166
Contact: Larry Gooden VP
Tel: 314-351-5500
Email: larry.gooden@kieselco.com
Website: www.thekieselcompany.com
Dist fuels & lubricants, emergency response services to chemical & petroleum product releases, railroad tank car cleaning, barge cleaning, non-hazardous & hazardous waste disposal, demolition & petroleum-contaminated waste water treatment & disposal. (Woman, estab , empl 48, sales $75,010,000, cert: City)

1969 TransChemical, Inc.
419 East Desoto Ave
Saint Louis, MO 63147
Contact: Marilyn Stovall FitzGerald President
Tel: 314-231-6905
Email: marilyn.stovall@transchemical.com
Website: www.transchemical.com
Dist chemicals. (Woman, estab 1973, empl 25, sales $26,000,000, cert: WBENC)

1970 Wallis Oil Company
106 E Washington St
Cuba, MO 65453
Contact: Dave Anthes Managing Dir
Tel: 573-885-2277
Email: dave.anthes@wallisco.com
Website: www.wallisco.com
Dist petroleum. (Woman, estab 1968, empl 550, sales $266,169,874, cert: State)

North Carolina

1971 A-1 Supply Company
638 Person St
Fayetteville, NC 28301
Contact: Sales
Tel: 910-323-3871
Email: sales@a1supplycorp.com
Website: www.a1supplycorp.com
Microfiber, Secondary Containment Units, Mold & Algae Cleaners, Remendiation Products, Absorbents, Absobent pads, Loose Absorbents, Sorb-sox and Booms, Spill kits, Air Care, Floor Care, Skin Care, Insecticides & Herbicides (Woman, estab 1990, empl 4, sales $1,000,000, cert: State)

1972 Continental Chemicals, LLC
4525 Park Rd Ste B-202
Charlotte, NC 28209
Contact: Brandon Lowery Natl Acct Exec
Tel: 704-535-1215
Email: blowery@continentalchemicals.com
Website: www.continentalchemicals.com
Dist chemicals & raw materials. (Nat Ame, estab 1975, empl 5, sales $30,100,000, cert: NMSDC)

1973 NDR Energy Group, LLC
4822 Albemarle Rd Ste 209
Charlotte, NC 28205
Contact: Solomon RC Ali CEO
Tel: 888-756-0555
Email: solomon.ali@ndrenergy.us
Website: www.ndrenergy.us
Dist natural gas, propane, refined products, fuels & energy efficient lighting, asset management services. (AA, estab 2005, empl 7, sales $65,000,000, cert: NMSDC)

1974 PHT International Inc.
8133 Ardrey Kell Road Ste 204
Charlotte, NC 28277
Contact: Ansley Proctor Cockerham Acct Rep
Tel: 704-246-3480
Email: acockerham@phtchemical.com
Website: www.phtchemical.com
Mfr & source fine chemicals, organic intermediates & API's. (Minority, Woman, estab 1993, empl 112, sales $88,900,000, cert: NMSDC, WBENC)

1975 PolySi Technologies, Inc.
5108 Rex McLeod Dr
Sanford, NC 27330
Contact: Lynn Richardson Operations Mgr
Tel: 919-775-4989
Email: lynn@polysi.com
Website: www.polysi.com
Mfr silicone, synthetic greases & silicone fluids, industrial packaging, retail packaging, contract filling & custom packaging. (Woman, estab 1995, empl 25, sales $7,000,000, cert: WBENC)

1976 Red Star Oil Company
802 Purser Dr
Raleigh, NC 27603
Contact: Paula Milliron Acct Mgr
Tel: 919-772-1944
Email: paula@redstaroil.com
Website: www.redstaroil.com
Deliver gasolines, diesel, non highway fuel, bio fuel, kerosene. Sell motor oils, provide fuel polishing. (Minority, estab 1969, empl 30, sales $38,489,046, cert: State)

1977 Texican Natural Gas Company
7301 Carmel Executive Park Dr Ste 316
Charlotte, NC 28226
Contact: Aubrey Hilliard President
Tel: 704-544-7121
Email: ahilliard@texican.com
Website: www.Texican.com
Dist Natural gas, fuel oil, propane, Natural gas consulting. (Hisp, estab 1985, empl 38, sales $500,000,000, cert: NMSDC)

New Jersey

1978 Ash Ingredients, Inc.
65 Harristown Rd, Ste 307
Glen Rock, NJ 07452
Contact: Phetmany Falconi Acct Mgr
Tel: 201-689-1322
Email: phet@ashingredients.com
Website: www.ashingredients.com
Mfr over 81 complex Intermediates for customers with CDA's in place. (Minority, Woman, estab 1999, empl 4, sales , cert: State, City)

1979 Assaycell Technologies LLC
36 Chestnut St
Avenel, NJ 07001
Contact: Dir
Tel: 732-429-0199
Email: info@assaycell.com
Website: www.assaycell.com
Dist biochemical reagents, bacterial & mammalian cell culture media, reagents, assaykits, molecular biology reagents, plastic ware glassware, laboratory supplies, technical consultation. (Minority, Woman, estab 2017, empl 2, sales $120,000, cert: State, SDB)

1980 Bel-Ray Co.
PO Box 526
Wall, NJ 07719
Contact: Bob Shrewsbury Acct Mgr
Tel: 270-585-9005
Email: rshrewsbury@belray.com
Website: www.belray.com
Mfr & dist high performance lubricants made for the Mining, Industrial & Powersports markets world wide. (Woman, estab 1946, empl 150, sales , cert: State)

1981 BKM Resources, Inc. Global Chemicals
PO Box 327
Eatontown, NJ 07724
Contact: Nancy Engkilterra President
Tel: 732-264-2300
Email: nengkilterra@bkmresources.com
Website: www.bkmresources.com
Dist commodity & specialty chemicals. (Woman/AA, estab 1986, empl 10, sales $7,000,000, cert: NMSDC)

1982 Elan Chemical Co., Inc.
268 Doremus Ave
Newark, NJ 07105
Contact: Isabel Couto VP
Tel: 973-344-8014
Email: icouto@elan-chemical.com
Website: www.elan-chemical.com
Natural benzaldehyde, flavors, natural ingredients, synthetic ingredients, vanilla, extracts, acetaldehyde, ethyl benzoate, iso amyl alcohol, aldehydes, natural esters, ethyl caproate, acetic acid, natural aromatic chemicals, ethyl-2-methyl. (Woman, estab 1985, empl 50, sales , cert: State, WBENC)

1983 Foodtopia, Inc.
      11 Harrisotwn Rd, Ste 101
      Glen Rock, NJ 07452
      Contact: Tae Kim GM
      Tel: 201-444-8810
      Email: tkim@foodtopiausa.com
      Website: www.foodtopiausa.com
Food Additives, Nutritional Raw Materials, Amino Acids, Sweeteners, Food Chemicals (As-Pac, estab 1997, empl 7, sales $4,000,000, cert: State)

1984 GJ Chemical
      40 Veronica Ave
      Somerset, NJ 08873
      Contact: Fiore Masci Sr Acct Mgr
      Tel: 973-589-4176
      Email: customerservice@gjchemical.com
      Website: www.gjchemical.com
Mfr & dist raw chemical. (Woman, estab 1974, empl 75, sales $30,000,000, cert: WBENC)

1985 Global Essence Inc.
      8 Marlen Dr
      Hamilton, NJ 08691
      Contact: Jeanna Johnson VP Sales
      Tel: 732-677-1100
      Email: jjohnson@globalessence.com
      Website: www.globalessence.com
Dist flavor & fragrance raw materials: essential oils, organic essential oils, oleoresins, concretes, absolutes an&d synthetic aroma chemicals. (Woman, estab 1993, empl 34, sales $54,700,000, cert: State, WBENC)

1986 INDOFINE Chemical Company
      121 Stryker Ln Bldg 30, Ste 1
      Hillsborough, NJ 08844
      Contact: Sujata Moton VP
      Tel: 908-359-6778
      Email: indofine@indofinechemical.com
      Website: www.indofinechemical.com
Provide custom synthesis, contract research & process development. (Woman/As-Ind, estab 1981, empl 8, sales $1,000,000, cert: NMSDC, WBENC)

1987 Kingchem
      5 Pearl Ct
      Allendale, NJ 07401
      Contact: Daniel Kukovski Diversity Supplier Mgr
      Tel: 201-825-9988
      Email: d.kukovski@kingchem.com
      Website: www.kingchem.com
Mfr fluoro-organic compounds. (As-Pac, estab 1994, empl 13, sales $69,780,000, cert: NMSDC)

1988 Su International Group, Inc.
      1430 Rte 206, Ste 210
      Bedminster, NJ 07921
      Contact: Dan Downs Project Mgr
      Tel: 908-901-0102
      Email: ddowns@suintl.com
      Website: www.suintl.com
Mfr chemicals: synthetic vitamins, food chemical, & artificial sweeteners. (Minority, Woman, estab 1996, empl 6, sales $18,946,253, cert: NMSDC, NWBOC)

1989 Vitusa Products Inc.
      343 Snyder Ave
      Berkeley Heights, NJ 07922
      Contact: Angela Grande CEO
      Tel: 908-665-2900
      Email: agrande@vitusaproducts.com
      Website: www.vitusaproducts.com
Provide food grade products: Glycerine, Sodium Bicarbonate, Ammonium Bicarbonate, Triacetin, Food Grade Phosphates & Acids. (Woman, estab , empl , sales $95,000,000, cert: WBENC)

New York

1990 Ampak Co., Inc.
      1890 Palmer Ave, Ste 203
      Larchmont, NY 10538
      Contact: Cindy Sturm Business Devel
      Tel: 914-833-7070
      Email: csturm@ampakcompany.com
      Website: www.ampakcompany.com
Dist amino acids, antioxidants, preservatives, cellulosics, hight intensity sweeteners, humectants, hydrocolloids, phosphates, colors, vitamins & minerals. (As-Ind, estab 1978, empl 22, sales $85,041,406, cert: NMSDC)

1991 Crescent Chemical Co., Inc.
      2 Oval Dr
      Islandia, NY 11749
      Contact: President
      Tel: 631-348-0333
      Email: creschem@aol.com
      Website: www.crescentchemical.com
Dist pesticides & herbicides. (Woman, estab 1947, empl 8, sales $3,000,000, cert: City, WBENC)

1992 Infinite Energy Corp d/b/a Definite Energy Group
      410 Park Ave, 15th Fl
      New York, NY 10022
      Contact: Deborah Pinto President
      Tel: 212-759-7426
      Email: dpinto@definiteenergy.com
      Website: www.definiteenergy.com
Dist petroleum products. (Woman, estab 1994, empl 2, sales $16,814,844, cert: State, City, WBENC)

1993 M&R Energy Resources Corporation
      259 Main St
      Cornwall, NY 12518
      Contact: Melissa Massimi CEO
      Tel: 845-534-5462
      Email: mmassimi@mandrenergy.com
      Website: www.mandrenergy.com
Dist natural gas: residential, commercial, retail, hospitals & municipalities. (Woman, estab 2002, empl 10, sales $15,000,000, cert: City, WBENC)

1994 Tra-Lin Corp.
      248 Buell Road
      Rochester, NY 14624
      Contact: Linda Fedele President
      Tel: 585-254-6010
      Email: lindafedele@rochester.rr.com
      Website: www.samsonfuel.com
Dist fuel & additives. (Woman, estab 1984, empl 10, sales $663,110, cert: State)

Ohio

1995 Accurate Lubricants & Metalworking Fluids Inc.
PO Box 3807
Dayton, OH 45401
Contact: Marilyn Kinne President
Tel: 937-461-9906
Email: mgkinne@acculube.com
Website: www.acculube.com
Sales & technical support of industrial lubricants, metalworking fluids, water treatment chemicals & ancillary sales & services. (Woman, estab 0, empl , sales , cert: WBENC)

1996 American Merchandising Services
13308 Euclid Ave
Cleveland, OH 44112
Contact: Micheal King President
Tel: 216-249-2626
Email: mkingams@aol.com
Website: www.americanmerchandisingservices.com
Industrial chemicals, maintenance chemicals & supplies, safety items, fuels, oils & ice-melters. (AA, estab 1977, empl 7, sales , cert: NMSDC)

1997 Calvary Industries, Inc.
9233 Seward Rd
Fairfield, OH 45014
Contact: Austin Morelock New Business Dev Mgr
Tel: 513-874-1113
Email: acmorelock@calvaryindustries.com
Website: www.calvaryindustries.com
Mfr industrial & inorganic chemicals. (Nat Ame, estab 1983, empl 120, sales $78,000,000, cert: NMSDC)

1998 Coolant Control, Inc.
5353 Spring Grove Ave
Cincinnati, OH 45217
Contact: Jorge Costa Owner
Tel: 513-471-8770
Email: jcosta@coolantcontrol.com
Website: www.coolantcontrol.com
Site chemical management services, mfr emulsifiers, corrosion inhibitors, cleaners, washers, coolants, coolant additives & odor control. (Hisp, estab 1975, empl 29, sales , cert: NMSDC)

1999 Creekwood Energy Partners, LLC
312 Walnut St Ste 3540
Cincinnati, OH 45202
Contact: Ron DeLyons CEO
Tel: 513-762-7808
Email: ron.delyons@creekwoodadvisors.com
Website: www.creekwoodenergy.com
Fuel procurement & supply chain mgmt: diesel, biodiesel & biodiesel blended fuels. (AA, estab 2004, empl 1, sales , cert: State, City, NMSDC)

2000 Global Environmental Products
4624 Interstate Dr
Cincinnati, OH 45406
Contact: Mike Mamaligas President
Tel: 513-984-5444
Email: info@gepltd.com
Website: www.gepltd.com
Dist absorbents, oil & chemical spill cleanup products. (AA, estab 2002, empl 5, sales $1,200,000, cert: NMSDC)

2001 Hightowers Petroleum Company
3577 Commerce Dr
Middletown, OH 45005
Contact: Stephen L. Hightower President
Tel: 513-423-4272
Email: steve@hightowerspetroleum.com
Website: www.hightowerspetroleum.com
Dist & transport fuel & petroleum products: gasoline, diesel fuel, lubricants, oils, greases, speciality chemicals. (AA, estab 1985, empl 37, sales $219,922,573, cert: NMSDC)

2002 Lianda Corporation
8285 Darrow Rd Ste 200
Twinsburg, OH 44087
Contact: Lifang Mao President
Tel: 330-653-8341
Email: lmao@liandacorp.com
Website: www.liandacorp.com
Import & dist synthetic rubber & related chemicals. (Minority, Woman, estab 1995, empl 11, sales , cert: NMSDC)

2003 Next Generation Fuel, LLC
3589 Commerce Dr
Middletown, OH 45005
Contact: Bernita MCCann Hightower President
Tel: 888-410-6448
Email: bmccann@nxtgenfuel.com
Website: www.nxtgenfuel.com
Dist unleaded gasoline, high & low sulfur diesel fuels, bio-diesel, ethanol & fuel additives. (Woman/AA, estab 2013, empl 5, sales $8,494,467, cert: NMSDC, CPUC, WBENC)

2004 Orchem Corporation
4927 Beech St
Cincinnati, OH 45212
Contact: Denise Ramey COO
Tel: 513-874-9700
Email: denise.ramey@orchemcorp.com
Website: www.orchemcorp.com
Mfr cleaning & sanitation chemicals. (Woman/AA, estab 1996, empl 28, sales $4,200,000, cert: NMSDC)

2005 Phymet
75 N Pioneer Blvd
Springboro, OH 45066
Contact: Amy Minck President
Tel: 937-743-8061
Email: alachman@micropoly.com
Website: www.micropoly.com
Mfr MicroPoly, a solid lubricant system made of plastics & oil used in bearing lubrication and conveyor chain lubrication. (Woman, estab 1986, empl 18, sales $3,000,000, cert: WBENC)

2006 Stand Energy Corporation
1077 Celestial St. Ste 110
Cincinnati, OH 45202
Contact: Kate Bedinghaus
Tel: 513-621-1113
Email: kbedinghaus@standenergy.com
Website: www.standenergy.com
Manage & supply natural gas to thousands of manufacturers, hospitals, hotels, universities, government facilities and smaller businesses. (Woman, estab 1984, empl 28, sales $95,195,066, cert: WBENC)

2007 Stevenson Oil & Chemical Corp.
      30130 Lakeland Blvd
      Wickliffe, OH 44092
      Contact: Suzanne Harkey
      Tel: 440-943-3337
      Email: info@stevensonoil.com
      Website: www.stevensonoil.com
Dist industrial lubricants: engine oil, hydraulic oil, gear oil, cutting oil, metalworking fluid, turbine oil, general purpose lubricants, transmission oil, quenching oil, bio-friendly lubricants, grease & solvents. (Woman, estab 1969, empl 3, sales $1,904,092, cert: WBENC)

2008 Tedia Company, Inc.
      1000 Tedia Way
      Fairfield, OH 45014
      Contact: Jennifer Herber Key Accounts Mgr
      Tel: 513-889-6468
      Email: jherber@tedia.com
      Website: www.tedia.com
Mfr & dist high purity solvents & reagents: research, industrial & analytical applications. (Minority, Woman, estab 1975, empl 120, sales , cert: NMSDC)

2009 Zephyr Solutions, LLC.
      1050 Lear Industrial Pkwy
      Avon, OH 44011
      Contact: Matt Knotts Natl Acct Mgr
      Tel: 440-420-9907
      Email: mknotts@zephyrsolutions.com
      Website: www.zephyrsolutions.com
Aluminum helium tank, air inflators, regulators, helium tank safety equipment, balloon corrals, LED balloons. (Woman, estab 2008, empl 17, sales $30,000,000, cert: WBENC)

Oklahoma

2010 Advance Research Chemicals
      1110 W Keystone Ave
      Tulsa, OK 74015
      Contact: Mat Cleveland Sales Mgr
      Tel: 918-266-6789
      Email: mathercleveland@fluoridearc.com
      Website: www.fluoridearc.com
Inorganic fluorides (As-Ind, estab 1987, empl 125, sales $50,000,000, cert: NMSDC)

2011 Sage Energy Trading, LLC
      8023 E 63rd Pl, Ste 350
      Tulsa, OK 74133
      Contact: Cindy Hughes President
      Tel: 918-362-2310
      Email: chughes@sageenergytrading.com
      Website: www.sageenergytrading.com
Dist natural gas. (Woman, estab 2004, empl 2, sales $9,359,750, cert: WBENC)

2012 Tiger Natural Gas, Inc.
      1422 E 71st St, Ste J
      Tulsa, OK 74136
      Contact: Johnathan Burris VP Marketing
      Tel: 918-491-6998
      Email: diversity@tigernaturalgas.com
      Website: www.tigernaturalgas.com
Dist natural gas. (Minority, Woman, estab 1991, empl 46, sales , cert: NMSDC, WBENC)

Oregon

2013 Ames Research Laboratories, Inc.
      1891 16th St SE
      Salem, OR 97302
      Contact: VP sales
      Tel: 503-588-7000
      Email: ar@amesresearch.com
      Website: www.amesresearch.com
Mfr & dist waterproof elastomeric coatings. (Woman, estab 1994, empl 22, sales $5,000,000, cert: WBENC)

2014 YOLO Colorhouse LLC
      519 NE Hancock St, Ste B
      Portland, OR 97212
      Contact: Rick Barnard VP Operations
      Tel: 503-493-8275
      Email: rick@colorhousepaint.com
      Website: www.colorhousepaint.com
Premium paints: no-VOC, low-odor & earth friendly. (Woman, estab 2006, empl 11, sales $780,000, cert: WBENC)

Pennsylvania

2015 American Energy Supply Corporation
      1704 Chichester Ave
      Upper Chichester, PA 19061
      Contact: Kristen Baiocco President
      Tel: 610-494-4874
      Email: kb@fueloilnow.com
      Website: www.fueloilnow.com
Diesel Fuel Delivery and Fuel Tanks for rent or sale. (Woman, estab 2009, empl 9, sales $2,454,000, cert: WBENC)

2016 Biopeptek Pharmaceuticals LLC
      5 Great Valley Pkwy Ste 100
      Malvern, PA 19355
      Contact: John Zhang CEO
      Tel: 610-643-4881
      Email: johnzhang@biopeptek.com
      Website: www.biopeptek.com
Mfr custom peptides services. (As-Pac, estab , empl , sales $5,000,000, cert: NMSDC)

2017 Crystal Inc. PMC
      601 W Eighth St
      Lansdale, PA 19446
      Contact: Karen Roorda Exec Asst
      Tel: 215-368-1661
      Email: kroorda@pmc-group.com
      Website: www.crystalinc-pmc.com
Specialty & performance chemicals, sodium & potassium stearates, wax emulsions, specialty antifoams, rubber & plastics additives, process chemicals & cable filling jellies. (As-Pac, estab 1929, empl 80, sales , cert: NMSDC)

2018 Crystal, Inc.
      601 W 8th St
      Lansdale, PA 19446
      Contact: Lynne Currie Exec/Mktg Asst
      Tel: 215-368-1661
      Email: epalincrystal@pmc-group.com
      Website: www.pmc-group.com
Dist specialty & performance chemicals, sodium & potassium stearates, wax emulsions, specialty antifoams, rubber & plastics additives, process chemicals & cable filling jellies. (Minority, estab 1929, empl 80, sales , cert: NMSDC)

CHEMICALS

2019 EMSCO Scientific Enterprises, Inc.
      5070 Parkside Ave
      Philadelphia, PA 19131
      Contact: Roderick Clifford Assistant VP
      Tel: 215-477-5601
      Email: rpclifford2@emscoscientific.com
      Website: www.emscoscientific.com
Dist production & laboratory chemicals. (AA, estab 1980, empl 9, sales $19,800,000, cert: City, NMSDC)

2020 GRP Services
      PO Box 41
      Pittsburgh, PA 15221
      Contact: Ernest Groover President
      Tel: 412-271-5231
      Email: egroover@grpservices.net
      Website: www.grpservices.net
Natural gas brokerage, utility cost recovery, telecommunications svcs. (AA, estab 2002, empl 3, sales $100,000, cert: NMSDC)

2021 Muscle Products Corp.
      752 Kilgore Rd
      Jackson Center, PA 16133
      Contact: Sharon Murphy-Dittrich President
      Tel: 814-786-0166
      Email: sharon@mpclubricants.com
      Website: www.mpclubricants.com
Manufacture Lubricants & Greases, for General Industry & Automotive Use. (Woman, estab 1986, empl , sales , cert: WBENC)

2022 Naughton Energy Corp.
      Rte 940
      Pocono Pines, PA 18350
      Contact: Sean Naughton VP
      Tel: 570-646-0422
      Email: sean@naughtonenergy.com
      Website: www.naughtonenergy.com
Energy products, energy services & lubricants: gasoline, heating oil, diesel, marine, kerosene, jet, residual & re-refined oil, Anthracite, Bituminous & Synfuel, natural gas. (Minority, Woman, estab 1976, empl 8, sales $14,000,000, cert: State, City, NMSDC)

Puerto Rico

2023 Lanco Manufacturing Corp.
      Urb. Aponte 5
      San Lorenzo, PR 00954
      Contact: Nelson Soto Category Mgr
      Tel: 787-736-4221
      Email: nsoto@lancopaints.com
      Website: www.lancopaints.com
Paints (Water and Oil Based), Enamels, Caulking, Spackling, Wood Stains, Wood Fillers, Adhesive, Roof Sealers, Concrete Bonding Agents and Solvents(Paint removers, Lacquer Thinners, Mineral Spirits). (Hisp, estab 1978, empl 250, sales $69,320,794, cert: NMSDC)

2024 Sachs Chemical Inc.
      PO Box 191670 KM 0 02 LOT, 18 RR 175
      San Juan, PR 00725
      Contact: Laura Conde Accountant
      Tel: 787-745-2520
      Email: laura@sachschem.com
      Website: www.sachschem.com
Dist chemicals. (Hisp, estab 1986, empl 33, sales $32,000,000, cert: NMSDC)

South Carolina

2025 AmberTech Technologies LLC
      2037 Summerton Hwy
      Summerton, SC 29148
      Contact: Tom Massey Dir
      Tel: 803-696-1152
      Email: tmassey001@sc.rr.com
      Website: www.ambertech-global.com
A USDA certified 99% bio-based metal conditioner used in all lubrication applications to reduce friction and heat. (Woman, estab 2011, empl 7, sales $1,600,000, cert: NWBOC)

2026 Sims Petroleum Company, LLC
      1201 Main St, Ste 1840
      Columbia, SC 29201
      Contact: Wayne Sims CEO
      Tel: 803-600-7941
      Email: wsims@simspetroleum.com
      Website: www.simspetroleum.com
Dist Bulk Fuel Products; Gasoline, Diesel, Biodiesel, Ethanol and Jet Fuel. (AA, estab 2017, empl 1, sales $414,539, cert: State, NMSDC)

Tennessee

2027 CGS, Inc.
      14225 Hickory Creek Rd
      Lenoir City, TN 37771
      Contact: Joy McCabe President
      Tel: 865-988-9080
      Email: joym@cgs-inc.com
      Website: www.cgs-inc.com
Sales agency and distributor of natural gas distribution products, (Woman, estab 1986, empl 5, sales , cert: WBENC)

2028 Pioneer Air Systems, Inc.
      210 Flat Fork Rd
      Wartburg, TN 37887
      Contact: Sam Basseen CEO
      Tel: 423-346-6693
      Email: sam@pioneerair.com
      Website: www.pioneerair.com
Convert CO to CO_2 to compressed air, clean & dry Nitrogen, Natural Gas, Hydrogen, Helium, Ethylene, Seal Gas, OxyPurge, etc. (As-Ind, estab 1980, empl 25, sales , cert: NMSDC)

2029 Quality Adhesives LLC
      3791 Air Park
      Memphis, TN 38118
      Contact: curtis hunt President
      Tel: 901-375-3991
      Email: curtish@qualityadhesivesinc.com
      Website: www.qualityadhesivesinc.com
Mfr & dist hot melt & liquid adhesives. (AA, estab 1999, empl 8, sales $8,000,000, cert: NMSDC)

Texas

2030 2 Tier Wholesalers
       15305 Dallas Pkwy Ste 400
       Dallas, TX 75001
       Contact: Tiffany McDaniel VP of Sales
       Tel: 972-674-3856
       Email: tiffany@2tierwholesaleinc.com
       Website: www.2TierWholesalers.com
Dist industrial grade "green" absorbent products to facility, aircraft, transportation & aerospace maintenance departments. (Woman/AA, estab 2015, empl 10, sales , cert: State, NMSDC)

2031 Accredo Packaging, Inc.
       12682 Cardinal Meadow Dr
       Sugar Land, TX 77478
       Contact: Malcolm Cohn Dir of Sustainability
       Tel: 713-580-4872
       Email: mcohn@accredopkg.com
       Website: www.accredopackaging.com
Dist biopolymer resins. (As-Pac, estab 2007, empl 350, sales $305,000,000, cert: State, NMSDC)

2032 American Biochemicals
       2151 Harvey Mitchell Pkwy S Ste 221
       College Station, TX 77840
       Contact: Sr Research Scientist
       Tel: 979-696-8080
       Email: info@americanbiochemicals.com
       Website: www.americanbiochemicals.com
Organic synthesis of specialty compounds & advanced, novel small molecules, medicinal chemistry, organic chemistry. (As-Ind, estab 2013, empl 5, sales $250,000, cert: State)

2033 American Chemie, Inc.
       13706 Research Blvd Summit Exec Ctr, Ste 302
       Austin, TX 78750
       Contact: Mike Kamdar President
       Tel: 512-219-7400
       Email: mike@americanchemie.com
       Website: www.americanchemie.com
Dist Emulsifiers, Emollients, Esters, Fatty alcohols, Eco-Cert Natural Refined Shea Butter and other body Butters, Preservatives & Surfactants. (Woman/As-Ind, estab 1991, empl 9, sales $10,086,762, cert: State, NMSDC, WBENC)

2034 AmPac Chemical Company Inc.
       PO Box 272848
       Houston, TX 77277
       Contact: Sonia Fujimoto President
       Tel: 713-660-9383
       Email: sonia@ampacchemical.com
       Website: www.ampacchemical.com
Dist chemicals. (Minority, Woman, estab 1996, empl 1, sales $2,217,678, cert: City, NMSDC)

2035 Arrow Magnolia International, Inc.
       2646 Rodney Ln
       Dallas, TX 75229
       Contact: Tanya Shaw Chairwoman
       Tel: 972-247-7111
       Email: tshaw@arrowmagnolia.com
       Website: www.arrowmagnolia.com
Dist safety & first aid, floor care products, disinfectants, deodorants, solid waste chemicals, kitchen & restroom sanitation, machine & automotive products, insecticides, repellents, weed killers, grease & lubricants, boiler & water products. (Minority, Woman, estab , empl , sales , cert: NMSDC, WBENC)

2036 Atlantic Petroleum & Mineral Resources Inc.
       723 Main St, Ste 207
       Houston, TX 77002
       Contact: Donald Sheffield
       Tel: 713-223-2767
       Email: drsheffield@atlantic-petro.com
       Website: www.atlanticpetro.com
Dist branded & unbranded petroleum products. (AA, estab 2005, empl 8, sales $476,200, cert: State, City, NMSDC)

2037 Avalon Chemicals, Inc.
       10101 Southwest Frwy Ste 400
       Houston, TX 77074
       Contact: Vinay Deshmane President
       Tel: 713-219-1457
       Email: info@avalonchemicals.com
       Website: www.avalonchemicals.com
Phenolic antioxidants (BHT, TBHQ, BHA), antioxidants (DODPA). (As-Ind, estab 2002, empl 2, sales $1,260,000, cert: State, NMSDC)

2038 BHP Engineering & Construction, LP
       715 Oak Park Ave
       Corpus Christi, TX 78408
       Contact: Mary Pham Treasurer
       Tel: 361-693-6283
       Email: viki.pham@bhpeng.com
       Website: www.bhpeng.com
Engineering consulting design services for refinery & petrochemical industries. (Minority, estab 1983, empl 60, sales , cert: CPUC)

2039 Champion Fuel Solutions
       PO Box 210191
       Bedford, TX 76095
       Contact: Patti Russell President
       Tel: 877-909-9191
       Email: prussell@championfs.com
       Website: www.championfs.com
Dist gasoline & diesel fuel, biodiesel, kerosene, oils & lubricants. (Woman, estab 2010, empl 2, sales , cert: State, WBENC)

2040 Cole Chemical & Distributing, Inc.
       1500 S Dairy Ashford Ste 450
       Houston, TX 77077
       Contact: Rebecca Cooper President
       Tel: 713-465-2653
       Email: weborders@colechem.com
       Website: www.colechem.com
Mfr & dist thermoformed products. (Minority, Woman, estab 0, empl 0, sales $47,000,000, cert: State, City, NMSDC, WBENC)

2041 Dien, Inc.
       3510 Pipestone Rd
       Dallas, TX 75212
       Contact: Dian Davis President
       Tel: 214-905-1528
       Email: dian@dieninc.com
       Website: www.dieninc.com
Dist chemicals: industrial, food, solvents, greases & lubricants, pharmaceutical & personal care. (Minority, Woman, estab , empl , sales $46,627,700, cert: State, NMSDC)

2042 Diversified Chemical and Supply, Inc.
       PO Box 1297
       Humble, TX 77347
       Contact: Donna Rosenstein President
       Tel: 713-461-9610
       Email: dcsupply@sbcglobal.net
       Website: www.diversifiedchem.com
Dist janitorial & industrial chemicals & supplies. (Woman, estab 1990, empl 3, sales $2,508,119, cert: State, WBENC)

2043 Elevation Energy Group LLC
       PO Box 6036
       Austin, TX 78762
       Contact: Gwen Kyle President
       Tel: 317-333-7281
       Email: tri@elevationeg.com
       Website: www.elevationeg.com
Natural gas supply and associated services. (As-Pac, estab 2014, empl 15, sales , cert: NMSDC)

2044 Energy Utility Group, LLC
       1402 Clearview Loop
       Round Rock, TX 78664
       Contact: Melinda Zito O'Brien CEO
       Tel: 512-805-8321
       Email: melinda@energyutilitygroup.com
       Website: www.energyutilitygroup.com
Energy consulting & electricity & natural gas brokering company. (Woman, estab , empl , sales , cert: State, City, CPUC, WBENC)

2045 FSTI Inc.
       6300 Bridge Point Pkwy, Ste 1-200
       Austin, TX 78730
       Contact: Coulter Gibson Dir of Packaged Products
       Tel: 512-278-8800
       Email: cgibson@fstichem.com
       Website: www.fstichem.com
Dist chemicals. (Woman, estab 1998, empl 50, sales $19,100,000, cert: State, WBENC)

2046 Gasochem International LLC
       9509 Pemberton Crescent Dr
       Houston, TX 77025
       Contact: Charu Jain President
       Tel: 713-837-6116
       Email: charu@gasochem.com
       Website: www.gasochem.com
Dist chemicals: oilfield, water treatment, industrial, agricultural & pharmaceutical. (Minority, Woman, estab 2012, empl 2, sales $167,000, cert: State, WBENC)

2047 Genoa International
       2245 Texas Dr, Ste 300
       Sugar Land, TX 77479
       Contact: Pamela Kahn Principal
       Tel: 281-313-0120
       Email: pkahn@genoaint.com
       Website: www.genoaint.com
Specialty chemicals, surfactants, drilling fluids, solvents, lubricants & commodities. (Woman, estab 0, empl , sales $4,000,000, cert: State, WBENC)

2048 Global Amchem Inc.
       407 E Methvin, Ste 200
       Longview, TX 75606
       Contact: Debbie Scott Office Admin
       Tel: 903-236-0138
       Email: debbie@amcheminc.com
       Website: www.amcheminc.com
Dist solvents & chemicals. (Hisp, estab 1993, empl 6, sales $430,505, cert: State, NMSDC)

2049 GND Consulting & Supply LLC
       1836 Snake River Rd, Ste A
       Katy, TX 77449
       Contact: Jose Camacho Sales Mgr
       Tel: 832-415-4100
       Email: camachojo@gndsc.com
       Website: www.gndsc.com
Dist non-toxic, environmentally-safe cleaners, degreasers, solvents, lubricants & specialty chemical products. (Minority, Woman, estab 2011, empl 8, sales $603,242, cert: State, NMSDC, WBENC)

2050 New K-Stone Management, Inc.
       10718 Sentinel St
       San Antonio, TX 78217
       Contact: Dana Stone President
       Tel: 210-494-0507
       Email: dstone@kstoneinc.com
       Website: www.kstonesupply.com
Industrial chemicals for automotive, animal shelters, food processing plants, physical plant supplies & chemicals for lab animal research. (Woman, estab 1997, empl 15, sales $1,147,125, cert: State)

2051 One Nation Energy Solutions, LLC
       4404 Blossom St
       Houston, TX 77007
       Contact: Terry Pierce President
       Tel: 713-861-0600
       Email: tpierce@onenationenergy.com
       Website: www.onenationenergy.com
Dist & market gas & power. (Woman, estab 2003, empl 1, sales $68,601,802, cert: City, CPUC, WBENC)

2052 Oxyde Chemicals, Inc.
       225 Pennbright Dr Ste 101
       Houston, TX 77090
       Contact: Elva Rojas Sales agent
       Tel: 281-874-9100
       Email: rojase@oxydeusa.com
       Website: www.oxydeusa.com
Dist petrochemicals & plastics. (Hisp, estab 1950, empl 60, sales $650,000,000, cert: State, NMSDC)

2053 Premier Polymers LLC
      16800 Imperial Valley, Ste 200
      Houston, TX 77060
      Contact: Melwani Kwan Supply Chain Mgr
      Tel: 281-902-0909
      Email: mkwan@premierpolymers.com
      Website: www.premierpolymers.com
Dist Plastic Resin. (As-Pac, estab 2009, empl 22, sales , cert: State, NMSDC)

2054 Ricochet Fuel Distributors, Inc.
      1201 Royal Pkwy
      Euless, TX 76040
      Contact: Jason Cox Mktg Coord
      Tel: 800-284-2540
      Email: sales@ricochetfuel.com
      Website: www.ricochetfuel.com
Dist diesel, gasoline, oil, antifreeze & kerosene, fuel mgmt & monitoring programs. (Woman, estab 1988, empl 27, sales $63,847,000, cert: WBENC)

2055 SolvChem, Inc.
      1904 Mykawa
      Pearland, TX 77546
      Contact: Stacey Barrett Acct Mgr
      Tel: 832-300-4067
      Email: stacey_barrett@solvchem.com
      Website: www.solvchem.com
Dist aircraft chemicals, chemicals blends, calibrating fluids, purging fluids. (Hisp, estab 1980, empl 40, sales $2,707,198, cert: State, NMSDC)

2056 Sun Coast Resources, Inc.
      6405 Cavalcade, Building 1
      Houston, TX 77026
      Contact: Susan Tyler President
      Tel: 713-844-9600
      Email: styler@suncoastresources.com
      Website: www.suncoastresources.com
Dist petroleum products (gasoline, diesel, etc.). (Woman, estab 1985, empl 1270, sales $860,000,000, cert: WBENC)

2057 The Green Chemical Store, Inc.
      11837 Judd Ct, Ste 104
      Dallas, TX 75243
      Contact: President
      Tel: 972-429-1719
      Email: operations@thegreenchemicalstore.com
      Website: www.thegreenchemicalstore.com
Dist chemicals for building maintenance trades. (Woman, estab 2009, empl 5, sales $150,000, cert: WBENC)

2058 Tri-Chem Specialty Chemicals, LLC
      PO Box 2056
      Cresson, TX 76035
      Contact: CEO
      Tel: 972-745-6875
      Email: contact@tri-chem.net
      Website: www.tri-chem.net
Custom liquid & dry chemical blending, chemical & additive distribution. (Minority, Woman, estab 1989, empl 14, sales $4,777,000, cert: WBENC)

2059 XD Ventures, LLC
      2555 South Shore Blvd. Ste C
      League City, TX 77573
      Contact: Xan Difede President
      Tel: 832-557-6622
      Email: xan@fidelityfuels.com
      Website: www.fidelityfuels.com
Dist aliphatic solvents, mineral spirits & mineral seal oils. (Woman, estab 2014, empl 1, sales , cert: State, WBENC)

Utah

2060 CP Industries, LLC
      560 North 500 West
      Salt Lake City, UT 84116
      Contact: Erica Sellers President
      Tel: 801-521-0313
      Email: info@cpindustries.net
      Website: www.cpindustries.net
Mfr ice melting compounds, customer chemical blending, liquid & powder detergents. (Woman, estab 1949, empl 19, sales $5,510,415, cert: WBENC)

2061 FYVE STAR, Inc.
      1972 E Dan Dr
      Layton, UT 84040
      Contact: Celeste Gleave CEO
      Tel: 801-552-9100
      Email: celeste@fyvestar.com
      Website: www.fyvestar.com
Mfr & dist deicers. Calcium Chloride, Blends, Solar Salt, Water Conditioning Salts, primary supplier to the US Military on Liquid Runway & Aircraft Deicers. (Woman, estab 1993, empl 2, sales $400,000, cert: State)

2062 The Horrocks Company LLC dba Volu-Sol
      5095 West 2100 South
      Salt Lake City, UT 84120
      Contact: Celeste Horrocks Owner
      Tel: 801-974-9474
      Email: celeste.horrocks@volusol.com
      Website: www.volusol.com
Mfr chemicals, alcohols, reagents, diagnostic stains & counterstains. (Woman, estab 2013, empl 10, sales $470,000, cert: WBENC)

Virginia

2063 Coyanosa Gas Services Corporation
      1765 Greensboro Station Place Ste 900
      McLean, VA 22102
      Contact: Jerry Curry President
      Tel: 703-938-7984
      Email: jerry@coyanosagasservices.com
      Website: www.coyanosagasservices.com
Dist natural gas & energy utilization consulting. (AA, estab 1995, empl 3, sales $20,000,000, cert: NMSDC, CPUC, SDB)

2064 Creative Maintenance Solutions, LLC
      1171 Polk Rd
      Edinburg, VA 22824
      Contact: Nancy Barnett
      Tel: 540-984-8172
      Email: nancy@cmsolutionsus.com
      Website: www.cmsolutionsus.com
Dist polymer/epoxy & coatings. (Woman, estab , empl , sales , cert: State)

2065 Enspire Energy, LLC
134 N Battlefield Blvd
Chesapeake, VA 23320
Contact: julie hashagen Dir of Operations
Tel: 757-963-9123
Email: jhashagen@enspireenergy.com
Website: www.enspireenergy.com
Natural gas marketing & transportation. (Woman, estab 2005, empl , sales $979,376, cert: WBENC)

2066 James River Solutions
10487 Lakeridge Pkwy
Ashland, VA 23005
Contact: Elizabeth Austin Commercial Project Mgr
Tel: 804-358-9000
Email: eaustin@jrpetro.com
Website: www.JamesRiverPetroleum.com
Bulk Deliveries, Gasoline, Diesel, Dyed Diesel, Heating Oil, DEF, Mobile Fueling, Fleet Fueling Cards. (Woman, estab 2005, empl 61, sales $251,000,000, cert: State)

2067 Quad Chemical Corporation
1008 Old Virginia Beach Rd, Ste 500
Virginia Beach, VA 23451
Contact: Karin Harrigan Natl Acct Mgr
Tel: 757-422-2486
Email: kharrigan@quadchemical.com
Website: www.quadchemical.com
Dist bulk process manufacturing chemicals. (Woman, estab 1991, empl 6, sales , cert: WBENC)

Washington

2068 Allied Fuel LLC
2400 Harbor Ave SW, Ste 100
Seattle, WA 98126
Contact: James E Hasty President
Tel: 206-582-2020
Email: james@alliedfuel.net
Website: www.alliedfuel.net
Dist fuel. (AA, estab 2009, empl 5, sales $51,350,000, cert: NMSDC)

2069 Dunkin & Bush, Inc.
PO Box 97080
Kirkland, WA 98083
Contact: Deidre Dunkin President
Tel: 425-885-7064
Email: ddunkin@dunkinandbush.com
Website: www.dunkinandbush.com
Industrial painting, scaffolding, insulation, rigging, containment, lead abatement, shop coating aplication, concrete restoration, plural applied tank linings, abrasive blasting, specialty blasting, water jetting, high heat coating applications. (Woman, estab 2008, empl 300, sales , cert: WBENC)

2070 PetroCard, Inc.
PO Box 40
Kent, WA 98035
Contact: Tamara Torklep Dir Corporate Marketing
Tel: 253-867-3218
Email: ttorklep@petrocard.com
Website: www.petrocard.com
Cardlock, Mobile Fueling, Lubricants, Retail Gas Stations and Bulk Fuels. (Nat Ame, estab 1985, empl 187, sales $744,000,000, cert: NMSDC)

2071 Walla Walla Environmental
4 W Rees Ave
Walla Walla, WA 99362
Contact: Cassie Rothstrom CEO
Tel: 509-522-0490
Email: cassie@wwenvironmental.com
Website: www.wwenvironmental.com
Dist mildewcide, insecticide & flame retardant paint additives. (Woman, estab 1990, empl 16, sales , cert: WBENC)

Wisconsin

2072 ChemCeed LLC
1720 Prosperity Court
Chippewa Falls, WI 54729
Contact: Myra Detienne Sales Rep
Tel: 715-726-2300
Email: customerservice@chemceed.com
Website: www.chemceed.com
Dist chemicals in bulk tankwagons, drums, totes, or custom packaging, ethanols, alcohols, reagents, & other solvents. (Minority, Woman, estab 2009, empl 10, sales , cert: NMSDC, WBENC)

2073 H Benton Capital, LLC
4400 W Roosevelt Dr
Milwaukee, WI 53216
Contact: Christopher Kemp Managing Principal
Tel: 312-771-0085
Email: hbentoncapital@gmail.com
Website: www.micro-tread.com
Dist Micro-Tread anti-slip floor treatment. This product greatly reduces the risk of slipping on floors. (AA, estab 2005, empl 4, sales , cert: State)

2074 Power Lube Industrial LLC
4930 S 2nd St, Ste 300
Milwaukee, WI 53207
Contact: Sarah Herr Exec VP Sales
Tel: 800-635-8170
Email: sarah@powerlubeind.com
Website: www.powerlubind.com
Automatic lubrication equipment and supplies, Memolub, Greaseomatic, and ATS Electrolub single point and multi- point product lines. (Woman, estab 1998, empl 10, sales $2,200,000, cert: WBENC)

Wyoming

2075 LBI LLC
22 Plains
Buffalo, WY 82834
Contact: Dennis Quenneville Dir of Mktg
Tel: 307-684-9340
Email: dennis.lbi@vcn.com
Website: www.littlebitsinc.comdefault.aspx
Mfr products for toxic substance remediation & clean up: Dual Zorb, Pond Zorb & Acid Zorb. (Woman, estab 2007, empl 16, sales $302,037, cert: WBENC)

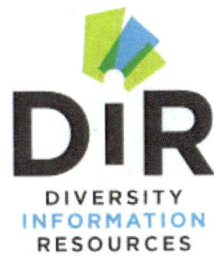

Driving Supplier Diversity Success since 1968.

1960's

1968 The "Buy Black Campaign" is founded by Peter and Rose Meyerhoff as a not-for-profit organization and prints its first directory of black-owned businesses in Minneapolis.

1968 The first Board of Directors is established and an office space is secured on Plymouth Ave. N. in Minneapolis.

1969 DIR publishes the "Buy Black" directory nationally.

1970's

1972 The "Buy Black" directory changes to "TRY US" and includes Black-, Hispanic-, Asian- and Native American-owned businesses.

1975 First edition of "Purchasing People in Major Corporations" directory is published.

1977 DIR's Board of Directors expands to include national corporations.

1980's

1986 DIR holds its first Supplier Diversity Seminars.

1990's

1992 First edition of the "Supplier Diversity Information Resources Guide" is published.

1995 DIR holds its first "Best Practices in Supplier Diversity Strategies and Initiatives"

1998 DIR creates an online, searchable database for its "Purchasing People in Major Corporations" directory.

2000's

2000 TRY US becomes Diversity Information Resources, Inc., to reflect the ongoing and ever-changing diverse-supplier categories.

2001 DIR hires SupplierGATEWAY as a technology partner.

2001 The "Buy Black" directory is now "National Minority and Women-Owned Business Directory" and includes certified women-owned businesses.

2006 DIR's verification and validation expertise expands to include Veteran-, Service-Disabled Veteran, and GLBT-owned businesses.

2010's

2011 DIR greatly expands online presence and redesigns identity to better reflect the open horizon for Supplier Diversity development.

2013 DIR celebrates its 45th Anniversary and looks forward to a thriving future!

2015 DIR responds to corporate and diverse-suppliers request for consolidated information and publishes a new directory and handbook: "The Business of Supplier Diversity".

CLEANING PRODUCTS, SUPPLIES & SERVICES

Manufacturers and distributors of maintenance supplies: all purpose cleaners, deodorizers, floor waxes, wax removers, oven cleaners, dishwashing & laundry detergents, soaps, hand cleaners, furniture & metal polishes, rug & upholstery shampoos, ammonia, janitorial services, etc. Janitorial services. NAICS Code 32

Arizona

2076 Maintenance Mart
      4648 N 7th Ave
      Phoenix, AZ 85013
      Contact: Shelley Krauss President
      Tel: 602-252-9402
      Email: shelley@maintenancemart.com
      Website: www.maintenancemart.com
Dist commercial janitorial supplies, tools, motorized equipment, paper, trash liners, walk-off mats, indoor & outdoor receptacles & ash urns. (Minority, Woman, estab 2000, empl 20, sales $7,200,000, cert: City)

California

2077 Ambiance Cosmetics Inc. dba CPR Cleaning Products
      928 N San Fernando Blvd J678
      Burbank, CA 91504
      Contact: Chelsey Sanderson Owner
      Tel: 310-482-2620
      Email: chelsey@ambiancecosmetics.com
      Website: www.cprcleaningproducts.com
CPR Cleaning Products: Leather, Carpet, Granite, Wood, Stainless Steel & Glass. (Woman, estab 2010, empl 8, sales $1,030,615, cert: WBENC)

2078 American Global Facility Services, Inc.
      6803 International Ave Ste A
      Cypress, CA 90630
      Contact: Evelyn Lee
      Tel: 213-382-6435
      Email: service@agfacilityservices.com
      Website: www.agfacilityservices.com
Janitorial services. (Woman/As-Pac, estab 2011, empl 20, sales $895,000, cert: NMSDC, CPUC, WBENC)

2079 Avery Group Inc.
      8941 Dalton Ave
      Los Angeles, CA 90047
      Contact: Leatora Morse President
      Tel: 310-217-1070
      Email: leatora@averygroup-inc.com
      Website: www.averygroup-inc.com
Mfr restroom hygiene products. (Woman/AA, estab 2003, empl 2, sales $100,000, cert: State, NMSDC)

2080 Ayota, LLC
      122 15th St, Ste 681
      San Diego, CA 92014
      Contact: Toya McWilliams Acct Mgr
      Tel: 914-548-6193
      Email: tm@ayotainternational.com
      Website: www.ayotainternational.com
Dist janitorial supplies. (Woman/AA, estab 2012, empl 3, sales , cert: State)

2081 BriteWorks, Inc.
      620 Commerical Ave.
      Covina, CA 91723
      Contact: Anita Ron President
      Tel: 626-337-0099
      Email: anitaron@briteworks.com
      Website: www.briteworks.com
Commercial & industrial janitorial services. General cleaning, construction cleaning, floor care & carpet care, window cleaning. (Minority, Woman, estab 1997, empl 130, sales $6,866,357, cert: NMSDC, CPUC, WBENC)

2082 Clean Sweep Group Inc
      8306 Wilshire Blvd Ste 7009
      Beverly Hills, CA 90211
      Contact: Leo Williams, II CEO
      Tel: 310-985-0504
      Email: leo.williams@csgiusa.com
      Website: www.csgiusa.com
Ultraviolet light disinfection & education services to Hospitals, nursing homes, professional sports facilities, cruise ships. (AA, estab 2011, empl 16, sales , cert: NMSDC)

2083 Continental Building Maintenance
      13316 Mapledale St
      Norwalk, CA 90650
      Contact: Sanggwon Kim President
      Tel: 562-926-7474
      Email: sgkim@continentalbm.com
      Website: www.continentalbm.com
Janitorial Services & Supplies. (As-Pac, estab 2003, empl 120, sales $2,950,000, cert: CPUC)

2084 Corporate Image Maintenance
      2700 S Main St, Ste D
      Santa Ana, CA 92707
      Contact: Gil Gamboa President
      Tel: 714-966-5325
      Email: corpimage@sbcglobal.net
      Website: www.cimservices.com
Janitorial services: office, industrial & warehouse, carpet cleaning, pressure washing & window cleaning. (Hisp, estab 1995, empl 70, sales $1,176,190, cert: State)

2085 Diamond Wipes International
      4651 Schaefer Ave
      Chino, CA 91710
      Contact: Rebecca Liu Natl Sales
      Tel: 909-230-9888
      Email: rliu@diamondwipes.com
      Website: www.diamondwipes.com
Mfr wiper based cleansing products: white board, furniture polishing wipes, antibacterial wipes, shoe shine, grease & graffiti remover wipes. (Minority, Woman, estab 1994, empl 88, sales $ 0, cert: WBENC)

2086 Eurow & O'Reilly Corp.
      51 Moreland Rd
      Simi Valley, CA 93065
      Contact: Martin Mair Dir Inside Sales
      Tel: 805-421-4310
      Email: mmair@eurow.com
      Website: www.eurow.com
Dist janitorial cleaning products. (Woman, estab 1983, empl 26, sales $40,000,000, cert: WBENC)

CLEANING PRODUCTS, SUPPLIES & SERVICES

2087 Global Building Services, Inc.
       25570 Rye Canyon Rd Ste F
       Valencia, CA 91355
       Contact: Charles Herrera Sr Dir operations
       Tel: 800-675-6643
       Email: charlesherrera@globalbuildingservices.com
       Website: www.globalbuildingservices.com
Janitorial services, building & grounds maintenance, window washing, floor care, pressure washing, parking lot maintenance, high dusting, green cleaning. (Hisp, estab 1986, empl 1200, sales $33,339,000, cert: NMSDC)

2088 Kim Gardner, Inc.
       1727 E 28th St
       Signal Hill, CA 90755
       Contact: Dori Bailey Dir Business Devel
       Tel: 562-988-7901
       Email: dori@mjmservices.com
       Website: www.mjmservices.com
Facility Support Services, Custodial, Waste Management, Pest Control/Grounds Maintenance Landscaping, Air Duct Cleaning, General Office Cleaning. (AA, estab 1986, empl 35, sales $605,000, cert: 8(a))

2089 Mar-Len Supply Inc.
       23159 Kidder St
       Hayward, CA 94545
       Contact: Shirley Winter Owner
       Tel: 510-782-3555
       Email: marlensupply@aol.com
       Website: www.marlensupply.com
Dist & service industrial cleaning equipment & cleaning agents. (Woman, estab 1956, empl 4, sales $1,000,000, cert: CPUC)

2090 NMS Management Inc.
       155 W 35th St Ste A
       National City, CA 91950
       Contact: Dir Business Devel
       Tel: 619-425-0440
       Email: cynthia@nmsmanagment.com
       Website: www.nms-management.com
Custodial services for military establishments, healthcare facilities, institutions of higher education, public housing agencies, public transportation authorities & federal, state & municipal agencies. (Hisp, estab 1985, empl 168, sales $3,822,801, cert: CPUC)

2091 Right Tek Enterprises
       1775 N Lee St
       Simi Valley, CA 93065
       Contact: Sandy Cohen Owner
       Tel: 877-208-3717
       Email: righttek@pacbell.net
       Website: www.righttekenterprises
Dist preventative maintenance cleaning products.. (Woman, estab 2001, empl 1, sales $272,000, cert: WBENC)

2092 SBM Management Services
       5241 Arnold Ave
       McClellan, CA 95652
       Contact: Dan Berardelli Dir Strategic Solutions
       Tel: - -
       Email: dberardelli@sbmcorp.com
       Website: www.sbmmanagement.com
Facilities support, janitorial, clean-room & laboratory sanitizing, general building maintenance, recycling & environmental awareness programs, move-add-change support services, vendor management. (Minority, estab 1982, empl 10000, sales $430,000,000, cert: NMSDC)

2093 SDI Systems Division, Inc.
       21 Morgan
       Irvine, CA 92618
       Contact: Jon Korbonski President
       Tel: 949-583-1001
       Email: sdi@sdinetwork.com
       Website: www.sdinetwork.com
Manufacture and distribute cleaning equipment & supplies. (Hisp, estab 2008, empl 20, sales $3,700,000, cert: NMSDC)

2094 SeaYu Enterprises Inc.
       236 West Portal
       San Francisco, CA 94127
       Contact: Quincy Yu CEO
       Tel: 415-566-9677
       Email: qyu@sea-yu.com
       Website: www.becleanandgreen.com
Natural cleaners, stain removers and odor eliminators that are effective, easy to use, biodegradable and safe for people, pets and the planet. (Minority, Woman, estab 2001, empl 2, sales , cert: NMSDC)

2095 Signature Building Maintenance, Inc.
       PO Box 110340
       Campbell, CA 95011
       Contact: Anna Murphy President
       Tel: 408-377-8066
       Email: anna@signaturefacilities.com
       Website: www.signaturefacilities.com
Facilities services, commercial janitorial services & general contractor interior improvements. (Woman, estab , empl , sales $8,125,433, cert: WBENC)

2096 Supply Solutions
       17625 Fabrica Way
       Cerritos, CA 92691
       Contact: Jeffrey Lerma CEO
       Tel: 888-901-5011
       Email: jlerma@casupplysolutions.com
       Website: www.casupplysolutions.com
Dist janitorial products, paper supplies, can liners, chemicals, and equipment. (Hisp, estab 2006, empl 27, sales $12,500,000, cert: NMSDC)

2097 Ultimate Maintenance Services, Inc.
       4237 Redondo Beach Blvd
       Lawndale, CA 90260
       Contact: Sherly Cstmr Service
       Tel: 310-542-1474
       Email: sherly@umscorporation.com
       Website: www.umscorporation.com
Janitorial services & construction clean up services. (Minority, Woman, estab 1990, empl 50, sales , cert: State)

2098 UNISERVE Facilities Services
       2363 S Atlantic Blvd
       Commerce, CA 90040
       Contact: Eugene Hwang Dir of Mktg
       Tel: 213-533-1000
       Email: ehwang@uniservecorp.com
       Website: www.uniservecorp.com
Janitorial services. (As-Pac, estab 1966, empl 750, sales $25,000,000, cert: NMSDC)

2099 US Metro Group, Inc.
      135 S State College Blvd, Ste 200
      Brea, CA 92821
      Contact: Phil Gregg Contracts Compliance
      Tel: 213-382-6435
      Email: phil.g@usmetrogroup.com
      Website: www.usmetrogroup.com/
Janitorial maintenance services. (As-Pac, estab 1975, empl 1000, sales $15,908,576, cert: NMSDC, CPUC)

2100 Western Indoor Environmental Services
      2345 Highbury Ave, Ste 19
      Los Angeles, CA 90032
      Contact: Tony Rosario Sr. Estimator
      Tel: 626-485-9255
      Email: info@westernindoor.com
      Website: www.westernindoor.com
Air Duct Cleaning Services, Kitchen Exhaust Cleaning Services. (Hisp, estab 2014, empl 25, sales , cert: State)

Colorado

2101 AFL Maintenance Group, Inc.
      1075 S. Yukon St, Ste 300
      Lakewood, CO 80226
      Contact: Bonnie Nash Business Devel
      Tel: 303-984-7400
      Email: b.nash@afsg-us.com
      Website: www.afsg-us.com
Facility maintenance, management & real estate services. (Woman/Hisp, estab 1989, empl 151, sales $26,573,622, cert: NMSDC)

Connecticut

2102 C & C Janitorial Supplies, Inc.
      665 New Britain Ave
      Newington, CT 06111
      Contact: Grace Cafe President
      Tel: 860-594-4200
      Email: gracec@ccsupplies.com
      Website: www.ccsupplies.com
Dist janitorial products, paper products & equip. (Minority, Woman, estab , empl , sales $ 0, cert: NMSDC, WBENC)

2103 Citra Solv, LLC
      188 Shadow Lake Rd
      Ridgefield, CT 06877
      Contact: Steve Zeitler Co-Founder
      Tel: 203-778-0881
      Email: szeitler@citrasolv.com
      Website: www.citrasolv.com
Plant-based ingredients, environmentally friendly cleaners and air fresheners. (Woman, estab 1996, empl 7, sales $15,000,000, cert: State)

2104 Horizon Services Company
      250 Governor St
      East Hartford, CT 06108
      Contact: Thomas Baerlein Sr Acct Exec
      Tel: 860-291-9111
      Email: tbaerlein@horizonsvcs.com
      Website: www.horizonsvcs.com
Custodial services, supply & management, window cleaning, clean room environmental svcs, hazardous material site labor, exterior cleaning & landscaping, post construction cleaning. (As-Pac, estab 1991, empl 412, sales $7,400,000, cert: State, NMSDC)

2105 KeeClean Management Inc.
      494 Bridgeport Ave Ste 180
      Shelton, CT 06484
      Contact: Keith Jang President
      Tel: 203-397-2532
      Email: keithjang@keeclean.com
      Website: www.keeclean.com
Commercial cleaning, custodial & janitorial services: floor care service, carpet cleaning, window washing services. (As-Pac, estab 2007, empl 5, sales $3,444,178, cert: State, City, NMSDC)

Delaware

2106 Star Building Services, Inc.
      106 Quigley Blvd
      New Castle, DE 19720
      Contact: Ernie Martin VP Sales & Mktg
      Tel: 302-983-0275
      Email: emartin@sbsclean.com
      Website: www.sbsclean.com
Janitorial Services, Medical Device Cleaning Services. (Woman, estab 1953, empl 300, sales , cert: WBENC)

Florida

2107 ABCO Products, Inc.
      6800 NW 36th Ave
      Miami, FL 33147
      Contact: Luis Janania Sales Mgr
      Tel: 786-223-0944
      Email: luisj@abcoproducts.com
      Website: www.abcoproducts.com
Dist cleaning supplies. (Hisp, estab 1979, empl 54, sales $24,000,000, cert: State, NMSDC)

2108 All Pro Janitorial Service Inc.
      3843 N Tanner Rd
      Orlando, FL 32826
      Contact: Glenda Lee President
      Tel: 407-649-8878
      Email: glenda@allprojan.com
      Website: www.procarpetcleanerorlando.com
Commercial janitorial cleaning, carpet cleaning, rug cleaning, upholstery cleaning, ceramic tile & grout cleaning, floor stripping, waxing, buffing & water restoration. (Woman/AA, estab 2000, empl 15, sales , cert: State, City, NMSDC)

2109 Clean Clean, Inc.
      3580 NW 56th St, Ste 106C
      Fort Lauderdale, FL 33309
      Contact: Gary Plancher Sales Mgr
      Tel: 954-777-9555
      Email: gplancher@cleancleaninc.com
      Website: www.cleancleaninc.com
Mfr personal wipes. (Woman/AA, estab 2004, empl 6, sales , cert: NMSDC)

2110 Cube Care Company
      6043 NW 167th St Ste A-23
      Miami Lakes, FL 33015
      Contact: Susana Robledo Founder & CEO
      Tel: 305-556-8700
      Email: susana@cubecare.com
      Website: www.cubecare.com
Janiorial Supplies, Window Treatments & Curtains, (Minority, Woman, estab 1999, empl 70, sales $6,685,526, cert: NMSDC, WBENC)

CLEANING PRODUCTS, SUPPLIES & SERVICES

2111 D&A Building Services, Inc.
321 Georgia Ave
Longwood, FL 32750
Contact: Albert Sarabasa CEO
Tel: 407-831-5388
Email: al@dabuildingservices.com
Website: www.dabuildingservices.com
Janitorial, window washing, pressure cleaning, caulking, carpet, cleaning, construction cleaning, seal buildings, light painting. (Hisp, estab 1985, empl 550, sales $8,200,000, cert: State, City)

2112 GEM Janitorial LLC
9031 Pembroke Rd
Pembroke Pines, FL 33025
Contact: Richard Addison President
Tel: 954-682-3594
Email: homeownersservicesfla@gmail.com
Website: www.gemjanitorialcorp.com
Cleaning, Commercial Remodeling and Repair, Painting, Pressure Cleaning, Carpentry, Doors & Windows Installation, Drywall Repairs and Installation, Flooring Installation. (Woman/AA, estab 2006, empl 6, sales $320,000, cert: NMSDC)

2113 Grosvenor Building Services Iinc.
3398 Pkwy Center Ct
Orlando, FL 32808
Contact: Lee McDaniel Business Devel Mgr
Tel: 407-292-3383
Email: lmcdaniel@grosvenorservices.com
Website: www.grosvenorservicescom
Janitorial Services. (Woman, estab 1984, empl 400, sales $6,000,000, cert: WBENC)

2114 Harvard Services Group, Inc.
201 S Biscayne Blvd FL 24
Miami, FL 33131
Contact: Nathalie Doobin CEO
Tel: 305-351-7300
Email: ndoobin@harvardservices.com
Website: www.harvardsg.com
Janitorial services & maintenance services. (Woman, estab 1986, empl 1500, sales $ 0, cert: WBENC)

2115 Jimco Maintenance Inc.
710 Commerce Dr, Ste 107
Venice, FL 34292
Contact: Lynn Moseley President
Tel: 800-392-8678
Email: lynn@jimcos.com
Website: www.jimcos.com
Janitorial services. (Woman, estab 1983, empl 90, sales $12,180,000, cert: WBENC)

2116 Merton Partners LLC
692 Solana Court
Marco Island, FL 34145
Contact: Nanette Rivera President
Tel: 609-773-0145
Email: wordehoff@mertonpartners.com
Website: www.mertonpartners.com
Operations Management Consultants: SPC; facilities; maintenance; engineering; construction; validation; manufacturing; yield; optimization (Minority, Woman, estab 2007, empl 50, sales $1,200,000, cert: NMSDC)

2117 RagsWarehouse & Cleaning Supplies
7221 NW 35th Ave
Miami, FL 33147
Contact: Luther Pierre Sales Mgr
Tel: 202-531-9225
Email: luther.pierre@ragswarehouse.com
Website: www.ragswarehouse.com
Dist wiping materials ideal for painters or cleaners. (Woman/AA, estab 2015, empl 2, sales , cert: State)

2118 SFM Services, Inc.
9700 NW 79th Ave
Hialeah Gardens, FL 33016
Contact: Christian Infante VP
Tel: 305-818-2424
Email: cinfante@sfmservices.com
Website: www.sfmservices.com
Complete janitorial services, landscape services, and security guard services. (Hisp, estab 1987, empl 480, sales $12,000,000, cert: NMSDC)

2119 Siboney Contracting Co.
1000 Southern Blvd, Ste 300
West Palm Beach, FL 33405
Contact: Dante Sevi VP
Tel: 561-832-3110
Email: dsevi@siboneycc.com
Website: www.siboneycc.com
Hauling fill and aggregates, hauling hurricane debris (Hisp, estab 1972, empl 8, sales $23,789,190, cert: City)

2120 The American Cleaning Services Inc
8270 Woodland Center Blvd.
Tampa, FL 33614
Contact: Marty Hales GM
Tel: 813-961-6970
Email: callus1st@americancleaningservice.com
Website: www.americancleaningservice.com
Complete janitorial services, commercial & construction. (Minority, Woman, estab 1989, empl 1, sales $367,000, cert: State)

2121 The Green Glider Company LLC
830 Harbor Cir
Palm Harbor, FL 34683
Contact: Tanya Lewis President
Tel: 727-504-9441
Email: info@gogreenglider.com
Website: www.gogreenglider.com
Green Glider Mop Pad, Reusable, Washable, Durable & Adjustable mop pad that fits onto virtually all of the Swiffer style/type mopping systems. (Woman, estab 2010, empl 1, sales $225,000, cert: WBENC)

2122 Treasure Enterprise, Inc.
11026 Oak Ridge Dr N
Jacksonville, FL 32225
Contact: Fidelis Odeh President
Tel: 904-683-8114
Email: info@treasureenterprise.com
Website: www.treasureenterprise.com
Janitorial maintenance, carpet cleaning, lawn services, roadside litter removal services, and the numerous services that we offer. (AA, estab 1998, empl 56, sales $1,250,000, cert: City)

Georgia

2123 5 Star Enterprise, Inc.
4705-G Bakers Ferry Rd SW
Atlanta, GA 30336
Contact: Tracey Felder President
Tel: 404-924-4290
Email: tfelder@5starchemicals.com
Website: www.5starchemicals.com
Mfr Green cleaning, soaps & detergent products, green certified chemicals. (Woman/AA, estab 2006, empl 10, sales $2,450,000, cert: WBENC)

2124 Anointed Professional Enterpises Inc.
233 Mitchell St SW, Ste 500
Atlanta, GA 30303
Contact: Alisa Clark President
Tel: 678-618-2434
Email: alisaclark@glorypcs.com
Website: www.glorypcs.com
Facilities services, carpet & upholstery cleaning, floors, windows, landscaping. (Woman/AA, estab 1996, empl 15, sales $53,374,800, cert: State)

2125 Frederick Hart Co. Inc.
4963 S Royal Atlanta Dr
Tucker, GA 30084
Contact: Dean-Paul Hart President
Tel: 404-373-4030
Email: deanpaul@compacind.com
Website: www.compacind.com/
Mfr cleaning products: garbage disposal cleaner & deodorizer, scented sink strainer, bathroom, kitchen, auto, cleaners, closet & air fresheners, kitchen gadgets. (AA, estab 1979, empl 15, sales $3,500,000, cert: NMSDC)

2126 General Building Maintenance, Inc.
3835 Presidential Pkwy Ste 200
Atlanta, GA 30340
Contact: Joe Woodson Sr VP
Tel: 770-457-5678
Email: marketing@gbmweb.com
Website: www.gbmweb.com
Janitorial svcs: carpet shampooing, stripping & waxing floors, marble & stone care, clean room cleaning & recycling. (As-Pac, estab 1983, empl 271, sales $ 0, cert: NMSDC)

2127 GMI Group, Inc.
130 Stone Mountain St
Lawrenceville, GA 30046
Contact: Kayla Dang CEO
Tel: 678-482-5288
Email: kayla.dang@gmigroupinc.com
Website: www.thegmigroup.com
Commercial janitorial cleaning, marble maintenance & restoration, ReKRETE waterless concrete cleaning, pressure washing, graffiti removal, construction clean up. (Minority, Woman, estab 2005, empl 72, sales $4,867,904, cert: NMSDC, WBENC)

2128 ShockTheory Interactive, Inc.
12705 Century Dr Ste C
Alpharetta, GA 30004
Contact: Sonja Williams VP
Tel: 877-747-4625
Email: sonja.williams@shocktheory.com
Website: www.shocktheory.com
(Woman/AA, estab 2003, empl 9, sales , cert: NMSDC)

2129 The Burks Companies, Inc.
2780 Bert Adams Road Ste 225
Atlanta, GA 30339
Contact: James Weisbrodt President & COO
Tel: 678-686-3203
Email: jweis@theburkscompanies.com
Website: www.theburkscompanies.com
Janitorial services. (AA, estab 1991, empl 181, sales $7,980,000, cert: NMSDC)

2130 WCS Maintenance Services, Inc.
669 Antietam Dr
Stone Mountain, GA 30087
Contact: Ricky Watkins CEO
Tel: 770-573-9238
Email: wcsmaintsvcinc@earthlink.net
Website: www.wcsmaintsvcinc.com
Janitorial Services; Floorcare and Carpet Cleaning services. (Woman/AA, estab 1997, empl 14, sales $ 0, cert: NMSDC)

Hawaii

2131 Building Maintenance Services, LLC
1541 S Beretania St, Ste 204
Honolulu, HI 96826
Contact: Barbara Beckmeier Owner
Tel: 808-983-1269
Email: barbara@bmsnationwide.com
Website: www.bmsnationwide.com
Janitorial services. (Woman, estab 2000, empl 45, sales , cert: WBENC)

Iowa

2132 Midwest Janitorial Service
1395 N Center Pt. Rd
Hiawatha, IA 52233
Contact: Aaron Schulze VP
Tel: 319-393-6162
Email: customerservice@mjsia.com
Website: www.midwestjanitorial.com
Commercial janitorial cleaning company, offering specialty services, carpet cleaning, floor care and window cleaning. (Woman, estab 1958, empl 650, sales $10,150,000, cert: NWBOC)

Illinois

2133 A&R Janitorial Service, Inc.
10127 w. Roosevelt Rd.
Westchester, IL 60154
Contact: Deborah Pintor Sr Exec VP
Tel: 708-656-8300
Email: dpintor@arjanitorial.com
Website: www.arjanitorial.com
Janitorial services, commercial cleaning, carpet care, floor care, power washing, snow removal, after construction cleanup & emergency response cleaning. (Minority, Woman, estab 1967, empl , sales $19,752,715, cert: City, NMSDC, WBENC)

CLEANING PRODUCTS, SUPPLIES & SERVICES

2134   B & B Maintenance, Inc.
        537 Capital Dr
        Lake Zurich, IL 60047
        Contact: Pamela Seiser VP Sales
        Tel: 847-550-6060
        Email: pseiser@bandbmaint.com
        Website: www.bandbmaint.com
Building maintenance: janitorial, window cleaning, & painting, carpet care, power washing, hard surfaced floor care, tile restoration, fire safety programs, porter service & support personnel. (Woman/Hisp, estab 1979, empl 550, sales , cert: City, NMSDC, WBENC)

2135   Clean Impressions Corp.
        127 N Northwest Hwy
        Palatine, IL 60067
        Contact: Teresa Garvin President
        Tel: 847-776-0706
        Email: cic@cleanimpressionscorp.com
        Website: www.cleanimpressionscorp.com
Janitorial service, building maintenance, floor care, stripping & refinishing floor tile, carpet cleaning, stone care, crystalizing & acoustical tile cleaning. (Woman, estab 1998, empl 40, sales , cert: WBENC)

2136   EBM, Inc (Executive Building Maintenance
        2238 Landmeier Rd
        Elk Grove Village, IL 60007
        Contact: Vtio M. D'Ambrosio Dir Sales
        Tel: 224-203-4090
        Email: vdambrosio@ebmclean.com
        Website: www.ebmcleaning.com
Janitorial services. (Woman, estab 1963, empl 450, sales $14,000,000, cert: State, City, WBENC, NWBOC)

2137   ELB Enterprises, Inc.
        4709 Bond Ave
        Alorton, IL 62207
        Contact: Rhonda Jones
        Tel: 618-394-1912
        Email: rjones@elb1inc.com
        Website: www.elbenterprisesinc.com
Dist janitorial supplies. (AA, estab 1993, empl 12, sales $ 0, cert: State, NMSDC)

2138   Emeric Facility Services
        918 S Green Bay Rd
        Waukegan, IL 60085
        Contact: Michael Ramirez Acct Exec
        Tel: 847-623-6912
        Email: mramirez@emericservices.com
        Website: www.emericservices.com
Janitorial services & carpet cleaning services. (Minority, Woman, estab 2011, empl 46, sales $932,000, cert: City, WBENC)

2139   IDSC, Inc.
        PO Box 1055
        Woodstock, IL 60098
        Contact: Milissa Dooley President
        Tel: 815-337-8066
        Email: milissa_ids@att.net
        Website: www.idscinc.com
Dist sanitation supplies & equipment, PPE, paper goods, maintenance supplies & equipment, hoses. (Woman, estab 1990, empl 7, sales $480,000, cert: WBENC)

2140   Jelmar LLC
        5550 W Touhy Ste 200
        Skokie, IL 60007
        Contact: Glenn Poticha VP Sales
        Tel: 800-323-5497
        Email: glenn@jelmar.com
        Website: www.jelmar.com
Dist cleaning products. (Woman, estab , empl , sales $36,745,934, cert: WBENC)

2141   LACOSTA Facility Support Services, Inc.
        440 W Bonner Rd
        Wauconda, IL 60084
        Contact: Jeffrey Johnson Natl Dir Business Dev
        Tel: 847-487-3103
        Email: sales@cms4.com
        Website: www.lacostaservices.com
Janitorial services, painting services, facility maintanance services. (Minority, Woman, estab 1988, empl 1700, sales $64,000,000, cert: NMSDC)

2142   United Building Maintenance, Inc.
        165 Easy St
        Carol Stream, IL 60188
        Contact: Amy Cabrera-Goddard Dir of Sales & Marketing
        Tel: 630-653-4848
        Email: agoddard@ubm-usa.com
        Website: www.ubm-usa.com
Janitorial, painting, pressure washing, snow removal, parking lot maintenance & landscape design. (Hisp, estab 1979, empl 1500, sales $63,800,000, cert: NMSDC)

2143   White Glove Janitorial Services & Supply, Inc.
        356 E Irving Park Rd
        Wood Dale, IL 60191
        Contact: Joyce Dickens Owner
        Tel: 630-766-7466
        Email: whtglove@msn.com
        Website: www.whiteglovejanitorialservices.com
Janitorial services: carpet cleaning, landscaping, power washing, food plant sanitation, floor scrubbing & supplies. (Woman, estab 1975, empl 105, sales $2,476,000, cert: City)

Indiana

2144   Suzy Q Cleaning Services
        2401 N Tibbs Ave
        Indianapolis, IN 46222
        Contact: Suzett Moffitt Owner
        Tel: 317-755-7664
        Email: suzettsuzett@gmail.com
        Website: www.suzyqcleaning.net
Janitorial, Ground and Building Maintenance, Commercial, Home-Maker Services, Renovation, Construction, Bridge, Road, Side Walk Repair. (Woman/AA, estab 2009, empl 10, sales , cert: State, City)

2145   Titan Associates, Inc. dba A.G. Maas Company
        8402 E 33rd St
        Indianapolis, IN 46226
        Contact: Cindy Schum President
        Tel: 317-632-8315
        Email: cindy@agmaas.com
        Website: www.agmaas.com
Dist Janitorial & Safety Supplies, Bathroom Partitions & Accessories, site Furnishings, Indoor/Outdoor Mats, Rock Salt, Ice Melt & Water Softener Salt, Breakroom Supplies, Office Supplies. (Woman, estab 1969, empl 4, sales $2,200,000, cert: City, WBENC)

CLEANING PRODUCTS, SUPPLIES & SERVICES

Kansas

2146 Complete Carpet Care Inc.
324 Fawn Valley Court
Lansing, KS 66043
Contact: Brad Turner President
Tel: 913-351-3550
Email: bradsmegastore@gmail.com
Website: www.notcompletewithoutyou.com
Professional carpet cleaning. (AA, estab 1993, empl 10, sales , cert: NMSDC)

Kentucky

2147 Facility Maintenance & Services Group
147 E Loudon Ave
Lexington, KY 40505
Contact: Frank HAll CEO
Tel: 859-554-6584
Email: info@facilitymsg.com
Website: www.facilitymsg.com
Janitorial, Facility Maintenance, Painting, Lawn Care, Pressure washing, High Dusting. (AA, estab 2015, empl 42, sales $1,000,019, cert: NMSDC)

2148 Superior Maintenance Co.
141 Howell Dr
Elizabethtown, KY 42701
Contact: Sid Shurn VP
Tel: 270-769-2553
Email: sid@smc.cc
Website: www.smc.cc
Janitorial & grounds maintenance, window cleaning, pest control, facility maintenance, HVAC, plumbing, chemicals, janitorial supplies & equip. (AA, estab 1988, empl 1200, sales , cert: NMSDC)

Louisiana

2149 Economical Janitorial & Paper Supplies
1420F Sams Ave, Ste F
Harahan, LA 70123
Contact: Suzie Migliore President
Tel: 504-464-7166
Email: suzie@economicaljanitorial.com
Website: www.econoomicaljanitorial.com
Dist janitorial supplies, paper supplies, janitorial equipment, food service supplies. (Woman, estab 1983, empl 85, sales $31,015,000, cert: WBENC)

Massachusetts

2150 ACP Facilitiy Services
1 Merrill St
Woburn, MA 01801
Contact: Joe Marchese VP
Tel: 301-606-8296
Email: jmarchese@acpfacility.com
Website: www.acpfacility.com
Facility Services, Green Cleaning Program, Day Cleaning & Porter Services, Paper Supply Programs, Floor & Carpet Care, Groundskeeping. (Woman/Hisp, estab 1986, empl 500, sales $12,500,000, cert: NMSDC)

2151 American Green Building Services, Inc.
190 Milton St
Dedham, MA 02026
Contact: Ariel Peguero CEO
Tel: 781-461-2500
Email: apeguero@agbservicesinc.com
Website: www.agbservicesinc.com
Janitorial services. (Hisp, estab 2010, empl 225, sales $2,060,117, cert: State)

2152 Dependable Facility Cleaning Services, LLC
1074 Hyde Park Ave, Ste 4
Hyde Park, MA 02136
Contact: Chuck Ojoko Managing Dir
Tel: 857-261-4582
Email: charles@dependablefacilitycleaning.com
Website: www.dependablefacilitycleaning.com
Commercial cleaning & janitorial services. (AA, estab 2015, empl 6, sales , cert: NMSDC)

2153 Milhench Supply Company
121 Duchaine Blvd
New Bedford, MA 02745
Contact: Angie Prevost Inside Sales
Tel: 508-995-8331
Email: angie@milhench.com
Website: www.milhench.com
Dist janitorial, paper, packaging & facility maintenance supplies. (Woman, estab 1932, empl 32, sales $16,315,760, cert: State, City)

2154 Moura's Cleaning Service, Inc.
349 Lunenburg St
Fitchburg, MA 01420
Contact: Andre Thibodeau Sales Mgr
Tel: 978-562-1839
Email: andre@mourascleaningservice.com
Website: www.mourascleaningservice.com
Janitorial services: floor strip & wax, restroom service, odor control service, concrete cleaning, carpet steam cleaning, upholstery steam cleaning, window cleaning, power washing of buildings. (Hisp, estab 1988, empl 150, sales $2,100,000, cert: State)

2155 Savin Products Co., Inc.
214 High St
Randolph, MA 02368
Contact: Dona D'Ambrosia President
Tel: 781-961-2743
Email: donamarie@savinproducts.com
Website: www.savinproducts.com
Mfr cleaning products. (Woman, estab 1968, empl 10, sales , cert: State)

2156 Unic Pro Inc.
415 Boston Tpk Ste 211B
Shrewsbury, MA 01545
Contact: Lilian Radke CEO
Tel: 877-881-8642
Email:
Website: www.unicpro.com
Commercial Business Cleaning Services, Commercial Carpet Cleaning, Floor Washing & Waxing, Green Cleaning Commercial Services, Industrial Cleaning Services, Nightly Office Cleaning, Post-Construction Cleaning. (Minority, Woman, estab 2007, empl 54, sales $2,450,000, cert: State, WBENC)

Maryland

2157 Associated Building Maintenance Co., Inc.
2140 Priest Bridge Court Ste 3
Crofton, MD 21114
Contact: Kurt Bender VP Sales
Tel: 410-721-1818
Email: kbender@abmcoinc.com
Website: www.abmcoinc.com/
Commercial general contract cleaning, window cleaning, carpet cleaning, snow removal, floor stripping & other building related services. (Woman, estab 1987, empl 1000, sales $25,599,000, cert: State)

2158 Bolana Enterprises, Inc.
      10739 Tucker St Ste 270
      Beltsville, MD 20705
      Contact: Valarie Dock President
      Tel: 301-595-2577
      Email: vdock@bolanainc.com
      Website: www.bolanainc.com
Green & sustainable janitoiral services, carpet cleaning, floor care, and garage cleaning. (Woman/AA, estab 2004, empl 355, sales $11,000,000, cert: NMSDC, WBENC)

2159 Busy Bee Cleaning Services, LLC
      1141 Fairview Rd
      Hagerstown, MD 21742
      Contact: Maurice Ramirez GM
      Tel: 240-217-9516
      Email: clean@allbusybee.com
      Website: www.allbusybee.com
Commercial & Residential Cleaning Services. (Hisp, estab 2011, empl 10, sales , cert: State)

2160 C.J. Maintenance, Inc.
      9254 Bendix Rd
      Columbia, MD 21045
      Contact: Tyler Yoon Acct Exec
      Tel: 410-720-5157
      Email: cjmaintenance@hotmail.com
      Website: www.cjmaint.com
Janitorial, custodial & housekeeping svcs: carpet cleaning, hard wood floors, marble floor restoration. (As-Pac, estab 1985, empl 700, sales $14,499,999, cert: State, NMSDC)

2161 Red Coats, Inc.
      4520 East-West Hwy
      Bethesda, MD 20814
      Contact: Page Pollock Dir of Reg Sales & Marketing
      Tel: 301-280-4414
      Email: ppollock@redcoats.com
      Website: www.redcoats.com
LEED compliant cleaning services. (Woman, estab 1960, empl 7000, sales $203,366,500, cert: WBENC)

2162 TruBlu Cleaning Pros, LLC
      1451 Rockville Pike Ste 250
      Rockville, MD 20852
      Contact: Ian Johnson CEO
      Tel: 240-685-6610
      Email: ijohnson@tublucleaning.com
      Website: www.tublucleaning.com
Commercial cleaning & janitorial services. (AA, estab 2022, empl 10, sales , cert: State)

2163 Viking Chemicals, Inc.
      2325 Banger St
      Baltimore, MD 21230
      Contact: Shannon Hodges VP
      Tel: 410-525-2100
      Email: shodges@vikingchem.com
      Website: www.vikingjanitorsupplies.com
Dist janatorial supplies: paper, floor care equipement, sweepers, vacuums, matting, brooms, brushes, trash cans & trash can liners. (Woman, estab 1974, empl 6, sales $2,206,148, cert: State, City)

Michigan

2164 Caravan Facilities Management, LLC
      1400 Weiss St
      Saginaw, MI 48602
      Contact: Victor Gomez Business Devel Mgr
      Tel: 989-798-0977
      Email: vg10@caravanfm.com
      Website: www.caravanfm.com
Facilities mgmt: janintorial, landscaping, snow removal, HVAC, fleet mgmt & building services. (Hisp, estab 1997, empl 2344, sales $139,000,000, cert: NMSDC)

2165 Caravan Technologies, Inc.
      3033 Bourke
      Detroit, MI 48238
      Contact: Robert Charleston CEO
      Tel: 313-341-2551
      Email: cti3033@aol.com
      Website: www.caravantech.com
Mfr industrial & commercial cleaning solutions, disinfecting agents & parts washer detergents. (AA, estab 1979, empl 10, sales $495,961, cert: NMSDC)

2166 CMS Sourcing Solutions
      29700 Harper Ave, Ste 2
      St. Clair Shores, MI 48082
      Contact: Cheryl A King Exec VP Sales
      Tel: 586-879-0669
      Email: cheryl.king@cmsgroup.us
      Website: www.cmsgroup.us
Janitorial services, management, labor, supplies, equipment & systems. (Woman, estab 2009, empl 150, sales $5,500,110, cert: NMSDC)

2167 Contract Direct, LLC
      24300 Southfield Rd, Ste 210
      Southfield, MI 48075
      Contact: Bill Dreyer Sr Corp Sales Exec
      Tel: 248-395-1199
      Email: elizabeth@contractdirect.net
      Website: www.contractdirect.net
Contract Cleaning Janitorial Services, Custodial Services, Food Plant Sanitation, Silo Cleaning. (Woman, estab 2002, empl 450, sales $15,000,000, cert: WBENC)

2168 DFM Solutions (Devon Facility Management LLC)
      777 Woodward Ave Ste 500A
      Detroit, MI 48226
      Contact: Chad Starnes Dir Business Devel
      Tel: 313-221-1510
      Email: cstarnes@dfm.solutions
      Website: www.dfm.solutions
Facility management, janitorial & building maintenance & industrial cleaning services. (Woman, estab 2007, empl 298, sales $45,000,000, cert: WBENC)

2169 Ipax Cleanogel, Inc.
      8301 Lyndon
      Detroit, MI 48238
      Contact: Veronika Maltsev CEO
      Tel: 313-933-4211
      Email: vmaltsev@ipax.com
      Website: www.ipax.com
Mfr & dist quality cleaning & maintenance products. (Woman, estab 1988, empl 12, sales $1,680,000, cert: WBENC)

2170 LCF - Farmer Group
 4581 S. Lapeer Road Ste G
 Lake Orion, MI 48359
 Contact: Forest Farmer President
 Tel: 248-322-7079
 Email: rfarmer@mti-farmergrp.com
 Website: www.thefarmergroup.com
Paints, cleaners, wipes, rags, paint-booth related products, cleaning supplies, oil, lubricants, janitorial and floor care. (AA, estab 1994, empl 7, sales $2,822,500, cert: NMSDC)

2171 Midwest Maintenance Services, Inc.
 3704 Trade Center Dr
 Ann Arbor, MI 48108
 Contact: Linda Johnson President
 Tel: 734-222-5902
 Email: linda@midwestms.com
 Website: www.midwestms.com
Janitorial services & building maintenance. (Woman, estab 1989, empl 35, sales , cert: WBENC)

2172 Perfection Commercial Services, Inc.
 905 N Church St
 Tekonsha, MI 49092
 Contact: Lori Smith Controller
 Tel: 888-933-3103
 Email: lori@pcsmichigan.com
 Website:
 www.perfectioncommercialservicesinc.com
Perfection Commercial Services provides janitorial services and supplies, which includes window and floor care. (Woman, estab 1991, empl 212, sales $5,785,000, cert: WBENC, NWBOC)

2173 Polstar Commercial Cleaning Services
 5124 Pontiac Trail
 Ann Arbor, MI 48105
 Contact: Kamil Krainski Sales Mgr
 Tel: 800-557-9120
 Email: kamil@polstar.us
 Website: www.polstar.us
Contract janitorial & commercial cleaning services, floor stripping & waxing, disinfection service, antimicrobial coatings, carpet cleaning. (Woman, estab 2000, empl 25, sales $903,146, cert: WBENC)

2174 Sparkle Janitorial Service
 4100 Woodward Ave, Ste 9
 Detroit, MI 48201
 Contact: Loretta Watson President
 Tel: 313-831-1535
 Email: watsonlorettam@sparklejani.com
 Website: www.saniglaze535.com
Complete janitorial service, window cleaning, carpet cleaning, construction clean-up, tile & grout restoration. (AA, estab 1989, empl 25, sales , cert: NMSDC)

2175 StarSource Management Services, Inc.
 39080 Webb Dr
 Westland, MI 48185
 Contact: Melvin Brown CEO
 Tel: 734-721-8540
 Email: sales@starsourceinc.com
 Website: www.starsourceinc.com
Dist uniforms, protective clothing, cutting tools, fasteners, janitorial chemical supplies, cleaning equipment, paper towels, plastic liners, welding supplies, automotive cleaning supplies, cooling tower chemicals, laundry services. (AA, estab , empl , sales $6,000,000, cert: NMSDC)

2176 Tri County Cleaning Supply, Inc.
 7109 Dan McGuire Dr
 Brigton, MI 48116
 Contact: Geri Gee President
 Tel: 810-229-6500
 Email: g.gee@tcclean.com
 Website: www.tcclean.com
Dist cleaning supplies. (Woman, estab 0, empl , sales $ 0, cert: WBENC)

Minnesota

2177 Allied National Services
 6066 Shingle Creek Pkwy #1105
 Minneapolis, MN 55430
 Contact: President
 Tel: 763-503-0707
 Email: sales@alliedns.com
 Website: www.alliedns.com
Contract cleaning services. Floor care Restroom sanitation. (AA, estab 2002, empl 541, sales $17,610,000, cert: City, NMSDC, 8(a))

2178 Diverse Maintenance Solutions Inc.
 1523 94th Lane NE
 Blaine, MN 55449
 Contact: Rita Dumra President
 Tel: 763-230-7488
 Email: rita.dumra@dmsimn.com
 Website: www.dmsimn.com
Dist maintenance supplies, janitorial supplies, rubbermaid products, paper products, equipment, office supplies & tools. (Woman/As-Ind, estab 1988, empl 7, sales $966,055, cert: NMSDC, WBENC)

2179 Innovative Chemical Corporation
 7769 95th St South
 Cottage Grove, MN 55016
 Contact: Shelly Meyers Sales Marketing Dir
 Tel: 651-649-1762
 Email: smeyers@iccmn.com
 Website: www.iccmn.com
Mfr eco friendly cleaning & maintenance products, green cleaning products. (As-Ind, estab 1994, empl 13, sales $2,000,000, cert: NMSDC)

2180 SDQ, Ltd.
 4737 County Rd 101, Ste 250
 Minnetonka, MN 55345
 Contact: Scott Bak VP
 Tel: 952-929-5263
 Email: scott@sdqltd.com
 Website: www.sdqltd.com
Janitorial svcs: cleaning, clean room clenaing, carpet cleaning, hard floor surface cleaning. (Woman, estab 1983, empl 250, sales $10,800,000, cert: WBENC)

Missouri

2181 HI-Gene
 1836 Linn St
 North Kansas City, MO 64116
 Contact: Barrie Evans Acct Mgr
 Tel: 816-472-4118
 Email: barrie@higenesjanitorial.com
 Website: www.higenesjanitorial.com
Janitorial services. (Woman, estab 1969, empl 275, sales $6,151,289, cert: NWBOC)

CLEANING PRODUCTS, SUPPLIES & SERVICES

2182 J&B Franchise Venture, Inc.
11684 Lilburn Park Rd
St. Louis, MO 63146
Contact: Janet Mann President
Tel: 314-989-9997
Email: janet.mann@jan-prousa.com
Website: www.stlouis.jan-pro.com
Janitorial services, commercial cleaning, carpet cleaning, floor cleaning services. (Woman, estab 2004, empl 8, sales $2,000,000, cert: State)

2183 Peistrup Paper Products, Inc.
1185 Research Blvd
St. Louis, MO 63132
Contact: Dennis Burjoski Acct Exec
Tel: 314-993-0970
Email: dburjoski@peistruppaper.com
Website: www.peistrup.com
Dist janitorial, paper & safety supplies. (Woman, estab 1960, empl 9, sales , cert: State, WBENC)

2184 Rockwell Labs Ltd.
1257 Bedford Rd
North Kansas City, MO 64116
Contact: Cisse Spragins CEO
Tel: 816-283-3167
Email: cspragins@rockwelllabs.com
Website: www.rockwelllabs.com
Mfr & dist pest management & biological cleaning products: baits for roaches, ants bed bugs & other crawling insects. (Woman, estab 1998, empl 11, sales $ 0, cert: NWBOC)

2185 Tier One Property Services
8601 E 63rd St
Kansas City, MO 64133
Contact: Joel Sanders Business Devel
Tel: 816-285-7439
Email: jsanders@tier1usa.com
Website: www.tier1usa.com
Janitorial services. (AA, estab 2011, empl 750, sales $27,200,000, cert: NMSDC)

2186 Wexford Labs, Inc.
325 Leffingwell Ave
Kirkwood, MO 63122
Contact: Mary Anne Auer CEO
Tel: 800-506-1146
Email: maryanne.auer@wexfordlabs.com
Website: www.wexfordlabs.com
Mfr hard surface, EPA registered disinfectants, floor care products, general purpose cleaners, hand soaps, alcohol hand sanitizers. (Woman, estab , empl , sales $2,966,970, cert: State)

Mississippi

2187 Jefferson Cleaning Services, LLC
06 Ray C. Nicks Rd
Jayess, MS 39641
Contact: Jan Jefferson President
Tel: 601-803-1601
Email: Jefferson.jan@gmail.com
Website: www.jeffersoncleaningservices.weebly.com
Commercial janitorial services, corporate buildings, post construction clean up, office space, hospitals, schools, daycares, retail centers, etc. (Woman/AA, estab 2014, empl 1, sales , cert: City, WBENC)

North Carolina

2188 Century Products LLC
404 Edwardia Dr
Greensboro, NC 27409
Contact: Evette Darden AVP Gov Accts
Tel: 336-292-8090
Email: edb@centuryproductsllc.com
Website: www.centuryproductsllc.com
Dist janitorial cleaning tools: mops, brooms, brushes for institutions & food industry. (AA, estab 1987, empl 21, sales $ 0, cert: NMSDC)

2189 Coverall Health Based Cleaning System
2401 Whitehall Park
Charlotte, NC 28273
Contact: Shannon Krieser Sr Lead Generation Sales Associate
Tel: 704-209-7113
Email: shannon.krieser@coverall.com
Website: www.coverall.com
Janitorial services. (Minority, estab 1985, empl 300, sales , cert: NMSDC)

2190 Elite Touch Cleaning Services, Inc.
4105-A Stuart Andrew Blvd
Charlotte, NC 28217
Contact: Mario Mendigana President
Tel: 704-266-0623
Email: mario@elitetouchcleaning.com
Website: www.elitetouchcleaning.com
Janitorial Services, Floor Maintenance, Carpet care, Construction clean up. (Hisp, estab 2007, empl 5, sales $1,668,000, cert: NMSDC)

2191 Green's Commercial Cleaning
4421 Stuart Andrew Blvd Ste 604
Charlotte, NC 28217
Contact: Kimberly Grace Dir of Sales
Tel: 704-201-6209
Email: kimberly@greenscommercialcleaning.com
Website: www.greenscommercialcleaning.com
Janitorial services, medical curtain cleaning, floor & carpet care, pressure washing & building maintenance. (AA, estab 2003, empl 165, sales $2,300,000, cert: City, 8(a))

2192 GrimeGuru Janitorial Service
1531 Westbrook Plaza Dr, Ste A
Winston-Salem, NC 27103
Contact: Brigitte Hampton President
Tel: 336-710-4406
Email: brigitte@grimeguru.com
Website: www.grimeguru.com
Janitorial Services. (AA, estab , empl , sales , cert: State, WBENC)

2193 JAC Janitorial Services
1101 Tyvola Rd, Ste 205
Charlotte, NC 28217
Contact: Jose Jaramillo Sales Mgr
Tel: 980-201-9099
Email: jjaramillo@jacjanitorialservice.com
Website: www.jacjanitorialservice.com
Cleaning services, hospitals, schools, business parks, government buildings, and more. (Hisp, estab 2006, empl 15, sales , cert: State, City)

2194 Solid Surface Care, Inc.
3820 Rose Lake Dr
Charlotte, NC 28217
Contact: Vanesah Noechel Business Devel
Tel: 202-281-7742
Email: vnoechel@solidcare.com
Website: www.solidcare.com
Stone, Terrazzo, Metal & Wood Maintenance and Restoration, Carpet & Upholstery Cleaning, Tile & Grout Maintenance & Restoration, High Performance Coatings & Concrete Refinishing. (Minority, estab 1996, empl 130, sales $16,604,415, cert: State, CPUC)

2195 Yu Ken Cut It Inc.
3121 Sweeten Creek Rd
Asheville, NC 28803
Contact: Jonathan Bae Marketing Mgr
Tel: 828-651-9770
Email: jonathanbae@yukencutit.com
Website: www.yukencutit.com
Janitorial services. (Minority, Woman, estab 1995, empl 300, sales $5,300,000, cert: NMSDC)

Nebraska

2196 Meylan Enterprises, Inc.
6225 S. 60th St
Omaha, NE 68117
Contact: Tori Peitz President
Tel: 402-339-4880
Email: tpeitz@meylan.net
Website: www.meylan.net
Industrial cleaning services to include; 10,000-40,000 psi high pressure waterblasting, vacuum services, blast wave services (explosives) and specialty projects. (Woman, estab , empl 160, sales , cert: WBENC)

New Jersey

2197 BRAVO! Building Services, Inc.
29 King George Road
Green Brook, NJ 08812
Contact: Frank S. Wardzinski COO
Tel: 732-465-0707
Email: fwardzinski@bravobuildingservices.com
Website: www.bravogroupservices.com
Janitorial svcs, day porters & matrons, HVAC, mail room services. (Minority, Woman, estab 1997, empl , sales $95,000,000, cert: NMSDC)

2198 Capstone Facilities Group LLC
609 Park Ave
Brielle, NJ 08730
Contact: Jrhosaboy President
Tel: 877-765-2242
Email: jrhosaboyj@gmail.com
Website: www.capstonefacilities.com
Dist foodservice, healthcare & janitorial disposables & equipment: paper towels, toilet paper, handsoap, cleaning chemicals, flatware, napkins. (AA, estab 2012, empl 3, sales , cert: NMSDC)

2199 CSS Building Services Inc
846 Livingston Ave
North Brunswick, NJ 08902
Contact: Liz Coury VP Internal Operations
Tel: 609-655-5000
Email: lcoury@cssbuildingservices.com
Website: www.cssbuildingservices.com
Janitorial, building maintenance. (Woman, estab 1976, empl 450, sales $40,000,000, cert: WBENC)

2200 Janel Inc.
7 Mountain Ave
Bound Brook, NJ 08805
Contact: Colleen McAteer President
Tel: 732-271-4700
Email: colleenm@janelinc.com
Website: www.janelonline.com
Dist cleaning products, assemble, test & repair electronic equipment. (Woman, estab 1960, empl 8, sales $2,897,219, cert: State, WBENC)

2201 Shore Manufacturing LLC
1709 Hwy 34 Unit 5
Wall, NJ 07727
Contact: William Vogel President
Tel: 732-894-9810
Email: williamjvogel@aol.com
Website: www.shoremfgllc.com
Mfr non woven disposable food service wipers. (Woman, estab 2013, empl 8, sales , cert: State, WBENC)

New Mexico

2202 Specialized Services, LLC
3150 Carlisle NE Ste, 6
Albuquerque, NM 87110
Contact: Faith St. Clair
Tel: 505-881-5237
Email: faith.specializedservices@gmail.com
Website: www.specializedservicesnm.com
Commercial maintenance, floor maintenance, strip & waxing, cleaning & disinfecting tile & grout. (Hisp, estab 2009, empl 26, sales $125,165,468, cert: NMSDC)

Nevada

2203 Kamco Industries LLC
6969 Speedway Blvd, Ste 107
Las Vegas, NV 89115
Contact: Delicia Liu President
Tel: 702-518-1253
Email: delicia@kamco-online.com
Website: www.kamco-online.com
Mfr & distribute nontoxic, plant-based industrial cleaner, EPA-registered disinfectant and foaming hand sanitizer. We also offer professional consultation for janitorial issues for hotels, (As-Pac, estab 2010, empl 1, sales $130,000, cert: State, NWBOC)

2204 Smalls Senibaldi Services LLC
4127 Falcons Flight Ave
North Las Vegas, NV 89084
Contact: Iris Senibaldi CEO
Tel: 702-636-1316
Email: iris@smaseni.com
Website: www.smaseni.com
Commercial & residential cleaning, janitorial services. (Woman/AA, estab 2013, empl 20, sales , cert: NMSDC)

2205 Smart Cleaning Solutions LLC
57 Spectrum Blvd
Las Vegas, NV 89101
Contact: Salvador Canales Mgr
Tel: 702-685-7055
Email: scanales@mysmartcleaningsolutions.com
Website: www.smartcleaningsolutionsllc.vom
Escalator Step Cleaning & Refurbishing, Powder Coating, Demarcations Lines, Commercial Cleaning, Industrial Cleaning, Power Wash, Custodial Services, Janitorial Services. (Minority, Woman, estab 2011, empl 38, sales $950,000, cert: State)

CLEANING PRODUCTS, SUPPLIES & SERVICES

2206 Spit Shine LLC
      2971 Vigilante Ct.
      North Las Vegas, NV 89081
      Contact: Wilbur LaSane Jr. Owner
      Tel: 702-586-7889
      Email: wilbur@spitshinelv.com
      Website: www.spitshinelv.com
Office cleaning, hard surface floor care, carpet cleaning, window cleaning, and graffiti clean-up. (AA, estab 2012, empl 10, sales $142,661, cert: CPUC, 8(a))

New York

2207 A&A Maintenance Enterprise, Inc.
      965 Midland Ave
      Yonkers, NY 10704
      Contact: Armando Rodriguez Jr. CEO
      Tel: 914-969-0009
      Email: arodriguez@aamaintenance.com
      Website: www.aamaintenance.com
Janitorial services. (Hisp, estab 1983, empl 2600, sales $23,000,000, cert: City, NMSDC)

2208 Alliance Supply, Inc.
      1743-48 St
      Brooklyn, NY 11204
      Contact: Sylvia President
      Tel: 347-564-0022
      Email: sylviasadv@yahoo.com
      Website: www.alliancesupply.net
Dist janitorial supplies & food service disposables. (Woman, estab 2005, empl 4, sales $850,000, cert: City)

2209 American Maintenance Janitorial Services &
      Supplies Co. Corp.
      1074 Home St
      Bronx, NY 10459
      Contact: Jessica Ortiz-Gonzalez Acct Mgr
      Tel: 718-409-0021
      Email: americanmaintenance3jss@gmail.com
      Website: www.americanmaint1807.com
Commercial janitorial services; custodial services floor & carpet care; construction cleanup; window cleaning; building maintenance. (Hisp, estab 2004, empl 25, sales $800,000, cert: State, City, NMSDC)

2210 Anthony's Janitorial/Maintenance Service Ltd.
      24-20 Jackson Ave
      Long Island City, NY 11101
      Contact: Anthony Fisher President
      Tel: 718-737-5806
      Email: anthonyjanitorialmaintenance@gmail.com
      Website: www.anthonysjanitorialmaintenance.com
Janitorial Supplies & Services. (AA, estab 2010, empl 100, sales , cert: City)

2211 Gilbert International Inc.
      1001 Ave of the Americas 12th Fl
      New York, NY 10018
      Contact: Kevin Gilbert President
      Tel: 212-628-5305
      Email: kevin@gilbertinternational.com
      Website: www.gilbertinternational.com
Integrated facilities services, janitorial & facilities support. (Minority, Woman, estab 1992, empl 266, sales $22,760,946, cert: State, City, NMSDC, WBENC)

2212 Global Traders, Inc.
      496 Powell St
      Brooklyn, NY 11212
      Contact: Charles Ossa President
      Tel: 347-240-9900
      Email: cossa@globaltradersusa.us
      Website: www.globaltradersusa.us
Cavicide surface disinfectant & decontaminant cleaner. (Woman/AA, estab 1999, empl 4, sales $400,000, cert: State, City)

2213 H. Weiss LLC
      12 Labriola Court
      Armonk, NY 10504
      Contact: Elizabeth Weiss Managing Member
      Tel: 914-273-4400
      Email: eweiss@hweiss.net
      Website: www.hweiss.net
Dist disposables, janitorial wares & supply items for the kitchen. (Minority, Woman, estab 2003, empl 46, sales $958,779,300, cert: WBENC)

2214 Premier Supplies
      460 W 34th St
      New York, NY 10001
      Contact: Brad Singer Dir Jan/San Div
      Tel: 732-240-6900
      Email: bsinger@premiersupplies.com
      Website: www.premiersupplies.com
Dist cleaning products & equipment. (Woman, estab 1962, empl 7, sales $1,250,000, cert: State)

2215 Quality Building Services
      801 Second Ave 8th Fl
      New York, NY 10017
      Contact: Andrea Barragan Research & Dev
      Tel: 212-883-0009
      Email: andrea.b@qbs.co
      Website: www.qualitybuildingservices.com
Janitorial services: offices, conference rooms, kitchens, bathrooms, lobbies and other common spaces. (Woman, estab 2000, empl 600, sales $50,050,000, cert: City, WBENC)

2216 Snappy Solutions
      106 Sycamore Dr
      East Hampton, NY 11937
      Contact: Fairlie President
      Tel: 212-748-9030
      Email: maureen@snappysolutions.com
      Website: www.snappysolutions.com
Dist janitorial, material maintenance products & safety products. (Woman, estab 2003, empl 2, sales $430,000, cert: WBENC)

Ohio

2217 ANS Inc.
      4400 Perkins Ave
      Cleveland, OH 44130
      Contact: Richard Harles Division Mgr
      Tel: 216-391-7000
      Email: rch@ansi.com
      Website: www.ansi.com
Highrise/Lowrise - Window Cleaning, Power Washing, Light & Fixture Cleaning & Changing, Metal Washing. (Woman, estab 1970, empl 80, sales $8,000,000, cert: WBENC)

CLEANING PRODUCTS, SUPPLIES & SERVICES

2218 Carpet Concepts, Inc.
9048 Sutton Pl
Hamilton, OH 45011
Contact: President
Tel: 513-772-7060
Email:
Website: www.carpetconcepts.net
Commercial carpet cleaning & preventive maintenance, pile lifting, odor neutralizing, clean panels & VCT flooring. (Woman, estab 1983, empl 24, sales $1,570,277, cert: WBENC)

2219 Cummins Facility Services, LLC
1798 Marion Cardington Rd E
Marion, OH 43302
Contact: Christa Cloud Business Devel Mgr
Tel: 740-726-9800
Email: sales@cumminsfs.com
Website: www.cumminsfs.com
Janitorial services, vendor management, building management, snow removal, ice melt, landscaping, security, floor work and carpet care (Woman, estab 1972, empl 500, sales $15,000,000, cert: WBENC)

2220 Ecoprocleaningsolutions Inc.
9001 Portage Pointe Dr, Ste R103
Streetsboro, OH 44241
Contact: Kevin White President
Tel: 330-689-8196
Email: kwhite@ecoprocleaningsolutions.com
Website: www.ecoprocleaningsolutions.com
Full service janitorial service, carpet cleaning; floor stripping; sanding; waxing; burnishing & window cleaning. (Minority, estab 2012, empl 1, sales $ 0, cert: NMSDC)

2221 J.T. Dillard, LLC dba ZayMat Distributors
25906 Emery Rd
Cleveland, OH 44128
Contact: Terrell Dillard President
Tel: 440-605-9000
Email: terrell.dillard@zaymat.com
Website: www.zaymat.com
Full-service commercial cleaning services. (AA, estab 2003, empl 6, sales $2,600,000, cert: State, NMSDC)

2222 Janitorial Services Inc.
5795 Canal Rd
Valley View, OH 44125
Contact: Ronald Martinez Jr. VP
Tel: 216-341-8601
Email: rmartinez@jsijanitorial.com
Website: www.jsijanitorial.com
Commercial Cleaning Services, Construction Cleaning, Window Washing, Wall Washing, Carpet Cleaning, Hard Surface Floor Care. (Hisp, estab 1972, empl 400, sales $ 0, cert: NMSDC)

2223 Link to Success dba HARKNESServices
947 E Johnstown Rd, Ste 127
Gahanna, OH 43230
Contact: Tara Harkness President
Tel: 888-959-4203
Email: tharkness@harknessservices.com
Website: www.harknesservices.com
Kitchen exhaust cleaning, Install hinges on fans, Install grease containment systems. (Woman/AA, estab 2011, empl 8, sales $41,222,200, cert: State, NMSDC)

2224 Ohio Services-CLE, LLC dba Jani-King of Cleveland
9075 Town Centre Dr, Ste 200
Broadview Heights, OH 44147
Contact: Joe Carollo President
Tel: 440-546-0000
Email: jcarollo@janikingcleveland.com
Website: www.janiking.com/cleveland
Janitorial services: general commercial cleaning, carpet cleaning, floor care, trash disposal, window cleaning, wall cleaning, etc. (Woman, estab 1991, empl 1000, sales $14,860,813, cert: WBENC)

Pennsylvania

2225 CSI International, Inc.
105 Terry Dr Ste 116
Newtown, PA 18940
Contact: Jamie Moore COO
Tel: 800-258-3330
Email: jmoore@csiinternational.com
Website: www.csiinternational.com
Janitorial Services, Integrated Facility Services, Building Operations & Maintenance Services. (Minority, Woman, estab 1994, empl 1915, sales $61,000,000, cert: WBENC)

2226 Homeland Industrial Supp
3045 McCann Farm Dr, Unit 102
Garnet Valley, PA 19060
Contact: Donna King CEO
Tel: 844-350-1550
Email: support@homelandindustrialsupply.com
Website: www.homelandindustrialsupply.com
Dist specialty maintenance products & janitorial supplies. (Woman, estab 2014, empl 11, sales $1,500,000, cert: State, City)

2227 Interstate Premier Services Corp
508 Prudential Rd Ste 600
Horsham, PA 19044
Contact: Brad Marg
Tel: 215-907-9857
Email: bmarg@interstatepremier.com
Website: www.interstatepremier.com
Building maintenance services. (Woman, estab 2019, empl 500, sales $7,000,000, cert: State, WBENC)

2228 T. Frank McCall's, Inc.
601 Madison St
Chester, PA 19013
Contact: Lisa Witomski President
Tel: 610-876-9245
Email: lisa@tfrankmccalls.com
Website: www.tfrankmccalls.com
Janitorial, maintenance & dist paper. (Woman, estab , empl 23, sales $ 0, cert: WBENC)

2229 Team Clean, Inc.
104 N 63rd St
Philadelphia, PA 19139
Contact: Donna Allie President
Tel: 267-514-8326
Email: dallie@team-clean.com
Website: www.team-clean.com
Janitorial cleaning, nightly office & commercial cleaning, hot water pressure washing, sanitizing garbage holding areas, window washing, carpet shampooing & full kitchen cleaning. (Woman/AA, estab 1989, empl 366, sales $17,271,812, cert: NMSDC, WBENC)

CLEANING PRODUCTS, SUPPLIES & SERVICES

Puerto Rico

2230 Action Service Corporation
      PO Box 364866
      San Juan, PR 00936
      Contact: Julie Garcia President
      Tel: 787-759-3737
      Email: julie@actionservicepr.com
      Website: www.actionservicepr.com
Janitorial, Groundkeeping & Security Services. (Woman/Hisp, estab 1978, empl 350, sales $6,000,000, cert: NMSDC, WBENC)

Rhode Island

2231 Universal Cleaning Concept LLC
      77 Burgess Ave
      East Providence, RI 02914
      Contact: Evanisio Oliveira Owner
      Tel: 401-952-2844
      Email: universalcc14@gmail.com
      Website: www.universalcleaning.org
Commercial office cleaning services. (AA, estab 2007, empl 14, sales , cert: State, 8(a), SDB)

South Carolina

2232 Clean Advantage, Inc.
      5 N Watson Rd
      Taylors, SC 29687
      Contact: Linda Black President
      Tel: 800-322-6641
      Email: linda@cleanadvantage.com
      Website: www.cleanadvantage.com
Mfr & package specialty cleaning products, private label packaging. (Woman, estab 1993, empl 25, sales $ 0, cert: WBENC)

2233 DeWhit, Inc.
      213 E Butler Rd, F2
      Mauldin, SC 29662
      Contact: Charles Whitner President
      Tel: 864-757-1560
      Email: cwhitner@dewhit.com
      Website: www.dewhit.com
Janitorial Services; Janitorial Equipment, Chemicals & Paper-Related Products. (AA, estab 1984, empl 110, sales $5,363,786, cert: NMSDC)

2234 Quality Touch Janitorial Service, Inc.
      7252 Investment Dr
      North Charleston, SC 29418
      Contact: John Brown President
      Tel: 843-552-7303
      Email: jbrown@qualitytouchjanitorial.com
      Website: www.wwwqualitytouchjanitorial.com
Janitorial services, general cleaning, construction cleanup & floor maintenance. (Woman/AA, estab , empl , sales $1,650,000, cert: State, City, SDB)

Tennessee

2235 Action Chemical, Inc.
      275 Cumberland St
      Memphis, TN 38112
      Contact: Charles E. Barnes President
      Tel: 901-522-8783
      Email: charles@actionjps.com
      Website: www.actionchemical.com
Dist janitorial supplies & equip, maintenance supplies & equip, industrial supplies, paper products, safety products, cleaning chemicals, odor control products, mops, brooms, brushes. (AA, estab 1994, empl 16, sales $5,481,460, cert: State, City, NMSDC)

2236 Fayette Janitorial Service LLC
      PO Box 866
      Sommerville, TN 38068
      Contact: Michael Kellon General Sales Mgr
      Tel: 901-465-1529
      Email: mburns@fayettejanitorialservice.com
      Website: www.fayettejanitorialservice.com
Janitorial services. (Woman, estab 1995, empl 15, sales $24,481,341, cert: CPUC, WBENC)

2237 Ladd Safety, LLC
      3901 Lighthouse Lane
      Lakeland, TN 38002
      Contact: Jessica Ladd Owner
      Tel: 901-268-2098
      Email: admin@laddsafety.com
      Website: www.laddsafety.com
Dist Safety PPE & Janitorial supplies. (Woman, estab 2016, empl 3, sales , cert: WBENC)

2238 Mason's Professional Cleaning Service, LLC
      1422 Menager Rd
      Memphis, TN 38106
      Contact: Dorothy Mason President
      Tel: 901-775-7778
      Email: dotm20032003@yahoo.com
      Website: www.masonprofessionalcleaningservicellc.com
Commercial janitorial cleaning services, carpet cleaning, hard surface flooring cleaning, pressure washing, groundskeeping/landscaping service. (Woman/AA, estab 2000, empl 21, sales $550,000, cert: State, City, NMSDC)

2239 Premiere Building Maintenance Corporation
      1416 McCalla Ave
      Knoxville, TN 37915
      Contact: Tom Poovey Dir of Business Dev
      Tel: 865-773-9524
      Email: tpoovey@premiberebuilding.com
      Website: www.premierebuilding.com
Full Janitorial Service, Maintenance & Facility Management (AA, estab 1996, empl 500, sales $13,900,000, cert: State, NMSDC)

2240 Reliable Building Solutions, Inc.
      6232 Airpark Dr
      Chattanooga, TN 37421
      Contact: Kathy Sok President
      Tel: 423-954-9834
      Email: ksok6322@aol.com
      Website: www.rbsi-online.com
Complete facility management: Janitorial, Floor maintenance, Emergency services, dist Janitorial supplies, equipment & chemicals. (Minority, Woman, estab 1992, empl 45, sales $2,800,000, cert: State)

2241 Universal Sanitizers and Supplies, Inc.
P.O. Box 50305
Knoxville, TN 37853
Contact: Emilia Rico-Munoz CEO
Tel: 865-573-7296
Email: emirico@msn.com
Website: www.universalsanitizers.com
Sanitation cleaners & sanitizers, conveyor lubricants, janitorial products, sanitation consulting, training & audits, contract cleaning, fogging, sanitation equipment, water treatment, environmental testing. (Minority, Woman, estab 1994, empl 15, sales $3,000,000, cert: WBENC)

Texas

2242 AHI Facility Services, Inc.
625 Yuma Ct
Dallas, TX 75208
Contact: Bethany Lorentzen Marketing Coord
Tel: 800-472-5749
Email: bethanylorentzen@ahifs.com
Website: www.ahifs.com
Janitorial svcs, carpet & floor care, minor & general maintenance, landscaping, groundskeeping, parking lot sweeping & striping, garage maintenance, window washing, power washing, document shredding, recycle programs. (Woman, estab 1968, empl 1500, sales $39,000,000, cert: WBENC)

2243 Aztec Facility Management, LP
11000 S Wilcrest, Ste 125
Houston, TX 77099
Contact: Andrea Bradshaw Proposal & Marketing Mgr
Tel: 281-668-9000
Email: andrea@aztec1.com
Website: www.aztecfacility.com
Facility management & support services: janitorial, grounds & preventive maintenance, pest control, parking lot maintenance, construction clean-up, property warehousing, environmental services. (Woman/AA, estab 1981, empl 900, sales $23,500,000, cert: State, NMSDC)

2244 Bell Janitorial Supplies & Services, Inc.
2828 Reward Ln
Dallas, TX 75220
Contact: Susan Morrissey President
Tel: 214-352-7775
Email: susan@belljanitorial.com
Website: www.belljanitorial.com
Dist janitorial supplies & services. (Woman, estab , empl , sales $ 0, cert: WBENC)

2245 CalGar Enterprises, LLC
3712 Arapaho Rd
Addison, TX 75001
Contact: Rick Calabrese
Tel: 972-437-6555
Email: rbraucht@calgar-ent.com
Website: www.calgar-ent.com
Maintenance & Detailed Cleaning of Cleanrooms, Data Center, Sub-Flooring Cleaning, Terminal Cleaning, Construction Clean Services, Site Preparation Contractors, Janitorial, Custodial, Green Cleaning, LEED. (Hisp, estab 2005, empl 30, sales $1,200,000, cert: State)

2246 Competitive Choice, Inc.
PO Box 35743
Houston, TX 77235
Contact: Aundrea Williams President
Tel: 832-724-5300
Email: aundrea@competitivechoice.net
Website: www.competitivechoice.net
Dist industrial maintenance & cleaning chemicals: lubricants, solvents, degreasers, hand cleaners & wipes, disinfectants, deodorizers, greases & oils, coil cleaners & pan tabs, drain & sewer maintainers, insecticdes & safety supplies. (Woman/AA, estab , empl , sales $700,000, cert: WBENC)

2247 Contractors Corner, LLC
9515 Maverick Point
San Antonio, TX 78240
Contact: Eduardo Garcia Owner
Tel: 210-462-3110
Email: agarcia@concorusa.com
Website: www.concorusa.com
Commercial janitorial services, floor care, strip & wax, buffing, polishing concrete floors & building maintenance services. (Hisp, estab 2009, empl 72, sales $1,000,000, cert: State)

2248 Entrust One Facility Services, Inc.
11142 Shady Trail
Dallas, TX 75229
Contact: Lupe Fernandez Marketing Coord
Tel: 972-669-8485
Email: lupe@entrust1.com
Website: www.entrust1.com
Janitorial Services, hard floor maintenance, carpet cleaning, marble restoration, powerwashing, window cleaning. (Minority, Woman, estab 1983, empl 600, sales , cert: State, NMSDC)

2249 Evelyn's Professional Janitorial Services, Inc.
1617 N Central Exprwy
Dallas, TX 75075
Contact: Tammy Pearce Business Devel Dir
Tel: 972-516-9550
Email: customerservice@alljanitorial.net
Website: www.alljanitorial.net
Janitorial service; window cleaning; power washing; floor maintenance; janitorial supplies; window cleaning equipment; window cleaning supplies; floor scrubbers; floor buffers; cleaning chemicals; floor sweepers; carpet vacuum. (Minority, Woman, estab 1992, empl 110, sales $1,258,040, cert: State, NMSDC, WBENC)

2250 Industrial Solution Company
2514 Oak Hill Dr
Arlington, TX 76006
Contact: Barbara Oldums Owner
Tel: 214-200-6535
Email: industrialsolutions513@yahoo.com
Website: www.indsolbo.com
Mfr Disposable Towel TUF Towels, Dist Cloth Towels, Gloves, Safety Supplies, Packaging Supplies & Janitorial Supplies. (Woman/AA, estab 2011, empl 2, sales , cert: State, City)

2251 La Med Facility Maintenance
      10815 Gulfdale
      San Antonio, TX 78216
      Contact: Eduardo Tijerina CEO
      Tel: 210-464-0107
      Email: edwardtij@hotmail.com
      Website: www.lamedfm.com
Facility maintenance, commercial cleaning, transportation. (Minority, Woman, estab 2011, empl 32, sales $1,250,987, cert: State)

2252 Lim Service Industries Inc.
      5829 W Sam Houston Pkwy N, Ste 907
      Houston, TX 77041
      Contact: Frank Gortot Jr. VP Business Dev
      Tel: 954-899-2257
      Email: f.gortot.exit@gmail.com
      Website: www.limsii.com
Janitorial nation wide. (As-Pac, estab 2013, empl 32, sales $6,000,000, cert: City, 8(a))

2253 M.A.N.S. Distributors, Inc.
      6719 Levelland Dr Ste 200
      Dallas, TX 75252
      Contact: Project Mgr
      Tel: 972-380-2062
      Email: sales@mans.us
      Website: www.mans.us
Dist industrial janitorial & maintenance supplies. (Minority, Woman, estab 1980, empl 5, sales $3,500,000, cert: State)

2254 MarFran Cleaning, LLC
      15502 Old Galveston Rd, Ste 718
      Webster, TX 77598
      Contact: Naomi Scales Managing Member
      Tel: 832-885-6692
      Email: naomi@marfrancleaning.com
      Website: www.marfrancleaning.com
Custodial/Janitorial Services, Landscaping Services, Carpet & Upholstery Cleaning, Facilities Maintenance Support, Painting & Flooring, Minor Construction, Remodeling & Renovations. (Woman/AA, estab 2006, empl 15, sales $543,650, cert: State, City, 8(a))

2255 MBE Cleaning LLC
      PO Box 152082
      Dallas, TX 75315
      Contact: Malachi Nance Owner
      Tel: 214-284-9206
      Email: mnance@mbacleaning.com
      Website: www.mbacleaning.com
Botanical & Eco-Friendly Crime & Trauma Scene Decontamination. (AA, estab 2011, empl 4, sales , cert: State)

2256 Prestige Maintenance USA Ltd.
      1808 10th St
      Plano, TX 75074
      Contact: Rachel Sanchez CEO
      Tel: 972-578-9801
      Email: rsanchez@prestigeusa.net
      Website: www.prestigeusa.net
Contract cleaning: retail, office, industrial & warehouse facilities. (Woman, estab 1976, empl 777, sales $ 0, cert: WBENC)

2257 Redlee/SCS, Inc.
      10425 Olympic Dr, Ste A
      Dallas, TX 75220
      Contact: John Gendreau CEO
      Tel: 214-357-4753
      Email: jgendreau@redleescs.com
      Website: www.redleescs.com
Commerical janitorial services, carpet cleaning, & hard surface flooring maintenance & restoration. (Nat Ame, estab 1982, empl 225, sales $30,353,905, cert: State, NMSDC)

2258 San Benito Textile Inc.
      201 N Travis St
      San Benito, TX 78586
      Contact: Carlos Sanchez Mgr
      Tel: 956-361-0282
      Email: jenny@sanbenitotextiles.com
      Website: www.sanbenitotextiles.com
Dist recycled wiping rags that clean grease, oil, petroleum, gasoline, chemicals & paint as well as buffing, polishing, & waxing. (Hisp, estab 1990, empl 15, sales , cert: NMSDC)

2259 SOYAC Industrial
      12514 Willow Breeze Dr
      Tomball, TX 77377
      Contact: Roberto Schnakofsky President
      Tel: 877-243-0445
      Email: roberto@soyacindustrial.com
      Website: www.soyacindustrial.com
Environmentally & Regulatory Friendly Solvents, Degreasers, Cleaners, Penetrating Lubricants. (Hisp, estab 2004, empl 3, sales $273,532, cert: State, City)

2260 Supply Sanitation Systems
      1450 Preston Forest Sq, Ste 209
      Dallas, TX 75230
      Contact: Sally Seegers Sales
      Tel: 972-458-2555
      Email: sallys@supplysystemsusa.com
      Website: www.supplysystemsusa.com
Mfr & dist cleaning chemicals. (Woman, estab 1992, empl 6, sales $ 0, cert: State)

2261 Texas Microfiber Incorporated
      2515 Tarpley Rd, Ste 118
      Carrollton, TX 75006
      Contact: President
      Tel: 800-742-2913
      Email: Sales@texasmicrofiber.com
      Website: www.texasmicrofiber.com
Mfr microfiber mop pads, microfiber mops, microfiber cloths, microfiber towels, telescopic microfiber high dusters & duster socks, aluminum mop handles & heads, cotton hand towels, cotton bar towels, logo cotton towels, logo microfiber towels. (Woman, estab 2010, empl 4, sales $725,000, cert: State, WBENC)

2262 The Entermedia Group, LLC
      900 RR620 S Ste C101-153
      Austin, TX 78734
      Contact: Lorraine Jordan CEO
      Tel: 512-553-8341
      Email: lorraine.jordan@tegteam.com
      Website: www.tegteam.com
(Woman/AA, estab 2010, empl 10, sales , cert: State, NMSDC, WBENC)

CLEANING PRODUCTS, SUPPLIES & SERVICES

2263 Total Building Maintenance, Inc.
PO Box 35669
Dallas, TX 75235
Contact: Erica Vasquez Office Mgr
Tel: 214-350-8293
Email: evasquez@totalbuildingmaintenance.com
Website: www.totalbuildingmaintenance.com
Commerical janitorial services. (Minority, Woman, estab 2005, empl 32, sales $2,500,000, cert: WBENC)

2264 XD Ventures, LLC
2555 South Shore Blvd. Ste C
League City, TX 77573
Contact: Xan Difede President
Tel: 832-557-6622
Email: xan@fidelityfuels.com
Website: www.fidelityfuels.com
Dist aliphatic solvents, mineral spirits & mineral seal oils. (Woman, estab 2014, empl 1, sales , cert: State, WBENC)

Virginia

2265 A&L Service Industries, Inc
10366A Democracy Lane
Fairfax, VA 22030
Contact: Andrea Sax President
Tel: 703-359-0555
Email: diversity@alsi.us.com
Website: www.alsi.us.com
Janitorial services, commercial & residential buildings, new construction cleanup, parking lot/garage cleaning, day porter service, carpet cleaning, window cleaning, floor restoration. (Woman, estab 1978, empl 62, sales $3,244,673, cert: State)

2266 Hutchins & Hutchins, Inc.
39 Hutchwood Lane
Waynessboro, VA 22980
Contact: Kristyn H Marketing Mgr
Tel: 540-949-6663
Email: marketing@yourcleanroomsupplier.com
Website: www.yourcleanroomsupplier.com/
Dist clean room supplies & safety apparel. (Woman, estab 1984, empl 17, sales $4,503,300, cert: State)

2267 Rock Solid Janitorial, Inc.
2705 W Mercury Ave
Hampton, VA 23666
Contact: Arvella Gardner President
Tel: 757-766-7223
Email: calltherock@aol.com
Website: www.rocksolidjanitorial.com
Certified green janitorial services: Complete Floor Care Services (hard surface and carpet), Day & Evening Custodial Support, Construction Cleanup. (AA, estab 1997, empl 226, sales $4,025,000, cert: State)

Washington

2268 AMEX Investments, LLC
730 West A St
Pasco, WA 99301
Contact: Deborah Bermudez Owner
Tel: 509-545-3903
Email: deb@acompletejanitorial.com
Website: www.acompletejanitorial.com
Cleaning supplies, chemicals, equipment & parts. (Minority, Woman, estab 2012, empl 6, sales $500,000, cert: State)

2269 Nexo Services LLC
12819 SE 38th St
Bellevue, WA 98006
Contact: Fatima Sotelo Principal
Tel: 206-518-3235
Email: patty@nexoservices.net
Website: www.nexoservices.net
Janitorial, Maintenance, Office, Industrial, Foodservice Supplies. (Minority, Woman, estab 2014, empl 1, sales , cert: State)

Wisconsin

2270 Lavelle Industries, Inc.
665 McHenry St
Burlington, WI 53105
Contact: Megan Schmidt Natl Acct Mgr
Tel: 262-757-2213
Email: mschmidt@lavelle.com
Website: www.lavelle.com
Mfr Korky brand toilet repair products: toilet flappers, toilet fill valves & flush valves. (Woman, estab , empl 450, sales , cert: WBENC)

2271 Modern Maintenance Building Services, Inc.
2125 S 162nd St
New Berlin, WI 53151
Contact: Steve Ogden VP Business Devel
Tel: 262-785-1962
Email: steven.o@mmbuildingservices.com
Website: www.mmbuildingservices.com
Complete janitorial services, General Cleaning, Carpet & Upholstery Cleaning, Hard Floor Care, Construction Cleaning, Parking Lot Cleaning. (Minority, Woman, estab 1984, empl 225, sales $ 0, cert: State, NMSDC)

2272 Performance Clean LLC
One Brewers Way
Milwaukee, WI 53214
Contact: Steven O'Connell General Mgr
Tel: 414-902-4439
Email: info@performanceclean.com
Website: www.performanceclean.com
Janitorial & building maintenance. (AA, estab 2001, empl 350, sales $4,381,330, cert: NMSDC)

2273 Rebel Green LLC
1009 Glen Oaks Lane
Mequon, WI 53092
Contact: Ali Florsheim Owner
Tel: 262-240-9992
Email: kristina@rebelgreen.com
Website: www.rebelgreen.com
Mfr & dist eco-friendly cleaning products that do not contain harsh chemicals. (Woman, estab 2009, empl 8, sales $7,000,000, cert: WBENC)

CONSTRUCTION: General Contractors

CONSTRUCTION: General Contractors
Companies listed are bonded general contractors who perform or will perform on a regional or national basis. NAICS Code 23

Alaska

2274 Teya Technologies, LLC
101 E 9th Ave, Ste 9B
Anchorage, AK 99501
Contact: Ronald Perry CEO
Tel: 907-339-4901
Email: ron.perry@teyatech.com
Website: www.teyatech.com
Construction, demolition, project management, custodial and janitorial services, administrative services, product manufacturing, housing maintenance. (Nat Ame, estab 2005, empl 46, sales $14,422,189, cert: NMSDC)

Alabama

2275 Dine Modular Construction, LLC
2515 11th Ave
Haleyville, AL 35565
Contact: Pam Morton Sr Project Mgr
Tel: 205-485-1267
Email: pparrish@dineconstruction.com
Website: www.dineconstruction.com
General construction: design/build construction, pre-engineered steel & modular buildings. (Minority, Woman, estab 2003, empl 6, sales $1,000,002, cert: WBENC)

Arizona

2276 Artic Air Heating & Cooling
1720 E Deer Valley, Ste 105
Phoenix, AZ 85024
Contact: Marcia Stewart President
Tel: 623-582-8004
Email: marcia@articac.com
Website: www.articac.com
Commercial design, build & instal HVAC systems. (Woman, estab 1984, empl 30, sales $5,260,000, cert: State, City)

2277 Caliente Construction, Inc.
485 W Vaughn St
Tempe, AZ 85283
Contact: Lorraine Bergman CEO
Tel: 480-894-5500
Email: lbergman@calienteconstruction.com
Website: www.calienteconstruction.com
Licensed commercial, residential and general engineering General Contractor. (Woman, estab 1991, empl 90, sales $69,838,941, cert: CPUC, WBENC)

2278 DAP Construction Management, LLC
516 W Vermont Ave
Phoenix, AZ 85013
Contact: Alicia Hernandez
Tel: 602-541-0229
Email: ahernandez@dapconstructionmgt.com
Website: www.dapconstructionmgt.com
General construction: self performing, rough framing, landscaping, roofing, painting, flooring & material supplies. (Minority, Woman, estab 2009, empl 2, sales $102,000, cert: State, City, WBENC)

2279 Eagle EGC dba Miura Contracting
4001 S Contractors Way, Ste 121
Tucson, AZ 85716
Contact: Liz Joye Office Mgr
Tel: 520-292-3939
Email: ljoye@miuracontracting.com
Website: www.miuracontracting.com/
General Contracting, horizontal construction projects & vertical construction projects. (Hisp, estab 2008, empl 13, sales $1,400,000, cert: City, 8(a), SDB)

2280 K&R Holdings, Inc.
2322 W Detroit Pl
Chandler, AZ 85224
Contact: Wayne Armoogam President
Tel: 480-236-2682
Email: warmoogam@lumawaresafety.com
Website: www.lumawaresafety.com
Dist & install photoluminescent egress systems for facilities. Requires no electricity, external power source or batteries to provide the illumination required for safe movement of employees. (As-Ind, estab 2007, empl 5, sales $100,000, cert: NMSDC)

2281 RJC Contracting, Inc.
2824 N Power Rd, Ste 113
Mesa, AZ 85215
Contact: Kristi Carpenter President
Tel: 480-357-0868
Email: kristi@rjccontracting.com
Website: www.rjccontracting.com
Civil construction, commercial building, professional engineering, concrete construction, inspecting, formwork & falsework design. (Woman, estab 1996, empl 6, sales , cert: City)

2282 Sentinel Fence and Contracting LLC
6908 East Thomas Road
Scottsdale, AZ 85251
Contact: Sharon Hamilton President
Tel: 602-828-4866
Email: sharonh@sentinelfence.com
Website: www.sentinelfence.com
General contracting, commercial renovations, high security fencing, gates, bollards, barriers & barricades. (Minority, Woman, estab 2002, empl 15, sales $3,219,351, cert: City, WBENC)

2283 Troon Inc.
16441 N 90th St
Scottsdale, AZ 85260
Contact: Ray Garcia President
Tel: 480-626-4300
Email: ray@trooninc.com
Website: www.trooninc.com
General contracting. (Hisp, estab 2002, empl 11, sales $11,000,000, cert: State)

California

2284 Ahtna Government Services Corporation
3100 Beacon Blvd.
West Sacramento, CA 95691
Contact: Craig O'Rourke President
Tel: 916-372-2000
Email: info@ahtnagov.com
Website: www.ahtnagov.com
General construction; construction mgmt; engineering; environmental engineering & remediation;. (Nat Ame, estab 1999, empl 120, sales $60,100,000, cert: CPUC)

CONSTRUCTION: General Contractors

2285 All American Lock
337 W Freedom Ave
Orange, CA 92865
Contact: William Judd Sales
Tel: 866-298-7200
Email: william@allamericanlock.com
Website: www.allamericanlock.com
Dist, install, service & repair Automatic, Storefront & Overhead doors, Hollow Metal & Wood Doors, Glass & Glazing, Dock Equip, CCTV & Access Control. (Woman, estab 1985, empl 30, sales $3,000,000, cert: WBENC)

2286 All American Rentals, Inc.
8136 Enterprise Dr
Newark, CA 94560
Contact: Mike Carter President
Tel: 510-713-7368
Email: mikec@allamericanrentals.com
Website: www.allamericanrentals.com
Construction, Industrial Equipment Rentals and Sales; Equipment Repairs & Preventative Maintenance Programs; Operator safety training & certifications; Transportation. (Woman/Hisp, estab 2000, empl 23, sales $4,541,765, cert: State)

2287 Anderson Burton Construction
121 Nevada St
Arroyo Grande, CA 93420
Contact: Joni Anderson President
Tel: 805-481-5096
Email: joni@andersonburton.com
Website: www.andersonburton.com/
General Engineering, Procurement, General Contracting, Energy (Woman, estab 1999, empl 155, sales $30,198,963, cert: CPUC)

2288 APW Construction, Inc.
15135 Salt Lake Ave
City of Industry, CA 91746
Contact: Mayra Oronia Contract Administrator
Tel: 626-333-0727
Email: moronia@acefencecompany.com
Website: www.acefencecompany.com
Construction: fences, gates, and guardrails. (Woman/As-Pac, estab 1988, empl 50, sales $9,000,000, cert: City)

2289 Aqual Corp.
7951 North Ave
Lemon Grove, CA 91945
Contact: Lanette McAfee Business Operations
Tel: 619-741-9028
Email: lanette@aqualcorp.com
Website: www.aqualcorp.com
Construction Management Cost Plus, GMP Design Build & Lump Sum, Multi Family Commercial & Industrial Tenant Improvements, Concrete, horizontal/vertical, drywall & taping, painting, framing, carpentry, tile, doors, plumbing. (AA, As-Pac, estab 2008, empl 4, sales $1,049,692, cert: NMSDC)

2290 Bjork Construction Co. Inc.
4420 Enterprise Place
Fremont, CA 94538
Contact: Jean Bjork President
Tel: 510-656-4688
Email: jbjork@bjorkconstruction.com
Website: www.bjorkconstruction.com
General contracting: self preforms, construction management, carpentry rough & finish, metal stud framing, sheetrock systems & painting. (Woman, estab 1988, empl 115, sales $22,000,000, cert: CPUC, WBENC)

2291 Cabral Roofing & Waterproofing Corp.
675 W. Terrace Dr
San Dimas, CA 91773
Contact: Desi Cabral PR/Sales
Tel: 323-832-9100
Email: desi@cabralroofing.com
Website: www.cabralroofing.com
General contracting: roofing & waterproofing (Hisp, estab 1997, empl 70, sales , cert: CPUC)

2292 Casco Contractors, Inc.
9850 Irvine Center Dr.
Irvine, CA 92618
Contact: Cheryl Osborn President
Tel: 949-679-6880
Email: cheryl@cascocontractors.com
Website: www.cascocontractors.com
General contracting, TI construction, construction management. (Woman, estab 2001, empl 44, sales $32,000,000, cert: CPUC, WBENC)

2293 Christian Brothers Mechanical Services, Inc.
11140 Thurston Lane
Mira Loma, CA 91752
Contact: Steve Knisley VP Service
Tel: 951-361-2247
Email: steve@cbhvac.com
Website: www.cbhvac.com
Commercial HVAC. (Nat Ame, estab 1985, empl 100, sales $18,500,000, cert: State)

2294 Commercial Site Improvements, Inc.
192 Poker Flat Rd
Copperopolis, CA 95228
Contact: Kim Batch Owner
Tel: 209-785-1920
Email: mainoffice@comimprovementsinc.com
Website: www.comsiteimprovementsinc.com
Construction maintenance & remodeling. (Woman, estab 2012, empl 50, sales $130,000,000, cert: CPUC)

2295 Excel Construction Services, Inc.
1950 Raymer Ave
Fullerton, CA 92833
Contact: Karen Ratzlaff CEO
Tel: 714-680-9200
Email: karen@excelconstruction.biz
Website: www.excelconstruction.biz
Commercial maintenance and construction services. (Woman, estab 2004, empl 125, sales $22,316,621, cert: WBENC)

2296 Fasone Construction inc
9124 Norwalk Blvd
Santa Fe Springs, CA 90670
Contact: Andrea N Garrido
Tel: 562-322-0828
Email: andrea@fasonegbc.com
Website: www.fasonegbc.com
Design & general construction contracting. (Minority, Woman, estab 1995, empl 21, sales $3,800,500, cert: City, CPUC, WBENC, 8(a))

CONSTRUCTION: General Contractors

2297 FS3, Inc.
    1201 Puerta del Sol, #314
    San Clemente, CA 92673
    Contact: Garrett Terlaak Principal
    Tel: 949-445-3734
    Email: garrett@fs3h.com
    Website: www.fs3h.com
Project Management, Construction Management, CPM Scheduling, Cost Estimating, Inspection, Constructibility Analysis, Risk Management (Hisp, estab 2011, empl 10, sales $1,200,000, cert: State)

2298 Health Education Services
    1000 Varian St, Ste A
    San Carlos, CA 94070
    Contact: Jenny Fernando
    Tel: 650-321-6500
    Email: jfernando@healtheducationservices.net
    Website: www.healtheducationservices.net
Health Education Services provides turnkey AED program implementation and management - sales, compliance, maintenance, database tracking, training. (Woman, estab 1979, empl 18, sales $900,000, cert: CPUC, WBENC)

2299 Heritage Global, Inc.
    230 N Maryland Ave, Ste 202
    Glendale, CA 91206
    Contact: Shawn Estep Dir, Business Devel
    Tel: 760-402-8688
    Email: shawn.estep@heritageglobal.com
    Website: www.heritageglobal.com
Commercial construction: new construction, renovation, retrofitting, mechanical, logistics, and HVAC services. (Nat-Ame, estab 2005, empl 15, sales $1,000,000, cert: NMSDC)

2300 Hollister Construction Company
    4065 E La Palma Ave Ste C
    Anaheim, CA 92807
    Contact: Holli Evelyn Carpenter President
    Tel: 714-632-1800
    Email: holli@hollico.net
    Website: www.hollico.net
General contracting, turn-key design & constuction services. (Woman, estab 1992, empl 12, sales $2,150,000, cert: CPUC, WBENC)

2301 Interior Plus, Inc.
    8620 Sorenson Ave, Ste 2
    Santa Fe Springs, CA 90670
    Contact: Stephen Muñoz President
    Tel: 562-464-6950
    Email:
    Website: www.interiorplusinc.us
General contracting, commercial & industrial interior construction & improvements, tenant improvements. (Hisp, estab 1992, empl 11, sales $2,261,918, cert: CPUC, 8(a))

2302 JOA Group
    260 Newport Center Dr Ste 100
    Newport Beach, CA 92660
    Contact: Scott Simpson Dir of Business Develop
    Tel: 949-251-0702
    Email: info@joagroup.com
    Website: www.joagroup.com
Program Management & Construction Management. (Hisp, estab 1996, empl 30, sales $6,099,191, cert: State, NMSDC, CPUC)

2303 KW Construction
    841 F St
    West Sacramento, CA 95605
    Contact: Dennis Horton Projects Est
    Tel: 916-372-8600
    Email: dhorton@kwc-usa.com
    Website: www.kwconstruction.us
General contracting: electric, plumbing, HVAC, painting, grading & paving, finish & rough carpentry. (Woman, estab 1989, empl 15, sales $4,072,182, cert: State)

2304 La Roza Construction, Inc.
    1181 Quarry Ln Ste 300
    Pleasanton, CA 94566
    Contact: Kelly Klein CEO
    Tel: 925-400-3772
    Email: Kelly@larozaconstruction.com
    Website: www.larozaconstruction.com
Commercial general contracting services. (Woman, estab 2002, empl 8, sales $4,600,000, cert: WBENC)

2305 Menco Pacific, Inc.
    15110 Keswick St.
    Van Nuys, CA 91405
    Contact: Jenna Lockstedt procurement Mgr
    Tel: 760-747-4405
    Email: jlockstedt@menco-pacific.com
    Website: www.menco-pacific.com
Construction services. (Hisp, estab 2007, empl 100, sales $20,500,000, cert: State, CPUC)

2306 MSH Construction Co., Inc.
    15301 Connector Lane
    Huntington Beach, CA 92649
    Contact: Lisa Moss President
    Tel: 714-899-9509
    Email: lmoss@mshconstruction.com
    Website: www.mshconstruction.com
General contractoring: tenant improvement & civil construction, concrete, demolition, grading & general maintanence labor. (Woman, estab 2003, empl 12, sales $6,679,909, cert: CPUC, WBENC)

2307 OST Trucks and Cranes, Inc.
    2951 N Ventura Ave
    Ventura, CA 93002
    Contact: L. Dennis Zermeno President
    Tel: 805-643-9963
    Email: ostcranes@aol.com
    Website: www.ostcranes.com
General & hazardous substance removal & remedial action, hydraulic cranes 5 to 140. (Hisp, estab 1947, empl 69, sales , cert: State, NMSDC, CPUC)

2308 Paradigm General Contractors
    1017 Macdonald Ave
    Richmond, CA 94801
    Contact: CEO
    Tel: 510-478-1121
    Email: KARLA@PARADIGMGC.COM
    Website: www.paradigmgc.com
General construction, construction mgmt svcs, tenant improvement & rennovation. (Woman, estab 1990, empl 17, sales , cert: WBENC)

CONSTRUCTION: General Contractors

2309 Petrochem Insulation, Inc.
2300 Clayton Road, Ste 1050
Concord, CA 94590
Contact: Ian Broste Business Devel Mgr
Tel: 707-644-7455
Email: ian.broste@petrocheminc.com
Website: www.petrocheminc.com
Insulation, Siding, Scaffolding, Fireproofing, Coatings & Linings, Removable Blankets, Tracing, and Lead & Asbestos Abatement. (Woman/Nat Ame, estab 1974, empl 900, sales $102,247,202, cert: NMSDC)

2310 ProWest Engineering, Inc.
1442 E Lincoln St Ste 360
Orange, CA 92865
Contact: Sherri Barrera Sales/Mktg Dir
Tel: 866-278-0572
Email: sherri@prowest-engineering.com
Website: www.prowest-engineering.com
General contracting, asphalt paving removal or maintainance, concrete repairs, seal/slurry coat, stenciling & re-striping & ADA compliant (Minority, Woman, estab 2005, empl 8, sales $1,500,000, cert: CPUC)

2311 Pub Construction, Inc.
23441 Golden Springs Dr, Ste 104
Diamond Bar, CA 91765
Contact: Chris Yi President
Tel: 909-455-0187
Email: pubconstruction@yahoo.com
Website: www.pubconstruction.com
General contracting services, building, carpet, flooring, tile, painting. (As-Pac, estab 2000, empl 13, sales $15,000,000, cert: NMSDC)

2312 Rock Industries Inc.
28338 Constellation Rd, Ste 206, Bldg. 900
Valencia, CA 93065
Contact: Russell Aboulafia Sales Tech
Tel: 661-257-2211
Email: raboulafia@rockconstruction.net
Website: www.buildwithrock.com
General Contractor, Electrical & Construction Supplies. (Hisp, estab 2004, empl 35, sales $18,000,000, cert: 8(a))

2313 Shames Construction Company, Ltd
5826 Brisa St, Ste E
Livermore, CA 94550
Contact: Carolyn Shames President
Tel: 925-606-3000
Email: cshames@shames.com
Website: www.shames.com
Commercial construction. (Woman, estab 1987, empl 48, sales $70,847,336, cert: CPUC)

2314 South City Construction Inc.
1111 Rancho Conejo Blvd Ste 205
Newbury Park, CA 91320
Contact: Andrew Solimine President
Tel: 805-376-2000
Email: a.solimine@southcityconstruction.com
Website: www.southcityconstruction.com
General contracting, construction management, program management, value engineering, scheduling, cost estimating. (Woman, estab 2011, empl 8, sales $100,000, cert: CPUC)

2315 The G Crew
225 E Broadway Ste 202
Glendale, CA 91205
Contact: Ella Daya VP
Tel: 818-240-4157
Email: info@thegcrew.com
Website: www.thegcrew.com
Inspection, Construction Management, & Project Support services (Minority, Woman, estab 2001, empl 9, sales , cert: CPUC)

2316 True Champions
5234 Cushman Pl, Ste 200
San Deigo, CA 92110
Contact: Kristi Vega Admin Mgr
Tel: 619-276-6999
Email: kristi@truechampions.net
Website: www.truechampions.net
General contracting, design build, concrete restoration/ protective coatings, waterproofing & commercial flooring. (Hisp, estab 1995, empl 23, sales , cert: State, CPUC)

2317 Vanir Construction Management, Inc.
4540 Duckhorn Dr, Ste 300
Sacramento, CA 95834
Contact: Dorene Dominguez Business Dev Dir
Tel: 916-575-8888
Email: melinda.guzman@vanir.com
Website: www.vanir.com
Construction management services. (Minority, Woman, estab 1980, empl 334, sales $129,308,942, cert: NMSDC, CPUC)

2318 WMB Financial Solutions
1999 Harrison St Ste 1800
Oakland, CA 94612
Contact: Franck Waota President
Tel: 510-210-8052
Email: fwaota@wmbgc.com
Website: www.wwww.wmbgc.com
General construction, tenant improvement & remodeling, design build, operation & maintenance real estate properties (Residential & commercial). (Woman/AA, estab 2004, empl 25, sales $3,700,000, cert: State, 8(a))

Colorado

2319 Alvarado Construction, Inc.
924 W Colfax Ave Ste 301
Denver, CO 80204
Contact: Jennifer Coons VP
Tel: 303-629-0783
Email: jcoons@alvaradoconstruction.com
Website: www.alvaradoconstruction.com
Commercial General Contracting, Construction Manager, Development, Design/Build & Property Management. (Woman/Hisp, estab 1976, empl 50, sales , cert: NMSDC, WBENC)

2320 B&M Construction, Inc.
3134 Beacon St
Colorado Springs, CO 80907
Contact: Barbara Myrick
Tel: 719-577-4550
Email: bmyrick@bmc-i.com
Website: www.bmc-i.com
Project Mgmt, Design-Build Services, Furniture Acquisition & Procurement, Electrical Design & Installation, Construction/Infrastructure, Tenant Finish/Renovation, Satellite Communications Repair & Overhaul. (Woman/ AA, estab 2005, empl 33, sales $13,000,000, cert: State, NMSDC, WBENC)

CONSTRUCTION: General Contractors

2321 Rhinotrax Construction, Inc.
1035 Coffman St
Longmont, CO 80501
Contact: Michele Noel President
Tel: 303-682-9906
Email: michelenoel@rhinotrax.com
Website: www.rhinotraxconstruction.com
General contracting: demolition, rough concrete, masonry, drywall & framing, doors & hardware, etc. (Woman, estab 2004, empl 12, sales $4,500,000, cert: City)

2322 Torix General Contractors a Tepa Company
5045 List Dr
Colorado Springs, CO 80919
Contact: Marvin Maples GM
Tel: 719-596-8114
Email: marvin.maples@tepa.com
Website: www.tepa.com
New construction & rennovations: design-build, general contracting & construction management. (Nat Ame, estab 1988, empl 180, sales $105,000,000, cert: NMSDC)

Connecticut

2323 Diggs Construction, LLC
1010 Wethersfield Ave Ste 201
Hartford, CT 06114
Contact: Derrick Diggs VP
Tel: 860-296-1664
Email: ddiggs@diggsconstruction.com
Website: www.diggsconstruction.com
Program Management, Construction Management, Contract Administration & General Contracting solutions. (AA, estab 1999, empl 35, sales $11,000,000, cert: State, NMSDC)

2324 TRI-CON Construction Managers, LLC
59 Amity Rd, Ste 11
New Haven, CT 06515
Contact: Larry Stewart Exec Project Mgr
Tel: 203-772-4229
Email: lmstewart@tri-con.org
Website: www.tri-con.org
Construction management, general contracting, project management, value engineering, contract administration, estimating,owners representation services. (AA, estab 2002, empl 11, sales , cert: State, NMSDC)

2325 West Reach Construction Company, Inc.
PO Box 1328
Manchester, CT 06045
Contact: Kerry Hainsey Owner
Tel: 860-649-7607
Email: westreachcon@wrconstruction.net
Website: www.westreachconstruction.com
General contracting, commercial, industrial construction. (Woman, estab 1987, empl 15, sales , cert: State, WBENC)

District of Columbia

2326 Columbia Enterprises
1018 7th St SE
Washington, DC 20003
Contact: President
Tel: 202-547-7979
Email:
Website: www.columbiadb.com
Construction management & general contracting services. (AA, estab 1993, empl 15, sales $5,200,000, cert: State, NMSDC)

2327 Drake Incorporated
4315 Sheriff Rd NE
Washington, DC 20019
Contact: Stephanie Y Drake CEO
Tel: 202-291-3174
Email: sdrake@drake-inc.com
Website: www.drake-inc.com
Construction, design / build & project management. (Woman/AA, estab 2002, empl 24, sales $7,088,479, cert: State)

2328 F&L Construction Inc.
2021 Martin Luther King Ave SE
Washington, DC 20020
Contact: Freddie Winston Estimator
Tel: 202-678-5788
Email: fwinston@falcinc.com
Website: www.falcinc.com
General construction services. (AA, estab 1991, empl 5, sales $1,350,000, cert: 8(a))

2329 Motir Services, Inc.
1508 E Capitol St, NE
Washington, DC 20003
Contact: Emmanuel Irono President
Tel: 202-371-9393
Email: eirono@motirservices.com
Website: www.motirservices.com
Industrial Building Construction, Commercial & Institutional Building, Office Moving/Relocation, Facilities Management, Janitorial Services. (Minority, estab 1994, empl 193, sales $17,635,639, cert: State, NMSDC, SDB)

2330 The ELOCEN Group
1341 H St, NE Ste 301
Washington, DC 20002
Contact: Taryn Lewis Dir of Operations
Tel: 202-644-8500
Email: tarynl@elocengroup.com
Website: www.elocengroup.com
Program & Project Management, Construction Management, Interior Design, Information Technology, Facilities/ Logistics, and Healthcare Facilities/Logistics/Management. (Woman/AA, estab 2007, empl 62, sales $20,089,894, cert: State, City, WBENC, 8(a))

Delaware

2331 M. Davis & Sons, Inc.
19 Germay Dr
Wilmington, DE 19804
Contact: Christina MacMillan VP Strategic Dev
Tel: 952-742-4096
Email: mdsregistrations@mdavisinc.com
Website: www.mdavisinc.com
Industrial construction company. (Woman, estab , empl 450, sales $82,717,195, cert: WBENC)

Florida

2332 Albu & Associates, Inc.
2711 W Fairbanks Ave
Winter Park, FL 32789
Contact: Jason Albu President
Tel: 407-788-1450
Email: jasonalbu@albu.biz
Website: www.albu.biz
General contracting, design build, construction management & consulting. (Hisp, estab 2001, empl 29, sales $37,809,180, cert: City, NMSDC)

CONSTRUCTION: General Contractors

2333 Arkren Inc.
6278 N Federal Hwy Ste 430
Fort Lauderdale, FL 33308
Contact: Mark Barati Sr VP
Tel: 954-210-8886
Email: mark@arkren.com
Website: www.arkren.com
Telecommunications, general construction(commercial and residential), design, Procurement, logistics, warehousing, transportation, temporary housing/life support, professional/craft labor, O&G/LNG. (Woman, estab 2013, empl 15, sales $960,000, cert: WBENC)

2334 Certified Constructors' Services Inc.
5330 Fairfield Dr
Crestview, FL 32536
Contact: Tommy Henderson Sr VP
Tel: 850-682-8953
Email: ccsithenderson@aol.com
Website: www.ccsipower.com
Provide onsite mechanical construction services for the Power Generating and General Industry. (Woman, estab 2004, empl 250, sales $42,000,000, cert: WBENC)

2335 Cortes Construction Services, LLC
720 Anclote Rd
Tarpon, FL 34689
Contact: Michael Corral VP
Tel: 727-937-4700
Email: mcorral@cortesconstruction.com
Website: www.cortesconstruction.com
Commercial construction company specializing in hotel renovations. (Hisp, estab 2004, empl 30, sales $5,178,771, cert: State)

2336 Dominion Builders, LLC
4942 S LeJeune Rd Ste 203
Coral Gables, FL 33146
Contact: Mark Gemignani President
Tel: 305-661-2700
Email: mgemignani@dominionbuild.com
Website: www.dominionbuild.com
General contracting services. (Nat Ame, estab 2008, empl 7, sales $5,000,000, cert: State, 8(a))

2337 Fine Line Construction contractors, Inc.
6500 Georgia Ave
Florida, FL 33405
Contact: Bob Waskiwicz VP
Tel: 561-582-7880
Email: bobw@finelinecontractors.com
Website: www.finelinecontractors.com
General contracting, commercial construction, commecial buildout, commercial renovations, interior remodel, building expansion, full buildout, interior improvements, warehouse expansion, warehouse renovations. (Woman, estab 2010, empl 15, sales $5,867,874, cert: WBENC)

2338 Hatcher Construction & Development, Inc.
3300 S Congress Ave Ste 15
Boynton Beach, FL 33426
Contact: William Hatcher
Tel: 561-752-4100
Email: hatchergc@bellsouth.net
Website: www.hatcher-construction.com
Commercial Institutional Bldg, General Contractor, Asphalt roofing, Asphalt Coating & Sealing, Concrete, Painting, spraying, or coating, Facilities Support Mgmt, Electrical, Residential Construction, multifamily, Landscaping. (AA, estab 1999, empl 7, sales $1,350,000, cert: State, 8(a))

2339 IBC, Inc. - International Builders & Consultants
5135 Starfish Ave
Naples, FL 34103
Contact: Brandy McCombs President
Tel: 816-220-0812
Email: brandy@ibcinc.biz
Website: www.IBCinc.biz
General contracting, install/repair drywall, cabinets, counter tops, doors, frames, hardware, paint and specailties. (Woman, estab 2008, empl 70, sales $12,500,000, cert: State, City)

2340 J & K Mechanical
2176 NW 82nd Ave
Miami, FL 33122
Contact: Jaime Monserrat VP
Tel: 305-278-7171
Email: jmonserrat@tropicac.com
Website: www.tropicmechanical.com
HVAC mechanical contractor, Engineering and design, New construction installation, Controls design, installation and programming. (Hisp, estab 2004, empl 56, sales $19,000,000, cert: State)

2341 J.L. Wallace, Inc.
9111 W College Pointe Dr
Fort Myers, FL 33919
Contact: Jerlad Wallace President
Tel: 239-437-1111
Email: info@jlwallaceinc.com
Website: www.jlwallaceinc.com
General Contractors/Construction Management. (Hisp, estab 1997, empl 18, sales $25,200,000, cert: NMSDC)

2342 JCQ Services, Inc
7200 Lake Ellenor Dr, Ste 130
Orlando, FL 32809
Contact: Eliana Fuguet Project Coord
Tel: 407-889-4944
Email: eliana@jcqservices.com
Website: www.jcqservices.com
Complete renovation subcontractor, flooring to ceiling & moving, storage & transportation & selective demolition. (Hisp, estab 2000, empl 25, sales $1,550,000, cert: State)

2343 LEGO Construction Co.
1011 Sunnybrook Rd Ste 905
Miami, FL 33136
Contact: Luis Garcia President
Tel: 305-381-8421
Email: lgarcia@legocc.com
Website: www.legocc.com
General Contractor. (Hisp, estab 2006, empl 40, sales $40,000,000, cert: State, SDB)

2344 Lemartec Corporation
11740 SW 80th St, 3rd Fl
Miami, FL 33183
Contact: Maira Suarez Mgr Strategic Partnerships
Tel: 305-273-8676
Email: cjaramillo@lemartec.com
Website: www.lemartec.com
EPC/EPCM, Design-Build, and Construction Management Firm. (Hisp, estab 1979, empl 88, sales $60,000,000, cert: NMSDC)

2345 Nakitare Builders LLC
      11806 Foxglove Dr
      Clermont, FL 34711
      Contact: Robert Mack GM
      Tel: 352-857-0000
      Email: buld2006@aol.com
      Website: www.sustainable-roofs.com
Construction services, inspections. (AA, estab 2006, empl 5, sales $390,000, cert: NMSDC)

2346 R L Burns Inc.
      1203 W Gore St
      Orlando, FL 32805
      Contact: Elizabeth Duncan
      Tel: 407-839-1131
      Email: eduncan@rlburnsinc.com
      Website: www.rlburnsinc.com
Construction management svcs: project management, consulting, cost estimating, pre-construction planning & design, schedule / CPM management, general construction, design/build, new construction, renovation. (AA, estab 1994, empl 9, sales $3,000,000, cert: City)

2347 Salomon Roofing & Construction
      689 W 26 St
      Hialeah, FL 33010
      Contact: Jared Susi President
      Tel: 305-883-1856
      Email: jared@salomonroofing.com
      Website: www.salomonroofing.com
New construction Roofing, re-roofing, repairs, and maintenance. Stucco, painting and waterproofing, window and door replacement, pavers, columns, interior partitions, and structural additions. (Hisp, estab 2000, empl 15, sales $4,300,000, cert: NMSDC)

2348 T&G Corporation
      8623 Commodity Circle
      Orlando, FL 32819
      Contact: Mark Knott Dir Business Devel
      Tel: 407-352-4443
      Email: officedepot@t-and-g.com
      Website: www.t-and-g.com
General contracting: facility operation/maintenance support services, commercial building, construction management & design-build services. (Hisp, estab 1987, empl 85, sales $23,214,524, cert: State, NMSDC)

2349 Thomco Enterprises Inc.
      745 Hollywood Blvd NW
      Fort Walton Beach, FL 32548
      Contact: Darryl Embrey President
      Tel: 850-244-0811
      Email: darryle@thomcoent.com
      Website: www.thomcoent.com
Construction, construction management, facility maintenance, renovations, upgrades, vertical construction, bank facility construction, commercial & government construction, development, project management. (AA, estab 1993, empl 35, sales $11,245,342, cert: State)

2350 Thornton Construction Company, Inc.
      13290 NW 42nd Ave
      Miami, FL 33054
      Contact: Nataly Guevara Business Devel Mgr
      Tel: 305-649-1995
      Email: nguevara@thornton-inc.com
      Website: www.thornton-inc.com
Contracting and construction management firm. (Hisp, estab 1998, empl 55, sales $55,978,278, cert: State)

2351 Validus Construction Services LLC
      7130 S Orange Blossom Trail Ste 111
      Orlando, FL 32809
      Contact: Nicole Wickens Owner
      Tel: 407-413-5022
      Email: validuscs@gmail.com
      Website: www.validuscs.net
New construction, remodel, remediation, design-build, renovation, office renovations, warehouse renovations, landscaping, parking lot, sidewalks, windows, doors, flooring, interiors, exteriors, HVAC, plumbing, electrical. (Woman, estab 2012, empl 9, sales $5,337,114, cert: WBENC)

2352 Veatic dba of Proxy Management Group
      2450 Smith St, Ste P
      Kissimmee, FL 34744
      Contact: Jon Andreasson Project Dev
      Tel: 888-474-2999
      Email: jandreasson@veatic.com
      Website: www.veatic.com
General Contractor, Site Development, Excavation, Retention, Disaster Response, Grading, Foundations, Underground Utilities, Demolition, Site Restoration, New Building Construction. (Hisp, estab 2008, empl 32, sales $3,801,885, cert: State, City, NMSDC)

Georgia

2353 5 Seasons Mechanical
      6971 Peachtree Industrial Blvd
      Peachtree Corners, GA 30092
      Contact: Adam Soyah CEO
      Tel: 770-727-5000
      Email: adam@fiveseasonsmechanical.com
      Website: www.5seasonsmechanical.com
Heating & Air Conditioning Service, Mechanical Design & Build Services, Indoor Air Quality Services. (AA, estab , empl , sales $5,500,000, cert: NMSDC)

2354 Bryson Constructors, Inc.
      2847 Main St, Ste 200
      East Point, GA 30344
      Contact: Steve Barnes CEO
      Tel: 404-762-1000
      Email: sbarnes@brysonconstructors.com
      Website: www.brysonconstructors.com
Design/build commercial construction. (AA, estab , empl , sales $7,351,431, cert: NMSDC)

2355 Colliers Facility Solutions, LLC
      1230 Peachtree St Ste 800
      Atlanta, GA 30309
      Contact: Holly Hughes CEO
      Tel: 404-574-1014
      Email: holly.hughes@colliers.com
      Website: www.colliers.com/atlanta
Facility management, project management, construction management, interior, exterior & maintenance, energy efficiency, systems optimization, risk mitigation & cost savings. (Woman, estab 2014, empl 160, sales $19,500,000, cert: WBENC)

2356　Pinnacle Services Group, Inc.
　　　10270 Oxford Mill Circle
　　　Alpharetta, GA 30022
　　　Contact: Jerry Peljovich President
　　　Tel:　770-355-7156
　　　Email: jerryp@psginc-ga.com
　　　Website: www.PSGinc-ga.com
General contracting. (Hisp, estab 2004, empl 5, sales $3,207,000, cert: State, City, NMSDC)

2357　Pioneer Construction, Inc.
　　　31 Park of Commerce Way Ste 100
　　　Savannah, GA 31405
　　　Contact: Whitney Butler Dir Mktg
　　　Tel:　912-650-1850
　　　Email: wbutler@pioneersavannah.com
　　　Website: www.pioneersavannah.com
General Contractors specializing in commercial construction. (Minority, Woman, estab 1994, empl 20, sales $10,000,000, cert: State)

2358　Quantum Installation Group
　　　889 Franklin Gateway, Ste 100
　　　Marietta, GA 30067
　　　Contact: Bob Turner VP Business Dev
　　　Tel:　706-506-2262
　　　Email: bob.turner@quantuminstall.com
　　　Website: www.quantuminstall.com
General construction contractor, millwork, fixture & decor installation contractor. (Woman/As-Pac, estab 2012, empl 150, sales , cert: NMSDC, WBENC)

2359　Synergy Development Partners, LLC
　　　83 Walton St, NW Ste 400
　　　Atlanta, GA 30303
　　　Contact: Brittany Montgomery Operations Mgr
　　　Tel:　404-254-4755
　　　Email: bmontgomery@synergydp.com
　　　Website: www.synergydp.com
General contracting, construction management, drywall, framing, renovation, restoration, roof repair, carpentry, flooring, paint, trim, tentant build-out & new construction. (Woman/AA, estab 2003, empl 15, sales $3,568,712, cert: City, NMSDC)

2360　The Chester Group, Inc.
　　　231 Peters St SW
　　　Atlanta, GA 30313
　　　Contact: Wallace Chester President
　　　Tel:　786-586-3941
　　　Email: wchester@thechestergroup.com
　　　Website: www.thechestergroup.com
General contracting & construction mgmt: renovation; design/build; maintenance; roofing; concrete placement; debris removal; fencing; asphalt resurfacing; masonry; interior build-out; windows; doors; painting; flooring; electrical. (AA, estab 2002, empl 1, sales $100,000, cert: State)

2361　Time Out Systems, Inc.
　　　308 Indian Creek Circle
　　　Adel, GA 31620
　　　Contact: Tim LeBlanc CFO
　　　Tel:　229-896-6190
　　　Email: admin@timeoutsystems.com
　　　Website: www.timeoutsystems.com
General Construction, Remolding, Roofing, Painting, Security, Surround Sound, Home Automation, Yard Maintenance, Door and Window Replacement, Blind Installation, Deck Construction. (Woman, estab 1991, empl 150, sales $13,000,000, cert: WBENC)

Hawaii

2362　Arita-Poulson General Contracting, LLC
　　　PO Box 1035
　　　Puunene, HI 96784
　　　Contact: John Evarts Sr Project Engineer
　　　Tel:　808-871-4787
　　　Email: jevarts@aritapoulson.com
　　　Website: www.aritapoulson.com
General Contracting. (As-Pac, estab 1986, empl 62, sales $50,000,000, cert: NMSDC)

Iowa

2363　Gethmann Construction Company, Inc.
　　　PO Box 160
　　　Marshalltown, IA 50158
　　　Contact: Jill Craft President
　　　Tel:　641-753-3555
　　　Email: jill@gethmann.com
　　　Website: www.gethmannconstruction.com
Concrete work, excavation, backfill, foundations, slabs, pads, elevated slabs, concrete demo, structural steel fab, crane rental & operators. (Woman, estab 1937, empl 67, sales $22,000,000, cert: WBENC)

Illinois

2364　A.M.C. Mechanical, Inc.
　　　11535 W 183rd Place Unit 106
　　　Orland Park, IL 60467
　　　Contact: Anthony Lopez VP
　　　Tel:　708-479-4678
　　　Email: tony@amc-mechanical.com
　　　Website: www.amc-mechanical.com
Mechanical contractor, commerical & industridal HVAC, boiler, power burners, process piping, refrigeration & controls. (Woman/Hisp, estab 2000, empl 11, sales $1,661,143, cert: State, City)

2365　Continental Painting and Decorating
　　　2255 S Wabash Ave
　　　Chicago, IL 60616
　　　Contact: Constance Williams President
　　　Tel:　312-225-6100
　　　Email: cwilliams@continentalpainting.com
　　　Website: www.continentalpainting.com
Painting, wallcovering, wood refinishing, drywall taping. (AA, estab 1994, empl 68, sales $11,700,000, cert: State, City, NMSDC)

2366　Cotter Consulting, Inc.
　　　100 S Wacker Dr Ste 920
　　　Chicago, IL 60606
　　　Contact: Anne Edwards-Cotter President
　　　Tel:　131-269-6120
　　　Email: a.cotter@cotterconsulting.com
　　　Website: www.cotterconsulting.com
Construction program & project management services. (Woman, estab 1990, empl 100, sales $18,650,000, cert: State, WBENC)

CONSTRUCTION: General Contractors

2367 CREA Construction
161 N Clark, Ste 4700
Chicago, IL 60601
Contact: Rea Johnson President
Tel: 312-371-3827
Email: rea1_23@yahoo.com
Website: www.creagc.com
Construction management, general contracting, estimating & engineering services. (Woman/AA, estab 2007, empl 10, sales $1,000,000, cert: State, NMSDC)

2368 GACC Video Electronics Inc.
700 Nicholas Blvd Ste 103
Elk Grove Village, IL 60007
Contact: Jennifer Chang Secretary
Tel: 312-733-5774
Email: jennifer@gaccvideo.com
Website: www.gaccvideo.com
(Minority, Woman, estab 2000, empl 3, sales $450,000, cert: City)

2369 Integrated Construction Technology Corp.
126 S Villa Ave
Villa Park, IL 60181
Contact: Les Shy President
Tel: 630-993-1800
Email: lshy@integratedusa.com
Website: www.integratedusa.com
Design & build construction, general contracting, property managment, supplies & services. (AA, As-Pac, estab 1994, empl 30, sales $18,000,000, cert: City)

2370 LiveWire Electrical Systems, Inc.
12900 S. Throop St
Calumet Park, IL 60827
Contact: Angela Drexel VP
Tel: 708-535-6001
Email: adrexel@livewire-systems.com
Website: www.livewire-systems.com
New Construction & renovations, phase electrical systems, Switchgear, Back up generators, Power systems for process/production. (AA, estab 2006, empl 65, sales $23,046,514, cert: State, NMSDC)

2371 Maman Corp.
346 W Colfax
Palatine, IL 60067
Contact: Rodney Pace Dir of Operations
Tel: 847-358-2688
Email: megan@maman-corp.com
Website: www.maman-corp.com
General contractors, commercial construction, project management. (Woman, estab 1997, empl 18, sales , cert: WBENC)

2372 Otis Construction Company
111 W Jackson Blvd Ste 1105
Chicago, IL 60604
Contact: Glenn Otis, Jr. President
Tel: 312-786-9877
Email: gotis@otiscc.com
Website: www.otiscc.com
Construction svcs: interior building alterations, commercial & industrial facilities, green construction & maintenance, specialty projects, facilities maintenance, emergency repairs. (AA, estab 1999, empl 4, sales $1,500,000, cert: NMSDC)

2373 Sumac Inc.
3701 N Ravenswood Ave Ste 202
Chicago, IL 60613
Contact: Liliana Gonzalez VP
Tel: 773-857-7906
Email: lgonzalez@sumacinc.com
Website: www.sumacinc.com
Architecture & construction management: architectural design, sustainable design, project scheduling, cost estimating, construction procurement, construction management services & general contracting. (Hisp, estab 2008, empl 10, sales $2,000,000, cert: NMSDC)

2374 The Landmark Group Companies LLC
6735 Vistagreen Way Ste 100
Rockford, IL 61107
Contact: Bob Sanches CEO
Tel: 815-639-0034
Email: bsanches@lmcos.com
Website: www.lmcos.com
Construction management of new & existing facilities. (Hisp, estab 2006, empl 8, sales $30,000,000, cert: NMSDC)

2375 Trinidad Construction, LLC
9850 190th St Ste N
Mokena, IL 60448
Contact: Brian Ortiz President
Tel: 773-429-4600
Email: bortiz@trinidadllc.com
Website: www.trinidadllc.com
General contracting, construction management. (Hisp, estab 2010, empl 75, sales $25,000,000, cert: NMSDC)

2376 Vistara Construction Services, Inc.
728 W Jackson Blvd, Ste 402
Chicago, IL 60661
Contact: Bina Nair President
Tel: 312-986-8660
Email: info@vistara.com
Website: www.vistara.com
General construction. (Woman/As-Ind, estab 1994, empl 10, sales , cert: City)

Indiana

2377 A & M Door, Inc.
5508 Elmwood Ave, Ste 303
Indianapolis, IN 46203
Contact: Bill Herron VP sales
Tel: 317-222-5897
Email: sales@aandmdoor.com
Website: www.aandmdoor.com
Furnish, install & service automatic doors. (Woman, estab 2006, empl 4, sales $443,000, cert: State)

2378 Custom Mechanical Systems, Corp.
691 Industrial Blvd
Bargersville, IN 46106
Contact: William Beach VP Business Dev
Tel: 617-803-0714
Email: wbeach@cms-corporation.com
Website: www.cms-corporation.com
New construction, renovations, energy & sustainability, building operations maintenance & repairs. (Hisp, estab 1996, empl 110, sales $42,753,323, cert: State, NMSDC)

CONSTRUCTION: General Contractors

2379 Finch Constructors, Inc.
5528 W 84th St
Indianapolis, IN 46268
Contact: Tammy Brooks Operations Mgr
Tel: 317-916-6770
Email: tbrooks@finchconstructors.com
Website: www.finchconstructors.com
Industrial, commercial & municipal construction & management services: mechanical piping, equipment erection, HVAC & electrical services. (AA, estab 2004, empl 42, sales $20,000,000, cert: NMSDC)

2380 Harmon Construction, Inc.
621 S State St
North Vernon, IN 47265
Contact: Ardell Mitchell Sr Project Mgr/Estimator
Tel: 812-346-2048
Email: ardell.mitchell@harmonconstruction.com
Website: www.harmonconstruction.com
Contracting, design-build capabilities. (AA, estab 1955, empl 81, sales $8,478,000, cert: State, NMSDC)

2381 K&S Construction Group, Inc.
9148 Louisiana St, Unit F
Merrillville, IN 46410
Contact: Vance R. Kenney CEO
Tel: 219-794-9550
Email: vkenney@k-sconstruction.com
Website: www.k-sconstruction.com
Heavy construction, construction mgmt, demolition, design build, excavation, reinforced concrete, concrete forming, sidewalk, curb, crushed granite, levees, revetments, carpentry, railroad construction, fencing, environmental. (AA, estab 1992, empl 25, sales $3,200,000, cert: State, NMSDC)

2382 Powers & Sons Construction Co, Inc.
2636 W 15th Ave
Gary, IN 46404
Contact: Kelly Powers Baria Dir Business Dev
Tel: 219-949-3100
Email: kbaria@powersandsons.com
Website: www.powersandsons.com
Construction services. (AA, estab 1967, empl , sales $30,390,330, cert: State, NMSDC)

2383 Shawnee Construction and Engineering
7701 Opportunity Dr
Fort Wayne, IN 46825
Contact: Matt Schenkel President
Tel: 260-489-1234
Email: matt@shawneeconstruction.com
Website: www.ShawneeConstruction.com
General contracting, new construction & remodeling, commercial & industrial. (Hisp, estab 1968, empl 42, sales $17,300,000, cert: State, City)

Kentucky

2384 AAECON General Contractors, LLC.
1147 Logan St
Louisville, KY 40204
Contact: Troy Ansert VP
Tel: 502-291-3976
Email: tansert@aacongc.com
Website: www.aacongc.com
Design/build, construction management & general construction. (AA, estab 2005, empl 33, sales , cert: NMSDC, 8(a))

Louisiana

2385 Lafayette Steel Erector
313 Westgate Rd
Lafayette, LA 70506
Contact: John Prudhomme President
Tel: - -
Email: janice@l-s-e.com
Website: www.LSEcrane.com
Crane, steel erection, precast erectors, equipment installation. (Nat Ame, estab 1957, empl 115, sales , cert: NMSDC)

Massachusetts

2386 Chicopee Industrial Contractors
107 N Chicopee St
Chicopee, MA 01020
Contact: Carol Campbell President
Tel: 413-538-7279
Email:
Website: www.chicopeeindustrial.com
Rigging, millwrighting, heavy equipment hauling, plant relocation, concrete, foundations, pre-fab building erection, demolition, welding, fabrication. (Woman, estab 1992, empl 20, sales $1,725,000, cert: WBENC)

2387 Essex Newbury North Contracting Corporation
65 Parker St, Unit 5
Newburyport, MA 01950
Contact: Delano Brooks President
Tel: 978-463-5414
Email: delano_br@yahoo.com
Website: www.essexnewburynorth.com
General Contracting, construction management, commercial & industrial construction, lead abatement & asbestos remediation, finish carpentry, commercial & institutional bldg construction, painting & wall coverings, site preparation. (AA, estab 1997, empl 400, sales $31,000,000, cert: State, City, NMSDC)

2388 General Air Conditioning and Heating Inc.
7 Gaston St
Dorchester, MA 02121
Contact: Felicia Pinckney Dir Business Dev
Tel: 617-427-7370
Email: FELICIA@GENERAL-AIR.NET
Website: www.genairheat.net
Mechanical Contractors, Heating, Air Conditioning, Plumbing, Refrigeration and Energy. (AA, estab 1985, empl 50, sales $29,000,000, cert: City)

2389 J&J Contractors, Inc.
101 Billerica Ave Bldg 5 Ste 2
North Billerica, MA 01862
Contact: Kamlesh Patel CEO
Tel: 978-452-9898
Email: kamp@jjcontractor.com
Website: www.jjcontractor.com
Construction management, general contracting & design/build. (As-Ind, estab 1997, empl 50, sales , cert: State)

CONSTRUCTION: General Contractors

Maryland

2390 Buch Construction Inc.
      11292 Buch Way
      Laurel, MD 20723
      Contact: Denise Buch Controller
      Tel: 301-369-3500
      Email: dbuch@buch.us.com
      Website: www.buchconstruction.com
General contracting, interior construction, carpentry, drywall, electric, painting, new construction, doors & hardware, structural steel. (Woman, estab 1984, empl 65, sales $6,210,000, cert: WBENC)

2391 Capital Brand Group, LLC
      12501 Prosperity Dr, Ste 400
      Silver Spring, MD 20904
      Contact: Max Brand President
      Tel: 301-358-1377
      Email: mbrand@capitalbrandgroup.com
      Website: www.capitalbrandgroup.com
Construction, Construction Management, A/E Services, Facility Management, Janitorial, Energy and Sustainability, landscaping, HVAC and Construction Services. (Hisp, estab 2013, empl 30, sales $3,512,178, cert: State, 8(a))

2392 Estime Enterprises, Inc.
      4640 Forbes Blvd Ste 100
      Lanham, MD 20706
      Contact: Lunique Estime President
      Tel: 301-731-8316
      Email: lestime@estimeinc.com
      Website: www.estimeinc.com
Construction management, renovation, environmental consulting services, green sustainable solutions (wind power generation, solar harvesting, triban antimicrobial systems, and photovoltaic roofing solutions). (AA, estab 1996, empl 35, sales $4,296,512, cert: State, NMSDC)

Michigan

2393 3LK Construction, LLC
      18401 S Weaver
      Detroit, MI 48228
      Contact: Lorenzo Walker President
      Tel: 313-493-9101
      Email: lorenzo@3lkconstruction.com
      Website: www.3lkconstruction.com
General Contracting, Construction Management, Painting, Special Coating & Wall Coverings. (AA, estab 1998, empl 20, sales $2,203,000, cert: NMSDC)

2394 Advanced Underground Inspection, LLC
      38657 Webb Dr
      Westland, MI 48185
      Contact: Jeana Moir Owner
      Tel: 734-721-0081
      Email: sheila_aui@yahoo.com
      Website: www.auinspection.com
Pipeline Rehabilitation/Sewer Repair, TV/Video Inspeciton, Drain/Sewer Cleaing, Mandreling/Grouting, Manhole Rehabilitation, High Pressure Waterblasting, Air Testing/Pipe Deflection, Industrial Services, Sewer Lining. (Woman/Hisp, estab 2001, empl 10, sales , cert: NMSDC, WBENC)

2395 Associated Design & Services, Inc.
      1177 Wadhams Rd, Bldg E
      Smiths Creek, MI 48074
      Contact: Mary Insley President
      Tel: 810-650-2809
      Email: minsley1@advnet.net
      Website: www.ads800callus.com/
Commercial Industrial & Structural Maintenance and Repairs, Millwrighting, Rotating Equipment and Mechanical Services. (Woman, estab 2003, empl 7, sales $831,602, cert: WBENC)

2396 Blaze Contracting, Inc.
      5640 St. Jean
      Detroit, MI 48213
      Contact: Gayl Turk Dir Business Dev
      Tel: 313-361-1000
      Email: gturk@blazecontracting.net
      Website: www.blazecontracting.com
Site Preparation Contractor; Excavation, Grading, Storm Sewer, Sanitary Sewer, Watermain, Water Detention Systems; (AA, estab 2000, empl 120, sales $19,000,000, cert: NMSDC)

2397 Commercial Construction Inc.
      7428 Kensington Rd
      Brighton, MI 48116
      Contact: ROBERT L. GARCIA President
      Tel: 248-685-3263
      Email: pgarcia@cci-rigging.com
      Website: www.cci-rigging.com
Millwright & migging contractor, install machinery, conveyors, robots, automation for automotive industry, industrial process. (Hisp, estab 1991, empl 40, sales $3,100,000, cert: NMSDC)

2398 Hale Contracting, Inc.
      18407 Weaver St
      Detroit, MI 48228
      Contact: Lawrence Hale President
      Tel: 313-272-9400
      Email: lawrence.hale@halecontracting.com
      Website: www.Halecontracting.com
General contracting. (AA, estab 0, empl , sales , cert: NMSDC)

2399 Hamilton Contracting
      30375 Northwestern Hwy Ste 102
      Farmington Hills, MI 48334
      Contact: Melissa Grundy Business Devel Exec
      Tel: 734-895-3547
      Email: mgrundy@hamilton-contracting.com
      Website: www.hamilton-contracting.com
General contracting: demolition, machinery installation & relocation, conveyor installation, structural installation, platform installation, automation installation, preventative maintenance & machine precision alignments. (Woman, estab 2011, empl 45, sales $5,400,000, cert: WBENC)

2400 Harris Design & Construction Services
      2512 W Grand Blvd, Ste 100
      Detroit, MI 48208
      Contact: Karl Harris CEO
      Tel: 313-444-3307
      Email: kharris@harrisdesignconstruction.com
      Website: www.harrisdesignconstruction.com
Architectural design & construction services. (AA, estab 2014, empl 1, sales $100,000, cert: NMSDC)

CONSTRUCTION: General Contractors

2401 Ideal Contracting, LLC
2525 Clark St
Detroit, MI 48209
Contact: Kevin Foucher VP
Tel: 313-843-8000
Email: kfoucher@idealcontracting.com
Website: www.idealcontracting.com
General contracting, construction management & design/build services. (Hisp, estab 1998, empl 325, sales $191,613,602, cert: NMSDC)

2402 Jenkins Construction, Inc.
985 E Jefferson, Ste 300
Detroit, MI 48207
Contact: Darwyn Parks Project Exec
Tel: 313-625-7200
Email: dparks@jenkinsconstruction.com
Website: www.jenkinsconstruction.com
Design/build, construction management, general contractor & excavation. (AA, estab 1989, empl 50, sales $65,000,000, cert: NMSDC)

2403 Optimum Contracting Solutions
2211 Devonshire Rd
Bloomfield Hills, MI 48302
Contact: Anamaria Tet Owner
Tel: 248-346-3069
Email: anamaria.optimum@att.net
Website: www.optimum1.net
General Contracting, Project Management, Residential Building & Remodeling Services, Commercial Remodeling Services, Roofing, Siding, Additions, Drywall, Rough and Finish Carpentry, Painting, Electrical, HVAC, Doors & window installation. (Woman, estab 2010, empl 10, sales $400,000, cert: WBENC)

2404 PAT USA, Inc.
2927 Waterview Dr
Rochester Hills, MI 48309
Contact: Fenar Mayes Sr Project Mgr
Tel: 248-299-2410
Email: fenar@pat-engineering.com
Website: www.pat-engineering.com
General contracting services, engineering & construction services. (Woman, estab 2011, empl 10, sales , cert: WBENC)

2405 Powerlink Electrical
217 Fisher Building
Detroit, MI 48202
Contact: Sherwood Merrill Chairman
Tel: 313-309-2020
Email: smerrill@powerlinkonline.com
Website: www.powerlinkonline.com
Facilities management, maintenance services, & construction. (AA, estab 2002, empl 350, sales $15,900,000, cert: NMSDC)

2406 R.B. Construction Company
6489 Metro Pkwy
Sterling Heights, MI 48312
Contact: Russell Beaver President
Tel: 586-264-9478
Email: rbeaver@rb-construction.com
Website: www.rb-construction.com
Construction, renovation, building, pre-engineered building, remodel. (Nat Ame, estab 1984, empl 7, sales $3,318,000, cert: NMSDC, 8(a))

2407 Rickman Enterprise Group, LLC
15533 Woodrow Wilson
Detroit, MI 48238
Contact: Lawrence Bost CEO
Tel: 313-454-4000
Email: lawrence@rickmanenterprise.com
Website: www.rickmanenterprise.com
Industrial Painting/Environmental, Flooring, Demo. (AA, estab 2007, empl 131, sales $10,000,000, cert: NMSDC)

2408 Sieler Construction
11119 E US 223
Blissfield, MI 49228
Contact: Jeff Sieler VP
Tel: 517-486-3050
Email: lue@sielerconstruction.com
Website: www.sielerconstruction.com
General Contracting, excavation, concrete, steel trades, steel fabrication, holding tanks, shut-down / machinery relocation, water & fire main repairs, water lines. (Woman, estab 2000, empl 12, sales , cert: WBENC)

2409 Stenco Construction Company, LLC
12741 Farmington Rd
Livonia, MI 48150
Contact: Nick Schallmo General Mgr
Tel: 734-427-8843
Email: nschallmo@stencoconstruction.com
Website: www.stencoconstruction.com
General contruction: interior finish, earthwork, concrete, steel & rigging projects. (As-Pac, estab 1998, empl 75, sales $33,650,000, cert: NMSDC)

2410 The Ideal Group
2525 Clark St
Detroit, MI 48209
Contact: Linzie Venegas Sales
Tel: 313-842-7290
Email: linzie@idealshield.com
Website: www.weareideal.com
Architectural & engineering svcs; general contracting & construction mgmt, rigging. Mfr, dist, fabricate & erect structural & misc steel. Patent for "Ideal Shield" Protective Guard Rail System. (Hisp, estab 1979, empl 120, sales , cert: NMSDC)

2411 Tooles Contracting Group LLC
500 Griswold St, Ste 1620
Detroit, MI 48226
Contact: Laura Ottman Mgr Business Devel
Tel: 313-221-8500
Email: laura.ottman@toolesgroup.com
Website: www.toolesgroup.com
Commercial & industrial construction, general contracting, construction & pogram management, equipment installation, self perform services & design build. (AA, estab 2002, empl 38, sales $119,996,211, cert: NMSDC)

2412 W-3 Construction Company
7601 Second Ave
Detroit, MI 48202
Contact: Walter E. Watson, Jr. CEO
Tel: 313-875-8000
Email: w3@w3group.net
Website: www.w3group.net
General contracting, project managers, self perform concrete, drywall & accoustical. (AA, estab 1987, empl 49, sales $19,950,000, cert: NMSDC)

2413 Zebing Solutions LLC
15617 Marksman Rd
Lanse, MI 49946
Contact: Arlan Friisvall President
Tel: 877-585-8171
Email: info@zebingsolutions.com
Website: www.zebingsolutions.com
Construction, electrical, mechanical & engineering services. (Nat Ame, estab 2011, empl 20, sales $500,000, cert: NMSDC)

Minnesota

2414 Air Corps Mechanical
13821 Industrial Park Blvd
Plymouth, MN 55441
Contact: Maggy Kottman President
Tel: 651-789-5400
Email: mkottman@aircorpmechanical.com
Website: www.aircorpmechanical.com
Design, installation, service commercial HVAC. (Woman, estab 1985, empl 22, sales $4,797,000, cert: WBENC)

2415 Go Fetsch Mechanical LLC
25884 Quail Ridge Trail
Lindstrom, MN 55045
Contact: Nikki Fetsch President
Tel: 763-432-2291
Email: nikki@gofetsch.com
Website: www.gofetsch.com
Commercial & residential heating & air conditioning. (Woman/Nat-Ame, estab 2004, empl 4, sales $480,000, cert: NMSDC)

2416 Loeffler Construction and Consulting, LLC
20520 Keokuk Ave, Ste 100
Lakeville, MN 55044
Contact: Doug Loeffler President
Tel: 952-955-9119
Email: dloeffler@loefflerconstruction.com
Website: www.loefflerconstruction.com
Construction and consulting services, new construction & remodeling projects. (Minority, Woman, estab 2010, empl 6, sales $21,922,187, cert: NMSDC)

2417 Meyer Contracting Inc.
11000 93rd Ave N
Minneapolis, MN 55369
Contact: Scott Kerzman CEO
Tel: 763-391-5959
Email: skerzman@meyercontractinginc.com
Website: www.meyercontractinginc.com
Water & sewer line construction, highway, street & bridge construction, site preparation, commercial & institutional building. (Minority, Woman, estab 1987, empl 41, sales $69,786,884, cert: NMSDC)

2418 Moltron Builders Inc.
2900 North 2nd St
Minneapolis, MN 55411
Contact: Patrick Buckner President
Tel: 612-354-2730
Email: patrick.buckner@moltronbuilders.com
Website: www.moltronbuilders.com
General Construction, Construction Management & Design Build. (AA, estab 2007, empl 5, sales , cert: State, City)

2419 Shaw-Lundquist Associates, Inc.
2757 W Service Rd
St. Paul, MN 55121
Contact: Hoyt Hsiao CEO
Tel: 651-454-0670
Email: hhsiao@shawlundquist.com
Website: www.shawlundquist.com
General construction & mgmt: commercial, industrial & institutional, multi-unit residential, tenant improvements, contract service work, etc. (As-Pac, estab 1974, empl 98, sales $185,879,100, cert: NMSDC)

2420 Shingobee Builders, Inc.
669 N Medina St
Loretto, MN 55357
Contact: Mike Melton President
Tel: 763-479-1300
Email: mmelton@shingobee.com
Website: www.shingobee.com
General construction. (Minority, Woman, estab 1980, empl 55, sales $49,882,025, cert: WBENC)

2421 Total Construction and Equipment, Inc.
10195 Inver Grove Trail
Inver Grove Heights, MN 55076
Contact: William Krech VP
Tel: 651-451-1384
Email: info@total-const.com
Website: www.total-const.com
General and electrical contracting, large facility maintenance. (Woman, estab 1972, empl 350, sales $53,000,000, cert: WBENC)

2422 Welsh Construction, LLC
4350 Baker Rd Ste 400
Minnetonka, MN 55343
Contact: Linda Solberg Corporate Services Dir
Tel: 952-897-7854
Email: lsolberg@welshco.com
Website: www.welshconstruct.com
General contracting, commercial new construction, office & industrial, expansions & renovations of existing office & industrial space. (Woman, estab 1977, empl 43, sales $73,308,502, cert: WBENC)

Missouri

2423 Amodu Engineering Solutions, LLC
1201 Garden Village Dr
Florissant, MO 63031
Contact: Anthony Osuma President
Tel: 314-249-8623
Email: aosuma@amodu-engineering.com
Website: www.amodu-engineering.com
Mechanical design & consulting services, electrical plumbing & fire protection systems, construction admin services. (AA, estab 2007, empl 5, sales $100,000, cert: State, City, NMSDC)

2424 Legacy Building Group
3242 S. KingsHwy
Saint Louis, MO 63139
Contact: Todd Weaver President
Tel: 314-361-3535
Email: weavert@legacybg.com
Website: www.legacybg.com
Doors & frames installation & concrete footings & foundations. (AA, estab 2003, empl 20, sales $7,123,000, cert: State, City, NMSDC)

CONSTRUCTION: General Contractors

2425 Mark One
      909 Troost
      Kansas City, MO 64106
      Contact: Rosana Privitera Biondo President
      Tel: 816-842-7023
      Email: rosana.priviterabiondo@markone.com
      Website: www.markone.com
General Electrical Construction, Fire Alarm, Security, CCTV, Utilities, Lighting, Electrical Engineering, Specialty Electrical Construction. (Woman, estab 1974, empl 250, sales $40,000,000, cert: State, WBENC)

2426 Pro Circuit, Inc.
      4925 Deramus Ave
      Kansas City, MO 64120
      Contact: Monica Bury President
      Tel: 816-474-9292
      Email: monicabury@procircuitinc.com
      Website: www.procircuitinc.com
Electrical, low voltage, Construction, design build, Service, industial, commercial, cabling, wiring, Motor control, panels, IR Scan, Power quality, Arc flash, data cabling, fiber, fire alarm, security, paging, water, wastewater, PLC, Controls. (Woman, estab 1993, empl 100, sales $17,706,683, cert: State, City, WBENC)

2427 Schweiger Construction Company
      8300 Troost Ave
      Kansas City, MO 64131
      Contact: Denise Holt VP
      Tel: 816-523-5875
      Email: dholt@schweigercc.com
      Website: www.schweigercc.com
General building construction & construction mgmt: critical facilities, office structures, food service facilities, new build, expansion, renovation. (Woman, estab , empl 50, sales $19,000,000, cert: WBENC)

2428 Tarlton Corporation
      5500 W Park Ave
      St. Louis, MO 63110
      Contact: Ted Guhr Dir Business Devel
      Tel: 314-633-3354
      Email: taguhr@tarltoncorp.com
      Website: www.tarltoncorp.com
General contracting & construction management. (Woman, estab 1945, empl , sales $207,000,000, cert: State, WBENC)

North Carolina

2429 Golden Sands General Contractors
      10924 Granite St, Ste 700
      Charlotte, NC 28273
      Contact: Jody Pinkston Project Coord
      Tel: 704-727-6000
      Email: jody.pinkston@goldensandsgc.com
      Website: www.goldensandsgc.com
Design/Build, New Construction, Tenant Improvements, Major & Minor Renovations, Dedicated Facilities Maintenance Department, Dedicated Disaster Recovery Department. (Woman, estab 1988, empl 167, sales $62,000,000, cert: WBENC)

2430 Holt Brothers Construction LLC
      421 Fayetteville St Stes 1300
      Raleigh, NC 27601
      Contact: Terrence Holt President
      Tel: 919-787-1981
      Email: terrence@holtbrothersinc.com
      Website: www.holtbrothersconstruction.com
Construction management, design-build & general contracting services. (AA, estab 2007, empl 22, sales $32,500,000, cert: State)

2431 Lakeside Project Solutions
      405 North Pilot Knob Rd
      Denver, NC 28037
      Contact: Ronnie Massingale Business Devel
      Tel: 704-483-3739
      Email: workorders@lakesideps.com
      Website: www.lakesideps.com
General Contracting, Drywall, Painting, Doors and Hardware, Carpentry, Ashpalt, Concrete. (Woman, estab 2009, empl 55, sales $42,000,000, cert: WBENC)

2432 Marand Builders, Inc.
      4534 Old Pineville Rd Ste A
      Charlotte, NC 28217
      Contact: Francisco Alvarado CEO
      Tel: 704-525-1824
      Email: falvarado@marandbuilders.com
      Website: www.marandbuilders.com
Commercial & industrial general contracting: demolition, new construction & renovations. (Hisp, estab 1999, empl 15, sales $75,822,000, cert: NMSDC)

2433 Metcon Inc.
      763 Comtech Dr
      Pembroke, NC 28372
      Contact: Aaron Thomas CEO
      Tel: 910-521-8013
      Email: athomas@metconus.com
      Website: www.metconus.com
General contracting, panelized metal studs & truss. (Nat Ame, estab 1999, empl 75, sales $24,180,330, cert: NMSDC)

2434 Miles McClellan Construction Co., Inc.
      2201-E Crownpoint Executive Dr
      Charlotte, NC 28227
      Contact: Melia Mauldin Sales & Marketing Coord
      Tel: 704-900-1170
      Email: melia.mauldin@mmbuildings.com
      Website: www.mmbuildings.com
Design & build, construction mgmt, general contracting, masonry. (AA, estab 1978, empl 75, sales $50,889,458, cert: State, NMSDC)

2435 Modern Construction Services, LLC
      5900 Harris Technology Ste D
      Charlotte, NC 28031
      Contact: Tracy Snowdy President
      Tel: 704-765-9937
      Email: tsnowdy@modernconstructionsvc.com
      Website: www.modernconstructionsvc.com
General Contractor & Facility Repairs, Interior demolition & up-fits, exterior refreshes, parking lot repairs/resurfacing, doors, windows, drywall, painting, rough & finish carpentry, ADA upgrades. (Woman, estab , empl 20, sales $5,300,000, cert: State, City, WBENC)

2436 Vega Construction Company, Inc.
147 Clover Ln
Mount Airy, NC 27030
Contact: Marlene Lopez Finance Officer
Tel: 336-756-3477
Email: mlopez@vega-constructionco.com
Website: www.vega-constructionco.com
Construction services. (Hisp, estab 2018, empl 48, sales $5,290,564, cert: State)

New Jersey

2437 A&A Industrial Piping
6 Gardner Rd
Fairfiled, NJ 07004
Contact: Jennifer Simmons Exec Asst
Tel: 973-882-2622
Email: jenn@a-agroup.com
Website: www.a-agroup.com
Install & services HVAC, Plumbing, Process Piping systems. (Woman, estab 1990, empl 45, sales $26,106,745, cert: WBENC)

2438 Carter Contracting Co. Corp.
PO Box 655
Union, NJ 07083
Contact: Robert McCoobery Project Mgr
Tel: 908-687-0075
Email: robert@cartercon.com
Website: www.cartercon.com
General contractor. (AA, estab 1978, empl 5, sales $10,000,000, cert: State)

2439 Ferreira Construction Co Inc.
31 Tannery Rd
Branchburg, NJ 08876
Contact: Megan Carton Dir of Mktg
Tel: 908-534-8655
Email: mcarton@ferreiraconstruction.com
Website: www.ferreiraconstruction.com
Utility Construction: Gas, Transmission and Distribution, Foundations, Water, Sewer, Fiber Optic. Heavy Civil Construction: Bridges, Highways, Airports, Excavation, Sitework
Marine Construction: Dredging, Seawalls, Docks/Piers (Hisp, estab 1988, empl 1000, sales $410,000,000, cert: State, CPUC)

2440 HC Constructors, Inc.
PO Box 855
Whitehouse Station, NJ 08889
Contact: Lisa Chowansky President
Tel: 908-534-3833
Email: lchowansky@hcconstructors.com
Website: www.hcconstructors.com
General contracting: Underground Excavation for Electrical & Telecommunication, Masonry, Bridgework, Sound Walls, Concrete - Wall, foundations & floors. (Woman, estab 1989, empl 15, sales $15,000,000, cert: WBENC)

2441 Hydro-Marine Construction Company, Inc.
1345 Route 38 West
Hainesport, NJ 08036
Contact: Castle President
Tel: 609-261-6353
Email: hmc@wjcastlegroup.com
Website: www.wjcastlegroup.com
Marine structures construction: repair, replace & maintain bulkhead & pier construction & rehabilitation, cable inspection & location, bridge undermining repairs, pile repair, underwater concreting, steel sheeting cofferdams. (Woman, estab 1997, empl 13, sales $2,000,000, cert: WBENC)

2442 Maysonet LLC
4 Orchard Terrace
Clark, NJ 07066
Contact: Mark Maysonet Managing Member
Tel: 732-396-0873
Email: info@maysonetllc.com
Website: www.maysonetllc.com
Commercial & residential construction: carpentry, drywall, framing, general contracting. (Hisp, estab 2005, empl 18, sales $751,588, cert: State)

2443 NC & Sons The Nicholson Corporation
201 Chambersbrook Rd
Branchburg, NJ 08876
Contact: Brandon Nicholson President
Tel: 908-575-0055
Email: accounting@nicholsoncorp.com
Website: www.nicholsoncorp.com
General contracting &construction management. (Minority, Woman, estab 1997, empl 225, sales $70,336,810, cert: State, NMSDC, WBENC)

2444 Wu & Associates, Inc.
100 Gaither Dr, Ste C
Mount Laurel, NJ 08054
Contact: Kirby Wu President
Tel: 856-857-1639
Email: info@wuassociates.com
Website: www.wuassociates.com
General contracting: govt, commercial, institutional & industrial, renovations, new construction, environ cleanups. (As-Pac, estab 1990, empl 25, sales $14,474,000, cert: State, NMSDC)

Nevada

2445 Kat@KMGSolutionsInc.com
7800 Via Costada St
Las Vegas, NV 89123
Contact: Kat Welniak CEO
Tel: 503-754-7592
Email: Kat@KMGSolutionsInc.com
Website: www.KMGSolutionsInc.com
General Contracting & Construction Management, Carpentry, Painting & Flooring. (Woman, estab 2002, empl 5, sales , cert: WBENC)

New York

2446 Abba Construction LLC
1133 Broadway Ste 401
New York, NY 10010
Contact: Jose Arias Owner
Tel: 212-727-2777
Email: jarias@abba-construction.com
Website: www.Abba-construction.com
Sapele Mahogany doors, Brazilian Mahogany Doors. (Hisp, estab 2007, empl 7, sales $650,000, cert: City)

2447 ACC Construction Corporation
519 Eighth Ave 7th Floor
New York, NY 10018
Contact: Michele Medaglia President
Tel: 212-686-9331
Email: mmedaglia@acc-construction.com
Website: www.acc-construction.com
General contracting & construction mgmt, phased, interior renovations. (Woman, estab 1984, empl 55, sales $28,748,041, cert: State, City, WBENC)

2448 Al-Pros Construction Inc.
109-20 121 St
South Ozone Park, NY 11420
Contact: Imran Ali Office Mgr
Tel: 718-848-3666
Email: iali@alprosconstruction.com
Website: www.alprosconstruction.com
General contracting & maintenance services. (As-Pac, estab 1995, empl 30, sales $500,000, cert: City)

2449 Brinco Mechanical Services, Inc.
111 Plainfield Ave
Floral Park, NY 11001
Contact: Renee Prager
Tel: 516-354-8707
Email: renee@brinco.com
Website: www.brinco.com
National Maintenance & service, HVAC & refrigeration work. (Woman, estab 1997, empl 40, sales $20,000,000, cert: WBENC)

2450 C.W. Brown Inc.
1 Labriola Court
Armonk, NY 10504
Contact: Erin Griffin Business Devel Mgr
Tel: 914-219-8323
Email: info@cwbrown.com
Website: www.cwbrown.com
General contracting/construction management. (Woman, estab 1984, empl 72, sales $48,000,000, cert: City, WBENC)

2451 Con Rac Construction Group LLC
1895 Walt Whitman Rd Ste 2
Melville, NY 11747
Contact: John Coleman EVO
Tel: 631-756-0101
Email: jcoleman@conracgroup.com
Website: www.conracgroup.com
General contracting & construction management. (Woman, estab 2010, empl 4, sales $13,009,136, cert: State, City)

2452 Construction and Service Solutions Corp.
216 Main Rd
Akron, NY 14001
Contact: Suzanne Witnauer President
Tel: 716-570-1352
Email: suzanne@csscbuilds.com
Website: www.csscbuilds.com
General contractor: drywall, doors & hardware, acoustic ceilings, siding, windows, cabinetry, countertops, framing, trim & finish carpentry installations. (Woman, estab 2002, empl 15, sales , cert: State, City, WBENC)

2453 Genesus One Enterprise, Inc.
43-24 54th Rd Ste 203
Maspeth, NY 11378
Contact: David Turner CEO
Tel: 718-361-7516
Email: office@genesusconstruction.com
Website: www.genesusconstruction.com
General contracting, construction management, interiors construction, site work, pavement, concrete, masonry, metal work & other trades. (AA, estab 1999, empl 16, sales $3,500,000, cert: State)

2454 Henegan Construction Co., Inc.
250 W 30th St
New York, NY 10001
Contact: MAUREEN HENEGAN CEO
Tel: 212-947-6441
Email: mahenegan@henegan.com
Website: www.henegan.com
Construction management & general contracting: interior building alterations, renovations & infrastructure upgrades. (Woman, estab 1959, empl 150, sales $238,724,000, cert: City, WBENC)

2455 Ideal Interiors Group, LLC
450 7th Ave, 21st Fl
New York, NY 10123
Contact: Ricardo Rivera President
Tel: - -
Email: kkolley@ideal-interiors.com
Website: www.ideal-interiors.com
Construction management, general contracting, and design/build services. (Hisp, estab 2008, empl 25, sales , cert: State, City, NMSDC)

2456 K-Pak Consulting, Inc.
29 Elves Ln
Levittown, NY 11756
Contact: Khurram Bajwa President
Tel: 718-813-7755
Email: bajwa@kpakconsulting.com
Website: www.kpakconsulting.com
General contracting: remodeling, renovations, carpentry, drywall, cement, flooring, masonry, demolition, painting, doors & windows. (As-Ind, estab 2012, empl 4, sales $169,960, cert: State)

2457 Mamais Contracting Corp.
256 West 124th St
New York, NY 10027
Contact: Mamais-Lorino President
Tel: 212-865-1666
Email: voula@mamais.com
Website: www.mamais.com
General contracting, high-end alterations & renovations, rapid repair services. (Woman, estab 1968, empl 142, sales $17,367,537, cert: City, WBENC)

CONSTRUCTION: General Contractors

2458 Milestone Construction Partners
100 Tech Park Dr, Ste C
Rochester, NY 14623
Contact: President
Tel: 585-247-5179
Email: info@milestoneconstructionpartners.com
Website: www.milestoneconstructionpartners.com
General contracting: commercial & multi-family projects. (Woman, estab 2001, empl 14, sales , cert: WBENC)

2459 Professional Retail Services
3249 Route 112 Ste 2 Bldg 4
Medford, NY 75028
Contact: Robbye Chasteen Natl sales/mktg
Tel: 888-834-2411
Email: rchasteen@profretail.com
Website: www.profretail.com
Commercial facility maintenance, construction & project services. (Woman, estab 2001, empl 51, sales $13,000,000, cert: WBENC)

2460 Theodore Williams Construction Company, LLC
641 Lexington Ave
New York, NY 10022
Contact: Shelby Johnson President
Tel: 212-593-9700
Email: sjohnson@twcc-llc.com
Website: www.twcc-llc.com
General contracting & construction management: interior buildouts, alterations, restorations & base building construction. (Woman, estab 1972, empl 24, sales $21,727,000, cert: WBENC)

2461 VRD Contracting, Inc.
25 Andrea Rd
Holbrook, NY 11741
Contact: Sapienza Exec VP
Tel: 631-956-7000
Email: joe@vrdcontracting.com
Website: www.vrdcontracting.com
General contracting & construction management services. (Woman, estab 1993, empl 60, sales $22,000,000, cert: State)

Ohio

2462 Allied Door Systems
23050 Miles Rd
Bedford Heights, OH 44128
Contact: Judith Lester President
Tel: 216-587-2100
Email: jlester@allieddoorsystems.com
Website: www.allieddoorsystems.com
Service & install automatic swinging, sliding, bi-folding revolving & manual pedestrian doors. (Woman, estab 1998, empl 8, sales $1,008,740, cert: City)

2463 Bambeck & Vest Associates, Inc.
49 E Fourth St, Ste 1020
Cincinnati, OH 45202
Contact: Ed Roark President
Tel: 513-621-5654
Email: ed@bambeckandvest.com
Website: www.bambeckandvest.com
General contracting, office renovations, new buildings, general repair work. (Woman, estab 1964, empl 35, sales $10,000,000, cert: WBENC)

2464 Better Built Construction Services, Inc.
PO Box 467
Middletown, OH 45042
Contact: Karen S. Tipton President
Tel: 513-727-8637
Email: ksh@betterbuiltcs.com
Website: www.betterbuiltcs.com
Pre-engineered steel building, steel erection. (Minority, Woman, estab 1995, empl 5, sales $1,245,340, cert: State)

2465 C&B Construction Company Ltd.
3713 Lee Rd
Cleveland, OH 44120
Contact: Barbara Coker President
Tel: 216-905-2617
Email: candbcont@sbcglobal.net
Website: www.candbconstoh.com
General construction, rehab, new construction, residential & commercial properties. (Woman/AA, estab 2007, empl 4, sales $990,000, cert: State)

2466 ConstructAbility, Inc.
24600 Center Ridge Rd Ste 295
Westlake, OH 44145
Contact: Brett P Luengo CEO
Tel: 440-835-2424
Email: inquiries@constructabilityinc.com
Website: www.ConstructAbilityInc.com
General Contracting, Construction Management, Program Management, budget estimating, value engineering, needs assessments, feasibility studies. (Hisp, estab , empl , sales $268,147, cert: State, City, 8(a))

2467 Construction Support Solutions, LLC
PO Box 48
Avon Lake, OH 44012
Contact: Anna Klee President
Tel: 440-541-6642
Email: anna.klee@constructionsupportsolutions.com
Website: www.constructionsupportsolutions.com
Construction management: scheduling, estimating, constructability review, contract administration, project controls, on site inspections & close out services. (Woman, estab 2008, empl 3, sales $250,000, cert: State, WBENC)

2468 Cook Paving & Construction Co., Inc.
4545 Spring Road
Brooklyn Heights, OH 44131
Contact: Linda Fletcher President
Tel: 216-267-7705
Email: linda.fletcher@cookpaving.com
Website: www.cookpaving.com
Construction management, underground utilities installation & maintenance telecommunication & electrical ductbank systems, directional boring, site development, commercial & heavy hwy hotmix asphalt & concrete paving, excavation & trenching. (Woman/AA, estab 1950, empl 100, sales , cert: State, City, NMSDC)

CONSTRUCTION: General Contractors

2469 D.A.G. Construction Company, Inc.
4924 Winton Rd
Cincinnati, OH 45232
Contact: Lindsay Wilhelm Mktg Dir
Tel: 513-542-8597
Email: lwilhelm@dag-cons.com
Website: www.dag-cons.com
General construction, construction management, design/build & renovations. (AA, As-Pac, estab 1990, empl 35, sales $21,000,000, cert: NMSDC)

2470 Dawn Incorporated
106 E Market St Ste 505
Warren, OH 44481
Contact: Dawn Ochman President
Tel: 330-652-7711
Email: dawn@dawnincorporated.com
Website: www.dawnincorporated.com
General contracting, pre-construction planning, quality control & customer service. (Woman, estab 1993, empl 15, sales $1,014,000, cert: State)

2471 Dynamix Engineering Ltd.
855 Grandview Ave, 3rd Fl
Columbus, OH 43215
Contact: Eugene Griffin President
Tel: 614-443-1178
Email: ggriffin@dynamix-ltd.com
Website: www.dynamix-ltd.com
Electrical, mechanical, plumbing, technology systems design; assessments & standard operating & maintenance procedures. (AA, estab 1997, empl 40, sales $11,700,000, cert: State, NMSDC)

2472 JWT&A LLC
3615 Superior Ave, Bldg 31-1J
Cleveland, OH 44114
Contact: John Todd President
Tel: 216-426-1580
Email: jwtassoc@sbcglobal.net
Website: www.jwta-construction.com
Construction management, general contractor, acoustical ceilings, drywall, drywall insulation, framing, gypsum board, metal studs & taping. (AA, estab 2005, empl 7, sales $969,473, cert: City)

2473 Kerricook Construction, Inc.
20355 Vermont St
Litchfield, OH 44253
Contact: Ann Smith Owner
Tel: 440-647-4200
Email: ann@kerricook.com
Website: www.kerricook.com
Ground-up construction, design build construction, tenant build-out construction, open store remodels, facilities maintenance. (Woman, estab 2003, empl 20, sales $5,393,450, cert: WBENC)

2474 MBJ Consultants, Inc.
30 W 3rd St, Ste 4M
Cincinnati, OH 45202
Contact: Monroe Barnes President
Tel: 513-631-9600
Email: mbarnes@mbjconsultants.com
Website: www.mbjconsultnats.com
General contracting & construction management. (AA, estab 1992, empl 30, sales $1,300,000, cert: NMSDC)

2475 McTech Corp.
8100 Grand Ave
Cleveland, OH 44104
Contact: Mark F. Perkins President
Tel: 216-391-7700
Email: mctechadmin@mctech360.com
Website: www.mctech360.com
General contracting, construction mgmt, design build, building renovation, restoration, roadway construction, waterline, sewerline. (AA, estab 1997, empl 45, sales , cert: NMSDC)

2476 Mel Lanzer Co.
2266 N Scott St
Napoleon, OH 43545
Contact: Lyndsey Lucas President
Tel: 419-592-2801
Email: llucas@mellanzer.com
Website: www.mellanzer.com
General contracting: renovations, additions, or new construction. (Woman, estab 1950, empl 30, sales $17,000,000, cert: WBENC)

2477 Northstar Contracting, Inc
26000 First St, Ste C
Westlake, OH 44145
Contact: Majid President
Tel: 216-999-7595
Email: nscontractingco@gmail.com
Website: www.nscontracting.net
General contracting services, interior & exterior painting, carpentry, drywall installation, windows/door replacement, concrete/masonry, roofing. (AA, estab 2002, empl 4, sales , cert: State)

2478 O'Rourke Wrecking Co.
660 Lunkenpark Dr
Cincinnati, OH 45226
Contact: Jeremy J. Hudson VP
Tel: 513-871-1400
Email: jhudson@orourkewrecking.com
Website: www.orourkewrecking.com
Demolition & dismantling services. (Woman, estab 1962, empl 100, sales $50,000,000, cert: WBENC, NWBOC)

2479 Ozanne Construction Co., Inc.
1625 E 25th St
Cleveland, OH 44114
Contact: Dominic L. Ozanne CEO
Tel: 216-696-2876
Email: dozanne1@ozanne.com
Website: www.ozanne.com
Multi-Diciplenary Construction Management; Construction Management Agency, Construction Management at Risk, Design-Build, Design-Bid-Build/General Contracting, Owner's Representative, Program Management, Task Order Contracting. (AA, estab 1956, empl 37, sales $50,000,000, cert: State, City, NMSDC)

2480 Precision Engineering & Contracting, Inc.
31340 Solon Rd, Stes 25 & 26
Solon, OH 44139
Contact: Sekhar Narendrula President
Tel: 440-349-1204
Email: kmoomaw@precisioneng.us
Website: www.precisioneng.us
Site work, demolition & construction. (As-Ind, estab 2001, empl 37, sales , cert: State)

CONSTRUCTION: General Contractors

2481 ProjDel Corporation
      One North Commerce Park Dr, Level G
      Cincinnati, OH 45215
      Contact: Eric Browne Principal
      Tel: 513-931-0900
      Email: brownee@projdel.com
      Website: www.projdel.com
Construction management, project management & construction technologies. (AA, estab 1995, empl 13, sales $1,500,000, cert: NMSDC)

2482 R L Hill Management, Inc.
      31875 Aurora Road
      Solon, OH 44139
      Contact: Ralphael Hill President
      Tel: 440-439-0490
      Email: pam@rlhillmgmt.com
      Website: www.rlhillmgmt.com
General contracting, construction management, architectural millwork, drywall, etc. (AA, estab 1998, empl 12, sales $1,744,631, cert: State, City)

2483 R.J. Runge Company, Inc.
      3539 NE Catawba Rd
      Port Clinton, OH 43452
      Contact: Amy Runge President
      Tel: 419-740-5781
      Email: arunge@rjrunge.com
      Website: www.rjrunge.com
Construction Management, CM at Risk, General Contracting, Scheduling, Cost Management, Pre Construction Services, Electrical Contractor, Carpentry, Concrete, Site Work, Rough Carpentry, Interior Finishes. (Woman, estab 2004, empl 30, sales $5,571,511, cert: State, City)

2484 Regency Construction Services Inc.
      14600 Detroit Ave, Ste 1495
      Lakewood, OH 44107
      Contact: Tari Rivera President
      Tel: 216-529-1188
      Email: riverat@regencycsi.com
      Website: www.regencycsi.com
General contracting & construction. (Woman, estab 1994, empl 70, sales $10,302,000, cert: City, WBENC)

2485 The Coniglio Co.
      4400 Commerce Ave.
      Cleveland, OH 44103
      Contact: Gwenay Reaze-Coniglio President
      Tel: 216-391-1800
      Email: coniglioco@aol.com
      Website: www.theconigliocompany.com
General contracting services, general trades, carpentry, custom cabinetry, pre-fabricated office structures. (Woman/AA, estab 1994, empl 20, sales $1,091,271, cert: City, NMSDC)

2486 Welling Inc.
      7781 Cooper Rd
      Cincinnati, OH 45242
      Contact: Amy Smith Acctg Mgr
      Tel: 513-793-6900
      Email: amy@wellinginc.com
      Website: www.wellinginc.com
Commercial Construction; install trash & linen chutes, security screens, interior window shading systems. (Woman, estab 1987, empl 6, sales $900,000, cert: WBENC)

2487 Wise Construction Management, Inc.
      1705 Guenther Rd
      Dayton, OH 45427
      Contact: David Abney President
      Tel: 937-854-0281
      Email: dfa@wiseconstructionco.com
      Website: www.wiseconstructionco.com
Construction management, design/build. (AA, estab 2001, empl 7, sales $804,000, cert: NMSDC)

Oklahoma

2488 DBG Construction, LLC
      PO Box 674
      Oklahoma City, OK 73101
      Contact: Deemah Ramadan Managing Partner
      Tel: 405-601-2700
      Email: info@dbgconstruction.com
      Website: www.dbgconstruction.com
Commercial Construction, Pre-Construction, Design/Build, General Contracting & Construction Management. (Woman, estab 2007, empl 15, sales $7,000,000, cert: WBENC)

2489 Red Stone Construction Services, LLC
      2738 E 51st St, Ste 140
      Tulsa, OK 74105
      Contact: Andrea L Gibson Natl Acct Exec
      Tel: 918-747-7410
      Email: andrea.gibson@redstonecs.com
      Website: www.redstonecs.com
Construction technology: BIM, 3D-based conceptual estimate, laser scanning existing building conditions & field validation, 3D visualization. (Nat Ame, estab 2009, empl 40, sales , cert: State, NMSDC)

2490 The Ross Group Construction Corporation
      510 E 2nd St
      Tulsa, OK 74120
      Contact: Tammy Pameticky Mgr Contracts Admin
      Tel: 918-234-7675
      Email: tammy.pameticky@withrossgroup.com
      Website: www.withrossgroup.com
General contracting, construction management & facilities maintenance services. (Nat Ame, estab 1979, empl 125, sales $88,398,046, cert: NMSDC)

Oregon

2491 Art Cortez Construction, Inc.
      15783 NW Dairy Creek Rd
      North Plains, OR 97133
      Contact: Art Cortez President
      Tel: 503-841-5732
      Email: art@artcortezconstruction.com
      Website: www.artcortezconstruction.com
Commercial construction, general contracting, steel frame construction & interior systems, MEP services. (Hisp, estab 2007, empl 25, sales $3,185,945, cert: State)

Pennsylvania

2492 84 Lumber Company
1019 Route 519
Eighty Four, PA 15330
Contact: Amy Criss Govt Sales
Tel: 724-228-8820
Email: amy.criss@84lumber.biz
Website: www.84lumber.com
General Construction Contracting Services. (Woman, estab 1954, empl 5000, sales $3,800,000,000, cert: WBENC)

2493 AHJ Construction, LLC
1208 Main St
Darby, PA 19023
Contact: Henry Robinson President
Tel: 215-900-3508
Email: hrobinson@ahjconstructionco.com
Website: www.ahjconstructionco.com
Commercial & industrial construction projects. (AA, estab 2010, empl 8, sales $360,235, cert: State)

2494 Berner Construction, Inc.
1101 Quarry Rd
Gap, PA 17527
Contact: Andrea Irey President
Tel: 717-442-3110
Email: andrea.irey@bernerconstruction.com
Website: www.bernerconstruction.com
Construction, environmental remediation, renovation, utility installation. (Woman, estab 2002, empl 25, sales $5,317,916, cert: WBENC)

2495 CD & Associates, Inc.
725 Skippack Pike, Ste 140
Blue Bell, PA 19422
Contact: Lisa Casiello President
Tel: 215-793-9069
Email: LCasiello@CDandAssociatesInc.com
Website: www.CDandAssociatesInc.com
Design & construction. (Woman, estab 1989, empl 24, sales $67,671,317, cert: WBENC)

2496 Crawford Consulting Services, Inc.
239 Highland Ave
East Pittsburgh, PA 15112
Contact: Crawford
Tel: 412-823-0400
Email: lschroeder@crawfordconsultingservices.com
Website: www.crawfordcs.com
Construction consulting services: cost estimating, value engineering, inspections, project (CPM) scheduling, project mgmt, construction mgmt, owner's representation & general construction. (Woman, estab 1993, empl 23, sales $1,050,000, cert: State, WBENC)

2497 DK Cleaning Contractors, LLC
6418 Woodland Ave Ste 1FF
Philadelphia, PA 19142
Contact: Chidozie Dike President
Tel: 610-883-3133
Email: cdike@dkconstructionservicesllc.com
Website: www.dkconstructionservicesllc.com
Project & Construction Management, Repair & Renovation, Drywall & Insulation, Painting & Wall Covering, Framing, Masonry, & Siding Contractors, Plumbing, HVAC, Electrical, Mechanical, Carpentry, Demolition, Site work. (AA, estab 2010, empl 5, sales $300,000, cert: City, 8(a))

2498 ecoservices, LLC
407 W Lincoln Hwy, Ste 500
Exton, PA 19341
Contact: Denenno President
Tel: 484-872-8884
Email: ldenenno@eco-pa.com
Website: www.eco-pa.com
Construction management / project management, industrial site rehabilitation, demolition, asbestos abatement, roof removal, lead & mold abatement & remediation. (Woman, estab 2009, empl 30, sales $5,293,485, cert: State, City)

2499 Northeast Construction Contractors, Inc.
4827 Wingate St
Philadelphia, PA 19136
Contact: April Slobodrian President
Tel: 215-624-3667
Email: info@northeastconstructioninc.com
Website: www.northeastconstructioninc.com
General construction management, construction related property maintenance, snow removal & general carpentry work, walls, wall coverings, FRP, ACT, ceilings, doors, windows, hardware, accessories, drywall, painting, electrical, interior. (Woman, estab 2004, empl 12, sales $1,520,000, cert: State)

2500 Perryman Building and Construction Services, Inc.
4548 Market St
Philadelphia, PA 19139
Contact: Angelo Perryman President
Tel: 215-243-4109
Email: admin@perrymanbc.com
Website: www.perrymanbc.com
Genenral construction: commercial interiors, building & project management services. (AA, estab 1998, empl 26, sales , cert: NMSDC, 8(a))

2501 Robert Ganter Contractors, Inc.
595 E Pumping Station Rd
Quakertown, PA 18951
Contact: Donna Ganter President
Tel: 215-538-3540
Email: dganter@gantercontractors.com
Website: www.gantercontractors.com
Architectural roofing & sheet metal servicing, commercial, industrial builders & architects. (Woman, estab 2000, empl 25, sales $37,735,416, cert: WBENC)

2502 Tracy Becker Construction, Inc.
7280 Dragonfly Lane
Macungie, PA 18062
Contact: Tracy Becker President
Tel: 610-421-8590
Email: tb@tbcinstalls.com
Website: www.tbcinstalls.com
General contracting & construction. (Woman, estab 1997, empl 15, sales $3,748,957, cert: WBENC)

2503 U.S Construction Group Inc.
6100 Henry Ave Ste 2N
Philadelphia, PA 19128
Contact: Yaw Danso President
Tel: 215-756-1364
Email: ydanso@usconstructgroup.com
Website: www.usconstructgroup.com
General Construction, Sitework, Utilities, Demolition, waste disposal, Hazardous waste disposal, Paving. (AA, estab 2008, empl 5, sales $517,000, cert: State, City, NMSDC)

2504 U.S. Facilities, Inc. PRWT Services Company
30 N 41st St Ste 400
Philadelphia, PA 19104
Contact: David Groomes Sr VP
Tel: 215-564-1448
Email: david.groomes@usfacilities.com
Website: www.usfacilities.com
Facilities support svcs, building operations & maintenance, subcontract mgmt svcs, project mgmt. (AA, estab 2000, empl 462, sales , cert: City, NMSDC)

Puerto Rico

2505 Aireko Construction, LLC
PO Box 2128
San Juan, PR 00922
Contact: Alejandro Nazario Business Dev Dir
Tel: 787-653-6300
Email: anazario@aireko.com
Website: www.aireko.com
Integrated construction & building maintenance services, planning, financing, building and servicing leading industrial, commercial & institutional facilities. (Hisp, estab 1963, empl 450, sales , cert: NMSDC)

2506 BNS Engineering Inc.
Rafael Cordero, Ste 140 HC 02 Box 14212
Gurabo, PR 00778
Contact: Bienvenido Negron
Tel: 787-745-4848
Email: b.negron@bns-eng.com
Website: www.bns-eng.com
Construction design/build, project management, equipment, maintenance, turnarounds, program/project management, procurement & safety. (Hisp, estab 2001, empl 25, sales $1,599,871, cert: NMSDC)

2507 CIC Construction Group, SE
PO Box 29726
San Juan, PR 00929
Contact: Jose Torrens VP
Tel: 787-287-3540
Email: jtorrens@cic-pr.com
Website: www.cicconstruction.com/
General contractors doing construction at pharmaceuticals, hotels, hospitals etc. (Hisp, estab 1983, empl 480, sales $70,743,703, cert: NMSDC)

2508 CPM PR, LLC
44 Road 20 Ste 201
Guaynabo, PR 00966
Contact: Francisco (Paco) Martínez Business Dev Mgr
Tel: 787-999-4000
Email: fmartinez@cpmintl.com
Website: www.cpmintl.com
Program, project & construction management & consulting services. (Hisp, estab 1991, empl 125, sales $9,849,191, cert: NMSDC)

2509 CR Quality Roofing of PR, Inc.
PO Box 334458
Ponce, PR 00924
Contact: Carlos Ramos President
Tel: 787-259-7721
Email: crqualityroofing@yahoo.com
Website: www.roofingcr.com
Roofing waterproofing, sales, installation, maintenance, renewable energy systems. (Hisp, estab 1990, empl 50, sales $1,834,674, cert: NMSDC)

2510 CSCG Inc.
PO Box 991
Aguada, PR 00602
Contact: Victor Jose Garcia Ruiz VP
Tel: 787-868-4030
Email: vgarciaruiz@cscginc.com
Website: www.cscginc.com
Pre construction: Conceptual Estimating, Budget Development, Project Phasing, General Contractor, Cost Monitoring & Control, Subcontractor Management, Safety Assurance, Quality Control, Civil and Structural Works. (Hisp, estab 2000, empl 60, sales $13,107,533, cert: NMSDC)

2511 Ideal Engineering Solutions, PSC
RR 3 Box 7266
Cidra, PR 00739
Contact: Ismael Robles President
Tel: 787-378-2948
Email: irobles.ies@gmail.com
Website: www.idealengineeringsolutions.com
General Construction, Electrical and Mechanical Installations, Instrumentation and Control Systems, Gypsum Board works. (Hisp, estab 2007, empl 5, sales $300,000, cert: NMSDC, 8(a))

2512 Jays and Fancy Interiors, Inc.
2A-16 Ave. Carlos Javier Andaluz
Bayamon, PR 00956
Contact: Gavin Davis
Tel: 787-786-9411
Email: gdavis@jaysandfancy.com
Website: www.jaysandfancy.com
General contracting, interior finishes, drywall, florring, etc. (Hisp, estab 2001, empl 25, sales $5,200,000, cert: NMSDC)

2513 JCD Engineering, Inc.
PO Box 192372
San Juan, PR 00919
Contact: Juan C. del Pino President
Tel: 787-787-7211
Email: jcdelpino@jcdengineering.com
Website: www.jcdengineering.com
Civil, electrical & mechanical engineering: concrete & steel small buildings, interiors work, hung ceilings, floors, gypsum board, electrical power & controls, fiber optics, local area networks (LAN), process & AHU control systems. (Hisp, estab 1996, empl 11, sales $1,327,000, cert: NMSDC)

South Carolina

2514 Benchmark Contracting, Inc.
215 E Bay St
Charleston, SC 29401
Contact: Jennifer Courville Dir of Business Dev
Tel: 843-628-5999
Email: courvillej@benchmarkcontracting.org
Website: www.BenchmarkContractingSC.com
General Contracting, Industrial, Commercial & Residential Construction. (AA, estab 1998, empl 20, sales $10,267,000, cert: State, City)

CONSTRUCTION: General Contractors

2515 Built Right Construction, LLC
      1524 Ashley River Rd
      Charleston, SC 29407
      Contact: Chris Pelletier Owner
      Tel: 843-882-7632
      Email: chris@brcsc.com
      Website: www.brcsc.com
Construction management, equipment rental, development, HVAC & plumbing & facility operations & maintenance. (Nat Ame, estab 2007, empl 10, sales $1,000,000, cert: State, City)

2516 CCCS International, LLC
      2414 Clements Ferry Rd
      Charleston, SC 29492
      Contact: Calvin Whitfield CEO
      Tel: 843-856-4874
      Email: cwhitfield@cccsinternational.com
      Website: www.cccsinternational.com
On-site construction management, project operations, site security, site clearing, site utilities, deep foundations, waterproofing & sealants, pre-treatment for mold & termites, concrete slab on grade, miscellaneous concrete, masonry. (Woman/AA, estab , empl , sales $2,500,000, cert: State, City, NMSDC, SDB)

2517 Greenwood, Inc.
      160 Milestone Way
      Greenville, SC 29615
      Contact: Sherry Harris Dir Sales/Marketing
      Tel: 540-298-2628
      Email: sharris@gwood.com
      Website: www.GreenWoodInc.com
Construction, maintenance & workforce solutions. (Woman, estab 1990, empl 680, sales $60,000,000, cert: WBENC)

2518 Landmark Construction Company, Inc.
      3255 Industry Dr
      North Charleston, SC 29418
      Contact: Sam Hayes Business Devel Dir
      Tel: 843-552-6186
      Email: shayes@landmark-sc.com
      Website: www.landmark-sc.com
Construction services: grading, drainage, utilities, paving (concrete and asphalt), foundations, steel erection, and vertical wall construction. (Woman, estab 1965, empl 135, sales $11,000,000, cert: City)

2519 Lipscomb Plant Services, Inc.
      160 Milestone Way Ste B
      Greenville, SC 29376
      Contact: Eric Burnette Business Devel
      Tel: 864-244-9669
      Email: eburnette@gwood.com
      Website: www.LIPSCOMBINC.COM
Industrial maintenance, construction, construction management & workforce solutions. (Woman, estab 2009, empl 4, sales $2,635,406, cert: WBENC)

Tennessee

2520 AHA Mechanical Contractors
      2010 Sycamore View Rd
      Memphis, TN 38134
      Contact: Donna Burlon Owner
      Tel: 901-383-2900
      Email: donna@ahamechanical.com
      Website: www.ahamechanical.com
Installation, repair & maintenance of heating, air conditioning & plumbing equipment. (Woman, estab 2006, empl 30, sales $3,224,000, cert: State, WBENC)

2521 Gipson Mechanical Contractors Inc.
      6863 E Raleigh LaGrange Rd
      Memphis, TN 38134
      Contact: Winston Gipson President
      Tel: 901-388-6149
      Email: info@gipsonmech.com
      Website: www.gipsonmech.com
Commercial and industrial mechanical, HVAC & Plumbing, installation, renovation & repair. (AA, estab 1983, empl 71, sales $20,000,000, cert: State, NMSDC)

2522 MC Builders, LLC
      2115 Chapman Rd Ste 131
      Chattanooga, TN 37421
      Contact: Linda Stooksbury Dir of Sales
      Tel: 423-355-8118
      Email: linda@mc-buildersllc.com
      Website: www.mcbuildersllc.construction
Retail, Restaurant, Multi-Family Housing, Property Management, Hospitals, Universities, Commercial and Industrial Building maintenance. (Woman, estab 2012, empl 36, sales $4,000,000, cert: WBENC)

2523 SRS, Inc.
      131 Saundersville Rd, Ste 210
      Hendersonville, TN 37075
      Contact: Charles Pickett CEO
      Tel: 615-230-2966
      Email:
      Website: www.srsincorp.com
Construction Management and Disaster Recovery Services (AA, estab 2001, empl 55, sales $16,974,636, cert: NMSDC)

Texas

2524 3i Construction, LLC
      400 N Saint Paul St Ste 700
      Dallas, TX 75201
      Contact: Micheal Williams VP Business Dev
      Tel: 214-231-0675
      Email: mwilliams@3iconstruction.com
      Website: www.3iconstruction.com
General commercial construction. (AA, estab 2001, empl 27, sales $22,146,587, cert: State, NMSDC)

2525 Air Mechanix, LLC
      PO Box 864772
      Plano, TX 75086
      Contact: Bobbi Pappas Owner
      Tel: 214-394-5520
      Email: bobbipappas@airmechanix.com
      Website: www.airmechanix.com
HVAC-R Service, Maintenance & Construction. (Woman, estab 2005, empl 7, sales $850,000, cert: State, WBENC)

CONSTRUCTION: General Contractors

2526 Alcatex, Inc. Data Center Design & Build
669 FM 1138 South
Royse City, TX 75189
Contact: President
Tel: 972-226-0047
Email:
Website: www.alcatex.com
Bio Computer Room/Data Center, Network Operations Center (NOC) Design, & Construction. (Woman, estab 1995, empl 15, sales $9,500,000, cert: State, WBENC)

2527 American Renewable Energy
3890 North Frwy, Unit F
Houston, TX 77022
Contact: JC Avila Mgr
Tel: 713-690-1116
Email: jca@arebuildingco.com
Website: www.arebuildingco.com
General contracting & design construction. (Minority, Woman, estab 2010, empl 20, sales $5,000,000, cert: WBENC, 8(a))

2528 Argent Associates, Inc.
2800 E Plano Pkwy Ste 400
Plano, TX 75074
Contact: Betty Manetta VP Supply Chain
Tel: 732-512-9009
Email: bmanetta@argentassociates.com
Website: www.argentassociates.com
Inventory mgmt, warehousing, dist, logistics, packaging, installation & commercial construction. (Woman/Hisp, estab 1998, empl 65, sales $320,157,842, cert: NMSDC, CPUC, WBENC)

2529 Beach Construction, Inc.
1271 Record Crossing
Dallas, TX 75235
Contact: Denice VanBuren
Tel: 214-920-9100
Email: denice@beachconstructiontx.com
Website: www.beachconstructiontx.com
Commerical general contracting. (Minority, Woman, estab 2002, empl 10, sales $2,740,000, cert: State)

2530 Bird Electric Enterprises, LLC
8787 IH 20
Eastland, TX 76448
Contact: Jeffrey Walter VP
Tel: 254-653-2950
Email: jwalter@birdelectricinc.com
Website: www.birdelectricinc.com
Distribution Line Construction, Maintenance and Repair. (AA, estab 2012, empl 275, sales $115,673,000, cert: NMSDC)

2531 Davitz Group
6220 Pine Ridge Blvd
McKinney, TX 75070
Contact: Earl Davis President
Tel: 972-746-6045
Email: tarad@davitzgroup.com
Website: www.davitzgroup.com
Construction, design / build, LEED project design & construction, building information modeling (BIM), large projects & small task orders, procurement services. (AA, estab 2006, empl 3, sales $2,000,000, cert: State, 8(a))

2532 Diversity Resources Group
101 E Park Blvd Ste 600
Plano, TX 75074
Contact: Wayne Lawrence President
Tel: 214-352-2284
Email: wlawrence@diversityroofing.com
Website: www.diversityroofing.com/
Construction management, commercial roofing services. (AA, Hisp, estab 2015, empl 80, sales , cert: State, NMSDC)

2533 DMG Commercial Construction Services, Inc.
3939 Beltline Rd Ste 540
Addison, TX 75001
Contact: Stephanie Hilburn President
Tel: 972-630-6900
Email: stephanie@dmginc.net
Website: www.dmginc.net
General contracting: renovations, finish out, additions & new build construction. (Woman, estab 2006, empl 17, sales $3,600,000, cert: State, WBENC)

2534 Elevated Solutions Team LLC
2550 Pacific Ave Ste 700
Dallas, TX 75226
Contact: Alonzo Hill Jr CEO
Tel: 972-850-8544
Email: listings@elevatedsolutionsteamllc.com
Website: www.elevatedsolutionsteamllc.com
Engineering & HVAC performance testing, installation of air and water-cooled packaged systems, preventive maintenance & inspections, piping & refrigeration leak repairs. (AA, estab 2021, empl 3, sales $306,000, cert: NMSDC)

2535 Falkenberg Construction Company, Inc.
2435 109th St
Grand Prairie, TX 75050
Contact: Trish Gomez Business Devel Mgr
Tel: 214-324-4779
Email: pag@falkenbertconstruction.com
Website: www.falkenbergconstruction.com
Commercial general contracting. (Hisp, estab , empl , sales $6,000,000, cert: State)

2536 High Plains Contactors and Management Group, Inc.
414 S. Dumas Ave.
Dumas, TX 79029
Contact: Michael Ramirez President
Tel: 806-935-5858
Email: michael.ramirez@highplainsmanagement.com
Website: www.highplainsmanagement.com
General construction, project management, plumbing, dry ice blasting & powder coating services. (Hisp, estab 2009, empl 12, sales $8,500,000, cert: State, 8(a))

CONSTRUCTION: General Contractors

2537 HJD Capital Electric, Inc.
5424 W Hwy 90
San Antonio, TX 78227
Contact: Heather Washburn Proposal Admin
Tel: 210-681-0954
Email: marketing@hjdcapital.com
Website: www.hjdcapital.com
Design Build, General construction, electrical, Plumbing, Sitework, SWPPP, Erosion control, Underground electrical, Overhead electrical, Datacomm, Telecommunications, Pole lighting bases, Electrical meters, Gas meters, Outside plant copper fiber. (Hisp, estab 1994, empl 150, sales $17,354,379, cert: State, City)

2538 Kings Aire, Inc.
1035 Kessler Dr
El Paso, TX 79907
Contact: Beama Hernandez Dispatcher
Tel: 915-592-2997
Email: service@kingsaire.com
Website: www.kingsaire.com
HVAC, Commercial & Residential, Installs, Maintainance & Repair Low Temp, Commercial Electrical, Duct Fabrication. (Hisp, estab 1980, empl 196, sales $15,921,442, cert: State)

2539 Largin Construction Services LLC
1959 Saratoga Blvd, Bldg. 10
Corpus Christi, TX 78417
Contact: Billy Largin VP
Tel: 361-723-1573
Email: billy@larginconstruction.com
Website: www.larginconstruction.com
General contracting: construction, new buildings, remodel & maintenance, new custom housing, remodel & repair, site work, concrete, masonry, metals, carpentry, environmental, doors & windows, finishes, specialties, equipment. (Woman, estab 2006, empl 25, sales $3,500,000, cert: State)

2540 Marvin Groves Electric Company, Inc.
PO Box 2305
Wichita Falls, TX 76307
Contact: Marvin Groves President
Tel: 940-767-2711
Email: m.groves@marvingroveselectric.com
Website: www.marvingroveselectric.com
Install electrical wiring for new and exist bldg. (Nat Ame, estab 1972, empl 13, sales , cert: State)

2541 Midwest Steel Company, Inc.
9825 Moers Rd
Houston, TX 77075
Contact: Christopher Given VP
Tel: 713-991-7843
Email: chrisgiven@midwest-steel.com
Website: www.midwest-steel.com
Dismantling & demolition contracting. (Woman, estab 1968, empl 89, sales $10,755,892, cert: State, WBENC)

2542 Minority Print Media, LLC
2646 South Loop West Ste 600
Houston, TX 77054
Contact: Barry Simmons Advertising Dir
Tel: 713-748-6300
Email: advertising@stylemagazine.com
Website: www.stylemagazine.com
educated Urban view inside the worlds of celebrity, business, fashion, beauty, health, travel, transportation, culinary, real estate,
arts, cultural and entertainment. (AA, estab 1989, empl 15, sales $539,868, cert: State, City, NMSDC)

2543 North American Commercial Construction, LP
11577 Goodnight Lane
Dallas, TX 75229
Contact: Lynn Dunlap Managing Partner
Tel: 972-620-9975
Email: lynn@naccolp.com
Website: www.naccolp.com
General Contractor. (Woman, estab 2004, empl 10, sales $12,000,000, cert: WBENC)

2544 Office Design Concepts, LLC
6750 Brittmoore Rd
Houston, TX 77041
Contact: Joseph Sylvan President
Tel: 713-849-3611
Email: admin@odc-llc.com
Website: www.odc-llc.com
Office furniture, carpet & flooring, moving services, furniture installation, and painting (AA, estab 1999, empl 5, sales , cert: State, NMSDC)

2545 Pecos Construction
8111 LBJ Freeway Ste 625
Dallas, TX 75251
Contact: Mitzi Green Business Devel Mgr
Tel: 214-299-4900
Email: mdgreen@pecosconstruction.com
Website: www.pecosconstruction.com
Pre-construction, construction management, general contracting, design-build projects, large projects & self-perform services. (AA, estab 2003, empl 20, sales $16,616,224, cert: State)

2546 Prim Construction LLC
252 Roberts Cut Off Rd
Fort Worth, TX 76114
Contact: Trent Prim COO
Tel: 817-885-7851
Email: tprim@primconstruction.com
Website: www.primconstruction.com
Commercial general contracting, end user/tenant improvement/retail, mission critical, corporate campuses, health care & institutional service providers. (Woman, estab 2007, empl 10, sales $10,000,000, cert: State, WBENC)

CONSTRUCTION: General Contractors

2547 Samaripa Oilfield Services, LLC
      2855 N Mechanic St
      El Campo, TX 77437
      Contact: Amy Samaripa President
      Tel: 979-257-9385
      Email: amy@samaripaofs.com
      Website: www.samaripaofs.com
Pressure washing services, oil & chemical spill clean up, disaster cleanup & disposal, construction site clean up & reclamation, general construction, general labor hands & transport of equipment and supplies. (Minority, Woman, estab 2011, empl 15, sales $850,000, cert: NMSDC, WBENC)

2548 Sun Builders Co.
      15012 FM 529 Rd
      Houston, TX 77095
      Contact: Mary Miller Sec/Treas
      Tel: 281-815-1020
      Email: mmiller@sunbuildersco.com
      Website: www.sunbuildersco.com
General Contractor. (Woman, estab 1979, empl 25, sales $16,919,787, cert: WBENC)

2549 Synergy Project Consultants, Inc.
      1801 Wyoming, Ste 204
      El Paso, TX 79902
      Contact: Mark Young COO
      Tel: 915-613-1442
      Email: mcyoung@spc-pm.com
      Website: www.spc-pm.com
General contracting, construction renovation & repairs, design-build construction, architectural, engineering design management, construction project management, commissioning. (Hisp, estab 2007, empl 29, sales $2,100,000, cert: State)

2550 Team 1 Texas LLC
      1716 S San Marcos, Ste 119
      San Antonio, TX 78207
      Contact: Wendy Persyn Owner
      Tel: 210-977-0500
      Email: wendyp@team1texas.com
      Website: www.team1texas.com
Construction management, commercial & institutional building. (Woman/Nat-Ame, estab 2018, empl 20, sales , cert: State, WBENC)

2551 Tejas Premier Building Contractor, Inc.
      9200 Broadway, Ste 120
      San Antonio, TX 78217
      Contact: Julissa Carielo President
      Tel: 210-821-5858
      Email: julissa@tejaspremierbc.com
      Website: www.tejaspremierbc.com
Commercial general contracting. (Minority, Woman, estab 2006, empl 15, sales $2,280,000, cert: WBENC)

2552 The Trevino Group, Inc.
      11410 Brittmoore Park
      Houston, TX 77041
      Contact: Erin Trevino Sec/Treas
      Tel: 713-863-8333
      Email: etrevino@trevinogroup.com
      Website: www.trevinogroup.com
General contracting, construction management, design/build. (Hisp, estab 1976, empl 65, sales $32,000,000, cert: State, NMSDC)

2553 UCS Group LLC
      5910 N. Central Expy Ste 900
      Dallas, TX 75206
      Contact: Henry Rodriguez Dir of Marketing Business Dev
      Tel: 214-349-1600
      Email: henryr@universaltx.com
      Website: www.universaltx.com
General contracting, tenant improvements, renovations, design & build, construction management, ground up, office space remodeling, restaurant build out. (Hisp, estab , empl , sales $5,000,000, cert: State, NMSDC)

2554 Vanguard Electrical Services, LLC
      12002 Forestgate Dr
      Dallas, TX 75243
      Contact: Dustin Sample Business Devel
      Tel: 214-534-0627
      Email: dsample@vesdfw.com
      Website: www.vesdfw.com
Commercial & Industrial Electrical Contractor, Design Build/Assist & Engineering. (Hisp, estab 2009, empl 115, sales $16,000,000, cert: State)

Virginia

2555 Bay Electric Co., Inc.
      627 36th St
      Newport News, VA 23607
      Contact: John F. Biagas President
      Tel: 757-595-2300
      Email: johnfbiagas@bayelectricco.com
      Website: www.bayelectricco.com
General contracting, design/build, electrical, security, technology & power quality solutions & services. (AA, estab 1962, empl 95, sales $62,173,000, cert: NMSDC)

2556 BFE Construction, Inc.
      7620 Whitepine Rd
      Richmond, VA 23237
      Contact: Travis Bowers President
      Tel: 804-714-2540
      Email: tbowers@bfe-llc.com
      Website: www.bfe-llc.com
General contracting: bonded, commercial. (AA, estab 1998, empl 19, sales , cert: State, NMSDC)

2557 Construction & Environmental Services of Virginia
      2817 Mark St
      Chesapeake, VA 23324
      Contact: Bambi Walters General Counsel
      Tel: 757-784-1978
      Email: bambi@vaconstructionllc.com
      Website: www.vaconstructionllc.com
Construction, general contractor, commercial, industrial, engineering, flooring, water quality, roofing, carpentry, training, compliance, inspection, design, environmental, alternative energy, renovation, repair. (Woman/Nat-Ame, estab 2007, empl 3, sales , cert: State)

2558 Davis & Green, Inc.
      PO Box 35418
      Richmond, VA 23235
      Contact: Teddi Bartlett Project Mgr
      Tel: 804-231-9684
      Email: teddi@dgelectrical.com
      Website: www.dgelectrical.com
Electrical Contractor, service and supplies. (Woman, estab 1985, empl 95, sales $11,400,000, cert: State, WBENC)

2559 Diamonds Management Group, Inc.
      10117 Residency Rd
      Manassas, VA 20110
      Contact: Glenn Bertrand President
      Tel: 703-257-0017
      Email: dmgincservices@outlook.com
      Website: www.diamondsmanagement.com/
General contracting. (AA, estab 1994, empl 4, sales $300,000, cert: State)

2560 J. R. Caskey, Inc.
      PO Box 305
      Oilville, VA 23129
      Contact: Ginger Caskey President
      Tel: 804-784-8001
      Email: gec@jrcaskey.com
      Website: www.jrcaskey.com
Engineering, Layout & Surveying, Clearing & Demolition, Earthwork, Grading & Excavation, Erosion & Sediment Control, Traditional Stormwater Management Systems, Low-Impact Development Systems, Underground Water & Sanitary Sewer Utilities. (Woman, estab 1985, empl 42, sales $6,630,000, cert: State)

2561 Prestige Construction Group, Inc.
      219 Turner Rd
      Richmond, VA 23225
      Contact: John Scott President
      Tel: 804-745-0000
      Email: johns@prestigeconstruction.com
      Website: www.prestigeconstruction.com
General contracting, construction management. (AA, estab 1991, empl 25, sales $10,919,532, cert: State)

2562 ProTech Restoration, LLC
      3730 Glenmore Rd
      Scottsville, VA 24590
      Contact: Frank Trimble President
      Tel: 434-960-4456
      Email: protechrestorationva@gmail.com
      Website: www.protechva.com
Disaster restoration & construction services. (Woman, estab 2015, empl 1, sales , cert: State)

2563 RMT Construction & Development Group, Inc.
      571 Southlake Blvd
      Richmond, VA 23236
      Contact: Warren Thomas VP Construction
      Tel: 804-464-2673
      Email: wthomas@rmt-construction.com
      Website: www.rmt.construction.com
Commercial & industrial construction. (Woman/AA, estab 2007, empl 10, sales $2,000,000, cert: State)

2564 T. K. Davis Construction, Inc.
      711 Dawn St
      Richmond, VA 23222
      Contact: Thomas Davis
      Tel: 804-321-7822
      Email: smosby@tkdavis.com
      Website: www.tkdavis.com
General contracting: commercial, light industrial, retail, medical, office, storage facilities, athletic facilities, multi-family, design build, construction mgmt. (AA, estab 2001, empl 9, sales $21,819,325, cert: State, NMSDC)

2565 United Unlimited Construction, Inc.
      213 East Clay St, Ste A
      Richmond, VA 23219
      Contact: Merlin Hargrove President
      Tel: 804-343-7266
      Email: mharuuc@cavtel.net
      Website: www.uucirichmondva.com
General contracting: painting, concrete, demolition, renovations & retrofit, masonry, carpentry, miscellaneous & structural steel. (AA, estab 1983, empl 32, sales $1,946,879, cert: State)

2566 Wunna Contracting Corporation
      43695 John Mosby Hwy
      Chantilly, VA 20152
      Contact: Darnell Ingram Business Devel Dir
      Tel: 703-957-4266
      Email: dingram@wunnacontracting.com
      Website: www.wunnacontracting.com
Concrete installation, rehabilitation & repair, building entrances; foundations, driveways; walkways; stairs; colums, walls, patios; landscape; retaining walls. (Minority, estab 2007, empl 30, sales $3,000,000, cert: State)

Washington

2567 A&D Quality Construction Company, LLC
      220 SW Sunset Blvd Ste E202
      Renton, WA 98057
      Contact: Annette Demps Owner
      Tel: 425-271-7751
      Email: annette@adqualityco.com
      Website: www.In-Work
General contractoring: commercial & residential construction, demolition, excavation, site clearing, grading, dirt removal, utilities, footing, foundation & concrete. (Woman/AA, estab 1991, empl 2, sales $270,000, cert: State)

2568 Apollo Mechanical Contractors
      1133 W. Columbia Dr
      Kennewick, WA 99336
      Contact: Janelle LaFlamme Business Devel
      Tel: 509-586-1104
      Email: janelle.laflamme@apollomech.com
      Website: www.apollomech.com
General contracting services. (Nat Ame, estab 1981, empl 1800, sales $625,000,000, cert: NMSDC)

2569 JTS Manage Services
      526 Yale Ave North, Ste A
      Seattle, WA 98109
      Contact: Douglas Hamilton Marketing Coord
      Tel: 206-861-8000
      Email: douglas@jtsmanageservices.com
      Website: www.jts-seattle.com/
Construction management & project controls. (Woman/AA, estab 1993, empl 10, sales $650,000, cert: State)

2570 Laboratory Design & Construction, Inc.
      6659 Kimball Dr Ste D404
      Gig Harbor, WA 98335
      Contact: Elia Grogan Sales Mgr
      Tel: 253-858-7835
      Email: elia@laboratorydesign.net
      Website: www.laboratorydesign.net
Build laboratory facilities. (Woman, estab 1996, empl 2, sales , cert: State)

CONSTRUCTION: General Contractors

2571 MACNAK Construction LLC
      2624 112th St S, Ste A1
      Lakewood, WA 98499
      Contact: Santiago Mateo Project Mgr
      Tel: 253-212-2378
      Email: smateo@macnak.com
      Website: www.macnak.com
General Construction Design-Build & Design-Bid-Build projects, site work, concrete, rough carpentry, finish carpentry, plumbing, mechanical, electrical, painting & roofing, fire alarm system & access control systems. (Minority, estab 2007, empl 35, sales $84,000,000, cert: State)

2572 RHD Enterprises, Inc.
      817 78th Ave SW
      Tumwater, WA 98501
      Contact: Rozanne Garman President
      Tel: 360-705-9459
      Email: rozanne@rhdenterprises.com
      Website: www.rhdenterprises.com
General contracting: marine/subsea construction, remodels, design/build services, new construcion, pre-engineered metal buildings, modular facilities, laboratory modernizations. (Minority, Woman, estab 2005, empl 25, sales $13,199,569, cert: NMSDC, WBENC, 8(a))

Wisconsin

2573 Arteaga Construction, Inc.
      4000 S Pine Ave
      Milwaukee, WI 53207
      Contact: Anthony Arteaga President
      Tel: 414-744-7944
      Email: anthony@arteagaconstruction.com
      Website: www.arteagaconstruction.com
General contracting: masonry, carpentry, concrete, demolition & HVAC. (Hisp, estab 1986, empl 75, sales $25,000,000, cert: State, NMSDC)

2574 Sirrah Construction & Co, LLC
      3430 N 53rd St
      Milwaukee, WI 53216
      Contact: James Harris Managing Member
      Tel: 414-442-7477
      Email: james@sirrahconstruction.net
      Website: www.sirrahconstruction.net
General contracting: flatwork concrete & asphalt paving, demolition services. (AA, estab 2005, empl 6, sales $1,250,000, cert: State, City)

> **COSMETICS**
> Formulate, manufacture & distribute face and eye products, hair care products, perfumes, hand and body lotions, wig cleaners and sprays, and cosmetics for men. NAICS Code 32

California

2575 Garcoa, Inc.
26135 Mureau Rd Ste 100
Calabasas, CA 91302
Contact: Deborah Reidy
Tel: 818-225-0375
Email: debbie@garcoa.com
Website: www.Garcoa.com
Mfr branded, private label, control label & branded external liquid fill health & beauty products. (Woman, estab 1983, empl 48, sales $126,000,000, cert: WBENC)

2576 La Canada Ventures Inc.
448 N San Mateo Dr
San Mateo, CA 94401
Contact: Susan Lin CEO
Tel: 650-340-8688
Email: drlin@susanlinmd.com
Website: www.md-factor.com
Provides innovative personal care products. (Woman/AA, estab 2006, empl 8, sales $7,500,000, cert: WBENC)

2577 Plantlife Natural Body Care
961 Calle Negocio
San Clemente, CA 92673
Contact: Nancy Baldini Sales Mgr
Tel: 888-708-7873
Email: nbaldini@plantlife.net
Website: www.plantlife.net
Mfr All Natural Organic Aromatherapy products. (Woman, estab 1994, empl 20, sales $3,000,000, cert: WBENC)

2578 Total Glow Enterprise
14320 Ventura Blvd 280
Sherman Oaks, CA 91423
Contact: EnJunaya Canton CEO
Tel: 747-204-8633
Email: hello@zuhuribeauty.com
Website: www.ZuhuriBeauty.com
Mfr clean beauty products, personal hygiene kits. (AA, estab 2015, empl 3, sales , cert: NMSDC)

Colorado

2579 Crossing Cultures LLC
1821 Lefthand Cir, Ste D
Longmont, CO 80501
Contact: Dennis O'Toole Natl Sales Mgr
Tel: 303-651-3678
Email: dennis@goddessgarden.com
Website: www.goddessgarden.com
Organic skincare products. (Woman, estab 2009, empl 12, sales $1,429,113, cert: WBENC)

District of Columbia

2580 Shea Yeleen Health and Beauty, LLC
417 H St NE Ste 2
Washington, DC 20002
Contact: Rahama Wright CEO
Tel: 202-285-3435
Email: rwright@sheayeleen.com
Website: www.sheayeleen.com
Natural & organic shea butter bodycare products. (Woman/AA, estab 2012, empl 1, sales , cert: NMSDC)

Florida

2581 High End Beauty Inc.
1120 Holland Dr, Ste 2
Boca Raton, FL 33487
Contact: CEO
Tel: 561-665-1968
Email: CustomerService@Highendbeauty.com
Website: www.highendbeauty.com
Dist hair, skin, cosmetics & nail products. (Woman, estab 2011, empl 6, sales , cert: WBENC)

2582 NAIWBE Natural As I Wanna Be
421 W Church St Ste 601
Jacksonville, FL 32202
Contact: President
Tel: 904-634-7607
Email: info@naiwbellc.net
Website: www.naiwbellc.net
Organic Skin Care Products. (Woman/AA, estab 2011, empl 3, sales $100,000, cert: State, City)

Indiana

2583 Elwood Staffing Services, Inc.
4111 Central Ave
Columbus, IN 47202
Contact: Kimberly Randall Dir Business Dev
Tel: 812-372-6200
Email: hope.lane@elwoodstaffing.com
Website: www.elwoodstaffing.com
Organic skincare products. (AA, estab 1980, empl 260, sales $95,010,000, cert: NMSDC)

Michigan

2584 Universal Products
854 Edgemont Park
Grosse Pointe Park, MI 48230
Contact: Jose Reyes CEO
Tel: 313-804-0042
Email: jose.reyes@universalproductsmarketing.com
Website: www.universalproductsmarketing.com
Health & beauty care, hair growth treatments and vitamin supplements. (Hisp, estab 1988, empl 6, sales $4,000,000, cert: NMSDC)

North Carolina

2585 TWT Distributing Inc.
11107-C S Commerce Blvd
Charlotte, NC 28273
Contact: Daniel Owens Business Devel Mgr
Tel: 704-588-1746
Email: dowens@twtdist.com
Website: www.twtdistributing.com
Dist African American & Hispanic health & beauty care products. (AA, estab 1993, empl 14, sales , cert: NMSDC)

New Jersey

2586 Custom Essence
53 Veronica Ave
Somerset, NJ 08873
Contact: Colin O'Such President
Tel: 732-249-6405
Email: cosuch@customessence.com
Website: www.CustomEssence.com
Manufacture Fragrance & Cosmetic Products. (As-Ind, estab 1985, empl 43, sales , cert: NMSDC)

2587 G&D Coffee Mud LLC
5 Mathews Ave
Riverdale, NJ 07457
Contact: Giovanna Cicillini Owner
Tel: 973-709-0090
Email: giovannaskincare@gmail.com
Website: www.gdnaturalskincare.com
Manufacture skin care moisturizers. (Woman, estab 2008, empl 2, sales , cert: State)

2588 Health & Natural Beauty Corp LLC
140 Ethel Rd, Ste W
Piscataway, NJ 08854
Contact: Alexandra DePierro Sales/Marketing Mgr
Tel: 732-640-1832
Email: a.depierro@sprinjene.com
Website: www.sprinjene.com
Mfr oral care products. SprinJene is our line of superior toothpastes combining the power of black seed oil, zinc, and xylitol. (AA, estab 2012, empl 11, sales , cert: State)

2589 US Organic Group Corp.
90 Dayton Ave. Ste 132 Bldg 18, Unit 1P
Passaic, NJ 07055
Contact: Leonard Moon President
Tel: 201-252-4269
Email: mij3461@us-organic.com
Website: www.us-organic.com
Mfr USDA certified organic topical & personal care products. (As-Pac, estab 2011, empl 7, sales $590,303, cert: NMSDC)

2590 Xenna Corporation
33 Witherspoon St Ste 200
Princeton, NJ 08542
Contact: Carol Buck CEO
Tel: 609-921-1101
Email: cbuck@xenna.com
Website: www.xenna.com
Dist personal care products for foot care & hair care. (Woman, estab 1996, empl 5, sales $3,355,705, cert: WBENC)

Ohio

2591 Shema Global, LLC
825 N Houk Rd
Delaware, OH 43015
Contact: mark butler Managing Dir
Tel: 740-953-0292
Email: contact@shemaglobal.com
Website: www.shemaglobal.com
Mfr & dist all natural hair & body care products. (Woman/AA, estab 2009, empl 2, sales , cert: State)

Tennessee

2592 Keystone Laboratories, Inc.
1103 Kansas St
Memphis, TN 38106
Contact: Melinda Menke Owner
Tel: 901-774-8860
Email: mmburns@earthlink.net
Website: www.keystone-labs.com
Personal care products, ethnic hair care, skin care, toiletries. (Woman, estab 1934, empl 21, sales $3,794,000, cert: WBENC)

Texas

2593 826 & Co. LLC
4301 Greatview Dr
Round Rock, TX 78665
Contact: Jaime Masters CEO
Tel: 913-284-5536
Email: jaime@826andco.com
Website: www.826andCo.com
Botanical-based aromatherapy, skin and hair care. (AA, estab 2010, empl 1, sales , cert: State)

2594 Clavél
4150 E Overland Trail
Abilene, TX 79601
Contact: Dason Williams EVP Sales & Marketing
Tel: 325-676-9655
Email: dason@clavel.com
Website: www.clavel.com
Private label skin, pain creams & scar creams. (Woman, estab 1988, empl 11, sales $2,854,152, cert: WBENC)

2595 Naterra International
13525 Denton Dr
Dallas, TX 75234
Contact: Dan Zarazan VP Sales & Mktg
Tel: 972-241-9665
Email: dan@naterra.com
Website: www.naterra.com
Mfr beauty products. (As-Pac, estab 1994, empl 51, sales , cert: NMSDC)

2596 NTE Legacy, LLC
2919 Commerce St, Ste 480
Dallas, TX 75226
Contact: Nathan Townsie CEO
Tel: 469-708-7546
Email: ntownsie@naturelovesyouskincare.com
Website: www.naturelovesyouskincare.com
Hand & Surface Sanitizer (Vegan), 4-in-1 Shave Oil, Moisturizing Rejuvenation Serum (Organic). (AA, estab 2016, empl 1, sales , cert: NMSDC)

2597 Synergy Bodycare LLC.
5653 Winding Woods Trail
Dallas, TX 75227
Contact: Rosie Hill CEO
Tel: 214-460-1500
Email: rosielh@synergibody.com
Website: www.synergibody.com
Performance Skin & Hair Care for women & men of all skin types, tones & hair. (Woman/AA, estab 2009, empl 1, sales , cert: State, NMSDC)

Virginia

2598 Tree Naturals Inc.
4204 Riding Place Rd
Richmond, VA 23223
Contact: LaTresha Sayles CEO
Tel: 804-514-4423
Email: customerservice@treenaturals.com
Website: www.treenaturals.com
Natural hair & body products. (Woman/AA, estab 2011, empl 1, sales , cert: State)

DETECTIVE & SECURITY AGENCIES

Provide civil, criminal and private investigations; security consulting services and security guard services. NAICS Code 54

Alaska

2599 NMS Security Services, LLC
800 E Domind Blvd, Ste 3-450
Anchorage, AK 99515
Contact: Patrick Hayes Exec Dir, Sales US
Tel: 952-233-4014
Email: patrick.hayes@nmsusa.com
Website: www.nmsusa.com
Security and investigative services. (Nat Ame, estab 1978, empl 2850, sales $187,737,520, cert: NMSDC)

Alabama

2600 Dothan Security Inc. dba DSI Security Services
600 W Adams St
Dothan, AL 36303
Contact: Boyd Clark Dir Sales/Marketing
Tel: 334-793-5720
Email: bclark@dsisecurity.com
Website: www.dsisecurity.com
Uniformed security officers. (Woman, estab 1969, empl 4000, sales $52,000,000, cert: WBENC)

2601 Employment Screening Services
2500 Southlake Park
Birmingham, AL 35244
Contact: Jared Balint Enterprise Sales Mgr
Tel: 314-282-0154
Email: jbalint@es2.com
Website: www.es2.com
Criminal checks, credit checks, drug testing, motor vehicle checks, electronic fingerprinting, education, employment & reference verifications. (Woman, estab 1994, empl 85, sales $12,500,000, cert: WBENC)

2602 Workable Solutions Investigative & Protective Services, LLC
5925 Carmichael Rd Ste D
Montgomery, AL 36117
Contact: Tyron Works CEO
Tel: 334-262-0432
Email: info@wsips.net
Website: www.workable-solutions.org/
Security Guards & Patrol Services, Investigation Services, Special Events Security, Background Investigations, CCTV Monitoring, Loss Prevention, Home Watch, Protection/Bodyguard Services, Security Training. (AA, estab 2009, empl 25, sales , cert: State)

Arizona

2603 Anderson Security Agency, Ltd.
PO Box 42690
Phoenix, AZ 85080
Contact: Kimberly Matich CEO
Tel: 602-331-7000
Email: kmatich@andersonsecurity.com
Website: www.andersonsecurity.com
Armed & unarmed uniformed security officers, executive protection service, patrol service, investigations & background checks. (Woman, estab 1994, empl 388, sales , cert: WBENC)

2604 Hope Capital LLC
PO Box 74554
Phoenix, AZ 85087
Contact: Sarah Hope CEO
Tel: 602-899-1606
Email: sarah@verticalidentity.com
Website: www.verticalidentity.com
Develop, implement & provide screening programs, background investigations, Employment Verification, Criminal Background Checks, Motor Vehicle Record Check, Government Watch Lists, Fingerprinting. (Minority, Woman, estab 2014, empl 6, sales , cert: WBENC)

2605 Law Enforcement Specialists, Inc.
PO Box 11656
Glendale, AZ 85318
Contact: Bonnie Lucas CEO
Tel: 623-825-6700
Email: bonnie@lesaz.com
Website: www.offdutypoliceofficers.com
Law Enforcement Officers off-duty armed, uniformed & plain clothes. (Woman, estab 1994, empl 8, sales $5,610,458, cert: WBENC)

California

2606 ABC Security Service, Inc.
1840 Embarcadero
Oakland, CA 94606
Contact: Ana Chretien President
Tel: 510-436-0666
Email: ana@abcsecurityservice.com
Website: www.abcsecurityservice.com
Security guard & patrol services. (Woman/Hisp, estab 1968, empl 199, sales $8,950,917, cert: State, City, NMSDC, CPUC, WBENC)

2607 American Eagle Protective Services Inc.
425 West Kelso St
Inglewood, CA 90301
Contact: Maria Moreno Business Devel
Tel: 213-427-0715
Email: officeadmi@aeprotectiveservices.com
Website: www.aeprotectiveservices.com
Security guard services & patrol services. (Woman/AA, estab 2012, empl 102, sales , cert: NMSDC, CPUC)

2608 American Executive Private Security Inc.
2930 W Imperial Hwy, Ste 518
Inglewood, CA 90303
Contact: Eric Hall President
Tel: 323-920-6463
Email: aeps.security@gmail.com
Website: www.aepsecurityservices.com
Security and patrol services. (AA, estab 2014, empl 36, sales $1,548,909, cert: NMSDC)

2609 American Professional Security, Inc.
2500 Wilshire Blvd Ste 1030
Los Angeles, CA 90057
Contact: Ibrahim Tchiany Mgr
Tel: 213-380-5558
Email: info@americanprofessionalsecurity.com
Website: www.americanprofessionalsecurity.com
Provides armed and unarmed guards nationwide. (Woman/AA, estab 1994, empl 100, sales $500,000, cert: State)

2610 Apex Investigative Services Inc.
      11171 Sun Center Dr Ste 120
      Rancho Cordova, CA 95670
      Contact: JR Robles CEO
      Tel: 916-858-2999
      Email: jr@apexpi.com
      Website: www.apexpi.com
Investigation svcs: surveillance, workers compensation fraud, liability, disability mgmt, sexual harassment, due diligence, SIU fraud, employee terminations, background investigation, discrimination, witness interviews, etc. (Hisp, estab 1997, empl 55, sales $1,555,730, cert: NMSDC)

2611 Diversified Risk Management
      8137 3rd ST. 2nd Fl
      Downey, CA 90241
      Contact: Patricia Kotze-Ramos President
      Tel: 800-810-9508
      Email: bids@drminc.us
      Website: www.diversifiedriskmanagement.com
Licensed investigation. (Woman, estab 2002, empl 10, sales $1,300,000, cert: State, CPUC, WBENC)

2612 Global Unit 1
      15603 Firmona Ave
      Lawndale, CA 90260
      Contact: Ferdinand Ndedi COO
      Tel: 310-760-1957
      Email: ferdinandd@globalunit1.com
      Website: www.globalunit1.com
Security guards, patrol services, access control, perimeter patrol, vehicle & bike patrol, special events & parties, control room surveillance, gate house & reception services. (Woman/AA, estab 2010, empl 500, sales , cert: State, City)

2613 Infortal Associates, Inc. dba Infortal Worldwide
      1590 The Alameda Ste 100
      San Jose, CA 95126
      Contact: Candice Tal CEO
      Tel: 408-298-9700
      Email: ctal@infortal.com
      Website: www.infortal.com
Global security & risk mitigation, risk management & investigation services, business due diligence, reputation due diligence, M&A, board advisory, international executive travel, competitive intelligence, FCPA due diligence. (Woman, estab 1985, empl 12, sales $1,159,505, cert: WBENC)

2614 Inter-Con Security Systems, Inc.
      210 S De Lacey Ave
      Pasadena, CA 91105
      Contact: Matthew Reeser VP
      Tel: 626-535-2639
      Email: solutionsdesign@icsecurity.com
      Website: www.icsecurity.com
Security services. (Hisp, estab 1973, empl 35000, sales $378,022,000, cert: State, NMSDC)

2615 JLR Invesitgations
      9375 Archibald Ave, Ste 103
      Rancho Cucamonga, CA 91730
      Contact: Ruth Riddle CEO
      Tel: 909-888-8880
      Email: ruth@jlrinvestigations.com
      Website: www.jlrinvestigations.com
Investigative services, Surveillance & Sub Rosa, Background Investigations, AOE/COE Statements & Field Interviews, Activity Checks, Mortgage fraud Investigations. (Woman/AA, estab 2004, empl 34, sales , cert: NMSDC)

2616 Locked on Referrals Protection Inc.
      4202 Atlantic Ave, Ste 212
      Long Beach, CA 90807
      Contact: Kris Potter CEO
      Tel: 562-552-7972
      Email: lorprotection@gmail.com
      Website: www.lorprotection.com
Security guard services. (Woman/AA, estab 2013, empl 30, sales , cert: NMSDC, CPUC)

2617 National Eagle Security, Inc.
      3200 Wilshire Blvd, Ste 1208
      Los Angeles, CA 90010
      Contact: Maria Castillo Business Devel
      Tel: 213-637-0200
      Email: nesbestone@yahoo.com
      Website: www.nationaleaglesecurity.com
Security Officers, Public Relations Officers, Vehicle Patrol. (AA, estab 2014, empl 45, sales $768,194, cert: NMSDC, CPUC)

2618 Pacific Protection Services, Inc.
      22144 Clarendon St, Ste 110
      Woodland Hills, CA 91367
      Contact: Bob Pina CEO
      Tel: 818-313-9369
      Email: bob.pina@pacific-protection.com
      Website: www.pacific-protection.com
Uniform unarmed, armed security guard services & Law Enforcement Experience Agents (ODO). (AA, estab 1984, empl 400, sales $5,123,267, cert: NMSDC, CPUC)

2619 RCI Associates
      5030 Business Center Dr Ste 280
      Fairfield, CA 94534
      Contact: Mitchell Brooks
      Tel: 866-668-4732
      Email: mbrooks@rciassociatesinc.com
      Website: www.rciassociatesinc.com
Corporate & Insurance Investigations, Security Consulting, Global Threat Management, Special Events & Specialized Unarmed & Armed Uniform Services. (Nat Ame, estab 2012, empl 5, sales $1,495,000, cert: NMSDC, 8(a))

2620 Reliant Protective Services LLC
      4125 Shelburn Ct
      Los Angeles, CA 90065
      Contact: Don Seawell CEO
      Tel: 213-500-8447
      Email: don.seawell@reliant-ps.com
      Website: www.reliant-ps.com
Armed/Unarmed Security Guard Service, Executive Protection Body Guard Services. (AA, estab 2009, empl 15, sales , cert: City)

2621 Rene Garza and Associates, Inc.
      2660 W. Shaw Lane, Ste 110
      Fresno, CA 93711
      Contact: Audra da Rosa President
      Tel: 559-399-3113
      Email: audra@rga-pi.com
      Website: www.rga-pi.com
Investigative Services: Workers Compensation, Criminal Defense, Pre-Employment Background & Reference Checks. (Hisp, estab 2009, empl 5, sales $284,000, cert: NMSDC)

DETECTIVE & SECURITY AGENCIES

2622 RMI International
8125 Somerset Blvd
Paramount, CA 90723
Contact: Roxanne Rodriguez President
Tel: 562-806-9098
Email: roxanner@rmiintl.com
Website: www.rodbat.com
Security svcs: armed & unarmed security, off-duty law enforcement protection, background screening, investigations, security system design & engineering, training, worldwide executive protection services. (Minority, Woman, estab 1996, empl 60, sales , cert: NMSDC)

2623 Servexo Protective Services
1515 W 190th St, Ste 170
Gardena, CA 90248
Contact: Nick Chaires Dir of Corporate Accts
Tel: 323-527-9994
Email: nchaires@servexousa.com
Website: www.servexo.com
Security Services, Security solutions. (AA, estab 2013, empl 300, sales $5,000,000, cert: NMSDC, CPUC)

2624 Spearhead Protection Inc.
PO Box 605
Antioch, CA 94509
Contact: Cherokee Martin Admin Asst
Tel: 925-308-7778
Email: cherokee.spearheadpro@hotmail.com
Website: www.spearheadpros.com
Security services. (AA, estab 2006, empl 22, sales $400,000, cert: State)

Colorado

2625 IBC
PO Box 1052
Arvada, CO 80001
Contact: Bob Linderman Dir Business Dev
Tel: 303-403-0807
Email: blinderman@industrialbuyers.com
Website: www.intelligentbackground.com
Employment background screening, workers comp credit identity, investigations. (Hisp, estab 1991, empl 35, sales , cert: NMSDC)

Florida

2626 American Guard Services, Inc.
7011 N Atlantic Ave, Ste 200
Cape Canaveral, FL 32920
Contact: John Boyle Dir Business Dev
Tel: 321-784-1893
Email: jboyle@americanguardservices.com
Website: www.americanguardservices.com
Security personnel for the maritime environment, government facilities, campus safety, commercial security, industrial security. (Woman/As-Ind, estab 1997, empl 2500, sales $20,300,000, cert: State)

2627 Darwin Securities, LLC
16350 Bruce B Downs, Ste 47178
Tampa, FL 33646
Contact: Michael Dastolfo Owner
Tel: 813-468-3504
Email: michael@darwinsecurities.com
Website: www.darwinsecurities.com
Private Investigation, Executive Protection & Process Service Agency. (As-Pac, estab 2005, empl 2, sales , cert: State)

2628 Drakonx, Inc.
127 Grand Ave
Coral Gables, FL 33133
Contact: Fernando Alvarez President
Tel: 866-224-1245
Email: info@drakonx.com
Website: www.drakonx.com
Private Investigations, Surveillance, Background Checks, Due Diligence, Skip Tracing, Executive Protection, Risk Assessments, Insurance Fraud, Employee Misconduct Investigations. (Hisp, estab 2003, empl 2, sales , cert: NMSDC)

2629 Westmoreland Protection Agency, Inc.
10194 NW 47th St
Sunrise, FL 33351
Contact: Paul Spence President
Tel: 954-318-0532
Email: pspence@wpafla.com
Website: www.wpafla.com
Security svcs: armed & unarmed security officers. (AA, estab 2002, empl 101, sales $2,901,382, cert: NMSDC)

Georgia

2630 ALL(n)1 Security Services, Inc.
3915 Cascade Rd, Ste 340
Atlanta, GA 30331
Contact: Mary Parker CEO
Tel: 404-691-4915
Email: rrobinson@alln1security.com
Website: www.allin1security.com
Security officers, off-duty police, background checks, motor vehicle reports, drug screening, security surveys, risk assessment analysis, consulting, seminars & workshops & security system designs, CCTV monitors. (Woman/AA, estab , empl , sales $20,000,000, cert: State, NMSDC, WBENC)

2631 Confidential Security Agency, Inc.
PO Box 55188
Atlanta, GA 30308
Contact: Patrice Adams VP
Tel: 404-888-0801
Email: padams@confidentialsecurityagency.net
Website: www.confidentialsecurityagency.net
Security guard protective services. (AA, estab 1972, empl 267, sales $6,000,000, cert: State, NMSDC)

2632 Ekeholm and Associates, LLC
550 Parkbrook Trace
Alpharetta, GA 30004
Contact: Kirsti Ekeholm Member
Tel: 877-219-0732
Email: info@screensafecheck.com
Website: www.ScreenSafeCheck.com
Background screening, pre-employment background checks, criminal records checks, credit history, motor vehicle driving records, identity trace, credential verification & healthcare sanction history searches. (Woman, estab 1998, empl 25, sales , cert: WBENC)

2633 ESA Investigations & Security, LLC
70 Whitaker Way
Midway, GA 31320
Contact: Gerard Easley President
Tel: 912-312-9510
Email: gerard.easley@gmail.com
Website: www.esainvestigations.com
Investigative and security solutions. (AA, estab 2020, empl 15, sales , cert: NMSDC)

2634 Global Bureau of Security & Investigations
      240 Auburn Ave
      Atlanta, GA 30303
      Contact: Robert Conley President
      Tel: 404-876-7273
      Email: chez@gbsillc.com
      Website: www.gbsillc.com
Full service private investigation & security firm. (AA, estab 2012, empl 8, sales , cert: NMSDC)

2635 Global Investigations Inc.
      PO Box 473
      Fayetteville, GA 30214
      Contact: Tracey Brown
      Tel: 770-477-9879
      Email: tbrown@globalpi.us
      Website: www.globalpi.us
Surveillance, background checks & liability cliams. (Woman/AA, estab 2003, empl 10, sales , cert: NMSDC)

2636 Hawque Protection Services, LLC.
      3017 Bolling Way
      Atlanta, GA 30305
      Contact: Chris Rich President
      Tel: 502-767-7479
      Email: chris@hawque.com
      Website: www.hpg.global
Military & LEO, GPS tracked movement, monitored & recorded, Licensed, Armed & Trained. (AA, estab 2019, empl 25, sales $400,000, cert: NMSDC)

2637 Safeguard Security Solutions LLC
      1781 Hwy 42 N
      McDonough, GA 30253
      Contact: Rahul Anand CEO
      Tel: 404-545-3023
      Email: mrandall@safeguardsecurityllc.com
      Website: www.safeguardsecurityllc.com
Security guards, staffing & janitorial services. (AA, estab 2010, empl 5, sales $348,000, cert: NMSDC, 8(a))

2638 The Cedalius Group LLC
      2900 Delk Rd, Ste 700
      Marietta, GA 30067
      Contact: Melissa Foiles CEO
      Tel: 404-963-9772
      Email: mfoiles@thecedaliusgroup.com
      Website: www.thecedaliusgroup.com
Background screening, criminal, credit reports an& d drug screening, talent selection research support, vendor/franchisee vetting & international searches. (Hisp, estab 2012, empl 5, sales , cert: NMSDC)

2639 The Guardian Protective Services, LLC
      2839 Church St
      Atlanta, GA 30344
      Contact: Jennifer Rocke VP Acctg/Business Dev
      Tel: 404-766-2611
      Email: jenniferr@theguardiansecurity.com
      Website: www.theguardiansecurity.com
Security guard service, armed & unarmed, security consultation & analysis, loss prevention, security concierge services, patrol services. (Woman/AA, estab 1998, empl 200, sales , cert: State)

Iowa

2640 3rd Degree Screening Inc.
      100 E. Broadway Ste 201
      Council Bluffs, IA 51503
      Contact: Jeanie Waters President
      Tel: 712-256-1701
      Email: jeanie.waters@3rddegreescreening.com
      Website: www.3rddegreescreening.com
International comprehensive background screening, verifications services & drug testing services. (Woman, estab 2012, empl 8, sales $646,000, cert: WBENC)

Illinois

2641 AGB Investigative Services, Inc.
      2033 W 95th St
      Chicago, IL 60643
      Contact: John Griffin Jr. President
      Tel: 773-445-4300
      Email: john,griffin@agbinvestigative.com
      Website: www.AGBinvestigativeservices.com
Asset protection, risk mitigation, computer forensics & network security, fraud management, assurance services, private security services. (AA, estab 1999, empl 100, sales $2,600,000, cert: State, City, 8(a))

2642 Allpoints Security & Detective, Inc.
      2112 E 71st St
      Chicago, IL 60649
      Contact: Rhone Llevelyn CCO
      Tel: 773-955-6700
      Email: lrhone@allpointssecurityinc.com
      Website: www.allpointssecurityinc.com
Armed/unarmed security guard & mobile patrol services. (Woman/AA, estab 2000, empl 210, sales $4,940,000, cert: State, City)

2643 Fact Finders Group, Inc.
      4747 Lincoln Mall Dr, Ste 300
      Matteson, IL 60443
      Contact: Kenneth Webb Sr. CEO
      Tel: 708-283-4200
      Email: kenwebb@factfindersgroup.com
      Website: www.factfindersgroup.com
Investigative & security consulting agency. (AA, estab 1996, empl 16, sales $1,000,000, cert: State, City, NMSDC, 8(a))

2644 Lincoln Security Services, LLC
      6735 W Archer Ave
      Chicago, IL 60638
      Contact: Gregory Ramirez Exec VP
      Tel: 773-796-7900
      Email: gramirez@lincolnsecurityllc.com
      Website: www.lincolnsecurityllc.com
Unarmed Security Guards, Security Guards in Vehicle Patrol and Off Duty Law Enforcement Officers. (Hisp, estab 2011, empl 451, sales $2,350,791, cert: City)

2645 Page Security Inc.
      9453 S Ashland Ave
      Chicago, IL 60620
      Contact: Henry Page COO
      Tel: 773-239-5256
      Email: pagesecurity@msn.com
      Website: www.pagesecurityagency.net
Armed & unarmed security guards, live scan fingerprinting & background. (AA, estab 2001, empl 100, sales $1,500,000, cert: State)

2646 Securatex Ltd.
651 W Washington Blvd Ste 105
Chicago, IL 60661
Contact: Patricia J. DuCanto
Tel: 708-536-3771
Email: pducanto@securatex.com
Website: www.securatex.com
Armed & unarmed physical security/guards, patrol services, background investigations, pre-employment screenings. (Woman, estab 1986, empl 838, sales $12,518,000, cert: State, City)

2647 Security Professionals of Illinois, Inc.
7120 Windsor Lake Pkwy Ste 102
Loves Park, IL 61111
Contact: Angela Larson Dir of Dev
Tel: 815-637-6950
Email: alarson@getspi.com
Website: www.getspi.com
Security risk management services & solutions. (Hisp, estab 2003, empl 50, sales , cert: State, City, 8(a))

Louisiana

2648 L&R Security Services, Inc.
3930 Old Gentilly Rd
New Orleans, LA 70126
Contact: Edward Robinson President
Tel: 504-943-3191
Email: ejrobinson@lrsecurity.com
Website: www.lrsecurity.com
Security guard & special events services. (AA, estab 1979, empl 250, sales , cert: NMSDC)

2649 Pinnacle Security & Investigation Inc.
332 N Jefferson Davis Pkwy
New Orleans, LA 70119
Contact: VP Dir of Business Dev
Tel: 504-934-1411
Email: info@securitybypinnacle.com
Website: www.securitybypinnacle.com
Security Guard Services, armed security, unarmed security, security patrols, CCTV monitoring, and security consulting. (Hisp, estab 2011, empl 175, sales $3,200,000, cert: NMSDC)

2650 Tracepoint, LLC
PO Box 24059
New Orleans, LA 70184
Contact: Kristi Barranco Owner
Tel: 504-284-2285
Email: kristi@tracepointllc.com
Website: www.tracepointllc.com
Background & drug screening. (Woman, estab 2012, empl 3, sales , cert: WBENC)

Maryland

2651 AU & Associates Inc.
3100 Ritchie Rd, Ste F
District Heights, MD 20747
Contact: Ade Uiyoshioria President
Tel: 301-909-0076
Email: adeu@auanda.com
Website: www.auanda.com
Personality Fitting & Proficiency Testing, In-Depth Background Research, Drug Screening & Urinalysis Testing, Prior Work History Inspections, Information Technology Solutions. (Woman/AA, estab 2003, empl 5, sales $1,094,799, cert: State)

2652 Bradley Technologies Inc.
8701 Georgia Ave Ste 804
Silver Spring, MD 20910
Contact: Angela Bradley President
Tel: 301-562-9201
Email: angelabradley@btisecurity.com
Website: www.btisecurity.com
Unarmed & armed guard security guard services, access control & monitoring services. (Woman/AA, estab 2000, empl 157, sales $9,116,610, cert: State, NMSDC, WBENC, 8(a))

2653 National Background Investigations, Inc.
PO Box 966
Stevensville, MD 21666
Contact: Lori Holmes Grail VP
Tel: 410-604-6200
Email: lori@nationalbackground.com
Website: www.nationalbackground.com
Pre & post employment screening, felony & misdemeanor court record searches, motor vehicle reports, credit profiles, sex offender registry, SSN tracing, employment verification, civil record searches. (Woman, estab 1996, empl 9, sales , cert: WBENC)

2654 PChange LLC
4400 Stamp Rd Ste 302
Temple Hills, MD 20748
Contact: Rosa Griffin
Tel: 240-619-3507
Email: r.griffin@pchangellc.com
Website: www.pchangellc.com
Guard services & patrol. (Woman/AA, Hisp, estab 2003, empl 165, sales $5,388,000, cert: State, City)

2655 Security 1 Solutions LLC
845 Quince Orchard Blvd Ste Q
Gaithersburg, MD 20878
Contact: Bruce Alexander President
Tel: 301-926-4957
Email: balexander@security1solutions.com
Website: www.security1solutions.com
Manned-guarding & related security solutions, Security staffing, Emergency response services, Special event security, Safety auditing & awareness, Security training, Conceptual security systems design. (AA, estab 2012, empl 80, sales $2,400,000, cert: State)

Michigan

2656 Del Ray Security
34215 Jefferson
Harrison Township, MI 48045
Contact: Rudy Garcia President
Tel: 586-415-4518
Email: delraypd@aol.com
Website: www.delraysecurity.com
Armed/unarmed security guard services. (Hisp, estab 1998, empl 25, sales $400,000, cert: NMSDC)

2657 Lagarda Security
2123 S Center Rd
Burton, MI 48519
Contact: Elena Rathburn Accounting specialist
Tel: 877-944-8400
Email: elenarathburn@lagardasecurity.com
Website: www.lagardasecurity.com
Security officers. (Woman, estab , empl , sales , cert: WBENC)

DETECTIVE & SECURITY AGENCIES

2658 Pyratech Security Systems, Inc.
      20150 Livernois
      Detroit, MI 48221
      Contact: Larry Teamer Sales
      Tel: 313-345-2000
      Email: larry@pyratechsecurity.com
      Website: www.pyratechsecurity.com
Security service: homeland security, alarm system design, uniformed security guards, private investigations, security & fire detection systems. (AA, estab 1993, empl 45, sales , cert: NMSDC)

2659 Tricon Security Group, LLC
      3011 W Grand Blvd, Ste 407
      Detroit, MI 48202
      Contact: Michael Whittaker CEO
      Tel: 877-641-2600
      Email: mwhittaker@rsigsecurity.com
      Website: www.triconsecurity.com
Uniformed security officers, loss prevention education, personal protection training, executive protective, event security. (AA, As-Pac, estab 2004, empl 1100, sales $10,000,000, cert: NMSDC)

Minnesota

2660 Guardem Security Group Inc.
      601 Carlson Pkwy, Ste 1050
      Minnetonka, MN 55305
      Contact: Daniel Claybrook CEO
      Tel: 888-314-0613
      Email: info@guardemsecuritygroup.com
      Website: www.guardemsecuritygroup.com
Security services, armed & unarmed security , cybersecurity, private protection & construction security. (AA, estab 2018, empl 18, sales , cert: NMSDC)

2661 Twin City Security, Inc.
      519 Coon Rapids Blvd
      Coon Rapids, MN 55433
      Contact: Jeff Flattum Reg Accounts/ Sales Mgr
      Tel: 763-784-4160
      Email: j.flattum@twincitysecurity.com
      Website: www.twincitysecurity.com
Armed & unarmed security guard services. (Woman, estab 1974, empl 650, sales , cert: State)

North Caroilina

2662 J.P. Investigative Group, Inc.
      9716-B Rea Rd, Ste 211
      Charlotte, NC 28277
      Contact: Joe Paonessa Co-Owner
      Tel: 704-243-1137
      Email: info@jpinvestigations.com
      Website: www.jpinvestigations.com
Video surveillance & special investigations for potentially fraudulent workers' compensation, property/casualty & general liability claims. (Woman, estab 2000, empl 15, sales $499,636, cert: State, WBENC)

2663 Professional Police Services Inc
      9731 Southern Pine Blvd Ste A
      Charlotte, NC 28273
      Contact: Candace Ratliff COO
      Tel: 704-442-9499
      Email: clratliff@pssprotection.com
      Website: www.pssprotection.com
Security guard & patrol services, law enforcement services, alarm response, crowd control, surveillance, escorts, personal protection. (Woman/AA, estab 2000, empl 95, sales , cert: State)

2664 Safe & Secure Worldwide Protection Group
      4925 W Market St Ste 1142
      Greensboro, NC 27409
      Contact: Lance Jones President
      Tel: 888-476-6388
      Email: chiefjones@safesecureworldwide.com
      Website: www.safesecureworldwide.com
Security guards, armed guards, loss prevention agents, executive protection agents. (Woman/AA, estab 2009, empl 157, sales , cert: NMSDC)

2665 Sunstates Security, LLC
      801 Corporate Center Dr Ste 300
      Raleigh, NC 27607
      Contact: Carol Drumheller Sales & Marketing Coordinator
      Tel: 919-987-1409
      Email: radams@sunstatessecurity.com
      Website: www.sunstatessecurity.com
Security services. (Woman, estab 1998, empl 2302, sales $58,957,564, cert: WBENC)

2666 TriMetro Security Services LLC
      224 E Holding Ave, Unit 935
      Wake Forest, NC 27588
      Contact: Terry Walser CEO
      Tel: 919-623-4354
      Email: terrywalser@trimetrosecurity.com
      Website: www.TriMetroSecurity.com
Guard staffing & patrol services. (AA, estab 2009, empl 9, sales , cert: State)

New Hampshire

2667 STANDA, Inc.
      41 Micah Terr
      Milton, NH 03851
      Contact: David G Duchesneau GM
      Tel: 603-652-7225
      Email: info@standa.com
      Website: www.standa.com
Security & Investigations consultant. (Woman, estab 1991, empl 8, sales $150,000, cert: State)

New Jersey

2668 Data Access Inc.
      999 McBride Ave Ste C205
      Woodland Park, NJ 07424
      Contact: Karen Jacobsen President
      Tel: 973-774-0030
      Email: karen@datascreening.com
      Website: www.datascreening.com
Background screening for pre-employment & tenant screening. (Woman, estab 1996, empl 5, sales $300,000, cert: State, City, WBENC)

2669 Motivated Security Services, Inc.
      34 W Main St Ste 204
      Somerville, NJ 08876
      Contact: Sheref Shahid VP Sales
      Tel: 908-526-1140
      Email: sshahid@motivatedsecurity.com
      Website: www.motivatedsecurity.com
Armed & unarmed uniform security officers. (Woman, estab 1969, empl 650, sales $16,300,000, cert: WBENC)

2670 We See You limited liability
116 N 2nd St Ste 208
Camden, NJ 08102
Contact: Raymond Jones President
Tel: 609-914-5775
Email: weseeyoullc@gmail.com
Website: www.we-see-you.net
Unarmed security & safety, uniformed & plain clothes, foot & vehicle patrols. (AA, estab 2010, empl 75, sales $761,000, cert: NMSDC, 8(a), SDB)

New York

2671 A.C. Roman & Associates, Inc.
1350 RXR Plaza West Tower
Uniondale, NY 11556
Contact: Kamil Podlinski VP of Operations
Tel: 516-596-3300
Email: info@romansearch.com
Website: www.romansearch.com
Insurance, corporate, fraud, surveillance & criminal investigation services. (Hisp, estab 1998, empl 70, sales $4,000,000, cert: City)

2672 AWICS Security & Investigations, Inc.
962 East 31 St
Brooklyn, NY 11210
Contact: Barrington Pinto President
Tel: 718-338-0882
Email: awicslisa@gmail.com
Website: www.iawics.com
Security, training, investigative & emergency management operations, armed & unarmed Peace Enforcement Officers, private investigators. (AA, estab 2000, empl 12, sales , cert: State)

2673 Bay Ridge Security Service, Inc.
110 Bay Ridge Ave
Brooklyn, NY 11220
Contact: Anthony La Bella
Tel: 718-238-2974
Email: alabella@bayridgesecurity.com
Website: www.bayridgesecurity.com
Uniformed & plainclothes security guard services, armed & unarmed, executive protection, vehicle patrol & armed transportation. (Woman, estab 1973, empl 175, sales $3,159,632, cert: State, City)

2674 BBG Consulting, LLC
8 Rosa Dr
White Plains, NY 10607
Contact: New Supplier Managing Dir
Tel: 917-727-1173
Email: cnbell@thebellbuskeygroup.com
Website: www.thebellbuskeygroup.com
Business Registry Checks, Fraud & Financial Investigations, BSA Investigations, Due Diligence Investigations, Litigation Checks, Asset Forfeiture Checks, Monitoring, Background Investigations, Law Enforcement, Security. (AA, estab 2012, empl 2, sales $100,000, cert: State, NMSDC)

2675 ISS Action, Inc.
158-12 Rockaway Blvd
Queens, NY 11434
Contact: Pamela Newman CEO
Tel: 718-978-3000
Email: cdcohen@issaction.com
Website: www.issaction.com
Armed & unarmed uniformed security guards. Aviation security, ramp security, mobile security. Security planning FCL Clearance Federal security contractor. (Woman, estab 1991, empl 200, sales $11,340,577, cert: State, City, 8(a))

2676 Johnson Security Bureau, Inc.
609 Walton Ave
Bronx, NY 10451
Contact: Jessica A. Johnson President
Tel: 718-402-3600
Email: info@johnsonsecuritybureau.com
Website: www.johnsonsecuritybureau.com
Watch, guard & patrol agency: armed & unarmed guard services. (Woman/AA, estab 1962, empl 120, sales $5,635,000, cert: City, NMSDC, WBENC)

2677 Lemire LLC
44 Wall St, Fl 12
New York, NY 10005
Contact: Christine O'Sullivan Analyst
Tel: 212-461-2158
Email: cosullivan@lemirellc.com
Website: www.lemirellc.com
Investigative due diligence, complex investigations, monitorships, background screening, sexual misconduct investigations, construction integrity monitoring & cyber forensics. (Woman, estab 2013, empl 10, sales , cert: State, City, WBENC)

2678 Miracle Security Inc.
193-49 Williamson Ave, Ste B
Queens, NY 11413
Contact: James Obayagbona President
Tel: 718-525-8030
Email: jambona193@aol.com
Website: www.miracle4security.com
Security guard services. (AA, estab 2005, empl 150, sales $200,000,000, cert: State)

Ohio

2679 National Alliance Security Agency, Inc.
7918 N Main St
Dayton, OH 45415
Contact: President
Tel: 937-387-6517
Email: administrative@nationalalliancesecurity.com
Website: www.nationalalliancesecurity.com
Uniformed armed & unarmed security guard services. (Woman, estab 2005, empl 92, sales $1,091,995, cert: State, WBENC)

2680 Safe Choice LLC
11811 Shaker Blvd, Ste 415
Cleveland, OH 44120
Contact: Anthony Spencer VP
Tel: 216-231-7233
Email: safechoice1@att.net
Website: www.Safechoicellc.com
Armed & Unarmed Security Guards & Police Officers, Public & Private Events, Traffic Control, Employee Investigations, Theft, Drug & Alcohol Testing, employee Removal Assistance, Body Guard Services. (Woman/AA, estab 2010, empl 382, sales $3,115,948, cert: State, SDB)

DETECTIVE & SECURITY AGENCIES

Oklahoma

2681 Superior Security
      4419 N. Bryan Ave.
      Shawnee, OK 74804
      Contact: Louis Maltos CEO
      Tel: 405-275-9072
      Email: lmaltos@superiorsecurityusa.com
      Website: www.superiorsecurityusa.com
Physical security, executive & personal protection, access control, CCTV cameras, life safety, on call emergency response, pre-employment screening, terrorism watch list searches, security guard analysis, crisis mgmt. (Hisp, estab 1994, empl 140, sales $8,000,000, cert: NMSDC)

2682 Wallace & Associates Protective Services, LLC
      3128 E Pine St
      Tulsa, OK 74115
      Contact: Virgil Wallace CEO
      Tel: 918-835-1456
      Email: virgilwllc@yahoo.com
      Website: www.wapsl.com
Protection services. (AA, estab 1993, empl 35, sales $50,000,000, cert: City)

Pennsylvania

2683 Century Security Services, Inc.
      6 Rose Lane
      Wilkes Barre, PA 18702
      Contact: President
      Tel: 800-927-0524
      Email: info@centurysecurityservices.com
      Website: www.centurysecurityservices.com
Armed & unarmed security officers, medical transports. risk assessment, general security consultation, private investigation, alarm & surveillance equipment. (Woman, estab 1984, empl 70, sales , cert: State)

2684 Gentile and Associates, Inc.
      3645 Brodhead Rd
      Monaca, PA 15061
      Contact: Christine Selden Principal
      Tel: 724-775-3511
      Email: cselden@gentilesecurity.com
      Website: www.gentilesecurity.com
Pre-employment background screening, risk management, workplace investigations, vulnerability analysis, executive protection, surveillance, security guards. (Woman, estab 2009, empl 314, sales $15,000,000, cert: WBENC)

2685 Peak Security Inc.
      103 Yost Blvd, Ste 100
      Pittsburgh, PA 15221
      Contact: Sales Consultant
      Tel: 412-349-0850
      Email: info@peaksecurityinc.com
      Website: www.peaksecurityinc.com
Armed & unarmed guard services, emergency operations planning & design, ID badging, security system services. (Woman, estab 1997, empl 150, sales , cert: State)

2686 Tactical Response Security Consulting Inc.
      3565 Sepviva St
      Philadelphia, PA 19134
      Contact: Luis Torres President
      Tel: 888-755-9111
      Email: tacresp@msn.com
      Website: www.tacticalresponsesecurity.com
Security & detective services, armed & unarmed security & investigative services. (Hisp, estab 2008, empl 50, sales $1,800,000, cert: NMSDC)

Puerto Rico

2687 One Corps, Inc
      PO Box 79767
      Carolina, PR 00984
      Contact: Sonia Fuentes
      Tel: 787-776-0062
      Email: sfuentes@one-corps.com
      Website: www.one-corps.com
Armed & Unarmed Security Guards, IP Monitoring, Cameras, Access Control, Fire Watch. (Hisp, estab 2007, empl 134, sales $2,641,716, cert: NMSDC)

South Carolina

2688 G&I Security Company, LLC.
      9444 Two Notch Rd Ste B-1
      Columbia, SC 29223
      Contact: Melvin Dewitt CEO
      Tel: 803-661-9221
      Email: info@gisecuritycompany.com
      Website: www.gisecuritycompany.com
Security services. (AA, estab 2011, empl 30, sales , cert: State)

Tennessee

2689 Metropolitan Security Inc. dba Walden Security
      100 E Tenth St Ste 400
      Chattanooga, TN 37402
      Contact: Lauren Tudor EVP Marketing & Sales
      Tel: 423-702-8200
      Email: marketinginfo@waldensecurity.com
      Website: www.waldensecurity.com
Security services. (Woman, estab 1990, empl 4550, sales $232,247,039, cert: WBENC)

2690 Phelps Security Inc.
      4932 Park Ave
      Memphis, TN 38117
      Contact: Andrew Phelps Business Mgr
      Tel: 901-365-9728
      Email: andy@phelpssecurity.com
      Website: www.phelpssecurity.com
Armed/unarmed security officers, commercial/residential patrols, investigations. (Woman, estab 1953, empl 375, sales $8,000,000, cert: WBENC)

2691 Security Walls LLC
      130 N Martinwood Rd
      Knoxville, TN 37923
      Contact: Juanita Walls Chief Mgr
      Tel: 865-546-2597
      Email: jwalls@securitywalls.net
      Website: www.securitywalls.net
Security & Protective Services: armed & unarmed, visitor/access control, SCIF security, intl visitor escort,, post & roving patrols, electronic security monitoring, CCTV systems, emergency plans. (Woman/AA, estab 2003, empl 376, sales $15,000,000, cert: State, City)

Texas

2692 Ameritex Guard Services
      100 N Central Expwy, Ste 350
      Richardson, TX 75080
      Contact: Christopher ONeal Sr Acct Exec
      Tel: 972-231-6395
      Email: isf972@earthlink.net
      Website: www.ameritexguardsaervices.com
Uniformed security guards. (Minority, Woman, estab 1994, empl 256, sales $7,400,000, cert: State, NMSDC)

2693 Asez Inc.
1716 S San Marcos, Ste 120
San Antonio, TX 78207
Contact: Robert Lozano CEO
Tel: 210-736-6200
Email: corporate@asezinc.com
Website: www.asezinc.com
Armed & unarmed security officers, security systems services, security alarm systems, fire alarm systems, access control, closed circuit television, alarm monitoring, intergraded system. (Hisp, estab 2000, empl 75, sales $2,575,000, cert: State, 8(a))

2694 Boutchantharaj Corporation
5705 Airport Freeway
Fort Worth, TX 76117
Contact: Kit Boutchantharaj President
Tel: 817-831-2000
Email: kit@dfwsecurityprotectiveforce.com
Website: www.dfwsecurityprotectiveforce.com
Provide unarmed & armed on-site security guard services. (As-Pac, estab 2000, empl 250, sales $7,000,000, cert: State, 8(a))

2695 Nationwide Investigations & Security, Inc.
2425 West Loop South, Ste 200
Houston, TX 77027
Contact: Allen G Hollimon CEO
Tel: 713-297-8830
Email: ahollimon@ntwinvestigations.com
Website: www.ntwinvestigations.com
Security guard services, investigations, dignitary protection, communications cabling, CCTV/CATV, alarms, automated controls, networking, home theaters. (AA, estab 1999, empl 123, sales , cert: State, NMSDC)

2696 Night Eyes Protective Services Inc.
2407 E Yandell, Ste C
El Paso, TX 79903
Contact: Barbara Rodriguez VP
Tel: 915-549-0501
Email: nebarb01@night-eyes.com
Website: www.night-eyes.com
Security officers/guards, patrol officers & armored courier services. (Hisp, estab 1999, empl 200, sales $3,400,000, cert: State, NMSDC)

2697 RGG Services Inc.
5959 Westheimer Rd, Ste 107
Houston, TX 77057
Contact: G. Gallardo President
Tel: 713-972-1719
Email: marketing@rggservices.org
Website: www.rggservices.org
Bilingual (English/Spanish) security guards, body guards, private investigators, civil process svcs. (Minority, Woman, estab 1978, empl 50, sales , cert: City)

2698 Ruiz Protective Service, Inc.
2646 Andjon Dr
Dallas, TX 75220
Contact: Sales Mgr
Tel: 214-357-0820
Email: info@myliedetect.com
Website: www.ruizservices.com
Security guard & patrol services: armed & unarmed guard services. (Hisp, estab 1998, empl 550, sales $6,000,000, cert: State)

2699 Thomas Protective Service, Inc.
PO Box 883
Kaufman, TX 75142
Contact: Larry Thomas Security Sales
Tel: 972-962-3686
Email: larry@thomasprotective.com
Website: www.securityguardservices.com
Armed & Unarmed Security Officers, Private Investigations, Alarm Systems & CCTV Systems. (Woman, estab 1981, empl 485, sales $15,000,000, cert: WBENC)

2700 Z-MAS International
2626 South Loop West, Ste 250
Houston, TX 77054
Contact: Janie Pinkney Managing Dir
Tel: 832-489-0960
Email: securitieszmas@outlook.com
Website: www.zmassecurity.wixsite.com
Certified, licensed, insured & bonded security officers, armed guards, unarmed guards, investigations. (AA, estab 2017, empl 5, sales , cert: State)

Virginia

2701 AIVI Global Inc.
6412 Brandon Ave, Ste 712
Springfield, VA 22150
Contact: Raphaela O'Brien President
Tel: 703-851-4521
Email: ella.obrien@aiviglobal.com
Website: www.aiviglobal.com
Security integration & engineering consulting, Physical Access Control installation & mgmt, Video installation, IP infrastructure & Security Investigations. (Minority, estab 2019, empl 4, sales , cert: State)

2702 Top Guard, Inc.
PO Box 55030
Norfolk, VA 23505
Contact: Chris Stuart VP
Tel: 757-722-3961
Email: cstuart@topguardinc.com
Website: www.topguardinc.com
Guard services, uniformed private security officers. (Woman, estab 1996, empl 575, sales $15,250,000, cert: State)

Washington

2703 Goldbelt Specialty Services LLC
200 W Thomas, Ste 420
Seattle, WA 98119
Contact: Gino DCafango Business Dev Mgr
Tel: 206-234-8759
Email: g.dcafango@gbss.us
Website: www.gbss.us
Security services: aromored transpot, vehicle, foot patrol & stationary security officers. (Nat Ame, estab 2005, empl 18, sales $996,994, cert: NMSDC)

2704 Oatridge Security Group Inc.
2111 South 90th St.
Tacoma, WA 98444
Contact: Colby Oatridge General Mgr
Tel: 253-212-3659
Email: colby@oatridgesecurity.com
Website: www.oatridgesecurity.com
Security Officers, Executive Protection, Patrol Officers, Concierges & Security Mgmt. (Hisp, estab 2003, empl 225, sales $12,000,000, cert: NMSDC)

EDUCATIONAL MATERIALS

> **EDUCATIONAL MATERIALS**
> Manufacturers and wholesale distributors of text books, films, tapes, posters, magazines and teaching guides. NAICS Code 42

California

2705 El Mundo Communications
      7444 E Chapman Ave Ste B
      Orange, CA 92869
      Contact: Martha Montoya Publisher
      Tel: 714-366-3225
      Email: martha@elmundous.com
      Website: www.elmundous.com
Spanish language newspaper. (Hisp, estab 1988, empl 7, sales $700,000, cert: NMSDC)

Florida

2706 Wilson Emergency Medical Training, LLC
      934 Walnut Creek Ln
      Kissimmee, FL 34759
      Contact: John Wilson President
      Tel: 646-246-2942
      Email: wilsonemt5@gmail.com
      Website: www.wilsonemt.com
Training & Certification: CPR AED & First Aid (AA, estab 2015, empl 10, sales , cert: State)

Indiana

2707 Briljent, LLC
      7999 Knue Road, Ste. 200
      Indianapolis, IN 46250
      Contact: Jennifer Duszynski Mgr Client Services
      Tel: 317-220-1563
      Email: jduszynski@briljent.com
      Website: www.briljent.com
Develop customized technical writing, education manuals, systems documentation, training & adult learner educational programs. (Woman, estab 1998, empl 120, sales $35,250,000, cert: State)

2708 HPC International, Inc.
      5261 Fountain Dr, Ste A
      Crown Point, IN 46307
      Contact: Lynn Bell CEO
      Tel: 219-922-4868
      Email: lbell@hpcinterantionalinc.com
      Website: www.hpcinternationalinc.com
Trade publishing: books, pamphlets, brochures, booklets, journals, newsletters, to comic books, e-zines, interactive DVD's, e-learning & web-based content. (AA, estab 1996, empl 20, sales , cert: NMSDC)

2709 MPM Marketing, Inc
      8918 Squire Ct
      Indianapolis, IN 46250
      Contact: Mary Pat McKee President
      Tel: 317-440-9376
      Email: marypat@mpmmarketinginc.com
      Website: www.indyboomer.com
Publish an annual visitor guides for several hospitals in Indiana, sell advertising & work with large marketing departments. (Woman, estab 2005, empl 1, sales , cert: State)

Massachusetts

2710 The Training Associates Corporation
      11 Apex Dr Ste 202A
      Marlborough, MA 01752
      Contact: Justin Barrett VP of Contracts & Compl
      Tel: 800-241-8868
      Email: JBarrett@TTACorp.com
      Website: www.thetrainingassociates.com
Learning & development talent & training solutions. Instructional Design, Learning Strategy, Corporate Coaching, Staff Augmentation, Direct Hire & Managed Learning Services. (Woman, estab 1994, empl 30, sales , cert: WBENC)

2711 Victory Productions, Inc.
      55 Linden St
      Worcester, MA 01609
      Contact: President
      Tel: 508-798-6218
      Email:
      Website: www.victoryprd.com
Develop educational products: print & electronic products in English and Spanish, concept development, design, editorial, translation, technology, & production. (Minority, Woman, estab 1996, empl 35, sales $5,500,000, cert: NMSDC, WBENC)

Minnesota

2712 Free Spirit Publishing Inc.
      6325 Sandburg Road, Ste 100
      Golden Valley, MN 55427
      Contact: April Neske Asst to President
      Tel: 612-338-2068
      Email: neske@freespirit.com
      Website: www.freespirit.com
Publish learning materials that support social & emotional development, counseling & educational needs, professional development, special needs, gifted & talented, counseling, bullying & conflict resolution, character education & service learning. (Woman, estab 1983, empl 31, sales $5,600,000, cert: WBENC)

New Jersey

2713 American Overseas Book Company, Inc.
      550 Walnut St
      Norwood, NJ 07648
      Contact: Peter Lieb Dir of Operations
      Tel: 201-767-7600
      Email: plieb@aobc.com
      Website: www.aobc.com
Dist books, CDs, DVDs & journal subscriptions. (Woman, estab 1969, empl 7, sales $4,500,000, cert: State)

2714 Horizon Group USA
      45 Technology Dr
      Warren, NJ 07059
      Contact: Penn Wilder VP Sales
      Tel: 908-810-1111
      Email: pwilder@hgusa.com
      Website: www.horizongroupusa.com/
broad array of activity kits, kids crafts, finished decor, fashion accessories and educational products. (As-Pac, estab , empl 340, sales $257,000,000, cert: NMSDC)

2715 Infopro Learning Inc
103 Morgan Ln, Ste 102
Plainsboro, NJ 08536
Contact: Ashhish Handa Regional VP Sales
Tel: 609-606-9012
Email: ash.handa@infoprolearning.com
Website: www.infoprolearning.com
Instructor Led/ Web Based/ Blended Training: Therapeutic Training, Sales Training, Product Training, Physician Training. (As-Ind, estab 2006, empl 1100, sales $262,418,117, cert: NMSDC)

New York

2716 Black Enterprise
130 Fifth Ave, 10 Fl
New York, NY 10011
Contact: Shareen Maison Staff Acct
Tel: 212-242-8000
Email: careers@blackenterprise.com
Website: www.blackenterprise.com
Publishing services. (AA, estab 1970, empl 100, sales $23,555,540, cert: State)

2717 Hudson Valley Press LLC
PO Box 2160
Newburgh, NY 12550
Contact: Chuck Stewart Editor
Tel: 845-562-1313
Email: sales@hvpress.net
Website: www.HudsonValleyPress.com
Minority newspaper that gives coverage to Orange, Dutchess, Westchester, Rockland, and Ulster Counties in the Hudson Valley of New York State. (AA, estab 1983, empl 3, sales $135,000, cert: State)

Pennsylvania

2718 AdMed, Inc.
122 Union Square Dr
New Hope, PA 18938
Contact: Joan Francy CEO
Tel: 215-485-8943
Email: joan.francy@admedinc.com
Website: www.admedinc.com
Integrated agency that blends medical writing, creative & learning expertise. (Woman, estab 1986, empl 40, sales $7,615,711, cert: WBENC)

Puerto Rico

2719 Seminarios Imagen, Inc.
PO Box 9118
San Juan, PR 00908
Contact: Ivis Davila President
Tel: 787-724-2548
Email: idavila@seminariosimagen.com
Website: www.seminariosimagen.com
Leader in bilingual corporate education. (Woman/Hisp, estab 2001, empl 5, sales $501,000, cert: NMSDC)

Texas

2720 Align4Profit, Inc.
5960 W Parker Blvd, Ste 278
Plano, TX 75093
Contact: Lezley Meggersee Office Mgr
Tel: 972-608-0400
Email: info@align4profit.com
Website: www.align4profit.com
Strategic & Tactical Learning Organization. (Woman, estab 1996, empl 6, sales $449,000, cert: State, WBENC)

2721 Minority Business News
13111 N Central Expressway, Ste 400
Dallas, TX 75044
Contact: Mia Smith Project Mgr
Tel: 214-369-3200
Email: mbnusa@globalxlr.com
Website: www.mbnusa.biz
Magazine/internet supplier diversity publishing. (AA, estab 1988, empl 10, sales $1,300,000, cert: NMSDC)

2722 Minority Opportunity News, Inc.
PO Box 763866
Dallas, TX 75376
Contact: Thurman Jones Publisher
Tel: 972-516-4191
Email: businessoffice@northdallasgazette.com
Website: www.northdallasgazette.com
Newspaper: advertising & media, paper & internet. (AA, estab 1991, empl 5, sales , cert: State)

2723 Southern Chinese Daily News LLC
11122 Bellaire Blvd
Houston, TX 77072
Contact: Mia Smith Project Mgr
Tel: 281-498-4310
Email: scdn@globalxlr.com
Website: www.scdaily.com/
Publishing, advertising. (As-Pac, estab 1978, empl 19, sales $2,327,224, cert: City, NMSDC)

2724 Tre Weekly Magazine
3202 N Shiloh Rd
Garland, TX 75044
Contact: Shayne Hohman Marketing Coord
Tel: 972-675-4383
Email: marketing@trenews.com
Website: www.baotreonline.com/
Circulates nearly 125,000 publications nationwide on a weekly basis. (As-Pac, estab 1997, empl 25, sales $1,600,000, cert: NMSDC)

Wisconsin

2725 Best Ed, LLC
10936 N Port Washington Rd, Ste 269 Ste 269
Mequon, WI 53092
Contact: June Perry-Stevens Co-Owner
Tel: 414-313-9762
Email: contact@bestedbusiness.com
Website: www.bestedbusiness.com
Dist school supplies, games, materials. (Woman/AA, estab 2004, empl 2, sales $525,000, cert: State, City, NMSDC)

ELECTRONIC ASSEMBLY

ELECTRONIC ASSEMBLY
Electro-mechanical job shops. Manufacturers of electro-mechanical devices: PC boards, wire harnesses, cables, circuit components, housing, power supplies, etc. (See also ELECTRONIC & ELECTRICAL DIST. and ELECTRONIC & ELECTRICAL MFG.) NAICS Code 33

Alabama

2726 Mtronics.com, Inc.
325 Electronics Blvd SW Ste C
Huntsville, AL 35824
Contact: Mary Fields Mgr, Quality Admin
Tel: 256-461-8883
Email: mary@mtronics.com
Website: www.mtronics.com
Mfr automotive electronic assemblies. (As-Ind, estab 1987, empl 61, sales $53,431,545, cert: NMSDC)

Arizona

2727 EDS Manufacturing Inc.
765 N Target Range Rd
Nogales, AZ 85621
Contact: Tony Milo VP Sales & Marketing
Tel: 520-287-9711
Email: tmilo@edsmanufacturing.com
Website: www.edsmanufacturing.com
Molding, wire harness assembly, automatic cut, strip & crimp. (Hisp, estab 1990, empl 1800, sales $45,687,820, cert: NMSDC)

California

2728 Aeroflite Enterprises
261 Gemini
Brea, CA 92821
Contact: Pamela DePape Sales Mgr
Tel: 714-773-4251
Email: pdepape@aeroflite.com
Website: www.aeroflite.com
Dist aerospace electronics, custom cable assemblies & electrical connectors assemblies. (Woman, estab 1977, empl 65, sales $20,000,000, cert: NWBOC)

2729 Black Diamond Manufacturing Company
755 Bliss Ave
Pittsburg, CA 94565
Contact: Barbara Williams Supplier Diversity Admin
Tel: 925-439-9160
Email: bwilliams@bwc.com
Website: www.blackdiamondmfg.com
Mechanical sub-assemblies, manufacture specialty parts, in-house manufacturing experiences & capabilities, single source solution for custom sub-assemblies. (Woman, estab 2008, empl 3, sales , cert: WBENC)

2730 Cal-Am Switch & Relay Co., Inc.
8837 Lankershim Blvd
Sun Valley, CA 91352
Contact: Max Beno COO
Tel: 818-252-0507
Email: lg@welcoelectronics.com
Website: www.welcoelectronics.com
Avionic components, batteries, bearings, bushings, cables assemblies, cable ties, capacitors, connectors, expando sleeve, fuses, circuit breakers, lacing cords, relays, resistors, semiconductors, switches, wire, cable, tubing. (Minority, Woman, estab 1971, empl 7, sales $1,250,000, cert: NMSDC)

2731 Calpak USA, Inc.
13750 Prairie Ave
Hawthorne, CA 90250
Contact: Danish Qureshi VP
Tel: 310-937-7335
Email: danish@calpak-usa.com
Website: www.calpak-usa.com
Electronic Design, Electronics Engineering, Contract Manufacturing Services (CMS), Electronic Manufacturing Services (EMS), PCB Layout, PCB Design, PCB Assembly. (As-Pac, estab 1978, empl 15, sales $2,400,000, cert: State, NMSDC, SDB)

2732 LeeMAH Electronics Inc.
1088 Sansome St
San Francisco, CA 94111
Contact: Brent Liebel Business Devel
Tel: 972-570-7170
Email: bliebel@leemah.com
Website: www.leemah.com
Cable harness, printed circuit board stuffing; SMT assembly. Machine-programmed auto. printed circuit board testing, coil winding, transformer production, radio frequency cables. Mfr for special communications systems. Custom injection molding. (As-Ind, estab 1971, empl 650, sales $46,000,000, cert: NMSDC)

2733 Micro Analog Inc.
1861 Puddingstone Dr
La Verne, CA 91750
Contact: Kim Bickmeier Dir of Sales
Tel: 909-392-8277
Email: kimbickmeier@micro-analog.com
Website: www.micro-analog.com
Mfr electronics: printed circuit board assembly PCBA, custom cable & wire harness assembly, box/system build. (Minority, Woman, estab 1991, empl 155, sales $15,698,000, cert: NMSDC)

2734 Sierra Proto Express, Inc.
1108 W Evelyn Ave
Sunnyvale, CA 94086
Contact: Greg Lawson Acct Rep
Tel: 408-735-7137
Email: gregl@protoexpress.com
Website: www.protoexpress.com

Mfr & assemble Printed Circuit Boards manufacturer, quick turn PCBs & medium production. (Minority, Woman, estab 1986, empl 353, sales , cert: NMSDC)

2735 Surface Art Engineering Inc
81 Bonaventura Dr
San Jose, CA 95134
Contact: Jennifer Lee CEO
Tel: - -
Email: sandy@surfaceart.com
Website: www.surfaceart.com

PCB assembly, system mfg, design analysis, test solutions. (As-Pac, estab 1996, empl 40, sales , cert: NMSDC)

Colorado

2736 Premier Manufactuirng and Supply Chain Services
7755 Miller Dr
Frederick, CO 80504
Contact: Edmond Johnson President
Tel: 303-776-4145
Email: ejohnson@pmscs.com
Website: www.pmscs.com

Contract mfr of printed circuit board assemblies for prototypes, production, sub assemblies, cable harness & test. (AA, estab 2000, empl 55, sales $12,000,000, cert: NMSDC)

Connecticut

2737 Accutron Inc.
149 Addison Rd
Windsor, CT 06095
Contact: Jim Foss Outside Sales Mgr
Tel: 860-683-8300
Email: jfoss@accutroninc.com
Website: www.accutroninc.com

Printed circuit board assembly, surface mount assembly, thru-hole assembly, box build assembly, ICT, functioanl testing, flying probe testing. (As-Pac, estab 1989, empl 130, sales $25,000,000, cert: NMSDC)

2738 ICDI Inc.
407 Brookside Rd
Waterbury, CT 06708
Contact: Steve Villodas President
Tel: 203-753-8551
Email: svillodas@icdi-inc.com
Website: www.icdi-inc.com

Contract mfr electronic high tech equip & systems, turnkey program mgmt, eng design, microprocessor systems, PC layout, PC board & automated surface-mount assembly, wave soldering, vapor degreasing, custom cables, ATE testing. (Hisp, estab 1975, empl 22, sales $3,019,307, cert: NMSDC)

Florida

2739 Circuitronix, LLC
3131 SW 42nd St
Fort Lauderdale, FL 33312
Contact: Ken Peterson VP Sales
Tel: 231-459-4670
Email: kenp@circuitronix.com
Website: www.circuitronix.com

Supplier of rigid, flexible and rigid-flexible printed circuit boards in small, medium and high volumes. (As-Pac, estab 2000, empl 20, sales $ 0, cert: NMSDC)

2740 Hyper IC Florida Inc.
5015 49th Ave N
Saint Petersburg, FL 33703
Contact: Nathalie Ouellet President
Tel: 727-822-7129
Email: nathalie@hypericflorida.com
Website: www.hypericflorida.com

Integrated Circuit. (Woman, estab 2008, empl 3, sales $ 0, cert: WBENC)

Georgia

2741 Roytec Industries LLC
306 Bell Park Dr
Woodstock, GA 30188
Contact: Amanda Chapman CEO
Tel: 770-926-5470
Email: mchapman@roytecind.com
Website: www.roytecind.com

Mfr electrical wire harnesses & electrical wire assemblies. (Woman, estab 1984, empl 500, sales $36,734,238, cert: WBENC)

Illinois

2742 Alpha Circuit Corporation
      730 N Oaklawn Ave
      Elmhurst, IL 60126
      Contact: Steven Ryan Business Dev
      Tel: 630-617-5555
      Email: stever@alphacircuit.com
      Website: www.alphacircuit.com
Mfr single sided, double sided & multilayer printed circuit boards. (As-Ind, estab 1981, empl 42, sales $3,200,000, cert: NMSDC)

2743 American Standard Circuits
      475 Industrial Dr
      West Chicago, IL 60185
      Contact: Anaya Vardya CEO
      Tel: 630-639-5444
      Email: anaya@asc-i.com
      Website: www.asc-i.com
Mfr quality rigid, metal-backed, flex & rigid-flex printed circuit boards, RF/microwave printed circuit boards. (As-Ind, estab 1988, empl 135, sales $31,000,000, cert: NMSDC)

2744 Casco Manufacturing, Inc
      600 Territorial Dr Unit C
      Bolingbrook, IL 60440
      Contact: David Cohen Sales Rep
      Tel: 630-771-9555
      Email: dc@cascomanufacturing.com
      Website: www.cascomanufacturing.com
Mfr custom cable assemblies, wiring harnesses, fiber-optic cables, patch cords, capabilities to solder, tin, and/or crimp our terminals. (Woman, estab 1997, empl 25, sales $3,100,000, cert: State)

2745 Circom, Inc.
      505 W Main St
      Bensenville, IL 60106
      Contact: Victor Bossov Business Devel Mgr
      Tel: 630-595-4460
      Email: vbossov@circominc.com
      Website: www.circominc.com
Printed circuit board assembly & electronic control design services, wire & cable harness assemblies, enclosures & panels. (Woman, estab 1968, empl 25, sales $5,200,000, cert: WBENC)

2746 Circuitronics LLC
      201 N Gables Blvd
      Wheaton, IL 60510
      Contact: Shelley Lara VP Sales
      Tel: 630-668-5407
      Email: shelleylara@yahoo.com
      Website: www.circuitronicsllc.com
Mfr high tech printed circuit boards, exotic materials and alternate finishes (As-Ind, estab 1993, empl 55, sales $18,000,000, cert: NMSDC)

2747 General Circuit Corporation
      1370 Lively Blvd
      Elk Grove Village, IL 60007
      Contact: Janice Rosario Sales/Mktg
      Tel: 847-758-8000
      Email: janice@deltapcb.com
      Website: www.Deltapcb.com
Mfr printed circuit boards: single, double & multi-layers in small, medium & high volumes. (As-Ind, estab 1996, empl 25, sales $4,600,000, cert: NMSDC)

2748 KLI Inc.
      304 Roma Jean Pkwy
      Streamwood, IL 60107
      Contact: Lisa Carso President
      Tel: 630-213-1283
      Email: support@kli-inc.com
      Website: www.kli-inc.com
Mfr electronic components; electronic assembly; main harness & cable to mil specs. (Minority, Woman, estab 1987, empl 15, sales $ 0, cert: State, NMSDC)

2749 Midwest Molding, Inc.
      1560 Hecht Dr
      Bartlett, IL 60103
      Contact: Sanjay Patel Dir of Purchasing
      Tel: 224-208-1110
      Email: sanjay.patel@mwmolding.com
      Website: www.mwmolding.com
Injection molding, insert molding, two shot molding, IMD molding, wire harness assembly & multi-component assembly. (As-Pac, estab 1996, empl 70, sales $ 0, cert: NMSDC)

Indiana

2750 Precision Wire Assemblies, Inc.
      551 E Main St
      Hagerstown, IN 47346
      Contact: Penny Wickes President
      Tel: 765-489-6302
      Email: penny@pwawire.com
      Website: www.pwawire.com
Mfr wire harnesses & assemblies, cable assemblies. (Woman, estab 1987, empl 75, sales $6,130,594, cert: State)

Kansas

2751 S and Y Industries, Inc.
606 Industrial Rd
Winfield, KS 67156
Contact: Dir Sales/Marketing
Tel: 620-221-4001
Email: info@sandyindustries.com
Website: www.sandyindustries.com

Printed circuit boards, wire harnesses, cable assemblies, connectors, surface mount. (Woman, estab 1984, empl 80, sales $7,660,639, cert: WBENC)

Massachusetts

2752 Cable Harness Resources, Inc.
One Robert Bonazzoli Ave
Hudson, MA 01749
Contact: Kim Nguyen
Tel: 978-562-4352
Email: knguyen@cableharnessresources.com
Website: www.cableharnessresources.com

Electrical wire harness& cable asembly, Mil-Spec source, cut, strip, tin, twist, splice, crimp, solder, coil, end-prep, connector/component installation. (Woman/As-Pac, estab 2008, empl 10, sales $800,000, cert: NMSDC)

Michigan

2753 Advanced-Cable, LLC
1179 Chicago Rd
Troy, MI 48083
Contact: Deanna Zwiesele Owner
Tel: 248-268-3167
Email: deanna@advanced-cable.com
Website: www.advanced-cable.com

Mfr custom cable assemblies (molded and non molded) & wire harnesses, dist bulk wire, cable & various electronic components. (Woman, estab 2012, empl 15, sales $2,000,000, cert: WBENC)

2754 American Hydrostatics Distribution Co.
6626 Sims Dr
Sterling Heights, MI 48313
Contact: Drew Parikh Business Devel
Tel: 248-649-2587
Email: dp@americanhydrostatics.com
Website: www.americanhydrostatics.com

Build small automation & assembly equipment, rebuild machines & general assembly services. (As-Pac, estab 1982, empl 25, sales $42,000,000, cert: NMSDC)

2755 Detroit Manufacturing Systems
12701 Southfield Rd Bldg A
Detroit, MI 48223
Contact: Sung Moon Business Devel Mgr
Tel: - -
Email: casey.smith@dmsna.com
Website: www.dmsna.com

Provide assembly and sub-assembly services. (Woman/AA, estab 2012, empl 1400, sales $900,000,000, cert: NMSDC)

2756 Embedded Logix Inc.
50644 Sabrina Dr
Shelby, MI 48315
Contact: Deborah McLeod President
Tel: 586-709-2025
Email: dmcleod@emlogix.net
Website: www.emlogix.net

Product design for automotive, commercial & medical, test equipment design, test consulting, service, connector build, harness build, assembly test equipment. Embedded design, embedded programming, labview programming. (Woman, estab 0, empl , sales $ 0, cert: WBENC)

2757 GM&T Engineering, Inc.
775 Davis St Ste 4
Plymouth, MI 48170
Contact: Carlos Gutierrez President
Tel: 734-679-8340
Email: cgutierrez@gmt-engineering.com
Website: www.gmt-engineering.com

Testing of Electrical Distribution Systems (Wire Harnesses, batteries), Engineering of EDS, Process and Product quality audits, Staffing and recruiting Wire Harnesses and prototypes
Testing tooling and equipment. (Hisp, estab 2005, empl 16, sales , cert: NMSDC)

2758 Newtech 3, Inc.
28373 Beck Rd Ste H7
Wixom, MI 48393
Contact: Gail Gyenese Dir of Sales
Tel: 248-912-1062
Email: ggyenese@newtech3inc.com
Website: www.newtech3.com

Mfr lower to mid volume wire harness & circuit board assemblies. (AA, estab 2009, empl 32, sales $3,965,000, cert: NMSDC)

2759 Orri Corporation
      5385 Perry Dr
      waterford, MI 48329
      Contact: Angelo Doa Sales
      Tel: 248-618-1104
      Email: Sales@orricorp.com
      Website: www.orricorp.com
Wire harnesses, cable assemblies, electrical test fixtures, robotic vision guidance software. (Woman, estab 2001, empl 12, sales $ 0, cert: WBENC)

2760 Saturn Electronics Corporation
      28450 Northline Rd
      Romulus, MI 48174
      Contact: Parthiv Trivedi Dir Business Dev
      Tel: 734-941-8100
      Email: parthiv@saturnelectronics.com
      Website: www.saturnelectronics.com
Printed circuit boards: prototype & production; 1 to 20 layers. (As-Ind, estab 1985, empl 190, sales $40,025,000, cert: NMSDC)

2761 Wolverine Assemblies, LLC
      30260 Oak Creek Dr
      Wixom, MI 48393
      Contact: Adam Claytor Sr Lead Analyst
      Tel: 248-822-8056
      Email: aclaytor@taghold.com
      Website: www.wolverine-llc.com/
Modular assembly, warehousing, sequencing, import & export, fabrication, machining, kitting, supply chain management, pre delivery inspection, repack and test, containment & sorting. (AA, estab 2010, empl 6, sales $12,000,000, cert: NMSDC)

2762 Wotko LLC
      229 South St
      Rochester, MI 48307
      Contact: Dustin Coon President
      Tel: 248-266-6016
      Email: dcoon@wotkollc.com
      Website: www.wotkollc.com
Custom cable & harness specialty products, prototype, fiber cables. (Nat Ame, estab 2013, empl 2, sales , cert: State)

Minnesota

2763 Aero Assemblies, Inc.
      12012 - 12th Ave S
      Burnsville, MN 55337
      Contact: Anthony Winick President
      Tel: 952-894-5552
      Email: tonyw@aeroassemblies.com
      Website: www.aeroassemblies.com
Contract manufacturing, wire rope assembly, electronic cable assembly, print finishing, bindery, eyeletting (As-Pac, estab 1972, empl 16, sales $3,000,000, cert: NMSDC)

2764 Quantronic Corporation
      8300 89th Ave N
      Brooklyn Park, MN 55445
      Contact: Gabriela Faouen Acct Mgr
      Tel: 763-425-2602
      Email: gfaouen@quantronic.net
      Website: www.quantronic.net
Surface Mount & Thru Hole Assemblies, Incircuit & Functional testing, Prototype & Product development, Circuit Board Rework & modifications, Complete Product & and sub assemblies, Packaging Solutions, Conformal Coating. (Hisp, estab 1995, empl 65, sales $15,000,000, cert: NMSDC)

New Jersey

2765 Delaire USA, Inc.
      1913 Atlantic Ave
      Manasquan, NJ 08736
      Contact: President
      Tel: 732-528-4520
      Email: sales@delaireusa.com
      Website: www.delaireusa.com
Mfr custom RF & fiber optic cables & assemblies, box level assemblies, precision soldering & testing. (Woman, estab 1994, empl 19, sales $ 0, cert: State, WBENC)

2766 Precision Graphics, Inc.
      21 County Line Rd
      Somerville, NJ 08876
      Contact: Alec Weissman VP
      Tel: 908-707-8880
      Email: aweissman@precisiongraphics.us
      Website: www.precisiongraphics.us
Mfr printed circuit board assemblies, surface mount, through hole, or RoHs processing. (Woman, estab 1971, empl 55, sales $13,000,000, cert: NWBOC)

Nevada

2767 Power Assemblies LLC
      7061 W Arby Rd Ste 120
      Las Vegas, NV 89113
      Contact: Patricia Knowles Owner
      Tel: 541-610-6494
      Email: gknowles@powerassemblies.com
      Website: www.powerassemblies.com
Assemble portable power & industrial products, flexible power cable assemblies, connectors, generator docking stations, enclosed variable speed drives & cam lock panels, custom portable power products ranging from 20A to 4000A. (Woman, estab 2006, empl 9, sales $350,000, cert: State, WBENC)

New York

2768 Hazlow Electronics
      49 St. Bridgets Dr
      Rochester, NY 14605
      Contact: Crain CEO
      Tel: 585-263-7852
      Email: rdwiz@aol.com
      Website: www.hazlow.com
Wire harnesses, printed circuit boards, cable assemblies, sub assembly. (Minority, Woman, estab 1971, empl 40, sales $3,500,000, cert: State, WBENC)

Pennsylvania

2769 American Cable Company
      1200 E Erie Ave
      Philadelphia, PA 19124
      Contact: Brian Thomas Dir of Operations
      Tel: 215-456-0700
      Email: bthomas@americancableco.com
      Website: www.americancableco.com
Mfr battery cables, wiring harness, grounding straps, panel assemblies & related components. (Hisp, estab 2009, empl 5, sales $15,000,000, cert: NMSDC, SDB)

2770 Contine Corporation
      1820 Nagle Rd
      Erie, PA 16510
      Contact: Constance Ellrich President
      Tel: 814-899-0006
      Email: cellrich@continedbe.com
      Website: www.continedbe.com
Mfr mechanical & electro mechanical assemblies. (Woman, estab 1981, empl 43, sales $9,175,996, cert: CPUC, WBENC)

2771 John A. Romeo & Associates, Inc.
      890 Pittsburgh Rd, Ste 7
      Butler, PA 16002
      Contact: Pamela Romeo CEO
      Tel: 724-586-6961
      Email: sales@jara-mfg.com
      Website: www.jara-mfg.com
Mfr Custom Cables, Wiring Harnesses & Electromechanical Assemblies. (Woman, estab 1990, empl 15, sales $1,506,698, cert: WBENC)

South Carolina

2772 North American Assemblies, LLC
      2222 Cale Yarborough Hwy
      Timmonsville, SC 29161
      Contact: William Rucker
      Tel: 248-342-6500
      Email: warucker@naa-llc.com
      Website: www.naa-llc.com
Mfg & assembly services. (AA, estab 2004, empl 17, sales $3,000,000, cert: NMSDC)

Texas

2773 Accurate Connections Inc.
      13801 Hutton Dr, Ste 100
      Farmers Branch, TX 75234
      Contact: President
      Tel: 972-484-8500
      Email: info@accurateconnections.com
      Website: www.accurateconnections.com
Cable assemblies, fiber optic & copper. (Woman, estab 2003, empl 26, sales $3,246,807, cert: State, WBENC)

2774 Arise Solutions Inc.
      5862 Cromo Ste 149
      El Paso, TX 79912
      Contact: Daniel Laing President
      Tel: 915-345-9134
      Email: sales@arisesolutions.biz
      Website: www.arisesolutions.biz
Custom designed wire harness, cable assembly, bulk wire, signal cable, specialty bolts, screws, Nut Rivets, Inserts, Fasteners, Spacers, Connectors & Fittings for automotive industry. (As-Pac, estab 2012, empl 5, sales $1,000,000, cert: State, NMSDC)

2775 Electro Plate Circuitry, Inc.
      1430 Century Dr
      Carrollton, TX 75006
      Contact: Nicolas Garcia President
      Tel: 972-466-0818
      Email: nickg@eplate.com
      Website: www.eplate.com
Mfr printed circuit boards: GF, GI, RF, insulators, heatsinks, blind buried vias, controlled impedance. (Hisp, estab 1981, empl 80, sales $9,000,000, cert: NMSDC)

2776 Electronic Assembly Services, Inc.
      4501 S Pinemont, Ste 108
      Houston, TX 77041
      Contact: Evelyn Fletcher CEO
      Tel: 713-686-4390
      Email: efletcher@easinchou.com
      Website: www.eashouston.com/

Custom electric & electronic assemblies & sub-assemblies: control panels, cable wire harnesses, electro-mechanical assemblies, printed circuit board assemblies, rack-mount assemblies. (Minority, Woman, estab 1987, empl 13, sales $1,500,000, cert: State, NMSDC)

2777 Galaxy Electronics Company
      201 E Arapaho Rd
      Richardson, TX 75081
      Contact: Will Moore Sales Mgr
      Tel: 972-234-0065
      Email: wmoore@galaxyee.com
      Website: www.galaxyee.com

Fiber optic & copper cable assembly. (As-Pac, estab 1988, empl 31, sales $ 0, cert: State, NMSDC)

2778 JVB Electronics dba Multilayer Technology
      3835 Conflans Rd
      Irving, TX 75061
      Contact: Johnnie Feathers Dir of Sales
      Tel: 972-790-0062
      Email: johnnie@multilayer.com
      Website: www.multilayer.com

Mfr printed circuit boards. (As-Ind, estab 1986, empl 45, sales , cert: State, NMSDC)

2779 Optical Interconnect
      2621 Summit Ave Ste 100
      Plano, TX 75074
      Contact: Steve Wade Acct Exec
      Tel: 214-239-3988
      Email: swade@opticalinterconnect.com
      Website: www.opticalinterconnect.com

Dist fiber optic cable assemblies, copper cable assemblies, rack/wall mount metal enclosures. (Woman, estab 2004, empl 15, sales , cert: State, WBENC)

2780 THT Electronics Company, Inc.
      6645 Fairway Dr
      Westworth Village, TX 76114
      Contact: Scott Sewell CEO
      Tel: 972-505-6769
      Email: scott.sewell@thtelec.com
      Website: www.thtpromo.com

Electronic components, cable assemblies. (Nat Ame, estab 1996, empl 6, sales $126,000, cert: State, NMSDC)

2781 Trendsetter Electronics
      2500 NE Inner Loop Bldg 1 Ste 105
      Georgetown, TX 78626
      Contact: Carol Williams President
      Tel: 512-310-8858
      Email: stacyb@trendsetter.com
      Website: www.trendsetter.com

Stocking programs & stocking replinishment, kitting, cable & harness assemblies, lead forming & modifying, part sleeving & custom transformers. (Woman, estab 1995, empl 12, sales $5,536,114, cert: WBENC)

2782 Trilogy Circuits, Inc.
      1717 Firman Dr Ste 200
      Richardson, TX 75081
      Contact: Mark T McCrocklin
      Tel: 972-907-2727
      Email: mark@trilogycircuits.com
      Website: www.trilogycircuits.com

Printed circuit board design/layout. (As-Pac, estab 2001, empl 27, sales $5,000,000, cert: State, NMSDC)

Wisconsin

2783 A1 Cable Solutions, Inc.
      665 Commercial Ave
      Waterloo, WI 53594
      Contact: Laurie Hoffmann President
      Tel: 608-444-3072
      Email: ljhoffmann@usa1cable.com
      Website: www.usa1cable.com

Battery Cables, Ground Straps, Wire Harnesses, Electro-mechanical Assemblies, Panel Assembly & Wiring, Prototypes, Testing & Reporting. (Woman, estab 2001, empl 2, sales , cert: WBENC)

ELECTRONICS & ELECTRICAL DIST.

Distribute a wide range of electrical or electronic products: battery chargers, communications equipment, video equipment, radios, measuring instruments, etc. (See also ELECTRONIC ASSEMBLY and ELECTRONICS & ELECTRICAL MFG.) NAICS Code 42

Arizona

2784 Aegis Electronic Group, Inc.
1465 North Fiesta Blvd. Ste 101
Gilbert, AZ 85233
Contact: Michelle Witt Technical Sales Rep
Tel: 480-635-8400
Email: michelle@aegiselect.com
Website: www.aegis-elec.com/
Dist industrial imaging equipment: cameras, lenses, monitors, cables, connectors, power supplies, frame grabbers, software, etc. (Woman, estab 1989, empl 17, sales $9,000,000, cert: WBENC)

2785 Spirit Distribution and Logistics, Inc.
23910 N 19th Ave Ste 26
Phoenix, AZ 85085
Contact: Vickie Wessel President
Tel: 480-998-1533
Email: v.wessel@spiritelectronics.com
Website: www.spiritelectronics.com
Dist passive components, memory products, obsolete & hard-to-find semiconductors & electromechanical devices. (Minority, Woman, estab 1979, empl 15, sales $29,307,000, cert: NMSDC, WBENC)

California

2786 AAA Electrical Supply, Inc.
1014 S Montebello Blvd
Montebello, CA 90640
Contact: Alfred J. Alvarez President
Tel: 323-721-2700
Email: zirma@aaaelectricalsupply.com
Website: www.aaaelectricalsupply.com
Dist electrical supplies: conduit fittings, wire, cable, steelboxes, weatherproof boxes, lighting, ballasts, hand tools, circuit breakers, panelboards, switchgear, transformers, wiring devices, lamps, incandescent, fluorescent, HID & LED lighting. (Hisp, estab 1988, empl 7, sales $3,426,300, cert: State, City, CPUC)

2787 Aeroflite Enterprises
261 Gemini
Brea, CA 92821
Contact: Pamela DePape Sales Mgr
Tel: 714-773-4251
Email: pdepape@aeroflite.com
Website: www.aeroflite.com
Dist aerospace electronics, custom cable assemblies & electrical connectors assemblies. (Woman, estab 1977, empl 65, sales $20,000,000, cert: NWBOC)

2788 American Industrial Control, Inc.
170 N Maple St Ste 104
Corona, CA 92880
Contact: Monica Pratt President
Tel: 951-520-0613
Email: monica@aicsupply.com
Website: www.aicsupply.com
Dist electrical supplies, mfr industrial control panels. (Woman/Hisp, estab 2000, empl 4, sales $1,010,254, cert: NMSDC, CPUC, WBENC)

2789 AREA51-ESG
51 Post
Irvine, CA 92618
Contact: Khanh Hoang OEM Sales
Tel: 949-387-0054
Email: khanh.hoang@area51esg.com
Website: www.area51esg.com
Dist electronic components, cables, hardware, mil spec hardware, rotables, expandables, etc. (As-Pac, estab 2000, empl 69, sales $60,571,568, cert: NMSDC)

2790 AutoCell Electronics
7311 Greenhaven Dr
Sacramento, CA 95831
Contact: Mark Hardwick Acct Mgr
Tel: 888-393-6668
Email: mark@autocell.net
Website: www.autocell.net
CFLs (compact fluorescent lights), linear fluorescent lights, LED (Light Emitting Diode) lights, indoor & outdoor hardwired light fixtures (luminaires), LED Desk Lamps. (As-Pac, estab 2000, empl 5, sales $2,000,000, cert: CPUC)

2791 Bright Light LED Inc.
7751 Alabama Ave, Warehouse 7-8
Canoga Park, CA 91304
Contact: Rami Vardi CEO
Tel: 310-987-6670
Email: rvardi@brightlightled.net
Website: www.brightlightled.net
Residential & commercial LED bulbs & fixtures. (Woman, estab 2008, empl 200, sales $2,050,000, cert: NMSDC)

2792 C Plus Electronics, Inc.
17842 Irvine Blvd. Ste B144
Tustin, CA 92780
Contact: Carrie Fill Purchasing
Tel: 714-783-7141
Email: carrie.fill@cpluselectronics.com
Website: www.cpluselectronics.com
Dist electronic components: ICs, passives; interconnect products, memory modules & other computer related products. (Minority, Woman, estab 2003, empl 15, sales $5,000,000, cert: NMSDC, SDB)

2793 Callor Sales, Inc
3850 Cedar Ave
Long Beach, CA 90807
Contact: Lori Nelson Owner
Tel: 562-426-6209
Email: lori.nelson@callorsales.com
Website: www.callorsales.com
Dist electrical, electronic & telecommunications materials & equipment. (Woman, estab 2005, empl 1, sales , cert: State)

2794 CE Supply
1111 W Victoria St
Compton, CA 90220
Contact: MobileVision Sales/Mktg
Tel: 310-735-2078
Email: customerservice@cesupply.com
Website: www.mobilevisionus.com/
Dist wireless & electronics accessories. (Minority, Woman, estab 1990, empl 3, sales $2,879,544, cert: CPUC, WBENC)

2795 DWY Inc.
911 S Primrose Ave, Ste I
Monrovia, CA 91016
Contact: Daniel Yohannes
Tel: 626-357-0500
Email: honeylyn@ecads-na.com
Website: www.ecads-na.com
Dist LED & solar products, energy saving LED bulbs & solar panels. (AA, estab 2001, empl 4, sales , cert: NMSDC)

2796 Forza Electronics
1110 S El Camino Real Ste C
San Clemente, CA 92672
Contact: James Cassano President
Tel: 949-276-8686
Email: james@forzaelectronics.com
Website: www.forzaelectronics.com
Dist electronics components, semiconductors, capacitors, resistors, switches, relays, connectors, diodes, computer peripherals, electromechanical devices. (Woman, estab 2006, empl 5, sales $794,000, cert: WBENC)

2797 FTS Lighting Services, Inc.
160 S. Cypress St
Orange, CA 92866
Contact: Michele Davidson President
Tel: 714-289-1957
Email: michele@ftslighting.com
Website: www.ftslighting.com
Energy Saving Lights & Analysis, LEDs, Induction, tubes, ballast, fixtures, aircraft, xenon, HID, Metal halide. (Minority, Woman, estab 2010, empl 1, sales $350,000, cert: State, CPUC, WBENC)

2798 Integra Electronics, Inc.
1363 Lewis St
Anaheim, CA 92805
Contact: Victor Montez President
Tel: 714-282-4990
Email: vicm@integrasmp.com
Website: www.integrasmp.com
Dist electronic components: Lampholders, Panel Mount indicator lights, incandescent & neon indicator lights, LED Panel lenses & Cable assemblies, Electro-Mechanial products. (Hisp, estab 1997, empl 11, sales $3,960,000, cert: State, NMSDC)

2799 MCV Technologies Inc.
6640 Lusk Blvd, Ste A102
San Diego, CA 92121
Contact: Edward Liang VP
Tel: 858-450-0468
Email: eliang@mcv-microwave.com
Website: www.mcv-microwave.com
MCV Microwave designs, manufactures and markets RF/Microwave Filter, Antenna, Dielectric Resonator and Microelectronic Circuit. Bandpass Filter, Notch Filter, Lowpass Filter, Highpass Filter, Duplexer, Triplexer, Multiplexer. (Minority, Woman, estab 1995, empl 25, sales $2,000,000, cert: CPUC)

2800 Meritke Electronics Corp.
5160 Rivergrade Rd.
Baldwin Park, CA 91706
Contact: Oliver Su President
Tel: 626-373-1728
Email: sales@meritekusa.com
Website: www.meritekusa.com
Dist electronics. (As-Pac, estab 1983, empl 36, sales $20,000,000, cert: NMSDC)

2801 Onesource Distributors, Inc.
3951 Oceanic Dr
Oceanside, CA 92056
Contact: Jeremy Schmidt Dir Diversity Devel
Tel: 760-966-4500
Email: jschmidt@1sourcesupplysolutions.com
Website: www.1sourcedist.com
Dist electrical related materials. (Hisp, estab 1983, empl 310, sales $250,000,000, cert: NMSDC)

2802 Perfect Parts Corporation
7545 Irvine Center Dr, Ste 200
Irvine, CA 92618
Contact: Lulu Jaff Owner
Tel: 949-209-1655
Email: lulu@perfectelectronicparts.com
Website: www.perfectelectronicparts.com
Dist electronic components. (Woman, estab 2013, empl 5, sales , cert: WBENC)

2803 RAK Technologies LLC
23122 Mountain Pine
Mission Viejo, CA 92692
Contact: Mark Meeks President
Tel: 949-633-9845
Email: mark@rak-techca.com
Website: www.raktechca.com
Dist electronic components: semiconductors, connectors, power, sensors, relays etc. (Nat Ame, estab 2007, empl 4, sales , cert: NMSDC)

2804 SilenX Corporation
10606 Shoemaker Ave Ste A
Santa Fe Springs, CA 90670
Contact: PK Karunphan Sales Mgr
Tel: 562-941-4200
Email: pkarun@silenx.com
Website: www.silenx.com
Replace & install energy-efficient LED light tubes. (As-Pac, estab 2004, empl 6, sales $2,077,409, cert: NMSDC)

2805 Steven Engineering, Inc.
230 Ryan Way
South San Francisco, CA 94080
Contact: Bonnie A. Walter VP Mktg
Tel: 800-258-9200
Email: bonnie_walter@steveneng.com
Website: www.stevenengineering.com
Dist electronic pneumatic products, electronic components, electrical parts, industrial automation & controls. (Woman, estab 1975, empl 123, sales $46,500,000, cert: CPUC, WBENC)

2806 telCade.Com
2914-24th Ave
San Francisco, CA 94132
Contact: Jerry Chan VP Sales
Tel: 408-955-9268
Email: jerry@telcade.com
Website: www.catalog.telcade.com/
Custom cable & wire harness, coaxial connector & cables, xDSL/ VDSL filter/splitter, connectors, optical cables & connectors, power cord, power supply adapter/chargers. (Minority, Woman, estab 1993, empl 168, sales $6,100,000, cert: CPUC)

2807 THISAI LLC
      1834 Blazewood St
      Simi Valley, CA 93063
      Contact: Ramalingam Subramaniam Owner
      Tel: 747-206-3886
      Email: ram@thisaillc.com
      Website: www.thisaillc.com
Electrical products, cables, switches, wire, lighting fixtures, metal products, sheet metal, laser cut, bent & fabricated. (Minority, estab 2015, empl 2, sales , cert: State)

2808 Unical Aviation Inc.
      4775 Irwindale Ave
      Irwindale, CA 91706
      Contact: Ray Daljeet Mgr
      Tel: 626-813-1901
      Email: rdaljeet@unical.com
      Website: www.unical.com
Kitts, connector, wire, hardware, flight component, Avionic, engine component, MROs. (As-Pac, estab 1990, empl 160, sales $2,000,000, cert: NMSDC)

2809 Waisun Corporation
      13321 Alondra Blvd, Ste D
      Santa Fe Springs, CA 90670
      Contact: Albert Hui President
      Tel: 562-394-6922
      Email: optolight@msn.com
      Website: www.optolight.com
Dist LED products, LED light bulbs, recess downlight, etc. (As-Pac, estab 1988, empl 8, sales , cert: CPUC)

Colorado

2810 Innov8 Solutions USA,LLC
      1500 W 47th Ave
      Denver, CO 80211
      Contact: Dan Montoya Dir of Sales operations
      Tel: 303-328-8888
      Email: dmontoya@innov8supplies.com
      Website: www.innov8solutions.com
Dist electrical & telecommunications supplies, warehouse services of cable stubbing, custom cutting, order fulfillment & kitting operations. (Hisp, estab 2001, empl 20, sales , cert: NMSDC)

District of Columbia

2811 Ideal Electrical Supply Corporation
      3515 V St NE
      Washington, DC 20018
      Contact: Cora Williams President
      Tel: 202-526-7500
      Email: cwilliams@idealelectric.com
      Website: www.idealelectric.com
Dist electrical, industrial, data & telecommunications, networking products, lighting tools & safety equipment. (Woman/AA, estab 1991, empl 17, sales $59,000,000, cert: NMSDC, WBENC)

Florida

2812 Aero Supply USA
      21941 US Hwy 19 N
      Clearwater, FL 33765
      Contact: Robert Ramirez Business Devel Mgr
      Tel: 727-754-4915
      Email: rramirez@aerosupplyusa.com
      Website: www.aerosupplyusa.com
Dist aerospace parts & electronic components. (Minority, Woman, estab 2012, empl 12, sales, cert: NMSDC, SDB)

2813 Aplusdealz LLC
      7860 W Commercial Blvd, Ste 833
      Lauderdale Lakes, FL 33351
      Contact: Andrew Patten Owner
      Tel: 305-495-5299
      Email: aplusdealzus@gmail.com
      Website: www.aplusdealz.com
Dist electronics. (AA, estab 2020, empl 1, sales $359,000, cert: State)

2814 Chase Components LLC
      647 Arnau Dr
      New Smyrna Beach, FL 32168
      Contact: Cristal Dongilli CEO
      Tel: 386-426-1367
      Email: cristal@chasecomponents.com
      Website: www.chasecomponents.com
Dist board level electronic components. (Woman, estab 2003, empl 10, sales $2,907,439, cert: WBENC)

2815 Efficient Lighting Technologies
      12555 Orange Dr Ste 4002
      Fort Lauderdale, FL 33330
      Contact: Jose Trevino Dir of Operations
      Tel: 954-623-7102
      Email: jtrevino@elt-us.com
      Website: www.elt-us.com
Dist LED light bulbs & linear fluorescent lamps. (Hisp, estab 2005, empl 22, sales $10,123,250, cert: NMSDC)

2816 LedZed International Inc.
      2240 Palm Beach Lakes Blvd
      West Palm Beach, FL 33409
      Contact: Helena Lahtinen CEO
      Tel: 954-629-0768
      Email: helena@ledzed.com
      Website: www.ledzed.com
Mfr & dist energy efficiency led lights. (Woman, estab 2011, empl 1, sales , cert: City)

2817 LXI Components Inc.
      2802 Leslie Road
      Tampa, FL 33619
      Contact: Wolmar Busche President
      Tel: 813-663-9682
      Email: wolmar.busche@lxicomponents.com
      Website: www.lxicomponents.com
Dist passive & interconnect electronic components. (AA, estab 1994, empl 10, sales $2,926,437, cert: NMSDC)

2818 The Bernd Group Inc.
      1251 Pinehurst Rd
      Dunedin, FL 34698
      Contact: Pilar Bernd President
      Tel: 727-733-0122
      Email: businessdevelopment@berndgroup.com
      Website: www.berndgroup.com
Material handling equip, safety products, hand & power tools, pumps & compressors, motors, generators, electrical hardware, batteries, lighting fixtures, lockers, bins, shelving, lab equip. (Minority, Woman, estab 1992, empl 66, sales , cert: NMSDC)

Georgia

2819 AC & DC Power Technologies
      125 Cavalier Ct
      Fayetteville, GA 30215
      Contact: Charles McCartha Office Mgr
      Tel: 404-361-3788
      Email: charles@acdcpowertechnologies.com
      Website: www.acdcpowertechnologies.com
Integrate, dist & engineer electrical systems: transformers, switchgear, batteries, generators, capacitor banks, resistors, ground fault protection, etc. (Minority, Woman, estab 1997, empl 14, sales $3,800,000, cert: State, NMSDC, WBENC)

2820 B & S Electric Supply Co., Inc
      4505 Mills Place
      S.W. Atlanta, GA 30336
      Contact: Clarence Robie
      Tel: 404-696-8284
      Email: c.robie@b-s-electric.com
      Website: www.bandselect.com
Dist electrical supplies. (AA, estab , empl , sales $ 0, cert: NMSDC)

2821 GC Electrical Solutions, LLC
      120 Cecil Court
      Fayetteville, GA 30214
      Contact: George Lottier President
      Tel: 770-716-5400
      Email: glottier@gcelectrical.com
      Website: www.gc-es.com
Dist electrical components: lamps, wire, conduit, panel boards, transformers, fixtures, wiring devices. (AA, estab 2003, empl 5, sales $ 0, cert: NMSDC)

2822 NAECO, LLC
      100 NAECO Way
      Peachtree City, GA 30269
      Contact: Steven Jones Dir Sales & Marketing
      Tel: 770-487-6006
      Email: stevej@naeco.net
      Website: www.naeco.net
Dist Electrical Contacts, Contact Assemblies, Tungsten based Heavy Metal Products & Machined Parts. (Minority, estab 1999, empl 25, sales $11,111,301, cert: NMSDC)

2823 Quality Standby Services, LLC
      1649 Sands Place SE Ste C
      Marietta, GA 30067
      Contact: Paul Whitaker General Mgr
      Tel: 770-916-1747
      Email: paul@qualitystandbyservices.com
      Website: www.qualitystandbyservices.com
Dist, install, maintain & test standby power systems: batteries, battery racks, chargers & spill containment. (Woman, estab 2006, empl 19, sales $8,558,834, cert: WBENC)

Illinois

2824 Electric Motor Corporation
      3865 N Milwaukee Ave
      Chicago, IL 60641
      Contact: Isabell Siegel President
      Tel: 773-725-1050
      Email: isabell@electricmotorcorp.us
      Website: www.electricmotorcorp.us
Electric motor repair. (Woman, estab 1960, empl 25, sales $2,488,000, cert: WBENC)

2825 Electro-Kinetics Inc.
      859 N Sivert Dr
      Wood Dale, IL 60191
      Contact: Aileen Sonderman President
      Tel: 630-595-6700
      Email: aileens@e-kinetics.com
      Website: www.e-kinetics.com
Dist electric & electronic components: sensors, relays, contactors, controls, fuses, fuse blocks, circuit breakers, solenoids, timers, transducers, boots/seals, cable cordsets, cable ties, connectors, cord grips, current operated switches. (Minority, Woman, estab 1957, empl 8, sales $2,400,000, cert: NMSDC, WBENC)

2826 Electro-Wire Inc.
      933 E Remington
      Schaumburg, IL 60173
      Contact: Mike Schmidt VP
      Tel: 847-944-1500
      Email: mschmidt@electrowire.com
      Website: www.electrowire.com
Dist wire & cable, cable assemblies, mechanical cable, harness assemblies & electromechanical sub-assemblies. (As-Pac, estab 1978, empl 100, sales $80,000,000, cert: NMSDC)

2827 Global Test Equipment Inc.
      1424 Centre Cir
      Downers Grove, IL 60515
      Contact: Jay Perry Acct Mgr
      Tel: 630-678-0400
      Email: jay@4gte.com
      Website: www.4gte.com
Dist, rent & lease electronic test equipment. (Woman, estab 2003, empl 4, sales $ 0, cert: WBENC)

2828 Go Green LED-Alternatives, LLC
      6621 State Route 71
      Yorkville, IL 60560
      Contact: Sandra Goeken CEO
      Tel: 630-802-4213
      Email: s.miles@gogreenled.com
      Website: www.gogreenled.com
LED, light, lighting, security, value added reseller, control systems, street lighti (Woman, estab 2008, empl 2, sales $2,937,513, cert: CPUC, WBENC)

2829 Gordon Electric Supply Co.
      1290 N Hobbie
      Kankakee, IL 60901
      Contact: Randy Molthan CFO
      Tel: 800-892-1866
      Email: rmolthan@gordonelec.com
      Website: www.gordonelectricsupply.com
Dist elelctrical supplies. (Woman, estab 0, empl 20, sales $8,500,000, cert: State, WBENC)

2830 Halogen Lighting Products Corp.
      PO Box 229
      Kaneville, IL 60144
      Contact: Gloria Stewart President
      Tel: 800-621-0001
      Email: info@halogen-lighting.com
      Website: www.halogen-lighting.com
LED & fluorescent industrial machine lights with with a wide range of wattages, lumens capable of operating in environments of 90 - 260 volts & some are compatible with 24VDC. (Woman, estab 1993, empl 5, sales , cert: City, NWBOC)

2831 Hinsdale Lighting
      777 N York Rd Ste 19
      Hinsdale, IL 60521
      Contact: David Laughter Warehouse Mgr
      Tel: 630-734-0662
      Email: hlighting@hinsdalelighting.com
      Website: www.hinsdalelighting.com
Lighting design, light fixture & light bulb distributor. (Woman, estab 2008, empl 6, sales $1,100,000, cert: WBENC)

2832 JP Simons & Co.
      1426 Brook Dr
      Downers Grove, IL 60641
      Contact: Jean Bradfield President
      Tel: - -
      Email: roger@jpsimons.net
      Website: www.jpsimons.com
Dist wiring devices & switches, electrical tapes, fittings, wire, cable & cords, transformers, electrical boxes, tools & testers, terminals & lugs, circuit breakers, fuses & terminal strips, cables ties, etc. (Woman, estab , empl 7, sales $10,000,000, cert: State)

2833 Midco Electric Supply
      7237 W 90th Pl
      Bridgeview, IL 60455
      Contact: Tony Niedospial Sales
      Tel: 888-446-4326
      Email: tony@midcoelectric.com
      Website: www.midcoelectric.com
Dist motor controls, fuses, wire & wiring devices, circuit breakers, switches, transformers, tie wraps, conduit & accessories, liquid tight & fittings, signal towers, PLC's, HMI's, relays, enclosures, timers, light fixtures, ballasts, batteries, tape, etc (Woman, estab 1979, empl 11, sales $13,500,000, cert: State, City, WBENC)

2834 Ottsie, LLC
      1412 Sioux Dr
      Ottawa, IL 61350
      Contact: Sally Rutledge Ott President
      Tel: 815-378-7841
      Email: ottsiesupply@gmail.com
      Website: www.ottsiesupply.com
Dist electrical & plumbing supplies, generators. (Woman, estab 2014, empl 1, sales $437,000, cert: State)

Indiana

2835 Diesel Electrical Equipment, Inc.
      139 N Griffith Blvd
      Griffith, IN 46319
      Contact: Susan Pappas President
      Tel: 219-922-1848
      Email: susan@dieselelectricalequipment.com
      Website: www.dieselelectricalequipment.com
Dist & service diesel electric locomotive components. (Woman, estab 0, empl , sales $ 0, cert: WBENC)

2836 First Electric Supply
      2225 N College Ave
      Indianapolis, IN 46205
      Contact: Tony Frost VP
      Tel: 317-931-3675
      Email: michaelb@firstelectricsupply.com
      Website: www.firstelectricsupply.com
Dist electrical components: ballats, batteries, cable, fuses, generators. (Woman/AA, estab 2004, empl 35, sales $60,000,000, cert: State, City, NMSDC)

2837 UV Solutions, LLC
      9118 Pinecreek Court
      Indianapolis, IN 46256
      Contact: Calvin Stewart CEO
      Tel: 317-345-9899
      Email: calvin@uvsolutions-indy.com
      Website: www.uvsolutions-indy.com
UV germicidal equipment & LED lighting. (AA, estab 2007, empl 3, sales $350,000, cert: State)

Kansas

2838 AJ Smith Enterprise Inc
      9320 Johnson Dr
      Merriam, KS 66203
      Contact: Leon Delmez
      Tel: 913-677-3008
      Email: leon.delmez@wattsuplighting.com
      Website: www.wattsuplighting.com
Dist lighting supplies: light bulbs, ballasts, sockets, fixtures, capacitors, starters, lenses, emergency batteries & emergency ballasts, lighting fixtures, LED bulbs & LED tape. (Hisp, estab 1985, empl 7, sales $3,000,000, cert: NMSDC)

Kentucky

2839 Asia-Link, Inc.
      12540 Westport Rd
      Louisville, KY 40245
      Contact: Andrew Lorenz Admin Mgr
      Tel: 502-394-3900
      Email: andrew.lorenz@asialnk.com
      Website: www.asialnk.com
Data & communication, coaxial cables & connectors, communication connectors & kits, data/LAN cables, telephone cords, voice & data connectors, wire terminals, insulation displacement connectors, shrink tubing. (Woman, estab 1986, empl 18, sales $16,000,000, cert: WBENC)

2840 BFW Inc.
      445 Baxter Ave, Ste 175
      Louisville, KY 40204
      Contact: Lynn Cooper President
      Tel: 502-899-1808
      Email: lynn@bfwinc.com
      Website: www.bfwinc.com
High intensity LED portable and tethered headlights and light sources. (Woman, estab 1994, empl 5, sales $4,200,000, cert: WBENC)

Massachusetts

2841 C & D Electronics
      28 Appleton St
      Holyoke, MA 01040
      Contact: Shelly Kubereit Acct Mgr
      Tel: 413-493-1217
      Email: skubereit@cdindustries.com
      Website: www.cdindustries.com
Dist electronic parts & equipment. (Woman/AA, estab 1982, empl 18, sales $11,000,000, cert: NMSDC)

ELECTRONICS & ELECTRICAL DIST.

2842 Eastern States Components, LLC dba ES Components
      108 Pratts Junction Rd
      Sterling, MA 01564
      Contact: Michelle Aubrey President
      Tel: 978-422-7641
      Email: maubrey@escomponents.com
      Website: www.escomponents.com
Dist electronic components. (Woman, estab 1981, empl 20, sales , cert: WBENC)

2843 Integrated Control Solutions Inc.
      28 Bridge Ave
      Scituate, MA 02066
      Contact: Tara Miller President
      Tel: 781-545-5100
      Email: icstara@comcast.net
      Website: www.icsonline.net
Japanese, Korean, and Chinese MRO parts. Omron, Fuji Electric, Mitsubishi, Idec Relays, motors, gear reducer, sensors, solenoids, breakers, switches, timers,counters (Woman, estab 1990, empl 3, sales $1,400,000, cert: WBENC)

2844 Port Electronics Corporation
      60 Island St
      Lawrence, MA 01840
      Contact: Louise Elliott Exec VP
      Tel: 603-894-6000
      Email: LElliott@PortNH.com
      Website: www.PortNH.com
Premier distributor and supply chain solutions supporting the Aerospace and Defense industries. (Minority, Woman, estab 1988, empl 10, sales $90,021,883, cert: NMSDC)

Maryland

2845 GreenerVolts
      801 N East St Ste 9A
      Frederick, MD 21701
      Contact: Business Devel
      Tel: 888-495-3629
      Email:
      Website: www.greenervolts.com
LED lighting, lighting controls, warehousing & fulfillment. (Hisp, estab 2010, empl 5, sales $1,800,000, cert: NMSDC)

2846 IVS Solutions, LLC
      1040 West St
      Laurel, MD 20707
      Contact: Brian Smith President
      Tel: 240-487-0295
      Email: brian.smith@ivssolutions.net
      Website: www.ivssolutions.net
IVS Solutions is a supplier diversity data management company that provides customized information technology solutions to manage and enrich supplier diversity data for corporations. Formed in 2011 to address industry needs of (AA, estab 2011, empl 2, sales , cert: NMSDC)

2847 MX4 Electronics, Inc.
      2203 Greenspring Dr
      Timonium, MD 21093
      Contact: Susan Grill Owner
      Tel: 410-252-1192
      Email: susan@mx4elect.com
      Website: www.mx4elect.com
Dist electronic components & accessories. (Woman, estab 1976, empl 3, sales $2,821,076, cert: State)

Michigan

2848 Arrow Motor & Pump Inc.
      692 Central Ave
      Wyandotte, MI 48192
      Contact: Gloria Marquess Inside Sales
      Tel: 734-285-5700
      Email: sales@arrowmotor.net
      Website: www.arrowmotor.net
Sales & repair electric motors, pumps & power transmission products, reducers, gearmotors, etc. (Woman, estab 1988, empl 14, sales $2,128,352, cert: WBENC)

2849 Bluecolt Lighting LLC
      4403 Concourse Dr STE B
      Ann Arbor, MI 48108
      Contact: Jaspreet Sawhney
      Tel: 734-864-5533
      Email: service@falconinnovations.com
      Website: www.bluecoltlighting.com
L.E.D. (Light Emitting Diode) lighting. (As-Ind, estab 2003, empl 9, sales $3,000,000, cert: NMSDC)

2850 Ebinger Manufacturing Company
      7869 Kensington Ct
      Brighton, MI 48116
      Contact: Janny Lu President
      Tel: 248-486-8880
      Email: emc@ebinger-mfg.com
      Website: www.ebinger-mfg.com
Dist electrical, plumbing, work gloves, HVAC & safety products. (Minority, Woman, estab 1974, empl 1, sales $ 0, cert: NMSDC)

2851 Empire Electric
      3575 Vinewood
      Detroit, MI 48208
      Contact: Bob Pauline vp
      Tel: 313-895-1920
      Email: bob@empireec.com
      Website: www.empirewc.com
Dist electrical, industrial & networking products. Mfr wire harnesses & cable assemblies. (AA, estab 2003, empl 10, sales $1,005,000,000, cert: NMSDC)

2852 Industrial Control Service, Inc.
      9267 Riley St
      Zeeland, MI 49464
      Contact: Dale Venema VP
      Tel: 800-087-8672
      Email: dale@industrialcontrol.com
      Website: www.industrialcontrol.com
Dist controls: Cognex, DVT, Banner, Turck, Sunx, X-Rite, Spectrum Illumination,Nerlite, RFID, Microscan, Eaton Cutler-Hammer, Parker, Danaher, IAI, Panasonic, Hyde Park, Giddings & Lewis, Nachi, Encoder Products, GE Industrial. (Nat Ame, estab 1975, empl 10, sales $5,157,803, cert: NMSDC)

2853 Manufacturing & Automation Cost Solutions, LLC
      28795 Goddard Rd, Bldg 6, Ste 201
      Romulus, MI 48174
      Contact: Kenneth M President
      Tel: 248-321-2433
      Email: kgutierrez@macostsolutions.com
      Website: www.macostsolutions.com
Dist non-production maintenance spare parts in the Electrical and Mechanical sector to support machines, robots, automation and clean rooms. (Hisp, estab 2016, empl 2, sales $500,000, cert: NMSDC)

ELECTRONICS & ELECTRICAL DIST.

2854 Sawyer Services Inc.
56851 Gratiot Ave
Chesterfield, MI 48051
Contact: Kim Sawyer Office Mgr
Tel: 586-646-5181
Email: electrical@sawyerservices.net
Website: www.sawyer-services.com
Design, installation, management & maintenance of facility lighting, electrical & sign systems to achieve significant energy cost savings and more efficient facility operations. (Minority, Woman, estab 2009, empl 20, sales $3,000,000, cert: NMSDC, WBENC)

2855 Strike Group LLC
18800 Fairway Dr, Ste 10
Detroit, MI 48221
Contact: Lane coleman President
Tel: 313-586-0003
Email: lanec@strikegroup.org
Website: www.strikegroup.org
Dist electrical products. (AA, estab 1998, empl 3, sales $3,200,000, cert: NMSDC)

2856 York Electric Motors, Inc.
611 Andre St
Bay City, MI 48706
Contact: Thomas Hunter Acct Mgr
Tel: 989-684-7460
Email: tomh@yorkelectric.com
Website: www.yorkelectric.com
Dist & svc electric motors, generators, transformers, inverters, pumps, etc. (Nat Ame, estab 1971, empl 37, sales $ 0, cert: NMSDC)

Minnesota

2857 Carlo Lachmansingh Sales, Inc.
4801 4th Ave S
Minneapolis, MN 55419
Contact: Carl Lachmansingh VP
Tel: 612-827-2211
Email: carlo@carloelectrical.com
Website: www.carloelectrical.com
Dist electrical supplies. (As-Ind, estab 1990, empl 2, sales $2,800,000, cert: State, 8(a))

2858 JCB Enterprises, Inc. dba Reluminate
1408 Northland Dr, Ste 105
Mendota Heights, MN 55120
Contact: Brigid Brady CEO
Tel: 612-378-1677
Email: brigid@reluminate.com
Website: www.reluminate.com
Commercial lighting service, interior & exterior lighting. (Woman, estab 2014, empl 10, sales $1,450,000, cert: WBENC)

2859 Recycle Technologies, Inc.
4000 Winnetka Ave North, Ste 210
Minneapolis, MN 55427
Contact: Lynn Petros CEO
Tel: 763-559-5130
Email: lynn@recycletechnologies.com
Website: www.recycletechnologies.com
Recycle fluorescent bulbs, ballasts, batteries, electronics, computers, mercury containing devices, & special industrial waste. (Woman, estab 1993, empl 18, sales $2,010,000, cert: WBENC)

Missouri

2860 Butler Supply, Inc.
965 Horan Dr
Fenton, MO 63026
Contact: Warren Baker Diversity Program Mgr
Tel: 314-952-7564
Email: wbaker@butlersupply.com
Website: www.butlersupply.com
Dist electrical, plumbing and telecommunications products and services. (Woman, estab , empl , sales $105,000,000, cert: State, WBENC)

2861 Communications & Electrical Supplies, Inc.
13288 Newt Dr
Neosho, MO 64850
Contact: Amanda Murphy Accounting Mgr
Tel: 417-451-1789
Email: amanda@ceslive.com
Website: www.ceslive.com
Dist tools & electrical equipment. (Woman, estab 1990, empl 8, sales $3,000,000, cert: WBENC)

2862 Cooling Components Inc.
69 N Gore Ave
Saint Louis, MO 63119
Contact: Morgan Brewster Dir of Sales
Tel: 314-772-8311
Email: morgan@coolingcomponents.com
Website: www.ccicoolingtowerparts.com
Dist, service, repair & erect cooling towers & related equipment. (Woman, estab 2000, empl 10, sales $ 0, cert: WBENC)

2863 Electronic Supply Co, Inc.
4100 Main St
Kansas City, MO 64111
Contact: Bob Niekamp Mgr
Tel: 816-931-0250
Email: bobn@eskc.com
Website: www.eskc.com
Dist electronic parts, wire/cable, tools, test equipment, security cameras & systems, access control systems, computer networking equipment. (Woman, estab 1952, empl 33, sales $17,300,000, cert: City)

2864 US Electronics Inc.
1590 Page Industrial Blvd
Saint Louis, MO 63132
Contact: Anil Arekapudi President
Tel: 314-423-7550
Email: anil@us-electronics.com
Website: www.us-electronics.com
Dist electrical & electronic components. Mfr electrical bulbs, Halogen, energy saving & LED bulbs. (As-Ind, estab 1995, empl 15, sales $2,200,000, cert: NMSDC)

North Carolina

2865 Tiger Controls Inc.
7615 Business Park Dr
Greensboro, NC 27409
Contact: Neeta Singh President
Tel: 336-889-6265
Email: neeta@tigercontrols.com
Website: www.tigercontrols.com
Dist electronic, electrical & industrial supplies. (Minority, Woman, estab , empl , sales $9,005,000, cert: NMSDC)

ELECTRONICS & ELECTRICAL DIST.

2866 Video & Security Specialists
2313 Wedgewood Dr
Matthews, NC 28104
Contact: Erika Gordon Partner
Tel: 704-821-9396
Email: egordon@carolina.rr.com
Website: www.videoandsecurityspecialists.com
Dist electrical & security products: alarm/security systems, fire alarm systems, structured wiring, access control, security cameras, networking, phone system, intercom & gates. (Woman, estab 1975, empl 7, sales $220,866, cert: State)

New Jersey

2867 Samson Electrical Supply Co Inc
1764 New Durham Road
South Plainfield, NJ 07080
Contact: Joan Cohen President
Tel: 732-393-7070
Email: yourdiversesupplier@samsonelectrical.com
Website: www.samsonelectrical.com
Dist electrical supplies. (Woman, estab 1949, empl 51, sales $40,200,000, cert: State, City, WBENC)

2868 Weissco Power Limited Liability Company
516 Route 513
Califon, NJ 07830
Contact: Stacy Weiss President
Tel: 908-832-2173
Email: sweiss@weisscopower.com
Website: www.weisscopower.com
DIst uninterruptible power supply products & services, preventative maintenance, emergency services, load testing, battery installation & removal, equipment removal & battery maintenance. (Woman, estab 1999, empl 10, sales $2,700,000, cert: State, WBENC)

Nevada

2869 Codale Energy Services & Supply, LLC
3920 W Sunset Rd, Ste A
Las Vegas, NV 89118
Contact: Oscar Aliaga President
Tel: 702-384-8500
Email: oscara@codaleess.com
Website: www.codaleess.com
Dist electrical supplies: commercial construction, hospitality MRO, solar, comm data, Outside plant, & Utility. (Hisp, estab 2010, empl 21, sales $21,500,000, cert: NMSDC)

New York

2870 Aurora Electric Inc.
141 Federal Circle
Jamaica, NY 11430
Contact: Veronica Rose President
Tel: 718-371-0385
Email: vrose@auroraelectric.org
Website: www.auroraelectric.org
Data communication & electrical installation & maintenance. (Woman, estab 1993, empl 17, sales $795,628, cert: State, City)

2871 Deep Roof Lighting
27 Hall St
Brooklyn, NY 11205
Contact: Jay Chen Exec
Tel: 718-243-9388
Email: deeproof@aol.com
Website: www.deeprooflighting.com
Software controlled patent daylight harvest dimming control system. Dimmanble LED, Dimmable and Non-dim Fluorescent, HID, Halogen Recess housings, Track lighting, Pendant lights, Flush mount ceiling. (As-Pac, estab 1997, empl 7, sales $2,000,000, cert: City)

2872 East Coast Metallic Tubing & Hardware Supply Corp
1951 Ocean Ave, Unit 4
Ronkonkoma, NY 11779
Contact: Ehmann CEO
Tel: 631-676-5570
Email: eastcoastmthsc@aol.com
Website: www.eastcoastmetallic.com/
Dist metallic & conduit hardware. (Woman, estab 2001, empl 2, sales , cert: State)

2873 Edge Electronics Inc.
75 Orville Dr.
Bohemia, NY 11716
Contact: Mitchel Auerbach VP Operations
Tel: 631-471-3343
Email: mauerbach@edgeelectronics.com
Website: www.edgeelectronics.com
Dist electronics. (Woman, estab 1990, empl 34, sales $33,009,000, cert: City, WBENC)

2874 Linrose Electronics Inc.
29 Cain Dr
Plainview, NY 11803
Contact: Debra Freedman President
Tel: 516-293-2520
Email: debra@linrose.com
Website: www.linrose.com
Dist CML - Led indicators. (Woman, estab 1964, empl 5, sales $510,000, cert: WBENC)

2875 North Shore Components Inc.
9 Sawgrass Dr
Bellport, NY 11713
Contact: David Hochhauser Acct Mgr
Tel: 631-504-6038
Email: davidh@nscomponents.com
Website: www.nscomponents.com
Dist IC's, semiconductors, capacitors, connectors, resistors, diodes, etc. (Woman, estab 2001, empl 22, sales $ 0, cert: WBENC)

2876 Serendipity Electronics, Inc.
152 E Main St
Huntington, NY 11743
Contact: Yovanna Camargo Acct Mgr
Tel: 631-424-2244
Email: yovannac@serendipityelectronics.com
Website: www.serendipityelectronics.com
Dist electronic components; capacitors, resistors, diodes, computer peripherals, active & passive components. (Woman, estab 1992, empl 9, sales $19,000,000, cert: WBENC)

ELECTRONICS & ELECTRICAL DIST.

2877 Southtown Electronics Inc.
75 Lake St
Hamburg, NY 14075
Contact: Heather Sidorowicz Owner
Tel: 716-648-6565
Email: heather@southtownav.com
Website: www.southtownav.com
Dist & install commercial Audio Video Technology Solutions: Audio Video Systems, Digital Signage, Electronics Sales (TVs, Speakers, Racking Equipment), Music Systems, interactive Rooms & Conference rooms. (Woman, estab 1984, empl 6, sales , cert: State)

2878 Venus Power-Com Supply, LLC
54-07 46th St
Maspeth, NY 11378
Contact: King President
Tel: 646-248-7050
Email: sheena@venussupply.com
Website: www.venussupply.com/
Dist electrical, data & power products. (Woman, estab 2014, empl 5, sales , cert: City, WBENC)

Ohio

2879 Daycoa, Incorporated
50 Walnut Rd
Medway, OH 45341
Contact: Tamela Chenault Sales Consultant
Tel: 937-849-1315
Email: tami@daycoa.com
Website: www.daycoa.com
Dist lighting products. (Woman, estab 1957, empl 14, sales $33,866,096, cert: WBENC)

2880 E-Z Electric Motor Service, Inc.
8510 Bessemer Ave
Cleveland, OH 44127
Contact: Demetrius Ledgyard VP Sales
Tel: 216-581-8820
Email: demetrius@ezelectricmotor.com
Website: www.ezelectricmotor.com
Dist & repair electric motors: complete rewinds, rebuild, machine shop services, repair pumps, & gearboxes, dynamic balancing. (AA, estab 1965, empl 16, sales , cert: State, NMSDC)

2881 Mars Electric
6655 Beta Dr, Ste 200
Mayfield Village, OH 44143
Contact: Michael Doris Exec VP
Tel: 440-946-2250
Email: mldoris@mars-electric.com
Website: www.mars-electric.com
Electrical dist: lighting (fixtures and lamps), distribution equipment, switches, conduit, wire, etc. (Woman, estab 1952, empl 160, sales $84,000,000, cert: City)

2882 Mirg Corporation
6270 Este Ave
Cincinnati, OH 45232
Contact: Michael Griffie President
Tel: 513-679-2020
Email: mgriffie@mirgcorp.com
Website: www.mirgcorp.com
Dist electrical supplies, electrical contracting. (AA, estab 1989, empl 9, sales $ 0, cert: State, NMSDC)

2883 Peak Electric, Inc.
320 N Byrne Rd
Toledo, OH 43607
Contact: Milton McIntyre President
Tel: 419-726-4848
Email: mmcintyre@peakelectrictoledo.com
Website: www.peakelectrictoledo.com
Dist lighting, LED indoor & outdoor, fixtures, lamps, ballast & components, switchgear, transformers, panelboards & disconnects, fuses, wire, conduits, fittings & boxes, telecommunication equip, high voltage equip. (Woman/AA, estab 2000, empl 3, sales $7,000,000, cert: State, City, NMSDC)

2884 Wheatley Electric Service Co.
2046 Ross Ave
Cincinnati, OH 45212
Contact: Dorothy Elsbrock President
Tel: 513-531-4951
Email: motor@fuse.net
Website: www.wheatleyelectric.com
Dist & repair electric motors & pumps, recondition, rebuild & re-design motors. (Woman, estab 1934, empl 9, sales $ 0, cert: WBENC)

Oklahoma

2885 Electro Enterprises, Inc.
3601 N I-35 Service Road
Oklahoma City, OK 73111
Contact: Nathan Little Dir Global Sales
Tel: 405-427-6591
Email: nathan.little@electroenterprises.com
Website: www.electroenterprises.com/
Dist interconnect, electro-mechanical, wire/cable and harness management systems, connector assembly, fiber optic cable assembly, kitting, marking, built to print, military packaging and labeling. (Minority, Woman, estab 1970, empl 227, sales $109,000,000, cert: State)

Oregon

2886 Super Stores Service
11170 SW 5th St
Beaverton, OR 97005
Contact: Mary Kroger Acct Mgr
Tel: 800-462-2370
Email: maryk@superstoresservice.com
Website: www.superstoresservice.com
Dist replacement parts for manual & electric pallet jacks used to handle palletized goods. (Woman, estab 1986, empl 20, sales $4,200,000, cert: WBENC)

Pennsylvania

2887 Decision Distribution America, Inc.
4548 Market St, Ste 215
Philadelphia, PA 19139
Contact: Bernie Hopewell President
Tel: 215-493-4400
Email: bernie@ddistribution.com
Website: www.ddistribution.com
Dist electrical, hvac, mechanical, plumbing, supplies & equipment. (AA, As-Pac, estab 2004, empl 7, sales $14,000,000, cert: State, NMSDC)

2888 DEW Electric, Inc.
      189 Enterprise Ln
      Connellsville, PA 15425
      Contact: Wendy Wiltrout CEO
      Tel: 724-628-9711
      Email: wendy@dewelectric.com
      Website: www.dewelectric.com
Dust & repair motors, electronic drives, gearboxes, generators, control panel fabrication. (Woman, estab 1993, empl 4, sales $935,000, cert: WBENC)

2889 Electrical Systems & Construction Supplies
      5131-37 N 2nd St, Bldg 12
      Philadelphia, PA 19120
      Contact: Bernard Hopewell CEO
      Tel: 215-324-3291
      Email: bhopewell@escsinc.net
      Website: www.escsinc.net
Dist electrical equipment, construction supplies, wire & cable & lighting. (AA, estab 2003, empl 3, sales $1,440,000, cert: State, City)

2890 Habsco Inc.
      12th St Bldg 240
      New Kensington, PA 15068
      Contact: George Hubbard CEO
      Tel: 724-337-9498
      Email: george@habscoinc.com
      Website: www.habscoinc.com
Dist Westinghouse Reactor Coolant Pump (RCP) & motor replacement components. (AA, estab , empl , sales $1,000,000, cert: NMSDC)

2891 Manna Supply, Inc.
      3015 Blackswift Rd
      East Norriton, PA 19403
      Contact: Elaine Prince President
      Tel: 610-222-4775
      Email: eprince@mannasupply.com
      Website: www.mannasupply.com
Dist electrical & electronic equipment & supplies: data & communications, network integration, telecom & conferencing, mechanical & general construction. (Minority, Woman, estab 1993, empl 6, sales $9,000,548, cert: WBENC)

2892 R. Scheinert & Sons, Inc.
      10092 Sandmeyer Ln
      Philadelphia, PA 19116
      Contact: Sheree Miller President
      Tel: 215-673-9800
      Email: sheree@scheinert.com
      Website: www.scheinert.com
Repair, rewind & dist AC & DC electric motors, pump repair & refurbish, new cooling tower technology, eliminating gearboxes, warranty center. (Woman, estab , empl 24, sales $6,000,000, cert: City, WBENC)

2893 Valenko Incorporated
      4124 Clendenning Rd
      Gibsonia, PA 15044
      Contact: Jim Perko VP
      Tel: 888-908-6322
      Email: info@valenko.com
      Website: www.valenko.com
Dist electrical products: custom transformers, panels, wire, cable, power distribution equipment, hand tools, conduit, couplings, cable assemblies, cable management, UPS, data center. (Woman, estab 2007, empl 5, sales $4,013,000, cert: State)

Puerto Rico

2894 Wholesale Electric Caribe Inc.
      PO Box 2057
      Barceloneta, PR 00617
      Contact: Miguel Barrios President
      Tel: 787-846-5755
      Email: sales@wecipr.com
      Website: www.wecipr.com
Dist electronic products: automation & control products. (Hisp, estab 1999, empl 43, sales $7,331,560, cert: NMSDC)

South Carolina

2895 Carolina Product Solutions, LLC
      PO Box 12901
      Florence, SC 29504
      Contact: Sean Tanner President
      Tel: 843-409-6922
      Email: stanner@cpsled.com
      Website: www.cpsled.com
LED Lighting. (Nat Ame, estab 2008, empl 4, sales $2,800,000, cert: NMSDC)

2896 Electritex
      321 Alliance Pkwy
      Williamston, SC 29697
      Contact: Tracie Craft President
      Tel: 864-226-4438
      Email: andersonoffice@electritex.com
      Website: www.electritex.com
Dist & service electric motors. (Woman, estab 1980, empl 20, sales , cert: WBENC)

Tennessee

2897 Brighter Days & Nites, Inc.
      2165 Troyer Aven
      Memphis, TN 38114
      Contact: Dorothy Sinclair CEO
      Tel: -   -
      Email: csallie@bdnincorp.com
      Website: www.bdnincorp.com
Dist electrical materials. (Woman/AA, estab 2003, empl 5, sales $13,000,000, cert: NMSDC, WBENC)

2898 Diversified Supply, Inc.
      210 N Highland Park Ave
      Chattanooga, TN 37404
      Contact: Janice Brown Sales Marketing Mgr
      Tel: 423-544-8964
      Email: jbrown@diversifiedsupply.com
      Website: www.diversifiedsupply.com
DIst electrical & instrument materials. (AA, estab 1987, empl 58, sales $ 0, cert: NMSDC)

2899 Edwards Supply Company
      315 Oak Ridge Turnpike
      Oak Ridge, TN 37830
      Contact: Tracie Miller CEO
      Tel: 865-483-1766
      Email: tracie@edwardssupply.com
      Website: www.edwardssupply.com
Dist electrical supplies: ballast, batteries, conduit, electric, electrical, janitorial, lamps, lighting, motors, tools, wire. (Minority, Woman, estab 1993, empl 23, sales $24,472,449, cert: NMSDC, WBENC)

Texas

2900 Advanced Equipment Co. dba Prime Distributing Co.
PO Box 946
Allen, TX 75013
Contact: Carole Booth Inside Sales
Tel: 972-562-0170
Email: caroleb@primedistributing.com
Website: www.primedistributing.com
Dist electronic components. (Woman, estab 1972, empl 8, sales $1,135,426, cert: WBENC)

2901 Arbor Electronics Inc.
4257 Arbor Creek Dr
Carrollton, TX 75010
Contact: Janice President
Tel: 972-939-7092
Email: janice@goarbor.com
Website: www.goarbor.com
Dist electronics. (Woman, estab 1999, empl 2, sales $850,000, cert: WBENC)

2902 BG Technologies of Austin, LLC
2301 Denton Dr, Ste A
Austin, TX 78758
Contact: Linda Gibson President
Tel: 512-336-2299
Email: linda@bg-technologies.com
Website: www.bg-technologies.com
Dist electronic components. (Woman, estab 2001, empl 6, sales $16,400,000, cert: State)

2903 Demand Lighting USA Inc
1321 Rutherford Lane Ste 150,
Austin, TX 78753
Contact: Gary Morrissey COO
Tel: 512-822-1100
Email: garymorrissey@demandlighting.com
Website: www.demandlighting.com
Dist DLC, Energy Star LED lighting solutions. (Woman, estab 2013, empl 15, sales $1,000,000, cert: State, WBENC, SDB)

2904 IDM Products
10500 Metric Dr, Ste 119
Dallas, TX 75243
Contact: Gerald Grimes President
Tel: 888-908-4580
Email: gerald@idmproducts.com
Website: www.idmproducts.com
Dist LED Lighting, Building Maintenance & Office Products, Industrial Products, Food Service Disposables and Healthcare Products. (AA, estab 2018, empl 4, sales $1,000,000, cert: NMSDC)

2905 Mavich LLC
525 Commerce St.
Southlake, TX 76092
Contact: Vincent Manfredini Operations
Tel: 682-503-4484
Email: vincent.manfredini@mavich.com
Website: www.mavich.com
Dist MRO & industrial supplies: electronic components, connectors, passives, resistors, etc. (Minority, Woman, estab 2010, empl 10, sales $3,000,000, cert: State)

2906 NOVA Electronic Materials LLC
1189 Porter Rd
Flower Mound, TX 75022
Contact: Lauri Boudreaux President
Tel: 972-478-7002
Email:
Website: www.novawafers.com
Dist silicon wafers & cleanroom consumables. (Woman, estab 1989, empl 5, sales $4,216,523, cert: State)

2907 Portable Power Systems Inc.
2890 Market Loop
Southlake, TX 76092
Contact: Jordan Hamill VP Sales
Tel: 303-460-8261
Email: sales@portablepower.com
Website: www.portablepower.com
Dist OEM battery and power products. (Woman/AA, Hisp, estab 1992, empl 13, sales $4,000,000, cert: State)

2908 Specialty Optical Systems, Inc.
10210 Forest Ln
Dallas, TX 75243
Contact: Terry Nelson
Tel: 214-340-8574
Email: sales@sossupply.com
Website: www.soslightbulbs.com
Dist lightbulbs: lamps & bulbs, ballasts & fixtures. (Woman, estab 1981, empl , sales $5,015,000, cert: WBENC)

2909 Supa Tech Inc.
17304 Preston Rd Ste 800
Dallas, TX 75252
Contact: Sue Glover President
Tel: 972-238-8958
Email: sglover@supatech.net
Website: www.supatech.net
Information technology products & printed circuit boards. (Minority, Woman, estab 1980, empl 3, sales $285,000, cert: State)

2910 Telecom Electric Supply Company
1304 Capital Ave
Plano, TX 75074
Contact: Christy Moses Sales Exec
Tel: 972-422-0012
Email: cmoses@tes85.com
Website: www.tes85.com
Dist electric, utility, construction & telecommunication supplies. (AA, estab , empl , sales $33,858,031, cert: State, NMSDC)

2911 Wholesale Electric Supply of Houston
4040 Gulf Fwy
Houston, TX 77004
Contact: Pam McKellop President
Tel: 713-749-8461
Email: khighland@wholesaleelectric.com
Website: www.wholesaleelectric.com
Dist electrical & data communications material. (Woman, estab 1949, empl 284, sales $ 0, cert: WBENC)

ELECTRONICS & ELECTRICAL DIST.

Virginia

2912 Bright Regards LLC
      5837 Governors Hill Dr
      Alexandria, VA 22310
      Contact: Yvonne Herrera President
      Tel: 703-349-1709
      Email: yvonne@brightregards.com
      Website: www.brightregards.com
Commercial LED, induction & solar lighting solutions. (Minority, Woman, estab 2014, empl 1, sales , cert: State)

2913 Delta Automation, Inc.
      2704 Charles City Rd
      Richmond, VA 23231
      Contact: Margarete Culley CEO
      Tel: 804-236-2800
      Email: plc@deltaautomation.com
      Website: www.deltaautomation.com
Industrial electronic control equipment, PLCs & drives. (Woman, estab 1996, empl 19, sales $ 0, cert: State)

2914 Jo Kell, Inc.
      1716 Lambert Ct
      Chesapeake, VA 23320
      Contact: Patricia Galiney Sales
      Tel: 904-260-8420
      Email: customerservice@jokell.com
      Website: www.jokell.com
Dist electrical apparatus & equipment, wiring supplies & related equipment. (Woman, estab 1977, empl 50, sales $30,383,075, cert: WBENC)

2915 Old Dominion Electrical Supply Co Inc
      2509 N Lombardy St
      Richmond, VA 23220
      Contact: Harold Parker President
      Tel: 804-344-5440
      Email: odessales@gmail.com
      Website: www.olddominionelectricalsupply.com
Dist electrical supplies: batteries, light bulbs, specialty lighting, circuit breakers, panel boxes, ballast, fuses, light fixtures, etc. (AA, estab 1983, empl 5, sales $4,457,015, cert: State, City)

2916 Reynolds Lighting Supply Co.
      606 Research Rd
      Richmond, VA 23236
      Contact: Valerie Reynolds President
      Tel: 804-897-2300
      Email: valarie@reynoldslighting.com
      Website: www.reynoldslighting.com
Dist replacement light bulbs, ballasts, fixtures, electrical & electronic items. (Woman, estab 1987, empl 7, sales $2,250,000, cert: State)

2917 The Mt. Olivet Group, LLC
      PO Box 56415
      Virginia Beach, VA 23456
      Contact: Jon McGlothian President
      Tel: 757-271-8681
      Email: jon@tmogllc.com
      Website: www.mtolivetgroup.com
Dist power, lighting, security & data products. (AA, estab 2007, empl 2, sales $475,000, cert: State)

Vermont

2918 Granite City Electric Supply
      14 Morse Rd
      Bennington, VT 05201
      Contact: Phyllis Papani Godwin Chair of the Board
      Tel: 617-472-6500
      Email: phyllisg@granitecityelectric.com
      Website: www.granitecityelectric.com
Dist electrical products. (Woman/As-Ind, estab 1923, empl 70, sales $90,000,000, cert: State)

Washington

2919 1 Industrial Source
      17627 E Lake Desire Dr SE
      Renton, WA 98058
      Contact: Tammie Cook Owner
      Tel: 206-354-4295
      Email: tammiecook@1industrialsource.com
      Website: www.1industrialsource.com
Supplier of LED lighting, hand dryers and other products used in electrical upgrades. (Woman, estab 2009, empl 1, sales , cert: State)

2920 Mobile Electrical Distributors, Inc.
      14050 Lake City Way NE
      Seattle, WA 98125
      Contact: Sales
      Tel: 206-363-2400
      Email:
      Website: www.mobileelec.com
Dist electrical supplies: ballasts, boxes, conduit & fittings, lighting, service gear, tools, testers, wire, wiring devices, motor controls, fuses, etc. (Woman, estab 1956, empl 11, sales $925,000, cert: State, WBENC)

Wisconsin

2921 Applied Sales & Installation Services, Inc.
      2900 Enloe St
      Hudson, WI 54016
      Contact: Tara Ferguson CEO
      Tel: 715-386-7214
      Email: tara@applied-sales.com
      Website: www.applied-sales.com
Sales, installation, and service of coolers, freezers, & all related refrigeration equipment. (Woman/As-Pac, estab 1995, empl 3, sales $3,500,000, cert: NMSDC)

2922 First American Engineered Solutions, LLC
      136 Jackson St, Ste C
      Oshkosh, WI 54901
      Contact: Gerald Morris President
      Tel: 920-231-8501
      Email: gmorris@firstamericanllc.com
      Website: www.firstamericanllc.com
Dist electronics, electrical equipment, industrial equipment & supplies, office equipment & supplies & ordnance. (Nat Ame, estab 1997, empl 12, sales $4,500,000, cert: NMSDC, 8(a))

ELECTRONICS & ELECTRICAL MFG.

ELECTRONICS & ELECTRICAL MFG.
Firms design, develop and make (turnkey) electro-mechanical devices on contract or market their own products such as power supplies, test equipment, guidance systems, robotics, radar, CMOS-IC, connectors, modems, military trainers, motors, etc. NAICS Code 33

Alabama

2923 Amphenol Tecvox, LLC.
      4900 Bradford Dr Ste 1
      Huntsville, AL 35805
      Contact: Ryan Brown Financial Analyst
      Tel: 256-417-4338
      Email: ryan.brown@tecvox.com
      Website: www.tecvox.com
Mfr finish electronic components, single, dual & multi channel headphones & remote contols, plastic & rubber products, metal stamping & cable assemblies. (Minority, estab 2002, empl 50, sales $3,300,000, cert: NMSDC)

2924 Global Manufacturing, Inc.
      248 N Main St
      Arab, AL 35016
      Contact: Kathy Bennefield Mgr
      Tel: 256-789-0948
      Email: kathy@globalmanufacturing.us
      Website: www.globalmanufacturing.us
Custom fabricated wire harnesses & cables, Data cables, MIL-SPEC, Coaxial, Power assemblies. (Hisp, estab 2014, empl 17, sales $1,824,260, cert: NMSDC)

Arizona

2925 Transtek Magnetics Inc.
      1900 W Grant Rd
      Tucson, AZ 85745
      Contact: Mary Yanez Office Mgr
      Tel: 520-792-4415
      Email: mary@ttkm.co
      Website: www.transtekmagnetics.com
Mfr & dist electronic components, custom magnetic coils, TableTop PowerStation, A/C, USB & wireless charging power to laptops, cell phones. (As-Pac, estab 1999, empl 1400, sales $30,000,000, cert: NMSDC)

California

2926 661 Electric
      3500 W Olive Ave Ste 300
      Burbank, CA 91505
      Contact: Raymond Moreno Principal
      Tel: 661-998-9061
      Email: office@661electric.com
      Website: www.661electric.com
Full-service electrical contractor. (Hisp, estab 2017, empl 15, sales $3,000,000, cert: NMSDC)

2927 A-1 Electric Service Co., Inc.
      4204 S Sepulveda Blvd
      Culver City, CA 90230
      Contact: Scott Pieper VP
      Tel: 310-204-1077
      Email: spieper@a-1electric.com
      Website: www.a-1electric.com
Electrical Contractor, design build services, Hi Voltage installations & preventive maintenance services. (Woman, estab 1997, empl 50, sales $1,600,000, cert: CPUC, WBENC)

2928 Absolute Sign, Inc
      10655 Humbolt St
      Los Alamitos, CA 90720
      Contact: Tish Scialampo Mgr
      Tel: 562-592-5838
      Email: tish@absolutesign.com
      Website: www.absolutesign.com
Design, manufacture, installation/removal, maintenance/repair of illuminated & non-illuminated signs and LED displays. (Woman, estab 1989, empl 15, sales , cert: WBENC, 8(a))

2929 Berkeley Integration Group dba Fiber.com
      2200 Powell St, Ste 1200
      Emeryville, CA 94608
      Contact: Sophia Mendoza-Hirano Account/Sales Mgr
      Tel: 510-227-5583
      Email: sophia@fiber.com
      Website: www.fiber.com
Fiber optic cables, connectors and accessories, fiber jumpers, patch cords, pigtails, multi-strand, armored, aerial, indoor/outdoor, plenum, LSZH. (As-Pac, estab 1989, empl 4, sales , cert: NMSDC)

2930 Bishop-Wisecarver Corporation
      2104 Martin Way
      Pittsburg, CA 94565
      Contact: Barbara Williams Supplier Diversity Admin
      Tel: 888-580-8272
      Email: bwilliams@bwc.com
      Website: www.bwc.com
Mfr linear & rotary motion components, custom engineering services, bearings, vee guide wheels, linear guides, linear actuator, custom machine shop, XYZ systems, gantry, rotary tables, custom assembly, linear slides, linear bearing, dualvee. (Woman, estab 1950, empl 64, sales $21,000,000, cert: WBENC)

2931 Calpak USA, Inc.
      13750 Prairie Ave
      Hawthorne, CA 90250
      Contact: Danish Qureshi VP
      Tel: 310-937-7335
      Email: danish@calpak-usa.com
      Website: www.calpak-usa.com
Electronic Design, Electronics Engineering, Contract Manufacturing Services (CMS), Electronic Manufacturing Services (EMS), PCB Layout, PCB Design, PCB Assembly. (As-Pac, estab 1978, empl 15, sales $2,400,000, cert: State, NMSDC, SDB)

2932 Century Wire & Cable
      7400 E Slauson Ave
      Commerce, CA 90040
      Contact: Bob Arthur Acct Exec
      Tel: 800-999-5566
      Email: arthur@centurywire.com
      Website: www.centurywire.com
Mfr electrical wire & cable products. (Hisp, estab 1965, empl 110, sales $40,000,000, cert: City)

2933 Doc Stephens Scientific
      5851 S Garth Ave
      Los Angeles, CA 90056
      Contact: David Stephens CEO
      Tel: 310-568-9082
      Email: david.stephens@dsscientific.com
      Website: www.dsscientific.com
Equipment & electronic manufacturing services related to infrared, visual cameras & imaging systems, RF & high speed fiber optic telecommunication circuits, sensor designs, silicon III-V semiconductor processing. (AA, estab 2014, empl 2, sales , cert: NMSDC)

2934 Evolve Manufacturing Technologies Inc
      47300 Bayside Pkwy
      Fremont, CA 94538
      Contact: Acct Analyst
      Tel: 510-690-8959
      Email: services@evolvemfg.com
      Website: www.evolvemfg.com
Contract manufacturer: assembly, precision & electro-mechanical products, component sourcing, turnkey supply chain management, prototyping, production, testing, product configuration. (Woman, estab 1998, empl 70, sales $20,000,000, cert: WBENC)

2935 Frontier Electronics
      667 E Cochran St
      Simi Valley, CA 93065
      Contact: Jeannie Gu President
      Tel: 805-522-9998
      Email: jeannie@frontierusa.com
      Website: www.frontierusa.com
Mfr electric coil, transformers & inductors. (Minority, Woman, estab 1985, empl 25, sales $5,400,000, cert: WBENC)

2936 Johnson-Peltier Electric
      12021 S Shoemaker Ave
      Santa Fe Springs, CA 90670
      Contact: Greg Kelley Business Devel
      Tel: 562-944-3408
      Email: gkelley@johnson-peltier.com
      Website: www.johnson-peltier.com
Industrial electrical contracting, including power distribution, medium & high voltage line work, control systems, instrumentation, and communication integration. (Nat Ame, estab 1957, empl 85, sales , cert: NMSDC, CPUC)

2937 KR Wolfe, Inc.
      10015 Maine Ave
      Lakeside, CA 92040
      Contact: Kasey Pitchford Dir of Client Relations
      Tel: 619-368-1544
      Email: kasey.pitchford@krwolfe.com
      Website: www.krwolfe.com
Low voltage systems installation & integration, design, layout & installation/integration of A/V & control systems. (Woman, estab 2007, empl 34, sales $5,500,000, cert: WBENC)

2938 Ledtronics, Inc.
      23105 Kashiwa Court
      Torrance, CA 90505
      Contact: Janelle Mika-Palmer Manufacturer Rep
      Tel: 630-243-0412
      Email: janemika@mikasales.com
      Website: www.ledtronics.com
Design & mfr light emitting diodes (LEDs). (Minority, estab 1983, empl 125, sales $12,470,700, cert: NMSDC, CPUC)

2939 Magnuson Products LLC
      1990 Knoll Dr Bldg A
      Ventura, CA 93003
      Contact: Nader Rayes Brand Mgr
      Tel: 805-765-5562
      Email: nader.rayes@magnusonproducts.com
      Website: www.magnusonsuperchargers.com
Design, fabrication & mfr superchargers. (Woman, estab 2010, empl 60, sales $14,649,000, cert: WBENC)

2940 Micro Analog Inc.
      1861 Puddingstone Dr
      La Verne, CA 91750
      Contact: Kim Bickmeier Dir of Sales
      Tel: 909-392-8277
      Email: kimbickmeier@micro-analog.com
      Website: www.micro-analog.com
Mfr electronics: printed circuit board assembly PCBA, custom cable & wire harness assembly, box/system build. (Minority, Woman, estab 1991, empl 155, sales $15,698,000, cert: NMSDC)

2941 Myers Power Products, Inc.
      2950 E Philadelphia St
      Ontario, CA 91761
      Contact: Diana Grootonk CEO
      Tel: 909-923-1800
      Email: diana.grootonk@myerspower.com
      Website: www.myerspower.com
Mfr low voltage & med voltage electrical distribution equipment, 5,15,27 & 38kv switchgear, LV switchgear, switchboards, panel boards, inverters, converters & electrical products & circuit breakers. (Woman, estab 2001, empl 500, sales $263,101,084, cert: CPUC, WBENC)

ELECTRONICS & ELECTRICAL MFG.

2942 NexEco Energy Conservation, Inc.
9370 Studio Court, Ste 168
Elk Grove, CA 95758
Contact: Nick Potter Acct Mgr
Tel: 855-711-6868
Email: nick@nexeco.net
Website: www.nexeco.net
Mfr energy efficient LED lighting products, LED Bulbs, LED Fixtures, LED Hardwired Interior Ceiling Fixture, LED Hardwired Exterior Porch lanterns, LED Hardwired Vanity Fixture. (Minority, Woman, estab 2016, empl 5, sales $800,000, cert: State)

2943 One-E-Way, Inc.
3016 E Colorado Blvd Ste 70848
Pasadena, CA 91107
Contact: Cedric Woolfork CFO/VP
Tel: 310-743-4081
Email: cedric@one-e-way.com
Website: www.wayvz.com/
Design & mgr electronic products. (AA, estab 2004, empl 5, sales , cert: NMSDC)

2944 Philatron Wire and Cable
15315 Cornet Ave
Santa Fe Springs, CA 90670
Contact: Phillip Ramos III GM
Tel: 562-802-2570
Email: p3@philatron.com
Website: www.philatron.com
Design & mfr electrical, electronic, instrumentation, control & communication wire & cable. (Hisp, estab 1974, empl 85, sales $24,000,000, cert: NMSDC)

2945 Pro-Lite
3505 Cadillac Ave, Bldg D
Costa Mesa, CA 92626
Contact: Andy Kaoh President
Tel: 714-668-9988
Email: ak@pro-lite.com
Website: www.pro-lite.com
Mfr LED signs & LED displays. (As-Pac, estab 1981, empl 400, sales , cert: CPUC)

2946 Solartech Power, Inc.
901 E Cedar St
Ontario, CA 91761
Contact: Sherry Fu Owner
Tel: 714-630-8880
Email: sherry.fu@solartechpower.com
Website: www.solartechpower.com
Mfr solar photovoltaic panels & equipment. (Minority, Woman, estab 2001, empl 10, sales $3,000,000, cert: CPUC)

2947 Steren Electronics International, LLC
6260 Sequence Dr Ste 110
San Diego, CA 92121
Contact: E'Lisa Jones Dir Business Devel
Tel: 800-266-3333
Email: elisa@steren.com
Website: www.sterenusa.com
Mfr voice, video & data connectivity solutions. (Hisp, estab 1978, empl 100, sales $56,000,000, cert: CPUC)

2948 Unicorp, Inc.
5780 Smithway St
Commerce, CA 90040
Contact: VP Business Dev
Tel: 323-890-9246
Email: customerservice@uninex.com
Website: www.uninex.com
LED lighting technology, Indoor & Outdoor Electric Lighting Fixtures, Residential Electrical Lighting Fixture, Commercial, Industrial, Institutional Electrical Lighting Fixture, Other Lighting Equipment. (As-Pac, estab 1989, empl 14, sales , cert: State, CPUC)

Colorado

2949 Colorado Lighting, Inc.
1831 E 73rd Ave
Denver, CO 80229
Contact: Christy Kidwell Contract/Sales Support
Tel: 303-288-3152
Email: quotes@cli-services.com
Website: www.coloradolighting.com
Electrical, Lighting, Sign Work, Fire Alarms, Energy Analysis, and Emergency Lighting service for commercial and retail facilities. (Woman, estab 1977, empl 70, sales $17,950,000, cert: WBENC)

2950 Premier Manufactuirng and Supply Chain Services
7755 Miller Dr
Frederick, CO 80504
Contact: Edmond Johnson President
Tel: 303-776-4145
Email: ejohnson@pmscs.com
Website: www.pmscs.com
Contract mfr of printed circuit board assemblies for prototypes, production, sub assemblies, cable harness & test. (AA, estab 2000, empl 55, sales $12,000,000, cert: NMSDC)

2951 Quality Concepts Manufacturing Inc.
1635 S Murray Blvd
Colorado Springs, CO 80911
Contact: Robert Millemon Program Mgr
Tel: 719-574-1013
Email: robert@qcmi.com
Website: www.qcmi.com
Electronic Manufacturing Services, Quick-turn prototyping, pre-production & full production support services, mechanical assembly. (Woman, estab 1988, empl 30, sales , cert: City)

Connecticut

2952 ICDI Inc.
407 Brookside Rd
Waterbury, CT 06708
Contact: Steve Villodas President
Tel: 203-753-8551
Email: svillodas@icdi-inc.com
Website: www.icdi-inc.com
Contract mfr electronic high tech equip & systems, turnkey program mgmt, eng design, microprocessor systems, PC layout, PC board & automated surface-mount assembly, wave soldering, vapor degreasing, custom cables, ATE testing. (Hisp, estab 1975, empl 22, sales $3,019,307, cert: NMSDC)

Florida

2953 123GermFree, LLC dba TrackedMobility
4537 Prime Terr
North Port, FL 34286
Contact: Cordell Jeter President
Tel: 888-976-2525
Email: cjeter@trackedmobility.us
Website: www.compositemotors.com
Design & mfr electrical motors & controllers. (AA, estab 2010, empl 1, sales , cert: State, NMSDC)

2954 CableNetwork Associates Inc.
4800 N Federal Hwy, Ste E300
Boca Raton, FL 33431
Contact: Marcela Gutierrez
Tel: 954-312-1200
Email: mgutierrez@cablenetwork.net
Website: www.cablenetwork.net
Mfr coax cable, drop & trunk cable. (Hisp, estab 1997, empl 300, sales $2,284,358,226, cert: NMSDC)

2955 ElectraLED, Inc.
12722 62nd St N Ste 200
Largo, FL 33773
Contact: Ryan Begin Marketing Mgr
Tel: 727-561-7610
Email: ryan.begin@electraled.com
Website: www.electraled.com
Mfr & dist LED light fixtures. (Woman, estab 2002, empl 18, sales , cert: WBENC)

2956 Mainstream IP Solutions, Inc.
6905 El Dorado Dr
Tampa, FL 33615
Contact: Arnie Solomon Acct Mgr
Tel: 813-549-7768
Email: asolomon@mcsoftampa.com
Website: www.mainstreamipsolutions.com
Electrical, structured cabling, audio-visual, security & fire alarm systems. (AA, estab 2010, empl 5, sales $250,000, cert: State, NMSDC, 8(a), SDB)

2957 PowerLogics, Inc.
1115 Marbella Plaza Dr
Tampa, FL 33619
Contact: Barbara Smith Sales Assoc
Tel: 813-645-2971
Email: barbarasmith@powerlogics.com
Website: www.powerlogics.com
Transient voltage surge suppression, uninterruptible power systems, power conditioning equip, battery replacements, generators, automatic transfer switches, AC & DC invertors. (Woman, estab 1981, empl 6, sales $4,000,000, cert: State)

Georgia

2958 Georgia Green Energy Services
335 Wilma Ct SW
Atlanta, GA 30331
Contact: Gavin Ireland CEO
Tel: 404-334-3323
Email: gireland@gagreenenergysvc.com
Website: www.gagreenenergysvc.com
Light retrofitting, LED lighting, occupancy sensors, solar power systems, alternative & renewable energy systems, Energy auditing, energy reduction reports, energy audits. (AA, estab 2007, empl 1, sales $1,099,000, cert: NMSDC, 8(a))

2959 Roytec Industries LLC
306 Bell Park Dr
Woodstock, GA 30188
Contact: Amanda Chapman CEO
Tel: 770-926-5470
Email: mchapman@roytecind.com
Website: www.roytecind.com
Mfr electrical wire harnesses & electrical wire assemblies. (Woman, estab 1984, empl 500, sales $36,734,238, cert: WBENC)

2960 Southern States, LLC
30 Georgia Ave
Hampton, GA 30228
Contact: Amit Modi Sr Reg Mgr
Tel: 770-946-4562
Email: a.modi@southernstatesllc.com
Website: www.southernstatesllc.com
Mfr high voltage electrical airbreak switchgear, power fuses, circuit switchers & capacitor bank switching devices. (As-Ind, estab , empl 300, sales , cert: NMSDC)

Hawaii

2961 American LED and Energy, Corp.
521 Ala Moana Blvd Ste M-329
Honolulu, HI 96813
Contact: Wailana Kamauu CEO
Tel: 808-626-5331
Email: info@al-e.com
Website: www.al-e.com
Semiconductor & Related Device Manufacturing, Indoor & Outdoor Electric Lighting Fixtures. (Nat-Ame, estab 2009, empl 4, sales $640,385, cert: NMSDC)

Illinois

2962 AC Gentrol, Inc.
100 S Fourth St
Chillicothe, IL 61523
Contact: Allan Capati President
Tel: 309-274-5486
Email: acapati@acgentrol.com
Website: www.acgentrol.com
Mfr specialized electrical controls systems. (Minority, Woman, estab , empl , sales $1,100,000, cert: State)

ELECTRONICS & ELECTRICAL MFG.

2963 Amitron, Inc.
2001 Landmeier Rd
Elk Grove Village, IL 60007
Contact: Thomas G. Massman Dir of North American Sales
Tel: 847-290-9800
Email: tomm@amitroncorp.com
Website: www.amitroncorp.com
Mfr Bare Printed Circuit Board, 1 to 30 layers, FR4, Thermal materials, Teflon, Rogers & exotic materials. (As-Ind, estab 1995, empl 140, sales , cert: NMSDC)

2964 Capsonic Group, LLC
460 S Second St Slot B-8
Elgin, IL 60123
Contact: George Albrecht Reg Sales Mgr
Tel: 847-888-7242
Email: georgea@capsonic.com
Website: www.capsonicgroup.com
Insert & composite molding: product design, prototype, automation. (AA, estab 1968, empl 225, sales , cert: NMSDC)

2965 CEC Industries Ltd.
599 Bond St
Lincolnshire, IL 60069
Contact: Michelle Draper
Tel: 847-599-6132
Email: michelle@cecindustries.com
Website: www.ceclighting.com
Mfr miniature halogen lamps, LED lamps, electronic turn signal flashers. (Minority, estab 1979, empl 66, sales , cert: NMSDC)

2966 KLI Inc.
304 Roma Jean Pkwy
Streamwood, IL 60107
Contact: Lisa Carso President
Tel: 630-213-1283
Email: support@kli-inc.com
Website: www.kli-inc.com
Mfr electronic components; electronic assembly; main harness & cable to mil specs. (Minority, Woman, estab 1987, empl 15, sales , cert: State, NMSDC)

2967 PowerVolt Inc. (DBA Ensign Corporation)
300 W Factory Rd
Addison, IL 60101
Contact: Ajay Sharma VP Sales & Mktg
Tel: 630-628-9999
Email: ajays@powervolt.com
Website: www.ensigncorp.com
Mfr power transformers & DC power supplies. (As-Ind, estab 1986, empl 39, sales $3,330,000, cert: NMSDC)

2968 Tempco Electric Heater Corp.
607 N Central Ave
Wood Dale, IL 60191
Contact: William Kilberry CFO
Tel: 630-350-2252
Email: williamkilberry@tempco.com
Website: www.tempco.com
Mfr thermal component products: electric heating elements, temperature controls, temperature sensors & turnkey process heating systems. (Hisp, estab 1972, empl 330, sales $28,500,000, cert: NMSDC)

2969 WarmlyYours.com Inc.
590 Telser Rd, Ste B
Lake Zurich, IL 60047
Contact: Julia BIllen President
Tel: 800-875-5285
Email: jbillen@warmlyyours.com
Website: www.WarmlyYours.com
Manufacturer Electric Radiant Floor Heating Systems. (Woman, estab 1999, empl 28, sales $14,441,282, cert: WBENC)

Indiana

2970 ATEC Electrical Contractors
419 Ransdell Rd
Lebanon, IN 46052
Contact: C. Shane Conner President
Tel: 765-482-8926
Email: s.conner@atec-electric.com
Website: www.atec-electric.com
Electrical and telecommunications sales, service and support, engineering, project management and sustainable energy consulting and installation. (Hisp, estab 2005, empl 25, sales $5,547,137, cert: NMSDC)

2971 Carson Manufacturing Company, Inc.
5451 N Rural St
Indianapolis, IN 46220
Contact: Barbara Ferguson President
Tel: 317-257-3191
Email: receptionist@carson-mfg.com
Website: www.carson-mfg.com
Contract mfg electromechanical assemblies & equipment, mfr emergency vehicle sirens, rotary switches & voting machines. Prototyping, testing, quick turns, stocking programs & turn-key capabilities. (Woman, estab 1946, empl 20, sales $2,500,000, cert: State, City)

2972 Continental Manufacturing, LLC
1524 Jackson St
Anderson, IN 46016
Contact: Chris Petty Natl Sales Mgr
Tel: 765-298-8030
Email: cpetty@solasray.com
Website: www.solasray.com
Mfr, design, engineer & test LED technology lighting solutions for commercial, industrial & educational applications. (Woman, estab 2007, empl 10, sales $900,000, cert: State, WBENC)

2973 Electric Motors and Specialties, Inc.
701 W King St
Garrett, IN 46738
Contact: Rick Moore President
Tel: 847-559-6132
Email: rmoore@emsmotors.com
Website: www.emsmotors.com
Design, mfg & application of shaded pole, PSC & electronically commutated unit bearing motors. (Woman, estab 1946, empl 200, sales , cert: WBENC)

Kentucky

2974 Dollar Aisle, LLC
165 Woods Dr
Brandenburg, KY 40108
Contact: rahul anand President
Tel: 502-303-4518
Email: dollaraisle@gmail.com
Website: www.wenlighting.com
Mfr led tube lights, wall packs, hig bays, led light bulbs etc. (As-Pac, estab 2011, empl 3, sales $650,000, cert: NMSDC)

Massachusetts

2975 Adcotron EMS
12 Channel St
Boston, MA 02210
Contact: Don MacNeil Business Devel Sales Rep
Tel: 617-598-3000
Email: donimac@comcast.net
Website: www.adcotron.com
Electronic mfg service, printed circuit board assembly, system integration, system assembly. (Woman/As-Pac, estab 1977, empl 100, sales $30,200,000, cert: State)

2976 International Coil, Inc.
15 Jonathan Dr Unit 1
Brockton, MA 02301
Contact: George Machadinho President
Tel: 508-580-8515
Email: gmachadinho@internationalcoil.com
Website: www.internationalcoil.com
Mfr Transformers (wire wound products) & Power Supplies. (AA, estab 1995, empl 12, sales $1,000,000, cert: State)

Maryland

2977 Armacost Lighting LLC
140 Baltic Ave
Baltimore, MD 21225
Contact: Terry Armacost President
Tel: 410-354-6000
Email: tarmacost@armacostlighting.com
Website: www.armacostlighting.com
Architectural quality LED lighting fixtures, LED tape lighting is ultra-thin, flexible, fully dimmable, can be cut to size or multiple strips. (Woman, estab 2009, empl 10, sales $3,700,000, cert: WBENC, NWBOC)

2978 JEM Engineering, LLC
8683 Cherry Ln
Laurel, MD 20707
Contact: Nancy Lilly CEO
Tel: 301-317-1070
Email: nlilly@jemengineering.com
Website: www.jemengineering.com
Design & prototype military & commercial antennas: HF to millimeter-wave, microstrip patch antennas & arrays, wire, aperture, broadband, active & low-observable antennas. (Minority, Woman, estab 2001, empl 30, sales , cert: State)

Michigan

2979 AG Manufacturing Inc.
319 Industrial Pkwy
Harbor Beach, MI 48441
Contact: Marlo Klaus Customer Service
Tel: 989-479-9590
Email: mklaus@agmanufacturing.com
Website: www.agmanufacturing.com
Mfr wire harnesses. (AA, estab 2004, empl 101, sales , cert: NMSDC)

2980 Amtech Electrocircuits, Inc.
701 Minnesota Dr
Troy, MI 48083
Contact: Jay Patel President
Tel: 248-583-1801
Email: jrp@amelectro.com
Website: www.amelectro.com
Electronic manufacturing services, contract manufacturer, printed circuit boards, wire harnesses & electronic assemblies. (As-Ind, estab 1997, empl 10, sales $800,000, cert: NMSDC)

2981 Eisen Electric Corporation
3340 Pinetree Rd
Lansing, MI 48911
Contact: Lokesh Kumar GM
Tel: 517-393-5850
Email: lkumar@eisennet.com
Website: www.eisennet.com
Mfr terminal screws, electrical fasteners & springs. (As-Ind, estab 1994, empl 72, sales $4,200,000, cert: NMSDC)

2982 Excel Electrocircuit Inc.
50 Northpointe Dr
Orion, MI 48359
Contact: Nipur Shah President
Tel: 248-373-0700
Email: sales@excelcircuits.com
Website: www.excelelectro.com
Mfr printed circuit boards. (As-Ind, estab 1970, empl 25, sales , cert: NMSDC)

2983 Hart Precision Products, Inc.
12700 Marion
Redford, MI 48239
Contact: Darlene Hart President
Tel: 313-537-0490
Email: d.hart@hart-precision.com
Website: www.Hart-Precision.com
Mfr precision components & assemblies for the Transportation Industry. (Woman, estab 1953, empl 48, sales $5,100,000, cert: WBENC)

2984 Industrial Control Repair - ICR Services
28601 Lorna Ave
Warren, MI 48092
Contact: Marlies Davis Business Devel
Tel: 586-582-1500
Email: mdavis@icrservices.com
Website: www.icrservices.com
Dist & repair industrial electronics: robots, PLCs drives, welders, encoders, temperature controls, displays, monitors, power sources, etc. (Hisp, estab 1992, empl 155, sales $80,000,000, cert: NMSDC)

2985 JA Quality Assurance Group, LLC
537 Bradford
pontiac, MI 48341
Contact: Julio Rodriguez CEO
Tel: 248-506-3316
Email: jrodriguez@jaqualityassurance.com
Website: www.jaqualityassurance.com
Mfr prototype harnesses. (Hisp, estab 2002, empl 469, sales $7,850,000, cert: NMSDC)

2986 JMC Electrical Contractor, LLC dba JMC Technologies
33651 Giftos
Clinton Township, MI 48035
Contact: Bob Locklear VP Technologies
Tel: 586-773-8026
Email: blocklear@jmcelectricllc.com
Website: www.jmcelectricllc.com
Electrical service, installation, Structured Cable, Fiber Optic Cable, Voice, Data, Security, CCTV, Intrusion Detection, Access Control, Audio/Visual, CATV, Wireless, Wi-Fi, DAS & Building Automation Systems installation. (Woman, estab 2010, empl 45, sales $6,000,000, cert: WBENC)

2987 Johnico LLC
400 Monroe St Ste 480
Detroit, MI 48226
Contact: John Economy Managing Partner
Tel: 248-895-7820
Email: johneconomy@yahoo.com
Website: www.americasgreenline.com
Commercial & industrial LED manufacturer. (Woman, estab 2011, empl 10, sales $3,500,000, cert: WBENC)

2988 Lotus International Company
6880 Commerce Blvd
Canton, MI 48187
Contact: Darren Ivey Dir Sales/Marketing
Tel: 734-245-0140
Email: divey@licus.com
Website: www.licus.com
Electrical & electro-mechanical contract mfg, wire harness, navigation CRT & LCD displays, aluminum & zinc die cast, electronics repair. (As-Ind, estab 1991, empl 200, sales $50,000,000, cert: NMSDC)

2989 Myron Zucker, Inc.
36825 Metro Ct
Sterling Heights, MI 48312
Contact: Mary Anderson Buyer
Tel: 586-979-9955
Email: dzobel@myronzucker.com
Website: www.myronzucker.com
Engineer & mfr low-voltage power products: power factor correction capacitors, harmonic filters & surge suppressors. (Woman, estab 1967, empl 10, sales $1,050,000, cert: WBENC)

2990 Newtech 3, Inc.
28373 Beck Rd Ste H7
Wixom, MI 48393
Contact: Gail Gyenese Dir of Sales
Tel: 248-912-1062
Email: ggyenese@newtech3inc.com
Website: www.newtech3.com
Mfr lower to mid volume wire harness & circuit board assemblies. (AA, estab 2009, empl 32, sales $3,965,000, cert: NMSDC)

2991 Orri Corporation
5385 Perry Dr
waterford, MI 48329
Contact: Angelo Doa Sales
Tel: 248-618-1104
Email: Sales@orricorp.com
Website: www.orricorp.com
Wire harnesses, cable assemblies, electrical test fixtures, robotic vision guidance software. (Woman, estab 2001, empl 12, sales , cert: WBENC)

Minnesota

2992 Electro Mechanical Industries (EMI)
13300 6th Ave N
Plymouth, MN 23606
Contact: Holly Hicks Sales/Mktg
Tel: 763-546-5998
Email: hhicks@e-m-i.com
Website: www.e-m-i.com
Low voltage switchgear, metal clad & metal enclosed medium voltage switchgear, paralleling switchgear, control panels, special wire ways, wall & floor ducts, pull boxes & sound-attenuated generator enclosures. (Woman, estab 1981, empl 36, sales $8,522,000, cert: WBENC)

2993 Telamco, Inc.
636 Industrial Dr SE
Lonsdale, MN 55046
Contact: Tracy Humann President
Tel: 507-744-5504
Email: tracy@telamcoinc.com
Website: www.telamcoinc.com
Mfr custom heat sealed membrane switches & quality assemblies. (Woman, estab 1968, empl 11, sales $1,500,000, cert: NWBOC)

Missouri

2994 Staco Electric Construction Co
11030 Hickman Mills Dr
Kansas City, MO 64134
Contact: Kristen Bilyeu Admin Asst
Tel: 1515-707-3513
Email: kbilyeu@stacoelectric.com
Website: www.stacoelectric.com
Commercial Electrical Contracting, Data centers, Manufacturing, Maintenance, Voice/Data services, Design/Build. (Woman, estab 1971, empl 120, sales $27,532,139, cert: NWBOC)

North Carolina

2995 Adams Electric Company
PO Box 958
Reidsville, NC 27323
Contact: Joy Jones Business Devel
Tel: 800-349-6283
Email: joyjones@adams-electric.com
Website: www.adams-electric.com
Electrical design-build, clean rooms, critical power, pharmaceuticals, health care, industrial & large commercial. (Woman, estab 1928, empl 300, sales $35,000,000, cert: State)

2996 American Tec Electric Company
      2234 Knowles St
      Kannapolis, NC 28083
      Contact: David Augustus Goodson President
      Tel: 704-787-3961
      Email: davidagoodson@americantecelectric.com
      Website: www.americantecelectric.com
Unlimited Licensed Electrical Contractor. (AA/Nat-Ame, estab 2015, empl 24, sales , cert: State, SDB)

2997 Cooper Electrical Construction
      1706 E Wendover Ave
      Greensboro, NC 27405
      Contact: Beverly Brown CEO
      Tel: 336-275-8439
      Email: beverly.brown@coopereic.com
      Website: www.coopereic.com
Electrical D/B, BIM, Prefabrication, Instrumentation & Controls, and Calibration services. (Woman, estab 1954, empl 120, sales $41,509,090, cert: WBENC)

2998 Freedom Industries, Inc.
      PO Box 7099
      Rocky Mount, NC 27804
      Contact: Jeff Groover VP Operations
      Tel: 252-984-0007
      Email: jgroover@freedomind.us
      Website: www.freedomind.us
Electrical, Mechanical, HVAC, Plumbing & Fabrication. (Woman, estab 2004, empl 105, sales $28,140,000, cert: State)

2999 TEC Electric, LLC
      6612G East WT Harris Blvd
      Charlotte, NC 28215
      Contact: Donald James President
      Tel: 704-394-5097
      Email: donald.james@harriselec.com
      Website: www.harriselec.com
Electical contracting, engineering, controls & conveyor installation. (AA, estab 2006, empl 15, sales $3,000,000, cert: NMSDC)

3000 Thermal Control Products
      6324 Performance Dr
      Concord, NC 28027
      Contact: Geoff Nilsen Commercial Sales Exec
      Tel: 704-454-7605
      Email: gnilsen@thermalcontrolproducts.com
      Website: www.thermalcontrolproducts.com
Mfr thermal & protective components, Protective shielding / robotics, Weld splatter shielding, Weld head covers, Gun Bags, Computer monitor protectors, Weld screens, Transport bags. (Woman, estab 1993, empl 40, sales , cert: State)

Nevada

3001 VaOpto, LLC
      5178 W Patrick Lane
      Las Vegas, NV 89118
      Contact: Charles Li Acct Mgr
      Tel: 702-517-5789
      Email: charles.li@vaopto.com
      Website: www.vaopto.com
Mfr LED lightings & LED fixtures. (As-Pac, estab 2010, empl 5, sales $6,000,000, cert: NMSDC)

New York

3002 Integrated Control Corporation
      748 Park Ave
      Huntington, NY 11743
      Contact: CEO
      Tel: 631-673-5100
      Email: sales@goicc.com
      Website: www.goicc.com
Mfr electronic control & communication devices, system integrated design. (Woman, estab 1986, empl 21, sales $6,100,000, cert: WBENC, NWBOC)

3003 PRMS Inc.
      3122 Expressway Dr S
      Islandia, NY 11749
      Contact: Ron Roybal President
      Tel: 631-851-7945
      Email: rroybal@prmsinc.com
      Website: www.prmsinc.com
Mfr & design electronic controls, interconnect devices, power distribution & power supplies. (Hisp, estab 1996, empl 10, sales $2,250,000, cert: State, 8(a))

Ohio

3004 Bryson/Tucker Electric, LLC
      50 Elmdale Rd
      Toledo, OH 43607
      Contact: Andrew Bryson Sales
      Tel: 419-536-2293
      Email: kerryp@brysontucker.com
      Website: www.brysontucker.com
Electrical Contractor-Commercial, Light Industrial. (AA, estab , empl 5, sales , cert: State)

3005 S & V Industries, Inc.
      3535 S Smith Rd
      Fairlawn, OH 44333
      Contact: Denise Uher Acct Exec
      Tel: 330-408-3078
      Email: denise.uher@svindustries.com
      Website: www.svindustries.com
Mfr gears, spur, helical, double helical, worm straight bevel, spiral bevel, herringbone, gear boxes, worm gear boxes, helical gear boxes, bevel helical gear boxes, custom or special gear boxes, geared motors. (As-Pac, estab 1993, empl 30, sales $40,000,000, cert: NMSDC)

3006 TelNet Technologies, LLC
      6455 Gano Rd Ste B
      West Chester, OH 45069
      Contact: Aaron Williams President
      Tel: 513-644-1478
      Email: ahw@telnettechnologies.com
      Website: www.telnettechnologies.com
Low voltage & commercial electrical installation, voice/data & electrical equipment. (AA, estab 2002, empl 20, sales $1,584,134, cert: State)

ELECTRONICS & ELECTRICAL MFG.

3007 Watkins Lighting & Sign Mtc, Inc.
300 Karl St
Berea, OH 44017
Contact: Tonia Watkins Owner
Tel: 440-243-3444
Email: tonia@watkinslighting.com
Website: www.watkinslighting.com
Lighting maintenance, LED lighting, Light poles service & installation, Interior and Exterior lighting. Sign Installation, Sign service, sign change. (Woman/Hisp, estab 2003, empl 6, sales $103,837,787, cert: State, City)

Oregon

3008 Powin Energy Corporation
20550 SW 115th Ave
Tualatin, OR 97062
Contact: Victor Liu Sales
Tel: 503-598-6659
Email: victorl@powinenergy.com
Website: www.powinenergy.com
Design & develop advanced battery management technology & manufactures battery energy storage solutions. (As-Pac, estab 2011, empl 43, sales , cert: NMSDC)

Pennsylvania

3009 AEC Group, Inc.
1735 Fifth Ave
McKeesport, PA 15132
Contact: Lori Pollack
Tel: 412-678-1440
Email: lpollack@theaecgroup.com
Website: www.aecgroup.com
Full service electrical contracting, installation of voice/data/fiber optic cable, network integration & business technology consulting services. (Woman, estab 1992, empl 115, sales , cert: WBENC)

3010 BS Cable Company, Inc.
334 Godshall Rd
Harleysville, PA 19438
Contact: Outside Sales
Tel: 215-513-4000
Email:
Website: www.bscable.com
Communication & computer cable mfg. Fiber Optics, Copper Cords. (Woman, estab 1984, empl 57, sales $5,185,430, cert: WBENC)

3011 Butler Technologies, Inc.
231 W Wayne St
Butler, PA 16001
Contact: Marilyn Suchy Sales Admin
Tel: 724-283-6656
Email: msuchy@butlertechnologies.com
Website: www.butlertechnologies.com
Mfr graphic overlays, membrane switches, labels, decals & printed electronics. (Woman, estab 1990, empl 61, sales $6,974,188, cert: WBENC)

3012 John A. Romeo & Associates, Inc.
890 Pittsburgh Rd, Ste 7
Butler, PA 16002
Contact: Pamela Romeo CEO
Tel: 724-586-6961
Email: sales@jara-mfg.com
Website: www.jara-mfg.com
Mfr Custom Cables, Wiring Harnesses & Electromechanical Assemblies. (Woman, estab 1990, empl 15, sales $1,506,698, cert: WBENC)

Puerto Rico

3013 Advanced Control Services, Inc.
425 Rd. 693, PMB 205, Ste 1
Dorado, PR 00646
Contact: Victor M. Taveras Operations Mgr
Tel: 787-502-8752
Email: victor@advcontrolservices.com
Website: www.advcontrolservices.com
Engineering & validation services, systems integration services, control panels, VFDs, electrical services, SCADA, HMI, instrumentation services. (Hisp, estab 1999, empl 7, sales $621,123, cert: NMSDC)

3014 AG Group Inc.
Centro Industrial Minellas, Carr. 174TH KM 3.0
Bayamon, PR 00959
Contact: Elliott Gonzalez Sales Mgr
Tel: 787-707-0022
Email: info@aggpr.com
Website: www.aggroupinc.com
Engineering, System Integration, Installations, Calibrations, Validations. (Hisp, estab 1997, empl 105, sales $7,892,343, cert: State, NMSDC)

3015 Hi-Tech Products Inc.
PO Box 4956
Carolina, PR 00984
Contact: Daisy Maldonado Admin Officer
Tel: 787-257-1707
Email: admin@hi-techproducts.com
Website: www.hi-techproducts.com
Mfr reps for industrial control products, electronics, electrical & pneumatics. (Hisp, estab 1991, empl 30, sales , cert: NMSDC)

3016 Invision Engineering Corp.
PO Box 6567
Mayaguez, PR 00681
Contact: Jose Vazquez President
Tel: 787-831-0070
Email: jvazquez@invisioneng.com
Website: www.invisioneng.com
Automation, Control System Design, System Integrations, Instrumentation, Calibrations & Installations, Electrical Installations, Computer System Validations, Software Validations, Software design. (Hisp, estab 2002, empl 35, sales $3,137,957, cert: NMSDC)

3017 Lord Electric company of PR, Inc.
      8 Simon Madera Ave. Rio Piedras, Parcelas Falu
      San Juan, PR 00924
      Contact: Manuel Rosabal CEO
      Tel: 787-758-4040
      Email: mrosabal@lordelectric.com
      Website: www.lordcg.com
Electrical, mechanical & piping contractors. (Hisp, estab 1959, empl 300, sales $26,200,000, cert: NMSDC)

South Carolina

3018 Amec, LLC
      4601 E White Horse Rd
      Greenville, SC 29611
      Contact: Kevin Lindsey Project Mgr
      Tel: 864-269-0222
      Email: kevin@amecllc.net
      Website: www.amecsc.net
Industrial & commercial electrical applications, industrial electrical maintenance, thermal imaging, de-energized maintenance, studies for lighting improvements, breaker testing, power analysis, installation of service entrance equipment. (Woman, estab 2009, empl 11, sales $838,385, cert: State)

3019 Arva, LLC
      3705 Centre Circle
      Fort Mill, SC 29715
      Contact: Shahil Amin Dir
      Tel: 803-336-2235
      Email: shahilamin@arva.us
      Website: www.hyliteledlighting.com/
Mfr energy-efficient, indoor & outdoor LED & Induction Lighting & Retrofit Kits. (Woman/As-Ind, estab 2010, empl 7, sales $1,200,000, cert: NMSDC)

Tennessee

3020 TLC Investments, LLC
      1244 Gallatin Pike S
      Madison, TN 37115
      Contact: Jami Hall CEO
      Tel: 615-885-0019
      Email: jhall@stonesriverelectric.com
      Website: www.stonesriverelectric.com
Provides electrical and lighting management and installation services on a national basis. (Woman, estab , empl , sales $44,750,424, cert: State, WBENC)

Texas

3021 Blackhawk Management
      1322 Space Park Dr Ste A220
      Houston, TX 77058
      Contact: Gabrielle Busby Admin
      Tel: 832-536-3703
      Email: busbyg@blackhawkmgmt.com
      Website: www.blackhawkmgmt.com
Electrical & mechanical engineering design services, prototyping, short production runs, printed circuit board design, 3D machining, digital, analog design, power electronics. (Minority, Woman, estab 1992, empl 24, sales $10,000,000, cert: WBENC, SDB)

3022 Electro Plate Circuitry, Inc.
      1430 Century Dr
      Carrollton, TX 75006
      Contact: Nicolas Garcia President
      Tel: 972-466-0818
      Email: nickg@eplate.com
      Website: www.eplate.com
Mfr printed circuit boards: GF,GI, RF, insulators, heatsinks, blind buried vias, controlled impedance. (Hisp, estab 1981, empl 80, sales $9,000,000, cert: NMSDC)

3023 FASIC Design LLC
      4105 Front Range Lane
      Austin, TX 78732
      Contact: Scott Buchanan Managing Member
      Tel: 214-298-7810
      Email: scott.buchanan@fasicdesigns.com
      Website: www.fasicdesigns.com
Design large to small semiconductor designs at low to large process nodes(350 nm to 4nm).
. (AA, estab 2008, empl 1, sales $151,366, cert: NMSDC)

3024 GCI Technologies
      1301 Precision Dr
      Plano, TX 75074
      Contact: Hinkki Chen CEO
      Tel: 972-423-8411
      Email: mike.beauchamp@gcitechnologies.com
      Website: www.gcitechnologies.com
Mfr magnetics: engineering, telecom, audio, power transformers, external power supplies, chokes, ferrite beads, cores. (As-Pac, estab 1982, empl 420, sales $25,000,000, cert: NMSDC)

3025 Krypton Solutions
      3060 Summit Ave 75074
      Plano, TX 75074
      Contact: Carol Primdahl Dir of Sales
      Tel: 214-882-2363
      Email: carol@krypton-solutions.com
      Website: www.krypton-solutions.com
Electronic contract manufacturer. (As-Pac, estab 2005, empl 51, sales $5,100,000, cert: State)

3026 PanAmerica Supply, Inc.
      21414 Provincial Blvd
      Katy, TX 77450
      Contact: Shaun Choi President
      Tel: 281-646-8472
      Email: sychoi@pasihouston.com
      Website: www.pasihouston.com
Mfr power cables (HV, Med XLPE), transformer (up to 230kV). (As-Pac, estab 2005, empl 3, sales $8,000,000, cert: City)

3027 Perau Power Technology, Inc.
      PO Box 540067
      Houston, TX 77254
      Contact: President
      Tel: 713-522-5808
      Email: information@peraupower.com
      Website: www.peraupower.com
Backup power supplies: telecommunications, computers, emergency equip, engineering, install, maintenance. (Woman, estab 2001, empl 1, sales , cert: WBENC)

3028 Roman Industries, Inc.
      10945 Estate Ln, Ste E115
      Dallas, TX 75238
      Contact: Shawn Quiroga Owner
      Tel: 214-503-3100
      Email: shawn@romanindustriesinc.com
      Website: www.romanindustriesinc.com
Mfr custom cable, dist power lugs & RF connectors. (Woman, estab 2008, empl 3, sales , cert: State)

3029 Southwest Synergistic Solutions, LLC
      215 N Center, Ste 701
      San Antonio, TX 78202
      Contact: Juan Cienfuegos Managing Member
      Tel: 956-645-5265
      Email: jc@everythingtactical.com
      Website: www.everythingtactical.com
Mfr & dist lighting solutions. (Hisp, estab 2010, empl 1, sales , cert: State)

3030 Telco Intercontinental Corporation
      9812 Whithorn Dr
      Houston, TX 77095
      Contact: Paolo Longo Dir of Sales
      Tel: 281-855-2218
      Email: plongo@telcointercon.com
      Website: www.telcointercon.com
Mfr electric motors, Permanent Magnet DC motor, PMDC, coreless, core-less DC, gearmotor, high speed, high torque, miniature, stepper, Brushless DC motor, BLDC, green energy efficient ECM motor, fan, blower. (As-Pac, estab 1985, empl 22, sales $19,000,000, cert: NMSDC)

3031 Texas Mgt Associates, Inc
      7001 Fairgrounds Pkwy
      San Antonio, TX 78238
      Contact: Dora Mendoza Business Devel
      Tel: 210-673-8422
      Email: dmendoza@t-m-a.com
      Website: www.t-m-a.com
Electrical engineering & mfg: cable harnesses, electrical components, test station fixtures, circuit boards, restraint test stations, electrical housings, both complex & simple. (Hisp, estab 1991, empl 20, sales $4,368,852, cert: State, NMSDC)

Virginia

3032 Atomized Products Group of Chesapeake, Inc.
      808 Curtis Saunders Ct
      Chesapeake, VA 23321
      Contact: Lee Puckett Exec VP/COO
      Tel: 757-793-2922
      Email: lee.puckett@atomizedproductsgroup.com
      Website: www.atomizedproductsgroup.com
Mfr & dist negative plate expander for lead-acid battery applications. (Woman, estab 2013, empl 13, sales , cert: WBENC)

Washington

3033 CETS LLC
      1441 N Northlake Way, Ste 211
      Seattle, WA 98103
      Contact: Tim Tracey Purchasing
      Tel: 206-588-1239
      Email: info@cetsinc.com
      Website: www.cetsinc.com
Develop & build new electrical systems; constructing additions, alterations & repairs, UL508 LISTED Open & Closed Industrial Panel, marine electrical construction services, electrical power distribution design & repair. (AA, estab 2013, empl 12, sales $1,500,000, cert: City, NMSDC)

3034 Charter Controls, Inc.
      1705 NE 64th Ave Ste B
      Vancouver, WA 98661
      Contact: Randy Ayala VP Industrial Sales
      Tel: 360-695-2161
      Email: randy@chartercontrols.us
      Website: www.chartercontrols.us
Design, engineer & mfr industrial control systems. (Woman, estab 2004, empl 15, sales $3,000,000, cert: State)

3035 Cherry City Electric
      8100 NE St. Johns Rd
      Vancouver, WA 98665
      Contact: Ray Ellis President
      Tel: 503-566-5600
      Email: rellis@cherrycityelectric.com
      Website: www.cherrycityelectric.com
Provide electrical construction, electrical remodels and electrical repair. Provide voice/data installations. (Woman, estab 1968, empl 275, sales $49,800,000, cert: WBENC)

3036 Eworld Solutions, Inc.
      19550 7th Ave NE
      Shoreline, WA 98155
      Contact: Nasir Junejo CEO
      Tel: 206-659-1988
      Email: nasir@eworldsolutions.com
      Website: www.eworldsolutions.com
Contractor placement for design and verification. Specializing in SystemVerilog, UVM and Mixed Signal verification. Consulting Service to audit verification and design environments, Consulting Service to create reusable template (As-Ind, estab 2010, empl 3, sales , cert: NMSDC)

3037 Reliable Investments LLC
      801 2nd Ave Ste 800
      Seattle, WA 98104
      Contact: Anthony Obiako President
      Tel: 800-918-4380
      Email: anthony@reliableinvestmentsllc.com
      Website: www.reliableinvestmentsllc.com
Procurement & supply chain management, field engineering, installation, repair, calibration and rental services. (AA, estab 2010, empl 3, sales $2,000,000, cert: State)

Wisconsin

3038 Arnev Products, Inc.
N1530 Spring Glen Rd
Keshena, WI 54135
Contact: Patricia Evensen President
Tel: 715-799-5944
Email: arnev@frontiernet.net
Website: www.arnev.com
Mfr decorative electrical hardware. (Woman, estab 1990, empl 2, sales $550,000, cert: State)

3039 Convenience Electronics, Inc.
4405 Triangle St
McFarland, WI 53558
Contact: J. Harry Lum President
Tel: 608-838-4300
Email: hlum@convenienceelectronics.com
Website: www.convenienceelectronics.com
Mfr custom computer cables & harnesses, fiber optic cables, molded cables, etc. (As-Pac, estab 1989, empl 45, sales $4,000,000, cert: NMSDC)

3040 Dairyland Electric Co, Inc.
12770 W. Custer Ave
Butler, WI 53007
Contact: Chris Martinez President
Tel: 262-783-1550
Email: cmartinez@dairylandelectric.com
Website: www.dairylandenergy.com/
Electrical construction, data & communication, cabling, testing & certifying, electrical, telecom, fiber, alarms & video installation. (Hisp, estab 1998, empl 11, sales , cert: State, NMSDC)

3041 Electrical Testing Solutions
2909 Green Hill Ct, Ste I
Oshkosh, WI 54904
Contact: Scott Banaski Business Devel Mgr
Tel: 920-420-2986
Email: sbanaski@electricaltestingsolutions.com
Website: www.electricaltestingsolutions.com
Power system components for low, medium voltage & parallel switchgear troubleshooting, commissioning, design, analysis, repair & testing. (Hisp, estab 2005, empl 25, sales $4,300,000, cert: State, NMSDC)

3042 Professional Power Engineering Company, LLC
W266 N7220 Kettle Ridge Ct
Sussex, WI 53089
Contact: Glenn Wilder President
Tel: 262-372-4220
Email: gwilder@ppecompany.com
Website: www.ppecompany.com
Uninterruptible power supply systems, generator sets, automatic transfer switches, batteries, battery racks & cabinets & preventive maintenance services. (AA, estab 2006, empl 3, sales $105,000, cert: NMSDC)

> **ENGINEERING SERVICES**
> Most of these firms are engaged in civil, structural and sanitation engineering services. May also do land surveying, environmental impact studies, testing and sampling, R&D, systems engineering, manufacturing, etc. Included are plant noise studies, digital design, radio active waste disposal, nuclear power. (See also ENVIRONMENTAL SERVICES). NAICS Code 54

Alabama

3043 Building & Earth Sciences, Inc.
5545 Derby Dr
Birmingham, AL 35210
Contact: Matt Adams Dir of Corp Client Dev - Principal
Tel: 205-836-6300
Email: madams@buildingandearth.com
Website: www.buildingandearth.com
Consulting Engineering, geotechnical, environmental & construction materials testing & special inspection services. (Minority, Woman, estab 1998, empl 215, sales $28,000,000, cert: City, WBENC)

3044 Manufacturing Technical Solutions, Inc.
7047 Old Madison Pike Ste 302
Huntsville, AL 35806
Contact: Emily Tanksley Contract Admin
Tel: 256-890-9090
Email: emily.tanksley@mts-usa.com
Website: www.mts-usa.com
Engineering and science, logistics, program management, business management, and information technology. (Woman, estab 2001, empl 135, sales $17,326,179, cert: WBENC)

3045 Mesa Associates Inc.
480 Production Ave
Madison, AL 35758
Contact: Darrell Christman Exec VP
Tel: 865-671-5401
Email: dchristman@mesainc.com
Website: www.mesainc.com
Civil, electrical, mechanical, structural engineering services: integration, surveying, transmission, substation, controls, panel build, telecommunication, fiber optic engineering, robotic vehicle payloads & devices. (Minority, Woman, estab 1988, empl 356, sales $36,000,000, cert: NMSDC, WBENC)

Arizona

3046 Airtelligence Inc.
16650 N 91st St Ste 108
Scottsdale, AZ 85260
Contact: President
Tel: 480-419-9466
Email:
Website: www.airtelligence.com
Laboratory controls, IAQ monitoring for control & reporting, OR Laminar Ceiling Systems, Airflow & Pressure Measuring devices, OR & Isolation room Pressure & Control systems. (Woman, estab 2012, empl 8, sales $3,500,000, cert: NWBOC)

3047 AllSource Global Management
4481 Campus Dr Ste A
Sierra Vista, AZ 85635
Contact: Cecilia Mata Owner
Tel: 520-458-1314
Email:
Website: www.agmaz.com
Training: Intelligence Analyst, Counter Intelligence, HUMINT, Joint Interrogation & Certification Course, Military Intelligence Basic Officer Leader Course (MI-BOLC), New Equipment Training Teams (NETT) in support of Distributive Common Ground Station-Army (DCGS-A). (Woman/As-Pac, estab 2005, empl 181, sales $10,041,256, cert: WBENC)

3048 G.D. Barri & Associates, Inc.
6860 W Peoria Ave
Peoria, AZ 85345
Contact: CEO
Tel: 623-773-0410
Email: gdbarri@gdbarri.com
Website: www.gdbarri.com
Engineering, management & technical support: environmental assessment, analysis, design, systems, baseline engineering, training, procedure development, quality assurance & quality control. (Woman/AA, estab 1989, empl 331, sales $54,435,707, cert: CPUC, WBENC)

California

3049 Abraxas Energy Consulting
811 Palm St
San Luis Obispo, CA 93401
Contact: Tyler Stafford Business Development Mgr
Tel: 805-547-2050
Email: tyler.stafford@abraxasenergy.com
Website: www.abraxasenergy.com
Energy auditing (Energy Star & ASHRAE levels 1,2,3), retro-commissioning, utility bill analysis, energy management training. (Hisp, estab 2001, empl 25, sales , cert: CPUC)

3050 Advanced Energy Products, Inc.
803 2nd St, Ste D
Davis, CA 95616
Contact: Bob Rispoli VP
Tel: 530-424-9348
Email: brispoli@advancedenergyproducts.com
Website: www.advancedenergyproducts.com
Provide energy efficient products. (Minority, estab 2004, empl 5, sales $17,015,000, cert: State)

3051 Aetypic, Inc.
7 Freelon St
San Francisco, CA 94107
Contact: Dennis Wong
Tel: 415-762-8388
Email: dennis.wong@aetypic.com
Website: www.aetypic.com
Architecture & engineering services: structural engineering, civil engineering, construction engineering & inspection, technology integration, & sustainable design. (As-Pac, estab 2011, empl 25, sales , cert: State, NMSDC)

3052 APOMed Systems, Inc.
      2033 Gateway Place, Ste 500
      San Jose, CA 95110
      Contact: Nicole Gebara Dir, Business Devel
      Tel: 408-420-1892
      Email: ngebara@apomedconsultants.com
      Website: www.apomedconsultants.com
Process Development, Facility & Technology Transfer, Master Validation, Process Verifications, IQ/ OQ / PQ, Quality System Regulations, QMS Audits & GMP. (As-Pac, estab 2003, empl 2, sales $13,000,000, cert: NMSDC)

3053 Blackstone Consulting, Inc.
      11726 San Vicente Blvd Ste 550
      Los Angeles, CA 90049
      Contact: Leila Arrants Admin Services Mgr
      Tel: 310-826-4389
      Email: Leila@blackstone-consulting.com
      Website: www.blackstone-consulting.com
Facilities Maintenance. (AA, estab 1991, empl 6000, sales $350,000,000, cert: NMSDC)

3054 Blair, Church & Flynn
      451 Clovis Ave, Ste 200
      Clovis, CA 93612
      Contact: David Mowry Principal
      Tel: 559-326-1400
      Email: dmowry@bcf-engr.com
      Website: www.bcf-engr.com
Engineering, land surveying, planning, civil engineering, landscape architecture & construction management. (Nat Ame, estab 1958, empl 49, sales $5,200,000, cert: CPUC)

3055 Calvada Surveying, Inc.
      411 Jenks Cir Ste 205
      Corona, CA 92880
      Contact: Armando Dupont President
      Tel: 951-280-9960
      Email: armando@calvada.com
      Website: www.calvada.com
Environmental site surveying & mapping, design topographic surveying & mapping, boundary surveys, construction staking, encumbrance mapping. (Hisp, estab 1989, empl 35, sales $4,200,000, cert: NMSDC, CPUC)

3056 Cynergy Professional Systems LLC
      23187 La Cadena, Ste 102
      Laguna Hills, CA 92653
      Contact: Cynthia Mason CFO
      Tel: 800-776-7978
      Email: jesse.lake@cynergy.pro
      Website: www.cynergy.pro
Full service engineering: communications systems, land mobile radio, microwave, aviation communications, marine radio, radio towers, computers, networking, data, all other communications systems engineering. APCO P25, Microwave, Satellite / SATCOM, Marine, Aviation Radio, & Remote Communications and Monitoring. (Hisp, estab 2009, empl 12, sales $25,000,000, cert: City, 8(a))

3057 DeltaTRAK Inc.
      6140 Stoneridge Mall Rd Ste 180
      Pleasanton, CA 94588
      Contact: Karen Bustillo
      Tel: 925-249-2250
      Email: dtsupplierdiversity@deltatrak.com
      Website: www.deltatrak.com
Thermal Mapping Analysis. (As-Pac, estab 1989, empl 200, sales $20,415,145, cert: NMSDC)

3058 Engineering/Remediation Resources Group, Inc.
      4585 Pacheco Blvd Ste 200
      Martinez, CA 94553
      Contact: Tyson Appel Sr Project Mgr
      Tel: 925-969-0750
      Email: tyson.appel@errg.com
      Website: www.errg.com
Engineering & remediation services, environmental, civil & geotechnical engineers, geologists, soil physicists, scientists, construction managers, construction superintendents, equipment operators, certified hazardous waste technicians. (Minority, Woman, estab 1997, empl 175, sales $81,494,792, cert: CPUC)

3059 Faith Com, Inc.
      3850 E Gilman St
      Long Beach, CA 90815
      Contact: Patricia Watts CEO
      Tel: 562-719-9300
      Email: patwatts@fcimgt.com
      Website: www.fcimgt.com
Consulting, strategic energy solutions for corporate, residential, commercial & industrial clients; government & municipal agencies. (Woman/AA, estab 1998, empl 50, sales $16,100,000, cert: State, City, NMSDC, CPUC, WBENC)

3060 GDSTA, LLC
      2000 Wyatt Dr, Ste 10
      Santa Clara, CA 95054
      Contact: Daphne Liu President
      Tel: 408-980-8399
      Email: daphneliu@gdsta.net
      Website: www.gdsta.net
Light emitting diode (LED) lighting & smart lighting devices, reduce carbon dioxide emission, energy usage, energy cost, lighting pollution, waste & return on investment (ROI). (Minority, Woman, estab 2009, empl 8, sales , cert: NMSDC)

3061 Global Software Resources, Inc.
      4447 Stoneridge Dr
      Pleasanton, CA 94588
      Contact: Keith Granucci Dir
      Tel: 925-249-2200
      Email: keith@gsr-inc.com
      Website: www.gsr-inc.com
Engineering services, plant floor operations. (As-Pac, estab 2003, empl 45, sales $4,000,000, cert: CPUC)

3062 Integrated Circuit Development, Inc.
      405 E Santa Clara St
      Arcadia, CA 91006
      Contact: George Johnson Dir Operations
      Tel: 626-599-8566
      Email: gjj@heateflex.com
      Website: www.heateflex.com
Deionized Water Heaters, In-Line Acid Heaters, Gas Heaters, Immersion Heaters, DI Water Heating Systems. (Hisp, estab 1974, empl 37, sales , cert: CPUC)

3063 Mercado Associates
      25583 Ave Stanford
      Valencia, CA 91355
      Contact: Lizandro Mercado Principal
      Tel: 661-753-9295
      Email: monicaf@mercadoassociates.com
      Website: www.mercadoassociates.com
Structural consulting engineering services. (Hisp, estab 1998, empl 5, sales $480,000, cert: State, NMSDC)

ENGINEERING SERVICES

3064 National Relocation Services, Inc. dba NRS, Inc.
2671 Pomona Blvd
Pomona, CA 91768
Contact: Irene Ito CEO
Tel: 909-869-5748
Email: icito@nrsca.com
Website: www.nrsca.com
Asset mgmt, online inventory, project & move mgmt, space planning, warehousing, inventory & bar coding, furniture installation, workstation, cubicle reconfiguration, furniture planning, CAD & CAFM. (Minority, Woman, estab 1994, empl 48, sales $4,373,000, cert: State, CPUC)

3065 Pari & Gershon Inc.
2053 Lincoln Ave Ste A
San Jose, CA 95125
Contact: Romena Jonas President
Tel: 408-966-7184
Email: rjonas@pgiinc.net
Website: www.pgicompany.com
Environmental Consulting, Engineering Design & Construction. (Woman, estab 2009, empl 5, sales $100,000, cert: State, WBENC)

3066 Pivox Corporation
3240 El Camino Real Ste 230
Irvine, CA 92602
Contact: Sean Shahin VP
Tel: 949-727-1400
Email: sean@pivox.com
Website: www.pivox.com
Remediation of soil & groundwater, demolition, project & construction management, permitting, design, feasibility study, treatment system installation (civil, mechanical, electril, and instrumentation). (Woman, estab 2004, empl 20, sales $8,000,000, cert: CPUC)

3067 Quest Project Controls, Inc.
114 W Colorado Blvd
Monrovia, CA 91016
Contact: Robyn Coates CEO
Tel: 626-639-2613
Email: robyn@thecmsolution.com
Website: www.thecmsolution.com
Project controls services & staff augmentation, project scheduling & planning, cost engineering, estimating & management of change. (Woman, estab 2002, empl 23, sales $1,959,183, cert: State, City, CPUC, WBENC)

3068 R.J. Roberts, Inc.
145 John Glenn Dr
Concord, CA 94520
Contact: Terri Van De Veire Acct Mgr
Tel: 925-689-8080
Email: van_t@robertscompanies.net
Website: www.robertscompanies.net
Consulting engineering services: civil, structural, electrical & mechanical. (Woman, estab 1978, empl 80, sales $9,712,761, cert: WBENC)

3069 RFE Engineering, Inc.
8680 Greenback Ln, Ste 107
Orangevale, CA 95662
Contact: Bob Eynck President
Tel: 916-989-3285
Email: reynck@rfeengineering.com
Website: www.RFEengineering.com
Surveying, boundary & topographic surveys, aerial control, ALTA/ACSM, parcel/subdivision maps, construction staking planning, military facility master planning, development feasibility analysis, zoning & use permits, master planning. (Hisp, estab 2003, empl 8, sales $640,000, cert: State, CPUC, 8(a))

3070 Solartech Power, Inc.
901 E Cedar St
Ontario, CA 91761
Contact: Sherry Fu Owner
Tel: 714-630-8880
Email: sherry.fu@solartechpower.com
Website: www.solartechpower.com
Mfr solar photovoltaic panels & equipment. (Minority, Woman, estab 2001, empl 10, sales $3,000,000, cert: CPUC)

3071 SW Safety Solutions Inc.
33278 Central Ave, Ste 102
Union City, CA 94587
Contact: Mike Kimberley Business Devel & Diversity Solutions Leader
Tel: 510-429-8692
Email: mkimberley@swsafety.com
Website: www.swsafety.com/
Manufacturing, R&D and hand health technologies to provide premium hand protection products that enhance worker performance. (Minority, Woman, estab 1984, empl 28, sales $102,000,000, cert: NMSDC, WBENC)

3072 TEC, Inc.
510 S. La Brea Ave.
Inglewood, CA 90301
Contact: Steven Youschak Sales
Tel: 949-450-8200
Email: syouschak@teccm.com
Website: www.teccm.com
Engineering & construction mgmt svcs: CPM scheduling, cost control, constructability review, claims analysis, design mgmt & contract administration. (AA, estab 1988, empl 32, sales , cert: NMSDC, CPUC)

3073 The CAD-Scan Connection
1111 Riverside Ave Ste 405
Paso Robles, CA 93446
Contact: Linda Martini Posner CEO
Tel: 805-237-9347
Email: lindap@cadscanconnection.com
Website: www.cadscanconnection.com
Engineering/architectural technical support services, Conversion to CAD architectural, engineering drawings to AutoCAD. Revit, Map 3D, ArcView,GIS, Large format Description scanning. (Woman, estab 1998, empl 3, sales , cert: CPUC)

ENGINEERING SERVICES

3074 The R.E.M. Engineering Co., Inc.
1575 N Lake Ave, Ste 204
Pasadena, CA 91104
Contact: Robert Milton, Jr. General Mgr
Tel: 626-296-7200
Email: remeng@remengr.com
Website: www.remengr.com
Engineering services: civil, structural, electrical & mechanical, design & design-build, scheduling, project status reporting, construction management. (AA, estab 1979, empl 7, sales $265,826, cert: State, CPUC)

3075 Vistam, Inc.
2375 Walnut Ave
Signal Hill, CA 90755
Contact: Arley Tamayo Sales
Tel: 562-912-7779
Email: art.tamayo@vistam.com
Website: www.vistam.com
Electrical engineering & testing services, substation maintenance & commissioning projects, scheduled maintenance programs. (As-Pac, estab 1992, empl 18, sales $1,752,000, cert: State)

3076 WRW Engineering
2104 Martin Way
Pittsburg, CA 94565
Contact: Barbara Williams Supplier Diversity Admin
Tel: 925-439-8272
Email: bwilliams@wrweng.com
Website: www.wrweng.com
Mechanical, electrical & software engineering, automated flexible testing stations, smart products & autonomous machines. (Woman, estab 2012, empl 2, sales , cert: WBENC)

3077 Zelos Consulting, LLC
2400 Wyandotte St Ste A
Mountain View, CA 94043
Contact: Sabrina Sirwet Business Devel Mgr
Tel: 650-462-1696
Email: sabrina.sirwet@zelos.com
Website: www.zelos.com
Turnkey & customized engineering: staffing services, payroll services, engineering project design services. (Minority, Woman, estab 1996, empl 40, sales $3,000,000, cert: CPUC, WBENC)

Colorado

3078 Amplidyne, Inc.
PO Box 462170
Aurora, CO 80016
Contact: Caroline Schneider Sales
Tel: 225-803-0208
Email: info@amplidyneco.com
Website: www.amplidyneco.com
Energy Consulting- energy audits, estimated energy/dollar savings, cash rebates, tax deductions, Solar Power Generation, Energy saving products and technologies. (As-Ind, estab 1988, empl 20, sales $1,600,000, cert: City)

3079 F&D International, LLC
5723 Arapahoe Ave Ste 1B
Boulder, CO 80303
Contact: Teri Ficken President
Tel: 303-652-3200
Email: teri@fdi-one.com
Website: www.fdi-one.com
F&Engineering, architecture & construction management, engineering consulting (civil & structural), facility condition assessments, site plans, construction consulting, architectural design & CAD drawings. (Woman, estab 2001, empl 10, sales $1,400,000, cert: WBENC)

3080 KIRA, Inc.
2595 Canyon Blvd Ste 240
Boulder, CO 80302
Contact: Constance O''Brien Sr Accountant
Tel: 303-402-1526
Email: cobrien@kira.com
Website: www.kira.com
Facilities maintenance and base operations support services contractor. (Nat Ame, estab 1987, empl 500, sales $49,524,857, cert: NMSDC)

3081 Samuel Engineering, Inc.
8450 E Crescent Pkwy, Ste 200
Greenwood Village, CO 80111
Contact: DJ Alemayehu CEO
Tel: 303-714-4840
Email: dj@samuelengineering.com
Website: www.samuelengineering.com
Engineering & architectural svcs: electrical, instrumentation, controls, civil, structural, process, chemical, mechanical, piping, HVAC. (Woman/AA, estab , empl 200, sales $2,934,704, cert: NMSDC)

Connecticut

3082 Butler America, LLC
2 Trap Falls Rd
Shelton, CT 06484
Contact: Cynthia Lashley Acct Exec
Tel: 765-464-5551
Email: clashley@butler.com
Website: www.butler.com
Engineering Solutions, Extensive recruiting network, rapid deployment, Turnkey Design Center development, Cost reduction. (Woman, estab 2009, empl 2500, sales $101,387,490, cert: WBENC)

Delaware

3083 Bethrant Industries LLC
7 Midfield Rd
New Castle, DE 19720
Contact: Ashly Bethrant President
Tel: 302-322-0521
Email: ashly17@comcast.net
Website: www.bethrantdesign.com
Design, engineering, CAD, graphics, illustration, rendering, prototype models & fixture fabrication, point of purchase displays, shelving design, exhibit booth & bathom furniture design. (Woman/AA, Hisp, estab 2016, empl 4, sales , cert: NMSDC)

3084 MBI, LLC
555 S Bay Rd
Dover, DE 19901
Contact: Jeff Bergstrom Dir of Business Develop
Tel: 610-269-6900
Email: ccarlin@mbius.net
Website: www.mbius.net
Cellular Cost Reduction Services, Energy Cost Reduction Services, Bank Fee Analysis & Cost Reduction Services (AA, estab 2002, empl 15, sales $2,000,000, cert: State, NMSDC)

3085 Mechanical Design Solutions, Inc.
5577 S DuPont Pkwy
Smyrna, DE 19977
Contact: Dianne Bingham President
Tel: 302-659-0233
Email: dbingham@mds13.com
Website: www.mds13.com
Mechanical, electrical & instrument system design & engineering, P&ID walkdown, verification, fabrication orthography, isometrics, bill of material & scopes of work, stress analysis (Rebis and AutoPIPE), PSV survey & modeling, Installation. (Minority, Woman, estab 1998, empl 6, sales $875,000, cert: State)

3086 Mountain Consulting, Inc.
103 S Bradford St
Dover, DE 19904
Contact: Kim Adams President
Tel: 302-744-9875
Email: kadams@mountainconsultinginc.com
Website: www.mountainconsultinginc.net
Engineering, land survey & technical services: Military Housing Privatization, Resident Construction Management, Contract Program Management, Title II Services, and Project Oversight. (Woman/AA, estab 2003, empl 5, sales , cert: State, NWBOC, 8(a))

Florida

3087 Brindley Pieters & Associates, Inc.
2600 Maitland Center Pkwy Ste 180
Maitland, FL 32751
Contact: Brindley Pieters President
Tel: 407-830-8700
Email: bpieters@bpa-engineers.com
Website: www.bpa-engineers.com
Civil & structural engineering svcs & construction management & inspection. (AA, estab 1991, empl 35, sales $6,234,839, cert: City)

3088 Centerline Services LLC
3311 NW 74th Ave, Unit 3311
Miami, FL 33122
Contact: Kenneth Plotkin CEO
Tel: 305-798-8182
Email:
Website: www.centerlinesvcs.com
Aviation contracting, logistics, maintenance & operations support in Latin America. (Hisp, estab 2013, empl 2, sales $3,282,309, cert: 8(a))

3089 Diversified Technology Consultants
650 Central Ave Unit 3
Sarasota, FL 34236
Contact: Robert Hammersley Program Mgr
Tel: - -
Email: robert.hammersley@teamdtc.com
Website: www.teamdtc.com
Civil, environmental, transportation, structures, water pollution control, solid/hazardous waste mgmt, survey, electrical, mechanical, construction inspection & admin, CADD svcs, landscape architecture. (As-Pac, estab 1979, empl 55, sales $6,724,276, cert: State)

3090 EAC Consulting, Inc.
815 NW 57th Ave, Ste 402
Miami, FL 33126
Contact: Enrique Crooks President
Tel: 305-264-2557
Email: eac@eacconsult.com
Website: www.eacconsult.com
Civil structural, bridge & highway design, construction engineering & inspection svcs. (AA, estab 1994, empl 34, sales , cert: State)

3091 EDF Company
8390 Currency Dr, Ste 4
Riviera Beach, FL 33404
Contact: Karla Watkins Dir
Tel: 561-863-6770
Email: karla@edfinc.com
Website: www.edfinc.com
Complex design & engineering support services to the Aerospace industry. Test Facilities & Test Equipment Design/Build for multiple Engine Test Programs, F100/F14, F119/F22, Joint Strike Fighter (JSF). (Woman, estab 1978, empl 25, sales $3,355,920, cert: WBENC)

3092 Engineered Design Services LLC
1035 S State Rd 7 Ste 315
Wellington, FL 33411
Contact: Craig McKenzie President
Tel: 561-600-1776
Email: craigmckenzie@edsengineers.com
Website: www.edsengineers.com
Mechanical & Electrical Engineering, Process Design, Pumping Systems, 3D Modeling, Food Grade Piping Design, Structural/Concrete
Vessel Design, Dry Material Handling, Material Conveying & Dust Collection. (AA, estab 2013, empl 4, sales $119,829, cert: State)

3093 Frazier Engineering, Inc.
6767 N. Wickham Road, Ste 304
Melbourne, FL 32940
Contact: Michelle Shoultz President
Tel: 321-253-8131
Email: mshoultz@fraziereng.com
Website: www.fraziereng.com
Civil, structural, environmental engineering & surveying: design, permitting & construction administration of site plans, utility improvements, water, sewer, reuse, drainage, roadway improvements, bridges. (Minority, Woman, estab 1992, empl 20, sales $17,700,000, cert: State, NMSDC)

ENGINEERING SERVICES

3094 GreenPath Energy Solutions
      3218 E Colonial Dr Ste G
      Orlando, FL 32803
      Contact: Samuel Graham CEO
      Tel: 321-948-3623
      Email: sgraham@greenpathes.com
      Website: www.greenpathenergysolutions.com
Energy monitoring, energy auditing, retro-commissioning, web-based energy dashboard management software. (AA, estab 2006, empl 3, sales $175,000, cert: State, City, NMSDC)

3095 Holland Engineering Inspection Services dba HEIS
      3900 Hollywood Blvd Ste 303
      Hollywood, FL 33021
      Contact: Catherine MacAskill CEO
      Tel: 954-626-0550
      Email: catherine@heisflorida.com
      Website: www.heisflorida.com/
Civil engineering inspections & certifications, 5-Year Surface Water Management Renewals, Stormwater Certifications, Stormwater Drainage Cleaning & Repairs, SSES. (Woman, estab 2016, empl 2, sales $400,000, cert: State)

3096 ITG Global, LLC
      11235 St. Johns Industrial Pkwy N Ste 2A
      Jacksonville, FL 32246
      Contact: Joseph Lukowski CEO
      Tel: 904-425-4760
      Email: almaferrante@itgtec.com
      Website: www.itgtec.com
Automation Design, PLC Programming, Software Development, Technologies Consulting, Motion Design, Robot programming, MES, OEE, Data Analytics, Condition Monitoring, Control System Design, UL 508A Panel Shop, Control Panel. (Minority, Woman, estab 2003, empl 27, sales $3,000,000, cert: NMSDC)

3097 RLJ Enterprises Inc. dba Genesis VII, Inc.
      1605 White Dr
      Titusville, FL 32780
      Contact: Robert Jordan CEO
      Tel: 321-383-4813
      Email: robert.jordan@genesisvii.com
      Website: www.genesisvii.com
Engineering, Logistics & Constructions Services, Design Engineering, 3D CAD, Reverse Engineering, Procurement (Wholesale Procurement), Facilities Management, Construction Management. (AA, estab 1989, empl 9, sales $3,900,000, cert: NMSDC, SDB)

3098 Sign Acquisition LLC dba American and Interstate Signcrafters
      130 Commerce Rd
      Boynton Beach, FL 33426
      Contact: Jonathan Bell
      Tel: 631-273-4800
      Email: jbell@aisigncrafters.com
      Website: www.aisigncrafters.com
Site surveys, recommendation books, permit procurement. (Woman, estab 1979, empl 97, sales $28,000,000, cert: WBENC)

3099 Southeastern Aerospace Services, LLC
      1816 SW 7th Ave
      Pompano Beach, FL 33060
      Contact: Julian Tucker Accountability Mgr
      Tel: 305-992-8257
      Email: sales@southeasternaerospace.com
      Website: www.southeasternaerospace.com
Certified FAA Repair Station, FAA 145 Cert 8SIR251C. Repair & overhaul military & commercial aircraft power generating units. (AA, estab 2016, empl 4, sales , cert: NMSDC)

3100 Southern Energy Solution Group, LLC
      2336 S East Ocean Blvd, Ste 204
      Stuart, FL 34996
      Contact: Oswald Hoffler Managing Member
      Tel: 772-919-2844
      Email: ohoffler@soenergy-grp.com
      Website: www.soenergy-grp.com
Renewable Energy Generation and RECs (AA, estab 2010, empl 5, sales $250,000, cert: CPUC)

Georgia

3101 BREED Enterprises, Inc.
      4501 Circle 75 Pkwy Ste A-1160
      Atlanta, GA 30339
      Contact: Bobby Reed CEO
      Tel: 678-324-0105
      Email: breed@breedenterprisesinc.com
      Website: www.breedenterprisesinc.com
LEED programs, LED lighting products. (AA, estab 2005, empl 45, sales $2,500,000, cert: State, NMSDC)

3102 Capital Inventory, Inc.
      9725 Main St
      Woodstock, GA 30188
      Contact: John Parham Dir of Client Development
      Tel: 770-928-7202
      Email: john.parham@capitalinventory.com
      Website: www.capitalinventory.com
Pharmacy inventory & pharmaceutical valuation (Woman, estab 1979, empl 65, sales $8,000,000, cert: NWBOC)

3103 Greenspeed Energy Solutions, LLC
      2148 Hills Ave NW Ste H
      Atlanta, GA 30318
      Contact: Thomas McNeill Business Devel Mgr
      Tel: 404-924-7400
      Email: tmcneill@greenspeedenergy.com
      Website: www.greenspeedenergy.com
Design/build energy services, audit & design, implementation (installation) of energy efficiency measures. (Minority, estab 2006, empl 20, sales $4,000,000, cert: State, NMSDC)

3104 Murzan Inc.
      2909 Langford Rd Ste 1-700
      Norcross, GA 30071
      Contact: Alberto Bazan VP
      Tel: 770-448-0583
      Email: albertobazan@murzan.com
      Website: www.murzan.com
Diaphragm Pumps, Transfer Pumps, Unloading Systems, Paw Pumps, Gizzard Pumps, Chicken Breast Pumps, CIP Systems, PLC Programming, Liver Pumps, Engineering Services. (Hisp, estab 1984, empl 50, sales $10,400,000, cert: NMSDC)

ENGINEERING SERVICES

3105 Present Energi LLC
411 S Greenwood St Ste B
LaGrange, GA 30240
Contact: Renee Warrick Managing Partner
Tel: 706-883-7336
Email: renee@presentenergi.com
Website: www.presentenergi.com

Solar Photovoltaic & Solar Thermal systems for residential, commercial, industrial & utility scale customers; engineering, project management & construction for large scale systems. (Woman, estab 2009, empl 2, sales , cert: WBENC)

3106 Prime Power Services
8225 Troon Circle
Austell, GA 30168
Contact: Addie Mathes President
Tel: 770-739-2300
Email: gmaddox@primepower.com
Website: www.primepower.com

Power generation svcs: maintenance & emergency response, testing, inspection, calibration & repair, rentals, installations, retrofit, commissioning, ngineering studies & analysis, support, investigation & consulting, training. (Woman, estab 1992, empl 50, sales $11,600,000, cert: WBENC)

3107 R2T, Inc.
580 W Crossville Road Stes 101-102
Roswell, GA 30075
Contact: Kimberly Ajy President
Tel: 770-569-7038
Email: kim.ajy@r2tinc.com
Website: www.r2tinc.com

Civil & environmental engineering & construction services: watershed/stormwater mgmt, conceptual planning, water & wastewater system design, design/build construction. (Woman/AA, estab 2005, empl 57, sales $6,810,190, cert: City, NMSDC, WBENC)

Iowa

3108 ACT Safe, LLC
4121 Gordon Dr
Sioux City, IA 51106
Contact: Lorna Puntillo Managing Member
Tel: 712-204-9274
Email: lorna@actsafellc.com
Website: www.actsafellc.com

Occupational Safety & Health (OSHA), Environmental (EPA) – Due Diligence & Remediation, Engineering (A&E), Construction services. (Woman, estab 2011, empl 12, sales $750,000, cert: City, 8(a))

Illinois

3109 Absolute Risk Management Strategies
416 Main St Ste 533
Peoria, IL 61602
Contact: Kelly Petersen CEO
Tel: 309-676-2767
Email: info@armshr.com
Website: www.armshr.com

Risk Management & Safety Education & Training. (AA, estab 2003, empl 2, sales $227,000, cert: State)

3110 Advanced Cad/Cam Service dba
EngineeringPeople
801 W Main St
Peoria, IL 61606
Contact: Jim Montelongo CEO
Tel: 309-621-5792
Email: jim@engineeringpeople.com
Website: www.engineeringpeople.com

Engineering service support, mechanical, electrical, hydraulic, structural, engineering staffing. (Hisp, estab 1991, empl 60, sales $5,700,000, cert: NMSDC)

3111 DeAmertek
300 Windsor Dr
Oak Brook, IL 60523
Contact: Dan Anderson Sales
Tel: 630-667-4687
Email: anderson@deamertek.com
Website: www.deamertek.com

Electrical Power Steering; AFS: Adaptive Front-lighting System and Fuel Delivery Modules (FDM). (As-Pac, estab 1997, empl 25, sales , cert: NMSDC)

3112 Environmental Systems Design, Inc.
233 south wacker Dr Ste 5300
Chicago, IL 60606
Contact: Tony Kempa Chief Marketing Officer
Tel: 312-580-0534
Email: akempa@esdglobal.com
Website: www.esdglobal.com

Consulting-engineering services. We deliver value by making building occupants more healthy and productive and your facility more cost effective, flexible, reliable, and sustainable. Utilizing an integrative design process, (As-Pac, estab 1967, empl 250, sales $53,537,753, cert: NMSDC)

3113 KAE Consultants, Inc.
1750 E Golf Rd Ste 490
Schaumburg, IL 60173
Contact: Karen Eng President
Tel: 847-605-0080
Email: keng@csmius.com
Website: www.csmius.com

Engineering & design services: project management, electrical, mechanical, packaging, automation engineering & CAD services. (Minority, Woman, estab 1983, empl 11, sales $5,309,251, cert: State, WBENC)

3114 Mat Holdings Inc
6700 Wildlife Way
Long Grove, IL 60047
Contact: Tatiana Sokolov Sr Tax Analyst
Tel: 847-821-9630
Email: tatiana.sokolov@matholdingsinc.com
Website: www.matholdingsinc.com

Global manufacturing, marketing and distribution company (As-Pac, estab 1984, empl 11000, sales , cert: NMSDC)

ENGINEERING SERVICES

3115 Milhouse Engineering and Construction, Inc.
333 S. Wabash Ave. Ste 1501
Chicago, IL 60604
Contact: William Whitaker Sr Business Mgr
Tel: 312-987-0061
Email: milhousebd@milhouseinc.com
Website: www.milhouseinc.com
Engineering design services, site civil, transportation, mechanical, electrical, plumbing, fire protection, water/waste water, preconstruction, quality assurance & control, post construction & construction. (AA, estab 2001, empl 200, sales $32,000,000, cert: NMSDC)

3116 Nest Builders
303 W Erie St Ste 510
Chicago, IL 60654
Contact: Victor Avila Principal
Tel: 312-915-0557
Email: vavila@dbhms.com
Website: www.dbhms.com
Engineering services: mechanical, electrical, plumbing & fire protection design. (Hisp, estab 2002, empl 60, sales , cert: City)

3117 PMA Consultants of Illinois LLC
333 W Wacker Dr, Ste 880
Chicago, IL 60606
Contact: Gui Ponce de Leon Managing Principal
Tel: 312-920-0404
Email: kflood@pmaconsultants.com
Website: www.pmaconsultants.com
Engineering consulting services: CPM scheduling, claims mitigation, change order management, contract document review, cost estimating, value engineering, training & expert analysis and testimony. (Hisp, estab 1971, empl 190, sales , cert: State, NMSDC)

3118 Prairie Engineers
107 N Main St, Ste 3C
Columbia, IL 62236
Contact: Michelle Chambliss Business Devel
Tel: 217-605-0403
Email: mchambliss@prairieengineers.com
Website: www.prairieengineers.com
Engineering services: planning, project management, civil engineering, water resources engineering, land surveying, land acquisition, environmental science & natural resources management & construction management. (Woman, estab 2010, empl 20, sales $2,000,000, cert: City, WBENC, 8(a))

3119 Primera Engineers
100 S Wacker Dr Ste 700
Chicago, IL 60606
Contact: Al Perla
Tel: 312-606-0910
Email: aperla@primeraeng.com
Website: www.primeraeng.com
Engineering design: mechanical, electrical, plumbing, fire protection, architecture, commissioning, structural, civil, telecommunications, utility distribution & substation engineering. (Hisp, estab 1987, empl 170, sales $21,910,784, cert: State, City, NMSDC)

3120 Quality Tools & Abrasives
605 Bonnie Lane
Elk Grove Village, IL 60007
Contact: Matthew Lombardo Sales Devel
Tel: 800-640-2110
Email: mattl@qualitytools.com
Website: www.qualitytools.com
Industrial distributor, supply chain integrator, fluid management, Six Sigma consulting, vending machines, engineering/process improvements. (Minority, estab 1974, empl 39, sales $24,000,000, cert: NMSDC)

3121 Solved Engineering
55 E Monroe, Ste 3800
Chicago, IL 60603
Contact: Edward William Prinicpal Engineer
Tel: 800-975-9723
Email: ewilliam@solvedeng.com
Website: www.solvedeng,com
Electrical Engineer & and Consulting, Engineering Design, Subject Matter Testimony & Engineering Calculation / Studies Service. (AA, estab 2015, empl 5, sales , cert: City, NMSDC, CPUC)

3122 Sterling Engineering, Inc.
Two Westbrook Corporate Center Ste 300
Westchester, IL 60154
Contact: Rama Kavaliauskas President
Tel: 630-993-3433
Email: rama@sterling-engineering.com
Website: www.sterling-engineering.com
Engineering & technical staff augmentation solutions. (Woman, estab 1969, empl 75, sales $2,691,294, cert: WBENC)

3123 Structure Designs, Inc.
309 W Washington St Ste 325
Chicago, IL 60606
Contact: Olufemi Oladeinde President
Tel: 312-551-9780
Email: oao@structuredesignsinc.com
Website: www.sdiengr.com
Civil Engineering, Structural Engineering, Architectural Engineering, Land Surveying, Construction management. (AA, estab 1994, empl 30, sales $12,500,000, cert: NMSDC, 8(a))

3124 Valdes Architecture and Engineering
100 W 22nd St
Lombard, IL 60148
Contact: Max Mather Business Devel Mgr
Tel: 630-792-1886
Email: mmather@valdeseng.com
Website: www.valdeseng.com/
Engineering svcs to process facilities, chemical, food, pharmaceutical, power & steel mfg plants in piping design, mechanical, civil & structural engineering, architecture & process engineering. (Hisp, estab 1992, empl 200, sales , cert: NMSDC)

Indiana

3125 AJ Quality Services, Inc.
   PO Box 764
   New Palestine, IN 46163
   Contact: Donna LaFon CEO
   Tel: 317-441-4305
   Email: donna.lafon@ajqualityservices.com
   Website: www.ajqualityservices.com
Containment, sorting & inspection for the automotive industry. (Woman, estab 2000, empl 35, sales $1,400,000, cert: WBENC)

3126 Allegiant International LLC
   450 E 96th St, Ste 500
   Indianapolis, IN 46240
   Contact: Tiffany Deardorff Key Account Mgr
   Tel: 574-551-6482
   Email: tiffany.deardorff@allegiantworks.com
   Website: www.allegiantworks.com
Advisory Services, Tactical Operations, Technical Services, Outsourcing Services & Strategic Alliances (Woman, estab 2007, empl 25, sales $49,000,000, cert: WBENC)

3127 Americas Engineers, Inc.
   1449 Kimber Ln, Ste 101
   Evansville, IN 47715
   Contact: KC Jain President
   Tel: 812-473-1905
   Email: kcjain@americasengineers.com
   Website: www.americasengineers.com
Civil engineering: surveying, site plans, drainage systems, grading & approach roads, access roads & storm water management. (As-Ind, estab 2004, empl 7, sales $1,200,000, cert: NMSDC)

3128 Consulting Management Inspection Design, Inc.
   1402 N Capitol Ave Ste 250
   Indianapolis, IN 46202
   Contact: Stacey L. Harrell Exec Admin Assist
   Tel: 317-917-4244
   Email: sharrell@cmidinc.com
   Website: www.cmidinc.com
Architectural, structural, mechanical, electrical, environmental, civil, commissioning & construction management & inspection services. (AA, estab 1996, empl 24, sales $3,500,000, cert: State, City)

3129 Continental, Inc.
   1524 Jackson St
   Anderson, IN 46016
   Contact: Paul Wysong CEO
   Tel: 765-778-9999
   Email: paul@continentalinc.com
   Website: www.continentalinc.com
Engineering Services, Drafting Services, Human Resources & Executive Search, Consulting Services (Woman, estab 1985, empl 147, sales $11,350,000, cert: WBENC)

3130 Falcon Manufacturing LLC
   164 S Park Blvd
   Greenwood, IN 46143
   Contact: Larry Waskom Exec VP
   Tel: 317-884-3600
   Email: lwaskom@falcon-manufacturing.com
   Website: www.falcon-manufacturing.com
Containment/Inspection, Repack/Kitting Operations, Global Sourcing & Procurement, Packaging and Parts Washing, Vendor-Managed Inventory (VMI), EDI Management, Customer Service. (As-Pac, estab 1991, empl 225, sales $120,000,000, cert: State, NMSDC)

3131 K & S Engineers, Inc.
   9715 Kennedy Ave
   Highland, IN 46322
   Contact: Debbie Pilawski President
   Tel: 219-924-5231
   Email: dpilawski@kandsengineers.com
   Website: www.kandsengineers.com
Geotechnical engineering & consulting, drilling soil borings & caissons, rock coring, lab & field testing of soil, concrete, asphalt & steel, environmental consulting & forensic investigation of construction materials. (As-Ind, estab 1984, empl 36, sales $4,515,115, cert: State, NMSDC)

Kansas

3132 Choson Resource LLC
   1999 N Amidon, Ste 100B
   Wichita, KS 67203
   Contact: Kim Silcott President
   Tel: 316-729-0312
   Email: kim@chosonresource.com
   Website: www.Chosonresource.com
Aerospace engineering & staffing services for the air, defense & space industries. (Minority, Woman, estab 2010, empl 4, sales $4,254,100, cert: NMSDC)

Kentucky

3133 LECGI Inc.
   13113 Eastpoint Park Blvd Ste D
   Louisville, KY 40223
   Contact: Don Liu President
   Tel: 502-425-1647
   Email: dliu@lecgi.us
   Website: www.lecgi.us
Engineering design & structural steel detailing, structural steel connection design & structural analysis of steel structures, handrails, and stairs for steel fabricators. (As-Pac, estab 2004, empl 10, sales $633,000, cert: State, 8(a))

3134 Pioneer Logistics Group, Inc.
   2208 Sieger Villa Ct
   Louisville, KY 40218
   Contact: Phillip Shoulders President
   Tel: 502-479-3546
   Email: pioneergroupse@msn.com
   Website: www.pioneergroupse.com
Logistics, inventory control management, warehouse services, facilities management, (AA, estab 2010, empl 25, sales $2,000,000, cert: NMSDC)

ENGINEERING SERVICES

Louisiana

3135 ARS Aleut Remediation, LLC
2609 N River Rd
Port Allen, LA 70767
Contact: Steve Shirley General Mgr
Tel: 225-381-2991
Email: sshirley@amrad.com
Website: www.amrad.com
Radiation protection, radiation survey, radioactive material decontamination, and radioactive material laboratory services. (Nat-Ame, estab 2013, empl 6, sales , cert: 8(a))

3136 Gulf South Engineering & Testing, Inc.
2201 Aberdeen St Ste B
Kenner, LA 70062
Contact: Chad Poche VP
Tel: 504-305-4401
Email: cpoche@gulfsoutheng.com
Website: www.gulfsoutheng.com
Geotechnical engineering, foundation engineering, soil borings, facility permitting, laboratory testing, construction materials testing & inspection, concrete testing, pile testing & inspection. (AA, estab 2010, empl 8, sales $550,000, cert: City)

3137 Omega Natchiq, Inc.
4418 Pesson Rd
New Iberia, LA 70560
Contact: Scott McKay GM Business Devel
Tel: 337-365-6028
Email: info@asrcenergy.com
Website: www.asrcenergy.com/
Turnkey Fabrication, Operations and Maintenance Services, Subsea Components, Construction Crews, and ASME Pressure Vessel Design and Fabrication. (Nat Ame, estab 1988, empl 450, sales $71,009,754, cert: NMSDC)

Massachusetts

3138 Corporate Environmental Advisors, Inc.
127 Hartwell St
West Boylston, MA 01583
Contact: Scott Soucy Health, Safety & Compliance
Tel: 800-358-7960
Email: contactus@cea-inc.com
Website: www.cea-inc.com/
Environmental engineering, consulting & contracting firm. (Woman, estab 1985, empl 20, sales $3,878,000, cert: State)

3139 Early Bird Power LLC
1 Adams St
Milton, MA 02186
Contact: Shaun Pandit CEO
Tel: 888-763-2759
Email: shaunpandit@earlybirdpower.com
Website: www.earlybirdpower.com
Facilitator of procurement services for electricity, natural gas, and renewable energy credits. Energy Consulting and risk management. (As-Ind, estab 2009, empl 1, sales $500,000, cert: State)

3140 Green International Affiliates, Inc.
100 Ames Pond Dr, Ste 200
Tewksbury, MA 01876
Contact: Adel Shahin Sr VP
Tel: 978-923-0400
Email: ashahin@greenintl.com
Website: www.greenintl.com
Consulting civil, environmental & structural engineers. (Minority, estab 1954, empl 28, sales , cert: State)

3141 RRMAE Engineering LLC
46 Loring Ave
Boxborough, MA 01719
Contact: Anton Edmund Owner
Tel: 508-517-4913
Email: anton.edmund@rrmaeengineering.com
Website: www.rrmaeengineering.com
Process Design, Process Improvement, Risk assessment, Process Validation, Validation, Commissioning & Qualification, Quality Engineering, Data analysis, Lean management, Process Automation. (As-Ind, estab 2013, empl 2, sales $267,000, cert: State)

Maryland

3142 Pivotal Practices Consulting
6301 Ivy Lane, Ste 800
Greenbelt, MD 20770
Contact: Patrina Clark Business Devel
Tel: 301-220-3179
Email: info@pivotalpractices.com
Website: www.pivotalpractices.com
Organizational climate assessments & engagements: surveys & diagnostic tools, improve individual, team & organizational performance. (Woman/AA, estab 2011, empl 10, sales $2,307,552, cert: NMSDC, WBENC, 8(a))

3143 Robotic Research, LLC
555 Quince Orchard Road, Ste 300
Gaithersburg, MD 20878
Contact: Alberto Lacaze President
Tel: 240-631-0008
Email: lacaze@roboticresearch.com
Website: www.roboticresearch.com
Robotics, intelligent control, sensor processing & specialized computer programming. (Hisp, estab 2002, empl 15, sales $3,000,000, cert: State)

3144 Site Resources, Inc.
14315 Jarrettsville Pike
Phoenix, MD 21131
Contact: Sharon Elliott Marketing Mgr
Tel: 410-683-3388
Email: selliott@siteresourcesinc.com
Website: www.siteresourcesinc.com
Civil engineering, landscape architecture & land planning services. (Woman, estab 1994, empl 28, sales $4,126,649, cert: State, City)

3145 Toole Design Group, LLC
8484 Georgia Ave
Silver Spring, MD 20910
Contact: Crystal Birmingham Exec Asst
Tel: 301-927-1900
Email: compliance@tooledesign.com
Website: www.tooledesign.com
Multimodal Transportation Planning & Engineering, Bicycle & Pedestrian Facilities, Greenway Designs, Safe Routes to Schools Studies and Programs, ADA Accessibility, Campus Planning, Street Design Guidelines. (Woman, estab 2003, empl 274, sales , cert: State, City, CPUC, WBENC)

Michigan

3146 4D Systems
4130 Market Place
Flint Twp, MI 48507
Contact: Jean-Pierre Rasaiah President
Tel: 248-535-0758
Email: jp.rasaiah@4dsysco.com
Website: www.4dsysco.com
Robotic Systems Build (Specializing in glass handling), Robot Programming (All applications), Robotic Simulation, Siemens software reseller, NX Design, Robcad Simulation, Process Simulate Simulation, Controls Design, Panel build. (As-Pac, estab 2010, empl 65, sales $8,000,000, cert: NMSDC)

3147 ABE Associates, Inc.
440 Burroughs St, Ste. 605
Detroit, MI 48221
Contact: Andre Brooks President
Tel: 313-961-5170
Email: andreb@abe-engineers.com
Website: www.abe-engineers.com
Architectural design, civil, environmental, fire protection, mechanical & structural engineering, project management, program management, drafting, surveying, construction inspection, land acquisition services. (AA, estab 1997, empl 3, sales $250,000, cert: State, NMSDC)

3148 Administrative Controls Management, Inc.
525 Avis Dr Ste 2
Ann Arbor, MI 48108
Contact: Patricia A. Mirek President
Tel: 734-995-9640
Email: mi@acmpm.com
Website: www.acmpm.com
Project Management, Process Implementation, Oversight Planning, Scheduling, Construction Management, Cost Engineering, Estimating. (Woman, estab 1985, empl 64, sales $10,200,000, cert: CPUC, WBENC)

3149 Advanced Safety & Energy (American Safety & Equipment, Inc.)
5055 Pilgrim Rd
Flint, MI 48507
Contact: Sandra Aulbrook CEO
Tel: 866-522-2300
Email: sandra.aulbrook@asesafety.com
Website: www.asesafety.com
Design capabilities, Risk Assessments, Installation of safety upgrades, OSHA & ANSI safety programs & training. (Woman/Hisp, estab 1999, empl 15, sales $1,300,000, cert: NMSDC)

3150 AMBE Engineering, LLC
15424 Prestwick Circle
Northville, MI 48168
Contact: Rashmi Zaveri VP
Tel: 734-667-3167
Email: rashmis@ambeeng.com
Website: www.ambeeng.com
Engineering: corrective actions implementations, design optimization, CAD/CAE design support, quality containment support. (Woman/As-Ind, estab 2001, empl 120, sales $8,000,000, cert: NMSDC, WBENC)

3151 Array of Engineers, LLC
2350 Oak Industrial Dr NE Ste 1
Grand Rapids, MI 49505
Contact: Stacy Paul CEO
Tel: 989-858-1855
Email: Stacy.paul@arrayofengineers.com
Website: www.arrayofengineers.com/
Lifecycle and certification process related to DO-178, MIL-STD-882E and similar standards. We specialize in all aspects of hardware and software design from conception through product realization. (Woman, estab 2018, empl 19, sales $1,200,000, cert: WBENC)

3152 Atier
24074 Gibson Dr
Warren, MI 48089
Contact: Patricia Schrenk Acct Mgr
Tel: 586-759-4240
Email: patti.schrenk@atierpro.com
Website: www.atierpro.com
Total Quality Management & Engineering Consulting, Quality & Industrial Engineering, Containment, Supplier Representation, ISO & TS Implementation Audits, Quality Inspection, Launch support, Scrap Reduction, Project Management. (AA, estab 2012, empl 100, sales $4,700,000, cert: NMSDC)

3153 Automotive Quality & Logistics, Inc.
14744 Jib St
Plymouth, MI 48170
Contact: Joe Nosek VP
Tel: 734-459-1670
Email: jnosek@aql-inc.com
Website: www.aql-inc.com
Sorting, inspection, containment, rework, engineering support, supplier development, technical staffing, warehousing. (Woman/As-Ind, estab 1994, empl 820, sales $22,000,000, cert: NMSDC, WBENC)

3154 Byce & Associates, Inc.
487 Portage St
Kalamazoo, MI 49007
Contact: Brenda Longman VP
Tel: 269-381-6170
Email: Accounting@byce.com
Website: www.byce.com
Structural, mechanical & electrical engineering design services. (Hisp, estab 1959, empl 34, sales , cert: NMSDC)

3155 CAD Engineering Resources, Inc.
6100 Auburn Rd
Shelby Township, MI 48317
Contact: Samantha Rutherford Mgr
Tel: -   -
Email: dmurphy@cergroupna.com
Website: www.cergroupna.com
Dimmensional support, CMM inpsection, 3rd party quality containment & rework, quality residency engineering, assembly and warehouseing. (Nat Ame, estab 2003, empl 600, sales $20,000,000, cert: NMSDC)

3156 Capitol Reproductions, Inc.
215 E 12 Mile Rd
Madison Heights, MI 48071
Contact: Laura Muresan GM
Tel: 313-564-4820
Email: lauram@capitolgroup.net
Website: www.capitolgroup.net
Engineering, CAD design & technical Illustration services. (Woman, estab 1946, empl 48, sales $6,750,000, cert: WBENC)

3157 CTI and Associates, Inc.
34705 W 12 Mile Rd Ste. 230
Farmington Hills, MI 48331
Contact: Jennifer Armstrong Admin
Tel: 248-486-5100
Email: jarmstrong@cticompanies.com
Website: www.cticompanies.com
Engineering consulting & construction management. (As-Ind, estab 1976, empl 150, sales $21,000,000, cert: NMSDC)

3158 Dakkota Integrated Systems, LLC
1875 Holloway Dr
Holt, MI 48842
Contact: Jessica Haughton Engineering Change Coordinator
Tel: 517-803-0755
Email: jessica.haughton@dakkotasystems.com
Website: www.dakkotasystems.com
Full-Service Interior Integration Management, Supplier Management, Assembly & Sequencing, JIT Product Delivery.
 (Woman/Nat Ame, estab 2001, empl 1114, sales $625,000,000, cert: NMSDC, WBENC)

3159 Detroit Engineered Products (DEP).
850 E Long Lake Rd
Troy, MI 48085
Contact: John Gelmisi Dir Business Devel
Tel: 248-219-9838
Email: john_gelmisi@depusa.com
Website: www.depusa.com
Reverse Engineering, Benchmarking, Scanning, Prototyping, Project Outsourcing, Offshore/Domestic Design support, and Technical Services. (As-Ind, estab 1998, empl 380, sales $18,000,000, cert: NMSDC)

3160 Doshi Associates, Inc.
5755 New King St Ste 210
Troy, MI 48098
Contact: Shailesh Doshi CEO
Tel: 248-247-3030
Email: shailesh.doshi@doshigroup.net
Website: www.doshigroup.net
Architecturel, civil, structural, mechanical & electrical engineering. (As-Pac, estab 1991, empl 30, sales $2,550,000, cert: NMSDC)

3161 Embedded Logix Inc.
50644 Sabrina Dr
Shelby, MI 48315
Contact: Deborah McLeod President
Tel: 586-709-2025
Email: dmcleod@emlogix.net
Website: www.emlogix.net
Product design for automotive, commercial & medical, test equipment design, test consulting, service, connector build, harness build, assembly test equipment. Embedded design, embedded programming, labview programming. (Woman, estab 0, empl , sales , cert: WBENC)

3162 Engineering Design Solutions PLC
5220 Lovers Lane, Ste LL-120
Portage, MI 49002
Contact: Irfan Ahmed, MSCE, PE President
Tel: 269-903-2652
Email: irfan.ahmed@enggdesigns.com
Website: www.enggdesigns.com
Manufacturing & industrial building design & CAD designing automobile facilities. (As-Ind, estab 2004, empl 8, sales $600,000, cert: NMSDC)

3163 ETCS Inc.
275 Executive Dr
Troy, MI 48083
Contact: Ravi Kapur Dir of Sales
Tel: 248-763-9467
Email: ravi@etcsinc.com
Website: www.etcsinc.com
Engineering, reverse engineering, tool design, staffing, offshore component sourcing. (Minority, estab 2003, empl 52, sales $4,826,000, cert: NMSDC)

3164 Feamold, Inc.
1441 W Long Lake Rd, Ste 240
Troy, MI 48098
Contact: Shrikant Oak President
Tel: 248-680-4628
Email: oak@feamold.com
Website: www.feamold.com
Engineering Consulting. (Minority, estab 1994, empl 5, sales , cert: NMSDC)

3165 Future Technologies, Inc.
2490 E Midland Rd
Bay City, MI 48706
Contact: Brent Waldie Applications Engineer
Tel: 989-686-6200
Email: brentw@futuretechnologies.com
Website: www.futuretechnologies.com
Custom leak testing systems, function testing equipment, welding & assembly automation & calibrated standard leaks. (Hisp, estab 1989, empl 33, sales , cert: NMSDC)

3166 Gala & Associates Inc.
31455 Southfield Rd
Beverly Hills, MI 48025
Contact: Chuni Gala President
Tel: 248-642-8610
Email: cgala@galaandassociates.com
Website: www.galaandassociates.com
Electrical, mechanical, structural, civil & architectural engineering svcs, CAD services. (As-Ind, estab 1987, empl 50, sales $6,000,000, cert: NMSDC)

ENGINEERING SERVICES

3167 Generalety, LLC
      5820 N Canton Center Rd Ste 140
      Canton, MI 48187
      Contact: Sheng-Dong Liu CEO
      Tel: 734-522-1488
      Email: sliu@generalety.com
      Website: www.generalety.com
Computer aided design (CAD) & computer aided engineering (CAE) services in the automotive industry. (As-Pac, estab 2003, empl 60, sales $1,250,000, cert: NMSDC)

3168 Global Supply Innovative Engineering LLC
      200 E Big Beaver
      Troy, MI 48083
      Contact: Dayle Farrimond VP
      Tel: -   -
      Email: dfarrimond@gsiengineering.com
      Website: www.gsiengineering.com
Injection Mold Building, Program Management, Engineering Sample Facility, Production Manufacturing Facility. (Woman, estab 2005, empl 7, sales $2,800,000, cert: WBENC)

3169 Gonzalez Aerospace
      29401 Stephenson Hwy
      Madison Heights, MI 48071
      Contact: Pablo Calzada NBD Dir
      Tel: 248-867-8212
      Email: pcalzada@gonzalezaerospace.com
      Website: www.gonzalezaerospace.com
Production Systems; Manufacturing Engineering, Program Management, Automated Assembly System Integration, Contingent Workforce Services. (Hisp, estab 1975, empl 130, sales $64,000,000, cert: NMSDC)

3170 Hybrid Design Services
      2479 Elliott Dr
      Troy, MI 48083
      Contact: James Pinon President
      Tel: 248-298-3400
      Email: jpinon@hybriddesignservices.com
      Website: www.hybriddesignservices.com
Engineering, design, prototyping, testing services specializing in hybrid vehicles & systems, electric vehicles & systems, HEV systems, EV systems, hybrid & electric vehicle R&D, high voltage systems, energy storage. (Hisp, estab 2007, empl 20, sales $2,000,000, cert: NMSDC)

3171 I*LOGIC, Inc.
      999 Tech Row
      Madison Heights, MI 48071
      Contact: Sharon Weatherspoon President
      Tel: 248-616-4506
      Email: sweatherspoon@goilogic.com
      Website: www.goilogic.com
Program management, containerization management, industrial engineering, material flow engineering, procurement services, design services & IT services. (Minority, Woman, estab 1995, empl 32, sales , cert: NMSDC, WBENC)

3172 Magnys Innovative Solutions LLC
      42500 W Eleven Mile Rd Ste B
      Novi, MI 48375
      Contact: Mary Willy Office Mgr
      Tel: 248-449-2600
      Email: mwilly@magnys.com
      Website: www.magnys.com
Design, oversee process, project engineering services, manufacturing engineering, 3-D simulation & PLC emulation software modeling. (AA, estab 1999, empl 210, sales $25,000,000, cert: NMSDC)

3173 MPS Group, Inc.
      38755 Hills Tech Dr
      Farmington Hills, MI 48331
      Contact: Bryon Lawrence Dir Sales/Marketing
      Tel: 313-841-7588
      Email: blawrence@mpsgrp.com
      Website: www.mpsgrp.com
Environmental Consulting & Engineering. (AA, estab 1995, empl 495, sales $46,200,000, cert: NMSDC)

3174 Optimal Computer Aided Engineering, Inc.
      47802 W Anchor Court
      Plymouth, MI 48170
      Contact: Song Young CEO
      Tel: 734-414-7933
      Email: ksrinivas@optimalinc.com
      Website: www.optimalinc.com
CAD/CAM/CAE/PDM services, contract engineering services & metrology product sales & support. (As-Pac, estab 1986, empl 100, sales $10,000,000, cert: NMSDC)

3175 PAT USA, Inc.
      2927 Waterview Dr
      Rochester Hills, MI 48309
      Contact: Fenar Mayes Sr Project Mgr
      Tel: 248-299-2410
      Email: fenar@pat-engineering.com
      Website: www.pat-engineering.com
General contracting services, engineering & construction services. (Woman, estab 2011, empl 10, sales , cert: WBENC)

3176 Process Control & Engineering Inc.
      1091 Centre Rd, Ste 290
      Auburn Hills, MI 48326
      Contact: Theresa Dies Treasurer
      Tel: 248-340-1888
      Email: tdies@pcemonarch.com
      Website: www.pcemonarch.com
Monitoring & Control System for process air & fluid parameters, VOC emissions, air and fluid handling equipment. Monitoring and Control system for: Process parameters: air velocities, humidity, temperature, fluid flows, viscosity, chemical parameters. (Minority, estab 1994, empl 15, sales $9,000,000, cert: NMSDC)

3177 Renaissance S & S Inc.
      26637 Golfview
      Dearborn Heights, MI 48127
      Contact: Smith Sylvester CEO
      Tel: 313-561-3897
      Email: rssgroup@sbcglobal.net
      Website: www.renaissancessgroup.com
Engineering consulting services. (AA, estab 1996, empl 4, sales , cert: NMSDC)

ENGINEERING SERVICES

3178 Sigma Associates, Inc.
1900 St. Antoine St
Detroit, MI 48226
Contact: Kathy Cotton Administrative Asst
Tel: 313-963-9700
Email: kcotton@sigmaassociates.com
Website: www.sigmaassociates.com
Multi-disciplinary engineering, architectural, program management, construction contract admin, design-build capabilities & information technology services. (Woman, estab 1978, empl 51, sales , cert: State, WBENC, SDB)

3179 SoundTech Inc.
3880 SoundTech Ct
Grand Rapids, MI 49512
Contact: Amy Sparks President
Tel: 616-575-0866
Email: asparks@soundtechinc.com
Website: www.soundtechinc.com
Engineer acoustic & thermal insulation solutions. (Woman, estab 1987, empl 90, sales $29,011,176, cert: WBENC)

3180 Universal Tool Equipment & Controls, Inc.
6525 Center Dr
Sterlng Heights, MI 48312
Contact: Bill Bartolotta VP
Tel: 586-268-4380
Email: bbartolotta@universaltecinc.com
Website: www.universaltecinc.com
Automation & welding systems, robotics, weld guns, vision systems, sealant systems, drawn arc welders, projection welders, material handling end effectors & welding fixtures. (Woman/AA, estab 2009, empl 29, sales $10,000,000, cert: WBENC)

3181 WFQ, Inc.
5751 S. Sheldon Rd
Canton, MI 48188
Contact: Jennifer McGuire Sales Acct Mgr
Tel: 734-512-6284
Email: jmcguire@wfqinc.com
Website: www.wfqinc.com
GP12/Launch support, Resident Liaison, Quality Engineering services, Containment, Inspection & Re-work Solutions Sequence, Kitting solutions, Warehousing. (Woman, estab 2013, empl 150, sales $5,780,000, cert: WBENC)

3182 Willie Horton Inc.
7784 Ronda Dr
Canton, MI 48187
Contact: Deryl Horton President
Tel: 248-855-2215
Email: dhorton@horton-inc.com
Website: www.horton-inc.com
Heat-treating, hardening, surface engineering, tool steel, mechcanical & electrical engineering. (AA, estab 2003, empl 20, sales , cert: NMSDC)

Minnesota

3183 EVS, Inc.
10025 Valley View Rd Ste 140
Eden Prairie, MN 55344
Contact: Andy Kim President
Tel: 952-646-0236
Email: akim@evs-eng.com
Website: www.evs-eng.com
Civil engineering, site development, surveying & environmental, permits, assessments & NEPA documentation. (As-Pac, estab 1979, empl 61, sales $7,432,378, cert: NMSDC)

3184 Fourth Factor Engineering, LLC
10636 Maryland Ave S
Bloomington, MN 55438
Contact: Elizabeth Becker President
Tel: 612-708-2562
Email: liz.becker@fourth-factor-engineering.com
Website: www.fourth-factor-engineering.com
Engineering analysis: system safety, software safety, human factors, reliability, maintainability, testability & logistics analysis. (Woman, estab 2010, empl 6, sales $1,049,233, cert: State, WBENC)

3185 Hansen Thorp Pellinen Olson, Inc.
7510 Market Place Dr
Eden Prairie, MN 55344
Contact: Tim Johnson Business Devel Dir
Tel: 952-829-0700
Email: tjohnson@htpo.com
Website: www.htpo.com
Engineering svcs: land surveying, civil engineering, landscape architecture design & construction. (Woman, estab 1980, empl 23, sales $2,876,105, cert: City)

3186 L.W. Survey Engineering & Design Company
1 E First St
Duluth, MN 55802
Contact: Richard Grogan Dir Business Dev
Tel: 218-722-8211
Email: r.grogan@lwsurvey.com
Website: www.lwsurvey.com
Engineering, drafting (AutoCAD), surveying, inspection, right of way, project management. (Nat Ame, estab 1998, empl 35, sales , cert: NMSDC)

3187 Questions & Solutions Engineering
1079 Falls Curve
Chaska, MN 55318
Contact: Rebecca Ellis
Tel: 612-309-0503
Email: rebecca.ellis@qseng.com
Website: www.QSEng.com
Commissioning program development, training & project execution, existing building troubleshooting, retro-commissioning, re-commissioning, HVAC system planning & implementing capital projects. (Woman, estab 2005, empl 4, sales $181,000, cert: City, WBENC)

3188 Sambatek
14800 28th Ave N, Ste 140
Plymouth, MN 55447
Contact: Erik Miller Sales
Tel: 763-476-6010
Email: emiller@sambatek.com
Website: www.sambatek.com
Civil engineering, land planning & surveying, water & waste water treatment process engineering, enviornmental assesments. (As-Pac, estab 1966, empl 46, sales $5,269,743, cert: State)

3189 SM Engineering Co.
9 Ninth Ave N
Hopkins, MN 55343
Contact: Wayne Peterson COO
Tel: 952-938-7407
Email: wayne@smeng.com
Website: www.smeng.com
Utility management: electricity, natural gas, water & sewer. (As-Ind, estab 1982, empl 13, sales $2,921,000, cert: NMSDC)

Missouri

3190 Ameri-Pac, Inc.
751 S 4th St
Joseph, MO 65501
Contact: Robert Colescott President
Tel: 816-233-4530
Email: bobc@ameri-pac.com
Website: www.ameri-pac.com
Mfr animal nutrition specialty products. (Woman, estab 1985, empl 45, sales , cert: WBENC)

3191 Civil Design Inc.
5220 Oakland Ave
St. Louis, MO 63110
Contact: Lori Daiber Business Devel Mgr
Tel: 314-916-1178
Email: ldaiber@civildesigninc.com
Website: www.civildesigninc.com
Civil & Site Engineering, Land Surveying, Water Resources, Infrastructure & Analytics. (Woman, estab 1996, empl 52, sales $5,800,000, cert: State, WBENC, NWBOC)

3192 David Mason & Associates, Inc.
800 S Vandeventer Ave
St. Louis, MO 63110
Contact: Taylor Mason Business Devel
Tel: 314-534-1030
Email: tmason@davidmason.com
Website: www.davidmason.com
Professional survey, civil & structural engineering services. (AA, estab 1989, empl 50, sales $48,327,574, cert: NMSDC)

3193 EFK Moen, LLC
13523 Barrett Pkwy Dr Ste 250
St. Louis, MO 63021
Contact: Darrell Eilers VP
Tel: 314-729-4104
Email: dleilers@efkmoen.com
Website: www.EFKMoen.com
Civil engineering & land surveying, roadway/highway engineering, bridge/structural design, site/development engineering, water/wastewater, traffic/transportation engineering. (Woman, estab 1998, empl 35, sales $2,700,000, cert: State)

3194 Peoria Contract Services, LLC
6428 Lipizzaner Dr
Imperial, MO 63052
Contact: Kyle Pogue CEO
Tel: 314-761-5470
Email: kyle@peoriacontractservices.com
Website: www.pcs-energy.com
Engineering, Electrical, Mechanical, Chemical, Process, Civil, Structural, Patented Modular Extrusion Process; ASME/API Storage Vessels; Bulk Material Handling/Storage; Automation; Piping Design & Pipe Supply; Hydraulic & Pneumatic. (Nat Ame, estab 2012, empl 5, sales , cert: State, NMSDC)

3195 Webb Engineering Services, Inc.
4670 Lansdowne Ave, Ste 111
St. Louis, MO 63116
Contact: Stanley Webb President
Tel: 314-351-0440
Email: webbs@webb-engineering.com
Website: www.webb-engineering.com
Mechanical, electrical, fire protection, plumbing, & civil design services. (AA, estab 1999, empl 8, sales $1,000,000, cert: City, 8(a))

North Carolina

3196 ENPULSE Energy Conservation, Inc.
100 N Elm St, Ste 138
Greensboro, NC 27401
Contact: Derrick Giles President
Tel: 336-370-1088
Email: info@enpulse.com
Website: www.enpulse.com
Engineering services, energy management, utility bill audits, engineering studies, measurement & verification, building commissioning (AA, estab 2002, empl 3, sales , cert: State, City)

3197 ImmunoReagents Inc.
6003 Chapel Hill Road Ste. 153
Raleigh, NC 27607
Contact: Ann Black CEO
Tel: 919-831-2240
Email: sales@immunoreagents.com
Website: www.immunoreagents.com
Mfr highly purified polyclonal antibodies used in the life sciences & immunodiagnostic industries. (Woman, estab 2005, empl 14, sales $1,636,402, cert: WBENC)

3198 John Davenport Engineering, Inc.
305 W Fourth St Ste 2A
Winston-Salem, NC 27101
Contact: Shari Mauk Chief Admin Officer
Tel: 336-744-1636
Email: smauk@davenportworld.com
Website: www.davenportworld.com
Roadway design, traffic signal design, transportation engineering, civil engineering, transportation planning, construction support, construction engineering & inspection, traffic data collection, turning movement counts. (AA, estab 2002, empl 21, sales $1,629,947, cert: State, City, 8(a))

3199 RDAF Energy Solutions
6201 Fairview Rd Ste 200
Charlotte, NC 28210
Contact: Rickey Hart Chairman
Tel: 980-205-1220
Email: rickey.hart@rdafenergy.net
Website: www.rdafenergy.net
Energy consulting & management, market & sell power, natural gas, renewable & sustainable energy & services. (AA, estab 2016, empl 5, sales $16,096,148, cert: NMSDC, CPUC)

3200 Sud Associates PA
1813 Chapel Hill Rd
Durham, NC 27707
Contact: Ish Sud President
Tel: 919-493-5277
Email: sudmain@sudassociates.com
Website: www.sudassociates.com
Energy svcs & studies: recycling process produced heat, energy conserving HVAC, electrical, plumbing. (Minority, estab 1980, empl 23, sales $2,000,000, cert: State, City)

ENGINEERING SERVICES

New Jersey

3201 3A Engineering & Validation LLC
 122 Lexington Ave
 Maplewood, NJ 07040
 Contact: Adebayo Boboye Principal Engineer
 Tel: 973-715-0541
 Email: adebayo.boboye@3a-engineering.com
 Website: www.3a-engineering.com
Engineering services, qualification, commissioning & validation of manufacturing processes & products. (AA, estab 2007, empl 1, sales $120,000, cert: NMSDC)

3202 Bluebix Solutions Inc
 6 Kilmer Rd Ste B1
 Edison, NJ 08817
 Contact: Roma Jenson
 Tel: 416-319-5486
 Email: roma.jenson@bluebixinc.com
 Website: www.bluebixinc.com
IT, finance, engineering, power utility, renewable energies, Education, pharma, and Healthcare. (Woman/As-Pac, estab 2019, empl 308, sales $12,000,000, cert: WBENC)

3203 Consolidated Energy Design, Inc.
 1933 Hwy 35 Ste 105
 Wall, NJ 07719
 Contact: Rey Montalvo President
 Tel: 732-681-8800
 Email: reym@cedinternational.com
 Website: www.fadrs.com
Smart Grid and Smart Micro Grid technology. (Hisp, estab 1987, empl 2, sales $101,432, cert: NMSDC)

3204 Economic Project Solutions, Inc.
 2 King Arthur Ct, Ste E
 North Brunswick, NJ 08902
 Contact: Sabrina Staats Mgr of Corporate Compliance
 Tel: 732-248-1110
 Email: sstaats@economicprojects.com
 Website: www.economicprojects.com
Construction consulting, facilities mgmt, move mgmt, OSHA fire & safety, property mgmt & technical design services. (Woman, estab 1997, empl 72, sales $21,172,800, cert: WBENC)

3205 IFSI General Contractor, Co.
 1245 Main St Apt 232
 Rahway, NJ 07065
 Contact: Rita (Joanie) George CEO
 Tel: 908-339-2842
 Email: sales@ifsgc.com
 Website: www.industrialfiberglassservices.com
Civil, Mechanical, FRP Repair & Installation. (Woman, estab 2000, empl 7, sales $3,000,000, cert: WBENC)

3206 inRange Solutions II, LLC
 695 Route 46 W, Ste 103
 Fairfield, NJ 07004
 Contact: Edwin Gomez President
 Tel: - -
 Email: ss@inrange-llc.com
 Website: www.inrangesolutions.com
DAS, Wireless and Telecom Design and Engineering, Site Acquisition, Real Estate Negotiation, Zoning and Permitting, Project Management, Architectural Engineering and Design, Electrical Engineering and Design, Mechanical Engineering and Design. (As-Pac, estab 2011, empl 24, sales $6,000,000, cert: State, City, NMSDC)

3207 KS Engineers, P.C.
 2 Riverfront Plaza 3rd Fl
 Newark, NJ 07102
 Contact: Kamal Shahid President
 Tel: 973-623-2999
 Email: info@kseng.com
 Website: www.kseng.com
Engineering, surveying & construction management. (As-Ind, estab 1991, empl 275, sales $25,000,000, cert: State, City, NMSDC)

3208 Matrix New World Engineering, Land Surveying and Landscape Architectur
 26 Columbia Trnpke 2nd Fl
 Florham Park, NJ 07932
 Contact: Jayne Warne, PE President
 Tel: 973-240-1800
 Email: jwarne@mnwe.com
 Website: www.matrixneworld.com
Environmental, geotechnical, civil engineering, survey & building facility consulting & engineering firm. (Woman, estab 1990, empl 200, sales $28,899,396, cert: State, City, WBENC)

3209 MFS Consulting Engineers & Surveyor, DPC
 2780 Hamilton Blvd
 South Plainfield, NJ 07080
 Contact: Jeffrey Clark Sr Project Admin
 Tel: 908-922-4622
 Email: jac@mfsengineers.com
 Website: www.MFSengineers.com
Site/civil, structural, geotechnical & foundation, environmental engineering, construction layout, sustainable design & construction management services. (Minority, estab 2009, empl 32, sales $4,403,207, cert: State, City, 8(a))

3210 Sovereign
 111 A North Gold Dr
 Robbinsville, NJ 08691
 Contact: Michael Hanlon Mgr
 Tel: 609-259-8200
 Email: mhanlon@sovcon.com
 Website: www.sovcon.com
Environmental consulting & remediation services, environmental, civil & geotechnical engineering; remediation system evaluation, optimization, design & construction/installation; environmental, land use & natural resources permitting. (As-Pac, estab 1999, empl 165, sales $35,466,433, cert: NMSDC)

New York

3211 Airosmith, Inc.
 318 West Ave
 Saratoga Springs, NY 12866
 Contact: Ann D'Alessandro VP Sales/Marketing
 Tel: 207-239-1641
 Email: adalessandro@airosmithdevelopment.com
 Website: www.airosmithdevelopment.com
Leasing, Zoning, Permitting & Project Management for Site Development services. (Woman, estab 2004, empl 130, sales $30,605,953, cert: State, WBENC)

ENGINEERING SERVICES

3212 Associated Renewable
1370 Broadway 5th Fl
New York, NY 10018
Contact: Manoj Patel CEO
Tel: 212-444-8214
Email: mbe@associatedrenewable.com
Website: www.associatedrenewable.com/
Energy management, cut energy costs, reduce energy wastage, meet regulatory requirements, building energy audits, install new energy-efficient equipment, supply electricity, natural gas & renewable energy. (As-Pac, estab 2010, empl 8, sales $420,000, cert: NMSDC)

3213 Atlantic Testing Laboratories, Limited
6431 US Hwy 11
Canton, NY 13617
Contact: Eric M. Van Alstyne Business Devel Mgr
Tel: 315-386-4578
Email: evanalstyne@atlantictesting.com
Website: www.atlantictesting.com
Subsurface investigations, water-based investigations, geotechnical engineering, construction materials engineering & testing, special inspection services, pavement engineering, nondestructive testing & environmental services. (Woman, estab 1967, empl 260, sales $16,190,692, cert: State, City)

3214 DESMAN, Inc. dba DESMAN Associates
3 W 35th ST 3rd Fl
New York, NY 10001
Contact: Anup Chhabra CFO
Tel: 212-686-5360
Email: achhabra@desman.com
Website: www.desman.com
Parking consulting, design, planning and restoration. (As-Ind, estab 1984, empl 100, sales $18,000,000, cert: NMSDC)

3215 Dose Engineering, PLLC
15 W 38TH ST Fl. 4, Ste 736
New York, NY 10018
Contact: Anostere Jean Principal
Tel: 646-715-2096
Email: ajean@dose-engineering.com
Website: www.dose-engineering.com
Engineering design, engineering design drawings, due diligence reports Mechanical: HVAC Electrical: Lighting and Power Plumbing Fire Alarm Fire Protection LEED: Leadership in Energy and Environmental (AA, estab 2009, empl 5, sales $300,000, cert: State, City, NMSDC)

3216 Energy Infrastructure Partners LLC
194 32nd St
Brooklyn, NY 11232
Contact: Renwick Paige CEO
Tel: 646-417-2390
Email: renwick.paige@energyinfrapartners.com
Website: www.energyinfrapartners.com
Energy Consultants, Energy Services. (AA, estab 2011, empl 35, sales $31,000,000, cert: State, City, NMSDC, CPUC)

3217 Environmental Design & Research, DPC
217 Montgomery St Ste 1000
Syracuse, NY 13202
Contact: Joanne Stewart Associate
Tel: 315-471-0688
Email: jstewart@edrdpc.com
Website: www.edrdpc.com
Landscape architecture, civil engineering, community planning, visualization, environmental regulatory, ecological, geographic information systems mapping & analysis, historic preservation, cultural resources, archeology. (Woman, estab 1979, empl 38, sales $4,500,000, cert: State)

3218 Foit-Albert Associates, Architecture, Engineering and Surveying, P.C.
215 W 94th St, Ste 517
New York, NY 10025
Contact: Gregory Carballada President
Tel: 716-856-3933
Email: cstoebe@foit-albert.com
Website: www.foit-albert.com
Architecture, Engineering, Environmental & Land Surveying Consulting. (Hisp, estab 1977, empl 70, sales $10,000,000, cert: State, City)

3219 Karp Strategies, LLC
26 Broadway
New York, NY 10004
Contact: Rebecca Karp CEO
Tel: 718-530-1728
Email: rebecca@karpstrategies.com
Website: www.karpstrategies.com
Urban strategy consultancy, community-economic development planning, community and stakeholder engagement, and real estate and urban planning. (As-Pac, estab 2015, empl 16, sales , cert: State, City)

3220 KLD Engineering PC
1601 Veterans Memorial Hwy Ste 340
Islandia, NY 11749
Contact: Kacie Larson HR & Contract Mgr
Tel: 631-524-5940
Email: klarsen@kldcompanies.com
Website: www.kldcompanies.com
Transportation Engineering Consultant. Professional Engineering services concentrated in three primary areas: (1) Traffic Engineering & ITS; (2) Evacuation & Emergency planning; (3) GIS & other support services to "1" & "2" (As-Ind, estab 1997, empl 25, sales , cert: State, City, CPUC)

3221 Outsource Consultants, Inc.
237 W 35th St, Fl 12A
New York, NY 10001
Contact: Diego Caballero President
Tel: 212-732-6933
Email: dcaballero@outsourceconsultants.com
Website: www.outsourceconsultants.com
Building code & zoning consultation, approvals, permit expediting, and sign offs. (Minority, estab 1993, empl 50, sales $5,500,000, cert: NMSDC)

ENGINEERING SERVICES

3222 Sabir, Richardson & Weisberg Engineers PLLC
      37 W 39th St, Ste 1005
      NYC, NY 10018
      Contact: Yvette Richardson Principal
      Tel: 646-863-6160
      Email: info@srw-eng.com
      Website: www.srw-eng.com
Engineering svcs: architectural, mechanical, electrical, fire protection & plumbing consulting. (Woman/AA, Hisp, estab 2004, empl 1, sales $2,018,954, cert: State, City)

3223 SI Engineering, P.C.
      107 Greenwich St 19th Fl
      New York, NY 10006
      Contact: Raim Izhar Sr Associate
      Tel: 212-354-5939
      Email: rizhar@siengineering.com
      Website: www.siengineering.com
Civil engineering design services, traffic engineering & planning, structural & transportation engineering, construction management highway, road, street & bridge, bridge & building condition inspection. (As-Ind, estab 2003, empl 115, sales $20,000,000, cert: State)

3224 SoundSense, LLC
      46 Newtown Lane Ste 1
      East Hampton, NY 11937
      Contact: Maryann Buquicchio Sr admin asst
      Tel: 631-324-2266
      Email: maryann@soundsense.com
      Website: www.soundsense.com
Acoustic consulting & design services, efficacy & compliance testing, site inspection services & innovative acoustical products. (Woman, estab 1981, empl 9, sales $2,623,444, cert: City, WBENC)

3225 Toll International LLC
      303 Fifth Ave Ste 211
      New York, NY 10016
      Contact: Nure M Aiza Bezares President
      Tel: 212-710-2633
      Email: nure.aiza@tollintl.com
      Website: www.tollintl.com
Construction experts, schedulers, construction managers, estimators, business consultants and information technology experts. (Hisp, estab 2005, empl 11, sales $2,410,000, cert: State, City, NMSDC)

3226 W. Allen Engineering PLLC
      400 Strawtown Rd
      West Nyack, NY 10994
      Contact: Wayne Allen Principal
      Tel: 646-398-7870
      Email: info@wallenengineering.com
      Website: www.wallenengineering.com
Civil & mechanical engineering, construction inspection/management services, contract admin, owner representation, cost estimating, lead based paint abatement, drafting, HVAC design. (AA, estab 1997, empl 12, sales $1,200,000, cert: State, City)

3227 Watts Engineering & Architecture, P.C.
      95 Perry St Ste 300
      Buffalo, NY 14203
      Contact: Edward Watts President
      Tel: 716-836-1540
      Email: ewatts@wattsengineers.com
      Website: www.wattsengineers.com
Civil, environmental, mechanical & electrical engineering & architecture consulting. (AA, estab 1986, empl 73, sales $6,800,000, cert: City, NMSDC)

3228 WM Group Services, LLC
      Two Penn Plaza Ste 552
      New York, NY 10121
      Contact: Hemant Mehta Controller
      Tel: 646-827-6400
      Email: hmehta@wmgroupeng.com
      Website: www.wmgroupeng.com
Study, Design, optimization of Central Utilities Systems: cooling, heating & power. (As-Pac, estab , empl , sales $2,697,396, cert: NMSDC)

Ohio

3229 Advanced Engineering Consultants, Ltd.
      1405 Dublin Road
      Columbus, OH 43215
      Contact: Lisa Huang President
      Tel: 614-486-4778
      Email:
      Website: www.aecmep.com
Mechanical, Electrical, Plumbing, Fire Protection, Technology engineering design & construction administration services. (Woman/As-Pac, estab 1998, empl 60, sales $11,500,000, cert: State, City)

3230 Airecon Manufacturing Corporation
      5271 Brotherton Court
      Cincinnati, OH 45227
      Contact: Josh Jacobs President
      Tel: 513-561-5522
      Email: josh@airecon.com
      Website: www.airecon.com
Design, fabricate & install industrial dust, mist & fume control equipment & systems, fume exhaust pneumatic conveying, supply & exhasut ventilation, clean air rooms & other industrial air handling systems. (Hisp, estab 1979, empl 40, sales $9,000,000, cert: NMSDC)

3231 AMG, Inc.
      1497 Shoup Mill Rd
      Dayton, OH 45414
      Contact: LeAnn Thompson VP Engineering
      Tel: 937-274-0736
      Email: jbaddour@amg-eng.com
      Website: www.amg-eng.com
Feasibility studies, conceptual design, capital cost esimtates, detailed design engineering, project management through construction management, commissioning. (Hisp, estab 1980, empl 40, sales $16,921,031, cert: NMSDC)

3232 Atmos360, Inc
      64 Circle Freeway Dr
      Cincinnati, OH 45246
      Contact: Icy Williams President
      Tel: 513-330-6688
      Email: iwilliams@atmos360.com
      Website: www.atmos360.com
Engineering & design of air system & custom/specialty fabricated products, Dust/Aerosol Control, Process Air, Central
Vacuum Cleaning, HVAC and Heated air Make-up Systems. (Woman/AA, estab 1989, empl 40, sales $17,000,000, cert: State, NMSDC, WBENC)

ENGINEERING SERVICES

3233 Balance Product Development, Inc.
3615 Superior Ave. Ste 4402B
Cleveland, OH 44114
Contact: Rene Polin President
Tel: 440-247-4711
Email: rene@balanceinc.com
Website: www.balanceinc.com
Industrial Design, product design, CAD development, prototype development, concept ideation, packaging design, graphic design, innovation, engineering, product research, ergonomic research, user interface design. (Hisp, estab 2004, empl 10, sales , cert: NMSDC)

3234 CAD Concepts, Inc.
2323 West 5th Ave Ste 120
Columbus, OH 43204
Contact: Joyce K Johnson
Tel: 614-485-0670
Email: certifications@ccitechs.com
Website: www.ccitechs.com
Engineering support services: CAD, GIS, field work & administrative services. (Woman, estab 1984, empl 26, sales , cert: State, WBENC)

3235 Crawford & Associates Services, LLC
100 E Campus View Blvd Ste 250
Columbus, OH 43235
Contact: Troy Crawford Principal
Tel: 614-557-1498
Email: tcrawford@cas-associates.com
Website: www.cas-associates.com
Commercial & Industrial Commissioning of Mechanical/Electrical/Plumbing Systems, Heating, Ventilating & Air Conditioning Systems & Building Automatic Temperature Control Systems. (AA, estab 2007, empl 5, sales $293,055, cert: 8(a))

3236 CTL Engineering, Inc.
2860 Fisher Rd
Columbus, OH 43204
Contact: C.K. Satyapriya President
Tel: 614-276-8123
Email: ctl@ctleng.com
Website: www.ctleng.com
Geotechnical, construction inspection, environmental, mining engineering, analytical chemistry, forensic science, metallurgy, product testing, research & development, roof engineering, existing structure evaluation, asbestos inspection. (Minority, estab 1928, empl 187, sales , cert: NMSDC)

3237 DLZ Industrial, LLC
6121 Huntley Rd
Columbus, OH 43229
Contact: Kurt Schmiegel CEO
Tel: 614-888-0040
Email: mbe@dlz.com
Website: www.dlz.com
Industrial surveying, close tolerance machinery surveying, setting & realignment, construction, topographical, hydrographic & property surveying. (Minority, estab 1989, empl 568, sales , cert: NMSDC)

3238 Moody Engineering, LLC
300 Spruce St Ste 200
Columbus, OH 43215
Contact: President
Tel: 614-280-8999
Email:
Website: www.moody-eng.com
Stormwater management, Site design, Sediment and erosion control, Roadway, Permits - NPDES, PTI, zoning, Vehicular access, Grading, Pedestrian traffic, Drainage, Parking lots, Wet and dry ponds, Utility design, Domestic water, Underground infrastructure. (AA, estab 2015, empl 10, sales $1,924,000, cert: State, City)

3239 Noble Technologies Corp. (DBA NobleTek)
1909 Old Mansfield Road
Wooster, OH 44691
Contact: Nathan Kramar Business Devel
Tel: 360-391-0055
Email: nathan.kramar@nobletek.com
Website: www.nobletek.com
3D CAD & Drafting. (As-Pac, estab 2009, empl 42, sales , cert: NMSDC)

3240 On Line Design, Inc.
12059 Sheraton Ln
Cincinnati, OH 45246
Contact: Kimberly Persiani Client Advisor
Tel: 513-476-3113
Email: Persiani.K@o-l-design.com
Website: www.o-l-design.com
Engineering & technical personnel: plant & capital projects, design/build equipment. (Woman, estab 1989, empl 50, sales $2,200,000, cert: WBENC)

3241 R Engineering Team, LLC
3100 E 45th St, Ste 306
Cleveland, OH 44127
Contact: Tom Roberts President
Tel: 216-361-2500
Email: rengineeringteam@gmail.com
Website: www.rengineeringteam.com
Consulting engineering in the disciplines of electrical engineering, mechanical engineering, construction administration, and computer CAD drafting. (AA, estab 2008, empl 7, sales $687,194, cert: State, City, NMSDC)

3242 Resource International
1740 St. Clair Ave
Cleveland, OH 44114
Contact: Brian Winslett Dir of Operations
Tel: 216-781-2820
Email: brianw@resourceinternational.com
Website: www.resourceintl.com
Civil engineering & engineering support services: environmental assessments, geotechnical engineering, surveying & construction material testing. (Minority, Woman, estab 1974, empl 100, sales $10,000,000, cert: WBENC)

3243 Thors, LLC
5054 Paramount Blvd.
Medina, OH 44256
Contact: Senthil Kumar Founder
Tel: 330-576-4448
Email: sales@thors.com
Website: www.thors.com
Mfg process training for procurement, design engineers & quality teams. (Minority, Woman, estab 2010, empl 11, sales , cert: NMSDC)

ENGINEERING SERVICES

3244 Williams Engineering LLC
1836 Dana Ave
Cincinnati, OH 45207
Contact: Kennard Williams President
Tel: 513-731-6400
Email: keino.williams@williamsengindesign.com
Website: www.williamsenginedesign.com
Engineering & mfg services, 3D CAD modeling & product development of machine tools, aerospace, medical and automotive aftermarket parts. (AA, estab 2005, empl 1, sales , cert: State)

Oklahoma

3245 Cameron Glass
3550 W Tacoma St
Broken Arrow, OK 74012
Contact: Angie Mann Customer Service Mgr
Tel: 918-307-4720
Email: angiem@camglass.com
Website: www.camglass.com
Glass fabrication, Glass bending, Tempering, Saftey glass, Screen printing. (Nat Ame, estab 1978, empl 120, sales $18,000,000, cert: NMSDC)

3246 Excellence Engineering, LLC
8670 S Peoria Ave
Tulsa, OK 74132
Contact: Deyona Hays CEO
Tel: 918-298-5500
Email: dee.hays@eeinco.com
Website: www.eeinco.com
Engineering, civil, structural, process, piping, mechanical, electrical, instrument, controls, startup & commissioning. (Woman, estab 2001, empl 40, sales , cert: WBENC)

Oregon

3247 Elcon Associates, Inc.
12670 NW Barnes Rd
Portland, OR 97229
Contact: Donna Freeman Marketing Mgr
Tel: 503-644-2490
Email: dfreeman@elcon.com
Website: www.elcon.com
Electrical energy: high voltage, project management, studies, cost estimating, and construction management, utility power systems, power distribution, PLC based control systems, energy management/SCADA. (As-Ind, estab 1975, empl 47, sales $5,600,000, cert: NMSDC)

Pennsylvania

3248 Advantus Engineers
300 Bilmar Dr Ste 150
Pittsburgh, PA 15205
Contact: Alicia Avick President
Tel: 412-489-9090
Email: aavick@advantusengineers.com
Website: www.advantusengineers.com
Facilities design engineering, commissioning, project management & construction management services for the commercial, institutional & light industrial markets. (Minority, Woman, estab 2004, empl 10, sales $550,000, cert: State, WBENC)

3249 Aquatech International Corporation
1 Four Coins Dr
Canaonsburg, PA 15317
Contact: Francis D'sa Reg Sales Mgr
Tel: 724-746-5300
Email: aic@aquatech.com
Website: www.aquatech.com
Mfr water & waste water treatment equip & systems. ASME tank & piping fabricators. (Minority, Woman, estab 1981, empl 450, sales $80,000,000, cert: NMSDC)

3250 Biopharm Project Solutions
119 Jaffrey Rd
Malvern, PA 19355
Contact: Surjit Sengha President
Tel: 484-614-0869
Email: surjs@biopharmprojects.com
Website: www.biopharmprojects.com
Process engineering, equipment, utilities & equipment cleaning/sterilization systems, automation engineering, project management & engineering staffing, equipment design engineering, factory testing, start-up. (As-Ind, estab 1987, empl 10, sales $2,500,000, cert: NMSDC)

3251 C & R Communications Group
2814 Guilford St
Philadelphia, PA 19152
Contact: Marc Carroll President
Tel: 215-480-0130
Email: marc.carroll@candrcommunicationsgroup.com
Website: www.candrcommunicationsgroup.com
Engineering, Procurement, Installation, and Certification of Communication Infrastructure Solutions. (Hisp, estab 2009, empl 15, sales , cert: NMSDC)

3252 Chester Engineers, Inc.
1555 Coraopolis Heights Rd
Moon Township, PA 15108
Contact: Elaine Talak Exec Asst
Tel: 412-809-6576
Email: etalak@chesterengineers.com
Website: www.chesterengineers.com
Engineering consulting services, construct. mgmt., water resource mgmt., scientific research & environmental mgmt. (AA, estab 1987, empl 200, sales $14,500,000, cert: NMSDC)

3253 Dawood Engineering, Inc.
2020 Good Hope Rd
Enola, PA 17025
Contact: Kristal Martinez
Tel: 717-732-8576
Email: kmartinez@dawood.cc
Website: www.dawood.cc
Civil Site Design, Survey & Mapping, Environmental Consulting, Mechanical & Electrical Engineering, Geotechnical Engineering
Structural Engineering. (Minority, estab 1992, empl 161, sales $20,100,000, cert: NMSDC)

ENGINEERING SERVICES

3254 Diversified Global Systems, LLC.
721 Arbor Way Ste 100
Blue Bell, PA 19422
Contact: Dale Hobbie Managing Dir
Tel: 703-963-4942
Email: dale.hobbie@diversifiedglobalsystems.com
Website: www.diversifiedglobalsystems.com
Finance, Site Development, Design, Engineering, Procurement Management, Construction Management (Pre-Construction and Construction), Project Management, Program Management & Operations & Maintenance services. (Nat Ame, estab 2016, empl 5, sales $265,000, cert: NMSDC)

3255 First Capital Engineering
48 S Richland Ave
York, PA 17404
Contact: Ann Luciani CEO
Tel: 717-845-3227
Email: annl@fcap.com
Website: www.fcap.com
Civil engineering, land surveying, landscape architecture, environmental & construction inspection services. (Woman, estab 1995, empl 17, sales $1,949,255, cert: State, WBENC)

3256 GAI Construction Monitoring Services, Inc. dba CMT Services Group
24 Portland Rd
Conshohocken, PA 19428
Contact: Valerie Moody President
Tel: 610-731-0430
Email: v.moody@cmtservicesgroup.com
Website: www.cmtservicesgroup.com
Geotechnical engineering, environmental consulting, construction materials testing, special inspections, engineering materials forensic investigations. (Woman, estab 1986, empl 23, sales $2,200,000, cert: WBENC)

3257 IES Engineers
1720 Walton Rd
Blue Bell, PA 19422
Contact: Lisa Wallis Mgr, Accounting & Administrative Services
Tel: 610-828-3078
Email: lwallis@iesengineers.com
Website: www.iesengineers.com
Engineering & environmental, health & safety consulting, regulatory compliance. (As-Ind, estab 1991, empl 30, sales $8,223,000, cert: NMSDC)

3258 RNDT, Inc.
228 Maple Ave
Johnstown, PA 15901
Contact: VP Technical Dir
Tel: 814-535-5448
Email: info@rndt.net
Website: www.rndt.net
Nondestructive testing services, radiographic, magnetic particle, liquid penetrant, ultrasonic & visual testing services. (Woman, estab 2002, empl 35, sales $5,800,000, cert: WBENC)

3259 Rodriguez Consulting LLC
1301 N 2nd St
Philadelphia, PA 19122
Contact: Yarelis Franco Marketing Coord
Tel: 215-839-8087
Email: yfranco@rodriguezconsulting.biz
Website: www.rodriguezconsulting.biz
Civil engineering, site design, environmental engineering, land surveying, traffic data collection and engineering, construction inspection & geographic information systems (GIS) services. (Hisp, estab 2007, empl 22, sales $909,000, cert: City, 8(a))

3260 Strother Enterprises Inc.
100 S Broad St Ste 2130
Philadelphia, PA 19110
Contact: Ernest L Strother CEO
Tel: 215-564-5538
Email: elstrother@strotherenterprises.com
Website: www.strotherenterprises.com
Food Service Management; Facilities Management; Commissary Services; Staffing and Training. Knowledge of government contracts, knowledge of compliance and regulatory standards and long-standing (AA, estab 1990, empl 26, sales $3,409,222, cert: State, City, NMSDC)

3261 TesTex, Inc.
535 Old Frankstown Rd, Ste A
Pittsburgh, PA 15239
Contact: Robert Gormley President
Tel: 412-798-8990
Email: r.gormley@testex-ndt.com
Website: www.testex-ndt.com
Electromagnetic NDT systems & services: inspect ferrous & non-ferrous components. (Minority, estab 1987, empl 50, sales $14,700,000, cert: NMSDC)

3262 TREC Group, Inc.
900 Old Marple Rd.
Springfield, PA 19064
Contact: Dir Business Devel
Tel: 610-328-6465
Email: info@trecgroup.com
Website: www.trecgroup.com
Mechanical, electrical & civil engineering, project management, construction management, drafting & AUTOCAD capabilities. (Woman, estab 2001, empl 11, sales , cert: State, WBENC)

3263 ValSource, Inc.
918A Horseshoe Pike
Downingtown, PA 19335
Contact: Deborah Stanton President
Tel: 610-269-2808
Email: dstanton@valsource.com
Website: www.valsource.com
Commissioning, Qualification and Validation Services (Woman, estab 1996, empl 220, sales $34,000,000, cert: WBENC)

ENGINEERING SERVICES

Puerto Rico

3264 Accurate Solutions & Designs, Inc.
PO Box 3745
Mayaguez, PR 00681
Contact: Roberto Acosta CEO
Tel: 787-833-2658
Email: racosta@asdpr.com
Website: www.asdpr.com
Consulting: electrical systems, process control & engineering, automation, programming, control panel manufacturing & custom solutions to industrial control needs. (Hisp, estab 1997, empl 13, sales $5,032,083, cert: NMSDC)

3265 Aireko Construction Management Services, LLC
PO Box 2128
San Juan, PR 00922
Contact: Alejandro Nazario Business Dev Dir
Tel: 787-653-4700
Email: emarrero@amscm.com
Website: www.amscm.com
Pre-construction management & financial Viability Planning, Project Development Services, Engineer, Procure & Construct, Capital Structuring & Performance Guarantees. (Hisp, estab 1999, empl 10, sales , cert: NMSDC)

3266 Applied Engineering Group & Company, Corp.
PO Box 361298
San Juan, PR 00936
Contact: Jose J. Maisonet Business Devel Mgr
Tel: 787-771-5071
Email: jose.maisonet@aegroup-pr.com
Website: www.aegroup-pr.com
Engineering consulting services. (Hisp, estab 2006, empl 10, sales $980,000, cert: NMSDC)

3267 CRB Caribe, LLP
BBVA Center Mail Box #21, 1738 Amarillo St Ste 314
San Juan, PR 00926
Contact: Tom Forester GM
Tel: 787-622-2720
Email: shirley.nieves@crbusa.com
Website: www.crbusa.com
Engineering & Architectural Consulting & Design Services, Construction and Use Permitting, Inspections and Construction Support (Hisp, estab 2004, empl 60, sales $8,729,275, cert: NMSDC)

3268 DC Engineering Group, PSC
FIrst Federal Savings Bldg, Ste 820 Ponce de Leon Ave 1519
San Juan, PR 00693
Contact: Daianyk Cordova CEO
Tel: 787-477-1789
Email: dcordova@dc-eng.com
Website: www.dc-eng.com
Project Management & Inspection Services During Construction. (Minority, Woman, estab 2011, empl 8, sales , cert: NMSDC)

3269 E&R Pharma and Industrial Consulting Corp.
Est. de Juana Diaz Laurel 158
Juana Diaz, PR 00795
Contact: Richard Montalvo President
Tel: 787-374-3722
Email: rmonta2155@aol.com
Website: www.erpharma.com
Validation, qualification, commissioning, regulatory compliance, training & staffing. (Woman/Hisp, estab 2004, empl 4, sales $276,720, cert: NMSDC)

3270 JCD Engineering, Inc.
PO Box 192372
San Juan, PR 00919
Contact: Juan C. del Pino President
Tel: 787-787-7211
Email: jcdelpino@jcdengineering.com
Website: www.jcdengineering.com
Civil, electrical & mechanical engineering: concrete & steel small buildings, interiors work, hung ceilings, floors, gypsum board, electrical power & controls, fiber optics, local area networks (LAN), process & AHU control systems. (Hisp, estab 1996, empl 11, sales $1,327,000, cert: NMSDC)

3271 José A. Batlle & Asociados C.S.P.
65 José Martí
San Juan, PR 00917
Contact: José A. Batlle Ojeda President
Tel: 787-753-6395
Email: jabatlle@jabapr.com
Website: www.jabapr.com
Filtration Plants & Sewage Treatment Plants, Pumping Station & Water Tanks, Architectural Services, Mechanical Engineering Services, Electrical Engineering Services, Surveying Services. (Hisp, estab 1972, empl 11, sales $1,000,000, cert: NMSDC)

3272 LabChemS
PO Box 1022
Boqueron, PR 00622
Contact: Efrain Rivera Torres CEO
Tel: 787-920-4657
Email: efrain.rivera@labchemspr.com
Website: www.labchemscorp.com/
Engineering Consulting, Manufacturing & Packaging Equipments, Facilities & Manufacturing Process Validation, Quality Engineering & Six Sigma tools. (Hisp, estab 2009, empl 10, sales $1,200,000, cert: NMSDC)

3273 NOVO Consulting Group LLC
PMB 9 6400
Cayey, PR 00737
Contact: Claritza Millan President
Tel: 787-413-7379
Email: cmillan@novo-pr.com
Website: www.novo-pr.com
Design Qualification, Engineering Studies, Installation Qualification, Operational Qualification, Performance Qualification, Process Verification/Validation, Project Management, Process Improvement/Optimization, Quality Assurance, CAPA, NCRs. (Minority, Woman, estab 2015, empl 2, sales , cert: NMSDC)

3274 PVSR Corporation
PO Box 1548
Vega Baja, PR 00694
Contact: Victor Ferrer GM
Tel: 787-547-7800
Email: victor.ferrer@pvsr.us
Website: www.pvsr.us
Validation Consulting Services, Calibration Services (Lab, Field and Analytical Calibration Services) Resources & Recruiting Services. (Hisp, estab 2004, empl 15, sales $700,954, cert: NMSDC)

ENGINEERING SERVICES

3275 SQS, Inc. (Successful Quality Systems)
Palmas Industrial Park Road 869 KM. 2.0 Street 4
Catano, PR 00962
Contact: Wilda Aguirre President
Tel: 787-275-2424
Email: wildaaguirre@sqswarehouse.com
Website: www.sqswarehouse.com
Specialized Storage & Inventory Management Services. (Woman/Hisp, estab 2003, empl 8, sales $2,500,000, cert: NMSDC)

3276 UNIPRO Architects Engineers LLP
PO Box 10914
San Juan, PR 00922
Contact: Jose R. Gonzalez Dir planning/Projects
Tel: 787-793-3950
Email: jgonzalez@uniproaep.net
Website: www.uniproaep.com
Architecture, civil engineering, structural engineering, mechanical engineering, electrical engineering, environmental engineering, construction management. (Hisp, estab 1980, empl 30, sales $3,200,000, cert: NMSDC)

3277 Visional Technology LLC
400 Calle Calaf, Ste 49
San Juan, PR 00918
Contact: Joyce Rotger President
Tel: 787-717-0881
Email: joycemar@visionaltechnology.com
Website: www.visionaltechnology.com
Engineering services, dimensional metrology solutions, vision systems, coordinate measurement machines (CMM), laser measurements, 3D scanning, reverse engineering & computer aided inspections. (Minority, Woman, estab 2013, empl 5, sales , cert: NMSDC)

3278 Water Treatment Specialists, Inc.
PO Box 11609 Caparra Heights
San Juan, PR 00922
Contact: Isabel Cavo controller
Tel: 787-788-8968
Email: isabel.cavo@wtspr.com
Website: www.wtspr.com
Mfr water filtering equipment & aqua ammonia solutions. (Hisp, estab 0, empl 12, sales $1,547,083, cert: NMSDC)

South Carolina

3279 Amee Bay LLC
915 Commerce Cir
Hanahan, SC 29410
Contact: William Messing Sr Program Mgr
Tel: 843-725-6800
Email: bmessing@ameebay.com
Website: www.ameebay.com
General/mechanical contracting, power & pressure process piping installation, repair mechanical systems on pressure vessels, conveyors & auxiliary systems. (Nat Ame, estab 2006, empl 184, sales $26,000,000, cert: State)

3280 AQuate II, LLC
508 Hampton St, Ste 204
Columbia, SC 29201
Contact: Deveda Hunter GM
Tel: 256-837-1774
Email: dhunter@aquate2.com
Website: www.aquate2.com
IT, engineering, base operations support, logistics, administrative, and technical support services. (Nat-Ame, estab 2013, empl 80, sales , cert: 8(a), SDB)

3281 Atlantic South Consulting Services
3030 Ashley Town Center Dr Ste 101A
Charleston, SC 29414
Contact: Adrian Williams
Tel: 843-266-3998
Email: awilliams@atlanticsouthconsulting.com
Website: www.atlanticsouthconsulting.com
Engineering, surveying, and right-of-way acquisition services, transportation & utility designs, site development & land planning, construction inspection & management services, easement. (AA, estab 2004, empl 6, sales $668,000, cert: State)

3282 Diverse Industries, Inc.
260 Morley Court, Ste A
Duncan, SC 29334
Contact: Laura Charles Office Mgr
Tel: 864-400-9741
Email: laurac@diverseii.com
Website: www.diverseii.com
We experience implementing solutions & fixes for many customers in a variety of industries. Contract Robot Programming, Panel View & Thin Client HMI's, Training, Robot & PLC, Vision, Robot Guidance, Inspection & Code Reading. (Woman, estab 2007, empl 40, sales $5,114,985, cert: State)

3283 Select Power Systems, LLC
569 S. Rutherford St.
Blacksburg, SC 29702
Contact: Kevin Roark HR Lead
Tel: 864-619-1274
Email: kevin.roark@selectpowersystems.com
Website: www.selectpowersystems.com
Engineering services, project management & construction management. (Woman, estab 2017, empl 37, sales $5,100,000, cert: WBENC)

3284 US&S, Inc.
50 Grand Ave
Greenville, SC 29607
Contact: Shontel Babb Regional Sales Mgr
Tel: 864-233-8035
Email: sbabb@usands.com
Website: www.usands.com
Facilities maintenance & support services. (AA, estab 2003, empl 137, sales $31,000,000, cert: State, NMSDC)

Tennessee

3285 GQSI
3777 Winchester Rd Ste 1
Memphis, TN 38118
Contact: Williette Graham President
Tel: 901-365-9566
Email: willgraham@gqsi.net
Website: www.gqsi.net
Engineering & technical services, medical devices, process & special processes equipment & validation, laser marking, CMM inspection services, product inspection, engineering support, supplier support services. (Woman/AA, estab 2005, empl 6, sales , cert: NMSDC)

Texas

3286 Aerolution Inc.
10803 Gulfdale, Ste 208
San Antonio, TX 78216
Contact: Kyle kim President
Tel: 210-524-9831
Email: kkim@aerolutioninc.com
Website: www.aerolution.com
Structural/Mechanical design & analysis, Aircraft system design & analysis, Complete CAD capabilities, Stress analysis & finite element modeling. (As-Pac, estab 2007, empl 12, sales $1,900,000, cert: 8(a))

3287 Aguirre Roden Inc.
10670 N Central Expressway 6th Fl
Dallas, TX 75231
Contact: Peter Aguirre, CFM SVP Program Devel
Tel: 972-789-2662
Email: paaguirre@aguirre.com
Website: www.aguirreroden.com
Architecture, mechanical, electrical & structural engineering, general contracting. (Hisp, estab 1960, empl 65, sales , cert: State, NMSDC)

3288 ALTECOR Engineering
3617 Flamingo Ave
McAllen, TX 78504
Contact: T. G. Altecor Sr Staff Engineer
Tel: 956-687-7389
Email: info@altecoreng.com
Website: www.altecoreng.com
Structural dynamics & control systems engineering, equipment-machinery installations, optimizations, maintenance, reliability. (Woman, estab 2007, empl 7, sales $100,000, cert: State)

3289 Analytical Food Laboratories, Inc.
865 Greenview Dr
Grand Prairie, TX 75050
Contact: Rebecca Pfundheller President
Tel: 972-336-0336
Email: becky@afltexas.com
Website: www.afltexas.com
Food Quality & Safety, Nutrition Value, Vendor Product Quality, Functional Foods/Dietary Supplement & Hospitality/Culinary segments. (Woman, estab 1992, empl 53, sales $4,180,000, cert: State, WBENC)

3290 Arias & Associates, Inc.
142 Chula Vista
San Antonio, TX 78232
Contact: Jeremy Arias VP
Tel: 210-308-5884
Email: purchaseorders@ariasinc.com
Website: www.ariasinc.com
Geotechnical engineering svcs, construction materials testing & observation, environmental svcs. (Hisp, estab 1996, empl 96, sales , cert: State, City, SDB)

3291 Bailey's Premier Services LLC
4200 S Hulen St Ste 668
Fort Worth, TX 76109
Contact: Tamiko Bailey Managing Member
Tel: 817-292-2423
Email: twbailey@baileyspremierservices.com
Website: www.baileyspremierservices.com
Aircraft maintenance/servicing, dist parts & mfg. Program Management, Process Improvement, Consulting, Contracts, EVMS. (Woman/AA, estab 2010, empl 19, sales , cert: State, NMSDC, 8(a))

3292 Balance Vibration Technologies, Inc.
2426 Lacy Ln
Carrollton, TX 75006
Contact: Savanna Cole President
Tel: 214-733-8771
Email: mferrante@balancevibration.com
Website: www.balancevibration.com
Vibration analysis, condition monitoring, motor current analysis, laser alignment, dynamic balancing service, spectrographic oil analysis, infrared thermography, ultrasound, electrical repair service, switchgear relay, ground fault testing. (Woman, estab 2005, empl 11, sales $2,983,487, cert: WBENC)

3293 Basal Solutions LLC
1301 Texas Ave Ste 122
Houston, TX 77002
Contact: Branden Morris
Tel: 713-393-8767
Email: branden@basalsolutionsllc.com
Website: www.basalsolutionsllc.com
Engineering & business management consulting, project management, develop, test & integrate 0-D/1-D dynamic mathematical models, create FMEA & DFMEA for various vehicle platforms, test script design & implementation. (AA, estab 2014, empl 10, sales , cert: State, NMSDC)

3294 Bastion Technologies, Inc.
17625 El Camino Real
Houston, TX 77058
Contact: Jorge Hernandez President
Tel: 281-283-9330
Email: jhernandez@bastiontechnologies.com
Website: www.bastiontechnologies.com
Engineering design, analysis, systems engineering, information technology applications, engineering research, mechanical engineering, structural engineering, safety & reliability engineering, systems safety, hazard analysis. (Hisp, estab 1998, empl 400, sales $42,711,000, cert: State, NMSDC)

3295 BEPC, Inc.
3240 Executive Dr
San Angelo, TX 76904
Contact: Liza Dennis Dir of New Business
Tel: 325-944-0169
Email: liza.dennis@bepcinc.com
Website: www.bepcinc.com
Engineering services: validations of equipment, processes, audit & qualification of external suppliers, quality systems & validations, R&D product design & testing. (Hisp, estab 2005, empl 460, sales $20,038,327, cert: State, NMSDC)

3296 Charles Gojer & Associates, Inc.
11615 Forest Central Dr, Ste 303
Dallas, TX 75243
Contact: Charles Gojer President
Tel: 214-340-1199
Email: cgojer@cgojer.com
Website: www.cgojer.com
Civil & structural engineering. (Hisp, estab 1973, empl 10, sales , cert: State, NMSDC)

ENGINEERING SERVICES

3297 Elements of Architecture, Inc.
1201 6th Ave Ste 100
Fort Worth, TX 76104
Contact: Debbie Fulwiler President
Tel: 817-333-2880
Email: info@elementsofarc.com
Website: www.elementsofarc.com
Architectural & engineering svcs: environmental, structure & facility, electrical, mechanical, fire protection, alarming. (Woman, estab 1996, empl 7, sales , cert: State, WBENC)

3298 Elevan LLC dba Elevate Systems
1919 NW Loop 410, Ste 200
San Antonio, TX 78213
Contact: Scott Gray CEO
Tel: 210-807-9981
Email: scott.gray@elevatesystems.com
Website: www.elevatesystems.com
Engineering and logistics services for Department of Defense Aging Weapon Systems, Subsystems, Components, Parts and Pieces. (Minority, Woman, estab 2012, empl 4, sales $1,100,000, cert: State, SDB)

3299 First Assured Quality Systems, LLC
PO Box 535812
Grand Prairie, TX 75053
Contact: Brittany Stovall President
Tel: 817-538-9240
Email: bstovall@assuredqualitysystems.com
Website: www.assuredqualitysystems.com
Quality Control Services- Containment, Sorting, Rework, Inspection, Liaison Support, Engineering Support & Launch Support. (Woman/AA, Hisp, estab 2013, empl 35, sales $2,872,632, cert: NMSDC, WBENC)

3300 Gap Engineering
21703 Kingsland Blvd, Ste 103
Katy, TX 77450
Contact: Mike Homma
Tel: 281-578-0500
Email: mhomma@gap-eng.com
Website: www.gap-eng.com
Engineering, design & drafting services, develop instrument Specs, Detail Design, Distributive Control Systems (DCS), Fieldbus, Programmable Logic Controllers (PLC), Safety Instrumented Systems (SIS), Fiber Optic Comm Networks. (As-Pac, estab 2004, empl 25, sales $2,800,000, cert: NMSDC, 8(a))

3301 GMR Protection Resources, Inc.
1629 Smirl Dr, Ste 200
Heath, TX 75032
Contact: Scott Crawford Sr Dir of Business Dev
Tel: 469-267-9144
Email: smcrawford@gmr1.com
Website: www.gmr1.com
ADA compliance inspections and risk/security assessments, security incident response assessments, security compliance reviews & crime report data development. (Woman, estab 1991, empl 105, sales $16,000,000, cert: WBENC)

3302 JAT Energy Services LLC
111 Soledad St, Ste 1900
San Antonio, TX 78205
Contact: Keith Allen President
Tel: 916-429-9096
Email: keith@jatenergies.com
Website: www.JATEnergies.com
Energy solutions, engineering & management firm, custom engineered solutions to reduce energy consumption in commercial & industrial spaces. (AA, estab 2012, empl 8, sales $500,000, cert: State, NMSDC)

3303 Johnson & Pace Inc.
1201 NW Loop 281, Ste 100
Longview, TX 75604
Contact: Linda Bennett President
Tel: 903-753-0663
Email: LindaB@johnsonpace.com
Website: www.johnsonpace.com
Engineering services: civil, mechanical, electrical, structural, architectural services, land surveying. (Woman, estab 1995, empl 45, sales $7,930,735, cert: State, WBENC)

3304 JQ Infrastructure, LLC
100 Glass St Ste 201
Dallas, TX 75207
Contact: Stephen Lucy Principal
Tel: 972-392-7340
Email: slucy@jqeng.com
Website: www.jqieng.com/
Surveying services, building, structures & components consulting, engineering consulting, civil engineering, concrete engineering, drainage engineering, foundation engineering, inspection, general/engineering. (As-Pac, estab 2003, empl 105, sales $6,471,893, cert: State, NMSDC)

3305 M.E.P. Consulting Engineers, Inc.
2928 Story Rd W
Irving, TX 75038
Contact: Camilla Beavers Admin Asst
Tel: 972-870-9060
Email: mail@mepce.com
Website: www.mepce.com
Mechanical, electrical, plumbing, fire protection & information technology design engineering & commissioning for aviation facilities, municipalities, educational facilities, government, health care & commercial facilities. (Woman, estab 1998, empl 14, sales $4,000,000, cert: State, WBENC)

3306 Maslowski Controls, LLC
1751 Hurd Dr, Ste 111
Irving, TX 75038
Contact: Jacqueline Sikorski President
Tel: 817-999-1662
Email: jsikorski@maslowskicontrols.com
Website: www.maslowskicontrols.com
Control System Engineering, PLC Programming, Historian, SCADA, HMI
Control Systems signal/instrumentation, troubleshooting, testing, simulation, staff training. (Woman, estab 2017, empl 3, sales , cert: WBENC)

ENGINEERING SERVICES

3307 Multatech
2821 W 7th St Ste 400
Fort Worth, TX 76107
Contact: Hong P. Chen President
Tel: 817-877-5571
Email: hchen@multatech.com
Website: www.multatech.com
mechanical, electrical, plumbing & civil consulting engineering services, architectural design services. (Hisp, estab 1986, empl 74, sales $11,048,061, cert: State, NMSDC)

3308 NSM Inc.
1535 Industrial Dr
Missouri City, TX 77489
Contact: Vini Gupta CEO
Tel: 281-880-8188
Email: sales@cornerstonevalve.com
Website: www.cornerstonevalve.vom
Custom Engineered Design and Manufacturing Solutions, Wide array of metallurgies, Temperature range -350F to 1500F, Metal seated bubble tight leakage, High cycling up to 1.5 million cycles per year. (As-Ind, estab 2019, empl 17, sales $4,500,000, cert: NMSDC)

3309 Oil Field Development Engineering
12121 Wickchester Lane, Ste 700
Houston, TX 77079
Contact: Jay Chen President
Tel: 281-679-9060
Email: jay.chen@ofdeng.com
Website: www.ofdeng.com
Project management, engineering and design for offshore and onshore oil and gas production and transportation facilities. (As-Pac, estab 2002, empl 64, sales , cert: State)

3310 Onyx Power and Gas LLC
13155 Noel Rd Ste 900
Dallas, TX 75240
Contact: Loraine Sutton Mgr
Tel: 214-871-5574
Email: vinnies@onyxpg.com
Website: www.onyxpg.com
Energy management and procurement; power sales; consultation. (AA, estab 2009, empl 14, sales , cert: State, NMSDC)

3311 Parra & Co., LLC
110 E Houston St, Fl 7
San Antonio, TX 78205
Contact: Veronica Parra
Tel: 210-819-4848
Email: vmparra@parracompany.com
Website: www.parracompany.com
Civil Engineering services: grant writing, planning, feasibility studies, preliminary engineering reports, platting, grading, stormwater & drainage management, utilities, permitting, construction inspection & project management. (Hisp, estab 2016, empl 12, sales $1,687,018, cert: State, City)

3312 SeaMax Corporation
3720 W Alabama St Ste 3108
Houston, TX 77027
Contact: Brendan Isidienu Structural Engineer
Tel: 713-584-3643
Email: ibrendan@seamax.org
Website: www.seamax.org
Engineering consulting, structural engineering & and design of offshore & onshore soil & gas structures. (AA, estab 2015, empl 10, sales , cert: NMSDC)

3313 Spencer Cole, LLC
1409 Wilderness Trail
Crowley, TX 76036
Contact: Carol Bell CEO
Tel: 703-725-7706
Email: carol.bell@spencercole.com
Website: www.spencercole.com
Product Lifecycle Development, Program Management, Training, Capture & Proposal support services & solutions. (AA, estab 2018, empl 3, sales , cert: State, 8(a))

3314 Sunland Group
10400 Westoffice Dr, Ste 116
Houston, TX 77042
Contact: Sales/Marketing
Tel: 713-467-8484
Email: info@sunlandgrp.com
Website: www.sunlandgrp.com
Design build: civil, structural, environmental engineering, architecture, design & construction surveying, value engineering. (Hisp, estab 1985, empl 85, sales $8,200,000, cert: State)

3315 Systems Integration, Inc.
7316 Business Pl
Arlington, TX 76001
Contact: Rhonda Smith Acct Mgr
Tel: 817-468-1494
Email: rsmith@sitexas.com
Website: www.sitexas.com
Engineering & Design, Reverse Engineering, Fabrication, Installation, Structural & Civil, Manufacturing, Machinery, Mechanical, CNC Machining, Electrical & Controls, Test Structures, Tooling. (Hisp, estab 1992, empl 20, sales $4,000,000, cert: State)

3316 Taylor & Hill, Inc.
9941 Rowlett
Houston, TX 77075
Contact: Natalie Langford Business Devel Mgr
Tel: 713-941-2671
Email: mwhittington@taylorandhill.com
Website: www.taylorandhill.com
Contract/direct hire personnel & in-house engineering services, computerized electronic measurement (AEMS) & high definition laser scanning for plant design purposes. (Hisp, estab 1974, empl 100, sales $16,300,000, cert: State, NMSDC)

3317 United Geo Technologies LLC
      7715 Mainland Dr, Ste 110
      San Antonio, TX 78250
      Contact: Patricia Ingram President
      Tel: 210-684-2147
      Email: pingram@unitedgeotech.com
      Website: www.unitedgeotech.com
Softcopy photogrammetric mapping, digital orthophotography, GIS services, geospatial database architecture, raster/vector data layer production, CAD to GIS data integration, remotely updating of GIS layers & solution development. (Woman, estab 2011, empl 6, sales , cert: State)

Virginia

3318 Alexton Incoporated
      7830 Backlick Rd Ste 405
      Alexandria, VA 22150
      Contact: Sophia Marnell President
      Tel: 703-405-6745
      Email: smarnell@alexton.com
      Website: www.alexton.com
Financial Management, Engineering, Information Technology, Business Support Services and Program/Project Management. (Woman, estab 2005, empl 20, sales $2,000,000, cert: 8(a))

3319 Ashe Consultants, PLLC
      950 Herndon Pkwy Ste 320
      Herndon, VA 20170
      Contact: Sharon M. Gorick, PE President
      Tel: 703-230-2500
      Email: sgorick@asheconsultants.com
      Website: www.asheconsultants.com
Mechanical, electrical & plumbing engineering design services for buildings. (Woman, estab 2008, empl 5, sales $130,660, cert: State, WBENC)

3320 Interspec, LLC
      464 S Independence Blvd Ste C-104
      Virginia Beach, VA 23452
      Contact: Sean Murphy Business Devel Dir
      Tel: 757-622-6299
      Email: murphys@interspecllc.net
      Website: www.interspecllc.net
Tank, piping & pressure vessel inspections, STI storage tank inspections, Non-Destructive Examination/Testing steel structures, Spill Prevention Control & Countermeasure (SPCC) plans, Oil Discharge Control Plans (ODCP. (Nat Ame, estab 2001, empl 22, sales $1,200,000, cert: State, 8(a))

3321 Lu Smith Engineers
      4604 Sadler Grove Way
      Glen Allen, VA 23060
      Contact: Dawen Lu President
      Tel: 804-519-9306
      Email: dlu6838@gmail.com
      Website: www.lsengineers.net
Building system commissioning services, energy modeling/audit services, geothermal system study & design, sustainable design/LEED consultation & administration, mechanical, electrical, plumbing & fire protection system design. (As-Pac, estab 2012, empl 12, sales $1,400,000, cert: State)

3322 MKAssociates, Inc.
      6593 Commerce Ct, Ste 100
      Warrenton, VA 20187
      Contact: Michelle Kilby-Miranda Principal
      Tel: 540-428-3550
      Email: info@mkassociates.com
      Website: www.mkassociates.com
Land surveying coordination. (Woman, estab 1998, empl 12, sales $350,000,000, cert: WBENC)

3323 Raul V. Bravo + Associates, Inc.
      1889 Preston White Dr Ste 202
      Reston, VA 20191
      Contact: Claudio Bravo VP
      Tel: 703-326-9092
      Email: procurement@rvba.com
      Website: www.RVBA.com
Rail Car Design, Mechanical, CADD, Electrical schematics, Telecommunication Design, Security Design, Electrical Diagrams Wiring, Smoke Detector Layout, CCTV & MATV Design, Power Supplies. (Hisp, estab 1979, empl 63, sales , cert: State)

3324 RMR Technology Group LLC
      7247 Archlaw Dr
      Clifton, VA 20124
      Contact: Terrie Rollins CEO
      Tel: 703-346-0631
      Email: trollins@rmrtechnologygroup.com
      Website: www.rmrtechnologygroup.com
Workforce Solutions, Technology Strategy, Transformation & Organization Change Innovation, Compliancy Solutions. (Woman/AA, estab 2003, empl 5, sales , cert: State, 8(a))

3325 T3 Design Corporation
      10340 Democracy Ln, Ste 305
      Fairfax, VA 22030
      Contact: Tandrumn Reid WBENC Liaison
      Tel: 770-813-0882
      Email: treid@t3design.us
      Website: www.streetsmarts.us
Transportation engineering, civil/site engineering, transportation planning, intelligent transportation systems, traffic engineering, survey services, subsurface utility engineering, data collection, geographic information systems & public involvement. (Woman, estab , empl , sales $9,500,000, cert: State)

3326 Unified Industries Inc.
      6551 Loisdale Ct Ste 400
      Springfield, VA 22150
      Contact: Tom Callahan
      Tel: 703-922-9800
      Email: callahan@uii.com
      Website: www.uii.com
Metrology & calibration services, life cycle logistics planning, supply chain support, ship outfitting, distance support, obsolescence analysis. (AA, estab 1970, empl 200, sales $16,045,000, cert: State)

ENGINEERING SERVICES

Washington

3327 CS3W Associates, Inc.
2821 167th Ave NE
Bellevue, WA 98008
Contact: Christopher Sims President
Tel: 425-922-5900
Email: csims@cs3w.com
Website: www.cs3w.com
Engineering & management services, electrical & structural/seismic engineering services, project management & analysis support. (AA, estab 1999, empl 8, sales $671,000, cert: State)

3328 Garry Struthers Associates, Inc.
3150 Richards Rd
Bellevue, WA 98005
Contact: Garry Struthers President
Tel: 425-519-0300
Email: garrys@gsassoc-inc.com
Website: www.gsassoc-inc.com
Engineering, construction, environmental science, facilities maintenance. (AA, estab 1988, empl 106, sales $21,000,000, cert: NMSDC)

3329 GeoTest Services, Inc.
741 Marine View Dr
Bellingham, WA 98225
Contact: Jeremy Wolf VP
Tel: 360-733-7318
Email: jeremyw@geotest-inc.com
Website: www.geotest-inc.com
Geotechnical engineering, environmental services, special inspection & materials testing, facilities, structures, roads, bridges & all types of infrastructure. (Woman, estab 1993, empl 33, sales $6,000,000, cert: State)

3330 Land Development Consultants, Inc.
14201 NE 200th St Ste 100
Woodinville, WA 98072
Contact: Frank Lemos President
Tel: 425-806-1869
Email: flemos@ldccorp.com
Website: www.ldccorp.com
Civil Engineering, Land Survey, Land Use Planning/Permitting, A/E Design, Commercial Site Design, Roadway Design, Drainage Design and Reporting, GIS ESRI Mapping, Water Systems. (Hisp, estab 2003, empl 40, sales $5,354,378, cert: State, NMSDC)

3331 Maniilaq Services, LLC
1700 7th Ave Ste 2100
Seattle, WA 98101
Contact: Michael Scott CEO
Tel: 206-715-7804
Email: michael_scott@comcast.net
Website: www.maniilaqservices.com
Facilities support services: IT, janitorial, housekeeping, security, food service & health professional staffing. (Nat-Ame, estab 2007, empl 45, sales $4,200,000, cert: 8(a))

3332 Professional CAD Services, Inc. dba PCSI Design
18916 N Creek Pkwy Ste 103
Bothell, WA 98011
Contact: Carlos Veliz CEO
Tel: 425-485-3420
Email: carlos@pcsidesign.com
Website: www.pcsidesign.com
Product design & engineering services focused on assisting companies to translate conceptual design into market-ready production products. Our product & solution offerings extend to many industries. (Hisp, estab 1997, empl 5, sales $1,116,889, cert: NMSDC)

3333 Tamazari Inc
487C Hotchkiss Rd
Colville, WA 99114
Contact: Leigh Stylos
Tel: 206-697-1984
Email: leigh.stylos@tamazari.com
Website: www.tamazari.com
ERP, MFG, engineering, CRM, sales operations. (Woman/Hisp, estab 2006, empl 26, sales $4,988,306, cert: NMSDC)

3334 WHPacific, Inc.
12100 NE 195th St Ste 300
Bothell, WA 98011
Contact: Carl Romig Dir ICS
Tel: 425-951-4000
Email: cromig@whpacific.com
Website: www.WHPacific.com
Accessibility/Universal Access, Aviation Planning & Design, Bridge Design and Rehabilitation, Civil Engineering, Commissioning, Community & Urban Design, Construction Inspection, Construction Management, Construction Management. (Nat Ame, estab 1981, empl 351, sales $55,249,100, cert: NMSDC)

Wisconsin

3335 Barrientos Design & Consulting, Inc.
205 W Highland Ave Ste 303
Milwaukee, WI 53203
Contact: President
Tel: 414-271-1812
Email: admin@barrientosdesign.com
Website: www.barrientosdesign.com
Architecture, structural engineering, civil & site engineering: industrial, office, training, warehousing, maintenance facilities, field operations, substations & power plant enclosures, space needs analysis, building programming, site selection. (Hisp, estab 1998, empl , sales $1,010,000, cert: NMSDC)

3336 Datasyst Engineering & Testing
S14 W33511 Hwy 18
Delafield, WI 53018
Contact: Rose Hoisington CFO
Tel: 800-969-4050
Email: mhoisington@datasysttest.com
Website: www.datasysttest.com
Mechanical & electrical equipment testing & engineering: medical, telecommunications, construction, mining & process, industrial, automotive. (Minority, Woman, estab 1990, empl 11, sales , cert: NMSDC)

3337 Fusion Integrated Solutions LLC
416 Security Blvd
Green Bay, WI 54313
Contact: Seaphes Miller CEO
Tel: 920-593-4200
Email: solutions@fusion-etc.com
Website: www.fusion-etc.com

Mechanical, civil & structural, electrical & process engineering & design svcs, project management, materials procurement, construction field supervision, electrical panel construction & custom machine design & manufacture. (AA, estab 2004, empl 60, sales $9,113,000, cert: State, NMSDC)

3338 ILLUME Advising, LLC
440 Science Dr, Ste 202 Ste 202
Madison, WI 53711
Contact: Don Smith
Tel: 608-807-7816
Email: don@illumeadvising.com
Website: www.illumeadvising.com

Energy Efficiency, Demand Response, Renewable & Smart Grid Program & Products Design, Planning, Research & Evaluation Consultants. (Woman, estab 2013, empl 38, sales $8,215,311, cert: State, CPUC, WBENC)

3339 K. Singh & Associates, Inc.
3636 N 124th St
Wauwatosa, WI 53222
Contact: Pratap Singh CEO
Tel: 262-821-1171
Email: gmiller@ksaconsultants.com
Website: www.ksaconsultants.com

Environmental engineering & management services, transportation, structural, environmental & civil engineering, land surveying & construction management. (As-Ind, estab 1987, empl 33, sales $3,000,000, cert: State)

3340 PSJ Engineering, Inc.
7665 N Port Washington Rd
Milwaukee, WI 53217
Contact: Parmjit Jaspal CEO
Tel: 414-352-2211
Email: jesse@psjengineering.com
Website: www.psjengineering.com

Consulting engineering svcs: heating, ventilation, air conditioning, plumbing & fire protection. (As-Pac, estab 1986, empl 13, sales $1,186,006, cert: State, City)

ENVIRONMENTAL SERVICES

Firms are engaged in underground and above ground storage tank removal and installation, assessment and remediation, lead and asbestos abatement, hazardous waste management, pollution, etc. NAICS Code 54

Alabama

3341 Action Environmental LLC
204 20th St N
Birmingham, AL 35203
Contact: Melissa Allen Admin Svcs Mgr
Tel: 813-909-0040
Email: melissa.allen@actn.com
Website: www.actn.com
Abatement Services, Emergency Services, Field Services, Oilfield Services, Waste Services. (AA, estab 2002, empl 300, sales $22,000,000, cert: NMSDC)

3342 Action Resources, Inc.
40 Country Rd 517
Hanceville, AL 35077
Contact: Samantha May Exec Asst
Tel: 205-271-4478
Email: smay@action-resources.com
Website: www.action-resources.com
Environmental Remediation Services; Hazardous & Specialty Transportation; In-Plant Services; Transportation Logistics; Municipal & Civil Services; Pipeline Services. (AA, estab 1995, empl , sales $119,000,000, cert: NMSDC)

3343 One Stop Environmental, LLC
4800 Division Ave
Birmingham, AL 35222
Contact: Elizabeth Hinson Marketing Dir
Tel: 205-595-8188
Email: ehinson@onestopenv.com
Website: www.onestopenv.com
Hazardous waste transport & disposal, confined space entry, emergency response, remediation, oil/water separator, lead/asbestos abatement. (Woman, estab 1999, empl 42, sales $4,000,000, cert: WBENC)

3344 Orrs Environmental, LLC
515 Sparkman Dr
Huntsville, AL 35756
Contact: Debra Sanders Mgr
Tel: 256-556-1220
Email: orrsenvironmental@gmail.com
Website: www.orrsenvironmental.com
Rail, air, water, trucking multimodal service, general & climate control warehousing, waste management assessments, spill response supplies & PPE, safety training, haz mat disposal & recycling services. (Woman/AA, estab 2004, empl 12, sales , cert: State)

3345 Slade Land Use, Environmental & Transportation Planning LLC
1500 1st Ave N, Unit 54
Birmingham, AL 35203
Contact: L'Tryce Slade Owner
Tel: 205-413-4685
Email: lslade@sladellc.com
Website: www.sladellc.com
General Contracting, Environmental Consulting, Geotechnical Services, Construction Material Testing, Urban Planning. (Woman/AA, estab 2006, empl 6, sales $644,986, cert: NMSDC, WBENC, 8(a))

3346 Vulcan Industrial Contractors Co., LLC
4625-A Valleydale Rd
Birmingham, AL 35242
Contact: Kristi Lawler CEO
Tel: 205-313-4766
Email: KLawler@vindco.com
Website: www.vindco.com
Asbestos & lead removal. (Woman, estab 1949, empl 727, sales $68,000,000, cert: WBENC)

Arizona

3347 Archaeological Consulting Services, Ltd.
424 W Broadway Rd
Tempe, AZ 85282
Contact: Margerie Green President
Tel: 480-894-5477
Email: mgreen@acstempe.com
Website: www.acstempe.com
Cultural resource services, class I to class III studies, testing, & data recovery, environmental services, biological assessments/evaluations, environmental project management, paleo environmental analysis, GIS mapping. (Woman, estab 1977, empl 34, sales $1,945,942, cert: State, City, CPUC)

3348 Beck Environmental and Remediation, Ltd.
772 S Holmes Rd
Apache Junction, AZ 85119
Contact: Julie Beck President
Tel: 480-671-1365
Email: julie.beck@earthlink.net
Website: www.beckenvironmental.com
Environmental assessments, site characterizations, remediation, air monitoring, hazardous materials management, environmental impact statements, health & safety, mitigation modeling. (Woman, estab 1998, empl 5, sales $292,915, cert: WBENC, 8(a))

3349 Darling Geomatics
9040 S Rita Rd, Ste 2350
Tucson, AZ 85747
Contact: Mary Darling CEO
Tel: 520-298-2725
Email: marydarling@darlingltd.com
Website: www.darlingltd.com
Environmental consulting. (Woman, estab 1997, empl 15, sales $2,000,000, cert: City, CPUC, WBENC)

3350 Gutierrez-Palmenberg, Inc.
2922 W Clarendon Ave
Phoenix, AZ 85017
Contact: Jason Weed Engineer
Tel: 602-234-0696
Email: jason.w@gpimail.com
Website: www.gpieng.com
Environmental consulting & engineering services, site characterizations, design, identifying potential environmental impacts of planned operations, remediation, monitoring and protecting valued resources. (Hisp, estab 1980, empl 25, sales $2,250,273, cert: NMSDC)

3351 The Green Way Environmental Group, LLC.
PO Box 5705
Scottsdale, AZ 85261
Contact: Chris McNally Business Dev Mgr
Tel: 480-639-0389
Email: chris@gweg-az.com
Website: www.greenway-environmental.com
Environmental, construction & restoration, sampling & clearance sampling of asbestos, lead based paint & microbial, environmental compliance, consulting, industrial hygiene & occupational safety. (Woman, estab 2010, empl 5, sales $616,000, cert: WBENC)

California

3352 Bainbridge Environmental Consultants, Inc.
12440 Firestone Blvd Ste 1022
Norwalk, CA 90650
Contact: Henry Alberto Moreno Owner
Tel: 714-247-0024
Email: mmoreno@bainbridge-env.com
Website: www.bainbridge-env.com
Environmental consulting services: hazardous materials, asbestos, lead-based paint, mold/fungi, radon, polychlorinated biphenyls (PCB's), volatile organic compounds (VOC's). (Hisp, estab 1992, empl 15, sales $1,200,000, cert: State, 8(a))

3353 BC Laboratories, Inc.
4100 Atlas Court
Bakersfield, CA 93308
Contact: Mark Ellis Business Devel Dir
Tel: 800-878-4911
Email: mark.ellis@bclabs.com
Website: www.bclabs.com
Analytical Services for Groundwater, Drinking Water, Wastewater, Soils & Air, Certified Testing Services, Sampling & Monitoring. (Woman, estab 1949, empl 97, sales $1,000,000,000, cert: CPUC)

3354 CAL Inc.
2040 Peabody Rd
Vacaville, CA 95687
Contact: David Esparza President
Tel: 707-446-7996
Email: desparza@cal-inc.com
Website: www.cal-inc.com
General contracting: Asbestos & Lead Abatement, Demolition, Remediation Services & Environmental & Safety Training. (Hisp, estab 1979, empl 40, sales $4,786,000, cert: CPUC)

3355 California Hazardous Services Inc
1431 E St Andrew Pl
Santa Ana, CA 92705
Contact: Tammy Taylor Sales Mgr
Tel: 714-434-9995
Email: bids@calhaz.com
Website: www.calhaz.com
Fuel tank service, cleaning, waste disposal, water intrusion pump-outs, environmental compliance tank testing, tank removals, tank installations, tank upgrades. (Woman, estab 1988, empl 24, sales $4,960,000, cert: CPUC, WBENC)

3356 EFR Environmental Services Inc.
PO Box 2669
Alpine, CA 91903
Contact: Laura L Harris President
Tel: 619-722-6781
Email: accounting@efrenviro.com
Website: www.efrenviro.com
Transport hazardous waste & non-hazardous waste, Drum, Rolloff Services, Bulk Services, Vacuum Services, Site Cleanups and Waste Categorization and Profiling. (Woman, estab 1999, empl 17, sales $2,506,684, cert: State, CPUC)

3357 Engineering/Remediation Resources Group, Inc.
4585 Pacheco Blvd Ste 200
Martinez, CA 94553
Contact: Tyson Appel Sr Project Mgr
Tel: 925-969-0750
Email: tyson.appel@errg.com
Website: www.errg.com
Engineering & remediation services, environmental, civil & geotechnical engineering, certified hazardous waste technicians. (Minority, Woman, estab 1997, empl 175, sales $81,494,792, cert: CPUC)

3358 FRS Environmental
1414 E Sixth St
Corona, CA 92879
Contact: President
Tel: 951-898-1888
Email: info@frsenvironmental.com
Website: www.frsenvironmental.com
Emergency response, containment & recommendation, hazardous waste mgmt & disposal, facility decontamination & remediation, analytical & testing svcs, lab pack svcs, vacuum pumping. (Woman, estab 1995, empl 10, sales $2,000,000, cert: WBENC)

3359 Future Power Corporation
66 Franklin St Ste 300
Oakland, CA 94607
Contact: Dahlia Moodie President
Tel: 510-647-8450
Email: dahlia@ecoptions.biz
Website: www.ecoptions.biz
Facility energy audits, energy savings solution recommendation & technology solution implementation. (Woman/AA, Hisp, estab 2008, empl 7, sales $1,175,198, cert: CPUC)

3360 GGG Demolition Inc.
1130 W Trenton Ave
Orange, CA 92867
Contact: President
Tel: 714-699-9350
Email:
Website: www.gggdemo.com
Structural Demolition, Asbestos/Lead Abatement, Mold Remediation, Soil Remediation.
Selective Demolition. (Woman, estab 2013, empl 150, sales $12,000,000, cert: CPUC, WBENC)

3361 Greenway Solid Waste & Recycling, Inc.
PO Box 1453
Claremont, CA 91711
Contact: Charles Elias VP
Tel: 909-518-7943
Email: celias@greenwayrecyclinginc.com
Website: www.greenwayrecyclinginc.com
Electronic waste recycling, nonhazardous waste treatment & disposal. (Minority, Woman, estab 2006, empl 3, sales $321,000, cert: State, 8(a))

3362 H2O Engineering, Inc.
189 Granada Dr
San Luis Obispo, CA 93401
Contact: Jeff Cedillos Sales Coord
Tel: 866-987-0303
Email: marketing@h2oengineering.com
Website: www.h2oengineering.com
Create tailored water treatment solutions for industrial process water, ultra-pure water, water reuse, and groundwater remediation. (Hisp, estab 2000, empl 16, sales $4,200,000, cert: NMSDC)

3363 Impact Absorbents, Inc.
5255 Traffic Way
Atascadero, CA 93422
Contact: Tammy Rayner Dir of Corporate Sales
Tel: 800-339-7672
Email: trayner@spillhero.com
Website: www.spillhero.com
Mfr & dist granular absorbents, sorbent pads, sorbents socks, spill clean up programs & products, non-hazardous, earth friendly. (Woman, estab 1992, empl 30, sales $5,300,000, cert: State)

3364 Integrated Science Solutions (ISSI)
      1777 N California Blvd Ste 305
      Walnut Creek, CA 94596
      Contact: Cecelia Mccloy President
      Tel: 925-979-1535
      Email: info@issi-net.com
      Website: www.issi-net.com
Earth & environmental science, engineering, regulatory compliance, occupational safety & health, homeland security, emergency response, & energy, water & natural resource development. (Woman, estab 1999, empl 40, sales $5,035,800, cert: CPUC, WBENC)

3365 Ninyo & Moore
      5710 Ruffin Rd.
      San Diego, CA 92123
      Contact: Elizabeth Brooks Corp Business Dev Mgr
      Tel: 858-576-1000
      Email: ebrooks@ninyoandmoore.com
      Website: www.ninyoandmoore.com
Geotechnical & environmental sciences consulting: geotechnical engineering, engineering geology, engineering geophysics, hydrogeology, soil & materials testing & environmental sciences. (Hisp, estab 1986, empl 492, sales $92,662,074, cert: City, NMSDC, CPUC)

3366 Northstar Environmental Remediation
      26225 Enterprise Ct
      Lake Forest, CA 92630
      Contact: Katherine Tweidt President
      Tel: 949-580-2800
      Email: ktweidt@cox.net
      Website: www.northstarremediation.com
Environmental consulting & remediation, soil & groundwater, equip fabrication, installation, & operation, permitting, consulting, soil & groundwater characterization, well installation, reporting, compliance activities. (Woman, estab 2002, empl 6, sales $1,250,000, cert: CPUC)

3367 Orange Coast Analytical, Inc.
      3002 Dow Ave, Ste 532
      Tustin, CA 92780
      Contact: Cindy Noorani President
      Tel: 714-832-0064
      Email: cindyn@ocalab.com
      Website: www.ocalab.com
Environmental & analytical testing laboratory, organic & inorganic testing-water, waste water, soil, air, industial, chemical & food products. (Woman, estab 1990, empl 15, sales $1,450,178, cert: State, CPUC)

3368 OST Trucks and Cranes, Inc.
      2951 N Ventura Ave
      Ventura, CA 93002
      Contact: L. Dennis Zermeno President
      Tel: 805-643-9963
      Email: ostcranes@aol.com
      Website: www.ostcranes.com
General & hazardous substance removal & remedial action, hydraulic cranes 5 to 140. (Hisp, estab 1947, empl 69, sales $ 0, cert: State, NMSDC, CPUC)

3369 Pari & Gershon Inc.
      2053 Lincoln Ave Ste A
      San Jose, CA 95125
      Contact: Romena Jonas President
      Tel: 408-966-7184
      Email: rjonas@pgiinc.net
      Website: www.pgicompany.com
Environmental Consulting, Engineering Design & Construction. (Woman, estab 2009, empl 5, sales $100,000, cert: State, WBENC)

3370 Piper Environmental Group, Inc.
      11600 California St
      Castroville, CA 95012
      Contact: Jane Piper CEO
      Tel: 831-632-2700
      Email: jpiper@peg-inc.com
      Website: www.peg-inc.com
Design ozone solutions, turn-key ozone trailer systems, ozone sparging systems. (Woman, estab 1992, empl 3, sales $1,483,616, cert: CPUC, WBENC)

3371 Pivox Corporation
      3240 El Camino Real Ste 230
      Irvine, CA 92602
      Contact: Sean Shahin VP
      Tel: 949-727-1400
      Email: sean@pivox.com
      Website: www.pivox.com
Remediation of soil & groundwater, demolition, project & construction management, permitting, design, feasibility study, treatment system installation (civil, mechanical, electril, and instrumentation). (Woman, estab 2004, empl 20, sales $8,000,000, cert: CPUC)

3372 RORE, Inc.
      5151 Shoreham Place
      San Diego, CA 92122
      Contact: Gita Murthy
      Tel: 858-404-7393
      Email: rore, inc.
      Website: www.roreinc.com
General & hazardous waste contracting, environmental investigation & remediation. (Woman/As-Ind, estab 2003, empl 70, sales $15,000,000, cert: State)

3373 SCA Environmental, Inc.
      320 Justin Dr
      San Francisco, CA 94112
      Contact: Christina Codemo President
      Tel: 415-882-1675
      Email: ccodemo@sca-enviro.com
      Website: www.sca-enviro.com
Environmental consulting services, O & M plans. (Woman, estab 1992, empl 11, sales $ 0, cert: WBENC)

3374 Spring Rivers Ecological Sciences LLC
      PO Box 153
      Cassel, CA 96016
      Contact: Maria Ellis Aquatic Ecologist
      Tel: 530-335-5446
      Email: maria@springrivers.com
      Website: www.springrivers.com
Aquatic ecology & resources consulting. (Woman, estab 1994, empl 15, sales $ 0, cert: CPUC)

3375 TERRA Solutions & Services, LLC
      3478 Buskirk Ave Ste 100
      Pleasant Hill, CA 94523
      Contact: Bruce Borup Owner
      Tel: 925-651-6388
      Email: bborup@sircorporation.com
      Website: www.terras2.com
Environmental engineering, Phase I & Phase II property assessment & site investigation,
underground storage tank assessment, removal, & site restoration services, environmental construction & remediation system installation. (Nat Ame, estab 2011, empl 11, sales $664,000, cert: CPUC)

3376 Thomas Land Clearing Company
2170 W Esther St
Long Beach, CA 90813
Contact: Bernice Antimo President
Tel: 562-436-6025
Email: tlc.demo@verizon.net
Website: www.jesdbes.com
Demolition, asbestos abatement, lead based paint removal & general land clearing. (AA, estab 1985, empl 5, sales $1,700,000, cert: State, CPUC)

3377 Three Squares International Inc.
1507 7th St, Ste 05
Santa Monica, CA 90401
Contact: Jaime Nack President
Tel: 310-403-6225
Email: jnack@threesquaresinc.com
Website: www.threesquaresinc.com
Environmental consulting, strategy, planning & implementation of sustainability initiatives. (Woman, estab 2008, empl 4, sales $500,000, cert: State, City, CPUC)

3378 Tycho Services, Inc.
3906 W. Burbank Blvd.
Burbank, CA 91505
Contact: Raj Chhina President
Tel: 818-840-9404
Email: raj@tychoservices.com
Website: www.tychoservices.com
Pre & post event clean-up & biohazard waste removal and clean-up. (As-Ind, estab 2009, empl 81, sales $1,600,000, cert: NMSDC, CPUC)

3379 UltraViolet Devices, Inc.
26145 Technology Dr
Valencia, CA 91355
Contact: Kathi Million Inside Sales Mgr
Tel: 661-295-8140
Email: marys@uvdi.com
Website: www.uvdi.com
Mfr & dist ultraviolet sanitation devices that purify surfaces, air and water. UV-C Disinfection. (Hisp, estab , empl , sales $ 0, cert: State, NMSDC)

3380 Veridian Environmental, Inc.
425 Merchant St, Ste 101
Vacaville, CA 95688
Contact: Charlotte R. Symms President
Tel: 707-449-4400
Email: csymms@veridianenv.com
Website: www.veridianenv.com
Quality assurance environmental chemistry consulting: human health & ecological risk assessment, lab audits & data validation, environmental data mgmt, QA/QC programs & documents, litigation. (Woman, estab 2001, empl 5, sales $210,000, cert: State, CPUC)

3381 West Coast Environmental Solutions
2650 Lime Ave
Signal Hill, CA 90755
Contact: Beatriz Esparza Business Devel Mgr
Tel: 562-448-9510
Email: beaesparza@westcoastes.com
Website: www.westcoastes.com
24-hour hazardous & non-hazardous emergency response spill cleanup; pipeline, facility, marine, rail, highway, container spills, river, stream, harbor, shoreline, drug lab, containment & protective booming, product skimming/ recovery & storage. (Woman, estab 2010, empl 35, sales $5,768,900, cert: CPUC)

3382 Wildscape Restoration, Inc.
2500 Channel Dr Ste A-1
Ventura, CA 93003
Contact: Noreen Cabanting Principal
Tel: 805-644-6852
Email: noreen@wildscaperestoration.com
Website: www.wildscaperestoration.com
Environmental consulting & contracting: habitat restoration, non-native invasive species removal, biological surveys & monitoring, permitting & environmental planning. (Minority, Woman, estab 2006, empl 8, sales $415,369, cert: State)

3383 Zero Waste Solutions Inc.
PO Box 1485
Newark, CA 94560
Contact: Shavila Singh CEO
Tel: 510-461-1433
Email: marketing@zerowastesolutions.com
Website: www.zerowastesolutions.com
Recycling services, waste management, janitorial services, waste reduction programs, construction recycling, construction debris, trash, hauling services. (Minority, Woman, estab 2002, empl 110, sales $17,500,000, cert: WBENC)

Colorado

3384 Colorado's Advanced Restoration Experts, LLC
PO Box 1592
Lyons, CO 80540
Contact: Theodore Pangilinan President
Tel: 303-588-6796
Email: theo@restorationwithcare.com
Website: www.restorationwithcare.com
Water damage mitigation, mold remediation, carpet cleaning, fire & smoke restoration, odor control & upholstery cleaning. (As-Pac, estab 2015, empl 12, sales $350,000, cert: State)

3385 Diamond T Services Inc.
112 N Rubey Dr Ste 101
Golden, CO 80403
Contact: Vanessa Ingalls CEO
Tel: 303-459-5499
Email: vanessa.ingalls@dtservices.com
Website: www.diamondtservices.com
Soil stabilization & welding solutions, access & environmental matting, primary & secondary containment, surface rentals, certified welding services for pipeline & well sites, fabrication, roustabout, heavy equipment, trucking & environmental services. (Woman, estab 2009, empl 30, sales $7,434,245, cert: WBENC)

3386 Impact Mitigation Consultants LLC.
9851 Castleridge Cir
Highlands Ranch, CO 80129
Contact: James Balman Owner
Tel: 720-285-9918
Email: james@imcnow.com
Website: www.imcnow.com
Environmental testing. Air quality, asbestos, mold, lead. Mitigation consulting Construction services not exceeding 2MMPlastic mold injection & design, IT development. (Nat Ame, estab 2016, empl 5, sales , cert: State)

3387 Property Doctors Inc.
14700 W 66th Place Unit 7
Arvada, CO 80004
Contact: Nancy Rees President
Tel: 888-456-0911
Email: information@property-drs.com
Website: www.property-drs.com
Asbestos abatement & removal, asbestos testing, asbestos consulting, carpet cleaning. (Woman, estab 2005, empl 12, sales $17,000,000, cert: City, WBENC)

3388 RDS Environmental, Inc.
11603 Teller St
Broomfield, CO 80020
Contact: Tammy Linton President
Tel: 303-444-5253
Email: tammy@rdsenvironmental.com
Website: www.rdsenvironmental.com
Environmental consulting, asbestos testing, mold testing, mold remediation/removal, radon testing, radon mitigation installation. (Woman, estab 1978, empl 6, sales $1,032,000, cert: WBENC)

3389 RMC Consultants, Inc.
12345 W Alameda Pkwy Ste 205
Lakewood, CO 80228
Contact: Richard Valdez President
Tel: 303-980-4101
Email: rvaldez@rmc-consultants.com
Website: www.rmc-consultants.net
Environmental consulting: science & engineering, project mgmt, planning & documentation, compliance, mine reclamation, heavy equipment operation, waste mgmt, remediation services. (Hisp, estab 1990, empl 56, sales $3,980,000, cert: State, City)

3390 TerraNext
155 S Madison, Ste 311
Denver, CO 80209
Contact: Martin President
Tel: 303-399-6145
Email: kmartin@terranext.net
Website: www.terranext.net
Environmental consulting & engineering: regulatory & historical reviews & compliance projects, phase I ESAs, NEPA, Section 106 reviews & remedial activity. (Woman, estab 1997, empl 45, sales $5,000,000, cert: WBENC)

Connecticut

3391 Material Management
363 New Britain Rd
Kensington, CT 06037
Contact: Karen Gamer Owner
Tel: 860-829-2000
Email: kg@materialmanagement.us
Website: www.materialmanagement.us
Recycling services: paper, plastics & metal. (Woman, estab 2002, empl 4, sales $16,000,000, cert: WBENC)

District of Columbia

3392 Windjammer Environmental
1001 G St NW Ste 800
Washington, DC 20001
Contact: Damien Hammond President
Tel: 888-270-8387
Email: hammond@wjenviro.com
Website: www.wjenviro.com
Indoor air Quality Surveys, Mold & Moisture Investigation, General Air & Waterborne Contaminate Sampling, Asbestos & Lead Mgmt Services, Environmental Health & Occupational Safety Services. (AA, estab 2012, empl 5, sales $350,000, cert: State, City, 8(a))

Delaware

3393 BrightFields, Inc.
801 Industrial St
Wilmington, DE 19801
Contact: Donald Short CFO
Tel: 302-656-9600
Email: dshort@brightfieldsinc.com
Website: www.brightfieldsinc.com
Environmental consulting svcs: phase I & II investigations, multi-media sampling, above & underground storage tanks, soil & groundwater remediation, brownfield redevelopment, asbestos & lead svcs. (Woman, estab 2003, empl 45, sales $5,907,000, cert: WBENC)

Florida

3394 Advantage Environmental Services, Inc.
2325 5th Ave N
St. Petersburg, FL 33713
Contact: Project Dir
Tel: 727-323-1902
Email:
Website: www.aesenv.com
Remediation, waste management & construction services. (Woman/AA, estab 1994, empl 3, sales $1,351,000, cert: State, City)

3395 Advisory Environmental Technologies, Inc.
4240 William Dr
Gulf Breeze, FL 32563
Contact: Gary Butler Business Development Mgr
Tel: 850-356-2365
Email: gbutler@aet-environmental.com
Website: www.aet-environmental.com
Environmental Remediation Services, Indoor Air Quality Remediation, Asbestos Abatement, Lead Abatement, Laboratory Services, Environmental & Safety Training Services. (Woman/Hisp, estab 2007, empl 4, sales $2,169,158, cert: 8(a))

3396 AirQuest Environmental, Inc.
6851 SW 45th St
Fort Lauderdale, FL 33314
Contact: Boyle President
Tel: 954-792-4549
Email: traci@airquestinc.com
Website: www.airquestinc.com
Environmental consulting: due diligence investigations, Phase I & II site assessments, mold & asbestos surveys, abatement mgmt, indoor air quality surveys, soil & groundwater assessment & remediation, etc. (Woman, estab 2002, empl 28, sales $6,575,064, cert: State, WBENC)

3397 Ambient Technologies, Inc.
4610 Central Ave
St. Petersburg, FL 33711
Contact: Carlos Lemos President
Tel: 727-328-0268
Email: ambtec@aol.com
Website: www.ambienttech.com
Environmental & geotechnical drilling, geophysics & utility designating services. (Hisp, estab 1992, empl 30, sales $3,000,000, cert: State, NMSDC)

3398 Clark Environmental, Inc.
      755 Prairie Industrial Pkwy
      Mulberry, FL 33860
      Contact: Beth Clark President
      Tel: 863-425-4884
      Email: bclark@clarkenvironmental.com
      Website: www.ThermalTreatment.com
Thermal treatment facility: dispose petroleum contaminated soil, waste processing, hazardous & non-hazardous waste disposal & transportation services. (Woman, estab 1991, empl 23, sales $ 0, cert: State)

3399 J. J. Sosa & Associates, Inc.
      6911 Pistol Range Rd, Ste 101A
      Tampa, FL 33635
      Contact: Josh Taxon President
      Tel: 813-888-6525
      Email: jjsosa@jjsosa.com
      Website: www.jjsosa.com
General contracting, industrial hygiene, asbestos abatement, environmental remediation. (Hisp, estab 1992, empl 45, sales , cert: State)

3400 Meryman Environmental, Inc.
      10408 Bloomingdale Ave
      Riverview, FL 33578
      Contact: Charles CEO
      Tel: 813-626-9551
      Email: meryman@merymanenvironmental.com
      Website: www.merymanenvironmental.com
Environmental consulting services: scientists, geologists, ecologists, forestry experts, & laboratory scientists. (Nat Ame, estab 1974, empl 9, sales $928,261, cert: State)

3401 OHC Environmental Engineering
      101 S. Hoover Blvd Unit 101
      Tampa, FL 33609
      Contact: James Rizk President
      Tel: 813-376-2005
      Email: ohcadmin@ohcnet.com
      Website: www.ohcnet.com
Environmental consulting: asbestos & lead surveys, indoor air quality investigations, phase I & II assessments, subsurface investigations, asbestos, lead & mold remediation & hazardous material management. (AA, estab 1983, empl 15, sales $2,000,000, cert: State)

3402 Pinnacle Environmental Management Support, Inc.
      2001 W Sample Rd, Ste 101
      Pompano Beach, FL 33064
      Contact: Cynthia Williams CEO
      Tel: -   -
      Email: nhaddy@pinnacleems.com
      Website: www.pinnacleems.com
Environmental claims management and cost-control services for petroleum-impacted sites. (Woman, estab 1995, empl 65, sales , cert: WBENC)

3403 Progressive Engineering & Construction, Inc.
      12402 N. 56th St
      Tampa, FL 33617
      Contact: Jill Doyle Office Admin
      Tel: 813-930-0669
      Email: jdoyle@progressiveec.com
      Website: www.progressiveec.com
Environmental engineering, construction management services, environmental feasibility/technology evaluations, remedial/closure strategy development, remedy construction & enhancement. (Woman, estab 1999, empl 9, sales $2,811,000, cert: WBENC)

3404 Pure Air Control Services, Inc.
      4911 Creekside Dr, Ste C
      Clearwater, FL 33760
      Contact: Alan Wozniak President
      Tel: 800-422-7873
      Email: awozniak@pureaircontrols.com
      Website: www.pureaircontrols.com
Indoor environmental svcs: IEQ training, building & home diagnostics, mold identification, industrial hygiene svcs, forensic IEQ testimony, IAQ-screen test kits, HVAC cleaning. (Hisp, estab 1982, empl 35, sales $2,500,000, cert: State, NMSDC)

3405 Spaulding Decon, LLC
      9420 Lazy Lane, E-9
      Tampa, FL 33614
      Contact: Laura Spaulding Owner
      Tel: 813-298-7122
      Email: spaulding911@yahoo.com
      Website: www.spauldingdecon.com
Bio-hazard clean up services. (Woman, estab 2005, empl 7, sales $1,500,000, cert: City, WBENC)

3406 Stone Environmental Services
      6151 Lake Osprey Dr
      Sarasota, FL 33946
      Contact: Anna Milantoni Owner
      Tel: 941-628-5693
      Email: amilantoni@stoneenvironmentalservices.com
      Website: www.stoneenvironmentalservices.com
Dist metal/plastic cleaning chemistry, refrigerants, disposal of non-hazardous & hazardous waste disposal, cleaning equipment. (Woman, estab 2001, empl 1, sales $446,000, cert: WBENC)

3407 Urban E Consulting, Inc.
      5630 E Powhatan Ave
      Tampa, FL 33610
      Contact: Dellinda Rabinowitz President
      Tel: 813-512-6998
      Email: dell@urbanerecycling.com
      Website: www.urbanerecycling.com
Provide, pick up, data destruction, recycling, and certification. (Woman, estab 2012, empl 24, sales $2,556,300, cert: WBENC)

Georgia

3408 Accura Analytical Laboratory, Inc.
      6017 Financial Dr
      Norcross, GA 30071
      Contact: Besa Trenova Business Dev
      Tel: 770-449-8800
      Email: besa@accura.com
      Website: www.accura.com
Environmental analytical lab svcs; inorganic, organic, geotechnical & radiochemical testing. (As-Ind, estab 1988, empl 35, sales $ 0, cert: State, City)

3409 Basha Services, LLC
      2336 Wisteria Dr Ste 510
      Snellville, GA 30078
      Contact: Neville Anderson President
      Tel: 678-344-1161
      Email: nanderson@bashaservices.com
      Website: www.bashaservices.com/
Environmental services: remediation, emergency & spill response, soil remediation, excavation & restoration, groundwater remediation, UST/AST closure, cleaning, inspection & installation. (AA, estab 2007, empl 11, sales , cert: State, NMSDC)

3410 Cape Environmental Management Inc.
500 Pinnacle Court, Ste 100
Norcross, GA 30071
Contact: Michael Healy Business Devel Mgr
Tel: 610-470-1189
Email: mhealy@cape-inc.com
Website: www.cape-inc.com
Environ remediation & consulting: base closures, USTS, ASTS, assessments, lead based paint, radon, asbestos, hazardous wastes, soil & groundwater. (Hisp, estab 1985, empl 455, sales $128,148,143, cert: NMSDC)

3411 Corporate Environmental Risk Management
1990 Lakeside Pkwy Ste 300
Tucker, GA 30084
Contact: Al Edwards Managing Dir
Tel: 678-999-0173
Email: certification@cerm.com
Website: www.cerm.com
Environmental mgmt & remediation, civil engineering & site dev, water resources mgmt, program & construction mgmt. (AA, estab 1995, empl 112, sales $2,960,000, cert: State)

3412 Environmental International Corporation
161 Kimball Bridge Rd Ste 100
Alpharetta, GA 30009
Contact: Phil Perley Tech Svcs Mgr
Tel: 770-772-7100
Email: pperley@eicusa.com
Website: www.eicusa.com
Environ compliance, site assessment, remedial investigation, feasibility study, soil & ground remediation, risk & hazard evaluation, litigation support, hazardous waste mgmt, etc. (Minority, Woman, estab 1994, empl 15, sales $1,000,000, cert: WBENC)

3413 Kemron Environmental Services, Inc.
1359-A Ellsworth Industrial Blvd
Atlanta, GA 30318
Contact: John Dwyer Exec VP
Tel: 404-636-0928
Email: mbe@kemron.com
Website: www.kemron.com
Environ svcs: site remediation, environ assessment, investigation & engineering, analytical svcs, geotechnical testing, treatability studies & technology evaluation. (Hisp, estab 1975, empl 165, sales $47,127,478, cert: NMSDC)

Illinois

3414 A3 Environmental, LLC.
3030 Warrenville Rd, Ste 418
Lisle, IL 60532
Contact: Tim Allen Business Devel
Tel: 630-507-9002
Email: Tim@A3E.com
Website: www.A3E.com
Environmental Due Diligence, Phase I & II Environmental, Record Search w/ Risk Assessment (RSRA), Transaction Screen Assessments (TSA), Preliminary Environmental Site Assessments. (Woman, estab 2015, empl 18, sales $2,600,000, cert: WBENC)

3415 All Service Contracting Corp.
2024 E Damon Ave
Decatur, IL 62526
Contact: CEO
Tel: 217-233-3018
Email: info@allservice.com
Website: www.allservice.com
Dist, remove & install filter media, water & waste water plants, industial & municipal. (Woman, estab 1996, empl 12, sales , cert: WBENC)

3416 Anderson & Egan, Co.
124 N Water St Ste 206
Rockford, IL 61107
Contact: Jennifer Anderson President
Tel: 815-962-9000
Email: janderson@andersonenveng.com
Website: www.andersonenveng.com
Air monitoring, asbestos abatements, environmental consulting & engineering, permitting assistance, underground storage tank removals, environmental site assessments. (Woman, estab 2003, empl 5, sales $469,000, cert: State, City)

3417 Endure, Inc.
360 Beinoris Dr
Wood Dale, IL 60191
Contact: Angelia Hopson Enviro Safety/Training
Tel: 630-616-9700
Email: ahopson@endure-inc.com
Website: www.endureinc.com
Safety, health & environmental consulting, training for regulatory compliance to OSHA, EPA & DOT requirements. (Woman/AA, estab 2010, empl 17, sales $1,845,500, cert: City, NMSDC)

3418 NES Incorporated
19015 Jodi Rd Unit B
Mokena, IL 60448
Contact: Kyla Lawson Secretary
Tel: 708-478-5497
Email: klawson@nesincorp.com
Website: www.nesincorp.com
Asbestos abatement, operations & maintenance, inspections & sampling, lead removal, mitigation, sampling & testing, mold remediation, inspections & sampling, hazardous materials clean-up & infrared investigations. (Hisp, estab 2000, empl 10, sales $1,800,000, cert: State, NMSDC)

Indiana

3419 Gurman Container & Supply Co.
800 N 3rd St
Terre Haute, IN 47807
Contact: Michael Roberts Sales Mgr
Tel: 800-448-7626
Email: mike@gurmancontainer.com
Website: www.gurmancontainer.com
Removal of used or damaged drums for reconditioning or disposal. (Woman, estab 1922, empl 13, sales $1,654,920, cert: State, WBENC)

3420 Hoosier Equipment Service, Inc.
8149 Network Dr
Plainfield, IN 46168
Contact: Anne DaVega VP Business Dev
Tel: 317-838-8988
Email: adavega@hoosierequipment.com
Website: www.hoosierequipment.com
Environmental services, underground & aboveground storage tank work (removals, installs, repairs), oil/water separator cleanouts, & environmental remediation work, excavate contaminated soil. (Woman, estab 1978, empl 13, sales $3,169,000, cert: WBENC)

3421 Keramida Environmental, Inc.
401 N College Ave
Indianapolis, IN 46202
Contact: Tim Higgins VP
Tel: 317-414-9862
Email: thiggins@keramida.com
Website: www.keramida.com
Environmental, health & safety engineering & consulting, remediation, site assessments, permitting. (Woman, estab 1988, empl 123, sales $21,043,881, cert: WBENC)

Kansas

3422 EMR, Inc.
2110 Delaware, Ste B
Lawrence, KS 66046
Contact: Connie Cook VP Mktg & Busines Devel
Tel: 785-842-9013
Email: ccook@emr-inc.com
Website: www.emr-inc.com
Environmental consulting: compliance, industrial hygiene, mold, asbestos, lead paint, UST/AST investigation, hazardous waste mgmt, recycling, soil & groundwater remediation. (Minority, Woman, estab 1988, empl 250, sales $44,000,000, cert: WBENC)

Kentucky

3423 Evergreen Environmental
7416 Hwy 329
Crestwood, KY 40014
Contact: Hollis Flora Project Mgr
Tel: 502-241-4171
Email: hflora@evgusa.com
Website: www.evgusa.com
Compliance plan dev, environmental process & RCRA audits, property audits, UST mgmt, hazard risk analysis, OSHA training & consulting, soil & groundwater remediation, permitting & closure plans, industrial cleaning, hazardous & waste mgmt, etc. (Woman, estab 1986, empl 26, sales $4,300,000, cert: WBENC)

3424 Specific Waste Industries
3600 Chamberlain Lane, Ste 104
Louisville, KY 40241
Contact: Victor Anderson President
Tel: 502-425-2770
Email: vanderson@a-solutionsinc.com
Website: www.specificwaste.com
Regulated Medical Waste Removal & Treatment, Pharmaceutical Waste (Haz and Non-Haz), Sharps Waste (Reusable Sharps Program). (AA, estab , empl , sales $500,000, cert: NMSDC)

Louisiana

3425 Quaternary Resource Investigations, LLC
13588 Florida Blvd
Baton Rouge, LA 70819
Contact: Mary Ruiz VP Sales
Tel: 225-292-1400
Email: info@qri.com
Website: www.qri.com
Litigation & strategy support; environmental sampling & lab data mgmt; groundwater geophysical svcs; remediation implementation; regulatory compliance; coastal & wetlands svcs. (Woman, estab 1986, empl 18, sales $31,000,000, cert: WBENC)

Massachusetts

3426 Capaccio Environmental Engineering Inc.
293 Boston Post Road West
Marlborough, MA 01752
Contact: Lisa Wilk President
Tel: 508-970-0033
Email: lwilk@capaccio.com
Website: www.capaccio.com
Environmental engineering & consulting services, compliance & permitting, occupational safety & health, environmental, health & safety mgmt systems. (Woman, estab , empl , sales $3,139,945, cert: State, WBENC)

3427 Corporate Environmental Advisors, Inc.
127 Hartwell St
West Boylston, MA 01583
Contact: Scott Soucy Health, Safety & Compliance
Tel: 800-358-7960
Email: contactus@cea-inc.com
Website: www.cea-inc.com/
Environmental engineering, consulting & contracting firm. (Woman, estab 1985, empl 20, sales $3,878,000, cert: State)

3428 CR Environmental Inc
639 Boxberry Hill Road
East Falmouth, MA 02536
Contact: Charlotte Cogswell President
Tel: 508-563-7970
Email: charlotte@crenvironmental.com
Website: www.crenvironmental.com
Ecological risk assessments & characterizations of terrestrial, wetland & aquatic habitats. (Woman, estab 1994, empl 7, sales $1,314,475, cert: State, City)

3429 Essex Newbury North Contracting Corporation
65 Parker St, Unit 5
Newburyport, MA 01950
Contact: Delano Brooks President
Tel: 978-463-5414
Email: delano_br@yahoo.com
Website: www.essexnewburynorth.com
General Contracting, construction management, commercial & industrial construction, lead abatement & asbestos remediation, commercial & institutional bldg construction. (AA, estab 1997, empl 400, sales $31,000,000, cert: State, City, NMSDC)

3430 Strategic Environmental
362 Putnam Hill Rd
Sutton, MA 01590
Contact: Ross Hartman Exec VP
Tel: 508-757-7782
Email: info@strategic-es.com
Website: www.strategic-es.com
Transportation & disposal management svcs: environmental testing & on-site field svcs, site clean-up & remediation, groundwater mgmt. (Woman, estab 2001, empl 48, sales $26,000,000, cert: WBENC)

Maryland

3431 ALL-SHRED, Inc.
4831 Winchester Blvd
Frederick, MD 21703
Contact: Emily Shaw Sr Acct Rep
Tel: 301-874-1480
Email: emilyshaw@allshredmd.com
Website: www.allshredmd.com
On-Site confidential document shredding. (Woman/Nat-Ame, estab 1999, empl 20, sales $380,000, cert: State)

3432 Environmental Health and Safety Solutions, LLC
13 Pheasant View Place
Parkton, MD 21120
Contact: Frank Damato Dir of Safety/Training
Tel: 904-556-6422
Email: fdamato@ehssgroup.com
Website: www.EHSSGroup.com
Environmental services, industrial hygiene monitoring services, air & noise monitoring surveys. (Woman, estab 2011, empl 5, sales $760,000, cert: State)

3433 Environmental, Engineering & Construction, Inc.
3303 Hubbard Rd
Landover, MD 20785
Contact: Norma Campos Business Development Mgr
Tel: 301-341-1000
Email: norma@eecinc.com
Website: www.eecinc.com
Asbestos abatement, Lead abatement, Mold remediation, demolition, painting, contaminated soil, and construction services (AA, estab 1993, empl 50, sales $760,001, cert: 8(a))

3434 SodexoMagic (Magic Food Provision, LLC)
9801 Washingtonian Blvd
Gaithersburg, MD 20878
Contact: Ken Holdman Dir Strategic Sales
Tel: 918-430-6514
Email: ken.holdman@sodexomagic.com
Website: www.sodexomagic.com
Food & catering services groundkeeping facilities and plant operations and maintenance, environmental & engineering services & laundry & linens. (AA, estab 2006, empl 4900, sales $283,400,000, cert: NMSDC)

3435 Turtle Wings Inc.
1771 Olive St
Capitol Heights, MD 20743
Contact: Elizabeth Wilmot President
Tel: 301-583-8399
Email: info@datakillers.com
Website: www.datakillers.com
Environmental services. (Woman, estab 2005, empl 13, sales $1,200,000, cert: State, WBENC)

Michigan

3436 Advanced Environmental Management Group, LLC
44339 Plymouth Oaks Blvd
Plymouth, MI 48170
Contact: Linda Leonard Office Admin
Tel: 734-354-9070
Email: admin@aemgroup.biz
Website: www.aemgroup.biz
Environmental permitting, compliance assessments, dispersion modeling, stack & ambient air testing, due diligence & remediation svcs, ISO 14001 EMS svcs, facility closure & decommissioning services, spill & contingency plans. (As-Ind, estab 1998, empl 11, sales, cert: NMSDC)

3437 A-Global Solution, LLC dba Environmental Services of North America, Inc.
10455 Ford Rd
Dearborn, MI 48126
Contact: Joe Coelho Owner
Tel: 313-945-7400
Email: jcoelho@esnainc.com
Website: www.esnainc.com
Facility svcs: waste disposal & recycling, snow removal, parking lot sweeping, power washing, janitorial services & supplies, landscaping, onsite & offsite document shredding, asbestos, lead based paint & mold, waste containers. (AA, estab , empl , sales, cert: NMSDC)

3438 Cadena, LLC.
1099 Highland Dr, Ste A
Ann Arbor, MI 48108
Contact: Armando Ojeda CEO
Tel: 734-418-1977
Email: aojeda@cadenaco.com
Website: www.cadenaco.com
Environmental services, lab data, Level II & Level IV validations, environmental laboratory audits, archiving environmental data. (Hisp, estab 2013, empl 2, sales $384,654, cert: NMSDC, CPUC)

3439 EKS Services Incorporated
7451 Third St
Detroit, MI 48202
Contact: Clarence E. Carpenter III CEO
Tel: 313-963-1433
Email: clarencecarpenter@eksservices.com
Website: www.eksservices.com
Environmental consulting & construction mgmt. (AA, estab 2000, empl 20, sales $1,500,000, cert: NMSDC)

3440 Environmental Compliance Office Inc.
3011 W Grand Blvd, Ste 420
Detroit, MI 48202
Contact: Vimala Anishetty, Ph.D. President
Tel: 313-285-8401
Email: vanishet@ecomain.com
Website: www.ecomain.com
Environmental engineering & consulting svcs: air, water, waste, auditing, reporting & training. (Minority, Woman, estab 2007, empl 4, sales $310,000, cert: WBENC)

3441 Environmental Testing and Consulting Inc.
38900 W Huron River Dr
Romulus, MI 48174
Contact: Patricia Stephen Business Devel Mgr
Tel: 734-955-6600
Email: sales@2etc.com
Website: www.2etc.com
Environmental consulting firm, asbestos, lead based paint, mold surveys, risk assessments, clearances, O&M plans, project management and training, indoor air quality assessments. (Woman, estab 1989, empl 75, sales $3,270,519, cert: WBENC)

3442 Infiniti Group International, LLC
241 Keelson Dr
Detroit, MI 48215
Contact: Melvin Gilmer Member
Tel: 586-995-5331
Email: mg@infinitigroup.us
Website: www.infinitigroupinternational.org
Environmental Products and Services. (AA, estab 2014, empl 2, sales , cert: NMSDC)

3443 Integrated Recycling Industries
PO Box 581
Wyandotte, MI 48192
Contact: Richard Pacheco President
Tel: 734-818-9835
Email: rpacheco.iri@gmail.com
Website: www.integratedrecyclingindustries.com
Recycle Ferrous and Non-Ferrous scrap metals, Cardboard and Plastics. (Hisp, estab 2015, empl 2, sales $100,000, cert: NMSDC)

3444 Merit Laboratories, Inc.
       2680 E Lansing Dr
       East Lansing, MI 48823
       Contact: Maya Murshak President
       Tel: 517-332-0167
       Email: mayamurshak@meritlabs.com
       Website: www.meritlabs.com
Environmental testing laboratory, RCRA remediation analytical, testing for soil, water & waste. We work with large and small industries, engineering firms, municipalities (Woman, estab 1987, empl , sales $ 0, cert: WBENC)

3445 MPS Group, Inc.
       38755 Hills Tech Dr
       Farmington Hills, MI 48331
       Contact: Bryon Lawrence Dir Sales/Marketing
       Tel: 313-841-7588
       Email: blawrence@mpsgrp.com
       Website: www.mpsgrp.com
Environmental Consulting & Engineering. (AA, estab 1995, empl 495, sales $46,200,000, cert: NMSDC)

3446 RTI Laboratories, Inc.
       33080 Industrial Rd
       Livonia, MI 48150
       Contact: Kae Trojanowski President
       Tel: 734-422-8000
       Email: ktrojanowski@rtilab.com
       Website: www.rtilab.com
Analytical testing laboratory: environmental, chemical & metallurgical testing, environmental compliance field sampling services. (Minority, estab 1986, empl 40, sales $5,000,000, cert: NMSDC, SDB)

3447 Unlimited Recycling, Inc.
       PO Box 363
       Richmond, MI 48062
       Contact: Maria Marin-McInturf President
       Tel: 586-784-4980
       Email: maria@unlimitedrecyclinginc.com
       Website: www.unlimitedrecyclinginc.com
Recycling svcs: spent electric lamps, batteries, electronic equip, mercury containing devices, hazardous & non-hazardous waste, oil, solvents, antifreeze. (Woman/Hisp, estab 1999, empl 7, sales , cert: NMSDC, WBENC)

3448 VMX International, LLC
       3011 W Grand Blvd Ste 2401
       Detroit, MI 48202
       Contact: Vickie Lewis CEO
       Tel: 313-875-9450
       Email: vlewis@vmxi.com
       Website: www.vmxi.com
International waste management & recycling services. (Woman/AA, estab 2001, empl 54, sales $3,140,800, cert: NMSDC, WBENC)

Minnesota

3449 EnviroBate, Inc.
       3301 E 26th Sttreet
       Minneapolis, MN 55406
       Contact: Dana Krakowski VP Sales & Marketing
       Tel: 612-437-5797
       Email: dkrakowski@envirobate.com
       Website: www.envirobate.com
Environmental remediation, asbestos & lead abatement, mold remediation & Indoor Air Quality (Duct Cleaning), hazardous waste disposal to include mercury, lead & PCB's. (Woman, estab 1991, empl 80, sales $14,000,000, cert: City, WBENC)

Missouri

3450 Ahrens Contracting, Inc.
       140 Lafayette Ave
       St. Louis, MO 63104
       Contact: Patricia Ahrens President
       Tel: 314-631-7799
       Email: pahrens@ahrenscontracting.com
       Website: www.ahrenscontracting.com
Hauling Dirt, Rubbish, Trash, Special Waste, Hazardous Waste, Clean Fill, etc. (Woman, estab , empl , sales $ 0, cert: WBENC)

3451 Cardinal Environmental Operations Corp.
       4518 Woodson Rd
       Saint Louis, MO 63134
       Contact: Paula Milligan President
       Tel: 314-890-2088
       Email: pmilligan@callcardinal.com
       Website: www.callcardinal.com
Asbestos abatement, lead abatement, environmental remediation, mold remediation, soil/water remediation, UST/AST removal & installation, duct cleaning services, consulting services, site assessments, demolition. (Woman, estab 1993, empl 25, sales $2,000,000, cert: State, City)

3452 CCI Environmental, Inc.
       6913 Noble Dr
       Hazelwood, MO 63024
       Contact: Mark Briguglio President
       Tel: 314-974-3893
       Email: marksbriguglio@gmail.com
       Website: www.ccienv.info
Asbestos abatement, inspections, testing, project management & estimating to air monitoring & project consulting. (Nat Ame, estab 1994, empl 7, sales $930,000, cert: State)

3453 Global Environmental, Inc.
       6439 Plymouth Ave Ste 119
       Wellston, MO 63133
       Contact: Vicki Dunn President/Owner
       Tel: 314-875-9501
       Email: vdunnglobal@ymail.com
       Website: www.globalabatement.com
Environmental remediation & consulting. (Woman/Nat-Ame, estab 1991, empl 10, sales $2,320,175, cert: State, 8(a))

3454 Haz-Waste, Inc.
       12951 Gravois Rd Ste 110
       St. Louis, MO 63127
       Contact: Kimberly Medlock VP
       Tel: 800-429-9783
       Email: kmedlock@haz-waste.com
       Website: www.haz-waste.com
Air pollution permitting, asbestos, abatement, byproduct mgmt, environmental audits, field service, industrial compliance, OSHA compliance, Phase I & II site work, plant closures, pollution prevention. (Woman, estab 1993, empl 34, sales $6,200,000, cert: WBENC)

3455 The Kiesel Company
4801 Fyler Ave
St. Louis, MO 63166
Contact: Larry Gooden VP
Tel: 314-351-5500
Email: larry.gooden@kieselco.com
Website: www.thekieselcompany.com
Dist fuels & lubricants, emergency response services to chemical & petroleum product releases, railroad tank car cleaning, barge cleaning, non-hazardous & hazardous waste disposal, demolition & petroleum-contaminated waste water treatment & disposal. (Woman, estab , empl 48, sales $75,010,000, cert: City)

Mississippi

3456 Advanced Environmental Consultants, Inc.
5430 Executive Place, Ste 2A
Jackson, MS 39206
Contact: DeJonnette Grantham-King CEO
Tel: 601-362-1788
Email: dgking@advancedenviroconsultants.com
Website: www.advancedenviroconsultants.com
Asbestos inspections, abatement & disposal, lead inspections, abatement & disposal, mold inspections, air monitoring, phase I site assessments. (Woman/AA, estab 1996, empl 10, sales $410,000, cert: WBENC)

North Carolina

3457 All Green Recycling Inc.
321 Atando Ave.
Charlotte, NC 28206
Contact: Carol Jegou CEO
Tel: 704-375-9676
Email: cjegou@all-green.com
Website: www.all-green.com
Environmental services. (Woman, estab 2012, empl 14, sales $500,000, cert: State)

3458 Environmental Process Solutions, PLLC
7000 Stinson Hartis Rd Ste F
Indian Trail, NC 28079
Contact: CEO
Tel: 980-202-2377
Email: info@epscharlotte.com
Website: www.EPSCharlotte.com
Environmental Consulting, Industrial wastewater treatment, engineering services. (Woman, estab 2010, empl 5, sales , cert: WBENC)

3459 Environmental Service Systems, LLC
5550 77 Center Dr. Ste 160
Charlotte, NC 28217
Contact: Ciara Lilly VP Diversity & Inclusion
Tel: 704-527-4099
Email: clilly@environmentalss.com
Website: www.environmentalss.com
Facility maintenance & janitorial services. (AA, estab 1998, empl 2500, sales $79,106,894, cert: NMSDC)

3460 FireWater CleanUp Crew Corp.
PO Box 78145
Greensboro, NC 27427
Contact: Jamal Mention President
Tel: 336-666-1913
Email: jamalmention@firewatercleanupcrew.com
Website: www.firewatercleanupcrew.com
Remediation/restoration services for smoke, fire & water damage. Trauma scene cleanup. (AA, estab 2016, empl 3, sales , cert: State)

3461 Porter Scientific Inc.
PO Box 1359
Pembroke, NC 28372
Contact: Freda Porter President
Tel: 910-521-0549
Email: fporter@porterscientific.com
Website: www.porterscientific.com
Environmental consulting services, assessments, remediation & cleanup, pollution prevention, regulatory compliance, water, sewer & solid waste project management. (Minority, Woman, estab 1997, empl 18, sales $3,458,000, cert: City)

3462 Reliable Solutions Construction, LLC dba Reliable Restorations
12220 Nations Ford Rd Ste A
Pineville, NC 28134
Contact: Johanna Suarez Operations Mgr
Tel: 704-909-7616
Email: johanna@reliablerestorations.net
Website: www.reliablerestorations.net
Disaster emergency response services, board ups, water extraction, fire & water damage restoration, odor & mold remediation, contents clean up & pack-outs, Non-Destructive Mold Remediation, Smoke & odor deodorization, Removal. (Minority, Woman, estab 2009, empl 15, sales $1,426,000, cert: State)

New Hampshire

3463 Absolute Resource Associates, LLC
124 Heritage Ave Unit 16
Portsmouth, NH 03801
Contact: Susan Sylvester President
Tel: 603-436-2001
Email: sues@absoluteresourceassociates.com
Website: www.absoluteresourceassociates.com
Environmental laboratory testing & indoor air quality assessments. (Woman, estab 1994, empl 25, sales $ 0, cert: WBENC)

New Jersey

3464 Advanced Indoor Air Quality Care
3 Kadel Dr
Mount Arlington, NJ 07856
Contact: Bobbi Maureen Monacelli President
Tel: 973-770-9636
Email: bobbim@uscleanblast.com
Website: www.uscleanblast.com
Dry ice blasting for power generation, combustible dust cleaning, mold remediation, fire restoration, Co2 blasting. (Woman, estab 1997, empl 8, sales $600,000, cert: WBENC)

3465 BGI Resources International Corporation
205 Barclay Pavilion W
Cherry Hill, NJ 08034
Contact: Bassey Akpan CEO
Tel: 856-888-2396
Email: info@bgiresourcesintl.com
Website: www.BGIResourcesIntl.com
Air, Water Soil Sampling, Phase I, II, III Projects, GIS Mapping, Preliminary Assessments. (AA, estab 2010, empl 3, sales , cert: State)

3466 Brinkerhoff Environmental Services, Inc.
1805 Atlantic Ave
Manasquan, NJ 08736
Contact: Laura Brinkerhoff CEO
Tel: 732-223-2225
Email: lbrinkerhoff@brinkenv.com
Website: www.brinkenv.com
Environmental services, Engineering, Site assessments, NEPA Evaluation Reports, Planning & Permitting, Wetland svcs, Brownfield Redevelopment, Underground Storage Tank mgmt, Geologic & Hydro-geologic. (Woman, estab 1989, empl 40, sales $7,505,209, cert: State, WBENC)

3467 Cornerstone EHS, LLC
PO Box 1102
Mullica Hill, NJ 08062
Contact: Marianne Payne President
Tel: 856-776-0455
Email: mpayne@cornerstoneehs.com
Website: www.cornerstoneehs.com
Environmental, health, safety consulting & services, EHS program development & management; comprehensive EHS compliance & management system auditing; EHS related training, management systems development & implementation. (Woman, estab 2011, empl 1, sales $332,065, cert: WBENC)

3468 Environmental Industrial Services Corp. of NJ
288 Oak Grove Rd
Swedesboro, NJ 08085
Contact: Robert Feller Business Devel
Tel: 856-467-5001
Email: rfeller@eisco4service.com
Website: www.eisco4action.com
Environmental remediation services, soil remediation, capping, stabilization, UST & AST cleaning & closure, subsurface exploratory/test pits, groundwater remediation, install systems, pump & treat, vapor extraction, vacuum enhanced recovery. (Woman, estab 1990, empl 55, sales $3,211,964, cert: State)

3469 Fortune Metal Group
900 Leesville Ave
Rahway, NJ 07065
Contact: Tina Chen Buyer
Tel: 732-388-0709
Email: tinac@fortunegroup.net
Website: www.fortunemetalrecycling.com
Full-service metal recycling facility. (As-Pac, estab 2006, empl 500, sales , cert: State)

3470 Fortune Metal Inc. of RI
900 Leesville Ave
Rahway, NJ 07065
Contact: Rick Gosselin Natl Sales Dir
Tel: 401-725-9100
Email: rickgosselin@fortunegroup.net
Website: www.fortunegroup.net
Buy & recycle scrap metals & plastics. (As-Pac, estab 1998, empl 128, sales $110,856,318, cert: NMSDC)

3471 Matrix New World Engineering, Land Surveying and Landscape Architectur
26 Columbia Trnpke 2nd Fl
Florham Park, NJ 07932
Contact: Jayne Warne, PE President
Tel: 973-240-1800
Email: jwarne@mnwe.com
Website: www.matrixneworld.com
Environmental, geotechnical, civil engineering, survey & building facility consulting & engineering firm. (Woman, estab 1990, empl 200, sales $28,899,396, cert: State, City, WBENC)

3472 Prestige Environmental, Inc.
220 Davidson Ave Ste 307
Somerset, NJ 08873
Contact: Girish Mehta President
Tel: 908-757-9700
Email: girish.mehta@prestige-environmental.com
Website: www.prestige-environmental.com
Environmental consulting & contracting svcs: site assessments & feasibility studies; removal & installation of petroleum tanks; soil & groundwater investigations; site remediation; design, installation & operation of remediation systems. (As-Ind, estab 1993, empl 6, sales $1,092,700, cert: State)

3473 Sovereign
111 A North Gold Dr
Robbinsville, NJ 08691
Contact: Michael Hanlon Mgr
Tel: 609-259-8200
Email: mhanlon@sovcon.com
Website: www.sovcon.com
Environmental consulting & remediation services, environmental, civil & geotechnical engineering; remediation system evaluation, optimization, design & construction/installation; environmental, land use & natural resources permitting. (As-Pac, estab 1999, empl 165, sales $35,466,433, cert: NMSDC)

Nevada

3474 The Westmark Group
2430 N Decatur Blvd Ste 140
Las Vegas, NV 89108
Contact: Leslie Mujica Dir of BD & gov affairs
Tel: 702-839-2960
Email: marketing@westmarkgroup.net
Website: www.westmarkgroup.net
Consulting & project management, environmental consulting, occupational safety & health services & waste management services. (Hisp, estab 1999, empl 25, sales $5,000,000, cert: State)

New York

3475 Abtron Associates Corp.
60A Corbin Ave
Bay Shore, NY 11706
Contact: Robert Green President
Tel: 631-392-1330
Email: rgreen@abtronassociatescorp.com
Website: www.abtronassociatescorp.com
Environmental hazards/non-hazards services. (AA, estab 1997, empl 30, sales $1,055,000, cert: NMSDC)

3476 American Demolition & Nuclear Decommissioning, Inc
PO Box 553
Grand Island, NY 14072
Contact: Bill Schaab VP
Tel: 866-699-5515
Email: bschaab@americandnd.com
Website: www.AmericanDND.com
Environmental Remediation & Decommissioning of both fossil and nuclear power facilities. Demolition, Wrecking, Razing, Demo, Demolish, D & D, DND, Salvage, Asset Recovery, Investment Recovery. (Minority, estab 2004, empl 50, sales $6,000,000, cert: NMSDC)

3477 American Environmental Assessment & Solutions
679 Lafayette Ave, 3rd Fl
Brooklyn, NY 11216
Contact: Antoinette Ollivierre Principal
Tel: 718-209-0653
Email: aollivierre@aeasinc.com
Website: www.aeasinc.com
Environmental services: Phase I, II and III Environmental Site Assessments (ESA), soil & groundwater investigation, remediation of contaminated sites, NYC E-designation investigation and compliance. (Woman/AA, estab 2006, empl 9, sales , cert: State, City)

3478 Chenango Contracting, Inc.
29 Arbutus Rd
Johnson City, NY 13790
Contact: Carl Burdick Project Mgr
Tel: 607-729-8500
Email: cburdick@chenangocontracting.com
Website: www.chenangocontracting.com
Supply & Install Environmental Geosynthetics. (Nat Ame, estab 1992, empl 45, sales , cert: State)

3479 CSA Central, Inc.
55 Broadway, 14th Fl
New York, NY 10006
Contact: Frederik Riefkohl Sr VP
Tel: 305-461-5484
Email: friefkohl@csagroup.com
Website: www.csagroup.com
Program & project mgmt, environmental services, architecture & engineering, Construction Management, Operation & Maintenance. (Hisp, estab 1995, empl 55, sales $4,963,359, cert: NMSDC)

3480 Environmental Design & Research, DPC
217 Montgomery St Ste 1000
Syracuse, NY 13202
Contact: Joanne Stewart Associate
Tel: 315-471-0688
Email: jstewart@edrdpc.com
Website: www.edrdpc.com
Landscape architecture, civil engineering, community planning, visualization, environmental regulatory, ecological, geographic information systems mapping & analysis, historic preservation, archeology. (Woman, estab 1979, empl 38, sales $4,500,000, cert: State)

3481 Foit-Albert Associates, Architecture, Engineering and Surveying, P.C.
215 W 94th St, Ste 517
New York, NY 10025
Contact: Gregory Carballada President
Tel: 716-856-3933
Email: cstoebe@foit-albert.com
Website: www.foit-albert.com
Architecture, Engineering, Environmental & Land Surveying Consulting. (Hisp, estab 1977, empl 70, sales $10,000,000, cert: State, City)

3482 Gianco Environmental Services Inc.
37 North Grand Boulevard
Brentwood, NY 11717
Contact: Michael Gianchetta VP
Tel: 631-952-9900
Email: michaelg@gianco.com
Website: www.gianco.com
Facilities management, hazard & non-hazard waste removal & recycling. (Woman, estab 2001, empl 4, sales $1,024,193, cert: WBENC)

3483 Innovative Recycling Technologies, Inc.
690 N Queens Ave
Lindenhurst, NY 11757
Contact: John Ewen Sales
Tel: 631-225-3044
Email: jewen@irtwaste.com
Website: www.irtwaste.com
Coordinating & implementing cost-effective, ihazardous & non-hazardous waste, waste classification, labelling, storage, transportation, and disposal solutions. (Woman, estab , empl , sales $ 0, cert: State, City)

3484 International Asbestos Removal, Inc.
68-08 Woodside Ave
Woodside, NY 11377
Contact: Karen Grando President
Tel: 718-335-0304
Email: kgrando@aol.com
Website: www.iaronline.com
Asbestos & lead removal, insulation, heat, cold, sound, firestopping, etc. (Woman, estab 1987, empl 25, sales $ 0, cert: WBENC)

3485 LEADCARE, Inc.
10-25 44th Ave
Long Island City, NY 11101
Contact: Sarah Attias-Dunn President
Tel: 718-706-8383
Email: dunn@leadcare.com
Website: www.leadcare.com
Environmental testing, consultating & remediation project management, asbestos, lead, mold & indoor air quality investigations. (Woman, estab 1992, empl 10, sales $1,100,000, cert: State, City)

3486 Mechanical Testing, Inc.
70 Lake Ave.
Saratoga Springs, NY 12866
Contact: Eileen Venn CEO
Tel: 518-450-7292
Email: eileenv@mechtest.com
Website: www.mechtest.com
Testing, Adjusting & Balancing of HVAC Systems, Indoor Air Quality Testing, Sound Testing, In Room/Space Pressure Relationship Testing, Duct Pressurization, SMACNA. (Woman, estab 1967, empl 27, sales $3,800,000, cert: State, WBENC)

3487 Miller Environmental Group, Inc.
538 Edwards Ave
Calverton, NY 11933
Contact: Carl Fiore VP Business Dev
Tel: 631-369-4900
Email: cfiore@millerenv.com
Website: www.millerenv.com
Environmental and Industrial Services Equipment, Emergency Response and Industrial Cleaning services. (Minority, estab 1971, empl 160, sales $30,000,000, cert: NMSDC)

3488 NPTS, Inc.
2060 Sheridan Dr
Buffalo, NY 14223
Contact: Hormoz Mansouri President
Tel: 716-876-8066
Email: rbroman@eiteam.com
Website: www.npts.net
Engineering consulting: nuclear, fossil, petrochem, risk assessment, thermohydraulic, design, outage mgmt, technical support svcs, etc. (As-Ind, estab 1983, empl 15, sales $1,521,462, cert: NMSDC)

ENVIRONMENTAL SERVICES

3489 Sienna Environmental Technologies, LLC
350 Elmwood Ave
Bufalo, NY 14222
Contact: Susanne Kelley President
Tel: 716-332-3134
Email: skelley@siennaet.com
Website: www.siennaet.com
Asbestos inspections & contamination assessments, lead-based paint inspection & risk assessment, indoor air quality, microbial & radon testing & investigative svcs, air, soil, dust, water & solid waste sampling. (Minority, Woman, estab 2000, empl 17, sales $2,000,000, cert: State, City)

3490 Universal Environmental Consulting, Inc.
900 Merchants Concourse Ste 214
Westbury, NY 11590
Contact: Lisa Giaquinto President
Tel: 800-552-0309
Email:
Website: www.uecny.com
Collection management of solid waste & recyclables. (Woman, estab 1995, empl 20, sales $33,785,084, cert: WBENC)

Ohio

3491 Ace Healthy Products LLC
907 W Fifth St
Dayton, OH 45402
Contact: Anthony Watson CEO
Tel: 866-891-5338
Email: acehealthyproducts11@gmail.com
Website: www.eaglewatchproducts.com/
Mfr unique and patented environmentally friendly products globally. (AA, estab 2015, empl 8, sales , cert: City)

3492 CAP-STONE & Associates, Inc.
748 Green Crest Dr
Westerville, OH 43081
Contact: Mary Sharrett President
Tel: 614-865-1874
Email: marysharrett@stoneenvironmental.com
Website: www.StoneEnvironmental.com
Assessment, Permitting, Design & Compliance, air, water, soil, waste streams, hazardous materials, storm water, natural resources, site civil, utilities, and structures. (Woman, estab 1989, empl , sales $1,400,000, cert: State, City, WBENC)

3493 CTL Engineering, Inc.
2860 Fisher Rd
Columbus, OH 43204
Contact: C.K. Satyapriya President
Tel: 614-276-8123
Email: ctl@ctleng.com
Website: www.ctleng.com
Geotechnical, construction inspection, environmental, mining engineering, analytical chemistry, forensic science, metallurgy, product testing, research & development, roof engineering, existing structure evaluation, asbestos inspection. (Minority, estab 1928, empl 187, sales $ 0, cert: NMSDC)

3494 Environmental and Safety Solutions, Inc.
544 Tohatchi Dr
Cincinnati, OH 45215
Contact: Cindy Tomaszewski President
Tel: 513-383-7703
Email: ctomaszewski@theessinc.com
Website: www.essinc.info
Enviromental, health & safety services. (AA, estab 2002, empl 9, sales $3,034,000, cert: State, NMSDC)

3495 Iron Eagle Enterprises, LLC
4991 Belmont Ave
Youngstown, OH 44505
Contact: M. McKenzie Business Devel
Tel: 330-759-2760
Email: mmckenzie@ironeagleent.com
Website: www.IronEagleEnt.com
Custom frac & storage tank rentals, Vacuum truck service—wet & dry materials, Professional cleaning—disposal wells, drains, holding tanks, frac tanks, Solid waste disposal & hauling—rentals of vac boxes & sealed top boxes. (Woman, estab 2010, empl 14, sales $4,500,000, cert: WBENC)

3496 MCFS Enterprises, Inc.
PO Box 30207
Middleburg Heights, OH 44130
Contact: Carrie Scaravelli Owner
Tel: 440-888-0497
Email: cscaravelli@cox.net
Website: www.rainbowintl.com/cleveland
Water & fire restoration, smoke & odor remediation, mold, lead & asbestos testing & abatement, hazardous waste specialist. (Woman, estab 2007, empl 5, sales $798,000, cert: State, City)

3497 Superior Environmental Corp.
1132 Luschek Dr
Cincinnati, OH 45241
Contact: Michael Weinstein Sr Project Mgr
Tel: 513-923-9000
Email: m.weinstein@superiorenvironmental.com
Website: www.superiorenvironmental.com
Environmental consulting: remedial design & implementation, property transfers. (Woman, estab 1989, empl 83, sales $12,200,000, cert: WBENC)

Oklahoma

3498 Natural Evolution, Inc.
5701 E 13th St
Tulsa, OK 74112
Contact: Chris Phillips CEO
Tel: 919-836-2995
Email: chris.phillips@naturalevolution.com
Website: www.naturalevolution.com
Electronics Recycling, Asset Disposition, Asset Recycling, Computer Recycling, IT asset disposition, Asset Revenue Recovery, Internet Auction Services. (Woman/Nat-Ame, estab 2002, empl 14, sales $982,046, cert: NMSDC)

Oregon

3499 Paul Carlson Associates, Inc.
5775 Jean Rd. Ste 101
Lake Oswego, OR 97035
Contact: Joel McCarthy Industrial Hygienist
Tel: 503-652-6040
Email: joelm@pcasafety.com
Website: www.pcasafety.com
HAZsolutions designed to manage hazardous materials and waste in retail. (Woman, estab 1988, empl 12, sales , cert: State)

Pennsylvania

3500   Environmental Data Validation, Inc.
1326 Orangewood Ave
Pittsburgh, PA 15216
Contact: Maxine Wright-Walters President
Tel: 412-341-5281
Email: mwalters@edv-inc.com
Website: www.edv-inc.com
Chemical & radiochemical data validation, environmental health & safety training, occupational health & safety consulting, industrial hygienist services, building inspections, environmental site assessments, risk assessment, hazard assessment. (Woman/AA, estab 1990, empl 8, sales $350,000, cert: State)

3501   Environmental Equipment + Supply, LLC
491-L Blue Eagle Ave, Ste L
Harrisburg, PA 17112
Contact: Lisa Reeves President
Tel: 717-901-8891
Email: reevesl@envisupply.com
Website: www.envisupply.com
Environmental equipment rental and sales. (Woman, estab 2018, empl 9, sales $1,260,211, cert: WBENC)

3502   Environmental Strategy Consultants, Inc.
1528 Walnut St Ste 1812-1818
Philadelphia, PA 19102
Contact: Lorna Velardi President
Tel: 215-731-4200
Email: lmv@envirostrat.com
Website: www.envirostrat.com
Environmental & safety management: air permitting & outsourcing, waste, emergency planning & safety & health services. (Woman, estab 1986, empl 5, sales $546,532, cert: WBENC)

3503   JD2 Environmental, Inc.
800 E Washington St
West Chester, PA 19380
Contact: Donna Hymes VP
Tel: 610-430-8151
Email: dhymes@jd2env.com
Website: www.jd2env.com
Environmental consulting: storage tank mgmt & remediation, phase I/II environmental site assessments & expert witness services. (Woman/AA, estab 2001, empl 15, sales $ 0, cert: WBENC)

3504   Keating Environmental Management, Inc.
835 Springdale Dr
Exton, PA 19341
Contact: Keith Choper President
Tel: 484-876-2200
Email: kchoper@kempartners.com
Website: www.kempartners.com
Engineering, environmental engineering and consulting, brownfields redevelopment, groundwater studies, subsurface evaluations, geology, remediation management, asbestos, site assessments and environmental auditing. (Woman, estab 1988, empl 13, sales $2,250,000, cert: State, City, WBENC)

3505   Niche Waste Reduction and Recycling Systems, Inc
PO Box 245246
Philadelphia, PA 19119
Contact: Maurice Sampson II CEO
Tel: 267-269-6912
Email: msampson@nicherecycling.com
Website: www.nicherecycling.com
Waste Management & recycling planning & consultation svcs: site survey/waste assessments, Waste Audits, Architectural Design Consultation for Waste Management, In-house container, brochure, poster training & orientation. (AA, estab 1995, empl 1, sales , cert: State)

3506   Novel Geo-Environmental, LLC
171 Montour Run Rd
Moon Township, PA 15108
Contact: Grace Aiken Office Mgr
Tel: 412-722-1970
Email: gaiken@ngeconsulting.com
Website: www.ngeconsulting.com
Environmental & geotechnical engineering consulting, Multi- Media Compliance Auditing, Permitting, Reporting & Plan Development, Environmental Management Systems Design & Implementation. (Woman, estab 2002, empl 34, sales $5,579,823, cert: State)

3507   Polaris Engineering, Inc.
5015 Preakness Pl
Bethlehem, PA 18020
Contact: Fidel Gonzalez President
Tel: 610-698-7185
Email: fidel@polarisengineeringinc.com
Website: www.polarisengineeringinc.com
Civil engineering: feasibility studies, roadways, storm water management facilities, water line design, sanitary sewer design, site layout & site grading. (Hisp, estab 2007, empl 2, sales , cert: State)

3508   SLM Waste & Recycling Services Inc.
80-90 N Main St
Sellersville, PA 18960
Contact: Susan V. Daywitt President
Tel: 888-847-4449
Email: sdaywitt@slmwaste.com
Website: www.slmwaste.com
Waste & recycling svcs: cardboard, plastics, aluminum, monitors & computer recycling. (Woman, estab 1998, empl 37, sales $12,939,507, cert: WBENC)

3509   W. K. Merriman, Inc.
7038 Front River Rd
Pittsburgh, PA 15225
Contact: Mary Ann Merriman CEO
Tel: 412-262-7024
Email: m.merriman@wkmerriman.com
Website: www.wkmerriman.com
Dist commodity chemicals & environmental technology, neutralize wastewater, reduce sluge & cost saving alternatives. (Woman, estab 1986, empl 6, sales $6,377,400, cert: WBENC)

Puerto Rico

3510 Altol Enterprises Management Corp.
PO Box 359
Mercedita, PR 00792
Contact: Juan Colon managing dir
Tel: 787-835-4242
Email: info@altolenterprises.com
Website: www.altolenterprises.com
Chemical & Environmental laboratory performing analyses for water, waste water, environmental samples, metals, RCRA, NPDES, combustible, solvents, soil & other as required. (Hisp, estab 1997, empl 27, sales $2,500,000, cert: NMSDC)

3511 RAC Enterprises, Inc.
Road 1, KM 24.8
Caguas, PR 00726
Contact: Vivian Carballo President
Tel: 787-789-9338
Email: rac@racsteeldrums.com
Website: www.racsteeldrums.com
Mfr steel drums, dist plastic, steel & stainless containers, sorbent products, secondary containment: spill pallets, drain seals. Stormwater management products, PPE & material handling, monitors. (Hisp, estab 1995, empl 15, sales $2,300,000, cert: NMSDC)

Rhode Island

3512 Full Circle Recycling
23 Green Hill Rd
Johnston, RI 02919
Contact: Maria Vinagro President
Tel: 401-464-5996
Email: maria@fullcircleri.com
Website: www.fullcirclerecyclingri.com
Full service recycling facility for metal, plastic, paper, fiber, and electronic post-industrial and post-consumer scrap materials and components. (Woman/AA, estab 2007, empl 30, sales , cert: WBENC)

South Carolina

3513 Air Hub, LLC
PO Box 2535
Mount Pleasant, SC 29465
Contact: Terri Sciarro Owner/Member
Tel: 843-343-3618
Email: tls@airhubllc.com
Website: www.airhubllc.com
Air permitting, air modeling, noise modeling & studies, stormwater pollution prevention plans (SWPPP), spill prevention control & countermeasure (SPCC), environmental consulting. (Woman, estab 2011, empl 1, sales , cert: State)

3514 Apollos Waters LLC
1964 Ashley River Rd, Ste E
Charleston, SC 29407
Contact: Kristi Snyder Owner
Tel: 765-427-3742
Email: kbsnyder@apolloswater.com
Website: www.apolloswater.com
Provide on-site recycling services: bailing cardboard, separating wood, paper & plastics, transporting liquid waste, refurbishing used cutting oils & fluids. (Woman, estab 2011, empl 8, sales $299,925, cert: WBENC)

Tennessee

3515 Bionomics, Inc.
PO Box 817
Kingston, TN 37763
Contact: Karen McCormick President
Tel: 865-220-8501
Email: karenbionomics@comcast.net
Website: www.bionomics-inc.com
Transportation & disposal of hazardous, radioactive & mixed waste. (Woman, estab 1988, empl 7, sales $4,000,000, cert: WBENC)

3516 EGSE Holdings, LLC. dba Emergency Response Team
195 Omohundro Pl, Unit H
Nashville, TN 37210
Contact: Kevin Seats Sales Assoc
Tel: 615-525-9075
Email: kseats@ertnashville.com
Website: www.fireandfloodexperts.com
Water Restoration, Fire & Smoke Mitigation, Mold Remediation. (AA, estab 2004, empl 5, sales $470,000, cert: State, NMSDC)

3517 iSustain Inc.
12249 Wildlife Place
Soddy Daisy, TN 37379
Contact: President
Tel: 423-668-0111
Email: huberda@me.com
Website: www.isustain.expert
Recycling & Waste Management. (Woman, estab 2014, empl 4, sales $2,653,697, cert: WBENC)

3518 Microbial Insights, Inc.
10515 Research Dr
Knoxville, TN 37932
Contact: Anita Biernacki VP Operations
Tel: 865-573-8188
Email: info@microbe.com
Website: www.microbe.com
Environmental biotechnology, bioremediation of chlorinated hydrocarbons, biofilm formation in drinking water systems. (Woman, estab 1992, empl 15, sales $2,951,477, cert: WBENC)

3519 Reliable Pharmaceutical Returns, LLC
1443 Donelson Pike
Nashville, TN 37217
Contact: Yafet Quashie President
Tel: 615-361-8856
Email: yafet@rpreturns.com
Website: www.rpreturns.com
Dispose of all pharmaceutical, documents, over the counter medication. Hazardous & non hazardous materials, return of expired pharmaceutical to manufacturer for credit. (AA, estab 0, empl 10, sales $2,861,666, cert: State, NMSDC, 8(a), SDB)

3520 Tioga Environmental Consultants, Inc.
      357 North Main St
      Memphis, TN 38112
      Contact: Larkin Myers VP
      Tel: 901-791-2432
      Email: lmyers@tiogaenv.com
      Website: www.tiogaenv.com
Lead based paint inspections, mold sampling, IAQ investigations, asbestos inspections, environmental sampling, soil & groundwater sampling, environmental compliance, SWPPP, SPCC Plans, waste water studies, erosion control. (Woman, estab 2009, empl 7, sales $730,000, cert: State, City)

Texas

3521 A1 Shredding Inc.
      PO Box 460085
      Houston, TX 77056
      Contact: Christopher Passmore President
      Tel: 832-545-3949
      Email: cpassmore@a1shreddinginc.com
      Website: www.a1shreddinginc.com
Document shredding, paper recycling, paper destruction & shredding, IT/computer services. (AA, estab 2007, empl 1, sales $ 0, cert: State)

3522 Alma Bell
      7425 Snow Ridge Dr
      Fort Worth, TX 76133
      Contact: Alma Bell
      Tel: 682-381-2153
      Email: admin@alblogisticspro.com
      Website: www.alblogisticspro.com
Nonhazardous solid waste & recycling commodities. (AA, estab 2021, empl 3, sales $140,000, cert: State, NMSDC)

3523 Architect for Life - A Professional Corporation
      2450 Louisiana St, Ste 400-233
      Houston, TX 77006
      Contact: Lolalisa King
      Tel: 888-986-7771
      Email: lking@architectforlife.com
      Website: www.architectforlife.com
Green consulting professional services, develop & manage energy efficient strategies, programs, & projects, retrofit strategies, benchmarking building energy performance, long-term energy management & water saving goals assessment. (Woman/AA, estab 1995, empl 12, sales , cert: City)

3524 Bocci Engineering, LLC
      12709 Pine Dr
      Cypress, TX 77429
      Contact: Lianne Lami Principal
      Tel: 713-575-2400
      Email: LBLami@bocciengineering.com
      Website: www.bocciengineering.com
Efficiency & Optimization, Renewable Resources, Combined Heat & Power, Distributed Generation, Central Plant Projects, Emissions Reduction, Waste Recovery, & Sustainability. Expect Engineering Excellence. (Woman, estab 2007, empl 13, sales , cert: CPUC, WBENC, SDB)

3525 Dougherty Sprague Environmental, Inc.
      3902 Industrial St Ste A
      Rowlett, TX 75088
      Contact: John Dougherty VP Marketing
      Tel: 972-412-8666
      Email: jdougherty@dsei.com
      Website: www.dsei.com
Environmental consulting, phase I & II site assessments, groundwater modeling, industrial compliance, UST removal & site clean-up, litigation support & expert witness testimony. (Woman, estab 1998, empl 25, sales $2,000,000, cert: State, WBENC)

3526 Lynx Ltd
      PO Box 591540
      Houston, TX 77259
      Contact: Darlene Sanchez VP
      Tel: 281-797-2546
      Email: darlene.sanchez@lynxltd.com
      Website: www.lynxltd.com
Environmental compliance & mechanical svcs: hazardous waste mgmt, hazardous waste permit compliance, environmental training, NPDES compliance, air quality compliance, spill response, NEPA review & compliance, asbestos & lead. (Hisp, estab 1998, empl 2, sales $119,640, cert: State, City)

3527 Nation Waste Inc.
      12006 Proctor St
      Houston, TX 77038
      Contact: Brendan Goodnough Cheif Marketing Officer
      Tel: 713-649-7776
      Email: bgood@nationwaste.us
      Website: www.nationwaste.us
Commercial waste disposal: Construction, Demolition, Commercial & Industrial Non-Hazardous Waste Removal, Portable Toilets & Recycling services. (Minority, Woman, estab 1997, empl 24, sales $3,200,000, cert: State, City)

3528 RNDI Companies, Inc.
      2255 Ridge Rd, Ste 216
      Rockwall, TX 75087
      Contact: Diana Cross President
      Tel: 214-771-3977
      Email: diana@rndicompanies.com
      Website: www.rndicompanies.com
Environmental services: asbestos, lead, mold remediation & abatement, demolition. (Minority, Woman, estab 2005, empl 20, sales $2,000,000, cert: State)

3529 Separation Systems Consultants, Inc.
      17041 El Camino Real, Ste 200
      Houston, TX 77058
      Contact: Helen Hodges President
      Tel: 281-486-1943
      Email: ssci@sscienvironmental.com
      Website: www.sscienvironmental.com
Risk-based corrective action, remediation & closure, engineering & consulting, waste mgmt, petroleum storage tank, environmental site assessments, health, safety & environmental compliance audits, plans, permits & training. (Woman, estab 1986, empl 23, sales $4,000,000, cert: State, WBENC)

ENVIRONMENTAL SERVICES

3530 SIA Solutions, LLC
17171 Park Row Ste 370
Houston, TX 77084
Contact: Mark Knight Program Mgr
Tel: 866-768-4625
Email: mjknight@siasolutions.com
Website: www.siasolutions.com
Environmental Consulting & Engineering, Asset Management & Energy Consulting, Environmental Remediation, Radiological Services, Hazardous, Toxic & Radioactive Waste (HTRW) Management. (As-Ind, estab 2012, empl 49, sales $2,100,000, cert: City, 8(a))

3531 Southern Global Safety Services, Inc.
2986 County Rd 180
Alvin, TX 77511
Contact: Julie Wernecke President
Tel: 281-331-3667
Email: possumloo@hotmail.com
Website: www.southernglobalsafetyservices.com
Environmental consulting: surveys identification & assesement, project design, specifications, indoor air quality testing, radon testing & mitigation, norm testing & hearing conservation. (Woman, estab 2001, empl 21, sales $3,127,872, cert: WBENC)

3532 TGE Resources, Inc.
8048 Northcourt Rd
Houston, TX 77040
Contact: Robin Franks President
Tel: 713-744-5800
Email: melanie.rivas@tgeresources.com
Website: www.tgeresources.com
Full Service Environmental and Consulting & Managment Services (Woman, estab 1994, empl 20, sales $2,360,000, cert: State, City, WBENC)

Virginia

3533 Aegis Environmental, Inc.
11511 Allecingie Pkwy
Richmond, VA 23235
Contact: Matthew Markee President
Tel: 804-378-6015
Email: mmarkee@aegisenv.com
Website: www.aegisenv.com
Air permitting & compliance, air dispersion modeling analyses, pollution control technology analyses, emissions estimates, environmental training & compliance, contingency planning, environmental mgmt systems dev & auditing. (Woman, estab 1996, empl 20, sales $3,000,000, cert: State)

3534 CMMD Enterprises, Inc.
7001 Loisdale Rd Ste C
Springfield, VA 22150
Contact: Carolyn Marina CEO
Tel: 703-646-2900
Email: carolyn.m@cmmdinc.com
Website: www.cmmdinc.com
Critical maintenance management & distribution, rotating process plant systems, wastewater treatment systems, potable water systems, chemical processes. (Woman/AA, estab 2001, empl 5, sales $483,000, cert: State, NMSDC)

3535 Environmental Waste Specialists, Inc.
4451 Brookfield Corporate Dr Ste 206
Chantilly, VA 20151
Contact: Dawn Walker Recycling Mgr
Tel: 703-502-0100
Email: dawn@ewsihazmat.com
Website: www.ewsihazmat.com
Package, transport, dispose & recycle hazardous & non-hazardous materials. (Woman/AA, estab 1994, empl 4, sales $1,700,000, cert: State)

3536 Froehling & Robertson, Inc.
3015 Dumbarton Rd
Richmond, VA 23228
Contact: Jackie Clingenpeel Exec Asst
Tel: 804-264-2701
Email: jclingenpeel@fandr.com
Website: www.fandr.com
Environmental services: phase I & II ESAs, EIRs, EIS, wetland & stream delineations, hazardous materials assessments, industrial hygiene svcs, asbestos & lead testing, environmental planning, property condition assessments. (Minority, Woman, estab , empl 400, sales $ 0, cert: State)

3537 Interspec, LLC
464 S Independence Blvd Ste C-104
Virginia Beach, VA 23452
Contact: Sean Murphy Business Devel Dir
Tel: 757-622-6299
Email: murphys@interspecllc.net
Website: www.interspecllc.net
Tank, piping & pressure vessel inspections, STI storage tank inspections, Non-Destructive Examination/Testing steel structures, Spill Prevention Control & Countermeasure (SPCC) plans, Oil Discharge Control Plans (ODCP. (Nat Ame, estab 2001, empl 22, sales $1,200,000, cert: State, 8(a))

3538 J. R. Caskey, Inc.
PO Box 305
Oilville, VA 23129
Contact: Ginger Caskey President
Tel: 804-784-8001
Email: gec@jrcaskey.com
Website: www.jrcaskey.com
Engineering, Layout & Surveying, Clearing & Demolition, Earthwork, Grading & Excavation, Erosion & Sediment Control, Traditional Stormwater Management Systems, Low-Impact Development Systems, Underground Water & Sanitary Sewer Utilities. (Woman, estab 1985, empl 42, sales $6,630,000, cert: State)

3539 Mac-Par Services, LLC
20 B Research Dr
Hampton, VA 23666
Contact: David Parham President
Tel: 866-622-7271
Email: dparham@macparservices.com
Website: www.macparservices.com
Interior demolition, material & debris hauling, lead paint & asbestos abatements, mold remediation & HVAC duct cleaning. (AA, estab 1999, empl 3, sales $370,000, cert: State)

3540 Sea Consulting Group
325 Mason Ave
Cape Charles, VA 23310
Contact: Ann Hayward Walker President
Tel: 757-331-1787
Email: ahwalker@seaconsulting.com
Website: www.seaconsulting.com
Environmental consulting. (Minority, Woman, estab 1983, empl 10, sales $ 0, cert: WBENC)

Washington

3541 Dunkin & Bush, Inc.
PO Box 97080
Kirkland, WA 98083
Contact: Deidre Dunkin President
Tel: 425-885-7064
Email: ddunkin@dunkinandbush.com
Website: www.dunkinandbush.com
Industrial painting, scaffolding, insulation, rigging, containment, lead abatement, shop coating aplication, concrete restoration, plural applied tank linings, abrasive blasting, specialty blasting, water jetting, high heat coating applications. (Woman, estab 2008, empl 300, sales $ 0, cert: WBENC)

3542 EHS-International, Inc.
1011 SW Klickitat Way, Ste 104
Seattle, WA 98134
Contact: Nancy Yee Marketing
Tel: 425-455-2959
Email: nancyy@ehsintl.com
Website: www.ehsintl.com
Environmental engineering & industrial hygiene svcs: workplace & environmental health & safety, hazards identification & removal, assessments & remediation, employee training & abatement management. (Hisp, estab 1996, empl 21, sales $1,489,983, cert: State)

3543 Environmental Assessment Services, LLC
350 Hills St Ste 112
Richland, WA 99354
Contact: Brett Tiller
Tel: 509-375-4212
Email: brett.tiller@easbio.com
Website: www.easbio.com
Environmental characterization, Spill Response & Natural Resource Damage Assessments, Hazardous Waste Site Remedial Investigations, Risk Assessments, & Environmental Surveillance, Ecological Characterization & Restoration. (Nat Ame, estab 2005, empl 44, sales $2,700,000, cert: NMSDC)

3544 GeoTest Services, Inc.
741 Marine View Dr
Bellingham, WA 98225
Contact: Jeremy Wolf VP
Tel: 360-733-7318
Email: jeremyw@geotest-inc.com
Website: www.geotest-inc.com
Geotechnical engineering, environmental services, special inspection & materials testing, facilities, structures, roads, bridges & all types of infrastructure. (Woman, estab 1993, empl 33, sales $6,000,000, cert: State)

Wisconsin

3545 K. Singh & Associates, Inc.
3636 N 124th St
Wauwatosa, WI 53222
Contact: Pratap Singh CEO
Tel: 262-821-1171
Email: gmiller@ksaconsultants.com
Website: www.ksaconsultants.com
Environmental engineering & management services, transportation, structural, environmental & civil engineering, land surveying & construction management. (As-Ind, estab 1987, empl 33, sales $3,000,000, cert: State)

3546 OGC Construction, LLC
W171 n10330 Wildrose Ln
Germantown, WI 53022
Contact: Michael Owens President
Tel: 414-383-4205
Email: mowens@ogcconstruction.com
Website: www.ogcconstruction.com
Hazardous waste removal remediation, construction lead asbestos abatement. (AA, estab 2005, empl 18, sales , cert: NMSDC)

3547 White Glove Environmental
8326 N Stevens Rd
Milwaukee, WI 53223
Contact: London Thomas President
Tel: 414-760-1733
Email: london@wgginc.net
Website: www.wgginc.net
Environmental services, safe abatement & removal. (AA, estab 2005, empl 11, sales , cert: NMSDC)

3548 White Glove Group, Inc.
8326 N Stevens Rd
Milwaukee, WI 53223
Contact: Joseph Njuguna Sales Dir
Tel: 414-760-1733
Email: joe@wgginc.net
Website: www.wgenvironmental.com
Environmental services, facility maintenance, demolition, construction & demolition waste recycling program mgmt, green construction final cleaning, LEED consulting, sustainable product procurement for new construction & existing buildings. (AA, estab 2003, empl 25, sales $700,000, cert: State)

FOOD PRODUCTS AND SERVICES

Products include coffees, teas, bottled water, water filtration units, milk and milk products, juices, soft drinks, candies, cookies, jellies, pastries, snacks, dressings, flavorings, sauces, spices, syrups, ethnic foods, fish, seafood & prepared meats, fruits & vegetables. NAICS Code 31

Alabama

3549 The Widget Development & Trading Company, LLC
10 S Perry St
Montgomery, AL 36104
Contact: David Martin President
Tel: 404-695-0141
Email: davidmartin@widgetdtc.com
Website: www.widgetdtc.com
Dist nuts, meats, sauces, baked goods. (Woman/AA, estab 2011, empl 2, sales , cert: NMSDC)

Arkansas

3550 My Brother's Salsa LLC
PO Box 922
Bentonville, AR 72712
Contact: Helen Lampkin Founder
Tel: 479-271-9404
Email: helen@mybrotherssalsa.com
Website: www.mybrotherssalsa.com
Produce 9 salsa varieties some available in multiple heat levels. Salsas range from smooth to textured consistencies with flavor profiles the span from earthy to smoky to sweet and savory. (Woman, estab 2003, empl 5, sales , cert: WBENC)

Arizona

3551 Sir Aubrey's Tea Company, Ltd
15941 N 77th St Ste 3
Scottsdale, AZ 85260
Contact: Kathryn Petty President
Tel: 480-607-5300
Email: kpetty@whiteliontea.com
Website: www.whiteliontea.com
White Lion Tea offers a collection of rare & beautiful teas from the world's finest gardens. (Woman, estab 1998, empl 8, sales $998,470, cert: WBENC)

California

3552 AG Commodties, Inc.
12815 Stevens Dr
Tustin, CA 92782
Contact: Theresa Bailey VP Business Dev
Tel: 612-839-3385
Email: ach112350@gmail.com
Website: www.agcommoditiesinc.com
Natural sweeteners & natural maltodextrins, rice maltodextrin, tapioca maltodextrin, rice syrups: brown & clarified, medium invert sugar cane syrup, clear tapioca syrups, organic sugar cane, organic glycerin, organic acacia powder, etc. (As-Ind, estab 2006, empl 10, sales $3,500,000, cert: NMSDC)

3553 Andytown LLC
3655 Lawton St
San Francisco, CA 94122
Contact: Lauren Crabbe Owner
Tel: 619-823-4359
Email: lauren@andytownsf.com
Website: www.andytownsf.com/
Coffee beans and ground coffee to companies large and small. (Woman, estab 2014, empl 55, sales $3,900,000, cert: WBENC)

3554 Asiana Cusine Enterprises (ACE Sushi)
22771 S. Western Ave
Torrance, CA 90501
Contact: Gary Chin CFO
Tel: 310-327-2223
Email: gary.chin@acesushi.com
Website: www.acesushi.com
Dist Sushi. (As-Pac, estab 1998, empl 35, sales , cert: City)

3555 Cacique, Inc.
14940 Proctor Ave
City of Industry, CA 91746
Contact: Bob Cashen Dir of Sales
Tel: 626-961-3399
Email: rcashen@caciqueinc.com
Website: www.caciqueinc.com
Mfr & dist food (dairy) products. (Hisp, estab 1973, empl 350, sales , cert: NMSDC)

3556 Carlos Steffens, Inc.
3061 Independence Dr, Ste E
Livermore, CA 94550
Contact: Carlos Steffens President
Tel: 925-838-2336
Email: carlos@steffenscorp.com
Website: www.steffenscorp.com
Industrial ingredient brokers, concentrated fruit juice products. (Hisp, estab 2000, empl 6, sales , cert: NMSDC)

3557 Creative Research Management
PO Box 7843
Stockton, CA 95267
Contact: Cheryl R. Mitchell President
Tel: 209-598-7565
Email: cheryl@crmcorp.net
Website: www.crmcorp.net
Produce Sucramask™, RiceLife® Brown Rice-Milk syrups, TherMoPectin and our line of GrainLife™ products including RiceLife® and CornLife™. (Woman, estab 2000, empl 3, sales $5,000,000, cert: NWBOC)

3558 C-Shore International Inc.
1010 N Central Ave
Glendale, CA 91202
Contact: Jacques Isaac CEO
Tel: 818-909-4684
Email: mirline@aol.com
Website: www.beantrader.com
Peas, beans, lentils, pre cooked flour, bread flour, wheat flour, dried malt extract roasted barley. (AA, estab 1988, empl 3, sales $ 0, cert: NMSDC)

3559 Encore Fruit Marketing, Inc.
      120 W Bonita Ave, Ste 204
      San Dimas, CA 91773
      Contact: Kandi Ashcraft VP Finance
      Tel: 909-394-5640
      Email: kashcraft@encorefruit.com
      Website: www.encorefruit.com
Acai, Acerola, Agave, Apple, Apricot, Aronia, Banana, Bilberry, Blackberry, Black Currant, Blueberry, Boysenberry, Cherry, Cranberry, Date (domestic), Dragon Fruit, Elderberry, Fig, Gac Fruit, Goji Berry, Grape, etc. (Woman, estab 1989, empl 15, sales $16,050,000, cert: WBENC)

3560 F. Gavina & Sons, Inc.
      2700 Fruitland Ave
      Vernon, CA 90058
      Contact: Angela Day Natl Sales Mgr
      Tel: 323-351-5616
      Email: Angela.Day@gavina.com
      Website: www.gavina.com
Coffee roasting, new blend development or matching of your current blend, brand & marketing support, brewing & espresso service & training. (Hisp, estab 1967, empl 265, sales $127,485,828, cert: NMSDC)

3561 Frieda's Inc.
      4465 Corporate Center Dr
      Los Alamitos, CA 90720
      Contact: Karen Caplan CEO
      Tel: 714-826-6100
      Email: karen.caplan@friedas.com
      Website: www.friedas.com
Specialty Fruits (including Fresh Tropicals and Dried Fruits), Specialty Vegetables (including cooking vegetables and leafy greens), Hispanic Fruits & Vegetables (including fresh & dried chile peppers), Asian Fruits & Vegetables. (Woman, estab 1962, empl 75, sales $46,000,000, cert: WBENC)

3562 Fusion Ranch, Inc. dba Fusion Jerky
      405 S Airport Blvd
      South San Francisco, CA 94080
      Contact: Kaiyen Mai CEO
      Tel: 650-589-8899
      Email: kaiyen@fusionranch.com
      Website: www.fusionjerky.com
Jerky, Sausage, Ham, Shredded Pork. (Minority, Woman, estab 2014, empl 46, sales , cert: NMSDC, WBENC)

3563 Got Broccoli, Inc.
      6201 Progressive Ave Ste 400
      San Diego, CA 92154
      Contact: Art Sanchez Dir
      Tel: 619-661-0909
      Email: art@gotbroccoli.com
      Website: www.frugo.com.mx
IQF Vegetables, Asparagus, Broccoli, Cauliflower, Celery, Cucumber, Jalapeno, Spinach, Kale. (Hisp, estab 2010, empl 2, sales $10,000,000, cert: NMSDC)

3564 Kruger Foods Inc.
      18362 E Hwy 4
      Stockton, CA 95215
      Contact: Kara Kruger CEO
      Tel: 209-941-8518
      Email: k.kruger@krugerfoods.com
      Website: www.krugerfoods.com
Pickles, Sweet Pickle Relish, Dill Pickle Relish, Hot Pepper Relish, Jalapeno Peppers (sliced, diced, whole), Banana Wax Peppers, Peppers, Giardinera. (Woman, estab 1930, empl 158, sales $65,400,000, cert: WBENC)

3565 Laxmi's Delights
      98 Brevensville Dr
      San Ramon, CA 94583
      Contact: Laxmi Hiremath Owner
      Tel: 925-833-0115
      Email: laxmihiremath@gmail.com
      Website: www.laxmisdelights.com
Organic flaxseed spreads. (Woman/As-Ind, estab 2000, empl 1, sales $100,000, cert: WBENC)

3566 National Raisin Company
      PO Box 219
      Fowler, CA 93625
      Contact: Joe Leon VP Business Dev
      Tel: 559-834-5981
      Email: jleon@nationalraisin.com
      Website: www.nationalraisin.com
High industrial specifications for confection, cereal & baking, using the California grown Natural Seedless Select and Small raisins, sugar coated raisins, glycerin infused raisins, juice concentrates, pastes and purees. (Woman, estab 1969, empl 450, sales , cert: WBENC, NWBOC)

3567 NC Moving & Storage Solutions
      3146 Corporate Pl
      Hayward, CA 94545
      Contact: Johanna Lobation Business Devel Mgr
      Tel: 510-385-4441
      Email: jlobaton@ncmss.com
      Website: www.ncmss.com
NC Moving & Storage Solutions is a full service household goods provider for both domestic and international moving services. We are an agent for North American Van Lines. (Minority, Woman, estab 2006, empl 19, sales $1,165,000, cert: NMSDC, CPUC, WBENC)

3568 NiuSource Inc.
      14266 Euclid Ave
      Chino, CA 91710
      Contact: Linda Lin General Mgr
      Tel: 909-631-2895
      Email: Linda.lin@niusource.com
      Website: www.NiuSource.com
Sweeteners business, like Aspartame, Sucralose, AceK, Stevia, Monk Fruit, Etc. (Woman/As-Pac, estab 2014, empl 15, sales $32,000,000, cert: NMSDC, WBENC)

3569 P.S. Let's Eat Inc.
      3943 Irvine Blvd, Ste 610
      Irvine, CA 92602
      Contact: Preya Patel Bhakta President
      Tel: 855-998-3554
      Email: preya@elliquark.com
      Website: www.elliquark.com
Produce German style Quark products. (Minority, Woman, estab 2011, empl 2, sales , cert: WBENC)

FOOD PRODUCTS AND SERVICES

3570 Peas of Mind LLC
      2339 3rd St Unit 53-3R
      San Francisco, CA 94107
      Contact: Jill Litwin CEO
      Tel: 415-504-2556
      Email: jill@peasofmind.com
      Website: www.peasofmind.com
Mfr healthy eating options. (Woman, estab 2005, empl 4, sales $2,800,000, cert: WBENC)

3571 Planet Popcorn, Inc.
      1616 E Wilshire Ave
      Santa Ana, CA 92705
      Contact: Sharla Gandy-Caldaronello CEO
      Tel: 949-278-1312
      Email: sharla@planetpopcorn.com
      Website: www.planetpopcorn.com
Hand-crafted gourmet popcorn. (Woman, estab 2005, empl 23, sales $2,009,000, cert: WBENC)

3572 Somax Inc.
      339 S Notre Dame Ave
      Orange, CA 92869
      Contact: Grace Knight Owner
      Tel: 714-633-6614
      Email: graceknight@sanluissausage.com
      Website: www.sanluissausage.com
Healthy, preservative free pork & chicken gourmet sausages. (Woman, estab 1991, empl 2, sales $2,200,286, cert: WBENC, NWBOC)

3573 Valley Lahvosh Baking Co.
      502 M St
      Fresno, CA 93721
      Contact: Lori Miller President
      Tel: 559-485-2700
      Email: customerservice@valleylahvosh.com
      Website: www.valleylahvosh.com
Mfr valley lahvosh crackerbreads & pita breads. (Woman, estab , empl , sales $8,578,874, cert: WBENC)

3574 Zego LLC
      912 Cole St, Ste 294
      San Francisco, CA 94117
      Contact: CEO
      Tel: 415-622-8115
      Email: customerservice@zegofoods.com
      Website: www.zegofoods.com
Mfr & dist Oats, Muesli, Sacha Inchi Protein Powder, Nutrition Bars, and Mix-Ins Trail Mix all free of the top 12 most common allergens and gluten. (Woman, estab 2013, empl 3, sales $410,000, cert: WBENC)

Colorado

3575 All American Seasonings, Inc.
      10600 E 54th Ave, Unit B & C
      Denver, CO 80239
      Contact: Andy Rodriguez President
      Tel: 303-623-2320
      Email: andyr@allamericanseasonings.com
      Website: www.allamericanseasonings.com
Custom blenders of food ingredients. (Hisp, estab 1968, empl 40, sales $18,000,000, cert: NMSDC)

3576 Mona's Granola and Cookies, Inc.
      651 Eldorado
      Broomfield, CO 80021
      Contact: Mona Gale CEO
      Tel: 727-420-0707
      Email: mona@monasinc.com
      Website: www.monasinc.com
All natural no white sugar nutrient rich granola cereal & ice cream toppings. (Woman, estab 1981, empl 27, sales $600,000, cert: WBENC)

3577 Toddy, LLC
      3706 Aldrin Dr
      Loveland, CO 80538
      Contact: Mike Skillins Key Acct Cstmr Advocacy
      Tel: 970-493-0788
      Email: diversity@toddycafe.com
      Website: www.toddycafe.com
Developed cold brewing solutions for food service, home users and also as consumer packaged goods. (Woman, estab 1964, empl 50, sales $14,324,000, cert: WBENC)

Connecticut

3578 Aleias Gluten Free Foods, LLC
      4 Pin Oak Dr
      Branford, CT 06405
      Contact: Kimberly Snow President
      Tel: 860-488-5556
      Email: contact@aleias.com
      Website: www.aleias.com
Marketing, Production & Sale of Gluten Free Foods. (Woman, estab 0, empl 38, sales , cert: WBENC)

3579 Aurora Product Inc.
      205 Edison Road
      Orange, CT 06477
      Contact: Stephanie Blackwell Business Devel
      Tel: 203-375-9956
      Email: sblackwell@auroraproduct.com
      Website: www.auroranatural.com
Natural & organic snacks: almonds, cashews, mixed nuts & peanuts, salted, unsalted & raw, dried fruits. (Woman, estab 1998, empl 225, sales $60,000,000, cert: WBENC)

3580 Carla's Pasta, Inc.
      50 Talbot Lane
      South Windsor, CT 06074
      Contact: Sandro Squatrito VP Business Dev
      Tel: 860-436-4042
      Email: abiel@carlaspasta.com
      Website: www.carlaspasta.com
Produce pasta & pesto products, Cheeseburger Ravioli, Buffalo Chicken Ravioli & Stromboli Ravioli. (Woman, estab 1978, empl 182, sales , cert: NWBOC)

3581 Gelato Giuliana, LLC
      240 Sargent Dr
      New Haven, CT 06511
      Contact: Deborah Cairo Mktg Mgr
      Tel: 203-772-0607
      Email: dcbottega@sbcglobal.net
      Website: www.gelatogiuliana.com
Mfr & dist gelato under our label Gelato Giuliana. (Woman, estab 2006, empl 10, sales $882,662, cert: State)

FOOD PRODUCTS AND SERVICES

3582 Heidi's Real Food LLC
47 Hillside Rd
Greenwich, CT 06830
Contact: Heidi Matonis Owner
Tel: 203-219-4202
Email: heidi@heidisrealfood.com
Website: www.heidisrealfood.com
Heidi's Meatless "Meat"balls also available in bulk for food service and prepared foods. (Woman, estab 2013, empl 1, sales , cert: WBENC)

3583 The Bites Company
PO Box 122
Westport, CT 06881
Contact: Dina Upton Owner
Tel: 203-296-2482
Email: sales@thebitescompany.com
Website: www.thebitescompany.com
All natural, round, bite size pieces of Biscotti in 5 flavors; almond, orange, lemon, cocoa & coffee. (Woman, estab 2011, empl 1, sales , cert: State)

District of Columbia

3584 Tribes-A-Dozen, LLC
PO Box 42063
Washington, DC 20015
Contact: Leah Hadad President
Tel: 202-684-8256
Email: leah@tribesadozen.com
Website: www.tribesadozen.com
Mfr three all-natural & kosher (OU) Voil! Hallah Egg Bread Mixes: Traditional, Wholey Wheat & Simply Spelt. (Woman, estab 2012, empl 1, sales , cert: WBENC)

3585 Village Tea Company Distribution Inc.
1342 Florida Ave., NW Ste 225-B
Washington, DC 20009
Contact: Janon Costley CEO
Tel: 888-406-1138
Email: janon@villageteaco.com
Website: www.villageteaco.com
100% organic & natural tea in biodegradable packaging, foodservice tea, bulk tea, tea dispensers, tea machines, packaged tea, tea in bags, loose leaf tea, loose tea, organic tea, natural tea. (AA, estab 2008, empl 12, sales , cert: NMSDC)

Florida

3586 ARA Food Corporation
8001 NW 60th St
Miami, FL 33166
Contact: Oscar Tanaka President
Tel: 305-592-5558
Email: marta@arafood.com
Website: www.arafood.com
Mfr plantain & cassava chips. (Hisp, estab 1975, empl 30, sales , cert: NMSDC)

3587 Brisk/RCR Coffee Company
507 N. 22nd St
Tampa, FL 33605
Contact: Richard Perez CEO
Tel: 813-248-6264
Email: customer@briskcoffee.com
Website: www.briskcoffee.com
Coffee importing, roasting, grinding, packaging & shipping. (Hisp, estab 1968, empl 30, sales , cert: State)

3588 COEX Coffee International Inc.
525 NW 27th Ave
Miami, FL 33125
Contact: Robert Menos Sr Trader
Tel: 305-459-5180
Email: lmones@coexgroup.com
Website: www.coexgroup.com
Coffee trading, importing green coffee from all major global coffee producing countries. (Hisp, estab 1980, empl 45, sales $415,000,000, cert: NMSDC)

3589 Delina Inc.
1068 Pine Branch Dr
Weston, FL 33326
Contact: President
Tel: 954-306-0628
Email: sales@delinainc.com
Website: www.delinainc.com
Dist asparagus spears, green pickled asparagus spears, cornichons, roasted red peppers, artichoke hearts, hearts of palm & organic coffee. (Minority, Woman, estab 1998, empl 2, sales , cert: City)

3590 GFIS
2525 Ponce de Leon Blvd Ste 300
Coral Gables, FL 33134
Contact: Andrea Cordova Mgr
Tel: 305-521-9094
Email: acordova@foodingredientsolution.com
Website: www.foodingredientsolution.com
Frozen, Aseptic, No pasteurized, Unpasteurized, IQF, Fruitm Vegetables, Puree, Juice, Concentrate, NFC, Single Straight, Organic, Conventional, Acai, Acerola, Apple, Blackberry, Blueberry, Cherry, Grapefruit, Guava, Kiwi, Lemon, Lime, Mango, and more. (Minority, Woman, estab 2016, empl 4, sales $1,500,000, cert: State)

3591 Henry Roberts BBQ Sauce
2001 Art Museum Dr
Jacksonville, FL 32207
Contact: Anthony Ammons VP
Tel: 904-591-8102
Email: anthony.ammons@gmail.com
Website: www.HenryRoberts.com
Bottle & distribute barbecue sauce & chow chow. (Woman/AA, estab 1985, empl 4, sales $160,000, cert: City)

3592 M&G Expresso, Inc
13311 SW 132 Ave, Unit 3
Miami, FL 33186
Contact: Gabriel Cortina VP
Tel: 786-200-9802
Email: mgexpressinc@gmail.com
Website: www.ladybeehoney.net
Dist Lady Bee Honey. (Minority, Woman, estab 2009, empl 3, sales $1,996,000, cert: NMSDC)

3593 MH Food Group LLC
1800 Sunset Harbour Dr, Ste P
Miami Beach, FL 33139
Contact: Calvin Harris President
Tel: 954-501-6215
Email: charris@mhfoodgroup.com
Website: www.mhfoodgroup.com
Pack & dist frozen fruit & industrial food ingredients. (Minority, Woman, estab 2014, empl 4, sales $1,000,000, cert: NMSDC)

FOOD PRODUCTS AND SERVICES

3594 Quirch Foods Co.
2701 S. LeJeune Rd. 12th Fl
Miami, FL 33134
Contact: Elijah Davis Natl Acct Sales Mgr
Tel: 305-691-3535
Email: elijah.davis@quirchfoods.com
Website: www.quirchfoods.com
Dist & export meat & seafood. (Hisp, estab 1967, empl 500, sales $747,373,931, cert: NMSDC)

3595 Sweet Additions, Inc.
4440 PGA Blvd, Ste 600
Palm Beach Gardens, FL 33410
Contact: Ken Valdivia President
Tel: 561-472-0178
Email: kvaldivia@sweetadditions.com
Website: www.sweetadditions.com
Mfr & dist cane & grain based sweeteners. (Hisp, estab 2004, empl 3, sales $5,000,000, cert: NMSDC)

Georgia

3596 82's, LLC
1475 Buford Dr Ste 403-227
Lawrenceville, GA 30043
Contact: Reginald Kelly Owner
Tel: 770-402-2226
Email: contact@kyvan82.com
Website: www.kyvan82.com
All Natural Honey Apple Salsa (Hot & Mild), Sesame Garlic BBQ Sauce, Sweet BBQ Sauce, Hot Sauce. (AA, estab 2008, empl 7, sales $100,000, cert: NMSDC)

3597 All A's Spices
504 Fair St SW Ste 2
Atlanta, GA 30313
Contact: Dondre Anderson CEO
Tel: 585-310-1970
Email: danderson@symphonychips.com
Website: www.symphonychips.com
Gluten-Free, Vegan-Friendly, Non GMO, No MSG, All-Natural Spices. (AA, estab 2010, empl 2, sales $240,000, cert: NMSDC)

3598 Brooksmade Gourmet Foods
8000 Avalon Blvd, Ste 100
Alpharetta, GA 30009
Contact: Antoinette Brooks Exec Asst
Tel: 770-231-2601
Email: antoinette.brooks@brooksmadegourmetfoods.com
Website: www.brooksmadegourmetfoods.com
Ketchups and seasonings. (AA, estab 2004, empl 10, sales $500,000, cert: NMSDC)

3599 Diaz Foods
5501 Fulton Industrial Blvd SW
Atlanta, GA 30336
Contact: Jorge Antona EVP
Tel: 404-344-5421
Email: jorge.antona@diazfoods.com
Website: www.diazfoods.com
Hispanic grocery distributor, grocery, frozen, dairy, meats & produce. (Hisp, estab 1980, empl 323, sales $168,000,000, cert: NMSDC)

3600 Fire & Flavor Grilling Co.
1160 S Milledge Ave, Ste 230
Athens, GA 30605
Contact: Davis Knox CEO
Tel: 706-369-9466
Email: davis@fireandflavor.com
Website: www.fireandflavor.com
Dist spices, seasonings, sauces, brines, grilling planks, wood chips, charcoal & fire starters. (Woman, estab 2003, empl 6, sales $5,000,000, cert: WBENC)

3601 H. Walker Enterprises, LLC
22 E Montgomery Crossroads
Savannah, GA 31406
Contact: Herschel Walker CEO
Tel: 912-961-0002
Email: hwrmi34@aol.com
Website: www.34promotions.com
Mfr & dist poultry, beef & pork food products. (AA, estab 2002, empl 4, sales $ 0, cert: NMSDC)

3602 JCPG LLC dba Popbar
4573 Bogan Meadows Ct
Buford, GA 30519
Contact: Charel Palmer Owner
Tel: 678-783-9688
Email: alpharetta@pop-bar.com
Website: www.pop-bar.com
Hand crafted, all natural and preservative free gelato, yogurt, vegan gelato and sorbet in a new way, on a stick! With 5 chocolate dippings. (AA, estab 2017, empl 15, sales , cert: City, NMSDC)

3603 Seeds of Nature, LLC
1456 Lechemin Dr
Snellville, GA 30078
Contact: Patricia Nowell Managing Member
Tel: 877-277-9260
Email: pnowell@prodigy.net
Website: www.seedsofnature.com
Premium Cocoa Beans sourced from Ivory Coast, Nigeria & Ghana. (Woman/AA, estab 2009, empl 3, sales $300,000, cert: NMSDC)

Iowa

3604 Young G's Barbecue Sauce, LLC
8211 Brookview Dr.
Urbandale, IA 50322
Contact: Gerald Young President
Tel: 515-331-8001
Email: youngsbbq@gmail.com
Website: www.ygsbbq.com
Young G's is a gluten free low sodium content with no high fructose corn syrup. (AA, estab 2010, empl 1, sales , cert: NMSDC)

Illinois

3605 Amazing Edibles Gourmet Catering, Inc.
2419 W 14th St Unit C
Chicago, IL 60608
Contact: Andrea Herrera President
Tel: 312-563-1600
Email: amazingedibles@aol.com
Website: www.amazingediblescatering.com
Full service caterer. We provide breakfast, brunch, lunch, dinner, snacks, and party options. (Minority, Woman, estab 1994, empl 10, sales $963,488, cert: State)

FOOD PRODUCTS AND SERVICES 3606-3617

3606 Baldwin Richardson Foods Co.
      One Tower Lane Ste 2390
      Oakbrook Terrace, IL 60181
      Contact: Cara Hughes Dir Sales/Marketing
      Tel: 630-607-1780
      Email: chughes@brfoods.com
      Website: www.brfoods.com
Mfr custom sauces, condiments, syrups, toppings & fillings. (AA, estab 1997, empl 287, sales $ 0, cert: NMSDC)

3607 Bell Marketing, Inc.
      10135 S Roberts Rd
      Palos Hills, IL 60465
      Contact: Mary Ann Bell President
      Tel: 708-598-8873
      Email: maryann@bellmarketing.com
      Website: www.bellmarketing.com
Fruit concentrates, purees, puree concentrates IQF frozen fruit, all natural colors from fruit & vegetable juice concentrates, extracts, ice cream inclusions. (Woman, estab 1986, empl 5, sales $10,000,000, cert: WBENC)

3608 Bitoy's Sweet Treats Inc.
      5957 W Chicago Ave
      Chicago, IL 60651
      Contact: Layla Bitoy Strategy Lead
      Tel: 877-424-8697
      Email: layla@bitoysbrands.com
      Website: www.bitoysbrands.com
Handcrafted gelato, popcorn, and confections. (AA, estab 2015, empl 4, sales , cert: State)

3609 CBC Sales, Inc.
      5117 S Normandy Ave
      Chicago, IL 60638
      Contact: Desiree Alonzo President
      Tel: 773-218-9563
      Email: desiree@cbcsalesinc.com
      Website: www.cicerobloodymary.com
Gourmet beverages, Craft Sodas & Bloody Mary Mixes, Salted Caramel Root beer, Bacon Bloody Mary Mix. (Woman, estab 2008, empl 1, sales $400,000, cert: WBENC)

3610 Chapin LLC
      1350 N Wells St Ste F109
      Chicago, IL 60610
      Contact: Jennifer Alexander Monzón
      Tel: 312-493-6976
      Email: jennifer@chapincoffee.com
      Website: www.ChapinCoffee.com
Specialty coffee, whole bean, ground & single serve (k-cup). (Hisp, estab 2013, empl 2, sales , cert: NMSDC)

3611 Compact Industries
      3945 Ohio Ave
      St. Charles, IL 60174
      Contact: Dan Matyus VP Business Dev
      Tel: 630-513-9600
      Email: matyus@compactind.com
      Website: www.compactind.com
Contract manufacturer of dry food products. (Woman, estab 1963, empl 120, sales $98,000,000, cert: WBENC)

3612 Cornfields, Inc.
      3898 Sunset Ave
      Waukegan, IL 60087
      Contact: JB Weiler VP Sales
      Tel: 847-263-7000
      Email: info@cornfieldsinc.com
      Website: www.cornfieldsinc.com
Mfr natural & organic snacks. (Woman, estab 1991, empl 60, sales $12,000,000, cert: WBENC)

3613 Cristina Foods, Inc.
      4555 S Racine Ave
      Chicago, IL 60609
      Contact: Cesar Dovalina President
      Tel: 312-829-0360
      Email: cdovalina@cristinafoods.com
      Website: www.cristinafoods.com
Dist fresh produce, frozen foods, spices, grocery & canned goods, meats, dairy, poultry, seafood, disposable paper & plastics. (Hisp, estab 1989, empl 42, sales $21,750,000, cert: NMSDC)

3614 DAMRON Corporation
      4433 W Ohio St
      Chicago, IL 60624
      Contact: Amariah Bradford Marketing Media Specialist
      Tel: 773-826-6000
      Email: amariahbradford@damroncorp.com
      Website: www.damroncorp.com
Healing Tea Leaves of the World brand of Specialty Tea - 25 ct. teabag cartons, quality fully equal to or better than National Brands. (AA, estab 1985, empl 50, sales $5,800,000, cert: City, NMSDC)

3615 Frey Produce
      RR 1 Box 89
      Keenes, IL 62851
      Contact: Renee Mattingly VP Sales & Mktg
      Tel: 618-835-2536
      Email: reneemattingly@freyproduce.com
      Website: www.freyproduce.com
Grow, pack & dist fresh fruits & vegetables: watermelons, cantaloupe, green bell peppers, sweet corn, pumpkins, squash, soybeans, wheat. (Woman, estab 1996, empl 20, sales $50,000,000, cert: WBENC)

3616 Harris Ice Company
      3927 W 5th Ave
      Chicago, IL 60624
      Contact: Walker Harris President
      Tel: 773-826-3110
      Email: harrisice1@sbcglobal.net
      Website: www.harrisicechicago.com
Mfr & deliver ice throughtout the City of Chicago and surrounding suburbs. (AA, estab 1970, empl 15, sales $1,423,175, cert: City, NMSDC)

3617 Mullins Food Products, Inc.
      2200 S 25th Ave
      Broadview, IL 60155
      Contact: Andy Camp Dir of Sales
      Tel: 708-344-3224
      Email: acamp@mullinsfood.com
      Website: www.mullinsfood.com
Custom mfr & package liquid condiments: sauces, salad dressings, ketchup, mayonnaise, picante sauce, salsa sauce, pizza sauce, asian style sauces, flavored syrups, icing. (Woman, estab 1934, empl 350, sales , cert: WBENC)

3618 Navisource Holdings LLC dba Golden Hill Foods LLC
      851 W Grand Ave 2nd Fl
      Chicago, IL 60642
      Contact: Demetrio Garcia VP Business Dev
      Tel: 312-226-5900
      Email: dgarcia@goldenhillfoods.com
      Website: www.goldenhillfoods.com
Import & dist dehydrated vegetables & spices. (Hisp, estab 2005, empl 6, sales $2,500,000, cert: NMSDC)

3619 Reggios' Pizza, Inc.
      340 W 83rd St
      Chicago, IL 60620
      Contact: Darryl Humphrey Sales & Marketing Dir
      Tel: 773-488-1411
      Email: dhumphrey@reggiospizzainc.com
      Website: www.reggios.com
Chicago Style Famous Buttercrust Pizza. (AA, estab 1972, empl 42, sales , cert: City)

3620 Stern Ingredients, Inc.
      1030 N State St #10BC
      Chicago, IL 60610
      Contact: Joni Stern President
      Tel: 773-472-0301
      Email: joni@sterningredients.com
      Website: www.sterningredients.com
Dist ingredients: confectionery, bakery, nutritional & snack food products. (Woman, estab 1990, empl 2, sales $434,255, cert: WBENC)

3621 Subco Foods
      1150 Commerce Dr
      West Chicago, IL 60185
      Contact: Nadia Attia Dir of Sales
      Tel: 630-231-0003
      Email: nattia@subcofoods.com
      Website: www.subcofoods.com
Dist dry food products: randed, private label & contract packaging, drink mixes, gelatin & puddings, coffee creamer, hot chocolate, cappuccino, cake mixes, gravy mixes, seasonings, pancake mixes, soup bases, rice products, nutraceuticals. (As-Pac, estab 1994, empl 90, sales $16,560,000, cert: NMSDC)

3622 Sulpice Better Bites
      PO Box 70
      Barrington, IL 60011
      Contact: Anne Shaeffer Founder
      Tel: 630-301-2345
      Email: anne@sulpicechocolat.com
      Website: www.sulpicechocolat.com
Milk chocolate with salt and almonds; dark chocolate with cinnamon and cayenne pepper; dark chocolate with ginger and lemon; 70% dark chocolate with sea salt; white chocolate with cake batter. (Woman, estab 2009, empl 2, sales $300,000, cert: WBENC)

3623 Suzy's Swirl
      703 Rockland Rd
      Lake Bluff, IL 60044
      Contact: Founder
      Tel: 224-544-5189
      Email: laine@suzysswirl.com
      Website: www.suzysswirl.com
Frozen desserts, liquor-infused frozen yogurts and sorbets. (Woman, estab 2012, empl 8, sales $350,000, cert: WBENC)

3624 The Edlong Corporation
      225 Scott St
      Elk Grove Village, IL 60007
      Contact: Gail Scott Exec Asst
      Tel: 847-631-6775
      Email: diversity@edlong.com
      Website: www.edlong.com
Dairy: cheese, butter, milk & cream, cultured, sweet & functional dairy. (Woman, estab , empl 100, sales , cert: WBENC)

3625 Thomas Imports LLC
      1327 W. Washington BLVD Ste 3D
      Chicago, IL 60607
      Contact: Chris Cottrell Sales
      Tel: 312-929-2699
      Email: ccottrell@isiahinternational.com
      Website: www.isiahimports.com
Corn tortillas, flour tortillas, flavored tortilla flour wraps; jalapeno wrap, tomato basil wrap, chipotle wrap, roasted garlic wrap, cheese, wraps corn chips, spices, chile peppers, canned sauces, frozen foods. (AA, estab 2016, empl 8, sales $ 0, cert: NMSDC)

3626 V&V Supremo Foods Inc.
      2141 S Throop St
      Chicago, IL 60608
      Contact: John Brandley Natl Sales Mgr
      Tel: 312-421-1020
      Email: johnb@vvsupremo.com
      Website: www.vvsupremo.com
Produce Hispanic cheese, creams & Chorizo. (Hisp, estab 1964, empl 184, sales $67,142,000, cert: NMSDC)

Indiana

3627 Williams, West & Witt's Product Co.
      3501 W Dunes Hwy
      Michigan City, IN 46360
      Contact: Joanne Tica Steiger Dir Business Dev
      Tel: 219-879-8236
      Email: jtsteiger@integrativeflavors.com
      Website: www.cooksdelight.com
Mfr healthy soup bases & innovative food flavor additives for the institutional, food service, corporate and government user channels. (Woman, estab 1938, empl 19, sales $2,500,000, cert: State, WBENC)

Louisiana

3628 Bridge Foods, Inc.
      PO Box 58698
      New Orleans, LA 70158
      Contact: Henry Chigbu President
      Tel: 504-254-9770
      Email: hchigbu@bridgefoods.com
      Website: www.ashantifoods.com
Condiments: hot sauce, wing sauce, steak sauce, worcestershire sauce, etc. (AA, estab 1993, empl 5, sales $15,000,000, cert: NMSDC)

Massachusetts

3629 600 lb Gorillas, Inc.
      558 Washington St
      Duxbury, MA 02332
      Contact: Paula White CEO
      Tel: 781-452-7273
      Email: paula@600lbgorillas.com
      Website: www.600lbgorillas.com
Dist premium frozen cookie dough. (Woman, estab 2000, empl 2, sales $3,000,000, cert: WBENC)

FOOD PRODUCTS AND SERVICES

3630 Adonai Spring Water Inc.
31 West St, Ste 4
Randolph, MA 02368
Contact: Gloria Olatunji President
Tel: 844-273-7672
Email: gloolat@aol.com
Website: www.adonaisprings.com
Bottled water 5 Gallons, Bottled Water Coolers, Point of Use Coolers, Drinking Water Fountains
Biodegradable & Compostable hot and cold cups, lids, straws, trays, napkins, plates, trays clamshells, Table top & Dinnerware. (Woman/AA, estab 2014, empl 2, sales , cert: State, WBENC)

3631 Boston Baking, Inc.
101 Sprague St
Boston, MA 02136
Contact: Julee Robey-Boschetto President
Tel: 617-364-6900
Email: julee@bostonbaking.com
Website: www.bostonbaking.com
Wholesale manufacturer of baked goods. (Woman, estab 2004, empl 54, sales $4,900,000, cert: City)

3632 Cape Cod Select LLC
73 Tremont St
Carver, MA 02330
Contact: Cindy Rhodes Owner
Tel: 508-866-1149
Email: crhodes@capecodselect.com
Website: www.capecodselect.com
Harvest, pack & dist cranberries. (Woman, estab 2009, empl 3, sales $ 0, cert: WBENC)

3633 Harbar LLC
320 Turnpike St
Canton, MA 02021
Contact: Keith Brennan Retail Sales Mgr
Tel: 800-881-7040
Email: kbrennan@harbar.com
Website: www.harbar.com
Mfr corn & flour tortillas. (Minority, Woman, estab 1986, empl 140, sales , cert: NMSDC)

3634 HimalaSalt - Sustainable Sourcing, LLC
1375 Boardman St
Sheffield, MA 01257
Contact: melissa kushi CEO
Tel: 413-446-8927
Email: melissa@himalasalt.com
Website: www.himalasalt.com
Dist pink Himalayan sea salt produced in our owned facility that is certified organic, Non-GMO, Gluten-Free, Kosher for Passover & powered by 156 solar panels. (Woman, estab 2006, empl 12, sales $2,500,000, cert: State)

3635 Jensay Co.
61 Maple St
Acton, MA 01720
Contact: Stephen Chen President
Tel: 978-929-9797
Email: stephenchen@joycechenfoods.com
Website: www.joycechenfoods.com
Asian, Chinese cooking sauces, oils, comdiments, spices & Asian frozen prepared food products. (As-Pac, estab 2006, empl 1, sales $950,000, cert: State)

3636 Monsoon Kitchens, Inc.
165 Memorial Dr Unit F
Shrewsbury, MA 01545
Contact: Lineman, Janice President
Tel: 508-842-0070
Email: jan@monsoonkitchens.co
Website: www.monsoonkitchens.com
Mfr Indian style frozen chicken entrees, vegetarian entress & appetizers. (As-Ind, estab 2003, empl 6, sales $5,000,000, cert: NMSDC)

3637 Nella Pasta LLC
859 Willard St Ste 400
Quincy, MA 02169
Contact: Leigh Foster Member
Tel: 860-888-9686
Email: nellapasta@gmail.com
Website: www.nellapasta.com
Pasta manufacturing. (Woman, estab 2009, empl 1, sales $145,879, cert: WBENC)

3638 R Square Desserts LLC
PO Box 990031
Boston, MA 02199
Contact: Susie Parish Co-Owner
Tel: 857-263-8833
Email: susie@batchicecream.com
Website: www.batchicecream.com
Ice cream made from real ingredients & without additives. (Woman, estab 2009, empl 5, sales , cert: WBENC)

3639 Signature Breads, Inc.
100 Justin Dr
Chelsea, MA 02150
Contact: Heidi Keathley VP Sales & Mktg
Tel: 617-819-3105
Email: heidi.keathley@signaturebreads.com
Website: www.signaturebreads.com
Mfr par-baked breads: dinner rolls, sandwich rolls, baguettes, ciabattas, breadsticks, pieggas & artisan breads, individual & bulk packaging, frozen or par-baked. (Hisp, estab 2006, empl 280, sales $48,000,000, cert: NMSDC)

3640 SJB Bagel Makers of Boston
77 Rowe St
Newton, MA 02466
Contact: Jeff Malich Dir of Sales
Tel: 617-213-8400
Email: jeff@finagleonline.com
Website: www.finagleabagel.com/
Artisan all natural bagel baker. We product 2 oz - 5 oz premium bagels. (Woman, estab 1992, empl 130, sales $12,000,000, cert: State, WBENC)

3641 VSR Enterprise, LLC
1675 Dorchester Ave
Boston, MA 02121
Contact: Vernon Barsatee CEO
Tel: 617-514-4711
Email: vernon@vsrenterprise.com
Website: www.vsrenterprise.com
Food Brokerage, Import & Export of consumer sized packaged (CPG), frozen foods, spices, dairy products, meats, health & beauty aids. (As-Pac, estab 2012, empl 2, sales , cert: NMSDC)

Maryland

3642 A Family Affair Productions, LLC
13679 Harvest Glen Way
Germantown, MD 20874
Contact: Lesley Riley CEO
Tel: 202-350-0448
Email: info@mamabiscuit.com
Website: www.mamabiscuit.com
Produce high-quality premium, clean label biscuits & baked goods. (AA, estab 2019, empl 5, sales $1,500,000, cert: NMSDC)

3643 Better and Best Corporation
1601 Knecht Ave
Halethorpe, MD 21227
Contact: Patricia Lobel President
Tel: 410-902-5701
Email: patricia.lobel@avenuegourmet.com
Website: www.avenuegourmet.com
Dist natural/organic products: sauces, marinades, fruit butters & spreads, cookies, crackers, cooking oils, vinegars, snacks, condiments & beverages. (Woman, estab 2000, empl 20, sales $ 0, cert: State)

3644 Caribbean Blue Organic Foods, LLC
6701 Democracy Blvd Ste 300
Bethesda, MD 20817
Contact: Lenore Travers President
Tel: 301-564-4322
Email: sales@caribbeanbluewater.com
Website: www.CaribbeanBlueWater.com
Caribbean Blue Natural Spring Water. (AA, estab 2011, empl 1, sales $185,000, cert: State)

3645 CharmedBar, LLC
120 Canfield Hill Dr
Gaithersburg, MD 20878
Contact: Debbi Ascher President
Tel: 202-430-5637
Email: debbi@charmedbar.com
Website: www.charmedbar.com
Kosher, baked fruit & nut bars, certified gluten free & grain free, dairy, soy, egg, refined sugars, GMOs, preservatives & artificial ingredients. (Woman, estab 2013, empl 2, sales $188,000, cert: WBENC)

3646 Collaborative Food & Beverage, LLC dba Mayorga Coffee
15151 Southlawn Ln
Rockville, MD 20850
Contact: Martin Mayorga President
Tel: 301-315-8093
Email: martin@mayorgacoffee.com
Website: www.mayorgacoffee.com
Roasted whole bean specialty coffees, ground "portion packed" specialty coffees, custom blends, private labeling. (Minority, Woman, estab 1997, empl 87, sales $17,500,000, cert: State)

3647 Demeter's Pantry dba GreenFood Associates LLC
419 Greenbrier Dr
Silver Spring, MD 20910
Contact: Maria Kardamaki Robertson Partner
Tel: 301-587-0048
Email: maria@demeterspantry.com
Website: www.thegreektable.net
Dist ethnic foods, Mediterranean (Greek prepared foods, entrées, side dishes & bean salad dishes. (Woman, estab 2003, empl 2, sales $490,058, cert: State)

3648 MAS Foods International, LLC
PO Box 2886
Montgomery Village, MD 20886
Contact: Michael Short Chief Managing Officer
Tel: 301-591-9728
Email: mshort@masfi.com
Website: www.masfi.com
Gourmet chicken sausage & personal chicken pizza made from halal products. (AA, estab 2004, empl 2, sales , cert: NMSDC)

3649 SodexoMagic (Magic Food Provision, LLC)
9801 Washingtonian Blvd
Gaithersburg, MD 20878
Contact: Ken Holdman Dir Strategic Sales
Tel: 918-430-6514
Email: ken.holdman@sodexomagic.com
Website: www.sodexomagic.com
Food & catering services groundkeeping facilities and plant operations and maintenance, environmental & engineering services & laundry & linens. (AA, estab 2006, empl 4900, sales $283,400,000, cert: NMSDC)

3650 SoFine Food
4825 Cordell Ave, Ste 200
Bethesda, MD 20814
Contact: Sophia Maroon CEO
Tel: 301-979-9555
Email: sophia@sofinefood.com
Website: www.dressitupdressing.com
Produce all-natural, shelf-stable vinaigrettes, called Dress It Up Dressing, gluten-free, sugar-free & vegan. (Woman, estab 2012, empl 2, sales , cert: WBENC)

3651 Soft Stuff Distributors, Inc.
8200 Preston Court Ste L
Jessup, MD 20794
Contact: Lois Gamerman President
Tel: 301-604-3300
Email: loisg@gosoftstuff.com
Website: www.gosoftstuff.com
Dist breads, bagels, cakes, cheesecakes, muffin batters & baked muffins, frozen doughs, preproofed danish & croisants, cookies-frozen doughs & prebaked, pizzas, soups fresh & frozen, catering dessert items. (Woman, estab 1989, empl 35, sales $10,500,000, cert: State, WBENC)

3652 Teddy Bear Fresh Produce, LLC
28595 Marys Ct
Easton, MD 21601
Contact: Mary Salins Owner
Tel: 410-829-7575
Email: mary@teddybearfresh.com
Website: www.teddybearfresh.com
Dist Fresh Produce & Dairy & Foodservice to School Systems, Health Care Facilities, Correctional Facilities, & Restaurants. (Woman, estab 2009, empl 120, sales $28,000,000, cert: State, WBENC)

Maine

3653 Bixby & Co., LLC
      248 Norport Ave Ste C
      Belfast, ME 04915
      Contact: Kate McAleer Owner
      Tel: 845-346-6591
      Email: kate@bixbyco.com
      Website: www.bixbyco.com
Mfr healthy gluten free candy bars. Produces three vegan flavors. Kosher certified. (Woman, estab 2011, empl 1, sales , cert: WBENC)

3654 Blue Sky Produce
      243 Tory Hill Rd
      Phillips, ME 04966
      Contact: Lynn Thurston Owner
      Tel: 207-684-2172
      Email: hope@tdstelme.net
      Website: www.blueskyproduce.com
Pesticide Free & Conventionally grown Frozen Wild Blueberries packed in 14 oz containers. (Woman, estab 1987, empl 6, sales , cert: WBENC)

Michigan

3655 Dual Sales & Associates, Inc.
      PO Box 725
      Grand Blanc, MI 48480
      Contact: Donna Bromm Owner
      Tel: 248-505-7128
      Email: donna@dualsales.com
      Website: www.dualsales.com
Dist shelled walnuts & pecans, specialty dried fruits. (Woman, estab 1993, empl 1, sales , cert: WBENC)

3656 Ebonex
      18400 Rialto
      Melvindale, MI 48122
      Contact: Shelly Toenniges Principal
      Tel: 313-388-0063
      Email: stoenniges@ebonex.com
      Website: www.keystoneuniversal.com
Dist baking ammonium carbonate: lump, chip or powder. (Woman, estab , empl 12, sales $ 0, cert: WBENC)

3657 Flamm Pickle & Packing Co., Inc.
      4502 Hipps Hollow Rd
      Eau Claire, MI 49111
      Contact: Dorothy Munao President
      Tel: 269-461-6916
      Email: dorothymunao@flammpickle.com
      Website: www.flammpickle.com
Mfr dill pickles & sweet pickle relishes. (Woman, estab , empl 16, sales $1,885,000, cert: WBENC)

3658 Jogue, Inc.
      14731 Helm Ct
      Plymouth, MI 48170
      Contact: Andrew Huber CFO
      Tel: 734-207-0100
      Email: andrew@jogue.com
      Website: www.jogue.com
Mfr dry flavors and beverage bases. (As-Ind, estab 1984, empl 48, sales $17,933,000, cert: NMSDC)

3659 The Alden Group
      31800 Northwestern Hwy Ste 355
      Farmington Hills, MI 48334
      Contact: Donald Bryant President
      Tel: 866-717-1077
      Email: dbryant@aldengroupinc.com
      Website: www.aldenoils.com
Wholesale food service for restaurants and distributors. Bulk product in bounding & shipment. (AA, estab 2007, empl 10, sales $8,200,000, cert: NMSDC)

Minnesota

3660 Aarthun Enterprises, LLC dba Taste of Scandinavia
      111 E County Rd F
      Vadnais Heights, MN 55127
      Contact: CFO
      Tel: 651-483-9242
      Email: office@tasteofscandinavia.com
      Website: www.tasteofscandinavia.com
Hand crafted Cakes & Tortes, Cupcakes & Cookies both traditional & custom request. (Woman, estab 2004, empl 118, sales $7,062,388, cert: WBENC)

3661 Catallia Mexican Foods, LLC
      2965 Lone Oak Circle
      Eagan, MN 55121
      Contact: Cathy Cruz Gooch President
      Tel: 651-647-6808
      Email: cathy@catallia.com
      Website: www.catallia.com
Mfr premium flour tortillas. (Woman/Hisp, estab 2005, empl 150, sales $ 0, cert: NMSDC)

3662 Healthy America, LLC
      13570 Grove Dr#372
      Maple Grove, MN 55311
      Contact: Sunil Kumar President
      Tel: 651-666-0375
      Email: sunil.kumar@theamazingchickpea.com
      Website: www.theamazingchickpea.com
Produce Chickpea Spread that tastes like peanut butter but does not contain any Nuts, Gluten Free and Dairy Free. "The Amazing Chickpea - Creamy", "The Amazing Chickpea - Crunchy","The Amazing Chickpea - Traditional". (As-Pac, estab 2016, empl 5, sales $200,000, cert: NMSDC)

3663 Sweet Harvest Foods Management Company
      15100 Business Pkwy
      Rosemount, MN 55068
      Contact: Joel Rengel Sales Dir
      Tel: 507-263-8599
      Email: jrengel@sweetharvestfoods.com
      Website: www.sweetharvestfoods.com
Mfr honey, ingredient honey, pancake syrup (table syrup), corn syrup & branded peanut butter. (Woman, estab 1923, empl 50, sales , cert: WBENC)

North Carolina

3664 Calvine's Coffee LLC
PO Box 3005
Matthews, NC 28106
Contact: John Williamson President
Tel: 800-545-8553
Email: john@cadprinting.biz
Website: www.calvinescoffee.com
Gourmet specialty roast blend of coffee beans from many origins around the world, including small farms and farmers. Our beans are roasted in small batches in a San Franciscan Artisan Roaster. (Woman/AA, estab 2015, empl 1, sales , cert: State)

3665 Dover Foods, Inc.
353 Banner Farm RD
Mills River, NC 28759
Contact: Kathy Milner Natl Acct Mgr
Tel: 828-890-8344
Email: kathy@americanqualityfoods.com
Website: www.aqf.com
Mfr & dist sugar free & gluten free dessert mixes: cookies, cream pie fillings, cheesecakes, gelatin, mousse mixes, drink mixes, cake mixes, frosting & pie shells. (Woman, estab 1994, empl 35, sales $5,000,000, cert: WBENC)

3666 FDY, Inc.
2459 Wilkinson Blvd Ste 300
Charlotte, NC 28208
Contact: Keith Haywood VP Sales & Mktg
Tel: 704-523-6605
Email: khaywood@fdyinc.com
Website: www.fdyinc.com
Food service mgmt: cafeteria, dining services, vending, catering, design. (Woman/AA, estab 1983, empl 275, sales $10,870,702, cert: City)

3667 High Country Springs LLC
PO Box 238
Pilot Mountain, NC 27041
Contact: Linda Tucker Partner
Tel: 336-374-7474
Email: ltucker@highcountrysprings.com
Website: www.highcountrysprings.com
Provide 5-gallon, 3-gallon & 1-gallon Spring, Distilled, RO (Reverse Osmosis), Deionized, and Fluoride Water, water dispensers & coffee service. (Woman, estab 1992, empl 10, sales $605,431, cert: State)

3668 MyThreeSons Gourmet, LLC
2309 Lafayette Ave
Greensboro, NC 27408
Contact: Cheryl Barnett President
Tel: 336-324-5638
Email: mtsgourmet@gmail.com
Website: www.mtsgourmet.com
Mfr natural gourmet pimento cheese spread. (Woman, estab 2010, empl 10, sales $3,800,000, cert: WBENC)

3669 Nirav Dye & Chemicals Inc.
6420 Rea Rd Ste A1-357
Charlotte, NC 28277
Contact: Shaili Doshi Dir
Tel: 704-509-1677
Email: shaili@niravgroup.com
Website: www.niravingredients.com
Dist food grade products, emulsifiers, functional ingredients, natural extracts and other ingredients. (As-Ind, estab 1994, empl 3, sales $25,000,000, cert: NMSDC)

3670 The Busha Group LLC
302 Lord Court
Cramerton, NC 28032
Contact: Julie Busha CEO
Tel: 704-879-4411
Email: jbusha@slawsa.com
Website: www.slawsa.com
Mfr Slawsa, slaw-salsa hybrid condiment, all natural, fat-free, cholesterol-free, gluten-free, low in sodium & kosher. (Woman, estab 2013, empl 1, sales $363,320, cert: WBENC)

3671 Tropical Nut & Fruit Co
1100 Continental Blvd
Charlotte, NC 28273
Contact: Angela Bauer Owner
Tel: 704-588-0400
Email: abauer@tropicalfoods.com
Website: www.tropicalfoods.com
Mfr & dist nuts, seeds, dried fruit, snack mixes, candy & specialty foods. (Woman, estab 1977, empl , sales $88,000,000, cert: WBENC)

New Hampshire

3672 Healthy Solutions Spice Blends, LLC
PO Box 1094
Hampton, NH 03843
Contact: Shelly Wolcott Mgr
Tel: 603-622-8744
Email: shelly@spiceblends.com
Website: www.spiceblends.com
Produce all natural, high quality, recipe ready spice blends. (Woman, estab 2013, empl , sales , cert: WBENC)

3673 Homefree, LLC
PO Box 491
Windham, NH 03087
Contact: Jill Robbins President
Tel: 603-898-0172
Email: info@homefreetreats.com
Website: www.homefreetreats.com
Mfr all natural or organic, ready-to-eat whole grain baked goods free of gluten & common food allergens. (Woman, estab 2009, empl 18, sales $624,408, cert: WBENC)

New Jersey

3674 Adrienne's Classic Creations, LLC
111 Patriots Ridge Dr
Deptford, NJ 08096
Contact: Adrienne Smith CEO
Tel: 856-313-3137
Email: adrienne@adriennecc.com
Website: www.adriennecc.com
Creation & sale of baked goods - regular sugar, all natural sugar replacement & gluten free. We sell to all retail, wholesale establishments, food service, and nursing homes/rehab facilities. (Woman/AA, estab 2006, empl 2, sales $225,000, cert: NMSDC)

FOOD PRODUCTS AND SERVICES

3675 Advanced Food Systems
      21 Roosevelt Ave
      Somerset, NJ 08863
      Contact: Al Rose Midwest Sales Mgr
      Tel: 732-873-6776
      Email: ajrose@charter.net
      Website: www.afsnj.com
Food ingredients: gums, starches, proteins, spices, flavors, lab services. (As-Pac, estab 1980, empl 40, sales $50,000,000, cert: NMSDC)

3676 Crispy Green Inc.
      10 Madison Rd
      Fairfield, NJ 07004
      Contact: Angela Liu President
      Tel: 973-679-4515
      Email: angela@crispygreen.com
      Website: www.crispygreen.com
Crispy Green Fruit product line is created using a sophisticated freeze-drying process where water is removed from the fresh fruit in a cold (freezing) vacuum condition, leaving behind the true essence of the fruit in a light and crispy texture. (Minority, Woman, estab 2004, empl 10, sales , cert: State)

3677 Harris Freeman & Co LP
      344 New Albany Rd
      Moorestown, NJ 08057
      Contact: Steve Sernka Natl Sales Mgr
      Tel: 856-793-0290
      Email: steve.sernka@harrisfreeman.com
      Website: www.HarrisTea.com
Manufacturer tea. (As-Ind, estab 1997, empl 129, sales , cert: NMSDC)

3678 JK Enterprise Solutions LLC
      1000 Delsea Dr Building I Unit 1
      Westville, NJ 08093
      Contact: Abdul Ahad Butt Owner
      Tel: 856-228-5934
      Email: ahad@jkens.com
      Website: www.jkens.com
Dist snack food products: Bud's Best Cookies, Uncle AL's Cremes, Lil Dutch maid wirecut cookies, Mayfair Candy Carnival, Select Sweets Candy, Daddy Rays fruit bars, Marco Polo Preserves, Caribbean Ice pops, Kisko Freezies. (As-Ind, estab 2014, empl 1, sales $187,000, cert: NMSDC)

3679 JVM Sales Corp.
      3401a Tremley Point Rd
      Linden, NJ 07036
      Contact: Justin Tomasino Owner
      Tel: 908-862-4866
      Email: justintomasino@aol.com
      Website: www.jvmsales.com
Provide Grated, Shredded & Shaved Cheeses, Hard Italian Cheese, Custom blended cheeses. (Woman, estab 1983, empl 200, sales $50,000,000, cert: WBENC)

3680 Soul Sisters Foods, Inc.
      41 Prince St, Ste B11
      Paterson, NJ 07505
      Contact: Betty Dixon President
      Tel: 973-742-8255
      Email: betty.dixon@unilever.com
      Website: www.soulroll.com
Retail frozen food, Soul Rolls: collard greens, marinated meats, cheddar cheese, onions, green peppers, and tomatoes, seasoned to perfection in a crispy flour tortilla. (Woman/AA, estab 2006, empl 2, sales , cert: WBENC)

3681 Suzanne's Specialties, Inc.
      421 Jersey Ave, Ste B
      New Brunswick, NJ 08901
      Contact: Susan Morano President
      Tel: 732-828-8500
      Email: suzspec@earthlink.net
      Website: www.suzannes-specialties.com
Mfr natural sweeteners: rice syrups, malt extracts, molasses, honey, agave syrup, invert, co-extracts, rice sweetener jellies, rice syrup based aerated toppings. (Woman, estab 1984, empl 25, sales $15,000,000, cert: WBENC)

3682 The Dessert Ladies
      266 Main Ave
      Stirling, NJ 07980
      Contact: Lindsay Smith Owner
      Tel: 908-340-7321
      Email: lindsay.smith@bienscc.com
      Website: www.dessertladies.com/
Custom edible gifts, hand-decorated, branded chocolate products & baked goods. (Woman, estab 2010, empl 10, sales $3,000,000, cert: WBENC)

3683 Undercover Chocolate Company LLC
      50 Williams Pkwy Ste B-2
      East Hanover, NJ 07936
      Contact: Michael Levy
      Tel: 973-665-8152
      Email:
      Website: www.undercoversnacks.com
Mfr snacks including our signature gluten-free, allergy friendly Chocolate Quinoa Crisps. (Woman, estab 0, empl , sales $1,000,000, cert: WBENC)

Nevada

3684 Tortillas Inc.
      2912 N Commerce St
      North Las Vegas, NV 89030
      Contact: Gustavo Gutierrez President
      Tel: 702-399-3300
      Email: gus@tortillasinc.com
      Website: www.tortillasinc.com
Corn tortillas, flour tortillas, flavored tortilla flour wraps; jalapeno wrap, tomato basil wrap, chipotle wrap, roasted garlic wrap, cheese, wraps corn chips, spices, chile peppers, canned sauces, frozen foods. (Hisp, estab 1979, empl 76, sales $8,000,000, cert: NMSDC)

New York

3685 Chocolate Promises, Inc.
      PO Box 694
      Merrick, NY 11566
      Contact: Zakalik Cindy President
      Tel: 516-299-6400
      Email: cindy@chocolatepromises.com
      Website: www.chocolatepromises.com
Personalized chocolate with edible images. We'll custom print your full color logo, picture, design and/or special message directly on delicious chocolate coins, lollipops, Belgian truffles and more. (Woman, estab 2012, empl 2, sales , cert: State, City, WBENC)

3686 Golden Glow Cookie Co. Inc.
       1844 Givan Ave
       Bronx, NY 10469
       Contact: Joan Florio Mgr
       Tel: 718-379-6223
       Email: ggcookies@aol.com
       Website: www.thecookiefactory.com
Wholesale bakery, cookies & other related bakery items in bulk, plastic clamshells & individually wrapped. (Woman, estab 1954, empl 15, sales , cert: City)

3687 IMK Products, Inc.
       244 Fifth Ave Ste D146
       New York, NY 10001
       Contact: Ilona Kovacs President
       Tel: 914-500-8127
       Email: imkproductsinc@gmail.com
       Website: www.truetastebar.com
Dist nutritional bars, organic/non gmo, no added sugar, vegan, gluten free, soy free, dairy free. (Woman, estab 2011, empl 2, sales , cert: WBENC)

3688 Lugo Nutrition Inc.
       51 N Broadway, Ste 2B
       Nyack, NY 10960
       Contact: Nick Lugo VP
       Tel: 302-573-2301
       Email: nlugo@lugonutrition.com
       Website: www.lugonutrition.com
Gelatin, beta carotene. Bitterness masking, sweetness enhancing, natural preservative/flavoring. (Hisp, estab 2010, empl 5, sales $4,500,000, cert: NMSDC)

3689 SFR&R Inc.
       9 Soundview Lane
       Sands Point, NY 11050
       Contact: Giovannina Bellino Owner
       Tel: 516-767-7286
       Email: goddess6x8@aol.com
       Website: www.flavorbombs.net
Mfr frozen cooking bases & foods. Low Sodium, Gluten Free, All Natural products. (Woman, estab 2008, empl 1, sales , cert: WBENC)

3690 Thunder Island Coffee Roasters, L.L.C.
       PO Box 1275
       Southampton, NY 11969
       Contact: Benjamin Haile CEO
       Tel: 631-204-1110
       Email: info@thunderislandcoffee.com
       Website: www.thunderislandcoffee.com
Coffee roasting and packaging. (Nat Ame, estab 2005, empl 4, sales , cert: State)

Ohio

3691 ABC Cookie Co., Inc.
       3 Nationwide Plaza
       Columbus, OH 43215
       Contact: Dee Tolber CEO
       Tel: 614-221-4442
       Email: dee@ablessedcookie.com
       Website: www.ablessedcookie.com
Fresh baked cookies, muffins, coffee cake, custom shaped, logo design cookies & custom gift items. (Woman/AA, estab 1990, empl 4, sales $185,000, cert: NMSDC)

3692 Super Bakery
       1667 E 40th St, Ste 1D3
       Cleveland, OH 44103
       Contact: Karen Cahill Corporate Admin
       Tel: 216-426-8989
       Email: karen.cahill@superbakery.com
       Website: www.superbakery.com
Baked goods. (AA, estab 1989, empl 27, sales , cert: NMSDC)

3693 Urban Food Concepts LLC
       852 E Highland Rd
       Macedonia, OH 44056
       Contact: Claude Booker President
       Tel: 330-908-0493
       Email: claude@simplysouthernsides.com
       Website: www.simplysouthernsides.com
Fully cooked & seasoned vegetables & side dishes. (Woman/AA, estab 2007, empl 3, sales $4,000,000, cert: State, NMSDC, WBENC)

3694 Whitehall, Inc.
       4760 Paddock Rd
       Cincinnati, OH 45229
       Contact: Shawn Higgins Dir of Natl Sales
       Tel: 513-242-1004
       Email: shiggins@klostermanbakery.com
       Website: www.klostermanbakery.com
Restaurant quality bread, buns & rolls in a unique, handy and more compact retail package. (Woman, estab , empl 560, sales $295,400,000, cert: WBENC)

Oregon

3695 Hood River Juice Company
       550 Riverside Dr
       Hood River, OR 97031
       Contact: David Ryan President
       Tel: 541-386-3003
       Email: davidr@hrjco.com
       Website: www.ryansjuice.com
Natural & organic apple juice, single strength, not from concentrate. (Hisp, estab 1982, empl 113, sales $35,000,000, cert: NMSDC)

3696 Lucky Foods, LLC
       7774 SW Nimbus Ave, Bldg 10
       Beaverton, OR 97008
       Contact: Tammy Jo President
       Tel: 503-641-6602
       Email: tammyjo@luckyfood.com
       Website: www.luckyfood.com
Asian foods. (Minority, Woman, estab 1985, empl 16, sales $1,547,000, cert: State)

Pennsylvania

3697 A.S.K. Foods Inc.
       71 Hetrick Ave
       Palmyra, PA 17078
       Contact: Liz Burkholder Reg Sales Mgr
       Tel: 717-838-6356
       Email: ldurr@askfoods.com
       Website: www.askfoods.com
Mfr prepared deli salads, entrees, side dishes, soups with no preservatives added. (Woman, estab 1947, empl 175, sales $42,200,000, cert: WBENC)

FOOD PRODUCTS AND SERVICES

3698 Casalingo LLC
6321 S Highlings Circle
Harrisburg, PA 17111
Contact: Monette Roberto Member
Tel: 717-805-5088
Email: monetteroberto@yahoo.com
Website: www.casalingofoods.com
Four Generation homemade local pasta sauce. (Woman, estab 2013, empl 2, sales , cert: WBENC)

3699 Dutch Gold Honey, Inc.
2220 Dutch Gold Dr
Lancaster, PA 17601
Contact: Jill Clark
Tel: 717-393-1716
Email: jclark@dutchgoldhoney.com
Website: www.dutchgoldhoney.com
Honey & maple syrup processing & packaging. (Woman, estab 1946, empl 75, sales , cert: WBENC)

3700 Enchanted Acres Farm, Inc.
200 N 8th St Ste 500
Reading, PA 19601
Contact: Kelley Huff President
Tel: 877-707-3833
Email: quality@enchantedacresfarm.net
Website: www.enchantedacresfarm.net
Mfr beverages: tea, coffee, cocoa. (Woman, estab 2002, empl 15, sales $700,000, cert: State)

3701 Fallon Trading Co., Inc.
3897 Adler Pl, Ste C150
Bethlehem, PA 18017
Contact: Michele Rossi Office Mgr
Tel: 610-867-5527
Email: michele@fallontrading.com
Website: www.fallontrading.com
Dist conventional and organic fruit and vegetable juice concentrates, purees, NFC, IQF, essences, powders, oils, flavors, colors, and extracts. (Woman, estab 1998, empl 4, sales , cert: WBENC)

3702 Gourmail Inc.
300 Elmwood Ave
Sharon Hill, PA 19079
Contact: Business Mgr
Tel: 610-522-2650
Email: info@jyotifoods.com
Website: www.jyotifoods.com
Ready to serve vegetarian entrees, soups and sauces for at-home cooking, packed in cans. Indian Dals (Legumes), in pouches. (Minority, Woman, estab 1979, empl 25, sales $30,000,000, cert: NMSDC)

3703 Sweet Street Desserts
722 Hiesters Lane
Reading, PA 19605
Contact: Anthony DiGirolamo CFO
Tel: 610-921-8113
Email: cathy.bitler@sweetstreet.com
Website: www.sweetstreet.com
Mfr frozen goumet desserts: cakes, pies, cheesecakes, dessert bars, bundt cakes, loaf cakes, cookies, scones, cupcakes & mousses. (Woman, estab , empl , sales , cert: WBENC)

3704 Zana Cakes, Inc.
12 W Willow Grove Ave, Ste 153
Philadelphia, PA 19118
Contact: Zana Billue President
Tel: 215-248-1575
Email: info@zanacakes.com
Website: www.zanacakes.com
Cakes & pies. (Woman/AA, estab 1988, empl 1, sales , cert: NMSDC)

Puerto Rico

3705 Able Sales Company
PO Box 11946
San Juan, PR 00936
Contact: Luis Silva CEO
Tel: 787-620-4141
Email: lsilva@ablesales.com
Website: www.ablesales.com
Confectionery Merchant Wholesalers (Hisp, estab 1988, empl 25, sales , cert: NMSDC)

South Carolina

3706 Charleston Gourmet Burger Company
4206 Sawgrass Dr
North Charleston, SC 29420
Contact: chevalo wilsondebriano Owner
Tel: 843-847-8369
Email: chevalo@charlestongourmetburger.com
Website: www.charlestongourmetburger.com
Charleston Gourmet Burger Marinade -blend of nine herbs & spices. (Woman/AA, Hisp, estab 2012, empl 2, sales $1,000,000, cert: NMSDC)

3707 Chef Belinda LLC dba Chef Belinda Spices
6 Mooney Court
Trenton, SC 29847
Contact: Belinda Smith-Sullivan President
Tel: 803-552-6450
Email: belinda@chefbelinda.com
Website: www.chefbelindaspices.com
Produce all-natural artisan spice blends. (Woman/AA, estab 2009, empl 3, sales , cert: NMSDC)

3708 Pino Gelato, LLC
1000 William Hilton Pkwy, Ste G-1
Hilton Head Island, SC 29928
Contact: Jessica Scott CEO
Tel: 843-842-2822
Email: marketing@pinogelato.com
Website: www.pinogelato.com
Premium gelato & sorbetto. (Woman, estab 2004, empl 6, sales $1,748,000, cert: WBENC)

3709 Spartanburg Meat Processing Co., Inc.
3003 N Blackstock Rd
Spartanburg, SC 29301
Contact: JoAnne LaBounty Business Devel
Tel: 864-621-1520
Email: eatbbqribsjl@aol.com
Website: www.eatbbqribs.com
Meat processing plant, pork, beef & chicken. Baby Back Ribs w/Sauce, Back Ribs, Pulled Pork w/Sauce, Pulled Chicken w/Sauce, Custom Proteins & Sauces. (Woman, estab 1999, empl 51, sales $17,128,586, cert: State, WBENC)

3710 Sweet Bottom Cookies
      PO Box 355
      Mt. Pleasant, SC 29466
      Contact: Michele Lewis President
      Tel: 843-693-7366
      Email: mlewis@sweetbottomcookies.com
      Website: www.SweetBottomCookies.Com
Privately brands & wholesales jumbo (3.5oz), soft, individually wrapped, fudge covered bottom cookies. (Woman, estab 2010, empl 4, sales , cert: WBENC)

3711 The Muffin Mam, Inc.
      3129 N Industrial Dr
      Simpsonville, SC 29681
      Contact: Greg Marshall VP Sales & Mktg
      Tel: 800-948-4268
      Email: gmarshall@muffinmam.com
      Website: www.muffinmam.com
Mfr custom baked Crème Cakes, Pound Cakes, Coffee Cakes, Gourmet Muffins, & Brownies. Use recycled & recycle able packaging. (Woman, estab 1990, empl 70, sales $24,500,000, cert: WBENC)

South Dakota

3712 Native American Natural Foods LLC
      287 Water Tower Rd
      Kyle, SD 57752
      Contact: Mark Tilsen President
      Tel: 605-455-2187
      Email: mtilsen@tankabar.com
      Website: www.tankabar.com
Gluten free, nitrate free, MSG free & hormone free Tanka Bar, Tanka Bites, and Tanka Sticks. (Minority, Woman, estab 2007, empl 12, sales $1,525,000, cert: NMSDC)

Tennessee

3713 Hardy Beverage LLC
      5815 E Shelby Dr
      Memphis, TN 38141
      Contact: Carolyn Hardy
      Tel: 901-779-2010
      Email: carolyn@hardybeverages.com
      Website: www.hardybeverages.com
Dist beverages. (Woman/AA, estab 2021, empl 12, sales $2,500,000, cert: NMSDC, WBENC)

Texas

3714 Artesia Springs LLC
      8130 Interchange Pkwy
      San Antonio, TX 78218
      Contact: Rudy Ramon President
      Tel: 210-637-5554
      Email: rudy@artesiasprings.com
      Website: www.artesiasprings.com
Bottled water in all sizes from 16.9 liters, 3 and 4 gallon disposable and 5 gallon recycable, Private label options, water coolers, water filtration options. (Woman/Hisp, estab 2004, empl 19, sales $1,400,000, cert: State, NMSDC)

3715 Behrnes Pepper Salts
      5313 E Side Ave
      Dallas, TX 75214
      Contact: Jan Olavarri Owner
      Tel: 214-724-0581
      Email: jan@behrnes.com
      Website: www.behrnes.com
Mfr pepper salts blends using Chipotle, Cayenne & Green Jalapeno. (Woman, estab 2012, empl 1, sales , cert: WBENC)

3716 Cadeco Industries, Inc.
      5610 Clinton Dr
      Houston, TX 77020
      Contact: Carlos deAldecoa President
      Tel: 713-670-0700
      Email: carlos@cadeco.cc
      Website: www.cadeco.cc
Bulk coffee processing, storage & distribution services. (Hisp, estab 1995, empl 45, sales $40,000,000, cert: State, NMSDC)

3717 Clint's Picante Inc.
      12 Thornhurst
      San Antonio, TX 78218
      Contact: Keri Poulter CFO
      Tel: 210-274-5916
      Email: keripoulter@yahoo.com
      Website: www.clintspicante.com
Mfr Salsa & BBQ sauce. (Woman, estab 1996, empl 2, sales $29,990,000, cert: State, City)

3718 Cookies by Design
      1865 Summit Ave Ste 607
      Plano, TX 75074
      Contact: Darylyn Phillips Natl Sales Coord
      Tel: 800-347-3110
      Email: dphillips@cookiesbydesign.com
      Website: www.cookiesbydesign.com
Customized, hand-decorated cookie baskets, cookie bouquets, cookie cakes, individual logo cookies, gourmet cookies, cupcakes, gluten free & sugar free. (Woman, estab 1983, empl 54, sales $28,000,000, cert: State, WBENC)

3719 Ezbake Technologies
      PO Box 270527
      Flowermound, TX 75027
      Contact: Rita Tolvanen CEO
      Tel: 888-287-8447
      Email: rita@ezbake.net
      Website: www.ezbaketechnologies.com
Dist baking ingredients, enzyme based dough conditioners, shelf life extenders & specialty conditioners for cookies, cakes, donuts, English muffins & low moisture products. (Woman, estab 1993, empl 4, sales $1,000,000, cert: WBENC)

3720 Global Coffee Company
      6161 Savoy Dr, Ste 821
      Houston, TX 77236
      Contact: Shaheed Momin President
      Tel: 713-222-2291
      Email: shaheed@globalcoffeecompany.com
      Website: www.javatogo.com
Coffee, cappuccino, slushy, iced tea, juices, soda, water, paper goods, etc. (As-Ind, estab 2007, empl 4, sales $1,596,400, cert: State, City, NMSDC)

FOOD PRODUCTS AND SERVICES

3721 Sociologie Wines Vintage LLC
      3901 Arlington Highlands Blvd Ste 200
      Arlington, TX 76018
      Contact: Mark Hansen Owner
      Tel: 832-871-7917
      Email: mark@sociologiewine.com
      Website: www.sociologiewine.com
Refreshing blends of delicious fruits & natural ingredients, Red Berry & Blushing Rose wine. (Woman/AA, estab 2012, empl 3, sales , cert: NMSDC)

3722 Synop LLC
      225 Matlage Way #1942
      Sugar Land, TX 77487
      Contact: Owner
      Tel: 512-705-5059
      Email:
      Website: www.cheezinos.com
Cheezinos goes from freezer directly to oven and it is ready to eat in minutes. (Woman/As-Pac, estab 2005, empl 2, sales $450,000, cert: WBENC)

3723 Twang Partners, Ltd.
      6255 WT Montgomery Rd
      San Antonio, TX 78252
      Contact: Patrick Trevino VP Business Dev
      Tel: 603-498-7078
      Email: ptrevino@twang.com
      Website: www.twang.com
Mfr premium-flavored salts, sugars & seasonings. (Hisp, estab 1986, empl 65, sales $ 0, cert: State, NMSDC)

Utah

3724 Amboseli Foods, LLC
      320 W 1550 N Ste L
      Layton, UT 84041
      Contact: Sylvia Kapsandoy CEO
      Tel: 801-471-4250
      Email: sylvia@amboselifoods.com
      Website: www.usimplyseason.com
Custom seasoning manufacturing services. (AA, estab 2013, empl 4, sales $250,000, cert: NMSDC)

Virginia

3725 A M King LLC
      13241 Otto Rd
      Woodbridge, VA 22193
      Contact: Adima Aniteye CEO
      Tel: 703-855-9822
      Email: amkingllc@gmail.com
      Website: www.queenvictoriaspunch.com
Mfr & dist fruit punches: The Queen-Grapefruit, Pineapple, Apple, Orange, The Duchess— Lemon, Pineapple, Apple, Orange, The Baroness—Pomegranate, Pineapple, Lemon, Lime, Agave. (Woman/AA, estab 2012, empl 2, sales , cert: State)

3726 Grandmas Garden
      7044 Sauvage Ln
      Gainesville, VA 20155
      Contact: Amy Weaver President
      Tel: 571-244-1443
      Email: amyweaver@grandmasgarden.us
      Website: www.grandmasgarden.us
All natural "Sweet" & "Spicy Sweet" gourmet relish: cabbage, peppers, tomatoes, onions & spices. (Woman, estab 2011, empl 2, sales , cert: State)

3727 Savaspice LLC
      6247 Glen Wood Loop
      Manassas, VA 20112
      Contact: Lova Mitchell Owner
      Tel: 703-895-4800
      Email: savaspice@gmail.com
      Website: www.savaspice.com
Madagascar vanilla & spices. (Woman/As-Ind, estab 2015, empl 1, sales , cert: State)

3728 Thompson Hospitality Services, LLC
      1741 Business Center Dr Ste 200
      Reston, VA 20190
      Contact: Genevieve Stona VP Joint Ventures
      Tel: 703-964-5500
      Email: gstona@thompsonhospitality.com
      Website: www.thompsonhospitality.com
Contract foodservice management, vending & facilities maintenance. (AA, estab , empl , sales $73,000,000, cert: NMSDC)

Washington

3729 Alexa's Catering Inc.
      10115 Main St
      Bothell, WA 98011
      Contact: Leigh Henderson President
      Tel: 425-483-6275
      Email: leigh@alexascafe.com
      Website: www.alexascafe.com
Full service catering services specializing in current American Cuisine. (Woman, estab 1991, empl 30, sales $1,800,000, cert: State)

3730 Kylie B's Pastry Case LLC
      4114 B Place NW, Ste 100
      Auburn, WA 98001
      Contact: Sabrina Bacungan Chief Mktg Officer
      Tel: 253-217-6131
      Email: sabrina@kyliebbakery.com
      Website: www.kyliebbakery.com
Hand-made traditional shortbread. (Minority, Woman, estab 2016, empl 4, sales , cert: WBENC)

3731 Lanier's Fine Candies
      5710 S Bangor St
      Seattle, WA 98178
      Contact: Herman Lanier CEO
      Tel: 206-723-6465
      Email: herman@laniersfinecandies.com
      Website: www.laniersfinecandies.com
Brittle candies: almond, cashew, peanut, pecan & macadamia, hand dipped in dark & milk chocolate. (AA, estab 2013, empl 2, sales , cert: NMSDC)

3732 Lynnae's Gourmet Pickles LLC
      3024 S Mullen #F
      Tacoma, WA 98466
      Contact: Lynnae Schneller President
      Tel: 253-226-2370
      Email: lynnae@lynnaesgourmetpickles.com
      Website: www.lynnaesgourmetpickles.com
Mfr all natural, high quality pickles with unique flavor combinations. (Woman, estab 2011, empl 3, sales $285,000, cert: State)

Wisconsin

3733 Fair Oaks Farms, LLC
7600 95th St
Pleasant Prairie, WI 53158
Contact: Michael Thompson Natl Acct Sales Mgr
Tel: 262-947-0320
Email: mthompson@osigroup.com
Website: www.fairoaksfarms.com

Dist meats. (AA, estab 1985, empl 260, sales $ 0, cert: NMSDC)

3734 Jeneil Biotech, Inc.
400 N Dekora Woods Blvd
Saukville, WI 53080
Contact: Stephen Beaver Sales
Tel: 262-268-6815
Email: s.beaver@jeneilbiotech.com
Website: www.jeneilbiotech.com

Mfr natural dairy flavors in pastes & powders, natural flavor aroma chemicals, soymilk powder, soy-cream cheese, fermentation, enzymolysis & distillation. (As-Ind, estab 1998, empl 43, sales $17,000,000, cert: NMSDC)

3735 Nanland LLC
5959 N Shore Acres Rd
New Franken, WI 54229
Contact: Nan Bush President
Tel: 920-562-9822
Email: nan@nanlandllc.com
Website: www.nanlandllc.com

Provides premium, single origin, organic coffee, 100% Arabica coffees from Peru, Nicaragua, Sumatra and Colombia packaged in 12 or 42 single serve cup boxes. (Woman, estab 2016, empl 2, sales , cert: WBENC)

FURNISHINGS

Manufacturers, distributors or importers of furniture for office and home. Also floor and window coverings, light fixtures, household and kitchen accessories such as wastebaskets, planters, dishes, vases, brooms, dustpans, etc. (See also GIFTWARE, ARTS & CRAFTS and OFFICE SUPPLIES categories. NAICS Code 42

Alabama

3736 E.S. Robbins Corp.
2802 E Avalon Ave
Muscle Shoals, AL 35661
Contact: Bonnie Donato Channel Marketing Mgr
Tel: 256-248-2494
Email: badonato@esrobbins.com
Website: www.esrchairmats.com
Dist office products & furnishings. Mfr polymer products. (Woman, estab 1967, empl 187, sales , cert: WBENC)

Arkansas

3737 Burris Inc.
113 S Arkansas Ave
Russellville, AR 72801
Contact: President
Tel: 479-968-4888
Email:
Website: www.burrisinc.com
Office supplies & office furniture, panel systems, custom millwork, office layout & design. (Woman, estab 1953, empl 15, sales $3,374,600, cert: WBENC)

Arizona

3738 Corporate Interior System
3311 E Broadway Rd, Ste A
Phoenix, AZ 85040
Contact: Lisa K Johnson President
Tel: 602-304-0100
Email: ljohnson@cisinphx.com
Website: www.cisinphx.com
Office Furniture Dealership, modular and system furniture and accessories, and installation of office furniture and accessories. (Woman, estab , empl , sales , cert: WBENC)

3739 Dave Scott & Associates, Inc.
PO Box 22115
Phoenix, AZ 85028
Contact: David R Scott Owner
Tel: 602-971-1600
Email: dave.scott@davescottassociates.com
Website: www.davescottassociates.com
Office Furniture, Health Care Furniture; Benches, receptacles, bike racks, ash urns; Millwork; Cell phone Charging Station Kiosks, Playgrounds, Design/space planning, Installation. (AA, estab 1999, empl 6, sales $1,360,539, cert: State, City, NMSDC)

3740 Elontec
5502 W Buckeye Rd, Ste 100
Phoenix, AZ 85043
Contact: Jessica Chappell Inside Sales Mgr
Tel: 602-759-5500
Email: jchappell@elontec.com
Website: www.elontec.com
Office furniture: cubicles, case goods, private offices, ect. Planning, design, procurement & installation. (Woman, estab 1997, empl 65, sales $5,200,000, cert: State, WBENC)

California

3741 Alternative Office Solutions
140 San Pedro Ave, Ste 110
Morgan Hill, CA 95037
Contact: Kevin Collier Sales Dir
Tel: 408-776-2036
Email: kevin@alt-office.com
Website: www.alt-office.com
Office space planning & installation of remanufactured Herman Miller AO1 and AO2 cubicles. (Woman, estab 1998, empl 19, sales $2,091,446, cert: CPUC)

3742 American Dawn Inc.
401 W Artesia Blvd
Compton, CA 90220
Contact: Mike Maloney Corp Secretary
Tel: 310-609-3222
Email: mmaloney@americandawn.com
Website: www.americandawn.com
Mfr & dist industrial & hospitality items: linens, towels, etc. (Minority, estab 1975, empl 200, sales , cert: NMSDC)

3743 Compact International
16161 Ventura Blvd, Ste 382
Encino, CA 91436
Contact: Robert Paul Mktg/Sales
Tel: 818-585-1374
Email: robert.paul@compactintl.com
Website: www.compactintl.com
Design, mfr & dist commercial furniture, folding chairs & tables. (AA, estab 1998, empl 4, sales $2,050,000, cert: State)

3744 Decor Interior Design
2937 E 4th St
Los Angeles, CA 90033
Contact: Principal
Tel: 310-289-2186
Email: info@designsbydecor.com
Website: www.designsbydecor.com
Interior Design, Custom Furniture, Window Treatments, Project Management, Interior Landscaping. (Woman/AA, estab 1997, empl 28, sales $552,000, cert: State, NMSDC, CPUC, WBENC)

3745 ECommerce Holdings, Inc.
201 Los Gatos Saratoga Rd, Ste 230
Los Gatos, CA 95030
Contact: Purnims Nandkishore President
Tel: 866-465-3294
Email: purnima@babychangingstations.com
Website: www.babychangingstations.com
Dist Koala baby changing stations & Bathroom Accessories: Fans, Mirrors, Medicine Cabinets, Soap Dishes, Towel Bars and Rings, Plumbing Fixtures & Parts. (Woman/As-Ind, estab 2009, empl 2, sales $840,866, cert: NMSDC, CPUC)

3746 Environments Plus, Inc.
1700 1st St
San Fernando, CA 91340
Contact: Regina Cordell Owner
Tel: 866-865-8120
Email: rcordell@epi-usa.com
Website: www.Environmentsplus.com
Office Furniture Installation, Reconfiguration, Liquidation, Furniture Storage, Design Services. (Woman, estab 1992, empl 45, sales, cert: CPUC, WBENC)

3747 HSE USA, Inc.
      5709 E 61st St
      Commerce, CA 90040
      Contact: Nelson Yip President
      Tel: 323-278-0888
      Email: nelson.yip@hseusa.com
      Website: www.hseusa.com
We carry a large selection of candles for the food-service and hospitality industries. (As-Pac, estab 2008, empl 10, sales $4,100,000, cert: NMSDC)

3748 Metro Contract Group
      1111 Broadway Ste 1650
      Oakland, CA 94607
      Contact: Dwight Jackson President
      Tel: 510-254-4281
      Email: dwight@metrocontractgroup.com
      Website: www.metrocontractgroup.com
Contract furniture dealer & design firm. (AA, estab 1993, empl 30, sales $3,010,000, cert: State, NMSDC, CPUC)

3749 MikaPak Inc.
      PO Box 4276
      Walnut Creek, CA 94596
      Contact: Helen Ma President
      Tel: 800-579-0880
      Email: helen@mikapak.com
      Website: www.mikapak.com
Sustainable, compostable products from plate wares, utensils, drink cups, food containers to packaging labels using renewable plant base raw materials. (Minority, Woman, estab 1995, empl 1, sales $279,000, cert: NMSDC)

3750 Murti LLC
      23896 Madison St
      Torrance, CA 90505
      Contact: Minal Mondkar President
      Tel: 310-614-3451
      Email: minalmondkar@auraseating.com
      Website: www.auraseating.com
Design-Manufacturer of Seating Products & accessories. Ergonomic Chairs, Tables, Training Room Tables, Trashcans, Glassboards, Floor glass mats
Hospitality Seating products. (Woman/As-Ind, estab 2010, empl 8, sales $926,000, cert: CPUC, WBENC)

3751 Office Design Group
      9963 Muirlands Blvd
      Irvine, CA 92618
      Contact: Katahy Habash Office Mgr
      Tel: 949-215-5557
      Email: kathy@officedesigngroup.com
      Website: www.officedesigngroup.com
Interior design, office furniture; wallcovering; carpet; signage; patio furniture; fitness equipment; and the delivery and installation of same. (Hisp, estab 1999, empl 5, sales $1,700,000, cert: NMSDC)

3752 Southwest Country
      17940 Ventura Blvd
      Encino, CA 91316
      Contact: Fred Fuchs Mgr
      Tel: 818-345-3900
      Email: webmaster@swcountry.com
      Website: www.cowboyindian.com
Mfr & dist southwest, western & country furniture, art & accessories. (Minority, Woman, estab 1989, empl 5, sales , cert: State, City)

3753 Systems Source Inc.
      4685 MacArthur Blvd. Ste 100
      Newport Beach, CA 92660
      Contact: Rosemarie Smith CEO
      Tel: 949-852-0920
      Email: bvente@systemsource.com
      Website: www.systemsource.com
Office furniture, modular furniture systems, demountable walls, design, installation, refinishing, reupholstery & service. (Woman, estab 1982, empl 215, sales $164,000,000, cert: CPUC, WBENC)

3754 Uniworld Omniport
      690 Garcia Ave Ste A
      Pittsburg, CA 94565
      Contact: Chris Smead Dir of Operations
      Tel: 925-439-3070
      Email: chris@bbopokertables.com
      Website: www.BBOPokerTables.com
Mfr & dist folding leg & furniture/dining/conference solid wood poker tables. (As-Pac, estab 2006, empl 5, sales $1,302,000, cert: NMSDC)

Colorado

3755 Premier Commercial Interiors, Inc.
      6830 N Broadway, Unit H
      Denver, CO 80221
      Contact: Brenda Jones President
      Tel: 303-466-8575
      Email: brendaj@pciwindowcoverings.com
      Website: www.pciwindowcoverings.com
Furnish & install window treatments (blinds, roller shades etc.) and projection screens. Clean & repair existing window treatments. (Woman, estab 2004, empl 9, sales , cert: WBENC)

3756 Workplace Elements LLC
      2501 Blake St
      Denver, CO 80205
      Contact: Cameron Gilbreath Controller
      Tel: 303-471-4334
      Email: cgilbreath@workplaceelements.com
      Website: www.workplaceelements.com
Office furniture, furniture storage, flooring, carpet, demountable walls, private office furniture. (Woman, estab 2008, empl 60, sales $38,000,000, cert: WBENC)

Connecticut

3757 De Clercq Office Group
      85 Willow St
      New Haven, CT 06511
      Contact: Deborah Hopewell Declercq President
      Tel: 203-230-9380
      Email: deb@dog-office.com
      Website: www.dog-office.com
Furniture related consulting services, pre-owned furniture & furniture rescue. (Woman, estab 2001, empl 6, sales $11,311,190, cert: WBENC)

3758 People Places and Spaces, LLC
      225 Asylum St
      Hartford, CT 06103
      Contact: Mark Nisbett CEO
      Tel: 860-386-8600
      Email: markn@pps-ct.com
      Website: www.pps-ct.com
Commercial office furniture, adaptable workspaces, and architectural interiors. (AA, estab 2018, empl 3, sales $8,280,210, cert: State, NMSDC)

3759 Workspace Consulting Group, LLC
      2777 Summer St, 2nd Fl
      Stamford, CT 06902
      Contact: Paulina Ribadeneyra Owner
      Tel: 203-548-0305
      Email: paulina@workspacecg.com
      Website: www.workspacecg.com
Office furniture and related consulting services. (Minority, Woman, estab 2010, empl 4, sales $1,591,348, cert: NMSDC)

Delaware

3760 Corporate Interiors, Inc.
      223 Lisa Dr
      New Castle, DE 19720
      Contact: Janice Leone President
      Tel: 302-345-7342
      Email: jleone@corporate-interiors.com
      Website: www.corporate-interiors.com
Sell and install office products. Manufacture & refabricate office furniture. Installation, reconfiguration & move services. (Woman, estab 1985, empl 189, sales $66,461,274, cert: WBENC)

Florida

3761 Above the Sill
      745 C Shamrock Blvd
      Venice, FL 34293
      Contact: Phillip Barone VP Sales & Mktg
      Tel: 941-492-3101
      Email: phil@abovethesill.net
      Website: www.abovethesill.net
Cubicle Curtains and track fabrication and installation, vertical blinds, roller shades, solar shades, mini blinds, faux wood blinds, solar panels, shutters, venetian blinds, etc. (Woman, estab 2004, empl 4, sales , cert: State)

3762 Berwin, Inc.
      3501 Commerce Pkwy
      Miramar, FL 33025
      Contact: Nancy Wolfe A/R Specialist
      Tel: 954-499-6677
      Email: nancy.wolfe@jcwhite.com
      Website: www.jcwhite.com
Design, dist, install & service office furniture, walls & floors. (Woman, estab 1978, empl 103, sales $43,000,000, cert: State, WBENC)

3763 Cadence Keen Innovations d/b/a CKI Solutions
      1645 Palm Beach Lakes Blvd #210
      West Palm Beach, FL 33401
      Contact: Gregg Saxton
      Tel: 561-249-2219
      Email: gregg.s@ckisolutions.us
      Website: www.ckisolutions.us
Bed doubling systems, mattress & pillow protectors, mattress protection systems, disposable luggage protection systems. (Woman, estab 1996, empl 6, sales $2,211,409, cert: NWBOC)

3764 Furniture Installation Solution Inc
      4740 NW 15th Ave Ste D
      Fort Lauderdale, FL 33309
      Contact: Donovan Williams Operations Mgr
      Tel: 954-638-2432
      Email: info@myfis.biz
      Website: www.myfis.biz
Install, reconfigure & relocate panel (cubicle) system & case good furniture. (AA, estab 2008, empl 10, sales $2,400,000, cert: NMSDC)

3765 HNM Enterprises, LLC
      1902 Cypress Lake Dr
      Orlando, FL 32837
      Contact: Juan Barney Business Devel Mgr
      Tel: 407-472-7575
      Email: jbarney@gohnm.com
      Website: www.gohnm.com
Dist & install furniture supplies, furniture, fixtures & equipment. (AA, estab 2004, empl 27, sales $16,900,000, cert: NMSDC)

Georgia

3766 Corporate Environments of GA, Inc.
      1636 Northeast Expressway
      Atlanta, GA 30329
      Contact: Sr Acct Mgr
      Tel: 404-679-8999
      Email: rstandard@ceofga.com
      Website: www.corporateenvironments.com
Dist office furniture. (Woman, estab 1973, empl 37, sales $47,200,000, cert: WBENC)

3767 Nance Carpet & Rug Inc.
      201 Nance Road
      Calhoun, GA 30701
      Contact: Trenna Smith Natl Accounts Specialist
      Tel: 706-629-7731
      Email: trenna.smith@nancecarpet.com
      Website: www.nancefloors.com
Dist area rugs, carpet remnants, carpet by the roll, carpet tiles & carpet base. (Woman, estab 1972, empl 300, sales $19,000,000, cert: WBENC)

3768 Table Decor International Inc.
      2748 S Cobb Industrial Blvd
      Smyrna, GA 30082
      Contact: Lynn Wells President
      Tel: 770-432-1156
      Email: tdi@tabledecor.com
      Website: www.tabledecor.com
Design & mfr specialty table lighting & unique centerpieces & table accessory items. (Woman, estab 1984, empl 5, sales $750,000, cert: WBENC)

3769 Zig Zag Inc.
      4300 Westpark Dr, SW
      Atlanta, GA 30336
      Contact: Gokul Nair CEO
      Tel: 347-558-6767
      Email: gokul@zzincorporation.com
      Website: www.zzincorporation.com
Mfr patio cushions, rugs, door mats & general safety items. (As-Ind, estab 2008, empl 10, sales $16,000,000, cert: NMSDC)

Illinois

3770 Corporate Concepts, Inc.
      500 Waters Edge, Ste 200
      Lombard, IL 60148
      Contact: Janet Szyszko Project Mgr
      Tel: 630-691-8800
      Email: jszyszko@corpconc.com
      Website: www.corpconc.com
Design services, space planning, and specifications, chair re-upholstery, furniture standards programs and financing consultation. (Woman, estab 1983, empl 55, sales $54,000,000, cert: WBENC)

3771 Phoenix Woodworking Corporation
      PO Box 459
      Woodstock, IL 60098
      Contact: Sandra Pierce President
      Tel: 815-338-9338
      Email: spierce@phoenixwoodworking.com
      Website: www.phoenixwoodworking.com
Custom & commercial cabinetry & casework, reception centers, filing cabinets, wooden lockers & millwork, custom desks & wooden store fixtures. (Woman, estab 1996, empl 10, sales , cert: State, WBENC)

3772 Resource One
      321 E Adams
      Springfield, IL 62701
      Contact: Cynthia Davis President
      Tel: 217-753-5742
      Email: cdavis@resourceoneoffice.com
      Website: www.resourceoneoffice.com
Dist office furniture, carpet, wallcovering, window treatments, refurbishment services, furniture, space-planning & interior design, furniture installation. (Woman, estab 1987, empl 22, sales $8,000,000, cert: State, WBENC)

Indiana

3773 Commercial Office Environments Inc.
      7301 Zionsville Road
      Indianapolis, IN 46268
      Contact: James Bednarski Acct Exec
      Tel: 317-876-9200
      Email: james@coeindy.com
      Website: www.coeindy.com
Furniture & storage equipment, design, install furniture & storage solutions. (Woman, estab 1989, empl 29, sales $13,000,000, cert: State)

3774 Lapsley Inc.
      1002 E Rudisill Blvd
      Fort Wayne, IN 46806
      Contact: Donita Mudd President
      Tel: 260-745-3265
      Email: dmudd@lapsleyinc.com
      Website: www.lapsleyinc.com
Furnish & install window treatments: blinds, shades, draperies, manual or motorized, projection screens, cubicle curtains & cubicle tracks. (Woman/AA, estab 2003, empl 4, sales $140,000, cert: State, 8(a))

3775 Office and Business Resources LLC
      244 McConnell Dr
      New Albany, IN 47150
      Contact: Kahy Brown President
      Tel: 502-333-8907
      Email: kbrown@officeandbusinessresources.com
      Website: www.officeandbusinessresources.com
Office furniture assembly & installation, furniture systems (cubicles), office relocations & interoffice relocations, space planning & design. (Woman, estab 2012, empl 4, sales , cert: NWBOC)

3776 TLS by Design, LLC
      10737 Sand Key Circle
      Indianapolis, IN 46256
      Contact: Jeff Day Dir
      Tel: 765-683-1971
      Email: sales@tlsbydesign.com
      Website: www.tlsbydesign.com
Mfr custom furniture. (Woman, estab 2002, empl 12, sales $780,000, cert: State, WBENC)

Kentucky

3777 Munson Business Interiors
      2307 River Rd
      Louisville, KY 40206
      Contact: Susan Lewis Acct Rep
      Tel: 502-588-7368
      Email: susan@mbifurniture.com
      Website: www.mbifurniture.com
Office furnishings, space planning, design, delivery, installation, project management, warehousing & inventory reports, repair & refinishing, reupholstery panels, chairs & custom furniture. (Woman, estab 1986, empl 21, sales $6,376,824, cert: NWBOC)

Louisiana

3778 Contract Furniture Group, LLC
      201 James Dr E
      Saint Rose, LA 70087
      Contact: Julio Rodriguez President
      Tel: 504-412-0080
      Email: julio@contractfurnituregroup.com
      Website: www.contractfurnituregroup.com
Design & install furniture systems modular furniture, freestanding casegoods, conference room furniture, break rooms, training rooms, healthcare furniture & high density filing systems. (Hisp, estab 2000, empl 20, sales , cert: NMSDC)

Massachusetts

3779 McElroy Scenic Services LLC
      PO Box 145
      Ashley Falls, MA 01222
      Contact: President
      Tel: 413-229-9920
      Email: info@mcelroyscenic.com
      Website: www.mcelroyscenic.com
Decor fabrication, set design & fabrication, custom displays, architectural models, exterior & interior signage, custom corporate furniture & staging, museum exhibits. (Woman, estab 1999, empl 7, sales $1,200,000, cert: State, WBENC)

3780 Wholesale Distribution
      PO Box 1497
      Cotuit, MA 02635
      Contact: Linda Sharp President
      Tel: 800-345-4027
      Email: linda@facilitiesfurniture.com
      Website: www.facilitiesfurniture.com
Dist folding, stack, office & classroom chairs, training & computer, cafeteria & classroom tables & desks, restroom fixtures & components, lockers, flags, communication boards. (Woman, estab 2001, empl 3, sales , cert: State, WBENC)

Maryland

3781 Contemporary Business Interiors, LLC
      1369 D Brass Mill Rd
      Belcamp, MD 21017
      Contact: Christi Member
      Tel: 410-272-5559
      Email: info@cbillc.com
      Website: www.cbillc.com
Dist business furniture: office, hospitality, bar & restaurant, medical, school, space planning & design, project mgmt, installation. (Woman, estab 2006, empl 3, sales $1,300,000, cert: State)

3782 Washington Office Interiors
12354 Carroll Ave
Rockville, MD 20852
Contact: Barbara Barry Prinicpal
Tel: 301-770-4327
Email: bbarry@washingtonoffice.com
Website: www.washingtonoffice.com
Full service contract furniture dealership. (Woman, estab 2005, empl 12, sales $11,300,000, cert: State)

Michigan

3783 Airea
3000 Town Center Ste 80
Southfield, MI 48075
Contact: Yulanda Trout Exec Asst
Tel: 248-226-3971
Email: ytrout@pistongroup.com
Website: www.aireainc.com
Modular walls & ceiling systems, raised-access flooring, floor covering, furniture & lighting. (AA, estab 1995, empl 28, sales $12,000,000, cert: NMSDC)

3784 Designer Installation Services, Inc.
9685 Harrison St, Ste 200
Romulus, MI 48174
Contact: Robert Corona President
Tel: 313-582-9310
Email: danielle.smith@designerinstallationservicesin.com
Website: www.designerinstallationservicesin.com
Dist commercial office furniture, flooring & ancillary items, installation, warehousing, asset management, delivery. (Hisp, estab 1979, empl 25, sales $4,000,000, cert: NMSDC)

3785 Hercules & Hercules, Inc.
19055 W Davison
Detroit, MI 48223
Contact: Belinda Jefferson President
Tel: 313-933-6669
Email: bjefferson@herculesandherculesinc.com
Website: www.herculesandherculesinc.com
Dist maintenance supplies & equip, office supplies & equip, office furniture. (AA, estab , empl , sales $7,000,000, cert: NMSDC)

3786 ISCG
612 N Main St
Royal Oak, MI 48067
Contact: Stephanie Chyz President
Tel: 248-399-1600
Email: schyz@iscginc.com
Website: www.iscginc.com
Contract furnishings (Haworth Preferred Dealer) & Floorcoverings, Facility Asset Management, Project & Move Management, Union & Non. (Woman, estab 1976, empl 21, sales $14,000,000, cert: WBENC)

3787 Remco Storage Systems, Inc.
2328 Livernois Road Ste 1070
Troy, MI 48083
Contact: Donna Tamburo-Wilson President
Tel: 248-362-0500
Email: donna@remcoequipment.com
Website: www.remcoequipment.com
Storage & retrieval systems: vertical lifts & carousels, electric lateral filing systems, movable shelving, rotary files, cabinets, records mgmt systems, color coded labels, custom filing systems, folders & indexes. (Woman, estab 1976, empl 7, sales $2,000,000, cert: WBENC)

3788 Star Textile, Inc.
2333 John B
Warren, MI 48091
Contact: Marketing
Tel: 586-758-2700
Email: info@startextile.com
Website: www.startextile.com
Provides bedding & draperies in the hospitality industry. (Woman, estab 1999, empl 60, sales $2,500,000, cert: WBENC)

Minnesota

3789 AIM Global Trading, LLC
11209 Commerce Dr N
Champlin, MN 55316
Contact: Mahtab Khan CEO
Tel: - -
Email: linenbay3@gmail.com
Website: www.aimglobaltrading.com
Mfr & dist 100% cotton terry towel & Polyester/Cotton Blended Bath Towels, Hand Towels, Wash Cloths, Bath Mats, Pool Towels, & Bar Mops. (As-Pac, estab 2014, empl 3, sales , cert: NMSDC)

3790 Ideal Commercial Interiors LLC
740 Portland Ave. Ste 1418
Minneapolis, MN 55414
Contact: Rick Harris CEO
Tel: 612-759-0955
Email: rick@icinteriors.net
Website: www.icinteriors.net
Office furniture, flooring, fixtures, design, space planning, installation, delivery & project management. (AA, estab 2012, empl 3, sales , cert: NMSDC)

3791 Kelly Computer Supply
2042 Wooddale Dr Ste 250
Woodbury, MN 55125
Contact: Bob Kelly President
Tel: 651-773-1109
Email: bobkelly@kellyrest.com
Website: www.kellyrest.com
Ergonomic equip; mfr "KellyRest" computer products: wrist & foot rests, adjustable copy holders, keyboard drawers & articulating keyboard trays; workstations. (Nat Ame, estab 1983, empl 10, sales , cert: State, NMSDC, CPUC)

3792 R and L Woodcraft, Inc
823 Industrial Park Dr SE
Lonsdale, MN 55046
Contact: Randall Rivers Business Devel
Tel: 507-744-2318
Email: randall@randlwoodcraft.com
Website: www.randlwoodcraft.com
Mfr commercial millwork & casework: cabinets, countertops, workstations, point of service counters, tables, booths, upholstered seating, running trim, trash recepticles, lockers & toilet partitions. (Woman, estab 1986, empl 22, sales $3,600,000, cert: WBENC)

Missouri

3793 Advanced Ergonomic Concepts Inc.
PO Box 460335
Saint Louis, MO 63146
Contact: Laurie Wall President
Tel: 314-994-0500
Email: aesales@advan-ergo.com
Website: www.advan-ergo.com
Furniture & ergonomic products dealer. (Woman, estab 1996, empl 2, sales $1,341,781, cert: State)

FURNISHINGS

3794 Spellman Brady & Company
8251 Maryland Ave, Ste 300
Saint Louis, MO 63105
Contact: Bruce Hentges VP
Tel: 314-669-3472
Email: bhentges@spellmanbrady.com
Website: www.spellmanbrady.com
Interior Design, Furniture & Artwork Procurement. (Woman, estab 1994, empl 24, sales , cert: State, City)

Mississippi

3795 Commercial Interiors, Inc.
4277 Espy Ave
Long Beach, MS 39560
Contact: President
Tel: 228-452-9540
Email: donna@cidesigns.net
Website: www.cidesigns.net
Commercial FF&E contractor. (Woman, estab 1990, empl 3, sales $555,647, cert: State)

3796 Durfold Corporation
102 Upton Dr
Jackson, MS 11111
Contact: Dawn Warren
Tel: 601-922-4144
Email: dwarren@durfold.com
Website: www.durfold.com
Mfr upholstered healthcare furniture: sleeper chairs & sofas, trendelenberg recliners, incliners, rocking chairs, gliders, bariatric seating, patient & guest seating, lounge seating, lobby furniture & ganged & tandem seating. (Woman, estab , empl , sales $3,200,000, cert: WBENC)

North Carolina

3797 DARRAN Furniture Industries, Inc.
2402 Shore St
High Point, NC 27263
Contact: Jennifer Hollingsworth President
Tel: 800-334-7891
Email: jlhollingsworth@darran.com
Website: www.darran.com
Mfr high quality, mid-market wood desk collections, conferencing solutions, reception stations & seating. (Woman, estab 1977, empl 195, sales $25,559,279, cert: WBENC)

3798 Excell Home Fashions Inc.
8511 Chatsworth Lane
Waxhaw, NC 28173
Contact: Acct Mgr
Tel: 704-564-2722
Email: bsinger@croscill-living.com
Website: www.croscill-living.com
Mfr Shower Liners, Shower Hooks, Shower Rods & Tub Mats. (Woman, estab 1932, empl 211, sales $200,000,000, cert: WBENC, NWBOC)

3799 Forms & Supply, Inc.
PO Box 563953
Charlotte, NC 28256
Contact: Amy Pyles Sr Sales Administrator
Tel: 704-598-8971
Email: amy.pyles@formsandsupply.com
Website: www.fsioffice.com
Furniture, office supplies. (Woman, estab 1962, empl 260, sales $80,000,000, cert: State, WBENC)

3800 Stuart Page Company, Inc.
1801 Stallings Rd
Matthews, NC 28104
Contact: Kimberly Page President
Tel: 704-545-0695
Email: kim@stuartpagecompany.com
Website: www.stuartpagecompany.com
Furnish and install commercial doors, toilet partitions, toilet accessories, lockers, wall protection, shelving, flags, flagpoles, etc. (Woman, estab 1991, empl 24, sales $37,000,000, cert: State, City)

New Jersey

3801 A Plus Installs LLC
29 Curtis St
Bloomfield, NJ 07003
Contact: Owner
Tel: 201-255-4412
Email: info@ainstallation.com
Website: www.ainstallation.com
Furnish & Install window treatments, drapery, cubical curtains, blinds, shades & window film for commercial & residential spaces. (Woman, estab 2014, empl 2, sales $666,000, cert: State, WBENC)

3802 Aldo Design Group
35 Hayward Ave
Carteret, NJ 07008
Contact: Aldo Jr. Benavides President
Tel: 732-969-9699
Email: aldo.benavides@aldodesigngroup.com
Website: www.aldodesigngroup.com
Flooring & interior products resource for retail & commercial customers, and homebuilders. (Woman/Hisp, estab 1972, empl 22, sales , cert: State)

3803 Business Environments
2001 Route 46 Ste 510
Parsippany, NJ 07054
Contact: John Gardner President
Tel: 973-335-7700
Email: jgardner@be-furniture.com
Website: www.befurniture.com
Office furniture dealer: Cad, project management, installation & refinishing. (Woman/AA, estab 2005, empl 18, sales $10,000,000, cert: State, WBENC)

3804 Concepts Office Furnishings, Inc.
280 N Midland Ave, Bldg J Unit 204
Saddle Brook, NJ 07663
Contact: Aida DeSoto President
Tel: 201-727-9110
Email: adesoto@conceptsoffice.com
Website: www.conceptsoffice.com
Contract office furniture & equipment, project management, furniture installations & re-configurations, refinishing & reupholstery. (Minority, Woman, estab 1973, empl 15, sales $3,200,000, cert: City)

3805 Contemporary Motives, Inc
445 US-202
Flemington, NJ 08822
Contact: Debbie Hill Dir of Business Dev
Tel: 908-806-4461
Email: dhill@interiormotives.net
Website: www.interiormotives.net
Commercial Interior Design Services, Planning, Design & installation, Fixtures, Decorative Drapery, Decorative Lighting, Office Furniture, Office Dividers, Office Desks, Chairs. (Woman, estab 2005, empl 11, sales $7,200,000, cert: WBENC)

3806 Global Installation Resources LLC
      18 Robert St
      Clifton, NJ 07014
      Contact: Krista Korinis President
      Tel: 973-494-9680
      Email: kkorinis@gi-resources.com
      Website: www.gi-resources.com
Installation services: office furniture, demountable walls, signage & laboratory case work installations & project management services. (Woman, estab 2002, empl 10, sales $1,345,540, cert: State, WBENC)

3807 Image Office Environments, LLC
      1122 Route 22 W
      Mountainside, NJ 07092
      Contact: Tricia Patricco President
      Tel: 908-301-0074
      Email: tpatricco@image-office.com
      Website: www.image-office.com
Interior constructions, raised flooring, moveable walls & furniture. (Woman, estab 2005, empl 6, sales $9,000,000, cert: State, WBENC)

3808 JC Office Consultants, LLC
      242 Union Ave
      Somerville, NJ 08876
      Contact: Jackie Orlando CEO
      Tel: 908-842-2150
      Email: jackie@jcofficeconsultants.com
      Website: www.jcofficeconsultants.com
Dist office furniture, installation & reconfiguration services. Space planning & CAD design. (Minority, Woman, estab 2009, empl 5, sales $1,900,000, cert: WBENC)

3809 Vaswani Inc
      75 Carter Dr
      Edison, NJ 08817
      Contact: Eric Clark Business Devel
      Tel: 877-376-4425
      Email: eric@vaswaniinc.com
      Website: www.vaswaniinc.com
Provide custom fixtures and furniture. (As-Ind, estab 1993, empl 120, sales $36,000,000, cert: NMSDC)

New York

3810 A.F.C. Industries, Inc.
      1316 133rd Pl, Ste 2
      Colege Point, NY 11356
      Contact: Donna Tannacore Govt Sales Acct Exec
      Tel: 718-747-0237
      Email: dtannacore@afcindustries.com
      Website: www.afcindustries.com
Ergonomic technical furniture & workstations: mission-critical control centers, data centers, medical, labs, military, etc. CPU rack systems & display mount hardware. (Woman, estab 1994, empl 95, sales $1,010,000, cert: State)

3811 Alianza Services LLC
      74 N Broadway 2nd Fl S
      Nyack, NY 10960
      Contact: Dawn Cannon VP
      Tel: 845-675-7337
      Email: dcannon@alianzacorp.com
      Website: www.alianzacorp.com
Dist furniture, budgeting, refurbishing, storage & asset management, rental solutions, service & repair. (Hisp, estab 2006, empl 6, sales $5,100,000, cert: NMSDC)

3812 Architectural Flooring Resources, Inc.
      135 W 27th St
      New York, NY 10001
      Contact: Mercedes Montano Project Coord
      Tel: 212-290-0200
      Email: mercedes@afrny.com
      Website: www.afrny.com
Carpet, carpet tile, vinyl, composition tile, wood (varies by species), cork, linoleum & specialty flooring. (Minority, Woman, estab 1993, empl 19, sales $7,896,224, cert: City, NMSDC, WBENC)

3813 County Draperies, Inc.
      64 Genung St
      Middletown, NY 10940
      Contact: President
      Tel: 845-342-9009
      Email: info@drape.com
      Website: www.drape.com
Mfr window & bedding products, hardware measuring & installtion. (Woman, estab 1987, empl 50, sales $4,520,000, cert: WBENC)

3814 Davies Office Refurbishing, Inc.
      40 Loudonville Rd
      Albany, NY 12204
      Contact: Evelyn Davies Owner
      Tel: 518-449-2040
      Email: evelyndavies@daviesoffice.com
      Website: www.daviesoffice.com
Remanufacture office furniture & office furniture asset mgmt. (Woman, estab 1975, empl 165, sales , cert: WBENC)

3815 Kittredge Equipment Company
      17 Pearce Ave
      Tonawanda, NY 14405
      Contact: Jeffrey Mackey COO
      Tel: 800-423-7082
      Email: jmackey@kittredgeequipment.com
      Website: www.kittredgeequipment.com
Dist kitchen equipment, smallwares, tabletop supplies, warewashing furniture. (Woman, estab , empl 93, sales $54,500,000, cert: City, WBENC)

3816 Meadows Office Supply Co., Inc.
      885 3rd Ave, 29th Fl
      New York, NY 10022
      Contact: Dina Radoncic Exec VP
      Tel: 212-741-0333
      Email: mofwbe@meadowsoffice.com
      Website: www.meadowsofficeinteriors.com
Dist Haworth furniture products. (Woman, estab 1967, empl 76, sales $81,500,000, cert: City, WBENC)

3817 Waldner's Business Environments, Inc.
      125 Route 110
      Farmingdale, NY 11735
      Contact: Meredith Stern President
      Tel: 631-844-9342
      Email: mstern@waldners.com
      Website: www.waldners.com
Dist & install office furniture. (Woman, estab 1939, empl 107, sales $92,800,000, cert: City, WBENC)

FURNISHINGS

Ohio

3818 APG Office Furnishings
PO Box 631850
Cincinnati, OH 45263
Contact: Connie L. Goins President
Tel: 513-239-6814
Email: cgoins@apgde.com
Website: www.apgof.com
Dist office furniture, space planning, design, project management services & product solutions. (Woman, estab 1969, empl 1, sales $50,000,000, cert: State, WBENC)

3819 Budget Office Interiors LLC
1771 E. 30th St
Cleveland, OH 44114
Contact: President
Tel: 216-566-1540
Email:
Website: www.budgetofficeinteriorsllc.com
New, used & refinished furniture: cubicles, workstations, space planning, desks, seating, conference rooms, training rooms, break rooms, home offices, telemarketing areas, reception areas, lateral & vertical filing. (Woman, estab 2005, empl 4, sales $292,229, cert: City)

3820 Clara I. Brown Interiors, Inc. (CIBI)
5305 Courtney Pl
Columbus, OH 43235
Contact: Clara I. Brown President
Tel: 614-224-9180
Email: jim@cibiinc.com
Website: www.cibiinc.com
Office Furniture, Carpet & Hard Flooring, Carpet Cleaning, Re-upholstery, Mill Work, De-mountable Walls, Wall Coverings, Window Treatments, Interior Design/Space Planning, Furniture Moves, Warehousing. (Minority, Woman, estab 1993, empl 12, sales $3,828,904, cert: NMSDC)

3821 Interior Services Incorporated dba Enriching Spaces
1360 Kemper Meadow Dr
Cincinnati, OH 45240
Contact: Dawn Schwartzman President
Tel: 513-851-0933
Email: dawn@enrichingspaces.com
Website: www.enrichingspaces.com
Furniture: office, Healthcare, School & University, Art & Accessories, Carpet Tile, Interior Design, Ergonomic Accessories, Ergonomic Chairs, Desks, Workstations. (Woman, estab 1982, empl , sales , cert: WBENC)

3822 King Business Interiors
1400 Goodale Blvd, Ste 102
Columbus, OH 43212
Contact: Darla King Owner
Tel: 614-430-0020
Email: darlaking@kbiinc.com
Website: www.kbiinc.com
Office furniture dealer. (Woman, estab 1998, empl , sales , cert: WBENC)

3823 Master Manufacturing Co, Inc.
9200 Inman Ave
Cleveland, OH 44105
Contact: Bob Ptacek VP Sales
Tel: 800-323-5513
Email: bptacek@mastermfgco.com
Website: www.mastermfgco.com
Mfr furniture casters & self-stick wheels; felt pads, surface protectors, wobble stoppers; furniture movers; door stops; ergonomic support cushions & wire mgmt channels & grommets. (Woman, estab 1951, empl , sales , cert: CPUC, WBENC)

3824 River City Furniture, LLC
6454 Centre Park Dr
West Chester, OH 45069
Contact: Carl Satterwhite President
Tel: 513-612-7303
Email: amy.andrews@thercfgroup.com
Website: www.thercfgroup.com
Design office layout, new furniture, installation, move management & asset management. (AA, estab 2003, empl 100, sales $43,900,000, cert: City, NMSDC)

3825 Vocon Partners, LLC
3142 Prospect Ave
Cleveland, OH 44115
Contact: Deb Donley President
Tel: 216-588-0800
Email: deb.donley@vocon.com
Website: www.vocon.com
Furniture coordination, graphic design. (Woman, estab 1987, empl 180, sales $30,000,000, cert: WBENC)

3826 Williams Interior Designs, Inc
4449 Easton Way, 2nd Floor
Columbus, OH 43219
Contact: Carolyn Williams Francis CEO
Tel: 614-418-7250
Email: carolyn@williamsinteriordesigns.com
Website: www.williamsinteriordesigns.com
Interior design, office furniture, office supplies & window treatments. (Woman/AA, estab 1985, empl 4, sales $2,000,000, cert: NMSDC)

Oregon

3827 Carriage Works, Inc.
1877 Mallard Ln
Klamath Falls, OR 97601
Contact: Barbara Evensizer President
Tel: 541-882-0700
Email: info@carriageworks.com
Website: www.carriageworks.com
Mfr carts: food, espresso, kiosks, beverage, bar, vending & display items. (Minority, Woman, estab 1971, empl 30, sales $4,000,000, cert: State)

3828 Dtocs LLC
14512 NW Cosmos St
Portland, OR 97229
Contact: Pallavi Pande Owner
Tel: 614-599-5679
Email: pal.pande@gmail.com
Website: www.dtocs.com
Tableware, Eco-friendly, Compostable & Biodegradable, Chemical-free & Non-toxic, Microwave & Oven Safe. (Woman/As-Pac, estab 2019, empl 1, sales $975,000, cert: State, WBENC)

Pennsylvania

3829 A. Pomerantz & Co. / Pomerantz Acquisition Corp.
123 S Broad St Ste 1260
Philadelphia, PA 19109
Contact: Elisa V. Feola VP Marketing
Tel: 215-408-2173
Email: feola@pomerantz.com
Website: www.pomerantz.com
Develop productive & efficient workplace environments. (AA, estab , empl 40, sales $37,700,000, cert: NMSDC)

3830 Alpha Office Supplies, Inc.
4950 Parkside Ave Ste 500
Philadelphia, PA 19131
Contact: Chester Riddick CEO
Tel: 215-226-2690
Email: chet.riddick@alphaos.com
Website: www.alphaos.com
Dist office furniture & supplies, paper, computers & accessories; desktop delivery, installation, space planning & project mgmt. (AA, estab 1985, empl 29, sales $26,000,000, cert: NMSDC)

3831 Corporate Facilities of New Jersey, LLC
2129 Chestnut St
Philadelphia, PA 19103
Contact: Amanda Chevalier Principal
Tel: 215-279-9999
Email: achevalier@cfinj-knoll.com
Website: www.cfi-knoll.com
Office furniture. (Minority, Woman, estab 2004, empl 26, sales , cert: NMSDC, WBENC)

3832 Peerless Wall and Window Coverings, Inc.
3490 William Penn Hwy
Pittsburgh, PA 15235
Contact: Bob Cherry Mgr
Tel: 412-823-7660
Email: sales@peerlesswallpaperandblinds.com
Website: www.peerlesswallpaperandblinds.com
Dist & install wallcoverings, window coverings, blinds, shades, shutters & draperies. (Woman, estab 1993, empl 6, sales $761,857, cert: State)

3833 Telrose Corporation
3801 Ridge Ave
Philadelphia, PA 19132
Contact: CEO
Tel: 215-229-0500
Email: support@telrosecorp.com
Website: www.telrosecorp.com
Dist office supplies, equipment & furniture. (AA, estab 1995, empl 19, sales $8,000,000, cert: City, NMSDC)

Puerto Rico

3834 Integrated Design Solutions
90 Carr 165, Ste 405
Guaynabo, PR 00968
Contact: Marlen Diaz VP
Tel: 787-706-0201
Email: mdiaz@ids-pr.com
Website: www.ids-pr.com
Office furniture dealer. (Hisp, estab 1999, empl 17, sales $5,800,000, cert: NMSDC)

South Carolina

3835 Advanced Window Fashions LLC
1956 Long Grove Dr Ste 5
Mt Pleasant, SC 29464
Contact: Larry McCrae Owner
Tel: 843-881-8858
Email: larry@charlestonblinds.com
Website: www.charlestonblinds.com
Provide quality window treatments: blinds, shutters, shades, draperies, valances, etc. (Woman, estab 2003, empl 6, sales $677,000, cert: State)

3836 Skutchi Designs Inc.
171 Gardner Lacy Rd
Myrtle Beach, SC 29579
Contact: Jeff Little Ecommerce
Tel: 843-410-0605
Email: jeff@skutchi.com
Website: www.skutchi.com
Mfr Office Furniture, Panels Systems, Wall Systems, Conference Tables, Acrylic Screens, Acoustical products, and Desks. We space plan, design and install nationwide. (Woman, estab 2005, empl 30, sales $5,000,000, cert: WBENC)

Texas

3837 B&H Total Office Solutions
120 Sam Bass Ridge Rd
Southlake, TX 76092
Contact: Jeannie Norris President
Tel: 817-430-8345
Email: jeannie@bhofficesolutions.com
Website: www.bhofficesolutions.com
New & used Furniture, refurbished cubicles, Space Planning, Furniture Moves. (Woman, estab 2006, empl 6, sales $650,000, cert: State)

3838 Business Interiors
1111 Valley View
Irving, TX 75061
Contact: Sally Smith President
Tel: 817-858-2000
Email: ssmith@businessinteriors.com
Website: www.businessinteriors.com
Office furniture sales & services: rental, used sales, installation, reconnfiguration, repair, touch up, carpet sales & installation, relocations, storage, design & space planning. (Woman, estab 1970, empl 140, sales $51,517,000, cert: WBENC)

3839 Facilities Connection, Inc.
240 E Sunset Rd
El Paso, TX 79922
Contact: Patty Holland Branch CEO
Tel: 915-833-8303
Email: phbranch@facilitiesconnection.com
Website: www.facilitiesconnection.com
Interior design, furniture layout, space planning, project management, office furniture installation, reconfiguration, relocation, interiors, assets maintenance. (Minority, Woman, estab 1987, empl 25, sales $27,000,000, cert: State)

3840 Facility Interiors Inc.
PO Box 201828
Dallas, TX 75320
Contact: Charles Griggsby President
Tel: 713-963-0678
Email: charlesg@fiinc.com
Website: www.facilityinteriors.com
Furniture installation, design, project management, move services, reconfigurations services. (Woman/AA, estab , empl , sales $80,000,000, cert: State, NMSDC, WBENC)

FURNISHINGS

3841 Intelligent Interiors, Inc.
16837 Addison Rd Ste 500
Addison, TX 75001
Contact: Mindy Casas President
Tel: 214-239-9886
Email: mcasas@intelligentinteriors.net
Website: www.intelligentinteriors.net
Contract office furniture, design, installation, repair refurbishing, carpet, window covering. (Minority, Woman, estab 1996, empl 12, sales $800,000, cert: State, NMSDC)

3842 Modular Installation Services, Inc.
8606 Wall St Ste 150
Austin, TX 78754
Contact: Monica Gould VP
Tel: 512-835-7706
Email: mpgould@modularinstall.com
Website: www.modularinstall.com
Commercial office furniture installation & reconfiguration services. (Hisp, estab 1996, empl 30, sales $1,300,000, cert: State)

3843 Neutral Posture, Inc.
3904 N. Texas Ave
Bryan, TX 77803
Contact: Rebecca Boenigk CEO
Tel: 979-778-0502
Email: rboenigk@np-us.com
Website: www.neutralposture.com
Mfr ergonomic, multipurpose, industrial seating & accessories. (Woman, estab 1989, empl 65, sales , cert: WBENC, 8(a), SDB)

3844 Quiltcraft Industries
1230 E Ledbetter Dr
Dallas, TX 75216
Contact: Janet Pearson President
Tel: 214-376-1841
Email: jpearson@quiltcraft.com
Website: www.quiltcraft.com
Mfr bedspreads, draperies, cubicle curtains, cubicle track, shower curtains, sheets, mattress pads, pillows, hardware, etc. (Minority, Woman, estab , empl , sales , cert: WBENC)

Virginia

3845 Alpha Stone Solutions
2251 Dabney Rd, Ste H
Richmond, VA 23230
Contact: Shion Fenty Acct Exec
Tel: 804-622-2068
Email: shion@alphastone.us
Website: www.alphastone.us
Dist granite products, furniture, fixtures & equipment for hotel industry. (Minority, Woman, estab 2000, empl 20, sales $2,800,000, cert: State)

3846 Finial Showcase, Inc.
720 Third St
Vinton, VA 24179
Contact: Whitney Snyder Corp Acct Mgr
Tel: 540-982-3593
Email: sales@finialshowcase.com
Website: www.finialshowcase.com
Dist accent tables, plant stands, quilt racks, coat racks, dvd/cd cabinets, stacking tables, umbrella stands, waste baskets, desks for home office, magazine racks, luggage racks, mirrors and wall decor, vases, decorative accessories, table lamps. (Woman, estab 1982, empl 5, sales $650,000, cert: WBENC)

3847 Votum Enterprises, LLC
3530 Post Office Rd Ste 5104
Midlothian, VA 23112
Contact: Mark Walton Dir Business Dev
Tel: 804-317-9660
Email: mark@votument.com
Website: www.votument.com
Provides cubicle, modular & systems furniture & related services, installations, reconfigurations, disassembly, moving & storage. (AA, estab 2009, empl 3, sales $257,000, cert: State, NMSDC)

3848 Apex Facility Resources, Inc.
20219 87th Ave S
Kent, WA 98031
Contact: John Williams Dir of Sales
Tel: 206-686-3357
Email: john@apexfacility.com
Website: www.apexfacility.com
Dist new & used office furnitures: liquidation, installation, project coordination, signage. (Woman, estab 1994, empl 35, sales , cert: WBENC)

3849 Home and Travel Solutions, LLC dba BedVoyage
18915 142nd Ave NE, Ste 230
Woodinville, WA 98072
Contact: CEO
Tel: 425-949-8216
Email: info@bedvoyage.com
Website: www.bedvoyage.com
Mfr eco-luxury bamboo bed linens, towels & blankets. (Woman, estab 2008, empl 7, sales $1,200,000, cert: NWBOC)

3850 CJ & Associates, Inc.
16915 West Victor Rd
New Berlin, WI 53151
Contact: Roberta Montague
Tel: 262-786-1772
Email: rmontague@cjassociatesinc.com
Website: www.cjassociatesinc.com
Dist, maintain, & repair furniture, Re-upholstery, reconfiguration, furniture moving. (Woman, estab 1984, empl 30, sales $16,000,000, cert: State, WBENC)

3851 Laacke & Joys LLC
3205 N 124th St
Brookfield, WI 53005
Contact: Joel Vento VP Sales & Mktg
Tel: 800-892-5563
Email: jsvento@conceptseating.com
Website: www.conceptseating.com
Mfr 24/7 intensive use ergonomic office chairs used for dispatch, security, control rooms, surveillance. (Woman, estab , empl 100, sales $9,000,000, cert: WBENC)

GIFTWARES, ARTS & CRAFTS
Manufacture, distribute and import merchandise as well as cooperatives which produce jewelry, carvings, baskets, greeting cards, etc. NAICS Code 42

California

3852 The Corporate Gift Service, Inc.
4120 W Burbank Blvd
Burbank, CA 91505
Contact: Lydia Eltringham Accounting Dept
Tel: 818-845-9500
Email: accounting@corpgiftservice.com
Website: www.thecorporategiftservice.com

Handmade Custom Gift Baskets, Embroidered Corporate Apparel, High End Corporate Gifts, Branded Promotional Products & Advertising Specialties. (Woman, estab 1990, empl 7, sales $1,600,000, cert: WBENC)

Florida

3853 Floral Group, Inc.
2291 NW 82 Ave
Miami, FL 33122
Contact: Dornett Mullings President
Tel: 305-477-5008
Email: dornett@floralgroup.net
Website: www.floralgroup.net

Fresh floral products to supermarket chains, foam arrangements, vase arrangements, hand-tied bouquets, rose bouquets, mixed bouquets. (Woman/AA, estab 2003, empl 12, sales $990,000, cert: NMSDC)

Georgia

3854 Barazzo, LLC
2221 Peachtree Rd NE Ste D357
Atlanta, GA 30309
Contact: Quiana Lloyd Member
Tel: 888-716-5785
Email: quiana@barazzo.com
Website: www.barazzo.com

Custom gift & accessory solutions, corporate brand identity & marketing solutions. (Woman/AA, estab 2009, empl , sales , cert: State, NMSDC, SDB)

3855 Gratitude Goodies, LLC
433 Canton Rd Ste 315
Cumming, GA 30040
Contact: Diane Campbell Owner
Tel: 770-886-9598
Email: diane@gratitudegoodies.com
Website: www.GratitudeGoodies.com

Gift basket with chocolate, savory & gift items. (Woman, estab 2009, empl 4, sales , cert: WBENC, NWBOC)

Illinois

3856 Brilliant Gifts LLC
1605 S Waukegan Rd
Waukegan, IL 60085
Contact: Nick Phillips Dir of Business Dev
Tel: 773-885-3532
Email: nick@brilliantmade.com
Website: www.brilliantmade.com

Curate and produce memorable gifts, branded merchandise and custom products, while providing our clients with a suite of tools to enable distribution, analytics, and ROI measurement. (Woman, estab 2015, empl 100, sales $25,000,000, cert: WBENC)

3857 Corporate Artworks, Ltd.
1300 Remington Rd, Ste H
Schaumburg, IL 60173
Contact: Denise Rippinger President
Tel: 847-843-3636
Email: corporateartwork@aol.com
Website: www.corporateartworks.com

Artwork sales & consulting. (Woman, estab 1988, empl 12, sales , cert: WBENC)

3858 Packed with Purpose
2000 W Addison St, Ste 127
Chicago, IL 60618
Contact: Kim Wasney VP Sales & Business Dev
Tel: 844-797-4438
Email: gifts@packedwithpurpose.gifts
Website: www.packedwithpurpose.gifts/

Corporate gifts. (Woman, estab 2016, empl 17, sales $8,697,260, cert: WBENC)

3859 Pearl's Girl Sweet Treats
15222 S LaGrange
Orland Park, IL 60463
Contact: Jacqueline Jackson Owner
Tel: 708-460-3960
Email: gojackiejackson@aol.com
Website: www.kilwins.com

Corporate gift baskets: gourmet caramel apples, handmade fudge, carmel corn, brittles, fine chocolates, dipped strawberries & confectins & 32 flavors of koshers icecream. (Woman/AA, estab 2007, empl 16, sales , cert: NMSDC)

3860 Planet Canit, LLC
843 Kimball Rd
Highland Park, IL 60035
Contact: Virginia Price
Tel: 847-433-1619
Email: vprice@planetcanit.com
Website: www.planetcanit.com

Custom decorative tin-ware packaging. (Woman, estab 2000, empl 1, sales , cert: WBENC)

GIFTWARES, ARTS & CRAFTS

3861 Vosges, Ltd.
      2211 N Elston St Ste 203
      Chicago, IL 60614
      Contact: Lesley Nosal Dir Corp Sales
      Tel: 773-388-5560
      Email: vosges@vosgeschocolate.com
      Website: www.vosgeschocolate.com
Corporate gifting & events, unique chocolate creations are infused with exotic spices, herbs, roots, flowers, fruits & nuts. (Woman, estab 1997, empl 85, sales $14,000,000, cert: City, WBENC)

Indiana

3862 Trans-Plants Inc.
      1260 S Senate Ave
      Indianapolis, IN 46225
      Contact: Christine Ernst President
      Tel: 317-972-6760
      Email: admin@trans-plantsindy.com
      Website: www.transplants-indy.com
Interior plants & maintenance, design & installation. Floral arrangements, gift baskets, corporate & individual gifts. (Woman, estab 1986, empl 10, sales $360,786, cert: City)

Kentucky

3863 Wall Street Greetings, LLC
      3265 Pincakrd Pike
      Versailles, KY 40383
      Contact: Susan Rice Natl Accounts Specialist
      Tel: 859-873-0877
      Email: april@wallstreetgreetings.com
      Website: www.wallstreetgreetings.com
Provide corporate greeting cards. (Woman, estab 1992, empl 33, sales $2,628,121, cert: WBENC)

Massachusetts

3864 Madison Floral, Inc.
      63B Innerbelt Rd
      Somerville, MA 02143
      Contact: Edison Chae President
      Tel: 781-648-2000
      Email: edison@madisonfloral.com
      Website: www.madisonfloral.com
Floral design: corporate functions, annual meetings, dinner affairs. (As-Pac, estab 2000, empl 5, sales $180,000, cert: State)

Maryland

3865 Copiosity, LLC
      8230 Georgia Ave, 2nd Fl
      Silver Spring, MD 20910
      Contact: Dianne Harrison Principal
      Tel: 301-608-9102
      Email: dcharrison@copiosityllc.com
      Website: www.copiositygreetings.com
Greeting products: holiday gift wrapping paper, bags, tags, and decorations; holiday greeting cards; graphic & decorative wall decals; celebration yard signs; and stylish seasonal garden products such as disposable table liners. (Woman/AA, estab 2010, empl 2, sales , cert: NMSDC)

Michigan

3866 Mahogani Collections LLC
      35323 Plymouth Rd
      Livonia, MI 48150
      Contact: Phyllis Mitchell Co-Owner
      Tel: 313-627-3513
      Email: mahoganicollections@aol.com
      Website: www.mahoganicollections.com
Mahogani Collections merchandise consists of necklaces, rings, earrings and bracelets for women and men. (AA, estab 2016, empl 2, sales , cert: WBENC)

Minnesota

3867 Schaaf Floral
      6554 University Ave NE
      Minneapolis, MN 55432
      Contact: Marcia Schaaf Owner
      Tel: 763-571-4600
      Email: flowers@schaaffloral.com
      Website: www.schaaffloral.com
Floral arrangement, gifts, etc. (Woman, estab 1970, empl 13, sales $806,748, cert: WBENC)

New Jersey

3868 Biens Chocolate Centerpieces Corp
      5a Stewart Ct
      Denville, NJ 07834
      Contact: Lindsay Smith Co-Founder
      Tel: 908-346-5983
      Email: order@bienscc.com
      Website: www.bienscc.com
Edible gifts for family celebrations, corporate representations & general sweet tooth cravings. (Woman, estab 2019, empl 10, sales $650,000, cert: WBENC)

3869 The Dessert Ladies
      266 Main Ave
      Stirling, NJ 07980
      Contact: Lindsay Smith Owner
      Tel: 908-340-7321
      Email: lindsay.smith@bienscc.com
      Website: www.dessertladies.com/

Custom edible gifts, hand-decorated, branded chocolate products & baked goods. (Woman, estab 2010, empl 10, sales $3,000,000, cert: WBENC)

New York

3870 Chocolate Promises, Inc.
      PO Box 694
      Merrick, NY 11566
      Contact: Zakalik Cindy President
      Tel: 516-299-6400
      Email: cindy@chocolatepromises.com
      Website: www.chocolatepromises.com

Personalized chocolate with edible images. We'll custom print your full color logo, picture, design and/or special message directly on delicious chocolate coins, lollipops, Belgian truffles and more. (Woman, estab 2012, empl 2, sales , cert: State, City, WBENC)

Ohio

3871 Independence Flowers & Gifts
      6495 Brecksville Rd
      Independence, OH 44131
      Contact: Laura Gmitro Owner
      Tel: 216-524-2800
      Email: indyflowers@yahoo.com
      Website: www.independenceflorist.com

Florist & gift shop, fruit baskets, gourmet baskets, custom baskets, floral arrangements & gifts. (Woman, estab 2009, empl 4, sales $280,000, cert: City)

3872 K&M International, Inc.
      1955 Midway Dr
      Twinsburg, OH 44087
      Contact: Prathap Shankar Sales
      Tel: 800-800-9678
      Email: ksprathap@kmtoys.com
      Website: www.wildrepublic.com

Mfr & dist Plush, Toys, Corporate Gifts and other distinctive gift products. (Woman/As-Ind, estab 1979, empl 130, sales , cert: NMSDC)

3873 Uniquely Lisa Designs dba Our Favorite Things Boutique
      12730 Larchmere Blvd
      Shaker Heights, OH 44120
      Contact: Lisa McGuthry CEO
      Tel: 216-536-7928
      Email: info@ourfavoritethingscle.com
      Website: www.ourfavoritethingscle.com

Boutique that features fine gift items and body products. (AA, estab 2019, empl 5, sales $139,000, cert: NMSDC)

Texas

3874 Dessert Gallery Bakery & Cafe
      PO Box 981034
      Houston, TX 77098
      Contact: Sara Brook Founder/CEO
      Tel: 713-960-4400
      Email: sara@dessertgallery.com
      Website: www.dessertgallery.com

Custom photo & logo cookies & cakes, catering- box lunches, office birthday cakes, corporate gifts. (Woman, estab 1995, empl 35, sales , cert: WBENC)

Washington

3875 Gifts by Design, Inc.
      66 S Hanford St Ste 100
      Seattle, WA 98134
      Contact: Andy Sroufe Acct Exec
      Tel: 206-286-6688
      Email: andy@giftsbydesign.net
      Website: www.giftsbydesign.net

Dist art objects, wearables, logo items, awards, baskets, etc. (Woman, estab 1988, empl 11, sales $2,950,000, cert: WBENC)

DIR
DIVERSITY INFORMATION RESOURCES

Top 10 Ways to Effectively (and Memorably) Reach Out to Supplier Diversity Professionals

DIVERSITY 411 — excerpts from DIR's Blog: www.diversityinforesources.blogspot.com

DIR works directly with diverse-owned suppliers, and helps to bring them to the procurement discussion table. Using this book is a fantastic first step. Keep in mind that these contacts and information are best used:
- to establish business relationships
- reinforce business matchmaking

After years of discussions with people on both sides of the procurement "fence," we offer our Top 10 Ways to make the most out of this resource:

#10: Don't send information blindly: Let the buyer ask you for samples, line cards and other company specific information.

#9: Let corporate contacts know what you've done and ask about the best next steps ("I've registered," "I've researched your products/services." etc.). Use references within their industry.

#8: Keep track of conversations: What was said. With whom. What to do next. Schedule follow-ups.

#7: Ask about a corporation's "prime suppliers". You may not be able to work directly with a global conglomerate, but you most likely are able to work with one of their prime suppliers ... ask about them!

#6: Take advantage of any "personal" time you can get. Utilize business events to their fullest potential, reconnecting face-to-face with contacts you meet locally or at national business fairs.

#5: Do your homework about regional outreach groups: Chambers of Commerce, Economic Development Agencies, state or regional divisions of national organizations. Check them all out and be tenacious about following up with their matchmaking opportunities.

#4: Practice your introductions, and have more than one 'ready'. Know what you're going to say to someone experienced or inexperienced in your industry. Educate efficiently!

#3: Do your due diligence in researching what a Supplier Diversity contact needs to bring your information forward to their procurement department. You'll often find their preferences and needs listed on their Web site's supplier diversity page.

#2: Develop targeted marketing lists, and be specific when following up ("Good to meet you at NMSDC on Monday," etc.). Recall a piece of information that distinguishes you from everyone else ("Thank you for commenting on the effectiveness of my capabilities brochure.").

#1: Use names and titles and use them correctly in all your correspondence. If you send an email that says "Dear Ray" to a Ramona, it'll be deleted at first glance.

HARDWARE & TOOLS DIST.

Distribute hardware: screw machine products, plumbing supplies, safety apparel, ladders, etc. (See also HYDRAULIC & COMPRESSED AIR EQUIPMENT and INDUSTRIAL EQUIPMENT & SUPPLIES). NAICS Code 42

Alabama

3876 Ram Tool & Supply Co., Inc.
      4500 5th Ave South Bldg A
      Birmingham, AL 35222
      Contact: Ashley Cato Accounts Receivable Rep
      Tel: 205-599-7085
      Email: ashley.cato@ramtool.com
      Website: www.ram-tool.com
Dist construction material, supplies & tools. (Woman, estab 1985, empl 804, sales , cert: WBENC)

Arizona

3877 Machine Works, LLC
      3832 E Illini St
      Phoenix, AZ 85040
      Contact: carter Trisha Sales/Office Mgr
      Tel: 602-426-1035
      Email: trisha.c@mworkllc.com
      Website: www.machineworksllc.com
Dist aerospace components & assemblies. (As-Pac, estab 1997, empl 12, sales $900,000, cert: NMSDC)

California

3878 ACF Components & Fasteners, Inc.
      31012 Huntwood Ave
      Hayward, CA 94544
      Contact: Bob Henriquez Exec VP
      Tel: 510-487-2100
      Email: bobh@acfcom.com
      Website: www.acfcom.com
Dist industrial fasteners, electronic component hardware, wire, industrial supplies, vmi, kitting, kits, fastener plating, fastener patching, fuses, screws, bolts, terminals. (As-Pac, estab 1976, empl 50, sales $13,000,000, cert: CPUC)

3879 B&B Socket Products, Inc.
      1919 Nancita Cir
      Placenta, CA 92870
      Contact: Robert Huke GM
      Tel: 714-985-4360
      Email: rchuke@bbsocket.com
      Website: www.bbsocket.com
Dist fasteners, hardware & electronic components. (Woman, estab 1976, empl 17, sales , cert: WBENC)

3880 Cordova Bolt, Inc.
      5601 Dolly Ave
      Buena Park, CA 90621
      Contact: Moses E. Cordova President
      Tel: 714-739-7500
      Email: info@cordovabolt.com
      Website: www.cordovabolt.com
Dist nuts, bolts, screws, washers, anchors, A325, A490, GR 2-5-8-L9, etc. (Hisp, estab 1975, empl 34, sales , cert: NMSDC, CPUC)

3881 Mackenzie Aircraft Parts, Inc.
      1400 Decision St
      Vista, CA 92081
      Contact: Toni Mackenzie President
      Tel: 760-727-3775
      Email: toni@macairparts.com
      Website: www.macairparts.com
Dist hardware, screws, nuts, bolts, rivets, washers, bearings & electrical parts. (Woman, estab 1979, empl 11, sales $2,500,000, cert: NWBOC)

3882 Satori Seal, Inc.
      8455 Utica Ave
      Rancho Cucamonga, CA 91730
      Contact: Anne Houlihan President
      Tel: 909-987-8234
      Email: anne@satoriseal.com
      Website: www.satoriseal.com
Dist o-rings, seals, custom molded seals, rotary shaft seals, PTFE seal tape, worm drive hose clamps, gaskets, washers, die cut gaskets, lathe cut gaskets. (Woman, estab 1971, empl 8, sales $2,749,793, cert: WBENC)

3883 STX, Inc. DBA Alta Industries
      418 Aviation Blvd, Ste E
      Santa Rosa, CA 95403
      Contact:
      Tel: 800-788-0302
      Email: info@altaindustries.com
      Website: www.altaindustries.com
Mfr & dist protective knee pads & elbow pads, tool belts for industrial, construction, safety, military & tactical markets. (Woman, estab , empl , sales $3,800,000, cert: NWBOC)

3884 Vampire Tools, Inc.
      47 Peters Canyon Rd
      Irvine, CA 92606
      Contact: Farooqui Ali Admin
      Tel: 949-449-5724
      Email: ali@vampiretools.com
      Website: www.vampiretools.com
Unique pliers for rusted, damaged, stripped screws/nuts/bolts extraction. (Minority, Woman, estab 2010, empl 7, sales $400,000, cert: NMSDC, CPUC)

3885 Widespread Industrial Supplies, Inc.
      1220 S Boyle Ave
      Los Angeles, CA 90023
      Contact: Josh Dorfman President
      Tel: 310-793-7315
      Email: josh.dorfman@widespreadind.com
      Website: www.widespreadind.com
Dist industrial supplies: fasteners, cutting tools, electrical, welding, chemical & safety related supplies, hand & power tools. (Woman, estab 2002, empl 4, sales $820,341, cert: State, City)

Florida

3886 Arrowhead Global, LLC
22033 US 19 N
Clearwater, FL 33765
Contact: Anthony Terranova Sales Mgr
Tel: 727-497-7340
Email: tony@arrowheadglobal.com
Website: www.arrowheadglobal.com
Dist aerospace, military & commercial fasteners, hardware, connectors, electronic components, aircraft parts, adhesives & information technology products & services. (Nat Ame, estab 2013, empl 10, sales $3,100,000, cert: NMSDC, 8(a))

3887 Consolidated Cordage Corp Inc.
1707 Avenida Del Sol
Boca Raton, FL 33432
Contact: Mike Perry Sales Mgr
Tel: 561-347-7247
Email: info@consolidatedcordage.com
Website: www.consolidatedcordage.com
Dist rope, cord, pull cord, twine, elastic shockcord, fall protection safety equip, multe tape, riggings, hoistings, etc. (Woman, estab 1993, empl 8, sales , cert: State, WBENC, NWBOC)

3888 Tropic Fasteners LLC
255 Semoran Comerce Pl
Apopka, FL 32703
Contact: Judy Watson President
Tel: 407-703-1582
Email: judy@tropicfast.com
Website: www.tropicfast.com
Dist fastener products. (Woman, estab 1995, empl 50, sales , cert: WBENC)

Georgia

3889 Stallings Industries Inc.
869 Pioneer Rd
Jasper, GA 30143
Contact: Trevor Wells Area Mgr
Tel: 706-253-0440
Email: trevor@stallingsindustries.com
Website: www.stallingsindustries.com
Dist Garlock gaskets, packings, expansion joints & oil seals, PPC mechanical seals & Teadit, aerosol fillers, "O" rings. (Woman, estab 1988, empl 6, sales , cert: WBENC)

Illinois

3890 Alin Machining Co, Inc. dba Power Plant Services
3131 W Soffel Ave
Melrose Park, IL 60160
Contact: Sonia Gandhi Sales Team Lead
Tel: 708-345-8600
Email: sonia@ppsvcs.com
Website: www.ppsvcs.com
Dist fasteners, studs, nuts, washers, bolts & pins, turbine valve parts, stems, discs & bushings, turbine blade mfg, turbine seals & packing, erosion shields. (As-Ind, estab 1998, empl 142, sales $42,000,000, cert: NMSDC)

3891 Hacha Products Corporation
801 North Main St 60187
Wheaton, IL 60187
Contact: Kimberly Meek CEO
Tel: 630-347-6093
Email: kmeek@hachaproducts.com
Website: www.hachaproducts.com
Wire devices: cable ties, wire nuts, clamps, nuts, bolts, fasteners, shrink tubing. (Minority, Woman, estab 2015, empl 2, sales $750,000, cert: NMSDC, WBENC)

Indiana

3892 Impex International Inc.
7114 Innovation Blvd
Fort Wayne, IN 46818
Contact: Nagin Shah President
Tel: 260-489-3030
Email: nshah@impexint.com
Website: www.impexint.com
Dist fasteners. (As-Ind, estab 1985, empl 6, sales , cert: NMSDC)

3893 Powell Tool Supply Co., Inc.
1338 Mishawaka Ave
South Bend, IN 46615
Contact: Cari Eaton CEO
Tel: 574-289-4811
Email: ceaton@powelltool.com
Website: www.powelltool.com
Dist industrial supplies: cutting tools, abrasives, chemicals, MRO supplies, material handling, janitorial, etc. (Woman, estab 1948, empl 20, sales $5,500,000, cert: WBENC)

3894 Quest Safety Products, Inc.
5720 W Minnesota St
Indianapolis, IN 46241
Contact: Sudhansu (Sam) Yadav President
Tel: 317-594-4500
Email: ar@questsafety.com
Website: www.QuestSafety.com
Dist safety products. (As-Pac, estab 1997, empl 34, sales $13,600,000, cert: NMSDC)

3895 Thompson Distribution Company
2225 N College Ave
Indianapolis, IN 46205
Contact: John Thompson President
Tel: 317-923-2581
Email: johnt@thomdist.com
Website: www.thomdist.com
Dist pipes, valves, pumps, fittings; plumbing, electrical & industrial supplies; fasteners, stainless steel. (AA, estab 2001, empl 14, sales , cert: State, NMSDC)

Kentucky

3896 Com Serv LLC
10201 Bunsen Way
Louisville, KY 40299
Contact: Shiva Dhanapal President
Tel: 502-553-1770
Email: sdhanapal@component-supply.com
Website: www.component-supply.com
Specialty screws & customs hardware, engineering special fasteners, tubing, plastic parts, plastic injection molds, jigs for paint line applications, jigs & fixtures, returnable containers/totes, stamping. (As-Ind, estab 2000, empl 7, sales $5,435,800, cert: NMSDC)

3897 Sandy Valley Fasteners, LLC
528 Broadway St
Paintsville, KY 41240
Contact: Christy Henry-Gregory CEO
Tel: 606-788-0222
Email: christy@sandyvalleyfasteners.com
Website: www.sandyvalleyfasteners.com

Dist commercial & aerospace fasteners & supplies: AN, MS, NAS washers, nuts, bolts, screws, rivets, nutplates, electrical connectors & backshells, tools, raw materials, fittings, tubing, bushings, etc. (Woman, estab 1999, empl 13, sales , cert: WBENC)

Louisiana

3898 Alta Max, LLC
246 Harbor Circle
New Orleans, LA 70126
Contact: Kevin Vorisek VP Seal Div
Tel: 504-948-8625
Email: kevin@altamax.net
Website: www.altamax.net

Security Seals & Plastic Caps, High Security Cable & Bolt Seals, Metal & Plastic Truck Seals, Drum Seals, Plastic Padlock Seals, Aluminum & Lead Head Seals, Plastic Tote Seals. (AA, estab 2001, empl 37, sales $9,700,000, cert: NMSDC)

3899 Best Bolt & Nut Corp.
2726 Lexington Ave
Kenner, LA 70062
Contact: Jason Mangiaracina GM
Tel: 504-469-3585
Email: jason@bestboltandnut.com
Website: www.bestboltandnut.com

Dist hardware. (Hisp, estab 1988, empl 20, sales , cert: NMSDC)

3900 Hardware Inc.
1500 Franklin Ave
Gretna, LA 70053
Contact: Cecilia Sogin President
Tel: 504-944-4610
Email: mro@hardwareincnola.com
Website: www.hardwareincnola.com

Dist hand tools, abrasives, fasteners, material handling, janitorial, construction tools & supplies. (Woman, estab 1989, empl 7, sales $4,900,000, cert: WBENC)

3901 Lightning Bolt and Supply
10626 S Choctaw Dr
Baton Rouge, LA 70815
Contact: Wesley Valverde VP Business Dev
Tel: 225-272-6200
Email: sharon@lightningboltandsupply.com
Website: www.lightningboltandsupply.com

Dist fasteners, nuts, bolts, hex bolts, lock nuts, lock washers, flat washers, fender washers, clips, retaining rings, hex head bolts, socket head cap screws, buttons, lug nuts, studs, double end studs, latches. (Woman, estab 1994, empl 15, sales , cert: WBENC)

Maryland

3902 Absolute Supply and Services, LLC
427 Council Bluffs Ct
Lusby, MD 20657
Contact: Paula Tilghman President
Tel: 301-440-6056
Email: ptilghman@absolutesupplyandservices.com
Website: www.absolutesupplyandservices.com

Dist HVAC, plumbing equipment & replacement parts. (Woman/AA, estab 2007, empl 1, sales $161,000, cert: WBENC)

3903 American General Contractor Inc.
1 Research Ct, Ste 450
Rockville, MD 20850
Contact: Linward Hope VP
Tel: 301-202-4511
Email: americangeneralmd@yahoo.com
Website: www.americangeneralmd.com

Dist construction materials, thermostats, tools, cement, sheet rock, led lights, hardware nails, screws, toilets, tile, all flooring, hand towels, paper towels. (Minority, Woman, estab 2012, empl 2, sales $107,000, cert: State)

3904 Atlantic Hardware Supply
8389 Ardwick Ardmore Rd
Hyattsville, MD 20785
Contact: Jon Gray VP
Tel: 240-249-6047
Email: jgray@atlantic-supply.com
Website: www.atlantic-supply.com

Dist hardware. (Woman, estab 2009, empl 6, sales , cert: State)

3905 B & B Lighting Supply, Inc.
PO Box 68084
Baltimore, MD 21215
Contact: Sharon Bradford CEO
Tel: 410-523-7300
Email: sbradford@bnblightingsupply.com
Website: www.bnblightingsupply.com

Dist lamps, relamping & energy mgmt, const mgmt & svcs, provision & professional. (Woman/AA, estab 1994, empl 2, sales $525,000, cert: State)

Michigan

3906 Ewie Co., Inc.
1099 Highland Dr
Ann Arbor, MI 48108
Contact: Shoki Mullick Dir of diversity
Tel: 734-971-6265
Email: shoki.mullick@ewie.com
Website: www.ewie.com

Dist cutting tools, abrasives, special tools, chemical/lubricants. (Minority, estab 1981, empl 253, sales $122,000,000, cert: NMSDC)

3907 Extreme Tooling LLC
48750 Structural Dr
Chesterfield, MI 48051
Contact: Kurt Schill President
Tel: 586-232-3618
Email: kschill@extremetooling.com
Website: www.extremetooling.com

Dist metal removal & industrial supplies, milling, drilling & industrial products. (Woman, estab 2003, empl 5, sales $3,683,821, cert: WBENC)

HARDWARE & TOOLS DIST.

3908 Marshall Sales Inc.
      14359 Meyers Rd
      Detroit, MI 48227
      Contact: Brian Tupiak Acct Mgr
      Tel: 313-491-1700
      Email: btupiak@marshallsales.com
      Website: www.marshallsales.com
Fasteners & fastener installation, tooling. (Woman, estab 1958, empl 9, sales $7,000,000, cert: State, WBENC)

3909 Materials Management Services Inc.
      13691 Girardin St
      Detroit, MI 48212
      Contact: Jack Long President
      Tel: 313-365-1290
      Email: jlong@mms-inc.com
      Website: www.mms-inc.com
Mfr & dist industrial work gloves of fabric & leather in a variety of styles. Also dist tools, tape, coolant, etc. (AA, estab 1994, empl 11, sales , cert: NMSDC)

3910 Mer Wil Industries, Inc.
      328 S Saginaw St, Ste 902
      Flint, MI 48502
      Contact: Deborah Love Sales Rep
      Tel: 810-239-0600
      Email: mwilliams@merwil.com
      Website: www.merwil.com
Dist hardware & building supplies. (AA, estab 1983, empl 2, sales , cert: State)

3911 National Industrial Supply Co.
      1201 Rochester Rd
      Troy, MI 48083
      Contact: Kathryn Harper President
      Tel: 248-588-1828
      Email: kathybrett@nischain.com
      Website: www.nischain.com
Dist chain, wire rope, nylons, hardware supplies, etc. (Minority, Woman, estab 1981, empl 20, sales $2,000,000, cert: NMSDC, WBENC)

3912 New Eagle, LLC
      3588 Plymouth Rd, Ste 271
      Ann Arbor, MI 48105
      Contact: Mickey Swortzel CEO
      Tel: 734-929-4557
      Email: mswortzel@neweagle.net
      Website: www.neweagle.net
Controls system solutions, tools, products & services. (Woman, estab 2008, empl 25, sales $3,874,600, cert: WBENC)

3913 Northern Industrial Products Corp.
      20380 Cornillie Dr
      Roseville, MI 48066
      Contact: Andrew Wilson General Mgr
      Tel: 586-293-9544
      Email: awilson@nipcorp.com
      Website: www.nipcorp.com
Dist industrial fasteners, tools, rack & shelving, etc. (AA, estab 1976, empl 17, sales $5,000,000, cert: NMSDC)

3914 Production Services Management, Inc.
      1255 Beach Court
      Saline, MI 48176
      Contact: Michael Henry Dir Diversity/Sustainability
      Tel: 917-690-0179
      Email: mhenry@psmicorp.com
      Website: www.psmicorp.com
Tool Commodity Management, Wholesaler, Integrator, etc. (As-Ind, estab 2004, empl 400, sales $184,000,000, cert: NMSDC)

3915 Reggie Mckenzie Industrial Materials, Inc.
      34401 Schoolcraft Rd Ste 200
      Livonia, MI 48150
      Contact: Dan Kapp Office Mgr
      Tel: 734-261-0844
      Email: dkapp@rmimi.com
      Website: www.reggiemckenzieindustrial.com
Dist MRO, Cutting Tools, Abrasives, Industrial Supplies, Industrial Materials. (AA, estab 2000, empl 3, sales $6,000,000, cert: NMSDC)

3916 Suburban Bolt and Supply Co.
      27670 Groesbeck
      Roseville, MI 48066
      Contact: Frank Woch Sales
      Tel: 586-775-8900
      Email: defense@suburbanbolt.com
      Website: www.suburbanbolt.com
Fasteners - Socket Products, Bolts, Screws, Pins, NAAMS, Nuts, Washers, Anchors, Cutting Tools - Drills, Taps, Counter Bores, Countersinks, Dies, Reamers, End Mills, Saw Blades, Abrasives- Coated Abrasives, Cut off Wheels, Flap Wheels and Discs. (Minority, estab 1971, empl 77, sales $14,004,169, cert: NMSDC)

Minnesota

3917 Bredemus Hardware Co Inc.
      1285 Sylvan St
      St. Paul, MN 55117
      Contact: Betty Bredemus CEO
      Tel: 651-489-6250
      Email: betty@bredemus.com
      Website: www.bredemus.com
Dist hardware, hollow metal doors, frames & wood doors. (Minority, Woman, estab 1955, empl 29, sales $5,000,000, cert: State, City)

3918 Wells Technology, Inc.
      4885 Windsor Ct NW
      Bemidji, MN 56601
      Contact: Wendy Knudson VP Contracts/Certifications
      Tel: 218-751-1412
      Email: wendy@wellstech.com
      Website: www.wellstech.com
Dist fasteners, brasives, power handtools, hardwares, paint, varnish & general line industrial supplies. (Nat Ame, estab 1989, empl 43, sales $132,890,629, cert: NMSDC, SDB)

Missouri

3919 AMC Industries, LLC
      4251 N Kentucky Ave
      Kansas City, MO 64117
      Contact: Adam French Dir of Sales
      Tel: 816-833-4249
      Email: adam@amc-industries.net
      Website: www.amc-industries.net
Dist pipes, valves, fittings, plumbing fixtures, HVAC equipment, HVAC accessories, toilet partitions & washroom accessories. (AA, estab 2001, empl 5, sales $4,400,000, cert: State, City, NMSDC)

North Carolina

3920 ARTU-USA, Inc.
      330 Fields Dr.
      Aberdeen, NC 28315
      Contact: Beverly Tate-Cooper President
      Tel: 910-944-1883
      Email: beverly@artu.com
      Website: www.artu.com/
Cutting tools, Multi-Purpose Drill Bits, PORC+ Drill Bits, Cobalt Drill Bits, Tungsten Carbide Grit Hole Saws & Saw Blades, SDS Drill Bits, Precision Multi-Purpose Drill Bits & Spline Shanks. (Woman, estab 1989, empl 6, sales $1,636,453, cert: State, CPUC, NWBOC)

3921 C & D Industrial Tools & Supplies Inc.
      2415 Penny Road Ste 101
      High Point, NC 27265
      Contact: Jerry Camp President
      Tel: 336-885-6675
      Email: jerry@cdi-tools.com
      Website: www.cdi-tools.com
Dist cutting tools: drills, end mills, reamers, taps & dies, precision tools, etc. (AA, estab 1988, empl 4, sales $2,500,000, cert: NMSDC)

3922 Edwards & West, Inc. dba Divspec
      605 Springfield Rd
      Kenilworth, NJ 07033
      Contact: Doug Burke NC Sales Mgr
      Tel: -   -
      Email: dougb@divspec.com
      Website: www.divspec.com
Dist threaded rod, strut, strut fittings, and fasteners. (Woman, estab 1980, empl 12, sales $5,913,389, cert: WBENC)

New Jersey

3923 Fastenation, Inc.
      120 Bright Rd Unit 2
      Clifton, NJ 07012
      Contact: Stephanie Cherepinsky Sales Rep
      Tel: 973-591-1277
      Email: stephanie@fastenation.com
      Website: www.fastenation.com
Distributor & Converter of VELCRO(R) Brand Fasteners (Die-Cutting, Packaging, Printing, etc.) (Woman, estab 1997, empl , sales $9,000,000, cert: WBENC)

3924 MF Supply Corp.
      164 Garibaldi Ave
      Lodi, NJ 07644
      Contact: Robin Lieberman President
      Tel: 973-777-5411
      Email: robin@mfsupply.com
      Website: www.mfsupply.com
Dist fasteners, Stainless Steel, Inserts & Keenserts, Socket products, Standoffs & Spacers & Mil-Spec fasteners. (Woman, estab 1974, empl 5, sales $823,000, cert: State)

New York

3925 Global Connection Co. of America, Inc.
      150-123 Powells Cove Blvd
      Whitestone, NY 11357
      Contact: Grace King President
      Tel: 718-767-5168
      Email: gk@madeinchina.net
      Website: www.glocoamerica.com
Dist hardware & tools. (Minority, Woman, estab 1992, empl 3, sales $2,107,046, cert: State, NMSDC)

3926 Henssgen Hardware Corporation
      PO Box 2078
      Queensbury, NY 12804
      Contact: Rachel Novak President
      Tel: 518-793-3593
      Email: rachel@henssgenhardware.com
      Website: www.henssgenhardware.com
Sources rigging hardware, Snap Hooks, Pulleys (both Fixed Eye and Swivel with Single Sheave and Double Sheave), Quick Links, Shackles, Wire Rope Clips, Drop Forged Clevis Grab & Clevis Slip Hooks. (Woman, estab 2000, empl 3, sales $548,000, cert: WBENC)

3927 NY Plumbing Wholesale & Supply, Inc.
      933 Columbus Ave
      New York, NY 10025
      Contact: Derek Price President
      Tel: 212-678-4900
      Email: derek@nyps1.com
      Website: www.nyps1.com
Dist plumbing fittings, fixtures, pipe, tools & accessories. (AA, estab 2009, empl 23, sales , cert: City)

3928 South Atlantic Marine Services
      342 Cold Spring Rd
      Syosset, NY 11791
      Contact: Linda Allen President
      Tel: 516-449-9000
      Email: southatlantic15@yahoo.com
      Website: www.southatlantic-services.com
Dist lubricants, greases, additives, hardware, bolts fasteners, tools, fittings, safety products, ropes, chains, hoses, twine, clamps rivet, cables, pumps, valves, bearings, tubing, welding supplies, cutting tools. (Woman, estab 2000, empl 2, sales $889,255, cert: State, City)

Ohio

3929 Bain Enterprises, LLC
4650 Allen Road Ste B
Stow, OH 44244
Contact: Owner
Tel: 513-378-4411
Email:
Website: www.bainenterprises.com
Dist Stanley handheld hydraulic & battery operated tools & accessories. (Woman, estab 2006, empl 2, sales $1,700,000, cert: WBENC)

3930 CJ Industrial Supply Inc.
15326 Waterloo Rd
Cleveland, OH 44110
Contact: Tom Frohwerk VP Sales
Tel: 216-481-4448
Email: tom@cjindustrial.com
Website: www.cjindustrial.com
Industrial hardware, Valves Pumps Steel Fabrication, OSHA Products, Plumbing, Electrical, Cutting Tools, Machine Shop Services, Abrasives, Hand Tools, Power Tools, VOC Compliant Chemicals & Paints, Steel. (Woman, estab 1995, empl 8, sales $2,000,000, cert: State, City)

3931 CryoPlus, Inc.
2429 N Millborne Rd
Wooster, OH 44691
Contact: Kathi Bond President
Tel: 330-683-3375
Email: kathicryo@aol.com
Website: www.cryoplus.com
Cutting tools, blades, knives, dies & punches. (Woman, estab 1994, empl 3, sales , cert: NWBOC)

3932 General Factory/ WD Supply
4811 Winton Rd
Cincinnati, OH 45232
Contact: Pat Priko Sales
Tel: 513-681-6300
Email: patp@gfwdsupply.com
Website: www.gfwdsupply.com
Dist MRO, welding, cutting tools, hand tools & safety. (Woman, estab 2007, empl 32, sales $12,500,000, cert: WBENC)

3933 Power Tool & Supply Co., Inc.
3699 Leharps Rd
Youngstown, OH 44515
Contact: Linda Richardson Dir Business Dev
Tel: 330-792-1487
Email: linda@powertoolandsupply.com
Website: www.powertoolandsupply.com
Dist power tools & supplies. (Woman, estab 1961, empl 18, sales , cert: State, WBENC)

3934 Queensgate Hardware & Security, Inc.
1025 Dalton Ave
Cincinnati, OH 45203
Contact: Sarah Back President
Tel: 513-929-0062
Email: sarah@queensgatehardware.com
Website: www.queensgatehardware.com
Dist commercial grade hardware, wood doors & frames, hollow metal doors & frames, access control systems, toilet partitions & accessories. (Woman, estab 2010, empl 3, sales $768,000, cert: WBENC)

3935 River City Building Solutions, LLC
19885 Detroit Rd, Ste 173
Cleveland, OH 44116
Contact: Peggy Powers President
Tel: 216-333-1491
Email: peggy@rivercitybuildingsolutions.com
Website: www.rivercitybuildingsolutions.com
Dist building materials, sustainable materials, paintings & coatings, roofing materials, flooring, HVAC, plumbing materials, electrical / telecommunications wiring. (Woman, estab 2011, empl 2, sales , cert: State, City)

South Carolina

3936 GT Industrial LLC Co.
846 Royle Rd
Ladson, SC 29456
Contact: Teresa Gore President
Tel: 843-873-0290
Email: teresag@gtindustrial.net
Website: www.gtindustrial.com/
Dist tools, cert kits, tape, adhesives, dust masks, respirators, marking crayons, flashlights, batteries, light bulbs. (Nat Ame, estab 1998, empl 6, sales $5,111,180, cert: NMSDC)

3937 Janeice Products Co. Inc
1084 Williston Road
Aiken, SC 29803
Contact: Vernal Sanders Mktg Mgr
Tel: 803-652-3025
Email: sales@janeiceproducts.com
Website: www.janeiceproducts.com
Dist MRO products: abrasives, cutting tools, fans, hand tools, hardware, ladders, lawn & garden, material handling equip & safety prods. (AA, estab 1995, empl 7, sales , cert: NMSDC)

Tennessee

3938 D & J Tool Supply, LLC
PO Box 9601
Knoxville, TN 37940
Contact: Deanna Maurer Owner
Tel: 865-546-0744
Email: deanna@djtoolsupply.com
Website: www.djtoolsupply.com
Dist metalworking & fabricating machinery, machine tool accessories, cutting tools, hand & power tools, metalworking fluids, abrasives, safety supplies, welding consumables. (Woman, estab 1999, empl 2, sales $386,641, cert: State)

Texas

3939 Power Tool Service Co., Inc.
3718 Polk St
Houston, TX 77003
Contact: JB Robertson VP
Tel: 713-228-0100
Email: sales@powertoolservice.com
Website: www.powertoolservice.com
Dist, rent & repair tool & equipment, calibration. (Minority, Woman, estab 1969, empl 18, sales , cert: State)

3940 PowerOne and Associates, LLC
      12320 Barker Cypress Rd Ste 600-300
      Cypress, TX 77429
      Contact: Gus Guerrero BDM
      Tel: 713-955-7888
      Email: gus@power-one-usa.com
      Website: www.powerone-usa.com
Dist High Temperature Pipe, Hose & Cable Wraps (Safety), MRO products, Hand Tools, Personal Safety Equipment (PSE), Power transmission equipment (Safety Couplings, Metal Bellows Coupling, Locking assemblies). (Hisp, estab 2008, empl 10, sales , cert: NMSDC)

3941 Powr-Guardian, Inc.
      1607 Falcon Dr, Ste 101
      DeSoto, TX 75115
      Contact: Von Miller President
      Tel: 972-228-9029
      Email: info@powrguardian.com
      Website: www.powrguardian.com
Dist & service batteries. (AA, estab 1988, empl 11, sales $1,375,000, cert: State)

Virginia

3942 Alkat Electrical Contractors, Inc.
      PO Box 6903
      Richmond, VA 23230
      Contact: Katherine Mickens
      Tel: 804-354-0944
      Email: katherinemickens@alkatelectric.com
      Website: www.alkatelectric.com
Integrated Build Systems, conduits, raceways, fittings, wire, cable, lugs, etc. (AA, estab 1983, empl 45, sales $4,780,000, cert: State, NMSDC)

3943 Apollo Energy Components Inc. t/a Apollo Supply
      2711 Lowesville Rd
      Arrington, VA 22922
      Contact: Christine Manley President
      Tel: 434-277-5556
      Email: apollonrg2711@aol.com
      Website: www.apolloenergycomponents.com
Dist fasteners, pipe fittings, valves, high pressure tube fittings, abrasives, grinding wheels, cutting tools, saw blades, aerosols. (Woman, estab 2009, empl 3, sales $122,080, cert: State)

3944 Machine Tools of Virginia, Inc.
      8147 Shady Grove Rd
      Mechanicsville, VA 23111
      Contact: Cindy Waddell President
      Tel: 804-569-6147
      Email: machinetoolsofva@hotmail.com
      Website: www.machinetoolsofvirginia.com
Dist machine tools: lathes & mills, CNC & standard, lathe & mill accessories, carbide cutting tools, compressors, grinders, drills, saws & fabrication equipment. (Woman, estab 2001, empl 4, sales , cert: State)

Washington

3945 The Part Works Inc.
      2900 4th Ave S
      Seattle, WA 98134
      Contact: Oly Welke Sales & Marketing Mgr
      Tel: 206-305-0448
      Email: oly@thepartworks.com
      Website: www.thepartworks.com
Dist plumbing supplies. (Woman, estab 1980, empl 25, sales $5,500,000, cert: City, WBENC)

HARDWARE & TOOLS MFG.

Manufacture fasteners and other screw machine products. Many manufacture tools and hand tools (See also HYDRAULIC & COMPRESSED AIR EQUIPMENT and INDUSTRIAL EQUIPMENT & SUPPLIES). NAICS Code 42

Arizona

3946 B&T Tool & Engineering Inc.
2618 E Washington St
Phoenix, AZ 85034
Contact: William Meras President
Tel: 602-267-1481
Email: bnttool@aol.com
Website: www.bnttool.us
Mfr & dist precision cutting tools. (Hisp, estab 1992, empl 21, sales $3,701,273, cert: NMSDC)

3947 Special Carbide Tools
3153 E 36th St
Tucson, AZ 85713
Contact: Jerry Gamboa CEO
Tel: 520-624-0007
Email: jerry@specialcarbide.com
Website: www.specialcarbide.com
Mfr special custom carbide cutting tools: standard drills, endmills & reamers. (Hisp, estab 1999, empl 18, sales $2,000,000, cert: NMSDC)

California

3948 Blue Sky Industries
595 Monterey Pass Rd
Monterey Park, CA 91754
Contact: Denis Gagnier Outside Sales Mgr
Tel: 213-620-9950
Email: dgagnier@blueskyindustries.com
Website: www.blueskyindustries.com
Cherry & Monogram blind rivets & blind bolts, Shear Pins & Collars Hi-locks, Standard Aerospace Bolts, Screws, Nuts & Washers, Single & Double Oversize fasteners, Bushings, Bearings, Spacers, & Shims. (As-Pac, estab 1995, empl 52, sales $15,000,000, cert: NMSDC)

3949 D Unique Tools Inc
5744 International
Oakland, CA 94621
Contact: Nanette Hunter President
Tel: 510-569-9961
Email: nanette@universalsquare.com
Website: www.universalsquare.com
Mfr & dist tools. (Woman/AA, estab 1991, empl 4, sales $125,536, cert: NMSDC)

Connecticut

3950 Chapman Manufacturing Company
471 New Haven Rd
Durham, CT 06422
Contact: Jason Camassar VP
Tel: 860-349-9228
Email: jason@chapmanmfg.com
Website: www.chapmanmfg.com
Mfr screwdriver kits. (Woman, estab 1936, empl 13, sales $683,000, cert: CPUC)

Florida

3951 AAW Products Inc.
825 Brickell Bay Dr Ste 246
Miami, FL 33131
Contact: Andre Woolery CEO
Tel: 305-330-6863
Email: andre@magnogrip.com
Website: www.magnogrip.com
Mfr magnetic work gear "MagnoGrip." MagnoGrip: wristbands, hammer holders, tool pouches & tool belts. (AA, estab 2005, empl 3, sales $4,500,000, cert: NMSDC)

3952 Limitless Investigative Solutions, L.L.C.
11160 Lost Creek Terrace Ste 205
Bradenton, FL 34211
Contact: Miguel Caraballo President
Tel: 678-458-8538
Email: miguel@limitlessinv.com
Website: www.limitlessinv.com
Solid carbide end mills, drills, reamers, burrs, inserts & specials, in house research & development, custom tool design for various applications, ools simulation software. (Hisp, estab 2017, empl 1, sales , cert: State)

3953 Raisman Corporation
5543 NW 72nd Ave
Miami, FL 33166
Contact: Sales
Tel: 786-581-3820
Email: sales@raisman.com
Website: www.raisman.com
Mfr trimmer heads, spindles, primer bulbs, fuel filters, oil pumps, spark plugs, shock absorbers, mufflers, carburetors, carburetor kits, etc. (Hisp, estab 1998, empl 120, sales $15,000,000, cert: State)

Illinois

3954 Foreman Tool & Mold Company
3850 Swenson Ave
St. Charles, IL 60174
Contact: Jeff Gardner Sales Mgr
Tel: 630-377-6389
Email: jgardner@foremantool.com
Website: www.foremantool.com

Complete 3D part design, Pro-E mold design & layout. (Hisp, estab 1984, empl 80, sales $ 0, cert: NMSDC)

3955 Pioneer Service Inc. - Addison, IL
542 W Factory Rd
Addison, IL 60101
Contact: Beth Swanson VP Sales & Mktg
Tel: 630-628-0249
Email: bswanson@pioneerserviceinc.com
Website: www.pioneerserviceinc.com/

Contract mfr screw machine products & centerless grinding services: shafts, axles, bolts, bushings, dowels, pins, rods, spacers, valve stems, deburring, drilling, flatting, grinding, knurling, slotting, tapping, threading, heat treating. (Woman, estab 1990, empl 40, sales $5,000,000, cert: CPUC, WBENC)

3956 Tag Tool Services, Inc.
3303 N Main St
East Peoria, IL 61611
Contact: Vonda Jones President
Tel: 309-694-2400
Email: vonda@countyline-tool.com
Website: www.countyline-tool.com

Cutting tool manufacturing & tool refurbishment, regrind Hobs, Shaper Cutters, Broach Bars, Drills, Rota Broaches, Port Tools, Gun Drills, End Mills, Taps, Reamers, Chamfer Tools, Special Form Tools. (Woman, estab 1984, empl 14, sales $1,200,000, cert: WBENC)

Massachusetts

3957 Electrical Safety Products LLC
375 Main St
Woburn, MA 01801
Contact: Tom Wilkie Dir of Sales
Tel: 781-249-5007
Email: tom.wilkie@electricalsafety-usa.com
Website: www.electricalsafety-usa.com

Mfr ASTM F-1505 certified insulated tools. (Woman, estab 2009, empl 4, sales , cert: WBENC)

Michigan

3958 2K Tool LLC
3025 Madison Ave SE
Wyoming, MI 49548
Contact: Kevin Smith Engineering Mgr
Tel: 616-452-4927
Email: kevin@2ktool.com
Website: www.2ktool.com

Moldmaker, machining, tooling, plastic injection molds, compression tooling, composite machining, casting machining part Injection molding. (Woman, estab 2004, empl 19, sales $9,500,000, cert: WBENC)

3959 Ideal Machine Tool Technologies, LLC
675 E Big Beaver Rd, Ste 105
Troy, MI 48083
Contact: Vincent H. Hylton Owner
Tel: 248-792-9061
Email: v.hylton@e-imtt.com
Website: www.e-imtt.com

Commodity management services, program management, engineering services, field services in the machine tool industry. (AA, estab 2010, empl 2, sales $ 0, cert: NMSDC)

3960 Micro Fixtures, Inc.
20448 Lorne
Taylor, MI 48180
Contact: Sue Rader Office Mgr
Tel: 313-382-9781
Email: microfixtures@msn.com
Website: www.MicroFixtures.com

Design & mfr tools, fixtures, gauges, prototype products. (Nat Ame, estab 1993, empl 4, sales $514,590, cert: NMSDC)

Minnesota

3961 Carbide Tool Services, Inc.
1020 Lund Blvd
Anoka, MN 55303
Contact: Julie Reiling President
Tel: 763-421-2210
Email: julie@carbidetool.com
Website: www.carbidetool.com

Mfr & repair indexable cutting tools, live tooling. (Minority, Woman, estab 1988, empl 40, sales $3,493,686, cert: WBENC)

North Dakota

3962 Posi Lock Puller, Inc.
805 Sunflower Ave
Cooperstown, ND 58425
Contact: Tamara Somerville VP
Tel: 701-797-2600
Email: t.somerville@posilock.com
Website: www.posilock.com

Mfr gear & bearing pullers. (Woman, estab 1977, empl 45, sales $3,900,000, cert: City)

New Jersey

3963 JDV Products, Inc.
22-01 Raphael St.
Fair Lawn, NJ 07410
Contact: Ron Vradenburg Sales Mgr
Tel: 201-796-1720
Email: ron@jdvproducts.com
Website: www.jdvproducts.com

Mfr & dist telecom tools: wire wrap & unwrap tools, semi-automatic wire wrap machines, wire strippers, hand & pneumatic power tools, industrial power bits, hand screwdrivers, tool balancer, torque wrenches & accessories, wire & plastics cutting tools. (Woman, estab 1995, empl 19, sales , cert: WBENC)

3964 SMG Services, LLC
462 W Lookout Ave
Hackensack, NJ 07601
Contact: CEO
Tel: 201-937-5378
Email: sweintraub@svcmgmt.com
Website: www.smgdiamondtools.com

Mfr Diamond Drill Bits, Diamond Plated drill Bits, Diamond Grinding Tools, Cutting Blades, Impregnated Inserts, Brazed Diamond Products, Diamond Core Drills, Diamond Solid Tools, Cstmr specs. (Woman/AA, estab 2009, empl 1, sales $765,000, cert: State)

3965 Sysmind LLC
38 Washington Rd
Princeton Junction, NJ 08550
Contact: Business Devel Specialist
Tel: 609-897-9670
Email: info@sysmind.com
Website: www.sysmind.com

Fabricate plastic components & fasteners for computer, aerospace, electronic, instrumentation, etc. applications. Prototype to production. Also stock molded nylon fasteners. (Woman/As-Ind, estab 1999, empl 456, sales $45,000,000, cert: NMSDC, WBENC)

New York

3966 American Pride Fasteners, LLC
195 S Fehr Way
Bay Shore, NY 11706
Contact: Lynda Zacpal President
Tel: 631-940-8292
Email: lynda@americanpridefasteners.com
Website: www.americanpridefasteners.com

Engineering & mfr miniature screws & miniature fasteners. (Minority, Woman, estab 2004, empl 24, sales $4,200,000, cert: City)

3967 Burnett Process, Inc.
545 Colfax St
Rochester, NY 14606
Contact: Melissa Shea-Brooks Marketing Dev Mgr
Tel: 585-254-8080
Email: burnettprocesscsr@cannonind.com
Website: www.burnettprocessinc.com

Mfr & dist ozone, pleated, particulate & HEPA filters. (AA, estab 1957, empl 39, sales $6,000,000, cert: NMSDC)

Ohio

3968 AKKO Fastener, Inc.
6855 Cornell Rd
Cincinnati, OH 45242
Contact: Art Huge Sales Mgr
Tel: 513-489-8300
Email: arthuge@comcast.net
Website: www.akkofastener.com

Mfr fastening products: machine screws, tapping screws, plascrews, thread cutting screws, & cold formed metal products. (Minority, Woman, estab 1967, empl 40, sales $7,000,000, cert: NMSDC)

3969 Cold Headed Fasteners & Assemblies, Inc.
1875 Harsh Ave SE
Massillon, OH 44646
Contact: Oscar Lee President
Tel: 330-833-0800
Email: o.lee@coldheaded.us
Website: www.coldheaded.us

Mfr fasteners & assemblies, sorting & packaging (As-Pac, estab 2002, empl 15, sales $ 0, cert: State)

3970 Custom Millcraft Corp.
9092 Le Saint Dr
Fairfield, OH 45014
Contact: Jody Corbett President
Tel: 513-874-7080
Email: jcorbett@custommillcraft.com
Website: www.custommillcraft.com

Mfr wood & plastic laminate store fixtures. (Woman, estab 1983, empl 45, sales $4,000,000, cert: WBENC)

3971 M.O.M. Tools, LLC
3659 Green Road Ste 304
Cleveland, OH 44122
Contact: Anthony Lockhart
Tel: 216-464-2992
Email: axlockhart@toolsbymom.com
Website: www.toolsbymom.com/

Mfr dual-head piercing tools & dies. (AA, estab 2003, empl 2, sales $ 0, cert: NMSDC)

3972 Master Manufacturing Co, Inc.
      9200 Inman Ave
      Cleveland, OH 44105
      Contact: Bob Ptacek VP Sales
      Tel: 800-323-5513
      Email: bptacek@mastermfgco.com
      Website: www.mastermfgco.com

Mfr furniture casters & self-stick wheels; felt pads, surface protectors, wobble stoppers; furniture movers; door stops; ergonomic support cushions & wire mgmt channels & grommets. (Woman, estab 1951, empl , sales , cert: CPUC, WBENC)

3973 Midwest Ohio Tool Company, Inc.
      215 Tarhe Trail
      Upper Sandusky, OH 43351
      Contact: Stephanie Kettels President
      Tel: 419-294-1987
      Email: skettels@midwestohio.com
      Website: www.midwestohio.com

Mfr custom cutting tools, metal cutting tools, milling cutters, specialized cutting tools, boring bars, tool holders, industrial tools. (Woman, estab 1954, empl 9, sales $500,000, cert: WBENC)

3974 RB Tool & Mfg Co.
      2680 Civic Center Dr
      Cincinnati, OH 45231
      Contact: Scott Schaeper Sales/Marketing Mgr
      Tel: 513-521-8292
      Email: scott@rbtoolandmfg.com
      Website: www.rbtoolandmfg.com

Mfr mills-horizontal and vertical, lathes-CNC and manuals, EDM-wire and sinker, welding, painting. (Woman, estab 1957, empl 40, sales $6,000,000, cert: WBENC)

3975 Steam Turbine Alternative Resources
      116 Latourette St
      Marion, OH 43302
      Contact: Ken Kubinski Sales Mgr
      Tel: 740-387-5535
      Email: ken@starturbine.com
      Website: www.starturbines.com

Mfr steam seals, packing, spill strips hardware, oil seals & deflectors, on-site field installation & machining sevices. (Woman, estab 1986, empl 40, sales $5,610,000, cert: WBENC)

3976 Stelfast Inc.
      22979 Stelfast Pkwy
      Strongsville, OH 44149
      Contact: Todd McRoberts Sales
      Tel: 877-619-8231
      Email: toddm@stelfast.com
      Website: www.stelfast.com

Import & manufacture fasteners. (As-Pac, estab 1973, empl 80, sales $31,500,000, cert: NMSDC)

3977 Talent Tool & Die, Inc.
      777 Berea Industrial Pkwy
      Berea, OH 44017
      Contact: Mylynh Vu President
      Tel: 440-239-8777
      Email: mylynh@talent-tool.com
      Website: www.talent-tool.com

Mfr dies, tools & fixtures; metal stamping & laser cutting. (As-Pac, estab 1989, empl 44, sales $ 0, cert: NMSDC)

3978 The M.K. Morse Company
      1101 11th St SE
      Canton, OH 44707
      Contact: Ryan Rhodes Customer Service
      Tel: 330-453-8187
      Email: rhodesr@mkmorse.com
      Website: www.mkmorse.com

Mfr saw blades, band saws, reciprocating saws, hole saws, hack saws and frames, wood boring bits, portable band saws, metal cutting circular saws & machines. Made from bimetal, carbon steel, carbide tipped & carbide grit. (Woman, estab 1963, empl 500, sales $84,000,000, cert: WBENC)

Oklahoma

3979 Hover Group, LLC
      416 Heritage Green Rd
      Edmond, OK 73003
      Contact: Nicole Hover CEO
      Tel: 405-437-8691
      Email: Nicole@hovergroup.net
      Website: www.hovergroup.net

Manufacturing and providing composite components, oil and gas downhole tools. (Woman, estab 2016, empl 5, sales $473,000, cert: WBENC)

Texas

3980 Arise Solutions Inc.
      5862 Cromo Ste 149
      El Paso, TX 79912
      Contact: Daniel Laing President
      Tel: 915-345-9134
      Email: sales@arisesolutions.biz
      Website: www.arisesolutions.biz

Custom designed wire harness, cable assembly, bulk wire, signal cable, specialty bolts, screws, Nut Rivets, Inserts, Fasteners, Spacers, Connectors & Fittings for automotive industry. (As-Pac, estab 2012, empl 5, sales $1,000,000, cert: State, NMSDC)

HARDWARE & TOOLS MFG.

3981 Danrick Industries Inc.
      850 Kastrin St
      El Paso, TX 79907
      Contact: Marco Herrera President
      Tel: 915-599-2988
      Email: marcoherrera@danrick.net
      Website: www.danrick.net
Mfr tooling & precision machining parts, fabrication of parts & components of terminal crimping. (AA, estab 2002, empl 22, sales $ 0, cert: State, NMSDC)

3982 EZKutter Company
      3617 Rabbit Lane
      Bryan, TX 77808
      Contact: Dora Loria Owner
      Tel: 979-778-0825
      Email: ezkutter@suddenlink.net
      Website: www.ezkutter-usa.com
Mfr hand held cutting tools used for cutting heavy plastic straps, strings & shrink wrapping. (Woman, estab 1992, empl 2, sales , cert: State)

3983 Versatech, LLC
      315 N Park Dr
      San Antonio, TX 78216
      Contact: Diana Grinman Admin
      Tel: 210-979-2823
      Email: dgrinman@pmtool.com
      Website: www.versatech-mfg.com
Advanced tooling, plastic injection molds, tools & dies fields. (Hisp, estab 2006, empl 5, sales , cert: NMSDC)

Virginia

3984 Master Gage & Tool Company
      112 Maplewood St
      Danville, VA 24543
      Contact: Debbye Lyle President
      Tel: 434-836-4243
      Email: debbyel@mastergt.com
      Website: www.mastergt.com
Calibration, specialized tooling & gaging products. (Woman, estab 1986, empl 26, sales $12,010,000, cert: WBENC)

Wisconsin

3985 R.J. Zeman Tool & Mfg. Co., Inc.
      W228 N575 Westmound Dr
      Waukesha, WI 53186
      Contact: Spencer Schreindl President
      Tel: 262-549-4400
      Email: sschreindl@zemantool.com
      Website: www.zemantool.com
Machining, design, mfr & inspect fixtures, special machines, gages, die cast dies, plastic injection molds, permanent molds, core boxes, patterns for sand casting & short and long-run production parts. (Woman, estab 1966, empl 48, sales $9,600,000, cert: WBENC)

3986 Valley Grinding & Mfg, / Mario Cotta America
      1717 Hamilton Ct
      Little Chute, WI 54140
      Contact: TJ Utschig President
      Tel: 800-750-7675
      Email: tju@valleygrinding.com
      Website: www.valleygrinding.com
Manufacturing, sharpening & servicing hard metal, tool steel and carbide cutting tools. (Minority, Woman, estab 1987, empl 84, sales $10,870,000, cert: WBENC)

HYDRAULIC & COMPRESSED AIR EQUIPMENT

Manufacturers and distributors of compressed air equipment, valves, gaskets, fittings, pumps, meters, hoses, special tools, pipe, etc. (See also HARDWARE & TOOLS, INDUSTRIAL EQUIPMENT & SUPPLIES, INDUSTRIAL MACHINES and MATERIAL HANDLING EQUIPMENT). NAICS Code 42

Alabama

3987 Elle Waterworks Supply, LLC
PO Box 205
Leeds, AL 35094
Contact: Courtney Myrick Owner
Tel: 205-352-3240
Email: cmyrick@ellewws.com
Website: www.ellewws.com
Dist valves: process, air, control, ductile iron pipe, steel pipe, pipe supports & hangers, couplings, adapters, pvc pipe & fittings, ductile iron fittings, hydrants, valve boxes, hardware, bolts, nuts, gaskets, safety equipment. (Woman, estab 2011, empl 2, sales $3,800,000, cert: State, WBENC)

Arizona

3988 Stenzel Sealing Solutions, LLC
16809 N 53rd Ave, Ste 5
Glendale, AZ 85306
Contact: Linda Stenzel Owner
Tel: 602-903-1250
Email: linda@azstenzel.com
Website: www.stenzelsealingsolutions.com
Fluid sealing solutions: Gaskets, Seals, Pump/Valve Packing, Duct/Pipe Expansion Joints, Valves, Pipe, Fittings, Flanges & Steam Traps. (Woman, estab 2012, empl 4, sales $1,925,914, cert: CPUC, WBENC)

California

3989 CLEAR Solutions, Inc.
942 Calle Amanecer, Ste D
San Clemente, CA 92673
Contact: Judy McMacking VP
Tel: 949-429-8922
Email: judy@clearsolutionscorp.com
Website: www.clearsolutionscorp.com
Dist filters, housings, water purification, process liquid filtration, HVAC, compressed air & gas filtration, gaskets, hose assemblies, tubing, quick disconnect fittings. (Woman, estab 2010, empl 6, sales , cert: WBENC)

3990 Dexen Industries, Inc.
9220 Norwalk Blvd
Santa Fe Springs, CA 90670
Contact: Yu-Shan Teng President
Tel: 562-699-8490
Email: info@dexen.com
Website: www.dexen.com
Mfr gas valves. (As-Pac, estab 1988, empl 17, sales $11,000,000, cert: CPUC)

3991 VIAIR Corporation
15 Edelman
Irvine, CA 92618
Contact: Alan Basham Dir of Operations
Tel: 949-585-0011
Email: alanb@viaircorp.com
Website: www.viaircorp.com
Dist Air Compressor, Air Tank, LED Light, Air accessories for automotive industry. (As-Pac, estab 1998, empl 32, sales $22,000,000, cert: NMSDC)

Colorado

3992 Die Cut Technologies/Denver Gasket
10943 Leroy Dr
Northglenn, CO 80233
Contact: Evelyn Meyers CEO
Tel: 303-452-4600
Email: evelyn@diecuttech.com
Website: www.diecuttech.com
Mfr gaskets, die cut parts & converted non-metallic materials. Also dist sponge, foam tapes rubber, bridge bearing pads, expansion joints, impact attenuators & adhesives, contract assembly & packaging svcs. (Hisp, estab 1961, empl 20, sales $2,524,000, cert: NMSDC, SDB)

Florida

3993 Amazon Hose and Rubber Company
4105 Seaboard Rd
Orlando, FL 32808
Contact: Jim Donlin President
Tel: 407-843-8190
Email: jimdonlin@amazonhose.com
Website: www.amazonhose.com
Dist industrial & hydraulic hoses & related fittings. (Woman, estab , empl 60, sales $12,698,846, cert: City, WBENC)

3994 Industrial Hose & Hydraulics, Inc.
2450 N Powerline Rd
Pompano Beach, FL 33069
Contact: Joanne R. Heckman Controller
Tel: 954-960-0311
Email: joeyheckman@industrialhose.com
Website: www.industrialhose.com
Dist hoses, fittings, clamps, adapters, fuel hose, hose reels, check valves, lubrication supplies, garden hose & pumps. (Woman, estab , empl , sales , cert: WBENC)

3995 Zabatt Engine Service, Inc.
4612 Hwy Ave
Jacksonville, FL 32254
Contact: Maria Sabatier AP & Credit Mgr
Tel: 904-421-9848
Email: maria@zabatt.com
Website: www.zabatt.com
Generator and Compressor distributor, specializing in sales, service, parts and installation of air compressors and generators. (Hisp, estab 1977, empl 104, sales $31,969,000, cert: State)

Illinois

3996 Bearings & Industrial Supply
431 Imen Ave
Addison, IL 60101
Contact: Sejal Khandwala Acct Exec
Tel: 630-628-1966
Email: Sejal@BearingsNow.Com
Website: www.bearingsnow.com
Dist bearings & power transmission products; pump & pump repair parts, HVAC & electrical parts. (As-Pac, estab , empl , sales , cert: NMSDC)

3997 Chambers Gasket & Manufacturing Co.
4701 W Rice St
Chicago, IL 60651
Contact: Heide Kenny President
Tel: 773-626-8800
Email: hkenny@chambersgasket.com
Website: www.chambersgasket.com
Gaskets; Washers; Strips; Spiral Wound Gaskets; Molded Gaskets; Waterjet cut parts; pressure sensitve adhesive added; kitting; special packaging. (Woman, estab 0, empl , sales , cert: WBENC)

3998 Cylinders Inc.
580 W 5th Ave
Naperville, IL 60563
Contact: Cynthia Crawford President
Tel: 630-357-5649
Email: cindy@cylindersinc.com
Website: www.cylindersinc.com
Repair & recondition hydraulic & pneumatic cylinders. (Woman, estab , empl 7, sales $1,440,992, cert: WBENC)

Indiana

3999 MIDpro Fluid Power and Automation
444 Johnson Ln
Brownsburg, IN 46112
Contact: Cynthia Torrance President
Tel: 317-852-5920
Email: ctorrance@midprofluidpower.com
Website: www.midprofluidpower.com
Pnuematic, hydraulic, electronic & air systems, conveyors, blowers, pumps, dryers, filtration, air tools, cylinders, valves, fittings, power units, PLC controllers, monitors & touch screens. (Woman, estab 1986, empl 11, sales $5,200,000, cert: WBENC)

Kentucky

4000 SealingLife Technology
1141 Red Mile Rd Ste 201
Lexington, KY 40504
Contact: Danette Wilder CEO
Tel: 859-977-6640
Email: wilderdj@sealinglife.com
Website: www.sealinglife.com
Fabricate, mfr & dist sealing, shielding & coating solutions, O-rings, gaskets, molded parts, extrusions, RFI/EMF shielding, vacuum coating & encapsulating. (Woman/AA, estab 2008, empl 9, sales $1,200,000, cert: NMSDC, SDB)

Louisiana

4001 Treco Stainless Solutions, LLC
366 Technology Lane
Gray, LA 70359
Contact: Brenna Treland Owner/Sales
Tel: 985-858-2880
Email: brenna@trecostainless.com
Website: www.trecostainless.com
Stainless Steel Compression fittings, Stainless Steel Instrumentation fittings, Tubing & Piping, Autoclave fittings (up to 60K PSI), Gauges, Hydraulic Hoses, Quick Connects. (Woman, estab 2014, empl 3, sales , cert: WBENC)

Maryland

4002 Phelps Industrial Products
6300 Washington Blvd
Elkridge, MD 21075
Contact: Gina Lehman CEO
Tel: 410-796-2222
Email: gmlehman@phelpsgaskets.com
Website: www.phelpsgaskets.com
Mfr, fabricator & dist Gaskets, Compression Packing, O' Rings, Molded Parts & Sealing Devices. (As-Pac, estab 1945, empl 15, sales , cert: State)

Michigan

4003 Chippewa Systems, Ltd.
32663 Coach
Chesterfield, MI 48047
Contact: Brian Barr VP
Tel: 586-772-1783
Email: chippewasystemsltd@gmail.com
Website: www.chippewasystems.com
Dist vacuum pumps, compressors, blowers, filters, air knives. (Minority, Woman, estab 1986, empl 3, sales $668,000, cert: NMSDC)

4004 Fluid Line Components, Inc.
638 S Rochester Rd
Clawson, MI 48017
Contact: Mary Schmitt CEO
Tel: 248-583-9070
Email: mary@fluidlinecomponents.com
Website: www.fluidlinecomponents.com
Dist air cylinders, air valves, air fittings, air filters, air gauges, air hoist, air hose, air manifolds, air motors, air drills, air presses, air tanks, air-oil tanks, anti-tie down, balancers, ball valves, ball vibrators, blow guns, brass pipe fittings (Woman, estab 1972, empl 4, sales $1,102,252, cert: WBENC)

4005 MCEM LLC
31153 Plymouth Rd
Livonia, MI 48150
Contact: BK Masti President
Tel: 517-881-1226
Email: bkm@mcem.co
Website: www.mcem.co
Lubricants, valves, conduit fittings. (As-Pac, estab 2011, empl 5, sales , cert: NMSDC)

4006 Service Manufacturing & Supply Co.
33380 Groesbeck Hwy
Fraser, MI 48026
Contact: Ryan Maggio General Mgr
Tel: 586-415-0455
Email: sales@servicemanufacturing.com
Website: www.servicemanufacturing.com
Hydraulic & pneumatic components & accessories, brass, steel, stainless steel, malleable & galvanized fittings, JIC 37 degree flare, push-on barbs, adaptors, solid & union barbs, pipe els & extension adaptors, hydraulic tubing. (Woman, estab 1957, empl 7, sales $1,154,683, cert: WBENC)

Minnesota

4007 Chrom Tech, Inc.
5995 W 149th St, Ste 102
Saint Paul, MN 55124
Contact: Jessica Kolsky Technical Sales Rep
Tel: 952-431-6000
Email: jessica@chromtech.com
Website: www.chromtech.com
Dist HPLC & GC instrumentation: autosampler vials, columns, filters, PEEK tubing & fittings, solid phase extraction cartridges, protein crash plates, positive pressure manifolds, evaporators, syringes. (Woman, estab 1985, empl , sales $10,538,000, cert: WBENC)

4008 Water Technology Resources
9201 E Bloomington Fwy, Ste Z
Bloomington, MN 55420
Contact: Sally Waldor President
Tel: 952-641-9004
Email: sallywaldor@wtrvalves.com
Website: www.wtrvalves.com
Mfr industrial valves. (Woman, estab 2009, empl 5, sales $1,000,000, cert: State)

North Carolina

4009 Raleigh-Durham Rubber & Gasket Co., Inc.
PO Box 90397
Raleigh, NC 27675
Contact: Judy Hooks President
Tel: 919-781-6817
Email: judyh@raleighdurhamrubber.com
Website: www.raleighdurhamrubber.com
Mfr & dist rubber gaskets. (Woman, estab , empl , sales , cert: WBENC)

4010 Smith Seal of NC
8441 Garvey Dr
Raleigh, NC 27616
Contact: Gertraud Smith President
Tel: 919-790-1000
Email: judysmith@smithseal.com
Website: www.smithseal.com
Dist hydraulic seals, gaskets & packings. (Woman, estab 1976, empl 13, sales , cert: WBENC)

New Jersey

4011 Liquid-Solids Separation Corp.
25 Arrow Rd
Ramsey, NJ 07446
Contact: Stacey Painter COO
Tel: 201-236-4833
Email: spainter@nafilter.com
Website: www.leemfiltration.com
Mfr pressure leaf filters and their components for oil seed processing, bio diesel fuel production, chemical processing and water treatment applications. (Woman, estab 1994, empl 42, sales $13,000,000, cert: WBENC)

4012 Sur-Seal, Inc.
12 Edgeboro Rd Unit 6
East Brunswick, NJ 08816
Contact: Donna King Accounting
Tel: 732-651-7070
Email: donnak@sur-sealinc.com
Website: www.sur-sealinc.com
Dist gaskets, gashet sheet, roll material, mechanical packing, compression packing, mechanical seals, pressure gauges & thermometers, hydraulic packings, o-rings, lantern rings, extrusions. (Woman, estab 1979, empl 11, sales $2,263,945, cert: State)

Ohio

4013 Trident Fluid Power, LLC
PO Box 368
Middletown, OH 45042
Contact: Sandy Ewen GM
Tel: 513-217-4999
Email: sewen@tridentfluidpower.com
Website: www.Tridentfluidpower.com
Replace, overhaul, manufacture, fluidpower components (cylinders, pumps, valves, systems), field service, trouble shoot, design, engineer, all coke oven equipment & operations, machine, welding, fabricating. (Woman, estab 2006, empl 17, sales $2,000,000, cert: WBENC)

Oklahoma

4014 PT Coupling Co.
PO Box 3909
Enid, OK 73702
Contact: James Matthew Parrish President
Tel: 580-237-4033
Email: credit03@ptcoupling.com
Website: www.ptcoupling.com
Mfr industrial hose couplings used in the transfer of fluid & dry products at medium to low pressure. (Nat Ame, estab 1951, empl 390, sales $60,000,000, cert: NMSDC)

Puerto Rico

4015 Pharmaceutical Processes Systems, Inc.
PO Box 31411
Manati, PR 00667
Contact: Eduardo Perez Sales Mgr
Tel: 787-854-5477
Email: eduardo.perez@ppspr.com
Website: www.ppspr.com
Dis process instrumentation, pumps, valves & equipment for chemical, food and beverage, pharmaceutical, power generation and water markets (Hisp, estab 1982, empl 10, sales , cert: NMSDC)

South Carolina

4016 Eastern Power Technologies, Inc.
11 Caledon Court
Greenville, SC 29615
Contact: Chet Chea Legal Counsel
Tel: 864-312-3840
Email: chet.chea@easternfirst.com
Website: www.easternpowertech.com
Dist industrial & commercial pipes, valves, fittings & commercial plumbing fixtures. (Woman, estab 2014, empl 15, sales , cert: WBENC)

4017 Filters South, Inc.
656 Wraggs Ferry Rd
Georgetown, SC 29440
Contact: Deborah Powell President
Tel: 843-833-1042
Email: dwillspowell@earthlink.net
Website: www.filterssouth.com
Dist filters: Air, HVAC, Oil, Hydraulic, Dust Collection, Water, Liquid, etc. (Woman, estab 1997, empl 2, sales , cert: State, City)

4018 Greenville Fluid System Technologies
      2516 River Rd
      Piedmont, SC 29673
      Contact: Greg Farley Sales Mgr
      Tel: 864-295-6700
      Email: greg.farley@swagelok.com
      Website: www.swagelok.com/columbiasc
Dist compression & pipe fittings, valves, hoses, tubing, pumps, gauges & regulators, Orbital welding equipment, tube benders, hydraulic swaging units. (Woman, estab 2001, empl 18, sales $3,200,000, cert: WBENC)

Texas

4019 Asociar, LLC
      2800 E Plano Pkwy Ste 400
      Plano, TX 75074
      Contact: Betty Manetta CEO
      Tel: 214-918-1013
      Email: bmanetta@asociar1.com
      Website: www.asociar1.com
Streamline Supply Chain Management
Total Equipment Rack Integration & Testing
Procure, Rack, Integrate, Deliver, Engineer
Warehousing & Logistics (Minority, Woman, estab 2012, empl 15, sales $185,000,000,000, cert: State, NMSDC, WBENC)

4020 Corley Gasket Company
      PO Box 271124
      Dallas, TX 75227
      Contact: Jody Anderson Office Mgr
      Tel: 214-388-7437
      Email: janderson@corleygasket.com
      Website: www.corleygasket.com
Mfr gaskets. (Woman, estab 1975, empl 19, sales $1,941,386, cert: CPUC)

4021 CVAL Innovations LLC
      9701 Raven Ln
      Irving, TX 75063
      Contact: Jinen Adenwala President
      Tel: 214-699-1326
      Email: jinen@cvalinnovations.com
      Website: www.cvalinnovations.com
Energy Consumption for Industrial and Commercial customers. We conduct Energy Efficiency Audits, recommend and implement the efficiency measures. (Woman/As-Ind, estab 2009, empl 5, sales $1,093,000, cert: State, NMSDC, SDB)

4022 El Paso Industrial Supplies
      119 N Cotton
      El Paso, TX 79901
      Contact: Antonio Herrera Sales Mgr
      Tel: 915-533-5080
      Email: sales@epis-usa.com
      Website: www.epis-usa.com
Dist pneumatic equipment & parts, sensors, sensors for safety, hydraulic equipments & parts, filters, HEPA filters, work mats, signal towers. (Hisp, estab 1988, empl 16, sales $4,000,000, cert: NMSDC)

4023 Indian Industries LP
      432 W Fork Dr
      Arlington, TX 76012
      Contact: Felipe Moncibaiz Sales
      Tel: 817-265-6731
      Email: info@indian-industries.com
      Website: www.indian-industries.com
Mfr custom gaskets & seals. (Nat Ame, estab 1977, empl 13, sales , cert: State, NMSDC)

4024 Industry Junction, Inc.
      3427 W. Kingsley Rd., Ste # 6 & 7
      Garland, TX 75041
      Contact: Rogelio Cabello President
      Tel: 972-926-3526
      Email: contact@industryjunction.com
      Website: www.industryjunction.com/
Dist fluid power valves, industrial Valves, mallable gittings, stainless steel fittings, hydra-sanitary products. (Hisp, estab 2011, empl 4, sales $4,400,000, cert: State, NMSDC)

4025 MARS Industries, LLC
      PO Box 560
      Cedar Creek, TX 78612
      Contact: Alvino Rosales President
      Tel: 512-303-4413
      Email: arosales@marsindustries.us
      Website: www.marsindustries.us
Dist pipe, fittings, valves, etc.for the construction of water & wastewater treatment facilities & water & wastewater utilities. (Hisp, estab 2001, empl 1, sales , cert: State, City)

4026 OG Energy Solutions LLC
      1836 Snake River Rd Ste A
      Katy, TX 77449
      Contact: Federico Zamar Reg Sales Rep
      Tel: 832-644-0121
      Email: fzsales@ogenergys.com
      Website: www.ogenergys.com
Pipes, tubes, fitting, flanges; Valves; Automation & Instrumentation (transducers, sensors, transmitters, panels); Heat Exchanger Equipment & Parts; Seals & Gaskets; Non-toxic, environmentally-safe cleaners, degreasers & solvents. (Minority, Woman, estab 2010, empl 8, sales $600,000, cert: WBENC)

4027 OnPoint, LLC
      13155 Noel Rd, Ste 900
      Dallas, TX 75240
      Contact: Amber B D'Amico Partner
      Tel: 972-918-5154
      Email: amber@onpointlighting.com
      Website: www.onpointlighting.com
Energy-efficient LED lighting, surveys, ROI analysis, best-of-breed American-made products, lighting design, installation & financing. (Hisp, estab 2011, empl 2, sales $750,000, cert: State)

4028 Petroleum Accessories, Inc.
      12500 Oxford Park Dr
      Houston, TX 77077
      Contact: Anna de Chabannes Technical Sales Dir
      Tel: 281-589-9337
      Email: hydraulics@paihouston.com
      Website: www.paihouston.com
Dist hydraulic components: filters, high pressure micro pumps & valves. (Woman, estab 1980, empl 5, sales $2,930,802, cert: WBENC)

HYDRAULIC & COMPRESSED AIR EQUIPMENT

4029 Piping Technology and Product Inc.
3701 Holmes Rd
Houston, TX 77051
Contact: Michael Rucker Business Devel Mgr
Tel: 713-731-0030
Email: info@pipingtech.com
Website: www.pipingtech.com
Custom Engineered Hot/Cold Insulated Pipe Shoes and Supports, Fabric Expansion Joints/Metal Bellows, ASME Certified Pressure Vessels, and ASME-U-Stamp rated Hydraulic and Mechanical Snubbers, Custom Engineered (As-Ind, estab 1978, empl 750, sales $60,000,000, cert: NMSDC)

4030 Professional Choice Fire & Security Systems
1815 N. Hampton Road
DeSoto, TX 75115
Contact: Dwanald Walker President
Tel: 972-298-2303
Email: dwanald@professionalchoicefire.com
Website: www.professionalchoicefire.com
Installation, service and repair for fire sprinkler, fire pump, fire alarm systems in the Dallas-Fort Worth metropolitan areas. * Testing, inspection and maintenance for fire alarm, sprinkler, fire pumps and backflow detetion equipment. * 24 hour central (AA, estab 2004, empl 6, sales $500,000, cert: State, NMSDC)

4031 Texas Seal Supply Co, Inc.
606 N Great Southwest Pkwy
Arlington, TX 76011
Contact: Carol Gallegos Ortega Mgr
Tel: 817-640-1193
Email: carols@texasseal.com
Website: www.texasseal.com
Dist seals: hydraulic, pneumatic, aerospace, oilfield. (Hisp, estab 1971, empl 13, sales , cert: NMSDC)

4032 The Valve Agency Inc.
5750 N Sam Houston Pkwy E
Houston, TX 77032
Contact: Brandon Wray Sales Engineer
Tel: 281-751-8891
Email: blw@thevalveagency.com
Website: www.thevalveagency.com
Valve Services. (Woman, estab 2013, empl 10, sales $4,000,000, cert: City, WBENC)

Virginia

4033 E&R Minority Supplier LLC
21290 Hedgerow Terr
Ashburn, VA 20147
Contact: Esvith Palomino-Quillama President
Tel: 703-932-5045
Email: epalomino@erminoritysupplier.com
Website: www.erminoritysupplier.com
Heavy highway material & industrial hydraulic hoses & fittings. (Hisp, estab 2011, empl 1, sales , cert: State)

Wisconsin

4034 Anderson Seal Inc.
16555 W Lincoln
New Berlin, WI 53151
Contact: Jennifer Hansen President
Tel: 262-821-0344
Email: jennifer@andersonseal.com
Website: www.andersonseal.com
Dist rubber o-rings, custom molded shapes, gaskets, oil seals, kit assemblies, inventory management. (Woman, estab 1990, empl 50, sales $27,000,000, cert: WBENC)

4035 Central Wisconsin Flex
8510 Enterprise Way
Weston, WI 54476
Contact: Carmen Sauer VP
Tel: 715-355-4344
Email: cenflex@cenflex.com
Website: www.cenflex.com
Flexible metal hose, braided metal hose, expansion joints, exhaust tubing and assemblies, laser cutting, plate rolling, fab shop, Teflon hoses, machining. (Minority, Woman, estab 1992, empl 37, sales $8,394,000, cert: NMSDC)

4036 Husco Automotive, LLC
2239 Pewaukee Rd
Waukesha, WI 53188
Contact: Jonathan Hassert Acct Mgr
Tel: 262-953-6400
Email: jon.hassert@huscoauto.com
Website: www.huscoauto.com
Design, develop & mfr electro-hydraulic solenoid valves & electro-magnetic solenoid actuators. (Hisp, estab 1946, empl 1015, sales $238,000,000, cert: NMSDC)

4037 Roeming Industries, Inc.
1133 W Liebau Rd
Mequon, WI 53092
Contact: Sandy Roeming Schumaker President
Tel: 262-243-5800
Email: sschumaker@roeming.com
Website: www.roeming.com
Contract sewing on vinyl, leather, Kevlar, fiberglass, plastics and fabric. Distributor of hydraulic packing, seals, and packing. Gasket cutting. Rubber to metal bonding. (Woman, estab 1955, empl 13, sales $1,600,000, cert: WBENC)

INDUSTRIAL EQUIPMENT & SUPPLIES

Manufacturers and distributors of food service and restaurant equipment, drive belts, aircraft parts, motors, industrial batteries, underground mining equipment, heaters, bearings, spark plug cleaner, traffic control signs, etc. (See also HARDWARE & TOOLS, HYDRAULIC & COMPRESSED AIR EQUIPMENT, INDUSTRIAL MACHINES and MATERIAL HANDLING EQUIPMENT). NAICS Code 42

Alabama

4038 Alabama Safety Products Inc.
150 Supply Room Rd
Oxford, AL 36203
Contact: Tracy Rouse President
Tel: 256-835-0963
Email: tracyr@alabamasafety.com
Website: www.alabamasafety.com
Dist safety supplies, safety audits, hand protections surveys, respirator fit-testing. (Minority, Woman, estab 1992, empl 8, sales , cert: NMSDC)

4039 CD Covenant Distributors International LLC
1400 Commerce Blvd Ste 12
Anniston, AL 36207
Contact: Rod Lemon CEO
Tel: 256-832-4385
Email: rlemon@cdcovenant.com
Website: www.cdcovenant.com
Dist MRO Products. (AA, estab 2001, empl 6, sales $254,000, cert: City, NMSDC, 8(a))

4040 Cornerstone Supply, Inc.
340 Production AVe
Madison, AL 35758
Contact: Bonnie Powers President
Tel: 256-461-4147
Email: bonnie@cornerstone-supply.com
Website: www.cornerstone-supply.com
Dist military fasteners, electronic components, MRO equipment & supplies. (Woman, estab 1996, empl 14, sales $6,500,000, cert: WBENC)

4041 Elle Waterworks Supply, LLC
PO Box 205
Leeds, AL 35094
Contact: Courtney Myrick Owner
Tel: 205-352-3240
Email: cmyrick@ellewws.com
Website: www.ellewws.com
Dist process valves, air valves, control valves, ductile iron pipe, steel pipe, pipe supports & hangers, couplings, adapters, pvc pipe & fittings, ductile iron fittings, hydrants, valve boxes, hardware, bolts, nuts, gaskets, safety equipment. (Woman, estab 2011, empl 2, sales $3,800,000, cert: State, WBENC)

4042 Rainbow Technology Corporation
261 Cahaba Valley Pkwy
Pelham, AL 35124
Contact: Larry Steeley VP
Tel: 800-637-6047
Email: lwsteeley@rainbowtech.net
Website: www.rainbowtech.net
Dist industrial equipment & supplies. (Woman, estab 1971, empl 32, sales $13,500,000, cert: State, CPUC)

4043 Vision Global Technology, Inc.
3512-B 6th Ave SE
Decatur, AL 35603
Contact: Frank Roberts Cstmr Devel
Tel: 877-753-3936
Email: frank@vgtcorp.com
Website: www.vgtcorp.com
Dist bulk R134A, 30 lb. cylinders & ISO tank & 12 oz. cans. (Woman/Nat Ame, estab 2003, empl 20, sales $20,000,000, cert: NMSDC)

Arkansas

4044 Welsco, Inc.
9006 Crystal Hill Rd
North Little Rock, AR 72113
Contact: Chris Layton President
Tel: 501-771-1204
Email: chris.layton@welsco.com
Website: www.Welsco.com
Welding gases and Supplies, industrial supplies and Spec gases. (Woman, estab 1941, empl 127, sales $40,000,000, cert: NWBOC)

Arizona

4045 Air Energy Systems & Services
4202 E Superior Ave, Ste 3
Phoenix, AZ 85040
Contact: Patricia Bewley Owner
Tel: 602-454-0210
Email: pbewley@aesas.com
Website: www.aesas.com
Dist & install commerical, industrial & HVAC air filters, energy products, IAQ products, UVC producst, energy audits. (Woman/Nat-Ame, estab 1997, empl 15, sales $2,300,000, cert: NMSDC, WBENC)

4046 Diversified Diamond Products
4634 E Mountain View Ct
Phoenix, AZ 85028
Contact: Mary Dillon CEO
Tel: 480-443-4899
Email: mdillon@diversifieddiamond.com
Website: www.diversifieddiamond.com
Dist safety supplies & equipment, vests, gloves, respirators, test meters, locks, cable protection, prescription safety glasses, fall protection, ear protection, face masks, cutting tools, abrasives, work holding, metal working. (Woman, estab 1989, empl 5, sales $1,295,404, cert: WBENC)

4047 Industrial Specialties Supply, Inc.
3941 E 29th St, Ste 606
Tucson, AZ 85711
Contact: Alan Davila Mgr
Tel: 520-745-5800
Email: indussupply@live.com
Website: www.indussupplyinc.com
Solenoid valves, PLC components, Conveyor belts, Steam traps, High Pressure Valves, Sanitary/Food grade fittings, valves & tubing, industrial concrete coatings, personal safety equipment, Gas detectors. (Hisp, estab 2001, empl 2, sales $1,438,845, cert: State, City)

INDUSTRIAL EQUIPMENT & SUPPLIES

California

4048 Able Industrial Products, Inc.
2006 S Baker
Ontario, CA 91761
Contact: Courtney Salvidar Sales/Mktg
Tel: 909-930-1585
Email: courtneys@able123.com
Website: www.able123.com
Mfr & convert thermal management materials: gap pads, interface pads & various non-metallic gaskets. (Woman/Hisp, estab 1974, empl 40, sales $3,800,000, cert: NMSDC)

4049 Advanced Mechatronics Solutions, Inc.
10030 Via De La Amistad
San Diego, CA 92154
Contact: Arnold Park Project Mgr
Tel: 619-661-5985
Email: arnold@ams-fa.com
Website: www.ams-fa.com
Dist automated factory equipment, design Modular Rack System. (As-Pac, estab 2002, empl 130, sales $4,306,000, cert: NMSDC)

4050 Anita Fire Hose Company Etc.
7937 North Ave, Ste B
Lemon Grove, CA 91945
Contact: Anita Barnes Owner
Tel: 619-462-3473
Email: anitafire@sbcglobal.net
Website: www.anitafirehosecompanyetc.com
Dist fire hoses, fire extinguishers, fire cabinets. (Woman, estab 2003, empl 7, sales , cert: State)

4051 Empire Safety & Supply
10624 Industrial Ave
Roseville, CA 95678
Contact: Monette Crawford CEO
Tel: 800-995-1341
Email: monette@empiresafety.com
Website: www.empiresafety.com
Dist environmental health & safety products. (Woman, estab 1992, empl 14, sales $6,000,000, cert: CPUC)

4052 FTG, Inc.
12750 Center Court Dr S Ste 280
Cerritos, CA 90703
Contact: Pino Pathak President
Tel: 562-865-9200
Email: pino@ftginc.com
Website: www.ftginc.com
Mfr air filters, oil filters, fuel filters, filtration products, custom engineered parts. (As-Pac, estab 1992, empl 20, sales $3,000,000, cert: NMSDC)

4053 Harris Industrial Gases
8475 Auburn Blvd
Citrus Heights, CA 95610
Contact: Tim Lettich GM
Tel: 916-725-2168
Email: tlettich@harrisgas.com
Website: www.harrisgas.com
Dist welding & industrial equipment & industrial gases. (Woman, estab 1936, empl 20, sales $5,000,000, cert: State, CPUC)

4054 Industrial Specialty Products
7400 Scout Ave, Ste C
Bell Gardens, CA 90201
Contact: Paula Mullan President
Tel: 562-806-2600
Email: info@gotoisp.com
Website: www.gotoisp.com
Dist industrial supplies: coatings, paints, chemicals, etc. (Woman, estab 1989, empl 6, sales $ 0, cert: WBENC)

4055 Liberty Glove, Inc.
433 Cheryl Lane
City of Industry, CA 91789
Contact: Ken Tran Natl Sales Mgr
Tel: 800-327-8333
Email: kentran@libertyglove.com
Website: www.libertyglove.com
Dist safety industrial products. (Minority, Woman, estab 1988, empl 70, sales , cert: NMSDC)

4056 Nathan Kimmel Company, LLC
1213 S Santa Fe Ave
Los Angeles, CA 90021
Contact: Carol Schary President
Tel: 213-627-8556
Email: carol@nathankimmel.com
Website: www.nathankimmel.com
Dist industrial supplies: mfr tarps, construction equipment & parts, motors, mixers, pumps, material handling, janitorial, electrical, pest control equipment, shipping supplies, safety equipment, shovels, tools. (Woman, estab 1996, empl 13, sales $4,740,000, cert: WBENC)

4057 Paramount Safety Supply
14516 Crenshaw Blvd
Gardena, CA 90249
Contact: Joel Pulgarin President
Tel: 866-200-2975
Email: info@paramountsafetysupply.com
Website: www.paramountsafetysupply.com
Personal Protective Equipment, Fall Protection Systems, Gas Monitors/Sniffers, Disaster Preparedness, Emergency Response Supplies, Confined Space Entry/Rescue, Rescue & Descent Systems, Construction Safety. (Hisp, estab 2015, empl 1, sales $500,000, cert: State, CPUC)

4058 R.J. Safety Supply Company Inc.
7320 Convoy Court
San Diego, CA 92111
Contact: Diane Rodriguez VP
Tel: 858-541-2880
Email: drodriguez@rjsafety.com
Website: www.rjsafety.com
Dist safety supplies: PPE products, respiratory, confined space, fall protection, blowers, first aid, gloves, boots, rainwear, protective clothing, hazardous material containers, signs, traffic control, safety cabinets, gas detectors. (Woman, estab 1959, empl 17, sales , cert: CPUC)

4059 Reese Enterprises
595 Tamarack Ave, Ste E
Brea, CA 92821
Contact: James Reese CEO
Tel: 714-447-8586
Email: reeseent@aol.com
Website: www.FOTOLum.com
Self-illuminating safety products, facilities. (AA, estab 1994, empl 4, sales $8,000,000, cert: NMSDC)

INDUSTRIAL EQUIPMENT & SUPPLIES

4060 Safetyvibe
2530 Corporate Pl, Ste A105
Monterey Park, CA 91754
Contact: Lila Don Owner
Tel: 626-281-8444
Email: bidops@safetyvibe.com
Website: www.safetyvibe.com
Dist industrial equipment & supplies. (Minority, Woman, estab 2003, empl 5, sales $1,950,000, cert: State)

4061 SafetyWeb Product Sales, LLC
11365 Sunrise Park Dr, Ste 200
Rancho Cordova, CA 95742
Contact: Giovanni Tufo Mktg Mgr
Tel: 916-386-4271
Email: orders@cargosafetyweb.com
Website: www.gladiatorcargonet.com
Certified cargo securement products. (AA, estab , empl 6, sales $1,667,704, cert: State, NMSDC, CPUC, 8(a))

4062 Vision Specialties, Inc.
10330 Regis Ct
Rancho Cucamonga, CA 91730
Contact: Donn DeMarzio VP
Tel: 800-499-8176
Email: donn.demarzio@visionspecialties.com
Website: www.visionspecialties.com
Mfr & dist Category Cable, HDMI Cable, Audio/Video Cable, Batteries, Injection Molding products & services. (Woman, estab 1995, empl 14, sales $6,000,000, cert: CPUC)

4063 Widespread Industrial Supplies, Inc.
1220 S Boyle Ave
Los Angeles, CA 90023
Contact: Josh Dorfman President
Tel: 310-793-7315
Email: josh.dorfman@widespreadind.com
Website: www.widespreadind.com
Dist industrial supplies: fasteners, cutting tools, electrical, welding, chemical & safety related supplies, hand & power tools. (Woman, estab 2002, empl 4, sales $820,341, cert: State, City)

Connecticut

4064 IBC - Industrial Supply Plus
2 Creamery Brook
East Granby, CT 06026
Contact: Ron Nunez CEO
Tel: 860-246-1618
Email: rnunez@industrialbuyers.com
Website: www.industrialbuyers.com
Dist maintenance, repair, operations, production, bearing & power transmission supplies, technical support, inventory control & mgmt, product support & service, consolidated invoicing & sales reporting, minority credits, standardization & rationalization. (Hisp, estab 1999, empl 15, sales $90,000,000, cert: NMSDC)

District of Columbia

4065 Van Tech Industries
1818 New York Ave Ste 214 C
Washington, DC 20002
Contact: Van Bond CEO
Tel: 301-642-7525
Email: vanbond@vantechindustries.com
Website: www.vantechindustries.com
Construction Supplies/Equipment. (AA, estab 1990, empl 1, sales $300,000, cert: NMSDC)

Florida

4066 Arroyo Process Equipment Inc.
1550 Centennial Blvd
Bartow, FL 33830
Contact: Diane Schleicher President
Tel: 863-533-9700
Email: diane@arroyoprocess.com
Website: www.arroyoprocess.com
Dist pumps, tanks, mixers, meters, filters, water treatment equip. (Woman, estab 1968, empl 32, sales $15,576,805, cert: NMSDC)

4067 O.T. Trans Inc.
201 Babock St
Melbourne, FL 32901
Contact: Dean Danner Business Dev Mgr
Tel: 321-259-9880
Email: ddanner@ottrans.com
Website: www.ottrans.com
Industrial machinery & equip, material handling, hand tools, wiring supplies, industrial supplies safety & rescue equip, tool & hardware boxes, abrasive materials, cabinets, lockers, bins & shelving, winches, hoists, cranes & derricks. (Hisp, estab 1993, empl 15, sales $5,000,000, cert: NMSDC)

4068 Silver Wings Aerospace
25400 SW 140th Ave
Princeton, FL 33032
Contact: Eduardo Montalvo President
Tel: 305-258-5950
Email: eddie@silverwingsaerospace.com
Website: www.silverwingsaerospace.com
Dist & repair aircraft parts. (Hisp, estab 2007, empl 16, sales $12,765,527, cert: NMSDC)

Georgia

4069 Control Specialties, Inc.
2503 Monroe Dr
Gainesville, GA 30507
Contact: Janice Moody CSR
Tel: 770-532-7736
Email: janice@control-specialties.com
Website: www.control-specialties.com
Dist pumps, instrumentation, filtration, controls, valves, energy audits, utility consultations. (Woman, estab 1987, empl 4, sales $1,965,970, cert: WBENC)

4070 H&S Supply Co., Inc.
528 N Main St
Moultrie, GA 31768
Contact: McKenzie Blanchett Sales
Tel: 229-985-4575
Email: mblanchett@hssupplyco.com
Website: www.hssupplyco.com
Dist plumbing & HVAC supplies, drilling supplies. (Nat Ame, estab 1969, empl 10, sales $40,000,000, cert: State)

4071 HeatRep, LLC
      400 Galleria Pkwy, Ste 1500
      Atlanta, GA 30339
      Contact: Owner
      Tel: 404-989-5457
      Email: sales@heatrep.com
      Website: www.heatrep.com
Industrial equipment supplies, heat exchangers, fired heaters, electric heaters, economizers, condensers, liquid filtration, gas filtration, strainers, automatic strainers, filter separators, knockout tanks, reactors, pulsation bottles, custom fabrication (Woman, estab 2011, empl 1, sales , cert: WBENC)

4072 KACO Supply Company
      1950 Lois Pointe Smyrna
      Georgia, GA 30080
      Contact: Kay Williams President
      Tel: 770-435-8902
      Email: kay.williams@kacosupplycompany.com
      Website: www.kacosupplycompany.com
Dist institutional food, paper & plastic products, janitorial supplies, kitchenwares & equipment. (Woman/AA, estab , empl , sales $1,449,460, cert: City, NMSDC)

4073 Stag Enterprise, Inc.
      383 Wilbanks Dr
      Ball Ground, GA 30107
      Contact: Rachel Niederer VP Operations
      Tel: 770-720-8888
      Email: racheln@stagenterprise.com
      Website: www.stagenterprise.com
Dist industrial supplies, slitting tapes. (Minority, Woman, estab 1993, empl 21, sales $22,000,000, cert: NMSDC, WBENC)

Illinois

4074 AMSYSCO, Inc.
      1200 Windham Pkwy
      Romeoville, IL 60446
      Contact: Neel Khosa VP
      Tel: 630-296-8383
      Email: nkhosa@amsyscoinc.com
      Website: www.amsyscoinc.com
Dist post-tensioning tendons used in concrete reinforcement, barrier cable used in parking garage restraint systems. (As-Pac, estab 1981, empl 30, sales $18,697,191, cert: NMSDC)

4075 Emergent Safety Supply
      1055 Kingsland Dr
      Batavia, IL 60510
      Contact: Jerry Hill VP
      Tel: 630-406-9666
      Email: jhill@emergentsafety.com
      Website: www.Emergentsafety.com
Dist PPE, FR Clothing, Traffic Safety Products, Safety Signage, Spill Containment, Repertory Products. (Woman, estab 1985, empl 28, sales $12,200,000, cert: State, WBENC)

4076 Equity Industrial
      2000 S 25th Ave Unit A
      Broadview, IL 60155
      Contact: Robert Butler President
      Tel: 708-450-0000
      Email: kevindonnelly@equityind.com
      Website: www.equityind.com
Dist industrial supplies. (AA, estab 1996, empl 7, sales $15,000,000, cert: NMSDC)

4077 Freedom Air Filtration Inc.
      1712 Arden Place
      Joliet, IL 60435
      Contact: Linda Freveletti President
      Tel: 877-715-8999
      Email: linda@freedomairfiltration.com
      Website: www.freedomairfiltration.com
HVAC supplies & services. (Woman, estab 2004, empl 5, sales $850,000, cert: WBENC)

4078 Inter-City Supply Co
      8830 S Dobson Ave
      Chicago, IL 60619
      Contact: Jackie Dyess President
      Tel: 773-731-8007
      Email: intercity@ameritech.net
      Website: www.intercity-supply.com
Dist janitorial, safety & food service. (AA, estab , empl , sales $11,000,000, cert: State, City, NMSDC)

4079 International Filter Manufacturing Corporation
      713 W Columbian Blvd
      Litchfield, IL 62056
      Contact: Cecilia Ewing Hayes President
      Tel: 217-324-2303
      Email: ifmpres@consolidated.net
      Website: www.ifm-corp.com
Mfr air filters for heavy-duty equip: transit vehicles, coal mining. Also dist HVAC, industrial & specailty filters. (Woman/AA, estab 1987, empl 35, sales $ 0, cert: NMSDC)

4080 ITA, Inc.
      150 Pierce Road, Ste 550 60143
      Itasca, IL 60143
      Contact: Ritu Agrawal Dir of Marketing
      Tel: 281-712-7608
      Email: ragrawal@itaoffice.com
      Website: www.itaoffice.com
Dist Industrial Equipment, Printers, Production Simulation Software, Hazardous & remote sensing robots, Oil filtration equipment, R&D Equipment, Chemiluminesent Oxidation Analyzers, Ferro Magnetic Detector, Automation MRO Products. (As-Pac, estab 1980, empl 10, sales $2,500,000, cert: NMSDC)

4081 Magid Glove & Safety Mfg. Co., LLC
      1300 Naperville Dr
      Romeoville, IL 60446
      Contact: Joe Staron Dir Corp Sales
      Tel: 888-380-9282
      Email: joestaron@magidglove.com
      Website: www.magidglove.com
Mfr, dist, import Work Gloves, Protective Clothing & Safety Equipment. (Minority, estab 1946, empl 3000, sales , cert: NMSDC)

4082 One Way Safety, LLC
      418 Shawmut Ave
      LaGrange, IL 60525
      Contact: Anne Callaghan Sales Mgr
      Tel: 708-579-0229
      Email: anne@onewaysafety.com
      Website: www.onewaysafety.com
Dist PPE, gas detection, fall protection, supplied air, respiratory equipment & uniforms, rescue teams, respiratory fit testing, safety training, safety equipment repair & rental, safety supervisors. (Woman, estab 2013, empl 20, sales $2,500,000, cert: WBENC)

INDUSTRIAL EQUIPMENT & SUPPLIES

4083 Permatron
    2020 Touhy Ave
    Elk Grove Village, IL 60007
    Contact: Leslye Sandberg President
    Tel: 847-434-1421
    Email: lsandberg@permatron.com
    Website: www.permatron.com
Mfr air filters, air intake filters, equipment protection filters. (Woman, estab 1957, empl 40, sales , cert: WBENC)

4084 Production Distribution Companies
    9511 S Dorchester ave
    Chicago, IL 60628
    Contact: Cleo Downs President
    Tel: 708-489-0195
    Email: cleo@pdcompanies.org
    Website: www.pdcompanies.org
Dist electrical, industrial supplies, tools & equipment. (AA, estab 2004, empl 9, sales $5,400,272, cert: City, NMSDC)

4085 Wabash Transformer (PowerVolt and Ensign Corp)
    300 W. Factory Rd.
    Addison, IL 60101
    Contact: Ajay Sharma VP Sales & Mktg
    Tel: 630-628-9999
    Email: ajays@wabashtransformer.com
    Website: www.wabashtransformer.com
Mfr power transformers: medical, dental, HVAC, controls, packaging & automation equipment. (As-Pac, estab 1966, empl 33, sales $3,200,000, cert: NMSDC)

Indiana

4086 Acorn Distributors, Inc.
    5820 Fortune Cir W
    Indianapolis, IN 46241
    Contact: Debbie Schulz Contract Coord
    Tel: 317-243-9234
    Email: dschulz@acorndistributors.com
    Website: www.acorndistributors.com
Dist disposable paper and plastic, janitorial supplies and equipment, chemicals, sanitary maintenance materials and foodservice supply products. (Woman, estab 1976, empl 128, sales $90,000,000, cert: State, City)

4087 Courtney Material Handling, Inc.
    PO Box 6925
    South Bend, IN 46660
    Contact: Beth Courtney President
    Tel: 574-231-0094
    Email: beth@cmhionline.com
    Website: www.cmhionline.com
Dist safety items: hard hats, vests, safety glasses, gloves, tools, fire & detection, bins, cabinets, carts, casters, chairs & stools. (Woman, estab 2003, empl 2, sales $213,673, cert: State)

4088 GM Supply Company, Inc.
    6321 E 30th St Ste 205
    Indianapolis, IN 46219
    Contact: Steven Batts Business Devel
    Tel: 317-898-3510
    Email: steveb@gmsupplyco.com
    Website: www.gmsupplyco.com
Integrated supply services, commodity management services, component assembly services, distribution of cutting tools, abrasives, safety supplies, MRO, packaging, tools, janitorial, electrical, plumbing, power transmission, bearings. (AA, estab 1992, empl 12, sales $22,000,000, cert: NMSDC)

4089 Gripp Inc.
    17322 Westfield Park Rd
    Westfield, IN 46074
    Contact: Judy Gripp President
    Tel: 317-896-3700
    Email: judyg@grippinc.com
    Website: www.grippinc.com
Dist, service, install & calibrate environmental monitoring equipment, open & and closed pipe flow monitoring & wastewater sampling. (Woman, estab 1992, empl 10, sales , cert: State, City)

4090 Powell Tool Supply Co., Inc.
    1338 Mishawaka Ave
    South Bend, IN 46615
    Contact: Cari Eaton CEO
    Tel: 574-289-4811
    Email: ceaton@powelltool.com
    Website: www.powelltool.com
Dist industrial supplies: cutting tools, abrasives, chemicals, MRO supplies, material handling, janitorial, etc. (Woman, estab 1948, empl 20, sales $5,500,000, cert: WBENC)

4091 Rfs Group
    PO Box 68506
    Indianapolis, IN 46268
    Contact: Ramon Morrison Principal
    Tel: 317-507-3165
    Email: rmorrison@meticulousdb.com
    Website: www.meticulousdb.com
Dist maintenance, janitorial & cleaning supplies, equipment & accessories. Also wholesale distributes office, foodservice and safety supplies. (AA, estab 2007, empl 6, sales $ 0, cert: State, City)

4092 Sullivan-Brough, Inc. dba SafetyWear
    1121 E Wallace St
    Ft Wayne, IN 46803
    Contact: Dan Brough President
    Tel: 800-877-3555
    Email: sales@safety-wear.com
    Website: www.safety-wear.com
Dist safety products & services. (AA, estab 1977, empl 30, sales , cert: NMSDC)

4093 Team Cruiser Supply LLC
    PO Box 88255
    Indianapolis, IN 46208
    Contact: Christopher Barney President
    Tel: 317-423-2430
    Email: mbarney@teamcruiser.com
    Website: www.tcsupplylogistics.com
Dist industrial products. (AA, estab 2013, empl 5, sales $3,345,000, cert: NMSDC)

4094 Worldwide Filters, LLC
    3318 Pagosa Court
    Indianapolis, IN 46201
    Contact: Dawn Codozor Sales Mgr
    Tel: 317-808-3719
    Email: frank@worldwidefilters.com
    Website: www.worldwidefilters.com
Dist filters: commercial, industrial & residential, HEPA filters, air, oil, hydraulic & fuel vehicle filters, water filtration systems. (AA, estab 2004, empl 5, sales $250,000, cert: NMSDC)

INDUSTRIAL EQUIPMENT & SUPPLIES

Kansas

4095 Sorella Group, Inc.
      14844 W 107th St
      Lenexa, KS 66215
      Contact: Shelia Ohrenberg President
      Tel: 913-390-9544
      Email: ap@sorellagroup.com
      Website: www.sorellagroup.com
Dist specialty products, bathroom partitions & accessories, flagpoles, lockers, fire protection specialties, mailboxes, shelving, mirrors & access flooring. (Woman, estab 2006, empl 30, sales $5,040,322,000, cert: State, City, WBENC, SDB)

4096 Touch Enterprises LLC
      117 N Cooper St
      Olathe, KS 66061
      Contact: Camilo Fernandez Sales Andmin
      Tel: 913-440-0770
      Email: cfernandez@touchenterprises.com
      Website: www.touchenterprises.com/shop
Dist industrial products, safety products, medical supplies, vet supplies, MRO supplies. (As-Pac, estab 2007, empl 15, sales $3,000,000, cert: NMSDC)

Kentucky

4097 Industrial Electronics LLC dba Indel-USA
      10312 Bluegrass Pkwy
      Louisville, KY 40299
      Contact: Vadim Nazarenko Owner
      Tel: 888-499-4877
      Email: indel@indel-usa.com
      Website: www.indel-usa.com
Repair, troubleshooting, retrofitting & design services for industrial electronic equipment. (Woman, estab 2005, empl 4, sales , cert: State)

4098 United American Supply, LLC
      100-C Dewey Dr
      Nicholasville, KY 40356
      Contact: Albert Taylor Managing Partner
      Tel: 859-881-1850
      Email: al@unitedamericansupply.com
      Website: www.unitedamericansupply.com
Dist safety supplies (PPE), machined parts & sanitary maintenance supplies. (AA, estab 2008, empl 8, sales $1,600,000, cert: NMSDC)

Louisiana

4099 Brewster Procurement Group, Inc.
      401 West Main St.
      Lafayette, LA 70501
      Contact: Pat Brewster, C.p.m. Principal
      Tel: 337-291-9009
      Email: pat@brewsterprocurement.com
      Website: www.brewsterprocurement.com
Dist MRO, mill & industrial supplies, electrical, tools, safety products, buyout services. (Minority, Woman, estab 1999, empl 8, sales $113,609,858, cert: NMSDC, WBENC)

4100 Precision Air & Liquid Solutions, LLC
      1905 W Thomas St, Ste D271
      Hammond, LA 70401
      Contact: Cynthia Bourg Chief Exec Mgr
      Tel: 504-208-1525
      Email: cyndibourg@precisionair-liquid.com
      Website: www.precisionair-liquid.com
Dist ventilation fans, fan parts, filtration, replacement filters, cartridges, housings, compressors, turbines & engines, dust, fume & mist control products & flow monitoring equipment. (Woman, estab 2003, empl 2, sales $550,000, cert: State, WBENC)

Massachusetts

4101 New England Die Cutting, Inc.
      96 Milk St
      Methuen, MA 01844
      Contact: Kimberly L Abare President
      Tel: 978-374-0789
      Email: kabare@nedc.com
      Website: www.nedc.com
Mfr gaskets, seals & insulators, die cutting, waterjet cutting & laser etching. (Woman, estab 1982, empl 28, sales $3,900,000, cert: WBENC)

Michigan

4102 Choctaw-Kaul Distribution Company
      3540 Vinewood
      Detroit, MI 48208
      Contact: Caitlin Johnson Customer Dev Mgr
      Tel: 313-895-3165
      Email: cjohnson@choctawkaul.com
      Website: www.choctawkaul.com
Mfr gloves & safety products. (Minority, estab 1998, empl 350, sales $107,000,000, cert: NMSDC)

4103 Extreme Tooling LLC
      48750 Structural Dr
      Chesterfield, MI 48051
      Contact: Kurt Schill President
      Tel: 586-232-3618
      Email: kschill@extremetooling.com
      Website: www.extremetooling.com
Dist metal removal & industrial supplies, milling, drilling & industrial products. (Woman, estab 2003, empl 5, sales $3,683,821, cert: WBENC)

4104 IMC Products, Inc.
      2743 Henry St, Ste 130
      Muskegon, MI 49441
      Contact: Irmgard Cooper President
      Tel: 877-625-8743
      Email: irmgard.cooper@imc-products.com
      Website: www.imc-products.com
Assembly & kit packaging, contract administration, warehouse & distribution. (AA, estab 1990, empl 12, sales $1,900,000, cert: NMSDC)

4105 JISI Group, LLC
      6043 18 Mile Rd
      Sterling Heights, MI 48314
      Contact: Amber Amato President
      Tel: 586-239-9016
      Email: a.amato@jisisupply.com
      Website: www.jisisupply.com
Concrete construction & repair products. (Woman, estab 2014, empl 2, sales $446,000, cert: WBENC)

4106 Mahar Tool Supply Company, Inc.
      7105 Nineteen Mile Rd
      Sterling Heights, MI 48314
      Contact: Dave Plosky Exec VP Sales
      Tel: 586-997-2584
      Email: dp@mahartool.com
      Website: www.mahartool.com
Dist industrial products & MRO supplies, commodity management, integrated supply, technical staffing, engineering support. (Woman, estab 1947, empl 142, sales $115,200,000, cert: WBENC)

4107 Master Pneumatic Detroit, Inc.
      6701 Eighteen Mile Road
      Sterling Heights, MI 48314
      Contact: Wendy Goscenski Mgr
      Tel: 586-254-1000
      Email: wgoscenski@aol.com
      Website: www.masterpneumatic.com
Mfr filters, regulators & lubrication systems for compressed air systems. (Woman, estab 1950, empl 56, sales $6,500,000, cert: WBENC)

4108 Midwest Safety Products of Michigan
      4929 E Paris SE
      Grand Rapids, MI 49512
      Contact: Vanh Miller CEO
      Tel: 616-554-5155
      Email: vanhm@midwestsafety.com
      Website: www.midwestsafety.com
Dist safety, first aid, janitorial, packaging supplies, Personal Protective Equipment, Gloves, Safety Glasses, Ear Plugs, Disposable Clothing, Respirators, Welding Supplies, Hardhats. (As-Pac, estab 1978, empl 32, sales $10,010,000, cert: NMSDC)

4109 National Integrated Systems
      4622 Runway Blvd
      Ann Arbor, MI 48108
      Contact: Jay Park Sales
      Tel: 313-817-0066
      Email: jpark@nisusa.com
      Website: www.nisusa.com
Dist coated pipe & components, used for modular pipe racking systems. (As-Pac, estab 2003, empl 10, sales $ 0, cert: NMSDC)

4110 Safety Services, Inc.
      5286 Wynn Rd
      Kalamazoo, MI 49048
      Contact: Kathryn Bowdish CEO
      Tel: 269-382-1052
      Email: info@safetyservicesinc.com
      Website: www.safetyservicesinc.com
Dist industrial safety equipment: personal protective equipment, gloves, first aid, fall protection, confined space equipment, handling, storage, instrumentation, spill control. (Minority, Woman, estab 1948, empl 28, sales $ 0, cert: WBENC)

4111 Simon Marketing Group, LLC
      4944 Cimarron Dr
      Bloomfield Township, MI 48302
      Contact: Carol Berg Managing Member
      Tel: 248-855-6647
      Email: carol@simonmarketinggroup.net
      Website: www.parkinglotsafetysolutions.com/
Dist parking lot maintenance safety supplies. (Woman, estab 2007, empl 4, sales , cert: WBENC)

4112 The Safety Source, LLC
      35320 Forton Court
      Clinton Township, MI 48035
      Contact: Elizabeth VanSickle President
      Tel: 866-688-7233
      Email: elizabeth@safetysourcellc.com
      Website: www.safetysourcellc.com
Dist industrial safety supplies, first aid supplies & miscellaneous MRO supplies. (Woman, estab 2006, empl 6, sales $2,200,000, cert: WBENC)

Minnesota

4113 Allied Electrical & Industrial Supply Company Inc.
      6112 14th St W
      St. Louis Park, MN 55416
      Contact: Valerie McKissack President
      Tel: 763-544-3600
      Email: vmckissack@allied-electrical.com
      Website: www.allied-electrical.com
Dist medical, industrial, electrical, safety, janitorial & construction supplies. (Woman/AA, estab 1994, empl 6, sales $832,000, cert: NMSDC)

4114 AMKA Global, LLC
      6441 Cecilia Circle
      Edina, MN 55439
      Contact: Bocar Kane CEO
      Tel: 952-495-4492
      Email: sales@amkasafety.com
      Website: www.amkasafety.com
Personal Protective products & work zone safety cones & equipment. (AA, estab 2006, empl 2, sales $129,000, cert: City)

4115 McClellan Sales Inc
      2851 84th Lane NE
      Blaine, MN 55449
      Contact: Brett Stangeland Operations Mgr
      Tel: 763-786-5350
      Email: brett@mcsales.com
      Website: www.mcsales.com
Dist safety PPE, tools & equipment. Gas detection supplier, repair & calibration services. (Woman, estab 2002, empl 5, sales $1,900,000, cert: WBENC)

4116 Safety Signs
      19784 Kenrick Ave
      Lakeville, MN 55044
      Contact: Sue Blanchard President
      Tel: 952-469-6700
      Email: sueblanchard@safetysigns-mn.com
      Website: www.safetysigns-mn.com
Traffic safety equipment and svcs specializing in traffic control, permanent signs, pavement striping, pavement stripe removals & safety apparel. (Woman, estab 1993, empl 28, sales , cert: State, City)

Missouri

4117 Alliance Industries LLC
      2959 N. Martin Ave
      Springfield, MO 65803
      Contact: Brenda Ryan President
      Tel: 417-863-6315
      Email: bryan@allianceind.com
      Website: www.allianceind.com
Remanufacture OEM torque converters. (Woman/AA, estab 2002, empl 20, sales $ 0, cert: NMSDC, WBENC)

INDUSTRIAL EQUIPMENT & SUPPLIES

4118 King Filtration Technologies, Inc.
      1255 Research Blvd
      Saint Louis, MO 63132
      Contact: Michael Miossi Energy Acct Mgr
      Tel: 800-999-8441
      Email: michael.miossi@kingfiltration.com
      Website: www.kingfiltration.com
Dist filtration products. (Woman, estab 1964, empl 20, sales $ 0, cert: WBENC)

4119 Stainless Integrity
      3431 E Bluff Point Dr
      Ozark, MO 65721
      Contact: Vickie Norton President
      Tel: 417-773-6383
      Email: vlnorton@stainlessintegrity.com
      Website: www.stainlessintegrity.com
Dist stainless steel nickel alloy ASME pressure vessels & tanks; bioreactor & fermenter skids; field repair; field modification & field erection, tank cleaning & inspection, powder hoppers & bins. (Woman, estab 2010, empl 1, sales $ 0, cert: WBENC)

Mississippi

4120 MS Rubber Company
      715 E McDowell Rd
      Jackson, MS 39204
      Contact: Susan Foster GM
      Tel: 601-948-2575
      Email: sfoster@msrubber.com
      Website: www.msrubber.com
Dist rubber hoses, hydraulic hoses, belting, plastic, gaskets, safety supplies, o'rings, general hoses, hose fittings, clamps, rubber tubing, matting, sheet packing, rainsuit, gloves & boots. (Woman, estab 1963, empl 14, sales $1,300,000, cert: CPUC, WBENC)

North Carolina

4121 EMI Supply
      5502 Cannon Dr
      Monroe, NC 28110
      Contact: Susan Richardson CEO
      Tel: 704-721-3641
      Email: srichardson@emisupply.com
      Website: www.emisupply.com
Dist electrical & industrial supplies: abrasives, adhesives, chemicals, cutting tools, safety, tapes. (Woman, estab 1990, empl 7, sales , cert: WBENC)

4122 GP Supply Company
      501 E Washington St
      Greensboro, NC 27401
      Contact: Antonio Wallace CEO
      Tel: 336-274-7615
      Email: awallace@gpsupplycompany.com
      Website: www.gpsupplycompany.com
Dist mechanical supplies, industrial supplies, commercial plumbing supplies, pipe, valves, fittings, fixtures. (AA, estab , empl , sales $14,000,000, cert: NMSDC)

New Hampshire

4123 Quintana Associates, Inc.
      8 Puzzle Lane
      Newton, NH 03858
      Contact: Jorge Cruz Sales & Acct Rep
      Tel: 978-689-4411
      Email: jorgec@qaisupply.com
      Website: www.quintanasupply.com
Dist industrial supplies: safety, janitorial, packaging, material handling equipment, office & clean room supplies. (Hisp, estab 1991, empl 20, sales $8,717,183, cert: NMSDC)

New Jersey

4124 Automotive and Industrial Equipment LLC
      43 Wilkeshire Blvd
      Randolph, NJ 07869
      Contact: Vijay Srinivasan President
      Tel: 973-343-6432
      Email: autoandindustrialinc@gmail.com
      Website: www.ai-equip.com
Dist materials, tools, equipment & supplies to laboratories, government facilities & private facilities. (As-Pac, estab 2011, empl 1, sales $375,891, cert: State)

4125 BKC Industries, Inc.
      3288 Delsea Dr Ste B
      Franklinville, NJ 08322
      Contact: Karen Harrison-Carter President
      Tel: 856-694-9400
      Email: bkcindustrial@comcast.net
      Website: www.bkcindustries.com
Dist industrial plant supplies, safety supplies, packaging materials & construction materials. (Woman/AA, estab 1998, empl 3, sales $1,200,000, cert: State, 8(a))

4126 Forty Nine Corp.
      PO Box 2325
      Paterson, NJ 07509
      Contact: Michael Temkin VP
      Tel: 201-791-0584
      Email: mct@49corp.com
      Website: www.49corp.com
Mfr safety, warning & protective flags, tapes & tarpaulins for electric utilities & telephone companies. (Woman, estab , empl , sales $500,000, cert: State, WBENC)

4127 Stillwell Hansen, Inc.
      PO Box 7820
      Edison, NJ 08818
      Contact: Carol Stillwell President
      Tel: 732-225-7474
      Email: carol@stillwell-hansen.com
      Website: www.stillwell-hansen.com
Mfrs rep HVAC Equipment, Computer Room Air Conditioning, UPS, Networking Equipment Racks, Fire Protection , Portable Air Conditioning, Service for HVAC, Computer Room, UPS, Fire Protection. (Woman, estab 1969, empl 70, sales $22,500,000, cert: State)

INDUSTRIAL EQUIPMENT & SUPPLIES

4128 The Olympic Glove & Safety Co. Inc.
75 Main Ave
Elmwood Park, NJ 07407
Contact: Jerry Lorenc Sales
Tel: 201-974-9320
Email: jlorenc@olympicglove.com
Website: www.olympicglove.com
Safety equipment. Gloves, safety glasses, safety goggles, disinfecting spray, hand sanitizer, disinfecting wipes, gas monitors, etc. (Woman, estab , empl 18, sales $18,000,000, cert: WBENC)

4129 Turtle & Hughes, Inc.
1900 Lower Rd
Linden, NJ 07036
Contact: Scott West President
Tel: 330-518-0874
Email: scott.west@turtle.com
Website: www.turtle.com
Dist MRO, industrial & electrical supplies & equipment. (Woman, estab 1923, empl 832, sales $760,000,000, cert: WBENC)

New York

4130 Active Fire Extinguisher Co., Inc.
5-16 47th Ave
Long Island City, NY 11101
Contact: Munich President
Tel: 718-729-0450
Email: m.munich@activefire.com
Website: www.activefire.com
Dist fire extinguishers, pre-engineered automatic kitchen range hood systems, cabinets, fire hoses. (Woman, estab 1942, empl 13, sales $2,600,000, cert: City)

4131 AMKO Trading
129-09 26th Ave Unit D
Flushing, NY 11354
Contact: Tae S Rim Sales Mgr
Tel: 718-505-8401
Email: trim@amkotrading.com
Website: www.amkotrading.com
Dist commercial kitchen equipment. Electric & Gas Rice cookers, Electric rice warmer, Steam pans, PC food pans, Noodle making machines, Stock pots. (Minority, Woman, estab 2001, empl 8, sales $1,000,000, cert: NMSDC)

4132 Harbison Bros., Inc.
32 Appenheimer Ave
Buffalo, NY 14214
Contact: Patricia Potts President
Tel: 716-892-3290
Email: pat@harbisonbros.com
Website: www.Harbisonbros.com
Dist reconditioned 55 gallon steel & poly drums, 275 & 330 gallon tote tanks. (Woman, estab , empl 17, sales $1,300,000, cert: WBENC)

4133 J.T. Systems, Inc.
8132 Oswego Rd, Rt 57
Liverpool, NY 13090
Contact: Jit Turakhia President
Tel: 315-622-1980
Email: info@jtsystemsinc.com
Website: www.jtsystemsinc.com
Mfr air pollution control equipment: cyclones, scrubbers & baghouses, fans, ventilation, blowers, etc. (As-Pac, estab 1980, empl 5, sales $ 0, cert: State)

4134 Legacy Construction, LLC
85 Milton Ave
Sag Harbor, NY 11963
Contact: Stephen Watson CFO
Tel: 917-560-5593
Email: swatson@twcurban.com
Website: www.twcurban.com
Dist construction material & supplies. (AA, estab 2004, empl 2, sales , cert: State)

4135 Mechanical Heating Supply, Inc.
476 Timpson Pl
Bronx, NY 10455
Contact: Frank Rivera President
Tel: 718-402-9765
Email: frank@mechheat.com
Website: www.mechheat.com
Dist heating equipment & supplies. (Hisp, estab 1989, empl 11, sales $12,800,000, cert: State)

4136 Mohawk Ltd.
3500 Bleachery Pl
Chadwicks, NY 13319
Contact: Linda Lane Dir of Mktg/Fleet
Tel: 315-570-6544
Email: lindal@mohawkltd.com
Website: www.mohawkltd.com
Equipment repair, refurbishment, calibration & product sales. (Woman, estab 1959, empl 32, sales $4,444,178, cert: State, WBENC)

4137 Nifty Concept
1159 Elton St
Brooklyn, NY 11239
Contact: Cedric Durant VP Project Devel
Tel: 800-830-1665
Email: cedricd@niftyaides.com
Website: www.niftyconcept.com
Janitorial supplies; Medical equipment & supplies; Office supplies and furniture.. (Woman/AA, estab 2014, empl 8, sales $1,850,000,000, cert: State, City)

4138 Strategic Procurement Group
36 Harbor Park Dr
Port Washington, NY 11050
Contact: Donna Kay President
Tel: 516-479-3778
Email: kayd@strategicprocurement.us
Website: www.strategicprocurement.us
Dist MRO supplies. (Minority, Woman, estab 2002, empl 10, sales $13,000,000, cert: NMSDC, WBENC)

4139 Wats International Inc.
200 Manchester Rd
Poughkeepsie, NY 12603
Contact: Josh Anselmo President
Tel: 845-473-2106
Email: josh.anselmo@watsinternational.com
Website: www.watsinternational.com
Dist janitorial, office & MRO supplies. (AA, estab 1980, empl 8, sales $ 0, cert: State, City, NMSDC)

Ohio

4140 889 Global Solutions
1943 W 5th Ave.
Columbus, OH 43212
Contact: Govt Sales Project Mgr
Tel: 614-235-8889
Email: info@889globalsolutions.com
Website: www.889globalsolutions.com
Healthcare Components & Equipment. Consumer Goods & Promotional Products. Industrial Products. (Minority, Woman, estab 2000, empl 20, sales $ 0, cert: State, NMSDC)

4141 Benchmark Industrial Supply, LLC
1913 Commerce Rd
Springfield, OH 45504
Contact: Ron Tenkman Natl Sales Mgr
Tel: 937-325-1001
Email: rtenkman@benchmarkindustrial.com
Website: www.benchmarkindustrial.com
Dist safety products & industrial supplies. (Woman, estab 2003, empl 18, sales $5,000,000, cert: State, WBENC)

4142 First Star Safety, LLC
310 South Cooper Ave
Cincinnati, OH 45215
Contact: President
Tel: 513-661-7827
Email: info@firststarsafety.com
Website: www.firststarsafety.com
Dist construction safety quipment: cones, barrels, safety vests, protective eye & ear wear. (Woman, estab 2005, empl 8, sales , cert: WBENC)

4143 Hydro Dyne Inc.
225 Wetmore Ave SE
Massillon, OH 44646
Contact: Kevin Boone Business Devel Mgr
Tel: 330-832-5076
Email: kevin@hydrodyneinc.com
Website: www.hydrodyneinc.com
Design, mfr & repair shell & tube heat exchangers, condensers, evaporators & feedwater heaters. (Woman, estab 1967, empl 30, sales $ 0, cert: WBENC)

4144 IPS Group LLC
3254 Hill Ave
Toledo, OH 43607
Contact: Michele Bighouse CEO
Tel: 419-241-5955
Email: ipsti@ipstreatment.com
Website: www.ipsgroupllc.com
Derusting, degreasing, washing, deburring, demagnetizing, descaling, pickling, rust inhibiting, surface passivation, chemical paint stripping, bonding removal, assembly, sorting & inspecting, repackaging & shipping. (As-Ind, estab 1994, empl 30, sales $900,000, cert: State, WBENC)

4145 National Access Design, LLC
1924 Losantiville Ave
Cincinnati, OH 45237
Contact: Cheryl White President
Tel: 513-351-3400
Email: cheryl@nationalaccessdesign.com
Website: www.nationalaccessdesign.com
Mfr double acting traffic/impact doors, strip doors, door jambs, blast cell doors, industrial/divider curtains, dock seals & equipment, dist FRP doors, cold storage doors, and air curtains. (Woman, estab 2011, empl 12, sales $ 0, cert: WBENC)

4146 Norfleet Distributors LLC
32493 Jefferson Dr
Solon, OH 44139
Contact: Garrick Norfleet Owner
Tel: 216-832-2038
Email: garrick.norfleet@norfleetdistributors.com
Website: www.norfleetdistributors.com
Construction safety equipment, hard hats, safety vests, etc. (AA, estab 2020, empl 2, sales $229,000, cert: NMSDC)

4147 PenCo Industrial Supply, Inc.
300 Industrial Pkwy, Unit D
Chagrin Falls, OH 44022
Contact: Penny Scocos President
Tel: 440-893-9506
Email: penny@pencosupply.com
Website: www.pencosupply.com
Dist MRO, safety & janitorial supplies: fasteners, cutting tools, abrasives, chemicals, eye & ear protection, gloves, respirators, toilet paper, paper towels, cleaning supplies & chemicals. (Woman, estab 2005, empl 5, sales $1,000,000, cert: WBENC)

4148 Quality Building Supplies For Industry, Inc.
17485 Saylor Ln
Grand Rapids, OH 43522
Contact: Edward haynes CEO
Tel: 419-832-2202
Email: qualitybldginc@aol.com
Website: www.qualitybuildingsupplies.com
Dist construction & industrial products: rebar, structural steel, piling, tools & hardware. (AA, estab 1978, empl 5, sales $2,300,000, cert: NMSDC)

4149 Superior Industrial Supply & Services Inc.
1717 Indianwood Circle Ste 200
Maumee, OH 43537
Contact: Stan McCormick President
Tel: 419-697-3700
Email: stan.mccormick@siss.cc
Website: www.superiorindustrialsupply.com
Dist janitorial chemicals & equipment, packaging supplies & equipment, paper supplies, mill & crib. (AA, estab 1972, empl 3, sales $ 0, cert: NMSDC)

4150 Tradex International Inc.
5300 Tradex Pkwy
Cleveland, OH 44102
Contact: Philip A. Baseil COO
Tel: 216-651-4788
Email: pab@tradexgloves.com
Website: www.tradexgloves.com
Dist gloves, aprons, shoe covers, bouffant caps, toilet seat covers & wipers. (Minority, estab 1988, empl 70, sales $ 0, cert: NMSDC)

Oklahoma

4151 Omni Packaging Corporation
12322 E 55th St
Tulsa, OK 74146
Contact: Roberta Jones President
Tel: 918-461-1700
Email: ar@omnipackaging.com
Website: www.omnipackaging.com
Dist adhesives/sealants, hose clamps, expansion joints, gaskets, matting, urethane, protective clothing, plastic, etc. (Minority, Woman, estab 1988, empl 65, sales $ 0, cert: NMSDC)

Pennsylvania

4152 ACHR Incorporated
      2148 Embassy Dr
      Lancaster, PA 17603
      Contact: Christi Henry President
      Tel: 717-617-7226
      Email: christi@achrincorporated.com
      Website: www.achrincorporated.com
HVAC & refrigeration parts & equipment, construction materials. (Woman, estab 2005, empl 2, sales $650,000, cert: WBENC)

4153 Arbill Industries, Inc.
      10450 Drummond Rd
      Philadelphia, PA 19154
      Contact: Renee Millett Sales Admin
      Tel: 215-501-8246
      Email: rmillett@arbill.com
      Website: www.arbill.com
Mfr & dist industrial safety products. (Woman, estab 1957, empl 76, sales $ 0, cert: WBENC)

4154 General Fire Equipment Company, Inc.
      220 Broadway Ave
      Aston, PA 19014
      Contact: Kim McDonnell Exec Asst
      Tel: 610-485-8200
      Email: kmcdonnell@generalfireequipment.net
      Website: www.GeneralFireEquipment.Net
Dist, Service & Inspect Fire Extinguishers, Fire Equipment & Fire Surpression Systems. (Woman, estab 1975, empl 23, sales $ 0, cert: City)

4155 Industrial Piping Systems, Inc.
      1250 Toronita St.
      York, PA 17402
      Contact: Christine Wardrop President
      Tel: 717-846-7473
      Email: christine.wardrop@ipspipe.com
      Website: www.ipspipe.com
Dist pipes, valves, fittings, pumps, heat exchangers, tube, industrial coatings, lubricants. (Woman, estab 1982, empl 56, sales $17,574,304, cert: WBENC)

4156 Shah Industrial Sales Inc.
      5824 Library Rd
      Bethel Park, PA 15102
      Contact: Barbara Shah President
      Tel: 412-831-1224
      Email: kara@shahind.com
      Website: www.shahind.com
Dist fasteners, seals, o-rings, gaskets. (As-Ind, estab 1988, empl 2, sales $280,000, cert: State, NMSDC)

4157 Supreme Safety Inc.
      21 Richard Road
      Warminster, PA 18974
      Contact: Annette Patchell President
      Tel: 215-259-1400
      Email: annette@supremesafetyinc.com
      Website: www.supremesafetyinc.com
Dist industrial safety supplies & equipment. (Woman, estab 2004, empl 4, sales $1,400,000, cert: State)

Puerto Rico

4158 Interport Trading Corp.
      PO Box 51958
      Toa Baja, PR 00950
      Contact: Antonio Cruz GM
      Tel: 787-788-8650
      Email: acruz@interportpr.com
      Website: www.interportpr.com
Dist & service fire prevention equip: extinguisher, hose, supresion systems, fire alarms, safety equip, gloves, coveralls, eye & ear protection, showers, boots. (Hisp, estab 1989, empl 10, sales $1,448,600, cert: NMSDC)

4159 Master Products Corp.
      Barrio Candelaria
      Toa Baja, PR 00949
      Contact: Zoila Rivera Sales & Logistics
      Tel: 787-740-5254
      Email: zrivera@mastergroup-pr.com
      Website: www.mastergroup-pr.com
Mfr QUIKRETE Brand cement mixes: Concrete Mixes, Mortars, Flooring Thin-Sets and Grouts, Fast-Setting, Non-Shrink. (Hisp, estab 2005, empl 75, sales $12,758,000, cert: NMSDC)

4160 New York Wiping & Industrial Products, Inc.
      698 Calle B
      San Juan, PR 00920
      Contact: Dr. Mario Julia President
      Tel: 787-273-6363
      Email: jsantos@nywiping.com
      Website: www.nywiping.com
Dist industrial supplies. (Hisp, estab 1989, empl 5, sales , cert: NMSDC)

South Carolina

4161 Atlan-Tec, Inc. (Atlantic Technical Sales & Svc)
      3215 Bryson Dr
      Florence, SC 29501
      Contact: Grace Patterson President
      Tel: 843-661-0415
      Email: atlreceivables@aol.com
      Website: www.atlan-tec.net
Dist industrial equipment. (Woman, estab 1991, empl 6, sales $3,156,683, cert: State)

4162 Bullzeye Equipment & Supply
      1383 Old Hwy 52
      Moncks Corner, SC 29461
      Contact: Kristie Collins Owner
      Tel: 843-499-2226
      Email: kcollins@bullzeyeequipment.com
      Website: www.bullzeyeequipment.com
Dist industrial products, welding supplies, janitorial supplies, safety supplies, packaging supplies, material handling supplies & construction supplies. (Woman, estab 2012, empl 1, sales , cert: State, SDB)

4163 Carolina Industrial Products, Inc.
      1872 Old Dunbar Rd
      West Columbia, SC 29172
      Contact: Dargon Gore President
      Tel: - -
      Email: dgore@cipbattery.com
      Website: www.cipbattery.com
Dist & service industrial batteries, chargers & handling equipment. (Woman, estab 1983, empl 45, sales $13,000,000, cert: WBENC)

INDUSTRIAL EQUIPMENT & SUPPLIES

4164 Charleston's Rigging and Marine Hardware Inc
PO Box 21255
Charleston, SC 29413
Contact: Jessica Sage President
Tel: 843-723-7145
Email: jsage@charlestonsrigging.com
Website: www.charlestonsrigging.com
Dist rigging & material handling equipment, industrial & safety products, fabricates custom wire rope, chain, & nylon slings. (Woman, estab 1982, empl 47, sales $10,000,000, cert: City)

4165 Indcon Inc.
105 Ben Hamby Dr., Ste E
Greenville, SC 29601
Contact: Collin Atkins Corporate Counsel
Tel: 864-298-8300
Email: collin@indconinc.com
Website: www.indconinc.com
Dist industrial maintenance products, lubrication quality, general equipment maintenance, equipment installation, concrete & industrial repair, maintenance tools & hardware. (Woman, estab 1998, empl 10, sales $6,000,000, cert: WBENC)

4166 Munaco Sealing Solutions, Inc.
5 Ketron Ct
Greenville, SC 29607
Contact: Jeff Adams Business Devel
Tel: 864-676-2055
Email: jeff@munaco-online.com
Website: www.munacosealing.com
Sealing solutions & precision components: gaskets, custom gaskets, metal seals, piston rings, metal gaskets, fiber gaskets, spiral-wound gaskets, rubber gaskets, silicone gaskets, elastomer o-rings, rubber o-rings, FKM, PTFE. (Woman, estab 1995, empl 13, sales $13,050,000, cert: WBENC)

4167 The Skinner Company
1519 Evans Pond Rd
Greenwood, SC 29649
Contact: Operations Mgr
Tel: 864-953-9618
Email:
Website: www.skinnerco.com
Dist pipeline clamps: emergency, band, pipe joint, pressed steel economy clamps. (Woman, estab , empl 7, sales $1,314,000, cert: WBENC)

Tennessee

4168 Dixon Services, Inc.
1315 Farmville Rd
Memphis, TN 38122
Contact: Charles Dixon President
Tel: 901-345-6608
Email: charlesrdixon@dixonservicesinc.com
Website: www.dixonservicesinc.com
Dist safety & industrial supplies. (Woman/AA, estab 2000, empl 10, sales , cert: City, NMSDC)

4169 eSpin Technologies, Inc.
7151 Discovery Dr
Chattanooga, TN 37416
Contact: Jay Doshi President
Tel: 423-267-6266
Email: jdoshi@exceedfilters.com
Website: www.eSpintechnologies.com
Mfr & dist low energy consuming, high performance HVAC air filters. (As-Ind, estab 1999, empl 27, sales $ 0, cert: NMSDC, 8(a))

4170 Porter-Walker LLC
115 Dyer St Ste 3
Columbia, TN 38401
Contact: Terrence Bybee Strategic Accounts Mgr
Tel: 931-560-2428
Email: tbybee@porter-walker.com
Website: www.porter-walker.com
Dist safety, industrial & MRO supplies, supply chain mgmt. (AA, estab , empl 41, sales $35,000,000, cert: State, NMSDC)

4171 Storage Systems Unlimited
3343 Aspen Grove Dr Ste 290
Franklin, TN 37067
Contact: Lars Anderson
Tel: 888-614-0004
Email: landerson@storagesystemsul.com
Website: www.storagesystemsul.com
Bins & Panels, Cabinets, Carts, Infection Protection, High Density Storage Systems, Shelving, Stainless Steel. (Woman, estab 1997, empl 20, sales , cert: WBENC)

4172 Superior Industrial Supply Co.
2675 Whitman Ave
Memphis, TN 38182
Contact: Rita Montesi CEO
Tel: 901-327-0450
Email: info@superiorindsupply.com
Website: www.superiorindsupply.com
Dist safety, industrial, janitorial, first aid supplies, fire protection & AED's. (Woman, estab 1981, empl 13, sales $2,500,000, cert: NWBOC)

4173 T G Inc.
615 Main St
Nashville, TN 37206
Contact: Joseph Towner VP Sales
Tel: 615-620-5100
Email: jtowner@t-g-inc.com
Website: www.t-g-inc.com
Dist industrial & electrical products, construction supplies, materials & equipment. (Woman/AA, estab 1999, empl 8, sales $2,000,000, cert: NMSDC)

Texas

4174 All-Tex Pipe & Supply, Inc.
9743 Brockbank
Dallas, TX 75220
Contact: Paul Borham Exec Asst
Tel: 214-389-2201
Email: paulb@alltexsupply.com
Website: www.alltexsupply.com
Dist pipe, valves & fittings: acid waste, carbon steel, cast iron, copper, CPVC, PVC, drainage, stainless steel. (Woman, estab 1973, empl 120, sales $78,039,000, cert: State, WBENC)

INDUSTRIAL EQUIPMENT & SUPPLIES

4175 Battery Consulting
4020 Christopher Way
Plano, TX 75024
Contact: MuMu Moorthi Owner
Tel: 214-929-6790
Email: mumu@battery-consulting.com
Website: www.battery-consulting.com
Dist batteries. (As-Pac, estab 2001, empl 2, sales $181,000, cert: State)

4176 CASADA Industrial
PO Box 203161
Austin, TX 78720
Contact: Ernest Anguiano Owner
Tel: 800-828-0934
Email: ernest@casada-industrial.com
Website: www.casada-industrial.com
Dist industrial supplies. (Hisp, estab 1993, empl 8, sales $ 0, cert: State)

4177 Daxwell
2825 Wilcrest Dr, Ste 500
Houston, TX 77042
Contact: Sam Zhang Advisor
Tel: 281-669-0622
Email: samuel.zhang@daxwell.com
Website: www.daxwell.com
Mfr & dist disposable products: gloves, dinnerware, foil & paper products. (As-Pac, estab 1996, empl , sales $69,982,944, cert: State)

4178 Dow-Caide Industrial, Inc.
1534 Sunset Lane
Duncanville, TX 75137
Contact: Michael Downs President
Tel: 972-421-8662
Email: dewaye@sbcglobal.net
Website: www.dowcaidesupply.com
Dist industrial supplies, industrial equipment, safety supplies, plastic wrap/sheeting, trashbags, corrugated boxes, lights/ballasts, food products, chemicals, paper products, tape, labels, packaging supplies & materials etc. (AA, estab 2011, empl 2, sales $424,660, cert: State, NMSDC)

4179 Duran Industries Inc.
504 Business Pkwy
Richardson, TX 75081
Contact: Richard Duran President
Tel: 972-238-7122
Email: rduran@duranco.com
Website: www.duranco.com/
Dist industrial, commercial, MRO, safety, scientific & lab products. (Hisp, estab 1995, empl 20, sales $14,050,000, cert: NMSDC)

4180 Evco Partners dba Burgoon Company
PO Box 1168
Galveston, TX 77553
Contact: Donna Hanson President
Tel: 409-766-1900
Email: office@burgooncompany.com
Website: www.burgooncompany.com
Dist industrial supplies & equipment, laboratory & medical supplies, heavy equipment. (Woman, estab 1988, empl 17, sales $20,981,530, cert: State, WBENC)

4181 Guardian Industrial Supply, LLC
10629 Metric Blvd
Austin, TX 78780
Contact: Christina Duncan Managing Member
Tel: 512-973-3500
Email: sales@guardian-industrial.com
Website: www.guardiancatalog.com
Dist industrial supplies: circuit breakers, motor starters, motor control products, transformers, fuses, safety switches, wiring devices, plug, receptacles, softstarters, variable frequency drives, transfer switches, controls, enclosures, contactors, etc. (Woman, estab 2006, empl 10, sales $3,193,459, cert: WBENC)

4182 HLF Distributing, Inc.
1213-B N Post Oak Rd
Houston, TX 77055
Contact: Sales
Tel: 713-932-9320
Email: info@huskybicycles.com
Website: www.huskybicycles.com
Dist industrial & commercial bicycles & tricycles: wheels, tires, tubes, chains, tools & lubricants. (Woman, estab 1993, empl 7, sales $2,600,000, cert: WBENC)

4183 I AM Safety
4565 FM 466
Seguin, TX 78155
Contact: Lynda President
Tel: 832-715-0375
Email: lynda@iamsafetytx.com
Website: www.iamsafetytx.com
Safety Training (OSHA), Fire, First Aid/CPR/BBP/AED, Safety Products. (Woman, estab 2011, empl 2, sales , cert: State, City)

4184 Industrial Water Services
4500 Turf Rd Cordillera de los Andes 5740-2,
El Paso, TX 79938
Contact: Ruben Diaz President
Tel: 915-849-0401
Email: rdiaz@industrialwaterservice.com
Website: www.industrialwaterservice.com
Industrial water equipment parts & service. (Hisp, estab 1997, empl 17, sales $3,800,000, cert: NMSDC)

4185 MagRabbit-Alamo Iron Works, LLC
PO Box 2341
San Antonio, TX 78298
Contact: Wayne Dennis Diversity Coord
Tel: 210-704-8520
Email: wdennis@aiwnet.com
Website: www.magrabbit-aiw.com
Dist industrial supplies, steel service & fabrication, hand & power tools, equipment repair & installation, logistics, transportation & freight forwarding. (As-Pac, estab 2004, empl 150, sales , cert: NMSDC)

4186 Romar Supply
2468 Fabens
Dallas, TX 75229
Contact: Ron Adair VP Operations
Tel: 214-357-2020
Email: rona@romarsupply.com
Website: www.romarsupply.com
Dist pipe, valves, fittings, steam controls, valve actuation, stainless piping products, sanitary stainless piping. (Woman, estab 1983, empl 42, sales $17,000,000, cert: State, WBENC)

INDUSTRIAL EQUIPMENT & SUPPLIES

4187 Safety Supply, Inc.
      12050 Crownpoint, Ste 160
      San Antonio, TX 78233
      Contact: Crystal Turner President
      Tel: 800-873-9033
      Email: CRYSTAL@SAFETYSUPPLYINC.COM
      Website: www.safetysupplyinc.com
Dist industrial safety apparel & equipment, fire service & rescue equipment, environmental & health products. (Woman, estab 1983, empl 11, sales $6,400,000, cert: State, WBENC)

4188 Supply Innovations Co, LLC
      200 Chihuahua St, Ste 100
      San Antonio, TX 78207
      Contact: Nancy Flack Mgr
      Tel: 210-225-3194
      Email: nancy@supplyinnovationsllc.com
      Website: www.supplyinnovationsllc.com
Dist industrial supplies: tapes, safety, tools, abrasives, packaging, material handling, hardware, janitorial, adhesive & aircraft supplies. (Woman, estab 2007, empl 4, sales $1,673,122, cert: State, WBENC)

4189 TKC Enterprises Inc. dba Batteries Plus
      2703 N Beltline Rd
      Irving, TX 75062
      Contact: Miguel Yan Owner
      Tel: 972-256-2073
      Email: miguel@battplus.net
      Website: www.batteriesplus.com
Dist batteries. (As-Pac, estab , empl , sales $100,000,000, cert: State, NMSDC)

4190 Track Trading Co. dba Exaco USA., Exaco Trading
      4209 Greystone Dr
      Austin, TX 78731
      Contact: Kim Cook President
      Tel: 512-345-1900
      Email: kim@exaco.com
      Website: www.exaco.com
Dist metal mixing blades, mixing paint & drywall. (Woman, estab 1987, empl 18, sales $10,000,000, cert: State, WBENC)

4191 VM Graphic Packaging & Safety Products LLC
      4413 Fairlake Dr
      Garland, TX 75043
      Contact: Verna Melton CEO
      Tel: 972-303-9102
      Email: vmgraph@flash.net
      Website:
         www.vmgraphicpkgandsafetyproducts.espwebsite.c
Dist style bags & textile bags, industrial supplies, part bags, brooms, trash containers, tilt trucks. (Woman/AA, estab 1988, empl 5, sales $2,015,489, cert: State)

4192 White-Tucker Company
      13895 Westfair East Dr
      Houston, TX 77041
      Contact: Controller
      Tel: 281-664-7444
      Email:
      Website: www.whitetucker.com
Dist industrial equipment & supplies. (Woman, estab , empl 24, sales $8,580,000, cert: WBENC)

Virginia

4193 17 Machinery, LLC
      3595 George Washington Mem Hwy
      Hayes, VA 23072
      Contact: Marie Knapp GM
      Tel: 804-642-9400
      Email: mknapp@17m2.com
      Website: www.17machinery.com
Industrial & marine pumps & parts, valves, filtration, fabricated process systems, dual laminate pipe, fittings & tanks (Woman, estab 2003, empl 2, sales $257,776, cert: WBENC)

4194 Can See Fire Service Co Inc. t/a Fire Solutions
      205 Haley Rd
      Ashland, VA 23005
      Contact: Edward Caldas VP Sales
      Tel: 804-752-2366
      Email: edward@firesolutionsinc.com
      Website: www.firesolutionsinc.com
Install, maintain, service, inspects, relocate & repair fire protection equipment. (Minority, Woman, estab 1987, empl 53, sales $4,901,793, cert: State, NMSDC, WBENC)

4195 Encompass Supply
      8000 Towers Crescent Dr Ste 1350
      Vienna, VA 22182
      Contact: Rudolph Burwell President
      Tel: 804-716-0546
      Email: info@encompasssupply.net
      Website: www.encompasssupply.net
Electrical and industrial supplies, electrical construction & industrial supplies. (AA, estab 2013, empl 3, sales $2,500,000, cert: State)

4196 Parker Battery, Inc.
      208 South St
      Franklin, VA 23851
      Contact: Shaun Parker Sales
      Tel: 800-569-6084
      Email: shaun@parkerbattery.com
      Website: www.parkerbattery.com
Dist batteries, starters & alternators for automotive, commercial & industrial applications. (Woman, estab 1990, empl 9, sales $2,000,000, cert: State)

4197 Weldex Sales Corporation
      PO Box 1
      Thaxton, VA 24174
      Contact: Robin Hartman President
      Tel: 540-586-9648
      Email: rhartman@weldexsales.com
      Website: www.weldexsales.com
Dist industrial electric forklift batteries & chargers. (Woman, estab 1980, empl 29, sales $3,000,000, cert: NWBOC)

Washington

4198 Birch Equipment Rental & Sales
PO Box 30918
Bellingham, WA 98228
Contact: Cara Buckingham Information Dir
Tel: 360-734-5744
Email: planning@birchequipment.com
Website: www.birchequipment.com
Dist & rent equipment & machines: aerators, carpet cleaners, boom ifts, large excavators & forklifts. (Woman, estab 1972, empl 75, sales $15,000,000, cert: WBENC)

4199 Emerald, Inc.
PO Box 14227
Seattle, WA 98168
Contact: President
Tel: 206-767-8909
Email: emeraldinc@msn.com
Website: www.emeraldinc.net
Kitchen Hood Cleaning, Fire Extinguisher Sales/Service, Kitchen Hood Fire System Sales/Service, Safety Equipment Sales. (Hisp, estab 1989, empl 5, sales $300,000, cert: State, City)

4200 Excel Gloves & Safety Supplies, Inc.
6808 26th St E, Ste 102
Fife, WA 98424
Contact: Irene Reyes CEO
Tel: 253-896-1195
Email: glovelady@excelgloves.com
Website: www.excelgloves.com
Import & dist gloves, safety, medical, janitorial & packaging supplies, (Minority, Woman, estab 1993, empl 8, sales $2,000,000, cert: State, NMSDC)

4201 Rohtek Automation LLC
9223 NE 174th Pl
Bothell, WA 98011
Contact: Oscar Rojas President
Tel: 425-318-2179
Email: orojas@rohtek.com
Website: www.rohtekautomation.com
Dist high tech mfg, operating & monitoring solutions. (Hisp, estab 2011, empl 2, sales , cert: State)

Wisconsin

4202 E. R. Abernathy Industrial Inc.
2000 Pewaukee Rd, Ste 0
waukesha, WI 53188
Contact: Edna Abernathy President
Tel: 262-446-3377
Email: edna@abernathyco.com
Website: www.abernathyco.com
Dist safety, construction, electrical & industrial supplies. (Woman/AA, estab 1991, empl 10, sales $1,354,000, cert: NMSDC)

INDUSTRIAL MACHINES

> **INDUSTRIAL MACHINES**
> Manufacturers and distributors of ovens, vacuum cleaners, air compressors, blasting machines, food processing equipment, paint mixers, tube flaring machines, etc. (See also HARDWARE & TOOLS, HYDRAULIC & COMPRESSED AIR EQUIPMENT, INDUSTRIAL MACHINES and MATERIAL HANDLING EQUIPMENT). NAICS Code 42

Arizona

4203 STRATCO, Inc.
14821 N 73rd St
Scottsdale, AZ 85260
Contact: Diane Graham CEO
Tel: 480-991-0450
Email: supplier.diversity@stratcoglobal.com
Website: www.stratcoglobal.com
Design blending & reaction equipment for grease, lubricants, bio-diesel & petrochemical industries. (Woman, estab 1928, empl 16, sales $5,621,643, cert: WBENC)

California

4204 Combustion Associates, Inc.
555 Monica Circle Corona
Corona, CA 92880
Contact: Preeti Chandan Sales/Mktg
Tel: 951-272-6999
Email: pchandan@cai3.com
Website: www.cai3.com
Food processing systems; integrated skid-mounted process systems; lube oil & gas systems; water heaters & industrial burners; modular aeroderivative power generation systems; packaged. (Woman/As-Ind, estab 1991, empl 45, sales $9,100,000, cert: NMSDC, CPUC)

4205 Lucio Family Enterprises, Inc.
2150 Prune Ave
Fremont, CA 94539
Contact: Sandra Garcia
Tel: 510-623-2323
Email: sgarcia@compactormc.com
Website: www.compactormc.com
Mfr waste & recycling equipment: compactors, containers, balers (all sizes), custom fabrication requests. (Minority, Woman, estab 2006, empl 18, sales $2,500,000, cert: NMSDC)

4206 Turbo Air, Inc.
1250 Victoria St
Carson, CA 90746
Contact: Laura Spears Natl Acct Mgr
Tel: 310-900-1000
Email: laura@turboairinc.com
Website: www.turboairinc.com
Mfr restaurant equipment: refrigerators/freezers, pizza prep tables, sandwich salad units, glass doors, microwave ovens, food warmers, sink tables, sushi cases & air conditioners. (Minority, estab 1997, empl 40, sales , cert: NMSDC)

Florida

4207 New England Machinery, Inc.
2820 62nd Ave E
Bradenton, FL 34203
Contact: Hans Weiden Sales Mgr
Tel: 941-755-5550
Email: hweiden@neminc.com
Website: www.neminc.com
Packaging equipment, Unscramblers, Orienters, Cappers, Retorquers, Pluggers, Pump Placers, Lidding. (Woman, estab 1974, empl 55, sales $15,000,000, cert: WBENC)

4208 Supergreen Inc.
4051 107th Circle N, Ste 1
Clearwater, FL 33762
Contact: Hoang Mai President
Tel: 727-459-3130
Email: mike.hoang@supergreenusa.com
Website: www.supergreenusa.com
Mfr Tankless Water Heaters. (As-Pac, estab 2013, empl 4, sales , cert: NMSDC)

Illinois

4209 AM Manufacturing Company
14151 Irving Ave
Dolton, IL 60419
Contact: Edward Mentz President
Tel: 708-841-0959
Email: lserafin@ammfg.com
Website: www.ammfg.com
Mfr dough processing equipment: dough dividers, dough rounders, pizza / tortilla presses, pizza crust dockers, proofers, cooling conveyors, bagel forming equipment. (Woman, estab 1961, empl 30, sales $7,000,000, cert: City)

4210 Apex Beverage Equipment Distribution Group, LLC.
450 Tower Blvd, Ste 200
Carol Stream, IL 60188
Contact: Christie Tierney President
Tel: 877-901-2739
Email: ctierney@totalapex.com
Website: www.totalapex.com
Dist beverage equipment, replacement parts & installation products. (Woman, estab 2008, empl 11, sales $14,000,000, cert: WBENC)

4211 Howe Corporation
1650 N Elston Ave
Chicago, IL 60642
Contact: Mary Howe President
Tel: 773-235-0200
Email: howeinfo@howecorp.com
Website: www.howecorp.com
Mfr Flake ice makers, refrigeration & ammonia pump out compressors & refrigeration pressure vessels. (Woman, estab , empl 37, sales $10,000,000, cert: WBENC)

INDUSTRIAL MACHINES

Indiana

4212 Cici Boiler Rooms Inc.
7811 Baumgart Rd
Evansville, IN 47711
Contact: Penny Duncan Administrative Asst
Tel: 812-867-0810
Email: penny@ciciboilers.com
Website: www.ciciboilers.com
Boilers, HVAC, Deareators, Water Heaters, Air Conditioning, New Equipment, Parts, Service, (Woman, estab 1965, empl 14, sales $4,900,000, cert: State)

Michigan

4213 Amigo Mobility International Inc.
6693 Dixie Hwy
Bridgeport, MI 48722
Contact: Gabriella DeVries Acct Mgr
Tel: 989-921-5073
Email: gdevries@myamigo.com
Website: www.myamigo.com
Provide electric handicap shopping carts to retailers. (Woman, estab 1968, empl 114, sales $12,400,000, cert: WBENC)

4214 Manufacturers/Machine Builders Services Co.
13035 Wayne Rd
Livonia, MI 48150
Contact: Glen Neal Managing Partner
Tel: 734-748-3706
Email: mmbswork2@sbcglobal.net
Website: www.mmbscorp
Build & service automated machines: pipe, wire, debug & install machines. (Minority, Woman, estab 2002, empl 16, sales $800,000, cert: NMSDC)

Missouri

4215 Erb Equipment Co., Inc.
200 Erb Industrial Dr
Fenton, MO 63026
Contact: Gregg Erb Dir of Sales
Tel: 636-349-0200
Email: greggerb@erbequipment.com
Website: www.erbequipment.com
Construction equipment, rent new & used equipment & repair parts, repair & maintenance, Backhoe, Wheel Loaders, Front loaders, excavators, dozers, crawler loaders, skid steer (bobcat), mini excavators & material handlers. (Woman, estab 1943, empl 230, sales $134,737,841, cert: WBENC)

4216 Productive Automoated Systems Corp. (PASCO)
2600 S Hanley Rd, Ste 450
St. Louis, MO 63144
Contact: Nate Mahoney Dir Finance & IT
Tel: - -
Email: nmahoney@pascosystems.com
Website: www.pascosystems.com
Design & Mfr rugged robotic automation systems and palletizers. (Woman, estab 1976, empl 50, sales $13,332,000, cert: State)

4217 TSA Sales Associates, LLC
3466 Bridgeland Dr
Bridgeton, MO 63044
Contact: Pamela Sanders Owner
Tel: 314-291-4400
Email: psanders@tsasales.com
Website: www.tsasales.com
Air pollution control equipment, dry bulk solids, handling equipment & storage silos & bins. Design dust, fume & mist collecion systems. (Woman, estab 2001, empl 5, sales $374,087, cert: State)

New Jersey

4218 Ana M Fisher dba A & A Glove & Safety Co.
20 Richey Ave
West Collingswood, NJ 08107
Contact: Ashton Goerge Sales
Tel: 800-854-0060
Email: ashton@aaglove.com
Website: www.aasafetyindustrial.com
Safety consulting & sourcing, industrial equipment. (Woman/Hisp, estab 1990, empl 5, sales $400,000, cert: State, City)

4219 Hop Industries Corp.
1251 Valley Brook Ave
Lyndhurst, NJ 07071
Contact: Melanie Harkin Sales Rep
Tel: 201-438-6200
Email: mharkin@hopindustries.com
Website: www.hopindustries.com
Laminating Supplies & Equipment: laminating rolls, laminating pouches, pouch laminators, roll laminators, Binding Supplies & Equipment: binding combs, twin wire binding, plastic coil binding. (As-Pac, estab 1977, empl 70, sales $43,697,760, cert: NMSDC)

Ohio

4220 ASD - Automation Systems & Design
6222 Webster St
Dayton, OH 45414
Contact: Sunny Kullar CEO
Tel: 937-387-0351
Email: sunny@asddayton.com
Website: www.asddayton.com
Build, design & integrate custom machines. (As-Ind, estab 2000, empl 14, sales $1,500,000, cert: NMSDC)

4221 OCS Process Systems
24142 Detroit Rd
Westlake, OH 44145
Contact: Beth Kloos CEO
Tel: 440-871-6009
Email: bkloos@ocsprocess.com
Website: www.ocsprocess.com
Engineer, design & install food processing systems: liquid & dry powder processing systems, heat transfer, mixing, batching systems, metering systems, distribution systems, COP, CIP, piping, pumps, valves, welding, fabrication & installation. (Woman, estab , empl 40, sales $7,500,000, cert: WBENC)

INDUSTRIAL MACHINES

Pennsylvania

4222 American Kitchen Machinery and Repair Co., Inc.
204 Quarry St
Philadelphia, PA 19106
Contact: Andrea Mahon President
Tel: 215-627-7760
Email: service@akmco.com
Website: www.akmco.com

Parts & service to commercial kitchen equipment: cooking equipment, sanitation & dishwashing equipment, preparation equipment & mixers, refrigeration equipment & ice machines. (Woman, estab 1953, empl 45, sales $7,000,000, cert: WBENC)

4223 D. Gillette Industrial Service, Inc.
46 N Main St
Bangor, PA 18013
Contact: CEO
Tel: 610-588-4939
Email: contact@deegindustries.com
Website: www.dgindustrialservices.com

Mfr & repair commercial equipment: oven rollers, packaging equip, bakery/food equip. (Minority, Woman, estab 2003, empl 12, sales $2,000,000, cert: 8(a))

4224 Gottscho Printing Systems, Inc.
740 Veterans Circle
Warminster, PA 18974
Contact: Aimee Hasson President
Tel: 267-387-3005
Email: sales@gottscho.com
Website: www.gottscho.com

Printing machines, marking machines, bar code printing, ink jet, coding & printing, blister pack printing, hot stamp, thermal printer, T1J printer, C1J printer, flexographic printer, platen printer, UV printer, digital coder, digital printer. (Woman, estab 2009, empl 12, sales , cert: WBENC)

South Carolina

4225 USS Rhino
50 Grand Ave, Ste D
Greenville, SC 29607
Contact: Deeann Holbird Accounting Clerk
Tel: 864-233-8035
Email: accounting@rhinoassembly.com
Website: www.rhinoassembly.com

Dist industrial machinery & equipment merchant. (AA, estab 2015, empl 2, sales , cert: NMSDC)

Texas

4226 Epcon Industrial Systems
PO Box 7060
The Woodlands, TX 77387
Contact: Shan Jamaluddin COO
Tel: 936-273-3300
Email: epcon@epconlp.com
Website: www.epconlp.com

Design, engineer & mfr air pollution control systems, oxidizers, afterburners, deoilers, washlines, spray booths, ovens & furnaces. (As-Pac, estab 1977, empl 99, sales $14,000,000, cert: State, NMSDC)

4227 PLP Enterprises, Inc.
PO Box 578
Blue Ridge, TX 75424
Contact: Phillip Pulliam VP
Tel: 972-752-4837
Email: ppulliam@aps-plp.com
Website: www.aps-plp.com

Build Plastic & Stainless Steel Chemical Delivery Systems, Valve Manifold Boxes, Chemical Process Tanks, Process Hoods, Drain Pans, Chemical Carts, Storage Cabinets. PLC Control Systems, Electrical Panels, Sump Systems. (Woman, estab 2000, empl 6, sales $1,100,000, cert: WBENC)

4228 RECS, Inc.
PO Box 520
Prosper, TX 75078
Contact: Elaine Underwood President
Tel: 972-346-3226
Email: recsmaterials@windstream.net
Website: www.richmondexpress.com

Heavy construction rental equipment: excavators, rock chrushers, bulldozers, motorgraders, dumptrucks, backhoes, wheel loader/w bucket & forks, dredging machines, automobile & pickup rental, truck & trailer rental, generators lightplants. (Minority, Woman, estab 1982, empl 25, sales $5,000,000, cert: State)

Virginia

4229 Crest Foodservice Equipment Company
605 Jack Rabbit Rd
Virginia Beach, VA 23451
Contact: Karen Ricketts Business Devel
Tel: 757-425-8883
Email: karen@cresteq.com
Website: www.crestfoodservice.com

Dist commercial kitchen equipment & ancillary items. (Woman, estab 1984, empl 36, sales $11,531,745, cert: State)

4230 E2C Group, LLC
1418 Jacquelin St
Richmond, VA 23220
Contact: Denise Fields Principal
Tel: 804-358-3334
Email: dif1@aol.com
Website: www.e2cgroup.com

Dist & install commercial foodservice equipment. (AA, estab 2004, empl 6, sales $2,200,000, cert: State)

4231 VMEK Group LLC
2719 Oak Lake Blvd
Midlothian, VA 23112
Contact: Adriana Lovvorn Operations Mgr
Tel: 804-349-9001
Email: adriana@vmek.com
Website: www.vmek.com

Build & support high speed industrial machines powered by advanced vision technology & machine design. (Minority, Woman, estab 2012, empl 9, sales , cert: NMSDC)

Wisconsin

4232 Accuracy Machine
201 Stange St.
Merrill, WI 54452
Contact: Kevin Keiser Project Mgr
Tel: 715-722-0825
Email: kevin.keiser@accuracymachine.com
Website: www.accuracymachine.com

Mfr machines & specialty parts: converting, printing, coating, paper, material handling, packaging, food grade machine, performance automotive, performance marine, aerospace & powertrain industries. (As-Pac, estab 1994, empl 10, sales , cert: State)

4233 Memmert USA, LLC
W355 S9075 Godfrey Ln
Eagle, WI 53119
Contact: Tina M. Binder CEO
Tel: 262-594-3941
Email: tslaboven@memmertusa.com
Website: www.memmertusa.com

Dist ovens, incubators, climate chambers, humidity chamber, vacuum ovens, water baths, oil baths, CO2 incubators, Paraffin Ovens, Climatic test chambers, sterilizers, glassware washers. (Woman, estab 2006, empl 4, sales $2,242,000, cert: WBENC)

4234 Quintec Integration, Inc.
1600 Paramount Dr
Waukesha, WI 53186
Contact: Tony Storniolo President
Tel: 262-754-5900
Email: tstorniolo@quintecconveyor.com
Website: www.quintecconveyor.com

Layout engineering, conveyor hardware, mechanical equipment, electrical controls & programming, mechanical & electrical installation, project management, field training of equipment. (Hisp, estab 1999, empl 7, sales $10,000,000, cert: State)

4235 Trester Hoist Equipment, Inc.
W136 N4863 Campbell Dr, Ste 6
Menomonee Falls, WI 53051
Contact: Robyn Vaupel President
Tel: 262-790-0700
Email: robyn@tresterhoist.com
Website: www.tresterhoist.com

Overhead lifting equipment & service. (Woman, estab 1995, empl 11, sales $5,000,000, cert: WBENC)

West Virginia

4236 Sisterville Tank Works, Inc.
1942 McCoy St
Sisterville, WV 26175
Contact: Jason Morgan Owner
Tel: - -
Email: sales@stwinc.com
Website: www.stwinc.com

Fabricate pressure vessels, heat exchangers, boilers, condensers, cryogenics, evaporators, hoppers, reactors, stills, strippers, tanks, towers, vaporizers, nitrators, columns, autoclaves. (Woman, estab , empl 50, sales , cert: WBENC)

INFORMATION TECHNOLOGY: Services

> **INFORMATION TECHNOLOGY: Services**
> Includes system engineering/design/research, consulting, programming, information/data management, data entry, microfilming, help desk, mobile applications, etc. (See also INFORMATION TECHNOLOGY: Systems/Machines and ENGINEERING, SPECIAL SERVICES). NAICS Code 54

Alaska

4237 Tuknik Government Services, LLC
      3800 Centerpoint Dr Ste 502
      Anchorage, AK 99503
      Contact: Navid Nekoui
      Tel: 301-802-3114
      Email: nnekoui@koniag.com
      Website: www.tuknikgs.com
Outsourced computer related services, IT support, software installation & security, physical security, program management. (Nat Ame, estab 2014, empl 2, sales , cert: NMSDC)

Alabama

4238 Ariel Information Technology Corporation
      1 Chase Corporate Center Ste 400
      Birmingham, AL 35244
      Contact: Terry Pennington
      Tel: 205-705-3100
      Email: tpennington@ariel-it.com
      Website: www.ariel-it.com
Information technology consulting, staff augmentation, business analysis, requirements management, software design, system design, software development, quality assurance testing, hardware & software procurement. (AA, estab 2009, empl 1, sales , cert: NMSDC)

4239 CompuCycle, Inc.
      8019 Kempwood Dr
      Houston, AL 77055
      Contact: Kelly Hess CEO
      Tel: 713-866-8026
      Email: khess@compucycle.com
      Website: www.compucycle.com
Local & national environmentally responsible IT asset disposal services & hard drive data destruction as well as data center decommissioning. (Woman, estab 1989, empl 85, sales $15,000,000, cert: State, WBENC)

4240 Daten System Consulting
      8225 Old Pascagoula Road 36582
      Theodore, AL 36582
      Contact: Catina Short
      Tel: 866-388-3856
      Email: cshort@datensys.com
      Website: www.datensystemconsulting.com
Information technology data centric consulting organization. (Woman/AA, estab 2013, empl 5, sales $396,000, cert: State, NMSDC, WBENC)

4241 Horizon Services Corporation
      4898 Valleydale Rd Ste B-3
      Birmingham, AL 35242
      Contact: Frank Davis CEO
      Tel: 205-249-8033
      Email: contracting@horizonamerica.net
      Website: www.horizonamerica.net
Technical products & services. (AA, estab 2001, empl 30, sales $5,200,000, cert: NMSDC)

4242 Never Ending Technology, Inc.
      2225 Drake Ave Sw Ste 8
      Huntsville, AL 35805
      Contact: Laquita Nelson CEO
      Tel: 256-213-1059
      Email: lnelson@net-incorporated.com
      Website: www.net-incorporated.com
IT management, network, servers, software, distance learning system, end user computer & mobile devices. (Woman/Nat-Ame, estab , empl 6, sales , cert: 8(a))

4243 Noetic Strategies, Inc.
      1300 Meridian St N Ste 3100
      Huntsville, AL 35801
      Contact: Michael Bertoldi VP Corp Development
      Tel: 256-489-4921
      Email: marketing@noeticstrategies.com
      Website: www.noeticstrategies.com
Cyber Systems Engineering, Supply Chain Security, Application Security Testing, Threat Assessment & Management, Computer Forensics, Information Assurance, Computer Network Defense, Test & Evaluation. (Woman/Nat-Ame, estab 2006, empl 65, sales $7,280,114, cert: WBENC, 8(a))

4244 RedKnot Resource Group, LLC
      120 19th St N, Ste 2067
      Birmingham, AL 35203
      Contact: Carol Pittman CEO
      Tel: 205-901-1386
      Email: carol@redknotresources.com
      Website: www.redknotresources.com
End-to-end outsourced vendor mgmt solution governing external business arrangements. (Woman, estab 2008, empl 8, sales $1,000,000, cert: WBENC)

4245 Safety Research Corporation of America, LLC
      133 Research Lane
      Dothan, AL 36305
      Contact: Susan Crump CEO
      Tel: 334-678-7722
      Email: scrump@srca.net
      Website: www.srca.net
Information technology services: software design & development database applications, websites & graphic design services. (Woman, estab 1993, empl 16, sales $2,517,535, cert: State)

Arkansas

4246 Celerit
      2200 N Rodney Parham, Ste 205
      Little Rock, AR 72212
      Contact: Terry Rothwell President
      Tel: 501-312-2900
      Email: info@celerit.com
      Website: www.celerit.com
IT consulting: full time personnel and custon application development. (Woman, estab 1985, empl 50, sales $ 0, cert: WBENC)

4247 Dacus Fence Co. Inc.
      2729 N Church St
      Jonesboro, AR 72401
      Contact: Frankie Dacus President
      Tel: 870-932-4100
      Email: frankie@dacusfence.com
      Website: www.Dacusfence.com
Design, install & support all computer and phone networks. (Hisp, estab 1995, empl 15, sales $4,020,000, cert: 8(a))

4248 Inteliblue
       15300 Governors Lake Dr
       Little Rock, AR 72223
       Contact: Priyanka kothakanti Mgr
       Tel: 501-251-8918
       Email: priya@inteliblue.com
       Website: www.inteliblue.com
IT Consulting/Staffing. (Woman, estab 2012, empl 1, sales , cert: State)

4249 Stratice, LLC
       3070 S. Champions Dr, Ste 102
       Rogers, AR 72758
       Contact: Robin Hampton
       Tel: 479-282-7337
       Email: stratice@mystratice.com
       Website: www.mystratice.com
Recruitment Gumption, LLC platform, facilitating seamless collaboration between companies and candidates. (Woman, estab 2015, empl 20, sales $5,000,000, cert: WBENC)

Arizona

4250 Business Partner Solutions Inc.
       7362 E Rovey Ave
       Scottsdale, AZ 85250
       Contact: Katherine Bluma CEO
       Tel: 858-337-9020
       Email: kat@businesspartnersolutions.com
       Website: www.businesspartnersolutions.com
Asset intelligence, encryption, strong authentication & application security & access control. (Woman, estab 2005, empl 7, sales $2,800,000, cert: WBENC, SDB)

4251 Clutch Solutions LLC
       2152 S Vineyard Ave, Building 1, Ste 120
       Mesa, AZ 85210
       Contact: Michael Burchell Strategic Diversity Partner
       Tel: 203-393-5234
       Email: mike.burchell@clutchsolutions.com
       Website: www.clutchsolutions.com
Information technology: IT Hardware and Software Value Added Reseller, Solution Architect/engineering, Cyber-Security, Unified Communications. (Nat Ame, estab 2017, empl 58, sales $200,000,000, cert: NMSDC)

4252 Creative Enterprise Solutions LLC (dba Beyond20)
       60 E. Rio Salado Pkwy Ste 900
       Tempe, AZ 85281
       Contact: Principal
       Tel: 866-856-3117
       Email: billing@beyond20.com
       Website: www.beyond20.com
Training (ITIL, ITSM, Agile, DevOps, Cyber etc.), Consulting & ServiceNow. (Woman/Hisp, estab 2006, empl 70, sales $10,000,000, cert: 8(a))

4254 Executive Technology Inc.
       4809 E Thistle Landing Dr Ste 100
       Phoenix, AZ 85044
       Contact: Linda Perkins Controller
       Tel: 480-346-7041
       Email: lperkins@exectechdirect.com
       Website: www.exectechdirect.com
Information technology products & services. (AA, estab 2001, empl 16, sales $ 0, cert: NMSDC)

4255 Native Technology Solutions Inc.
       7065 W Allison Rd
       Chandler, AZ 85226
       Contact: Mabel Tsosie
       Tel: 480-639-1234
       Email: mtsosie@gilarivertel.com
       Website: www.native-tech.net
Cabling & computing services, structured cabling, phone, security systems, video conferencing, & technology solutions. (Nat Ame, estab 2007, empl 14, sales $4,000,000, cert: State)

4256 QCM Technologies, Inc.
       9060 E Via Linda Ste 220
       Scottsdale, AZ 85258
       Contact: Lenny Aupperlee Sales Exec
       Tel: 602-412-3539
       Email: laupperlee@qcmtech.com
       Website: www.qcmtech.com
IT solutions & services, hardware, software & professional services, design, implement & support enterprise-wide IT solutions. (Hisp, estab 2001, empl 20, sales $12,651,000, cert: NMSDC)

4257 TDR Consulting Inc
       951 N Forest Ct
       Chandler, AZ 85226
       Contact: Dean Rosales
       Tel: 480-293-4959
       Email: deanrosales@tdrconsultinginc.com
       Website: www.tdrconsultinginc.com
Engineering consulting, systems engineering, specification dev, requirements traceability, derived requirements, schedule dev, milestone, performance & metrics reporting. (Hisp, estab 2013, empl 1, sales , cert: NMSDC)

4258 TIPS Consultants LLC
       1412 E Michelle Dr
       Phoenix, AZ 85022
       Contact: Dr. Charles Fisher CFO
       Tel: 713-307-3362
       Email: cfisher@tipsconsultants.com
       Website: www.tipsconsultants.squarespace.com
Engineering consultant & training services, Enterprise Project Management (EPM) & Earned Value Management (EVM) solutions. (Woman/AA, estab 2015, empl 3, sales , cert: State)

4259 XL Technology Group, LLC
       6895 E Camelback Rd Ste 118
       Scottsdale, AZ 85251
       Contact: Michael Brown Dir
       Tel: 602-324-7474
       Email: michael@xltechnologygroup.com
       Website: www.xltechnologygroup.com
IT staffing: IT implementations & staff augmentation (contract, contract to hire, & direct hire) . (AA, As-Pac, estab 2010, empl 20, sales $2,600,000, cert: NMSDC)

California

4260 314e Corporation
       6701 Koll Center Pkwy #340
       Pleasanton, CA 94566
       Contact: Alok Sharma COO
       Tel: 646-639-1035
       Email: alok@314ecorp.com
       Website: www.314e.com
IT consulting, staffing & managed services. (As-Ind, estab 2004, empl 350, sales $26,000,000, cert: NMSDC)

INFORMATION TECHNOLOGY: Services

4261 360 IT Professionals, Inc.
3031 Tisch Way, 110 Plaza West
San Jose, CA 95128
Contact: Manmeet Manace Business Devel Dir
Tel: 510-254-3300
Email: manmeet@360itpro.com
Website: www.360itpro.com/
Programming Languages, .net, Java, PHP, Android, IOS, Python, Ruby, Enterprise Resource Planning SAP, Oracle, Microsoft AX & GP, Program Managers, Project Managers, Business Analysts & Data. (As-Pac, estab 2013, empl 93, sales $8,948,501, cert: State, NMSDC, SDB)

4262 3K Technologies LLC
161 Mission Falls Ln Ste 201
Fremont, CA 94539
Contact: Krishna Chittabathini CEO
Tel: 408-716-5900
Email: krishna@3ktechnologies.com
Website: www.3ktechnologies.com
Information technology consulting services & staffing. (Woman/As-Ind, estab 2002, empl 65, sales $24,000,000, cert: CPUC)

4263 3S Global Business Solutions
7923 Nita Ave
Canoga Park, CA 91304
Contact: Sam Mookerjee Dir corp affairs
Tel: 818-453-4403
Email: sam.mookerjee@3sgbs.com
Website: www.3sgbs.com
Information technology resources, staff augmentation, project management, IT training, IT development/ maintenance outsourcing. (As-Ind, estab 2007, empl 12, sales $895,000, cert: State, City, CPUC)

4264 4WardTech Inc.
7317 El Cajon Blvd, Ste 111, La Mesa, CA 91942
La Mesa, CA 91942
Contact: Andrew Parker President
Tel: 757-876-1735
Email: andrew@4ward.tech
Website: www.4ward.tech
Information Technology solutions & services, Cloud Computing, Internet of Things (IoT), Bluetooth Low Energy (BLE) & Beacons, Machine Learning, Chatbots, Blockchain & DevOps. (AA, estab 2016, empl 2, sales $100,000, cert: NMSDC, SDB)

4265 ABOTTS Consulting Inc.
16755 Von Karman Ave Ste 200
Irvine, CA 92606
Contact: Malar Santiago Director
Tel: 630-444-7415
Email: Malar.Santiago@abotts.com
Website: www.abotts.com
Artificial Intelligence & Machine Learning Agile Methodology Consulting & Resourcing Blockchain Technology CRM & ERP Software Integration. (Woman/As-Ind, estab 2014, empl 75, sales $8,914,127, cert: NMSDC, WBENC)

4266 AccountSight
19925 Stevens Creek Blvd Ste 100
Cupertino, CA 95014
Contact: Anita Bist VP Business Dev
Tel: 408-560-3900
Email: abist@accountsight.com
Website: www.accountsight.com
AccountSight time tracking & resource planning software, SaaS solution, eSign Genie esignature software. (Woman/As-Ind, estab 2013, empl 20, sales , cert: NMSDC)

4267 Ace Technologies, Inc.
2880 Zanker Rd, Ste 208
San Jose, CA 95134
Contact: Jessy Jaiswal Mgr
Tel: 408-228-0240
Email: jessy@acetechnologies.com
Website: www.acetechnologies.com
Information technology: software consulting, software recruitment & staffing, SAP project consulting & staffing, application development, software maintenance. (Minority, Woman, estab , empl , sales $15,170,000, cert: WBENC)

4268 Adroit Resources Inc.
39500 Stevenson Place, Ste 202
Fremont, CA 94539
Contact: Prashant Sharma Sr Dir
Tel: 510-573-6102
Email: prashant@adroitresources.com
Website: www.adroitresources.com
Information Technology services. (Minority, Woman, estab 2011, empl 75, sales $7,000,000, cert: NMSDC, CPUC)

4269 Advancio Inc.
25050 Ave Kearny
Valencia, CA 91385
Contact: Roxette Lopez Strategic Partnership Specialist
Tel: 888-407-4030
Email: roxette@advancio.com
Website: www.advancio.com
Planning & design computer systems that integrate with computer hardware, software, and communication technologies. (Minority, Woman, estab 2010, empl 50, sales $5,600,000, cert: NMSDC, WBENC)

4270 AE & Associates, LLC
506 Queensland Circle
Corona, CA 92879
Contact: Lerma Veloso Accounting Mgr
Tel: 951-278-3477
Email: lerma.v@aemedcode.com
Website: www.aeandassociatesllc.com
Medical record coding services. (As-Pac, estab 2000, empl 150, sales , cert: NMSDC)

4271 Agama Solutions Inc.
39159 Paseo Padre Pkwy Ste 216
Fremont, CA 94538
Contact: Peter Kalra VP
Tel: 510-377-9959
Email: peter@agamasolutions.com
Website: www.agamasolutions.com
IT Consulting services in terms of Project based consulting and Staffing Services of various technical hard to find skills in the area of Information technology. (As-Pac, estab 2006, empl 200, sales $3,000,000, cert: State)

4272 Agile Global Solutions, Inc
193 Blue Ravine Rd Ste 160
Folsom, CA 95630
Contact: Vasudha Krishnan President
Tel: 916-353-1780
Email: raja@agileglobalsolutions.com
Website: www.agileglobal.com
IT services (staffing) & turnkey solutions. (Woman/As-Ind, estab 2003, empl 97, sales $10,787,727, cert: State, NMSDC)

INFORMATION TECHNOLOGY: Services

4273 AgileTalent, Inc.
1900 S Norfolk Ave.
San Mateo, CA 94403
Contact: Jay Singh
Tel: 650-931-2572
Email: jay.singh@agiletalentinc.com
Website: www.agiletalentinc.com
IT contract staffing & recruiting. (As-Ind, estab 2011, empl 48, sales $4,600,000, cert: NMSDC, CPUC)

4274 AgreeYa Solutions, Inc.
605 Coolidge Dr
Folsom, CA 95630
Contact: Ajay Kaul Managing Partner
Tel: 916-294-0075
Email: sales_americas@agreeya.com
Website: www.agreeya.com
IT consulting services, staff or project based. (Minority, Woman, estab 1999, empl 1800, sales $123,300,000, cert: NMSDC, CPUC)

4275 Ahtna Contractors, LLC
3680 Industrial Blvd Ste 600H
West Sacramento, CA 95691
Contact: Jessica Vela Admin Asst
Tel: 916-329-1591
Email: jvela@ahtna.net
Website: www.ahtnacontractors.com
IT Support. (Nat-Ame, estab 2005, empl 1, sales $376,178, cert: 8(a))

4276 AKRAYA, Inc.
2901 Tasman Dr Ste 106
Santa Clara, CA 95054
Contact: Sonu Ratra President
Tel: 408-907-6400
Email: sonu.ratra@akraya.com
Website: www.akraya.com
IT consulting - Java, Microsoft, databases, Peoplesoft, Oracle, Siebel, SAP, data warehousing. (Woman/As-Ind, estab 2001, empl 390, sales $33,430,000, cert: NMSDC, CPUC, WBENC)

4277 Alicon Group, Inc.
5405 Alton Pkwy, Ste 5A514
Irvine, CA 92604
Contact: Chris Metzger Operations Coord
Tel: 949-294-9634
Email: chris@alicongroup.com
Website: www.alicongroup.com
Oracle applications technology consulting. (Minority, Woman, estab 2001, empl 4, sales $3,980,000, cert: NMSDC, NWBOC)

4278 Allfon LLC
2746 Glendon Ave
Los Angeles, CA 90064
Contact: Roya Hosseinion President
Tel: 310-470-7868
Email: roya@allfon.com
Website: www.allfon.com
Systems integration, offshore development, outsourcing services. (Woman, estab 2000, empl 50, sales $5,390,928, cert: WBENC)

4279 Alpha Omega Solutions, Inc.
3070 Saturn St, Ste 200
Brea, CA 92821
Contact: Benny Wong President
Tel: 714-996-8760
Email: bennywong@aosolutions.com
Website: www.aosolutions.com
Computer software, computer consulting, financial consulting, automotive business consulting. (As-Pac, estab 1993, empl 8, sales $1,000,000, cert: NMSDC)

4280 AMBCO Electronics Corporation
15052 Redhill Ave, Ste D
Tustin, CA 92780
Contact: Ada Xiong CEO
Tel: 714-259-7930
Email: ada@ambco.com
Website: www.ambco.com
Audiometer Manufacturer. 5 year warranty on all Ambco Audiometers from date of purchased. We repair, service, and calibrate all makes of audiometers. (Woman/As-Pac, estab 1941, empl 6, sales $1,551,400, cert: State)

4281 Amick Brown LLC
2500 Old Crow Canyon Rd Ste 425
San Ramon, CA 94583
Contact: Karen Gildea Principal
Tel: 925-820-2000
Email: karen.gildea@amickbrown.com
Website: www.amickbrown.com
SAP BI Implementation, SAP HANA, SAP BI, Strategy and Roadmaps, SAP BI Production Support, SAP BI Installations and Upgrade, Reporting, Analytics & Dashboards, SAP BI Training Workshops, SAP BI Security. (Woman/As-Ind, estab 2010, empl 35, sales $7,335,144, cert: State, CPUC, WBENC)

4282 AmmMm Inc.
28364 S Western Ave, Ste 402
Rancho Palos Verdes, CA 90275
Contact: Malee Tansavatdi CEO
Tel: 310-294-1203
Email: malee@ammminc.com
Website: www.AmmMmInc.com
Web application & design, portals, online branding, database dev, intranet. (Minority, Woman, estab 2007, empl 20, sales $ 0, cert: NMSDC)

4283 Amp Inc.
1317 E Edinger Ave
Santa Ana, CA 92705
Contact: Lydia McDonald Sales Mgr
Tel: 800-778-7928
Email: lydia.mcdonald@ampinc.biz
Website: www.ampinc.biz
Design & deliver memory & storage solutions. (Woman, estab 2007, empl 34, sales $3,000,000, cert: CPUC)

4284 Apex Computer Systems, Inc.
13875 Cerritos Corporate Dr Unit A
Cerritos, CA 90703
Contact: Ira Klein Dir Partner Alliance
Tel: 562-926-6820
Email: sales@acsi2000.com
Website: www.acsi2000.com
Computer hardware maintenance & support, managed services, project management, accounting/ERP, EDI, data warehousing, (As-Pac, estab 1984, empl 52, sales $17,010,000, cert: State, NMSDC, CPUC, SDB)

4285 APN Software Services Inc.
      39899 Balentine Dr, Ste 385
      Newark, CA 94560
      Contact: Anisha Sodha
      Tel: 510-683-9043
      Email: anisha@apninc.com
      Website: www.apninc.com
IT staffing: contract, contract to hire & direct hire. (As-Ind, estab 1996, empl 300, sales $16,000,000, cert: NMSDC)

4286 Applied Computer Solutions
      15461 Springdale St.
      Huntington Beach, CA 92649
      Contact: Cathy Fancher Operations Mgr
      Tel: 714-861-2200
      Email: cathy.fancher@acsacs.com
      Website: www.acsacs.com
System integration, strategic solutions, enterprise infrastructure, Sun Microsystems, Cisco Systems, HDS, Veritas, Oracle, Network Appliance, Checkpoint, Symantec, StorageTek. (Woman, estab 1989, empl 25, sales $206,523,000, cert: CPUC, WBENC)

4287 ARRC Enterprises, Inc
      1600 Mill Rock Way
      Bakersfield, CA 93311
      Contact: Monique Rogers Corp Admin
      Tel: 661-281-4000
      Email: monique@arrc.com
      Website: www.arrc.com
Designs and develops computer, network, telecommunication & voice & data caling needs. (Woman, estab 1992, empl 45, sales $6,000,000, cert: State)

4288 Ashunya Inc
      642 n. eckhoff St
      orange, CA 92868
      Contact: Melanie Merchant CEO
      Tel: 714-385-1900
      Email: melaniem@ashunya.com
      Website: www.ashunya.com
Information technology: hardware & software, LAN/WAN wiring, project mgmt, post implementation svcs. (Minority, Woman, estab 1993, empl 8, sales $3,000,000, cert: WBENC)

4289 Automae
      7111 Garden Grove Blvd
      Garden Grove, CA 92841
      Contact: Mbuyi Khuzadi CEO
      Tel: 714-816-3000
      Email: mbuyi@mail.automae.com
      Website: www.automae.com
Technical services: hardware design, systems engineering, software engineering, system safety & health management. (AA, estab 1997, empl 3, sales , cert: City)

4290 Automation Anywhere, Inc.
      633 River Oaks Pkwy
      San Jose, CA 95134
      Contact: Jayme Newell Strategic Partnerships
      Tel: 703-728-6887
      Email: jayme.newell@automationanywhere.com
      Website: www.automationanywhere.com
Automation platform that provides powerful features to automate complex business tasks. It is used to automate such processes that are repetitive, rule-based, and manually performed by humans. (As-Pac, estab 2010, empl 3100, sales , cert: NMSDC)

4291 Aviana Global Technologies, Inc.
      915 W Imperial Hwy Ste 100
      Brea, CA 92821
      Contact: Donna Sanchez Staffing Consultant
      Tel: 714-256-9756
      Email: donnas@avianaglobal.com
      Website: www.avianaglobal.com
Enterprise planning, reporting, OLAP analysis, dashboards, scorecards, analytics & statutory regulations. (As-Pac, estab 1994, empl 30, sales $53,822,829, cert: CPUC)

4292 Axelliant LLC
      21250 Hawthorne Blvd, Ste 500
      Torrance, CA 90503
      Contact: Mohsin Khan Procurement Mgr
      Tel: 310-377-2881
      Email: mohsin.khan@axelliant.com
      Website: www.axelliant.com
IT Solutions, Cyber Security, Date Center/ Networking, to Mobility, Cloud Life Cycle Management & UC / Collaboration. (Minority, estab 2016, empl 10, sales , cert: NMSDC)

4293 Axiom Global Technologies, Inc.
      220 North Wiget Lane
      Walnut Creek, CA 94598
      Contact: Mohit Arora
      Tel: 925-393-5800
      Email: mohit.arora@axiomglobal.com
      Website: www.axiomglobal.com
Application development, staff augmentation, document management. (Woman/As-Ind, estab 2001, empl 70, sales $6,000,000, cert: NMSDC)

4294 BayInfotech LLC
      11501, Dublin Blvd Ste 200
      Dublin, CA 94568
      Contact: Maulik Shyani Sr Acct Mgr
      Tel: 408-480-8501
      Email: maulik@bay-infotech.com
      Website: www.bay-infotech.com
Contingent Staffing, Beeline, Infrastructure Management: End-to-End Management, Application, Network, Security, Data Center, Service Desk. (Minority, Woman, estab 2011, empl 15, sales $1,101,000, cert: NMSDC, CPUC, WBENC)

4295 BayOne Solutions
      4637 Chabot Dr Ste 250
      Pleasanton, CA 94588
      Contact: Mohammed Ismail Sr Mgr MSP/VMS Program
      Tel: 925-399-0595
      Email: mismail@bayone.com
      Website: www.bayonesolutions.com
IT & Engineering - Development, testing, Mobile Apps, infrastructure, Analytics, Creative/Product & Data Science/Machine Learning. (Minority, estab 2012, empl 187, sales $54,000,000, cert: NMSDC)

4296 Beta Soft Systems Inc.
      42808 Christy St Ste 101
      Fremont, CA 94538
      Contact: Bob Hemnani Sr Sales Mgr
      Tel: 510-744-1700
      Email: bob@betasoftsystems.com
      Website: www.betasoftsystems.com
IT Services & solutions, recruitment, business development, software development & service delivery. (As-Pac, estab 2005, empl 300, sales , cert: State)

INFORMATION TECHNOLOGY: Services

4297 BeyondCurious, Inc.
3767 Overland Ave, Ste 115
Los Angeles, CA 90034
Contact: Nikki Barua CEO
Tel: 310-210-1907
Email: nbarua@beyondcurious.com
Website: www.beyondcurious.com
Design & technology, mobile interfaces. (Woman/As-Ind, estab 2011, empl 9, sales $2,289,210, cert: NMSDC)

4298 Bullock's Techology Solutions
11465 Escoba Pl
San Diego, CA 92127
Contact: Zikomo Bullock COO
Tel: 858-663-9176
Email: zbullock@bts-llc.biz
Website: www.bts-llc.biz
Program & project management, strategic business consulting, business intelligence & data integration, IV&V, staff augmentation. (Woman/As-Pac, estab 2004, empl 6, sales $600,000, cert: State)

4299 California Creative Solutions, Inc.
13475 Danielson St, Ste 220
Poway, CA 92064
Contact: Raminder Singh Accountant
Tel: 858-208-4131
Email: mbeprogram@ccsglobaltech.com
Website: www.ccsglobaltech.com
Information & Technology, software engineering, systems analysis, integration, and development. (As-Ind, estab 1997, empl 400, sales $21,600,000, cert: NMSDC)

4300 California Electronic Asset Recovery
3678 LeMay St
Mather, CA 95655
Contact: Stacey Henrikson Corporate Acct Mgr
Tel: 916-952-1711
Email: shenrikson@cearinc.com
Website: www.cearinc.com
Electronic asset recovery & recycling, Total Solution IT Asset Management & Disposition, E-Waste/E-Asset, ITAD, Data Sanitization, Recovery, Destruction/Shred, Test, Repair, Reporting. (As-Pac, estab 2000, empl 58, sales $11,000,000, cert: CPUC)

4301 Celer Systems, Inc.
1024 Iron Point Rd, Ste 100
Folsom, CA 95630
Contact: Sree Gaddam VP
Tel: 916-220-2093
Email: sree.gaddam@celersystems.com
Website: www.celersystems.com
IT consulting services, project mgmt, end to end, application dev, testing services, database mgmt, data warehouse, staff augmentation. (Minority, Woman, estab 2007, empl 25, sales $3,000,000, cert: NMSDC)

4302 Central Computer Systems Inc.
3777 Stevens Creek Blvd
Santa Clara, CA 95051
Contact: Heidi Co CEO
Tel: 408-248-5888
Email: heidi@centralcomputer.com
Website: www.CentralComputers.com
Custom-build computer systems, repair services, IT services, networking, notebook repair, corporate sales, local government sales, education sales & retail consumer sales. (Minority, Woman, estab 1986, empl 80, sales $25,000,000, cert: NMSDC, WBENC)

4303 Cerna Solutions, LLC
3304 Febo Ct
Carlsbad, CA 92009
Contact: Michelle Yu CEO
Tel: 442-222-0303
Email: michelle@cernasolutions.com
Website: www.cernasolutions.com
IT consulting services. (Minority, Woman, estab 2012, empl 6, sales , cert: NMSDC)

4304 Certified Independent Adjusters, Inc.
25000 Ave Stanford Ste 224
Valencia, CA 91390
Contact: Roosevelt Jackson Owner
Tel: 800-501-6032
Email: rosey@gociai.com
Website: www.gociai.com
(AA, estab 2010, empl 350, sales , cert: NMSDC)

4305 Clovity Inc.
11501 Dublin Blvd, Ste 200
Dublin, CA 94568
Contact: Bhawna Vats Dir Operations
Tel: 925-264-6360
Email: certifications@clovity.com
Website: www.clovity.com/
IoT-as-a-Service platform provider powered by CSensorNet and Digital Transformation professional and managed services provider in IoT Digital, Cloud and Data. (As-Pac, estab 2008, empl 100, sales , cert: NMSDC)

4306 Consult Our Sorce, LLC
2121 26th St, Ste 202
San Francisco, CA 94107
Contact: Bruin Gerber Business Dev Exec
Tel: 937-925-1336
Email: Bruin@consultoursource.com
Website: www.consultoursource.com
ITIL (Information Technology Infrastructure Library), TOGAF (The Open Group Architecture Framework), Project Management (PMP, Agile), Management Consulting Services, Information Security Consulting, Managed Services. (Hisp, estab 2014, empl 5, sales $937,564, cert: NMSDC)

4307 CPAC Inc.
4749 E. Wesley Dr
Anaheim, CA 92807
Contact: Kara Mack Natl Acct Mgr
Tel: 800-778-2722
Email: kmack@cpacinc.com
Website: www.cpacinc.com
Technical support, IT solutions. (Woman, estab 1993, empl 30, sales $20,000,000, cert: CPUC)

4308 Cyber Professionals Inc dba Encore Software
2025 Gateway Pl, Ste 385
San Jose, CA 95110
Contact: Radha Krishnan Managing Partner
Tel: 408-573-7337
Email: rkrishnan@encoress.com
Website: www.encoress.com
Mobility, social commerce, Cloud & analytics IT services. (As-Ind, estab 1998, empl 500, sales $10,679,387, cert: NMSDC)

INFORMATION TECHNOLOGY: Services

4309 Danta Technologies
561 Rush Dr
San Marcos, CA 92078
Contact: President
Tel: 619-862-3415
Email: office@dantatechnologies.net
Website: www.dantatechnologies.net
IT applications, Infrastructure, IBM WebSphere, Oracle, Sales Force, IOS developer, Network engineer, Big Data, Hadoop, Java, Angular JS, Node JS, etc. (As-Pac, estab 2013, empl 25, sales $864,000, cert: NMSDC)

4310 Delta Computer Consulting, Inc.
25550 Hawthorne Blvd Ste 106-108
Torrance, CA 90505
Contact: Alisa Spiegel VP Sales
Tel: 310-541-9440
Email: A.Spiegel@deltacci.com
Website: www.deltacci.com
Human Capital Recruiting & Deployment, IT Staff Recruiting & Augmentation. (Woman, estab 1987, empl 165, sales $28,000,000, cert: WBENC, NWBOC)

4311 Dew Software, Inc.
983 Corporate way
Fremont, CA 94539
Contact: Suresh Deopura President
Tel: 510-490-9995
Email: suresh@dewsoftware.com
Website: www.dewsoftware.com
Provide software consultants for short/long term in legacy systems, develop projects at offsite or offshore. (Minority, estab 1997, empl 25, sales $3,400,000, cert: CPUC)

4312 DFI Technologies, LLC
1065 National Dr Ste 1
Sacramento, CA 95834
Contact: Vieng Phouthachack Technical Sales Engineer
Tel: 916-568-1234
Email: vieng@dfitech.com
Website: www.dfitech.com
High performance computing solutions: Digital Signage, Interactive Kiosk, Gaming, Industrial Automation, Medical Device/Healthcare, Transportation. (As-Pac, estab 1985, empl 70, sales , cert: State)

4313 Digital Mountain
4633 Old Ironsides Dr Ste 401
Santa Clara, CA 95054
Contact: Julie Lewis CEO
Tel: 866-344-3627
Email: supplierdiversity@digitalmountain.com
Website: www.digitalmountain.com
Web-based filtering & review (FileQuest), electronic evidence collection, electronic discovery (including tape restoration), computer forensics, data breach management & expert witness services. (Woman, estab 2003, empl 5, sales $2,006,316, cert: State, CPUC, WBENC)

4314 Digitive LLC
1879 Lundy Ave Ste 219
San Jose, CA 95131
Contact: Terrina Butler
Tel: 917-913-0891
Email: michael@godigitive.com
Website: www.godigitive.com
Salesforce & Cloud Solutions, Supply Chain & Logistics Automation & AI, Digital Technology & Data Mgmt. (As-Ind, estab 2019, empl 150, sales $35,000,000, cert: NMSDC)

4315 E-Base Technologies, Inc.
39159 Paseo Padre Pkwy Ste 206
Fremont, CA 94538
Contact: Archana Kaushik President
Tel: 510-790-2547
Email: archana@ebasetek.com
Website: www.ebasetek.com
IT staffing: contract, contract-to-hire & permanent positions. (Woman/As-Ind, estab 2000, empl 69, sales $6,012,054, cert: WBENC)

4316 eJangar, Inc.
13700 Altin Pkwy, Ste 154
Irvine, CA 92618
Contact: Ayesh Natekal President
Tel: 800-259-9578
Email: ayesha@ejangar.com
Website: www.ejangar.com
IT services: staffing, project mgmt, Cloud architect, SFDC Consultants, Sharrepoint Developers, Salesforce developers, .Net, Java, Offshore Development from India, Onsite Services. (Woman/As-Ind, estab 2009, empl 25, sales , cert: CPUC)

4317 En Pointe IT Solutions, LLC
2121 Rosecrans Ave, Ste 4310 Ste 4310
El Segundo, CA 90245
Contact: Brian Huber Natl Acct Mgr
Tel: 424-220-6700
Email: brian.huber@enpointeits.com
Website: www.enpointeits.com
Provides software, hardware and IT Services. (Minority, estab 2016, empl 25, sales $150,000,000, cert: State, NMSDC, CPUC, WBENC)

4318 En Pointe Technologies Sales, Inc.
18701 S Figueroa St
Gardena, CA 90248
Contact: Michael Rapp VP Sales & Mktg
Tel: 310-337-5200
Email: helpdesk@enpointe.com
Website: www.enpointe.com
IT products & professional services. (Minority, Woman, estab 1993, empl 1200, sales $347,000,000, cert: NMSDC, WBENC)

4319 Engage Integrated Systems Technology
770 L St, Ste 950
Sacramento, CA 95814
Contact: Louis Collins President
Tel: 916-449-3977
Email: pam@engageist.com
Website: www.engageist.com
Project/Program Management, Independent Validation & Verification Systems, Design/Development Database Design & Upgrades, Disaster Recovery Planning & Business Continuity Services. (AA, estab 1997, empl 20, sales $500,000, cert: State)

4320 eTouch Systems
6627 Dumbarton Circle
Freemont, CA 94555
Contact: Amit Shah VP
Tel: 510-795-4800
Email: ashah@etouch.net
Website: www.etouch.net
Information technology services - QA, Automation, Manual, Functional, Performance, Specialized testing, Mobile testing, etc. (As-Ind, estab 1997, empl 700, sales $70,000,000, cert: NMSDC)

INFORMATION TECHNOLOGY: Services

4321 EUS IT Solutions, LLC
      19327 Broadacres Ave
      Carson, CA 90746
      Contact: Donald Hale CEO
      Tel: 562-731-2244
      Email: donhale@eusitsolutions.com
      Website: www.eusitsolutions.com
IT consulting, IT Support, pc/laptop/workstation support, Hardware/Software support, smartphone support, tablet support, network support, printer support, cloud support, do projects. (AA, estab 2012, empl 5, sales , cert: NMSDC)

4322 EYP, Inc.
      235 E Broadway Ste 800-B
      Long Beach, CA 90802
      Contact: Troy DuCre CEO
      Tel: 310-684-3022
      Email: tducre@eypinc.com
      Website: www.eypinc.com
Workforce Management, IT & engineering contract services, Software as a Service (SaaS), Talent Mgmt & Learning Mgmt, Mgmt Consulting, Business Process Improvement. (AA, estab 2011, empl 3, sales $146,000, cert: NMSDC)

4323 Flexon Technologies Inc.
      7901 Stoneridge Dr, Ste 390
      Pleasanton, CA 94588
      Contact: Sandeep Singh VP Sales
      Tel: 510-648-8878
      Email: ken@flexontechnologies.com
      Website: www.flexontechnologies.com
Our offerings are designed to cater to the entire range of clients' technology needs. (As-Ind, estab 2015, empl 52, sales $1,500,000, cert: NMSDC)

4324 Global IT Services
      180 Promenade Circle, Ste 300
      Sacramento, CA 95834
      Contact: Shavinder (Shawn) Phagura President
      Tel: 916-414-0311
      Email: sphagura@globalitsvcs.com
      Website: www.globalitsvcs.com
IT Staffing Services, Cloud & IT Consulting, and Skilled Staffing Solutions. (As-Ind, estab 2014, empl 15, sales $910,000, cert: State, NMSDC, SDB)

4325 GoAhead Solutions LLC.
      400 Oyster Point Blvd Ste 407
      South San Francisco, CA 94080
      Contact: Jaime Mendoza CEO
      Tel: 650-873-7255
      Email: jaime@goaheadsolutions.com
      Website: www.goaheadsolutions.com
IT Staff Augmentation, Consulting Services, Oracle Software Resell & Oracle Audit Representation. (Hisp, estab 2001, empl 46, sales $12,469,516, cert: NMSDC)

4326 Gray Systems, Inc.
      3160 Camino del Rio S, Ste 308
      San Diego, CA 92108
      Contact: Michelle Gray President
      Tel: 619-285-5848
      Email: mggray@graysys.com
      Website: www.graysys.com
Outsource information technology & programming professionals: project managers, helpdesk, programming & development, R&D, LAN administrators. (Woman/AA, estab 1991, empl 30, sales $5,000,000, cert: WBENC)

4327 Grove Technical Resources
      9035 Rosewood Ave
      West Hollywood, CA 90048
      Contact: Debra Polister President
      Tel: 786-390-7119
      Email: dpolister@grovetr.com
      Website: www.grovetr.com
Technical staffing & consulting services. (Woman, estab 2005, empl 2, sales , cert: CPUC, WBENC)

4328 HB Computers, Inc.
      17131 Beach Blvd, Ste B
      Huntington Beach, CA 92647
      Contact: Madiha Rajput CEO
      Tel: 714-916-9294
      Email: amir@hbcomputerz.com
      Website: www.hbcomputerz.com
Test & manage networks cables. (Woman/As-Ind, estab 2005, empl 10, sales , cert: WBENC)

4329 Heritage Global Solutions, Inc.
      230 N Maryland Ave Ste 202
      Glendale CA, CA 91206
      Contact: Jeff Estep President
      Tel: 949-501-1038
      Email: jeff.estep@heritageglobal.com
      Website: www.heritageglobal.com
IT solutions, staff augmentation. (Nat Ame, estab 2003, empl 19, sales $2,000,000, cert: State)

4330 Horologiii, Inc.
      270 Corte Colina
      Novato, CA 94949
      Contact: Rod Nash President
      Tel: 510-764-8500
      Email: rod@horologiii.com
      Website: www.horologiii.com
Energy Consulting Services & Information Technology. (AA, estab 2002, empl 1, sales , cert: CPUC)

4331 IDEAON
      1855, Gateway Blvd Ste 170
      Concord, CA 94520
      Contact: Shankar Krishna Dir
      Tel: 925-465-2175
      Email: shankar@ideaoninc.com
      Website: www.ideaoninc.com
Custom Computer Programming Services, Technology Staffing, eLearning, Virtual Training Development. (As-Ind, estab 2003, empl 5, sales $1,500,000, cert: NMSDC)

4332 IGIS Technologies Inc.
      10393 San Diego Mission Rd Ste 212
      San Diego, CA 92108
      Contact: Andres Abeyta CEO
      Tel: 619-640-2330
      Email: abeyta@igist.com
      Website: www.igist.com
GIS consulting, training & application develop. (Hisp, estab 1997, empl 11, sales $1,000,000, cert: CPUC)

4333 IMPEX Technologies, Inc.
      880 Apollo St Ste 315
      El Segundo, CA 90245
      Contact: Rajiv Shah President
      Tel: 310-320-0280
      Email: rshah@impextechnologies.com
      Website: www.impextechnologies.com
Computer hardware, software, consulting & project mgmt, enterprise storage systems, enterprise backup, regulatory compliance, business continuance & disaster recovery, security solutions & networking. (As-Ind, estab 1992, empl 10, sales $3,000,000, cert: NMSDC)

INFORMATION TECHNOLOGY: Services

4334 Infobahn Softworld, Inc.
2010 N 1st St, Ste 470
San Jose, CA 95131
Contact: Nitin Chandra VP Sales
Tel: 408-855-9616
Email: nchandra@infobahnsw.com
Website: www.infobahnsw.com
Technology, professional services and staffing solutions. (Minority, Woman, estab 1996, empl 200, sales $28,100,000, cert: NMSDC, CPUC)

4335 Information Design Consultants, Inc.
222 W 6th St, Ste 400
San Pedro, CA 90731
Contact: President
Tel: 310-707-2532
Email: informationdesign@idcinc.net
Website: www.idcinc.net
Project Management; Systems Integration (Woman/AA, estab 2002, empl 1, sales $ 0, cert: CPUC, WBENC)

4336 Infosoft Inc.
7891 Westwood Dr, Ste 113
Gilroy, CA 95020
Contact: Raj Chopra VP
Tel: 408-659-4326
Email: rchopra@infosoft-inc.com
Website: www.infosoft-inc.com
Information technology staffing & consulting. (As-Ind, estab 2000, empl 130, sales $16,330,000, cert: NMSDC)

4337 Infoyogi LLC
2320 #A Walsh Ave
Santa Clara, CA 95051
Contact: Sriram Sundaravaradan Mktg Mgr
Tel: 408-850-1700
Email: info@infoyogi.com
Website: www.infoyogi.com
Information technology, custom computer programming services, systems design services. (As-Ind, estab 1995, empl 15, sales , cert: CPUC)

4338 Integrated Spatial Solutions, Inc.
13879 Penn St
Whittier, CA 90602
Contact: Julie Henry COO
Tel: 562-693-2253
Email: jhenry@issi-gis.com
Website: www.issi-gis.com
Application devel, internet map services, systems integration, strategic planning, needs assessment, data conversion, database design, GIS mapping. (Woman, estab 1999, empl 7, sales $841,279, cert: CPUC)

4339 Intelecox inc
4660 La Jolla Village Dr Ste 100
San Diego, CA 92122
Contact: Jay Arora VP Professional Services
Tel: 408-320-4269
Email: diversity@intelecox.com
Website: www.intelecox.com
IT Staff Augmentation, IT projects, IT Managed Services, Software Development, Temp Staffing. (As-Pac, estab 2010, empl 37, sales $2,100,000, cert: NMSDC)

4340 Intelliswift Software, Inc.
39600 Balentine Dr, Ste 200
Newark, CA 94560
Contact: Payal Kanaiya VP Strategic Initiatives
Tel: 510-370-2619
Email: payal.kanaiya@intelliswift.com
Website: www.intelliswift.com
Systems integration & software services. (As-Pac, estab 2001, empl 1100, sales $80,224,959, cert: NMSDC)

4341 International Word Processing Services, Inc.
PO Box 5053
Downey, CA 90241
Contact: Mary Jones CEO
Tel: 562-900-8359
Email: mary.jones@intlword.com
Website: www.intlword.com
Technical word processing, transcription & employment placement. (Woman/AA, estab 1994, empl 2, sales , cert: State, City, CPUC)

4342 Intrinsyx Technologies
350 N Akron Rd, Bldg.19-102
Moffett Field, CA 94035
Contact: Nabil Afifi Business Coordinator
Tel: 510-266-2721
Email: nabil@intrinsyx.com
Website: www.intrinsyx.com
Information technology solutions. (Woman/As-Ind, estab 2000, empl 50, sales $7,137,776, cert: State, NMSDC)

4343 IP International, Inc.
1510 Fashion Island Blvd, Ste 104
San Mateo, CA 94404
Contact: Margaret Schaninger CEO
Tel: 650-403-7840
Email: info@infoplusintl.com
Website: www.infoplusintl.com
IT consulting services: project mgmt & PMO, ERP, help desk & contact center, cost mgmt savings, bill audit & mgmt, ordering & provisioning, business case development, RFP & RFI creation, vendor mgmt & selection. (Woman, estab 1986, empl 50, sales $15,000,000, cert: CPUC, WBENC)

4344 IsComp Systems Inc.
5777 W Century Blvd, Ste 560
Los Angeles, CA 90045
Contact: Joshlyn Black Sr Acct Exec
Tel: 310-641-3260
Email: jblack@iscompsystems.com
Website: www.iscompsystems.com
Unix system integration, systems engineering, software develop, database mgmt. (AA, estab 1986, empl 20, sales $ 0, cert: CPUC)

4345 iTalent Corporation
27 Devine St Ste 20
San Jose, CA 95110
Contact: Silvia Quintanilla Dir
Tel: 408-428-2641
Email: silvia@italentdigital.com
Website: www.italentdigital.com
Global technology consulting services, Software Development Solutions, Innovative & Flexible Consulting Project Resource Solutions, Specialized Practices, Managed Services, Social Knowledge Management, Change Management. (Minority, Woman, estab 2005, empl 150, sales $25,000,000, cert: NMSDC, WBENC)

4346 JAUST Consulting Partners Inc.
3150 Almaden Exprwy Ste 215
San Jose, CA 95118
Contact: Gail D'Silva Founder
Tel: 408-805-0901
Email: gail@jaustpartners.com
Website: www.jaustpartners.com
IT solutions, ERP, CRM, SCM, Analytics & Web services, development & application integration. (Woman/Hisp, estab 2005, empl 8, sales $ 0, cert: NMSDC)

4347 Kaygen, Inc.
      15420 Laguna Canyon Road Ste 270
      Irvine, CA 92618
      Contact: Rashmi Chaturvedi President
      Tel: 949-203-5100
      Email: rashmi.chaturvedi@kaygen.com
      Website: www.kaygen.com
Oracle Enterprise Resource Planning (ERP). (Minority, Woman, estab 2003, empl 45, sales $13,000,000, cert: State, City, NMSDC, WBENC)

4348 Kutir Corporation
      37600 Central Ct, Ste 280
      Newark, CA 94560
      Contact: Prathiba Kalyan Sr Business Mgr
      Tel: 510-870-0227
      Email: prathiba@kutirtech.com
      Website: www.kutirtech.com
Contract & permanent staffing, custom software development, business & technology consulting, systems integration, technical support, admin, testing & support, data warehousing, business intelligence. (As-Ind, estab 2003, empl 40, sales $3,400,000, cert: NMSDC, CPUC, 8(a))

4349 Laboratory Data Consultants, Inc.
      2701 Loker Ave. West Ste 220
      Carlsbad, CA 92010
      Contact: Laura Soeten Exec Admin
      Tel: 760-827-1100
      Email: Lsoeten@lab-data.com
      Website: www.lab.data.com
Data validation and data management services. (As-Pac, estab 1991, empl 36, sales $3,940,313, cert: CPUC)

4350 LocalBizNetwork
      3141 Stevens Creek Blvd, Ste 358
      San Jose, CA 95117
      Contact: Indu Jayakumar President
      Tel: 408-741-8184
      Email: info@localbiznetwork.com
      Website: www.localbiznetwork.com
Custom software applications: Internet, Internet based online survey forms, computation of survey data, Internet marketing, SEO, Internet publishing, blogging, website development & hosting. (Woman/As-Ind, estab 2002, empl 22, sales , cert: CPUC)

4351 LogixService, Inc.
      1383 Calle Avanzado
      San Clemente, CA 92673
      Contact: Van Boone CEO
      Tel: 949-400-6083
      Email: vboone@amtek.net
      Website: www.amtek.net
Computer Support Services: IBM, HP, DELL, Compaq, Gateway, EMC, NetApp, Cisco, etc. (AA, estab 1980, empl 12, sales $2,100,000, cert: State, NMSDC)

4352 Luminous Tec LLC
      15481 Red Hill Ave, Ste B
      Tustin, CA 92780
      Contact: Uma Sharma Dir new business devel
      Tel: 949-630-0448
      Email: usharma@luminoustec.com
      Website: www.luminoustec.com
IT & non IT staffing & consulting services: project managers, business & technical architects, business analysts, applications development resources, systems integration specialists. (Minority, Woman, estab 2006, empl 5, sales $750,000, cert: CPUC)

4353 MalikCo
      900 E. Hamilton Ave Ste 100
      Campbell, CA 95008
      Contact: Stephynie Malik CEO
      Tel: 408-879-7447
      Email: smalik@malikco.com
      Website: www.malikco.com
Information technology svcs, software consulting, architecture, integration & implementation staff consulting. (Minority, Woman, estab 2003, empl 112, sales $461,000,000, cert: WBENC)

4354 Meijun LLC
      9888 Carroll Centre Rd Ste#210
      San Diego, CA 92126
      Contact: Huy Ly
      Tel: 619-333-8698
      Email: hly@meijun.cc
      Website: www.meijun.cc
Web development & marketing agency, custom software solutions, web & mobile development, design & strategy, digital marketing services, SEO, content marketing & marketing automation integration. (As-Pac, estab 2011, empl 5, sales , cert: NMSDC, CPUC)

4355 Metabyte Inc.
      39350 Civic Center Dr Ste 200
      Fremont, CA 94538
      Contact: Unni Krishnan Business Devel Mgr
      Tel: 510-494-9700
      Email: unnik@metabyte.com
      Website: www.metabyte.com
IT Services, High Technology & ISV, Life Sciences & Healthcare, Manufacturing & Logistics, Banking & Financial Services, Speciality Retail, Telecom & Media. (As-Pac, estab 1993, empl 235, sales $ 0, cert: NMSDC)

4356 Method360, Inc
      One Post St, Ste 550
      San Francisco, CA 94104
      Contact: Heather Swanson Operations Mgr
      Tel: 415-956-6360
      Email: hswanson@method360.com
      Website: www.method360.com
Business Intelligence & Enterprise Application initiatives. (Hisp, estab 2001, empl 60, sales , cert: NMSDC, CPUC)

4357 Microland Electronics Corporation
      1883 Ringwood Ave
      San Jose, CA 95131
      Contact: Liny Yu Sales Rep
      Tel: 800-632-1688
      Email: linyy@microlandusa.com
      Website: www.microlandusa.com
Computing technology products, services and solutions, mass storage solutions, controllers, high-end systems, peripherals and components. (As-Pac, estab 1986, empl 57, sales $67,000,000, cert: NMSDC)

4358 Millennium Franchise Group
      1432 Broadway
      Oakland, CA 94612
      Contact: Tony Beaman President
      Tel: 510-454-9955
      Email: tony.beaman@hackingsolutions.com
      Website: www.millsolgroup.com
Cyber security solutions - penetration testing, vulnerability scanning, risk analysis, compliance, application security, network security, wireless security. (AA, estab 2013, empl 5, sales $950,000, cert: NMSDC, CPUC, 8(a))

INFORMATION TECHNOLOGY: Services

4359 Mission Critical Technologies, Inc.
2041 Rosecrans Ave Ste 220
El Segundo, CA 90245
Contact: Patti Converse
Tel: 310-246-4455
Email: patti_converse@mctinc.com
Website: www.mctinc.com
Technology solutions: relational database, application design & implementation, custom software dev, outsourcing, offsite dev projects, graphic design & development. (Woman, estab 1993, empl 50, sales , cert: WBENC)

4360 Mobilematics, Inc.
2528 Qume Dr, Ste 2
San Jose, CA 95131
Contact: Dominick Borrello Business Devel Mgr
Tel: 408-609-1220
Email: dominick@mobilematics.us.com
Website: www.mobilematics.us.com
IT hardware & software, training, configuration, etc. (Minority, Woman, estab 2012, empl 5, sales $100,000,000, cert: State, NMSDC, WBENC)

4361 MSRCOSMOS LLC
6200 StoneRidge Mall Rd, Ste 300
Pleasanton, CA 94588
Contact: Rajkumar Bogam Lead Sales
Tel: 321-332-6344
Email: rajj@msrcosmos.com
Website: www.msrcosmos.com
IT services, mobile application, web applications, cloud solutions, analytics, infrastructure management & offshore consulting. (Woman, estab 2008, empl 84, sales $6,000,000, cert: WBENC)

4362 Mudrasys Inc.
6200 Stoneridge Mall Rd, Ste 300
Pleasanton, CA 94588
Contact: Narsi Ayyagari CEO
Tel: 925-353-3888
Email: narsi@mudrasys.com
Website: www.mudrasys.com
AWS Cloud Transformation, Salesforce, ERP Tech, Gen AI, Solution Studio, Artificial Intelligence, Architectures & Engineering. (Woman/As-Ind, estab 2009, empl 59, sales $4,200,000, cert: NMSDC, CPUC)

4363 NexInfo Solutions, Inc.
1851 E First St Ste 900
Santa Ana, CA 92705
Contact: Kate Duffy Client Relations
Tel: 714-955-6970
Email: kate.duffy@nexinfo.com
Website: www.nexinfo.com
ERP solutions, PLM solutions, Supply Chain Planning, Software implementations, Manged Services, Technical consulting, Functional consulting, Techno Functional Consulting, business process design, Global order promising. (As-Ind, estab 1999, empl 300, sales , cert: NMSDC)

4364 Northbound LLC
961 E Arques Ave
Sunnyvale, CA 94085
Contact: Leena Menon Operations Mgr
Tel: 408-333-9885
Email: supplierdiversity@northboundllc.com
Website: www.northboundllc.com
IT contract & full-time placement services. (Woman/As-Ind, estab 1998, empl 150, sales $ 0, cert: NMSDC)

4365 Omni2max, Inc.
1202 Morena Blvd, Ste 100
San Diego, CA 92110
Contact: Javonda Franklin Business Devel Mgr
Tel: 619-269-1663
Email: javonda.franklin@omni2max.com
Website: www.omni2max.com
Information Assurance, Information Technology, Logistics, Engineering, Contract Management, Help Desk Management & CRM, Systems Engineering, Program Management & Performance Based Acquisition. (AA, estab 2009, empl 25, sales $1,500,000, cert: State, 8(a))

4366 Omnikron Systems Inc.
20920 Warner Center Lane Ste A
Woodland Hills, CA 91367
Contact: Robin Borough President
Tel: 818-223-4115
Email: robin.borough@omnikron.com
Website: www.Omnikron.com
Applications development (ERP), database, reporting, business intelligence, operations, infrastructure, security & business personnel. (As-Pac, estab 1980, empl 50, sales $8,000,000, cert: CPUC)

4367 OrangePeople
300 Spectrum Dr Ste 400
Irvine, CA 92618
Contact: Natasha Myers VP
Tel: 949-667-1762
Email: natasha.myers@orangepeople.com
Website: www.orangepeople.com
Business strategy, architecture & program management. (As-Pac, estab 2006, empl 70, sales $1,800,000, cert: NMSDC)

4368 Partner Engineering and Science, Inc.
1990 E Grand Ave, Ste 100
El Segundo, CA 90245
Contact: Sean Rakhshani Principal
Tel: 800-419-4923
Email: srakhshani@partneresi.com
Website: www.partneresi.com
Software engineering, modeling & simulation, research & development & consulting services. (Woman, estab 2006, empl 120, sales $22,700,000, cert: WBENC)

4369 Perlinski & Company
30025 Alicia Pkwy, Ste 107
Laguna Niguel, CA 92677
Contact: Isabel Perlinski CEO
Tel: 949-481-5482
Email: isabel.perlinski@perlinskico.com
Website: www.perlinskico.com
Provide management consulting. (Minority, Woman, estab 1989, empl 2, sales $244,250, cert: NMSDC, WBENC, 8(a))

4370 Pinpoint Resource Group, LLC
1960 E Grand Ave Ste 1260
El Segundo, CA 90245
Contact: Felix Lin President
Tel: 310-356-8123
Email: felix@pinpoint.jobs
Website: www.pinpoint.jobs
Information technology staffing: consultants & direct hire, systems analysts, project managers & management personnel. (As-Pac, estab 2004, empl 15, sales $4,500,000, cert: NMSDC)

INFORMATION TECHNOLOGY: Services

4371 PM Business Holdings LLC
733 Hindry Ave, Ste C205
Inglewood, CA 90301
Contact: Derrick Ferguson CEO
Tel: 310-242-3171
Email: pmbh14@gmail.com
Website: www.brilliantmindssolutions.com
Computer Systems Design Services, employment placement & executive search services (AA, estab 2012, empl 1, sales , cert: NMSDC)

4372 Premium Technologies, Inc.
PO Box 757
Palm Desert, CA 92261
Contact: Stanway Wong President
Tel: 760-340-4603
Email: stanwong@premium-technologies.com
Website: www.premium-technologies.com/
Computer software design & dev, data integration, physical asset mgmt, computerized maintenance mgmt system (CMMS) & enterprise asset mgmt (EAM). (As-Pac, estab 1993, empl 1, sales , cert: NMSDC, CPUC)

4373 Primitive Logic Inc.
704 Samsone St
San Francisco, CA 94111
Contact: COO
Tel: 415-248-0847
Email:
Website: www.primitivelogic.com
Digital & Business Strategy, Customer Experience Management, Customer Relationship Management & Digital Marketing, Enterprise Analytics. (Woman, estab 1984, empl 60, sales $34,000,000, cert: CPUC, WBENC)

4374 Progressive Technology Solutions
500 E Calaveras
Milpitas, CA 95035
Contact: Rumi Bordoloi Account/Relationship Mgr
Tel: 408-507-7106
Email: hr@ptsol.com
Website: www.ptsol.com
Business, Functional Technical consultants and permanent staff/workforce, SAP, Oracle, Internet Technology, Data Management and Analysis, ETL and Datawarehousing, Release and Change Management. (Woman/As-Ind, estab 2002, empl 50, sales $6,650,000, cert: NMSDC)

4375 Propane Studio
1153 Mission St
San Francisco, CA 94103
Contact: Neil Chaudhari CXO
Tel: - -
Email: neil@propanestudio.com
Website: www.propanestudio.com
Websites & Applications, Responsive Websites, Tech Arch Consulting, E-Commerce Dev, UX Prototyping & Testing, Mobile & Online Applications, Content Strategy & Migration, CMS Consulting, Strategic Digital Consulting. (As-Ind, estab 2003, empl 20, sales $5,000,000, cert: NMSDC)

4376 Prospance Inc
4221 Business Center Dr. Ste - 1
Fremont, CA 94538
Contact: Santhosh Sundaram Dir Client Service
Tel: 510-240-7085
Email: santhosh.s@prospanceinc.com
Website: www.prospanceinc.com
Short and long term IT services in the mainstream and emerging technologies. (Minority, Woman, estab 2009, empl 178, sales $25,000,000, cert: NMSDC, CPUC)

4377 Prosum, Inc.
2201 Park Place, Ste 102
El Segundo, CA 90245
Contact: Ravi Chatwani CEO
Tel: 310-426-0609
Email: ravi.chatwani@prosum.com
Website: www.prosum.com
Technology staffing services, technology consulting services, technology product sales. (Minority, estab 1996, empl 250, sales $38,000,000, cert: NMSDC, CPUC)

4378 Qsolv Inc.
1735 N First St, Ste 302
San Jose, CA 95112
Contact: President
Tel: 408-429-0918
Email:
Website: www.qsolv-inc.com
Cloud Automation Services, Network management and Networking products, virtualization, automation and orchestration solutions. (Minority, Woman, estab 1999, empl 150, sales $ 0, cert: NMSDC, WBENC)

4379 QualityWorks Consulting Group, LLC
6018 S Citrus Ave
Los Angeles, CA 90043
Contact: Aurelia Crews VP Sales
Tel: 310-467-5122
Email: sales@qualityworkscg.com
Website: www.qualityworkscg.com
Automated & manual web & mobile testing, Integrated automation test frameworks for web & mobile, DevOps/Continuous Integration Support, API/microservices testing, Agile QA coaching & training. (Woman/AA, estab 2010, empl 40, sales $2,287,690, cert: NMSDC, WBENC)

4380 RaviG Inc. dba Salient Global Technologies
510 Garcia Ave, Ste E
Pittsburg, CA 94565
Contact: Ravikanth Ganapavarapu President
Tel: 925-526-1234
Email: rganapa@salientglobaltech.com
Website: www.salientglobaltech.com
End-to-end business applications & IT infrastructure. (As-Pac, estab 1999, empl 45, sales $8,323,350, cert: NMSDC)

4381 Raycom Data Technologies, Inc.
1320 E Imperial Ave
El Segundo, CA 90245
Contact: Ayaz Pandhiani President
Tel: 310-322-5113
Email: ayaz@raycomdtech.com
Website: www.raycomdtech.com
Document archiving software, document management services, document scanning, conversion services, microfiche & microfilm. (As-Pac, estab 1978, empl 10, sales $1,165,000, cert: State)

4382 Related Technologies, Inc.
81 Blue Ravine Rd Ste 230
Folsom, CA 95630
Contact: Cheryl Borgonah Mgr
Tel: 916-357-5902
Email: cherylb@relatedtech.com
Website: www.relatedtech.com/
Technical & Functional SAP consultants & Subject Matter Experts, implementations, upgrades, enhancements & support. (Woman/As-Ind, estab 2002, empl 150, sales , cert: CPUC)

4383 RJT Compuquest
       222 N Sepulveda Blvd. Ste 2250
       El Segundo, CA 90245
       Contact: Vivek Bhatia Sr Accounts Exec
       Tel: 310-421-1297
       Email: vivek@rjtcompuquest.com
       Website: www.rjtcompuquest.com
IT solutions, SAP, Oracle, WB, web development, CRM & archiving solutions, staff augmentation. (As-Pac, estab 1996, empl 300, sales $46,000,000, cert: NMSDC)

4384 RKG Technologies Inc
       11 Antietam
       Irvine, CA 92620
       Contact: Raju Gottimukkala President
       Tel: 949-910-1262
       Email: grkraju@hotmail.com
       Website: www.rkgtech.com
Strategic consulting, staffing & staff augmentation, training, vendor mgmt & outsourcing. (As-Ind, estab 2004, empl 20, sales $465,000, cert: City, NMSDC, CPUC)

4385 RPM Engineers, Inc.
       102 Discovery
       Irvine, CA 92618
       Contact: Raymond Phua Principal
       Tel: 949-450-1229
       Email: marisolv@rpmpe.com
       Website: www.rpmpe.com
Engineering services. (As-Pac, estab 1993, empl 17, sales $1,727,000, cert: State)

4386 SA Technologies Inc.
       5201 Great America Pkwy, Ste #441 Ste 441
       Santa Clara, CA 95054
       Contact: Priyanka Joshi President
       Tel: 408-986-0152
       Email: priyanka.joshi@satechglobal.com
       Website: www.satechglobal.com
Information technology consulting & staffing. (Woman/As-Ind, estab , empl , sales $10,800,000, cert: NWBOC)

4387 SD Shredding, Inc.
       7263 Engineer Rd Ste C
       San Diego, CA 92111
       Contact: Todd M Hoover CFO
       Tel: 858-492-9600
       Email: todd.hoover@proshred.com
       Website: www.proshred.com
On-site document & computer hard drive shredding. (Woman, estab 2010, empl 3, sales $200,000, cert: WBENC)

4388 Shimento Inc.
       1350 Hayes St, Ste B4
       Benecia, CA 94510
       Contact: Raj Sharma President
       Tel: 877-211-8708
       Email: jake.gaetti@shimento.com
       Website: www.shimento.com
Staff augmentation, IT services & direct hire. (As-Ind, estab 2009, empl 80, sales $12,000,000, cert: NMSDC)

4389 Shirubaa Inc
       209 E Java Dr Unit 6041
       Sunnyvale, CA 94089
       Contact: Babi Thapa CEO
       Tel: 408-306-6101
       Email: babi@shirubaa.com
       Website: www.shirubaa.com
Cloud technology, Storage Solution & Data Center Management. (Woman/As-Ind, estab 2011, empl 11, sales , cert: NMSDC, WBENC)

4390 Sidebench Studios
       10317 Washington Blvd.
       Culver City, CA 90232
       Contact: Nate Schier Dir of Staff & Co-Founder
       Tel: 808-294-5948
       Email: nate@sidebench.com
       Website: www.sidebench.com
App design, development & strategy. (As-Pac, estab 2012, empl 13, sales $1,342,459, cert: NMSDC, CPUC)

4391 Sigmaways, Inc
       39737 Paseo Padre Pkwy
       Fremont, CA 94538
       Contact: Prakash Sadasivam Founder & CEO
       Tel: 510-713-7800
       Email: info@sigmaways.com
       Website: www.sigmaways.com
Software product, technology innovation & staff augmentation. (As-Ind, estab 2006, empl 85, sales $8,300,000, cert: NMSDC)

4392 Sohum Inc
       1055 Minnesota Ave, Ste 6
       San Jose, CA 95125
       Contact: Vandana Patil President
       Tel: 408-265-2391
       Email: marketing@sohum.biz
       Website: www.sohum.biz
Software UX design, web & mobile, Software Design & Development, Cloud based software deployment & monitoring. (Woman/As-Ind, estab 1998, empl 5, sales $300,000, cert: State)

4393 Solugenix Corporation
       7700 Irvine Center Dr Ste 800
       Irvine, CA 92618
       Contact: Dir
       Tel: 949-266-0938
       Email: info@solugenix.com
       Website: www.solugenix.com
Application Lifecycle Management: Project & Requirements Management, Custom Application Development, Testing & Quality Assurance, Change & Release Management, Level 2 & Level 3 Production Support. (As-Ind, estab 2004, empl 52, sales $27,583,910, cert: NMSDC)

4394 Source Diversified, Inc.
       1206 Vista Cantora
       San Clemente, CA 92672
       Contact: Alfred Ortiz President
       Tel: 949-940-0450
       Email: aortiz@sourced.com
       Website: www.sourced.com
Command & control systems, security alerting systems, flight test support svcs, aircraft system integration, software dev, construction automation software, network installation, mission control room support svcs. (Hisp, estab 1987, empl 3, sales $ 0, cert: State)

4395 SPK and Associates, LLC
       5011 Scotts Valley Dr
       Scotts Valley, CA 95030
       Contact: Michael Roberts VP Sales & Marketing
       Tel: 888-310-4540
       Email: mroberts@spkaa.com
       Website: www.spkaa.com
IT, Infrastructure, implementation, support, training, data migration, Staffing, Large Data Storage/Management, Network Management, Product Development, Software Programming, Web Administrators (Woman, estab 2003, empl 17, sales $2,882,705, cert: WBENC)

INFORMATION TECHNOLOGY: Services

4396 SRS Consulting Inc.
39465 Paseo Padre Pkwy, Ste 1100
Fremont, CA 94538
Contact: Aswath Panduranga Business Devel Mgr
Tel: 510-252-0625
Email: aswath@srsconsultinginc.com
Website: www.srsconsultinginc.com
IT Development, Custom Software Development, R&D/Product Development/Re-engineering, Testing and Quality Assurance, Network Security Services, ERP/EAI consulting & implementation, CRM, SCP, BPM, CMS, DMS, e-Governance, Mobile Security. (Woman/As-Ind, estab 2002, empl 250, sales $46,000,000, cert: NMSDC, WBENC)

4397 Stratitude
6601 Koll Center Pkwy, Ste 132
Pleasanton, CA 94566
Contact: Khannan Sankaran CEO
Tel: 510-461-3981
Email: khannan@stratitude.com
Website: www.stratitude.com
IT services, implementation & staffing, software advisory, design, development & testing services, SAP, Microsoft, Java, Salesforce.com , Netsuite, Pega BPM, Guidewire Temenos, Veeva. (As-Ind, estab 2006, empl 36, sales $3,600,000, cert: NMSDC)

4398 Sun MicroSolutions Inc.
29 Avanzare St
Irvine, CA 92606
Contact: Ruchi Mitra CEO
Tel: 949-387-9878
Email: ruchi@sunmicrousa.com
Website: www.sunmicrousa.com
IT consulting, staffing & training. (Minority, Woman, estab 2000, empl 5, sales $540,000, cert: City)

4399 Sunny City Enterprises, Inc.
959 Mount Whitney Ct
Chula Vista, CA 91913
Contact: Francisco Esparza President
Tel: 619-250-5970
Email: francisco.esparza@sbcitpros.com
Website: www.sbcitpros.com
IT & Telecom services, Technology Services, Software Solutions & Applications, Staffing Augmentation. (Hisp, estab 2007, empl 10, sales $1,500,000, cert: NMSDC, CPUC)

4400 Sunrise Global Solutions, Inc.
30 Monroe, Ste 101
Irvine, CA 92620
Contact: Neetu Sadhwani President
Tel: 949-331-3678
Email: neetu@sunrisegroupinc.com
Website: www.sunrisegroupinc.com
IT Consulting, Computer related services. (Woman/As-Pac, estab 2008, empl 2, sales $450,000, cert: CPUC, WBENC)

4401 SupplierGATEWAY LLC
20 Corporate Park Ste 118
Irvine, CA 92606
Contact: Adenuga Solaru CEO
Tel: 949-525-9205
Email: ade.solaru@suppliergateway.com
Website: www.suppliergateway.com
IT solutions & consulting svcs: end-to-end collaborative supply chain solution. (AA, estab 1997, empl 15, sales $2,500,000, cert: NMSDC, CPUC)

4402 Svitla Systems, Inc.
100 Meadowcreek Dr, Ste 102
Corte Madera, CA 00949
Contact: Khrystyna Zahorodnichok Dir Enterprise Accounts
Tel: 650-741-1387
Email: k.zahorodnichok@svitla.com
Website: www.svitla.com
Support and help desk support. (Woman, estab 2003, empl 300, sales $12,037,432, cert: WBENC)

4403 Sycomp a Technology Company., Inc.
950 Tower Lane Ste 1785
Foster City, CA 94404
Contact: Stacy Hunter
Tel: 650-312-8174
Email: shunter@sycomp.com
Website: www.sycomp.com
Design, implement & deliver complex, heterogeneous Infrastructure, Software & Security technology solutions. (Minority, Woman, estab 1994, empl 80, sales $120,000,000, cert: NMSDC)

4404 SysIntelli, Inc.
9466 Black Mountain Road, Ste. 200
San Diego, CA 92126
Contact: CEO
Tel: 858-271-1600
Email: info@sysintelli.com
Website: www.sysintelli.com
Software Development Life Cycle, Re-engineering & Legacy Migration, Database Administration, Quality Assurance Testing & Validation, E-Commerce, Data Processing, Software Maintenance & Support. (As-Ind, estab 2005, empl 55, sales $16,690,351, cert: NMSDC)

4405 Systems Integration Solutions, Inc.
1255 Treat Blvd. Ste 100
Walnut Creek, CA 94597
Contact: Nick Bata Reg acct dir
Tel: 952-220-7549
Email: nbata@sisinc.com
Website: www.sisinc.com
IT consulting & executive search services. (Minority, estab 1990, empl 150, sales $30,000,000, cert: CPUC)

4406 Tap3Solutions
2279 Eagle Glen Pkwy, Ste 112-444
Corona, CA 92883
Contact: Catrina Snell-Rehder President
Tel: 949-229-1910
Email: catrina@tap3solutions.com
Website: www.Tap3Solutions.com
Information technology & human capital solutions. (Woman/AA, estab 2015, empl 2, sales , cert: State, City)

4407 TechLink Systems, Inc.
2 Embarcadero Center Ste 2240
San Francisco, CA 94111
Contact: Shannon Proverbs Mgr Business Dev
Tel: 415-732-7580
Email: sproverbs@techlinksystems.com
Website: www.techlinksystems.com
Information technology, engineering, scientific & biotech, application development. (Minority, Woman, estab 1998, empl 141, sales $23,560,181, cert: NMSDC, WBENC)

INFORMATION TECHNOLOGY: Services

4408   Technossus LLC
4000 MacArthur Blvd Ste 100
Newport Beach, CA 92660
Contact: Dave LaJeunesse Dir of Sales
Tel: 949-769-3522
Email: info@technossus.com
Website: www.technossus.com
Custom software develop, Microsoft technology stack, application development, desktop, enterprise & web-based, mobile applications, SharePoint & Dynamics CRM, proprietary systems development & enhancement. (As-Ind, estab 2008, empl 25, sales $4,700,000, cert: NMSDC)

4409   Tellus Solutions, Inc
3350 Scott Blvd 34A
Santa Clara, CA 95054
Contact: HR/Business Dev
Tel: 408-850-2942
Email: contact@tellussol.com
Website: www.tellussol.com
Information technology services. (Minority, Woman, estab 2005, empl 67, sales $5,320,000, cert: NMSDC, WBENC, 8(a))

4410   TESCRA
2440 Camino Ramon, Ste 263
San Ramon, CA 94583
Contact: Pradeep Kumar Marketing Exec
Tel: 925-415-5290
Email: pradeepkumar.g@tescra.com
Website: www.tescra.com
Systems integration & ERP solutions, enterprise solutions. (Minority, Woman, estab 2002, empl 220, sales $16,000,000, cert: NMSDC)

4411   The LSC Group, Inc.
200 Spectrum Center Dr 3rd Fl
Irvine, CA 92618
Contact: Troy Humphrey CEO
Tel: 800-572-9280
Email: troy.humphrey@yourlscgroup.com
Website: www.yourlscgroup.com
Electronic Discovery, Data Collection, Data Processing, Data Production, Forensic Date Discovery, Litigation Support, Records Management, Early Case Assessment, Webhosting, Project Management, Consulting. (AA, estab 2007, empl 1, sales $125,000, cert: NMSDC, CPUC)

4412   Thomas Gallaway Corporation
100 Spectrum Center Dr Ste 700
Irvine, CA 92618
Contact: Shari Jones Client Vendor Relations
Tel: 949-716-9500
Email: vendorbids@technologent.com
Website: www.technologent.com
Sun Microsystems hardware & service, multi vendor support, Finisar, Sharkrak, Storedge Tek, Oracle & Veritas. (Woman, estab 2002, empl 265, sales $651,000,000, cert: WBENC)

4413   Thoughtpowers LLC
1919 Williams St Ste 215
Simi Valley, CA 93065
Contact: Surendra Kulkarni President
Tel: 805-433-4950
Email: surendra@thoughtpowers.com
Website: www.thoughtpowers.com
Custom Application IT development & management, IT consulting services, IT resources, technical resources. (Minority, estab 2008, empl 1, sales $ 0, cert: NMSDC)

4414   Trabus
3547 Camino Del Rio South
San Diego, CA 92108
Contact: Arthur Salindong Principal
Tel: 619-220-8000
Email: art@trabus.com
Website: www.trabus.com
Providing Disruptive Advances in Wireless, Cybersecurity and Artificial Intelligence (As-Pac, estab 2010, empl 30, sales $ 0, cert: NMSDC)

4415   Trident Consulting
2410 Camino Ramon, Ste 183
San Ramon, CA 94583
Contact: Shabana Siraj CEO
Tel: 925-683-5166
Email: Farhaan@Tridentconsultinginc.com
Website: www.Tridentconsultinginc.com
IT staffing and technology company. (Woman/As-Ind, estab 2005, empl 80, sales $12,908,447, cert: State, NMSDC, WBENC)

4416   Trinus Corporation
225 South Lake Ave, Ste 1080
Pasadena, CA 91101
Contact: Harshada Kucheria President
Tel: 818-246-1143
Email: harshada_kucheria@trinus.com
Website: www.trinus.com
IT consulting & implementation services, business consulting, systems integration & outsourcing. (Woman/As-Ind, estab 1995, empl 250, sales $ 0, cert: NMSDC, CPUC, WBENC, SDB)

4417   Two Shea Consulting, Inc.
1009 Oak Hill Rd, Ste 202
Lafayette, CA 94549
Contact: Maureen Shea CEO
Tel: 925-962-7432
Email: maureen@twoshea.com
Website: www.twoshea.com
IT consulting & recruiting services. (Woman, estab 2000, empl 25, sales $5,000,000, cert: City, WBENC)

4418   Two Way Direct, Inc.
3262 Grey Hawk Ct
Carlsbad, CA 92010
Contact: Ron Bevard
Tel: 866-938-5586
Email: ron@twowaydirect.com
Website: www.twowaydirect.com
First Net for first responders. (Hisp, estab 2006, empl 30, sales $3,000,000, cert: NMSDC)

4419   VARITE, Inc.
111 North Market St, Ste 730
San Jose, CA 95113
Contact: Adarsh Katyal CEO
Tel: 408-977-0700
Email: katyal@varite.com
Website: www.varite.com
Technical consulting & staffing, customized onshore, near shore & offshore solutions. (As-Ind, estab 2000, empl 49, sales $9,500,000, cert: NMSDC, CPUC)

4420 Versa Shore Inc.
      1999 S Bascom Ave Ste 700
      Campbell, CA 95008
      Contact: Shawn Rao CEO
      Tel: 408-874-8330
      Email: shawnrao@versashore.com
      Website: www.versashore.com
IT Consulting, staffing, Microsoft APS, Data warehousing, big data, business intelligence, Oracle, Birst, Tableau, Sql Server, Hadoop, MongoDB, Java & IT mgmt skills. (As-Ind, estab 2003, empl 10, sales $3,000,000, cert: NMSDC)

4421 Vertisystem Inc.
      39300 Civic Center Dr, Ste 230
      Fremont, CA 94538
      Contact: Shaloo Jeswani Sr BDM
      Tel: 702-241-5131
      Email: shaloo@vertisystem.com
      Website: www.vertisystem.com
Staff Augmentation, Full-Time Placements, contract to Hire, IT Projects & Consulting. (Minority, Woman, estab 2008, empl 120, sales $20,000,000, cert: City, CPUC)

4422 Vidhwan Inc dba E-Solutions, Inc.
      2 N Market St Ste 400
      San Jose, CA 95113
      Contact: Eric Kumar Acct Mgr
      Tel: 408-239-4647
      Email: eric.kumar@e-solutionsinc.com
      Website: www.e-solutionsinc.com
IT & ITES staffing, recruitment & deployment: permanent, contract, contract to hire & project based staffing. (Woman/As-Ind, estab 2003, empl 450, sales $22,800,000, cert: NMSDC, CPUC)

4423 Virtual Computing Technology
      7767 Calle Andar
      Carlsbad, CA 92009
      Contact: Cigi Oakley CEO
      Tel: 760-436-0922
      Email: coakley@vcomptech.com
      Website: www.vcomptech.com
Authorized IBM Business Partner, Value Added Reseller (VAR) for IBM, hardware, software & services. (Woman, estab 2010, empl 9, sales $550,000, cert: State)

4424 Visionary Integration Professionals, LLC
      80 Iron Point Cir, Ste 100
      Folsom, CA 95630
      Contact: Stephen Carpenter VP Admin
      Tel: 916-985-9625
      Email: scarpenter@vipincorp.com
      Website: www.trustvip.com
Assists govt agencies use IT to increase productivity & revenue, improve performance, and reduce costs. (Woman/Hisp, estab 1996, empl 410, sales $30,000,000, cert: State, CPUC)

4425 Volante Enterprise Consulting
      3863 Millbrae Terr
      Perris, CA 92571
      Contact: Sheila Volante CEO
      Tel: 310-256-9639
      Email: sheilavolante@volantenc.com
      Website: www.volantenc.com
Scheduling Mgmt, Risk Mgmt, Systems Consulting, Microsoft Project Server, Microsoft Project Professional, Configuration, Office 365 + SharePoint Configuration, Project Management Office Setup & Maintenance. (Woman/AA, estab 2014, empl 2, sales , cert: State)

4426 VXI Global Solutions, LLC
      220 W 1st St 3rd Floor
      Los Angeles, CA 90012
      Contact: Annette Timmins Sales Support
      Tel: 213-637-1300
      Email: annette.timmins@vxi.com
      Website: www.vxi.com
Business process & information technology outsourcing, call center & BPO services, software development, quality assurance testing & infrastructure outsourcing. (As-Pac, estab 1998, empl 30000, sales $ 0, cert: NMSDC)

4427 Webbege, Inc.
      7851 Mission Center Ct Ste 108
      San Diego, CA 92108
      Contact: Francis Geraci President
      Tel: 619-786-7075
      Email: frank.geraci@webbege.com
      Website: www.webbege.com
Web Design, Development, and Online Marketing. (Hisp, estab 2011, empl 7, sales $300,000, cert: NMSDC)

4428 WINTEC Software Corporation
      3333 Bowers Ave, Ste 189
      Santa Clara, CA 95054
      Contact: Narender Ramarapu CEO
      Tel: 408-988-1600
      Email: narender@winteccorp.com
      Website: www.winteccorp.com
Scientific Applications & Testing, Disaster Recovery, Business Continuity Planning & Large Database Implementation & Maintenance. (As-Ind, estab 1998, empl 56, sales $3,320,000, cert: 8(a))

4429 WMBE Payrolling, dba TargetCW
      9475 Chesapeake Dr
      San Diego, CA 92123
      Contact: Dave Bakkeby SVP Business Devel
      Tel: 858-810-8038
      Email: dave.bakkeby@targetcw.com
      Website: www.targetcw.com
Payrolling of contingent workers identified by our clients. Employer of record for temporary workers and contractors already sourced across the US and overseas. (Woman, estab 2009, empl 12, sales , cert: State)

4430 Worksters
      97 S 2nd St, Ste 100
      San Jose, CA 95113
      Contact: Ania Kaminska Sr. Technical Liaison
      Tel: 650-458-0600
      Email: ania@worksters.com
      Website: www.worksters.com
Hardware & software solutions, Product Installation & Implementation, Vulnerability Assessment, Penetration Testing. (Woman, estab 2011, empl 10, sales , cert: 8(a))

4431 Xavient Information Systems, Inc.
      2125 Madera Rd, Ste B
      Simi Valley, CA 93065
      Contact: Melissa Montejano Dir Admin
      Tel: 805-955-4140
      Email: melissa@xavient.com
      Website: www.xavient.com
Application development & integration, testing & quality assurance, IT infrastructure support, application support, core telecom engineering services. (As-Pac, estab 2003, empl 2200, sales $40,000,000, cert: NMSDC)

INFORMATION TECHNOLOGY: Services

4432 Xinnovit Inc.
      21001 San Ramon Valley Blvd, Ste A4-103
      San Ramon, CA 94583
      Contact: Client Relations Mgr
      Tel: 925-236-2310
      Email:
      Website: www.xinnovit.com
Information technology services: application development, systems & database management, data warehousing & quality assurance. (Woman/As-Ind, estab 2002, empl 165, sales $12,000,000, cert: NMSDC)

4433 Yadari Enterprises
      728 Texas St, Ste 3
      Fairfield, CA 94533
      Contact: Tara Lynn Gray President
      Tel: 707-398-6478
      Email: tara@yadari.com
      Website: www.yadari.com
Web develop, databasese, report writing, business intelligence, visual data displays, mgmt consulting, graphic design, electronic health record, diagnostic imaging systems, laboratory systems, pharmacy systems. (Woman/AA, estab 2004, empl 3, sales $310,000, cert: State, CPUC)

4434 Zebra-net Incorporated
      9995 Muirlands Blvd
      Irvine, CA 92618
      Contact: Jeanie Reese Recruiter
      Tel: 949-900-6110
      Email: Jeanie.Reese@Zebra-net.com
      Website: www.zebra-net.com
Information technology staffing. (Woman, estab 1996, empl 11, sales $5,635,048, cert: WBENC)

Colorado

4435 Aspen Capital Company, Inc.
      530 North Jefferson Ave Unit A
      Loveland, CO 80537
      Contact: Peggy Tomcheck
      Tel: 303-716-2898
      Email: plapp@aspencapitalcompany.com
      Website: www.aspencapitalcompany.com
Custom asset tracking & invoicing solutions, educational laptop program lease structures, consignment solutions, electronic invoicing & billing processes, web based equipment stores. (Woman, estab 2001, empl 8, sales $10,385,908, cert: WBENC)

4436 Aureus Tech Systems, LLC
      17593 E Euclid Ave
      Aurora, CO 80016
      Contact: Sujata Bhattarai CEO
      Tel: 816-373-1979
      Email: sujata@aureustechsystems.com
      Website: www.aureustechsystems.com
Customized & needs-based reporting dashboard, Web-based, & and near real-time reporting tools, overall performance optimization reducing lag times & frivolous resource allocation. (Woman/As-Ind, estab 2008, empl 35, sales $2,316,830, cert: WBENC)

4437 BCM Global Technologies Consultants, Inc.
      9457 S University Blvd, Ste 329
      Highlands Ranch, CO 80126
      Contact: President
      Tel: 866-761-8880
      Email: info@bcmglobaltech.com
      Website: www.bcmglobaltech.com
Provide technical resources & solutions. (Woman/AA, estab 2008, empl 20, sales $1,550,000, cert: NMSDC, WBENC, NWBOC, 8(a))

4438 Bross Group LLC
      200 Union Blvd, Ste 200
      Lakewood, CO 80228
      Contact: Cathy Fligger Sr Acct Exec
      Tel: 303-945-2700
      Email: sales@brossgroup.com
      Website: www.brossgroup.com
Information technology consulting & staffing. (Woman, estab 2004, empl 50, sales $3,094,000, cert: WBENC, NWBOC)

4439 Data Destruction LLC
      96 Inverness Dr E Ste K
      Englewood, CO 80112
      Contact: Ginger Patrick President
      Tel: 303-388-3282
      Email: ginger@data-destruction.com
      Website: www.data-destruction.com
Destroy data, hard drives & back-up tapes, mobile hard drive shredding, digital media. (Woman, estab 2014, empl 5, sales , cert: WBENC)

4440 DCM Technology Solutions, Inc.
      17011 Moorside Dr
      Parker, CO 80134
      Contact: Leslie Kleyweg President
      Tel: 303-325-5202
      Email: info@dcmsolution.com
      Website: www.dcmsolution.com
IT services: staffing, low voltage wiring, networking & computer repair/maintenance. (Woman, estab 2002, empl 5, sales $550,000, cert: WBENC)

4441 iBeta, LLC
      2675 S ABilene St, Ste 300
      AURORA, CO 80014
      Contact: Curt Dusing II Sales & Marketing Exec
      Tel: 303-627-1110
      Email: cdusing@ibeta.com
      Website: www.ibeta.com
Testing services: test engineering, automated & manual, functionality , performance, stress & load, hardware & software, data conversion, usability, console certification, handheld. (Hisp, estab 1999, empl 141, sales $4,500,000, cert: NMSDC)

4442 Istonish
      5500 Greenwood Plaza Blvd
      Greenwood Village, CO 80108
      Contact: Shannon Hickey Business Devel Exec
      Tel: 720-529-4550
      Email: shickey@istonish.com
      Website: www.istonish.com
Technical resources: staff augmentation, perm placement, vendor mgmt svcs, IT solutions, project based svc. (Minority, Woman, estab 1990, empl 100, sales $6,883,874, cert: NMSDC, WBENC)

4443 Managed Business Solutions
      12325 Oracle Blvd, Ste 200
      Colorado Springs, CO 80921
      Contact: Jane Kovalik Marketing Mgr
      Tel: 719-314-3400
      Email: diversity@mbshome.com
      Website: www.mbshome.com
IT managed svcs: IT infrastructure support, multi-vendor/platform system admin, storage mgmt & admin, SAN engineering & design, server consolidation, open view service desk support, project mgmt, data center operations & mgmt. (Nat Ame, estab 2009, empl 7, sales $23,513,000, cert: NMSDC)

4444 Maven Companies
　　　 1880 Office Club Pointe
　　　 Colorado Springs, CO 80920
　　　 Contact: Manish Kochhar President
　　　 Tel:　719-884-0102
　　　 Email: diversity@mavenco.com
　　　 Website: www.mavenco.com
IT consulting, Project Management & Business Analysis (PM Coordination, Change and Release Management, Process Analysis), ERP Development & Support (Oracle, PeopleSoft, SAP),Business Intelligence (Business Objects, Cognos, Microstrategy, Crystal Reports). (As-Pac, estab 2003, empl 30, sales $3,000,000, cert: NMSDC)

4445 Merlin Techncial Solutions
　　　 7730 E Belleview Ave, Ste A306
　　　 Greenwood Village, CO 80111
　　　 Contact: Linda Somogyi Sr Alliance Mgr
　　　 Tel:　303-221-0797
　　　 Email: lsomogyi@merlints.com
　　　 Website: www.merlints.com
Information technology products, innovative financing programs & access to numerous contract vehicles. (Hisp, estab 1997, empl 35, sales $　0, cert: 8(a))

4446 netRelevance LLC
　　　 4865 Hidden Rock Rd
　　　 Colorado Springs, CO 80908
　　　 Contact: Rick Limas Dir Business Dev
　　　 Tel:　719-488-5742
　　　 Email: rick.limas@netrelevance.com
　　　 Website: www.netrelevance.com
Wireless Network Site Surveys, Design, Installation & Support, Network Equipment Installations and Startup, Computer Room and Data Center Design and Installation, Copper and Fiber Cabling, Performing Network refresh/upgrades, IP Surveillance. (Hisp, estab 2007, empl 9, sales $2,679,948, cert: NMSDC)

4447 Rearden Logic Inc.
　　　 2010 E 17th Ave Unit 1
　　　 Denver, CO 80206
　　　 Contact: Kristopher Schehr Principal
　　　 Tel:　720-515-3289
　　　 Email: kschehr@reardenlogic.com
　　　 Website: www.reardenlogic.com
Offensive Cyber, Defensive Cyber, Networks, Reverse Engineering, TS//SCI, Software Defined Radio SDR, FPGA, TCP/IP, Coding. (Hisp, estab 2013, empl 5, sales $537,000, cert: 8(a))

4448 Sedulus Group LLC
　　　 19511 Good Life View
　　　 Calhan, CO 80808
　　　 Contact: Julian Candia CEO
　　　 Tel:　719-505-8419
　　　 Email: julian.candia@cyberlogistix.com
　　　 Website: www.cyberlogistix.com
Cybersecurity expertise and operations. (Hisp, estab 2019, empl 3, sales , cert: NMSDC)

4449 The 'Apps' Consultants Inc.
　　　 6909 S Holly Circle Ste 350
　　　 Centennial, CO 80112
　　　 Contact: Kiran Pingali President
　　　 Tel:　303-502-5407
　　　 Email: kiran@appsconsultants.com
　　　 Website: www.appsconsultants.com
IT consulting, ERP/ CRM & Business Intelligence. (Woman/As-Ind, estab 2005, empl 4, sales $546,846, cert: City)

4450 V3Gate, LLC
　　　 555 Middle Creek Pkwy, Ste 120
　　　 Colorado Springs, CO 80921
　　　 Contact: Lindsay Dumanch Business Devel Mgr
　　　 Tel:　855-483-4283
　　　 Email: lumanch@v3gate.com
　　　 Website: www.v3gate.com/
IT solutions provider for the US Public Sector, healthcare, and education. (Hisp, estab 2007, empl 36, sales $314,000,000, cert: NMSDC)

Connecticut

4451 Agilus Global Services, LLC
　　　 35 E Main St, Ste 352
　　　 Avon, CT 06001
　　　 Contact: Dennis Williams CEO
　　　 Tel:　860-404-0476
　　　 Email: dwilliams@agilusglobal.com
　　　 Website: www.agilusglobalservices.com
IT consulting/staffing & recruiting services. (AA, estab 2015, empl 1, sales , cert: NMSDC)

4452 Aquinas Consulting, LLC
　　　 154 Herbert St
　　　 Milford, CT 06460
　　　 Contact: Haruthay "Pam" Rasmidatta CEO
　　　 Tel:　203-876-7822
　　　 Email: info@aquinasconsulting.com
　　　 Website: www.aquinasconsulting.com
IT & engineering consulting & staffing. (Woman/As-Pac, estab 2000, empl 173, sales $31,746,822, cert: State)

4453 Aspire Systems
　　　 36 Mill Plain Rd
　　　 Danbury, CT 06811
　　　 Contact: Laura Del Corpo VP Business Dev
　　　 Tel:　732-406-4284
　　　 Email: laura@aspiresystem.com
　　　 Website: www.aspiresystem.com
Information Technology, Staff Augmentation, Technology Deployment & Enterprise support. (As-Pac, estab 2002, empl 45, sales $5,000,000, cert: NMSDC)

4454 Dudas IT Resources & Advisory, Inc.
　　　 117 Butternut Lane
　　　 Stamford, CT 06903
　　　 Contact: Liz Chait CEO
　　　 Tel:　203-653-2739
　　　 Email: liz@zarit.com
　　　 Website: www.zarit.org
Information technology staffing & consulting services. (Woman, estab 2005, empl 8, sales $6,389,623, cert: WBENC)

4455 eRichards Consulting LLC
　　　 1381 Burr St Ste 390
　　　 Fairfield, CT 06824
　　　 Contact: Doreen F. Gebbia President
　　　 Tel:　203-944-0816
　　　 Email: dgebbia@erichards.com
　　　 Website: www.eRichards.com
IT consulting: strategic assessment, internet strategy, application development, project management, IT governance, web development & staff augmentation. (Woman, estab 1996, empl 3, sales $　0, cert: WBENC)

INFORMATION TECHNOLOGY: Services

4456 InfoLynx Services, Inc.
      325 Danbury Rd
      New Milford, CT 06776
      Contact: Uelysee Scantling Dir of Sales
      Tel: 860-210-1203
      Email: contact@infolynx.com
      Website: www.infolynx.com
Technical services: project mgmt, technical configuration, system & application engineering, performance tuning, desktop support. (AA, estab 1994, empl 75, sales $6,200,000, cert: State)

4457 iTech Solutions, Inc.
      20 Stanford Dr
      Farmington, CT 06032
      Contact: Salil Sankaran President
      Tel: 703-638-1346
      Email: salil.sankaran@itechsolutions.com
      Website: www.itechsolutions.com
Information technology staffing, consulting & recruting services. (Woman, estab 1995, empl 115, sales $14,092,608, cert: NMSDC, WBENC)

4458 JANUS Software, Inc. (dba JANUS Associates)
      2 Omega Dr
      Stamford, CT 06907
      Contact: Patricia Fisher President
      Tel: 203-251-0200
      Email: patfisher@janusassociates.com
      Website: www.janusassociates.com
Information & telecommunications security solutions; risk analysis & disaster recovery planning; computer forensics & fraud investigations; information mgmt strategies; identity authentication software. (Woman, estab 1988, empl 20, sales , cert: WBENC)

4459 Nadicent Technologies LLC
      2389 Main St
      Glastonbury, CT 06033
      Contact: Frank Gomes Dir
      Tel: 860-659-2600
      Email: frank.gomes@nadicent.com
      Website: www.nadicent.com
Advanced Managed Security, Conferencing, Video, Web & Audio, Cloud Services, Disaster Recovery, Help Desk Services, Microsoft Azure, Office 365 Enterprise Suites, Data Centers, Colocation, Infrastructure. (As-Pac, estab 2003, empl 10, sales $9,000,000, cert: NMSDC)

4460 OutSecure Inc.
      Shelton Pointe, 2 Trap Falls Rd Ste 401
      Shelton, CT 06484
      Contact: Pamela Gupta President
      Tel: 203-816-8061
      Email: pamela.gupta@outsecure.com
      Website: www.outsecure.com
Cyber Security assessment & security programs, risk assessments. (As-Pac, estab 2003, empl 7, sales $300,000, cert: NMSDC)

4461 PCC Technology Group
      2 Barnard Lane
      Bloomfield, CT 06002
      Contact: Jo Gumbs Marketing Coord
      Tel: 860-466-7261
      Email: jomal.gumbs@pcctg.com
      Website: www.pcctg.com
Software development. (AA, As-Pac, estab 1995, empl 50, sales , cert: NMSDC)

4462 Safety Management Systems, Inc.
      5 Eversley Ave, Ste 306
      Norwalk, CT 06851
      Contact: Business Dev Mgr
      Tel: 203-838-8877
      Email: info@sms360.com
      Website: www.sms360.com
Develop SMS360, enables organizations to manage its EHS program. (Woman, estab 2004, empl 9, sales $451,000, cert: State, WBENC)

4463 Saisystems International
      5 Research Dr
      Shelton, CT 06484
      Contact: Chirag Modi VP Technology Services
      Tel: 203-929-0790
      Email: cmodi@saisystems.com
      Website: www.saisystems.com
Informatation technology consulting: disaster recovery planning, dataware & database mgmt systems, quality assurance svcs. (Woman/As-Ind, estab 1987, empl 350, sales $12,306,249, cert: State, NMSDC)

4464 Source IT Technologies, LLC
      24 East Ave, Ste 244
      New Canaan, CT 06840
      Contact: Serica King CEO
      Tel: 203-252-0439
      Email: sking@sourceittech.com
      Website: www.sourceittech.com
Technology solutions. (Woman, estab 2012, empl 7, sales $8,696,000, cert: WBENC)

4465 Stratoserve LLC
      18 Colonial Ct
      Cheshire, CT 06410
      Contact: Subroto Roy President
      Tel: 203-768-5690
      Email: subroto.roy@stratoserve.com
      Website: www.stratoserve.com
Consulting, research & training . (As-Pac, estab 2005, empl 1, sales , cert: NMSDC)

4466 TCA Consulting Group, Inc.
      39 New London Tpke, Ste 220, Glen Lochen Center
      Glastonbury, CT 06033
      Contact: Kelly Beard
      Tel: 484-574-3561
      Email: kelly@tcagroupmail.com
      Website: www.tcagroup.com
Administrative Services; Information Management Services; Information Technology. (AA, estab , empl 150, sales $10,713,771, cert: State)

4467 Technosteps LLC
      3 Hayes Ave Unit B
      Norwalk, CT 06855
      Contact: Narayan Venugopal President
      Tel: 703-864-4848
      Email: narayan.venugopal@technosteps.com
      Website: www.technosteps.com
IT Staffing. (As-Ind, estab 2012, empl 3, sales $189,000, cert: State)

INFORMATION TECHNOLOGY: Services

4468 The Computer Company, Inc.
15 Commerce Dr
Cromwell, CT 06416
Contact: Eileen Hasson President
Tel: 860-635-0500
Email: ehasson@www.computercompany.net
Website: www.computercompany.net
Network engineering, internet connectivity, system firewalls & security, remote system monitoring, IT outsourcing, custom programming & integration. (Minority, Woman, estab 1995, empl 22, sales $3,750,000, cert: State, NMSDC)

4469 The Computer Support People, LLC
16 River St Upper Level
Norwalk, CT 06850
Contact: Cassandre Jean Business Devel
Tel: 203-653-4643
Email: cassandre.jean@tcsp360.com
Website: www.tcsp360.com
Managed Computer Services. Computer Software & Hardware support. (Hisp, estab 2005, empl 8, sales $419,362, cert: State, NMSDC)

4470 The Wellspring Group, Inc.
4 Research Dr, Ste 402
Shelton, CT 06484
Contact: Amy Dain Vincelette President
Tel: 203-261-1616
Email:
Website: www.wellspringgrp.com
Information technology staffing & project management: temps, contract-to-hire, direct-hire. (Woman, estab 2001, empl 59, sales $7,000,000, cert: WBENC)

4471 Transcend Business Solutions, LLC
30 Grassy Plain St, Unit 5A
Bethel, CT 06801
Contact: Linda Rowan President
Tel: 203-790-5222
Email: info@transcendbus.com
Website: www.transcendbus.com
IT consulting firm & employment recruiting. (Woman, estab 2003, empl 10, sales $850,000, cert: WBENC)

4472 Virpie Inc
1 Reservoir Office Pk #208, 1449 Old Waterbury
Southbury, CT 06488
Contact: Shre Thammana President
Tel: 203-264-0999
Email: shre@virpietech.com
Website: www.virpietech.com
Information technology staffing, storage area network design, architecture & administration, disaster recovery, database developers & administrators, senior & project management. (As-Pac, estab 1997, empl 150, sales $4,725,000, cert: NMSDC)

4473 VisionPoint LLC
152 Rockwell Rd
Newington, CT 06111
Contact: Louise Mastroianni Acct Mgr
Tel: 860-436-9673
Email: visionpointct@gmail.com
Website: www.visionpointllc.com
Technology acquisition, integration, design, installation, technical meeting support & service. (Woman, estab 2003, empl 24, sales $7,002,015, cert: WBENC)

District of Columbia

4474 Analytica LLC
1705 DeSales St, NW Ste 400
Washington, DC 20036
Contact: VP Business Dev
Tel: 202-470-4806
Email:
Website: www.analytica.net
Business Intelligence & Analytics, Information Management, Software Development, Financial Management & Analysis, Program Management Support, Cyber Security & Intelligence, GIS Mapping Solutions, IT and Finance Staff Augmentation. (Hisp, estab 2007, empl 19, sales $7,000,000, cert: State)

4475 Centricity Technology Partners, Inc.
621 Quackenbos St NW
Washington, DC 20011
Contact: CEO
Tel: 202-696-5270
Email:
Website: www.centricity-us.com
Cloud, Mobile & SOA Application Development, Enterprise Architecture, Program/Project Management, Architecture & Engineering, Business Process Reengineering, Operations & Maintenance, IT Governance, Independent Validation & Verification. (Woman/AA, estab 2012, empl 4, sales $1,661,362, cert: WBENC, 8(a))

4476 E-Logic, Inc.
1025 Connecticut Ave NW Ste 1000
Washington, DC 20036
Contact: Luis F Padilla CEO
Tel: 202-499-7837
Email: lpadilla@e-logic.us
Website: www.e-logic.us
IT Hardware, Software, System Integration. (Hisp, estab 2007, empl 20, sales $8,500,000, cert: 8(a), SDB)

4477 Logistics Systems Incorporated
1100 G St Nw Ste 410
Washington, DC 20005
Contact: Henry Jennings SVP Business Devel
Tel: 202-347-0821
Email: henry.jennings@logistics-sys.com
Website: www.logistics-sys.com
Integrated logistics management & life cycle support, information technology services & program management. (AA, estab , empl 125, sales $15,000,000, cert: 8(a))

4478 MSys Inc.
1025 Connecticut Ave, NW Ste 1000
Washington, DC 20036
Contact: Raj Thiyagarajan Dir
Tel: 202-629-0353
Email: register@msysinc.com
Website: www.msysinc.com
Software consulting, custom programming & development, web development. (As-Ind, estab 1994, empl 67, sales $5,787,890, cert: NMSDC)

INFORMATION TECHNOLOGY: Services

4479 Optimus Technologies, LLC
700 12th St NW Ste 700
Washington, DC 20005
Contact: Donald Jones CEO
Tel: 202-263-7370
Email: djones@optimustech.net
Website: www.optimustech.net
Document scanning, records mgmt & retention, electronic data processing, computer forensics, foreign language document conversion, web hosting, backup tape restoration, document printing. (AA, estab 2005, empl 20, sales $8,000,000, cert: NMSDC)

4480 Orgro
20 F St NW Ste 700
Washington, DC 20001
Contact: Aditya Dahagam Founder
Tel: 202-505-1431
Email: connect@orgro.team
Website: www.orgro.team
ITSM & ITIL process improvement, Software/Application Development, IT Business Analytics, BPR, Quality Assurance, Systems Engineering, IT & Organizational Strategy. (As-Ind, estab , empl , sales $ 0, cert: State, NMSDC, 8(a), SDB)

4481 Peak Technology Solutions, Inc.
1627 K St, NW, Ste 400
Washington, DC 20006
Contact: Mohammad Tariq President
Tel: 202-776-7196
Email: mtariq@peaktsinc.com
Website: www.peaktsinc.com
COTS implementation, system integration, database design & application development services, Geographic Information System (GIS) solutions, and web enabled automation. (Minority, estab 2002, empl 9, sales $645,948, cert: State)

4482 Sylver Rain Consulting
1120 Connecticut Ave NW, Ste 421
Washington, DC 20036
Contact: LaToya White President
Tel: 202-792-6722
Email: lwhite@sylverrainconsulting.com
Website: www.sylverrain.com
Custom Software Development, Systems Implementation, 508 Compliance testing & remediation. (Woman/AA, estab , empl 20, sales $1,000,000, cert: 8(a))

4483 The ELOCEN Group
1341 H St, NE Ste 301
Washington, DC 20002
Contact: Taryn Lewis Dir of Operations
Tel: 202-644-8500
Email: tarynl@elocengroup.com
Website: www.elocengroup.com
Program & Project Mgmt, Construction Mgmt, Interior Design, IT, Facilities/Logistics & Healthcare Facilities/Logistics/Management. (Woman/AA, estab 2007, empl 62, sales $20,089,894, cert: State, City, WBENC, 8(a))

4484 vTech Solution Inc
1100 H St NW Ste 750
Washington, DC 20005
Contact: Soudeepya Chinni Client Relation Specialist
Tel: 202-919-8964
Email: info@vtechsolution.com
Website: www.vtechsolution.com
IT staffing, permanent & temporary. (As-Ind, estab 2006, empl 49, sales $38,800,000, cert: State, NMSDC, SDB)

Delaware

4485 Alpha Technologies USA, Inc.
704 N King St
Wilmington, DE 19801
Contact: Harry Virk CEO
Tel: 302-304-8421
Email: Communications@alphait.us
Website: www.alphaIT.us
Information technology staffing & consulting, project mgmt, software devel, systems integration, datacenter mgmt. (Minority, estab 1997, empl 200, sales $8,924,288, cert: NMSDC)

4486 DecisivEdge LLC
131 Continental Dr Ste 409
Newark, DE 19713
Contact: Michele Frayler
Tel: 302-299-1570
Email: michele.frayler@decisivedge.com
Website: www.decisivedge.com
Business consulting & technology services, business architecture & performance, business analytics, data warehouse strategy, design, development & governance, marketing analytics development. (As-Ind, estab 2007, empl 41, sales $4,739,862, cert: NMSDC)

4487 Frontier Technologies, Inc.
1521 Concord Pike Ste 302
Wilmington, DE 19803
Contact: Reshma Moorthy President
Tel: 302-225-2530
Email:
Website: www.ftiusa.com
Develop & deploy integrated business solutions: front office apps, IT staff augmentation, CRM, supply chain mgmt & computer telephony. (Woman/As-Ind, estab 1989, empl 15, sales $20,000,000, cert: NMSDC, WBENC)

4488 LiivData Inc.
1201 N Orange St Ste 7065
Wilmington, DE 19801
Contact: Dominic Francis Oguejiofo CEO
Tel: 302-235-3040
Email: dom.francis@liivdata.com
Website: www.liivdata.com
Information & systems integration, communications services, Voip technology. (AA, estab 2010, empl 15, sales $3,850,000, cert: State)

Florida

4489 A. Harold and Associates, LLC
7595 Baymeadows Way
Jacksonville, FL 32256
Contact: Andrew Harold, Jr. President
Tel: 904-535-2290
Email:
Website: www.aha-llc.com
Engineering, Training, E-learning, Software, Instructional Systems Development, Aviation Systems, V-22, H-60, F/A-18, FMS, Project Management. (AA, estab 2003, empl 260, sales $27,521,267, cert: SDB)

INFORMATION TECHNOLOGY: Services

4490 AC4S Technologies
       4017 W. Martin Luther King Blvd
       Tampa, FL 33614
       Contact: Kristin Jackson Operations
       Tel: 813-432-4320
       Email: kristin.jackson@ac4sconsulting.com
       Website: www.ac4stechnologies.com
Integrated video conferencing, email, CRM solutions, sharing & synchronizing documents. (AA, estab 2013, empl 6, sales , cert: NMSDC)

4491 Action 9-A, Inc.
       10416 New Berlin Rd
       Jacksonville, FL 32226
       Contact: William Valentino President
       Tel: 904-696-9191
       Email: action9a@earthlink.net
       Website: www.action9astorage.com
Moving totes/dollies rentals; specialized equipment for modular furniture; breakdown and reconfiguration for modular furniture systems; corporate moving and storage (Hisp, estab 1999, empl 12, sales $800,000, cert: NMSDC)

4492 Advanced IT Concepts, Inc.
       1351 Sundial Point
       Winter Springs, FL 32708
       Contact: Gabriel Ruiz President
       Tel: 407-914-2484
       Email: eve.maldonado@aitcinc.com
       Website: www.aitcinc.com
Telecommunications & Information Technology services. (Hisp, estab 2006, empl 51, sales $24,860,693, cert: City, 8(a))

4493 Almond Consulting Group
       5472 Baytowne Place
       Oviedo, FL 32765
       Contact: Derrick Henry President
       Tel: 407-602-8540
       Email: derrick.henry@almondconsulting.com
       Website: www.almondconsulting.com
Information technology consulting solutions: Project Management, Information Assurance, Certification & Accreditation & Process Improvement. (AA, estab 2001, empl 1, sales , cert: State, City, NMSDC)

4494 Amzur Technologies, Inc.
       405 N Reo St Ste 110
       Tampa, FL 33609
       Contact: Bala Nemani CEO
       Tel: 813-600-4060
       Email: supplier@amzur.com
       Website: www.amzur.com
Information technology, information security, anti-virus, firewalls, operating systems, IT services, Web e-commerce, LAN / WAN, network management, staff augmentation, servers, workflow, imaging, asset management. (Woman/Nat-Ame, estab 2004, empl 200, sales $22,173,714, cert: State, NMSDC)

4495 Auritas
       4907 International Pkwy, Ste 1001
       Sanford, FL 32771
       Contact: Anne Cross Dir of Mktg
       Tel: 407-834-8324
       Email: rfp@auritas.com
       Website: www.auritas.com
SAP Consulting Services & Project Management services, Data Lifecycle Management. (Minority, Woman, estab 2003, empl 200, sales $7,400,000, cert: WBENC)

4496 Beacon Systems, Inc.
       3928 Coral Ridge Dr
       Coral Springs, FL 33065
       Contact: Brian Tupiak Contracts Admin
       Tel: 954-426-1171
       Email: info@beacongov.com
       Website: www.beacongov.com
IT training & support, security systems, program mgmt, performance consulting, software & program training, systems security, systems & networking engineering support, web design & dev. (Minority, Woman, estab 2005, empl 20, sales $500,000, cert: State, NMSDC)

4497 BlueStreak Learning, LLC
       PO Box 110435
       Naples, FL 34108
       Contact: Jennifer De Vries President
       Tel: 630-842-1865
       Email: info@bluestreaklearning.com
       Website: www.bluestreaklearning.com
Technology-based training programs: needs assessments, e-learning strategy, LMS selection, course development svcs, evaluation/ROI analysis. (Woman, estab 2003, empl 3, sales $500,000, cert: WBENC)

4498 Braille Works International, Inc.
       941-942 Darby Lake St
       Seffner, FL 33584
       Contact: Marketing
       Tel: 813-654-4050
       Email: JEFF@BRAILLEWORKS.COM
       Website: www.brailleworks.com
Braille, large print, audio & computerized documents. (Woman, estab 1994, empl 12, sales $1,250,000, cert: WBENC)

4499 Business Information Technology Solutions.Com
       100 S. Orange Ave Ste 800
       Orlando, FL 32801
       Contact: Amy Seaman Acct Exec
       Tel: 407-363-0024
       Email: amy@abtsolutions.com
       Website: www.abtsolutions.com
IT staffing. (Woman, estab 2000, empl 25, sales $4,700,000, cert: State, City)

4500 C&C International Computers & Consultants, Inc.
       7777 N Davie Rd Ext Ste 100 A
       Hollywood, FL 33024
       Contact: Bill James President
       Tel: 954-450-0023
       Email: bjames@ccintercomputers.com
       Website: www.ccintercomputers.com
Value Added Reseller (VAR) Services, Support Services & IT Staffing, Computer Installations, Product Rollouts & Deployments, Consulting Services & Project Management, Onsite & Remote Help Desk Support. (Woman/AA, estab 1995, empl 27, sales , cert: State, City, NMSDC)

4501 Corporate Subscription Management Services, LLC
       5763 N Andrews Way
       Fort Lauderdale, FL 33309
       Contact: Julie Auslander Chief Cultural Officer
       Tel: 201-307-9900
       Email: jsauslander@couranto.com
       Website: www.couranto.com/
Customizable, end-to-end information, contract, and license management solution, publisher negoigations, information asset consulting, custom information hub. (Woman, estab 2003, empl 22, sales $19,985,377, cert: WBENC)

INFORMATION TECHNOLOGY: Services

4502 Corpotel, Inc
      2800 Glades Circle Ste. 146
      Weston, FL 33327
      Contact: Elias Benaim Sales
      Tel: 954-364-7045
      Email: ebenaim@corpotel.com
      Website: www.corpotel.com
Telecom expense mgmt, call accounting, multi-store telecom svcs, call center software dev, bilingual call center outsourcing. (Hisp, estab 2001, empl 15, sales $1,000,000, cert: NMSDC)

4503 Craig Technical Consulting, Inc.
      150 N Sykes Creek Pkwy
      Merritt Island, FL 32952
      Contact: Greg Sheppard Dir Business Dev
      Tel: 321-613-5620
      Email: greg.sheppard@craigtechinc.com
      Website: www.craigtechinc.com
Software Design & Devel, Systems Engineering & Integration, Multidisciplinary Engineering, Training & Courseware Devel, Modeling & Simulation, IT Support & Integrated Logistics Support. (Minority, Woman, estab 1999, empl 300, sales $30,000,000, cert: NMSDC, WBENC, SDB)

4504 Curia Document Solutions LLC
      815 North Homestead Blvd. Ste #646
      Homestead, FL 33030
      Contact: Lourdes Cox President
      Tel: 888-516-5193
      Email: sales@curiausa.com
      Website: www.curiausa.com
On-site & Off-site Document Production & Reprographics, Imaging Services, On-site & Offsite Scanning & Data Conversion, Document Utilization & Coding, Document Clustering for Review Prioritization. (Minority, Woman, estab 2011, empl 5, sales $100,000, cert: State)

4505 Damasco Design Inc
      7136 Crescent Creek Way
      Coconut Creek, FL 33073
      Contact: Jorge Castillo President
      Tel: 954-361-6600
      Email: jorge@damascodesign.com
      Website: www.damasco.io
Web Application solutions & Cloud systems integration. (Hisp, estab 2013, empl 1, sales , cert: State)

4506 DataSavers of Jacksonville, Inc.
      888 Suemac Rd
      Jacksonville, FL 32254
      Contact: Charlene Sullivan CEO
      Tel: 800-884-9538
      Email: charlene.sullivan@datasaversfl.com
      Website: www.datasaversusa.com
Records storage & management, disaster recovery planning & services, media storage & rotations, copying services, optical imaging. (Woman, estab 1989, empl 22, sales $3,444,025, cert: WBENC)

4507 Dbsys Inc.
      5224 W State Rd 46, Ste 369
      Sanford, FL 32771
      Contact: Matthew Hudson Field Tech/Mktg
      Tel: 497-322-7832
      Email: matt@dbsys.com
      Website: www.dbsys.com
Hardware Solutions, PCs, Notebooks, Storage & File Servers Networking Solutions, Certified Novell Engineer (CNE), supportWindows, Sales Solutions. (Woman, estab 1990, empl 13, sales $2,200,000, cert: State)

4508 Digital Hands
      400 N Tampa St 17th Fl
      Tampa, FL 33602
      Contact: Karen Krymski Dir strategic initiatives
      Tel: 877-229-8020
      Email: kkrymski@digitalhands.com
      Website: www.digitalhands.com
Outsourced IT managed services: IT security, enterprise data security, data loss prevention, endpoint security, infrastructure security & management. (Woman, estab 2001, empl 25, sales $2,225,000, cert: WBENC)

4509 Easy Verification Inc.
      7050 W Palmetto Park Rd Ste 15-256
      Boca Raton, FL 33433
      Contact: Lisa Bruno President
      Tel: 877-904-7770
      Email: lbruno@easyverification.com
      Website: www.easyverification.com
4506-T Fulfillment, IRS Tax Transcript Verification, Income Verification, SSN & ID Validation, Web-based verification application. (Woman, estab 2006, empl 3, sales , cert: State, SDB)

4510 Ebyte Technologies, Inc.
      7855 NW 12th St Ste 214 & 212
      Miami, FL 33126
      Contact: Mgr Business Devel
      Tel: 786-358-9300
      Email: infomiami@ebytetechnologies.com
      Website: www.ebytetechnologies.com
Technology staffing, placing contract, project solutions & permanent placement opportunities. (Woman/As-Ind, estab 2009, empl 70, sales $5,400,000, cert: City)

4511 Employer Management Solutions, Inc.
      5550 W Executive Dr Ste 450
      Tampa, FL 33609
      Contact: Jennifer Johnston
      Tel: 813-287-2486
      Email: jjohnston@consultems.com
      Website: www.consultems.com
Info technology svcs: enterprise wide initiatives; vendor selection, software implementation & project planning svcs. (Woman, estab 1998, empl 30, sales $4,000,000, cert: WBENC)

4512 Enterprise Risk Management, Inc.
      800 S Douglas Rd, North T s940
      Coral Gables, FL 33134
      Contact: Suzanne Siberon Sr Business Devel
      Tel: 305-447-6750
      Email: ssiberon@emrisk.com
      Website: www.ermprotect.com
IT Security Design & Implementation, Vulnerability Assessments, Penetration Testing, Social Engineering, Incident Response Planning, Business Continuity Planning Disaster Recovery (Minority, Woman, estab 1998, empl 18, sales $2,543,700, cert: State, City, 8(a))

4513 ExecuSys, Inc.
      551 S Apollo Blvd, Ste 104
      Melbourne, FL 32901
      Contact: Eddie Haralson President
      Tel: 321-253-0077
      Email: eharalson@execusys.com
      Website: www.execusys.com
Software engineering & information technology services, financial management systems support & range operations cost modelling solutions. (AA, estab 1993, empl 20, sales $2,155,571, cert: State)

INFORMATION TECHNOLOGY: Services

4514 Freedom Solutions LLC
19046 Bruce B Downs Blvd, Ste 108
Tampa, FL 33647
Contact: Kelli Covel Dir Business Dev
Tel: 404-713-7777
Email: kcovel@freedomsolutionsllc.com
Website: www.freedomsolutionsllc.com
IBM Business partner, dist IBM software & hardware, aintenance, programming services & installation services. (AA, estab 2002, empl 18, sales $12,000,000, cert: NMSDC)

4515 GDKN Corporation
9700 Stirling Road Ste 110
Cooper City, FL 33024
Contact: Gary Dhir VP
Tel: 954-985-6650
Email: gdhir@gdkn.com
Website: www.gdkn.com
Staffing: information technology, engineering, professional, administrative & clerical, IT consulting, custom application development. (As-Ind, estab 1993, empl 400, sales $18,000,000, cert: NMSDC)

4516 Global Gateway Solutions Inc.
8201 Peters Rd Ste 1000
Plantation, FL 33324
Contact: Jacqueline Sutherland CEO
Tel: 877-447-4627
Email: asutherland@callggs.com
Website: www.callggs.com
Outsourced contact center solutions, customer service, sales, and collections. (Woman/AA, estab 2007, empl 450, sales $14,113,423, cert: NMSDC, WBENC)

4517 Global Information Technology
8905 Regents Park Dr Ste 210
Tampa, FL 33647
Contact: Aruna Ajjarapu VP
Tel: 813-973-1061
Email: araj@git-org.com
Website: www.git-org.com
IT developers, DBA's, project managers & architects. (Minority, Woman, estab 1995, empl 300, sales $36,000,000, cert: State)

4518 ITG Global, LLC
11235 St. Johns Industrial Pkwy N Ste 2A
Jacksonville, FL 32246
Contact: Joseph Lukowski CEO
Tel: 904-425-4760
Email: almaferrante@itgtec.com
Website: www.itgtec.com
Automation Design, PLC Programming, Software Development, Technologies Consulting, Motion Design, Robot programming, MES, OEE, Data Analytics, Condition Monitoring, Control System Design, UL 508A Panel Shop, Control Panel. (Minority, Woman, estab 2003, empl 27, sales $3,000,000, cert: NMSDC)

4519 ITTConnect Inc.
9021 Southern Orchard Rd N
Davie, FL 33328
Contact: Fabio Back CEO
Tel: 954-732-8277
Email: fabio.back@ittconnect.com
Website: www.ittconnect.com
IT Recruiting / Direct Hire / Placement, IT Staffing / Temporary Contractors. (Hisp, estab 2017, empl 2, sales $ 0, cert: State, NMSDC)

4520 Kolter Solutions
175 Middle St
Lake Mary, FL 32746
Contact: Kim Carr Partner
Tel: 407-583-9483
Email: kcarr@koltersolutions.com
Website: www.koltersolutions.com
Information Technology Staff Augmentation, Project Teams, Application Design and Development (Java, C/C++, .NET/C#), Business Analysis/Project Management/Program Management, Quality Assurance, Infrastructure/Network/Security. (Woman, estab 2010, empl 28, sales $1,300,000, cert: WBENC)

4521 Lancesoft, Inc.
8804 Fazio Ct Ste 120
Tampa, FL 33647
Contact: Philip J Kalafut VP Healthcare Advisory
Tel: 813-449-1301
Email: phil.kalafut@lancesoft.com
Website: www.lancesoft.com
IT software, staffing & project execution. (Minority, Woman, estab 2000, empl 2000, sales $90,000,000, cert: NMSDC)

4522 LebenTech Innovative Solutions Inc.
PO Box 670832
Coral Springs, FL 33067
Contact: Lennox Bennett President
Tel: 954-796-7107
Email: lennox_bennett@lebentech.com
Website: www.lebentech.com
Technology consultation svcs: CAD designs, product development, RAMS analysis, R&D, FRACAS implementation, product validation, reliability testing. (AA, estab 2004, empl 6, sales , cert: State)

4523 Lodestar Solutions, Inc.
3212 W Harbor View Ave
Tampa, FL 33611
Contact: Heather Cole President
Tel: 813-415-2910
Email: hcole@lodestarsolutions.com
Website: www.lodestarsolutions.com
IBM business analytics/Cognos reseller & IBM support renewals, IBM Cognos licenses, TM1, Cognos business intelligence, FSR, SPSS, Varicent & Cognos planning. (Woman, estab 2004, empl 11, sales $3,949,751, cert: WBENC)

4524 MAS Global Consulting, LLC
3030 N Rocky Point Dr W S730
Tampa, FL 33607
Contact: Supplier Diversity
Tel: 727-474-3212
Email: SupplierDiversityMAS@masglobalconsulting.com
Website: www.masglobalconsulting.com
Custom Agile Software Development, Cloud Moderinzation, Data/AI Solutions. (Woman/Hisp, estab 2013, empl 150, sales $12,208,602, cert: NMSDC, WBENC)

INFORMATION TECHNOLOGY: Services

4525 N2 Services Inc
13241 Bartram Park Blvd Ste 2301
Jacksonville, FL 32258
Contact: Neminathan Ammaiyappan President
Tel: 904-703-4245
Email: nemi@n2sglobal.com
Website: www.n2sglobal.com
Software design, devel, analysis a& nd consulting services, internet application devel, E-Commerce solutions, Web 2.0, n-tier architecture & rapid application devel. (As-Pac, estab 2004, empl 140, sales $6,580,000, cert: NMSDC)

4526 Noise Consulting Group, Inc.
9280 Bay Plaza Blvd Ste 705
Tampa, FL 33619
Contact: Gina Hannah CEO
Tel: 315-491-0771
Email: gina.hannah@noisetcd.com
Website: www.noisetcd.com
IT staffing, consulting & systems integration, technology solutions & systems integration & implementation services. (Woman/AA, estab 2007, empl 38, sales $1,900,000, cert: State)

4527 Ospro Systems, LLC
1327 LaFayette St Ste C
Cape Coral, FL 33904
Contact: Prasad Kasireddy BDM-Recruitment
Tel: 239-309-0319
Email: prasad@osprosys.com
Website: www.osprosys.com
Software Implementations, Software Changes, Custom Software Development, Software validation/Testing, Maintenance and Support
Project Management, E-commerce, B2B, B2C, Custom Web Development, Application Web. (Woman/As-Ind, estab 2004, empl 70, sales $2,000,000, cert: State, NMSDC)

4528 Professional Materials Management
4210 Saltwater Blvd
Tampa, FL 33615
Contact: Julie Floen President
Tel: 813-249-0834
Email: julie@pm2online.com
Website: www.pm2online.com
Inventory management planning, inventory project implementation services, database building. (Woman, estab , empl , sales $ 0, cert: WBENC)

4529 Professional Translating Services, Inc.
44 W Flagler St, Ste 1800
Miami, FL 33130
Contact: Alexandra Hunt Natl Business Dev
Tel: 305-371-7887
Email: ahunt@protranslating.com
Website: www.protranslating.com
Translate documents, films & websites, interpreting services & equipment for multilingual meetings. (Minority, Woman, estab 1973, empl 100, sales $8,800,000, cert: NMSDC)

4530 Qualex Consulting Services, Inc.
1111 Kane Concourse Ste 320
Bay Harbor Island, FL 33154
Contact: Mark Miller Govt Sales
Tel: 877-887-4727
Email: mark.miller@qlx.com
Website: www.qlx.com
Software solutions & consulting services. (Minority, Woman, estab 1995, empl 26, sales $4,700,000, cert: State, WBENC)

4531 RADgov Inc.
6750 N Andrews Ave, Ste 200
Fort Lauderdale, FL 33309
Contact: Mark Smith Sr Business Mgr
Tel: 954-691-4588
Email: msmith@radgov.com
Website: www.radgov.com
IT planning services, system planning, development & implementation, electronic commerce, training & support, program mgmt. (Minority, Woman, estab 2005, empl 247, sales $2,900,000, cert: NMSDC, WBENC)

4532 RIK Data Solutions Inc.
8875 Hidden River Pkwy Ste 300
Tampa, FL 33637
Contact: Chris Kambhampati Principal Architect
Tel: 941-527-1464
Email: krk@rds-us.com
Website: www.rds-us.com
Datacenter Systems Integration, Cloud Brokerage Services, Software Development. (Minority, Woman, estab 2012, empl 6, sales $1,540,000, cert: NMSDC)

4533 Rudram Engineering, Inc.
845 Executive Lane Ste 200
Rockledge, FL 32955
Contact: Patel Alkesh President
Tel: 321-735-4159
Email: alkesh.patel@rudramengineering.com
Website: www.rudramengineering.com
System design, development, verification & validation, EMI analysis, Concept analysis, trade studies, emerging technology research, Software development, embedded system support, Interface identification, definition, design and system safety. (As-Ind, estab , empl 20, sales $1,454,900, cert: State, NMSDC, 8(a), SDB)

4534 SDI International Corp
2500 N Military Trail,STE. 318
Boca Raton, FL 33431
Contact: Carmen Castillo President
Tel: 561-288-4079
Email: sdidiversity@sdintl.com
Website: www.sdintl.com
Staffing & business solutions, staff augmentation, e-vendor mgmt services. (Minority, Woman, estab 1992, empl 1500, sales $600,000,000, cert: NMSDC, WBENC)

4535 Securance LLC
13904 Monroes Business Park
Tampa, FL 33635
Contact: Paul Ashe President
Tel: 877-578-0215
Email: supplydiv@securanceconsulting.com
Website: www.securanceconsulting.com
Independent technology risk consulting & IT auditing services. (AA, estab 2002, empl 12, sales $ 0, cert: NMSDC)

4536 SGF US Inc.
501 Golden Isles Dr, Ste 205
Hallandale Beach, FL 33009
Contact: Kevin Cabrera Acct Mgr
Tel: 954-454-7676
Email: kcabrera@sgfglobal.com
Website: www.sgfglobal.com
Technical recruiting & staffing. (Hisp, estab 1997, empl 90, sales $21,929,723, cert: NMSDC)

INFORMATION TECHNOLOGY: Services

4537	SGS Technologies
	6817 Southpoint Pkwy, Ste 2104
	Jacksonville, FL 32216
	Contact: Arun Venkatesan CEO
	Tel:	904-332-4534
	Email: bids@sgstechnologies.net
	Website: www.sgstechnologies.net
Custom Software Applications Devel, Mobile Apps Devel, Website Design, Digital Marketing, SEO, Salesforce Implementation, CRM, SharePoint Devel. (As-Pac, estab 2003, empl 150, sales $15,000,000, cert: State, NMSDC)

4538	Simplified Technologies, LLC
	6310 Techster Blvd, Ste 2
	Fort Myers, FL 33966
	Contact: Darius Joseph Owner
	Tel:	239-210-9645
	Email: darius@simplifiedtech.biz
	Website: www.simplifiedtech.biz
Network & systems integration, Windows Servers Business Server, SQL Server, Exchange Server, Windows Desktop, Microsoft Office & Office 365. (AA, estab 2010, empl 10, sales , cert: State)

4539	Sonoi Solutions LLC
	800 6th St N
	St. Petersburg, FL 33701
	Contact: Vienggeun Gertsch President
	Tel:	727-341-5100
	Email: vienggeun.gertsch@sonoisolutions.com
	Website: www.sonoisolutions.com
IT aggregation, logistics & technical services for supply chain diversification. (Minority, Woman, estab 2013, empl 2, sales , cert: NMSDC, WBENC)

4540	SpendCheQ, Inc.
	3171 Jasmine Dr
	Delray Beach, FL 33483
	Contact: Mary Ellen Mitchell President
	Tel:	561-870-3171
	Email: mmitchell@spendcheq.com
	Website: www.spendcheq.com
Integrated supply chain & procurement solutions, Catalog Management, Inventory Data Management, Supplier Information Management & Spend Analysis. (Woman, estab 2014, empl 19, sales , cert: State, WBENC)

4541	SurfBigData LLC
	4474 Foxtail Ln
	Weston, FL 33331
	Contact: Andrew Li CEO
	Tel:	954-353-5599
	Email: service@surfbigdata.com
	Website: www.surfbigdata.com
Enterprise Workflow Analysis, Information Technology, Architecture & System Integration, Dev/Ops & Agile Scrum Plan & Management, Web Application Development, Central Information Repository Design, Big Data Platform design. (As-Pac, estab 2015, empl 6, sales $480,000, cert: State)

4542	Synergy Technologies, LLC
	9600 W Sample Rd, Ste 207
	Coral Springs, FL 33065
	Contact: Srikaanth Bollampally Program Mgr
	Tel:	954-775-0064
	Email: sri.b@synergytechs.net
	Website: www.synergyteks.com
Diverse end-to-end IT solutions. (Woman/As-Ind, estab 2006, empl 65, sales $5,000,000, cert: NMSDC, WBENC)

4543	System Soft Technologies, Inc
	3000 Bayport Dr Ste 840
	Tampa, FL 33607
	Contact: Sreedhar Veeramachaneni CEO
	Tel:	727-723-0801
	Email: v.sreedhar@sstech.us
	Website: www.sstech.us
Software development & IT services. (As-Pac, estab 2000, empl 800, sales $67,964,203, cert: State, NMSDC)

4544	Tech Army, LLC
	7777 Davie Road Extension Ste 303B
	Hollywood, FL 33024
	Contact: Jay Narang CEO
	Tel:	954-372-2698
	Email: sales@techarmy.com
	Website: www.techarmy.com
IT consulting and staffing augmentation. (As-Ind, estab 2016, empl 18, sales $ 0, cert: NMSDC, 8(a))

4545	Techno-Transfers of Florida, Inc.
	4609 NW 26th Ave
	Boca Raton, FL 33434
	Contact: Virginia Mendiola Dir
	Tel:	561-212-2383
	Email: vmendiola@techno-transfers.com
	Website: www.techno-transfers.com
IT personnel for temporary contract, temp-to-perm roles & full-time positions. (Minority, Woman, estab 1992, empl 6, sales $350,000, cert: State)

4546	Tec-Link
	16350 BB Downs Blvd, Ste 48942
	Tampa, FL 33646
	Contact: Derek Holmes President
	Tel:	813-929-3222
	Email: derek@tec-link.com
	Website: www.tec-link.com
Information technology professional services & consulting. (AA, estab 1999, empl 20, sales $2,000,000, cert: NMSDC)

4547	The Ashvins Group, Inc.
	6161 Blue Lagoon Dr Ste 340
	Miami, FL 33126
	Contact: Ivette Boyd Partner, Proj Mgr
	Tel:	305-264-4442
	Email: iboyd@ashvinsgroup.com
	Website: www.ashvinsgroup.com
Consulting, software validation, software quality audits. (Woman, estab 2000, empl 20, sales $940,000, cert: WBENC)

4548	The Goal Inc.
	1408 N. Westshore Blvd Ste 705
	Tampa, FL 33607
	Contact: Mary Kate Gowl Managing Dir Business Dev
	Tel:	813-319-7015
	Email: mgowl@thegoalinc.com
	Website: www.thegoalinc.com
Technology Consulting, Software Development, Security Services, and our Government Practice. (Hisp, estab 1998, empl 250, sales $34,000,000, cert: NMSDC, SDB)

4549 Tropical Surveillance & Investigations, Inc.
      1813 N Tampa St
      Tampa, FL 33602
      Contact: JC Dominguez
      Tel: 813-282-0074
      Email: jc@tsilegal.com
      Website: www.tsilegal.com
Process serving & document reproduction. (Minority, Woman, estab 2003, empl 15, sales $1,100,000, cert: NMSDC)

4550 Vitaver and Associates, Inc.
      401 East Las Olas Boulevard Ste 1400
      Fort Lauderdale, FL 33301
      Contact: Pablo Vitaver CEO
      Tel: 954-382-0075
      Email: pablo@vitaver.com
      Website: www.vitaver.com
IT staff augmentation & software outsourcing. (Hisp, estab 1993, empl 15, sales $8,309,079, cert: State)

4551 Wayfinder, LLC
      7300 Biscayne Blvd, Ste 200
      Miami, FL 33138
      Contact: Chinmoy Raval CEO
      Tel: 305-496-8663
      Email: letstalk@wayfinder-ux.com
      Website: www.wayfinder-ux.com
Digital application design, website design and product development. (As-Ind, estab 2004, empl 5, sales $2,300,000, cert: NMSDC)

4552 Widescope Consulting And Contracting Services LLC
      14466 Kandi Ct
      Largo, FL 33774
      Contact: Donald Jackson VP of Operations
      Tel: 813-374-5205
      Email: donald.jackson@widescopeccs.com
      Website: www.widescopeccs.com
IT, Cyber Security, Submarine Fiber optic cable route survey, engineering, professional services & consulting. (AA, estab 2014, empl 6, sales , cert: 8(a))

Georgia

4553 1Source International, LLC
      925 Woodstock Rd Ste 150
      Roswell, GA 30075
      Contact: Margaret Tinsley VP Operations
      Tel: 770-733-1202
      Email: mtinsley@1source-intl.net
      Website: www.1sourceinternational.com
Audio, video & conferencing solutions. (Woman, estab 2000, empl 11, sales $6,000,000, cert: WBENC)

4554 24X7SYSTEMS, Inc.
      1080 Holcombe Bridge Rd Bldg 200, Ste 150
      Roswell, GA 30076
      Contact: Ranjan Dattagupta EVP
      Tel: 678-234-2711
      Email: ranjan@24x7systems.com
      Website: www.24x7systems.com
Information Technology solutions, Resource Sourcing, PM, Entr Arch, Application (As-Ind, estab 2000, empl 20, sales $4,000,000, cert: NMSDC, 8(a))

4555 3i People, Inc.
      5755 N Point Pkwy Ste 234
      Alpharetta, GA 30022
      Contact: Buvi Raj CMO
      Tel: 678-628-4810
      Email: rbuvi@3ipeople.com
      Website: www.3ipeople.com
IT consulting, application dev, project mgmt & contract staffing. (As-Pac, estab 2002, empl 220, sales $13,500,000, cert: NMSDC)

4556 Accretive Technologies, Inc.
      330 Research Ct Ste 250
      Norcross, GA 30092
      Contact: Claire Ehrhardt President
      Tel: 678-328-2440
      Email: claire@accretive.com
      Website: www.accretive.com
Information technology consulting & placement services. (Woman, estab 1997, empl 17, sales $1,857,679, cert: WBENC)

4557 ACS Solutions
      2400 Meadowbrook Pkwy
      Duluth, GA 30096
      Contact: Akshay Reddy Dir Business Dev
      Tel: 630-605-4731
      Email: akshay.reddy@acsicorp.com
      Website: www.acsicorp.com
IT services: staffing, payrolling, vendor management services, consulting & business solutions. (As-Ind, estab 1998, empl 17000, sales $683,000,000, cert: NMSDC)

4558 Adroix Corp DBA CodeForce 360
      3970 Old Milton pkwy, Ste 200 Ste 200
      Alpharetta, GA 30005
      Contact: Dickson-Lemond VP Sales
      Tel: 470-407-4189
      Email: amandad@codeforce.com
      Website: www.codeforce.com/
IT Staffing & Talent Management. (As-Ind, estab 2010, empl 250, sales $30,000,000, cert: NMSDC)

4559 Alegna Technologies, Inc.
      3355 Lenox Rd NE
      Atlanta, GA 30326
      Contact: Angela Cabrera CEO
      Tel: 770-855-3328
      Email: acabrera@AlegnaTechnologies.com
      Website: www.AlegnaTechnologies.com
IoT- Artificial Intelligence (AI) & Remote-Early Warning Smart Solutions. (Hisp, estab 2011, empl 17, sales $1,273,000, cert: State)

4560 Aligned Partner Group LLC
      2101 Reynolds Walk Trl
      Greensboro, GA 30642
      Contact: Luke Maslow CEO
      Tel: 470-869-1388
      Email: luke@apgemergingtech.com
      Website: www.apgemergingtech.com
Build lowcode, nocode, mobile, web, and voice software platforms. (Hisp, estab 2018, empl 14, sales $662,000, cert: NMSDC)

4561 Allstaff Technical Solutions
      1954 Airport Road Ste 220
      Atlanta, GA 30341
      Contact: Justin Katz VP Business Devel
      Tel: 678-281-3063
      Email: jkatz@allstafftech.com
      Website: www.allstaffsolutions.net/
Infrastructure Support, Cyber Security, Application Development, and Engineering. (Woman, estab 1991, empl 176, sales $14,000,000, cert: WBENC)

4562 Analysts International Corporation (AIC)
      2400 Meadowbrook Pkwy
      Duluth, GA 55435
      Contact: Vicki Bien Sr Dir Mktg/Sales
      Tel: 800-800-5044
      Email: diversitysupplier@aictalent.com
      Website: www.analysts.com
Information technology (IT) services. (As-Ind, estab 1966, empl 350, sales $695,000,000, cert: NMSDC)

4563 Applications Technology Group, Inc.
      5825 Glenridge Dr, Bldg3, Ste 101
      Atlanta, GA 30328
      Contact: Trelaine Business Devel Mgr
      Tel: 404-552-0191
      Email: tnunnally@atgworks.com
      Website: www.atgwork.com
Technical & staffing services. (Minority, Woman, estab 2004, empl 105, sales $3,000,000, cert: NMSDC)

4564 Arete Technology Solutions, Inc. dba STATEMENT
      3379 Peachtree Road NE Ste 555
      Atlanta, GA 30326
      Contact: Kendall Flagg Principal
      Tel: 800-640-5589
      Email: kendall.flagg@statementcorp.com
      Website: www.statementcorp.com
Software & IT consulting, Architecture Custom software development Automated Testing Continuous Development and Integration Oracle Database Development noSql Development Services Native tablet/mobile iOS. (AA, estab 2007, empl 12, sales $1,641,519, cert: NMSDC)

4565 Arion Systems, Inc.
      2741 Calloway Ct
      Duluth, GA 30097
      Contact: Michael Brewington II President
      Tel: 770-569-3434
      Email: michael.brewington@arioncorp.com
      Website: www.ArionCorp.com
Implementation & systems integration consulting: business applications & ERP products, PeopleSoft, SAP, Oracle, Siebel, technology solutions, financials, supply chain mgmt, human capital mgmt, enterprise performance mgmt. (Woman/AA, estab 2003, empl 10, sales $2,000,000, cert: NMSDC)

4566 Armedia LLC
      200 Galleria Pkwy, Ste 440
      Atlanta, GA 30339
      Contact: Andre Staten Global Sales Dir
      Tel: 678-945-4417
      Email: astaten@armedia.com
      Website: www.armedia.com
Enterprise content management (ECM): design, implementation, collaboration, web publishing, workflow, digital asset management & compliance. (AA, estab 2002, empl 30, sales $10,000,000, cert: NMSDC)

4567 ASAP Solutions Group, LLC
      3885 Holcomb Bridge Rd
      Norcross, GA 30092
      Contact: Nancy Williams CEO
      Tel: 770-246-1718
      Email: nancy@myasap.com
      Website: www.myasap.com
IT staff augmentation. (Woman, estab 1989, empl 800, sales $60,000,000, cert: CPUC, WBENC)

4568 Bellsoft
      PO Box 743622
      Atlanta, GA 30374
      Contact: Kannan Ramanathan Dir Client Services
      Tel: 888-545-7639
      Email: kannanr@ameri100.com
      Website: www.ameri100.com/
Implement ERP solutions: JD Edwards, SAP & PeopleSoft. (Minority, estab 1996, empl 350, sales $30,000,000, cert: NMSDC)

4569 Blaze Information Systems Inc.
      13026 Dartmore Ave
      Alpharetta, GA 30005
      Contact: Smita Deshpande CEO
      Tel: 877-877-5293
      Email: smita.deshpande@blazeinfosys.com
      Website: www.blazeinfosys.com
Onsite Technical Support, Onsite Temporary Technology Staffing, Remote Temporary Technology Staffing, End-To-End e-Business Solutions. (Minority, Woman, estab 2009, empl 5, sales $116,000, cert: State)

4570 BlueFletch LLC
      621 North Ave NE Ste A-150
      Atlanta, GA 30308
      Contact: Richard Makerson Managing Partner
      Tel: 855-529-6349
      Email: invoices@bluefletch.com
      Website: www.bluefletch.com
Mobile software development, program leadership, business analysis, mobile web application development, legacy integration, MDM management & cloud infrastructure integration. (AA, estab 2008, empl 34, sales $2,906,767, cert: NMSDC)

4571 BMC Solutions, Inc.
      3391 Town Point Dr, Ste 300
      Kennesaw, GA 30144
      Contact: George Hergen Mgr Business Devel
      Tel: 770-514-6704
      Email: ghergen@bmcsolutions.com
      Website: www.BMCSolutions.com
Computer support & services: maintenance, design, implemeny & support networks. (Woman, estab 1990, empl 130, sales $34,645,320, cert: WBENC)

4572 Capricorn Systems, Inc.
      3569 Habersham At Northlake Bldg K
      Tucker, GA 30084
      Contact: Charles Goldman VP Sales
      Tel: 678-514-1080
      Email: cgoldman@capricornsys.com
      Website: www.capricornsys.com
Software consulting: staff augmentation, turnkey custom application develpment & permanent placements, on site, offsite & off-shore. (Minority, estab 1991, empl 155, sales $3,250,000, cert: NMSDC)

INFORMATION TECHNOLOGY: Services

4573 Cellworx LLC
      1005 Alderman Ste 110
      Alpharetta, GA 30005
      Contact: Chandrasekhar Anchala
      Tel: 678-254-9094
      Email: csanchala@celworx.com
      Website: www.celworx.com
Wireless & wireline technology design, development, validation & realization, Software Defined Network, Cloud & Virtualization. (As-Ind, estab 2008, empl 10, sales $500,000, cert: NMSDC, CPUC)

4574 Charter Global Inc.
      One Glenlake Pkwy Ste 525
      Altanta, GA 30328
      Contact: Dev Shah Client Engagement Mgr
      Tel: 770-326-9933
      Email: dshah@charterglobal.com
      Website: www.charterglobal.com
Software consulting svcs: client server, web based, e-commerce. (Minority, estab 1994, empl 1100, sales $45,000,000, cert: NMSDC)

4575 CI2, Inc.
      200 Galleria Pkwy, Ste 1200
      Atlanta, GA 30339
      Contact: Sharon Mendon VP bus devel
      Tel: 770-425-2267
      Email: info2@ci2.com
      Website: www.ci2.com
Systems integration & engineering, telecommunications mgmt. (Woman/AA, estab 1993, empl 83, sales $25,000,000, cert: State, City, NMSDC)

4576 Competent Systems Inc.
      4080 McGinnis Ferry Rd Ste 1504
      Alpharetta, GA 30005
      Contact: Sridhar Konkala Mgr
      Tel: 678-691-7120
      Email: skonkala@competentsystems.com
      Website: www.competentsystems.com
Information Technology Consulting, Development, Outsourcing & Technology Staffing. (As-Pac, estab 2004, empl 150, sales $15,000,000, cert: NMSDC)

4577 Concept Software & Services Inc
      11600 Atlantis Place Ste E
      Alpharetta, GA 30022
      Contact: Ravindra Bhave CEO
      Tel: 770-300-9486
      Email: ravi@concept-inc.com
      Website: www.concept-inc.com
Software solutions, IT consulting, application outsourcing & enterprise consulting services. (As-Ind, estab 1998, empl 57, sales $7,682,520, cert: NMSDC)

4578 Corpnet Consulting LLC
      2300 Lakeview Pkwy, Ste 700
      Alpharetta, GA 30009
      Contact: Faisal Ansari Managing Principal
      Tel: 678-795-1612
      Email: corpnet@corpnetconsulting.com
      Website: www.corpnetconsulting.com
Information security & risk management consultancy services, IT platform integration services. (Minority, Woman, estab 2008, empl 15, sales $1,300,000, cert: WBENC)

4579 Datamatics Consultants Inc.
      3505 Duluth Park Ln Ste 200
      Duluth, GA 30096
      Contact: Frank Kulendran Business Devel Mgr
      Tel: 770-232-9460
      Email: frank@datamatics.us
      Website: www.datamatics.us
Business process management, financial management, CRP, ERP, consulting & strategy, architecture & integration, custom systems dev, supply chain mgmt, knowledge mgmt, IT strategy, re-engineering & migration services, maintenance. (As-Ind, estab 1993, empl 95, sales $10,000,000, cert: NMSDC)

4580 Dataset, Inc.
      145 Noble Ct Ste 100
      Alpharetta, GA 30005
      Contact: Azhar Syed President
      Tel: 678-240-0771
      Email: azhar_syed@dataset-inc.com
      Website: www.datasetcorp.com
Professional consulting services, software & hardware installation, software training & temporary contractors. (As-Ind, estab 1994, empl 7, sales $3,009,031, cert: NMSDC)

4581 Datum Software Inc.
      12000 Findley Road, Ste 350
      Johns Creek, GA 30097
      Contact: Ram Moorthy President
      Tel: 678-740-0265
      Email: ram@datumsoftware.com
      Website: www.datumsoftware.com
Software application devel, system integration & IT staffing svcs. (Woman/As-Ind, estab 1992, empl 45, sales $5,702,565, cert: NMSDC, WBENC)

4582 Diversant, LLC
      2400 Meadowbrook Pkwy
      Duluth, GA 30096
      Contact: Spencer Smith Business Dev Mgr
      Tel: 732-222-1250
      Email: ssmith@diversant.com
      Website: www.diversant.com
IT staffing and diversity products, IT staff augmentation, direct hire, contract. (AA, estab 2010, empl 27000, sales $1,700,000,000, cert: NMSDC)

4583 Dominus Gray, LLC
      1273 Mackintosh Park NW
      Atlanta, GA 30318
      Contact: Odie Gray CEO
      Tel: 404-360-7453
      Email: odie.gray@dominusgray.com
      Website: www.dominusgray.com
Cybersecurity & IT Diversity Staffing Services as well as the development and administration of cyber security workforce development. (AA, estab 2020, empl 1, sales , cert: NMSDC)

4584 DW Practice, LLC
      5901 Peachtree Dunwoody Rd Ste C-160
      Atlanta, GA 30328
      Contact: Rajani Koneru President
      Tel: 678-999-8197
      Email: raj.koneru@dwpractice.com
      Website: www.dwpractice.com
Software development services, product development services & IT staffing services. (As-Pac, estab 1998, empl 30, sales $4,000,000, cert: NMSDC)

INFORMATION TECHNOLOGY: Services

4585   Edge Solutions, LLC
        131 Roswell St C-101
        Alpharetta, GA 30009
        Contact: Julie Ison Haley CEO
        Tel: 888-861-8884
        Email: jhaley@edge-solutions.com
        Website: www.edge-solutions.com
Data center solutions (hardware & software), Application development tools, cloud computing, virtualization, network security, data storage, backup and recovery, archiving, professional & managed services. (Woman, estab 2008, empl 32, sales $71,000,000, cert: WBENC)

4586   Elgia, Inc.
        11675 Rainwater Dr
        Alpharetta, GA 30009
        Contact: Sandra Jackson Marketing Mgr
        Tel: 678-242-4000
        Email: sjackson@elgia.com
        Website: www.elgia.com
Web conferencing applications, WebEx & Live Meeting, software applications. (Woman/AA, estab 2001, empl 20, sales $1,031,000, cert: WBENC)

4587   Enrich Inc
        3655 Brookside Pkwy Ste 265
        Alpharetta, GA 30022
        Contact: Paul Herron VP-Sales & Marketing
        Tel: 770-667-0510
        Email: info@enrich.com
        Website: www.enrich.com
Software deployment lifecycle in Oracle EBS. (Minority, Woman, estab 2004, empl 200, sales $17,624,212, cert: NMSDC)

4588   Entellimetrix LLC
        445 Victorian Lane
        Johns Creek, GA 30097
        Contact: Magha Devan Partner
        Tel: 678-779-7673
        Email: mdevan@entellimetrix.com
        Website: www.entellimetrix.com
Data Management, Business Intelligence and Analytics Services, Teradata, Informatica, DataStage. (Woman/As-Ind, estab 2012, empl 17, sales $2,450,000, cert: State, City, CPUC, 8(a))

4589   Exalt Integrated Technologies LLC
        PO Box 888161
        Atlanta, GA 30356
        Contact: Donald Maycott VP
        Tel: 678-920-3019
        Email: dmaycott@exaltit.com
        Website: www.exaltit.com
Network business consulting, organizational assessment, IT strategic planning, telecommunications services, security assessment, intrusion detection, firewall & DMZ implementation & management. (Woman/AA, estab 2004, empl 15, sales $1,750,000, cert: NMSDC)

4590   Fabulous Sites, Inc.
        160 Clairemont Ave, Ste 555
        Decatur, GA 30030
        Contact: Laron Walker President
        Tel: 404-478-2050
        Email: walkerla@sciberus.com
        Website: www.sciberus.com
Information technology consulting & software development. (AA, estab 2006, empl 5, sales $1,447,158, cert: NMSDC, 8(a))

4591   Firmament Solutions
        510 Plaza Dr
        College Park, GA 30349
        Contact: Adrian Andrews
        Tel: 770-742-0385
        Email: aandrews@firmamentsolutions.com
        Website: www.firmamentsolutions.com
Managed IT Services, Network Services, CAT3 & CAT6 Install, Hosting Software Service, Break FIX, Fiber Patch Panel, Cloud Services, ISP Services, Conduit/Surface Mount, IT Asset Mgmt, App Support, Voice/Mobile. (AA, estab 2013, empl 10, sales , cert: State, City, NMSDC)

4592   Focused HR-Solutions, LLC
        400 Galleria Pkwy, Ste 1500
        Atlanta, GA 30309
        Contact: Ross Falik President
        Tel: 678-385-6120
        Email: rfalik@fhr-solutions.com
        Website: www.fhr-solutions.com
IT staffing: software development, project management, development, networking. (Woman, estab 2002, empl 71, sales , cert: WBENC)

4593   Global Resource Manangement, Inc.
        5400 Laurel Springs Pkwy Ste 902
        Suwanee, GA 30024
        Contact: Naheed Syed CEO
        Tel: 678-456-6992
        Email: naheed1@grmi.net
        Website: www.grmi.net
IT consulting, telecommunications & staff augmentation. (Minority, Woman, estab 1993, empl 70, sales $2,600,000, cert: NMSDC, WBENC)

4594   Global Technology Services Group, Inc.
        2850 Barrett Lakes Blvd NW Ste 500
        Kennesaw, GA 30144
        Contact: Jacqueline Holland CEO
        Tel: 404-551-5189
        Email: jacqui@gtservices.net
        Website: www.gtservices.net
IT Asset Management, Auditing, Inventory Mgmt, Warehouse & Logistics, Project Mgmt & Deployment, Reverse Logistics & Asset Recovery, NSA Level Data Security, Depot Technology Hardware Repair & Refurbishment. (Woman, estab 2010, empl 44, sales $8,947,059, cert: State, WBENC)

4595   GTS, Inc.
        1325 Satellite Blvd Bldg 1600, Ste 1601
        Suwanee, GA 30024
        Contact: Dinesh Raturi President
        Tel: 770-497-8637
        Email: dinesh@gtsamerica.com
        Website: www.gtsamerica.com
IT staff augmentation, permanent & contract, software development, requirement analysis & design, outsourcing. (Woman/As-Ind, estab 1998, empl 150, sales $16,500,000, cert: NMSDC, WBENC)

4596   Heagney Logan Group, LLC
        2002 Summit Blvd Ste 300
        Atlanta, GA 30319
        Contact: Jeannette Weigelt Principal
        Tel: 404-267-1351
        Email: info@heagneylogan.com
        Website: www.heagneylogangroup.com
Management Consulting, IT Consultant Staffing, Project Management, ERP Consulting, Remote Development, Contract Technical Staffing. (AA, estab 2009, empl 3, sales $924,954, cert: State, NMSDC)

INFORMATION TECHNOLOGY: Services

4597 HireGenics, Inc.
      2400 Meadowbrook Pkwy
      Duluth, GA 30096
      Contact: Nancy Budmayr Program Dir
      Tel: 651-470-5240
      Email: nancy.budmayr@hiregenics.com
      Website: www.hiregenics.com
Technology consulting & solutions: onsite, near-shore, off-shore, business intelligence, e-business, database technologies, ERP, CRM. (As-Ind, estab 1998, empl 10000, sales $683,000,000, cert: NMSDC)

4598 IBEX IT Business Experts LLC
      3295 River Exchange Dr, Ste 550
      Sandy Springs, GA 30092
      Contact: Maggie Carter Sales Dir
      Tel: 678-752-7542
      Email: mcarter@ibexexperts.com
      Website: www.ibexexperts.com
IT Service Mgmt, Enterprise Governance, Project Management, IT Security Management. (Woman/AA, estab , empl , sales $7,500,000, cert: NMSDC, WBENC, 8(a))

4599 Impel Professional Consulting, LLC
      7058 Wind Run Way
      Stone Mountain, GA 30082
      Contact: Jerome Potts Business Dev Dir
      Tel: 678-410-9245
      Email: info@impelprofessional.com
      Website: www.impelprofessional.com
Design & develop end-to-end integrated IT Solutions in ERP, BI, CRM Assessment for ERP systems and Business process improvements for SAP IT Road Maps and Best Practices. (Woman/AA, estab 2016, empl 2, sales , cert: State, WBENC)

4600 INDU LLC dba intiGrow
      2760 Peach tree Ind. Blvd, Ste D
      Duluth, GA 30097
      Contact: Mike Evans Business Dev Exec
      Tel: 678-666-4365
      Email: mike@intigrow.com
      Website: www.intigrow.com
Managed Security Services, Identity & Access Management, Federated Identity Management, Single Sign On (E-SSO and SSO), Intrusion Detection & Prevention, Vulnerability Assessment & Penetration Testing. (As-Pac, estab 2006, empl 580, sales $13,000,000, cert: NMSDC)

4601 Information Technology Consulting Company
      190 Bluegrass Valley Pkwy Ste B7
      Alpharetta, GA 30005
      Contact: Gary Kallenbach Sr Procurement Advisor
      Tel: 614-207-9475
      Email: gkallenbach@itc2.net
      Website: www.itc2.net
IT resource & infrastrucute consulting. (Hisp, estab 2006, empl 15, sales $ 0, cert: NMSDC)

4602 InfoSmart Technologies Inc.
      5400 Laurel Springs Pkwy Ste 706
      Suwanee, GA 30024
      Contact: Karun Kevin Reddy President
      Tel: 678-584-5635
      Email: kevin@infosmarttech.com
      Website: www.infosmarttech.com
Software consulting, project management, participation & subcontracting, partnership, staff augumentation, software programming, design & area. (As-Ind, estab 1998, empl 75, sales $6,700,000, cert: NMSDC)

4603 Intellectual Concepts LLC
      3300 Buckeye Rd, Ste 601
      Atlanta, GA 30341
      Contact: DeLois Babiker CEO
      Tel: 202-321-4560
      Email: dbabiker@intellectualconcepts.net
      Website: www.intellectualconcepts.com
Information management technology, full life-cycle IT services, communication, content, collaboration & conferencing, contract administration, asset management & IT acquisition services. (Woman/AA, estab 2004, empl 7, sales $817,000, cert: City, NMSDC, WBENC, 8(a))

4604 IT Division, Inc.
      5955 Pkwy North Blvd Unit A
      Cumming, GA 30040
      Contact: Jamie Crosby Dir of Sales
      Tel: 678-649-3022
      Email: jamiec@itdivisioninc.com
      Website: www.itdivisioninc.com
IT staffing & services, application development, application testing & infrastructure services. (Minority, Woman, estab 2006, empl 165, sales $9,332,282, cert: State)

4605 K.L. Scott & Associates LLC
      235 Peachtree St NE Ste 400
      Atlanta, GA 30303
      Contact: Keith Scott CEO
      Tel: 404-692-5552
      Email: keith.scott@klscottassociates.com
      Website: www.klscottassociates.com
Information technology & management consulting, data analytics, analysis, and business growth strategy, Business Process Management (BPM) & (Re)engineering. (AA, estab 2013, empl 10, sales , cert: NMSDC)

4606 Kavi Software Inc.
      250 Gladeside Path
      Suwanee, GA 30024
      Contact: Jegannathan Mehalingam President
      Tel: 678-358-4861
      Email: mjegann@kavisoft.net
      Website: www.kavisoft.net
IT services & temporary staffing: application security implementation. (As-Ind, estab 1999, empl 25, sales $1,500,000, cert: NMSDC)

4607 Lanin Technologies
      730 Stuart Ct
      Alpharetta, GA 30004
      Contact: Mariano Saldana VP Operations
      Tel: 678-620-8210
      Email: msaldana@lanintech.com
      Website: www.lanintech.com
Software development, IT services, custom software development; primarily web, mobile applications & SAP. (Hisp, estab 2015, empl 3, sales , cert: NMSDC)

4608 Management Decisions, Inc. - MDI Group
      35 Technology Pkwy S Ste 150
      Norcross, GA 30092
      Contact: Joel McCreight Client Business Devel
      Tel: 770-416-7949
      Email: jmccreight@mdigroup.com
      Website: www.mdigroup.com
IT staffing & contracting, project mgmt, vendor mgmt, direct hire, IT staffing. (Woman, estab , empl , sales $45,800,000, cert: WBENC, NWBOC)

4609 McNeal Professional Services, Inc.
      2593 Kennesaw Due W Rd Ste 200
      Kennesaw, GA 30144
      Contact: Leslie McNeal Dir Business Dev
      Tel: 770-218-2000
      Email: leslie.mcneal@mcnealpro.com
      Website: www.mcnealpro.com
Technical staffing, wireless engineering svcs. (Woman/AA, estab 2001, empl 50, sales $5,600,000, cert: WBENC)

4610 Metasys Technologies
      3460 Summit Ridge Pkwy, #401
      Duluth, GA 30096
      Contact: Romeen Sheth President
      Tel: 678-523-1798
      Email: info@metasysinc.com
      Website: www.metasysinc.com
Information technology svcs: e-business application devel & integration, staff augmentation. (Minority, estab 2000, empl 495, sales $40,900,000, cert: NMSDC)

4611 Milletech Systems Inc.
      11539 Park Woods Cir, Ste 201
      Alpharetta, GA 30005
      Contact: Nasir Mujawar VP
      Tel: 770-619-0095
      Email: nmujawar@milletechinc.com
      Website: www.milletechinc.com
IT services: staffing & consultants, outsourcing, ERP solutions & implementation, application support, upgrades, custom application devel, training, QA & testing, systems integration. (Woman/As-Ind, estab 2000, empl 46, sales $3,900,000, cert: NMSDC)

4612 Next Level Business Services Inc.
      221 Roswell St Ste 150
      Alpharetta, GA 30009
      Contact: Theresa Jackson Dir Strategic Business
      Tel: 678-438-0195
      Email: theresa.jackson@nlbtech.com
      Website: www.nlbservices.com
IT Consultancy and BPO Services. (As-Ind, estab 2007, empl 6000, sales $378,000,000, cert: NMSDC)

4613 Nineteen Eleven Solutions Inc.
      12850 Hwy 9 Ste 600-247
      Alpharetta, GA 30004
      Contact: Daud Haseeb Principal
      Tel: 404-644-3702
      Email: daud@1911solutions.com
      Website: www.nineteenelevensolutions.com/
IT Staffing, ERP (Oracle, PeopleSoft, & SAP), Open Source & Big Data (Hadoop). (AA, estab 2010, empl 9, sales $275,000, cert: NMSDC)

4614 Nutech Systems Inc.
      2675 Paces Ferry Rd Ste 460
      Atlanta, GA 30339
      Contact: Nachu Anbil President
      Tel: 770-434-7063
      Email: nanbil@nutech-inc.com
      Website: www.nutech-inc.com
IT staff augmentation, IT solutions, software development life cycle, support & infrastructure. (As-Ind, estab 1995, empl 120, sales $20,400,000, cert: NMSDC)

4615 Ocher Technology Group
      130 Prospect Pl
      Alpharetta, GA 30005
      Contact: Vijay Vasudevan CEO
      Tel: 678-521-6329
      Email: vijay_vasudevan@ochertech.com
      Website: www.ochertech.com
IT consulting & staffing. (As-Ind, estab 2007, empl 55, sales $4,945,175, cert: NMSDC)

4616 Olivine LLC
      970 Peachtree Industrial Blvd. Ste 100
      Suwanee, GA 30024
      Contact: Rajeev Maddur Sr Acct Mgr
      Tel: 770-596-5155
      Email: rajeevm@olivinellc.com
      Website: www.olivinellc.com
IT Consulting Services, Contract, Contract to Hire and Direct hire placements. (As-Ind, estab 2006, empl 20, sales , cert: NMSDC)

4617 Open Systems Inc.
      6495 Shiloh Rd, Ste 310
      Alpharetta, GA 30005
      Contact: Karen Ashley Sr Recruiting Mgr
      Tel: 770-752-8600
      Email: karen.ashley@opensystemsinc.com
      Website: www.opensystemsinc.com
IT consulting & custom software development. (Minority, estab 1994, empl 300, sales $15,165,059, cert: NMSDC)

4618 Orpine Inc.
      5865 N Point Pkwy, Ste 320
      Alpharetta, GA 30022
      Contact: Krish Subbiah Partner
      Tel: 770-475-1445
      Email: krish@orpine.com
      Website: www.orpine.com/
Custom application development services, key information, performance, strategies & Operations. (As-Ind, estab 2006, empl 163, sales $18,170,000, cert: NMSDC)

4619 Paramount Software Solutions, Inc
      4030 Old Milton Pkwy
      Alpharetta, GA 30005
      Contact: Srinivas Kumar Business Devel Mgr
      Tel: 770-872-7829
      Email: srinivas@paramountsoft.net
      Website: www.paramountsoft.net/
IT Staffing, IT Consulting, Software outsourcing % development services. (As-Ind, estab 1997, empl 120, sales $178,777,000, cert: NMSDC)

4620 Paramount Software Solutions, Inc.
      4030 Old Milton Pkwy
      Alpharetta, GA 30005
      Contact: Lokesh Shiv Sr Business Exec
      Tel: 770-857-8348
      Email: lokesh@paramountsoft.net
      Website: www.paramountsoft.net
Research and Emerging Technologies. (Minority, estab 1997, empl 200, sales , cert: NMSDC)

INFORMATION TECHNOLOGY: Services

4621 PIE Technology Consulting
559 Commons Park Lane
Tucker, GA 30084
Contact: Wesner Charlotin Dir of Operations
Tel: 877-866-2677
Email: wesnerc@pietconsulting.com
Website: www.pietconsulting.com
Planning, design & implement Microsoft products: Active Directory, Exchange, Lync/Skype for Business, SharePoint, and Office 365. (AA, estab 2014, empl 7, sales $554,276, cert: NMSDC)

4622 Precedent Technologies LLC
3330 Cumberland Blvd SE, Ste 500
Atlanta, GA 30339
Contact: Patrick Carley
Tel: 770-303-0223
Email: pfcarley@precedent-tech.com
Website: www.precedent-tech.com
Strategic IT consulting & project mgmt, voice over IP telephone systems installation & support, web services, network design, installation and support, internet security software/services. (AA, estab 2006, empl 3, sales $196,000, cert: NMSDC)

4623 Premier Software Solutions
3707 Main St, Ste 201
College Park, GA 30337
Contact: Paul Gupta President
Tel: 678-643-3034
Email: pgupta@presoftsolutions.com
Website: www.presoftsolutions.com
IT Solutions & Services, Cisco Security, Data Analytics & Visualization. (Woman/As-Ind, estab 2008, empl 5, sales $3,050,000, cert: 8(a))

4624 Primus Software Corporation
3061 Peachtree Industrial Blvd Ste 110
Duluth, GA 30097
Contact: Satish Anand President, Project Sevices
Tel: 678-336-1871
Email: supplier.diversity@primussoft.com
Website: www.primussoft.com
J2EE technology implementation, web services, IBM Websphere, MS .NET Web svcs, data warehousing, Oracle & SYBASE, project management, ERP, CRM and SCM technologies. (Minority, Woman, estab 1996, empl 220, sales $27,000,000, cert: NMSDC, WBENC)

4625 Professional Technology Integration, Inc.
5425 Peachtree Pkwy NW
Peachtree Corners, GA 30092
Contact: Walter Lee Jones, III CEO
Tel: 877-643-6038
Email: walter.jones@professionaltechintegration.com
Website: www.professionaltechintegration.com
Information technology consulting: software, database application development. (AA, estab 2001, empl 1, sales $180,000, cert: NMSDC)

4626 Prosys Information Systems
6025 The Corners Pkwy Ste 120
Norcross, GA 30092
Contact: Becky Brown Acct Exec
Tel: 404-663-1403
Email: becky.brown@prosysis.com
Website: www.prosysis.com
IP telephony & wireless, network integration, outsourcing solutions & technical staff augmentation. (Woman, estab 1997, empl 425, sales $776,000,000, cert: WBENC)

4627 PSR Associates, Inc.
3350 Riverwood Pkwy Ste 1900
Atlanta, GA 30339
Contact: Ernest Ball SVP
Tel: 404-618-0206
Email: eball@psrassociates.com
Website: www.psrassociates.com
Information technology, program management, project management, staff augmentation, web portal, customer relationship management, IT resources, program testing. (As-Pac, estab 2003, empl 43, sales $7,900,000, cert: NMSDC)

4628 Pyramid Consulting, Inc.
3060 Kimball Bridge Rd Ste 200
Alpharetta, GA 30022
Contact: Lara Lundy Exec VP Client Relations
Tel: 678-514-3500
Email: pcistaffing@pyramici.com
Website: www.pyramidci.com
Information technology consulting: staff augmentation, turnkey IT projects. (As-Ind, estab 1996, empl 1150, sales $283,000,000, cert: NMSDC)

4629 Rapid IT, Inc.
4080 McGinnis Ferry Rd, Ste 1206
Atlanta, GA 30005
Contact: Goutham Goli President
Tel: 678-366-3820
Email: contracts@rapiditinc.com
Website: www.rapiditinc.com
Information Technology. (As-Ind, estab 2006, empl 120, sales $ 0, cert: NMSDC)

4630 Renovo Data, Inc.
3121 Maple Dr Ste 200
Atlanta, GA 30305
Contact: Charlotta Vinson President
Tel: 404-935-6363
Email: cvinson@renovodata.com
Website: www.renovodata.com
Data backup & disaster recovery solutions: replication services, virtualization, consulting services. (Minority, Woman, estab 2005, empl 9, sales $2,000,000, cert: NMSDC, NWBOC)

4631 ResiliEnt Business Solutions, LLC
11175 Cicero Dr, Ste 100
Alpharetta, GA 30022
Contact: CEO
Tel: 678-242-5242
Email: infoservices@resilientbiz.com
Website: www.resilientbiz.com
SDLC, Business Intelligence, Enterprise Data Management/Reporting, Data Modeling, Governance, warehousing, cleansing, WebFOCUS, WebQuery, ScoreCards, Dashboards Cognos, MicroStrategy, Mobile Development. (Woman, estab 2004, empl 6, sales $1,153,725, cert: WBENC)

4632 RiVi Consulting Group LLC
2475 Northwinds Pkwy, Ste 200
Alpharetta, GA 30009
Contact: Bhushan Mocherla CIO/partner
Tel: 678-643-8133
Email: bmocherla@rivigroup.com
Website: www.rivigroup.com
Technology solutions: SAP, Peoplesoft & Oracle. (Woman/As-Ind, estab 2002, empl 45, sales $6,217,522, cert: NMSDC, WBENC, 8(a))

INFORMATION TECHNOLOGY: Services

4633 RTX Technology Partners, LLC
400 Perimeter Center Terr NE Ste 900
Atlanta, GA 30346
Contact: M. Hans Delly Managing Dir
Tel: 404-551-5609
Email: m.hans.delly@rtxpartners.com
Website: www.rtxpartners.com
Global management & technology consulting: business strategy, technology planning & architecture & business process optimization. (AA, estab 2007, empl 25, sales $6,500,000, cert: NMSDC)

4634 Scintel Technologies Inc.
6340 Sugarloaf Pkwy Ste 200
Duluth, GA 30097
Contact: Shailesh Patel Acct Mgr
Tel: 678-775-6874
Email: s.patel@scintel.com
Website: www.scintel.com
Application outsourcing & enterprise consulting solutions. (As-Ind, estab 2003, empl 400, sales $17,500,000, cert: NMSDC)

4635 Scope IT Consulting
3235 Satellite Blvd Bldg 400, Ste 300
Duluth, GA 30096
Contact: Nadir Noorani Principal, Consultant
Tel: 912-580-5929
Email: nadir.noorani@scopeitconsulting.com
Website: www.scopeitconsulting.com
Business Process Management, Project Management, Mobility Solutions, BigData Solutions, Cloud Solutions. (Woman/As-Ind, estab 2015, empl 16, sales , cert: NMSDC, WBENC)

4636 Secure Traces LLC
270 Prospect Pl
Alpharetta, GA 30005
Contact: Natraj Subramaniam
Tel: 404-918-8226
Email: natraj@securetraces.com
Website: www.securetraces.com
Cyber Security, IT Data Management, Networking, Applications, Cloud Services, ETL Services. (As-Ind, estab 2018, empl 40, sales , cert: State)

4637 Serenity Infotech, Inc.
950 Scales Rd, Ste 104
Suwanee, GA 30024
Contact: Srini Vangimalla Partner
Tel: 770-242-9966
Email: srini@serenityinfotech.com
Website: www.serenityinfotech.com
Software solutions & consulting services. (As-Pac, estab 1997, empl 120, sales $13,000,000, cert: NMSDC)

4638 Six Consulting, Inc.
5900 Windward Pkwy, Ste 230
Alpharetta, GA 30005
Contact: Sam Yehya VP
Tel: 470-395-0200
Email: sa@sixconsultingcorp.com
Website: www.sixconsultingcorp.com
Custom Application Development & Maintenance, Business Intelligence & Data Warehousing, Enterprise Resource Planning, Business Process Management, Enterprise Content Management. (As-Ind, estab 2007, empl 72, sales $5,472,009, cert: NMSDC)

4639 Smartecute LLC
1266 Wt Paces ferry Rd Ste 196
Atlanta, GA 30327
Contact: Sheldon Mundle CEO
Tel: 404-939-6303
Email: sheldon@smartecute.com
Website: www.smartecute.com
IT Consulting, IT Advisory, IT Network & Wireless Access Points, IT Unified Communications, Voice Communications & Data, PeopleSoft ERP Consulting, Telecommunications, IT Project Management. (AA, estab 2010, empl 2, sales , cert: NMSDC)

4640 Softech Int'l Resources, Inc.
3300 Holcomb Bridge Rd, Ste 216 30092
Norcross, GA 30092
Contact: Balaji HR
Tel: 770-447-8002
Email: supplier@softintl.com
Website: www.softintl.com
IT consulting, project mgmt, analysis, architectural design, object modeling, application devel. (Woman/As-Ind, estab 1995, empl 40, sales $7,415,369, cert: NMSDC)

4641 Softpath System, LLC
3985 Steve Reynolds Blvd Bldg C
Norcross, GA 30093
Contact: Sushumna Roy Jalajam President
Tel: 404-315-1555
Email: supplier@softpath.net
Website: www.softpath.net
IT services: business intelligence & data warehousing. (Minority, Woman, estab 1999, empl 618, sales $53,000,000, cert: City, NMSDC, CPUC, WBENC)

4642 Stellar Consulting Solutions, LLC
2475 NorthWinds Pkwy, Ste 200
Alpharetta, GA 30009
Contact: Varun Jhanjee CEO
Tel: 678-777-7411
Email: varun@stellarconsulting.com
Website: www.stellarconsulting.com
Onsite Technology Staff Augmentation, Contract, Contract to Hire & Permanent Placements, C Level executive search. (As-Ind, estab 2015, empl 11, sales $2,500,500, cert: NMSDC)

4643 STONE Resource, LLC
9755 Dogwood Rd Ste 350
Roswell, GA 30075
Contact: Kelley Gardner Dir Operations
Tel: 678-646-5488
Email: kgardner@stoneresource.net
Website: www.stoneresource.net
Information Technology staffing: Project Management, Business Analysts, Developers, Architects, System Engineers. (AA, estab 2010, empl 85, sales $16,000,000, cert: NMSDC)

4644 Strategic Systems & Technology Corporation
3325 Paddocks Pkwy Ste 250
Suwanee, GA 30024
Contact: Magan McQuiston CEO
Tel: 678-389-7200
Email: magan.mcquiston@sstid.com
Website: www.sstid.com
Computer database, peripherals, printers, application systems, terminals, network interface hardware, terminal remote job entry. (Woman, estab , empl 29, sales $6,200,000, cert: WBENC)

INFORMATION TECHNOLOGY: Services

4645 Sun Technologies, Inc.
3700 Mansell Rd
Alpharetta, GA 30022
Contact: Beena George Dir Client Relations
Tel: 770-418-0434
Email: supplierdiversity@suntechnologies.com
Website: www.suntechnologies.com
IT staffing & IT projects. (Minority, Woman, estab 1996, empl 793, sales $40,060,616, cert: NMSDC, WBENC)

4646 Symbioun Technologies, Inc.
4501 Circle 75 Pkwy D4200
Atlanta, GA 30339
Contact: Raj Muppalla Relationship Mgr
Tel: 408-385-1078
Email: srinik@symbiountech.com
Website: www.symbiountech.com
Information technology consulting, staffing services. (As-Ind, estab 1993, empl 140, sales $7,900,000, cert: NMSDC)

4647 Synergy America, Inc.
6340 Sugarloaf Pkwy, Ste 200
Duluth, GA 30097
Contact: Mike Williams CEO
Tel: 770-923-9300
Email: mike@synergyamerica.com
Website: www.synergyamerica.com
IT services: BPO, healthcare, ERP, e-business, & client server environments. (As-Ind, estab 1993, empl 50, sales $ 0, cert: NMSDC, 8(a))

4648 TechBios, Inc.
11800 Amberpark Dr, Ste 130
Alpharetta, GA 30004
Contact: Larry Parker President
Tel: 770-569-2721
Email: lparker@techbios.com
Website: www.techbios.com
Information technology contract & permanent staffing; professional, administrative & clerical staffing, help desk & customer svc, software engineering, LAN/WAN installation, maintenance, & support, configuration mgmt & desktop deployment. (AA, estab 2000, empl 18, sales $1,466,970, cert: State, NMSDC)

4649 TechNet Resources
4080 McGinnis Ferry Rd Ste 604
Alpharetta, GA 30005
Contact: Kyle Hardy Sr Acct Mgr
Tel: 678-242-3044
Email: khardy@tnri.net
Website: www.tnri.net
Information technology & information services, contractors & full time. (Woman, estab 1997, empl 147, sales $17,000,000, cert: WBENC)

4650 Technical Communication Concepts Inc.
179 Fulton Ct
Peachtree City, GA 30269
Contact: Yamasia Evans CEO
Tel: 404-234-1468
Email: yamasia@technicalcomm.com
Website: www.technicalcomm.com
A/V production to bring your ideas into fruition with top-of-the-line service. (AA, estab 1998, empl 4, sales $464,769, cert: NMSDC)

4651 The Danby Group, LLP
3060-A Business Park Dr
Norcross, GA 30071
Contact: Genie Ragin Managing Partner
Tel: 770-416-9844
Email: genie@danbygroup.com
Website: www.danbygroup.com
Automatic identification technology (AIT) design & integration, bar code printing stations. (Woman, estab 1982, empl 11, sales $10,000,000, cert: WBENC)

4652 The Ian Thomas Group, LLC
2870 Peachtree Rd, Ste 417
Atlanta, GA 30305
Contact: Kevin Mobley CEO
Tel: 404-993-5698
Email: info@ianthomasgroup.com
Website: www.ianthomasgroup.com
Software performance engineering (SPE): software performance testing, engineering analysis & optimization, database analysis & tuning & operational support. (AA, estab 2007, empl 15, sales $1,451,588, cert: NMSDC, 8(a))

4653 The REIA Corporation
3348 Fieldwood Dr
Smyrna, GA 33080
Contact: Darnell Clarke CEO
Tel: 770-432-6974
Email: darnell@reiacorp.com
Website: www.reiacorp.com
Systems software application devel& integration, security mgmt & compliance, custom devel, help desk & IT support project & risk mgmt. (Woman/AA, estab 1992, empl 46, sales $5,868,000, cert: State, City, 8(a))

4654 Think Development Systems
6000 Live Oak Pkwy, Ste 102
Norcross, GA 30093
Contact: P I Joy President
Tel: 770-723-7777
Email: joy@thinkdevelopment.com
Website: www.thinkdevelopment.com
Software development & IT consulting, offshore development, wireless application. (Minority, Woman, estab 1998, empl 47, sales $3,085,109, cert: City, NMSDC)

4655 Unicorn Technologies, LLC
4080 McGinnis Ferry Rd Ste 1203
Alpharetta, GA 30005
Contact: Sunil Savili President
Tel: 678-825-8143
Email: sales@unicorntek.com
Website: www.unicorntek.com
IT solutions & staffing services, Fit Gap Analysis, Application Development, Implementation, Upgrades, Quality Assurance, Maintenance & Support, Project Management. (Woman/As-Ind, estab 2012, empl 60, sales $3,700,000, cert: State, WBENC, SDB)

4656 Universal Business Solutions, LLC
4080 McGinnis Ferry Rd Ste 803
Alpharetta, GA 30005
Contact: Jan O'Brien VP Recruitment & Sales
Tel: 770-416-9900
Email: jobrien@ubsolutions.com
Website: www.ubsolutions.com
IT svcs & solutions: ERP & CRM systems, application systems, web systems, e-business, security & threat evaluation, telecommunications, telephony consulting, call & contact centers, infrastructure design, project mgmt. (Nat Ame, estab 1995, empl 34, sales $ 0, cert: SDB)

4657 VDart Inc.
11180 State Bridge Rd, Ste 302
Alpharetta, GA 30022
Contact: Bruce Hay VP Business Dev
Tel: 309-657-8528
Email: supplier.registration@vdartinc.com
Website: www.vdartinc.com
High growth, global digital solutions, product development and professional services. (Minority, estab 2007, empl , sales $158,580,118, cert: NMSDC)

4658 Virtue Group
5755 N Point Pkwy, Ste 85
Alpharetta, GA 30022
Contact: Lakshmi Manthena President
Tel: 678-578-4554
Email: lmanthena@virtuegroup.com
Website: www.virtuegroup.com
IT professionals: contract, contract-to-hire & direct hire basis. (Woman/As-Ind, estab 2002, empl 250, sales $23,400,000, cert: NMSDC)

4659 VisionSoft International, Inc.
1842 Old Norcross Rd
Lawrenceville, GA 30044
Contact: Jay Kumar Dir-Marketing
Tel: 770-682-2899
Email: jay@vsiiusa.com
Website: www.vsiiusa.com
On-site software consulting, fixed-price dev services, off shore development. (Minority, Woman, estab 1996, empl 150, sales $5,400,000, cert: NMSDC)

4660 Whitty IT Solutions LLC
260 Peachtree St, NW Ste 2200
Atlanta, GA 30303
Contact: Mrs. Charlie Whitfield CEO
Tel: 404-823-6955
Email: charlie@whittyapps.com
Website: www.whittyit.solutions
Software engineering & integration, architecture, design, development & project management, mobile software solutions. (Woman/AA, estab 2011, empl 2, sales , cert: WBENC, 8(a))

4661 XentIT, LLC
5425 Peachtree Pkwy
Norcross, GA 30092
Contact: Tariq Alvi President
Tel: 678-906-4046
Email: talvi@xentit.com
Website: www.xentit.com
Value Added Reseller, System Integrator & Cloud Managed Service provider. (As-Ind, estab 2006, empl 7, sales $2,247,000, cert: NMSDC)

4662 Xtreme Solutions, Inc.
1170 Peachtree St, Ste 1875
Atlanta, GA 30309
Contact: Phyllis Newhouse Project Mgr
Tel: 404-883-2000
Email: pnewhouse@xtremesolutions-inc.com
Website: www.xtremesolutions-inc.com
Engineering & technology services. (Woman/AA, estab 2002, empl 140, sales , cert: NMSDC)

Iowa

4663 Advanced Technology Solutions, Inc.
416 Creek Side Dr
Fairfax, IA 52404
Contact: Debra Kiwala President
Tel: 319-845-5177
Email: debra.kiwala@ats-inc.org
Website: www.ats-inc.org
IT consulting: software devel, system & network engineers, project managers, etc. (Minority, Woman, estab 1997, empl 85, sales $3,233,188, cert: State)

4664 Certintell, Inc.
317 6th Ave Ste 901
Des Moines, IA 50309
Contact: Benjamin Lefever Sales
Tel: 515-802-1281
Email: benjamin@certintell.com
Website: www.certintell.com
Online & on-demand healthcare delivery services, software & remote monitoring that benefit patients, hospitals, employers, payers, physician practice groups & accountable care organizations. (AA, estab 2014, empl 6, sales , cert: NMSDC)

4665 ePATHUSA
1075 Jordan Creek Pkwy Ste 295
West Des Moines, IA 50266
Contact: Hari Nallure VP
Tel: 515-974-6778
Email: hnallure@epathusa.net
Website: www.epathusa.net
Salesforce & ServiceNow development & configuration. (Minority, estab 2005, empl 45, sales $9,000,000, cert: NMSDC, 8(a))

4666 PC Pitstop LLC
2515 W 22nd St
Sioux City, IA 51103
Contact: Scott Palmer Sales Consultant
Tel: 712-233-4015
Email: scottp@pcpitstop.com
Website: www.pcpitstop.com/
Security optimization software, PC Matic. (As-Pac, estab 1999, empl 32, sales $11,913,000, cert: NMSDC)

Idaho

4667 In Time Tec, LLC
580 E Corporate Dr
Meridian, ID 83642
Contact: Skyler Simmons Sr Partner Mgr
Tel: 208-258-2424
Email: skyler.simmons@intimetec.com
Website: www.intimetec.com
Long-term strategic technology partnerships. (Minority, estab 2009, empl 1200, sales $33,598,977, cert: NMSDC)

Illinois

4668 3Core Systems, Inc.
75 Executive Dr, Ste 401I
Aurora, IL 60504
Contact: Shyam Reganti Dir PreSales
Tel: 630-748-8800
Email: shyam.reganti@3coresystems.com
Website: www.3coresystems.com
IT services, solutions & consulting, ERP, CRM, DW/BI (Data Warehousing & Business Intelligence), Application Devel & Mgmt. (Minority, estab 2004, empl 45, sales $9,100,000, cert: State)

INFORMATION TECHNOLOGY: Services

4669 A1PlusSoft, Inc.
222 W Merchandise Mart Plaza, Ste 1212
Chicago, IL 60654
Contact: Balaji Rengamannar CEO
Tel: 630-935-6938
Email: brengamannar@a1plussoft.com
Website: www.a1plussoft.com
PCI Compliance assessment, Staff Augmentation, Information & Cloud security consulting, Legacy system transformation/modernization, Data & EMV Migration, Testing & Technical Writing. (As-Ind, estab 2002, empl 5, sales $518,000, cert: State, City, NMSDC)

4670 About Xtreme LLC
401 N Michigan Ave Ste 1200
Chicago, IL 60611
Contact: Yasoob Ahmed Dir Business Devel
Tel: 815-603-5521
Email: yasoob.ahmed@axtcorp.com
Website: www.axtcorp.com
Cloud IT Consulting, Microsoft Azure, Amazon AWS, and SalesForce, Office 365, Dynamics 365, SharePoint, SCCM, AI Chatbots, Knowledge Mining, Big Data, and Analytics, Azure and AWS IAAS. (As-Ind, estab 2016, empl 12, sales $1,000,000, cert: NMSDC)

4671 Accede Solutions Inc.
164 Ela Rd
Inverness, IL 60067
Contact: Garvita Sethi Managing Partner
Tel: 844-522-2333
Email: garvita@accedesol.com
Website: www.accedesol.com
IT, Healthcare, Finance & HR staffing & consulting. Enterprise Resource Planning (ERP) Customer relationship management (CRM) Human Resource Management System (HRMS) Software configuration Management (SCM) System. (Minority, Woman, estab 2005, empl 32, sales $ 0, cert: City, WBENC)

4672 Acility, LLC
410 N Michigan Ave Ste 750
Chicago, IL 60611
Contact: John Lee Dir, Business Devel
Tel: 312-948-9929
Email: jlee@acility.com
Website: www.acility.com
Multisite property management services industry through its remarkable smartphone platform, Cloud-based technology. (AA, estab 2014, empl 425, sales $150,000,000, cert: NMSDC)

4673 Advansoft International Inc.
415 W Golf Rd Ste 55
Arlington Heights, IL 60005
Contact: John Ashwin Business Devel Mgr
Tel: 224-323-1707
Email: jjashwin@adso.com
Website: www.adso.com
Supplier to direct clients and major SAP implementation partners. (Woman, estab 1998, empl 261, sales $22,600,000, cert: WBENC)

4674 Ageatia Technology Consultancy Services Inc
949 N Plum Grove Road
Schaumburg, IL 60173
Contact: Chuck Srinivasan President
Tel: 847-517-8415
Email: csrinivasan@ageatia.com
Website: www.ageatia.com
E-gov, systems integration, database admin, software, implementation, software services, Legacy data, conversions, software devel, custom devel, web devel, systems outsourcing & support, technical support, enterprise, Oracle, Microsoft, PeopleSoft, SAP. (Minority, Woman, estab 2005, empl 300, sales $30,000,000, cert: City, NMSDC)

4675 AJT Technology Designs Inc
1423 Bangor Ln
Aurora, IL 60504
Contact: Todd Hill President
Tel: 321-223-4760
Email: todd.hill@ajttechnology.com
Website: www.ajttechnology.com
Information & communications technology planning, design & integration services for IT. (AA, estab 2014, empl 3, sales $349,477, cert: State, City, 8(a))

4676 ALC Enterprises, Inc.
111 E Wacker Dr, Ste 1200
Chicago, IL 60601
Contact: President
Tel: 312-819-8888
Email: info@teamwerks.com
Website: www.teamwerks.com
Technology consulting, e-business applications. (Woman/As-Ind, estab 1997, empl 30, sales $2,000,000, cert: WBENC)

4677 Alert IT Solutions Inc.
1230 Golfview Dr
Woodridge,, IL 60517
Contact: Joe Puthen President
Tel: 630-854-3762
Email: jputhen@alertitsolutions.com
Website: www.AlertITSolutions.com
IT staffing, consulting, and training services. (As-Ind, estab 2006, empl 12, sales $177,000, cert: State)

4678 Aloha Document Services, Inc.
141 W. Jackson Blvd. S-A100A
Chicago, IL 60604
Contact: Virginia Peak President
Tel: 312-542-1300
Email: ginger@alohaprintgroup.com
Website: www.alohaprintgroup.com
Litigation copying, oversize & digital imaging, presentation, marketing & training materials, multi-media duplication & electronic archiving. (Woman, estab 2002, empl 16, sales $2,600,000, cert: City, WBENC)

4679 Ameex Technologies Corp.
1701 E Woodfield Rd, Ste 710
Schaumburg, IL 60173
Contact: Arockia Preethi Marketing Analyst
Tel: 847-563-3064
Email: vendor.registration@ameexusa.com
Website: www.ameexusa.com/
Develop content management solutions, web development, maintenance & enhanced services. (As-Pac, estab 2007, empl 180, sales $8,000,000, cert: NMSDC)

INFORMATION TECHNOLOGY: Services

4680 AmorServ LLC
      2340 W Touhy Ave Ste B
      Chicago, IL 60645
      Contact: Otse Amorighoye CEO
      Tel: 312-414-0430
      Email: o.amorighoye@amorserv.com
      Website: www.amorserv.com
Turn-key technology service and solutions, white labelled on-demand / on-site solutions. (AA, estab 2016, empl 10, sales $593,000, cert: City, NMSDC)

4681 Aonsoft International, Inc
      1600 Golf Rd, Ste 1270
      Rolling Meadows, IL 60008
      Contact: Siddiq Ahmed President
      Tel: 847-999-4060
      Email: siddiq@aonsoft.com
      Website: www.aonsoft.com
IT Consulting Services & Staff Augmentation Services. (As-Ind, estab 2007, empl 14, sales $661,000, cert: NMSDC)

4682 Aptude, Inc.
      1601 North Bond St, Ste 316
      Naperville, IL 60563
      Contact: Guy De Rosa Principal
      Tel: 630-692-6700
      Email: accounts@aptude.com
      Website: www.aptude.com
Remote data capturing applications, ebusiness solutions, customer relationship mgmt solutions, data warehousing & business intelligence, content svcs, CAD/CAM integration, knowledge mgmt solutions. (As-Ind, estab 2001, empl 100, sales $15,300,000, cert: State, City)

4683 ARBA Technology, Inc.
      2760 Forgue Dr Ste 104
      Naperville, IL 60564
      Contact: Kathy de la Torre Dir Sales/Marketing
      Tel: 630-620-8566
      Email: kathy@arbapro.com
      Website: www.arbapro.com
Point of Sale (POS), inventory management & cashless payment solutions. (Woman/As-Pac, estab 2007, empl 17, sales $881,670, cert: NMSDC)

4684 Ascent Innovations, LLC
      475 N Martingale Rd Ste 820
      Schaumburg, IL 60173
      Contact: Sohena Hafiz President
      Tel: 847-572-8000
      Email: solutions@ascent365.com
      Website: www.ascent365.com
Dynamics AX & Dynamics CRM Consulting, Implementation, Development, Integration, Support, Upgrades, Data Migration, SYSPRO ï¿½ Implementation & Integration, ERP/CRM Integration. (Minority, Woman, estab 2009, empl 32, sales $780,000, cert: State, WBENC, 8(a))

4685 Aura Innovative Technology
      223 W Jackson Blvd, Ste 1112
      Chicago, IL 60606
      Contact: James Chen President
      Tel: 312-342-4292
      Email: mmrcela@aurachicago.com
      Website: www.aurachicago.com
Microsoft & AWS consulting & custom software/integration development. (As-Pac, estab 2011, empl 15, sales , cert: City, NMSDC)

4686 Aurora Solutions, Inc.
      1051 Perimeter Dr, Ste 510
      Schaumburg, IL 60173
      Contact: Sanjeev Srivastava Business Devel
      Tel: 847-274-7777
      Email: sanjeev@auroraworldwide.com
      Website: www.auroraworldwide.com
Data Mining & Business Analytics, ECommerce & Custom Application Development. (Minority, Woman, estab 1997, empl 30, sales $3,500,000, cert: NMSDC, 8(a))

4687 BitWise Inc.
      1515 Woodfield Rd Ste 930
      Schaumburg, IL 60173
      Contact: Michael Palermo New Business Mgr
      Tel: 847-969-1500
      Email: john.broshar@bitwiseglobal.com
      Website: www.bitwiseglobal.com
Application development, system maintenance & support, IT consulting. (As-Pac, estab 1996, empl 600, sales $30,000,000, cert: NMSDC)

4688 Bourntec Solutions, Inc.
      1701 E Woodfield Rd Ste 636
      Schaumburg, IL 60173
      Contact: Srujana Gudur President
      Tel: 224-232-5090
      Email: ssurya@bourntec.com
      Website: www.bourntec.com
Information technology remote Oracle support services, on-site Oracle implementation & application development services. (Woman/As-Ind, estab 1994, empl 33, sales $4,500,000, cert: State, NMSDC)

4689 BTR Solutions, LLC
      1300 Thorndale
      Elk Grove Village, IL 60007
      Contact: Business Devel Mgr
      Tel: 630-594-2011
      Email: JOEP@SIPIAR.COM
      Website: www.sipiar.com
IT Asset Disposition, remarket, redeploy, perform DOD level Data Security. (Woman, estab 1988, empl 300, sales , cert: WBENC, NWBOC)

4690 CeLeen LLC
      325 E Main St
      Belleville, IL 62220
      Contact: Charleen Hickey President
      Tel: 618-222-1600
      Email: charleen.hickey@celeengroup.com
      Website: www.celeengroup.com
Information technology & business improvement solutions. (Woman, estab 2010, empl 7, sales $816,526, cert: State, 8(a), SDB)

4691 Clerysys Incorporated
      10600 W Higgins Rd, Ste 711
      Rosemont, IL 60018
      Contact: Nicole Lim Business Dev Exec
      Tel: 847-768-0314
      Email: info@clerysys.com
      Website: www.clerysys.com
Application design & devel, ERP, business intelligence, systems integration, quality assurance, content mgmt & web-based applications, SAP R/3 implementation svcs, ERP, CRM, SRM, PLM, BI & data warehousing. (As-Pac, estab 2005, empl 450, sales $10,000,000, cert: NMSDC)

INFORMATION TECHNOLOGY: Services

4692 Cogent Data Solutions LLC
2500 W Higgins Rd Ste 1165
Hoffman Estates, IL 60169
Contact: Sumanth Yalavarthy VP IT
Tel: 866-666-1877
Email: sumanth@cogentdatasolutions.com
Website: www.cogentdatasolutions.com
IT services, IT project base & contract staff augmentation, Information management, Infrastructure Management, Data Warehousing, Business Intelligence, QA Testing, Web Development, EHR & EMR. (Woman/As-Ind, estab 2007, empl 89, sales $5,400,000, cert: State, NMSDC, WBENC)

4693 Com2 Computers and Technologies
1196C S Main St
Lombard, IL 60148
Contact: Saheem Baloch CEO
Tel: 630-544-1708
Email: com2@com2computer.com
Website: www.com2computer.com
IT asset recovery & remarketing, electronic recycling, IT technical service. (Woman/As-Ind, estab 2002, empl 10, sales $62,150,000, cert: NMSDC)

4694 Compact Solutions, LLC.
Two TransAm Plaza Dr Ste 400
Oakbrook Terrace, IL 60181
Contact: Pankaj Agrawal President
Tel: 312-493-9911
Email: pankaj.agrawal@compactsolutionsllc.com
Website: www.compactsolutionsllc.com
Enterprise wide data integration, data management & quality initiatives, data migration/consolidation, data synchronization, master data management & cross-enterprise information integration. (As-Ind, estab 2002, empl 54, sales $5,550,000, cert: NMSDC)

4695 Complex Network Solutions
7747 W 96th Pl
Hickory Hills, IL 60457
Contact: Eduardo Lopez President
Tel: 708-233-6222
Email: elopez@complexnetwork.com
Website: www.complexnetwork.com
IT services, routing switching & wireless, desktop & server support. (Hisp, estab 2005, empl 7, sales $ 0, cert: NMSDC)

4696 CosaTech, Inc.
1415 W 22nd St, Tower Fl
Oak Brook, IL 60523
Contact: Ann Le VP
Tel: 630-684-2331
Email: ann.le@cosatech.com
Website: www.cosatech.com
Information technology services: systems integration & applications, development, quality assurance, managed services, IT staff augmentation, onsite, offsite & offshore applications dev & maintenance. (Minority, Woman, estab 1988, empl 350, sales $25,000,000, cert: NMSDC)

4697 CRSGroup, Inc.
One Pierce Place Ste 325 West
Itasca, IL 60143
Contact: Yolanda Gaines Business Solutions Mgr
Tel: 630-202-5348
Email: YGAINES@CRSCORP.COM
Website: www.crscorp.com
Information technology consulting. (AA, estab 1994, empl 311, sales $17,500,000, cert: State, City, NMSDC)

4698 Cube Hub Inc.
600 N Commons Dr Ste 109
Aurora, IL 60504
Contact: Sunil Bakhshi Business Devel Mgr
Tel: 630-746-1239
Email: sunil@cube-hub.com
Website: www.cube-hub.com
Technology, Training, Staffing & Professional Services, Staffing/Recruiting services, Software Development, IT, Engineering, Professional, Marketing, Healthcare, Clinical, Scientific, Finance/Audit, Telecommunication, etc. (Minority, Woman, estab 2014, empl 28, sales $3,580,640, cert: NMSDC)

4699 Cyberbridge Intl. Inc. dba Creospan Inc.
1515 E Woodfield Rd, Ste 350
Schaumburg, IL 60173
Contact: Praj Shah President
Tel: 847-598-1101
Email: praj.shah@creospan.com
Website: www.creospan.com
Software solutions consulting. (Woman/As-Ind, estab 1999, empl 125, sales $12,500,000, cert: NMSDC)

4700 Data Defenders, LLC
10 W 35th St, Ste 9F5-1
Chicago, IL 60616
Contact: Lester McCarroll Business Devel Mgr
Tel: 312-224-8831
Email: lester.mccarroll@data-defenders.com
Website: www.data-defenders.com
Information Security, Managed Technology, Applied Computer Forensics & Professional Services solutions. (AA, estab 2005, empl 14, sales $400,000, cert: City)

4701 DivIHN Integration Inc.
2800 W Higgins Rd Ste 240
Hoffman Estates, IL 60169
Contact: Shantanoo A Govilkar VP
Tel: 224-704-1704
Email: sgovilkar@divihn.com
Website: www.divihn.com
Computer software consulting, staff augmentation, custom software design & development, data management solutions & services. (As-Ind, estab 2002, empl 55, sales $11,200,000, cert: NMSDC)

4702 Edgilent Corp.
700 Cooper Ct Ste AF
Schaumburg, IL 60173
Contact: Raj Ponnuswamy President
Tel: 847-839-7388
Email: rponnuswamy@edgilent.com
Website: www.edgilent.com
Information technology svcs: application development, outsourcing & consulting. (As-Pac, estab 2003, empl 20, sales $2,500,000, cert: NMSDC)

4703 Edify Technologies, Inc.
1952 Mc Dowell Rd, Ste 112
Naperville, IL 60563
Contact: Acct Exec
Tel: 630-932-9308
Email: info@edifytech.com
Website: www.edifytech.com
Software development & consulting, business process automation, SharePoint consulting, custom .NET solutions, testing & quality assurance, project management, staffing, offshore development. (As-Pac, estab 2002, empl 65, sales $4,000,000, cert: State, NMSDC)

INFORMATION TECHNOLOGY: Services

4704 Electronic Knowledge Interchange, Co.
      33 W Monroe St, Ste 1050
      Chicago, IL 60603
      Contact: Jose Cruz
      Tel: 312-762-0129
      Email: jcruz@eki-consulting.com
      Website: www.eki-consulting.com
Technology solutions: web portals, e-commerce, knowledge management, employee intranets, workgroup collaboration & process automation technologies. (AA, estab 1996, empl 91, sales $17,105,910, cert: State, City, NMSDC)

4705 Entelli Consulting LLC
      900 N Arlington Hts. Road Ste 170
      Itasca, IL 60143
      Contact: Suzy Carlson Dir of Sales
      Tel: 847-348-7780
      Email: scarlson@entelli.com
      Website: www.entelli.com/
Contract technical IS consulting. (Minority, Woman, estab 1999, empl 35, sales $1,600,000, cert: WBENC)

4706 Enterprise Solutions Inc
      500 E. Diehl Road Ste 130
      Naperville, IL 60563
      Contact: Ishrat Jan VP
      Tel: 408-385-1731
      Email: ishratjan@enterprisesolutioninc.com
      Website: www.enterprisesolutioninc.com
IT & engineering staffing, direct hire, contract to hire & contract positions. (As-Ind, estab 2000, empl 350, sales $ 0, cert: NMSDC, CPUC)

4707 Evanston Technology Partners, Inc.
      56 East 47th St
      Chicago, IL 60653
      Contact: Emmanuel Jackson President
      Tel: 312-348-5122
      Email: ejackson@evanstontec.com
      Website: www.evanstontec.com
Implement & integrate object storage data (partner to Cleaversafe). Unified & Real Time Communications platform including Telehealth. (AA, estab , empl , sales $120,000, cert: NMSDC)

4708 Evolutyz Corp.
      1560 Wall St Ste 105
      Naperville, IL 60563
      Contact: Adriana Perez Dir of Sales
      Tel: 312-275-5735
      Email: adriana@evolutyz.com
      Website: www.evolutyz.com
Application Development, ERP, Mobile Apps, ETL/ BI/ DW, Quality Assurance & Testing, Professional Services, Staff Augmentation. (Minority, Woman, estab 2011, empl 25, sales $6,051,748, cert: NMSDC)

4709 Excelsior Consulting Services
      PO Box 325
      Clarendon Hills, IL 60514
      Contact: Dileta Sapokaite Business Mgr
      Tel: 973-447-2575
      Email: dileta@excelsiorconsulting.net
      Website: www.excelsiorconsulting.net
IT staff & contracting resources. (Minority, Woman, estab 2004, empl 2, sales $790,000, cert: State, WBENC, 8(a))

4710 Frontier Technologies LLC
      1601 Bond St, Ste 305
      Naperville, IL 60563
      Contact: Richard Ewbank Sales Exec
      Tel: 630-687-1606
      Email: richard@frontiertechllc.com
      Website: www.frontiertechllc.com/
IT consulting services. (Minority, Woman, estab 2002, empl 146, sales , cert: State)

4711 Galmont Consulting, LLC
      70 W Madison St, Ste 1400
      Chicago, IL 60602
      Contact: Jeri Smith President
      Tel: 312-214-3261
      Email: jerig@galmont.com
      Website: www.galmont.com
Software quality assurance, testing & tool automation. (Woman, estab 2000, empl 50, sales $5,700,000, cert: WBENC)

4712 Genius Business Solutions, Inc.
      1711 5th Ave, Ste 2
      Moline, IL 61265
      Contact: Sarthak Joshi Founder & CEO
      Tel: 309-269-2551
      Email: Shivaji@GeniusBSI.com
      Website: www.GeniusBSI.com
IT & Engineering Services Consulting, Software licensing, Implementation & Support SAP, Oracle & Windchill, Custom software development, Quality assurance & Testing, End User Training, Strategic Staffing. (As-Ind, estab 2004, empl 70, sales $6,015,657, cert: NMSDC)

4713 Harrington Technology & Associates, Inc dba HTA Technology Security
      30 S Wacker Dr, 22 Fl
      Chicago, IL 60606
      Contact: Michelle Chaudry CEO
      Tel: 708-862-6348
      Email: mchaudry@hta-inc.com
      Website: www.hta-inc.com
Technology & information security consulting: risk assessments, protection, independent verification & validation, vulnerability assessments & penetration testing, computer forensics, network & security remediation. (Woman/AA, estab 2001, empl 29, sales $2,778,000, cert: WBENC)

4714 HOBI International, Inc.
      1202 Nagel Blvd
      Batavia, IL 60510
      Contact: Cathy Hill CEO
      Tel: 630-761-0500
      Email:
      Website: www.hobi.com
Recycle electronics, reverse logistics, IT & cellular asset management, resale & re-marketing, data security, data erasure, equipment removal & environmentally safe recycling. (Woman, estab 1992, empl 250, sales $42,000,000, cert: WBENC)

4715 Indusa Technical Corp.
      1 TransAm Plaza Dr Ste 350
      Oakbrook Terrace, IL 60181
      Contact: Hemant Shah Dir Business Dev
      Tel: 865-769-0715
      Email: hemant.shah@indusa.com
      Website: www.indusa.com
Information technology consulting & software solutions. (As-Ind, estab 1989, empl 100, sales $ 0, cert: NMSDC)

INFORMATION TECHNOLOGY: Services

4716 Innovative Systems Group, Inc.
799 Roosevelt Rd Ste 109
Glen Ellyn, IL 60137
Contact: Jordan Myers Acct Mgr
Tel: 312-861-1745
Email: jordanm@innovativesys.com
Website: www.innovativesys.com/
Information systems consulting, full life cycle systems, application dev & support, business systems analysis, QA & testing svcs, database architecture & admin, network & systems admin, CRM & enterprise systems. (As-Pac, estab 1991, empl 250, sales $20,000,000, cert: City)

4717 Intellisys Technology, LLC
1000 Jorie Blvd Ste 200
Oak Brook, IL 60523
Contact: Raju Iyer Managing Partner
Tel: 630-928-1111
Email: riyer@intellisystechnology.com
Website: www.intellisystechnology.com
IT consulting: system integration, application development, QA & testing, embedded system technology & staff augmentation. (As-Ind, estab 1998, empl 300, sales $6,000,000, cert: State)

4718 Iyka Enterprises, Inc.
PO Box 3534
St. Charles, IL 60174
Contact: Poonam Gupta-Krishnan President
Tel: 630-372-3900
Email: poonam@iyka.com
Website: www.iyka.com
Custom application software & IT consulting. (Woman/As-Ind, estab 2000, empl 25, sales $500,000, cert: WBENC)

4719 JRE & Associates Inc.
46 E 26th St
Chicago, IL 60616
Contact: Jeffrey Edwards CEO
Tel: 312-326-4327
Email: jedwards@jreitsolutions.com
Website: www.jreitsolutions.com
Logical Identity Controls, Access Control Systems Telecommunications & Network Security, Computer Operations, Security Mgmt, Cryptography & PKI Infrastructure Support (AA, estab 2009, empl 3, sales $150,000, cert: State)

4720 KBS
12549 S Laramie Ave
Alsip, IL 60803
Contact: Anthony R. Kitchens President
Tel: 708-720-5981
Email: tonyk@kbs.us.com
Website: www.kbsgc.com
Technology products & svcs: desktop & notebook support, network admin, voice, video, data & electricity cabling, RFID tagging, WLAN, LAN, wireless cameras, help desk & end-user technical support. (AA, estab 1992, empl 22, sales $16,710,521, cert: NMSDC)

4721 Kristine Fallon Associates, Inc.
11 E Adams St, Ste 1100
Chicago, IL 60603
Contact: Angelica Martinez Marketing Coord
Tel: 312-360-9600
Email: amartinez@kfa-inc.com
Website: www.kfa-inc.com
Information technology consulting services, Building Information Modeling (BIM / COBie), electronic project mgmt & collaboration systems, Facility Mgmt Systems & Transit Asset Management database solutions. (AA, estab 1993, empl 11, sales $ 0, cert: City)

4722 LCS Entertainment LLC
4545 S Drexel
Chicago, IL 60653
Contact: Chrishon Lampley CEO
Tel: 773-330-2440
Email: chrishon@lovecorkscrew.com
Website: www.lovecorkscrew.com
(Woman/AA, estab 2014, empl 5, sales , cert: NMSDC, WBENC)

4723 Lead IT Corporation
1999 Wabash Ste 210
Springfield, IL 62704
Contact: Ira Neuman Sales Mgr
Tel: 217-726-7250
Email: ira.neuman@leaditgroup.com
Website: www.leaditgroup.com
IT staffing & HR, executive search, consulting, computer programming, IT management, technical consulting. (Minority, Woman, estab 2005, empl 232, sales $23,712,000, cert: State)

4724 LG Associates Inc. dba Asen Computer Associates
900 N National Pkwy, Ste 155
Schaumburg, IL 60173
Contact: Liza Brigham Acct Mgr
Tel: 847-995-1300
Email: lbrigham@asen.com
Website: www.asen.com/
Information technology & engineering consulting. (Woman, estab 1975, empl 137, sales $5,985,000, cert: WBENC)

4725 MG Automation, Inc.
537 N Sycamore Ln
North Aurora, IL 60542
Contact: Michael Graham President
Tel: 630-336-2577
Email: m.graham@mgautomation-inc.com
Website: www.mgautomation-inc.com
IT services, Automation, SCADA, Controls, Robotics, and Machine Learning. (Woman/AA, estab 2004, empl 2, sales $160,276, cert: State, NMSDC)

4726 Midwest Solution Providers, Inc.
21720 W Long Grove Rd, Ste C-227
Deer Park, IL 60010
Contact: Raj Andathode Principal Consultant
Tel: 224-520-1510
Email: raj@midwest-sp.com
Website: www.midwest-sp.com
IT Consulting, Database design, database programming, ETL, solutions using Informatica, Oracle, Teradata, Java, Web-Services & custom applications. (As-Ind, estab 2004, empl 1, sales , cert: NMSDC)

4727 Mu Sigma Inc.
3400 Dundee Rd Ste 160
Northbrook, IL 60062
Contact: Shelly Singh Head Sales
Tel: 847-620-9419
Email: shelly.singh@mu-sigma.com
Website: www.mu-sigma.com
Provide data science solutions. (As-Ind, estab , empl , sales $70,000,000, cert: NMSDC)

INFORMATION TECHNOLOGY: Services

4728 MVC Consulting Inc.
      203 N LaSalle St
      Chicago, IL 60601
      Contact: Greg Mummert Recruiting Mgr
      Tel: 312-606-5555
      Email: greg.mummert@mvc-consulting.com
      Website: www.mvc-consulting.com
IT consulting svcs: business intelligence/data warehousing, compliance, ERP, CRM sales force automation, change mgmt & project based consulting projects. (Woman, estab 1981, empl 30, sales $2,800,000, cert: WBENC)

4729 MZI Group Inc.
      1937 W Fulton St
      Chicago, IL 60612
      Contact: Nicole Klimenko VP
      Tel: 312-492-8740
      Email: nicole@mzigroup.com
      Website: www.mzigroup.com
Electrical, Mechanical, and Building Services Contractor (Hisp, estab 1999, empl 110, sales $35,877,000, cert: City, NMSDC)

4730 National Tek Services, Inc.
      PO Box 6
      Libertyville, IL 60048
      Contact: Terry Sharkey President
      Tel: 847-850-1201
      Email: info@tekservinc.com
      Website: www.tekservinc.com
Information technology solutions. (Woman, estab 2003, empl 6, sales $1,200,000, cert: WBENC)

4731 Netrion Global Solutions, Inc
      451 Dunham Rd Ste 202
      St. Charles, IL 60174
      Contact: Heather Thompson VP Business Operations
      Tel: 630-510-3000
      Email: heather.thompson@netrion.com
      Website: www.netrion.com
IT svcs: ERP implimentation, e-commerce solutions, database development, project mgmt. (As-Ind, estab 1989, empl 21, sales $1,950,000, cert: NMSDC)

4732 Next Generation, Inc.
      800 West 5th Ave Ste 202
      Naperville, IL 60563
      Contact: Darrell Higueros President
      Tel: 312-739-0520
      Email: dhigueros@nxtgeninc.com
      Website: www.nxtgeninc.com
Customizations, implementation & support Enterprise Resource Planning software. (Hisp, estab 2001, empl 15, sales $2,100,000, cert: State)

4733 OnShore Technology Group, Inc.
      505 N Lake Shore Dr Ste 220
      Chicago, IL 60611
      Contact: Valarie King- Bailey CEO
      Tel: 312-321-6400
      Email: vkbailey@onshoretech.com
      Website: www.onshoretech.com
Applied technology products & svcs: engineering, e-govt support, advanced strategic & tactical mktg svcs, digital media production, enterprise business intelligence solutions, digital home networking. (Woman/AA, estab 2004, empl 6, sales $1,534,540, cert: City, NMSDC, WBENC)

4734 Pace Systems, Inc
      2040 Corporate Ln
      Naperville, IL 60563
      Contact: Nick Taylor
      Tel: 630-395-2191
      Email: ntaylor@pace-systems.com
      Website: www.pace-systems.com
Information technology services & sales. Citrix networking design & consulting. Physical & network security consulting. (As-Pac, estab 1983, empl 32, sales $30,000,000, cert: State, City, NMSDC)

4735 Plego Technologies
      5002 Main St Ste 203
      Downers Grove, IL 60515
      Contact: Dir of Business Dev
      Tel: 630-796-2074
      Email:
      Website: www.Plego.com
Web apps development, enterprise web design, systems integration, mobile app development, business intelligence & staff augmentation. (Minority, estab 2002, empl 20, sales $1,890,332, cert: NMSDC)

4736 Premier Systems, Inc
      14489 John Humphrey Ste 202 Ste 202
      Orland Park, IL 60462
      Contact: Tariq Khan Acct Mgr
      Tel: 708-349-9200
      Email: tkhan@premiersystemsinc.com
      Website: www.premiersystemsinc.com
IT consulting & staffing, project mgmt, systems programming & admin: IBM mainframe midrange, client server, PeopleSoft, SAP & Microsoft based systems; e-commerce devel. (As-Pac, estab 1993, empl 30, sales $2,713,000, cert: City, NMSDC)

4737 PTS Consulting Services LLC
      1700 Park St, Ste 212
      Naperville, IL 60563
      Contact: Reshma Multani Client Servicing Mgr
      Tel: 630-635-8328
      Email: reshma.multani@ptscservices.com
      Website: www.ptscservices.com
IT consulting and Business Consulting Services. (As-Pac, estab 2012, empl 50, sales $7,000,000, cert: NMSDC)

4738 Purple Consulting
      2539 Lexington Lane
      Naperville, IL 60540
      Contact: Purnima Parashar Principal
      Tel: 630-303-2706
      Email: purnima@consultpurple.com
      Website: www.consultpurple.com
Permanent placement of Software Engineers, Network Engineers, Analysts. Positions like Systems Engineers, Project Managers, Trading Engineers, IT Analysts, Business Analysts, Software Engineers, Sales. (Woman/As-Ind, estab 2014, empl 5, sales , cert: City)

4739 Q1 Technologies, Inc.
      750 Shoreline Dr
      Aurora, IL 60504
      Contact: Krishna Bansal Sr Dir
      Tel: 630-536-8202
      Email: krishna.bansal@q1tech.com
      Website: www.q1tech.com
Enterprise software implementation, application integration & tech/functional support, software devel. (As-Pac, estab 2002, empl 50, sales $7,204,257, cert: State, NMSDC)

INFORMATION TECHNOLOGY: Services

4740 Quinnox Inc.
400 N. Michigan Ave Ste 1300
Chicago, IL 60611
Contact: Amar Sowani Sr Mgr
Tel: 312-219-6517
Email: amars@quinnox.com
Website: www.quinnox.com
Information technology consulting & staff augmentation services. (As-Ind, estab , empl , sales $52,000,000, cert: NMSDC)

4741 Radian Compliance LLC
3 Grant Square, Ste 243
Hinsdale, IL 60521
Contact: Sally Smoczynski Managing Partner
Tel: 630-305-7100
Email: Info@radiancompliance.com
Website: www.radiancompliance.com
ISO Management Systems for Information Security, Cybersecurity, Service Management, Quality Management, Business Continuity, Private Security, Environmental Management, Privacy Information Management, and Supply Chain Security. (Woman, estab 2003, empl 15, sales $1,000,000, cert: WBENC)

4742 RK Management Consultants, Inc.
One Tower Lane Ste 2540
Oakbrook Terrace, IL 60181
Contact: Nidhi Kapoor President
Tel: 630-202-3768
Email: nidhi@rkmcinc.com
Website: www.rkmcinc.com
Information technology solutions & professional consulting services, e-commerce & web dev, network infrastructure & support, software mgmt svcs, client server & mainframe computing environments. (Minority, Woman, estab 1988, empl 70, sales $8,200,000, cert: NMSDC, WBENC)

4743 RL Canning Inc.
8700 W. Bryn Mawr Ste 120N
Chicago, IL 60631
Contact: Rachel Canning President
Tel: 773-693-1900
Email: rachel@rlcanning.com
Website: www.rlcanning.com
Information technology consulting & staffing services. (Minority, Woman, estab 1999, empl 48, sales $5,000,000, cert: State, City, WBENC)

4744 S & F Software Solutions Inc.
285 Victor Lane
Lake Zurich, IL 60047
Contact: Asma Farhin
Tel: 847-726-2571
Email: afarhin@sandfbizsolutions.com
Website: www.sandfbizsolutions.com
Project Management, Program/Project Management Office (PMO), Enterprise Risk Management, Business Process Re-engineering (BPR), Strategic Business Analysis, Data Management, Enterprise Quality Management. (Minority, Woman, estab 2011, empl 2, sales , cert: State, NMSDC, WBENC)

4745 Sayers Technology
825 Corporate Woods Pkwy
Vernon Hills, IL 60061
Contact: Adam Shipp Reg Sales Mgr
Tel: 404-695-2707
Email: ashipp@sayers.com
Website: www.sayers.com
IT Solutions, Servers & Storage, Virtualization, Security & Mobility, Networking & Professional Services. Storage, Servers, Cloud, Virtualization, Networking, Data Management, Archiving & Disaster Recovery Security. (AA, estab 1984, empl , sales , cert: NMSDC)

4746 SDA Consulting, Inc.
3011 W 183rd St
Homewood, IL 60430
Contact: Shawn Anderson President
Tel: 708-372-8809
Email: sda@sdaci.com
Website: www.sdaci.com
Technical consulting, staffing, support, development & training, business software, Oracle EBS, PeopleSoft, JDE, Siebel, Hyperion, Microsoft, SAP, custom software. (Woman/AA, estab 2004, empl 66, sales $9,185,610, cert: State, NMSDC)

4747 SDI Presence LLC
200 East Randolph, Ste 3550
Chicago, IL 60601
Contact: Dawn Pfeiffer Sr Proposal Mgr
Tel: 312-580-7563
Email: dpfeiffer@sdipresence.com
Website: www.sdipresence.com
Traditional or cloud-based systems life-cycle, concept development, systems integration & long-term support. (As-Ind, estab 2015, empl 250, sales , cert: State, NMSDC)

4748 Silveredge Business Systems, Ltd.
4 Westbrook Center, Ste 1020
Westchester, IL 60154
Contact: Sue Boers President
Tel: 708-449-7738
Email: office@silveredgeconsulting.com
Website: www.silveredgeconsulting.com
Computer consulting services, project management, ERP Implementation, programming, websites, EDI, staff augmentation & outsourcing. (Woman, estab 1987, empl 30, sales $7,309,357, cert: WBENC)

4749 SNtial Technologies, Inc.
150 N. Michigan Ave Ste 2800
Chicago, IL 60601
Contact: Leon Francisco President
Tel: 630-452-4735
Email: leon.francisco@sntialtech.com
Website: www.sntialtech.com
IT services, custom software development, systems integration & re-engineering. (As-Pac, estab 2001, empl 8, sales $1,000,000, cert: City, NMSDC)

4750 Softal Technologies LLC
318 W Adams St Ste 1600
Chicago, IL 60606
Contact: Marina Perla CEO
Tel: 872-895-7955
Email: mperla@mojotrek.com
Website: www.mojotrek.com
Nearshoring, staff augmentation, technology staffing, tech recruitment. (Woman, estab 2010, empl 8, sales $6,170,497, cert: WBENC)

4751 Swoon Group
300 South Wacker Dr Ste 300
Chicago, IL 60606
Contact: Joseph Matalone EVP
Tel: 312-450-8700
Email: joe.matalone@swoonstaffing.com
Website: www.swoonstaffing.com
Technical staffing. (Woman, estab , empl , sales $80,000,000, cert: WBENC)

4752 Synchronous Solutions, Inc.
211 W Wacker Dr Ste 300
Chicago, IL 60606
Contact: John Sterling CEO
Tel: 312-252-3700
Email: jsterling@synch-solutions.com
Website: www.synch-solutions.com
Implementations, integrations & upgrades, ERP software products, Oracle-PeopleSoft & SAP, functional & technical Consulting, database admin, application integration, training, project mgmt, strategic IT outsourcing. (AA, estab 1998, empl 75, sales $14,000,000, cert: State, City, NMSDC)

4753 Synectics Inc.
135 S LaSalle St Ste 2050
Chicago, IL 60603
Contact: Melissa Lounds Dir of Global Accounts
Tel: 312-629-1020
Email: m_lounds@synectics.com
Website: www.synectics.com/
Information technology consulting, staff augmentation. (Woman, estab 1984, empl 300, sales $19,300,000, cert: CPUC, WBENC)

4754 System Solutions, Inc.
3630 Commercial Ave
Northbrook, IL 60062
Contact: Oliver Patterson Sr Acct Mgr
Tel: 847-272-6160
Email: oliver.patterson@thessi.com
Website: www.THESSI.COM
Information technology: enterprise solution products & architecture, consulting, staffing, network design & implementation, hardware & software procurement, onsite installation services. (As-Pac, estab 1987, empl 20, sales $24,000,000, cert: State, NMSDC)

4755 TechCircle, Inc.
500 N Michigan Ave Ste 600
Chicago, IL 60611
Contact: Aakash Gajera President
Tel: 312-767-5653
Email: agajera@techcircleinc.com
Website: www.techcircleinc.com
Information technology consulting & staff augmentation services, project/program management, business system analysis, quality assurance, verification & validation. (As-Ind, estab 2015, empl 4, sales $300,000, cert: State, NMSDC)

4756 Technical Source, Inc.
1447 E Rosita Dr
Palatine, IL 60074
Contact: President
Tel: 847-705-1730
Email: jgutwein@computerrelocation.com
Website: www.computerrelocation.com
Project Management Information Technology, IT Management, Help Desk & Support Disaster Recovery. (Woman, estab 1999, empl 54, sales $1,025,201, cert: City, WBENC)

4757 Teklink International Inc.
4320 Winfield Rd Ste 215
Warrenville, IL 60563
Contact: Douglas Heck VP
Tel: 630-881-9026
Email: douglas.heck@tli-usa.com
Website: www.tli-usa.com
Data Analytics Services and Business Intelligence Consulting Services. (As-Pac, estab 1998, empl 78, sales $ 0, cert: NMSDC)

4758 teksoft ventures, inc.
127 Ridge Lane
Geneva, IL 60134
Contact: Janet Konn President
Tel: 630-232-9630
Email: jan.konn@teksoftventures.com
Website: www.teksoftventures.com
SAP training & education services, live classroom education & web based remote education. (Woman, estab 1996, empl 50, sales $5,000,000, cert: WBENC)

4759 The Silicon Blackgroup, LLC
110 W Superior St, Ste 2001
Chicago, IL 60504
Contact: Nikolina Akinula Business Success Mgr
Tel: 312-298-9892
Email: nikolina@thesiliconblackgroup.com
Website: www.thesiliconblackgroup.com
Cybersecurity, Security Compliance, Strategic Advisory and IT Project Recovery Management. (AA, estab 2020, empl 10, sales , cert: NMSDC)

4760 Total Response Technology, LLC
1921 Richfield Ave
Highland Park, IL 60035
Contact: Sandra Bast President
Tel: 312-513-0478
Email: sandra@trt-llc.com
Website: www.totalresponsetechnology.com
Implement or maintain IT investments. (Minority, Woman, estab 2009, empl 20, sales $1,400,000, cert: City, WBENC)

4761 TransTech, LLC
248 Spring Lake Dr
Itasca, IL 60143
Contact: Cynthia Conroy Sales Admin
Tel: 630-228-8880
Email: cconroy@transtechit.com
Website: www.transtechit.com
Informational technology staffing solutions. (Woman, estab 1990, empl 100, sales $34,600,000, cert: WBENC)

4762 Tranzact Technologies, Inc.
360 W Butterfield Rd Ste 400
Elmhurst, IL 60126
Contact: LeAnn DeFalco Sales Asst
Tel: 630-833-0890
Email: diversity@tranzact.com
Website: www.tranzact.com
Sourcing and Spend Management, Constellation TMS, Supply Chain Edge, Risk Monitoring, Advanced Data mining & reporting. (Woman, estab 1984, empl 250, sales $74,228,000, cert: WBENC)

4763 UFC Technology, Inc.
      1900 E Golf Rd, Ste 950
      Schaumburg, IL 60173
      Contact: Lisa Smith-Maxam President
      Tel: 908-336-8831
      Email: lisa@the-staffroom.com
      Website: www.ufctechnology.com/
Contingent Workforce Staffing and IT Consulting services. (As-Pac, estab 2013, empl 30, sales , cert: CPUC)

4764 VIVA USA Inc.
      3601 Algonquin Rd Ste 425
      Rolling Meadows, IL 60008
      Contact: Vasanthi Ilangovan President
      Tel: 847-368-0860
      Email: vilangovan@viva-it.com
      Website: www.viva-it.com
IT svcs, custom software dev, IT staffing, offsite & offshore IT project outsourcing. (Woman/As-Ind, estab 1996, empl 380, sales $30,000,000, cert: State, NMSDC, CPUC, WBENC)

4765 Von Technologies, LLC
      1193 Old Creek Ct
      Woodridge, IL 60517
      Contact: Michelle Vondrasek President
      Tel: 630-985-8474
      Email: vondrasek.michelle@vontechnologies.com
      Website: www.vontechnologies.com
Network solutions: infrastructure design, implementation, management, refresh, software & hardware configuration, wireless solutions. (Woman, estab 2006, empl 23, sales , cert: State, WBENC)

4766 Wavicle Data Solutions
      1111 W 22nd St Ste 270
      Oak Brook, IL 60523
      Contact: Olivia Landry Business Development Rep
      Tel: 630-756-2632
      Email: olivia.landry@wavicledata.com
      Website: www.wavicledata.com
Cloud data & analytics solutions, modern data architectures & fuel advanced analytics, machine learning, and artificial intelligence initiatives. (As-Ind, estab 2013, empl 550, sales $43,000,000, cert: NMSDC)

Indiana

4767 Alliance Group Technologies Company-Calumet, Inc.
      911 Broad Ripple Ave, Ste B
      Indianapolis, IN 46220
      Contact: Michael Weir Dir-Business Dev
      Tel: 317-254-8285
      Email: mweir@alliancegrouptech.com
      Website: www.alliancegrouptech.com
Engineering consulting & technical staffing solutions. (As-Pac, estab 1975, empl 215, sales $ 0, cert: NMSDC)

4768 Anchor Point Technology Resources, Inc
      9510 N Meridian St Ste 200
      Indianapolis, IN 46260
      Contact: Rachael Schatko President
      Tel: 317-225-4141
      Email: rachael.schatko@anchorpointtr.com
      Website: www.anchorpointtr.com/
Engineering & IT solutions, IT staffing, contract, C2D, Permanent Placement, Engineering Staffing & Executive Placement. (Woman, estab 2004, empl 60, sales $14,886,000, cert: State)

4769 Bottom-Line Performance, Inc.
      PO Box 155
      New Palestine, IN 46163
      Contact: Kirk Boller President
      Tel: 317-861-5935
      Email: kirk_boller@bottomlineperformance.com
      Website: www.bottomlineperformance.com
E-learning, classroom-based training. (Woman, estab , empl , sales $1,500,000, cert: WBENC)

4770 CIMCOR Inc.
      8252 Virginia St
      Merrillville, IN 46410
      Contact: Robert Johnson President
      Tel: 219-736-4400
      Email: johnson.robert@cimcor.com
      Website: www.cimcor.com
Protect critical IT infrastructure from malicious exposure. (AA, estab 1997, empl 15, sales $1,359,269, cert: NMSDC)

4771 Data Integration Consulting, Inc.
      7399 N. Shadeland Ave Ste 312
      Indianapolis, IN 46250
      Contact: Tim Thompson President
      Tel: 317-894-2623
      Email: tthompson@dataic.com
      Website: www.dataic.com
IT consulting, web application devel, desktop application devel, computer programming, network design & administration, database design & administration. (AA, estab 2003, empl 1, sales , cert: State)

4772 Esource Resources, LLC
      7114 Lakeview Pkwy W Dr
      Indianapolis, IN 46268
      Contact: Eddie Rivers CEO
      Tel: 317-863-0423
      Email: erivers@esourceresources.net
      Website: www.esourceresources.net
IT staffing, placement, computer & software consulting, virtualization, systems integration, web and graphic design resources, software licensing. (AA, estab 2002, empl 8, sales $15,133,940, cert: State, NMSDC)

4773 GuideSoft Inc. dba Knowledge Services
      5875 Castle Creek Pkwy N Dr Ste 400
      Indianapolis, IN 46250
      Contact: Cindy Davis Dir
      Tel: 317-578-1700
      Email: cindyd@knowledgeservices.com
      Website: www.knowledgeservices.com
IT staffing; IT training development. project mgmt, application development, tier I-III help desk & desktop support. (Woman, estab 1994, empl 130, sales $13,186,909, cert: State)

4774 Guilford Group LLC
      615 W Carmel Dr, Ste 130
      Carmel, IN 46032
      Contact: Rajan Kapur Dir
      Tel: 317-814-1060
      Email: rajkapur@guilfordgroup.com
      Website: www.guilfordgroup.com
Information technology consulting, IT project management, enterprise application development, mobile development, data management, staffing, cloud storage, systems integrations, web development & graphic design resources. (As-Ind, estab 2003, empl 30, sales $2,922,823, cert: State, NMSDC)

INFORMATION TECHNOLOGY: Services

4775 GyanSys Inc.
      702 Adams St
      Carmel, IN 46032
      Contact: Padmaja Una Chairman
      Tel: 317-332-3290
      Email: padma.una@gyansys.com
      Website: www.gyansys.com
Global systems integration: SAP & Microsoft products, mobile platforms. (Woman/As-Ind, estab , empl , sales $17,000,000, cert: State, WBENC)

4776 JumpStart Point of Arrival, LLC
      9801 Fall Creek Rd, Ste 410
      Indianapolis, IN 46256
      Contact: Ek-Leng Chua-Miller CEO
      Tel: 317-777-1995
      Email: ek-leng@jumpstartpoa.biz
      Website: www.jumpstartpoa.biz
Statistical analysis, data analysis, database marketing, data mining, statistical modeling, regression analysis (Minority, Woman, estab 2005, empl 2, sales $442,000, cert: State, NMSDC, WBENC)

4777 LHP Software, LLC
      1888 Poshard Dr
      Columbus, IN 47203
      Contact: Kandace Yamcharern Mgr Payment Process
      Tel: 812-418-6331
      Email: kandace.y@lhpes.com
      Website: www.lhpsoftware.com
Custom software solutions: embedded software, communication software, internet software, testing. (As-Pac, estab 2001, empl 210, sales $26,893,359, cert: NMSDC)

4778 Lucidia IT
      6525 E 82nd St, Ste 103
      Indianapolis, IN 46250
      Contact: Janet Stiller CEO
      Tel: 317-953-9800
      Email: anikirk@lucidiait.com
      Website: www.lucidiait.com/
Data Center Technologies, Cloud Connectivity, Collaboration, End User Technology, Enterprise Networking, Cybersecurity and Project Management. (Woman, estab 2018, empl 11, sales $5,000,000, cert: WBENC)

4779 Morse Communications Inc.
      8207 Linden Ave
      Munster, IN 46321
      Contact: Tim Kerrick Sr Acct Mgr
      Tel: 219-314-6029
      Email: tkerrick@morsecom.com
      Website: www.morsecom.com
Systems integration, communications, networking & electronic safety & security. (Woman, estab 1994, empl 75, sales $17,000,000, cert: State)

4780 Phelco Technologies, Inc.
      9801 Fall Creek Rd Ste 131
      Indianapolis, IN 46256
      Contact: Tasha Phelps CEO
      Tel: 317-898-0334
      Email: tasha@phelco.com
      Website: www.phelco.com
Network infrastructure, disaster recovery, off-site data backup, web development. (Woman/AA, estab 1997, empl 1, sales , cert: State)

4781 Pinnacle Mailing Products, LLC
      7701 W Kilgore Ave, Ste 5
      Yorktown, IN 47396
      Contact: Kimberly Laffoon Owner
      Tel: 765-405-1194
      Email: kimlaffoon@pinnaclemailing.com
      Website: www.pinnaclemailingproducts.net
Address correction & shipping software solutions. (Woman, estab 2009, empl 6, sales $195,000, cert: State)

4782 RCR Technology Corporation
      251 N Illinois St Ste 1150, North Tower
      Indianapolis, IN 46204
      Contact: Robert Reed CEO
      Tel: 317-624-9500
      Email: rreed@rcrtechnology.com
      Website: www.rcrtechnology.com
Information technology consulting, network design, application services & project management. (AA, estab 1997, empl 150, sales $18,000,000, cert: State, City, NMSDC)

4783 Ryan Consulting Group, Inc.
      7914 N Shadeland Ave
      Indianapolis, IN 46250
      Contact: Hubert Goodman COO
      Tel: 317-541-9300
      Email: sales@consultrcg.com
      Website: www.consultrcg.com/
Information technologies, systems integration, design & consulting. (AA, estab 2001, empl 123, sales $25,990,253, cert: NMSDC)

4784 Sondhi Solutions LLC
      47 S Pennsylvania St Ste 400
      Indianapolis, IN 46204
      Contact: Justin Harris Principal
      Tel: 3122-222-2222
      Email: jmurphy@sondhisolutions.com
      Website: www.sondhisolutions.com
Application Development Services, Client-Server Development, Database Development Legacy System & Application Conversions Systems. (As-Ind, estab 2008, empl 95, sales $12,000,000, cert: State, NMSDC)

4785 STLogics
      1119 Keystone Way Ste 301
      Carmel, IN 46032
      Contact: Priya Prasad President
      Tel: 800-505-0357
      Email: hr@stlogics.com
      Website: www.stlogics.com
IT consulting, staff augmentation, managed IT solutions, project management, web & software development, quality assurance, Java applications, sharepoint, SAP, ERP, datawarehouse & network administration. (Woman/As-Ind, estab 2004, empl 120, sales , cert: NMSDC)

4786 Women Impact Tech, LLC
      4602 Saint Georges Ct
      Floyds Knobs, IN 47119
      Contact: Amy LaScola VP, Operations
      Tel: 330-685-3358
      Email: lisa.englehart@womenimpacttech.com
      Website: www.womenimpacttech.com
Digital platform for organizations to showcase roles within a diverse tech community, enhancing visibility. (Woman, estab 2022, empl 25, sales $289,027,541, cert: WBENC)

Kansas

4787 3 Fuerzas Technology Solutions, LLC
      14013 Outlook
      Overland Park, KS 66223
      Contact: Shawn Hashmi VP Program Management
      Tel: 913-744-1163
      Email: shashmi@edzsystems.com
      Website: www.edzsystems.com
Software Development, IT Consulting Services, Intelligent Resource Management System (Intelligent RMS. (Minority, Woman, estab 2015, empl 5, sales $201,000, cert: NMSDC)

4788 Cyber Research Group
      2623 N Woodridge Ct
      Wichita, KS 67226
      Contact: Mershard Frierson VP of Business Dev
      Tel: 316-941-8269
      Email: mfrierson@cyberresearchgroup.com
      Website: www.cyberresearchgroup.com
Cyber Research Group specializes in cyber security & IT infrastructure support. (AA, estab 2012, empl 5, sales $350,000, cert: 8(a))

4789 DW Training and Development Incorporated
      6019 Hauser Dr
      Shawnee, KS 66216
      Contact: Jill Evans VP Sales & Mktg
      Tel: 913-268-4400
      Email: jill@technicallytraining.com
      Website: www.technicallytraining.com
Technical writing & database development. (Woman, estab 2001, empl 2, sales $1,970,000, cert: WBENC)

4790 Evolv Solutions, LLC.
      7300 West 110th St Ste 700
      Overland Park, KS 66210
      Contact: Eric Harland VP
      Tel: 913-469-8900
      Email: eharland@evolvsolutions.com
      Website: www.evolvsolutions.com
IT & document mgmt solutions, project mgmt & outsourcing, enterprise solutions, web devel, system integration, tech communication, office assessment, asset mgmt, etc. (AA, estab 2001, empl 8, sales $7,849,351, cert: NMSDC)

4791 Global Control Systems, Inc.
      11605 S Alden St
      Olathe, KS 66062
      Contact: Manual David President
      Tel: 913-681-9261
      Email: sales@gcsks.com
      Website: www.webcontrolsystems.com
Systems integration, configuration & programming, SCADA system & industrial networks, intelligent batch mgmt systems, process equipment, packaging systems, robotics systems, vision systems, material handling controls. (Hisp, estab 2000, empl 8, sales $1,027,400, cert: City, NMSDC)

4792 IT Consulting Services, Inc.
      901 Kentucky St Ste 105
      Lawrence, KS 66044
      Contact: Kishor Gohel COO
      Tel: 913-972-2321
      Email: kgohel@itcscorp.net
      Website: www.itcscorp.net
Software Engineering: Application Devel (Web, non-Web, Mobile, SharePoint, e-commerce), Legacy systems & data migration, System Integration (SOA based & FOSS Custom Solutions). (Woman/As-Ind, estab 2004, empl 6, sales , cert: State, 8(a))

4793 JMA Chartered
      10551 Barkley St Ste 400
      Overland Park, KS 66212
      Contact: Sanjay Chopra Dir of Western Region
      Tel: 913-722-3252
      Email: schopra@jmait.com
      Website: www.jma-it.com
IT: systems integration, IT infrastructure planning, IT facilities mgmt, network design & implementation, IT security audits & staff supplementation. (As-Pac, estab 1994, empl 250, sales $13,900,000, cert: NMSDC, CPUC)

4794 Perfect Output, LLC
      9200 Indian Creek Pkwy Ste 400
      Overland Park, KS 66210
      Contact: Angela Pease VP Business Dev
      Tel: 913-317-8400
      Email: apease@perfectoutput.com
      Website: www.perfectoutput.com
Document output devices: printers, fax machines, & digital multi-functional devices, develop & implement document management strategies. (AA, estab 1997, empl 70, sales $ 0, cert: State, NMSDC, CPUC)

4795 Technology Group Solutions, LLC
      8551 Quivira Road
      Lenexa, KS 66215
      Contact: Lenora Payne CEO
      Tel: 913-451-9900
      Email: lpayne@tgs-mtc.com
      Website: www.tgs-mtc.com
IT solutions. (Woman/AA, estab 2005, empl 79, sales $87,407,949, cert: NMSDC, WBENC)

4796 Veracity Consulting, Inc.
      15516 W 81st St, Ste 195
      Lenexa, KS 66219
      Contact: Angela Hurt CEO
      Tel: 913-579-9242
      Email: angela.hurt@engageveracity.com
      Website: www.veracityconsulting.us
IT contracting services: process improvement, PMO, project Mgt, custom computer programming, systems administration & information security. (Minority, Woman, estab 2006, empl 26, sales , cert: WBENC)

Kentucky

4797 AnITConsultant, LLC
      PO Box 22998
      Owensboro, KY 42304
      Contact: Whaylon Coleman Owner
      Tel: 270-883-1450
      Email: it@anitconsultant.com
      Website: www.anitconsultant.com
IT solutions & consulting services, Game Development (Unity3d), Social Media Consulting, Microsoft Application Dev, Mobile & Tablet Apps. (AA, estab 2010, empl 1, sales , cert: State)

4798 DSSI Group Holding, LLC
      9300 Shelbyville Rd, Ste 402
      Lousiville, KY 40222
      Contact: Robin Wright King Supplier Diversity Dir
      Tel: 248-208-8364
      Email: rking@directsourcing.com
      Website: www.directsourcingsolutions.com
Indirect Purchasing infrastructure for Strategic Sourcing, Catalog Development, and Purchase-to-Pay transaction processing. (As-Pac, estab 2001, empl 76, sales $88,000,000, cert: NMSDC)

4799 Etisbew Technology Group Inc.
      7031 Glen Arbor Dr
      Florence, KY 41042
      Contact: Raj Pakala CEO
      Tel: 502-386-4999
      Email: bizteam@etisbew.com
      Website: www.etisbew.com
E-Business solutions, e-business strategy, architecture & process automation, web based applications development & maintenance. (As-Pac, estab 2000, empl 150, sales $5,321,106, cert: NMSDC)

4800 GlowTouch LLC
      9931 Corporate Campus Dr, Ste 1400
      Louisville, KY 40223
      Contact: Victoria Karrer Exec Admin
      Tel: 502-410-1732
      Email: victoria@glowtouch.com
      Website: www.glowtouch.com
Technology Outsourcing: custom software development, product development, systems integration, mobile applications, QA, testing, and network monitoring. (Woman/As-Ind, estab 2006, empl 2300, sales $27,909,083, cert: NMSDC, WBENC)

4801 V-Soft Consulting Group Inc.
      101 Bullitt Lane Ste 205
      Louisville, KY 40222
      Contact: Vincel Anthony Natl Business Dev Mgr
      Tel: 502-425-8425
      Email: vanthony@vsoftconsulting.com
      Website: www.vsoftconsulting.com
Information technology staffing & consulting services: temporary, contract & permanent placement. (Minority, Woman, estab 1997, empl 230, sales $ 0, cert: NMSDC)

Louisiana

4802 A-B Computer Solutions, Inc.
      PO Box 1851
      Mandeville, LA 70470
      Contact: Jason Brady President
      Tel: 985-624-3092
      Email: jasonb@a-bcomputers.com
      Website: www.a-bcomputers.com
Information technology solutions & consulting. (Woman, estab 1997, empl 13, sales $3,060,000, cert: WBENC)

4803 Barrister Global Services Network Inc
      42548 Happywoods Road
      Hammond, LA 70403
      Contact: Melissa Dobson Dir of Service Solutions
      Tel: 985-365-0806
      Email: mdobson@barrister.com
      Website: www.barrister.com
Information technology services. (Woman, estab , empl 147, sales $ 0, cert: WBENC)

4804 ComTec Consultants Inc.
      2400 Veterans Memorial Blvd Ste 205
      Kenner, LA 70062
      Contact: Vijay Saradhi VP
      Tel: 972-338-3533
      Email: vijay@comtecinfo.com
      Website: www.comtecinfo.com
Information technology & business process services. (Woman/As-Ind, estab 1996, empl 635, sales $62,550,319, cert: NMSDC)

4805 MSF Global Solutions, LLC
      201 St. Charles Ave, Ste 2500
      New Orleans, LA 70170
      Contact: Marseyas Fernandez CEO
      Tel: 504-872-0641
      Email: marseyas@msfglobal.net
      Website: www.msfglobal.net
Geospatial & location based software & data development, mobile website & app development, staffing & training support services, data & business intelligence services, web & custom software design & development services. (AA, estab 2003, empl 5, sales $400,000, cert: NMSDC)

4806 VINFORMATIX L.L.C.
      801 North Boulevard Ste 120
      Baton Rouge, LA 70802
      Contact: Kelli Cagle Dir Business Devel
      Tel: 504-401-0533
      Email: kcagle@vinformatix.com
      Website: www.vinformatix.com
Custom-built software applications for web & mobile platforms (including OS/Android/Windows mobile apps), software lifecycle services, requirements analysis, design, coding, testing, QA/QC, training & maintenance. (Minority, Woman, estab 2008, empl 27, sales $1,073,605, cert: WBENC)

Massachusetts

4807 Advans IT Services, Inc.
      65 Boston Post Rd W Ste 390
      Marlborough, MA 01752
      Contact: Paul Angelo CRM Mgr
      Tel: 508-624-9900
      Email: pangelo@advansit.com
      Website: www.AdvansIT.com
IT infrastructure, project management & software development & offshore support. (As-Pac, estab 2009, empl 205, sales $21,000,000, cert: State, NMSDC)

4808 Advoqt, LLC
      10 Guest St Ste 290
      Boston, MA 02135
      Contact: Reinier Moquete Founder & CEO
      Tel: 617-307-7770
      Email: info@advoqt.com
      Website: www.advoqt.com
Systems integration & technology advisory firm focused on Hybrid Cloud Computing. (Hisp, estab 2012, empl 10, sales , cert: State)

4809 Aquent LLC
      501 Boylston St 3rd Fl
      Boston, MA 02116
      Contact: Jennifer Cousins Dir Staffing Solutions Dev
      Tel: 202-808-0557
      Email: jcousins@aquent.com
      Website: www.aquent.com
Graphic designers, web designers, production artists, presentation graphics experts, writers & project managers: freelance, permanent & temporary-to-permanent basis. (Minority, Woman, estab 1986, empl 890, sales $500,000,000, cert: NMSDC)

INFORMATION TECHNOLOGY: Services

4810 Cambridge Computer Services, Inc.
271 Waverley Oaks Ste 301
Waltham, MA 02452
Contact: Business Operations Customer Advocate
Tel: 781-250-3000
Email: bizops@cambridgecomputer.com
Website: www.cambridgecomputer.com
Data storage & data protection solutions: SAN, NAS, backup, cloud, solid state, archiving solutions, research data management, scientific workflow, metadata, tiered storage, chargebacks, archiving & cloud storage. (Woman, estab , empl , sales $ 0, cert: State, WBENC)

4811 Continental Resources Inc.
175 Middlesex Tpke
Bedford, MA 01730
Contact: Louis Novakis DPO
Tel: 781-533-0450
Email: lnovakis@conres.com
Website: www.conres.com
Global IT solutions provider. (Woman, estab 1962, empl 328, sales $410,000,000, cert: WBENC)

4812 CTS Services Inc.
260 Maple St
Bellingham, MA 02019
Contact: Michelle Carlow President
Tel: 508-528-7720
Email: mcarlow@ctsservices.com
Website: www.ctsservices.com
Computer, printer & peripheral repair: touch screen displays, barcode scanning equip, receipt printer. (Woman, estab 1989, empl 22, sales $2,775,000, cert: State)

4813 Cube Intelligence Corporation
12 Brattle Lane
Arlington, MA 02474
Contact: Hemant Verma President
Tel: 617-275-8254
Email: hsverma@cubeic.com
Website: www.cubeic.com
IT consulting and Staffing augmentationsvcs: data warehousing, data integration, data profiling, data quality, master data management, ODS, Operational Data Stores, Data Mart, Star Schema. (As-Ind, estab 2001, empl 2, sales $178,654, cert: State, NMSDC, 8(a))

4814 Deerwalk, Inc.
430 Bedford St
Lexington, MA 02420
Contact: Jeffrey Gasser President
Tel: 781-325-1775
Email: jgasser@deerwalk.com
Website: www.deerwalk.com
Global data analytics, big data technology & web based data analytics applications, healthcare data analytics, population mgmt & controlling healthcare costs. (As-Ind, estab 2010, empl 400, sales $7,450,000, cert: NMSDC)

4815 Distributed Technology Associates
1740 Massachusetts Ave
Boxborough, MA 01719
Contact: Sanjay Tikku President
Tel: 978-274-0462
Email: office@dtainc.us
Website: www.dtainc.us
Database & systems services, database & systems, Oracle & SQL Server databases, Linux, Solaris & Windows platforms. (As-Ind, estab 1997, empl 7, sales $2,114,602, cert: State, NMSDC)

4816 Dnutch Associates, Inc.
301 Broadway
Methuen, MA 01844
Contact: Stephen Payne CEO
Tel: 978-687-1500
Email: spayne@dnutch.com
Website: www.dnutch.com
Networking & systems integration solutions. (Woman/AA, estab 1993, empl 8, sales $550,000, cert: State, WBENC)

4817 Hawkins Point Partners LLC
7 Technology Dr
North Chelmsford, MA 01863
Contact: Heather Morris Kyer Sr Principal
Tel: 781-640-0893
Email: hmorriskyer@hawkinspointpartners.com
Website: www.hawkinspointpartners.com
IT consulting, outsourcing reset, application modernization, information management, mobile solutions & enterprise architecture & integration. (Woman, estab 2012, empl 5, sales , cert: State, WBENC)

4818 Inspiration Zone, LLC
Two Heritage Dr, Ste 302
Quincy, MA 02171
Contact: Juliette Mayers CEO
Tel: 617-328-0953
Email: info@inspirationzonellc.com
Website: www.inspirationzonellc.com
Multicultural Marketing & Leadership Development. (AA, estab 2011, empl 1, sales $130,000, cert: State, NMSDC)

4819 Integration Technology, Inc.
167 Washington St Ste 32
Norwell, MA 02061
Contact: Sean Stewart Acct mgr
Tel: 781-569-4949
Email: sean.stewart@it-inc.us
Website: www.integration-technology.com
IT, SAP staffing and consulting services (Woman, estab 1998, empl 4, sales $1,300,000, cert: State)

4820 IntePros Incorporated
750 Marrett Road Ste 301
Lexington, MA 02421
Contact: Jeffrey Anderson Branch Mgr
Tel: 612-916-7387
Email: janderson@intepros.com
Website: www.intepros.com
Provide contracted IT consultants, software development lifecycle, network infrastructure & security. (Woman, estab 1996, empl 350, sales $55,400,000, cert: WBENC)

4821 Interactive Tactical Group
55 Wallace St
Somerville, MA 02144
Contact: Michael Quan President
Tel: 617-500-7520
Email: mike@tacticalvr.com
Website: www.tacticalvr.com
Interactive panoramic imaging for military, security & industrial organizations. DotProduct3D hand held 3D scanner, DotProduct3D hand held 3D scanner, DPI-7, uses Android tablet & Kinect sensor. (As-Pac, estab 2000, empl 1, sales $150,500, cert: State, NMSDC)

INFORMATION TECHNOLOGY: Services

4822 Iterators LLC
50 Milk St, Fl 16
Boston, MA 02109
Contact: Jill Willcox Managing Member
Tel: 617-909-0564
Email: jwillcox@iteratorstesting.com
Website: www.Iteratorstesting.com
Accessibility Testing, Website and Mobile App Testing: Manual, Accessibility, Automation, Manual Functional and Regression Testing, Automated Regression Testing. (Woman, estab 2017, empl 5, sales $264,000, cert: WBENC)

4823 M & R Consultants Corporation
700 Technology Park Dr Ste 203
Billerica, MA 01821
Contact: Sales Dir
Tel: 781-273-5050
Email: info@mrccsolutions.com
Website: www.mrccsolutions.com
IT consulting: software engineering, client server technology, internet & intranet, network admin, project mgmt, product dev. (As-Ind, estab 1996, empl 700, sales $20,000,000, cert: State)

4824 Martindale Associates, Inc.
65 Avco Rd, Unit M
Bradford, MA 01835
Contact: Laurie Hall President
Tel: 978-372-2120
Email: lmh@martindaleassoc.com
Website: www.martindaleassoc.com
Automated machine & process control systems, data acquisition systems, barcode data collection, inventory & asset tracking, RFID, mobile device management, handheld computers & systems integration. (Minority, Woman, estab 1976, empl 7, sales $1,525,041, cert: State)

4825 On Track Consulting
317 Eliot St
Milton, MA 02186
Contact: Janet McCloskey President
Tel: 617-653-1409
Email: jmccloskey@ontrackconsult.com
Website: www.ontrackconsult.com
Information mgmt services, big data, data warehousing, business intelligence & data management. (Woman, estab 1997, empl 1, sales $3,157,077, cert: State, WBENC)

4826 Online Computer Prodcuts, Inc.
672 Pleasant St
Norwood, MA 02062
Contact: Harry Butters Acct Mgr
Tel: 781-255-9100
Email: hbutters@online-computer.com
Website: www.online-computer.com
Information technology support products, services & solutions. (Woman, estab 1987, empl 24, sales $14,075,000, cert: WBENC)

4827 Onyx Spectrum Technology, Inc. dba Shearwater EM
78 Fisher Ave
Boston, MA 02120
Contact: Adrienne R. Benton President
Tel: 617-407-2826
Email: abenton@onyxspectrum.com
Website: www.onyxspectrum.com
Technical consulting services: data analysis, information security, business process improvement & regulatory concerns. (Woman/AA, estab 2004, empl 5, sales $726,000, cert: State)

4828 ResourceSoft, Inc.
33 Boston Post Rd W Ste 230
Marlborough, MA 01752
Contact: Pyi Phyo VP
Tel: 508-787-0882
Email: pyi@resourcesoft.com
Website: www.resourcesoft.com
Custom computer programming svcs: MS .NET, JAVA/J2EE, quality assurance. (Minority, Woman, estab 1999, empl 55, sales $5,711,183, cert: State, NMSDC)

4829 Scitics Inc.
436 Central St
Acton, MA 01720
Contact: Joan Yu President
Tel: 978-844-1258
Email: jyu@sciticsinc.com
Website: www.sciticsinc.com
Data analytic services, data exploration & discovery, data processing, hosting & related services, custom computer programming services, dashboard & customized business intelligence reports, predictive modeling. (Minority, Woman, estab 2010, empl 3, sales $128,170, cert: State, WBENC)

4830 Scout Exchange LLC
501 Boylston St, Ste 3101
Boston, MA 02116
Contact: Farla Russo Dir of Admin
Tel: 617-535-4561
Email: frusso@goscoutgo.com
Website: www.goscoutgo.com
Integrated with Applicant Tracking System (ATS). (As-Pac, estab 2013, empl 58, sales , cert: NMSDC)

4831 Shred King Corporation
60 McGrath Hwy
Quincy, MA 02169
Contact: Donald Cornell GM
Tel: 617-221-1600
Email: info@shred-king.com
Website: www.shred-king.com
Document destruction services. (Woman, estab 2006, empl 10, sales , cert: State)

4832 Sigma Systems, Inc.
293 Boston Post Rd W Ste 301 Ste 100
Mar, MA 01752
Contact: Nate Fischer Dir
Tel: 508-925-3233
Email: nfischer@sigmainc.com
Website: www.sigmainc.com
IT consulting, project mgmt, application dev, network mgmt, database mgmt & support, staffing services, custom application dev, data warehousing, business intelligence, CRM, ERP, EAI, quality assurance, systems admin, web dev & custom MIS. (Minority, Woman, estab 1994, empl 97, sales $4,000,000, cert: State, NMSDC)

4833 SJB Enterprises, Inc. dba Sandra Network
25 Goodale St
Peabody, MA 01960
Contact: Sandra Batakis President
Tel: 978-535-0202
Email: wbe@sandranetwork.com
Website: www.sandranetwork.com
IT consulting: PC repair, training & networks. (Woman, estab 1998, empl 5, sales $671,895, cert: State, WBENC)

INFORMATION TECHNOLOGY: Services

4834 Softlinx, Inc.
      100 Riverpark Dr
      North Reading, MA 01864
      Contact: Helen Kim Contract Mgr
      Tel: 978-881-0575
      Email: hkim@softlinx.com
      Website: www.softlinx.com
Software, IT development, consulting & training. (Woman/As-Pac, estab 1993, empl 15, sales $1,530,000, cert: NMSDC, WBENC)

4835 Solidus Technical Solutions, LLC
      17 Forsythia Rd
      Leominster, MA 01453
      Contact: Jill Blagsvedt Business Devel Specialist
      Tel: 866-765-4387
      Email: solidussmallbd@solidus-ts.com
      Website: www.solidus-ts.com
Software & systems engineering, life cycle, radar, sensors, fault tolerant, mission planning, intelligence systems, embedded software, networking, integration & test. (Woman, estab 2001, empl 95, sales $ 0, cert: WBENC)

4836 Soltrix Technology Solutions Inc.
      860 Worcester Road Ste 215
      Framingham, MA 01702
      Contact: Raghu Nandan President
      Tel: 774-293-1293
      Email: raghu.nandan@soltrixsolutions.com
      Website: www.soltrixsolutions.com
Custom software application design & development services. (Woman/As-Ind, estab 2007, empl 3, sales , cert: State)

4837 Stellar Corporation
      594 Marrett Rd
      Lexington, MA 02421
      Contact: Swapan Roy President
      Tel: 781-863-0101
      Email: sroy@stlr.net
      Website: www.stlr.net
Software custom application development, reengineering, database engineering, structural engineering (As-Pac, estab 2002, empl 7, sales $614,678, cert: State)

4838 Stemac Inc
      30 Evergreen Dr
      Bridgewater, MA 02324
      Contact: Jane McCarthy President
      Tel: 508-331-1410
      Email: jane@stemacinc.com
      Website: www.stemacinc.com
IT placement, pre screened Supply Chain & SAP Talent, Customer Service & Consultative. (Woman, estab 2013, empl 2, sales $400,000, cert: WBENC)

4839 TalentBurst, Inc
      679 Worcester Road
      Natick, MA 01760
      Contact: Jamie Jacobs Dir of Strategic Partnerships
      Tel: 614-382-8840
      Email: jamie.jacobs@talentburst.com
      Website: www.talentburst.com
Information technology staff augmentation, lifesciences, business & regulatory compliance, accounting, finance & IT solutions services. (Minority, estab 2002, empl 1405, sales $84,700,000, cert: NMSDC)

4840 Tanisha Systems Inc.
      75 Federal St Ste 1330
      Boston, MA 02110
      Contact: Gorav Aggarwal VP
      Tel: 617-729-0260
      Email: gaggarwal@tanishasystems.com
      Website: www.tanishasystems.com
Custom application development & end-to-end IT services. (As-Ind, estab 2002, empl 80, sales $9,700,000, cert: State)

4841 tCognition, Inc.
      70 Kemble St Ste 100
      Boston, MA 02119
      Contact: Manoj Shinde CEO
      Tel: 617-438-4819
      Email: Manoj.Shinde@tCognition.com
      Website: www.tCognition.com
IT/software consulting & outsourcing services. (As-Ind, estab 2003, empl 65, sales $3,159,484, cert: State, NMSDC)

4842 Vernance, LLC
      745 Atlantic Ave
      Boston, MA 02111
      Contact: Pedro Marcano CEO
      Tel: 936-647-3376
      Email: pmarcano@vernance.com
      Website: www.vernance.com
Cyber & Physical Security Risk Mgmt consulting services. (Hisp, estab 2014, empl 3, sales $350,000, cert: State, NMSDC)

Maryland

4843 5 Star Consulting Group, LLC.
      3261 Old Washington Rd Ste 2020
      Waldorf, MD 20602
      Contact: Lethia Dargin President
      Tel: 301-216-3839
      Email: ldargin@5starconsultinggrp.com
      Website: www.5StarConsultingGrp.com
Systems Integration & Design, Computer Integration, SCCM, Software deployment, Software packaging, Server maintenance, troubleshooting, configuration & build. IT Consulting, software & hardware support. (Woman/AA, estab 2013, empl 5, sales , cert: State, SDB)

4844 Acela Technologies, Inc.
      5115 Pegasus Ct, Ste A
      Frederick, MD 21704
      Contact: Carole Derringer CEO
      Tel: 301-846-9060
      Email: cderringer@acelatechnologies.com
      Website: www.acelatechnologies.com
Wireless solutions engineering & integration, wireless internet services, VoIP, VoWiFi, wireless video surveillance. (AA, estab 2002, empl 20, sales $3,834,797, cert: State)

4845 Advanced Engineering Design, Inc.
      6525 Belcrest Road Ste 426
      Hyattsville, MD 20782
      Contact: Reginald Waters CEO
      Tel: 301-683-2112
      Email: rwaters@aedworld.com
      Website: www.aedworld.com
Central office & data center engineering services: site surveys, computer-aided-design drafting, equipment inventories & assessments, records development & space planning. (AA, estab 1991, empl 60, sales $2,480,000, cert: State, NMSDC)

INFORMATION TECHNOLOGY: Services

4846 Alliance Technology Group, LLC
7010 Hi Tech Dr
Hanover, MD 21076
Contact: Lauren Russ Corporate Admin
Tel: 410-712-0270
Email: Lauren.Russ@alliance-it.com
Website: www.alliance-it.com
End-to-end storage technology solutions, computer, monitor & printer repair, network peripherals, system upgrades, backup & recovery engineering, data storage assessments. (Woman, estab 1987, empl 83, sales $36,903,700, cert: WBENC)

4847 ALTEK Information Technology, Inc.
241 E Fourth St, Ste 205
Frederick, MD 21701
Contact: Anne Lipman CEO
Tel: 301-695-4440
Email: cardinalhealth@al-tekinc.com
Website: www.al-tekinc.com
Information technology staffing & project management: contract, contract to hire or direct hire. (Woman, estab 2004, empl 150, sales $15,000,000, cert: State, WBENC)

4848 Altus Technology Solutions
1121 Annapolis Rd, Ste 211
Odenton, MD 21113
Contact: David Brashear President
Tel: 443-321-2069
Email: dbrashear@altusts.com
Website: www.altusts.com
Mission-critical services & solutions, IT network management, operations & maintenance, cyber security, software & application testing. (AA, estab 2004, empl 32, sales $5,618,000, cert: 8(a))

4849 Applications Alternatives, Inc.
PO Box 4238
Upper Marlboro, MD 20775
Contact: David Kiasi-Barnes
Tel: 301-350-4752
Email: david.kiasi@appalt.com
Website: www.appalt.com
Information technology applications consulting in the area of informational survey processing. (AA, estab 1987, empl 2, sales , cert: State)

4850 Applied Development LLC
7 S Front St Ste 200
Baltimore, MD 21202
Contact: Kimberly Citizen
Tel: 410-571-4016
Email: kcitizen@applied-dev.com
Website: www.applied-dev.com
Process improvement, automation, analytics & cyber security, project management, business process improvement, strategic communications, cybersecurity & administrative support. (Woman/AA, estab 2011, empl 12, sales $687,000, cert: State, City, NMSDC, WBENC, 8(a))

4851 Avance IT Solutions LLC
7 Gondola View Court
Woodstock, MD 21163
Contact: Antoinette Gardner CEO
Tel: 443-955-5107
Email: partner@avanceits.com
Website: www.avanceitsolutions.com
IT consulting services, project mgmt, training, technology assessments, programming, helpdesk, testing & deployment. (Woman/AA, estab 2007, empl 5, sales , cert: State)

4852 BITHGROUP Technologies, Inc.
113 W Monument St
Baltimore, MD 21201
Contact: Robert Wallace President
Tel: 410-962-1188
Email: robertwallace@bithgroup.com
Website: www.bithgroup.com
Information Technology Consulting, Network Engineering, Application Development, Wireless Infrastructure Development, e-learning (AA, estab 1992, empl 60, sales $ 0, cert: State)

4853 Business Integra Technology Solutions, Inc.
6550 ROCK SPRING DR Ste 600
Bethesda, MD 20817
Contact: Jay Fernandez Sr Dir Business Dev
Tel: 732-887-5611
Email: Jay.Fernandez@businessintegra.com
Website: www.businessintegra.com
Staff augmentation services, information technology consulting. (Minority, Woman, estab 2001, empl 650, sales $115,000,000, cert: WBENC)

4854 CAEI Inc.
9256 Bendix Rd, Ste 102
Columbia, MD 21045
Contact: Derrick Burnett Sr Business Devel Exec
Tel: 443-319-5381
Email: dburnett@caeiinc.com
Website: www.caeiinc.com
Help Desk and Customer Service call center, Personnel and management, in addition to our Help Desk Tier I, Tier II and Tier III experience and past performance. (AA, estab 2011, empl 125, sales $6,500,000, cert: State, NMSDC)

4855 Carson Solutions, LLC
16701 Melford Blvd. Ste. 431
Bowie, MD 20715
Contact: Eugene Carson President
Tel: 800-480-7132
Email: eugene@carsonsolutionsllc.com
Website: www.carsonsolutionsllc.com
Information technology solutions & administrative support. (AA, estab 2000, empl 10, sales $1,850,000, cert: State)

4856 Cyber Management Systems
11504 Eastern Red Cedar Ave
Clinton, MD 20735
Contact: Cory Coleman CEO
Tel: 301-613-3717
Email: corycoleman@cybermss.com
Website: www.cybermanagementsystems.com
Information Technology consulting, Enterprise IT Systems Monitoring, Management Consulting & IT Consulting. (AA, estab 2014, empl 1, sales , cert: State)

4857 Cybern Consulting Group, LLC
13615 Triadelphia Mill Rd
Clarksville, MD 21029
Contact: Serif Mumuney President
Tel: 410-379-0545
Email: serif.mumuney@cyberngroup.com
Website: www.cyberngroup.com
Develop applications using Business Process Management tools running on finely tuned Databases. (AA, estab 2004, empl 8, sales $400,050, cert: State, 8(a))

INFORMATION TECHNOLOGY: Services

4858 Dakota Consulting Inc.
       1110 Bonifant St Ste 310
       Silver Spring, MD 20910
       Contact: Lokesh Sayal VP
       Tel: 240-645-0229
       Email: contracts@dakota-consulting.com
       Website: www.dakotaconsulting.com
Information technology management, telecommunications & networking. (Woman, estab 2015, empl 150, sales $19,000,000, cert: State)

4859 DB Commercial Group LLC
       8401 Colesville Rd Ste 310
       Silver Spring, MD 20910
       Contact: Kim Harwell CEO
       Tel: 301-363-2790
       Email: kim.harwell@dbcommercialgroup.com
       Website: www.dbcommercialgroup.com
IT Services, Staff Augmentation, Systems Engineering, Cyber Security, Application Development, Cloud Computing & Multimedia Services. (AA, estab 2014, empl 20, sales $10,000,000, cert: NMSDC)

4860 Dhaivat Maharaja Enterprises Inc.
       6 Latimore Ct
       Reisterstown, MD 21136
       Contact: Dhaivat Maharaja CEO
       Tel: 443-650-8287
       Email: dhaivat.maharaja@dhaivat.com
       Website: www.dhaivat.com
Enterprise resource planning (ERP), customer relationship management (CRM), Cloud architecture, unified computing system (UCS), online course development, service-oriented architecture (SOA). (As-Pac, estab 2006, empl 3, sales , cert: State)

4861 Digital Foundation Computer Consulting Services Co
       3195 Old Washington Rd Ste 2108
       Waldorf, MD 20602
       Contact: Abdullah Baytops Dir Business Devel
       Tel: 888-754-0341
       Email: abdul@thedigitalcorp.com
       Website: www.thedigitalcorp.com
Application software development, Help-Desk support services, Oracle/SQL Server database administration & development & web design integrations. (AA, estab 2001, empl 4, sales $185,000, cert: 8(a))

4862 Diverse Concepts, Inc.
       1131 Benfield Blvd, Ste K
       Millersville, MD 21108
       Contact: CEO
       Tel: 443-698-1052
       Email:
       Website: www.dciits.com
Web Development and Design, System Engineering, Network Engineering, Information Assurance, Disaster Recovery, Program Management, (AA, estab 2002, empl 20, sales $1,520,000, cert: State)

4863 DK Consulting, LLC
       8955 Guilford Road Ste 240
       Columbia, MD 21046
       Contact: Dana Kerr CEO
       Tel: 443-552-5851
       Email: contacts@dkconsult.net
       Website: www.dkconsult.net
Management & technological solutions services. (Woman, estab 2003, empl 9, sales $818,570, cert: State, City, WBENC)

4864 Encore Solutions Inc.
       12300 Twinbrook Pkwy, Ste 330
       Rockville, MD 20852
       Contact: Gary Lewis President
       Tel: 301-998-6191
       Email: glewis@encore-solu.com
       Website: www.encore-solu.com
Technology solutions: systems engineering, acquisition & logistics support, program mgmt & admin services, records information mgmt. (Woman/AA, estab 2001, empl 3, sales $502,789, cert: State, NMSDC, WBENC)

4865 ERPMatrix LLC
       3620 Turbridge Dr
       Burtonsville, MD 20866
       Contact: Shams Abedin Managing Partner
       Tel: 240-396-4380
       Email: sa@erpmatrix.com
       Website: www.erpmatrix.com
Staffing, enterprise architecture/integration, software devel, database & IT support. (As-Ind, estab 2005, empl 4, sales $178,191, cert: State)

4866 Infinite Computer Solutions Inc.
       15201 Diamondback Dr Ste 125
       Rockville, MD 20850
       Contact: John Stritzl Dir Sales
       Tel: 215-262-8027
       Email: partnership@infinite.com
       Website: www.infinite.com
Applications devel, network engineering/operations, help desk support; e-business, client/server & mainframe solutions; network & system migrations; LAN/WAN/MAN svcs. (As-Ind, estab 2001, empl , sales , cert: NMSDC)

4867 Information Protection Solutions
       1997 Annapolis Exchange Pkwy Ste 300
       Annapolis, MD 21401
       Contact: Todd Chamberlain CEO
       Tel: 240-345-4212
       Email: info@ips314.com
       Website: www.ips314.com
Cyber Security, Cloud security, Continuous Monitoring Strategies, Cyber Security Policy Development, System Hardening Implementation, Vulnerability Analysis Information Assurance. (AA, estab 2014, empl 3, sales , cert: State, NMSDC, 8(a))

4868 Information Security Enterprise Consulting, LLC
       6701 Democracy Blvd
       Bethesda, MD 20814
       Contact: Jason Peterson CEO
       Tel: 301-337-2527
       Email: jpeterson@isec-cybersecurity.com
       Website: www.isec-cybersecurity.com
Cyber security, design, develop, deploy, operate & maintain defensive security measures. (AA, estab 2007, empl 20, sales $2,500,200, cert: State, NMSDC)

4869 International Computer Systems, Inc.
       9111 Edmonston Rd, Ste 403
       Greenbelt, MD 20770
       Contact: Tan Aslam President
       Tel: 301-614-3989
       Email: tanaslam@ics-systems.us
       Website: www.ics-systems.us
Systems engineering, satellite ground systems design & dev, raw data processing systems, system specification, interface control documents, system integration & test, independent verification & test, operations & maintenance, system admin. (Woman/As-Ind, estab 1997, empl 2, sales , cert: WBENC)

INFORMATION TECHNOLOGY: Services

4870   JuneGem Technologies, Inc.
       3601 Hamilton St Ste 201
       Hyattsville, MD 20782
       Contact: Stephanie Thomas Business Devel Mgr
       Tel: 301-864-2321
       Email: hr@junegemtech.com
       Website: www.junegemtech.com
Information Technology and Enterprise Resource Planning (ERP) solutions, project management, business process engineering, and software & systems development. (Woman/AA, estab 2011, empl 10, sales , cert: State)

4871   Jupiter LLC
       12021 Eaglewood Ct
       Silver Spring, MD 20902
       Contact: E Alex Jupiter President
       Tel: 240-316-2943
       Email: alexj@jupitercybsec.com
       Website: www.jupitercybsec.com
Risk assessment, analysis & management; control vulnerability assessment, data & functional specification; IS/IT security scope management, features, architecture & design; cyber incident response planning; software capability maturity assessment. (AA, estab 2013, empl 3, sales , cert: State, City)

4872   MASAI Technologies Corporation
       201B Broadway St
       Frederick, MD 21701
       Contact: Masai Troutman CEO
       Tel: 301-694-2751
       Email: masai@masai-tech.com
       Website: www.masai-tech.com
Staffing & Enterprise Resource Planning (ERP) SAP Software System Integration, implementation & operational services. (AA, estab 1997, empl 15, sales $2,000,000, cert: State, NMSDC)

4873   NucoreVision, Inc
       4601 Forbes Blvd, Ste 310
       Lanham, MD 20706
       Contact: Yolanda Murphy
       Tel: 301-577-3999
       Email: ymurphy@nucorevision.com
       Website: www.nucorevision.com
Cybersecurity, Agency IT Operations, IT Program / Project Management, Management Consulting, IT Services & Solutions. (AA, estab 1996, empl 25, sales $1,900,000, cert: NMSDC)

4874   Nu-Pulse Technologies, Inc.
       21 Industrial Park Dr Ste 101
       Waldorf, MD 20602
       Contact: E. Renee Ingram President
       Tel: 301-374-2534
       Email: ringram@nu-pulse.com
       Website: www.nu-pulse.com
Information technology svcs: software design & devel, LAN/WAN design & implementation, database design & devel, project mgmt. IT security, fire protection engineering, voice guidance exit systems, electronic door locks. (AA, estab 1998, empl 39, sales $3,000,000, cert: State)

4875   Omega Micro Services
       PO Box 1271
       Bowie, MD 20721
       Contact: Paulson Obiniyi CEO
       Tel: 240-602-8624
       Email: info@omicroservices.com
       Website: www.omicroservices.com
Technical Services and Consulting, Enterprise Architecture, Data & Media Sanitization, Web site Design and development, Project and Program Management, Staffing Augmentation, Content Production, Enterprise Content Management. (AA, estab 2007, empl 2, sales , cert: State)

4876   Open Technology Group
       8403 Colesville Rd, Ste 760
       Silver Spring, MD 20910
       Contact: Leon Burns CEO
       Tel: 301-588-1600
       Email: lburn@otghq.com
       Website: www.otghq.com
Software development & maintenance support for applications & databases on internet/intranet websites. (AA, estab 1991, empl 55, sales $9,000,000, cert: 8(a))

4877   Pa Na Solutions Inc.
       3504 Waterford Mill Rd
       Bowie, MD 20721
       Contact: Brahim Zahar VP
       Tel: 703-348-6436
       Email: bzahar@panasolutions.com
       Website: www.panasolutionas.com
IT Svcs: Program Management, Finance, Scheduling, Methodology, Tools, Network Engineering, Strategy & Planning, Assessment, Architecture & design services, Integration & deployment, Optimization, & Device Support, Video Engineering. (AA, estab 2006, empl 28, sales $4,218,518, cert: State, 8(a))

4878   Peyak Solutions, Inc.
       9250 Bendix Rd N, Ste 150
       Columbia, MD 21045
       Contact: Leah Conover CEO
       Tel: 800-958-2188
       Email: leah.conover@peyaksolutions.com
       Website: www.peyaksolutions.com
IT consulting & support services: network design, procurement & installation, desktop, internet & database application dev, project & program management, hardware recycling & confidential data destruction. (Minority, Woman, estab 2007, empl 2, sales $195,000, cert: State, City, 8(a))

4879   Planned Systems International, Inc.
       10632 Little Patuxent Pkwy, Ste 200
       Columbia, MD 21044
       Contact: Terry Lin CEO
       Tel: 410-964-8000
       Email: tlin@plan-sys.com
       Website: www.plan-sys.com/
Providing Healthcare IT, management consulting, IT solutions & services. (As-Pac, estab 1988, empl 350, sales $105,101,730, cert: State)

4880 Pn Automation
       1521 S Edgewood St
       Baltimore, MD 21227
       Contact: Nitin Baviskar COO
       Tel: 410-409-6730
       Email: nitin@pnautomation.com
       Website: www.pnautomation.com
Software development & IT service. (As-Ind, estab 2004, empl 25, sales $600,000, cert: State)

4881 Pramac Engineering LLC
       2000 Astilbe Way
       Odenton, MD 21113
       Contact: Kevin Ruffin CEO
       Tel: 410-409-9772
       Email: kfruffin@pramacengineering.com
       Website: www.pramacengineering.com
Java and C/C++ object oriented design & devel, web applications Model/View/Controller (MVC) devel, Niagara Files devel, Commercial Off the Shelf (COTS) Integration, Systems Integration & 508 Compliance application. (AA, estab 2017, empl 1, sales $121,000, cert: State)

4882 Radiant Infotech
       5520 Research Park Dr, St 100
       Catonsville, MD 21228
       Contact: Sumant Kapoor COO
       Tel: 443-846-2525
       Email: sumant@radiantt.com
       Website: www.radiantt.com
Data Management & Analytics, Agile Software Engineering & DevOps & Management Consulting services. (Woman/As-Ind, estab 2008, empl 20, sales $2,000,000, cert: 8(a))

4883 Realistic Computing, Inc.
       5707 Calverton St
       Baltimore, MD 21228
       Contact: Sequoia Ramsey CEO
       Tel: 410-744-8144
       Email: sramsey@realistic-computing.com
       Website: www.realistic-computing.com
IT support services, network installation, cabling, data & voice. (Woman/AA, estab 2000, empl 3, sales $200,000, cert: WBENC)

4884 Reliable Government Solutions Inc.
       3002 Gazebo Ct
       Silver Spring, MD 20904
       Contact: Chieu Le President
       Tel: 800-767-0896
       Email: chieule@rgsfederal.com
       Website: www.rgsfederal.com
Data warehouse, development, architecture & admin, financial applications, IT audits, JCIDS documentation, network admin & security, testing, program & project mgmt, equirements analysis, SME, training, web development. (As-Pac, estab 2001, empl 5, sales $317,842, cert: City)

4885 Rescon Inc.
       4526 Cheltenham Dr,
       Bethesda, MD 20814
       Contact: Prem Singh CEO
       Tel: 301-330-5265
       Email: resconinc@aol.com
       Website: www.resconisit.com
IT technology consulting & staffing, project management, software architects, programmers, systems admin, network engineers, software quality assurance. (As-Ind, estab 1998, empl 14, sales $2,000,000, cert: State)

4886 Resourcesys Inc.
       8850 Columbia 100 Pkwy Ste 304
       Columbia, MD 21045
       Contact: Kolluri VP Sales
       Tel: 609-721-4446
       Email: anna@resourcesys.com
       Website: www.resourcesys.com
IT contract staffing resources: Oracle Java & .NET technologies. (Woman/As-Ind, estab 1999, empl 20, sales $1,800,000, cert: WBENC)

4887 Right Choice Computers & Networks, LLC
       PO Box 5324
       Capitol Heights, MD 20791
       Contact: Pamela Mitchell President
       Tel: 301-839-4905
       Email: contactus@rchoicecn.com
       Website: www.rchoicecn.com
Software & applications, mainframe Legacy Systems, networks topologies, computer hardware & accessories, help desk & support, network installation. (Woman/AA, estab 1994, empl 1, sales , cert: State)

4888 RTH Solutions LLC
       10320 Little Patuxent Pkwy, Ste 200
       Columbia, MD 21044
       Contact: Tanisha Lockett COO
       Tel: 240-638-1222
       Email: tanisha.lockett@rthsolutions.com
       Website: www.rthsolutions.com
Management consulting, staffing & training, business & IT Service Management process consulting, ITIL, Project Management, Cyber Resilia, DevOps, Lean IT, and Scrum. (Woman/AA, estab 2006, empl 2, sales , cert: State, WBENC, NWBOC)

4889 Shakthy Information Systems, Inc.
       13910 Falconcrest Rd
       Germantown, MD 20874
       Contact: Susheela Palaniswamy CEO
       Tel: 240-355-6184
       Email: hr@shakthy.com
       Website: www.shakthy.com
Custom software development services & solutions. (Minority, Woman, estab 2000, empl 5, sales $350,000, cert: State)

4890 Sympora Technologies
       5431 Woodland Blvd Ste B
       Oxon Hill, MD 20745
       Contact: Dean Matthews President
       Tel: 800-568-9965
       Email: dean.matthews@sympora.com
       Website: www.sympora.com
Software development, information technology, web-based training & information security services. (AA, estab 2000, empl 3, sales $158,325, cert: State)

4891 The Aspen Group, Inc.
       1100 Wayne Ave Ste 1200
       Silver Spring, MD 20910
       Contact: Christina Fitts Exec VP
       Tel: 410-308-0629
       Email: cfitts@theaspengroupinc.com
       Website: www.theaspengroupinc.com
Information technology consulting & services. (Woman/AA, estab 1988, empl 400, sales $38,481,357, cert: NMSDC, WBENC)

INFORMATION TECHNOLOGY: Services

4892 The net.America Corporation
      16201 Trade Zone Ave, Unit 112
      Upper Marlboro, MD 20774
      Contact: Yasmin Hines Business Devel Analyst
      Tel: 301-218-4559
      Email: yasmin.hines@netamerica.net
      Website: www.discovernetamerica.com
IT solutions, contact centers & help desk, information technology, health services, program management, peer review & grants management. (Woman/AA, estab 2000, empl 51, sales $8,226,437, cert: State, WBENC)

4893 The Squires Group
      128 Lubrano Dr, Ste 102
      Annapolis, MD 21401
      Contact: Nancy Squires CEO
      Tel: 410-224-7779
      Email: nancy@squiresgroup.com
      Website: www.squiresgroup.com
ERP staffing & consulting svsc: process reengineering, change mgmt, implementation, upgrades & web-enabled integration. (Woman, estab 1994, empl 75, sales $ 0, cert: WBENC)

4894 TMCS, LLC
      6910 Wade Ave Ste A
      Clinton, MD 20735
      Contact: Tynnetta McBeth CEO
      Tel: 301-686-8417
      Email: tmcbeth@tmcsllc.com
      Website: www.tmcsllc.com
Technical & management consulting, design & implementation of LAN/WAN solutions, security, communicatons & mobility, virtual data center solutions, hardware & software resales. (Minority, Woman, estab 2008, empl 3, sales $160,000, cert: State, 8(a))

4895 Unatek, Inc.
      1100 Mercantile Lane Ste 115-A
      Largo, MD 20774
      Contact: Charles Iheagwara Dir
      Tel: 301-583-4629
      Email: ciheagwara@unatek.com
      Website: www.unatek.com
Information technology consulting. (AA, estab 1996, empl 15, sales $1,860,000, cert: State, 8(a))

4896 Vangel Inc.
      3020 Nieman Ave
      Baltimore, MD 21230
      Contact: Valerie Androutsopoulos Principal
      Tel: 410-644-2600
      Email: valerie@vangelinc.com
      Website: www.vangelinc.com
Data destruction & recycling services: on-site & off-site paper shredding, off-site non-paper storage, media shredding. (Woman, estab 1988, empl 15, sales $1,642,150, cert: State)

4897 Victory Global Solutions, Inc.
      5950 Symphony Woods Rd, Ste 211
      Columbia, MD 21044
      Contact: Angela Brown CEO
      Tel: 410-884-9310
      Email: abrown@victorygs.com
      Website: www.victorygs.com
Information technology & networking integration services, systems engineering, integration & consulting. (Woman/AA, estab 2001, empl 30, sales $26,000,000, cert: State, WBENC)

4898 VVL Systems & Consulting, LLC
      8840 Stanford Blvd Ste 1550
      Columbia, MD 21045
      Contact: Vinnie Lima Managing Dir
      Tel: 410-864-8659
      Email: vlima@vvlsystems.com
      Website: www.vvlsystems.com
Information technology & consulting, cloud services, infrastructure & end-user optimization. (Hisp, estab 2008, empl 6, sales $950,000, cert: State, 8(a))

4899 Web Traits, Inc.
      9423 Eagleton Lane
      Montgomery Village, MD 20886
      Contact: Bhaskar Roy President
      Tel: 240-731-6120
      Email: bhaskar.roy@web-traits.com
      Website: www.web-traits.com/
Information systems security & operations (ISSO), cyber security, network operations management, virtualization, certification & accreditation (C&A), independent verification & validation (IV&V). (Minority, estab 2007, empl 7, sales $960,000, cert: State, 8(a))

Maine

4900 CST2000 dba iCST IT Solutions
      100 Brickhill Ave Ste C, Lower Level
      South Portland, ME 04106
      Contact: Sasha Asdourian Finance Mgr
      Tel: 207-221-2952
      Email: finance@i-cst.com
      Website: www.i-cst.com
Software testing & IT solutions: ASP, client server, database, IT staffing, .NET, internet, Java, network admin, mainframe, migration, etc. (As-Pac, estab 1997, empl 70, sales $6,050,000, cert: State)

Michigan

4901 Acro Service Corporation
      39209 W. Six Mile Rd.
      Livonia, MI 48152
      Contact: Todd Kearns Marketing & Proposal Mgr
      Tel: 734-591-1100
      Email: acrocorp@acrocorp.com
      Website: www.acrocorp.com
Staff augmentation: engineering, IT. Outsourcing; offshore application dev; IT, engineering, project mgmt consulting. (Minority, estab 1982, empl 1, sales $371,000,000, cert: NMSDC)

4902 All About Technology
      6450 Michigan Ave
      Detroit, MI 48210
      Contact: Willie Brake Mgr
      Tel: 313-965-5543
      Email: isupply@all-about-technology.com
      Website: www.all-about-technology.com
Computer Sales, Service, Training & Upgrades. Data Backup & Recovery, Wireless Networking, Microsoft, Adobe, Quicken, Value Added Reseller, Computer Insurance, Website Maintenance & Design. (AA, estab 2001, empl 7, sales $210,000, cert: State, NMSDC, SDB)

4903 Allegiance Technologies Inc.
      140 Edgelake Dr
      Waterford, MI 48327
      Contact: Matthew Montpas President
      Tel: 248-425-0252
      Email: matt.montpas@allegiance-tech.com
      Website: www.allegiance-tech.com
SAP consulting & implementation. (Hisp, estab 1998, empl 10, sales $594,447, cert: NMSDC)

INFORMATION TECHNOLOGY: Services

4904 AltaFlux Corporation
3250 W Big Beaver Rd Ste 342
Troy, MI 48084
Contact: John Morrison Natl Sales Mgr
Tel: 248-850-2298
Email: john.morrison@altaflux.com
Website: www.altaflux.com
Complete SaaS Solutions, Cloud Computing Solutions, Specialized Technology Staffing, SAP, Oracle, Google Apps, Dell Boomi, OrangeScape (Minority, Woman, estab 2006, empl 48, sales $5,000,000, cert: NMSDC)

4905 Altimetrik Corp
1000 Town Ctr Ste 700
Southfield, MI 48075
Contact: Iain McKendrick Dir of Automotive & Mfg
Tel: 248-281-2500
Email: imckendrick@synovainc.com
Website: www.altimetrik.com
IT Staffing, Managed Programs, Offshore, Creative Technical Outsourcing, Projects and Solution Service offerings. (Minority, estab 2012, empl 6000, sales , cert: NMSDC)

4906 Argus Logistics, LLC
3290 W. Big Beaver Rd. Ste 300
Troy, MI 48304
Contact: Jeff Lau President
Tel: 248-731-4724
Email: jlau@argussolutions.net; jparslow@argussolutions.n
Website: www.arguslogistics.com
Route & mode optimizations, Logistics Consulting, RFQ/RFP builder, Claims mgmt, Carrier & supplier compliance mgmt. EDI, ERP integration, Supply chain design, Visibility, Predictive Analytics. (As-Pac, estab 2004, empl 250, sales , cert: NMSDC)

4907 Blue Chip Talent
43252 Woodward Ave, Ste 240
Bloomfield Hills, MI 48302
Contact: Steve Gaura Sr Dir of IT Services
Tel: 248-630-7170
Email: steveg@bctalent.com
Website: www.bctalent.com
Information technology project based services, project management, staff augmentation services & security consulting. (Woman, estab 1994, empl 220, sales $26,500,000, cert: WBENC)

4908 Broadgate Inc.
830 Kirts Blvd, Ste 400
Troy, MI 48084
Contact: Kashi Kotha Dir
Tel: 248-918-0110
Email: kashi@broadgateinc.com
Website: www.broadgateinc.com
IT Profetional services, consulting, project services & software development. (Woman/As-Ind, estab 2006, empl 70, sales $5,000,000, cert: NMSDC)

4909 BSC Solutions, Inc.
1000 John R. Rd, Ste 203
Troy, MI 48083
Contact: Jody Kapale Business Devel Mgr
Tel: 810-449-3640
Email: jody@bsc-us.com
Website: www.BSCSolutionsInc.com
ERP Implementation & support PeopleSoft, Oracle, SAP, CRM - Siebel & Salesforce, Staff Augmentation/Custom Application Dev, Java, .Net, C#, EDI, Data Warehousing, BI, Big Data, Cloud based applications. (As-Ind, estab 1999, empl 200, sales $11,143,000, cert: NMSDC)

4910 CADworks Solutions, Inc.
43422 W Oaks Dr, Ste 326
Novi, MI 48377
Contact: James Vaughn Jr. President
Tel: 248-910-9988
Email: jamesv@cadwrx.com
Website: www.cadwrx.com
CAD systems integration, lifecycle mgmt consulting. (AA, estab 1995, empl 5, sales $153,000, cert: NMSDC)

4911 CAEtech International, Inc.
43000 W 9 Mile Rd, Ste 305
Novi, MI 48375
Contact: Vic Havele President
Tel: 248-342-7661
Email: havelev@caetech.com
Website: www.caetech.com
Contract & direct placement staffing svcs, engineering svcs, IT svcs. (As-Ind, estab 1989, empl 55, sales $ 0, cert: NMSDC)

4912 Ciber Global, LLC
3270 West Big Beaver Road
Troy, MI 48084
Contact: Neal King Sr Client Partner
Tel: 603-661-0146
Email: nking@ciber.com
Website: www.ciber.com
Software Eng., Systems Eng., Software and Systems Test, Configuration Mgmt, Systems Anaylsis, Intelligence, Data Warehousing, Business Intelligence, Network Security, Network Engineering, Information Technology (As-Ind, estab 1974, empl 11000, sales $ 0, cert: NMSDC)

4913 CnC Controls
5745 W Maple #217
West Bloomfield, MI 48322
Contact: Abizer Rasheed President
Tel: 248-681-7722
Email: arasheed@cnccontrolsusa.com
Website: www.cnccontrolsusa.com
Information technology: installation, repairs & maintenance services. (Woman/As-Ind, estab 1983, empl 10, sales $2,102,000, cert: NMSDC, WBENC)

4914 Cogent Integrated Business Solutions, Inc.
2855 Coolidge Hwy Ste 112
Troy, MI 48084
Contact: Srini Thonta Dir SAP Solutions
Tel: 248-649-4444
Email: sthonta@cogentibs.com
Website: www.cogentIBS.com
IT services & solutions, SAP services. (Minority, Woman, estab 2005, empl 30, sales $3,795,325, cert: WBENC)

4915 Communications Professionals, Inc.
2265 Livernois Rd
Troy, MI 48083
Contact: Andrew Wallace CEO
Tel: 248-557-0100
Email: awallace2@cpgp.com
Website: www.cpgp.com
Information technology: development, implementation & application, hardware, software & technological analysis. (AA, estab 1997, empl 15, sales $15,000,000, cert: NMSDC)

INFORMATION TECHNOLOGY: Services

4916 CompuSoft Integrated Solutions, Inc.
       31500 W 13 Mile Rd Ste 200
       Farmington Hills, MI 48334
       Contact: Pratap Koganti CEO
       Tel: 248-538-9494
       Email: pkoganti@compusoft-is.com
       Website: www.compusoft-is.com
Internet & intranet, e-commerce dev, ERP, Oracle, SAP, PeopleSoft, client/server software. (As-Ind, estab 1997, empl 80, sales $8,500,000, cert: State, NMSDC)

4917 Computech Corporation
       W 100 Kirby St
       Detroit, MI 48202
       Contact: Sai Kancharla Project Mgr
       Tel: 248-622-1420
       Email: sai.kancharla@computechcorp.com
       Website: www.computechcorp.com
Information technology staffing & project svcs: custom programming, enterprise resource planning, CRM, ebusiness, database programming. (Minority, estab 1996, empl 250, sales , cert: NMSDC)

4918 Custom Business Solutions, Inc.
       40480 Grand River Ave, Ste 107
       Novi, MI 48375
       Contact: Jeff Burton President of Sales
       Tel: 248-478-5300
       Email: burtonj@custom-it.com
       Website: www.custom-it.com
IT consulting, project mgmt, system & app architecture, disaster recovery & business continuity, business process engineering, software devel, network design & support, internet & web technologies, ERP systems. (Woman, estab 1995, empl 75, sales $4,042,000, cert: WBENC)

4919 Dechen Consulting Group, Inc.
       37000 Grand River Ave., Ste. 330
       Farmington Hills, MI 48335
       Contact: Raj Dechen President
       Tel: 248-346-4590
       Email: rdechen@dcg-us.com
       Website: www.dcg-us.com/
IT professional staffing & project-based implementation, PeopleSoft, SAP & Oracle software application packages, staff augmentation services, design, develop & implement Business Intelligence. (As-Ind, estab 1998, empl 100, sales $11,000,000, cert: NMSDC)

4920 Emergent Systems Corp.
       3 Parklane Blvd Ste 1120 West
       Dearborn, MI 48126
       Contact: Saleem Qureshi VP- Engineering
       Tel: 313-996-8285
       Email: saleemq@emergentsys.com
       Website: www.EmergentSys.com
Engineering, design, product devel & styling, CAD/CAM/CAE consulting, software development, engineering design staffing, tooling design, offshore capability, engineering software products, KBE, knowledge management. (As-Ind, estab 1997, empl 40, sales $7,000,000, cert: NMSDC)

4921 Epitec
       24800 Denso Dr Ste. 150
       Southfield, MI 48033
       Contact: Kelleen Young
       Tel: 469-454-3649
       Email: businessdevelopment@epitec.com
       Website: www.epitec.com
IT staff augmentation. (AA, estab 1978, empl 1000, sales $75,000,000, cert: NMSDC)

4922 ESM Group LLC
       43422 W Oaks Dr, Ste 298
       Novi, MI 48377
       Contact: Jayme Rossiter President
       Tel: 248-921-7452
       Email: jrossiter@esmonline.com
       Website: www.esmonline.com
Information technogy services & staffing. (Woman, estab 1992, empl 23, sales $1,800,000, cert: WBENC)

4923 Excel Technical Services, Inc.
       200 Kirts Blvd Ste A
       Troy, MI 48084
       Contact: Pat Kirby Managing Dir
       Tel: 248-310-9413
       Email: patkirby@exceltechnical.com
       Website: www.exceltechnical.com
Technical staffing & document management svcs, supplier quality & development. (Hisp, estab 1998, empl 30, sales $2,500,000, cert: NMSDC)

4924 GDI Infotech, Inc.
       3775 Varsity Dr
       Ann Arbor, MI 48108
       Contact: Vishal Chaubal Dir
       Tel: 734-477-6900
       Email: vishal@gdii.com
       Website: www.gdii.com
Enterprise information technology consulting & services. (As-Ind, estab 1993, empl 125, sales $10,200,000, cert: NMSDC)

4925 HRU Technical Resources
       3451 Dunckel Road Ste 200
       Lansing, MI 48911
       Contact: Todd Briggs VP Business Dev
       Tel: 517-272-5888
       Email: briggs.todd@hru-tech.com
       Website: www.hru-tech.com
Engineering, IT, design, mfg, technical staffing services: contract or direct hire. (Woman, estab 1980, empl 215, sales $20,500,517, cert: WBENC)

4926 HTC Global Services Inc.
       3270 W Big Beaver
       Troy, MI 48084
       Contact: Gary Gozdor Dir
       Tel: 763-245-0746
       Email: kevin.kraft@htcinc.com
       Website: www.htcinc.com
Information technology services and solutions, Business Process Services. (As-Pac, estab 1990, empl 11000, sales $450,000,000, cert: NMSDC)

4927 ICONMA, LLC
       850 Stephenson Hwy Ste 612
       Troy, MI 48083
       Contact: Lauren Diener Sales Operations Mgr
       Tel: 888-451-2519
       Email: rfp@iconma.com
       Website: www.iconma.com
IT consultant staffing: contract, contract to hire & fulltime.
 (Woman, estab 2000, empl 2985, sales $188,000,000, cert: WBENC)

INFORMATION TECHNOLOGY: Services

4928 IGI Detroit dba Villc, LLC
      1020 Metro Dr
      Commerce, MI 48390
      Contact: Pat Hernandez President
      Tel: 248-624-6520
      Email: pat@werigi.com
      Website: www.werigi.com
Large scale, ultra high resolution systems for advanced visualization applications and commercial AV systems. (Hisp, estab 2003, empl 1, sales $ 0, cert: NMSDC)

4929 Iknowvate Technologies, Inc.
      17197 N Laurel Park Dr, Ste 307
      Livonia, MI 48152
      Contact: Sriram Rajakumar Sales Dir
      Tel: 734-432-0634
      Email: rkumar@iknowvate.com
      Website: www.iknowvate.com
IT staff augmentation, application dev, maintenance & support, project mgmt, real time embedded systems, e-strategize, portals, implement & deploy SCM, CRM, ERP packaged solutions, business intelligence solutions. (As-Pac, estab 2001, empl 40, sales $2,000,000, cert: NMSDC)

4930 Infomatics Inc.
      31313 Northwestern Hwy, Ste 219
      Farmington Hills, MI 48334
      Contact: Ragan Raghunathan Founder
      Tel: 248-865-0300
      Email: rajan@infomatinc.com
      Website: www.infomatinc.com
Information technology staffing, web technologies, Java, J2EE , ERP/CRM-Oracle, SAP, database administration, Oracle, DB2 SQL Server, content management. (Minority, Woman, estab 1998, empl 225, sales $25,000,000, cert: NMSDC)

4931 Information Systems Resources
      1800 Bailey St
      Dearborn, MI 48124
      Contact: Eric Levy Business Devel Mgr
      Tel: 313-274-6400
      Email: elevy@is-resources.com
      Website: www.is-resources.com
Computer asset mgmt services, professional services, lifecycle mgmt, dist hardware & software.
 (AA, estab 1989, empl 48, sales $4,856,426, cert: NMSDC, CPUC)

4932 Internet Operations Center, Inc.
      200 Galleria Officentre Ste 109
      Southfield, MI 48034
      Contact: Rhonda Hall Business Dev Mgr
      Tel: 248-204-8800
      Email: thayward@iocenter.net
      Website: www.iocenter.net
Managed internet service provider, web development, help center, EDI, TPP appilcation development. (As-Pac, estab 1996, empl 56, sales $ 0, cert: NMSDC)

4933 IP Consulting, Inc.
      3635 29th St
      Kentwood, MI 49512
      Contact: Cherri Mosey VP
      Tel: 616-855-9967
      Email: cherri.mosey@ipconsultinginc.com
      Website: www.ipconsultinginc.com
Information technology solutions, design, implementation & support services. (Hisp, estab 2006, empl 10, sales $1,400,000, cert: NMSDC, 8(a))

4934 IPS Technology Services
      363 W Big Beaver Rd Ste 100
      Troy, MI 48084
      Contact: Pradip Sengupta CEO
      Tel: 248-835-9895
      Email: info@ipstechnologyservices.com
      Website: www.ipstechnologyservices.com
Information technology services: customer systems development, CAD/CAM/CAE/PDM svcs, systems integration, HR technology implementation, consulting, & ERP implementation. (As-Pac, estab 2000, empl 22, sales $1,200,000, cert: NMSDC)

4935 JRD Systems, Inc.
      42450 Hayes Rd Ste 3
      Clinton Township, MI 48038
      Contact: Melissa Husmillo
      Tel: 586-416-1500
      Email: contact@jrdsi.com
      Website: www.jrdsi.com
Information technology solutions, services, & staffing. (Minority, estab 2000, empl 80, sales $5,500,000, cert: State, NMSDC)

4936 Logic Solutions, Inc.
      2929 Plymouth Rd Ste 207
      Ann Arbor, MI 48105
      Contact: Grace Lee CFO
      Tel: 734-930-0009
      Email: grace@logicsolutions.com
      Website: www.logicsolutions.com
Custom web based software development & integration. (As-Pac, estab 1995, empl 104, sales $8,261,867, cert: NMSDC)

4937 Millennium Software Inc.
      2000 Town Center Dr Ste, 300
      Southfield, MI 48075
      Contact: Anu Anand President
      Tel: 248-213-1800
      Email: anu@webmsi.com
      Website: www.webmsi.com
IT consulting, project developemnt, contract programming, web designing. (Woman/As-Pac, estab 1996, empl 165, sales $23,129,824, cert: NMSDC, WBENC)

4938 Miracle Software Systems
      45625 Grand River Ave
      Novi, MI 48374
      Contact: Pandu Byroj IT SALES LEAD
      Tel: 234-233-1851
      Email: pbyroj@miraclesoft.com
      Website: www.miraclesoft.com/
IT consulting: SAP, Oracle, PeopleSoft, JDEdwards, Solaris, J2EE. webMethods, MQ, EAI, Cognos, MicroStrategy, VB, ASP,.Net, SQL, Siebel, Informatica, TIBCO, Vitria, etc. (Minority, estab 1994, empl 2750, sales $100,000,000, cert: NMSDC)

4939 Netlink Software Group
      999 Tech Row
      Madison Heights, MI 48071
      Contact: Bob Pniewski Exec Dir NA Sales
      Tel: 248-535-3250
      Email: bpniewski@netlink.com
      Website: www.netlink.com
IT Business solutions: Automotive, High Tech, Health Care. Education. Solutions experience in Portals, Intranet/Extranet, Software Applications, Exchanges Wireless, eLearning, Program Management (As-Ind, estab 1997, empl 112, sales $ 0, cert: NMSDC)

INFORMATION TECHNOLOGY: Services

4940 Ocean Inc. dba Omega Systems
      5324 Plainfield Ave NE
      Grand Rapids, MI 49525
      Contact: Nadeem Hamid President
      Tel: 616-361-6677
      Email: nadeem.hamid@oceaninc.com
      Website: www.oceaninc.com
Computer solutions, components, notebooks, printers, assembly, packing & configuration, web development, web hosting, surveillance camera solutions & installation. (As-Ind, estab 1984, empl 8, sales $600,000, cert: NMSDC)

4941 Ojibway, Inc.
      3720 High St
      Ecorse, MI 48229
      Contact: James Richardson Acct Exec
      Tel: 248-526-0555
      Email: jrichardson@theojibwaygroup.com
      Website: www.theojibwaygroup.com
Information technology, leasing & financial services, computer equipment & services. (Nat Ame, estab 1988, empl 13, sales $3,500,000, cert: NMSDC)

4942 Open Systems Technologies DE, LLC
      605 Seward NW, Ste 101
      Grand Rapids, MI 49504
      Contact: David Gerrity Exec Dir
      Tel: 616-574-3500
      Email: dgerrity@ostusa.com
      Website: www.ostusa.com
Resell computer hardware & software, business process solutions, data center solutions, application development, managed services. (Nat Ame, estab 1997, empl 110, sales $68,873,026, cert: NMSDC)

4943 OpenLogix Corporation
      28345 Beck Rd Ste 308
      Wixom, MI 48393
      Contact: Rick Pardy Acct Mgr
      Tel: 919-200-4333
      Email: mbe@open-logix.com
      Website: www.open-logix.com
SOA, business integration, portals & business intelligence, SAP, WebSphere, web svcs, webMethods, Java/J2EE, Informatica, business objects.. (As-Ind, estab 2006, empl 45, sales $18,000,000, cert: NMSDC)

4944 Paskon, Inc.
      25899 W 12 Mile Rd Ste 380
      Southfield, MI 48034
      Contact: Sharath Konanur CEO
      Tel: 248-440-2334
      Email: sharath@paskon.com
      Website: www.paskon.com
Business & Technology Consulting, SAP Development Implementations. (Hisp, estab 1999, empl 50, sales $3,530,000, cert: NMSDC)

4945 Peer Solutions Group, Inc.
      30777 Northwestern Hwy Ste 107
      Farmington Hills, MI 48334
      Contact: Mohamed Irfan Peeran CEO
      Tel: 248-522-7767
      Email: mpeeran@peersolutionsgroup.com
      Website: www.peersolutionsgroup.com
IT Consulting Staffing, Recruiting, Project Management, Technology Consulting. (As-Ind, estab 2002, empl 60, sales $5,412,715, cert: NMSDC)

4946 PeoplePlus software Inc.
      3131 South State St. Ste 250
      Ann Arbor, MI 48108
      Contact: Tom Bastian Solutions Consultant
      Tel: 734-531-6620
      Email: tbastian@peopleplussoftware.com
      Website: www.peopleplussoftware.com
Software design & development, SaaS cloud supply chain software. IT staffing, Mobile app development. (Minority, Woman, estab 2007, empl 35, sales $1,500,000, cert: NMSDC)

4947 Preferred Data Systems, LLC
      39100 Country Club Dr Ste 200
      Farmington Hills, MI 48331
      Contact: Chad Muncy
      Tel: 248-522-4442
      Email: cmuncy@pdsnetworking.com
      Website: www.pdsnetworking.com
IT networking infrastructure & consulting services. (Minority, Woman, estab 1982, empl 12, sales $510,000, cert: NMSDC)

4948 Prince Technology Solutions, Inc.
      51221 Schoenherr, Ste 106
      Shelby Township, MI 48315
      Contact: Tigi Duraku CEO
      Tel: 810-512-4253
      Email: jessica@princetechnology.com
      Website: www.princetechnology.com
IT consulting services, contract & permanent. (Woman, estab 1998, empl 50, sales $4,500,000, cert: WBENC)

4949 PROLIM Global Corporation
      30445 Northwestern Hwy Ste 380
      Farmington Hills, MI 48334
      Contact: Prabhu Patil President
      Tel: 248-522-6959
      Email: prabhu.patil@prolim.com
      Website: www.prolim.com
IT & PLM solutions & consulting services. (As-Ind, estab 2005, empl 350, sales $ 0, cert: NMSDC)

4950 Pro-Motion Technology Group
      29755 Beck Rd
      Wixom, MI 48393
      Contact: Brian Flewelling Acct Mgr
      Tel: 248-668-3100
      Email: hello@promotion.tech
      Website: www.promotion.tech
Audiovisual technology solutions. (Woman, estab 2002, empl 45, sales $25,000,000, cert: WBENC)

4951 Ragha Systems, LLC
      8390 Warwick Groves Ct
      Grand Blanc, MI 48439
      Contact: Veera R Thota CEO
      Tel: 810-694-6551
      Email: vthota@raghasys.com
      Website: www.raghasys.com
IT solutions. (Woman/As-Ind, estab 2002, empl 4, sales $240,000, cert: NMSDC, WBENC)

4952 Ramsoft Systems, Inc..
      29777 Telegraph Rd Ste 2250
      Southfield, MI 48034
      Contact: Rama Gudivada COO
      Tel: 248-354-0100
      Email: rama@ramsoft.net
      Website: www.ramsoft.net
IT solutions, staff augmentation: onsite, offsite, nearshore, offshore projects. (Minority, Woman, estab 1993, empl 100, sales $ 0, cert: NMSDC)

INFORMATION TECHNOLOGY: Services

4953 Rapid Global Business Solutions, Inc.
1200 Stephenson Hwy
Troy, MI 48083
Contact: Vivek Thakur Business Dev Mgr
Tel: 248-589-1135
Email: vt@rgbsi.com
Website: www.rgbsi.com
Engineering svcs: staffing, mechanical, electrical & electronics, mfg, automotive, design & release, embedded systems, systems modeling & simulation, CAD/CAM/CAE/PIM svcs, software dev, contract & permanent. (Minority, estab 1997, empl 1800, sales $80,000,000, cert: NMSDC)

4954 Real World Technologies Inc.
28423 Orchard Lake Rd Ste 203
Farmington Hills, MI 48334
Contact: Vishnu Jampala President
Tel: 248-987-6008
Email: vishnujam@rwts.net
Website: www.rwts.net
IT solutions & Business Analyst solutions, Application development, Enterprise resource planning, Data-Warehousing, Customer Relationship Management, Business Analysis, Project Management. (As-Pac, estab 2005, empl 40, sales $3,155,012, cert: State, NMSDC, SDB)

4955 Rumba Solutions, LLC
44648 Mound Rd, Ste 190
Sterling Heights, MI 48314
Contact: Jibu Joseph Managing Dir
Tel: 248-978-3674
Email: jibu.joseph@rumbasolutions.com
Website: www.rumbasolutions.com
Application development, staff augmentation & consulting services, Mobile, Web Applications (Cloud and On premise), IoT, Identity & Access Management, Portal Development. (As-Ind, estab 2010, empl 50, sales , cert: NMSDC)

4956 Skansoft Inc.
4681 Amberwood Ct
Rochester, MI 48306
Contact: Srividya Sadasivam President
Tel: 248-276-4770
Email: srividya@skandasoftinc.com
Website: www.skandasoftinc.com
Integrated information technology consulting & placement services, IT professionals. (Woman/As-Ind, estab 2006, empl 11, sales $1,118,340, cert: NMSDC)

4957 SoftCorp International, Inc.
2838 E Long Lake Ste 236
Troy, MI 48085
Contact: Raja Puli President
Tel: 248-918-2224
Email: vinod@softcorpinc.com
Website: www.softcorpinc.com
Staff augmentation, permanent & temporary IT resources. (As-Ind, estab 1997, empl 87, sales $6,100,000, cert: NMSDC)

4958 SoftPath Technologies LLC
16801 Newburgh Rd, Ste 112
Livonia, MI 48154
Contact: Rohith Thumma Reg Sales Mgr
Tel: 248-522-7011
Email: supplier@softpathtech.com
Website: www.softpathtech.com
Global Staffing, Technology, Services & Consulting. (As-Ind, estab 2006, empl 150, sales $6,012,589, cert: NMSDC)

4959 SunSoft Technologies Inc.
21772 Manchester Ct
Farmington Hills, MI 48335
Contact: Rashmi Upadhyaya President
Tel: 248-426-9805
Email: rashmiu@sunsoft.us
Website: www.sunsofttechnologies.com
Engineering & IT staffing. (Minority, Woman, estab 2000, empl 45, sales $3,705,233, cert: NMSDC, WBENC)

4960 Synergy Computer Solutions, Inc,
30700 Telegraph Rd Ste 2615
Bingham Farms, MI 48025
Contact: Ruslan Avshalumov Accountant
Tel: 248-723-7220
Email: ravshalumov@synergycom.com
Website: www.synergycom.com
Information techology & engineering consulting & staffing: implementation & integration, infrastructure support, web solutions, project mgmt, data warehousing, EDI, off shore devel. (As-Pac, estab 1995, empl 250, sales $16,000,000, cert: NMSDC)

4961 Synova Inc.
1000 Town Center Ste 700
Southfield, MI 48075
Contact: Iain McKendrick Dir of Automotive & Mfg
Tel: 248-281-2500
Email: imckendrick@synovainc.com
Website: www.synovainc.com
IT Staffing, Managed Programs, Offshore, Creative Technical Outsourcing, Projects and Solution Service offerings. (As-Pac, estab 1998, empl 1800, sales $117,000,000, cert: NMSDC)

4962 Syntel Inc.
525 E Big Beaver 3rd Fl
Troy, MI 48083
Contact: ShyamSundar Dittakavi Dir- Lifesciences
Tel: 602-391-8868
Email: vendor_registration@syntelinc.com
Website: www.syntelinc.com
IT lifecycle solutions, applications outsourcing, development, enhancements, maintenance, integration & technology transformation & support. (Minority, estab , empl , sales $923,828,000, cert: NMSDC)

4963 Systems Technology Group, Inc. (STG)
3001 W Big Beaver Rd Ste 500e
Troy, MI 48084
Contact: Anup Popat CEO
Tel: 248-712-6702
Email: apopat@stgit.com
Website: www.stgit.com
Application software development outsourcing svcs: onsite & offshore. (Minority, estab 1985, empl 600, sales $102,000,000, cert: NMSDC)

4964 Systems Technology International, Inc.
39555 Orchard Hill Pl, Ste 530
Novi, MI 48375
Contact: Rodney Tesarz Dir of Sales
Tel: 248-735-3900
Email: rodney.tesarz@sti-world.com
Website: www.sti-world.com
Information technology & engineering: contract staffing, off shore services, software development & testing, engineering design & diagnostics. (AA, estab , empl , sales $7,500,000, cert: NMSDC)

INFORMATION TECHNOLOGY: Services

4965 Technosoft Corporation
      1 Towne Square 6th Fl
      Southfield, MI 48076
      Contact: Radhakrishnan Gurusamy CEO
      Tel: 248-603-2666
      Email: supplierdiversity@technosoftcorp.com
      Website: www.technosoftcorp.com
Information technology staffing, IT consulting, system integration & business process outsourcing. (Minority, Woman, estab 1996, empl 4000, sales $123,867,758, cert: NMSDC)

4966 Tekshapers Inc.
      2018 Harbor Village Ave
      Keego Harbor, MI 48320
      Contact: Nalini Kolli President
      Tel: 248-470-5733
      Email: nalini@tekshapers.com
      Website: www.tekshapers.com
Software development, consulting services. (Woman, estab , empl , sales $ 0, cert: NMSDC)

4967 Touch World, Inc.
      31500 W 13 Mile Rd Ste 101
      Farmington Hills, MI 48334
      Contact: Gordon McKenna President
      Tel: 248-539-3700
      Email: gordon.mckenna@touchworld.com
      Website: www.touchworld.com
Computer software consulting & staff agumentation svcs: ERP, Client Server, Microsoft, UNIX, workflow, supply chain mgmt, ILVS, EDI , barcoding, RFID, Gentran, Future 3, Harbinger, Mercator, Trinary, AS 400, mainframe products. (As-Pac, estab 1996, empl 17, sales $1,550,000, cert: NMSDC)

4968 Trillium Teamologies Inc.
      219 S Main St
      Royal Oak, MI 48067
      Contact: Greg Stanalajczo COO
      Tel: 248-584-2080
      Email: stano@trilliumteam.com
      Website: www.trilliumteam.com
IT solutions: 2D & 3D animations, web dev, flash animations, IT consulting, e-commerce, project mgmt, systems integration & software dev, etc. (Woman, estab 1996, empl 63, sales $ 0, cert: WBENC)

4969 TTi Global
      6001 N. Adams Road Ste 185
      Bloomfield Hills, MI 48304
      Contact: April Bousamra Controller
      Tel: 248-853-5550
      Email: abousamra@tti-global.com
      Website: www.tti-global.com
Training design, development & delivery, outsourcing services, staffing services. (Woman, estab 1976, empl 780, sales $38,100,000, cert: WBENC)

4970 Unified Business Technologies Inc.
      315 Indusco Ct
      Troy, MI 48083
      Contact: Allyssia Gutierrez Sales Rep
      Tel: 248-677-9550
      Email: allyssia.gutierrez@ubtus.com
      Website: www.emd.ubtus.com
Software consulting services & staffing. (Minority, Woman, estab 1997, empl 150, sales , cert: WBENC)

4971 V2Soft Inc.
      300 Enterprise Court
      Bloomfield Hills, MI 48302
      Contact: Varchasvi Shankar President
      Tel: 248-904-1702
      Email: vs@v2soft.com
      Website: www.v2soft.com
Software business solutions, consulting, contract services & staff augmentation, project outsourcing, offshore development. (Minority, estab 1998, empl 1200, sales $37,000,000, cert: NMSDC)

4972 Vigilant Technologies
      1050 Wilshire Dr Ste 307
      Troy, MI 48084
      Contact: Sameera buksh VP
      Tel: 248-396-2665
      Email: sameera@vigilant-inc.com
      Website: www.vigilant-inc.com
Oracle Managed Services, Oracle Professional Services, Oracle Talent, Staff Augmentation, QA Testing, Oracle Licensing. (Woman/As-Ind, estab 1999, empl 69, sales $12,574,008, cert: NMSDC)

4973 Vision Information Technologies, Inc.
      3031 W Grand Blvd, Ste 600
      Detroit, MI 48202
      Contact: Christine Rice President
      Tel: 313-420-2000
      Email: info@visionit.com
      Website: www.visionit.com
IT staffing, e-business consulting & web application dev. (Hisp, estab 1997, empl 1000, sales $209,000,000, cert: NMSDC)

4974 Vivek Systems, Inc.
      2163 Avon Industrial Dr
      Rochester Hills, MI 48309
      Contact: Bose Vivek President
      Tel: 248-293-1070
      Email: bvivek@viveksystems.com
      Website: www.viveksystems.com
CAD/engineering solution company. (As-Ind, estab , empl , sales $1,080,000, cert: NMSDC)

4975 WebRunners, Inc. dba W3R Consulting
      1000 Town Center Ste 1150
      Southfield, MI 48044
      Contact: CEO
      Tel: 248-358-1002
      Email: info@w3r.com
      Website: www.w3r.com
Infrastructure planning & design, custom hosting solutions, directory svcs design, systems admin, middleware & database support, metrics tools, monitoring & reporting, firewall mgmt & security, VPN architecture, application integration. (AA, estab 1995, empl 400, sales $36,500,000, cert: NMSDC)

4976 Weldon Enterprise Global IT, LLC
      3031 W Grand Blvd, Ste 695
      Detroit, MI 48202
      Contact: Markeith Weldon CEO
      Tel: 313-687-4990
      Email: mweldon@weglobalit.com
      Website: www.weglobalit.com
IT managed services, technical staffing & non technical staffing. (AA, estab 2011, empl 10, sales $1,000,000, cert: NMSDC)

4977 WIT Inc.
      900 Tower Dr Ste 325
      Troy, MI 48098
      Contact: Quaid Saifee President
      Tel: 248-641-5900
      Email: quaid@witinc.com
      Website: www.witinc.com
Web site design & development, internet branding, graphic design, content management solutions, database design & consulting, web application development, training, web collaboration. (As-Ind, estab 1996, empl 20, sales $2,500,000, cert: NMSDC)

4978 Youngsoft Inc.
      49197 Wixom Tech Dr Ste B
      Wixom, MI 48393
      Contact: Chris Reaume Dir of Sales Operations
      Tel: 248-675-1200
      Email: chrisr@youngsoft.com
      Website: www.youngsoft.com
Information technology services: staffing support, consulting, solution design & development. (As-Ind, estab 1996, empl 130, sales $11,690,000, cert: NMSDC)

Minnesota

4979 Aldis Systems, Inc.
      119 N 2nd St
      Minneapolis, MN 55401
      Contact: Barb Condit CEO
      Tel: 612-805-8811
      Email: barb@aldissystems.com
      Website: www.DAM-it.com
Digital Asset Management (DAM) software, hardware, and cloud solutions. (Woman, estab 2009, empl 15, sales $1,501,000, cert: WBENC)

4980 AMI Imaging Systems, Inc.
      7815 Telegraph Rd
      Bloomington, MN 55438
      Contact: Leah Swartzbaugh VP
      Tel: 952-828-0080
      Email: leahs@ami-imaging.com
      Website: www.ami-imaging.com
Content mgmt, document imaging, scanning, imaging systems, workflow, process automation, remittance processing, aperture card scanning, microfilm & microfiche scanning, large format & roll film scanning. (Woman, estab 1982, empl 15, sales , cert: WBENC)

4981 Analytiks International, Inc.
      10 S Fifth St Ste 720
      Minneapolis, MN 55402
      Contact: Mike Regan Marketing & Sales
      Tel: 612-305-4312
      Email: mregan@aii-3.com
      Website: www.aii-3.com
SAS consulting & resource placement services. (As-Ind, estab 2004, empl 6, sales $200,000, cert: NMSDC)

4982 Arrowhead Promotion & Fulfillment Co., Inc.
      1105 SE 8th St
      Grand Rapids, MN 55744
      Contact: Katie Prokop Christmas CEO
      Tel: 218-327-1165
      Email: katie@apfco.com
      Website: www.arrowheadpromotion.com
Software development, customized reporting, fulfillment activities. (Woman, estab 1983, empl 250, sales $13,000,000, cert: WBENC)

4983 Backbone Consultants
      50 S 6th St Ste 1360
      Minneapolis, MN 55402
      Contact: Operations & Acct Mgr
      Tel: 612-568-7167
      Email: info@backboneconsultants.com
      Website: www.backboneconsultants.com
IT Audit Outsource & Co-source, IT Risk Assessment & Advisory, IT Sourcing Risks, Information Security Risk Assessment, Financial Institutions Data Privacy (GLBA) Reviews. (Minority, estab 2008, empl 13, sales $1,897,914, cert: State)

4984 Barnes Business Solutions, Inc.
      4857 Island View Dr
      Mound, MN 55364
      Contact: Maria Barnes President
      Tel: 630-715-4452
      Email: mbarnes@barnesbusinesssolutions.com
      Website: www.BarnesBusinessSolutions.com
Custom programming services, Microsoft Access databases, SQL Server databases, Microsoft Excel tools & macros, Microsoft Office integration, Windows-based software solutions. (Woman, estab 2008, empl 1, sales $139,235, cert: WBENC)

4985 BCforward
      7701 France Ave S, Ste 325
      Edina, MN 55435
      Contact: Kortney Cartwright District Branch Mgr
      Tel: 954-540-4064
      Email: kortney.cartwright@bcforward.com
      Website: www.bcforward.com
IT consulting & staffing. (AA, estab , empl , sales $2,500,000, cert: NMSDC)

4986 BPK Inc.
      12800 Whitewater Dr, Ste 100
      Minnetonka, MN 55439
      Contact: Rajeev Bhatia CEO
      Tel: 612-293-7585
      Email: rajeev@bpktech.com
      Website: www.bpktech.com
IT Consulting, Agile, Software Development, IT Services, Financial consulting, Staff augmentation, Staffing solutions, Java, .Net, Project Manager, Sap, SQ, Investment management, Wealth management. (As-Ind, estab 2006, empl 10, sales $4,000,000, cert: NMSDC)

4987 BTM Global Consulting LLC
      330 S Second Ave Ste 450
      Minneapolis, MN 55401
      Contact: Lesli Hines President
      Tel: 612-238-8801
      Email: lesli.hines@btmgcs.com
      Website: www.btmgcs.com
Custom application development, software development, integration, implementation. (As-Pac, estab 2004, empl 85, sales $5,100,000, cert: NMSDC)

4988 Business Technology Solutions, Inc.
      7441 Windmill Dr
      Chanhassen, MN 55317
      Contact: Brian Hugh President
      Tel: 612-208-7287
      Email: brian.hugh@btsbiz.com
      Website: www.btsbiz.com
Information systems integration/development, project management, business/system analysis, large-scale application/infrastructure upgrades, packaged software evaluation/selection & database performance analysis & tuning. (As-Pac, estab 1996, empl 2, sales $290,804, cert: State)

INFORMATION TECHNOLOGY: Services

4989 Cetus Digital LLC
      15646 Michele Ln
      Eden Prairie, MN 55346
      Contact: Pervej Alam CEO
      Tel: 763-360-9024
      Email: pervej.alam@cetusdigital.com
      Website: www.cetusdigital.com
Product Management: Domain expertise & Principals, Road-mapping, Backlog development & release strategy, Incremental Agile maturity improvement. (As-Ind, estab 2021, empl 10, sales $1,400,000, cert: State)

4990 Charter Solutions, Inc.
      3033 Campus Dr Ste N160
      Plymouth, MN 55441
      Contact: Alexander Wittig Sales Exec
      Tel: 763-230-6100
      Email: alex.wittig@chartersolutions.com
      Website: www.chartersolutions.com
Information technology solutions, mgmt consulting, application dev, system integration & staffing. (Woman, estab 1997, empl 55, sales $4,000,000, cert: WBENC)

4991 Clarity Tek, Inc.
      2859 Aspen Lake Dr NE
      Blaine, MN 55449
      Contact: Abida Banu President
      Tel: 612-567-0835
      Email: abida.banu@claritytek.com
      Website: www.claritytek.com/
Placement, Recruiting, IT Consulting, IT Services, Staff augmetation, IT Contractor Services, Software development services, Software maintenance services. (Minority, Woman, estab 2012, empl 4, sales , cert: City)

4992 CrossUSA Inc.
      13754 Frontier Court Ste 106
      Burnsville, MN 55337
      Contact: John Beesley Dir Business Devel
      Tel: 952-432-3775
      Email: jbeesley@cross-usa.com
      Website: www.cross-usa.com
Mainframe application support & development, remote staff augmentation, legacy application support. (Woman, estab 1999, empl 75, sales $6,379,503, cert: WBENC)

4993 Crown CyberSystems
      160 Birchwood Ave
      St. Paul, MN 55110
      Contact: Austin Kasper Mgr of Client Partnerships
      Tel: 612-207-7423
      Email: akasper@crowncybersystems.com
      Website: www.crowncybersystems.com/
IT Solutions, managed IT Department Services. (Woman, estab 2010, empl 10, sales $6,000,000, cert: WBENC)

4994 CS Solutions, Inc.
      7525 Mitchell Road Ste 106
      Eden Prairie, MN 55344
      Contact: Sonia Stephen Staffing Mgr
      Tel: 651-271-4477
      Email: sonia@cssoln.com
      Website: www.cssolutionsinc.com
IT consulting, staff augmentation, project outsourcing, solution design & develop, data warehousing & admin, e-commerce security, web develop. (As-Ind, estab 1996, empl 30, sales $1,200,000, cert: NMSDC)

4995 Denysys Corporation
      2400 Blaisdell Ave Ste 202
      Minneapolis, MN 55404
      Contact: Philip Denny President
      Tel: 612-869-7617
      Email: philip.denny@denysys.com
      Website: www.denysys.com
Information technology, administrative & management consulting services. (AA, estab 1991, empl 35, sales $4,100,540, cert: State)

4996 Enclipse Corp.
      331 2nd Ave S Ste 703
      Minneapolis, MN 55401
      Contact: Mohammed Halim Client Mgr
      Tel: 612-360-4713
      Email: halimm@enclipse.com
      Website: www.enclipse.com
Managed svcs & solutions design & development: identifying organizational strategies & objectives, design, develop & implement end-to-end software solutions. (As-Pac, estab 2002, empl 128, sales $10,000,000, cert: NMSDC)

4997 Genisys Technologies, Inc.
      3545 Plymouth Blvd, Ste 115
      Plymouth, MN 55447
      Contact: Mohan Dhavileswarapu CEO
      Tel: 763-205-4883
      Email: mohan@genisystechnologies.com
      Website: www.genisystechnologies.com
Management, IT staffing & solutions, business information, system design, planning, development & implementation. (As-Ind, estab 2013, empl 15, sales $2,000,000, cert: NMSDC)

4998 Horizontal Integration, Inc.
      1660 Hwy 100 Ste 200
      St. Louis Park, MN 55416
      Contact: Craig Blake Dir Staffing Operations
      Tel: 612-392-7581
      Email: finance@horizontalintegration.com
      Website: www.horizontalintegration.com
IT staff augmentation, software design & devel, e-commerce, crm apps, enterprise arcitecture & enterprise app integration, business performance mgmt app, custom business apps, web app information architecture. (As-Pac, estab 2003, empl 632, sales $101,000,000, cert: NMSDC)

4999 Icon IT Group
      3025 Hatbor Ln N, Ste 324
      Plymouth, MN 55447
      Contact: Shaik Ahmed President
      Tel: 612-207-4778
      Email: ahmed@iconitgroup.com
      Website: www.iconitgroup.com
E-verify Software Development, Web Technologies, ERP Packages, Data Warehousing, Business Intelligence, Business Analysis & Quality Assurance. (As-Ind, estab 2013, empl 11, sales $1,200,000, cert: NMSDC)

5000 ILM Professional Services, Inc.
      5221 Viking Dr Ste 300
      Edina, MN 55435
      Contact: Lee Ann Villella Acct Exec
      Tel: 952-960-2220
      Email: leeann.villella@ilmservice.com
      Website: www.ilmservice.com
Integrated, custom web & mobile apps, consulting, project outsourcing on & offsite. (Minority, Woman, estab 2002, empl 30, sales $4,100,000, cert: NMSDC, WBENC)

INFORMATION TECHNOLOGY: Services

5001 Infinity Systems, Inc.
PO Box 43925
Brooklyn Park, MN 55443
Contact: Michael Perkins Dir of Business Dev
Tel: 612-819-3940
Email: mperknoll@aol.com
Website: www.isimetrics.com
Internet security software. (AA, estab 1993, empl 10, sales , cert: NMSDC)

5002 Javen Technologies, Inc.
8030 Old Cedar Ave, Ste 225
Bloomington, MN 55425
Contact: Venkat Kota CEO
Tel: 952-698-4454
Email: vkota@javentechnologies.com
Website: www.javentechnologies.com
Oracle, SQL, QA, .Net, Java, Data warehousing, ERP (Peoplesoft, SAP, Oracle Apps) PM, RedPrairie, BA, System admins. (Minority, Woman, estab 2003, empl 80, sales $24,100,000, cert: NMSDC, WBENC)

5003 Jeevtek Inc.
7160 Cahill Rd, Ste 238
Edina, MN 55439
Contact: President
Tel: 612-440-0123
Email: go@jeevtek.com
Website: www.jeevtek.com/
IT staff augmentation & custom software development services, Java, J2EE, web applications, eCommerce, databases, SQL, ERP (Oracle, SAP), .NET, Cloud etc. (Woman/As-Ind, estab 2015, empl 2, sales $230,000, cert: City, WBENC)

5004 JOBMA LLC
13911 Ridgedale Dr, Ste 230
Minnetonka, MN 55305
Contact: Krishna Kant Head of Global Business
Tel: 952-546-3300
Email: krishnak@jobma.com
Website: www.jobma.com/
Cloud based video interview platform, artificial intelligence recruiting, video resumes, and automated recruiting, (Nat Ame, estab 2013, empl 35, sales , cert: NMSDC)

5005 KCS
2395 Ariel St N, Ste A
Saint Paul, MN 55109
Contact: Dorothy C. Richburg CEO
Tel: 651-777-9119
Email: drichburg@keystonecs.com
Website: www.kcscorp.com
IT consulting, technical services, IT training. (Woman/AA, estab 1987, empl 45, sales $9,894,985, cert: State)

5006 Net Anchor, Inc.
202 N 22nd Ave
Minneapolis, MN 55411
Contact: Keni Fegbeboh
Tel: 612-425-2200
Email: kenfegb@netanchor.com
Website: www.netanchor.com
Software & hardware procurement, Help desk support, IT Managed Services, IT Staff Augmentation, Remote monitoring, IT Network Architecture, Network Design & Installation, IT Infrastructure & Data Center, Custom hardware software application development. (AA, estab 2006, empl 1, sales , cert: NMSDC)

5007 New Horizons Computer Learning Ctr Minnesota
2915 Commers Dr Ste 500
Eagan, MN 55121
Contact: Sammy Peterson Dir of Operations
Tel: 651-900-7203
Email: speterson@newhorizonsmn.com
Website: www.newhorizonsmn.com
IT training. (Woman, estab 2010, empl 18, sales $3,554,749, cert: WBENC)

5008 Performix
7400 Metro blvd Ste 390
Edina, MN 55439
Contact: Sunil Bafna Owner
Tel: 952-893-0143
Email: priya@performixbiz.com
Website: www.performixbiz.com
Software consulting, application integration, database integration, ecommerce application, enterprise application. (Minority, estab 1997, empl 13, sales $1,650,000, cert: State, NMSDC)

5009 Pinnacle Consulting Solutions
17761 Cascade Dr
Eden Prairie, MN 55347
Contact: Ranja Tarafder CEO
Tel: 952-292-4556
Email: ranja@pinnacleconsultingsolutions.com
Website: www.pinnacleconsultingsolutions.com
IT staffing & consulting, Project/Program Management, ITIL Process Management, Application Development, Software Development Life Cycle, Database Design & Development, Business Intelligence, Business Analysis/Data Analysis. (Woman/As-Ind, estab 2014, empl 2, sales $150,000, cert: NMSDC, WBENC)

5010 Pleasant Consulting, LLC
9145 Lyndale Ave S
Bloomington, MN 55420
Contact: Marty Pleasant President
Tel: 952-484-4373
Email: marty@pleasantconsulting.com
Website: www.pleasantconsulting.com
Contract & temporary IT staff, contract to hire staff. (Woman, estab 2012, empl 17, sales $900,000, cert: WBENC)

5011 Procellis Technology Inc.
1330 Lagoon Ave 4th Fl
Minneapolis, MN 55408
Contact: Damian Young CEO
Tel: 612-430-9505
Email: damian.young@procellis.com
Website: www.procellis.com
IT services, servers, storage, virtualization, backup, disaster recovery & cloud services. (AA, estab 2013, empl 19, sales $5,000,000, cert: NMSDC)

5012 SDK Software Inc aka Sudhko Inc.
810 Lilac Dr North Ste #116
Golden Valley, MN 55422
Contact: Hema Arumilli President
Tel: 763-657-7272
Email: sdkhr@sdksoft.com
Website: www.sdksoft.com
Software development svcs, staff augmentation & project mgmt. (Woman/As-Ind, estab 1993, empl 100, sales $13,350,000, cert: City, NMSDC)

INFORMATION TECHNOLOGY: Services

5013 Select Source International
13911 Ridgedale Dr, Ste 230
Minnetonka, MN 55305
Contact: Mandeep Sodhi CEO
Tel: 952-546-3300
Email: sales@selectsourceintl.com
Website: www.SelectSourceIntl.com
Temporary Staffing, IT Staffing & Services, Engineering Services, Financial Services, Govt Services, Retail Services, Energy & Utility Services, App Devel, Mobile Devel. (Nat Ame, estab 2000, empl 771, sales , cert: NMSDC)

5014 TAJ Technologies, Inc.
7900 International Dr Ste 405
Bloomington, MN 55425
Contact: K.C. Sukumar President
Tel: 651-405-7411
Email: kcs@tajtech.com
Website: www.tajtech.com
E-business solutions, e-commerce applications, client/server programming, on-site, off-site & offshore. (As-Ind, estab 1987, empl 208, sales $22,829,532, cert: NMSDC)

5015 Tanson Corp.
8317 Pillsbury Ave S
Bloomington, MN 55420
Contact: Prema Patil President
Tel: 612-237-5148
Email: prema@tansoncorp.com
Website: www.tansoncorp.com
Offer strategic IT staffing, staff augmentation, and direct placement in application development, business intelligence, web solution, quality assurance, & databases. (Woman/As-Ind, estab 2005, empl 20, sales $1,152,872, cert: WBENC)

5016 Technology Solutions Group LLC
60 S 6th St Ste 2800
Minneapolis, MN 55402
Contact: Alexandra Farnsworth CEO
Tel: 888-733-4599
Email: ali@tsg-mn.com
Website: www.tsg-mn.com/
BI/Data Mining, IoT & Software Development, Business Intelligence, BI/Data mining, Analytics, Internet of Things, Mobile App Development, Software Development, Web Development, QA/testing. (Woman, estab 2013, empl 1, sales $616,140, cert: WBENC)

5017 The MACRO GROUP, Inc.
1200 Washington Ave S Ste 350
Minneapolis, MN 55415
Contact: Dawn Kuzma Marketing Dir
Tel: 612-206-3382
Email: dkuzma@macrogroup.net
Website: www.macrogroup.net
Project/Program Mgmt, Business Analysis, Process Improvement, Web App Devel, App Integration, Electronic Content Mgmt/Electronic Document Mgmt, Technical Analysis & Design, Client/Service App Devel. (Woman, estab 1987, empl 35, sales $3,700,000, cert: City)

5018 The Sartell Group, Inc.
800 Hennepin Ave, Ste 400
Minneapolis, MN 55403
Contact: Mary Jacobs Dir of Sales
Tel: 612-548-3101
Email: mjjacobs@sartellgroup.com
Website: www.sartellgroup.com
Customized software development. (Woman, estab 1998, empl 16, sales $3,571,250, cert: WBENC)

5019 Titan Data Group Inc.
6043 Hudson Rd, Ste 399-E
Woodbury, MN 55125
Contact: Viswanathan Subramanian President
Tel: 651-493-0039
Email: vish@titandata.com
Website: www.titandata.com
Business strategy, IT consulting, process improvement & technology development. (Woman/As-Ind, estab 2002, empl 20, sales $3,917,883, cert: NMSDC)

5020 Transcomp Inc. DBA: Evolve Systems
2974 Rice St
St. Paul, MN 55113
Contact: Marnie Ochs-Raleigh CEO
Tel: 651-628-4000
Email: info@evolve-systems.com
Website: www.evolve-systems.com
Web development, shopping carts, event management interfaces, Content Management Systems (CMS) & payment forms. (Woman, estab 1993, empl 15, sales $1,128,000, cert: WBENC)

5021 TSG Server and Storage
10 2nd St NE, Ste 214
Minneapolis, MN 55413
Contact: Mike DuBois COO
Tel: 612-465-0800
Email: info@tsg-usa.com
Website: www.tsg-usa.com
Solution Integrator & infrastructure, Hyper-converged infrastructure, cloud and security, networking, storage, server & software, cloud storage, back up & recovery, cybersecurity, IBM Power Systems, IBM Storage. (As-Pac, estab 2001, empl 11, sales , cert: State, City)

5022 Twin Cities Solutions, Inc.
PO Box 21975
Eagan, MN 55121
Contact: Scott Miller CFO
Tel: 952-583-0367
Email: smiller@twincs.com
Website: www.twincs.com
IT consulting: .Net developers, Java developers, business analysts & project managers. (Woman, estab 2000, empl 10, sales $970,000, cert: State)

5023 UpNet Technologies, Inc.
7825 Washington Ave S Ste 450
Minneapolis, MN 55439
Contact: Kevin Amys Controller
Tel: 952-944-2345
Email: kevin.amys@upnettec.com
Website: www.upnettec.com
Information technologies: EDI, XML, CIDX, EDIFACT and Rosetta net. (Minority, Woman, estab 2000, empl 25, sales $3,200,000, cert: WBENC)

5024 Virtelligence, Inc
6216 Baker Road Ste 100
Eden Prairie, MN 55346
Contact: Akhtar Chaudhri CEO
Tel: 952-548-6600
Email: achaudhri@virtelligence.com
Website: www.virtelligence.com
Management consulting & technology solutions: project mgmt, enterprise software dev & integration, business intelligence & data warehousing, application outsourcing, staffing. (Minority, estab , empl , sales , cert: NMSDC)

INFORMATION TECHNOLOGY: Services

5025 Virtual Matrix Corporation (dba 1 Source, Inc.)
7200 France Ave S Ste 324
Edina, MN 55435
Contact: Bill Hohn Dir
Tel: 952-835-6400
Email: hohnb@vmatrixcorp.com
Website: www.1Source.net
IT staffing/consulting, SAP (HANA certified), ABAP, Java, PHP, Oracle, Microsoft products (.NETs). (As-Ind, estab 2002, empl 78, sales $3,500,000, cert: State, City, NMSDC)

5026 Visual Consultants, Inc.
4900 Hwy 169 N, Ste 307
New Hope, MN 55428
Contact: Bala Akkina VP
Tel: 763-533-1000
Email: bala@visual-consultants.com
Website: www.visual-consultants.com
IT solutions, enterprise IT applications development & IT consulting services. (Minority, Woman, estab 2003, empl 42, sales $3,500,000, cert: NMSDC)

5027 Word Tech Secretarial Service Inc.
6825 York Place N
Minneapolis, MN 55429
Contact: Patty Mesenbrink President
Tel: 612-349-9214
Email: patty@wordtechtranscription.com
Website: www.wordtechtranscription.com
Audio Transcription, Digital transcription, Video transcription, transcription, document preparation, audio and video transcription. (Woman, estab 1986, empl 3, sales $ 0, cert: State, City, SDB)

5028 Xylo Technologies Inc.
2434 Superior Dr NW Ste 105
Rochester, MN 55901
Contact: Dharani Ramamoorthy President
Tel: 507-289-9956
Email: dharani@xylotechnologies.com
Website: www.xylotechnologies.com
IT consulting, web & client/server technolgies, custom software development & system integration services. (As-Pac, estab 2000, empl 60, sales $7,043,821, cert: NMSDC)

5029 YFI Technologies
1422 Thomas Ave
Saint Paul, MN 55104
Contact: Reynaldo Lyles President
Tel: 651-645-4987
Email: rlyles@yourfutureimage.com
Website: www.YFItechnologies.com
Mobile & wireless solutions: PDA's, palm devices, custom software design, mobile database synchronization, IT consulting & staff augmentation. (AA, estab 1994, empl 8, sales , cert: NMSDC)

Missouri

5030 Advanced Resources Group, Inc.
687 Trade Center Blvd Ste 110
Chesterfield, MO 63005
Contact: Sonya Gotto CEO
Tel: 636-777-4141
Email: tgeolat@advr.com
Website: www.advr.com
Contract engineers & IT consultants. (Woman, estab 2002, empl 450, sales $22,300,000, cert: WBENC)

5031 Applications Engineering Group
12300 Old Tesson Rd, Ste 100-G
St. Louis, MO 63128
Contact: Chris Rakel VP Operations
Tel: 314-842-9110
Email: chris.rakel@aeg-inc.com
Website: www.aeg-inc.com
Provide contract, contract to hire & direct hire IT employment services. (Hisp, estab 1992, empl 35, sales , cert: State)

5032 Ares Construction Co, LLC
4900 Lawn Ave
Kansas City, MO 64130
Contact: Quinton Fears CEO
Tel: 816-285-5933
Email: qfears@aresconst.com
Website: www.aresconst.com
Electrical contracting, satellite dishes, computer consulting, network design & installation, web design, data recovery, customer training, structured cabling & phone systems. (AA, estab 2002, empl 7, sales , cert: State, City)

5033 Byrne Software Technologies, Inc.
16091 Swingley Ridge Rd Ste 200
Chesterfield, MO 63017
Contact: Tom Allen VP
Tel: 636-537-2505
Email: tra@byrnesoftware.com
Website: www.byrnesoftware.com
IT consulting & software development; custom applications, web sites, Windows applications. (Woman, estab 1985, empl 55, sales $6,538,000, cert: State)

5034 Communitronics Corp.
970 Bolger Court
Fenton, MO 63026
Contact: Rita Leitensdorfer CEO
Tel: - -
Email: rital@communitronics.com
Website: www.communitronics.com
Audio Visual Systems, VTC Systems, Secure/Non-Secure VTC, Enterprise Collaboration, Video/Media Walls, Project Engineering, Custom AV Applications, Service Contracts, FTEs, Information Assurance Compliance (Woman, estab 1969, empl 11, sales $2,000,000, cert: State, NWBOC)

5035 ComSolutions Inc.
26 Forest Club Dr
Chesterfield, MO 63005
Contact: President
Tel: 504-224-9475
Email:
Website: www.comsolutionsusa.com
Help Desk Support , Website Development, Cloud & On premise Software Solutions, Backup & Disaster recovery Planning & Monitoring. (Woman, estab 2017, empl 17, sales $3,100,000, cert: NWBOC)

5036 Data Dynamics, Inc.
500 Oak Leaf Manor Court Ste 1
St. Louis, MO 63021
Contact: Thomas Van Cleave Mgr Business Devel
Tel: 314-607-3758
Email: thomas.vancleave@datadynamics-inc.com
Website: www.datadynamics-inc.com
IT consulting, software development, web applications, mobile apps, web sites& custom software development, infrastructure, PCs, server, networks, routers, etc. (Minority, Woman, estab 1996, empl 2, sales $195,836, cert: State)

INFORMATION TECHNOLOGY: Services

5037 Datasoft Global LLC
      128 Enchanted Pkwy, Ste 206
      Manchester, MO 63021
      Contact: Parveen Pattan CEO
      Tel: 636-724-9979
      Email: parveen.pattan@datasoftglobal.net
      Website: www.datasoftglobal.net
IT consulting & staffing solutions. (As-Ind, estab , empl 21, sales $1,780,000, cert: State, NMSDC)

5038 Digital Partners Incorporated
      8008 Carondelet Ave Ste 103
      Saint Louis, MO 63105
      Contact: Matina Koester President
      Tel: 314-863-8008
      Email: matina@dpipro.com
      Website: www.dpipro.com
System Integration. (Woman, estab 1994, empl 11, sales $8,500,000, cert: WBENC)

5039 Document Imaging Systems of St. Louis
      1463 S Vandeventer Ave
      St. Louis, MO 63110
      Contact: Adrienne Williams President
      Tel: 314-531-0167
      Email: awilliams@disrepro.com
      Website: www.disrepro.com
Blueprint document reproduction, project collaboration & document management solutions. (Woman/AA, estab 1995, empl 8, sales $4,095,761, cert: State, City, NMSDC)

5040 ECCO Select Corporation
      1601 Iron St, Ste 200
      North Kansas City, MO 64116
      Contact: Jeanette Prenger President
      Tel: 816-960-3800
      Email: registrations@eccoselect.com
      Website: www.eccoselect.com
Project management, security consulting, network security admin, system security audits. (Minority, Woman, estab , empl , sales $28,172,000, cert: State, NMSDC, WBENC)

5041 Ferguson Consulting Inc.
      1350 Timberlake Manor Pkwy Ste 450
      Chesterfield, MO 63017
      Contact: Paul Woolverton VP Govt Sector
      Tel: 636-728-4408
      Email: pwoolverton@fergcons.com
      Website: www.fci-engr.com
IT solutions. (Woman estab 1993, empl 110, sales $ 0, cert: State)

5042 Geodata IT
      555 Washington Ave, Ste 310
      St. Louis, MO 63101
      Contact: Justin Bennett President
      Tel: 217-390-8085
      Email: justin@geodatait.com
      Website: www.geodatait.com
Agile Software Development, Data Center Consolidation & Cloud Services, Big Data & Data Analytics, Systems Engineering & Integration, Program & Project Management, Enterprise Content Management, Data & Information Engineering. (Hisp, estab 2012, empl 4, sales $120,000, cert: NMSDC, 8(a))

5043 Information Technology Group
      316 Delaware
      Kansas City, MO 64105
      Contact: CEO
      Tel: 816-421-6472
      Email:
      Website: www.itgllc.net
IT staffing svcs, supplier mgmt, fixed price staffing, project outsourcing. (Woman, estab 1999, empl 78, sales $2,000,000, cert: WBENC)

5044 Ingenuity Consulting Partner, Inc.
      410 B SE 3rd St, Ste 102
      Lee's Summit, MO 64081
      Contact: Brenda Riggs CEO
      Tel: 816-272-8145
      Email: briggs@ingenuityconsulting.com
      Website: www.ingenuityconsulting.com
Software development & application integration, web & mobile applications. (Woman, estab 2002, empl 22, sales $1,155,578, cert: State)

5045 Kelly Mitchell Group, Inc.
      8229 Maryland Ave
      Clayton, MO 63105
      Contact: Cassandra Sanford
      Tel: 314-727-1700
      Email: cassandra.sanford@kellymitchell.com
      Website: www.kellymitchell.com
Technology consulting: staff augmentation, project solutions, managed outsourcing & strategic consulting. (Woman, estab 1998, empl 2000, sales $90,000,000, cert: CPUC, WBENC)

5046 NextGen Information Services Inc.
      906 Olive St Ste 600
      Saint Louis, MO 63101
      Contact: Christy Herschbach Admin Asst
      Tel: 314-588-1212
      Email: supplierdiversity@nextgen-is.com
      Website: www.nextgen-is.com
IT consulting services: project mgmt, custom application dev, legacy transition svcs & staff augmentation, staff augmentaion. (Minority, Woman, estab 1997, empl 300, sales $ 0, cert: State, City, WBENC)

5047 Pace Solutions, Inc.
      1065 Executive Pkwy Ste 225
      St. Louis, MO 63141
      Contact: Clint Kleinsorge Dir Business Devel
      Tel: 314-560-9641
      Email: clint@pacesi.com
      Website: www.pacesi.com
Information Technology staffing & consulting services. (Minority, Woman, estab 2011, empl 55, sales $5,000,000, cert: NWBOC)

5048 Programmer Resources International Inc.
      221 Clarkson Executive Park
      Ellisville, MO 63011
      Contact: Deanna Wickey Business Devel Mgr
      Tel: 636-256-7172
      Email: deanna@prijbs.com
      Website: www.prijbs.com
IT professionals & innovative technology solutions. (AA, estab 1997, empl 350, sales $29,600,000, cert: NMSDC)

5049 PSRI TecHnologies LLC
      113 Eastland Dr
      Jefferson City, MO 65101
      Contact: Natasha Conley President
      Tel: 573-636-9696
      Email: cconley@psritech.com
      Website: www.psritech.com
Information technology/staff augmentation, project management & call center/help desk operations. (Woman/AA, estab 2001, empl 5, sales $197,053, cert: State)

5050 Quanteq, Inc.
      10 Strecker Rd, Ste 1170
      Ellisville, MO 63011
      Contact: Juan Kuanfung CEO
      Tel: 314-329-7799
      Email: jkuanfung@quantequsa.com
      Website: www.quantequsa.com
Software service solutions: information systems & technology life-cycle, project mgmt, requirement & business studies, package evaluation, system design & dev, system & software integration, database admin, custom programming svcs. (Hisp, estab 1997, empl 1, sales , cert: State, City)

5051 Rose International, Inc.
      16305 Swingley Ridge Rd Ste 350
      Chesterfield, MO 63017
      Contact: Sabina Bhatia CEO
      Tel: 636-812-4000
      Email: sales@roseint.com
      Website: www.roseint.com
Information systems consulting, software devlopment, computer programming & maintenance. (Minority, Woman, estab 1993, empl 7000, sales $424,000,000, cert: State, NMSDC, CPUC, WBENC)

5052 Saigan Technologies Inc.
      2300 Main St Ste 900
      Kansas City, MO 64108
      Contact: Julie Robertson Client Engagement Mgr
      Tel: 816-303-1301
      Email: diversity@saigantech.com
      Website: www.saigantech.com
Information technology IT services & solutions. (Minority, Woman, estab 2004, empl 31, sales $1,701,826, cert: State, NMSDC, WBENC)

5053 ServeKool Technologies LLC
      287 Arbor Trails Dr
      Ballwin, MO 63021
      Contact: Lovelina Bhagat President
      Tel: 636-207-8055
      Email: info@servekool.com
      Website: www.servekool.com
Custom software development, application support outsourcing & staffing services. (Woman/As-Ind, estab 2013, empl 2, sales , cert: NMSDC)

5054 Strategic Staffing Solutions
      120 S. Central Ave
      St. Louis, MO 63105
      Contact: Denice Olson VP
      Tel: 630-546-1784
      Email: gscharf@strategicstaff.com
      Website: www.strategicstaff.com
Information technology consulting. (Woman, estab 1990, empl 2700, sales $642,000,000, cert: WBENC)

5055 Systems Service Enterprises, Inc.
      77 Westport Plaza, Ste 500
      St. Louis, MO 63146
      Contact: Susan Elliott Exec Acct Mgr
      Tel: 314-439-4700
      Email: susan.elliott@sseinc.com
      Website: www.sseinc.com
Information technology svcs: desktop computer solutions, technical support, hardware & software installation. (Woman, estab 1966, empl 115, sales $ 0, cert: WBENC)

5056 TechGuard Security LLC
      28 Hawk Ridge Blvd, Ste 107
      Lake St. Louis, MO 63367
      Contact: Carla Stone CEO
      Tel: 636-489-2230
      Email:
      Website: www.techguard.com
IT networking & security services: vulnerability assessments; policy development; secure network infrastructure design; security awareness training; intrusion detection; business continuity/disaster recovery; 24x7 incident response. (Woman, estab 2000, empl 45, sales $7,550,000, cert: State)

5057 TechnoSmarts, Inc.
      16090 Swingley Ridge Rd Ste 330
      St.Louis, MO 63017
      Contact: Rao Vallabhaneni President
      Tel: 636-519-0814
      Email: rao@technosmarts.com
      Website: www.technosmarts.com
IT consulting & staffing services. (As-Ind, estab 1997, empl 30, sales $ 0, cert: NMSDC)

5058 TurnGroup Technologies, LLC
      2811 Locust St
      St. Louis, MO 63103
      Contact: Kim St. Onge Business Dev Mgr
      Tel: 314-289-8734
      Email: kim@turngroup.com
      Website: www.turngroup.com
Database development, hardware/software support, internet solutions, LAN/WAN, programming, website development. (AA, estab 2002, empl 9, sales , cert: City)

5059 Unitech Consulting, LLC dba Chameleon
      3207 Washington Ave
      St. Louis, MO 63103
      Contact: Mary Burgess Business Devel Specialist
      Tel: 314-773-7200
      Email: sales@chameleonis.com
      Website: www.chameleonis.com
Program management, software development & integration & infrastructure support services. (Hisp, estab 2003, empl 75, sales $7,742,000, cert: NMSDC)

Mississippi

5060 Omni Sourcing, Inc.
      1230 Raymond Road; Box 6
      Jackson, MS 39204
      Contact: John Perkins President
      Tel: 713-628-6929
      Email: jperkins@omnisourcing.net
      Website: www.omnisourcing.net
Systems integration & quality management, service assurance mgmt & testing, sourcing value creation, business & technology performance improvement, program & project mgmt. (AA, estab 2012, empl 30, sales $3,600,000, cert: NMSDC)

North Carolina

5061 3 Birds Marketing, LLC
505-B W Franklin St
Chapel Hill, NC 27516
Contact: Layton Judd President
Tel: 919-913-2750
Email: layton@3birdsmarketing.com
Website: www.3birdsmarketing.com
Technology, software, integrated marketing platform, marketing, digital marketing, multichannel marketing, email marketing, email newsletters, digital newsletters, social media management, social media marketing. (Woman, estab 2009, empl 60, sales $3,769,500, cert: WBENC, NWBOC)

5062 Active Ergonomics, Inc.
6501 Creedmoor Rd Ste 101
Raleigh, NC 27613
Contact: Shannon A Powell President
Tel: 919-676-8211
Email: spowell@actergo.com
Website: www.actergo.com
Office ergonomic software to help increase worker productivity and reduce repetitive stress injuries. (Minority, Woman, estab 1997, empl 4, sales $934,000, cert: State, NMSDC, WBENC)

5063 Advantco International LLC
8601 Six Forks Road Ste 120
Raleigh, NC 27615
Contact: Kimthanh Le VP
Tel: 919-518-8298
Email: ktdole@advantco.com
Website: www.advantco.com
Pre-built adapters for integrating SAP & Oracle systems with other leading enterprise platforms (As-Pac, estab 2007, empl 10, sales $100,000, cert: State)

5064 Alliance of Professionals & Consultants, Inc.
8200 Brownleigh Dr
Raleigh, NC 27617
Contact: Troy Roberts President
Tel: 919-510-9696
Email: troberts@apcinc.com
Website: www.apcinc.com
Requirements analysis, network architecture definitions & enhancements, information technology, hardware & software upgrades, modifications, installation, operation & maintenance. (Nat Ame, estab 1993, empl , sales $65,872,532, cert: NMSDC)

5065 Arayal Consulting, LLC
5448 Apex Peakway, Ste 160
Apex, NC 27502
Contact: Thomas Mathew Owner
Tel: 917-406-3261
Email: tom.mathew@arayalconsulting.com
Website: www.arayalconsulting.com
Program / Project Management, Process Improvement, Portfolio Management, Performance Management, Quality Assurance. (As-Ind, estab 2014, empl 4, sales $1,150,000, cert: NMSDC)

5066 Artisan Management LLC
825 Merrimon Ave
Asheville, NC 28804
Contact: Tim Mitrovich CEO
Tel: 828-276-2440
Email: tim@artisan-studios.com
Website: www.artisan-studios.com
Digital Innovation. (AA, estab 2019, empl 60, sales $10,000,000, cert: NMSDC)

5067 Banerasoft Inc.
5710 W Gate City Blvd Ste K, 279
Greensboro, NC 27407
Contact: Brenda Zamzow Sales & Customer Relations Mgr
Tel: 864-787-5408
Email: akshata@banerasoft.biz
Website: www.banerasoft.com
Technology Consulting/Outsourcing, Software Devel, App Devel for all iOS & Android devices, Data Analytics & Business Intelligence, QA & Solutions Integration. (As-Ind, estab 2012, empl 35, sales , cert: NMSDC)

5068 Barrchin, Inc.
326 Morgan Brook Way
Rolesville, NC 27571
Contact: Janet Barrett President
Tel: 919-630-5128
Email: jbarrett@barrchin.com
Website: www.barrchin.com
Information Technology (IT) & Management consulting. (Woman/AA, estab 2013, empl 4, sales $ 0, cert: State, City)

5069 Carolina IT Professionals, Inc.
243 W Catawba Ave
Mount Holly, NC 28120
Contact: VP Mktg
Tel: 704-827-8102
Email: gus.brown@citpinc.com
Website: www.citpinc.com
Information technology staff augmentation, solutions & consulting, permanent placements. (Woman, estab 2001, empl 160, sales $19,009,811, cert: WBENC)

5070 Clark-Powell Associates, Inc.
920 Blairhill Rd
Charlotte, NC 28217
Contact: C. Gibson Sales
Tel: 704-525-4223
Email: cgibson@clark-powell.com
Website: www.clark-powell.com
Design, integration & maintenance of AV systems for presentation, videoconferencing, video broadcast & production. (Woman, estab 1983, empl 62, sales $20,000,000, cert: State)

5071 Clinton Gaddy Inc.
717 Green Valley Rd Ste 200
Greensboro, NC 27408
Contact: Gaddy Will CEO
Tel: 336-355-8708
Email: Wmgaddy@gsostaffing.com
Website: www.gsostaffing.com
Contract IT Staffing/Temporary Labor: Systems Analyst, API Development, Data Analyst, Software Developers, DevOps, Lead Architects, IT Audit Managers, Change Management, Incident/Change Management, Technical Lead, IT Directors, Solution Architect. (AA, estab 2017, empl 8, sales $319,000, cert: State)

5072 COMNet Group, Inc.
      301 McCullough Dr, Ste 400
      Charlotte, NC 28262
      Contact: Ana Sai President
      Tel: 704-323-7762
      Email: ana@comnetgroup.com
      Website: www.comnetgroup.com
IT Technology & training services: ERP, offshoring/ outsourcing, agile program management & complex software development & delivery. (Woman/As-Ind, estab 2005, empl 20, sales $400,000, cert: NMSDC, WBENC)

5073 CrossComm, Inc.
      PO Box 673
      Durham, NC 27702
      Contact: Beverly Williams Business Operations Mgr
      Tel: 919-667-9432
      Email: beverlywilliams@crosscomm.com
      Website: www.crosscomm.com
Mobile & web application develop, custom iOS, Android, Web & Augmented Reality/Virtual Reality apps. (As-Pac, estab 2000, empl 8, sales $975,000, cert: NMSDC)

5074 Data Bridge Consultants LLC
      101 N Tryon St, Ste 1260
      Charlotte, NC 28246
      Contact: Sola Daves Principal Partner
      Tel: 980-319-7635
      Email: sola.daves@databridgeconsultants.com
      Website: www.databridgeconsultants.com
Big data and Artificial Intelligence Consulting, staffing/ BPO. (AA, estab 2013, empl 8, sales $11,300,000, cert: NMSDC)

5075 DD Consulting and Management
      13016 Eastfield Rd Ste 200-272
      Huntersville, NC 28078
      Contact: Walter Great
      Tel: 704-909-2970
      Email: walter@ddconsultingservice.com
      Website: www.DDConsultingservice.com
IT consulting, data storage, data backup, physical surveillance data, digital evidence & security-sensitive digital data. (AA, estab 2001, empl 3, sales , cert: NMSDC)

5076 DynPro
      7412 Chapel Hill Rd
      Raleigh, NC 27607
      Contact: Michael Kallam VP-Business Dev
      Tel: 919-747-7114
      Email: mkallam@dynpro.com
      Website: www.dynpro.com
Design & implement internet applications & web-enable, enterprise solutions, SAP, People Soft & Oracle application mgmt outsourcing, technical svcs, staff augmentation, project mgmt, help desk support. (Minority, estab 1996, empl 90, sales $3,695,000, cert: NMSDC)

5077 Empores LLC
      11020 David Taylor Dr
      Charlotte, NC 28262
      Contact: Satish Prasad Ramamurthy VP Business Dev
      Tel: 703-409-4945
      Email: satish@emporesllc.com
      Website: www.emporesllc.com
Voltage optimization, intelligent PF correction, KVAR improvements, cloud based energy monitoring & automatic techniques. (Minority, estab 2012, empl 5, sales , cert: State, City)

5078 Golden Tech Systems Inc.
      2704 Twinberry Ln
      Waxhaw, NC 28173
      Contact: Pushpinder Garcha President
      Tel: 704-236-2939
      Email: pushpinder@golden-tech-systems.com
      Website: www.golden-tech-systems.com
Enterprise Application Devel, n-tier Web Devel, Systems Integration, SCRUM Devel, Cyber Security, Migration Strategies. (As-Ind, estab 2007, empl 5, sales $753,550, cert: State, City, NMSDC, 8(a))

5079 IBG Global Consulting
      333 W Trade St
      Charlotte, NC 28202
      Contact: Diondre Lewis President
      Tel: 866-611-3604
      Email: ellie@ibgsoftware.com
      Website: www.ibgsoftware.com
IT Resource Procurement, Application Development, Software Architecture, Project Mangement. (AA, estab 2008, empl 50, sales $10,850,000, cert: NMSDC)

5080 Infestus Inc.
      PO Box 222
      McLeansville, NC 27301
      Contact: Glasco Taylor CEO
      Tel: 202-794-7280
      Email: glasco.taylor@calibertec.com
      Website: www.calibertec.com/
IT staffing: Cyber Security, Data Center(Virtualization, Storage, SAN, Networking, Server Hardware, Linux, etc), Infrastructure Networking. (AA, estab 2014, empl 5, sales $200,000, cert: NMSDC)

5081 IT People Corporation
      One Copley Pkwy. Ste 216
      Morrisville, NC 27560
      Contact: Sai Nidamarty Business Dev
      Tel: 919-806-3535
      Email: sai@itpeoplecorp.com
      Website: www.itpeoplecorp.com
Information technology staffing, consulting & outsourcing services. (Minority, Woman, estab 1999, empl 153, sales $7,459,294, cert: State, NMSDC, WBENC)

5082 Marketing Resource Solutions LLC
      725 W Main St, Ste E
      Jamestown, NC 27282
      Contact: Melita Vick Natl Accts Svc Mgr
      Tel: 336-510-7523
      Email: info@marketingresourcesolutions.com
      Website: www.marketingresourcesolutions.com
Remote Executive Assistance, Database & CRM support, Basic Internet Research, Data management, Website content management, Sales & Customer support, Social Media Optimization Services, Office management. (Woman, estab 2003, empl 160, sales , cert: NMSDC)

5083 Paula P. White and Associates, Inc dba
      DataMasters
      PO Box 14548
      Greensboro, NC 27415
      Contact: Dana White Dir Operations
      Tel: 336-373-1461
      Email: dwhite@datamasters.com
      Website: www.datamasters.com
IT staffing, contract, staff augmentation & permanent or direct hire positions. (Woman, estab 1971, empl 25, sales $2,500,000, cert: State)

INFORMATION TECHNOLOGY: Services

5084 Pinnacle Tek LLC
1920 E NC Hwy 54 Ste 150,
Durham, NC 27713
Contact: Caitlin Hales
Tel: 984-646-5111
Email: caitlin@pinnacletek.net
Website: www.pinnacletek.net/
IT Solutions/Services, recruiting/staffing needs, Full Time/Contract/SOW. (Woman/As-Pac, estab 2016, empl 50, sales $5,490,622, cert: State, WBENC)

5085 QCentric Consultants, LLC
624 Tyvola Rd, Ste 103-177
Charlotte, NC 28217
Contact: Nuradin Kariye Managing Partner
Tel: 800-260-5728
Email: admin@qcentricconsultants.com
Website: www.qcentricconsultants.com
IT staffing & technology solutions. (AA, estab 2009, empl 45, sales , cert: State)

5086 Refulgent Technologies Inc.
112 South Tryon St Ste 1270
Charlotte, NC 28284
Contact: Horace Worley President
Tel: 704-405-4238
Email: horace.worley@refulgent-tech.com
Website: www.refulgent-tech.com
IT consulting & staffing services, application development & staffing. (Minority, Woman, estab 2005, empl 22, sales $1,157,433, cert: NMSDC)

5087 Sajiton LLC
301 McCullough Dr Ste 400
Charlotte, NC 28262
Contact: Nicole Williams Managing Dir
Tel: 888-828-7991
Email: nicole.williams@sajiton.com
Website: www.sajiton.com
Custom Mobile & Web Application Development, Big Data, Data Analytics, Data Engineering, Data Integration, Master Data Management. Data Encryption, Data Security in the Cloud & On Premise - CyberSecurity. (Woman/AA, estab 2014, empl 1, sales , cert: NMSDC, WBENC)

5088 Saponi Industries, Inc.
3229 Goslen Dr
Pfafftown, NC 27040
Contact: Deborah Bare Owner
Tel: 336-770-5321
Email: lynn@saponi-industries.com
Website: www.saponi-industries.com
Universal life, whole life, term life, accident, critical illness, dental, cancer and long term care. (Minority, Woman, estab 2010, empl 2, sales , cert: NMSDC)

5089 Spectraforce Technologies, Inc.
500 W Peace St
Raleigh, NC 27603
Contact: Julianne Howard Dir Client Relations
Tel: 919-280-3064
Email: supplierdiversity@spectraforce.com
Website: www.spectraforce.com
IT/Clinical/Scientific/Engineering contingent staffing and IT Application Development and Maintenance services. (As-Ind, estab 2004, empl 2500, sales $112,000,000, cert: NMSDC)

5090 STATProg Inc.
421 Fayetteville St, Ste 1100
Raleigh, NC 27601
Contact: Dany Guerendo Christian President
Tel: 919-987-2015
Email: statprogadmin@statproginc.com
Website: www.statproginc.com
Research and Development, and/or Life Sciences departments. Statistical Programming and Analysis using SAS as software. (Woman/AA, estab 2012, empl 2, sales $162,000, cert: NMSDC, WBENC)

5091 Stonelaurel Consulting, Inc.
1515 Mockingbird Ln, Ste 800
Charlotte, NC 28209
Contact: Ted Shelton Global Accounts Dir
Tel: 704-333-8878
Email: bnymellon@stonelaurel.com
Website: www.stonelaurel.com
Information Technology & Management Consulting. (AA, estab 1994, empl 100, sales $7,786,344, cert: NMSDC)

5092 Technology Concepts & Design, Inc.
4510 Weybridge Ln
Greensboro, NC 27407
Contact: Lisa Cain CFO
Tel: 336-232-5800
Email: l_cain@tcdi.com
Website: www.tcdi.com
Advanced application & system design services, eDiscovery, review & production & large-scale case management products & services to help effectively manage and reduce costs associated with significant litigation and investigations. (As-Pac, estab 1988, empl 69, sales , cert: NMSDC)

5093 Third Law Enterprises, LLC
517 S Front St
Wilmington, NC 28401
Contact: Michael Gilbert Managing Partner
Tel: 910-477-3772
Email: mgilbert@thirdlawenterprises.com
Website: www.thirdlawenterprises.com
Data Center Solutions (Computer hardware, software, implementation services), Servers, Storage, Networking, Cloud solutions (on premise, off premise) and Hybrid Cloud Solutions, Personal Computing (PCs, Notebooks, Backup drives). (Hisp, estab 2004, empl 2, sales $220,000, cert: State)

5094 United Global Technologies
338 S. Sharon Amity Road
Charlotte, NC 28202
Contact: Manny Rodriguez Market Mgr
Tel: 980-270-6636
Email: mrodriguez@ugtechnologies.com
Website: www.ugtechnologies.com
Systems integration & IT/engineering services. (Woman, estab 2005, empl 120, sales $21,400,000, cert: State)

5095 VDC Technologies
513 New Bridge St Ste 600
Jacksonville, NC 28540
Contact: Vactronia Russell CEO
Tel: 910-353-1492
Email: support@vdctechs.com
Website: www.vdctechs.com
IT solutions. (Woman/AA, estab , empl , sales , cert: State)

INFORMATION TECHNOLOGY: Services

North Dakota

5096 Razor Consulting Solutions, Inc.
5625 51st Ave S
Fargo, ND 58104
Contact: Laura Hale
Tel: 651-357-7907
Email: laura.hale@gotorazor.com
Website: www.gotorazor.com
BPO (Business Process Outsourcing), business intelligence & analytics, project management, accounting & finance, marketing & custom application design & development. (Woman/Nat-Ame, estab 2010, empl 181, sales $31,082,991, cert: NMSDC, WBENC, 8(a))

New Hampshire

5097 Advanced Presentation Systems dba CCS
132 Northeastern Blvd
Nashua, NH 03062
Contact: Chris Gamst VP
Tel: 978-256-2001
Email: cgamst@ccsprojects.com
Website: www.ccsnewengland.com
Audio visual system design, integration, sales, service & installation for boardrooms, conference rooms, training rooms & auditoriums. (Woman/As-Ind, estab 1998, empl 23, sales $ 0, cert: State)

5098 Apollo Professional Solutions, Inc.
29 Stiles Rd Ste 302
Salem, NH 03079
Contact: Bruce Thomason VP
Tel: 866-277-3343
Email: bthomason@apollopros.com
Website: www.apollopros.com
Recruited & payrolled engineering & information technology temporary personnel. (Woman, estab 1983, empl 20, sales $12,000,000, cert: State, WBENC)

5099 Dataservinc
1 Tara Blvd, Ste 102
Nashua, NH 03062
Contact: Anil Kumar VP Business Dev
Tel: 603-557-0600
Email: contact@dataservinc.com
Website: www.dataservinc.com
IT staffing & IT software development. (Woman/As-Ind, estab 2005, empl 100, sales $7,000,000, cert: State)

5100 Digital Prospectors Corp.
100 Domain Dr Ste 103
Exeter, NH 03833
Contact: Chris Roos Principal
Tel: 603-772-2700
Email: croos@dpcit.com
Website: www.dpcit.com
Permanent & temporary IT staffing. (Woman, estab 1999, empl 120, sales $50,201,563, cert: WBENC)

5101 Paramount Technology Solutions LLC
63 Emerald St, Ste 442
Keene, NH 03431
Contact: Beth Wright Dir of Finance & Admin
Tel: 281-617-1400
Email: beth.wright@acuitycloudsolutions.com
Website: www.acuitycloudsolutions.com
Computer software consulting services. (Woman, estab 2008, empl 25, sales , cert: WBENC)

5102 Universal Software Corporation
20 Industrial Park Dr
Nashua, NH 03062
Contact: Sonu Khanna Sr Mgr
Tel: 603-324-4004
Email: sonuk@universal-sw.com
Website: www.universal-sw.com
Information technology: staff augmentation, project mgmt, project & offshore outsourcing, embedded systems & hardware design, Oracle/MS SQL, .Net framework, open source tools, WinNT, Solaris, Unix, Linux. (As-Pac, estab 1992, empl 58, sales $ 0, cert: State)

New Jersey

5103 1st Choice Financial Group LLC
1121 Asbury Ave
Asbury Park, NJ 07712
Contact: Kathrina Nease CEO
Tel: 717-599-1907
Email: knease@1stchoicefg.com
Website: www.1stchoicefg.com
Information technology solutions & program/project management. (Woman, estab 2006, empl 10, sales $500,000, cert: State)

5104 20/20 Solutions, Inc.
33 Wilson Dr Unit D
Sparta, NJ 07871
Contact: Jody Torre President
Tel: 973-383-8703
Email: j.torre@20-20solutions.com
Website: www.20-20solutions.com
Website development, website management, search engine optimization, website design, website hosting, computer programming, computer repair, computer training, computer equipment, computer maintenance, computer support. (Woman, estab 1999, empl 10, sales $450,000, cert: WBENC)

5105 22nd Century Technologies, Inc.
1 Executive Dr Ste 285
Somerset, NJ 08873
Contact: Eva Gaddis-McKnight Contracts Admin
Tel: 732-537-9191
Email: com@tscti.com
Website: www.tscti.com
Computer programming & consulting, IT support. (As-Pac, estab 1997, empl 4230, sales $284,132,720, cert: State, NMSDC)

5106 2iSolutions Inc.
1012 Ellis Pkwy
Edison, NJ 08820
Contact: Praveen Kumar CEO
Tel: 732-212-7436
Email: vendor@2isolutions.com
Website: www.2isolutionsus.com
SAP Solutions: Comprehensive SAP services covering various modules. (Woman/As-Ind, estab 2005, empl 250, sales $2,621,186, cert: NMSDC, WBENC)

INFORMATION TECHNOLOGY: Services

5107 Actuan Global LLC
    4 Debra Ct
    Scotch Plains, NJ 07076
    Contact: Talib Morgan President
    Tel: 908-443-1180
    Email: talib.morgan@actuanglobal.com
    Website: www.actuanglobal.com
Digital innovation & technology consulting, mobile, personalization, marketing automation, content management, social media, data & digital systems. (AA, estab 2011, empl 1, sales , cert: NMSDC)

5108 Adaptive Tech Resources Inc.
    4400 Route 9 South Ste 1000
    Freehold, NJ 07728
    Contact: Roland Williams CEO
    Tel: 732-683-0800
    Email: roland.williams@atrstaffing.com
    Website: www.atrstaffing.com
IT consulting/contract & full time staffing services. (AA, estab 1996, empl 3, sales $862,000, cert: NMSDC)

5109 Aequor Technologies Inc.
    377 Hoes Lane
    Piscataway, NJ 08854
    Contact: Ramesh Nair VP
    Tel: 408-480-6241
    Email: ramesh@aequor.com
    Website: www.aequor.com
Software Development, Maintenance & Support, Software Reengineering & Migration, Software Testing, Application Integration. (As-Ind, estab 1998, empl 300, sales $5,350,000, cert: NMSDC)

5110 Agnosco Technologies Inc.
    6 Thornhill Dr
    Lumberton, NJ 08048
    Contact: Kiran Khan Operations Mgr
    Tel: 877-933-5439
    Email: kiran@agnoscotech.com
    Website: www.agnoscotech.com
Information technology recruitment consultancy services: permanent, temporary & contract positions, executive search & outplacement services & solutions. (Minority, Woman, estab 2013, empl 50, sales , cert: State)

5111 AIT Global Inc.
    228 Route 34
    Matawan, NJ 07747
    Contact: Mittal Shah VP
    Tel: 732-997-9917
    Email: mittals@aitglobalinc.com
    Website: www.aitglobalinc.com
IT Staffing & Solutions, Contract, Contract to Hire or Full-time Placements. (Woman/As-Ind, estab 2003, empl 135, sales $14,800,000, cert: NMSDC, WBENC)

5112 AITA Consulting Services Inc.
    6-80 Towne Center Dr
    North Brunswick, NJ 08902
    Contact: Aisha Thomas Business Devel Mgr
    Tel: 732-658-4471
    Email: hello@aishathomas.com
    Website: www.aitacs.com
IT staffing services, Corp To Corp, W2, 1099, contract, full time, contract to hire, Business Intelligence, Big Data, Web development, J2EE, Microsoft technologies, Quality Assurance & Oracle Applications, SAP, Mobile Apps. (Woman/As-Ind, estab 2006, empl 182, sales $ 0, cert: NMSDC, WBENC)

5113 Algoriom Inc.
    292 Main St, Ste 6
    Hackensack, NJ 07601
    Contact: Kamlesh Ranka President
    Tel: 201-489-3500
    Email: kamlesh.ranka@algoriom.com
    Website: www.algoriom.com
Big Data Platform & Maintenance, Statistical Data Analytics Tools & predictive analytics, Custom-designed Deep Learning Models, Artificial Intelligence Platforms. (As-Ind, estab 2019, empl 15, sales $1,500,000, cert: NMSDC)

5114 Alliance Sourcing Network Inc
    40 Galesi Dr Ste 2
    Wayne, NJ 07470
    Contact: CEO
    Tel: 201-438-2005
    Email: information@asn-corp.com
    Website: www.asn-corp.com
IT consulting services: application design, client server design, database admin & hardware design & support, network admin. (Woman, estab 2006, empl 26, sales $10,893,853, cert: WBENC)

5115 American Software LLC
    29-31 Freeman St, Ste D-1
    Newark, NJ 07105
    Contact: Manmohan Uttarwar CEO
    Tel: 785-317-0071
    Email: info@american-software.com
    Website: www.american-software.com
IT Staffing, Software Reseller, IT Services, Custom Programming, IT Consulting, Digital transformation, IT Product design, IT & Software Development, Applications support. (As-Ind, estab 2013, empl 4, sales $518,265, cert: State)

5116 AMMKCORP
    19 Emily Place
    Hamilton, NJ 08690
    Contact: Virginia Madonia President
    Tel: 610-955-4993
    Email: madonia@ammkcorp.com
    Website: www.ammkcorp.com
Technology solution services, managed outsourcing & staff augmentation. (Woman, estab 2002, empl 15, sales $9,000,000, cert: WBENC)

5117 AppliedInfo Partners, Inc.
    28 World's Fair Dr
    Somerset, NJ 08873
    Contact: Betty Lau CEO
    Tel: 732-507-7316
    Email: blau@appliedinfo.com
    Website: www.appliedinfo.com
Software & web dev, computer & IT products & services, marketing communications. (Minority, Woman, estab 1990, empl 50, sales $10,000,000, cert: NMSDC, WBENC)

5118 APTIVA Corp.
    100 Franklin Square Dr, Ste 210
    Somerset, NJ 08873
    Contact: Paula Philip Sr VP
    Tel: 732-391-1055
    Email: info@applesandorangespr.com
    Website: www.aptivacorp.com
IT Solutions and services. (As-Ind, estab 2007, empl 80, sales $8,000,000, cert: NMSDC)

INFORMATION TECHNOLOGY: Services

5119 Arborsys Group
3131 Princeton Pike, Bldg 4, Ste 210
Lawrenceville, NJ 08648
Contact: Vasu Ranganathan Partner/President
Tel: 609-843-0225
Email: vranganathan@arborsys.com
Website: www.arborsys.com
Business & IT consulting, content lifecycle mgmt, collaboration, business process management, portal solutions & electronic records management. (Woman/As-Ind, estab 2004, empl 20, sales $5,300,000, cert: State, NMSDC)

5120 Argo Navis IT
155 Glen Alpin Rd
Morristown, NJ 07960
Contact: CEO
Tel: 973-285-1202
Email: bridgens@argonavisit.com
Website: www.argonavisit.com
Global audio & web conferencing services. Resell HP hardware. (Woman, estab 2003, empl 1, sales $270,000, cert: WBENC)

5121 Artech L.L.C.
360 Mt. Kemble Ave Ste 2000
Morristown, NJ 07960
Contact: Vinu Varghese AVP, New Business Development
Tel: 206-679-9001
Email: rfp@artech.com
Website: www.artech.com
Network infrastructure mgmt, web applications dev, content mgmt, design, internet infrastructure design devel & maintenance, multitier architecture, client server, software applications, systems devel & support. (Woman/As-Ind, estab 1992, empl 11500, sales $902,000,000, cert: State, NMSDC, WBENC)

5122 Astir IT Solutions
50 Cragwood Rd Ste 219
South Plainfield, NJ 07080
Contact: Robert Markowitz Exec VP
Tel: 908-279-8670
Email: bobm@astirit.com
Website: www.astirit.com
IT consulting, staffing & outsourced software development. (Minority, Woman, estab 2001, empl 300, sales $30,700,000, cert: State, NMSDC)

5123 Atlas Data Systems DBA Atlas
400 Connell Dr Ste 6000
Berkeley Heights, NJ 07922
Contact: Lisa Wickey Acct Exec
Tel: 908-519-8013
Email: lisa.wickey@chooseatlas.com
Website: www.chooseatlas.com
Information technology consulting: internet, e-commerce, infrastructure & RDMS consulting. (Woman, estab 1998, empl 350, sales $31,900,000, cert: State, WBENC)

5124 Aumtech, Inc.
710 Old Bridge Turnpike
East Brunswick, NJ 08816
Contact: Tom Porter COO
Tel: 732-254-1875
Email: tporter@aumtech.com
Website: www.aumtech.com
IVR & VoIP network solution: speech recognition, touchtone input, VXML programming tools. (Minority, estab 1988, empl 38, sales $2,120,000, cert: NMSDC)

5125 Avenues International Inc.
4 Restrick Court
Princeton Junction, NJ 08550
Contact: Anupam Gupta Dir
Tel: 609-945-1160
Email: anupam@avenuesinc.com
Website: www.avenuesinc.com
IT consulting services: Data Analytics, Business Intelligence, Data Warehousing, Big Data Solution & Management Reporting Solutions. (As-Ind, estab 1994, empl 15, sales $1,870,000, cert: NMSDC)

5126 Axtria Inc.
300 Connell Dr, 5th Floor
Berkeley Heights, NJ 07922
Contact: Maria Poulos Principal
Tel: 1-201-2859
Email: maria.poulos@axtria.com
Website: www.axtria.com
Data analytics, understanding data & training in the latest technologies. (As-Ind, estab , empl , sales $29,600,000, cert: NMSDC)

5127 Blue Planet Solutions Inc.
36 Route 10 W, Ste E
East Hanover, NJ 07936
Contact: Pradeep Darbhe Resource Mgr
Tel: 973-581-1500
Email: pradeep@blueplanetsolutions.com
Website: www.blueplanetsolutions.com
Outsource software development & maintenance, contract programmers, offshore programming. (Woman/As-Ind, estab 1997, empl 20, sales $ 0, cert: State)

5128 BNG Consulting, Inc.
12 Sandhill Ct
Jamesburg, NJ 08831
Contact: Biswatosh Guha VP
Tel: 732-631-0003
Email: guha@bngconsulting.com
Website: www.bngconsulting.com
Business intelligence, data warehousing, reporting/ ETL tools, database admin, support, development, maintenanance, enhancements, architecture & design, data modeling. (As-Pac, estab 2003, empl 65, sales $7,000,000, cert: State)

5129 Boomer Technology Group, Inc.
475 Wall St Ste 257
Princeton, NJ 08540
Contact: Derris Boomer CEO
Tel: 732-800-2058
Email: sales@boomertechnologygroup.com
Website: www.boomertechnologygroup.com
Human Capital Management, Human Resources & Payroll Software. (AA, estab 2018, empl 1, sales $294,000, cert: NMSDC)

5130 Brillio, LLC
100 Town Square Pl, Ste 308
Jersey City, NJ 07310
Contact: Gautam Arni VP Sales
Tel: 201-744-5759
Email: gautam@brillio.com
Website: www.brillio.com
Business Technology Consulting, progam mgmt, analytics,cost optimization. (As-Ind, estab 2013, empl 2000, sales , cert: NMSDC)

5131 Cardinal Technology Solutions Inc.
1100 Cornwall Rd, Ste 113
Monmouth Junction, NJ 08852
Contact: Dir
Tel: 732-821-7400
Email: nfo@cardinalts.com
Website: www.cardinaltsinc.com
IT and Engineering Staffing and consulting services. (As-Ind, estab 2004, empl 22, sales $8,000,000, cert: NMSDC)

5132 Caresoft Inc.
220 Lincoln Blvd Ste 300
Middlesex, NJ 08846
Contact: Dhaval Desai Business Dev Mgr
Tel: 732-764-9500
Email: ddesai@caresoftinc.com
Website: www.caresoftinc.com
Information technology staff augmentation. (Minority, estab 1994, empl 189, sales $9,000,000, cert: NMSDC)

5133 Cavalier Workforce, Inc
379 Thornall St 6th Fl
Edison, NJ 08837
Contact: Parag Shroff VP- Delivery
Tel: 201-215-2160
Email: parag@cavalierworkforce.com
Website: www.cavalierworkforce.com/
Technology staffing & consulting. (As-Pac, estab 2007, empl , sales $13,000,000, cert: State, NMSDC)

5134 CBS Technologies
191 Main St
Hackensack, NJ 07601
Contact: President
Tel: 201-843-8070
Email: info@cbstechnologies.com
Website: www.cbstechnologies.com
Business analysis, software & hardware architectures, vendor software selection, hosting, application, database support, security, business processes, portals, intranets & extranets. (AA, estab 1996, empl 12, sales $800,000, cert: City)

5135 Chenoa Information Services, Inc.
10 Parsonage Rd Ste 312
Edison, NJ 08837
Contact: Michael Fortino EVP Client Solutions
Tel: 732-549-6800
Email: mfortino@chenoainc.com
Website: www.chenoahealth.com
Information technology solutions & staff augmentation. (As-Ind, estab 1998, empl 600, sales $17,000,000, cert: State, NMSDC)

5136 CNC Consulting
50 E Palisades Ave Ste 422
Englewood, NJ 07631
Contact: Fred Seltzer Business Devel Mgr
Tel: 201-541-9122
Email: fseltzer@cncconsult.com
Website: www.cncconsulting.com
IT professionals for consulting contracts. (AA, estab 1996, empl 25, sales $3,000,000, cert: State)

5137 Cognixia Inc.
110 Allen Rd
Basking Ridge, NJ 06584
Contact: Irina Borovitskaya Associate VP
Tel: 973-559-9121
Email: irina.borovitskaya@cognixia.com
Website: www.cognixia.com
IT and business training courses. (Minority, estab 2018, empl 20, sales , cert: NMSDC)

5138 Collabera
110 Allen Road
Basking Ridge, NJ 07920
Contact: Brittany Tipton Exec VP
Tel: 973-889-5200
Email: ar@collabera.com
Website: www.collabera.com
Information technology & management svcs, customized software solutions, business solutions, implementation, maintenance, support, etc. (Minority, estab 1996, empl 3000, sales $400,000,000, cert: NMSDC)

5139 Combined Computer Resources, Inc.
120 Wood Ave S, Ste 408
Iselin, NJ 08830
Contact: Laura Palamara Controller
Tel: 732-632-2502
Email: laurap@combinedcomputer.com
Website: www.combinedcomputer.com
Information technology consulting: data processing, right-to-hire & full time placement services. (Woman, estab 1994, empl 107, sales $16,500,000, cert: State)

5140 Communication Experts, Inc.
51 Cragwood Rd Ste 304
South Plainfield, NJ 07080
Contact: Shirish R. Nadkarni CEO
Tel: 908-512-9129
Email: srn@comexpinc.com
Website: www.comexpinc.com
Software products & services. (As-Ind, estab 2003, empl 8, sales $1,704,000, cert: NMSDC)

5141 Compunnel Software Group, Inc.
103 Morgan Lane Ste 102
Plainsboro, NJ 08536
Contact: Lalitha Reddy AVP Finance & Legal Operations
Tel: 609-606-9010
Email: contracts@compunnel.com
Website: www.compunnel.com
IT Staffing, eLearning, Application Development, Off shore DEvelopment Facility in India. (Minority, estab 1994, empl 1028, sales $262,418,117, cert: NMSDC)

5142 CompuPlus International Inc.
94 Lilac Lane
Paramus, NJ 07652
Contact: David Wei President
Tel: 626-755-0607
Email: davidw@cp-intl.com
Website: www.cp-intl.com
IT staffing & IT consulting, recruitment & service. (As-Pac, estab 1990, empl 7, sales $1,625,219, cert: State)

INFORMATION TECHNOLOGY: Services

5143 Compu-Vision Consulting Inc.
2050 Route 27 Ste 202
North Brunswick, NJ 08902
Contact: Rahul Gupta HR Mgr
Tel: 732-422-1500
Email: rahul.gupta@compuvis.com
Website: www.compuvis.com
Information technology consulting, IT staffing & related services. (Minority, Woman, estab 1998, empl 50, sales $7,250,000, cert: NMSDC, WBENC, NWBOC)

5144 Comrise Technology, Inc.
90 Woodbridge Center Dr Ste 360
Woodbridge, NJ 07730
Contact: Michael Ferrara Dir of Operations
Tel: 732-203-6236
Email: mferrara@comrise.com
Website: www.comrise.com
Staff supplementation, IT mgmt consulting, project outsourcing & recruiting svcs. (As-Pac, estab 1984, empl 150, sales $19,000,000, cert: NMSDC)

5145 Connexions Data Inc.
241 Main St, Ste 206
Hackensack, NJ 07601
Contact: Raghu Menon CFA
Tel: 201-210-8938
Email: raghu.menon@cdatainc.com
Website: www.cdatainc.com
Information technology consulting & integration services, SAP, Oracle & Cloud computing. (As-Ind, estab 2004, empl 48, sales , cert: State)

5146 Corporate Training Group, Inc.
120 Wood Ave S Ste 405
Iselin, NJ 08830
Contact: Kathleen Harvey Sr Acct Exec
Tel: 732-635-9033
Email: kharvey@ctgtraining.com
Website: www.ctgtraining.com
Technical & business end user training on Microsoft, Java, J2EE, Linux, Oracle solutions. (Woman, estab 1991, empl 8, sales $2,000,000, cert: State, WBENC)

5147 Cosmic Software Technology, Inc.
14 Benedek Rd
Princeton, NJ 08540
Contact: Ranvir Sinha CEO
Tel: 609-430-8284
Email: ranvir@cosmic-usa.com
Website: www.cosmic-usa.com
System programming, database analysis, design, dev & admin, documentation & content mgmt, software analysis & design, system analysis & architecture, systems integration, interface design & dev, ERP/CRM implementations. (As-Ind, estab 1999, empl 15, sales $950,000, cert: State)

5148 Crave InfoTech LLC
15 Corporate Place S Ste 104
Piscataway, NJ 08854
Contact: President
Tel: 253-310-5371
Email: shrikant@craveinfotech.com
Website: www.craveinfotech.com
Global software and technology services. (Minority, Woman, estab 2007, empl 75, sales $2,439,000, cert: State, NMSDC, CPUC, WBENC)

5149 Crescens Inc.
1200 Route 22 East, Ste 2000-2176
Bridgewater, NJ 08807
Contact: Sophia Samuel President
Tel: 732-305-2858
Email: supplier@crescensinc.com
Website: www.crescensinc.com
IT consulting, application development, maintenance, product engineering services, testing, business intelligence, packaged applications & staffing. (Minority, Woman, estab 2002, empl 25, sales $550,000, cert: State, NMSDC)

5150 Crystal Data LLC
1 Eves Dr Ste 145
Marlton, NJ 08053
Contact: CEO
Tel: 732-766-9292
Email: info@crystaldatasystems.net
Website: www.crystaldatasystems.net
IT Staffing & Services. (Minority, Woman, estab 2008, empl 40, sales $3,009,933, cert: State, City, WBENC)

5151 Cyber Security Consulting Ops
309 Fellowship Rd, East Gate Center, Ste 200
Mt. Laurel, NJ 08054
Contact: Tony Wittock Dir/CTO
Tel: 888-588-9951
Email: tonyw@cybersecurityconsultingops.com
Website: www.cybersecurityconsultingops.com/
Hardware and software security services. (AA, estab 2017, empl 5, sales , cert: NMSDC)

5152 cyberThink, Inc.
685 Route 202/206 Ste 101
Bridgewater, NJ 08807
Contact: Raj Thind Dir
Tel: 908-429-8008
Email: rajveer.thind@cyberthink.com
Website: www.cyberthink.com
IT auditing & assessment, project mgmt, app devel & integration, infrastructure architecture & deployment, database modeling, data warehousing, business intelligence, quality assurance, ebusiness, collaboration & knowledge mgmt, network & sys admin. (Minority, estab 1996, empl 407, sales $42,800,000, cert: State, NMSDC)

5153 Cygnus Professionals Inc.
3490 US Hwy # 1,
Princeton, NJ 08540
Contact: Gurudas Sarkar CEO
Tel: 732-423-1785
Email: gurudas@cygnuspro.com
Website: www.cygnuspro.com
Business-IT transformation solutions and consulting. (As-Pac, estab 2010, empl 250, sales $25,000,000, cert: State)

5154 Databased Solutions Inc.
1200 Route 22 E Ste 2000
Bridgewater, NJ 08807
Contact: Ila Choudhary President
Tel: 732-309-0872
Email: ila.choudhary@dbsiservices.com
Website: www.dbsiservices.com
IT svcs, staffing augmentation, IT products. (As-Ind, estab 1995, empl 50, sales $4,400,000, cert: NMSDC)

INFORMATION TECHNOLOGY: Services

5155 DataEdge Consulting, Inc.
101 Morgan Ln Ste 203B
Plainsboro, NJ 08536
Contact: Siva N Kolli VP Operations
Tel: 609-275-4500
Email: Shiv@DataEdgeConsulting.com
Website: www.DataEdgeConsulting.com
Provide broad-based ERP, Web technology and management consulting services. (As-Ind, estab 2007, empl 30, sales $4,000,000, cert: NMSDC)

5156 Datanomics, Inc.
991 US Hwy 22 West Ste 201
Bridgewater, NJ 08807
Contact: Lori Vail CEO
Tel: 908-707-8200
Email: vail@datanomics.com
Website: www.datanomics.com
IT staffing, helpdesk, desktop support, administration, technical writers, validation specialists, business/systems analysts, programmers, mainframe, client/server, & web. (Woman, estab 1982, empl 100, sales , cert: State)

5157 Diverse Lynx LLC
300 Alexander Park, Ste 200
Princeton, NJ 08540
Contact: Hemanth Durvasula Sr Business Dev Mgr
Tel: 732-452-1006
Email: hemanth@diverselynx.com
Website: www.diverselynx.com
Information technology staffing services. (Woman/As-Ind, estab 2002, empl 100, sales $18,000,000, cert: WBENC)

5158 Element Technologies Corporation
1100 Cornwall Rd Ste 113
Monmouth Junction, NJ 08852
Contact: Shirish Sharma CEO
Tel: 973-495-6965
Email: skashyap@elementtechnologies.com
Website: www.elementtechnologies.net/
Domain Competency, Global presence, Cost effective Delivery Model. (As-Ind, estab 2001, empl 300, sales $11,000,000, cert: State, NMSDC)

5159 EmployVision, Inc.
1100 Cornwall Road Ste 115
Monmouth Junction, NJ 08854
Contact: Ash Geria Managing Dir
Tel: 732-422-7100
Email: ash@emplolyvision.com
Website: www.employvision.com
Information technology, recruitment, RPO, IT consulting, staffing. (Minority, Woman, estab 2005, empl 10, sales $3,445,280, cert: NMSDC)

5160 Enin Systems, Inc.
666 Plainsboro Rd
Plainsboro, NJ 08536
Contact: Raj Vendra VP
Tel: 615-710-8582
Email: su@eninsystems.com
Website: www.eninsystems.com/
IT Services, Consulting and Business Solutions. (Woman/As-Pac, estab 2019, empl 60, sales , cert: State, NMSDC, WBENC)

5161 eTeam, Inc.
1001 Durham Ave Ste 201
South Plainfield, NJ 07080
Contact: Ann Thakur Dir Strategic Accounts
Tel: 732-248-1900
Email: rfp@eteaminc.com
Website: www.eteaminc.com
IT, Business Consulting, Management Consulting. (Minority, estab 1999, empl 1300, sales $93,586,862, cert: State, NMSDC, CPUC)

5162 Evergreen Technologies, LLC
2050 Route 27 Ste 202
North Brunswick, NJ 08902
Contact: Elan Kling Sr Acct Mgr
Tel: 732-422-1500
Email: elank@evergreentechnologies.com
Website: www.evergreentechnologies.com
Provides top-notch IT talent with a depth of knowledge in the latest cutting-edge technologies. (Minority, Woman, estab 1998, empl 80, sales $3,154,475, cert: State, NMSDC, WBENC)

5163 Excelgens, Inc.
5 East Main St Ste 6B
Denville, NJ 07834
Contact: Pankaj Sharda CEO
Tel: 973-943-1739
Email: pankaj@excelgens.com
Website: www.excelgens.com
Information technology solutions & services. (Woman/As-Pac, estab 2011, empl 430, sales $19,355,458, cert: NMSDC, WBENC)

5164 ExterNetworks Inc.
10 Corporate Place S, Ste 1-05
Piscataway, NJ 08854
Contact: Abdul Moiz Sr Dir
Tel: 908-751-0875
Email: mmoiz@externetworks.com
Website: www.externetworks.com
Staff augmentation, IT professional services, managed services. (Minority, Woman, estab 2001, empl 205, sales $20,000,000, cert: CPUC, WBENC)

5165 Fabergent, Inc.
63 Ramapo Valley Rd, Ste 214
Mahwah, NJ 07430
Contact: Ratna Silpa Gorantla President
Tel: 201-378-0036
Email: ratna@fabergent.com
Website: www.fabergent.com
Contract & full-time positions IT staffing in Java, .Net, SharePoint, SAP, Oracle, BI, Analytics, networking & IT security. (Minority, Woman, estab 2005, empl 125, sales , cert: State)

5166 Fortidm Technologies LLC
103 Carnegie Center Ste 300
Princeton, NJ 08540
Contact: Hariram Hari President
Tel: 609-851-7190
Email: chari@fortidm.com
Website: www.fortidm.com
IT Program management, information security advisory, identity & access management, secured SDLC, vulnerability management services. (Woman/As-Ind, estab 2005, empl 9, sales $900,000, cert: State, City, 8(a), SDB)

INFORMATION TECHNOLOGY: Services

5167 Fourth Technologies Inc.
      1816 Springdale Road
      Cherry Hill, NJ 08003
      Contact: Ravi Shankar CEO
      Tel: 856-751-4848
      Email: ravi@fortek.com
      Website: www.fortek.com
IT Solutions & Staffing; Customized, cost-effective, reliable solutions; SEI-CMM assessed & quality conscious; Resource Management Group. (As-Ind, estab 1987, empl 200, sales $ 0, cert: NMSDC)

5168 Futran Solutions Inc.
      2025 Lincoln Hwy STE 110, Edison, NJ 08817 Ste 110
      Edison, NJ 08817
      Contact: Jyoti Vazirani President
      Tel: 908-279-3112
      Email: apankaj@futransolutions.com
      Website: www.futransolutions.com
IT services, information technology services. (Minority, estab 2010, empl 150, sales $7,000,000, cert: State, NMSDC)

5169 FYI Systems Inc.
      3799 Route 46 E
      Parsippany, NJ 07054
      Contact: Mindy Zaziski
      Tel: 973-909-0390
      Email: colleen.luzaj@fyisolutions.com
      Website: www.fyisolutions.com
IT solutions: corporate performance mgmt, business intelligence, analytics, data warehousing, web dev, systems integration, project mgmt, applications support, testing, etc. (Woman, estab 1984, empl 100, sales $14,500,000, cert: WBENC)

5170 Global IT Solutions, Inc.
      200 Centennial Ave Ste 200
      Middlesex, NJ 08846
      Contact: William Moore President
      Tel: 732-667-3578
      Email: info@globalitsolutionscorp.com
      Website: www.globalitsolutionscorp.com
Software development life cycle. (AA, estab 2008, empl 2, sales , cert: State, NMSDC)

5171 Globalnest LLC
      281 State Route 79, Ste 208
      Morganville, NJ 07751
      Contact: Durga P Mikkilineni Partner
      Tel: 732-333-1901
      Email: durgam@globalnest.com
      Website: www.globalnest.com
IT staffing, software development & design. (Minority, estab 2005, empl 170, sales $12,000,000, cert: NMSDC, CPUC)

5172 Government Systems Technologies, Inc.
      3159 Schrader Rd
      Dover, NJ 07801
      Contact: Prashanth Kalnad Mgr Finance & Contracts
      Tel: 973-361-2627
      Email: accounting@gstiusa.com
      Website: www.gstiusa.com
Consulting services, software products, full service SAP implementations & offshore development and support. (Woman/As-Ind, estab 2002, empl 46, sales $16,367,405, cert: NMSDC)

5173 Hired by Matrix, Inc.
      266 Harristwon Rd Ste 202
      Rochelle Park, NJ 07452
      Contact: Jennifer Catanese Supplier Diversity & Business Devel
      Tel: 201-587-0777
      Email: jcatanese@hiredbymatrix.com
      Website: www.hiredbymatrix.com
IT consulting svcs & permanent placements. (Woman, estab 1986, empl 275, sales $23,000,000, cert: WBENC)

5174 iii Technologies Inc.
      100 Horizon Center Blvd, Ste 100
      Hamilton, NJ 08691
      Contact: Deepak Mandrekar President
      Tel: 609-901-8000
      Email: drman@iiitech.com
      Website: www.iiitech.com
IT & SAP transformation projects, SAP program management, project management, architecture & implementation consulting. (As-Ind, estab 2005, empl 1, sales $150,000, cert: State, NMSDC)

5175 InfoQuest Consulting Group Inc.
      68 Culver Road Ste 106
      Monmouth Junction, NJ 08852
      Contact: Vinita Lobo Business Mgr
      Tel: 609-409-5151
      Email: vinita@infoquestgroup.com
      Website: www.infoquestgroup.com
IT contract staffing: ERP, CRM, business intelligence, infrastructure management, industry verticals. (Minority, Woman, estab 1994, empl 40, sales $4,000,000, cert: NMSDC)

5176 Inforeem
      One Quality Pl
      Edison, NJ 08820
      Contact: Bhal Deshpande CEO
      Tel: 732-494-4100
      Email: bhal@inforeem.com
      Website: www.inforeem.com
IT consulting services. (As-Pac, estab 2004, empl 40, sales $3,000,000, cert: State)

5177 Innospire Systems Corporation
      281 State Route 79
      Morganville, NJ 07751
      Contact: Raj Durai President
      Tel: 732-858-1740
      Email: vrm@innospire.com
      Website: www.innospire.com
IT consulting, custom application development & advanced analytics solutions, Predictive Analytics, Enterprise Performance Management, Mobile & Custom Application development. (As-Ind, estab 1996, empl 5, sales $355,480, cert: NMSDC)

5178 Instaknow.com, Inc.
      180 Talmadge Rd, Ste 32
      Edison, NJ 08817
      Contact: Paul Khandekar CEO
      Tel: 908-650-9598
      Email: pkhandekar@instaknow.com
      Website: www.instaknow.com
Artificial Intelligence software solutions. (As-Ind, estab 1999, empl 3, sales $293,478, cert: NMSDC, CPUC)

5179 Integration International Inc.
1081 Parsippany Blvd, Ste#101
Parsippany, NJ 07054
Contact: Rahul Chitte
Tel: 973-796-2300
Email: rahul.chitte@i3intl.com
Website: www.i3intl.com
IT infrastructure planning & implementation, software dev, ERP design & deployment, offshore software development & network monitoring. (Minority, estab 2000, empl 400, sales $23,000,000, cert: NMSDC)

5180 Intellyk Inc.
15 Corporate Place S Ste 450
Piscataway, NJ 08854
Contact: Vineet Kumar CEO
Tel: 732-399-9510
Email: vineet@intellyk.com
Website: www.intellyk.com/
IT consulting and technology professional services. (As-Pac, estab 2007, empl 200, sales $13,000,000, cert: State, NMSDC)

5181 International Digital Systems
400 Kelby St, 6th Fl
Fort Lee, NJ 07024
Contact: Anthony Han CEO
Tel: 201-983-7700
Email: ahan@idigitalsystems.com
Website: www.idigitalsystems.com
Server, Network management, Helpdesk, Desktop Support. Microsoft .Net C# based system development. Data Cabling, Data Center build up, SAN, NAS, Server & Network Hardware Resell. (As-Pac, estab 2005, empl 20, sales $1,883,584, cert: State)

5182 International Technology Solutions, Inc.
2000 Cornwall Road Ste 220
Monmouth Junction, NJ 08852
Contact: Brian Armstrong Dir Business Dev
Tel: 732-754-7019
Email: brian@itcsolutions.com
Website: www.itcsolutions.com
Information technology consulting & software development services. (Minority, estab 1998, empl 165, sales $ 0, cert: NMSDC)

5183 Intuity Technologies, LLC
One Gateway Center Ste 2600
Newark, NJ 07102
Contact: Max Bhavnani VP Operations
Tel: 201-880-0774
Email: mbhavnani@intuitytech.com
Website: www.intuitytech.com
IT Services, Oracle Hyperion tool-set (Essbase, Planning, HFM, DRM/MDM Financial Reporting) & Oracle Business Intelligence (OBIEE, Staff Augmentation, Implementations, Infrastructure, Performance Tuning. (As-Ind, estab 2005, empl 12, sales $1,100,000, cert: State)

5184 iQuanti, Inc.
111 Town Square Place Ste 710
Jersey City, NJ 07310
Contact: Vish Sastry CEO
Tel: 718-223-3403
Email: supplier@iquanti.com
Website: www.iquanti.com/
Web analytics, web development, web design, online marketing, search engine optimization, pay per click. (As-Ind, estab 2008, empl 205, sales $5,867,132, cert: NMSDC)

5185 Iris Software Inc.
200 Metroplex Dr, Ste 300
Edison, NJ 08817
Contact: Jonathan Fabros Dir
Tel: 732-393-0034
Email: jfabros@irissoftinc.com
Website: www.irissoftware.com
Information technology services. (Minority, estab 1994, empl 200, sales $180,000,000, cert: NMSDC)

5186 ISES, Inc
372 Rte 22 West
Whitehouse Station, NJ 08889
Contact: Kathleen Sullivan Dir
Tel: 800-447-4737
Email: ksullivan@isesincorporated.com
Website: www.isesincorporated.com
IT consulting: esolutions & ecommerce, B2B, knowledge mgmt, customer relationship mgmt, application dev & support, database dev & admin, data warehousing, telecommunications. (Woman, estab 1980, empl 142, sales $20,000,000, cert: WBENC)

5187 IT by Design
120 Wood Ave S Ste 608
Iselin, NJ 08830
Contact: Kam Attwal CEO
Tel: 646-380-0688
Email: kkaila@itbd.net
Website: www.itbd.net
Infrastructure management, virtualization/cloud computing, data center hosting, managed backups, implementations/migrations & 24x7x365 Live Help Desk. (Woman/As-Ind, estab 2003, empl 100, sales $3,000,000, cert: WBENC)

5188 IT Staffing, Inc.
5 Bliss Court Ste 200
Woodcliff Lake, NJ 07677
Contact: Jerry G. Myers Dir Business Dev
Tel: 201-505-0493
Email: jerry.myers@itstaffinc.com
Website: www.itstaffinc.com
Strategic contract sourcing, consulting, staff augmentation, managed teams & outsourcing. (Minority, Woman, estab 1998, empl 78, sales $11,500,000, cert: State)

5189 IT Trailblazers
2050 Route 27, Ste 203
North Brunswick, NJ 08902
Contact: Chris Jones Business Head
Tel: 732-227-1772
Email: chris@ittblazers.com
Website: www.ittblazers.com
Information Technology Consulting, onsite and offshore capabilities. (As-Ind, estab 1999, empl 100, sales $37,000,000, cert: State)

5190 ITM Information & Technology Management
6 Kilmer Rd
Edison, NJ 08817
Contact: Jeffrey Snow Business Devel Mgr
Tel: 732-339-9801
Email: jeffs@itmsys.com
Website: www.itmsys.com
Computer consulting, applications development, QA, infrastructure support, SAP implimentation, database administration, maintenance & support, data warehousing, technical support. (Minority, Woman, estab 1989, empl 40, sales $2,750,000, cert: State, NMSDC)

INFORMATION TECHNOLOGY: Services

5191 Kamptos Technologies, LLC
88 Dellwood Rd
Edison, NJ 08820
Contact: Vijaya Kodali Owner
Tel: 848-250-5062
Email: ramesh@kamptos.com
Website: www.kamptos.com
IT Resources and SAP, IT support services, IT Staffing. (As-Ind, estab 2011, empl 5, sales $900,000, cert: NMSDC, 8(a))

5192 Kavayah Solutions Inc.
5 Independence Way, Ste 360
Princeton, NJ 08540
Contact: Vivek Casula Principal
Tel: 609-919-9797
Email: vivek.casula@kavayahsolutions.com
Website: www.kavayahsolutions.com
Enterprise application management (development and maintenance) & project management services, technology solutions, staff augmentation. (As-Ind, estab 2006, empl 10, sales $1,224,316, cert: State)

5193 LexHarbor, LLC
1974 State Route 27
Edison, NJ 08817
Contact: Akshat Tewary Dir
Tel: 626-427-2674
Email: info@lexharbor.com
Website: www.lexharbor.com
Information technology services. (As-Ind, estab 2007, empl 2, sales $100,000, cert: NMSDC)

5194 Link2consult, Inc.
1 Bridge Plaza Ste 275
Fort Lee, NJ 07024
Contact: Peter McCree President
Tel: 201-308-9101
Email: peter.mccree@link2consult.com
Website: www.link2consult.com
Information technology consulting: PeopleSoft, human resources & finance solutions. (AA, estab 1992, empl 35, sales $5,800,000, cert: State, NMSDC, CPUC)

5195 Logistic Solutions Inc.
216 Stelton Rd Ste 2
Piscataway, NJ 08854
Contact: Al Limaye President
Tel: 732-743-2300
Email: al.limaye@logistic-solutions.com
Website: www.logistic-solutions.com
Information technologies, Mobile (iPhone, Android, Blackberry/RIM) content aggregation services. (As-Pac, estab 1990, empl 715, sales $140,000,000, cert: NMSDC)

5196 Maestro Technologies, Inc.
510 Thornall St Ste 375
Edison, NJ 08837
Contact: Kamal Bathla Managing Dir
Tel: 908-458-8600
Email: kamal.s.bathla@maestro.com
Website: www.maestro.com
Actuarial Sciences, Big Data & Technologies, Data Science, IT Services. (Woman/As-Ind, estab 2003, empl 63, sales $6,800,000, cert: State, City, NMSDC)

5197 Makro Technologies, Inc.
One Washington Park, Ste 1303
Newark, NJ 07102
Contact: Pritesh Dholakia Business Devel
Tel: 973-481-0100
Email: pritesh.dholakia@makrocare.com
Website: www.makrocare.com
Information technology, IT staffing services. (As-Ind, estab 1996, empl 650, sales $45,000,000, cert: State)

5198 Marlabs Inc.
One Corporate Place S
Piscataway, NJ 08854
Contact: Danielle Jennings Assoc Business Dev Mgr
Tel: 732-694-1000
Email: danielle.jennings@marlabs.com
Website: www.marlabs.com
Information technology services & solutions: IT strategy consulting, resources & staff augmentation, application dev, business intelligence solutions, SAP & Oracle, ERP/CRM systems, data warehousing. (As-Pac, estab 1996, empl 2100, sales $92,000,000, cert: NMSDC)

5199 MARVEL INFOTECH Inc.
45 Knightsbridge Rd Ste 101
Piscataway, NJ 08854
Contact: Venkat Sales
Tel: 732-906-0444
Email: vbokka@marvelinfotech.com
Website: www.marvelinfotech.com
Information technology staffing, consulting. (As-Pac, estab 2000, empl 25, sales $1,850,000, cert: NMSDC)

5200 MashPoint, LLC
100 Wood Ave S Ste 109
Iselin, NJ 08830
Contact: KJ Saini President
Tel: 732-515-7171
Email: kjsaini@mashpoint.com
Website: www.mashpoint.com
Staffing services, data management, data quality, data security, business intelligence, web & mobile development & internet marketing services. (As-Ind, estab 2011, empl 55, sales , cert: NMSDC)

5201 Masterex Technologies, Inc.
379 Princeton-Hightstown Rd, Bldg 2
Cranbury, NJ 08512
Contact: Sunny Gupta Business Devel Mgr
Tel: 302-632-9532
Email: info@masterexinc.com
Website: www.Masterexinc.com
IT staffing, application development, project management, framework, on-shore & offshore testing & QA services. (Woman/As-Ind, estab 2002, empl 60, sales $5,000,000, cert: State)

5202 Mercury Systems, Inc.
5 Independence Way Ste 140
Princeton, NJ 08540
Contact: Wing Li Administrative Mgr, VP
Tel: 609-937-2801
Email: wli@mercurysystemsinc.com
Website: www.mercurysystemsinc.com
Consulting, IT Staffing & IT Placement services. (As-Pac, estab 1999, empl 170, sales $10,000,000, cert: State)

INFORMATION TECHNOLOGY: Services

5203   microMEDIA Imaging Systems, Inc.
       300-2 Route 17 South, Ste 4
       Lodi, NJ 07644
       Contact: Joseph Wise President
       Tel: 973-685-5164
       Email: jwise@imagingservices.com
       Website: www.imagingservices.com
Document conversion & scanning services, Data Capture, Data Migration, Document Hosting. (Woman, estab 1993, empl 85, sales $3,200,000, cert: State, City)

5204   Millennium Info Tech. Inc.
       101 Morgan Lane Ste 204
       Plainsboro, NJ 08536
       Contact: Ramana Krosuri President
       Tel: 609-750-7120
       Email: ramana@mitiweb.com
       Website: www.mitiweb.com
Application Development, Business Analysis/Project Management, Business Intelligence, Data/Database Management, Document Management, ERP, ETL, Information Security/Compliance, Migration Services. (As-Ind, estab 1999, empl 150, sales $9,500,000, cert: State)

5205   Mindlance, Inc.
       1095 Morris Ave
       Union, NJ 07083
       Contact: Vik Kalra Co-Founder & Managing Dir
       Tel: 201-386-5400
       Email: cws@mindlance.com
       Website: www.mindlance.com
IT contigent staffing, offshore recruitment, IT permanent placement, software, semiconductor, finance & insurance. (As-Ind, estab 1999, empl 5000, sales $300,000,000, cert: NMSDC)

5206   MKI Group, LLC dba IS3 Solutions
       740 Broad St Ste 1
       Shrewsbury, NJ 07702
       Contact: John Marshall President
       Tel: 732-945-0403
       Email: sraffetto@is3sol.com
       Website: www.is3sol.com
Information technology solutions, Services & Staffing programs. (AA, estab 2010, empl 220, sales , cert: NMSDC)

5207   Momento USA LLC
       440 Benigno Blvd Unit A, 2nd Fl
       Bellmawr, NJ 08031
       Contact: Hasheem Himmati Dir
       Tel: 856-432-4774
       Email: info@momentousa.com
       Website: www.momentousa.com
Project Management, Application Development, Business Analysis, Systems Analysis, System Design, ERP, Database Administration, Systems Engineering, Systems Maintenance, Systems Testing, Systems Architecture, Systems Administration. (As-Pac, estab 2009, empl 28, sales $2,128,413, cert: NMSDC)

5208   MSquare Systems Inc.
       35 Journal Sq, Ste 415
       Jersey City, NJ 07306
       Contact: Muthu Natarajan President
       Tel: 201-290-6728
       Email: info@msquaresystems.com
       Website: www.msquaresystems.com
IT consulting services. (As-Pac, estab 2005, empl 5, sales $403,967, cert: NMSDC)

5209   Mutex Systems Inc.
       50 Cragwood Rd Ste 224
       South Plainfield, NJ 07080
       Contact: Bill Scharnikow BDM
       Tel: 908-822-8515
       Email: bill.scharnikow@mutexsystems.com
       Website: www.mutexsystems.com
IT staff augmentation & consulting services. (Minority, Woman, estab 1999, empl 100, sales $10,000,000, cert: State)

5210   NatSoft Corporation
       27 Worlds Fair Dr
       Somerset, NJ 08873
       Contact: Rakesh Kotha Business Devel Mgr
       Tel: 732-939-2969
       Email: rakeshkv@natsoft.us
       Website: www.natsoft.us
Software development, IT consulting, Enterprise application development, ERP implementation & support, Quality assurance services on offshore/Onsite/Nearshore model. (As-Pac, estab 2004, empl 300, sales , cert: State)

5211   NCS Technologies, Inc.
       15 Corporate Place S Ste 200
       Piscataway, NJ 08854
       Contact: Michael Giannotti Sales
       Tel: 732-562-8880
       Email: mgiannotti@ncstech.com
       Website: www.ncstech.com
Data warehousing, business intelligence, enterprise architecture, process engineering & enterprise security. (Hisp, estab 1984, empl 155, sales $29,000,000, cert: NMSDC)

5212   Neo Tech Solutions, Inc.
       1 Cragwood Rd Ste 301
       South Plainfield, NJ 07080
       Contact: CEO
       Tel: 917-385-8717
       Email: info@neotechusa.com
       Website: www.neotechusa.com
IT, telecommunications, program & project management: ASP.NET, ASP, HTML, DHTML, VBScript, JavaScript, SOAP, ADO.NET, ActiveX, ADO, RDO, DAO, MTS, ODBC, OLEDB, MSOffice, MS-Visual Source Safe, VB.NET, C#, C++, Cobol, VB 6.0,XML, XSLT, SQL. (As-Ind, estab 1996, empl 63, sales , cert: NMSDC)

5213   Neotecra, Inc.
       200 Craig Rd Ste 109
       Manalapan, NJ 07726
       Contact: Nirmal Goswamy VP
       Tel: 212-693-3353
       Email: nirmal@neotecra.com
       Website: www.neotecra.com
IT staffing & consulting, data communication, system programming & administration, client-server application development. (Minority, Woman, estab 2000, empl 90, sales $4,020,000, cert: State)

INFORMATION TECHNOLOGY: Services

5214 NetTarius Technology Solutions, LLC
35 College Dr
East Orange, NJ 07017
Contact: Derrick Law President
Tel: 973-788-1955
Email: sdiversity@nettarius.net
Website: www.nettarius.com
Business Strategy, Technology Design & Integration, Fiber Wireless Broadband, Data Network, Video Technology, Web & Application Development, Cloud Services, Installation & Support. (AA, estab 2003, empl 5, sales $300,000, cert: NMSDC)

5215 New Instruction, LLC
615 Valley Rd
Upper Montclair, NJ 07043
Contact: Dir of Training
Tel: 973-744-3339
Email: training@newinstruction.com
Website: www.newinstruction.com/
Instructor-led technology training: systems & software engineering, project management, programming languages, internet security, telecommunications & networking, management & leadership skills. (Woman, estab 1978, empl 4, sales $1,000,000, cert: WBENC)

5216 NewAgeSys, Inc.
4390 US Hwy 1
Princeton, NJ 08540
Contact: Gintu Mary Eapen Business Devel Mgr
Tel: 609-919-9800
Email: contact@newagesys.com
Website: www.newagesys.com
Validation & quality mgmt svcs, custom application devel, SAP upgrade & support svcs, information security, infrastructure services. (Woman/As-Ind, estab 1994, empl 285, sales $21,000,000, cert: NMSDC, WBENC)

5217 NexAge Technologies USA Inc.
75 Lincoln Hwy Ste 104
Iselin, NJ 08830
Contact: Suresh Kumar CEO
Tel: 732-494-4944
Email: minoritymanager@nexageusa.com
Website: www.nexageusa.com
IT staffing & consulting, software applications. (As-Pac, estab 2001, empl 65, sales $ 0, cert: State, NMSDC)

5218 NIKSUN Inc.
100 Nassau Park Blvd 3rd Fl
Princeton, NJ 08540
Contact: Christopher Dervishian VP Operations
Tel: 609-936-9999
Email: cdervish@niksun.com
Website: www.niksun.com
Develop real time & forensics-based cybersecurity, network performance management & mobility solutions. (As-Ind, estab 1997, empl 175, sales , cert: NMSDC)

5219 NPD Global Inc.
3 Lincoln Hwy Ste 102
Edison, NJ 07018
Contact: Nagesh Davuluri President
Tel: 732-902-6342
Email: ndavuluri@npdglobal.com
Website: www.npdglobal.com
IT staffing & recruiting services. (Nat Ame, estab 2006, empl 30, sales $6,000,000, cert: NMSDC)

5220 Optima Global Solutions, Inc.
3113 Princeton Pike Bldg. 3, Ste 207
Lawrenceville, NJ 08648
Contact: Rajesh Sinha Federal Business Specialist
Tel: 609-586-8811
Email: rajesh@optimags.com
Website: www.optimags.com
IT staffing, BPM, Data Warehousing, Business Intelligence, Microsoft & Enterprise Mobility. (As-Ind, estab 2001, empl 10, sales $3,186,483, cert: NMSDC, 8(a))

5221 PamTen Inc.
5 Independence Way, Ste # 180
Princeton, NJ 08540
Contact: Satish Kommareddy Acct Mgr
Tel: 609-643-4228
Email: satish.kommareddy@pamten.com
Website: www.pamten.com
IT Strategy, Planning, Program/Project Management, Business Process Management. (Woman/As-Ind, estab 2002, empl 160, sales $13,500,000, cert: State, City, NMSDC)

5222 Paxton Consultants Limited Liability Company
50 Brandywine Rise
Green Brook, NJ 08812
Contact: Anand Emmanuel CEO
Tel: 831-210-8850
Email: anand.emmanuel@paxtonconsultants.com
Website: www.paxtonconsultants.com
Information Technology (IT) Consulting & Staffing Solutions. (As-Ind, estab 2007, empl 2, sales , cert: State)

5223 Peri Software Solutions
570 Broad St
Newark, NJ 07102
Contact: Rosemarie Lederer Sr Acct Mgr
Tel: 973-735-9500
Email: rlederer@perisoftware.com
Website: www.perisoftware.com
Open source solutions, IT staff augmentation, offshore business outsourcing, custom application development. (Minority, Woman, estab 1999, empl 700, sales $12,631,398, cert: NMSDC)

5224 Pioneer Data Systems, Inc.
379 Thornall St
Edison, NJ 08837
Contact: Naushad Mulji Dir
Tel: 732-603-0001
Email: nmulji@pioneerdata.com
Website: www.pioneerdata.com
Client-server, e-business, data warehousing, CRM & ERP. (As-Ind, estab 1995, empl 100, sales $5,000,000, cert: NMSDC)

5225 Platys Group
100 Franklin Square Dr
Somerset, NJ 08873
Contact: Darren Cobb VP Business Dev
Tel: 908-888-6007
Email: dcobb@platysgroup.com
Website: www.platygroup.com
IT consulting & software solutions. (Minority, Woman, estab 2008, empl 140, sales $10,000,000, cert: State)

5226   Presafe Technologies, LLC
       PO Box 5872
       Somerset, NJ 08875
       Contact: Robert V Jones CEO
       Tel: 732-887-2442
       Email: rvjones@presafetech.com
       Website: www.presafetech.com
Cybersecurity architecture & design; Secure network planning & design, enterprise system design, network builds, migration upgrades; Data center planning design, consolidation migrations & relocations; network & performance mgmt. (AA, estab 2010, empl 2, sales , cert: State)

5227   Princeton Web Systems Inc.
       1901 N Olden Ave Ext, Ste 8A
       Ewing, NJ 08618
       Contact: Bhavesh Senedhun CEO
       Tel: 888-485-9040
       Email: bhavesh@princetonwebsystems.com
       Website: www.princetonwebsystems.com
Custom software development, software & application development, website design, mobile app development, IT staff augmentation, staffing & networking solutions. (Minority, estab 2014, empl 25, sales $1,000,000, cert: State)

5228   Rang Technologies Inc.
       15 Corporate Place S
       Piscataway, NJ 08854
       Contact: Gary Sacks Sr VP
       Tel: 732-947-4119
       Email: sales@rangtech.com
       Website: www.rangtech.com/
Analytics & Data Science solutions & comprehensive IT staffing services. (As-Ind, estab 2005, empl 474, sales $25,004,426, cert: State, NMSDC)

5229   Rangam Consultants Inc.
       270 Davidson Ave Ste 103
       Somerset, NJ 08873
       Contact: Hetal Parikh President
       Tel: 908-704-8843
       Email: rci@rangam.com
       Website: www.rangam.com
IT staffing & outsourced web application development services. (Minority, Woman, estab 1995, empl 712, sales $42,500,000, cert: State, City, NMSDC, WBENC)

5230   Rapid Response Computer Service Inc.
       2313 Route 33
       Robbinsville, NJ 08691
       Contact: Terry Ikey Owner
       Tel: 609-945-2389
       Email: tikey@rapidresponsecs.com
       Website: www.rapidresponsecs.com
Software development, website design, network installation & support & compuer repair. (Woman, estab 2004, empl 12, sales $750,000, cert: State)

5231   RCI Technologies
       1133 Green St
       Iselin, NJ 08830
       Contact: Gereld Boffa Exec VP
       Tel: 732-382-3000
       Email: gereld@rci-technologies.com
       Website: www.rci-technologies.com
Custom software development & IT staffing, consulting services. (Minority, Woman, estab 1983, empl 63, sales $8,000,000, cert: State, City, WBENC)

5232   Real Soft Inc.
       68 Culver Road Ste 100
       Monmouth Junction, NJ 08852
       Contact: Joel Jerva VP
       Tel: 609-409-3636
       Email: joel@realsoftinc.com
       Website: www.realsoftinc.com
Software development, consulting & staffing, offshore resources, turnkey dev, voice solutions, IVR, VXML. (Minority, estab 1991, empl 450, sales $30,000,000, cert: NMSDC)

5233   RedSalsa Technologies, Inc.
       12 Roszel Rd Ste A-204
       Princeton, NJ 08540
       Contact: Kiran Vallurupalli CEO
       Tel: 609-243-9603
       Email: k_vallurupalli@redsalsa.com
       Website: www.redsalsa.com/
IT consulting services: internet & e-business consulting, system integration, custom application development & application management. (Minority, estab 1993, empl 120, sales $ 0, cert: NMSDC)

5234   Reliant Tech., Inc.
       2137 Route 35 Ste 365
       Holmdel, NJ 07733
       Contact: Subhash Kothari President
       Tel: 732-583-6244
       Email: skothari@relianttech.com
       Website: www.relianttech.com
Application development, technical training, Sun Solaris, HP UX certified. (Minority, estab 1985, empl 30, sales $3,000,000, cert: State)

5235   Revision Technologies Inc.
       10 Station Place, Ste 3
       Metuchen, NJ 08840
       Contact: Raja Balan President
       Tel: 732-261-9239
       Email: raja.balan@revisiontek.com
       Website: www.revisiontek.com
Data Center Design, support, maintenance.Networking, IP and SAN products, Project management, Storage Area Networking architect, planning, implementation, system analysis, Big Data, Cloud implementation & support services. (As-Ind, estab 2006, empl 4, sales $17,792,057, cert: NMSDC)

5236   Samiti Technologies, Inc.
       2 Lincoln Hwy Ste 401
       Edison, NJ 08820
       Contact: Akash Kulshrestha Client Relationship Specialist
       Tel: 732-516-0066
       Email: rfp@samitimail.com
       Website: www.samititechnology.com
Software development & consulting services. (Minority, Woman, estab 2003, empl 70, sales $11,796,921, cert: State, NMSDC)

INFORMATION TECHNOLOGY: Services

5237 Satnam Data Systems, Inc.
      220 Davidson Ave Ste 318
      Somerset, NJ 08873
      Contact: Parita Patel Dir Business Dev
      Tel: 732-961-8383
      Email: parita@satnam.com
      Website: www.satnam.com
Technology Consulting, Professional & Outsourcing services., Staff Augmentation Services, Custom Development Services, Software Integration Services, Custom Solution Services, Business Applications, Database Development. (Minority, Woman, estab 1994, empl 23, sales $6,500,000, cert: State, NMSDC, CPUC)

5238 Scadea Solutions Inc
      100 Franklin Square Dr Ste 304
      Somerset, NJ 08873
      Contact: Sreekanth Akkapalli CEO
      Tel: 609-937-6699
      Email: sreekanth@scadea.net
      Website: www.scadea.net
ERP, Consulting & Outsourcing Services. (Woman/As-Ind, estab 2011, empl 150, sales $9,000,000, cert: WBENC)

5239 Scalable Systems Inc.
      15 Corporate Place S Ste 222
      Piscataway, NJ 08854
      Contact: Suman Bajaj Acct Mgr
      Tel: 732-333-3191
      Email: sumanb@scalable-systems.com
      Website: www.scalable-systems.com
Software consulting, development & IT outsourcing, offshore & onshore software solutions & integration services. (As-Ind, estab 2005, empl 30, sales $3,000,000, cert: State, NMSDC)

5240 Scalar Solutions, LLC.
      330 Changebridge Rd, Ste 101
      Pinebrook, NJ 07058
      Contact: Mariana C Mgr Sales
      Tel: 973-767-3260
      Email: sales@scalarsol.com
      Website: www.scalarsol.com
IT consulting/staffing, end-to-end IT services, Software Development Services (Java, Dot Net Platform), Database & Data warehouse development (SQL Server, Oracle, MPP Systems, Cloud, Hadoop Big data), Database Administration. (As-Ind, estab 2013, empl 2, sales , cert: State)

5241 SEAL Consulting Inc.
      105 Fieldcrest Ave 4th FL, Raritan Plaza 3
      Edison, NJ 08837
      Contact: John Beaumont VP
      Tel: 732-947-4901
      Email: info@sealconsult.com
      Website: www.sealconsult.com/
Systems integration, implementation services & staffing: ERP, APO, SEM, BW and SRM. (As-Ind, estab 1996, empl 400, sales $50,000,000, cert: NMSDC)

5242 Seven Seven Softwares, Inc.
      217 E Main St
      Rockaway, NJ 07866
      Contact: Adela Sering VP / Global HR Dir
      Tel: 973-586-1817
      Email: dsering@77soft.com
      Website: www.77soft.com
Information technology, business process outsourcing & call center services. (Minority, Woman, estab 1996, empl 335, sales $ 0, cert: NMSDC)

5243 Silicon Alley Group, Inc.
      1 Austin Ave. 2nd Fl
      Iselin, NJ 08830
      Contact: Terrance L Sprinkle Business Devel Mgr
      Tel: 732-326-1600
      Email: tsprinkle@sag-inc.com
      Website: www.sag-inc.com
Information technology services & solutions. (Minority, Woman, estab 2003, empl 30, sales $1,901,608, cert: State, 8(a))

5244 Smart Information Management Systems Inc
      103 Morgan Lane
      Plainsboro, NJ 08536
      Contact: Bharath Medisetty Sr Recruitment Exec
      Tel: 609-269-2732
      Email: bharath.medisetty@smartims.com
      Website: www.SmartIMS.com
Information Management Systems, Software Consulting, Recruitment & Staffing, Quality Assurance Testing & Certification, Custom application development services. (Woman/As-Ind, estab 1994, empl 450, sales $23,000,000, cert: State, City, NMSDC)

5245 Smart IT Frame LLC
      220 Davidson Ave Ste 313
      Somerset, NJ 08873
      Contact: Chezhian Krishnamurthy COO
      Tel: 201-201-1243
      Email: Krishna.murthy@smartitframe.com
      Website: www.smartitframe.com
Built in "SMART Intelligent Business Automation Platform" Using RPA / Bots integrated with AI-ML Optical Character Recognition(OCR) and Business Process Management (BPM) to automate diversified Business Process Management use cases across various Industri (Woman/As-Ind, estab 2012, empl 1000, sales $35,000,000, cert: NMSDC, WBENC)

5246 Smart Source Technologies, Inc.
      622 Georges Rd Ste 203
      North Brunswick, NJ 08902
      Contact: Shaan Kelly Acct Rep
      Tel: 732-729-7700
      Email: subcontract@smartsourcetec.com
      Website: www.smartsourcetec.com
IT staffing, application & web development, database administration & development, data warehousing & systems administration, business analyst & project management. (Minority, Woman, estab 1999, empl 52, sales $6,000,000, cert: State)

5247 Software Professional Solutions, Inc.
      1315 Hwy 34 2nd Fl
      Farmingdale, NJ 07727
      Contact: Suzanne Schlesinger President
      Tel: 732-751-8770
      Email:
      Website: www.spshome.com
Custom software solutions: develop & implementation, system upgrades, software conversions & system integrations. (Woman, estab 1995, empl 40, sales $ 0, cert: WBENC)

INFORMATION TECHNOLOGY: Services

5248 Software Synergy, Inc.
151 Hwy 33 E Ste 252
Manalapan, NJ 07726
Contact: Rose Oxley CEO
Tel: 732-617-9300
Email: rmo@ssi-corp.com
Website: www.ssi-corp.com
Information technology: automate key business processes, modernize legacy systems, integrate multi system & technology environments, data translations. (Woman, estab 1990, empl 10, sales $1,500,000, cert: WBENC)

5249 Software Technology, Inc.
100 Overlook Center Ste 200
Princeton, NJ 08540
Contact: Scott Mandel VP Sales
Tel: 609-858-0630
Email: scott.mandel@stiorg.com
Website: www.stiorg.com
IT staffing services. (Minority, Woman, estab 2004, empl 45, sales , cert: NMSDC)

5250 Solutions3 LLC
637 Wyckoff Ave
Wyckoff, NJ 07481
Contact: Dianne McKim Exec Business Admin
Tel: 845-365-0675
Email: dianne.mckim@solutions3llc.com
Website: www.solutions3llc.com
Enterprise Network & Systems Management (architecture and implementation), IT Service Management, Service Desk & associated process definitions (Incident & Problem Management, Change & Configuration Management). (Woman, estab 2003, empl 18, sales $2,707,834, cert: State)

5251 Source One Technical Solutions, LLC
1952 Rte 22 East
Bound Brook, NJ 08805
Contact: Linda Ake President
Tel: 732-748-8643
Email: lake@source1tek.com
Website: www.source1tek.com
Information technology staffing services, consulting & permanent placement. (Woman, estab 2003, empl 56, sales $4,036,000, cert: WBENC)

5252 SPHERE Technology Solutions
525 Washington Blvd. Ste 2635
Jersey City, NJ 07310
Contact: Dir
Tel: 201-659-6204
Email: CHELSEA.WHITE@SPHERECO.COM
Website: www.sphereco.com
Data Governance, Security & Compliance centering on structured & un-structured data. (Woman, estab 2009, empl 22, sales $6,448,680, cert: State, WBENC)

5253 Spruce Technology, Inc.
1149 Blloomfield Ave, Ste G
Clifton, NJ 07012
Contact: Srini Penumella CEO
Tel: 781-413-5527
Email: spenumella@sprucetech.com
Website: www.sprucetech.net
Information technology consulting svcs: systems deployment, server infrastructure, technology deployment, network infrastructure, executive, management & general support. (As-Ind, estab 2006, empl 69, sales $42,000,000, cert: State, NMSDC)

5254 Sunrise Systems, Inc.
105 Fieldcrest Ave, Ste 504
Edison, NJ 08837
Contact: Sandy Baldino Sr Acct Exec
Tel: 732-395-4446
Email: sandy@sunrisesys.com
Website: www.sunrisesys.com
IT systems integration, systems integration. (As-Ind, estab 1990, empl 500, sales $ 0, cert: NMSDC)

5255 Synergem, Inc.
2323 Randolph Ave
Avenel, NJ 07001
Contact: Amy Silverman President
Tel: 732-225-0001
Email: amysilverman@synergem.com
Website: www.synergem.com
Duplicate DVD's, CD's & USBs, custom packaging, custom printing, fulfillment & distribution. (Woman, estab 1985, empl 26, sales $7,344,330, cert: WBENC)

5256 Systemart, LLC
140 Littleton Rd, Ste 303
Parsippany, NJ 07054
Contact: Nitin Shah President
Tel: 973-917-4834
Email: mbe@systemart.com
Website: www.systemart.com
IT related services, custom software dev, business process mgmt svcs. (Woman/As-Ind, estab 1999, empl 75, sales $5,000,000, cert: NMSDC)

5257 SystemGuru,Inc.
900 Rte 9 N Ste 205
Woodbridge, NJ 07095
Contact: Nitin Sohal Business Dev Mgr
Tel: 732-326-3951
Email: nitin.sohal@systemguru.com
Website: www.systemguru.com
Web enabled application development, data modeling & enterprise data architecture, application design & architecture. (As-Pac, estab 2000, empl 100, sales $8,907,001, cert: City)

5258 Technology Concepts Group International, LLC
150 Maple Ave Ste 306
Somerset, NJ 08873
Contact: Elizabeth Shelton Office Mgr
Tel: 732-659-6035
Email: eshelton@technologyconcepts.com
Website: www.technologyconcepts.com
E-business solutions, web design & hosting, systems integration, desktop support. (Woman/AA, estab 2008, empl 7, sales $21,000,000, cert: NMSDC, WBENC)

5259 TechnoSphere, Inc.
21 Addison Rd
Bergenfield, NJ 07621
Contact: Aureo Capiral President
Tel: 201-384-7400
Email: aureo.capiral@technosphere.com
Website: www.technosphere.com
IT staffing, contracting, contract programming svcs. (As-Pac, estab 1994, empl 26, sales $4,171,947, cert: State, NMSDC)

INFORMATION TECHNOLOGY: Services

5260 Technovision, Inc.
10 Stuyvesant Ave
Lyndhurst, NJ 07071
Contact: Anju Aggarwal President
Tel: 732-381-0200
Email: anju@etechnovision.com
Website: www.etechnovision.com
IT Consulting. (Woman/As-Ind, estab 1995, empl 35, sales $3,000,000, cert: State, WBENC)

5261 The Sourcium Group
833 Blanch Ave
Norwood, NJ 07648
Contact: Gabriella Lombardi CEO
Tel: 201-447-1777
Email: gabriella.lombardi@sourcium.net
Website: www.sourcium.net
IT procurement, project management, desktop svcs, staff augmentation. (Woman, estab 2002, empl 12, sales $ 0, cert: WBENC)

5262 Triveni Group LLP
71 Union Ave, Ste 208
Rutherford, NJ 07070
Contact: Jwalit Shah CEO
Tel: 307-203-3888
Email: Pratap.singh@triveniconsulting.com
Website: www.triveniit.com
Full-service software consulting. (As-Pac, estab 2011, empl 55, sales , cert: NMSDC)

5263 Twintron Data Systems Inc.
26 Woodbrook Rd
Voorhees, NJ 08043
Contact: Dayal Nagasuru President
Tel: 856-952-8506
Email: dayal.nagasuru@twintron.com
Website: www.twintron.com
IT services (Java, C++, SQL, Big Data, .NET, Web Applications). (As-Ind, estab 2004, empl 5, sales $500,000, cert: NMSDC)

5264 Urooj LLC
301 Route 17N Ste 800
Rutherford, NJ 07070
Contact: Salman Mohammed CEO
Tel: 201-966-7861
Email: salman@urooj.net
Website: www.urooj.net
IT solutions, IT staffing, project architecture, design & analysis, project administration & management, web paradigm, e-commerce & web applications, networking & system administration, RF engineering, database admin & management. (As-Ind, estab , empl , sales $2,154,929, cert: City, NMSDC)

5265 US Tech Solutions, Inc.
10 Exchange Place
Jersey City, NJ 07302
Contact: Michelle Vanetti Legal/Compliance Mgr
Tel: 201-719-9953
Email: Michelle@ustechsolutions.com
Website: www.ustechsolutions.com
IT solutions: consulting, outsourcing, software development, engineering, systems integration, ERP, customer relationship management, supply chain mngt, product development, & electronic commerce. (As-Ind, estab 2000, empl 11500, sales $530,000,000, cert: NMSDC)

5266 V Group Inc.
379 Princeton Hightstown Road Bldg 3, Ste 2A, Cranbury, NJ 08512
Contact: Monika Rohila CEO
Tel: 609-371-5400
Email: certifications@vgroupinc.com
Website: www.vgroupinc.com/
Software development consulting, networking, database admin, systems admin. (Minority, Woman, estab 1999, empl 35, sales $6,256,810, cert: WBENC)

5267 Vedicsoft Solutions Inc.
100 Wood Ave, Ste 200
Iselin, NJ 08830
Contact: Sam Vaghela Strategic Business Alliance Mgr
Tel: 732-906-3200
Email: sam@vedicsoft.com
Website: www.vedicsoft.com
IT technologies: ERP, data warehousing, web & client/server technologies. (As-Ind, estab 1999, empl 300, sales $54,000,000, cert: NMSDC)

5268 Vega Consulting Solutions, Inc.
3 Romaine Rd
Mountain Lakes, NJ 07046
Contact: Carol Jones Dir Business Dev
Tel: 973-335-7800
Email: cjones@vegaconsulting.com
Website: www.vegaconsulting.com
Information technology consulting svcs. (Woman, estab 1994, empl 70, sales $ 0, cert: WBENC)

5269 Ventures Unlimited Inc.
309 Fellowship Rd, Ste 200
Mount Laurel, NJ 08054
Contact: Rajesh Varma President
Tel: 201-377-5954
Email: rvarma@vui-inc.com
Website: www.vui-inc.com
IT consulting services: enterprise application services, product life cycle management, business process modeling. (Minority, estab 2004, empl 162, sales $4,500,000, cert: State, NMSDC, 8(a))

5270 Vichara Technologies Inc.
5 Marine View Plaza Ste 312
Hoboken, NJ 07030
Contact: Atul Jain CEO
Tel: 201-850-1912
Email: payables@vichara.com
Website: www.vichara.com
Software development services for financial institutions, banks & asset management firms, hedge funds, private equity firms. (As-Pac, estab 2000, empl 15, sales $7,259,788, cert: NMSDC)

5271 VNB Consulting Services, Inc.
100 Menlo Park Ste 302B
Edison, NJ 08837
Contact: Nirav Shah Dir HR & Finance
Tel: 732-474-0700
Email: info@vnbconsulting.com
Website: www.vnbconsulting.com
IT services, Business Intelligence, Analytics, CRM, Marketing & Application Integration solutions. (As-Ind, estab 2007, empl 25, sales $2,000,000, cert: State)

5272 WisEngineering, LLC
      3159 Schrader Rd
      Dover, NJ 07801
      Contact: Cheryl Hall President
      Tel: 973-783-1000
      Email: chall@wisengineering.com
      Website: www.wisengineering.com
Management information systems, close combat systems, combat ammo systems. (Woman/AA, estab 1998, empl 32, sales $6,338,536, cert: State, NMSDC, WBENC)

5273 XL Impex Inc DBA Atika Technologies
      5 Independence Way Ste 300
      Princeton, NJ 08540
      Contact: Ashish Dua President
      Tel: 732-907-9001
      Email: ash@atikaservices.com
      Website: www.atikatech.com
CRM recruiting, staff augmentation, IT services & Digital Marketing. (As-Pac, estab 2008, empl 22, sales $1,770,777, cert: NMSDC)

5274 Xybion Corporation & Subsidiaries
      105 College Road East
      Princeton, NJ 08540
      Contact: Nagraj Lanka Business Dev Dir
      Tel: 609-512-5790
      Email: nlanka@xybion.com
      Website: www.xybion.com
Compliance/software & services solutions, data migration, data content & compliance management, enterprise asset management, pre-clin/R&D, quality management, validation/software testing & IT consulting services. (As-Ind, estab 1977, empl 33, sales $7,751,400, cert: State, NMSDC)

5275 Z&A Infotek Corporation
      35 Waterview Blvd 2nd Fl
      Parsippany, NJ 07054
      Contact: John Pezzullo EVP
      Tel: 917-751-2299
      Email: johnp@znainc.com
      Website: www.znainc.com
Information technology, consulting & software, ERP & CRM, web enabling applications, RDBMS, project management, network infrastructure tools & management. (As-Ind, estab 2003, empl 90, sales $7,500,000, cert: NMSDC, 8(a))

New Mexico

5276 Westwind Computer Products
      5655 Jefferson St NE, Ste B
      Albuquerque, NM 87109
      Contact: Brigetta Koepke Supplier Diversity AE
      Tel: 505-345-4720
      Email: diversity@wwcpinc.com
      Website: www.wwcpinc.com/
Mobility & End User Computing, Enterprise Storage Solutions, Blade and Rack Server Integration, Large Deployment Rollouts, VDI design and pilots, Cyber Security, Control & Command Solutions, AV Solutions, VOIP / VTC. (Hisp, estab 1992, empl 56, sales $20,000,000, cert: NMSDC)

Nevada

5277 A.R. Acosta, Ltd. dba Alisa Acosta Business Conslt
      18124 Wedge Pkwy
      Reno, NV 89511
      Contact: Alisa Acosta President
      Tel: 702-203-4382
      Email: alisaa@earthlink.net
      Website: www.AlisaAcostaConsulting.com
Business consulting: process reengineering, documentation, process mapping, project management, develop training curriculum & conducting training. (Minority, Woman, estab 1998, empl 1, sales , cert: State, 8(a))

5278 Agilea Solutions, Inc.
      6671 S.Las Vegas Blvd Ste D, Ste 210
      Las Vegas, NV 89119
      Contact: Marce Roth CEO
      Tel: 866-800-1897
      Email: contact@agileasolutions.com
      Website: www.agileasolutions.com
IT consulting firm, systems integration, implement & support enterprise software applications. (Woman/As-Pac, estab 2005, empl 75, sales $14,110,000, cert: NMSDC, WBENC)

5279 American Project Management LLC
      11700 W Charleston Blvd, Ste 170-315
      Las Vegas, NV 89135
      Contact: Jane Lee Managing Partner
      Tel: 702-220-4562
      Email: jlee@apmlasvegas.com
      Website: www.apmlasvegas.com
Project Scheduling & Cost Control, Earned Value Management System (EVMS) Implementation, Computer Programming & Embedded Software Development Services & Staff Augmentation. (Minority, Woman, estab 2003, empl 2, sales , cert: NMSDC, NWBOC)

5280 Blue Fields Digital LLC
      3172 N Rainbow Blvd, Ste 1120
      Las Vegas, NV 89108
      Contact: Akilah Kamaria Data Security Consultant
      Tel: 949-344-2996
      Email: akilahk@bluefieldsdigital.com
      Website: www.bluefieldsdigital.com
Cybersecurity solutions, security risk assessments, third-party risk management, security engineering & cyber security awareness training. (Woman/AA, estab 2015, empl 2, sales , cert: City)

5281 Ingenarius, Inc.
      29 N 28th St, Ste 14E
      Las Vegas, NV 89101
      Contact: Ishmael Thomas President
      Tel: 702-763-1419
      Email: ishmaellthomas@ingenarius.com
      Website: www.solutions.oracle.com/scwar/scr/Partner/SCP
Software product life cycle (SPLC) services & enterprise Java software development services, embedded, mobile, big data & the Internet of Things (IoT), analysis, design, construction, operation, configuration & maintenance. (AA, estab 2013, empl 1, sales , cert: State)

INFORMATION TECHNOLOGY: Services

5282   Intelligent Image Management Inc.
2850 W Horizon Ridge Pkwy Ste 200
Henderson, NV 89052
Contact: Shuvo Rahman VP Business Dev
Tel: 801-906-9517
Email: shuvo@iimdirect.com
Website: www.capturedata.com
Business Process Outsourcing (BPO) & document management, data entry, indexing, data conversion, data mining, call center, post scan processing, back office. (As-Ind, estab 1999, empl 3, sales $5,000,000, cert: NMSDC)

5283   Link Tech, LLC
9505 Hillwood Dr Ste 150
Las Vegas, NV 89134
Contact: Banko SBDE
Tel: 702-233-8703
Email: debbieb@linktechconsulting.com
Website: www.linktechconsulting.com
Information Technology; CAD; Computer Facilities Management Services; Management Consulting Services (Woman, estab 2000, empl 82, sales $15,193,470, cert: WBENC)

5284   OCAA Solutions LLC
170 S Green Valley Pkwy, Ste 300
Henderson, NV 89012
Contact: Foma Odje
Tel: 702-900-2733
Email: odje@ocaasolutions.com
Website: www.ocaasolutions.com
Identity Management Solutions, Single Sign-On Solutions, Custom Software Development, Enterprise Architecture Design, Technical Writing, Remote DBA Services, Business Analysis, Personal GPS Trackers. (AA, estab 2011, empl 3, sales $500,446, cert: NMSDC)

5285   XIOSS, Inc.
4730 S. Fort Apache Rd Ste 300
Las Vegas, NV 89147
Contact: Susie Galyardt Founder, President
Tel: 952-941-4000
Email: susie.galyardt@xioss.com
Website: www.xioss.com
IT storage solutions: data & network architecture, data management, infrastructure management, systems architecture & disaster recovery. (Woman, estab 2008, empl 11, sales $1,100,000, cert: WBENC)

New York

5286   A-1 Technology Inc.
115 Broadway, 13th Fl
New York, NY 10006
Contact: Ishwari Singh President
Tel: 212-397-7481
Email: ishwari.singh@a1technology.biz
Website: www.a1technology.com
Website design, iPhone programming, mobile programming, application development, database, networking, quality assurance. (As-Ind, estab 2001, empl 45, sales $4,500,000, cert: City)

5288   Ask IT Consulting Inc
33 Peachtree St., Ste 100
Holtsville, NY 11742
Contact: Gupta President
Tel: 631-649-1313
Email: manisha.gupta@askitc.com
Website: www.askitc.com
Information technology services. (Woman/As-Ind, estab 2008, empl 10, sales $ 0, cert: State, City, SDB)

5289   ATS Associates LLC
50 Clinton St Ste 205
Hempstead, NY 11550
Contact: Arjun Shah President
Tel: 877-944-3339
Email: arjun.s@atsassociates.net
Website: www.atsassociates.net
Information technology solutions with a specialization in software. (As-Ind, estab , empl 2, sales $1,200,000, cert: City, 8(a), SDB)

5290   Avani Technology Solutions Inc.
687 Lee Road Ste 208
Rochester, NY 14606
Contact: Sameer Penakalapati President
Tel: 585-507-0386
Email: sameer.k@avanitechsolutions.com
Website: www.avanitechsolutions.com
IT Consulting, Software Programming, Application Management, Application Maintenance Outsourcing, IT Staff Augmentation. (As-Ind, estab 2008, empl 325, sales $18,514,969, cert: NMSDC, 8(a))

5291   BruteForce Solutions Inc
545 8th Ave, Ste 540
New York, NY 10018
Contact: Khurshedur Rahman President
Tel: 212-658-0277
Email: info@bruteforcesolution.com
Website: www.bruteforcesolution.com
Staffing & consulting, Information Technology (IT) solutions. (As-Ind, estab 2010, empl 14, sales $1,093,686, cert: State)

5292   Cerami & Associates, Inc.
404 Fifth Ave 8th Fl
New York, NY 10018
Contact: Jennifer Guzman Project Financial Coord
Tel: 212-370-1776
Email: info@ceramiassociates.com
Website: www.ceramiassociates.com
Acoustical, Audiovisual, Information Technology & Security Consulting Services. (Woman, estab , empl , sales $15,400,000, cert: City, WBENC)

5293   Citadel NY Inc.
62 William St 6th Fl
New York, NY 10005
Contact: Imranova Sr Acct Mgr
Tel: 212-931-8830
Email: sevda@citadelny.com
Website: www.citadelny.com
Information Technology Design; Computer Consulting; Information management computer systems integration design services. (Woman, estab 1998, empl 12, sales $10,913,532, cert: State)

INFORMATION TECHNOLOGY: Services

5294 Compulink Technologies, Inc.
214 W 29th St Ste 201
New York, NY 10001
Contact: Rafael Arboleda CEO
Tel: 212-695-5465
Email: rafael@compu-link.com
Website: www.compu-link.com
Cabling, network consulting, wireless networks, fiber optic cabling, LAN/WAN, computer hardware, software. (Minority, Woman, estab 1989, empl 15, sales $5,000,000, cert: State, City)

5295 Connect Technology Solutions
550 W Old Country Rd, Ste 307
Hicksville, NY 11801
Contact: Donna Chaimanis President
Tel: 516-433-7707
Email: donnac@connectts.com
Website: www.connectts.com
Information technology consulting & staffing services: technical staffing, executive recruiting, project mgmt, process reengineering, networking & system admin, software development & web design. (Woman, estab 1998, empl 30, sales $1,084,139, cert: State)

5296 Controls and Automation Consultants LLC
100 N Main St, Ste L06
Elmira, NY 14901
Contact: Tangela Nixon CEO
Tel: 800-430-4021
Email: tnixon@controls-automation.com
Website: www.controls-automation.com
IT Staffing, Hybrid Technical Staffing TM, Project Management & Control, Electrical Engineering, Automation Engineering. (AA, estab 2005, empl 4, sales $1,000,000, cert: State, NMSDC)

5297 Corporate Computer Solutions
55 Halstead Ave
Harrison, NY 10528
Contact: Larry Grippo VP Sales
Tel: 914-835-1105
Email: lgrippo@corporatecomputersol.com
Website: www.corporatecomputersol.com
Computer-based business solutions. (Woman, estab 1986, empl 18, sales $12,000,000, cert: State, City, WBENC)

5298 Crossfire Consulting
1940 Commerce St
Yorktown Heights, NY 10598
Contact: Paul Byrne VP Sales
Tel: 914-302-2900
Email: jessica@crossfireconsulting.com
Website: www.crossfireconsulting.com
IT Consulting, Development & Staff Augmentation, consulting, program management & onshore outsourcing. (Woman, estab 2000, empl 25, sales $ 0, cert: City, CPUC, WBENC, NWBOC)

5299 Datrose
660 Basket Rd
Webster, NY 14580
Contact: Eunice Sonneville Operations Partner
Tel: 585-217-0225
Email: esonneville@datrose.com
Website: www.datrose.com
Facilities support mgmt svcs: mailing-repro & steno; computer hardware & software; programming; data processing; systems design. (AA, estab 1976, empl 219, sales $14,765,522, cert: NMSDC)

5300 Deltronix Technologies Inc.
251 New Karner Road
Albany, NY 12205
Contact: Snekalatha Jegadeesan President
Tel: 518-713-5140
Email: hr@deltronixtech.com
Website: www.deltronixtech.com
IT Staff Augmentation: Java, .NET, Siebel, SAP, Peoplesoft, CRM, Database, Kofax, Testing etc. (Minority, Woman, estab 2012, empl 15, sales $888,071, cert: State)

5301 Derive Technologies
40 Wall St
New York, NY 10005
Contact: Bill Eggers Sr VP
Tel: 212-363-1111
Email: beggers@derivetech.com
Website: www.derivetech.com
Hardware fullfillment, computer integration service, iinfrastructure, desktop & printer support. (As-Ind, estab 1986, empl 110, sales $85,000,000, cert: NMSDC)

5302 Doddi Information Technologies
24 Picture Lane
Hicksville, NY 11801
Contact: David Trotman Dir Business Devel
Tel: 646-330-5354
Email: david.trotman@dodditech.com
Website: www.dodditech.com
Professional Services and Software development. (As-Ind, estab 2013, empl 10, sales , cert: State, City, NMSDC)

5303 Donnelly & Moore Corporation
75 Carolina Dr
New City, NY 10956
Contact: Tracy Stein CEO
Tel: 845-304-8344
Email: tracys@donmor.com
Website: www.donmor.com
IT consulting & full time IT staffing: GUI dev, internet & intranet application dev, quality assurance testing, help desk & desk top support, database dev & administration. (Minority, Woman, estab 1997, empl 50, sales $10,000,000, cert: State, City, NMSDC)

5304 Eclaro International, Inc.
450 7th Ave Ste 1102
New York, NY 10123
Contact: Tom Sheridan Principal
Tel: 212-695-2922
Email: tsheridan@eclaro.com
Website: www.eclaroit.com
Information technology staffing & software development services. (As-Pac, estab , empl , sales $23,100,000, cert: State, City, NMSDC)

5305 eiWorkflow Solutions, LLC
125 Wolf Rd
Albany, NY 12205
Contact: John Andrew CEO
Tel: 518-240-1155
Email: info@eiworkflowsolutions.com
Website: www.eiworkflowsolutions.com
Cloud software consulting, Workflow Management, Customer Service Management, Customer Relationship Management & Human Resource Management. (As-Ind, estab 2006, empl 7, sales $450,000, cert: NMSDC)

INFORMATION TECHNOLOGY: Services

5306 Elite Technical Services, Inc.
      3281 Veterans Memorial Hwy Ste E17
      Ronkonkoma, NY 11779
      Contact: Donna Keller President
      Tel: 631-256-1399
      Email: dkeller@elitetechnical.com
      Website: www.elitetechnical.com
Technical consultants & staff augmentation services: information technology, networking & engineering. (Woman, estab 1992, empl 88, sales $14,500,000, cert: State, WBENC)

5307 emedia, LLC
      274 Madison Ave Ste 1202
      New York, NY 10017
      Contact: Shari Lowsky Dir Client Relations
      Tel: 212-774-6100
      Email: slowsky@emediaweb.com
      Website: www.emediaweb.com
Design, build, integrate & maintain custom software applications, Enterprise Resource Planning (ERP) systems, Enterprise Content Management (ECM) systems, Customer Relationship Management (CRM) systems. (Woman, estab 1996, empl 8, sales $1,000,000, cert: State, City, WBENC)

5308 Episerve Corp.
      266 Midwood St
      Brooklyn, NY 11225
      Contact: Sony Titus President
      Tel: 917-921-2644
      Email: info@episervecorp.com
      Website: www.episervecorp.com
Training, consulting, system integration & managed services. (Woman/AA, estab 2003, empl 6, sales $245,000, cert: City)

5309 Espirit Systems, LLC
      14 Penn Plaza Ste 2105
      New York, NY 10122
      Contact: Sales
      Tel: 212-631-0188
      Email: amcclean@eliteconsulting.com
      Website: www.eliteconsulting.com
Application architect & dev, database dev, network admin & architects, systems admin, business analysts, mainframe. (AA, estab 1997, empl 10, sales $5,000,000, cert: State)

5310 Expinfo, Inc.
      1621 Central Ave
      Albany, NY 12205
      Contact: CEO
      Tel: 518-459-4100
      Email: nys@expinfo.com
      Website: www.expinfo.com
Information technology staffing, HR consulting, custom computer programming, computer systems design, web development & graphic design, custom application development. (Minority, Woman, estab 2005, empl 21, sales $1,800,000, cert: State, City)

5311 Fair Pattern Inc.
      1460 Broadway
      New York, NY 10036
      Contact: Simon Islam Managing Dir
      Tel: 800-906-1656
      Email: simon@fairpattern.com
      Website: www.fairpattern.com
IT staffing, web & mobile application, software engineering & project management. (As-Ind, estab 2015, empl 22, sales $650,000, cert: NMSDC)

5312 Fast Lane Interactive
      PO Box 987
      New York, NY 11225
      Contact: Shalonda Hunter Founder
      Tel: 646-389-8495
      Email: contactus@flitimes.com
      Website: www.flitimes.com
Digital Media & Advertising, Content Devel, Web, Mobile, Tablet Device Devel & Services, Software Devel, Web Security, Information Security, Cloud Services (Email, Web Storage, Telecomm, Data Center Migration). (Woman/AA, estab 2015, empl 5, sales , cert: NMSDC)

5313 Financial Technologies Inc
      305 Madison Ave, Ste 4600
      New York, NY 10165
      Contact: Young Lee CEO
      Tel: 212-485-9842
      Email: hlee@sciostrategy.com
      Website: www.telochain.com/
IT consulting services, web/mobile applications & back end data management & integration solutions. (Minority, Woman, estab 2006, empl 3, sales $527,935, cert: State)

5314 GCom Software, Inc.
      24 Madison Ave
      Albany, NY 12203
      Contact: Rebecca Fischer Acct Mgr
      Tel: 518-869-1671
      Email: PreSales@gcomsoft.com
      Website: www.gcomsoft.com
IT Staff Augmentation, fixed cost deliverable, project based services, Web based application development, Data warehousing, Network support, server , security, virtualization, Quality/Testing. (As-Ind, estab 2005, empl 130, sales , cert: State)

5315 GENESYS Consulting Services, Inc.
      1 Marcus Blvd, Ste 102
      Albany, NY 12205
      Contact: Leo Pfohl VP
      Tel: 518-459-9500
      Email: leo@genesysonline.com
      Website: www.genesysonline.com
IT consulting services, design, develop, implement & maintain technology solutions. (Woman, estab 1987, empl 84, sales $12,500,717, cert: State, City)

5316 Globalquest
      435 Lawrence Bell Dr, Ste 7
      Williamsville, NY 14221
      Contact: Lynn Dearmyer Business Devel Mgr
      Tel: 716-635-9820
      Email: ldearmyer@globalquestinc.com
      Website: www.globalqueststaffing.com
IT staffing: contract, contract-to-hire, direct & payroll. (Woman, estab 1994, empl 120, sales $24,000,000, cert: State, City)

5317 Granwood Inc
       61-43 186th St
       Fresh Meadows, NY 11365
       Contact: Glen Greene Managing Dir
       Tel: 718-640-2828
       Email: ggreene@granwoodinc.com
       Website: www.granwoodinc.com
Information technology consulting & staffing. (AA, estab 2005, empl 11, sales $1,200,000, cert: State, City, NMSDC)

5318 ImageWork USA LLC
       170 Hamilton Ave, Ste 301
       White Plains, NY 10601
       Contact: Bikkal President
       Tel: 914-681-0700
       Email: cbikkal@imagework.com
       Website: www.imagework.com
Full life Cycle Recruitment - IT services - Information Technology; Documentation Scanning; Printing; Computing. (Minority, Woman, estab 2009, empl 1, sales , cert: State, City)

5319 Indotronix International Corporation
       687 Lee Rd, Ste 250
       Rochester, NY 14606
       Contact: Venkat S Mantha President
       Tel: 845-473-1137
       Email: bd@iic.com
       Website: www.iic.com
Software applications, e-business initiatives, IT consulting, customer interaction management. (As-Ind, estab 1986, empl 1250, sales $85,000,000, cert: State, NMSDC, CPUC)

5320 InnoSoul, Inc.
       24 Fairfield Ave
       Albany, NY 12205
       Contact: Rashi Shamshabad President
       Tel: 518-400-0425
       Email: innosoul@gmail.com
       Website: www.innosoul.com
Software Product Development & IT Consulting Services, IT Staffing. (Minority, Woman, estab 2003, empl 20, sales $4,000,000, cert: State, City, WBENC)

5321 Integrated Systems Management
       303 S Broadway, Ste 101
       Tarrytown, NY 10591
       Contact: Dave Business Dev Mgr
       Tel: 914-332-5590
       Email: ndave@ismnet.com
       Website: www.omnimd.com
IT solution services & IT staffing: network security, ERP, CRM softwares. (Minority, Woman, estab 1989, empl 35, sales $5,550,000, cert: State)

5322 Jasper Solutions Inc.
       21 Melville Rd
       Huntington Station, NY 11746
       Contact: Anshuman Patel President
       Tel: 631-514-8106
       Email: contracts@jaspersolutions.com
       Website: www.jaspersolutions.com
Enterprise storage, network monitoring, security, private & public Cloud, networking, disaster recovery, application integration, data warehousing, data mining, database implementation, virtualization, hybrid Cloud, Cisco. (As-Ind, estab 2002, empl 3, sales $300,000, cert: State)

5323 Jean Martin Inc.
       551 Fifth Ave, Ste 1425
       New York, NY 10176
       Contact: Shawn Kumar CEO
       Tel: 212-883-1000
       Email: shawnk@jeanmartin.com
       Website: www.jeanmartin.com
Information technology consulting services. (As-Ind, estab 1997, empl 150, sales $16,000,000, cert: City)

5324 JSL Computer Services, Inc.
       447 E Allen St
       Hudson, NY 12534
       Contact: Ed Grossman VP
       Tel: 518-828-7761
       Email: ed@jslinc.com
       Website: www.jslinc.com
E-commerce, web design & dev, JAVA, systems programming, analysis & business requirements, project mgmt, software testing & quality assurance, documentation, database design, data modeling & warehousing, network engineering. (Woman, estab 1978, empl 33, sales $3,610,079, cert: City, WBENC)

5325 KDI Technology Solutions, Inc
       412 Broadway 2nd Fl
       New York, NY 10113
       Contact: John Thomas President
       Tel: 646-724-0875
       Email: jthomas@kditek.com
       Website: www.kditek.com
Database design & development, mobile applications, web development, business & systems analysis. (AA, estab 2007, empl 1, sales $100,000, cert: State, City)

5326 Keystats Inc
       81 Pondfield Rd
       Bronxville, NY 10708
       Contact: Bilal Karriem President
       Tel: 914-337-6883
       Email: bkarriem@keystatsinc.com
       Website: www.keystatsinc.com
Statistically driven analytic solutions (AA, estab 1999, empl 11, sales $100,000, cert: City, NMSDC)

5327 Maureen Data Systems, Inc.
       307 W 38th St Ste 1801
       New York, NY 10018
       Contact: Robert Irvin Dir govt channels
       Tel: 646-744-1000
       Email: rirvin@mdsny.com
       Website: www.mdsny.com
Systems integrator & VAR, UC, Cloud computing, virtualization & storage, networking & security. (Woman, estab 1994, empl 24, sales $8,500,000, cert: State, City, WBENC)

5328 Mola Group Corporation
       450 Park Ave S Fl 3
       New York, NY 10016
       Contact: Emmanuel Ola-Dake Managing Dir
       Tel: 646-217-0727
       Email: contact@molaprise.com
       Website: www.molaprise.com
Cybersecurity Solutions, Threat Detection. (AA, estab 2014, empl 15, sales $5,000,000, cert: State, City, NMSDC)

INFORMATION TECHNOLOGY: Services

5329 Motivate Design, LLC
       111 John St, Ste 450
       New York, NY 10038
       Contact: Laura Haykel Client Experience Dir
       Tel: 646-400-5108
       Email: laura@motivatedesign.com
       Website: www.motivatedesign.com
Build high-performing websites, mobile applications, SaaS or enterprise platforms using our fully-outsourced or staff augmentation. (Minority, Woman, estab 2009, empl 15, sales $4,000,000, cert: NMSDC, WBENC)

5330 Navatar Consulting Group Inc.
       44 Wall St, 12 Fl
       New York, NY 10005
       Contact: Mgr operations
       Tel: 212-461-2140
       Email: billing@navatargroup.com
       Website: www.navatargroup.com
On-demand CRM, ERP & supply chain. (As-Pac, estab 2002, empl 25, sales $820,000, cert: State)

5331 Netfast Technology Solutions Inc.
       589 8th Ave 22nd Fl
       New York, NY 10018
       Contact: Navid Nawaz Mgr
       Tel: 212-792-5200
       Email: nnawaz@netfast.com
       Website: www.netfast.com
Information security consulting & network integration. (As-Pac, estab 1994, empl 25, sales $13,800,000, cert: City, NMSDC)

5332 New York Technology Partners
       332 Jefferson Rd
       Rochester, NY 14623
       Contact: VP
       Tel: 585-300-4720
       Email:
       Website: www.nytp.com
Software consulting, onsite, offsite, and offshore, IT & Business Consulting, IT Integration, Project Management. (As-Pac, estab 1999, empl 280, sales $4,000,000,000, cert: NMSDC)

5333 NewVolt Solutions, Inc.
       260 E Main St Ste 6335
       Rochester, NY 14604
       Contact: Christopher Fallon
       Tel: 585-451-6241
       Email: admin@newvoltsolutions.com
       Website: www.newvoltsolutions.com
Devel robust, full-stack analytics applications. (As-Pac, estab 2021, empl 2, sales $510,000, cert: NMSDC)

5334 Panther Solutions, LLC
       1001 Lee Rd
       Rochester, NY 14606
       Contact: Robert Kleinschmidt Dir Natl Accounts
       Tel: 414-336-8217
       Email: robert_kleinschmidt@panthersolutions.com
       Website: www.flowercitygroup
Account management, custom data programming. (AA, estab 2005, empl 45, sales $32,000,000, cert: NMSDC)

5335 Perpetual Solutions LLC
       134 W 29th St, 607
       New York, NY 10001
       Contact: Amish Gandhi CEO
       Tel: 212-904-1497
       Email: b2bsales@perpetualny.com
       Website: www.perpetualny.com
Software User Experience Mobile Development Computer Services, Technology & Engineering Services. (As-Ind, estab 2012, empl 8, sales $1,650,000, cert: NMSDC)

5336 Pride Healthcare, LLC
       420 Lexington Ave 30th Fl
       New York, NY 10170
       Contact: Bhavin Shah Dir
       Tel: 212-235-5309
       Email: bhavin.shah@pride-health.com
       Website: www.pride-health.com
Staff Augmentation, Vendor Management, IT Hardware Procurement Services and Business Processing Outsourcing. (Hisp, estab 2003, empl 350, sales $358,000,000, cert: NMSDC)

5337 Quantilus Inc.
       115 Broadway Ste 1202
       New York, NY 10006
       Contact: Debarshi Chaudhury Dir Business Dev
       Tel: 212-768-8900
       Email: debarshi.chaudhury@quantilus.com
       Website: www.quantilus.com/
IT Strategy, Implementation, Custom Development, Machine Vision, Publishing, Education, Artificial Intelligence, Natural Language Processing3. (As-Ind, estab 2004, empl 22, sales $7,213,447, cert: State, City, NMSDC)

5338 RMK Consulting, Inc.
       2 Oregon Hollow Rd
       Armonk, NY 10504
       Contact: Debra DeWitt Acct Exec
       Tel: 914-765-0075
       Email: info@rmkconsulting.com
       Website: www.rmkconsulting.com
BPO & IT consulting, outsourcing & consulting services for staff augmentation, managed services & project sourcing solutions, on-site, near-site & off-shore staffing/delivery models. (Woman, estab 1998, empl 127, sales $30,000,000, cert: WBENC)

5339 RMS Computer Corp.
       1185 Ave of the Americas Fl 32
       New York, NY 10036
       Contact: Carole Klang
       Tel: 212-840-8666
       Email: carolee@rmscorp.com
       Website: www.rmscorp.com
Contract Information technology professionals: hardware, software, application development, networking, e-commerce, client server & mainframe environments. (Woman, estab 1985, empl 250, sales $ 0, cert: WBENC)

INFORMATION TECHNOLOGY: Services

5340   Sharp Decisions, Inc.
1040 Ave of the Americas 9th Fl
New York, NY 10018
Contact: Edward McCann Managing Dir
Tel: 212-403-7557
Email: hdteam@sharpdecisions.com
Website: www.sharpdecisions.com
Computer consulting: staff augmentation & contract programming, systems integration, data networks design, development & implementation, business continuity planning, security & firewall design & dev, vendor product evaluation. (Woman, estab 1990, empl 330, sales $60,000,000, cert: NWBOC)

5341   Siwel Consulting, Inc.
213 W 35th St Ste 12 W
New York, NY 10001
Contact: Michael LaPayower Sr Accountant
Tel: 212-691-9326
Email: mlapayower@siwel.com
Website: www.siwel.com
Information technology: contract & fulltime staffing, IBM Premier VAR, ELA & software license, asset management, Linux, VOIP, VMware, server, storage & networking. (Woman, estab 1992, empl 30, sales $52,780,000, cert: WBENC)

5342   Softpath Systems Inc.
75 Maiden Lane, Ste 903
New York, NY 10038
Contact: Shiv Mgr
Tel: 212-405-1894
Email: shiv@softpathsystems.com
Website: www.softpathsystems.com
IT & supply chain staffing. (As-Pac, estab 1997, empl 150, sales , cert: State)

5343   Software Guidance & Assistance, Inc.
200 White Plains Road
Tarrytown, NY 10591
Contact: Craig Rydell Business Devel Mgr
Tel: 914-366-5950
Email: craigr@sgainc.com
Website: www.sgainc.com
IT professionals: programmers, analysts, senior project managers, operating systems, programming, networking, application software & hardware skills & certifications. (Woman, estab 1981, empl 652, sales $78,218,000, cert: City, WBENC)

5344   Software People Inc.
738 Smithtown Bypass, Ste 202
Smithtown, NY 11787
Contact: Sandeep Jain Sr VP
Tel: 631-863-0299
Email: sandeep.jain@softwarepeople.us
Website: www.softwarepeople.us
ERP implementation, systems analysis, system & database admin, web design & application, client/server implementation, relational database design, systems conversion/ migration, electronic data interchange. (Woman/As-Ind, estab 1998, empl 5, sales $2,869,583, cert: State)

5345   Source Of Future Technology (SOFT), Inc.
333 Hudson St Ste 202
New York, NY 10013
Contact: Cathy Grubiak President
Tel: 212-633-1515
Email: cgrubiak@soft-inc.com
Website: www.softinc.com
Computer technology solutions: project life cycle. (Woman, estab 1981, empl 75, sales $6,000,000, cert: State, WBENC)

5346   Sphynx Software Solutions LLC
59 Lafayette Ave Ste 2D
Brooklyn, NY 11217
Contact: Yonas Keflemariam CEO
Tel: 917-705-5548
Email: yonas@sphynxsoftware.com
Website: www.sphynxsoftware.com
Technology solutions, enterprise architecture, local & offshore software development resources & technical staff augmentation. (AA, estab 2007, empl 3, sales , cert: City, NMSDC)

5347   StudioLabs LLC.
247 W 30th St Ste 12A
New York, NY 10001
Contact: Liz Young CEO
Tel: 646-880-6892
Email: liz@studiolabs.com
Website: www.studiolabs.com
Websites, online software, mobile applications, digital ads, online tools & digital marketing products. (Woman, estab 2003, empl 27, sales $3,999,300, cert: WBENC)

5348   Sutherland Global Services
1160 Pittsford-Victor Rd
Pittsford, NY 14534
Contact: Steve Sandt Business Devel Mgr
Tel: 585-586-5757
Email: sandts@sutherlandglobal.com
Website: www.sutherlandglobal.com
Business process outsourcing & call ctr svcs: technical & customer support, systems integration & application development. (As-Ind, estab 1986, empl 33000, sales $500,500,000, cert: NMSDC)

5349   SVAM International Inc.
233 East Shore Rd, Ste 201
Great Neck, NY 11023
Contact: Manav Bhasin Managing Dir
Tel: 516-466-6655
Email: manav@svam.com
Website: www.svam.com
IT staff augmentation, custom software dev, web enabling technologies, workflow automation, content management. (As-Pac, estab 1994, empl 600, sales $100,000,000, cert: State, NMSDC)

5350   Sygma Technology Solutions, Inc.
300 W 135th St, Ste 5J
New York, NY 10030
Contact: Stuart Holland President
Tel: 917-507-1500
Email: stuart.holland@sygmatechnology.com
Website: www.sygmatechnology.com
Custom software development, integrated technology, technology system solutions, application software development, business information technology, business software development. (AA, estab 2005, empl 20, sales , cert: State, NMSDC, 8(a))

INFORMATION TECHNOLOGY: Services

5351 Techolution LLC
      3 World Financial Center 24th Fl
      New York, NY 10281
      Contact: Zachary Kissel Office Mgr
      Tel: 201-417-7240
      Email: zak@techolution.com
      Website: www.techolution.com
Digital transformation: web & mobile, migrating server farms & applications to the cloud (public or private). (As-Pac, estab 2014, empl 50, sales $1,500,000, cert: NMSDC)

5352 Trivision Group Inc.
      118-21 Queens Blvd Ste 401
      Forest Hills, NY 11375
      Contact: Vijay Shenoy CEO
      Tel: 212-869-5455
      Email: contracts@trivisioninc.com
      Website: www.trivisioninc.com
Contract staffing solutions, Project Management and Information Technology Consulting Services, system design, programming, and testing, to post-implementation support and maintenance. (As-Pac, estab 2003, empl 17, sales $1,000,000, cert: State, City)

5353 TTI of USA
      601 Bangs Ave
      Asbury Park, NJ 07712
      Contact: CEO
      Tel: 646-495-9019
      Email: LK@TTIOFUSA.COM
      Website: www.ttiofusa.com
IT staff augmentation. (Woman, estab 1996, empl 240, sales $20,182,200, cert: WBENC)

5354 URimagination, Inc.
      18 E 41st St Ste 1703
      New York, NY 10017
      Contact: Alf Baez CEO
      Tel: 212-729-9558
      Email: info@urimagination.com
      Website: www.urimagination.com
Information technology solutions: custom application development, systems integration, maintenance spanning. (Hisp, estab 2007, empl 7, sales $500,000, cert: City, NMSDC)

5355 Vernalis Group Inc
      353 Lexington Ave, Ste 1604
      New York, NY 10016
      Contact: Nanda Rajasek COO
      Tel: 647-923-1903
      Email: nanda.rajasek@vernal.is
      Website: www.vernalisengg.com
Global software & engineering solutions, Microsoft, IBM, JEE, openSource, Mobile, Business Intelligence, Enterprise Application Integration. (As-Ind, estab 2012, empl 300, sales $4,440,000, cert: NMSDC)

5356 VQV Services LLC
      204 Forrest Pointe Dr
      East Greenbush, NY 12061
      Contact: Khuhsbooben Patel President
      Tel: 201-920-6170
      Email: khush@vqvservices.com
      Website: www.vqvservices.com
Quality Engineer, Validation Engineer, Qualification Specialist, Information Technology consultants. (Minority, Woman, estab 2016, empl 2, sales , cert: State)

5357 Xperteks Computer Consultancy, Inc.
      132 West 36th St 10th Fl
      New York, NY 10018
      Contact: Marcial Velez CEO
      Tel: 212-206-6262
      Email: mvelez@xperteks.com
      Website: www.xperteks.com
Apple, PC & network managed services, IT services. (Hisp, estab 2002, empl 17, sales $2,500,000, cert: City, NMSDC)

Ohio

5358 Accelerated Business Results an A Fox Corporation
      1530 Sycamore Ridge Dr
      Maineville, OH 45039
      Contact: Amy Fox Owner
      Tel: 513-774-8608
      Email: amy.fox@acceleratedbr.com
      Website: www.acceleratedbr.com/what-we-do/
Customized content development, design & develop instructor-led training programs, e-Learning solutions & blended learning solutions. (Woman, estab 2002, empl 11, sales $1,678,119, cert: WBENC)

5359 AespaTech, LLC
      23800 Commerce Park, Ste A
      Beachwood, OH 44122
      Contact: President
      Tel: 216-928-1919
      Email: info@aespatech.com
      Website: www.aespatech.com
Information Technology Consulting & Training Services. (Woman/As-Pac, estab 2014, empl 10, sales $3,500,000, cert: State, City, WBENC, 8(a))

5360 Alego Health
      24651 Center Ridge Rd Ste 400
      Westlake, OH 44145
      Contact: Jonathan Levoy VP
      Tel: 440-617-6516
      Email: jlevoy@alegohealth.com
      Website: www.alegohealth.com
Healthcare IT, EMR Training, EMR Implementation, EMR Analysts, Hardware Support, Hardware, Software, IT Analysts, IT, Mobile Technology (Woman, estab 2004, empl 127, sales $11,500,000, cert: WBENC)

5361 American Business Solutions, Inc.
      8850 Whitney Dr
      Lewis Center, OH 43035
      Contact: Nitin Sharma Sr Mgr, Business Devel
      Tel: 877-781-2274
      Email: nitin@absi-usa.com
      Website: www.absi-usa.com
Technology Services & Solutions, Business Intelligence & Database Management, Organizational Change Management, Mobile Application Development, Project Management & Support, Quality Assurance & Testing, Cloud Computing Services. (As-Ind, estab 1998, empl 85, sales $19,000,000, cert: State, NMSDC)

INFORMATION TECHNOLOGY: Services

5362 Analytical Solutions by Kline
      7546 Ridge Rd
      Parma, OH 44129
      Contact: Cynthia Kline Owner
      Tel: 440-829-9275
      Email: cak@ask-consulting.org
      Website: www.ASK-consulting.org
Database Development (Oracle, IDMS, DB2), Data Migration, Data Architecture, Database Design & Analysis, Application Architecture. (Woman, estab , empl 12, sales $1,394,000, cert: City)

5363 Arbelos Partners LLC
      3386 Lawton Ln
      Pepper Pike, OH 44124
      Contact: Djifa Amefia Managing Partner
      Tel: 216-369-9272
      Email: info@arbelospartners.com
      Website: www.arbelospartners.com
Consulting, System Implementation & Integration services. (AA, estab 2012, empl 1, sales $160,000, cert: State, NMSDC)

5364 Ardent Technologies Inc.
      6234 Far Hills Ave
      Dayton, OH 45459
      Contact: Vas Appalaneni President
      Tel: 937-312-1345
      Email: ohbids@ardentinc.com
      Website: www.ardentinc.com
ITservices & project management, software development & maintenance, systems analysis, turnkey project implementations, data services, project outsourcing services. (As-Ind, estab 2000, empl 90, sales $12,984,147, cert: State, SDB)

5365 Ascendum
      10290 Alliance Rd
      Blue Ash, OH 45242
      Contact: Mark Vornwald Dir
      Tel: 513-792-5100
      Email: mark.vornwald@ascendum.com
      Website: www.ascendum.com
IT solutions, technology-inspired solutions to business-driven challenges. (As-Pac, estab 2008, empl 2000, sales $110,000,000, cert: State, NMSDC)

5366 Avantia, Inc.
      9655 Sweet Valley Dr, Ste 1
      Valley View, OH 44125
      Contact: Jeff Ladd Controller
      Tel: 216-901-9366
      Email: jladd@avantia-inc.com
      Website: www.avantia-inc.com
Information technology consulting & systems development. (Woman, estab 2000, empl 35, sales $9,240,331, cert: WBENC)

5367 Barcode Industrial Systems, Inc.
      8044 Montgomery road Ste 700
      Cincinnati, OH 45236
      Contact: Juan Merchan Business Devel Mgr
      Tel: 513-772-5252
      Email: contracts@bislabels.com
      Website: www.BISLabels.com
Mobile data transaction systems, wireless & batch data capture applications: inventory, shipping, receiving & warehouse mgmt via Internet. (AA, Hisp, estab 1990, empl 16, sales $1,010,000, cert: NMSDC)

5368 Cadre Computer Resources Co.
      201 E 5th St, Ste 1800
      Cincinnati, OH 45202
      Contact: Kristen Norris Marketing
      Tel: 513-762-7350
      Email: kristen.norris@cadre.net
      Website: www.cadre.net
Network & information security solutions, design, assessment, installation, training & support of information security systems. (Woman, estab 2001, empl 47, sales $43,383,000, cert: WBENC, NWBOC)

5369 CB Tech
      1491 Polaris Pkwy Ste 291
      Columbus, OH 43240
      Contact: Josh Harris Sr Dir of Business Dev
      Tel: 614-339-8550
      Email: info@cbtechnow.com
      Website: www.cbtechnow.com
IT services & document management solutions. (AA, estab 1990, empl 15, sales $28,300,000, cert: NMSDC)

5370 CGB Tech Solutions Inc
      2310 Superior Ave Ste 105
      Cleveland, OH 44114
      Contact: Jennifer Brunkow Owner
      Tel: 216-373-9449
      Email: jen@cgbtech.com
      Website: www.cgbgtech.com
Network Infrastructure planning, procurement, installation & troubleshooting, server monitoring, evaluation, troubleshooting and repair, User endpoint (desktop/laptop) troubleshooting, remote or in-person Help Desk services. (Woman, estab 2003, empl 17, sales $1,000,000, cert: City)

5371 Chagrin Consulting Services Inc.
      1795 South Belvoir Blvd.
      South Euclid, OH 44121
      Contact: Ann Allard President
      Tel: 216-514-3301
      Email: ahallard@chagrinconsulting.com
      Website: www.chagrinconsulting.com
Information technology consulting & staffing. (Woman, estab 1993, empl 12, sales $2,451,851, cert: WBENC)

5372 ClemCorp
      714 E Monument Ave
      Dayton, OH 45402
      Contact: Kevin Clemons CEO
      Tel: 937-531-6645
      Email: kevin.clemons@clemcorp.com
      Website: www.ClemCorp.com
IT solution & services: rational capabilities, enterprise architecture, GCSS, web dev, graphic design, document mgmt, network design & admin, software dev, project mgmt, system design, life cycle application support. (AA, estab 2005, empl 12, sales , cert: State, 8(a))

5373 Corbus, LLC
      1129 Miamisburg Centerville Rd
      West Carrollton, OH 45449
      Contact: Jerry Teuschler Dir Strategic Sales Dev
      Tel: 513-703-2929
      Email: corbusconnects@corbus.com
      Website: www.corbus.com
Software development, offshore IT support, testing & quality solutions, staff augmentation. (Minority, estab 1994, empl 600, sales , cert: NMSDC)

INFORMATION TECHNOLOGY: Services

5374 Cybervation, Inc.
4150 Tuller Rd, Ste 204
Dublin, OH 43017
Contact: Purba Majumder President
Tel: 614-818-9061
Email: pmajumder@cybervationinc.com
Website: www.cybervationinc.com
Technology Services, Website Development, custom Software Programming, Graphics Design, Animation, Video, Transcription, Data Entry & Internet Marketing. (Minority, Woman, estab 1998, empl 32, sales $ 0, cert: State, NMSDC, WBENC)

5375 Cynergies Solutions Group
26301 Curtiss-Wright Pkwy Ste 400
Richmond Heights, OH 44143
Contact: Debbie Holy President
Tel: 440-565-0168
Email: debbie_holy@cynergies.net
Website: www.cynergies.net
Information technology staffing: consulting, contracting, permanent, executive placement, contract-to-hire, software devel & training. (Woman, estab 1997, empl 62, sales $ 0, cert: WBENC)

5376 Dedicated Tech Services, Inc.
545 Metro Pl S Ste 100
Dublin, OH 43017
Contact: Patty E Lickliter President
Tel: 614-695-5990
Email: sales@dtsdelivers.com
Website: www.dtsdelivers.com
Application Design & Development, Service Oriented Architecture (SOA), Database Design & Development, Client/Server & N-Tier Development, Web & Web Service Development, Data Warehousing Solutions. (Woman, estab 2008, empl 41, sales $1,930,000, cert: WBENC, NWBOC)

5377 Deemsys Inc.
800A Cross Pointe Rd
Columbus, OH 43230
Contact: RT Rajan
Tel: 614-322-9929
Email: raj@deemsysinc.com
Website: www.deemsysinc.com
Application design, development & implementation, Systems integration/consolidation, Re-engineering, Implementation, Feasibility & requirement analysis. (Woman/As-Ind, estab 2004, empl 82, sales $7,550,000, cert: State, NMSDC)

5378 DevCare Solutions
131 N High St Ste 640
Columbus, OH 43215
Contact: Ron Vogel Dir Business Dev
Tel: 614-285-2714
Email: rvogel@devcare.com
Website: www.devcare.com
On-site/offshore development of software solutions & Staff Augmentation consultants. (Minority, Woman, estab 1995, empl 380, sales $22,000,000, cert: State, NMSDC, WBENC)

5379 Echo Imaging Inc.
2645 Wooster Rd
Rocky River, OH 44116
Contact: Barbara Milloy President
Tel: 440-356-4720
Email: barbara@echoimg.com
Website: www.echoimg.com
Replication svcs: CD-R, CD-ROM, DVD-R, mini CD's, business card CD's & diskette duplication, full color custom printed packaging. (Woman, estab 1997, empl 1, sales $801,642, cert: WBENC)

5380 ERP Analysts, Inc
425 Metro Place N Ste 510
Dublin, OH 43017
Contact: Cory Drescher Dir
Tel: 727-424-4427
Email: jvyas@erpagroup.com
Website: www.erpagroup.com
Project management, ERP Applications. Database Management & Administration, Performance Tuning. (AA, As-Pac, estab 2003, empl 500, sales $88,000,000, cert: State, 8(a))

5381 Expeed Software LLC
659 Lakeview Plaza Blvd, Ste K
Worthington, OH 43085
Contact: Rao Chejarla President
Tel: 614-371-4791
Email: rao.chejarla@expeedsoftware.com
Website: www.expeedsoftware.com
Custom Application Development, Mobile Application Development, Application Integration, Data Warehousing and Business Intelligence, Independent Software, Verification/Quality Assurance, Project Management. (As-Pac, estab 2008, empl 35, sales $735,000, cert: State, NMSDC)

5382 Expert Technical Consultants, Inc.
3831 Attucks Dr Ste A
Powell, OH 43065
Contact: Betty Keck President
Tel: 614-430-9113
Email: betty@etci.net
Website: www.etci.net
Information systems consulting, Complete Project Life Cycle Management, Application Development, Database Management and Administration, Web-Enhanced Solutions, Maintenance and Support, & Staff Augmentation & Outsourcing. (Woman/Hisp, estab 1991, empl 10, sales $1,500,000, cert: State)

5383 Fiducia TechneGroup LLC
3838 Eileen Dr
Cincinnati, OH 45209
Contact: Alma Bartos CEO
Tel: 513-418-8217
Email: amartinez@fiduciatg.com
Website: www.fiduciatg.com
Engineering Services, Reliability (Products, Processes and Software), Implement Reliability Life Cycle Management & Benchmarking. (Minority, Woman, estab 2014, empl 2, sales $100,000, cert: NMSDC, WBENC)

INFORMATION TECHNOLOGY: Services

5384 Flairsoft, Ltd.
7720 Rivers Edge Dr Ste 200
Columbus, OH 43235
Contact: Sharon Fraley Sr Business Devel Mgr
Tel: 614-207-0764
Email: sharon.fraley@flairsoft.net
Website: www.flairsoft.net
Information Technology, e-Business, Professional Services, Systems Integration & Business Process Re-Engineering. (Minority, estab 2001, empl 100, sales $8,000,000, cert: NMSDC)

5385 Global Associates, Inc.
7160 Corporate Way
Dayton, OH 45459
Contact: Kevin Toshok Dir Solutions Sales
Tel: 937-312-1204
Email: ktoshok@gassociates.com
Website: www.gassociates.com
IT Consulting, Staff Augmentation, Project Outsourcing & Offshore software design & testing. (Minority, Woman, estab 1996, empl 8, sales $15,000,000, cert: NMSDC)

5386 Halcyon Solutions, Inc.
5880 Innovation Dr.
Dublin, OH 43016
Contact: Shaun Frecska VP
Tel: 614-339-5608
Email: sfrecska@halcyonit.com
Website: www.halcyonit.com
IT consulting and staffing agency. (As-Ind, estab 1992, empl 125, sales $ 0, cert: State, NMSDC)

5387 IdentiPhoto Company Ltd.
1810 Joseph Lloyd Pkwy
Willoughby, OH 44094
Contact: Pamela Johnson GM
Tel: 440-306-9000
Email: pam@identiphoto.com
Website: www.identiphoto.com
Badging, tracking, verification systems, photo ID systems ID badges, ID software ID supplies, ID badge attachments, ID cards, visitor management software/systems, card printers, perimeter management systems, smart cards, proximity. (Woman, estab 1969, empl 15, sales $2,252,840, cert: WBENC)

5388 Integrated Solutions and Services
4055 Executive Park Dr, Ste 450
Cincinnati, OH 45241
Contact: Clarence McGill
Tel: 513-769-3913
Email: rmcgill@iss-unlimited.com
Website: www.iss-unlimited.com
Information technology hardware integration, network server mgmt, help desk svcs, LAN/WAN, database dev & mgmt, system application support. (AA, estab 1999, empl 5, sales $ 0, cert: State)

5389 IT Reserves, LLC
40 Hutchinson Ave, Ste 403
Columbus, OH 43235
Contact: Pierre Ilyamukuru CEO
Tel: 469-416-8910
Email: pierre.aimable@itreserves.com
Website: www.itreserves.com/
IT and software development, Digital Consulting Services, Experience Design Services, Application Development & Maintenance. (AA, estab 2020, empl 5, sales $300,000, cert: NMSDC)

5390 JASStek, Inc.
555 Metro Place N Ste 100
Dublin, OH 43017
Contact: Praveen Tummalla Business Devel Mgr
Tel: 614-808-3600
Email: praveen@jasstek.com
Website: www.jasstek.com
Information technology consulting, project staffing, IT staffing, contract programming, contract consultants, technology consultants & contract to hire consultants. (Minority, Woman, estab 2012, empl 9, sales , cert: State, NMSDC, WBENC)

5391 Lightwell Inc.
565 Metro Place S Ste 220
Columbus, OH 43017
Contact: Bryan Scott Acct Exec
Tel: 614-310-2700
Email: bryan.scott@lightwellinc.com
Website: www.lightwellinc.com
EDI, B2B integration, order management, ecommerce, business management, and supply chain management services. (Woman, estab 1998, empl 225, sales $39,000,000, cert: WBENC)

5392 Logic Soft, Inc.
5900 Sawmill Rd, Ste 200
Dublin, OH 43017
Contact: Louis Viciedo Business Dev Mgr
Tel: 614-884-5544
Email: louis.viciedo@logicsoftusa.com
Website: www.logicsoftusa.com
IT Managed Services, monitor program activity, detailed program analysis & benchmarking, invoicing, robust supplier management & total workforce solutions. (As-Ind, estab 1997, empl 50, sales $15,000,000, cert: State)

5393 LRSolutions, LLC
5743 Edgepark Dr
Brook Park, OH 44142
Contact: Linda Gutekunst CEO
Tel: 440-476-9492
Email: linda@lrsolutions.net
Website: www.LRSolutions.net
IT staffing & solutions: permanent placement, staff augmentation & project-based solutions. (Woman, estab 2006, empl 8, sales $500,000, cert: State, NWBOC)

5394 Marinar Technology Co LLC dba VantageOne Software
33801 Curtis Blvd, Ste 112
Eastlake, OH 44095
Contact: Erica Martin CEO
Tel: 440-354-1458
Email: erica.francis@vantageonesoftware.com
Website: www.vantageonesoftware.com
IT service engineers & technicians, infrastructure expansion, data migration, system security, disaster planning or basic workstation & server optimization. (Woman, estab 1994, empl 14, sales $975,000, cert: WBENC)

INFORMATION TECHNOLOGY: Services

5395 Marketing & Engineering Solutions
      625 Bear Run Lane
      Lewis Center, OH 43035
      Contact: Hiten Shah President
      Tel: 740-201-8112
      Email: hshah@mesinc.net
      Website: www.mesinc.net
Information technology, outsourcing, customer survey processing, database maintenance, OCR & ICR data processing, call center, data processing, data entry, rebate processing. (As-Ind, estab 1999, empl 110, sales $2,700,000, cert: NMSDC)

5396 MAX Technical Training Inc.
      4900 Pkwy Dr
      Cincinnati, OH 45040
      Contact: Patricia Miller CEO
      Tel: 513-322-8888
      Email: patricia@maxtrain.com
      Website: www.maxtrain.com
IT programmers & developers training. (Woman, estab 1998, empl 12, sales $1,950,556, cert: WBENC)

5397 Mediascript, LLC
      3982 Powell Rd, Ste 235
      Powell, OH 43065
      Contact: Angela Horne CEO
      Tel: 614-551-3549
      Email: angela@mediascriptllc.com
      Website: www.mediascriptllc.com
Media webinar technology: distance education, online learning & training. (Woman, estab 2009, empl 3, sales $175,000, cert: WBENC)

5398 MurTech Consulting LLC
      4807 Rockside Rd, Ste 250
      Independence, OH 44131
      Contact: Ailish Murphy President
      Tel: 216-328-8580
      Email: amurphy@murtechconsulting.com
      Website: www.murtechconsulting.com
Information technology consulting & placement services. (Woman, estab 2000, empl 25, sales $14,200,000, cert: WBENC)

5399 Myca Multimedia and Training Solutions, LLC
      4555 Lake Forest Dr Ste 650
      Cincinnati, OH 45242
      Contact: Patricia Massey President
      Tel: 513-608-6033
      Email: pmassey@mycagroup.com
      Website: www.mycalearning.com
Interactive & engaging eLearning tools, computer & cloud-based eLearning courseware on harassment prevention, culture & inclusion, bullying. (Woman, estab 1991, empl 15, sales $984,166, cert: WBENC)

5400 N-ovation Technology Group
      10 W. 2nd St Ste 2201
      Dayton, OH 45402
      Contact: Dwayne Coker CEO
      Tel: 937-886-4850
      Email: sales@n-ovationtech.com
      Website: www.n-ovationtech.com
Network Design, Architecture & Integration services, Data Center Solutions, Cyber Security, Wireless DAS deployment, Cloud strategy, Infrastructure Program Management, Process Management & Quality Assurance, Vendor Management. (AA, estab 2015, empl 5, sales $10,000,000, cert: City, NMSDC)

5401 Precise Infotech Inc.
      7315 Royal Portrush Dr
      Solon, OH 44139
      Contact: Kashifa Ahmed President
      Tel: 440-265-0402
      Email: kahmed@preciseinfotech.com
      Website: www.preciseinfotech.com
Software development & consulting. (Minority, Woman, estab 2004, empl 2, sales $274,121, cert: State)

5402 Promark Custom Solutions LLC
      8 Prestige Plaza, Ste 110
      Springboro, OH 45342
      Contact: Lisa Johnson President
      Tel: 937-557-0333
      Email: ljohnson@promarkcs.com
      Website: www.promarkcs.com
Office Productivity, Cyber Security, Security Certifications, IT Certifications, IT Skills, and Business Skills. (Woman, estab 1995, empl 1, sales , cert: WBENC)

5403 R.Dorsey & Company, Inc.
      400 W Wilson Bridge Rd Ste 105
      Worthington, OH 43085
      Contact: Joyce Dorsey CEO
      Tel: 614-486-8900
      Email: jcdorsey@dorseyplus.com
      Website: www.dorseyplus.com
Network Architecture, Application Architecture, Service Oriented Architecture, Data Warehouse, Hosting, Security, Data Backup, Outsourcing (Woman, estab 1996, empl 30, sales $ 0, cert: WBENC, 8(a))

5404 Solutions For You Inc.
      470 Olde Worthington Rd Ste 200
      Westerville, OH 43082
      Contact: Robert Johnson
      Tel: 614-410-6648
      Email: robertj@sfyi.com
      Website: www.sfyi.com
Information Technology consulting: Full cycle product development, Business Analysis, Quality Assurance, Project Management, Security (data, network, database), Open Source (language, tools, software), data analysis, Electronic Data Interchange. (Woman/AA, estab 1999, empl 4, sales $423,027, cert: State, City, NMSDC)

5405 StarTech Consulting, Inc.
      6746 Rivercrest Dr, Ste 100
      Cleveland, OH 44141
      Contact: Joe Bains President
      Tel: 440-546-9500
      Email: jbains@startech-consult.com
      Website: www.startech-consult.com
Staff Augmentation, Web & Mobile apps, Database development/administrators, Project Managers, Business Analysts, Quality Assurance, etc. (As-Ind, estab 1998, empl 6, sales $2,107,771, cert: State)

5406 Strategic Systems, Inc.
      475 Metro Place South Ste 450
      Dublin, OH 43017
      Contact: Kaushal Vadada Dir of Operations
      Tel: 614-973-7979
      Email: kaushal@strsi.com
      Website: www.strsi.com
IT Staff Augmentation, Project Management, Hybrid Staff Aumentation, Contract to Hire, and Platform Development/Delivery. (Woman/As-Ind, estab 2004, empl 175, sales $19,000,000, cert: State, NMSDC)

5407   SYSTEMIAN LLC
       555 Metro Place N, Ste 100
       Plain City, OH 43064
       Contact: Wilson Fernando President
       Tel: 614-390-9660
       Email: wilson@systemian.com
       Website: www.systemian.com
IT services, Enterprise Architecture, Intelligent Automation, Cloud Adoption and Migration, Talent Management. (As-Pac, estab 2020, empl 12, sales , cert: NMSDC)

5408   TechSoft Systems, Inc.
       10296 Springfield Pike Ste 400
       Cincinnati, OH 45215
       Contact: Clifford A. Bailey President
       Tel: 513-772-5010
       Email: cabailey@techsoftsystems.com
       Website: www.techsoftsystems.com
IT Consultants/Staffing, On-Site Support (desktop, network, help desk), Remot Support, Manages Services, Hardware & Software purchasing. (AA, estab 1983, empl 10, sales $904,328, cert: City, NMSDC)

5409   Texcel, Inc.
       4415 Euclid Ave
       Cleveland, OH 44103
       Contact: Herman Atkins President
       Tel: 216-514-1818
       Email: batkins@texcelinc.net
       Website: www.texcelinc.net
Digital document rendering. IBM cloud solutions. (AA, estab , empl , sales $6,000,000, cert: State, City, NMSDC)

5410   TMH Solutions LLC
       4176 Menderes Dr
       Powell, OH 43065
       Contact: Theresa Harris President
       Tel: 614-581-4450
       Email: theresa@tmhsolutions.com
       Website: www.tmhsolutions.com
Resell software & services, management & information technology solutions. (Woman/AA, estab 2010, empl 5, sales $5,100,000, cert: State, NMSDC, WBENC)

5411   TPSi, LLC
       11590 Century Blvd
       Cincinnati, OH 45246
       Contact: Matt Bender President
       Tel: 877-682-5300
       Email: mbender@tpsinc.com
       Website: www.tpsinc.com
Technical staffing & engineering services. (Woman, estab 2000, empl 25, sales $2,300,000, cert: WBENC)

5412   UNICON International, Inc.
       241 Outerbelt St
       Columbus, OH 43213
       Contact: Bobby Cameron Dir Client Services
       Tel: 614-861-7070
       Email: bcameron@unicon-intl.com
       Website: www.unicon-intl.com
Information technology solutions. (Minority, Woman, estab 1990, empl 300, sales $31,000,000, cert: City, NMSDC, WBENC)

5413   United Software Group Inc.
       565, Metro Place South, Ste 110
       Dublin, OH 43017
       Contact: Vetri Palaniappan Business Devel Dir
       Tel: 614-588-8530
       Email: vetri.p@usgrpinc.com
       Website: www.usgrpinc.com
Software consulting services. (As-Ind, estab 2002, empl 200, sales $69,000,000, cert: State, NMSDC)

5414   Vertex Computer Systems, Inc
       25700 Science Park Dr Ste 280
       Beachwood, OH 44122
       Contact: Reshmy Kesavadas Office of Supplier Diversity
       Tel: 479-903-6827
       Email: vertex.rfp@vertexcs.com
       Website: www.vertexcs.com
IT development & outsourced services: web, database & middleware. (Woman/As-Ind, estab 1989, empl 200, sales $12,425,234, cert: NMSDC, WBENC)

5415   Warwick Communications, Inc.
       405 Ken Mar Pkwy
       Broadview Heights, OH 44147
       Contact: Heidi Murphy Principal
       Tel: 216-787-0300
       Email: hmurphy@warwickinc.com
       Website: www.warwickinc.com
Information technology managed services, telephone systems, VOIP systems, cloud/hosted systems, wireless systems, data switching equipment, call recording software, support desk services, call accounting systems, call center software. (Woman, estab 1960, empl 40, sales $6,245,000, cert: City)

5416   Western Reserve Technology
       34194 Aurora Rd, Ste 200
       Solon, OH 44139
       Contact: Kim Cahuas Owner
       Tel: 440-498-9500
       Email: kim@gowrt.com
       Website: www.gowrt.com
Oracle Business Intelligence Enterprise Edition. (Minority, Woman, estab 2005, empl 1, sales $1,100,000, cert: State, NMSDC)

Oklahoma

5417   Delaware Resource Group of Oklahoma LLC
       3220 Quail Springs Pkwy
       Oklahoma City, OK 73134
       Contact: Meredith Kemp Program Mgmt Assistant
       Tel: 405-721-7776
       Email: meredith.kemp@drgok.com
       Website: www.drgok.com/
Contract instruction services, computer based training, curriculum development & maintenance, computer training materials devel & contract operations maintenance svcs. (Nat Ame, estab 2002, empl 200, sales $21,569,317, cert: NMSDC)

INFORMATION TECHNOLOGY: Services

5418 Lynnco Supply Chain Solutions
      2448 E 81st St, Ste 2600
      Tulsa, OK 74137
      Contact: Wendy Buxton President
      Tel: 918-664-5540
      Email: wendy.buxton@lynnco-scs.com
      Website: www.lynnco-scs.com
Supply Chain Analytics, Planning and Execution, Supply Chain Metrics, Continuous Improvement with Lean Methodologies, Supplier Fulfillment & Compliance Programs, Freight Procurement & Optimization. Logistics Management. (Minority, Woman, estab 1991, empl 65, sales $70,000,000, cert: NMSDC, WBENC)

5419 Xyant Technology, Inc.
      710 ASP Ave Ste 500
      Norman, OK 73069
      Contact: Sowmya Sridhar President
      Tel: 405-209-7371
      Email: sowmyas@xyant.com
      Website: www.xyant.com
IT consulting & staff augmentation solutions: application implementation & deployment, maintenance & support, networking svcs, migration upgrades. (As-Pac, estab 1995, empl 50, sales $2,000,000, cert: NMSDC)

Oregon

5420 BahFed
      1000 SW Broadway Ste 1110
      Portland, OR 97205
      Contact: Ken Paul President
      Tel: 503-208-8410
      Email: govsales@bahfed.com
      Website: www.bahfed.com
IT products, commodities & support solutions. (As-Ind, estab 2011, empl 20, sales $97,000,000, cert: State)

5421 Cayuse Technologies, LLC
      72632 Coyote Rd
      Pendleton, OR 97801
      Contact: Heather Collins Dir Business Dev
      Tel: 541-278-8200
      Email: heather.collins@cayusetechnologies.com
      Website: www.cayusetechnologies.com
Technology Platforms: Java and .NET-Operating Systems: UNIX and Windows-Programming Languages: Java, J2EE, PL/SQL, ASP, C, C+, C++, C#, VB, COBOL, TAL, TACL-Open Source Frameworks; Hibernate, Spring. (Nat Ame, estab 2006, empl 240, sales $15,063,354, cert: State, NMSDC)

5422 Everest Consultants, Inc.
      1500 NW Bethany Blvd Ste 235
      Beaverton, OR 97006
      Contact: Ranya Edupuganti President
      Tel: 503-643-3990
      Email: ranya@everestinc.com
      Website: www.everestinc.com
Software consulting, offshore software dev, systems integration & IS/IT staff augmentation. (Minority, Woman, estab 1993, empl 65, sales $9,500,000, cert: NMSDC)

5423 iBridge LLC
      12725 SW Millikan Way, Ste 300
      Beaverton, OR 97005
      Contact: Desh Urs President
      Tel: 503-906-3930
      Email: bids@ibridgellc.com
      Website: www.ibridgellc.com/
Digitizing, converting, data processing all forms of information, electronic, paper, microfilm, voice or video, e cleanse, format & verify data. (As-Ind, estab 2004, empl 16, sales $ 0, cert: State)

5424 Martin's Got You Covered
      PO Box 3764
      Portland, OR 97208
      Contact: Donald Martin President
      Tel: 503-289-0278
      Email: donald@martinsgotyoucovered.com
      Website: www.martinsgotyoucovered.com/
Computer hardware & software, custom-build laptops, notebooks, tablet pcs, monitors, modems, presentation equipment, servers. (AA, estab 2002, empl 1, sales $ 0, cert: State)

5425 Mavensoft Technologies
      15248 NW Greenbrier Pkwy
      Beaverton, OR 97006
      Contact: Acct Mgr
      Tel: 503-629-4855
      Email: sales@mavensoft.com
      Website: www.mavensoft.com
IT services, software development, QA, Cloud Engineering, Project Management, Java, .NET, PHP, Angular JS, HP ALM, Selenium, BI Analytics, E-commerce, IBM Websphere, SAP Hybris, Oracle ATG, Magento. (As-Ind, estab 2004, empl 30, sales $2,400,000, cert: NMSDC)

5426 Protech Excellens Inc.
      1500 NW Bethany Blvd Ste 200
      Beaverton, OR 07006
      Contact: Ben Condol CEO
      Tel: 866-688-8843
      Email: ben@protechexcellens.com
      Website: www.protechexcellens.com
Oracle Databases, Oracle Middleware, Oracle applications, Oracle Engineered Systems, Oracle storage, Oracle support. PeoleSoft, Fusion, EBS, CRM. (Minority, Woman, estab 2007, empl 2, sales $170,000, cert: State)

5427 Rapid External Solutions, Inc.
      9450 SW Gemini Dr Ste 61944
      Beaverton, OR 97008
      Contact: Vic Gupta Dir
      Tel: 617-616-0986
      Email: info@r-e-s.com
      Website: www.r-e-s.com
ERP Applications staffing: Oracle, SAP, PeopleSoft, JDE, Siebel, Microsoft. (As-Ind, estab 2009, empl 13, sales $11,000,000, cert: NMSDC)

5428 Triad Technology Group
      10300 SW Greenburg Rd, Ste 560
      Portland, OR 97223
      Contact: Regina Shapiro Acct Mgr
      Tel: 503-293-9547
      Email: kelley@go2triad.com
      Website: www.triadtechnology.com
Information technology staffing & recruiting services. (Hisp, estab 1989, empl 30, sales $3,700,000, cert: State)

INFORMATION TECHNOLOGY: Services

Pennsylvania

5429 Abator Information Services, Inc.
615 South Ave
Pittsburgh, PA 15221
Contact: Joanne Peterson CEO
Tel: 412-271-5922
Email: joanne@abator.com
Website: www.abator.com/
Information technology & systems projects. (Woman, estab 1983, empl 9, sales $1,297,485, cert: State, WBENC)

5430 ABOUT-Consulting LLC
330 Kennett Pike, Ste 205
Chadds Ford, PA 19317
Contact: Frances Gatto CEO
Tel: 610-388-9455
Email: fgatto@about-consulting.com
Website: www.about-consulting.com
Project mgmt, internet, intranet & extranet design & dev, business apps & databases, help desk, network systems engineering, architecture & admin, operations & technical svcs. (Woman, estab 2002, empl 20, sales $3,000,000, cert: WBENC)

5431 Advanced Integration Group Inc.
1 McCormick Rd Ste A
McKees Rocks, PA 15136
Contact: Donna Chappel President
Tel: 412-722-0065
Email: dchappel@aigcontrols.com
Website: www.aigcontrols.com
IT & engineering professionals: consultants, contractors & temp to perm personnel. (Woman, estab 1997, empl 35, sales $2,750,000, cert: WBENC)

5432 AptoTek Inc.
2026 Milta Hill Rd
Romansville, PA 19320
Contact: Joe Johnbosco CEO
Tel: 610-241-2603
Email: joe.johnbosco@aptotek-inc.com
Website: www.aptotek-inc.com
Custom Application Development, CRM Solutions, IT staff augmentation, IT outsource Services, Application/software support & maintenance contracts, IT strategy solutions. (As-Ind, estab 2015, empl 1, sales , cert: NMSDC)

5433 Aspect Consulting, Inc.
20140 Valley Forge Cir
King of Prussia, PA 19406
Contact: Nicole Gantzhorn Business Devel Rep
Tel: 610-783-0600
Email: ngantzhorn@aspect-consulting.com
Website: www.aspect-consulting.com
Technical Staffing, Data Mgmt, Business Intelligence, Configuration, Data Warehouse Development, Database Administration, Oracle, SQL Server, Custom Software Development, Application Design & Architecture. (Woman, estab 1994, empl 40, sales $5,300,000, cert: WBENC)

5434 Cognis IT Advisors LLC
1735 Market St Ste A-485
Philadelphia, PA 19103
Contact: Mike Thomas CEO
Tel: 215-557-4455
Email: mthomas@cognisit.com
Website: www.cognisit-advisors.com
Information Technology (IT) Services. (AA, estab 2007, empl 4, sales $489,000, cert: NMSDC)

5435 Computer Enterprises, Inc.
1000 Omega Dr Ste 1150
Pittsburgh, PA 15205
Contact: Joe Esposito Solutions Sales Dir
Tel: 412-680-4880
Email: jesposito@ceiamerica.com
Website: www.ceiamerica.com
Software consulting & system integration services, custom applications & systems software programming services & Internet systems consulting services. (AA, As-Pac, estab , empl 620, sales $71,947,000, cert: NMSDC)

5436 ConnectedSign, LLC
120A W Airport Rd
Lititz, PA 17543
Contact: Loren Bucklin President
Tel: 866-833-2723
Email: lbucklin@connectedsign.com
Website: www.connectedsign.com
Digital Signage Software, Navori Tycoon Software, Digital Signage Hardware, Digital Signage Content, Website Development and Content, Kiosks Software, Kiosks Hardware, Kiosks Content. (Woman, estab 2003, empl 12, sales $1,000,000, cert: WBENC)

5437 CREDO Technology Solutions, Inc.
110 Sunset Ave Ste 101
Harrisburg, PA 17112
Contact: Missy Flexman Dir of Marketing & Communications
Tel: 717-657-7017
Email: mflexman@credotsinc.com
Website: www.credotsinc.com
IT project solutions, ERP software implementations & upgrades. (As-Ind, estab 2010, empl 42, sales $3,130,000, cert: State, NMSDC)

5438 DecisionOne Corporation
640 Lee Road 3rd Fl
Wayne, PA 19087
Contact: Karen Strickler Sr Proposal Specialist
Tel: 610-296-6183
Email: karen.strickler@decisionone.com
Website: www.decisionone.com
Outsourced remote solutions & support desk services, technology centers, hardware & software asset services, forward/reverse logistics & supply chain management services. (As-Ind, estab 1969, empl 800, sales $101,755,000, cert: NMSDC)

5439 Eminent Group, Inc
2 Walnut Grove Rd Ste 130
Horsham, PA 19044
Contact: Katherine Moore CEO
Tel: 267-387-6487
Email: kmoore@egiusa.com
Website: www.egiusa.com
Transportation Management Systems Implementation, Global Trade Management Systems Implementation, Outsourcing:
Transportation Operational Planning, Transportation Optimization. (Woman, estab 2002, empl 38, sales $7,104,089, cert: WBENC)

INFORMATION TECHNOLOGY: Services

5440 Futura Services, Inc.
515 Pennsylvania Ave Ste 100
Fort Washington, PA 19034
Contact: Dominic Sambucci COO
Tel: 215-639-9540
Email: dsambucci@futuraservices.net
Website: www.futuraservices.net
Help desk support, spare pool, asset management, staging, kitting, hardware roll-outs & imaging. (Woman, estab 1992, empl 45, sales $9,000,000, cert: WBENC)

5441 Genzeon Corporation
559 W Uwchlan Ave Ste 120
Exton, PA 19341
Contact: Brendan OHayre COO
Tel: 203-516-1109
Email: brendan.ohayre@genzeon.com
Website: www.genzeon.com
Technology solutions, custom application development, performance engineering & human capital solutions. (Minority, estab 1999, empl 150, sales $17,500,000, cert: NMSDC)

5442 Hanabi Networks Systems, LLC
150 N Radnor Chester Rd, Ste F200
Radnor, PA 19087
Contact: Tariq Yusufzai VP Business Dev
Tel: 484-381-0698
Email: tyusufzai@ehanabi.com
Website: www.ehanabi.com
Analyze, design, install, configure, manage & repair global network infrastructure & application components. (As-Pac, estab 2016, empl 2, sales $120,000, cert: NMSDC)

5443 iBusiness Solution, LLC
5000 Lenker St
Mechanicsburg, PA 17050
Contact: Narendra Ghuge
Tel: 717-724-7865
Email: sales@ibusinesssolution.com
Website: www.ibusinesssolution.com
IT consulting, technology services, staffing & outsourcing. (As-Ind, estab 2000, empl 54, sales $9,000,000, cert: State, NMSDC)

5444 ID Discovery, Inc.
18 Mainland Rd
Harleysville, PA 19438
Contact: Amanda Mortimer Business Dev
Tel: 215-230-4130
Email: amanda.mortimer@id-llc.com
Website: www.id-llc.com
Strategic Project Management, Data Management, Product Commercialization, eDiscovery, Cyber Security, IT consulting and Information Governance solutions. (Woman, estab 2012, empl 30, sales , cert: WBENC)

5445 ImageTech Systsems, Inc.
3913 Hartzdale Dr
Camp Hill, PA 17011
Contact: RJ Oommen Principal
Tel: 717-761-5900
Email: rjo@imagetechsys.com
Website: www.imagetechsys.com
Enterprise Content Management (ECM) & Business Process automation technologies. (As-Ind, estab 1994, empl 7, sales $2,000,000, cert: State, NMSDC)

5446 Independent Computer Consulting Group, Inc.
1 Ivybrook Blvd Ste 177
Warminster, PA 18974
Contact: Mihir Shah Sr Business Dev Mgr
Tel: 215-675-9149
Email: mshah@iccg.com
Website: www.iccg.com
LX, SA, M3 products implementation, upgrades & support, WMS/PkMS, WMOS, SCALE, DOM implementations, upgrades & support, Business Intelligence, Qlik, Cognos & Micro Strategy
SAP suite of applications. (Woman/As-Ind, estab 1988, empl 100, sales , cert: WBENC)

5447 Iron Lady Enterprises Inc.
1943 Poplar St, 2nd Fl
Philadelphia, PA 19130
Contact: Dianna Montague CEO
Tel: 267-973-8626
Email: dianna.montague@ironladyenterprises.com
Website: www.ironladyenterprises.com/
Ironworking services: welding & repair bridges & structural units. (Woman/AA, estab 2011, empl 2, sales , cert: City, NMSDC)

5448 JCW Computer Consulting, LLC
7478 Rhoads St, Ste C
Philadelphia, PA 19151
Contact: Carl Johnson Sales Assoc
Tel: 215-879-6701
Email: carl@jcwcc.com
Website: www.jcwcc.com
Computer consulting: Microsoft, IBM & Compaq solutions, workstation & server product lines. (AA, estab 1992, empl 3, sales $ 0, cert: City, NMSDC)

5449 KORYAK Consulting, Inc.
2003 Kinvara Dr
Pittsburgh, PA 15237
Contact: Suresh Ramanathan CEO
Tel: 412-364-6600
Email: sramanathan@koryak.com
Website: www.koryak.com
Management & IT consulting: business & IT strategy dev, supply chain enhancement, E-business integration, Oracle app implementation & outsourcing, systems dev & integration. (As-Ind, estab 2000, empl 25, sales $3,000,000, cert: State, NMSDC)

5450 Lim, Norris & Associates
12 Fox Hunt Cir
Plymouth Meeting, PA 19462
Contact: Yvonne Norris President
Tel: 610-825-6730
Email: ynorris@limnorris.com
Website: www.limnorris.com
Information technology, strategic planning & organization design. (Minority, Woman, estab 1994, empl 3, sales $953,000, cert: City)

INFORMATION TECHNOLOGY: Services

5451 Logix Guru LLC
      3821 Old William Penn Hwy
      Murrysville, PA 15668
      Contact: Singh Ajmani Business Devel Mgr
      Tel: 724-733-4500
      Email: ajmani@logixguru.com
      Website: www.logixguru.com
IT consulting & staff augmentation, engineering, administrative, information technology. (As-Ind, estab 2000, empl 20, sales $4,200,000, cert: State, NMSDC)

5452 M.A.P. Consulting Services, Inc.
      520 South 3rd St
      Philadelphia, PA 19147
      Contact: CEO
      Tel: 215-315-4175
      Email: info@mapconsult.com
      Website: www.mapconsult.com
IT staffing & consulting, ERP & EDI specialists, project mgmt expertise, data warehousing. (Woman, estab 1997, empl 2, sales $201,000, cert: WBENC)

5453 Mastech Digital Technologies, Inc.
      1305 Cherrington Pkwy Bldg 210, Ste 400
      Moon Township, PA 15108
      Contact: Michael Kosar Dir of MSP
      Tel: 412-787-9559
      Email: Michael.kosar@mastechdigital.com
      Website: www.mastechdigital.com
IT services: usiness intelligence, data warehousing, architecture & web svcs, enterprise resource planning, custom applications, dev & maintenance, migration, re-engineering, project mgmt, ebusiness solutions. (Minority, estab , empl 750, sales $123,400,000, cert: NMSDC)

5454 Minitab Inc.
      1829 Pine Hall Rd
      State College, PA 16801
      Contact: Justin Callahan Sr Reg Mgr Commercial Sales
      Tel: 814-238-3280
      Email: jcallahan@minitab.com
      Website: www.minitab.com
IT products and services. (Minority, Woman, estab 1983, empl 350, sales $ 0, cert: WBENC)

5455 Momentum, Inc.
      2120 Market St Ste 100
      Camp Hill, PA 17011
      Contact: Scott Reilly Exec Dir
      Tel: 717-214-8000
      Email: momentum@m-inc.com
      Website: www.m-inc.com
IT & management consulting, process improvement, project management & implementation support. (Woman, estab 1998, empl 54, sales $9,304,338, cert: State, City)

5456 Ohm Systems, Inc.
      955 Horsham Rd Ste 205
      Horsham, PA 19044
      Contact: Praful Patel President
      Tel: 215-309-6233
      Email: ppatel@ohmsysinc.com
      Website: www.ohmsysinc.com
Software development, support, maintenance, R&D, web, consulting, FAA, telecom, protocols, client/server, java. (Minority, estab 1998, empl 65, sales $6,500,000, cert: NMSDC)

5457 OPTiMO Information Technology LLC
      240 Market St, Ste 112
      Bloomsburg, PA 17815
      Contact: Michael Miguelez CEO
      Tel: 877-564-8552
      Email: mmiguelez@optimo-it.com
      Website: www.optimo-it.com
Web & Mobile app devel, UI/UX system integration, database development, agile project/program mgmt, digital forensic investigations & eDiscovery processing. (Hisp, estab , empl 50, sales $5,000,000, cert: 8(a))

5458 Partner's Consulting, Inc.
      2004 Sproul Road, Ste 206
      Broomall, PA 19008
      Contact: Delivery & Engagement Mgr
      Tel: 215-939-6294
      Email: info@partners-consulting.com
      Website: www.partners-consulting.com
Information technology recruiting for full-time, temp-to-perm & contract positions. (Woman, estab 2006, empl 40, sales $6,000,000, cert: State, WBENC)

5459 Pierson Computing Connection, Inc.
      10 Long Ln
      Mechanicsburg, PA 17050
      Contact: Debra Pierson President
      Tel: 717-796-0493
      Email: deb@pierson.it
      Website: www.pierson.it
Project mgmt, multi-site IT & related installations, printers, cash registers, PC equipment, cabling, networking equipment, etc. (Woman, estab 1993, empl 47, sales $16,900,000, cert: State, WBENC)

5460 Plumlogix LLC
      7035 Schantz Rd #150
      ALLENTOWN, PA 18106
      Contact: Shoaib Chaudhary CEO
      Tel: 732-688-9552
      Email: Sherjeelc@plumlogix.com
      Website: www.plumlogix.com
Salesforce, Web/App Development, UI/UX. (As-Pac, estab 2016, empl 45, sales $2,400,000, cert: NMSDC)

5461 Probitas Technology Inc.
      3544 N Progress Ave Ste 104
      Harrisburg, PA 17110
      Contact: Benjamin Williams President
      Tel: 717-773-4208
      Email: sales@probitastek.com
      Website: www.probitastek.com
Computer networking design, installation & maintenance, electronic security. (AA, estab 2004, empl 8, sales $600,000, cert: State, City)

5462 PRWT Services, Inc.
      1835 Market St Ste 800
      Philadelphia, PA 19103
      Contact: Rose Braverman SVP Strategic Planning & Operations
      Tel: 215-569-8810
      Email: rose.braverman@prwt.com
      Website: www.prwt.com
Information & document processing; lockbox processing; call ctr customer care & service; facilities mgmt; web & telephone-based fulfillment; telecommunications construction; help desk functions & toll collections operations. (AA, estab 1988, empl 1000, sales $69,800,000, cert: City, NMSDC)

INFORMATION TECHNOLOGY: Services

5463 Raise Tech Solutions, LLC
606 Liberty Ave, 3rd Fl
Pittsburgh, PA 15222
Contact: John R Thomson President
Tel: 412-267-3069
Email: contact@raisets.com
Website: www.RaiseTS.com
IT Services and Consulting. (AA, estab 2017, empl 10, sales , cert: NMSDC)

5464 River Development Corporation
2005 Garrick Dr
Pittsburgh, PA 15235
Contact: Cheryl McAbee
Tel: 412-243-2005
Email: crmcabee@riverdevcorp.com
Website: www.riverdevcorp.com
Records storage: off site, web access inventory, media vault storage & delivery, scan & index, data vaulting, shredding. (Woman, estab 1996, empl 4, sales , cert: State, City, NMSDC)

5465 RST Solutions Inc.
1005 Azlen Lane Ste 114
Chalfont, PA 18914
Contact: Rajan Kaistha VP
Tel: 610-613-8699
Email: rajan@rstsolutions.com
Website: www.rstsolutions.com
ERP services, implementations, upgrade, integrations, JDE Mobile Apps, FRICE/COMLI, etc. (Woman/As-Ind, estab 2003, empl 18, sales $5,000,000, cert: WBENC)

5466 ShazTEK LLP
500 Office Center Dr, Ste 400
Fort Washington, PA 19034
Contact: Zak Khan Dir Sales
Tel: 267-507-3168
Email: zkhan@shaztek.com
Website: www.shaztek.com
Analyze business impact, costs, and regulatory requirements to build a technology roadmap. (As-Ind, estab 2011, empl 27, sales $18,225,000, cert: NMSDC)

5467 Sigma Resources LLC
7950 Saltsburg Rd
Pittsburgh, PA 15239
Contact: Sandy Kaleida VP Consulting
Tel: 412-712-1019
Email: skaleida@sigma-resources.com
Website: www.sigma-resources.com
IT consulting services. (Minority, Woman, estab 1998, empl 24, sales $9,000,000, cert: State, WBENC)

5468 SoftNice Inc.
5050 Tilghman St, Ste 115
Allentown, PA 18104
Contact: Zubin Pardiwala Mgr Business Devel
Tel: 201-603-2635
Email: zubin@softnice.com
Website: www.softnice.com
Global Consulting and IT services. (As-Pac, estab 2001, empl 600, sales $18,007,269, cert: NMSDC)

5469 SoftSages, LLC
17 Mystic Lane, Ste 2A
Malvern, PA 19355
Contact: Jiraj Ruparelia VP
Tel: 484-604-0603
Email: jiraj@softsages.com
Website: www.softsages.com
Software Development Consultants, programming, Database Developments, Networking & mobile development, custom software & security solutions. (Woman/As-Pac, estab 2005, empl 25, sales $8,000,000, cert: State, NMSDC, WBENC)

5470 solutions4networks, Inc.
1501 Reedsdale St Ste 2001
PIttsburgh, PA 15233
Contact: Michele McGough CEO
Tel: 412-638-4341
Email: michele@s4nets.com
Website: www.s4nets.com
Data, voice, wireless & network security consulting: network assessments & design, security assessments, IPv6 planning, MPLS, QoS, project mgmt, product selection, RFP devel. (Woman, estab 2000, empl 25, sales $8,430,000, cert: State, WBENC)

5471 SwitchLane Inc.
5 Christy Dr Ste 303
Chadds Ford, PA 19317
Contact: Meera Kalyani President
Tel: 267-297-0790
Email: meera@switchlane.com
Website: www.switchlane.com
IT staffing & consulting services. (Woman, estab 2010, empl 10, sales $1,312,407, cert: State, WBENC)

5472 Symphony Enterprises LLC
PO Box 16140
Pittsburgh, PA 15242
Contact: Head Sales & Business Dev
Tel: 412-212-0135
Email: sales@symphonyenterprises.com
Website: www.symphonyenterprises.com
IT staffing & consulting services. (Minority, Woman, estab 2004, empl 4, sales $ 0, cert: State)

5473 Synergy EnterPrize, LLC
1150 First Ave, Ste 501
King of Prussia, PA 19406
Contact: Jonathan Ngah Principal
Tel: 610-945-1737
Email: information@synergy-ia.com
Website: www.synergy-ia.com
Audit Support, Information Technology Management & Governance, Business Process Improvement, Project Management, Fraud Risk & Vulnerability Assessment solutions. (AA, estab 2011, empl 10, sales $1,500,000, cert: NMSDC, 8(a))

5474 Systems Staffing Group Inc.
910 E. Main St Ste 201
Norristown, PA 19401
Contact: Beth Verman CEO
Tel: 610-668-8101
Email: bverman@systemsstaffinggroup.com
Website: www.systemsstaffinggroup.com
Information technology staffing: consultants & permanent employees. (Woman, estab 2000, empl 30, sales $15,000,000, cert: WBENC)

5475 Tan Check Consolidated, Inc.
2 Silver Trail Circle Ste 101
Newtown, PA 18940
Contact: Rebecca Smith Sr Acct Mgr
Tel: 215-860-5031
Email: rsmith@tcci.com
Website: www.tcci.com
IT Staffing, Information Technology Management, Consulting, Permanent Placement, Temp to Perm, Executive Search, Software Development. (Woman, estab 2001, empl 75, sales $6,850,000, cert: State, WBENC)

5476 Techwave Consulting Inc.
1 E Uwchlan Ave
Exton, PA 19341
Contact: Jalpesh Thaker Mgr
Tel: 484-873-4602
Email: infona@techwave.net
Website: www.techwave.net/
Software consulting & staffing services: SAP (BI, BO, BPC, BPM & BW), Oracle (OBIEE), Cognos & BPM products & services. (Woman/As-Ind, estab 2004, empl 150, sales $11,000,000, cert: State)

5477 TreCom Systems Group
99 November Dr
Camp Hill, PA 17011
Contact: Phillip Gring COO
Tel: 717-319-0711
Email: pgring@trecomsystems.com
Website: www.trecomsystems.com
Information technology consulting svcs: software dev & design, enterprise architecture, training, help desk, programming, networking, documentation, software testing, staff augmentation, contract programming, Oracle authorized reseller. (AA, estab 2009, empl 58, sales $7,000,000, cert: State, NMSDC)

5478 Tri-force Consulting Services Inc.
650 North Cannon Ave
Lansdale, PA 19446
Contact: Manish Gorawala President
Tel: 215-362-2611
Email: mgorawala@triforce-inc.com
Website: www.triforce-inc.com/
Information technology consulting: Java, J2EE, .NET, QA & open source technologies based business applications solutions. (Minority, estab 2000, empl 40, sales $6,285,927, cert: State, City, NMSDC)

5479 TriLogic Corporation
161 Hillpointe Dr
Canonsburg, PA 15317
Contact: Gary Grabowski Operations Mgr
Tel: 724-745-0200
Email: ggrabowski@tri-logic.com
Website: www.tri-logic.com
Design, install & maintain LAN/WANs; wireless networking, IP telephony, virtual private networks. (AA, estab 1981, empl 35, sales $ 0, cert: NMSDC)

5480 Urban Harvest Partnership, LLC
6050 Osage Ave
Philadelphia, PA 19143
Contact: Jonathan Ford Principal
Tel: 610-482-4284
Email: ford@uhpwireless.com
Website: www.uhpwireless.com/
Technology services: desktop & network services, secure wireless networking, cabling services, voice, data & audio/video installations. (AA, estab 2003, empl 7, sales $960,000, cert: NMSDC)

5481 Velocity Works, LLC
12330 Perry Hwy, Ste 115
Wexford, PA 15090
Contact: Dionisio Lopez CEO
Tel: 412-398-2679
Email: al@velocityworks.io
Website: www.velocityworks.io
Technical staffing and software engineering consulting to the financial services, healthcare and robotics industries. (Hisp, estab 2018, empl 30, sales $3,625,433, cert: NMSDC)

5482 YIKES, Inc.
204 E Girard Ave
Philadelphia, PA 19125
Contact: Mia Levesque Co-Owner
Tel: 215-238-8801
Email: info@yikesinc.com
Website: www.yikesinc.com
Web design & development services, WordPress, Custom web design, website maintenance, ecommerce, web/database integration, ColdFusion, custom-built web-based applications, content management systems. (Minority, Woman, estab 1996, empl 5, sales $664,693, cert: City, WBENC)

5483 Zodiac Solutions Inc.
270 Lancaster Ave Ste h-2
Malvern, PA 19355
Contact: VP Operations
Tel: 484-550-6482
Email: info@zodiac-solutions.com
Website: www.zodiac-solutions.com
IT staff augmentation , IT solutions services, managed services, project management, software development, knowledge process outsourcing, management consulting. (As-Ind, estab 2011, empl 70, sales $4,751,993, cert: NMSDC)

Puerto Rico

5484 Barquin & Associates Inc.
452 Ponce de Leon Ave Ste 520
San Juan, PR 00918
Contact: Ramon Carlos Barquin VP
Tel: 787-296-9768
Email: rbarquin3@barquin.com
Website: www.barquin.com
Information technology services, data warehousing, business intelligence, knowledge management, and information architecture. (Hisp, estab 1994, empl 84, sales $8,000,000, cert: State)

INFORMATION TECHNOLOGY: Services

5485 Beryllium Corporation
PO Box 5938
Caguas, PR 00726
Contact: Jorge Normandia CEO
Tel: 787-744-5729
Email: info@berylliumpr.com
Website: www.berylliumpr.com
Custom Software Design & Development, Pharmaceutical/Medical Devices Industries, Manufacturing Execution Systems Integrators. (Hisp, estab 1998, empl 8, sales $756,288, cert: NMSDC)

5486 Ingellicom Corp
1510 F.D. Roosevelt Ave.
Guaynabo, PR 00965
Contact: Heber Irizarry CEO
Tel: 939-401-0505
Email: contact@ingelli.com
Website: www.ingelli.com
Enterprise Software Development, Web Application, Cloud Platform Solutions, Mobile Applications. (Hisp, estab 2006, empl 37, sales $1,900,000, cert: 8(a))

5487 Integrated Services for Productivity & Validation
Acuarela St, Ste 3A Urb Munoz Rivera
Guaynabo, PR 00969
Contact: Luis Baez Principal
Tel: 787-789-4778
Email: lmbaez@is-pv.com
Website: www.is-pv.com
Technology, Management, Systems & Productivity Improvement projects. (Hisp, estab 2007, empl 25, sales $2,280,441, cert: NMSDC)

5488 Integrated Technology & Compliance Services
PMB 470 Box 4956
Caguas, PR 00726
Contact: Ismael Aviles COO
Tel: 939-579-3846
Email: ismael.aviles@itcspr.com
Website: www.itcspr.com
Information Technology Consulting & cGMP Validation Consulting & Compliance services. (Hisp, estab 2005, empl 10, sales $977,456, cert: NMSDC)

5489 JC Automation, Corp.
Calle D #27-C Urb. Los Maestros
Humacao, PR 00791
Contact: Juan Senquiz GM
Tel: 787-719-7315
Email: jsenquiz@jcapr.cmom
Website: www.jcapr.com
IT Management, Compliance & Manufacturing System Services, Application Design & Development, Systems Integration. (Hisp, estab 1997, empl 40, sales $4,700,000, cert: NMSDC)

5490 Mirus Consulting Group Corp
PO Box 851
Humacao, PR 00792
Contact: Giovanni Gomez Dir
Tel: 787-285-0992
Email: ggomez@miruspr.com
Website: www.miruspr.com
Computer system validation & information technology consulting services. (Hisp, estab 2001, empl 25, sales $2,900,000, cert: NMSDC)

5491 PACIV Inc.
PO Box 363232
San Juan, PR 00936
Contact: Jose Calderon VP of Operations
Tel: 787-721-5290
Email: calderonj@paciv.com
Website: www.paciv.com
Automation, instrumentation (installation, calibration, procurement), panel construction, computer system validation (CSV), Commissioning & Qualification (C&Q) & Project Management. (Hisp, estab 1997, empl 45, sales $4,724,109, cert: NMSDC)

5492 PharmaBioServ US, Inc. (PBSV)
545 West Germantown Pike 6 Road 696
Dorado, PR 00646
Contact: Armando Morales US Operations Dir
Tel: 787-278-2709
Email: info@pharmabioserv.com
Website: www.pharmabioserv.com
Data Processing, Hosting, and related Services, Internet Publishing and Broadcasting and Web Search Portals, Engineering Services. (Hisp, estab 1993, empl 150, sales $14,000,000, cert: NMSDC)

5493 Real Physics, Inc.
1056 Munoz Riviera Ave Ste 903
San Juan, PR 00927
Contact: Pedro Torres President
Tel: 787-469-1359
Email: ptorres@realphysics.net
Website: www.realphysics.net
Project management, IT consulting, outsourcing, appraisal, validation, aerial photography, scheduling services, quality & logistics audits. (Hisp, estab 2007, empl 3, sales , cert: NMSDC)

5494 Weil Group, Inc.
Urb. Villa Blanca Calle Aquamarina #78 Ste 1
Caguas, PR 00725
Contact: Milagros del R Gonzalez GM
Tel: 787-633-0025
Email: clopez@weilgroup.com
Website: www.weilgroup.com
Temporary employment agency, outsourcing IT & automation services: management and/or admin, help desk, servers, WAN, email system, desktop, maintenance, backup & restore. (Hisp, estab 1994, empl 215, sales $12,000,000, cert: NMSDC)

Rhode Island

5495 Artifex Technology Consulting, Inc.
614 George Washington Hwy
Lincoln, RI 02865
Contact: Jenna Schmidt President
Tel: 401-723-6644
Email: jenna@artifextech.com
Website: www.artifextech.com
Custom software solutions & graphic design. (Woman, estab 2002, empl 13, sales $2,380,350, cert: WBENC)

5496   CSG LLC
        98 Slope Ave
        Wakefield, RI 02879
        Contact: Meridith Voshell Acct Exec
        Tel: 770-377-8955
        Email: mvoshell@csg-llc.co
        Website: www.csg-llc.co
Information Technology strategies. (Woman, estab 2017, empl , sales , cert: WBENC)

5497   Granger Warburton Consulting, LLC
        79 West St
        East Greenwich, RI 02818
        Contact: Bethany Warburton Principal Consultant
        Tel: 401-965-1288
        Email: bethany@grangerwarburton.com
        Website: www.grangerwarburton.com
Learning management system design & deployment, elearning creation, software application development, project management, business analysis, change management, documentation & process design. (Woman, estab 2013, empl 2, sales $127,000, cert: State)

South Carolina

5498   Blue Eye Soft Corp.
        44 Pkwy Commons Way
        Greer, SC 29650
        Contact: Srikanth Kodeboyina Managing Partner
        Tel: 864-479-0888
        Email: sri@blueyesoft.com
        Website: www.blueyesoft.com
IT Consulting Software solutions, BI Analytics, CRM, Scalable Architecture, Health IT, Program& Project Management, Human Resource Consulting. (As-Pac, estab 2017, empl 14, sales $479,000, cert: NMSDC)

5499   Datasoft Technologies Inc.
        34 Pkwy Commons Way
        Greer, SC 29650
        Contact: Manyapu Alka President
        Tel: 864-849-9022
        Email: amanyapu@datasoft-tech.com
        Website: www.datasoft-tech.com
Software devel & consulting: system integration, engineering & architecture, project mgmt, analysis & design. (Minority, estab 1994, empl 41, sales $4,000,000, cert: State, NMSDC)

5500   Globalpundits Technology Consultancy Inc.
        4715D Sunset Blvd
        Lexington, SC 29072
        Contact: Manoj Devulapalli President
        Tel: 803-354-9400
        Email: manoj@globalpundits.com
        Website: www.globalpundits.com
Computer programming services, software design services, project management, business analysts, database administrations, contract engineering, mechanical engineers, stress engineers, electrical engineers, aeronautical engineers, CAD. (Minority, estab 2000, empl 106, sales $13,000,000, cert: State, NMSDC)

5501   Native American Industrial Solutions L.L.C.
        358 Lumbee Circle
        Pawleys Island, SC 29585
        Contact: Jeremy Meyers CEO
        Tel: 845-702-8323
        Email: jeremy.meyers@nais-llc.com
        Website: www.nais-llc.com
Cyber Security, Software Integration. (Nat-Ame, estab 2013, empl 10, sales $4,100,000, cert: 8(a))

5502   Resource Partners, LLC
        4975 Lacross Rd Ste 153
        North Charleston, SC 29406
        Contact: Rosemary Audrey CEO
        Tel: 843-554-2533
        Email: awhetsell@consultrp.net
        Website: www.consultrp.net
Health IT software & hardware solutions, optimal workflow, technology & reimbursement strategies. (Woman/AA, estab 2005, empl 8, sales $575,000, cert: City, NMSDC, WBENC)

5503   Synesis International, Inc.
        30 Creekview Ct
        Greenville, SC 29615
        Contact: Ricardo Studart President
        Tel: 864-288-1550
        Email: rstudart@synesisintl.com
        Website: www.synesisintl.com
Information technology: ERP, MES, business analytics, EDI, bar code & quality control systems. (Hisp, estab 1994, empl 28, sales $3,500,000, cert: NMSDC)

5504   Technology Solutions Inc.
        PO Box 212098
        Columbia, SC 29221
        Contact: Cathy Hill President
        Tel: 803-359-6079
        Email: cathy@tsisc.com
        Website: www.tsisc.com
IT services: contracted programming, analysis, design, development, database analysis & design, technical writing, PC/technical support, systems programming, help desk, LAN/WAN, etc. (Woman, estab 1989, empl 75, sales $ 0, cert: WBENC)

Tennessee

5505   Conch Technologies, Inc.
        6750 Poplar Ave, Ste 711
        Memphis, TN 38138
        Contact: Ray Scott VP Natl Sales
        Tel: 901-827-5183
        Email: contact@conchtech.com
        Website: www.conchtech.com
IT consultants & contract programming, pc/client servers, internet/intranet, B2B & e-commerce. (Minority, Woman, estab 2004, empl 55, sales $1,700,000, cert: State)

5506   Resource Regeneration LLC dba S3 Asset Mgmt
        1309 Elm Hill Pike
        Nashville, TN 37210
        Contact: Rod McDaniel CEO
        Tel: 615-873-4466
        Email: rmcdaniel@s3rs.com
        Website: www.s3rs.com
E-Waste Recycling, IT Equipment, Asset Recovery Resale, Data Security. (AA, estab 2006, empl 20, sales $500,000, cert: NMSDC)

5507 Stragistics Technology
6263 Poplar Ave, Ste 603
Memphis, TN 38119
Contact: Scott Swanson Business Devel Specialist
Tel: 901-799-0402
Email: sswanson@stragistics.com
Website: www.stragistics.com

Technology solutions, data integration, migration, eCommerce, infrastructure management, proprietary software, SDLC, systems integration. (Woman/AA, estab 1997, empl 8, sales $379,010, cert: State, City, NMSDC, WBENC)

5508 Zycron, Inc.
413 Welshwood Dr
Nashville, TN 37211
Contact: Rochelle Taylor VP Operations
Tel: 615-251-9588
Email: rtaylor@zycron.com
Website: www.zycron.com

System integration, technical consulting, supplemental staffing, configuration mgmt, software analysis, system design & facilities mgmt. (AA, estab 1991, empl 300, sales $29,245,696, cert: State)

Texas

5509 4Consulting, Inc.
1221 Abrams Rd, Ste 326
Richardson, TX 75081
Contact: Vivek Anand President
Tel: 972-333-0041
Email: vivek@4ci-usa.com
Website: www.4ci-usa.com

Consulting services: IT project mgmt, workforce mgmt, custom application dev, process mgmt, .NET technology, J2EE, Legacy, ERP, CRM, business process analyst, SME, data security, infrastructure mgmt. (Minority, Woman, estab 2000, empl 188, sales $15,780,000, cert: WBENC)

5510 AACANN Mechanical, Inc.
12718 Robert E. Lee
Houston, TX 77044
Contact: Larry Cannon President
Tel: 281-458-2258
Email: aacann@ymail.com
Website: www.aacann.com

Service, repair, installation, maintenance and zone comfort controls/design of HVACR systems designed for industrial and offshore accommodations along with process cooling systems. (AA, estab 1982, empl 4, sales $642,000, cert: NMSDC)

5511 Accolite Inc.
16479 Dallas North Pkwy, Ste 350
Addison, TX 75001
Contact: Matthew McKinley VP Business Dev
Tel: 469-235-9316
Email: matthew.mckinley@accolite.com
Website: www.accolite.com

Contingent staffinng services: contract, contract to hire & permanent candidates for IT. (As-Pac, estab 2006, empl 280, sales $12,000,000, cert: State, NMSDC)

5512 Ace Delivery
7308 Gaines Mill Ln
Austin, TX 78745
Contact: Tammie Garcia Office Mgr
Tel: 512-326-3553
Email: viaace1@gmail.com
Website: www.acedeliveryatx.com

Deliver medical products to all hospitals & supply chains. (Minority, Woman, estab 1980, empl 7, sales $947,931, cert: City)

5513 Addison Stuart
566 Homewood Dr
Coppell, TX 75019
Contact: Christina Kolassa Owner
Tel: 847-707-0429
Email: ckolassa@addisonstuart.com
Website: www.addisonstuart.com

Information technology, PPM implementation using CA Clarity & Oracle PPM tools. (Woman, estab 2012, empl 4, sales $200,000, cert: WBENC)

5514 Adonius Corp.
23503 Swinging Bow
San Antonio, TX 78261
Contact: Catherine Morse President
Tel: 210-305-5663
Email: cmorse@adonius.com
Website: www.adonius.com

Healthcare transition logistics consulting services. (Woman, estab 2014, empl 6, sales $1,274,000, cert: WBENC)

5515 Advent Global Solutions, Inc
12777 Jones Rd, Ste 445
Houston, TX 77070
Contact: Chet Mann VP Client Services
Tel: 281-640-8934
Email: chet.mann@adventglobal.com
Website: www.adventglobal.com/

ERP implementation, IT development & systems integration, SAP technology. (As-Ind, estab 1997, empl 1500, sales $182,000,000, cert: NMSDC)

5516 Akisha Networks, Inc.
5868 A-1 Westheimer Rd, Ste 224
Houston, TX 77057
Contact: Ronald Smith VP
Tel: 713-840-7424
Email: info@akisha.net
Website: www.akisha.net

Digital Systems Integration: designs, builds & manages IP convergence solutions. (AA, estab 2001, empl 8, sales $395,776, cert: NMSDC)

5517 All Business Machines, Inc. dba AttainIt
2028 E Ben White Blvd Ste 230
Austin, TX 78741
Contact: Mackenzie Evers Business Devel Mgr
Tel: 916-325-7800
Email: sales@attainit.net
Website: www.attainit.net

Provide high-quality products & services to government agencies & federal prime contractors. (Woman, estab 2001, empl 21, sales $29,090,791, cert: CPUC, WBENC, 8(a))

INFORMATION TECHNOLOGY: Services

5518 Alphaworks LLC
  1600 10th St, Ste B
  Plano, TX 75074
  Contact: Don R Joe Operations Mgr
  Tel: 972-509-8837
  Email: rodney.joe@alphaworksnow.com
  Website: www.alphaworksnow.com
IT hardware, software & services: HP, Oracle, SAP, Cisco & TDi. (As-Pac, estab 2010, empl 16, sales $3,000,000, cert: NMSDC)

5519 Al-Razaq Computing Services
  6001 Savoy, Ste 505
  Houston, TX 77036
  Contact: Vicki Semander Contract Vehicle Spec
  Tel: 713-839-9613
  Email: vsemander@al-razaqcomputing.com
  Website: www.al-razaqcomputing.com
Database mgmt, systems network integration, computer hardware & software, educational product dev & training, financial mgmt, budget dev & execution package, software dev & computer programming. (AA, estab 1993, empl 48, sales $3,167,414, cert: State, NMSDC)

5520 American Information Technology Corp.
  14285 Midway Rd, Ste 100
  Addison, TX 75001
  Contact: Heather Hamann Contract Mgr
  Tel: 319-362-2601
  Email: heather@aitcusa.com
  Website: www.aitcusa.com
Computer Consulting. (As-Ind, estab 1995, empl 102, sales $5,000,000, cert: State, NMSDC)

5521 American Unit, Inc.
  2901 N Dallas Pkwy Ste 333
  Plano, TX 75093
  Contact: Ramana Mgr
  Tel: 972-398-3335
  Email: ravi@americanunit.com
  Website: www.americanunit.com
Enterprise & e-business implementation, upgrade, & production support services. (As-Pac, estab 2003, empl 365, sales $30,000,000, cert: NMSDC)

5522 Amsys Innovative Solutions
  10101 Southwest Frwy, Ste 570
  Houston, TX 77074
  Contact: Khalid Z. Parekh CEO
  Tel: 713-484-7786
  Email: psharma@amsysis.com
  Website: www.amsysis.com
IT Staffing, Software Programming, Infrastructure, Maintenance & Support, Project Management, Fiber Optic Cable Installation. (As-Ind, estab 2006, empl 30, sales $5,000,000, cert: City, NMSDC)

5523 Amtek Consulting LLC
  18170 Dallas Pkwy Ste 104
  Dallas, TX 75287
  Contact: Satya Movva President
  Tel: 214-680-6111
  Email: smovva@amtekconsulting.com
  Website: www.amtekconsulting.com
IT consulting services, system design & implementation, client-Server solutions, application development, systems maintenance/operations support. (As-Ind, estab 2004, empl 47, sales $1,461,360, cert: City, NMSDC)

5524 Anblicks
  5055 Keller Springs Rd, Ste 160
  Dallas, TX 75254
  Contact: Srinivas V VP Projects
  Tel: 214-254-4633
  Email: sri@anblicks.com
  Website: www.anblicks.com
Cloud Data Analytics. (As-Pac, estab 2003, empl 300, sales $13,500,000, cert: NMSDC)

5525 Applied Training Resources Inccorporated
  6405 Cypresswood Dr, Ste 250
  Spring, TX 77379
  Contact: Rose Bradshaw Controller
  Tel: 281-370-9540
  Email: rbradshaw@atrco.com
  Website: www.atrco.com
Lifecycle management systems: procedure & policy management, editing, procedure workflow (MOC), periodic review, incident investigation, action tracking & integrated learning management. (Woman, estab 1990, empl 43, sales $6,580,266, cert: WBENC)

5526 ARC Government Solutions, Inc
  9211 Waterford Centre Blvd Ste 202
  Austin, TX 78758
  Contact: Anne Fielding Dir Finance
  Tel: 512-452-0651
  Email: anne.fielding@arc-gs.com
  Website: www.arc-gs.com
IT services, staffing and solutions. (Woman, estab 1984, empl 43, sales $104,628,999, cert: State)

5527 Argus Talent, LLC
  11739 Willcrest
  Houston, TX 77031
  Contact: Zeyn Patel President
  Tel: 713-465-5985
  Email: info@argustalent.com
  Website: www.argustalent.com
Document Management, Records Management and Electronic Content Management (ECM) systems, custom computing services, system design services, and staff augmentation services. (As-Ind, estab 1989, empl 20, sales $500,000, cert: State, NMSDC)

5528 Armstrong Archives LLC
  1515 Crescent Dr
  Carrollton, TX 75006
  Contact: Sherri Taylor President
  Tel: 972-242-7179
  Email: staylor@aarchives.com
  Website: www.armstrongarchives.com
Secure & Reliable Record Storage, Document Storage, Document Management, Document Scanning, Paper Shredding & Distribution. (Woman, estab 1996, empl 13, sales $ 0, cert: WBENC)

5529 Aspiryon, LLC
  711 Nolana, Ste 103-F
  McAllen, TX 78504
  Contact: Neil Crisman GM
  Tel: 919-900-8622
  Email: sales@aspiryon.net
  Website: www.aspiryon.net
Plan & implement information security solutions. (Minority, Woman, estab 2011, empl 12, sales $2,000,000, cert: State)

INFORMATION TECHNOLOGY: Services

5530 Assent Solutions LLC
      27311 Bentridge Park Ln
      Katy, TX 77494
      Contact: Venkata Reka VP
      Tel: 713-853-9288
      Email: reka@assentsolutions.com
      Website: www.assentsolutions.com
Information Technology Consulting, Staffing Augmentation, IT Staffing Services, Custom Software Application Development, Web Development. (Woman/As-Ind, estab 2009, empl 10, sales $588,751, cert: City)

5531 Associates Systems LLC
      750 S Mac Arthur Blvd Ste 100
      Coppell, TX 75019
      Contact: Pavan Akula Dir of Sales
      Tel: 972-241-4436
      Email: pavan.akula@associatessystems.com
      Website: www.associatessystems.com
Information technology solutions & services. (Minority, Woman, estab 2002, empl 40, sales , cert: State, NMSDC)

5532 Austin Tele-Services Partners, LP dba Genesis ATS
      4209 S Industrial Dr Ste 300
      Austin, TX 78744
      Contact: Patrick Manning VP Business Dev
      Tel: 512-437-3041
      Email: pmanning@genesis-ats.com
      Website: www.genesis-ats.com
IT, Networking, Telecommunications & Computer related equipment & services. (Hisp, estab 2003, empl 45, sales $25,000,000, cert: State, NMSDC)

5533 AustinCSI LLC
      7950 Legacy Dr Ste 750
      Plano, TX 75024
      Contact: Karen Moree Found & CEO
      Tel: 972-677-6464
      Email: karen.moree@austincsi.com
      Website: www.austincsi.com
Project & Portfolio Delivery (Organizational Change Management, Agile Transformation, DevOps Transformation, Digital Transformation, Big Data, Internet of Things (IoT), Cybersecurity, Process Innovation, Governance, Metrics & Exec Dashboards, Data Center. (Woman, estab 2007, empl 201, sales $31,000,000, cert: WBENC)

5534 Bastion Technologies, Inc.
      17625 El Camino Real
      Houston, TX 77058
      Contact: Jorge Hernandez President
      Tel: 281-283-9330
      Email: jhernandez@bastiontechnologies.com
      Website: www.bastiontechnologies.com
Engineering design, analysis, systems engineering, information technology applications, engineering research, mechanical engineering, structural engineering, safety & reliability engineering, systems safety, hazard analysis. (Hisp, estab 1998, empl 400, sales $42,711,000, cert: State, NMSDC)

5535 Bestica, Inc.
      3463 Magic Dr Ste 303
      San Antonio, TX 78229
      Contact: Harvinder Singh CEO
      Tel: 210-614-4198
      Email: harvinder@bestica.com
      Website: www.bestica.com
IT consulting & staffing firm. (As-Ind, estab 2005, empl 198, sales $7,500,000, cert: NMSDC, 8(a))

5536 Bravo Technical Resources, Inc.
      5301 Alpha Road Ste 80-37
      Dallas, TX 75204
      Contact: Bettina Jones Strategic Acct Mgr
      Tel: 214-422-3620
      Email: bjones@bravotech.com
      Website: www.bravotech.com
IT & engineering staffing: contract, contract to hire, direct hire. (Woman, estab 1996, empl 180, sales $28,500,000, cert: WBENC)

5537 BroadAxis Inc.
      2591 Dallas Pkwy Ste 300
      Frisco, TX 75034
      Contact: Nazish Imran Technical Recruiter
      Tel: 215-280-1992
      Email: nazish@broadaxis.com
      Website: www.broadaxis.com
Technology solutions, infrastructure & security projects, IT projects & staffing. (As-Ind, estab 2014, empl 5, sales , cert: State, NMSDC)

5538 Calpion Inc.
      4835 Lyndon B Johnson Freeway Ste 515
      Dallas, TX 75244
      Contact: Thomas John President
      Tel: 469-242-6056
      Email: thomas@calpion.com
      Website: www.calpion.com
IT consulting & staffing, software development, SAP testing & consulting, Cloud based server & IT resources. (As-Ind, estab 2004, empl 50, sales $2,400,000, cert: State, NMSDC)

5539 Can-Am Wireless LLC dba Can-Am IT Solutions
      1333 Corporate Dr, Ste 110
      Irving, TX 75038
      Contact: Johan Rahardjo Dir of Engineering
      Tel: 866-976-4177
      Email: johan.rahardjo@canamitsolutions.com
      Website: www.canamitsolutions.com
Telecommunications and Information Technology Hardware & Software. (As-Pac, estab 2001, empl 7, sales $1,020,000, cert: NMSDC)

5540 Caravan Consulting, LLC
      16947 Old Pond Dr
      Dallas, TX 75248
      Contact: Richard Bird Mgr
      Tel: 469-525-6518
      Email: rbird@caravanconsulting.com
      Website: www.caravanconsulting.com
Infrastructure Architecture, Data Modeling, Database Management, ETL Architecture & Development, Data Warehouse Architecture & Development. (AA, estab 2009, empl 1, sales $318,000, cert: NMSDC)

5541 Castillo & Associates
      6942 FM 1960 E., Ste 290
      Humble, TX 77346
      Contact: Mike Castillo President
      Tel: 281-852-7487
      Email: mike.a.castillo@cainfotech.com
      Website: www.cainfotech.com
Engineering & technical support services: network infrastructure, telecommunications systems & services, enterprise application support & IT risk analysis. (Hisp, estab 1998, empl 16, sales $3,200,000, cert: State, City)

INFORMATION TECHNOLOGY: Services

5542　CBI Consulting Group
　　　9609 Asheboro St
　　　Frisco, TX 75035
　　　Contact: Heriberto Estrada President
　　　Tel:　956-559-0454
　　　Email: heriberto.estrada@cbiconsultinggroup.com
　　　Website: www.cbiconsultinggroup.com
IT professional services, SAP solutions, implementation, system upgrades, education, support, and custom development. (Hisp, estab 2014, empl 5, sales $350,000, cert: State, NMSDC)

5543　CES Network Services, Inc.
　　　PO Box 810256
　　　Dallas, TX 75381
　　　Contact: Enrique Flores President
　　　Tel:　972-241-3683
　　　Email: ehflores@cesnetser.com
　　　Website: www.cesnetser.com
Network engineering services, LAN, WAN & MAN, cell site planning & desig, RFI / EMI analysis, CADD services, satellite design, microwave radio, topographic map studies, digital terrain studies. (Hisp, estab 1988, empl 11, sales $6,200,000, cert: State, City)

5544　CESCO, Inc.
　　　11969 Plano Rd Ste 130
　　　Dallas, TX 75243
　　　Contact: Billie Bryant Schultz CEO
　　　Tel:　214-824-8741
　　　Email: bbryant@cesco-inc.cm
　　　Website: www.cesco-inc.net
Dist & service fax, printers & copiers, pens, paper, furniture, etc. (Woman, estab , empl , sales $4,900,000, cert: State, WBENC)

5545　Cima Solutions Group, Ltd.
　　　118 Lynn Ave Ste 300
　　　Lewisville, TX 75057
　　　Contact: John Alday President
　　　Tel:　972-499-8261
　　　Email: jalday@cimasg.com
　　　Website: www.cimasg.com
IT optization & business continuity. (Hisp, estab 2005, empl 11, sales $2,374,624, cert: State, City, NMSDC)

5546　Cimarron Software Services, Inc.
　　　18050 Saturn Lane, Ste 280
　　　Houston, TX 77058
　　　Contact: Jeannie Crowell CEO
　　　Tel:　281-226-5100
　　　Email: jcrowell@cimarroninc.com
　　　Website: www.cimarroninc.com
Information technology support: computer operations, systems engineering, networking, verification testing, systems analysis & software engineering. (Woman, estab 1981, empl 215, sales $37,477,460, cert: WBENC)

5547　CIS Cenergy International Services
　　　12650 Crossrroads Park Dr
　　　Houston, TX 77065
　　　Contact: June Ressler President
　　　Tel:　713-965-6200
　　　Email: christine.lujan@cenergyintl.com
　　　Website: www.cenergyintl.com
Information technology consulting services: outsourcing, software development, PC repairs & network support, training, project mgmt, GIS consulting, web development, system support, repair & maintenance. (Woman, estab 2006, empl 20, sales , cert: WBENC)

5548　ClearRES LLC
　　　800 E Campbell Rd Ste 170
　　　Richardson, TX 75081
　　　Contact: Dhanya Yalamanchi CEO
　　　Tel:　214-455-7860
　　　Email: dhanya@clearres.com
　　　Website: www.ClearRES.com
IT services & solutions, fixed priced projects, strategic staffing, onshore, offshore developed centers. (Nat Ame, estab 2015, empl 3, sales $100,000, cert: State, NMSDC)

5549　Cognitive Technologies, Inc.
　　　115 Wild Basin Rd S Ste 104
　　　Austin, TX 78746
　　　Contact: Karen McGraw CEO
　　　Tel:　512-380-1204
　　　Email: kmcgraw@cognitive-technologies.com
　　　Website: www.cognitive-technologies.com
Project management, project recovery, business process redesign, implementation planning, change management, testing. (Woman, estab 2001, empl 10, sales $800,000, cert: City)

5550　Compass Technology Group, LLC
　　　14001 N Dallas Pkwy, Ste 1200
　　　Dallas, TX 75240
　　　Contact: Rebecca Zarski Managing Partner
　　　Tel:　214-679-0133
　　　Email: rzarski@compasstgp.com
　　　Website: www.compasstechnologygroup.com
IT staffing & recruiting: contract, contract to hire & direct placement of IT resources. (Woman, estab 2008, empl 10, sales $800,000, cert: WBENC)

5551　CompNova LLC.
　　　300 N Coit Rd Ste 340
　　　Richardson, TX 75080
　　　Contact: Charles Reddy VP
　　　Tel:　214-227-9458
　　　Email: charlesr@compnova.com
　　　Website: www.compnova.com
IT Staff Augmentation, ERP Consulting, Customer Relationship Management (CRM), Evaluation & Implementation, Data Warehouse/DSS/EIS, Development Data, Architecture Development, (Minority, Woman, estab 1995, empl 1600, sales $85,000,000, cert: State, NMSDC)

5552　CompQsoft, Inc.
　　　505N Sam Houston Pkwy East Ste 682
　　　Houston, TX 77060
　　　Contact: Franklin Benjamin Business Devel Mgr
　　　Tel:　832-932-8732
　　　Email: franklinb@compqsoft.com
　　　Website: www.compqsoft.com
Mobile computing solutions, custom programming, network support, e-commerce solutions, QA testing svcs, staffing, on-site training. (As-Ind, estab 1997, empl 170, sales $12,000,000, cert: NMSDC)

5553　Consultis
　　　8700 Tesoro Dr, Ste 360
　　　San Antonio, TX 78217
　　　Contact: Barbara Fleming CEO
　　　Tel:　210-930-1640
　　　Email: info@consultis.com
　　　Website: www.consultis.com
Information technology staffing, staff augmentation, outsourcing & direct hires. (Woman, estab 1984, empl 150, sales $13,000,000, cert: WBENC)

INFORMATION TECHNOLOGY: Services

5554   Corporate Records Management Inc.
        3141 Hansboro Ave
        Dallas, TX 75233
        Contact: Denise Chadima Owner
        Tel: 214-333-3453
        Email: denise@crmfiles.com
        Website: www.crmfiles.com
Record storage, archiving, secured shredding, back up tape rotation. (Woman, estab 1998, empl 12, sales $764,220, cert: State)

5555   Critical Start LLC
        6100 Tennyson Pkwy Ste 250
        Plano, TX 75024
        Contact: Tera Davis Managing Dir
        Tel: 214-810-6760
        Email: tera.davis@criticalstart.com
        Website: www.criticalstart.com
Network security products & services: risk, compliance, governance; threat management & incident response. (Woman, estab 2012, empl 10, sales , cert: State)

5556   Cybersoft Technologies Inc.
        4422 FM 1960 W, Ste 300
        Houston, TX 77068
        Contact: Milind Sethi
        Tel: 281-453-8504
        Email: milind.sethi@cybersoft.net
        Website: www.cybersoft.net
IT Business solutions: ERP, WEB Technologies, EAI, Microsoft Technologies, Data Management. (As-Ind, estab 1996, empl 50, sales $7,000,000, cert: State, NMSDC)

5557   Dallas Digital Services, LLC
        5316 Bransford Dr
        Colleyville, TX 76034
        Contact: Howie Evans VP
        Tel: 817-577-8794
        Email: howie.evans@ddserv.com
        Website: www.ddserv.com
IT storage products: Fibre Channel & iSCSI devices, data center design solutions, Quantum, OverlandStorage, EMC, SUN, Tek-Tools, Qlogic, Legato, Cisco, NEOScale. (Woman, estab 1996, empl 14, sales $10,000,000, cert: WBENC)

5558   Decca Consulting LLC
        14090 SW Freeway Ste 300
        Sugar Land, TX 77478
        Contact: Nayeem Amin Managing Partner
        Tel: 832-561-0634
        Email: amin@deccaconsulting.com
        Website: www.deccaconsulting.com
IT staffing & solutions. (Woman/As-Ind, estab 2007, empl 25, sales $1,850,000, cert: State, NMSDC)

5559   Decision Tree Technologies
        306 Thunderbird Ln
        El Paso, TX 79912
        Contact: Bryyan Ritter Client Mgr
        Tel: 512-294-0604
        Email: ritter@dtreetech.com
        Website: www.dtreetech.com
Data center, contact center, IT security, networking & related IT technologies. (Woman, estab 1989, empl 10, sales $8,100,000, cert: State)

5560   Defense Support Services, Inc.
        3212 Bishop Dr
        Arlington, TX 76010
        Contact: Deon Moses President
        Tel: 817-261-0233
        Email: dmoses@dss-inc.net
        Website: www.dss-inc.net
Aircraft hardware logistics & distribution, IT design & services, communications. (AA, estab 1998, empl 15, sales $3,000,000, cert: NMSDC)

5561   Digital Consulting & Software Services, Inc.
        2277 Plaza Dr Ste 275
        Sugar Land, TX 77479
        Contact: Patricia Patterson CEO
        Tel: 713-982-8034
        Email: pmpatter@dcss.com
        Website: www.dcss.com
Management consulting, professional technical serivces. (Woman, estab , empl , sales $30,241,907, cert: WBENC)

5562   Direct Line To Compliance, Inc.
        9555 W Sam Houston Pkwy S, Ste 333
        Houston, TX 77099
        Contact: Micha Adeeko Business Devel Mgr
        Tel: 713-777-3522
        Email: michael.adeeko@dl2c.com
        Website: www.dl2c.com
Software & consulting (ColorCodeIT and ChameleonDocs), form automation, electronic document handling & compliance program software. (Woman/AA, estab 2008, empl 17, sales $1,363,745, cert: State, NMSDC)

5563   Diversified Technical Services, Inc.
        433 Executive Center Blvd
        El Paso, TX 79902
        Contact: Mgr Business Dev
        Tel: 915-544-7997
        Email: jeffz@dts.net
        Website: www.dtsi.com
Information technology services, Oracle Enterprise Resource Planning (ERP), Development & Administration, Enterprise Scale Applications Design. (Hisp, estab 1980, empl 155, sales $22,000,000, cert: NMSDC)

5564   doc2e-file,Inc.
        4500 S. Wayside Dr, Ste 102
        Houston, TX 77087
        Contact: Sherry McManus President
        Tel: 713-649-2006
        Email: sherrymcmanus@doc2e-file.com
        Website: www.doc2e-file.com
Document scanning & indexing, e-records mgmt, systems & equipment. (Woman, estab , empl , sales $ 0, cert: State, WBENC)

5565   Doyensys, Inc.
        2591 Dallas Pkwy, Ste 300
        Frisco, TX 75034
        Contact: Chithra Gopalan President
        Tel: 972-992-4220
        Email: sales@doyensys.com
        Website: www.doyensys.com
Information Technology Staffing and Services in technologies inlcuding but not limited to SAP, Oracle , Siebel, peoplesoft, Java, Dot net, IBM Mainframe (Minority, Woman, estab 2006, empl 4, sales $185,000, cert: City)

INFORMATION TECHNOLOGY: Services

5566 Dynamic Computing Services
3307 Northland Dr, Ste 250
Austin, TX 78731
Contact: Jenelle Thomas Dir Business Dev
Tel: 800-345-1275
Email: jenelle@dcshq.com
Website: www.dcshq.com
Information technology placements services. (Woman, estab 1990, empl 152, sales $13,926,270, cert: WBENC)

5567 ECOM Consulting, Inc.
2828 W Parker Rd Ste 224
Plano, TX 75075
Contact: Baku Kshatriya President
Tel: 972-578-0191
Email: baku@ecomconsultinginc.com
Website: www.ecomconsultinginc.com
Technical consulting services & staff augmentation. (As-Ind, estab 1995, empl 72, sales $ 0, cert: State, NMSDC)

5568 eConsulting Partners Global, Inc
10000 North Central Exprwy Ste 400
Dallas, TX 75231
Contact: Jade Tran Principal
Tel: 214-680-0982
Email: jade.tran@ecpgi.com
Website: www.ecpgi.com
System Integration, Enterprise Application Architecture, Service-Oriented Architecture, and IT Security (Cyber Security, Information Assurance, Computer Forensics). (Minority, Woman, estab 2006, empl 20, sales , cert: State)

5569 eDataWorld LLC
2770 Main St Ste 229
Frisco, TX 75033
Contact: Bhujang Karakavalasa Dir
Tel: 206-504-8739
Email: bhujang.k@edataworld.com
Website: www.edataworld.com
IT consulting, software development & service. (Minority, Woman, estab 2005, empl 100, sales $2,000,000, cert: NMSDC)

5570 ElectroSystems Engineers Inc.
4141 Pinnacle St, Ste 208
El Paso, TX 79902
Contact: Benita R Munoz Dir of Operations
Tel: 915-587-7902
Email: brmunoz@esei.com
Website: www.esei.com
Information technology, integrated solutions, telecommunications engineering, software design, management & consulting, test & evaluation support & intelligence training. (Hisp, estab 1994, empl 20, sales $1,441,208, cert: NMSDC)

5571 Endata Corporation
3217 Thorne Hill Ct
Richardson, TX 75082
Contact: Ricardo Rossi CTO
Tel: 214-603-4456
Email: ricardo@endata.com
Website: www.endata.com
Information Technology Professional Services, machine learning, sentiment analysis, predictive data analytics, web & app development, artificial intelligence for web, mobile & cloud applications. (Minority, Woman, estab 1997, empl 2, sales $370,808, cert: State, NMSDC)

5572 Enovox Technical Group, LLC
1775 St. James Place, Ste 120
Houston, TX 77584
Contact: Michael Wilson President
Tel: 832-736-5869
Email: mike@enovox.com
Website: www.enovox.com
IT consulting & technology services, telecommunication services, telecommunication/network equipment, program/project management & outsourcing. (AA, estab 2011, empl 2, sales $100,000, cert: State, City)

5573 Enterprise IT Experts LLC dba EITE LLC
4017 Duclair Dr
McKinney, TX 75070
Contact: Ravi Vegesna Managing Partner
Tel: - -
Email: ravi@eitellc.com
Website: www.enterpriseitexperts.com
Information Technology & Computer Software services: Enterprise Architecture, SAP Implementations, Upgrades, Technology Upgrades, Microsoft Technologies - Sharepoint & Office 365, Cloud Architecture, Integration & Custom development. (As-Ind, estab 2011, empl 228, sales $8,700,000, cert: State, NMSDC)

5574 Enterprise Logic, Inc.
7457 Harwin Dr, Ste 208
Houston, TX 77036
Contact: Ajay Thomas CEO
Tel: 832-489-1851
Email: admin@enterprise-logic.com
Website: www.enterprise-logic.com
Staffing company that focuses on staffing all types of IT Skills. (As-Ind, estab 2000, empl 200, sales , cert: City, NMSDC)

5575 ERP Logic
7423 Las Colinas Blvd Ste 103
Irving, TX 75063
Contact: Caldwell Velnambi CEO
Tel: 972-401-3771
Email: caldwell@erplogic.com
Website: www.erplogic.com
SAP-ERP Implementation, Customization, Integration, Business Process, Re-Engineering, Application Development, Management and Staff Augmentation (As-Ind, estab 2009, empl 45, sales $3,000,000, cert: NMSDC)

5576 Expedien Inc.
2925 Richmond Ave Ste 1200
Houston, TX 77098
Contact: Jiten K Agarwal Dir
Tel: 832-607-5335
Email: jkumar@expedien.net
Website: www.expedien.net/
Business Intelligence, Data Warehousing, Data Integration, Data Migration, Data conversion, Master Data Management, SAP, SAP BW, EAI, SAP Netweaver, SAP Portal, Oracle Financials, Application Development, Business Objects. (Woman/As-Ind, estab 2002, empl 72, sales $15,873,000, cert: NMSDC)

INFORMATION TECHNOLOGY: Services

5577 Fermat Software LLC
9800 N Lamar Blvd Ste 319
Austin, TX 78753
Contact: Mahvish Qureshi CEO
Tel: 512-814-5086
Email: mahvish@fermatsoftware.com
Website: www.fermatsoftware.com
UX, User Experience, Enterprise, Desktop, Cloud, Applications, Tools, Mobile, AWS, Azure, Database, Oracle, mySQL, Artificial Intelligence, Machine Learning, Cyber Security, etc. (As-Ind, estab 2015, empl 15, sales $2,600,000, cert: State)

5578 Fidelis Companies, LLC
2800 N Dallas Pkwy Ste 250
Plano, TX 75093
Contact: Bryce Shields Business Dev Mgr
Tel: 972-392-9230
Email: bshields@fideliscompanies.com
Website: www.fideliscompanies.com
IT Consulting for Oracle, PeopleSoft, Hyperion, SAP. (Woman, estab 2000, empl 50, sales $ 0, cert: State, WBENC)

5579 Fuse Solutions Inc.
4100 Midway Rd Ste 2120
Carrollton, TX 75007
Contact: Jay Jordan COO
Tel: 214-687-7393
Email: jay@fusesolutions.com
Website: www.fusesolutions.com
Strategic consulting, enterprise service delivery, vendor & asset management. (Woman, estab 2014, empl 25, sales , cert: State, WBENC)

5580 Genesis Networks Enterprises, LLC
600 N Loop 1604 E
San Antonio, TX 78232
Contact: Jason McGinnis Dir-Vendor Engagements
Tel: 770-329-6538
Email: jason.mcginnis@genesisnet.com
Website: www.genesisnet.com
Software development, software testing, systems integrator, proto-type development, security, system application mgmt, application mgmt, business process flow, event mgmt, exception mgmt. (Hisp, estab 2001, empl 771, sales $1,100,000,000, cert: State, NMSDC, CPUC)

5581 Gill Digital Services, LLC
4100 Spring Valley Road, Ste 920
Dallas, TX 75244
Contact: Barbara Gill President
Tel: 214-653-8352
Email: bgill@gilldigital.com
Website: www.gilldigital.com
Document Scanning, Database Software, Disaster Recovery Services, Court Reporting (Woman, estab , empl , sales $ 0, cert: State, WBENC)

5582 Global IT, Inc.
1303 W Walnut Hill Ln Ste 360
Irving, TX 75038
Contact: Sales
Tel: 972-871-9292
Email: info@globalitinc.com
Website: www.globalitinc.com
Information technology: ERP packages, SAP, Oracle Apps & PeopleSoft. (As-Ind, estab 1999, empl 182, sales $13,400,000, cert: State)

5583 GS Infovision LLC dba Global Systems LLC
1200 Walnut Hill Lane, Ste 2220
Irving, TX 75038
Contact: Shekhar Gupta VP
Tel: 214-717-4344
Email: account@globalsyst.com
Website: www.globalsyst.com
IT Consulting, Staffing, BPO, IT Consulting, temporary, contract, temp to perm & permanent staffing solutions. (Minority, Woman, estab 2005, empl 110, sales $11,000,000, cert: NMSDC)

5584 Hacware, Inc.
1212 E Arapaho Rd Ste 204
Richardson, TX 75081
Contact: Tiffany Ricks CEO
Tel: 214-662-8332
Email: hello@hacware.com
Website: www.hacware.com
Mobile applications and emerging technology solutions. (AA, estab 2017, empl 8, sales , cert: WBENC)

5585 iBizSoft
9300 Wade Blvd Ste 301
Frisco, TX 75035
Contact: Sandeep Kuttiyatur President
Tel: 214-705-3623
Email: vendor@ibizsoftinc.com
Website: www.ibizsoftinc.com
Enterprise application services: system integration & solution development for Oracle ERP, CRM, Endeca & ATG implementation. (As-Ind, estab 2001, empl 100, sales $6,000,000, cert: State)

5586 Independent Professional Management
9525 Katy Freeway, Ste 435
Houston, TX 77024
Contact: Sheila McIlnay CEO
Tel: 713-973-7400
Email: contact@ipm-inc.com
Website: www.ipm-inc.com
IT Staffing, SAP programers, developers & consultants. (Woman, estab 1992, empl 9, sales $ 0, cert: State, WBENC)

5587 Infobeam Technologies LLC
1333 Corporate Dr, Ste 262
Irving, TX 75038
Contact: Jay Gajavelli Dir
Tel: 972-365-9928
Email: jay.gajavelli@infobeamtech.com
Website: www.infobeamtech.com
IT consulting. (As-Pac, estab 2009, empl 15, sales , cert: State)

5588 Infolob Solutions, Inc.
909 Lake Carolyn Pkwy Ste 120
Irving, TX 75039
Contact: Vijay Cherukuri CEO
Tel: 972-535-5559
Email: vijay@infolob.com
Website: www.infolob.com
Database services, RAC, Exadata, SOA, Oracle Fusion, Ebusiness, OBIEE, BI, DW, OLTP, networking, J2EE, replication. (Woman/As-Ind, estab 2009, empl 130, sales $50,000,000, cert: State, NMSDC)

INFORMATION TECHNOLOGY: Services

5589 InfoVision Consultants, Inc.
800 E Campbell Road Ste 388
Richardson, TX 75081
Contact: John Mendez Practice Head & Dir
Tel: 972-234-0058
Email: john.mendez@infovision.com
Website: www.infovision.com/
IT solutions: staffing, consulting & outsourcing. (As-Ind, estab 1995, empl 300, sales $26,550,000, cert: NMSDC)

5590 Innovation Network Technologies Corporation
5729 Lebanon Rd, Ste 144
Frisco, TX 75034
Contact: Cathy Davis Accounting Mgr
Tel: 972-624-1222
Email: cdavis@innetworktech.com
Website: www.innetworktech.com
Computer Hardware, Computer Software, Licenses, Subscriptions, A10, A10 Network, F5, Accedian, Cloud Monitoring, Virtualization, OPTIV, Alert Logic, Algosec, Firewall Management, Analyzer, Security Policy, AlienVault, Managed SIEM, Securematics. (Hisp, estab 2009, empl 15, sales $3,922,715, cert: WBENC)

5591 Inoditech LLC, dba Camino Information Services
14340 Torrey Chase Blvd Ste 210
Houston, TX 77014
Contact: Lam Nguyen CEO
Tel: 281-742-9560
Email: lam.nguyen@caminois.com
Website: www.caminois.com
Custom software development & mobile applications. (Minority, Woman, estab 2012, empl 22, sales $1,273,000, cert: State, NMSDC)

5592 Instant Data Technologies
85 NE Loop 410, Ste. 405
San Antonio, TX 78216
Contact: Bede Ramcharan CEO
Tel: 210-344-0012
Email: bramcharan@indatatech.com
Website: www.indatatech.com
Physical inventory, RFID technology, asset valuation & tracking, supplier integration, barcoding, asset procurement, tagging & management, inventory mgmt software. (AA, As-Pac, estab 2001, empl 31, sales $11,999,837, cert: State, NMSDC, SDB)

5593 Intras LLC
101 E Park Ste 769
Plano, TX 75074
Contact: Elvan Jones
Tel: 972-422-1022
Email: elvanj@intras-it.com
Website: www.intras-it.com
Global integrator of technology solutions, technology hardware & applications develop, IT products, IT Services, IT Consulting & IT Managed services. (AA, estab 2010, empl 10, sales $3,000,000, cert: State, NMSDC)

5594 IPM Asset Solutions, Inc.
9525 Katy Freeway Ste 435
Houston, TX 77024
Contact: Andy Bishop VP Resource Management
Tel: 713-973-7400
Email: andy.bishop@ipm-inc.com
Website: www.ipmasset.com
Asset management & tracking utilizing bar code & Radio Frequency Identification (RFID) technology. (Woman, estab 2006, empl 9, sales , cert: State, WBENC)

5595 JB Software and Consulting, Inc.
333 E. Bethany Dr Ste J130
Allen, TX 75002
Contact: Uzma Shereen CEO
Tel: 469-878-3639
Email: info@jbsac.com
Website: www.jbsac.com
Information technology services & staff augmentation. (Minority, Woman, estab 2004, empl 38, sales $6,000,000, cert: NMSDC, CPUC, WBENC)

5596 KEDAR Integration Services, Inc.
405 State Hwy 121 Bypass Ste A250
Lewisville, TX 75067
Contact: Charles Sales
Tel: 972-317-3577
Email: charles@kedarit.com
Website: www.kedarit.com
IT financial management, cost optimization; business process management; lean transformation; and training. (AA, estab , empl , sales $586,858, cert: State)

5597 Krasamo Inc.
1201 W 15th St, Ste 200
Plano, TX 75075
Contact: Melissa Amoros President
Tel: 214-418-3347
Email: sales_team_00@krasamo.net
Website: www.krasamo.com
Internet-of-Things & Digital Transformation. (Hisp, estab 2010, empl 47, sales $3,200,000, cert: WBENC)

5598 Kreative Zeno Systems, Inc.
12019 Colwick
San Antonio, TX 78216
Contact: Thomas Dooley VP
Tel: 877-768-1574
Email: tomd@kreativesystemsinc.com
Website: www.kreativesystemsinc.com
Provide SCSI disk drive assemblies. (Woman, estab 2010, empl 7, sales , cert: State)

5599 LMG Technology Services, LLC
134 Vintage Park Blvd, Ste A-791
Houston, TX 77070
Contact: Lloyd Gauthier CEO
Tel: 832-465-4641
Email: Lloyd@Lmgtechnology.com
Website: www.lmgtechnology.com
Information technology. (AA, estab 2006, empl 2, sales , cert: State, City, NMSDC)

5600 Managed Staffing Inc
15851 Dallas Pkwy | Ste 450, Addison
Dallas, TX 75001
Contact: Mark Miller Sr Mgr
Tel: 469-608-7015
Email: mark@managedstaffing.com
Website: www.managedstaffing.com
IT consulting: contract, contract to hire, or direct placement, outsourcing. (Minority, Woman, estab 2007, empl 300, sales $39,300,000, cert: NMSDC, WBENC)

INFORMATION TECHNOLOGY: Services

5601 MB Five Consulting LLC
      8013 Blue Hole Ct
      McKinney, TX 75070
      Contact: Andre Ketter Mgr
      Tel: 972-895-2414
      Email: aketter@mb5consulting.com
      Website: www.mb5consulting.com
IT Services & Industrial Automation services, desktop & server support, Networking & software development. (AA, estab 2014, empl 1, sales $220,000, cert: State, NMSDC)

5602 McNeely Technology Solutions, Inc.
      PO Box 38545
      Dallas, TX 75238
      Contact: Mary Elizabeth McNeely President
      Tel: 214-349-9994
      Email: mmcneely@mcneelytech.com
      Website: www.mcneelytech.com
Database administration & database software development. (Woman, estab 2005, empl 7, sales $476,928, cert: WBENC)

5603 Milner & Schooley LLC
      14000 S Hwy 95
      Coupland, TX 78615
      Contact: Sheri Milner Mgmt Services
      Tel: 512-914-4061
      Email: slmilner@milnerschooley.com
      Website: www.milnerschooley.com
Information technology svcs: ERP CIS/CRM. (Woman, estab 2005, empl 2, sales $165,000, cert: State)

5604 Mshana Group LLC dba AriesPro
      19901 Southwest Frwy
      Sugar Land, TX 77479
      Contact: Shivani Sangari Dir Business Dev
      Tel: 281-410-6930
      Email: shivani.sangari@ariespro.com
      Website: www.ariespro.com
Information technology consulting: SAP, HANA, BW, ERP, CRM, SCM, Business Objects, FICO, Oracle, Teradata, Big Data, Microsoft, IBM, Java, Microstrategy, Cognos, Hadoop, DB2, DataStage, Informatica, Netezza, Tivoli, Unix, WebSphere. (Woman/As-Ind, estab 2011, empl 5, sales $460,000, cert: City)

5605 MTech Partners, LLC
      1464 E. Whitestone Blvd, Ste #1001
      Cedar Park, TX 78613
      Contact: Tommy Hodinh President
      Tel: 512-993-5730
      Email: tommy.hodinh@mtechpartners.net
      Website: www.mtechpartners.net
Global Digital Transformation services, Legacy Modernization to Distributed Platform, ERP Integration and DevOps Support, SalesForce Cloud Development and Migration, IOT Engineering Design. (AA, estab 2020, empl 1001, sales $23,245,422, cert: NMSDC)

5606 My Business Matches, Inc.
      110 Broadway St, Ste 70
      San Antonio, TX 78205
      Contact: Karla Gomez Dir Business Devel
      Tel: 210-858-7379
      Email: kgomez@mybusinessmatches.com
      Website: www.mybusinessmatches.com
Customizable & innovative online engagement tool. (Hisp, estab 2010, empl 16, sales $900,000, cert: 8(a))

5607 National Systems America, L.P.
      6860 Dallas Pkwy Ste 200
      Plano, TX 75024
      Contact: Mukesh Shah Managing Partner
      Tel: 972-212-7434
      Email: manager@nsiamerica.com
      Website: www.nsiamerica.com
Softwareconsulting: data processing, software development, system integration, client services & quality assurance analysis. (As-Ind, estab 1996, empl 85, sales $9,839,031, cert: NMSDC)

5608 New Renewable Energy Technologies, LLC dba NERETEC
      4102 Amhurst Dr
      Highland Village, TX 75077
      Contact: Phil Fosso Principal
      Tel: 217-299-7789
      Email: fosso@neretec.com
      Website: www.neretec.com
Project Management, Application Development, Technology Migration/Upgrade, Application Maintenance and Support, IT Assessments/Planning, Independent Verification and Validation, Business Intelligence/Data Warehouse, Service Oriented, Architecture (SOA). (AA, estab 2010, empl 2, sales $154,000, cert: State)

5609 NewData Strategies
      5339 Alpha Rd Ste 200
      Dallas, TX 75240
      Contact: Kristen Scott Dir of Sales
      Tel: 972-735-0001
      Email: tpope@newdata.com
      Website: www.newdata.com
Information technology consulting, placement & education. (Woman, estab 1989, empl 70, sales $7,384,599, cert: WBENC)

5610 Next Generation Technology Inc.
      6060 N Central Exprwy, Ste 560
      Dallas, TX 75206
      Contact: Ray Richardson President
      Tel: 214-800-2893
      Email: rrichardson@nexgentech.us
      Website: www.nexgentech.us
Resell Hewlett Packard products, UPS back-up power for Liebert, APC & Powerware, digital video surveillance systems, IT consulting. (AA, estab 2003, empl 5, sales $ 0, cert: State, SDB)

5611 Object Information Services, Inc.
      1755 North Collins Blvd #220
      Richardson, TX 75080
      Contact: Mohammad Hafizullah President
      Tel: 214-335-6632
      Email: mhafiz@objectinformation.com
      Website: www.objectinformation.com
Information technology recruiting. (As-Ind, estab 1995, empl 42, sales $3,449,325, cert: NMSDC)

5612 ObjectWin Technology, Inc.
      19219 Katy Freeway, Ste 275
      Houston, TX 77094
      Contact: Pete Adams Sales
      Tel: 832-485-1566
      Email: mbe@objectwin.com
      Website: www.objectwin.com
IT services & staffing, Partners with Microsoft, Oracle SAP. (Minority, estab 1997, empl 220, sales $28,000,000, cert: NMSDC)

INFORMATION TECHNOLOGY: Services

5613   Omega Business Systems
        PO Box 8297
        Fort Worth, TX 76124
        Contact: Norman Labrosse President
        Tel: 817-492-4249
        Email: norman@omegabiz.com
        Website: www.omegabiz.com
Network solutions & technical services. (As-Ind, estab 1992, empl 6, sales $2,000,000, cert: State, City, NMSDC, SDB)

5614   Oveana
        123 W Mills Ave, Ste 400
        El Paso, TX 79901
        Contact: Bill Randag Business Devel
        Tel: 915-533-0549
        Email: bill.randag@oveana.com
        Website: www.oveana.com
Document mgmt, data processing, mail room processing, scanning, data storage, data entry, data capture & destruction, call center. (Minority, Woman, estab 2013, empl 2200, sales , cert: State)

5615   OverNite Software Inc.
        1212 N Velasco, Ste 110
        Angleton, TX 77515
        Contact: David Stark Mktg Dir
        Tel: 979-849-2002
        Email: david.stark@overnitecbt.com
        Website: www.overnitecbt.com
Computer-based performance systems. (Hisp, estab 1995, empl 55, sales , cert: State)

5616   Pinnacle Technical Resources, Inc.
        5501 Lyndon B. Johnson Frwy, Ste 600
        Dallas, TX 75240
        Contact: Monica Watkins Managing Dir
        Tel: 214-995-6648
        Email: monica.watkins@pinnacle1.com
        Website: www.pinnacle1.com
Nearshore software development in latin america. (Minority, Woman, estab 1996, empl 3606, sales $306,000,000, cert: WBENC)

5617   Precision Task Group, Inc.
        9801 Westheimer, Ste 803
        Houston, TX 77042
        Contact: James Morris General Mgr
        Tel: 713-781-7481
        Email: massey@ptg.com
        Website: www.ptg.com
IT staff augmentation. (Hisp, estab 1980, empl 615, sales $25,000,000, cert: NMSDC)

5618   PriceSenz LLC
        4615 Al Razi St
        Irving, TX 75062
        Contact: Bijith Moopen CEO
        Tel: 469-817-3804
        Email: bijith@pricesenz.com
        Website: www.pricesenz.com
Digital Technology Services, application modernization, system rationalization, system strategy, Data & staff augmentation. (As-Ind, estab 2015, empl 38, sales $1,430,638, cert: NMSDC)

5619   Principle Information Technology
        9301 Southwest Fwy Ste 475
        Houston, TX 77074
        Contact: Nickell Cheruku President
        Tel: 832-434-4016
        Email: reddy@principleinfotech.com
        Website: www.principleinfotech.com
SAP Services, Oracle Service, Big Data, Cloud Mobility, Luxon. (As-Pac, estab 2009, empl 157, sales $ 0, cert: State, City, NMSDC, 8(a))

5620   Promacsolution Inc.
        9916 Bundoran Dr
        Austin, TX 78717
        Contact: Srinivas Ande Dir
        Tel: 310-733-3076
        Email: srinivas@promacsolution.com
        Website: www.promacsolution.com
IT consulting, SOA Architecture, Web Services, ERP, Data warehousing, SAP, Oracle HRMS, .NET,J2EE etc. (Woman/As-Ind, estab 2004, empl 5, sales $143,086, cert: State)

5621   Prudent Technologies and Consulting Inc.
        1505 LBJ Freeway Ste 327
        Dallas, TX 75234
        Contact: Mario Guerra VP
        Tel: 414-491-9056
        Email: mguerra@prudentconsulting.com
        Website: www.prudentconsulting.com
IT consultants & staffing: Oracle, SAP, PeopleSoft, .Net, Java, Hyperion, Documentum, Clarity, Crystal Reports, Testing, Mercury Tools, Compuware Tools, .Net, C#, Oracle, Oracle ERP, SQL, etc. (As-Ind, estab 1998, empl 70, sales $5,000,000, cert: NMSDC)

5622   Pure Business Solutions, LLC
        219 Gessner Rd
        Houston, TX 77024
        Contact: Andrea Hite CEO
        Tel: 713-750-9500
        Email: ahite@purebizsolns.com
        Website: www.purebizsolns.com
IT Operations Management Software, IT Service Management, Discovery, Configuration Management Database, Application & Service Modeling, IT Operations & Business Analytics, Performance and Availability Management. (Woman, estab 2015, empl 1, sales , cert: State, WBENC)

5623   Quality High-Tech Services, Inc.
        11807 Forestgate Dr
        Dallas, TX 75243
        Contact: Mary Rogers President
        Tel: 972-231-6696
        Email: m.rogers@qht.com
        Website: www.QHT.com
IT services and repairs. (Woman, estab 1987, empl 17, sales $2,492,492, cert: State)

5624   RD Data Solutions
        2340 E Trinity Mills Ste 349
        Carrollton, TX 75006
        Contact: Reuben D'Souza CEO
        Tel: 972-899-2334
        Email: reuben.dsouza@rddatasolutions.com
        Website: www.rddatasolutions.com
Technology staffing: SAP & ERP. (Minority, Woman, estab 2002, empl 26, sales $25,000,000, cert: State, NMSDC)

INFORMATION TECHNOLOGY: Services

5625 Reed Global Networks, Inc.
1354 N Loop 1604 E
San Antonio, TX 78232
Contact: Tina Younts Mgr Supplier Diversity Dev
Tel: 210-489-6601
Email: tina.younts@reedglobalnetworks.com
Website: www.reedglobalnetworks.com
End-to-end technology solutions, design, installation, monitoring, and maintenance technology infrastructure. (AA, estab 2021, empl 8, sales $20,000,000, cert: NMSDC)

5626 ReMedi Health Solutions LLC
20333 TX-249, Ste 224
Houston, TX 77070
Contact: Sandeep Hyare CEO
Tel: 832-966-0430
Email: diversity@remedihs.com
Website: www.remedihs.com/
Healthcare IT management and consulting, end-to-end, physician-centric EHR implementation and training, including system selection advisory, system optimization, integration and testing. (As-Ind, estab 2013, empl 12, sales $4,000,000, cert: State, City, NMSDC)

5627 Remedy Technological Services, L.P.
501 N 4th St
Killeen, TX 76541
Contact: Christopher Walton VP & Legal Counsel
Tel: 254-213-4740
Email: cwalton@centextech.com
Website: www.centextech.com
Information Technology, Software Engineering, Project Management, Database Management, ERP Solutions, Data Warehouse & Business Intelligence, Web & App Development, Internet Marketing & Network Administration. (As-Ind, estab 2006, empl 50, sales $1,300,000, cert: State, 8(a))

5628 Research Analysis and Maintenance, Inc.
9440 Viscount Blvd, Ste 200
El Paso, TX 79925
Contact: Richard Jones Contracts Admin
Tel: 915-592-7047
Email: jonesr@ramincorp.com
Website: www.ramincorp.com
IT services, networking & telecommunications, software development, systems integration & information management. (Woman, estab 1982, empl 650, sales $62,000,000, cert: State)

5629 Resolve Tech Solutions
15851 Dallas Pkwy, Ste 1103
Addison, TX 75001
Contact: Business Devel Mgr
Tel: 703-995-7377
Email: info@resolvetech.com
Website: www.resolvetech.com
Information Technology Staffing, Consulting Services and Implementation. (As-Ind, estab 1996, empl 25, sales $3,000,000, cert: State)

5630 RSI Solutions Inc.
3607 Summer Ranch Dr
Katy, TX 77494
Contact: Principal
Tel: 832-506-0868
Email: contactus@rsisolutions.net
Website: www.rsisolutions.net
Enterprise Resource Planning (ERP) based solutions to both public and private sector entities, SAP BW, HANA. (As-Ind, estab 2011, empl 2, sales $254,000, cert: State, SDB)

5631 Sandtx International Corp.
6551 Paredes Line Rd
Brownsville, TX 78526
Contact: Sandra Carrete
Tel: 956-546-9009
Email: sandra@sandtexusa.com
Website: www.sandtexusa.com
In-house built ERP that specializes in keeping control of and tracking your orders. (Woman/Hisp, estab 1993, empl 25, sales $10,050,000, cert: WBENC)

5632 Saratoga Software Solutions, Inc.
555 Republic Dr. Ste 200
Plano, TX 75074
Contact: Arlene Carter President
Tel: 469-301-1515
Email: arlene.carter@teamsaratoga.com
Website: www.saratogasoftwaresolutions.com
IT staff augmentation: contract, contract-to-hire & permanent. (Woman, estab , empl , sales $1,400,000, cert: State)

5633 Shirley Hollywood & Associates, Inc.
17585 State Hwy 19 Ste 100
Canton, TX 75103
Contact: Stacie Hollywood-Baber President
Tel: 972-287-8834
Email: stacie@shirleyhollywoodinc.com
Website: www.shirleyhollywoodinc.com
SAP curriculum devel & training delivery resources. (Woman, estab 1996, empl 5, sales $5,000,000, cert: WBENC)

5634 Simplistek, LLC
5050 Quorum Dr, Ste 700
Dallas, TX 75254
Contact: Xavier Hurd VP Talent Acquisition
Tel: 469-675-3594
Email: xhurd@simplistekit.com
Website: www.simplistekit.com
ERP Implementation & support, business process improvement, utilities business consulting & staff augmentation for all areas of Information Technology (IT). (Minority, estab 2014, empl 3, sales $1,200,000, cert: State, NMSDC)

5635 Smart IT Pros, Inc.
2305 Ridge Rd Ste 101D
Rockwall, TX 75087
Contact: David Thomas Dir Sales
Tel: 734-238-1553
Email: dave.thomas@smartitpros.com
Website: www.smartitpros.com
IT & Business Services, Application & Business process services. (Minority, Woman, estab 2012, empl 65, sales $3,566,788, cert: NMSDC, WBENC)

INFORMATION TECHNOLOGY: Services

5636 Smartbridge
      2000 W Sam Houston Pkwy S
      Houston, TX 77042
      Contact: William Wong Marketing Dir
      Tel: 713-360-2500
      Email: innovations@smartbridge.com
      Website: www.smartbridge.com
Technology consulting services, strategy, implementation, and support to bring each client's digital agenda to reality. (As-Pac, estab 2003, empl 55, sales $14,000,000, cert: State, NMSDC)

5637 SOAL Technologies, LLC
      10900 Research Blvd, Ste. 160C-40
      Austin, TX 78759
      Contact: Ahmed Moledina CEO
      Tel: 512-270-6700
      Email: amoledina@soaltech.com
      Website: www.soaltech.com
Information technology development & consulting. (As-Ind, estab 2009, empl 40, sales $10,600,000, cert: City)

5638 Software Professionals, Inc.
      1029 Long Prairie Road Ste A
      Flower Mound, TX 75022
      Contact: Reena Batra CEO
      Tel: 972-355-0054
      Email: reena@spius.net
      Website: www.spius.net
Systems integration & computer programming svcs: client/server & mainframe environ; facilities mgmt, help desk support & training; business re-engineering & total quality mgmt. (Minority, Woman, estab 1992, empl 100, sales $15,000,000, cert: NMSDC, WBENC)

5639 Softway Solutions, Inc.
      7324 Southwest Frwy Ste 1600
      Houston, TX 77074
      Contact: Robert Goady VP Client Services
      Tel: 281-914-4381
      Email: robert@softwaysolutions.com
      Website: www.softway.com
Website design & development, Internet marketing services, graphics design & multimedia. (As-Pac, estab 2003, empl 65, sales $5,800,000, cert: NMSDC)

5640 Sontesa Technologies Inc.
      2101 Cedar Springs Rd, Ste 1050
      Dallas, TX 75201
      Contact: Jewel Hale CEO
      Tel: 972-534-2023
      Email: procurement@sontesa.com
      Website: www.sontesa.com
Telecom Network and System Design. (Woman/AA, estab 2007, empl 4, sales , cert: NMSDC, WBENC)

5641 SPAR Information Systems
      7800 Dallas Pkwy, Ste 120
      Plano, TX 75024
      Contact: Abraham Regan VP IT Talent Acquisition
      Tel: 201-528-5324
      Email: abraham.regan@sparinfosys.com
      Website: www.sparinfosys.com
IT Services. (Minority, Woman, estab 2012, empl 380, sales $30,000,000, cert: State)

5642 Storage Assessments LLC
      PO Box 864017
      Plano, TX 75086
      Contact: Carolyn Chambers CEO
      Tel: 972-578-2708
      Email: cc@storageassessments.com
      Website: www.storageassessments.com
Resell, design & support computer storage related products: database, backup & recovers, disaster recovery & file management. (Woman, estab 2003, empl 6, sales $4,774,271, cert: State, WBENC)

5643 Stratium Consulting Group, Inc.
      14785 Preston Rd Ste 550
      Dallas, TX 75013
      Contact: James Gayle Principal
      Tel: 972-789-5566
      Email: opportunities@stratiumconsulting.com
      Website: www.stratiumconsulting.com
Information mgmt services, document management, records management, web portals, digital asset management, business intelligence, data warehouse, enterprise search and integrations with backend systems. (As-Pac, estab 2009, empl 20, sales , cert: State, NMSDC)

5644 Swift Pace Solutions, Inc
      600 E John Carpenter Frwy Ste 175
      Irving, TX 75062
      Contact: Pratima Upadhya Client Partner
      Tel: 972-714-0000
      Email: pratima@spsolinc.com
      Website: www.spsolinc.com
IT Services Consulting, Oracle Gold Partner, SAP Partner, Horton Works Partner Migrate, Integrate & Build Custom Apps. (Woman/As-Ind, estab 2013, empl 12, sales $2,000,000, cert: State, NMSDC)

5645 Systemware Professional Services, Inc.
      15601 Dallas Pkwy, Ste 1000
      Dallas, TX 75001
      Contact: Marisa Hammond VP
      Tel: 972-239-0200
      Email: marisa.hammond@systemware.com
      Website: www.systemware.com
Application system dev, life cycle turnkey solutions, system life cycle development methodology, testing svcs, application support & maintenance. (Woman, estab 1991, empl 100, sales $8,480,000, cert: WBENC)

5646 Talent Logic Inc.
      2313 Timber Shadows Dr Ste 200
      Kingwood, TX 77339
      Contact: Hilda Roper VP
      Tel: 281-358-1858
      Email: hroper@talentlogic.com
      Website: www.talentlogic.com
Computer consulting & programming svcs. (As-Ind, estab 1984, empl 300, sales $17,500,000, cert: NMSDC)

5647 Technology Asset LLC
      789 N Grove Rd, Ste 103
      Richardson, TX 75081
      Contact: Tom Earley Reg Sales Mgr
      Tel: 972-318-2600
      Email: tearley@globalassetonline.com
      Website: www.globalassetonline.com
Eco-Friendly IT lifecycle management. (Minority, Woman, estab 2010, empl 40, sales $12,500,000, cert: State)

5648 Technology for Education
       658 Alliance Pkwy
       Hewitt, TX 76643
       Contact: Brandy Mynar-Olson Sales Mgr
       Tel: 254-741-2450
       Email: sales@tfeconnect.com
       Website: www.tfe-wordpress.tfeconnect.com
Structured cabling & networking, Data Center, IP Communications, Audio Visual & Physical Security. (Woman, estab 1998, empl 50, sales $31,709,451, cert: State, WBENC)

5649 TechTrans International, Inc.
       2200 Space Park Dr, Ste 410
       Houston, TX 77058
       Contact: Joel Anderson VP
       Tel: 281-335-8000
       Email: janderson@tti-corp.com
       Website: www.tti-corp.com
International logistics, translation, interpretation, language training, and global support. (Woman, estab 1993, empl 145, sales $13,843,636, cert: NWBOC)

5650 Techway Services
       12880 Valley Branch Ln Ste 120
       Farmers Branch, TX 75234
       Contact: Cathi Coan CEO
       Tel: 855-832-4929
       Email: cathi@techwayservices.com
       Website: www.techwayservices.com
E-data destruction services & used computer asset remarketing. (Woman, estab 2004, empl 52, sales $607,751,300, cert: State, WBENC)

5651 Tek Leaders, Inc
       4975 Preston Park Blvd, Ste 500, Plano 75093
       Plano, TX 75093
       Contact: VP Enterprise Accounts
       Tel: 214-244-3753
       Email: hr@tekleaders.com
       Website: www.tekleaders.com
IT Services, IT Staffing, Data Analytics and Business Intelligence. (As-Pac, estab 2008, empl 150, sales $20,000,000, cert: NMSDC)

5652 TELA Technologies, Inc.
       10310 Harwin Dr. East Wing
       Houston, TX 77036
       Contact: Jaime Flores President
       Tel: 713-863-1411
       Email: jflores@telatechnologies.com
       Website: www.telatechnologies.com
Document management solutions, electronic document storage & retrieval solutions. (Hisp, estab 2003, empl 15, sales $1,050,000, cert: State, NMSDC)

5653 The Ternio Group LLC
       8285 El Rio Ste 120
       Houston, TX 77054
       Contact: Luis Romero Principal
       Tel: 210-519-7933
       Email:
       Website: www.terniogroup.com
Consulting & project management services: supply chain, logistics, distribution, medical-surgical & pharmacy inventory management, consignment, resource management, data processing, data cleansing, e-commerce, ERP. (Hisp, estab 2012, empl 10, sales $1,960,000, cert: State)

5654 Themesoft Inc.
       13601 Preston Rd, Ste W860
       Dallas, TX 75240
       Contact: Pascal Vinoth Dir
       Tel: 972-474-8787
       Email: vinoth@themesoft.com
       Website: www.themesoft.com
Custom Software Development & Consulting, Java, J2EE, SAP, Networking, Infrastructure, QA, Project Management. (Woman/As-Ind, estab 2004, empl 200, sales $42,845,261, cert: State, NMSDC, WBENC)

5655 Third Term Inc.
       6 Meadowridge Pl
       The Woodlands, TX 77381
       Contact: Carolina Denkler Project Mgr
       Tel: 713-357-6666
       Email: carolina.denkler@thirdtermlearning.com
       Website: www.thirdtermlearning.com
eLearning, computer based training, web based Training, Learning Management Systems, LMS. (Hisp, estab 2013, empl 2, sales $266,000, cert: NMSDC)

5656 Traveling Coaches Inc.
       2805 Dallas Pkwy Ste 150
       Dallas, TX 75093
       Contact: Lyndi Lockhart Acct Mgr
       Tel: 214-742-6224
       Email: llockhart@travelingcoaches.com
       Website: www.travelingcoaches.com
Software, consulting, integration & training. (Woman, estab 1995, empl 35, sales $10,637,000, cert: State, WBENC)

5657 Tunabear, Inc.
       13155 Noel Rd Ste 900
       Dallas, TX 75240
       Contact: James Knowles
       Tel: 888-923-8889
       Email: james@tunabear.com
       Website: www.tunabear.com
Staff Augmentation, Project Management, Upgrades, Implementation, Development, Strategy Development, Infrastructure Planning, Training / Change Management, Technologies, Peoplesoft, Hyperion / Data Warehousing. (As-Pac, estab 2010, empl 6, sales $1,444,000, cert: City)

5658 Valbrea Technologies, Inc.
       PO Box 1516
       Addison, TX 75001
       Contact: President
       Tel: 972-661-2268
       Email: info@valbrea.com
       Website: www.valbrea.com
Custom software development, database solutions, custom applications & programming services. (Woman, estab 1999, empl 14, sales , cert: WBENC)

5659 VCM Technologies, Inc.
       25 Highland Park Village, Ste 100-149
       Dallas, TX 75205
       Contact: CEO
       Tel: 817-571-6335
       Email: info@beaconsystems.com
       Website: www.beaconsystems.com
Information technology staff augmentation, SAP consultants. (Woman, estab 2002, empl 6, sales $14,200,000, cert: WBENC)

5660 Vensiti Inc
300 East Royal Lane Ste 104
Irving, TX 75039
Contact: Vijaya Saradhi Sr Dir Staffing
Tel: 972-887-7995
Email: saradhi.v@vensiti.com
Website: www.vensiti.com
Information tehcnology staffing & consulting services. (Woman/As-Ind, estab 2004, empl 52, sales $4,340,000, cert: State)

5661 Verge Information Technologies, Inc.
1305 Cheyenne Trail
Corinth, TX 76210
Contact: Mark McLaughlin Operations Mgr
Tel: 940-279-1390
Email: mark@vergeit.com
Website: www.vergeit.com
Information technology & IS consulting & staff augmentation. (Nat Ame, estab 2000, empl 25, sales $5,342,852, cert: State, NMSDC)

5662 ViewTech Group, LLC
1332 Crampton St
Dallas, TX 75207
Contact: Jessica Landestrait CEO
Tel: 817-717-9600
Email: support@viewtechgroup.com
Website: www.viewtechgroup.com
Business Intelligence consulting & comprehensive digital signage solutions, integrated design, hardware procurement and installation, software implementation and ongoing maintenance. (Woman, estab 2018, empl 20, sales $2,251,558, cert: WBENC)

5663 Virtuo Group Corporation
6700 Woodlands Pkwy Ste 230-322
The Woodlands, TX 77382
Contact: Theresa Blackwell CEO
Tel: 281-298-8571
Email: tblackwell@virtuogroup.com
Website: www.virtuogroup.com
PMO, Cyber Security, application modernization, migration & consolidation technology services. (Woman/AA, estab 2001, empl 35, sales $ 0, cert: City, NMSDC)

5664 VKNetworks IT Solutions
638 Quail Run Dr
Murphy, TX 75094
Contact: Dr. Rajan Subramanian President
Tel: 469-323-3345
Email: drrajs@vknetworks.com
Website: www.vknetworks.com
IT/SAP Staffing & Consulting, SAP Projects, AM, AD. Big Data. (Woman/As-Ind, estab 1999, empl 10, sales , cert: State)

5665 Wave Technologies
2340 E Trinity Mills Rd Ste 240
Carrollton, TX 75006
Contact: Phillip Radcliff VP Business Dev
Tel: 972-820-6950
Email: pradcliff@wavehitech.com
Website: www.wavehitech.com
Voice, data, cabling, inside & outside plant design, PC's, network appliances, servers, printers, routers, switches & network design, systems integration, network admin & configuration mgmt, database dev, email & calendaring, systems upgrades & support. (Woman, estab 1990, empl 12, sales $3,000,000, cert: State)

5666 Wise Men Consultants Inc
1500 S Dairy Ashford Ste 285
Houston, TX 77077
Contact: Rosa Delgado-Batchan Dir of Operations
Tel: 281-953-4511
Email: rosa.batchan@wisemen.com
Website: www.wisemen.com
IT staffing, project mgmt, team leads, onshore & offshore custom software development. (Minority, Woman, estab 1997, empl 220, sales $ 0, cert: NMSDC, WBENC)

5667 XBI Tech Corporation
7670 Woodway Dr, Ste 370
Houston, TX 77063
Contact: Trieu Nguyen CEO
Tel: 713-999-1286
Email: trieu.nguyen@xbitech.com
Website: www.xbitech.com
Comprehensive web development & management services: web design & development, accessibility, web content management, web training, maintenance & support, web application/software development & business intelligence. (As-Pac, estab 2007, empl 5, sales $1,300,000, cert: State)

5668 Xpediant Solutions
2425 W Loop South
Houston, TX 77027
Contact: Suparna Mahesri Dir
Tel: 713-335-5550
Email: qusai@xpediantsolutions.com
Website: www.xpediantsolutions.com
Digital experience consulting and systems integration, Cloud installation, configuration and staffing support. (As-Ind, estab 2001, empl 25, sales $4,800,000, cert: City)

5669 XTGlobal, Inc.
2701 N Dallas Pkwy, Ste 550
Plano, TX 75093
Contact: Ananth Ramaswamy President
Tel: 972-755-1800
Email: ananth@xtglobal.com
Website: www.xtglobal.com
Professional design, development, integration & support services: Microsoft. NET, SQL, BizTalk, SharePoint, .NET Web-based & Desktop Application development. (As-Ind, estab 1998, empl 170, sales $26,500,000, cert: State, NMSDC)

5670 YASME Soft Inc.
1212 Corporate Dr Ste 150
Irving, TX 75038
Contact: Sandeep Kilaru President
Tel: 214-529-3693
Email: sam@yasmesoft.com
Website: www.yasmesoft.com
IT consulting solution services: Oracle, SAP, Microsoft & IT staff augmentation. Application devel, maintenance & support, enterprise applications, practices, consulting. (As-Ind, estab 2007, empl 70, sales $6,000,000, cert: State, NMSDC)

5671 Zepol Productions, Inc. dba KiloTech
1991 Rawhide Dr
Round Rock, TX 78681
Contact: Michael Jones Strategic Acct Exec
Tel: 512-831-3663
Email: michael.jones@kilotechusa.com
Website: www.kilotechusa.com
Information technology sales and services. (Hisp, estab 2011, empl , sales $8,500,000, cert: NMSDC, 8(a))

Virginia

5672 Aarisha Inc.
11890 Sunrise Valley Dr Ste 201
Reston, VA 20191
Contact: Shailesh Akhouri President
Tel: 703-579-8510
Email: supplier@aarisha.com
Website: www.aarisha.net
Software development life cycle, Oracle Fusion Middle ware Administration, Oracle Fusion Middle ware Development, Oracle Database Administration, Business Intelligence and Data warehousing, Software Development. (As-Pac, estab 2005, empl 6, sales $1,059,708, cert: NMSDC)

5673 ACI Solutions Inc.
131 E Broad St
Falls Church, VA 22046
Contact: Jovan Silva Business Devel Mgr
Tel: 703-766-4070
Email: jsilva@acisolutions.net
Website: www.acisolutions.net
Information technology, data & voice networking products & services. (AA, As-Pac, estab 2001, empl 25, sales , cert: NMSDC)

5674 Advanced Computer Concepts
7927 Jones Branch Dr Ste 600 N
Mclean, VA 22102
Contact: Mark Braxton Sr Acct Exec
Tel: 571-395-4117
Email: bill@acconline.com
Website: www.acconline.com
IT hardware, software sales & network engineering services, wireless network design & implementation, IT security, IT storage systems, VOIP design & implementation. (Woman, estab 1982, empl 45, sales $55,000,000, cert: WBENC)

5675 Affigent, LLC
13873 Park Center Rd Ste 127
Herndon, VA 20171
Contact: Joe Clagett Acct Exec
Tel: 301-305-9513
Email: joe.clagett@affigent.com
Website: www.affigent.com
Dist IT product & systems integration. (Nat Ame, estab 2004, empl 5, sales $ 0, cert: NMSDC)

5676 AhaApps LLC
11608 Timberton Ct
Glen Allen, VA 23060
Contact: Satish Reddy CEO
Tel: 804-366-9979
Email: satish@ahaapps.com
Website: www.ahaapps.com
Design & build mobile applications for iOS (iPhone, iPad), Android phone & tablets, web applications, ASP.NET, ASP.NET MVC, Ruby on Rails, Java, Salesforce.com implementation & integration. (As-Pac, estab 2010, empl 15, sales $245,146, cert: State, NMSDC)

5677 Alliant Global Strategies Inc.
4607 W. Broad St
Richmond, VA 23230
Contact: James Wallace
Tel: 804-283-2203
Email: jwallace@alliantglobalstrategies.com
Website: www.alliantglobalstrategies.com
Business process outsourcing (BPO) & technology training solutions. (AA, estab 2011, empl 5, sales $137,000, cert: State, NMSDC)

5678 Alltech International, Inc.
8298-B Old Courthouse Rd
Vienna, VA 22182
Contact: Nathan Sanders Client Svcs Mgr
Tel: 703-506-1222
Email: alltech-raytheon@alltech.net
Website: www.alltech.net
Applications Development & Engineering, Systems Administration & Engineering, Database Development & Administration, Security & Training. (Woman/Hisp, estab 1993, empl 150, sales $18,000,000, cert: State)

5679 Alpha Omega Integration LLC
1749 Old Meadow Rd, Ste 400
McLean, VA 22102
Contact: Sujani Rangareddy CEO
Tel: 571-435-5656
Email: sujani.rangareddy@alphaomegaintegration.com
Website: www.alphaomegaintegration.com
Digital services, big data, emerging technologies & cloud solutions. (Woman/As-Pac, estab 2010, empl 90, sales , cert: 8(a))

5680 Ampcus Inc.
14900 Conference Ctr Dr, Ste 500
Chantilly, VA 20151
Contact: Donna Howell Sr VP
Tel: 703-429-0550
Email: donna.howell@ampcus.com
Website: www.ampcus.com
Information technology and application development services that are aligned with our clients business objectives. (Woman/As-Pac, estab 2004, empl 2400, sales $150,000,000, cert: State, NMSDC, CPUC, WBENC)

5681 Anselux LLC
       3104 Douglasdale Rd
       Richmond, VA 23221
       Contact: Fidel Aghomo CTO
       Tel: 425-922-8023
       Email: fidela@anselux.com
       Website: www.anselux.com
IT Consulting Services, Custom Business Software Solutions, Web Application Development. (AA, estab 2004, empl 4, sales , cert: State, NMSDC)

5682 Apex CoVantage
       198 Van Buren St Ste 200
       Herndon, VA 20170
       Contact: Mike Lohneis Dir Proposal & Contract
       Tel: 703-709-3000
       Email: mlohneis@apexcovantage.com
       Website: www.apexcovantage.com
Process engineering, knowledge & content management, imaging, document management, forms processing & digital assets creation, engineering: data conversion, purification & conflation, work order posting, inspections, audits. (As-Ind, estab 1988, empl 2500, sales , cert: State, NMSDC)

5683 Applied Integrity Consulting, LLC
       40646 Weaver Ct
       Leesburg, VA 20175
       Contact: Loan Clarke CEO
       Tel: 703-868-3886
       Email: lclarke@aic-llc.us
       Website: www.aic-llc.us
Enterprise IT & Software Engineering support and services. Expertise in Microsoft technologies. (Minority, Woman, estab 2011, empl 2, sales , cert: State)

5684 Astyra Corporation
       411 East Franklin St, Ste 105
       Richmond, VA 23219
       Contact: Lee Rattigan VP Strategy & Dev
       Tel: 804-433-1117
       Email: lrattigan@astyra.com
       Website: www.astyra.com
IT staff augmentation & IT solutions: Medicaid & HIPAA application development & project management. (AA, estab 1997, empl 150, sales $15,000,000, cert: State, NMSDC, SDB)

5685 Atlantic Resource Group, Inc.
       4880 Cox Rd, Ste 105
       Glen Allen, VA 23060
       Contact: Deborah J. Dowdy President
       Tel: 804-262-4400
       Email: Debbie.Dowdy@AtlanticResource.com
       Website: www.AtlanticResource.com
Information technology, staff augmentation & project mgmt. (Woman, estab 1990, empl 45, sales $ 0, cert: WBENC)

5686 Avineon, Inc.
       1430 Spring Hill Road Ste 300
       McLean, VA 22102
       Contact: Charles Erdrich VP Business Devel
       Tel: 703-671-1900
       Email: cerdrich@avineon.com
       Website: www.avineon.com
Information technology, geospatial, and engineering support services. (As-Pac, estab 1992, empl 142, sales $36,021,678, cert: State, CPUC)

5687 Balance Technology Group, Inc.
       8136 Old Keene Mill Rd Ste A207
       Springfield, VA 22152
       Contact: Tracy Betts CEO
       Tel: 703-451-8675
       Email: tracy.betts@balanceinteractive.com
       Website: www.balanceinteractive.com
Web design & development agency. (Woman, estab 1997, empl 13, sales $1,600,000, cert: WBENC)

5688 Benten Technologies
       13996 Parkeast Circle 105
       Herndon, VA 20171
       Contact: President
       Tel: 703-788-6560
       Email:
       Website: www.bententech.com
IT consulting. (As-Pac, estab 2000, empl 4, sales $2,050,615, cert: State)

5689 Betis Group. Inc.
       1420 Beverly Rd, Ste 330
       McLean, VA 22205
       Contact: Hernan Cortes CEO
       Tel: 703-532-2008
       Email: hcortes@betis.com
       Website: www.betis.com
Staff augmentation and technology deployments, systems integration services. (Hisp, estab 1995, empl 36, sales $22,000,000, cert: State, NMSDC)

5690 Biswas Information Technology Solutions Inc.
       2612 Litchfield Dr
       Herndon, VA 20171
       Contact: Sumita Biswas
       Tel: 202-203-0982
       Email: sbiswas@b-itsinc.com
       Website: www.b-itsinc.com
Database centric applications, dbase mgmt & development. (Minority, Woman, estab 2006, empl 5, sales $383,733, cert: NMSDC, WBENC, 8(a))

5691 BlueAlly Technology Solutions, LLC
       8609 Westwood Center Dr Ste 100
       Vienna, VA 22182
       Contact: Hope Jepson Proposal & Certification Mgr
       Tel: 919-249-1509
       Email: hjepson@blueally.com
       Website: www.blueally.com
Big Data, Business Intelligence, Micro Strategy cognos, project management office model. (As-Pac, estab , empl , sales $46,000,000, cert: NMSDC)

5692 Burke Consortium, Incorporated
       5500 Cherokee Ave, Ste 510
       Alexandria, VA 22312
       Contact: Thomas Nodeen COO
       Tel: 703-941-0600
       Email: tnodeen@bcinow.com
       Website: www.bcinow.com
Information technology solutions, software development, cyber security, independent verification & validation. (Woman, estab 1982, empl 44, sales $10,500,000, cert: WBENC)

INFORMATION TECHNOLOGY: Services

5693 Capital Legal Solutions dba Capital Novus
10521 Rosehaven St Ste 300
Fairfax, VA 22030
Contact: Ramesh Purohit Business Dev Mgr
Tel: 703-226-1500
Email: rpurohit@capitalnovus.com
Website: www.capitalnovus.com
Forensic data collection from project sites around the world, data preservation, processing, and presentation, web hosting services & loading (Minority, Woman, estab 2002, empl 250, sales $21,560,000, cert: State, WBENC)

5694 Cetan Corp.
1001 Scenic Pwy, Ste 203
Chesapeake, VA 23323
Contact: Brad Scott President
Tel: 757-548-6420
Email: brad.scott@cetancorp.com
Website: www.cetancorp.com
Enterprise and Business Service Management (BSM) software and services. (Nat Ame, estab 2007, empl 16, sales $ 0, cert: State, NMSDC)

5695 Cheshil Consultants, Inc.
8136 Old Keene Mill Rd, Ste B-201
Springfield, VA 22152
Contact: Chet Bhimani President
Tel: 703-569-8763
Email: cvbhimani@ccione.com
Website: www.ccione.com
Information technology consulting. (As-Ind, estab 1991, empl 13, sales $1,226,303, cert: State)

5696 CompuGain LLC
13241 Woodland Park Rd, Ste 100 Ste 100
Herndon, VA 20171
Contact: Manita Hota VP Client Dev
Tel: 703-956-7005
Email: srinivasa.chowdary@compugain.com
Website: www.compugain.com
Application development, business intelligence, data management, systems integration, project management, support & maintenance services. (Minority, estab 2000, empl 500, sales $100,000,000, cert: NMSDC)

5697 Conviso Inc.
312 E Main St, Ste 200
Luray, VA 22835
Contact: Uday Malhan President
Tel: 703-980-7074
Email: umalhan@convisoinc.com
Website: www.convisoinc.com
Application Development & Maintenance lication security & applications portfolio rationalization, .NET, Java, PeopleSoft, Systems Integration. (As-Ind, estab 2010, empl 18, sales $1,590,000, cert: State)

5698 CoreLogix Consulting Incorporation
1900 Campus Commons Dr Ste 100
Reston, VA 20191
Contact: Inderbir Singh President
Tel: 703-665-0813
Email: inder@clx-inc.com
Website: www.clx-inc.com
IT & management consulting services. (As-Ind, estab 2011, empl 25, sales $1,400,000, cert: State)

5699 CurtMont Global Services, Inc.
9501 Hull St Rd, Ste D
Richmond, VA 23236
Contact: Curtiss Stancil President
Tel: 804-982-9349
Email: cstancil@curtmont.com
Website: www.curtmont.com
Contracted foodservices, facility management, and transportation support services through our operating companies (CurtMont Foodservices and TransitServcorp). We are minority owned certified in 20 states in the USA. (AA, estab 2014, empl 105, sales , cert: State)

5700 Cyber Clarity Inc.
15722 Ryder Court
Haymarket, VA 20169
Contact: Ed Kraemer VP
Tel: 571-982-6710
Email: ed@cyberclarity.com
Website: www.cyberclarity.com
Cyber Intelligence, Operational Continuity, Computer network Defense, Incident Response & Compliance. (Woman, estab 2011, empl 12, sales $1,700,000, cert: State, City)

5701 Cynet Systems Inc.
21000 Atlantic Blvd #700
Sterling, VA 20166
Contact: Arpit Paul VP Strategy & Partnerships
Tel: 571-442-1007
Email: arpitp@cynetsystems.com
Website: www.cynetsystems.com
IT & engineering staffing consulting, direct/full time hiring, contract (temp hiring) or contract to hire services. (Minority, estab 2010, empl 1200, sales $65,000,000, cert: NMSDC)

5702 Data Concepts
4405 Cox Rd Ste 140
Glen Allen, VA 23060
Contact: Dennis Woomer Dir Business Dev
Tel: 804-968-4700
Email: dennis.woomer@dataconcepts-inc.com
Website: www.dataconcepts-inc.com/
Application development, Microsoft, Java & Mobile technologies.. (Minority, Woman, estab 1997, empl 20, sales $15,000,000, cert: State)

5703 Data-Clear
4201 Wilson Blvd. #110-265
Arlington, VA 22203
Contact: Carolyn Carlson President
Tel: 703-499-3816
Email: info@data-clear.com
Website: www.data-clear.com
Data analytics, hygiene & online communications solutions. (Woman/As-Pac, estab 2010, empl 2, sales $278,000, cert: State, 8(a))

5704 DayBlink
1595 Spring Hill Road Ste 300
Vienna, VA 22182
Contact: Michael Wong CEO
Tel: 703-869-1309
Email: minority.supplier@dayblink.com
Website: www.dayblink.com
IT, Procurement, Contact Center, Finance, HR, Marketing, and Supply Chain. (As-Pac, estab 2013, empl 63, sales $13,720,845, cert: NMSDC)

INFORMATION TECHNOLOGY: Services

5705   Deque Systems, Inc.
       2121 Cooperative Way Ste 210
       Reston, VA 20191
       Contact: Preety Kumar CEO
       Tel: 703-225-0380
       Email: preety.kumar@deque.com
       Website: www.deque.com
IT consulting & services. (Woman/As-Ind, estab 1999, empl 25, sales $1,745,001, cert: State, WBENC)

5706   Desktop Service Center, Inc.
       111 N 17th St
       Richmond, VA 23219
       Contact: Philise Conein CEO
       Tel: 804-249-8720
       Email: info@techead.com
       Website: www.techead.com
IT staff augmentation svcs, web & graphics training, website devel, Linux platform. (Woman, estab 1988, empl 299, sales $13,000,000, cert: State, WBENC)

5707   Digilent Consulting, LLC
       2612 Amanda Ct
       Vienna, VA 22180
       Contact: Vinny Raj Managing Dir
       Tel: 412-657-2219
       Email: vinnyraj@digilentconsulting.com
       Website: www.digilentconsulting.com
SMAC (Social, Mobile, Analytics and Cloud), Cyber Security expertise/capabilities. (Woman/As-Ind, estab 2006, empl 5, sales $450,000, cert: State, NMSDC)

5708   Digital Intelligence Systems, LLC dba Dexian DISYS
       8270 Greensboro Dr Ste 1000
       McLean, VA 22102
       Contact: Tara Winn COO
       Tel: 818-481-5556
       Email:
       Website: www.dexian.com
Non-IT/Professional Staffing Firm, Implementations & Roll Outs, Strategic Counseling, Support & Maintenance, Instance Consolidation, Upgrades. (As-Ind, estab 1994, empl 12241, sales $1,234,014,477, cert: NMSDC, CPUC)

5709   DISYS Solutions, Inc.
       4151 Lafayette Center Dr Ste 600
       Chantilly, VA 20151
       Contact: Vinu Luthra COO
       Tel: 703-802-0500
       Email: supplier.diversity@disyssolutions.com
       Website: www.disyssolutions.com
Information technology products & services. (As-Ind, estab 2010, empl 45, sales $62,000,000, cert: State)

5710   End to End Computing
       1800 Diagonal Rd Ste 600
       Alexandria, VA 22301
       Contact: Esteve Mede Principal
       Tel: 833-720-7770
       Email: emede@eecomputing.com
       Website: www.eecomputing.com
Vendor agnostic solutions, infrastructure solution, network architectureand design, network security architecture, unified communications, data center design, Cloud data center design, information assurance, policy implementation & procedure. (AA, estab 2012, empl 31, sales $3,800,000, cert: State)

5711   Enterprise ITech Corp.
       10014 Manor Pl
       Fairfax, VA 22032
       Contact: Pals Nagaraj
       Tel: 703-731-7881
       Email: pnagaraj@enterpriseitech.com
       Website: www.enterpriseitech.com
Full Software Development Lifecycle, Business Analytics, Business Intelligence, Enterprise Web Development, Enterprise Legacy System Modernization, Mobile application development, Database Design, Data Warehouse ETL. (As-Ind, estab 2000, empl 2, sales $300,000, cert: State, NMSDC)

5712   EsteemLogic
       722 E Market St
       Leesburg, VA 20176
       Contact: K. Francis CEO
       Tel: 571-235-9284
       Email: kfrancis@esteemlogic.com
       Website: www.esteemlogic.com
IT consulting and training firm that implements sustainable, scalable solutions to ensure organizations optimize engagement with its people, customers and the communities they serve. (AA, estab 2017, empl 2, sales , cert: State, WBENC)

5713   eTechSecurityPro, LLC
       851 French Moore Jr. Blvd
       Abingdon, VA 24210
       Contact: Alain Sadeghi CTO
       Tel: 202-587-2750
       Email: alain@etechsecurity.com
       Website: www.etechsecurity.com
Health IT Patient Registration, History & Secure Access Control Solution, Security Auditing Services. (Woman, estab 2004, empl 14, sales $1,200,000, cert: State)

5714   ETELIC Inc.
       5388 Twin Hickory Rd
       Glen Allen, VA 23059
       Contact: Mark Murphy President
       Tel: 866-240-3395
       Email: mark.murphy@etelic.com
       Website: www.etelic.com
Computer programming svcs: systems design, facilities management, consulting, database & data warehouse. (As-Pac, estab 2004, empl 20, sales $2,400,000, cert: State, NMSDC)

5715   EvereTech LLC
       2705 Main Sail Ct
       Henrico, VA 23233
       Contact: Andrew Everett Principal
       Tel: 804-986-9998
       Email: andrew.everett@everetech.com
       Website: www.everetech.com
Systems Administration & Engineering , Network Design, Network Administration & Network Engineering, Software Development & Engineering, Project Management, COTS/GOTS Systems Integration & Configuration. (AA, estab 2014, empl 7, sales $300,000, cert: State)

INFORMATION TECHNOLOGY: Services

5716 eWaste Tech Systems, LLC
      501 E Franklin St Ste 726
      Richmond, VA 23219
      Contact: Felipe Wright Managing Member
      Tel: 804-716-3577
      Email: fwright@ewastetech.com
      Website: www.ewastetech.com
Green Information technology sustainability & asset mgmt, data destruction & disposition services, electronic waste disposal. (AA, estab 2012, empl 16, sales , cert: State, NMSDC)

5717 Eyak Technology
      22980 Indian Creek Dr Ste 400
      Dulles, VA 20166
      Contact: Susan Stepanski Business Development Mgr
      Tel: 703-481-0050
      Email: susan.stepanski@eyaktek.com
      Website: www.eyaktek.com
IT products, Information Assurance, help desk, networking, storage solutions, satellite and LMR communications, wireless, physical security, critical infrastructure design & construction. (Nat-Ame, estab 2002, empl 170, sales $225,000,000, cert: 8(a))

5718 Force 1 Global, LLC
      1050 Temple Ave Ste 214
      Colonial Heights, VA 23834
      Contact: DeAlteman Beasley CEO
      Tel: 804-723-1164
      Email: dbeasley@force1global.com
      Website: www.force1global.com
Staffing, outsourcing & technology integration. (AA, estab 2014, empl 1, sales , cert: State, NMSDC)

5719 G2 Global Solutions, LLC
      202 Church St SE Ste 538
      Leesburg, VA 20176
      Contact: Elizabeth Lauren Galati CEO
      Tel: 703-349-7787
      Email: lgalati@g2gs.net
      Website: www.g2gs.net
Cyber Exploitation, Information Technology Services, Intelligence. (Minority, Woman, estab 2012, empl 86, sales $8,000,000, cert: State, 8(a), SDB)

5720 G2 Ops Inc.
      205 Business Park Dr
      Virginia Beach, VA 23462
      Contact: Robert Gregorio COO
      Tel: 757-965-8330
      Email: bobg@g2-ops.com
      Website: www.g2-ops.com
Model based systems engineering & cybersecurity, acquiring data, modeling systems & processes, identifying cyber vulnerabilities, performing analyses, identifying capability gaps and/or areas for improvement. (Woman, estab 2005, empl 15, sales $2,200,000, cert: State, WBENC)

5721 Geologics Corporation
      5285 Shawnee Rd, Ste 300
      Alexandria, VA 22312
      Contact: John Hildreth Dir Consulting Services
      Tel: 978-524-8152
      Email: jhildreth@geologics.com
      Website: www.geologics.com
Technical services: systems engineering, spacecraft, space systems, software dev, science applications. (Hisp, estab 1989, empl 500, sales $79,434,480, cert: NMSDC)

5722 Global Geographic Inc.
      11511 Cavalier Landing Ct
      Fairfax, VA 22030
      Contact: Sameer Chandra VP
      Tel: 703-594-5181
      Email: schandra@globalgeographic.com
      Website: www.globalgeographic.com
IT Services, resourcing, customized software devel, program & project mgmt. (As-Pac, estab 2006, empl 3, sales , cert: State, NMSDC)

5723 Gupton & Associates, Inc.
      901 N Pitt St Ste 230
      Alexandria, VA 22314
      Contact: Clara Lee Client Engagement Mgr
      Tel: 703-419-3048
      Email: clarablee@guptonassociates.com
      Website: www.guptonassociates.com
Program/Project Mgmt; Application Architecture; Information Assurance/Cyber Security; Network Services; Virtualization & Consolidation; Cloud Computing; Engineering Svcs; Data Analysis & Generation. (Woman, estab 2002, empl 5, sales $19,200,000, cert: State)

5724 Hanusoft Inc.
      7206 Impala Dr, Ste 214
      Richmond, VA 23228
      Contact: Bala Kamuju President
      Tel: 804-484-2400
      Email: kamuju@hanusoftinc.com
      Website: www.hanusoftinc.com
Computer related services, implementation requirements, computer applications, implementing customize hardware systems, updating & modifying existing programs. (As-Ind, estab 2005, empl 46, sales $4,816,708, cert: State)

5725 HarmonyTech
      2010 Corporate Ridge Ste 700
      McLean, VA 22102
      Contact: Nat Vinod President
      Tel: 703-405-4587
      Email: nat.vinod@harmonytech.com
      Website: www.harmonytech.com
SQL/NoSQL/XML development, Microsoft Dynamics, Sharepoint, Secure Enterprise Search. (As-Ind, estab 1995, empl 30, sales $3,500,000, cert: 8(a))

5726 HyperGen Inc.
      7810 Carvin St
      Roanoke, VA 24019
      Contact: Sherry Dyer VP Sales
      Tel: 540-992-6500
      Email: sales@hypergeninc.com
      Website: www.hypergeninc.com
PeopleSoft® functional & technical consulting svcs: implementation, upgrade, system analysis, custom developed. (Woman, estab 1992, empl 25, sales $5,000,000, cert: State, WBENC)

INFORMATION TECHNOLOGY: Services

5727 Idexcel, Inc.
       459 Herndon Pkwy, Ste 10
       Herndon, VA 20170
       Contact: Prasad Alapati President
       Tel: 703-230-2600
       Email: palapati@idexcel.com
       Website: www.idexcel.com
Staff augmentation, software development, network design, systems integration & business process improvement. (Minority, estab 1998, empl 615, sales $44,289,871, cert: NMSDC)

5728 Inficare, Inc.
       22375 Broderick Dr Ste 225
       Dulles, VA 20166
       Contact: Sumar Mathur President
       Tel: 703-945-1800
       Email:
       Website: www.inficaretech.com
IT consulting, staff augmentation. (As-Ind, estab 2001, empl 465, sales $29,000,000, cert: State)

5729 Infomatics Corporation
       23465 Rock Haven Way, Ste 100
       Dulles, VA 20166
       Contact: Shahil Shariff CEO
       Tel: 703-786-4824
       Email: jeff@infomaticscorp.com
       Website: www.infomaticscorp.com
Digital Transformation, Application Modernization. (Woman/As-Ind, estab 2005, empl 67, sales $15,000,000, cert: State)

5730 Inoventures, LLC/SciMetrika, LLC
       7601 Lewinsville Road Ste 101
       McLean, VA 22102
       Contact: Meena Krishnan CEO
       Tel: 703-917-6622
       Email: meenak@inoventures.com
       Website: www.inoventures.com
Information Technology, Big Data, Software Engineering and Development, Systems Integration, Cloud Migration, and Talent Acquisition. (Minority, estab 2008, empl 53, sales $4,550,315, cert: WBENC)

5731 Integrated Support Systems Inc (ISSi)
       PO Box 2402
       Arlington, VA 22202
       Contact: Frank Duron CEO
       Tel: 703-892-6100
       Email: fduron@integratedsupport.com
       Website: www.integratedsupport.com
Web design, develop & content mgmt, imaging, form conversion, records & docuemnt mgmt, workflow & litigation solutions, systems integration & custom solutions. (Hisp, estab 1984, empl 22, sales $2,334,042, cert: NMSDC)

5732 IntellectFaces, Inc.
       23397 Minerva Dr
       Ashburn, VA 20148
       Contact: Kishore Kochi CEO
       Tel: 703-340-6445
       Email: kkochi@intellectfaces.com
       Website: www.intellectfaces.com
IT and managed services. (Woman/As-Pac, estab 2011, empl 10, sales $854,791, cert: NMSDC, WBENC, 8(a))

5733 iQuasar, LLC
       6 Pidgeon Hill Dr Ste 305
       Sterling, VA 20165
       Contact: Amin Bhat Chief Business Officer
       Tel: 703-962-6001
       Email: amin.bhat@iquasar.com
       Website: www.iquasar.com
Information technology solutions & services, IT consulting, staffing & recruitment services. (As-Pac, estab 2004, empl 15, sales $2,070,152, cert: State, NMSDC)

5734 IT Data Consulting LLC
       11951 Freedom Dr, Ste 1300
       Reston, VA 20190
       Contact: Benny Asnake CEO
       Tel: 202-999-9184
       Email: benny@it-dc.com
       Website: www.it-dc.com
Enterprise Business Solutions, Enterprise Data Management, Cloud/Web/Mobile/Database Solution Development, Systems Integration, Staff Augmentation & Program Management. (AA, estab 2010, empl 8, sales $570,000, cert: 8(a), SDB)

5735 iWorks Corporation
       1889 Preston Shite Dr Ste 100
       reston, VA 20191
       Contact: Jothi Radhakrishnan Sr VP
       Tel: 571-485-2004
       Email: jradhakrishnan@iworkscorp.com
       Website: www.iworkscorp.com
Information technology consulting & staff augmentation. (As-Ind, estab 2005, empl 9, sales $8,000,000, cert: State)

5736 JPI Technology LLC
       9720 Capital Court, Ste 301
       Manassas, VA 20155
       Contact: Haris Perwaiz VP
       Tel: 703-828-5651
       Email: harris@jpitechnology.com
       Website: www.jpitechnology.net
Information consulting, contracting, application development, e-commerce/ERP, application integration, infrastructure & staff augmentation. (Minority, Woman, estab 2011, empl 9, sales $1,300,000, cert: State)

5737 Key Concepts Knowledgebase LLC
       4031 University Dr
       Fairfax, VA 22030
       Contact: Kim de Peiza President
       Tel: 703-966-1364
       Email: kdepeiza@keyknowledgebase.com
       Website: www.keyknowledgebase.com
Technical and customer centric documentation, SOPsService Desk supportLAN/WAN Infrastructure and Systems Administration supportSoftware Web Development, SOA development, mobile computing, Web 2.0 (AA, estab 2004, empl 10, sales $450,000, cert: NMSDC, 8(a))

5738 Knowledge Connections, Inc.
       610 Herndon Pkwy Ste 900A
       Herndon, VA 20170
       Contact: Marion Bonhomme-Knox President
       Tel: 571-203-9120
       Email: marion.bk@theknowledgeconnection.com
       Website: www.knowledgeconnector.com
Systems engineering & telecommunications. (Woman/AA, estab 1996, empl 150, sales $4,000,000, cert: State)

INFORMATION TECHNOLOGY: Services

5739 Knowledge Information Solutions, Inc.
      227 South Rosemont Road
      Virginia Beach, VA 23452
      Contact: Terry Kreamer CFO
      Tel: 757-463-0033
      Email: terry.kreamer@kisinc.net
      Website: www.kisinc.net
Information technology products & services: inside/outside plant cabling & wireless solutions, security systems, telephone systems, computer products & services, web development, data base dev & mgmt, network architecture & engineering. (Minority, Woman, estab 1983, empl 100, sales $30,200,000, cert: State)

5740 Loyola Enterprises Inc.
      2984 S Lynnhaven Rd Ste 101
      Virginia Beach, VA 23452
      Contact: Benito Loyola President
      Tel: 757-498-6118
      Email: benito@loyola.com
      Website: www.Loyola.com
TS/SCI, Modeling & Simulation Information Technology, Web Portal and Multimedia. (Hisp, estab 1991, empl 30, sales $7,325,312, cert: State)

5741 MAI Enterprises, Inc.
      PO Box 1194
      Annandale, VA 22003
      Contact: Bonnie Norem President
      Tel: 703-750-2228
      Email: bonnie@maienterprises.com
      Website: www.maienterprises.com
System engineering, graphic illustration, desktop publishing, proposals, tech editing & writing, computer hardware & software products. (Woman, estab 1986, empl 15, sales $763,400, cert: State)

5742 Meta Dimensions Inc.
      7115 Leesburg Pike, Ste 213
      Falls Church, VA 22043
      Contact: Amit Prakash
      Tel: 571-969-4140
      Email: amit@metadim.com
      Website: www.metadim.com
Analytics service, Big Data Lake, Data Visualization, Enterprise Information Management, Intelligent Enterprise Roadmap, Master Data Management. (Minority, Woman, estab 2007, empl 85, sales $2,064,955, cert: State, NMSDC, WBENC)

5743 MicroAutomation, Inc.
      5870 Trinity Pkwy, Ste 600
      Centreville, VA 20120
      Contact: Suresh Gursahaney CEO
      Tel: 703-543-2100
      Email: Sgursahaney@microautomation.com
      Website: www.microautomation.com
Computer telephony integration, speech recognition, interactive voice response, reporting, workforce mgmt & digital recording. (Minority, estab 1991, empl 34, sales $7,900,000, cert: NMSDC)

5744 MicroTechnologies, LLC
      8330 Boone Blvd, Ste 600
      Vienna, VA 22182
      Contact: Aaron Drabkin SVP Contracts
      Tel: 703-891-1073
      Email: adrabkin@microtech.net
      Website: www.MicroTech.net
Program mngt, database mgnt & admin, change mgnt & process re-engineering, sys eng svcs, info sys sustainment & support, IT svcs & solns, collaboration svcs & info sharing apps, network solns & sys modernization, & IT enterprise transformation. (Hisp, estab 2004, empl 420, sales $780,000,000, cert: State, NMSDC)

5745 Mindseeker, Inc.
      20130 Lakeview Center Plaza, Ste 320
      Ashburn, VA 20147
      Contact: Cassie Kelly VP Client Services & Operations
      Tel: 304-549-9281
      Email: ckelly@mindseeker.com
      Website: www.mindseeker.com
Information Technology, Financial, Clerical and Enterprise Performance Management services and solutions. (Woman, estab , empl 234, sales $2,000,000, cert: State, WBENC)

5746 Mosaic Solutions, Inc.
      209 Elden St, Ste 204
      Herndon, VA 20170
      Contact: Vikash Nangalia program Mgr
      Tel: 703-707-1680
      Email: vikash@mosaic-us.com
      Website: www.mosaic-us.com/
Systems integration, program mgmt, enterprise resource mgmt, customer relationship mgmt, data mgmt, database admin & warehousing, knowledge mgmt, networking, desktop & help desk svcs, business process outsourcing & supply chain mgmt. (As-Ind, estab 1996, empl 17, sales $1,170,660, cert: NMSDC)

5747 NETHOST, Inc.
      1750 Tysons Blvd. Ste 1500
      McLean, VA 22102
      Contact: Ikram Koreshi CEO
      Tel: 571-236-0781
      Email: ikoreshi@nethostus.com
      Website: www.nethostus.com
Network systems & data communication, engineering, business processes, ERP & CRM functional areas & technical consulting. (As-Ind, estab 2002, empl 3, sales $300,000, cert: State)

5748 NetVision Resources
      2201 Cooperative Way Ste 600
      Herndon, VA 20171
      Contact: Sunny Nangia Dir Resource Management
      Tel: 703-342-4284
      Email: snangia@netvisionresources.com
      Website: www.netvisionresources.com
Information technology svcs: staff augmentation, on-site, off-site & off-shore software development. (Minority, estab 1999, empl 100, sales , cert: NMSDC)

5749   NexThreat
        7686 Richmond Hwy Ste 116
        Alexandria, VA 22306
        Contact: Ruben Gavilan CEO
        Tel: 202-796-1676
        Email: ruben@nexthreat.com
        Website: www.Nexthreat.com
Cyber Security. Emerging SIEM Tool Optimization (Splunk, Qradar, Arcsight Partner), Insider Threat Detection, Incident Response, SOC/NOC Support Services, Continuous Data Analytics, IA, IT Security, Vulnerability Assessments. (Hisp, estab 2016, empl 15, sales $1,000,000, cert: State)

5750   Nirvana International Inc.
        2108 Gunnell Farms Dr
        Vienna, VA 22181
        Contact: Pritish Nawlakhe President
        Tel: 571-215-0072
        Email: pritish@nirvana-international.com
        Website: www.nirvana-international.com
Oracle EBS/ERP Solutions, INFOR Solutions, Program & Project Management, Staff Augmentation, PCI Compliant Credit Card Solutions, Business Intelligence & Analytics solutions, Social Media Integration. (Woman/As-Ind, estab 2012, empl 5, sales $158,000, cert: State)

5751   Pan Asia Resources Pte Ltd.
        44031 Pipeline Plaza Ste 305
        Ashburn, VA 20147
        Contact: Aparnaa Vinod President
        Tel: 571-269-2778
        Email: aparnaa@panasiagroup.net
        Website: www.panasiaresources.com
Information Technology, Marketing & Telecommunications. (Woman/As-Ind, estab 2003, empl 35, sales , cert: State)

5752   Pantheon Inc.
        1801 Robert Fulton Dr Ste 160
        Reston, VA 20191
        Contact: Sarah Johnson Sales Dir
        Tel: 469-387-9775
        Email: sarah.johnson@pantheon-inc.com
        Website: www.odyssey-automation.com
Technology consulting services, Cloud engineering services. SAP services, Salesforce consulting services, Cyber Security services, Web development services, IT staff augmentation services, TaaS services, Customer Technology Solutions. (Woman/As-Pac, estab 1997, empl 1200, sales $247,000,000, cert: NMSDC, NWBOC)

5753   PeopleNTech LLC
        8133 Leesburg Pike, Ste 220
        Vienna, VA 22182
        Contact: Chandra Sharma Dir Business Dev
        Tel: 703-982-7034
        Email: chandra.sharma@email.peoplentech.com
        Website: www.peoplentech.com
IT & Engineering solutions, Development, Outsourcing & Consulting. (Minority, Woman, estab 2005, empl 57, sales $9,600,000, cert: State, City, NMSDC)

5754   Pretek Corporation
        800 Corporate Dr Ste 301
        Stafford, VA 22554
        Contact: Exec Dir
        Tel: 703-855-7148
        Email: info@pretek.com
        Website: www.pretek.com
Enterprise architecture, agile application development, DevOps, enterprise data management, IT infrastructure, systems engineering, and security. (Woman/As-Ind, estab 2002, empl 25, sales $2,800,000, cert: State, 8(a))

5755   Protege LLC
        12359 Sunrise Valley Dr Ste 260
        Reston, VA 20191
        Contact: Shyam Monaysar Sr Business Devel Mgr
        Tel: 703-953-2535
        Email: shyam@protegellc.com
        Website: www.protegellc.com
Web/Application Development (.Net, Java, J2EE, JSP, HTML, DHTML, CSS, Ajax, Flash, C#, C++, C), Web Services(WebLogic, WebSphere, Apache, TeamSite, Windows Administration), SharePoint (Developers, Administrators). (Woman/As-Ind, estab 2004, empl 60, sales $3,500,000, cert: State)

5756   Qassurance Technology Inc.
        5821 Maybrook Court
        Glen Allen, VA 23059
        Contact: Gurushyam Mony CEO
        Tel: 814-441-9634
        Email: support@qassurancetechnology.com
        Website: www.qassurancetechnology.com
Information technology consulting services. (As-Ind, estab 2012, empl 2, sales $145,000, cert: State)

5757   QSACK & Associates, Inc.
        2111 Wilson Blvd, Ste 700
        Arlington, VA 22201
        Contact: C. Anthony Cusack CEO
        Tel: 703-351-5035
        Email: cac@qsack1.com
        Website: www.qsack1.com
Professional, information technology & business support services, systems integration; information assurance; systems security services; information technology services, program & project management. (AA, estab 2001, empl 35, sales $3,879,000, cert: State)

5758   Savi Solutions, Inc.
        8200 Greensboro Dr, Ste 900
        McLean, VA 22102
        Contact: Smita Iyer CEO
        Tel: 571-258-7602
        Email: siyer@savisolutions.biz
        Website: www.savisolutions.biz
Strategic Planning, Program/Project Management, Merger & Acquisition Support, Systems Implementation (ERP/CRM/SCM), Cloud Based Implementation Solutions, Business Requirement Analysis, System Design and Development. (Minority, estab 2010, empl 3, sales $552,551, cert: WBENC)

INFORMATION TECHNOLOGY: Services

5759 Secured Network Solutions, Inc.
929 Ventures Way Ste 113
Chesapeake, VA 23320
Contact: Alphonzo Barney President
Tel: 757-819-7647
Email: abarney@teamsns.com
Website: www.teamsns.com
Telecommunications & information technology: cabling, design, install, fiber optics single/multi-strand, fiber fusion & splicing, LAN/WAN/wireless network engineering, drafting & information systems security. (AA, estab 2006, empl 11, sales , cert: State)

5760 Shivan Technologies, Inc.
12818 Owens Glen Dr
Fairfax, VA 22030
Contact: Rekha Bathula President
Tel: 703-595-6879
Email: contact@stgxinc.com
Website: www.stgxinc.com
Information Technology (IT), Network Management, Computer Facilities Management, Program Management, Consulting, Administrative & Professional Support Services, Information Assurance, Enterprise Architecture, Cloud. (Minority, Woman, estab 2007, empl 4, sales , cert: State, 8(a))

5761 SilTek, Inc.
13454 Sunrise Valley Dr Ste 250
Herndon, VA 20171
Contact: Silvia M. Park President
Tel: 703-620-9130
Email: info@siltek.com
Website: www.siltekinc.com
Computer hardware, IT svcs, systems integration, computer training. (Minority, Woman, estab 1997, empl 1, sales , cert: State)

5762 SMART Resources, Inc.
10442 Patterson Ave
Richmond, VA 23238
Contact: Van Williams Principal
Tel: 804-864-9150
Email: vanw@smartva.net
Website: www.smartva.net
Information Technology and Human Resources Consulting Services. (Woman, estab 2007, empl 28, sales $13,800,000, cert: State)

5763 Solvitur Systems LLC
202 Church St SE Ste 526
Leesburg, VA 20176
Contact: Ade Odutola Managing Dir
Tel: 703-348-3544
Email: aodutola@solvitursystems.com
Website: www.solvitursystems.com
Regulatory Compliance & Security Assessments, Privacy Impact Analysis, Cloud Security Services, FedRAMP, CSA, Assessment & Authorization: FISMA, FISCAM, DIACAP, FFIEC, PCI, HIPAA, ISO 27001/27002, Independent Verification & Validation. (AA, estab 2007, empl 5, sales $230,000, cert: State, 8(a))

5764 Spurgetech, LLC
21580 Atlantic Blvd, Ste 220B
Sterling, VA 20166
Contact: Susetha Balabishegan President
Tel: 703-652-6576
Email: susetha@spurgetech.com
Website: www.spurgetech.com
Information Technology Consulting, contract & permanent staffing solutions, On-site, off-site or remote, ERP Resources, SAP, Oracle & Peoplesoft. (Minority, Woman, estab 2006, empl 5, sales $900,000, cert: State, WBENC)

5765 Stanton Secure Technologies, LLC
2054 S Shirlington Rd
Arlington, VA 22204
Contact: Lisa Wallace CEO
Tel: 703-568-0553
Email: johnson@sst-llc.com
Website: www.sst-llc.com
Information Assurance services, training & security management, Cyber Security Program Management, Assessment & Authorization, Security Engineering, Remediation Solutions, Security Awareness & Training. (Woman/AA, estab 2005, empl 2, sales $180,000, cert: State)

5766 Summit Information Solutions, Inc.
3957 Westerre Pkwy Ste 120
Richmond, VA 23233
Contact: Vickie Quigg Communications & Marketing Mgr
Tel: 804-201-4356
Email: vickie.quigg@summitis.com
Website: www.summitis.com
Enterprise Architecture; Change Management; Information Technology; SCORM; Virtual; 3D; Training; Atomic Layering; ALD; Banking; Finance; Aerospace Engineering; Big Data; Data Analytics; Resource Management; Portfolio Management; Cloud; Procurement; AGIL. (Minority, Woman, estab 2002, empl 37, sales $8,326,000, cert: NMSDC)

5767 Sygna Technologies Inc
4000 Legato Rd Ste 1100
Fairfax, VA 22033
Contact: Paul Shakya President
Tel: 571-445-4800
Email: paul@sygnatechnologies.com
Website: www.sygnatechnolgies.com
Temporary contract IT Staffing. (Minority, estab 2014, empl 1, sales , cert: State)

5768 Symposit LLC
4809 Eisenhower Ave Ste B3
Alexandria, VA 22304
Contact: Allen R Bermudez President
Tel: 571-224-4739
Email: bobby.bermudez@symposit.com
Website: www.symposit.com
Cloud Solutions & Applications, Cloud Office Productivity, Integration, Email Migration Services, Virtual Machines, Virtual Desktop Infrastructure Windows & Linux Servers Network. (Hisp, estab 2009, empl 6, sales $400,000, cert: 8(a))

INFORMATION TECHNOLOGY: Services

5769 Synapse Business Systems
11350 Random Hills Rd, Ste 800
Fairfax, VA 22030
Contact: Shivani Kaushal Sales Head
Tel: 703-782-0007
Email: hr@synapsebsystems.com
Website: www.synapsebsystems.com
Staff Augmentation, Experienced, dedicated and qualified core staffs, Network of IT Professional, Systematic and well-defined process to recruit and hire new talent. (Minority, Woman, estab 2013, empl 63, sales $2,911,046, cert: WBENC)

5770 Synaptein Solutions Inc.
1568 Spring Hill Road Ste 402
Mclean, VA 22102
Contact: Sharad Dayma CEO
Tel: 703-209-2350
Email: sharad.d@synap-one.com
Website: www.synapteinsolutions.com
Staff Augmentation & Resource Planning Services, BPM Solutions, Product Development, Customer Support, Professional Services, Enterprise Solutions Provider, Business Intelligence & DSS, Off-& and On-site. (As-Ind, estab 2011, empl 15, sales $1,196,000, cert: State, NMSDC, 8(a))

5771 Talteam,Inc
13800 Coppermine Rd Ste 120
Herndon, VA 20171
Contact: Bobby Toe Exec VP
Tel: 571-315-4958
Email: bobbyt@talteam.com
Website: www.talteam.com
IT professional Services, Salesforce & Java technologies. (Minority, Woman, estab 2011, empl 100, sales $9,000,000, cert: WBENC)

5772 Team Askin Technologies, Inc
13135 Lee Jackson Memorial Hwy Ste 340
fairfax, VA 22033
Contact: steve askin COO
Tel: 703-230-0111
Email: steve.askin@teamaskin.com
Website: www.teamaskin.com
Software engineering & development, electronic commerce (Internet and Intranet Web Sites, G2C,G2G), Java Applets, XML, Graphical User Interface (GUI), Front Page, Cold Fusion, Dreamweaver. (Minority, Woman, estab 1992, empl 50, sales $9,000,000, cert: State, WBENC)

5773 Technalink, Inc.
8000 Towers Crescent Dr Ste 600
Vienna, VA 22182
Contact: Alka Dhillon CEO
Tel: 703-627-1916
Email: adhillon@technalink.net
Website: www.technalink.net
Informaiton technology staffing solutions. (Woman/As-Ind, estab 2000, empl 20, sales $ 0, cert: WBENC)

5774 Technology Assurance Group, Inc.
2114 Tomlynn St
Richmond, VA 23230
Contact: Angela Taylor CEO
Tel: 804-323-7480
Email: ahtaylor@tagva.com
Website: www.tagva.com
Systems integration: LAN/WAN, VP & wireless networks, bandwidth mgmt tools, file & directory svcs, storage, messaging, databases, IP telephony, desktop support. (Woman, estab 2002, empl 10, sales $850,000, cert: State)

5775 Terralogic Integrated Systems Analysts, Inc.
2001 N Beauregard St Ste 600
Alexandria, VA 22311
Contact: Tony Swetich Business Devel Mgr
Tel: 313-416-1741
Email: tony.s@terralogic.com
Website: www.terralogic.com
Computer Systems Services, Project Management, Process Engineering, Site Planning, Safety Engineering, PC Deployments, Hardware/Software Upgrades, Deskside Support, Help desk, Asset Management, Hardware Maintenance. (As-Ind, estab 1980, empl 1000, sales $11,000,000, cert: NMSDC)

5776 Total System Services US, Inc.
1900 Campus Commons Dr #100
Reston, VA 20191
Contact: Aniths Paalepu
Tel: 703-732-6063
Email: anithapaalepu@tsysus.com
Website: www.tsysus.com
IT consulting solutions, distributed operating & computing systems, storage, networking, systems knowledge. (Minority, Woman, estab 2012, empl 3, sales , cert: NMSDC)

5777 Unicom Government, Inc.
2553 Dulles View Dr Ste 100
Herndon, VA 20171
Contact: Margaret Dooley Systems Integrator
Tel: 703-502-2937
Email: maggie.dooley@unicomgov.com
Website: www.unicomgov.com
Integration, Logistics, Warehouse Warehousing, Cloud Computing, IT Products Computers, laptops Desktops Servers Switches Cables Software, Supply Chain Outsourcing, procurement, Financial Services Leasing. (As-Pac, estab 1986, empl 199, sales $193,000,000, cert: NMSDC)

5778 USM Business Systems, Inc.
14175 Sullyfield Circle Ste 400
Chantilly, VA 20151
Contact: Joshua R. SVP Business Dev
Tel: 832-881-7903
Email: joshuar@usmsystems.com
Website: www.usmsystems.com
Staffing & implementation solutions, computer software programming, application dev, web dev, data warehouse dev & ERP implementations. (As-Ind, estab 1999, empl 400, sales $45,000,000, cert: State)

INFORMATION TECHNOLOGY: Services

5779 Vigintis LLC
      4000 Legato Rd, Ste 1100
      Fairfax, VA 22033
      Contact: Subodh Dash President
      Tel: 703-395-3044
      Email: subodh.dash@vigintis.us
      Website: www.vigintis.us
Agile Program & Project Management Software Engineering, Product Development Solution Architecture, Technology Consulting System, Application Integration Cloud Solutions. (As-Pac, estab 2004, empl 3, sales $460,000, cert: 8(a))

5780 VisionOnline, Inc.
      1984 Isaac Newton Square W Ste 202
      Reston, VA 20190
      Contact: Ned Malik President
      Tel: 703-626-5662
      Email: ned.malik@visiononline.com
      Website: www.visiononline.com
Information Technology: software engineering, systems integration, web design & information assurance services. (Woman, estab 1998, empl 25, sales $3,500,000, cert: State)

5781 Weiatech, LLC
      22584 Hammersmith Pl
      Ashburn, VA 20148
      Contact: Akomala Akouete Operation Dir
      Tel: 703-665-9603
      Email: aakouete@weiatech.com
      Website: www.weiatech.com
Information technology equipment, solutions, and services. (AA, estab 2016, empl 5, sales , cert: State)

5782 Worldgate, LLC
      1760 Reston Pkwy Ste 312
      Reston, VA 20190
      Contact: Katelyn Montgomery Dir Client Services
      Tel: 703-349-0493
      Email: kmontgomery@worldgatellc.com
      Website: www.worldgatellc.com
IT systems integration consulting, technology platforms, operating systems & infrastructures, data warehouse, business intelligence, ERP, project managment, call center/service desk. (Woman, estab 2002, empl 20, sales $1,200,000, cert: State, WBENC)

5783 Zeva Inc
      10300 Eaton Place Ste 305
      Fairfax, VA 22030
      Contact: Sam I Shihadeh Dir Diversity & Inclusion
      Tel: 301-518-3705
      Email: sshihadeh@zeva.us
      Website: www.zevainc.com
Cloud Services, Public Key Ennoblement (PKE), Identity, Credentialing and Access Management. (Woman, estab 2005, empl 55, sales $10,000,000, cert: WBENC)

5784 Zillion Technologies, Inc.
      20745 Williamsport Pl Ste 150
      Ashburn, VA 20147
      Contact: Kimberlee Sours Business Devel Mgr
      Tel: 703-592-6949
      Email: kimberlee@zilliontechnologies.com
      Website: www.zilliontechnologies.com
Business consulting & technology solutions, strategic outsourcing & application management. (As-Ind, estab 2002, empl 350, sales $38,000,000, cert: NMSDC, SDB)

5785 Zirtex Systems Corporation
      7371 Atlas Walk Way, Ste 152
      Gainesville, VA 20155
      Contact: Rajeev Jessani President
      Tel: 800-536-4982
      Email: rjessani@zirtexsystems.com
      Website: www.zirtexsystems.com
Management consulting & technology services. (As-Ind, estab 2006, empl 2, sales $328,832, cert: NMSDC)

5786 Zolon Tech Solutions, Inc.
      13921 Park Center Rd, Ste 500
      Herndon, VA 20171
      Contact: Goutham Amarneni President
      Tel: 703-636-7370
      Email: supplier.diversity@zolon.com
      Website: www.zolontech.com
Information technology consulting services: integration, modification, unification, secure & customized, applications & enterprise software solutions. (Minority, estab 1998, empl , sales $66,000,000, cert: NMSDC)

Vermont

5787 iTech US, Inc.
      20 Kimball Ave, Ste 303N
      South Burlington, VT 05403
      Contact: Kishore Khandavalli CEO
      Tel: 802-383-1500
      Email: kk@itechus.com
      Website: www.itechus.com
Software consulting services, application development, business process outsourcing solutions & offshore project development. (As-Pac, estab 2001, empl 1150, sales $53,000,000, cert: NMSDC)

Washington

5788 Advanced Technology Computers, Inc.
      824 Grimes Rd
      Bothell, WA 98012
      Contact: Andre Tyson Owner
      Tel: 425-486-6045
      Email: andre@atcdirect.com
      Website: www.atcdirect.com
Information technology systems integration. (AA, estab , empl 3, sales , cert: 8(a))

5789 Amaxra, Inc.
      2509 152nd Ave NE Ste E
      Redmond, WA 98052
      Contact: Rosalyn Arntzen President
      Tel: 425-749-7471
      Email: supplierdiversity@amaxra.com
      Website: www.amaxra.com
Program Management & Management. (Woman, estab 2007, empl 45, sales $6,003,345, cert: WBENC)

5790 Amreli Technology Solutions, LLC
      17530 NE Union Hill Rd, Ste 290
      Redmond, WA 98052
      Contact: Atul Hirpara CEO
      Tel: 425-881-6971
      Email: atul@amrelitech.com
      Website: www.amrelitech.com
IT intelligence, dashboards & scorecards, software, integration of disparate systems & applications. (As-Pac, estab 2004, empl 32, sales $3,400,000, cert: State, NMSDC)

INFORMATION TECHNOLOGY: Services

5791   Attunix Corporation
        405 114th Ave SE Ste 110
        Bellevue, WA 98004
        Contact: Matt O'Donnell CEO
        Tel: 206-774-3163
        Email: matto@attunix.com
        Website: www.attunix.com
Custom Development, Portals & Web, Cloud Integration, and Mobile Solutions, Program Management. (Hisp, estab 2006, empl 12, sales $1,935,000, cert: State, NMSDC)

5792   Axelerate
        13401 Bel Red Rd, Ste B8
        Bellevue, WA 98005
        Contact: Sr Client Services Mgr
        Tel: 425-429-6720
        Email: info@axelerate.com
        Website: www.axelerate.com
IT consulting & staffing. (Woman, estab 2003, empl 5, sales , cert: WBENC)

5793   BiSoft Consultancy Services
        16310 NE 80th St, Ste 104
        Redmond, WA 98052
        Contact: Balaji Udayshankar CEO
        Tel: 401-450-1672
        Email: bala@bisoftllc.com
        Website: www.bisoftllc.com
Information technology svcs, website design, wed development & maintenance, SEO optimization, application software. (As-Ind, estab 2015, empl 1, sales $2,000,000, cert: NMSDC)

5794   Chameleon Technologies, Inc.
        520 Kirkland Way Ste 101
        Kirkland, WA 98033
        Contact: Principal
        Tel: 425-827-1173
        Email: sales@chameleontechinc.com
        Website: www.chameleontechinc.com
Technical staffing: software testers, software developers, network engineers & admins, database admins & developers, project mgrs, business & systems analysts, technical writers, etc. (Minority, Woman, estab 2000, empl 30, sales $722,000, cert: WBENC)

5795   Eastside Groups LLC
        P.O.Box 165
        Mercer Island, WA 98040
        Contact: Jessie Wang Owner
        Tel: 206-466-6649
        Email: main@catandena.com
        Website: www.catandena.com
Software solutions, financial applications, web sites & web services, from stand-alone scale to enterprise scale. (Minority, Woman, estab 2014, empl 1, sales , cert: State)

5796   ELYON International Inc.
        1111 Main St, Ste 405
        Vancouver, WA 98660
        Contact: Carmen Nazario President
        Tel: 360-696-5892
        Email: carmen@elyoninternational.com
        Website: www.elyoninternational.com
Consulting & technology svcs: software devel, systems integration, offshore solutions delivery, etc. (Minority, Woman, estab 1997, empl 148, sales $23,000,000, cert: State, NMSDC, WBENC)

5797   General Microsystems Inc.
        3220 118th Ave SE
        Bellevue, WA 98005
        Contact: Earl Overstreet President
        Tel: 425-644-2233
        Email: earl@gmi.com
        Website: www.gmi.com
Information technology: systems, storage management solutions. (AA, estab 1983, empl 13, sales $32,330,000, cert: State, NMSDC)

5798   Hansell Tierney, Inc.
        2955 80th AVE SE #103
        Mercer Island, WA 98040
        Contact: Acct Mgr
        Tel: 206-232-3080
        Email: info@hanselltierney.com
        Website: www.hanselltierney.com
IT consulting services & recruiting. (Woman, estab 2001, empl 35, sales $2,800,000, cert: State)

5799   i9 Systems, Inc.
        16928 NE 38th Place
        Bellevue, WA 98008
        Contact: Sukhjot Basi CEO
        Tel: 206-412-7918
        Email: basi@i9systems.com
        Website: www.i9systems.com
Staffing, consulting, software development & testing, program/project management, database & network administrations, business requirements, full software development life cycle. (Woman/As-Ind, estab 1999, empl 16, sales $500,000, cert: State)

5800   Idea Entity Corporation
        16625 Redmond Way Ste M 009
        Redmond, WA 98052
        Contact: John Strathy CFO
        Tel: 425-454-2905
        Email: john.strathy@ideaentity.com
        Website: www.ideaentity.com
Project, staff, development, testing, onsite, offsite, offshore, application developmen, custom application development & packaged solution integration. (As-Ind, estab 2006, empl 45, sales , cert: State, NMSDC)

5801   InConsulting Inc.
        12901 181st Ave NE
        Redmond, WA 98052
        Contact: Aparna Mahadevan CEO
        Tel: 425-880-5996
        Email: services@inconsultinginc.com
        Website: www.inconsultinginc.com
Information staffing & placement, IT services, Consulting, Systems planning, Web Design & development. (Woman/As-Ind, estab 2010, empl 40, sales , cert: State)

5802   Kaasm, LLC
        900 1st Ave S, Ste 302
        Seattle, WA 98134
        Contact: Shawn Sandoval President
        Tel: 206-735-3882
        Email: shawns@kaasm.com
        Website: www.kaasm.com
SCADA software, Industrial computers, networking components, alarm notification software & Enterprise Asset Management. (Hisp, estab 2013, empl 3, sales $150,000, cert: City, NMSDC)

INFORMATION TECHNOLOGY: Services

5803 Kathcart Open Systems & Consulting, Inc.
17311 135th Ave NE, Ste B500
Woodinville, WA 98072
Contact: CEO
Tel: 425-402-0258
Email: info@dimension-systems.com
Website: www.dimension-systems.com
Information technology consulting services. (Woman, estab 1993, empl 20, sales $42,000,000, cert: WBENC)

5804 Martirx Infotech LLC
1017 4th Ave E Ste 6
Olympia, WA 98506
Contact: Narasimha Varakantham CEO
Tel: 360-545-4089
Email: reddy@matrixinf.com
Website: www.matrixinf.com
Information technology services, contingent workforce staffing solutions, technology support, consulting & development, software to hardware. (Woman/As-Ind, estab 2014, empl 3, sales $105,253, cert: State)

5805 New Era Contract Sales Inc.
5838 S Adams St
Tacoma, WA 98409
Contact: Brenda Valentine President
Tel: 253-272-3553
Email: brenda@newerasalesteam.com
Website: www.newerasalesteam.com
Customized purchasing software. (Woman, estab 1988, empl 9, sales $15,200,000, cert: WBENC)

5806 Nvelup Consulting
19125 North Creek Pkwy Ste 120
Bothell, WA 98011
Contact: Chris Barrios CEO
Tel: 206-419-2584
Email: chris@nvelupconsulting.com
Website: www.nvelupconsulting.com
Performance Management (Budgeting, Planning & Forecasting) & Business Intelligence (Data Analysis & Reporting) solutions. (Minority, estab 2014, empl 15, sales $936,000, cert: State, NMSDC, SDB)

5807 Online Training Solutions, Inc.
PO Box 951
Bellevue, WA 98009
Contact: Joan Preppernau President
Tel: 888-308-6874
Email: biz@otsi.com
Website: www.otsi.com
Publishing & programming services. (Woman, estab 1987, empl 13, sales $1,120,873, cert: WBENC)

5808 P2 Solutions Group LLC
2296 W Commodore Way, Ste 300
Seattle, WA 98199
Contact: Tonjia Borland
Tel: 206-226-8433
Email: tborland@p2solutionsgroup.com
Website: www.p2solutionsgroup.com
Technical, system administrator, programming, developer, engineering, finance, marketing & project management staff. (Hisp, estab 2002, empl 120, sales $10,600,000, cert: City, NMSDC)

5809 PeopleTech Group
15809 Bear Creek Pkwy Ste 410
Redmond, WA 09082
Contact: Exec VP
Tel: 425-444-6174
Email:
Website: www.peopletech.com
ERP Services, Oracle, PeopleSoft, SAP, Microsoft Dynamics, Implementation, Upgrade, Application Development, Testing & Consulting, Big Data, DWH & BI, OBIEE, BO, Micro Strategy, Microsoft. (Minority, Woman, estab 2006, empl 1200, sales $22,000,000, cert: NMSDC)

5810 Prowess Consulting, LLC
5701 Sixth Ave S Ste 374
Seattle, WA 98108
Contact: Aaron Suzuki CEO
Tel: 206-443-1117
Email: info@prowesscorp.com
Website: www.prowesscorp.com
Content program management, technical content development & editing, training content development, IT & content systems management & digital marketing services. (As-Pac, estab 2003, empl 80, sales $11,800,000, cert: State, NMSDC)

5811 Redapt, Inc.
14051 NE 200th St. Bldg D
Woodinville, WA 98072
Contact: Rick Cantu CEO
Tel: 425-882-0400
Email: agreen@redapt.com
Website: www.redapt.com
Business Transformation Cloud native apps, Application Development, Refactoring, Security Best Practices. (Minority, estab 1996, empl 220, sales $350,050,000, cert: NMSDC)

5812 S3Global Consulting Services, LLC
10532 82nd Ave Court SW
Lakewood, WA 98498
Contact: Morris Sterling III, MBA CEO
Tel: 877-470-1900
Email: morris.sterling@s3goglobal.com
Website: www.s3goglobal.com
Information technology & business-based enterprises, project, program & product management, technical writing & communications, continuous process improvement, business analysis & intelligence. (Woman/AA, estab 2012, empl 5, sales , cert: State, City)

5813 ScrumPoint
1110 112th Ave Northeast Ste 350
Bellevue, WA 98052
Contact: Michael Mpare President
Tel: 509-714-4842
Email: michael@scrumpoint.com
Website: www.scrumpoint.com
Custom software applications, SSIS & SSRS management, SharePoint portals, custom web applications, Windows Azure Cloud Services. (AA, estab 2011, empl 6, sales $ 0, cert: NMSDC)

INFORMATION TECHNOLOGY: Services

5814 Tam Partners Consulting, LLC
      18350 204th Ave NE
      Woodinville, WA 98077
      Contact: Lisa Tam Founder
      Tel: 425-998-8401
      Email: lisatam@tpartnerscg.com
      Website: www.tpartnerscg.com
Engineering: Power BI, Excel Power Pivot, ETL, SSIS, SSAS, T-SQL, Data Marts, Data Warehouse, SQL Server Management Studio, Business Intelligence Development StudioBig Data Analytics: JSon, HiveQL, Microsoft Azure HDInsight | Cloud Hadoop, Azure Managem (Woman, estab 2016, empl 1, sales $114,784, cert: WBENC)

5815 TripleNet Technologies, Inc.
      1122 E Pike St, Ste 509
      Seattle, WA 98122
      Contact: Hans Gomez President
      Tel: 206-260-8998
      Email: hansgomez@triplenettech.com
      Website: www.triplenettech.com
IT staffing, network architecture & design, software development, wireless network design & implementation, data storage plan, disaster recovery. (Hisp, estab 1997, empl 18, sales $500,000, cert: State, City, NMSDC)

5816 TSS Redmond
      8461 154th Ave NE, Bldg G
      Redmond, WA 98052
      Contact: Lisa Roeder CEO
      Tel: 425-749-3030
      Email: lroeder@tssredmond.com
      Website: www.tssredmond.com
Software, computer, technical development, soft skills, project management, business development & leadership training. (Woman, estab 2000, empl 20, sales $700,000, cert: State)

5817 Zones, LLC
      1102 15th St SW Ste 102
      Auburn, WA 98001
      Contact: Bruce Heather Field Acct Mgr - Sales West
      Tel: 253-205-3227
      Email: bruce.heather@zones.com
      Website: www.zones.com
Information technology products & services, resell computer hardware & software. (As-Ind, estab 1986, empl 2744, sales $2,900,000,000, cert: State, NMSDC)

Wisconsin

5818 Abaxent, LLC
      N28W23050 Roundy Dr Ste 200
      Pewaukee, WI 53072
      Contact: Adonica Randall President
      Tel: 262-650-6500
      Email: arandall@abaxent.com
      Website: www.abaxent-global.com
Information technology services, project management, software development, network engineering & consulting/design. (Woman/AA, estab 2002, empl 10, sales $14,000,000, cert: State, NMSDC, WBENC)

5819 Comcentia, LLC
      1025 W Glen Oaks Lane Ste 211
      Mequon, WI 53092
      Contact: Darrell Caldwell President
      Tel: 414-871-1100
      Email: info@comcentia.com
      Website: www.comcentia.com
IT Consulting, Custom Applications & Database Development, Custom web based or windows desktop application development, Application Management of Existing Systems, Ongoing & and ad hoc changes. (AA, estab 2006, empl 6, sales $612,112, cert: NMSDC, 8(a))

5820 CTL Resources (Caribou Thunder)
      8558 N County Rd K
      Hayward, WI 54843
      Contact: Rita Peterson Owner
      Tel: 719-412-3754
      Email: rita@ctlresources.com
      Website: www.ctlresources.com
Project Management, Process Re-engineering, Process Change, Enterprise application integration, Engineering. (Minority, Woman, estab , empl , sales $10,000,000, cert: NMSDC)

5821 Excel Global Solutions Inc.
      2727 N Grandview Blvd Ste 117
      Waukesha, WI 53188
      Contact: Jerry Sorci VP
      Tel: 262-347-4911
      Email: jerry.sorci@excelglobalsolution.com
      Website: www.excelglobalsolution.com
IT services, solutions & products, Big Data Predictive intelligence Product, Automated Application Testing Product, Vehicle Maintenance Management Product. (Minority, Woman, estab 2010, empl 250, sales , cert: State)

5822 Genome International Corporation
      8000 Excelsior Dr Ste 202
      Madison, WI 53717
      Contact: Sue Seshadri HR Mgr
      Tel: 608-833-5855
      Email: sue@genome.com
      Website: www.genome.com
IT staffing, technical consulting, enterprise application developement. (Minority, Woman, estab 1992, empl 120, sales $9,100,000, cert: WBENC)

5823 Malleswari Inc.
      11512 N Port Washington Rd, Ste 101-I
      Mequon, WI 53092
      Contact: Trinadha Pattem
      Tel: 262-308-3480
      Email: trinadha@malleswari.com
      Website: www.malleswari.com
End to End SAP ERP/SRM/BI/Mobile Technology Solutions. (Woman/As-Ind, estab 2004, empl 5, sales $2,350,227, cert: State, City, NMSDC)

INFORMATION TECHNOLOGY: Services

5824 Valicom Corp
2923 Marketplace Dr Ste 104
Fitchburg, WI 53719
Contact: Marketing
Tel: 800-467-7226
Email: sales@valicomcorp.com
Website: www.valicomcorp.com
IT & telecom invoice audit & management: RFP facilitation, contract negotiation & management, network design & engineering, help desk, invoice payment & general ledger coding. (Woman, estab 1991, empl 20, sales $ 0, cert: State, WBENC)

5825 Vanguard Computers, Inc.
13100 W Lisbon Rd, Ste 100
Brookfield, WI 53005
Contact: Owner
Tel: 262-317-1900
Email: sales@vanguardinc.com
Website: www.vanguardinc.com
Dist, svc & rent computer equipment & peripherals; network configuration, installation & maintenance. (Minority, Woman, estab 1982, empl 39, sales $ 0, cert: WBENC)

5826 Wissen Infotech Inc
2325 Parklawn Dr Ste G
Waukesha, WI 53186
Contact: Upendra Rachupaly Operations Mgr
Tel: 262-510-2900
Email: upendra.rachupally@wisseninfotech.com
Website: www.wisseninfotech.com
IT services, onsite, offsite & offshore service, End to end Mobility application, development, Analytics, Cloud Management, Media & Entertainment, Embedded Systems, Big data & Hadoop.
Enterprise Resource Planning, Remote Infrastructure Management (As-Ind, estab 2001, empl 800, sales $12,000,000, cert: State)

West Virginia

5827 Fusion Plus Solutions Inc.
17 Cherokee Dr
Moundsville, WV 26041
Contact: Mark Thomas Dir
Tel: 732-250-9048
Email: mark@fusionplusinc.com
Website: www.fusionplusinc.com
IT Staff Augmentation, Information Technology Solutions, Consulting/Staffing Services, System Integration, Software Products. (Minority, Woman, estab 2009, empl 1000, sales , cert: State)

INFORMATION TECHNOLOGY: Supplies

Manufacture or distribute magnetic media supplies such as, disketts, paper, printers, fascimilies, toner cartridges, keyboards, computer peripherials. NAICS Code 42

Arizona

5828 Centacor, Inc.
135 Chilton Dr
Chandler, AZ 85225
Contact: Troy Bryan Mgr
Tel: 480-899-9500
Email: info@centacor.com
Website: www.centacor.com
IT products & services. (AA, estab 2009, empl 4, sales , cert: NMSDC)

5829 Cybergear, Inc.
4711 E Falcon Dr Ste 202
Mesa, AZ 85215
Contact: President
Tel: 480-926-6470
Email: sales@cybergearUSA.com
Website: www.cybergearusa.com
Dist computer hardware, consumer electronics, electronic test & measurement, computer software & software licensing, POS/bar code equipment, wireless voice/data products & services. (Woman, estab 1998, empl 2, sales , cert: City, WBENC)

5830 ESI Ergonomic Solutions, LLC
4030 E Quenton Dr Ste 101
Mesa, AZ 85215
Contact: Carol Keogh CEO
Tel: 480-517-1871
Email: ckeogh@esiergo.com
Website: www.esiergo.com
Mfr & dist articulating arms, keyboard platforms, flat screen monitor arms & ergonomic accessories. (Woman, estab 1988, empl 25, sales $15,000,000, cert: NWBOC)

5831 Herco Technology div. of Hernandez Companies
3734 E Anne St
Phoenix, AZ 85040
Contact: Mike Pena Acct Exec
Tel: 602-438-7825
Email: info@hernandezcompanies.com
Website: www.hernandezcompanies.com/
Dist computer & networking cable & cable accessories: fiber optic cables, coaxial, custom assemblies, racks, shelving, wire mgmt, Cat5E patch cables. (Minority, Woman, estab 1975, empl 75, sales , cert: NMSDC)

5832 Identico Print Services (DBA Print.Save.Repeat.com)
4942 S 71st St
Mesa, AZ 85212
Contact: Nathan Carter Business Devel
Tel: 800-587-1173
Email: orders@printsaverepeat.com
Website: www.printsaverepeat.com
Mfr pressure sensitive labels & laser printer toner cartridges. (Hisp, estab 1986, empl 51, sales $17,938,582, cert: NMSDC)

5833 Swift Office Solutions
2429 W 12th St Ste#6
Tempe, AZ 85281
Contact: Edward Swift President
Tel: 480-966-2100
Email: eswift@sosnet.com
Website: www.sosnet.com
Dist computers, hardware, software, and office products. (Minority, estab 1981, empl 9, sales $5,000,000, cert: NMSDC)

California

5834 Alliant Event Services
196 University Pkwy
Pomona, CA 91768
Contact: Heather Milianak Sr Sales Mgr
Tel: 909-354-4469
Email: hmilanak@asn-corp.com
Website: www.AlliantEvents.com
Rental technology & event production solutions: laptop & desktop computers, printers, copiers, audio-visual, sound & lighting products. (As-Ind, estab 2003, empl 38, sales $4,150,000, cert: State)

5835 CDCE Inc.
22755-G Savi Ranch Pkwy
Yorba Linda, CA 92887
Contact: Kim Hufford Natl Acct Mgr
Tel: 714-282-8881
Email: khufford@cdce.com
Website: www.cdce.com
Wireless, computer vehicle installations, ruggedized notebooks & tablets. (Woman, estab 1984, empl 25, sales , cert: CPUC, WBENC)

5836 ComputerSuppliers.Com
7377 Convoy Court, Ste A
San Diego, CA 92111
Contact: Jay Satpute Bids Specialist
Tel: 858-268-7370
Email: bids@computersupplies.com
Website: www.computersupplies.com
Dist inks, toners, monitor filters, furniture, pens, printers, ribbons, and storage media such as DVD, CD, LTO, SDX, AIT, 4mm & 8mm cartridges. (Woman/As-Ind, estab 2002, empl 7, sales $6,000,000, cert: City)

5837 Conversions Technology
1740 Emerson Ave
Oxnard, CA 93033
Contact: Kevin Williams VP Sales
Tel: 800-596-2037
Email: kevin@conversiontechnology.com
Website: www.ConversionsTechnology.com
Mfr & dist cable accessory & PC peripheral components. (Minority, Woman, estab 2006, empl 25, sales $1,000,000, cert: CPUC)

5838 GC Micro Corporation
3910 Cypress Dr
Petaluma, CA 94954
Contact: Ashley Kidd Acct Mgr
Tel: 800-426-4276
Email: bg@gcmicro.com
Website: www.gcmicro.com
Dist personal computers, microcomputer hardware, software, peripherals, IBM, HP, AST, Epson authorized dealer. (Minority, Woman, estab 1986, empl 35, sales , cert: State, NMSDC, CPUC, WBENC)

INFORMATION TECHNOLOGY: Supplies

5839 Gear One Enterprise
34450 Calle Sereno
Temecula, CA 92592
Contact: Brad Barnes Sr Acct Mgr
Tel: 949-276-7924
Email: brad@gearonecom.com
Website: www.gearonecom.com
Network peripherals & connectivity products: optical transceivers, network memory, media converters & cable solutions. (Woman, estab 2012, empl 6, sales $1,511,024, cert: WBENC)

5840 Kambrian Corporation
2707 E Valley Blvd
West Covina, CA 91792
Contact: Cathy Hsieh CEO
Tel: 626-374-3933
Email: cathyh@kambrian.com
Website: www.kambrian.com
Resell IT products: software, hardware & services. (Minority, Woman, estab 2009, empl 7, sales $10,469,102, cert: NMSDC, WBENC, 8(a))

5841 MelroseMAC, Inc.
6614 Melrose Ave
Hollywood, CA 90038
Contact: Jonathan Strayhorn CEO
Tel: 323-937-4600
Email: jon@mac330.com
Website: www.melrosemac.com
Resell Apple products. (Woman, estab 2003, empl 80, sales $55,000,000, cert: CPUC, WBENC)

5842 Mobile ID Solutions, Inc.
1574 N Batavia St, Ste 1
Orange, CA 92867
Contact: Rick Fahilga Acct Exec
Tel: 714-922-1134
Email: rfahilga@mobileidsolutions.com
Website: www.mobileidsolutions.com
Mobile Computers, printers. Barcode Printers, Scanners, verifiers. ID Card Printers and supplies. IP Cameras. Cellular Routers, modem, POS Equipment, Satellite phones. (As-Pac, estab 2004, empl 9, sales $4,800,000, cert: NMSDC)

5843 On-Site LaserMedic Corp.
21540 Prairie St, Unit D
Chatsworth, CA 91311
Contact: Gail Solomon CEO
Tel: 818-772-6911
Email: sd@onsitelasermedic.com
Website: www.onsitelasermedic.com
Laser printer, fax & deskjet service & repair, dist toner. (Woman, estab 1992, empl 46, sales $5,318,472, cert: WBENC)

5844 Paris Laser Printer Repair
16224 Gundry Ave
Paramount, CA 90723
Contact: Arthur Milton Owner
Tel: 562-634-4499
Email: parisprinters@sbcglobal.net
Website: www.parisprinterrepair.com
Laser printer repair. (AA, estab 2001, empl 3, sales $550,000, cert: State)

5845 Performance Designed Products
14144 Ventura Blvd Ste 200
Sherman Oaks, CA 91423
Contact: Theresa Harrell Natl Acct Mgr
Tel: 479-445-8612
Email: theresa.harrell@pdp.com
Website: www.pdp.com
Design & mfr video game peripherals & accessories. (Woman, estab 1990, empl 200, sales , cert: WBENC)

5846 PNH Technology, Inc.
15375 Barranca Pkwy Ste F-108
Irvine, CA 92618
Contact: Thacher Grauer Office Mgr
Tel: 949-614-4102
Email: thacher@pnhtech.com
Website: www.pnhtech.com
Dist servers, rack, tower, blades, memory, hard drives, server accessories, storage (SAN, NAS, DAS), storage accessories. networking switches, routers, firewalls, network accessories, desktops, PCs & laptops. (As-Pac, estab 2008, empl 6, sales $3,000,000, cert: State)

5847 RC & JT Inc. dba Computer Masters
6185 Cornerstone Court Ste 103
San Diego, CA 92121
Contact: Jessie Thorell Acct Mgr
Tel: 858-444-2966
Email: jthorell@computermastersinc.com
Website: www.computermastersinc.com
Dist computer hardware, software, printers, supplies & networking products & services. (Minority, Woman, estab 1990, empl 4, sales , cert: State)

5848 Saitech Inc.
42640 Christy St
Fremont, CA 94538
Contact: Ernesto Juarez Business Devel
Tel: 510-440-0256
Email: ernesto@esaitech.com
Website: www.saitechincorporated.com/
Dist telecom, network & computer components & equipment. (Minority, estab 2002, empl 18, sales $18,721,958, cert: NMSDC, CPUC)

5849 Source Graphics
1530 N. Harmony Circle
Anaheim, CA 92807
Contact: Sy Hussaini Sr Acct Mgr
Tel: 714-701-1500
Email: sy.h@sourcegraphics.com
Website: www.sourcegraphics.com
Dist & svc plotter scanners, printers & digitizers. (As-Pac, estab 1989, empl 10, sales , cert: CPUC)

5850 Southland Technology Inc.
8053 Vickers St
San Diego, CA 92111
Contact: Jack Lowrey Acct Exec
Tel: 858-634-4136
Email: jlowrey@southlandtechnology.com
Website: www.southlandtechnology.com
Computer, computer hardware, software, cables, peripherals, IT, information technology, audio, video, A/V, sound systems, servers, storage, virtualization, fiber cables, workstations, notebooks, voip, projectors, monitors. (Minority, Woman, estab 2001, empl 43, sales $45,000,000, cert: CPUC)

INFORMATION TECHNOLOGY: Supplies

5851   Varitek, Inc.
       1100 E. Orangethorpe Ave Ste 195
       Anaheim, CA 92801
       Contact: Moe Moalemi VP
       Tel: 714-224-0361
       Email: moalemi@varitekinc.com
       Website: www.varitekinc.com
Dist & service network solutions, computers, printers, barcode printers, plotters, point of sale, copiers, faxes, office equipment consumables. (Minority, Woman, estab 1982, empl 12, sales $1,030,000, cert: State)

5852   ViewSonic Corporation
       381 Brea Canyon Rd
       Walnut, CA 91789
       Contact: Julie Yao Legal Assistant
       Tel: 909-444-8613
       Email: legal@viewsonic.com
       Website: www.viewsonic.com
Dist visual display technology products: liquid crystal displays, LCD, monitors, cathode ray tube, CRT, monitors, projectors, LCD TVs, plasma displays, tablet personal computers & PCs, wireless monitors. (As-Pac, estab 1987, empl 700, sales $1,093,000,000, cert: NMSDC)

5853   Zetta Pros - Total IT Solutions
       2201 E Willow St, Ste D232
       Signal Hill, CA 90755
       Contact: Sarom Hong CEO
       Tel: 562-252-3673
       Email: sarom.hong@zettapros.com
       Website: www.zettapros.com
Computers, hardware, software, printers, computer peripherals, cables. (Minority, Woman, estab 2005, empl 4, sales $600,000, cert: NMSDC, CPUC, 8(a))

Colorado

5854   Image Projections West, Inc.
       14135 E 42nd Ave Ste 40
       Denver, CO 80239
       Contact: Kedar Morarka CEO
       Tel: 888-576-9477
       Email: josephf@ipwusa.com
       Website: www.ipwusa.com
Mfr advance technology toner cartridges. (Woman/As-Ind, estab 1996, empl 172, sales $31,200,000, cert: NMSDC, WBENC)

5855   SK&T Integration Inc.
       10495 S. Progress Way
       Parker, CO 80112
       Contact: Kathy Lawson President
       Tel: 720-851-9108
       Email: info@skandt.com
       Website: www.skandt.com
Dist stock & custom labels, ribbons, bar code & specialty printers, asset tracking & inventory management systems, bar coding software, scanners, mobile computers & wireless switches. (Woman, estab , empl , sales $3,200,000, cert: WBENC)

5856   Systec101
       1027 Fenwick Dr
       Fort Collins, CO 80524
       Contact: Murat Yildirim Owner
       Tel: 970-646-2706
       Email: murat.yildirim@systec101.com
       Website: www.systec101.com
Dist networking equipment, manufacture & resell, cat5e, cat6, cat6a cables & accessories. (Minority, estab 2012, empl 3, sales $277,000, cert: State)

5857   Hartford Toner & Cartridge
       6 Wapping Rd
       Broad Brook, CT 06016
       Contact: Timothy Golubeff Sr Sales
       Tel: 860-292-1280
       Email: tgolubeff@hartfordtoner.com
       Website: www.hartfordtoner.con
Dist toner & cartridges. (Woman, estab 1998, empl 9, sales $1,000,100, cert: State)

District of Columbia

5858   Borrowed Time Enterprises, Inc.
       4460 Alabama Ave, SE
       Washington, DC 20019
       Contact: Vanessa Brooks CEO
       Tel: 202-581-0406
       Email: borrowedte@rcn.com
       Website: www.btenterprise.us
Dist computers, parts, software & hardware, office supplies, digital signage & content management software installation & services. (Woman/AA, estab 1999, empl 1, sales $127,000, cert: State, City)

5859   Mall Lobby.com, Inc.
       1775 Eye St, NW Ste 1150
       Washington, DC 20006
       Contact: Lang Maith CEO
       Tel: 301-807-2422
       Email: lang.maith@malllobby.com
       Website: www.malllobby.com
Dist computers, software, network equipment, office products, electronics, cellular phones, pagers, merchant accounts, microfilm/microfiche, CD/DVD production, etc. (AA, estab 1995, empl 15, sales $500,000, cert: State)

Delaware

5860   Laser Tone, Inc.
       24 S W Front St
       Milford, DE 19963
       Contact: Debra Cromer President
       Tel: 302-422-2323
       Email: emailus@laser-tone.net
       Website: www.lasertoneinc.com
Laser printer service, repairs, preventive maintenance & supplies, toner supplies. (Woman, estab 1989, empl 13, sales , cert: State)

INFORMATION TECHNOLOGY: Supplies

Florida

5861 BIT DIRECT
       2202 N Westshore Blvd, Ste 200
       Tampa, FL 33607
       Contact: Duane Turner Sr VP& GM
       Tel: 813-343-0879
       Email:
       Website: www.bitdirect.com
Dist audio & headsets, digital cameras, LCD & plasma TV's & projectors, handheld computers, removable media, optical dives, keyboards & mice, software & licenses, flash drives, cables, hard drives, media tapes, computer furniture. (Woman, estab 2002, empl 11, sales $700,000,000, cert: City, WBENC)

5862 Card Quest, Inc.
       6630 Rowan Rd
       New Port Richey, FL 34655
       Contact: Shannon Capshaw President
       Tel: 727-816-8401
       Email: sales@cardquest.com
       Website: www.cardquest.com
Dist proximity cards, readers, photo ID printers, ribbons, accessories, cards. (Woman, estab 2001, empl 4, sales $750,000, cert: State)

5863 ICG Software Corporation
       2860 W State Rd 84 Ste 113
       Fort Lauderdale, FL 33312
       Contact: Tiffany Nutt Office Mgr
       Tel: 305-933-9100
       Email: info@icgsoftware.us
       Website: www.icgsoftware.us
Mfr Point of Sale Software & Hardware. (Minority, Woman, estab 2010, empl 5, sales $200,000, cert: State)

5864 Innovative Software Solution
       3762 NW 124th Ave
       Coral Springs, FL 33065
       Contact: Kareline Duverge Office Mgr
       Tel: 954-800-7552
       Email: kduverge@isoftwaresolution.com
       Website: www.isoftwaresolution.com
Mfr ink & toner cartridges. Authorized distributors of HP, Lexmark & Ricoh products & supplies, general office supplies, toner & ink cartridges. (Woman/AA, estab 2012, empl 15, sales $1,590,000, cert: State, NMSDC)

5865 Keiki Enterprises LLC
       200 Crandon Blvd Ste 327
       Key Biscayne, FL 33149
       Contact: Karina Diaz VP
       Tel: 305-361-0623
       Email: karina@dsignage.net
       Website: www.dsignage.net
We are system integrator specialized in providing reliable digital signage with dynamic and/or interactive solutions for the health care industry by representing the best software and hardware manufacturers in the digital signage (Minority, Woman, estab , empl , sales $441,317, cert: City)

5866 LRE Inc. dba Lee Ryder Lamination
       6187 NW 167th St Unit H-10
       Miami, FL 33015
       Contact: Lee Ryder President
       Tel: 305-893-2762
       Email: office@leeryder.com
       Website: www.leeryder.com
Computerized photo id systems & supplies: Hid Global, Edisecure, Magicard, Eltron, Fargo, Nisca, Zebra, Evolis, Datacard. retractable id badge reels, laminator, pouch laminator, roll laminator, laminating pouches, laminating roll (Woman, estab 1980, empl 2, sales $350,000, cert: State, City)

5867 R&D Systems Group, Inc.
       19140 SW 24th St
       Miramar, FL 33029
       Contact: Patricia Garcia Acct Exec
       Tel: 305-528-9402
       Email: pgarcia@rdsgi.com
       Website: www.rdsgi.com
Resell IBM software & hardware. (Minority, Woman, estab 2004, empl 6, sales $400,000, cert: NMSDC)

5868 Solares Electrical Services, Inc.
       10421 NW 28th St Ste D105
       Miami, FL 33172
       Contact: A. Solares President
       Tel: 305-717-6184
       Email: asolares@solareselectrical.com
       Website: www.solareselectrical.com
Electrical, Communication, Lightning Protection, Utilites. Experience in Toll Collection Equipment, wiring and testing. (Hisp, estab 1997, empl 40, sales $3,500,000, cert: State)

5869 Telecom Resources of America, Inc.
       205 Goolsby Blvd
       Deerfield Beach, FL 33442
       Contact: Toni Mastrullo President
       Tel: 954-427-1104
       Email: toni@telrecusa.com
       Website: www.telrecusa.com
Dist data switch & networking products, space parts & peripherals. (Woman, estab 2000, empl 3, sales , cert: WBENC)

5870 Touchpoint Inc.
       7200 Lake Ellenor Dr, Ste 101
       Orlando, FL 32809
       Contact: Jim Soloway Sr Acct Mgr
       Tel: 407-977-0507
       Email: jsoloway@touchpoint-inc.com
       Website: www.touchpoint-inc.com
Dist computer equipment, supplies, PC's, laptops, servers, storage, security, etc. (Woman, estab 1999, empl 18, sales , cert: WBENC)

Georgia

5871 Eastern Data, Inc.
       4386 Park Dr
       Norcross, GA 30093
       Contact: JoAnn Pfeiffer Natl Accounts Mgr
       Tel: 770-279-8888
       Email: jo.pfeiffer@ediatlanta.com
       Website: www.ediatlanta.com
Dist computer systems, components & peripherals. (Minority, Woman, estab 1997, empl 27, sales $20,906,578, cert: NMSDC, WBENC)

5872 Worldwide Audio Visual Services Inc
       5040 Bakers Ferry Rd SW
       Atlanta, GA 30336
       Contact: Bradford McWhorter CEO
       Tel: 404-745-9842
       Email: brad@atlanta-audiovisual.com
       Website: www.atlantaav.com
Audio visual equipment, audio reinforcement, video production, lighting design & corporate set design. (AA, estab 2005, empl 8, sales $374,970, cert: NMSDC)

5873 XentIT, LLC
       5425 Peachtree Pkwy
       Norcross, GA 30092
       Contact: Tariq Alvi President
       Tel: 678-906-4046
       Email: talvi@xentit.com
       Website: www.xentit.com
Value Added Reseller, System Integrator & Cloud Managed Service provider. (As-Ind, estab 2006, empl 7, sales $2,247,000, cert: NMSDC)

Iowa

5874 Qualmar Technology Group, LLC
       10201 University Ave
       Clive, IA 50325
       Contact: Marshall Payne CEO
       Tel: 515-554-8161
       Email: marshall.payne@qualmar.com
       Website: www.qualmar.com
Resell Hardware/Sofware. (AA, estab 2012, empl 1, sales $100,000, cert: NMSDC)

Illinois

5875 Flexaco, Inc.
       936 W Lake St
       Roselle, IL 60172
       Contact: Donna Fiedler President
       Tel: 630-529-4510
       Email: Donnafiedler@flexaco.com
       Website: www.flexaco.com
Dist flexographic & rotogravure printers: 10 color printing, 2 color backside printing, surface & reverse printing, laminating, shrink sleeves, lidding material, paper, poly, foil & poly. (Woman, estab 1981, empl 5, sales $1,000,000, cert: WBENC)

5876 Liberty Laser Solutions
       375 Commercial St
       Marseilles, IL 61341
       Contact: President
       Tel: 800-570-1987
       Email: sales@libertylasersolutions.com
       Website: www.libertylasersolutions.com
Mfr & dist laser, ink jet & MICR products. (Woman, estab 1996, empl 42, sales $3,700,000, cert: WBENC)

5877 Mercommbe Inc.
       2101 Estes Ave
       Elk Grove Village, IL 60007
       Contact: Eric Moe Sales
       Tel: 847-290-0368
       Email: eric@mercommbe.com
       Website: www.mercommbe.com
Dist datacom & networking products; fiber optic, structured wiring, low voltage cable & connectors. (Minority, Woman, estab 1989, empl 7, sales $5,686,000, cert: State, City, NMSDC, WBENC)

5878 MNJ Technologies Direct, Inc.
       1025 Busch Pkwy
       Buffalo Grove, IL 60089
       Contact: Holly Hayward
       Tel: 312-591-5167
       Email: hhayward@mnjtech.com
       Website: www.mnjtech.com
Dist computer hardware, software & peripheral products. (Woman, estab 2002, empl 85, sales $25,000,000, cert: WBENC)

5879 RPT Toner LLC
       475 Supreme Dr
       Bensenville, IL 60106
       Contact: Jamie Sr VP Sales/Mktg
       Tel: 630-694-0400
       Email: jamie@rpttoner.com
       Website: www.rpttoner.com
Re-manufacture laser toner cartridges. (As-Ind, estab , empl , sales $10,770,000, cert: NMSDC)

Indiana

5880 AfterMarket Services
       2910 S CR-500 E
       Greencastle, IN 46135
       Contact: JL Freeman Sr. VP of Operations
       Tel: 317-714-2181
       Email: ams@aftermarketservices.net
       Website: www.aftermarketservices.net
Repair & service laser printers, repair/upgrade servers, pc's, laptops & install wired/wireless networks. (Woman, estab 2003, empl 5, sales , cert: State)

5881 ASAP Identification Security, Inc.
       212 W 10th St, Ste F-100
       Indianapolis, IN 46202
       Contact: Sheila Brown President
       Tel: 317-488-1030
       Email: sbrown@asapident.com
       Website: www.asapident.com
Photo ID printers, supplies, service, software and accessories. (Woman, estab 1982, empl 3, sales , cert: State, WBENC)

5882 Convenient Tape & Supplies LLC
       545 Industrial Dr
       Carmel, IN 46032
       Contact: Jennifer Pippen President
       Tel: 317-846-0335
       Email: jencts1@sbcglobal.net
       Website: www.sundsales.com
Distributors of point-of-sale (pos) paper rolls, cash register rolls, printer ribbons, toner cartridges, ink-jet cartridges, printer cleaning supplies, scale labels, industrial bar code labels, pos printers to small computer printer users. (Woman, estab 2002, empl 3, sales $244,000, cert: State)

Kansas

5883 Inland Associates, Inc.
       18965 W 158th St
       Olathe, KS 66062
       Contact: Peggy Meader President
       Tel: 913-764-7977
       Email: pmeader@inlandassoc.com
       Website: www.inlandassoc.com
Dist computer peripherals, data communications equipment. (Woman, estab 1969, empl 7, sales $4,000,000, cert: WBENC)

INFORMATION TECHNOLOGY: Supplies

Louisiana

5884 Dempsey Business Systems of Louisiana
      1201 3rd St Ste 210
      Alexandria, LA 71301
      Contact: Freddie Price, Sr. President
      Tel: 318-704-6061
      Email: fprice@dempseybus.com
      Website: www.dempseybus.com
Dist Computer & Computer Peripheral equip & software, custom computer programing services, computer systems design services, computer facilities management services, information technology value added reseller. (AA, estab 2004, empl 1, sales $278,789, cert: NMSDC)

5885 The Lazers Edge LLC
      2168 Airline Dr, Ste C
      Bossier City, LA 71111
      Contact: Sandra Nix Owner
      Tel: 318-742-6232
      Email: nix@lazers-edge.com
      Website: www.lazers-edge.com
Remanufactured Toner cartridges, laser printer service & repair. (Woman, estab 1989, empl 7, sales , cert: City)

Massachusetts

5886 Alpha Identification, Inc.
      7 Spanish River Rd
      Grafton, MA 01519
      Contact: Frank Ng Treasurer
      Tel: 508-839-6144
      Email: alphaidinc@gmail.com
      Website: www.alphaidinc.com
Dist photo ID equip & supplies for employee & student ID badges: Polaroid films, cameras, laminators, die-cutters, etc. (Woman/As-Pc, estab 1987, empl 2, sales $918,810, cert: State, City, CPUC)

5887 Encore Images
      21 Lime St
      Marblehead, MA 01945
      Contact: Laurel Mervis President
      Tel: 781-631-4568
      Email: laurel.mervis@encoreimages.com
      Website: www.encoreimages.com
Remanufacture toner cartridges: monochrome & color laser printers, copiers & facsimile machines. (Woman, estab 1989, empl 14, sales $2,020,000, cert: State)

5888 Pro AV Systems, Inc.
      275 Billerica Road Ste 3
      Chelmsford, MA 01824
      Contact: President
      Tel: 978-692-5111
      Email:
      Website: www.proavsi.com
Dist audiovisual products & installation. (Woman/As-Ind, estab 2006, empl 58, sales $16,100,000, cert: State)

5889 Roxbury Technology Corp
      3368 Washington St
      Jamaica Plain, MA 02130
      Contact: Elizabeth Williams President
      Tel: 617-524-1020
      Email: info@roxburytechnology.com
      Website: www.roxburytechnology.com
Mfr & dist premium toner cartridges and imaging supplies. (Woman/AA, estab 1994, empl 55, sales $12,000,000, cert: NMSDC)

Maryland

5890 Laser Printers Plus
      PO Box 264
      Greenbelt, MD 20768
      Contact: Sales
      Tel: 301-933-9007
      Email: info@laserprintersplus.com
      Website: www.laserprintersplus.com
Dist new & remanufactured laser & toner cartridges, drum units, fusers, ribbons, developers, parts. (As-Ind, estab 1998, empl 4, sales $500,000, cert: State)

Michigan

5891 Data Ranger Computer Products
      507 E Main St
      Manchester, MI 48158
      Contact: Andrea Ranger Owner
      Tel: 734-428-8551
      Email: andrea@datarangercomputerproducts.com
      Website: www.datarangercomputerproducts.com
Dist computer, pos, barcoding & imaging supplies, hardware/equipment & peripherals, toner, ink, ribbons, back-up media, paper, labels, custom forms, printers, cables, scanners, networking hardware, monitors, computers, etc. (Woman, estab 2002, empl 2, sales , cert: WBENC)

5892 JEM Tech Group
      23537 Lakepointe Dr.
      Clinton Township, MI 48036
      Contact: Shelley Deane Sr Technology Consultant
      Tel: 586-783-3400
      Email: s.deane@jemtechgroup.com
      Website: www.jemtechgroup.com
Dist IT products: toners, tape backup media, printers, cables, monitors, bar code readers, backup libraries, furniture, switches, hubs, racks, projectors, hardware & software, etc. (Woman, estab 1979, empl 14, sales $10,400,000, cert: WBENC)

5893 M.O.R.E. Computer Supplies, LLC
      384 Park
      Troy, MI 48083
      Contact: Jim Williams CEO
      Tel: 248-733-9011
      Email: jw@more-office.biz
      Website: www.more-office.biz
Dist computer supplies. (AA, estab 2001, empl 9, sales $16,000,000, cert: NMSDC)

5894 Micro Wise, Inc.
      21421 Hilltop Dr, Unit 4
      Southfield, MI 48034
      Contact: Dan Mamman Sales Mgr
      Tel: 248-350-0066
      Email: dan@microwise.net
      Website: www.microwise.net
Resell computers, servers & networking gear, POS, access-control, PC repairs, upgrades, service, leasing & disposal. (Minority, Woman, estab 1989, empl 9, sales , cert: NMSDC)

INFORMATION TECHNOLOGY: Supplies

5895 Mikan Corporation
      1271 Industrial, Ste 3
      Saline, MI 48176
      Contact: Maggie Stevens President
      Tel: 734-944-9447
      Email: maggie@mikancorp.com
      Website: www.mikancorp.com
Remanufacture laser toner cartridges. (Woman, estab 1990, empl 7, sales $1,726,617, cert: WBENC)

5896 Open Systems Technologies DE, LLC
      605 Seward NW, Ste 101
      Grand Rapids, MI 49504
      Contact: David Gerrity Exec Dir
      Tel: 616-574-3500
      Email: dgerrity@ostusa.com
      Website: www.ostusa.com
Resell computer hardware & software, business process solutions, data center solutions, application development, managed services. (Nat Ame, estab 1997, empl 110, sales $68,873,026, cert: NMSDC)

5897 PFA Recycling, Inc.
      50150 E Russell Schmidt
      Chesterfield, MI 48051
      Contact: Peter Feamster VP Business Dev
      Tel: 586-949-5788
      Email: pfeamster92@gmail.com
      Website: www.pfa-recycling.com
Recycle plastic consumer goods, ink jet cartridges. (Hisp, estab 1991, empl 20, sales $3,306,104, cert: NMSDC)

5898 The Computer Group, Inc.
      32985 Hamilton Ct Ste 135
      Farmington Hills, MI 48331
      Contact: Phillip Ingram President
      Tel: 248-888-6900
      Email: phil@compgroup.com
      Website: www.compgroup.com
Computer systems, copy machines, computer peripherals, computer software networking products. (AA, estab 1982, empl 9, sales $525,000, cert: NMSDC)

Minnesota

5899 All Media Supplies, Inc.
      4902 NE Tri Oak Circle S
      Wyoming, MN 55092
      Contact: Rita Morse President
      Tel: 763-413-1907
      Email: shelly@allmediasuppliesinc.com
      Website: www.allmediasuppliesinc.com
Dist magnetic computer products: 4MM,8MM,CD-Rom, labels & racking. (Woman, estab 1997, empl 5, sales $729,000, cert: WBENC)

5900 Best Datacom, Inc.
      8405 First Ave NE
      Stacy, MN 55079
      Contact: Doug Anderson Acct Mgr
      Tel: 715-398-0342
      Email: doug@best-datacom.com
      Website: www.best-datacom.com
Computer & network hardware & peripheral products, copper & fiber cable assemblies, cabinets/racks & computer/network enclosures. (Minority, Woman, estab 2007, empl 3, sales $264,000, cert: NMSDC)

5901 CaDan Technologies
      4131 Old Sibley Memorial Hwy Ste 200
      Eagan, MN 55122
      Contact: Tom Kreiling Sales
      Tel: 952-278-0560
      Email: sales@cadan.com
      Website: www.cadan.com
Computer hardware, software & services, new & refurbished hardware, hardware/software installations, new site setups or site tear downs. (Woman, estab 1992, empl 32, sales $9,300,000, cert: WBENC)

5902 Magnetic Products and Services, Inc.
      7600 Boone Ave N. Ste 1
      Minneapolis, MN 55428
      Contact: Michelle Morey VP
      Tel: 800-447-1277
      Email: mmorey@mpsinc.org
      Website: www.mpsinc.org
Dist electrical products & computer supplies: magnetic tapes, cartridges, optical disks, etc. (Woman, estab 1989, empl 14, sales $9,520,000, cert: WBENC)

Missouri

5903 Desktop Color Systems
      1675 Larkin Williams Rd
      Fenton, MO 63122
      Contact: Maryann Gephardt CEO
      Tel: 636-343-4600
      Email: info@dtcolor.com
      Website: www.dtcolor.com
Resell imaging supplies & office equipment hardware, service agreements, break-fix & warranty service. (Woman, estab 1993, empl 5, sales $1,546,000, cert: WBENC)

5904 Huber & Associates, Inc.
      1400 Edgewood Dr
      Jefferson City, MO 65109
      Contact: Elizabeth Huber CEO
      Tel: 573-634-5000
      Email: ehuber@teamhuber.com
      Website: www.teamhuber.com
Dist IBM hardware, software, maintenance & services. (Woman, estab 1986, empl 80, sales , cert: WBENC)

North Carolina

5905 Carolina Cartridge Systems, Inc.
      516 E Hebron St
      Charlotte, NC 28273
      Contact: CEO
      Tel: 704-347-2447
      Email:
      Website: www.ccsinside.com
Mfr toner cartridges. (Woman, estab 1991, empl 35, sales $2,200,000, cert: State, WBENC)

5906 Key Services, Inc.
      3921 Westpoint Blvd
      Winston-Salem, NC 27103
      Contact: Lisa Hodges VP & Quality Assurance Mgr
      Tel: 336-397-2129
      Email: arice@key-services.com
      Website: www.key-services.com
Dist & repair computer hardware & software, displays, touchscreens, printers, scanners, barcoding products & networking equipment. (Woman, estab 1976, empl , sales $2,749,120, cert: WBENC)

INFORMATION TECHNOLOGY: Supplies

5907 Stay Online Corp.
      3301 Bramer Dr
      Raleigh, NC 27604
      Contact: Jim Higgins GM
      Tel: 919-510-5464
      Email: jim@stayonline.com
      Website: www.stayonline.com/
Power and data products. (Minority, Woman, estab 1987, empl 13, sales $6,050,000, cert: NMSDC)

New Hampshire

5908 110 Technology LLC
      27 Technology Way
      Nashua, NH 03060
      Contact: Gary Nicoll Sales Mgr
      Tel: 603-886-2800
      Email: sales@110technology.com
      Website: www.110technology.com
Resell IT products: Hewlett Packard, IBM, Dell, Apple, Microsoft, Cisco, 3Com, APC, Philips, Xerox, NEC, Infocus, Intel, Viewsonic. (Minority, Woman, estab 2004, empl 8, sales $11,000,000, cert: NMSDC, WBENC)

5909 Tape Services, Inc.
      15 Londonderry Rd, Unit 11
      Londonderry, NH 03053
      Contact: Bryan Webb Sales Mgr
      Tel: 603-425-2202
      Email: bwebb@tapeservices.com
      Website: www.tapeservices.com/
Pro Audio; Back Up Tape; Data Media;Hard Drives; Computer Media; Digital Media; Pro Tape; Professional Media; Recording Media; Computer Media; Data Migration; DBeta; DVCam; DVCPro; Glyph; G-Tech. (Woman, estab 1989, empl 8, sales $4,314,589, cert: WBENC)

New Jersey

5910 Baanyan Software Services, Inc.
      399 Thornall St Fisrt Fl
      Edison, NJ 08837
      Contact: VP Sales
      Tel: 732-595-9006
      Email: nshah@baanyan.com
      Website: www.baanyan.com
IT staffing, ERP, BI, Data Warehousing, Cloud and Mobile Computing, and Big Data. (Minority, Woman, estab 2009, empl 100, sales $7,091,695, cert: City, NMSDC)

5911 DATA Inc. USA
      72 Summit Ave
      Montvale, NJ 07645
      Contact: Deepali Schwarz Dir Corporate Affairs
      Tel: 201-802-9800
      Email: dschwarz@dataincusa.com
      Website: www.datainc.biz
IT solutions: staff augmentation & custom application development solutions. (As-Pac, estab 1983, empl 400, sales $49,079,601, cert: State, NMSDC)

5912 First Call Services, Inc.
      121 Chestnut St
      Roselle Park, NJ 07204
      Contact: Fred Bonda President
      Tel: 908-620-1240
      Email: firstcallsvcs@live.com
      Website: www.firstcallservicesinc.com
Repair & service office machines, scanners, micro-graphics, computers, printers & shredders. dist toners, ribbons, drums, fuser units & additional parts. (Hisp, estab 1995, empl 10, sales , cert: State)

5913 High Point Solutions
      5 Gail Ct
      Sparta, NJ 07871
      Contact: Rich McDonald Acct Mgr
      Tel: 973-940-6516
      Email: rmcdonald@highpt.com
      Website: www.highpoint.com
Resell networking products: Cisco, Juniper, Bay, Fore, IBM, Lucent, Extreme, Nortel, Cables, memory, Digital Link, Paradyne. (Hisp, estab 1997, empl , sales $170,000,000, cert: City)

New York

5914 BXI Consultants, Inc.
      33 Peuquet Pkwy
      Tonawanda, NY 14150
      Contact: Ingrid Charlton President
      Tel: 716-693-0343
      Email: icharlton@bxiconsultants.com
      Website: www.bxiconsultants.com
Xerox copying, printing & scanning. (Minority, Woman, estab 1993, empl 15, sales , cert: State)

5915 Garic Inc.
      68 35th St Ste C653
      Brooklyn, NY 11232
      Contact: Patrick OKeefe Principal
      Tel: 646-487-0105
      Email: patrick@garicinc.com
      Website: www.garicinc.com
Technology leasing & computer remarketing, financial services, computer & telecommunications equipment, computers, telephone systems, switches, networks, peripherals, etc. (AA, Hisp, estab 2000, empl 7, sales $5,000,000, cert: State, City, NMSDC)

5916 Gholkar's, Inc.
      7321 State Rt 251
      Victor, NY 14564
      Contact: Preeya Gholkar President
      Tel: 585-924-2050
      Email: info@gholkars.com
      Website: www.gholkars.com
Dist computer supplies: magnetic media, CAD plotter paper, ribbons, barcode labels, & ribbons. (As-Ind, estab 1988, empl 7, sales $3,400,000, cert: State)

5917 GT Business Supplies LLC
      115-13 Linden Blvd
      South Ozone park, NY 11420
      Contact: Jodhan Basanta Managing Dir
      Tel: 718-659-9165
      Email: jodhanb@gttoner.com
      Website: www.gttoner.com
Dist printers, ink cartridges & toners. (Hisp, estab 2003, empl 4, sales $400,000, cert: City)

5918 Hugo Neu Recycling, LLC
      249 E Sandford Blvd
      Mount Vernon, NY 10550
      Contact: Joseph Claiborne Dir sourcing
      Tel: 917-566-8464
      Email: info@hugoneu.com
      Website: www.hugoneurecycling.com
IT asset disposal & advance electronic e-waste recycler. (Minority, Woman, estab 2009, empl 90, sales , cert: NMSDC, WBENC)

5919 Minoria Tech LLC
      326 Broad St
      Utica, NY 14476
      Contact: Robles President
      Tel: 315-628-0021
      Email: rose@minoriatech.com
      Website: www.minoriatech.com/
Dist computer, hardware, software, and peripherals value added reseller. (Minority, Woman, estab 2017, empl 3, sales $854,026, cert: State, City, WBENC)

5920 New Computech, Inc.
      39 Broadway Ste 1630
      New York, NY 10006
      Contact: Abraham President
      Tel: 212-406-1801
      Email: mona@newcomputech.com
      Website: www.newcomputech.net
Resell computer hardware & software products. (Woman/AA, estab 1996, empl 12, sales $1,500,000, cert: City, WBENC)

5921 Pioneer Business Systems
      165 W 29th St
      New York, NY 10001
      Contact: James Breland Dir Business Devel
      Tel: 212-594-2614
      Email: jamesb@pioneercopier.com
      Website: www.pioneercopier.com
Lease, rentals, purchase copiers, prints, scanners, MFP equipment, wide format printers. Service copiers, printers, fax & MFP equipment. (As-Pac, estab , empl , sales $13,500,000, cert: City, NMSDC)

5922 Sidewinder Holdings, Inc.
      245 Mineola Blvd
      Mineola, NY 11501
      Contact: Stacey Rose President
      Tel: 516-742-1700
      Email: srose@cartridgeworldusa.com
      Website: www.cartridgeworldusa.com/store76
Dist laser, toner & inkjet cartridges for printers, copiers & fax machines. (Woman/AA, estab 2005, empl 5, sales $211,429, cert: City, NMSDC)

Ohio

5923 Integrated Business Supplies Inc.
      17381 Old Tannery Trail
      Chagrin Falls, OH 44023
      Contact: Judy Wardley VP
      Tel: 440-498-3888
      Email: judyw@misibs.com
      Website: www.askibs.com
Dist computers & equipment, office machines, supplies, paper, furniture, vellum. (Woman, estab 1990, empl 5, sales $546,600, cert: State, City)

5924 SpaceBound, Inc.
      280 Opportunity Way
      LaGrange, OH 44050
      Contact: Cindi Duesler Sales Mgr
      Tel: 440-355-8008
      Email: govtbids@spaceboundsolutions.com
      Website: www.spaceboundsolutions.com
Computer hardware, software, peripherals, accessories, electronics, office supplies, office equipment, audio, video, cameras, phones telephone, etc. (Woman, estab 1987, empl 38, sales $34,000,000, cert: WBENC)

5925 Tape Central, Inc.
      7020 Huntley Rd, Ste C
      Columbus, OH 43229
      Contact: Jeff Alan Commercial Sales
      Tel: 866-701-0098
      Email: southeasternmedia@juno.com
      Website: www.tapecentral.com
Dist digital cameras, video cameras & camcorders, lighting, cables, microphones, LCD & Plasma TV-monitors, projectors, duplicators, CD - DVD disk printers, toner and ink, plus pro video & audio tape, CDR, Blu-Ray & DVD media, cases & sleeves. (Woman, estab 2001, empl 10, sales $6,820,168, cert: WBENC)

5926 WMG, LLC
      PO Box 3115
      Dayton, OH 45401
      Contact: William Michael Green CEO
      Tel: 937-268-0773
      Email: info@wmgreensales.com
      Website: www.WMGreensales.com
Office equipment, hardware & doftware multifunctional devices, copiers, scanners, plotters & faxes. (AA, estab 2011, empl 1, sales $1,250,000, cert: State, City, NMSDC)

Pennsylvania

5927 Parmetech, Inc.
      137 W Eagle Ave
      Havertown, PA 19083
      Contact: Ana Fernandez-Parmet President
      Tel: 610-446-4000
      Email: afparmet@parmetech.com
      Website: www.parmetech.com
Dist printers, scanners, multifuction machines & storage devices. (Minority, Woman, estab 1991, empl 23, sales $4,900,000, cert: NMSDC, WBENC)

Rhode Island

5928 NetCablesPlus Inc.
      PO Box 7815
      Cumberland, RI 02864
      Contact: John Rodrigues President
      Tel: 401-475-6040
      Email: sales@netcablesplus.com
      Website: www.netcablesplus.com
Network & PC cables & accessories, ethernet, fiber optic, USB, firewire. (Hisp, estab 2004, empl 3, sales $135,000, cert: State)

Tennessee

5929 Columbia Data Systems, Inc.
      2002 Oakland Pkwy
      Columbia, TN 38401
      Contact: Julie Baker President
      Tel: 931-381-4660
      Email: julie.baker@edge.net
      Website: www.cdsmicro.com
Dist & service computer & peripherals. (Woman, estab 1983, empl 3, sales $308,690, cert: State)

INFORMATION TECHNOLOGY: Supplies

5930 Guy Brown, LLC
      7111 Commerce Way
      Brentwood, TN 37027
      Contact: Lauren Dooros Sales & Marketing Mgr
      Tel: 615-777-1500
      Email: lauren.dooros@guybrown.com
      Website: www.guybrown.com
Mfr recycled laser toner cartridges & office products. (Minority, Woman, estab 1997, empl 45, sales $204,877,006, cert: NMSDC, WBENC)

5931 Laser Recharge Inc.
      485 E South St Ste 100
      Collierville, TN 38017
      Contact: John Ferris VP
      Tel: 901-853-0742
      Email: jferris@laser-recharge.com
      Website: www.laser-recharge.com
Laser Printers, Ink Jet Printers, Copiers, Fax, Machines, Multi Function Machines, Scanners, Digital Senders, Plotters, Printer & Copier Supplies, Printer Repair Service. (Woman, estab 1986, empl 11, sales $2,780,000, cert: State)

5932 RLB Procurement
      1180 Gunter Smith Rd
      Pulaski, TN 38478
      Contact: Cassandara Moore Sales
      Tel: 931-548-1170
      Email: cassandara@rlbprocurement.com
      Website: www.rlbprocurement.com
Systems, switches, servers, software, computers, printers, toners, inks, security cameras, monitors, displays, storage, cables, automation, racks & IT related products. (Woman, estab 2006, empl 3, sales , cert: WBENC)

5933 Unistar-Sparco Computers, Inc.
      7089 Ryburn Dr
      Millington, TN 38053
      Contact: SooTsong Lim CEO
      Tel: 901-872-2272
      Email: lim@sparco.com
      Website: www.sparco.com
IT solutions, hardware, computer systems, desktops, notebooks, thin clients, tablet PCs, PDAs, workstations, rack-mount servers, blade servers, monitors, displays, Plasma TVs, LCD monitors, flat-screen monitors, LCD TVs. (As-Pac, estab 1992, empl 35, sales $38,700,641, cert: NMSDC)

Texas

5934 ARDETECH Industries, Inc.
      11526 Pagemill Rd
      Dallas, TX 75243
      Contact: Sales Rep
      Tel: 800-821-5678
      Email:
      Website: www.ardetech.com
Dist IT products, cable assemblies, computer peripherals, data & telecomm supplies. (Woman, estab 1996, empl 14, sales $2,415,008, cert: State, WBENC)

5935 CompuPro Global
      15720 Park Row Ste 400
      Houston, TX 77084
      Contact: Randy Pfeiffer VP Business Dev
      Tel: 713-934-9633
      Email: ginnib@compuproglobal.com
      Website: www.compuproglobal.com
Dist computer tape, computer media, computer accessories, hardware, toner, wide format printer supplies (Woman, estab 1999, empl 9, sales $5,600,000, cert: State, WBENC)

5936 Designs That Compute
      1778 N Plano Rd, Ste 211B
      Richardson, TX 75081
      Contact: Gregg Coapman Technical Sales Consultant
      Tel: 214-276-0124
      Email: sales@visionality.com
      Website: www.visionality.com
Videoconferencing & audio/visual solutions, digital signage, interactive whiteboards & displays, video walls, projectors/screens, audio/speakers, recording, streaming video. (Woman, estab 1986, empl 14, sales $5,400,000, cert: State)

5937 ELP Enterprises, Inc.
      9346 Rosstown Way
      Houston, TX 77080
      Contact: Martha Ceballos CEO
      Tel: 832-969-9947
      Email: mceball@aol.com
      Website: www.elpenterprisesinc.com
Dist computer supplies. (Minority, Woman, estab 1999, empl 2, sales $813,923, cert: City, NMSDC, WBENC)

5938 JHJ Computer Supplies, Inc.
      3901 Arlington Highlands Blvd. Ste 200
      Arlington, TX 76018
      Contact: Jessie Jones President
      Tel: 817-861-0888
      Email: jhampton@jhjcs.com
      Website: www.jhjcs.com
Dist computer supplies: printers, keyboards, flash drives, ink & toner cartridges, magnetic media, media storage, anti-glare screens, mouse pads, optical mouse devices, wireless devices, computer bags, USB cables. (Woman/AA, estab 2007, empl 3, sales $116,336, cert: State)

5939 Meridian Office Systems, Inc.
      4113 Lindbergh Dr
      Addison, TX 75001
      Contact: Jeff Emery Mgr
      Tel: 972-690-3661
      Email: jemery@meridianoffice.com
      Website: www.meridianoffice.com
Sell, lease, rent, repair, service & maintenance office copiers, laser printers & multifunction color copiers. (Minority, Woman, estab 1994, empl 15, sales $3,200,000, cert: State)

5940 OAS Computer Supplies
      3333 Earhart Dr, Ste 120
      Carrollton, TX 75006
      Contact: Sales Exec
      Tel: 972-267-8020
      Email: sales@oas-supplies.com
      Website: www.oas-supplies.com
Resell office supplies & computer supplies. (Woman, estab 1986, empl 12, sales $150,500,000, cert: State)

5941 Patriot Group, Ltd.
      5000 Terminal St
      Bellaire, TX 77401
      Contact: Lois Livingston Acct Mgr
      Tel: 713-664-1172
      Email: llivingston@patriotgroup.com
      Website: www.patriotgroup.com
Dist business equipment, equipment supplies, service and support. (Woman, estab 1979, empl 22, sales $5,137,000, cert: State)

5942 RLS Interests, Inc.
      10402 Harwin Dr
      Houston, TX 77036
      Contact: Michael Chang
      Tel: 713-933-0934
      Email: directron@globalxlr.com
      Website: www.directron.com
DIY computer components, CPUs, memory, hard drives, optical drives, hardware & software, pre-built systems, notebooks, netbooks, tablets, peripherals & accessories. (As-Pac, estab 1990, empl 157, sales $51,100,000, cert: NMSDC)

5943 Southwest Office Systems, Inc.
      13960 Trinity Blvd
      Fort Worth, TX 76040
      Contact: Debbie Sorrells COO
      Tel: 817-730-8000
      Email: rjasper@sostexas.com
      Website: www.sostexas.com
Copiers, printers, print management, plotters, digital white boards. (Hisp, estab , empl , sales $10,819,775, cert: State, City, NMSDC)

5944 TAPEANDMEDIA.com, LLC
      450 Colorado Dr
      Cedar Creek, TX 78612
      Contact: Bennie Wallace VP
      Tel: 877-938-0901
      Email: bennie@tapeandmedia.com
      Website: www.tapeandmedia.com
Dist blank media: computer back-up tapes, video tapes, audio tapes, DVD's, CD's, DVD/CD cases. (Woman, estab 2000, empl 6, sales $5,000,000, cert: State)

5945 Zepol Productions, Inc.
      1991 Rawhide Dr
      Round Rock, TX 78681
      Contact: Trevor Babyak COO
      Tel: 512-293-0936
      Email: trevor.babyak@aompartner.com
      Website: www.aompartner.com
Information technology sales & services. (Hisp, estab 2010, empl 6, sales $2,000,000, cert: NMSDC, 8(a))

Virginia

5946 Advanced Business Software Consulting LLC dba NCN
      11890 Sunrise Valley Dr, Ste 515
      Reston, VA 20191
      Contact: Sharon Muniz CEO
      Tel: 703-298-2468
      Email: sharon@ncntechnology.com
      Website: www.ncntechnology.com
Mobile & web application development, SharePoint services. (Minority, Woman, estab 2006, empl 3, sales $520,000, cert: State, WBENC, 8(a), SDB)

5947 Computer Upgrade King, LLC
      1555 Standing Ridge Dr Ste A-1
      Powhatan, VA 23139
      Contact: Robert Robinson VP
      Tel: 800-985-9364
      Email: sales@computerupgradeking.com
      Website: www.computerupgradeking.com
Computers (laptops, desktops), Custom Desktops, Components, Cases, Laser Etching. (Minority, Woman, estab 2008, empl 45, sales $846,956, cert: State)

Washington

5948 EC Corporation Export
      22307 Marine View Dr S
      Des Moines, WA 98198
      Contact: Patricio Mendoza Mgr
      Tel: 206-878-3321
      Email: patricio@eccomputer.com
      Website: www.eccomputer.com
Computers Peripherals, Cartridges, Office Supply, External hard drives, Keyboard, Mouse, Monitors, Software, Licenses, Office Supplies, PC'S. (Hisp, estab 1991, empl 4, sales $250,000, cert: State)

5949 Evergreen Computer Products Inc
      2720 1st Ave S
      Seattle, WA 98134
      Contact: Barbara Anderson VP
      Tel: 206-624-3722
      Email: banderson@evergreencomp.com
      Website: www.evergreencomp.com
Printer repair services. (Woman/AA, estab 1977, empl 10, sales $10,116,295, cert: State, NMSDC)

Wisconsin

5950 Cartridge Savers, Inc.
      2801 Coho St Ste 206
      Madison, WI 53713
      Contact: Thomas Wangard President
      Tel: 608-663-5126
      Email: tom.w@cartridgesavers.com
      Website: www.cartridgesavers.com
Dist remanufactured & new laser printer toner cartridges, laser printers. (Hisp, estab 1994, empl 8, sales $6,843,995, cert: State, NMSDC)

5951 Vanguard Computers, Inc.
      13100 W Lisbon Rd, Ste 100
      Brookfield, WI 53005
      Contact: Owner
      Tel: 262-317-1900
      Email: sales@vanguardinc.com
      Website: www.vanguardinc.com
Dist, svc & rent computer equipment & peripherals; network configuration, installation & maintenance. (Minority, Woman, estab 1982, empl 39, sales , cert: WBENC)

INFORMATION TECHNOLOGY: Systems/Machines

Design, manufacture, lease and/or distribute information processing systems, machines and components. Many of these firms also distribute information processing supplies. (See also INFORMATION TECHNOLOGY: Services and INFORMATION TECHNOLOGY: Supplies). NAICS Code 33

Arizona

5952 Electronic Responsible Recyclers, LLC
730 E Southern Ave
Mesa, AZ 85204
Contact: Christopher Ko CEO
Tel: 602-688-5800
Email: chris@er2.com
Website: www.ER2.com
Provide technology & computer hardware installation, imaging, disposal, and recycling services. (As-Pac, estab 2010, empl 78, sales $11,300,000, cert: NMSDC)

California

5953 CB Technologies, Inc.
750 The City Dr South Ste 225
Orange, CA 92868
Contact: Dwanna Lynch Dir/ Corporate Relations
Tel: 714-573-7733
Email: dwanna.lynch@cbtechinc.com
Website: www.cbtechinc.com
Information technology hardware. (Woman, estab 2001, empl , sales $1,400,000, cert: CPUC, WBENC)

5954 CCIntegration, Inc.
2060 Corporate Ct
San Jose, CA 95131
Contact: Stephanie Stoller Dir Business Dev
Tel: 408-228-1314
Email: stephanie.stoller@ccintegration.com
Website: www.ccintegration.com
Technology, Computer, Server, Storage, Networking, Rack, On-site Service, Integration, Global Logistics, Hardware Engineering Support, Life Cycle Management, Appliance, System Platform, Dell, Lenovo, Supermicro, HPe. (As-Pac, estab 1985, empl 81, sales $108,000,000, cert: WBENC)

5955 DuraTech USA, Inc.
6765 Westminster Blvd Ste 314
Westminster, CA 92683
Contact: Skip Howland Govt Business Dev
Tel: 831-419-8179
Email: showland@duratechusa.com
Website: www.Duratechusa.com
Dist semi rugged & MIL-STD 810F laptops, rugged & submersible tablet pc's. (Minority, Woman, estab 2005, empl 3, sales $2,500,000, cert: State)

5956 Elgin Micro
14271 Jeffrey Rd Ste 247
Irvine, CA 92620
Contact: Daniel Laterneau Sales Dir
Tel: 949-878-7461
Email: dan@elginmicro.com
Website: www.elginmicro.com
Dist HP, IBM, SUN Microsystems (Oracle), Dell, Cisco, Emulex, Qlogic, Juniper, EMC, NetApp, Nortel, Lenovo, Toshiba, Acer, Operating systems, Security, Applications, Design, Accounting, Training & Utilities. (Minority, Woman, estab 2012, empl 8, sales , cert: NMSDC)

5957 JE Components Inc.
8709 Aviation Blvd
Inglewood, CA 90301
Contact: Joni Paulo President
Tel: 310-645-6021
Email: joni@jecom.com
Website: www.jecom.com
Resell PC & network hardware. (Minority, Woman, estab 1995, empl 7, sales , cert: NMSDC, NWBOC)

5958 Performance Designed Products
14144 Ventura Blvd Ste 200
Sherman Oaks, CA 91423
Contact: Theresa Harrell Natl Acct Mgr
Tel: 479-445-8612
Email: theresa.harrell@pdp.com
Website: www.pdp.com
Design & mfr video game peripherals & accessories. (Woman, estab 1990, empl 200, sales , cert: WBENC)

5959 Premio, Inc.
918 Radecki Court
City of Industry, CA 91748
Contact: Debby Dodd Mktg Mgr
Tel: 626-839-3128
Email: debby.dodd@premioinc.com
Website: www.premioinc.com
Oem Systems, desktop PCs, servers. (Minority, Woman, estab , empl , sales , cert: CPUC)

5960 RICOM
26062 Merit Circle Bldg. 108
Laguna Hills, CA 92653
Contact: Isaac Buchanan Acct Exec
Tel: 949-788-9939
Email: isaac@ricom.net
Website: www.shopricom.com
Computers: Cisco; IBM; Hewlett Packard; Emulex; Sun Microsystems; Dell; EMC; Nimble Storage; F5 Networks; VMware; citrix. (Minority, Woman, estab 1998, empl 9, sales $13,000,000, cert: NMSDC, CPUC, WBENC)

Colorado

5961 CounterTrade Products Inc.
7585 W 66th Ave
Arvada, CO 80003
Contact: Angela Dumm Dir of Contracts & Security
Tel: 303-424-9710
Email: adumm@countertrade.com
Website: www.COUNTERTRADE.COM
Dist computer porducts: IBM, Compaq, Hewlett Packard, Epson, Toshiba, Microsoft, Novell, Apple, Citrix, Viewsonic & 3COM. (Woman, estab 1985, empl 45, sales $275,000,000, cert: WBENC)

INFORMATION TECHNOLOGY: Systems/Machines

5962 SF&B, LLC
      9585 Niwot Rd
      Longmont, CO 80504
      Contact: Mgr
      Tel: 703-297-7447
      Email: support@sfbllc.com
      Website: www.sfbllc.com
Dist top-tier computer hardware. (Woman, estab 2011, empl 4, sales , cert: WBENC)

Connecticut

5963 PCNet, Inc.
      100 Technology Dr
      Trumbull, CT 06611
      Contact: VP Finance/Operations
      Tel: 203-452-8559
      Email: teric@pcnet-inc.com
      Website: www.pcnet-inc.com
Network systems integrator; e-commerce, Internet/Intranet; resell of personal computer products & svcs. (Hisp, estab 1993, empl 65, sales $26,000,000, cert: NMSDC)

Florida

5964 United Data Technologies
      8825 NW 21 Terrace
      Doral, FL 33172
      Contact: Mariana Lugaro Mgr Sales Operations
      Tel: 305-882-0435
      Email: sales.operations@udtonline.com
      Website: www.udtonline.com
Dist, install & repair IT equipment: desktops, laptops, servers, printers, switches, peripherals, & audio visual equipment. (Hisp, estab 1995, empl 94, sales , cert: State)

Georgia

5965 American Megatrends Inc.
      5555 Oakbrook Pkwy, Ste 200
      Norcross, GA 30093
      Contact: Srivatsan Ramachandran Dir Business Dev
      Tel: 770-246-8600
      Email: srivatsanr@ami.com
      Website: www.ami.com
Mfr key hardware & software solutions, StorTrends, IP Storage Area Network (IP-SAN) and Network Attached Storage (NAS) solutions, Aptio and AMIBIOS system software and firmware, MegaRAC remote management software & firmware. (As-Ind, estab 1985, empl 1345, sales $10,000,000, cert: NMSDC)

5966 Eastern Data, Inc.
      4386 Park Dr
      Norcross, GA 30093
      Contact: JoAnn Pfeiffer Natl Accounts Mgr
      Tel: 770-279-8888
      Email: jo.pfeiffer@ediatlanta.com
      Website: www.ediatlanta.com
Dist computer systems, components & peripherals. (Minority, Woman, estab 1997, empl 27, sales $20,906,578, cert: NMSDC, WBENC)

Illinois

5967 Hagerman & Company Inc.
      505 Sunset Ct
      Mount Zion, IL 62549
      Contact: Sandy Hagerman President
      Tel: 217-972-7268
      Email: sandyhagerman@hagerman.com
      Website: www.hagerman.com
Platinum Autodesk Reseller, System Integrator and Consultant. (Woman, estab 1985, empl 89, sales $43,800,000, cert: WBENC)

5968 Koi Computers Inc.
      200 W North Ave
      Lombard, IL 60148
      Contact: Ayde Chavez Acct Rep
      Tel: 630-627-8811
      Email: ayde@koicomputer.com
      Website: www.koicomputer.com
Dist computers, servers, printers, copiers, digital imaging & networking equipments. (Minority, Woman, estab 1995, empl 6, sales $7,500,000, cert: State)

5969 Sayers Technology
      825 Corporate Woods Pkwy
      Vernon Hills, IL 60061
      Contact: Adam Shipp Reg Sales Mgr
      Tel: 404-695-2707
      Email: ashipp@sayers.com
      Website: www.sayers.com
IT Solutions, Servers & Storage, Virtualization, Security & Mobility, Networking & Professional Services. Storage, Servers, Cloud, Virtualization, Networking, Data Management, Archiving & Disaster Recovery Security. (AA, estab 1984, empl , sales , cert: NMSDC)

Indiana

5970 Professional Information Systems
      232 S Linda St
      Hobart, IN 46342
      Contact: Paulette Hill President
      Tel: 219-947-4349
      Email: paulette@proinfosys.com
      Website: www.proinfosys.com
Hardware & software, build customize computers or prebuilt computers. (Woman, estab 1992, empl 4, sales $172,000, cert: State, 8(a))

5971 Qumulus Solutions LLC
      101 N Michigan St Ste 300
      South Bend, IN 46601
      Contact: Russell Ford President
      Tel: 574-208-6772
      Email: rford@qumulussolutions.com
      Website: www.qumulussolutions.com
Resell servers, storage, data backup hardware & software. (AA, estab 2010, empl 7, sales $644,000, cert: State, NMSDC)

Kansas

5972 ProActive Solutions Inc.
      5625 Foxridge Dr
      Shawnee Mission, KS 66202
      Contact: Dean Thiede Exec VP
      Tel: 913-948-8000
      Email: dthiede@proactivesolutions.com
      Website: www.proactivesolutions.com
IBM Hardware Power, System i, AS400, System p, RS6000, System x, Storage, SAN, Lotus, Domino, Notes, Websphere, Tivoli, TSM, VMWare, virtualization, Disaster Recovery, DR, High Availability, HA, Business Continuity, BC, Linux, (Woman, estab 1996, empl 30, sales $45,029,277, cert: CPUC, WBENC)

Massachusetts

5973 Concord Information Systems, LLC
      165 Middlesex Turnpike Ste 201
      Bedford, MA 01730
      Contact: Suzanne Hiniker Partner
      Tel: 781-863-7200
      Email: suzy@concordinfo.com
      Website: www.concordinfo.com
Computers, laptops, tablets, servers, monitors, printers, networking hardware, cloud & email services & technical consulting services. (Woman, estab 1994, empl 10, sales $10,000,000, cert: State)

5974 Fenco Global Industries Corp.
      1 Federal St
      Springfield, MA 01105
      Contact: Fenella Sitati President
      Tel: 413-308-8800
      Email: fenella@winningtek.com
      Website: www.winningtek.com
Technology hardware for application security, datacenters & cloud virtualization, F5 Networks, VMware, Palo Alto, Cisco Networks, RedHat, Microsoft, NetApp, EMC, HP, IBM, Dell & ExtraHop. (Woman/AA, estab 2009, empl 5, sales $450,000, cert: NMSDC)

Michigan

5975 Dynamic Computer Corporation
      23400 Industrial Park Court
      Farmington Hills, MI 48335
      Contact: Tami Schultz VP Business Dev
      Tel: 248-473-2200
      Email: tschultz@dynamictech.solutions
      Website: www.dynamictech.solutions
Dist IT equipment: HP/Compaq, Dell, IBM, Microsoft, Symantec & Gateway. (Minority, Woman, estab 1979, empl 24, sales $29,500,000, cert: NMSDC, WBENC)

New Hampshire

5976 Worldcom Exchange Inc.
      43 Northwestern Dr
      Salem, NH 03079
      Contact: Matt Good
      Tel: 603-893-0900
      Email: matt.good@wei.com
      Website: www.wei.com
Dist computer hardware, integration & installation, enterprise storage, servers & PC solutions. (Hisp, estab 1989, empl , sales $265,000,000, cert: NMSDC)

New Jersey

5977 CPI (USA) Inc.
      6 Doreen Court
      Edison, NJ 08820
      Contact: Deepak Advani
      Tel: 732-494-0007
      Email: dadvani@cpiusainc.com
      Website: www.cpiusainc.com
Workstations, Laptops, Servers, Tablets, Multifunction Printers, Held Workstations, CCTV Phone Systems (Panasonic, Mitel), Enterprise Business, Industry Standard Servers and Options Routers & Add On, Switches & Add On, UPS & Generators. (Minority, Woman, estab 1997, empl 2, sales $375,000, cert: NMSDC)

New York

5978 Empire Electronics Inc.
      103 Fort Salonga Rd
      Northport, NY 11768
      Contact: Krista Fisher
      Tel: 631-544-9111
      Email: kfisher@empireusa.com
      Website: www.empireusa.com
Dist information technology equip, computer hardware & components. (Woman, estab 1983, empl 6, sales $10,400,000, cert: City, WBENC)

5979 Ergonomic Group, Inc.
      200 Robbins Ln
      Jericho, NY 11753
      Contact: David Ferguson Sr Acct Exec
      Tel: 516-746-7777
      Email: dave.ferguson@ergogroup.com
      Website: www.ergogroup.com
Resell computer equipment, peripherals & computer related services. (Woman, estab 1984, empl , sales , cert: WBENC)

Ohio

5980 Northern Technical Group LLC
      14500 Industrial Ave N
      Maple Heights, OH 44137
      Contact: Mary Fink President
      Tel: 216-662-0561
      Email: mfink@northerntechnicalgroup.com
      Website: www.northerntechnicalgroup.com
IT Asset Management, removal, audit, sanitizing, remarketing & recycling of computer related asset. (Woman, estab 2003, empl 17, sales $921,316, cert: NWBOC)

Texas

5981 Computize Inc.
      80 E. McDermott Dr.
      Allen, TX 75002
      Contact: Bennie Moore Sr Sales Dir
      Tel: 972-437-3100
      Email: benniem@computize.com
      Website: www.computize.com
Resell computers. (Minority, Woman, estab 1982, empl 125, sales $4,000,000, cert: WBENC)

5982 M&A Technology Inc.
      2045 Chenault Dr
      Carrollton, TX 75006
      Contact: Donna Shepard Exec VP
      Tel: 469-767-6657
      Email: dshepard@macomp.com
      Website: www.macomp.com
Custom intergration, servers, workstation, high performance intergrating, data center, on line back up, disater recovery. (AA, estab 1984, empl 55, sales $75,000,000, cert: State)

5983 Via Technology
      906 Fredericksburg Rd
      San Antonio, TX 78201
      Contact: Manuel Rosabal President
      Tel: 210-227-7726
      Email: manuelv@800viatech.com
      Website: www.800viatech.com
Hardware, software, peripherals, storage. (Minority, Woman, estab 1995, empl 10, sales $1,400,000, cert: State)

Virginia

5984 GovSmart, Inc.
      706 Forest St
      Charlottesville, VA 22903
      Contact: Jason Gaviria Owner
      Tel: 434-326-5656
      Email: jason@govsmart.com
      Website: www.govsmart.com
Authorized Reseller of IT Technology. (As-Pac, estab 2009, empl 50, sales $155,000,000, cert: State, 8(a), SDB)

5985 US21, Inc.
      2721 Prosperity Ave, Ste 300
      Fairfax, VA 22031
      Contact: Bassel Shubassi Business Devel Mgr
      Tel: 703-560-0021
      Email: info@us21.com
      Website: www.us21.com
Dist IT hardware: SMB & Enterprise. (Woman, estab 1998, empl 20, sales $10,000,000, cert: State)

> **INSURANCE COMPANIES**
> Firms carry life, accident, auto and health insurance policies. Most are licensed in several states. NAICS Code 52

California

5986   Definiti Healthcare Management
       26445 Rancho Pkwy South
       Lake Forest, CA 92630
       Contact: Mike Guerrero CEO
       Tel: 949-716-1890
       Email: mike.guerrero@definiti.net
       Website: www.definiti.net
National Workers Compensation Cost Containment provider. (Woman/Hisp, estab 2002, empl 27, sales $3,300,000, cert: NMSDC, CPUC)

5987   Merriwether & Williams Insurance Services
       550 Montgomery St Ste 550
       San Francisco, CA 94111
       Contact: Donna Hart CEO
       Tel: 415-986-3999
       Email: dhart@imwis.com
       Website: www.imwis.com
Commercial insurance marketing & placements, surety bonding, OCIP, third party administration. (Woman/AA, estab 1997, empl 35, sales $2,292,090, cert: NMSDC, CPUC)

5988   Sovereign Employee Benefits, Inc.
       10630 Town Center Dr, Ste 113
       Rancho Cucamonga, CA 91730
       Contact: Katie King Owner
       Tel: 909-948-7779
       Email: melissadickson@sebins.com
       Website: www.sebins.com
Insurance brokerage services: group medical, customized employee benefit packages, liability, workers' comp & consulting services. (AA, estab 1982, empl 10, sales , cert: CPUC)

Florida

5989   Epiphany Insurance Company LLC
       6073 NW 167 St, Ste C7
       Hialeah, FL 33015
       Contact: Martine Miller Mgr
       Tel: 305-783-1487
       Email: epiphanyinsures@gmail.com
       Website: www.epiphanyinsures.com
Health and Life Insurance, Group Benefits, Supplemental Benefits, Dental & Vision. (Woman/AA, estab 2017, empl 4, sales , cert: State, SDB)

5990   Havens & Company
       586 Bay Villas Lane
       Naples, FL 34108
       Contact: Diane Green COO
       Tel: 978-283-4366
       Email: dgreen@havensandcompany.com
       Website: www.havensandcompany.com
Designing & negotiating benefits programs for life, accident, disability, dental, vision, along with retiree, voluntary, and executive benefits. (Woman, estab 2007, empl 6, sales $2,807,521, cert: WBENC)

5991   Leslie Saunders Insurance Agency, Inc.
       1535 N Dale Mabry Hwy
       Lutz, FL 33548
       Contact: Leslie Saunders President
       Tel: 813-949-8964
       Email: lsaunders@lsimi.com
       Website: www.lesliesaunders.com
Insurance agency: property casualty; employee benefits; life, health, STD, LTD & disablity insurance. (Woman, estab 1988, empl 7, sales , cert: WBENC)

Georgia

5992   Atlanta Life Insurance Company
       191 Peachtree St. Ste 2500
       Atlanta, GA 30303
       Contact: Howard Stephenson President
       Tel: 404-654-8842
       Email: hstephenson@atlantalife.com
       Website: www.atlantalife.com
Financial services, employee benefits, reinsurance, asset mgmt, etc. (AA, estab 2001, empl 68, sales $343,000,000, cert: NMSDC)

5993   Benalytics Consulting Group, LLC
       1850 Pkwy Place SE Ste 730
       Marietta, GA 30067
       Contact: Charles Atkinson Principal
       Tel: 770-420-0525
       Email: catkinson@benalytics.com
       Website: www.benalytics.com
Benefit consulting & insurance brokerage services. (AA, estab 2005, empl 12, sales , cert: NMSDC, 8(a), SDB)

5994   JLM Risk Management Group
       201 17th St Ste 300
       Atlanta, GA 30363
       Contact: Joseph L Moore
       Tel: 404-874-2929
       Email: jmoore@jlmriskmgmt.com
       Website: www.jlmriskmgmt.com
Property, casualty, life & employee benefits insurance brokerage. Risk management, claims management & loss control consultation. (AA, estab 1996, empl 7, sales $600,000, cert: NMSDC)

5995   Premier Benefit Consultants, Inc.
       2470 Windy Hill Rd Ste 300
       Marietta, GA 30068
       Contact: Maureen Jurgelas President
       Tel: 678-794-8104
       Email: maureen@premierbenefit.com
       Website: www.Premierbenefit.com
Insurance agency & consulting: group medical, dental, vision plans, LTD, STD, life insurance, AD&D, etc. (Woman, estab 2000, empl 4, sales $240,000, cert: WBENC)

Illinois

5996   CS Insurance Strategies
       542 S Dearborn St
       Chicago, IL 60605
       Contact: Charles Smith CEO
       Tel: 312-566-9700
       Email: csmith@csstrategy.com
       Website: www.csstrategy.com
Comprehensive risk management, commercial insurance & group employee benefit solutions. (AA, estab 2006, empl 4, sales $500,000, cert: City)

INSURANCE COMPANIES

5997 Insurers Review Services, Inc.
225 N Michigan Ave Ste 902
Chicago, IL 60601
Contact: Alvin Robinson President
Tel: 312-938-0900
Email: arobin3172@aol.com
Website: www.insurersreviewservices.com
Insurance coverages, employee benefits, property coverages, special events, travel accident insurance & expatriate benefits. (AA, estab 1983, empl 5, sales $450,000, cert: State, City, NMSDC)

5998 Lambent Risk Management Services, Inc.
33 N. La Salle St Ste 1150
Chicago, IL 60602
Contact: Shirley Evans-Wofford CEO
Tel: 866-419-1415
Email: shirley_evans@lambent-rms.com
Website: www.lambent-rms.com
Insurance brokerage: property & casualty, third party theft, construction builders risk, insurance bonding, travel accident, healthcare & life, 401(k). (Woman/AA, estab 2000, empl 21, sales $2,433,496, cert: State, City)

5999 Prairie States Enterprises, Inc.
101 West Grand Ave., Ste 404
Chicago, IL 60654
Contact: Felicia Wilhelm CEO
Tel: 312-464-1888
Email: fwilhelm@prairieontheweb.com
Website: www.prairieontheweb.com
Health benefit plan administration svcs: medical, dental, vision, health savings account & eeimbursement accounts, short term disability, subrogation, COBRA&HIPAA certifications. (Woman, estab 1989, empl 64, sales $5,000,000, cert: WBENC)

6000 Risk & Insurance Management Services, Inc.
80 Burr Ridge Pkwy, Ste 121
Burr Ridge, IL 60527
Contact: Elizabeth Rodriguez-Spreck President
Tel: 630-655-0800
Email: lspreck@21chc.com
Website: www.21chc.com
Risk mgmt & insurance consulting svcs: employee benefits, group health, property & casualty, workers' comp, liability, product liability, auto, short-term disability, long-term disability, third-party claims admin svcs, healthcare & managed care. (Minority, Woman, estab 1991, empl 23, sales $2,282,406, cert: WBENC)

Louisiana

6001 1st Team Insurance Agency
3745 Choctaw Dr
Baton Rouge, LA 70805
Contact: Harold Williams Owner
Tel: 225-806-6923
Email: hwilliams@1stteaminsurance.com
Website: www.1stteaminsurance.com
Property & casualty insurance, property management, public relations, lobbying. (AA, estab 2005, empl 3, sales $350,000, cert: State)

6002 Hammerman and Gainer, Inc.
2400 Veterans Blvd Ste 510
Kenner, LA 70062
Contact: Kelisha Garrett Business Devel/PMO
Tel: 504-982-5030
Email: kelishag@hgi-global.com
Website: www.hgi.global
Risk management & insurance consulting services. (AA, estab 1929, empl 85, sales $38,000,000, cert: NMSDC)

Michigan

6003 Armstrong/Robitaille/Riegle, Inc.
2950 S State St Ste 350
Ann Arbor, MI 48104
Contact: Laurie Riegle President
Tel: 734-665-5900
Email: lriegle@arrinsurance.com
Website: www.arrinsurance.com
Commercial Insurance, Financial & Employee Benefit Services. (Woman, estab 1994, empl 9, sales $1,305,893, cert: WBENC)

6004 Brownrigg Companies LTD
840 W Long Lake Rd Ste 100
Troy, MI 48098
Contact: Nancy Brownrigg CEO
Tel: 248-373-5580
Email: nbrownrigg@brownrigg.com
Website: www.brownrigg.com
Specialty insurance. (Woman, estab 1990, empl 14, sales $11,000,000, cert: WBENC)

6005 Custom Results Corporate Consulting LLC
101 W Big Beaver Rd Ste 115
Troy, MI 48084
Contact: Diane Christensen President
Tel: 248-572-1160
Email: diane@customresults.com
Website: www.customresults.com
Insurance, design, implementation, service & communication of Employee Benefit Plans & Retiree Medicare Advantage plans. (Woman, estab 2001, empl 6, sales , cert: WBENC)

6006 Employee Solve
725 S Adams Ste L-140
Southfield, MI 48009
Contact: Kenneth Hurtt, RHU, REBC President
Tel: 248-438-0096
Email: info1@employeesolve.com
Website: www.employeesolve.com
Health & welfare plans for employer groups. (AA, estab 1987, empl 6, sales $3,000,000, cert: NMSDC)

6007 Goss LLC
600 Renaissance Ctr, Ste 1200
Detroit, MI 48243
Contact: Vincent Davis Dir of Mktg
Tel: 313-446-9636
Email: vdavis@gossllc.com
Website: www.gossllc.com
Commercial risk & risk consulting svcs: group benefits, property, casualty, liability, E&O, D&O, workers comp, business auto, etc. (AA, estab 2001, empl 7, sales $37,150,000, cert: State, NMSDC)

6008 Laurie Sall & Associates
      201 West Big Beaver Road #300
      Troy, MI 48084
      Contact: Laurie Sall President
      Tel: 248-641-2755
      Email: laurie@lauriesall.com
      Website: www.lauriesall.com
Life, disability & health insurance. (Minority, Woman, estab 1980, empl 3, sales $8,532,047, cert: NMSDC, WBENC)

6009 ReviewWorks
      21500 Haggerty Rd Ste 250
      Northville, MI 48167
      Contact: Carolyn Lahousse President
      Tel: 248-848-5067
      Email: carolyn_lahousse@reviewworks.com
      Website: www.reviewworks.com
Medical cost containment solutions & disability services for workers' compensation, LTD & auto injury related claims & claimants. (Woman, estab 1989, empl 70, sales $11,650,921, cert: WBENC)

6010 The Dearborn Agency
      22691 Michigan Ave
      Dearborn, MI 48124
      Contact: Wendy Beaver Sales Mgr
      Tel: 313-562-8373
      Email: wendyb@dearbornagency.com
      Website: www.dearbornagency.com
Insurance. (Woman, estab 1924, empl 10, sales , cert: WBENC)

6011 Yee & Associates LLC
      20789 Harper
      Harper Woods, MI 48225
      Contact: Matthew Yee Member
      Tel: 313-886-6770
      Email: matthew@bakerhopp.com
      Website: www.bakerhopp.com
Property & casualty life and health insurance agency. (As-Pac, estab 2002, empl 1, sales , cert: NMSDC)

Minnesota

6012 Integrated Benefits Group, Inc.
      601 Carlson Pkwy Ste 1097
      Hopkins, MN 55305
      Contact: Deborah J. Dybdahl CEO
      Tel: 952-449-5290
      Email: deborah@integratedbenefitsgroup.com
      Website: www.integratedbenefitsgroup.com
Auto/home, legal, long term care, critical illnesss, supplemental disability, retirement planning, PET, etc. (Woman, estab 1992, empl 16, sales $550,000, cert: WBENC)

Ohio

6013 Cox Financial Corporation
      105 E Fourth St
      Cincinnati, OH 45202
      Contact: Ethan Cox CEO
      Tel: 513-621-1771
      Email: ethancox@coxfinco.com
      Website: www.coxfinco.com
Long Term & Short Term Disability Plans. (AA, estab 1972, empl 12, sales $1,436,689, cert: NMSDC)

6014 Pinkney-Perry Insurance Agency, Inc.
      2143 Stokes Blvd
      Cleveland, OH 44106
      Contact: Patricia L. Welcome VP
      Tel: 216-795-1995
      Email: pwelcome@pinkney-perry.com
      Website: www.pinkney-perry.com
Insurance. (AA, estab 0, empl , sales , cert: NMSDC)

Pennsylvania

6015 Benefits Plus Consulting Group
      1807 Pine St 1st Fl
      Philadelphia, PA 19103
      Contact: Norma Romero-Mitchell CEO
      Tel: 215-564-0288
      Email: norma@consultbenefitsplus.com
      Website: www.benefitsplusconsulting.com
Benefits consulting & advisory services, insurance, long term care. (Minority, Woman, estab 1993, empl 8, sales $403,180, cert: NMSDC, WBENC)

Rhode Island

6016 Axiom Actuarial Consulting
      26 Knapton St
      Barrington, RI 02806
      Contact: Carlos Fuentes President
      Tel: 860-550-0740
      Email: carlos-fuentes@axiom-actuarial.com
      Website: www.axiom-actuarial.com
Broad actuarial consulting services in healthcare, retirement, life and employee benefits. (Hisp, estab 2008, empl 4, sales , cert: State, 8(a))

Tennessee

6017 Diversity Benefits
      230 N 4th Ave, Ste 162
      Nasville, TN 37219
      Contact: David Carter President
      Tel: 615-515-3329
      Email: davidc@diversitybenefits.net
      Website: www.diversitybenefits.net
Health insurance/self-funded health plans, Prescription drug coverage, Reinsurance ,Dental insurance, Vision insurance, Life and AD&D insurance, Disability insurance, Voluntary benefits, Retirement plans. (AA, estab 2012, empl 2, sales , cert: NMSDC)

Texas

6018 CPR Insurance Group LLC
      600 E John Carpenter Frwy Ste 365
      Irving, TX 75062
      Contact: Les Titus President
      Tel: 972-887-3660
      Email: ltitus@cprins.com
      Website: www.cprins.com
Insurance claims: property, liability/casualty & auto claims. (AA, Hisp, estab 2013, empl 19, sales $1,200,000, cert: State)

LABORATORY/SCIENTIFIC SUPPLIES & SERVICES

Manufacture or distribute products or provide services for scientific laboratories. Products include glassware, disposables, chemicals, safety items. etc.
NAICS Code 33

California

6019 Accurate C&S Services Inc
8105 Edgewater Dr Ste 225
Oakland, CA 94621
Contact: Regina Jones President
Tel: 510-394-3985
Email: rjones@accuratescreens.com
Website: www.accuratescreens.com
Drug & alcohol testing. (Woman/AA, estab 2006, empl 12, sales $2,765,000, cert: NMSDC, WBENC)

6020 Advanced ImmunoChemical, Inc.
111 W Ocean Blvd, 4th Fl
Long Beach, CA 90802
Contact: President
Tel: 562-434-4676
Email: order@advimmuno.com
Website: www.advimmuno.com
Mfr laboratory reagents for In vitro diagnostics & research, Cardiac Disease, Tumor Markers, Metabolic Syndrome, Inflammation, Emerging Infectious Diseases, Biowarfare Threats, Hormones, Autoimmune Disease, Neuroscience. (Woman, estab 1986, empl 2, sales , cert: WBENC)

6021 BIO PLAS, Inc.
4340 Redwood Hwy Ste A1
San Rafael, CA 94903
Contact: Jeananne McGrath VP
Tel: 415-472-3777
Email: jam@bioplas.com
Website: www.bioplas.com
Mfr disposable laboratory supplies. (Woman, estab 1977, empl 10, sales , cert: State)

6022 Brylen Technologies
275 Orange Ave
Santa Barbara, CA 93117
Contact: Barbara Tzur President
Tel: 805-692-9300
Email: barbara.tzur@brylen.com
Website: www.brylen.com
Calibration & testing laboratory, clean room & clean bench certifications, calibration is electro-magnetic, thermodynamics, dimensional, angle, & mechanical areas, calibrate equipment. (Woman, estab 1985, empl 10, sales $572,850, cert: State)

6023 Comprehensive Drug Testing, Inc. (CDT, Inc.)
PO Box 11869
Santa Ana, CA 92711
Contact: Kim Jasper President
Tel: 800-440-3784
Email: kimj@cdtsolutions.com
Website: www.cdtsolutions.com
Substance abuse program management, drug testing, collections, laboratory, education. (Woman, estab 1985, empl 13, sales $2,400,000, cert: State, CPUC)

6024 Core Diagnostics
3535 Breakwater Ave
Hayward, CA 94545
Contact: Krishnamurthy Balachandran CEO
Tel: 650-532-9500
Email: balachandran@corediagnostics.net
Website: www.corediagnostics.net
Biomarker analysis & translational research support, Phase III clinical trial samples. (As-Ind, estab 2009, empl 12, sales $3,259,000, cert: NMSDC)

6025 CP Lab Safety
14 Commercial Blvd, Ste 113
Novato, CA 94949
Contact: Jessica Kurtz Cstmr Service
Tel: 415-883-2600
Email: info@cplabsafety.com
Website: www.calpaclab.com
Mfr environmentally conscious laboratory safety products & dist leading lab supply brands. (Woman, estab 1996, empl 6, sales $3,069,392, cert: State, 8(a))

6026 Discount Lab Supplies
3201 Verdant Way
San Jose, CA 95117
Contact: Stacey Blanding President
Tel: 408-246-4024
Email: stacey@discountlabs.com
Website: www.discountlabs.com
Dist lab products: cryogenic storage vessels, DI water systems, furnaces, harvey sterilizers, incubators, NANOpure water systems, ovens, rotators & rockers, spectrophotometers, turner fluorometers, ultrasonic cleaners. (Minority, Woman, estab 2004, empl 1, sales , cert: NMSDC)

6027 Fulgent Therapeutics LLC
4978 Santa Anita Ave Ste 205
Temple City, CA 91780
Contact: Joe Roach VP
Tel: 626-350-0537
Email: joeroach@fulgentdiagnostics.com
Website: www.fulgentdiagnostics.com
Hereditary genetic testing. (As-Pac, estab 2013, empl 30, sales $1,000,000, cert: NMSDC)

6028 InterWorking Labs, Inc.
PO Box 66190
Scotts Valley, CA 95067
Contact: Judy Jones Marketing Mgr
Tel: 831-460-7010
Email: info@iwl.com
Website: www.iwl.com
Network Emulation for testing Products. (Woman, estab 1993, empl 10, sales $800,000, cert: WBENC)

6029 Orange Coast Analytical, Inc.
3002 Dow Ave, Ste 532
Tustin, CA 92780
Contact: Cindy Noorani President
Tel: 714-832-0064
Email: cindyn@ocalab.com
Website: www.ocalab.com
Environmental & analytical testing laboratory, organic & inorganic testing-water, waste water, soil, air, industial, chemical & food products. (Woman, estab 1990, empl 15, sales $1,450,178, cert: State, CPUC)

LABORATORY/SCIENTIFIC SUPPLIES & SERVICES

6030   Phamatech, Inc.
       10151 Barnes Canyon Rd
       San Diego, CA 92121
       Contact: Jodee Callaghan Natl Sales Consultant
       Tel: 888-635-5840
       Email: jodee@phamatech.com
       Website: www.phamatech.com
Drug testing laboratory. (As-Pac, estab 1991, empl 185, sales $22,277,000, cert: NMSDC)

6031   Pure Lab Solutions, Inc.
       4901 Morena Blvd, Ste 118
       San Diego, CA 92117
       Contact: Pam Wammes President
       Tel: 619-840-5858
       Email: pwammes@purelabsolutions.com
       Website: www.purelabsolutions.com
Dist Sartorius lab equipment, ultrapure water purification & lab bench scales. (Woman, estab 2012, empl 2, sales , cert: WBENC)

6032   The Andwin Corp.
       6636 Variel Ave
       Canoga Park, CA 91303
       Contact: Arnie Shedlow Sr VP Sales
       Tel: 818-999-2828
       Email: jpalaganas@andwin.com
       Website: www.andwinsci.com
Dist medical & lab supplies & product kits: boxes, labels, bar codes, instruction inserts & kit components. (Woman, estab 1950, empl 98, sales $32,000,000, cert: WBENC)

Connecticut

6033   PRO Scientific Inc.
       99 Willenbrock Rd
       Oxford, CT 06478
       Contact: Holly Archibald Sales Dir
       Tel: 203-267-4600
       Email: sales@proscientific.com
       Website: www.proscientific.com
Mfr PRO Scientific laboratory equipment, PRO homogenizers, mixers, shakers & stirrers. Dist Andreas Hettich Centrifuges. (Woman, estab 1992, empl 15, sales , cert: State)

Florida

6034   Algon Corporation
       12000 SW 132 Court
       Miami, FL 33186
       Contact: Eduardo Suarez-Troconis Dir
       Tel: 305-253-6901
       Email: edal@algon.com
       Website: www.algon.com
Chemical raw materials, laboratory supplies & machine parts. (Woman/Hispanic, estab 1989, empl 24, sales $20,570,883, cert: NMSDC)

6035   Kramer Laboratories, Inc.
       400 University Dr Ste 400
       Coral Gables, FL 33134
       Contact: Myrna Patterson Sales Mgr
       Tel: 800-824-4894
       Email: mpatterson@kramerlabs.com
       Website: www.kramerlabs.com
Fungi Nail Brand, Safetussin CD Cough Relief/Nasal Decongestant Formula, Safetussin DM Cough Formula. (Minority, Woman, estab 1987, empl 14, sales , cert: NMSDC, WBENC)

6036   VetMeds, Inc.
       8950 SW 74th Court Ste 2201
       Miami, FL 33156
       Contact: President
       Tel: 786-220-3634
       Email: vetmeds@gmx.com
       Website: www.vetmedsinc.com
Dist medical equipment, medical apparel, wound care supplies, medical furniture, exam room supplies, extrication-patient transport equipment, surgical gloves, IV therapy & laboratory supplies. (Woman/AA, estab 2012, empl 5, sales , cert: State)

Massachusetts

6037   Cross-Spectrum Acoustics Inc
       PO Box 90842
       Springfield, MA 01139
       Contact: Herbert Singleton Managing Partner
       Tel: 413-315-5770
       Email: dbe@csacoustics.com
       Website: www.csacoustics.com
Acoustical consulting, noise and vibration control, sound measurements, noise & vibration mitigation. (AA, estab 2003, empl 1, sales , cert: State)

Maryland

6038   Quality Biological, Inc.
       7581 Lindbergh Dr
       Gaithersburg, MD 20879
       Contact: Basile Whitaker VP Operations
       Tel: 301-840-9331
       Email: whitakerb@qualitybiological.com
       Website: www.qualitybiological.com
Mfr tissue culture & molecular biology products, bacteriological plates, dist Corning glass & plastics, Corning lab equipment, Microflex gloves & JT Baker chemicals. (Woman/AA, estab 1983, empl 24, sales , cert: NMSDC)

6039   Trinity Sterile, Inc.
       201 Kiley Dr
       Salisbury, MD 21801
       Contact: Crystal Lutz VP Sales
       Tel: 410-860-5123
       Email: crystal.lutz@trinitysterile.com
       Website: www.trinitysterile.com
Production & sterilization equipment: clinical kits, trays or instruments. (As-Ind, estab , empl , sales , cert: NMSDC)

Michigan

6040   Forensic Fluids Laboratories Inc.
       225 Parsons St
       Kalamazoo, MI 49007
       Contact: Bridget Lemberg CEO
       Tel: 269-492-7700
       Email: blemberg@forensicfluids.com
       Website: www.Forensicfluids.com
Drug testing & screening. (Woman, estab 2005, empl 60, sales $19,861,000, cert: WBENC)

LABORATORY/SCIENTIFIC SUPPLIES & SERVICES

6041 RTI Laboratories, Inc.
      33080 Industrial Rd
      Livonia, MI 48150
      Contact: Kae Trojanowski President
      Tel: 734-422-8000
      Email: ktrojanowski@rtilab.com
      Website: www.rtilab.com
Analytical testing laboratory: environmental, chemical & metallurgical testing, environmental compliance field sampling services. (Minority, estab 1986, empl 40, sales $5,000,000, cert: NMSDC, SDB)

6042 Structural Testing Laboratory
      397 Washington St, Ste B
      Brighton, MI 48116
      Contact: Tracy LaCroix Owner
      Tel: 734-476-9882
      Email: sales@stlbrighton.com
      Website: www.stlbrighton.com
Vibration & shock testing services for automotive, aerospace & defense, transportation & packaging & military. (Nat Ame, estab 2005, empl 3, sales , cert: NMSDC)

Minnesota

6043 LKT Laboratories, Inc.
      545 Phalen Blvd
      Saint Paul, MN 55130
      Contact: Luke Lam President
      Tel: 651-644-8424
      Email: llam@lktlabs.com
      Website: www.lktlabs.com/
Mfr biochemicals for life science research, inhibitors, activators, modulators, and many other high purity small molecules, phytochemical isolation and analysis. (As-Pac, estab 1990, empl 11, sales $1,300,000, cert: NMSDC)

Missouri

6044 HERA Laboratory Planners
      411 N. Tenth St, Ste 400
      St. Louis, MO 63101
      Contact: Laurie Sperling President
      Tel: 314-289-9202
      Email: lauries@herainc.com
      Website: www.herainc.com
Laboratory planning, design, programming & equipment planning. (Woman, estab 1996, empl 22, sales $8,113,716, cert: State, WBENC)

6045 Taylor Scientific
      950 Hanley Industrial Ct
      St. Louis, MO 63144
      Contact: Jill Taylor President
      Tel: 800-727-0467
      Email: jill@taylorscientific.com
      Website: www.taylorscientific.com
Dist laboratory supplies. (Woman, estab 1972, empl 12, sales , cert: WBENC)

North Carolina

6046 Clinical Choice LLC
      5574 Garden Village Way Ste D400
      Greensboro, NC 27410
      Contact: Minerva Loran President
      Tel: 336-841-0919
      Email: mloran@clinicalchoice.com
      Website: www.clinicalchoice.com
Lab supplies, cleaning brushes, bite blocks, filters for the reprocessing scope washing machines, Endo supplies, SafeCap Endoscope Transport Trays, ScopeVault Endoscope Storage Cabinets, OneTab Powder and Liquid detergent. (Minority, Woman, estab 2001, empl 7, sales $3,751,424, cert: NMSDC)

6047 LJP Lab LLC
      495-S Arbor Hill Rd
      Kernersville, NC 27284
      Contact: Thomas Stith President
      Tel: 336-992-3902
      Email: tstith@ljplab.com
      Website: www.ljplab.com
Urine drug screen & confirmation services. (As-Pac, estab 2017, empl 6, sales $500,000, cert: State)

Nebraska

6048 Midland Scientific Inc.
      10651 Chandler Rd, Ste 102
      La Vista, NE 68128
      Contact: Shane Hanzlik
      Tel: 402-346-8352
      Email: shanzlik@midlandsci.com
      Website: www.midlandsci.com
Dist lab supplies & equipment. (Woman, estab , empl , sales $48,000,000, cert: WBENC)

New Jersey

6049 AGC Products Inc.
      3740 NW Blvd
      Vineland, NJ 08360
      Contact: Subu Natesan CEO
      Tel: 856-692-4435
      Email: snatesan@andrews-glass.com
      Website: www.andrews-glass.com
Mfr specialty & precision glass products for industrial & scientific applications. (As-Ind, estab 1948, empl 40, sales $4,000,000, cert: State, NMSDC)

6050 BioRepository Resources, LLC
      755 Central Ave, Unit 3
      New Providence, NJ 07974
      Contact: Catherine Chin CEO
      Tel: 908-790-8890
      Email: cchin@brr.us.com
      Website: www.brr.us.com
Long term storage of biological & clinical trial samples: blood, plasma, urine, tissue, biomarkers, retain drug product, API, pathology slides, blocks. (Minority, Woman, estab 2008, empl 2, sales , cert: State)

LABORATORY/SCIENTIFIC SUPPLIES & SERVICES

6051 Laboratory Disposable Products
1 Como Court
Towaco, NJ 07082
Contact: Cindy Beatty President
Tel: 973-335-2966
Email: mail@labdisposable.com
Website: www.labdisposable.com
Laboratory Disposable Products. (Woman, estab 1979, empl 10, sales $3,549,720, cert: City, WBENC)

6052 Neta Scientific Inc.
4206 Sylon Blvd
Hainesport, NJ 08036
Contact: Winfred Sanders, PhD President
Tel: 609-265-8210
Email: sales@netascientific.com
Website: www.netascientific.com
Dist laboratory instruments & supplies safety & environmental supplies. (Woman/AA, estab 1999, empl 45, sales , cert: State, NMSDC, WBENC)

6053 Sarchem Laboratories, Inc.
5012 Industrial Rd
Farmingdale, NJ 07727
Contact: Arun Kumar VP
Tel: 732-938-2777
Email: arun.kumar@sarchemlabs.com
Website: www.sarchemlabs.com
Custom Synthesis, Process development from concept to lab scale preparation, Contract Research and Development. Supply small scale diagnostic reagents, chemical reagents and EPA samples in customer required ampules. (Woman/As-Ind, estab 1984, empl 6, sales $1,215,000, cert: NMSDC)

Ohio

6054 DHDC Engineering Consulting Services, Inc.
2390 Advanced Business Center Dr
Columbus, OH 43228
Contact: Savvas Sophocleous President
Tel: 614-527-7656
Email: sophocleous@dhdcinc.com
Website: www.dhdcinc.com
Laboratory testing services, geotechnical (engineering, drilling, and laboratory) & subsurface utility engineering (SUE). (As-Pac, estab 2012, empl 15, sales $500,000, cert: State)

6055 Midtown Scientific, Inc.
4415 Euclid Ave, Ste 343
Cleveland, OH 44103
Contact: Darlene Darby Baldwin CEO
Tel: 216-431-0110
Email: ddarbywatt@aol.com
Website: www.midtownscientific.com
Dist scientific laboratory research supplies & equipment, chemicals. (Woman/AA, estab 2002, empl 4, sales , cert: City)

Pennsylvania

6056 MB Research Laboratories
1765 Wentz Rd
Spinnerstown, PA 18968
Contact: Betty Salyer Accounts Receivable
Tel: 215-536-4110
Email: blandis@mbresearch.com
Website: www.mbresearch.com
Contract Research Toxicology Laboratory. (Hisp, estab 1972, empl 28, sales , cert: WBENC)

Puerto Rico

6057 Instrumed Services Corp.
10th St O 14 Castellana G
Carolina, PR 00983
Contact: Luis Peña President
Tel: 787-257-9249
Email: luis.pena@instrumed.net
Website: www.instrumed.net
Sales, Service, Validation and Calibration of Laboratory Equipments. (Minority, Woman, estab 1999, empl 10, sales , cert: NMSDC)

6058 J.C. Gonzalez, Inc.
2 St KM 178.2 Interior BO. Minillas Alto
San German, PR 00683
Contact: Julio C. Gonzalez Santiago CEO
Tel: 787-892-0047
Email: sales@jcgonzalezinc.com
Website: www.jcgonzalezinc.com
Dist & service scientific & research equipment, laboratory equipment & consumables, microscopes, stereoscopes, freezers, refrigerators. (Hisp, estab 2001, empl 6, sales $865,047, cert: NMSDC, SDB)

6059 MentorTechnical Group, Corp.
PO Box 6857
Caguas, PR 00726
Contact: Luis David Soto President
Tel: 787-743-0897
Email: jose.gonzalez@mentortg.com
Website: www.mentortg.com
Calibration, Instrumentation, and Control Systems Laboratory. (Hisp, estab 2000, empl 450, sales $27,500,000, cert: NMSDC)

6060 Pharma Consulting Corp.
Ave Amalia Paoli HL 5 7MA SECC Levittown
Toa Baja, PR 00949
Contact: Charil Pabon President
Tel: 787-784-9595
Email: pharmaconsultingcorp@gmail.com
Website: www.pharmapcc.com
Laboratory Products & Equipment Sales & Services. (Woman/Hisp, estab 2003, empl 17, sales $700,000, cert: NMSDC)

6061 R & G Clean Room Laboratory, Inc.
Ave Esmeralda #53 PMB 112
Guaynabo, PR 00969
Contact: Ruben Gomez President
Tel: 787-993-1781
Email: rgomez@crlrd.com
Website: www.cleanroomlab.com
Laboratory & clean room products to Biotech, Medical Devices, Animal Research & Pharmaceutical. (Hisp, estab 2007, empl 10, sales $700,000, cert: NMSDC)

South Carolina

6062 Professional Healthcare Services LLC
1007 Pendleton St
Greenville, SC 29601
Contact: Doris Haley President
Tel: 864-505-6747
Email: dhaley@phsonline.com
Website: www.phsonline.com
Alcohol & drug screening, pre employment physicals & health screening & health fairs, injury management programs & medical case management, On Site nursing care. (Woman/AA, estab 1998, empl 7, sales $259,000, cert: NMSDC)

Tennessee

6063 Safety Plus, LLC
PO Box 2549
Chattanooga, TN 37409
Contact: Alexa Wardlaw VP/Member
Tel: 423-822-0487
Email: alexa@safetyplusllc.com
Website: www.safetyplusllc.com
Safety solutions: fume hood, biosafety cabinet & clean air bench testing & maintenance, employee training, lab design & equipment recommendations. (Woman, estab 2005, empl 7, sales $284,017, cert: WBENC)

6064 Scientific Sales, Inc.
130 Valley Ct St
Oak Ridge, TN 37830
Contact: Ember Murphy President
Tel: 865-483-9332
Email: emurphy@scisale.com
Website: www.scisale.com
Dist laboratory supplies, equipment, chemicals, safety, industrial & environmental products. (Minority, Woman, estab 1987, empl 30, sales , cert: State, NMSDC)

6065 The Premier Group
4600 Cromwell Ave, Ste 101
Memphis, TN 38118
Contact: JW Gibson CEO
Tel: 901-346-9002
Email: jwgibson@gibsoncompanies.com
Website: www.gibsoncompanies.com
Dist medical supplies, laboratory & scientific equipment & related supplies. (AA, estab 1991, empl 7, sales $8,692,576, cert: NMSDC)

Texas

6066 Affirmative Biosolutions
PO Box 2274
Stafford, TX 77497
Contact: Seble Woubshet Owner
Tel: 713-256-8996
Email: abiosolutions@hotmail.com
Website: www.abiosolutions.com
Dist laboratories, medical & industrial products (Woman/AA, estab 2010, empl 3, sales , cert: State, City)

6067 Duran Industries Inc.
504 Business Pkwy
Richardson, TX 75081
Contact: Richard Duran President
Tel: 972-238-7122
Email: rduran@duranco.com
Website: www.duranco.com/
Dist industrial, commercial, MRO, safety, scientific & lab products. (Hisp, estab 1995, empl 20, sales $14,050,000, cert: NMSDC)

6068 Fox Scientific, Inc.
8221 East FM 917
Alvarado, TX 76009
Contact: Jetta Lewis Sales
Tel: 800-369-5524
Email: paisleyg@foxscientific.com
Website: www.foxscientific.com
Dist laboratory supplies, equipment & chemicals. (Hisp, estab 1988, empl 21, sales $5,420,000, cert: State, City, NMSDC)

6069 Products Unlimited, Inc.
PO Box 339
Justin, TX 76247
Contact: Raithel Susan Sales Mgr
Tel: 940-648-3073
Email: sraithel@products-unlimited.com
Website: www.products-unlimited.com
Dist medical, lab & safety supplies & equipment. (Woman, estab 1992, empl 7, sales $5,020,000, cert: State)

LEGAL SERVICES
Legal counsel, process services, patent agents, public notaries, paralegal services, court reporting, litigation, mediation, law firms. NAICS Code 54

California

6070 Apogee Law Group, P.C.
      100 Sprectrum Center Dr Ste 900
      Irvine, CA 92618
      Contact: Francisco Rubio President
      Tel: 949-862-8484
      Email: frubio@goapogee.com
      Website: www.apogeelawgroup.com
Specialize in patents, trademarks, and corporate law. (Hisp, estab 2015, empl 6, sales $820,000, cert: NMSDC)

6071 Baer Reed
      8 Sunburst
      Irvine, CA 92603
      Contact: Danielle Buglino SVP
      Tel: 516-658-5003
      Email: dbuglino@baerreed.com
      Website: www.baerreed.com
Virtual Paralegals, Virtual Assistants, Legal Assistants, Global Shared Services, Legal Billing, Management & Review, Ediscovery, Real Estate Law, Contract Analysis, AI Support, Due Diligence, Document Review & Foreign Language Review, Legal Research, Litigation / Internal Investigation, Deposition Summaries, Paper Document Collection, Privilege Review, Lease Abstraction, Mortgage Compliance & Operational Support, AI / Digital Business Transformation Services, Back Office Support Services, Content Moderation & Social Media Monitoring (Woman, estab 2011, empl 85, sales $1,038,084, cert: NWBOC)

6072 Banker's Hill Law Firm, A.P.C.
      160 Thorn St, Ste 200
      San Diego, CA 92103
      Contact: Carlos Alvarez Tostado Marketing Rep
      Tel: 619-230-0330
      Email: carlosa@bhlflaw.com
      Website: www.bhlflaw.com
Personal injury, immigration law, criminal defense, bankruptcy, and family law. (AA, estab 1991, empl 12, sales $3,154,988, cert: NMSDC)

6073 Behmke Reporting & Video Services
      160 Spear St Ste 300
      San Francisco, CA 94105
      Contact: Paula Behmke Owner
      Tel: 415-597-5600
      Email: paula.behmke@behmke.com
      Website: www.behmke.com
Court reporting, realtime reporting, legal videography, litigation support services with local, state, and nationwide coverage. Cetralized scheduling and billing. (Woman, estab 1989, empl 7, sales $2,168,392, cert: CPUC, WBENC)

6074 Ben Hyatt Corporation
      17835 Ventura Blvd Ste 310
      Encino, CA 91316
      Contact: Mitch Hyatt VP
      Tel: 888-272-0022
      Email: mhyatt@benhyatt.com
      Website: www.benhyatt.com
Court reporting, litigation support services. (Woman, estab 1998, empl 10, sales $3,300,000, cert: WBENC)

6075 California Deposition Reporters
      599 S Barranca
      Covina, CA 91723
      Contact: Jamie Kirk President
      Tel: 800-274-1996
      Email: jamie@caldepo.com
      Website: www.caldepo.com
Court reporting, deposition transcription, videography for depositions, legal depositions, civil trial reporting, video conferencing. (Woman, estab 1979, empl 15, sales $1,687,887, cert: State, CPUC)

6076 Carol Nygard & Associates
      2295 Gateway Oaks Dr, Ste 170
      Sacramento, CA 95833
      Contact: John Nygard VP Business Dev
      Tel: 877-438-7787
      Email: john@walnutcreekcourtreporter.com
      Website: www.nygardreporting.com
Full-service court reporting agency specializing in complex litigation 24/7. (Woman, estab 2000, empl 5, sales $1,257,000, cert: State)

6077 CIR Law Offices International
      2650 Camino Del Rio N, Ste 308
      San Diego, CA 92108
      Contact: Amanda Cinq-Mars Business Devel Mgr
      Tel: 858-496-8909
      Email: acinq-mars@cirlaw.com
      Website: www.cirlaw.com/
Business law, International law, Intellectual Property counseling and Litigation. (Hisp, estab 1997, empl 35, sales $2,608,078, cert: NMSDC)

6078 EcoTeal, Inc.
      18685 Main St, 101-144
      Huntington Beach, CA 92648
      Contact: Maria Tettman President
      Tel: 714-375-5700
      Email: mtettman@ecoteal.com
      Website: www.ecoteal.com
Accident Investigation & Reporting, Acquisitions & Divestitures, Construction Safety, Emergency Preparedness & Response, Energy Efficiency & Conservation. (Woman, estab 2012, empl 1, sales $100,000, cert: City, CPUC)

6079 Kupferstein Manuel LLP
      865 S Figueroa St Ste 3338
      Los Angeles, CA 90017
      Contact: Phyllis Kupferstein Managing Partner
      Tel: 213-988-7531
      Email: pk@kupfersteinmanuel.com
      Website: www.kupfersteinmanuel.com
Trial law firm specializing in employment & general business litigation. (Woman, estab 2014, empl 3, sales $1,406,238, cert: WBENC)

6080 Kusar Court Reporters & Legal Services, Inc.
111 W Ocean Blvd Ste 1200
Long Beach, CA 90802
Contact: Amber Kusar Contract Mgr
Tel: 800-282-3376
Email: info@kusar.com
Website: www.kusar.com
Court reporters specializing in complex litigation & medmal. (Woman, estab 1983, empl 12, sales $3,600,000, cert: City, CPUC, WBENC)

6081 Lafayette & Kumagai LLP
1300 Clay St Ste 810
Oakland, CA 94612
Contact: Clara Marigmen Office Admin
Tel: 415-357-4600
Email: cmarigmen@lkclaw.com
Website: www.lkclaw.com
Civil litigation law firm, motion practice, jury trials, appeals, mediations, arbitrations, other ADR procedures and hearings. (AA, As-Pac, estab 1994, empl 15, sales $3,285,704, cert: NMSDC, CPUC)

6082 Livingston Law Firm, A Professional Corporation
1600 S Main St, Ste 280
Walnut Creek, CA 94596
Contact: Renee Livingston President
Tel: 925-952-9880
Email: rlivingston@livingstonlawyers.com
Website: www.livingstonlawyers.com
Provide high quality, cost efficient legal services, product liability litigation. (Woman, estab 2000, empl 11, sales $1,976,196, cert: CPUC, WBENC)

6083 Nemovi Law Group APC
2173 Salk Ave Ste 250
Carlsbad, CA 92008
Contact: Genail Nemovi President
Tel: 760-585-7066
Email: gmn@nemovilawgroup.com
Website: www.nemovilawgroup.com
Commercial Real Estate Transactions, End to End Commercial & Residential Mortgage, Default Legal Services (state and regulatory compliance consulting, foreclosure, title, bankruptcy, eviction, litigation). (Woman/AA, estab 2018, empl 10, sales $475,000, cert: State, NMSDC, WBENC)

6084 Parker Law Group, Inc.
27815 Barbate
Mission Viejo, CA 92692
Contact: Claudia Parker CEO
Tel: 949-916-9910
Email: cparker@parkerlawgroup.com
Website: www.parkerlawgroup.com
Transactional business legal services. (Woman/As-Pac, Hisp, estab 2008, empl 2, sales , cert: NMSDC)

6085 Sideman & Bancroft LLP
1 Embarcadero Center #2200
San Francisco, CA 94111
Contact: Ellen Kahn
Tel: 415-392-1960
Email: ekahn@sideman.com
Website: www.sideman.com
Legal services, civil, business, real estate, professional liability, intellectual property and tax litigation; trademarks, copyrights, domain names, brand protection, technology licensing and transfers; corporate; mergers, acquisitions, joint ventures, strategic alliances; commercial contracts; real estate transactions; tax planning; business crimes defense. (Woman, estab , empl , sales , cert: WBENC)

6086 Urrabazo Law, P.C.
2029 Century Park E Ste 400
Los Angeles, CA 90067
Contact: Donald Urrabazo President
Tel: 310-388-9099
Email: durrabazo@ulawpc.com
Website: www.ulawpc.com
Full range of complex litigation matters, contractual and commercial disputes. (Hisp, estab 2011, empl 6, sales $1,500,000, cert: NMSDC, CPUC)

6087 Wang & Chang
255 California St Ste 525
San Francisco, CA 94111
Contact: Justin Chang Partner
Tel: 415-599-2828
Email: justin@wangchanglaw.com
Website: www.wangchanglaw.com
Litigation matters, complex commercial cases, class actions, and civil lawsuits. (As-Pac, estab 2011, empl 4, sales $1,300,000, cert: NMSDC)

6088 Wilson Turner Kosmo LLP
550 West C St, Ste 1050
San Diego, CA 92101
Contact: Robin Wofford Partner
Tel: 619-236-9600
Email: rwofford@wilsonturnerkosmo.com
Website: www.wilsonturnerkosmo.com
Legal services: employment law, product liability, contract disputes, real property litigation, health care, warranty, first amendment, trade secret & trust litigation. (Woman/AA, estab 1991, empl 55, sales $11,770,943, cert: CPUC, WBENC)

6089 Yang Professional Law Corporation
80 S. Lake Ave, Ste 820
Pasadena, CA 91101
Contact: Rey Shung President
Tel: 626-921-4300
Email: ryang@yangpc.com
Website: www.yangpc.com
Civil litigation, insurance defense, personal injury, premises liability, product liability, insurance, subrogation, indemnity, employment, automobile, labor, transportation. (As-Pac, estab 2014, empl 3, sales $350,000, cert: NMSDC, CPUC)

LEGAL SERVICES

6090 Zuber Lawler & Del Duca LLP
      350 S Grand Ave, 32nd Floor
      Los Angeles, CA 90071
      Contact: Tom Zuber Managing Partner
      Tel: 213-596-5620
      Email: contact@zuberlaw.com
      Website: www.zuberlaw.com
IP, environment, class action, and commercial litigation. (As-Pac, estab 2003, empl 54, sales $14,565,000, cert: NMSDC, CPUC)

6091 Zumizi Corp, dba iDepo Reporters
      898 N Pacific Coast Hwy, Ste 475
      El Segundo, CA 90245
      Contact: Tina Mason-Hicks Dir of Operations
      Tel: 323-393-3768
      Email: tm@idepureporters.com
      Website: www.idepureporters.com
Full-service court reporting & record retrieval, document retrieval, process service, subpoenas, depositions, court stenographic reporting, transcriptions, legal videography and translation/interpreter services. (As-Pac, estab 2013, empl 10, sales $2,894,115, cert: NMSDC)

Colorado

6092 Campbell Litigation, P.C.
      730 17th St, Ste 740
      Denver, CO 80202
      Contact: Michelle Campbell VP Operations
      Tel: 303-536-1833
      Email: michelle@campbell-litigation.com
      Website: www.campbell-litigation.com/
Employment, labor and commercial litigation defense trial lawyers. (AA, estab 2015, empl 5, sales $1,000,000, cert: NMSDC)

6093 Fair Measures, Inc.
      PO Box 22939
      Denver, CO 80222
      Contact: Jo-Ann Birch President
      Tel: 800-458-2778
      Email: jbirch@fairmeasures.com
      Website: www.fairmeasures.com
Legal services and training on management law for line Mgrs, business owners, Human Resource professionals and lawyers. (Woman, estab , empl , sales $640,000, cert: WBENC)

6094 Gibson Arnold & Associates, Inc.
      518 17th St, Ste 1125
      Denver, CO 80202
      Contact: Elizabeth Dahill Exec VP
      Tel: 303-595-3655
      Email: denver@gibsonarnold.com
      Website: www.gibsonarnold.com
Natl legal recruiting: attorneys, paralegals, and legal support staff. (Woman, estab 1981, empl 16, sales $5,228,089, cert: WBENC)

6095 Wells, Anderson & Race, LLC
      1700 Broadway, Ste 1020
      Denver, CO 80290
      Contact: Jaime Heveron CFO
      Tel: 303-830-1212
      Email: jheveron@warll.com
      Website: www.warllc.com
Litigation and appeals for local, regional and national clients. (Woman, estab 1995, empl 28, sales , cert: WBENC)

Connecticut

6096 Reardon Scanlon LLP
      45 S Main St, Ste 305
      Hartford, CT 06107
      Contact: Katherine Scanlon Managing Partner
      Tel: 860-955-9450
      Email: katherine.scanlon@reardonscanlon.com
      Website: www.reardonscanlon.com
Insurance industry litigation boutique. (Woman, estab 2012, empl 3, sales $899,950, cert: WBENC)

6097 Varunes & Assocaites, P.C.
      5 Grand St
      Hartford, CT 06106
      Contact: Anita Varunes President
      Tel: 860-541-1675
      Email: avarunes@varuneslaw.com
      Website: www.varuneslaw.com
Liability defense litigation & workers' compensation defense litigation. (Woman, estab 2006, empl 9, sales $996,810, cert: WBENC)

District of Columbia

6098 Garrison & Sisson, Inc.
      1620 Eye St, NW Ste 501
      Washington, DC 20006
      Contact: Kathy Charlwood
      Tel: 202-429-5630
      Email: kcharlwood@g-s.com
      Website: www.g-s.com
Attorney Referral and Placement. (Woman, estab 1986, empl 8, sales $1,565,495, cert: WBENC)

6099 Ifrah PLLC
      1717 Pennsylvania Ave, NW Ste 650
      Washington, DC 20006
      Contact: Kyle Ueyama Legal Asst
      Tel: 202-524-4140
      Email: kyle@ifrahlaw.com
      Website: www.ifrahlaw.com
Successful defense strategies, successfully manage, navigate and negotiate federal investigations. (Hisp, estab 2009, empl 7, sales $4,500,000, cert: City)

6100 Livesay IP Law, PLLC
   888 16th St, NW, Ste 800
   Washington, DC 20006
   Contact: Margo Livesay Owner
   Tel: 202-684-8685
   Email: Margo@Livesay-IP.com
   Website: www.Livesay-IP.com
Patent attorney services - patent prosecution, opinion work, due diligence, litigation support, software-related inventions, systems, architectures. (Woman, estab 2009, empl 1, sales $186,590, cert: WBENC)

6101 The O'Riordan Bethel Law Firm, LLP
   1314 19th St NW
   Washington, DC 20036
   Contact: Carol O'Riordan Managing Partner
   Tel: 202-822-1720
   Email: coriordan@oriordan-law.com
   Website: www.oriordan-law.com
Trial, appellate, ADR, counseling & drafting, administrative, civil & criminal law; fiduciary matters, government procurement, Title VII, construction, Sarbanes Oxley. (Woman/AA, estab 1997, empl 5, sales $649,874, cert: State, City, WBENC, 8(a))

Florida

6102 Alvin K. Brown, P.A.
   1001 3rd Ave West Ste 375
   Bradenton, FL 34203
   Contact: Alvin Brown President
   Tel: 941-953-2825
   Email: alvin@akbrownlaw.com
   Website: www.brownandbrown.legal/
Security assessments, risk assessments, security training, investigation & litigation svcs. (AA, estab 2002, empl 1, sales , cert: State)

6103 DeMahy Labrador & Drake PA (DLD Lawyers)
   806 Douglas Rd 12th Fl
   Coral Gables, FL 33134
   Contact: Greg Victor Partner
   Tel: 305-443-4850
   Email: gvictor@dldlawyers.com
   Website: www.dldlawyers.com
Trial practice for large corporations. (Hisp, estab 1984, empl 56, sales $10,000,000, cert: NMSDC)

6104 Hudson & Calleja LLC
   355 Alhambra Circle Ste 801
   Coral Gables, FL 33134
   Contact: Alexis Calleja Attorney Majority Shareholder
   Tel: 305-444-6628
   Email: acalleja@hudsoncalleja.com
   Website: www.hudsoncalleja.com
Legal services. (Woman/Hisp, estab 2011, empl 20, sales $1,700,000, cert: NMSDC, WBENC)

6105 Leon Cosgrove, LLC
   255 Alhambra Circle, Ste 800
   Coral Gables, FL 33134
   Contact: Maricarmen Ortega Firm Admin
   Tel: 305-740-1975
   Email: mortega@leoncosgrove.com
   Website: www.leoncosgrove.com
Complex litigation. (Hisp, estab 2013, empl 23, sales , cert: NMSDC)

6106 Levi G. Williams, Jr., P.A.
   12 SE 7th St Ste 700
   Fort Lauderdale, FL 33301
   Contact: Levi Williams President
   Tel: 954-463-1626
   Email: levi@leviwilliamslaw.com
   Website: www.leviwilliamslaw.com
Business Consulting, Litigation, Mediation, Administrative Hearings, Employment, Wage, Civil Rights, Sexual Harassment, Contracts, Negligence, Third Party Litigation, Premises Liability, Negotiations, Bonds, Mergers. (AA, estab 2011, empl 2, sales $300,000, cert: NMSDC)

6107 Losey PLLC
   450 S Orange Ave, Ste 550
   Orlando, FL 32801
   Contact: M. Catherine Losey Managing Partner
   Tel: 407-986-0406
   Email: closey@losey.law
   Website: www.losey.law
Legal services, litigations, arbitrations, and negotiations, manage cybersecurity risks, manage data breach response. (Woman, estab 2016, empl 5, sales $949,437, cert: WBENC)

6108 Marrero & Wydler
   2600 Douglas Rd, PH-4
   Coral Gables, FL 33113
   Contact: Oscar Marrero President
   Tel: 305-446-5528
   Email: oem@marrerolegal.com
   Website: www.marrerolegal.com
Litigation management. (Hisp, estab 2002, empl 6, sales $833,348, cert: State, NMSDC)

6109 Mint Legal Solutions
   150 South Pine Island Rd Ste 300
   Plantation, FL 33324
   Contact: Zully Vergel President
   Tel: 954-241-1300
   Email: zully@mintlegalsolutions.com
   Website: www.mintlegalsolutions.com
Electronic discovery & litigation support. (Woman/Hisp, estab 2017, empl 5, sales , cert: State, WBENC)

6110 Orange Legal Inc.
   633 E Colonial Blvd
   Orlando, FL 32803
   Contact: Kim Henderson Corporate Acct Mgr
   Tel: 404-400-6289
   Email: kim.henderson@orangelegal.com
   Website: www.orangelegal.com
Litigation support and unmatched customer service to the legal community, court reporting, process service, interpreting, videography. (Woman, estab , empl , sales $15,542,932, cert: State, City)

6111 Phipps Reporting, Inc.
   1615 Forum Place, Ste 500
   West Palm Beach, FL 33401
   Contact: Christine Phipps Owner
   Tel: 888-811-3408
   Email: christine@phippsreporting.com
   Website: www.phippsreporting.com
Court reporting. (Woman, estab 2010, empl 10, sales $2,862,699, cert: NWBOC)

LEGAL SERVICES

6112 Quintairos, Prieto, Wood, and Boyer
      255 S Orange Ave Ste 900
      Orlando, FL 32801
      Contact: Frank Alvarez Attorney/Partner
      Tel: 407-872-6011
      Email: frank.alvarez@qpwblaw.com
      Website: www.QPWBlaw.com
Workers compensation appeals. (Woman/Hisp, estab 1998, empl 125, sales $17,012,551, cert: NMSDC)

6113 Roig Lawyers
      1255 S Military Trail Ste 100
      Deerfield Beach, FL 33442
      Contact: Michael Rosenberg Managing Partner
      Tel: 954-462-0330
      Email: mrosenberg@roiglawyers.com
      Website: www.roiglawyers.com
Defense law firm, premises liability; workers' compensation; wrongful death. (Hisp, estab 2000, empl 300, sales $19,452,441, cert: NMSDC)

6114 Romaguera Law Group, PA
      11911 US Hwy 1, Ste 303
      North Palm Beach, FL 33408
      Contact: Raul Romaguera President
      Tel: 561-472-1077
      Email: rromaguera@romagueralaw.com
      Website: www.romagueralaw.com
Professional liability, Products liability, Specialty risk liability, Breach of contract, Slip & fall. (As-Ind, estab 2013, empl 4, sales $691,239, cert: NMSDC)

6115 Sanchez-Medina, Gonzalez, Quesada, et al.
      201 Alhambra Circle Ste 1205
      Miami, FL 33134
      Contact: Emilia Quesada Partner
      Tel: 305-377-1000
      Email: equesada@smgqlaw.com
      Website: www.smgqlaw.com
Legal services. (Hisp, estab 2007, empl 40, sales , cert: NMSDC)

6116 Steven C. Fraser, P.A.
      221 W Hallandale Beach Blvd, Ste 201
      Hallandale Beach, FL 33009
      Contact: Steve Fraser Managing Dir
      Tel: 305-809-6781
      Email: sfraser@fraserlawfl.com
      Website: www.fraserlawfl.com
Civil trial lawyers. We handle all kinds of claims, defense and liability cases throughout Florida in county, state and federal. (AA, estab 2008, empl 2, sales , cert: State)

6117 Torricella Law, PLLC
      4551 Ponce de Leon Blvd
      Coral Gables, FL 33146
      Contact: Roberto A. Torricella, Jr. Managing Member
      Tel: 786-693-6644
      Email: Robert@TorricellaPastor.com
      Website: www.TorricellaLaw.com
Civil & commercial litigation: business, insurance, aviation, real estate, professional liability, employment & general liability litigation. (Hisp, estab 2014, empl 4, sales , cert: NMSDC)

6118 Van Ness Law Firm, PLC
      1239 E Newport Center Dr, Ste 110
      Deerfield Beach, FL 33442
      Contact: John Van President
      Tel: 954-571-2031
      Email: compliance@vanlawfl.com
      Website: www.vanlawfl.com
Law Firm, Commercial & Real Estate Litigation. (AA, estab 2004, empl 75, sales , cert: NMSDC)

Georgia

6119 Benefits Law Group, PK Keesler, PC
      945 E Paces Ferry Rd Ste 2515
      Atlanta, GA 30326
      Contact: Patricia Keesler Owner
      Tel: 404-995-9505
      Email: pkeesler@benefitslawgroup.com
      Website: www.benefitslawgroup.com
Law firm: employee benefits & executive compensation matters. (Woman, estab 1996, empl 8, sales , cert: WBENC)

6120 Friese Legal, LLC
      1100 Spring St NW, Ste 730
      Atlanta, GA 30309
      Contact: Stephanie Friese Aron Managing Partner
      Tel: 404-876-4880
      Email: stephanie@frieselegal.com
      Website: www.frieselegal.com
Commercial real estate transactions, including multi-family development, acquisitions, dispositions, and leasing and asset management of commercial properties. (Woman, estab 2001, empl 6, sales $350,000, cert: WBENC)

6121 Lee, Hong, Degerman, Kang & Waimey, APC
      133 Main St
      LaGrange, GA 30240
      Contact: Bernard Ham Partner
      Tel: 706-298-0134
      Email: bham@lhlaw.com
      Website: www.lhlaw.com
Intellectual property, business & corporate transactions, commercial litigation, products liability, labor & employment, international arbitration, banking & financial services & real estate. (As-Pac, estab 1991, empl 70, sales $17,290,000, cert: NMSDC, CPUC)

6122 Moser Law Co LLC
      112 Krog St NE, Ste 26
      Atlanta, GA 30307
      Contact: Theresia Moser Owner
      Tel: 404-537-5339
      Email: tmoser@moserlawco.com
      Website: www.moserlawco.com
Employment Lawyers & Litigators. (Woman, estab 2014, empl 5, sales $250,000, cert: WBENC, NWBOC)

6123 Patrick Law Group, LLC
       3705 Canyon Ridge Ct, NE
       Atlanta, GA 30319
       Contact: Founder
       Tel: 404-437-6731
       Email: info@patricklawgroup.com
       Website: www.patricklawgroup.com
Construction Law and Commerical Contracting. We have prepared and negotiated hundreds of design, architect, construction, procurement and other contracts. (Woman, estab 2006, empl 4, sales $1,281,125, cert: WBENC)

6124 Pursley Friese Torgrimson, LLP
       1230 Peachtree St., NE Ste 1200
       Atlanta, GA 30309
       Contact: Maxine Buchman Office Mgr
       Tel: 404-665-1226
       Email: marketing@pftlegal.com
       Website: www.pftlegal.com
Commercial real estate transactions & eminent domain litigation. (Woman, estab 2013, empl 15, sales $1,853,288, cert: WBENC)

6125 Rutherford & Christie LLP
       225 Peachtree St South Tower, Ste 1750
       Atlanta, GA 30303
       Contact: Carrie Christie Managing Partner
       Tel: 404-522-6888
       Email: clc@rclawllp.com
       Website: www.rutherfordchristie.com
Defense litigation, general liability, employment, construction, contracts, constitutional law, aviation, products liability & workers' compensation. (Woman, estab 1999, empl 12, sales $2,600,000, cert: WBENC)

6126 Shingler Lewis LLC
       1230 Peachtree St Ste 1075
       Atlanta, GA 30309
       Contact: Joyce Gist Lewis Managing Partner
       Tel: 404-907-1999
       Email: jlewis@shinglerlewis.com
       Website: www.shinglerlewis.com
General liability defense, employment discrimination defense, and commercial litigation. (Woman/AA, estab 2012, empl 4, sales $510,000, cert: NMSDC)

Hawaii

6127 Carlsmith Ball LLP
       1001 Bishop St, Ste 2100
       Honolulu, HI 96809
       Contact: Michael Dolan COO
       Tel: 808-523-2500
       Email: mdolan@carlsmith.com
       Website: www.carlsmith.com
Real estate & land use, corporate, litigation, energy & environmental. (Woman/As-Pac, estab , empl 180, sales $32,450,000, cert: CPUC)

Iowa

6128 MWH Law Group LLP
       1501 42nd St Ste 465
       West Des Moines, IA 50266
       Contact: Kerrie Murphy Managing Partner
       Tel: 515-453-8509
       Email: kerrie.murphy@mwhlawgroup.com
       Website: www.mwhlawgroup.com
Corporate & Transactional, Real Estate, Contract Support, Employment & Labor Law, Litigation, Intellectual Property. (AA, estab 2016, empl 14, sales $2,563,000, cert: NMSDC)

Illinois

6129 Advitam IP, LLC
       160 N Wacker Dr, 2nd Fl
       Chicago, IL 60606
       Contact: Michele Katz Founding Partner
       Tel: 312-332-7700
       Email: MKatz@AdvitamIP.com
       Website: www.advitamip.com
Intellectual property, patent & trademark prosecution & litigation, copyright & domain name registration. (Woman, estab 2012, empl 4, sales , cert: WBENC)

6130 Chico & Nunes, P.C.
       333 W. Wacker Dr. Ste 1420
       Chicago, IL 60606
       Contact: Marcus Nunes Partner
       Tel: 312-463-1000
       Email: mnunes@chiconunes.com
       Website: www.chiconunes.com
Legal Services, Government Relations Services. (Hisp, estab 2004, empl 33, sales , cert: NMSDC)

6131 Clayborne, Sabo, and Wagner LLP
       525 W Main St Ste 105
       Belleville, IL 62220
       Contact: John Sabo Partner
       Tel: 618-239-0187
       Email: jsabo@cswlawllp.com
       Website: www.cswlawllp.com
Legal services. (AA, estab 2013, empl 10, sales $1,580,000, cert: State, NMSDC)

6132 Grant Law, LLC
       230 W Monroe St Ste 240
       Chicago, IL 60606
       Contact: Maurice Grant Principal
       Tel: 312-551-0111
       Email: Mgrant@grantlawllc.com
       Website: www.grantlawllc.com
Commercial and Corporate Litigation: Real Estate, Commercial Lending and Corporate Services, Employment Law, Estate Planning. (Woman/AA, estab 2004, empl 6, sales $315,000, cert: NMSDC)

6133 Heavner Beyers & Mihlar LLC
       PO Box 740
       Decatur, IL 62525
       Contact: Faiq Mihlar Managing Member
       Tel: 217-422-1719
       Email: faiqmihlar@hsbattys.com
       Website: www.hsbattys.com
Law firm representing leading financial corporations, middle & small-market clients. (Woman, estab 1978, empl 143, sales $11,771,967, cert: WBENC)

6134 Johnson Blumberg & Associates
       230 W Monroe Ste 1125
       Chicago, IL 60606
       Contact: Kenneth Johnson Sr Partner
       Tel: 312-541-9713
       Email: ken@johnsonblumberg.com
       Website: www.johnsonblumberg.com
Legal services. (Minority, estab 0, empl , sales , cert: NMSDC)

6135 LAW Ventures, Ltd.
       2970 Maria
       Northbrook, IL 60062
       Contact: Lori Ward President
       Tel: 847-791-1396
       Email: lori@lawventuresltd.com
       Website: www.lawventruesltd.com
Services provided leasing, management, acquistions, disposition, cost anaysis, re posistioning, sale lease back, nvestment and auction services. (Woman, estab 2004, empl 2, sales , cert: State)

6136 McClain & Canoy, LLC
       10 S Riverside Plaza Ste 875
       Chicago, IL 60606
       Contact: Salina Canoy Managing Member
       Tel: 312-474-6030
       Email: salina@mcclaincanoy.com
       Website: www.mcclaincanoy.com
Comprehensive legal services, transactional matters concerning health care, regulatory compliance, information privacy & security, health care information technology, government affairs, public policy. (Woman/AA, estab 2015, empl 5, sales $702,892, cert: State, NMSDC)

6137 McCormack Schreiber Legal Solutions Inc.
       303 W Madison St Ste 1725
       Chicago, IL 60606
       Contact: Amy McCormack Co-President
       Tel: 312-827-6470
       Email: amy@mslegalsolutions.com
       Website: www.thelawrecruiters.com
Contract attorney staffing firm. (Woman, estab 2007, empl 12, sales $458,579, cert: WBENC)

6138 Reyes Kurson, Ltd.
       328 S Jefferson St Ste 909
       Chicago, IL 60661
       Contact: Amy Kurson Managing Partner
       Tel: 312-332-0055
       Email: akurson@rkchicago.com
       Website: www.rkchicago.com
Boutique law firm. (AA, As-Pac, Hisp, estab 2005, empl 14, sales , cert: NMSDC)

6139 Sanchez Daniels & Hoffman, LLP
       333 W Wacker Dr Ste 500
       Chicago, IL 60606
       Contact: Heather D. Erickson Partner
       Tel: 312-641-1555
       Email: herickson@sanchezdh.com
       Website: www.sanchezdh.com
Mid-sized civil defense litigation firm with over 35 attorneys. (Hisp, estab 1987, empl 70, sales $9,480,000, cert: City, NMSDC)

6140 Valentine Austriaco & Bueschel, P.C.
       105 W Adams St 35th Fl
       Chicago, IL 60603
       Contact: Aurora Austriaco Partner
       Tel: 312-288-8285
       Email: aaustriaco@vablawfirm.com
       Website: www.vablawfirm.com
Resolve & litigate business disputes, real estate related matters, employment law, commercial litigation, contract dispute. (Woman, estab 2016, empl 8, sales $500,000, cert: WBENC)

6141 Victoria Legal + Corporate Services
       2 N. LaSalle St Ste 1615
       Chicago, IL 60602
       Contact: Victoria Rock CEO
       Tel: 312-443-1025
       Email: victoria@victorialcs.com
       Website: www.VictoriaLCS.com
Court reporting, complex litigation, accurate, verbatim transcripts, comprehensive services. (Woman, estab 1981, empl 4, sales $1,034,478, cert: State, WBENC)

Indiana

6142 Delaney & Delaney LLC
       3640 N Washington Blvd
       Indianapolis, IN 46205
       Contact: Kathleen Delaney President
       Tel: 317-920-0400
       Email: kathleen@delaneylaw.net
       Website: www.delaneylaw.net
Law Firm (Woman, estab 0, empl , sales $1,500,000, cert: State)

Kansas

6143 Barbera & Watkins, LLC
       6701 W 64th St., Ste 315
       Overland Park, KS 66202
       Contact: Natalie Stice Office Mgr
       Tel: 913-677-3800
       Email: nstice@bwaerolaw.com
       Website: www.bwaerolaw.com
Legal Services. (Woman, estab 2008, empl 7, sales , cert: State, WBENC)

Louisiana

6144 Courington Kiefer & Sommers, LLC
      650 Poydras St Ste 2105
      New Orleans, LA 70130
      Contact: Valerie Matherne Member
      Tel: 504-524-5510
      Email: vmatherne@courington-law.com
      Website: www.courington-law.com
Defending cases in Louisiana, Mississippi, and Texas. (Woman, estab 2011, empl 29, sales $3,854,117, cert: WBENC)

Massachusetts

6145 Fitzhugh & Mariani LLP
      155 Federal St, Ste 1700
      Boston, MA 02110
      Contact: Amy Crowley Partner
      Tel: 617-695-2330
      Email: acrowley@fitzhughlaw.com
      Website: www.fitzhughlaw.com
Environmental law, employment law, products liability, personal injury and general corporate litigation. (Woman/AA, estab 1986, empl 22, sales $1,700,000, cert: NMSDC)

6146 Schwartz Hannum PC
      11 Chestnut St Ste 11
      Andover, MA 01810
      Contact: Sara Goldsmith Schwartz President
      Tel: 978-623-0900
      Email: schwartz@shpclaw.com
      Website: www.shpclaw.com
Labor and Employment law firm representing employers with respect to a full spectrum of labor and employment issues, including Immigration-related matters. (Woman, estab 1995, empl 24, sales $5,639,572, cert: State, WBENC)

6147 The Wagner Law Group
      99 Summer St. 13th Fl
      Boston, MA 02110
      Contact: Marcia Wagner Cheif Marketing Officer
      Tel: 617-357-5200
      Email:
      Website: www.wagnerlawgroup.com
Employee benefits, estate planning, employment, labor and human resources and investment management. (Woman, estab 1996, empl 38, sales $7,709,000, cert: WBENC)

6148 West Hill Technology Counsel, Inc.
      900 Cummings Center Ste 206-T
      Beverly, MA 01915
      Contact: Louise Kennedy President
      Tel: 978-338-4082
      Email: llkennedy@westhillcounsel.com
      Website: www.westhillcounsel.com
Boutique business and technology law firm. (Woman, estab 2008, empl 9, sales $563,930, cert: State, WBENC)

Maryland

6149 A&E Enterprises II
      18403 Woodfield Rd, Ste A
      Gaithersburg, MD 20879
      Contact: Torri Schaffer President
      Tel: 301-869-5081
      Email: torri@torrilegalservices.com
      Website: www.torrilegalservices.com
Serve court papers, skip tracing & document retrieval. (Woman, estab 1998, empl 6, sales $831,388, cert: State)

6150 For The Record, Inc.
      10760 Demarr Rd
      White Plains, MD 20695
      Contact: Sara Vance CFO
      Tel: 800-921-5555
      Email: svance@ftrinc.net
      Website: www.ftrinc.net
Court reporting, transcription, legal video and litigation support. (Woman, estab 1991, empl 12, sales $2,265,600, cert: State, WBENC)

6151 Rahman LLC
      10025 Governor Warfield Pkwy Ste 212
      Columbia, MD 21044
      Contact: Mohammad Rahman Owner
      Tel: 443-283-7000
      Email: rahman@rahmanllc.com
      Website: www.rahmanllc.com
Intellectual property, patents, trademarks, copyrights, trade secrets, legal, strategy, valuation, IP. (As-Ind, estab 2008, empl 3, sales , cert: State, NMSDC)

6152 Taylor & Ryan, LLC
      1777 Reisterstown Rd CommereCenter E, Ste 265
      Pikesville, MD 21208
      Contact: Frances Taylor Member
      Tel: 410-486-5800
      Email: ftaylor@taylor-ryan.com
      Website: www.taylor-ryan.com
Immigration legal services to employers of all sizes. (Woman, estab 2005, empl 6, sales $851,000, cert: State)

Michigan

6153 A.K.Adams, PLC dba A|Squared Legal Group, PLC
      615 Griswold Ste 714
      Detroit, MI 48226
      Contact: Alari Adams Managing Member
      Tel: 313-702-2222
      Email: aa@asquaredlegal.com
      Website: www.asquaredlegal.com
Provide legal counseling to businesses for litigation and transactional matters pertaining to business law, labor/employment law, and human resources management. (Woman/AA, estab 2014, empl 2, sales $100,000, cert: NMSDC, WBENC)

6154 Americlerk, Inc. dba Lumen Legal
1025 N. Campbell Rd
Royal Oak, MI 48067
Contact: Iris Dalfrey VP Southern Region
Tel: 281-853-9295
Email: idalfrey@lumenlegal.com
Website: www.lumenlegal.com

Contract Legal Services, Secondments, Process Assessment, Spend Optimization, Document Review, Six Sigma Project Management, Lumen Review Center, Legal Spend Analysis with Sky Analytics, Document Automation. (Woman, estab 1993, empl 25, sales $8,000,000, cert: WBENC)

6155 Apis LLC
2216 Northlawn Blvd
Birmingham, MI 48009
Contact: Turkia Mullin CEO
Tel: 313-468-4932
Email: tmullin@apisconsultinggroup.com
Website: www.apisconsultinggroup.com

Corporate transactional attorney providing legal, financial and business consulting advice and support, drafting and negotiating all aspects of a deal, including all agreements for such transactions. (Woman, estab 2013, empl 1, sales , cert: WBENC)

6156 Banas and Associates PLLC
330 Hamilton Ste 350
Birmingham, MI 48009
Contact: Leslie Banas Managing Member
Tel: 248-203-5400
Email: leslie.banas@banaslegal.net
Website: www.banaslegal.net

Commercial real estate and corporate legal services; negotiation and documentation of office leases; sales and purchases of manufacturing and warehouse facilities; construction contracts and tenant build. (Woman, estab 2009, empl 4, sales $400,000, cert: WBENC)

6157 Bush Seyferth PLLC
3001 W Big Beaver Rd
Troy, MI 48084
Contact: Cheryl Bush President
Tel: 248-822-7800
Email: bush@bsplaw.com
Website: www.bsplaw.com

Law Firm; legal services (Woman, estab 0, empl , sales $5,344,367, cert: WBENC)

6158 LegalEase Solutions LLC
2301 Platt Rd, Ste 20
Ann Arbor, MI 48104
Contact: Teri Whitehead VP Global Strategy
Tel: 866-534-6177
Email: teri.whitehead@lgles.com
Website: www.legaleasecorporate.com

Customized legal support, including legal research and drafting service, compliance support, contract lifecycle management, transactional and litigation support. (Minority, estab 2005, empl 6, sales $80,000,000, cert: NMSDC)

6159 Lewis & Munday
2490 First Natl Bldg
Detroit, MI 48226
Contact: Gerald W. Helms Controller
Tel: 313-961-2550
Email: ghelms@lewismunday.com
Website: www.lewismunday.com

Law firm, legal services. (AA, estab 1972, empl 31, sales , cert: NMSDC)

6160 Rona M. Lum, P.C., dba Law Offices of Rona M. Lum
691 N Squirrel Rd Ste 185
Auburn Hills, MI 48326
Contact: Rona Lum, Esq. President
Tel: 248-340-1854
Email: rlum@corpimmigration.us
Website: www.corpimmigration.us

Immigration Law - corporate and business immigration related matters. (Woman, estab 0, empl , sales , cert: WBENC)

6161 Skye Suh, PLC.
32000 Northwestern Hwy, Ste 260
Farmington Hills, MI 48334
Contact: Skye Suh Managing Member
Tel: 248-932-8844
Email: ssuh@skyesuhplc.com
Website: www.skyesuhplc.com

Law firm, legal services. (Woman/As-Pac, estab 2002, empl 8, sales , cert: NMSDC)

6162 Sowell Law Partners PLLC
300 River Place Dr Ste 5500
Detroit, MI 48207
Contact: Leamon R. Sowell Managing Partner
Tel: 313-964-7900
Email: lrsowell@sowellpartners.com
Website: www.sowellpartners.com

Mergers, acquisitions, joint ventures & strategic alliances. (AA, estab 2000, empl 5, sales $300,000, cert: NMSDC)

Minnesota

6163 Blackwell Burke P.A.
431 S 7th St Ste 2500
Minneapolis, MN 55415
Contact: Kandy Branch FIRM Admin
Tel: 612-343-3200
Email: info@blackwellburke.com
Website: www.blackwellburke.com

Law Firm (AA, estab 2006, empl 34, sales $6,250,000, cert: NMSDC)

6164 Depo International
1330 Jersey Ave South
Minneapolis, MN 55426
Contact: CEO
Tel: 763-591-0535
Email:
Website: www.depointernational.com

Court reporting, videography, digital litigation tools, online repository, trial consulting, videoconferencing on a national/international level. (Woman, estab 2008, empl 15, sales $2,420,000, cert: WBENC)

6165 Fondungallah & Kigham, LLC
      2499 Rice St, Ste 145
      Saint Paul, MN 55113
      Contact: Mike Essien Attorney
      Tel: 651-482-0520
      Email: messien@fondlaw.com
      Website: www.fondlaw.com
Legal services: Intellectual property; immigration & nationality law; business & corporate law; business & commercial litigation; employment issues; int'l law. (AA, estab 2005, empl 3, sales $650,000, cert: State, NMSDC)

6166 Hollingsworth Davis, LLC
      8500 Normandale Lake Blvd Ste 320
      Minneapolis, MN 55437
      Contact: Tracey Dotter Exec Dir
      Tel: 952-854-2700
      Email: info@hdpatlaw.com
      Website: www.hdpatlaw.com
U.S. and international patent procurement, strategic patent portfolio, legal analysis & opinion work, pre-litigation. (Woman, estab 2005, empl 12, sales $2,600,000, cert: WBENC)

6167 Hope Law PLLC
      4999 France Ave S, Ste 245
      Minneapolis, MN 55410
      Contact: Rosanne Hope President
      Tel: 612-669-7017
      Email: roseanne@hopelawoffice.com
      Website: www.hopelawoffice.com
Commercial real estate law firm. (Woman, estab 2015, empl 4, sales $212,880, cert: WBENC)

6168 Igbanugo Partners Int'l Law Firm, PLLC
      250 Marquette Ave Ste 1075
      Minneapolis, MN 55401
      Contact: Herbert Igbanugo CEO
      Tel: 612-746-0360
      Email: higbanugo@igbanugolaw.com
      Website: www.igbanugolaw.com
U.S. Immigration & Nationality Law & International Trade Law limited to Sub-Saharan Africa. (AA, estab 2006, empl 13, sales $1,011,828, cert: NMSDC)

6169 Integrity Medicolegal Enterprises
      4800 Olson Memorial Hwy Ste 250
      Minneapolis, MN 55422
      Contact: Amy Berg President
      Tel: 763-398-5300
      Email: amy@integrityme.com
      Website: www.integrityme.com
Independent Medical Exams, workers compensation, liablity and disablity claims, Peer Reviews. (Woman, estab 2002, empl 50, sales $20,000,000, cert: WBENC)

6170 J. Selmer Law, P.A.
      500 Washington Ave S Ste 2010
      Minneapolis, MN 55415
      Contact: James Selmer Managing Partner
      Tel: 612-338-6005
      Email: jselmer@jselmerlaw.com
      Website: www.jselmerlaw.com
Defense law firm specializing in litigation and appellate practice, civil litigation process, from initial case evaluation through appellate proceedings. (AA, estab 1983, empl 10, sales $747,769, cert: NMSDC)

6171 Kelly & Berens, P.A. dba Berens & Miller, P.A.
      80 S Eighth St
      Minneapolis, MN 55402
      Contact: Barbara Podlucky Berens President
      Tel: 612-349-6171
      Email:
      Website: www.berensmiller.com
Law firm, legal services. (Woman, estab 1989, empl 10, sales $2,280,000, cert: WBENC)

6172 Nightowl Document Management Services, Inc.
      724 N First St
      Minneapolis, MN 55401
      Contact: Andrea Wallack CEO
      Tel: 612-337-0448
      Email: awal2652@msn.com
      Website: www.nightowldiscovery.com
Full service litigation support, single-source solution for both paper and electronic document collections. (Woman, estab 1991, empl 100, sales $3,800,000, cert: WBENC)

6173 Nwaneri Law Firm, PLLC
      1885 University Ave W, Ste 222
      St. Paul, MN 55104
      Contact: Patrick Nwaneri Managing Partner
      Tel: 651-917-0633
      Email: nwaneri@nwaneri.com
      Website: www.nwaneri.com
Professional legal services. (AA, estab 2002, empl 5, sales $153,743, cert: State, City, NMSDC)

Missouri

6174 Boggs, Avellino, Lach & Boggs
      9326 Olive Blvd Ste 200
      St. Louis, MO 63131
      Contact: Beth Boggs Managing Partner
      Tel: 314-726-2310
      Email: bbblawyers@aol.com
      Website: www.balblawyers.com
Legal services in Missouri & southern Illinois. (Woman/AA, estab 1999, empl 45, sales $5,000,000, cert: City, WBENC)

6175 Optitek, Inc.
      2001 S Hanley Rd Ste 250
      Brentwood, MO 63144
      Contact: Ricki McGuire President
      Tel: 314-644-2880
      Email: ricki@optitek.com
      Website: www.optitek.com
Electronic remittance processing, electronic lockbox services, forms processing, legal services & electronic document management systems. (Woman, estab 1992, empl 30, sales $1,796,300, cert: WBENC)

6176 Taylor and Associates, Inc.
      711 N 11th St
      St. Louis, MO 63101
      Contact: Deborah Weaver CEO
      Tel: 314-644-2191
      Email: dweaver@alaris.us
      Website: www.alaris.us/
Court Reporting, Video Depositions, Video Conferencing, digital video services, video-to-text synchronization. (Woman, estab 1985, empl 63, sales , cert: State, WBENC)

North Carolina

6177 Stanek Lemon Crouse + Meeks, PA
982 Trinity Rd
Raleigh, NC 27607
Contact: Ron Baker Patent Attorney
Tel: 919-944-4006
Email:
Website: www.staneklemon.com
Intellectual property & technology law. (Woman, estab 2019, empl 7, sales , cert: WBENC)

New Jersey

6178 Hudson Reporting & Video Inc.
90 Woodbridge Center Dr Ste 240
Woodbridge, NJ 07095
Contact: Geeta Sundrani Communications Specialist
Tel: 732-906-2078
Email: geeta@hudsonreporting.com
Website: www.hudsonreporting.com
Boutique court reporting agency servicing the legal industry. (Woman/As-Ind, estab 1998, empl 6, sales $2,541,000, cert: NMSDC, WBENC)

6179 Johnson & Associates
280 Amboy Ave
Metuchen, NJ 08840
Contact: Al Gil VP Business Dev
Tel: 848-229-2254
Email: agil@johnsonlegalpc.com
Website: www.johnsonlegalpc.com
Law Firm, Corporate & Business Law, Litigation, Immigration, Appeals, Real Estate, Bankruptcy, Municipal Court. (AA, estab 2012, empl 42, sales , cert: NMSDC)

6180 Kim Winston LLP
1307 White Horse Rd, Ste 601
Voorhees, NJ 08043
Contact: Jae Kim Partner
Tel: 856-520-8991
Email: yjaekim@kimwinston.com
Website: www.kimwinston.com
Intellectual property law firm, legal services for patents, patent prosecution, patent procurement, trademarks, trademark prosecution, copyright, intellectual property litigation, patent litigation, trademark litigation, copyright litigation, trademark. (As-Pac, estab 2013, empl 14, sales $850,000, cert: NMSDC)

6181 Love and Long, LLP
108 Washington St
Newark, NJ 07102
Contact: Lisa Love Partner
Tel: 215-546-8433
Email: llove@lovandlonglaw.com
Website: www.loveandlonglaw.com
Commercial transactions. (Woman/AA, estab 1992, empl 5, sales $500,000, cert: State, NMSDC)

6182 Rosenberg & Associates
425 Eagle Rock Ave, Ste 201
Roseland, NJ 07068
Contact: Catherine Kane VP Operations
Tel: 973-618-2101
Email: ckane@trantech.net
Website: www.rosenbergandassociates.com
Court reporting, litigation support, trial presentation, stenographic transcription services, audiography, videography, video conferencing, interpreting, database consulting. (Woman, estab 1973, empl 48, sales , cert: WBENC)

6183 RVM Enterprises, Inc.
525 Washington Blvd. 25th Fl
Jersey City, NJ 07310
Contact: Cheryl A. Brunetti Exec Chairwoman
Tel: 212-693-1525
Email: cbrunetti@rvminc.com
Website: www.rvminc.com
Litigation, litigation support, ediscovery, e-discovery, Information Governance, Managed Review, document review , ESI Processing , ESI Hosting, data hosting, Kcura, Relativity, clearwell, Predictive Coding, Legal, Litigation Consulting (Woman, estab 1996, empl 62, sales $15,000,000, cert: State, City, WBENC)

6184 Wall & Tong, LLP
25 James Way
Eatontown, NJ 07724
Contact: Robert Traina Business Mgr
Tel: 732-542-2280
Email: rtraina@walltong.com
Website: www.walltong.com
Patent, Trademark & related Intellectual Property Legal Services. (As-Pac, estab 2009, empl 15, sales $3,993,003, cert: CPUC)

6185 Wong Fleming
821 Alexander Rd, Ste 200
Princeton, NJ 08540
Contact: Linda Wong CEO
Tel: 609-951-9520
Email: lwong@wongfleming.com
Website: www.wongfleming.com
Employment Law, Civil Rights, Commercial Law, Real Estate, Education Law, Intellectual Property, and International Law. (Woman/As-Pac, estab 1994, empl 65, sales $2,590,897, cert: NMSDC, WBENC)

New Mexico

6186 Ortiz & Lopez, LLC
PO Box 4484
Albuquerque, NM 87196
Contact: Kermit Lopez Patent Attorney
Tel: 505-314-1312
Email: klopez@olpatentlaw.com
Website: www.olpatentlaw.com
Patent & other intellectual property legal services. (Hisp, estab 2001, empl 8, sales $1,000,000, cert: NMSDC)

New York

6187 A. Kershaw, PC//Attorneys & Consultants
161 Grove St, Ste 200
Tarrytown, NY 10591
Contact: Anne Kershaw Owner
Tel: 914-332-0438
Email: anne.kershaw@akershaw.com
Website: www.akershaw.com
Litigation management consulting, providing innovative and impartial analysis and recommendations for the management of all aspects of volume litigation. (Woman, estab 1999, empl 1, sales , cert: WBENC)

6188 B&N Legal Interpreting, Inc.
350 Fifth Ave, 59th Floor
New York, NY 10118
Contact: Livingston Buchanan President
Tel: 866-661-1053
Email: lbuchanan@bninterpreting.com
Website: www.bninterpreting.com
Provides interpreting, translation and sign language services to court reporting agencies, law firms, fortune 100 & 500 companies, individuals for all language needs. (AA, estab 2004, empl 2, sales , cert: City)

6189 Brune & Richard LLP
80 Broad St, 30th Fl
New York, NY 10004
Contact: Laurie Edelstein Managing Attorney, San Francisco Office
Tel: 212-668-1900
Email: info@brunelaw.com
Website: www.bruneandrichard.com
Securities fraud, breach of contract, trade secrets, intellectual property, successor liability, & consumer class actions. (Woman, estab 1998, empl 30, sales $15,000,000, cert: WBENC)

6190 Burgher Gray Jaffe LLP
535 Fifth Ave 16th Fl
New York, NY 10017
Contact: Ron Llewellyn Managing Partner
Tel: 646-513-3231
Email: rllewellyn@grayhaile.com
Website: www.burghergray.com
Boutique corporate law firm, corporate services & middle market transactions, partnership, stockholders & operating agreements, corporate governance & securities law advice, angel & venture capital investments, securities offerings, mergers, acquisitions, divestitures, joint ventures. (AA, estab 2006, empl 4, sales $360,000, cert: State, NMSDC)

6191 Complete Discovery Source Inc.
345 Park Ave Level B
New York, NY 10154
Contact: Bibi Bacchus
Tel: 212-813-7005
Email: bbacchus@cdslegal.com
Website: www.cdslegal.com
eDiscovery services, litigation support, and software supporting planning, early case assessment, information governance, processing and production, software, data analytics, review hosting, managed review, and cross-border. (As-Ind, estab , empl , sales $39,601,399, cert: City, NMSDC)

6192 David Carrie LLC
155 E 55th St Ste 4K
New York, NY 10022
Contact: Carrie Printz Managing Dir
Tel: 212-308-6560
Email:
Website: www.davidcarrie.com
Full-service legal search firm. (Woman, estab 2003, empl 7, sales , cert: WBENC)

6193 Drohan Lee LLP
489 Fifth Ave
New York, NY 10017
Contact: Vivian Drohan Partner
Tel: 212-710-0000
Email: vdrohan@dlkny.com
Website: www.dlkny.com
Boutique law firm with capabilities to provide legal services in corporate, contract transactions and litigation. (As-Pac, Hisp, estab 2007, empl 5, sales $1,400,000, cert: State, City)

6194 Frank, Frank, Goldstein & Nager, PC
330 West 38th St Ste 701
New York, NY 10018
Contact: Jocelyn Nager President
Tel: 212-686-0100
Email: jnager@ffgnesqs.com
Website: www.ffgnesqs.com
Collection of bad debt, commercial & consumer. (Woman, estab 2000, empl 12, sales $1,405,280, cert: City)

6195 Green Point Technology Services LLC
555 Theodore Fremd Ave Ste A102
Rye, NY 10580
Contact: Shirley Sharma President
Tel: 212-913-0500
Email: shirley@greenpointglobal.com
Website: www.greenpointglobal.com/
Legal and Compliance, Regulatory Tracking, Publishing & Editorial services, Software Development, Professional development. (Woman/As-Ind, estab 2001, empl 350, sales , cert: State)

6196 JG Advisory Services LLC
200 E 27th St
New York, NY 10016
Contact: Judith Gross Principal
Tel: 917-375-6852
Email: judy@jgadvisory.com
Website: www.jgadvisory.com
Specialty consulting related to hedge funds, legal/regulatory/compliance issues. (Woman, estab 2005, empl 1, sales $200,000, cert: City)

6197 Johnson Liebman, LLP
305 Broadway Ste 801
New York, NY 10007
Contact: Robert Johnson Partner
Tel: 212-619-6744
Email: robert.johnson@johnsonliebman.com
Website: www.johnsonliebman.com
Insurance defense firm, handle defense & subrogation cases. (AA, estab 1999, empl 6, sales $875,000, cert: City)

6198 Law Office of Marian Polovy
192 Lexington Ave, Ste 903
New York, NY 10016
Contact: Marian Polovy Owner
Tel: 212-696-0133
Email: marianpolovy@aol.com
Website: www.lawofficeofmarianpolovy.com

Law firm-trial attorneys, defense negligence, product liability, general liability, defense medical malpractice, employment law and general civil litigation. (Woman, estab 1983, empl 4, sales $635,382, cert: State, City)

6199 Lee Anav Chung White Kim Ruger & Richter LLP
156 Fifth Ave Ste 303
New York, NY 10010
Contact: Annie Chen Legal Asst
Tel: 212-271-0664
Email: anniechen@lacwkrr.com
Website: www.leeanavchung.com

Legal advice & representation on complex legal matters. (As-Pac, estab 2003, empl 30, sales $3,100,000, cert: NMSDC)

6200 Pittleman & Associates
336 E 43rd St
New York, NY 10017
Contact: Linda Pittleman Chairman
Tel: 212-370-9600
Email: lindap@pittlemanassociates.com
Website: www.pittlemanassociates.com

Placement of attorneys. (Woman/Hisp, estab 1993, empl 7, sales $1,625,000, cert: NMSDC)

6201 QuisLex, Inc.
126 E 56th St
New York, NY 10022
Contact: Adam Beschloss Exec Dir Client Solutions
Tel: 917-512-4447
Email: adam.beschloss@quislex.com
Website: www.quislex.com

Premier legal services, multi-shore capabilities. (As-Ind, estab 2004, empl 9, sales $30,500,000, cert: NMSDC)

6202 Rozario & Associates, P.C.
55 Broadway 20th Fl
New York, NY 10006
Contact: Rovin Rozario Managing Partner
Tel: 212-301-2770
Email: rrozario@rozariolaw.com
Website: www.rozariolaw.com

Provide superior client service, high-quality legal services. (AA, estab 2005, empl 9, sales $821,000, cert: NMSDC)

6203 Schoeman Updike Kaufman & Gerber LLP
551 Fifth Ave 12th Fl
New York, NY 10176
Contact: Beth L. Kaufman Managing Partner
Tel: 212-661-5030
Email: bkaufman@schoeman.com
Website: www.schoeman.com

Litigation (employment, commercial, personal injury and product liability) & real estate (commercial transactions and leasing, financing). (Woman/As-Pac, Hisp, estab 1969, empl 39, sales $5,054,048, cert: State, City)

6204 Silverman Shin & Byrne PLLC
88 Pine St, 22nd Fl
New York, NY 10005
Contact: Gerard Crowe Partner
Tel: 212-779-8600
Email: gcrowe@silverfirm.com
Website: www.silverfirm.com

Corporate/Commercial, Insurance/Tort defense. (Woman/AA, As-Pac, Hisp, estab 1986, empl 46, sales $9,188,231, cert: NMSDC)

6205 Yorkson Legal, Inc.
800 2nd Ave 804, 8th Fl
New York, NY 10017
Contact: Gail Reichwald Managing Dir
Tel: 212-265-1400
Email: greichwald@yorkson.com
Website: www.yorkson.com

Legal staffing & recruiting serves. (Woman, estab 2003, empl 10, sales $6,207,569, cert: WBENC)

6206 Younkins & Schecter LLP
420 Lexington Ave Ste 2050
New York, NY 10170
Contact: Mardi Schecter Partner
Tel: 212-286-0040
Email: mschecter@ys-law.com
Website: www.ys-law.com

Legal Counsel & Prosecution; Legal Services; Property Management Services; Real Estate Agents. (Woman, estab 1996, empl 12, sales , cert: City, WBENC)

Ohio

6207 Curtin & Associates, LLP
159 S Main St, Ste 920
Akron, OH 44308
Contact: Cynthia K. Curtin President
Tel: 330-376-7245
Email: dbudny@curtinlawfirm.com
Website: www.curtinlawfirm.com

Tort Litigation; emphasis on defense. (Woman, estab 2003, empl 9, sales $1,200,000, cert: WBENC)

6208 DCR Denmark Court Reporting Agency, LLC
810 Sycamore St, 3rd Fl
Cincinnati, OH 45202
Contact: Angela Denmark CEO
Tel: 513-254-8753
Email: angela@dcragency.com
Website: www.dcragency.com

Independent, freelance court reporting agency. (Woman/AA, estab 2006, empl 1, sales , cert: State)

6209 Giffen & Kaminski, LLC
1300 E Ninth St Ste 1600
Cleveland, OH 44114
Contact: Karen Giffen Partner
Tel: 216-621-5161
Email: kgiffen@thinkgk.com
Website: www.thinkgk.com

Legal Services; Arbitration; Mediation; Creditor's Rights; Business Torts; Criminal Defense; White Collar Criminal Defense; Employment Law; Employment Litigation; Immigration Law; Product Liability; Real Estate. (Woman, estab 2004, empl , sales , cert: WBENC)

6210 Litigation Management, Inc.
6000 Parkland Blvd
Mayfield Heights, OH 44124
Contact: Megan Pizor Exec Dir
Tel: 440-484-2000
Email: megan.pizor@lmiweb.com
Website: www.lmiweb.com
Comprehensive management & analysis: defense of claims, individual lawsuits, mass torts or class actions where health, illness or injury . (Woman, estab 1984, empl 600, sales , cert: WBENC)

6211 Perez & Morris LLC
8000 Ravine's Edge Ct, Ste 300
Columbus, OH 43235
Contact: Juan Jose Perez Partner
Tel: 614-431-1500
Email: jperez@perez-morris.com
Website: www.perez-morris.com
Legal services. (Hisp, estab 1997, empl 29, sales $2,350,000, cert: NMSDC)

6212 Safety Controls Technology Inc.
6993 Pearl Rd
Middleburg Heights, OH 44130
Contact: Annette Plavny GM
Tel: 440-449-6000
Email: APlavny@sct.us.com
Website: www.sct.us.com
Occupational Health & Safety Services. (Woman, estab 1999, empl 50, sales $500,000,000, cert: City, WBENC)

6213 Thacker Martinsek LPA
2330 One Cleveland Ctr 1375 E 9th St
Cleveland, OH 44114
Contact: John Larger President
Tel: 216-456-3840
Email: jlarger@TMLPA.com
Website: www.thackermartinsek.com
Business & commercial litigation, insurance recovery, litigation management, employment law, intellectual property & civil rights. (Woman, estab 2010, empl 33, sales $6,590,743, cert: WBENC)

6214 Walker & Jocke Co., LPA
231 S Broadway
Medina, OH 44256
Contact: Patricia A. Walker President
Tel: 330-721-0000
Email: paw@walkerandjocke.com
Website: www.walkerandjocke.com
Patents, trademarks & copyrights, infringement analysis, claim mitigation & infringement defense, IT agreements, software licensing, outsourcing agreements, electronic funds transfer agreements, hosting agreements & SaaS arrangements. (Woman, estab 1993, empl 13, sales $3,518,153, cert: WBENC, NWBOC)

Oregon

6215 Gordon & Polscer LLC
9755 SW Barnes Rd Ste 650
Portland, OR 97225
Contact: Diane Polscer Managing Partner
Tel: 503-242-2922
Email: dpolscer@gordon-polscer.com
Website: www.gordon-polscer.com
Represent insurers, corporate, business clients for: Insurance Coverage Advice & Litigation; Civil Litigation; Extra-contractual Claim Advice & Litigation; Class-Action Defense. (Woman, estab 0, empl , sales $5,253,027, cert: WBENC)

Pennsylvania

6216 Assigned Counsel Inc.
950 W Valley Rd Ste 2600
Wayne, PA 19087
Contact: Bob Murphy President
Tel: 610-964-8300
Email: nabrams@assignedcounsel.com
Website: www.assignedcounsel.com
Provide attorneys on a temporary, temp-to-perm and direct hire basis to corporate law departments, non-profit organizations, federal agencies, and law firms. (AA, estab , empl , sales $5,084,003, cert: NMSDC)

6217 Ellen Freeman Immigration Law Group
303 Timber Court
Pittsburgh, PA 15238
Contact: Ellen Freeman Managing Partner
Tel: 412-822-6500
Email: efreeman@freemanimmigration.com
Website: www.freemanimmigration.com
A full-service immigration law firm. (Woman, estab 2019, empl 4, sales $750,000, cert: WBENC)

6218 Griesing Law, LLC
1880 John F. Kennedy Boulevard Ste 1800
Philadelphia, PA 19103
Contact: Francine Griesing Managing Member
Tel: 215-618-3720
Email: fgriesing@griesinglaw.com
Website: www.griesinglaw.com
Complex business transactions & high stakes litigation. (Woman, estab 2010, empl 15, sales , cert: WBENC)

6219 JURISolutions, Inc.
1500 Joh F Kennedy Blvd Ste 1850
Philadelphia, PA 19102
Contact: Fawn Linn Operations
Tel: 215-383-3517
Email: flinn@jsl-hq.com
Website: www.jurisolutions.com
Legal services & recruitment. (Woman, estab 1997, empl 125, sales $14,085,967, cert: CPUC, WBENC)

LEGAL SERVICES

6220 Parrish Law Offices
       788 Washington Rd
       Pittsburgh, PA 15228
       Contact: Debra Parrish Partner
       Tel: 412-561-6250
       Email: debbie@dparrishlaw.com
       Website: www.dparrishlaw.com
Legal support for provider and beneficiary appeals of denied claims, Federal court litigation; appeals of post-payment overpayment determinations (Woman, estab 2000, empl 4, sales $833,635, cert: WBENC)

6221 Summit Court Reporting, Inc.
       1500 Market St 12th Fl - East Tower
       Philadelphia, PA 19102
       Contact: Yvette Samuel President
       Tel: 215-665-5633
       Email: ysamuel@summitreporting.com
       Website: www.summitreporting.com
Court Reporting & Legal Video & Videoconference Services. (Woman, estab 1993, empl 4, sales $958,498, cert: State)

6222 The Axelrod Firm, PC
       1125 Walnut St
       Philadelphia, PA 19107
       Contact: Sheryl Axelrod President
       Tel: 215-461-1768
       Email: saxelrod@theaxelrodfirm.com
       Website: www.theaxelrodfirm.com
Assist individuals, businesses and non-profit organizations with appellate, commercial, real estate, estate planning and bodily injury / product liability lawsuit needs. (Woman, estab 2007, empl 4, sales $386,272, cert: State, WBENC)

6223 Tiagha & Associates, Ltd.
       2112 Walnut St
       Philadelphia, PA 19103
       Contact: Kahiga Tiagha Attorney At Law
       Tel: 215-543-7970
       Email: info@tiaghalaw.com
       Website: www.tiaghalaw.com
Corporate & Real Estate transactional services. (AA, estab 2009, empl 7, sales , cert: NMSDC)

6224 Walker Nell Partners Inc.
       1515 Market St, Ste 820
       Philadelphia, PA 19102
       Contact: Wayne Walker CEO
       Tel: 215-569-1660
       Email: WalkerNell@walkerNell.com
       Website: www.WalkerNell.com
Litigation Support & Insolvency, Restructuring, Valuation & Fiduciary Services; Accounting. (AA, estab 2004, empl 7, sales $249,000, cert: City, NMSDC)

Puerto Rico

6225 Del Toro & Santana
       Plaza 273, Ste 900
       San Juan, PR 00917
       Contact: Roberto Santana Sr Partner
       Tel: 787-754-8700
       Email: rsantana@dtslaw.com
       Website: www.dtslaw.com
Litigation & counseling. (Hisp, estab 1984, empl 12, sales $1,400,000, cert: NMSDC)

6226 Estrella LLC
       PO Box 9023596
       San Juan, PR 00902
       Contact: Alberto Estrella Managing Member
       Tel: 787-977-5050
       Email: agestrella@estrellallc.com
       Website: www.estrellallc.com
Legal Services. (Hisp, estab 1974, empl 31, sales $4,622,484, cert: NMSDC)

6227 Fiddler Gonzalez & Rodriguez, PSC
       PO Box 363507
       San Juan, PR 00936
       Contact: Kenneth Bury General Admin
       Tel: 787-759-3145
       Email: kcbury@fgrlaw.com
       Website: www.fgrlaw.com
Full-service law firm with well established practice areas encompassing nearly all areas of law. With over 100 lawyers, the firm is one of the largest in the Caribbean and Latin America. (Hisp, estab 1932, empl 209, sales , cert: NMSDC)

Texas

6228 Akula & Associates, P.C.
       4835 LBJ Freeway Ste 750
       Dallas, TX 75244
       Contact: Kavitha Akula Marketing Mgr
       Tel: 972-241-4698
       Email: kavitha.akula@akulalaw.com
       Website: www.akulalaw.com
Intellectual Property Business & Transactional Law. (Minority, Woman, estab 2007, empl 9, sales $500,000, cert: State)

6229 Bennett Law Office, PC
       132 W Main St
       Lewisville, TX 75057
       Contact: Tamera H. Bennett President
       Tel: 972-436-8141
       Email: info@tbennettlaw.com
       Website: www.tbennettlaw.com
Intellectual Property Law, Trademark Law, Copyright Law, Entertainment Law. (Woman, estab 2001, empl 2, sales , cert: State)

6230 Brewer & Lormand, PLLC
      5910 N Central Expressway, Ste 730
      Dallas, TX 75206
      Contact: Ruth Brewer Managing Partner
      Tel: 214-420-6001
      Email: rbrewer@brewerlormand.com
      Website: www.brewerlormand.com
Legal Services, Attorneys, Lawyers. (Woman, estab 2008, empl 11, sales $1,140,687, cert: State, WBENC)

6231 Callier & Garza, L.L.P.
      4900 Woodway, Ste 700
      Houston, TX 77056
      Contact: Bernardo Garza Partner
      Tel: 713-439-0248
      Email: garza@callierandgarza.com
      Website: www.callierandgarza.com
The firm specializes in representing large entities, private and government, insured and self insured, in State and Federal co urtsin the following areas: (1) Employment Litigation (including age, gender, race, ADA and FLA (AA, Hisp, estab 1985, empl 8, sales $1,650,000, cert: State, NMSDC)

6232 Carter Scholer Arnett Hamada & Mockler PLLC
      8150 N Central Expressway Ste 500
      Dallas, TX 75206
      Contact: Helen Gilliland Partner
      Tel: 214-550-8188
      Email: helen@carterscholer.com
      Website: www.carterscholer.com
Legal Services (Woman/AA, As-Ind, As-Pac, estab 2012, empl 14, sales $6,000,000, cert: NMSDC)

6233 Cluso Investigation LLC
      4500 Mercantile Plaza Dr Ste 106
      Fort Worth, TX 76137
      Contact: Sharon Sutila CEO
      Tel: 817-422-2289
      Email: ssutila@cluso.com
      Website: www.cluso.com
Provides comprehensive reports for fraud prevention, asset recovery, collection, skip tracing, litigation & employment screening. (Woman, estab 2008, empl 10, sales $923,433, cert: State, WBENC)

6234 ELS ESQ. LLC
      400 N Ervay St No. 131612
      Dallas, TX 75201
      Contact: E. Lynette Stone Attorney
      Tel: 972-383-9499
      Email: inquire@elsesq.com
      Website: www.elsesq.com
Legal services (commercial litigation). (Woman/AA, estab 2008, empl 1, sales $150,000, cert: WBENC)

6235 Estes Thorne Ewing & Payne PLLC
      3811 Turtle Creek Blvd. Ste 2000
      Dallas, TX 75219
      Contact: Lisa Bys Dir of Administration
      Tel: 214-599-4000
      Email: lbys@estesthorne.com
      Website: www.estesthorne.com
Legal Services. (Woman, estab 2008, empl 21, sales $5,000,000, cert: WBENC)

6236 Farrow-Gillespie & Heath LLP
      1700 Pacific Ave Ste 3700
      Dallas, TX 75201
      Contact: Liza Farrow-Gillespie Managing Partner
      Tel: 214-361-5600
      Email: liza@fghlaw.net
      Website: www.fghlaw.com
Employment law; employment litigation and arbitration defense; internal employment investigations; internal audits; employee handbooks; contract preparation and review; personal injury defense; advertising (Woman, estab 2007, empl 22, sales $1,761,000, cert: CPUC, WBENC)

6237 Henjum Goucher Reporting Services, LP
      2777 N Stemmons Fwy, Ste 1025
      Dallas, TX 75207
      Contact: Kristin Neerhof Dir Business Dev
      Tel: 214-521-1188
      Email: kneerhof@hglitigation.com
      Website: www.hglitigation.com
Deposition provider with over 35 years in the litigation support industry. (Woman, estab 1979, empl 33, sales , cert: WBENC)

6238 Janik Vinnakota LLP
      8111 LBJ Freeway, Ste 790
      Dallas, TX 75251
      Contact: Shelbye Harbour Office Admin
      Tel: 214-390-9999
      Email: sharbour@jvllp.com
      Website: www.jvllp.com
Litigation Services, State and Federal for intellectual property, business, and contract disputes, Business Legal Services, Business Formation, Contracts and Legal Agreements, Business Liability Consulting and Diligence. (Minority, estab 2016, empl 7, sales $950,000, cert: State, NMSDC)

6239 Lehtola & Cannatti PLLC
      5001 Spring Valley Rd, Ste 400 E
      Dallas, TX 75244
      Contact: Patricia Lehtola Managing Member
      Tel: 972-383-1515
      Email: plehtola@lc-lawfirm.com
      Website: www.lc-lawfirm.com
Legal services. (Minority, Woman, estab 0, empl , sales , cert: NMSDC)

6240 Lindsay Law
      11700 Preston Rd, Ste 660-167
      Dallas, TX 75230
      Contact: John Lindsay Principal Attorney
      Tel: 214-736-4306
      Email: supplier@inventiveiplaw.com
      Website: www.inventiveiplaw.com
Provides intellectual property law services, namely patent, copyright, trademark, and technology services. The firm focuses on the legal aspects of analysis, protection. (AA, estab 2009, empl 2, sales , cert: CPUC)

LEGAL SERVICES 6241-6250

6241 Owens Hervey PLLC
      901 Main St, Ste 3612
      Dallas, TX 75202
      Contact: Maurice Owens Jr Member
      Tel: 214-741-2288
      Email: mowens@owenshervey.com
      Website: www.owenshervey.com
Civil litigation & trial experience. (AA, estab 2008, empl 3, sales $254,446, cert: State)

6242 Reeves & Brightwell LLP
      221 W 6th St
      Austin, TX 78701
      Contact: Beverly Reeves President
      Tel: 512-334-4501
      Email: breeves@reevesbrightwell.com
      Website: www.reevesbrightwell.com
Commercial Litigation firm. (Woman, estab 0, empl , sales , cert: WBENC)

6243 State Tax Group, LLC
      5050 Quorum Dr, Ste 700
      Dallas, TX 75254
      Contact: Richard Fleming
      Tel: 972-492-9841
      Email: rfleming@statetaxgroup.com
      Website: www.statetaxgroup.com
State audit representation, sales tax compliance review, tax refund reviews, litigation support, dispute resolution, sampling analysis & evaluation, voluntary disclosures. (AA, estab 2005, empl 4, sales $518,000, cert: NMSDC)

6244 Stratos Legal Services
      4299 San Felipe, Ste 350
      Houston, TX 77027
      Contact: Bert Farris Exec. VP
      Tel: 713-481-2180
      Email: bfarris@stratoslegal.com
      Website: www.stratoslegal.com
Litigation support: court reporting, videography, interpreters, records retrieval, process serving, and electronic discovery. (Woman/Hisp, estab 2005, empl 40, sales $8,100,000, cert: WBENC)

6245 The Law Office of Kathryn N Karam
      2200 Southwest Frwy Ste 400
      Houston, TX 77098
      Contact: Kathryn Karam President
      Tel: 832-582-0620
      Email: katie@immisolver.com
      Website: www.immisolver.com
Law firm: internal I-9 audit, immigration liabilities of a merger or acquisition. (Woman, estab 2013, empl 4, sales , cert: WBENC)

6246 The Marker Group, Inc.
      13105 Northwest Frwy
      Houston, TX 77040
      Contact: Hillary Johnson GM
      Tel: 713-460-9070
      Email: supplierdiversity@marker-group.com
      Website: www.marker-group.com
Litigation support services, medical record (MR) collection, MR retrieval, MR review, record analysis, reprographics, scanning, subpoenas, litigation management, chronologies, oral despositions, evidentiary chain of custody, real time reporting. (Woman, estab 1985, empl 289, sales $33,542,107, cert: WBENC)

6247 We Muv U, LLC
      3948 Legacy Dr Ste 106
      Plano, TX 75023
      Contact: Jessica Oliver Dir
      Tel: 214-208-1313
      Email: jessica@wmull.com
      Website: www.wmull.com
Manage trial logistics for corporations in a manner that minimizes cost and maximizes desired productivity. (AA, estab 2014, empl 5, sales $225,000, cert: NMSDC)

Virginia

6248 Gavin Law Offices, PLC
      2500 Gaskins Rd, Ste B
      Richmond, VA 23238
      Contact: Pamela Gavin Managing Member
      Tel: 804-784-4427
      Email: pgavin@gavinlawoffices.com
      Website: www.gavinlawoffices.com
Legal services, intellectual property (transfers, licensing, protection, enforcement, commercial transactional services, entertainment focused legal services, litigation, trademark preclearance and prosecution, managing trademark portfolios. (Woman, estab 2004, empl 9, sales $1,345,216, cert: State, WBENC)

6249 Guidance Law Firm, P.C.
      440 Monticello Ave, Ste 1834
      Norfolk, VA 23510
      Contact: Lamont Maddox President
      Tel: 757-454-2045
      Email: lmaddox@guidancelaw.com
      Website: www.guidancelaw.com
Legal services, contract review, contract drafting, document review, regulatory compliance, corporate governance, policy drafting, policy review, corporate transactions, general business law, negotiations, settlements, consulting. (AA, estab 2010, empl 1, sales , cert: State, NMSDC)

Washington

6250 Focal PLLC
      900 1st Ave S, Ste 201
      Seattle, WA 98134
      Contact: Venkat Balasubramani Owner/Partner
      Tel: 206-718-4250
      Email: info@focallaw.com
      Website: www.focallaw.com
Boutique law firm specializing in internet and technology-related issues. (As-Ind, estab 2009, empl 11, sales $666,153, cert: NMSDC)

6251   Mayner Business Law, P.S.
       19495 SE 57th Pl
       Issaquah, WA 98027
       Contact: Andrea Mayner Owner
       Tel: 425-996-7335
       Email: andrea@maynerlaw.com
       Website: www.maynerlaw.com
Legal services. (Woman, estab 2008, empl 1, sales $287,385, cert: WBENC)

Wisconsin

6252   Bell & Manning, LLC
       2801 W Beltline Hwy Ste 210
       Madison, WI 53713
       Contact: Callie Bell Shareholder
       Tel: 608-661-3590
       Email: cbell@bellmanning.com
       Website: www.bellmanning.com/
Intellectual property, with an emphasis on U.S. and international patents. (Woman, estab 2010, empl 6, sales $1,312,916, cert: WBENC)

6253   JAC Consulting LLC dba The Champagne Group
       2233 N Summit Ave Ste 315
       Milwaukee, WI 53202
       Contact: Jacquie Champagne President
       Tel: 414-704-0602
       Email: jacquie@champagnegrp.com
       Website: www.champagnegrp.com
Executive search, legal services. (Woman, estab 2015, empl 1, sales , cert: WBENC)

6254   Midwest Legal and eData Services, Inc.
       7625 S Howell Ave
       Oak Creek, WI 53154
       Contact: Shawn Olley Owner
       Tel: 414-764-2772
       Email: solley@mwedata.com
       Website: www.mwedata.com
Provides experienced paralegals on an as-needed basis charged at an hourly rate. (Woman, estab 1989, empl , sales , cert: WBENC)

MATERIAL HANDLING EQUIPMENT

Manufacturers or distributors of handtrucks, hoists, dollies, conveyors, racks, forklifts, etc. (See also HARDWARE & TOOLS, HYDRAULIC & COMPRESSED AIR EQUIPMENT, INDUSTRIAL EQUIPMENT & SUPPLIES and INDUSTRIAL MACHINES. NAICS Code 42

Alabama

6255 Southeastern Conveyor Services, Inc.
870 Minor Pkwy
Birmingham, AL 35224
Contact: Stephanie Weeks President
Tel: 205-785-6884
Email: stephanie.weeks@southeasternconveyorservices.com
Website: www.southeasternconveyorservices.com
Conveyor solutions for all types of conveyor systems, belt sales, belt vulcanizing, change-outs and replacement, mechanical splices, new installations, wiper replacements, roller change-outs. (Woman, estab 2014, empl 15, sales $1,800,000, cert: WBENC)

6256 Springer Equipment Co., Inc.
4263 Underwood Industrial Dr
Birmingham, AL 35210
Contact: Annette Springer CEO
Tel: 205-951-3675
Email: annettes@springerequip.com
Website: www.SpringerEquipment.com
New & used forklift equipment sales, service, parts rentals & leasing. (Woman, estab 1992, empl 52, sales $19,225,692, cert: WBENC)

California

6257 Bench-Tek Solutions, LLC
525 Aldo Ave
Santa Clara, CA 95054
Contact: Maria Castellon CEO
Tel: 408-653-1100
Email: mcastellon@bench-tek.com
Website: www.bench-tek.com
Custom workbenches, materials handling & storage. (Minority, Woman, estab , empl , sales $4,000,000, cert: NMSDC, WBENC)

6258 Can Lines Engineering
9839 Downey-Norwalk Rd
Downey, CA 90241
Contact: Erik Koplien
Tel: 800-233-4597
Email: erik.koplien@canlines.com
Website: www.canlines.com
Engineer, design, fabricate, install & service container & material operational & conveying systems. (Hisp, estab 1960, empl 100, sales , cert: NMSDC)

6259 ELA Enterprises
1813 Lexington Dr
Fullerton, CA 92835
Contact: President
Tel: 714-738-0397
Email: info@elaent.com
Website: www.elaent.com
Design & mfr custom material handling solutions: dollies, service carts, platform trucks, hand trucks, electric tugs, tow vehicles, trailers, food containers, packaging for transportation & storage solutions. (Minority, Woman, estab 2006, empl 2, sales $115,000, cert: CPUC, WBENC)

6260 McMurray-Stern Inc.
15511 Carmenita Rd
Santa Fe Springs, CA 90670
Contact: Edward Stern Design Consultant
Tel: 562-623-3000
Email: pferro@mcstern.com
Website: www.mcmurraystern.com
Design build specialty contractor offering storage, work space and records management solutions, warehouse & industrial racking, storage systems & material handling equipment. (Woman, estab 1984, empl 50, sales $16,000,000, cert: CPUC, WBENC)

6261 Quality Material Handling
900 W Foothill Blvd
Azusa, CA 91702
Contact: Hector Pinto President
Tel: 626-812-9722
Email: info@qmhinc.com
Website: www.qmhinc.com
Material handling equipment distribution & services, pallet racking, boltless shelving, yard ramps, warehouse racks, pallet rack installation, city permits, high pile & fire permits. (Hisp, estab 1991, empl 40, sales , cert: CPUC)

Colorado

6262 Advanced Manufacturing Technology For Bottles, Inc
3920 Patton Ave
Loveland, CO 80538
Contact: Jamie Maier Accounting
Tel: 970-612-0315
Email: jmaier@amtcolorado.com
Website: www.amtcolorado.com
Mfr conveyor systems, integrated systems, conveyors, controls & mechanical & electrical installation services, primarily for the packaging industry. (Woman, estab 1996, empl 57, sales , cert: WBENC)

Connecticut

6263 Warner Specialty Products, Inc.
40-B Montowese Ave
North Haven, CT 06473
Contact: Jack Norton VP
Tel: 203-691-9030
Email: amy@warnerspecialty.com
Website: www.warnerspecialty.com
Dist material handling & ergonomic equipment solutions. (Woman, estab 1991, empl 8, sales $4,228,000, cert: WBENC)

Florida

6264 Teknia Networks & Logistics, Inc.
10451 66th St N
Pinellas Park, FL 33782
Contact: Jorge Monsalve President
Tel: 813-918-8417
Email: laura@teknialogistics.com
Website: www.TEKNIANETWORKS.COM
Rent machinery, copiers, printers, material handling machines, forklifts, racking systems, power generators. (Hisp, estab 2010, empl 10, sales $5,000,000, cert: NMSDC)

6265 The Bernd Group Inc.
1251 Pinehurst Rd
Dunedin, FL 34698
Contact: Pilar Bernd President
Tel: 727-733-0122
Email: businessdevelopment@berndgroup.com
Website: www.berndgroup.com
Material handling equip, safety products, hand & power tools, pumps & compressors, motors, generators, electrical hardware, batteries, lighting fixtures, lockers, bins, shelving, lab equip. (Minority, Woman, estab 1992, empl 66, sales , cert: NMSDC)

6266 TriFactor Solutions, LLC
2401 Drane Field Rd
Lakeland, FL 33811
Contact: JJ Phelan Managing Member
Tel: 863-646-9671
Email: jjphelan@trifactor.com
Website: www.trifactor.com
Material handling systems, services, parts & integrations: conveyors, racking, palletizers, diverters, storage systems, pallets, work stations. (Woman, estab 2007, empl 25, sales $756,831, cert: State, WBENC)

Georgia

6267 Atlanta Caster & Equipment
1810-E Auger Dr
Tucker, GA 30084
Contact: John Brumbaugh Govt Sales Mgr
Tel: 770-492-0682
Email: atlantacaster@atlantacaster.com
Website: www.atlantacaster.com
Dist casters, wheels & non-powered material handling equipment. (Woman, estab 1986, empl 8, sales $2,010,000, cert: WBENC)

6268 Material Handling Inc.
PO Box 1045
Dalton, GA 30722
Contact: William Gleaton CFO
Tel: 706-278-1104
Email: billgleaton@mhiusa.net
Website: www.mhiusa.net
New & used lift trucks, lift truck parts, service, maintenance, rental & leasing. (As-Ind, estab 1975, empl 93, sales $33,707,229, cert: NMSDC)

Illinois

6269 Kamflex Conveyor Corporation
2312 Oak Leaf St
Joliet, IL 60436
Contact: Grant Branch III President
Tel: 800-323-2440
Email: gbranch@kamflex.com
Website: www.kamflex.org
Mfr sanitary machinery: conveyors (bucket, trough, vertical lift & conveyors), robotic integration (product picking and assembly, case packing vision guided), palletizers, stretch wrappers, case erectors. (AA, estab 1974, empl 72, sales $13,000,000, cert: NMSDC)

6270 Midway Industrial Equipment Inc..
660 Heartland Dr
Sugar Grove, IL 60554
Contact: Dawn Adams President
Tel: 630-466-7700
Email: dawn@midwaylift.com
Website: www.midwaylift.com
Material Handling Services, sales, service, rental & parts for forklifts, scrubbers, aerial. (Minority, Woman, estab 2003, empl 42, sales $11,200,000, cert: State)

6271 Stevenson Crane Service, Inc.
410 Stevenson Dr
Bolingbrook, IL 60440
Contact: John Edmonson President
Tel: 630-972-9199
Email: john@stevensoncrane.com
Website: www.stevensoncrane.com
Material handling equipment: truck cranes, carrydeck cranes, crawler cranes, rough terrain cranes, material & personnel hoists, material handlers, scissor lifts & boom lifts. (Woman, estab 1989, empl 85, sales $17,779,999, cert: WBENC)

Indiana

6272 Handling Technologies, Inc.
51024 Portage Rd
South Bend, IN 46628
Contact: Randy Trowbridge Natl Acct Mgr
Tel: 706-495-7683
Email: rtrowbridge@handlingtechnologies.com
Website: www.handlingtechnologies.com
Dist material handling products - shelving, racking systems, decking, conveyor systems, shop equipment (i.e., carts, bins, tables, hoists). (Woman, estab 1982, empl 10, sales $5,000,000, cert: WBENC)

6273 Harriman Material Handling
511 N Range Line Rd
Morristown, IN 46161
Contact: Ashley Larochelle President
Tel: 765-763-8985
Email: ashlar@harrimanmaterialhandling.com
Website: www.HarrimanMaterialHandling.com
Overhead Cranes, Hoists, Jib Cranes, Monorails, Gantry Cranes, Custom Lifting Devices, Slings/Rigging, Fall Protection Equipment, Crane Components & Parts, Dock Equipment, Storage Equipment, Drum Handling Equipment (Woman, estab 2004, empl 5, sales $3,528,300, cert: WBENC)

MATERIAL HANDLING EQUIPMENT

6274 Meyer Material Handling Products Inc.
PO Box 47366
Indianapolis, IN 46247
Contact: Carolyn F. Meyer Chairman
Tel: 317-786-9214
Email: cfmeyer@meyermat.com
Website: www.meyermat.com
Material handling equipment. (Woman, estab 1974, empl 11, sales , cert: WBENC)

Michigan

6275 Dynamic Conveyor Corp
5980 Grand Haven Rd
Muskegon, MI 49441
Contact: Tracy Powers Business Devel
Tel: 800-640-6850
Email: tpowers@dynamicconveyor.com
Website: www.dynamicconveyor.com
Quality built radius turns, metal detection, clean room, water tanks, cooling fans, box filling, split belt, ergonomic tilt, etc. (Woman, estab 1991, empl 24, sales $5,700,000, cert: WBENC)

6276 ECI Unlimited, Inc.
110 Trealout Dr Ste 102
Fenton, MI 48430
Contact: Lance Stokes President
Tel: 810-354-2775
Email: powertrain@ecienv.com
Website: www.ecipowertrain.webs.com
Install & refurbish material handling & machine loading & unloading equipment: chain conveyors, roller conveyors, pallet conveyors, accumulating conveyors, overhead conveyors, inverted conveyors, skillet conveyors, assembly machines. (AA, estab 1993, empl 4, sales , cert: NMSDC)

6277 Econobuild, LLC
21060 Bridge St
Southfield, MI 48033
Contact: Ramiro Salazar Managing Member
Tel: 248-799-7500
Email: rsalazar@econobuild.com
Website: www.econobuild.com
Material handling equip: flow-thru racks, rack systems, industrial carts, fork-free environment, plant engineering, facility improvements. (As-Pac, estab 1999, empl 15, sales $3,100,000, cert: NMSDC)

6278 Jarvis Handling Equipment Co.
PO Box 140767
Grand Rapids, MI 49514
Contact: Susan Smith President
Tel: - -
Email: ssmith@jarvishandling.com
Website: www.jarvishandling.com
Dist material handling equipment: racks, containers, modular offices mezzanines, and all basics and essentials, i.e. pallet trucks, carts, drum dumpers, lockers, work benches, etc. (Woman, estab 1966, empl 1, sales $1,010,000, cert: WBENC)

6279 Kenowa Industries
11405 E Lakewood Blvd
Holland, MI 49424
Contact: Dan Houle Sales Mgr
Tel: 616-392-7080
Email: dan.houle@kenowa.com
Website: www.kenowa.com
Fabricate material handling racks, baskets, workstations, containers, work-in-process carts, dollies, signboards, mezzanines, steel containers, tubs, steel skids, steel pallets, stands, shelf units. (Hisp, estab 1979, empl 26, sales $3,964,542, cert: NMSDC)

6280 Quality Design Services, Inc.
3914 Highwood Pl
Okemos, MI 48864
Contact: Ashish Manek Business Dev Mgr
Tel: 614-946-4749
Email: ashish.manek@qdsautomation.com
Website: www.qdsautomation.com
System Integration: Engine Assembly Lines, Transmission Assembly Lines, Axle Assembly Lines, Transfer Machines, Test Systems, Washers, Conveyor Systems, Hydraulic Systems, Lubrication Systems. (As-Ind, estab 1990, empl 22, sales , cert: NMSDC)

6281 Technical Conveyor Group, Inc.
5918 Meridian Blvd, Ste 2
Brighton, MI 48116
Contact: Rob Tarrien President
Tel: 810-229-5811
Email: rtarrien@tcginc.org
Website: www.tcginc.org
Material handling systems: floor conveyors, overhead/inverted power & free systems, chain-on-edge systems, AGV, electrified monorails, indexing systems, AS/AR systems. (Nat Ame, estab 2000, empl 5, sales $650,956, cert: NMSDC)

6282 Ultimation Industries LLC
27930 Groesbeck Hwy
Roseville, MI 48066
Contact: Jacqueline Canny CEO
Tel: 586-771-1881
Email: jcanny@ultimationinc.com
Website: www.ultimationinc.com
Design, mfr & install assembly line equipment & services, automation devices & conveyor systems, tire & wheel mounting & inflation devices, tire processing lines, TPMS & soaping machines. (Woman, estab 1989, empl 14, sales $4,855,120, cert: WBENC)

6283 Valmec Inc.
1274 S Holly Rd
Fenton, MI 48430
Contact: Krystn Tatus CEO
Tel: 810-629-8750
Email: valmec@comcast.net
Website: www.valmecinc.com
Material handling & packaging, conveyors, returnable packaging, installation, tear-outs & complete system integration. (Woman, estab 1971, empl 5, sales $1,344,664, cert: WBENC)

Minnesota

6284 J & B Equipment Company, Inc.
8200 Grand Ave S
Bloomington, MN 55420
Contact: David Heggem VP/COO
Tel: 952-884-2040
Email: office@jbeq.com
Website: www.jbeq.com
Design & sell engineered overhead crane & monorail systems; hoists; lift tables; specialty carts; and engineered ergonomic material handling systems. (AA, As-Pac, estab 1961, empl 10, sales , cert: NMSDC)

Missouri

6285 C&B Lift Truck Service, Inc.
6250 Knox Industrial Dr
High Ridge, MO 63049
Contact: Melinda Barbaglia Owner
Tel: 314-781-5438
Email: sales@cbforklift.com
Website: www.cbforklift.com
Dist & service forklifts, aerial/scissor lifts, sweepers, scrubbers, golf carts, dollies, dock equipment, warehouse & distribution equipment (Woman, estab 1976, empl 12, sales $1,000,000, cert: State)

6286 Millennium Industrial Equipment, LLC
1475 Legacy Circle
Fenton, MO 63026
Contact: Tony Estopare President
Tel: 314-574-2047
Email: testopare@miequipment.com
Website: www.miequipment.com
Bulk Solids (Dry) Material Handling, Air Handling, and Air Pollution Control Equipment. (As-Pac, estab 2002, empl 4, sales $630,862, cert: State)

6287 Warehouse One Inc.
7800 E 12th St
Kansas City, MO 64126
Contact: Mary L Jacoby President
Tel: 816-255-2250
Email: garys@wh1.com
Website: www.wh1.com
Dist lifts, hoists, conveyors, racks, cabinets, storage, furniture, work benches, lockers, file cabinets, ladders, shelving, bins, casters, industrial compactors, dock boards, ramps, dollies, platform trucks, etc. (Woman, estab , empl , sales $12,000,000, cert: WBENC)

North Carolina

6288 Guna Enterprises, Inc.
1104 Commercial Ave
Charlotte, NC 28205
Contact: Sales
Tel: 704-358-8787
Email: info@gandrcasters.com
Website: www.gandrcasters.com
Mfr industrial, institutional, special & custom made casters, wheels & floor locks. (Woman/As-Ind, estab 1994, empl 60, sales $2,400,000, cert: State)

6289 MYCA Material Handling Solutions, Inc.
223 E. Chatham St, Ste 102
Cary, NC 27511
Contact: Maria Ezell CFO
Tel: 919-378-9409
Email: mezell@mycagroup.com
Website: www.mycamaterialhandling.com
Material handling equipment, lift trucks, safety programs & safety equipment, training, warehouse systems, conveyor systems. (Woman, estab , empl , sales $4,600,000, cert: WBENC)

6290 WARP Services, LLC
1316 Providence Rd
Charlotte, NC 28207
Contact: Dr. Patrick LaRive CEO
Tel: 888-547-9277
Email: patrick@warprobotics.com
Website: www.warprobotics.com
Intall, repair & replace conveyors, motors, compressors, electrical safety equipment, material handling, industrial robotics, laser navigation, anything mechanical or electrical. (Woman/AA, estab 2005, empl 4, sales $298,000, cert: State, NWBOC)

New Jersey

6291 Hu-Lift Equipment
400 Apgar Dr, Unit F
Somerset, NJ 08873
Contact: Ming Gang Guo Mgr
Tel: 908-874-5585
Email: mgguo@hu-liftusa.com
Website: www.hu-liftusa.com
Dist material handling products: lift table, cart, platform trucks, furniture movers, skid lifters, highlifts, scale jacks, hydraulic jacks, skates,
pallet trucks, industrial class portable air conditioners, pallet tilters, forklift jacks. (As-Pac, estab 1999, empl 5, sales , cert: State)

Ohio

6292 Caster Connection, Inc.
2380 International St
Columbus, OH 43228
Contact: Joe Lyden Dir of Sales
Tel: 800-544-8978
Email: joe.lyden@casterconnection.com
Website: www.casterconnection.com
Mfr & dist institutional & industrial casters and wheels, hand trucks, pallet jacks, dollies & manual materials handling products. (Minority, Woman, estab 1987, empl 36, sales , cert: WBENC)

6293 Darana Hybrid
345 High St, STE 510
Hamilton, OH 45011
Contact: Darryl Cuttell CEO
Tel: 513-785-7540
Email: development@daranahybrid.com
Website: www.daranahybrid.com
Industrial electrical & mechanical installations of processing, packaging, and conveyor equipment systems and machinery for the food & beverage industry. (Nat Ame, estab 1995, empl 50, sales , cert: NMSDC)

MATERIAL HANDLING EQUIPMENT

6294 WHM Equipment Co.
11775 Enterprise Ave
Cincinnati, OH 45241
Contact: Joan Morgan President
Tel: 513-771-3200
Email: joan@whmequipment.com
Website: www.whmequipment.com
Design, fabricate & assemble conveyors & material handling systems. (Woman, estab 1968, empl 12, sales $1,920,869, cert: WBENC)

Pennsylvania

6295 Shingle Belting
420 Drew Court
King of Prussia, PA 19406
Contact: Bob Frasetto
Tel: 610-239-6667
Email: bfrasetto@shinglebelting.com
Website: www.shinglebelting.com
Dist industrial conveyors & power transmission belting. (Woman, estab 1979, empl 31, sales , cert: WBENC)

Tennessee

6296 Kenco Group
2001 Riverside Dr
Chattanooga, TN 37406
Contact: Lindsey Shrader Business Dev Mgr
Tel: 706-766-9554
Email: lindsey.shrader@kencogroup.com
Website: www.kencogroup.com
Fleet management program, material handling fleet, regardless of OEM, we offer battery and charger maintenance. (Woman, estab 1950, empl 5737, sales $947,075,000, cert: WBENC)

Texas

6297 Design Associates International, Inc
11615 Forest Central Dr, Ste 101
Dallas, TX 75243
Contact: Lucia Fredenburgh President
Tel: 214-720-6083
Email: luciaf@daiinc.com
Website: www.daiinc.com
Dist materials handling equipment: casters, wheels, carts, dollies, hand trucks, facilities planning & design. (Woman/Hisp, estab 1994, empl 8, sales $1,250,000, cert: State)

6298 Mighty Lift Inc.
PO Box 14998
Houston, TX 77221
Contact: Helen Fu President
Tel: 713-668-0263
Email: helenfu@mightylift.com
Website: www.mightylift.com
Dist pallet jacks, lifting tables, hand trucks, casters and wheels, wire containers, wire partitions, pallet racks & guard rails, electric personnel & burden carriers & scooters. (Minority, Woman, estab 2002, empl 15, sales $4,042,931, cert: State, NMSDC, WBENC)

6299 Permian Machinery Movers Inc.
2200 W Interstate 20
Odessa, TX 79763
Contact: Robert M. Chavez President
Tel: 432-333-1777
Email: robert@permianmachineryinc.com
Website: www.permianmachineryinc.com
Dist, rent & lease forklifts. (Hisp, estab 1981, empl 45, sales $11,100,000, cert: State)

6300 Texas Storage Systems
PO Box 751632
Houston, TX 77075
Contact: Karen Cato Owner
Tel: 713-991-1089
Email: tssinc@ymail.com
Website: www.catoindustries.com
Material handling & warehouse equipment. (Woman/AA, estab 2010, empl 5, sales $100,000, cert: State)

Washington

6301 Washington Liftruck
700 S Chicago
Seattle, WA 98108
Contact: Jeff Darling VP
Tel: 206-762-2040
Email: darling@forkliftsamerica.com
Website: www.washingtonlift.com
Dist forklifts & material handling equipment. (Woman, estab 1973, empl 34, sales $21,260,000, cert: City, WBENC)

> **MEASURING INSTRUMENTS**
> Manufacturers and distributors of counters and timers, X-ray spectrometers, voltage and frequency indicators, gas analyzers, thermocouples, thermometers, etc. (See also ELECTRONIC categories and HARDWARE & TOOLS). NAICS Code 42

Alabama

6302 Technical Maintenance, Inc.
 117 Jetplex Circle, Ste C4
 Madison, AL 35758
 Contact: Scott Chamberlain Quality Mgr
 Tel: 256-772-4115
 Email: scott.chamberlain@tmicalibration.com
 Website: www.tmicalibration.com
Calibrate test & measurement equipment (Minority, Woman, estab 1991, empl 162, sales $22,700,000, cert: WBENC)

California

6303 Alloy Valves and Control
 3210 S Susan St
 Santa Ana, CA 92704
 Contact: Phyllis Abrams Dir Sales/Marketing
 Tel: 714-427-0877
 Email: pabrams@avcovalve.com
 Website: www.avcovalve.com
Design & mfr ball valves & flow measurement products, manual & automated ball valve assemblies. (Woman, estab 2000, empl 15, sales , cert: CPUC)

6304 Brylen Technologies
 275 Orange Ave
 Santa Barbara, CA 93117
 Contact: Barbara Tzur President
 Tel: 805-692-9300
 Email: barbara.tzur@brylen.com
 Website: www.brylen.com
Calibration & testing laboratory, clean room & clean bench certifications, calibration is electro-magnetic, thermodynamics, dimensional, angle, & mechanical areas, calibrate equipment. (Woman, estab 1985, empl 10, sales $571,850, cert: State)

6305 RHF, Inc.
 16202 Keats Circle
 Westminster, CA 92683
 Contact: Robert Friesen President
 Tel: 714-848-9367
 Email: rhf.radar@earthlink.net
 Website: www.radaretc.com
Repair & calibration of speed radar & lidar equipment. (Woman, estab 1983, empl 3, sales $300,000, cert: State)

6306 STB Electrical Test Equipment, Inc.
 1666 Auburn Ravine Rd
 Auburn, CA 95603
 Contact: Patricia Tavare President
 Tel: 530-823-5111
 Email: pat@stbinc.com
 Website: www.stbinc.com
Mfr phasing voltmeters, voltage detectors, voltage sensors, ground detectors, clamp-on ammeters, phase rotation meters, ground cable testers, drain tools. (Woman, estab 1979, empl 6, sales $1,329,220, cert: State, CPUC)

6307 Vanguard Instruments Company, Inc.
 1520 S. Hellman Ave
 Ontario, CA 91761
 Contact: Timm Smith Natl Sales Mgr
 Tel: 513-477-2965
 Email: timm.s@vanguard-instruments.com
 Website: www.vanguard-instruments.com
Mfr measuring & testing electricity & electrical signal instruments. (As-Pac, estab 1993, empl 11, sales , cert: CPUC)

Connecticut

6308 Environics, Inc.
 69 Industrial Park Rd E
 Tolland, CT 06084
 Contact: Cathy Dunn CEO
 Tel: 860-872-1111
 Email: cdunn@environics.com
 Website: www.environics.com
Design, mfr, dist & service computerized gas flow instruments, gas mixing systems, gas on-demand systems, gas calibration systems, gas dilution systems, gas flow management systems. (Woman, estab 1986, empl 20, sales $3,000,000, cert: State)

Florida

6309 Diverse Services USA, Inc.
 11111 N 46th St
 Tampa, FL 33617
 Contact: Michael Schmidt VP
 Tel: 813-988-6000
 Email: michael.schmidt@diverseservicesusa.com
 Website: www.diverseservicesusa.com
Mfr & install all signs: interior, exterior, graphics, LED message centers, millwork (counters, cabinetry), architectural imaging (ACM panel systems, awnings) and lighting (general illumination, specialty/accent, energy savings (Hisp, estab 2009, empl 650, sales $152,000,000, cert: NMSDC)

Georgia

6310 Georgia Time Recorder Co., Inc.
722 Collins Hill Rd Ste H-283
Lawrenceville, GA 30046
Contact: Andrea Drath President
Tel: 770-441-2879
Email: andrea@georgiatime.com
Website: www.gtrbusinesssystems.com

Time & Attendance, Time clocks, Wireless Synchronized clocks & master clocks, Temperature Sensors, temp/humidity sensors, CO_2 sensors, emergency lighting, event monitoring. (Woman, estab 1982, empl 6, sales $550,000, cert: WBENC)

Illinois

6311 B&B Instruments, Inc.
145 W Taft Dr
South Holland, IL 60473
Contact: Bob Samoska Owner
Tel: 708-596-1700
Email: bobsamoska@bbinstruments.com
Website: www.bbinstruments.com

Dist pressure, temperature, level, flow, humidity gauges & instrumentation, NiST shop calibrations, testing type calibrators. (As-Pac, estab 1972, empl 8, sales , cert: NMSDC)

Indiana

6312 AFC International Inc
PO Box 894
DeMotte, IN 46310
Contact: Pamela Seneczko President
Tel: 219-987-6825
Email: pjseneczko@afcintl.com
Website: www.afcintl.com

Gas detectors, respiratory protection, detector tubes, self contained breathing apparatus, heat stress monitors, CO detectors, toxic gas detectors. (Woman, estab 1992, empl 6, sales $3,000,000, cert: WBENC)

6313 The CREW Corporation
PO Box 254
Brownsburg, IN 46112
Contact: Kathy Adkins President
Tel: 317-713-7777
Email: kadkins@crewcorp.com
Website: www.crewcorp.com

Validation services: qualification testing & validation, change control, FAT & SAT, IQ/OQ/PQ protocols & execution, instrument calibration, supporting documentation. (Woman, estab 1995, empl 38, sales $2,970,000, cert: WBENC)

Michigan

6314 Hines Industries, Inc.
793 Airport Blvd.
Ann Arbor, MI 48108
Contact: Beverly Monge Sales Admin
Tel: 734-769-2300
Email: ddonall@hinesindustries.com
Website: www.hinesindustries.com

Balancing machines, rebuild balancing equipment & balancing instrumentation services, balancing equipment design innovation & manufacturing process improvement. (Woman, estab 1971, empl 25, sales $8,400,000, cert: WBENC)

6315 M & B Holdings, LLC
5594 E Ten Mile Rd
Warren, MI 48091
Contact: Brian McMillan GM
Tel: 586-427-9971
Email: bmcmillan@gsnscorp.com
Website: www.gsnscorp.com

Gage Commodity Management, Gage Purchasing, Gage Design & Manufacturing. (As-Ind, estab 2005, empl 31, sales $4,420,017, cert: NMSDC)

6316 Omni-Tech Sales, Inc.
31189 Schoolcraft Rd
Livonia, MI 48150
Contact: Deborah Denne CEO
Tel: 734-425-5730
Email: omnitech_sales@ameritech.net
Website: www.omnitech-sales.com

Dist precision measuring equipment, CMM's, Vision Systems, Roundness & Form Measurement, Surface Finish equipment & fixturing, Hardness Testers, Optical Comparators. (Woman, estab 1988, empl 6, sales $3,975,637, cert: WBENC)

6317 River City Metrology LLC
2215 29th St SE, Ste B1
Grand Rapids, MI 49508
Contact: Victor Barker Owner
Tel: 616-530-4899
Email: vbarker@rcmetrology.com
Website: www.rcmetrology.com

Dimensional Inspection, CMM calibration & sales, Dimensional inspection product sales. (As-Pac, estab 2004, empl 5, sales , cert: NMSDC)

6318 Standard Scale & Supply Co.
      25421 Glendale
      Redford, MI 48239
      Contact: John Bowman GM
      Tel: 313-255-6700
      Email: jbowman@standardscale.com
      Website: www.standardscale.com
Dist & service weight-based measuring equipment & accessories. (Hisp, estab 1946, empl 12, sales , cert: NMSDC)

North Carolina

6319 Cooper Electrical Construction
      1706 E Wendover Ave
      Greensboro, NC 27405
      Contact: Beverly Brown CEO
      Tel: 336-275-8439
      Email: beverly.brown@coopereic.com
      Website: www.coopereic.com
Electrical D/B, BIM, Prefabrication, Instrumentation & Controls, and Calibration services. (Woman, estab 1954, empl 120, sales $41,509,090, cert: WBENC)

6320 Measurement Controls, Inc.
      PO Box 562775
      Charlotte, NC 28256
      Contact: Paresh Patel President
      Tel: 704-921-1101
      Email: sales@measurementcontrols.com
      Website: www.measurementcontrols.com
Refurbish, mfr & dist rotary, diaphragms & turbine gas meters, meter sets with regulators, filters & by-pass, install index, connections, swivels, nuts, & washers, electro mechanical correctors, dust caps & blind disc. (As-Ind, estab 1999, empl 9, sales $400,000, cert: State, City, NMSDC)

Ohio

6321 AVM Industries
      30505 Bainbridge Rd, Ste 100
      Solon, OH 44139
      Contact: Linda Holt Dir
      Tel: 440-349-1849
      Email: lholt@hawthornmc.com
      Website: www.avminc.com
Mfr & dist climate control actuators & counterbalancing systems for the automotive, commercial & aftermarket industries. (As-Pac, estab 2006, empl 376, sales $34,000,000, cert: NMSDC)

6322 Cooper Atkins
      11353 Reed Hartman Hwy Ste 110
      Cincinnati, OH 45241
      Contact: Sr VP Sales
      Tel: 847-373-2033
      Email: gmarcus@cooper-atkins.com
      Website: www.cooper-atkins.com
Wireless temperature / environmental monitoring systems, software, hardware, installation & support. (Woman, estab , empl , sales , cert: WBENC)

6323 Intek, Inc.
      751 Intek Way
      Westerville, OH 43082
      Contact: Audrey Myers Customer Service Assoc.
      Tel: 614-895-0301
      Email: amyers@intekflow.com
      Website: www.intekflow.com
Mfr & dist thermal low flow meters & switches, measures liquid flow rates, also mfr RheoVac line of vacuum monitoring equipment. (As-Pac, estab 1976, empl 17, sales , cert: City)

6324 Precision Gage & Tool Co.
      375 Gargave Rd
      Dayton, OH 45449
      Contact: Victoria Mack Admin
      Tel: 937-866-9666
      Email: vmack@pgtgage.com
      Website: www.pgtgage.com
Custom grind gauges. (Woman/AA, estab , empl 16, sales , cert: WBENC)

Oregon

6325 Component Design Northwest, Inc.
      PO Box 10947
      Portland, OR 97296
      Contact: Krissy McKay VP
      Tel: 503-225-0900
      Email: krissy@cdnw.com
      Website: www.cdn-timeandtemp.com
Thermometers & timers. (Woman, estab 1983, empl 7, sales $4,700,100, cert: WBENC)

Puerto Rico

6326 American Test & Balance
      PO Box 366584
      San Juan, PR 00936
      Contact: David Rosa President
      Tel: 787-781-7654
      Email: d.rosa@american-test.com
      Website: www.american-test.com
Testing, adjusting and balancing (TAB) services for heating, ventilating and air conditioning systems. We also provide Cleanroom Performance Testing (CPT) services. (Hisp, estab 1994, empl 21, sales , cert: NMSDC)

MEASURING INSTRUMENTS

6327 Instrumentation Corps, Inc.
PO Box 2116
Barceloneta, PR 00617
Contact: Juan Oliveras President
Tel: 787-970-0746
Email: jaoliver@instrumentationcorps.com
Website: www.instrumentationcorps.com
Process instrumentation & weight scales sales, installation, configuration, calibration & certification svcs, equipment repair & technical services. (Hisp, estab 1998, empl 40, sales $4,851,214, cert: NMSDC)

6328 MentorTechnical Group, Corp.
PO Box 6857
Caguas, PR 00726
Contact: Luis David Soto President
Tel: 787-743-0897
Email: jose.gonzalez@mentortg.com
Website: www.mentortg.com
Calibration, Instrumentation, and Control Systems Laboratory. (Hisp, estab 2000, empl 450, sales $27,500,000, cert: NMSDC)

6329 PAS Technologies, Inc.
9 Pedro Arzuaga W
Carolina, PR 00984
Contact: Alfredo Agelviz President
Tel: 787-775-2237
Email: alfredo.agelviz@pastechnologies.com
Website: www.pastechnologies.com
Dist & service instrumentation & control products. (Hisp, estab 1993, empl 3, sales $1,300,000, cert: NMSDC)

Wisconsin

6330 Precision Metrology, Inc.
7350 N Teutonia Ave
Milwaukee, WI 53209
Contact: Carol Shipley President
Tel: 414-351-7420
Email: carol@precisionmetrology.com
Website: www.precisionmetrology.com
Calibrate & repair precision measuring instruments. (Woman, estab , empl , sales , cert: WBENC)

MEDICAL SUPPLIES & SERVICES

Manufacturers and distributors of over the counter drugs, dental supplies, diagnostic equipment and supplies, glass containers, labwear, veterinary products, latex, hospital supplies & apparel, etc. NAICS Code 32

Alabama

6331 NuAngel Inc.
14717 Friend Rd
Athens, AL 35611
Contact: Teresa Carroll President
Tel: 256-729-5000
Email: info@nuangel.com
Website: www.NuAngel.com
Mfr breastfeeding & infant items: washable nursing pads, biodegradable disposable nursing pads, burp cloths, washable baby wipes, receiving blankets, bra extenders. (Woman, estab 1990, empl 10, sales $450,000, cert: WBENC)

6332 VELOX Integration Services, LLC
600 S Court St, Ste 322
Montgomery, AL 36104
Contact: Sherrell Love CEO
Tel: 334-233-3328
Email: sherrell@veloxintegration.com
Website: www.veloxintegration.com
Dist medical supplies & equipment, construction management. (Woman/AA, estab 2014, empl 2, sales , cert: State)

Arizona

6333 Magnum Medical LLC
3265 N Nevada St
Chandler, AZ 85225
Contact: Omar Hameed Mktg Dir
Tel: 800-336-9710
Email: ohameed@magnummed.com
Website: www.magnummed.com
Dist medical equip: handheld surgical dental instruments, hemostats, scissors, needle holders, etc. (As-Ind, estab 1984, empl 9, sales $3,000,000, cert: NMSDC)

California

6334 Abell Marketing Group, Inc.
15057 Avenida De Las Flores
Chino Hills, CA 91709
Contact: James Lohan Project Mgr
Tel: 909-456-8905
Email: james@abellmarketinggroup.com
Website: www.abellmarketinggroup.com
Protective clothing & medical/industrial nitrile, vinyl & latex gloves. (Woman, estab 1998, empl 2, sales $375,000, cert: WBENC)

6335 Active Potential Inc.
7898 Ostrow St Ste G
San Diego, CA 92111
Contact: CEO
Tel: 858-292-4128
Email:
Website: www.activepotentialmedical.com
Emergency & Exam room supplies, Emergency preparedness, Ergonomics, Eye protection & accessories, Fall protection, Fire protection, Safety storage, Work wear, Gloves & hand protection, Hearing protection, First aid supplies. (Woman/AA, estab 2006, empl 7, sales $247,300, cert: NMSDC, CPUC)

6336 Alcam Medical Inc.
1760 Chicago Ave, Ste L-21
Riverside, CA 92507
Contact: Cameron Stewart VP
Tel: 866-847-7187
Email: cameron@alcammedical.com
Website: www.alcammedical.com
Orthotic & Prosthetic Service: upper & lower extremity prosthetics, custom orthotics, diabetic shoes, compression garments, cranial helmets, knee braces, back braces, pediatric orthotics, mastectomy bras. (AA, estab 2006, empl 69, sales $8,100,000, cert: CPUC)

6337 Alfa Scientific Designs
13200 Gregg St
Poway, CA 92064
Contact: Jeanette Christian Marketing & Communications
Tel: 858-513-3888
Email: jchristian@alfascientific.com
Website: www.alfascientific.com
Mfr superior quality, rapid, point-of-care health tests. (Woman/As-Pac, estab 1996, empl 95, sales $10,000,000, cert: NMSDC)

6338 American Healthcare Products, Inc.
1028 Westminster Ave
Alhambra, CA 91803
Contact: Tony Djie
Tel: 626-588-2788
Email: tony@uniseal.net
Website: www.uniseal.net
Dist medical & industrial grade disposable latex, vinyl, nitrile & synthetic gloves. (As-Pac, estab 1991, empl 12, sales , cert: NMSDC)

6339 Ames Medical Equipment, Inc.
301 N Jackson Ave, Ste 7A
San Jose, CA 95133
Contact: Mike Patel Treasurer
Tel: 408-942-9000
Email: mspatel101@hotmail.com
Website: www.Alliancemedsupply.com
Dist durable medical equipment & supplies. (Minority, Woman, estab 2005, empl 2, sales , cert: State)

MEDICAL SUPPLIES & SERVICES

6340 BioMed Resources Inc.
6646 Doolittle Ave
Riverside, CA 92503
Contact: Lisa Liu CEO
Tel: 310-323-3888
Email: lisal@bmres.com
Website: www.bmres.com
Dist specimen containers, transfer pipettes, conical tubes, irrigation syringes, lab jackets, lab coats, isolation gowns & cover gowns. (Minority, Woman, estab 2002, empl 15, sales $4,300,000, cert: NMSDC)

6341 Broadline Medical, Inc.
2100 Atlas Rd, Ste E
Richmond, CA 94806
Contact: Georgia W. Richardson President
Tel: 510-662-5270
Email: grichardson@broadline.com
Website: www.broadline.com
Dist disposable medical apparel: headwear, footwear, labcoats & lab jackets, OR towels, lap sponges, gowns & non sterile kits. (Woman/AA, estab 1994, empl 10, sales $3,000,000, cert: NMSDC)

6342 Clariti Eyewear, Inc.
940 Ajax Ave
City of Industry, CA 91748
Contact: Dominique Yonemoto President
Tel: 800-372-6372
Email: gene@claritieyewear.com
Website: www.claritieyewear.com
Eyeglasses, Optical frames, Eyeglass frames, Eyewear, Sunglasses, Eyeglass cases, Cleaning cloths, Cleaning Kit. (Minority, Woman, estab 1993, empl 14, sales $3,219,627, cert: State, NMSDC)

6343 Duncan & Duncan Medical, Inc.
911 Marina Way S Unite E2
Richmond, CA 94804
Contact: Luta Duncan President
Tel: 510-799-0100
Email: glovesbylu@aol.com
Website: www.duncanmeds.com
Medical, surgical, laboratory supplies & equipment, medical books, cleaning supplies, housekeeping supplies, apparel, gloves, incontinence, textiles, orthopedic , nutritional & feeding supplies, personal hygiene, physical therapy. (Woman/AA, estab 2011, empl 3, sales $429,000, cert: CPUC)

6344 EMS Safety Services, Inc.
1046 Calle Recodo Ste K
San Clemente, CA 92673
Contact: Marian Lepore CEO
Tel: 800-215-9555
Email: bids@emssafety.com
Website: www.emssafetyservices.com
Training curriculums & products: CPR, AED, First Aid & Bloodborne Pathogens. (Minority, Woman, estab 1993, empl 18, sales $2,700,000, cert: NMSDC, CPUC, WBENC)

6345 Flying Medical USA
18187 Valley
La Puente, CA 91744
Contact: Conrad Reveles Sales Exec
Tel: 855-227-3080
Email: sales3@flyingmedusa.com
Website: www.flyingmedusa.com
Mfr medical supplies: band aid, ice packs, finger splints, etc. (As-Pac, estab 2008, empl 4, sales , cert: State)

6346 Hand and Hand Medical
822 Wakefield Dr
Oakdale, CA 95361
Contact: Sharon Devereaux CEO
Tel: 209-322-2699
Email: dwight@handandhand.com
Website: www.handandhandmed.com
Dist surgical post-op "JP Drain" Management Systems, unique effective product, US Patent Awarded 2015. (Woman, estab 2016, empl 3, sales $750,000, cert: WBENC)

6347 J2 Medical Supply
28790 W Chase
Valencia, CA 91355
Contact: Roland Williams Dir Contracts & Compliance
Tel: 855-615-8633
Email: heather.alnimri@j2medicalsupply.com
Website: www.raelife.co
Mfr & dist high-quality medical solutions. (AA, estab 2020, empl 5, sales $6,728,535, cert: NMSDC)

6348 Kili Summit Corporation
102 Cross St Ste 220
San Luis Obispo, CA 93401
Contact: Cinde Dolphin CEO
Tel: 916-768-1690
Email: cinde@medicaldraincarrier.com
Website: www.medicaldraincarrier.com
Manage JP wound-care drains after mastectomy, cancer, cardiac and organ transplant surgeries. (Woman, estab 2015, empl 2, sales , cert: WBENC)

6349 Legend Medical Devices Inc.
16714 E Johnson Dr
City of Industry, CA 91745
Contact: Mark Sevilla Dir of Sales
Tel: 626-350-9733
Email: msevilla@legendmd.com
Website: www.legendmd.com
Mfr & dist CPAP, anesthesia, respiratory care & infection control products. (Minority, Woman, estab 2006, empl 8, sales $1,500,000, cert: CPUC)

6350 Medi Max Tech
2805 E Ana St
East Rancho Dominguez, CA 90221
Contact: Natl Contracting Mgr
Tel: 716-868-6108
Email: Support@MediMaxTech.com
Website: www.medimaxtech.com
Dist electrosurgical pencils: Telescopic Smoke and Ergonomic Pencils. (Minority, Woman, estab 2012, empl 10, sales , cert: NMSDC, WBENC)

6351 Medical Receivables Solutions, Inc.
      802 Wilmington
      Fairfield, CA 94533
      Contact: Aleshia Hunter President
      Tel: 415-377-3775
      Email: aleshia@medicalreceivables.net
      Website: www.medicalreceivables.net
Account receivables & medical billing shortage, Medical Receivables Solutions. (Woman/AA, estab 2002, empl 7, sales $250,000, cert: CPUC)

6352 Plus One Lab Works Inc.
      2872 Walnut Ave, Ste C
      Tustin, CA 92780
      Contact: Jason Vi Mgr
      Tel: 714-558-8009
      Email: jason@plusonelab.com
      Website: www.plusonelab.com
Dist disposable products for use in labs, clean rooms, hospitals, dental & medical offices. (As-Pac, estab 2010, empl 5, sales , cert: NMSDC)

6353 ProTrials Research, Inc.
      333 W San Carlos St Ste 800
      San Jose, CA 95110
      Contact: Jodi Andrews CEO
      Tel: 650-864-9180
      Email: jandrews@protrials.com
      Website: www.protrials.com/
Project Management, Clinical Trial Monitoring, Regional Clinical Trial Monitoring, Clinical Training, SOP Development. (Woman, estab 1996, empl 160, sales $27,000,000, cert: WBENC)

6354 Shen Wei USA Inc.
      33278 Central Ave, Ste 102
      Union City, CA 94587
      Contact: James Lee President
      Tel: 510-429-8692
      Email: james@shenweiusa.com
      Website: www.shenweiusa.com
Mfr latex & non-latex disposable gloves. (Minority, Woman, estab 1984, empl 20, sales $45,234,000, cert: WBENC)

6355 Small Beginnings, Inc.
      17229 Lemon St Ste B2
      Hesperia, CA 92345
      Contact: Kelly Brockelmeyer Exec Admin
      Tel: 760-949-7707
      Email: kelly@small-beginnings.com
      Website: www.small-beginnings.com
Mfr Neonatal Intensive Care Unit disposable products: diapers, photo-therapy masks, suction devices, pacifiers, & meconium aspirators. (Woman, estab 2001, empl 8, sales $1,071,101, cert: WBENC)

6356 Special Respiratory Care, Inc.
      18327 NAPA St
      Northridge, CA 91325
      Contact: Don Reiter President
      Tel: 818-717-8807
      Email: dreiter@src-medical.com
      Website: www.src-medical.com
Dist, rent and service respiratory, anesthesia and critical care products. Portable ventilators, BiPaps/CPAPs/BiLevels, airway clearance devices, high flow humidification systems, ventilation monitors, pulse oximeters, intubation products, patient circuit (Woman, estab 1982, empl 33, sales $6,000,000, cert: WBENC)

6357 Strive Well-Being, Inc.
      5920 Friars Rd, Ste103
      San Diego, CA 92108
      Contact: Amit Sangani President
      Tel: 619-684-5700
      Email: reg@strive2bfit.com
      Website: www.strive2bfit.com
Onsite Physical Activity Classes, Onsite Stress Management Classes, Musculoskeletal Strengthening Classes, Fitness Center Staffing & Management, Fitness & Wellness Program Management, Fitness Facility Design & Development. (As-Ind, estab 2008, empl 40, sales $1,500,000, cert: City, NMSDC, 8(a))

6358 Tampon Tribe
      2609 Brighton Ave
      Los Angeles, CA 90018
      Contact: Martha Schultz
      Tel: 310-592-3193
      Email: martha.schultz@tampontribe.com
      Website: www.tampontribe.com
Dist sanitary, period products. (Hisp, estab 2016, empl 3, sales $986,778, cert: CPUC)

6359 Teco Diagnostics Inc.
      1268 N Lakeview Ave
      Anaheim, CA 92807
      Contact: Lewis Cabrera Dir of Sales
      Tel: 714-463-1111
      Email: lewis@tecodiagnostics.com
      Website: www.tecodiag.com
Mfr vitro clinical diagnostic tests and instruments. (As-Pac, estab 1987, empl 50, sales $7,000,000, cert: NMSDC)

6360 The Andwin Corp.
      6636 Variel Ave
      Canoga Park, CA 91303
      Contact: Arnie Shedlow Sr VP Sales
      Tel: 818-999-2828
      Email: jpalaganas@andwin.com
      Website: www.andwinsci.com
Dist medical & lab supplies & product kits: boxes, labels, bar codes, instruction inserts & kit components. (Woman, estab 1950, empl 98, sales $32,000,000, cert: WBENC)

6361 Total Resources International
      420 S Lemon Ave
      Walnut, CA 91789
      Contact: Andre Dela Victoria Sales Mgr
      Tel: 909-594-1220
      Email: andrev@totalresourcesintl.com
      Website: www.totalresourcesintl.com
Mfr First Aid Kits & Emergency Survival Essentials. (As-Pac, estab 1990, empl 150, sales $13,000,000, cert: NMSDC)

6362 Trademark Plastics, Inc.
      807 Palmyrita Ave
      Riverside, CA 92507
      Contact: Gilbert McMoran Sales Mgr
      Tel: 909-941-8810
      Email: gmcmoran@trademarkplastics.com
      Website: www.TrademarkPlastics.com
Mfr plastic, medical components. (Woman, estab 1989, empl 150, sales $14,000,000, cert: WBENC)

Colorado

6363 LifeHealth LLC
      5951 S Middlefield Rd, Ste 102
      Littleton, CO 80123
      Contact: Margot Langstaff Managing Partner
      Tel: 303-730-1902
      Email: margot@lifehealthcorp.com
      Website: www.lifehealthcorp.com
Clinical health care services & solutions. (Woman, estab 2004, empl 5, sales $870,000, cert: State, WBENC)

6364 Mountainside Medical Colorado, LLC
      6165 Lookout Rd
      Boulder, CO 80301
      Contact: Susan Neidecker President
      Tel: 303-222-1271
      Email: sneidecker@mountainsidemed.com
      Website: www.mountainsidemed.com
Contract manufacturing for complex, tight-tolerance medical products, Multi-axis Machining Assembly, Wire EDMCNC, Swiss type machining centers, Laser welding & Laser marking, Finishing Metal Forming. (Woman, estab 2006, empl 90, sales $12,731,416, cert: WBENC)

6365 Relius Medical LLC
      615 Wooten Rd Ste 150
      Colorado Springs, CO 80915
      Contact: Lauralee Martin Owner
      Tel: 719-725-6444
      Email: lmartin@reliusmed.com
      Website: www.reliusmed.com
Orthopedic Medical Device Manufacturer: Implants, External Fixation Devices, Instrumentation. (Woman, estab 2014, empl 125, sales $1,010,907,952, cert: WBENC)

6366 The Medcom Group, Ltd.
      541 East Garden Dr, Unit Q
      Windsor, CO 80550
      Contact: Steven Barnett
      Tel: 970-674-3032
      Email: novation@medcomgroup.com
      Website: www.medcomgroup.com
Dist orthopedic rehabilitative equipment. (Woman, estab , empl , sales $2,500,000, cert: WBENC)

Connecticut

6367 PL Medical Co., LLC
      117 West Dudley Town Road
      Bloomfield, CT 06002
      Contact: Rahul Kanwar Owner
      Tel: 860-243-2100
      Email: r.kanwar@plmedical.com
      Website: www.plmedical.com
Dist IV lines (sets), surgical blades, opthalmic products, x-ray film, x-ray envelopes, safety instruments. (Woman/As-Ind, estab 1998, empl 8, sales $2,172,116, cert: NMSDC)

Delaware

6368 Med-Tech Equipment, Inc.
      2207 Concord Pike Ste 135
      Wilmington, DE 19803
      Contact: David Gentile VP
      Tel: 800-322-2609
      Email: info@buymedtech.com
      Website: www.buymedtech.com
Dist, service & maintain sport medicine modalities & training equipment: Electrotherapy Ultrasound, Stim, Laser and Combo units, Hydrotherapy Whirlpools, Traction/Decompression Systems, Treatment Tables, Extremity Testing Systems. (Woman, estab 1989, empl 2, sales $250,000, cert: State)

6369 QPS, LLC
      3 Innovation Way Ste 240
      Newark, DE 19711
      Contact: Lily Rosa Sr Dir Business Dev
      Tel: 302-369-5601
      Email: lily.rosa@qps.com
      Website: www.qps.com
GLP/GCP compliant CRO supporting discovery, preclinical and clinical drug development. We provide quality services to pharmaceutical and biotechnology clients worldwide. (As-Pac, estab 1995, empl 251, sales $19,999,999,998, cert: NMSDC)

6370 Sivad PPE, LLC
      703 Carson Dr
      Bear, DE 19701
      Contact: Lenzie Davis CEO
      Tel: 313-285-9821
      Email: Sivad@sivadppe.com
      Website: www.sivadppe.com
Dist durable PPE & Janitorial supply chain, UV-C Disinfection. (AA, estab 2020, empl 30, sales $47,000,000, cert: City, NMSDC)

Florida

6371 AccurReg, Inc.
      4400 SW 95th Ave
      Davie, FL 33328
      Contact: Andrea Milonas Office Mgr
      Tel: 954-641-6400
      Email: amilonas@regulatory.com
      Website: www.regulatory.com
Medical device, pharmaceutical, OTC & biologic industry consulting svcs. Software, process, and analytical validation; Warning Letter & Consent Decree remediation. (Woman, estab 1987, empl 8, sales $9,108,707, cert: WBENC)

MEDICAL SUPPLIES & SERVICES

6372 Advanced Surgical Technologies, Inc.
901 SW Martin Downs Blvd, 200A
Palm City, FL 34990
Contact: Barbara Alfaro President
Tel: 561-801-2314
Email: balfaro@astlaser.com
Website: www.astlaser.com
Medical laser rental and related supplies. (Hisp, estab 2017, empl 16, sales $4,245,000, cert: NMSDC, 8(a))

6373 American Medicals
8900 Corporate Square Court
Jacksonville, FL 32216
Contact: B G Bihani President
Tel: 904-636-9451
Email: bg.bihani@americanmedicals.com
Website: www.americanmedicals.com
Mfr & dist medical, surgical & healthcare products. (As-Ind, estab 2001, empl 3, sales , cert: State)

6374 American Purchasing Services
10315 USA Today Way
Miramar, FL 33025
Contact: Akhil Agrawal President
Tel: 305-364-0888
Email: akhil.agrawal@american-depot.com
Website: www.american-depot.com
Dist medical supplies. (Minority, estab , empl , sales , cert: NMSDC)

6375 Anexa Biomedical, Inc.
40423 Air Time Ave
Zephyrhills, FL 33542
Contact: Lenny Budloo President
Tel: 813-780-7927
Email: lenny@anexabiomedical.com
Website: www.anexabiomedical.com
Mfr USP Sterile Saline & Sterile Water solutions. (Hisp, estab 2010, empl 8, sales , cert: State)

6376 Asset Surplus Reallocation LLC (SurgiShop)
8910 N Dale Mabry Hwy
Tampa, FL 33614
Contact: Spencer Geer
Tel: 855-720-2285
Email: spencer.geer@surgishop.com
Website: www.surgishop.com
Dist surgical disposables. (Hisp, estab 2018, empl 30, sales , cert: State)

6377 Care-Full Products
3905 Tampa Rd, Ste 432
Oldsmar, FL 34677
Contact: Colleen Meloff President
Tel: 813-602-2824
Email: cmeloff@carefullproducts.com
Website: www.carefullproducts.com
Mfr CareFull Catch disposable specimen cup holder. (Woman, estab 2015, empl 1, sales , cert: NWBOC)

6378 Customed USA, LLC
10805 Southport Dr
Orlando, FL 32824
Contact: Milexis Torres Dir of Sales
Tel: 407-850-5558
Email: milexis.torres@prhospital.com
Website: www.customedhealing.com
Dist hospital, medical supplies, imaging products, custom surgical products. (Hisp, estab 2010, empl 240, sales , cert: NMSDC)

6379 Dazmed, Inc.
508 NW 77th St
Boca Raton, FL 33487
Contact: Amio Das President
Tel: 561-414-3733
Email: amio@dazmed.com
Website: www.dazmed.com
Prescription drug, over-the counter, cosmetics, and prescription drug re-packager. (As-Ind, estab 2011, empl 11, sales , cert: State)

6380 ECI Holdings, LLC dba Exam Coordinators Network
6111 Broken Sound Pkwy NW Ste 207
Boca Raton, FL 33487
Contact: Barbara Levine CEO
Tel: 561-922-5200
Email: supplierdiversity@ecnime.com
Website: www.ecnime.com
Claim evaluation services, independent medical examinations, functional capacity evaluations, fitness for duty exams, 2nd opinion exams & medical file, film & bill reviews. (Woman, estab 1999, empl 75, sales $16,300,000, cert: WBENC)

6381 EncompasUnlimited, Inc.
2219 Whitfield Park Dr
Sarasota, FL 34243
Contact: Marybeth Flynn VP
Tel: 941-751-3385
Email: marybeth@encompasunlimited.com
Website: www.encompasunlimited.com
Dist endoscopy accessories, specimen caddies, multiple glove dispenser boxes, endoscopy wedges & headrests. (Woman, estab 1977, empl 4, sales $2,400,000, cert: NWBOC)

6382 Global Sourcing, LLC
2415 Albany Ave
Tampa, FL 33607
Contact: Tom Irby VP Strategic Partnerships
Tel: 512-293-8709
Email: tom.irby@globalsourcingppe.com
Website: www.globalsourcingppe.com
Dist PPE items, N95 masks, ASTM level 1,2,3 surgical masks, face shields, surgical gowns level 1/2/3/4, nitrile FDA 510k exam gloves, latex gloves, vinyl gloves, show covers/boots, alcohol EPA list N wipes, hand sanitizers. (Woman, estab 2020, empl 20, sales $25,500,000, cert: WBENC)

6383 Healthcare Supply Solutions, Inc.
13949 Alvarez Rd Ste 100
Jacksonville, FL 32218
Contact: Lara Cheek
Tel: 904-638-5520
Email: lcheek@hssone.com
Website: www.hssone.com
Dist healthcare products & services. (Hisp, estab 2008, empl 14, sales $10,000,000, cert: NMSDC)

6384 HNM Medical USA
20855 Northeast 16th Ave, Ste C15
Miami, FL 11111
Contact: Yoav Anisz President
Tel: 866-291-8498
Email: yanisz@hnmmedical.com
Website: www.hnmmedical.com
Dist medical equipment and supplies. (Hisp, estab , empl , sales $7,000,000, cert: NMSDC)

6385 Kramer Laboratories, Inc.
400 University Dr Ste 400
Coral Gables, FL 33134
Contact: Myrna Patterson Sales Mgr
Tel: 800-824-4894
Email: mpatterson@kramerlabs.com
Website: www.kramerlabs.com
Fungi Nail Brand, Safetussin CD Cough Relief/Nasal Decongestant Formula, Safetussin DM Cough Formula. (Minority, Woman, estab 1987, empl 14, sales , cert: NMSDC, WBENC)

6386 Lifeline Pharmaceuticals LLC
1301 NW 84th Ave Ste 101
Miami, FL 33126
Contact: Benjamin Rivera Jr SVP
Tel: 877-430-6337
Email: ben@lifelinepharm.com
Website: www.lifelinepharm.com
Dist medical supplies & equipment, medical-surgical products, specialty pharmaceuticals, anesthesia, controlled medications, blood & plasma products, generic & branded chemotherapy products, vaccines, albumin, IVIG. (AA, estab 2006, empl 37, sales $29,000,000, cert: State, NMSDC)

6387 Lipotriad LLC
219 Via Emilia
Palm Beach Gardens, FL 33418
Contact: Joan McCabe CEO
Tel: 203-561-0970
Email: joan@lipotriad.com
Website: www.lipotriadvitamins.com
Eye vitamins for eye health. (Woman, estab 2009, empl 13, sales $2,000,000, cert: WBENC, NWBOC)

6388 Medgluv Inc
4100 Coral Ridge Dr Ste 100
Coral Springs, FL 33065
Contact: Jerry Leong CEO
Tel: 954-586-5309
Email: jleong@medgluv.com
Website: www.medgluv.com
Mfr & dist examination gloves. (As-Pac, estab 2001, empl 6, sales $8,000,000, cert: State, NMSDC)

6389 Medical Support International, LLC
2626 Sawyer Terr
Wellington, FL 33414
Contact: Edgar Rivera CEO
Tel: 561-337-4866
Email: edgar.rivera@medsupportintl.com
Website: www.medsupportintl.com
Dist medical, dental, veterinary, surgical & hospital supplies & equipment. (Hisp, estab 2009, empl 2, sales , cert: NMSDC)

6390 Med-Lab Supply Co. Inc
800 Waterford Way Ste 950
Miami, FL 33126
Contact: Lucas Diaz VP Sales
Tel: 800-330-3183
Email: lucas.diaz@med-lab.com
Website: www.med-lab.com
Dist & service Siemens medical equipment. (Hisp, estab 1964, empl 79, sales $25,000,000, cert: NMSDC)

6391 Mellow Enterprises LLC
201 SW 63rd Ave
Plantation, FL 33317
Contact: Helen F Litsky President
Tel: 954-312-7175
Email: me@mellowllc.com
Website: www.voacorp.com/mellowenterprises.net
Safety & fire related training, medical supplies. (Woman/AA, estab 2010, empl 1, sales , cert: City)

6392 Ocean (Caribbean) Distributors, Inc.
4300 Oak Cir
Boca Raton, FL 33431
Contact: Cynthia Jerry President
Tel: 561-465-5411
Email: cynthia@oceancaribbeaninc.com
Website: www.oceancaribbeaninc.com
Dist medical supplies & equipment. (Woman/AA, estab 2012, empl 3, sales $230,257, cert: State, WBENC, 8(a))

6393 Surgimed Corporation
1303 NW 78th Ave
Doral, FL 33126
Contact: Luis Arias VP
Tel: 305-594-1121
Email: larias@surgimedcorp.com
Website: www.surgimedcorp.com/
Dist endotracheal tubes, stylets, guedels, suction catheters, tracheostomy tubes, endobroncheal tubes, foley catheters, urinary collection bags, leg bags, urine meters, pediatric urine collectors, foley Catheterization trays, irrigation syringes & trays. (Hisp, estab 1981, empl 13, sales $4,000,000, cert: NMSDC)

6394 Syna Medical
1035 Collier Center Way Ste 5
Naples, FL 34110
Contact: Arlene Norris Natl Sales Dir
Tel: 917-428-8309
Email: anita@synamedical.com
Website: www.synamedical.com
Mfr medical devices, nitrile exam gloves. (Woman, estab 2021, empl 10, sales $150,000, cert: WBENC)

6395 US Medical International LLC
      6989 NW 82nd Ave
      Miami, FL 33166
      Contact: Ryan Kissane Sales/Operations Mgr
      Tel: 305-468-3248
      Email: ryan@usmedicalintl.com
      Website: www.usmedicalintl.com
Mfr & dist disposable medical supplies. (Hisp, estab 2009, empl 3, sales , cert: State, NMSDC)

6396 ValorPoint, LLC
      7827 Chase Meadows Dr E
      Jacksonville, FL 32256
      Contact: Markus hardy CEO
      Tel: 904-321-7007
      Email: mark.hardy@valorpointllc.com
      Website: www.valorpointllc.com
Dist Personal Protective Equipment (PPE) for government and non-government entities. (AA, estab 2016, empl 2, sales , cert: NMSDC)

6397 VetMeds, Inc.
      8950 SW 74th Court Ste 2201
      Miami, FL 33156
      Contact: President
      Tel: 786-220-3634
      Email: vetmeds@gmx.com
      Website: www.vetmedsinc.com
Dist medical equip, medical apparel, wound care supplies, medical furniture, exam room supplies, extrication-patient transport equip, surgical gloves, IV therapy & laboratory supplies. (Woman/AA, estab 2012, empl 5, sales , cert: State)

Georgia

6398 American Clinics for Preventive Medicine
      1343 Terrell Mill Rd Ste 100
      Marietta, GA 30067
      Contact: Juanita Cato Office Assistant
      Tel: 767-836-3477
      Email: americanclinicpm@gmail.com
      Website: www.acpm.net
Provide physical exams, alternative medical treatment options, nutritional infusion therapy, high dose Vitamin C infusions, primary prevention exams, alternative complimentary cancer therapies, detoxification programs. (AA, estab 1985, empl 10, sales , cert: State)

6399 Attain Med, Inc.
      5825 Glenridge Dr NE Bldg 4, Ste 106
      Atlanta, GA 30328
      Contact: Charles Stafford VP Diversity Partnerships
      Tel: 770-288-2466
      Email: charles.stafford@attainmed.com
      Website: www.attainmed.com
Dist pharmaceuticals. (Minority, estab , empl , sales $8,000,000, cert: NMSDC, 8(a))

6400 Black Knight Medical, LLC
      50 Hurt Plaza SE, Ste 803
      Atlanta, GA 30303
      Contact: Ron Thomas President
      Tel: 877-767-3792
      Email: ron@blackknightmedical.com
      Website: www.blackknightmedical.com
Dist medical supplies. (AA, estab 2017, empl 4, sales $5,900,000, cert: City)

6401 Canterbury Pointe LLC
      3350 Riverwood Pkwy, Ste 1900
      Atlanta, GA 30339
      Contact: Diane Dixon Principal
      Tel: 770-633-2570
      Email:
      Website: www.cpointellc.com
Medical Supplies, Pharmacy Benefit Management, Energy Management & Insurance Services. (Woman/AA, estab 2015, empl 1, sales , cert: WBENC)

6402 Doc-Development, Inc., LLC
      2500 Park Central Blvd Ste A6
      Decatur, GA 30035
      Contact: Willa Lewis Contract Mgr
      Tel: 678-509-1501
      Email: wlewis@doc-development.com
      Website: www.doc-development.com
Medical Equipment & Supply, Industrial & Safety Supply, Janitorial Cleaning & Chemical Solutions. (AA, estab 2001, empl 15, sales $550,000, cert: 8(a))

6403 MedX Diagnostic Solutions, LLC
      2004 Eastview Pkwy Ste 108
      Conyers, GA 30013
      Contact: Gerald Patterson COO
      Tel: 770-278-0199
      Email: gpatterson@medxghs.com
      Website: www.medxghs.com
Dist healthcare materials, supplies, furniture, diagnostic kits, biomedical equipment services & repairs. (Woman/AA, estab 2014, empl 3, sales , cert: NMSDC)

6404 U.S. Imaging, Inc.
      2234 Bryant Place Court
      Marietta, GA 30066
      Contact: Sherman Weston President
      Tel: 404-934-9054
      Email: sweston@bellsouth.net
      Website: www.usimagingsite.com
Dist bio-medical, medical supplies & medical imaging equipment. (AA, estab , empl , sales $949,000, cert: NMSDC)

6405 Unyter Enterprises
      6065 Pkwy North Dr Ste 200
      Cumming, GA 30040
      Contact: Rayfus D'Yana President
      Tel: 678-500-9568
      Email: drayfus@unyter.com
      Website: www.unyter.com
Dist pharmaceuticals, medical/surgical supplies & equipment. (AA, estab 2009, empl 10, sales , cert: City)

6406 Vanguard Safety Company LLC
      PO Box 608
      Savannah, GA 31402
      Contact: Howard Genser Jr. Exec VP/COO
      Tel: 912-236-1766
      Email: howardg@vanguardsafetyco.com
      Website: www.vanguardsafetyco.com
Dist occupational health & safety products. (AA, estab 1985, empl 21, sales $8,700,000, cert: NMSDC)

6407 WellSol Medical Inc.
1261 LaVista Rd, Ste D1
Atlanta, GA 30324
Contact: William Moylan CFO/COO
Tel: 855-935-5765
Email: bill@wellsolmed.com
Website: www.wellsolmed.com
Dist medical equipment. (Hisp, estab 2015, empl 4, sales , cert: NMSDC)

Illinois

6408 AllCare, Inc.
2580 Foxfield Rd Ste 101
St. Charles, IL 60174
Contact: Dong, Brian VP
Tel: 630-830-7486
Email: brian@allcaredirect.com
Website: www.allcaredirect.com
Towels & Lap Sponges, IV Site Management, Surgical Gowns & Drapes, Wound Care. (As-Pac, estab , empl , sales $5,000,000, cert: NMSDC)

6409 Ekla Corporation
1707 Quincy Ave, Ste 127
Naperville, IL 60419
Contact: Jeff Prendergast President
Tel: 630-258-6242
Email: jeff@eklacorp.com
Website: www.eklacorp.com
Medcal surgical and equipment supplies and services. (Minority, Woman, estab , empl , sales $7,100,000, cert: City, WBENC)

6410 ESM Products LLC
245 W Roosevelt Rd, Bldg 10, Ste 71
West Chicago, IL 60185
Contact: Roger Sudnick VP Sales
Tel: 630-965-4569
Email: rsudnick@trademanagementpartners.com
Website: www.esmproducts.com
Provides high quality, low cost PPE. (Woman, estab 2012, empl 6, sales $3,000,000, cert: WBENC)

6411 Global Medical Services LLC
707 Davis Rd, Ste 102B
Elgin, IL 60123
Contact: Kelvin Udogu CEO
Tel: 224-238-3273
Email: kudogu@gmail.com
Website: www.globalmedsllc.com
Dist Pharmaceuticals & Medical equipment. (Woman/AA, estab 2009, empl 5, sales $450,000, cert: 8(a))

6412 Goodhealth Medical Products
14818 Drexel Ave
Dolton, IL 60419
Contact: David Wilson President
Tel: 708-841-1700
Email: info@goodhealthmed.com
Website: www.goodhealthmed.com
Dist medical, dental, and surgical supplies. (AA, estab 2001, empl 15, sales $2,000,000, cert: State, NMSDC)

6413 JERO Medical Equipment & Supplies, Inc.
4108 W Division St
Chicago, IL 60651
Contact: President
Tel: 312-829-5376
Email:
Website: www.jeromedical.com
Mfr disposbable wearing apparels, kit assembler, 1st aid, disaster, admission. (AA, estab 1987, empl 24, sales $4,000,000, cert: City)

6414 Medefil, Inc.
405 Windy Point Dr
Glendale Heights, IL 60139
Contact: Praveen Aggarwal Exec VP
Tel: 630-682-4600
Email: manoj@medefilinc.com
Website: www.medefilinc.com
Mfr prefilled syringes filled with saline & hepain for IV flush. (As-Ind, estab , empl , sales , cert: NMSDC)

6415 Medgyn Products Inc.
PO Box 3126
Oak Brook, IL 60522
Contact: Susan Bendle Finance & HR Mgr
Tel: 630-627-4105
Email: sbendle@medgyn.com
Website: www.medgyn.com
Provides high-quality medical devices: sterile disposable medical devices, stainless steel instruments, equipment, diagnostic test kits & various OB/GYN procedure kits. (As-Ind, estab 1983, empl 50, sales , cert: NMSDC)

6416 Medical Applications Specialists, Inc.
579 Warbler Dr
Bolingbrook, IL 60440
Contact: George Brown President
Tel: 630-739-1373
Email: gbrown@medappspec.com
Website: www.medappspec.com
Radiology CT & Nuclear Medicines imaging services, radiology equipment/supplies, sales & service. (AA, estab 1994, empl 7, sales $62,754,548, cert: State, City)

6417 Nexus Pharmaceuticals, Inc.
400 Knightsbridge Pkwy
Lincolnshire, IL 60069
Contact: Chris Conroy Dir Natl Accouts
Tel: 847-996-3790
Email: cconroy@nexuspharma.net
Website: www.nexuspharma.net
Mfr sterile generic injectable pharmaceuticals. (Minority, Woman, estab , empl , sales $750,000, cert: NMSDC, WBENC)

6418 Saris and Things Inc.
3836 Mistflower Ln
Naperville, IL 60564
Contact: Shital Daftari CEO
Tel: 630-346-6531
Email: shital@sntbiotech.com
Website: www.sntbiotech.com
NIOSH N95, CDC & EAU KN95, Hand Sanitizers, Covid Tests, Swabs, VTM Kits, Cryovial Tubes, Extraction Tubes, Covid Antigen Tests. (Woman/As-Ind, estab 2011, empl 12, sales $5,500,000, cert: City, WBENC)

Indiana

6419 Bryton Corporation
4001 Methanol Ln
Indianapolis, IN 46268
Contact: James Waldrop Controller
Tel: 317-334-8700
Email: j.waldrop@brytoncorp.com
Website: www.brytoncorp.com
Mfr & dist medical equipment, supplies & accessories. (Woman, estab 1981, empl 40, sales $9,000,000, cert: City)

6420 Hapak Enterprises Inc.
PO Box 21
Crawfordsville, IN 47933
Contact: Shannon Payne Mgr Operations
Tel: 765-364-0490
Email: shannon.payne@currtech.net
Website: www.currtechinc.com
Bio-Check® BioHazard wipes & Benchliners. (Woman, estab 1994, empl 50, sales $15,000,000, cert: WBENC)

Kentucky

6421 Blu Pharmaceuticals
301 Robey St
Franklin, KY 42134
Contact: Bill Luster Contract Mgr
Tel: 270-586-6386
Email: jfurlong@blurx.us
Website: www.blurx.us
Mfr & dist generic pharmaceuticals. (Minority, Woman, estab 2006, empl 15, sales $39,613,667, cert: State)

6422 Marian Medical, Inc.
319 Westport Dr
Louisville, KY 40207
Contact: Lisa Stewart Clinical Sales Mgr
Tel: 502-425-6363
Email: lisa@marianmedicalonline.com
Website: www.marianmedicalonline.com
Neonatal products: Enteral System, Urinary Catheters, Urinary Collection Kit, Circumcision Tray, Chest Tube Kit, Exchange Transfusion Tray, Blood Administration Syringe Sets, PICC Procedure Kits. (Woman, estab , empl , sales , cert: City)

Louisiana

6423 AOSS Medical Supply, Inc.
4971 Central Ave
Monroe, LA 71203
Contact: Claudia Sikes President
Tel: 318-325-8290
Email: claudia@aossmedical.com
Website: www.aossmedicalsupply.com
Dist medical supplies. (As-Pac, estab 1979, empl 46, sales $18,000,000, cert: NMSDC)

Massachusetts

6424 Asaman, Inc.
258 Bodwell St
Avon, MA 02322
Contact: Marie Vrakking VP Operations
Tel: 508-588-2008
Email: mvrakking@asaman.com
Website: www.asaman.com
Dist Source Comparator Drugs for Clinical Trials and Analytical testing. (AA, estab 1995, empl 22, sales $17,900,000, cert: State, NMSDC)

6425 Genesis Medical Products, Inc.
40 Farm Hill Rd
Wrentham, MA 02093
Contact: Kevin Kelliher Principal
Tel: 877-933-5437
Email: genesismedical@aol.com
Website: www.iGenesisMedical.com
Dist neonatal, pediatric, labor & delivery soft goods. (Woman, estab 1996, empl 10, sales $300,000, cert: State)

6426 Intelimas Corporation
177 Huntington Ave
Boston, MA 02115
Contact: Charles Mwangi CEO
Tel: 781-388-3300
Email: charles@intelimas.com
Website: www.intelimas.com
Mfr & dist devices, mfr pharmaceutical, generic injectables, pharmaceutical & medical courier, non-emergency medical transportation. (AA, estab 2020, empl 44, sales $22,000,000, cert: NMSDC)

6427 Medical Monofilament Manufacturing
121 Camelot DR
Plymouth, MA 02360
Contact: Michelle Hardiman Mgr
Tel: 508-746-7877
Email: micki@medicalmonofilament.com
Website: www.medicalmonofilament.com
Mfr in-line, precision monofilaments. (Woman, estab 1999, empl , sales $1,965,403, cert: WBENC)

6428 Shinemound Enterprise Inc.
17A Sterling Rd
North Billerica, MA 01862
Contact: Gloria Shiao VP
Tel: 978-436-9980
Email: info@shinemound.com
Website: www.shinemound.com
Mfr latex & non-latex products: disposable PVC, synthetic, vinyl & nitrile, CPE & PE gloves. (As-Pac, estab 1988, empl 6, sales , cert: State)

6429 WestCarb Enterprises, Inc.
122 Florida St
Springfield, MA 01109
Contact: Morrell Thomas President
Tel: 866-507-1576
Email: mt@westcarb.com
Website: www.westcarb.com
Industrial, Hospitality, Medical, Office, Material Handling, Janitorial, Cleanroom & Safety Supplies. (Woman/AA, estab 2002, empl 5, sales , cert: State)

MEDICAL SUPPLIES & SERVICES

6430 Westnet Inc.
55 North St
Canton, MA 02021
Contact: Gordon Thompson CEO
Tel: 781-828-7772
Email: gordon@westnetmed.com
Website: www.westnetmed.com
Dist medical/surgical supplies & equipment; life science products & industrial paper. (AA, estab 1994, empl 37, sales , cert: NMSDC)

Maryland

6431 1st Needs Medical LLC
7003 Glenn Dale Rd Ste 151
Glenn Dale, MD 20769
Contact: Vernon White Partner
Tel: 301-928-2557
Email: info@1stneedsmedical.com
Website: www.1stneedsmedical.com
Durable Medical Equipment & daily use medical supplies. (AA, estab 2014, empl 2, sales , cert: State, NMSDC)

6432 Lifeline Medical Services, Inc.
2955 Mercy Lane
Cheverly, MD 20785
Contact: Eze Nwoji President
Tel: 301-386-0000
Email: eze@lifelinemeds.com
Website: www.lifelinemedicalsupplies.com
Dist automatic sanitary shoe dispenser, hand held EKG monitor, ambulatory product, bathroom product, gloves, dental supplies, woundcare supplies, diagnostics equipment, medical apparels hospital beds & accessories. (AA, estab 2003, empl 4, sales $385,000, cert: State)

6433 Universal Medical Associates, Inc.
111 Hamlet Hill Rd Ste 710
Baltimore, MD 21210
Contact: Renee Parks
Tel: 443-765-9366
Email: reneeparks@universalmedicalassociates.com
Website: www.UniversalMedicalAssociates.com
Medical & surgical implants, osteobiologics & regenerative medicine products, Osteobiologics, Sports Medicine Allografts, Synthetic Biologics &
Regenerative Tissue products. (AA, estab 2010, empl 3, sales $621,930, cert: NMSDC)

Michigan

6434 Heritage Vision Plans, Inc.
One Woodward Ave Ste 2020
Detroit, MI 48226
Contact: Leonard T. Barnes VP Sales & BD
Tel: 313-863-1633
Email: lbarnes@heritagevisionplans.com
Website: www.heritagevisionplans.com
Optical goods & services: eye exams, frames, lenses & contact lenses. (AA, estab 1975, empl 18, sales $11,154,350, cert: NMSDC)

6435 J and B Medical Supply Company Inc.
50496 W Pontiac Trail
Wixom, MI 48393
Contact: Julian Shaya Exec VP
Tel: 800-737-0045
Email: jshaya@jandbmedical.com
Website: www.jandbmedicalsupply.com
Dist Medical Surgical & Emergency Medical Supplies. (Woman, estab 1996, empl 500, sales , cert: WBENC)

6436 MMS Holdings Inc.
6880 Commerce Blvd
Canton, MI 48187
Contact: Prasad M. Koppolu EVP & COO
Tel: 734-245-0310
Email: pkoppolu@mmsholdings.com
Website: www.mmsholdings.com
Clinical research, regulatory submission support for the pharmaceutical, biotech and medical device industries. (Minority, Woman, estab 2005, empl 362, sales $82,294,495, cert: NMSDC)

6437 OCS Inc.
916 Fremont St
Bay City, MI 48708
Contact: Amy Swackhamer Dir of communications
Tel: 989-714-0719
Email: amy@ocsmgt.com
Website: www.ocsmgt.com
Medical & vocational management, occupational therapy consultating & cost containment services. (Woman, estab 2010, empl 12, sales $1,000,000, cert: WBENC)

6438 TerryWorldWide, LLC
6505 Grandville Ave
Detroit, MI 48228
Contact: Terry Willis CEO
Tel: 313-974-8341
Email: terry@terryworldwide.com
Website: www.terryworldwide.com
Dist CanAm Medical/SiO2 Ultra Thin Liquid Glass Coatings. (AA, estab 2010, empl 1, sales , cert: NMSDC)

6439 The Black Moon Group dba BMG Medical Supply
6026 Kalamazoo Ave, Ste 237
Grand Rapids, MI 49508
Contact: Bill McCurdy CEO
Tel: 616-275-9109
Email: bmccurdy@theblackmoongroup.com
Website: www.BMGmed.com
Dist Medline and McKesson Medical Supply and Equipment. (AA, estab 2015, empl 5, sales , cert: NMSDC)

6440 Veteran Medical Products, Inc.
813 Franklin St SE
Grand Rapids, MI 49507
Contact: Roosevelt Tillman President
Tel: 616-451-8486
Email: rt@veteranmedical.com
Website: www.veteranmedical.com
Disposable medical supplies. (AA, estab 2005, empl 2, sales $100,000, cert: NMSDC)

Minnesota

6441 Global International LLC
P.O.BOX 240385
Apple Valley, MN 55124
Contact: Ambrose Kpoto Dir Strategic Partnership
Tel: 612-404-1051
Email: ambrose@fgmmedical.com
Website: www.fgmmedical.com
Dist medical, dental, and pharmaceuticals. (AA, estab 2014, empl 30, sales $3,000,000, cert: NMSDC)

6442 NavasDRSTi, LLC
1714 Basswood Court
Carver, MN 55315
Contact: Yog Ohneswere CEO
Tel: 888-628-2860
Email: yohnes@navadrsti.com
Website: www.navadrsti.com
Electro-Surgical Units, Cardio-Vascular & Cardiology Equipment & Instruments, Radiology, Ultrasound, Diagnostic Imaging & Testing Equipment, Orthopedic Devices, Implants & Tools, Surgical Equipment, Instruments, Supplies & Disposables. (As-Ind, estab 2016, empl 2, sales , cert: State)

6443 Ulmer Pharmacal
1614 Industry Ave W
Park Rapids, MN 56470
Contact: Brent Swanson CFO
Tel: 218-732-2656
Email: bswanson@lobanaproducts.com
Website: www.ulmerpharmacal.com
Mfr premium cleaning & infection control products, patient lubricating jellies & skin care products.. (Woman, estab 2013, empl 10, sales $520,000, cert: State)

Missouri

6444 Emed Medical Company
11551 Adie Rd
Maryland Heights, MO 63043
Contact: Eric Bailey President
Tel: 314-291-3633
Email: SJONES@EMEDMEDICAL.COM
Website: www.emedmedical.com
Dist medical & pharmaceutical products. (AA, estab , empl , sales $26,000,000, cert: State, NMSDC)

6445 I.V. House, Inc.
418 Seven Gables Ct
Chesterfield, MO 63017
Contact: Angela Cressey
Tel: 314-453-9200
Email: angela@ivhouse.com
Website: www.ivhouse.com
Mfr & dist I.V. House Ultra Dressings & Ultra Domes, IV site protectors for all ages. (Woman, estab , empl , sales , cert: State)

6446 Metro Medical Equipment & Supply, Inc.
500 NW Plaza Dr
Saint Ann, MO 63074
Contact: Karen Moore CEO
Tel: 341-383-2879
Email: karen.moore@metromedicalequip.com
Website: www.metromedicalequip.com
Dist medical & surgical supplies. (As-Pac, estab 1985, empl 8, sales $1,100,000, cert: State)

6447 RDB Enterprises II LLC
10011 E 67th St
Raytown, MO 64133
Contact: Robert Branscumb President
Tel: 888-626-1577
Email: rmeeks7@aol.com
Website: www.RDBENTERPRISESLLC.COM
Dist medical supplies, first-aid, safety, lab equip, food services & industrial supplies. (AA, estab 1991, empl 35, sales , cert: City)

6448 SimmCo Distribution
4813 Lee Ave
St. Louis, MO 63115
Contact: Shaun Simms President
Tel: 314-389-3630
Email: info@simmcodistribution.com
Website: www.simmcodistribution.com
Dist Medical Devices, Medical Supplies & Pharmaceuticals. (AA, estab 2012, empl 5, sales , cert: State, City)

North Carolina

6449 MYCO Medical Supplies, Inc.
2015 Production Dr
Apex, NC 27539
Contact: Sanjiv Kumar President
Tel: 919-460-2535
Email: kkennedy@mycomedical.com
Website: www.mycomedical.com
Dist medical supplies, needles, blunt fill needles, blood collection sets, sutures, syringes, PPE, blades and scalpels. (Minority, estab 1993, empl 22, sales , cert: NMSDC)

6450 Playtime Edventures LLC
9905 Running Cedar Ln
Indian Trail, NC 28079
Contact: Kevin Gatlin CEO
Tel: 704-806-5692
Email: playtimebedsheets@gmail.com
Website: www.PlaytimeEdventures.com
Interactive therapy bed sheets for hospitalized children. (AA, estab 2014, empl 4, sales , cert: NMSDC)

6451 Seniors Medical Supply, Inc.
540 W Elm St
Graham, NC 27253
Contact: Gavin Coble President
Tel: 336-227-0730
Email: seniorsmedical@bellsouth.net
Website: www.seniorsmedicalsupply.net
Dist medical equipment: power & manual wheelchairs, canes, commodes, walkers, lift chairs, surgical equipment & supplies, hospital beds & sheets, oxygen, wound care products, compression therapy, ED pumps, diabetic shoes. (Woman/AA, estab 2004, empl 6, sales $345,789, cert: WBENC)

MEDICAL SUPPLIES & SERVICES

New Jersey

6452 Amneal Pharmaceuticals
      400 Crossing Blvd 3rd Fl
      Bridgewater, NJ 08807
      Contact: Brown Massey Dir Sales
      Tel: 908-947-3120
      Email: bmassey@amneal.com
      Website: www.amneal.com
Develop, mfg & dist generic pharmaceutical products. (As-Ind, estab 2002, empl 4727, sales , cert: NMSDC)

6453 BLOXR Solutions LLC
      PO Box 5148
      North Branch, NJ 08876
      Contact: John Buday Customer Service
      Tel: 801-590-9880
      Email: order@bloxr.com
      Website: www.bloxr.com
Mfr radiation protection cream and apparel. (Minority, Woman, estab 2015, empl 14, sales , cert: WBENC)

6454 Case Medical, Inc.
      50 West St
      Bloomfield, NJ 07003
      Contact: Sandy Swerdloff President
      Tel: 201-313-1999
      Email: sswerdloff@casemed.com
      Website: www.casemed.com
Develope Custom Case packs for Health Care Providers (HCP). (Woman, estab 1992, empl 164, sales $23,814,575, cert: WBENC)

6455 Cenmed Enterprises
      121 Jersey Ave
      New Brunswick, NJ 08901
      Contact: Rizwan Chaudhry Operations
      Tel: 732-447-1100
      Email: rizwan@cenmed.com
      Website: www.cenmed.com
Dist medical supplies, laboratory supplies, hospital supplies, surgical supplies, emt supplies, safety supplies, fire supplies. (Woman/As-Ind, estab 1992, empl 25, sales $8,400,000, cert: State, City, NMSDC, WBENC, SDB)

6456 Discovery ChemScience LLC
      66 Witherspoon St, Ste 1100
      Princeton, NJ 08542
      Contact: Qun Sun President
      Tel: 609-475-5097
      Email: qsun@dischemsci.com
      Website: www.dischemsci.com
Provide discovery, medicinal chemistry & custom synthesis CRO services. (As-Pac, estab 2004, empl 2, sales $2,900,000, cert: NMSDC)

6457 Earth2Earth LLC
      8 Promenade Place
      Voorhees, NJ 08043
      Contact: Sita Rentala Owner
      Tel: 856-843-1441
      Email: earth2earth45@gmail.com
      Website: www.earth2earthonline.com
PPE products to the Health Care Industry, as well as Biodegradable Toothbrushes to Dentists and Environmentalists. Our products are made from renewable resources that include plant fiber, bamboo, sugar cane, unbleached, and recycled items. (Woman/As-Ind, estab 2018, empl 5, sales , cert: City, WBENC)

6458 Eastmed Enterprises, Inc.
      11 Brandywine Dr
      Marlton, NJ 07039
      Contact: Supti Putatunda President
      Tel: 856-797-0131
      Email: mona.p@eastmedent.com
      Website: www.eastmedent.com
Mfr & dist laryngoscope systems, airway management & intubation products. (Woman/As-Ind, estab 1987, empl 4, sales , cert: WBENC)

6459 IBS Solutions Corporation
      9 Peach Tree Hill Rd
      Livingston, NJ 07039
      Contact: Matthew ODoherty Strategic Acct Dir
      Tel: 973-994-8000
      Email: matto@pittplastics.com
      Website: www.ibssolutionsgroup.com
Dist can liners and medical waste bags. (As-Pac, estab 2011, empl 10, sales $45,000,000, cert: NMSDC)

6460 NCT Holdings, Inc.
      212 Carnegie Center Blvd Ste 301
      Princeton, NJ 08540
      Contact: Duane Clark Dir Business Devel
      Tel: 609-945-0101
      Email: dclark@wcgclinical.com
      Website: www.wcgclinical.com
Clinical Trials, rater training, certification and data review. (Woman, estab 2005, empl , sales $15,000,000, cert: WBENC)

6461 NEXT Medical Products Company, LLC
      45 Columbia Road
      Branchburg, NJ 08876
      Contact: John Buday Dir CS & Sales Support
      Tel: 800-458-4254
      Email: jbuday@nextmedicalproducts.com
      Website: www.nextmedicalproducts.com
Mfr Clear Image & LithoClear Ultrasound Gel brands, sterile & non-sterile single patient packets. (Woman/As-Pac, estab 2012, empl 13, sales $5,000,000, cert: WBENC)

6462 Precision Medical Devices, Inc.
        121 Jersey Ave
        New Brunswick, NJ 08901
        Contact: Lynn Indyk Business Devel Mgr
        Tel: 732-447-2587
        Email: lindyk@pmdmfg.com
        Website: www.pmdinstruments.com
Mfr medical devices, instrument systems & clinical products, surgical instruments. (As-Ind, estab 2008, empl 6, sales $275,000, cert: NMSDC)

6463 Siris Pharmaceutical Services
        75 North St Ste 1
        Bloomsbury, NJ 08804
        Contact: Andrew Voigt Business Devel
        Tel: 908-479-1331
        Email: andrewv@sirispharma.com
        Website: www.sirispharma.com
Clinical packaging, distribution, drug storage, and drug returns/destruction services. (Woman, estab 2001, empl 12, sales $672,000, cert: WBENC)

6464 TSK Products, Inc.
        12 Windsor Dr
        Eatontown, NJ 07724
        Contact: Eric Klein VP
        Tel: 732-982-1090
        Email: esklein@tskproducts.com
        Website: www.tskproducts.com
Dist products that improve safety, for both patients & staff, plus improves comfort for patients receiving treatment. (Minority, Woman, estab 2000, empl 3, sales $989,849, cert: State, City)

6465 United Medical Supplies Inc.
        25 Craig Place
        North Plainfield, NJ 07059
        Contact: Raman Alaigh CEO
        Tel: 908-757-0075
        Email: rayalaigh@unitedmedsupplies.com
        Website: www.unitedmedsupplies.com
Dist synthetic, latex & nitrile exam gloves, walkers, wheelchairs, bathroom accessories, bath benches, commodes, rollators, crutches, disposable medical supplies, alternating pressure relief mattress, overlay mattress. nebulizers, oxygen tubing. (Minority, Woman, estab 2007, empl 4, sales , cert: State)

New Mexico

6466 R & M Government Services
        650 Montana Ave, Ste A
        Las Cruces, NM 88001
        Contact: Sharon Guerrero VP
        Tel: 575-522-0430
        Email: sharon@rmgovernmentservices.com
        Website: www.rmgovernmentservices.com
Abaxis Veterinary Diagnostics, Vetscan, ACR Mechanical Construction A-dec Dental Chairs, Handpieces, Delivery Systems. (Minority, Woman, estab 2011, empl 8, sales , cert: WBENC)

Nevada

6467 PPE Catalog LLC
        2300 W Sahara Ave Ste. 800
        Las Vegas, NV 89102
        Contact: Michael Gordon Chairman
        Tel: 702-856-4459
        Email: michaelgordon@ppecatalog.com
        Website: www.ppecatalog.com
Dist PPE equipment and supplies, disinfectant wipes, and other disinfectant products, sanitizing products, NIOSH N95 respirators, N95 masks. (Woman, estab 2020, empl 5, sales $3,500,000, cert: WBENC)

New York

6468 Alpha Medical Distributor, Inc.
        60-B Commerce Place Unit B
        Hicksville, NY 11801
        Contact: Jonathan Lee President
        Tel: 516-681-5290
        Email: alphameddis@aol.com
        Website: www.MortuarySuppliesUSA.com
Dist body bags, cadaver bags, transport bags & mortuary supplies. (Woman/As-Pac, estab 2000, empl 4, sales $500,000, cert: State)

6469 BFFL Co., LLC
        20 Kensington Rd
        Scarsdale, NY 10583
        Contact: Elizabeth Thompson CEO
        Tel: 914-713-8550
        Email: drelizabeth@bfflco.com
        Website: www.bfflco.com
Surgical Bras, surgical vests, compression bras, comfort & recovery garments, compression wear, hospital gowns, orthopedic dressings. (Woman, estab 2011, empl 5, sales $1,549,736, cert: WBENC)

6470 Danlee Medical Products, Inc.
        6075 E Molloy Rd, Ste 5 Bldg. 5
        Syracuse, NY 13211
        Contact: Joni Walton operations
        Tel: 315-431-0143
        Email: joni@danleemedical.com
        Website: www.danleemedical.com
Mfr custom hook-up kits, boxer shorts & endoscopy shorts, disposable pouches for holter & event recording, disposable scrubs & disposable blood pressure cuff liners. (Woman, estab 1994, empl 13, sales $2,900,000, cert: State, City, WBENC)

6471 JLGJ Trading, Inc.
        65 East Bethpage Rd Ste 400
        Plainview, NY 11803
        Contact: Edie Berntson VP Sales
        Tel: 888-222-2237
        Email: edie@jlgjtrading.com
        Website: www.ourcaresupplies.com
Dist medical supplies. (Woman, estab 2004, empl 4, sales , cert: NWBOC)

MEDICAL SUPPLIES & SERVICES

6472 Sidra Medical Supply Inc
474 Meacham Ave
Elmont, NY 11003
Contact: Muhammad Momen President
Tel: 516-226-3449
Email: momen@sidramedicalsupply.com
Website: www.sidramedicalsupply.com
Manufacturing; Medical equipment & supplies; Surgical appliances; First aid & safety equipment, (As-Ind, estab 2015, empl 2, sales $750,000, cert: State)

6473 Silarx Pharmaceuticals, Inc.
19 West St
Spring Valley, NY 10977
Contact: George Hauss RA/QA coord
Tel: 845-325-4020
Email: ghauss@silarx.com
Website: www.silarx.com
Mfr liquid generic pharmaceutical & nutritional supplements. (As-Ind, estab 1985, empl 40, sales $11,130,742, cert: NMSDC)

6474 SPS Medical Supply Corp.
6789 W Henrietta Rd
Rush, NY 14543
Contact: Mariann Hughes Dir of Sales & Marketing
Tel: 585-359-0130
Email: mhughes@spsmedical.com
Website: www.spsmedical.com
Mfr & dist sterility assurance products: biological & chemical indicators, integrators, bowie dick tests, autoclave tape, pouches & record keeping products. (Woman, estab , empl , sales , cert: WBENC)

6475 XGen Pharmaceuticals DJB, Inc.
300 Daniel Zenker Dr
Horseheads, NY 14845
Contact: Liz Carbon Dir Natl Accounts
Tel: 607-562-2700
Email: ecarbon@xgenpharmadjb.com
Website: www.xgenpharmadjb.com
Provide affordable generic equivalents that enhance patient care, today and tomorrow. (Woman, estab , empl 55, sales $57,250,000, cert: WBENC)

Ohio

6476 889 Global Solutions
1943 W 5th Ave.
Columbus, OH 43212
Contact: Govt Sales Project Mgr
Tel: 614-235-8889
Email: info@889globalsolutions.com
Website: www.889globalsolutions.com
Healthcare Components & Equipment. Consumer Goods & Promotional Products. Industrial Products. (Minority, Woman, estab 2000, empl 20, sales , cert: State, NMSDC)

6477 C&M Medical Supply, Inc.
8600 S Wilkinson Way, Ste C
Perrysburg, OH 43551
Contact: Creston Tarrant President
Tel: 419-872-0033
Email: ctarrant@cmmedicalsupply.com
Website: www.cmmedicalsupply.com
Diagnostic & respiratory equipment & supplies, advanced woundcare, latex, vinyl & nitrile exam gloves, ultrasound & electro medical products, portable EKG, spirometry, holter, blood pressure & oximetry. (AA, estab 2005, empl 8, sales $486,000, cert: State, NMSDC)

6478 Cincinnati Sub-Zero Products, LLC
12011 Mosteller Rd
Cincinnati, OH 45241
Contact: Matt McCurdy Natl Accts Mgr
Tel: 513-772-8810
Email: mmccurdy@genthermcsz.com
Website: www.cszindustrial.com
Hyper-Hypothermia systems for use in hosptials before during & after surgery. Patient temperature controlled. (Woman, estab 1940, empl 200, sales , cert: City)

6479 Kadiri Health, LLC
PO Box 746
Yellow Springs, OH 45387
Contact: Christopher Cox Owner, Sr Consultant
Tel: 310-435-5455
Email: ccox@kadirihealth.com
Website: www.kadirihealth.com
Dist medical, laboratory, scientific, diagnostic, & research equipment, supplies & furniture. (AA, estab , empl , sales , cert: NMSDC)

6480 Medical Resources
8377 Green Meadows Dr N Ste C
Lewis Center, OH 43035
Contact: Randy Reichenbach VP
Tel: 740-201-3300
Email: Randy@MedicalResources.com
Website: www.MedicalResources.com
Mfr Stainless Steel Products for Healthcare Facilities: blanket warming cabinets, instrument cabinets, instrument stands, back tables, and endoscope cabinets. (Woman, estab 1987, empl 18, sales $8,400,000, cert: State, NWBOC)

6481 MediGreen Medical Supplies & Services, LLC
340 Echo Valley Dr
Vandalia, OH 45377
Contact: Veronica Green Owner
Tel: 937-776-3113
Email: veronica.green@medigreenmedsupplies.com
Website: www.medigreenmedsupplies.com
Disposable Gowns, Apparel, Patient Care Items, Operating Room/ER Items Gloves. (Woman/AA, estab 2012, empl 1, sales , cert: State, City)

MEDICAL SUPPLIES & SERVICES

6482 Premium Contractor Solution LLC
2601 W Stroop Rd, Ste 500
Moraine, OH 45439
Contact: Dexiang Bao Sales Dir
Tel: 216-527-4338
Email: dbao@premiumcontractorsolution.com
Website: www.premiumcontractorsolution.com
Provide PPE, N95 mask, KN95 mask, Gowns, Thermometer, surgical mask, cotton face mask, Ventilator, gloves and etc. (Woman, estab 2014, empl 15, sales $4,134,000, cert: WBENC)

6483 Procura Select
30700-E Carter St
Solon, OH 44139
Contact: Patricia Palermo President
Tel: 440-248-1622
Email: ppalermo@procuraselect.com
Website: www.procuraselect.com
Dist medical carts, shelving, storage & organization products. (Woman, estab 2014, empl 3, sales , cert: WBENC)

6484 Reidy Medical Supply, Inc.
PO Box 713079
Cincinnati, OH 45271
Contact: Ted Stitzel President
Tel: 330-686-4485
Email: tstitzel@reidymed.com
Website: www.reidymed.com
Dist disposable medical supplies. (Woman, estab 1992, empl 26, sales $9,000,000, cert: WBENC)

6485 SGM Contracting Inc.
9485 Root Rd
North Ridgeville, OH 44039
Contact: Regina Morris Owner
Tel: 216-337-0742
Email: ginamorris@sgmcontracting.com
Website: www.sgmcontracting.com
Engineered medical support systems: cath, x-ray, surgical & exam light supports, operable walls & specialty support systems. (Woman, estab 2008, empl 3, sales $265,000, cert: City)

6486 Transworld Supply Network, LLC
3850 Winning Stakes Way
Mason, OH 45040
Contact: Christopher Che President
Tel: 513-229-7595
Email: dsmith@transworldsn.com
Website: www.transworldsn.com
Global importer of healthcare disposables. (AA, estab 2018, empl 3, sales $10,000,000, cert: NMSDC)

Oklahoma

6487 Mobile Cardiac Imaging LLC
7018 South Utica Ave
Tulsa, OK 74136
Contact: Kristy Yang Sr Operations Mgr
Tel: 918-744-1001
Email: kyang@mcidiagnostics.com
Website: www.mcidiagnostics.com
Dist medical and laboratory products, services, and equipment. (AA, estab 1998, empl 27, sales $4,900,000, cert: NMSDC)

6488 NeoChild
8213 SW 23rd Place
Oklahoma City, OK 73128
Contact: Chad Kennard VP Operations
Tel: 888-887-6428
Email: chad@neochild.com
Website: www.neochild.com
Neonatal specialty products. (Woman, estab , empl , sales $3,200,000, cert: WBENC)

Oregon

6489 Ascent Group Medical LLC
1631 NE Broadway St, Ste 308
Portland, OR 97211
Contact: Nuradin Kariye CEO
Tel: 888-386-1112
Email: nuradin@ascentgroupmedical.com
Website: www.ascentgroupmedical.com
Dist medical surgical supplies, equipment & medical staffing. (AA, estab 2011, empl 1, sales , cert: State)

6490 Panga Eco-Friendly Dental Supply
2269 SE Lindenbrook Ct
Milwaukie, OR 97222
Contact: Ingrid Adeogun Owner
Tel: 503-523-9442
Email: ingrid@wearepanga.com
Website: www.wearepanga.com
Mfr & dist eco-friendly dental products: Tongue Scraper, Bamboo Toothbrush, eco-friendly floss. (AA, Hisp, estab 2019, empl 1, sales , cert: WBENC)

Pennsylvania

6491 Actuated Medical, Inc.
310 Rolling Ridge Dr
Bellefonte, PA 16823
Contact: Rachael Bernier President
Tel: 814-380-2879
Email: rachael.bernier@actuatedmedical.com
Website: www.actuatedmedical.com/face-shield.html
Provide reusable face shield with a reinforced headband & manufacture a face shield attachment for hard hats. (Woman, estab , empl 22, sales $4,480,000, cert: WBENC)

6492 Coleman Laboratories
1150 First Ave, Ste 501
King of Prussia, PA 19406
Contact: Le-Jun Yin President
Tel: 267-644-7767
Email: lejun.yin@colemanlabs.com
Website: www.colemanlabs.com
Develop & mfr IV status monitors. The LM series Fluid Level Monitor is a passive sensing device that alarms when the infusion fluid level is low. The device provides both visual and audible alarms when preset condition is met. (As-Pac, estab 2010, empl 4, sales $200,000, cert: NMSDC)

6493 Regulatory and Quality Solutions LLC
2790 Mosside Blvd Ste 800
Monroeville, PA 15146
Contact: Maria Fagan CEO
Tel: 877-652-0830
Email: accounting@rqteam.com
Website: www.rqteam.com
Medical device regulatory & quality consulting support organization. (Woman, estab 2008, empl 100, sales $15,200,000, cert: WBENC)

6494 SlateBelt Safety
1694 Southlawn Dr
Lancaster, PA 17603
Contact: Robert D Williams President
Tel: 888-642-0001
Email: robert@slatebeltsafety.com
Website: www.slatebeltsafety.com
Dist occupational safety prescription eyewear. (AA, estab 2006, empl 21, sales $1,000,000, cert: NMSDC)

6495 UMF Medical
1316 Eisenhower Boulevard
Johnstown, PA 15904
Contact: Eileen Melvin Dir Marketing & Cstmr Care
Tel: 814-266-8726
Email: emelvin@umfmedical.com
Website: www.umfmedical.com
Mfr exam tables, podiatry chairs, Procedure Chairs, phlebotomy chairs, power & manual exam tables, treatment & orthopedic tables, pediatric examination tables, clinical casework, modular cabinetry, stools, side chairs, treatment & supply cabinets. (Woman, estab , empl , sales $16,000,000, cert: WBENC)

Puerto Rico

6496 Cesar Castillo, Inc.
361 Calle Angel Buonomo St Tres Monjitas Industrial Pk
Hato Rey, PR 00917
Contact: Luis Vazquez VP
Tel: 787-999-1616
Email: lvazquez@cesarcastillo.com
Website: www.cesarcastillo.com
Dist pharmaceutical products, health & beauty care, consumer goods, Specialty Pharmaceutical Products to Physicians and Specialty Pharmacies. (Hisp, estab 1946, empl 400, sales $177,000,000, cert: NMSDC)

6497 J.C. Gonzalez, Inc.
2 St KM 178.2 Interior BO. Minillas Alto
San German, PR 00683
Contact: Julio C. Gonzalez Santiago CEO
Tel: 787-892-0047
Email: sales@jcgonzalezinc.com
Website: www.jcgonzalezinc.com
Dist & service scientific & research equipment, laboratory equipment & consumables, microscopes, stereoscopes, freezers, refrigerators. (Hisp, estab 2001, empl 6, sales $865,047, cert: NMSDC, SDB)

6498 Steri-Tech Inc.
Road 701 Km. 0.7, Salinas Ind. Park
Salinas, PR 00751
Contact: Juan Arguelles Managing Dir
Tel: 787-824-4040
Email: jarguelles@steri-tech.com
Website: www.steri-tech.com
Dist cleanroom products & contract sterilization services. (Hisp, estab 1986, empl 30, sales $3,020,000, cert: NMSDC)

South Carolina

6499 AlphaVets, Inc.
15A Liberty St E
York, SC 29745
Contact: Cynthia Spragg President
Tel: 803-548-6800
Email: cindys@alphavets.com
Website: www.alphavets.com
Dist medical equipment. (Woman, estab 2019, empl 7, sales $5,817,176, cert: State, WBENC)

6500 Bennett Wholesale Distributors LLC
300 Long Point Ln Ste 220-O
Columbia, SC 29229
Contact: Jameel Bennett Owner
Tel: 800-650-0616
Email: jb@bennettwholesale.com
Website: www.bennettwholesale.com
Dist medical supplies / equipment and laboratory services. (AA, estab 2003, empl 1, sales $250,000, cert: NMSDC)

6501 Cambridge Marketing, Inc.
PO Box 4481
Rock Hill, SC 39732
Contact: Carol Ballard Owner
Tel: 803-328-3167
Email: carolcmi@aol.com
Website: www.cambridgemarketingcorp.com
Dist hospital products: custom sterile kits, suture removal kits & ER kits. (Minority, Woman, estab 1983, empl 2, sales $326,813, cert: State)

6502 Carolina Diagnostic Solutions
100 Old Cherokee Rd Ste F 301
Lexington, SC 29072
Contact: Amanda Clark President
Tel: 803-360-3410
Email: amanda@carolinadxsol.com
Website: www.carolinadiagnosticsolutions.com/
Pulmonary diagnostic related equipment, supplies, consultation & clinical service, body box/ plethysmography, gas measurement (FRC lung volumes, diffusing capacity), Spirometry equipment, handheld spirometer, portable spirometer. (Woman, estab 2014, empl 2, sales , cert: State)

6503 Pediatric Medical Solutions
      974 Harbortowne Rd
      Charleston, SC 29412
      Contact: Heather Able Owner
      Tel: 843-762-6769
      Email: theableco@aol.com
      Website: www.pediatricmedicalsolutions.com
Snuggle Wraps, Pediatric Elbow Immobilizers, are the cool and comfortable solution to keep little hands safely away! Snuggle Wraps are the world's best elbow immobilizers! (Woman, estab 1998, empl 2, sales $155,000, cert: City)

6504 Rhino Medical Supply
      649 Rosewood Dr, Ste B
      Columbia, SC 29201
      Contact: Elliott Haynie COO
      Tel: 404-704-7961
      Email: info@rhinomedicalsuppy.com
      Website: www.rhinomedicalsupply.com/
Dist Personal Protective Equipment (PPE), medical devices, and disinfectants. (AA, estab 2020, empl 10, sales $8,500,000, cert: NMSDC)

Tennessee

6505 Arch Plastics Packaging, LLC
      2010 Polymer Dr
      Chattanooga, TN 37421
      Contact: Shital Rali Sales/Mktg Exec
      Tel: 423-553-7751
      Email: srali@archplasticsllc.com
      Website: www.archplasticsllc.com
Dist high quality HDPE & PET bottles. (Woman/As-Ind, estab 2006, empl 94, sales $12,000,000, cert: NMSDC, NWBOC)

6506 Direct Medical Supplies, LLC
      7285 Winchester Rd Ste 104
      Memphis, TN 38125
      Contact: Robert E Williams GM
      Tel: 901-461-5379
      Email: robert@directmedicalofamerica.com
      Website: www.directmedicalsuppliesonline.com
Dist medical equipment & supplies: vinyl gloves, masks, shoes, wheelchairs, hospital beds, motorized wheelchairs, walkers, canes, commodes, rollators, wound dressings, diabetic test supplies, etc. (AA, estab 1999, empl 4, sales $425,000, cert: State)

6507 Global Industrial Components Inc.
      705 S College St
      Woodbury, TN 37190
      Contact: David W. Vance Automtive Product Mgr
      Tel: 615-563-5120
      Email: dvance@gic-co.com
      Website: www.gic-co.com
Dist medical kits, ER kits, roadside emergency kits, dental & medical supplies & equipment, component hardware. (Hisp, estab 1994, empl 47, sales $14,900,000, cert: NMSDC)

6508 Innovate Medical, LLC
      2210 Buffalo Rd
      Johnson City, TN 37604
      Contact: Susan Johnston Owner
      Tel: 423-461-3558
      Email: susanj@innovatemed.com
      Website: www.innovatemed.com
Medical rubber products: tourniquets, esmark bandages, exercise bands, dental dams & component parts. (Woman, estab 2001, empl , sales $11,231,046, cert: WBENC)

6509 International Medical & Laboratory Supply, LLC
      9093 Valkrie Lane
      Lakeland, TN 38002
      Contact: Michael Tharps VP
      Tel: 901-377-0191
      Email: michaeltharps@bellsouth.net
      Website: www.internationalmedlab.com
Dist medical, safety, automotive, print management & labopratory supplies. (AA, estab 2004, empl 2, sales , cert: NMSDC)

6510 MRP, LLC dba Aquabiliti & AmUSA
      5209 Linbar Dr Ste 640
      Nashville, TN 11111
      Contact: Timir Patel CEO
      Tel: 615-833-2633
      Email: accounts@aquabiliti.com
      Website: www.aquabiliti.com
Mfr terminally sterilized pre-filled flush syringes used for maintaining IV (intravenous) catheter patency. (Minority, estab 2005, empl 25, sales $8,016,000, cert: NMSDC)

6511 Princeton Medical Group, Inc.
      1601 Championship Blvd Ste 233
      Franklin, TN 37064
      Contact: Terry Rust VP Marketing & Sales
      Tel: 601-594-9495
      Email: tcrust50@gmail.com
      Website: www.princetonmedical.net
Dist surgical instruments. (Woman, estab 1991, empl 20, sales $1,400,000, cert: WBENC)

6512 The Premier Group
      4600 Cromwell Ave, Ste 101
      Memphis, TN 38118
      Contact: JW Gibson CEO
      Tel: 901-346-9002
      Email: jwgibson@gibsoncompanies.com
      Website: www.gibsoncompanies.com
Dist medical supplies, laboratory & scientific equipment & related supplies. (AA, estab 1991, empl 7, sales $8,692,576, cert: NMSDC)

Texas

6513 Accel Lifestyle LLC
      2014 Bailey St
      Houston, TX 77006
      Contact: Megan Eddings CEO
      Tel: 832-980-0875
      Email: megan@accelunite.com
      Website: www.accelunite.com
Designed a new style of reusable isolation gowns. (Woman, estab 2020, empl 3, sales , cert: State, WBENC)

6514 Adair Visual, Inc.
      3550 W 7th St
      Fort Worth, TX 76107
      Contact: Alyce Jones President
      Tel: 817-377-3500
      Email: melanie@adaireyewear.com
      Website: www.adaireyewear.com
Protective eyewear & surgical loupes. (AA, estab 1980, empl 6, sales $1,484,023, cert: State, NMSDC)

6515 Affirmative Biosolutions
      PO Box 2274
      Stafford, TX 77497
      Contact: seble woubshet Owner
      Tel: 713-256-8996
      Email: abiosolutions@hotmail.com
      Website: www.abiosolutions.com
Dist laboratories, medical & industrial products (Woman/AA, estab 2010, empl 3, sales , cert: State, City)

6516 Alea Health dba Kersh Health
      2600 Technology Dr, Ste 100
      Plano, TX 75074
      Contact: Bruce Brown VP Advanced Clinical Services
      Tel: 469-241-2500
      Email: program.coordinator@aleahealth.com
      Website: www.kershhealth.com
Population health management, Health Risk Assessment, Diabetes Disease Management, Weight Loss, Stop Smoking, Activity Monitoring, Wellness Programs. (Nat Ame, estab 2015, empl 37, sales , cert: City)

6517 BayLab USA
      2230 LBJ Frwy, Ste 100
      Dallas, TX 75234
      Contact: Joseph Petroni VP Operations
      Tel: 214-907-2527
      Email: joseph.petroni@baylabusa.com
      Website: www.baylabusa.com
Medical device & supplies, designing, manufacturing, sourcing disposable medical & surgical supplies. (As-Pac, estab 2019, empl 27, sales $15,000,000, cert: WBENC)

6518 Bracane Company, Inc.
      1201 W. 15th St. Ste 330
      Plano, TX 75075
      Contact: Cheryl Barrett Admin
      Tel: 888-568-4271
      Email: mail@bracaneco.com
      Website: www.bracaneco.com
Dist medical supplies: lab equipment, Iv pumps, hospital beds, lab kits and supplies. (Woman/AA, estab 2002, empl 12, sales , cert: NMSDC, WBENC)

6519 Dalton Medical Corp.
      4259 McEwen Rd
      Farmers Branch, TX 75244
      Contact: Jennifer Yu COO
      Tel: 469-329-5200
      Email: jennifery@daltonmed.net
      Website: www.daltonmedical.com
Dist bariatric wheelchairs; walking aids, rollators, forearm rollators, walkers, and U-shape moving walkers with seat; cane stand; knee walker; foot pillow; acrylic medicine organizer; DryAid incontinence supply, protective underwear. (As-Pac, estab 1993, empl 25, sales $4,500,000, cert: State, NMSDC)

6520 Glove Ventures LLC
      11325 Cash Rd
      Stafford, TX 77477
      Contact: Alishah Momin COO
      Tel: 281-301-5277
      Email: alishah@usagloves.com
      Website: www.usagloves.com
Mfr exam-grade nitrile gloves. (As-Ind, estab 2021, empl 11, sales , cert: NMSDC)

6521 GTL Supply Solutions, LLC
      101C N Greenville Ave, Ste 423
      Allen, TX 75002
      Contact: Famira Green Inside Sales Acct Mgr
      Tel: 972-359-7300
      Email: fgreen@gtlsolutions.com
      Website: www.gtlsolutions.com
Dist medical supplies & equipment. (Woman/AA, estab 2007, empl 10, sales $2,300,000, cert: State)

6522 Jackson & Associates, Inc.
      8633 Schumacher Ln
      Houston, TX 77063
      Contact: Saul Szub President
      Tel: 713-777-1155
      Email: saul@dealmedical.com
      Website: www.dealmedical.com
Dist medical, dental, surgical, pharmaceuticals, beauty, health & safety supplies & equipment. (Hisp, estab 1998, empl 6, sales $1,210,000, cert: State, City)

6523 MDD Marketing Inc.
      5773 Woodway, Ste 214
      Houston, TX 77057
      Contact: Jennifer Hess Acct Mgr
      Tel: 713-647-8240
      Email: jennifer.hess@sterlingtonmedical.com
      Website: www.aedtoday.com
AEDs and Manual Defibrillators. (Woman, estab 2000, empl 7, sales $2,000,000, cert: State)

6524 Mpulse Healthcare, LLC
      54 Sugar Creek Center Ste 300
      Sugarland, TX 77478
      Contact: Tyrone Dixon CEO
      Tel: 281-277-4410
      Email: tdixon@mpulsehealth.com
      Website: www.mpulsehealth.com
Dist medical, veterinary, dental, athletic & scientific supplies, products & equipment. (AA, estab 2005, empl 2, sales $100,000, cert: State, NMSDC)

6525 MRC - Medical Research Consultants
      10550 Richmond Ave Ste 310
      Houston, TX 77042
      Contact: Gretchen Watson CEO
      Tel: 713-528-6326
      Email: gwatson@mrchouston.com
      Website: www.mrchouston.com
Medical litigation support services: nurse reviews, mass tort expertise, record retrieval & document management. (Woman, estab 1983, empl 268, sales $9,102,297, cert: WBENC)

MEDICAL SUPPLIES & SERVICES

6526 Prestige Ameritech LTD
7201 Iron Horse Blvd
North Richland Hills, TX 76180
Contact: Elizabeth Givens
Tel: 817-427-7200
Email: elizabeth@prestigeam.com
Website: www.prestigeameritech.com
Mfr surgcal masks & face shields. (Nat Ame, estab , empl , sales $7,000,000, cert: State)

6527 Products Unlimited, Inc.
PO Box 339
Justin, TX 76247
Contact: Raithel Susan Sales Mgr
Tel: 940-648-3073
Email: sraithel@products-unlimited.com
Website: www.products-unlimited.com
Dist medical, lab & safety supplies & equipment. (Woman, estab 1992, empl 7, sales $5,020,000, cert: State)

6528 Taylor Distribution Group, LLC
8117 Preston Rd Ste 300
Dallas, TX 75225
Contact: Artura Taylor President
Tel: 214-890-9200
Email: artura@tdgsci.com
Website: www.tdgscientific.com
Dist pharmaceuticals, medical, surgical, industrial dispenser paper products & laboratory equipment, supplies, chemicals & instruments. (Woman/AA, estab 2009, empl 14, sales $2,581,860, cert: State, NMSDC, WBENC)

6529 VM Cardio Vascular Inc.
4235 Centergate St
San Antonio, TX 78217
Contact: Sara Weyman President
Tel: 800-247-6294
Email: info@vossmedicalproducts.com
Website: www.vossmedicalproducts.com
Manufacture & dist disposable surgical products used in open heart surgeries, bypass graft markers, vein clamps & cannulas. (Woman, estab 2005, empl 4, sales $409,000, cert: WBENC)

6530 Zeitgeist Expressions, Inc.
1222 N Main Ste 740
San Antonio, TX 78212
Contact: Patricia Adams President
Tel: 210-271-7411
Email: padams@zeitgeistexpressions.com
Website: www.zwgroup.net
Employee assistance programs, critical incident debriefing, chaplains, MINT programs, counselors, psychiatrists, psychologists, nurses, social workers & educators. (Woman/AA, estab 2001, empl 47, sales $14,000,000, cert: WBENC)

Utah

6531 Acquire Med LLC
528 N Kays Dr, Ste 1
Kaysville, UT 84037
Contact: Austin Wood Dir of Contracts
Tel: - -
Email: sales@acquiremed.com
Website: www.acquiremed.com
Dist Urology disposables & surgical equipment rental. (Woman, estab 2013, empl 4, sales $3,325,000, cert: WBENC)

6532 CAO Group, Inc.
4628 W Skyhawk Dr
West Jordan, UT 84084
Contact: Michael Tippets
Tel: 801-256-9282
Email: pilot@caogroup.com
Website: www.caogroup.com
Mfr & develop veterinary, dental, medical & forensic products & solutions. (As-Pac, estab 2000, empl 50, sales , cert: NMSDC)

Virginia

6533 Best Medical International Inc.
7643 Fullerton Rd
Springfield, VA 22153
Contact: Lauri Luxton Corporate Counsel
Tel: 800-336-4970
Email: lauri@teambest.com
Website: www.bestmedical.com
Dist brachytherapy solutions. (As-Pac, estab 1977, empl 104, sales $14,000,000, cert: NMSDC)

6534 Evident, Inc.
739 Brooks Mill Rd
Union Hall, VA 24176
Contact: Michael Grimm President
Tel: 800-576-7606
Email: michael@evident.cc
Website: www.ShopEVIDENT.com
Crime scene & forensic identification products: fingerprint products, evidence supplies, DNA collection materials, identification equipment, & crime scene kits for police & law enforcement. (Woman, estab 1992, empl 15, sales , cert: State)

6535 Global PPE Inc.
11490 Commerce Park Dr, Ste 400
Reston, VA 20191
Contact: Andrew Treanor SVP
Tel: 703-488-6912
Email: inquiry@global-ppe.com
Website: www.global-ppe.com
Dist certified diagnostic, testing kits, medical consumables, surgical masks & respirators, gloves, face shields, protective eyewear, surgical gowns, shoe coverings. (As-Ind, estab 2020, empl 30, sales $15,000,000, cert: State)

6536 JKICT, Inc.
       11240 Waples Mill Rd Ste 400
       Fairfax, VA 22030
       Contact: Jay Kim President
       Tel: 703-474-4924
       Email: jeakuk@gmail.com
       Website: www.jkict.net
Digital X-Ray Imaging System, High frequency X-Ray generator, Digital Radiology System, ECG Electrodes, ESU Pencils, ESU Plates, TENS/EMS Units, Cutaneous Electrodes, Robotic Assisted Gait Training System. (As-Pac, estab 2008, empl 2, sales , cert: State)

6537 M.E.Z Distributors LLC
       45910 Transamerica Plaza Ste 104
       Sterling, VA 20166
       Contact: Adeel Shah President
       Tel: 703-821-6760
       Email: adeel@sterlingsurgical.com
       Website: www.sterlingsurgical.com
Dist medical supplies, medical equipment & equipment maintenance/service. (Minority, estab , empl , sales $1,700,000, cert: State)

6538 Reliant Medical Supply
       1431 Abingden Road
       W. Chesterfield, VA 23236
       Contact: stacey worthington Owner
       Tel: 804-814-3180
       Email: staceyworthington@reliantmedicalsupply.com
       Website: www.reliantmedicalsupply.com
Dist medical supplies. (Woman, estab 2008, empl 2, sales , cert: State)

6539 Triton Light Medical, LLC
       8412 MacAndrew Terr
       Chesterfield, VA 23838
       Contact: Kennon Artis Principal
       Tel: 804-543-8137
       Email: kennon@tritonlightmedical.com
       Website: www.tritonlightmedical.com
Dist our proprietary line of instruments crafted in Tuttlingen, Germany, the global center of first-quality, surgical-grade instruments and operating room (OR) equipment. (AA, estab 2017, empl 1, sales , cert: State, NMSDC)

Washington

6540 Anesthesia Equipment Supply, Inc.
       24301 Roberts Dr.
       Black Diamond, WA 98010
       Contact: Michelle Norrie President
       Tel: 253-631-8008
       Email: michelle@aesol.com
       Website: www.aesol.com
Dist custom medical equipment. (Woman, estab 1967, empl 15, sales , cert: WBENC)

6541 Cassel Communications, Inc.
       1402 140th Place NE
       Bellevue, WA 98007
       Contact: Lewis Barnes SVP
       Tel: 917-862-2324
       Email: lewis@casselpackaging.com
       Website: www.casselpackaging.com
Dist standard & custom designed body fluid/waste transport specimen bags. (Woman/AA, estab 1989, empl 5, sales $2,000,000, cert: NMSDC)

6542 Summit Imaging
       15000 Woodinville Redmond Rd Bldg B, Ste 800
       Woodinville, WA 98072
       Contact: Jessica Curtiss Customer Outreach Coord
       Tel: 866-586-3744
       Email: sales@mysummitimaging.com
       Website: www.mysummitimaging.com
Ultrasound transducers & parts. (As-Ind, estab 2006, empl 41, sales , cert: NMSDC)

Wisconsin

6543 Alpha Source Inc.
       6619 W Calumet Rd
       Milwaukee, WI 53223
       Contact: Norine Carlson-Weber
       Tel: 800-654-9845
       Email: norine.carlson-weber@alphasource.com
       Website: www.alphasource.com
Mfr medical batteries, dist medical lighting, diagnostic instruments, repair parts for medical equipment. (Woman, estab 1986, empl 40, sales $18,219,000, cert: WBENC)

6544 Fox Converting, Inc.
       PO Box 12795
       Green Bay, WI 54307
       Contact: Accounting Mgr
       Tel: 920-434-5272
       Email:
       Website: www.foxconverting.com
Sterilization Bags/Envelopes, Swabs -Sterilizable, CSR Sterilizer Wraps, Hospital Bedside Disposal Bags, X-Ray Envelopes. (As-Pac, estab 1960, empl 60, sales $15,150,000, cert: State)

METAL CASTING
Non-ferrous foundries and molds. (Also see six other METAL categories). NAICS Code 33

California

6545 JDH Pacific Inc.
      14821 Artesia Blvd.
      La Mirada, CA 90638
      Contact: David Unger Sales Mgr
      Tel: 562-207-1764
      Email: dunger@jdhpacific.com
      Website: www.jdhpacific.com
Cast & forged components. (As-Pac, estab 1989, empl 35, sales $19,000,000, cert: NMSDC)

6546 KFM International Industries, Inc.
      20277 Valley Blvd, Ste L
      Walnut, CA 91789
      Contact: Dennis Boribor Engineer
      Tel: 626-369-9556
      Email: dennis@kfmii.com
      Website: www.kfmii.com
Casting: Sand Cast, Die Casting, Investment Casting & Permanent Mold Forging: Hot & Cold Formed Sheet Metal Stamping Machining: CNC,Turning & Milling Powder Metal. (Minority, Woman, estab 2000, empl 6, sales $2,700,000, cert: City, CPUC)

Illinois

6547 Calumet Brass Foundry, Inc.
      14610 Lakeside Ave
      Dolton, IL 60419
      Contact: Dawn Stromberg President
      Tel: 708-344-7874
      Email: dawn@calumetbrassfoundry.com
      Website: www.calumetbrassfoundry.com
Mfr bushings, bearings, liners & guides, bronze sand casting, foundry. (Minority, Woman, estab , empl , sales , cert: WBENC)

Michigan

6548 Aerostar Manufacturing
      28275 Northline Rd
      Romulus, MI 48174
      Contact: Robert Johnson VP
      Tel: 734-942-8440
      Email: rjohnson@aerostarmfg.com
      Website: www.aerostarmfg.com
CNC machining assembly, prototyping, machine castings & forgings, sand casting. (As-Pac, estab 1970, empl 200, sales , cert: NMSDC)

6549 Allied Technology Inc.
      6830 Metro Plex Dr
      Romulus, MI 48174
      Contact: Annie Shen President
      Tel: 734-728-6688
      Email: ati.purchasing@alliedtech-eng.com
      Website: www.alliedtech-eng.com
Castings, forgings, cold forming products, stampings and screw machine products. (As-Pac, estab 1999, empl 12, sales $7,000,000, cert: NMSDC)

6550 GK Tech, LLC
      3331 W Big Beaver Rd Ste 106
      Troy, MI 48084
      Contact: Kelly Choi
      Tel: 248-494-1960
      Email: kellychoi@gktechusa.com
      Website: www.gktechllc.com
Marketing specialist, consulting, business development, forging, die-casting, stamping, spring, magnesium pulley, rubber bushing, fasteners, machining, plastic injection molding. (Minority, Woman, estab 2015, empl 3, sales , cert: NMSDC)

6551 Lucerne International
      40 Corporate Dr
      Auburn Hills, MI 48326
      Contact: Karen Ryan Finance Mgr
      Tel: 248-674-7210
      Email: kryan@lucerneintl.com
      Website: www.lucerneintl.com
Advanced metal forming components & assemblies, body structures, chassis systems & powertrain systems. Mfg aluminum & steel forgings, stampings, aluminum & zinc die castings & steel. (Woman, estab 1993, empl 58, sales , cert: WBENC)

6552 New Products Corporation
      448 North Shore Dr
      Benton Harbor, MI 49022
      Contact: Kristy Lovejoy VP
      Tel: 269-925-2161
      Email: kristy.lovejoy@newproductscorp.com
      Website: www.newproductscorp.com
Custom, precision, high-pressure aluminum and zinc die casting. (Woman, estab , empl 50, sales , cert: WBENC)

6553 Precision Components Manufacturing, LLC
      35855 Stanley
      Sterling Heights, MI 48312
      Contact: Tommy Longest CEO
      Tel: 586-939-8500
      Email: tommy@pcmfettes.com
      Website: www.pcmfettes.com
Mfr cast tooling, castings iron/aluminum, steel forging, fully machined castings & assembly, ferrous & non-ferrous products, forging, sand & die casting. (AA, estab 2009, empl 30, sales $7,000,000, cert: NMSDC)

METAL COATING
Includes plating, polishing, spray painting, metal finishing, paint stripping, de-oiling, anodizing, etc. (Also see six other METAL categories). NAICS Code 33

Arizona

6554　Best Finishing, Inc.
　　　7670 E Broadway Blvd Ste 203
　　　Tucson, AZ 85710
　　　Contact: Chris Schlesinger President
　　　Tel:　520-546-7763
　　　Email: chris@bestfinishing.com
　　　Website: www.bestfinishing.com
Metal finishing, polishing & buffing: aluminum castings, exhaust systems, metal moldings, body hardware, stampings, aluminum heads & blocks, magnesium components, closures. (Woman, estab 2000, empl 5, sales $1,000,000, cert: WBENC)

California

6555　Dean Baldwin Painting, LP
　　　2395 Bulverde Rd Ste 105
　　　Bulverde, CA 78163
　　　Contact: Rick Smith Dir Business Dev
　　　Tel:　830-438-5340
　　　Email: ricks@deanbaldwinpainting.com
　　　Website: www.deanbaldwinpainting.com
High quality aircraft painting: commercial, regioanl, military and VIP corporate aircraft. (Woman/Hisp, estab 1972, empl 560, sales $28,800,000, cert: State, NMSDC, WBENC)

Florida

6556　AmeriCoat Corporation
　　　2935 Barneys Pumps Pl
　　　Lakeland, FL 33812
　　　Contact: Shrikant Desai President
　　　Tel:　863-667-1035
　　　Email: americoatusa@yahoo.com
　　　Website: www.ameri-coat.com
Powder coating, fluoropolymers, metal finishing, coating, blasting, stripping. (As-Ind, estab 1995, empl 5, sales , cert: State)

Illinois

6557　Advance Coating Solutions
　　　748 E Sunnyside Ave
　　　Libertyville, IL 60048
　　　Contact: Joseph Webb CEO
　　　Tel:　847-732-1118
　　　Email: joseph@acsco.us
　　　Website: www.acsco.us
Epoxy coating solutions. (AA, estab 2008, empl 7, sales , cert: State, NMSDC)

Indiana

6558　Advanced Nitriding Solutions, LLC
　　　1688 Lammers Pike
　　　Batesville, IN 47006
　　　Contact: Megumi Owens Dir of Sales
　　　Tel:　812-932-1010
　　　Email: sales@ans-ion.net
　　　Website: www.ans-ion.net
Commercial Heat Treating specializing in Nitriding, Internal Metallurgical Lab (NADCAP) Sand Blasting (Woman, estab 2004, empl 8, sales $2,700,000, cert: WBENC)

Massachusetts

6559　The Falmer Associates, Inc.
　　　96 Swampscott Road Unit 10
　　　Salem, MA 01970
　　　Contact: Stacy Ames President
　　　Tel:　978-745-4000
　　　Email: sames@falmer.com
　　　Website: www.falmer.com
Machining, grinding & thermal spray coating svcs: metal, ceramic & carbide coatings, wear, corrosion, erosion, galling, thermal insulation or conduction, electrical insulation or conduction, anti-skid. (Woman, estab 1961, empl 4, sales $400,000, cert: WBENC)

Michigan

6560　Dhake Industries
　　　15169 Northville Rd
　　　Plymouth, MI 48170
　　　Contact: Arjun Dhake VP
　　　Tel:　734-420-0101
　　　Email: adhake@dhakeindustries.com
　　　Website: www.dhakeindustries.com
Mfr automotive coatings. (As-Ind, estab 1979, empl 25, sales $12,000,000, cert: NMSDC)

6561　Great Lakes Finishing, Inc.
　　　510 W Hackley Ave
　　　Muskegon, MI 49444
　　　Contact: Diana Bench President
　　　Tel:　231-733-9566
　　　Email: dbench@greatlakesfinishinginc.com
　　　Website: www.greatlakesfinishinginc.com
Alkaline and Chloride zinc plating. Barrel plating for small parts. Rack plating for parts up to 12' long. Two automatic lines. RoHS compliant. Chromates: bright, yellow, black and olive drab. (Woman, estab 2002, empl 12, sales $1,000,000, cert: WBENC)

6562 Jackson Tumble Finish
      1801 Mitchell St
      Jackson, MI 49203
      Contact: Denise L. Losey President
      Tel: 517-787-0368
      Email: denise@jacksontumble.com
      Website: www.jacksontumble.com

Zinc phosphate, fine, med, heavy grain; calcium modified fine grain phosphate, manganese phosphate, phos. and lube, black oxide, tumble and vibratory deburr, shot blast, glass bead, acid pickle, wash/degrease, and passivate, sort and packaging. (Woman, estab 1956, empl 45, sales $4,700,000, cert: WBENC)

Minnesota

6563 Coating Solutions, Inc.
      13525 Fenway Blvd N
      Hugo, MN 55038
      Contact: Kimberly Northrop CFO
      Tel: 651-762-5700
      Email: knorthrop@coatingsolutions.com
      Website: www.coatingsolutions.com

DuPont teflon industrial coatings. (Woman, estab 1995, empl 7, sales , cert: WBENC)

New Jersey

6564 Karnak Corporation
      330 Central Ave
      Clark, NJ 07066
      Contact: Sarah Jane Jelin President
      Tel: 800-526-4236
      Email: sjjelin@karnakcorp.com
      Website: www.karnakcorp.com

Protective roof coatings, reflective roof coatings, aluminum coatings, elastomeric coatings, Energy Star & LEED compliant coatings, dampproofing, waterproofing, flashing cements, primers, sealants, membranes, reinforcing fabrics. (Woman, estab 1933, empl 97, sales $60,000,000, cert: WBENC)

Ohio

6565 Cleveland Die & Mfg. Co.
      20303 First Ave
      Middleburg Heights, OH 44130
      Contact: Marty Curry Sales/Engineering
      Tel: 440-243-3404
      Email: mcurry@clevelanddie.com
      Website: www.clevelanddie.com/

Ecoat & powder coat line, automatic & single hit presses, spot & robotic welders, CNC machining. (Hisp, estab 1973, empl 300, sales $24,000,000, cert: NMSDC)

6566 Great Lakes Maintenance, Inc.
      1213 Maple Ave.
      Hamilton, OH 45011
      Contact: Marilyn Barlow President
      Tel: 513-423-0800
      Email: glmbarlow@hotmail.com
      Website: www.greatlakesmtce.com

Tank linings & coatings, abrasive blasting, industrial & maintenance painting, leak repair to live gas, water, sludge, fume exhaust & liquor piping, secondary containment coatings & repairs, fiberglass repairs & fabrications. (Minority, Woman, estab 1997, empl 14, sales $14,000,000, cert: State, NMSDC, WBENC)

6567 Herbert E. Orr Comany, Inc.
      335 W Wall St
      Paudling, OH 45879
      Contact: Greg Johnson President
      Tel: 419-399-4866
      Email: gjohnson@heorr.com
      Website: www.heorr.com

Hot Forged Wheel Wrenches; Jack Tool Kits; Hood Support Rods; E-Coat Painting & powder coating; wire forms (pnuematic and CNC); assembly and kitting. (Woman, estab 1957, empl 51, sales $12,656,024, cert: WBENC)

6568 Steelcote, Inc.
      215 Eastview Dr
      Brooklyn Hts., OH 44131
      Contact: Mohan Kapahi President
      Tel: 216-635-2585
      Email: mohan_kapahi@steelcoteinc.com
      Website: www.steelcoteinc.com

Anti-corrosion coatings on metal stampings & assemblies. (As-Ind, estab 2002, empl 9, sales $1,000,000, cert: NMSDC)

South Carolina

6569 JBE, Inc.
      512 Hartland Dr
      Hartsville, SC 29551
      Contact: John Miller Dir Business Devel
      Tel: 843-332-0589
      Email: johnmiller@jbeinc.net
      Website: www.jbeinc.net

Metal finishing; preplate finishing; abrasive blasting, manual & auto buffing, plating needs, chrome, decorative & hard, brite & electroless, silver & tin. Pre-eng bldgs; structure steel & metal fab. Sub-assembly for auto field. (AA, estab 1982, empl 40, sales $348,000,000, cert: NMSDC)

METAL COATING

Tennessee

6570 Y&W Technologies LLC
      2883 Director Cove
      Memphis, TN 38131
      Contact: Willis Yates President
      Tel: 901-396-3380
      Email: wyates@ywtech.com
      Website: www.ywtech.com

Chrome plating, titanium anodizing, metal finishing, electroplating, laser marking, critic & nitric passivation. (AA, estab 2001, empl 20, sales $1,200,000, cert: NMSDC)

Texas

6571 Carrco Painting Contractors, Inc.
      10944 Alder Cir
      Dallas, TX 75238
      Contact: Rudy Cox Business Dev Mgr
      Tel: 214-624-7560
      Email: rcox@carrcopainting.com
      Website: www.carrcopainting.com

Painting, pressure cleaning, wallcovering, drywall repair, epoxy and urethane floor, specialty coating, wall and ceiling coating, protective coating, Cool Seal Roof Coating & Industrial Painting (Hisp, estab 1994, empl 250, sales $8,000,000, cert: State, City)

6572 Cimcon Finishing, LLC
      2314 Executive Dr
      Garland, TX 75041
      Contact: Mike Gilbert VP Sales
      Tel: 972-840-0934
      Email: mike@cimconfinishing.com
      Website: www.cimconfinishing.com

Electroplate: hard anodize, anodize, chemfilm, electroless nickel, nickel, tin, zinc, powder coat. (AA, estab 1994, empl 48, sales $3,200,000, cert: NMSDC)

6573 Texas Finishing Company
      PO Box 59445
      Dallas, TX 75229
      Contact: Carolyn Beard President
      Tel: 972-416-2961
      Email: cbeard@texasfinishing.com
      Website: www.texasfinishing.com

Paint application & custom metal fabrication. (Woman, estab 1982, empl 45, sales , cert: State, WBENC)

Washington

6574 Dunkin & Bush, Inc.
      PO Box 97080
      Kirkland, WA 98083
      Contact: Deidre Dunkin President
      Tel: 425-885-7064
      Email: ddunkin@dunkinandbush.com
      Website: www.dunkinandbush.com

Industrial painting, scaffolding, insulation, rigging, containment, lead abatement, shop coating aplication, concrete restoration, plural applied tank linings, abrasive blasting, specialty blasting, water jetting, high heat coating applications. (Woman, estab 2008, empl 300, sales , cert: WBENC)

> **METAL FABRICATION**
> Includes tanks and tank liners, steel containers, aircraft framework parts, electronic chassis, work stands, ornamental ironwork, fences, sheet metal components, etc. (Also see six other METAL categories). NAICS Code 33

Alabama

6575 Majestic Solutions, Inc.
241 Production Ave
Madison, AL 35758
Contact: Grace Lo President
Tel: 256-772-3232
Email: grace@majesticsolutionsinc.net
Website: www.majesticsolutionsinc.net
Mfr institutional metal furniture & security products: lockers, bunk beds, electronic enclosures, dayroom tables, access panel, shelves, storage cabinets, railings, stairs, wire mesh partition/fence, tubings. (Minority, Woman, estab 2004, empl 10, sales $1,000,000, cert: State, City, SDB)

Arizona

6576 Vics Welding Company, LLC
8376 N El Mirage Rd Bldg 3
El Mirage, AZ 85335
Contact: Victor Valencia President
Tel: 623-925-5696
Email: vic@vicswelding.com
Website: www.vicswelding.com
Metal fabrication, field welding, structural, piping, ASME pressure vessel repair or manufacturing, aerospace welding. (Minority, Woman, estab 1996, empl 6, sales $970,000, cert: City)

California

6577 A-1 Truck and Equipment, Inc.
1588 Los Angeles Ave
Ventura, CA 93004
Contact: Dan Poole President
Tel: 805-659-1817
Email: dan@a1truck.com
Website: www.a1truck.com
Rotating equip repair, body repair, truck, trailers & equip blasting & paint repairs, metal fab & welding. (Hisp, estab 2008, empl 30, sales $2,200,000, cert: NMSDC)

6578 Architectural Mailboxes
123 W Torrance Blvd Ste 201
Redondo Beach, CA 90277
Contact: Vanessa Troyer CEO
Tel: 310-374-5700
Email: vanessa@architecturalmailboxes.com
Website: www.architecturalmailboxes.com
Manufacturers of sheet metal, die casting, and extrusion. (Woman/Hisp, estab 2000, empl 12, sales , cert: NMSDC, WBENC)

6579 Bueno Enterprises
25589 Seaboard Ln
Hayward, CA 94545
Contact: Lydia Bueno Sec/Treas
Tel: 510-782-2225
Email: lydia@metalspecialists.com
Website: www.metalspecialists.com
Precision sheet metal, laser cutting, machining & powder coat painting, fabricate metal parts. (Hisp, estab 1988, empl 10, sales , cert: CPUC)

6580 Columbia Sanitary Products, Inc.
1622 Browning
Irvine, CA 92606
Contact: Paul Escalera
Tel: 847-559-6132
Email: p.escalera@columbiasinks.com
Website: www.columbiasinks.com
Mfr stainless steel products: sinks, wash stations, sink accessories, faucets, heavy-duty forks, shovels, scoops, valves, knife sterilizers & trays. (Woman, estab 1949, empl 8, sales , cert: State)

6581 CX Enterprise Inc.
14408 Iseli Rd
Santa Fe Springs, CA 90670
Contact: Steve Chin Mgr
Tel: 562-407-1088
Email: stevechin@cxenterprise.com
Website: www.cxenterprise.com
Steel strapping. (Minority, Woman, estab 1991, empl 5, sales $1,771,000, cert: CPUC)

6582 Pacific HVAC Depot Corporation
3029 Teagarden St
San Leandro, CA 94577
Contact: Phyllis La Voy CEO
Tel: 510-346-6500
Email: pacifichvacdepot@aol.com
Website: www.pacifichvacdepot.com
Dist hardcast duct sealants, coils & condensers, sheet metal products, fittings & heat ducts. (Woman/Hisp, estab 2000, empl 6, sales $2,300,000, cert: WBENC)

6583 Scott Engineering, Inc.
5051 Edison Ave
Chino, CA 91710
Contact: CFO/COO
Tel: 909-594-9637
Email: info@scott-eng.com
Website: www.scott-eng.com
Mfr medium voltage custom fabricated mild steel, stainless steel, & aluminum electrical cabinets & metal fabricated products. (Hisp, estab 1967, empl 75, sales $14,990,887, cert: CPUC)

6584 Tanfel
1945 Camino Vida Roble, Ste J
Carlsbad, CA 92008
Contact: Greg Lange Owner
Tel: 760-720-9632
Email: glange@tanfel.com
Website: www.tanfel.com
Custom metal parts: stamping, extrusion, casting, metal injection molding, machining, turning, prototype to large production with warehousing capabilities. (Hisp, estab 2008, empl 5, sales , cert: NMSDC)

6585 THISAI LLC
1834 Blazewood St
Simi Valley, CA 93063
Contact: Ramalingam Subramaniam Owner
Tel: 747-206-3886
Email: ram@thisaillc.com
Website: www.thisaillc.com
Electrical products, cables, switches, wire, lighting fixtures, metal products, aluminum, sheet metal, laser cut, bent & fabricated. (Minority, estab 2015, empl 2, sales , cert: State)

6586 West Coast Form Grinding
      2548 S Fairview St
      Santa Ana, CA 92704
      Contact: Adrian Calderon President
      Tel: 714-540-5621
      Email: adrian@precisioncorepins.com
      Website: www.precisioncorepins.com
Mfr mold components, core pins, sleeves, ejector pins, luer taper pins. (Hisp, estab 2005, empl 10, sales $1,222,670, cert: NMSDC)

Colorado

6587 Excalibur Machine & Sheet Metal
      208 W Buchanan St, Unit C
      Colorado Springs, CO 80907
      Contact: Douglas McDaniel Plant Mgr
      Tel: 719-520-5404
      Email: doug@excaliburmfg.com
      Website: www.excaliburmfg.com/
Precision machining & sheet metal fabrication, welding, assembly, powder coating. (Hisp, estab 1989, empl 25, sales $2,600,000, cert: NMSDC)

Connecticut

6588 Turbo America Technology, LLC
      1400 Old North Colony Rd
      Meriden, CT 06450
      Contact: Liliane Yebarth
      Tel: 860-970-8777
      Email: liliane@turboamericatech.com
      Website: www.turboamericatech.com
Mfr & repair Industrial Gas Turbine components. (Hisp, estab 2014, empl 5, sales $341,000, cert: NMSDC)

Florida

6589 Blue Water Dynamics LLC dba Dougherty Mfg.
      301 S Old County Rd
      Edgewater, FL 32132
      Contact: Davey Carroll Sales Dir
      Tel: 386-316-5939
      Email: dcarroll@dougherty-mfg.com
      Website: www.doughertymanufacturing.com
Fabricate metals (aluminum, steel & stainless steel) & composites/FRP, engineering, design, tooling, prototyping & manufacturing. (Woman, estab 2010, empl 46, sales $2,500,000, cert: State, WBENC)

6590 Coastal Steel Inc.
      870 Cidco Rd
      Cocoa, FL 32926
      Contact: Dale Coxwell
      Tel: 321-632-8228
      Email: dcoxwell@coastalsteelmfg.com
      Website: www.coastalsteel.com
Complex & Iconic Structures, Ride & Show, Machining, CMM (Zeiss Contra G2 & FERO). (Nat Ame, estab 1976, empl 90, sales $14,000,000, cert: State, NMSDC)

6591 Cool Tactics LLC
      910 S 8th St, Ste 302
      Fernandina Beach, FL 32034
      Contact: Dana Brodsky President
      Tel: 904-420-0070
      Email: contact@cooltactics.com
      Website: www.cooltactics.com
Installs Insulated Metal Panels (IMPs), underfloor insulation systems, and specialty doors for cold storage and food processing facilities, refrigerated warehouses. (Woman, estab 2019, empl 7, sales , cert: WBENC)

Georgia

6592 Harbor Enterprises, LLC
      1207 Sunset Dr
      Thomasville, GA 31792
      Contact: Brandy Spradlin CEO
      Tel: 229-226-0911
      Email: sba@harborenterprisesllc.com
      Website: www.survive-a-storm.com
Wood & metal fab, mfr solid steel above ground safe rooms & underground storm shelters. (Nat Ame, estab 2009, empl 25, sales $5,500,000, cert: NMSDC, 8(a))

Iowa

6593 Air Control, Inc.
      80 14th Ave N
      Clinton, IA 52732
      Contact: Mary Connell President
      Tel: 563-243-7228
      Email: marypat@acifabricators.com
      Website: www.acifabricators.com
HVAC contracting, specialty steel fabrication, tank fabrication. (Woman, estab 1956, empl 45, sales $8,000,000, cert: WBENC, 8(a))

6594 EIP Manufacturing, LLC
      2677 - 221st St
      Earlville, IA 52041
      Contact: Kathy Krapfl VP Sales & Mktg
      Tel: 800-942-2226
      Email: kkrapfl@eipmfg.com
      Website: www.eipmfg.com
Steel fab, structural steel, rebar. (Woman, estab 1975, empl 45, sales $7,700,000, cert: State)

Idaho

6595 Burly Products, Inc.
      3999 St. Joe Ave
      Post Falls, ID 83854
      Contact: Stephani Morris Admin Asst
      Tel: 208-262-9531
      Email: stephani@burlyproducts.com
      Website: www.burlyproducts.com
Design & mfr steel & aluminum products. (Nat Ame, estab 2006, empl 18, sales , cert: State)

Illinois

6596 Ace Metal Craft
      484 Thomas Dr
      Bensenville, IL 60106
      Contact: Kevin Bailey Sales
      Tel: 847-455-1010
      Email: kevin.bailey@acemetal.com
      Website: www.acemetal.com
Structural Metal Fabrication (Woman, estab 1960, empl 150, sales $10,000,000, cert: WBENC)

6597 American Chrome Chicago Company, Inc.
      518 W Crossroads Pkwy
      Bolingbrook, IL 60440
      Contact: Linda Hou President
      Tel: 630-685-2200
      Email: linda.hou@americanchrome.com
      Website: www.americanchrome.com
Dist chrome, stainless steel & PC/ABS chrome products, mirrors, exhaust products, clam shells for catalytic converters, shock absorbers & components, rubber products / bushings, u-joints, grease caps, air tubes, clutch control rods. (Minority, Woman, estab 1983, empl 26, sales $11,695,000, cert: NMSDC, WBENC)

6598 Combined Metals of Chicago LLC
      2401 W Grant Ave
      Bellwood, IL 60104
      Contact: John Dicello Dir Diversity Devel
      Tel: 708-547-8800
      Email: johnd@combmet.com
      Website: www.combmet.com
Stainless steel: flat rolled stainless steel strip, sheet & foil. (As-Pac, estab 1975, empl 279, sales , cert: NMSDC)

6599 Great Lakes Metals
      8920 S Octavia
      Bridgeview, IL 60455
      Contact: Donna Herpich President
      Tel: 708-430-0500
      Email: glmcdonna@aol.com
      Website: www.greatlakesmetals.com
Steel & metal svcs. (Woman, estab 1994, empl 6, sales , cert: WBENC)

6600 KSO Metalfab, Inc.
      250 Roma Jean Pkwy
      Streamwood, IL 60107
      Contact: Dora Kuzelka President
      Tel: 630-372-1200
      Email: dkuzelka@kso.com
      Website: www.kso.com
Precision sheet metal fabrication: short to large runs. (Woman, estab 1973, empl 33, sales $3,700,000, cert: State)

6601 Patel International
      30 N River Rd Ste 102
      Des Plaines, IL 60016
      Contact: Steve Gordon Sales Rep
      Tel: 847-795-3006
      Email: sgordon@patelintl.com
      Website: www.sejasmi.com
Injection molding, aluminum die casting. (As-Ind, estab 2005, empl 65, sales $8,000,000, cert: NMSDC)

6602 Premier Manufacturing Corporation
      3008 Malmo Dr
      Arlington Heights, IL 60005
      Contact: Susan Fischer President
      Tel: 847-640-6644
      Email: sfischer@premiermfgcorp.com
      Website: www.Premiermfgcorp.com
Sheet metal fabrication: punching, forming, welding, painting, powder coating & assembly. (Woman, estab 1999, empl 9, sales $920,000, cert: WBENC)

6603 Rockford Specialties Company
      5601 Industrial Ave
      Rockford, IL 61111
      Contact: Lisa Stankey President
      Tel: 815-877-6000
      Email: lisas@rswire.com
      Website: www.rockfordspecialties.com
Mfr wire, tube & sheet metal custom displays & components, counter racks, free standing floor displays, wire dividers & aisle extenders, plating & powder painting, laser cutting, forming & welding, MIG, TIG, resistance & robotic welding. (Woman, estab 1979, empl 45, sales $10,780,000, cert: WBENC)

6604 W.E.B. Production & Fabricating, Inc.
      448 N Artesian Ave
      Chicago, IL 60612
      Contact: Maureen Kendziera President
      Tel: 312-733-6800
      Email: maureenk@webproductionandfabricating.com
      Website: www.webproductionandfabricating.com
Welding, shearing, bending, punching, stamping, & drilling, MIG & TIG welding, aluminum, stainless steel, carbon steel, guardrails & metal stair frames. (Woman, estab 1993, empl 24, sales $3,068,370, cert: State)

6605 Young Technology Inc.
      900 W. Fullerton Ave.
      Addison, IL 60101
      Contact: Young Sohn President
      Tel: 630-690-4320
      Email: youngsohn@ytinc.com
      Website: www.ytinc.com
Mfr molded rubber, plastic & forged steel: shifter knobs, bezels, decorative molding & cable components, leather wrapped & chrome plated. (As-Pac, estab 1985, empl 350, sales $6,000,000, cert: NMSDC)

Indiana

6606 Circle City Rebar, LLC
      4002 Industrial Blvd
      Indianapolis, IN 46254
      Contact: Heidi Russo Controller
      Tel: -   -
      Email: hrusso@circlecityrebar.com
      Website: www.circlecityrebar.com
Supplier and Fabricator of concrete reinforcing steel bars (rebar) in all sizes; plain and epoxy coated. (AA, estab 2005, empl 14, sales $7,541,942, cert: NMSDC)

6607 Diversified Quality Services of Indiana, LLC
      1315 W 18th St
      Anderson, IN 46016
      Contact: Sharon Montgomery CEO
      Tel: 765-644-7712
      Email: sharon.montgomery@dqsicorp.com
      Website: www.dqsicorp.com
Design, prototyping, production, modification & repair steel racks, containers & dunnage. (AA, estab 2003, empl 123, sales $5,000,000, cert: NMSDC)

6608 Eagle Magnetic Company Inc.
      7417 Crawfordsville Rd
      Indianapolis, IN 46214
      Contact: Ron Jaggers VP Inside Sales
      Tel: 317-297-1030
      Email: rjaggers@eaglemagnetic.com
      Website: www.eaglemagnetic.com
Magnetic shielding, precision sheet metal fabrication, precision machining. (Woman, estab 1970, empl 39, sales $3,275,000, cert: State)

6609 Electric Metal Fab, Inc.
      4889 Helmsburg Rd
      Nashville, IN 47448
      Contact: Mandy Chittum President
      Tel: 812-988-9353
      Email: mandy@electricmetalfab.com
      Website: www.electricmetalfab.com
Mfr Stainless Steel Equip for the Pharmaceutical & Food Industries, turn-key conveyor systems for production lines, specialty products. Cabinets, Carts, Tables, Racks, Platforms, Lab Furnishings, etc. (Woman, estab 1993, empl 16, sales $1,177,089, cert: WBENC)

METAL FABRICATION

6610 Indiana Bridge
1810 S Macedonia Ave
Muncie, IN 47302
Contact: Sheryl Bronnenberg Mgr
Tel: 765-288-1985
Email: sheryl.bronnenberg@indianabridge.net
Website: www.indianabridge.net
Steel fabrication and erection services. (As-Pac, estab 2001, empl 47, sales $6,348,823, cert: NMSDC)

6611 Indiana Bridge-Midwest Steel, Inc.
1810 S Macedonia Ave
Muncie, IN 47307
Contact: Sheryl Bronnenberg Office Mgr
Tel: 765-288-1985
Email: sheryl@indianabridge.net
Website: www.indianabridge.net/
Fabricate structural steel & rack structures, design build & erection services. (As-Pac, estab , empl 35, sales $26,790,376, cert: NMSDC)

6612 Irons Metal Processing LLC
1605 Adler Cir Ste I
Portage, IN 46368
Contact: Earmon Irons CEO
Tel: 219-764-9999
Email: earmon@ironsmetalprocessing.com
Website: www.ironsmetalprocessing.com
Processed metal products. (AA, estab 2007, empl 3, sales , cert: NMSDC)

6613 Lacay Fabrication and Mfg Inc.
52941 Glenview Dr
Elkhart, IN 46514
Contact: Ann Filley President
Tel: 574-288-4678
Email: ann@lacayfab.com
Website: www.lacayfab.com
Mfr material handling racks, Baskets, Industrial & Production Welding, Machining, Robotic Welding, Stamping, Custom Fabrication, Prototyping. (Woman, estab 1975, empl 70, sales , cert: WBENC)

6614 Refractory Service Corp.
4900 Cline Ave
East Chicago, IN 46312
Contact: Laura Bianchi Eikenmeyer President
Tel: 219-397-7108
Email: laura@refractoryservice.net
Website: www.refractoryservice.net
Mfr high temperature refractories: lances & precast shapes (Woman, estab 1979, empl 85, sales $15,092,895, cert: WBENC)

6615 Royalty Investments, LLC
2476 E US Hwy 50
Seymour, IN 47274
Contact: Marshall Royalty Member
Tel: 812-358-3534
Email: mroyalty@cranehillmachine.com
Website: www.cranehillmachine.com
Machining, fabricating & assembly: steel, aluminum & plastic components. Design, engineering & coating applications. (Woman, estab 1989, empl 30, sales $3,714,618, cert: State, WBENC)

6616 The Phillips Company, Inc.
6330 East 100 South
Columbus, IN 47201
Contact: Valerie Phillips CEO
Tel: 812-378-3797
Email: valeriephillips@thephillipscompany.com
Website: www.thephillipscompany.com
Cast iron & aluminum parts: pulleys, lube pumps, oil coolers, wire harnesses, water pumps, blocks, heads, gear covers. (Woman/AA, estab 1986, empl 47, sales $2,800,000, cert: NMSDC)

Kansas

6617 American Energy Products, Inc.
1105 Industrial St
Lansing, KS 66043
Contact: Gail Watson President
Tel: 913-351-3388
Email: administrator@americanenergyinc.com
Website: www.americanenergyinc.com
Mfr metal products: corrugated seal plate, seal skirting, dip seal plate, drip screen, wire cloth, drip lips, wareplate, scrubber modules, coal piping, pyrite hoppers, ducting work, seal trough, water trough, telescopic coal chutes. (Woman, estab 2000, empl 3, sales $1,200,000, cert: WBENC)

6618 Industrial Metal Fabrication, Inc.
1401 S Spencer
Newton, KS 67114
Contact: Jere Dean Sales Mgr
Tel: 316-650-4068
Email: jere@imfinc.com
Website: www.imfinc.com
Welding, submerged arc, metal plate and sheet rolling, shearing, laser cutting, fabrication, Spouting, Millwright Crew, Transitions, Feed Funnel, Steam Vent, Platform, Pipe Support, Hopper, Silo, Cover Plate, Manhole, ,Weldment, Industrial Bed, Bin. (Woman, estab 2002, empl 41, sales $5,851,062, cert: WBENC)

6619 PTMW, Inc.
5040 NW US Hwy 24
Topeka, KS 66618
Contact: Ashley Bettis President
Tel: 785-232-7792
Email: abettis@ptmw.com
Website: www.ptmw.com
OEM metal fabrication & assembly: metal parts, enclosures & cases, assembly & powdercoating. (Woman, estab 1983, empl 250, sales $55,000,000, cert: CPUC, WBENC)

Louisiana

6620 JRE LLC dba Ascension Roofing and Sheet Metal
2140 S Philippe Ave
Gonzales, LA 70737
Contact: Rebecca Evans President
Tel: 225-647-3576
Email: rebevans@ascensionrsm.com
Website: www.ascensionrsm.com
Metal fabrication: stainless steel, carbon steel, galvanized metal & specialty alloys. (Woman, estab 1954, empl 31, sales $2,260,000, cert: WBENC)

METAL FABRICATION

Massachusetts

6621 Heat Exchanger Products Corp.
55 Industrial Park Rd
Hingham, MA 02043
Contact: Tracy Hennigan Bonnyman President
Tel: 781-749-0220
Email: hepco@heatexchangerproducts.com
Website: www.HeatExchangerProducts.com
Mfr tube plugs for condensers, heat exchangers, boilers in sizes 5/8" up to 1 1/4" in materials; Brass, 316 and 314 Stainless Steel, Titanium and Ultem & Non-Metallic High Performance Polymer plug. (Woman, estab 1985, empl 5, sales , cert: WBENC)

6622 Wrobel Engineering Co., Inc.
154 Bodwell St
Avon, MA 02322
Contact: Michael Long General/QA Mgr.
Tel: 508-586-8338
Email: mlong@wrobeleng.com
Website: www.wrobeleng.com
Mfr precision sheet metal fabricated parts per customer specs, precision machining, milling & turning, metal stamping, long & short runs, tool & die making, assembly mechanical & electrical, welding all materials. (Woman, estab 1976, empl 86, sales $14,800,000, cert: State, City)

Maryland

6623 Waltons Welding & Fabrication, Inc.
155 Prospect Dr
Huntingtown, MD 20639
Contact: Fay Walton President
Tel: 301-855-2944
Email: metalfab@waltonswelding.net
Website: www.waltonswelding.com
Metal fabrication: elctrode welding, mig welding, tig welding, aluminum welding, stainless steel welding, tourch cutting, saw cutting, plasma cutting, shear cutting, drilling, rolling, bending, sanding, grinding, tapping & punching. (Woman, estab 2000, empl 5, sales $154,007, cert: State)

Michigan

6624 Aaron's Fabrication, Inc.
48001 Structural Dr
Chesterfield, MI 48051
Contact: Sue Bursteinowicz President
Tel: 586-883-0652
Email: sue@aaronsfabrication.com
Website: www.aaronsfabrication.net
Structural fabrication, handrails, platforms, stringers, Tube fabrication, Welding Assemblies. (Woman, estab 2014, empl 7, sales $80,000,000, cert: WBENC)

6625 Airodyne Industries, Inc.
95 E 10 Mile Rd
Madison Heights, MI 48071
Contact: Celeste Herpel President
Tel: 248-548-3336
Email: caherpel@airodyne.com
Website: www.airodyne.com
Mfr & dist aerodynamic & fuel-saving devices. (Woman, estab 2004, empl 3, sales $1,265,000, cert: WBENC)

6626 Anderson Express, Inc.
580 W Sherman Blvd
Muskegon Heights, MI 49444
Contact: Angel Ball HR Mgr
Tel: 231-733-6001
Email: aball@andersonexpressinc.com
Website: www.andersonexpressinc.com
Rapid tooling & tooling prototypes for small & medium projects. (Woman, estab 2011, empl 17, sales , cert: WBENC)

6627 Clips & Clamps Industries
15050 Keel St
Plymouth, MI 48170
Contact: Jeff Aznavorian President
Tel: 734-455-0880
Email: jaznavorian@clipsclamps.com
Website: www.clipsclamps.com
Metal forming, progressive dies, four slide, CNC wire forming, tool building, MIG & TIG welding, tapping, riveting, automated assemblies, prototyping & production volumes, engineering services, design services, sales support. (Woman, estab 1954, empl 62, sales , cert: WBENC)

6628 DGH Enterprises, Inc. dba K-O Products Co.
1225 Milton St
Benton Harbor, MI 49022
Contact: Barbara Herrold CEO
Tel: 269-925-0657
Email: barbaraherrold@koproducts.com
Website: www.koproducts.com
Metal stampings, welded & fabricated assemblies, electrical & mechanical assemblies, metal hardware, metal truck parts & assemblies, metal stamped components for auto, appliances, off-road equipment, metal welding, mig welding, spot welding. (Woman, estab 1938, empl 28, sales $5,700,000, cert: WBENC)

6629 Gill Industries Inc.
5271 Plainfield Ave
Grand Rapids, MI 49525
Contact: Regina Wilk Sales Acct Mgr
Tel: 616-559-2700
Email: rwilk@gill-industries.com
Website: www.gill-industries.com/
Stamped weldments & structural assemblies, seat, chassis, body & powertrain structural assemblies, folding head restraint & seat mechanisms. (Woman, estab 1964, empl 1923, sales $340,000,000, cert: WBENC)

6630 Globe Tech LLC.
101 Industrial Dr
Plymouth, MI 48170
Contact: Amanda Menchinger President
Tel: - -
Email: mmenchinger@globe-tech.biz
Website: www.globe-tech.biz
Machining, fabrication & welding, metal stamping. (Woman, estab 2009, empl 72, sales , cert: WBENC)

6631 Harbin Steel
440 Burroughs St, Ste 133
Detroit, MI 48202
Contact: Anthony Harbin President
Tel: - -
Email: anthony@harbinsteel.com
Website: www.harbinsteel.com
Miscellaneous/structural steel fabrication & installation. (AA, estab 2016, empl 1, sales , cert: NMSDC)

6632 HDN F&A, Inc. dba F&A Fabricating
104 Arbor St
Battle Creek, MI 49015
Contact: Hiep Nguyen President
Tel: 269-965-3268
Email: hiep.nguyen@fa-fabricating.com
Website: www.fa-fabricating.com
Custom sheet metal fabrication, food grade stainless steel, dist sheet metal, tubing. (As-Pac, estab 1956, empl 25, sales $3,000,000, cert: NMSDC)

6633 I F Metalworks
14009 Achyl
Warren, MI 48313
Contact: Karen Arondoski President
Tel: 586-776-8311
Email: karen@ifmetalworks.com
Website: www.ifmetalworks.com
Welding, fabrication, design, weldments, assemblies, prototype, short & long run, decorative, railings, staircases, ballisters, custom furniture, artistic works, architectural, trailers, foodservice production equipment, racks & repair. (Woman, estab 2002, empl 10, sales $425,000, cert: WBENC)

6634 International Robot Support, Inc.
24521 N River Rd
Mt. Clemens, MI 48043
Contact: David Emlaw President
Tel: 586-783-8000
Email: demlaw@irobotsupport.com
Website: www.irobotsupport.com
Custom metal fabrication & CNC machining services. (As-Pac, estab , empl 15, sales $1,727,000, cert: NMSDC)

6635 International Specialty Tube
6600 Mt. Elliott
Detroit, MI 48124
Contact: Jason VanDeVen Sales Mgr
Tel: 313-841-6900
Email: quality@istube.com
Website: www.istube.com
Mfr stainless steel tubing for automotive exhaust. (AA, estab 0, empl , sales $29,000,000, cert: NMSDC)

6636 JLC Group LLC
287 Executive Dr
Troy, MI 48083
Contact: William Chen Dir Ph.D.
Tel: 248-792-3281
Email: wchen@jlcgroupllc.com
Website: www.jlcgroupllc.com
Dist casting parts, forging parts & machine finished parts, plastic injected molds & plastic parts. (Minority, Woman, estab 2010, empl 5, sales , cert: WBENC)

6637 Jorgensen Steel Machining & Fabrication
101 Spires Pkwy
Tekonsha, MI 49092
Contact: Matt Jorgensen President
Tel: 517-767-4600
Email: mjorgensen@jorgensen-usa.com
Website: www.jorgensen-usa.com
Design & manufacture contract machinery & contour formed products for the aviation, space & defense industries. (Nat Ame, estab 2001, empl 26, sales $6,334,000, cert: State, NMSDC)

6638 Midbrook Industrial Washers Inc.
2080 Brooklyn Rd
Jackson, MI 49204
Contact: Rodney Sims Govt & diversity Sales
Tel: 517-787-3481
Email: rsims@midbrookindustrial.com
Website: www.midbrookindustrial.com
Custom sheet metal fabrication. (Woman/AA, As-Pac, estab 2012, empl 70, sales , cert: WBENC)

6639 Mintech LLC
PO Box 428
Niles, MI 49120
Contact: Minnie Warren President
Tel: 269-683-4551
Email: minnie@mintechllc.com
Website: www.mintechllc.com
Metal fabrication, stamping, light assembly, sort, vibratory deburring, rollforming. (Woman, estab 0, empl , sales , cert: WBENC)

6640 MNP Corporation
44225 Utica Rd
Utica, MI 48317
Contact: Donna DeSantis Dir Special Applications
Tel: 586-254-1320
Email: donna.desantis@mnp.com
Website: www.mnp.com
Mfr Specialty Fasteners & Engineered Cold Formed Components. Heat Treatment, Plating Stampings, Powder Metal, Machining. Fastener Design and Testing, Steel processing, Rod and Wire, Flat roll slitting (Woman, estab 1970, empl 540, sales $160,000,000, cert: WBENC)

6641 Rochester Tube Products, Ltd.
51366 Fischer Park Dr
Shelby Township, MI 48316
Contact: Jennie Preston Dir of Mktg
Tel: 586-726-4816
Email: jennie@rochestertube.com
Website: www.rochestertube.com
Fabricate steel parts; specifically tube. (Woman, estab 1973, empl 25, sales , cert: WBENC)

6642 Rose-A-Lee Technologies, Inc
7448 19 Mile Rd
Sterling Heights, MI 48314
Contact: Julie Wood Dir Business Dev
Tel: 586-799-4555
Email: jwood@rosealeetechnologies.com
Website: www.rosealeetechnologies.com
CAD design (surface and solid modeling), stamping, assembly/kitting, tube bending, welding (mig, tig, stud arc), etc. (Woman, estab 2013, empl 2, sales , cert: WBENC)

6643 Santanna Tool &Design LLC
25880 Commerce Dr
Madison Hgts, MI 48071
Contact: Jamilce & Newton President
Tel: 248-541-3500
Email: jsnewton@santannatool.com
Website: www.santannatool.com
Design & mfr conveyors, tooling & welding. (Minority, Woman, estab , empl , sales $1,376,927,385, cert: NMSDC, WBENC)

6644 The Ideal Group
      2525 Clark St
      Detroit, MI 48209
      Contact: Linzie Venegas Sales
      Tel: 313-842-7290
      Email: linzie@idealshield.com
      Website: www.weareideal.com
Architectural & engineering svcs; general contracting & construction mgmt, rigging. Mfr, dist, fabricate & erect structural & misc steel. Patent for "Ideal Shield" Protective Guard Rail System. (Hisp, estab 1979, empl 120, sales , cert: NMSDC)

6645 Thompson Marketing, LLC
      15890 Sturgeon CT
      Roseville, MI 48066
      Contact: Derek Thompson President
      Tel: 248-761-6802
      Email: derek@tmsglobalservices.com
      Website: www.tmsglobalservices.com
Mfr shipping racks & fixtures. (AA, estab 1999, empl 7, sales $370,000, cert: NMSDC)

6646 Vari-Form, Inc.
      17199 North Laurel Park, Ste #322
      Livonia, MI 48152
      Contact: Derek W. Ochodnicky Acct Specialist
      Tel: 248-641-2816
      Email: dochodnicky@vari-form.com
      Website: www.vari-form.com
Advanced tube hydro-forming technology, laser cut, assembly & various welding applications, instrument panel beams, radiator enclosures, roof rails & front end structures. (As-Ind, estab 1989, empl 402, sales , cert: NMSDC)

6647 W.S Molnar Company dba SlipNOT Metal Safety Flooring
      2545 Beaufait St
      Detroit, MI 48207
      Contact: Christina Molnar Metrose President
      Tel: 313-923-0400
      Email: info@slipnot.com
      Website: www.slipnot.com
Mfr non slip metal products (Woman, estab , empl , sales $20,700,000, cert: WBENC)

Minnesota

6648 Electrical Builders, Inc.
      2720 1 1/2 St S
      St. Cloud, MN 56301
      Contact: Jessica Netter Ducharme President
      Tel: 320-257-9008
      Email: jnetter@electricalbuilders.com
      Website: www.electricalbuilders.com
Turnkey Substation Construction, Iso Phase and Aluminum Bus Welding (Woman, estab 1974, empl 65, sales $12,500,000, cert: WBENC)

6649 Ironpines Welding Inc.
      1544 64th St SW
      Pequot Lakes, MN 56472
      Contact: Steve Verville Owner
      Tel: 218-820-4190
      Email: sverville@ironpineswelding.com
      Website: www.ironpineswelding.com
Welding, metal fabrication, Plate work, sheetmetal welding, pipe welding & fabrication, (Woman, estab 2012, empl 2, sales , cert: State)

6650 JML Fabrication, LLC
      21054 Chippendale Ct
      Farmington, MN 55024
      Contact: Margo Lackore President
      Tel: 612-444-3025
      Email: margo@jmlfabrication.com
      Website: www.jmlfabrication.com
Aluminum welding, Aluminum Fabrication, Stainless steel welding, Stainless steel fabrication, Steel welding, Steel fabrication, Certified Welding, Bending, Shearing. MIG/TIG welding, Flux core welding, large structural steel fabrication. (Minority, Woman, estab 2004, empl 7, sales $2,400,000, cert: WBENC)

6651 Jones Metal Inc.
      3201 3rd Ave
      Mankato, MN 56001
      Contact: John Clifford Natl Business Devel
      Tel: 507-625-4436
      Email: jclifford@jonesmetalinc.com
      Website: www.jonesmetalinc.com
Metal fabrication, laser technology, water jet, saw, punch presses, press brakes, rollers & machining capabilities. (Woman, estab 1942, empl 100, sales $12,000,000, cert: WBENC)

6652 LAI International, Inc.
      4255 Pheasant Ridge Dr NE #405
      Minneapolis, MN 55449
      Contact: Terri Lambert Dir Sales
      Tel: 480-469-4170
      Email: tlambert@laico.com
      Website: www.laico.com
Cutting-Edge Precision Component Manufacturing. (AA, estab 1979, empl 287, sales $73,113,237, cert: NMSDC)

6653 Wyoming Machine, Inc.
      30680 Forest Blvd
      Stacy, MN 55079
      Contact: Lori Tapani President
      Tel: 651-462-4156
      Email: ltapani@wyomingmachine.com
      Website: www.wyomingmachine.com
Precision metal fabrication: aser cutting, CNC punching, forming & welding. (Woman, estab 1974, empl 65, sales , cert: WBENC)

Missouri

6654 Sinclair Industries, Inc.
      1317 Kentucky Ave
      St. Louis, MO 63110
      Contact: Jagdish Hinduja President
      Tel: 314-535-6335
      Email: sinclair.inc@sbcglobal.net
      Website: www.snclr.com
Metal fabrication. (As-Ind, estab 1978, empl 9, sales $1,200,000, cert: City)

North Carolina

6655 QMF Metal & Electronic Solutions, Inc.
324 Berry Garden Rd
Kernersville, NC 27284
Contact: Raymond Polomski Sales Assoc
Tel: 336-992-6501
Email: rpolomski@qmf-usa.com
Website: www.qmf-usa.com
Custom sheet metal fabrication, punching, forming, welding, robotic welding, machining, hardware installation, wet and powder coat painting, silk screening, mechanical & electronic assembly. (Woman, estab 1978, empl 75, sales $7,000,000, cert: WBENC)

6656 Structural Steel of Carolina, LLC
1720 Vargrave St
Winston-Salem, NC 27107
Contact: Mary Brewer President
Tel: 336-725-0521
Email: mbrewer@steelofcarolina.com
Website: www.steelofcarolina.com
Fab & erect structural & miscellaneous steel. (Woman, estab 2004, empl 85, sales $20,000,000, cert: State)

New Jersey

6657 Central Metals, Inc.
1054 S 2nd St
Camden, NJ 08103
Contact: Susan Vilotti President
Tel: 856-963-5844
Email: vilotti@aol.com
Website: www.centralmetals.com
Steel fabrication, structural steel, miscellaneous metals, ornamental metals, railings, stairs & iron. (Woman, estab 1981, empl 57, sales $29,770,000, cert: WBENC, NWBOC)

6658 Holtec International
1 Holtec Blvd
Camden, NJ 08104
Contact: Jordan Landis Sales & Marketing Mgr
Tel: 856-797-0900
Email: j.landis@holte.com
Website: www.holtecinternational.com
Design & mfr storage systems for wet & dry spent nuclear fuel, takes, vessels, hoists, cranes. (As-Ind, estab , empl , sales $99,000,000, cert: NMSDC)

New York

6659 ASP Industries
9 Evelyn St
Rochester, NY 14606
Contact: Robert Uerkvitz Acct Exec
Tel: 585-254-9130
Email: robert@aspindustries.com
Website: www.aspindustries.com
Sheet metal fabrication, laser, welding, machine. (Woman, estab 1980, empl 25, sales , cert: State)

6660 Bailey Manufacturing Co., LLC
10987 Bennett State Rd
Forestville, NY 14062
Contact: John Hines President
Tel: 716-965-2731
Email: bailey03@netsync.net
Website: www.baileymfgcollc.com
Metal Stamping, Sheet Metal Fabrication, Welding, Multi-Part Assemblies, Zinc Plating, Rust Proofing, Quality Inspection, E-Coat Painting. (AA, estab 2002, empl 100, sales $8,500,000, cert: NMSDC)

6661 Technical Welding Fabricators LLC
27 Thatcher St
Albany, NY 12207
Contact: Carole Boyer Owner
Tel: 518-463-2229
Email: caroleboyer@aol.com
Website: www.technicalweldingfabricators.com
Metals & structural steel, railings, columns, beams, repairs. (Woman, estab 2006, empl 5, sales $1,600,000, cert: State)

Ohio

6662 Armor Metal Group
4600 Mason-Montgomery Rd
Mason, OH 45040
Contact: John Ravana Inside Sales
Tel: 800-543-7417
Email: jravana@witt.com
Website: www.witt.com
Fabrication, burn, grind, machining, lathe, blanchard, surface, roll, laser, form, weld, paint, blast. (Woman, estab 1950, empl 250, sales $51,000,000, cert: WBENC)

6663 Aster Industries
275-299 N Arlington St
Akron, OH 44305
Contact: Kaitlyn Oplinger Admin Asst
Tel: 330-762-7965
Email: kmoplinger@asterind.com
Website: www.asterind.com
Custom millwork manufacturing, commercial booth seating, interior design, stainless steel fabrication, and full construction management. (Woman, estab 1990, empl 25, sales $6,000,000, cert: WBENC)

6664 Extol of Ohio, Inc.
208 Republic St
Norwalk, OH 44857
Contact: Andrea Buggele Inside Sales
Tel: 419-668-2072
Email: andrea@extolohio.com
Website: www.extolohio.com
Fabricate & dist thermally efficient, non-wicking rigid pipe insulation products & accessories. (Woman, estab 1985, empl 50, sales $22,919,925, cert: WBENC)

6665 Fabrication Group LLC
3453 W 140th St
Cleveland, OH 44111
Contact: Patricia Setlock President
Tel: 216-251-1125
Email: patty@fabricationgroup.com
Website: www.fabricationgroup.com
Metal fabrications, welded assemblies, guardrails, handrails, bollards, stair railings, cutting, shearing, roll forming, punch presses, sheet metal fabrication equipment. (Woman, estab 2008, empl 10, sales $433,345, cert: WBENC)

6666 Ferragon Corporation
11103 Memphis Ave
Cleveland, OH 44144
Contact: Luis J. Gonzalez Mgr
Tel: 216-671-6161
Email: lgonzalez@ferrousmetalprocessing.com
Website: www.ferrousmetalprocessing.com
Hot roll steel toll processing: pickle, slit, level, shear, decamber & warehousing. (Hisp, estab 1983, empl 144, sales $16,200,000, cert: NMSDC)

6667 Forest City Erectors, Inc.
8200 Boyce Pkwy
Twinsburg, OH 44087
Contact: Eric Swinehart Project Mgr
Tel: -   -
Email: eswinehart@forestcityerectors.com
Website: www.forestcityerectors.com
Structural Steel & Steel Erection, Precast erection, Tower crane & personnel hoist erection & dismantle, Blast furnace rebuilds/repairs. (Woman, estab 1960, empl 45, sales $27,500,000, cert: City)

6668 GOJO Industries, Inc.
1 Gojo Plz
Akron, OH 44311
Contact: Kerry Bingham Sr Corporate Accounts Dir
Tel: 330-255-6000
Email: binghamk@gojo.com
Website: www.gojo.com
Miscellaneous Fabricated Metal Product Manufacturing. (Woman, estab 1946, empl 3500, sales , cert: WBENC)

6669 Journey Steel, Inc.
7655 Production Dr
Cincinnati, OH 45237
Contact: Barbara Smith President
Tel: 513-731-2930
Email: bsmith@journeysteel.com
Website: www.journeysteel.com/
Remodeling & Expanding: retrofit piping, staircases, overhead walkways. Structural & Mechanical Erector: mechanical devices & assorted equipment supported & erected. (Woman/AA, estab 2009, empl 4, sales $3,900,000, cert: State, NMSDC, WBENC)

6670 KeYAH International Trading, LLC
4655 Urbana Rd
Springfield, OH 45502
Contact: Ramon Vasquez VP
Tel: 937-399-3140
Email: rvasquez@keyahint.com
Website: www.keyahint.com
Die cut, RF weld/sonic weld, automotive interior trim components, sub-assemblies. (Minority, Woman, estab 2000, empl 85, sales $2,000,000, cert: WBENC)

6671 Magni-Power Company
5511 Lincoln Way E
Wooster, OH 44691
Contact: Kim Coblentz New Business Dev Mgr
Tel: 330-264-3637
Email: kcoblentz@magnipower.com
Website: www.magnipower.com
Metal fabrication & stamping: process steel, aluminum, stainless steel, CNC punching, forming, laser cutting, robotic welding, in-house powder coating & assembly. (As-Ind, estab 1948, empl 230, sales $27,000,000, cert: NMSDC)

6672 MCM Ind. Co., Inc.
22901 Millcreek Blvd., Ste 250
Highland Hills, OH 44122
Contact: Gloria Reljanovic Owner
Tel: 216-292-4708
Email: greljanovic@mcmindustries.com
Website: www.mcmindustries.com
Mfr, dist & import finished steel & plastic parts: precision & bicycle chains, non-metal chains, steel ball bearings. (Minority, Woman, estab 1986, empl 50, sales , cert: NMSDC)

6673 Middletown Tube Works, Inc.
2201 Trine St
Middletown, OH 45044
Contact: Angela Phillips CEO
Tel: 513-727-0080
Email: aphillips@middletowntube.com
Website: www.middletowntube.com
Mfr as-welded steel tubes for Automotive, Appliance, HVAC and Packaging industries. (Woman, estab 0, empl , sales , cert: WBENC)

6674 Mid-West Materials, Inc.
3687 Shepard Rd
Perry, OH 44081
Contact: Scott Dennis Sales Rep
Tel: 440-259-5200
Email: scott.dennis@midwestmaterials.com
Website: www.midwestmaterials.com
Flat rolled steel service center, hot rolled, hot rolled, pickled & oiled & coated steel in commercial quality, high strength-low alloy & low through high carbon chemistries. (Woman, estab 1952, empl 50, sales $50,000,000, cert: State)

6675 Morrison Metalweld Process Corporation
3685 Stutz Dr, Ste 102
Canfield, OH 44406
Contact: Robin Eisenbrei CEO
Tel: 330-702-5188
Email: robin@morrisonmetalweld.com
Website: www.morrisonmetalweld.com
Railroad track & crane rail welding services & products. (Woman, estab 1929, empl 9, sales , cert: WBENC)

6676 Shelby Welded Tube
5578 State Route 61 North
Shelby, OH 44875
Contact: Kelly Kleman Sales
Tel: 419-347-1720
Email: kkleman@shelbytube.com
Website: www.shelbytube.com
Dist welded steel tubes. (Woman, estab 1967, empl 81, sales $22,000,000, cert: WBENC)

6677 Thieman Quality Metal Fab, Inc.
05140 Dicke Rd
New Bremen, OH 45869
Contact: Ben Wissman Sales Mgr
Tel: 419-629-2612
Email: bwissman@thieman.com
Website: www.thieman.com
Engineering: AutoCAD, 2000i, Solid Edge & Metamation CAD/CAM Software, Welding:
MIG, TIG, Robotic & Spot welding, Fabrication: Sawing, Machining, Drilling, Hy Def Plasma, Turret Punch, Lasers, Press Break. (Woman, estab 1951, empl 90, sales $16,200,000, cert: NWBOC)

6678 Tylok International, Inc.
1061 E 260th St
Euclid, OH 44132
Contact: Michael Palinkas VP Sales
Tel: 216-261-7310
Email: mpalinkas@tylok.com
Website: www.tylok.com
Mfr stainless steel, brass & steel tube fittings, pipe & weld fittings, ball valves, needle valves, manifolds & double block & bleed valves. (Woman, estab 1955, empl 75, sales $8,600,000, cert: WBENC)

Oregon

6679 General Sheet Metal Works, Inc.
PO Box 1490
Clackamas, OR 97015
Contact: Carol Duncan President
Tel: 503-650-0405
Email: carol@gsmw.com
Website: www.gsmw.com
Sheet metal fabrication, installation, design & support. (Woman, estab 1932, empl 40, sales $7,620,093, cert: WBENC)

Pennsylvania

6680 Cromedy Construction Corporation
5702 Newtown Ave
Philadelphia, PA 19120
Contact: Bill Cromedy President
Tel: 215-437-7606
Email: bcromedy@cromedyconstruction.com
Website: www.cromedyconstruction.com
HVAC, Sheetmetal (AA, estab 2004, empl 15, sales $14,000,000, cert: State, NMSDC, 8(a))

6681 Flexospan Steel Buildings, Inc.
PO Box 515
Sandy Lake, PA 16145
Contact: Karla Black Exec Asst
Tel: 724-376-7221
Email: karla@flexospan.com
Website: www.flexospan.com
Mfr metal roofing and siding panels, matching trims, decking, structural components, custom engineered metal buildings, as well as complete self storage building packages. (Woman, estab 1969, empl 44, sales $10,872,000, cert: WBENC)

6682 General Carbide Corporation
1151 Garden St
Greensburg, PA 15601
Contact: Carrie Gartland Admin Exec
Tel: 800-245-2465
Email: sales@generalcarbide.com
Website: www.generalcarbide.com
Mfr tungsten carbide preforms & blanks used in wear resistant, cutting & metal forming operations. (Woman, estab 0, empl , sales , cert: WBENC)

6683 Specialty Steel Supply Co., Inc.
225 Lincoln Hwy
Fairless Hills, PA 19030
Contact: Green-Campbell President
Tel: 215-949-8800
Email: pat@225steel.com
Website: www.225steel.com
Dist steel beams, angles shapes & plates, fabricate to specs & prototypes. (Woman, estab 1993, empl 10, sales $1,600,000, cert: WBENC)

Puerto Rico

6684 Alonso & Carus Iron Works, Inc.
PO Box 566
Cataño, PR 00963
Contact: Jorge L Ramos, Jr. VP
Tel: 787-788-1065
Email: jramosjr@alonsocarus.com
Website: www.alonsocarus.com
Structural Steel odd-shaped buildings, conventional buildings, steel bridges. Storage tanks for portable water, firewater, waste water and fuel oil. (Hisp, estab 1961, empl 135, sales $12,000,000, cert: NMSDC)

6685 RAC Enterprises, Inc.
Road 1, KM 24.8
Caguas, PR 00726
Contact: Vivian Carballo President
Tel: 787-789-9338
Email: rac@racsteeldrums.com
Website: www.racsteeldrums.com
Mfr steel drums, dist plastic, steel & stainless containers, sorbent products, secondary containment: spill pallets, drain seals. Stormwater management products, PPE & material handling, monitors. (Hisp, estab 1995, empl 15, sales $2,300,000, cert: NMSDC)

South Carolina

6686 J.I.T. Manufacturing, Inc.
428 Oglesby Lane
Cowpens, SC 29330
Contact: Dan Hunter Production / Sales Mgr.
Tel: 864-463-0581
Email: dan@jitmanufacturing.com
Website: www.jitmfg.net
Laser cutting, welding, forming, CNC punching, CNC machines, fabrication, sheetmetal, powdercoating, pressbrakes, modifications, spot welding, control boxes, mounting plates, brackets, CAD programing, Cad design. (Woman, estab 1992, empl 22, sales $2,910,792, cert: City, WBENC)

6687 Lamar's Fabrication, Inc.
210 Ashley Circle
North Augusta, SC 29841
Contact: Michael Lamar CEO
Tel: 706-513-1992
Email: michael.lfab@gmail.com
Website: www.LamarsFabrication.com
Process Pipe, Structural Steel, Carbon steel, Stainless steel, Chromemoly, Inconel, Hastelloy, GTAW, SMAW, FCAW, CNC Plasma cutting, C.A.D. Detailing and Design, 3D Modeling. (AA, estab 2008, empl 2, sales , cert: State, City, NMSDC)

Tennessee

6688 Manufacturers Industrial Group, LLC
228 Rush St
Lexington, TN 38351
Contact: Andre Gist CEO
Tel: 731-967-6442
Email: agist@migllc.com
Website: www.migllc.com
Metal, fabrication, assembly, structural steel, rebar, concrete, reinforcement, welding, racks, metal containers, formed wire and bent tube. (AA, estab 1998, empl 407, sales , cert: State, NMSDC)

Texas

6689 A & A Aero Structures Inc.
800 Schneider Bldg M
Cibolo, TX 78108
Contact: Ronald D Atkins Owner
Tel: 210-566-3660
Email: ron@aaaerostructures.com
Website: www.aaaerostructures.com
Fabricate, assemble & mfr aircraft parts & components. (AA, estab 2007, empl 4, sales , cert: State)

METAL FABRICATION

6690 Advanced Turbine Solutions LLC
      15653 N Brentwood
      Channelview, TX 77530
      Contact: Tim Donohue InterNatl Sales Mgr
      Tel: 314-494-1900
      Email: donohuet@atshouston.com
      Website: www.ATSHouston.com
Fabrication, piping, structural & skids, welding, carbon steel to exotic metals. (As-Pac, estab 2010, empl 12, sales $2,850,000, cert: NMSDC)

6691 All Steel Fabrication Inc.
      501 N Houston St
      Fort Worth, TX 76164
      Contact: Patty Robbins President
      Tel: 817-877-0082
      Email: patty@allsteelfabinc.com
      Website: www.allsteelfabinc.com
Platforms for working around aircraft, large tanks, weld mild steel, A588 Core, stainless Steel & Aluminum. (Woman/Nat-Ame, estab 1990, empl 10, sales $874,579, cert: State)

6692 GABS LLC
      1011 Regal Row
      Dallas, TX 75247
      Contact: Dot Haymann CEO
      Tel: 972-354-6512
      Email: dhaymann@guard-all.com
      Website: www.guard-all.com
Engineer, design & manufacture steel framed, tension fabric buildings for a multitude of applications. (Woman, estab 2011, empl 45, sales $4,990,000, cert: State, WBENC)

6693 GST Manufacturing, Ltd.
      4201 Janada St
      Haltom City, TX 76117
      Contact: Sharrian Lamberth Owner
      Tel: 817-520-2320
      Email: info@gstmanufacturing.com
      Website: www.gstmanufacturing.com
Metal fabrication, in plant maintenance. (Woman, estab 2000, empl 250, sales $50,800,000, cert: State)

6694 Hanstine LLC
      14027 Memorial Dr, Ste 145
      Houston, TX 77079
      Contact: Shawn Gao Sales Mgr
      Tel: 281-712-1588
      Email: shawn.gao@sorogo.com
      Website: www.sorogo.com
Hardware cloth, chainlink fence, barbed wire, welded mesh, hexagonal wire mesh, field fence, horse fence, yard fence, metal wires, window screens (Minority, Woman, estab 2009, empl 2, sales , cert: WBENC)

6695 Harris Composites, Inc.
      600 Holmes Dr
      Granbury, TX 76048
      Contact: Debra Harris CEO
      Tel: 817-279-9546
      Email: hci@itexas.net
      Website: www.harriscomposites.com
Mfr & produce all size composite parts. (Woman, estab 2000, empl 25, sales $3,500,000, cert: State, WBENC)

6696 Llano River Fence Company, LLC
      11418 Lake June Rd
      Balch Springs, TX 75180
      Contact: Ashanti Smith President
      Tel: 972-286-4316
      Email: asmith@llanoriverfence.com
      Website: www.llanoriverfence.com
Custom iron products: gates, iron doors, handrails, & puppy panels, fencing, automatic gates installation & automatic gate operator maintenance. (Woman/AA, estab 2006, empl 13, sales $1,250,000, cert: State)

6697 Magni-Fab Southwest Company
      PO Box 578
      Howe, TX 75459
      Contact: Wayne Swineford Dir Sales/Marketing
      Tel: 903-532-5533
      Email: wswineford@mfsw.net
      Website: www.magnifab.com
Sheet metal fabrication, shearing, CNC punching, laser cutting, stamping, forming, sawing, spot welding, arc welding, robotic welding, powder coating. (As-Pac, estab 1971, empl 105, sales $10,350,000, cert: NMSDC)

6698 MagRabbit-Alamo Iron Works, LLC
      PO Box 2341
      San Antonio, TX 78298
      Contact: Wayne Dennis Diversity Coord
      Tel: 210-704-8520
      Email: wdennis@aiwnet.com
      Website: www.magrabbit-aiw.com
Dist industrial supplies, steel service & fabrication, hand & power tools, equipment repair & installation, logistics, transportation & freight forwarding. (As-Pac, estab 2004, empl 150, sales , cert: NMSDC)

6699 Quality Fabrication & Design
      955 Freeport Pkwy Ste 400
      Coppell, TX 75019
      Contact: Alex Pier President
      Tel: 972-304-3266
      Email: alexpier@quality-fabrication.com
      Website: www.quality-fabrication.com
Mfr custom stainless steel & mild steel equipment: conveyors, drags, belts & bucket, structural steel platforms, waterjet cutting & complete food processing lines. (Hisp, estab 1987, empl 65, sales $6,000,000, cert: State, NMSDC)

6700 Royberg Inc.
      315 North Park Dr
      San Antonio, TX 78216
      Contact: Dwight Bowen
      Tel: 210-525-0094
      Email: dbowen@pmtool.com
      Website: www.precision-group.com
Provide metal cutting machine tools & services. (Woman, estab 1985, empl 60, sales $10,000,000, cert: WBENC)

6701 Texas Finishing Company
      PO Box 59445
      Dallas, TX 75229
      Contact: Carolyn Beard President
      Tel: 972-416-2961
      Email: cbeard@texasfinishing.com
      Website: www.texasfinishing.com
Paint application & custom metal fabrication. (Woman, estab 1982, empl 45, sales , cert: State, WBENC)

METAL FABRICATION

Virginia

6702 Metal Tech Inc.
2629 Richard Ave NE
Roanoke, VA 24012
Contact: Natasha Crowder Project estimator
Tel: 540-798-4193
Email: metaltech@cox.net
Website: www.metaltechincorporated.com
Custom metal fabrication: sandblasting, punching, machine cutting, CNC plasma cutting, water jet cutting, pipe bending, ornamental bender machine, surface preparation & coating. (Woman, estab 1996, empl 2, sales $150,000, cert: State)

6703 Shickel Corporation
115 Dry River Rd
Bridgewater, VA 22812
Contact: Don Crawford Sales Mgr
Tel: 540-828-2536
Email: donc@shickel.com
Website: www.shickel.com
Custom metal fabricating, engineering, design, project management, welding, fabrication, precision machining, finishing & installation services. (Woman, estab 1938, empl 80, sales $11,200,000, cert: State)

6704 Valley Industrial Piping, Inc.
P O Box 1751
Waynesboro, VA 22980
Contact: Michelle Carter President
Tel: 540-942-4469
Email: michelle@valleypipes.com
Website: www.valleypipes.com
Industrial maintenance, fabricate & install process skid systems, pressure vessels, tank installation & repair, structural steel, carbon & stainless steel platforms, mezzanines, ladders & stairways, piping, in-line instrumentation & equipment installation (Woman, estab 2004, empl 10, sales $984,906, cert: State, WBENC)

Vermont

6705 Vermont Precision Tools, Inc.
10 Precision Ln
Swanton, VT 05488
Contact: Monica Greene President
Tel: 802-868-4246
Email: mgreene@vermontprecisiontools.com
Website: www.vermontprecisiontools.com
Mfr high quality precision ground medical burr blanks for the OEM medical industry. (Woman, estab 1968, empl 190, sales $32,527,681, cert: WBENC)

Washington

6706 JIT Manufacturing
19510 144th Ave NE, Ste E 7
Woodinville, WA 98072
Contact: Duane Parrish Sales Mgr
Tel: 425-487-0672
Email: duanep@jit-mfg.com
Website: www.jit-mfg.com
Aerospace Sheet Metal Manufacturing, complete parts, Punching, Laser, Bending, Forming, Hardware & Assembly, Finish, Chem Treat, Paint, Primer. (Woman, estab 1985, empl 60, sales , cert: State)

Wisconsin

6707 Church Metal Spinning Company
5050 N 124th St
Milwaukee, WI 53225
Contact: Brenda Birno President
Tel: 414-461-6460
Email: markv@churchmetal.com
Website: www.churchmetal.com
Metal fabrications including metal stampings, metal spun, laser cut, press brake parts. Also, complete assembly and welding of multi-part components. (Woman, estab 1944, empl 30, sales $6,600,000, cert: State)

6708 Creative CNC LLC
16620 W Rogers Dr
New Berlin, WI 53151
Contact: Janet Murphy President
Tel: 262-347-3939
Email: jmurphy@creativecnc.net
Website: www.creativecnc.net/
Mfr metal parts: aerospace, medical, automotive, turbomachinery, etc. (Woman, estab 2010, empl 3, sales , cert: WBENC)

6709 Metal-Era, Inc.
1600 Airport Rd
Waukesha, WI 53188
Contact: Jody Delie Channel Marketing Mgr
Tel: 800-373-9156
Email: info@metalera.com
Website: www.metalera.com
Mfr perimeter edge metal for the low sloped commercial roofing industry. (Hisp, estab 1980, empl 148, sales $36,700,000, cert: State, NMSDC)

6710 Ridgway LLC dba The Price Erecting Co.
10910 W Lapham St
Milwaukee, WI 53214
Contact: Fred Quilling Estimator
Tel: 414-778-0300
Email: fquilling@priceerecting.com
Website: www.priceerecting.com
Equipment installation & removal, steel erection, fabrication & machining. (Minority, estab , empl 40, sales $9,000,000, cert: State)

6711 Safeway Sling USA, Inc.
6209 Industrial Ct
Greendale, WI 53129
Contact: Susan Szymczak President
Tel: 414-421-7303
Email: sales@safewaysling.com
Website: www.safewaysling.com
Mfr nylon & polyester web lifting slings, polyester round slings, alloy chain slings, wire rope slings, metal mesh slings & tie down assemblies. (Woman, estab 1980, empl 36, sales $6,800,000, cert: WBENC)

METAL STAMPING
Services include forming, welding, tapping, tooling, tube fabrication and bending, etc. (Also see six other METAL categories). NAICS Code 33

California

6712 Proformance Manufacturing, Inc.
      1922 Elise Circle
      Corona, CA 92879
      Contact: Tim Borth Technical Sales Mgr
      Tel: 951-279-1230
      Email: tborth@proformancemfg.com
      Website: www.proformancemfg.com
Precision metal stampings, deep draw parts & machined components. Components formed from flat sheet stock are produced in mechanical & hydraulic presses. (Hisp, estab 1987, empl 21, sales $2,200,000, cert: NMSDC)

6713 Tanfel
      1945 Camino Vida Roble, Ste J
      Carlsbad, CA 92008
      Contact: Greg Lange Owner
      Tel: 760-720-9632
      Email: glange@tanfel.com
      Website: www.tanfel.com
Custom metal parts: stamping, extrusion, casting, metal injection molding, machining, turning, prototype to large production with warehousing capabilities. (Hisp, estab 2008, empl 5, sales , cert: NMSDC)

Connecticut

6714 Hylie Products, Inc.
      669 Straits Tpke
      Watertown, CT 06795
      Contact: Bill Thompson CEO
      Tel: 860-274-5447
      Email: donna@hylie.com
      Website: www.hylie.com
Mfr high-volume, customer-specific, high-precision, quality-critical, metal stampings & progressively drawn eyelets, four-slide stamped & formed parts. (Woman, estab 1963, empl 17, sales $2,500,000, cert: WBENC)

6715 WCES, Inc.
      225 S Leonard St
      Waterbury, CT 06708
      Contact:
      Tel: 203-573-1325
      Email: sales@waterburycontract.com
      Website: www.waterburycontract.com
Deep drawn eyelets & metal stampings, die design & manufacture, long run production, assembly, finishing & plating. (Woman, estab , empl , sales , cert: WBENC)

Georgia

6716 Dixien LLC
      5286 Circle Dr
      Lake City, GA 30260
      Contact: Alex Garcia VP Mktg
      Tel: 404-366-7427
      Email: agarcia@dixien.com
      Website: www.dixien.com
Stamping 100 ton to 1000 ton, welded sub-assemblies, tooling, plastic injection molding, blow molding & vaccum forming. (Hisp, estab 1961, empl 400, sales $25,000,000, cert: NMSDC)

Illinois

6717 Altak Inc.
      250 Covington Dr
      Bloomingdale, IL 60108
      Contact: Steve Janas Sales Mgr
      Tel: - - - 308
      Email: rtakayama@arktechno.com
      Website: www.altakinc.com
Wire Harness manufacturing, Switch Assembly manufacturing, Spring manufacturing, Stampings - 30 to 800 ton, Wire Forms, IATF 16949 and ISO 9001 certified. (As-Pac, estab 1980, empl 400, sales $37,000,000, cert: NMSDC)

6718 North Star Stamping & Tool, Inc.
      1264 Industrial Dr
      Lake in the Hills, IL 60156
      Contact: Catherine O'Brien
      Tel: 847-658-9400
      Email: nstar9400@aol.com
      Website: www.northstarstampingandtool.com
Metal stamping & assembly: 32 ton press to 200 ton press. (Woman, estab 1993, empl 9, sales , cert: WBENC)

6719 Reliable Machine Company
      1327 10th Ave
      Rockford, IL 61104
      Contact: Gloria Pernacciaro CEO
      Tel: 815-968-8803
      Email: gloriap@reliablemachine.com
      Website: www.reliablemachine.com
Metal Stampings, Part Production Capabilities: Deep draw up to 5 inches, Flat stampings, Stampings with multiple geometric forms, Secondary operations (piercing, staking, trimming and forming). (Woman, estab 1921, empl 40, sales $8,000,000, cert: WBENC)

Indiana

6720 Lacay Fabrication and Mfg Inc.
      52941 Glenview Dr
      Elkhart, IN 46514
      Contact: Ann Filley President
      Tel: 574-288-4678
      Email: ann@lacayfab.com
      Website: www.lacayfab.com
Mfr material handling racks, Baskets, Industrial & Production Welding, Machining, Robotic Welding, Stamping, Custom Fabrication, Prototyping. (Woman, estab 1975, empl 70, sales , cert: WBENC)

Kentucky

6721 Lincoln Manufacturing USA, LLC
      102 Industrial Park Dr
      Stanford, KY 40484
      Contact: Tetsuya Hatta President
      Tel: 606-365-3016
      Email: blunsford@lincolnmfg.com
      Website: www.lincolnmfg.com
Metal stamping services. (As-Pac, estab 1996, empl 150, sales $24,000,000, cert: State)

METAL STAMPING

Massachusetts

6722 Springfield Spring
311 Shaker Rd
Longmeadow, MA 01028
Contact: Norman Rodriques President
Tel: 413-525-6837
Email: pat@springfieldspring.com
Website: www.springfieldspring.com
Mfr precision engineered compression springs, torsion springs, extension springs, wire forms, fourslide-produced stampings, assemblies. (Hisp, estab 1942, empl 39, sales $7,200,000, cert: NMSDC)

Michigan

6723 Allied Technology Inc.
6830 Metro Plex Dr
Romulus, MI 48174
Contact: Annie Shen President
Tel: 734-728-6688
Email: ati.purchasing@alliedtech-eng.com
Website: www.alliedtech-eng.com
Castings, forgings, cold forming products, stampings and screw machine products. (As-Pac, estab 1999, empl 12, sales $6,000,000, cert: NMSDC)

6724 Apex Spring & Stamping
11420 First Ave
Grand Rapids, MI 49544
Contact: Doug Furness Sales/Eng Mgr
Tel: 616-453-5463
Email: djf@apexspring.com
Website: www.apexspring.com
4 slide & vertislide, CNC winders, stamping presse to 110 ton & various assembly equipment, in-house tool room, proto-type capability. (Minority, estab 1977, empl 40, sales $12,000,000, cert: NMSDC)

6725 Atlas Tool Inc.
29880 Groesbeck Hwy
Roseville, MI 48066
Contact: Douglas Flanagan Business Devel Mgr
Tel: 586-778-3570
Email: doug@atlastool.com
Website: www.atlastool.com
Stamping dies, service parts production, prototype parts, machining, engineering, die repair. (Woman, estab 1962, empl 200, sales , cert: WBENC)

6726 Delaco Steel Corporation
8111 Tireman, Ste 1
Dearborn, MI 48126
Contact: Michael Roualet VP Quality
Tel: 313-491-1200
Email: mike.roualet@delacosteel.com
Website: www.delacosteel.com
Dist & process steel & aluminum. Blanking, warehousing, slitting, stampings, etc. (Woman/Hisp, estab 1974, empl 650, sales , cert: NMSDC, WBENC)

6727 DGH Enterprises, Inc. dba K-O Products Co.
1225 Milton St
Benton Harbor, MI 49022
Contact: Barbara Herrold CEO
Tel: 269-925-0657
Email: barbaraherrold@koproducts.com
Website: www.koproducts.com
Metal stampings, welded & fabricated assemblies, electrical & mechanical assemblies, metal hardware, metal truck parts & assemblies, metal stamped components for auto, appliances, off-road equipment, metal welding, mig welding, spot welding. (Woman, estab 1938, empl 28, sales $5,700,000, cert: WBENC)

6728 Die Cad Group
3258 Clear Vista Court NE
Grand Rapids, MI 49525
Contact: Bobbie Blanton President
Tel: - - -2705
Email: bobbie@diecadgroup.com
Website: www.diecadgroup.com
Product & process simulation, tool & die design, mold design, special purpose machine design, transfer press simulation, die details sourcing, metal stamping die design, metal stamping process development, stamped parts formation. (Woman, estab 1995, empl 41, sales $8,150,746, cert: WBENC)

6729 GK Tech, LLC
3331 W Big Beaver Rd Ste 106
Troy, MI 48084
Contact: Kelly Choi
Tel: 248-494-1960
Email: kellychoi@gktechusa.com
Website: www.gktechllc.com
Marketing specialist, consulting, business development, forging, die-casting, stamping, spring, magnesium pulley, rubber bushing, fasteners, machining, plastic injection molding. (Minority, Woman, estab 2015, empl 3, sales , cert: NMSDC)

6730 Globe Tech LLC.
101 Industrial Dr
Plymouth, MI 48170
Contact: Amanda Menchinger President
Tel: - - -2278
Email: mmenchinger@globe-tech.biz
Website: www.globe-tech.biz
Machining, fabrication & welding, metal stamping. (Woman, estab 2009, empl 72, sales , cert: WBENC)

6731 Lapeer Metal Stamping Companies, Inc.
930 S Saginaw St
Lapeer, MI 48446
Contact: Joe Wierbicki VP Sales
Tel: 810-664-8588
Email: jwierbicki@lapeermetal.com
Website: www.lapeermetal.com
Mfr metal stampings & assemblies: seat frame assemblies, dash panels assemblies, heat shields, fuel tank straps, pedals, brake, clutch, latches & hinges, crossmembers, air bag components & structural body components. (Hisp, estab 1960, empl 500, sales $101,781,836, cert: NMSDC)

METAL STAMPING

6732 Lucerne International
      40 Corporate Dr
      Auburn Hills, MI 48326
      Contact: Karen Ryan Finance Mgr
      Tel: 248-674-7210
      Email: kryan@lucerneintl.com
      Website: www.lucerneintl.com
Advanced metal forming components & assemblies, body structures, chassis systems & powertrain systems. Mfg aluminum & steel forgings, stampings, aluminum & zinc die castings & steel. (Woman, estab 1993, empl 58, sales , cert: WBENC)

6733 Metalbuilt LLC
      50171 E Russell Schmidt
      Chesterfield, MI 48051
      Contact: Don Wood
      Tel: 586-786-9106
      Email: dwood@metalbuiltllc.com
      Website: www.metalbuiltllc.com
Prototype Stampings, Die development, Laser Cutting, engineering simulation, Short run production. (Woman, estab 2006, empl 35, sales $6,050,000, cert: WBENC)

6734 Mico Industries, Inc.
      2929 32nd St SE
      Kentwood, MI 49512
      Contact: Tracy DeKlein VP Technical Sales
      Tel: 616-245-6426
      Email: tdeklein@micoind.com
      Website: www.micoindustries.com
Mfr metal stampings, welding, assemblies. (Hisp, estab 1983, empl 75, sales $12,000,000, cert: NMSDC)

6735 MNP Corporation
      44225 Utica Rd
      Utica, MI 48317
      Contact: Donna DeSantis Dir Special Applications
      Tel: 586-254-1320
      Email: donna.desantis@mnp.com
      Website: www.mnp.com
Mfr Specialty Fasteners & Engineered Cold Formed Components. Heat Treatment, Plating Stampings, Powder Metal, Machining. Fastener Design and Testing, Steel processing, Rod and Wire, Flat roll slitting (Woman, estab 1970, empl 540, sales $160,000,000, cert: WBENC)

6736 Motor City Stamping
      47783 N Gratiot Ave
      Chesterfield Twp, MI 48051
      Contact: Paul Lachowicz Controller
      Tel: 586-949-8420
      Email: plachowicz@mcstamp.com
      Website: www.mcstamp.com
Medium stampings & multi-welded assemblies. (Minority, Woman, estab 1969, empl 350, sales $48,000,000, cert: WBENC)

6737 Proos Manufacturing, Inc.
      1037 Michigan St NE
      Grand Rapids, MI 49503
      Contact: Amy Engelsman CEO
      Tel: 616-454-5622
      Email: aengelsman@proos.com
      Website: www.proos.com
Metal stampings & assemblies. (Woman, estab , empl , sales , cert: WBENC)

6738 PTM Corporation
      6560 Bethuy
      Fair Haven, MI 48023
      Contact: Nicole Robinson Sales
      Tel: 248-670-2650
      Email: nrobinson@ptmcorporation.com
      Website: www.ptmcorporation.com
Metal stamping, production up to 600 ton, prototype/low volume up to 1000 ton, tool design & build, laser, EDM, CNC, welding & assemblies. (Woman, estab 1972, empl 196, sales $60,000,000, cert: WBENC)

6739 Rose-A-Lee Technologies, Inc
      7448 19 Mile Rd
      Sterling Heights, MI 48314
      Contact: Julie Wood Dir Business Dev
      Tel: 586-799-4555
      Email: jwood@rosealeetechnologies.com
      Website: www.rosealeetechnologies.com
CAD design (surface and solid modeling), stamping, assembly/kitting, tube bending, welding (mig, tig, stud arc), etc. (Woman, estab 2013, empl 2, sales , cert: WBENC)

6740 Roth-Williams Industries Inc. dba Lunar Industries
      34335 Groesbeck Hwy
      Clinton Township, MI 48035
      Contact: Patricia Williams President
      Tel: 586-792-0090
      Email: pat@lunarind.com
      Website: www.lunarind.com
Design & mfr custom tooling, fixtures, gages, stamping dies, prototype parts & stamped metal parts. (Woman, estab 1966, empl 9, sales $670,000, cert: NWBOC)

6741 Sequoia Tool
      44831 N Groesbeck Hwy
      Clinton Township, MI 48036
      Contact: James Coates Acct Mgr
      Tel: 586-463-4400
      Email: bcoates@sequoiatool.net
      Website: www.sequoiatool.net
Mfr prototype sheet metal stampings & assemblies, low volume production and short run svcs. (Nat Ame, estab 1988, empl 65, sales $10,000,000, cert: NMSDC)

Minnesota

6742 Bokers Inc.
      3104 Snelling Ave
      Minneapolis, MN 55406
      Contact: Linda Demma CFO
      Tel: 800-448-7492
      Email: ldemma@bokers.com
      Website: www.bokers.com
Mfr precision metallic & non-metallic stampings & washers. (Woman/AA, estab , empl 110, sales , cert: WBENC)

6743 Top Tool Company
      3100 84th Lane Northeast
      Blaine, MN 55449
      Contact: Duane Kari Sales Mgr
      Tel: 763-786-0030
      Email: dakari@toptool.com
      Website: www.toptool.com
Dies, precision metal stampings & wire EDM, exotic & precious metals, platinum, iridium, titanium, MP35N, copper alloys, phos bronze, gold & silver plating. (Woman, estab 1966, empl 30, sales $4,427,000, cert: State)

Missouri

6744 Thiel Tool & Engineering Co., Inc.
4622 Bulwer Ave
St. Louis, MO 63147
Contact: Gary Shamel Sales Mgr
Tel: 314-241-6121
Email: gshamel@thieltool.com
Website: www.thieltool.com
Automotive stampings & sub-assemblies. (Woman, estab 1945, empl 42, sales $10,000,000, cert: WBENC)

New York

6745 Bailey Manufacturing Co., LLC
10987 Bennett State Rd
Forestville, NY 14062
Contact: John Hines President
Tel: 716-965-2731
Email: bailey03@netsync.net
Website: www.baileymfgcollc.com
Metal Stamping, Sheet Metal Fabrication, Welding, Multi-Part Assemblies, Zinc Plating, Rust Proofing, Quality Inspection, E-Coat Painting. (AA, estab 2002, empl 100, sales $8,500,000, cert: NMSDC)

6746 Cannon Industries, Inc.
525 Lee Rd
Rochester, NY 14606
Contact: Reggie Cannon President
Tel: 585-254-8080
Email: rcannon@cannonind.com
Website: www.cannonind.com
Sheet metal fabrication, welding fabrication, laser & plasma cutting, metal stamping, CNC machining & turning, mechanical assembly, spot welding. (AA, estab 1979, empl 104, sales $16,000,000, cert: NMSDC)

Ohio

6747 Die-Mension Corporation
3020 Nationwide Pkwy
Brunswick, OH 44212
Contact: Karen Thompson President
Tel: 330-273-5872
Email: karen@diemension.com
Website: www.diemension.com
Mfr & design precision progressive die & metal stampings. (Woman, estab 1985, empl 8, sales $1,500,000, cert: WBENC)

6748 GB Manufacturing Company
100 Adams St
Delta, OH 43515
Contact: Teresa Elling Sales
Tel: 419-822-5323
Email: apetree@gbmfg.com
Website: www.gbmfg.com
Stamping, laser blanking, fabrication & assembly, tool making, robotic & hand welding, spot welding, press braking, productin machining, prototyping. (Minority, estab 1975, empl 85, sales $24,500,000, cert: NMSDC)

6749 Green Rock Lighting, LLC
3175 W 33rd St
Cleveland, OH 44109
Contact: Tina Haddad CEO
Tel: 216-651-6446
Email: thaddad@greenrocklighting.com
Website: www.greenrocklighting.com
Laser cutting, wire bending & forming, press brake, spinning, stamping, mig, tig & stick welding, spot welding, machining, destructive & non-destructive testing, packaging & assembly. (Woman, estab 2011, empl 20, sales , cert: State, WBENC)

6750 Hamlin Acquisition, LLC dba Hamlin Steel Products
2741 Wingate Ave
Akron, OH 44314
Contact: Lal Tekchandani President
Tel: 330-753-7791
Email: jkunczt@hnmetalstamping.com
Website: www.hamlinsteel.com
Small to medium size metal stampings, assembly & robotic welding capabilities. (As-Ind, estab 1953, empl 95, sales $15,000,000, cert: NMSDC)

6751 Hamlin Newco, LLC
2741 Wingate Ave
Akron, OH 44314
Contact: Rick Sadd Sales Mgr
Tel: 216-924-5449
Email: ricksadd@gmail.com
Website: www.hnmetalstamping.com/
Metal stampings & welded assemblies with presses up to 800 tons for the automotive industry. (As-Pac, estab 1945, empl 105, sales $16,000,000, cert: NMSDC)

6752 Magni-Power Company
5511 Lincoln Way E
Wooster, OH 44691
Contact: Kim Coblentz New Business Dev Mgr
Tel: 330-264-3637
Email: kcoblentz@magnipower.com
Website: www.magnipower.com
Metal fabrication & stamping: process steel, aluminum, stainless steel, CNC punching, forming, laser cutting, robotic welding, in-house powder coating & assembly. (As-Ind, estab 1948, empl 230, sales $27,000,000, cert: NMSDC)

6753 Mohr Stamping, Inc.
22038 Fairgrounds Rd
Wellington, OH 44090
Contact: Amber Mohrman CEO
Tel: 440-647-4316
Email: sales@mohrstamping.com
Website: www.mohrstamping.com
Metal Stampings, Die design and Build, Assembly. (Woman, estab 1967, empl 25, sales $4,000,000, cert: WBENC)

6754 Select Industries Corp
60 Heid Ave
Dayton, OH 45404
Contact: Timothy Gonyeau Corp Acct Mgr
Tel: 586-337-1006
Email: tgonyeau@select.org
Website: www.select.org

TC clutch & damper assemblies; stamped components; stamped steel synchronizer cores & cone sets, 3-pin synchronizer rings with Gylon friction material for the heavy truck market. (Woman, estab 1970, empl 130, sales $35,400,000, cert: WBENC)

6755 Tech-Matic Industries, Inc.
17941 Englewood Dr
Middleburg Heights, OH 44130
Contact: Kathleen Byrnes President
Tel: 440-826-3191
Email: kbyrnes@tc-tm.com
Website: www.tc-tm.com

Metal stamping for automotive industry. (Woman, estab 1985, empl 9, sales $4,000,000, cert: WBENC)

6756 Wrena, LLC dba Angstrom-USA, LLC
265 Lightner Rd
Tipp City, OH 45371
Contact: Nagesh Palakurthi CEO
Tel: 937-667-4403
Email: pyenger@wrenallc.com
Website: www.angstrom-usa.com

Stampings, tubular products, machining, welding, robotic welding, steel forgings (Warm & Cold), aluminum forgings, assemblies, plastic injection molding, needle bearings, starter assemblies (As-Pac, estab 2011, empl 46, sales , cert: NMSDC)

6757 Zip Tool & Die Inc.
12200 Sprecher Ave
Cleveland, OH 44135
Contact: Victor De Leaon CEO
Tel: 216-267-1117
Email: vdeleon@tritonduro.com
Website: www.ziptool.com

Engineering, Prototyping, Metal Forming, Metal Stamping & Tool & Die solutions. (Hisp, estab 1968, empl 10, sales $650,000, cert: NMSDC)

Pennsylvania

6758 Spalding Automotive, Inc.
1011 Cedar Ave
Croydon, PA 19021
Contact: Vincent Florio Business Devel
Tel: 215-826-4061
Email: vflorio@spaldingautomotive.com
Website: www.spaldingautomotive.com

Metal stampings, roll form components, welding, mechanical assemblies & design & build tooling. (Hisp, estab 1987, empl 75, sales $18,518,000, cert: NMSDC)

6759 Tottser Tool and Manufacturing
1630 Republic Rd
Huntingdon Valley, PA 19006
Contact: Linda Macht President
Tel: 215-357-7600
Email: lmacht@tottser.com
Website: www.tottser.com

Metal stampings, tool & die. (Woman, estab 0, empl , sales , cert: WBENC)

Wisconsin

6760 Church Metal Spinning Company
5050 N 124th St
Milwaukee, WI 53225
Contact: Brenda Birno President
Tel: 414-461-6460
Email: markv@churchmetal.com
Website: www.churchmetal.com

Metal fabrications including metal stampings, metal spun, laser cut, press brake parts. Also, complete assembly and welding of multi-part components. (Woman, estab 1944, empl 30, sales $6,600,000, cert: State)

6761 Universal Die & Stampings
735 15th St
Prairie du Sac, WI 53555
Contact: Karl Andersson Sales Mgr
Tel: 608-643-2477
Email: kanders@unidie.com
Website: www.unidie.com

Precision, high volume metal stamping, full tooling. (Woman, estab 1967, empl 32, sales $6,000,000, cert: City)

METAL, GENERAL MACHINING

Job shops, prototypes, short and long run production work. Tool and dies, jigs and fixtures, electro-mechanical assemblies, etc. (Also see six other METAL categories). NAICS Code 33

Alabama

6762 Theonics Inc.
      12525 Memorial Pkwy SW
      Huntsville, AL 35803
      Contact: Shelley Coxwell President
      Tel: 256-885-3500
      Email: shelley.coxwell@theonicsinc.com
      Website: www.theonicsinc.com
Precision machining, CMM inspection & assembly of complex hardware. (Woman, estab 2012, empl 31, sales $1,300,000, cert: WBENC)

Arkansas

6763 Conway Machine, Inc.
      192 Commerce Rd
      Conway, AR 72032
      Contact: Anthony Davis President
      Tel: 501-327-1311
      Email: tonyd@conwaymachine.com
      Website: www.ConwayMachine.com
Precision milling & turning machining. (Woman, estab 1970, empl 25, sales $2,400,000, cert: WBENC)

Arizona

6764 Pivot Manufacturing
      2602 E Magnolia
      Phoenix, AZ 85034
      Contact: Steve Macias President
      Tel: 602-306-2923
      Email: smacias@klmanufacturing.com
      Website: www.pivotmfg.com
CNC machining: metals & plastics. (Hisp, estab 2000, empl 17, sales $36,000,010, cert: NMSDC)

6765 State Technology & Manufacturing
      2555 E University Dr
      Phoenix, AZ 85034
      Contact: Ruben Cadena CEO
      Tel: 602-275-0990
      Email: ruben@azsip.com
      Website: www.azsip.com
Machinng, mill, lathe, CNC, welding, fab, dist steel, copper, brass, bronze, stainless steel, aluminum. (Hisp, estab 2003, empl 21, sales $3,000,000, cert: State, City, NMSDC)

California

6766 3D Machine Company, Inc.
      4790 E Wesley Dr
      Anaheim, CA 92807
      Contact: Maria Falcusan President
      Tel: 714-777-8985
      Email: costel@3dmachineco.com
      Website: www.3dmachineco.com
CNC machining, 5-axis CNC capability, CAD/CAM software, precision-machined parts & assemblies. (Woman, estab 1996, empl 35, sales , cert: CPUC)

6767 ACC Precision, Inc.
      321 Hearst Dr
      Oxnard, CA 93030
      Contact: Arturo Alfaro GM
      Tel: 805-278-9801
      Email: aalfaro@accprecision.com
      Website: www.accprecision.com
Quality precision manufacturing & assembly. (Hisp, estab 1998, empl 22, sales $1,867,833, cert: 8(a))

6768 Acutek US
      1488 E Valencia Dr
      Fullerton, CA 92831
      Contact: Charley Yoo Owner
      Tel: 714-278-0912
      Email: cyoo@acutekus.com
      Website: www.acutekus.com
CNC milling, turning: aluminum, steel, titanium, copper, brass. 3 & 4 axis programming tooling fixtures, electronic file transfer. (As-Pac, estab 2003, empl 60, sales $10,700,000, cert: CPUC)

6769 Aranda Tooling, Inc.
      15301 Springdale St
      Huntington Beach, CA 92649
      Contact: Gerrard Connolly GM
      Tel: 714-379-6565
      Email: gerrard.connolly@arandatooling.com
      Website: www.arandatooling.com
Medium to high production metal stamping, assembly, robotic welding, tooling, EDM, prototypes. (Hisp, estab 1975, empl 125, sales , cert: NMSDC)

6770 Azachorok Contract Services LLC
      320 Grand Cypress Ave Ste 502
      Palmdale, CA 93551
      Contact: Gene Souza Mgr
      Tel: 661-951-6566
      Email: gsouza@azachorok.com
      Website: www.azcsllc.com
Precision CNC machining & turnning, aircraft structures, machined housings, castings, aluminum, steel, titanium, copper, brass etc. (Nat Ame, estab 1998, empl 12, sales $550,000, cert: 8(a), SDB)

6771 Bay Tank and Boiler Works
      825 W 14th St
      Eureka, CA 95501
      Contact: Amandy Massey Office Mgr
      Tel: 707-443-0934
      Email: info@btmetals.com
      Website: www.baytankandboilerworks.com
Carbon Steel Products Stainless Steel Products Aluminum Products Rebar Industrial Fasteners (Stock and Custom) We specialize in Made in the USA Certified Welding Drilling, Milling, Plasma Cutting, Oxy Fuel Cutting, laser Forming, Press (Woman, estab 1956, empl 7, sales $500,000, cert: CPUC, WBENC)

METAL, GENERAL MACHINING

6772 Dinucci Corporation
1057 Shary Cir
Concord, CA 94518
Contact: Gabriela Dinucci COO
Tel: 925-798-3946
Email: gabriela@dinuccicorp.com
Website: www.dinuccicorp.com
Machine shop; computerized mfg & precision prototypes. (Minority, Woman, estab 1978, empl 25, sales $4,227,662, cert: NMSDC)

6773 Fabtronics, Inc.
5026 Calmview Ave
Baldwin Park, CA 91706
Contact: David K. Thompson VP Operations
Tel: 626-962-3293
Email: contact@fabtronics.com
Website: www.fabtronics.com
Precision sheet metal mfg, CNC turret punching, spot welding, enclosures, tubular frame weldments, skins & chassis. (Hisp, estab 1976, empl 14, sales $3,500,000, cert: NMSDC)

6774 Hunter Hawk, Inc.
1842 Taft St
Concord, CA 94521
Contact: Sandy Hunter President
Tel: 925-798-4950
Email: sandy@hunterhawk.com
Website: www.hunterhawk.com
Precision mechanical components, fabrication, reverse engineering, documentation, critical inventory & equipment boxes. (Woman, estab 1994, empl 4, sales $1,886,100, cert: State, CPUC, WBENC)

6775 Infinity Precision Inc.
6919 Eton Ave
Canoga Park, CA 91303
Contact: President
Tel: 818-447-3008
Email: sales@ipinc-usa.com
Website: www.ipinc-usa.com
Hydroforming, Machined parts per print, CAD/CAM/ CNC Machining, 5-Axiss Water Jet Cutting, Honing, Sheet Metal Fabrication (Woman, estab 1996, empl 19, sales $2,338,000, cert: WBENC)

6776 Ingels Engineering Inc.
1828 Evergreen St
Duarte, CA 91010
Contact: Enilde Ingels VP
Tel: 626-256-1967
Email: eeemachineshop@earthlink.net
Website: www.ingelsengineeringservices.com
Machining & engineering consulting services, specialized medical devices, prototype works, short run productions in Stainless Steel, Aluminum, Delrin, Brass, Copper or plastics. (Minority, Woman, estab 1997, empl 7, sales $230,000, cert: State, City)

6777 JB Manufacturing
2814 Aiello Dr Ste D
San Jose, CA 95111
Contact: Jim Ogawa GM
Tel: 408-281-9994
Email: jim@jb-mfg.com
Website: www.jb-mfg.com
CNC milling & turning, 5 CNC vertical mills & 1 CNC lathe. (As-Pac, estab 1985, empl 4, sales $325,000, cert: NMSDC)

6778 KFM International Industries, Inc.
20277 Valley Blvd, Ste L
Walnut, CA 91789
Contact: Dennis Boribor Engineer
Tel: 626-369-9556
Email: dennis@kfmii.com
Website: www.kfmii.com
Casting: Sand Cast, Die Casting, Investment Casting & Permanent Mold Forging: Hot & Cold Formed Sheet Metal Stamping Machining: CNC,Turning & Milling Powder Metal. (Minority, Woman, estab 2000, empl 6, sales $2,500,000, cert: City, CPUC)

6779 LT CNC Machining, Inc.
7945 Silverton Ave, Ste 1103
San Diego, CA 92126
Contact: Liem Phan President
Tel: 858-586-7705
Email: liem@ltmachininginc.com
Website: www.ltmachininginc.com
CNC milling & machining. (Minority, Woman, estab 2006, empl 7, sales $800,000, cert: State)

6780 M&L Precision Machining
18655 Madrone Pkwy
Morgan Hill, CA 95037
Contact: Mike Sullivan Business Specialist
Tel: 408-436-3955
Email: mikes@mlprecision.com
Website: www.mlprecision.com
Precision machining done with over 55 mills and multiple lathes. (Woman, estab 1971, empl 110, sales $18,000,000, cert: WBENC)

6781 QMP Inc.
25070 Ave. Tibbitts
Valencia, CA 91355
Contact: Freddy Vidal CEO
Tel: 661-294-6860
Email: sales@qmpusa.com
Website: www.qmpusa.com
Mfr water filtration systems and components, injection molding and machine shop. (Woman/Hisp, estab 1994, empl 44, sales , cert: NMSDC)

6782 Qualitask, Inc.
2840 E Gretta Lane
Anaheim, CA 92806
Contact: Som Suntharaphat President
Tel: 714-237-0900
Email: soms@qualitask.net
Website: www.qualitask.com
CNC Milling & Turning, Research & Development, Prototype & Production Machining, Jigs & Fixtures, steel, stainless steel, titanium, aluminum, plastics. (As-Pac, estab 1992, empl 30, sales $1,187,381, cert: NMSDC)

METAL, GENERAL MACHINING

6783 Spec-Metal Inc.
PO Box 660536
Arcadia, CA 91066
Contact: Evelyn Chen
Tel: 626-301-7969
Email: evelync@spec-metal.com
Website: www.Spec-Metal.com

Machine metal precision machined parts: aluminum, brass, copper, carbon steel & stainless steel. Engineering design, product development, manufacturing, logistics & customer service. (Minority, Woman, estab 2008, empl 4, sales $2,600,000, cert: NMSDC)

Colorado

6784 Custom Machining Corporation
2090 W College Ave
Englewood, CO 80110
Contact: Terri Yount-Ross
Tel: 303-762-0333
Email: terri.ross@cmc1.net
Website: www.cmc1.net

Can lining machining. (Woman, estab 0, empl , sales , cert: WBENC)

6785 Excalibur Machine & Sheet Metal
208 W Buchanan St, Unit C
Colorado Springs, CO 80907
Contact: Douglas McDaniel Plant Mgr
Tel: 719-520-5404
Email: doug@excaliburmfg.com
Website: www.excaliburmfg.com/

Precision machining & sheet metal fabrication, welding, assembly, powder coating. (Hisp, estab 1989, empl 25, sales $2,600,000, cert: NMSDC)

6786 Mountainside Medical Colorado, LLC
6165 Lookout Rd
Boulder, CO 80301
Contact: Susan Neidecker President
Tel: 303-222-1271
Email: sneidecker@mountainsidemed.com
Website: www.mountainsidemed.com

Contract manufacturing for complex, tight-tolerance medical products, Multi-axis Machining Assembly, Wire EDMCNC, Swiss type machining centers, Laser welding & Laser marking, Finishing Metal Forming. (Woman, estab 2006, empl 90, sales $12,731,416, cert: WBENC)

Connecticut

6787 Precision Metal Products, Inc.
307 Pepes Farm Rd
Milford, CT 06460
Contact: Sean O'Brien VP
Tel: 203-877-4258
Email: seanobrien@pmpinc.biz
Website: www.pmpinc.biz

CNC milling, CNC Swiss, CNC turning, wire EDM, stamping. (Woman, estab 1975, empl 145, sales $19,000,000, cert: WBENC)

Florida

6788 Custom Manufacturing & Engineering, Inc.
3690 70th Ave North
Pinellas Park, FL 33781
Contact: Fred Munro VP
Tel: 727-547-9799
Email: fmunro@custom-mfg-eng.com
Website: www.custom-mfg-eng.com

Subassemblies, turn-key, integrated test systems & process equip. (Woman, estab 1997, empl 40, sales $10,300,000, cert: WBENC)

6789 KN Machine & Tool, Inc.
3125 Jupiter Park Circle Ste 4
Jupiter, FL 33458
Contact: Ron Passino Operations Mgr
Tel: 561-748-3035
Email: ron@knmachine.com
Website: www.knmachine.com

High Speed Machining on Milling machines capable of handling parts up 40"x20"x20".
Turning w/ Live Tooling up to 2-5/8" Bar Capacity and up to 12" O.D. Turning. (As-Pac, estab 2000, empl 10, sales $1,300,000, cert: State)

6790 Tychon, Inc.
2360 Clark St, Unit J
Apopka, FL 32703
Contact: Cindy Wiley President
Tel: 407-293-7601
Email: tychon_machining@hotmail.com
Website: www.tychoninc.com

CNC manufacturing, close tolerance, precision machining, CNC mills & CNC lathes. (Woman, estab 2003, empl 3, sales $339,648, cert: WBENC)

Georgia

6791 Omni Machine Works, Inc.
30-A Chamisa Rd
Covington, GA 30016
Contact: Claudia Engelbracht President
Tel: 404-861-9035
Email: claudia@omnimachineworks.com
Website: www.omnimachineworks.com

Full service machine shop, custom machine manufacturer & engineering/design resource. (Woman, estab 0, empl , sales , cert: WBENC)

Iowa

6792 Indoshell Precision Technologies, LLC
435 Precision Pkwy
Story City, IA 50248
Contact: Ramki Ramakrishan Owner
Tel: - -
Email: paul.diggins@isptglobal.com
Website: www.isptglobal.com

Precision machine aluminum and steel, CNC Turning Centers and Swiss Turning Centers; Multi axis CNC HMC and VMC Machining Centers with pallet changers; as well as lapping, honing and grinding work centers. (As-Ind, estab 2009, empl 75, sales $12,000,000, cert: NMSDC)

Illinois

6793 ADC LP
 1720 Wolf Rd
 Wheeling, IL 60090
 Contact: Patrick Tang President
 Tel: 847-541-3030
 Email: ptang@adclp.com
 Website: www.adclp.com
High pressure aluminum die casting, CNC machining, automated assembly. (As-Pac, estab 1991, empl 243, sales $35,000,000, cert: NMSDC)

6794 Craftsman Custom Metals, LLC
 3838 N River Rd
 Schiller Park, IL 60176
 Contact: William Johnson Business Devel Mgr
 Tel: 847-655-0040
 Email: wjohnson@ccm.com
 Website: www.ccm.com
Custom chassis & enclosures, cabinets, brackets, structural components, OEM's & EMS's, prototype development, precision milling, metal stamping, testing, weilding, engineering support, mechanical & electro-mechanical assembly. (Hisp, estab 1953, empl 65, sales $10,000,000, cert: NMSDC)

6795 Edmik Inc.
 3850 Grove Ave
 Gurnee, IL 60031
 Contact: Heidi Knill VP
 Tel: 847-263-0460
 Email: edmik@edmik1.com
 Website: www.edmik1.com/
Production, custom tooling, machinery & engineering, CAD/CAM, contract & production assembly, industrial appliances, machining & tooling services. (Minority, Woman, estab 1957, empl 32, sales $3,200,000, cert: NMSDC)

6796 KrisDee & Associates, Inc.
 755 Schneider Dr
 South Elgin, IL 60177
 Contact: Hermann VP
 Tel: 847-608-8300
 Email: gregg.m@krisdee.com
 Website: www.krisdee.com
Precision machining of non ferrous prismatic components. (Nat Ame, estab 1983, empl 65, sales $14,000,000, cert: NMSDC)

6797 Lakeview Precision Machining, Inc.
 751 Schneider Dr
 South Elgin, IL 60177
 Contact: President
 Tel: 847-742-7170
 Email: sales@lakeviewprecision.com
 Website: www.lakeviewprecision.com
CNC precision machining. (Woman, estab 2006, empl 15, sales $1,600,000, cert: WBENC)

6798 Machined Products Co.
 2121 Landmeier Rd
 Elk Grove Village, IL 60007
 Contact: Mohammed Qureshi President
 Tel: 847-718-1300
 Email: mirna@machinedproducts.com
 Website: www.machinedproducts.com
Machine iron, steel & aluminum. (As-Ind, estab 1958, empl 100, sales , cert: NMSDC)

6799 Mennie's Machine Company
 10549 Mennie Ln
 Mennie, IL 61326
 Contact: Mark Stengel Dir Sales
 Tel: 815-339-2226
 Email: markstengel@mennies.com
 Website: www.mennies.com
Supplier of precision machined components and assemblies. (Woman, estab 1970, empl 175, sales $34,100,000, cert: WBENC)

6800 Microtech Machine Company, Inc.
 222 Camp McDonald Rd
 Wheeling, IL 60090
 Contact: Elizabeth A. Iwanicki CEO
 Tel: 847-870-0707
 Email: microcamp@aol.com
 Website: www.microtech-machine.com
Engineering services & precision machined prototype & production components, precision machining, machine design & building, assembly & welding. (Woman, estab 1984, empl 22, sales $4,000,000, cert: NWBOC)

6801 Monnex Precision Inc.
 476 Diens Dr
 Wheeling, IL 60090
 Contact: James E. Wallace Sr. President
 Tel: 847-478-1800
 Email: jwallace@monnex.net
 Website: www.monnex.net
Metals, die casting, stampings & fasteners. (AA, As-Pac, estab 1985, empl 620, sales $5,000,000, cert: NMSDC)

6802 Multitech Industries, Inc.
 350 Village Dr
 Carol Stream, IL 60188
 Contact: Nick S. Anastopoulos Business Acct Mgr
 Tel: 630-784-9200
 Email: nick@multitechind.com
 Website: www.multitechind.com
Wire forms, castings, forgings, stampings, machining, cold-heading. (As-Ind, estab 1993, empl 60, sales $100,000,000, cert: NMSDC)

6803 Pioneer Service Inc. - Addison, IL
 542 W Factory Rd
 Addison, IL 60101
 Contact: Beth Swanson VP Sales & Mktg
 Tel: 630-628-0249
 Email: bswanson@pioneerserviceinc.com
 Website: www.pioneerserviceinc.com/
Contract mfr screw machine products & centerless grinding services: shafts, axles, bolts, bushings, dowels, pins, rods, spacers, valve stems, deburring, drilling, flatting, grinding, knurling, slotting, tapping, threading, heat treating. (Woman, estab 1990, empl 40, sales $5,000,000, cert: CPUC, WBENC)

METAL, GENERAL MACHINING 6804-6814

6804 Precise Products Inc.
3286 Talbot Ave
Warrenville, IL 60555
Contact: Ernest Tucker CEO
Tel: 630-393-9698
Email: sales@preciseproductsinc.com
Website: www.precise-products-inc.com
Automatic screw & CNC machined parts. (AA, estab 1966, empl 30, sales $3,000,000, cert: NMSDC)

6805 Tuson Corporation
475 Bunker Court
Vernon Hills, IL 60061
Contact: Michael Jin Sales Mgr
Tel: 847-816-8800
Email: michael-jin@tuson.com
Website: www.tuson.com
Precision CNC machining, powdered metal, forging, casting, gear, hydraulic relief valve assembly, pump, motor & cylinder components, electric motor. (As-Pac, estab 1987, empl 200, sales $29,000,000, cert: NMSDC)

Indiana

6806 A&A Custom Automation, Inc.
2125 Bergdolt Rd
Evansville, IN 47711
Contact: Bill Frey Sales Rep
Tel: 812-464-3650
Email: bfrey@aacustomautomation.com
Website: www.AAcustomautomation.com
Precision CNC machining, steel fabrication, design, mfg & rebuild automated equipment, mechanical & electrical engineering. (Woman, estab 1989, empl 55, sales , cert: NWBOC)

6807 Accutech Mold & Machine, Inc.
2817 Goshen Rd
Fort Wayne, IN 46808
Contact: Darrin Geiger VP
Tel: 260-471-6102
Email: dgeiger@accutechmoldinc.com
Website: www.accutechmoldinc.com
Plastic injection molding, Insert plastic injection molder of cables/connectors, rapid prototype tooling builder/injection molding, production machining of brass, aluminum & metals, prototype machining of brass, aluminum & metals. (Woman, estab 1996, empl 70, sales $3,000,000, cert: WBENC)

6808 AMG Engineering & Machining, Inc.
4030 Guion Ln
Indianapolis, IN 46268
Contact: Chris Chadd Business Devel
Tel: 317-329-4000
Email: cchadd@amgindy.com
Website: www.amgindy.com
Mfr & design machined components, fluid controls & connectors, adapters, fittings, plugs, check valves, gas regulators & pressure relief valves. (AA, estab 1989, empl 46, sales , cert: NMSDC)

6809 Brinly-Hardy Company
3230 Industrial Pkwy
Jeffersonville, IN 47130
Contact: Scott Whitehouse Sales Mgr
Tel: 812-218-7219
Email: swhitehouse@brinly.com
Website: www.brinly.com
Bending & forming, welding, powder painting, assembly & packaging. (Woman, estab , empl 150, sales $28,000,001, cert: WBENC)

6810 Exacto, Inc. of South Bend
1137 S Lafayette Blvd
South Bend, IN 46601
Contact: Barbara Jordan CEO
Tel: 574-288-4716
Email: bjordan@exacto-inc.com
Website: www.exacto-inc.com
CNC turning, CNC milling, OD/ID grinding, lapping & honing (Woman, estab 1970, empl 52, sales $4,000,000, cert: WBENC)

6811 Mercer Machine
1421 S Holt Rd
Indianapolis, IN 46241
Contact: Joe Robinson VP Sales
Tel: 317-441-0877
Email: jrobinson@mercermachine.net
Website: www.mercermachine.net
CNN machining. (Woman, estab 1954, empl 20, sales $2,000,000, cert: WBENC)

6812 Precision Cadcam, Inc.
8446 Brookville Rd
Indianapolis, IN 46239
Contact: Darryl Williams President
Tel: 317-353-8058
Email: precisioncadcam@sbcglobal.net
Website: www.pccinc.org
Precision maching and molding, tool & dies. (AA, estab 2004, empl 2, sales $170,000, cert: NMSDC)

6813 Royalty Investments, LLC
2476 E US Hwy 50
Seymour, IN 47274
Contact: Marshall Royalty Member
Tel: 812-358-3534
Email: mroyalty@cranehillmachine.com
Website: www.cranehillmachine.com
Machining, fabricating & assembly: steel, aluminum & plastic components. Design, engineering & coating applications. (Woman, estab 1989, empl 30, sales $3,714,618, cert: State, WBENC)

Louisiana

6814 Vast Industries
108 Venus St Ste 200
Morgan City, LA 70380
Contact: Yvette Archuleta-Tudury Owner
Tel: 985-312-1592
Email: yvette@vast-ind.com
Website: www.Vast-Ind.com
Wire EDM & precision machined parts manufacturing, custom product design, reverse engineering & aluminum & steel fabrication. (Minority, Woman, estab 2007, empl 7, sales $600,000, cert: NMSDC, WBENC, 8(a))

Massachusetts

6815 Boulevard Machine & Gear
       326 Lockhouse Road
       Westfield, MA 01085
       Contact: Susan Kasa President
       Tel: 413-788-6466
       Email: tanya@boulevardmachine.com
       Website: www.boulevardmachine.com/
Mfr aerospace, defense, paper & commercial parts, precision machining, CNC turning, lathe & milling, manual lathes & millers, grinding, splines, rack cutting, turning, honing, stamping & assembly. (Woman, estab 1954, empl 22, sales , cert: WBENC)

6816 Fitz Machine Inc.
       4 Railroad Ave
       Wakefield, MA 01880
       Contact: Kathleen Fitzgerald President
       Tel: 781-245-5966
       Email: kathleen@fitzmachine.com
       Website: www.fitzmachine.com
Precision CNC machined components, multi axis capabilities, prototype & production machining, long & short production runs, in-house tooling design. (Woman, estab 1994, empl 15, sales $1,300,000, cert: WBENC)

6817 M&K Engineering
       66 Concord St
       North Reading, MA 01864
       Contact: Gene Ungvarsky Business Dev Mgr
       Tel: 978-276-1973
       Email: gene@mkeng.com
       Website: www.mkeng.com
Precision machining: CNC & swiss screw CNC. (Woman, estab 1990, empl 28, sales $4,464,492, cert: NMSDC)

6818 PremaTech Advanced Ceramics
       2 Coppage Dr
       Worcester, MA 01603
       Contact: Thomas Shearer Dir Business Dev
       Tel: 508-791-9549
       Email: info@prematechac.com
       Website: www.PremaTechAC.com
Fabricate technical ceramics, sapphire, composite & exotic materials, machining & grinding, ceramic components, refractories, cordierite, kiln furniture, porous metal parts, stainless steel, bronze & titanium filters, zinc, zinc selenide. (Woman, estab 1980, empl 35, sales $3,525,000, cert: WBENC)

6819 Wrobel Engineering Co., Inc.
       154 Bodwell St
       Avon, MA 02322
       Contact: Michael Long General/QA Mgr.
       Tel: 508-586-8338
       Email: mlong@wrobeleng.com
       Website: www.wrobeleng.com
Mfr precision sheet metal fabricated parts per customer specs, precision machining, milling & turning, metal stamping, long & short runs, tool & die making, assembly mechanical & electrical, welding all materials. (Woman, estab 1976, empl 86, sales $14,800,000, cert: State, City)

Maryland

6820 FlexFit Hose LLC
       7948 E. Baltimore St.
       Baltimore, MD 21224
       Contact: Arjun Radhakrishnan Managing Partner
       Tel: 410-327-0758
       Email: sales@flexfithose.com
       Website: www.ffhose.com
CNC Swiss machining, MNT, Female NPT, Female JIC, Tube Adaptors, Tri-Clamps, Mini Tri-Clamps. (AA, estab 2008, empl 4, sales $1,400,000, cert: NMSDC, SDB)

6821 Ray Machine Inc.
       12 Lynbrook Rd
       Baltimore, MD 21220
       Contact: Dan Solomon General Mgr
       Tel: 410-686-6955
       Email: dsolomon@rayamch.com
       Website: www.raymachine.com
CNC & conventional machining; precision sheet metal fab, welding, mechanical & elec assembly, etc. (As-Ind, estab 1950, empl 42, sales $4,711,000, cert: NMSDC)

Michigan

6822 2K Tool LLC
       3025 Madison Ave SE
       Wyoming, MI 49548
       Contact: Kevin Smith Engineering Mgr
       Tel: 616-452-4927
       Email: kevin@2ktool.com
       Website: www.2ktool.com
Moldmaker, machining, tooling, plastic injection molds, compression tooling, composite machining, casting machining part Injection molding. (Woman, estab 2004, empl 19, sales $9,500,000, cert: WBENC)

6823 Accu-Shape Die Cutting, Inc.
       4050 Market Place Dr
       Flint, MI 48507
       Contact: Joe Brooks New Business Dev
       Tel: 810-230-2445
       Email: joebrooks@accushape.com
       Website: www.accushape.com
Large parts a specialty up to 84" x 75" in size with kiss cutting capability from larger roll stock. Lamination of pressure sensitive adhesives up to 54" wide. Slitting and Sheeting of rolled goods up to 85" wide. (AA, estab 1998, empl 36, sales $3,200,000, cert: NMSDC)

6824 Action Tool & Machine Inc.
       5976 Ford Ct
       Brighton, MI 48116
       Contact: Doug Lademan Dir minority bus dev
       Tel: 810-229-6300
       Email: actiontool@actiontoolmachine.com
       Website: www.actiontoolmachine.com
Machining & assembly svcs: build-to-print, part-to-print reverse engineering svcs. (As-Pac, estab 1993, empl 30, sales $3,700,000, cert: NMSDC)

METAL, GENERAL MACHINING

6825 Adaptive Manufacturing Solutions
      G-4206 S Saginaw St
      Burton, MI 48529
      Contact: Debbie Sippell HR Mgr
      Tel: 810-743-1600
      Email: dsippell@ams-miti.com
      Website: www.ams-miti.com
Design & engineering, fabrication, dies, molds, fixtures & gauges, manufacturing, metrology, packaging, material handling, special machines, and precision machining. (Woman, estab 2007, empl 13, sales $649,009, cert: WBENC)

6826 Aerostar Manufacturing
      28275 Northline Rd
      Romulus, MI 48174
      Contact: Robert Johnson VP
      Tel: 734-942-8440
      Email: rjohnson@aerostarmfg.com
      Website: www.aerostarmfg.com
CNC machining assembly, prototyping, machine castings & forgings, sand casting. (As-Pac, estab 1970, empl 200, sales , cert: NMSDC)

6827 ALBAH Manufacturing Technologies Corp.
      1985 Ring Rd
      Troy, MI 48083
      Contact: Kofi Adomako VP
      Tel: 519-972-7222
      Email: kadomako@albah.com
      Website: www.albah.com
Automation & robotics, machine load/unload, material handling, assembly, dispensing, palletizing & material removal. (Woman/AA, estab 1992, empl 27, sales $5,000,000, cert: NMSDC)

6828 Alphi Manufacturing, LLC
      576 Beck St
      Jonesville, MI 49250
      Contact: Ed Carter Dir Diversity Devel
      Tel: -   -
      Email: ecarter@crownegroupllc.com
      Website: www.alphimfg.com/
Fabrication (bending, piercing, end forming, miter cutting, welding) of ferrous and non-ferrous tubalur products. Fabricated exhaust components, Fabricated structural components. (Nat Ame, estab 1959, empl 125, sales $19,939,913, cert: NMSDC)

6829 Aluminum Blanking Company, Inc
      360 W Sheffield
      Pontiac, MI 48340
      Contact: Michael Rutkowski VP Finance & Admin
      Tel: 248-338-4422
      Email: mrutkowski@albl.com
      Website: www.albl.com
Leveling, Blanking, lubing, edge-trimming and slitting of Aluminum, Stainless and other surface sensitive materials. (Woman, estab 1979, empl 120, sales $9,864,397, cert: WBENC)

6830 Aztec Manufacturing Corporation
      15378 Oakwood Dr
      Romulus, MI 48174
      Contact: Richard Johnson President
      Tel: 734-942-7433
      Email: rjohnson@aztecmfgcorp.com
      Website: www.aztecmfgcorp.com
Machined aluminum, ductile iron castings & forgings. (Hisp, estab 1983, empl 55, sales $25,000,000, cert: NMSDC)

6831 Casemer Tool
      2765 Metamora Rd
      Oxford, MI 48371
      Contact: Ray Wrubel Sales
      Tel: 248-860-3689
      Email: Ray@casemer.com
      Website: www.casemer.com
CNC machining, large diameter turning 32" x 120 ", bridge Mill 59" x 119" (Woman, estab 1979, empl 85, sales $15,000,000, cert: WBENC)

6832 Chippewa Industries, Inc.dba Thaymar Medical
      1223 Greenleaf Dr
      Royal Oak, MI 48067
      Contact: Jeff St. Louis President
      Tel: 248-266-1206
      Email: jstlouis@thaymar.com
      Website: www.thaymar.com
CNC Machining, vertical and horizontal 3 Axis, 4 Axis and 5 Axis CNC machining capabilities. We provide Billet, Sand Castings, Metal Castings, Aluminum Castings, Investment Castings, Plaster Casting, Die Casting, Prototype, and Short to Medium Production. (Nat Ame, estab 2015, empl 25, sales $6,000,000, cert: NMSDC)

6833 CKS Precision Machining
      700 E Soper Rd
      Bad Axe, MI 48413
      Contact: Frank Gerbig Dir of Sales
      Tel: 989-269-9702
      Email: fgerbig@geminigroup.net
      Website: www.ckstool.com
CNC machining: lathe, mill, grind & heat treating. (Woman, estab 1979, empl 100, sales $15,709,000, cert: WBENC)

6834 Clips & Clamps Industries
      15050 Keel St
      Plymouth, MI 48170
      Contact: Jeff Aznavorian President
      Tel: 734-455-0880
      Email: jaznavorian@clipsclamps.com
      Website: www.clipsclamps.com
Metal forming, progressive dies, four slide, CNC wire forming, tool building, MIG & TIG welding, tapping, riveting, automated assemblies, prototyping & production volumes, engineering services, design services, sales support. (Woman, estab 1954, empl 62, sales , cert: WBENC)

METAL, GENERAL MACHINING

6835 CNC Products Inc.
      2126 S 11th St
      Niles, MI 49120
      Contact: President
      Tel: 269-684-5500
      Email: orders@cncproductsinc.com
      Website: www.cncproductsinc.com/
CNC machining. (Woman, estab 2019, empl 18, sales $2,500,000, cert: WBENC)

6836 Costello Enterprises, LLC
      56358 Precision Dr
      Chesterfield Township, MI 48051
      Contact: Tom Orban VP
      Tel: 586-615-6307
      Email: torban@costelloenterprises.com
      Website: www.costelloenterprises.com
CNC machining & dimensional inspection services. (Hisp, estab 2000, empl 25, sales , cert: NMSDC)

6837 Costello Machine LLC
      56358 Precision Dr
      Chesterfield, MI 48051
      Contact: Frank Keena Operations Mgr
      Tel: 586-749-0136
      Email: fkeena@costellomachine.com
      Website: www.costellomachine.com
Precision machining, boring mill & assemblies. (Hisp, estab 2000, empl 25, sales $3,500,000, cert: NMSDC)

6838 Dalany Metal Products Inc.
      4450 13th St
      Wyandotte, MI 48192
      Contact: Al Yglesias President
      Tel: 734-282-6666
      Email: al.yglesias@dalany.com
      Website: www.dalany.com
Machine formed metal parts: cold heading, rod heading, wire forming, stampers & screw machine, grooves, reamed holes, cross holes, plating. (Hisp, estab 2004, empl 9, sales $525,000, cert: NMSDC)

6839 Dienamic Tool Corporation
      4541 Patterson Ave SE
      Kentwood, MI 49512
      Contact: Rogelio (Roger) Ramirez President
      Tel: 616-954-7882
      Email: rramirez@dienamictoolcorp.com
      Website: www.dienamictoolcorp.com
Die Build, Reverse Engineering, CNC Machining, Fixture Build. (Hisp, estab 1998, empl 16, sales $1,856,444, cert: NMSDC)

6840 Dowding Industries
      503 Marilin
      Eaton Rapids, MI 48827
      Contact: Roger Cope VP Sales
      Tel: 517-663-5455
      Email: roger@willowhill.net
      Website: www.dowdingindustries.com
CNC machining, milling & boring. (Woman, estab 1965, empl 150, sales , cert: WBENC)

6841 GK Tech, LLC
      3331 W Big Beaver Rd Ste 106
      Troy, MI 48084
      Contact: Kelly Choi
      Tel: 248-494-1960
      Email: kellychoi@gktechusa.com
      Website: www.gktechllc.com
Marketing specialist, consulting, business development, forging, die-casting, stamping, spring, magnesium pulley, rubber bushing, fasteners, machining, plastic injection molding. (Minority, Woman, estab 2015, empl 3, sales , cert: NMSDC)

6842 Jolico/J-B Tool, Inc.
      4325 22 Mile Rd
      Utica, MI 48317
      Contact: Patricia Wieland President
      Tel: 586-739-5555
      Email: pwieland@jolico.com
      Website: www.jolico.com
CNC turning, vertical, multipallet machining, welding, suface, wet & blanchard grinding. (Woman, estab 1963, empl 38, sales , cert: WBENC)

6843 KJL Industries, Inc.
      44057 Phoenix Dr
      Sterling Heights, MI 48314
      Contact: Kristin Wikol President
      Tel: 586-803-1818
      Email: kwikol@kjlindustries.com
      Website: www.kjlindustries.com
Precision machining, tight tolerance, complex parts. (Woman, estab 1984, empl 15, sales $2,000,000, cert: WBENC)

6844 Maya Jig Grinding & Gage Co.
      20770 Parker Rd
      Farmington Hills, MI 48336
      Contact: Jeff Beier VP
      Tel: 248-471-0802
      Email: jbeier@mayagage.com
      Website: www.MayaGage.com
Automatic gages, variable gages, functional gages, hand gages, masters, fixtures & tooling. (Woman, estab 1976, empl 20, sales $3,000,000, cert: WBENC)

6845 PGS Incorporated
      2565 Industrial Row Dr
      Troy, MI 48084
      Contact: Vicki Kafura Exec Admin
      Tel: 248-280-1142
      Email: vkafura@pgsinc.net
      Website: www.pgsinc.net
Prototype, product machining, assembly, steel & plastic component washing & cleaning, sorting, gage/testing, kitting & crisis manufacturing management. (Woman, estab 1983, empl 17, sales $3,844,800, cert: WBENC)

6846 Pioneer Machine & Tech
      1167 East 10 Mile Rd
      Madison Heights, MI 48071
      Contact: Jeffery Harris President
      Tel: 248-546-4451
      Email: jharris@pioneermachinetech.com
      Website: www.pioneermachinetech.com
Machining: custom & precision machining, fabrication, grinding & repair of components & fixtures. (AA, estab 1998, empl 15, sales $1,500,000, cert: NMSDC)

METAL, GENERAL MACHINING 6847-6857

6847 Precision Components Manufacturing, LLC
35855 Stanley
Sterling Heights, MI 48312
Contact: Tommy Longest CEO
Tel: 586-939-8500
Email: tommy@pcmfettes.com
Website: www.pcmfettes.com
Mfr cast tooling, castings iron/aluminum, steel forging, fully machined castings & assembly, ferrous & non-ferrous products, forging, sand & die casting. (AA, estab 2009, empl 30, sales $7,010,000, cert: NMSDC)

6848 Robinson Industries, Inc.
3051 W Curtis Rd
Coleman, MI 48618
Contact: Marvin Ries Sales
Tel: 989-465-6111
Email: mries@robinsonind.com
Website: www.robinsonind.com
Custom design & mfg, vacuum forming, injection molding, extrusion, tool & die shop. (Woman, estab 1950, empl 200, sales $28,348,370, cert: WBENC)

6849 Sequoia Tool
44831 N Groesbeck Hwy
Clinton Township, MI 48036
Contact: James Coates Acct Mgr
Tel: 586-463-4400
Email: bcoates@sequoiatool.net
Website: www.sequoiatool.net
Mfr prototype sheet metal stampings & assemblies, low volume production and short run svcs. (Nat Ame, estab 1988, empl 65, sales $10,000,000, cert: NMSDC)

6850 Set Enterprises, Inc.
38600 Van Dyke Ave Ste 325
Sterling Heights, MI 48093
Contact: Antoinette Turner Mgr Corp Communication
Tel: 586-573-3600
Email: aturner@setenterprises.com
Website: www.setenterprises.com
Metal processing services, blanking, slitting & warehousing of metal products. (AA, estab 0, empl 310, sales , cert: NMSDC)

6851 Steadfast Engineered Products, LLC
775 Woodlawn Ave
Grand Haven, MI 49417
Contact: Jay Cutie Managing Partner
Tel: 616-846-4747
Email: jcutie@steadfastep.com
Website: www.steadfastep.com
Screw machine products, turned parts. (AA, Hisp, estab 1986, empl 12, sales $6,000,000, cert: NMSDC)

6852 Sure Solutions LLC
5385 Perry Dr
Waterford, MI 48329
Contact: Art Huge Sales
Tel: 248-674-7210
Email: info@suresolutionsmbe.com
Website: www.suresolutionsmbe.com/
Stampings, plating, coatings, roll forming, machining, castings, forgings, assembly, packaging, warehousing & distribution, containment. (Minority, Woman, estab 1990, empl 25, sales $8,250,000, cert: WBENC)

6853 Systrand Manufacturing Corporation
19050 Allen Rd
Brownstown, MI 48329
Contact: Jim Meadows Dir of Finance
Tel: 734-479-8100
Email: jim.meadows@systrand.com
Website: www.systrand.com
High volume production machining: cast iron, aluminum, steel & powdered metal components. (Minority, Woman, estab 1982, empl 200, sales $65,000,000, cert: NMSDC, WBENC)

6854 Trutron Corporation
274 Executive Dr
Troy, MI 48083
Contact: Lisa Kingsley President
Tel: 248-583-9166
Email: lkingsley@trutron.com
Website: www.trutron.com
Precision machining, CNC turning, milling, grinding: pressure plates, valve plates, wafer plates, cam rings, rotors, housings, manifolds, radial rings, levers, sleeves, actuator pistons, tooling & gauging. (Woman, estab 1967, empl 26, sales $5,239,911, cert: WBENC)

6855 United Manufacturing Network Inc.
12 Lincoln St
Mt. Clemens, MI 48043
Contact: Cathy DeNardo President
Tel: 586-468-7443
Email: cathydenardo@comcast.net
Website: www.unitedmanufacturingnetwork.com
Design & build fixtures & gages, tool & dies injection molds, molded parts & rapid prototype CNC machining, turning, milling & boring mill OD, ID, surface & centerless grinding, precision jig grinding & wire EDM. (Woman, estab 2004, empl 3, sales $104,202, cert: WBENC)

6856 West Michigan Flocking
78277 County Road 378
Covert, MI 49043
Contact: Garrett Fox VP Sales
Tel: 269-639-1634
Email: gfox@wmflocking.com
Website: www.wmflocking.com
Object flocking, injection molding, in-line attachment assembly, sub assembly & sonic welding. (AA, estab 1978, empl 50, sales $4,500,000, cert: NMSDC)

6857 Witco Inc.
6401 Bricker Rd
Avoca, MI 48006
Contact: Tom Kean Sales Engineer
Tel: 810-387-4231
Email: tomk@witcoinc.com
Website: www.witcoinc.com
CNC precision machine parts: milling, turning, grinding, gear shaping & assembly. (Woman, estab 1977, empl 60, sales $7,000,000, cert: WBENC)

6858 Zoatex
      25580 Brest Road
      Taylor, MI 48180
      Contact: Hamid Servati Partner
      Tel: 734-697-5555
      Email: hservati@zoatex.com
      Website: www.zoatex.com
Manufacturing & machining, powertrain devel, emissions, durability testing, project mgmt, prototyping. (AA, estab 2002, empl 20, sales $12,000,000, cert: NMSDC)

Minnesota

6859 LAI International, Inc.
      4255 Pheasant Ridge Dr NE #405
      Minneapolis, MN 55449
      Contact: Terri Lambert Dir Sales
      Tel: 480-469-4170
      Email: tlambert@laico.com
      Website: www.laico.com
Cutting-Edge Precision Component Manufacturing. (AA, estab 1979, empl 287, sales $73,113,237, cert: NMSDC)

6860 Mack Engineering Corporation
      3215 E 26th St
      Minneapolis, MN 55406
      Contact: Jennifer Salisbury President
      Tel: 612-721-2471
      Email: info@mackengineering.com
      Website: www.mackengineering.com
Mfr precision-machined components utilizing a dock to stock quality system. (Woman, estab 1943, empl 30, sales , cert: WBENC)

6861 Metal Craft Machine & Engineering, Inc.
      13760 Businesss Center Dr
      Elk River, MN 55330
      Contact: Trisha Mowry CEO
      Tel: 763-441-1855
      Email: trisha@metal-craft.com
      Website: www.metal-craft.com
Contract manufacturing & engineering design: CNC milling & turning, multi-tasking machining, 7-axis CNC grinding, wire EDM, swiss gundrilling, laser & GTAW (Tig.), welding blasting, deburring, & finishing. (Woman, estab 1978, empl 185, sales , cert: WBENC)

6862 Miller Machine Company
      14105 Commerce Dr
      Becker, MN 55308
      Contact: Cynthia Wahl President
      Tel: 763-263-0091
      Email: cyndiw@millermachinecompany.com
      Website: www.millermachinecompany.com
CNC mills & lathes, brown & sharpe screw machines, automatice saws, bridgeports, hardinges. (Woman, estab 1944, empl 15, sales $1,764,305, cert: WBENC)

6863 Modern Manufacturing & Engineering, Inc.
      9380 Winnetka Ave N
      Brooklyn Park, MN 55445
      Contact: Nancy Lien Berndt President
      Tel: 612-781-3347
      Email: nancyl@mmeincmn.com
      Website: www.mmeincmn.com
Precision custom machining, milling, turning, grinding, assembly, plating, painting. (As-Pac, estab 1958, empl 156, sales , cert: NMSDC)

6864 Northern U & S, Inc. dba Quali-Mac, Inc.
      9208 James Ave S, Ste 11
      Bloomington, MN 55431
      Contact: Shawn Thai President
      Tel: 952-881-6677
      Email: shawnt@qualimac-inc.com
      Website: www.qualimac-inc.com
Precision, CNC machining, metal/plastic machining, turning, vertical milling, protoype, production machining. (As-Pac, estab 1974, empl 7, sales $400,000, cert: NMSDC)

6865 Permac Industries, Inc.
      14401 Ewing Ave S
      Burnsville, MN 55306
      Contact: Mike Bartizal VP
      Tel: 952-746-0289
      Email: mbartizal@permacindustries.com
      Website: www.permacindustries.com
Precision machining: CNC lathe, swiss & screw machined custom components. (Woman, estab 1966, empl 30, sales $5,000,000, cert: WBENC)

6866 Riverside Manufacturing, Inc.
      14280 Sunfish Lake Blvd NW
      Ramsey, MN 55303
      Contact: Mic Wieshaar President
      Tel: 763-274-2193
      Email: riversidemnf@earthlink.net
      Website: www.riversidemnf.com
CNC machining, complex horizontal machining. (Nat Ame, estab 1997, empl 15, sales $3,450,000, cert: NMSDC)

New Hampshire

6867 Maclean Precision Machine
      1928 Village Rd
      Madison, NH 03849
      Contact: Deborah Folsom President
      Tel: 603-367-9011
      Email: d.folsom@macleanprecision.com
      Website: www.macleanprecision.com
Precision machining, tight tolerance parts, Titanium, Inconel, Stainless Steel, Aluminum, Castings, Bar Stock & Plate. (Woman, estab 1977, empl 33, sales $3,800,000, cert: NWBOC)

METAL, GENERAL MACHINING

New Jersey

6868 Arlington Machine & Tool
      90 New Dutch Ln
      Fairfield, NJ 07004
      Contact: Susan Blanck President
      Tel: 973-276-1377
      Email: sblanck@arlingtonmachine.com
      Website: www.arlingtonmachine.com
CNC machining & turning, manufacturing, assemblies & systems. (Woman, estab 1963, empl 100, sales $16,000,000, cert: State, WBENC)

6869 Computa-Base Machining
      411 N Grove St
      Berlin, NJ 08009
      Contact: Agustin Rosado President
      Tel: 856-767-3509
      Email: cbmpresident@computabase.com
      Website: www.computabase.com
Close tolerance, special metals, nickel, inconell, kamenell, etc. (Hisp, estab 1981, empl 20, sales $1,000,000, cert: NMSDC, SDB)

6870 Kaizen Technologies Inc.
      1 Lincoln Hwy, Ste 10
      Edison, NJ 08820
      Contact: Prakash Bahumanyam VP
      Tel: 732-452-9555
      Email: prakashb@kaizentek.com
      Website: www.kaizentek.com
Precision machining, tooling, jigs & fixtures. (As-Ind, estab 1995, empl 150, sales $11,000,000, cert: State)

6871 Progressive Machinery Inc.
      19 E Centre St
      Nutley, NJ 07110
      Contact: VP Finance
      Tel: 833-776-6224
      Email: info@pro-machinery.com
      Website: www.pro-machinery.com
CNC milling and turning, grinding, welding, die & mold fabrication, multi-slide forming & assembly on Bihler machines & CMM inspections, molding, stamping forming, punching, cutting, welding, tapping, inserting, assembling, and sheet metal fabrication. (Woman, estab 2009, empl 10, sales $1,500,000, cert: State, WBENC)

New Mexico

6872 Las Cruces Machine, Mfg. & Engineering
      6000 S Main, Ste B
      Mesilla Park, NM 88047
      Contact: Rod Mitchell President
      Tel: 575-526-1411
      Email: rmitchell@lascrucesmachine.com
      Website: www.lascrucesmachine.com
CNC precision machining capabilities. (Woman, estab 1975, empl 40, sales $3,907,000, cert: WBENC)

New York

6873 Cannon Industries, Inc.
      525 Lee Rd
      Rochester, NY 14606
      Contact: Reggie Cannon President
      Tel: 585-254-8080
      Email: rcannon@cannonind.com
      Website: www.cannonind.com
Sheet metal fabrication, welding fabrication, laser & plasma cutting, metal stamping, CNC machining & turning, mechanical assembly, spot welding. (AA, estab 1979, empl 104, sales $16,000,000, cert: NMSDC)

6874 Greno Industries Inc.
      PO Box 542
      Schenectady, NY 12301
      Contact: Joe Vainauskas VP Operations
      Tel: 518-393-4195
      Email: jvainauskas@greno.com
      Website: www.greno.com
Contract OEM machining, milling & turning services, CAD/CAM capabilities, modern equipment. (Woman, estab 1961, empl 65, sales $15,500,000, cert: WBENC)

6875 Ingleside Machine Company, Inc.
      1120 Hook Rd
      Farmington, NY 14425
      Contact: Gary Veomett
      Tel: 585-924-3046
      Email: office@inglesidemachine.com
      Website: www.Inglesidemachine.com
CNC milling, turning, sheet metal fabrication, welding, finishing & assembly. (Woman, estab 1974, empl 85, sales , cert: State)

6876 Park Enterprises
      226 Jay St
      Rochester, NY 14608
      Contact: Robert Amo Sales
      Tel: 716-393-7106
      Email: rob@questsls.com
      Website: www.parkent.com
CNC machining, screw machining, prototypes, electrical assemblies. (As-Pac, estab 1991, empl 160, sales $20,000,000, cert: NMSDC)

Ohio

6877 Action Precision Products Inc.
      100 E North Ave Box 188
      Pioneer, OH 43554
      Contact: Linda Heisler President
      Tel: 419-737-2348
      Email: linda@actionprecision.com
      Website: www.actionprecision.com
Machining: low volume, high tolerance blue print items, steel, brass, bronze & plastics, CNC turning, milling & grinding operations. (Woman, estab 1972, empl 10, sales $1,020,000, cert: WBENC)

METAL, GENERAL MACHINING

6878 Cleveland Die & Mfg. Co.
20303 First Ave
Middleburg Heights, OH 44130
Contact: Marty Curry Sales/Engineering
Tel: 440-243-3404
Email: mcurry@clevelanddie.com
Website: www.clevelanddie.com/
Ecoat & powder coat line, automatic & single hit presses, spot & robotic welders, CNC machining. (Hisp, estab 1973, empl 300, sales $24,000,000, cert: NMSDC)

6879 Covert Manufacturing, Inc.
328 S East St
Galion, OH 44833
Contact: Steve Lamontagne VP Sales
Tel: 419-468-1761
Email: stevel@covertmfg.com
Website: www.covertmfg.com
CNC Machine Shop specializing in the machining of castings, Forgings, and Bar. Heavy Truck parts, engine components, suspension components, driveline components, Braking systems. (Woman, estab 1967, empl 140, sales , cert: WBENC)

6880 EnKon, LLC dba Broadway
6344 Webster St
Dayton, OH 45414
Contact: Jodi Walters Member
Tel: 937-890-2221
Email: jodi.walters@enkonllc.com
Website: www.broadwaymold.com
Injection molds, components, mold repairs, Precision Fabrication,
CNC Machining, welding, turning, Electrode manufacturing, EDM'ING, Wire EDM, Polish, Milling, OD, ID, and surface grinding, Design. (Woman, estab 1955, empl 12, sales , cert: WBENC)

6881 GB Manufacturing Company
100 Adams St
Delta, OH 43515
Contact: Teresa Elling Sales
Tel: 419-822-5323
Email: apetree@gbmfg.com
Website: www.gbmfg.com
Stamping, laser blanking, fabrication & assembly, tool making, robotic & hand welding, spot welding, press braking, productin machining, prototyping. (Minority, estab 1975, empl 85, sales $24,500,000, cert: NMSDC)

6882 Green Rock Lighting, LLC
3175 W 33rd St
Cleveland, OH 44109
Contact: Tina Haddad CEO
Tel: 216-651-6446
Email: thaddad@greenrocklighting.com
Website: www.greenrocklighting.com
Laser cutting, wire bending & forming, press brake, spinning, stamping, mig, tig & stick welding, spot welding, machining, destructive & non-destructive testing, packaging & assembly. (Woman, estab 2011, empl 20, sales , cert: State, WBENC)

6883 Kaskell Manufacturing, Inc.
240 Hiawatha Trail
Springboro, OH 45066
Contact: Brian Harris VP
Tel: 937-704-9700
Email: bharris@kaskellmfg.com
Website: www.kaskellmfg.com
CNC machining, milling & turning. (Woman, estab 2000, empl 12, sales $1,250,000, cert: WBENC)

6884 Lewis Unlimited, Inc.
165 Jackson Dr
Cleveland, OH 44022
Contact: Joseph Lewis, Jr. President
Tel: 216-514-8282
Email: jlewis@lewisunlimited.com
Website: www.lewisunlimited.com
CNC precision machined components, multi axis machining centers, single & multi-spindle screw products, CNC Swiss machined components. (AA, estab 1991, empl 10, sales $6,043,537, cert: State, NMSDC)

6885 Magni-Power Company
5511 Lincoln Way E
Wooster, OH 44691
Contact: Kim Coblentz New Business Dev Mgr
Tel: 330-264-3637
Email: kcoblentz@magnipower.com
Website: www.magnipower.com
Metal fabrication & stamping: process steel, aluminum, stainless steel, CNC punching, forming, laser cutting, robotic welding, in-house powder coating & assembly. (As-Ind, estab 1948, empl 230, sales $27,000,000, cert: NMSDC)

6886 Mantych Metalworking, Inc.
3175 Plainfield Rd
Dayton, OH 45432
Contact: Bill Sewell Sales
Tel: 937-258-1373
Email: bill@mantych.net
Website: www.mantych.net
Precision CNC machining & sheet metal fabrication. (Woman, estab 1971, empl 34, sales $8,000,000, cert: WBENC)

6887 Ohio Transitional Machine & Tool Inc.
3940 Castener St
Toledo, OH 43612
Contact: Marten Whalen President
Tel: 419-476-0820
Email: ohiotransitional@hotmail.com
Website: www.ohiotransitional.com
CNC milling & turning, wire EDM, boringmill, general machining, blanchard grinding, 3D machining, jigs & fixtures, prototypes, R&D, welding, painting & assembly. (Nat Ame, estab 1985, empl 10, sales $800,000, cert: NMSDC)

6888 Vantage Agora
23811 Chagrin Blvd Ste 244
Beachwood, OH 44122
Contact: Sudhir Achar President
Tel: 888-246-7211
Email: sudhir@vantageagora.com
Website: www.vantageagora.com
Mfr turned parts, machining, hot & cold forging, printing, precision parts. (As-Ind, estab 2004, empl 19, sales $3,697,558, cert: NMSDC)

6889 Wrena, LLC dba Angstrom-USA, LLC
265 Lightner Rd
Tipp City, OH 45371
Contact: Nagesh Palakurthi CEO
Tel: 937-667-4403
Email: pyenger@wrenallc.com
Website: www.angstrom-usa.com
Stampings, tubular products, machining, welding, robotic welding, steel forgings (Warm & Cold), aluminum forgings, assemblies, plastic injection molding, needle bearings, starter assemblies (As-Pac, estab 2011, empl 46, sales , cert: NMSDC)

Oregon

6890 Browns Machine
90500B Hwy 99N
Eugene, OR 97402
Contact: Kevin Brown President
Tel: 541-344-1466
Email: kevin@brownsmachine.com
Website: www.brownsmachine.com
Custom machining, first article inspections, material certifications. (Nat Ame, estab 2003, empl 31, sales , cert: State)

6891 Hy Speed Machining, Inc.
353 California Ave
Grants Pass, OR 97526
Contact: Rachel Chamberland HR Mgr
Tel: 541-476-0769
Email: rachelc@hyspeedmachining.com
Website: www.hyspeedmachining.com
Machine shop specializing in machined parts; all materials; close tolerance, high volume. (Minority, Woman, estab 1984, empl 19, sales $3,049,034, cert: State)

Pennsylvania

6892 Acutec Precision Aerospace Inc.
13555 Broadway
Meadville, PA 16335
Contact: Rich Shaffer Sr Acct Mgr
Tel: 814-763-3214
Email: rshaffer@acutecprecision.com
Website: www.acutecprecision.com
Milling, turning, grinding, honing, lapping, EDM & light assembly of aluminum, titanium, stainless steel, inconel, hastalloy, hastx, plastics. (Woman, estab 1988, empl 385, sales $100,000,000, cert: WBENC)

6893 Agape Precision Manufacturing, LLC
320 Circle of Progress Dr Ste 108
Pottstown, PA 19464
Contact: Dana Wolfe President
Tel: 484-824-3134
Email: dana.wolfe@agapeprecision.com
Website: www.agapeprecision.com
Machining, fabrication, bending, assemblies, hardware, some special processes, brackets, prototyping, metals, delron, plastics, aerospace manufacturing. (Woman, estab 2006, empl 11, sales $1,100,000, cert: State)

6894 Amity Industries
491 Old Swede Rd
Douglassville, PA 19518
Contact: Monica Lubinsky CEO
Tel: 610-385-6075
Email: mlubins@amityindustries.com
Website: www.amityindustries.com
Custom fabrication, machining & assembly. (Nat Ame, estab 1973, empl 45, sales $10,000,000, cert: NMSDC)

6895 Atlas Machining & Welding, Inc.
777 Smith Lane
Northampton, PA 18067
Contact: Andrew Weiss Project Mgr
Tel: 610-262-1374
Email: info@atlasmw.com
Website: www.atlasmw.com
CNC machine & steel fabrication, vertical & horizontal boring mills, vertical machine centers, lathes & turning. (Woman, estab 1981, empl 65, sales $13,000,000, cert: NWBOC)

6896 C.A. Spalding, Co.
1011 Cedar Ave
Croydon, PA 19021
Contact: Javier Kuehnle CEO
Tel: 215-850-5777
Email: nteubert@spaldingautomotive.com
Website: www.caspalding.com
High-precision forming, laser cutting & bracket machining. (Hisp, estab 1938, empl 30, sales $18,231,344, cert: NMSDC)

6897 D & R Machine Co.
1330 Industrial Hwy
Southampton, PA 18966
Contact: Nelson Redante Mgr Business Dev
Tel: 215-526-2080
Email: nelsonredante@drmachine.com
Website: www.drmachine.com
Mfr precision machine parts to cstmr specs. (Hisp, estab 1971, empl 38, sales , cert: NMSDC)

Rhode Island

6898 East Bay Manufacturing
400 Franklin St
Bristol, RI 02809
Contact: Randy Medina General Mgr
Tel: 401-254-2960
Email: randy@eastbaymfg.com
Website: www.eastbaymfg.com
CNC machining & fabrication resources. (Hisp, estab 1985, empl 14, sales , cert: State)

South Carolina

6899 Bunty, LLC
444 Fairforest Way
Greenville, SC 29607
Contact: Rajeev Jindal President
Tel: 864-567-0498
Email: rajeev@buntyllc.com
Website: www.buntyllc.com
Precision machined components, assemblies, metal fabrication, jigs & fixtures, forgings, castings, dies, re-engineered OEM parts, CNC milling, CNC turning. (As-Pac, estab 2000, empl 10, sales $1,600,000, cert: NMSDC)

6900 J.I.T. Manufacturing, Inc.
428 Oglesby Lane
Cowpens, SC 29330
Contact: Dan Hunter Production / Sales Mgr.
Tel: 864-463-0581
Email: dan@jitmanufacturing.com
Website: www.jitmfg.net
Laser cutting, welding, forming, CNC punching, CNC machines, fabrication, sheetmetal, powdercoating, pressbrakes, modifications, spot welding, control boxes, mounting plates, brackets, CAD programing, Cad design. (Woman, estab 1992, empl 22, sales $2,910,792, cert: City, WBENC)

6901 Secondary Solutions, Inc.
101 Northeast Dr
Spartanburg, SC 29303
Contact: Mark Mahaffey Sales
Tel: 864-494-5337
Email: markmahaffey@secondarysolutionsinc.net
Website: www.ssiservesyou.net
Machining, fabrication, drilling, tapping, grinding, warehousing, assembly, boring, wire marking, wire harness assembly, 3rd party inspection services, buffing, polishing, packaging. (Woman, estab 1997, empl 10, sales $550,000, cert: WBENC)

Tennessee

6902 Engineered Mechanical Systems
118 Parmenas Lane
Chattanooga, TN 37405
Contact: Brenna Fairchild CEO
Tel: 423-624-3300
Email: brenna@emsfab.com
Website: www.emsfab.com
Design & build custom machines/equipment, multiple lasers & CNC sheet metal machines, certified welders. (Minority, Woman, estab 1990, empl 67, sales $13,000,000, cert: WBENC)

6903 Gonzalez Group LLC
237 Kraft St
Clarksville, TN 37040
Contact: Felix Gonzalez CEO
Tel: 517-542-2928
Email: fg@gonzalezmfg.com
Website: www.gonzalezmfg.com
Mfr precision turned machined parts. (Hisp, estab 1974, empl 135, sales $14,000,000, cert: NMSDC)

6904 Southern Precision Machining, LLC
220 Calsonic Way
Shelbyville, TN 37160
Contact: President
Tel: 931-685-9057
Email: info@spm-precisionmachining.com
Website: www.spm-precisionmachining.com
3, 4, & 5 axis CNC machining: aluminum, stainless steel & titanium components. (Minority, Woman, estab 2005, empl 30, sales $4,500,000, cert: WBENC)

Texas

6905 365 Machine Inc.
27890 Commercial Park Lane
Tomball, TX 77375
Contact: Billy Helveston VP Sales & Mktg
Tel: 281-378-7811
Email: billy@365-machine.com
Website: www.365-machine.com
Precision CNC machining, 4 CNC lathes, 5 CNC mills, horizontal mill. (Woman, estab 2013, empl 13, sales $1,200,000, cert: State, WBENC)

6906 Best Sheet Metal Solutions
923 KCK Way, Ste A
Cedar Hill, TX 75104
Contact: Jacob Bell Owner
Tel: 214-384-1951
Email: jacob@bestsheetmetalsolutions.com
Website: www.bestsheetmetalsolutions.com
Close Tolerance CNC Machining, CNC Vertical Machining Center & Haas CNC Horitzonal Turning Center (Lathe), Machine Heat Sinks, Buss bar, Surfacing, Profiling, Casting Molds, (AA, estab 2008, empl 3, sales $150,000, cert: NMSDC)

6907 Buks Tool Company, Inc.
6410-X Langfield Rd
Houston, TX 77092
Contact: Danielle Buks President
Tel: 713-974-5187
Email: danielle@bukstool.com
Website: www.bukstool.com
CNC Machining, Conventional machining, coordinate measuring machine, welding, grinding, boring, jig bore, tooling, design, EDM, sawing, hydrostatic pressure testing, high pressure pumps, components & assemblies. (Woman, estab 1978, empl 22, sales , cert: WBENC)

6908 Clay Precision, Ltd.
1102 FM 1417 NE
Sherman, TX 75090
Contact: J. Diann Spencer President
Tel: 903-891-9022
Email: jspencer@clayprecision.com
Website: www.clayprecision.com
Milling, turning, 4th axis capabilities, fixturing, plastic weldment, assemblies, heat treating, grinding, dock-to-stock quality, fabrication of custom metal and plastic machined parts and assemblies, prototypes, exotic metals, exotic plastics. (Woman, estab 1996, empl 11, sales $1,293,930, cert: State, WBENC)

METAL, GENERAL MACHINING

6909 Coastal Machine & Mechanical, LLC
14004 S Hwy 288B
Angleton, TX 77515
Contact: Mike Adams GM
Tel: 979-848-8900
Email: madams@coastalmandm.com
Website: www.coastalmandm.com
Custom machining & fabrication, millwright & welding services, maintenance services & balancing, rebuild pumps, gearboxes, ASME "R" stamp certificate. (Hisp, estab 2010, empl 28, sales , cert: State)

6910 Cutting Source Precision, Inc.
14011 Fm 529 Bldg B
Houston, TX 77065
Contact: Larry Boyd Dir Govt Sale
Tel: 281-859-2900
Email: info@cspmachine.com
Website: www.cspmachine.com
Machining, CNC milling & turning, waterjet saw cutting, carbon, aluminum, stainless, Monel, Inconel, Ferrilum, Titanium, Delrin, & Duplex. (Woman, estab 2000, empl 20, sales $1,900,000, cert: WBENC, NWBOC)

6911 Gretna Machine Shop, Inc.
3450 Lang Rd
Houston, TX 77092
Contact: Aerospace Div. Mgr.
Tel: 713-690-7328
Email:
Website: www.gretnamachine.com
CNC turning machines, CAD/CAM software programming, Sawing, Marking, Deburring services, Real-time order tracking, Worldwide Packaging & Delivery. (Minority, Woman, estab 1980, empl 85, sales , cert: WBENC)

6912 Guzman Manufacturing, Inc.
4206 Industrial St
Rowlett, TX 75088
Contact: Annabell Acuna Office Mgr
Tel: 972-475-3003
Email: info@gzmfg.com
Website: www.gzmfg.com
Machine shop: precision sheet metal, spot welding, CNC, etc. (Hisp, estab 1975, empl 15, sales , cert: State)

6913 Mentco Inc.
15926 University Oak
San Antonio, TX 78249
Contact: Matt Weber Sr Mgr
Tel: 210-494-3100
Email: matt.weber@mentco.com
Website: www.mentcoinc.com
Mfr high precision, tight tolerance machined parts from bar stock, castings or forgings. Stainless Steel, (all grades), Inconel, Monel, Hastelloy, 15-5PH, 17-4PH, Titanium, Aluminum, Copper, Brass, Bronze. (As-Ind, estab 2006, empl 55, sales , cert: State, NMSDC)

6914 QMF Steel, Inc.
3846 IH-30 East
Campbell, TX 75422
Contact: Sherrill Lester President
Tel: 903-455-3618
Email: sherrill@qmfsteel.com
Website: www.qmfsteel.com
CNC plate saw precision cutting, CNC plasma cutting, CNC machining, CNC lathe/turning, bundle cutting, threading, polishing: aluminum, stainless, hot roll, cold roll, alloy, magnesium, brass, copper & other metal products. (Woman, estab 1994, empl 49, sales $15,000,000, cert: State, WBENC)

6915 Spring International
23594 Dogwood Trail Dr Ste A
Hockley, TX 77447
Contact: President
Tel: 281-966-5109
Email: support@springintl.net
Website: www.springintl.net
Machining, turn key, assembly, coat. etc. (Woman/AA, estab 2014, empl 5, sales $500,000, cert: State)

6916 Standard Industrial Products Company
12610 Galveston Rd
Webster, TX 77059
Contact: Walter Gomez Dir Operation & Mktg
Tel: 281-480-8711
Email: wgomez@sipco-mls.com
Website: www.sipco-mls.com
Engineering, Electro Mechanical Design, Validation & System Integration, CNC Milling, CNC Turning, Sawing, Mechanical System assembly & integration, Gearing - Design, Sourcing, Assembly & System Integration. (Hisp, estab 1984, empl 15, sales $2,099,000, cert: NMSDC)

6917 Systems Integration, Inc.
7316 Business Pl
Arlington, TX 76001
Contact: Rhonda Smith Acct Mgr
Tel: 817-468-1494
Email: rsmith@sitexas.com
Website: www.sitexas.com
Engineering & Design, Reverse Engineering, Fabrication, Installation, Structural & Civil, Manufacturing, Machinery, Mechanical, CNC Machining, Electrical & Controls, Test Structures, Tooling. (Hisp, estab 1992, empl 20, sales $4,000,000, cert: State)

6918 VLJ Inc. dba Smith Tool & Mfg.
116 Regency Dr
Wylie, TX 75098
Contact: Kevin Hefley Sales Mgr
Tel: 972-442-4673
Email: smithtoolsales@airmail.net
Website: www.smithtoolmfg.com
Precision sheet metal mfg, stamping, tool & die, laser cutting, spinning, maching, turning. (Woman, estab 2001, empl 35, sales $570,000, cert: State)

METAL, GENERAL MACHINING

Virginia

6919   High-Tech Machine Mfg, Inc.
11010 Trade Rd
North Chesterfield, VA 23236
Contact: Cheryl P Cacciotti President
Tel: 804-794-8640
Email: sales@hightechmachineinc.com
Website: www.htmachineinc.com
Production machining, swiss screw machine, CNC milling & turning, stock & release program. (Woman, estab 1984, empl 10, sales $1,100,000, cert: State, WBENC)

6920   HUB Corporation
2113 Salem Ave SW
Roanoke, VA 24016
Contact: Hubert Humphrey CEO
Tel: 540-342-3505
Email: hhumphrey@hubcorp.net
Website: www.hubcorp.net
Custom manufacturing CNC specializing in true 5-axis contour programming and machining with the ability to make incredibly complex shapes. (AA, estab 1957, empl 20, sales $5,000,000, cert: NMSDC)

6921   Metal Tech Inc.
2629 Richard Ave NE
Roanoke, VA 24012
Contact: Natasha Crowder Project estimator
Tel: 540-798-4193
Email: metaltech@cox.net
Website: www.metaltechincorporated.com
Custom metal fabrication: sandblasting, punching, machine cutting, CNC plasma cutting, water jet cutting, pipe bending, ornamental bender machine, surface preparation & coating. (Woman, estab 1996, empl 2, sales $150,000, cert: State)

Washington

6922   Premier Manufacturing
1711 N Madison
Liberty Lake, WA 99019
Contact: Britt La Chance Sales Dir
Tel: 509-993-6800
Email: britt@premier-manufacturing.com
Website: www.premier-manufacturing.net
Mfr precision sheet metal products. (Woman, estab 2001, empl 100, sales $8,486,433, cert: WBENC)

Wisconsin

6923   American Metal Technologies LLC
8213 Durand Ave
Sturtevant, WI 53177
Contact: San Santharam President
Tel: 262-633-1756
Email: san@amermetals.com
Website: www.amermetals.com
Precision CNC machining & assembly: ferrous & non-ferrous components, fluid retention components, FEAD brackets & vibration dampening products. (As-Pac, estab 2000, empl 142, sales $25,500,000, cert: NMSDC)

6924   Bothe Associates Inc.
6901-46th St
Kenosha, WI 53144
Contact: Laura Bothe VP
Tel: 262-656-1860
Email: lbothe@bothe.com
Website: www.bothe.com
Machine shop & assembly: prototype, short & long run metal & plastic parts, high tolerance, tooling lathes, mills. (Woman, estab 1950, empl 42, sales $5,876,062, cert: WBENC)

6925   Cardinal Components, Inc.
N59W13500 Manhardt Dr
Menomonee Falls, WI 53051
Contact: Leann Kurey President
Tel: 262-437-1510
Email: nelsonm@cardinalcomponents.com
Website: www.cardinalcomponents.com
Dist Metal Components: Rivet-Nut Fasteners; Precision Machining: CNC Turning and Milling; Metal Fabrication: Brake Press, Laser, Stamping and Welding-Spot; Wire Forming and Springs. (Woman, estab 1983, empl 17, sales $7,000,100, cert: CPUC)

6926   Mantz Automation
1630 Innovation Way
Hartford, WI 53027
Contact: Gary Sonnenburg Sales Rep
Tel: 262-224-7528
Email: tnewman@mantzautomation.com
Website: www.mantzautomation.com
Machining components: alloys, design & build tooling, gages, fitures, CNC machinery, 5 axis machinng centers with large envelope of 60" x 120" x 48". (Minority, Woman, estab 1986, empl 105, sales $22,300,000, cert: State)

6927   R.J. Zeman Tool & Mfg. Co., Inc.
W228 N575 Westmound Dr
Waukesha, WI 53186
Contact: Spencer Schreindl President
Tel: 262-549-4400
Email: sschreindl@zemantool.com
Website: www.zemantool.com
Machining, design, mfr & inspect fixtures, special machines, gages, die cast dies, plastic injection molds, permanent molds, core boxes, patterns for sand casting & short and long-run production parts. (Woman, estab 1966, empl 48, sales $9,600,000, cert: WBENC)

6928   Stanek Tool Corporation
2500 S Calhoun Rd
New Berlin, WI 53151
Contact: Paul Bartkowiak VP Workholding
Tel: 262-786-0120
Email: pbartkowiak@stanektool.com
Website: www.stanektool.com
Design & build machining fixtures, plastic molds, & precision machined parts & assemblies. (Woman, estab 1924, empl 50, sales $10,000,000, cert: WBENC)

METAL RAW STOCK

Includes distributors of metal sheets, plates, rods, pipe, etc. Many can provide cutting and other metal processing services. (Also see six other METAL categories). NAICS Code 33

California

6929 California Metal & Supply Inc.
10230 Freeman Ave
Santa Fe Springs, CA 90670
Contact: Kenneth Minkyu Lee President
Tel: 800-707-6061
Email: klee@californiametal.com
Website: www.CaliforniaMetal.com

Titanium, Inconel, Aluminum, Stainless, Magnesium Sheet, Plate, Bar, Tube & Tubing, Pipe, Tubing: Stainless, Carbon Steel, Aluminum, Brass, Valves. (As-Pac, estab 1984, empl 12, sales $60,000,000, cert: NMSDC)

6930 Global Steel Alliance Corp.
14241 E Firestone Blvd, Ste 400
La Mirada, CA 90638
Contact: Keith Shiozaki President
Tel: 562-293-4086
Email: keith@steel-alliance.net
Website: www.steel-alliance.net

Dist carbon steel pipe. (As-Pac, estab 2008, empl 1, sales $2,779,880, cert: NMSDC, CPUC)

6931 International Metal Source
17605 Fabrica Way Ste E & F
Cerritos, CA 90703
Contact: Jaymee Del Rosario Founder/CEO
Tel: 714-676-5669
Email: jaymee@imetalsource.com
Website: www.imetalsource.com

Dist Aluminum, Nickel, Titanium, Stainless Steel, High-Temperature & Specialty Steels, Ferrous, Non-Ferrous & Non-Metallic Raw Material in Sheet, Plate, Rod, Bar, Extrusions, Tubes & Formed Shapes. (Minority, Woman, estab 2009, empl 10, sales $889,000, cert: CPUC, SDB)

6932 Southern California Metals, Inc.
9900 Bell Ranch Dr
Santa Fe Springs, CA 90670
Contact: Alisa Thorpe President
Tel: 562-941-1616
Email: alisa@socalmetals.com
Website: www.socalmetals.com

Dist alloys, steels, stainless steels, titanium, nickel based alloys, aluminum & copper alloys in plate, sheet, bar, extrusion, forgings & castings, plastic lexan sheets, aviation rivets, nuts, fasteners, screws & seat tracks. (Woman, estab 1995, empl 15, sales $4,001,000, cert: State, CPUC)

Florida

6933 Aluminum Distributing, Inc. dba ADI Metal
2930 SW Second Ave
Fort Lauderdale, FL 33315
Contact: Betsy McGee President
Tel: 954-523-6474
Email: betsy@adimetal.com
Website: www.adimetal.com

Dist aluminum for the marine and industrial markets. (Woman, estab 1958, empl 16, sales $5,300,000, cert: State, WBENC)

6934 ASM Aerospace Specifications Metals, Inc.
2501 NW 34th Place, B28
Pompano Beach, FL 33069
Contact: Douglas Bridges VP
Tel: 954-977-0666
Email: dbridges@aerospacemetals.com
Website: www.aerospacemetals.com

Dist raw materials: aircraft quality metals, sheet, plate, rod, wire, bar, tubing & extruded shapes. (Minority, Woman, estab 2001, empl 14, sales $7,000,000, cert: NMSDC)

6935 Manzi Metals, Inc.
15293 Flight Path Dr
Brooksville, FL 34604
Contact: Dorsey Peterson Small Business Special
Tel: 352-277-5852
Email: dpeterson@manzimetals.com
Website: www.manzimetals.com

Dist aerospace & commercial metals: aluminum, stainless, alloy steel, copper, brass, titanium, high temps in sheet, plate, bar, rod, hex, tube, etc. forgings, castings, ingots, billets.
(Woman/AA, estab 1993, empl 10, sales $3,600,000, cert: State, City, NMSDC, SDB)

Illinois

6936 Elgiloy Specialty Metals
1565 Fleetwood Dr
Elgin, IL 60123
Contact: Margaret Wilson Wire Sales Rep
Tel: 847-695-1900
Email: margaretw@elgiloy.com
Website: www.elgiloy.com

Strip, wire, rod & bar specialty alloys; various gauges/diameters and widths. Strip: rolling, slitting, annealing. Wire/bar/rod: drawing, annealing. In-house lab. (As-Pac, estab 1975, empl 75, sales , cert: NMSDC)

6937 HL Metals, LLC
910 Spruce St
Winnetka, IL 60093
Contact: Hui Lin Lim President
Tel: 312-590-3360
Email: hlim@hlmetalsllc.com
Website: www.hlmetalsllc.com
Dist P1020 aluminum sows/aluminum sheet ingot. (Minority, Woman, estab 2007, empl 1, sales $55,000,000, cert: CPUC, NWBOC)

6938 National Material Trading, LLC
1965 Pratt Blvd
Elk Grove Village, IL 60007
Contact: Jim Osborne Dir of Minority Dev
Tel: 847-806-4742
Email: josborne@nmlp.com
Website: www.nationalmaterialtrading.com
Dist carbon flat rolled steel. (As-Pac, estab 1964, empl 299, sales $370,000,000, cert: NMSDC)

6939 North States Steel Corp.
12255 Hwy 173
Hebron, IL 60034
Contact: Sandra Myers President
Tel: 815-648-1500
Email: smyers@northstatessteel.com
Website: www.northstatessteel.com
Hot rolled, cold rolled, aluminum stainless steel sheets. (Woman, estab 1971, empl 25, sales $14,000,000, cert: State, WBENC, SDB)

6940 S & S International, Inc.
457 St. Paul Blvd
Carol Stream, IL 60188
Contact: Rich Isom Sr Acct Exec
Tel: 708-805-5701
Email: icemanandfamily1@msn.com
Website: www.ssistainless.com
Dist stainless steel: sheet, plate, strip, coil, bars, structural shapes, square & rectangular tubing, pipe & fittings, aluminum sheet, strip & coil. (Minority, estab 1991, empl 105, sales $30,000,000, cert: NMSDC)

Indiana

6941 Circle City Rebar, LLC
4002 Industrial Blvd
Indianapolis, IN 46254
Contact: Heidi Russo Controller
Tel: - -
Email: hrusso@circlecityrebar.com
Website: www.circlecityrebar.com
Supplier and Fabricator of concrete reinforcing steel bars (rebar) in all sizes; plain and epoxy coated. (AA, estab 2005, empl 14, sales $7,541,942, cert: NMSDC)

6942 Eagle Steel Products, Inc.
5150 Loop Rd
Jeffersonville, IN 47130
Contact: Gary Shumate GM Sales
Tel: 812-282-7090
Email: gshumate@eaglesteelproducts.com
Website: www.eaglesteelproducts.com
Mfr strip steel; flat rolled products, blanking; covered barge & rail loading & unloading svcs, warehousing, etc. (Woman/As-Pac, estab 1982, empl 83, sales $32,000,000, cert: NMSDC)

Michigan

6943 Delaco Steel Corporation
8111 Tireman, Ste 1
Dearborn, MI 48126
Contact: Michael Roualet VP Quality
Tel: 313-491-1200
Email: mike.roualet@delacosteel.com
Website: www.delacosteel.com
Dist & process steel & aluminum. Blanking, warehousing, slitting, stampings, etc. (Woman/Hisp, estab 1974, empl 650, sales , cert: NMSDC, WBENC)

6944 Ferrous Processing & Trading
2920 Scotten
Detroit, MI 48210
Contact: Kristy Boismier President
Tel: 313-567-9710
Email: kristy.boismier@fptscrap.com
Website: www.fptscrap.com
Process, distribute & recycle scrap metals. (AA, estab 0, empl , sales , cert: NMSDC)

6945 H&H Metal Source
1909 Turner Ave NW
Grand Rapids, MI 49504
Contact: JR Hartman Operations Mgr
Tel: 616-364-0113
Email: jr@hhmetalsource.com
Website: www.hhmetalsource.com
Flat rolled steel in coil or blanks. (Woman, estab 1992, empl 30, sales $38,000,000, cert: WBENC)

6946 Instramed
3071 Commerce Dr. Ste. C
Ft. Gratiot, MI 48059
Contact: Cori Bonkoske Office Mgr
Tel: 800-451-5840
Email: allinfo@instramedinc.com
Website: www.instramedinc.com
Scrap metal & recyclable materials, ferrous & non-ferrous scrap metal. (Woman, estab 1987, empl , sales , cert: NWBOC)

6947 Marwol Metals, Ltd.
PO Box 252464
West Bloomfield, MI 48325
Contact: VP
Tel: 248-356-3444
Email: info@marwolmetals.com
Website: www.marwolmetals.com

Dist & buy ferrous & non-ferrous scrap metals. (Woman, estab 1981, empl 2, sales $950,000, cert: WBENC)

6948 National Material Co.
1505 N Dixie Dr, Ste 2
Monroe, MI 48162
Contact: John Allen Sales Rep
Tel: 734-384-9720
Email: jballen53@msn.com
Website: www.nmcmonroe.com

Steel coil, sheet, blank, painted steel, galvanized, aluminum,stainless HSLA, CS, DS. (As-Pac, estab 0, empl 0, sales $750,000,000, cert: NMSDC)

6949 Scion Steel
21555 Mullin Ave
Warren, MI 48089
Contact: Micky Tschirhart VP
Tel: 800-288-2127
Email: mtschirhart@scionsteel.com
Website: www.scionsteel.com

Full line steel service center - processed & fabricated to order. (Hisp, estab 1984, empl 51, sales , cert: NMSDC)

6950 Torch Steel Sales LLC
18501 Krause St
Riverview, MI 48193
Contact: Cristina Simone Owner
Tel: 734-783-2018
Email: csimone@torchsteelsales.com
Website: www.torchsteelsales.com

Steel service center: slitting, blanking, shearing, & slearing of non-ferrous flat rolled steel products, Hot Rolled, Cold Rolled, Hot Dipped Galvanized, Electro Galvanized, Galvanneal, & Aluminized. (Woman, estab 2013, empl 2, sales $700,600, cert: WBENC)

North Carolina

6951 Accro-Met, Inc.
3406 Westwood Industrial Dr
Monroe, NC 28110
Contact: Andrea Doolittle Sales
Tel: 704-283-2111
Email: alm@accromet.com
Website: www.accromet.com

Dist metal: stainless, nickel, aluminum, copper, brass, bronze, sheet, plate, bar, shapes. (Woman, estab 1988, empl 15, sales $6,000,000, cert: WBENC)

New Jersey

6952 L-E-M Plastics& Supply Inc.
255 Highland Cross
Rutherford, NJ 07070
Contact: Ellen Pietrowitz-Phillips President
Tel: 201-933-9150
Email: ellenp@l-e-mplastics.com
Website: www.l-e-mplastics.com

Fabriate & dist raw material plastic & rubber, Sheet, rod, tubing & film cut to size. Machining of all plastic, build to print. Steel rule die punching of thin plastic & rubber. (Woman, estab 1974, empl 12, sales $1,200,000, cert: WBENC)

Ohio

6953 CT Metal Source
9551 St Christine Ct
Sylvania, OH 43560
Contact: Chad Crooks President
Tel: 419-779-6172
Email: ccrooks@ctmetalsource.com
Website: www.ctmetalsource.com

Dist metal castings, rail car parts, vent registers & steel coils. (Hisp, estab 2005, empl 5, sales $7,000,000, cert: NMSDC)

6954 Ferrolux Metals Co. of Ohio, LLC
8055A Highland Pointe Pkwy
Macedonia, OH 44056
Contact: Mark Nester GM
Tel: 330-468-1008
Email: mnester@ferrolux.com
Website: www.ferrolux.com

Dist flat rolled processed steel, Cold rolled, Coated, Slitting & Inspection, Storage, Transportation. (Hisp, estab 2004, empl 22, sales , cert: NMSDC)

6955 Mid-West Materials, Inc.
3687 Shepard Rd
Perry, OH 44081
Contact: Scott Dennis Sales Rep
Tel: 440-259-5200
Email: scott.dennis@midwestmaterials.com
Website: www.midwestmaterials.com

Flat rolled steel service center, hot rolled, hot rolled, pickled & oiled & coated steel in commercial quality, high strength-low alloy & low through high carbon chemistries. (Woman, estab 1952, empl 50, sales $50,000,000, cert: State)

6956 Nu Tek Steel, LLC
6180 American Road
Toledo, OH 43612
Contact: Sarah Bates President
Tel: 419-724-0891
Email: sarah.bates@ntsteel.net
Website: www.ntsteel.net

Steel services: slitting, pickling, blanking, leveling, special bar quality, construction & medical. (Woman/AA, estab 2000, empl 10, sales $4,300,000, cert: State, WBENC)

Virginia

6957 United Scrap Metal
2900 Terminal Ave
Richmond, VA 23234
Contact: Owen Tomlinson Recycling Consultant
Tel: 434-430-1039
Email: otomlinson@unitedscrap.com
Website: www.unitedscrap.com

Metal recycling. (Woman, estab 1978, empl 170, sales , cert: WBENC)

> **METAL, WIRE PRODUCTS**
> See six other METAL categories. NAICS Code 33

California

6958 Top-Shelf Fixtures
       5263 Schaefer Ave
       Chino, CA 91710
       Contact: Michelle Burguan Controller
       Tel: 909-627-7423
       Email: sprochnow@topshelffixtures.com
       Website: www.topshelffixtures.com
Wire fabrication: sheet metal & structural steel for gondola shelving. (Hisp, estab 2002, empl 123, sales $8,500,000, cert: NMSDC)

Georgia

6959 Healthier & Happier, Inc.
       1853 Whitehall Forest Ct.
       Atlanta, GA 30316
       Contact: Jing Carter-Lu President
       Tel: 678-900-6617
       Email: jing.carter-lu@healthier-happier.com
       Website: www.healthier-happier.com
Dist wire rope, steel rope, carbon spring steel wire, bead wire, hose wire, plastic coated wire rope, PC stranded wire, bunched wire, galvanized stranded wire & zinc-plated steel wire. (Minority, Woman, estab 2003, empl 2, sales $120,000, cert: City)

Illinois

6960 Altak Inc.
       250 Covington Dr
       Bloomingdale, IL 60108
       Contact: Steve Janas Sales Mgr
       Tel: - - -308
       Email: rtakayama@arktechno.com
       Website: www.altakinc.com
Wire Harness manufacturing, Switch Assembly manufacturing, Spring manufacturing, Stampings - 30 to 800 ton, Wire Forms, IATF 16949 and ISO 9001 certified. (As-Pac, estab 1980, empl 400, sales $37,000,000, cert: NMSDC)

6961 Solar Spring & Wire Forms
       345 Criss Circle
       Elk Grove Village, IL 60007
       Contact: Aida Carrera Dir of Global Sales
       Tel: 847-437-7838
       Email: acarrera@solarspring.com
       Website: www.solarspring.com
Mfr springs, wire forms & stampings. (Hisp, estab 1979, empl 110, sales $11,100,000, cert: NMSDC)

Louisiana

6962 Vast Industries
       108 Venus St Ste 200
       Morgan City, LA 70380
       Contact: Yvette Archuleta-Tudury Owner
       Tel: 985-312-1592
       Email: yvette@vast-ind.com
       Website: www.Vast-Ind.com
Wire EDM & precision machined parts manufacturing, custom product design, reverse engineering & aluminum & steel fabrication. (Minority, Woman, estab 2007, empl 7, sales $600,000, cert: NMSDC, WBENC, 8(a))

Massachusetts

6963 Springfield Spring
       311 Shaker Rd
       Longmeadow, MA 01028
       Contact: Norman Rodriques President
       Tel: 413-525-6837
       Email: pat@springfieldspring.com
       Website: www.springfieldspring.com
Mfr precision engineered compression springs, torsion springs, extension springs, wire forms, fourslide-produced stampings, assemblies. (Hisp, estab 1942, empl 39, sales $7,200,000, cert: NMSDC)

Ohio

6964 Herbert E. Orr Comany, Inc.
       335 W Wall St
       Paudling, OH 45879
       Contact: Greg Johnson President
       Tel: 419-399-4866
       Email: gjohnson@heorr.com
       Website: www.heorr.com
Hot Forged Wheel Wrenches; Jack Tool Kits; Hood Support Rods; E-Coat Painting & powder coating; wire forms (pnuematic and CNC); assembly and kitting. (Woman, estab 1957, empl 51, sales $12,656,024, cert: WBENC)

6965 Mid West Fabricating
       313 N Johns St
       Amanda, OH 43102
       Contact: Dave Gallimore Business Devel
       Tel: 740-969-4411
       Email: dgallimore@midwestfab.com
       Website: www.midwestfab.com
Cold formed rod & wire products, fasteners, CNC wireforming, cold forming. (Woman, estab 1945, empl 200, sales $32,000,000, cert: WBENC)

Oklahoma

6966 Ebsco Spring Company, Inc.
4949 S 83rd Ave E
Tulsa, OK 74145
Contact: Todd Pfeifer Sales
Tel: 918-628-1680
Email: toddp@ebscospring.com
Website: www.ebscospring.com
Mfr & engineer custom, high quality compression, extension & torsion springs. (Woman, estab 1940, empl 75, sales $6,500,000, cert: WBENC)

Pennsylvania

6967 LEM Products, Inc.
147 Keystone Dr
Montgomeryville, PA 18936
Contact: Nicole Adamczyk Sales
Tel: 800-220-2400
Email: nadamczyk@lemproductsinc.com
Website: www.lemproductsinc.com
Mfr wire identification safety products: wire marker cards & books, voltage markers, transformer marking, hand writeable cable markers, laser coded bar codes, lockout tags, roll
dispensers, heat shrinkables, etc. (Woman, estab 1967, empl 38, sales $5,500,000, cert: CPUC, WBENC)

6968 R.A.W. Consulting, LLC
126 Mervis Dr
Beaver Falls, PA 15010
Contact: Robert Washington President
Tel: 724-384-1559
Email: rawconsultantsllc@gmail.com
Website: www.R-A-W-LLC.com
Distribution & warehousing of Stainless & alloy tubing, Cold rolled wire, Metal grating, Deformed wire. (AA, estab 2013, empl 3, sales $309,996, cert: State, NMSDC)

Puerto Rico

6969 Industrial Fittings & Valves
PO Box 2329
Toa Baja, PR 00951
Contact: Jose Merino President
Tel: 787-251-0840
Email: jmerino@infiva.com
Website: www.infiva.com
Dist industrial valves & fittings. (Hisp, estab 1985, empl 30, sales $6,093,000, cert: NMSDC)

Texas

6970 M3 Associates, Inc.
PO Box 224075
Dallas, TX 75222
Contact: Yvonne Newhouse President
Tel: 214-339-2117
Email: yvonne@m3associatesinc.com
Website: www.m3associatesinc.com
Distributor of wire, cable, tubing, sleeving, solder sleeves, heat shrink molded, shapes, boots (Woman/AA, estab 1988, empl 5, sales , cert: State)

Virginia

6971 Jo Kell, Inc.
1716 Lambert Ct
Chesapeake, VA 23320
Contact: Patricia Galiney Sales
Tel: 904-260-8420
Email: customerservice@jokell.com
Website: www.jokell.com
Dist electrical apparatus & equipment, wiring supplies & related equipment. (Woman, estab 1977, empl 50, sales $30,383,075, cert: WBENC)

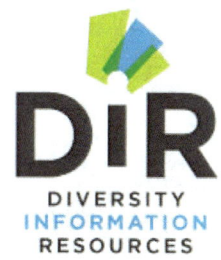

Driving Supplier Diversity Success since 1968.

1960's

1968 The "Buy Black Campaign" is founded by Peter and Rose Meyerhoff as a not-for-profit organization and prints its first directory of black-owned businesses in Minneapolis.

1968 The first Board of Directors is established and an office space is secured on Plymouth Ave. N. in Minneapolis.

1969 DIR publishes the "Buy Black" directory nationally.

1970's

1972 The "Buy Black" directory changes to "TRY US" and includes Black-, Hispanic-, Asian- and Native American-owned businesses.

1975 First edition of "Purchasing People in Major Corporations" directory is published.

1977 DIR's Board of Directors expands to include national corporations.

1980's

1986 DIR holds its first Supplier Diversity Seminars.

1990's

1992 First edition of the "Supplier Diversity Information Resources Guide" is published.

1995 DIR holds its first "Best Practices in Supplier Diversity Strategies and Initiatives"

1998 DIR creates an online, searchable database for its "Purchasing People in Major Corporations" directory.

2000's

2000 TRY US becomes Diversity Information Resources, Inc., to reflect the ongoing and ever-changing diverse-supplier categories.

2001 DIR hires SupplierGATEWAY as a technology partner.

2001 The "Buy Black" directory is now "National Minority and Women-Owned Business Directory" and includes certified women-owned businesses.

2006 DIR's verification and validation expertise expands to include Veteran-, Service-Disabled Veteran, and GLBT-owned businesses.

2010's

2011 DIR greatly expands online presence and redesigns identity to better reflect the open horizon for Supplier Diversity development.

2013 DIR celebrates its 45th Anniversary and looks forward to a thriving future!

2015 DIR responds to corporate and diverse-suppliers request for consolidated information and publishes a new directory and handbook: "The Business of Supplier Diversity".

> **OFFICE SUPPLIES**
> Manufacturers and distributors of office supplies and equipment: rubber stamps, writing implements, binders and portfolios, business forms, calculators, envelopes, tape, ink, office machines and furniture, paper and maintenance products, paper recycling, paper conversion, toner cartridges, printers, etc. NAICS Code 42

Alabama

6972   E.S. Robbins Corp.
        2802 E Avalon Ave
        Muscle Shoals, AL 35661
        Contact: Bonnie Donato Channel Marketing Mgr
        Tel: 256-248-2494
        Email: badonato@esrobbins.com
        Website: www.esrchairmats.com
Dist office products & furnishings. Mfr polymer products. (Woman, estab 1967, empl 187, sales , cert: WBENC)

Arkansas

6973   Burris Inc.
        113 S Arkansas Ave
        Russellville, AR 72801
        Contact: President
        Tel: 479-968-4888
        Email:
        Website: www.burrisinc.com
Office supplies & office furniture, panel systems, custom millwork, office layout & design. (Woman, estab 1953, empl 15, sales $3,374,600, cert: WBENC)

6974   Goddess Products, Inc.
        6142 Getty Dr
        North Little Rock, AR 72117
        Contact: Andrew Sigeti Acct Mgr
        Tel: 501-372-4002
        Email: asigeti@ussco.com
        Website: www.goddessproductsinc.com
Dist office products, office equipment, office furniture, computer peripherals, janitorial supplies & safety equipment. (Woman/AA, estab 2006, empl 5, sales $375,000, cert: WBENC)

California

6975   AM Copiers Inc.
        301 Wake Ave Ste 113
        El Centro, CA 92243
        Contact: Jethro Marrujo Admin
        Tel: 760-352-6007
        Email: amarrujo@amcopiers.com
        Website: www.amcopiers.com
Office equipment, maintenance service & repair. (Hisp, estab 1987, empl 6, sales $422,875, cert: State)

6976   American Textile Systems, Inc. DBA American Paper
        13151 Midway Place
        Cerritos, CA 90703
        Contact: Mike Khan VP Corporate Markets
        Tel: 562-229-0036
        Email: mike@amtexsys.com
        Website: www.amtexsys.com
Healthcare & hospitality related textile & paper products. (As-Ind, estab 1993, empl 25, sales $20,000,000, cert: State)

6977   Big Red Print Solutions, LLC
        2100 Sawtelle Blvd Ste 201
        Los Angeles, CA 90025
        Contact: Rudy Wrabel Dir
        Tel: 213-985-7201
        Email: rudy@bigredink.com
        Website: www.bigredink.com
Dist office equipment, supplies & technology products. (Minority, Woman, estab 2010, empl 7, sales $1,100,000, cert: NMSDC, CPUC)

6978   DD Office Products, Inc
        5025 Hampton St
        Los Angeles, CA 90058
        Contact: John Kim GSA Contract Admin
        Tel: 323-973-4569
        Email: johnk@libertypp.com
        Website: www.libertypp.com
Dist office paper. (As-Ind, estab 2001, empl 14, sales $36,617,778, cert: NMSDC)

6979   Garza Industries
        1870 N Glassell St
        Orange, CA 92865
        Contact: James Garza
        Tel: 714-769-2777
        Email: james@garzaindustries.com
        Website: www.garzaindustries.com
Dist office supplies: copy paper, laser toner cartridges, fax & copier supplies, furniture, direct mail svcs, commercial printing, corporate apparel, promotional items. (Minority, Woman, estab 1991, empl 35, sales , cert: CPUC)

6980   Kleenslate Concepts, LP
        14997 Camage Ave, Unit B
        Sonora, CA 94370
        Contact: Julia Rhodes CEO
        Tel: 209-588-0375
        Email: julia@kleenslate.com
        Website: www.kleenslate.com
Dist attachable white board markers erasers, white board products (Minority, Woman, estab 2001, empl 12, sales , cert: WBENC)

6981   Z Venture Capital Frontiers, Inc.
        1625 W Vernon Ave
        Los Angeles, CA 90062
        Contact: Karim Zaman President
        Tel: 323-596-4690
        Email: karim@thezamangroup.com
        Website: www.thezamangroup.com
Dist office supplies, inkjet, laser, toner cartridge, thermal fax ribbon. (AA, estab 1997, empl 2, sales $1,300,000, cert: State, City, CPUC)

Colorado

6982   Eon Office
        60 Tejon St
        Denver, CO 80223
        Contact: Jeniffer Beam VP Sales
        Tel: 720-570-5400
        Email: jbeam@eonoffice.com
        Website: www.eonoffice.com
Office Supplies, Furniture and Design, Printing, Breakroom, Janitorial (Woman, estab 2001, empl 86, sales , cert: WBENC)

6983 Faison Office Products, Inc
      12508 E Briarwood Ave Ste 1A
      Centennial, CO 80012
      Contact: Bonnie Key Exec Coordinator
      Tel: 303-340-3672
      Email: bkey@faisonopc.com
      Website: www.faisonopc.com
Dist office supplies & furniture; word processing & data processing supplies & furniture. (AA, estab 1981, empl 55, sales $45,000,000, cert: NMSDC)

District of Columbia

6984 The Hamilton Group
      4406 Gault Place NE
      Washington, DC 20019
      Contact: Kaari Hamilton President
      Tel: 202-689-4304
      Email: kayhhpbp@verizon.net
      Website: www.thehamiltongroupllc.net
Dist office supplies, advertisement & promotional products, office equipment & clothing wearables. (Woman/AA, estab 2007, empl 1, sales $731,000, cert: City, NMSDC, WBENC)

Florida

6985 Apex Office Products, Inc.
      5209 N Howard Ave
      Tampa, FL 33603
      Contact: Aurelio Llorente, Jr President
      Tel: 800-227-1563
      Email: allorentejr@apexop.com
      Website: www.apexofficeproducts.com
Dist office supplies & furniture, data supplies & furniture, paper products, rubber stamps. (Minority, Woman, estab 1981, empl 55, sales , cert: State, NMSDC)

6986 Konie Cups International, Inc.
      9001 NW 105th Way
      Medley, FL 33178
      Contact: Fiorella Roversi Sales Analyst
      Tel: 786-337-7967
      Email: fiorellaroversi@koniecups.com
      Website: www.koniecups.com
Mfr paper cone cups & funnels. (Hisp, estab 1991, empl 56, sales $9,223,670, cert: NMSDC)

6987 Mammoth Office Products, LLC
      7351 Southampton Terr
      Boynton Beach, FL 33436
      Contact: Lynn Pilato Owner
      Tel: 561-251-8662
      Email: Info@MammothOfficeProducts.com
      Website: www.mammothofficeproducts.com
Office products & supplies. (Woman, estab 2012, empl 1, sales $200,000, cert: WBENC)

6988 MarkMaster, Inc.
      11111 N 46th St
      Tampa, FL 33617
      Contact: Deborah Jordan Sales Rep
      Tel: 813-988-6000
      Email: sales@markmasterinc.com
      Website: www.markmasterinc.com
Mfr rubber stamps, engraved & screened signage & badges; industrial marking equip. (Hisp, estab 1933, empl 65, sales $8,700,993, cert: NMSDC)

Georgia

6989 ABC Laser USA, Inc.
      6000 G Unity Dr
      Norcross, GA 30092
      Contact: Kammie Lee Acct Mgr
      Tel: 770-448-5867
      Email: kmichell@abclaserusa.com
      Website: www.abclaserusa.com
Office Supplies, Ink, Toner, Furniture, Paper, Disc, Printers, Faxes, Pens, Pencils, Maintenance, Service, Janitorial Supplies, Cleaners, Toilet Paper, Paper Towels, Recycle Toner, Hewlett Packard, Lexmark, Dell, Canon. (Woman/As-Pac, estab 1996, empl 6, sales , cert: City)

6990 Interface Consulting Services, LLC
      4525 Flat Shoals Pkwy Ste 405
      Decatur, GA 30034
      Contact: Anthony Sylvester CEO
      Tel: 404-243-4954
      Email: anthony@interface-cs.com
      Website: www.interface-cs.com
Provide quality consulting advice & paper solutions. (AA, estab 2008, empl 3, sales $20,000,000, cert: NMSDC)

6991 Peachtree Supplies, Inc.
      233 Peachtree St NE, Ste 1265
      Atlanta, GA 30303
      Contact: Al Graham President
      Tel: 404-963-2410
      Email: agraham@peachtreesupplies.com
      Website: www.peachtreesupplies.com
Office supplies, furniture, ink & toner, paper, cleaning supplies, technology. (Woman/AA, estab 2009, empl 10, sales $1,350,000, cert: NMSDC)

6992 South Coast Paper LLC
      2300 Windy Ridge Pkwy, Ste 830
      Atlanta, GA 30339
      Contact: LaJoia Broughton Supplier Diversity
      Tel: 770-933-3411
      Email: supplierdiversity@southcoastpaper.com
      Website: www.southcoastpaper.com
Mfr & convert uncoated, coated, photographic & digital paper grades, cut, wrap, package, palletize & ship product. (AA, estab 2000, empl 49, sales $18,000,000, cert: NMSDC)

Iowa

6993 American Diversity Business Solutions
      9834 Hickory Dr
      Urbandale, IA 50322
      Contact: Joe Riggsbee Sr Acct Exec
      Tel: 515-276-1232
      Email: jriggsbee@americanmin.com
      Website: www.americandiv.com
Dist custom business forms, office supplies, & promotional items. (Woman, estab 1992, empl 15, sales $23,941,250, cert: WBENC)

6994 Bailey Office Equipment, Inc.
      123 E 2nd St
      Ottumwa, IA 52501
      Contact: Linda Gardner President
      Tel: 800-728-0407
      Email: linda@baileyoffice.com
      Website: www.baileyoffice.com
Dist office supplies, business machines, office furniture, cleaning supplies, safety equipment & breakroom essentials. (Woman, estab 1925, empl 10, sales $2,798,000, cert: WBENC)

OFFICE SUPPLIES

Illinois

6995 Chicago Green Office Company dba National Office Works, Inc.
7930 S Madison St
Burr Ridge, IL 60527
Contact: Joanna Davidson President
Tel: 312-455-9343
Email: joanna.davidson@nationalofficeworks.com
Website: www.nationalofficeworks.com
Dist office supplies. (Woman, estab , empl , sales $750,000, cert: State, WBENC)

6996 Gorilla Paper Inc.
1125 Lunt Ave
Elk Grove Village, IL 60007
Contact: Su Chang Lim President
Tel: 773-789-8113
Email: suchang@gorillapaper.com
Website: www.gorillapaper.com
POS Thermal Paper rolls, carbonless paper rolls, & related Ink Ribbons. (As-Pac, estab 2009, empl 3, sales $18,598,936, cert: NMSDC)

6997 Logsdon Office Supply
111 S Fairbank
Addison, IL 60101
Contact: Jack Dern VP
Tel: 847-593-8282
Email: jdern@logsdonofficesupply.com
Website: www.logsdonofficesupply.com
Dist office supplies. (AA, estab 1966, empl 25, sales $7,000,000, cert: City, NMSDC)

6998 Norwood Paper
7001 W 60th St
Chicago, IL 60674
Contact: Laura Martin Natl Accts Mgr
Tel: 773-788-1508
Email: laura@norwoodpaper.com
Website: www.norwoodpaper.com
Dist non-box related packaging chipboard, skid liners, dust covers, interleavers, divider sheets, pallet liners, pallet pads. (Woman, estab 1972, empl 1, sales $8,000,000, cert: WBENC)

6999 Pointe International
234 Oakwood Road
Lake Zurich, IL 60047
Contact: Sheila Liao President
Tel: 847-550-7001
Email: sheila.liao@pointecompany.com
Website: www.pointecompany.com
Mfr & dist wooden case pencils, mechanic pencils, desk stapler, office supplies & promotional items. (Minority, Woman, estab 1997, empl 12, sales $1,800,000, cert: NMSDC, WBENC)

7000 Taylor Made Business Solutions LLC
318 W. Adams St 16th Fl
Chicago, IL 60606
Contact: Evonne Taylor CEO
Tel: 312-803-5635
Email: etaylor@tmbsllc.com
Website: www.TMBSLLC.com
Dist general office supplies, office furniture, break room & janitorial supplies. (Woman/AA, estab 2011, empl 3, sales $2,762,000, cert: State, NMSDC)

7001 Working Hands, Inc.
39W254 Sheldon Ct
Geneva, IL 60134
Contact: Maureen Vedder President
Tel: 630-270-1097
Email: maureen@workinghandsinc.com
Website: www.workinghandsinc.com
GBC equipment & supplies, copier tabs, laminating rolls & pouches, clear presentation covers, black composition back covers prepunched, binding coils, 3 ring clear view binders, plain or mylar docucopy copier tabs. (Woman, estab 2003, empl 2, sales $250,000, cert: NWBOC)

Indiana

7002 Kramer & Leonard, Inc.
312 Roberts Rd
Chesterton, IN 46304
Contact: Mary Fox President
Tel: 219-926-1171
Email: mfox@kramerleonard.com
Website: www.kramerleonard.com
Office products, office supplies, computer supplies, office furniture, commercial interior design services, copier sales, copier service. (Woman, estab 0, empl , sales , cert: State, WBENC)

7003 OfficeWorks Services LLC
12000 Exit Five Pkwy
Fishers, IN 46037
Contact: Joyce Posson VP Admin
Tel: 317-577-3519
Email: jposson@officeworks.net
Website: www.officeworks.net
Dist office furniture & material handling equip. (Hisp, estab 1984, empl 60, sales $43,000,000, cert: State, NMSDC)

7004 Rite Quality Office Supplies, Inc.
710 N Washington St
Kokomo, IN 46901
Contact: Douglas Vaughn President
Tel: 765-459-4788
Email: riteq@netusa1.net
Website: www.ritequality.com
Dist office & janitorial supplies & office furniture. (AA, estab 1989, empl 10, sales , cert: State, NMSDC)

Kansas

7005 Supplies Express LLC
626 S 10th St
Manhattan, KS 66502
Contact: Enrique Garibay Managing Partner
Tel: 785-341-2123
Email: suppliesexpressllc@gmail.com
Website: www.suppliesexpress.us
Mfr the world's only water-resistant paper drinking straws, import water-resistant paper grocery bags. (Hisp, estab 2017, empl 4, sales , cert: State)

Massachusetts

7006 B2B Holdings Inc
168 Sutton St
Uxbridge, MA 01569
Contact: Randy Bloem Sr Accounts Mgr
Tel: 508-839-6144
Email: rbloem@mygotosource.com
Website: www.mygotosource.com
Dist office products, office furniture, promotional products/branded apparel & identification supplies. (Woman, estab 2018, empl 4, sales $150,000, cert: WBENC)

OFFICE SUPPLIES

Maryland

7007 Rudolph's Office & Computer Supply, Inc.
5020 Campbell Blvd Ste C
Baltimore, MD 21014
Contact: Henry Dow VP Sales
Tel: 410-931-4150
Email: henry@rudolphsupply.com
Website: www.rudolphsupply.com
Dist office, computer & janitorial supplies, custom stamps, office furniture, space planning. (Woman, estab 1980, empl 60, sales $1,600,000, cert: State)

7008 Sue-Ann s Office Supply, Inc.
4147 Hayward Ave
Baltimore, MD 21215
Contact: Beverly Williams CEO
Tel: 410-664-6226
Email: bwms@sueannsofficesupply.com
Website: www.sueannsofficesupply.com
Dist office products; office furniture; workstations; computer products. (Woman/AA, estab 1986, empl 5, sales $1,503,484, cert: State, City)

Michigan

7009 AVE Solutions
1155 Brewery Park Blvd., #350
Detroit, MI 48207
Contact: Carol Kirkland Exec VP
Tel: 313-347-8592
Email: carol@avesolutions.net
Website: www.avesolutions.net
Dist office supplies, office furniture, office equipment, audio visual equipment, computer equipment & supplies, printer equipment & supplies, paper, janitorial supplies, first aid supplies. (Woman/AA, estab 1990, empl 6, sales , cert: NMSDC, WBENC)

7010 Caracal Products & Services Inc.
6500 E Warren Ave
Detroit, MI 48207
Contact: Rebecca Miller Dir Sales/Marketing
Tel: 877-898-2847
Email: edis@caracalcorp.com
Website: www.caracalcorp.com
Paper (roll, cut, coated, uncoated), Print Management, office supplies, PPE (to include disposable and cloth 3-ply customizable masks, hand sanitizer, disinfectant spray, wipes, air filters), surgical apparel. (AA, estab 2004, empl 42, sales $81,000,000, cert: NMSDC)

7011 Hercules & Hercules, Inc.
19055 W Davison
Detroit, MI 48223
Contact: Belinda Jefferson President
Tel: 313-933-6669
Email: bjefferson@herculesandherculesinc.com
Website: www.herculesandherculesinc.com
Dist maintenance supplies & equip, office supplies & equip, office furniture. (AA, estab , empl , sales $7,000,000, cert: NMSDC)

7012 Integrated Supply Chain Solutions LLC
21056 Bridge St
Southfield, MI 48033
Contact: Cassaundra Bing President
Tel: 248-354-3445
Email: cbing@iscsupplysolutions.com
Website: www.iscsupplysolutions.com
Office products and print management services. (Woman/AA, estab 2008, empl 30, sales $11,000,000, cert: NMSDC, WBENC)

7013 KamarOE
1280 E Big Beaver Ste A
Troy, MI 48083
Contact: Devin Durrell
Tel: 866-996-8952
Email: devind@kamaroe.com
Website: www.kamaroe.com
Dist office supplies. (AA, estab 2005, empl 15, sales , cert: NMSDC)

7014 Nationwide Envelope Specialists, Inc.
1259 Doris Rd
Auburn Hills, MI 48326
Contact: David Dzuris Sales
Tel: 248-373-0111
Email: sales@nespn.com
Website: www.nespn.com
Printed & plain envelopes: special sizes & windows; commercial, booklet & open-end. (Hisp, estab 1990, empl 16, sales $5,200,000, cert: NMSDC)

7015 Paperworks, Inc.
15477 Woodrow Wilson St
Detroit, MI 48238
Contact: Katrece Business Unit Mgr
Tel: 800-243-1424
Email: customerservice@pwi-inc.com
Website: www.dchem.com
Dist paper & paper related products & office supplies. (AA, estab 1981, empl 23, sales $26,000,000, cert: NMSDC)

7016 Remco Storage Systems, Inc.
2328 Livernois Road Ste 1070
Troy, MI 48083
Contact: Donna Tamburo-Wilson President
Tel: 248-362-0500
Email: donna@remcoequipment.com
Website: www.remcoequipment.com
Storage & retrieval systems: vertical lifts & carousels, electric lateral filing systems, movable shelving, rotary files, cabinets, records mgmt systems, color coded labels, custom filing systems, folders & indexes. (Woman, estab 1976, empl 7, sales $2,000,000, cert: WBENC)

7017 RM International Resource Group. Ltd.
22759 Heslip Dr
Novi, MI 48375
Contact: Reuben Levy President
Tel: 877-637-6468
Email: rlevy@rmintrg.com
Website: www.rmintrg.com
Dist office supplies & furniture. (AA, estab 1998, empl 1, sales $800,000, cert: NMSDC)

7018 Rubber Stamps Unlimited, Inc.
334 S Harvey St
Plymouth, MI 48170
Contact: Maryellen Lewandowski President
Tel: 888-451-7300
Email: mlew@thestampmaker.com
Website: www.thestampmaker.com
Custom rubber stamps, self inking stamps, date stamps, seals, embossers & signs in one day. (Woman, estab 1993, empl 12, sales $3,306,000, cert: WBENC)

7019 Swift Computer Supply, Inc.
      37676 Enterprise Court
      Farmington Hills, MI 48331
      Contact: Henry Swift President
      Tel: 248-489-9250
      Email: meberle@smartofficedeals.com
      Website: www.shopSOSnow.com
Office supplies, furniture, printing, promotional items, janitorial & break room supplies. (AA, estab 1985, empl 1, sales $467,200, cert: NMSDC)

7020 Workplace Integrators
      30700 Telegraph, Ste 4800
      Bingham Farms, MI 48025
      Contact: Joe Eatman President
      Tel: 248-430-2345
      Email: jeatman@wp-int.com
      Website: www.wp-int.com
Dist office supplies: paper, writing instruments, folders, technology products, fastners, etc. (AA, estab 1938, empl 1, sales $50,000,000, cert: NMSDC)

Minnesota

7021 Crown Marking, Inc.
      4270 Dahlberg Dr
      Golden Valley, MN 55422
      Contact: Gregg Prest Treasurer
      Tel: 763-543-8243
      Email: gprest@crownmarking.com
      Website: www.crownmarking.com
Mfr & dist rubber & photopolymer stamps, daters, embossers & related stamping supplies. (Woman, estab 1928, empl 9, sales $5,000,000, cert: WBENC)

7022 ecoThynk
      607 Dayton Ave
      Saint Paul, MN 55012
      Contact: Gale Ward President
      Tel: 612-605-4885
      Email: gale@ecoenvelopes.com
      Website: www.ecothynk.com
Mfr reusable envelopes. (Woman, estab 2002, empl 5, sales $210,000, cert: WBENC)

7023 Innovative Office Solutions, LLC
      151 E Cliff Rd
      Burnsville, MN 55337
      Contact: Kathy Hovde Sr Acct Exec, Sales & Diversity
      Tel: 952-808-9900
      Email: khovde@innovativeos.com
      Website: www.innovativeos.com
Dist office, school, janitorial supplies & furniture. (Woman, estab 2001, empl 213, sales $100,000,000, cert: WBENC)

Missouri

7024 Missouri Office Systems & Supplies, Inc.
      941 W 141st Terrace Ste B
      Kansas City, MO 64145
      Contact: Virgie Dillard President
      Tel: 816-761-5152
      Email: vld@8asupplier.com
      Website: www.8asupplier.com
Dist office supplies, furniture, ethernet, media, printers, software, hardware, ribbons, fax, scanners, computers, typewriters, routers, hubs, toners, servers. (Woman/AA, estab 1993, empl 9, sales $8,775,113, cert: State, City, NMSDC)

7025 Offices Unlimited Inc.
      2127 William St
      Cape Girardeau, MO 63703
      Contact: Celeste "Sally" LeGrand Owner
      Tel: 573-332-0202
      Email: sally@officesunlimited.com
      Website: www.officesunlimited.com
Office supplies, stationary, office furniture, office partitions, panel systems, office equipment, copiers, faxes, toners, medical supplies, break room furniture, break room foods, janitorial products. (Woman, estab 2001, empl 6, sales $2,000,000, cert: State)

North Carolina

7026 American Product Distributors, Inc.
      8350 Arrowridge Blvd
      Charlotte, NC 28273
      Contact: Ray Kennedy CEO
      Tel: 704-522-9411
      Email: registration@americanproduct.com
      Website: www.americanproduct.com
Dist office imaging supplies, remanufactured toner cartridges, cut sheet paper, wide format paper, rolled paper & ribbons, business & manufacturing labels. (AA, estab 1992, empl 50, sales $40,000,000, cert: NMSDC)

7027 Kennedy Office Supply Inc.
      4211-A Atlantic Ave
      Raleigh, NC 27604
      Contact: Linda McCotter Accounting Mgr
      Tel: 919-878-5400
      Email: lmccotter@kennedyoffice.com
      Website: www.kennedyofficesupply.com
Dist office supplies, breakroom products, technology & janitorial supplies. (Woman, estab 1960, empl 50, sales $13,200,000, cert: State)

7028 New Generation Product, Inc.
      5736 North Tryon St Ste 223B
      Charlotte, NC 28213
      Contact: Donald Allen Black President
      Tel: 704-596-5327
      Email: don.black@newgenproduct.com
      Website: www.NewGenProduct.com
Provide biomass papers made from recycled agricultural fibers. (AA, estab 2010, empl 1, sales , cert: State, CPUC)

New Hampshire

7029 Gorham Paper and Tissue LLC
      72 Cascade Flats
      Gorham, NH 03581
      Contact: Greg Kane VP Sales & Mktg
      Tel: 603-342-3300
      Email: greg.kane@gorhampt.com
      Website: www.gorhampt.com
Mfr recycled & virgin fiber towel & tissue products. (Woman, estab 2012, empl 130, sales $50,000,000, cert: WBENC)

New Jersey

7030 Corporate Diversity Solutions
      615 Franklin Turnpike Ste 5
      Ridgewood, NJ 07450
      Contact: Stacey Scarpa President
      Tel: 201-444-1506
      Email: stscarpa@corporatediversitysolutions.com
      Website: www.corporatediversitysolutions.com
Dist stationery & office supplies. (Woman, estab 2009, empl 7, sales $4,300,000, cert: WBENC)

7031 CSS Building Services Inc.
12 Stults Rd, Ste 132
Dayton, NJ 08810
Contact: Vic Tartara Sales
Tel: 732-246-0554
Email: lcoury@cssbuildingservices.com
Website: www.cssofficesupply.com
Dist office supplies. (Hisp, estab 2004, empl 25, sales , cert: WBENC)

7032 Lotus Connect LLC
221 River St Ste 9
Hoboken, NJ 07030
Contact: Andre Cepeda CEO
Tel: 201-606-1444
Email: acepeda@lotusconnect.org
Website: www.lotusconnect.org
Dist Medical supplies; Office supplies; Janitorial supplies. (Hisp, estab 2018, empl 5, sales $1,984,230, cert: State, City, NMSDC)

7033 Officemate International Corporation
90 Newfield Ave
Edison, NJ 08837
Contact: Sharon Kiefer Natl Sales Mgr
Tel: 732-225-7422
Email: skiefer@officemate.com
Website: www.officemate.com
Mfr & dist office supply products. (As-Pac, estab 1978, empl 100, sales , cert: NMSDC)

7034 Thayer Distribution, Inc.
333 Swedesboro Ave
Gibbstown, NJ 08027
Contact: Nicholas diRenzo Dir sales/mktg
Tel: 856-687-0000
Email: nick@thayerdist.com
Website: www.thayerdist.com
Confectionery wholesalers, break room products, office coffee, candy, snacks, chips, creamer, sugar, k-cups. (Hisp, estab 1987, empl 100, sales , cert: State, City, NMSDC)

7035 The Fisher Group
PO Box 1653
Dover, NJ 07802
Contact: Irving Fisher Managing Partner
Tel: 973-442-3000
Email: irving@fisherpaper.net
Website: www.fisherpaper.net
Dist paper. (AA, estab 2000, empl 4, sales $3,556,001, cert: NMSDC)

New Mexico

7036 Desert Paper & Envelope Company, Inc.
2700 Girard Blvd NE
Albuquerque, NM 87107
Contact: VP Finance
Tel: 800-228-2298
Email: info@desertpaper.com
Website: www.desertpaper.com
Mfr & print envelopes. (Minority, Woman, estab 1973, empl 40, sales $5,435,600, cert: NMSDC, WBENC)

7037 Midway Office Supply Inc.
5900 Midway Park Blvd NE
Albuquerque, NM 87109
Contact: Mike Sei President
Tel: 505-345-3414
Email: mikesei@midwayos.com
Website: www.midwayos.com
Dist office supplies. (As-Pac, estab 1980, empl 10, sales $9,000,000, cert: NMSDC)

7038 Roses Southwest Paper, Inc.
1701 2nd St SW
Albuquerque, NM 87102
Contact: James Hinkle NSM
Tel: 734-968-8103
Email: jmhinkle@aol.com
Website: www.rosessouthwest.com
Mfr sanitary paper products: hard roll towels, multi fold towels, jumbo roll toilet tissue, standard roll toilet tissue, facial tissue, seat covers, dispenser napkins, dinner napkins, cocktail napkins, kitchen roll towels. (Hisp, estab 1984, empl 215, sales $58,980,000, cert: NMSDC)

7039 Stride Inc.
1021 Carlisle Blvd SE
Albuquerque, NM 87106
Contact: Kerry Bertram President
Tel: 505-232-3201
Email: info@stridewrite.com
Website: www.stridewrite.com
Writing instruments & binders, hinged lid cigar boxes. (Woman, estab , empl , sales $7,000,000, cert: WBENC)

7040 Stride, Inc.
1021 Carlisle Blvd SE
Albuquerque, NM 87106
Contact: Kerry Bertram President
Tel: 505-232-3201
Email: kerry@strideinc.com
Website: www.strideinc.com
Mfr & dist writing instruments, binders & office products: pens & markers for wood finishes, parts marking, black light, crafts, photographic, cosmetics, cleaning devices & voter marking pens. (Woman, estab 1988, empl 11, sales $2,778,019, cert: State, WBENC)

New York

7041 Asian & Hispanic Trading & Consulting Inc.
37 West 39th St Ste 503
New York, NY 10018
Contact: Suzanne Cohon Business Devel
Tel: 212-252-8988
Email: suzanne@asc-to.com
Website: www.aandhtc.com
Dist office supplies, furniture, computer equipment, and promotional products. (Minority, Woman, estab 2016, empl 3, sales $295,000, cert: State, City)

7042 Ebony Office Products, Inc.
10-17 44th Ave
Long Island City, NY 11101
Contact: Michael Ukhueduan Dir Business Dev
Tel: 718-706-8200
Email: info@ebonyproducts.com
Website: www.ebonyofficeusa.com
Dist office supplies, office furniture, computer supplies, printing services. (AA, estab 1982, empl 10, sales $1,500,000, cert: State, City)

7043 FM Office Express dba FM Resources
One Woodbury Blvd
Rochester, NY 14604
Contact: Fabricio Morales President
Tel: 585-238-2895
Email: fmorales@fmop.com
Website: www.fmop.com
Dist office supplies, office furniture, janitorial supplies & computer supplies. (Hisp, estab 1995, empl 92, sales $50,000,000, cert: State)

7044 Impact Enterprises, Inc.
11 Horse Hill Lane
Warwick, NY 10990
Contact: Ralph Salisbury Sr VP
Tel: 845-988-1900
Email: rsalisbury@impactenterprises.com
Website: www.impactenterprises.com
Mfr custom binder covers, award covers, presentation folders, portfolio covers, sales kits & other custom covers. (Woman, estab 1987, empl 8, sales $2,500,000, cert: WBENC)

7045 Mrs. Paper
31 West 34th St, Ste 8044
New York, NY 10001
Contact: Marion Hindenburg President
Tel: 212-532-7777
Email: marion@mrspaper.com
Website: www.mrspaper.com
Dist copy & computer paper, janitorial/sanitary supplies & advertising specialties. (Woman, estab 1982, empl 3, sales $4,082,000, cert: City, WBENC)

7046 Proftech LLC
200 Clearbrook Rd
Elmsford, NY 10523
Contact: Jose Montiel President
Tel: 800-937-8354
Email: jmontiel@proftech.com
Website: www.proftech.com
Dist office supplies; computer supplies; packaging supplies; drafting & art supplies; furniture; janitorial supplies; remanufactured toner cartridges. (Hisp, estab 1998, empl 55, sales , cert: State, City, NMSDC)

7047 Royal Automation Supplies
1982 Crotona Pkwy
Bronx, NY 10460
Contact: David Changar VP
Tel: 718-842-5900
Email: royalautomation@aol.com
Website: www.royalautomation.com
Dist paper & office supplies. (As-Ind, estab 1954, empl 5, sales $1,200,000, cert: City, NMSDC)

7048 S & B Computer & Office Products Inc.
17 Wood Road Ste 700
Round Lake, NY 12151
Contact: Brittany Woods-Holmes President
Tel: 518-877-9500
Email: info@royalflashphotobooths.com
Website: www.sbcomputers-office.com
Dist office & computer supplies, office furniture & promotional products. (Minority, Woman, estab 1989, empl 9, sales $5,695,685, cert: State)

7049 Seating, Inc.
PO Box 898
Nunda, NY 14517
Contact: Emily Hart Dir Business Dev
Tel: 585-468-2875
Email: emily@seatinginc.com
Website: www.seatinginc.com
Mfr quality ergonomic office seating for business and government buyers in the form of task, swivel, executive, multi-purpose, stacking, and nesting chairs as well as stools. (Woman, estab 1987, empl 25, sales $4,315,077, cert: City, WBENC)

Ohio

7050 BoLinds Solutions Services, Inc.
850 Euclid Ave, Ste 1314
Cleveland, OH 44114
Contact: Sales
Tel: 216-479-0290
Email: service@bolinds.com
Website: www.bolinds.com
Dist office products, office furniture, remanufactured & compatible toner cartridges, fax machines & office equipment repair. (Woman/AA, estab 1990, empl 6, sales , cert: State, NMSDC)

7051 Office Partners, LLC
826 E Edgerton
Bryan, OH 43506
Contact: Cookie Lehman President
Tel: 419-636-7260
Email: cookie1@bright.net
Website: www.officepartnersonline.com
Office products. (Hisp, estab 2002, empl 3, sales , cert: NMSDC)

7052 Quality Ribbons and Supplies Co.
2769 Commercial Rd
Cleveland, OH 44113
Contact: Jacqueline Litz Owner
Tel: 216-579-6200
Email: jackielitz@qr-s.com
Website: www.qr-s.com
Dist office, computer & janitorial supplies & small equip. (Woman, estab 1982, empl 5, sales , cert: City)

7053 SeaGate Office Products, Inc.
1044 Hamilton Dr
Holland, OH 43528
Contact: Connie Leonardi President
Tel: 419-861-6161
Email: cleonardi@seagateop.com
Website: www.seagteop.com
Dist office supplies: copy & writing paper, pens, post it notes, toner cartridges, ink, stamps, computer supplies, promotional items, mugs, golf balls and, pens, uniforms, desk accessories, binder clips, pencils, staples, tape & dispensers. (Woman, estab 1985, empl 14, sales $5,300,000, cert: WBENC)

7054 The Millcraft Paper Company
6800 Grant Ave
Cleveland, OH 44105
Contact: Lisa Rogala Corporate Business Dev
Tel: 216-441-5500
Email: rogalal@millcraft.com
Website: www.millcraft.com
Paper converting, mfr envelopes, printing, inventory management. (Woman, estab 1920, empl 225, sales $139,988,865, cert: WBENC)

7055 World Pac Paper, LLC
1821 Summit Rd, Ste 317
Cincinnati, OH 45237
Contact: Edgar Smith CEO
Tel: 513-779-9595
Email: elsmith@worldpacpaperllc.com
Website: www.worldpacpaperllc.com
Dist printing & packaging papers. (AA, estab 2004, empl 22, sales $3,563,898, cert: NMSDC)

OFFICE SUPPLIES

Pennsylvania

7056 Alpha Office Supplies, Inc.
 4950 Parkside Ave Ste 500
 Philadelphia, PA 19131
 Contact: Chester Riddick CEO
 Tel: 215-226-2690
 Email: chet.riddick@alphaos.com
 Website: www.alphaos.com
Dist office furniture & supplies, paper, computers & accessories; desktop delivery, installation, space planning & project mgmt. (AA, estab 1985, empl 29, sales $26,000,000, cert: NMSDC)

7057 Ardian Group, Inc.
 7 Creek Pkwy, Ste 710
 Boothwyn, PA 19342
 Contact: Jeffrey Shelton COO
 Tel: 610-459-4975
 Email: jlshelton@ardiangroup.com
 Website: www.ardiangroup.com
Dist photo & nonphoto badges: clips, laminates, lanyards, software, laminators, etc. (Woman/As-Pac, estab 1999, empl 20, sales $3,177,000, cert: WBENC)

7058 Legacy Information Systems, LLC
 601 Upland Ave Ste218
 Brookhaven, PA 19015
 Contact: Gaylord Neal Chairman
 Tel: 800-547-5820
 Email: info@tplegacy.com
 Website: www.tplegacy.com
Office & Business Products. (AA, estab 2005, empl 11, sales , cert: City, NMSDC)

7059 Max International
 2360 Dairy Rd
 Lancaster, PA 17603
 Contact: Tiffanie Shaud Mktg Dir
 Tel: 800-233-0222
 Email: tjs@maxintl.com
 Website: www.maxintl.com
Roll paper converting: standard & special sizes, slittering, 4-color printing. (Woman, estab 1992, empl 22, sales $7,500,000, cert: WBENC)

7060 SUPRA Office Solutions, Inc.
 5070 PArkside Ave Ste 3200
 Philadlephia, PA 19131
 Contact: COO
 Tel: 855-777-8772
 Email: ken.carter@supraos.com
 Website: www.supraos.com
Office supplies, office furniture, janitorial & break-room, paper & paper products, technology items, medical & chemical supplies. (AA, estab 2011, empl 16, sales $19,000,000, cert: State, NMSDC)

7061 Telrose Corporation
 3801 Ridge Ave
 Philadelphia, PA 19132
 Contact: CEO
 Tel: 215-229-0500
 Email: support@telrosecorp.com
 Website: www.telrosecorp.com
Dist office supplies, equipment & furniture. (AA, estab 1995, empl 19, sales $8,000,000, cert: City, NMSDC)

South Carolina

7062 Ebony Holding
 1204 Lexington Ave Unit 1, A-2
 Irmo, SC 29063
 Contact: Pam Heirs Acct Exec
 Tel: 803-798-7777
 Email: pamh@jmgrace.com
 Website: www.jmgrace.com
Office Supplies, Office Furniture, Business Machines, Printing, Promotional Items, Embroidered Apparel, Janitorial Supplies, Breakroom Items, Safety Equipment. (Woman/AA, estab 2013, empl 7, sales $590,692, cert: State)

Tennessee

7063 DevMar Products, LLC
 1865 Air Lane Dr
 Nashville, TN 37210
 Contact: Sharon W. Reynolds CEO
 Tel: 615-232-7040
 Email: sharaon@devmarproducts.com
 Website: www.devmarproducts.com
Janitorial supplies; chemicals; personal paper; MRO; biohazard spill kits/risk management; safety; Clean Up; Safety Sweep; green; sustainable; Ada[t ASB; Oil & Gas; Automotive; Healthcare; Furniture; Chemicals; Forest Products & Paper; Wholesale Dist. (Woman/AA, estab 2007, empl 5, sales $1,000,000, cert: NMSDC, WBENC)

7064 Guy Brown, LLC
 7111 Commerce Way
 Brentwood, TN 37027
 Contact: Lauren Dooros Sales & Marketing Mgr
 Tel: 615-777-1500
 Email: lauren.dooros@guybrown.com
 Website: www.guybrown.com
Mfr recycled laser toner cartridges & office products. (Minority, Woman, estab 1997, empl 45, sales $204,877,006, cert: NMSDC, WBENC)

Texas

7065 Dallas Paper & Packaging
 880 Gerault Rd
 Flower Mound, TX 75028
 Contact: Nemosthenes Baker Owner
 Tel: 817-422-3089
 Email: nemo@dallaspaperpackaging.com
 Website: www.dallaspaperpackaging.com
Dist toner & ink cartridges, trash bags, food gloves, white T-shirts, grey sweat pants, shirts, drinking water carts, janitorial supplies, ribbons, first aid kits, popcorn, hazard & medical supplies. (AA, estab 1984, empl 2, sales $745,963, cert: State, NMSDC)

7066 Derrah Morrison Enterprises, LLC
 1120 Toro Grande Blvd Bldg 2, Ste 208
 Cedar Park, TX 78613
 Contact: Chelsea Derrah CEO
 Tel: 512-879-3088
 Email: cderrah@dme-vet.com
 Website: www.dme-vet.com
resell recycled copy paper, office products, industrial supplies, and medical-surgical products and equipment. (Woman, estab 2009, empl 2, sales $47,611,687, cert: WBENC)

OFFICE SUPPLIES

7067 EIS Office Solutions, Inc.
      5803 Sovereign Dr, Ste 214
      Houston, TX 77036
      Contact: Judy Lanum Acct Exec
      Tel: 713-484-7300
      Email: judy.lanum@secor.cc
      Website: www.eisoffice.net
Provide OEM & Compatible printer ink & toner cartridges, office supplies. (As-Pac, estab 2004, empl 11, sales $1,700,000, cert: State)

7068 General Office Plus
      1020 W 8th Ave
      Amarillo, TX 79101
      Contact: Loretta Redmon President
      Tel: 806-373-2877
      Email: lredmon@generalofficeplus.com
      Website: www.general-officesupply.com
Dist office supplies, machines, furniture. (Woman, estab 1948, empl 15, sales $1,803,887, cert: State)

7069 Houdal Corporation dba 2M Business Products
      2630 Nova Dr
      Dallas, TX 75229
      Contact: Shabbir Mamdani President
      Tel: 972-484-0000
      Email: cs@2mbp.com
      Website: www.2mofficesupplies.com
Dist office supplies, computer supplies, office furniture, new & remanufactured toner cartridges. rubber stamps, printing. (As-Ind, estab 1980, empl 3, sales $980,770, cert: NMSDC)

7070 J R Rodriguez International Corporation
      4541 Leston St
      Dallas, TX 75247
      Contact: Jim Lohr Natl Acct Mgr
      Tel: 214-905-5086
      Email: jim@interconpaper.com
      Website: www.interconpaper.com
Printing paper in rolls & sheets: offset, gloss & matte/dull, board (C1S and C2S), Hi-Brite, groundwood coated, newsprint, digital sizes, cut size xerographic, slitting & rewinding. (Hisp, estab 1998, empl 61, sales $25,100,000, cert: NMSDC)

7071 Lee Office Solutions
      202 Travis ST, Ste 205
      Houston, TX 77002
      Contact: Cathleen Nguyen Exec Asst
      Tel: 713-227-1010
      Email: cathleen@leeofficesolutions.com
      Website: www.leeofficesolutions.com
Dist office supplies & products, electronics, furniture, paper, facilities mgmt & system design. (As-Pac, estab 1970, empl 5, sales $308,647, cert: NMSDC)

7072 Limitless Office Products
      1778 N Plano Rd Ste 114
      Richardson, TX 75081
      Contact: Mita Guha President
      Tel: 214-764-4092
      Email: mg@limitlessofficeproducts.com
      Website: www.LimitlessOfficeProducts.com
Dist office products: printer, copier, fax, ink & laser cartridges, digital cameras, digital storage devices, paper, pens, pencils, file folders etc. (Woman/As-Ind, estab 2005, empl 2, sales , cert: State, NMSDC)

7073 Longhorn Office Products, Inc.
      2210 Denton Dr. Ste. 109
      Austin, TX 78758
      Contact: Marcia Winkler CEO
      Tel: 512-672-4567
      Email: mswinkler@longhornop.com
      Website: www.longhornop.com
Dist office products & furniture. (Woman, estab 1999, empl 13, sales $2,386,005, cert: State, City, WBENC)

7074 P.D. Morrison Enterprises, Inc.
      1120 Toro Grande Blvd Bldg 2, Ste 208
      Cedar Park, TX 78613
      Contact: P.D. Morrison CEO
      Tel: 512-879-3070
      Email: pd@pdme.com
      Website: www.pdme.com
Dist office & computer supplies, office furniture. (AA, estab 1994, empl 10, sales , cert: NMSDC)

7075 Pearle, Inc.
      3660 Richmond Ave Ste 370
      Houston, TX 77046
      Contact: Erskine Black Jr. President
      Tel: 832-304-9571
      Email: eblack@pearle-inc.com
      Website: www.pearle-inc.com
Dist disposable paper goods. (AA, estab 2013, empl 1, sales , cert: State, City, NMSDC)

7076 R.W. Gonzalez Office Products, Inc.
      600 Congress Ave 14th Fl
      Austin, TX 78701
      Contact: Pamela Gonzalez VP
      Tel: 512-717-6623
      Email: diversity@gonzalezop.com
      Website: www.MBEpartners.com
Dist office products. (Hisp, estab 2002, empl 7, sales , cert: State, NMSDC)

7077 Reliant Business Products, Inc
      10641 Haddington Dr, Ste 100
      Houston, TX 77043
      Contact: Steven Woodall VP Sales & IT
      Tel: 713-980-7140
      Email: stevenw@rbp.com
      Website: www.rbp.com
Office Products, Office Supplies, Industrial Supplies, HS&E, MRO, Office Furniture, Coffee Service, Break Room Supplies, Printing. (Nat Ame, estab 1984, empl 17, sales $7,000,000, cert: State, NMSDC)

7078 Summus Industries, Inc.
      245 Commerce Green Blvd Ste 155
      Sugar Land, TX 77478
      Contact: Rodney Craig CEO
      Tel: 281-640-1765
      Email: rcraig@summusindustries.com
      Website: www.summusindustries.com
Dist office supplies. (AA, estab 1997, empl 21, sales $21,000,000, cert: State, City, NMSDC)

7079 Tejas Office Products, Inc.
      1225 W 20th St
      Houston, TX 77008
      Contact: Stephen M. Fraga President
      Tel: 713-864-6004
      Email: stephenf@tejasoffice.com
      Website: www.tejasoffice.com
Dist office products. (Hisp, estab 1962, empl 50, sales , cert: NMSDC)

OFFICE SUPPLIES

7080 Today's Business Solutions
1920 N Memorial Way
Houston, TX 77007
Contact: Priscilla Luna President
Tel: 713-861-8508
Email: priscilla@tbsconnection.com
Website: www.tbsknows.com
Dist office supplies. (Hisp, estab 2003, empl 25, sales $19,000,000, cert: State, NMSDC)

Virginia

7081 Access Office Products
6 W Cary St
Richmond, VA 23220
Contact: AJ Scott President
Tel: 804-767-7211
Email: aj@accessofficeproducts.com
Website: www.AccessOfficeProducts.com
Dist office supplies, technology & furniture. (AA, estab 2009, empl 2, sales $119,231, cert: State, NMSDC)

7082 Ball Office Products, LLC
2218 Tomlyn St
Richmond, VA 23230
Contact: Melissa Ball Managing Member
Tel: 804-204-1774
Email: melissa@ballop.com
Website: www.ballop.com
Dist business furniture & office supplies. (Woman, estab 2000, empl 17, sales $7,050,591, cert: State, WBENC)

7083 Corporate Office Solutions, LLC
4094 Majestic Ln, Ste 33
Fairfax, VA 22033
Contact: Katrina Funkhouser President
Tel: 703-352-2029
Email: kf@cosdirect.com
Website: www.cosdirect.com
Dist computer products, office equipment & supplies, printer service, computer repair, networking & office furniture. (Woman/As-Ind, estab 1996, empl 8, sales $2,386,109, cert: State)

7084 Snap Office Supplies, LLC
9710 Farrar Court Ste M
Richmond, VA 23236
Contact: Andy Todd VP Sales
Tel: 804-794-9387
Email: andy@snapsupplies.com
Website: www.snapsupplies.com
Dist Office & Point-of-Sale supplies. (Woman, estab 1980, empl 7, sales $1,500,000, cert: State)

7085 TSRC, Inc.
PO Box 1810
Ashland, VA 23005
Contact: David Johnson Acct Mgr
Tel: 804-412-1200
Email: djohnson@thesupplyroom.com
Website: www.thesupplyroom.com
Dist office supplies & furniture. (Woman, estab 1986, empl 187, sales $45,000,000, cert: State)

Washington

7086 American Paper Converting Inc.
1845 Howard Way
Woodland, WA 98674
Contact: Lydia Work President
Tel: 360-225-0488
Email: Storneby@americanpaperco.com
Website: www.americanpaperco.com
Mfr paper towel, bathroom tissue & napkins. (Minority, Woman, estab 1997, empl 60, sales $32,185,106, cert: NMSDC)

PACKAGING & PACKING SERVICES & SUPPLIES

Contract packaging and crating, shrink or blister packaging and bagging. Manufacturers and distributors of foam packaging, rope and twine, bottles, shrink wrap, corrugated cardboard boxes or bags of various materials such as paper, plastic, etc. NAICS Code 32

Alabama

7087 ARD Logistics, LLC
10098 Brose Dr
Vance, AL 35490
Contact: Courtney Waters Sales & Marketing Rep
Tel: 205-393-5207
Email: cwaters@ardlogistics.com
Website: www.ardlogistics.com
Distribution operations: sequencing, sub-assembly, warehousing, inventory mgmt, shipping & receiving materials handling maintenance, packaging & repackaging, transportation mgmt, transportation svcs. (AA, estab 1998, empl 900, sales $68,717,549, cert: NMSDC)

7088 Containers Plus, Inc.
3068 Alabama Hwy 53
Huntsville, AL 35806
Contact: Ajesh Khanijow Business Devel
Tel: 256-746-8002
Email: akhanijow@containersplusUSA.com
Website: www.containersplusUSA.com
Wooden crates, pallets, cardboard boxes, heat shrink, milspec packaging, packaging, RFID, UID, Mil-std-129, mil-std-2073, warehousing, logistics, hazmat packaging. (As-Pac, estab 2014, empl 5, sales $180,000, cert: NMSDC)

7089 Coxco, Inc.
3603 Pine Lane SE
Bessemer, AL 35022
Contact: Renee Cox President
Tel: 205-428-6223
Email: renee@coxcoinc.com
Website: www.coxcoinc.com
Dist wooden & plastic pallets, new & reconditioned, custom packaging. (Woman, estab 1983, empl 4, sales $6,000,000, cert: WBENC)

7090 Prystup Packaging Products
430 North Industrial PArk Dr
Livingston, AL 35470
Contact: Corey Hayden Technical Sales Engineer
Tel: 205-499-9397
Email: chayden@prystup.com
Website: www.prystup.com
Mfr folding paper cartons: food, consumer goods & electronics. (Minority, Woman, estab 1980, empl 160, sales $38,000,000, cert: WBENC)

7091 The Trinity Design Group, LLC
1107 Dowzer Ave
Pell City, AL 35125
Contact: Fernando Valentin CEO
Tel: 205-338-6888
Email: fvalentin@thetrinitydesigngroup.com
Website: www.thetrinitydesigngroup.com
Design, mfr & copack packaging, corrugated, paper, plastics, point of purchase & promotional materials. (AA, Hisp, estab 2004, empl 15, sales $2,028,500, cert: NMSDC)

Arkansas

7092 Alliance Rubber Company, Inc.
210 Carpenter Dam Rd
Hot Springs, AR 71901
Contact: Sheryl Koller Natl Accounts
Tel: 501-262-2700
Email: skoller@alliance-rubber.com
Website: www.rubberband.com/
Mfr & dist mailing, packaging & shipping products. (Woman, estab 1923, empl , sales $35,529,619, cert: WBENC)

7093 Sigma Supply North America
824 Mid America Blvd
Hot Springs, AR 71913
Contact: Brooke Griffin Natl Acct Mgr
Tel: 501-760-1151
Email: supplierdiversity@sigmasupply.com
Website: www.sigmasupply.com
Packaging solutions, turnkey solution for warehouse equipment, bulk storage, individual shipment packaging, labeling & inventory control. (Woman, estab 2003, empl 371, sales $380,900,000, cert: WBENC)

Arizona

7094 All-Pac Distributng LLC
4859 E Gleneagle Dr
Chandler, AZ 85249
Contact: Adam Snow Sales Mgr
Tel: 480-861-0842
Email: asnow@allpaconline.com
Website: www.allpaconline.com
Mfr & dist returnable plastic packaging, injection molding, compression molding. (Woman, estab 2001, empl 3, sales $1,150,000, cert: NWBOC)

7095 La Fiesta Label & Packaging Systems
6162 W Detroit St
Chandler, AZ 85226
Contact: Kirk Valadez VP Operations
Tel: 480-785-3900
Email: kvaladez@lafiestalabel.com
Website: www.lafiestalabel.com
Mfr shrink sleeves, unsupported film pouches & packets, pressure sensitive labels, fold out coupons, cartons, static cling, consecutive number, UV & laminate coating. (Hisp, estab 1985, empl 20, sales $ 0, cert: NMSDC)

California

7096 ACME Bag Inc Dba The Bulk Bag Company
14730 Northam St, La Mirada, CA,
La Mirada, CA 90638
Contact: John Willoughby Natl Sales Dir
Tel: 866-517-4699
Email: john@thebulkbagcompany.com
Website: www.thebulkbagcompany.com
Soilsaver Rolls, SOD Staples, Construction Fabrics, Landscaping Fabrics & Tarps, Agriculture Packaging, FIBC Bags & Woven Polypropyline Bags, Sand Bags- Burlap & WPP, Treated Burlap Sqares, Silt Fences, Truncated Wire Baskets. (As-Pac, estab 1975, empl 24, sales $20,000,000, cert: NMSDC)

PACKAGING & PACKING SERVICES & SUPPLIES

7097 ALOM Technologies Corporation
48105 Warm Springs Blvd
Fremont, CA 94539
Contact: Lisa Dolan VP Supply Chain Strategy
Tel: 510-360-3600
Email: customerservice@alom.com
Website: www.alom.com
Fulfillment, assembly, contract packaging, video & audio tape duplication, CD & DVD duplication (Woman, estab 1997, empl 284, sales $108,800,000, cert: WBENC)

7098 American Supply
PO Box 2322
Chino, CA 91710
Contact: Vonn Castillo Business Devel Mgr
Tel: 949-216-0468
Email: vcastillo@myamericansupply.com
Website: www.myamericansupply.com
Mfr & customize bags & covers, janitorial, housekeeping, promotional & OEM products. Mfr replacement cart bags, laundry bags, caddy bags, laundry truck liners, hair dryer bags, etc. (Woman/As-Pac, estab 2013, empl 5, sales $300,000, cert: CPUC)

7099 Atlantis Paper & Packaging
13405 Benson Ave
Chino, CA 91710
Contact: James Montano Sales Rep
Tel: 909-591-1809
Email: james@atlantispkg.com
Website: www.atlantispkg.com
Dist packaging products & machinery, corrugated boxes, stretch wrap, poly bags, ice pages, tape, cold storage, pallets, etc. (Hisp, estab 1984, empl 15, sales $15,000,000, cert: NMSDC)

7100 Blue Lake Packaging Inc.
2100 Geng Rd, Ste 210
Palo Alto, CA 94303
Contact: Boxia Schmidt Business Development Mgr
Tel: 650-665-3001
Email: boxia.schmidt@bluelakepackaging.com
Website: www.bluelakeecolife.com
Sustainable packaging design; sustainable materials; biodegradable or compostable packaging boxes; sustainable molded fiber packaging solution; recyclable packaging bags; recyclable packaging boxes. (Woman/As-Pac, estab 2018, empl 20, sales $400,000, cert: WBENC)

7101 Future Commodities Int'l Inc.
10676 Fulton Ct
Rancho Cucamonga, CA 91730
Contact: Matthew Lim VP Operations
Tel: 909-987-4258
Email: mlim@bestpack.com
Website: www.bestpack.com
Mfr & import carton sealing equipment, carton sealing tape. (As-Pac, estab 1984, empl 14, sales $10,200,000, cert: NMSDC)

7102 Industrial Container Corporation
2015 Acacia Court
Compton, CA 90220
Contact: Josh Rodgers Operations
Tel: 310-763-3550
Email: sales@industrialcontainer.com
Website: www.industrialcontainer.com
Packaging design services & protective packaging, Customer Design/CAD Documentation, Prototyping, Performance Certification, Manufacturing Responsibility, Total Quality control, Supply Chain Management, Maquiladora/JIT & warehousing. (Hisp, estab 1971, empl 35, sales $ 0, cert: NMSDC)

7103 PKG Packaging
311 Hearst Dr
Oxnard, CA 93030
Contact: Carlos Rodriguez Customer Service Mgr
Tel: 805-278-6648
Email: c.rodriguez@pkgpackaging.com
Website: www.pkgpackaging.com
Design, mfr & dist packaging material. (Minority, Woman, estab 1987, empl 10, sales $3,805,000, cert: NMSDC, WBENC)

7104 Premier Packaging/Assembly div of Haringa Inc.
14422 Best Ave
Santa Fe Springs, CA 90670
Contact: Vicki Haringa CEO
Tel: 562-802-2765
Email: vharinga@premierpkg.com
Website: www.premierpkg.com
Packaging services. (Woman, estab 1987, empl 6, sales $13,882,899, cert: WBENC)

7105 Thoro Packaging
1467 Davril Cir
Corona, CA 92880
Contact: Andrea Percy Marketing Liaison
Tel: 951-278-2100
Email: apercy@thoropkg.com
Website: www.thoropkg.com
Mfr & print custom folding cartons. (Woman, estab 1967, empl 184, sales $29,750,000, cert: WBENC)

7106 TransPak
520 N. Marburg Way
San Jose, CA 95133
Contact: Sharon Spina Strategic Accounts Mgr
Tel: 408-590-6543
Email: sharon.spina@transpak.com
Website: www.transpak.com
Mfr wood crates & crating systems, custom packaging solutions, logistics, transportation & rigging services. (Woman, estab 1952, empl 800, sales $120,000,000, cert: WBENC)

7107 Uniq Seal, LLC
5753-G Santa Ana Canyon Rd
Anaheim, CA 92807
Contact: Jacek Zdzienicki VP Sales
Tel: 714-299-5899
Email: jacek@nafm.com
Website: www.nafm.com
Contract sleeving & shrink labeling, multi-pack assemblies, shrink overwrap, tray assembly, re-packing & special assemblies, casing & cartoning, displays assembly, packaging R&D, fulfillment. (Minority, Woman, estab 1993, empl 7, sales $3,500,000, cert: NMSDC)

7108 World Centric
      101 H St, Ste M
      Petaluma, CA 94956
      Contact: Matt Mgr, Natl Accounts
      Tel: -   -
      Email: mattw@worldcentric.org
      Website: www.worldcentric.org
Sustainable, Compostable, Plant-based foodservice disposables (As-Ind, estab , empl , sales $36,000,000, cert: NMSDC)

Colorado

7109 Craters and Freighters
      331 Corporate Circle, Ste J
      Golden, CO 80401
      Contact: Chad Brockmeyer Natl Sales Mgr
      Tel: 720-287-7805
      Email: chad@cratersandfreighters.com
      Website: www.cratersandfreighters.com
Custom wood crating, plastic hard cases and freight services. (Woman, estab 1990, empl 12, sales $55,000,000, cert: WBENC)

7110 Die Cut Technologies/Denver Gasket
      10943 Leroy Dr
      Northglenn, CO 80233
      Contact: Evelyn Meyers CEO
      Tel: 303-452-4600
      Email: evelyn@diecuttech.com
      Website: www.diecuttech.com
Mfr gaskets, die cut parts & converted non-metallic materials. Also dist sponge, foam tapes rubber, bridge bearing pads, expansion joints, impact attenuators & adhesives, contract assembly & packaging svcs. (Hisp, estab 1961, empl 20, sales $2,524,000, cert: NMSDC, SDB)

7111 Rocky Mountain Pioneer, LLC
      13802 E 33rd Pl, Unit B
      Aurora, CO 80011
      Contact: Diane Hamilton Acct Mgr
      Tel: 303-371-6070
      Email: diane@pioneerdenver.com
      Website: www.hpcorporategroup.com
Custom & stock packaging materials: corrugated boxes, folding carton, bubble, foam protective packaging, shrink & stretch films, banding & tapes, fulfillment services. (Woman, estab 2004, empl 9, sales $5,000,000, cert: WBENC)

7112 Summit Container Corporation
      901Synthes Ave
      Monument, CO 80132
      Contact: Adam Walker CEO
      Tel: 719-481-8400
      Email: awalker@summitcontainer.com
      Website: www.summitcontainer.com
Packaging solutions, custom packaging, warehousing, distribution, assembly & kitting, (AA, estab 1989, empl 200, sales , cert: NMSDC)

7113 Universal Packaging Corp
      11440 E 56th Ave
      Denver, CO 80239
      Contact: Karen Millwater VP
      Tel: 303-373-2523
      Email: kmillwater@upc-solutions.com
      Website: www.upc-solutions.com
Dist industrial packaging supplies: bubble, foam, tape, stretch, shrink wrap, banding, bags, cable ties, boxes, styrofoam, rolled corrugated, mailing tubes, etc. (Woman, estab 1980, empl 13, sales $8,000,000, cert: City)

Connecticut

7114 Eastern Bag & Paper Company, Inc.
      200 Research Dr
      Milford, CT 06460
      Contact: Meredith Reuben CEO
      Tel: 203-878-1814
      Email: mreuben@ebpsupply.com
      Website: www.ebpsupply.com
Dist paper, packaging & allied products. (Woman, estab , empl 270, sales $196,987,948, cert: WBENC)

7115 Flexo Converters USA, Inc.
      1200 Northrop Rd
      Meridan, CT 06450
      Contact: Emily Gerrard Mktg/Sales Mgr
      Tel: 203-639-7070
      Email: egerrard@flexobags.com
      Website: www.flexobags.com
Mfr twisted handle paper shopping & merchandise bags. (Minority, estab 1994, empl 51, sales $15,000,000, cert: NMSDC)

7116 New England Packaging Co. LLC
      119 Sherman Ct
      Fairfield, CT 06824
      Contact: Mark Hyman President
      Tel: 203-256-2350
      Email: mark@zero-contact.com
      Website: www.zero-contact.com
Dist corrugated & paper products. (Hisp, estab 1997, empl 6, sales $200,000, cert: NMSDC)

7117 Penmar Industries, Inc.
      35 Ontario St
      Stratford, CT 06615
      Contact: Ed Rodriguez President
      Tel: 203-853-4868
      Email: eddy@penmar-industries.com
      Website: www.penmar-industries.com
Mfr & convert custom labels & tapes, dist packaging materials, carton sealing tapes, cartons & shipping room supplies. (Hisp, estab 1964, empl 15, sales $2,900,000, cert: NMSDC)

Florida

7118 3 Points Packaging LLC
      3505 NW 123rd St
      Miami, FL 33167
      Contact: Noel Bosh President
      Tel: 305-624-8343
      Email: info@3pointspackaging.com
      Website: www.3PointsPackaging.com
Packaging & janitorial products. (AA, estab 2011, empl 2, sales $660,000, cert: NMSDC)

7119 All American Containers, Inc
9330 NW 110th Ave
Miami, FL 33178
Contact: Richard Cabrera VP Int'l Division
Tel: 305-913-0624
Email: richardc@americancontainers.com
Website: www.americancontainers.com
Dist packaging supplies. (Woman/Hisp, estab 1991, empl 284, sales $ 0, cert: NMSDC)

7120 Containers Unlimited, Inc.
636 Volterra Blvd
Kissimmee, FL 34759
Contact: C. Eric Jones President
Tel: 678-833-4575
Email: cjones@containersunlimited.net
Website: www.containersunlimited.net
Dist stock & custom boxes & packaging materials. (AA, estab 1999, empl 4, sales $2,729,551, cert: SDB)

7121 Diverse Solution and Supplies
7305 Lismore Ct.
Orlando, FL 32835
Contact: Carolyn Griffin President
Tel: 407-256-2653
Email: carolyn.griffin@div-erse.com
Website: www.div-erse.com
Dist packaging & facility supplies: stretch wrap, corrugated, tapes, cushioning, bundling material, void fill, floor cleaning equipment, mats, bags, etc. (Woman, estab 2013, empl 2, sales $279,000, cert: WBENC)

7122 FlexSol Packaging Corp.
1531 NW 12th Ave
Pompano Beach, FL 33069
Contact: Bonni O'Connell Dir Sales/Marketing
Tel: 800-325-7740
Email: bonnio@flexsolpackaging.com
Website: www.flexsolpackaging.com
Mfr flexible packaging & value-added plastic films, custom bags & film, shrink & hood films, performance & barrier films & can liners. (As-Pac, estab 2009, empl 425, sales , cert: NMSDC)

7123 National Packaging, LLC
6346-65 Lantana Rd, Ste 126
Lake Worth, FL 33463
Contact: Kerry Lowe Mgr
Tel: 561-968-4420
Email: klowe@nationalpack.net
Website: www.nationalpack.net
Flexible packaging, Bag films. (Woman/AA, estab 2006, empl 2, sales , cert: NMSDC)

7124 Soule Medical
4322 Pet Ln
Lutz, FL 33559
Contact: Tim Goode Natl Accounts Mgr
Tel: 800-999-2928
Email: tim.goode@soulemedical.com
Website: www.soulemedical.com
Dist packaging products: crates, corrugated cartons, military type board, hard & soft cases, foams, bubble, tapes, poly bags, ect. (Woman, estab 1957, empl 31, sales $10,000,000, cert: WBENC)

7125 Totalpack, Inc.
2151 NW 72nd Ave
Miami, FL 33122
Contact: Robert Kweller GM
Tel: 305-597-9955
Email: robert@totalpack.com
Website: www.totalpack.com
Mfr & dist boxes, custom printed tapes & labels, double studs, fittings with ring polyfilm, stretchfilm & cargo straps & tapes. (Minority, Woman, estab 1990, empl 24, sales $ 0, cert: WBENC)

Georgia

7126 Alliance Packaging Group, Inc.
940 Sherwin Pkwy, Ste 100
Buford, GA 30517
Contact: Michelle Calvert CEO
Tel: 770-309-1012
Email: mcalvert@alliancepkggroup.com
Website: www.alliancepkggroup.com
Packaging, janitorial & shipping supplies. (Woman, estab 2007, empl 5, sales $2,733,290, cert: WBENC)

7127 E. Smith Box, Inc.
1875 Rockdale Industrial Blvd
Conyers, GA 30012
Contact: Jaquacer Middlebrooks President
Tel: 770-388-7787
Email: sales@esmithbox.com
Website: www.esmithbox.com
Mfr corrugated boxes. (AA, estab 1987, empl 35, sales $1,300,000, cert: NMSDC)

7128 FilmLOC Inc.
4190 Thurmon Tanner Pkwy
Flowery Branch, GA 30542
Contact: Shirl Handly President
Tel: 404-892-8778
Email: shirl@filmloc.com
Website: www.filmloc.com
Mfr placards for labeling & re-labeling reusable containers, totes & pallets, shelves, equipment, racking, manufactured goods in process, shipping crates. (Woman, estab 2002, empl 5, sales $749,359, cert: WBENC)

7129 Flexstar Packaging, Inc.
1902 Kimberly Park Dr
Dalton, GA 30720
Contact: Alan DaCosta GM
Tel: 706-272-3575
Email: alan@flexstarinc.com
Website: www.flexstarinc.com
Packaging, flexographic. (Woman, estab 2005, empl 21, sales $2,680,000, cert: WBENC)

7130 Meristem Packaging Company LLC
5090 Old Ellis Point
Roswell, GA 30076
Contact: Paige Mesaros Supply Chain Mgr
Tel: 770-998-7120
Email: pmesaros@meristempkg.com
Website: www.meristempkg.com
Packaging, folding cartons/boxes, plastic bags & styrofoam coolers. (AA, Hisp, estab 2009, empl 5, sales $7,444,000, cert: NMSDC)

PACKAGING & PACKING SERVICES & SUPPLIES

7131 Palmetto Industries International, Inc.
      6001 Horizon West Pkwy
      Grovetown, GA 30813
      Contact: Purvis King VP
      Tel: 706-737-7995
      Email: customerservice@palmetto-industries.com
      Website: www.palmetto-industries.com
Mfr & dist polymer & paper packaging products. (Minority, estab , empl , sales $20,000,000, cert: NMSDC)

7132 SquarePac LTD
      7115 Oak Ridge Pkwy Ste 110
      Austell, GA 30168
      Contact: Walter Griggs CFO
      Tel: 770-617-5688
      Email: admin@squarepac.us
      Website: www.squarepac.us
Returnable packaging & material handling solutions, eco-friendly containers & packaging, totes, pallets & metal racks. (AA, estab 2013, empl 8, sales $ 0, cert: NMSDC, SDB)

Illinois

7133 Action Bag Company
      1001 Entry Dr.
      Bensenville, IL 60640
      Contact: Martha Quintero
      Tel: 866-349-8853
      Email: mquintero@actionbag.com
      Website: www.actionhealth.com
Printed bags, bags, retail packaging products, printed promotional products, promotional items, packaging supplies, labels, tissue paper, gift cards, specialty packaging, custom bags, custom printed items, rush orders, in-stock products. (Woman, estab , empl , sales $ 0, cert: City, WBENC)

7134 Advertising Resources, Inc. (ARI Packaging)
      11601 S Central Ave
      Alsip, IL 60803
      Contact: Sheldon Ross Dir Business Devel
      Tel: 773-230-0884
      Email: sross@ari-packaging.com
      Website: www.ari-packaging.com
Assembly, Packing, Distribution, Tracking & Reporting, Bundling & Multi-Packs, Bagging & Filling. (AA, estab 2000, empl 100, sales $81,500,000, cert: NMSDC)

7135 Alta Packaging, Inc.
      150 Chaddick Dr
      Wheeling, IL 60090
      Contact: Jill Zienkiewicz
      Tel: 847-215-2582
      Email: jillz@altapackaging.com
      Website: www.altapackaging.com
Dist industrial packaging supplies. (Woman, estab 1995, empl 10, sales $5,276,581, cert: WBENC)

7136 AREM Container & Supply Co.
      6153 W Mulford Unit D
      Niles, IL 60714
      Contact: Brian Shifrin VP
      Tel: 847-673-6184
      Email: brian@aremcontainer.com
      Website: www.aremcontainer.com
Dist shipping, packaging & warehouse supplies: corrugated boxes & sheets, chipboard, poly bags, bubble & foam wrap, tape & spray adhesives, stretch wrap, kraft paper, padded mailers, bubble mailers, poly courier bags, chipboard mailers, etc. (Woman, estab 1961, empl 7, sales $2,182,000, cert: WBENC)

7137 BAF Packaging, LLC
      1053 E. 95th St.
      Chicago, IL 60619
      Contact: Valerie Matthews President
      Tel: 888-225-8221
      Email: vam@bafpack-rite.com
      Website: www.bafpack-rite.com
Contract Packaging, shrink wrap packaging, Light industrial assembly, Fulfillment, Distribution warehouse capabilities. (Woman/AA, estab 2013, empl 3, sales $350,000, cert: NMSDC)

7138 Cano Container Corporation
      3920 Enterprise Court
      Aurora, IL 60504
      Contact: Juventino Cano President
      Tel: 630-585-7500
      Email: juventino@canocontainer.com
      Website: www.canocontainer.com
Mfr corrugated shipping containers. (Hisp, estab 1986, empl 2, sales $20,000,000, cert: NMSDC)

7139 Carter Paper & Packaging, Inc.
      3400 SW Washington St
      Peoria, IL 61607
      Contact: Mike Krost Sales
      Tel: 309-637-7711
      Email: mike@carterpaper.com
      Website: www.erpaper.com
Dist paper & plastic packaging, bags, towels, wipers, tissue, VCI paper, loose fill, foam, tape, adhesives & specialty items. (Woman, estab 1957, empl 18, sales $ 0, cert: WBENC)

7140 Commercial Bag Company
      1 Paper Chase
      Normal, IL 61761
      Contact: Rachel Bowling
      Tel: 309-862-0144
      Email: rbowling@commercialpackaging.com
      Website: www.commercialpackaging.com
Flexible Packaging, stand up pouches, Bulk Bags/Totes, Woven Poly Bags, Multiwall Bags. (Woman, estab , empl , sales $95,000,000, cert: WBENC)

7141 Cross Packaging Supply, Inc.
      968 Dundee Ave Ste B
      Elgin, IL 60120
      Contact: AJ Loredo President
      Tel: 847-780-7225
      Email: aloredo@crosspackaging.com
      Website: www.crosspackaging.com
Packaging supplies (boxes, paper, tape, stretch film, bubble wrap, poly bags, bubble mailers, mailers, labels, can liners, etc). (Hisp, estab 2013, empl 2, sales $500,000, cert: NMSDC)

PACKAGING & PACKING SERVICES & SUPPLIES

7142 Dynamic Packaging
1248 W Jackson Blvd, Ste 2E
Chicago, IL 60607
Contact: Elson Seale President
Tel: 312-374-4445
Email: elson@dynam-pak.com
Website: www.dynam-pak.com
Dist industrial & janitorial supplies: corrugated boxes, tape, stretch-film, shrink-film, poly-bags, bubble wrap. (Woman/AA, estab 2014, empl 5, sales $250,000, cert: NMSDC)

7143 Food Packaging Consultants, Inc.
1601 Pleasant Ct
Libertyville, IL 60048
Contact: Laura Boucher President
Tel: 708-883-7240
Email: laura@pripackaging.com
Website: www.pripackaging.com
Flexible & rigid packaging & food processing materials. (Woman, estab 2004, empl 1, sales $3,535,219, cert: WBENC)

7144 H&H Sorting Services
1021 St. Charles St
Elgin, IL 60120
Contact: Jeanne Hintz President
Tel: 847-741-8479
Email: jeanne@hhsort.com
Website: www.hhsort.com
Sorting & inspection, assembly, packaging, labeling of fasteners & molded plastics & other pre-manufactured parts. (Woman, estab 1989, empl 48, sales $1,737,436, cert: WBENC)

7145 Magenta LLC
15160 New Ave
Lockport, IL 60441
Contact: Stephanie Smith Business Dev Exec
Tel: 630-737-9606
Email: ssmith@magentallc.com
Website: www.magentallc.com
Design, development & mfr injection molded components—primarily packaging— closures and containers. (Woman, estab 1969, empl 81, sales $14,900,000, cert: WBENC)

7146 Midwest Mailing & Shipping Systems Inc.
3006 Gill St, Ste A
Bloomington, IL 61704
Contact: Dave Rappa VP Sales
Tel: 309-661-1144
Email: dave@midwestmailing.com
Website: www.midwestmailing.com
Dist mailing systems, folder inserters, letter openers, inbound letter & parcel tracking systems, shipping systems, addressing systems, CASS/PAVE certified software, electronic scales, shredders, pressure sealers, bursters, collators, etc. (Woman, estab 1988, empl 9, sales $1,650,000, cert: WBENC)

7147 Montenegro Paper, Ltd.
25 E Main St. Ste 205
Roselle, IL 60172
Contact: Ed Enciso President
Tel: 630-894-0350
Email: mbe@montenegro-inc.com
Website: www.montenegro-inc.com
Dist commercial printing paper & packaging supplies. (Hisp, estab 1996, empl 6, sales $23,173,000, cert: State, City, NMSDC)

7148 Morris Packaging
211 N Williamsburg Dr, Ste A
Bloomington, IL 61701
Contact: Penny Steinwagner Sales & Marketing
Tel: 309-663-9100
Email: psteinwagner@morrispkg.com
Website: www.morrispkg.com
Flexible packaging manufacturer. (Nat Ame, estab 2004, empl 263, sales $100,000,000, cert: NMSDC)

7149 Numeridex, Inc.
632 Wheeling Rd
Wheeling, IL 60090
Contact: Alberto Hoyos President
Tel: 847-541-8840
Email: debbie@numeridex.com
Website: www.numeridex.com
Dist labeling & bar code products: thermal transfer printers, labels, ribbons, scanners, packaging & shipping supplies, corrugated cartons, stretch film, carton sealing tape. (Hisp, estab 1967, empl 10, sales $2,370,000, cert: NMSDC)

7150 Planned Packaging of Illinois Corp.
19558 S Harlem Ave Ste 5
Frankfort, IL 60423
Contact: Jack Callham Exec VP
Tel: 815-277-5270
Email: jack@ppoic.com
Website: www.ppoic.com
Dist industrial packaging supplies: corrugated boxes, film, foams, pallets, etc. (AA, estab 2001, empl 30, sales , cert: NMSDC)

7151 Poly-Pak and Ship, Inc.
2021 Illini Ave
Vandalia, IL 62471
Contact: JoAnn Boggs President
Tel: 618-283-2397
Email: joannboggs@polypakusa.com
Website: www.polypakusa.com
Warehousing, packaging, labeling, addressing, mailing, distribution printed matter, direct mail svcs. (Woman, estab 1985, empl 85, sales $2,658,671, cert: State, City, WBENC)

7152 Primary Resources Inc.
405 Busse Road
elk Grove Village, IL 60007
Contact: Enza Fragassi President
Tel: 847-808-7684
Email: enza@primarypkg.com
Website: www.primaryresources.net
Corrugated packaging, fibre board slip sheets, folding cartons, corrugated, chip partitions, flexible films, barrier bags, pouches, bundling, film products, shrink, stretch, polyethylene, labels, tamper evident products, bio-degradable materials. (Minority, Woman, estab 2001, empl 10, sales , cert: NMSDC)

7153 Scout Sourcing, Inc.
2340 South River Road Ste 309
Des Plaines, IL 60018
Contact: Anne Cowherd President
Tel: 917-428-8184
Email: acowherd@scoutsourcinginc.com
Website: www.scoutsourcinginc.com
Dist paper & packaging. (Woman, estab 2006, empl 6, sales $95,000,000, cert: WBENC)

PACKAGING & PACKING SERVICES & SUPPLIES

7154 Service Packaging Design, Inc.
      6238 Lincoln Ave
      Morton Grove, IL 60053
      Contact: Norman Croft President
      Tel: 847-966-6556
      Email: ncroft@servicepackaging.com
      Website: www.servicepackaging.com
Mfr & dist corrugated boxes, wood products, tags & labels, gum & poly tape, stretch wrap. (AA, estab 1982, empl 7, sales $1,250,000, cert: NMSDC)

7155 Skyline Container Corporation
      9755 W 143rd St
      Orland Park, IL 60462
      Contact: Dawn Souliotis President
      Tel: 708-460-7965
      Email: dawn@skyline99.com
      Website: www.skyline99.com
Dist corrugated boxes. (Woman, estab 1990, empl 5, sales $1,697,049, cert: City, WBENC)

7156 TransWorld Plastic Films, Inc.
      150 N 15th St
      Rochelle, IL 61068
      Contact: Rodolfo Hernandez Business Devel
      Tel: 815-561-7117
      Email: rhernandez@transworldplasticfilms.com
      Website: www.transworldplasticfilms.com
Polyethylene film for the automotive, tire & rubber industries used in the manufacturing & packaging process. (Minority, Woman, estab 2007, empl 31, sales , cert: NMSDC, WBENC)

7157 Trinity Graphic & Packaging Solutions, LLC
      28W031 Greenview Ave
      Warrenville, IL 60555
      Contact: Hardy Leonard President
      Tel: 630-393-7550
      Email: len.hardy@trinitygraphic.net
      Website: www.trinitygraphic.net
Dist thermal transfer ribbons, thermal transfer printers, thermal transfer print heads, printed labels, warehouse labels, promotional labels. (AA, Nat Ame, estab 2001, empl 1, sales , cert: State)

Indiana

7158 AIM Solutions, Inc.
      PO Box 340
      McCordsville, IN 46055
      Contact: John Laakso Dir
      Tel: 239-316-0004
      Email: john.laakso@aimsolutionsinc.net
      Website: www.aimsolutionsinc.net
Packaging & shipping supplies, pallets, boxes, film, bubble sheet stock, package automation engineering, foam, packaging equipment, plastic trays, labeling products & equipment, tape. (As-Pac, estab 2006, empl 7, sales $1,500,000, cert: State)

7159 Brown Tape Products Company
      8909 Sargent Rd
      Indianapolis, IN 46256
      Contact: Janice Brown President
      Tel: 866-276-9682
      Email: janbrown@browntapeproducts.com
      Website: www.browntapeproducts.com
Adhesive tape, cardboard boxes, mailers, steel banding, plastic banding, banding tools, stretch film, bubble pack, foam packaging, tape dispensers, newsprint, nylon cable ties, rolled corrugated, packing slip envelopes, plastic bags. (Woman, estab 1984, empl 5, sales $1,000,000, cert: City)

7160 Morales Group, Inc.
      5628 W 74th St
      Indianapolis, IN 46278
      Contact: Seth Morales Sales Mgr
      Tel: 317-334-0950
      Email: smorales@moralesgroup.net
      Website: www.moralesgroup.net
Assembly, packaging & warehousing services, Point of Purchase display assembly, Kitting, Literature collation, insertion, Sort/rework. (Hisp, estab 2003, empl 28, sales $14,900,000, cert: NMSDC)

7161 MSW (Mahomed Sales & Warehousing, LLC)
      8258 Zionsville Rd
      Indianapolis, IN 46268
      Contact: Keith Kanipe Sr VP
      Tel: 317-472-5800
      Email: kkanipe@whse.com
      Website: www.whse.com
Assembly, Sub-assembly Packaging, Kitting, Warehousing, Supply Chain Mgmt & Sorting services. (As-Ind, estab 1996, empl 110, sales $87,000,000, cert: NMSDC)

7162 Premier Business Solutions
      3202 N Kenmore
      South Bend, IN 46628
      Contact: President
      Tel: 574-232-8840
      Email: PBSAdmin@premierbus.com
      Website: www.premierbus.com
Fulfillment & marketing services: product & literature fulfillment, rebate & free offer processing, network programs, lead mgmt programs, pick pack, warehousing & inventory management.
We help our clients execute all facets of their marketing plan. (Woman, estab 2001, empl 15, sales $ 0, cert: WBENC)

7163 The Servants, Inc.
      3145 Lottes Dr
      Jasper, IN 47546
      Contact: Jerome Balbach Controller
      Tel: 812-634-2201
      Email: jerome@servants.com
      Website: www.servants.com
Corrugated packaging & packaging accessories. (Woman/AA, estab 1973, empl 55, sales $10,000,000, cert: NWBOC)

7164 Vesta Ingredients, Inc.
5767 Thunderbird Rd
Indianapolis, IN 46236
Contact: Richard Pinner Client Relationship Mgr
Tel: 317-397-9004
Email: richard@vestaingredients.com
Website: www.vestaingredients.com
Contract manufacturing & packaging. (As-Pac, estab 1997, empl 20, sales $10,000,010, cert: NMSDC)

Kansas

7165 Pitt Plastics, Inc. dba IBS Solutions
PO Box 356
Pittsburg, KS 66762
Contact: Randy Orscheln VP Sales, Strategic Accounts
Tel: 800-835-0366
Email: randyo@pittplastics.com
Website: www.pittplastics.com
Dist bags: can liners & poly bags, rolls or flat pack. (Nat Ame, estab 1971, empl 450, sales , cert: NMSDC)

Kentucky

7166 CSS Distribution Group, Inc.
3600 Chamberlain Ln Ste 216
Louisville, KY 40241
Contact: Sandy Allemang CEO
Tel: 502-423-1011
Email: sandya@customersourcingsolutions.com
Website: www.customersourcingsolutions.com
Dist packaging tape, edge protector, pallets, packaging & automation equipment, forklift software tracking program. (Woman, estab 2006, empl 12, sales $2,200,000, cert: WBENC)

7167 Kyana Packaging & Industrial Supply, Inc.
2501 Ampere Dr
Louisville, KY 40291
Contact: Kimberly Osborne CEO
Tel: 502-992-3333
Email: kim@kyanaind.com
Website: www.kyanaind.com
Dist packaging & shipping supplies: boxes, tape, stretch wrap, bubble wrap, strapping, adhesives, air pillow machines, stretch wrappers, strapping machines, automatic tape machines, shrink wrap equipment & film, poly bags, plastic films. (Woman, estab 1976, empl 37, sales $9,737,350, cert: WBENC)

7168 P3 Protective Packaging Products
PO Box 3583
Louisville, KY 40201
Contact: Anne Sizemore VP
Tel: 502-357-6872
Email: annes@p3products.com
Website: www.p3products.com
Expendable/Returnable Packaging & design. Retail package supplier/distributor. (Woman, estab 2001, empl 22, sales $7,000,000, cert: WBENC)

Massachusetts

7169 Lancaster Packaging, Inc.
560 Main St, Ste 2
Hudson, MA 01749
Contact: Marianne Lancaster President
Tel: 978-562-0100
Email: mlancaster@lancasterpackaging.com
Website: www.lancasterpackaging.com
Dist bank tamper evident bags, file storage boxes, corrugated materials, stretch wrap, shipping supplies. (Woman/AA, estab 1989, empl 10, sales $10,320,151, cert: WBENC)

Maryland

7170 Vac Pac, Inc.
150 W Ostend St, Ste 160
Baltimore, MD 21230
Contact: Hessa Tary CEO
Tel: 410-685-5181
Email: hessa.tary@vacpacinc.com
Website: www.vacpacinc.com
Print & convert flexible packaging, poly, polyprop, polyester, cellophane, nylon
high temeprature. (Woman, estab 1949, empl 25, sales $4,000,000, cert: WBENC)

Michigan

7171 Aldez Containers, LLC
4260 Van Dyke, Ste 109
Almont, MI 48003
Contact: Diane Pattison VP
Tel: 586-243-0596
Email: dpattison@aldezcontainers.com
Website: www.aldezcontainers.com
Mfr corrugated packaging & dunnage, service parts packaging. (Woman/Hisp, estab 1998, empl 78, sales $10,000,000, cert: NMSDC)

7172 Bay Corrugated Container, Inc.
1655 W 7th St
Monroe, MI 48161
Contact: Judy Thoma Exec Admin
Tel: 734-243-5400
Email: jthoma@baycorr.com
Website: www.baycorr.com
Mfr corrugated boxes/folding cartons, corrugated pallets, corrugated interior packaging materials, stretchwrap, chipboard, board coatings, linerboard/fine paper, stickers, labels, etc. (Minority, Woman, estab 1964, empl 250, sales $65,027,000, cert: NMSDC, WBENC)

7173 Contract Source & Assembly Inc.
5230 33rd St SE
Grand Rapids, MI 49512
Contact: Bryce Cooper
Tel: 616-897-2185
Email: bryce@contractmi.com
Website: www.contractmi.com
Light Manufacturing & Contract Assembly, Contract Packaging & Inventory Management, Supply Chain Management, Inspection & Re-work. (As-Pac, estab 2001, empl 13, sales $18,000,000, cert: NMSDC)

PACKAGING & PACKING SERVICES & SUPPLIES

7174 Diversity Products
32031 Howard St
Madison Heights, MI 48071
Contact: Darlene Fleser Operations Dir
Tel: 248-585-1200
Email: dfleser@diversityproducts.com
Website: www.diversityproducts.com
Packaging engineering support, cost reduction, vendor consolidation, packaging program mgmt, returnable container repair, cleaning & tracking, inventory management. (Woman/AA, estab 1998, empl 35, sales $9,000,000, cert: NMSDC)

7175 Galaxy Forest Products LLC
1655 W 7th St
Monroe, MI 48161
Contact: Judy Thoma Exec Admin
Tel: 734-243-5400
Email: jthoma@galaxyforestproducts.com
Website: www.galaxtforestproducts.com
Packaging materials, pulp, microflute, consumer boxes, corrugated containers, slip sheets, folding cartons, corner/angle protectors, dunnage packaging. (Minority, Woman, estab 2005, empl 1, sales $2,058,358, cert: State, NMSDC)

7176 Genesee Packaging, Inc (The Genesee Group)
2010 N. Dort Hwy, PO Box 7716
Flint, MI 48506
Contact: Ken Miller Sales Mgr
Tel: 248-514-1883
Email: kmiller@genpackaging.com
Website: www.genpackaging.com
Packaging supplies & services. (Woman, estab 1979, empl 125, sales $190,000,000, cert: WBENC)

7177 Global Strategic Supply Solutions
34450 Industrial Rd
Livonia, MI 48150
Contact: Lisa Williams-Lunsford CEO
Tel: 734-525-9100
Email: lisa@gs3global.com
Website: www.gs3global.com
Warehousing Operations, Consigned Packaging, Order Fulfillment and Distribution, Kit Building, Assembly. (Woman/AA, estab 2010, empl 50, sales $ 0, cert: WBENC)

7178 Integrated Packaging Company
6400 Harper Ave
Detroit, MI 48211
Contact: Jeffrey Laney Strategic Accounts Mgr
Tel: 612-802-1736
Email: jeff.laney@ipcboxes.com
Website: www.ipcboxes.com
Packaging solutions, packaging & displays, Design, Concept & Development. (AA, estab 1992, empl 30, sales $20,000,000, cert: NMSDC)

7179 James Group International
4335 W Fort St
Detroit, MI 48209
Contact: Lorron James Sales Mgr
Tel: 313-842-4543
Email: lorron.james@jamesgroupintl.com
Website: www.jamesgroupintl.com
Logistics, sequencing, warehousing & distribution, deconsidation, re-packing, sub-assembly, inventory management. (AA, estab 1971, empl 171, sales $30,000,000, cert: NMSDC)

7180 Macomb Wholesale Supply Corp.
17730 E 14 Mile Rd
Fraser, MI 48026
Contact: Catherine David President
Tel: 586-415-7400
Email: online@macombwholesale.com
Website: www.macombwholesale.com
Dist Packaging, Safety, Janitorial & Facility Maintenance Supplies, corrugated, poly bags, tape, paper, chemical, packaging, gloves, safety & facility cleaning supplies. (Woman, estab 1988, empl 10, sales $2,500,000, cert: WBENC)

7181 Packaging Integration, LLC
13235 Avalon Ct
Brighton, MI 48116
Contact: Scott Bradford President
Tel: 248-437-1900
Email: scott.bradford@packagingintegration.com
Website: www.packagingintegration.com
Dist packaging materials. (Hisp, estab 2005, empl 5, sales $5,000,000, cert: NMSDC)

7182 Patriot Packaging Solutions and Consulting
269 Walker St, Ste 522
Detroit, MI 48207
Contact: Jay Jackson VP
Tel: 313-580-1538
Email: jay.jackson@patriotgm1.com
Website: www.patriotpackagingsolutionsconsuting.com
Packaging services: corrugated box, bulk boxes, displays, single face, bubble wrap, stretch wrap, trays, sheets, tape & labels. (AA, estab 2011, empl 4, sales $500,250, cert: NMSDC)

7183 Peach State Packaging Solutions
8803 Cairn Hwy
Elk Rapids, MI 49629
Contact: Lisa McCririe President
Tel: 819-599-2594
Email: lmccririe@peachstatepackagingsolutions.com
Website: www.peachstatepackagingsolutions.com
Dist packaging supplies. (Woman, estab 2006, empl 1, sales $800,000, cert: WBENC)

7184 Pro-Pak Products, Ltd.
17580 Helro Dr
Fraser, MI 48026
Contact: Nancy Stachnik President
Tel: 586-415-1500
Email: propakltd@aol.com
Website: www.propakproductsltd.com
Packaging supplies & services. (Woman, estab 1993, empl 5, sales , cert: NWBOC)

7185   Qualfon Solutions, Inc,
       13700 Oakland Ave
       Highland Park, MI 48203
       Contact: Alisha McNary SVP Customer Solutions Group
       Tel: 877-261-0804
       Email: alisha.mcnary@qualfon.com
       Website: www.qualfon.com
Fulfillment, Literature & Product Fulfillment, Kitting/Production Support, B2B & B2C fulfillment support, Sampling Packaging & Fulfillment Support, Trade Show, Convention, Event Fulfillment, Promotional Offer/Rebate Support " Inventory Management. (Hisp, estab 2021, empl 16000, sales $379,030,000, cert: NMSDC)

7186   Quixerve Corporation
       341 N Helmer Rd
       Springfield, MI 49037
       Contact: Linda Gillett President
       Tel: 269-441-0700
       Email: lgillett@quixerve.com
       Website: www.quixerve.com
Printing, Labeling, Packaging, Fulfillment, Warehousing, Inventory Control, Distribution. (Woman, estab 2003, empl 3, sales $225,000, cert: WBENC)

7187   Ryan Industries, Inc.
       30369 Beck Rd
       Wixom, MI 48382
       Contact: Brenda Ryan President
       Tel: 248-926-5254
       Email: bryan@ryanind.net
       Website: www.ryanind.net
Warehousing, packaging, light assembly, kitting, distribution, rework. (Woman/AA, estab 1995, empl 10, sales $ 0, cert: NMSDC, WBENC)

7188   Sibley Laboratories LLC
       8816 Charbane St
       White Lake, MI 48386
       Contact: Kathleen Sibley Managing Partner
       Tel: 248-363-3972
       Email: ksibley@sibleylabs.com
       Website: www.sibleylabs.com
Dist ergonomically safe trash collection receptacles & trash bags. (Woman, estab 2001, empl 3, sales $ 0, cert: WBENC)

7189   STEWART Industries, LLC
       150 McQuiston Dr
       Battle Creek, MI 49037
       Contact: Matt Amos Business Dev Mgr
       Tel: 269-998-0608
       Email: mamos@stewartindustriesusa.com
       Website: www.stewartindustriesusa.com
Third party inspection, sorting, rework, light assembly, packaging. (AA, estab 2000, empl 60, sales $37,615,000, cert: NMSDC)

7190   Tabb Packaging Solutions
       41605 Ann Arbor Rd Ste 2
       Plymouth, MI 48170
       Contact: Julie Kavulich Business Devel Mgr
       Tel: 734-254-0251
       Email: jkavulich@tabbpackaging.com
       Website: www.tabbpackaging.com
Post Consumer Recycled Materials, HDPE & PET, Primary Processing Operations, Market Color Concentrates & Additives, Packaging Materials & Label Substrate (IML), Virgin & PCR Pre-blend Resins. (Woman, estab 2007, empl 7, sales , cert: WBENC)

7191   Total Packaging Solutions LLC
       900 Wilshire Dr STE 202
       Troy, MI 48084
       Contact: Liz Dzuris Owner
       Tel: 248-505-4419
       Email: servie@totalpkgsolutions.com
       Website: www.totalpackaging.biz
Mfr custom returnable & expendable packaging. (Woman, estab 2005, empl 3, sales $708,000, cert: WBENC)

7192   Venchurs, Inc.
       800 Liberty St
       Adrian, MI 49221
       Contact: Erica Wilt Program Mgr
       Tel: 517-264-4392
       Email: esellers@venchurs.com
       Website: www.venchurs.com
Custom package design & flexible packaging solutions. Global Sourcing, Supply Chain Management, Inventory Management, Packaging, Warehousing & Distribution. (Hisp, estab 1973, empl 86, sales $ 0, cert: NMSDC)

7193   World Corrugated Container
       PO Box 840
       Albion, MI 49224
       Contact: Tara Saumier Human Resources
       Tel: 517-629-9400
       Email: tsaumier@worldcorrugated.com
       Website: www.worldcorrugated.com
Mfr & dist corrugated containers. (Minority, Woman, estab 1991, empl 40, sales $7,900,000, cert: WBENC)

Minnesota

7194   Independent Packing Services, Inc.
       7600 32nd Ave N
       Crystal, MN 55427
       Contact: Joseph Wallace President
       Tel: 763-425-7155
       Email: jwallace@ipsipack.com
       Website: www.ipsipack.com
Mfr industrial crating for domestic & export shipments; electronics & fragile artwork. (AA, estab 1976, empl 60, sales $ 0, cert: NMSDC)

7195   Polybest, Inc.
       2962 Cleveland Ave N
       Roseville, MN 55113
       Contact: Zongzhao Li President
       Tel: - -
       Email: johnli@polybestinc.com
       Website: www.polybestinc.com
Mfr packaging materials such as all kinds of plastic and compostable bags, hazard trash bags, disposal bags, trash canliners, wrapping film, etc. (As-Pac, estab 2006, empl 4, sales $2,007,686, cert: NMSDC)

7196 Promotion Management Center, Inc.
31205 Falcon Ave
Stacy, MN 55079
Contact: DeAnn Monson Business Devel
Tel: 612-801-7921
Email: dmonson@pmci.com
Website: www.pmci.com
Fulfillment, direct mail, sweepstakes, packaging. (Woman, estab 1983, empl 40, sales $3,000,000, cert: WBENC)

7197 SeaChange Print Innovations
14505 27th Ave N
Plymouth, MN 55447
Contact: Nancy Servais Business Devel
Tel: 763-586-3700
Email: nancy.servais@seachangem.com
Website: www.seachangemn.com
Folding carton & marketing print production, Folding Carton Packaging, Marketing Printing, Commercial Printing, Direct Mail Printing, Digital Printing. (Woman, estab 2014, empl 90, sales $13,100,000, cert: WBENC)

7198 TJ's Packaging Inc
19950 177th St NW
Big Lake, MN 55309
Contact: Kristy Murray COO
Tel: 763-241-2022
Email: jfarrington@tjpackaging.com
Website: www.tjpackaging.com
Packaging supplies & automated packaging equipment. (Woman, estab 1998, empl 4, sales $1,862,202, cert: WBENC)

Missouri

7199 Bennett Packaging of Kansas City, Inc.
220 NW Space Center Cir
Lee's Summit, MO 64064
Contact: Traci Strickert Dir of Marketing
Tel: 816-379-5001
Email: traci.strickert@bpkc.com
Website: www.BennettKC.com
Design & mfr corrugated boxes, point-of-purchase displays, co-packing, fulfillment, warehousing & distribution. (Woman, estab 1987, empl 240, sales $65,153,256, cert: WBENC)

7200 Crossroads USA
14004 Century Lane
Grandview, MO 64030
Contact: Jason Begnaud Dir of Sales
Tel: 816-767-8008
Email: service@bestwaylogistics.com
Website: www.bestwaylogistics.com/
Single source packaging & shipping solutions nationwide. (Woman, estab 2000, empl 14, sales $5,050,000, cert: WBENC)

7201 Engineered Packaging Systems, Inc.
16141 Westwoods Business Park
Ellisville, MO 63021
Contact: Debra Debra Runtzel-Young CEO
Tel: 636-227-8600
Email: info@packeps.com
Website: www.packeps.com
Full service packaging machinery and packaging materials or consumables, CAD layout drawings, installation, service, shrink film, stretch film, tapes, adhesives, cartons, custom printed bags, powder filling, liquid filling, labeling machines and labels. (Woman, estab 2004, empl 11, sales $9,000,000, cert: WBENC)

7202 Swan Packaging Inc.
PO Box 1558
St. Louis, MO 63026
Contact: President
Tel: 314-771-9777
Email: info@swanpackaginginc.com
Website: www.swanpackaginginc.com
Dist shrink sleeves, lidding films, printed rollstock & pouches, rotogravure & flexographic printing, multilayer films, extrusion & off-line lamination, films, paper & foil. (Woman, estab 1999, empl 6, sales $3,519,000, cert: WBENC)

Mississippi

7203 Innpack LLC
10511 High Point Rd
Olive Branch, MS 38654
Contact: Jin Ahn CFO
Tel: 901-949-4977
Email: jahn@innpack.com
Website: www.innpack.com
Mfr & dist packaging solutions: burlap, cotton, PP woven, laminated & FBIC bags. (As-Pac, estab 1997, empl 20, sales $9,000,000, cert: NMSDC)

North Carolina

7204 Carolina Industrial Resources, Inc
4303 Oak Level Rd
Rocky Mount, NC 27803
Contact: Margaret Hoyle President
Tel: 800-849-1819
Email: tphoyle@cir-poly.com
Website: www.cir-poly.com
Dist polyethylene plastic packaging products. (Woman, estab 1986, empl 359, sales $155,000,000, cert: WBENC)

7205 Packrite, LLC
PO Box 2438
High Point, NC 33688
Contact: Kevin Spencer Business Devel
Tel: - -
Email: mark@packrite.net
Website: www.packrite.net
Single face-lamination corrugated products. (Woman, estab 2008, empl 90, sales $28,262,000, cert: WBENC)

7206 PolySi Technologies, Inc.
5108 Rex McLeod Dr
Sanford, NC 27330
Contact: Lynn Richardson Operations Mgr
Tel: 919-775-4989
Email: lynn@polysi.com
Website: www.polysi.com
Mfr silicone, synthetic greases & silicone fluids, industrial packaging, retail packaging, contract filling & custom packaging. (Woman, estab 1995, empl 25, sales $7,000,000, cert: WBENC)

7207 SLR Designs, LLC
11220 Elm Lane, Ste 200
Charlotte, NC 28277
Contact: Linda Tilley Managing Member
Tel: 704-546-8448
Email: linda@slrdesignsllc.com
Website: www.slrdesignsllc.com
Design & dist customer packaging, PVC, mPE & phthalate free materials. (Woman, estab 2011, empl 4, sales $3,247,681, cert: WBENC)

7208 Southern Film Extruders, Inc.
2319 English Rd
High Point, NC 27265
Contact: John Barnes VP Finance
Tel: 800-334-6101
Email: sales@southernfilm.com
Website: www.southernfilm.com
Extrudes polyethylene packaging films using LDPE, LLDPE, HDPE & Metallocene resins: shrink film, film for bags, laminations etc. (Hisp, estab 1965, empl 150, sales $65,000,000, cert: NMSDC)

Nebraska

7209 Frontier Bag Company, Inc
2520 Grant St
Omaha, NE 68111
Contact: Rendell Gines Reg Sales Mgr
Tel: 402-342-0992
Email: jplee@frontierbagco.com
Website: www.frontierbagco.com
Dist plastic bags & packaging, film wrap & shrink wrap. (Woman/AA, estab 1946, empl 15, sales $1,430,000, cert: WBENC)

New Jersey

7210 Accurate Box Company
86 Fifth Ave
Paterson, NJ 07524
Contact: Samara Schlossman Sales & Mktg Mgr
Tel: 973-345-2000
Email: sschlossman@accuratebox.com
Website: www.accuratebox.com
Litholaminated E, B & F flute packaging & displays. (Woman, estab 1944, empl 315, sales $138,000,000, cert: WBENC)

7211 Alpha Industries Inc. dba Sigma Stretch Film
Page and Schuyler
Lyndhurst, NJ 07071
Contact: John Buchan Mgr strategic accts
Tel: 214-799-3975
Email: johnbuchan@sigmaplastics.com
Website: www.sigmaplastics.com
Mfr custom barrier & sealant mono & co-ex blown films for dry, frozen, refrigerated & liquid food applications.. (As-Pac, estab 1997, empl 70, sales $57,500,000, cert: NMSDC)

7212 Creative Packaging Solutions Corporation
5 W First St
Keyport, NJ 07735
Contact: Coni Lefferts President
Tel: 732-335-3700
Email: info@packaging-usa.com
Website: www.packaging-usa.com
Dist packaging containers, parts & components: bottles, jars, flexible tubes, rigid tubes aand canister, caps, sprayers, lotion pumps, folding boxes, rigid gift set up boxes, ribbons, thermoformed blisters and trays. (Woman, estab 2003, empl 2, sales $176,677, cert: State, WBENC)

7213 G&T Trading International
128 Circle Ave
Clifton, NJ 07011
Contact: George Chen President
Tel: 973-340-8003
Email: philipgttic@gmail.com
Website: www.gttic.com
Dist stretch film, wooden pallets, chipboard, stretch film equip, annual equipment audits, shrink film, shrink wrap & bundling equip, carton sealing & bagging equip, supporting films & tapes. (As-Pac, estab 1977, empl 6, sales $23,987,513, cert: State, NMSDC)

7214 Glopak Corporation
132 Case Dr
South Plainfield, NJ 07080
Contact: Elyne Williams Sales Dir
Tel: 908-753-8735
Email: glopakinc@aol.com
Website: www.glopakcorp.com
Dist plastic bags & liners. (Woman/AA, estab 1966, empl 33, sales $ 0, cert: NMSDC)

7215 Kampack, Inc
100 Frontage Rd
Newark, NJ 07114
Contact: Patrick J Fox Strategic Accounts Mgr
Tel: 804-370-0351
Email: pat.fox@kampackinc.com
Website: www.kampackinc.com
Mfr corrugated packaging. (Woman/Hisp, estab 1959, empl 250, sales $60,000,000, cert: State, NMSDC, WBENC)

7216 Modpak, Inc.
317 Godwin Ave
Midland Park, NJ 07432
Contact: CEO
Tel: 201-493-7677
Email: Modpak@Aol.Com
Website: www.modpakinc.com
Packaging & printing. (Woman, estab 1977, empl 4, sales $ 0, cert: WBENC)

PACKAGING & PACKING SERVICES & SUPPLIES

7217 Pro Pack Inc.
500 W Main St
Wyckoff, NJ 07481
Contact: Peter Quercia CEO
Tel: 201-337-1001
Email: peter@shrinkfilm.com
Website: www.shrinkfilm.com
Packaging materials, form, fill & seal systems, doy-pack systems, metal detectors & check weighers, labeling systems, clip & twist systems, shrink wrappers, carton sealers, stretch wrappers, strapping machines, conveyors, band sealers, filling systems. (Woman, estab 1976, empl 10, sales $4,000,000, cert: WBENC)

7218 Products Distribution, Inc.
7 Santa Fe Way Ste 701
Cranbury, NJ 08512
Contact: Dawn Dunbar President
Tel: 609-655-1341
Email: requests@productsdistribution.com
Website: www.productsdistribution.com
Warehousing, distribution, fulfillment, assembly, kitting, pick pack, container unloading, palletizing, ingredient storage, bulk storage, EDI, custom assembly, display assembly, GWP assembly, rack storage, raw material storage. (Woman, estab 1979, empl 7, sales $1,119,000, cert: WBENC)

7219 Quality Packaging Specialists International, LLC
2030 US 130 N
Florence, NJ 08518
Contact: Jeff Lemke Sales Exec
Tel: 609-239-0503
Email: jlemke@qpsiusa.com
Website: www.qpsiusa.com
Packaging & fulfillment, merchandising displays, contract packaging, logistics & distribution services. (AA, estab 1972, empl 1500, sales $300,000,000, cert: NMSDC)

7220 RKS Plastics Inc.
100 Jersey Ave
New Brunswick, NJ 08903
Contact: Sudhir Shah President
Tel: 800-635-9959
Email: srshah@rksplastics.com
Website: www.rksplastics.com
Dist polyethylene & polyproylene bags, drum/box liners, sheeting & tubing, zipper lock bags, anti-static bags, printed bags, wicket/staple pack, stretch wrap & tapes. In addition, we also offer design services. (AA, As-Pac, estab 1993, empl 7, sales $4,223,000, cert: NMSDC)

7221 SunFlex Packagers Inc.
2 Commerce Dr
Cranford, NJ 07016
Contact: Manny Patel CEO
Tel: 908-709-1500
Email: mannypatel@sunflexpackagers.com
Website: www.sunflexpackagers.com
Convert & dist flexible packaging material: roll form, bags & specialty pouches. (As-Ind, estab 2002, empl 15, sales $5,900,000, cert: NMSDC)

Nevada

7222 West Pack Industries, LLC.
2225 E Greg St, Ste 107
Sparks, NV 89431
Contact: James Alford General Mgr
Tel: 775-351-3345
Email: james@westpackcopack.com
Website: www.westpackcopack.com/
Flexible packaging, contract packaging, dry product filling, mixing, blending. Stand up pouch filling, Vertical Form Fill Seal filling, volume metric filling, scale filling. Snack Foods, candy, confectionery, powdered beverages. (Nat Ame, estab 2003, empl 44, sales $1,850,000, cert: NMSDC)

New York

7223 Aluf Plastics div. of API Industries, Inc.
2 Glenshaw St
Orangeburg, NY 10962
Contact: Tom Cross VP Retail Sales
Tel: 845-365-2200
Email: tom.c@alufplastics.com
Website: www.alufplastics.com
Mfr plastic bags. (Woman, estab 1977, empl 314, sales , cert: WBENC)

7224 Berry Industrial Group, Inc.
30 Main St
Nyack, NY 10960
Contact: Debra Berry CEO
Tel: 845-353-8338
Email: debra.berry@berryindustrial.com
Website: www.berryindustrial.com
Mfr, recycle & dist industrial shipping pallets. (Woman, estab 1984, empl 7, sales $22,636,656, cert: WBENC)

7225 Bluepack
215 John Glenn Dr
Amherst, NY 14228
Contact: Helen Ma President
Tel: 716-923-0032
Email: hma@bluepackinc.com
Website: www.bluepackinc.com
Mfr printed & unprinted shrink labels, neck bands & safety seals. We have 8 color flexo and rotogravure presses. (Minority, Woman, estab 1999, empl 65, sales $10,000,000, cert: NMSDC)

7226 Cross River Medical LLC dba Proforma Edge
282 Katonah Ave #132
Katonah, NY 10536
Contact: Bruce Browning
Tel: 914-380-7510
Email: bruce.browning@proforma.com
Website: WWW.THEPROFORMAEDGE.COM
Commercial printing, packaging, direct mail, branded merchandise programs, uniform & apparel programs, online ordering, fulfillment. (As-Pac, estab 2010, empl 8, sales $3,545,000, cert: NMSDC)

7227 Diamond Packaging
       111 Commerce Dr
       Rochester, NY 14623
       Contact: Dennis Bacchetta Dir of Marketing
       Tel: 585-334-8030
       Email: sales@diamondpkg.com
       Website: www.diamondpackaging.com
Contract mfg & packaging services: automatic cartoning, bagging bar coding, blister sealing, EAS source tagging, flexible packaging, form, fill & seal, fulfillment, labeling, POP displays, product assembly, RF sealing, shrink wrapping & skin packaging. (Woman, estab , empl 230, sales $59,180,000, cert: WBENC)

7228 Global Packaging Solutions LLC
       70 E Sunrise Hwy Ste 611
       Valley Stream, NY 11581
       Contact: Mitchell Sloane Managing Dir
       Tel: 516-256-7416
       Email: msloane@glopackllc.com
       Website: www.glopackllc.com
Bags, plastic bags, reusable bags, trash liners, shopping bags. (AA, estab 2011, empl 5, sales $3,500,000, cert: State)

7229 Golden Group International, Ltd.
       305 Quaker Rd
       Patterson, NY 12563
       Contact: Transue President
       Tel: 845-440-5220
       Email: jackiet@goldengroupinternational.com
       Website: www.goldengroupinternational.com
Mfr & dist bags, dispensers, receptacles and cabinets. (Woman, estab 2009, empl 8, sales , cert: WBENC)

7230 Howell Packaging
       79 Pennsylvania Ave
       Elmira, NY 14904
       Contact: Katherine Roehlke CEO
       Tel: 607-734-6291
       Email: khr@howellpkg.com
       Website: www.howellpkg.com
Mfr printed folding cartons and thermo-formed plastic components internally. (Woman, estab , empl 240, sales $41,000,000, cert: WBENC)

7231 Ongweoweh Corp
       5 Barr Road
       Ithaca, NY 14850
       Contact: Brett Bucktooth Supplier Diversity Mgr
       Tel: 607-266-7070
       Email: supplierdiversity@ongweoweh.com
       Website: www.ongweoweh.com
Mfr & dist wooden pallets & specialty containers. (Nat Ame, estab 1978, empl 96, sales $252,000,000, cert: NMSDC)

7232 Star Poly Bag Inc.
       200 Liberty Ave.
       Brooklyn, NY 11207
       Contact: Rachel Posen President
       Tel: 718-384-3130
       Email: rachel@starpoly.com
       Website: www.starpoly.com
Mfr poly bags. (Woman, estab 1961, empl 15, sales $3,550,000, cert: State, City, WBENC)

7233 The Standard Group
       1010 Northern Blvd Ste 236
       Great Neck, NY 11021
       Contact: James Gregory Acct Exec
       Tel: 718-310-5512
       Email: jamesg@thestandardgroup.com
       Website: www.thestandardgroup.com
Folding carton, specialty printed packaging & paperboard converter. (Hisp, estab 1932, empl 130, sales $35,000,000, cert: NMSDC)

7234 Universal Packaging Systems
       6080 Jericho Turnpike
       commack, NY 11725
       Contact: David Boone Natl Acct Mgr
       Tel: 404-554-0770
       Email: dboone@paklab.com
       Website: www.paklab.com
Contract manufacturing & flexible film, extended gamut flexographic printing of roll stock & pouches with gussets & fitments. (AA, estab 1987, empl 600, sales $116,400,000, cert: NMSDC

Ohio

7235 Accel inc.
       9000 Smith's Mill Road
       New Albany, OH 43054
       Contact: Chairwoman
       Tel: 614-656-1100
       Email:
       Website: www.accel-inc.com
Contract packaging & fulfillment svcs: design, sourcing, assembly, shrink-wrapping, warehousing, dist & e-fulfillment svcs. (Woman, estab 1995, empl 375, sales $25,890,000, cert: WBENC)

7236 Allied Shipping and Packaging Supplies
       3681 Vance Road
       Moraine, OH 45439
       Contact: Shelly Heller President
       Tel: 937-222-7422
       Email: sheller@asapi.com
       Website: www.asapi.com
Dist packaging supplies: special size boxes, printed boxes, printed tape, special inserts or cell partitions, printed poly bags or special size poly bags. (Woman, estab 1982, empl 12, sales $4,034,225, cert: WBENC)

7237 Arrowhead Packaging Services
       PO Box 1284
       Perrysburg, OH 43551
       Contact: Brian Deiger VP Sales
       Tel: 419-344-7373
       Email: brian@apackserv.com
       Website: www.apackserv.com
Packaging & packaging services, fulfillment operations, sequencing, storage & logistics. (AA, estab 2010, empl 2, sales $120,000, cert: NMSDC)

7238 Bickley Innovations, LLC
       607 Redna Terr, Ste 700
       Cincinnati, OH 45215
       Contact: Kendra Alexander President
       Tel: 513-655-6074
       Email: information@bickleyllc.com
       Website: www.bickleyllc.com
Dist packaging & industrial supplies. (Woman/AA, estab 2015, empl 1, sales , cert: NMSDC, WBENC)

7239 Borinquen Container Corp.
541 Grant St
Mansfield, OH 44903
Contact: Mary President
Tel: 787-898-5000
Email: mary@orflo.com
Website: www.borinquengroup.com
Corrugated and Solid Fiber Box Manufacturing. (Hisp, estab 1969, empl 20, sales , cert: NMSDC)

7240 Custom Paper Tubes
15900 Industrial Pkwy
Cleveland, OH 44135
Contact: Emily Miller Marketing Mgr
Tel: 216-362-2964
Email: emiller@custompapertubes.com
Website: www.custompapertubes.com
Produce sustainable, recyclable & biodegradable packaging for all types of products. (Woman/AA, Hisp, estab 1964, empl 25, sales $5,500,000, cert: WBENC, SDB)

7241 Forest City Companies, Inc.
3607 W 56th St
Cleveland, OH 44102
Contact: Anthony Galang
Tel: 216-634-9000
Email: tgalang@forestcityco.com
Website: www.forestcityco.com
Military packaging service & supplies, laser marking services, wood boxes, export packing & crating, hazmat packaging service & supplies, induatrial sewing, bellows, insulated blankets. (Minority, estab 1993, empl 14, sales $3,600,000, cert: NMSDC)

7242 Fre-Flo Distribution
3700 Inpark Circle
Dayton, OH 45414
Contact: Theodore R. Ross, III President
Tel: 937-233-1997
Email: tross@freflo.com
Website: www.freflo.com
Warehousing, distribution, containment, quality inspection, assembly, sub-assembly, power-washing returnable containers, reworking, components recovery, packaging, labeling, kitting, pick & pack, bulk repacking. (AA, estab 1991, empl 26, sales $1,495,883, cert: State, NMSDC)

7243 Joshen Paper and Packaging
5800 Grant Ave
Cuyahoga Heights, OH 44105
Contact: Anthony Salyers
Tel: 216-441-5600
Email: greiser@joshen.com
Website: www.joshen.com
Dist packaging supplies, bags, office supplies, custom printing, sanitation, chemicals & floor care programs. (Woman, estab 1988, empl 152, sales $180,500,000, cert: NWBOC)

7244 LEFCO Worthington, LLC
18451 Euclid Ave
Cleveland, OH 44112
Contact: Larry Fulton President
Tel: 216-432-4422
Email: larry.fulton@lefcoworthington.com
Website: www.LEFCOWorthington.com
Dist wooden crates, OSB Boxes, custom pallets, sub-assembly & packaging services. (AA, estab 2003, empl 30, sales $3,600,000, cert: State, NMSDC)

7245 TrueChoicePack Corp.
9565 Cincinnati Columbus Road
Cincinnati, OH 45069
Contact: Rakesh Rathore COO
Tel: 513-759-5540
Email: info@truechoicepack.com
Website: www.truechoicepack.com
Mfr environmentally friendly green packaging products, biodegradable & compostable food service packaging & disposable products. (Woman/As-Ind, estab 2008, empl 10, sales $50,560,000, cert: NMSDC, WBENC)

7246 Vista Industrial Packaging, Inc.
4700 Fisher Rd
Columbus, OH 43228
Contact: Michael Houser Business Devel
Tel: 614-372-9951
Email: mhouser@vistaindustrialpackaging.com
Website: www.vistaindustrialpackaging.com
Contract or co-packaging, hand assembly work, shrink wrapping, build POP displays, HazMat packing, kit or giftset assembly, auto or manual bagging, ticketing, sorting, returns processing, pick and pack, QA, warehousing, direct shipments, distribution. (Woman, estab 1983, empl 70, sales $ 0, cert: WBENC)

Oregon

7247 Standard Bag Manufacturing Company
1800 SW Merlo Dr
Beaverton, OR 97003
Contact: Rita Fung Controller
Tel: 503-616-7307
Email: rfung@standardbag.com
Website: www.standardbag.com
Mfr bags: sewn open mouth, pinch bottom open mouth & pinch block bottom bags. (As-Pac, estab 1985, empl 140, sales $ 0, cert: NMSDC)

7248 Yoshida Foods International
8440 NE Alderwood Rd, Ste A
Portland, OR 97220
Contact: Junki Yoshida Sales Mgr
Tel: 503-872-8450
Email: junki.yoshida@yoshida.com
Website: www.yoshidafoodsinternational.com
Liquid hot-fill bottling, industrial packaging, portion packaging. (As-Pac, estab 1982, empl 241, sales $ 0, cert: NMSDC)

Pennsylvania

7249 Alpine Packaging Inc.
4000 Crooked Run Rd
North Versailles, PA 15137
Contact: Jan Lehigh President
Tel: 412-664-4000
Email: jlehigh@alpinepackaging.com
Website: www.alpinepackaging.com
Packaging supplies & services. (Woman, estab 1972, empl 33, sales $761,368,117, cert: WBENC)

PACKAGING & PACKING SERVICES & SUPPLIES

7250 Carlisle Packaging Company, Inc.
750 Claremont Rd
Carlisle, PA 17013
Contact: Ed Schimmel CEO
Tel: 717-249-2444
Email: eschimmel@carlislecontainer.net
Website: www.carlislecontainer.net
Mfr corrugated packaging & displays. (Woman, estab 1965, empl 40, sales $7,173,000, cert: State, WBENC)

7251 Evco Industries, Inc.
126 Talbot Ave
Holmes, PA 19043
Contact: Kathleen Evans President
Tel: 610-586-9842
Email: kitty@evcoindustries.com
Website: www.evcoindustries.com
Dist industrial packaging products: adhesives, adhesive applicating equipment, marking/coding equipment & drying systems. (Woman, estab 1979, empl 8, sales $2,230,099, cert: WBENC)

7252 Kalstar Enterprises, LLC
PO Box 931
Scranton, PA 18501
Contact: Adam Zaranski Dir Client Solutions
Tel: 973-553-5370
Email: adam.zaranski@kalstar.com
Website: www.kalstar.com
Packaging, kitting other labor services to manufacturing companies. (Woman, estab 2004, empl 206, sales $33,600,000, cert: WBENC)

7253 S&G Corrugated Packaging
195 Slocum St
Swoyersville, PA 18704
Contact: Earl Sampson CEO
Tel: 570-287-1718
Email: sgcorrugated@verizon.net
Website: www.s-gcorrugatedpackaging.com
Mfr corrugated cartons & corrugated sheets: assembled partitions, corrugated trays, half slotted cartons, one & five panel folders, scored sheets, coated pads, telescoping cartons, die cutting items, slip sheets, packaging tapes. (AA, estab 2007, empl 10, sales , cert: NMSDC)

7254 Secure Applications, LLC
419 West Market St Ste C
Bethlehem, PA 18018
Contact: Gina Uzzolino President
Tel: 732-874-0954
Email: guzzolino@secureapplications.net
Website: www.secureapplications.net
Packaging materials for Product Security, Tamper Evident, Non-Tamper Evident tapes & labels, security bags, stretch film & Temperature Monitoring Systems for cold chain applications as well as security containers & seals. (Woman, estab 2011, empl 2, sales $110,000, cert: State, CPUC)

7255 Union Packaging, LLC
6250 Baltimore Ave
Yeadon, PA 19050
Contact: Michael K. Pearson President
Tel: 610-622-7001
Email: mpearson@unionpkg.com
Website: www.unionpkg.com
Mfr folding cartons, paperboard printing & converting. (AA, estab 1999, empl 82, sales $9,287,115, cert: NMSDC)

7256 Wexler Packaging Products, Inc.
777-M Schwab Rd
Hatfield, PA 19440
Contact: Tara Utain VP Sales
Tel: 800-878-3878
Email: tara@wexlerpackaging.com
Website: www.wexlerpackaging.com
Packaging products. (Woman, estab 1997, empl 20, sales $ 0, cert: WBENC)

Puerto Rico

7257 3A Press
PO Box 47
Lajas, PR 00667
Contact: Marie Rosado President
Tel: 787-899-0110
Email: mrosado@3apress.com
Website: www.3apress.com
Mfr & print pharmaceutical, commercial & folding cartons, inserts, stitched & perfect bound booklets/magazines, printed literature. (Hisp, estab 1996, empl 126, sales $11,200,000, cert: NMSDC)

7258 Flexible Packaging Company, Inc.
KM 5 1 BO Guaragua RR 176 Bayamon Gardens Station
Bayamon, PR 00959
Contact: Esteban Serrano Sales Mgr
Tel: 787-622-7225
Email: eserrano@flepak.com
Website: www.flepak.com
Flexible packaging solutions. (Hisp, estab 1976, empl 170, sales , cert: NMSDC)

7259 Inter-Strap Packaging Systems
PO Box 12367
San Juan, PR 00914
Contact: Antonio Fernández GM
Tel: 787-771-5230
Email: afernandez@inter-strap.com
Website: www.inter-strap.com
Dist packaging equipment & materials. (Woman/Hisp, estab 1991, empl 18, sales $6,317,564, cert: NMSDC)

7260 Johnny Rullan & Co.,
Road # 1 Km. 20.9 RR-3 Box 3710
San Juan, PR 00926
Contact: Julio Pizarro Accounting Clerk
Tel: 787-789-3050
Email: accountsreceivable@johnnyrullan.com
Website: www.johnnyrullan.com
Packaging equipment sales & service. (Hisp, estab 1970, empl 25, sales , cert: NMSDC)

Rhode Island

7261 Banneker Industries, Inc.
582 Great Rd, Ste 101
North Smithfield, RI 02896
Contact: Joe Cefalo Sales & Marketing Mgr
Tel: 603-819-6966
Email: marketing@banneker.com
Website: www.banneker.com
Supply chain management services: e-business services, assembly & packaging, bar coding, dist packaging materials, third party logistics (3PL), warehousing, material flow & inventory management. (Woman/AA, estab 1991, empl 72, sales $10,072,400, cert: NMSDC, WBENC)

South Carolina

7262 Alpha Pack LLC
      PO Box 30266
      Charleston, SC 29417
      Contact: Carver Wright Jr. Owner
      Tel: 843-737-3931
      Email: wright.pkg@alphapackllc.com
      Website: www.alphapackllc.com
Flexible packaging, polybags, shrink bags, printed bags, tubing, vci bags, sheeting & can liners. (AA, estab 2012, empl 2, sales , cert: NMSDC)

7263 Milagro Packaging LLC
      60 Fairview Church Rd
      Spartanburg, SC 29306
      Contact: Jill McCurry President
      Tel: 864-578-0085
      Email: jillm@concept-pkg.com
      Website: www.milagro-pkg.com
Mfr corrugated & solid fiber boxes, polystyrene foam products & urethane foam products. (Hisp, estab 2001, empl 425, sales $94,873,435, cert: NMSDC)

7264 Progressive Packaging
      1224 Old Stage Rd
      Greenville, SC 29681
      Contact: Mark Hutcherson Sales Exec
      Tel: 864-271-8106
      Email: hutcherson64@gmail.com
      Website: www.progpack.com
Corrugated packaging, boxes, sheet plant, assembly. (Woman, estab 1996, empl , sales $19,000,000, cert: WBENC)

7265 Solution Packaging LLC
      2131 Woodruff Rd, Ste 196
      Greenville, SC 29607
      Contact: Joe Nichol VP Sales
      Tel: 864-313-9595
      Email: joe@solutionplastics.net
      Website: www.solutionplastics.net
Mfr & dist polyethylene based end product & solutions, packaging, poly film, etc. (Minority, Woman, estab 2013, empl 2, sales , cert: WBENC)

7266 WDS, Inc.
      1414 Village Harbor Dr
      Lake Wylie, SC 29710
      Contact: Jennfer Maier CEO
      Tel: 803-619-0301
      Email: jennifer.maier@womends.com
      Website: www.womends.com
Dist industrial supplies: paper products, chipboard, films & plastics. (Woman, estab 2007, empl 180, sales $186,000,000, cert: WBENC)

Tennessee

7267 DSI Warehouse Inc
      1315 Farmville Rd
      Memphis, TN 38122
      Contact: Debbie Martin President
      Tel: 901-345-6608
      Email: debbiemartin@dsiwarehouse.com
      Website: www.dsiwarehouseandstorage.com
Warehousing & Storage, Packing & Crating, Packaging & Labeling, Kitting Pack Svcs, Storage & Handling Equipment & Supplies, Distribution Fulfillment. (Woman/AA, estab 2013, empl 20, sales $1,455,421, cert: NMSDC, WBENC)

7268 Interstate Packaging Corp.
      2285 Hwy 47 N
      White Bluff, TN 37187
      Contact: Marketing Dir
      Tel: 615-797-9000
      Email: ldoochin@interstatepkg.com
      Website: www.interstatepkg.com
Flexible packaging, labels, bags, and pouches. (Woman, estab 1969, empl 210, sales $42,000,000, cert: WBENC)

7269 Johnson Bryce, Inc.
      5405 Hickory Hill
      Memphis, TN 38141
      Contact: Ron Purifoy CEO
      Tel: 901-942-6522
      Email: rpurifoy@johnsonbryce.com
      Website: www.johnsonbryce.com
Mfr flexible packaging. (AA, estab 1991, empl 25, sales $27,500,000, cert: NMSDC)

7270 OTB Container, LLC
      1380 Poplar Ave
      Memphis, TN 38104
      Contact: Daniel Coates President
      Tel: 901-270-5407
      Email: daniel@otbcontainer.com
      Website: www.otbcontainer.com
Supplies corrugated shipping boxes. (AA, estab 2015, empl 5, sales $589,000, cert: NMSDC)

7271 Puffy Stuff
      9 Music Square S, Ste 376
      Nashville, TN 37203
      Contact: Sales
      Tel: 877-833-9872
      Email: info@puffystufftn.com
      Website: www.puffystufftn.com
Mfr 100% biodegradable packing peanuts. (Woman, estab 2000, empl 20, sales , cert: State)

7272 RD Plastics
      PO Box 111300
      Nashville, TN 37222
      Contact: Jeffrey D. Loveless VP Natl Accts
      Tel: 615-781-0007
      Email: jeffl@rdplastics.com
      Website: www.rdplastics.com
Bags: biohazard ziplock, clear ziplock, adhesive closure, specimen transport, open end, security seals, pill crushers, personal belonging. (Woman, estab , empl , sales $16,502,500, cert: WBENC)

7273 Remar Inc
      6200 E. Division St
      Lebanon, TN 37090
      Contact: Lee Whittaker President
      Tel: 720-601-4785
      Email: lwhittaker@remarinc.com
      Website: www.remarinc.com
Dist blister packaging, fin seal wrap, shrink wrap, inventory mgmt, point of purchase displays, media replication, direct mail services, turn key or component projects. (Hisp, estab , empl 150, sales $ 0, cert: State, NMSDC)

7274 TSS Industrial Packaging, LLC
PO Box 3181
Jackson, TN 38303
Contact: Michelle Boyd CEO
Tel: 888-424-1946
Email: mboyd@tssip.com
Website: www.tssip.com
Dist industrial packaging materials: industrial sewing thread & yarn for closing bags, crepe paper sewing tape, pull tape, twine, slip sheets, pallet covers, stretch film & stretch wrap. (Woman, estab 2006, empl 4, sales $3,803,124, cert: State, WBENC)

7275 Worldwide Label & Packaging LLC
158 Madison Ave Ste 101
Memphis, TN 38103
Contact: Anthony Norris President
Tel: 901-454-9290
Email: anorris@worldwidebg.com
Website: www.worldwidebg.com
Mfr printed packaging: pressure sensitive labels, flexible packaging & continuous roll forms. (AA, estab 2000, empl 26, sales $5,000,000, cert: NMSDC)

Texas

7276 Age Industries, Ltd.
3601 County Rd, Ste 316C
Cleburne, TX 76031
Contact: Max Walls GM/VP Packaging Div
Tel: 281-799-0935
Email: max@ageindustries.com
Website: www.ageindustries.com
Mfr & dist packaging products. (Woman, estab 1974, empl 247, sales $72,000,000, cert: WBENC)

7277 American Carton Company
607 S Wisteria St
Mansfield, TX 76063
Contact: Sales Rep
Tel: 817-473-2992
Email:
Website: www.americancarton.com
Mfr Folding Carton, Full Graphics Prepress Services. (Woman, estab 1992, empl 45, sales $8,000,000, cert: State, WBENC)

7278 Austin Foam Plastics, Inc.
2933 AW Grimes Blvd
Pflugerville, TX 78660
Contact: Lisa Carnett Project Leader
Tel: 512-251-6300
Email: lisa.carnett@a-f-p.com
Website: www.a-f-p.com
Packaging Design & testing; logistics; sustainable solutions; mfr corrugated boxes, wood crates & pallets, custom cases. (Woman, estab 1978, empl 228, sales $ 0, cert: WBENC)

7279 B.A.G. Corp.
1155 Kas Dr. Ste 170
Richardson, TX 75081
Contact: Sherlene A Wegner Marketing Assistant
Tel: 214-340-7060
Email: sherlene@bagcorp.com
Website: www.bagcorp.com
Bulk handling & supply chain solutions. (Woman, estab 1969, empl 100, sales $70,000,000, cert: WBENC)

7280 Boxes 4 U, Inc.
1405 E Plano Pkwy
Plano, TX 75074
Contact: Nikki Hernandez VP
Tel: 972-516-0002
Email: nikki@boxes4u.com
Website: www.boxes4u.com
Corrugated boxes and packaging materials. Shipping boxes, heavy duty boxes, cardboard sheets, bubblewrap, tape, stretch film, packing paper, kraft paper, styrofoam peanuts, biodegradeable peanuts, biodegradeable bubble, custom boxes, etc. (Hisp, estab 1991, empl 11, sales $ 0, cert: State, 8(a))

7281 Castle Business Solutions, LLC
2777 North Stemmons Frwy Ste 1242
Dallas, TX 75207
Contact: Sharon King CEO
Tel: 214-599-2880
Email: sharon@castlebusinesssolutions.net
Website: www.castlebusinesssolutions.com/
Directory & mailing list publishing, direct mail advertising, packaging & labeling services, warehousing & storage, custom computer programming services, data processing, hosting & related services. (Woman/AA, estab 2010, empl 3, sales $615,880, cert: State, NMSDC)

7282 CCA Distributions
12832 Tierra Karla Dr
El Paso, TX 79938
Contact: Carlos Camarena Owner
Tel: 915-239-1870
Email: carlos@ccadistributions.com
Website: www.ccadistributions.com
Dist Packaging Material: Stretch Film, Kraft Paper, Tape, Poly Strapping, Metal Strapping, Boxes, Kraft Paper Tubes, Chipboard. Poly Sheeting, Poly Bags, and more. (Minority, Woman, estab 2007, empl 2, sales , cert: State, NMSDC)

7283 Diamond Display Group Partners, Inc.
2637 Summit Ave Ste 303
Plano, TX 75074
Contact: Glenn Towery Business Devel Mgr
Tel: 972-636-0781
Email: glenn@ddg-corp.com
Website: www.diamonddisplaygroup.com
Corrugated & permanent displays & packaging, shipper style corrugated displays & POS signage, styrene, foamboard, vinyl, acrylic and metal. (Woman, estab 2003, empl 5, sales , cert: State, WBENC)

7284 Formers International, Inc.
3533 Preston Ave
Pasadena, TX 77505
Contact: Corina Carmona Business Dev Mgr
Tel: 281-998-9570
Email: corina@formers.com
Website: www.formers.com
Mfr bag forming assemblies: vertical form, fill & seal packaging machines. (Hisp, estab 1975, empl 39, sales $ 0, cert: City)

7285 Guardian Packaging Industries, LP
      3615 Security St
      Garland, TX 75042
      Contact: President
      Tel: 214-349-1500
      Email:
      Website: www.guardianpackaging.com
Design & manufacture protective packaging, Polyurethanes, Polyethylenes, Expanded Polystyrene, Rigid Urethanes and all Military Spec Foams, corrugated box shop. (Woman, estab 2005, empl 35, sales $3,900,000, cert: State, WBENC)

7286 Harris Packaging Corporation
      1600 Carson St
      Haltom City, TX 76117
      Contact: Jana Harris-Bickford CEO
      Tel: 817-429-6262
      Email: janab@harrispackaging.com
      Website: www.harrispackaging.com
Mfr corrugated & folding carton trays & boxes. (Woman, estab 1976, empl 130, sales $22,000,000, cert: WBENC)

7287 International Print & Packaging, Inc.
      951 Hwy 183 N.
      Liberty Hill, TX 78642
      Contact: Shelly Armstrong Digital Solutions Specialist
      Tel: 512-515-6333
      Email: shelly@dle-corp.com
      Website: www.ipp-corp.com
Mfr flexible packaging: labels, stickers, decals, shrink film, printed film, lidding materials, POP products, displays, table tents, shelf strips, hang tags, folding cartons, self sufficient manufacturing, inhouse graphics design department. (Woman, estab 1996, empl 90, sales $ 0, cert: State)

7288 Komplete Group, Inc.
      202 N Great Southwest Pkwy
      Grand Prairie, TX 75050
      Contact: Tariq Usmani Diversity Coord
      Tel: 214-252-8102
      Email: tusmani@kpak.com
      Website: www.kpak.com
Food copackaging, packaging equipment & supplies, thermoforming, commercial printing. (As-Pac, estab 1995, empl 150, sales , cert: State, NMSDC)

7289 New Century Packaging Systems, LLC
      401 N Carrol Ave, Ste 124
      Southlake, TX 76092
      Contact: Vanessa Brown General Mgr
      Tel: 972-725-0311
      Email: vbrown@newcenturypkg.net
      Website: www.newcenturypkg.net
Dist packaging materials & packaging equipment. (AA, estab 1972, empl 4, sales $1,900,000, cert: NMSDC)

7290 Southwest Packaging Solutions, LLC
      2472 Southwell Rd
      Dallas, TX 75229
      Contact: Edgar Sotelo President
      Tel: 903-440-3628
      Email: edgar@southwestpackaging.net
      Website: www.southwestpackaging.net
Contract packaging services, printed registered film packaging services, warehousing, display building, bundling, reverse logistics, blister pack, skin pack, mfg consulting for improved efficiencies. (Hisp, estab 2009, empl 30, sales $1,800,000, cert: NMSDC)

7291 Starpak Ltd.
      9690 W Wingfoot Rd
      Houston, TX 77041
      Contact: Catherine Beers Customer Service Dir
      Tel: 713-329-9183
      Email: cbeers@starpakltd.com
      Website: www.starpakltd.com
Converter and printer of flexible films for packaging of Food and Beverage products (Hisp, estab 2003, empl 350, sales $106,196,322, cert: NMSDC)

7292 Superbag USA Corp.
      9291 Baythorne Dr
      Houston, TX 77041
      Contact: Woody Hunt VP Sales
      Tel: 713-462-1173
      Email: whunt@superbag.com
      Website: www.superbag.com
Dist high density polyethylene grocery, retail bags & woven polypropylene bags. (Hisp, estab 1999, empl 250, sales $149,000,000, cert: NMSDC)

7293 TCP Universal
      3536 Hwy 6 South, Ste 118
      Sugarland, TX 77478
      Contact: Pep Ly President
      Tel: 281-966-8208
      Email: pep.ly@tcpuniversal.com
      Website: www.tcpuniversal.com
Can Liners, Biohazard Bags, Composite Bags, Ice Bags, Poly Bags, Produce Bags. (Minority, Woman, estab 2015, empl 3, sales , cert: State, City)

Washington

7294 Kalani Packaging, Inc.
      2525 W Casino Rd, Ste 8C
      Everett, WA 98204
      Contact: Shelly Dickson
      Tel: 425-347-0330
      Email: shelly@kalanipkg.com
      Website: www.kalanipkg.com
Dist packaging supplies: tape, stretch wrap, shipping labels, poly bags & sheeting, boxes, bubble wrap & custom printed labels. Also dist janitorial supplies, boxes & bags. (As-Pac, estab 2000, empl 12, sales , cert: NMSDC)

Wisconsin

7295 Chryspac - Quality Custom Solutions
130 W Edgerton Ave Ste 130
Milwaukee, WI 53207
Contact: Warren Scurlock Business Devel Mgr
Tel: 414-372-0541
Email: Sales@Chryspac.com
Website: www.chryspac.com

Packaging & assembly: quality inspection, containment sorting, assembling, re-work, reclamation, shrink wrapping & labeling. (AA, estab 2000, empl 50, sales $816,456, cert: NMSDC)

7296 Pac Basic
S10744 State Road 93
Eleva, WI 54738
Contact: Mindy Pedersen President
Tel: 715-552-1722
Email: mpedersen@pacbasic.com
Website: www.pacbasic.com

Packaging, corrugated, molded pulp & other various protective materials. (Woman, estab 2007, empl 4, sales $1,978,000, cert: WBENC)

7297 Packaging Specialties Inc.
W130 N10751 Washington Dr
Germantown, WI 53022
Contact: Hugh Ahn President
Tel: 262-512-1261
Email: hahn@packaging-specialties.com
Website: www.packaging-specialties.com

Dist packaging systems & materials. (As-Pac, estab 1973, empl 30, sales $ 0, cert: NMSDC)

7298 TechniSource Services Group
1025 S Moorland Rd 2057
Brookfield, WI 53005
Contact: Elizabeth Tran President
Tel: 800-864-2317
Email: james@technisourcegroup.com
Website: www.technisourcegroup.com

Dist packaging products & services: stretch films, shrink film, poly films, carton sealers, erectors, stretch wrappers, tapes & adhesives, corrugated & fiber boxes. (Minority, Woman, estab 1994, empl 50, sales $25,000,000, cert: NMSDC)

7299 Twin River LLC
2721 Harvey St
Hudson, WI 54016
Contact: Kathy Enerson President
Tel: 715-381-3067
Email: kathyb@twinriverllc.com
Website: www.twinriverllc.com

Packaging, fulfillment, high-speed shrink wrapping, blister pack, clamshells, poly & paper banding, labeling, barcoding, kitting, assembly, distribution, warehousing, POP displays, quality inspections & mailings. (Woman, estab 2009, empl 8, sales $357,450, cert: WBENC)

> **PHOTOGRAPHY, MOTION & STILL**
> Commercial photographers. Includes aerial photography, topographic mapping, film processors, photo labs, corporate and professional photography.
> NAICS Code 54

California

7300 Lightbox Libraries
320 Hedge Rd
Menlo Park, CA 94025
Contact: Cindy Lee Founder
Tel: 650-298-4759
Email: cindy.lee@lightboxlibraries.com
Website: www.lightboxlibraries.com
Custom photography & video production. (Minority, Woman, estab 2011, empl 2, sales $1,954,051, cert: NMSDC)

7301 Number 3 Inc.
108 W 2nd St, Ste 706
Los Angeles, CA 90012
Contact: Kal Yee
Tel: 323-646-8764
Email: kal@kalyee.com
Website: www.kalyee.com
Photography & videography. (As-Pac, estab 2000, empl 2, sales $100,000, cert: CPUC)

Florida

7302 APImaging, Inc.
19 SW 6th St
Miami, FL 33130
Contact: Diana Herrera VP Sales
Tel: 305-373-4774
Email: dianah@apimaging.com
Website: www.apimaging.com
Photo imaging & photo finishing services, commercial printing, studio photography, self adhesive signs & graphics, directional signs, posters, point of purchase signs, graphic displays, graphic design, trade shows & exhibits. (Woman/Hisp, estab 2013, empl 22, sales , cert: WBENC)

7303 Kerrick Williams Photography LLC
811 Hickory Glen Dr
Seffner, FL 33584
Contact: Kerrick Williams Owner
Tel: 813-571-3768
Email: kerrick@kerrickwilliams.com
Website: www.KerrickWilliams.com
Corporate Photography, Video Production: special event coverage, advertising, marketing archival. Onsite printing, Executive portraits, Head Shots, group functions. (AA, estab 1992, empl 1, sales , cert: State, City, NMSDC)

Illinois

7304 McLaren Photographic LLC
1482 Armstrong Court
Elk Grove Village, IL 60007
Contact: Fiona McLaren Owner
Tel: 847-668-8615
Email: fmclaren@mclarenphotographic.com
Website: www.mclarenphotographic.com
HD video, time-lapse, commercial photography, gigapanography & virtual mobile tours, commercial photographic services with portable studios & editing capabilities. (Woman, estab 2009, empl 1, sales , cert: WBENC)

7305 Powell Photography, Inc.
531 S Plymouth Court, Ste 101
Chicago, IL 60605
Contact: Victor Powell President
Tel: 312-922-6366
Email: vpowell@powellphotography.com
Website: www.powellphotography.com
Photography, photography services, digital imaging & retouching, photo composition, video, multi-media & graphics pre-production. (AA, estab 1976, empl 3, sales $440,000, cert: State, NMSDC)

7306 Yates Enterprises
213 N Stetson Ave
Chicago, IL 60601
Contact: Owen Donnelly VP Operations
Tel: 419-308-9938
Email: owen@yatesprotect.com
Website: www.yatesprotect.com
(AA, estab 2013, empl 10, sales $2,000,000, cert: NMSDC)

Massachusetts

7307 Melvin's Photo
34 Frank st
Watertown, MA 02472
Contact: Melvin Guante Owner
Tel: 617-942-3432
Email: melvin@melvinsphoto.com
Website: www.Melvinsphoto.com
Portrait photographic studios, still or video photography, business portrait, commercial, real estate & corporate event. (AA, Hisp, estab 2001, empl 1, sales , cert: State)

Michigan

7308 Stage 3 Productions
1532 N. Opdyke Rd Ste 700
Auburn Hills, MI 48326
Contact: Andre LaRoche President
Tel: 248-955-1250
Email: andre@stage3.com
Website: www.stage3.com
Commercial, advertising photography, digital imaging, illustration, graphic design, stage rental. (AA, estab 1984, empl 8, sales , cert: NMSDC)

Minnesota

7309 Code Creative Services
6001 Code Ave
Edina, MN 55436
Contact: Erin Schwind Owner
Tel: 952-922-8348
Email: erin@codecreativeservices.com
Website: www.codecreativeservices.com
Photography production, Estimating, Crew Sourcing, Location Scouting, Casting, Talent Negotiations, Budget Management, Catering, Travel Arrangements, Props, Permits & Insurance & Billing. (Woman, estab 2012, empl 1, sales $120,262, cert: WBENC)

Nevada

7310 Infinity Enterprises, Inc.
3347 S Highland Dr, Ste 304
Las Vegas, NV 89109
Contact: Audrey Dempsey President
Tel: 702-837-1128
Email: audrey@infinity-photo.com
Website: www.infinity-photo.com
Photography & graphic design: conventions & special events, food, corporate headshots, products & architecture, private sittings, weddings & retouching, web & print design, company branding, logo design & marketing, video editing. (Woman, estab 1993, empl 5, sales $532,467, cert: WBENC)

7311 Square Shooting
1800 Industrial Rd, Ste 103
Las Vegas, NV 89102
Contact: Jennifer Burkart Managing Partner
Tel: 702-721-9893
Email: jennifer@squareshooting.com
Website: www.squareshooting.com
Commercial photography, professional photographer, executive portrait photography, architecture, interior design, editorial, food & cocktail photography, advertising, fashion, lifestyle, resort, product, photography studio. Established in 2013, Square (Woman, estab 2013, empl 2, sales , cert: WBENC)

New York

7312 5th Avenue Digital
231W 29th St, Ste 1006
New York, NY 10001
Contact: Caitlin Elby Corporate Sales Assoc
Tel: 212-741-6427
Email: caitlin@5thavenuedigital.com
Website: www.5thavenuedigital.com
Corporate photography: promotional & marketing events, meetings & conventions, galas & award ceremonies, headshots, group photos & product shots. (Woman, estab 2008, empl 5, sales $2,560,552, cert: WBENC)

7313 Adrienne Nicole Productions, LLC
14 Dekalb Ave 3rd Fl
Brooklyn, NY 11201
Contact: Adrienne Nicole Exec Producer
Tel: - -
Email: info@producedbyanp.com
Website: www.producedbyanp.com
Videography, aerial video, drone video photography, drone photography, progress photos, story development, pre-production, post-production, motion graphics and animation, casting, photography, progress photos. (Woman/AA, estab 2011, empl 1, sales $986,000, cert: State, City, NMSDC)

7314 E. Lee White Photography, LLC
116 Duane St, 3rd F
New York, NY 10007
Contact: E. Lee White President
Tel: 917-584-8000
Email: lee@leewhite.com
Website: www.leewhite.com
Advertising photography, executive portraits. (AA, estab 2004, empl 1, sales , cert: NMSDC)

7315 SPA Digital Images, Ltd.
54 W 39th St, 16th fl
New York, NY 10018
Contact: Kelly Murphy President
Tel: 917-420-0940
Email: janine@spadigital.com
Website: www.spadigital.com
Commercial digital photography & digital retouching services. (Woman, estab 1994, empl 15, sales $5,165,450, cert: WBENC)

Washington

7316 Mike Nakamura Photography LLC
7414 337th Place SE
Fall City, WA 98024
Contact: Mike Nakamura Owner
Tel: 425-260-4033
Email: mike@mikenakamuraphotography.com
Website: www.mikenakamuraphotography.com/
Headshots, event & lifestyle photography, aerial & commercial photography. (As-Pac, estab 2013, empl 1, sales $110,000, cert: NMSDC)

Wisconsin

7317 Image Studios, Inc.
1100 S Lynndale Dr
Appleton, WI 54914
Contact: Molly Mader Operations Mgr
Tel: 920-738-4080
Email: molly@imagestudios.com
Website: www.imagestudios.com
Commercial Photography, Video Production, Computer Generated Imagery (CGI), Editing, Retouching, Aerial Photography, Post Production. (Woman, estab 1965, empl 18, sales $2,148,000, cert: State, WBENC)

PLASTIC PRODUCTS

Manufacturers and distributors of plexiglass, plastic, rubber and fiberglass products. Products range from supplies to aircraft and automobile parts, housewares and apparel accessories. NAICS Code 42

Arizona

7318 4front Tooling LLC dba 4front Manufacturing
3820 E Watkins St
Phoenix, AZ 85034
Contact: Joseph Baiz Owner
Tel: 480-966-1088
Email: joebaiz@4frontmfg.com
Website: www.4frontmfg.com
Plastic injection mold making, molding prototype & production, stampings, assembly & decorating. (Hisp, estab 2008, empl 20, sales $2,595,172, cert: NMSDC)

7319 All-Pac Distributng LLC
4859 E Gleneagle Dr
Chandler, AZ 85249
Contact: Adam Snow Sales Mgr
Tel: 480-861-0842
Email: asnow@allpaconline.com
Website: www.allpaconline.com
Mfr & dist returnable plastic packaging, injection molding, compression molding. (Woman, estab 2001, empl 3, sales $1,150,000, cert: NWBOC)

California

7320 Benchmark Displays LLC
75-145 St. Charles Place Ste 5
Palm Desert, CA 92211
Contact: Bonnie Miller VP Sales
Tel: 760-775-2424
Email: bonnie@benchmarkdisplays.com
Website: www.benchmarkdisplays.com
Mfr soft & hard vinyl store merchandising products, acrylic pos displays & fixtures, stock & custom molded & fabricated plastic literature holders. (Woman, estab 2009, empl 3, sales $349,750, cert: WBENC)

7321 Fairway Injection Molding Systems, Inc.
20109 Paseo Del Prado
Walnut, CA 91789
Contact: David Cockrell VP General Mgr
Tel: 909-595-2201
Email: dcockrell@fairwaymolds.com
Website: www.fairwaymolds.com
Plastic injection molding. (As-Pac, estab 2006, empl 72, sales , cert: NMSDC)

7322 L.W. Reinhold Plastics
8763 Crocker St
Los Angeles, CA 90003
Contact: Everett Woolum Engineering Mgr
Tel: 562-862-2714
Email: brenda@rpiplastics.com
Website: www.rpiplastics.com
Injection molded thermosets & thermoplastics, compression molded thermosets & transfer molded thermoset, prototyping, machining. (Minority, Woman, estab 1943, empl 26, sales $1,800,000, cert: NMSDC)

7323 MJB Plastics, Inc.
6615 E Pacifc Coast Hwy, Ste 270
Long Beach, CA 90803
Contact: Martin Brunn VP
Tel: 562-431-3337
Email: martybrunn@mjbplastics.com
Website: www.mjbplastics.com
Dist plastic materials. (Minority, Woman, estab 1993, empl 6, sales , cert: WBENC)

7324 Plastek Cards, Inc.
24412 S Main St Ste 104
Carson, CA 90745
Contact: Mark Robinson Dir of Marketing
Tel: 888-762-2737
Email: mark.robinson@plastekcards.com
Website: www.plastekcards.com
Blank, white PVC plastic cards with & without a magnetic strip, high coercivity Hi-Co or low coercivity Lo-Co. (As-Pac, estab 2004, empl 51, sales , cert: NMSDC)

7325 Plastikon Industries, Inc.
688 Sandoval Way
Hayward, CA 94544
Contact: Ron Yerrick Sales Specialist
Tel: 989-525-3310
Email: ryerrick@plastikon.com
Website: www.plastikon.com
Custom injection molding of thermal plastic products & packaging. (Nat Ame, estab 1984, empl 100, sales $38,000,000, cert: NMSDC)

7326 Prestige Mold
11040 Tacoma Dr
Rancho Cucamonga, CA 91730
Contact: Curt Corte Tech Sales
Tel: 909-980-6600
Email: curt.corte@prestigemold.com
Website: www.prestigemold.com
Mfr precision plastic injection molds. (Woman, estab 2004, empl 65, sales $11,000,000, cert: WBENC)

7327 Trademark Plastics, Inc.
807 Palmyrita Ave
Riverside, CA 92507
Contact: Gilbert McMoran Sales Mgr
Tel: 909-941-8810
Email: gmcmoran@trademarkplastics.com
Website: www.TrademarkPlastics.com
Mfr plastic, medical components. (Woman, estab 1989, empl 150, sales $14,000,000, cert: WBENC)

7328 Weldon Works, Inc.
1650 Mabury Rd
San Jose, CA 95133
Contact: Jennifer Easom CEO
Tel: 408-251-1161
Email: jenn@weldonworks.com
Website: www.weldonworks.com
Plastic Fabrication & Signage, Interior & Exterior Signs, ADA Signage, Lobby Signs, Window Graphics & Lettering, Menu Boards, Isle Signage, Banner, Stencils, Reflective Road Work/ Parking Signs, Full Color Digital Printing. (Woman, estab 1982, empl 3, sales $100,000, cert: State)

7329 Wright Engineered Plastics, Inc.
3663 N Laughlin Road Ste 201
Santa Rosa, CA 95403
Contact: Mike Nellis VP Mfg
Tel: 707-575-1218
Email: mnellis@wepmolding.com
Website: www.wepmolding.com
Plastic injection molding & contract manufacturing. (Woman, estab 1970, empl 48, sales $5,040,000, cert: CPUC)

7330 Yamada Enterprises Inc.
14070 Montfort Ct
San Diego, CA 92128
Contact: Hidehiko Yamada President
Tel: 858-248-1928
Email: hyamada@ugoplastics.com
Website: www.ugoplastics.com
Outsourcing plastic parts mfg. Plastic injection machine sales. Packaging machine sales. SMT surface mount technology machines sales. Consultation production machines. Cartner, Caser, palletizer. Conveyors. (As-Pac, estab 2013, empl 2, sales $300,000, cert: NMSDC)

Connecticut

7331 Technical Industries, Inc.
336 Pinewoods Rd
Torrington, CT 06790
Contact: Susan O. Parent CEO
Tel: 860-489-2160
Email: susan.parent@technicalindustriesinc.com
Website: www.technicalindustriesinc.com
Mfr plastic injection molded parts. (Woman, estab 1994, empl 30, sales $4,700,000, cert: WBENC)

Florida

7332 Alice Ink, Inc. dba Plastec Industries
350 SE First St
Delray Beach, FL 33483
Contact: Susan Yeager VP
Tel: 561-272-0018
Email: susan@plastecproducts.com
Website: www.plastecproducts.com
Plastic manufacturing. (Woman, estab 1981, empl 12, sales $18,000,000, cert: State)

7333 American Tool and Mold LLC
1700 Sunshine Dr
Clearwater, FL 33765
Contact: Phil Gaitan Dir of Sales
Tel: 727-447-7377
Email: pgaitan@a-t-m.com
Website: www.atmmolding.com
Design & construct complex, precision, multi-cavity plastic injection molding, thin-wall, stack, hot runner, unscrewing & two-shot molds built with the latest methods & technologies available. (Woman, estab 1992, empl 220, sales , cert: WBENC)

7334 Plastec USA Inc.
7752 NW 74th Ave
Miami, FL 33166
Contact: Julio Mejia Dir Reg Sales
Tel: 513-708-9091
Email: julio.mejia@mejiatechnologies.com
Website: www.plastecusa.com
Dist plastics processing machinery, ancillary equip, spare parts & MRO services, chemicals & plastic goods. (Hisp, estab 1985, empl 23, sales $20,000,000, cert: NMSDC)

7335 Precision Tool and Mold, Inc.
12050 44th St N
Clearwater, FL 33762
Contact: Sherry Mowery President
Tel: 727-573-4441
Email: sherry@precisiontoolmoldinc.com
Website: www.precisiontoolmoldinc.com
Design build & run plastic injection molded parts. Small to medium sized molds. Assembly work, pad printing, over molding & insert molding. (Woman, estab 1981, empl 30, sales $2,665,365, cert: WBENC)

Georgia

7336 Citation Plastics, LLC
5828 Riverstone Circle
Atlanta, GA 30339
Contact: Gregory Collingwood President
Tel: 248-798-7705
Email: gregcollingwood@citationplastics.com
Website: www.citationplastics.com
Dist Plastic Resins: High Density Polyethylene (HDPE)- Polypropylene (PP)- Talc & Glassed Filled Polypropylene- Glass Filled Nylon 6 & 66 (AA, estab 1998, empl 7, sales $189,000, cert: NMSDC)

7337 Dixien LLC
5286 Circle Dr
Lake City, GA 30260
Contact: Alex Garcia VP Mktg
Tel: 404-366-7427
Email: agarcia@dixien.com
Website: www.dixien.com
Stamping 100 ton to 1000 ton, welded sub-assemblies, tooling, plastic injection molding, blow molding & vaccum forming. (Hisp, estab 1961, empl 400, sales $25,000,000, cert: NMSDC)

7338 Joyce Fabrication LLC dba Custom Plastics & More
2625 Jason Industrial Pkwy Ste 700
Winston, GA 30187
Contact: Gail Moore President
Tel: 770-577-0661
Email: gailmoore@customplasticsandmore.com
Website: www.customplasticsandmore.com
Rigid plastic fabrication, hand cut sheet plastic; die stamped parts, CNC or hand routed plastic. (Woman, estab 2004, empl 4, sales $318,365, cert: WBENC)

7339 Marglen Industries
1748 Ward Mountain Rd
Rome, GA 30161
Contact: Ben McElrath President
Tel: 706-295-5621
Email: bmcelrath@marglen.us
Website: www.marglen.us
Recycle PET plastic containers, convert recycled PET water & soda bottles into cleaned washed flake, then convert the clean washed flake into a FDA approved, high IV, melt filtered pellet that can be used to make new bottles. (Woman, estab 1971, empl 150, sales $62,513,555, cert: WBENC)

7340 Standridge Color Corp.
1196 E Hightower Trail
Social Circle, GA 30025
Contact: Sherry Waters President
Tel: 770-464-3362
Email: swaters@standridgecolor.com
Website: www.standridgecolor.com
Mfr pellitized plastic pellets and color concentrates for the plastics industry. (Woman, estab 0, empl 1, sales , cert: WBENC)

7341 United Seal & Rubber Co. Inc.
7025 C Amwiler Industrial Dr
Atlanta, GA 30360
Contact: Kathy Alonso VP/General Mgr
Tel: 770-729-8880
Email: kalonso@unitedseal.com
Website: www.unitedseal.com
Mfr seals, gaskets, custom molded rubber parts, EMI Shielding products, lathe cut seals, extrusions, rubber to metal bonded parts, spliced & vulcanized parts. (Hisp, estab 1974, empl 28, sales $8,000,000, cert: NMSDC, SDB)

Iowa

7342 Engineered Plastic Components Inc.
1408 Zimmerman Dr S
Grinnell, IA 50112
Contact: Jeremy Barger Sales
Tel: 641-236-3100
Email: jbarger@epcmfg.com
Website: www.epcmfg.com
Mfr wire harness cover caps, injection molding. (As-Ind, estab 1998, empl 500, sales $200,000,000, cert: NMSDC)

Illinois

7343 Amtec Molded Products, Inc.
1355 Holmes Road Unit A
Elgin, IL 60123
Contact: Adithya Jayakar Sales Mgr
Tel: 815-226-0187
Email: adithyaj@amtecmolded.com
Website: www.amtecmolded.com
Plastic injection molding, insert molding, pad printing & sub-assemblies. (As-Ind, estab 1998, empl 35, sales $3,862,500, cert: NMSDC)

7344 Best Foam Fabricators, Inc.
9633 S Cottage Grove
Chicago, IL 60628
Contact: Aqui Hasty Mktg Mgr
Tel: 773-721-1006
Email: aqui@bff.com
Website: www.bff.com
Mfr thermoforming, high speed die cutting, heat sealing, CNC machining & injection molding. (Woman/AA, estab 1981, empl 60, sales $14,750,000, cert: NMSDC)

7345 Cope Plastics Inc.
PO Box 368
Godfrey, IL 62002
Contact: Bryan Cox COO
Tel: 618-467-7351
Email: bcox@copeplastics.com
Website: www.copeplastics.com
Plastic stock shapes (rod, sheet & tube) distribution & fabrication. (Woman, estab 1946, empl 350, sales $86,000,000, cert: NWBOC)

7346 E James & Co.
6000 S Oak Park Ave
Chicago, IL 60638
Contact: Mike Romano
Tel: 773-788-1881
Email: mike.romano@ejames.com
Website: www.ejames.com
Mfr & dist rubber & plastic products: V belts, rubber hose, plastic hose & hose assemblies. (Hisp, estab 1955, empl 14, sales $2,200,000, cert: NMSDC)

7347 Ebco
1330 Holmes Rd
Elgin, IL 60123
Contact: Bill Bernardo Sales
Tel: 847-531-9500
Email: bbernardo@ebcoinc.com
Website: www.ebcoinc.com
Rubber products: molded, extruded, rubber bonded, metal vibration isolators & plastic extrusions. (Hisp, estab 1951, empl 48, sales $20,000,000, cert: NMSDC)

7348 First American Plastics Molding Enterprise
810 Progressive Ln
South Beloit, IL 61080
Contact: Steven McGaw Sales Engineer
Tel: 815-624-8538
Email: info@firstamericanplastic.com
Website: www.firstamericanplastic.com
Custom plastic injection molding. (Nat Ame, estab 1993, empl 130, sales $12,000,000, cert: NMSDC)

7349 HST Materials, Inc.
1631 Brummel Ave
Elk Grove Village, IL 60007
Contact: Kathryn Miller President
Tel: 847-640-1803
Email: kmiller@hstmaterials.com
Website: www.hstmaterials.com
Custom die-cutting & fabrication of non-metallics, including sponge & dense rubber, plastic, films & tapes used as gaskets & sealing devices. (Woman, estab 1987, empl 20, sales $4,428,617, cert: WBENC)

7350 LSL Industries, Inc.
5535 N Wolcott Ave
Chicago, IL 60640
Contact: Jerry Czaja
Tel: 773-878-1100
Email: jerry.czaja@lslhealthcare.com
Website: www.lslhealthcare.com
Mfg plastics & procedural kit assembly & packaging. (As-Ind, estab , empl , sales , cert: NMSDC)

7351 Magenta LLC
15160 New Ave
Lockport, IL 60441
Contact: Stephanie Smith Business Dev Exec
Tel: 630-737-9606
Email: ssmith@magentallc.com
Website: www.magentallc.com
Design, development & mfr injection molded components-primarily packaging— closures and containers. (Woman, estab 1969, empl 81, sales $14,900,000, cert: WBENC)

PLASTIC PRODUCTS

7352 Matrix IV, Inc.
610 E Judd St
Woodstock, IL 60098
Contact: Patrica Miller President
Tel: 815-338-4500
Email: pmiller@matrix4.com
Website: www.matrix4.com
Mfr injection molded parts, 3D printing, design & engineering. (Woman, estab 1976, empl 25, sales $2,450,000, cert: WBENC)

7353 Midwest Insert Composite Molding & Assembly Corp.
3940 Industrial Ave
Rolling Meadows, IL 60008
Contact: Chirag Patel President
Tel: 847-818-8444
Email: chirag.pate@micmolding.com
Website: www.micmolding.com
Mfr plastic injection molded products. (Minority, estab 2015, empl 23, sales $2,526,000, cert: NMSDC)

7354 Thermal-Tech Systems, Inc.
750 W Hawthorne Lane
West Chicago, IL 60185
Contact: Joe Majchrowski Sales
Tel: 630-639-5115
Email: jm@thermal-tech.com
Website: www.thermal-tech.com
Dist plastic injection molders, service and repair of manifolds. (Woman, estab 1986, empl 10, sales $2,500,000, cert: WBENC)

7355 TransWorld Plastic Films, Inc.
150 N 15th St
Rochelle, IL 61068
Contact: Rodolfo Hernandez Business Devel
Tel: 815-561-7117
Email: rhernandez@transworldplasticfilms.com
Website: www.transworldplasticfilms.com
Polyethylene film for the automotive, tire & rubber industries used in the manufacturing & packaging process. (Minority, Woman, estab 2007, empl 31, sales , cert: NMSDC, WBENC)

7356 Young Technology Inc.
900 W. Fullerton Ave.
Addison, IL 60101
Contact: Young Sohn President
Tel: 630-690-4320
Email: youngsohn@ytinc.com
Website: www.ytinc.com
Mfr molded rubber, plastic & forged steel: shifter knobs, bezels, decorative molding & cable components, leather wrapped & chrome plated. (As-Pac, estab 1985, empl 350, sales $6,000,000, cert: NMSDC)

Indiana

7357 A. H. Furnico, Inc.
6425 English Ave. Unit 1A
Indianapolis, IN 46278
Contact: Benjamin Liu President
Tel: 317-802-9363
Email: ben.liu@ahfurnico.com
Website: www.ahfurnico.com
Polystyrene extruded mouldings with PVC veneers. (As-Pac, estab 1999, empl 5, sales $3,880,000, cert: NMSDC)

7358 Accutech Mold & Machine, Inc.
2817 Goshen Rd
Fort Wayne, IN 46808
Contact: Darrin Geiger VP
Tel: 260-471-6102
Email: dgeiger@accutechmoldinc.com
Website: www.accutechmoldinc.com
Plastic injection molding, Insert plastic injection molder of cables/connectors, rapid prototype tooling builder/injection molding, production machining of brass, aluminum & metals, prototype machining of brass, aluminum & metals. (Woman, estab 1996, empl 70, sales $3,000,000, cert: WBENC)

7359 Calico Precision Molding, LLC
1211 Progress Rd
Fort Wayne, IN 46808
Contact: Nancy Rivera Sales Rep
Tel: 260-484-4500
Email: nancyr@calicopm.com
Website: www.calicopm.com/
Custom plastic injection molding. (AA, estab 2001, empl 28, sales , cert: NMSDC)

7360 Hi-Tech Foam Products, LLC
One Technology Way
Indianapolis, IN 46268
Contact: John Metaxas VP
Tel: 317-615-1515
Email: jmetaxas@hitechfoam.com
Website: www.hitechfoam.com
Convert, design, package, mold, form, cut & route foam rubber. Laminating foam to foam, foam to corrugated, foam to plastic. Protective, cushioning, acoustical, thermal, polyethylene, polyurethane, crosslink, EVA, EDPM rubber. (AA, estab , empl 35, sales $6,000,000, cert: NMSDC)

7361 Hoosier Molded Products
3603 Progress Dr
South Bend, IN 46628
Contact: Brian Johnson Sales Mgr
Tel: 574-235-7900
Email: johnson@hoosiermp.com
Website: www.hoosiermp.com
Mfr quality injecting molded products. (Hisp, estab 1996, empl 100, sales $14,000,000, cert: NMSDC)

7362 Lorentson Manufacturing Co., Inc.
PO Box 932
Kokomo, IN 46903
Contact: John Routt VP / COO
Tel: 765-452-4425
Email: jroutt@lorentson.com
Website: www.lorentson.com
Design & build plastic injection molds, injection molding machines. (Woman, estab 1949, empl 100, sales $16,000,000, cert: WBENC)

7363 Tomken Plastic Technologies, Inc.
4601 N Superior Dr.
Muncie, IN 47303
Contact: Kevin Undem Sales/Engineering
Tel: 765-284-2472
Email: kevinu@tomkenplastics.com
Website: www.tomkenplastics.com
Precision plastic injection molding, tooling, & injection molding. (Woman, estab 1960, empl 40, sales $6,000,000, cert: WBENC)

7364 Vidal Plastics, LLC
 318 Main St Ste 207
 Evansville, IN 47708
 Contact: Alfonso Vidal President
 Tel: 812-431-8075
 Email: alfonso@vidalplastics.com
 Website: www.vidalplastics.com
Dist resins, from prime raw materials to recycled compounds. (Minority, estab 2009, empl 2, sales , cert: NMSDC)

Kentucky

7365 Foam Design Inc.
 444 Transport Ct
 Lexington, KY 40511
 Contact: Chris Harrod Sales Engineer
 Tel: 502-682-8562
 Email: charrod@foamdesign.com
 Website: www.foamdesign.com
Commercial & industrial foam conversion capabilities & design, intricate parts cut to precise tolerances. (Woman, estab 1974, empl 102, sales $18,500,000, cert: WBENC)

Louisiana

7366 Noble Plastics Inc.
 318 Burleigh Lane
 Grand Coteau, LA 70541
 Contact: Sandy Rowell Inside Sales
 Tel: 337-662-5374
 Email: sandy@nobleplastics.com
 Website: www.nobleplastics.com
SPE, MAPP, ASME, Product design, Contract manufacturing, Scientific molding, Inspection, Assembly & fulfillment, Automation systems. (Woman, estab 2000, empl 30, sales $4,900,000, cert: WBENC)

Massachusetts

7367 Polyneer, Inc.
 259D Samuel Barnet Blvd
 New Bedford, MA 02745
 Contact: Nancy DeOliveira Customer Service
 Tel: 508-998-5225
 Email: ndeoliveira@polyneer.com
 Website: www.polyneer.com
Design & mfg polymeric products. (Hisp, estab 2001, empl 39, sales $2,600,000, cert: NMSDC)

7368 TPE Solutions, Inc.
 3 Patterson Rd
 Shirley, MA 01464
 Contact: Jonas Angus President
 Tel: 978-425-3033
 Email: jonas.angus@tpesinc.com
 Website: www.tpesinc.com
Design, mfr & dist Thermoplastic elastomers (TPEs). (AA, estab 2004, empl 5, sales $3,000,000, cert: NMSDC)

Michigan

7369 Accu-Mold, LLC
 7622 S Sprinkle Rd
 Portage, MI 49002
 Contact: Dave Felicijan President
 Tel: 269-323-0388
 Email: davidf@accu-moldinc.com
 Website: www.accum-moldinc.com
Overmold & two shot mold, hybrid metal/plastic parts, high & low pressure plastic injection molds, machined plastic or metal parts, SLA plastic parts, metal-to-plastic conversions. (Nat Ame, estab 1977, empl 15, sales $4,118,893, cert: NMSDC)

7370 Agape Plastics, Inc.
 11474 1st Ave NW
 Grand Rapids, MI 49534
 Contact: Jeff Powers Sales Admin
 Tel: 616-735-4091
 Email: jpowers@agapeplastics.com
 Website: www.agapeplastics.com
Plastic Injection molder serving the automotive and furniture industries. (Woman, estab 1975, empl 150, sales , cert: WBENC)

7371 Albar Industries
 780 Whitney Dr
 Lapeer, MI 48446
 Contact: Glenn Curtis President
 Tel: 810-667-0150
 Email: gcurtis@albar.com
 Website: www.albar.com
Mfr & paint blow-molded, injection-molded & compression molded plastic parts, stamped metal parts for the automotive industry. (Woman, estab 1969, empl 250, sales , cert: WBENC)

7372 Ammex Plastics
 725 Ternes Dr
 Monroe, MI 48162
 Contact: David Ayala President
 Tel: 734-241-9622
 Email:
 Website: www.ammexplastics.com
Mfr & design plastic injection molded parts. (Hisp, estab 1999, empl 17, sales $3,300,000, cert: NMSDC)

7373 Argent International
 41016 Concept Dr
 Plymouth, MI 48170
 Contact: Tomas Flores Sales Mgr
 Tel: 734-582-9800
 Email: tflores@argent-international.com
 Website: www.argent-international.com
Die cut foam, felt, fabric adhesive. (Woman, estab 1976, empl 120, sales , cert: WBENC)

7374 Atlantic Precision Products
 51234 Filomena Dr
 Shelby Township, MI 48315
 Contact: Rob Pryomski General Mgr
 Tel: 586-532-9420
 Email: rpryomski@atlanticpp.com
 Website: www.atlanticpp.com
Custom injection molding, functional/decorative plastics, insert molding, welding, sonic, vibration, heatstaking, assembly. Fully certified CMM Lab with color approval capabilities. (Minority, Woman, estab 2004, empl 26, sales $5,200,000, cert: NMSDC)

PLASTIC PRODUCTS

7375 CG Plastics, Inc.
5349 Rusche Dr NW
Comstock Park, MI 49321
Contact: Shelly Miller CFO
Tel: 616-308-7838
Email: shelly.miller@commercialtool.com
Website: www.cgplastics.com
Tryout, sampling and production plastic injection molding. Capabilities for design and manufacturing of plastic injection molds and custom molding. Gauge & Fixture, Automation, 6-axis robots, Large 5-axis CNC machining. (Woman, estab 0, empl , sales , cert: WBENC)

7376 Colonial Plastics, Inc
51734 Filomena Dr
Shelby Township, MI 48315
Contact: Michele Simo
Tel: 586-991-5150
Email: mms@colgrp.com
Website: www.colgrp.com
Injection molds, compression molds, blow molds, vacuum molds, prototype molds, hybrid molds, bridge molds, production molds, machining, assemblies, tryouts, product developement, product design & sorting. (Woman, estab 1988, empl 110, sales $8,200,000, cert: WBENC)

7377 Concordant Healthcare Solutions, Inc.
200 E. Big Beaver
Troy, MI 48083
Contact: James P Young CEO
Tel: 248-321-3899
Email: jyoung@concordanthealth.com
Website: www.concordanthealth.com
NCQA Certified in Patient Centered Medical Home Recognition for PCPs and Specialists. Staff training in cultural competency and communication skills. Improve hospital HCAHPS total performance scores. (AA, estab 2009, empl 8, sales , cert: NMSDC)

7378 Diversified Engineering & Plastics
1801 Wildwood Ave
Jackson, MI 49202
Contact: Anita Quillen President
Tel: 517-789-8118
Email: aquillen@deplastics.com
Website: www.wwww.deplastics.com
Plastic Injection Molding, Design/Engineering Services, Plastic Part Assembly. (Minority, Woman, estab 2010, empl 130, sales $14,497,480, cert: NMSDC)

7379 DN Plastics
1415 Steele Ave SW
Grand Rapids, MI 49507
Contact: Raj Agrawal President
Tel: 616-942-6060
Email: raj@dnplasticscorp.com
Website: www.dnplasticscorp.com
Polymer compounding for custom & toll manufacturing, Thermoplastic Elastomers (TPE), Thermoplastic Olefins (TPO) & filled Polypropylene compounds. (As-Ind, estab 0, empl 1, sales , cert: NMSDC)

7380 Eagle Fasteners
185 Park Dr
Troy, MI 48083
Contact: Theresa C. Srock President
Tel: 248-373-1441
Email: tsrock@eaglefasteners.com
Website: www.eaglefasteners.com
Custom injection molded plastic parts, design & fabricate tooling. (Woman, estab 1976, empl 9, sales , cert: WBENC)

7381 Elite Mold & Engineering
51548 Filomena Dr
Shelby Township, MI 48315
Contact: Daniel Mandeville Sales Engineer
Tel: 586-314-4000
Email: dj@teameliteonline.com
Website: www.teameliteonline.com
Dist close tolerance plastic parts for the automotive, consumer product, electronic & medical device industries. (Nat Ame, estab 1982, empl 34, sales $3,576,887, cert: NMSDC)

7382 Engineered Plastic Products
699 James L. Hart Pkwy
Ypsilanti, MI 48197
Contact: Aschandria Fisher Business Mgr
Tel: 734-483-2500
Email: afisher@eppmfg.com
Website: www.eppmfg.com
Injection molded plastic assembly & sequencing. (AA, estab 1987, empl 500, sales $50,000,000, cert: NMSDC)

7383 Gemini Plastics, Inc.
4385 Garfield St
Ubly, MI 48475
Contact: Melanie Cappello Mgr Business Devel
Tel: 248-435-7271
Email: melaniecappello@geminigroup.net
Website: www.geminigroup.net
Mfr engineered plastic extrusion products: transportation, medical, lawn & garden, consumer, & appliance. (Woman, estab 1972, empl 110, sales $60,000,000, cert: WBENC)

7384 Jenerxx Inc.
307 West Sixth St Ste 209
Royal Oak, MI 48067
Contact: Paul Chaplin Acct Mgr
Tel: 810-225-1600
Email: paul@jenerxx.com
Website: www.jenerxx.com
Dist injection grade resins ranging from engineered plastics to commodities. (Woman, estab 2000, empl 5, sales $760,000, cert: WBENC)

7385 JLC Group LLC
287 Executive Dr
Troy, MI 48083
Contact: William Chen Dir Ph.D.
Tel: 248-792-3281
Email: wchen@jlcgroupllc.com
Website: www.jlcgroupllc.com
Dist casting parts, forging parts & machine finished parts, plastic injected molds & plastic parts. (Minority, Woman, estab 2010, empl 5, sales , cert: WBENC)

7386 Latin American Industries, LLC
1036 Ken-O-Sha Industrial Dr SE
Grand Rapids, MI 49508
Contact: Scott Bigger General Mgr
Tel: 616-301-1878
Email: sbigger@laiinc.net
Website: www.laiinc.net
Plastic injection molding & assembly, molding machines. (Minority, Woman, estab 2000, empl 10, sales $1,000,000, cert: NMSDC)

7387 Molding Concepts, Inc.
6700 Sims St
Sterling Heights, MI 48313
Contact: Norman Fouts President
Tel: -   -
Email: slfouts@moldingconcepts.com
Website: www.moldingconcepts.com

Plastic injection molds & parts, plastic parts, CNC machining, 3D printing, Additive manufacturing, Prototype, Short run, Production, High heat resin. (Woman, estab 1987, empl 9, sales $800,000, cert: WBENC)

7388 Premier Plastic Resins, Inc.
3079 S Baldwin Rd
Orion, MI 48359
Contact: Michelle Cloutier Sales Engineer
Tel: 877-777-4514
Email: mcloutier@premierplasticresins.com
Website: www.premierplasticresins.com

Dist thermoplastic resins for injection molding. ABS, Nylon, Polycarbonate, PBT, Acetal. Automotive approved grades. Prime branded materials available, such as DuPont, Sabic, Covestro, etc. (Woman, estab 2007, empl 5, sales $1,200,000, cert: WBENC)

7389 Primera Plastics
3424 Production Court
Zeeland, MI 49464
Contact: Noel Cuellar President
Tel: 616-748-6248
Email: noelc@primera-inc.com
Website: www.primera-inc.com

Plastic injection molding & assembly. (Hisp, estab 1994, empl 140, sales , cert: NMSDC)

7390 Quality Assured Plastics, Inc.
1200 Crandall Pkwy
Lawrence, MI 49064
Contact: Annette Crandall President
Tel: 269-674-3888
Email: acrandall@qapinc.com
Website: www.qapinc.com

Custom injection molding, insert/overmolding, & assembly capabilities, molding commodity & engineering resins, Nylon, TPE, ABS, PEEK, Valox, Polystyrene, HDPE, TPO & Polypropylene. (Woman, estab 1986, empl 60, sales $5,200,000, cert: WBENC)

7391 Sejasmi Industries, Inc.
6100 Bethuy
Fair Haven, MI 48023
Contact: Nichole Roemer Production Control
Tel: 586-725-5300
Email: nicholer@us.sejasmi.com
Website: www.us.sejasmi.com

Contract manufacturer of plastic injection molded parts & light assemblies. (As-Ind, estab 2007, empl 50, sales , cert: NMSDC)

7392 Sur-Flo Plastics & Engineering, Inc.
24358 Groesbeck Hwy
Warren, MI 48089
Contact: Jean Douglass IT Security Mgr
Tel: 586-859-6050
Email: jdouglass@sur-flo.com
Website: www.sur-flo.com

Custom injection molded component or assembly: Plastic Injection Molding, Engineering, Program Management, Assembly, Quality. (Woman, estab 1977, empl 207, sales , cert: NMSDC)

7393 Western Diversified Plastics LLC
53150 N Main St
Mattawan, MI 49071
Contact: George Kawwas Dir of Business Dev
Tel: 269-668-3377
Email: george.kawwas@westerndp.com
Website: www.westerndp.com

Mfr close tolerance injection & insert molded electromechanical components, engineering grade plastic resin. (AA, estab 2005, empl 75, sales , cert: NMSDC)

7394 Williamston Products, Inc.
845 Progress Ct
Williamston, MI 48895
Contact: Nigam Tripathi President
Tel: 517-655-2131
Email: nigam@wpius.com
Website: www.wpius.com

Blow mold, injection mold, foaming, hand wrapping, cutting, trim, sewing, lamination, prototyping, assembly. (As-Ind, estab 2006, empl 450, sales $42,000,000, cert: NMSDC)

Minnesota

7395 Classic Acrylics Inc.
11040 Industrial Circle NW
Elk River, MN 55330
Contact: Kathy Berg Sales Exec
Tel: 763-241-5221
Email: kberg@classicacrylics.com
Website: www.classicacrylics.com

Plastic fabrication: POP & POS displays, acrylic cereal boxes, literature & brochure holders, advertising & specialty items, sign holders, screened acrylic signs, display cases, food service bins, LED lighting. (Hisp, estab 1998, empl 22, sales $3,754,000, cert: NMSDC)

7396 Lakeview Industries
1225 Lakeview Dr
Chaska, MN 55318
Contact: DeDe Bennett inside Sales
Tel: 952-368-3500
Email: dbennett@lakeviewindustries.com
Website: www.lakeivewindustries.com

Dist molded rubber products & fabricate flexible products. (Woman, estab 1974, empl 49, sales $1,000,000, cert: WBENC)

7397 Proto Edge Inc.
8550 Revere Lane N Ste 228
Maple Grove, MN 55369
Contact: Louis Roberts President
Tel: 612-432-4303
Email: lou@protoedge.com
Website: www.protoedge.com

Dist metal & plastic parts for existing and new product development engineered designs, focused on a wide range of processes and materials. (AA, estab 2011, empl 3, sales $125,000, cert: NMSDC)

7398 Thermotech, Inc.
      1302 S 5th St
      Hopkins, MN 55343
      Contact: Andrea Hinrichs
      Tel: 734-634-1816
      Email: andrea.hinrichs@thermotech.com
      Website: www.thermotech.com
Mfr precision plastic parts, thermoplastic molding, thermoset molding, insert molding, two-shot molding, micromolding & assembly. (As-Ind, estab 1949, empl 522, sales $83,000,000, cert: NMSDC)

7399 TMI Coatings, Inc.
      3291 Terminal Dr
      St. Paul, MN 55121
      Contact: Tracy Gliori President
      Tel: 651-452-6100
      Email: tmi@tmicoatings.com
      Website: www.tmicoatings.com
Protective coatings & linings, spray on urethane foam insulation, chemical resistant floor coverings & containment dike linings. (Woman, estab 1985, empl 75, sales $12,162,000, cert: WBENC)

North Carolina

7400 Central Carolina Products
      250 W Old Glencoe Rd
      Burlington, NC 27217
      Contact: Jason Greenhill President
      Tel: 336-226-0005
      Email: jgreenhill@isotechintl.com
      Website: www.centralcarolinaproducts.com
Plastic injection molding: assembly & finishing capabilities. (Hisp, estab 1993, empl 72, sales , cert: NMSDC)

7401 Core Technology Molding Corp.
      2911 E. Gate City Blvd
      Greensboro, NC 27410
      Contact: Brandon Frederick Mfg Engineer
      Tel: 919-273-3408
      Email: brandon.frederick@coretechnologycorp.com
      Website: www.coretechnologycorp.com
Product concept & design services, CAD part & mold design, Mold Flow analysis, Prototyping, raw material selection & testing, New all-electric injection molding machines ranging from 200 ton to 400 ton. (AA, estab 2007, empl 25, sales $10,000,000, cert: NMSDC)

7402 Raleigh-Durham Rubber & Gasket Co., Inc.
      PO Box 90397
      Raleigh, NC 27675
      Contact: Judy Hooks President
      Tel: 919-781-6817
      Email: judyh@raleighdurhamrubber.com
      Website: www.raleighdurhamrubber.com
Mfr & dist rubber gaskets. (Woman, estab , empl , sales , cert: WBENC)

7403 RubberMill, Inc.
      9897 Old Liberty Rd
      Liberty, NC 27298
      Contact: Shawn Baldwin Sales Mgr
      Tel: 704-458-2653
      Email: sbaldwin@rubbermill.com
      Website: www.rubbermill.com
OEM custom parts manufactured from solid and sponge rubber, foams, and nonwovens. Gaskets and Seals, Custom Molded Parts, Acoustical Insulation Parts, Urethane Products, Balls, Lab Stoppers, Cleanout Balls. (Woman, estab 1987, empl 56, sales $11,000,000, cert: WBENC)

7404 Sky Leap LLC
      PO Box 16368
      Chapel Hill, NC 27516
      Contact: Lili Engelhardt CEO
      Tel: 919-338-2580
      Email: office@skyleapllc.com
      Website: www.skyleapllc.com
Mfr & design injected molded tool organizers for tools: wrenches, screw drivers, pliers, and sockets. (Minority, Woman, estab 2013, empl 2, sales $425,000, cert: NMSDC)

Nebraska

7405 Lenco, Inc. - PMC
      10240 Deer Park Rd
      Waverly, NE 68462
      Contact: Clarke McGuire VP
      Tel: 402-786-2000
      Email: cmcguire@pmc-group.com
      Website: www.lencopmc.com
Dist defect-free molded & assembled products, injection molding. (As-Ind, estab 1963, empl 160, sales , cert: State, NMSDC)

New Jersey

7406 L-E-M Plastics& Supply Inc.
      255 Highland Cross
      Rutherford, NJ 07070
      Contact: Ellen Pietrowitz-Phillips President
      Tel: 201-933-9150
      Email: ellenp@l-e-mplastics.com
      Website: www.l-e-mplastics.com
Fabriate & dist raw material plastic & rubber, Sheet, rod, tubing & film cut to size. Machining of all plastic, build to print. Steel rule die punching of thin plastic & rubber. (Woman, estab 1974, empl 12, sales $1,200,000, cert: WBENC)

7407 Sigma Extruding Corp. DBA Sigma Stretch Film
      808 Page Ave, Bldg 8 Bldg 8
      Lyndhurst, NJ 07071
      Contact: Maria Samuelson
      Tel: 201-507-9100
      Email: maria.samuelson@sigmaplastics.com
      Website: www.sigmastretchfilm.com
Mfr plastics. (As-Pac, estab 1988, empl 354, sales $396,000,000, cert: NMSDC)

7408 Sysmind LLC
      38 Washington Rd
      Princeton Junction, NJ 08550
      Contact: Business Devel Specialist
      Tel: 609-897-9670
      Email: info@sysmind.com
      Website: www.sysmind.com
Fabricate plastic components & fasteners for computer, aerospace, electronic, instrumentation, etc. applications. Prototype to production. Also stock molded nylon fasteners. (Woman/As-Ind, estab 1999, empl 456, sales $45,000,000, cert: NMSDC, WBENC)

New York

7409 Extreme Molding LLC
25 Gibson St
Watervliet, NY 12189
Contact: Joanne Moon Managing Partner
Tel: 518-266-6261
Email: joanne@extrememolding.com
Website: www.extrememolding.com
Injection molding: silicone, TPE, floropolymers, teflon, polycarbonate, polypropelene, Ultem, CAD design, material selection assistance, rapid prototyping, overmolding, compression molding, packaging. (Woman, estab 2002, empl 20, sales $1,000,000, cert: State)

7410 Mechanical Rubber Products Company, Inc.
77 Forester Ave, Ste 1
Warwick, NY 10990
Contact: Cedric Glasper President
Tel: 845-986-2271
Email: alisa.sherow@mechanicalrubber.com
Website: www.mechanicalrubber.com
Mfr elastomeric (rubber) products. (AA, estab 1995, empl 21, sales $945,000, cert: NMSDC)

Ohio

7411 Advanced Engineering Solutions Incorporated
250 Advanced Dr
Springboro, OH 45066
Contact: Scott Paulson Business Dev
Tel: 937-743-6900
Email: spaulson@aesi-usa.com
Website: www.advancedinternational.com
Tooling, CNC, punch press, subassembly, automated equipment, injection molded plastics. (Minority, Woman, estab 1995, empl 35, sales $2,250,000, cert: NMSDC)

7412 Axium Plastics LLC
9005 Smiths Mill Rd N
Johnstown, OH 43031
Contact: Tammy Hoffman Business Devel Mgr
Tel: 678-464-2259
Email: thoffman@axiumplastics.com
Website: www.axiumplastics.com
Extrusion Blow Molding, Injection Stretch Blow Molding, Injection Molding, Modeling, Design, Silk Screening, Pressure Sensitive Labeling (As-Ind, estab 2010, empl 250, sales $102,000,000, cert: NMSDC)

7413 Composite Technologies LLC
401 N Keowee St
Dayton, OH 45404
Contact: Karen Pierce Sales & Marketing Mgr
Tel: 937-228-2880
Email: kpierce@ctcplastics.com
Website: www.ctcplastics.com
Mfr plastic pallets made from 100% recycled plastic, compression & injection molding, of plastic parts made from recycled & virgin materials. (As-Pac, estab 1994, empl 150, sales $27,000,000, cert: NMSDC)

7414 EnKon, LLC dba Broadway
6344 Webster St
Dayton, OH 45414
Contact: Jodi Walters Member
Tel: 937-890-2221
Email: jodi.walters@enkonllc.com
Website: www.broadwaymold.com
Injection molds, components, mold repairs, Precision Fabrication, CNC Machining, welding, turning, Electrode manufacturing, EDM'ING, Wire EDM, Polish, Milling, OD, ID, and surface grinding, Design. (Woman, estab 1955, empl 12, sales , cert: WBENC)

7415 Ernie Green Industries
2030 Dividend Dr
Columbus, OH 43228
Contact: Bill Dunlevy VP Sales & Marketing
Tel: 614-949-1714
Email: bdunlevy@egindustries.com
Website: www.egi.net/
Plastic injection molding, paint, pad print, silk screen, hot stamp, graphic emblems, sonic welding, chrome plating, assembly, bar code labeling, shrink wrap & kit/unitized packaging. (AA, estab 1987, empl 450, sales $28,000,000, cert: NMSDC)

7416 HESS Advanced Technology, Inc.
PO Box 17669
Dayton, OH 45417
Contact: Frederick Edmonds CEO
Tel: 937-268-4377
Email: fred.edmonds@gmail.com
Website: www.plastikleen.net
Mfr protective coatings: surveillance cameras, lens/domes, PC's, laptops, PDA's, plasma screens & anti-microbial skin protector. (AA, estab , empl , sales $825,000, cert: NMSDC)

7417 Industry Products Company
500 Statler Rd
Piqua, OH 45356
Contact: Aaron Blakely Sales Specialist
Tel: 937-778-0585
Email: ablakely@industryproductsco.com
Website: www.industryproductsco.com
Mfr precision die-cut & formed products, gasket & sealing products, rubber-coated steel & alloys, compressed fiber, cork, neoprene, phenolic, nylon, Mylar, felts, PE, PP, rubber, etc. (Woman, estab 1966, empl 450, sales $80,000,000, cert: WBENC)

7418 MVP Plastics, Inc.
15005 Enterprise Way
Middlefield, OH 44062
Contact: Darrell McNair President
Tel: 440-834-1790
Email: darrellm@mvpplastics.com
Website: www.mvpplastics.com
Custom injection molding, decorating & assembly of plastics components. (AA, estab 2009, empl 30, sales $20,000,000, cert: NMSDC)

7419 PMC SMART Solutions LLC
9825 Kenwood Rd Ste 302
Cincinnati, OH 45242
Contact: Lisa Jennings CEO
Tel: 513-557-5222
Email: ljennings@pmcsmartsolutions.com
Website: www.pmcsmartsolutions.com
Development engineering, contract manufacturing & injection molding services for medical device, transportation & commercial electronics markets. (Woman, estab 1929, empl 200, sales $33,000,000, cert: WBENC)

7420 Polymer Technologies
1835 James Pkwy
Heath, OH 43056
Contact: Sharad Thakkar President
Tel: 740-929-5500
Email: sharad@polymertechnologiesinc.com
Website: www.polymertechnologiesinc.com
Provide reprocessed & wide spec resins, form, film. powder, parts & return back in certified pellet form. (As-Ind, estab 2002, empl 38, sales $7,000,000, cert: NMSDC)

7421 Shirley K's Storage Trays LLC
PO Box 2519
Zanesville, OH 43702
Contact: Devin Hall Sales & Marketing Coord
Tel: 740-868-8140
Email: devin.hall@shirleyks.com
Website: www.shirleyks.com
Mfr storage products, high-impact polystyrene or high-density polyethylene; labeling tags, casters, locking lids & imprinting. (Woman, estab 2013, empl 8, sales $1,410,400, cert: WBENC)

7422 Tom Smith Industries, Inc.
500 Smith Dr
Clayton, OH 45315
Contact: James Pugh Sales Mgr
Tel: 937-832-1555
Email: jpugh@tomsmithindustries.com
Website: www.tomsmithindustries.com
Design & build plastic injection molds. Custom injection molding of thermoplastics; assemble computer components. (Woman, estab 1980, empl 85, sales $25,367,000, cert: WBENC)

7423 Triple Diamond Plastics, Inc.
405 N Pleasantview Dr
Liberty Center, OH 43532
Contact: Josh Purdy VP
Tel: 941-484-7750
Email: josh.purdy@tdplastics.com
Website: www.tdplastics.com
Mfr structural foam, multiple plastic pallets & collapsible bins, large plastic contract products. (Woman, estab 2005, empl 35, sales $3,500,000, cert: WBENC)

Oklahoma

7424 DA/PRO Rubber Inc.
601 N Poplar Ave
Broken Arrow, OK 74012
Contact: Gretchen Brauninger CEO
Tel: 918-258-9386
Email: gbrauninger@daprorubber.com
Website: www.daprorubber.com
High quality rubber, TPE & plastic custom components, diaphragms, seals, connectors, custom molded shapes, rubber-to-metal parts & molded to precision tolerances. (Woman, estab 1961, empl 320, sales , cert: WBENC)

Oregon

7425 Griffith Rubber Mills
2625 NW Industrial
Portland, OR 97296
Contact: Rick McClain Corporate Quality Mgr
Tel: 503-226-6971
Email: rickm@griffithrubber.com
Website: www.griffithrubber.com
Custom rubber products (Woman, estab , empl 250, sales , cert: NWBOC)

7426 Warm Springs Composite Products
Highway 26, Bldg 8
Warm Springs, OR 97761
Contact: Charles Currier CFO
Tel: 541-553-1143
Email: curriercw@bendnet.com
Website: www.wscp.com
Composite panel mfg & product development: thermal setting, thermal plastic, radio frequncy & cold pressing processes. (Nat-Ame, estab 1994, empl 50, sales $6,200,000, cert: 8(a))

Pennsylvania

7427 Accudyn Products Inc.
2400 Yoder Dr
Erie, PA 16506
Contact: Leanne Sheldon President
Tel: 814-833-7615
Email: lsheldon@accudyn.com
Website: www.accudyn.com
Various high tolerance plastics parts: Appliance, Automotive, Business Equipment, Electronics, Heating and Cooling, and Medical. (Woman, estab 0, empl , sales , cert: WBENC)

7428 Pittsburgh Plastics Manufacturing
140 Kriess Rd
Butler, PA 16001
Contact: Emily Crawford Acct Mgr
Tel: 724-789-9300
Email: ecrawford@pittsburghplastics.com
Website: www.pittsburghplastics.com
Polyurethanes, TPEs, Silicones, Hydrogels & Foams. (Woman, estab 1977, empl 100, sales , cert: WBENC)

7429 PMC-Polymer Products Company, Inc.
100 Station Ave
Stockertown, PA 18083
Contact: Don Barber Business Mgr
Tel: 610-759-3690
Email: donbarber@pmc-group.com
Website: www.polymerproductscompany.com/index.htm
Design & develop additive masterbatches & ignition resistant thermoplastic compounds. (As-Ind, estab 1965, empl 75, sales $25,500,000, cert: NMSDC)

Puerto Rico

7430 Vassallo International
1000 St 506
Cotolaurel, PR 00780
Contact: Rafael Vassallo CEO
Tel: 787-848-1515
Email: faelo@vassalloindustries.com
Website: www.vassallointernational.com
Lines of PVC & plastics, Water Tanks. (Minority, Woman, estab 1962, empl 90, sales $15,000,000, cert: NMSDC)

South Carolina

7431 Milagro Packaging LLC
60 Fairview Church Rd
Spartanburg, SC 29306
Contact: Jill McCurry President
Tel: 864-578-0085
Email: jillm@concept-pkg.com
Website: www.milagro-pkg.com
Mfr corrugated & solid fiber boxes, polystyrene foam products & urethane foam products. (Hisp, estab 2001, empl 425, sales $94,873,435, cert: NMSDC)

Tennessee

7432 Innovative Plastics
2900 Old Franklin Rd
Antioch, TN 37013
Contact: Tom Florence Sales
Tel: 404-402-8062
Email: tomf4plastics@aol.com
Website: www.innovative-plastics.com
Custom thermoform & RF contract packaging: PVC, PETG, Styrene, Barex & HDPE. (Woman, estab 1985, empl 350, sales , cert: NWBOC)

7433 Precision Molding Inc.
5500 Roberts Matthews Hwy
Sparta, TN 38583
Contact: Ray Sachs Sales
Tel: 931-738-8376
Email: ray.sachs@precision-molding.com
Website: www.precision-molding.com
High-Pressure injection, inserts & blow molding. (Woman, estab 1987, empl 200, sales $20,000,000, cert: WBENC)

Texas

7434 Belco Manufacturing Company, Inc.
2303 Taylor's Valley Rd
Belton, TX 76513
Contact: Steve Macy President
Tel: 254-933-9000
Email: sales@belco-mfg.com
Website: www.belco-mfg.com
Industrial fiberglass reinforced plastics products. (Woman, estab 0, empl , sales , cert: WBENC)

7435 CamLow, LLC
105 S Friendswood Dr, Ste B
Friendswood, TX 77546
Contact: Karen Wiest President
Tel: 281-474-2613
Email: kawiest@camlow.com
Website: www.camlow.com
Polyurethane spray foam insulation, closed cell spray foam, open cell spray foam, roof spray foam insulation, hurricane protection, hurricane panels, storm panels, storm shutters, roll down shutters, accordian shutters, stainless steel screens. (Woman, estab 2005, empl 4, sales $317,000, cert: State, City)

7436 Chemplast, Inc.
1002 Texas Pkwy, Ste A
Stafford, TX 77477
Contact: Jubin Alexander Business Dev Mgr
Tel: 281-208-2585
Email: jubin@chemplastinc.com
Website: www.chemplastinc.com
Plastic Injection Molding with high performance Engineering Grade Plastics, Compression Molding, Thermoforming, Parts Assembly. (As-Ind, estab 2000, empl 47, sales $15,000,000, cert: NMSDC, CPUC)

7437 Clay Precision, Ltd.
1102 FM 1417 NE
Sherman, TX 75090
Contact: J. Diann Spencer President
Tel: 903-891-9022
Email: jspencer@clayprecision.com
Website: www.clayprecision.com
Milling, turning, 4th axis capabilities, fixturing, plastic weldment, assemblies, heat treating, grinding, dock-to-stock quality, fabrication of custom metal and plastic machined parts and assemblies, prototypes, exotic metals, exotic plastics. (Woman, estab 1996, empl 11, sales $1,293,930, cert: State, WBENC)

7438 Idea Planet, LP
6001 Summerside Dr Ste 204
Dallas, TX 75252
Contact: Michael Flecker President
Tel: 972-380-9867
Email: mflecker@ideaplanetinc.com
Website: www.ideaplanetinc.com
Plastic injected molding, resin, metal & glass manufacturing. (Woman, estab 1999, empl 18, sales $19,000,000, cert: WBENC)

7439 King's Eco Plastics, LLC
4001 W Military Hwy
McAllen, TX 78503
Contact: Owen Stewart President
Tel: 956-631-1115
Email: ostewart@kingsecoplastics.com
Website: www.kingsecoplastics.com
Custom-molded plastics, product assembly & finishing services. (Woman/AA, As- Pac, estab 1986, empl 75, sales $8,109,000, cert: NMSDC, WBENC)

7440 Mexican Technologies Co
8650 Yermoland Dr
El Paso, TX 79907
Contact: Alfredo Baca Sales Mgr
Tel: 915-595-2285
Email: abaca@uniqueproductsinc.com
Website: www.uniqueproductsinc.com
Die cutting, converting, lamination, plastic fabrication, extrusion & coextrusion, slitting, sewing. (Hisp, estab 2002, empl 20, sales , cert: State)

7441 Nicor Inc.
100 Commons Rd, Ste 7-355
Dripping Springs, TX 78620
Contact: Jeff Cook VP Sales & Mktg
Tel: 707-484-0835
Email: jeffacook@nicorinc.net
Website: www.nicorinc.net
Custom injection molding, polymer replacement meter pit lids that are traffic rated. (Woman, estab 1988, empl 5, sales $2,000,000, cert: State)

PLASTIC PRODUCTS

7442 Precision Mold & Tool Group
315 N Park Dr
San Antonio, TX 78216
Contact: Domingo Auces Dir of Marketing
Tel: 210-525-0094
Email: dhauces@pmtool.com
Website: www.precision-group.com
Injection molding & mold making. (Woman, estab 1985, empl 36, sales $6,505,000, cert: WBENC)

7443 Premier Polymers LLC
16800 Imperial Valley, Ste 200
Houston, TX 77060
Contact: Melwani Kwan Supply Chain Mgr
Tel: 281-902-0909
Email: mkwan@premierpolymers.com
Website: www.premierpolymers.com
Dist Plastic Resin. (As-Pac, estab 2009, empl 22, sales , cert: State, NMSDC)

Utah

7444 Kaddas Enterprises, Inc.
255 N. Apollo Rd. Ste 500
Salt Lake City, UT 84116
Contact: Patrick Scott Dir of Sales
Tel: 801-972-5400
Email: patricks@kaddas.com
Website: www.kaddas.com
Custom Thermoforming, Pressure Forming, Hand Fabrication, 5-Axis CNC Router, Master CAM, Solid Works Modeling, 3-Axis CNC Router, vacuum formed or hand fabricated polymer solutions. (Woman, estab 1966, empl 28, sales $4,296,559, cert: CPUC, WBENC)

Virginia

7445 Dynaric Inc.
5740 Bayside Rd
Virginia Beach, VA 23455
Contact: Kenny Samdahl Cstmr Service
Tel: 757-363-5851
Email: kens@dynaric.com
Website: www.dynaric.com
Mfr plastic strapping & strapping systems. (Hisp, estab 1973, empl 150, sales $122,000,000, cert: NMSDC)

7446 Polyfab Display Company
14892 Persistence Dr
Woodbridge, VA 22191
Contact: Al Parker Owner
Tel: 703-497-4577
Email: al@polyfab-display.com
Website: www.polyfab-display.com
Mfr & dist acrylic fabricated products: point-of-purchase displays (countertop, wall-mount, slatwall and free-standing), fixtures, signage, protective covers & medical device holders. (AA, estab 1987, empl 15, sales $1,189,000, cert: State, NMSDC)

Wisconsin

7447 Custom Service Plastics, Inc.
1101 S Wells St
Lake Geneva, WI 53147
Contact: Minoo Seifoddini President
Tel: 262-248-9557
Email: john@csplastics.com
Website: www.csplastics.com
Plastics injection molding: autotmotive & non automaotive parts & assemblies. (Minority, Woman, estab 0, empl 160, sales $12,000,000, cert: WBENC)

7448 Molded Dimensions, Inc.
701 Sunset Rd
Port Washington, WI 53074
Contact: Sue Bialzik Cstmr Service
Tel: 262-284-9455
Email: sue@moldeddimensions.com
Website: www.moldeddimensions.com
Rubber & polyurethane custom molded components. (Woman, estab 1952, empl 70, sales $12,500,000, cert: WBENC)

7449 Shell Plastics LLC
1010 Valley Rd
Plymouth, WI 53073
Contact: Mary Beth Dellger President
Tel: 920-893-6281
Email: marybeth@shellplastics.com
Website: www.shellplastics.com
Job Shop, Plastic Fabrication, Screen Printing, Vacuum Forming, CNC routing, Heat Bending, Cold Bending, Flame Polishing, Solvent Bonding, Laminating, Spray Painting, Die Cutting, Buffing, Drape Forming, Assembly, Packaging, Fulfillment. (Woman, estab 1953, empl 15, sales $2,924,884, cert: State)

7450 SMC Ltd.
330 SMC Dr
Somerset, WI 54025
Contact: Eugene Puckhaber Corporate Controller
Tel: 978-422-6800
Email: eugene.puckhaber@smcltd.com
Website: www.smcltd.com
Contract manufacturing & molding services, design, engineering, thermoplastic molding including insert & two-shot, micro molding. (As-Ind, estab 1989, empl 700, sales , cert: State, NMSDC)

PRINTING & ENGRAVING

Full service printers with layout, composition, binding and trimming, digital, multi-color, large format, etc. Also included are silkscreen printers, nameplate and trophy engravers, manufacturers or distributors of labels, decals and pressure sensitive materials. NAICS Code 32

Alabama

7451 Advanced Label Worx
1006 Larsen Dr
Oak Ridge, AL 37830
Contact: Lana Sellers President
Tel: 865-966-8711
Email: lsellers@advancedlabelworx.com
Website: www.advancedlabelworx.com
Flexographic pressure-sensitive labels, specialty converting, die-cut components, digital imprinting. (Woman, estab 1968, empl 120, sales , cert: WBENC)

7452 Precision Graphics Inc.
4121 Lewisburg Rd
Birmingham, AL 35207
Contact: Robert Grant President
Tel: 205-841-2072
Email: robertg@precisiongraphicsinc.net
Website: www.precisiongraphicsinc.net
Design, layout, printing, mailing, warehouse, direct mail, packaging, die cut. (Minority, Woman, estab 2002, empl 25, sales $3,529,600, cert: WBENC)

Arizona

7453 Courier Graphics Corporation
2621 S 37th St
Phoenix, AZ 85034
Contact: Renee Teper Acct Exec
Tel: 602-437-9700
Email: renee_teper@couriergraphics.com
Website: www.couriergraphics.com
Commercial printing. (Woman, estab 1975, empl 70, sales $13,789,000, cert: WBENC)

7454 Sapphire Printing Group, Inc.
3800 N. 38th Ave
Phoenix, AZ 85019
Contact: Kenn Gary Dir of Sales
Tel: 714-941-9534
Email: kenng@sapphireprinting.com
Website: www.sapphireprinting.com
Commercial web printing, mailing & fulfillment services. (Woman, estab 2004, empl 115, sales $22,000,000, cert: CPUC)

California

7455 3V Signs & Graphics, LLC
434 Pacific Coast Hwy
Hermosa Beach, CA 90254
Contact: Pat Dacy Sec/Treas
Tel: 310-372-0888
Email: pat@3vsigns.com
Website: www.3Vsigns.com
Laser cutting & engraving various materials, large format latex ink printer, UV flatbed printer. (Woman/Hisp, estab 2010, empl 5, sales $186,000, cert: City)

7456 Acme Press Inc., dba California Lithographers
2312 Stanwell Dr
Concord, CA 94520
Contact: VP
Tel: 925-682-1111
Email:
Website: www.Calitho.com
Commercial printing, digital printing, fulfillment, mailing, packaging. (Woman, estab 1976, empl 75, sales $11,530,100, cert: WBENC)

7457 Advantage Mailing, LLC.
1600 N Kraemer Blvd
Anaheim, CA 92806
Contact: Nicholas Lancione Natl Acct Dir
Tel: 414-379-5210
Email: nlancione@advantageinc.com
Website: www.advantageinc.com
Printing, Mailing, Fulfillment. (As-Pac, estab 1994, empl 450, sales $95,000,000, cert: NMSDC)

7458 Alpha Printing & Graphics, Inc.
12758 schabarum ave
irwindale, CA 91706
Contact: Kelly Ngo VP Sales
Tel: 626-851-9800
Email: kelly.ngo@alphaprinting.com
Website: www.alphaprinting.com
Commercial & digital printing. (Minority, Woman, estab 1995, empl 20, sales $3,000,000, cert: CPUC)

7459 Clear Image Printing, Inc.
12744 San Fernando Road Bldg 2
Sylmar, CA 91342
Contact: Gene Byrne Dir Mktg/Sales
Tel: 818-630-7670
Email: eugene@clearimageprinting.com
Website: www.clearimageprinting.com
Offset sheet fed & digital printing, Brochures, Catalogues, Direct mail campaigns, Special Packaging, Books, Foil stamping, Die-cutting, Posters, Large Format Banners, Graphic Design, Modern-Media. (As-Pac, estab 2008, empl 45, sales $5,005,000, cert: CPUC)

7460 Digital Mania, Inc.
455 Market St Ste 180
San Francisco, CA 94105
Contact: Darius Meykadeh CEO
Tel: 415-896-0500
Email: copymat@copymatsf.com
Website: www.copymat1.com
Indoor & outdoor signs, brochures, booklets, RFPs, oversized prints, desktop publishing & design, mailing services, newsletters, name tents, name badges, conference materials, etc. (As-Ind, estab 1994, empl 20, sales $4,000,000, cert: City)

7461 Digital Services Enterprises
40 Tesla, Ste B
Irvine, CA 92618
Contact: Sales Mgr
Tel: 949-387-6200
Email: orders@sirspeedyprinter.com
Website: www.sirspeedyprinter.com
Offset printing, digital printing, color copies, photocopying, promotional products, Signs, banners, posters, floor graphics, direct mail, fulfillment, high speedy copies, training manuals, human resource manuals, direct marketing. (Woman, estab 1974, empl 17, sales $2,757,000, cert: CPUC)

7462 Essence Printing
       151 Mitchell Ave
       South San Francisco, CA 94080
       Contact: Bau-Lin Yueh President
       Tel: 650-952-5072
       Email: baulin@essenceprinting.com
       Website: www.essenceprinting.com
Printing: marketing material, brochures, datasheets, newsletters, tradeshow posters, business cards, letterheads, etc. (As-Pac, estab 1976, empl 60, sales , cert: CPUC)

7463 Financial Statement Services, Inc.
       3300 S Fairview St
       Santa Ana, CA 92704
       Contact: Jennifer Dietz CEO
       Tel: 714-436-3300
       Email:
       Website: www.fssi-ca.com
Printing, mailing & electronic invoices, statements, bills & marketing communications. (Woman, estab 1980, empl 187, sales $5,000,000, cert: WBENC)

7464 Fong & Fong Printers and Lithographers
       3009 65th St
       Sacramento, CA 95820
       Contact: Karen Cotton Controller
       Tel: 916-739-1313
       Email: kcotton@fongprinters.com
       Website: www.fongprinters.com
Commercial printing services: sales literature, brochures, folders, packaging, annual reports, data sheets, direct mail & posters. (Minority, Woman, estab 1962, empl 51, sales $12,000,000, cert: CPUC)

7465 Fruitridge Printing and Lithograph
       3258 Stockton Blvd
       Sacramento, CA 95820
       Contact: Karen Young VP
       Tel: 916-452-9213
       Email: karen@fruitridge.com
       Website: www.fruitridge.com
Commercial offset and digital printing, in house bindery & mailing capabilities. (Woman, estab 1970, empl 35, sales $5,100,000, cert: CPUC)

7466 Gibraltar Graphics
       5075 Brooks St
       Montclair, CA 91763
       Contact: Hector Rosado Sales Mgr
       Tel: 909-624-6171
       Email: hectorr@gprint4u.com
       Website: www.gPrint4u.com
Printing, inhouse bindery, heatset web presses, pick up and delivery, brochures, envelopes, laser forms, newsletters, booklets, scratch pads, laser forms, (Hisp, estab 1989, empl 18, sales $410,000, cert: CPUC)

7467 Image Quest Plus, LLC
       215 No Marengo Ave. Third Floor
       Pasadena, CA 91101
       Contact: Margaret Floyd Member
       Tel: 626-744-1333
       Email: margaret@iqcopy.com
       Website: www.iqcopy.com
Photocopy services: document reproduction, scanning & imaging, color copies, wideformat printing, binding, off-site document reproduction. (Woman/AA, estab 1998, empl 5, sales $661,441, cert: NMSDC, CPUC)

7468 Impact Printing
       23278 Bernhardt St
       Hayward, CA 94545
       Contact: Sarah Elder VP Sales
       Tel: 510-783-7977
       Email: impactprint@impactprint.com
       Website: www.impactprint.com
Digital & offset printing, full bindery, graphics. (Minority, Woman, estab 1985, empl 25, sales $2,500,000, cert: CPUC)

7469 Ink Link, Incorporated
       351 Oak Place, Ste J
       Brea, CA 92821
       Contact: Linda Brooking CEO
       Tel: 714-256-9700
       Email: linda@myinklink.com
       Website: www.myinklink.com
Commercial printing: banners, signs, displays, floor graphics. (Woman, estab 2003, empl 4, sales $850,000, cert: State, CPUC, WBENC)

7470 International Diversified Marketing, Inc.
       18277 Pasadena St., Ste B102
       Lake Elsinore, CA 92530
       Contact: Jan Northcutt President
       Tel: 714-550-4971
       Email: jn@comfortfirst.us
       Website: www.ComfortFirstProducts.com
Comfort First Filtered Diffuser™If you want to go GREEN and save energy, improve employee comfort and health, all while improving indoor air quality, this diffuser is the solution you've been looking for. (Woman, estab 2003, empl 3, sales $458,000, cert: WBENC)

7471 Lester Lithograph Inc. (dba Castle Press)
       1128 N Gilbert St
       Anaheim, CA 92801
       Contact: Larry Lester Retired
       Tel: - -
       Email: amy@castlepress.com
       Website: www.castlepress.com
Commercial printing. (Woman, estab 1980, empl 45, sales $5,500,000, cert: CPUC, WBENC)

7472 Marina Graphic Center, Inc.
       12903 Cerise Ave
       Hawthorne, CA 90250
       Contact: Sr Acct Exec
       Tel: 310-970-1777
       Email:
       Website: www.marinagraphics.com
Commercial Printing, Pre-Press, Offset Printing, Digital Printing, Mail fulfillment & Mailing services, Full Bindery, Letterpress, Die Cutting & Embossing. (Woman, estab 1964, empl 125, sales $14,000,000, cert: WBENC)

7473 Metropolitan West, Inc.
       130 Pine Ave Ste 400
       Long Beach, CA 90802
       Contact: Kelly Taylor CEO
       Tel: 562-426-7701
       Email: nikki@metwest.com
       Website: www.metwest.com
Dist film products: solar, safety, anti-graffiti, designer, custom & digital film. (Woman, estab 1992, empl 5, sales $1,200,000, cert: WBENC)

PRINTING & ENGRAVING

7474 Monarch Litho, Inc.
      1501 Date St
      Montabella, CA 90640
      Contact: Gerry Lewis Acct Exec
      Tel: 323-727-0300
      Email: gerry.lewis@monarchlitho.com
      Website: www.monarchlitho.com
Printing svcs: small & large format sheet fed press; digital pre-press (Hisp, estab 1974, empl 275, sales , cert: NMSDC, CPUC)

7475 PGI Pacific Graphics International
      14938 Nelson Ave
      City of Industry, CA 91744
      Contact: Rick Wasson President
      Tel: 626-336-7707
      Email: rwasson@pacgraphics.com
      Website: www.pacgraphics.com
Printing & graphics, business forms, etc. (Minority, Woman, estab 1989, empl 20, sales $3,600,372, cert: NMSDC, CPUC, SDB)

7476 Photomation
      2551 W La Palma Ave
      Anaheim, CA 92801
      Contact: Francisco Flores Production Mgr/Sales
      Tel: 714-236-2121
      Email: fflores@photomation.com
      Website: www.photomation.com
Digital Graphics, Trade show, Digital Imaging, Photographics prints, Banners, POP displays, Standees, Wallcovering, Large wall Murals, Lobby art, Custom framing, Awards and recognition, office décor. (Woman, estab 1955, empl 21, sales , cert: State, CPUC, WBENC)

7477 Summit Graphics Inc.
      11354 Burbank Blvd, Ste A
      North Hollywood, CA 91601
      Contact: Jorge Ververa VP Diversity
      Tel: 818-753-5075
      Email: jorge@summit-graphics.net
      Website: www.summit-graphics.net
Medium to large runs in offset, digital & large format printing: mailers, brochures, catalogues, booklets, bindery, die-cutting, packaging, coallating, hand fulfillment. (Hisp, estab 2001, empl 4, sales $1,436,504, cert: State, NMSDC)

7478 Transworld Printing Services, Inc.
      2857 Transworld Dr
      Stockton, CA 95206
      Contact: Daphyne Brown CEO
      Tel: 209-982-1511
      Email: daphyne@tpslabels.com
      Website: www.tpslabels.com
Flexographic & digital label manufacturer. (Woman/AA, estab 1996, empl 15, sales $2,065,000, cert: NMSDC, NWBOC)

Colorado

7479 DT Investments Inc. dba Beacon Printing Inc.
      2161 S Platte River Dr
      Denver, CO 80223
      Contact: Terri Witt CEO
      Tel: 303-922-4384
      Email: beacon.sales@qwestoffice.net
      Website: www.beaconprintingdenver.com
Printing services, large format sheetfed, digital, full color, PMS color, pocket folders, post cards, letterhead, envelopes, posters, booklets, annual reports, forms, rack cards, pamphlets, catalogs, tabs, loose leaf, inserts. (Minority, Woman, estab 1995, empl 10, sales $1,200,000, cert: City)

7480 Mar-Tek Industries, Inc.
      3545 S Platte River Dr, Ste G
      Englewood, CO 80110
      Contact: Irene Smith President
      Tel: 303-789-4067
      Email: irene@mar-tekind.com
      Website: www.mar-tekind.com
Mfr & dist screen printed & digital graphic labels, decals, overlays. (Woman, estab 1987, empl 45, sales $4,500,000, cert: WBENC)

Connecticut

7481 Enhance a Colour Corp.
      43b Beaver Brook Road
      Danbury, CT 06810
      Contact: Lenore Nespoli Sales Mgr
      Tel: 203-748-5111
      Email: lnespoli@eacgs.com
      Website: www.eacgs.com
Large format digitally printed graphics, printing dyesub fabrics & carpets up to 16' wide, UV printing, full color & white ink direct to rigid and flexible substrates, pressure sensitive, regular & mesh substrates. (Woman, estab 1988, empl 32, sales $4,014,058, cert: WBENC)

7482 Kool Ink/Sir Speedy Printing
      21 Old Windsor Rd
      Bloomfield, CT 06002
      Contact: Mark Jacobs Owner
      Tel: 860-242-0303
      Email: mark@sirspeedy.cc
      Website: www.sirspeedy.com
Offset printing, copying, black & white, color, scanning, posters banners & signs. (AA, estab 2001, empl 15, sales $3,500,000, cert: State, NMSDC)

7483 Turnstone Inc. dba Alphagraphics
      915 Main St
      Hartford, CT 06103
      Contact: VP Sales
      Tel: 860-247-3766
      Email: us667@alphagraphics.com
      Website: www.hartford.alphagraphics.com
Brochures, Reports, Training books, Posters, Reports, mailings. Forms, labels, Flyers, Design Services. Fulfillment, Signs & banners, marketing material. (Woman, estab 1989, empl 23, sales $3,100,000, cert: WBENC)

Florida

7484 Alpha Press, Inc.
      3804 N John Young Pkwy, Ste 2
      Orlando, FL 32804
      Contact: John Latoree VP
      Tel: 407-299-2121
      Email: sales@apiprint.net
      Website: www.apiprint.net
Four color press: brochures, business cards, envelopes, pamplets, magazines & publications. (Woman/Hisp, estab 1996, empl 5, sales $870,000, cert: City)

7485 Amazon Services Inc.
      7186 SW 47th St
      Miami, FL 33155
      Contact: Cristina Serralta Founder/CEO
      Tel: 305-663-0585
      Email: cristina@amazonprinters.com
      Website: www.amazonprinters.com
Commercial printers with in-house bindery: booklet making, continuous forms, logo, graphics, invoices, checks, brochures, flyers, digital printing, quick printing, envelopes, stationery, cards, and more. (Minority, Woman, estab 1987, empl 12, sales , cert: WBENC)

7486 APImaging, Inc.
      19 SW 6th St
      Miami, FL 33130
      Contact: Diana Herrera VP Sales
      Tel: 305-373-4774
      Email: dianah@apimaging.com
      Website: www.apimaging.com
Photo imaging & photo finishing services, commercial printing, studio photography, self adhesive signs & graphics, directional signs, posters, point of purchase signs, graphic displays, trade shows & exhibits. (Woman/Hisp, estab 2013, empl 22, sales , cert: WBENC)

7487 Bellak Color
      PO Box 227656
      Miami, FL 33222
      Contact: Manny Fernandez VP
      Tel: 305-854-8525
      Email: manny@bellak.com
      Website: www.bellak.com
Commerical sheet-fed printing - print publications, magazines, brochures, rack brochures, catalogs, stationery packages, POS pieces, postcards, pamplets, invitations, folders. (Hisp, estab 1960, empl 47, sales $6,500,000, cert: NMSDC)

7488 Colonial Press International, Inc.
      3690 NW 50th St
      Miami, FL 33142
      Contact: Jeff Statler EVP Corporate Sales
      Tel: 540-347-1402
      Email: jstatler@colonialpress.com
      Website: www.colonialpressintl.com
Printing svcs: web & sheet fed, 4-6 color, brochures, rack cards, magazines, etc. (Hisp, estab 1952, empl 120, sales $31,000,000, cert: NMSDC)

7489 Graphic Designs International LLC
      7941 SW Jack James Dr
      Stuart, FL 34997
      Contact: Kimberly Amsalem
      Tel: 772-287-0000
      Email: marketing@gdigraphics.com
      Website: www.gdigraphics.com
Graphic Design/Sales Services, Markings/Decals for Public Safety Vehicles. (Woman, estab 2019, empl 18, sales $1,606,818, cert: City, WBENC)

7490 Innovative Printing & Graphics
      310 S Federal Hwy
      Boynton Beach, FL 33435
      Contact: Amy Bernard Sales Assoc
      Tel: 561-742-2977
      Email: info@ipgprinting.com
      Website: www.ipgprinting.com
Commercial printing: full color, magazines, NCR forms, pocket folders, postcard mailers, letterhead, invitations, etc. (Woman, estab 2006, empl 9, sales $250,000, cert: City)

7491 Lawton Printers, Inc.
      649 Triumph Court
      Orlando, FL 32804
      Contact: Kimberly Lawton Koon President
      Tel: 407-260-0400
      Email: kimberly@lawtonprinters.com
      Website: www.LawtonPrinters.com
Printing ; offset, digital & wide-format printing equipment. (Woman, estab , empl 27, sales $3,600,000, cert: State, WBENC)

7492 Martin Litho, Inc.
      505 N Rome Ave
      Tampa, FL 33606
      Contact: Martin Saavedra CEO
      Tel: 813-254-1553
      Email: martin@martinlitho.com
      Website: www.mlicorp.com
Commercial sheet-fed, multi-color printing. (Minority, Woman, estab 1970, empl 42, sales $5,116,143, cert: State, NMSDC)

7493 Quadco Printing & Signs
      8953 NW 23rd St
      Doral, FL 33172
      Contact: Jorge Quadreny President
      Tel: 305-519-1234
      Email: jorge@quadcoonline.com
      Website: www.quadcoonline.com
Full color printing services, advertising specialties, promotional items, trade show & retractable banner stands. (Hisp, estab 1982, empl 8, sales $140,000,000, cert: State)

7494 Sol Davis Printing, Inc.
      5205 N Lois Ave
      Tampa, FL 33614
      Contact: Solomon E. Davis President
      Tel: 813-353-3609
      Email: soldavis.print@verizon.net
      Website: www.soldavisprinting.com
Offset printing: 1, 2, 3 & 4 color process, graphic design, typesetting & bindery services. (Woman/AA, estab 1999, empl 9, sales , cert: State, City, NMSDC)

7495 Vista Color Corporation
      1401 NW 78th Ave
      Miami, FL 33126
      Contact: Catherine Finnemore Sr Acct Exec
      Tel: 305-635-2000
      Email: cfinnemore@vistacolor.com
      Website: www.vistacolor.com
Pre-press & printing svcs. (Hisp, estab 1968, empl 120, sales $22,000,000, cert: NMSDC)

Georgia

7496 Advanced Barcode & Label Technologies, Inc.
      3300 E Ponce de Leon Ave Ste I
      Scottdale, GA 30079
      Contact: Elizabeth Davey President
      Tel: 404-671-3150
      Email: edavey@ablt.com
      Website: www.ablt.com
Mfr barcode labels with & without sequential numbering used for inventory tracking, product identification & logistic tracking. (Woman, estab 1985, empl 9, sales , cert: WBENC)

7497 American Reprographics Corporation
      7800 Jett Ferry Rd
      Atlanta, GA 30350
      Contact: Mindy Godwin President
      Tel: 770-394-2465
      Email: mindy@arcinatlanta.com
      Website: www.arcinatlanta.com
Full service printing: business cards, letterhead, envelopes, check stock, brochures, mailings, graphic design services. (Woman, estab 1978, empl 3, sales , cert: WBENC)

7498 Barcode Warehouse
      101 Smoke Hill Lane Ste 130
      Woodstock, GA 30188
      Contact: Margie Benton VP Sales Operations
      Tel: 888-422-9249
      Email: mbenton@barcodewarehouse.biz
      Website: www.barcodewarehouse.biz
Mfr labels & tags, full color product branding labels, blank labels & tags for variable data printing. (Woman, estab 2004, empl 18, sales $4,225,778, cert: WBENC)

7499 Basiqa, LLC
      1555 Oakbrook Dr Ste 135
      Norcross, GA 30093
      Contact: Winston Dzose VP Digital Marketing
      Tel: 678-824-6460
      Email: winston@basiqa.com
      Website: www.basiqa.com
Direct mail, advertising, material preparation services for mailing or other direct distribution, digital printing. (AA, estab 2009, empl 16, sales $3,000,000, cert: NMSDC)

7500 Dixie Graphics
      2074 E Park Dr NE
      Conyers, GA 30013
      Contact: Denise Hindle COE
      Tel: 770-972-2354
      Email: dhindle@dixiegraphicsinc.com
      Website: www.dixiegraphicsinc.com
Commercial offset printing & large format, graphics design & full mail room capabilities. (Woman, estab 1980, empl 14, sales $2,012,337, cert: WBENC)

7501 Fuentes Enterprises, Inc
      2605 Park Central Blvd
      Decatur, GA 30035
      Contact: Monica Maldonado CEO
      Tel: 770-987-7400
      Email: monica@weareipcomm.com
      Website: www.weareipcomm.com
Commercial printing, graphic design, posters, billboards, marketing collateral materials, annual reports, ads, etc. (Minority, Woman, estab 1984, empl 12, sales $1,649,328, cert: NMSDC)

7502 LittKare, LLC
      200 Cobb Pkwy N Ste 130
      Marietta, GA 30062
      Contact: Littie Brown President
      Tel: 770-693-1767
      Email: lbrown@speedpro.com
      Website: www.speedpromarietta.com
Large format digital printing: banners, posters, signs, trade show displays & banner stands, vehicle wraps, vinyl lettering, wall, window & floor graphics, stickers & decals. (Woman/AA, estab 2010, empl 2, sales $373,880, cert: NMSDC, WBENC)

7503 Matoaka Enterprises, LLC
      2455 Bridlewood Dr
      Smyrna, GA 30080
      Contact: Julie Custalow Owner
      Tel: 404-932-6825
      Email: julie@matoaka.com
      Website: www.matoaka-ent.com
Large format graphics, banners, signs, window clings, vehicle wraps, LEED certified wall paper, custom printed litho & digital printing, custom printed promotional items, apparel. (Minority, Woman, estab 2010, empl 1, sales $181,611, cert: NMSDC)

7504 NorthStar Print, LLC
      6050 Peachtree Pkwy Ste 240359
      Norcross, GA 30092
      Contact: Jacki Suckow President
      Tel: 770-490-6251
      Email: jacki@northstarprint.net
      Website: www.northstarprint.net
Print & promotional products, marketing materials, traditional business forms, POP items, promotional items & just-in-time digital printing, distribution & kitting services. (Woman, estab 1991, empl 8, sales $3,000,000, cert: NWBOC)

7505 PrinTech Label Corporation
      2550 Collins Springs Dr
      Smyrna, GA 30080
      Contact: Kelly Weaver CFO
      Tel: 404-792-1133
      Email: kelly@printechlabel.com
      Website: www.printechlabel.com
Pressure senstive labels, custom printed tags, 4 color process, 6 color capability, hot stamp labels, cold foil labels, UL registered label vendor, IRC's, IRC, redeemable coupons, silver coupon, thermal transfer blanks, direct thermal blanks. (Minority, Woman, estab 1993, empl 14, sales $1,701,002, cert: WBENC)

7506 Printing and Marketing Services, Inc.
      1500 Southland Circle, Ste A
      Atlanta, GA 30318
      Contact: Brian McDaniel Sr Acct Mgr
      Tel: 404-724-9080
      Email: bmcdaniel@alphagraphics.com
      Website: www.us756.alphagraphics.com
Printing: digital color, digital black & white, offset printing, envelopes, stationery, large format signs & banners. (AA, estab 2015, empl 13, sales $1,695,647, cert: NMSDC)

7507 The Printing People, Inc.
      3427 Oakcliff Rd. Ste 112
      Doraville, GA 30340
      Contact: Misael Millan VP
      Tel: 770-452-7561
      Email: misa@printingpeople.com
      Website: www.printingpeople.com
Commercial offset & digital printing: brochures, postcards, catalogs, posters, folders, manuals & stationery. (Hisp, estab 1980, empl 13, sales $1,400,000, cert: NMSDC)

Iowa

7508 Promotion Support Services, Inc.
      1320 W Kimberly Rd
      Davenport, IA 52806
      Contact: Terance VanWinkle Dir
      Tel: 563-362-6002
      Email: tvanwinkle@pss-inc.net
      Website: www.pss-inc.net
Offset printing, Digital printing (static & variable), Commercial printing, Transactional print & mail services, Transcription Services, Data capture, Medical Transcription, Outbound call center, warehousing, Fulfillment, Kitting. (Woman, estab 1989, empl 56, sales $5,600,000, cert: WBENC)

Illinois

7509 American Marketing Services and Consultants Inc.
939 Tower Rd
Mundelein, IL 60060
Contact: Dan Van Erden EVP
Tel: 847-566-4545
Email: dvanerden@amscinc.com
Website: www.amscinc.com
Full service lettershop, data processing, Cass certification & postal presorting, high volume simplex & duplex lasering. (Woman, estab 1979, empl 75, sales $9,800,000, cert: State)

7510 AmeriPrint Corporation
1401 W Diggins St
Harvard, IL 60098
Contact: Taylor Schulty Marking & Sales Dir
Tel: 800-366-8573
Email: taylors@ameriprint.com
Website: www.ameriprint.com
Continuous forms & checks, snap sets, laser cut-sheets, booked & padded sets, integral card forms & labels, decals, re-positionable labels, key tags, magnets, thermal labels, barcoding, jumbo numbering & rolls. (Woman, estab 1990, empl 63, sales $8,603,265, cert: NWBOC)

7511 Clyde Printing Company
3520 S Morgan
Chicago, IL 60609
Contact: Colleen Woulfe President
Tel: 773-847-5900
Email: clydeprint@sbcglobal.net
Website: www.clydeprinting.com
Sheet fed commercial printing, conventional & digital printing, fullfillment & mailing. (Woman, estab 1942, empl 10, sales $792,852, cert: WBENC)

7512 ComGraphics Inc.
329 W 18th St, 10 Fl
Chicago, IL 60616
Contact: Lydia Erickson CFO
Tel: 312-226-0900
Email: lydiae@cgichicago.com
Website: www.cgichicago.com
Digital printing svcs, folding & inserting operations, internet hosting, statement processing, web statement, laser svcs, invoicing, marketing & fulfillment, data archiving, scanning svcs, direct mail. (Woman, estab 1980, empl 55, sales , cert: WBENC)

7513 Consolidated Printing Company
5942 N Northwest Hwy
Chicago, IL 60631
Contact: Marilyn Jones President
Tel: 773-631-2800
Email: marilyn@consolidatedprinting.net
Website: www.consolidatedprinting.net
Commercial printing includes: design, computer to plate, color digital, offset short & long run: advertising materials, annual reports, banners, brochures, booklets, buttons, business cards, conference materials, digital printing, door hangers. (Woman, estab 1973, empl 15, sales , cert: WBENC)

7514 D&D Business Inc. dba DDI Printing
7830 Quincy St
Willowbrook, IL 60527
Contact: Darmi Parikh CEO
Tel: 630-734-1455
Email: darmi@ddimage.com
Website: www.ddimage.com
Graphic design, Commercial colored printing, digital printing, full bindery & fullfillment. (Woman/As-Ind, estab 1994, empl 5, sales $560,000, cert: State, City, NMSDC)

7515 Krick Enterprises, Inc.
1548 Ogden Ave
Downers Grove, IL 60515
Contact: President Sales & Marketing
Tel: 630-515-1085
Email: info@signsnowdownersgrove.com
Website: www.signsnowdownersgrove.com
Graphic Design & Layout, commercial & digital printing. Signs & Posters, Brochures, Business Cards, Training Manuals & materials, Promotional items. (Minority, Woman, estab 1991, empl 7, sales $600,000, cert: State, NMSDC)

7516 M & R Graphics
2401 Bond St
University Park, IL 60466
Contact: Keith Reimel VP
Tel: 708-534-6621
Email: kreimel@mrgraphics.biz
Website: www.mrgraphics.biz
Mfr pressure sensitive labels & flexographic printing. (Woman/AA, estab 1989, empl 17, sales , cert: NMSDC)

7517 Master Marketing International
280 Gerzverske Lane
Carol Stream, IL 60188
Contact: Rene Asselmeier Sr Sales Exec
Tel: 630-653-5525
Email: rasselmeier@magnetstreet.com
Website: www.magnetstreet.com
Magnet printing, high-end stationary products, digital printer and mail house. (Woman, estab 1990, empl 66, sales $10,800,000, cert: WBENC)

7518 MOTR GRAFX, LLC
225 Larkin Dr Unit 5
Wheeling, IL 60090
Contact: Lissette Herin VP/Partner
Tel: 847-529-7454
Email: Lherin@motrgx.com
Website: www.motrgrafx.com
Print/media production, design, print, finishing, fulfillment & distribution, digital, sheet fed, large format, web printing, screen printing, direct mail, POP/packaging services. (Minority, Woman, estab 2011, empl 10, sales $2,980,000, cert: City, NMSDC, WBENC)

7519 Orion Offset
236 E Northwest Hwy
Palatine, IL 60067
Contact: President
Tel: 847-776-2300
Email: info@orionoffset.com
Website: www.orionoffset.com
Commercial printers, design, pre-press, digital printing, mailing, fulfillment. (Woman, estab 1993, empl 9, sales , cert: WBENC)

7520 Richards Graphic Communications, Inc.
2700 Van Buren St
Bellwood, IL 60104
Contact: Mary Lawrence President
Tel: 708-731-2103
Email: maryl@rgcnet.com
Website: www.rgcnet.com
Printing & communications, creative concept development, language translations, digital imaging, printing, finishing & mailing. (Woman, estab 1925, empl 23, sales $4,400,000, cert: State, WBENC)

7521 Shree Ganesha, Inc.
311 S Wacker Dr
Chicago, IL 60606
Contact: Tina Kuvadia Production Mgr
Tel: 312-408-1080
Email: printxpress@printx-press.com
Website: www.printx-press.com
Offset printing, copying, binding, large format, digital printing & graphic designing capabilities. (Minority, Woman, estab 2008, empl 9, sales , cert: City)

7522 Signcraft Screenprint, Inc.
100 AJ Harle Dr
Galena, IL 61036
Contact: Sandy Redington President
Tel: 815-777-3030
Email: sandy@signcraftinc.com
Website: www.signcraftinc.com
Custom screen printing, mfr pressure sensitive decals, signs & anti-skid plates. (Woman, estab 1947, empl 133, sales $11,500,000, cert: NWBOC)

7523 Sunrise Hitek Service, Inc.
5915 N Northwest Hwy
Chicago, IL 60631
Contact: Mark Finch VP
Tel: 773-792-8880
Email: mfinch@sunrisedigital.us
Website: www.sunrisehitek.com
Large format printing; displays, exhibit boards, POP displays, signs, floor graphics, etc. (As-Pac, estab 1987, empl 15, sales $3,700,000, cert: State, NMSDC)

7524 THM Creative, Inc. dba Advanced Imaging Inc.
1944 University Lane
Lisle, IL 60532
Contact: Tim Donnell Sales
Tel: 630-969-1300
Email: tim@aiprolab.com
Website: www.aiprolab.com
Digital Color Lab, Photographic Printing & Processing, Enlargements to 30x40, Inkjet/Giclee Printing, Online Order Fulfillment. (Minority, Woman, estab 1994, empl 6, sales , cert: NMSDC)

7525 Wyka LLC d/b/a Edison Graphics
1515 S Mt. Prospect Rd
Des Plaines, IL 60018
Contact: Larae J. Breitenstein CEO
Tel: 847-298-0740
Email: larae@edison-graphics.com
Website: www.edison-graphics.com
Printing svcs: 6 colors & coater sheet fed printing, in-house finishing, cutters, MBO folders, stitcher, digital printing & wide format printing. (Woman, estab 1998, empl 14, sales $3,215,000, cert: WBENC)

Indiana

7526 Fineline Printing Group
8081 Zionsville Rd
Indianapolis, IN 46268
Contact: Richard Miller President
Tel: 317-802-1964
Email: richardm@finelineprintinggroup.com
Website: www.FinelinePrintingGroup.com
Commercial sheetfed printing, inhouse bindery, mailing svcs, prepress svcs: scanning, design, ctp & high end color corrections. (Minority, Woman, estab 1981, empl 59, sales $11,500,000, cert: State, NMSDC)

7527 International Label Mfg.
1925 S 13th St
Terre Haute, IN 47802
Contact: Lisa Gonzales VP
Tel: 800-525-8469
Email: lisagonzales@internationallabelmfg.com
Website: www.internationallabelmfg.com
Custom label mfr & commercial printer. (Woman, estab 1972, empl 18, sales , cert: State, WBENC)

7528 Miles Printing Corporation
4923 W 78th St
Indianapolis, IN 46268
Contact: Exec VP
Tel: 317-870-6145
Email: ap@miles2.mystagingwebsite.com
Website: www.milesprinting.com
Commercial printing, offering digital, multi-color UV sheet-fed, large format printing, complete bindery, mailing & fulfillment capabilities. (Woman, estab 2006, empl 38, sales $13,600,000, cert: State, WBENC)

7529 Nicholson Printing Inc.
209 Eastern Blvd
Jeffersonville, IN 47130
Contact: Chris Nicholson VP
Tel: 812-283-1200
Email: chris@nicholsonprinting.com
Website: www.nicholsonprinting.com
Commercial & quick printing, graphic design, full-color printing, digital color, digital black & white, copying, letterheads, envelopes, business cards, business forms, carbonless forms, time cards, folders, books. (Woman, estab 1979, empl 12, sales $1,118,000, cert: State)

7530 Offset House Printing, Inc.
9374 Castlegate Dr
Indianapolis, IN 46256
Contact: Jay Williamson Acct Mgr
Tel: 317-849-5155
Email: jwilliamson@offsethouse.biz
Website: www.offsethouseinc.com
Commercial printing, graphic design & direct mail. (Woman, estab 1964, empl 13, sales , cert: State)

7531 Printing Inc of Louisville Kentucky
1600 Dutch Lane Ste A
Jeffersonville, IN 47130
Contact: Kelly Abney Mgr Business Devel
Tel: 502-368-6555
Email: wbe@prettyincredible.com
Website: www.prettyincredible.com
Print, fulfillment, distribution, marketing consulting, project management, direct mail with management of distributions, inventory & fulfillment of literature, bindery & kit packing. (Woman, estab 1971, empl 19, sales $3,000,000, cert: State)

7532 Thomas E. Slade, Inc.
      6220 Vogel Road
      Evansville, IN 47715
      Contact: Lisa Slade President
      Tel: 812-437-5233
      Email: tom@sladeprint.com
      Website: www.sladeprint.com
Printing, graphic design, website design, wide format posters & banners, mailing, promotional products, letterhead, envelopes, business cards, labels, tags, inserts, marketing services, augmented reality, QR codes for tracking, signs. (Woman, estab 1993, empl 17, sales $2,500,000, cert: State)

7533 Town & Country Printing
      1001 E Summit St
      Crown Point, IN 46307
      Contact: Debera Hinchy President
      Tel: 219-924-0441
      Email: dhinchy@tandcii.com
      Website: www.townandcountryprinting.com
Commercial printing - offset & digital. Traditional, large/grand format printing. Full color business cards, stationery, notepads, banners, indoor and outdoor signage, brochures, booklets, wall and floor graphics, decals (window, wall, floor). (Woman, estab 1970, empl 18, sales $1,800,000, cert: WBENC)

7534 UN Communications Group, Inc.
      1429 Chase Court
      Carmel, IN 46032
      Contact: Denise Purvis President
      Tel: 317-218-8262
      Email: dpurvis@uncommgroup.com
      Website: www.uncommgroup.com
Commercial, digital & wide format print services, mailing services, brochures, catalogs & annual reports, banners, vehicle wraps & tradeshow signage. (Woman, estab 1975, empl 32, sales $4,500,000, cert: State, City, WBENC)

7535 Valley Screen Process Company, Inc.
      58740 Executive Dr
      Mishawaka, IN 46544
      Contact: Karen Barnett CEO
      Tel: 574-256-0901
      Email: karenb@valleyscreen.com
      Website: www.valleyscreen.com
Commercial screen & digital printing. (Woman, estab 1967, empl 50, sales $7,445,882, cert: WBENC)

Kansas

7536 Total Print Solutions, Inc.
      3220 W 121st Terr
      Leawood, KS 66209
      Contact: Constance Kingsley President
      Tel: 913-481-7393
      Email: ckingsley@tpsmidwest.com
      Website: www.tpsmidwest.com
Commercial printing, pharma labels, digital print, magazine type publications, business forms, direct mail, warehousing & distribution. (Minority, Woman, estab 2000, empl 2, sales $800,000, cert: State, NMSDC)

Kentucky

7537 EDJ Inc.
      8158 Mall Rd
      Florence, KY 41042
      Contact: Maureen Schuler President
      Tel: 859-525-1199
      Email: maureen.schuler@fastsigns.com
      Website: www.fastsigns.com/226
Banners, posters, foam boards, decals, site signs, dimensional logos, coroplast signs, now hiring signs, production boards, & tradeshow products and graphics. (Woman, estab 1995, empl 5, sales $856,000, cert: WBENC)

7538 Multi-Craft Litho, Inc.
      131 E Sixth St
      Newport, KY 41072
      Contact: Debbie Simpson President
      Tel: 859-655-8863
      Email: dsimpson@multi-craft.com
      Website: www.multi-craft.com
Commercial printing: pocket folders, annual reports, posters, brochures, sell sheets, packaging, etc. (Woman, estab 1955, empl 50, sales $9,500,000, cert: WBENC)

Louisiana

7539 Advanced Graphic Engraving, LLC
      3105 Melancon Rd
      Broussard, LA 70518
      Contact: Monica Duplantis Mgr
      Tel: 337-364-1991
      Email: monica@tagsfast.com
      Website: www.tagsfast.com
Industrial Engraving: Safety Signage, Architectural signage, Vinyl signs & decals, Master/Well Control Panels, Sub Sea Well Control Panels, Flow Schematics, Data Tags, Operating Instruction Tags, Dual Language Tags, Angle Indicators, Crane Hand Signals. (Woman, estab 1997, empl 21, sales $2,000,000, cert: WBENC)

7540 Walle Corporation
      600 Elmwood Park Blvd
      Harahan, LA 70123
      Contact: Dave Taylor Business Devel
      Tel: 504-734-8000
      Email: dave_taylor@walle.com
      Website: www.walle.com
Lithographic & flexographic label printing. (Woman, estab , empl 175, sales , cert: WBENC)

Massachusetts

7541 Adam Graphic Corporation
      16 Mason Ave Unit 4
      North Attleboro, MA 02760
      Contact: Nancy Ruo President
      Tel: 508-699-2089
      Email: nancy@adamgraphic.com
      Website: www.adamgraphic.com
Printing, print management, forms, envelopes, marketing brochures, folders, binders, ID cards, labels, commerical print, digital print, signage, mailings, fulfillment, kitting, warehousing, on-line ordering, promotional products. (Woman, estab 1985, empl 5, sales $1,193,045, cert: State, WBENC)

7542 CSW Inc.
      45 Tyburski Rd
      Ludlow, MA 01056
      Contact: Scott Ellison VP Sales
      Tel: 800-800-9522
      Email: scotte@cswgraphics.com
      Website: www.cswgraphics.com
Packaging pre press, design, flexo plates, cutting dies. (Woman, estab 1936, empl 150, sales $16,160,013, cert: State, WBENC)

7543 Gangi Printing, Inc.
      17 Kensington Ave
      Somerville, MA 02145
      Contact: Stephen Gangi Sales
      Tel: 617-776-6071
      Email: steve@gangiprinting.com
      Website: www.gangiprinting.com
Promotional printing & book binding services, printed apparel, trade show displays & direct mail pieces. (Woman, estab 1972, empl 9, sales $1,200,000, cert: State)

7544 Print & More Associates
      143 North St
      Mattapoisett, MA 02739
      Contact: Fred Ford Sales Rep
      Tel: 617-899-3664
      Email: frford@p-massociates.com
      Website: www.p-massociates.com
Commercial printing, stationary, brochures, catalogs, window displays, POP, floor mats & banners. (AA, estab 2005, empl 6, sales $1,000,000, cert: NMSDC)

7545 Pyramid Printing and Advertising Inc
      58 Mathewson Dr
      Weymouth, MA 02189
      Contact: Bill Scheufele Sales Rep
      Tel: 781-337-7609
      Email: bill@pyramidprinting.net
      Website: www.pyramidprinting.net
Multicolor offset & digital graphics. (Woman, estab 1978, empl 14, sales $1,400,000, cert: State)

7546 Schmidt Printing, Inc.
      237 Chandler St
      Worcester, MA 01609
      Contact: Ariel Schmidt Dir Sales/Marketing
      Tel: 508-752-7600
      Email: ariel@schmidtprinting.ink
      Website: www.schmidtprinting.ink
Eight Color Offset Printing, HP Indigo Printing, Variable Data Printing, Stochastic Screening, Online Remote Proofing, In-House Mailing Services, Full Service Bindery & Fulfillment. (Hisp, estab 2011, empl 2, sales , cert: NMSDC)

7547 Shafiis' Inc.
      PO Box 215
      East Longmeadow, MA 01028
      Contact: Jennifer Shafii CEO
      Tel: 413-224-2100
      Email: jennifer@tigerpress.com
      Website: www.tigerpress.com
Custom printing, digital prepress, packaging & bindery services. (Woman, estab 1985, empl 70, sales $8,800,000, cert: State)

7548 Spotlight Graphics, Inc.
      9-B Whalley Way
      Southwick, MA 01077
      Contact: Diane Demarco Sales
      Tel: 413-998-3232
      Email: info@SpotlightGraphicsInc.com
      Website: www.SpotlightGraphicsInc.com
Large format printing. (Woman, estab 2013, empl 5, sales $165,000, cert: State, WBENC)

7549 Standard Modern Company, Inc.
      186 Duchaine Blvd.
      New Bedford, MA 02745
      Contact: Bob Crowell Sales
      Tel: 508-586-4300
      Email: bcrowell@standardmodern.com
      Website: www.standardmodern.com
Commercial printing. (Woman, estab 1974, empl 44, sales $7,596,467, cert: WBENC)

7550 Starburst Printing & Graphics
      300 Hopping Brook Rd
      Holliston, MA 01764
      Contact: Jason Grondin VP
      Tel: 800-244-8396
      Email: jgrondin@starburstprinting.com
      Website: www.starburstprinting.com
Printing svcs: prepress, digital & offset & post press services. (Hisp, estab 1988, empl 22, sales $2,600,000, cert: State, NMSDC)

7551 Summit Press Inc.
      63 Sixth St
      Chelsea, MA 02150
      Contact: Lenore DelVecchio President
      Tel: 617-889-3991
      Email: lsava@summitpress.com
      Website: www.summitpress.com
Printing services: 2-6 color sheetfed. (Woman, estab 1961, empl 22, sales $2,910,000, cert: State)

7552 The Matlet Group
      30 Industrial Way
      Wilmington, MA 01887
      Contact: Sheldon Ross Dir of Natl Accounts
      Tel: 401-834-3007
      Email: sross@thematletgroup.com
      Website: www.thematletgroup.com
Printing & graphic services. (As-Pac, estab 2005, empl 408, sales $99,498,000, cert: NMSDC)

Maryland

7553 Alpha Graphics, Inc.
      1750 Union Ave, Unit B
      Baltimore, MD 21211
      Contact: Christine Walsh President
      Tel: 410-727-1400
      Email: cwalsh@alphagrap.com
      Website: www.alpha-graphics.net
Large format printing: banners & signs, posters, mounting, laminating, framing, graphic design, menu boards, point of purchase, adhesive vinyl, cut vinyl, trade show display (Woman, estab 1972, empl 7, sales $853,948, cert: State, City, WBENC)

PRINTING & ENGRAVING

7554 Art & Negative Graphics, Inc.
4621 Boston Way Ste C
Lanham, MD 20706
Contact: Adrienne Myers Strategic Acct Exec
Tel: 301-459-8911
Email: amyers@artneg.com
Website: www.artneg.com
Prepress, digital & offset printing; full bindery; mailing services; storage and fulfillment. (Woman, estab 1981, empl 42, sales $6,425,530, cert: State, WBENC)

7555 Black Classic Press
3921 Vero Rd Ste F
Halethorpe, MD 21227
Contact: Principal
Tel: 410-242-6954
Email:
Website: www.bcpdigital.com
Printing svcs: ultra short-run book & document printing, digital. (AA, estab 1978, empl 9, sales $1,500,000, cert: State)

7556 Britt's Industries Inc.
40 HUDSON ST STE 112
Annapolis, MD 21401
Contact: President
Tel: 410-266-8100
Email: contact@wosbprinting.com
Website: www.wosbprinting.com
Commercial printing, offset, digital, prepress, graphic design, business cards, envelopes, letterhead, brochures, pamphlets. (Woman/As-Pac, estab 1976, empl , sales $784,035, cert: WBENC, 8(a))

7557 Centaur Graphics LLC
12109 Glissans Mill Rd
Union Bridge, MD 21791
Contact: Carl wurzer VP Sales
Tel: 202-297-7575
Email: carl@centaurgraphics.com
Website: www.centaurgraphics.com
Commercial Printing, Direct Mail Printing, Digital Printing, Labels, Envelopes, Fulfillment, Warehousing, Logistics, Mailing , corrugated boxes, packaging, assembly, print on demand, web to print, saddle stich, perfect bound. (Woman, estab 1994, empl 4, sales $784,000, cert: WBENC)

7558 IVY Services, LLC
PO Box 20092
Baltimore, MD 21284
Contact: Tammy Boccia VP
Tel: 410-235-1489
Email: tboccia@ivy-services.com
Website: www.ivy-services.com
Offset printing: letterhead, envelopes, business cards, brochures, flyers, string & button, metal clasp, latex, peel & seal, tear strip & shrink wrapping. (Woman, estab 2004, empl 2, sales $5,511,950, cert: State, WBENC)

7559 Strouse
1211 Independence Way
Westminster, MD 21157
Contact: Scott Chambers Business Devel Mgr
Tel: 410-848-1611
Email: dchambers@strouse.com
Website: www.strouse.com
Rotary die-cutting, slitting, 6 color printing, laminations. (Woman, estab 1986, empl 70, sales $18,500,000, cert: WBENC)

Michigan

7560 Argent Tape & Label, Inc.
41016 Concept Dr, Ste A
Plymouth, MI 48170
Contact: Lynn Perenic President
Tel: 734-582-9955
Email: lperenic@argent-label.com
Website: www.argent-label.com
Custom tape & label solutions. (Woman, estab 1995, empl 20, sales $14,000,000, cert: WBENC)

7561 Graphic Resource Group
528 Robbins Dr
Troy, MI 48083
Contact: Allen Pyc President
Tel: 248-588-6100
Email: apyc@graphicresource.com
Website: www.graphicresource.com
Large format digital & screen printing, offset printing on plastics, promotional products. (Woman, estab 1990, empl 20, sales , cert: WBENC)

7562 Graywolf Printing
757 S Eton St
Birmingham, MI 48009
Contact: Max Grayvold President
Tel: 248-540-5930
Email: graywolf@ameritech.net
Website: www.graywolfprinting.com/
Printing services. (Nat Ame, estab 0, empl 0, sales $772,368, cert: NMSDC)

7563 Hatteras Printing, Inc.
12801 Prospect St
Dearborn, MI 48126
Contact: Rebecca McFarlane VP
Tel: 313-624-3300
Email: bmcfarlane@4hatteras.com
Website: www.4hatteras.com
Commercial printing. (Woman, estab 1977, empl 70, sales , cert: WBENC)

7564 Imax Company Inc.
22326 Woodward Ave
Ferndale, MI 48220
Contact: Jay Williams President
Tel: 248-629-9680
Email: jay@imaxprinting.com
Website: www.imaxprinting.com
Commercial printing, offset full color printing, multi page booklets, manuals, business cards, brochures, sales sheets, envelopes, posters, postcards, flyers, rack cards, special shapes (die cutting). (AA, estab 2009, empl 5, sales $879,852, cert: NMSDC)

7565 Impact Label Corp.
3434 S Burdick St
Kalamazoo, MI 49001
Contact: Jill Jones Acct Mgr
Tel: 269-381-4280
Email: jillj@impactlabel.com
Website: www.impactlabel.com
Labels, domed labels,tamper evident labels, nameplates, tags, polycarbonate overlays, control panel overlays, warning labels, product identification, serial numbers, security tags, inventory tags, asset labels, ingredient labels. (Woman, estab 1964, empl 50, sales , cert: WBENC)

PRINTING & ENGRAVING

7566 Kimprint, Inc. dba Progressive Printing
1326 Goldsmith
Plymouth, MI 48170
Contact: Bruce Price vp
Tel: 734-459-2960
Email: sales@progressiveprint.com
Website: www.progressiveprint.com
Full color printing: flyers, brochures, postcards, directmail, stock & color consulting. (Woman, estab 1989, empl 20, sales $2,300,000, cert: WBENC)

7567 New Echelon
280 S Southbound Gratiot Ave
Mt. Clemens, MI 48043
Contact: Michael Arnold President
Tel: 586-307-8001
Email: mcarnold@newechelon.com
Website: www.newechelon.com
Printing, bindery, big color output services. (AA, estab 1996, empl 8, sales , cert: NMSDC)

7568 SMTAutomation LLC
15895 Sturgeon St
Roseville, MI 48066
Contact: Omar Guzman
Tel: 586-585-1428
Email: omguzman@smtautomationllc.com
Website: www.smtautomationllc.com
Outsourcing services, Laser Marking, 3D Printing, Engineering Services. (Hisp, estab 2017, empl 35, sales $6,300,000, cert: NMSDC)

7569 Stylerite Label Corporation
2140 Avon Industrial Dr
Rochester Hills, MI 48309
Contact: Danielle J. Kay Sales Exec
Tel: 419-367-3772
Email: dkay@styleritelabel.com
Website: www.styleritelabel.com
Mfr Tags & Forms, short to long runs, 4 color process up to 8 colors, rolls, sheets, singles, fan-folded, continuous, printing on adhesive side of labels, lamination, UV varnish. (Woman, estab 1989, empl 25, sales $6,200,000, cert: WBENC)

7570 The MardonGroup LLC
701 Woodward Heights Ste 128
Ferndale, MI 48220
Contact: Shawn Torrence VP Business Dev
Tel: 248-336-3376
Email: s.torrence@mardongroup.com
Website: www.mardongroup.com
Sheet-Fed Printing, Digital Printing, Design, Creative, Layout, Desktop Publishing, Binding, Envelopes, Mail list Processing, List Rental/Purchase, Offline Finishing, Digital/Mobile marketing. (AA, estab 2005, empl 15, sales , cert: NMSDC)

Minnesota

7571 Booth Publications Ink
1217 Seminole Ave
West St Paul, MN 55118
Contact: Jason Booth CEO
Tel: 651-338-8140
Email: jason@boothpublications.com
Website: www.boothpublications.com
Print services: off-set (web & sheet fed), digital, large format & plastic card printing. (Nat Ame, estab 1999, empl 6, sales $3,000,000, cert: NMSDC)

7572 Bromley Printing, Inc.
514 Northdale Blvd
Minneapolis, MN 55448
Contact: Elizabeth Bromley President
Tel: 763-767-0000
Email: elizabeth@bromleyprinting.com
Website: www.bromleyprinting.com
Printing, graphic design & marketing, multi-color printing, digital printing, in-house pre-press, graphic design, bindery & mailing services. (Woman, estab 1986, empl 10, sales , cert: WBENC)

7573 Bywater Business Solutions LLC
800 Washington Ave SE Ste 203
Minneapolis, MN 55414
Contact: Christopher Ferguson CEO
Tel: 763-244-1090
Email: chris@bywater.co
Website: www.bywater.co
Printing: envelopes, labels, letterhead, notecards, folders, business forms, booklets, checks, business cards, direct mail, signs, annual reports, post-it notes. (Hisp, estab 2009, empl 3, sales $185,000, cert: State)

7574 Char-Dell Sign Co.
1017 109th Ave NE
Blaine, MN 55434
Contact: Charlette Grandell VP
Tel: 763-784-8252
Email: ken.grandell@fastsigns.com
Website: www.fastsigns.com/337
Wide Format Digital Printing, Banners, Banner Stands, Trade Show Booths, Trade Show Graphics, ADA & OSHA Compliant, Safety & Identification Materials, Presentation Materials, Posters, Name Tags, Large & Small Vehicle. (Woman, estab 1998, empl 4, sales $400,000, cert: City)

7575 Cimarron Graphics
15400 28th Ave N
Plymouth, MN 55447
Contact: Barbara Schulz CEO
Tel: 952-697-3400
Email: barb@cimgraphics.com
Website: www.cimgraphics.com
Commercial sheet fed & digital printing: brochures, postcards, catalogs, business forms, calendars, tabs, magnets, greeting cards, envelopes, letterhead, labels, annual reports, flyers, header cards, inserts, pocket folders. (Woman, estab 2004, empl 15, sales $1,598,609, cert: State)

7576 Clear Lake Press, Inc.
300 16th Ave SE
Waseca, MN 56093
Contact: Phyllis Beschnett CEO
Tel: 507-835-4430
Email: pbeschnett@clearlakepress.com
Website: www.clearlakepress.com
Marketing & printing solutions, sheet-fed, digital & variable, fulfillment, design services, collateral development & direct marketing, outdoor advertising & customized apparel services. (Woman, estab 1988, empl 34, sales $4,099,574, cert: WBENC)

7577 Dan Dolan Printing
2301 E Hennepin Ave
Minneapolis, MN 55413
Contact: Jeanne Dolan CEO
Tel: 612-379-2311
Email: jeannedolan@dolanprinting.com
Website: www.dolanprinting.com
Printing & marketing services: offset/lithographic printing, digital printing, large format printing, signage, banners, publication, textile printing, light boxes, trade show displays, pamphlet, printed packaging. (Woman, estab 1985, empl 28, sales $6,434,227, cert: WBENC)

7578 Docunet Corporation
2435 Xenium Ln N
Plymouth, MN 55441
Contact: Wendy Morical President
Tel: 800-936-2863
Email: wnm@docunetworks.com
Website: www.docunetworks.com
Digital printing: black & white, color, database management, direct mail & fulfillment. (Woman, estab 1991, empl 12, sales $1,790,000, cert: WBENC)

7579 Highlight Printing Inc.
3839 Washington Ave N
Minneapolis, MN 55412
Contact: Lisa Bickford President
Tel: 612-522-7600
Email: lisab@highlightprinting.com
Website: www.highlightprinting.com
Offset & digital 1-4 color printing, high-impact high-touch projects, thermography, design, direct mail, warehousing, kitting, niche fulfillment, distribution, work-flow system, saddle stitching, wire-o binding, binding. (Woman, estab , empl , sales $1,205,000, cert: WBENC)

7580 Ideal Printers
645 Olive St
Saint Paul, MN 55130
Contact: Emily Stevenson Acct Rep
Tel: 651-855-1064
Email: emily.stevenson@idealprint.com
Website: www.idealprint.com
Commercial sheetfed printing: 1-6 color & aqueous coating, brochures, newsletters, annual reports, posters, catalogs, packaging, stationary products. (Woman, estab 1979, empl 85, sales $12,625,028, cert: WBENC)

7581 IntegriPrint, Inc.
309 12th Ave S
Buffalo, MN 55313
Contact: Jacqueline Wurm Owner
Tel: 763-682-3750
Email: jackie@integriprint.com
Website: www.integriprint.com
Printing, graphic design & mailing services. (Woman, estab 1994, empl 5, sales $590,338, cert: WBENC)

7582 Lightning Printing dba Wallace Carlson Co.
10825 Greenbrier Rd
Minnetonka, MN 55305
Contact: Ann Turbeville CEO
Tel: 952-277-1210
Email: ann@wc-print.com
Website: www.wc-print.com
Printing svcs: 1-6color offset, sheetfed, aqueous coating, full color & B/W digital printing, mailing & fullfillment services. (Woman, estab 1984, empl 47, sales $9,128,000, cert: WBENC)

7583 Northstar Imaging Services, Inc.
1325 Eagandale Court Ste 130
Eagan, MN 55121
Contact: Martha Smyre CEO
Tel: 651-686-0477
Email: planroom@northstarimaging.com
Website: www.northstarimaging.com
Reprographic svcs, large & small format, plotting, scanning, color imagery & document mgmt. (Woman, estab 1997, empl 5, sales $6,500,000, cert: State, City)

7584 SeaChange Print Innovations
14505 27th Ave N
Plymouth, MN 55447
Contact: Nancy Servais Business Devel
Tel: 763-586-3700
Email: nancy.servais@seachangem.com
Website: www.seachangemn.com
Folding carton & marketing print production, Folding Carton Packaging, Marketing Printing, Commercial Printing, Direct Mail Printing, Digital Printing. (Woman, estab 2014, empl 90, sales $13,100,000, cert: WBENC)

7585 Team One Printing, Inc.
635 Ninth St SE, Ste 180
Minneapolis, MN 55414
Contact: Grace Wong President
Tel: 612-481-5907
Email: grace@teamoneprinting.com
Website: www.teamoneprinting.com
Commercial print & display graphics: manuals, directories, catalogs, direct mail pieces, portable trade show displays, banner stands, wall murals, vehicle graphics, sign & banner graphics, large format posters. (Minority, Woman, estab 2006, empl 3, sales , cert: NMSDC)

Missouri

7586 Complete Solutions LLC
2233 N Village
St. Charles, MO 63303
Contact: Donna Gastreich Owner
Tel: 314-640-6633
Email: dgastreich@complete-solutionsllc.com
Website: www.complete-solutionsllc.com
Printing svcs: letterhead, business cards, envelopes, invoices, BOL, labels, tags, folders, binders, index tabs, brochures, catalogs & checks, direct mail services, promotional products & advertising specialty items. (Woman, estab 2008, empl 1, sales , cert: State, City)

7587 Isringhaus Printing LLC
11012 Lin Valle Dr, Ste D
Affton, MO 63123
Contact: Patricia Isringhaus Owner
Tel: 314-416-9955
Email: patti@isringhausprinting.com
Website: www.isringhausprinting.com
Commercial printing services. (Woman, estab 2002, empl 6, sales $600,000, cert: State, WBENC)

7588 Modern Litho-Print Co.
6009 Stertzer Rd
Jefferson City, MO 65101
Contact: Debra Patterson Cstmr Service
Tel: 573-635-6119
Email: debra@modernlitho.com
Website: www.modernlitho.com
Printing: annual reports, newsletters, books, magazines, promotional materials, labels, etc. (Woman, estab 1937, empl 88, sales $14,500,000, cert: State)

7589 PrintCOR Solutions
      826 Heatherhaven Dr
      Ballwin, MO 63011
      Contact: Kelly Kohn Owner
      Tel: 636-891-9900
      Email: customerservice@printcorsolutions.com
      Website: www.printcorsolutions.com
Labels/tags: blank stock labels, barcode pre-printed labels, numbered barcode labels, thermal ribbons, integrated labels, piggy back labels, full color labels, die cut labels & custom labels. (Woman, estab 2006, empl 2, sales $1,500,000, cert: State)

7590 PrintFlex Graphics
      2201 January Ave
      St. Louis, MO 63110
      Contact: Elizabeth Pecha-Poelker CEO
      Tel: 800-406-7093
      Email: eap@print-flex.com
      Website: www.printflexgraphics.com
Promotional printing: instant redeemable coupons, dry release, folded & placed booklets, USDA & FDA direct food contact printing. (Woman, estab 1995, empl 35, sales $6,128,000, cert: State, NWBOC)

Mississippi

7591 Ranger Distributing, Inc dba Ranger Label
      286 Commerce Park Dr
      Ridgeland, MS 39157
      Contact: Bob Anger VP
      Tel: 601-898-1380
      Email: banger@rangerlabel.com
      Website: www.rangerlabel.com
Prime 8 color pressure sensitive labels, blank thermal labels, complete color process controls. (Woman, estab 1979, empl 14, sales $3,000,000, cert: WBENC)

North Carolina

7592 DocuSource of North Carolina
      2800 Slater Rd
      Morrisville, NC 27560
      Contact: Michael Chorba President
      Tel: 919-459-5909
      Email: mchorba@docusourceofnc.com
      Website: www.docusourceofnc.com
Commercial digital printing, bindery, fulfillment & distribution services. (Woman, estab 2002, empl 46, sales $8,000,000, cert: State)

7593 Labels, Tags & Inserts, Inc.
      2302 Air Park Dr
      Burlington, NC 27215
      Contact: Rhonda Baker President
      Tel: 336-227-8485
      Email: rhondab@lti-us.com
      Website: www.labelstagsandinserts.com
Flexographic printing services: pressure sensitive labels, shrink film sleeves, vinyl labels, scratch off labels, tamper-evident labels, clear labels, hot foil labels, embossed labels, holographic labels. (Woman, estab 1995, empl 27, sales $7,000,000, cert: WBENC)

7594 PharmaPress, Inc.
      3360 Old Lexington Rd
      Winston-Salem, NC 27107
      Contact: Terri Roth President
      Tel: 973-376-6625
      Email: pharmapress@gmail.com
      Website: www.pharmapressinc.com
Mfr inserts, outserts, booklets, pamphlets, cards and pads. (Woman, estab 2004, empl 164, sales $2,400,000, cert: State)

7595 Progressive Business Solutions, Inc.
      508 New Hope Rd
      Raleigh, NC 27610
      Contact: Tim Catlett President
      Tel: 919-255-6500
      Email: tcatlett@progform.com
      Website: www.progform.com
Commercial printing, business forms, promotional products, copy & computer paper, web ordering capabilities, office supplies, forms mgmt & warehouse dist. (AA, estab 1988, empl , sales $6,000,000, cert: NMSDC)

7596 Southern Print & Imaging, Inc.
      9311-D Monroe Rd
      Charlotte, NC 28270
      Contact: Barbara Jones President
      Tel: 704-708-5818
      Email: barbara@allegracharlotte.com
      Website: www.allegracharlotte.com
Offset & digital printing, mail services, list sourcing, direct mail, brochures, flyers, newsletters, postcards, booklets & promotional products. (Woman, estab 2004, empl 4, sales $411,000, cert: City)

New Jersey

7597 4 Banner Inc. (DBA Alchemy Printing)
      125 5th Ave
      Paterson, NJ 07524
      Contact: Brett Haikins Production Coordinator
      Tel: 973-341-1311
      Email: jobs@4banner.com
      Website: www.4banner.com
Large format printing: vinyl banners, mesh banners, dye sublimation fabric banners, trade show displays, banner stands, flatbed UV printing. (As-Pac, estab 2010, empl 6, sales $550,000, cert: NMSDC)

7598 A+ Letter Service
      200 Syracuse Ct
      Lakewood, NJ 08701
      Contact: Elizabeth Fricke Sales Support Sspecialist
      Tel: 732-905-2010
      Email: aplus@aplusletter.com
      Website: www.aplusletter.com
Print mailing inserts, postcards, brochures, marketing fulfillment, four-color digital printing, mailing services. (Woman, estab 1986, empl 75, sales $5,000,000, cert: State)

7599 AJ Images.com
      259 E First Ave
      Roselle, NJ 07203
      Contact: Lisa Greebel
      Tel: 908-241-6900
      Email: lisa@ajimages.com
      Website: www.ajimages.com
Commercial printing: brochures, newsletters, annual reports, magazines, technical pieces, posters, postcards, bill stuffers, direct mail, price lists & catalogs. (Woman, estab 1967, empl 23, sales $4,500,000, cert: State)

7600 American Plus Printers, Inc.
      2604 Atlantic Ave Ste 300
      Wall, NJ 07719
      Contact: President
      Tel: 732-528-2170
      Email:
      Website: www.americanplusprinters.com
Commercial printing, design & mailing capabilities. (Woman, estab 2002, empl 10, sales $1,150,000, cert: State)

PRINTING & ENGRAVING 7601-7611

7601 Arna Marketing
      60 Readington Road
      Branchburg, NJ 08876
      Contact: Jakob Hegna Sales Rep
      Tel: 908-231-1100
      Email: jhegna@arnamarketing.com
      Website: www.arnamarketing.com
Digital printing: mailings, brochures, flyers, booklets, envelopes, letterhead, business cards, newsletters, coupons, etc. (Woman, estab 2005, empl 80, sales $40,000,000, cert: WBENC)

7602 Capital Printing Corporation
      420 South Ave
      Middlesex, NJ 08846
      Contact: Brett Russo
      Tel: 732-560-1515
      Email: brettr@capitalprintingcorp.com
      Website: www.capitalprintingcorp.com
Printing services, die cutting & binding, automated in-line gluing & inserting, warehouse & mailing abilities. (Woman, estab 1983, empl 85, sales $15,100,000, cert: WBENC)

7603 CCG Marketing Services
      14 Henderson Dr
      West Caldwell, NJ 07006
      Contact: Steve Stern Sr Acct Exec
      Tel: 973-808-0009
      Email: sstern@corpcomm.com
      Website: www.ccgms.com
Printing, offset, digital with variable data, web 1:1 mktg, Digital Print Tech, Sales Collateral & Promotional Materials, Sales Force Support, Order Fulfillment. (Woman, estab , empl , sales $20,000,000, cert: WBENC)

7604 CRW Graphics
      9100 Pennsauken Hwy
      Pennsauken, NJ 08110
      Contact: Kathleen Chinnici Acct Dir
      Tel: 800-820-3000
      Email: kchinnici@crwgraphics.com
      Website: www.crwgraphics.com
Digital & critical color prepress services & printing: 1 to 6 colors, bindery, fulfillment & mailing services. (Woman, estab 1993, empl 90, sales $15,500,000, cert: WBENC)

7605 Direct Mail Depot
      200 Circle Dr N
      Piscataway, NJ 08854
      Contact: Terrie Stonack President
      Tel: 305-819-1065
      Email: tstonack@dtsdirectmail.com
      Website: www.directmaildepot.com
Postal services, digital printing, finishing, lettershop services, data processing, mail tracking & handling & fulfillment services (Woman/Hisp, estab 1999, empl 150, sales $14,300,000, cert: State)

7606 Federal Business Products Inc.
      150 Clove Road, 5th Floor 5th Fl
      Little Falls, NJ 07424
      Contact: Angela Stubbs President
      Tel: 973-272-7066
      Email: astubbs@feddirect.com
      Website: www.feddirect.com
Print, direct mail data & fulfillment services: data processing, sheet digital print, continuous form printing to 10 colors, continuous form laser (simplex, duplex, MICR) & inkjet personalization, bindery, fulfillment lettershop mailing services. (Woman, estab , empl , sales $15,663,435, cert: WBENC)

7607 FrontEnd Graphics Inc.
      1951 Old Cuthbert Road, Ste 414
      Cherry Hill, NJ 08034
      Contact: Elizabeth Maul President
      Tel: 856-547-1600
      Email: bettymaul@frontendgraphics.com
      Website: www.frontendgraphics.com
Layout, design, database mgmt, large project mgmt, digital photography, large output, direct to plate & press, finishing, distribution, kitting, mailing. Sheet fed, web, envelopes, label, manual, technical illustration, book publishing. (Woman, estab 1983, empl 13, sales $1,300,000, cert: WBENC)

7608 HighRoad Press, LLC
      220 Anderson Ave
      Moonachie, NJ 07074
      Contact: Hallie Satz CEO
      Tel: 201-708-6900
      Email: hallie@highroadpress.com
      Website: www.highroadpress.com
Printing: web & sheet fed, offset sheet fed printing up to 8/C aqueous coating, offset half web didde press, coldset web & offset full web, packaging & DVD packaging. (Woman, estab 2004, empl 45, sales $10,000,000, cert: State, WBENC)

7609 Industrial Labeling Systems, Inc.
      50 Kulick Rd
      Fairfield, NJ 07004
      Contact: Keith Meyer Reg Sales Mgr
      Tel: 973-882-9688
      Email: kmeyer@e-ilsi.com
      Website: www.e-ilsi.com
Mfr & dist pressure-sensitive labels, prime labels, mailing labels, product ID labels, direct thermal labels, supermarket thermal scale labels, coupons, bar codes, tub labels, retail shelf marketing labels. (As-Pac, estab 1997, empl 23, sales $3,500,000, cert: State)

7610 Mahin Impressions, Inc. DBA Kirkwood Mahin
      600 Meadowlands Pkwy
      Secaucus, NJ 07094
      Contact: Sharon Mahin President
      Tel: 201-870-6300
      Email: smahin@kirkwood-mahin.com
      Website: www.kirkwood-mahin.com/
Offset & digital printing, digital & xerograhpy services, large format, finishing, binding, fullfillment & mailing. (Woman, estab 1983, empl 250, sales $20,000,000, cert: WBENC, SDB)

7611 Mountain Printing Company Inc.
      PO Box 608
      Berlin, NJ 08009
      Contact: Mark DiClementi Dir of Operations
      Tel: 856-767-7600
      Email: mark@mountainprinting.com
      Website: www.mountainprinting.com
Commerical, packaging & digial printing services: bindery, pre-press, press, bindery, coatings, die cutting, foil stamping, embossing, box manufacturing & mailing capabilities. (Woman, estab 1962, empl 25, sales $2,499,116, cert: State)

PRINTING & ENGRAVING

7612 P/EK Press
      7 Essex Rd
      Scotch Plains, NJ 07076
      Contact: Ann Kahn Owner
      Tel: 908-305-1960
      Email: annelizabethkahn@gmail.com
      Website: www.pekpress.com
Commercial printing & graphic design: NCR forms, Brochures, Stationery, Posters, Direct Mail, Letterhead, Envelopes, Business Cards, Postcards, Note Cards, Presentation Folders, Pads. (Woman, estab 1989, empl 1, sales $126,000, cert: State)

7613 Positive Publications LLC
      65 Madison Ave Ste 510
      Morristown, NJ 07960
      Contact: Susan Poeton COO
      Tel: 973-218-0310
      Email: spoeton@positivepublications.us
      Website: www.positivepublications.us
Publishing, magazines, guides, pamphlets, periodicals, reprints, newsletters & e-newsletters. (Woman, estab 1998, empl 8, sales $827,880, cert: State)

7614 Primary Colors Graphics Inc.
      629 Grove St 7th Fl
      Jersey City, NJ 07310
      Contact: Cecilia Chin Controller
      Tel: 201-526-9300
      Email: cecilia@primarycolorsgraphics.com
      Website: www.primarycolorsgraphics.com
Commercial Offset Printing, Lithographic Printing, business cards, posters, finishing, trimming, die-cut, score, foil stamping, embossing. (As-Pac, estab 2012, empl 12, sales $1,303,673, cert: State)

7615 Riegel Printing Inc.
      One Graphics Dr
      Ewing, NJ 08628
      Contact: Brian Haley President
      Tel: 609-771-0555
      Email: brian.haley@riegelprintinginc.com
      Website: www.riegelprintinginc.com
Commercial printing svcs: pre-press, bindery, one to six color. (Woman, estab 1935, empl 75, sales $28,000,000, cert: WBENC)

7616 RJ Graphics, Inc.
      206 Crown Point Rd
      West Deptford, NJ 08086
      Contact: John Iannelli Dir
      Tel: 856-848-1986
      Email: jiannelli@rjgraphicsprinting.com
      Website: www.rjgraphicsprinting.com
Commercial sheet-fed printing, digital printing, fulfillment, direct mail & web creative services. (Woman, estab 1979, empl 22, sales $3,300,000, cert: WBENC)

7617 Sheroy Printing
      220 Entin Rd
      Clifton, NJ 07014
      Contact: Robert Sternau Dir New Business Dev
      Tel: 973-242-4040
      Email: roberts@onesourcenj.com
      Website: www.onesourcenj.com
Graphic communications, mktg collateral, annual reports, catalogs, presentation kits, packaging, wide format point-of-purchase materials, direct mail & publications. (Woman, estab 1984, empl 65, sales $2,000,000, cert: State)

7618 Wheal-Grace Corporation
      300 Ralph St
      Belleville, NJ 07109
      Contact: Emil Salvini Dir of Marketing
      Tel: 973-450-8100
      Email: salvini@wheal-grace.com
      Website: www.wheal-grace.com
Printing: corporate literature, product information, news magazines, business cards, letterheads, portfolios, posters. (Woman, estab 1946, empl 16, sales $11,301,000, cert: State)

New Mexico

7619 Captiva Group
      3838 Bogan Ave NE
      Albuquerque, NM 87109
      Contact: Jane Fernandez VP Business Dev
      Tel: 505-872-2200
      Email: jfernandez@thecaptivagroup.com
      Website: www.thecaptivagroup.com
Four color offset commercial printing; newsletters, business forms, envelopes, posters, books, etc. (Hisp, estab 1981, empl 100, sales $22,000,000, cert: NMSDC)

7620 R.W. Chavez, Inc.
      1361 Flight Way SE
      Albuquerque, NM 87106
      Contact: Nate Tapia Sales
      Tel: 505-264-2453
      Email: nate@stixon.com
      Website: www.stixon.com
Commercial flexographic printing & mfr labels, pressure sensitive labels. (Minority, Woman, estab 1985, empl 15, sales $2,800,000, cert: NWBOC)

Nevada

7621 Haig's Quality Printing
      6360 Sunset Corporate Dr
      Las Vegas, NV 89120
      Contact: Garo Atamian VP
      Tel: 702-966-1000
      Email: gatamian@haigsprinting.com
      Website: www.haigsprinting.com
Commercial print & mail shop, offset & digital. (Woman, estab 1996, empl 25, sales $3,500,000, cert: WBENC)

New York

7622 Ampie Enterprises, Inc.
      100 College Ave Ste 130
      Rochester, NY 14607
      Contact: Tina Paradiso President
      Tel: 585-482-4400
      Email: tinap@imprintablesolutions.com
      Website: www.imprintablesolutions.com
Envelopes, forms, carbonless sheets, reports, brochures & informational collateral. (Woman, estab 2013, empl 8, sales $1,500,000, cert: State)

7623 Bell Imaging Inc.
      2055 Cruger Ave, Ste 5E
      Bronx County, NY 10462
      Contact: Megan Blackburn Sales Mgr
      Tel: 862-262-6128
      Email: mblackburn@bellimagingonline.com
      Website: www.bellimagingonline.com
Printing services, 1 to 6 color, commercial & direct mail, bindery, pre-press, fullfilment. (AA, estab 2004, empl 8, sales , cert: NMSDC)

PRINTING & ENGRAVING

7624 Brigar XPress Solutions Inc, dba Digital XPress
5 Sand Creek Rd
Albany, NY 12205
Contact: Tracy Terry VP Sales
Tel: 518-437-5349
Email: tracy@dxp1.com
Website: www.dxp1.com
Print and mail services, offset, digital, and large format printing. (Woman, estab 1988, empl 72, sales $9,435,127, cert: State)

7625 Classic Labels Inc.
217 River Ave
Patchogue, NY 11772
Contact: Steven Ayala President
Tel: 718-463-0256
Email: sayala@classiclabels.com
Website: www.classiclabels.com
Specialty pressure sensitive labels. (Hisp, estab 1979, empl 100, sales , cert: NMSDC)

7626 Dakota Print and Premiums LLC
150 Barton Road
White Plains, NY 10605
Contact: Stuart Standard President
Tel: 914-831-9101
Email: stuart@fuseprinting.com
Website: www.fuseprinting.com
Promotional products, commercial printing, wide format & transit advertising, vehicle wraps, directories, transit & marketing tools provider, screen printing, banners, posters, postcards, journals, award items, etc. (Woman/AA, estab 2004, empl 3, sales $606,000, cert: State, City, NMSDC)

7627 Duggal Visual Solutions
63 Flushing Ave, Bldg 25
Brooklyn, NY 11205
Contact: George Whalen CFO
Tel: 212-242-7000
Email: cm@duggal.com
Website: www.duggal.com
Digital Sheet Fed Print, Wide Format Print, Photographic Print, 3D Print, Painting, Mounting, Laser cutting, Routering, Finishing, Framing, Digital Display, Lightboxes, SEG Graphics, Digital Animation, Beauty Graphics. (As-Ind, estab 1963, empl 400, sales $92,000,000, cert: State, City, NMSDC)

7628 Fred Weidner & Daughter Printers
15 Maiden Ln, Ste 1601
New York, NY 10038
Contact: Cynthia Weidner President
Tel: 212-964-8676
Email: cynthia@fwdprinters.com
Website: www.fwdprinters.com
Printing services. (Woman, estab , empl 6, sales , cert: State)

7629 Graphic Arts Inc.
11 Bertel Ave
Mount Vernon, NY 10550
Contact: Wayne Purveille
Tel: 914-663-8395
Email: wp@graphicartsinc.net
Website: www.graphicartsinc.net
Design & print brochures, newsletters, pamphlets, pocket folders, annual reports, sheets catalog mailing inserts, etc. (Woman/AA, estab 1994, empl 9, sales , cert: State, City, NMSDC)

7630 Millennium Signs & Display, Inc.
90 W Graham Ave
Hempstead, NY 11550
Contact: Saj Khalfan President
Tel: 516-292-8000
Email: saj@msdny.com
Website: www.msdny.com
Signs and Graphics; Point of Purchase Displays; Large Format Digital Printing; Wayfinding Signage; 3-Dimensional Letters and Logos; Lenticular Graphics; Laser & Waterjet Cutting; Architectural Signage. (Minority, estab 2008, empl 28, sales $5,255,000, cert: City, NMSDC)

7631 Minority Graphics Inc.
4202 Third Ave
Brooklyn, NY 11232
Contact: President
Tel: 212-255-4355
Email: alec@minoritygraphics.com
Website: www.minoritygraphics.com
Offset & digital printing, fulfillment. (Woman/AA, estab 2004, empl 3, sales $190,000, cert: City, NMSDC)

7632 No Other Impressions, Inc.
27 Tower Dr
Rochester, NY 14623
Contact: Elaine McCarthy CEO
Tel: 585-436-8500
Email: elaine@nootherimpressions.com
Website: www.nootherimpressions.com
Commercial color printing & fullfillment, digital & offset printing process. Complete in house bindery & fullfillment services. (Woman, estab 1990, empl 15, sales $1,800,000, cert: WBENC)

7633 North American D.F., Inc.
280 Watchogue Rd
Staten Island, NY 10314
Contact: Debbie Ayala President
Tel: 718-698-2500
Email: debbie@northamericandf.com
Website: www.northamericandf.com
Commercial printing: 8 color, web & sheet fed, business forms, brochures, booklets, business stationary, folders, direct mailers, posters labels. (Woman, estab 1992, empl 10, sales $3,000,000, cert: State, City, WBENC)

7634 Panther Graphics Inc.
465 Central Ave
Rochester, NY 14605
Contact: Henry Ehindero Sales Mgr
Tel: 585-546-7163
Email: henry@panthergraphics.net
Website: www.panthergraphics.net
Commercial printing: brochures, coupons, marketing & promotional materials, large format printing, folding cartons, kit packing & distribution.
 (AA, estab 1993, empl 25, sales $1,035,000, cert: City)

Ohio

7635 Associated Visual Communications, Inc.
200 Cherry Ave NE
Canton, OH 44702
Contact: Raymond J Gonzalez President
Tel: 330-452-4449
Email: rgonzalez@avcprint.com
Website: www.avcprint.com
Printing services: screen, digital & offset. (Hisp, estab 1979, empl 32, sales $2,814,501, cert: NMSDC)

7636 Bridge Media, LLC
      1457 E 252nd St Ste 100
      Euclid, OH 44117
      Contact: Craig Brooks, Sr. President
      Tel: 216-526-3044
      Email: craig@bridge-ohio.com
      Website: www.bridge-ohio.com
Printing: professional business cards, brochures & promotional materials, annual reports & glossy publications. (AA, estab 2008, empl 4, sales , cert: State)

7637 Cannell Graphics
      5787 Linworth Rd
      Worthington, OH 43085
      Contact: Phil Ferguson CEO
      Tel: 614-330-9110
      Email: pferguson@cannellgraphics.biz
      Website: www.cannellgraphics.biz
Large & small digital, screen, offset format, mounting & laminating, scanning, document management, litigation support, copier services. (Woman/AA, estab 1964, empl 7, sales , cert: State, NMSDC)

7638 Commodity Management Services CMS
      7233 Freedom Ave. NW
      North Canton, OH 44720
      Contact: Curt Keels Business Dev Exec
      Tel: 614-207-2707
      Email: ckeels@cmsprintsolutions.com
      Website: www.cmsprintsolutions.com
Printing: business forms, print mgmt, print solutions, labels. (AA, estab 1999, empl 525, sales $72,893,797, cert: NMSDC)

7639 Copy King, Inc.
      3333 Chester Ave
      Cleveland, OH 44114
      Contact: Peg Walsh President
      Tel: 216-861-3377
      Email: peg@copy-king.com
      Website: www.copy-king.com
Digital & offset press printing, binding, in house graphic design services, digital color printing, posters & large format printing, business cards. (Woman, estab 1995, empl 21, sales , cert: City)

7640 Corporate Document Solutions, Inc.
      11120 Ashburn Rd
      Cincinnati, OH 45240
      Contact: Mary Percy President
      Tel: 513-595-8200
      Email: mpercy@cdsprint.com
      Website: www.cdsPRINT.com
Design & pre-press services, layout compatibility, graphic file resolution, press imaging sizes & preferred file submission methods, black & white printing. (Woman, estab 1992, empl 18, sales $2,000,000, cert: WBENC)

7641 Dana Graphics, Inc.
      PO Box 42219
      Cincinnati, OH 45242
      Contact: Debbie Coad Mgr, cstmr service
      Tel: 513-351-4400
      Email: debbie@danalink.com
      Website: www.danalink.com
Graphic design, commercial & digital printing. (Woman, estab 1980, empl 8, sales $387,000, cert: WBENC)

7642 Dancor Inc.
      2155 Dublin Rd
      Columbus, OH 43228
      Contact: Michael Michalski Controller
      Tel: 614-737-3221
      Email: mmichalski@dancorinc.com
      Website: www.dancorinc.com
Commercial printing. (Woman, estab 0, empl , sales $8,041,000, cert: WBENC)

7643 DINATCO Inc.
      814 Morrison Rd
      Gahanna, OH 43230
      Contact: Tony Segarra President
      Tel: 614-367-1910
      Email: tony-segarra@crossbowsystems.net
      Website: www.crossbowsystems.net
Design and Installation Services, Technology Infrastructure Engineering, and Media Services. Our core competency is voice and data structural cable infrastructure design and installation. (Hisp, estab 2009, empl 8, sales , cert: State)

7644 Hooven-Dayton Corporation
      511 Byers Rd
      Miamisburg, OH 45342
      Contact: Evan Arrindell VP Sales & Marketing
      Tel: 937-233-4473
      Email: diversesupplier1@hoovendayton.com
      Website: www.hoovendayton.com
Print & convert pressure sensitive labels, coupons & custom specific solutions. (AA, estab 1935, empl 101, sales $24,899,000, cert: NMSDC)

7645 IC3D
      1697 Westbelt Dr
      Columbus, OH 43228
      Contact: Michael Cao CEO
      Tel: 614-260-5631
      Email: michael@ic3dprinters.com
      Website: www.ic3dprinters.com/
3D printing services, prototyping & low volume manufacturing. (As-Pac, estab 2012, empl 10, sales $500,000, cert: NMSDC)

7646 Identification Systems, Inc. dba Identity Systems,
      1324 Stimmel Road
      Columbus, OH 43223
      Contact: DeeDee Warden Acct Exec
      Tel: 614-448-1741
      Email: dwarden@identitysystemsinc.com
      Website: www.identitysystemsinc.com
Commercial screen printing: vinyl, styrene, ABS & engraveable stock. Mfr name badges, signage, architectural signage, signage systems inserts, accordion/ spiral signs, engraved signs, nameplates, equipment tags, decals, plaques. (Woman, estab 1986, empl 34, sales $3,626,392, cert: WBENC)

7647 JSCS Group, Inc. dba Market Direct
      3478 Hauck Road, Ste C
      Cincinnati, OH 45241
      Contact: Stephanie Harmon President
      Tel: 513-563-4900
      Email: stephanie@marketdirectinc.com
      Website: www.marketdirectinc.com
Printing: offset & digital on-demand, direct marketing, direct mailing & fulfillment, mailing, target list development & management, graphic design. (AA, estab 2004, empl 5, sales $130,000, cert: NMSDC)

7648 RPI Color Service, Inc.
      1950 Radcliff Dr
      Cincinnati, OH 45204
      Contact: Karen Rellar EVP Mktg/Communications
      Tel: 513-471-4040
      Email: karen.rellar@rpigraphic.com
      Website: www.rpigraphic.com
Off-set & digital printing, large & small format printing, die cutting, bindery & finishing, on demand printing, signage, packaging, sales samples, prototyping, displays, mailing services, point of sale materials, web-based tools. (Woman, estab 1969, empl 50, sales $8,500,000, cert: WBENC)

7649 Swimmer Printing dba Alphagraphics
      1701 E 12th St
      Cleveland, OH 44114
      Contact: Judith Swimmer President
      Tel: 216-623-1005
      Email: us320@alphagraphics.com
      Website: www.J2MedicalSupply.com
One to four color offset printing, B&W & color copy services, Mailing services, Digital archiving, Poster & banner printing, Prepress & design services, Finishing & bindery services. (Woman, estab 1991, empl 9, sales $1,400,000, cert: City)

7650 Ten 10 Design LLC
      119 Main St
      Chardon, OH 44024
      Contact: Casey Zulandt Owner
      Tel: 440-286-4367
      Email: casey@ten10design.com
      Website: www.ten10design.com
Printing (offset and digital), promotional items, ad specialties, mailing services, labels & decals,
graphic design, web design. (Woman/AA, estab 2009, empl 5, sales $3,093,663, cert: State, NMSDC, WBENC)

7651 Three Leaf Productions, Inc.
      261 West Johnstown Road Ste 200
      Gahanna, OH 43230
      Contact: Ron Stokes President
      Tel: 614-626-4941
      Email: rstokes@three-leaf.com
      Website: www.three-leaf.com
Commercial & large digital format printing: retail packaging, point of purchase displays, banners & signs, fulfillment services, pick & pack, kitting, promotional premiums. (AA, estab 1995, empl 15, sales $10,271,000, cert: State, NMSDC)

Oklahoma

7652 OakTree Software, Inc.
      1437 S Boulder Ave, Ste 300
      Tulsa, OK 74119
      Contact: Tony Floyd Business Devel
      Tel: 918-584-7900
      Email: tony.floyd@oaktreesoftware.com
      Website: www.oaktreesoftware.com
IT Consulting, training and services (Woman, estab 1995, empl 100, sales $10,000,000, cert: WBENC)

Oregon

7653 Industrial Safety Solutions Corporation
      14791 SE 82nd Dr
      Clackamas, OR 97015
      Contact: Rhonda Evans President
      Tel: 503-303-5958
      Email: revans@industrialsafetysolution.com
      Website: www.industrialsafetysolution.com
Industrial labeling systems, in-house pipe marking, 5S, Kaizen & general directional labeling. (Minority, Woman, estab 2004, empl 6, sales $854,257, cert: State)

7654 PrintSync, Inc.
      6775 SW 111th Ave, Ste 10
      Beaverton, OR 97008
      Contact: President
      Tel: 503-520-2000
      Email: customerservice@printsync.com
      Website: www.printsync.com
Printing & copying, direct mail & fulfillment. (Woman, estab 1991, empl 10, sales $2,048,000, cert: WBENC)

Pennsylvania

7655 Brenneman Printing, Inc.
      1909 Olde Homestead Lane
      Lancaster, PA 17601
      Contact: Dir Sales/Marketing
      Tel: 717-299-2847
      Email: ed.nevling@brennemaninc.com
      Website: www.brennemaninc.com
Commercial printing: offset printing 1-5 colors, thermography, digital printing, variable data printing, inkjet addressing, mailing services, inserting, database management, online ordering storefronts, mail list acquisition, custom distribution services. (Woman, estab 1969, empl 30, sales , cert: State, WBENC)

7656 Chaucer Press, Inc.
      535 Stewart Rd
      Hanover Township, PA 18706
      Contact: Patricia Frances CEO
      Tel: 570-825-2005
      Email: pfrances@chaucerpress.com
      Website: www.chaucerpress.com
Printed packaging & on-pack promotional materials: pressure-sensitive, cut & extended content labels, folding cartons, inserts, on-serts, blister cards, sleeves, foilstamping, embossing, screen printing, structural design. (Woman, estab 1965, empl 49, sales $15,000,000, cert: WBENC)

7657 Diamond Graphics Inc.
      456 Acorn Lane
      Downingtown, PA 19335
      Contact: Barbara Martin Owner
      Tel: 610-269-7010
      Email: barb@diamondgraphicsprint.com
      Website: www.diamondgraphicsprint.com
Commercial Printing, Direct Mail, Web Offset, Brochures, Pharmaceutical inserts, Letters, Flyers, Circulars, Instruction Manuals, Note Pads, Inserts, Reply Cards, Order Cards. (Woman, estab 1999, empl 40, sales $6,500,000, cert: WBENC)

7658 Graphic Arts, Incorporated
      2867 East Alleghany Ave
      Philadelphia, PA 19134
      Contact: Fred Binder Acct Exec
      Tel: 215-382-5500
      Email: fbinder@galitho.com
      Website: www.galitho.com
Full color sheet fed printing: finish, fulfill & mail. (Woman, estab 1928, empl 100, sales $6,135,881, cert: City, WBENC)

7659 Innovation Marketing Communications LLC
      232 Conestoga Rd
      Wayne, PA 19154
      Contact: George Slater Major Accounts Mgr
      Tel: 215-802-2885
      Email: gslater@phoenixlitho.com
      Website: www.innomc.com
Creative, offset & digital printing, wide format, physical & virtual events, warehousing & web-to-print solutions. (As-Pac, estab 1973, empl 92, sales $20,500,000, cert: NMSDC)

7660 Lizzie Bullets LLC dba KDC
      2100 Babcock Blvd.
      Pittsburgh, PA 15209
      Contact: Kristine King CEO
      Tel: 412-446-2784
      Email: kking@printpgh.com
      Website: www.printpgh.com
Print and communication: digital printing, conventional/commercial offset printing & wide format signage & banners, design, data archiving, direct mail, variable data and web-to-print services. (Woman, estab 2005, empl 22, sales $2,650,000, cert: WBENC)

7661 Migu Press Inc.
      260 Ivyland Rd
      Warminster, PA 18974
      Contact: Ken Bucker New Business Dev
      Tel: 215-957-9763
      Email: kenb@migu4u.com
      Website: www.migu4u.com
Commercial printing. (Woman, estab 1988, empl 28, sales , cert: State, WBENC)

7662 Movad
      801 Bristol Pike
      Bensalem, PA 19020
      Contact: Terri Gasbarra Business Devel
      Tel: 215-638-2679
      Email: bhanf@gostrata.com
      Website: www.movadcorp.com
Digital & offset printing, mailing services, bindery & finishing, fulfillment, variable data printing, database services, graphic design & pre-press, online ordering & proofing. (Woman, estab 1986, empl 11, sales $1,500,000, cert: WBENC)

7663 PAP Technologies, Inc.
      1813 Colonial Village Ln
      Lancaster, PA 17601
      Contact: Michael Robinson President
      Tel: 717-399-3333
      Email: mrobinson@paptech.net
      Website: www.paptech.net
Printing, warehousing, distribution, fulfillment & machine automation, electrical control panels. (AA, estab 1988, empl 54, sales , cert: State, NMSDC)

7664 TMMPROMOS.COM dba The Artifactori
      140 Christopher Ln, Ste 101
      Harleysville, PA 19438
      Contact: Victoria Magagna President
      Tel: 215-513-1693
      Email: tori@theartifactori.com
      Website: www.theartifactori.com
Commercial Printing, Large-Format Printing, Direct mail, Fulfillment, Warehousing, and Custom Distribution, Branded Promotional Products, and Custom Apparel. (Woman, estab 2014, empl 3, sales $617,000, cert: WBENC)

7665 Triangle Press Inc.
      6720 Allentown Blvd
      Harrisburg, PA 17112
      Contact: Tammy Shelley VP
      Tel: 717-541-9315
      Email: tammy@trianglepress.net
      Website: www.trianglepress.net
Graphic design, wide format printing, digital printing, variable data, 5-color offset printing, fulfillment & delivery. (Woman, estab 1970, empl 21, sales $3,175,100, cert: WBENC)

7666 Unity Printing Co., Inc.
      5848 State Route 981
      Latrobe, PA 15650
      Contact: Lori Askins President
      Tel: 724-537-5800
      Email: lori@unipakcorp.net
      Website: www.UnityPrinting.com
Digital Printing, Offset Printing, Direct Mail, services, Variable Data Services, Warehousing. (Woman, estab 1979, empl 40, sales $3,660,000, cert: WBENC)

7667 Universal Printing Company LLC
      1205 O'Neill Hwy
      Dunmore, PA 18512
      Contact: Margaret McGrath CEO
      Tel: 570-342-1243
      Email: mah@universalprintingcompany.com
      Website: www.universalprintingcompany.com
Commercial printing, fulfillment, 4, 8 & 10 color presses with roll-to-sheet capabilities. (Woman, estab 1995, empl 150, sales $32,396,000, cert: WBENC)

Puerto Rico

7668 3A Press
      PO Box 47
      Lajas, PR 00667
      Contact: Marie Rosado President
      Tel: 787-899-0110
      Email: mrosado@3apress.com
      Website: www.3apress.com
Mfr & print pharmaceutical, commercial & folding cartons, inserts, stitched & perfect bound booklets/magazines, printed literature. (Hisp, estab 1996, empl 126, sales $11,200,000, cert: NMSDC)

South Carolina

7669 National Beverage Screen Printers, Inc
12000 Main St
Williston, SC 29853
Contact: Janet Roberson President
Tel: 803-266-5272
Email: jroberson@nbsinc.net
Website: www.nbsinc.net
Screen printing, digital printing, plastic injection & metal fabrication. (Woman, estab 1984, empl 38, sales $7,000,000, cert: WBENC)

7670 Print Solutions Inc.
1273 Bowater Rd
Rock Hill, SC 29732
Contact: Wyman Wilson Acct Rep
Tel: 803-366-1510
Email: wyman.wilson@printsolutions.org
Website: www.printsolutions.org
Thermal Products, Printheads, Ribbons, Labels & Tags, Continuous Labels & Tags Laser Labels & Tags Custom, Stock Labels & Tags. (Woman, estab 2001, empl 3, sales $325,000, cert: State)

Tennessee

7671 A-1 Printing Services
810 E Brooks Rd
Memphis, TN 38116
Contact: Frazer Windless President
Tel: 901-396-2023
Email: fwindless@a1printingsvc.com
Website: www.a1printingsvc.com
Commercial sheet-fed printing. (AA, estab 1988, empl 12, sales $1,500,000, cert: NMSDC)

7672 Graphic Label Solutions
2407 Pulaski Hwy
Columbia, TN 38401
Contact: Bob Offord VP
Tel: 931-490-0019
Email: bob.offord@abrandcompany.com
Website: www.graphiclabelsolutions.com/
Labels, decals, overlays, nameplates, membrane switches, RFID, EAS. (Woman, estab 2002, empl 5, sales $5,000,000, cert: State, WBENC)

7673 O'Ryan Group
4010 Pilot Dr, Ste 108 Ste 108
Memphis, TN 38118
Contact: Sara O'Ryan Acct Exec
Tel: 901-794-4610
Email: sara@oryangroup.com
Website: www.oryangroup.com
Printing, screen printing, offset printing, web printing, digital printing, hardware, structural, POP, kit packing, installation. (Woman, estab 1997, empl 52, sales $44,000,000, cert: WBENC)

7674 Tec-Print, LLC
4600 Cromwell Ave, Ste 101
Memphis, TN 38118
Contact: Lynn Higgs Business Devel Mgr
Tel: 865-471-1846
Email: lhiggs@nashua.com
Website: www.tec-print.com
Printing: labels, tickets, cash register receipts, brochures, pamphlets, forms, digital off-set or roll fed web, etc. (AA, estab 2004, empl 23, sales $896,000, cert: NMSDC)

7675 Women in Printing, LLC
2285 Hwy 47 N
White Bluff, TN 37187
Contact: Teri Doochin President
Tel: 615-797-9811
Email: tdoochin@womeninprinting.com
Website: www.womeninprinting.com
Flexographic & offset printing, films & laminated structures, labels, coupons, blister-board, offset and rotary printing, finished pouches & bags. (Woman, estab 2004, empl 15, sales $2,500,000, cert: WBENC)

7676 Worldwide Label & Packaging LLC
158 Madison Ave Ste 101
Memphis, TN 38103
Contact: Anthony Norris President
Tel: 901-454-9290
Email: anorris@worldwidebg.com
Website: www.worldwidebg.com
Mfr printed packaging: pressure sensitive labels, flexible packaging & continuous roll forms. (AA, estab 2000, empl 26, sales $5,000,000, cert: NMSDC)

Texas

7677 AC Printing LLC
3400-1 S Raider Dr
Euless, TX 76040
Contact: Robert Bolt Sales
Tel: 817-267-8990
Email: acpsales@acprinting.com
Website: www.acprinting.com
Commercial printing. (As-Ind, estab 1989, empl 40, sales $7,790,014, cert: State, NMSDC, SDB)

7678 Advanced Business Graphics, Inc.
680 S Royal Lane, Ste 200
Coppell, TX 75019
Contact: Sales Sales
Tel: 972-471-3740
Email: abgi@abgi.com
Website: www.abgi.com
Printed products-business forms, checks, labels, commercial printing, promotional items, packaging, printer supplies, presentation materials. (Woman, estab 1995, empl 8, sales $5,884,880, cert: State, WBENC)

7679 Alliance of Diversity Printers, LLC
15950 Dallas Pkwy Ste 400
Dallas, TX 75248
Contact: Terri Quinton CEO
Tel: 214-856-8368
Email: terri@adp-llc.com
Website: www.adp-llc.com
Print management solution. (Woman/AA, estab 2008, empl 12, sales $12,700,000, cert: State, NMSDC, WBENC)

7680 Bayside Printing Co, Inc
160 Lockhaven Dr
Houston, TX 77073
Contact: David Solis VP Business Dev
Tel: 281-209-9500
Email: david@baysideprinting.com
Website: www.baysideprinting.com
Commercial multi-color printing: prepress, multiple sheet fed presses, 6 color, coaters, in-house bindery, die cutting & assembly, mailing & fulfillment. (Minority, Woman, estab 1973, empl 30, sales $7,000,000, cert: NMSDC, WBENC)

7681 Best Press Inc.
      4201 Airborn Dr
      Addison, TX 75001
      Contact: Bobby Yocum Marketing/Business Develop
      Tel: 972-930-1000
      Email: admin@bestpress.com
      Website: www.bestpress.com
Commercial printing. (Woman, estab 1993, empl 100, sales $13,200,000, cert: State, WBENC)

7682 Creative Menus & Folders, LLC dba Texas Covers
      409 Old Hwy 80
      Olden, TX 76466
      Contact: Renee Ferguson Asst Production Mgr
      Tel: 254-653-2775
      Email: reneeferguson@texascovers.com
      Website: www.texascovers.com
Presentation/Executive Binders, folders, business cards, printing (screen, digital, offset, foil stamp, deboss, specialty color cast printing, plastic ID badge holders, ID badges, name tags, souvenir printing, banners, signage, laminating, caps. (As-Pac, estab 2015, empl 19, sales , cert: NMSDC)

7683 Digi-Color, LP
      4414 Hollister
      Houston, TX 77040
      Contact: Barkla Tully Managing Partner
      Tel: 713-934-9800
      Email: barkla@digi-color.com
      Website: www.digi-color.com
Digital printing; climate-controlled warehousing & fulfillment, mailing, on-line inventory management - ordering & reporting, on-demand 4 color & black/white digital printing, document management services, binding & finishing, packaging, kitting. (Woman, estab 2004, empl 20, sales $4,525,142, cert: State, WBENC)

7684 Dragonfly Group
      1015 Amesbury Dr
      Murphy, TX 75094
      Contact: Laura McClain President
      Tel: 972-742-2215
      Email: laura@thedragonflygroup.net
      Website: www.thedragonflygroup.net
Print production & creative design: litho, UV, web, silkscreen, digital & flexo printing, full bindery, finishing, diecutting, assembly, kitting & fulfillment. (Minority, Woman, estab 2004, empl 1, sales $1,163,510, cert: WBENC)

7685 Dream Big Media Solutions dba Alphagraphics 114
      7801 Mesquite Bend Dr
      Irving, TX 75063
      Contact: Sam Reed Owner
      Tel: 972-570-0868
      Email: us114@alphagraphics.com
      Website: www.us114.alphagraphics.com
Printing, graphic design, marketing, and signage, envelopes, brochures, blueprints, business cards, digital printing, letterhead, forms, postcards, stationery, banners, signs, wall graphics. (AA, estab 1984, empl 5, sales $1,047,076, cert: State, NMSDC)

7686 Dynamic Color Graphics
      PO Box 161758
      Fort Worth, TX 76161
      Contact: Kathy Bowers President
      Tel: 817-520-6631
      Email: kathy@dynamiccolorgraphics.com
      Website: www.dynamiccolorgraphics.com
Printing: large format digital printing, banners, posters, trade show graphics, booths, vehicle graphics, floor graphics, murals, fine art reproduction, digital photo lab. (Woman, estab 2000, empl 19, sales $9,403,342, cert: State)

7687 Exalt Printing Solutions
      1628 W Crosby Rd, Ste 104
      Carrollton, TX 75006
      Contact: Lisa Marta CEO
      Tel: 972-245-3858
      Email: lisa@exaltprinting.com
      Website: www.exaltprinting.com
Printing, promotional & office products, forms, labels, brochures, checks, direct mail. (Woman, estab , empl , sales $8,150,000, cert: State, WBENC)

7688 FBC Enterprises, Inc.
      5110 Rondo Dr
      Fort Worth, TX 76106
      Contact: Teresa McClain Sales Rep
      Tel: 817-740-1951
      Email: tmcclain@customgs.com
      Website: www.customgs.com
Commercial printing, web & sheetfed, bindery svcs: direct mail, booklets, catalogs, posters, pocket folders, door hangers & brochures, hand assembly, kitting, custom distribution & fulfillment. (Woman, estab 1990, empl 45, sales $4,500,000, cert: WBENC)

7689 Global Bridge Infotech Inc.
      5525 N Macarthur Blvd, Ste 670
      Irving, TX 75038
      Contact: Vishnu Sethuraman Swarna Dir Business Dev
      Tel: 972-550-9400
      Email: vishnu@gbitinc.com
      Website: www.gbitinc.com
Commercial, full-color web offset printing, sheet-fed, digital design & print. (As-Ind, estab 2006, empl 97, sales $9,000,000, cert: State, NMSDC)

7690 ISSGR, Inc. dba ImageSet
      6611 Portwest Dr Ste 190
      Houston, TX 77024
      Contact: President
      Tel: 713-869-7700
      Email: sales@imageset.com
      Website: www.imageset.com
Digital printing, large format graphics, premedia & graphic design. (Woman, estab 1985, empl 31, sales $4,325,248, cert: WBENC)

7691 Label Systems, Inc.
      4111 Lindberg Dr
      Addison, TX 75001
      Contact: Amy Van Brunt President
      Tel: 972-387-4512
      Email: amy@labelsystemsinc.com
      Website: www.labelsystemsinc.com
Mfr custom labels, flexography, hot stamping & silkscreening, promotional products & incentive programs (Woman, estab 1994, empl 10, sales $350,000, cert: State, WBENC)

7692 Marfield Corporate Stationery
1225 E Crosby Rd Ste B-1
Carrollton, TX 75006
Contact: Andrea Rowe SVP-Sales
Tel: 877-245-9122
Email: accounting@marfield.com
Website: www.marfield.com
Printing, engraving, embossing, foil stamping: business cards, letterheads & envelopes. (Woman, estab 1968, empl 17, sales $2,100,000, cert: State, WBENC)

7693 Market Hut dba United Graphics
1130 Ave H East Ste 300
Arlington, TX 76011
Contact: Lisa Hoffman
Tel: 817-701-3639
Email: lhoffman@unitedgraphics.com
Website: www.unitedgraphics.com
Commercial Printing, Direct Mail, POP, POS, kitting, fulfillment, variable data, database marketing production, packaging. (Woman, estab 2003, empl 40, sales $8,500,000, cert: WBENC)

7694 Mastercraft Printed Products & Services
2150 Century Circle
Irving, TX 75062
Contact: Eoff Suzanne VP
Tel: 214-455-4148
Email: txmx1144@yahoo.com
Website: www.mbfi.com
Commercial print, direct mail, operational forms, ASI speciality items, document retention, kitting, fulfillment, warehousing, logistics. (Woman, estab 1979, empl 45, sales $15,200,000, cert: WBENC)

7695 Nicholas Earth Printing, LLC
7021 Portwest Dr. Ste 100
Houston, TX 77024
Contact: Marvin (Bob) Nicholas President
Tel: 713-880-0195
Email: bnicholas@nicholasearth.com
Website: www.nicholasearth.com
Sheetfed printing, UV & aqueous coating, web printing & inline, digital prepress & computer to plate, digital archiving, bindery, fulfillment, outdoor advertising. (Woman/AA, estab 2003, empl 18, sales , cert: State)

7696 Nieman Printing
10615 Newkirk St
Dallas, TX 75220
Contact: James Quinonez Acct Rep
Tel: 214-458-8011
Email: jq@niemanprinting.com
Website: www.niemanprinting.com
Digital pritning: short runs press, large press up to 12 colors with UV or AQ on paper or plastic. (Woman, estab 1984, empl 160, sales $22,000,000, cert: State, WBENC)

7697 Parker Business Forms, Inc.
7395 Frint Dr
Beaumont, TX 77705
Contact: Heather Camp VP
Tel: 409-842-5251
Email: heather@parkerbf.com
Website: www.parkerbf.com
Commercial & industrial printing: letterheads, envelopes, thank you cards, note cards, Christmas Cards, carbonless forms - invoices, purchase orders, shipping manifest, etc., full color(shortand long run). (Woman, estab 0, empl 20, sales $6,000,000, cert: WBENC)

7698 Peacock Press LLC
538 Shepherd
Garland, TX 75042
Contact: Ru Patel COO
Tel: 972-272-7764
Email: ru@peacockpress.net
Website: www.peacockpress.net
Digital printing, offset printing, complete finishing capabilities. (As-Ind, estab 2003, empl 15, sales $2,500,000, cert: State, NMSDC)

7699 Technology Media Group
1262 Viceroy Dr
Dallas, TX 75247
Contact: Amanda Clarke Business Devel
Tel: 214-267-0535
Email: amandaclarke@tmguniverse.com
Website: www.tmguniverse.com
Offset print, digital print, high speed web printing, signage, wearables, screenprint, embroidery, promotional, warehousing, fulfillment, graphic design, envelope manufacturing, foil stamp, die cut. (Woman, estab 1986, empl 75, sales $9,000,000, cert: State)

Virginia

7700 BBR Print Inc.
807 Oliver Hill Way
Richmond, VA 23219
Contact: Brooke Rhodes Cstmr Service
Tel: 804-901-2535
Email: brooke@jamesriverpress.com
Website: www.bambooink.com
Printing services: in-house art dept, offset press & copy svcs, bindery. (Woman, estab 1997, empl 15, sales $1,143,000, cert: State)

7701 Grubb Printing & Stamp Co.
3303 Airline Blvd, Ste 1G
Portsmouth, VA 23701
Contact: Darla Alexander Sales Rep
Tel: 757-465-7855
Email: darla@grubbprint.com
Website: www.grubbprint.com
Commercial printing. (Woman, estab , empl 16, sales $17,002,000, cert: State)

7702 JoMoCo Studio LLC
8416 Staples Mill Rd
Richmond, VA 23228
Contact: Joe Coleman Mgr
Tel: 804-262-3555
Email: engraving@jomocostudio.com
Website: www.jomocostudio.com
Engraving: stainless steel, brass, aluminum & plastic signs, nameplates, name badges, labels, legends, tags, awards & plaques, vinyl signs, braille signs, acrylic awards & laser engraved metals & glass. (Woman, estab 1985, empl 3, sales $523,155, cert: State)

7703 Premier Reprographics, Inc.
4701-A Eisenhower Ave
Alexandria, VA 22304
Contact: Vickie Banks CEO
Tel: 703-370-6612
Email: vickie@premierrepro.com
Website: www.premierrepro.com
Digital printing, copying, binding, scanning, posters, manuals, newsletters, reports, proposals, marketing collateral, presentations, laminating, blueprinting, drymounting, large & small format color. (Woman/AA, estab 1993, empl 10, sales $1,000,000, cert: State)

Washington

7704 Angel Screen Printing, Inc.
8459 S 208th St, Bldg N
Kent, WA 98031
Contact: Rex Korrell Mktg Mgr
Tel: 206-755-7737
Email: rex@angelscreenprinting.net
Website: www.angelscreenprinting.net
Screen printing and Embroidery services. (Woman/As-Pac, estab 2004, empl 8, sales $672,896, cert: State, NMSDC)

7705 EE Printing. LLC
8258 S 192nd St
Kent, WA 98032
Contact: Tory Nguyen
Tel: 425-656-1250
Email: tory@eeprinting.com
Website: www.eeprinting.com
From one color to full color, offset to digital, business forms, business cards, stationary, bulk volume envelopes, signs, posters, manuals, books, NCR forms, flyer, brochures. (Minority, Woman, estab 2007, empl 3, sales $190,752, cert: State, NMSDC)

7706 Risque Inc.
1122 N State St
Bellingham, WA 98225
Contact: Nadeem Israr President
Tel: 360-738-1280
Email: nadeem@copysource.com
Website: www.copysource.com
Printing services: digital printing, poster printing, offset printing, copying, publishing, etc. (Minority, Woman, estab 1990, empl 15, sales $1,200,000, cert: State)

Wisconsin

7707 Crossmark Graphics, Inc.
16100 W Overland Dr
New Berlin, WI 53151
Contact: Tammy Rechner President
Tel: 262-821-1343
Email: trechner@crossmarkgraphicsinc.com
Website: www.crossmarkgraphicsinc.com
Print communication, litho, UV printing, lenticular, POS, digital, PURLs, fulfillment/kit packing & web-to-print. (Woman, estab 1987, empl 48, sales $12,703,065, cert: WBENC)

7708 Flex Pre-Press, Inc.
6812 S 112th St
Franklin, WI 53132
Contact: Burt Tabora President
Tel: 414-427-8833
Email: btabora@flexprepress.com
Website: www.flexprepress.com
Photopolymer printing plates, DuPont WaterProofs, color keys, film negatives, analog & digital proofing, high-end color separations, photo retouching, package design, file management & printing, digital plates. (Hisp, estab 1995, empl 15, sales $1,100,000, cert: State, NMSDC)

7709 H.Derksen & Sons Co., Inc.
250 Industrial Dr
Omro, WI 50310
Contact: Mike Willeford VP
Tel: 920-685-4000
Email: mike@hderksen.com
Website: www.hderksen.com
Pressure sensitive labels, wide format digital printing, business forms, computer paper, paper & packaging products, mobility solutions, bar code label printers, bar coding software. (Nat Ame, estab , empl 11, sales $8,000,000, cert: NMSDC)

7710 Industrial Graphics Inc.
304 Industrial Dr
Fredonia, WI 53021
Contact: Teri Swenson Acct Mgr
Tel: 262-692-2424
Email: tswenson@igc-image.com
Website: www.industrialgraphics.com
Digital Printing, Screen Printing, Creative Services, Cad Cut Lettering, Fleet Wrapping, Advertising, Point of Purchase Displays, Priting on Metals, Prototyping, High Volume Sourcing, Architectural Decorating, Wall Paper Printing, Ceiling Tile Printing. (Woman, estab 1969, empl 20, sales $2,750,000, cert: State)

7711 Kubin-Nicholson Corporation
8440 N 87th St
Milwaukee, WI 53224
Contact: Margaret Rees CEO
Tel: 414-586-4300
Email: rees.p@kubin.com
Website: www.kubin.com
Commerical printed products: billboards, banners, transit posters, in store signs, floor graphics, wall scapes, vehicle wraps, building wraps, POP displays. (Woman, estab 1935, empl 63, sales $16,000,000, cert: State)

7712 Promo Print Solutions Inc.
420 S Koeller St, Ste 208
Oshkosh, WI 54902
Contact: Paula Condor President
Tel: 920-233-7900
Email: paula.condor@promoprintsolutions.com
Website: www.promoprintsolutions.com
Print collateral: in-store promotions, sales promotions, commerical printing, giveaways & sampling. (Woman, estab 2000, empl 4, sales $2,087,395, cert: WBENC)

7713 Red Oak Label, LLC
2923 S 160th St
New Berlin, WI 53151
Contact: President
Tel: 262-780-9797
Email: CustomerService@RedOakLabel.com
Website: www.redoaklabel.com
Pressure sensitive flexographic labels & tags. (Woman, estab 1997, empl 6, sales $510,900, cert: WBENC)

PROFESSIONAL SERVICES: Financial

Provide various financial consulting services: auditing/tax, 401K, pension and employee benefits, risk and injury management insurance, asset management and investment advice, money management, collection services, certified public accounting firms, etc. NAICS Code 54

Alaska

7714 Delta Leasing LLC
8101 Dimond Hook Dr
Anchorage, AK 99507
Contact: Sam Amato VP
Tel: 907-771-1300
Email: lmorgan@deltaleasing.com
Website: www.deltaleasing.com

Commercial leasing services of vehicles, equipment for oil & gas, construction, mining, (Nat Ame, estab 2002, empl 32, sales $13,000,000, cert: NMSDC)

Alabama

7715 MSB Analytics, Inc.
4970 Corporate Dr NW, #100
Huntsville, AL 35805
Contact: Tharon Honeycutt President
Tel: 256-726-4729
Email: tharon.honeycutt@msbainc.com
Website: www.msbainc.com

Financial & Accounting Management. (AA, estab , empl 18, sales $1,000,000, cert: 8(a))

7716 Optimum Financial Corporation
1300 Meridian St Ste 12
Huntsville, AL 35801
Contact: Thomas Parker Dir Business Dev
Tel: 256-539-3994
Email: tparker@optimumcorp.com
Website: www.optimumcorp.com

Administrative & financial support svcs, revenue cycle, mgmt consulting, asset mgmt, budgeting, const analysis, data entry, debt collection and records management. (AA, estab 1995, empl 20, sales $1,000,000, cert: NMSDC)

California

7717 Advertising Audit Services International, LLC
32663 Red Maple St Ste 100
Union City, CA 94587
Contact: Pankaj Sewal Chief Auditing Officer
Tel: 415-828-0779
Email: psewal@adauditservintl.com
Website: www.adauditservintl.com

Contract compliance audits & analysis: vendor compliance, financial accounting accuracy & advertiser best practices. (As-Ind, estab 2005, empl 5, sales $3,000,000, cert: NMSDC)

7718 Amerivet Securities, Inc.
26550 Silverado Court
Moreno Valley, CA 92555
Contact: Steven Kay President
Tel: 888-960-0644
Email: skay@amerivetsecurities.com
Website: www.amerivetsecurities.com

Securities business, commodities business & registered investment advisory business. (AA, estab 1993, empl 29, sales $9,408,484, cert: CPUC)

7719 Blaylock Van, LLC
350 Frank H Ogawa Plaza 10th Fl
Oakland, CA 94612
Contact: Tarrell Gamble VP
Tel: 510-208-6100
Email: tgamble@brv-llc.com
Website: www.brv-llc.com

Investment banking & financial services: corporate debt & equity underwriting, equity research, share repurchase, pension sales & trading & municipal finance. (AA, estab 1991, empl 48, sales , cert: State, NMSDC)

7720 Cadence Leasing, Inc
3848 W Carson St Ste 212
Torrance, CA 90503
Contact: Bruce Humiston Dir of Sales & Marketing
Tel: 310-784-8484
Email: BruceH@CadenceLeasing.com
Website: www.cadence-rg.com

National Financial Services. (AA, estab 2002, empl 12, sales $17,733,843, cert: CPUC)

7721 Coast to Coast Financial Solutions Inc.
101 Hodencamp Rd Ste 120
Thousand Oaks, CA 91360
Contact: John Mastro Dir
Tel: 888-877-4700
Email: jmastro@c2cfsi.com
Website: www.c2cfsi.com

Debt collection services. (AA, estab 2002, empl 14, sales $1,412,059, cert: NMSDC)

7722 Consumer Financial Service Corporation
1500 Park Ave Ste 116
Emeryville, CA 94608
Contact: Loy Sheflott President
Tel: 510-596-4100
Email: lsheflott@consumerfinancial.com
Website: www.consumerfinancial.com

Financial services. (Woman, estab 1994, empl 30, sales $1,100,000, cert: WBENC)

7723 Corporate Tax Incentives
PO Box 2770
Rancho Cordova, CA 95670
Contact: Shawn Battle Controller
Tel: 916-366-0144
Email: ebarajas@ctillc.com
Website: www.ctillc.com

State & federal tax incentives, provide complete business incentives consulting services. (AA, As-Pac, estab 2008, empl 44, sales $10,542,392, cert: NMSDC)

7724 Garnier Group and Associates
10679 Westview Pkwy, 2nd Fl.
San Diego, CA 92126
Contact: Winslow Garnier President
Tel: 858-530-2468
Email: winslow@garniergroup.com
Website: www.garniergroup.com

Equipment finance leasing, appraisal services, computer leasing, analytical lab instrumentation leasing. (AA, estab 2003, empl 19, sales $7,023,000, cert: NMSDC, CPUC)

7725 Great Pacific Securities
      151 Kalmus Dr Ste H-8
      Costa Mesa, CA 92626
      Contact: Christopher Vinck-Luna CEO
      Tel: 714-619-3000
      Email: cvinck@greatpac.com
      Website: www.greatpac.com
Financial svcs: equity & fixed income execution, debt underwriting, equity underwriting & corporate buy backs. (Hisp, estab 1990, empl 30, sales $13,926,000, cert: State, City, NMSDC, CPUC)

7726 Jules & Associates, Inc.
      515 S Figeroa St, Ste 1950
      Los Angeles, CA 90071
      Contact: Vincent Alexander Sr acc exec
      Tel: 213-362-5600
      Email: vincea@julesandassociates.com
      Website: www.julesandassociates.com
Equipment finance corporate acquisitions. (Hisp, estab 1989, empl 31, sales $ 0, cert: CPUC)

7727 Liberty Commercial Finance
      250 El Camino Real, Ste 110
      Tustin, CA 92780
      Contact: Frank Jansen Sr Acct Mgr
      Tel: 949-484-7611
      Email: fjansen@libertycommercial.com
      Website: www.libertycommercial.com
Commercial equipment finance company. (Minority, Woman, estab 2017, empl 10, sales $75,000,000, cert: NMSDC)

7728 LNL Solutions LLC
      423 W Adams Ave
      Alhambra, CA 91801
      Contact: Philip Li Dir of Finance
      Tel: 424-256-5894
      Email: info@lnl-solutions.com
      Website: www.lnl-solutions.com
Middle market & boutique accounting & financial services. (As-Pac, estab 2013, empl 2, sales , cert: State, City, NMSDC)

7729 Pacific Rim Capital, Inc.
      525 Technology Dr Ste 400
      Irvine, CA 92618
      Contact: Tom Budnick VP Sales
      Tel: 949-389-0800
      Email: sales@pacrimcap.com
      Website: www.pacificrimcapital.com
Lease financing: materials handling & IT equip, also dist new & reconditioned IT hardware. (AA, estab 1990, empl 90, sales $42,568,153, cert: NMSDC)

7730 Receivables Solutions, Inc.
      2910 Inland Empire Blvd Ste 100
      Ontario, CA 91764
      Contact: Regina Cameron
      Tel: 909-360-8140
      Email: rcameron@rsinc.us
      Website: www.rsinc.us
National accounts receivable management (ARM), 1st party collections (pre-charge off), 3rd party collections & billing. (Woman/AA, estab 2015, empl 2, sales , cert: CPUC)

7731 Sequoia Financial Services
      28632 Roadside Dr Ste 110
      Agoura Hills, CA 91301
      Contact: Olivia Romero Business Dev Dir
      Tel: 818-409-6000
      Email: secon@sequoiafinancial.com
      Website: www.sequoiafinancial.com
Collection services. (Woman/AA, estab 1991, empl 73, sales $3,000,000, cert: CPUC, WBENC)

7732 Southern California Leasing Inc.
      180 E Main, Ste 204
      Tustin, CA 92780
      Contact: Barbara Griffith President
      Tel: 714-573-9804
      Email: bgriffith@socalleasing.com
      Website: www.socalleasing.com
Equipment leasing & financing. (Woman, estab 1992, empl 7, sales $1,200,000, cert: WBENC)

7733 Strategic Partners Consultants
      8889 W Olympic Blvd, Ste 1000
      Beverly Hills, CA 90211
      Contact: Brenda West CEO
      Tel: 310-870-7055
      Email: brenda.west@strategicpartnersconsultants.com
      Website: www.strategicpartnersconsultants.com/page/168/1
Consulting & outsourcing, Bank Regulatory Compliance issues, Internal Audit functions & Risk Assessment activities. (Woman, estab 2014, empl 3, sales , cert: WBENC)

7734 The Gilson Group, LLC
      2967 Michelson Dr Ste G102
      Irvine, CA 92612
      Contact: Catherine Doll CEO
      Tel: 949-830-3499
      Email: catherine@thegilsongroup.com
      Website: www.TheGilsonGroup.com
Accounting, mergers, financial analysis, due diligence, internal controls, general ledger, forecasting, cash flow, process improvement, Quickbooks, SOX, SEC, cost accounting, financial reporting, internal audit, risk management, GAAP. (Woman, estab 2006, empl 20, sales $502,000, cert: WBENC)

7735 The Zamzow Group, Inc.
      264 S La Cienega Blvd, Ste 1120
      Beverly Hills, CA 90211
      Contact: Brenda Zamzow President
      Tel: 310-551-3000
      Email: wbe@thezamzowgroup.com
      Website: www.thezamzowgroup.com
Accounting services. (Woman, estab 2003, empl 20, sales $1,600,000, cert: State, City)

7736 Venpalia LLC
      1331 N Cuyamaca St, Ste G
      El Cajon, CA 92020
      Contact: Liza Amog Principal
      Tel: 619-788-3781
      Email: liza@venpalia.com
      Website: www.venpalia.com
Finance, risk management. (Minority, Woman, estab 2010, empl 1, sales $150,000, cert: NMSDC, CPUC)

Colorado

7737 Aspen Capital Company, Inc.
       530 North Jefferson Ave Unit A
       Loveland, CO 80537
       Contact: Peggy Tomcheck
       Tel: 303-716-2898
       Email: plapp@aspencapitalcompany.com
       Website: www.aspencapitalcompany.com
Custom asset tracking & invoicing solutions, educational laptop program lease structures, unique iPad refresh programs, consignment solutions, electronic invoicing & billing processes, web based equipment stores. (Woman, estab 2001, empl 8, sales $10,385,908, cert: WBENC)

Connecticut

7738 Argus Investors' Counsel, Inc.
       1266 E Main St 4th Fl
       Stamford, CT 06902
       Contact: Sharon Wagoner President
       Tel: 203-316-9000
       Email: clesko@argusinvest.com
       Website: www.argusinvest.com
Manage portfolios: pensions, endowments & foundations. (Woman, estab 1960, empl 6, sales $ 0, cert: WBENC)

7739 SCG Capital Leasing, LLC
       74 West Park Place
       Stamford, CT 06901
       Contact: Sam Goichman Sr Vice President
       Tel: 917-597-8568
       Email: sgoichman@scgwbe.com
       Website: www.scgwbe.com/
Equipment Leasing, Operating Leases. (Woman, estab 2005, empl 20, sales $30,000,000, cert: WBENC)

7740 Soundview Capital Solutions
       116 Washington Ave
       North Haven, CT 06473
       Contact: John Abella CEO
       Tel: 203-821-7830
       Email: johnabella@soundviewcapitalsolutions.com
       Website: www.soundviewcapitalsolutions.com
Third-party leasing specializing in technology financing. (Hisp, estab 2009, empl 3, sales $100,000, cert: NMSDC)

District of Columbia

7741 McKissack & McKissack of Washington, Inc.
       901 K St, NW 6th Fl
       Washington, DC 20001
       Contact: Pamela Prue Marketing & Proposal Mgr
       Tel: 202-347-1446
       Email: registrations@mckinc.com
       Website: www.mckinc.com
Budget preparation, scheduling, programming, scope preparation, financial consulting. (Woman/AA, estab 1990, empl 130, sales $24,010,225, cert: State, City, NMSDC, WBENC)

Delaware

7742 Faw Casson
       160 Greentree Dr, Ste 203
       Dover, DE 19904
       Contact: Tammy Ordway Dir of ES
       Tel: 302-674-4305
       Email: tjo@fawcasson.com
       Website: www.fawcasson.com
Employee benefit plan audits, business valuations, fraud services, EBP audits, agreed-upon procedures, internal audit staffing & tax services. (Woman, estab 1944, empl 39, sales $6,460,702, cert: WBENC)

Florida

7743 Advantium Capital, LLC
       12555 Orange Dr, Ste 1003
       Davie, FL 33330
       Contact: Souren Sarkar CEO
       Tel: 214-771-7568
       Email: ssarkar@advantiumcapital.com
       Website: www.advantiumcapital.com
Full suite mortgage fulfillment & compliance services. (As-Pac, estab 2012, empl 25, sales $2,036,335, cert: State, NMSDC)

7744 AMI Risk Consultants
       1336 SW 146th Court
       Miami, FL 33184
       Contact: Actuary Analyst/Admin
       Tel: 305-173-1589
       Email: cingo@comcast.net
       Website: www.amirisk.com
Property/casualty actuarial & risk management consulting. (As-Pac, estab 1992, empl 7, sales , cert: NMSDC)

7745 Carter-Health LLC
       4201 Vineland Road Ste I-13-14
       Orlando, FL 32811
       Contact: Rodney Carter President
       Tel: 407-296-6689
       Email: rodney@carterhealth.com
       Website: www.carter-health.com
Carter-Health is a turn-key solutions provider for creating sterile environments for I.V. compounding facilities. Our expertise in this area assists healthcare facilities in meeting the stringent requirements of (AA, estab 2007, empl 5, sales $2,500,000, cert: NMSDC)

7746 Commonwealth Capital Corp
       4532 US Hwy 19 Ste 200
       New Port Richey, FL 34652
       Contact: Kim Springsteen-Abbott Business Devel
       Tel: 800-249-3700
       Email: kspringsteen@ccclease.com
       Website: www.ccclease.com
Equipment leasing: IT, telecom & medical equipment. (Woman, estab 1978, empl 45, sales $10,000,000, cert: WBENC)

7747 Empower Benefits Inc. dba Corestream
       3606 Enterprise Ave, Ste 304
       Naples, FL 34104
       Contact: Neil Vaswani CEO
       Tel: 917-686-5886
       Email: info@corestream.com
       Website: www.corestream.com
Provides consolidated payroll deduction, voluntary benefits portals, employee discount shopping portals, group auto insurance real time comparative quoting, online enrollment and voluntary benefits brokerage. (As-Ind, estab 2006, empl 30, sales , cert: NMSDC)

7748 Enfusion, Inc.
       2429 Grand Teton Circle
       Winter Park, FL 32792
       Contact: Anita White CEO
       Tel: 407-802-0006
       Email: anita@enfusionfinance.com
       Website: www.enfusionfinance.com
Financial intelligence consulting, expense & cost management. (Woman/AA, estab 2007, empl 1, sales , cert: WBENC)

7749 Risk & Re-Insurance Solutions Corporation
      1500 San Remo Ave Ste 247B
      Coral Gables, FL 33146
      Contact: Steven Pacholick VP
      Tel: 770-437-8880
      Email: spacholick@rrisc.com
      Website: www.rrisc.com
Risk management, advisory & risk financing needs to corporate & governmental clients. (Hisp, estab 2001, empl 10, sales $2,550,000, cert: NMSDC)

Georgia

7750 Accountant In A Minute
      1781 Chadds Lake Dr
      Marietta, GA 30068
      Contact: Alison Nicholson President
      Tel: 404-804-5778
      Email: alison.nicholson@aimaccountingservices.com
      Website: www.aimaccountingservices.com
Accounting Services: Reconciliations Statement reconciliations & Expenses Bank reconciliations, Recording transactions Financial Statement preparation & tutorials Month, Quarter close support, Audit support (Failing Audits) System Migration. (Woman, estab 2017, empl 2, sales $100,000, cert: NWBOC)

7751 Corporate Reports, Inc.
      3610 Piedmont Rd NE Ste 200
      Atlanta, GA 30305
      Contact: Angela King Controller
      Tel: 404-233-2230
      Email: angela.king@corporatereport.com
      Website: www.corporatereport.com
Annual (financial) & sustainability/corporate responsibility/citizenship reporting. (Woman, estab , empl , sales $3,500,000, cert: WBENC)

7752 Harris Group Services, Inc.
      PO Box 2244
      Alpharetta, GA 30023
      Contact: Marine Harris CEO
      Tel: 404-243-5600
      Email: contact@harrisgs.com
      Website: www.harrisgs.com
Project management & support, accounting & finance services, audit support svcs, business analysis & communication, financial compliance & reviews, asset management & valuation. (Woman/AA, estab 2009, empl 3, sales , cert: WBENC)

7753 Infinite Financial Concepts, LLC
      PO Box 953
      Stone Mountain, GA 30086
      Contact: Amin Hassan President
      Tel: 678-933-5304
      Email: amin@ifc326.com
      Website: www.ifc326.com
Accounting & financial reporting. (AA, estab 2011, empl 1, sales , cert: City)

7754 Real Property Tax Advisors
      3525 Piedmont Rd, Ste 7-300
      Atlanta, GA 30305
      Contact: Anne Sheehan CEO
      Tel: 404-816-2050
      Email: asheehan@realpropertytaxadvisors.com
      Website: www.realpropertytaxadvisors.com
Property tax consulting services. (Woman, estab 1972, empl 45, sales , cert: WBENC)

7755 Resurgens Risk Management, Inc.
      1201 Peachtree St NE
      Atlanta, GA 30361
      Contact: Clifton McKnight, Sr. Asst VP
      Tel: 678-298-5119
      Email: cmcknight@rrmgt.com
      Website: www.rrmgt.com
Human resources consulting services, financial products, employee benefits, commercial property & liability insurance & consultative services. (AA, estab 1987, empl 33, sales $3,000,000, cert: NMSDC)

7756 RiverStone Associates, LLC
      750 Olde Clubs Dr
      Alpharetta, GA 30022
      Contact: Monty Brinkley President
      Tel: 770-656-7820
      Email: mbrinkley@riverstone-us.com
      Website: www.riverstone-us.com
Professional svcs: internal audit, accounting, IT security, process improvement & risk management solutions. (AA, estab 2007, empl 2, sales , cert: State)

Illinois

7757 A3B, LLC
      100 S Saunders Rd, Ste 150
      Lake Forest, IL 60045
      Contact: Betsey Robinson President
      Tel: 847-574-7227
      Email: betsey@a3bllc.com
      Website: www.a3bllc.com
Accounting & Finance Consulting Services, business process improvements resulting in cost savings, financial accounting reporting & analysis, financial transformation of shared services centers, management of change. (Woman/AA, estab 2013, empl 3, sales , cert: NMSDC, WBENC)

7758 Adelfia LLC
      400 E Randolph Str Ste 705
      Chicago, IL 60601
      Contact: Stella Marie Santos
      Tel: 312-240-9500
      Email: sbsantos@adelfiacpas.com
      Website: www.adelfiacpas.com
Assurance & advisory services: financial audit, compliance examination, internal audit, agreed-upon procedures, tax services, tax preparation, payroll tax returns, tax notices/audit assistance, tax planning, accounting services. (Minority, Woman, estab 2011, empl 30, sales $541,996, cert: State, City, NMSDC)

7759 Ariel Investments
      200 E Randolph St Ste 2900
      Chicago, IL 60601
      Contact: Gary L. Rozier Sr VP
      Tel: 312-726-0140
      Email: grozier@arielinvestments.com
      Website: www.arielinvestments.com
Financial management services. (AA, estab 1983, empl , sales $54,074,660, cert: NMSDC)

PROFESSIONAL SERVICES: Financial

7760 Barbee Tax Consulting, LLC
18700 Wolf Rd Ste 206
Mokena, IL 60448
Contact: Prentice Barbee President
Tel: 708-945-8334
Email: pbarbee@barbeetax.com
Website: www.barbeetax.com
Certified tax, accounting, and affordable care act (ACA) provider to corporate taxpayers. Compliance, contract services, tax preparation, assistance with state audits and notices, research and planning, and much more. (AA, estab 2013, empl 1, sales $145,680, cert: NMSDC, 8(a))

7761 Benford Brown & Associates LLC
8334 S Stony Island Ave
Chicago, IL 60617
Contact: Kim Ellen Partner
Tel: 773-731-1300
Email: kellen@benfordbrown.com
Website: www.benfordbrown.com
Auditing, accounting, tax & small business consulting services. (Woman/AA, estab 1996, empl 7, sales $1,005,155, cert: State, NMSDC, WBENC)

7762 Cabrera Capital Markets, LLC
10 S LaSalle St Ste 1050
Chicago, IL 60603
Contact: William Feeley Managing Dir
Tel: 312-236-8888
Email: mfeeley@cabreracapital.com
Website: www.cabreracapital.com
Investment banking services, domestic & international equity brokerage, taxable fixed income brokerage, mergers & acquisitions. (Hisp, estab 2001, empl 74, sales $25,109,305, cert: State, NMSDC)

7763 Davenport Capital Management
312 N Clark St Ste 500
Chicago, IL 60654
Contact: Thomas Davenport Managing Partner
Tel: 312-445-6406
Email: thomas@davenportcap.com
Website: www.davenportcap.com
Merchant banking, strategic advisory & investments. (AA, estab 2014, empl 4, sales $800,000, cert: NMSDC)

7764 E.C. Ortiz & Co., LLP
333 S Des Plaines St, Ste 2-N
Chicago, IL 60661
Contact: Edilberto C. Ortiz Managing Partner
Tel: 312-876-1900
Email: ecortiz@ecortiz.com
Website: www.ecortiz.com
Auditing, accounting, consulting, taxation, employee benefit plan audits, management services & financial advice. (As-Pac, estab 1974, empl 65, sales $3,968,725, cert: State, City, NMSDC)

7765 Global Capital, Ltd.
205 W. Wacker Dr. Ste 730
Chicago, IL 60606
Contact: Terri McNally President
Tel: 312-846-6918
Email: brian@globelease.com
Website: www.globalcapitalltd.com
Equipment leasing & financing: aircraft, rails, trailers, vehicles, computers, manufacturing & construction equipment. (Woman, estab 1999, empl 7, sales $34,465,113, cert: WBENC)

7766 Holland Capital Management LLC
303 West Madison Ste 700
Chicago, IL 60606
Contact: Valerie King Dir of Marketing
Tel: 312-553-4830
Email: vking@hollandcap.com
Website: www.hollandcap.com
Equity & fixed income institutional management. (Minority, Woman, estab 1991, empl 22, sales $6,966,000, cert: State, NMSDC)

7767 Loop Capital Markets
111 W Jackson Blvd Ste 1901
Chicago, IL 60604
Contact: Sidney Dillard Partner
Tel: 312-356-5008
Email: nancy.ziagos@loopcapital.com
Website: www.loopcapital.com
Corporate debt & issuances, sub notes, floating rate notes, bonds, securities, credit cards, equity, common stock, variable rate debt, etc. (AA, estab 1997, empl 150, sales , cert: NMSDC)

7768 MWM Consulting Group Inc.
55 E Jackson Blvd Ste 1000
Chicago, IL 60604
Contact: Managing Principal
Tel: 312-987-9097
Email: mail@mwmcg.com
Website: www.mwmcg.com
Actuarial analysis, valuations & administriative svcs. (Woman, estab 1993, empl 12, sales $2,350,000, cert: WBENC)

7769 Sierra Forensic Group
30 S Wacker Dr Ste 2200
Chicago, IL 60606
Contact: Adrian Sierra CEO
Tel: 312-674-7100
Email: adrian.sierra@sfg-global.com
Website: www.sfg-global.com
Forensic accounting & investigative services. (Hisp, estab 2005, empl 8, sales $327,688, cert: NMSDC)

Indiana

7770 Engaging Solutions, LLC
3965 N Meridian St Ste 1B
Indianapolis, IN 46208
Contact: Debbie Wilson Managing Principal
Tel: 317-283-8300
Email: debbie@engagingsolutions.net
Website: www.engagingsolutions.net
Fiscal Mgmt & Accountability, Financial Compliance Audits, Program Audits, Financial Reviews, Compilations, Agreed Upon Procedures, Internal Controls Reviews, Tax Preparation, Ta Audit Representation. (Woman/AA, estab 2005, empl 26, sales $2,009,000, cert: State)

7771 Moore Accounting, LLC
9465 Counselors Row, Ste 200
Indianapolis, IN 46240
Contact: April Moore Owner
Tel: 317-504-0296
Email: afreeman@mooreacctg.com
Website: www.mooreacctg.com
Accounting, Tax, Payroll, Tier 2 Audit Services, Davis Bacon & Related Acts, Long-Term Care, Mental Health, Transportation, A133, Echos, Housing Authority, Section 8, Tax Credit Housing, Public Housing. (Woman/AA, estab 2010, empl 3, sales , cert: State, City, WBENC)

7772 Putnam Industries Inc.
      4582 NW Plaza W Dr# 100
      Zionsville, IN 46077
      Contact: Jim Pickens President
      Tel: 317-275-3153
      Email: jpickens@putnamindustriesinc.com
      Website: www.putnamindustriesinc.com
Equipment leasing & finance: computers, software, hardware, copiers, office furniture, fleet vehlices, medical equipment, trucks, buses, lighting, HVAC systems, bulldozers, forklifts, heavy machinery, telephone systems, alarm systems. (AA, estab 2007, empl 5, sales $3,836,816, cert: NMSDC)

7773 Solace Risk Management
      9247 N Meridian St Ste 221
      Indianapolis, IN 46260
      Contact: Charles Moorer President
      Tel: 317-423-3947
      Email: charles.moorer@srm-cs.com
      Website: www.srm-cs.com
Designs comprehensive fully insured & self-insured risk financing & risk management programs. (AA, estab 2011, empl 3, sales , cert: State, NMSDC)

7774 Thomas & Reed, LLC
      148 E. Market St Ste 300
      Indianapolis, IN 46204
      Contact: Stephen A Reed
      Tel: 317-955-6933
      Email: tclemons@trllc-cpa.com
      Website: www.trlllc-cpa.com
Certified public accounting: auditing, reviews, compilations, controllership, bookkeeping, financial software system installation & training, payroll, staff outsourcing, rate analysis, Davis Bacon Compliance, contract compliance. (Woman/AA, estab 2004, empl 3, sales $267,340, cert: City)

Kansas

7775 Asset LifeCycle, LLC
      PO Box 19286
      Topeka, KS 66619
      Contact: President
      Tel: 785-272-8288
      Email:
      Website: www.assetlc.com
Asset disposition, electronics asset remarketing & recycling solutions. (Woman, estab 2004, empl 10, sales $450,000, cert: WBENC)

Massachusetts

7776 Spafford Leasing Associates, Inc.
      1350 Main St Ste 318
      Springfield, MA 01103
      Contact: Angela Flebotte CEO
      Tel: 413-526-0975
      Email: angelaf@spafford.com
      Website: www.spafford.com
Equipment leasing, computer systems, hospital equipment, copiers, telephone systems, computer software, manufacturing equipment, for lease terms ranging from 3-7 years. (Woman, estab 1989, empl 2, sales $500,000, cert: WBENC)

Maryland

7777 AdNet/AccountNet, Inc.
      757 Frederick Rd Ste 102
      Catonsville, MD 21228
      Contact: Betsy Cerulo CEO
      Tel: 410-715-4040
      Email: bcerulo@adnetp3.com
      Website: www.adnetp3.com
Accounting/Financial, Information Tecnology, Human Resources and Administrative staffing. (Woman, estab 1990, empl 23, sales $2,000,000, cert: State, WBENC)

7778 Beasley Financial Group LLC
      4815 Coyle Rd, Ste 103
      Owings Mills, MD 21117
      Contact: Marcus Beasley CEO
      Tel: 877-265-1264
      Email: mbeasley@beasleyfinancialgroup.com
      Website: www.beasleyfinancialgroup.com
Financial advisory, brokerage & consulting: 401(k) retirement plans, life, health, dental, disability & long term care insurance benefit plans. (Woman/AA, estab 2005, empl 3, sales , cert: State)

7779 Beyond The Bottom Line, Inc.
      1300 Mercantile Lane Ste 139
      Largo, MD 20774
      Contact: Corinda Davis President
      Tel: 301-322-4083
      Email: bblinc@beyondbottomline.com
      Website: www.beyondbottomline.com
Budget formulation, execution & monitoring processes, data mining to compile raw data to help clients recognize significant facts, relationships, trends, patterns, exceptions & anomalies. (Woman/AA, estab 2003, empl 16, sales $1,202,364, cert: State)

7780 EurekaFacts, LLC
      51 Monroe St, PE-10
      Rockville, MD 20850
      Contact: Jorge Restrepo Dir Business Devel
      Tel: 240-403-1646
      Email: certifications@eurekafacts.com
      Website: www.eurekafacts.com
Research design, rigorous data collection, & advanced analytic & statistical services. (Hisp, estab 2003, empl 23, sales $4,281,146, cert: NMSDC)

7781 Gonzalez, Hawkins & Johnson LLC
      PO Box 2705
      Upper Marlboro, MD 20772
      Contact: Alejandro Gonzalez Partner
      Tel: 240-865-6052
      Email: agonzalez@ghjaccounting.com
      Website: www.ghjaccounting.com
Federal Financial Consulting. (Woman/AA, Hisp, estab 2008, empl 3, sales , cert: State, 8(a))

7782 IMB Development Corporation, LLC
      7201 Wisconsin Ave., Ste 440
      Bethesda, MD 20814
      Contact: Tarrus Richardson CEO
      Tel: 240-507-1660
      Email: trichardson@imbdc.com
      Website: www.imbdc.com
Enterprise risk management & insurance solutions, supplier diversity strategy & capacity building, M&A advisory & direct private equity investing. (AA, estab 2010, empl 6, sales $2,012,892, cert: State, NMSDC)

7783 New Century Advisors, LLC
      2 Wisconsin Circle, Ste 940
      Chevy Chase, MD 20815
      Contact: Ellen Safir President
      Tel: 240-395-0550
      Email: esafir@ncallc.com
      Website: www.newcenturyadvisors.com
Investment Management Services. (Woman, estab 2002, empl 14, sales $4,695,000, cert: WBENC)

7784 Premier Group Services, Inc
      7404 Executive Pl
      Lanham, MD 20706
      Contact: Joye Sistrunk Principal
      Tel: 301-577-6444
      Email: joyes@pgs-cpa.com
      Website: www.pgservicesinc.com
CPA & management: audits, fraud, waste & abuse support, government contracting consulting & audits, temporary accounting staff, attestation services, business consulting, budgeting, taxes & payroll, financial forecasting & projections. (Woman/AA, estab 2005, empl 5, sales $139,000, cert: State, 8(a))

7785 SB & Company, LLC.
      200 International Cir, Ste 5500
      Hunt Valley, MD 21030
      Contact: Stacy Wenzl Principal of Practice Dev
      Tel: 410-584-9302
      Email: swenzl@sbandcompany.com
      Website: www.sbandcompany.com
Accounting services. (Woman/AA, estab 2005, empl 95, sales $14,050,000, cert: State, NMSDC)

7786 The CTS Group, LLC
      13407 Tamarack Rd
      Silver Spring, MD 20904
      Contact: Calvin L. Scott, Jr. Managing Member
      Tel: 301-801-1193
      Email: cscott@ctsgroupllc.com
      Website: www.ctsgroupllc.com
Comprehensive accounting & advisory business services, account maintenance, financial management, budget development & analysis, interim outsourcing, transaction analysis, transaction processing, data analysis & summarization. (AA, estab 2007, empl 1, sales $175,000, cert: State, 8(a))

7787 TSC Enterprise
      5211 Auth Rd Ste 100
      Suitland, MD 20746
      Contact: Salome Tinker Managing Partner
      Tel: 240-455-7848
      Email: sjtinker@tsccpas.com
      Website: www.TSCcpas.com
Certified public accounting, FIAR, audit readiness, tax, financial transition, compliance, assurance, management consulting, A133, yellow book, cost recovery, performance reviews, financial system implementation, financial support & staffing. (Woman/AA, estab 2001, empl 6, sales $250,000, cert: WBENC)

Maine

7788 Absolute Credit LLC
      175 Exchange St, Ste 225
      Bangor, ME 04401
      Contact: President
      Tel: 800-680-5000
      Email: info@absolutecreditllc.com
      Website: www.AbsoluteCreditLLC.com
Nationwide collections. (Woman, estab 2006, empl 28, sales $980,000, cert: WBENC)

Michigan

7789 Baron Wealth Management
      3150 Livernois Rd, Ste 250
      Troy, MI 48083
      Contact: Beth Zilka Operations Mgr
      Tel: 248-251-0161
      Email: bzilka@baron-wealth.com
      Website: www.baron-wealth.com
Comprehensive wealth management services, income tax, retirement, cash flow, estate, investment, compensation, benefits & insurance planning. (Woman, estab 2010, empl 6, sales $ 0, cert: WBENC)

7790 Centennial Securities Advisory Services
      515 Ship St, Ste 211
      Saint Joseph, MI 49085
      Contact: Jim Roberts President
      Tel: 269-982-4188
      Email: jim@jrcent.com
      Website: www.jrcent.com
Wealth management, investments, investing, 401k, IRA, pension, foundation, financial advisor. (Minority, estab 2014, empl 3, sales $300,000, cert: NMSDC)

7791 Chippewa Capital LLC
      3190 Tri Park Dr
      Grand Blanc, MI 48439
      Contact: Thomas Barrett VP
      Tel: 810-579-0579
      Email: thomas.barrett@macarthurcorp.com
      Website: www.chippewacapital.com
Equipment leasing, painting, trucking, warehousing & distribution. (Nat Ame, estab 2000, empl 35, sales $2,000,000, cert: NMSDC)

7792 First Independence Bank
      44 Michigan Ave
      Detroit, MI 48226
      Contact: Rhonda Pugh Branch Admin
      Tel: 313-256-8400
      Email: rhondapugh@firstindependence.com
      Website: www.firstindependence.com
Banking services. (AA, estab 1970, empl 62, sales $13,737,000, cert: NMSDC)

7793 Gonzales Financial Consulting, LLC
      4707 Charest
      Waterford, MI 48327
      Contact: Rogelio Gonzales Managing Member
      Tel: 810-706-1687
      Email: roy@gonzalesfc.com
      Website: www.gonzalesfc.com
Retirement plan consulting services, insurance coverage review, broker management & risk management support services, commercial liability, property, general liability, worker's compensation. (Hisp, estab 2015, empl 4, sales , cert: NMSDC)

7794 KCM Technical Inc.
      850 Stephenson Hwy, Ste 603
      Troy, MI 48083
      Contact: Pamela Williford President
      Tel: 877-996-3749
      Email: cjohnson@kcmtech.net
      Website: www.kcmtech.net
Offers Payroll, Accounting & Help Supply Services. (AA, estab 2005, empl 350, sales , cert: NMSDC)

7795 L J Ross Associates, Inc.
      4 Universal Way
      Jackson, MI 49204
      Contact: Kaylyn Todd Marketing & Business Dev Mgr
      Tel: 517-544-9100
      Email: kaylyn@ljross.com
      Website: www.ljross.com
Debt collection: consumer & commercial debts. (Woman, estab 1992, empl 60, sales $8,012,319, cert: WBENC)

7796 Lakefront Capital, LLC
      28175 Haggerty Rd
      Novi, MI 48377
      Contact: Sandy Fuchs Dir Ops & Client Service
      Tel: 248-994-9001
      Email: sandy.fuchs@lakefrontts.com
      Website: www.lakefrontts.com
Lease financing & portfolio management. (As-Pac, estab 2002, empl 8, sales $10,000,000, cert: NMSDC)

7797 Minority Alliance Capital, LLC
      6960 Orchard Lake Rd Ste 306
      West Bloomfield, MI 48322
      Contact: Tim McCormick VP- Sales
      Tel: 248-236-5182
      Email: mccormick.t@mac-leasing.com
      Website: www.mac-leasing.com
Equipment leasing: computer & software, office furniture & fixtures, production & process control. (AA, estab 1999, empl 14, sales $248,000,000, cert: NMSDC)

7798 Optimal Leasing LLC
      4301 Orchard Lake Rd, Ste 180-173
      West Bloomfield, MI 48323
      Contact: Larry Robinson CEO
      Tel: 248-738-2699
      Email: larry@optimalleasingcompany.com
      Website: www.optimalleasingcompany.com
Third party lease financing of capital equipment. (AA, estab 1996, empl 50, sales , cert: NMSDC)

7799 Renaissance Capital Alliance
      5440 Corporate Dr, Ste 275
      Troy, MI 48098
      Contact: Kyle Bell Natl Acct Mgr
      Tel: 248-821-1811
      Email: kylebell@rcalliance.com
      Website: www.rcalliance.com
Equipment leasing: materials handling, lift trucks, transportation & warehousing equipment; fleet mgmt services. (AA, estab 2001, empl 13, sales $50,000,000, cert: NMSDC, CPUC)

Minnesota

7800 Amare & Associates LLC dba ABA Tax Accounting
      10670 Hawthorn Trail
      St. Paul, MN 55129
      Contact: Amare Berhie CEO
      Tel: 866-936-0430
      Email: amare@abataxaccounting.com
      Website: www.abataxaccounting.com
Finance & accounting outsourcing svcs: transaction processing & staffing services. (AA, estab 1989, empl 2, sales , cert: State, City, NMSDC)

7801 Certes Financial Pros, Inc.
      5775 Wayzata Blvd, Ste 550
      St. Louis Park, MN 55416
      Contact: Sally Mainquist President
      Tel: 952-345-4141
      Email: getalife@certespros.com
      Website: www.certespros.com
Provide high-end financial professionals on an interim & project basis. (Woman, estab 1994, empl 170, sales $12,000,000, cert: State)

7802 Diversified Adjustment Service, Inc.
      600 Coon Rapids Blvd
      Coon Rapids, MN 55433
      Contact: Michelle Wendell Admin Asst
      Tel: 763-783-2334
      Email: diversity@diversifiedadjustment.com
      Website: www.diversifiedadjustment.com
Managed collection svcs: accounts recievable mgmt & credit reporting, debt collection, pre-collect & skip-tracing svcs. (Woman, estab 1981, empl 60, sales $14,400,000, cert: CPUC, WBENC)

Missouri

7803 Stern Brothers & Co.
      8000 Maryland Ave, Ste 800
      Saint Louis, MO 63105
      Contact: Lisa Liebschutz Marketing
      Tel: 314-727-5519
      Email: lliebschutz@sternbrothers.com
      Website: www.sternbrothers.com
Full service investment bank. Lines of business include public and project finance, corporate and equity finance, sales and trading. (Woman, estab 1985, empl 42, sales $20,766,637, cert: WBENC)

North Carolina

7804 Falcon Square Capital, LLC
      4000 Westchase Blvd
      Raleigh, NC 27607
      Contact: Melissa Pendergrass CEO
      Tel: 919-825-1534
      Email: mpendergrass@falconsquarecapital.com
      Website: www.falconsquarecapital.com
Trading, research, portfolio construction, transition management, client commission arrangements & other institutional brokerage services. (Woman, estab 2013, empl 16, sales $1,711,975, cert: WBENC)

7805 Innovation Partners LLC
5950 Fairview Road, Ste 140
Charlotte, NC 28210
Contact: Anthony Lawrence Principal
Tel: 704-708-5461
Email: alawrence@innovationpartnersllc.com
Website: www.innovationpartnersllc.com
Deferred compensation plans, retirement planning, actuarial, pension funds, investment banking, reinsurance, securities portfolio management, risk management, asset portfoilo management, underwriting services. (Woman/AA, estab 2007, empl 20, sales $1,500,000, cert: NMSDC)

7806 Tryon Clear View Group, LLC
816 W Mills St
Columbus, NC 28722
Contact: Mary Thompson Exec VP
Tel: 314-255-6279
Email: mthompson@tryonclearview.com
Website: www.tryonclearviewgroup.com
Detect & recover overpayments to vendors, improved financial & operational practices & procedures. (Woman, estab , empl 13, sales $2,200,000, cert: WBENC)

New Jersey

7807 Allen, Maxwell & Silver, Inc.
17-17 Route 208 N Ste 340
Fair Lawn, NJ 07401
Contact: Lisa Freidman CEO
Tel: 201-871-0044
Email: lisa@amscollections.com
Website: www.amscollections.com
Commercial collections. (Woman, estab 1992, empl 38, sales $2,650,000, cert: WBENC)

7808 Ateeca Inc.
107 B1 Corporate Blvd,
South Plainfield, NJ 07080
Contact: Adam Lee Sr Business Dev
Tel: 908-427-5591
Email: gdavis@ateeca.com
Website: www.ateeca.com/
Payroll services. (Minority, Woman, estab 2005, empl 180, sales $6,830,000, cert: NMSDC, WBENC)

7809 Broad Street Capital Markets LLC
494 Broad St Ste 206
Newark, NJ 07102
Contact: Andrew Adderly CEO
Tel: 862-367-9930
Email: mdejesus@broadscm.com
Website: www.broadscm.com
Investment Banking & Securities Dealing, Investment Advice, Administrative Management & General Management Consulting. (AA, Hisp, estab 2000, empl 8, sales $ 0, cert: State, NMSDC)

7810 Business Processes Redefined, LLC
155 Passaic Ave, Ste 470
Fairfield, NJ 07004
Contact: President
Tel: 800-470-6622
Email: customerservice@bprllc.com
Website: www.bprllc.com
Collection services. (Woman, estab 2007, empl 12, sales $500,000, cert: WBENC)

7811 Enhanced Due Diligence Advisory, Inc.
910 Garden St
Hoboken, NJ 07030
Contact: Wayne Chau
Tel: 973-727-7248
Email: wchau@eddadvisory.com
Website: www.eddadvisory.com
Risk assessment of domestic/international assets, compliance, audit & logistics strategy. (As-Pac, estab 2015, empl 3, sales , cert: State, NMSDC)

7812 First Credit Services, Inc.
9 Wills Way
Piscataway, NJ 08854
Contact: Rajesh Chhabria CEO
Tel: 732-305-8301
Email: rchhabria@fcsbpo.com
Website: www.firstcreditonline.com
Collection & business process outsourcing, past-due A/R for medium & large businesses. (As-Ind, estab 1993, empl 50, sales $6,934,493, cert: NMSDC)

7813 Runnymede Capital Management, Inc.
10 Wilrich Glen Rd
Morristown, NJ 07960
Contact: Andrew Wang Sr VP
Tel: 973-267-6886
Email: awang@runnymede.com
Website: www.runnymede.com
Manages investment portfolios of institutions (Taft-Hartley, captive insurance, public pension fund, corporate, non-profit) & high-net-worth individuals. (As-Pac, estab 1993, empl 8, sales $1,500,000, cert: NMSDC)

Nevada

7814 ReCredit
1925 Village Center Circle Ste 150-11
Las Vegas, NV 89134
Contact: Katrina Screen Owner
Tel: 650-539-0800
Email: katrina@thepremierconcierge.com
Website: www.recredit.co/bp/
Offers a turn-key solution to personal debt and credit matters by providing financial literacy education via our digital content, phone consultations and our credit services work, which produces maximum credit score improvement. (Minority, Woman, estab 2016, empl 15, sales , cert: NMSDC, SDB)

New York

7815 BCA Watson Rice LLP
5 Penn Plaza, 15th Fl
New York, NY 10001
Contact: Bennie Hadnott Managing Partner
Tel: 212-447-7300
Email: blhadnott@bcawatsonrice.com
Website: www.bcawatsonrice.com
Financial auditing services, retirement plan audits, forensic accounting services, internal control services & tax compliance services. (AA, As-Pac, estab 1982, empl 299, sales $4,597,538, cert: State)

PROFESSIONAL SERVICES: Financial

7816 C.L. King & Associates, Inc.
      410 Park Ave
      New York, NY 10022
      Contact: Jason Freed Sales
      Tel: 212-364-1834
      Email: jcf@clking.com
      Website: www.clking.com
Investment banking services, stock (equity) underwriting, bond (fixed income/debt) underwriting, mergers & acquisitions advisory, securities sales, trading & distribution, stock buybacks & pension fund asset mgmt. (Woman, estab 1972, empl 125, sales $45,242,635, cert: WBENC)

7817 CastleOak Securities, L.P.
      110 E 59th St, 2nd Fl
      New York, NY 10022
      Contact: Philip Ippolito CFO
      Tel: 646-521-6700
      Email: ochukwu@castleoaklp.com
      Website: www.castleoaklp.com
Primary & secondary sales & trading of fixed income, equity, municipal & money market securities. (AA, estab , empl , sales $23,087,000, cert: NMSDC)

7818 CAVU Securities, LLC.
      52 Vanderbilt Ave. Ste 403
      New York, NY 10017
      Contact: Karin Sheehy Managing Dir
      Tel: 212-916-3855
      Email: ksheehy@cavusecurities.com
      Website: www.cavusecurities.com
Full service brokerage, investment banking & funds distribution. (AA, estab 2013, empl 12, sales $1,500,000, cert: NMSDC, CPUC)

7819 Corporate Leasing Associates, Inc.
      21 Morris Ave
      Rockville Center, NY 11570
      Contact: Mitch Gelnick Diversity Sales
      Tel: 212-732-5571
      Email: mitch@corplease.com
      Website: www.corplease.com
Operating lease structures, lease purchase, sale & leaseback, step down & step up payments, balloon payments, single investor leases, etc. (Woman, estab 1982, empl 6, sales $4,654,218, cert: State, CPUC, WBENC)

7820 DACK Consulting Solutions
      2 William St Ste 202
      White Plains, NY 10601
      Contact: Aleksandra Chancy CEO
      Tel: 914-686-7102
      Email: ggayle@dackconsulting.com
      Website: www.dackconsulting.com
Cost consulting, estimating, scheduling & project management services. (Woman/AA, estab 1997, empl 24, sales $1,000,000, cert: State, City)

7821 Delta Risk Capital Group LLC
      860 Fifth Ave (2L)
      New York, NY 10065
      Contact: Shanker Merchant Principal
      Tel: 212-961-6825
      Email: shanker.merchant@deltariskcapital.com
      Website: www.DeltaRiskCapital.com
Model Validation Services pursuant to FHFA Requirements & Dodd-Frank Financial Regulations, Valuation on Securities, Residential & Commercial Mortgages, Mortgage & Asset backed securities, Investment Banking, Capital Raising. (As-Pac, estab , empl , sales , cert: NMSDC)

7822 Divine Capital Markets
      39 Broadway, 36 Fl
      New York, NY 10006
      Contact: Hughes Sales
      Tel: 212-344-5867
      Email: dani@divinecapital.com
      Website: www.divinecapital.com
Investment banking, underwriting & distributions, research, corporate share repurchase programs, proprietary VWAP trading, municipal & corporate bonds, international equities. (Woman, estab 1997, empl 12, sales $13,900,000, cert: WBENC)

7823 Elmark Group, Inc.
      499 7th Ave 22 N Tower
      New York, NY 10018
      Contact: President
      Tel: 212-856-9888
      Email: info@marcusjobs.com
      Website: www.marcusjobs.com
Contingency & retained accounting & finance search services, financial reporting, general accounting, accounting policy, internal audit, SOX compliance, risk management, financial & strategic analysis. (Woman, estab 1991, empl 5, sales $1,243,000, cert: WBENC)

7824 EXIGIS LLC
      589 8th Ave Fl 8
      New York, NY 10018
      Contact: Armand Alvarez CEO
      Tel: 800-928-1963
      Email: sales@exigis.com
      Website: www.exigis.com
Risk management services, risk, insurance & business process automation technology. (Hisp, estab 2002, empl 35, sales $1,550,000, cert: NMSDC)

7825 KBL, LLP Certified Public Accountants & Advisors
      110 Wall St, 11th Fl
      New York, NY 10005
      Contact: Richard Levychin Partner
      Tel: 212-785-9700
      Email: rlevychin@kbl.com
      Website: www.kbl.com
Audit & assurance, agreed-upon procedures, compilation & review procedures, business process outsourcing, risk mgmt & advisory services, cross border international practices business services, tax compliance. (AA, estab 1994, empl 50, sales $5,000,000, cert: NMSDC)

7826 Lebenthal Holdings, LLC
      521 Fifth Ave Fl 15
      New York, NY 10175
      Contact: Steven Willis Sr managing dir
      Tel: 877-425-6006
      Email: swillis@lebenthal.com
      Website: www.lebenthalcapitalmarkets.com
Underwrites securities, equity & corporate debt underwriting. (Woman, estab 2007, empl 38, sales $13,179,068, cert: WBENC)

7827 Masterpiece Accounting Services LLC
      2 Hamilton Ave Ste 206
      New Rochelle, NY 10801
      Contact: Ibanessa Hogan Principal
      Tel: 914-661-2798
      Email: i.hogan@masterpieceaccounting.com
      Website: www.masterpieceaccounting.com
Accounting & bookkeeping services, tax preparation & QuickBooks consulting. (Minority, Woman, estab 2010, empl 1, sales , cert: State, WBENC)

PROFESSIONAL SERVICES: Financial

7828 Mitchell & Titus LLP
1 Battery Parkm Plaza, Fl 27
New York, NY 10004
Contact: Irene Davis CFO
Tel: 312-325-7422
Email: IDavis@MitchellTitus.com
Website: www.mitchelltitus.com
Certified public accounting & mgmt consulting. (AA, estab 1974, empl 200, sales $17,000,000, cert: State, NMSDC)

7829 Samuel A. Ramirez & Company, Inc.
61 Broadway 29th Fl
NewYork, NY 10006
Contact: Lawrence Goldman Managing Dir
Tel: 212-248-1214
Email: larry.goldman@ramirezco.com
Website: www.ramirezco.com
Investment banking & capital markets, distribution, brokerage, corporate share repurchase & research services. (Hisp, estab , empl 150, sales $72,950,961, cert: State, City, NMSDC)

7830 Sunrise Credit Services, Inc.
260 Airport Plaza
Farmingdale, NY 11735
Contact: Benjamin Carroccio Sr VP/ General Counsel
Tel: 800-208-8565
Email: bcarroccio@sunrisecreditservices.com
Website: www.SunriseCreditServices.com
Credit & collection services. (Woman, estab 1974, empl 425, sales $15,500,000, cert: WBENC)

7831 SWS Capital Management, LLC (formerly Williams Capital Management, LLC
100 Wall St, 18th Floor
New York, NY 10005
Contact: Lorna Maye Administrative Mgr
Tel: 212-461-6500
Email: lmaye@swscapitalmanagement.com
Website: www.swscapitalmanagement.com
Investment svcs: cash management & short-term fixed income investment strategies. (AA, estab 2002, empl 11, sales $1,073,590, cert: City, NMSDC)

7832 Tigress Financial Partners LLC
114 W 47th St
New York, NY 10036
Contact: George Orr
Tel: 212-430-8700
Email: gorr@tigressfp.com
Website: www.tigressfp.com
Financial services: rtesearch, trade execution, asset management, corporate advisory & investment banking. (Woman, estab 2010, empl 9, sales $100,000, cert: State, City, WBENC)

7833 Topeka Capital Markets Inc.
40 Wall St, Ste 1702
New York, NY 10005
Contact: Sylvester McClearn COO
Tel: 212-709-5706
Email: sm@topekacapitalmarkets.com
Website: www.topekacapitalmarkets.com
Agency-only trading domestic & international equities, traders, sales traders & research analysts. (AA, estab 2010, empl 28, sales , cert: City, NMSDC)

7834 Torres Llompart, Sanchez Ruiz LLP
Bowling Green Station
New York, NY 10274
Contact: Frank Sanchez-Ruiz Partner
Tel: 646-214-1064
Email: fsanchez@tlsr.com
Website: www.tlsr.com
CPAs & business consulting: auditing, tax & corporate advisory, operational studies, mgmt advisory, risk mgmt, marketing consulting, franchising services, international commerce. (Hisp, estab 1989, empl 35, sales $2,410,000, cert: City, NMSDC)

7835 Tribal Capital Markets, LLC
405 Lexington Ave 54th Fl
New York, NY 10174
Contact: Sean Harte CEO
Tel: 212-850-2295
Email: sharte@tribalcap.com
Website: www.tribalcap.com
Client focused services, Fixed Income trading, Equity trading. (Nat Ame, estab 1995, empl 14, sales $4,000,000, cert: NMSDC)

7836 VJN Associates. LLC
39-38 Bell Blvd, Ste 202
Bayside, NY 11361
Contact: Victor Chin Operations Mgr
Tel: - -
Email: victorc@vjnassociates.com
Website: www.vjnassociates.com
Assurance, accounting, book keeping, audits both financial & compliance. (Minority, Woman, estab 2012, empl 10, sales , cert: City, NMSDC)

Ohio

7837 Chard Snyder
3510 Irwin Simpson Rd
Mason, OH 45040
Contact: Deborah Meek
Tel: 513-754-3121
Email: deborah.meek@chard-snyder.com
Website: www.chard-snyder.com
Flexible Spending Accounts, Health Reimbursement Accounts, Health Savings Account, Parking and Transportation Accounts, COBRA and Billing Administration. (Woman, estab 1988, empl , sales $ 0, cert: WBENC)

7838 Kaiser Consulting, LLC
818 Riverbend Ave
Powell, OH 43065
Contact: Lori Kaiser CEO
Tel: 614-300-1088
Email: lkaiser@kaiserconsulting.com
Website: www.kaiserconsulting.com
Financial & accounting consulting. (Woman, estab 1994, empl 63, sales $4,440,000, cert: WBENC)

7839 Kanu Asset Managment, LLC
4015 Executive Park Dr Ste 402
Cincinnati, OH 45241
Contact: Enyi Kanu CEO
Tel: 513-769-2700
Email: ktrent@kanuinvestments.com
Website: www.kanuasset.com
Registered Investment Advisory Firm (RIA) - Investments, Wealth Mgmt, Financial Planning, Insurance, Portfolio Mgmt, Institutional Consulting & Advisory Services. (AA, estab 1996, empl 5, sales , cert: NMSDC)

7840 McCarthy, Burgess & Wolff
       26000 Cannon Rd
       Cleveland, OH 44146
       Contact: Paul Joseph Dir Business Devel
       Tel: 440-735-5100
       Email: paul.joseph@mbandw.com
       Website: www.mbandw.com
Commercial collections & receivables. (Woman, estab 2000, empl 203, sales $17,200,000, cert: WBENC)

7841 Parms & Company, LLC
       585 S Front St Ste 220
       Columbus, OH 43215
       Contact: John Parms
       Tel: 614-224-3078
       Email: jparms@parms.com
       Website: www.parms.com
Auditing, accounting, agreed-upon procedures, forensic accounting, consulting & tax-related services. (AA, estab 1983, empl 14, sales $1,335,851, cert: State, NMSDC)

7842 Richardson and Associates, LLC
       427 Appaloosa Ct
       Cincinnati, OH 45231
       Contact: Sherri Richardson Owner
       Tel: 513-772-8348
       Email: sherri@richardsonandassociates.com
       Website: www.richardsonandassociates.com
Accounting services, audits, writing policies & procedures. (Woman/AA, estab 2007, empl 12, sales , cert: State, NMSDC, WBENC)

7843 The Pension & Retirement Group LLC
       5900 Roche Dr Ste 435
       Columbus, OH 43229
       Contact: Curtis Clark Managing Partner
       Tel: -   -
       Email: cclark@thepensionandretirementgroup.com
       Website: www.thepensionandretirementgroup.com
Financial Wellness, Retirement Planning, Insurance, Investments, 401(k) & 403(b) Plan Management, Retirement Income Planning, Supplement Benefits, Securities, Mutual Funds, IRA's. (AA, estab 2005, empl 3, sales $500,000, cert: NMSDC)

Oklahoma

7844 First Financial Network, Inc.
       9211 Lake Hefner Pkwy, Ste 200
       Oklahoma City, OK 73120
       Contact: John A. Morris President
       Tel: 405-748-4100
       Email: jmorris@ffncorp.com
       Website: www.ffncorp.com/
Turnkey solutions to loan disposition. (Woman, estab , empl , sales $ 0, cert: WBENC)

Pennsylvania

7845 Milligan & Company LLC
       105 N 22nd St, 2nd Fl
       Philadelphia, PA 19103
       Contact: Angela Giunta Dir of Marketing
       Tel: 215-496-9100
       Email: agiunta@milligancpa.com
       Website: www.milligancpa.com
Consulting & certified public accounting. (AA, estab 1985, empl 45, sales $6,400,000, cert: State)

7846 Relevante, Inc
       1235 Westlakes Dr Ste 280
       Berwyn, PA 19312
       Contact: William Brassington CEO
       Tel: 484-403-4100
       Email: wbrassington@relevante.com
       Website: www.relevante.com
Accounting & technology consultants. (As-Ind, estab 2002, empl 130, sales $6,100,000, cert: NMSDC)

Puerto Rico

7847 Alvarado Tax & Business Advisors LLC
       PO Box 195598
       San Juan, PR 00918
       Contact: Miguel Rodriguez Admin
       Tel: 787-620-7744
       Email: mrodriguez@alvatax.com
       Website: www.alvatax.com
Tax & business consulting, outsourcing, business operations, government compliance resolution issues, financial management, business, development, business continuation & succession, business governance. (Hisp, estab 2002, empl 32, sales $5,506,828, cert: NMSDC)

Texas

7848 Bley Investment Group
       4200 S Hulen, Ste 519
       Fort Worth, TX 76109
       Contact: Laura Bley President
       Tel: 817-732-2442
       Email: laurab@bleyinvestments.com
       Website: www.bleyinvestments.com
Financial services. (Woman, estab 1990, empl 7, sales $565,000, cert: State, WBENC)

7849 CAET Project Management Consultants
       1139 Keller Pkwy Ste B
       Keller, TX 76248
       Contact: President
       Tel: 817-741-6546
       Email: info@caetpmc.com
       Website: www.caetpmc.com
Owner Representation & Financial Consulting, project budgeting, cost estimation, Assist & develop contract strategies, Conduct requests for proposals (RFPs) & manage process for receipt & review. (Woman, estab 2016, empl 5, sales $150,000, cert: State, WBENC)

7850 Credit Systems International, Inc.
       1277 Country Club Lane
       Fort Worth, TX 76112
       Contact: Kathy Faith Strategic Devel Dir
       Tel: 800-405-7546
       Email: kathy@creditsystemsintl.com
       Website: www.creditsystemsintl.com
Provides debt collection services. (Woman, estab 1980, empl 70, sales $708,000,000, cert: State, City)

7851 Davis & Davis Professional Services Firm LLC
       12300 Ford Rd, Ste 290
       Dallas, TX 75234
       Contact: Chanel Davis Partner
       Tel: 972-488-5000
       Email: chanel.davis@davisanddavisllc.com
       Website: www.DavisandDavisLLC.com
Sales tax consultants, state tax audit consulting & audit defense. (Woman/AA, estab , empl , sales $1,376,000, cert: NMSDC, WBENC)

7852 DWG CPA PLLC
      5100 Westheimer, Ste 200
      Houston, TX 77056
      Contact: Darrell Groves Managing Dir
      Tel: 281-201-8348
      Email: info@dwgcpatx.com
      Website: www.dwgcpatx.com
Tax, accounting, auditing & financial management. (AA, estab 2005, empl 2, sales , cert: State, NMSDC)

7853 Galosi LLC
      16800 Dallas Pkwy, Ste 210
      Dallas, TX 75248
      Contact: J. Wayne Trimmer EVP
      Tel: 972-267-9907
      Email: wayne.trimmer@galosi.com
      Website: www.galosi.com
Cost of Money, Audit Discounts, Credit Memo Errors, Defective or Spoiled Goods Audit, Duplicate Payments, Errors Involving Returns. (Hisp, estab 2001, empl 27, sales $2,100,000, cert: State, NMSDC)

7854 Goldman, Imani & Goldberg, Inc.
      9894 Bissonnet St Ste 900
      Houston, TX 77036
      Contact: Karl Miller Dir of Marketing & Client Dev
      Tel: 713-395-5120
      Email: kmiller@giginconline.com
      Website: www.giginconline.com
Collection programs, accounts receivable management, third party recovery. (AA, estab 2003, empl 26, sales $2,800,000, cert: NMSDC, 8(a))

7855 Harris & Dickey, LLC.
      4127 Wycliff Ave
      Dallas, TX 75219
      Contact: Kelly Harris Partner
      Tel: 972-672-7597
      Email: kelly.harris@harris-dickey.com
      Website: www.harris-dickey.com
Accounting, finance, tax, internal audit, technology risk & special project assistance. (Woman, estab 2010, empl 12, sales $1,662,658, cert: State, City, WBENC)

7856 Innovative Regulatory Risk Advisors LLC
      3131 McKinney Ave, Ste 0600
      Dallas, TX 75204
      Contact: Brian Robinson, J.D. Managing Member
      Tel: 214-784-5030
      Email: brian.r@innovativeriskadvisors.com
      Website: www.innovativeriskadvisors.com
Business Advisory, Healthcare Compliance, Risk Management. (AA, estab , empl 25, sales $920,000, cert: State, 8(a), SDB)

7857 JN3 Global Enterprises LLC
      3302 Far View Dr
      Austin, TX 78730
      Contact: James Nowlin CEO
      Tel: 512-501-1155
      Email: Assistant@egpventures.com
      Website: www.excelglobalpartners.com/
Corporate financial strategy & implementation. (AA, estab 2007, empl 20, sales $5,920,000, cert: State, NMSDC, CPUC)

7858 Kipling Jones & Co., Ltd.
      1200 Smith St Ste 1600
      Houston, TX 77002
      Contact: Robbi Jones President
      Tel: 713-353-4688
      Email: rjones@kiplingjones.com
      Website: www.kiplingjones.com
Investment banking, financial advisory, bond underwriting & guidance. (Woman/AA, estab 2008, empl 7, sales $500,000, cert: State, City)

7859 McConnell & Jones LLP
      4828 Loop Central Dr, Ste 1000
      Houston, TX 77081
      Contact: Lori Jamail Marketing Dir
      Tel: 713-968-1600
      Email: info@mjlm.com
      Website: www.mcconnelljones.com
Financial statement audits, benefit plan audits, tax returns, compilations, accounting & bookkeeping services, SEC compliance services & single audits. (AA, estab , empl , sales $14,048,077, cert: NMSDC)

7860 Pharos Financial Services LP
      3889 Maple Ave Ste 400
      Dallas, TX 75219
      Contact: Vince Mullins Program Mgr Pharos/DFS-Del
      Tel: 770-330-9105
      Email: cswain@pharosfinancial.com
      Website: www.pharosfinancial.com
Financial loan & lease products. (AA, estab 2002, empl 20, sales , cert: State, NMSDC)

7861 PMB Precision Medical Billing Inc.
      8203 Willow Place Dr S Ste 230
      Houston, TX 77070
      Contact: Petria McKelvey CEO
      Tel: 713-672-7211
      Email: petria@precisionmedicalbilling.com
      Website: www.precisionmedicalbilling.com
Revenue recovery & collections services. (Woman/AA, estab 1995, empl 13, sales $1,611,635, cert: State, WBENC)

7862 PRO Consulting Services, Inc.
      500 Lovett Blvd Ste 250
      Houston, TX 77006
      Contact: Victor Juarez CEO
      Tel: 713-523-1800
      Email: vjuarez@proconsrv.com
      Website: www.proconsrv.com
Accounts receivables management services, commercial collections. (Hisp, estab 1992, empl 90, sales $4,500,000, cert: NMSDC)

7863 Real Time Resolutions, Inc.
      1349 Empire Central Dr Ste 150
      Dallas, TX 75247
      Contact: Mark Hutto SVP Business Dev
      Tel: 214-599-6557
      Email: client.services@rtresolutions.com
      Website: www.realtimeresolutions.com
Financial services & asset recovery: auto, credit card, mortgages, direct demand accounts, student loans, installment loans & commercial loans. (Woman, estab 2000, empl 320, sales , cert: WBENC)

7864 Standberry Enterprises, Inc.
      5956 Sherry Lane, Ste 2000
      Dallas, TX 75225
      Contact: Gwendolyn Evans President
      Tel: 972-914-3597
      Email: gse@thestatetaxexperts.com
      Website: www.thestatetaxexperts.com
Tax compliance services, fixed asset reviews. (Woman/AA, estab 2000, empl 5, sales $250,000, cert: NMSDC, WBENC)

Utah

7865 Merrimak Capital Company LLC
      823 Norfolk Ave
      Park City, UT 84060
      Contact: Dan Crowl VP Human Resources
      Tel: 415-475-4100
      Email: rfq@merrimak.com
      Website: www.merrimak.com
Financing solutions: operating leases, capital leases, lease lines, sale leasebacks & technology refresh leases. (Woman, estab 1991, empl 42, sales $150,655,616, cert: CPUC, WBENC)

Virginia

7866 BME Ventures LLC
      PO Box 2675
      Ashburn, VA 20146
      Contact: Bianca Ellis Owner
      Tel: 571-342-7774
      Email: bellis@projacctworkflow.com
      Website: www.projacctworkflow.com
Accounting, bookkeeping, and consulting services. (Woman/AA, estab 2019, empl 1, sales , cert: NMSDC, WBENC)

7867 Integrated Finance and Accounting Solutions, LLC
      4310 Prince William Pkwy, Ste 405
      Woodbridge, VA 22192
      Contact: Tracy Jones Business Development Mgr
      Tel: 314-267-5847
      Email: tjones@ifaasolutions.com
      Website: www.ifaasolutions.com
Business Re-engineering, Process Improvement, Financial Data Analysis, Internal Control Monitoring, Program, Planning, Budget & Execution. (Woman/AA, estab 2007, empl 29, sales $1,000,000, cert: 8(a))

7868 Kodiak Finance LLC
      8000 Towers Crescent Dr Ste 1350
      Vienna, VA 22182
      Contact: Marcy Dilworth President
      Tel: 703-266-9199
      Email: mdilworth@kodiakfinance.com
      Website: www.kodiakfinance.com
Computer leasing & sales, asset management. (Minority, Woman, estab 2004, empl 10, sales $560,357, cert: NMSDC, WBENC)

7869 RER Solutions Inc.
      950 Herndon Pkwy, Ste 200
      Herndon, VA 20170
      Contact: Errin Green CEO
      Tel: 703-742-6789
      Email: errin.green@rer-solutions.com
      Website: www.rer-solutions.com
Comprehensive business, real estate & financial mgmt. services, asset sale support, due diligence, portfolio management systems, technical & admin support personnel, financial modeling, document & records management, risk management. (Woman/AA, estab 1989, empl 27, sales $2,633,597, cert: State, 8(a))

7870 Technology Ventures
      7930 Jones Branch Dr Ste 310
      McLean, VA 22102
      Contact: John Earl Dir Business Dev
      Tel: 703-917-1650
      Email: jearl@tventures.net
      Website: www.tventures.net
IT & Financial Staffing, Government & Consulting Services, Financial Services, Healthcare Communications, Consumer & Retail. (As-Ind, estab 1998, empl 150, sales , cert: State)

Washington

7871 Adekoya Business Consulting LLC
      33021 Hoyt Rd SW
      Federal Way, WA 98023
      Contact: Andre Adekoya CEO
      Tel: 206-817-9775
      Email: andrew@adekoyabc.com
      Website: www.adekoyabc.com
Business solutions, strategic financial planning & analysis, audits, market (digital) competitive analytics & revenue growth opportunities identification, resource planning, process re-engineering & system implementation. (AA, estab 2013, empl 5, sales $425,000, cert: State)

Wisconsin

7872 One Accord, LLC
      PO Box 241763
      Milwaukee, WI 53224
      Contact: Shanna Reid President
      Tel: 414-855-6342
      Email: smreid@oneaccord.biz
      Website: www.oneaccord.biz
Risk management & reinsurance brokerage. (Woman/AA, estab 2002, empl 3, sales , cert: State, City)

PROFESSIONAL SERVICES: Human Resources

Provide training and seminars on a variety of human resources topics: diversity, supplier diversity programs, team building, customer relations, staff development, wellness programs, policy and procedure manuals, coaching, etc. NAICS Code 54

Alabama

7873 C. Edward Lewis & Associates
3415 Buckboard Rd
Montgomery, AL 36116
Contact: Charles Lewis President
Tel: 334-272-3365
Email: charleslewis@celewisohs.com
Website: www.celewisohs.com
EEO & human resources training & consulting. (AA, estab 2004, empl 2, sales , cert: NMSDC)

7874 EAP Lifestyle Management, LLC
805 Daphne Ave Ste B
Daphne, AL 36526
Contact: Patricia Vanderpool Owner
Tel: 800-788-2077
Email: pvanderpool@eaplifestyle.com
Website: www.eaplifestyle.com
Employee assistance program & work/life svcs, substance abuse professional svcs, workplace training & presentation, continuing education, critical incident stress svcs. (Woman, estab 1998, empl 12, sales , cert: WBENC)

Arizona

7875 HR Wise, LLC
8399 E Indian School Rd Ste 101
Scottsdale, AZ 85251
Contact: Gregory O'Keefe CEO
Tel: 480-626-2109
Email: gokeefe@hrwisellc.com
Website: www.hrwisellc.com
Payroll, Payroll Services, Human Resource Management, Talent Management, Benefits Administration, Time and Attendance, Human Capital Management, HR Business Process Outsourcing (HRBPO). (Hisp, estab 2008, empl 6, sales $290,000, cert: NMSDC, 8(a))

California

7876 Accurate Background
7515 Irvine Center Dr
Irvine, CA 92618
Contact: Matthew Schneider Enterprise Acct Exec
Tel: 949-609-2277
Email: mschneider@accuratebackground.com
Website: www.accurate.com
Background screening: criminal background checks, drug screening, fingerprinting, verifications, & compliance services. (Hisp, estab 1997, empl 1700, sales $350,000,000, cert: NMSDC)

7877 AccuSource, Inc.
30650 Rancho California Road Ste D406-215
Temecula, CA 92591
Contact: Cynthia Woods VP Sales & Mktg
Tel: 888-649-6272
Email: diversity@accusource-online.com
Website: www.accusource-online.com
Screening services: criminal backgrounds checks, social security traces, DMV records, drug testing, international criminal & reference, employment verfications, domestic employment verification, license verification, I-9 compliance. (Woman, estab 1999, empl 30, sales $4,603,876, cert: WBENC)

7878 A-Check Global
1501 Research Park Dr
Riverside, CA 92507
Contact: Mike Primbsch Dir of Marketing
Tel: 951-750-1501
Email: diversity@acheckglobal.com
Website: www.acheckglobal.com
Screening services: background & drug-screening. (Woman/AA, estab 1998, empl 209, sales $24,200,000, cert: NMSDC, CPUC, WBENC)

7879 Certified Credit Reporting, Inc.
28202 Cabot Rd Ste 245
Laguna Niguel, CA 92677
Contact: Russ Donnan
Tel: 800-769-7615
Email: russ.donnan@certifiedcredit.com
Website: www.certifiedcredit.com
Background Screening, Broker Screening, Tenant Screening. (Woman, estab 1985, empl 63, sales $26,043,657, cert: WBENC)

7880 ClearPath Management Group, Inc
165 N Maple Ave #1930 Ste 102
Manteca, CA 95336
Contact: ClearPath WM Corporate Services Mgr
Tel: 209-239-8700
Email: wbe@clearpathwm.com
Website: www.clearpathwm.com
Contractor payroll, employer of record service, Contingent workforce management, business process outsourcing, Independent contractor compliance. (Woman, estab 2010, empl 16, sales $49,491,482, cert: WBENC)

7881 E. L. Goldberg & Associates
950 Siskiyou Dr
Menlo Park, CA 94025
Contact: Edie Goldberg CEO
Tel: 650-854-0854
Email: edie@elgoldberg.com
Website: www.elgoldberg.com
Human Resources Management Consulting, Talent Management, Performance Management, Career Management, Succession Planning, Selection, Leadership Development, Competency Modeling, Benchmarking, HR Strategic Planning. (Woman, estab 2001, empl 1, sales $300,000, cert: CPUC)

7882 Employers Choice Online Inc.
9845 Painter Ave. Ste B
Whittier, CA 90605
Contact: Jesus Ariel Lopez Procure Contracts Mgr
Tel: 562-319-0413
Email: bids@ecoinc.us
Website: www.employerschoicescreening.com
Employment background checks, drug testing, physical exams & Form 1-9 services. (Hisp, estab 2011, empl 20, sales $2,034,818, cert: NMSDC, CPUC, 8(a), SDB)

7883 Executive Office Services
PO Box 6621
Oakland, CA 94603
Contact: Detria Mixon HR consultant
Tel: 510-830-9721
Email: dmixon@exeservice.biz
Website: www.exeservice.biz
Full service executive human resources business consulting services. (Woman/AA, estab 2008, empl 1, sales , cert: NMSDC, CPUC)

7884 Global Protective Services, Inc.
24973 Ave Stanford
Valencia, CA 91355
Contact: Gene Biscailuz President
Tel: 661-295-1241
Email: gbiscailuz@globalprotectiveservices.com
Website: www.globalprotectiveservices.com
Extensive background check, interview & drug testing before being considered for employment. (Hisp, estab 2008, empl 50, sales $1,000,000, cert: State)

7885 HR Allen Consulting Services
6065 Sundale Way Ste. 98
Fair Oaks, CA 95628
Contact: Michael Allen President
Tel: 916-370-7849
Email: mallen@hrallenconsulting.com
Website: www.hrallencs.com
Human resource consulting & outsourcing. (AA, Hisp, estab 2005, empl 10, sales , cert: State)

7886 Private Eyes, Inc
2700 Ygnacio Valley Rd, Ste 100
Walnut Creek, CA 94598
Contact: Sandra James CEO
Tel: 925-927-3333
Email: sandra@pebackgroundchecks.com
Website: www.privateeyesbackgroundchecks.com
Pre-employment screening, employment background investigations. (Woman, estab 1999, empl 45, sales $6,500,000, cert: WBENC)

7887 RehabWest, Inc. (RWI)
277 Rancheros Dr Ste 190
San Marcos, CA 92025
Contact: CEO
Tel: 760-759-7500
Email: info@rehabwest.com
Website: www.RehabWest.com
Workers' compensation, risk management & human resources. (Woman, estab 1977, empl 55, sales $6,200,000, cert: WBENC)

7888 Translating Services, Inc.
22141 Ventura Blvd Ste 210
Woodland Hills, CA 91364
Contact: Mel Menendez President
Tel: 310-453-3302
Email: mel@lazar.com
Website: www.lazar.com
Translation, interpreting. (Woman, estab 1999, empl 8, sales $ 0, cert: WBENC)

Colorado

7889 Champion Business Services
2668 Dexter St
Denver, CO 80207
Contact: Carol Sales
Tel: 303-873-9147
Email: info@championbusiness.com
Website: www.championbusiness.com
Clerical support svcs, help supply svcs, Ccmputer pogramming, data entry processing & preparation, business svcs, clerical skills training, facilities management support svcs. (Woman/AA, estab 1986, empl 3, sales , cert: WBENC)

7890 Employee Development Systems, Inc.
7300 S Alton Way Ste 5J
Centennial, CO 80112
Contact: Sherman Updegraff Managing Dir
Tel: 800-282-3374
Email: sherm@edsiusa.com
Website: www.employeedevelopmentsystems.com
Personal training: self-confidence, understanding behavioral styles, communication skills, listening skills, self-motivation & personal accountability. (Woman, estab , empl , sales $ 0, cert: NWBOC)

7891 FirstIdea, Inc.
19029 E Plaza Dr, Ste 200
Parker, CO 80134
Contact: Annette Alvarez President
Tel: 303-840-3346
Email: info@firstidea.org
Website: www.firstidea.org
Human Resources consulting and recruitment services. (Woman/Hisp, estab 1989, empl 9, sales $600,000, cert: NMSDC, WBENC)

7892 PayTech, Inc.
7979 E Tufts Ave Ste 1000
Denver, CO 80237
Contact: Julie Knabenshue
Tel: 303-617-0030
Email: jknabenshue@paytech.com
Website: www.paytech.com
Global Payroll & HRIS consulting. (Woman, estab 1999, empl , sales $20,000,000, cert: WBENC)

District of Columbia

7893 HR Strong
1140 3rd St NE Ste 2028
Washington, DC 20002
Contact: Talitha Beverly Principal
Tel: 855-975-2873
Email: talitha@hrstrong.biz
Website: www.hrstrong.biz
Talent retention, upskilling, and reskilling initiatives. (AA, estab 2014, empl 3, sales $300,000, cert: NMSDC, 8(a))

7894 Lenserf & Co. Inc.
700 12th St NW Ste 700
Washington, DC 20005
Contact: Jean-Claude Fresnel, Jr.
Tel: 410-961-5800
Email: jc@lenserfco.com
Website: www.lenserfco.com
HR Consulting services (AA, estab 2008, empl 7, sales $900,000, cert: NMSDC)

Florida

7895 DDM Professional Leasing Services
2100 Ponce de Leon Ave Ste 1260
Coral Gables, FL 33134
Contact: Magda Vargas Dir Region North America
Tel: 305-495-6889
Email: mvargas@bmapr.com
Website: www.bmagroupglobal.com
HR Consulting: BPO, Headhunting, Culture-Fit Staffing, Temporary/Contract Employees, Outplacement, Training and Development, Engagement Survey, Employee Values Survey, Behavioral assessments. (Woman/Hisp, estab 2000, empl 20, sales $11,178,587, cert: WBENC)

7896 First Choice Background Screening
4611 S. University Dr Box 314
Davie, FL 33328
Contact: Nicole Morales
Tel: 888-222-9688
Email: sales@firstchoicebackground.com
Website: www.firstchoicebackground.com
Pre-employment background screening & drug testing, criminal history, motor vehicle records, social security verification, credit report. (Minority, Woman, estab 1996, empl 48, sales $4,600,000, cert: NMSDC, WBENC)

7897 HRSS Consulting Group
125 E Merritt Island Cswy Ste 107 246
Merritt Island, FL 32952
Contact: Karen Gregory President
Tel: 321-576-1314
Email: kgregory@hrssconsultinggroup.com
Website: www.hrssconsultinggroup.com
Organizational development and talent management. (Woman, estab 2012, empl 6, sales $230,000, cert: State, WBENC)

7898 Midwest Background Inc.
200 Central Ave, Ste 820
St. Petersburg, FL 33701
Contact: Syan Kazi Dir of Business Dev
Tel: 727-592-8275
Email: media@mbiworldwide.com
Website: www.mbiworldwide.com
Background screening & hiring solutions. (Woman, estab 1998, empl 27, sales $2,700,000, cert: NWBOC)

7899 Moten Tate, Inc.
301 E. Pine St Ste 250
Orlando, FL 32801
Contact: Kenneth Moten CEO
Tel: 407-843-3277
Email: kmoten@motentate.com
Website: www.motentate.com
Human resource management: staffing, HR project mgmt, reward strategies, employee development & HR outsourcing. (AA, estab 1997, empl 100, sales $3,400,000, cert: State, NMSDC)

7900 OP4 Security Solutions
902 S Federal Hwy Unit 7
Lake Worth Beach, FL 33460
Contact: Anthoneyl Weedman
Tel: 866-383-6510
Email: info@weedmaninc.com
Website: www.op4risk.com
Background Check Services. (Woman/AA, estab 2015, empl 2, sales , cert: WBENC)

7901 Resource Management 1, LLC
520 N Semoran Blvd
Orlando, FL 32807
Contact: Leyla Eagle Dir strategic alliance
Tel: 800-508-0048
Email: leagle@rmi-solutions.com
Website: www.helpmewithhr.com
Payroll, workers compensation, regulatory compliance, risk management and benefits administrations. (Hisp, estab 1995, empl 45, sales $114,000,000, cert: State, NMSDC)

7902 Sobriety On the Sea / Danette Arthur MD PA
4302 Hollywood Blvd 125
Hollywood, FL 33021
Contact: Danette Arthur MD President
Tel: 954-923-7333
Email: sos@doctorsos.org
Website: www.DrArthur.org
Pre-employment & random drug testing services. (Woman/AA, estab 2001, empl 4, sales $140,000, cert: State)

7903 Suncoast Compliance Services, LLC
16765 Fishhawk Dr, Ste 325
Lithia, FL 33547
Contact: Vincent McGrew President
Tel: 813-653-4559
Email: vroy.mcgrew@usamdt.com
Website: www.usamdt.com/westcentralflorida
Pre-employment background screening, drug-free workplace policy devel & implementation, on-site drug & alcohol testing, Employer Assistance Program referral, supervisor training for DOT & non-DOT employees. (AA, estab 2012, empl 1, sales , cert: State, NMSDC)

7904 The Management Edge, Inc.
      12360 66th St, Ste S
      Largo, FL 33773
      Contact: Patty Dunn Dir ops/finance
      Tel: 727-588-9481
      Email: patty.dunn@mgtedge.com
      Website: www.themanagementedge.com
Organization dev, team building & partnering, executive & staff dev, training & coaching, conflict resolution, consensus building. (Woman, estab 1986, empl 18, sales $908,000, cert: State, WBENC)

7905 The Right Method, LLC
      16307 Baycross Dr
      Lakewood Ranch, FL 34202
      Contact: Dhomonique Murphy
      Tel: 833-744-4888
      Email: info@TheRightMethod.com
      Website: www.TheRightMethod.com
Workforce solutions, HR consulting, employee engagement, performance management, workforce optimization, labor force planning, workforce development, human capital solutions, talent management. (Woman/AA, estab 2013, empl 11, sales $1,000,201, cert: NMSDC, WBENC)

Georgia

7906 Assessment Plus, Inc.
      2180 Satellite Blvd Ste 400
      Duluth, GA 30097
      Contact: Brielle Fetrow Project Coord
      Tel: 770-925-3990
      Email: brielle.fetrow@assessmentplus.com
      Website: www.assessmentplus.com
Employee opinion surveys, customers satisfaction surveys, leadership development, 360-degree feedback assessments, executive & leadership coaching, exit interviews & team assessments. (Woman, estab 1984, empl 14, sales $650,000, cert: WBENC)

7907 Career Connection, Inc.
      1170 Peachtree St Ste 1200
      Atlanta, GA 30309
      Contact: Cody Stowers
      Tel: 404-814-5282
      Email: cstowers@ccicareers.com
      Website: www.ccicareers.com
Staff augmentation, workforce solutions, permanent placement, recruitment, personnel management, HR services, administrative management, call center, customer support, IT support, Information technology, facilities management. (Woman, estab 1986, empl 1000, sales $40,000,000, cert: WBENC)

7908 CyQuest Business Solutions, Inc.
      3645 Market Place Blvd Ste 130
      East Point, GA 30344
      Contact: DeVan Brown CEO
      Tel: 404-761-6699
      Email: devan@cyquesthr.com
      Website: www.cyquesthr.com
HR outsourcing solutions: compensation, employee benefits, retirement plans, HRIS systems, payroll processing, employee recruitment & retention. (AA, estab 2004, empl 8, sales $107,500, cert: State, NMSDC)

7909 eVerifile.com Inc.
      900 Circle 75 Pkwy Ste 1550
      Atlanta, GA 30339
      Contact: Jennifer Brown VP Business Dev
      Tel: 404-585-4487
      Email: jennifer.brown@everifile.com
      Website: www.everifile.com
Criminal background investigations, action notification and/or information analytics & grading, US Government watch searches, certificate & license verification, motor vehicle reports, employment & reference verification. (AA, estab , empl , sales $12,000,000, cert: NMSDC)

7910 InfoMart
      1582 Terrell Mill Rd
      Marietta, GA 30067
      Contact: Michelle Summers Supplier Diversity Admin
      Tel: 770-984-2727
      Email: infomartwbe@backgroundscreening.com
      Website: www.backgroundscreening.com
Background checks, criminal history searches, reference checks, education verification, professional license certification, drug screening, business reports, credit/driving history. (Woman, estab 1989, empl 140, sales $19,376,578, cert: WBENC, NWBOC)

7911 IPROVEIT.COM
      6340 Sugarloaf Pkwy Ste 200
      Duluth, GA 30097
      Contact: Vaughn Harvey President
      Tel: 770-239-1707
      Email: vharvey@iproveit.com
      Website: www.iproveit.com
Background screening, investigations, fingerprint services, fingerprint equipment. (AA, estab 2005, empl 3, sales $315,000, cert: NMSDC)

7912 JNX Partners, LLC
      2935 Haynes Club Cir
      Grayson, GA 30017
      Contact: Judy Swanier President
      Tel: 770-982-0043
      Email: judy.swanier@jnxpartners.com
      Website: www.jnxpartners.com
Executive staffing, HR & career transition: sourcing, screening, testing, hiring & retention practices, coaching & support. (Woman/AA, estab 2005, empl 3, sales , cert: WBENC)

7913 McPherson, Berry & Associates, Inc.
      4158 S River Ln Ste 110
      Ellenwood, GA 30294
      Contact: LaSonya Berry CEO
      Tel: 800-325-5269
      Email: lasonya@mcphersonberryassoc.com
      Website: www.mcphersonberry.com
Human Rrsource training, consulting & team building event planning. (Woman/AA, estab 2000, empl 3, sales $250,000, cert: NMSDC, WBENC)

PROFESSIONAL SERVICES: Human Resources

7914 Springboard Benefits, LLC
695 Pylant St NE Ste 232
Atlanta, GA 30306
Contact: Amy Parkman CEO
Tel: 205-790-1060
Email: aparkman@springboardbenefits.com
Website: www.springboardbenefits.com
Project management & consulting, employee on-boarding & off-boarding, hire to retire, new hires, open enrollment, ACA, variable hour tracking, medicare exchange & early termination exchanges. (Woman, estab 2014, empl 6, sales $250,000, cert: WBENC)

7915 Steelbridge Solutions, Inc
2451 Cumberland Pkwy Ste 3228
Atlanta, GA 30339
Contact: Susan Richards President
Tel: 404-259-0865
Email: susan.richards@steelbridgesolutions.com
Website: www.SteelBridgeSolutions.com
Human Capital Consulting, Human Resource Consulting, Business Transformation Consulting, Change Management Consulting, Human resource Information System Consulting, HR Transformation, HR Strategy, HR Technology. (Woman, estab 2013, empl 1, sales $900,000, cert: WBENC)

Illinois

7916 Clark Consulting Group, Inc.
1220 South Blvd
Evanston, IL 60202
Contact: Dr. Marilyn A. Clark CEO
Tel: 847-332-1778
Email: contact@ccg-solutions.com
Website: www.ccg-solutions.com
Human resource development consulting: organizational development, learning & development & career development. (Woman/AA, estab 2002, empl 2, sales $150,000, cert: WBENC)

7917 Executive Coaching Connections
1000 Skokie Blvd, Ste 340
Wilmette, IL 60091
Contact: Kathy Green President
Tel: 847-920-0190
Email: info@executivecoachingconnections.com
Website: www.executivecoachingconnections.com
Organizational development, executive coaching, leadership acceleration, introspection guide, development planning template. (Woman, estab 1995, empl 30, sales $0, cert: WBENC)

7918 Ossanna Corporation
48 Hawthorne Lane
Barrington Hills, IL 60010
Contact: Mariaelena Estrada Office/Contracts Mgr
Tel: 847-255-2800
Email: mestrada@ossanna.com
Website: www.ossanna.com
Human resource professionals: consulting, option-to-hire & permanent basis. (Woman, estab 1988, empl 16, sales $3,313,000, cert: State, WBENC)

7919 Quantum Associates Inc.
459 Lambert Tree Ave
Highland Park, IL 60035
Contact: Willie L. Carter President
Tel: 847-919-6127
Email: wcarter@quantumassocinc.com
Website: www.quantumassocinc.com
Operations management, process redesign, team building & team problem solving. (AA, estab 1999, empl 4, sales $215,000, cert: NMSDC)

Indiana

7920 HR Alternative Consulting, Inc.
10641 Medinah Dr
Indianapolis, IN 46234
Contact: Ann Fisher President
Tel: 317-852-3590
Email: afisher@hralternativeconsulting.com
Website: www.hralternativeconsulting.com
Customized human resources services. (Woman, estab 2003, empl 2, sales , cert: State, City)

7921 Work-Comp Management Services
760 Park East Blvd #5
Lafayette, IN 47905
Contact: Julie Ott Owner
Tel: 765-447-7473
Email: jott@workcompms.com
Website: www.workcompms.net
On-site occupational health services, work comp case management, pre-employment random drug screening, certified collections. (Woman, estab 1996, empl 55, sales $3,600,000, cert: WBENC)

Louisiana

7922 Debra Gould & Associates, Inc.
PO Box 871211
New Orleans, LA 70187
Contact: Debra Gould President
Tel: 504-244-6576
Email: djgould@gouldassoc.com
Website: www.gouldassoc.com
Diversity, change management, team building, leadership, project management, Six Sigma & communication. (Woman/AA, estab 1996, empl 2, sales , cert: WBENC)

Maryland

7923 Full Disclosure
2 Industrial Park Dr Ste B
Waldorf, MD 20602
Contact: Felicia Denman President
Tel: 877-214-4717
Email: fdenman@full-disclosure.org
Website: www.full-disclosure.org
Preemployment screening, background checks, criminal records, employment verification, education verification, terrorist watch list, reference check, civil records, professional license verification. (Woman/AA, estab 2006, empl 1, sales , cert: State)

PROFESSIONAL SERVICES: Human Resources

7924 HR Anew, Inc.
6350 Stevens Forest Rd Ste 250
Columbia, MD 21046
Contact: Melanie Freeman President
Tel: 410-381-5220
Email: mfreeman@hranew.com
Website: www.hranew.com
Human resource management & consulting, training & professional development, management & employee coaching, recruitment & hiring, executive search, staff augmentation, event & conference planning, employee relations. (Woman/AA, estab 1999, empl 17, sales $2,200,000, cert: State)

7925 Managed Care Advisors
2 Wisconsin Cir, Ste 800
Chevy Chase, MD 20815
Contact: Lisa Firestone President
Tel: 301-951-4344
Email:
Website: www.managedcareadvisors.com
Consulting svcs: employee health benefits, workers compensation, disability, case, claims management. (Woman, estab 1997, empl 5, sales $ 0, cert: WBENC)

7926 Rickinson Marketing Inc.
302 Treemont Way
Rockville, MD 20850
Contact: Janette Rickinson President
Tel: 240-683-6550
Email: janette@therickinsongroup.com
Website: www.therickinsongroup.com
Market research consulting, qualitative & quantative research. (Woman, estab 1998, empl 2, sales $450,000, cert: WBENC)

Michigan

7927 Aha! Leadership LLC
49425 Deer Run
Northville, MI 48167
Contact: Robyn Marcotte President
Tel: 248-882-2354
Email: robyn.marcotte@ahaleadership.com
Website: www.ahaleadership.com
Leadership Training & Development, Human Resources Consulting Services; Customer Service Training & Development. (Woman, estab 0, empl , sales $ 0, cert: WBENC)

7928 Ashlor Management Corporation
3710 Davison Rd
Flint, MI 48506
Contact: Charles Kuta President
Tel: 810-275-0690
Email: charles@ashlorstaffing.com
Website: www.ashlorstaffing.com
Human resources, staffing, payroll & complete benefit administration. (Hisp, estab 2015, empl 5, sales , cert: NMSDC)

7929 The Orsus Group, Inc.
3155 W Big Beaver Rd Ste 216
Troy, MI 48084
Contact: Brandon Meagher Business Devel Mgr
Tel: 248-530-3685
Email: bmeagher@theorsusgroup.com
Website: www.theorsusgroup.com
Employment screening: criminal checks, sex offender registry, employment & education verification, motor vehicle records, credit checks, sanctions checks, drug screening, prohibited parties. (AA, estab 2007, empl 22, sales $900,000, cert: NMSDC)

Minnesota

7930 Inclusion, Inc.
126 N 3rd St Ste 412
Minneapolis, MN 55401
Contact: Shirley Engelmeier CEO
Tel: 612-339-2202
Email: shirley@inclusion-inc.com
Website: www.inclusion-inc.com
Diversity & inclusion strategies: web based survey, diversity & inclusion assesment, customized skills based training, changing business behaviors, micro-inequities & on-the-job application. (Woman, estab 2001, empl 21, sales , cert: WBENC)

Missouri

7931 Discreet Check, LLC
655 NE Swann Circle
Lees Summit, MO 64086
Contact: Owner
Tel: 816-600-6200
Email: info@DiscreetCheck.com
Website: www.discreetcheck.com
Global Criminal Background Checks, National Criminal Background Checks, National Background Screenings, National Drug Testing. (Woman, estab 2012, empl 1, sales , cert: CPUC, WBENC)

7932 Hicks-Carter-Hicks, LLC
12747 Olive Blvd, Ste 300
St. Louis, MO 63141
Contact: Gloria Carter-Hicks CEO
Tel: 314-260-7587
Email: info@h-c-h.com
Website: www.h-c-h.com
Performance improvement consulting: mgmt & human resources, performance coaching, training & dev, facilitation, keynote presentations. (Woman/AA, estab 1999, empl 5, sales $ 0, cert: NMSDC, WBENC)

North Carolina

7933 Benefit Advocates, Inc.
514 S Stratford Rd
Winston-Salem, NC 27103
Contact: Mary Kesel President
Tel: 336-721-2029
Email: mkesel@benefitadvocates.net
Website: www.benefitadvocates.net
Health Advocacy and billing claim assistance. Work with HR in managing employees health benefits and medicare. (Woman, estab 2001, empl 10, sales $500,000, cert: WBENC, 8(a))

PROFESSIONAL SERVICES: Human Resources

7934 CareerUnlocked, Inc.
626 N Graham St, Ste 203
Charlotte, NC 28202
Contact: Andrew Lee President
Tel: 919-264-1288
Email: andrew@careerunlocked.com
Website: www.Careerunlocked.com
Human resources consulting, business process improvements, executive search, professional and management development training & talent management. (AA, estab 2015, empl 1, sales , cert: State)

7935 Mind Your Business Inc.
500 Beverly Hanks Ctr
Hendersonville, NC 28792
Contact: Christina Beckworth Contract Specialist
Tel: 828-698-9900
Email: mail@mybinc.com
Website: www.mybinc.com
Pre-employment screening: background investigation, civil, federal & state criminal checks, motor vehicle records, credit history, social security traces, employment/education verifications, workers compensation, drug testing, professional licenses checks (Woman, estab 1996, empl 15, sales $1,600,000, cert: WBENC)

New Jersey

7936 Diversified Consulting Consortium, LLC
5 Tenalfy Rd, Ste 404
Englewood, NJ 07631
Contact: Antonette Alonso
Tel: 908-669-4633
Email: talonso@diversifiedconsultingconsortium.com
Website: www.diversifiedconsultingconsortium.com
Human resources management consulting, training, investigations, diversity management, affirmative action, employee coaching & counseling, labor relations. (Woman/AA, Hisp, estab 2012, empl 6, sales , cert: NMSDC)

7937 Fintech Consulting LLC DBA ApTask
120 Wood Ave South, Ste 300
Iselin, NJ 08830
Contact: Taj Haslani Founder
Tel: 212-256-9131
Email: joshua@aptask.com
Website: www.aptask.com
Staffing, workforce solutions, strategic outsourcing. (As-Ind, estab 2010, empl 367, sales $32,000,000, cert: NMSDC)

7938 SHIFT Employment Law Training, LLC
26 Main St, Ste 301
Chatham, NJ 07928
Contact: Regina Feeney Dir of Operations
Tel: 800-790-5030
Email: regina@shiftelt.com
Website: www.shiftelt.com
Online HR Compliance Training courses. (Woman, estab 2015, empl 14, sales $1,788,000, cert: WBENC)

Nevada

7939 ActOne Government Solutions, Inc.
8330 W Sahara Ave, Ste 290
Las Vegas, NV 89117
Contact: Millton Perkins SVP
Tel: 866-493-8343
Email: GovNotices@A1GovernmentSolutions.com
Website: www.A1GovernmentSolutions.com
General HR consulting/solutions related to the lifecycle of an employee, Diversity/Equity & Inclusion, commodities. (Woman/AA, estab 2015, empl , sales , cert: NMSDC, WBENC)

New York

7940 Can-Am Consultants Inc.
208 Mill St
Rochester, NY 14614
Contact: Cathryn Bell CEO
Tel: 585-777-4040
Email: carrie.bell@can-amconsultants.com
Website: www.can-amconsultants.com
Recruitment & Payroll, Recruitment, Staffing & Payroll of Engineering, Technical & IT Personnel. (Woman, estab 2003, empl 150, sales $19,494,834, cert: State)

7941 Corporate Screening Consulting, LLC
4201 N Buffalo Rd Ste 10
Orchard Park, NY 14127
Contact: Maria DiPirro President
Tel: 716-583-4629
Email: mdipirro@corpscreen.com
Website: www.corpscreen.com
Risk management advisory services, Risk Avoidance consulting, litigation support, corporate compliance, due diligence, fraud analysis, background investigations & loss prevention program design. (Woman, estab 2007, empl 3, sales $250,000, cert: State)

7942 People Primary LLC
3935 50th St
Woodside, NY 11377
Contact: Darus Ng Founder
Tel: 917-446-2643
Email: darus@peopleprimary.com
Website: www.peopleprimary.com
Interim HR Leadership Support, Fractional Organizational Effectiveness & Talent Management Support. (Woman, estab 2021, empl 1, sales $250,000, cert: WBENC)

Ohio

7943 Amerisearch Background Alliance
2529 S Ridge Rd E
Ashtabula, OH 44004
Contact: Kelley Groff Sales & Marketing
Tel: 800-569-6133
Email: kelleygroff@hotmail.com
Website: www.amerisearchbga.com
Background screening, electronic I-9s solutions, drug screening, behavioral assessments & information services. (Woman, estab 2006, empl 11, sales $750,000, cert: WBENC)

PROFESSIONAL SERVICES: Human Resources

7944 Crimcheck
       150 Pearl Rd
       Brunswick, OH 44212
       Contact: Michelle Ackley EA to CEO
       Tel: 877-992-4325
       Email: mackley@crimcheck.com
       Website: www.crimcheck.net
Pre-employment screening & background checks. (As-Pac, estab 1991, empl 77, sales $15,759,628, cert: NMSDC)

7945 Global to Local Language Solutions, LLC
       1776 Mentor Ave Ste 319
       Cincinnati, OH 42512
       Contact: Grace Bosworth President
       Tel: 513-526-5011
       Email: grace@g2local.com
       Website: www.g2local.com
Interpreting/translation services, interpreter training & language training. (Woman, estab 2009, empl 3, sales , cert: State, WBENC)

7946 Strategic Performance Systems, LLC
       2206 Highland Ave
       Cincinnati, OH 45219
       Contact: Deborah Heater CEO
       Tel: 513-602-6200
       Email: debheater@strategicperformancesystems.com
       Website: www.strategicperformancesystems.com
Employee Development: management, leadership, compliance & risk reduction strategies, Human Resources Best Practices: effective human resources functions, Diversity Climate Assessments. (Woman/AA, estab 2013, empl 1, sales $130,000, cert: State)

7947 Stryker Green, LLC
       1240 Sharonbrook Dr
       Twinsburg, OH 44087
       Contact: Sandy Moore CEO
       Tel: 330-963-9985
       Email: sjohnson@strykergreen.com
       Website: www.strykergreen.com
Human Resource Solutions consulting & managed services. (Woman/AA, estab 2012, empl 2, sales , cert: NMSDC)

7948 TriCor Employment Screening
       110 Blaze Industrial Pkwy
       Berea, OH 44017
       Contact: Gary Becher Co-Owner
       Tel: 800-818-5116
       Email: gbecher@tricorinfo.com
       Website: www.tricorinfo.com
Employment screening, background checks, personal & business credit reports, social security number verifications, driving records, criminal & civil record searches, verifications of educational degrees, terrorist checks & drug screening. (Woman, estab 1998, empl 18, sales $3,252,000, cert: WBENC)

Pennsylvania

7949 Advance Sourcing Concepts, LLC
       3000 McKnight East Dr Ste 201
       Pittsburgh, PA 15237
       Contact: Judith Bernhard President
       Tel: 412-415-5081
       Email: jbernhard@ascpeople.com
       Website: www.ascpeople.com
Human Resources contract & sourcing. (Woman, estab 2005, empl 4, sales $1,200,000, cert: State, WBENC)

7950 American Personnel Managers and Consultants, Inc.
       3607 Rosemont Ave, Ste 101
       Camp Hill, PA 17011
       Contact: Pat Gingrich CEO
       Tel: 717-465-5637
       Email: patg@apmci.com
       Website: www.amerijob.com
Staffing, Human Resource Management, Consulting, Testing & Training, Procurement, Information Technology Staffing, Project Management. (Woman, estab 1998, empl 45, sales $3,000,000, cert: State)

7951 BRODY Professional Development
       115 West Ave Ste 114
       Jenkintown, PA 19046
       Contact: Laura Gabor Accounting Department
       Tel: 215-886-1688
       Email: laura@BrodyPro.com
       Website: www.BrodyPro.com
Training & coaching. (Woman, estab 1983, empl 15, sales $2,520,316, cert: WBENC)

7952 Career Concepts, Inc.
       Arborcrest 2, 721 Arbor Way
       Blue Bell, PA 19422
       Contact: Sharon Imperiale CEO
       Tel: 610-941-4455
       Email: simperiale@cciconsulting.com
       Website: www.cciconsulting.com
Management consulting, human resources, outplacement/career transition, recruiting, managerial & executive coaching, leadership development, training. (Woman, estab 1988, empl 40, sales $7,000,000, cert: State, WBENC)

7953 Exude, LLC
       325 Chestnut St Ste 1000
       Philadelphia, PA 19106
       Contact: Marcos Lopez CEO
       Tel: 215-875-8730
       Email: mlopez@exudeinc.com
       Website: www.exudeinc.com
Employee Benefits, Human Resources & Risk Management Consulting. (Hisp, estab 2013, empl 2, sales $293,231, cert: State, NMSDC)

PROFESSIONAL SERVICES: Human Resources

7954 FCF Schmidt Public Relations
600 W Germantown Pike, Ste 380
Plymouth Meeting, PA 19462
Contact: Maribeth Schmidt President
Tel: 610-941-0395
Email: mschmidt@fcfschmidtpr.com
Website: www.fcfschmidtpr.com
Strategic, integrated business-to-business & consumer public relations programs: technical writing, media relations, special events management, public service. (Woman, estab 1989, empl 43, sales $8,700,000, cert: WBENC)

7955 Strategic Benefit Solutions
204 Rivercrest Dr
Phoenixville, PA 19460
Contact: Le Phan CEO
Tel: 609-957-5309
Email: lphan@sbscompanies.com
Website: www.sbscompanies.com
Strategic Benefit Solutions is a full service consulting firm for voluntary worksite benefit solutions with a proven track record of delivering successful benefit solutions that deliver the results you and your employees require. (Minority, Woman, estab 2011, empl 6, sales $500,000, cert: NMSDC)

7956 The Bradley Partnerships, Inc.
207 Malbec Lane Ste 100
Wexford, PA 15090
Contact: Lois Bradley President
Tel: 724-779-8170
Email: lois@bradleypartnerships.com
Website: www.bradleypartnerships.com
Organizational & human resource consulting services. (Woman, estab 2002, empl 6, sales $325,000, cert: State, City, WBENC, 8(a))

7957 The JPI Group LLC
1700 Market St, Ste 1005
Philadelphia, PA 19103
Contact: Paul Douglas Exec
Tel: 267-688-9606
Email: paul@thejpigroup.com
Website: www.thejpigroup.com
HR Consulting Services for Technology & Software Development. (Woman/AA, estab 2012, empl 6, sales $16,925,273, cert: NMSDC, WBENC)

7958 Tri-Starr Services of Pennsylvania, Inc.
2201 Oregon Pike
Lancaster, PA 17601
Contact: Basil Gordon
Tel: 717-560-2111
Email: basil@tristarrjobs.com
Website: www.tristarrjobs.com
Payroll Services, Customized VMS, On site program management. (Woman, estab 1989, empl 130, sales $6,000,000, cert: WBENC)

Puerto Rico

7959 Smart Option Search
PO Box 194088
San Juan, PR 00917
Contact: Melissa Concepcion Esterrich President
Tel: 787-767-2373
Email: mconcepcion@smartoptionsearch.com
Website: www.smartoptionsearch.com
Recruiting and Human Resources Consulting. (Minority, Woman, estab 2000, empl 10, sales $398,000, cert: NMSDC)

South Carolina

7960 RL Enterprise & Associates, LLC
319 Garlington Rd Ste D-3
Greenville, SC 29615
Contact: Rick Harris CEO
Tel: 864-234-8788
Email: rharris@rlenterprisellc.com
Website: www.rlenterprisellc.com
Human resource lifecycle from candidate placement through career development, and even outplacement, in unfortunate circumstances. (AA, estab 2006, empl 21, sales $11,800,000, cert: NMSDC)

7961 Sunkiko
280 Hindman Rd
Travelers Rest, SC 29690
Contact: Sonja Milisic President
Tel: 864-660-6958
Email: sonja@sunkiko.com
Website: www.sunkiko.com
Outsourced solutions for payroll, benefits, HR, workers' comp, tax reporting and more. (Woman, estab 2009, empl 3, sales $356,408, cert: WBENC)

Texas

7962 24/7 Background Checks LLC
11520 N Central Expressway Ste 230
Dallas, TX 75243
Contact: Jones Ajatuaewo President
Tel: 214-206-3565
Email: jones@criminal411.com
Website: www.criminal411.com
Pre employment screening services: driving records, education & employment verification. (Woman/AA, estab 2004, empl 25, sales $600,000, cert: State, NMSDC)

7963 AGResearch International, LLC
PO Box 460
McKinney, TX 75070
Contact: Patti T. Mayer President
Tel: 214-842-4540
Email: patti.mayer@agresearch.info
Website: www.agresearch.info
Human capital services, benchmarking studies. (Woman, estab 2002, empl 15, sales $1,450,278, cert: State, WBENC)

PROFESSIONAL SERVICES: Human Resources

7964 Aspire HR, Inc.
5151 Belt Line Rd Ste 1125
Dallas, TX 75254
Contact: Kevin Vonderschmidt Managing Partner
Tel: 972-372-2815
Email: kvonder@aspirehr.com
Website: www.aspirehr.com
HR services for SAP ERP HCM solutions, implementations, upgrades & support, payroll, HR renewal, data conversions & migrations. (Woman, estab 1998, empl , sales , cert: WBENC)

7965 Bashen Corporation
2603 Augusta Dr, Ste 200
Houston, TX 77057
Contact: Janet Bashen CEO
Tel: 800-994-1554
Email: sales@bashencorp.com
Website: www.bashencorp.com
HR consulting services: EEO compliance administration, EEO investigations/ position statements & investigative reports, workplace training, affirmative action planning, diversity strategies, risk management. (Woman/AA, estab 2013, empl 20, sales $1,578,181, cert: NMSDC, WBENC)

7966 Brook Consultants Inc.
2500 N Dallas Pkwy Ste 180
Plano, TX 75093
Contact: Matt Jones VP Sales
Tel: 972-473-8918
Email: sales@brookvms.com
Website: www.brookvms.com
Human Resource Management services, Contractor onboarding, competence evaluation, E-Verify & background checks. (Woman, estab 2006, empl 125, sales $60,000,000, cert: WBENC)

7967 Cruvel Data Analytics
6315 Liberty ct
Frisco, TX 75035
Contact: Jose Owner
Tel: 214-250-8937
Email: jvel2572@gmail.com
Website: www.cruvel.com
Translation & interpretation services. (Hisp, estab 2018, empl 6, sales , cert: City)

7968 DIVERSA LLC
7003 Viscount Blvd Ste 103
El Paso, TX 79925
Contact: Eleanor Euler VP Business Devel
Tel: 915-781-2665
Email: eleanor.euler@ihcus.com
Website: www.diversaus.com
HR Solutions with focus on MSP services. (Woman/Hisp, estab 2009, empl 8, sales $16,158,922, cert: NMSDC, WBENC)

7969 Excellian Inc.
2301 Ohio Dr, Ste 285
Plano, TX 75093
Contact: Linda Labrada HR Services & Business Dev
Tel: 972-499-0525
Email: llabrada@excellian.com
Website: www.excellian.com
Human Resources | Payroll | Training | Coaching | Management Consulting | Diversity & Inclusion. (Woman/AA, estab 2014, empl 20, sales , cert: NMSDC, WBENC)

7970 G&A Partners
4801 Woodway Ste 210
Houston, TX 77056
Contact: David Vasquez VP
Tel: 713-784-1181
Email: dvasquez@gnapartners.com
Website: www.gnapartners.com
Professional Employer Organization (PEO) & Human Resources Outsourcing & Consulting. (Hisp, estab 1995, empl 175, sales $131,230,000, cert: State)

7971 Human Capital International, LLC dba Integrated Human Capital
7300 Viscount Blvd Ste 103
El Paso, TX 79925
Contact: Rosa Santana CEO
Tel: 915-781-2665
Email: rosa.santana@ihcus.com
Website: www.ihcus.com
HR consulting, temporary staffing, professional & executive placement, payroll svcs, skill testing, vendor mgmt, on-site staff mgmt. (Minority, Woman, estab 2002, empl 34, sales $16,171,166, cert: State, NMSDC, WBENC)

7972 KAS Consulting Group
3625 North Hall Ste 610
Dallas, TX 75219
Contact: Keith Scott CEO
Tel: 214-528-3326
Email: keith@kasconsulting.com
Website: www.kasconsulting.com
Human resources consulting, direct staffing & placement svcs, outplacement svcs, performance mgmt & appraisals, leadership & performance coaching. (AA, estab 2002, empl 3, sales $1,000,000, cert: State)

7973 Pursuit of Excellence Inc.
10440 N Central Expwy Ste 1250
Dallas, TX 75231
Contact: Glenda Scott Finance Admin
Tel: 214-452-7881
Email: gscott@pursuitofexcellenceinc.com
Website: www.pursuitofexcellenceinc.com
Outsourcing for Human Resources/Payroll. (Minority, Woman, estab 1995, empl 6, sales , cert: State)

Virginia

7974 Helios HR LLC
1925 Isaac Newton Sq E Ste 200
Reston, VA 20190
Contact: VP Finance
Tel: 703-860-3882
Email: ekrause@helioshr.com
Website: www.helioshr.com
HR Effectiveness & Compliance Analysis, Employee Assimilation & Onboarding, Employee Regulation Requirements, Policy Maintenance, Employee Relations & Retention, Maintain & Implement Employee Performance Management. (Woman, estab 2001, empl 20, sales $3,670,154, cert: State, WBENC)

7975 Human Capital Consultants, LLC
4201 Wilson Blvd Ste 320
Arlington, VA 22203
Contact: Milton Hall President
Tel: 202-601-1080
Email: SupplierDiversity@humancapitalllc.com
Website: www.humancapitalllc.com
Employee benefit consulting & workplace diversity training. (AA, estab 2004, empl 14, sales $2,497,097, cert:)

7976 RKL Resources
6933 Commons Plaza Ste 245
Chesterfield, VA 23831
Contact: Tawanda Johnson Owner
Tel: 804-638-5991
Email: tjohnson@rklresources.com
Website: www.rklresources.com
Human resources solutions: recruitment, training, organizational development, employee relations & audits. (Woman/AA, estab 2013, empl 2, sales $552,167, cert: State)

7977 ScreenThem Background Investigations
PO Box 7600
Alexandria, VA 22307
Contact: Robin Farmer President
Tel: 703-360-5000
Email: rfarmer@beltrante.com
Website: www.screenthem.com
Pre-employment & background checks. (Woman/AA, estab 1977, empl 6, sales $385,649, cert: State, NMSDC)

West Virginia

7978 Edwards Management Consultants, Inc.
110 S. George St Ste 1
Charles Town, WV 25414
Contact: Christine Edwards President
Tel: 703-349-1412
Email: christinec@edwardsemc.com
Website: www.edwardsemc.com
HR Advisor/Consulting Services, HR Support Services, Recruitment - Short/Long Term Entry Level/Mid to Senior Level Candidates Managenment and Performance Management. (Woman/AA, estab 2005, empl 5, sales , cert: NMSDC)

PROFESSIONAL SERVICES: Management Consulting

Provide general management consulting services: survey research, economic forecasting, transportation studies, facilities and program management, strategic planning, training and development. NAICS Code 54

Alabama

7979 Blazin' Inc.
702 Blake Bottom Rd
Huntsville, AL 35806
Contact: Lanona Sykes CEO
Tel: 256-746-8223
Email: lsykes@blazin1.com
Website: www.blazin1.com
Accounts Receivable management, business mgmt consulting, database mgmt, and teaming consulting. (Woman/AA, estab 1998, empl 4, sales $250,000, cert: State)

7980 Paragon Management Group
PO Box 687
Cotondale, AL 35453
Contact: Ty Jones President
Tel: 205-409-2948
Email: tjones@paragon-mgmt.com
Website: www.paragon-mgt.com
Management consulting, supply chain management strategy, operations, technology & organization solutions. (Woman/AA, estab 2006, empl 5, sales $180,000, cert: NMSDC)

7981 Terrell & Associates, LLC
2210 S Tallassee Dr
Tallassee, AL 36078
Contact: Shandra Terrell President
Tel: 334-283-5156
Email: sterrell@terrellassociates.net
Website: www.terrellassociates.net
Training: diversity, difficult people, teamwork, customer service, speaking engagements, research & evaluation, etc. (Woman/AA, estab 2001, empl 1, sales , cert: NWBOC)

Arizona

7982 Banda Group International, LLC
1799 E Queen Creek Rd Ste 1
Chandler, AZ 85286
Contact: Elisonia Valle Marketing & Communications
Tel: 480-636-8734
Email: elisoniav@bandagroupintl.com
Website: www.bandagroupintl.com
Safety management, risk management, project management, training & associated engineering disciplines. (Hisp, estab 2003, empl 88, sales $9,049,000, cert: NMSDC, SDB)

7983 BLeadersEdge LLC
721 N 106th St
Mesa, AZ 85207
Contact: Michael Nadeau President
Tel: 480-269-7438
Email: mike@bleadersedge.com
Website: www.bleadersedge.com
Personal, team, and organizational leadership development growth (ERG's, BRG's, AG's, PM's), increased team engagement, and continued leadership development. (Nat Ame, estab 2019, empl 1, sales , cert: NMSDC)

7984 Tax Roof, LLC dba JT Project Management Office
1 E Washington St Ste 500
Phoenix, AZ 85004
Contact: Dionne Joseph Thomas President
Tel: 623-374-6455
Email: admin@taxroof.com
Website: www.jtprojectmanagementoffice.com
Program/Project Management & Implementation, Initiation; Planning; Execution; Monitoring & Control; Closing. (Woman/AA, estab 2011, empl 2, sales , cert: State, City, WBENC)

California

7985 Agile Sourcing Partners, Inc.
2385 Railroad St
Corona, CA 92880
Contact: Gabriela Lozano CEO
Tel: 951-279-4154
Email: glozano@agilesp.com
Website: www.agilesp.com/
Procurement, warehousing, assembly, logistics, managing suppliers, and professional staff augmentation. (Woman/Hisp, estab 2006, empl 200, sales $222,512,779, cert: State, NMSDC, WBENC)

7986 Alorica Inc.
5 Park Plaza Ste 1100
Irvine, CA 92614
Contact: Kyle Baker VP Sales
Tel: 949-527-4600
Email: kyle.baker@alorica.com
Website: www.alorica.com
Business process outsourcing, customer management solutions. (As-Pac, estab , empl 22000, sales $570,000,000, cert: State, NMSDC, CPUC)

7987 Being Present Inc
8601 Sunland Blvd, Ste 53
Sun Valley, CA 91352
Contact: Sonya Shelton CEO
Tel: 818-473-5323
Email: sonya@executiveleader.com
Website: www.ExecutiveLeader.com
Management consulting & executive coaching services. (Minority, Woman, estab 2006, empl 4, sales $970,003, cert: NMSDC, WBENC)

7988 causeIMPACTS
5301 W 119th Pl
Inglewood, CA 90304
Contact: Jessica Daugherty Principal
Tel: 714-390-6301
Email: jessica@causeimpacts.com
Website: www.causeimpacts.com
Social impact strategy consulting. (Woman, estab 2015, empl 2, sales $500,000, cert: WBENC)

7989 Celerity Consulting Group, Inc.
2 Gough St, Ste 300
San Francisco, CA 94103
Contact: Yinna Wong CEO
Tel: 415-986-8850
Email: ywong@consultcelerity.com
Website: www.consultcelerity.com
Litigation & business consulting: strategic planning, quality control processes. (Woman, estab 2001, empl 98, sales $16,604,529, cert: CPUC)

PROFESSIONAL SERVICES: Management Consulting

7990 Dilan Consulting Group
550 15th St Ste M-13
San Francisco, CA 94103
Contact: Eugene Dilan CEO
Tel: 415-937-0621
Email: office@dilanconsulting.com
Website: www.dilanconsulting.com
Organizational Development & Change. (Hisp, estab , empl , sales $1,004,136, cert: NMSDC)

7991 Directed Action, Inc.
222 W 6th St. Ste 400
San Pedro, CA 90732
Contact: Kevin Keane President
Tel: 310-707-2504
Email: kevin.keane@directedaction.com
Website: www.directedaction.com
Comprehensive approach to drive strategic transformations: Assess, Communicate, and Transform or ACT. (Woman, estab 2005, empl 18, sales $540,000,000, cert: WBENC)

7992 Elia Erickson, LLC
11620 Wilshire Blvd. 9th Fl
Los Angeles, CA 90025
Contact: Lisa Elia CEO
Tel: 310-479-0217
Email: team@expertmediatraining.com
Website: www.expertmediatraining.com
Media training, presentation training, public speaking training, communication consulting, business coaching, publicity training. (Woman, estab 1999, empl 1, sales $128,741, cert: State, City, CPUC)

7993 Emerson Human Capital Consulting, Inc.
2199 Harbor Bay Pkwy
Alameda, CA 94502
Contact: Tricia Emerson CEO
Tel: 510-545-4435
Email: temerson@emersonhc.com
Website: www.emersonhc.com
Training, diversity training & workshops, change management, organizational design, communications, intercultural svcs, process design, IT implementation, user acceptance. (Woman, estab 2001, empl 35, sales $7,459,817, cert: WBENC)

7994 Extron-Knurr USA
496 S Abbott Ave
Milpitas, CA 95035
Contact: Cobey Cross Business Devel Mgr
Tel: 510-353-0177
Email: diversity@extroninc.com
Website: www.knurrUSA.com
Product Assembly, Warehousing, Order Fulfillment, Returns Management, and Repairs. (As-Ind, estab 1999, empl 65, sales $ 0, cert: CPUC)

7995 ICE Safety Solutions Inc.
47703 Fremont Blvd
Fremont, CA 94538
Contact: Pamela ISom CEO
Tel: 877-743-8423
Email: accounting@getice.com
Website: www.getice.com
Safety training: CPR, first aid, ERT, AED, forklift, Fire safety, fire extinguisher training, safety consulting & curriculum dev. (Woman/AA, Hisp, estab , empl , sales $1,800,000, cert: NMSDC, CPUC, WBENC)

7996 Imani Lee, Inc.
11297 Senda Luna Llena Bldg. B
San Diego, CA 92130
Contact: Lee Martin CEO
Tel: 858-523-9733
Email: translations@imanilee.com
Website: www.imanilee.com
Translation & Localization, Transcription, Transcreation, Interpreting, International Social Media Mgmt, Consulting Services, Language & Culture training, Subtitling & Voiceover, Educational Curriculum Devel. (AA, estab 2002, empl 10, sales $1,526,000, cert: NMSDC, CPUC)

7997 Julianna Hynes & Associates
1638 Freed Circle
Pittsburg, CA 94565
Contact: Julianna Hynes Principal
Tel: 925-207-1578
Email: julianna@juliannahynes.com
Website: www.juliannahynes.com
Executive coaching & leadership development services. (Woman/AA, estab 2003, empl 1, sales $139,599, cert: WBENC)

7998 K'ontinuous Technologies, Inc.
1304 W 2nd St, Ste 346
Los Angeles, CA 90026
Contact: Steve Buchanan President
Tel: 213-334-3951
Email: sbuchanan@kontinuoustech.com
Website: www.kontinuoustech.com
Program Management Oversight, Program/Project Definition & Direction, Program/Project Tracking & Documentation, Technical Resource Allocation, Client/Vendor Relations, Change Management, Risk Management. (AA, Hisp, estab 2015, empl 1, sales , cert: State)

7999 LKG-CMC, Inc.
707 Wilshire Blvd, Ste 3600
Los Angeles, CA 90017
Contact: Kathy Simons vp
Tel: 213-892-0789
Email: ksimons@lkgcmc.com
Website: www.lkgcmc.com
Project controls & configuration mgmt consulting: document control, cost control & estimating, scheduling & business continuity planning. (Woman, estab 1987, empl 70, sales $ 0, cert: CPUC)

8000 LUZ, Inc.
555 Montgomery St Ste 720
San Francisco, CA 94111
Contact: Katie Levenstein Marketing Specialist
Tel: 415-981-5890
Email: register@luz.com
Website: www.luz.com
Translation & localization solutions. (Woman, estab , empl , sales $29,000,000, cert: WBENC)

8001 McKallen Medical
9253 Hermosa Ave
Rancho Cucamonga, CA 91730
Contact: Sade Stephenson
Tel: 747-225-6776
Email: mckallenmedical@gmail.com
Website: www.mckallenmedicaltraining.com
Nurse Education Consulting, Leadership Training, Customer Service Training, American Heart Association Training. (Woman/AA, estab 2018, empl 5, sales $524,000, cert: WBENC)

8002 Nesso Strategies
      4142 Adams Ave Ste 103-256
      San Diego, CA 92116
      Contact: Judy Hissong President
      Tel: 619-546-7885
      Email: judy@nessostrategies.com
      Website: www.NessoStrategies.com
Speaking, training, consulting & facilitation, communication & conflict management, leadership development, accountability, diversity & inclusion. (Woman, estab 2009, empl 3, sales $240,000, cert: City, CPUC)

8003 OneSource Supply Solutions (OSS)
      3951 Oceanic Dr
      Oceanside, CA 92506
      Contact: John Maybeery Exec VP
      Tel: -   -
      Email: jmayberry@1sourcesupplysolutions.com
      Website: www.1sourcesupplysolutions.com
Supply chain solutions to industry leading utilities, contractors and manufacturers. (Hisp, estab 2010, empl 60, sales $295,000,000, cert: NMSDC)

8004 Osceola Consulting llc
      One Blackfield Dr, Ste 410
      Tiburon, CA 94920
      Contact: Neda Najibi VP Business Operations
      Tel: 800-986-1960
      Email: nnajibi@osceolac.com
      Website: www.osceolac.com
Management consulting, business process consulting, information technology procurement, & computer & data processing services. (Nat Ame, estab 2006, empl 27, sales $6,103,929, cert: NMSDC, CPUC)

8005 ROI Communication Inc.
      5274 Scotts Valley Dr Ste 207
      Scotts Valley, CA 95066
      Contact: Tricia Deeter VP Finance
      Tel: 831-430-0170
      Email: accounting@roico.com
      Website: www.roico.com/index.html
Strategy & planning, leader & manager communication, measurement, benchmarking & analysis, employee experience, change communication, creative & visual design, sales communication, communication architecture. (Woman, estab 2001, empl 73, sales $ 0, cert: WBENC)

8006 Ruiz Strategies
      1900 Ave of the Stars Ste 1800
      Los Angeles, CA 90067
      Contact: Michele Ruiz CEO
      Tel: 310-853-3605
      Email: inquiries@ruizstrategies.com
      Website: www.ruizstrategies.com
Strategic communications, change mgmt, reputational management, internal communications, and unconscious bias training and assessments. (Woman/Hisp, estab 2011, empl 10, sales $1,200,000, cert: NMSDC, CPUC, WBENC)

8007 SCMSP (dba) of Spotswood Consulting
      92 Corporate Park Ste 812
      Irvine, CA 92606
      Contact: Derek Spotswood President
      Tel: 800-716-2360
      Email: derek@scmsp.com
      Website: www.scmsp.com
Management consulting, business & technology solutions. (AA, estab 2006, empl 20, sales $2,200,000, cert: NMSDC, 8(a))

8008 Wentworth Consulting Group, LLC
      4616 Dolores Ave
      Oakland, CA 94602
      Contact: Audrey Waidelich Business Mgr
      Tel: 510-482-6278
      Email: info@wentworthconsulting.com
      Website: www.wentworthconsulting.com
Training, leadership development, organization development, executive coaching, instructional design, workplace mediation & meeting facilitation. (Woman, estab 2011, empl 1, sales $890,200, cert: CPUC, WBENC)

Colorado

8009 in3corp Inc.
      1750 30th St, Ste 216
      Boulder, CO 80301
      Contact: Patricia Gilpin Acct Coord
      Tel: 303-448-1191
      Email: gilpin@in3corp.com
      Website: www.in3corp.com/
Audit supplier invoice payments, reinforce existing best practices, identify new optimization strategies. (Hisp, estab 2000, empl 79, sales $2,200,000, cert: NMSDC)

8010 LFL International Inc.
      4 W Dry Creek Circle Ste 100
      Littleton, CO 80120
      Contact: Loretta Lovell CEO
      Tel: 303-791-8405
      Email: lflinc@aol.com
      Website: www.LFLINC.com
Professional, administrative & anagement support services: program/, project & construction management services. (Woman/AA, estab 1990, empl 1300, sales $3,150,000, cert: City, NMSDC)

8011 Sanchez, Tennis & Associates, LLC
      470 Fountaintree Ln
      Boulder, CO 80304
      Contact: Anita Sanchez Dir
      Tel: 303-449-5921
      Email: anita@sancheztennis.com
      Website: www.SanchezTennis.com
Organizational development consulting. (Minority, Woman, estab 1976, empl 2, sales $230,000, cert: NMSDC)

Connecticut

8012 Daniel Penn Associates, LLC
      151 New Park Ave, Ste 106
      Hartford, CT 06106
      Contact: Tony Rodriguez President
      Tel: 860-232-8577
      Email: info@danielpenn.com
      Website: www.danielpenn.com
Mgmt consutling firm, consulting svcs, productivity improvement, supply chain optimization, lean mfg, maintenance mgmt, supplier diversity, mfr systems improvement. (Hisp, estab 1978, empl 11, sales $ 0, cert: State, NMSDC)

PROFESSIONAL SERVICES: Management Consulting

8013 Framework LLC
      1 Atlantic St, Ste 405
      Stamford, CT 06901
      Contact: Cecile Girard COO
      Tel: 203-563-0644
      Email: cgirard@framework-llc.com
      Website: www.framework-llc.com
Develop & integrate sustainable business strategy & practices & communicate performance to stakeholders. (Woman, estab 2003, empl 6, sales , cert: WBENC)

8014 HOPET Engineering Services LLC
      151 New Park Ave
      Hartford, CT 06106
      Contact: Rosa Valenzuela President
      Tel: 860-251-9587
      Email: rosa@hopetengineeringservices.com
      Website: www.hopetengineeringservices.com
Project management & engineering, government & commercial contracts project management, supply chain, value stream mapping, sourcing strategies, earned value management systems, risk mitigation plans & root cause analysis. (Minority, Woman, estab 2013, empl 1, sales , cert: State)

8015 N-Touch Strategies, LLC
      263 Tresser Blvd, 9 Fl
      Stamford, CT 06901
      Contact: Natasha Williams Managing Partner
      Tel: 855-686-8247
      Email: nwilliams@ntouchstrategies.com
      Website: www.ntouchstrategies.com
Strategic management, Initiate & Accelerate growth, Improve organizational efficiency, Leadership Development. (Woman/AA, estab 2010, empl 17, sales $2,250,000, cert: NMSDC, WBENC, 8(a))

District of Columbia

8016 H Rizvi Consulting Inc.
      1345 S Capitol St SW 807
      Washington, DC 20003
      Contact: Hamid Rizvi President
      Tel: 832-640-7374
      Email: hamid.rizvi@hrizviconsulting.com
      Website: www.hrizviconsulting.com
Consulting, Administrative, and Training Services. (Minority, estab 2017, empl 0, sales $ 0, cert: NMSDC)

8017 Nexlevel Consulting Services, LLC
      611 Pennsylvania Ave SE Ste 197
      Washington, DC 20003
      Contact: Tammy Davis CEO
      Tel: 202-417-7495
      Email: tldavis@nexlevelconsultingllc.com
      Website: www.nexlevelconsultingllc.com/
Training, Organizational Change Management, Communications (Woman/AA, estab 2006, empl 3, sales $500,000, cert: NMSDC, 8(a))

Delaware

8018 DecisivEdge LLC
      131 Continental Dr Ste 409
      Newark, DE 19713
      Contact: Michele Frayler
      Tel: 302-299-1570
      Email: michele.frayler@decisivedge.com
      Website: www.decisivedge.com
Business consulting & technology services, business architecture & performance, business analytics, data warehouse strategy, design, development & governance, marketing analytics development. (As-Ind, estab 2007, empl 41, sales $4,739,862, cert: NMSDC)

8019 Jackson LMS and Associates Inc.
      1328 W 4th St
      Wilmington, DE 19805
      Contact: Samuel Jackson Dir
      Tel: 678-477-8355
      Email: sam@jacksonlms.com
      Website: www.jacksonlms.com
Change Management, Communications and Training, Program and Project Management, Customer Relationship Management, IT Project Portfolio Management, Vendor Evaluation and Selection, Certified Technologists/Staffing, Regulatory Support. (AA, estab 2012, empl 2, sales $500,000, cert: CPUC)

Florida

8020 A3i, Inc.
      600 Rinehart Rd Ste 2156
      Lake Mary, FL 32746
      Contact: Elizaveta Markelova Project Coord
      Tel: 888-234-6735
      Email: emarkelova@a3inow.com
      Website: www.a3inow.com
Management Consulting (Hisp, estab 2015, empl 65, sales $4,400,000, cert: NMSDC)

8021 Advaion LLC
      1560 Sawgrass Corporate Pkwy 4th Fl
      Sunrise, FL 33323
      Contact: Pavan Satyaketu Operations Mgr
      Tel: 954-331-7969
      Email: bhuvan@advaion.com
      Website: www.advaion.com
Transaction & risk solutions, acquisition integration svcs, risk assessment, Sarbanes-Oxley section svcs, process & control documentation, entity level controls review, corporate governance. (Minority, Woman, estab 2003, empl 10, sales $1,900,000, cert: NMSDC)

8022 Aikerson Consulting Group, Inc.
      66 W Flagler St Fl 9
      Miami, FL 33130
      Contact: LaShanya Aikerson CEO
      Tel: 888-384-3357
      Email: lashanyaga@gmail.com
      Website: www.AikersonConsulting.com
Training, speaking, coaching, talent development, and meeting facilitation services. (Woman/AA, estab 2004, empl 1, sales $467,707, cert: NMSDC, WBENC)

PROFESSIONAL SERVICES: Management Consulting

8023 American Sign Language Services Corporation
3700 Commerce Blvd Ste. 216
Kissimmee, FL 34741
Contact: Julian Ignatowski CFO
Tel: 407-518-7900
Email: gabrielle@aslservices.com
Website: www.aslservices.com
Interpretation services, sign language, onsite interpreting, Video Relay Services (VRS) & Video Remote Interpreting (VRI). (Minority, Woman, estab 1997, empl 125, sales $8,750,000, cert: State, NMSDC)

8024 Argos Global Partner Services, LLC
240 Crandon Blvd. Ste 201
Key Biscayne, FL 33149
Contact: Luciana Ciuchini CEO
Tel: 305-365-1096
Email: lciuchini@argosus.com
Website: www.argosgps.com
Supply chain solutions, sourcing, consolidation, import, export, purchasing, quality control, logistics and warehousing. (Woman/Hisp, estab 2005, empl 15, sales $20,120,630, cert: NMSDC, WBENC)

8025 Blue Isis LLC
525 Caribbean Dr E
Summerland Key, FL 33042
Contact: Dawn Mahan CEO
Tel: 717-412-1900
Email: dmahan@blueisisllc.com
Website: www.blueisisllc.com
Project management consulting & talent development services, management consulting services, program management, portfolio management, governance, budgeting, forecasting, strategic planning, resource management. (Minority, Woman, estab 2009, empl 10, sales $1,000,000, cert: State)

8026 Caraballo Consulting & Associates, LLC
11312 NW 65 St
Doral, FL 33178
Contact: Lourdes Cordeiro Dir New Business Dev
Tel: 305-204-2493
Email: lourdes@caraballoconsulting.com
Website: www.caraballoconsulting.com
Regulatory Compliance & Submissions, Clinical, Quality Assurance, Manufacturing, Project Management, Black Belt, Lean Manufacturing, Engineering & Specialized Engineering. (Minority, Woman, estab 2015, empl 10, sales , cert: NMSDC)

8027 CMA Enterprise Incorporated
207 Laurel Oak Lane Ste B
Davie, FL 33325
Contact: Gail Birks Williams President
Tel: 954-476-3525
Email: cma@cma-ent.com
Website: www.cma-ent.com
Management consulting, business process re-engineering, supplier/corporate diversity initiatives, employee relations, training. (Woman/AA, estab 1990, empl 2, sales $ 0, cert: State, WBENC)

8028 Corporate Fitness Works, Inc.
1200 16TH ST N
Saint Petersburg, FL 33705
Contact: Ken Viglio Sr Dir of Business Dev
Tel: 727-522-2900
Email: kviglio@teamcfw.com
Website: www.corporatefitnessworks.com/
Manage customized fitness centers & wellness programs, feasibility studies, facility layout & design, equipment recommendations. (Minority, Woman, estab 1988, empl 370, sales $9,587,182, cert: NMSDC, CPUC, WBENC)

8029 Enhance Performance Consulting, Inc.
1724 Bella Lago Dr
Clermont, FL 34711
Contact: Donnie Cochran CEO
Tel: 404-277-1950
Email: dcec1@outlook.com
Website: www.donniecochran.com/
Leadership Development Keynote, Motivational Teaching, Team Building & Development Strategies. (AA, estab 2000, empl 2, sales , cert: State)

8030 Government Business Solutions
12905 SW 132nd St, Ste 4
Miami, FL 33186
Contact: Lourdes Martin-Rosa President
Tel: 786-293-1601
Email: lourdes@govbizsolutions.com
Website: www.govbizsolutions.com
Educate small businesses on procuring federal, state & local government contracts. (Minority, Woman, estab 2002, empl 6, sales , cert: State, WBENC, 8(a))

8031 HMB Enterprises LLC
5401 S Kirkman Rd, Ste 310
Orlando, FL 32819
Contact: Harry Bailey President
Tel: 678-887-7670
Email: hbailey@hmbenterprises.net
Website: www.hmbenterprises.net
Healthcare Risk Management System (HRMS), Airborne Pathogen Elimination system, Purlalizer. (AA, estab 2005, empl 5, sales $425,000, cert: State, NMSDC)

8032 Impresiv Health
145 Bellagio Way
Sanford, FL 32771
Contact: Marcus Fontaine President
Tel: 305-407-0218
Email: mfontaine@impresivhealth.com
Website: www.impresivhealth.com
Accreditation Readiness, Care Management, Program Development, Regulatory Compliance Readiness, Clinical & Non-Clinical Managed, Care Training, System Redesign, Process & Workflow Improvement. (AA, estab 2015, empl 17, sales $2,500,000, cert: State)

8033 Maria R Pearson Inc dba Own Your World
101 Del Sol Circle
Tequesta, FL 33469
Contact: Maria Pearson President
Tel: 772-287-5833
Email: mariapearson@ownyourworld.net
Website: www.OwnYourWorld.net
Training & management consulting: communication, presentation skills, leadership effectiveness, time mgmt, process & system improvement. (Minority, Woman, estab 1993, empl 1, sales , cert: State)

8034 Premier Remodeling Services, Inc.
5703 Red Bug Lake Rd, Ste 328
Winter Springs, FL 32708
Contact: Geoff Gilpin
Tel: 407-489-8510
Email: ggilpin@premiergroupadvisors.com
Website: www.premiergroupadvisors.com
Policy, Planning & Program Support, Information Mgmt, Human Capital Optimization, Education & Training, Infrastructure Management, Sustainability Planning, Engineering & Technical Assistance, Supplier Mgmt. (AA, estab 2006, empl 8, sales $1,500,000, cert: NMSDC, 8(a))

8035 Program Evaluation Services Inc.
5521 Oak Hollow Dr
Titusville, FL 32780
Contact: Gina Beckles CEO
Tel: 321-243-4809
Email: ginabeckles@cfl.rr.com
Website: www.programevaluationservices.com
Program evaluation & performance measurement, analytical & administrative services. (Woman/AA, estab 2006, empl 2, sales , cert: NMSDC)

8036 Strategic Defense Solutions, LLC
8902 N Dale Mabry Hwy Ste 111
Tampa, FL 33614
Contact: Lauren Souders Exec Asst
Tel: 813-443-0658
Email: Lauren.souders@strategicdefensesolutions.com
Website: www.strategicdefensesolutions.com
Strategic/Deliberate Planning, Program/Project Management, Senior Operations Analyst, Facility Management Technician Support. (AA, estab 2006, empl 39, sales $3,000,000, cert: 8(a))

8037 Trustee Capital LLC
100 S Ashley Dr, Ste 600
Apollo Beach, FL 33572
Contact: Andre Fair CEO
Tel: 813-397-3648
Email: info@trusteecap.com
Website: www.trusteecap.com
Business valuations and custom analytics solutions. (AA, estab 2017, empl 2, sales , cert: NMSDC)

8038 Wightman & Associates LLC
720 W Montrose St
Clermont, FL 34711
Contact: Louis Dommer III CFO
Tel: 757-574-4386
Email: ldommer@wightman-associates.com
Website: www.Wightman-Associates.com
Training & organizational development products & services. (Woman, estab 2011, empl 12, sales $836,000, cert: State)

Georgia

8039 Asil White Enterprises, Inc.
642 Concord Lake Circle Se
Smyrna, GA 30082
Contact: Lisa L White President
Tel: 404-786-8931
Email: lw@thinkaweinc.com
Website: www.thinkaweinc.com
Instructional design, training materials, professional & mgmt dev training, coaching, time mgmt , organizational dev, performance improvement, project mgmt. (Woman/AA, estab 2004, empl 1, sales , cert: State)

8040 BDM2
235 Peachtree St, Ste 400
Atlanta, GA 30303
Contact: Missy Pitcher CEO
Tel: 404-301-5879
Email: missy.pitcher@bdmsquared.com
Website: www.bdmsquared.com
Project Delivery; PMO Creation and Management; and Project Planning for Rapid Ignition Project Startup and Launching. (AA, estab 2016, empl 8, sales $284,000, cert: NMSDC)

8041 Horizon Leadership, Inc.
3295 River Exchange Dr Ste 560
Norcross, GA 30092
Contact: Cindy Larkin President
Tel: 770-552-5511
Email: clarkin@horizonleadership.com
Website: www.horizonleadership.com
Facilitation, presentation & influencing skills, teambuilding, change management, coaching skills, etc. (Woman, estab 2002, empl 4, sales $2,300,000, cert: WBENC)

8042 LBJR Consulting LLC
2942 Darlington Run
Duluth, GA 30097
Contact: Lavoska Barton President
Tel: 678-662-9159
Email: lbarton@lbjrconsulting.com
Website: www.lbjrconsulting.com
Project Management & Planning, Cost management & Control, Budget prioritization & Management, Vendor Management & Control, Financial / Variance Analysis of projects, Process Management, Six Sigma Black Belt. (AA, estab 2005, empl 4, sales , cert: State)

8043 LEAP Leadership
1011 Carriage Lane SE
Smyrna, GA 30082
Contact: Kim Radford Partner
Tel: 404-414-8624
Email: kr@leaplead.com
Website: www.leaplead.com
Leadership education, executive coaching & organizational development services. (Woman/AA, estab 2009, empl 3, sales $590,405, cert: NMSDC)

8044 Peerless Performance, LLC
9040 Roswell Road Ste 460
Atlanta, GA 30350
Contact: LeeAnne Canecchio Acct Dir
Tel: 404-551-5181
Email: leeannecanecchio@peerlessperformance.net
Website: www.peerlessperformance.net
Performance Improvement, Culture Engineering Agency. (Woman, estab 2017, empl 8, sales $550,000, cert: WBENC)

8045 The Cadence Group, Inc.
1095 Zonolite Rd Ste 105
Atlanta, GA 30306
Contact: Tina Teree Baker President
Tel: 404-874-0544
Email:
Website: www.cadence-group.com
Information management: acquire, organize & disseminate information. (Woman, estab 1988, empl 46, sales $2,890,048, cert: WBENC)

8046 The Intuition Consulting Firm, LLC.
      2870 Peachtree Rd NW Ste 404
      Atlanta, GA 30305
      Contact: Roy Broderick Jr President
      Tel: 404-861-2661
      Email: team@authentiqueagency.com
      Website: www.authentiqueagency.com
Multicultural integration and programming. (AA, estab 2016, empl 25, sales $1,500,000, cert: NMSDC)

8047 Translation Station, Inc.
      3460 Chamblee Dunwoody Way
      Chamblee, GA 30341
      Contact: Lindsey Cambardella CEO
      Tel: 770-234-9387
      Email: lindsey@translationstation.com
      Website: www.translationstation.com
Foreign language translation: technical, legal, medical documents, benefits, software localization, website translation, interpretation for meetings, conferences, courts, depositions, conflict resolution, etc. (Woman, estab 1998, empl 10, sales $703,000, cert: WBENC)

8048 Tricia Browning Design Group
      102 Westside Dr
      LaGrange, GA 30240
      Contact: Tim Donahue
      Tel: 706-883-7741
      Email: tdonahue@nimlok-westgeorgia.com
      Website: www.nimlok-westgeorgia.com
Trade Show booths, Exhibits, Graphic Design, Display Advertising, Commercial Photography, Advertising Services, Design Services (Woman, estab 1996, empl 8, sales $2,180,000, cert: WBENC)

8049 VetWorks LLC
      5865 N Point Pkwy, Ste 320 Ste 320
      Alpharetta, GA 30022
      Contact: Avilala Thanuja HR Mgr
      Tel: 770-561-3929
      Email: Thanuja@vetworksus.com
      Website: www.vetworksus.com/
Design & implement customized recruiting solutions that deliver proven, dependable Leaders and Technicians transitioning from the military. (Woman/AA, estab 2008, empl 100, sales $1,062,323, cert: NMSDC, WBENC)

8050 VYD and Associates, LLC
      3306 Blanton Dr
      Scottdale, GA 30079
      Contact: Vonetta Daniels CEO
      Tel: 404-966-8411
      Email: vonetta.daniels@gmail.com
      Website: www.vydandassociates.com
Management consulting: business strategy, business process engineering, supply chain management, revenue cycle & cost optimization; program performance measurement & evaluation, strategic planning, budget & performance. (Woman/AA, estab 2010, empl 1, sales , cert: NMSDC, WBENC, 8(a))

Hawaii

8051 Native Hawaiin Veterans LLC
      3375 Koapaka St, Ste F238-20
      Honolulu, HI 96819
      Contact: Rebecca McKee Sr Program Mgr
      Tel: 808-792-7528
      Email: rebecca.mckee@nativehawaiianveterans.com
      Website: www.nativehawaiianveterans.com
Homeland Security, Emergency Management, Information Technology, Communication Equipment, Professional Staff Augmentation, Munitions and Explosives of Concern (MEC) Remediation, and Strategic Communications/Creative Services. (Minority, estab 2004, empl 190, sales $ 0, cert: NMSDC)

Illinois

8052 Administrative Resource Options Inc.
      200 W Adams St Ste 2000
      Chicago, IL 60606
      Contact: Alecia McClung CEO
      Tel: 312-634-0300
      Email: ammcclung@aroptions.com
      Website: www.aroptions.com
Managed & on-site services outsourcing, customized workplace & workspace solutions, print & document management, mail center, front of office, conference room services. (Woman, estab 1990, empl 394, sales $22,827,215, cert: WBENC)

8053 Artesian Collaborative
      77 W Washington St Ste 1500
      Chicago, IL 60602
      Contact: Sunitha Chandy, PsyD Founder
      Tel: 773-980-9679
      Email: connect@artesiancollaborative.com
      Website: www.artesiancollaborative.com
Corporate training, consultation & coaching services. (Woman/As-Ind, estab 2017, empl 6, sales $760,393, cert: City, NMSDC, WBENC)

8054 B2B Strategic Solutions, Inc.
      150 N Michigan Ave Ste 2800
      Chicago, IL 60601
      Contact: Donna Bryant President
      Tel: 312-368-1700
      Email: info@b2bssi.com
      Website: www.b2bssi.com
Management consulting, information technology, technical training, strategic planning, professional development, leadership, customer service, training, business writing. (Woman/AA, estab 2003, empl 20, sales $1,254,000, cert: State, NMSDC)

8055 CGN & Associates, Inc.
      415 SW Washingotn
      Peoria, IL 61602
      Contact: Patrick Dierker Associate Partner
      Tel: 309-495-2100
      Email: patrick.dierker@cgnglobal.com
      Website: www.cgnglobal.com
Business consulting: operations, execution & technology mgmt, analysis, design & implementation of complex operational transformations, strategy development, solution design, implementation & optimization techniquies. (As-Pac, estab 1995, empl 125, sales $ 0, cert: State, NMSDC)

PROFESSIONAL SERVICES: Management Consulting

8056 EMS Consulting
477 W Happfield Dr
Arl, IL 60004
Contact: Liz Kistner President
Tel: 224-465-1115
Email: lkistner@enrollmentmarketingsolutions.com
Website: www.emsconsultgroup.com
Project & program management consulting. (Woman, estab 2006, empl 1, sales $ 0, cert: WBENC)

8057 Executive Consultants United, LLC
180 N Stetson Ave, Ste 3500
Chicago, IL 60601
Contact: Wheeler Coleman CEO
Tel: 312-268-5829
Email: wcoleman@ec-united.com
Website: www.ec-united.com
Data Strategy / Roadmap, Advanced Analytics, Reporting, Dashboards & Scorecards, Data Strategies, Data Lakes, Data Platforms & Data Management, Data Scientists & DBAs Specialists, Analytics (Consumer, Provider, etc.) (AA, estab 2016, empl 10, sales $1,020,000, cert: NMSDC)

8058 Hendon Group, Inc.
165 Robincrest Ln
Lindenhurst, IL 60046
Contact: Ira M. Hendon President
Tel: 847-245-8722
Email: imh@hendon-group.com
Website: www.hendon-group.com
Program and Project Leadership Professional Services and Consulting. (AA, estab 2006, empl 1, sales , cert: State, NMSDC)

8059 Kairos Consulting Worldwide
935 West Chestnut Ste 455
Chicago, IL 60642
Contact: Managing Principal
Tel: 312-757-5197
Email: info@kairosworldwide.com
Website: www.kairosworldwide.com
Technology consulting: change management & process reengineering, process management, strategic planning & project management. (Woman/AA, estab 2004, empl 1, sales , cert: State, WBENC)

8060 MarketZing Inc.
875 N Michigan Ave Ste 3100
Chicago, IL 60611
Contact: Aleen Bayard Principal
Tel: 312-794-7880
Email: aleen@aleenbayard.com
Website: www.marketzing.org
Change management project design & execution, culture & values alignment work, strategic planning facilitation & implementation support, employee engagement and team effectiveness, organizational & leadership development. (Woman, estab 1999, empl 1, sales $350,000, cert: WBENC)

8061 MJ Learning Inc.
605 S Maple Ave
Oak Park, IL 60304
Contact: Sarah Gee CEO
Tel: 708-613-5401
Email: sarah@mjlearning.com
Website: www.mjlearning.com
Professional & management development training. (Woman, estab 2010, empl 5, sales $500,000, cert: WBENC)

8062 Multilingual Connections, LLC
847 Chicago Ave, Ste 250
Evanston, IL 60202
Contact: Jill Bishop CEO
Tel: 773-292-5500
Email: jill@mlconnections.com
Website: www.multilingualconnections.com
Translation/interpretation services (all languages), workplace language training (Spanish and ESL - English as a Second Language), diversity training and workplace harassment prevention training and leadership development. (Woman, estab 2005, empl 25, sales $3,122,086, cert: WBENC)

8063 Nancy Conner Consulting, LLC
1235 Berry Lane
Flossmoor, IL 60422
Contact: Nancy Conner CEO
Tel: 847-456-5601
Email: nancy@nancyconner.com
Website: www.nancyconner.com
Supply chain, supplier development business partnerships, negotiation, community outreach & advocacy. (Woman, estab 2016, empl 1, sales , cert: WBENC)

8064 PTS Consulting Services LLC
1700 Park St, Ste 212
Naperville, IL 60563
Contact: Reshma Multani Client Servicing Mgr
Tel: 630-635-8328
Email: reshma.multani@ptscservices.com
Website: www.ptscservices.com
IT consulting and Business Consulting Services. (As-Pac, estab 2012, empl 50, sales $7,000,000, cert: NMSDC)

8065 RGMA
980 N Michigan Ave Ste 1230
Chicago, IL 60611
Contact: Ralph Moore President
Tel: 312-419-7250
Email: ralphmoore@rgma.com
Website: www.rgma.com
Provides supplier diversity services to drive shareholder value in an increasingly diverse, global economy. (AA, estab 1979, empl 6, sales , cert: City, NMSDC)

8066 Sandstorm Design
4422 N Ravenswood Ave Ste 50
Chicago, IL 60640
Contact: Amanda Heberg VP Business Dev
Tel: 773-348-4200
Email: aheberg@sandstormdesign.com
Website: www.sandstormdesign.com
Internal Communications, Annual Reports. (Woman, estab 1998, empl 14, sales $ 0, cert: WBENC)

8067 TrainSmart, Inc.
1600 Golf Rd, Ste 1200
Rolling Meadows, IL 60008
Contact: President
Tel: 847-991-8181
Email: inquiries@trainsmartinc.com
Website: www.trainsmartinc.com
Computer training, performance solutions, team building, customer service, leadership skills, manufacturing quality training, needs analysis, instructural design, assessments, programming. (Woman, estab 1994, empl 6, sales $1,500,000, cert: WBENC)

PROFESSIONAL SERVICES: Management Consulting

8068   Trilogy Consulting Group, Inc.
       2021 Midwest Rd, Ste 200
       Oak Brook, IL 60523
       Contact: Kathy Martin-Smith VP
       Tel: 630-953-6278
       Email: kmartin-smith@trilogy-consulting.com
       Website: www.trilogy-consulting.com
Health plan administration reviews & audits. (Woman, estab 1995, empl 3, sales $679,217, cert: State, WBENC)

8069   Trinal, Inc.
       329 W 18th St, Ste 401
       Chicago, IL 60616
       Contact: Gladys Rodriguez GM
       Tel: 312-738-0500
       Email: info@trinalinc.com
       Website: www.trinalinc.com
Strategic business management consulting, procurement policy development & economic development program monitoring. (Woman/AA, Hisp, estab 1997, empl 14, sales , cert: State)

8070   Tristana R Harvey Career Planning & Consulting Series LLC
       5135 S Kenwood Ave, Box 504
       Chicago, IL 60615
       Contact: Tristana Harvey Owner
       Tel: 312-351-0272
       Email: tristana_harvey@harveycareerplanning.com
       Website: www.harveycareerplanning.com
Counseling, coaching & consulting, training programs that create awareness, increase education & produce behavior change. (Woman/AA, estab 2010, empl 2, sales $125,000, cert: State, City, 8(a))

8071   Universal. Innovative. Intelligent, Inc.
       PO Box 1711
       Bolingbrook, IL 60440
       Contact: Kimberly Johnson President
       Tel: 630-981-1931
       Email: kjohnson@universal3i.com
       Website: www.myfavoritethings-u3i.com
Management & marketing consulting. (Woman/AA, estab 2003, empl 1, sales , cert: State)

8072   Vaughn Management LLC
       125 S. Wacker Dr Ste 300
       Chicago, IL 60606
       Contact: Stephen Vaughn President
       Tel: 312-924-2902
       Email: svaughn@cerasolutions.com
       Website: www.cerasolutions.com
Management Services Business: Engineering, Accounting, Research & Management Services Sector, Building Inspection, Administrative Management Services (AA, estab 2018, empl 25, sales $2,523,000, cert: NMSDC)

8073   Vitalizing Business Solutions
       7547 S Emerald Ave
       Chicago, IL 60620
       Contact: Fatemah Ateyah
       Tel: 773-303-2017
       Email: fateyah@vitalizebus.com
       Website: www.vitalizebus.com
Project Management Professional (PMP) ISO Lean Six-Sigma(LSS). (AA, estab 2016, empl 5, sales $705,819, cert: 8(a))

8074   ZOI Incorporated
       2114 Rugen Rd, Unit A
       Glenview, IL 60026
       Contact: Susanna Alvarado CEO
       Tel: 847-834-4787
       Email: info@zoiinc.com
       Website: www.zoiinc.com
Project, Product and Logistics Management, Change Management, and Training Development, e-Commerce, Cloud, Cognitive & Data Analysis. (Woman/Hisp, estab 2011, empl 5, sales $115,000, cert: NMSDC, WBENC)

Indiana

8075   Advanced Systems
       508 Sunshine Dr
       Valparaiso, IN 46385
       Contact: Christy Poturkovic Reg Sales Mgr
       Tel: 317-845-5017
       Email: christyp@successstrategiesllc.com
       Website: www.processspecialist.com
Business consulting services, education & training: process improvement, strategic planning, leadership development, management & supervision training, sales training, customer service training, quality improvement. (Woman, estab 1997, empl 1, sales , cert: City)

8076   Bulldog Consulting Services
       PO Box 65
       Leo, IN 46765
       Contact: Sharon Miller President
       Tel: 517-455-7016
       Email: smiller@bulldogmeansbusiness.com
       Website: www.BulldogMeansBusiness.com
Process Assessment, Process Improvements, Program/Project Management, Process Documentation, and Training. (Woman, estab 2007, empl 3, sales $200,000, cert: State)

8077   Intrinz Inc.
       12175 Visionary Way
       Fishers, IN 46038
       Contact: Patricia Musariri Gurnell President
       Tel: 317-288-2267
       Email: patricia.musariri@intrinzincorp.com
       Website: www.intrinzincorp.com/
Project Management, Corporate Treasury, Corporate Tax, International Business, Global Sourcing, Language Translation, Business Strategy & Business Consulting Services. (Woman/AA, estab 2011, empl 5, sales $1,250,000, cert: NMSDC)

8078   Prairie Quest Consulting
       4211 Hobson Court Ste A
       Fort Wayne, IN 46815
       Contact: Martha Martin Program Mgr
       Tel: 260-420-7374
       Email: mmartin@pqcworks.com
       Website: www.pqcworks.com
Project mgmt: application development, business case analysis, conceptual & functional process design, project plans, budgets, tracking assessment & metrics. (Woman, estab 2004, empl 150, sales $12,340,945, cert: WBENC)

PROFESSIONAL SERVICES: Management Consulting

8079 Raymond Young & Associates, LLC
10705 Club Chase
Fishers, IN 46037
Contact: Raymond Young President
Tel: 317-459-0797
Email: rayyoungjr@msn.com
Website: www.raymondyoungassociates.com
Business consulting, planning, business preformance, competitive analysis, service quality & retention, project management & six sigma principals. (AA, estab 2007, empl 1, sales , cert: State)

Kentucky

8080 Catalyst Learning Co.
310 W Liberty St, Ste 403
Louisville, KY 40202
Contact: Elizabeth LaRue Accountant
Tel: 502-584-7737
Email: elarue@catalystlearning.com
Website: www.catalystlearning.com
Provides proven learning & development tools. (Woman, estab 1994, empl 14, sales , cert: NWBOC)

Louisiana

8081 Agilify LLC
7117 Florida Blvd
Baton Rouge, LA 70806
Contact: Ezra Hodge CFO
Tel: 800-557-1719
Email: Procurement@agilifyus.com
Website: www.agilifyus.com
Management consulting, Project, Program and Portfolio, Business Process Documentation & Requirements Analysis, Portfolio and Project Governance. (Woman/As-Pac, estab 2016, empl 50, sales $8,600,000, cert: NMSDC, WBENC)

8082 Henry Consulting LLC
1010 Common St Ste 2500
New Orleans, LA 70112
Contact: Allen Square Dir
Tel: 504-529-9890
Email: allen.square@henryconsulting.net
Website: www.henryconsulting.net
Management consulting services. (AA, estab 2001, empl 15, sales $1,941,921, cert: NMSDC)

Massachusetts

8083 3D Leadership Group LLC
396 Washington St, Ste 207
Wellesley, MA 02481
Contact: Sue Williamson Co-Founder
Tel: 781-453-9800
Email: sue.williamson@3dleadershipgroup.com
Website: www.3dleadershipgroup.com
Executive Coaching, Team Coaching, Transition Coaching, Leadership Workshops, Assessments. (Woman, estab 2008, empl 2, sales $1,528,044, cert: WBENC)

8084 Chrysalis Coaching & Consulting
595 E Fourth St Ste 1
Boston, MA 02127
Contact: Karen Carmody President
Tel: 617-283-8705
Email: kcarmody@chrysaliscoachingconsulting.com
Website: www.chrysaliscoachingconsulting.com/
Corporate coaching, organizational effectiveness, & corporate wellness services. (Woman, estab 2012, empl 1, sales , cert: WBENC)

8085 Communication Management, Inc.
5 Perkins Glen
Eastham, MA 02642
Contact: Joseph Perkins President
Tel: 508-255-3789
Email: jperkins@cmiglobal.com
Website: www.cmiglobal.com
Communications skills, training, onsite & online business writing & presentation skills training programs. (AA, estab 1991, empl 1, sales , cert: State, NMSDC)

8086 Culture Coach International
259 Walnut St, Ste 17
Newton, MA 02460
Contact: Kari Heistad CEO
Tel: 617-795-1688
Email: admin@culturecoach.biz
Website: www.CultureCoach.biz
Consulting, strategic planning & training. (Woman, estab 1998, empl 10, sales , cert: WBENC)

8087 EnVision Performance Solutions
9 Pond View Cir
Sharon, MA 02067
Contact: Irene Stern Frielich President
Tel: 617-877-2719
Email: irene.frielich@envision-performance.com
Website: www.envision-performance.com/
Custom instructional design & training development services; needs assessment, curriculum development, instructor-led classes, virtual classes, elearning, on-the-job training, performance support. (Woman, estab 1998, empl 1, sales $448,000, cert: State, WBENC)

8088 Incite, Inc.
14 St. Charles St
Boston, MA 02116
Contact: Beth Rogers President
Tel: 617-521-9050
Email: brogers@pointtaken.net
Website: www.pointtaken.net
Custom communication skills training workshops; Presentation Skills, Facilitation Skills, Negotiation Skills. (Woman, estab 1997, empl 4, sales $1,800,000, cert: WBENC)

8089 Synterex, Inc.
122 Rosemary Rd
Dedham, MA 02026
Contact: Jeanette Towles President
Tel: 617-905-1522
Email: bizdev@synterex.com
Website: www.synterex.com
Clinical & regulatory consulting: agile methodology, automation & artificial intelligence (AI)-driven technologies. (Woman, estab 2016, empl 32, sales $7,229,000, cert: WBENC)

8090 The Asaba Group
220 N Main St, Ste 102
Natick, MA 01760
Contact: Katrice Rivers Business Mgr
Tel: 508-655-8100
Email: krivers@asabagroup.com
Website: www.asabagroup.com
Strategic assessments, strategic support services, organizational improvement. (AA, estab 1999, empl 10, sales $1,000,000, cert: NMSDC)

PROFESSIONAL SERVICES: Management Consulting

Maryland

8091 Andean Consulting Solutions International, LLC
11140 Rockville Pike Ste 100-155
Rockville, MD 20852
Contact: Andres Echeverri President
Tel: 202-618-1455
Email: andres@acsitranslations.com
Website: www.acsitranslations.com
Language translation & interpretation services in over 60 languages. (Hisp, estab 2011, empl 2, sales $585,000, cert: State, 8(a))

8092 Applied Development LLC
7 S Front St Ste 200
Baltimore, MD 21202
Contact: Kimberly Citizen
Tel: 410-571-4016
Email: kcitizen@applied-dev.com
Website: www.applied-dev.com
Process improvement, automation, analytics & cyber security, project management, business process improvement, strategic communications, cybersecurity & administrative support. (Woman/AA, estab 2011, empl 12, sales $687,000, cert: State, City, NMSDC, WBENC, 8(a))

8093 BETAH Associates, Inc.
199 E. Montgomery Ave. Ste 100
Rockville, MD 20815
Contact: Meisha Robinson Marketing & Proposals Coordinator
Tel: 301-657-4254
Email: mrobinson@betah.com
Website: www.betah.com
Professional, technical & communications consulting: social marketing & outreach, management consulting, technical assistance, research & evaluation, communications & media relations, event planning. (Woman/AA, estab 1988, empl 105, sales $ 0, cert: WBENC)

8094 Cheseldine Management Consulting, LLC
PO Box 1307
Leonardtown, MD 20650
Contact: Margaret Cheseldine CEO
Tel: 301-475-2272
Email: margiec@md.metrocast.net
Website: www.cheseldine.org
Management consulting, asset, property & construction management. (Woman, estab 2008, empl 11, sales $512,000, cert: State)

8095 Destiny Management Services, LLC
8737 Colesville Rd Ste 710
Silver Spring, MD 20910
Contact: Donna Mitchell President
Tel: 301-650-0047
Email: donnam@destinymgmtsvcs.com
Website: www.destinymgmtsvcs.com
Management Consulting, Business Solutions, Information Technology, Staff Augmentation, Compliance Reviews, Contacts Management, Human Capitol Development. (Woman/AA, estab 1996, empl 10, sales $1,300,000, cert: State, WBENC)

8096 DPN Group, LLC
516 N Charles St Ste 303
Baltimore, MD 21201
Contact: Andrea Jackson Principal
Tel: 410-905-4036
Email: ajackson@dpngroup.net
Website: www.dpngroup.net
Management consulting: public outreach, supplier diversity & inclusion consulting, strategic planning, workforce development, performance evaluation, policy development, & compliance monitoring. (Woman/AA, estab 2008, empl 4, sales $204,000, cert: State)

8097 Ivy Planning Group, LLC
15204 Omega Dr, Ste 110
Rockville, MD 20850
Contact: Cynthia Featherson President
Tel: 301-963-1669
Email: cfeatherson@ivygroupllc.com
Website: www.ivygroupllc.com
Diversity consulting & training, strategic planning, change mgmt, customer service, executive coaching, assessments & surveys, knowledge mgmt, performance measurement & mgmt, training & development. (Woman/AA, estab 1990, empl 30, sales $ 0, cert: WBENC)

8098 Lord and Tucker Management Consultants, LLC
4140 Holbrook Ln
Huntingtown, MD 20639
Contact: Dawn Tucker President
Tel: 866-517-0477
Email: info@ltmctraining.com
Website: www.ltmctraining.com
Staff development & training: life skills, career development & entrepreneurship, customer service, time mgmt, organizational dev, financial mgmt, budgeting, resume writing & interview skills. (Woman/AA, estab 2004, empl 1, sales , cert: State)

8099 Mitaja Corporation
8115 Maple Lawn Blvd, Ste 350
Fulton, MD 20759
Contact: Harnish Amin Dir of Sales
Tel: 301-332-0649
Email: mpatel@mitajacorp.com
Website: www.mitajacorp.com
Staff Augmentation, RPO, Managed Services, Managed Projects & Consulting Services. (As-Pac, estab 2014, empl 50, sales $3,000,000, cert: 8(a))

8100 Muse GME Enterprises LLC
2 Wisconsin Circle, Ste 700
Chevy Chase, MD 20815
Contact: Gwen Muse-Evans CEO
Tel: 301-244-4947
Email: g.museevans@gmeenterprises.net
Website: www.gmeenterprises.net
Organizational governance, program review and development, professional and management development, quality management, strategic planning, committee establishment, regulatory compliance, risk governance. (Woman/AA, estab 2014, empl 3, sales $154,300, cert: State, WBENC, SDB)

PROFESSIONAL SERVICES: Management Consulting

8101 Performance Development Corporation
17308 Twin Ridge Court
Silver Spring, MD 20905
Contact: Sharon Fountain President
Tel: 301-421-0118
Email: sharon@sharonfountain.com
Website: www.SharonFountain.com
Training: interpersonal competence, communication, feedback, assertiveness, conflict management, self-esteem/self confidence, leadership/management/supervisory skills, team building, organizational skills, time management/managing multiple priorities. (Woman, estab 1980, empl 1, sales , cert: NWBOC)

8102 Sheila Lee & Associates, LLC - Learning Everywhere
1518 W Pratt St
Baltimore, MD 21223
Contact: Sheila S. Lee CEO
Tel: 410-233-6922
Email: sheilalee@learningeverywhere.com
Website: www.learningeverywhere.com
Organizational development, curriculum design & training. (Woman/AA, estab 2005, empl 8, sales $ 0, cert: State, NMSDC, WBENC)

8103 Starr and Associates LLC
10707 Heather Glen Way
Bowie, MD 20720
Contact: Jamal Starr CEO
Tel: 888-727-3017
Email: jamalstarr@starrconsultant.com
Website: www.starrconsultant.com
Management consulting practices and technologies to improve productivity and reduce costs. (AA, estab 2004, empl 30, sales $ 0, cert: NMSDC)

8104 The Fehlig Group, LLC
1 Arch Pl, Ste 421
Gaithersburg, MD 20878
Contact: Mary Fehlig President
Tel: 240-912-9422
Email: maryfehlig@fehliggroup.com
Website: www.fehliggroup.com
Corporate Social Responsibility, Corporate Social Responsibility Development, Sustainability Action Plans, Award Applications, Local, National, Global: Great Place To Work Strategy & Recognition, Green Business Strategy & Recognition, Capacity Building. (Woman, estab 1993, empl 1, sales $435,227, cert: WBENC)

8105 The Stroud Group
9130 Red Branch Rd, Ste S
Columbia, MD 21045
Contact: Theo Bell VP Business Dev
Tel: 410-964-2222
Email: theo@stroudgroup.com
Website: www.stroudgroup.com
Procurement & project management services. (Woman, estab 1987, empl 22, sales $22,000,000, cert: WBENC)

Michigan

8106 American Resource Training System, Inc.
453 M L King Blvd
Detroit, MI 48201
Contact: Sharon McWhorter President
Tel: 313-832-2787
Email: slm@arts-usa.com
Website: www.arts-usa.com
Human Performance & Management Consulting. (Woman/AA, estab 1983, empl 5, sales $122,215, cert: NMSDC, 8(a))

8107 ASG Renaissance
27655 Middlebelt Rd Ste 140
Farmington Hills, MI 48334
Contact: Maureen Michaels Acct Mgr
Tel: 248-477-5432
Email: mmichaels@asgren.com
Website: www.asgren.com
Consulting svcs: information technology, public relations, engineering, mktg, minority technical assistance programs, etc. (Minority, Woman, estab 1987, empl 200, sales $206,586,000, cert: NMSDC, WBENC)

8108 Bigelow Family Holdings LLC
3223 15 Mile Rd
Sterling Heights, MI 48310
Contact: President
Tel: 586-306-8962
Email: info@mettleops.com
Website: www.mettleops.com
Program management, engineering, and business development. (Woman, estab 2013, empl 10, sales , cert: WBENC, 8(a))

8109 BTS Consulting & Training LLC
211 N. First St Ste 200
Brighton, MI 48116
Contact: Mary Temple Managing Partner
Tel: 586-322-3065
Email: mary.temple@btsmichigan.com
Website: www.btsmichigan.com/
Designs, develops & delivers customized training solutions, instructional design, course development, training delivery, project and curriculum management, conference and event coordination, travel administration. (Woman, estab 1991, empl 10, sales $2,600,000, cert: WBENC)

8110 Coach for Higher
2015 Geddes Ave
Ann Arbor, MI 48104
Contact: Nan Owner
Tel: 734-255-7833
Email: nan@coachforhigher.com
Website: www.CoachForHigher.com
Executive & Leadership Coaching Services for Individuals, Teams & Organizations. (Woman, estab 2010, empl 1, sales , cert: WBENC)

8111 DSSI LLC
40 Oak Hollow St Ste 225
Southfield, MI 48033
Contact: Kathy Young
Tel: 248-208-8340
Email: kyoung@directsourcing.com
Website: www.directsourcing.com
Purchasing services. (As-Ind, estab 2000, empl 100, sales $110,000,000, cert: NMSDC)

8112 Focused Coaching LLC
2022 Liberty HTS
Ann Arbor, MI 48103
Contact: Lisa Pasbjerg CEO
Tel: 734-663-0420
Email: lpasbjerg@focusedcoaching.net
Website: www.focusedcoaching.net
Leadership development, executive coaching, assessment & facilitation services. (Woman, estab 2006, empl 1, sales $104,000, cert: WBENC)

PROFESSIONAL SERVICES: Management Consulting

8113 Global LT, Inc.
      1871 Woodslee Dr
      Troy, MI 48083
      Contact: Chris Brotherson VP Sales
      Tel: 248-786-0999
      Email: CBrotherson@global-lt.com
      Website: www.Global-LT.com
English, foreign language, cross-cultural, diversity training; relocation translation, interpreting svcs; video/film narration. (AA, estab 1979, empl , sales $25,000,000, cert: NMSDC)

8114 GSHA Quality Services
      PO Box 1452
      Ann Arbor, MI 48103
      Contact: CEO
      Tel: 734-263-7399
      Email:
      Website: www.gshasolutions.org
Quality management services, stabilize processes, reduce cost, reduce waste, improve effectiveness, and efficiency to achieve sustainable, transformational performance improvements. (Woman/AA, estab 2009, empl 8, sales $400,000, cert: NMSDC, WBENC)

8115 Innovative Learning Group, Inc.
      1130 Coolidge Hwy
      Troy, MI 48084
      Contact: Gayle Holsworth Performance Consultant
      Tel: 248-544-1568
      Email: gayle.holsworth@innovativelg.com
      Website: www.innovativeLG.com
Human performance consulting, needs assessment, training design & development, evaluation. (Woman, estab 2004, empl 17, sales $5,000,000, cert: WBENC)

8116 Jim Roberts Enterprises LLC
      515 Ship St Ste 211
      Saint Joseph, MI 49085
      Contact: Jim Roberts President
      Tel: 269-982-4188
      Email: jim@jimrobertsenterprises.com
      Website: www.jimrobertsenterprises.com
Management consulting, financial, facility management, real estate & project management consulting services. (Minority, estab 2004, empl 1, sales $163,000, cert: NMSDC)

8117 Learning Designs, Inc.
      6001 North Adams, Ste 100
      Bloomfield Hills, MI 48304
      Contact: Julie Gieraltowski Operations Mgr
      Tel: 248-269-0808
      Email: jgieral@learningdesigns.com
      Website: www.learningdesigns.com
Training & consulting: performance consulting, instructional design, training delivery, technology solutions & evaluation. (Woman, estab 1984, empl 18, sales $2,029,000, cert: WBENC)

8118 LWH Enterprises
      1515 W. Wackerly St.
      Midland, MI 48640
      Contact: Anne Herron VP
      Tel: 989-835-5811
      Email: aherron@allisinfo.com
      Website: www.allisinfo.com
Business research, market research, business intelligence, marketing services, IT support. (Minority, Woman, estab 1979, empl 17, sales $1,884,979, cert: WBENC)

8119 OMNEX
      315 E Eisenhower Pkwy Ste 110
      Ann Arbor, MI 48108
      Contact: Jason Hicks Pulishing Coord
      Tel: 734-761-4940
      Email: jhicks@omnex.com
      Website: www.omnex.com
Consulting & training services in Quality, Environmental, Health & Safety standards-based management systems, ISO 9001:2000, ISO 14000, ISO/TS 16949:2002 & QOS. (As-Ind, estab 1985, empl 200, sales $2,000,001, cert: NMSDC)

8120 Pyramid Quality Solutions & Innovations, Inc.
      2075 West Big Beaver Ste 415
      Troy, MI 48084
      Contact: Ossie Nunn CEO
      Tel: 248-577-1356
      Email: onunn@pqsiinc.com
      Website: www.pqsiinc.com
Quality & industrial engineering consulting: sequencing (JIT), rework & repair svcs, manuals & procedures, kitting & assembly, supplier representation, logistics, quality standards implementation, error & mistake proofing, etc. (AA, estab 2002, empl 150, sales $3,450,000, cert: NMSDC)

8121 Richalin Digue, LLC
      46036 Michigan Ave Ste 201
      Canton, MI 48188
      Contact: Richalin Digue Mgr
      Tel: 313-213-3103
      Email: rich.digue@rnd-engineering.com
      Website: www.rnd-engineering.com
Marketing & project management. (AA, estab 2004, empl 2, sales $800,000, cert: NMSDC)

8122 Syncreon.US Inc.
      2851 High Meadow Circle Ste 250
      Auburn Hills, MI 48326
      Contact: Oswald Reid CEO
      Tel: 248-377-4700
      Email: oswald.reid@syncreon.com
      Website: www.syncreon-us.com
Supply chain management, material follow-up & transportation management and cross-dock. Complex material handling and material integration. (AA, estab 2000, empl 1100, sales $671,200,000, cert: NMSDC)

8123 Utility Reduction Analysts, Inc.
      12935 S West Bay Shore Dr Ste 240
      Traverse City, MI 49684
      Contact: Jennifer Wynn Stoll President
      Tel: 888-586-2121
      Email: jwstoll@utilityreduction.com
      Website: www.utilityreduction.com
Full service utility cost reduction company. Our thorough analysis provides information on rates/tariffs, promotions, refund processing, market opportunities, consumption patterns, & available deregulation options. (Woman, estab 1991, empl 5, sales $410,000, cert: WBENC)

8124 Vani Quality Quest, Inc.
41000 Woodward Ave Ste 350
Bloomfield Hills, MI 48304
Contact: Jagdish Vani President
Tel: 248-733-0000
Email: jvani@vqqinc.com
Website: www.vqqinc.com
Containment inspection, rework svcs, SQI consulting & training, problem solving, customer liaison, QC employee staffing services. (As-Pac, estab 1992, empl 60, sales $ 0, cert: NMSDC)

8125 VAS Consulting Services
33228 W 12 Mile Rd
Farmington Hills, MI 48334
Contact: Glenn Stafford President
Tel: 248-553-6603
Email: gstafford@vas4.com
Website: www.vas4.com
Consulting services: develop minority supplier programs, strategic alliances & joint ventures. (AA, estab 2001, empl 1, sales $250,000, cert: NMSDC)

Minnesota

8126 Alliant Consulting, Inc.
555 7th St W, Ste 101
Saint Paul, MN 55102
Contact: CFO
Tel: 651-291-0607
Email: solutions@alliantconsulting.com
Website: www.alliantconsulting.com
Operational assessment, redesign & implementation to improve service, quality & productivity (Woman, estab 1997, empl 4, sales $505,200, cert: WBENC)

8127 Beehive Strategic Communication GBC
PO BOX 11373
Saint Paul, MN 55111
Contact: Rebecca Martin SVP Culture & Talent
Tel: 651-789-2236
Email: rmartin@beehivepr.biz
Website: www.beehivepr.biz
Strategic planning, competitive intelligence, brand positioning, crisis management, media coaching, communications. (Woman, estab 1998, empl 14, sales $3,000,000, cert: WBENC)

8128 CultureBrokers, LLC
1610 5th St NE
Minneapolis, MN 55413
Contact: Lisa Tabor President
Tel: 651-321-2167
Email: lisa@culturebrokers.com
Website: www.culturebrokers.com
Diversity & inclusion services, diversity recruitment, cultural competence training, strategic planning, inclusion initiatives, employee engagement and retention, community relations, community engagement, equity initiatives. (Woman/AA, estab 2005, empl 1, sales , cert: City)

8129 ECM Instructional Systems
5816 11th Ave S
Minneapolis, MN 55417
Contact: Michael Mazyck President
Tel: 888-685-0877
Email: mazyck@ecminstructionalsystems.com
Website: www.ecminstructionalsystems.com
Instructional design, training, professional development & evaluation services, Learning & Development. (AA, estab 2004, empl 4, sales , cert: State, City)

8130 Hollstadt & Associates, Inc.
1333 Northland Dr, Ste 220
Mendota Heights, MN 55120
Contact: Molly Jungbauer CEO
Tel: 952-898-6813
Email: mjungbauer@hollstadt.com
Website: www.hollstadt.com/
Management & technology consulting: portfolio, program & project management, business analysis, training programs. (Woman, estab 1990, empl 200, sales $26,053,034, cert: WBENC)

8131 JIT Energy Services
23505 Smithtown Rd Ste 280
Excelsior, MN 55331
Contact: Jamie Aragon CEO
Tel: 952-474-3410
Email: jamie.a@jitservicesinc.com
Website: www.jitservicesinc.com
Energy efficiency consulting & energy mgmt services. (Minority, Woman, estab 1991, empl 12, sales $173,840,860, cert: NMSDC, WBENC)

8132 MDA Leadership Consulting
150 S 5th St, Ste 3300
Minneapolis, MN 55402
Contact: Linda Barrett Dir Business Svcs
Tel: 612-332-8182
Email: info@mdaleadership.com
Website: www.mdaleadership.com
Talent management, leadership development, organizational performance (Woman, estab 1981, empl 31, sales $4,422,000, cert: State)

8133 Nelson Consulting LLC
1330 Lagoon Ave 4th Fl
Minneapolis, MN 55408
Contact: Owner
Tel: 612-460-5250
Email: info@pivotstrategies.com
Website: www.pivotstrategies.com
Communications strategy, organizational change management, reputation management, sustainability, corporate social responsibility, (Woman, estab 2015, empl 12, sales $1,500,000, cert: WBENC)

8134 ON Point Next Level Leadership
5775 Wayzata Blvd, Ste 700
Minneapolis, MN 55416
Contact: Pam Borton CEO
Tel: 612-418-7776
Email: pam@onpointnextlevel.com
Website: www.onpointnextlevel.com
Leadership development, strategic succession planning and innovative training. (Woman, estab 2015, empl 3, sales , cert: WBENC)

8135 Risk Management Consulting Services, LLC.
35 Pineview Lane N
Plymouth, MN 55441
Contact: Gwen McFadden Managing Partner
Tel: 952-544-0354
Email: gwen@rmcsllc.com
Website: www.riskconsultingservices.net
Insurance placement, insurance & risk management consulting services, RFP/RFQ consulting, insurance placement, risk management consulting, due diligence projects, claims consulting & management. (Woman/AA, estab 1997, empl 2, sales $150,000, cert: NMSDC, 8(a))

PROFESSIONAL SERVICES: Management Consulting

8136 Talencio, LLC
708 N 1st St Ste 341
Minneapolis, MN 55401
Contact: Paula Norbom President
Tel: 612-703-4236
Email: pnorbom@talencio.com
Website: www.talencio.com
Accounting & Finance, Clinical Research, Data Analysis & Statistics, Engineering, Health Care Policy & Reform, Human Resource Management, Informatics, Information Technology, Interim Leadership, Lean & Six Sigma, Marketing, Operations. (Woman, estab 2008, empl 6, sales $1,037,000, cert: WBENC)

8137 The Improve Group
700 Raymond Ave Ste 140
St. Paul, MN 55114
Contact: Leah Goldstein Moses Founder & CEO
Tel: 651-315-8919
Email: leah@theimprovegroup.com
Website: www.theimprovegroup.com
Professional services: evaluation, strategic planning, management consulting & facilitation. (Woman, estab 2000, empl 11, sales $973,523, cert: WBENC)

8138 Vuelta Management Group, LLC
1507 Chelmsford St
Saint Paul, MN 55108
Contact: Scott Hamilton President
Tel: 651-329-8609
Email: shamilton@vueltamanagement.com
Website: www.vueltamanagement.com
Project Management; Process Improvement; Lean Six Sigma; Supply Chain Management; Inventory Management; Purchasing; Production Management. (Hisp, estab 2009, empl 1, sales $162,117, cert: State, NMSDC)

Missouri

8139 Kwame Building Group, Inc.
1204 Washington Ave, Ste 200
Saint Louis, MO 63103
Contact: Joshua Randall VP
Tel: 314-862-5344
Email: jrandall@kwamebuildinggroup.com
Website: www.kwamebuildinggroup.com
Program & construction mgmt services: project scheduling, estimating, cost controls, document controls, value engineering, quality assurance & project inspection. (AA, Hisp, estab 1991, empl 75, sales $6,100,000, cert: City)

8140 Mustardseed Cultural & Environmental Services, LLC
222 W Gregory Blvd, Ste 211
Kansas City, MO 64114
Contact: Timberlyn Smith, CHMM President
Tel: 816-333-2424
Email: tsmith@m-c-e-services.net
Website: www.m-c-e-services.net
Environmental, safety & cultural resource management consulting. (Woman/AA, estab 2003, empl 5, sales $227,305, cert: State, City)

8141 P/Strada, LLC
406 W 34th st.
Kansas City, MO 64111
Contact: Patrice Manuel CEO
Tel: 816-256-4577
Email: pat@pstrada.com
Website: www.pstrada.com
Organizational development & homeland security consulting. (Woman/AA, estab 2001, empl 42, sales $3,370,000, cert: State, City, NMSDC)

8142 Project Controls Group, Inc.
2 Campbell Plaza, Bldg C
St. Louis, MO 63139
Contact: Viola Pancratz Principal
Tel: 314-647-0707
Email: vpancratz@projectcontrolsgroup.com
Website: www.projectcontrolsgroup.com
Cost engineering & estimating, CPM scheduling, claims analysis, document control, claims analysis, construction management, program management. (AA, estab 2003, empl 22, sales $1,430,353, cert: State, NMSDC)

8143 PryCor Technologies, LLC
20 S Sarah St
St. Louis, MO 63108
Contact: Seqwana Pryor CEO
Tel: 302-528-0965
Email: ceo.prycortechnologies@gmail.com
Website: www.prycortechnologies.com
Management consulting & training: Lean Six Sigma & operational excellence. (Woman/AA, estab 2016, empl 1, sales , cert: WBENC)

8144 Standing Partnership
1610 Des Peres Rd Ste 200
St. Louis, MO 63131
Contact: Melissa Lackey CEO
Tel: 314-469-3500
Email: mlackey@standingpartnership.com
Website: www.standingpartnership.com
Strategy, corporate social responsibility (CSR), public affairs, internal communications and issues and crisis management. (Woman, estab 1991, empl 26, sales $3,824,984, cert: WBENC)

Mississippi

8145 AGF Enterprise LLC
1060 E Countyline Rd Ste 3A-104
Ridgeland, MS 39157
Contact: Anthony Fairley Managing Partner
Tel: 601-500-2325
Email: anthonygf@agfenterprise.com
Website: www.agfenterprise.com
Learning Management System (LMS), Tracking & Reporting Easily track goal progress, knowledge gains, ROI, Regulatory Compliance Train, assess, and report for compliance purposes. (AA, estab 2013, empl 1, sales $376,000, cert: NMSDC)

PROFESSIONAL SERVICES: Management Consulting

North Carolina

8146 Aseptic Haven LLC
3330 Black Jack Simpson Rd
Greenville, NC 27858
Contact: Felicia Richardson Owner
Tel: 252-258-5935
Email: feliciarichardson@aseptichaven.com
Website: www.aseptichaven.com
Consulting & training services, Life Sciences, Workforce Development, Inclusion & Diversity. (Woman/AA, estab 2014, empl 1, sales , cert: State)

8147 Flynn Heath Holt Leadership, LLC
309 E Morehead St, Ste 230
Charlotte, NC 28202
Contact: Maggie Norris COO
Tel: 704-632-6712
Email: mnorris@flynnheath.com
Website: www.flynnheath.com/
Development programs and workshops, executive coaching and speaking. (Woman, estab , empl , sales $4,415,000, cert: WBENC)

8148 LMK Clinical Research Consulting, LLC
9815 J Sam Furr Rd
Huntersville, NC 28078
Contact: Isaiah Howard Dir of Marketing
Tel: 704-464-3291
Email: isaiah.howard@lmkclinicalresearch.com
Website: www.lmkclinicalresearch.com
Strategic development, project management & quality control of documents & content that support clinical development. (Woman/AA, estab 2013, empl 10, sales , cert: WBENC)

8149 Proficient Learning LLC
1508 Military Cutoff Rd Ste 304
Wilmington, NC 28403
Contact: Pamela Marinko CEO
Tel: 910-795-1376
Email: pam.marinko@proficientlearning.com
Website: www.proficientlearning.com
Instructor-led, virtual, eLearning & mobile learning solutions. (Woman, estab 2005, empl 23, sales $3,200,000, cert: WBENC)

8150 Tactegra
18 Cabarrus Ave W
Concord, NC 20825
Contact: Leanne Kinsella Dir Business Devel
Tel: 704-793-0800
Email: info@tactegra.com
Website: www.tactegra.com
Management consulting, program/project management, IT project support services, staff augmentation & process management. (AA, Hisp, estab 2007, empl 50, sales $3,700,000, cert: NMSDC)

8151 The Future Procurement Group, LLC
3513 McPherson St
Waxhaw, NC 28173
Contact: Silas Carter
Tel: 203-913-9598
Email: scarter@thefutureprocurementgroup.com
Website: www.thefutureprocurementgroup.com
Consulting Services, Strategic Sourcing, Procurement Management, Supplier Diversity, Program Devel, Training, Vendor Management, - Supplier Evaluation, Process Review & Analysis, Cost Management, Management Consulting. (AA, estab 2011, empl 1, sales , cert: NMSDC)

8152 The Thrower Group, LLC.
11204 Waightstill Way
Charlotte, NC 28277
Contact: Baron Thrower CEO
Tel: 704-215-4946
Email: baron.thrower@thethrowergroupllc.com
Website: www.thethrowergroupllc.com
Management consulting firm. (AA, estab 2010, empl 35, sales , cert: NMSDC)

New Jersey

8153 Ally Solutions Group LLC
12 Lower Center St
Clinton, NJ 08809
Contact: Egina Dir of Talent
Tel: 908-968-0908
Email: seagert@asgna.com
Website: www.allysolutionsgroup.com
Building Change Leadership, Change Management & Enterprise Change. (Woman, estab 2006, empl 20, sales $2,616,789, cert: WBENC)

8154 Bardess Group Ltd.
15 Morey Ln, Ste 100
Randolph, NJ 07869
Contact: Barbara Pound President
Tel: 973-584-9100
Email: bspound@bardess.com
Website: www.bardess.com
Mgmt consulting; data management, business performance management, IT, business planning & process improvement, reveune & asset management. (Woman, estab 1997, empl 25, sales $ 0, cert: State, WBENC)

8155 BTII Institute
414 Eagle Rock Ave Ste 100 D
West Orange, NJ 07052
Contact: Sharon Bussey Managing Partner
Tel: 973-325-9001
Email: Sharon.Bussey.SD@BTIIInstitute.com
Website: www.btiiglobal.com
Consulting & training, Project Management, Professional Development & Microsoft. (Woman/AA, estab 2009, empl 5, sales $300,000, cert: NMSDC)

8156 Candid Services
80 Pine St
Bridgewater, NJ 08807
Contact: Meghana Patel CEO
Tel: 732-874-1345
Email: contact@candidcorp.com
Website: www.candidcorp.com
Pharmaceutical & medical device consulting services, computer system validation, non compartmental analysis (NCA), Clinical data analysis & handling, SAS programming & Regulatory Affairs consulting. (Minority, Woman, estab 2015, empl 2, sales , cert: WBENC)

8157 Davis & Company, Inc.
11 Harristown Rd
Glen Rock, NJ 07452
Contact: David Pitre VP Sonsulting Svcs
Tel: 201-445-5100
Email: david.pitre@davisandco.com
Website: www.davisandco.com
Communication consulting & implementation, strategic planning & research, implementation, writing & design. (Woman, estab 1984, empl 17, sales $3,350,000, cert: State, WBENC)

8158   Microexcel Inc.
       One Harmon Plaza, 10th Fl
       Secaucus, NJ 07094
       Contact: Ayub Qhadri President
       Tel: 201-787-4562
       Email: ayub.qhadri@microexcel.com
       Website: www.microexcel.com
Global management consulting, technology services & outsourcing. (As-Ind, estab 2001, empl 75, sales $28,000,000, cert: State)

8159   Munnlane LLC
       3000 Atrium Way
       Mount Laurel, NJ 08054
       Contact: Jenna Wolfson
       Tel: 856-275-6103
       Email: jenna@munnlaneworkplace.com
       Website: www.munnlaneworkplace.com
Furniture Procurement Management, Asset Management, Budget Management, Project Management, Technology Management,, Permitting, FF&E Management, Change Management. (Woman, estab 2021, empl 6, sales $1,300,000, cert: WBENC)

8160   QualComp Consulting Services LLC
       675 US Hwy One Ste B203
       North Brunswick, NJ 08902
       Contact: Victor Arriaran Principal
       Tel: 800-511-8758
       Email: victor.arriaran@qualcomp.com
       Website: www.qualcomp.com
Quality systems design & implementation, audit & inspection readiness, complaint remediation, process control & process improvement, risk management , design control, root cause analysis, Corrective & Preventive Action. (Hisp, estab 2010, empl 4, sales $1,521,586, cert: NMSDC)

8161   The Forefront Group
       26 Sunflower Circle
       Lumberton, NJ 08048
       Contact: Bonnie Keith Owner
       Tel: 609-265-1825
       Email: bkeith@theforefrontgroup.com
       Website: www.theforefrontgroup.com
Admin management consulting, education support svcs, professional & management development training. (Woman, estab 2002, empl 10, sales , cert: WBENC)

8162   Trascent Management Consulting LLC
       460 US Hwy 22 West
       Whitehouse Station, NJ 08889
       Contact: Neha Patel Dir Finance
       Tel: 973-641-8806
       Email: npatel@trascent.com
       Website: www.trascent.com
Corporate Real Estate & Facilities management consulting. (As-Ind, estab 2014, empl 45, sales , cert: NMSDC)

8163   Vitiello Communications Group
       825 Georges Rd Ste 6
       North Brunswick, NJ 08902
       Contact: Nadine Green COO
       Tel: 732-238-6622
       Email: nadine.green@vtlo.com
       Website: www.vtlo.com
Communications, employee engagement, strategic change & leadership communications. (Woman, estab 1990, empl 20, sales $3,600,000, cert: WBENC)

8164   Wet Cement, Inc.
       18 Yardley Manor Dr
       Matawan, NJ 07747
       Contact: Jennifer Willey CEO
       Tel: 917-334-3653
       Email: info@wet-cement.com
       Website: www.wet-cement.com/
Coach and train on powerful presenting, public speaking and pitching skills to drive sales and develop talent. (Woman, estab 2017, empl 3, sales $120,000, cert: WBENC)

Nevada

8165   American Project Management LLC
       11700 W Charleston Blvd, Ste 170-315
       Las Vegas, NV 89135
       Contact: Jane Lee Managing Partner
       Tel: 702-220-4562
       Email: jlee@apmlasvegas.com
       Website: www.apmlasvegas.com
Project Scheduling & Cost Control, Earned Value Management System (EVMS) Implementation, Computer Programming & Embedded Software Development Services & Staff Augmentation. (Minority, Woman, estab 2003, empl 2, sales , cert: NMSDC, NWBOC)

8166   Operations Service Systems
       9716 Terrace Green Ave
       Las Vegas, NV 89117
       Contact: Susan Beyer President
       Tel: 800-878-6906
       Email: sue@suebeyer.com
       Website: www.suebeyer.com
Training & development: operations, dev, customer service & results oriented training systems. (Woman, estab 2000, empl 2, sales $255,000, cert: WBENC)

8167   Purpose & Action, LLC
       3225 McLeod Dr, Ste 100
       Las Vegas, NV 89121
       Contact: Miguel de Jesus President
       Tel: 760-438-9907
       Email: miguel@coachmiguel.com
       Website: www.coachmiguel.com
Business management, global sales/marketing. (Hisp, estab 2011, empl 1, sales , cert: NMSDC)

New York

8168   Action Resources
       PO Box 278
       Gardiner, NY 12525
       Contact: Nancy Pompeo President
       Tel: 845-895-2643
       Email: nancy@actionresources.com
       Website: www.actionresources.com
Account Development Strategies, Assessments & Profiles, Business Acumen, Career Development, Change Management, Client Relationship Development, Coaching Skills. (Woman, estab 1985, empl 1, sales $2,577,067, cert: WBENC)

8169 AIOPX Management Consulting
      1007 La Quinta Dr
      Webster, NY 14580
      Contact: David Powe Partner & Lead Consultant
      Tel: 585-627-1716
      Email: dpowe@aiopx.com
      Website: www.aiopx.com
Operation Excellence (OpEx): lean, six sigma, total quality, practical process improvement & the Toyota production system. (AA, estab 2012, empl 1, sales $125,000, cert: NMSDC)

8170 Axiom Consulting LLC
      126 W Main St
      Endicott, NY 13760
      Contact: Wayne McCray CEO
      Tel: 800-563-2758
      Email: info@4axiomcorp.com
      Website: www.4axiomcorp.com
MRO sales, business process outsourcing, staffing, training. (AA, estab 2001, empl 150, sales $6,000,000, cert: NMSDC)

8171 Carlin Solutions, LLC
      237 Flatbush Ave Ste 128
      Brooklyn, NY 11217
      Contact: Carla Franklin Managing Dir
      Tel: 917-463-3592
      Email: carla@carlinsolutions.com
      Website: www.carlinsolutions.com
Requirements analysis, staff augmentation, program management, project management, operational improvement, management consulting, Strategic Planning, Business Development, Strategic Market Analysis. (Woman/AA, estab 2003, empl 3, sales $414,000, cert: City, NMSDC, WBENC)

8172 Chapman Lean Enterprise
      81 Rock Hill Rd
      Rochester, NY 14618
      Contact: Christopher Chapman President
      Tel: 585-406-7804
      Email: cdchapman1@chapmanlean.com
      Website: www.chapmanlean.com
Lean process improvement training & consultation services. (AA, estab 2010, empl 1, sales , cert: NMSDC)

8173 Galica, LLC
      620 Park Ave, Ste 216
      Rochester, NY 14607
      Contact: Carlos Perez Principal
      Tel: 585-319-9301
      Email: galicaehs@gmail.com
      Website: www.galicaehs.com
Bilingual (Spanish/English) Strategy Support & Lean Facilitation. (Hisp, estab 2009, empl 1, sales , cert: State, NMSDC)

8174 Gillespie Associates, Ltd.
      1501 East Ave Ste 200
      Rochester, NY 14610
      Contact: Karen Barrow President
      Tel: 585-287-8191
      Email: kbarrow@gillespieassociates.com
      Website: www.gillespieassociates.com
Performance consulting, customized training & development, sales performance institute, e-learning solutions, web-based learning, technical documentation, business process documentation.
 (Woman, estab 1989, empl 9, sales $1,292,286, cert: State, WBENC)

8175 Green Silk Associates, LLC
      10440 Queens Blvd., Ste 5J
      Forest Hills, NY 11375
      Contact: Deb Seidman President
      Tel: 917-445-2443
      Email: dseidman@greensilkassociates.com
      Website: www.greensilkassociates.com
Organizational effectiveness & leadership development services, innovation, planning, problem-solving meeting/offsite facilitation; team development; organization design; executive coaching; & talent management consulting. (Woman, estab 2009, empl 1, sales , cert: State, City)

8176 Hyun & Associates, Inc.
      222 Riverside Dr, #3B
      New York, NY 10025
      Contact: Jane Hyun President
      Tel: 917-327-0992
      Email: jhyun@hyunassociates.com
      Website: www.hyunassociates.com
Leadership, diversity training & coaching services. (Minority, Woman, estab 1997, empl 3, sales $275,000, cert: NMSDC)

8177 Impact Consulting, LLC
      1177 Ave of the Americas
      New York, NY 10036
      Contact: Lucy Sorrentini Founder & CEO
      Tel: 973-727-1574
      Email: team@impactconsultingus.com
      Website: www.impactconsultingus.com
Leadership & organizational development, consulting, coaching & training services. (Minority, Woman, estab 2015, empl 6, sales $1,038,000, cert: State, City, NMSDC, WBENC)

8178 International Institute for Learning, Inc. (IIL)
      110 E 59th St, 31st Fl
      New York, NY 10022
      Contact: Amy Gershen
      Tel: 212-758-0177
      Email: amy.gershen@iil.com
      Website: www.iil.com
Project management, six sigma & MSP training & consulting services. (Woman, estab 1991, empl 87, sales $1,300,000,000, cert: WBENC)

8179 JDR Consulting, LLC
      4305 Broadway Ste 41
      New York, NY 10033
      Contact: John Rivers CEO
      Tel: 917-324-2443
      Email: jrivers@jdrconsulting.net
      Website: www.jdrconsulting.net
Management consulting, program & project management, systems & and accounting services. (AA, estab 2004, empl 9, sales $6,000,000, cert: State, NMSDC)

8180 Jennifer Brown LLC
      20 E 9th St, Ste 4U
      New York, NY 10003
      Contact: Jennifer Brown CEO
      Tel: 917-769-1599
      Email: info@jenniferbrownconsulting.com
      Website: www.jenniferbrownconsulting.com
Leadership consulting, HR training, coaching, speaker, communications, diversity, global, teams, facilitator, facilitation, career planning, leaders, inclusive, inclusion, innovative, innovation, empowered, empowerment. (Woman, estab 2004, empl 15, sales $1,400,000, cert: City, WBENC)

8181 JR Language Translation Services, Inc.
2112 Empire Blvd, Ste 1C
Rochester, NY 14580
Contact: d'Empaire Language Solutions Specialist
Tel: 877-771-0145
Email: info@jrlanguage.com
Website: www.jrlanguage.com
Document Translation - Web site and software localization - Scripts - Manuals - Brochures - Contracts. (Minority, Woman, estab 2006, empl 8, sales $1,680,371, cert: State, WBENC)

8182 KGM Consulting Inc.
30 Wall St
New York, NY 10005
Contact: Martell Admin
Tel: 212-791-1555
Email: mmcgovern@kgmcon.com
Website: www.kgmit.com
Technology management solutions: echnology project mgmt, circuit provisioning mgmt & voice systems admin, carrier & telecom expense mgmt svcs, staff augmentation. (Woman, estab 1996, empl 30, sales $3,952,677, cert: City, WBENC)

8183 KnowledgeSources Consulting Inc.
23 W 73rd St Ste 1103
New York, NY 10023
Contact: Peggy Decker Principal
Tel: 212-362-1606
Email: peggy@knowledgesources.com
Website: www.knowledgesources.com
Employee/Financial Advisor Learning & Development; Customer Events.
Specifically: employee engagement, organizational development, professional development, training, coaching, facilitating. (Woman, estab 2009, empl 1, sales $400,000, cert: WBENC)

8184 Shaheen & Associates, Inc.
37 Maple Ave
Armonk, NY 10504
Contact: William Shaheen COO
Tel: 914-273-9000
Email: w.shaheen@shaheeninc.com
Website: www.shaheeninc.com
Telecom auditing & cost-containment services. (Woman, estab 1988, empl 8, sales $2,400,000, cert: WBENC)

8185 The Caswood Group, Inc.
811 Ayrault Rd, Ste 2
Fairport, NY 14450
Contact: Isabel Casamayor President
Tel: 585-425-0332
Email: icasamayor@caswood.com
Website: www.caswood.com
Specialty sales teams, analytics, data collection & management, sample management. (Woman, estab 1996, empl 38, sales $5,054,073, cert: WBENC)

8186 The Madison Consulting Group, Inc.
41 Madison Ave 31st Fl
New York, NY 10010
Contact: Fisher Consultant & Marketing Mgr
Tel: 212-532-0703
Email: n.carrington@tmcginc.com
Website: www.tmcginc.com
Training & consulting: executive coaching, organizational consulting & strategic resourcing. (Woman, estab 1993, empl 11, sales $1,103,130, cert: City, WBENC)

8187 The Real Advice Plus LLC
108 5th Ave, Ste 20-B
New York, NY 10011
Contact: Tony Brown President
Tel: 718-812-8856
Email: tbrown@t-rap.com
Website: www.t-rap.com
Management consulting, executive search consulting, diversity consulting & career development coaching services. (AA, estab 2006, empl 1, sales , cert: State, City)

Ohio

8188 Alegre, Inc.
3101 W Tech Rd
Miamisburg, OH 45342
Contact: Don Phillips Business Dev Mgr
Tel: 937-885-6786
Email: dphillips@alegreinc.com
Website: www.alegreinc.com
Supply chain mgmt, program mgmt, customer engineering & quality interface, warehousing & distribution processes, sorting & containment, rework processes, light assembly processes. (Woman/As-Pac, estab 1992, empl 30, sales $20,000,000, cert: NMSDC)

8189 APB & Associates, Inc.
55 Erieview Plaza Ste 328
Cleveland, OH 44114
Contact: Andre Bryan President
Tel: 216-541-2900
Email: abryan@apbandassociates.com
Website: www.apbandassociates.com
Document management services, office technology, organizational design, business process improvement, telecommunications & office automation consulting. (AA, estab 2004, empl 12, sales $2,200,000, cert: State, NMSDC, SDB)

8190 Arnold Solutions, LLC
4228 E 178th St
Cleveland, OH 44128
Contact: Reginald E. Arnold CEO
Tel: 216-533-2837
Email: arnoldsolutionsllc@gmail.com
Website: www.arnoldsolutionsllc.com
Consulting, administrative & innovative leadership, Federal Law, HR, PMP, Fleet Management, IT, BPM, Supply Chain Management, Strategic Analysis, Construction Management, Contract Procurement. (Woman/AA, estab 2014, empl 2, sales , cert: State, City)

8191 ATS Training and Consulting Co
1991 Crocker Rd Ste 340
Westlake, OH 44145
Contact: P. Rani Maddali President
Tel: 440-249-0095
Email: pm@ats-tc.com
Website: www.ats-tc.com
Training & consulting services: lean, Six Sigma, supply chain, organizational devel, change mgmt, team building & executive coaching. (Woman/As-Ind, estab 2001, empl 20, sales $1,060,000, cert: NMSDC, WBENC, 8(a))

PROFESSIONAL SERVICES: Management Consulting   8192-8203

8192 Berkshire Group Inc.
2711 W Market St, Ste 5310
Akron, OH 44334
Contact: Janet Kendall White CEO
Tel: 800-556-5549
Email: janet@berkshire-leadership.com
Website: www.berkshire-leadership.com
Consulting & leadership development, strategic planning, process & profit improvement; training & development; executive coaching & facilitation. (Woman, estab 1993, empl 4, sales $309,000, cert: WBENC)

8193 C H Smith & Associates dba Scale Strategic Solution
1329 E Kemper Rd, Ste 4218E
Cincinnati, OH 45246
Contact: Calista Smith President
Tel: 513-252-8129
Email: chs@scalestrategicsolutions.com
Website: www.scalestrategicsolutions.com
Management consulting and evaluation services for the public and non-profit sectors. (Woman/AA, estab 2011, empl 3, sales $290,354, cert: WBENC)

8194 Compass Consulting Services, LLC
PO Box 221347
Beachwood, OH 44122
Contact: Tameka Taylor President
Tel: 216-299-7335
Email: tameka@compassconsultingservices.com
Website: www.compassconsultingservices.com
Organizational development, diversity & inclusion management, conflict management, communication, leadership development, team building. (Woman/AA, estab 2008, empl 2, sales $170,000, cert: State, NMSDC, WBENC)

8195 Diverse Supply Chain Partner, LLC
4132 E Village Dr
Mason, OH 45040
Contact: Cheryl El-Alfi President
Tel: 513-274-8035
Email: cheryl@diversepartner.com
Website: www.diversepartner.com
Strategic business development consulting services to help diverse business enter & grow within the corporate supply chain. (Woman, estab 2014, empl 1, sales , cert: WBENC)

8196 Driven to Succeed LLC
PO Box 104
Lewis Center, OH 43035
Contact: Kristin Harper CEO
Tel: 740-233-1145
Email: Kristin@Driventosucceedllc.com
Website: www.DriventoSucceedLLC.com
Market research & consulting. (Woman/AA, estab 2018, empl 25, sales , cert: NMSDC, WBENC)

8197 Equilibrium Perceptum LLC
11839 Pearl Rd, Ste 101
Strongsville, OH 44136
Contact: Ramana Gaddamanugu
Tel: 216-278-1866
Email: ramana@epfocus.com
Website: www.epfocus.com
Management consulting services: systems & process reviews, strategy documentation, risk management / risk assessments / risk analysis assistance, data analysis, data review, data preparation. (As-Pac, estab 2014, empl 1, sales , cert: State, City)

8198 G. Stephens Inc.
133 N Summit St
Akron, OH 44304
Contact: Glen Stephens President
Tel: 330-762-1386
Email: marketing@gstephensinc.com
Website: www.gstephensinc.com
Estimating, Project Management. (AA, estab 1992, empl 37, sales $6,000,000, cert: State)

8199 GPI Enterprises Inc.
3637 Medina Rd, Ste 60
Medina, OH 44256
Contact: Christopher Murillo President
Tel: 330-321-2461
Email: chris.murillo@e-gpi.com
Website: www.e-gpi.com
Management consulting services, process analysis/ development, data analysis, project management & IT support. (Hisp, estab 2001, empl 16, sales $1,050,000, cert: State, 8(a))

8200 Howse Solutions LLC
17325 Euclid Ste 2030
Cleveland, OH 44112
Contact: Christopher Howse President
Tel: 440-318-4720
Email: chowse@howsesolutions.com
Website: www.howsesolutions.com
Experience leading analysts, developers, and project teams; and defining, creating, and delivering business solutions. (AA, estab , empl 1, sales $255,000, cert: State, City, SDB)

8201 Improve Consulting & Training Group LLC
4600 Euclid Ave Ste 320
Cleveland, OH 44103
Contact: Ellen Burts-Cooper Sr Managing Partner
Tel: 216-539-8737
Email: ellen@improveconsulting.biz
Website: www.improveconsulting.biz
Leadership development & continuous improvement. (Woman/AA, estab 2005, empl 10, sales $700,000, cert: State)

8202 Integrity Development
8050 Beckett Center Dr Ste 317
West Chester, OH 45069
Contact: Eric Ellis CEO
Tel: 513-874-6836
Email: ericellis@integritydev.com
Website: www.integritydev.com
Diversity training, leadership development, conflict mgmt, strategic planning, cultural assessment, executive coaching & team building. (AA, estab 1991, empl 6, sales , cert: NMSDC)

8203 Monterey Consultants, Inc.
5335 Far Hills Ave, Ste 311
Dayton, OH 45429
Contact: Gary Munoz President
Tel: 937-436-4536
Email: gary.munoz@mcix.com
Website: www.mcix.com
Management consulting, organizational development & business process improvement, strategic planning, change management, process improvement, outreach & marketing & customer service. (Hisp, estab , empl , sales $2,704,856, cert: NMSDC)

8204 Pep Promotions
151 W Fourth St Ste 700
Cincinnati, OH 45202
Contact: Dave Kroeger President
Tel: 513-826-3871
Email: kroegerd@peppromotions.com
Website: www.peppromotions.com
Project management, promotional programs. (AA, estab 2004, empl 125, sales $11,000,000, cert: NMSDC)

8205 SimpleQuE, Inc.
249 S Garber Dr
Tipp City, OH 45371
Contact: Jim Lee President
Tel: 740-305-0868
Email: jlee@simpleque.com
Website: www.simpleque.com
Management consulting services. (As-Pac, estab 2005, empl 26, sales $2,100,000, cert: NMSDC)

8206 Sritech Global Inc.
341 S 3rd St, Ste 100
Columbus, OH 43215
Contact: Sheela Kunduru President
Tel: 614-477-2944
Email: ksheela@sritechglobal.com
Website: www.sritechglobal.com
Business process consulting, Business process improvement, Enterprise process & product quality assurance, Independent verification & validation. (Minority, Woman, estab 2013, empl 1, sales $339,640, cert: State, WBENC)

8207 SRM & Associates, LLC
1123 Firth Ave
Worthington, OH 43085
Contact: Victoria Schneider President
Tel: 614-505-1209
Email: vschneider@srm-consulting.net
Website: www.srm-consulting.net
Risk Management Consulting services, Safety & Environmental Consulting, Process Safety Management, Risk Management Planning, Safety & Environmental Program Development, Auditing & Training. (Woman, estab 2011, empl 4, sales $370,000, cert: WBENC)

8208 The CADD Department, Inc.
13916 Euclid Ave Ste 5
East Cleveland, OH 44112
Contact: Wayne Grant CEO
Tel: 216-269-5901
Email: wgrant@thecaddept.net
Website: www.thecaddept.net
Progressive civil / structural engineering, construction supervision & surveying, design, surveying & construction phase services. (AA, estab 2007, empl 4, sales , cert: State, City)

Oklahoma

8209 CDR Assessment Group, Inc.
1644 S Denver Ave
Tulsa, OK 74119
Contact: President
Tel: 918-488-0722
Email: cdrinfo@cdrassessmentgroup.com
Website: www.cdrassessmentgroup.com
Mfr CDR 3-Dimensional Assessment Suite® accurately revealing a leader's Character, Risk Factors for Derailment, and Drivers & Reward Needs. (Woman, estab 1998, empl 5, sales $ 0, cert: WBENC)

8210 Gina Sofola & Associates, Inc.
5801 Broadway Extension Ste 310
Oklahoma City, OK 73118
Contact: Gina Sofola President
Tel: 203-613-9471
Email: gsofola@sofolaassociates.com
Website: www.sofolaassociates.com
Project mgmt: facility mgmt, transportation, strategic planning, engineering & feasibility studies, cost control, scheduling, building assessment, document mgmt, contract admin, interior design, transportation analysis, environmental assessment. (Woman/AA, estab 1999, empl 20, sales $ 0, cert: State)

Oregon

8211 71 & Change
2402 NE 45th Ave
Portland, OR 97213
Contact: Katie Whitbeck Director
Tel: 503-816-6824
Email: katie@71andchange.com
Website: www.71andchange.com
ChangeAnalytics™ is a powerful tool that enables you to manage, communicate & visualize change throughout an organization. (Woman, estab 2016, empl 32, sales $5,000,000, cert: WBENC)

Pennsylvania

8212 ACS Learning Inc.
400 Woodcrest Rd
Wayne, PA 19087
Contact: Sharon Levitch
Tel: 610-724-4896
Email: sharon@acslearning.com
Website: www.acslearning.com
Bundle learning & development solutions. (Woman, estab 1993, empl 1, sales $1,500,000, cert: WBENC)

8213 Clarity Concepts Inc.
240 Dechert Dr
Gulph Mills, PA 19406
Contact: Jane Downey President
Tel: 610-825-3705
Email: janedowney@clarityconceptsinc.com
Website: www.clarityconceptsinc.com
Customized training programs.Leadship training. Personal branding.Team development.Risk management services. (Woman, estab 1996, empl 2, sales $220,000, cert: WBENC)

8214 Evolve Advisors I, LLC
85 Overhill Rd
Bala Cynwyd, PA 19004
Contact: Peri Higgins President
Tel: 610-420-5535
Email: phiggins@evolveadvisors.com
Website: www.evolveadvisors.com
Management consulting, assess, baseline, restructure & redesign business processes. (Woman/AA, estab 2012, empl 3, sales $108,000, cert: NMSDC, WBENC)

8215   Innovative Business Products & Services, LLC
       514 Firethorne Dr
       Monroeville, PA 15146
       Contact: Harvey Smith, Sr. CEO
       Tel: 412-894-3132
       Email: ibpshssr@outlook.com
       Website: www.artistecard.com/ibps
Diversity, inclusion & sensitivity training, recruiting diversity talent services; diversity website review; diversity mission/vision statement development; & re-entry of ex-offenders into job market services. (Woman/AA, estab 2015, empl 7, sales , cert: NMSDC)

8216   KnowledgeStart, Inc.
       300 King St
       Pottstown, PA 19464
       Contact: Bryan Yingst Internet Dir
       Tel: 610-650-0448
       Email: byingst@knowledgestart.com
       Website: www.knowledgestart.com
Diversity & Inclusion training. (Minority, estab 2001, empl 12, sales $850,000, cert: NMSDC)

8217   Lapine Group, Inc.
       8200 Greensboro Dr Ste 900
       McLean, PA 22102
       Contact: Judy Honig Managing Partner
       Tel: 703-940-6005
       Email: lapineinfor@lapinegroup.com
       Website: www.lapinegroup.com
Management consulting. (Woman, estab 2006, empl 10, sales $3,770,000, cert: WBENC)

8218   Lima Consulting Group, LLC
       40 Lloyd Ave Ste 108B
       Malvern, PA 19335
       Contact: Paul Lima Managing Partner
       Tel: 212-671-0309
       Email: plima@limaconsulting.com
       Website: www.LimaConsulting.com
Administrative Management & General Management Consulting, Marketing Consulting, Process, Physical Distribution & Logistics Consulting. (Hisp, estab 2004, empl 26, sales $739,087, cert: NMSDC)

8219   Quacoapit LLC
       7121 Lynford St
       Philadelphia, PA 19149
       Contact: Chea Kunwon CEO
       Tel: 267-315-5147
       Email: ckunwon@quacoapit.com
       Website: www.quacoapit.com
Quality & Compliance Consulting Services. (AA, estab 2017, empl 3, sales , cert: NMSDC)

8220   Quality Solutions Now, Inc.
       3251 Olympic Dr
       Emmaus, PA 18049
       Contact: Brette Travaglio President
       Tel: 610-462-4090
       Email: brette@qualitysolutionsnow.com
       Website: www.qualitysolutionsnow.com
Strategic, on-demand support & tactical project management svcs, product launch, regulatory compliance, large-scale change, process improvement. (Woman, estab 2004, empl 1, sales $2,064,000, cert: NWBOC)

8221   Sustainable Solutions Corporation
       155 Railroad Plaza Ste 203
       Royersford, PA 19468
       Contact: Tara Radzinski CEO
       Tel: 610-569-1047
       Email: tara@sustainablesolutionscorporation.com
       Website: www.sustainablesolutionscorporation.com
Sustainable Buildings & Operations, Corporate Sustainability, Training & Education, Seminars. (Woman, estab 2001, empl 16, sales $882,045, cert: WBENC)

8222   Talson Solutions, LLC
       41 N. 3rd St
       Philadelphia, PA 19106
       Contact: Robert S. Bright President
       Tel: 215-592-9634
       Email: rbright@talsonsolutions.com
       Website: www.talsonsolutions.com
Independent contract audits & compliance reviews, project risk analysis, due diligence services & project reporting. (AA, estab 2001, empl 4, sales $330,000, cert: NMSDC)

8223   TayganPoint Consulting Group
       1118 General Washington Memorial Blvd. Ste 210
       Washington Crossing, PA 08977
       Contact: CEO
       Tel: 215-302-2500
       Email: info@tayganpoint.com
       Website: www.tayganpoint.com
Consulting services: business process improvement, strategy development & execution, change management & communications, program management. (Woman, estab 2009, empl 69, sales $18,700,000, cert: WBENC)

8224   The Claiborne Consulting Group, Inc.
       1800 JFK Blvd, Ste 300
       Philadelphia, PA 19103
       Contact: Julian Gray VP HR, Staffing GM
       Tel: 914-388-4165
       Email: julian.gray@claibornecg.com
       Website: www.claibornecg.com
Management Consulting Services: Business Process Re-engineering, Business Case Development, Software Selection, Organization Change Management, Technical Content Writing, Startup Consultation, Digital Brand Management. (AA, As-Pac, estab 2015, empl 10, sales , cert: NMSDC)

8225   Veris Associates, Inc. dba VerisVisalign
       PO Box 245
       West Point, PA 19486
       Contact: Trisha Daly Office Mgr
       Tel: 267-649-5007
       Email: trishadaly@verisvisalign.com
       Website: www.verisvisalign.com
Consulting & training: process engineering, compliance consulting & corporate learning. (Woman, estab 2003, empl 38, sales $3,500,000, cert: State, WBENC)

8226 XCELLAS, LLC
275 Dilworth Ln
Langhorne, PA 19047
Contact: Maria T. Alvarez CEO
Tel: 215-287-9488
Email: maria.alvarez@xcellas.com
Website: www.xcellas.com
Consulting assessment & requirements, project management solution strategies, implementation & optimization. (Minority, Woman, estab 2013, empl 10, sales $1,308,715, cert: State, NMSDC, WBENC)

Puerto Rico

8227 Development Management & Consulting Group, Inc.
PO Box 142343
Arecibo, PR 00614
Contact: Eduardo Hernandez Principal Engineer
Tel: 787-897-0830
Email: eduardo.hernandez@dmcginc.com
Website: www.dmcginc.com
Validation Master Planning/Management, Commissioning & Qualification (C&Q), Decommissioning & Records Management, GMP Documentation Review / Generation, Cleaning & Process/Packaging Validation. (Hisp, estab 2000, empl 44, sales $4,089,547, cert: NMSDC)

8228 ECHO Consulting Group
PMB 274 200 Ave. Rafael Cordero Ste 140
Caguas, PR 00907
Contact: Sales
Tel: 787-226-6803
Email: plx-puertorico@pharmalex.com
Website: www.echo-cg.com
Project Management, Process Validation, Cleaning Validation, Equipment/Systems/Utilities Validation, Computer Validation, Packaging Process Validation, Standard Operating Procedures, Regulatory Compliance. (Woman/Hisp, estab 2002, empl 20, sales $2,212,776, cert: NMSDC)

8229 Impactivo LLC
PMB 140 1357 Ashford Ave
San Juan, PR 00907
Contact: Maria Fernanda Levis-Peralta CEO
Tel: 787-993-1508
Email: maria.levis@gmail.com
Website: www.impactivo.com
Systems Research, Policy Analysis, Strategic Planning & Financial Sustainability, Community Health Needs Assessment, Strategic Planning, Data Driven Decision Making, Project Planning, Technical Assistance, Performance Improvement. (Minority, Woman, estab 2010, empl 5, sales $ 0, cert: NMSDC)

8230 Integrated Management & Controls, Inc.
PO Box 229
Manati, PR 00674
Contact: Ismael Jaime President
Tel: 787-462-4739
Email: ismael.jaime@imanagementcontrols.com
Website: www.imanagementcontrols.com
Program Management, Portfolio Management, Project Management, Construction Management, Project Controls, Cost Control, Planning, Scheduling, Document & Contract Management, Engineering, Design, Qualification Schedule, Design Schedules. (Hisp, estab 2014, empl 3, sales $390,000, cert: NMSDC)

8231 Process Excellence & Engineering Consultants Inc
Zona Industrial Las Palmas Calle 4, Edificio, Ste 8
Catano, PR 00962
Contact: Michael Garcia Business Devel Dir
Tel: 787-565-9970
Email: info@peec-inc.com
Website: www.peec-inc.com
Six Sigma, Process Excellence, Lean Manufacturing, Validation, IQ, OQ, PQ, CAPA, Installation Qualification, Operational Qualification, Process Qualification, Commissioning, Computer Systems (Hisp, estab 2006, empl 25, sales $400,000, cert: NMSDC)

Rhode Island

8232 Granger Warburton Consulting, LLC
79 West St
East Greenwich, RI 02818
Contact: Bethany Warburton Principal Consultant
Tel: 401-965-1288
Email: bethany@grangerwarburton.com
Website: www.grangerwarburton.com
Learning management system design & deployment, elearning creation, software application development, project management, business analysis, change management, documentation & process design. (Woman, estab 2013, empl 2, sales $127,000, cert: State)

South Carolina

8233 180 Management Group, LLC
301 Halton Rd, C-2
Greenville, SC 29607
Contact: Miriam Dicks CEO
Tel: 864-605-7111
Email: mdicks@180managementgroup.com
Website: www.180managementgroup.com
Healthcare management support services. (Woman/AA, estab 2014, empl 4, sales , cert: State)

8234 C E McKenzie & Associates, LLC
724 S Shelmore Blvd Ste 100
Mount Pleasant, SC 29464
Contact: Janice Timpson Office Mgr
Tel: 843-849-1122
Email: jtimpson@cemallc.com
Website: www.cemallc.com
Program Administration and General Management Consultant Services. (AA, estab 2000, empl 35, sales $1,900,000, cert: 8(a))

8235 DESA, Inc
400 Percival Rd
Columbia, SC 29206
Contact: Diane Sumpter CEO
Tel: 803-256-3212
Email: dianes@desainc.com
Website: www.desainc.com
Conference management, construction management, facilities management, business services. (Woman/AA, estab 1986, empl 75, sales $1,811,901, cert: State)

PROFESSIONAL SERVICES: Management Consulting

8236 Elevate USA Inc
509 Colony Dr
Ridgeland, SC 29936
Contact: Delvon Survine President
Tel: 843-441-6478
Email: delvon@elevate4success.com
Website: www.elevate4success.com
Workforce management, training, and consulting, customized solutions, interactive training, executive coaching, account management, and online learning solution delivery. (Woman, estab 2008, empl 12, sales $600,000, cert: State, WBENC)

8237 Sharp Business Consulting Services LLC
1320 Main St Ste 300
Columbia, SC 29210
Contact: Mitchell Wyatt CEO
Tel: 803-600-7941
Email: mitchell.wyatt@gmail.com
Website: www.sharpbusinessconsulting.com
Growth & market penetration, profitability, repeat clients, customer service & strong community presence. (AA, estab 2006, empl 23, sales $1,642,774, cert: State, 8(a))

Tennessee

8238 Delta Consulting Group, Inc
9033 Garden Arbor Dr. Ste 210
Germantown, TN 38138
Contact: Tina DeCosta-Fortune CEO
Tel: 901-473-1708
Email: tdfortune@dcgmemphis.com
Website: www.dcgmemphis.com
Business management, technology consulting & resource management services. (Woman/Hisp, estab 2003, empl 17, sales $2,670,000, cert: State)

8239 PEOPLE3, Inc.
91 Antioch Pike, Ste 603
Nashville, TN 37211
Contact: Candace Warner CEO
Tel: 615-340-6896
Email: candace@people3.co
Website: www.people3.co
Provides diversity and inclusion training, workshops, and inclusion-centered consulting. (Woman, estab 2016, empl 5, sales , cert: WBENC)

8240 Performance Consulting Group, Inc.
100 Saddle Springs Blvd Ste 100
Thompsons Station, TN 37179
Contact: Marcy Willerton VP
Tel: 303-709-3889
Email: mwillerton@eperformax.com
Website: www.eperformax.com
Provide customer service & BPO to support English-speaking customers from the US, Canada & Australia. (Woman, estab 2000, empl 6000, sales $65,900,000, cert: WBENC)

8241 Remnant Management Group Inc.
2550 Meridian Blvd Ste 200
Franklin, TN 37067
Contact: Stephanie Beard CEO
Tel: 615-403-1567
Email: info@remnantgroup.com
Website: www.theremnantgroup.com
Employee development training & construction management services, leadership training & development, workforce development, curriculum selection & customization, construction management workforce development. (Woman/AA, estab 2006, empl 5, sales , cert: State)

Texas

8242 Accendo International, LLC
4535 Shetland Ste 300
Houston, TX 77027
Contact: Spencer Bynes Managing Partner
Tel: 800-656-1788
Email: erin@accendointernational.com
Website: www.AccendoInternational.com
Executive Coaching, Career Development, Organizational Development, Leadership Development, Team Building, Workforce Planning, Sales Training, Recruitment Strategy. (Woman, estab 2009, empl 6, sales , cert: WBENC)

8243 Access Sciences Corporation
1900 West Loop South Ste 1450
Houston, TX 77027
Contact: Todd Brown
Tel: 713-664-4357
Email: tbrown@accesssciences.com
Website: www.accesssciences.com
Information & records mgmt, enterprise content mgmt & regulatory compliance, information management consulting & outsourcing. (Woman, estab 1985, empl 62, sales $ 0, cert: State, WBENC)

8244 AHRMDCO International LLC
14405 Walters Road Ste 1002
Houston, TX 77014
Contact: Roderick Lemon President
Tel: 713-589-3688
Email: rlemon@ahrmdcoint.com
Website: www.ahrmdcoint.com
Organizational development: customer service, time mgmt, partenering & team building, supervisor, executive coaching, project mgmt, web & graphic design, employee assessment surveys & interviewing techniques. (AA, estab 2002, empl 20, sales , cert: State, NMSDC)

8245 Alexander and Davis Consulting
5927 Almeda Rd Unit 21405
Houston, TX 77004
Contact: Ranessa Davis CEO
Tel: 713-232-0455
Email: info@alexanderanddavis.com
Website: www.AlexanderAndDavis.com
Engineering, project management, marketing, sales and business management. (AA, estab 2014, empl 15, sales , cert: City)

PROFESSIONAL SERVICES: Management Consulting

8246 Alfa Management Solutions LLC
1228 Grant Ave
Lantana, TX 76226
Contact: Frank Wilson Managing Dir
Tel: 214-642-5907
Email: fwilson@aflams.com
Website: www.alfams.com
Critical Path Method Scheduling & Control, Project & Program Management Support, Develop, Implement & Monitor Schedule, Report Progression of Program/ Projects. (AA, estab 2007, empl 2, sales $313,500, cert: 8(a))

8247 Austin Texas Mediators LLC
4500 Williams Dr. Ste 212-111
Georgetown, TX 78633
Contact: Barbara Allen Owner
Tel: 512-966-9222
Email: info@motexas.com
Website: www.mediatorsoftexas.com
Train the trainer; sensitivity training; sexual harassment in the workplace training; non-confrontational communication skills training; conflict resolution in the work place. (Woman, estab 2014, empl 15, sales , cert: State, WBENC)

8248 Beacon Training Services Inc.
1229 Mohawk Trail
Richardson, TX 75080
Contact: Diana Stein Managing Principal
Tel: 972-404-0069
Email: diana@beacontraining.com
Website: www.beacontraining.com
Computer/technical, management/supervisory, professional development & project management training. (Woman, estab 1987, empl 4, sales $1,000,000, cert: State, WBENC)

8249 Brittain-Kalish Group, LLC
PO Box 8577
Fort Worth, TX 76124
Contact: Heather Randolph Consultant
Tel: 817-991-0705
Email: bkg@theupconsultants.com
Website: www.brittainkalishgroup.com
Management consulting firm comprised of trusted advisors, valued resources and trainers who strategically collaborate to create optimal results in a timely manner. (Woman, estab 2010, empl 3, sales , cert: WBENC)

8250 Caldwell Everson PLLC
2777 Allen Pkwy, Ste 950
Houston, TX 77019
Contact: Faye Caldwell Managing Partner
Tel: 713-654-3000
Email: fcaldwell@caldwelleverson.com
Website: www.caldwelleverson.com
Management employment, drug-testing, commercial, product liability & general civil litigation. (Woman, estab 1997, empl 6, sales $940,180, cert: State, WBENC)

8251 Career Management International, Inc.
4801 Woodway Dr Ste 300 East
Houston, TX 77056
Contact: Jim Tye CEO
Tel: 713-623-8780
Email: jimt@careermanagement.com
Website: www.careermanagement.com
Career transition & outplacement; training; team building & organizational development. (Woman, estab 1975, empl 18, sales $3,000,000, cert: City, WBENC)

8252 Deirdre Sanborn & Associates
4321 Bretton Bay Lane
Dallas, TX 75287
Contact: Deirdre Sanborn Owner
Tel: 214-308-1408
Email: deirdre@deirdresanborn.com
Website: www.deirdresanborn.com
Executive Coaching, Leadership Coaching, Team Integration, Team Management & Strategic consulting. (Woman, estab 2014, empl 3, sales , cert: WBENC)

8253 DiversityInPromotions, Inc.
5057 Keller Springs Rd Ste 300
Addison, TX 75001
Contact: Rodney Woods
Tel: 469-718-5589
Email: rwoods@diversityinpromotions.com
Website: www.diversityinpromotions.com
Program Assessment, Strategic Planning, Policy Development, Metrics Development, Communication Plan (Internal & External), Mentor/Protege Development, Government Reporting (Subcontract Plan). (AA, estab 1998, empl 18, sales $1,200,000, cert: State, NMSDC)

8254 D'Onofrio Consulting Partners
1700 Post Oak Blvd
Houston, TX 77056
Contact: Margaret D'Onofrio Principal
Tel: 713-963-3673
Email: margaret@donofrioconsultingpartners.com
Website: www.donofrioconsultingpartners.com
Coaching for individuals, teams & organizations. (Woman, estab 2007, empl 1, sales $1,168,885, cert: WBENC, NWBOC)

8255 Dramatic Conclusions, LLC
3900 Vitruvian Way Ste 231
Addison, TX 75001
Contact: Pam Boyd Owner
Tel: 469-855-0543
Email: pam@dramaticconclusions.com
Website: www.dramaticconclusions.com
Management & employee training & consulting. (Woman, estab 1999, empl 1, sales , cert: State, WBENC)

8256 FFG Strategic Consulting LLC
363 N. Houston Pkwy E Ste 1100
Houston, TX 77060
Contact: Colette Lewis
Tel: 832-412-2524
Email: colette.lewis@ffgsconsulting.com
Website: www.ffgsconsulting.com
Program/project management, engineering consulting, technical resources, project planning, construction management, project scheduling, project controls, system engineering, six sigma methodology analysis, mechanical engineering. (Woman/AA, estab 2011, empl 5, sales , cert: State, NMSDC, WBENC)

8257 Hybrid Teams, Inc.
3023 Cape Buffalo Trail
Frisco, TX 75034
Contact: Mac Choi President
Tel: 847-530-9034
Email: info@hybridteams.com
Website: www.hybridteams.com
Enterprise content management professional services, document management, consulting services. (As-Pac, estab 2006, empl 3, sales $306,000, cert: NMSDC)

PROFESSIONAL SERVICES: Management Consulting

8258 JFE International Consultants, Inc.
18705 Stoneridge Dr
Dallas, TX 75252
Contact: J. Francisco Escobar President
Tel: 214-728-6903
Email: francisco@jfeintl.com
Website: www.jfeintl.com
Management consulting, contract diagnostics, compensation principles, negotiations, performance evaluations & measurements, internal/external process audits. (Hisp, estab 2003, empl 1, sales $214,595, cert: NMSDC)

8259 Jill Hickman Companies
1721 Palomino Ln
Kingwood, TX 77339
Contact: Jill Hickman President
Tel: 281-358-8580
Email: jill@jillhickman.com
Website: www.jillhickman.com
Training & development services: leadership, supervision, consultative sales, customer service & team building, pre-employment assessment, executive advisement, strategic planning. (Minority, Woman, estab 1998, empl 1, sales $141,956, cert: WBENC)

8260 Languages Houston
1001 S Dairy Ashford Ste 100
Houston, TX 77077
Contact: Elena Tsilina CEO
Tel: 832-359-4226
Email: info@languageshouston.com
Website: www.languageshouston.com
Foreign language classes & translation services. (Woman, estab 2015, empl 20, sales , cert: State, WBENC)

8261 Lone Star Interpreters LLC
2800 Post Oak Blvd, Ste 1400 Ste 4100
Houston, TX 77056
Contact: Marie Mills CEO
Tel: 832-399-2100
Email: marie.mills@lonestarinterpreters.com
Website: www.lonestarinterpreters.com
Language services in over 200 languages: Translation & Localization, Transcription, Interpretation: On Site, Telephonic & Video, Voice Prompt Translating, Voice Prompt Recording. (Woman/AA, estab 2007, empl 40, sales $2,480,000, cert: State)

8262 Michael Resource Group LLC
1325 Daja Lane Ste 604
Grand Prairie, TX 75050
Contact: Brandon Russell Sales
Tel: 888-313-8688
Email: brussell@mrgroupllc.com
Website: www.mrgroupllc.com
Management Consulting. (AA, estab 2014, empl 4, sales $100,000, cert: State, NMSDC)

8263 Mind The Gap, LLC
901 Parkwood Ct
McKinney, TX 75070
Contact: Beth Anagnos Principal
Tel: 314-378-6426
Email: betha@mindthegapcoaching.com
Website: www.mindthegapcoaching.com
Leadership coaching, customized coaching programs for all levels of leadership. (Woman, estab 2007, empl 5, sales , cert: WBENC)

8264 Mohr Partners, Inc.
14643 Dallas Pkwy Ste 1000
Dallas, TX 75254
Contact: Robert Shibuya CEO
Tel: 214-907-8094
Email: robert.shibuya@mohrpartners.com
Website: www.mohrpartners.com
Portfolio management, lease administration, horizon business intelligence, research and site selection, incentive practices, and project management. (As-Pac, estab 1986, empl 120, sales $29,056,140, cert: NMSDC)

8265 Niche Assurance LLC
9894 Bissonnet St
Houston, TX 77036
Contact: Peter Kiilu
Tel: 281-636-2749
Email: peter.kiilu@nicheconsult.net
Website: www.nicheconsult.net
Financial & IT risk management, business performance improvement, Internal control design & implementation, Sarbanes-Oxley Act compliance, FCPA compliance, internal audits, I.T. audits, cyber security, SAP security. (AA, estab 2007, empl 4, sales $150,000, cert: State, NMSDC)

8266 Obsidian Technical Communications, Ltd.
3522 White Oak Dr
Houston, TX 77007
Contact: Erik Pettine Dir of Sales
Tel: 281-732-5940
Email: erikp@obsidianlearning.com
Website: www.obsidianlearning.com
Consulting: job performance, end-user performance support, custom training strategy & development, documentation, e-learning, knowledge mgmt & change mgmt. (Woman, estab 1998, empl 26, sales $3,700,000, cert: WBENC)

8267 PABULUM Consulting, LLC
1002 Gemini St Ste 225D
Houston, TX 77058
Contact: Ferrel Bonner CEO
Tel: 713-538-4719
Email: ferrelbonner@pabulumconsulting.com
Website: www.pabulumconsulting.com
Military Intelligence, Security & Emergency Management, Special Operations & Tactical Communications. (AA, estab 2007, empl 4, sales $150,000, cert: State, City, 8(a))

8268 Peck Training Group LLC
907 Glen Rose Dr
Allen, TX 75013
Contact: Holly St John Peck President
Tel: 214-495-9499
Email: holly@pecktraining.com
Website: www.pecktraining.com
Professional development training & coaching. (Woman, estab 1985, empl 2, sales $325,000, cert: WBENC)

PROFESSIONAL SERVICES: Management Consulting

8269 Phoenix Translations
2110 White Horse Trail
Austin, TX 78757
Contact: Deborah Wright CEO
Tel: 512-343-8389
Email: service@phoenixtranslations.com
Website: www.phoenixtranslations.com
Technical translation services. (Woman/AA, Hisp, estab 2000, empl , sales $2,500,000, cert: State, WBENC)

8270 Phronetik
5851 Legacy Circle 6th Fl
Plano, TX 75024
Contact: Tania Martin-Mercado President
Tel: 877-844-3575
Email: taniame@phronetik.com
Website: www.phronetik.com
Research & Development, Technical Support, Interoperability, Patient Portal Development, Privacy & Security, Clinical Documentation, Mobile Health, Decision Support Systems, Telemedicine, Custom Development. (Minority, Woman, estab 2013, empl 11, sales , cert: WBENC)

8271 Possible Missions, Inc.
150 W Parker Rd., Ste 602
Houston, TX 77076
Contact: Paula Mendoza CEO
Tel: 713-271-3746
Email: paula@possiblemissions.com
Website: www.possiblemissions.com
Project management solutions, plan, execute & complete projects within budget and on schedule. (Minority, Woman, estab 2001, empl 33, sales $2,100,000, cert: State, City, NMSDC, WBENC, 8(a))

8272 Proje Inc.
6942 FM 1960 E, Ste 362
Humble, TX 77346
Contact: Violet Stephens President
Tel: 832-293-5633
Email: info@projeinc.com
Website: www.projeinc.com
Project Management Leadership & analytical thinking, Crisis Management, Integration & Consolidation, Risk Analysis & Adjustment, Medicare Advantage. (Woman, estab 2004, empl 38, sales $8,800,119, cert: WBENC)

8273 Risk Mitigation Worldwide
9800 Northwest Frwy Ste 600
Houston, TX 77092
Contact: Michele Ward VP Business Dev
Tel: 713-864-9997
Email: michele@legalwatch.com
Website: www.legalwatch.com
Training & consulting services: communications to minimize & avoid potential lawsuits, claims & internal disputes. (Woman/AA, estab 1997, empl 6, sales $ 0, cert: State, NMSDC, WBENC)

8274 RWG Consulting, Inc.
2560 King Arthur Blvd. Ste 124-34
Dallas, TX 75056
Contact: Anton Gates Managing Partner
Tel: 972-386-7601
Email: agates@rwgconsulting.com
Website: www.rwgconsulting.com
Training, Instructional Design, Project Management, Organizational Change Management, SAP Training Development, Staff Augmentation, Business Process Optimization, Contract to Hire. (AA, estab 2013, empl 15, sales $900,000, cert: State, NMSDC)

8275 Sales Trac Coaching & Mgmt Development
10012 SIlvertree Dr
Dallas, TX 75243
Contact: David Tyson CEO
Tel: 214-215-1108
Email: davidt@salestrac.net
Website: www.salestrac.net
Leadership Development & Performance Management, Management training, Sales Management training, sales training, service focused training, customer service training
Generational training. (AA, estab 2007, empl 1, sales , cert: State, NMSDC)

8276 Seilevel Partners, LP
3410 Far West Blvd Ste 265
Austin, TX 78731
Contact: Christine Wollmuth
Tel: 512-527-9952
Email: cwollmuth@seilevel.com
Website: www.seilevel.com
Business analysis consulting, business analyst staffing, assessment, mentoring & training. (As-Ind, estab 2000, empl 30, sales , cert: State, NMSDC)

8277 Sirius Solutions, LLLP
1233 West Loop South Ste 1800
Houston, TX 77027
Contact: Kathy Pattillo Dir Business Devel
Tel: 713-888-0488
Email: kpattillo@sirsol.com
Website: www.sirsol.com
Management consulting: finance, internal audit, information technology, accounting, risk, operations, process improvement, strategy & tax. (Woman, estab 1998, empl 230, sales , cert: WBENC, NWBOC)

8278 Taylor Smith Consulting, LLC
16800 Greenspoint Park Dr, STE 155N
Houston, TX 77060
Contact: Tracy Smith CEO
Tel: 713-937-3111
Email: staylor@taylorsmithconsulting.com
Website: www.taylorsmithconsulting.com
Business Development, Training, Call/Customer Service Center Operations, Staffing, Contracting Services. (Woman/AA, estab 2006, empl 1200, sales $18,001,317, cert: State, City, NMSDC)

PROFESSIONAL SERVICES: Management Consulting

8279 The Conxsis Group, Inc.
1910 McCartney Court
Arlington, TX 76012
Contact: Abdul Shakir President
Tel: 817-348-0060
Email: ashakir@conxsis.com
Website: www.conxsis.com
Environmental consulting, financial, economic, business consulting, large & small business teaming, M/WBE Programs, marketing & business development. (AA, estab 2002, empl 16, sales , cert: State)

8280 The I4 Group Consulting, LLC
1206 Rio Grande Ct
Allen, TX 75013
Contact: Charles Maddox Sr. Business Dir
Tel: 612-207-2751
Email: charles.sr@thei4group.com
Website: www.thei4group.com
Training & coaching for Scaled Agile, Agile, and IT business process improvement, Lean Six Sigma, project management training & certification. (AA, estab 2013, empl 42, sales $8,250,120, cert: NMSDC, 8(a))

8281 The Tagos Group, LLC
8 E Greenway Plaza Ste 1340
Houston, TX 77046
Contact: Maria Traver Office Mgr
Tel: 713-850-7031
Email: mtraver@tagosgroup.com
Website: www.tagosgroup.com
Business consulting, services & products: supply chain mgmt, transportation & logistics mgmt, speciality maintenance & call center operations. (AA, estab 2007, empl 9, sales $500,000, cert: NMSDC)

8282 Tray-Tec, Inc.
2598 Wilson Rd
Humble, TX 77396
Contact: Darrell Fowler VP
Tel: 281-441-7314
Email: traytec@traytec.com
Website: www.traytec.com
Installers of process equipment such as trays, packings, distributors in towers, reactors, and drums. We perform installation and repairs of nozzles, and we perform vessel shell repairs. (Hisp, estab 2005, empl 20, sales $10,000,000, cert: State)

Virginia

8283 3DIF LLC
47 E Queens Way Ste 204-C
Hampton, VA 23669
Contact: Indy Freeman CEO
Tel: 757-905-0631
Email: indy.freeman@3dif.co
Website: www.3dif.co
Professional & Management Consulting Services, Staff Augmentation and Job Placement Services, i3DReadiness Training & Custom Facilitation Solutions and Events Management & Custom Branded Products to individuals, businesses, organizations and local, state (Minority, Woman, estab 2011, empl 3, sales , cert: State)

8284 A. Reddix & Associates Inc.
1215 N Military Hwy, Ste 754
Norfolk, VA 23502
Contact: Contracts Dir
Tel: 757-410-7704
Email: info@ardx.net
Website: www.ardx.net
Workforce training & technical assistance, innovative information technology & security solutions & support, collaborative conferencing & events management, quality, compliance & revenue audits, policy documentation & management. (Minority, Woman, estab 2006, empl 105, sales , cert: State)

8285 AEi International LLC
7686 Richmond Hwy, Ste 118
Alexandria, VA 22306
Contact: Jenna Reese CEO
Tel: 410-988-3966
Email: jenna.reese@aeiintl.com
Website: www.aeiintl.com
Management consulting & technology, strategic consulting, digital experience & enterprise technology, staff augmentation. (Woman/AA, estab 2007, empl 12, sales $1,200,000, cert: 8(a))

8286 Aerobodies Fitness Company, Inc.
950 N Washington St Ste 311
Alexandria, VA 22314
Contact: CEO
Tel: 703-402-8477
Email: contact@aerobodies.com
Website: www.aerobodies.com
Program management services, acquisition support, organizational development, and occupational health services to federal and private sector agencies. (AA, estab 1997, empl 25, sales $750,000, cert: WBENC, 8(a))

8287 Assura, Inc.
7814 Carousel Ln, Ste 202
Richmnod, VA 23294
Contact: Karen Cole CEO
Tel: 804-672-8714
Email: karen.cole@assuraconsulting.com
Website: www.assurainc.com
Consulting: Governance, Risk & Compliance (GRC), Enterprise Risk Management (ERM), cyber-security, business continuity planning & Information Technology (IT) audit. (Woman, estab , empl , sales , cert: State, WBENC)

8288 Burton-Fuller Managment
4905 Radford Ave Ste 105
Richmond, VA 23230
Contact: Vicki Funk Office Mgr
Tel: 804-217-6380
Email: support@burtonfuller.com
Website: www.burtonfuller.com
Management consulting. (Woman, estab 1989, empl 5, sales $ 0, cert: State)

PROFESSIONAL SERVICES: Management Consulting

8289 C.W. Hines and Associates, Inc.
344 Churchill Cir, Sanctuary Bay
White Stone, VA 22578
Contact: Cheryl Hudson President
Tel: 804-435-8844
Email: turtlecwh@aol.com
Website: www.cwhinesassociates.org
Management training & consulting: performance excellence coaching, diversity, teambuilding, leadership development, communications, customer service, strategic thinking, strategic planning, supervisory effectiveness, executive coaching, mediation. (Woman/AA, estab , empl , sales $850,000, cert: State, City)

8290 Capitol Management Consulting Services, Inc.
1600 Chain Bridge Rd
McLean, VA 22101
Contact: Akshat Prasad President
Tel: 571-318-6404
Email: akshat@capitolmcs.com
Website: www.capitolmcs.com
Management consulting, organizational governance, performance optimization, strategy, technology, and training services. (Minority, estab 2011, empl 7, sales $687,678, cert: NMSDC, 8(a))

8291 DP Distribution & Consulting, LLC
12240 Hunting Horn Lane
Rockville, VA 23146
Contact: Darren Reeves President
Tel: 804-307-7706
Email: dreeves@dpdconline.com
Website: www.dpdconline.com/
Quality Assurance & Regulatory for Manufacturing, Auditing, 510K, FDA regulation. (Woman, estab 2000, empl 1, sales $300,000, cert: State)

8292 EMY Consulting LLC
13406 Poplar Woods
Chantillly, VA 20151
Contact: Elena Yearly President
Tel: 703-943-8129
Email: eyearly@emyconsulting.biz
Website: www.emyconsulting.biz
Management consulting solutions. (Woman, estab 2013, empl 1, sales $201,000, cert: State, WBENC)

8293 Evans Inc.
2750 Property Ave, Ste 425
Fairfax, VA 22031
Contact: Sue Evans Founder
Tel: 703-663-2480
Email: info@evansconsulting.com
Website: www.evansincorporated.com
Business process consulting, change mgmt & reengineering, enterprise IT investment analysis & integration, ethical leadership training, process & data modeling, performance mgmt, competency framework changes & development, user interface. (Woman, estab 1993, empl 10, sales $1,500,000, cert: WBENC)

8294 FM Solutions, PLLC
901 E Byrd St Ste 1210
Richmond, VA 23219
Contact: Wendy Henley Principal
Tel: 804-288-3173
Email: wendyh@fmsolutions-us.com
Website: www.fmsolutions-us.com
Project & program mgmt, facilities mgmt, consulting & supplemental staffing, space allocation analyses & programming, strategic space & facilities planning, relocation mgmt. (Woman, estab 2003, empl 4, sales $394,143, cert: State)

8295 Intelligent Decision Systems, Inc.
5870 Trinity Pkwy
Centreville, VA 20120
Contact: Joe Collins VP Business Devel
Tel: 703-766-9631
Email: bd@idsi.com
Website: www.idsi.com
Human Performance Management, Research, analysis & assessment studies. (Woman, estab 1995, empl 133, sales $15,000,000, cert: WBENC)

8296 KAPAX Solutions LLC
44308 Navajo Dr
Ashburn, VA 20147
Contact: Katrecia Nolen President
Tel: 571-239-0653
Email: katrecia.nolen@kapaxsolutions.com
Website: www.kapaxsolutions.com
Professional services & management consulting, strategic planning, system integration & project management support services. (Woman/AA, estab 2011, empl 1, sales , cert: State)

8297 KickStart Specialists, LLC
11809 Crown Prince Circle
Henrico, VA 23238
Contact: Robert Riley Principal
Tel: 855-454-2578
Email: rriley@kickstartspecialists.com
Website: www.kickstartspecialists.com
Leadership development & training; roles & responsibilities, business objectives, business case evaluation, teambuilding; project & program management consulting; project board training; health checks. (Woman, estab 2011, empl 2, sales , cert: State)

8298 Mindseeker, Inc.
20130 Lakeview Center Plaza, Ste 320
Ashburn, VA 20147
Contact: Cassie Kelly VP Client Services & Operations
Tel: 304-549-9281
Email: ckelly@mindseeker.com
Website: www.mindseeker.com
Information Technology, Financial, Clerical and Enterprise Performance Management services and solutions. (Woman, estab , empl 234, sales $2,000,000, cert: State, WBENC)

8299 OmniTek Consulting, Inc.
8260 Greensboro Dr Ste 120
McLean, VA 22102
Contact: Matthew Donahue GM
Tel: 240-344-7914
Email: support@omnitekconsulting.com
Website: www.omnitekconsulting.com/
Consulting, Contingent, and Professional Service Engagements: Program & Project Management, Business Process Management (BPM), Change Management & Training, Systems Implementation & Integration, Business Analytics & Data Management. (As-Pac, estab 2005, empl 41, sales $3,736,515, cert: NMSDC)

8300 Project Management and Consulting LLC
512 Lafayette Boulevard, Ste 2
Fredericksburg, VA 22401
Contact: Bryan Rock CEO
Tel: 800-971-3194
Email: brock@pmcllcva.com
Website: www.pmcva.com
Business management & consulting business consulting, minority-owned business consulting. (AA, estab 2007, empl 1, sales $195,000, cert: State)

8301 Savi Solutions, Inc.
8200 Greensboro Dr, Ste 900
McLean, VA 22102
Contact: Smita Iyer CEO
Tel: 571-258-7602
Email: siyer@savisolutions.biz
Website: www.savisolutions.biz
Strategic Planning, Program/Project Management, Merger & Acquisition Support, Systems Implementation (ERP/CRM/SCM), Cloud Based Implementation Solutions, Business Requirement Analysis, System Design and Development. (Minority, estab 2010, empl 3, sales $552,551, cert: WBENC)

8302 The Perspectives Group
7620 Little River Turnpike Ste 205
Annandale, VA 22003
Contact: Dir Business Dev
Tel: 703-837-1197
Email: info@theperspectivesgroup.com
Website: www.theperspectivesgroup.com
Public participation & outreach, advisory boards & governance, collaboration, facilitation, graphic design, mediation & dispute resolution, message development, policy development, process design, strategic planning, training & education. (Woman, estab 1991, empl 6, sales $990,000, cert: State)

8303 TMS Consulting LLC
2776 S Arlington Mill Dr Ste 114
Arlington, VA 22206
Contact: Tafadzwa Matinenga President
Tel: 703-864-9965
Email: info@tmsconsultingservices.us
Website: www.tmsconsultingservices.us
Global management consulting. (Woman/AA, estab 2015, empl 3, sales , cert: State)

8304 Visions2000 Inc.
312 Tides Run
Yorktown, VA 23692
Contact: Che Henderson VP
Tel: 757-898-5010
Email: che@visions2000inc.com
Website: www.visions2000inc.com
Consulting & training solutions: diversity, leadership, teambuilding, change management, life work planning & job search assistance. (Woman/AA, estab 1990, empl 2, sales , cert: NMSDC)

Washington

8305 ANOPS Limited
1420 Fifth Ave, Ste 2200
Seattle, WA 98101
Contact: Miriam Schwarz President
Tel: 206-219-1605
Email: anops@anops.com
Website: www.anops.com
Management consulting, project management, and talent placement solutions. (Woman/AA, estab 1999, empl 12, sales $967,830, cert: State)

8306 Blueprint Consulting Services, LLC
350 106th Ave NE, 2nd Fl
Bellevue, WA 98004
Contact: Ryan Neal President
Tel: - -
Email: ryanh@bpcs.com
Website: www.bpcs.com
Business management and technology solutions. (Nat Ame, estab 2013, empl 650, sales , cert: NMSDC)

8307 Brightwork Consulting, Inc.
200 W Mercer St, Ste 108
Seattle, WA 98119
Contact: Shannan Epps CEO
Tel: 206-659-0643
Email: info@brightworkhealthit.com
Website: www.brightworkhealthit.com
Risk management, solution deployment, smart decisions, and change management. (Woman, estab 2017, empl 15, sales $4,000,000, cert: WBENC)

8308 Cascade Management and Consulting
26211 178th St SE
Monroe, WA 98272
Contact: Amy Hoyt Owner
Tel: 206-778-4322
Email: info@cascademgtconsulting.com
Website: www.cascademgtconsulting.com
Project & program management, IT & global rollouts, business continuity/disaster recovery, brand integrity, change management & collaborative communications. (Woman, estab 2015, empl 1, sales , cert: State)

8309 Eagle Hill Consulting
10400 NE 4th St
Bellevue, WA 98004
Contact: Jordan Henry Dir Seattle Office
Tel: 301-980-2910
Email: jhenry@eaglehillconsulting.com
Website: www.eaglehillconsulting.com/seattle
Management consulting services, change management, organizational design, human capital management, strategy, and business process improvement. (Woman, estab 2003, empl 185, sales $30,000,000, cert: WBENC, NWBOC)

8310 Groundwork Tech, LLC
      PO Box 489
      Bellevue, WA 98004
      Contact: Jeff Foster Principal
      Tel: 425-209-0588
      Email: jeff@groundworktech.com
      Website: www.groundworktech.com
Professional Management Services, consulting services & resources to enhance, re-engineer & develop customer business. (AA, estab 2014, empl 3, sales $180,000, cert: State)

8311 Humbition Consulting, LLC
      4123 NE 9th Pl
      Renton, WA 98059
      Contact: Steven Sun Managing Partner
      Tel: 206-618-2080
      Email: ssun@humbitionconsulting.com
      Website: www.humbitionconsulting.com
Program Leadership, Innovation & Planning, Technology Operations, Financial & Insights. (Woman/As-Pac, estab 2019, empl 5, sales $1,491,154, cert: NMSDC, WBENC)

8312 Lions & Tigers
      PO Box 46386
      Seattle, WA 98146
      Contact: Ashley Jude COO
      Tel: 503-610-8684
      Email: ashjud@lions-tigers.com
      Website: www.lions-tigers.com
Project management, communications, marketing, workforce design solutions. (Woman, estab 2018, empl 23, sales $13,022,532, cert: WBENC)

8313 Rafael A Colon Voices Internacional
      5145 Illahee Ln NE
      Olympia, WA 98516
      Contact: Rafael Colon President
      Tel: 360-459-7228
      Email: rafael@voicesinternacional.com
      Website: www.voicesinternacional.com
Consulting, training, organizational operations & administration, leadership & management development, program development & management, communication effectiveness & meeting facilitation, peak performance & team unity practices. (Hisp, estab 1994, empl 1, sales $217,500, cert: State, NMSDC)

8314 Rivet Consulting LLC
      2212 Queen Anne Ave N, Ste 127
      Seattle, WA 98109
      Contact: Courtney Klein Managing Partner
      Tel: 888-201-1422
      Email: courtney@rivetconsulting.com
      Website: www.rivetconsulting.com
Project Managers, Program Managers, Marketing Managers, Marketing Coordinators, Financial Analysts, Business Analysts, Social Media Experts, Search Marketing Experts, Data Analysts, Market Researchers, Marketing Communications Managers. (Woman, estab 2013, empl 30, sales , cert: WBENC)

Wisconsin

8315 Advantage Research, Inc.
      W162N11840 Fond Du Lac Ave
      Germantown, WI 53022
      Contact: Adam Hale Dir of Research & Business Dev
      Tel: 262-502-7001
      Email: ahale@advantageresearchinc.com
      Website: www.advantageresearchinc.com
Awareness, attitude and usage studies; Customer satisfaction, retention and loyalty studies. (Woman, estab 1992, empl 7, sales $ 0, cert: WBENC)

8316 Cross Management Services, Inc.
      1815 N 4th St
      Milwaukee, WI 53212
      Contact: Demeke Meri President
      Tel: 414-449-4920
      Email:
      Website: www.cross-management.com
Supplier & workforce diversity consulting, real estate development management. (Woman/AA, estab 1999, empl , sales $436,000, cert: NMSDC)

8317 Urban Strategies US LLC DBA SMCG
      759 N Milwaukee St Ste 414
      Milwaukee, WI 53202
      Contact: Jim Milner CEO
      Tel: 414-221-9500
      Email: jmilner@sectormanagement.biz
      Website: www.sectormcg.com
Leadership development, assessing/shaping organizational culture, stretching leadership capacity & accelerating the development of those who follow through effective coaching. (AA, estab 2002, empl 3, sales , cert: State, NMSDC)

PROFESSIONAL SERVICES: Public Relations/Marketing

Provide services including business research and marketing plans, data collection and analysis, meeting planning, needs assessments, corporate imaging enhancement, focus groups, fundraising, technical writing, media relations, etc. NAICS Code 54

Alabama

8318 Marketry Inc.
      1630 29th Ct S
      Birmingham, AL 35209
      Contact: Gillian Waybright Business Mgr
      Tel: 205-802-7252
      Email: gwaybright@marketryinc.com
      Website: www.marketryinc.com
Qualitative marketing research: focus groups, ethnography, online discussions, online video focus groups, interviews, dyads, triads, observational research, ideation, shop-a-longs, online bulletin boards, video diaries. (Woman, estab 1995, empl 5, sales , cert: WBENC)

8319 PM Group, Inc.
      4324 Midmost Dr
      Mobile, AL 36685
      Contact: Juan Peasant
      Tel: 251-445-7804
      Email: juan@pmgroupnow.com
      Website: www.TheCultureExperts.com
Branding & Marketing, Social Media Marketing, creative & design development, print, web development & video production. (AA, estab 2004, empl 3, sales $226,910, cert: NMSDC)

Arizona

8320 Denise Meridith Consultants Inc.
      1201 E Palo Verde Dr
      Phoenix, AZ 85014
      Contact: Denise Meridith CEO
      Tel: 602-763-9900
      Email: denisemeridithconsultants@cox.net
      Website: www.denisemeridithconsultants.com
Public relations, marketing, lobbying, human resources management, training, organizational development. (Woman/AA, estab 2001, empl 1, sales , cert: City)

8321 EventPro Strategies, Inc.
      7373 N. Scottsdale Road, Ste B-120
      Scottsdale, AZ 85283
      Contact: Kelly Springs-Kelley Dir of Marketing
      Tel: 480-449-4100
      Email: kkelley@eventprostrategies.com
      Website: www.eventprostrategies.com
Marketing, public relations & promotional events. (Woman, estab 1999, empl 32, sales $6,700,000, cert: WBENC)

8322 Hospitality Solutions Corporation
      2937 East Broadway Rd
      Phoenix, AZ 85040
      Contact: Sheldon Ross President
      Tel: 813-538-0244
      Email: sross@hospitalitysolutionscorp.com
      Website: www.hospitalitysolutionscorp.com
Trade Show Displays & Event production. (AA, estab 2003, empl 2, sales $234,000, cert: NMSDC)

8323 JVJ Can 22 Corp
      3260 N Hayden, Ste 210
      Scottsdale, AZ 85251
      Contact: Michelle Candelaria CEO
      Tel: 480-626-7919
      Email: mc@cts10.com
      Website: www.CTS10.com
SEO Search Engine Optimization, Social Media Management, Reputation monitoring. (Minority, Woman, estab 2016, empl 7, sales , cert: NMSDC)

8324 Katherine Christensen & Associates, Inc.
      107 S Southgate Dr
      Chandler, AZ 85226
      Contact: Katherine Christensen, CMP, DMCP President
      Tel: 480-893-6110
      Email: kc@kc-a.com
      Website: www.kc-a.com
Meeting management, trade association management & public relations. (Woman, estab 1992, empl 12, sales $731,957, cert: WBENC)

8325 Morrissey & Associates, LLC
      PO Box 25967
      Scottsdale, AZ 85255
      Contact: Neysa Morrissey CEO
      Tel: 480-515-2688
      Email: admin@morrisseytravel.com
      Website: www.MorrisseyTravel.com
Meeting, Event & Travel, Site Research & Selection, Analysis & Cost Containment Solutions, Contract Negotiations & Risk Mitigation, Strategic Meetings Mgmt (SMM); Program Itinerary & Agenda Devel, Housing & Registration, Trade Show Mgmt. (Minority, Woman, estab 2007, empl 1, sales $151,168, cert: State, WBENC, 8(a))

8326 Scarritt Group
      7620 N Hartman Ln, Ste 100
      Tucson, AZ 85743
      Contact: Adrienne Williams CEO
      Tel: 520-529-0000
      Email: Edson.Ribeiro@scarrittgroup.com
      Website: www.scarrittgroup.com
Meeting planning: contract negotiations, budgeting, registration, invitations, online registration, confirmation & welcome packets, name badges, etc. (Woman, estab 2000, empl 23, sales $4,100,000, cert: WBENC)

8327 The Event Concierge
      3218 E Bell Rd, Ste 142
      Phoenix, AZ 85032
      Contact: Julie Wong President
      Tel: 602-569-5333
      Email: julie@eventconcierge.com
      Website: www.eventconcierge.com
Event Planning and Meeting Management. (Minority, Woman, estab 2005, empl 2, sales $330,029, cert: State, City, WBENC)

8328 The Translation Team
      4960 S Gilbert Rd, Ste 1-115
      Chandler, AZ 85249
      Contact: Micaela Novas Owner
      Tel: 720-394-0109
      Email: micaela.novas@thetranslationteam.com
      Website: www.thetranslationteam.com
Spanish translations, multicultural communication. (Woman/Hisp, estab 2014, empl 1, sales $936,000, cert: CPUC, WBENC)

PROFESSIONAL SERVICES: Public Relations/Marketing

California

8329 Acento Advertising, Inc.
11400 West Olympic Blvd 12th Fl
Los Angeles, CA 90064
Contact: Donnie Broxson CEO
Tel: 310-843-8300
Email: dbroxson@acento.com
Website: www.acento.com
Integrated marketing programs for the U.S. Hispanic & total market segments. (Hisp, estab 1983, empl 30, sales $32,067,933, cert: NMSDC, CPUC)

8330 Acme Arts Inc.
19709 Horseshoe Dr
Topanga, CA 90290
Contact: Scott Ferguson Partner
Tel: 310-455-1413
Email: scott@sferguson.com
Website: www.sferguson.com
Marketing communications services, copywriting, creative direction, strategic brand consulting, original music, complete production for educational & promotional corporate videos. (Minority, Woman, estab 1990, empl 2, sales $234,000, cert: CPUC, WBENC)

8331 Afaf Translations, LLC
15655 Liberty St
San Leandro, CA 94578
Contact: Afaf Steiert President
Tel: 510-684-4586
Email: afaf@afaftranslations.com
Website: www.afaftranslations.com
Translation, interpreting, voice-over, desktop publishing, transcription, localization, language proficiency evaluations & cultural consultation. (Woman/AA, estab 2004, empl 2, sales , cert: WBENC)

8332 AfterViolet Inc.
1100 Glendon Ave Ste 1715
Los Angeles, CA 90024
Contact: Christopher Bodmer Innovation Consultant
Tel: 917-331-5637
Email: cab@afterviolet.com
Website: www.afterviolet.com
Innovation & branding, Product, service & experience design, Marketing & innovation strategy, Graphic design services, Consumer research. (Hisp, estab 2013, empl 6, sales $243,857, cert: NMSDC)

8333 Alter Agents
617 S Olive St, Ste 1010
Los Angeles, CA 90014
Contact: Angela Woo Co-Founder
Tel: 213-612-0356
Email: angela@alteragents.com
Website: www.alteragents.com
Market research & brand strategy, brand building, targeting, marketing strategy/development, product development, shopper insights & in-market performance. (Woman, estab 2010, empl 10, sales , cert: NWBOC)

8334 AP42
2303 Camino Ramon, Ste 280
San Ramon, CA 94583
Contact: Imelda Alejandrino CEO
Tel: 925-901-1100
Email: info@ap42.com
Website: www.ap42.com
Create ads, direct marketing programs, website content, logo design, email blasts, collateral materials. (Woman/As-Pac, estab 2001, empl 7, sales $720,000, cert: WBENC, NMSDC)

8335 Artisan Creative Inc.
1830 Stoner Ave Ste 6
Los Angeles, CA 90025
Contact: Katty Douraghy President
Tel: 310-312-2062
Email: kattyd@artisancreative.com
Website: www.artisancreative.com
Design & development solutions: marketing, advertising, communications & production teams in the digital, broadcast, mobile & print space. (Woman, estab 1996, empl 15, sales $3,000,000, cert: WBENC)

8336 Bleu Marketing Solutions
101 Lucas Valley Road Ste 300
San Rafael, CA 94903
Contact: Jennifer Giordano Acct Dir
Tel: 415-345-3317
Email: jgiordano@bleusf.com
Website: www.bleumarketing.com
Direct marketing, strategy & consulting, media planning & procurement, design & creative implementation, marketing program systems & IT support. (Woman, estab 2001, empl 25, sales $2,500,000, cert: WBENC)

8337 Blue Beyond Consulting, Inc
20211 Patio Dr Ste 235
Castro Valley, CA 94546
Contact: Lynn Martin Head of Finance
Tel: 510-714-9879
Email: lynn@bluebeyondconsulting.com
Website: www.bluebeyondconsulting.com
Visual Communications Customization. (Woman, estab 2006, empl 75, sales , cert: WBENC)

8338 BrandGov
125 Humphrey Lane
Vallejo, CA 94591
Contact: K Patrice Williams President
Tel: 800-215-0280
Email: supplier@brandgov.com
Website: www.brandgov.com
Brand Strategy & Lobbying, Integrated Branding & Marketing Solutions, Supplier Diversity Outreach, Website & Mobile Application Development, Logo Development, Brochures, Graphic Designs, Technical Procurement. (Woman/AA, estab 2007, empl 4, sales , cert: NMSDC, CPUC)

8339 Briabe Media, Inc.
634A Venice Blvd
Venice, CA 90291
Contact: James Briggs CEO
Tel: 310-694-3283
Email: james.briggs@briabemedia.com
Website: www.briabemedia.com
Multicultural mobile marketing solutions, SMS & MMS campaigns, mobile advertising & mobile website development. (AA, Hisp, estab 2006, empl 15, sales $3,000,000, cert: NMSDC)

8340 Captura Group
408 Nutmeg St
San Diego, CA 92103
Contact: Walter Boza GM
Tel: 619-681-1856
Email: diversity@capturagroup.com
Website: www.capturagroup.com/
Strategic, data-driven consulting with digital first in-language and in-culture marketing services. (Hisp, estab 2001, empl 16, sales $4,800,000, cert: WBENC)

PROFESSIONAL SERVICES: Public Relations/Marketing

8341 CCS/PR, Inc.
2888 Loker Ave East Ste 316
Carlsbad, CA 92010
Contact: Gayle Mestel President
Tel: 760-929-7514
Email: gaylem@ccspr.com
Website: www.ccspr.com/
Marketing communications & services: case studies, magazine articles, press releases/kits, video scripts, website content, blogs, PPTs, newsletters, marketing collateral, testimonial quotes, brochures, pitches. (Woman, estab 1966, empl 6, sales $1,405,334, cert: WBENC)

8342 Chica Intelligente LLC
5757 Wilshire Blvd
Los Angeles, CA 90036
Contact: Katrina Jefferson Owner
Tel: 323-360-4191
Email: katrina@chicaintelligente.com
Website: www.chicaintelligente.com
Digital marketing, enhance or develop digital marketing programs through integrated experiential Marketing, online branding & increase target audience. (Woman/AA, Hisp, estab 2013, empl 2, sales , cert: CPUC)

8343 CLC Publicidad dba Sherpa Marketing Solutions
4528 Stern Ave
Sherman Oaks, CA 91423
Contact: Carlos Cordoba President
Tel: 818-635-7318
Email: ccordoba@sherpa-marketing.com
Website: www.sherpa-marketing.com/
Consumer research & insights into the Hispanic population, qualitative & quantitative research services. (Hisp, estab 1996, empl 5, sales $1,500,000, cert: State, CPUC)

8344 Coast to Coast Conferences & Events
100 W Broadway Ste 250
Long Beach, CA 90802
Contact: Michelle Manire President
Tel: 562-980-7566
Email: michelle@ctcconferences.com
Website: www.ctcconferences.com
Meeting & event management: site selection, contract negotiations, housing, on line registration, transportation, on site services, on site registration, exhibit management, event planning & destination management. (Woman, estab 1994, empl 4, sales $700,000, cert: State, WBENC)

8345 Cook & Schmid, LLC
740 13th St, Ste 502
San Diego, CA 92101
Contact: Jon Schmid President
Tel: 619-814-2370
Email: jschmid@cookandschmid.com
Website: www.cookandschmid.com
Public relations, advertising and marketing agency. (Minority, estab 2006, empl 10, sales $1,006,305, cert: NMSDC, CPUC)

8346 Corporate Translations, Inc.
222 N. Pacific Coast Hwy., Ste 2000
El Segundo, CA 90245
Contact: Toni Andrews President
Tel: 310-376-1400
Email: projects@corporatetranslations.com
Website: www.CorporateTranslations.com
Provides native-speaking, technical language translation, multilingual document publishing, audio/video production & certified interpreting. (Woman, estab 1995, empl 10, sales $1,205,000, cert: State, CPUC)

8347 Culturati Research & Consulting, Inc.
12625 High Bluff Dr, Ste 218
San Diego, CA 92130
Contact: Lisa Raggio Acct Exec
Tel: 858-750-2600
Email: lisa.raggio@culturatiresearch.com
Website: www.CulturatiResearch.com
Market research, custom research solutions. (Minority, Woman, estab 2004, empl 18, sales $1,000,000,000, cert: CPUC)

8348 DM Connect LLC
4223 Glencoe Ave, Ste A-130
Marina Del Rey, CA 90292
Contact: Dawn Perdew Managing Partner
Tel: 800-778-2990
Email: accounting@dumontproject.com
Website: www.thedumontproject.com
Marketing Consulting Services. (Woman, estab 2008, empl 23, sales $1,700,000, cert: WBENC)

8349 DoubleShot Creative, LLC
499 Seaport Court Ste 205
Redwood City, CA 94063
Contact: Kathy Hutton VP Strategy
Tel: 415-992-7468
Email: kathy@doubleshotcreative.com
Website: www.doubleshotcreative.com
Creative & strategic marketing services, executive communications, marketing strategy and implementation, presentations, videos, messaging, campaign strategy, event creative concepts, social media, blogs, professional bios. (Woman, estab 2007, empl 2, sales $1,000,000, cert: WBENC)

8350 Duarte Communications, Inc.
3200 Coronado Dr
Santa Clara, CA 95054
Contact: Nancy Duarte CEO
Tel: 650-625-8200
Email: nancy@duarte.com
Website: www.duarte.com/
Presentation Development, Speaker Coaching, Communication Strategy and Presentation Coaching, graphic design, management consulting, and marketing research (Woman, estab 1994, empl 117, sales $20,000,000, cert: WBENC)

8351 Elevate Planning
13575 Zivi Ave
Chino, CA 91710
Contact: Viviana Salvia Owner
Tel: 951-217-1028
Email: viviana@elevateplanning.com
Website: www.elevateplanning.com
Experiential marketing & event planning. (Woman, estab 2003, empl 1, sales , cert: WBENC)

8352 Everfield Consulting, LLC
2075 W 235th Pl
Torrance, CA 90501
Contact: Delbara Dorsey Partner
Tel: 310-251-7165
Email: deldorsey@everfieldconsulting.com
Website: www.everfieldconsulting.com
Marketing Consulting Services, Administrative & Mgmt, Display Advertising, Advertising, Public Relations, Media Buying, Direct Mail Advertising, Advertising Material Distribution Services. (Woman/AA, As-Pac, estab 2011, empl 2, sales , cert: State, City, CPUC)

PROFESSIONAL SERVICES: Public Relations/Marketing

8353 ExpoMarketing Group LLC
2741 Dow Ave
Tustin, CA 92780
Contact: Laurie Pennacchi CEO
Tel: 949-777-1051
Email: laurie@expomarketing.com
Website: www.expomarketing.com
Trade show exhibits: custom rental & custom-built exhibits, portable exhibits & peripherals, large format graphics, program management & logistics, & in-house design & creative services. (Woman, estab 1991, empl 13, sales $2,596,339, cert: CPUC, WBENC)

8354 Freddie Georges Production Group
15362 Graham St
Huntington Beach, CA 92649
Contact: Melanie Chomchavalit CFO
Tel: 714-367-9260
Email: mchomchavalit@fgpg.com
Website: www.freddiegeorges.com
Trade show & special events: design, fabrication, project mgmt, rental solutions & logistical support. (Woman, estab 2001, empl 24, sales $7,079,500, cert: WBENC)

8355 HispaniSpace LLC
2100 W Magnolia Blvd Ste A/B
Burbank, CA 91506
Contact: Mario X. Carrasco Partner
Tel: 818-843-0220
Email: mario@thinknowresearch.com
Website: www.thinknowresearch.com
Online market research solutions for the U.S. Hispanic consumer. (Hisp, estab 2010, empl 8, sales $1,583,661, cert: NMSDC, CPUC)

8356 Hunter-Blyden, Katherine
PO Box 94893
Pasadena, CA 91104
Contact: Katherine Hunter-Blyden Managing Dir
Tel: 626-344-8730
Email: khb@katherinehunterblyden.com
Website: www.khbmarketinggroup.com
Develop marketing strategies, evaluate marketing channels & tactics & define programs that align with growth profitable goals. (Woman/AA, estab 2012, empl 1, sales , cert: CPUC)

8357 Ilana Ashley Events
24226 Park Granada
Calabasas, CA 91302
Contact: Ilana Rosenberg CEO
Tel: 818-963-8670
Email: ilana@ilanaashleyevents.com
Website: www.IlanaAshleyEvents.com
Full-service event production, plan and design corporate events, gala affairs, holiday parties, soirées, weddings, and other social events. (Woman, estab 2013, empl 2, sales $108,476, cert: WBENC)

8358 Innovate Marketing Group
300 S Raymond Ave
Pasadena, CA 91105
Contact: Amanda Ma CEO
Tel: 626-817-9588
Email: amanda@innovatemkg.com
Website: www.innovatemkg.com
Experiential event & production agency, product launch, conferences, meetings, sponsorship activations, award & galas. (Minority, Woman, estab 2014, empl 3, sales , cert: NMSDC, CPUC, WBENC)

8359 JR Resources
1130 Camino Del Mar Ste H
Del Mar, CA 92014
Contact: Waren Katz Acct Exec
Tel: 858-481-1074
Email: warren@jrresources.com
Website: www.jrresources.com
Promotional products & marketing services. (Woman, estab 1991, empl 10, sales $4,151,500, cert: CPUC, WBENC)

8360 Language Select, LLC.
7590 N Glenoaks Blvd, Ste 100
Los Angeles, CA 91504
Contact: Paolo Santa
Tel: 818-394-3407
Email: psantamaria@languageselect.com
Website: www.languageselect.com
Simultaneous & consecutive interpreting services. (Hisp, estab , empl , sales $11,700,000, cert: NMSDC)

8361 Latin Nation Live LLC
3245 N San Fernando Rd
Los Angeles, CA 90065
Contact: Ricardo Gieseken President
Tel: 213-924-5683
Email: ricardo@lnlagency.com
Website: www.lnlagency.com
Experiential Marketing, Diversity Marketing, Tastemaker/influencer marketing, Event production, Government affairs/tradeshows, Asset design & procurement, Brand Strategy, Brand Devel, Shopper Marketing. (Hisp, estab 2008, empl 10, sales $1,000,000, cert: NMSDC)

8362 Liehr Marketing & Communications, Inc.
1899 Western Way Ste 400A
Torrance, CA 90501
Contact: Elisa Liehr President
Tel: 310-781-3727
Email: eliehr@lmconline.net
Website: www.lmconline.net
Marketing & research, copywriting, design, interactive, video, web development, design & programing. (Woman, estab 1987, empl 6, sales $780,000, cert: WBENC)

8363 Luth Research
1365 4th Ave
San Diego, CA 92101
Contact: Candice Hinds Assoc Business Dev Mgr
Tel: 619-234-5884
Email: chinds@luthresearch.com
Website: www.luthresearch.com
Market research, enhanced data & data collection solutions, qualitative & quantitative research methodologies. (Woman, estab 1977, empl 90, sales , cert: WBENC)

8364 Marketing Maven Public Relations, Inc.
2390 C Las Posas Rd, Ste 479
Camarillo, CA 93010
Contact: John Carnett Dir Business Dev
Tel: 310-994-7380
Email: john@marketingmavenpr.com
Website: www.marketingmavenpr.com
Public Relations, Hispanic Marketing, Social Media Management, Digital Advertising, Deep Dive Research, Brand Analysis, Graphic Design, Media Traning, Clip Tracking, Event Execution. (Minority, Woman, estab 2009, empl 13, sales $1,259,534, cert: State, CPUC, WBENC, 8(a), SDB)

PROFESSIONAL SERVICES: Public Relations/Marketing

8365 Meeting Planners Plus
3069 Taylor Way
Costa Mesa, CA 92626
Contact: Rosa McArthur President
Tel: 714-668-1126
Email: rlmcarthur@meetingplannersplus.com
Website: www.meetingplannersplus.com
Meeting & special event management; tradeshow production, seminars, conferences, retreats, board meetings. (Woman/AA, estab 1993, empl 1, sales , cert: CPUC)

8366 Meijun LLC
9888 Carroll Centre Rd Ste#210
San Diego, CA 92126
Contact: Huy Ly
Tel: 619-333-8698
Email: hly@meijun.cc
Website: www.meijun.cc
Web development & marketing agency, custom software solutions, web & mobile development, design & strategy, digital marketing services, SEO, content marketing & marketing automation integration. (As-Pac, estab 2011, empl 5, sales , cert: NMSDC, CPUC)

8367 Multi-Cultural Convention Services Network (MCCSN)
212 Sweetwood St
San Diego, CA 92114
Contact: Clara Carter CEO
Tel: 619-265-2561
Email: info@mccsn.com
Website: www.mccsn.com
Meeting & event management, hotel sourcing & contract negotiations & business consulting services. (Woman/AA, estab 2004, empl 1, sales , cert: CPUC)

8368 Netpace Inc.
5000 Executive Pkwy, Ste 530
San Ramon, CA 94583
Contact: Omar Khan President
Tel: 925-543-7760
Email: rfp@netpace.com
Website: www.netpace.com
Lead generation and brand awareness, web development and design practices. (As-Ind, estab 1996, empl 120, sales $22,771,314, cert: NMSDC)

8369 Nostrum, Inc.
401 E Ocean Blvd Ste M101
Long Beach, CA 90802
Contact: Alice Kijak VP
Tel: 562-437-2200
Email: alicekijak@verizon.net
Website: www.nostruminc.com
Strategic marketing communications: advertising, direct marketing, brand optimization, concept development, creative & print production services. (Woman, estab 1981, empl 9, sales $2,452,000, cert: WBENC)

8370 Outward Media, Inc.
9229 Sunset Blvd, Ste 410
Los Angeles, CA 90069
Contact: Paula Chiocchi President
Tel: 310-274-5312
Email: paula@outwardmedia.com
Website: www.outwardmedia.com
Email marketing; creative design, deployment, statistical reporting & campaign management. (Woman, estab 1998, empl 8, sales $5,000,000, cert: WBENC)

8371 Parle Enterprises, Inc.
800 Airport Blvd, Ste 21
Burlingame, CA 94010
Contact: Mary Shulenberger CEO
Tel: 415-467-3100
Email: mary@parle.com
Website: www.parle.com
Media, marketing sponsorships, advertising, oppportunity programs, promotional marketing. (Minority, Woman, estab 1997, empl 8, sales $1,400,000, cert: NMSDC, CPUC)

8372 ProExhibits
48571 Milmont Dr
Fremont, CA 94538
Contact: Acct Exec
Tel: 916-364-9013
Email: msanzone@proexhibits.com
Website: www.proexhibits.com
Trade show exhibit & events. (Woman, estab 1987, empl 40, sales $1,040,000, cert: CPUC)

8373 Purpose Generation LLC
535 Mission St 14th Fl
San Francisco, CA 94105
Contact: Nellie Morris Co-Founder
Tel: 917-243-4777
Email: nellie@purposegeneration.com
Website: www.purposegeneration.com/
Millennial marketing, market research, millennials, gen Y, project management, consulting, strategy, consumer insights, quantitative research, product sampling, product co-creation, quantitative research, influencer strategy. (Woman, estab 2013, empl 4, sales $758,280, cert: WBENC, NWBOC)

8374 RED Company
10323 Los Alamitos Blvd
Long Beach, CA 90720
Contact: President
Tel: 562-498-1270
Email: hello@redcompany.com
Website: www.redcompany.com
Meeting & event planning: site review, contract negotiation, vendor relations, sponsorship cultivation to onsite management, ground transportation, registration services, staffing, hotel block/rooming lists, hospitality, activities. (Woman, estab 2007, empl 22, sales $11,600,000, cert: WBENC)

8375 Red Kite Business Advisors LLC
3525 Del Mar Heights Rd, Ste 202
San Diego, CA 92130
Contact: Principal
Tel: 858-232-4555
Email: info@redkitecorp.com
Website: www.redkitesite.com
Marketing, advertising, public speaking, seminars, workshops, strategic planning, brand assessment & development, integrated campaign strategies, media plan development, online & traditional marketing. (Minority, Woman, estab 2007, empl 1, sales , cert: CPUC, WBENC)

PROFESSIONAL SERVICES: Public Relations/Marketing

8376   RevOne Design, Inc.
       1649B Adrian Rd
       Burlingame, CA 94010
       Contact: Sean Carlin Dir Business Dev
       Tel: 650-468-2996
       Email: sean@revonedesign.com
       Website: www.revonedesign.com
Graphic & Production Design, Photography & Photo Retouching, Digital/Web & Print Communications, Creative Concepting & Campaign Design & Copywriting. (Minority, Woman, estab 2011, empl 7, sales $300,000, cert: NMSDC, WBENC)

8377   RMD Group Inc.
       2311 E South St
       Long Beach, CA 90805
       Contact: Laura Milanes COO
       Tel: 562-866-9288
       Email: laura@rmdgroupinc.com
       Website: www.rmdgroupinc.com
Experiential Marketing, Digital & Social Media, Large Format Graphic Printing, Vehicle Fabrication, Trade Show Design, Trade Show Booth Builder, Millwork, Data Collection. (Hisp, estab 1993, empl 25, sales $6,000,000, cert: NMSDC)

8378   Samantha Smith Productions LLC
       2325 Third St Ste 407
       San Francisco, CA 94107
       Contact: Samantha Smith Owner
       Tel: 415-626-7925
       Email: samantha@samanthasmithproductions.com
       Website: www.samanthasmithproductions.com
Meeting & event planning. (Woman, estab 2003, empl 5, sales $1,500,000, cert: WBENC)

8379   Sax Productions Inc.
       1055 W 7th St 33rd Fl PH
       Los Angeles, CA 90017
       Contact: Tamara Keller COO
       Tel: 213-232-1682
       Email: tamara@saxproductions.com
       Website: www.saxproductions.com
Brand marketing & storytelling, digital strategy, innovation & public relation. (Woman/AA, estab 2012, empl 6, sales , cert: NMSDC, WBENC)

8380   Shiloh Event Management
       PO Box 2772
       Santa Clara, CA 95050
       Contact: Huong Burrow Dir of Events
       Tel: 408-899-5464
       Email: huong@shiloh-events.com
       Website: www.shiloh-events.com
Event strategies, event production, event marketing solutions & event management services. (As-Pac, estab 2013, empl 3, sales , cert: NMSDC)

8381   Specialized Marketing Services, Inc.
       3421 W Segerstrom Ave
       Santa Ana, CA 92704
       Contact: John Snook Exec VP
       Tel: 714-955-5450
       Email: jsnook@teamsms.com
       Website: www.teamsms.com
Strategic marketing devel, copywriting, print mgmt, database mgmt/processing, mailing svcs, warehousing, fulfillment/hand assembly, internet application, telemarketing. (Minority, Woman, estab 1988, empl 23, sales $8,161,000, cert: WBENC)

8382   Stage 4 Solutions, Inc.
       4701 Patrick Henry Dr, #19
       Santa Clara, CA 95054
       Contact: Niti Agrawal CEO
       Tel: 408-868-9739
       Email: niti@stage4solutions.com
       Website: www.stage4solutions.com
Marketing & strategy consulting svcs: strategic business & product plan devel, focused sales tools, competitive analyses, new product introduction management & interim marketing staffing solutions. (Woman/As-Ind, estab , empl , sales , cert: NMSDC, WBENC)

8383   Strategic Business Communications
       12175 Dearborn Pl
       Poway, CA 92064
       Contact: Jim Hernandez President
       Tel: 858-679-1805
       Email: jhernandez@sbcinc.com
       Website: www.sbcinc.info
Sales & Marketing Training & Consulting, Meeting & Event Planning. (As-Pac, estab 1987, empl 10, sales $2,400,000, cert: NMSDC)

8384   Sundial Marketing Research, Inc.
       30 Center St
       San Rafael, CA 94901
       Contact: Nancy Kelber President
       Tel: 415-200-1461
       Email: nancy@sundialresearch.com
       Website: www.sundialresearch.com
Market research to the medical device, pharmaceutical & biotechnology industries. (Woman, estab 2010, empl 6, sales $2,500,000, cert: WBENC)

8385   The Mark USA, Inc.
       4482 Barranca Pkwy, Ste 220
       Newport Beach, CA 92663
       Contact: Traci Shirachi CEO
       Tel: 949-396-6053
       Email: tshirachi@themarkusa.com
       Website: www.themarkusa.com
Research and evaluation through innovative data collection, analytics, and visualization in order to help clients achieve better outcomes and demonstrate the impact of an organization. (Woman/As-Pac, estab 2007, empl 15, sales $1,250,000, cert: NMSDC, WBENC)

8386   Undisclosed Location, Inc
       5761 Sonoma Mountain Rd
       Santa Rosa, CA 95404
       Contact: Barbara Gorder President
       Tel: 415-295-4920
       Email: barbara.gorder@unlo.com
       Website: www.unlo.com
Marketing, advertising & communications solutions, strategic brand advertising, mobile marketing consulting & content devel, website devel, packaging design, presentation consulting & event promotions. (Woman, estab 2003, empl 10, sales $1,000,000, cert: WBENC)

8387   Valencia, Perez & Echeveste
       1605 Hope St, Ste 250
       South Pasadena, CA 91030
       Contact: Patricia Perez President
       Tel: 626-403-3200
       Email: patricia@vpepr.com
       Website: www.vpepr.com
Public relations & marketing communications. (Hisp, estab 1987, empl 25, sales , cert: NMSDC)

PROFESSIONAL SERVICES: Public Relations/Marketing

8388 Vic Salazar Enterprises, LLC
2514 Jamacha Rd, Ste 502-21
El Cajon, CA 92019
Contact: Vic Salazar President
Tel: 619-517-4744
Email: vicsalazar@cox.net
Website: www.vicsalazar.com
Public Relations, Hispanic Marketing, Video Production, Media Training, Advertising, Crisis Communications, Hard Drive Storage, Printing, Labeling, Promotional Items, Event Production. (Hisp, estab 2008, empl 1, sales , cert: CPUC)

Colorado

8389 Egg Strategy, Inc.
1360 Walnut St Ste 102
Boulder, CO 80302
Contact: Matthew Sommers Dir of Operations
Tel: 303-546-9311
Email: boulderinfo@eggstrategy.com
Website: www.eggstrategy.com
Marketing consulting, innovation, brand strategy, market research, consumer insight. (Woman, estab 2005, empl 50, sales $10,000,000, cert: WBENC)

8390 MorSports & Events, Inc.
3333 S Bannock St Ste 790
Englewood, CO 80110
Contact: Betsy Mordecai President
Tel: 720-381-5000
Email: betsy@morevents.com
Website: www.morevents.com
Event planning, meeting coordination & hospitality mgmt. (Woman, estab 1996, empl 13, sales $6,000,000, cert: WBENC)

8391 Translation Excellence
2620 S Parker Rd Ste 210
Aurora, CO 80014
Contact: Nisar Nikzad President
Tel: 720-325-0459
Email: info@translationexcellence.com
Website: www.translationexcellence.com
Translation, interpretation, interpretation equipment & language classes. (As-Ind, estab 2010, empl 5, sales $422,000, cert: City, 8(a))

8392 Vladimir Jones
PO Box 387
Colorado Springs, CO 80901
Contact: Trudy Rowe CFO
Tel: 719-473-0704
Email: trowe@vladimirjones.com
Website: www.vladimirjones.com
Marketing services: strategic planning, research, advertising & public relations, creative development & production, television, print, radio, out of home, digital & on-line communications, media planning & buying, account planning. (Woman, estab 1970, empl 71, sales $21,863,320, cert: NWBOC)

Connecticut

8393 Adams & Knight, Inc.
80 Avon Meadow Lane
Avon, CT 06001
Contact: SVP Financial Services
Tel: 860-676-2300
Email: none@none.com
Website: www.adamsknight.com
Integrated marketing: research, strategy, brand development, advertising, design, collateral development, public relations, social media, experiential, event marketing. (Woman, estab 1987, empl 39, sales $8,547,385, cert: State)

8394 BCM Media
30 Old Kings Hwy S
Darien, CT 06820
Contact: S. McKenna Managing Dir
Tel: 203-326-1477
Email: smckenna@bcmmedia.biz
Website: www.bcmmedia.biz/
Advertising, Media Consulting & Planning, Negotiations, B2B Advertising, B2C Advertising, Trade Advertising, Multimedia Planning and Buying, Global Media Planning, National Media Planning, Local Media Planning, Public Relations. (Woman, estab 2013, empl 9, sales $855,047, cert: WBENC)

8395 Domo Domo IMG
28 Castle Meadow Road
Newtown, CT 06470
Contact: Deb Adams Founder & CCO
Tel: 203-270-3515
Email: judy@domomarketing.com
Website: www.domomarketing.com
Brand strategy & optimization, strategic positioning, new product launches, line extensions, NPD innovation, trend & market analyses. (Woman, estab 1997, empl 10, sales $845,000, cert: WBENC)

8396 Peralta Illustration & Design LLC
431 Howe Ave
Shelton, CT 06484
Contact: Ramon Peralta
Tel: 203-513-2222
Email: ramon@peraltadesign.com
Website: www.peraltadesign.com
Digital interactive design: web development, web applications, corporate identity & marketing, branding. (Hisp, estab 2003, empl 6, sales , cert: NMSDC)

8397 Survey Launch Co.
494 Bridgeport Ave. Unit 101-345
Shelton, CT 06484
Contact: Francis O'Donnell Head of Sales
Tel: 203-497-2560
Email: insights@surveylaunch.com
Website: www.surveylaunch.com
Research methodologies & statistical methods, cluster/segmentation, regression, key drivers, TURF, classification & typing tools. (Woman, estab 1996, empl 6, sales $733,678, cert: State)

8398 Touchpoint Integrated Communications, LLC
16 Thorndal Circle
Darien, CT 06820
Contact: Karen Kluger CEO
Tel: 203-665-7705
Email: kkluger@tpointmedia.com
Website: www.tpointmedia.com
Communication: broadcast, print, digital, social, mobile, email, direct mail, out of home & alternative. (Woman, estab 2005, empl 40, sales $9,591,292, cert: WBENC)

8399 TruEvents LLC
PO Box 893
Madison, CT 06443
Contact: CEO
Tel: 203-980-3495
Email: Info@BE-TRU.com
Website: www.be-tru.com
Marketing, Graphic Design, Creative Design, Web, Retail Packaging, Retail Strategy, Digital, Digital Store Displays, Retail POS, Merchandising,
Tradeshows, Meeting Production, Event Production, Ideation, Strategy. (Woman, estab 2000, empl 4, sales $2,082,729, cert: WBENC)

District of Columbia

8400 JPA Health Communications
1101 Connecticut Ave NW Ste 600
Washington, DC 20036
Contact: Carrie Jones Principal
Tel: 202-591-4000
Email: carrie@jpa.com
Website: www.jpa.com
Public Relations, Health Communications, Influencer Relations (Media relations, advocacy engagement, social & digital media, policy & issues advocacy, stakeholder engagement). (Woman, estab 2007, empl 21, sales $7,700,000, cert: NWBOC)

8401 Premier Consultants International, Inc.
1020 16th St NW Ste 201
Washington, DC 20036
Contact: Renard H. Marable
Tel: 202-319-1211
Email: rmarable@premiercon.com
Website: www.premiercon.com
Marketing & business development services. (AA, estab 2000, empl 1, sales , cert: State, City)

8402 Scott Circle Communications, Inc.
1307 New York Ave NW Ste 702
Washington, DC 20005
Contact: Laura Gross President
Tel: 202-695-8225
Email: lgross@scottcircle.com
Website: www.scottcircle.com
Public relations & event-planning. (Woman, estab 2006, empl 11, sales $1,614,156, cert: WBENC)

8403 SEW, Inc.
717 D St NW Ste 300
Washington, DC 20004
Contact: Thedis Miller CEO
Tel: 202-403-4739
Email: tmiller@4sew.com
Website: www.4sew.com
Human capital mgmt svcs, customer relationship mgmt (CRM) & [roject mgmt (PMP), large team operations support, business planning, executive coaching, administrative support. (Woman/AA, estab 2004, empl 1, sales $104,000, cert: NMSDC)

8404 Washingtonian Custom Media
1828 L St NW, Ste 200
Washington, DC 20036
Contact: James Byles President
Tel: 202-862-3500
Email: jbyles@washingtonian.com
Website: www.washingtoniancustommedia.com
Communications strategy, print & digital publications, magazines, brochures, white papers, annual reports, content development, content strategy, audience development, writing, editing, website design, graphic design, website development. (Woman, estab 1965, empl 80, sales $10,000,000, cert: WBENC)

Delaware

8405 Barron Marketing Communications
833 Washington St
Wilmington, DE 19801
Contact: Patricia D. Barron President
Tel: 302-658-1627
Email: pbarron@barronmarketing.com
Website: www.barronmarketing.com
Mktg print communications: direct mail, catalogs, displays, premiums, POS, broadcast, packaging, media, outdoor. (Woman, estab 1976, empl 9, sales $1,000,000, cert: State)

Florida

8406 A-Plus Meetings and Incentives
901 Ponce de Leon Blvd. Ste 600
Coral Gables, FL 33134
Contact: Jay Klein COO
Tel: 786-888-3203
Email: jklein@aplusmeetings.com
Website: www.aplusmeetings.com
Meeting planning, online registration, venue selection, audio-visual management, production development, airline travel, ground transportation & hospitality desk staffing. (Woman, estab 1993, empl 21, sales $10,382,504, cert: CPUC, WBENC)

8407 Avenue Event Group LLC
501 N Orlando Ave Ste 313-312 Orlando, FL 32789
Orlando, FL 32801
Contact: Sean Hughes Marketing
Tel: 650-784-0175
Email: sean@avenueeventgroup.com
Website: www.avenueeventgroup.com
National event planning & logistics services: Venue Selection, Meeting Logistics, Hotel Coordination, Group Transportation, Vendor Procurement, Unique Entertainment. (Woman, estab 2013, empl 5, sales $1,300,000, cert: WBENC)

8408 BodenPR Inc.
7791 NW 46th St
Doral, FL 33166
Contact: Sara Garibaldi
Tel: 305-639-6770
Email: credentials@bodenagency.com
Website: www.bodenagency.com
Storyboarding & script development, post-production. (Woman/Hisp, estab 2008, empl 40, sales $9,100,000, cert: State, WBENC)

PROFESSIONAL SERVICES: Public Relations/Marketing

8409 Chasm Communications, Inc.
13045 W Linebaugh Ave Ste 101
Tampa, FL 33626
Contact: Jennifer Williams President
Tel: 813-283-0908
Email: jwilliams@chasmcommunications.com
Website: www.chasmcommunications.com
Marketing & web design, app design, digital marketing & traditional print marketing. (Woman, estab 2006, empl 7, sales $845,317, cert: WBENC)

8410 Cordova Marketing Group
2702 Wright Ave
Winter Park, FL 32789
Contact: Tom Cordova President
Tel: 321-972-8181
Email: tom@covacova.com
Website: www.covacova.com
Multi-culutral Marketing, Sponsorship, Broadcasting, Naming Rights, Events, Ticket Sales, Community Outreach, Executive Recruitment. (Hisp, estab 1998, empl 2, sales $375,000, cert: NMSDC)

8411 Creative Zing Promotion Group
189 S Orange Ave Ste 1130a
Orlando, FL 32801
Contact: Pamela D Aniello President
Tel: 407-514-0044
Email: pamela@creativezing.com
Website: www.creativezing.com
Integrated marketing & promotions, complex contest & sweepstakes administration. (Woman, estab 2007, empl 9, sales $1,300,000, cert: WBENC)

8412 CRG Global, Inc.
3 Signal Ave, Ste B
Ormong Beach, FL 32174
Contact: Anastasia Mentavlos VP Sensory
Tel: 386-677-5644
Email: am@cssdatatelligence.com
Website: www.crgglobalinc.com
Custom market research services. (Woman, estab 1989, empl 530, sales $28,446,000, cert: WBENC)

8413 Detail Planners, LLC
1452 Distant Oaks Dr
Wesley Chapel, FL 33543
Contact: Anita Jentzen CEO
Tel: 813-991-1348
Email:
Website: www.detailplanners.com
Plan & manage corporate meetings & events. (Woman, estab 2004, empl 5, sales $1,900,000, cert: WBENC)

8414 Diper Designers LLC
7306 Exchange Dr
Orlando, FL 32809
Contact: Ricardo Contreras Business Devel Mgr
Tel: 407-208-2226
Email: rcontreras@diper.com
Website: www.diper.com
Designing & build customized exhibit displays; booths, pavilions, corporate events, retail stores, kiosks, among others. (Hisp, estab 1999, empl 19, sales $516,352, cert: City)

8415 Executive Meeting Management, Inc.
6996 Piazza Grande Ave Ste 314
Orlando, FL 32835
Contact: Heather Wilson President
Tel: 407-399-7681
Email: hwilson@execmm.com
Website: www.execmm.com
Meeting management. (Woman, estab 2004, empl 1, sales $1,026,779, cert: WBENC)

8416 Fortes Laboratories
1005 W Busch Blvd Ste 101
Tampa, FL 33612
Contact: Steven Seigel CFO
Tel: 813-390-6536
Email: info@forteslabs.com
Website: www.forteslabs.com
Drug testing, national forensic, toxicology laboratory, drug & alcohol testing. (Woman, estab 1994, empl 15, sales , cert: State)

8417 Fusion Communications, Inc.
8725 NW 18 Terrace, Ste 103
Miami, FL 33172
Contact: Annabel Beyra Partner
Tel: 786-574-2330
Email: annabel@fusioncomminc.com
Website: www.fusioncomminc.com
Public relations agency. (Minority, Woman, estab 2006, empl 5, sales $1,279,242, cert: NMSDC)

8418 HAS Art Solutions LLC
3139 Philips Hwy, Ste 100
Jacksonville, FL 32207
Contact: Heather Sams President
Tel: 904-503-9800
Email: hasams@hasartsolutions.com
Website: www.HASartsolutions.com
Art consulting, art design, and procurement. (Woman, estab 2010, empl 7, sales $355,000, cert: State)

8419 Imagine Enterprises International
8600 Commodity Circle, Ste 109
Orlando, FL 32819
Contact: Heidi Brumbach CEO
Tel: 407-409-7310
Email: heidi@technischcreative.com
Website: www.technischcreative.com
Event Planning & Production, Venue Research & Selection, Venue Negotiation & Contracting, Room Block Management, Speaker Selection, Event Marketing, Food & Beverage Management, Event Registration, Audio Visual. (Woman, estab 1999, empl 4, sales , cert: WBENC)

8420 Ingenium Research Boutique, Inc.
8057 Solitaire Ct
Orlando, FL 32836
Contact: Maria Parra President
Tel: 407-309-2742
Email: mlparra@ingeniumresearch.com
Website: www.ingeniumresearch.com
Qualitative marketing research, focus groups, ethnographic interviews, in-depth interviews, shop-alongs, qualitative techniques. (Minority, Woman, estab 2011, empl 2, sales $500,000, cert: WBENC)

PROFESSIONAL SERVICES: Public Relations/Marketing

8421   Inktel Direct
       13975 NW 58th Ct
       Miami Lakes, FL 33014
       Contact: Jason Schlenker VP Business Dev
       Tel: 305-523-1129
       Email: jason.schlenker@inktel.com
       Website: www.inktel.com
Direct marketing: call center, fulfillment, direct mail, database marketing. (Hisp, estab 1997, empl 580, sales , cert: NMSDC)

8422   ITC Translations USA Inc.
       900 E Indiantown Rd, Ste 302
       Jupiter, FL 33477
       Contact: Allison Paxton Business Dev Mgr
       Tel: 561-746-6242
       Email: a.paxton@itcglobaltranslations.com
       Website: www.itcglobaltranslations.com
Technical, scientific & communication translation services in over 25 languages. (Woman, estab 1999, empl 68, sales $8,600,000, cert: WBENC)

8423   Key Lime Interactive
       8750 NW 36th St, Ste 475
       Doral, FL 33178
       Contact: Ania Rodriguez
       Tel: 305-809-0555
       Email: accounting@keylimeinteractive.com
       Website: www.keylimeinteractive.com
Qualitative & quantitative research, usability testing, mobile research, card sorting, remote intercept testing, expert reviews, ethnography, competitive benchmarking, eye tracking, shop along. (Minority, Woman, estab 2009, empl 17, sales $3,686,319, cert: NMSDC, WBENC)

8424   Lingua Franca Translations, LLC
       1111 Brickell Ave Ste 1140
       Miami, FL 33156
       Contact: Marcela Arbelaez CEO
       Tel: 305-913-7193
       Email: marcela.arbelaez@lftranslations.com
       Website: www.lftranslations.com
Translations, interpretations & transcriptions into and from over 240 languages. (Minority, Woman, estab 2011, empl 3, sales $138,000, cert: NMSDC)

8425   M. Gill & Associates, Inc.
       4770 Biscayne Blvd, Ste 1050
       Miami, FL 33137
       Contact: Marie Gill President
       Tel: 305-576-7888
       Email: info@mgillonline.com
       Website: www.mgillonline.com
Management & public relations consulting. (Woman/AA, estab 1990, empl 10, sales , cert: State)

8426   Media Global Group, LLC
       2000 Ponce de Leon Blvd
       Coral Gables, FL 33134
       Contact: Maria Gonzalez-Pacheco CEO
       Tel: 786-431-4555
       Email: mgonzalez@mggmedia.com
       Website: www.mggmedia.com
Digital Media Outlets & Out-of-Home (OOH), TV, Radio & Print Media. (Minority, Woman, estab 2008, empl 10, sales $3,600,000, cert: NMSDC)

8427   Nobles Research, Inc.
       8321 Golden Prairie Dr
       Tampa, FL 33647
       Contact: Kevin Nobles President
       Tel: 813-977-7700
       Email: kevin@noblesresearch.com
       Website: www.noblesresearch.com
Qualitative research. (AA, estab 2001, empl 1, sales $270,000, cert: NMSDC)

8428   Orlando Conference Management Group, Inc.
       13124 Sunkiss Loop
       Windermere, FL 34786
       Contact: Lori Lombardi Ryan President
       Tel: 407-948-5706
       Email: llr@ocmg.net
       Website: www.ocmg.net
Meeting management, logistics & events planning. (Woman, estab 1993, empl 2, sales , cert: State, WBENC)

8429   Paragon Events, Inc.
       352 NE 3rd Ave
       Delray Beach, FL 33444
       Contact: Renee Radabaugh CEO
       Tel: 561-243-3073
       Email: info@paragon-events.com
       Website: www.paragon-events.com
Meeting & special events. (Woman, estab 1989, empl 12, sales $5,514,280, cert: WBENC)

8430   Pierson Grant Public Relations
       6301 NW 5th Way, Ste 2600
       Fort Lauderdale, FL 33309
       Contact: President
       Tel: 954-776-1999
       Email: info@piersongrant.com
       Website: www.piersongrant.com
Public relations planning; media relations; publicity; crisis communications; creating & managing community relations programs; writing newsletters, brochures, speeches; graphic design. (Woman, estab 1995, empl 15, sales $1,840,898, cert: WBENC)

8431   Prestige Auto Specialists
       4250 St. Charles Way
       Boca Raton, FL 33434
       Contact: Marcello Serrato President
       Tel: 954-428-6689
       Email: mserrato@prestigeautous.com
       Website: www.prestigeautous.com
Event production, media fleet management, marketing & communication. (Hisp, estab 1985, empl 30, sales $52,000,000, cert: NMSDC)

8432   Quest Corporation of America
       17220 Camelot Court
       Land O'Lakes, FL 34638
       Contact: Sharlene Francois President
       Tel: 813-926-2942
       Email: corporate@usa.com.com
       Website: www.QCAusa.com
Public relations, partnering, marketing, creative services, media, publications, printing, aerial photography, advertising, technology support, web design & data storage, transportation support svcs. (Woman, estab 1995, empl 14, sales $3,075,300, cert: State)

PROFESSIONAL SERVICES: Public Relations/Marketing

8433 RBB Public Relations LLC
355 Alhambra Cir Ste 800
Coral Gables, FL 33134
Contact: Marsha Rhymer Controller
Tel: 305-448-7450
Email: marsha.rhymer@rbbpr.com
Website: www.rbbpr.com
Marketing, Public Relations. (Woman, estab 2001, empl 81, sales $6,401,984, cert: WBENC)

8434 Republica, LLC
2153 Coral Way 5th Fl
Miami, FL 33145
Contact: Jorge A. Plasencia CEO
Tel: 786-347-4700
Email: jp@republica.net
Website: www.republica.net
Branding, advertising, promotions, digital and communications company. (Hisp, estab 2006, empl 100, sales $14,500,000, cert: State, NMSDC)

8435 ROUGE 24, Inc.
5279 Grande Palm Cir
Delray Beach, FL 33484
Contact: Todd Victor Dir of Accounts
Tel: 561-213-0260
Email: todd.victor@rouge24.com
Website: www.rouge24.com
Brand Strategy, Identity Design, Packaging, Style Guides, Adaptation, Process Management, Marketing Materials, In-Store Signage. (Woman, estab 2009, empl 1, sales $2,500,000, cert: WBENC)

8436 T. Mak's International, Inc.
2100 Corporate Sq Blvd, Ste 100
Jacksonville, FL 32216
Contact: Shannon Stoddard GBD
Tel: 904-855-4188
Email: shannon@2100tmaks.com
Website: www.2100tmaks.com
Mfr, international sourcing, advertising & marketing, custom promotional products, advertising signage. (Minority, Woman, estab 1985, empl 11, sales $2,200,000, cert: WBENC)

8437 Trickey Jennus, Inc.
5300 W Cypress St Ste 285
Tampa, FL 33607
Contact: Kathie Craft Comella COO
Tel: 813-831-2325
Email: kathie@trickeyjennus.com
Website: www.trickeyjennus.com
Strategy review & rational, collaborative account planning, strategic media planning, specialized direct marketing, campaign development, web services, social media strategy, creative services. (Woman, estab 2005, empl 7, sales $1,015,266, cert: State)

8438 Vistra Communications, LLC
18315 N US Hwy 41
Lutz, FL 33549
Contact: Brian A. Butler President
Tel: 813-961-4700
Email: brian@consultvistra.com
Website: www.ConsultVistra.com
Public relations, strategic communications, homeland security, information technology, management consulting, training & curriculum development. (AA, estab 2007, empl 112, sales $22,716,235, cert: City, NMSDC, 8(a))

8439 Wragg & Casas Public Relations, Inc.
3191 Coral Way 607
Miami, FL 33145
Contact: Ramon Casas President
Tel: 305-372-1234
Email: rcasas@wraggcasas.com
Website: www.wraggcasas.com
Strategic counseling, media relations, reputation & crisis management, brand visibility & public affairs. (Hisp, estab 1991, empl 8, sales $1,200,000, cert: NMSDC)

Georgia

8440 B. King's Audio Visual Services
3175 Thrasher Cir
Decatur, GA 30032
Contact: Bernard King CEO
Tel: 404-286-0829
Email: bkingsav@bellsouth.net
Website: www.bk-av.com
Production, Meeting Planning, Show Coordinating, Installations,etc. (AA, estab 1995, empl 10, sales , cert: NMSDC)

8441 Benchmarc360, Inc.
6340 Sugarloaf Pkwy Ste 200
Atlanta, GA 30097
Contact: CEO
Tel: 678-291-0011
Email:
Website: www.benchmarc360.com
Strategic solutions, strategic event marketing, conference, meeting & event mgmt, destination mgmt, trade shows, incentive programs, site selection & contract negotiations. (Woman, estab , empl , sales $32,800,000, cert: NWBOC)

8442 BLH Consulting, Inc.
502 Pryor St Ste 301
Atlanta, GA 30312
Contact: Betsy Helgager Hughes
Tel: 404-688-0415
Email: betsy@blhconsulting.net
Website: www.blhconsulting.net
Multicultural public relations & marketing services. (Woman/AA, estab 2002, empl 2, sales $350,000, cert: WBENC)

8443 CMT Agency
1417 Dutch Valley Place Ste A
Atlanta, GA 30324
Contact: Shelly Justice CEO
Tel: 404-233-4644
Email: sjustice@cmtagency.com
Website: www.cmtagency.com
Spokesmodels, event staffing, brand ambassadors, product demonstrators, celebrity look-a-likes & corporate presenters. (Woman, estab 2001, empl 11, sales $2,119,677, cert: WBENC)

8444 Colour One O One, Inc.
4995 Avalon Ridge Pkwy Ste 100
Norcross, GA 30071
Contact: Taylor Lepera Sales Assoc
Tel: 404-350-1700
Email: tlepera@studio101.com
Website: www.colour101.com
Strategic marketing programs for the retail, food, beverage, sports & entertainment industries. (Woman, estab 1983, empl 9, sales $697,000, cert: WBENC)

PROFESSIONAL SERVICES: Public Relations/Marketing

8445 Creative Juice LLC
      75 Marietta St, Ste 503
      Atlanta, GA 30303
      Contact: Octavia Gilmore Owner
      Tel: 404-947-8599
      Email: octavia@itscreativejuice.com
      Website: www.itscreativejuice.com
Graphic design & web design services, logo, branding, print design, infographics, brochures, tradeshow graphics, marketing, web design & development, Wordpress, email marketing, copy writing, blogging, local SEO & motion graphics. (Woman/AA, Hisp, estab 2013, empl 4, sales $315,000, cert: City)

8446 CyberAnalysis, LLC
      427 Rhodes House Dr
      Suwanee, GA 30024
      Contact: Jeanne Eidex President
      Tel: 770-614-6334
      Email: jeidex@eidexgroup.com
      Website: www.cyberanalysisllc.com
Market research: questionnaire design, data collection, data analysis, reports, presentations, recommendations. (Woman, estab 1999, empl 5, sales , cert: WBENC)

8447 EventEssentials, LLC
      1227 Rockbridge Rd Ste 208-238
      Stone Mountain, GA 30087
      Contact: Qualena Odom-Royes President
      Tel: 404-642-6064
      Email: qualena@eventsessential.com
      Website: www.eventsessential.com
Marketing, branding & messaging, special events, meetings, corporate sponsorships, event promotion & production, best practices, public relations. (Woman/AA, estab 2002, empl 2, sales $125,055, cert: NMSDC)

8448 Folio, Inc. Design & Illustration
      1145 Zonolite Rd NE, Ste 2
      Atlanta, GA 30306
      Contact: Margaret Lisi
      Tel: 404-888-6599
      Email: margaret@stir-marketing.com
      Website: www.stir-marketing.com
Marketing & communications services, create content & media, employee engagement/change management & event marketing. (Woman, estab 1993, empl 10, sales $1,200,000, cert: WBENC)

8449 Full Circle Events
      6070 Black Water Trail
      Atlanta, GA 30328
      Contact: Sally Silverman Owner
      Tel: 404-236-0440
      Email: sally.fullcircle@comcast.net
      Website: www.fullcircleeventsinc.com
Event, meeting & conference planning. (Woman, estab 2002, empl 5, sales $416,897, cert: WBENC)

8450 Global Organization and Planning Services, LLC
      2727 Skyview Dr. Unit 76
      Lithia Springs, GA 30122
      Contact: Vanessa Whitehead Managing Dir
      Tel: 770-574-4415
      Email: vanessa@globalorganizationplanning.com
      Website: www.globalorganizationplanning.com
Event planning & mgmt services: business meetings, conferences, tours, trips, receptions, cruises, accommodations & travel, program & agenda devel, logistics mgmt. (Woman/AA, estab 2002, empl 20, sales , cert: State, City)

8451 Grow Now, LLC
      1320 Ellsworth Industrial Blvd NW
      Atlanta, GA 30318
      Contact: Bob McNeil CEO
      Tel: 404-254-3281
      Email: b.mcneil@grownowllc.com
      Website: www.grownowllc.com
Marketing communications, advertising, promotional marketing, public relations & activations. (AA, estab 2013, empl 24, sales $8,600,000, cert: State, NMSDC)

8452 Insights Marketing
      3131 Piedmont Rd. Ste 205
      Atlanta, GA 30305
      Contact: Keshia Walker President
      Tel: 404-872-9899
      Email: kw@insights-mpc.com
      Website: www.insights-mpc.com
Multi-cultural research development & analysis, marketing, promotion, special event program development & execution. (Woman/AA, estab 1998, empl 10, sales $390,000, cert: NMSDC, WBENC)

8453 IROK Solutions, Inc.
      4002 Hwy 78, Ste 530-192
      Snellville, GA 30039
      Contact: Kunmi Oluleye President
      Tel: 770-982-1000
      Email: kunmi@shebafoods.com
      Website: www.shebafoods.com
Marketing consulting. (Woman/AA, estab 2000, empl 4, sales , cert: WBENC)

8454 Juice Studios
      1123 Zonolite Rd, Ste 7B
      Atlanta, GA 30306
      Contact: Co-Owner
      Tel: 404-817-9369
      Email: Atlanta@TheJuiceStudios.com
      Website: www.thejuicestudios.com
Meeting planning & special events. (Woman, estab 2004, empl 1, sales $2,560,189, cert: WBENC)

8455 LightPath OM LLC dba strut AGENCY
      1235 Oriole Dr, SW
      Atlanta, GA 30311
      Contact: Tashion Macon, PhD, MBA President
      Tel: 404-855-4568
      Email: tashion@strutagency.com
      Website: www.strutagency.online
Creative design, cross-cultural communications, and consumer marketing strategy. (Woman/AA, estab 2008, empl 15, sales , cert: NMSDC, WBENC)

8456 Maveryck Marketing Group, LLC
      3726 Upton Ct
      Ellenwood, GA 30294
      Contact: Keith Philpot Managing Member
      Tel: 770-681-0731
      Email: kphilpot@maveryckmarketing.com
      Website: www.maveryckmarketing.com
Strategic market planning & implementation. (AA, estab 2005, empl 1, sales , cert: NMSDC)

PROFESSIONAL SERVICES: Public Relations/Marketing

8457 McDowell Information Group Public Relations LLC.
233 Mitchell St, Ste 500
Atlanta, GA 30303
Contact: Anita Carlyle Sr Managing Partner
Tel: 844-462-3693
Email: acarlyle@mccevents.ca
Website: www.mcdowellpr.com
Public relations, Web Development, Voice Overs, Military/Corporate engagement, Minority Community Relations, Stage Productions, lighting & Event Planning. (AA, estab 2014, empl 10, sales , cert: NMSDC)

8458 Modo Modo Agency LLC
3175 Northside Pkwy NW Bldg 300, Ste 700
Atlanta, GA 30327
Contact: Moira Vetter CEO
Tel: 770-436-3100
Email: moira@modomodoagency.com
Website: www.modomodoagency.com
Marketing, brand development, thought leadership, lead generation, internal communications, publications, web sites, integrated marketing campaigns, direct response. (Woman, estab 2007, empl 15, sales $1,535,000, cert: WBENC)

8459 National Business Advisory Group, Inc.
540 Powder Springs St, Ste C16
Marietta, GA 30064
Contact: Silah Williams CEO
Tel: 770-974-8100
Email: swilliams@mynbag.com
Website: www.mynbag.com
Market research & strategy consulting services. (AA, estab 2011, empl 5, sales $150,000, cert: NMSDC)

8460 Outsource Events, Inc.
1647 Emory Place Dr, NE
Atlanta, GA 30329
Contact: President
Tel: 404-982-1640
Email: info@blackironbystro.com
Website: www.outsourceevents.com
Event & meeting planning. (Woman, estab 2003, empl 2, sales $156,620, cert: WBENC)

8461 Phase 3 Marketing and Communications
280 Interstate North Circle SE, Ste 300
Atlanta, GA 30339
Contact: Jim Cannata EVP Strategic Growth
Tel: 404-367-9898
Email: jim.cannata@phase3mc.com
Website: www.phase3mc.com
Integrated marketing services from ideation to execution, including creative, digital, public relations- and large-format printing and warehousing and distribution. (As-Pac, estab 2001, empl 167, sales $28,000,000, cert: NMSDC)

8462 Printing Systems, LLC
2759 Delk Rd, Ste 2300
Marietta, GA 30067
Contact: Sherrica Davis New Business Specialist
Tel: 404-855-3021
Email: sdavis@printingsys.com
Website: www.printingsys.com
Target marketing success, increase return on investments and impact CRM through increasing consumer databases & identifying consumer purchasing habits. (AA, estab 2002, empl 7, sales $2,300,000, cert: NMSDC)

8463 Q&A Entertainment Inc.
1514 E Cleveland Ave Ste 116
East Point, GA 30344
Contact: Sheila Merritt Dir New Business Dev
Tel: 404-762-5665
Email: smerritt@qandaentertainment.com
Website: www.QandAEntertainment.com
Event production & marketing services: production & management, marketing & promotion, ideation & creation & sponsorships. (Woman, estab 1999, empl 3, sales $830,788, cert: WBENC)

8464 Sojo, Inc.
4400 N Point Pkwy Ste 153
Alpharetta, GA 30022
Contact: Sophie Gibson President
Tel: 770-360-6330
Email: sophie.gibson@sojoinc.com
Website: www.sojoinc.com
Technology marketing, marketing communications. (Woman/AA, estab 2001, empl 11, sales $2,300,000, cert: NMSDC)

8465 Southeast Exhibits and Events
1000 Marietta St Ste 124
Atlanta, GA 30318
Contact: Jamal Lewis President
Tel: 470-865-2007
Email: info@southeastexhibit.com
Website: www.Southeastexhibit.com
Trade show exhibits & design. (Woman/AA, estab 2014, empl 5, sales , cert: NMSDC)

8466 SPAR Solutions, LLC
360 Interstate North Pkwy SE Ste 220
Atlanta, GA 30339
Contact: Swami Ganapathy Dir Solutions Consulting
Tel: 855-772-7765
Email: sganapathy@sparsolutions.com
Website: www.sparsolutions.com
CRM Solutions, Marketing, Customer Service, Field Service, Contract Management . Contact Centers, Telephony, Email, Chat, Social Media Complex business process automation & mgmt Systems Integratio (As-Ind, estab 2003, empl 60, sales $3,670,000, cert: NMSDC)

8467 TDEFERIAMEDIA, Inc.
9795 Talisman Dr
Johns Creek, GA 30022
Contact: Antenor Tony President
Tel: 404-630-0639
Email: contact@tdeferiamedia.com
Website: www.tdeferiamedia.com
Marketing, branding consulting & creative production, ethnic market study & plans, media buying, translation & interpretation in Spanish, digital & social media expertise. (Hisp, estab 2007, empl 1, sales $140,000, cert: NMSDC)

8468 The Capre Group
115 Perimeter Center Place Ste 1120
Atlanta, GA 30346
Contact: Kim Gavlak Controller
Tel: 678-443-2280
Email: kgavlak@capregroup.com
Website: www.capregroup.com
Strategic marketing consulting. (Woman, estab 2001, empl 14, sales $4,750,000, cert: WBENC)

PROFESSIONAL SERVICES: Public Relations/Marketing

8469 The Crafton Group, Inc.
1107 Lanier Blvd Atlanta
Georgia, GA 30306
Contact: Crafton Langley President
Tel: 404-873-3019
Email: crafton.langley@thecraftongroup.com
Website: www.thecraftongroup.com
Marketing & communications: research, strategy, branding, design, advertising, promotion, product development, media. (Woman, estab 1996, empl 15, sales , cert: City, WBENC)

8470 V & L Research and Consulting, Inc.
3340 Peachtree Rd Ste 1800
Atlanta, GA 30326
Contact: Dydra Virgil Principal
Tel: 770-908-0003
Email: vlresearch@mindspring.com
Website: www.vlresearch.com
Market research: focus groups; in-depth interviews; Ethnographies, telephone & intercept surveys. (Woman/AA, estab 1991, empl 2, sales $492,052, cert: WBENC)

8471 VonCreations, Inc.
2886 Branchwood Dr
East Point, GA 30344
Contact: Yvonne J. Wiltz CEO
Tel: 404-347-1054
Email: vonco3@bellsouth.net
Website: www.voncreations.com
Meeting planning & management, conferences, special events & marketing campaigns. (Woman/AA, estab 1989, empl 2, sales $145,279, cert: NMSDC, WBENC, 8(a))

Idaho

8472 Milligan Events
1116 S Vista Ave #189
Boise, ID 83705
Contact: Milligan Events Owner
Tel: 208-387-0770
Email: diversitymatters@milliganevents.com
Website: www.milliganevents.com
Event & meeting planning & logistics. (Woman, estab 1994, empl 8, sales $756,972, cert: WBENC)

Illinois

8473 Aeffect, Inc.
740 Waukegan Rd Ste 400
Deerfield, IL 60015
Contact: CEO
Tel: 847-267-0169
Email: info@aeffect.com
Website: www.aeffect.com
Marketing research & consulting: Integrated Marketing Communications, Quantitative & Qualitative Research, Brand Tracking, Multi-Mode Surveys. (Woman, estab 1994, empl 20, sales , cert: WBENC)

8474 Bamboo Worldwide Inc.
30 N Racine Ave, Ste 300
Chicago, IL 60607
Contact: Tracy Thirion President
Tel: 773-227-4848
Email: tracyt@bambooinc.com
Website: www.bambooworldwide.com
Branding, innovation & market research. (Woman, estab , empl , sales $1,700,545, cert: WBENC)

8475 Beaman Public Relations, Inc.
401 N Michigan Ave, Ste 1300
Chicago, IL 60611
Contact: Robin Beaman President
Tel: 312-751-9689
Email: rbeaman@beamaninc.com
Website: www.beamaninc.com
Public relations, marketing & advertising services. (Woman/AA, estab 1996, empl 7, sales $1,084,431, cert: State, City, NMSDC, WBENC)

8476 Belle Communications
1390 Jaycox Rd
Chicago, IL 60673
Contact: Kate Finley CEO
Tel: 614-304-1463
Email: kate@bellecommunication.com
Website: www.bellecommunication.com/
Digital public relations and social media agency. (Woman, estab 2013, empl 16, sales $1,112,921, cert: WBENC)

8477 Classical Marketing LLC
2300 Cabot Dr Ste 390
Lisle, IL 60532
Contact: Susan Mazanek Managing Partner
Tel: 847-969-9006
Email: smazanek@classicalmarketing.com
Website: www.classicalmarketing.com
Marketing programs in Business to Business and Business to Consumer categories for clients in retail, financial services, automotive, health care. (Woman, estab 1999, empl 8, sales $1,700,687, cert: WBENC)

8478 Creative & Response Research Services, Inc.
500 N Michigan Ave, 12th Fl
Chicago, IL 60611
Contact: Robbin Jaklin CFO
Tel: 312-828-9200
Email: robbinj@crresearch.com
Website: www.crresearch.com
Custom market research, internet surveys, phone surveys, focus groups, qualitative & quantitative research. (Woman, estab 1960, empl 120, sales $23,268,888, cert: State, WBENC)

8479 Customer Lifecycle, LLC
1112 W Boughton Rd, Ste 365
Bolingbrook, IL 60440
Contact: Principal
Tel: 630-412-8989
Email: info@customerlifecycle.us
Website: www.customerlifecycle.us
Full-service qualitative and quantitative market research, plan, support and deploy customer satisfaction and loyalty research and align the stages of the customer lifecycle to improve customer loyalty. (Woman, estab 2008, empl 16, sales , cert: WBENC)

8480 Data Research Inc.
2525 Cabot Dr Ste 107
Lisle, IL 60532
Contact: Leslie Gunner Losh President
Tel: 630-281-8307
Email: lgunnerlosh@mindseyeresearch.com
Website: www.mindseyeresearch.com
Market research services. (Woman, estab 1982, empl 46, sales $3,600,000, cert: WBENC)

PROFESSIONAL SERVICES: Public Relations/Marketing

8481 DCC Marketing, LLC
2130 N 22nd St
Decatur, IL 62526
Contact: Kara Demirjian Huss President
Tel: 217-421-7580
Email: ksd@dccmarketing.com
Website: www.dccmarketing.com
Integrated marketing, communications and digital services. (Woman, estab 2000, empl 10, sales $1,200,000, cert: State, WBENC)

8482 Elemento L2, LLC
401 S LaSalle St, Ste 1501
Chicago, IL 60605
Contact: Ivan Lopez Managing Dir
Tel: 312-465-2355
Email: chemistry@elementol2.com
Website: www.elementol2.com
Multicultural marketing, experiential, PR, shopper & digital marketing. (Hisp, estab 2011, empl 15, sales $1,048,333, cert: NMSDC)

8483 Eved Services, Inc.
4811 Oakton St, Ste 250
Skokie, IL 60077
Contact: Alexis Feczko Dir of Sales Operations
Tel: 773-764-7000
Email: sales@eved.com
Website: www.eved.com/
Event services, destination management, technology services. (Woman, estab 2004, empl 25, sales $8,100,000, cert: WBENC)

8484 Fridkin Valo, Inc. dba TPG Live Events
210 N Cass Ave, Ste A
Westmont, IL 60559
Contact: Christina Piedlow CEO
Tel: 630-353-1308
Email: cpiedlow@tpgliveevents.com
Website: www.tpgliveevents.com
Event management and marketing expertise, creativity. (Woman, estab 1994, empl 9, sales $3,835,057, cert: WBENC)

8485 Frontline Public Strategies, Inc.
100 E. Washington St
Springfield, IL 62701
Contact: Kim Robinson President
Tel: 217-528-3434
Email: kimrobinson@frontline-online.net
Website: www.frontline-online.net
Public relations, marketing, event planning & public affairs. (Woman, estab 2001, empl 12, sales $1,200,000, cert: State, WBENC)

8486 Gerard Design, Inc.
28371 Davis Pkwy
Warrenville, IL 60555
Contact: Carolyn Gerard President
Tel: 630-355-0775
Email: carolyn@gerarddesign.com
Website: www.gerarddesign.com
Strategic Branding and Design, Communications, Graphic Design. (Woman, estab 0, empl , sales , cert: WBENC)

8487 Group O, Inc.
4905 77th Ave
Milan, IL 61264
Contact: Mike De La Cruz Sr VP Business Dev & Diversity
Tel: 210-213-2258
Email: supplierdiversity@groupo.com
Website: www.groupo.com
Single source integrated marketing solutions, customer loyalty, rebate administration & fulfillment, gift cards, inbound & outbound call center services, 4-color printing, print personalization, direct mail & fulfillment. (Hisp, estab 1974, empl 1200, sales $900,424,000, cert: NMSDC)

8488 Ivan Carlson & Associates
2224 W Fulton
Chicago, IL 60612
Contact: Tina Carlson President
Tel: 312-829-4616
Email: tina@ivancarlson.com
Website: www.ivancarlson.com
Event production & management, logistics, staging, sound & lighting. (Woman, estab 1974, empl 25, sales $3,370,000, cert: WBENC)

8489 JAK Graphic Design, LLC
4949 Forest Ave
Downers Grove, IL 60515
Contact: Jill Kerrigan Founder & CEO
Tel: 630-512-0500
Email: jill@jakcd.com
Website: www.jakcd.com
Creative concepting, design and final art production in both print and digital channels including, direct mail, internal corporate employee communications, POP, emails, landing pages, animated and static banner ads, wireframes and web. (Woman, estab 1995, empl 6, sales $1,500,000, cert: WBENC)

8490 JRS Consulting, Inc.
1316 Gregory Ave
Wilmette, IL 60091
Contact: Jenny Schade President
Tel: 847-920-1701
Email: jenny.schade@JRSConsulting.net
Website: www.JRSconsulting.net
Market research, management consulting, marketing & internal & external communications initiatives. (Woman, estab 2002, empl 1, sales , cert: WBENC)

8491 JumpGarden Consulting, LLC
1534 Washington Ave
Wilmette, IL 60091
Contact: Sheila Cahnman President
Tel: 312-286-0119
Email: sheila@jumpgardenllc.com
Website: www.jumpgardenllc.com
Healthcare design, planning & marketing solutions. (Woman, estab 2014, empl 1, sales , cert: State, City, WBENC)

PROFESSIONAL SERVICES: Public Relations/Marketing

8492 K.O. Strategies
2903 N Wolcott Ave, Ste B
Chicago, IL 60657
Contact: Kate O'Malley CEO
Tel: 312-307-4206
Email:
Website: www.kostrategies.com
Strategic communications, public affairs, stakeholder relations, crisis leadership & strategic planning/presentations. (Woman, estab 2006, empl 1, sales , cert: WBENC)

8493 Kathy Schaeffer and Associates, Inc.
17 N State St, Ste 1690
Chicago, IL 60602
Contact: Kathy Schaeffer President
Tel: 312-251-5100
Email: kschaeffer@ksapr.com
Website: www.ksapr.com
Public relations. (Woman, estab 1994, empl 5, sales , cert: City)

8494 L3 Agency
1452 E 53rd
Chicago, IL 60615
Contact: Larvetta Loftin CEO
Tel: 312-268-5207
Email: larvetta.loftin@l3eventeurs.com
Website: www.thel3agency.com
Marketing and communications, digital content creation, PR, advertising, brand experiences, corporate sponsorship, community outreach, and social philanthropy. (Woman/AA, estab 2000, empl 4, sales , cert: NMSDC)

8495 Liberty Lithographers, Inc.
18625 W Creek Dr
Tinley Park, IL 60477
Contact: Angela Hipelius CEO
Tel: 708-633-7450
Email: ahipelius@libertycreativesolutions.com
Website: www.libertycreativesolutions.com
Marketing services: graphic design, direct mail campaigns, research, promotions & loyalty campaigns, marketing collateral, advertising, web design, brand development, corporate identity. (Woman, estab 1964, empl 65, sales $12,000,001, cert: WBENC)

8496 Live Marketing
1201 N Clark St
Chicago, IL 60610
Contact: Alyssa Lavik Relationship Mgr
Tel: 312-787-4800
Email: alavik@livemarketing.com
Website: www.livemarketing.com
Trade show engagement strategies. (Woman, estab 1978, empl 175, sales $7,100,000, cert: WBENC)

8497 Magnolia Insights
350 N Orleans St, Ste 9000N
Chicago, IL 60654
Contact: Tania Haigh CEO
Tel: 646-768-4279
Email:
Website: www.magnoliainsights.com
Integrated marketing communications agency. (Hisp, estab 2014, empl 5, sales , cert: NMSDC)

8498 Marketing Innovators International Inc.
9701 W Higgins Rd Ste 400
Rosemont, IL 60018
Contact: Merrie Marinovich Acct Exec
Tel: 847-696-1111
Email: mmarinovich@marketinginnovators.com
Website: www.marketinginnovators.com
Employee recognition award programs. (Woman, estab 1978, empl 70, sales , cert: WBENC)

8499 Mary O'Connor & Company
220 W River Dr
St. Charles, IL 60174
Contact: Mary O'Connor President
Tel: 630-443-4300
Email: moconnor@mocandco.com
Website: www.mocandco.com
Meeting & event mgmt, online event registration, program dev, employee training & dev, speaker svcs, hotel mgmt, transportation, food & beverage mgmt. (Woman, estab 1995, empl 17, sales $3,400,000, cert: WBENC)

8500 Matrex Exhibits
301 S Church St
Addison, IL 60101
Contact: VP Business Dev
Tel: 630-628-2233
Email:
Website: www.matrexhibits.com
Tradeshow exhibits, design, construction & mgmt, graphic design & production, tradeshow svcs. (Woman, estab 1987, empl 66, sales $27,000,000, cert: WBENC)

8501 Mekky Media Relations
913 S. I-Oka Ave
Mount Prospect, IL 60056
Contact: Bill Rossi COO
Tel: 312-315-0181
Email: supplierdiversity@mekkymedia.com
Website: www.mekkymedia.com
Public relations firm. (Woman, estab 2016, empl 5, sales $1,125,901, cert: WBENC)

8502 Metaphrasis Language and Cultural Solutions, LLC
1147 W Ohio, Ste 306
Chicago, IL 60714
Contact: Elizabeth Colon President
Tel: 815-464-1423
Email: ecolon@metaphrasislcs.com
Website: www.metaphrasislcs.com
Language services, interpretation, translation & corporate trainings. (Minority, Woman, estab 2007, empl 6, sales , cert: State, WBENC)

8503 MHJohnson & Associates, Inc.
1918 S Michigan Ave Ste 302
Chicago, IL 60616
Contact: Marilyn Johnson Principal
Tel: 312-949-9164
Email: marilyn@mhjohnson.com
Website: www.mhjohnson.com
Marketing management, program, product development & mgmt, organizational development. (Woman/AA, estab 2001, empl 2, sales $225,000, cert: WBENC)

PROFESSIONAL SERVICES: Public Relations/Marketing

8504 ModelPeople Inc
301 W Grand Ave Ste 139
Chicago, IL 60654
Contact: Claire Brooks President
Tel: 858-755-7150
Email: cbrooks@modelpeopleinc.com
Website: www.modelpeopleinc.com
Qualitative research, ethnographic research, consumer research, deep insights research, consumer video production, consumer brand consulting. (Woman, estab 2000, empl 3, sales $1,400,000, cert: WBENC)

8505 Neiger Design, Inc.
1515 Sherman Ave
Evanston, IL 60201
Contact: President
Tel: 847-328-1328
Email: info@neigerdesign.com
Website: www.neigerdesign.com
Graphic design, marketing & communications: website design, annual reports, logos & corporate identity, brochures, employee communications, packaging, magazine & book design. (Woman, estab 1989, empl 6, sales , cert: WBENC)

8506 PACO Communications, Inc. dba PACO Collective
400 S. Green St Unit H
Chicago, IL 60607
Contact: Ozzie Godinez CEO
Tel: 312-281-2040
Email: marketing@pacocollective.com
Website: www.pacocollective.com
Hispanic marketing, advertising, public relations & community outreach, web design & development. (Hisp, estab 2006, empl 40, sales $19,900,000, cert: NMSDC)

8507 PCH Communications
600 W Fluton Fl 4
Chicago, IL 60661
Contact: Alice Pollard SVP Operations
Tel: 312-384-1906
Email: alice@discovercg.com
Website: www.commongroundmgs.com
Advertising/Marketing, Strategic Planning/Development, Creative, Public Relations, Event Marketing, Multicultural Marketing, Digital Marketing , Shopper/Retail Marketing, Content Development, Research Promotions. (AA, Hisp, estab 2014, empl 256, sales $35,276,000, cert: NMSDC)

8508 Production Partners Company LLC
911 Rock Spring Rd
Naperville, IL 60565
Contact: Haves McNeal CEO
Tel: 312-735-1486
Email: haves@pp-co.biz
Website: www.pp-co.biz
Marketing Communications. (AA, estab 2017, empl 5, sales , cert: NMSDC)

8509 Public Communications Inc.
1 E Wacker Dr Ste 2450
Chicago, IL 60601
Contact: Pamela Oettel CFO/COO
Tel: 312-558-1770
Email: poettel@pcipr.com
Website: www.pcipr.com
Develop integrated communications strategies: Advocacy Programs, Board Counsel, Branding & Positioning, Competitive Analysis, Consumer Marketing, Conservation & Wildlife Issues, Crisis/Issues Management & Monitoring. (Woman, estab 1962, empl 50, sales $6,111,500, cert: State, WBENC)

8510 Quicksilver Associates, Inc.
18 W Ontario St
Chicago, IL 60654
Contact: Diane MacWilliams President
Tel: 312-943-7622
Email: dianem@quicksilvernow.com
Website: www.quicksilvernow.com
Print, video, meeting planning, production, web & interactive media. (Woman, estab 1976, empl 22, sales $4,600,000, cert: WBENC)

8511 Rabin Research Company
6177 N Lincoln Ave #369
Chicago, IL 60659
Contact: Michelle Elster President
Tel: 312-527-5010
Email: melster@rabin-research.com
Website: www.rabinroberts.com
Social Media Ethnography, Database Marketing Analytics, Secondary Research (Woman, estab 1963, empl 8, sales $1,200,000, cert: WBENC)

8512 Reilly Connect
625 N Michigan Ave Ste 1705
Chicago, IL 60611
Contact: Kim Smith President
Tel: 312-600-6780
Email: ksmith@tcgad.com
Website: www.tcgad.com
Social media marketing, brand activation & events, video production, public relations. (Woman, estab 1996, empl 5, sales , cert: WBENC)

8513 Research Explorers, Inc
1111 New Trier Ct
Wilmette, IL 60091
Contact: Lisa Gaines McDonald President
Tel: 847-853-0237
Email: lisa@researchexplorers.com
Website: www.reserachexplorers.com
Market research & consulting services: qualitative research, focus groups, in-depth interviews, ethnographies, brain storming & idea generation sessions. (Woman/AA, estab 1994, empl 1, sales $305,087, cert: City, NMSDC)

8514 Revel Global Events
1402 N Western Ave
Chicago, IL 60622
Contact: Dir of Sales
Tel: 773-292-9100
Email: hello@therevelgroup.com
Website: www.revelglobalevents.com
Event planning & production, experiential events. (Woman, estab 2007, empl 15, sales $3,000,000, cert: WBENC)

8515 Signature Media Group Talk
1327 W Washington Blvd
Chicago, IL 60607
Contact: Pam Redwood President
Tel: 312-226-5552
Email: pam@smgspeakers.com
Website: www.smgspeakers.com
Public communications, speakers bureau, brand creation awareness, client advertising, ad management, creative services, custom publishing, event planning, media planning, media relations, corporate communications. (Woman/AA, estab 2009, empl 2, sales $400,000, cert: State, City)

PROFESSIONAL SERVICES: Public Relations/Marketing

8516 Simple Truth Communication Partners Inc
314 W Superior St Ste 300
Chicago, IL 60654
Contact: Rhonda Kokot Managing Partner
Tel: 312-376-0360
Email: m.person@yoursimpletruth.com
Website: www.yoursimpletruth.com
Brand strategy & positioning, B2B, sales force & corporate/internal communications. (Woman, estab 1988, empl 20, sales $9,803,864, cert: WBENC)

8517 Strategic Marketing, Inc.
350 S Northwest Hwy Ste 304
Park Ridge, IL 60068
Contact: Leslie Reinhardt Controller
Tel: 847-720-7500
Email: lreinhardt@smialcott.com
Website: www.smialcott.com
Marketing research services. (Woman, estab 1980, empl 23, sales $7,636,812, cert: WBENC)

8518 The Wynning Experience
2325 South Michigan Ave
Chicago, IL 60616
Contact: Lead Event Planner
Tel: 312-800-3605
Email: hello@thewynningexperience.com
Website: www.thewynningexperience.com
Event & meeting mgmt. (Woman/AA, estab 1996, empl 5, sales $400,000, cert: NMSDC, WBENC)

8519 Total Event Resources
1920 N Thoreau Dr Ste 105
Schaumburg, IL 60173
Contact: Lynnea Walsh Dir of Operations
Tel: 847-397-2200
Email: lwalsh@total-event.com
Website: www.total-event.com
Corporate communications, event production, entertainment [roduction, meeting management, experiential learning & destination management. (Woman, estab 1995, empl 15, sales $3,320,000, cert: WBENC)

8520 Wedgeworth Business Communications
2215 Enterprise Dr, Ste 1506
Westchester, IL 60154
Contact: Pamela G. Wedgeworth President
Tel: 708-223-0019
Email: pamela@wedgeworthbiz.com
Website: www.wedgeworthbiz.com
Visual communications: video production, multimedia creation, print & electronic collateral, event coordination. (Woman/AA, estab 1999, empl 2, sales $320,000, cert: City, WBENC)

Indiana

8521 Avant Healthcare
630 W Carmel Dr
Carmel, IN 46032
Contact: Jeff Sears Exec Dir
Tel: 317-208-3600
Email: info@avanthc.com
Website: www.AvantHC.com
Peer-to-peer marketing for pharmaceutical and biotechnology companies, creating comprehensive communication strategies & plans. (Woman, estab 1994, empl 200, sales $22,000,000, cert: WBENC)

8522 Coles Marketing Communications
3950 Priority Way Ste 106
Indianapolis, IN 46240
Contact: Barbara Coles President
Tel: 317-571-0051
Email: bcoles@colesmarketing.com
Website: www.colesmarketing.com
Marketing communications services: graphic design, web design, e-communications, public relations, media relations, word of mouth marketing, videography, photography. (Woman, estab 1985, empl 10, sales $1,250,000, cert: State, City)

8523 TalentCode Management Group
1801 S Liberty Dr, Ste 300
Bloomington, IN 47403
Contact: Melanie Hoffman Business Devel
Tel: 888-381-7248
Email: melanie.hoffman@employbridge.com
Website: www.employbridge.com
Staffing services. (Minority, estab 1997, empl 3000, sales $3,000,000,000, cert: NMSDC)

Kansas

8524 A.S.K. Associates, Inc.
1505 Kasold Dr
Lawrence, KS 66047
Contact: Kenneth Martinez President
Tel: 800-315-4333
Email: kenm@askusa.com
Website: www.askusa.com
Conference, convention, trade show, meeting, seminar support services. (Minority, Woman, estab 1979, empl 15, sales $6,600,000, cert: WBENC)

8525 Advantage Marketing Inc.
10026 W Westlakes Ct
Wichita, KS 67205
Contact: Cori K Kohlmeier President
Tel: 316-729-0500
Email: cori@admarkict.com
Website: www.admarkict.com
Design, marketing, and communication. (Hisp, estab 2013, empl 16, sales $6,750,000, cert: NMSDC)

8526 Exhibit Arts, LLC
326 N Athenian
Wichita, KS 67203
Contact: Beth Harshfield Managing Member
Tel: 316-264-2915
Email: beth@exhibitarts.net
Website: www.exhibitarts.net
Exhibit design, fabrication & management, project management, conference support services, warehousing & fulfillment center services. (Minority, Woman, estab 2000, empl 160, sales $18,843,000, cert: NMSDC, NWBOC)

8527 Meeting Excellence, Inc.
7300 West 110th St Ste 700
Overland Park, KS 66210
Contact: Kory Oplinger Dir of Sales
Tel: 913-693-4675
Email: koplinger@meeting-excellence.com
Website: www.meeting-excellence.com
Corporate meetings, events & incentive travel services. (AA, estab 2003, empl 4, sales $1,113,929, cert: NMSDC)

8528 Sassafras Marketing, Inc.
      13600 Santa Fe Trail Dr
      Lenexa, KS 66215
      Contact: Jenny Holton CEO
      Tel: 913-888-7400
      Email: creativejobs@sassafrasmarketing.co
      Website: www.sassafrasmarketing.com
Marketing, customer/consumer promotions & B2B communication. (Woman, estab 2000, empl 8, sales $1,342,000, cert: WBENC)

8529 The Lexinet Corporation
      701 N Union
      Council Grove, KS 66846
      Contact: Lindsey Boyer President
      Tel: 620-767-7000
      Email: indseyb@lexinetcorporation.com
      Website: www.lexinetcorporation.com
Marketing campaigns & programs, custom personalized variable data printed direct mail, fully-integrated marketing centers, complete multi-channel solutions. (Woman, estab 1991, empl 18, sales $3,100,000, cert: WBENC)

Kentucky

8530 ConvenePro
      1792 Alysheba Way Ste 160
      Lexington, KY 40509
      Contact: Delphine Hepp Acct Dir
      Tel: 859-276-0065
      Email: dhepp@convenepro.com
      Website: www.convenepro.com
Event management, marketing & communications, live speaker programs, conferences & trade shows, promotional presentations, satellite broadcasts/webcasts, live & virtual training workshops, product training. (Woman, estab 1995, empl 50, sales , cert: NWBOC)

8531 Corporate World Public Relations
      4017 Whiteblossom Estates Ct
      Louisville, KY 40241
      Contact: Ray Callender, Jr. VP
      Tel: 678-592-8516
      Email: ray.callender@corpworldpr.com
      Website: www.corpworldpr.com
Exhibits design & management services. (AA, estab , empl , sales $262,000, cert: NMSDC)

8532 Digital Business Solutions, Inc.
      517 S Fourth St
      Louisville, KY 40202
      Contact: Cynthia Masters CEO
      Tel: 502-562-7895
      Email: rfp@dbswebsite.com
      Website: www.dbswebsite.com
Web & digital development, design, strategy & marketing, websites, apps, mobile, hosting, interactive infographics, SEO, digital business strategy, lead generation online marketing. (Woman, estab 2000, empl 20, sales $1,700,000, cert: WBENC)

8533 Intrinzic Marketing & Design
      One Levee Way, Ste 3121
      Newport, KY 41071
      Contact: Tami Beattie Office Mgr
      Tel: 859-292-5061
      Email: tami@intrinzicinc.com
      Website: www.intrinzicinc.com
Marketing & design: marketing, design & interactive svcs, creative concepting, campaign dev, graphic design, copywriting, public relations, website design, email marketing & media planning. (Woman, estab 1989, empl 12, sales , cert: WBENC)

8534 Mackey Group LLC
      2250 Mackey Pike
      Nicholasville, KY 40356
      Contact: Nancy Wiser President
      Tel: 859-887-0866
      Email: nancy@wiserstrategies.com
      Website: www.wiserstrategies.com
Public relations, marketing, market research, corporate relations, crisis planning & response, media relations, branding creative services, writing, graphic design, photography, video production & editing, print production management. (Woman, estab 2011, empl 1, sales $300,000, cert: WBENC)

8535 New West LLC
      9630 Ormsby Station Rd
      Louisville, KY 40223
      Contact: Melvin Graham Managing Dir
      Tel: 888-867-7811
      Email: mgraham@newwestagency.com
      Website: www.newwestagency.com
Advertising, Public Relations, Brand Strategy, Website & Mobile App Development, Social Media, Multicultural Marketing, SEO/SEM/PPC, Event Planning & Video Production. (AA, estab 2002, empl 28, sales $5,500,000, cert: NMSDC)

Massachusetts

8536 Causemedia, Inc.
      50 Hunt St Ste 140
      Watertown, MA 02472
      Contact: Donna Latson Gittens Principal
      Tel: 617-558-6850
      Email: info@causemedia.com
      Website: www.moreadvertising.com
Communications, advertising & marketing agency. (Woman/AA, estab 1997, empl 8, sales $4,636,330, cert: State, NMSDC, WBENC)

8537 Color Media Group, LLC
      4 Copley Pl, Ste 120
      Boston, MA 02116
      Contact: Josefina Bonilla President
      Tel: 617-266-6961
      Email: josefina@colorboston.com
      Website: www.colormagazineusa.com
Web advertising, signature events, event management, strategic marketing initiatives, new markets, media buying services, public relations. (Minority, Woman, estab 2007, empl 3, sales $289,000, cert: State)

PROFESSIONAL SERVICES: Public Relations/Marketing

8538   Conover + Gould Strategic Communications, Inc.
       69 Milk St Ste 101
       Westborough, MA 01581
       Contact: Heather Conover CEO
       Tel: 508-789-9273
       Email: hconover@conovergould.com
       Website: www.conovergould.com
Public relations & marketing communications, environmental communications & event management. (Woman, estab 1984, empl 9, sales $1,528,016, cert: State)

8539   Consolidated Marketing Services, Inc.
       841 Woburn St
       Wilmington, MA 01887
       Contact: Andrew Bausman key acct Mgr
       Tel: 800-474-5756
       Email: abausman@cmsassociates.com
       Website: www.cmsassociates.com
Marketing svcs: fulfillment, printing, mailing, promotional products, graphics & catalogs. (Woman, estab , empl , sales $4,000,000, cert: WBENC)

8540   EMI Strategic Marketing Inc.
       15 Broad St
       Boston, MA 02109
       Contact: Paul OBrien VP Finance
       Tel: 617-224-1101
       Email: pobrien@emiboston.com
       Website: www.emiboston.com
Marketing services. (Woman, estab 1989, empl 45, sales $7,000,000, cert: State, WBENC)

8541   Global Link Language Services, Inc.
       71 Commercial St Ste 218
       Boston, MA 02109
       Contact: Carol Ann Managing Dir
       Tel: 617-451-6655
       Email: cmichel@gleneagleadv.com
       Website: www.languagetranslate.com
Intl communication svcs: translation, interpretation, localization, multilingual typesetting & desktop publishing. (Woman, estab 1996, empl 4, sales $650,000, cert: State)

8542   Grand Design, Inc.
       42 Chestnut St Ste 2
       Salem, MA 01970
       Contact: Debra Glabeau Principal
       Tel: 978-741-0112
       Email: dglabeau@greatisland.com
       Website: www.greatisland.com
Graphic design & marketing communications solutions, brand development, logos & corporate identity systems, naming & taglines, collateral & brochures, websites, email & direct mail programs, print advertising, sales kits. (Woman, estab 1982, empl 4, sales $223,742, cert: State)

8543   Inspired Marketing
       20 Maple St 4th Fl, Ste 1
       Springfield, MA 01103
       Contact: Lauren Mendoza Office Mgr
       Tel: 413-303-0101
       Email: lauren@inspiredmarketing.biz
       Website: www.inspiredmarketing.biz
Marketing, Event Planning, Social Media, Media Buying, Advertising, Graphic Design (Woman, estab 2009, empl 6, sales $632,920, cert: WBENC)

8544   Kelley Chunn & Associates
       184 Dudley St, Ste 106
       Boston, MA 02119
       Contact: Kelley Chunn Principal
       Tel: 617-427-0997
       Email: kc4info@aol.com
       Website: www.kelleychunn.com
Multicultural marketing & public relations services. (Woman/AA, estab 1991, empl 1, sales $160,000, cert: State)

8545   NXTevent, Inc.
       60 K St, 4th Fl
       Boston, MA 02127
       Contact: Joanne O'Connell General Mgr
       Tel: 617-904-9053
       Email: connect@nxtevent.com
       Website: www.nxtevent.com
Event & destination management. (Woman, estab 2001, empl 8, sales $2,447,766, cert: State, WBENC)

8546   The Castle Group, Inc.
       38 Third Ave Ste 200
       Charlestown, MA 02129
       Contact: Wendy Spivak Treasurer
       Tel: 617-337-9535
       Email: wspivak@thecastlegrp.com
       Website: www.thecastlegrp.com/
Public relations & events management. (Woman, estab 1996, empl 23, sales $5,300,000, cert: WBENC)

8547   Twirling Tiger Press Inc.
       7 Jeffrey Road
       Franklin, MA 02038
       Contact: Maureen Joyce President
       Tel: 508-520-3258
       Email: mjoyce@twirlingtigermedia.com
       Website: www.twirlingtigermedia.com
Writing & graphic design, creation of design & imagery, development, scheduling & trafficking, & content generation, advertising, printing, promotions, publications, RFPs & proposals, social media, websites, white papers. (Woman, estab 2013, empl 2, sales $270,000, cert: WBENC)

Maryland

8548   Bates Creative Group, LLC
       1119 East West Hwy
       Silver Spring, MD 20910
       Contact: Debra Bates Schrott President
       Tel: 301-495-8844
       Email: debbie@batescreative.com
       Website: www.batescreative.com
Branding & Identity, Magazine Design & Redesign, Event Marketing, Marketing Collateral, Web Design & Development, iPad UI Design, Annual Reports, Media Kits. (Woman, estab 2003, empl 11, sales , cert: WBENC)

8549   BrightKey, Inc.
       60 West St Ste 300
       Annapolis, MD 21401
       Contact: Krystal Dyer Business Solutions
       Tel: 301-604-3305
       Email: businessdevelopment@brightkey.net
       Website: www.brightkey.net/
Marketing research, strategy & creative services. (Woman, estab 1988, empl 600, sales $34,212,531, cert: WBENC)

PROFESSIONAL SERVICES: Public Relations/Marketing

8550 Hargrove Inc.
One Hargrove Dr
Lanham, MD 20706
Contact: Meghan Muniz Natl Sales Exec
Tel: 301-306-3000
Email: meghanmuniz@hargroveinc.com
Website: www.hargroveinc.com
Events, exhibits & trade shows: venue selection, staffing, design, menu development, security, building of stages, set design, AV & lighting services. (Woman, estab 1946, empl 225, sales $73,000,000, cert: WBENC)

8551 Humdinger Enterprises LLC
PO Box 4542
Crofton, MD 21114
Contact: Alexis Jenkins Managing Member
Tel: 410-279-0205
Email: alexis@humdingerenterprise.com
Website: www.humdingerenterprises.com
Event planning: festivals, concerts, meetings, award shows & broadcast events. (Woman, estab 2008, empl 5, sales $230,681, cert: State)

8552 JDC Events, LLC
8720 Georgia Ave Ste 801
Silver Spring, MD 20910
Contact: Jennifer Collins President
Tel: 240-512-4219
Email: jennifer@jdc-events.com
Website: www.jdc-events.com
Meeting & event management: custom-designed logistical solutions, guidance & communications, meetings, conferences & special events. (Woman/AA, estab 1997, empl 4, sales $2,040,000, cert: NMSDC, WBENC, 8(a))

8553 McMillon Communications, Inc.
12902 Argyle Circle
Fort Washington, MD 20744
Contact: Doris McMillon CEO
Tel: 301-292-9141
Email: Doris@McMillonCommunications.com
Website: www.mcmilloncommunications.com
Marketing support solutions, public relations & strategic partnership development. (Woman/AA, estab 1986, empl 1, sales $4,528,979, cert: State, WBENC)

8554 Mjach Designs
5100 Buckeystown Pike Ste 250
Frederick, MD 21704
Contact: Admin
Tel: 410-366-0505
Email: rose@mjachdesigns.com
Website: www.mjachdesigns.com
Graphic design, marketing & communications, web design & implementation, print production, marketing & advertising, public relations, media planning & buying, research & copywriting. (Woman, estab 2003, empl 5, sales $336,640, cert: State, City)

8555 MultiLingual Solutions, Inc.
11 N Washington St Ste 300
Rockville, MD 20850
Contact: Paul Keys VP Business Dev
Tel: 301-424-7444
Email: pkeys@mlsolutions.com
Website: www.mlsolutions.com
Document Translation, On-site and Remote Interpretation, Website & Software Localization, Multicultural Marketing & Advertising, Language, Cultural & Executive Training & Curriculum Devel, Desktop Publishing. (Minority, Woman, estab 2002, empl 162, sales $9,729,040, cert: NMSDC, WBENC)

8556 Pensari, LLC
107 Theodora Court
Forest Hill, MD 21050
Contact: Hans Plate
Tel: 410-588-5465
Email: hans.plate@pensari.com
Website: www.pensari.com
Market research specializing in healthcare research, qualitative & quantitative research. (Hisp, estab 2013, empl 1, sales , cert: NMSDC)

8557 Slice, Inc dba SliceWorks
20301 Highland Hall Dr
Montgomery Village, MD 20886
Contact: Kathleen Rabil CEO
Tel: 301-519-8101
Email: kathi@slice-works.com
Website: www.slice-works.com
Graphic design, marketing strategy consulting, marketing communications & campaign devel, social media strategy consulting & execution, website design & devel, brand consulting, publication layout & design. (Woman, estab 1997, empl 4, sales $445,690, cert: WBENC)

8558 Sutter Design, Inc. dba The Sutter Group
4640 Forbes Blvd. Ste 160A
Lanham, MD 20706
Contact: Karen Sutter President
Tel: 301-459-5445
Email: karen@sutter-group.com
Website: www.sutter-group.com
Marketing, advertising & public relations: brand, creating logos, corporate collateral, websites, direct mail & e-marketing campaigns, advertising & public relations. (Woman, estab 1987, empl 8, sales $1,000,000, cert: State)

8559 The Hannon Group, LLC
10002 Edgewater Terr, Ste 100
Fort Washington, MD 20744
Contact: Sandra Wills Hannon President
Tel: 301-839-2744
Email: info@thehannongroup.com
Website: www.thehannongroup.com
Public relations, strategic planning, market research, materials development, communications training & consulting services. (Woman/AA, estab 1991, empl 2, sales $2,404,262, cert: WBENC)

8560 TMNcorp
8720 Georgia Ave, Ste 206
Silver Spring, MD 20910
Contact: Nhora Barrera Murphy President
Tel: 301-565-0770
Email: nbarrera@tmncorp.com
Website: www.tmncorp.com
Communication & social marketing, advertising, media relations, research & evaluation & cultural adaptation services. (Minority, Woman, estab 1999, empl 20, sales $4,850,000, cert: State)

8561 Transient Identiti, Inc.
11 Webster Hill Ct
Clarksburg, MD 20871
Contact: Albert Thompson Dir Brand Strategy
Tel: 301-792-8535
Email: albert@transientidentiti.com
Website: www.transientidentiti.com
Digital Marketing: mobile, social, display, search, apps, email, advanced targeting. (AA, estab 2002, empl 7, sales $424,000, cert: NMSDC)

PROFESSIONAL SERVICES: Public Relations/Marketing

8562 What Works Studio LLC
       8 Market Pl, Ste 300
       Baltimore, MD 21202
       Contact: Brooke Allen CEO
       Tel: 410-800-0788
       Email: hello@whatworksstudio.com
       Website: www.whatworksstudio.com
Full service creative marketing agency, digital, social media, and content marketing. (Woman, estab 2009, empl 2, sales $560,557, cert: City, WBENC)

Michigan

8563 Airfoil Public Relations, Inc.
       336 N Main St
       Royal Oak, MI 48067
       Contact: Sharon Neumann SVP Finance & Admin
       Tel: 248-304-1400
       Email: neumann@airfoilgroup.com
       Website: www.airfoilgroup.com
Marketing communications. (Woman, estab 2000, empl 37, sales $7,200,000, cert: WBENC)

8564 Archer Corporate Services
       6703 Haggerty Ste B
       Belleville, MI 48111
       Contact: Dennis Archer Dir of Operations
       Tel: 734-713-3100
       Email: diversity@theacsadvantage.com
       Website: www.theacsadvantage.com
Marketing support svcs: B2B fulfillment, rebates, direct response, sweepstakes, customer service, merchandising. (AA, estab 2004, empl 25, sales $15,400,000, cert: NMSDC)

8565 BPI Communications, LLC
       13700 Oakland Ave
       Highland Park, MI 48203
       Contact: Jim Suddendorf EVP Sales/mlktg
       Tel: 313-957-5459
       Email: j.suddendorf@bpicommunications.com
       Website: www.bpicommunications.com
Fulfillment & direct marketing solutions. (AA, estab 2005, empl 10, sales $107,000,000, cert: NMSDC)

8566 Bromberg & Associates, LLC
       3141 Caniff St.
       Hamtramck, MI 48212
       Contact: Carly Priehs Business Devel Specialist
       Tel: 313-871-0080
       Email: carly@brombergtranslations.com
       Website: www.brombergtranslations.com
Translations & interpretations: over 60 languages. (Woman, estab 1999, empl 20, sales , cert: WBENC)

8567 Collaborative Advantage Marketing
       2987 Franklin St
       Detroit, MI 48207
       Contact: Sales Rep
       Tel: 248-723-0793
       Email: accounting@camtrade.com
       Website: www.camtrade.com
Category Management Quality Assurance Programs Total Product Design Business Analysis Brand Management Full Service Marketing Headquarter Selling. (Woman, estab 1999, empl 18, sales , cert: WBENC)

8568 Harris Marketing Group, Inc.
       102 Pierce St
       Birmingham, MI 48009
       Contact: Wendy Vadnais Finance Dir
       Tel: 248-723-6300
       Email: wvadnais@harris-hmg.com
       Website: www.harris-hmg.com/
Integrated marketing campaigns, loyalty programs, brand advertising, targeted direct mail, fulfillment, media, public relations, training materials, website development, event marketing & viral marketing. (Woman, estab 1976, empl 10, sales $4,425,995, cert: WBENC)

8569 Maestro LLC
       7107 Elm Valley Dr
       Kalamazoo, MI 49009
       Contact: Tagg Petersen Dir Business Dev
       Tel: 800-319-2122
       Email: tagg@meetmaestro.com
       Website: www.meetmaestro.com
Training, brand consulting, management consulting services, solution based contractors. (Woman, estab 2007, empl 31, sales $7,612,178, cert: WBENC)

8570 RSVP Premier Group, LLC
       900 Wilshire Dr Ste 202
       Troy, MI 48084
       Contact: Tamika Brown CEO
       Tel: 248-663-4107
       Email: tbrown@rsvppremier.com
       Website: www.rsvppremier.com
Event planning & management, meeting planning, conference planning, incentive trips, trade shows/expos, event design & dÃ©cor, event production, celebrity entertainment, talent & speaker booking. (Woman/AA, estab 2002, empl 4, sales $109,450, cert: WBENC)

8571 Skyline Exhibits West Michigan
       4768 Danvers Dr. SE
       Kentwood, MI 49512
       Contact: Eloy Cantu President
       Tel: 616-301-8708
       Email: cantul@skylinewm.com
       Website: www.skyline.com
Trade show marketing, seminars, workshops. (Hisp, estab 2004, empl 5, sales $900,000, cert: NMSDC)

8572 Smith-Dahmer Associates, LLC
       116 State St
       Saint Joseph, MI 49085
       Contact: Lori Stanwood Dir Key Accounts
       Tel: 269-983-4748
       Email: loristanwood@smithdahmer.com
       Website: www.smithdahmer.com
Marketing research & consulting, custom qualitative & quantitative methodologies, innovation & design research processes. (Woman, estab 1995, empl 30, sales $9,000,000, cert: WBENC)

8573 Special D Events, Inc.
       535 Woodward Heights
       Ferndale, MI 48220
       Contact: Carol Galle CEO
       Tel: 248-336-8600
       Email: administrator@specialdevents.com
       Website: www.specialdevents.com
Corporate event planning. (Woman, estab 1992, empl 17, sales $2,200,000, cert: WBENC)

PROFESSIONAL SERVICES: Public Relations/Marketing

8574 Strategic Market Research Group, Inc.
      37129 Saint Martins St
      Livonia, MI 48152
      Contact: Ami Nienus President
      Tel: 734-452-9104
      Email: ami@smrginc.com
      Website: www.smrginc.com
Market research. (Woman/As-Ind, estab 2007, empl 1, sales , cert: WBENC)

8575 Vista Latinos LLC
      6582 Horncliffe
      Clarkston, MI 48346
      Contact: Terry Beltran-Miller President
      Tel: 248-978-7491
      Email: tbm@vistalatinos.com
      Website: www.VistaLatinos.com
Marketing consulting services. (Minority, Woman, estab 2005, empl 1, sales $150,000, cert: WBENC)

8576 Wilson-Taylor Associates, Inc.
      242 Lighthouse Circle
      Manistee, MI 49660
      Contact: Joanne Cleaver President
      Tel: 231-291-1275
      Email: jycleaver@wilson-taylorassoc.com
      Website: www.wilson-taylorassoc.com
Content strategy & execution, writing, editing, research, website content, digital publishing, strategic communication consulting, communication training, career training, media training, communication coaching. (Woman, estab 1998, empl 2, sales $110,000, cert: WBENC)

Minnesota

8577 Advent Creative Group
      7101 York Ave S, Ste 240
      Edina, MN 55435
      Contact: Mary Younggren Owner
      Tel: 952-746-5668
      Email: maryy@adventcreativegroup.com
      Website: www.adventcreativegroup.com
Advertising, communications, creative, marketing & interactive hiring resources, contract & full-time basis. (Woman, estab 2007, empl 4, sales $606,822, cert: WBENC)

8578 AllOut Marketing, Inc.
      5775 Wayzata Blvd Ste 700
      St. Louis Park, MN 55416
      Contact: Ruth Lane CEO
      Tel: 952-404-0800
      Email: ruthlane@alloutsuccess.com
      Website: www.alloutsuccess.com
Medical marketing consulting, market research, web development, graphic design, event management & public relations. (Woman/Hisp, estab 1995, empl 8, sales $722,000, cert: State)

8579 Amplio Marketing, Inc.
      7385 Mark St
      Greenfield, MN 55357
      Contact: Naomi Teske President
      Tel: 763-477-6910
      Email: naomi@ampliomarketing.com
      Website: www.ampliomarketing.com
Print communications, In-Store Point-of-Purchase, Brochures, Sell Sheets, Sales Tools, Training Materials, Direct Mail. (Woman, estab 2001, empl 2, sales $2,800,000, cert: WBENC)

8580 Art Partners Group, LLC
      3529 Raleigh Ave
      St Louis Park, MN 55416
      Contact: Brian Knudsvig Principal
      Tel: 952-548-6643
      Email: bknudsvig@artpartners.com
      Website: www.artpartners.com
Artwork, graphics & displays. Consulting, design, production & installation. (Woman, estab 2006, empl 10, sales $1,350,000, cert: WBENC)

8581 Azul 7, Inc.
      800 Hennepin Ave Ste 700
      Minneapolis, MN 55403
      Contact: Sara O'Brien Business Devel Lead
      Tel: 612-767-4335
      Email: hello@azul7.com
      Website: www.azul7.com
Build better brands, products & services, strategy & innovation consulting, research, digital product & service design along with innovation process training. (Woman, estab 2007, empl 16, sales $1,868,437, cert: WBENC)

8582 Char Mason & Associates, LLC, dba Mason Creative
      695 Mount Curve Blvd
      Saint Paul, MN 55116
      Contact: Owner
      Tel: 651-698-2678
      Email: char@masoncreative.biz
      Website: www.masoncreative.biz
Event planning agency. (Woman, estab 2000, empl 1, sales $117,469, cert: State)

8583 Creative Connections
      4049 Blackhawk Rd
      Eagan, MN 55122
      Contact: Marianne Badar Ohman Owner
      Tel: 651-261-7886
      Email: marianne@creativeconnections.net
      Website: www.creativeconnections.net
Communications consulting, marketing communications project management, conference, meeting, tradeshow & event planning & production, team leadership, teambuilding training & services. (Woman, estab 1998, empl 1, sales , cert: City)

8584 D.Trio Marketing Group
      401 N Third St, Ste 480
      Minneapolis, MN 55401
      Contact: Fred Driver Business Dev Dir
      Tel: 612-436-0401
      Email: fdriver@dtrio.com
      Website: www.dtrio.com
Direct marketing, strategy, creative, list, DP, print and lettershop production, fulfillment & graphic design services. (Woman, estab 2000, empl 12, sales $3,500,000, cert: WBENC)

8585 deZinnia, Inc.
      1032 W 7th St
      St. Paul, MN 55102
      Contact: Michele Boone CEO
      Tel: 651-695-1041
      Email: sbboone@dezinnia.com
      Website: www.dezinnia.com
Program management, graphic design, marketing, marketing communications, digital architecture. (Woman, estab 1993, empl 14, sales $1,322,045, cert: State, City, WBENC)

PROFESSIONAL SERVICES: Public Relations/Marketing

8586 Five Star Productions
      7400 Metro Blvd
      Minneapolis, MN 55439
      Contact: Cindy Black President
      Tel: 952-831-7309
      Email: cjblack@fivestarproductions.net
      Website: www.fivestarproductions.net
Full-service production and event management, national sales meetings and conventions; recognition, incentive, and awards programs; entertainment and keynote speakers; product launches; philanthropic and special events. (Woman, estab 1989, empl 3, sales $1,300,000, cert: WBENC)

8587 Futura Marketing, Inc.
      9531 W 78th St Ste 250
      Eden Prairie, MN 55344
      Contact: Kelly Wold Smith President
      Tel: 952-843-5400
      Email: kelly@futuramarketing.com
      Website: www.futuramarketing.com
Marketing svcs: strategic planning, project management & creative design. (Woman, estab 1999, empl 13, sales $1,146,520, cert: WBENC)

8588 Group Ventures Inc.
      1770 James Ave S, Ste 2
      Minneapolis, MN 55403
      Contact: Ann Wellmuth President
      Tel: 612-821-0511
      Email: ann@groupventuresinc.com
      Website: www.groupventuresinc.com
Event & meeting planning, coordination & execution of incentive trips, sales & organizational meetings, board of directors meetings, conventions & tradeshows. (Woman, estab 1997, empl , sales $14,000,000, cert: WBENC)

8589 KDG InterActive, Inc.
      8010 Demontreville Trail
      Lake Elmo, MN 55042
      Contact: Lynette Kramer President
      Tel: 651-748-8480
      Email: lynette@kdg.com
      Website: www.kdg.com
Design & develop interactive marketing, education & training solutions. (Woman, estab 1991, empl 11, sales $1,200,000, cert: WBENC)

8590 LEE Branding
      945 Broadway St NE Ste 280
      Minneapolis, MN 55413
      Contact: Terri Lee CEO
      Tel: 612-843-8477
      Email: terri@leebranding.com
      Website: www.leebranding.com
Consumer-minded, strategic brand development. (Woman, estab 2011, empl 15, sales $4,100,000, cert: WBENC)

8591 Neka Creative LLC
      PO Box 211481
      Saint Paul, MN 55121
      Contact: Rosemary Ugboajah President
      Tel: 651-207-9656
      Email: rosemaryu@nekacreative.com
      Website: www.nekacreative.com
Brand development, Competitive Analysis, Brand Audits, Qualitative Research, Quantitative Research, Strategic Positioning, Brand Development, Culture Plans, Brand Workshops, Brand Blueprints, Marketing/Communication. (Woman/AA, estab 2009, empl 1, sales , cert: NMSDC)

8592 Nina Hale Inc.
      100 S 5th St, Ste 2000
      Minneapolis, MN 55402
      Contact: Sarah Petit Sales & Marketing Mgr
      Tel: 612-392-2427
      Email: businessinquiry@ninahale.com
      Website: www.ninahale.com
Digital direct marketing; search engine optimization (SEO), paid placement, social media consulting, analytics & reporting, local search. (Minority, Woman, estab , empl , sales $14,000,000, cert: WBENC)

8593 One 2 One Marketing Inc.
      12101 12th Ave South
      Burnsville, MN 55337
      Contact: Elaine Grundhauser CEO
      Tel: 952-567-2730
      Email: elaine.g@one2onemktg.com
      Website: www.one2onemktg.com
Strategic promotional programs. (Woman, estab 1995, empl 9, sales $1,606,966, cert: WBENC)

8594 Perkins & Associates, LLC
      400 Grovaland Ave, Ste 2309
      Minneapolis, MN 55403
      Contact: Frank Perkins Owner
      Tel: 612-810-8361
      Email: frank@perkinsbridge.com
      Website: www.perkinsbridge.com
Marketing & business development. (AA, estab 2000, empl 1, sales $125,000, cert: City, NMSDC)

8595 Showcraft, Inc.
      1357 Larc Industrial Blvd
      Burnsville, MN 55337
      Contact: Jeryl Beaulieu President
      Tel: 952-890-4200
      Email: jeryl@showcraft.com
      Website: www.showcraft.com
Trade show exhibits, events & environments. (Minority, Woman, estab 1996, empl 14, sales $500,000, cert: WBENC)

8596 SmartBase Solutions LLC
      411 Washington Ave N
      Minneapolis, MN 55401
      Contact: Kris Lynch CEO
      Tel: 612-767-9940
      Email: klynch@smartbasesolutions.com
      Website: www.smartbasesolutions.com
Database marketing solutions, measure, analyze, & improve marketing & sales activities. (Woman, estab 2005, empl 20, sales , cert: WBENC)

8597 Tartan Marketing, Inc.
      10467 93rd Ave N
      Maple Grove, MN 55369
      Contact: Margie MacLachlan CEO
      Tel: 763-391-7575
      Email: info@tartanmarketing.com
      Website: www.tartanmarketing.com
Integrated marketing, strategy. (Woman, estab 1999, empl 14, sales $2,038,340, cert: WBENC)

PROFESSIONAL SERVICES: Public Relations/Marketing

8598 The Research Edge LLC
1821 University Ave W, Ste N177
St. Paul, MN 55104
Contact: Cheryl Powers President
Tel: 651-644-6006
Email: cheryl@theresearchedge.com
Website: www.theresearchedge.com
Marketing research services, focus groups, in-depth interviews, qualitative research, quantitative research, phone surveys, online surveys, online focus groups, customized market research services full-service market research services. (Woman, estab 1995, empl 5, sales $303,360, cert: WBENC)

8599 The Social Lights, LLC
610 SE 9th St, Ste 101
Minneapolis, MN 55414
Contact: Emily Pritchard CEO
Tel: 612-803-8833
Email: emily@thesocial-lights.com
Website: www.thesociallights.com
Strategy development, creative production, influencer management, media buying, and social media management. (Woman, estab 2011, empl 40, sales $4,632,928, cert: WBENC)

8600 Touch Of Magic Inc.
PO Box 9311
St. Paul, MN 55109
Contact: Lori Hurley Chief Entertainment Officer
Tel: - -
Email: lori@atouchofmagicentertainment.com
Website: www.atouchofmagicentertainment.com
Event planning, Corporate Events, Holiday Parties, Banquets, Trade Shows, Sales Meetings, Festivals, Fairs, Mitzvahs, Team Building, Schools, Churches, etc. (Woman, estab 1986, empl 2, sales $250,000, cert: WBENC)

8601 Treat and Company, LLC
1315 Glenwood Ave
Minneapolis, MN 55405
Contact: Lisa Duchene
Tel: 612-455-6705
Email: Lisa.Duchene@TreatAndCompany.com
Website: www.TreatandCompany.com
Brand Identity & Voice, Packaging Systems, Event Ideation, Campaign Devel, Signage & Wayfinding, Photography & Retouching, Illustration, Production, Mktg Collateral. (Woman, estab 2006, empl 6, sales , cert: WBENC)

8602 Tunheim
8009 34th Ave South
Minneapolis, MN 55425
Contact: Ginny Melvie Sr Exec Assistant/Consultant
Tel: 952-851-1600
Email: gmelvie@tunheim.com
Website: www.tunheim.com
Public Relations, Public Affairs, Strategic Communications, Crisis Communications, Branding - Marketing, Research & Opinion Polling. (Woman, estab 1990, empl 25, sales $5,000,000, cert: WBENC)

8603 Type A Events, LLC
10701 Red Circle Dr
Minnetonka, MN 55343
Contact: CEO
Tel: 763-682-4846
Email: events@typeaevents.com
Website: www.typeaevents.com
Strategic event management. (Woman, estab 2009, empl 40, sales $9,000,000, cert: WBENC)

8604 Visions, Inc.
8801 Wyoming Ave N
Brooklyn Park, MN 55445
Contact: Jon Otto President
Tel: 763-425-4251
Email: jon.otto@visionsfirst.com
Website: www.visionsfirst.com
Web design, print design, advertising & promotion, corporate identification, logo branding, packaging, interactive media, flash animation, video & special effects, 3D animation, web-based applications. (Nat Ame, estab 1985, empl 109, sales $14,207,330, cert: NMSDC)

Missouri

8605 Brighton Agency, Inc.
7711 Bonhomme Ave Ste 100
Saint Louis, MO 63105
Contact: Tina VonderHaar CEO
Tel: 314-726-0700
Email: accounting@brightonagency.com
Website: www.brightonagency.com
Strategic planning, brand development, digital marketing & production, marketing consulting, public relations, advertising, promotions, media planning, audio & video production, event marketing, online, mobile & app development. (Woman, estab 1989, empl 71, sales $9,030,143, cert: State, WBENC)

8606 Credit Financial Group Inc.
141 Chesterfield Business Pkwy
Chesterfield, MO 63005
Contact: Vincent Andaloro President
Tel: 636-536-5344
Email: vince@latinpak.com
Website: www.latinpak.com
Direct marketing services. (Hisp, estab 1996, empl 11, sales $1,600,000, cert: State, NMSDC)

8607 Decision Insight Inc.
2940 Main St
Kansas City, MO 64108
Contact: Tami Kaegi Office Mgr
Tel: 816-221-0445
Email: info@decisioninsight.com
Website: www.decisioninsight.com
Market research services. (Woman, estab 1983, empl 22, sales $3,440,000, cert: WBENC)

8608 Moxi Events, LLC
1904 Grassy Ridge Rd
Saint Louis, MO 63122
Contact: Jaime Ratino Acct Mgr
Tel: 615-454-2008
Email: jratino@moxievents.com
Website: www.moxievents.com
Corporate event planning, meetings, conferences, incentive programs & special events. (Woman, estab 2008, empl 7, sales $267,125, cert: WBENC)

8609 Mozaic Management, Inc.
      5257 Shaw Ave Ste 204
      St. Louis, MO 63110
      Contact: Mary Ann Gibson CEO
      Tel: 314-446-6400
      Email: mgibson@mozaicltd.com
      Website: www.mozaicltd.com
Marketing communications: strategic brand consulting, concept & design, creative execution, digital photography, illustration, photo retouching, interactive web services, art production, prepress, large format digital printing, sales promotion, etc. (Woman, estab 2003, empl 130, sales $30,000,000, cert: WBENC)

8610 MT & Associates, LLC
      222 S Meramec Ave, Ste 202
      St. Louis, MO 63105
      Contact: Mishely Tisius President
      Tel: 314-896-0275
      Email: mt@mtapractice.com
      Website: www.mtapractice.com
Sign language interpreting services. (Woman, estab 2013, empl 5, sales , cert: State, City, WBENC)

8611 Pixie Stuff LLC
      18 Brighton Way
      Clayton, MO 63105
      Contact: Jennifer Hein Chief Business Officer
      Tel: 314-368-4730
      Email: jennifer@hiredink.com
      Website: www.hiredink.com
Develop outreach programs that engage, educate and empower your target audience. (Woman, estab 2003, empl 10, sales $800,000, cert: State, WBENC)

8612 Stakeholder Insights, LLC
      319 N 4th St Ste 820
      St. Louis, MO 63102
      Contact: Lisa Richter Managing Principal
      Tel: 314-454-1923
      Email: lisa@stakeholderinsights.com
      Website: www.stakeholderinsights.com
Market & employee research services, supports branding, change management, competitive intelligence, customer experience, employee engagement and retention, message testing, public opinion & website usability. (Woman, estab 2006, empl 3, sales $408,312, cert: WBENC)

8613 The Vandiver Group, Inc.
      16052 Swingley Ridge Road Ste 210
      St. Louis, MO 63017
      Contact: Donna Vandiver CEO
      Tel: 314-991-4641
      Email: tvg@vandivergroup.com
      Website: www.vandivergroup.com
Strategic communications & public relations, corporate image & reputation management, branding, market research & training. (Woman, estab 1993, empl 10, sales $1,432,900, cert: State, WBENC)

North Carolina

8614 3 Birds Marketing, LLC
      505-B W Franklin St
      Chapel Hill, NC 27516
      Contact: Layton Judd President
      Tel: 919-913-2750
      Email: layton@3birdsmarketing.com
      Website: www.3birdsmarketing.com
Integrated marketing platform, marketing, digital marketing, multichannel marketing, email marketing, email newsletters, digital newsletters, social media management, social media marketing. (Woman, estab 2009, empl 60, sales $3,769,500, cert: WBENC, NWBOC)

8615 ABZ Creative Partner
      1300 S Mint St, Ste 100
      Charlotte, NC 28203
      Contact: President
      Tel: 704-374-1072
      Email: worksmart@abzcreative.com
      Website: www.abzcreativepartners.com
Marketing communications & graphic design. (Woman, estab 1982, empl 11, sales , cert: State)

8616 Avantgarde Translations
      5960 Fairview Rd Ste 400
      Charlotte, NC 28210
      Contact: Jael Williams Administrative Asst
      Tel: 704-496-2735
      Email: submissions@avantgardetranslations.com
      Website: www.avantgardetranslations.com
Translating written material, interpretation services, revising, editing, proofreading & laying out translated documents, cultural consulting. (Woman/AA, estab 2004, empl 3, sales $200,789, cert: NMSDC, WBENC)

8617 Bellomy Research, Inc.
      175 Sunnynoll Ct
      Winston-Salem, NC 27106
      Contact: Glen Kelley Sr Dir of Admin
      Tel: 336-721-1140
      Email: glen.kelley@bellomy.com
      Website: www.bellomyresearch.com
Marketing research services: design, data collection, analysis, interpretation, reporting & delivering point-of-view. (Woman, estab 1977, empl 100, sales $14,600,000, cert: State)

8618 Confero, Inc.
      535 Keisler Dr Ste 204
      Cary, NC 27518
      Contact: Elaine Buxton President
      Tel: 919-469-5200
      Email: ebuxton@conferoinc.com
      Website: www.conferoinc.com
Mystery shopping & customer satisfaction studies, training, brand management. (Woman, estab 1987, empl 23, sales $2,670,000, cert: WBENC)

8619 Content Spectrum
      1832 Folly Gate Ct
      Charlotte, NC 28262
      Contact: David Springston Owner
      Tel: 980-309-1465
      Email: contentspectrum@gmail.com
      Website: www.contentspectrum.net
Copywriting, Editing, Graphic design (banners, fliers, magazines, newsletters, posters, etc.), Translation services, Website development & maintenance. (Woman/AA, estab 2015, empl 1, sales , cert: NMSDC)

PROFESSIONAL SERVICES: Public Relations/Marketing

8620 It's My Affair, LLC
8711 Walden Ridge Dr
Charlotte, NC 28216
Contact: Kenneth Fields President
Tel: 704-394-4928
Email: kffields@it-henhouse.com
Website: www.itsmyaffair.com
Special events & meeting management: meetings, conferences, tradeshow management, grand openings, corporate recognition, launch parties, incentives. (Woman/AA, estab 2002, empl 2, sales , cert: WBENC, 8(a))

8621 Lockman-Brooks Marketing Services, LLC
6135 Park Dr S Ste 510
Charlotte, NC 28210
Contact: Linda Lockman-Brooks President
Tel: 704-293-5666
Email: linda@lockmanbrooks.com
Website: www.lockmanbrooks.com
Strategic marketing consulting: commununity relations & outreach, leadership consulting, communications planning & project management. (Woman/AA, estab 1998, empl 1, sales , cert: NMSDC)

8622 Lyerly Agency
4819 Park Rd
Charlotte, NC 28209
Contact: Elaine Lyerly CEO
Tel: 704-525-3937
Email:
Website: www.lyerly.com
Advertising, marketing, public relations & interactive svcs. (Woman, estab 1977, empl 4, sales $976,184, cert: State, City)

8623 TCG Events
2923 S. Tryon St Ste 230
Charlotte, NC 28203
Contact: Travis Holmes President
Tel: 704-376-1943
Email: info@tbsfreightmanagement.com
Website: www.tcgevents.com
Event planning & production, video production, graphic design and art direction, conference management, entertainment production, incentive programs, corporate awards programs, destination management. (Woman, estab 1985, empl 5, sales $2,400,000, cert: WBENC)

8624 The Media Pro
4613 Hunters Creek Lane
Raleigh, NC 27606
Contact: Jill Hammergren Owner
Tel: 919-805-1061
Email: jill@themediapro.biz
Website: www.themediapro.biz
Media, marketing & communications, visual storytelling, creative writing, videos, animations & graphic, live TV, network programming, PSAs, video, film, e-learning, government, training & & multimedia purposes. (Woman, estab 1987, empl 0, sales , cert: WBENC)

8625 The Special Event Company
6112 Saint Giles St
Raleigh, NC 27612
Contact: Ly Nguyen Dir Business Devel
Tel: 919-459-8785
Email: bp@recredit.co
Website: www.specialeventco.com/
Event & meeting management. (Woman, estab 2001, empl 15, sales $5,000,000, cert: WBENC)

Nebraska

8626 Bozell and Jacobs LLC
1022 Leavenworth St
Omaha, NE 68102
Contact: Robin Donovan President
Tel: 402-965-4300
Email: rdonovan@bozell.com
Website: www.bozell.com
Marketing Communications, Branding, Digital Marketing, Interactive Design & Development, Social Media, Media, Public Relations, Market Research, Data Analytics. (Woman, estab 1921, empl 38, sales $3,200,000, cert: WBENC)

New Jersey

8627 AG Marketing & Consulting Group
554 W Broad St 1st Fl Rear
Westfield, NJ 07090
Contact: April Gregory President
Tel: 908-456-5700
Email: april@aprilgregoryinc.com
Website: www.agmarketingconsulting.com
Brand development, event marketing & marketing planning, social media & web implementation services. (Woman/AA, estab 2000, empl 3, sales $250,000, cert: State)

8628 Baldwin & Obenauf, Inc.
50 Division St Ste 401
Somerville, NJ 08876
Contact: Joanne Obenauf Founder
Tel: 908-685-1510
Email: jmobenauf@baldwinandobenauf.com
Website: www.bnoinc.com
Marketing & communications, strategic, creative & production, brand strategy, identity packages, advertising, print & digital collateral, web & mobile sites, corporate intranets, mobile apps, social media campaigns, videos. (Woman, estab 1981, empl 46, sales $7,824,663, cert: State, WBENC)

8629 Breakthrough Marketing Technology
110 E. Shearwater Court Ste 11
Jersey City, NJ 07305
Contact: Elaine Harris President
Tel: 201-604-3600
Email: elaine@breakthroughgroup.com
Website: www.breakthroughgroup.com
Marketing, strategic planning, market research, learning, coaching, implementation planning. (Woman/AA, estab 2002, empl 13, sales $432,000, cert: State, WBENC)

8630 BUZZRegistration
3525 Quakerbridge Rd Ste 908
Hamilton, NJ 08619
Contact: Michael Rayner CEO
Tel: 888-202-2262
Email: michaelr@buysmart-gsa.com
Website: www.buzzregistration.com
Registration management services. (Woman, estab 2011, empl 25, sales $4,647,794, cert: WBENC)

PROFESSIONAL SERVICES: Public Relations/Marketing

8631 Cajam Marketing, Inc.
8 Haviland Dr
Millstone Twp, NJ 08535
Contact: Kathy Gould President
Tel: 609-371-1325
Email: kgould@cajammarketing.com
Website: www.cajammarketing.com
Offline & online marketing initiatives through analytics. (Woman, estab 2001, empl 5, sales $400,000, cert: State)

8632 Classic Conferences Inc.
1 University Plaza, Ste 310
Hackensack, NJ 07601
Contact: Andrea Strauss President
Tel: 201-343-1999
Email: astrauss@classicconferences.com
Website: www.classicconferences.com
Corporate meeting & event planning. (Woman, estab 1990, empl 7, sales $20,000,000, cert: WBENC)

8633 Command Marketing Innovations
70 Outwater Lane
Garfield, NJ 07026
Contact: Michele Murphy Acct Exec
Tel: 201-835-4588
Email: mmurphy@commandmi.com
Website: www.commandmarketinginnovations.com
Best in-class, data-driven, print & multi-channel based marketing solutions. (Woman, estab 2016, empl 25, sales $14,000,000, cert: WBENC)

8634 Decentxposure LLC
75 Gorge Rd
Edgewater, NJ 07020
Contact: Joseph Confreda VP Finance
Tel: 201-313-1100
Email: jconfreda@dxagency.com
Website: www.dxagency.com
Digital marketing, strategy, creative, media, content, CRM, research & insights, and e-commerce (Minority, Woman, estab 2004, empl 45, sales $14,896,000, cert: NMSDC, WBENC)

8635 Diagnocine LLC
370 Golf Pl
Hackensack, NJ 07601
Contact: Jessica Suh CEO
Tel: 201-681-7263
Email: orders@diagnocine.com
Website: www.diagnocine.com
Sales, Marketing, Distribution & Consulting. (As-Pac, estab 2008, empl 13, sales $15,000,000, cert: State)

8636 Digital Brand Expressions
100 Overlook Center 2nd Fl
Princeton, NJ 08540
Contact: Veronica Fielding President
Tel: 609-688-8558
Email: vfielding@digitalbrandexpressions.com
Website: www.digitalbrandexpressions.com
Search engine marketing consultancy & services firm. Focus: search engine marketing/optimization/advertising and/or search engine image protection. (Woman, estab 2002, empl 10, sales $860,000, cert: WBENC)

8637 Distinctive Marketing, Inc.
516 Bloomfield Ave
Montclair, NJ 07042
Contact: Diane Spencer
Tel: 973-746-9114
Email: dmiassociates@verizon.net
Website: www.distinctivemktg.com
Marketing research, focus groups, telephone surveys, event planning & mgmt, consulting, etc. (Woman/AA, estab 1990, empl 12, sales , cert: State)

8638 Diversity Marketing and Communications
28 Washington St, Ste 103 Ste 103
East Orange, NJ 07017
Contact: Susan Cohen Managing Partner
Tel: 973-377-0300
Email: susan.cohen@diversitymc.com
Website: www.diversitymc.com
Marketing & advertising, public relations, special events management, crisis communications & partnership alliance development. (Woman, estab 2004, empl 5, sales $286,787, cert: State, WBENC)

8639 Executive Meetings & Incentives, Inc.
685 US Hwy 202/206 N 2nd Fl
Bridgewater, NJ 08876
Contact: Larry Hambro Business Devel
Tel: 908-864-5800
Email: rgiaimo@eminj.com
Website: www.eminj.com
Meeting planning, global, full service meeting, event & incentive planning, logistic services. (Woman, estab 1982, empl 18, sales $2,746,000, cert: State)

8640 FirstEye Media Works
59 Lincoln Park Ste 375
Newark, NJ 07102
Contact: Kimberlee Williams CEO
Tel: 973-494-9705
Email: kwilliams@femworksllc.com
Website: www.femworksllc.com
Integrated campaigns, events & custom campaign photography. (Woman/AA, estab 2004, empl 5, sales $503,611, cert: NMSDC, WBENC)

8641 Focus USA, Inc
95 North State Route 17 Ste 109
Paramus, NJ 07652
Contact: Meg Ugenti Corporate Dir of Sales & Marketing
Tel: 201-489-2525
Email: megu@focus-usa.com
Website: www.focus-usa.com
Direct & data marketing services, consumer & business database aggregator, buyer behavior profiling, data & email appending, email marketing, digital solutions, mobile marketing, social media marketing. (Woman, estab 1994, empl 14, sales $3,840,000, cert: WBENC)

8642 Global Planners, Inc.
3525 Quakerbridge Rd Ste 909
Hamilton, NJ 08619
Contact: Megan Buzzetta CEO
Tel: 609-689-0001
Email: wbereg@globalplanners.com
Website: www.globalplanners.com
Meeting & event coordination, contract negotiation, on line attendee registration, on site staff support, site selection, travel agency. (Woman, estab 2000, empl 14, sales $3,368,000, cert: WBENC)

PROFESSIONAL SERVICES: Public Relations/Marketing

8643 HAP Marketing Services, Inc.
1511 Wayside Rd
Tinton Falls, NJ 07724
Contact: Lorenzo Fernandez Managing Partner
Tel: 732-982-8222
Email: lorenzo.fernandez@hapmarketing.com
Website: www.hapmarketing.com
Advertising, public relations, promotional items, graphics design. (Hisp, estab 1984, empl 24, sales $5,063,096, cert: State)

8644 InGroup, Inc.
PO Box 206
Midland Park, NJ 07432
Contact: Marlene Bauer President
Tel: 201-612-1230
Email: mbaur@ingroupinc.com
Website: www.ingroupinc.com
Strategy & customized support services for marketing programs, outreach communications & public relations. (Woman, estab 1995, empl 5, sales $461,884, cert: State, City, SDB)

8645 Iris Communications LLC
11 Belaire Dr
Roseland, NJ 07068
Contact: Barbara Bochese Managing Dir
Tel: 973-902-7027
Email: bbochese@iriscommunications.org
Website: www.iriscommunications.org
Marketing services, corporate communications & branding, presentations-internal/corporate, brand deliverables, educational/training, video production & animation, website design & development, media planning & buying. (Woman, estab 2011, empl 12, sales , cert: State, NWBOC)

8646 Magee Enterprises, LLC dba Event1Source
68 Abbond Court
Plainfield, NJ 07063
Contact: Dion Magee Co-Owner
Tel: 888-299-2250
Email: dion@event1source.com
Website: www.event1source.com
Event management & meeting sourcing. (Woman/AA, estab 1994, empl 2, sales $195,000, cert: State)

8647 Marketsmith Inc.
2 Wing Dr
Cedar Knolls, NJ 07927
Contact: Smith President
Tel: 973-889-0006
Email: nmichael@marketsmithinc.com
Website: www.marketsmithinc.com
Media: strategic consulting; media planning, buying & optimization; traditional; programmatic display; mobile; paid social; social CRM. (Woman, estab 1999, empl 72, sales $9,417,082, cert: WBENC)

8648 MarketView Research Group, Inc.
115 River Rd, Ste 105
Edgewater, NJ 07020
Contact: Gail Apkarian President
Tel: 201-840-5300
Email: sales@mvrg.com
Website: www.mvrg.com
Quantitative marketing research. (Woman, estab 1989, empl 35, sales $8,021,000, cert: State, WBENC)

8649 Meadowlands Consumer Center Global Marketing Resea
301 Rt. 17N Ste 503
Rutherford, NJ 07070
Contact: Andrea C. Schrager CEO
Tel: 201-865-4900
Email: info@consumercenters.com
Website: www.consumercenters.com
Qualitative market research & strategic consulting: study design, strategy development, branding & new product R & D. (Woman, estab 1984, empl 50, sales $5,200,000, cert: State, WBENC)

8650 Meeting Logistics, LLC
890 Mountain Ave
New Providence, NJ 07974
Contact: President
Tel: 908-771-0804
Email:
Website: www.mtglogistics.com
Meeting, event, convention mgmt, trade show support, incentive programs, special events, advisory boards, awards, educational & training programs. (Woman, estab 2000, empl 5, sales $1,933,790, cert: WBENC)

8651 MMI Inc.
350 W Passaic St
Rochelle Park, NJ 07662
Contact: Michele McKenna President
Tel: 201-556-1188
Email: info@MarketAnalytics.com
Website: www.marketanalytics.com
International research: customer, competitive & market intelligence solutions, qualitative & quantitative solutions. (Woman, estab 2002, empl 10, sales $1,200,000, cert: State, WBENC)

8652 Mona Terrell & Associates LLC
1610 Division Ave
Piscataway, NJ 08854
Contact: Mona Terrell President
Tel: 732-752-4690
Email: mona@monaterrell.com
Website: www.monaterrell.com
Corporate communications, public relations, public affairs, social responsibility & sustainability programs. (Woman/AA, estab 2009, empl 1, sales $150,000, cert: State, WBENC)

8653 Paragon Productions Inc.
1900 Shadow Brook Dr
Wall Township, NJ 07719
Contact: Susanne Ardolino President
Tel: 732-282-9088
Email: susanne@paragonproductionsinc.com
Website: www.paragonproductionsinc.com
Marketing & communications, Design, Scheduling, Staging, Audio Visual, Guest Speaker & Entertainment requirements. (Woman, estab 1995, empl 4, sales $895,000, cert: State)

8654 Raare Solutions LLC
4 Lorettacong Dr
Lake Hopatcong, NJ 07849
Contact: Business Dev Dir
Tel: 800-693-2994
Email: sales@raaresolutions.com
Website: www.raaresolutions.com
CRM & customer data analysis, marketing campaign design & management services, focusing on luxury brands. (Woman, estab 2004, empl 17, sales $2,100,000, cert: WBENC)

PROFESSIONAL SERVICES: Public Relations/Marketing

8655 Smith Design Associates Inc.
      8 Budd St
      Morristown, NJ 07960
      Contact: Jenna Smith President
      Tel: 973-429-2177
      Email: jenna@smithdesign.com
      Website: www.smithdesign.com
Brand Identity & Package Design, Seamless Account + Project Management, Visual Strategy + Positioning, Verbal Expression + Brand Package Design, Design Production + Realization.
Visual (Woman, estab 1978, empl 25, sales $7,200,000, cert: State, WBENC)

8656 Snap Creative Marketing
      425 Sand Shore Rd
      Hackettstown, NJ 07840
      Contact: Roberta Rivinius Managing Partner
      Tel: 908-441-6220
      Email: roberta@snapcreativemarketing.com
      Website: www.snapcreativemarketing.com
Campaign Development & Strategy, Brand Management, Direct Mail & Fulfillment, Lettershop/Mailhouse, Print Production, Multicultural Marketing, Graphic Design, Web Development & Interactive Design, Social Media & TV & Radio Production, Promotions. (Woman, estab 2013, empl 21, sales $13,800,000, cert: WBENC)

8657 Stokes Creative Group, Inc.
      1666 Route 206
      Vincentown, NJ 08088
      Contact: Diane Konopka President
      Tel: 609-859-8400
      Email: diane@stokescg.com
      Website: www.stokescg.com
Marketing agency, public outreach, videography, marketing, advertising, and photography. (Woman, estab 1989, empl 32, sales $2,970,811, cert: WBENC)

8658 Strategic Research I
      101 Morgan Lane
      Plainsboro, NJ 08536
      Contact: Venky Jagannathan Principal
      Tel: 609-751-5231
      Email: venky.jagan@srinsights.com
      Website: www.srinsights.com
Pharmaceutical Marketing Research, Marketing Consulting, Big Data Analysis. (As-Ind, estab 2006, empl 20, sales , cert: State)

8659 Taurus Market Research
      1810 Englishtown Rd
      Old Bridge, NJ 08857
      Contact: Beth Kamenitz Dir Client Dev
      Tel: 732-251-7772
      Email: beth@taurusresearch.com
      Website: www.taurusresearch.com
Qualitative & quantitative market research: concept, product, packaging & advertising testing, one-on-one in-depth interviewing, intercept/exit interviewing, ethnographies & consumer panels, in-house recruiting. (Woman, estab 1992, empl 53, sales $1,000,000, cert: City)

8660 The Lane Group LLC
      14-25 Plaza Rd North Ste 3N
      Fair Lawn, NJ 07410
      Contact: Tracey Lane President
      Tel: 201-398-9230
      Email: tlane@tlgmeetings.com
      Website: www.tlgmeetings.com
Event & meeting planning, production & management (Woman, estab 2000, empl 15, sales $2,226,800, cert: State, WBENC)

8661 TMW Enterprises, Inc.
      76 Park Ave
      Flemington, NJ 08822
      Contact: President, Exec Producer
      Tel: 908-638-6070
      Email: tmwinfo@tmwenterprises.com
      Website: www.tmwenterprises.com
Audio visual equipment & staging services: sales meetings, product launches & award ceremonies. (Woman, estab 1992, empl 6, sales $2,650,000, cert: WBENC)

8662 Trimensions Inc.
      One Engle St
      Englewood, NJ 07631
      Contact: Maria Maceri President
      Tel: 201-816-8820
      Email: mmaceri@trimensionsinc.com
      Website: www.trimensionsinc.com
Printed material for sales & promotional purposes, design & manufacturing of displays, direct mail, packaging, detail aids & interactive pieces. (Woman, estab 1975, empl 6, sales $4,500,000, cert: WBENC)

8663 Vanadams Sports Group LLC
      623 Eagle Rock Ave Ste 317
      West Orange, NJ 07052
      Contact: Van Adams Principal
      Tel: 888-435-8006
      Email: vadams@vanadamssports.com
      Website: www.VanAdamsSports.com
Marketing Athletes & Events, Consulting, Event Development, national events and promotions, contract negotiations, budget creation. (Woman/AA, estab 2004, empl 1, sales $225,000, cert: State)

8664 VS Research LLC
      411 Hackensack Ave, 10 Fl
      Hackensack, NJ 07601
      Contact: Steven Segal CFO
      Tel: 201-498-9333
      Email: steven@vsresearch.com
      Website: www.vsresearch.com
Qualitative & quantitative market research. (Woman, estab 1997, empl 9, sales , cert: WBENC)

8665 Websignia
      60 Park Place Ste 404
      Newark, NJ 07102
      Contact: Steve Jones CEO
      Tel: 973-732-4750
      Email: diversity@websignia.net
      Website: www.websignia.net
Digital marketing, visual design for web & print, digital marketing & custom web & mobile applications. (AA, estab 2003, empl 13, sales $670,000, cert: NMSDC)

PROFESSIONAL SERVICES: Public Relations/Marketing

New Mexico

8666 Slow Life Games, LLC
9 Piedras Negras
Santa Fe, NM 87505
Contact: Jason Zeaman President
Tel: 505-603-8930
Email: jason@handcraftedlearning.com
Website: www.HandcraftedLearning.com
Design & develop custom training: virtual webinars, in-person classroom, and stand alone eLearning. (Minority, Woman, estab 2011, empl 2, sales $716,617, cert: NMSDC, WBENC)

Nevada

8667 Ad Hoc Communication Resources, LLC
6 Benevolo Dr
Henderson, NV 89011
Contact: Shelli Ryan President
Tel: 702-567-1115
Email: shelli@adhoccr.com
Website: www.adhocCR.com
Business & corporate management consulting svcs: editing, technical writing, public realtions, news & publicity, product launches, media outreach, industry analyst outreach, whitepapers, press releases. (Woman, estab 1996, empl 2, sales $304,129, cert: WBENC)

8668 Fresh Wata, LLC
3905 W Diablo Dr, Ste 100
Las Vegas, NV 89118
Contact: Tricia Costello President
Tel: 913-269-3849
Email: tricia@freshwata.com
Website: www.freshwata.com
Create extraordinarily meaningful brand moments that drive connection, engagement and dialogue. (Woman/AA, estab , empl , sales $10,400,000, cert: WBENC)

8669 INTU Corporation
7065 W Ann Rd, Ste 130-332
Las Vegas, NV 89130
Contact: Joanna Lai Project Coord
Tel: 702-656-4503
Email: events@intucorporation.com
Website: www.intucorporation.com
Chair massage therapy, corporate wellness, spa oasis, casino gaming, luxury poolside services, sporting sky boxes, golf tournaments, themed parks, special events. (Woman, estab 2005, empl 150, sales , cert: WBENC)

8670 MYS LLC
1000 N Green Valley Pkwy, Ste 440-592
Henderson, NV 89074
Contact: Laura Silva Project Dir
Tel: 800-933-9720
Email: info@mysfirm.com
Website: www.mysfirm.com
Project management & brand management services, strategic marketing services, print & digital media. (Woman/AA, Hisp, estab 2014, empl 2, sales $122,600, cert: NMSDC, WBENC)

New York

8671 Adrea Rubin Marketing Inc.
19 W 44th St Ste 1415
New York, NY 10036
Contact: Jennifer Vilkelis CFO
Tel: 212-983-0020
Email: jenniferv@adrearubin.com
Website: www.adrearubin.com
Direct marketing. (Woman, estab 1990, empl 14, sales , cert: WBENC)

8672 Beardwood&Co. LLC
40 Wooster St, 4th Fl
New York, NY 10013
Contact: Partner
Tel: 212-334-5689
Email: hello@beardwood.com
Website: www.beardwood.com
Branding & design, qualitative research, naming & voice, logos, packaging structures, packaging graphics, point-of-purchase displays, point-of-purchase advertising, brand books, brand guidelines. (Woman, estab 2004, empl 12, sales $2,294,723, cert: WBENC)

8673 BuzzBack Market Research dba Buzzback LLC
989 Sixth Ave
New York, NY 10036
Contact: Andrea Levene SVP Finance & Admin
Tel: 646-315-7575
Email: info@buzzback.com
Website: www.buzzback.com
Full service market research. (Woman, estab 2000, empl 37, sales , cert: WBENC)

8674 Buzzword PR Corp.
34 N 6th St
Brooklyn, NY 11249
Contact: Eva Dilmanian Owner
Tel: 718-599-2591
Email: eva@buzzwordpr.com
Website: www.buzzwordpr.com
Media relations. (Minority, Woman, estab 2003, empl 1, sales , cert: WBENC)

8675 CBA Research Corp.
59 Clubhouse Ln
Scarsdale, NY 10583
Contact: Judy Bernstein VP Qualitative Insights
Tel: 914-478-9355
Email: judy_bernstein@cba-link.com
Website: www.cba-link.com
Qualitative marketing research, focus groups, insights, moderating, analysis, ethnographies, depth interviews, shop-alongs, brand imagery, new product development, concept/messaging. (Woman, estab 1967, empl 3, sales $1,063,279, cert: WBENC)

8676 Company 20, Inc.
555 Eighth Ave Ste 2201
New York, NY 10018
Contact: Michele Lasky VP
Tel: 212-784-6453
Email: michelelasky@company20.com
Website: www.company20.com
Event marketing; planning; mgmt; consulting; production; charity fundraisers; celebrity; athlete foundations; cause-related; sports; special events; corporate meetings; consumer promotions; incentives; hospitality. (Woman, estab 2005, empl 5, sales $2,085,000, cert: WBENC)

PROFESSIONAL SERVICES: Public Relations/Marketing

8677 Complemar Partners
500 Lee Rd Ste 200
Rochester, NY 14606
Contact: President
Tel: 585-647-5890
Email: info@complemar.com
Website: www.complemar.com
Marketing & sales communication programs. (Woman, estab 2004, empl 65, sales $5,195,389, cert: WBENC)

8678 Converge Marketing Services, LLC
33 E 33rd St 3rd Fl
New York, NY 10016
Contact: Maarten Terry President
Tel: 203-536-9414
Email: maartent@convergedirect.com
Website: www.convergemarketingservices.com
Media buying, planning & strategy, print production services & paper procurement. (AA, estab 2017, empl 17, sales , cert: NMSDC)

8679 D Exposito & Partners, LLC
875 6th Ave, 25th Fl
New York, NY 10001
Contact: Louis Maldonado Managing Dir
Tel: 646-747-8814
Email: lmaldonado@dex-p.com
Website: www.newamericanagency.com
Hispanic Marketing Solutions, Spanish language, In-Culture and English language communications programs to reach America's Hispanics no matter where they live, work or play. (Minority, Woman, estab 2005, empl 28, sales $5,077,000, cert: State, NMSDC, WBENC)

8680 Design & Source Productions, Inc.
143 W 29th St 3rd Fl
New York, NY 10001
Contact: Laura Tufariello President
Tel: 212-265-8632
Email: laura@dsnyc.com
Website: www.design-and-source.com
Design & develop branded & private label products, custom creative packaging solutions. (Woman, estab 1996, empl 7, sales $8,400,000, cert: City, WBENC)

8681 DEVLINHAIR Production Inc.
120 Wooster Dr 3rd Fl
New York, NY 10012
Contact: Dorothy Devlin Co-Founder
Tel: 212-941-9009
Email: supplier-diversity@devlinhair.com
Website: www.devlinhair.com
Corporate event planning: meetings, conferences, internal sales/mktg campaigns, film, video training programs, interactive media. (Woman, estab 1991, empl 13, sales $14,938,324, cert: WBENC)

8682 Drury Design Dynamics, Inc.
275 7th Ave Ste 2001
New York, NY 10001
Contact: Liza Handman VP Creative Devel Group
Tel: 212-576-1314
Email: l.handman@drurydesign.com
Website: www.drurydesign.com
Planning & production of meetings, learning & performance (training) programs, corporate. (Woman, estab 1981, empl 35, sales $20,000,000, cert: WBENC)

8683 Ebony Marketing Systems, Inc.
79 Alexander Ave, Ste 31-A
Bronx, NY 10454
Contact: K. Fuentes Operations Dir
Tel: 718-742-0006
Email: kfuentes@ebonysystems.com
Website: www.ebonysystems.com
Market research studies & services. (Woman/AA, estab 2011, empl 1, sales $650,000, cert: City, NMSDC)

8684 Eclipse Direct Marketing LLC
173 Mineola Blvd Ste 402
Mineola, NY 11501
Contact: Kris Thelen CEO
Tel: 212-931-8344
Email: kthelen@eclipsedm.com
Website: www.eclipsedm.com
Tracking & analytics, strategy planning with marketing departments. (Woman, estab 2003, empl 7, sales $1,600,000, cert: WBENC)

8685 Egami Group, Inc.
212 W. 35th St 10th Fl
New York, NY 10001
Contact: Teneshia Jackson CEO
Tel: 917-720-5580
Email: teneshia@egamigroup.com
Website: www.egamigroup.com
Maketing consulting, branding, events, custom community programs, campaigns & new products. (Woman/AA, estab 2004, empl 12, sales $401,000, cert: NMSDC, WBENC)

8686 Extrovertic Communications, LLC
30 W 21st St 3rd Fl
New York, NY 10010
Contact: Dorothy Wetzel CEO
Tel: 646-312-6001
Email: dorothy@extrovertic.com
Website: www.extrovertic.com
Creative (print, video and digital), relationship marketing, patient education, social media, & marketing consulting. (Woman, estab 2009, empl 27, sales $7,933,003, cert: WBENC)

8687 Foglamp Research Corp.
100 Greenwich Rd
Bedford, NY 10506
Contact: Kate Horn CEO
Tel: 914-682-4127
Email: kate.horn@foglampresearch.com
Website: www.foglampresearch.com
Due diligence, reputational risk inquiries, surveys, interviews & local market intelligence research in emerging & frontier markets. (Woman, estab 2013, empl 3, sales $237,811, cert: WBENC)

8688 Gammon & Associates
152 Madison Ave, Ste 400
New York, NY 10016
Contact: Fred Gammon President
Tel: 212-725-6710
Email: admin@thegroagency.com
Website: www.thegroagency.com
Branding and Package Design Agency. (AA, estab 1988, empl 13, sales $1,771,414, cert: NMSDC)

PROFESSIONAL SERVICES: Public Relations/Marketing

8689 Greater Than One Inc.
      395 Hudson St
      New York, NY 10014
      Contact: Elizabeth Izard Apelles CEO
      Tel: 917-549-4202
      Email: eapelles@gthegtogroup.com
      Website: www.thegtogroup.com
Marketing services: strategies, assessments, metrics analytics, consumer research, behavior analytics, communications planning, engagement. (Woman, estab 2000, empl 120, sales $28,000,000, cert: WBENC)

8690 Human Touch Translations Ltd.
      1010 Northern Boulevard Ste 208
      Great Neck, NY 11021
      Contact: President
      Tel: 646-358-4972
      Email: enagy@humantouchtranslations.com
      Website: www.humantouchtranslations.com
Translation servivces, 120 languages, interpreting documents, technical documents, legal documents, scientific papers, journal and magazine articles, educational materials, medical documents, market research surveys. (Woman, estab 2010, empl 5, sales , cert: State, WBENC)

8691 Imagine 360 Marketing
      340 E 64th St Ste 17N
      New York, NY 10065
      Contact: President
      Tel: 212-313-9616
      Email: info@i360m.com
      Website: www.i360m.com
Strategic marketing and innovative design to increase brand awareness, acquire new business and retain existing customers. (Woman, estab 2005, empl 7, sales , cert: WBENC)

8692 Intstrux LLC
      15 W 39th St, 13th Fl
      New York, NY 10018
      Contact: Sanjiv Mody CEO
      Tel: 646-688-2782
      Email: sanjiv.mody@pixacore.com
      Website: www.pixacore.com
Digital communication, strategy & implementation services, marketing, training, corporate communication, live events initiatives. (As-Ind, estab 2007, empl 30, sales $7,577,436, cert: NMSDC)

8693 Ivy Cohen Corporate Communications, Inc.
      2098 Frederick Douglass Blvd. Ste 10M
      New York, NY 10026
      Contact: Ivy Cohen CEO
      Tel: 212-399-0026
      Email: ivy@ivycohen.com
      Website: www.ivycohen.com
Branding, promotions, corporate communications & organizational issues. (Woman, estab 2001, empl 1, sales $326,063, cert: City, WBENC)

8694 Jeannette McClennan LLC
      109 W 118th St
      New York, NY 10026
      Contact: Jeannette McClennan President
      Tel: 917-842-0364
      Email: jeannette@mcclennangroup.com
      Website: www.mcclennangroup.com
Digital products and marketing programs for its corporate clients quickly and cost-effectively. (AA, estab 2004, empl 50, sales , cert: WBENC)

8695 Keeper of the Brand
      894 Otsego Rd
      West Hempstead, NY 11552
      Contact: Donyshia Boston-Hill CEO
      Tel: 917-697-1699
      Email: db@keeperofthebrand.com
      Website: www.keeperofthebrand.com/
Marketing Plans & Strategies, Media Buying, TV, Radio, Print & Digital Solutions, Broadcast Media Distribution, Brand Development, Consumer Insight, Copyright, Transactional Engagement, Programming & Campaign Mgmt, Graphic Design, Creative Services. (Woman/AA, estab 2013, empl 6, sales , cert: State, NMSDC, WBENC)

8696 Kipany Productions, Ltd.
      32 E 39 St
      New York, NY 10016
      Contact: Salman Ali President
      Tel: 212-883-8300
      Email: rfp@kipany.com
      Website: www.kipany.com
Marketing communication svcs: direct response TV sales & outbound telemarketing; video, print, Internet direct mktg/web design & placement. (Woman, estab 1979, empl 30, sales , cert: WBENC)

8697 Kupcha Marketing Services
      2 Hayes Rd
      Amity Harbor, NY 11701
      Contact: Elizabeth Kupcha President
      Tel: 917-432-9481
      Email: liz@kupchamkt.com
      Website: www.kupchamkt.com
Marketing consulting: proposal management, presentation preparation/coaching, publicity & event planning. (Woman/AA, estab 2010, empl 1, sales , cert: State, City)

8698 Language Bank, Inc.
      143 W 95th St
      New York, NY 10025
      Contact: Juho Rana Procurement Specialist
      Tel: 212-213-3336
      Email: jhrana@alanguagebank.com
      Website: www.alanguagebank.com
Multilingual content management, translation, interpretation, multimedia services & cultural consulting. (As-Pac, estab 1999, empl 10, sales $3,300,000, cert: State, NMSDC)

8699 Lightbeam Communications Corp
      1787 Madison Ave, Ste 710
      New York, NY 10035
      Contact: Roben Allong CEO
      Tel: 917-498-1738
      Email: robena@lightbeamnyc.com
      Website: www.lightbeamnyc.com
Qualitative research. (Woman/AA, estab 2009, empl 1, sales $284,000, cert: City)

8700 LilyGild Ltd.
      199 Carlton Ave
      Brooklyn, NY 11205
      Contact: Ann Chitwood Co-President
      Tel: 718-797-4656
      Email: ilygild@lilygild.com
      Website: www.lilygild.com
Communications svcs: event, meeting & media production. (Woman, estab 1991, empl 3, sales $890,323, cert: WBENC)

PROFESSIONAL SERVICES: Public Relations/Marketing

8701 MedEdNow, LLC
29 W 35th St Ste 10A
New York, NY 10001
Contact: Alexis Pone VP Strategy & Business Dev
Tel: 646-674-9549
Email: apone@medednow.com
Website: www.medednow.com
Marketing; medical education; medical communication; content development & medical writing; brand strategy; brand planning; sales training; global; conferences and society meetings; symposia and product theaters. (Woman, estab 2001, empl 35, sales $12,952,301, cert: WBENC)

8702 Meeting Management Associates, Inc.
16 W State St
Sherburne, NY 13460
Contact: Lisa Denton Dir Sales
Tel: 607-674-2666
Email: lisa@mma-inc.com
Website: www.mma-inc.com
Manage conventions, tradeshows, meetings, special events & develop promotional, specialty items. Housing, electronic registrations, registrations via phone, travel arrangements, sales correspondence, exhibit routing, labor management. (Woman, estab 1994, empl 17, sales $1,355,199, cert: WBENC)

8703 Mico Promotions, Inc.
1350 6th Ave, 4th Fl
New York, NY 10019
Contact: Maia Michaelson President
Tel: 212-255-5785
Email: maia@micopromotions.com
Website: www.micopromotions.com
Creative and art studio services. (Woman, estab 1992, empl 5, sales $1,295,287, cert: WBENC)

8704 Mirror Show Management
855 Hard Rd
Webster, NY 14580
Contact: Devon Donatello Marketing & Sales Enablement Specialist
Tel: 585-232-4020
Email: supplierdiversity@msmxp.com
Website: www.msmxp.com
Exhibit design & management firm. (Woman, estab 1993, empl 50, sales $20,000,000, cert: WBENC)

8705 Novatek Communications, Inc.
500 Helendale Road Ste 280
Rochester, NY 14609
Contact: Amy Castronova CEO
Tel: 585-482-4070
Email: patty.setchell@novatekcom.com
Website: www.novatekcom.com
User & service writing, computer-based training, e-learning & multimedia. (Woman, estab 1989, empl 29, sales $1,504,910, cert: State, WBENC)

8706 Percepture
104 W 40th St.
New York, NY 10018
Contact: Thor Harris CEO
Tel: 800-707-9190
Email: supplierdiversity@percepture.com
Website: www.percepture.com
Public relations & marketing. (AA, estab 2004, empl 4, sales $3,389,825, cert: State)

8707 Sage Advertising LLC
71 Atkinson Rd
Rockville Centre, NY 11570
Contact: Jodi O'Sullivan Owner
Tel: 516-320-9225
Email: jodi@sage-agency.com
Website: www.sage-agency.com
Marketing strategies & materials, print, collateral, digital, trade show & video production. (Woman, estab 2008, empl 5, sales $454,000, cert: WBENC)

8708 Site Solutions Worldwide
1023 Route 146
Clifton Park, NY 12065
Contact: Nathalie Whitton President
Tel: 518-399-7181
Email: nathalie@sswmeetings.com
Website: www.sitesolutionsworldwide.com
Meeting svcs: site selection, meeting management, contract negotiations, online registration, speaker coordination, exhibitor coordination & on-site meeting management. (Woman, estab 2001, empl 14, sales $8,764,783, cert: State, WBENC)

8709 Spiral Design Studio, LLC
135 Mohawk St
Cohoes, NY 12047
Contact: Lauren Payne Managing Partner
Tel: 518-326-1135
Email: lauren@spiraldesign.com
Website: www.spiraldesign.com
Graphic design, advertising, marketing, website design, web page design, responsive design, mobile website design, internet marketing, digital marketing, email marketing, branding, logo design, corporate identity, print design, print marketing. (Woman, estab 1989, empl 10, sales $948,500, cert: State, WBENC)

8710 Strategic Marketing & Promotions, Inc.
10 N Main St
Pearl River, NY 10965
Contact: Greg Caglione President
Tel: 845-623-7777
Email: gcaglione@smpglobal.com
Website: www.smpglobal.com
Mfr, design & produce point of purchase display fixtures, signage, retail consumer packaging. Assembly, fulfillment, inventory management, distribution center. (Woman, estab 2001, empl 85, sales $5,000,000, cert: State)

8711 The CementBloc
32 Old Slip 15th Fl
New York, NY 10005
Contact: Art Chavez Partner
Tel: 646-829-2002
Email: achavez@thebloc.com
Website: www.thebloc.com
Global branding, full-service professional promotion, medical strategy, patient education, payer strategy, digital strategy & communications planning/execution. (Woman, estab 2000, empl 175, sales $41,900,000, cert: WBENC)

8712 The Mixx
350 7th Ave Ste 1403
New York, NY 10001
Contact: Olympia Lambert Client Services Dir
Tel: 212-695-6663
Email: hi@themixxnyc.com
Website: www.themixxnyc.com
Strategic branding, messaging & marketing firm: corporate identity & brand platforms, brand collateral, annual reports & Bbochures, advertising campaigns, direct mail campaigns, web design & development, multi-media marketing plans. (Woman, estab 1996, empl 18, sales $16,968,000, cert: WBENC)

8713 The Mundial Group, Inc.
28 E 28th St
New York, NY 10016
Contact: Felix Sencion
Tel: 212-213-1400
Email: billing@mundialgroup.net
Website: www.mundialsportsnetwork.com
Marketing; Print Sport Publication; Print Advertising; Digital Advertidsing: display, flash, mobile, pre-roll, branded content production (Hisp, estab 1999, empl 11, sales , cert: NMSDC)

8714 The Thomas Collective LLC
37 w 28th st 12th floor
New York, NY 10001
Contact: Erin Donley Special Projects Coordinator
Tel: 212-229-2294
Email: edonley@thethomascollective.com
Website: www.thethomascollective.com
Marketing communications, Brand Development, Public Relations & Digital/Social Media. (Woman, estab 2004, empl 20, sales $700,000, cert: WBENC)

8715 TITANIUM Worldwide LLC
350 7th Ave Ste 1403
New York, NY 10001
Contact: Streisand Chief Financial Operations Officer
Tel: 646-952-8440
Email: accounting@titaniumww.com
Website: www.titaniumww.com
Media, marketing, communications & consulting: Branding/Creative/Strategy, Content/Messaging, Digital/Social/Mobile, Film/Video Production, Event Marketing, Business Intelligence, Data Warehousing, Development/Deployment. (Woman, estab 2014, empl 4, sales , cert: WBENC)

8716 UX Design Collective LLC
672 Carroll St, Unit 3
Brooklyn, NY 11215
Contact: Ariel Rey Head of Product & Projects
Tel: 929-352-4489
Email: services@uxdesigncollective.com
Website: www.uxdesigncollective.com
Design websites, mobile apps, strategize, design, and build thoughtful, transformative digital products. (As-Pac, estab 2017, empl 4, sales , cert: State, City, WBENC)

8717 View Finders Market Research
11 Sandra Ln
Pearl River, NY 10965
Contact: Janet Gaines Owner
Tel: 845-735-7022
Email: jgaines@view-finders.com
Website: www.view-finders.com
Focus group management, consumer & business research, advertising testing, product definition, concept development, attitudinal research, usage testing, customer satisfaction & new product development. (Woman, estab 1983, empl 25, sales $700,000, cert: WBENC)

8718 Weinman Schnee Morais, Inc.
250 W 57th St Ste 2212
New York, NY 10107
Contact: Cynthia Weinman Principal
Tel: 212-906-1900
Email: cweinman@wsm-inc.com
Website: www.wsm-inc.com
Marketing research, 50% qualitative & 50% quantitative. (Woman, estab 1993, empl 12, sales , cert: WBENC)

8719 Yorkville Marketing Consulting LLC
425 E 79 St Ste 11M
New York, NY 10075
Contact: Dina Shapiro CEO
Tel: 646-284-2481
Email: dina.shapiro@yorkvilleconsulting.com
Website: www.YorkvilleConsulting.com
Corporate Brand Strategy, Marketing, Organization Planning, Marketing Capabilities, Training. (Woman, estab 2013, empl 1, sales , cert: WBENC)

8720 Zebra Strategies
421 7th Ave Ste 1100
New York, NY 10001
Contact: Denene Jonielle Rodney CEO
Tel: 212-244-3960
Email: denene@zstrategies.net
Website: www.zebrastrategies.com
Qualitative market research services. (Woman/AA, estab 2001, empl 10, sales $1,541,000, cert: NMSDC, WBENC)

Ohio

8721 Abercrumbie Group
10301 Giverny Blvd
Cincinnati, OH 45241
Contact: Claudia Abercrumbie President
Tel: 513-733-1555
Email: claudia@theabercrumbiegroup.com
Website: www.theabercrumbiegroup.com
Event management. (Woman/AA, estab 2005, empl 1, sales $350,000, cert: WBENC)

8722 Acadia Lead Management Services Inc.
4738 Gateway Circle Ste A100
Kettering, OH 45440
Contact: Tami Randall Mgr
Tel: 888-605-3194
Email: tlr@acadialms.com
Website: www.acadialms.com
Customized industry data, marketing information & sales leads, lead qualification, lead nurturing, marketing dashboard & lead management. (Woman, estab 1999, empl 21, sales $958,835, cert: WBENC)

8723 Affordable Language Services
      8944 Blue Ash Road
      Cincinnati, OH 45242
      Contact: Kristi Reynek CEO
      Tel: 513-745-0888
      Email: kreynek@affordablelanguages.com
      Website: www.affordablelanguages.com
Translation & interpreting services, voice-over & transcription. (Woman, estab 2000, empl 14, sales $2,209,000, cert: WBENC)

8724 Baker Creative Ltd.
      386 Main St
      Groveport, OH 43125
      Contact: Michele Cuthbert Principal
      Tel: 614-836-3845
      Email: mbaker@baker-creative.com
      Website: www.baker-creative.com
Graphic Design, Marketing Consulting, Advertising, Public Relations, Display Advertising. (Minority, Woman, estab 2003, empl 10, sales , cert: State, WBENC, SDB)

8725 Bascom & Adams Business Solutions, LLC
      1209 Hill St North Ste 227
      Pickerington, OH 43147
      Contact: Christine Adams President
      Tel: 614-252-7880
      Email: chrisadams@bascomadams.com
      Website: www.bascomadams.com
Marketing communications, public relations, special events, outreach & engagement. (Woman/AA, estab 2002, empl 1, sales , cert: State, City)

8726 Charm Consulting
      2957 Cranbrook Dr
      Cincinnati, OH 45251
      Contact: Toyia Montgomery CEO
      Tel: 513-290-6357
      Email: charmconsulting3@gmail.com
      Website: www.charmconsulting3.com
Branding, public relations & event services. (Woman/AA, estab 2014, empl 3, sales , cert: State)

8727 EVOLUTION Creative Solutions
      7107 Shona Dr Ste 110
      Cincinnati, OH 45237
      Contact: Robert Miller Sales Rep
      Tel: 513-864-3761
      Email: bob.miller@evo-creative.com
      Website: www.evo-creative.com
Marketing plans, graphic design & production, website creation & maintenance, and social media. (Woman, estab 2011, empl 6, sales , cert: WBENC)

8728 Exhibit Concepts Inc.
      700 Crossroads Ct
      Vandalia, OH 45377
      Contact: Ellen Kaminski VP Sales and Marketing
      Tel: 937-535-0224
      Email: ekaminski@exhibitconcepts.com
      Website: www.exhibitconcepts.com
Strategic design, graphic design and production, engineering and fabrication, program management, custom, rental, hybrid, modular exhibits, interior nvironments, events, museum design, fabrication. (Woman, estab 1978, empl 106, sales $280,000,000, cert: WBENC)

8729 Gong Gong Communications
      746 Green Crest Dr
      Westerville, OH 43081
      Contact: Amanda Sage CEO
      Tel: 614-388-8918
      Email: amanda@gonggongcommunications.com
      Website: www.gonggongcommunications.com
Corporate, non-profit event planning & marketing, Offline & online experiential marketing campaigns, Target social media & e-mail marketing campaigns, Podcast production & promotion. (Woman, estab 2009, empl 3, sales , cert: WBENC)

8730 Illumination Research, Inc.
      5947 Deerfield Blvd Ste 203
      Mason, OH 45040
      Contact: Karri Bass President
      Tel: 513-774-9588
      Email: kbass@illumination-research.com
      Website: www.illumination-research.com
Qualitative market research. (Woman, estab 0, empl 29, sales $6,593,000, cert: WBENC)

8731 Incite Visual Communications
      PO Box 1017
      Milford, OH 45150
      Contact: Michael Perry Business Dev Dir
      Tel: 513-575-5100
      Email: mike@incitevisual.com
      Website: www.incitevisual.com
Branding/marketing design, Branding, Package Design, Print & Digital Sales/Marketing Assets, Point of Sale materials, Product Sell Sheets, FSI, Event Promotional assets. (Woman, estab 2001, empl 2, sales $186,000, cert: WBENC)

8732 Market Inquiry, Inc.
      5825 Creek Rd
      Cincinnati, OH 45242
      Contact: Cathy Noyes Owner
      Tel: 513-794-1088
      Email: cathy@marketinquiry.com
      Website: www.marketinquiry.com
Qualitative & quantitative research. (Woman, estab 1995, empl 20, sales $1,164,000, cert: WBENC)

8733 MMP LLC
      7588 Central Parke Blvd, Ste 321
      Mason, OH 45040
      Contact: Linda Dektas Owner
      Tel: 513-234-0560
      Email: linda@creativestorm.com
      Website: www.creativestorm.com
Websites, ads-print & broadcast, brochures, logo design, digital marketing, direct mail, social media, promotions, displays, promotional items & apparel. (Woman, estab 1999, empl 5, sales $1,000,000, cert: WBENC)

8734 Modern Technique, LLC
      1050 Lear Industrial Pkwy
      Avon, OH 44011
      Contact: Kristi Blosser President
      Tel: 440-497-8547
      Email: kristi@whatsyourtechnique.com
      Website: www.whatsyourtechnique.com
Advertising, digital & mobile media development, website design, SEO & email marketing, broadcast & social media planning & devel, mobile app devel & mobile marketing. (Woman, estab 2012, empl 4, sales $250,000, cert: WBENC)

PROFESSIONAL SERVICES: Public Relations/Marketing

8735 Partners In Planning One Inc.
7061 Larkspur Lane
Liberty Township, OH 45044
Contact: Nancy Caine President
Tel: 513-755-1091
Email: ncainepip@aol.com
Website: www.partnersinplanning.org
Meeting planning & event svcs: food & beverage negotiation, budget control, meeting set up & contract negotiations. (Woman, estab 1997, empl 1, sales , cert: WBENC)

8736 Power Presentations, Inc.
8225 Brecksville Rd, Ste 100
Brecksville, OH 44141
Contact: Cate Huff Finance/Admin Mgr
Tel: 440-526-4400
Email: ch@power-presentations.com
Website: www.power-presentations.com
Communication and presentations skills training for all types of communication, standing, seated and virtual. (Woman, estab 1993, empl 7, sales , cert: WBENC)

8737 Quez Media Marketing
1138 Prospect Ave E
Cleveland, OH 44115
Contact: Jose Vasquez CEO
Tel: 216-910-0202
Email: info@quezmedia.com
Website: www.quezmedia.com
Marketing communications, online storefronts, data services, creative services, print. (Hisp, estab 2009, empl 17, sales $1,646,098, cert: State, City, NMSDC)

8738 R/P Marketing Public Relations
1500 Timberwolf Dr
Holland, OH 43528
Contact: Robin Walters VP Business Dev
Tel: 614-428-6056
Email: rwalters@r-p.com
Website: www.r-p.com
Marketing, advertising & public relations services. (Woman, estab 1993, empl 25, sales $5,559,217, cert: WBENC)

8739 Rhonda Crowder & Associates LLC
1465 E 112th St
Cleveland, OH 44106
Contact: Wayne Dailey Creative Dir
Tel: 216-352-3330
Email: wayne@rhondacrowderllc.com
Website: www.rhondacrowderllc.com
Communications, content creation, graphic design, fundraising & media relations services. (Woman/AA, estab 2011, empl 5, sales , cert: State)

8740 SCANVenger Hunt LLC
1275 Kinnear Rd
Columbus, OH 43212
Contact: Sean Fields Dir Business Dev
Tel: 800-975-5161
Email: sean@scanvengerhunt.biz
Website: www.scanvengerhunt.biz
Event services, event applications, registration badges for attendees. (AA, estab 2012, empl 3, sales $155,000, cert: NMSDC)

8741 Various Views Research, Inc.
11353 Reed Hartman Hwy, Ste 200
Cincinnati, OH 45241
Contact: Doug van der Zee Dir Business Dev
Tel: 513-387-2208
Email: dvanderzee@variousviews.com
Website: www.variousviews.com
Market research, qualitative research methodologies, focus groups, in-depth interviews & product tests. (Woman, estab 2007, empl 75, sales $3,500,000, cert: WBENC)

8742 Visibility Marketing, Inc.
24700 Chagrin Blvd Ste 306
Beachwood, OH 44122
Contact: Montrie Rucker Adams Visibility Officer
Tel: 440-684-9920
Email: mra@visibilitymarketing.com
Website: www.visibilitymarketing.com
Marketing communications & public relations, public & media relations services & strategic marketing campaigns. (Woman/AA, estab 2000, empl 2, sales , cert: State, City, WBENC, 8(a))

Oklahoma

8743 Bullseye Database Marketing, LLC
5546 S 104th East Ave
Tulsa, OK 74146
Contact: Deborah Kobe Norris CEO
Tel: 918-587-1731
Email: dnorris@bullseyedm.com
Website: www.bullseyedm.com
Direct marketing, direct mail, email, mobile & social media, strategic campaign direction, creative services, on-time, on-budget, error-free production, response tracking & analysis. (Woman, estab 1988, empl 8, sales $1,638,390, cert: WBENC)

Oregon

8744 Paulette Carter Design, Inc. (PCD Group)
5257 NE MLK Jr Blvd, Ste 301
Portland, OR 97211
Contact: Danielle Bastron Controller
Tel: 503-525-2989
Email: danielle@pcdgroup.com
Website: www.pcdgroup.com
Marketing svcs: custom websites, intranets & online applications, content mgmt, customer relationship mgmt tools, custom work flow & productivity applications, e-commerce, systems & data integration. (Woman, estab 1996, empl 12, sales , cert: WBENC)

8745 Stewart Marketing Group, LLC
905 N Harbour Dr, Unit 3
Portland, OR 97217
Contact: Michael Stewart President
Tel: 503-270-7857
Email: michael@stewartmarketinggroup.com
Website: www.stewartmarketinggroup.com
Conference & event planning, training & seminar materials, travel & hospitality, point of purchase displays, media & CD/DVD disc storage, office supplies. (AA, estab 2006, empl 1, sales $130,000, cert: State)

8746 The Kingfisher Group, LLC
       10260 SW Greenburg Rd Ste. 400
       Portland, OR 97223
       Contact: Mary Lou Kayser CEO
       Tel: 503-567-8730
       Email: mlk@maryloukayser.com
       Website: www.maryloukayser.com
Content Marketing Strategies, Visual Strategic Planning, Creativity & Innovation, Training & Development, Presentation Skills Development. (Woman, estab 2012, empl 1, sales , cert: State)

Pennsylvania

8747 2nd Spark Consulting LLC
       31 E Butler Ave 1st Fl
       Ambler, PA 19002
       Contact: Stefanie Freeling Finance Mgr
       Tel: 215-948-3055
       Email: sfreeling@2ndspark.com
       Website: www.2ndspark.com
Marketing consulting & creative advertising, customer insights, situation analysis, war games, portfolio architecture strategy, buying process, positioning, messaging, branding, campaign development, media planning, tactical planning. (Minority, Woman, estab 2009, empl 20, sales $1,726,022, cert: WBENC)

8748 aiaTranslations LLC
       4387 W. Swamp Rd
       Doylestown, PA 18902
       Contact: Molly Naughton President
       Tel: 908-955-5201
       Email: molly.naughton@aiatranslations.com
       Website: www.aiaTranslations.com
Specializing in healthcare & life science translation. (Woman, estab 2010, empl 4, sales $1,500,000, cert: WBENC)

8749 Albrecht Events LLC
       209 Providence Ln
       Lansdale, PA 19446
       Contact: Ashley Albrecht Managing Dir
       Tel: 215-699-3784
       Email: aalbrecht@albrechtevents.com
       Website: www.albrechtevents.com
Corporate meeting, event planning & destination management services. (Woman, estab 2005, empl 1, sales $171,228, cert: WBENC)

8750 Apex Impact Marketing LLC
       1720 Kendarloren Dr Ste. 714
       Jamison, PA 18929
       Contact: Howard Wilensky Partner
       Tel: 215-489-5460
       Email: howard@focusmx.com
       Website: www.focusmx.com
Marketing Strategy, Digital Strategy & Planning Websites, Microsites, Landing Pages, Creative & Design (Wordpress,Kentico, Sitecore, .NET), eCRM Programs, Social Media Campaigns, Mobile & Tablet Applications, Online Advertising. (Woman, estab 2009, empl 14, sales , cert: WBENC)

8751 Bosha Design Inc.
       921 Childs Ave
       Drexel Hill, PA 19026
       Contact: Barbara Bosha President
       Tel: 610-622-4422
       Email: BarbBosha@boshadesign.com
       Website: www.boshadesign.com
Print & web graphic design: corp communications, business collateral, annual reports, web design & dev, identity systems, brochures, newsletters, advertising, exhibits & signage. (Woman, estab 1986, empl 5, sales $85,019,107, cert: WBENC)

8752 Brandwidth Solutions, LLC
       108 Samantha Lane
       Lansdale, PA 19446
       Contact: Debra Harrsch CEO
       Tel: 215-997-8575
       Email: dharrsch@brandwidthsolutions.com
       Website: www.brandwidthsolutions.com
Marketing communications, digital, 3D interactive, video & social media. (Woman, estab 2005, empl 7, sales $718,392, cert: WBENC)

8753 Chelsea Partners Inc.
       108 Arch St Ste 1202
       Philadelphia, PA 19106
       Contact: Tempa Berish President
       Tel: 215-603-7300
       Email: tempa@chelseapartners.com
       Website: www.chelseapartners.com
Graphic design, printing (digital, flat sheet and web), presort mailing svcs & fulfillment. (Woman, estab 1998, empl 13, sales $2,120,795, cert: State, City, WBENC)

8754 Community Marketing Concepts, Inc.
       7300 City Ave Ste 330
       Philadelphia, PA 19151
       Contact: Daud Hadi Public Relations
       Tel: 215-871-0900
       Email: johnpaul@communitymarketingconcepts.com
       Website: www.communitymarketingconcepts.com
Public relations & marketing, research, strategic development, social & issue management programs, brand messaging, publicity & media placement, event planning, corporate & community relations, sponsorships, graphic & web design. (Woman/AA, estab 1998, empl 10, sales $2,400,000, cert: State, City, NMSDC)

8755 DaBrian Marketing Group
       500 Penn St, Ste 201
       Reading, PA 19602
       Contact: Daniel Laws, Jr. President
       Tel: 610-743-5602
       Email:
       Website: www.dabrianmarketing.com
Digital marketing agency, original and strategic digital marketing solutions. (AA, estab 2008, empl 9, sales $949,000, cert: State, NMSDC)

8756 Direct Marketing Alliance Inc.
       104 Park Dr
       Montgomeryville, PA 18936
       Contact: Ted Gramiak VP
       Tel: 215-619-8800
       Email: tgramiak@directma.com
       Website: www.directma.com
Direct marketing fulfillment services, direct mail package production. (Woman, estab 2003, empl 45, sales $6,000,000, cert: WBENC)

PROFESSIONAL SERVICES: Public Relations/Marketing

8757 Eitzen Creative LLC
202 Dudley Ave
Narberth, PA 19072
Contact: Pamela Eitzen President
Tel: 610-660-0220
Email: pam@eobcreative.com
Website: www.eobcreative.com
Graphic design, strategic communications, branding, advertising, video, animation, corporate & employee communications, corporate identity, investor relations materials, websites, exhibit design. (Woman, estab 2012, empl 3, sales $268,944, cert: WBENC)

8758 Fox Specialties, Inc. dba Encompass Elements
2750 Morris Rd Ste C
Lansdale, PA 19446
Contact: Nadine Hodges New Business Dev
Tel: 267-209-4133
Email: nhodges@encompasselements.com
Website: www.encompasselements.com
Marketing communications. (Woman, estab 1995, empl 65, sales $34,000,000, cert: WBENC)

8759 Lead Dog, Inc.
305 S Chester Rd
Swarthmore, PA 19081
Contact: Mary Susan Milbourne, CMM CEO
Tel: 610-690-5184
Email: marysusan@leaddogonline.com
Website: www.leaddogonline.com
Plan & manage meetings, conferences & special events: budget dev, site selection, attendee registration, multimedia presentations. (Woman, estab 1997, empl 3, sales $275,232, cert: WBENC)

8760 Linguis-Techs, Inc.
408 Executive Dr
Langhorne, PA 19047
Contact: Lisa O'Rourke Dir of Finance
Tel: 215-860-8152
Email: lisa@sommerconsulting.com
Website: www.sommerconsulting.com
Qualitative marketing research, strategy & motivational profile of target audiences on conscious, unconscious & emotional levels. (Minority, Woman, estab 1991, empl 11, sales $3,855,315, cert: NMSDC, WBENC)

8761 Markitects, Inc.
107 W Lancaster Ave, Ste 203
Wayne, PA 19087
Contact: Francine Carb CEO
Tel: 610-687-2200
Email: fcarb@markitects.com
Website: www.markitects.com
Strategic marketing, branding, public relations & communications. (Woman, estab 1994, empl 12, sales $2,000,000, cert: WBENC)

8762 Maven Communications, LLC
123 S Broad St Ste 1645
Philadelphia, PA 19109
Contact: Jessica Sharp Principal
Tel: 215-434-7190
Email: jsharp@mavenagency.com
Website: www.mavenagency.com
Public relations: strategic planning, community affairs, issues management, crisis communications & planning, internal communications, product & corporate launches, spokesperson & media training. (Woman, estab 2006, empl 4, sales $315,839, cert: WBENC)

8763 MFR Consultants, Inc.
128 Chestnut St
Philadelphia, PA 19106
Contact: Maria Roberts CEO
Tel: 215-238-9270
Email: mfrizelle@mfrconsultants.com
Website: www.mfrconsultants.com
Strategic marketing, multimedia, graphic design, web & application development, management consulting. (Woman/AA, estab 1989, empl 15, sales $4,114,966, cert: State, WBENC)

8764 MOD Worldwide
1429 Walnut St Fl 2
Philadelphia, PA 19102
Contact: Nina Stanley President
Tel: 215-732-7666
Email: nina@modworldwide.com
Website: www.modworldwide.com
Brand, marketing, digital, 3D visualization, graphic design, digital media, internet marketing, film, website development, production, visual effects, and print production. (Woman, estab 2002, empl 20, sales $3,000,000, cert: City, WBENC)

8765 Modern Graphics
118 Dickerson Rd Ste B
North Wales, PA 19454
Contact: Diane Connor President
Tel: 215-619-4700
Email: dconnor@modernsbc.com
Website: www.modernsbc.com
Branding, web design, collateral & digital literature, logo design, graphic design, internal & external corporate communications. (Woman, estab 1999, empl 8, sales $2,100,000, cert: WBENC)

8766 Rector Communications, Inc.
2300 Chestnut St, Ste. 360
Philadelphia, PA 19103
Contact: Marion Rector President
Tel: 215-963-9661
Email: marion@rector.com
Website: www.rector.com
Corporate Communications, Employee Communications, Branding, Business Development, Marketing Services, Management Consulting, Graphic Design & Annual Reports. (Woman, estab 1983, empl 5, sales $654,514, cert: City, WBENC)

8767 Slice Communications, LLC
234 Market St, Fl 4
Philadelphia, PA 19106
Contact: Brian McDonnell Business Devel
Tel: 215-600-0050
Email: bmcdonnell@slicecommunications.com
Website: www.slicecommunications.com/
PR & social media, stories, editorials, research, data, trends, case studies, events & digital assets. (Woman, estab 2008, empl 15, sales , cert: City, WBENC)

8768 SPRYTE Communications
200 S Broad St, Ste 1160
Philadelphia, PA 19102
Contact: Lisa Simon CEO
Tel: 215-545-4715
Email: lsimon@sprytecom.com
Website: www.sprytecom.com
Public relations & marketing consulting. (Woman, estab 1990, empl 6, sales $1,527,267, cert: State, WBENC)

8769 The Melior Group, Inc.
1528 Walnut St, Ste 1414
Philadelphia, PA 19102
Contact: Linda McAleer President
Tel: 215-545-0054
Email: lmcaleer@meliorgroup.com
Website: www.meliorgroup.com
Marketing research & consulting, analysis, implications & recommendations. (Woman, estab 1982, empl 10, sales $1,500,000, cert: State)

Puerto Rico

8770 Maremar Design, Inc.
Urb Casa Linda Court 20 B St
Bayamon, PR 00959
Contact: Marina Rivon President
Tel: 787-731-8795
Email: marina@maremar.com
Website: www.maremar.com
Graphic design, corporate identity, logos, stationary, graphic standards manual, design consultancy, sales literature, collateral, point of purchase, annual peports, corporate profiles, brochures, newsletters. (Minority, Woman, estab 1997, empl 2, sales , cert: NMSDC)

Rhode Island

8771 Advertising Ventures, Inc. dba (add)ventures
20 Risho Ave
East Providence, RI 02914
Contact: Joseph R Miech COO
Tel: 401-453-4748
Email: jmiech@addventures.com
Website: www.addventures.com
Marketing, branding, public relations, advertising, graphic & interactive design. (Hisp, estab 1989, empl 42, sales $9,891,991, cert: State)

8772 FAVOR Design + Communications
582 Great Rd Ste 201
North Smithfield, RI 02896
Contact: Rene Payne Principal
Tel: 508-272-0522
Email: rene@favordesignco.com
Website: www.favordesignco.com
Graphic & web design services, branding, creative direction, brand identity, content creation, copywriting, positioning, book design, packaging, interactive design, product design, typography, editorial, environmental retail. (Woman/AA, estab 2004, empl 1, sales $335,817, cert: WBENC)

8773 Katie Schibler & Associates LLC
5875 Post Rd, Unit 1
East Greenwich, RI 02818
Contact: Katie Schibler Founder
Tel: 401-398-0830
Email: partnerships@schiblerandassociates.com
Website: www.katieschibler.com
Project Management, Event Planning, Marketing Consulting, Social Media Planning, Social Media Strategy, Copywriting, Sales Strategy, Strategic Planning, Partnership Consulting, PR/Media Relations. (Woman, estab 2011, empl 4, sales , cert: WBENC)

8774 North Star Marketing, Inc.
1130 Ten Rod Rd Ste D-208
North Kingstown, RI 02852
Contact: April Williams President
Tel: 401-294-0133
Email: april@fortheloveofmarketing.com
Website: www.fortheloveofmarketing.com
Marketing & PR: direct mail, advertising, strategy, email marketing & public relations. (Woman, estab 1997, empl 10, sales $708,613, cert: State, WBENC)

Tennessee

8775 Behind the Scenes
7850 Stage Hills Blvd Ste 103
Bartlett, TN 38133
Contact: Dusky Project Mgr
Tel: 901-937-3926
Email: dusky@btsmemphis.com
Website: www.btsmemphis.com
Procurement, warehousing, mail merge & related activities, event & production management. (Woman, estab 2000, empl 17, sales $2,000,000, cert: WBENC)

8776 Bytes of Knowledge, Inc.
1212 6th Ave N
Nashville, TN 37208
Contact: Nancy Bass Lead Visual Artist, eLearning
Tel: 615-383-9005
Email: sales@bytesofknowledge.com
Website: www.bytesofknowledge.com
Website design, mobile & software development, brand support, social marketing, digital elearning, business strategy, network design & maintenance & entrepreneur consulting. (Woman, estab 1995, empl 22, sales $2,964,288, cert: WBENC)

8777 Miller Tanner Associates, LLC
2070 Lebanon Rd
Lebanon, TN 37087
Contact: Dawn Barnes Dir Global Sales
Tel: 615-466-2600
Email: dawn@millertanner.com
Website: www.millertanner.com
Global meeting & event planning. (Woman, estab 1997, empl 50, sales $26,000,000, cert: WBENC)

8778 Shelton Communications Group, Inc.
111 E Jackson Ave, Ste 201
Knoxville, TN 37915
Contact: Gwen Meadows Accounting Asst
Tel: 865-524-8385
Email: gmeadows@sheltongrp.com
Website: www.sheltongrp.com
Green advertising; green marketing; consumer research; environmental research. (Woman, estab 0, empl , sales , cert: WBENC)

Texas

8779 70kft, LLC
325 N. St. Paul St Ste 3000
Dallas, TX 75201
Contact: Tiffany Bryant
Tel: 214-653-1600
Email: tiffany@70kft.com
Website: www.70kft.com
Design, public relations & digital marketing disciplines. (AA, estab 2003, empl 25, sales $3,251,230, cert: State, NMSDC)

PROFESSIONAL SERVICES: Public Relations/Marketing

8780 Akorbi Translations, LLC
6010 W Spring Creek Pkwy, Ste 238
Plano, TX 75024
Contact: Genny Bobadilla Compliance Officer
Tel: 214-256-9222
Email: gbobadilla@akorbi.com
Website: www.akorbi.com
Multilingual business solutions in more than 140 languages. (Hisp, estab 2016, empl 60, sales $36,000,000, cert: NMSDC)

8781 All About Events
7810 Chinon Circle
Houston, TX 77071
Contact: Elmer Rogers Owner
Tel: 713-723-1618
Email: elmer@allaevents.com
Website: www.allaevents.com
Event planning, ceremonies, conferences, conventions, exhibitions, fundraisers, meetings, receptions, seminars & trade shows. (Woman/AA, estab 2005, empl 2, sales , cert: State, City, NMSDC)

8782 American Installation and Management, LLC
1407 Woodridge Circle
Euless, TX 76040
Contact: Gary Springer Sales
Tel: 817-803-3302
Email: gary@aimgraphicsco.com
Website: www.aimgraphicsco.com
Print, display & installation management. (Woman, estab 2011, empl 2, sales $300,000, cert: State)

8783 Boone DeLeon Communications, Inc.
3100 S Gessner, Ste 110
Houston, TX 77063
Contact: Leo De Leon Jr President
Tel: 713-952-9600
Email: leo@boonedeleon.com
Website: www.boonedeleon.com
Marketing, advertising, public relations, promotions, retail overlays, couponing & sampling, Spanish translations. (Hisp, estab 1979, empl 7, sales $1,656,911, cert: State, City)

8784 BrandEra, Inc.
219 S Main St Ste 301
Fort Worth, TX 76104
Contact: Elizabeth Owens Principal
Tel: 817-927-7750
Email: bo@branderamarketing.com
Website: www.branderamarketing.com
Strategic planning, sales/promotional initiatives, advertising, press materials, designing/maintaining websites, marketing materials, planning special events. (Woman, estab 2004, empl 4, sales $935,118, cert: State, WBENC)

8785 Consumer and Market Insights, LLC (CMI)
3010 Lyndon B Johnson Fwy Ste 1200
Dallas, TX 75234
Contact: Royalyn Reid CEO
Tel: 972-939-9500
Email: madisen@thecmiteam.com
Website: www.thecmiteam.com
Market research, training & strategic event planning. (Woman/AA, estab 1998, empl 16, sales , cert: State, NMSDC, WBENC, SDB)

8786 CS Creative
9108 Chancellor Row
Dallas, TX 75247
Contact: Cindy Slayton President
Tel: 214-905-8008
Email: cindy@cs-creative.com
Website: www.cs-creative.com
Graphic design svcs: corporate communications, identity devel & mgmt. (Woman, estab 1989, empl 17, sales $1,886,000, cert: WBENC)

8787 Dallas Fan Fares, Inc.
14900 Landmark Blvd. Ste 300
Dallas, TX 75254
Contact: Christine Spradling
Tel: 972-239-9969
Email: cspradling@fanfares.com
Website: www.fanfares.com
Corporate meeting, incentive trips & sporting event planning. (Woman, estab 1980, empl 35, sales $14,412,000, cert: WBENC)

8788 DirecToHispanic, LLC
4909 N McColl Rd
McAllen, TX 78504
Contact: Lauren Boyle
Tel: 562-624-4680
Email: lauren.boyle@directohispanic.com
Website: www.directohispanic.com
Marketing promotions agency. (Hisp, estab 2004, empl 12, sales $2,700,000, cert: NMSDC)

8789 Elias Events, LLC
6214 Beverly Hill, Ste 24
Houston, TX 77057
Contact: Deborah Elias President
Tel: 713-334-1800
Email: deborah@eliasevents.com
Website: www.eliasevents.com
Meeting planning, production schedules, resource & staff management, marketing & communications strategy & delivery, graphic design, public relations, marketing/press collateral, website development & social media support. (Woman, estab 1998, empl 2, sales $10,111,567, cert: City)

8790 ETC Group, Inc.
1112 Copeland Rd Ste 400
Arlington, TX 76011
Contact: Bill Nichols vp
Tel: 817-462-0103
Email: bnichols@etconline.net
Website: www.etconline.net
Corporate travel management, groups, meeting & incentive, promotional marketing. (Woman, estab 1989, empl 25, sales $40,000,000, cert: State, WBENC)

8791 Event Source Professionals, inc.
4109 Gateway Court 300
Colleyville, TX 76034
Contact: Dara Hall EVP
Tel: 817-267-6698
Email: dara@espinc-usa.com
Website: www.espinc-usa.com
Executive meeting, corporate conference & event planning services, travel, site selection, trade shows, exhibits, security, destination management, online and/or onsite registration. (Woman, estab 1988, empl 4, sales $2,489,000, cert: WBENC)

PROFESSIONAL SERVICES: Public Relations/Marketing

8792 EventLink International, Inc.
5910 N Central Expressway Ste 1665
Dallas, TX 75206
Contact: Teri Abram Sales
Tel: 214-750-9229
Email: tabram@eventlinkintl.com
Website: www.eventlinkintl.com
Global corporate event management: conferences, incentive trips, sales kick-offs, conventions, trade shows, business meetings, user conferences, retreats, leadership forums, etc. (Woman, estab 1998, empl 4, sales $330,000, cert: WBENC)

8793 Focus Latino
720 Barton Creek Blvd
Austin, TX 78746
Contact: Guy Antonioli President
Tel: 512-306-7393
Email: gcafocuslatino@austin.rr.com
Website: www.focuslatino.com
Qualitative Research & Strategic Planning, Focus Groups, Triads, Dyads, IDIs, Ethnographies (In-Homes & Shop-Alongs) & Quanti-Qualis. (Minority, Woman, estab 1996, empl 5, sales $814,366, cert: State)

8794 Garcia Baldwin Inc.
8647 Wurzbach Rd Ste J100
San Antonio, TX 78240
Contact: Yvonne Garcia CEO
Tel: 210-222-1933
Email: ygarcia@mvculture.com
Website: www.mvculture.com
Market & advertising, promotions/merchandising, event marketing, market research creative services, media strategies. (Minority, Woman, estab 1998, empl 42, sales $12,791,077, cert: State, NMSDC, WBENC, NWBOC)

8795 Global Exhibit Management
PO Box 331641
Fort Worth, TX 76163
Contact: President
Tel: 817-370-1400
Email: info@globalexhibitmanagement.com
Website: www.globalexhibitmanagement.com
Exhibit & event svcs: rental or purchase options, design & project management. (Woman, estab 2002, empl 10, sales $737,681, cert: State, WBENC)

8796 Impact Strategies Consultants
PO Box 266232
Houston, TX 77207
Contact: Debny Greenlee President
Tel: 713-446-4600
Email: debny@impact06.com
Website: www.impact06.com
Business development, diversity marketing, meeting & special events planning. (Woman/AA, estab 2006, empl 12, sales , cert: WBENC)

8797 Integrated Focus
6523 Embers Rd
Dallas, TX 75248
Contact: Valerie Pelan President
Tel: 214-454-5376
Email: vpelan@integratedfocus.com
Website: www.integratedfocus.com
Leadership management, sales training, branding, sales marketing integration. (Woman, estab 2004, empl 1, sales , cert: WBENC)

8798 Integrity International, Inc.
11767 Katy Frwy, Ste 750
Houston, TX 77079
Contact: Susan Lake Project Mgr
Tel: 877-955-0707
Email: info@tarrenpoint.com
Website: www.tarrenpoint.com
Documentation consulting, project mgmt, content devel, graphic design, technical illustration, desktop publishing, editing & quality assurance, indexing, localization & translation. (Woman, estab 1994, empl 63, sales $6,000,000, cert: State, WBENC)

8799 Ivie & Associates, Inc.
601 Silveron Blvd
Flower Mound, TX 75028
Contact: Jodi Marsh SVP Communications & Business Dev
Tel: 972-899-4723
Email: jodi.marsh@ivieinc.com
Website: www.ivieinc.com
Advertising & marketing support services: print procurement, print mgmt, media, creative, digital, communication/PR services, shopper marketing, kitting & fulfillment, staffing, publishing, CRM. (Woman, estab 1993, empl 650, sales $1,065,000,000, cert: WBENC)

8800 J.O. Agency
440 S Main St
Fort Worth, TX 76104
Contact: Business Dev Mgr
Tel: 817-335-0100
Email:
Website: www.joagency.com
Full service marketing, public relations and advertising: branding, public relations, graphic design, market research, marketing campaigns, digital marketing, etc. (Woman, estab 1998, empl 10, sales $950,825, cert: WBENC)

8801 K. Fernandez and Associates LLC
10601 RR 2222 Ste R13
Austin, TX 78730
Contact: Karla Fernandez Parker CEO
Tel: 210-614-1052
Email: karla@kfernandez.com
Website: www.kfernandez.com
Marketing services. (Minority, Woman, estab 1996, empl 11, sales $2,640,615, cert: State)

8802 Listo Translating Services & More LLC
830 S Mason Rd, Ste B2-A
Katy, TX 77450
Contact: Roxana Heredia CEO
Tel: 832-592-9264
Email: roxana@listotranslating.com
Website: www.houston-translation.com/
Translation & interpretation services. (Minority, Woman, estab 2012, empl 2, sales $150,000, cert: State, City, NMSDC)

8803 LNT 3 Group
545 E John Carpenter Frwy Ste 300
Irving, TX 75062
Contact: Marqueax Price President
Tel: 214-650-9966
Email: marqueax.price@lnt3group.com
Website: www.lnt3group.com
Marketing, e-communications, business development & new media services & support. (Woman/AA, estab 2010, empl 1, sales , cert: State)

PROFESSIONAL SERVICES: Public Relations/Marketing

8804 Magic Moments Parties and Events
4760 Preston Rd Ste 244-257
Frisco, TX 75034
Contact: Courtney Rai VP Sales & Mktg
Tel: 214-688-9900
Email: courtney@magicmomentsevents.com
Website: www.magicmomentsevents.com
Event planning, custom design & décor, floral design, event lighing, drapery, theme decor, props, interactive LED dance floor, custom artwork. (Woman, estab 2004, empl 12, sales $550,000, cert: WBENC)

8805 Malkoff Promotions
4904 Stony Ford Dr
Dallas, TX 75287
Contact: Lynne Malkoff President
Tel: 972-248-4354
Email: lynne@lmpspecialties.com
Website: www.lmpspecialties.com
Marketing & promotional solutions. (Woman, estab 1989, empl 5, sales , cert: State, WBENC)

8806 Mobius Partners Enterprise Solutions
1711 Citadel Plaza
San Antonio, TX 78209
Contact: Arlene Watson Principal
Tel: 216-621-9653
Email: arlene@mobiusgrey.com
Website: www.mobiusgrey.com
Design & visual communications, marketing development & branding. (Woman/AA, Hisp, estab 2002, empl 4, sales $33,600,000, cert: State, NMSDC)

8807 MSR Group, Inc.
3060 Communications Pkwy, Ste 200
Plano, TX 75093
Contact: Lauren Dunnaway Dir Sales & Marketing
Tel: 214-291-2920
Email: lauren.dunnaway@infinxglobal.com
Website: www.infinixglobal.com
Meeting management, Site selection, negotiation & venue contracting. (Woman, estab 1994, empl 25, sales $14,787,000, cert: State, WBENC)

8808 n8 Solutions
18650 Martinique
Houston, TX 77058
Contact: Dawn Magnan Owner
Tel: 281-333-3428
Email: dawn@n8s.cc
Website: www.n8s.cc
Marketing communications, marketing plans, packaging, advertising, sales materials & public relations, design brochures, trade show displays, point-of-purchase, billboards, direct mail, ads, corporate identity logos and standards, catalogs. (Woman, estab 1996, empl 3, sales $700,000, cert: WBENC)

8809 Open Channels Group, LLC
1320 S. University Dr Ste 220
Fort Worth, TX 76107
Contact: Tonya Veasey CEO
Tel: 817-332-0404
Email: info@ocgpr.com
Website: www.ocgpr.com
Public Relations, Multicultural Strategy Development, Integrated Communications, Digital Strategies, Public Involvement, Advertising & Marketing. (Woman/AA, estab 2005, empl 20, sales $1,794,160, cert: NMSDC)

8810 Outreach Strategists LLC
2727 Allen Pkwy., Ste 1300
Houston, TX 77019
Contact: Mustafa Tameez Managing Dir
Tel: 713-247-9600
Email: marketing@outreachstrategists.com
Website: www.outreachstrategists.com
Corporate & strategic communications, messaging, government affairs, public relations & marketing, ethnic & media relations, advocacy, constituent engagement, community outreach, graphic design, crisis management. (As-Ind, estab 2003, empl 5, sales $500,000, cert: State)

8811 Planning Professionals, Ltd.
1210 W McDermott Ste 111
Allen, TX 75013
Contact: Mollie Wallace CEO
Tel: 469-854-6991
Email: mwallace@planningprofessionals.com
Website: www.planningprofessionals.com
Web dev, logistical support, hotel site selection, electronic mktg, on-site staffing, food & beverage selection, contract negotiation, transportation, airfare, event marketing, signs, graphics, premiums & giveaways, mail fulfillment. (Woman, estab 1994, empl 12, sales $6,265,000, cert: WBENC)

8812 Production & Event Services, Inc.
9425 Sandy Ln
Manvel, TX 77578
Contact: Cindy Kutch President
Tel: 281-585-0569
Email: cindy@eventsplanning.com
Website: www.EventsPlanning.com
Special event services: sound, lighting, staging, theme decor, drapery, entertainment, catering, event planning, production & show management. (Woman, estab 2003, empl 10, sales , cert: WBENC)

8813 Regali Inc.
518 N Interurban St
Richardson, TX 75081
Contact: Renee Dutia President
Tel: 972-726-8830
Email: renee@regaliinc.com
Website: www.regaliinc.com
Diversified global marketing & technology services, integrating promotional programs, creative development & technology. (Woman/As-Ind, estab 1989, empl 7, sales , cert: State, NMSDC)

8814 Rutherford Enterprises, Inc.
17304 Preston Rd Ste 1020
Dallas, TX 75252
Contact: Al Rutherford President
Tel: 214-438-1185
Email: alrutherford@teamrutherford.net
Website: www.teamrutherford.net
Convention, meeting & event planning, event management, communications, sourcing & site selection, housing management, attrition mitigation exhibit & logistics management, senior executive travel support. (AA, estab 1998, empl 10, sales $1,032,594, cert: NMSDC)

PROFESSIONAL SERVICES: Public Relations/Marketing

8815 Sanders Wingo Advertising, Inc.
      303 N Oregon Auite 1200
      El Paso,, TX 79901
      Contact: Leslie Wingo President
      Tel: 915-533-9583
      Email: lwingo@sanderswingo.com
      Website: www.sanderswingo.com
Strategic planning, account planning, public relations, research, brand creation, account services, media planning, buying & creative services. (AA, Hisp, estab 1958, empl 76, sales $27,800,000, cert: NMSDC)

8816 Sissy Siero Voiceover & Media LLC
      1907 Frazier Ave
      Austin, TX 78704
      Contact: Sissy Siero
      Tel: 512-560-6772
      Email: Admin@sissysiero.com
      Website: www.sieromedia.com
Multimedia communications. (Woman, estab 2016, empl 5, sales $1,600,000, cert: WBENC)

8817 Steel Digital Studios, Inc.
      6414 Bee Cave Rd, Ste B
      Austin, TX 78746
      Contact: Andrea Wallace Business Dev Dir
      Tel: 800-681-8809
      Email: andrea.wallace@steelbranding.com
      Website: www.steelbranding.com
Family targeted marketing. (Woman, estab 2000, empl 25, sales $4,321,750, cert: State, WBENC)

8818 Strategar LLC
      3100 Independence Pkwy, Ste 311-204
      Plano, TX 75075
      Contact: Yareli Esteban CEO
      Tel: 972-948-3781
      Email: yareli@strategar.com
      Website: www.strategar.com
Marketing services: marketing, advertising, translations, web development, creative services, SEM, traditional media, content production & support of promotional events. (Minority, Woman, estab 2013, empl 3, sales , cert: State)

8819 Studio B Dallas, LLC
      2719 Randal Lake lane
      Spring, TX 77388
      Contact: MJ Moreau President
      Tel: 281-528-7000
      Email: mj@studiobdallas.com
      Website: www.studiobdallas.com
Strategic design, brand identity, packaging, retail store design & restaurant store design & merchandising. (Woman, estab 2009, empl 1, sales $165,000, cert: City)

8820 Studio J Designworks LLC
      7750 N. Macarthur Blvd Ste 120-356
      Irving, TX 75063
      Contact: Gina Jacobson Owner
      Tel: 972-556-0511
      Email: gina.jacobson@studiojdesignworks.com
      Website: www.studiojdesignworks.com
Visual communication solutions, branding, tag line development, trade show & event marketing, copywriting & copy editing, flash animation & development. (Woman, estab 2008, empl 2, sales , cert: State, WBENC)

8821 T3
      1801 N Lamar Blvd
      Austin, TX 78701
      Contact: Gay Gaddis Founder & CEO
      Tel: 512-499-8811
      Email: austin.hegarty@t-3.com
      Website: www.t-3.com
Integrated marketing solutions. (Woman, estab 1989, empl 150, sales , cert: WBENC)

8822 Tandem Axle Inc. dba Mixed Media Creations
      2300 Rockbrook Dr Ste D
      Lewisville, TX 75067
      Contact: Whitney Stockstill Operations Mgr
      Tel: 972-221-1600
      Email: whitney@mailmmc.com
      Website: www.mixedmediacreations.com
Graphic Design, Large-Scale Design, Web Development, Digital Media, Photography / Videography, Printing Services, Creative Consultation, Copywriting / Editing, Marketing Campaigns, Branded Merchandise. (Woman, estab 2007, empl 27, sales $2,800,000, cert: State, WBENC)

8823 Teneo Linguistics Company, LLC
      4700 Bryant Irvin Ct. Ste 301
      Fort Worth, TX 76107
      Contact: Hana Laurenzo CEO
      Tel: 817-441-9974
      Email: hana@tlctranslation.com
      Website: www.tlctranslation.com
Foreign language translation & interpreting services. (Woman, estab , empl , sales $1,400,000, cert: State, WBENC)

8824 The Backshop, Inc. DBA Mercury Mambo
      1107 S 8th St
      Austin, TX 78704
      Contact: Liz Arreaga Partner
      Tel: 512-447-4440
      Email: liz@mercurymambo.com
      Website: www.mercurymambo.com
Research & strategic planning, sales promotions, shopper marketing, retail merchandising, online/social media, field management, brand advertising experiential marketing, bilingual local market staffing. (Minority, Woman, estab 1999, empl 3, sales $1,062,732, cert: NMSDC, WBENC)

8825 The ID Development Group
      8811 Teel Pkwy, Ste 100 - 5233
      Frisco, TX 75035
      Contact: Julian Dorise President
      Tel: 214-295-5414
      Email: jdorise@iddevelop.com
      Website: www.iddevelop.com
Project designs, creative interior environments, tradeshow events & marketing campaigns. (AA, estab 2010, empl 5, sales , cert: NMSDC)

8826 The Maxcel Company
      6600 LBJ Freeway Ste 109
      Dallas, TX 75240
      Contact: Gwenna Brush President
      Tel: 972-644-0880
      Email: gwenna.brush@maxcel.net
      Website: www.maxcel.net
Plan & manage meetings, conventions & incentive travel programs. (Woman, estab 1995, empl 6, sales , cert: State, WBENC)

PROFESSIONAL SERVICES: Public Relations/Marketing

8827 Trilogy LLC
      5601 Democracy Dr Ste 105
      Plano, TX 75024
      Contact: Jeff Hoedebeck VP Business Dev
      Tel: 972-473-8911
      Email: jeffh@trilogymktg.com
      Website: www.trilogymktg.com
Experiential marketing: product sampling, product demonstrations, product merchandising & sponsorship activations. (AA, Hisp, estab 2002, empl 10, sales $3,500,000, cert: State, NMSDC)

8828 Ultimate Ventures
      4400 Beltway Dr
      Addison, TX 75001
      Contact: Val Lenington VP
      Tel: 972-732-8433
      Email: val@ultimateventures.com
      Website: www.ultimateventures.com
Special events, transportation, conference & convention services, corporate meeting & team building, inbound incentive programs & customized sightseeing tours. (Woman, estab 1993, empl 12, sales , cert: WBENC)

8829 Ward Creative Communications, Inc.
      PO Box 701219
      Houston, TX 77270
      Contact: Deborah Buks President
      Tel: 713-869-0707
      Email: dbuks@wardcc.com
      Website: www.wardcc.com
Media, community & employee relations; public affairs; marketing communications, graphic design; special events; crisis management. (Woman, estab 1990, empl 1, sales $1,200,000,000, cert: State)

8830 Winkler Public Relations
      PO Box 73404
      Houston, TX 77273
      Contact: Kathleen Winkler CEO
      Tel: 713-259-0189
      Email: kathy@winklerpr.com
      Website: www.winklerpr.com
Public relations services, crisis mgmt, media training. (Woman, estab 2003, empl 2, sales , cert: WBENC)

Utah

8831 Andavo Meetings & Incentives
      5588 S Green St Ste 300
      Salt Lake City, UT 84123
      Contact: Jessica Perez
      Tel: 720-398-5504
      Email: jessica.perez@andavomeetings.com
      Website: www.andavomeetings.com
Meetings, incentives & event planning & management. (Woman, estab 1982, empl 162, sales $36,989,079, cert: WBENC)

8832 Andinas dba/ Inlingua Utah
      602 E 300 S
      Salt Lake City, UT 84102
      Contact: Don Durham Business Devel
      Tel: 801-355-3775
      Email: don@inlinguautah.com
      Website: www.inlinguautah.com
Language classes, interpretation & translation services, translate websites, technical & legal documents. (Woman/Hisp, estab 1996, empl 15, sales $1,013,000, cert: NMSDC)

8833 Craig Enterprises, Inc. dba CommGap
      7069 S Highland Dr Ste 201
      Salt Lake City, UT 84121
      Contact: Lelani Craig CEO
      Tel: 801-944-4049
      Email: info@commgap.com
      Website: www.commgap.com
Machine translation, Ai, generative Ai, Communications, interpretation, document translation, voice-over, website development. (Woman/Hisp, estab 2000, empl 18, sales $4,200,000, cert: WBENC)

8834 Lexicon & Line LLC
      2527 E 5950 S
      Ogden, UT 84403
      Contact: Mary Johnstun
      Tel: 801-842-2682
      Email: mary@roadmapresearchglobal.com
      Website: www.roadmapresearchglobal.com
Market research, insights, data, data collection, polling, online surveying, survey, research, study, research, study, technical writing, business writing training, professional writing training, editing (Woman, estab 2014, empl 10, sales $1,000,000, cert: WBENC)

Virginia

8835 360 Virtual Assistance, LLC
      905 22nd St
      Newport News, VA 23607
      Contact: Natalie Robertson CEO
      Tel: -   -
      Email: sales@360virtualassistance.com
      Website: www.360virtualassistance.com
Integrated document preparation, multimedia creation, content design, layout, printing, optical scanning, research, technical writing. (AA, estab 2013, empl 1, sales , cert: State, NMSDC)

8836 All About Presentation, LLC
      707 E Main St Ste 1615
      Richmond, VA 23219
      Contact: Andrea M. Lyons CEO
      Tel: 804-381-4002
      Email: andrea@allaboutpresentation.com
      Website: www.allaboutpresentation.com
Event management: plan, design, manage and produce corporate events. (Woman/AA, estab 2007, empl 5, sales , cert: State, NMSDC)

8837 Bare International Inc.
      3702 Pender Dr, Ste 305
      Fairfax, VA 22030
      Contact: Lynne Brighton Sr VP
      Tel: 703-995-3132
      Email: lbrighton@bareinternational.com
      Website: www.bareinternational.com
Mystery shopping, employee surveys, video mystery shopping. (Woman, estab 1987, empl 300, sales $16,000,000, cert: WBENC)

8838 Candice Bennett & Associates, Inc.
      9621 Masey McQuire Ct
      Lorton, VA 22079
      Contact: Candice Bennett President
      Tel: 703-919-6231
      Email: clb@candicebennett.com
      Website: www.candicebennett.com
Market research, communications, organizational assessment & development. (Woman, estab 2003, empl 7, sales $619,866, cert: State, WBENC)

PROFESSIONAL SERVICES: Public Relations/Marketing

8839 Customer Relationship Metrics
      100 Glenn Dr, Ste A-11
      Sterling, VA 20164
      Contact: Dr. Jodie Monger President
      Tel: 410-643-1136
      Email: jmonger@metrics.net
      Website: www.metrics.net
Automated, email & website customer surveys, metrics designs, customer satisfaction & loyalty programs, data collection, analysis, reporting & consulting. (Woman, estab 1993, empl 14, sales $3,500,000, cert: WBENC)

8840 DGS Create, Inc.
      6400 Arligton Blvd
      Falls Church, VA 22042
      Contact: Christine Francis Owner
      Tel: 703-776-1919
      Email: christine@printdgs.com
      Website: www.dgscreate.com
Graphic design, digital printing, mailing & e-mailing services & online communication channels. (Woman, estab 2012, empl 21, sales $1,854,501, cert: NMSDC)

8841 Elizabeth Coffey Design
      1616 Claremont Ave
      Richmond, VA 23227
      Contact: Elizabeth Coffey Principal
      Tel: 804-266-2193
      Email: ecoffey@elizabethcoffeydesign.com
      Website: www.estrategicdesign.com
Graphic design solutions, brochures, publications, catalogs, advertisements, direct mail, websites, displays and banners, invitations, logos & identity packages. (Woman, estab 2000, empl 1, sales , cert: State)

8842 Exhibit Edge Inc.
      4315-A Walney Road
      Chantilly, VA 20151
      Contact: Bev Gray President
      Tel: 703-230-0000
      Email: bev.gray@exhibitedge.com
      Website: www.exhibitedge.com
Trade show exhibit services: design & fabricate custom exhibits, rent trade show displays & exhibits, large format graphics & banners. (Woman, estab 1992, empl 20, sales $3,450,000, cert: WBENC)

8843 Frontline Marketing LLC
      2248 Dabney Rd, Ste J
      Richmond, VA 23230
      Contact: Henry Howells President
      Tel: 804-359-2422
      Email: h.howells@frontline-exhibits.com
      Website: www.frontline-exhibits.com
Mfr, design & dist trade show & outdoor event exhibits & office environments. (Woman, estab 1992, empl 5, sales $635,000, cert: State)

8844 Johnson, Inc.
      201 W Broad St Ste 600
      Richmond, VA 23220
      Contact: Andre Dean Corp VP
      Tel: 804-644-8515
      Email: adean@johnsonmarketing.com
      Website: www.johnsonmarketing.com
Marketing & communications. (AA, estab 1993, empl 15, sales $2,750,000, cert: State)

8845 KTL Communications LLC
      5055 Seminary Rd, 1220 Unit
      Alexandria, VA 22311
      Contact: Amir Khan Owner
      Tel: 703-662-0465
      Email: amir@ktl-communications.com
      Website: www.ktl-communications.com
Language Service Provider (LSP), translation, in person interpretation, DTP, localization, language tutoring & language authentication services. (Minority, Woman, estab 2013, empl 2, sales , cert: State)

8846 LeapFrog Solutions, Inc.
      3201 Jermantown Rd Ste 350
      Fairfax, VA 22030
      Contact: Kathleen Jerabek Contracts & Pricing Mgr
      Tel: 703-273-7900
      Email: kjerabek@leapfrogit.com
      Website: www.leapfrogit.com
Strategic marketing communications: web site design, graphic design, branding/marketing campaigns, multi-media, corporate collateral materials. (Woman, estab 1996, empl 11, sales $893,494, cert: State, WBENC)

8847 Montage Marketing Group, LLC
      8000 Westpark Dr Ste 480
      McLean, VA 22102
      Contact: Mercedita Roxas-Murray CEO
      Tel: 703-215-4201
      Email: mroxasmurray@montagemarketinggroup.com
      Website: www.montagemarketinggroup.com
Full cycle integrated experiential marketing: Audience intelligence/data & market analysis, Strategy development, campaign conceptualization, creative development, experiential design. (Minority, Woman, estab 2015, empl 3, sales $1,900,000, cert: State, NMSDC, WBENC, 8(a))

8848 National Events LLC
      4003 Westfax Dr, Ste L
      Chantilly, VA 20151
      Contact: Ruth Crout CEO
      Tel: 703-961-1105
      Email: RCrout@nationaleventsllc.com
      Website: www.nationaleventsllc.com
Strategic event planning, comprehensive event management, and all-inclusive event production services for private, corporate, government, and not-for-profit organizations. (Woman, estab 2003, empl 8, sales $2,154,730, cert: WBENC)

8849 Nexus Direct, LLC
      101 W Main St Ste 400
      Norfolk, VA 23510
      Contact: Suzanne Nowers CEO
      Tel: 757-340-5960
      Email: suzanne@nexusdirect.com
      Website: www.nexusdirect.com
Direct marketing, marketing spend, strategy, creative, messaging, production, media buying, data analytics, processing, modeling & overall analysis & attribution of the direct marketing program results. (Woman, estab 2004, empl 30, sales $6,243,833, cert: WBENC)

PROFESSIONAL SERVICES: Public Relations/Marketing

8850 Omega World Travel
3102 Omega Office Park
Fairfax, VA 22031
Contact: Jackie Olt Marketing & PR Specialist
Tel: 703-359-0200
Email: jolt@owt.net
Website: www.OmegaTravel.com
Full service travel agency. Meeting Planning & Strategic Meetings Management Services. (Minority, Woman, estab 1972, empl 475, sales $1,400,000,000, cert: WBENC)

8851 ORI
171 Elden St Ste 160
Herndon, VA 20170
Contact: Kathleen Benson CEO
Tel: 571-257-3205
Email: kathyb@oriresults.com
Website: www.ORIresults.com
Strategic research planning, sample & questionnaire design, qualitative & quantitative research, data collection, technology-based online research, data coding & entry, database mgmt & integration, statistical analysis & interpretation. (Woman, estab 1988, empl 75, sales $22,971,050, cert: WBENC)

8852 Rhudy & Co. Communications and Marketing, Inc.
14342 Lander Rd
Midlothian, VA 23113
Contact: Michele Rhudy President
Tel: 804-897-0762
Email: michele@rhudy.biz
Website: www.rhudy.biz
Public relations, communications & marketing consulting: strategic communications planning, media relations, writing services. (Woman, estab 2003, empl 16, sales $2,200,000, cert: State, WBENC)

8853 The Dominion Group Marketing Research & Consulting
1800 Alexander Bell Dr Ste 515
Reston, VA 20191
Contact: Susan Wyant President
Tel: 703-234-2360
Email: swyant@thedominiongrp.com
Website: www.thedominiongrp.com
Marketing research, competitive intelligence, & consulting, qualitiative methodologies. (Woman, estab 1993, empl 7, sales $2,934,757, cert: WBENC)

8854 The InnovateHers
713 Huntsman Rd
Sandston, VA 23150
Contact: Tasha Chambers Principal
Tel: 804-263-0491
Email: info@theinnovatehers.com
Website: www.theinnovatehers.com
PR Communications Plans, News Releases, Crisis Communications, Executive Speeches, Media Monitoring, Community Engagement Events. (Woman/AA, estab 2017, empl 1, sales , cert: State)

Washington

8855 Artitudes Design Inc
700 NW Gilman Blvd Ste e103-451
Issaquah, WA 98027
Contact: Andrea Heuston CEO
Tel: 425-369-3030
Email: andrea@artitudes.com
Website: www.artitudes.com
Tailored graphic design & motion graphics, presentation design. (Woman, estab 1995, empl 4, sales $673,000, cert: WBENC)

8856 Blue Crest Creative, LLC
5108 S Myrtle St
Seattle, WA 98118
Contact: Troy Shelby Creative Dir
Tel: 800-476-0128
Email: shelbyt@bluecrestcreative.com
Website: www.bluecrestcreative.com
Corporate Identity Design, Branding, Logo, Letterhead, Business Cards, Print Design, Brochures, Invitations, Direct Mail, Newsletters, Internet Design, Architecture planning, Web Design, eNewsletters, Maintenance, SharePoint. (AA, estab 2011, empl 1, sales $105,600, cert: City, NMSDC)

8857 Dynamic Events Inc
6715 NE 63rd St
Vancouver, WA 98661
Contact: Tim Fish Dir Sales/Marketing
Tel: 503-686-1498
Email: tfish@dynamicevents.com
Website: www.dynamicevents.com
Professional event management company committed to strategic management and execution of our global client's requirements, extraordinary service and cutting edge planning.
Area (Woman, estab 1998, empl 40, sales $5,000,000, cert: WBENC)

8858 Elite Meetings & Events of Washington
2606 81st Court NW
Gig Harbor, WA 98332
Contact: Eileen Higgins President
Tel: 866-734-9990
Email: ehiggins@emeworldwide.com
Website: www.emeworldwide.com
Meetings, trade shows & incentives, event planning. (Woman, estab 1998, empl 3, sales $25,000,000, cert: WBENC)

8859 Green Cat Dzine, Inc.
5412 101st St SW
Mukilteo, WA 98275
Contact: Elisabeth Rumpelsberger President
Tel: 206-406-8329
Email: liz@greencatdzine.com
Website: www.greencatdzine.com
Graphic design: print, online (web), environmental graphics, strategic branding, promotions, online development, logo work, posters, brochures, invitations, tradeshow exhibit designs. (Woman, estab 2001, empl 1, sales $148,000, cert: State)

PROFESSIONAL SERVICES: Public Relations/Marketing

8860 PRR, Inc.
1501 4th Ave, Ste 550
Seattle, WA 98101
Contact: Rachel Novotny Business Devel
Tel: 206-623-0735
Email: bd@prrbiz.com
Website: www.prrbiz.com
Public relations, marketing, market research, social & digital media, graphic design, facilitation, public involvement & advertising services. (Minority, Woman, estab 1981, empl 86, sales , cert: State)

8861 SHWorldwide
100 W Harrison St
Seattle, WA 98119
Contact: Rey Rodriguez
Tel: 206-923-8564
Email: ReyR@SHWorldwide.com
Website: www.SHWorldwide.com
Event services, destination management & virtual production. (Woman, estab 1978, empl 25, sales , cert: WBENC)

Wisconsin

8862 Madison Avenue Worldwide LLC
113 N Iowa St
Dodgeville, WI 53533
Contact: Sara Rahn
Tel: 608-354-6879
Email: accounting@madisonavenueworldwide.com
Website: www.madeveww.com
Graphic Design, Production Art, Powerpoint Presentations, Adaptational Design, Print Collateral Design, Custom Logo Items, Trade Show Graphics, Digital Display Ads, Fulfillment, Warehouse, Shipping. (Woman, estab 2008, empl 21, sales , cert: WBENC)

8863 Market Probe, Inc.
2655 N Mayfair Rd
Milwaukee, WI 53226
Contact: Bonnie Lockwood Sr VP
Tel: 414-778-6000
Email: info@marketprobe.com
Website: www.marketprobe.com
Market research & cstmr satisfaction research svcs. (As-Ind, estab 1976, empl 125, sales $40,000,000, cert: State, NMSDC)

8864 Mazur/Zachow, Inc.
1025 S Moorland Rd Ste 300
Brookfield, WI 53005
Contact: Michele Conway President
Tel: 262-938-9244
Email: michelec@mazurzachow.com
Website: www.mazurzachow.com
Data collection services, marketing research studies, focus groups, IDI's, ethnographic studies, in-home product placements & music tests. (Woman, estab 1983, empl 16, sales , cert: WBENC)

8865 Meetings & Incentives Worldwide, Inc.
10520 7 Mile Road
Caledonia, WI 53108
Contact: Dan Tarpey VP Sales & Marketing
Tel: 773-851-0908
Email: dtarpey@meetings-incentives.com
Website: www.meetings-incentives.com
Global strategic meeting & event management, strategic meeting management implementation, global strategic sourcing & contracting, attendee management. (Woman, estab 1967, empl 350, sales $90,000,000, cert: WBENC)

8866 Revelation, LLC
222 N Midvale Blvd Ste 18
Madison, WI 53705
Contact: Brian Lee President
Tel: 608-622-7767
Email: brian@experiencerevelation.com
Website: www.experiencerevelation.com
Public relations, media buying, ad buying, advertising, social media consulting, internet marketing, web marketing & speaking engagements. (As-Pac, estab 2010, empl 3, sales $170,000, cert: NMSDC)

8867 Rivera & Associates, Inc.
1543 S 14th St
Milwaukee, WI 53204
Contact: Michael Rivera CEO
Tel: 414-736-1255
Email: michael.rivera@riveraprfirm.com
Website: www.riveraprfirm.com
Public Relations, Marketing, Strategic Communication, Multicultural Marketing, Public Information & Outreach, Media Relations, Language Translations, Management Consulting, Brand Awareness, Environmental Marketing. (Hisp, estab , empl , sales , cert: State)

8868 The Dieringer Research Group, Inc.
200 Bishops Way
Brookfield, WI 53005
Contact: Shelley Ahrens Chief Customer Officer
Tel: 262-432-5231
Email: shelley.ahrens@thedrg.com
Website: www.thedrg.com
Customer Experience, Brand Awareness, Product Development, and Market Opportunity. (Woman, estab 1974, empl 74, sales $6,720,000, cert: WBENC)

West Virginia

8869 CRA Communications LLC
601 Morris St Ste 301
Charleston, WV 25301
Contact: Susan Lavenski CEO
Tel: 304-342-0161
Email: slavenski@charlesryan.com
Website: www.charlesryan.com
Account Management, Planning, Advertising, Branding, Communications, Crisis Communications, Graphic Design, Media Buying, Media Relations, Media Training, Message Development, Public Relations, Social Media, Strategy. (Woman, estab 2015, empl 25, sales $6,402,960, cert: WBENC)

PROFESSIONAL SERVICES: Staffing Services

Firms provide temporary and permanent personnel placement, contract and direct hire, personnel consulting, training and employment services. NAICS Code 54

Alabama

8870 Providence Staffing LLC
15 Windsweep Ct, Ste 114
Phenix City, AL 36870
Contact: Albert Williams President
Tel: 706-358-8926
Email: albertwilliams@get2worknow.com
Website: www.get2worknow.com
Broad-based staffing and recruiting solutions, temporary, temp-to-hire, and permanent employees. (AA, estab 2018, empl 4, sales , cert: State)

8871 RecruitSource, Inc.
3532 Seventh Ct S
Birmingham, AL 35222
Contact: Jane Smith CEO
Tel: 205-322-6822
Email: jsmith@recruitsource.org
Website: www.rsi-services.com
Contract management services: staff augmentation, advertising & marketing. (Woman, estab 2001, empl 4, sales , cert: WBENC)

8872 SK Services, LLC
45281 US Hwy 78
Lincoln, AL 35096
Contact: Sonya Jacks President
Tel: 205-763-1818
Email: job4u@skstaffing.com
Website: www.skstaffing.com
Staffing, temp to hire & contingent staffing. (Woman, estab 2010, empl 9, sales , cert: WBENC)

8873 Tech Providers, Inc.
2117 Magnolia Ave S
Birmingham, AL 35205
Contact: Eleanor Estes CEO
Tel: 205-930-9664
Email: eleanorestes@techproviders.com
Website: www.techproviders.com
Permanent IT staffing needs, IT software developers, IT systems or database administrators, financial staffing & engineering staffing. (Woman, estab 1998, empl 135, sales $10,701,387, cert: WBENC)

Arkansas

8874 Temporaries Plus, Inc.
601 E Eighth Ave
Pine Bluff, AR 71601
Contact: Kayla Cheatwood Sales
Tel: 870-535-5507
Email: kcheatwood@ateamtemp.com
Website: www.ateamtemp.com
Temporary staffing services. (Woman/AA, estab 1995, empl 7, sales $5,300,000, cert: WBENC)

Arizona

8875 All About People
4422 E Indian School Rd
Phoenix, AZ 85018
Contact: Kendra Rightsell Business Devel Mgr
Tel: 602-453-4253
Email: krightsell@allaboutpeople.net
Website: www.allaboutpeople.net
Temporary & executive level staffing. (AA, estab 2002, empl 20, sales $12,235,511, cert: NMSDC)

8876 All About People, Inc.
4422 East Indian School Road
Phoenix, AZ 85018
Contact: Charles Mitchell CEO
Tel: 602-955-1212
Email: charles@allaboutpeople.net
Website: www.allaboutpeople.net/
Temporary & executive level staffing. (AA, estab 2002, empl 87, sales , cert: NMSDC)

8877 Axis Employment Services
7000 N 16th St, Ste 120-501
Phoenix, AZ 85020
Contact: Tran Tran CEO
Tel: 602-301-8115
Email: tran@axisemployment.com
Website: www.axisemployment.com
Temp-to-hire & direct hire searches, drug testing, Criminal/County searches, software testing, education & employment verification. (Minority, Woman, estab 2002, empl 6, sales $2,130,000, cert: State, City)

8878 AZ Construction Resources, Inc., dba AZCR Staffing
2601 W Dunlap Ave Ste #4
Phoenix, AZ 85021
Contact: Kim Jones Dir of Sourcing
Tel: 602-870-3515
Email: kjones@azcrstaffing.com
Website: www.azcrstaffing.com
Temporary and Temp to Perm Employees to the Industrial, Oil & Construction Industries (Minority, Woman, estab 2006, empl 100, sales $11,093,000, cert: NMSDC, WBENC)

8879 Bridgeport Resources, LLC
930 W Watson Dr
Tempe, AZ 85283
Contact: Diana Lemos-Marquez
Tel: 480-456-6031
Email: diana@bridgeportresources.com
Website: www.bridgeportresources.com
Direct placement staffing service, Finance, Accounting, Administration, Customer Service, Education, Engineering, IT, Healthcare, Management, Manufacturing, Sales/Marketing, Human Resources. (Minority, Woman, estab 2013, empl 2, sales , cert: NMSDC)

8880 Creative Human Resources Concepts LLC
4710 E Falcon Dr, Ste 125
Mesa, AZ 85215
Contact: Rosa Roy President
Tel: 480-654-4606
Email: rosa@chrc4work.com
Website: www.chrc4work.com
Staffing: contract, full-time, part-time, temporary, long & short-term. (Minority, Woman, estab 1997, empl 205, sales $1,723,389, cert: NMSDC, CPUC, WBENC)

8881 DuffyGroup, Inc.
      4727 E Union Hills Dr, Ste 200
      Phoenix, AZ 85050
      Contact: Kathleen Duffy Ybarra President
      Tel: 602-942-7112
      Email: kduffy@duffygroupinc.com
      Website: www.duffygroupinc.com
Executive search, sourcing, HR contracting & direct hire, short-term, extended assignments. (Woman, estab 1991, empl 25, sales $2,600,000, cert: WBENC)

8882 Egnite LLC
      4747 E Elliot Rd Bldg 29, Ste 600
      Phoenix, AZ 85044
      Contact: Alex Luevano VP
      Tel: 602-931-5000
      Email: alex.luevano@egniteinc.com
      Website: www.egniteinc.com
Direct placement, contract, contract to hire & project solutions. (Minority, Woman, estab 2007, empl 5, sales $325,000, cert: State)

8883 Elsner Human Resources
      7409 E Chaparral Rd Ste A110
      Scottsdale, AZ 85250
      Contact: Krisanne Elsner CEO
      Tel: 480-657-8638
      Email: ke@southwestrecruiting.com
      Website: www.elsnerhr.com
Recruiting, talent acquisition, executive search. (Woman, estab 2003, empl 1, sales $115,000, cert: WBENC)

8884 JBN & Associates, LLC.
      4040 E Camelback Rd Ste 280
      Phoenix, AZ 85018
      Contact: Dainiz Alvarez Exec Search Mgr
      Tel: 480-344-2822
      Email: info@jbnassociates.com
      Website: www.jbnassociates.com
Recruiting firm, direct/perm placements, executive search & C-level positions. (Woman, estab 1999, empl 12, sales , cert: WBENC)

8885 Safe T Professionals LLC
      241 S Washington St
      Chandler, AZ 85249
      Contact: Anna Martinez CEO
      Tel: 800-502-9481
      Email: info@safetpros.com
      Website: www.safetpros.com
Safety staff augmentation and consulting services. (Woman/Hisp, estab 2011, empl 57, sales $8,700,000, cert: NMSDC)

8886 Scott Business Group, LLC
      668 N 44th St Ste 300
      Phoenix, AZ 85008
      Contact: Milagros Gonzalez-Scott
      Tel: 480-694-2619
      Email: millie@scottbiz.net
      Website: www.scottbiz.net
Contract & temporary staffing. (AA, estab 2003, empl 105, sales $3,451,356, cert: State, City, NMSDC)

8887 Source Group Professionals
      4729 E Sunrise Dr Ste 244
      Tucson, AZ 85718
      Contact: GM
      Tel: 520-870-5114
      Email: info@sourcegrouppros.com
      Website: www.sourcegrouppros.com
Staffing services. (Woman, estab 2003, empl 35, sales $1,273,000, cert: WBENC)

California

8888 24-Hour Medical Staffing Services, LLC
      21700 East Copley Dr Ste 270
      Diamond Bar, CA 09765
      Contact: Linda Stone VP Sales & Client Delivery
      Tel: 909-895-8960
      Email: linda@24-hrmed.com
      Website: www.24-hrmed.com
Temporary healthcare staffing services to clients on permanent, per diem, travel, and local contract assignment. (Minority, Woman, estab 2000, empl 150, sales $8,678,030, cert: NMSDC)

8889 3 Bridge Networks LLC
      601 Montgomery St Ste 715
      San Francisco, CA 94111
      Contact: Caleb Hill Managing Partner
      Tel: 415-692-6944
      Email: caleb.hill@3bridgenetworks.com
      Website: www.3bridgenetworks.com
Recruiting services, direct hire & temporary consults ranging from staff to VP levels within Accounting & Finance. (As-Pac, estab 2011, empl 7, sales , cert: NMSDC, CPUC)

8890 A.P.R., Inc. (Alpha Professional Resources)
      100 E Thousand Oaks Blvd Ste 240
      Thousand Oaks, CA 91360
      Contact: Rick C. Ramirez VP Operations
      Tel: 805-371-5644
      Email: rick@alphaprotemps.com
      Website: www.alphaprotemps.com
Technical IT personnel on contract or contract to hire or permanent. (AA, Hisp, estab 1993, empl 155, sales $15,605,246, cert: NMSDC, CPUC)

8891 Absolute Employment Solutions, Inc.
      PO Box 2446
      Culver City, CA 90231
      Contact: Penelope Sherman- Hunt President
      Tel: 323-931-6262
      Email: phunt@absoluteemploymentsolutions.com
      Website:www.absoluteemploymentsolutions.com
Staffing services: direct-hire, temporary-to-hire & temporary. (Woman/AA, estab 2001, empl 3, sales $350,000, cert: State, CPUC, SDB)

8892 Accelon Inc.
      2410 Camino Ramon, Ste 194
      San Mateo, CA 94583
      Contact: Kelda Williams Acct Mgr
      Tel: 925-216-5735
      Email: kelda@acceloninc.com
      Website: www.AccelonInc.com
Staffing, managed services, project management and application development. (As-Pac, estab 2014, empl 65, sales $52,300,000, cert: NMSDC, CPUC)

8893 Agile1
      1999 W 190th St
      Torrance, CA 90504
      Contact: Bobbi Babcock Regional Vice President
      Tel: 480-209-0374
      Email: bbabcock@agile1.com
      Website: www.agile-1.com
Workforce management, human capital management, talent acquisition and contingent staffing services, payrolling, and 1099 independent contractor compliance. (Woman/AA, estab 1978, empl , sales $971,113,334, cert: NMSDC, CPUC, WBENC)

PROFESSIONAL SERVICES: Staffing Services

8894 AgileTalent, Inc.
1900 S Norfolk Ave.
San Mateo, CA 94403
Contact: Jay Singh
Tel: 650-931-2572
Email: jay.singh@agiletalentinc.com
Website: www.agiletalentinc.com
IT contract staffing & recruiting. (As-Ind, estab 2011, empl 48, sales $4,600,000, cert: NMSDC, CPUC)

8895 Allstem Connections, Inc.
327 W Broadway
Glendale, CA 91204
Contact: Penni Rich VP
Tel: - -
Email: prich@ain1.com
Website: www.allstemconnections.com
Specialty recruiting & staffing, temp, temp-to-permanent & direct hire in STEM (Science, Technology, Engineering and Mathematics) positions. (Woman/AA, estab 2018, empl 2800, sales $965,741,349, cert: NMSDC, WBENC)

8896 AppleOne Employment Services
327 W Broadway
Glendale, CA 91204
Contact: Lea Murga Sr Dir Business Devel
Tel: 714-404-6068
Email: lmurga@ain1.com
Website: www.appleone.com
Contingent Workforce Services and Technologies: Managed Service Program
Recruitment, Process Outsourcing,
Workforce Consulting Technology:
Vendor Management System Applicant. (Woman/AA, estab 1963, empl 1535, sales $1,038,404,566, cert: NMSDC, WBENC)

8897 APR Consulting, Inc.
1370 Valley Vista Dr Ste 280
Diamond Bar, CA 91765
Contact: Daniel Benninghoff VP
Tel: 909-396-5375
Email: dbenninghoff@aprconsulting.com
Website: www.aprconsulting.com
Supporting Managed Staffing (MSP)/Vendor Management, System (VMS) Programs, Direct Hire Search, Contract Labor. (Minority, Woman, estab 1980, empl 1382, sales $75,000,000, cert: NMSDC, CPUC, WBENC)

8898 ATR International, Inc.
1230 Oakmead Pkwy Ste 110
Sunnyvale, CA 94085
Contact: Angelique Alvarez Chief Diversity Relations Officer
Tel: 408-328-8085
Email: angeliques@atr1.com
Website: www.atrinternational.com
Temporary employment svcs. (Minority, Woman, estab 1988, empl 100, sales $96,000,000, cert: NMSDC)

8899 Bench International Search Inc.
120 S Doheny Dr
Beverly Hills, CA 90211
Contact: Mary Kelley CFO
Tel: 310-854-9900
Email: mkelley@benchinternational.com
Website: www.benchinternational.com
Executive search services. (Woman, estab 1974, empl 23, sales $8,865,478, cert: WBENC)

8900 Berkhemer Clayton
241 S Figueroa St Ste 300
Los Angeles, CA 90012
Contact: Exec Admin
Tel: 213-621-2300
Email: Info@berkhemerclayton.com
Website: www.berkhemerclayton.com
Executive search firm. (Woman, estab 1994, empl 8, sales , cert: CPUC, WBENC)

8901 Bratton & Co., Inc. DBA Hyperdrive Agile
1547 Palos Verdes Mall, Ste 198
Walnut Creek, CA 94597
Contact: Mary Louie Owner
Tel: 925-330-6970
Email: mary@brattoninc.com
Website: www.hyperdriveagile.com
Temporary staffing: administration, project management, technology, marketing & public relations. (Minority, Woman, estab 2009, empl 2, sales $3,000,000, cert: WBENC)

8902 Canon Recruiting Group LLC
26531 Summit Circle
Santa Clarita, CA 91351
Contact: Recruiting Mgr
Tel: 661-252-7400
Email: Careers@canonrecruiting.com
Website: www.canonrecruiting.com
Identification, evaluation & recruit Executives, Professionals, IT Technical, Accounting, Environmental & Industrial staffing. (Woman, estab 1980, empl 300, sales $15,000,000, cert: WBENC)

8903 Coneybeare Inc.
2003 N Broadway
Santa Ana, CA 92706
Contact: Victoria Betancourt President
Tel: 714-547-8546
Email: vicky@coneybeare.com
Website: www.coneybeare.com
Staffing services: technical, skilled industrial, administrative, clerical & professional. (Woman, estab 1986, empl 5, sales , cert: WBENC)

8904 Crowdstaffing, a Zenith Talent Company
6030 Hellyer Ave Ste 100
San Jose, CA 95138
Contact: Bret Bass Dir Content Strategy
Tel: 844-467-2300
Email: bret@crowdstaffing.com
Website: www.crowdstaffing.com
Staffing & recruiting: software and OS, hardware, QA & automation, IT, mobile applications & platforms & professional. (As-Ind, estab 2000, empl 25, sales $14,000,000, cert: NMSDC)

8905 Dawson & Dawson Staffing Inc.
26522 La Alameda Ste 110
Mission Viejo, CA 92691
Contact: Kathy Dawson President
Tel: 949-421-3966
Email: kathy.dawson@dawsondawsoninc.com
Website: www.dawsondawsoninc.com
National search & staffing employment services. (Woman, estab 2008, empl 14, sales $3,544,239, cert: WBENC)

PROFESSIONAL SERVICES: Staffing Services

8906 Delta Computer Consulting, Inc.
25550 Hawthorne Blvd Ste 106-108
Torrance, CA 90505
Contact: Alisa Spiegel VP Sales
Tel: 310-541-9440
Email: A.Spiegel@deltacci.com
Website: www.deltacci.com
Human Capital Recruiting & Deployment, IT Staff Recruiting & Augmentation. (Woman, estab 1987, empl 165, sales $28,000,000, cert: WBENC, NWBOC)

8907 Domar Companies, LLC
14742 Beach Blvd, Ste 256
La MIrada, CA 90638
Contact: Don Martinez CEO
Tel: 714-674-0391
Email: martinezd@domarcompanies.com
Website: www.domarcompanies.com
Executive search recruiting Hispanic & Multicultural Diversity Executives & Professionals. (Minority, Woman, estab 2011, empl 8, sales $27,500,000, cert: CPUC)

8908 Enterprise Resource Services, Inc.
400 Continental Blvd Ste 6170
El Segundo, CA 90245
Contact: Ladie Ella Daya Natl Acct Mgr
Tel: 424-888-3771
Email: ella@ersstaffing.com
Website: www.ersstaffing.com
Staffing, payroll & IT consulting services: temp, temp-to-hire & direct hire. (As-Pac, estab 2001, empl 25, sales $3,851,150, cert: CPUC)

8909 Full Umbrella Talent LLC
1877 Seigneur Ave
Los Angeles, CA 90032
Contact: Alex Smith Co-Founder
Tel: 757-237-2089
Email: alex@full-umbrella.com
Website: www.full-umbrella.com
Permanent & temp placement recruiting svcs. (Woman, estab 2021, empl 2, sales $913,521, cert: WBENC)

8910 Genesis Professional Staffing, Inc.
2600 West Olive Ave 5th Fl
Burbank, CA 91505
Contact: Marcus T. Moore CEO
Tel: 818-333-5153
Email: marcus.moore@gpstaffing.com
Website: www.gpstaffing.com
Staffing: permanent hires, temp-to-hire, temporary placement, payrolling & consulting. (AA, estab 2003, empl 25, sales , cert: NMSDC)

8911 Government Staffing Associates
101 Howard St, Ste 490
San Francisco, CA 94105
Contact: Steven Strawser Owner
Tel: 415-692-6905
Email: sf@govstaff.org
Website: www.govstaff.org
Temporary, contract & permanent staffing solutions. (As-Pac, estab 2009, empl 11, sales $833,429, cert: City, NMSDC, CPUC)

8912 Grove Technical Resources
9035 Rosewood Ave
West Hollywood, CA 90048
Contact: Debra Polister President
Tel: 786-390-7119
Email: dpolister@grovetr.comb
Website: www.grovetr.com
Technical staffing & consulting services. (Woman, estab 2005, empl 2, sales , cert: CPUC, WBENC)

8913 Hart Employment Services
220 S Kenwood St Ste 320
Glendale, CA 91205
Contact: Rhonda Minarcin President
Tel: 626-405-0778
Email: gsa@hartjobs.com
Website: www.hartjobs.com
Staffing services. (Woman, estab 1988, empl 6, sales $1,833,485, cert: WBENC)

8914 Harvest Technical Services
1839 Ygnacio Valley Rd, Ste 390
Walnut Creek, CA 94598
Contact: Renee Bush Sales
Tel: 925-937-4874
Email: renee@harvtech.com
Website: www.harvtech.com
Temporary technical staffing personnel. (Woman, estab 1997, empl 85, sales $12,018,213, cert: WBENC)

8915 HBL Search
118 Prospect Ave Ste 4
Long Beach, CA 90803
Contact: Halvern Logan President
Tel: 562-754-6925
Email: halvern@hblsearch.com
Website: www.hblsearch.com
Staffing: accountants, finance, banking, IT, engineering, sales & HR. (AA, estab 2013, empl 1, sales , cert: NMSDC)

8916 Human Potential Consultants, LLC
454 E Carson Plaza Dr, Ste 102
Carson, CA 90746
Contact: Garnett Newcombe CEO
Tel: 310-756-1560
Email: drnewcombe@aol.com
Website: www.hpcemployment.org
Staffing services: administrative, janitorial, warehouse & production service workers. (Woman/AA, estab 1997, empl 7, sales $580,000, cert: City, NMSDC, WBENC)

8917 Inconen Corporation
6133 Bristol Pkwy Ste 232
Culver City, CA 90230
Contact: Gordon Ross CEO
Tel: 310-410-1931
Email: register@inconen.com
Website: www.inconen.com
Temporary employees & pay-rolled employees. (As-Ind, estab 1978, empl 120, sales $13,351,317, cert: NMSDC, CPUC)

8918 Inconen Temporary Services, Inc.
6133 Bristol Pkwy Ste 225
Culver City, CA 90230
Contact: Gordon Ross CEO
Tel: 310-216-6715
Email: gordon@e-its.com
Website: www.e-its.com
Staffing svcs: temporary, payroll svcs, engineers & IT professionals. (As-Ind, estab 1996, empl 25, sales $1,592,435, cert: NMSDC, CPUC)

8919 Integrated Talent Solutions, Inc. dba Vivo
    7901 Stoneridge Dr Ste 440
    Pleasanton, CA 94588
    Contact: Marilyn Weinstein CEO
    Tel: 925-271-6800
    Email: info@vivoinc.com
    Website: www.vivoinc.com
Staffing services: contract, contract-to-hire & full-time/direct positions. (Woman, estab 2006, empl 15, sales $5,100,000, cert: WBENC)

8920 Integritas Resources, Inc.
    12304 Santa Monica Blvd. Ste 300
    Los Angeles, CA 90025
    Contact: Lindy Huang Werges CEO
    Tel: 310-584-7295
    Email: lhwerges@integritasresources.com
    Website: www.integritasresources.com
Executive search, recruitment & staffing, direct hire, contract, contract-to-hire, temporary, or project basis. (Minority, Woman, estab 2014, empl 3, sales $646,557, cert: City, NMSDC, CPUC, WBENC)

8921 Invero Group
    8560 Vineyard Ave Ste 504
    Rancho Cucamonga, CA 91730
    Contact: Daniel Phillips President
    Tel: 909-373-8120
    Email: daniel@inverogroup.com
    Website: www.inverogroup.com
Staffing & recruiting: temporary, direct hire & contingent staffing solutions. (Woman, estab 2001, empl 75, sales $1,988,644, cert: WBENC)

8922 Josephine's Professional Staffing, Inc.
    2158 Ringwood Ave
    San Jose, CA 95131
    Contact: Josephine Hughes CEO
    Tel: 408-943-0111
    Email: josephine@jps-inc.com
    Website: www.jps-inc.com
Staffing svcs: temp, contract, yemporary-to-hire, full-time placement, payroll svcs, vendor-on-site. (Minority, Woman, estab 1988, empl 10, sales $3,248,000, cert: State, NMSDC, WBENC)

8923 Kavaliro
    5401 Old Redwood Hwy Ste 104
    Petaluma, CA 94954
    Contact: Timothy M. Harrington Managing Dir
    Tel: 704-525-3457
    Email: tharrington@kavaliro.com
    Website: www.kavaliro.com
Staffing services: Information Technology (IT); Engineering; Finance & Accounting; Administrative & Professional; & Project Solutions & Delivery. (Minority, Woman, estab 2003, empl 200, sales $41,700,000, cert: NMSDC, CPUC)

8924 Lighthouse Management Group Inc.
    1650 The Alameda
    San Jose, CA 95126
    Contact: Nirav Shah Managing Dir
    Tel: 408-579-6200
    Email: nirav.shah@lighthousemg.com
    Website: www.lighthousemg.com
Staffing, temporary & temp-to-hire, senior-level consulting & management professionals. (As-Ind, estab 2006, empl 20, sales $8,500,000, cert: NMSDC)

8925 Loan Administration Network Inc.
    18952 MacArthur Blvd Ste 315
    Irvine, CA 92612
    Contact: Charlene Nichols President
    Tel: 949-752-5246
    Email: charlene_nichols@lani.com
    Website: www.lani.com
Temporary, Temp-to-Hire, Direct Hire staffing services: Accounting, Finance, Healthcare, Banking, Credit Unions, Title, Escrow, Mortgage industries. Clerical, mid-level, Management, Executive positions. (Woman, estab 1992, empl 12, sales $5,600,000, cert: CPUC)

8926 Login Consulting Services
    300 Continental Blvd Ste 405
    El Segundo, CA 90245
    Contact: Carolyn Hernandez Regional Dir
    Tel: 310-607-9091
    Email: carolyn.hernandez@loginconsult.com
    Website: www.loginconsult.com
Provide supplemental staff to the information systems community. (Woman, estab 1994, empl 60, sales $2,500,000, cert: WBENC)

8927 Marquee Workforce Solutions, Inc.
    338 Via Vera Cruz, Ste 140
    San Marcos, CA 92078
    Contact: Emily Salanio CEO
    Tel: 949-271-0502
    Email: workforcesolutions@marqueewfs.com
    Website: www.marqueewfs.com
Workforce solutions. (Minority, Woman, estab 2013, empl 43, sales $12,000,000, cert: NMSDC)

8928 MIDCOM
    1275 N Manassero St
    Anaheim, CA 92807
    Contact: Anastacia Warunek VP
    Tel: 714-507-3723
    Email: stacy@midcom.com
    Website: www.midcom.com
Recruit & place technical & professional personnel. (Woman, estab 1979, empl 635, sales $120,000,000, cert: CPUC, WBENC)

8929 Mynela Staffing LLC
    17777 Center Court Dr N Ste 600
    Cerritos, CA 90703
    Contact: CEO
    Tel: 562-246-5317
    Email:
    Website: www.mynela.com
Healthcare staffing services, per diem, temp & direct hire services of physicians, nurses, clinical, allied & administrative staff. (Minority, estab 2015, empl 75, sales $2,000,000, cert: NMSDC)

8930 netPolarity, Inc.
    900 E Campbell Ave
    Campbell, CA 95008
    Contact: Jeremy Schiff Sr Acct Mgr
    Tel: 408-200-3230
    Email: jeremys@netpolarity.com
    Website: www.netpolarity.com
Temporary staffing, staff augmentation, contingent workforce staffing for information technology, project management, application development, professional services, marketing, finance and accounting. (Minority, Woman, estab 2000, empl 500, sales $55,000,000, cert: NMSDC, CPUC)

PROFESSIONAL SERVICES: Staffing Services

8931 NetSource, Inc.
PO Box 590665
San Francisco, CA 94159
Contact: VP Sales
Tel: 415-831-3681
Email: resumes@netsourceweb.com
Website: www.netsourceweb.com
Placement, contracting & consulting services. (Woman, estab 1997, empl 50, sales $800,000, cert: State, CPUC, WBENC)

8932 Occasions Staffing Solutions, LLC
2191 S El Camino Real, Ste 206
Oceanside, CA 92821
Contact: Derek Rippy President
Tel: 760-439-7500
Email: derek@occasionsstaffing.com
Website: www.occasionsstaffing.com
Temporary staffing requirements for Warehouse, Customer Service, Data Entry, Convention Services. (AA, estab 2017, empl 12, sales , cert: NMSDC)

8933 Partners In Diversity, Inc.
690 E Green St Ste 101
Pasadena, CA 91101
Contact: Arlene Apodaca President
Tel: 626-793-0020
Email: arlene.apodaca@p-i-d.biz
Website: www.partnersindiversity.com
Staffing support: clerical & non-clerical. (Minority, Woman, estab 2002, empl 10, sales $14,130,878, cert: State, CPUC, WBENC)

8934 Patricia J. Mayer & Associates, LLC
2395 Lake Meadow Cir
Martinez, CA 94553
Contact: Patricia Mayer CEO
Tel: 925-689-1440
Email: pattmayer@earthlink.net
Website: www.pjmstaffing.com
Staffing services: temporary & permanent employees. (Woman, estab 2003, empl 1, sales $1,000,000, cert: WBENC)

8935 Peoples Choice Staffing, Inc.
1269 W Pomona Rd, Ste 107
Corona, CA 92882
Contact: Denise Peoples CEO
Tel: 951-735-0550
Email: dapeoples@peopleschoicestaffing.com
Website: www.peopleschoicestaffing.com
Staffing: temporary, temporary-Hire or full-time placement services. (Woman/AA, estab 2003, empl 200, sales $19,037,280, cert: NMSDC, CPUC)

8936 PFITECH
17011 Beach Blvd, Ste 9
Huntington Beach, CA 92647
Contact: Sean Scully Reg Sales Mgr
Tel: 310-824-1800
Email: sean.scully@PFITECH.COM
Website: www.PFITECH.com
Staffing and desktop solutions. (Hisp, estab 2001, empl 200, sales $16,318,677, cert: NMSDC, CPUC)

8937 Pivotal Search Partners
2531 Greenwich St
San Francisco, CA 94123
Contact: President
Tel: 415-323-6339
Email:
Website: www.pivotalsearchpartners.com
Staffing Solutions: IT, Engineering & Accounting & Finance, Direct Hire, Contract & Contract to Hire & VSP / MSP Contingent Workforce staffing solutions. (As-Ind, estab 2012, empl 6, sales $538,000, cert: NMSDC, CPUC)

8938 PM Business Holdings LLC
733 Hindry Ave, Ste C205
Inglewood, CA 90301
Contact: Derrick Ferguson CEO
Tel: 310-242-3171
Email: pmbh14@gmail.com
Website: www.brilliantmindssolutions.com
Computer Systems Design Services, employment placement & executive search services (AA, estab 2012, empl 1, sales , cert: NMSDC)

8939 POGO Inc.
6265 Greenwich Dr Ste 103
San Diego, CA 92122
Contact: Reg Dir
Tel: 858-587-4970
Email:
Website: www.getpogo.com
Temporary staffing services. (Woman, estab 2011, empl 7, sales $2,500,000, cert: CPUC, WBENC)

8940 Premier Staffing, Inc
3595 Mt Diablo Blvd Ste 340
Lafayette, CA 94549
Contact: Andrew Melgar Acct Mgr
Tel: 415-362-2211
Email: andrewm@premiertalentpartners.com
Website: www.premiertalentpartners.com/
Direct-hire & temporary/contract staffing. (Woman, estab , empl , sales $6,778,631, cert: WBENC)

8941 Proven Solutions Inc
9444 Waples St Ste 440
San Diego, CA 92121
Contact: Louis Song Sr Partner
Tel: 858-412-1122
Email: lsong@provenrecruiting.com
Website: www.provenrecruiting.com
Consulting, staffing & solutions. (As-Pac, estab 2007, empl 49, sales $16,800,000, cert: NMSDC, CPUC)

8942 PTS Advance Life Sciences
2860 Michelle Dr, Ste 150
Irvine, CA 92606
Contact: Jayne Gill Managing Dir
Tel: 949-268-4021
Email: jayne.gill@ptsadvance.com
Website: www.ptsadvance.com
Engineering & professional staffing: petrochemical, power, transportation & infrastructure. (Woman, estab 1995, empl 200, sales $28,000,000, cert: WBENC)

PROFESSIONAL SERVICES: Staffing Services

8943 Quality Driver Solutions, Inc.
      320 S Milliken Ave, Ste A
      Ontario, CA 91761
      Contact: Angelica Dazhan Reg Mgr
      Tel: 510-453-4655
      Email: angelica@qualitydriversolutions.com
      Website: www.qualitydriversolutions.com
Full service staffing: temps, temp to hire, long term dedicated & direct hire placements. (Hisp, estab 2004, empl 23, sales , cert: NMSDC)

8944 RennickBarrett Recruiting, Inc.
      82-408 Brewster Dr
      Indio, CA 92203
      Contact: Vinette Morris President
      Tel: 760-863-0076
      Email: vinette@rennickbarrett.com
      Website: www.rennickbarrett.com
Direct & temporary/contract labor, high level, hard to fill positions at the senior and executive management levels. (Woman/AA, estab 2008, empl 4, sales $1,246,000, cert: City)

8945 SearchPros
      6363 Auburn Blvd
      Citrus Heights, CA 95621
      Contact: Myla Ramos CEO
      Tel: 916-721-6000
      Email: myla@spstaffing.com
      Website: www.spstaffing.com
Human capital staffing & solutions: temporary staffing, contract to hire, long-term contract, project staffing, direct hire, payrolling services, retained searches, outplacement services. (Woman/AA, As- Pac, estab 2005, empl 100, sales $20,000,000, cert: NMSDC)

8946 SuperbTech, Inc.
      5800 Hannm Ave Ste 150
      Culver City, CA 90230
      Contact: Jan Davis President
      Tel: 310-645-1199
      Email: jdavis@superbtechinc.com
      Website: www.superbtechinc.com
Staffing:contract, temporary & permanent placement. (Woman/AA, estab 1998, empl 7, sales , cert: CPUC, WBENC)

8947 TEKtalent Inc.
      26250 Industrial Blvd, Ste 110
      Hayward, CA 94545
      Contact: Kishore Pallapothu CEO
      Tel: 510-256-7311
      Email: joeparker@tektalentinc.com
      Website: www.tektalentinc.com
End-to-end recruitment and service solutions. (Woman/As-Ind, estab 2015, empl 25, sales , cert: NMSDC, WBENC)

8948 The ACT 1 Group, Inc.
      1999 W 190th St
      Torrance, CA 90504
      Contact: Gary Randazzo Dir of Natl Communications
      Tel: 800-383-1965
      Email: hrcg-rfxmanager@act-1.com
      Website: www.act1group.com
Staffing, payrolling & workforce mgmt svcs: financial, energy, healthcare & high technology industries. (Woman/AA, estab 1978, empl 1535, sales $476,000,000, cert: NMSDC, CPUC)

8949 The Mice Groups, Inc.
      1730 S Amphlett Blvd Ste 100
      San Mateo, CA 94402
      Contact: Sofia Gomez VP Recruiting & Strategy
      Tel: 650-655-7655
      Email: sofia@micegroups.com
      Website: www.micegroups.com
IT contract, contract-to-hire & full-time employment positions. (Hisp, estab 2000, empl 100, sales $100,000,000, cert: NMSDC, CPUC)

8950 TheraEx Rehab Services, Inc.
      1191 Central Blvd Ste E
      Brentwood, CA 94513
      Contact: Rey Rivera President
      Tel: 707-342-5200
      Email: info@theraexstaffing.com
      Website: www.theraexstaffing.com
Healthcare staffing: Registered Nurses (RN), Licensed Vocational Nurses (LVN), Certified Nurse Assistants (CNA), Physical therapist (PT), Occupational Therapist (OT). (As-Pac, estab 2009, empl 64, sales $3,545,324, cert: NMSDC)

8951 Tiffany Stuart Solutions, Inc.
      390 Diablo Rd. Ste 220
      Danville, CA 94526
      Contact: President
      Tel: 925-855-3600
      Email: AR@Go2Dynamic.com
      Website: www.go2dynamic.com
Temporary contractors, temp to hire & direct hire. (Woman, estab 1997, empl 100, sales $5,200,000, cert: CPUC, WBENC)

8952 Two Roads Professional Resources, Inc.
      5122 Bolsa Ave, Ste 112
      Huntington Beach, CA 92649
      Contact: Tammy Gottschalk President
      Tel: 714-901-3804
      Email: tgotts@2roads.com
      Website: www.2roads.com
Provide temporary staffing in the technical, engineering, and information technology services. (Woman, estab 1996, empl 125, sales $12,168,000, cert: CPUC)

8953 Vertisystem Inc.
      39300 Civic Center Dr, Ste 230
      Fremont, CA 94538
      Contact: Shaloo Jeswani Sr BDM
      Tel: 702-241-5131
      Email: shaloo@vertisystem.com
      Website: www.vertisystem.com
Staff Augmentation, Full-Time Placements, contract to Hire, IT Projects & Consulting. (Minority, Woman, estab 2008, empl 120, sales $20,000,000, cert: City, CPUC)

8954 Vidhwan Inc dba E-Solutions, Inc.
      2 N Market St Ste 400
      San Jose, CA 95113
      Contact: Eric Kumar Acct Mgr
      Tel: 408-239-4647
      Email: eric.kumar@e-solutionsinc.com
      Website: www.e-solutionsinc.com
IT & ITES staffing, recruitment & deployment: permanent, contract, contract to hire & project based staffing. (Woman/As-Ind, estab 2003, empl 450, sales $22,800,000, cert: NMSDC, CPUC)

PROFESSIONAL SERVICES: Staffing Services

8955 Vitesse Recruiting & Staffing, Inc.
      1432 Edinger Ave, Ste 100
      Tustin, CA 92780
      Contact: Kim N. Zastrow President
      Tel: 714-210-5959
      Email: knzastrow@vitesserecruiting.com
      Website: www.VitesseRecruiting.com
Temporary or permanent human resources employment services. (Minority, Woman, estab 2000, empl 3, sales , cert: State, CPUC)

8956 Vobecky Enterprises, Inc.
      134 N. Vermont Ave.
      Glendora, CA 91741
      Contact: Bianca Vobecky President
      Tel: 626-852-5800
      Email: bianca@vobecky.com
      Website: www.vobecky.com
Program Management, Staff Augmentation, Project Staffing, Office Administrative Services. (Woman/AA, estab 2006, empl 7, sales $7,774,576, cert: City, NMSDC, CPUC, WBENC)

8957 Voigt & Associates, Inc.
      22981 Sonriente Trail
      Coto de Caza, CA 92679
      Contact: Barbara Voigt President
      Tel: 949-766-1100
      Email: bvoigt@voigtinc.com
      Website: www.voigtinc.com
Executive search services. (Woman, estab 2005, empl 1, sales $1,200,000, cert: CPUC)

8958 Whitham Group Executive Search
      8130 Luisa Way
      Windsor, CA 95492
      Contact: President
      Tel: 888-238-1273
      Email: Info@WhithamGroup.com
      Website: www.WhithamGroup.com
Executive search & recruiting specializing in Utilities, Renewable Energy & Environmental Services. (Woman, estab 2010, empl 2, sales $1,174,000, cert: CPUC, WBENC)

8959 Workforce Solutions Group
      26090 Towne Centre Dr
      Foothill Ranch, CA 92679
      Contact: Colleen Jones COO
      Tel: 949-588-5812
      Email: cjones@wsgcorp.com
      Website: www.workforcesolutionsgroup.com
Staffing & direct hire: contract, temporary & direct hire placement. (Minority, Woman, estab 2002, empl 11, sales , cert: City, NWBOC)

8960 WorkSquare West
      4401 Crenshaw Blvd, Ste 220
      Los Angeles, CA 90043
      Contact: Natasha White President
      Tel: 323-294-9675
      Email: natasha@worksquare.com
      Website: www.worksquare.com
Recruiting,Temporary to Permanente Staffing Firm (Woman/AA, estab 2008, empl 4, sales , cert: NMSDC)

8961 Xtra Pair of Hands
      4307 San Joaquin Plz
      Newport Beach, CA 92660
      Contact: Kym Smith Managing Partner
      Tel: 404-825-4398
      Email: info@xtrapairofhands.com
      Website: www.xtrapairofhands.com
Staffing & recruiting: temp, temp-to-hire & direct hire placements. (Woman/AA, estab 2007, empl 4, sales $250,000, cert: State, CPUC)

8962 Zempleo, Inc.
      4000 Executive Pkwy Ste 240, Bishop Ranch 8
      San Ramon, CA 94583
      Contact: Sabrina Chisholm VP
      Tel: 925-284-0377
      Email: schisholm@zempleo.com
      Website: www.zempleo.com
Temporary staffing, payrolling & direct hire services. (Hisp, estab 2005, empl 1000, sales $62,860,000, cert: NMSDC, CPUC)

8963 Zenex Partners Inc
      4699 Old Ironsides Dr Ste 230
      Santa Clara, CA 95054
      Contact: Martin Dass Dir of Marketing & Client
      Tel: 408-863-1158
      Email: martin@zenexpartners.com
      Website: www.zenexpartners.com
Boutique staffing services promoting diversity & inclusivity in the workforce. (Woman/As-Pac, estab 2003, empl 170, sales , cert: WBENC)

Colorado

8964 Action Staffing Solutions
      1409 W 29th St
      Loveland, CO 80538
      Contact: Robin Fischer CEO
      Tel: 970-667-4202
      Email: robin@myactionstaffing.com
      Website: www.myactionstaffing.com
Temporary to permanent employee placement, contract personnel, long-term, executive placement, direct hire, on-site management. (Woman/AA, estab 2008, empl 7, sales $1,500,000, cert: State, City, 8(a))

8965 EGS, Inc.
      333 W Hampden Ave, Ste 530
      Englewood, CO 80111
      Contact: Susan Fenske President
      Tel: 303-477-6800
      Email: susan@egs-partners.com
      Website: www.egs-partners.com
Provide staffing & consulting assistance to public and private sector organizations. (Woman, estab 2002, empl 120, sales $12,000,000, cert: WBENC)

8966 Equity Staffing Group, Inc.
      8310 S. Valley Hwy Ste 135
      Englewood, CO 80112
      Contact: Stacey L Moore Operations Mgr
      Tel: 720-897-8714
      Email: stacey.moore@equitystaffing.com
      Website: www.equitystaffing.com
Staffing, consulting, contingent, or direct-hire workforce solutions. (Nat Ame, estab 2009, empl 60, sales $85,617,000, cert: NMSDC)

8967 IntelliSource
1899 Wynkoop St Ste 900
Denver, CO 80202
Contact: Matt Pollard SVP
Tel: 303-692-1100
Email: mpollard@intellisource.com
Website: www.intellisource.com
Staffing solutions, temporary, temp to perm, project management, outsourcing, contract & direct hire. (Woman, estab 1999, empl 300, sales , cert: WBENC)

8968 Job Store, Inc.
7100 E Hampden Ave Ste A
Denver, CO 80224
Contact: Julie DeGolier President
Tel: 303-757-7686
Email: julie@jobstorestaffing.com
Website: www.jobstorestaffing.com
Tempoary office, clerical admin support, accounting & technical & light industrial personnel. (Woman, estab 1974, empl 14, sales $8,400,419, cert: WBENC)

8969 Lakeshore Talent, LLC
5251 DTC Pkwy, Ste 400
Denver, CO 80111
Contact: Mary Clark President
Tel: 303-483-1100
Email: mclark@lakeshoretalent.com
Website: www.lakeshoretalent.com
Staffing and recruiting, contract, contract to hire, direct hire and payroll services. (Woman, estab 2017, empl 15, sales $10,529,849, cert: WBENC)

8970 MHa Technical Staffing, Inc.
7475 Dakin St, Ste 350
Denver, CO 80221
Contact: Thomas R. Leyba VP Operations
Tel: 303-428-1728
Email: t.leyba@martinez-hromada.com
Website: www.mhatech.com/
Temporary eng support personnel: civil, electrical, structural, mechanical, HVAC, programmers, subcontract, construction mgmt, designers & drafters. (Hisp, estab 1992, empl 65, sales , cert: City, NMSDC)

8971 Nexus Staffing Solutions Corp.
4701 Marion St, Ste 307
Denver, CO 80216
Contact: Barbara Butler Business Devel Mgr
Tel: 303-736-2008
Email: bonnie@nexusstaffingllc.com
Website: www.nexusstaffingllc.com/
Staffing: Engineering, Construction & Call Centers. (Woman, estab 2010, empl 12, sales , cert: WBENC)

8972 Prestige Staffing, Inc.
1873 S Bellaire St, Ste 320
Denver, CO 80222
Contact: President
Tel: 303-691-0111
Email: contactus@prestigecareer.com
Website: www.prestigecareer.com
Permanent, contract & temp positions. (Woman, estab 2003, empl 2, sales $350,000, cert: WBENC)

8973 Primesource Staffing
400 S. Colorado Blvd, Ste 400
Denver, CO 80246
Contact: Dennis Hatcher Controller
Tel: 303-869-2990
Email: dhatcher@primesourcestaffing.com
Website: www.primesourcestaffing.com
Staffing services. (Woman, estab 1996, empl 27, sales $20,600,000, cert: WBENC)

8974 The Maris Group
2696 S Colorado Blvd, Ste 595
Denver, CO 80222
Contact: Kathryn Ake Principal
Tel: 303-778-1962
Email: info@marisgroup.com
Website: www.marisgroup.com
Staffing: contract, marketing & communications. (Woman, estab 1999, empl 2, sales $2,500,000, cert: WBENC)

Connecticut

8975 CYMA Systems Inc.
360 Tolland Turnpike Ste 2D
Manchester, CT 06042
Contact: Nisha Sunil HR Mgr
Tel: 860-791-6356
Email: hr@cymasys.com
Website: www.cymasys.com
Professional staffing & solutions. (As-Ind, estab 2006, empl 179, sales $16,800,000, cert: NMSDC)

8976 Horizon Staffing Services
1169 Main St
East Hartford, CT 06108
Contact: Jennie Icard Business Solutions Consultant
Tel: 860-282-6124
Email: sales@horizonstaff.com
Website: www.horizonstaff.com
Full service staffing: Temporary, Long-term, Permanent, Nationwide Payroll Service & On-site management. (Woman/As-Ind, estab 1995, empl 45, sales $7,500,000, cert: NMSDC)

8977 JOBPRO Temporary Services, Inc.
36 Main St
East Hartford, CT 06118
Contact: Catherine Beck President
Tel: 800-404-7795
Email: cbeck@job-pro.com
Website: www.jobproworks.com
Staffing: temporary, temp-to-hire & direct placements: office, accounting, light industrial & technical niches. (Woman, estab 1981, empl 10, sales , cert: State)

8978 Key Alliance Staffing, LLC
406 Farmington Ave
Farmington, CT 06032
Contact: Sandra Hathaway
Tel: 860-676-7733
Email: shathaway@keyalliancestaff.com
Website: www.kas-consulting.com
Staffing: contract, contract to hire, or direct hire personnel. (Woman, estab 2008, empl 32, sales $2,586,000, cert: State)

PROFESSIONAL SERVICES: Staffing Services

8979 MY HR Supplier
 1266 E Main St Ste 700R
 Stamford, CT 06902
 Contact: Omer Mutaqi COO
 Tel: 203-274-8595
 Email: omutaqi@myhrsupplier.cm
 Website: www.myhrsupplier.com
Human capital talent: IT, administrative & office support, clerical & accounting. (Woman/As-Ind, estab 2011, empl 53, sales , cert: State, NMSDC)

8980 Skylightsys, LLC
 175 Capital Blvd Ste 402
 Rocky Hill, CT 06067
 Contact: Shalu Arora President
 Tel: 860-289-9096
 Email: arora@skylightsys.com
 Website: www.skylightsys.com
Staffing services. (Woman/As-Ind, estab 2005, empl 9, sales , cert: State)

8981 Stratoserve LLC
 18 Colonial Ct
 Cheshire, CT 06410
 Contact: Subroto Roy President
 Tel: 203-768-5690
 Email: subroto.roy@stratoserve.com
 Website: www.stratoserve.com
consulting, research and training for the following NAICS codes:541720,541613,611430 and is committed to provide quick and measurable value to its clients. (As-Pac, estab 2005, empl 1, sales , cert: NMSDC)

8982 Talus Partners, LLC
 321 Main St
 Farmington, CT 06032
 Contact: Steve Massucci Mgr
 Tel: 860-678-4410
 Email: accounting@taluspartners.com
 Website: www.taluspartners.com
IT, Engineering & Accounting contract & direct hire staffing. Certified Project Managers, Web Developers, Analysts. (Woman, estab 2011, empl 35, sales $5,500,000, cert: NWBOC)

8983 The Good Search, LLC
 4 Valley Rd
 Westport, CT 06880
 Contact: CEO
 Tel: 203-227-8615
 Email: info@tgsus.com
 Website: www.tgsus.com
Retained search & recruitment research, strategic recruitment initiatives of internal search teams. (Woman, estab 1999, empl 1, sales $662,398, cert: State, WBENC)

8984 Walt Medina & Associates, LLC
 1224 Mill St Bldg D, Ste 200
 East Berlin, CT 06023
 Contact: Walt Medina CEO
 Tel: 860-357-5002
 Email: wm@waltmedina.com
 Website: www.waltmedina.com
Healthcare recruiting, recruit military personnel (veterans). (Hisp, estab 2003, empl 2, sales $400,000, cert: NMSDC)

District of Columbia

8985 Adept Professional Staffing Inc.
 1629 K St, NW Ste 300
 Washington, DC 20006
 Contact: Elizabeth Joseph CEO
 Tel: 301-883-4308
 Email: tavares@adeptprostaffing.com
 Website: www.adeptprostaffing.com
Recruitment service for Accounting, Legal & Administrative Assistants, Permanent & Temporary placements. (Woman/AA, estab 2010, empl 1, sales $795,000, cert: State, WBENC, 8(a))

8986 JustinBradley, Inc.
 1725 I St, NW Ste 300
 Washington, DC 20006
 Contact: Andrew Chase EVP
 Tel: 202-457-8400
 Email: asc@justinbradley.com
 Website: www.JustinBradley.com
Recruiting & staff augmentation. (Woman, estab 2002, empl 65, sales $5,566,000, cert: WBENC)

8987 Midtown Personnel, Inc.
 1130 Connecticut Ave. NW Ste 1101
 Washington, DC 20036
 Contact: Proposal Mgr
 Tel: 202-887-4747
 Email: Accounting@themidtowngroup.com
 Website: www.themidtowngroup.com
Staffing services: direct hire, temp to hire, temporary, executive search. (Woman, estab 1989, empl 35, sales $15,400,000, cert: WBENC)

8988 National Associates, Inc.
 1130 Connecticut Ave, NW Ste 530
 Washington, DC 20036
 Contact: Oscar Hannaway President
 Tel: 202-223-7606
 Email: ohannaway@naipersonnel.com
 Website: www.naipersonnel.com
Permanent & temporary staffing: administrative, clerical, professional, technical & light industrial. (AA, estab 1987, empl 18, sales $9,600,000, cert: NMSDC)

8989 Pat Taylor and Associates, Inc.
 1101 17th St, NW Ste 707
 Washington, DC 20036
 Contact: Pat Taylor President
 Tel: 202-466-5622
 Email: pat@pattaylor.com
 Website: www.pattaylor.com
Temporary, temp to perm & permanent employment of attorneys, law clerks, paralegals, legal technology & court reporting services. (Woman, estab 1992, empl 6, sales $1,400,000, cert: WBENC)

Florida

8990 Airetel Staffing, Inc.
 PO Box 915864
 Longwood, FL 32791
 Contact: Mike Tomaso Natl Aquisitions Mgr
 Tel: 407-788-2015
 Email: mt@airetel.com
 Website: www.airetel.com
Full-time, contract & contract-to-hire staffing solutions. (Woman, estab 2000, empl 10, sales $3,570,000, cert: WBENC)

PROFESSIONAL SERVICES: Staffing Services

8991 Albion Healthcare Staffing
      10162 W Sample Rd
      Coral Springs, FL 33065
      Contact: Francisco Arteaga Division Dir
      Tel: 954-796-3336
      Email: francisco@albionbiomed.com
      Website: www.albionstaffing.com
Staffing services for Pharmaceutical & Medical Device companies. (Woman, estab 2005, empl 5, sales , cert: State)

8992 All Team Franchise Corp
      PO Box 21644
      Tampa, FL 33622
      Contact: Robert Lieberman
      Tel: 646-241-2368
      Email: Bdonoghue@allteamstaffing.com
      Website: www.allteamstaffing.com
Provide staff to Set up, Break Down, Clean, Cook, Prep, All Food Service Work. (Woman, estab 1991, empl 1400, sales $20,000,000, cert: WBENC)

8993 Alpha1 Staffing/Search Firm, LLC.
      3350 SW 148th Ave, Ste 220
      Miramar, FL 33027
      Contact: Garrie Harris President
      Tel: 954-734-2744
      Email: gharris@alpha1staffing.com
      Website: www.alpha1staffing.com
Staffing solutions, recruitment, assessment, training, development, and career management, to outsourcing and workforce consulting. (Woman/AA, estab 2007, empl 500, sales $13,000,000, cert: NMSDC)

8994 Apsis Solutions Inc.
      1120 E Kennedy Blvd Ste 232
      Tampa, FL 33602
      Contact: Angela Colonello
      Tel: 813-999-4853
      Email: acolonello@apsissolutionsinc.com
      Website: www.apsissolutionsinc.com
Provide certified IT personnel: temp, part-time, contract, or full time positions. (AA, estab 2012, empl 10, sales $300,000, cert: State, City)

8995 Ascendo Resources, LLC
      500 West Cypress Creek Road Ste 230
      Fort Lauderdale, FL 33309
      Contact: Melissa Mitchell Partner
      Tel: 321-251-3762
      Email: mmitchell@ascendo.com
      Website: www.ascendo.com
Executive recruiting & temporary staffing, temporary & project opportunities. (Hisp, estab 2009, empl 100, sales $39,000,000, cert: NMSDC)

8996 Bear Staffing Services Corporation
      10501 Six Mile Cypress Pkwy, Ste 104
      Fort Myers, FL 33966
      Contact: Gary Johnson CEO
      Tel: 856-848-0082
      Email: gjohnson@bearstaff.com
      Website: www.bearstaff.com
Temporary, temp to hire & direct hire staffing services. (Woman, estab , empl 475, sales , cert: WBENC)

8997 BioStaff Solutions Inc.
      4007 Blushing Rose Court
      Oviedo, FL 32766
      Contact: Jim Owens
      Tel: 407-542-6006
      Email: jowens@biostaffsolutions.com
      Website: www.biostaffsolutions.com
Provide clinical staffing services: contract, contract to hire & direct placements in SAS Programming, Clinical Programming, Biostatistics, Clinical Data Management, Pharmacovigilance, Clinical Monitoring. (Minority, Woman, estab 2014, empl 3, sales , cert: NMSDC)

8998 Career Center, Inc.
      1236 NW 18th Ave
      Gainesville, FL 32609
      Contact: Carolynn Buchanan Owner
      Tel: 352-378-2300
      Email: cbuchanan@tempforce.net
      Website: www.tempforcegainesville.com
Staffing: temporary, temp to perm & direct hire. (Woman, estab , empl , sales $934,261, cert: State, City)

8999 Career Solutions International Inc.
      400 Lexington Green Lane
      Sanford, FL 32771
      Contact: Suzette DiMascio CEO
      Tel: 866-484-4752
      Email: suzette@csigroup.net
      Website: www.csigroup.net
Executive search & recruiting services. (Woman, estab 2002, empl 8, sales $3,400,000, cert: WBENC)

9000 CareersUSA, Inc.
      6501 Congress Ave Ste 200
      Boca Raton, FL 33487
      Contact: Jennifer Johnson Exec VP & General Counsel
      Tel: 561-995-7000
      Email: jjohnson@careersusa.com
      Website: www.careersusa.com
Temporary, temp-to-hire, direct hire placements & payrolling services. (Woman, estab 1981, empl 10000, sales $32,000,000, cert: State, WBENC)

9001 Fast Dolphin Inc
      12555 Orange Dr Ste 4059
      Davie, FL 33330
      Contact: Ramon Osuna
      Tel: 954-376-4578
      Email: ramon.osuna@fastdolphin.com
      Website: www.fastdolphin.com
IT staffing providing bilingual & trilingual experts that speak English, Spanish and/or Portuguese. (Hisp, estab 2004, empl 150, sales $14,200,000, cert: NMSDC)

9002 Future Force Personnel
      15800 NW 57th Ave
      Miami Lakes, FL 33014
      Contact: Adela Gonzalez CEO
      Tel: 407-851-0039
      Email: adela@futureforcepersonnel.com
      Website: www.futureforcepersonnel.com
Temporary, temp to hire & direct hire placements. (Minority, Woman, estab 1992, empl 15, sales $17,500,000, cert: NMSDC)

PROFESSIONAL SERVICES: Staffing Services

9003 Garcia & Ortiz Staffing, LLC
888 Executive Center Dr W, Ste 101
St. Petersburg, FL 33702
Contact: Jeremy Lavin Operations Mgr
Tel: 727-342-1007
Email: jlavin@garciaortiz.com
Website: www.garciaortiz.com
Staffing: accounting, finance & banking professionals on a temporary, project & permanent basis. (Hisp, estab 2005, empl 5, sales $900,000, cert: State)

9004 GDKN Corporation
9700 Stirling Road Ste 110
Cooper City, FL 33024
Contact: Gary Dhir VP
Tel: 954-985-6650
Email: gdhir@gdkn.com
Website: www.gdkn.com
Staffing: information technology, engineering, professional, administrative & clerical, IT consulting, custom application development. (As-Ind, estab 1993, empl 400, sales $18,000,000, cert: NMSDC)

9005 Genesis Global Recruiting
3000 SW 148 Ave, Ste 116
Miramar, FL 33027
Contact: Jim Cochran Dir of Recruiting
Tel: 800-780-2232
Email: jcochran@genesis-global.com
Website: www.genesis-global.com
Staffing & workforce solutions: direct hire, temporary workforce & contract consulting. (Minority, Woman, estab 1999, empl 167, sales $16,500,000, cert: WBENC)

9006 Genoa Employment Solutions, Inc
1560 Sawgrass Corporate Pkwy
Sunrise, FL 33323
Contact: Walter Ruf CEO
Tel: 954-604-6056
Email: wruf@genoausa.com
Website: www.genoausa.com
Staffing services: engineering, IT, office support, human resources & purchasing. (Hisp, estab 2009, empl 162, sales $15,000,000, cert: NMSDC)

9007 GlobalVise Inc.
10335 Cross Creek Blvd Ste 8
Tampa, FL 33647
Contact: Sanjay Mehta President
Tel: 813-333-0400
Email: sanjay@globalvise.com
Website: www.globalvise.com
Permanent, temporary & contract staffing solutions. (As-Ind, estab 2008, empl 8, sales $2,758,764, cert: State, NMSDC, 8(a))

9008 Hamilton-Malone Corp
31958 US 19 N
Palm Harbor, FL 34684
Contact: Eileen McQuown President
Tel: 727-781-7747
Email: eileen@accordstaff.com
Website: www.accordstaff.com
Temporary & temp to hire staffing, executive search. (Woman, estab 1993, empl 4, sales $80,000,000, cert: State)

9009 Hanker Systems, Inc.
5401 W Kennedy Blvd, Ste 100
Tampa, FL 33609
Contact: Shravan Bommireddy Business Dev Mgr
Tel: 813-710-1444
Email: ranjithk@hankersystems.com
Website: www.HankersystemsInc.com
Permanent and Temporary staffing. (As-Ind, estab 2013, empl 62, sales $4,000,000, cert: State)

9010 Innovative Systems Group of Florida, Inc. dba ISGF
100 E Pine St Ste 605
Orlando, FL 32801
Contact: Thomas Bryan Managing Partner
Tel: 407-481-9580
Email: tbryan@isgf.com
Website: www.isgf.com
Temporary, contract, contract to hire, direct hire staffing & recruitment in information technology, accounting & finance, sales & marketing. (As-Pac, estab 1996, empl 30, sales $3,210,000, cert: State, City, NMSDC, CPUC)

9011 I-Tech Personnel Services, Inc.
5627 Atlantic Blvd, Ste 1
Jacksonville, FL 32207
Contact: Marco Tran President
Tel: 904-381-1911
Email: mtran@itechpersonnel.com
Website: www.itechpersonnel.net
Staffing svcs: clerical, technical professionals & light industrial, temporary to permanent, direct hire placement & on-site management. (As-Pac, estab 1998, empl 125, sales $3,580,000, cert: State, NMSDC)

9012 Key Technical Resources, Inc.
5763 N Andrews Way
Fort Lauderdale, FL 33309
Contact: President
Tel: 954-771-1554
Email:
Website: www.keytechnical.com
Full time, contract & temporary placement: information technology, accounting & finance. (Woman, estab 1999, empl 15, sales $1,828,000, cert: WBENC)

9013 KeyStaff, Inc.
3540 Forest Hill Blvd Ste 203
West Palm Beach, FL 33406
Contact: Jessica Irons Business Devel
Tel: 561-688-9184
Email: jirons@mykeystaff.com
Website: www.mykeystaff.com/
IT/technical staffing solutions. (Woman, estab 1990, empl 60, sales $50,000,000, cert: State, WBENC)

9014 Mihnovich Consulting LLC
44 Prospect Ln
Ponte Vedra, FL 32081
Contact: Amanda Mihnovich CEO
Tel: 631-538-5008
Email: amanda@privatelabelstaff.com
Website: www.privatelabelstaff.com
Contract Recruitment, Talent Acquisition Program Management, Contract Professional Staffing, Executive Search, Permanent Placement, Full-Time Placement, Direct Hire, IT Staffing. (Woman, estab 2020, empl 6, sales , cert: WBENC)

PROFESSIONAL SERVICES: Staffing Services

9015 Nurses And Medical Staffing Agency LLC
      37 N Orange Ave, Ste 328
      Orlando, FL 32801
      Contact: Triffina Brown Admin
      Tel: 954-608-7971
      Email: admin@wholecaremedicalstaffing.com
      Website: www.wholecaremedicalstaffing.com/
Medical Staffing provides healthcare facilities (hospitals, rehabilitation center, nursing care centers, Assisted living facilities) in Florida with local nursing staff. (AA, estab 2021, empl 14, sales , cert: State)

9016 Premier Advisors Staffing and Sales, LLC
      7138 Spikerush Ct
      Lakewood Ranch, FL 34202
      Contact: Richard Burns President
      Tel: 313-869-8868
      Email: rburns@premierhealthcareadvisors.com
      Website: www.premierhealthcareadvisors.com
Staffing and Recruiting. (AA, estab 2015, empl 1, sales $1,000,000, cert: State, NMSDC)

9017 Pro-Staffing Agency
      981 W Commercial Blvd
      Fort Lauderdale, FL 33309
      Contact: Marie Morency Owner
      Tel: 954-530-2894
      Email: marie@pro-staffinggroup.com
      Website: www.pro-staffinggroup.com
Recruiting, staffing & business management. (Woman/AA, estab 2016, empl 2, sales , cert: NMSDC)

9018 Qualese, LLC
      3035 Honeysuckle Rd
      Largo, FL 33770
      Contact: Roberto Filippelli President
      Tel: 727-488-6373
      Email: roberto.filippelli@qualese.com
      Website: www.qualese.com
Recruiting & staffing agency. (Hisp, estab 2015, empl 1, sales , cert: NMSDC)

9019 Rapid Staffing, Inc.
      PO Box 602
      Valrico, FL 33595
      Contact: Lani Harless President
      Tel: 813-651-1242
      Email: lani@rapidstaffing.com
      Website: www.rapidstaffing.com
Staffing services: temporary & temporary to permanent employees. (Minority, Woman, estab 2002, empl 5, sales $2,227,174, cert: State, NMSDC)

9020 Resource Employment Solutions
      5900 Lake Ellenor Dr, Ste 100
      Orlando, FL 32809
      Contact: Eddy Dominguez VP Business Dev
      Tel: 321-234-9363
      Email: eddy_d@resourceemployment.com
      Website: www.resourceemployment.com
Employment agency, staffing services & recruitment company. (Hisp, estab 1995, empl 35000, sales $111,000,000, cert: NMSDC)

9021 Search Wizards, Inc.
      15 Paradise Plaza Ste 261
      Sarasota, FL 34239
      Contact: Miranda Hinshaw CEO
      Tel: 941-932-4108
      Email: miranda@searchwizards.com
      Website: www.searchwizards.com
Staffing: IT, finance & human resources, contract, contract-to-hire & full time. (Woman, estab 2000, empl 71, sales $35,000,000, cert: WBENC)

9022 Spherion Corporation
      8130 Baymeadows Way W Ste 103
      Jacksonville, FL 32256
      Contact: Shelley Sherman Sr Mgr Qualification
      Tel: 904-448-9102
      Email: info@spherion.com
      Website: www.spherion.com
National staffing: temp, temp to perm & direct placement staffing. (Woman, estab 1946, empl 1500, sales $14,089,000, cert: WBENC)

9023 Staffing By Choice LLC
      7975 NW 154th St, Ste 380
      Miami Lakes, FL 33016
      Contact: Matthew Marsh VP Business Acquisition
      Tel: 954-417-5627
      Email: mmarsh@cpabychoice.com
      Website: www.staffingbychoice.com
Staffing, recruiting & executive search services: accounting, finance, sales & operations professionals, permanent, temp to perm & contract roles. (As-Pac, estab 2002, empl 7, sales $360,000, cert: NMSDC)

9024 Techno-Transfers of Florida, Inc.
      4609 NW 26th Ave
      Boca Raton, FL 33434
      Contact: Virginia Mendiola Dir
      Tel: 561-212-2383
      Email: vmendiola@techno-transfers.com
      Website: www.techno-transfers.com
IT personnel for temporary contract, temp-to-perm roles & full-time positions. (Minority, Woman, estab 1992, empl 6, sales $350,000, cert: State)

9025 The CALER Group, Inc.
      23337 Lago Mar Cir
      Boca Raton, FL 33433
      Contact: Colleen Perrone President
      Tel: 561-394-8045
      Email: cperrone@calergroup.com
      Website: www.calergroup.com
Executive recruiting. (Woman, estab 1995, empl 6, sales $1,200,000, cert: WBENC)

9026 The Fountain Group, LLC
      4505 Woodland Corporate Blvd Ste 200
      Tampa, FL 33614
      Contact: Rachel Slowey VP
      Tel: 813-439-8393
      Email: rachel.slowey@thefountaingroup.com
      Website: www.thefountaingroup.com
Match top contingent talent with Fortune 100 to Fortune 500 companies. Life Sciences, Clinical, Engineering, IT. (Woman, estab 2001, empl 1000, sales $91,000,000, cert: WBENC)

PROFESSIONAL SERVICES: Staffing Services

9027 TransHire
3601 W Commercial Blvd Ste 12
Fort Lauderdale, FL 33309
Contact: Yvonne Rasbach President
Tel: 954-484-5401
Email: yvonne@transhiregroup.com
Website: www.TransHiregroup.com
Staffing svcs: office, clerical, admin support, word processing, light industrial, on-site mgmt programs & payrolling svcs, temp, contract & permanent placement. (Minority, Woman, estab 1984, empl 9, sales $21,575,122, cert: State, NMSDC)

9028 Victoria & Associates Career Services, Inc.
8181 NW 36 St, Ste 22
Miami, FL 33166
Contact: Victoria Villalba President
Tel: 305-477-2233
Email: victoria@victoriaassociates.com
Website: www.victoriaassociates.com
Staffing svcs: temporary, temporary to hire, direct hire, vendor on premise, payrolling, background checks, etc. (Minority, Woman, estab 1992, empl 6, sales , cert: WBENC)

9029 Vinali LLC
2860 Delaney Ave
Orlando, FL 32806
Contact: Acct Mgr
Tel: 407-574-2000
Email:
Website: www.vinalistaffing.com/
Permanent and temporary staffing services across technology, accounting, logistics and healthcare. (Minority, Woman, estab 2016, empl 15, sales $5,000,000, cert: State, WBENC)

Georgia

9030 Allyon, Inc.
3066 Mercer University Dr
Chamblee, GA 30341
Contact: Samuel Cohen Federal Account Mgr
Tel: 678-922-0479
Email: scohen@allyon.com
Website: www.allyon.com
IT staffing: temp-to-perm, or direct hire. (Woman, estab 2009, empl 150, sales $29,097,363, cert: WBENC)

9031 Apex Veteran Staffing, Inc.
2910 School Side Way
Lawrenceville, GA 30044
Contact: Brian Herbert President
Tel: 404-287-2855
Email: bherb@aveteranstaffing.com
Website: www.aveteranstaffing.com
Temporary, Permanent and Contracting of employees, staff augmentation. (AA, estab 2010, empl 31, sales $270,000, cert: State)

9032 Apollos Partners LLC
PO Box 49755
Atlanta, GA 30359
Contact: Bryan Payne Managing Partner
Tel: 404-437-7500
Email: bryan@apollospartners.com
Website: www.apollospartners.com
Direct-hire placements, accounting & finance positions. (AA, estab 2009, empl 1, sales $225,000, cert: NMSDC)

9033 ARK Temporary Staffing, LLC
221 Scenic Hwy
Lawrenceville, GA 30046
Contact: Alvin Keitt Business Devel Mgr
Tel: 770-962-5099
Email: akeitt@arktempstaffing.com
Website: www.arktempstaffing.com
Staffing services providing reliable, quality Temporary and Permanent personnel for business and government agencies. (Woman/AA, estab 2004, empl 100, sales $4,324,547, cert: NMSDC)

9034 Ashton Staffing, Inc
3590 Cherokee St Ste
Kennesaw, GA 30144
Contact: Jennifer Coon-Leeper Major Accounts Mgr
Tel: 770-419-1776
Email: jleeper@ashtonstaffing.com
Website: www.ashtonstaffing.com
Direct hire & contract recruiting: technology, financial, management. (Woman, estab 1995, empl 35, sales $16,100,000, cert: WBENC)

9035 ASK Staffing, Inc.
6495 Shiloh Road Ste 300
Alpharetta, GA 30005
Contact: Manish Karani President
Tel: 770-813-8947
Email: mkarani@askstaffing.com
Website: www.askconsulting.com/
Permanent placement & information technology staff augmentation. (Minority, Woman, estab 1995, empl , sales $22,000,000, cert: NMSDC, WBENC)

9036 Bison Data Systems, Inc.
5425 Peachtree Pkwy
Peachtree Corners, GA 30092
Contact: Wesley Owens CEO
Tel: 888-242-5737
Email: sscott@bisonstaffing.com
Website: www.bisonstaffing.com
Staffing, Technology, Light, Industrial & Health Care industries. (AA, estab 2014, empl 37, sales $12,000,000, cert: NMSDC)

9037 Blue Ocean Ventures LLC
2814 Spring Rd Ste 116
Atlanta, GA 30339
Contact: Robert Jordan
Tel: 404-279-2777
Email: robert.jordan@blue-oceanventures.com
Website: www.blue-oceanventures.com
Recruiting, permanent hire & staffing. (AA, estab 2012, empl 10, sales , cert: NMSDC)

9038 Boomers Consulting, LLC
PO Box 246
Lithonia, GA 30058
Contact: Pamela Garr Managing Dir
Tel: 678-476-8243
Email: info@boomersconsultingllc.com
Website: www.boomersconsultingllc.com
Talent acquisition & consulting, staffing/recruiting services. (Woman/AA, estab 2011, empl 1, sales , cert: State, City)

PROFESSIONAL SERVICES: Staffing Services

9039 COMFORCE
2400 Meadowbrook Pkwy
Duluth, GA 30096
Contact: Shivani Sardana Recruiter
Tel: 678-648-7422
Email: shivani.sardana@comforce.com
Website: www.comforce.com
Contingent staffing, information technology consulting & human resource outsourcing solutions. (As-Ind, estab 1962, empl 500, sales $438,000,000, cert: NMSDC)

9040 Corporate Temps, Inc.
5950 Live Oak Pkwy Ste 230
Norcross, GA 30093
Contact: Shawn Menefee President
Tel: 770-934-1710
Email: shawn@corporatetemps.com
Website: www.corporatetemps.com
Temporary & permanent staffing. (AA, estab 1991, empl 250, sales $11,670,618, cert: State, City, NMSDC)

9041 CorTech
710 Morgan Falls Road
Atlanta, GA 30350
Contact: JP Rogers Sr VP Sales
Tel: 770-628-0268
Email: jrogers@cor-tech.net
Website: www.cor-tech.net
Recruiting svcs: technical, professional services, vendor mgmt (VMS). (Hisp, estab 1999, empl 7500, sales $260,543,521, cert: NMSDC)

9042 Diversified Staffing & Consulting Group LLC
75 Cliftwood Dr
Atlanta, GA 30328
Contact: Monica Fox President
Tel: 404-459-3380
Email: monica@diversifiedscg.com
Website: www.diversifiedscg.com
Provide Temp, Temp to Perm & Direct Hire personnel in all fields. (Woman, estab 2010, empl 6, sales , cert: City)

9043 DoverStaffing
2451 Cumberland Pkwy Ste 3418
Atlanta, GA 30339
Contact: Sanquinetta Dover CEO
Tel: 770-434-3040
Email: sdover@doverstaffing.com
Website: www.doverstaffing.com
Staffing, training, call center svcs. (Woman/AA, estab 1996, empl 200, sales , cert: NMSDC)

9044 EC London & Associates
101 Marietta St NW, Ste 3310
Atlanta, GA 30303
Contact: Edward C. London CEO
Tel: 404-688-6607
Email: elondon@bellsouth.net
Website: www.eclondon.com
Facilities support & staffing services. (AA, estab 1981, empl 50, sales $1,821,984, cert: City)

9045 Ellsworth Healthcare Staffing LLC
160 Clairemont Ave, Ste 200
Decatur, GA 30030
Contact: Terri Lawson-Adams CEO
Tel: 404-806-8164
Email: tadams@ehstaffing.com
Website: www.ehstaffing.com
Healthcare staffing. (Woman/AA, estab 2016, empl 10, sales $920,000, cert: NMSDC, WBENC)

9046 Enterprise Project Solutions Group Corporation
204 Kobuk Court
Canton, GA 30114
Contact: Dir of Sales
Tel: 678-592-2256
Email: sales@epsgcorp.com
Website: www.epsgcorp.com
Staff Augmentation (Woman, estab 2005, empl 5, sales $1,500,000, cert: WBENC)

9047 Excel Staffing Inc.
1174 Grimes Bridge Rd Ste 100
Roswell, GA 30075
Contact: Khushnood Elahi Sales/ Marketing Mgr
Tel: 678-461-8701
Email: k.elahi@4esi.com
Website: www.4esi.com
Staffing svcs: sales & marketing, executive, accounting & finance, engineering & manufacturing, industrial, office professionals, IT managed svcs & e-business svcs. (As-Ind, estab 2001, empl 10, sales $9,000,000, cert: NMSDC)

9048 FirstPro Inc.
PO Box 420559
Atlanta, GA 30342
Contact: Michelle Kennedy Dir of Mktg
Tel: 404-250-7179
Email: m.kennedy@firstproinc.com
Website: www.firstproinc.com
Executive search, professional placement & staffing: accounting, administrative, call center, clerical, collections, finance, healthcare, human resources, information technology, legal, light industrial, life sciences, management consulting. (Woman, estab 1986, empl 125, sales $31,900,000, cert: WBENC)

9049 Futurewave Systems Inc.
5 Concourse Pkwy Ste 3000
Roswell, GA 30075
Contact: Raj Prabhu CEO
Tel: 678-640-1167
Email: raj.prabhu@futurewavesystems.com
Website: www.futurewavesystems.com
Staffing services. (As-Ind, estab 2006, empl 267, sales $3,292,000, cert: NMSDC)

9050 Global Personnel Solutions, Inc.
1143 Laney Walker Blvd
Augusta, GA 30901
Contact: Giselle Brown Acct Mgr
Tel: 706-722-4222
Email: gbrown@gapersonnel.com
Website: www.globalpersonnelsol.com
Full service staffing services. (Woman/AA, estab 1987, empl 10, sales $4,475,681, cert: NMSDC)

9051 GSquared Group, LLC
3180 Northpoint Pkwy, Ste 301
Alpharetta, GA 30005
Contact: Joan Guillory CEO
Tel: 404-698-1810
Email: contactus@gsquaredgroup.com
Website: www.gsquaredgroup.com
Contract, contract-to-hire & direct hire positions. (Woman, estab 2010, empl 25, sales , cert: WBENC)

PROFESSIONAL SERVICES: Staffing Services

9052 Heagney Logan Group, LLC
2002 Summit Blvd Ste 300
Atlanta, GA 30319
Contact: Jeannette Weigelt Principal
Tel: 404-267-1351
Email: info@heagneylogan.com
Website: www.heagneylogangroup.com
Mgmt Consulting, IT Staffing, Project Mgmt, ERP Consulting, Remote Devel, Contract Technical Staffing. (AA, estab 2009, empl 3, sales $924,954, cert: State, NMSDC)

9053 Healthcare Resources Staffing Agency
2107 N Decatur Rd, Ste 256
Decatur, GA 30033
Contact: Terrilyn Ferguson Dir
Tel: 770-820-7874
Email: terri@hrsagency.com
Website: www.hrsagency.com
Medical staffing: Nurses, Therapists, Nursing Assistants. (AA, estab 2016, empl , sales $1,100,000, cert: NMSDC)

9054 Homrich, Klein & Associates
3500 Lenox Rd
Atlanta, GA 30326
Contact: Amy Dresser Principal
Tel: 404-541-9010
Email: adresser@hkasearch.com
Website: www.hkasearch.com
Accounting & financial recruiting. (Woman, estab 2003, empl 5, sales $1,000,400, cert: WBENC)

9055 Infinite Resouce Solutions
2400 Herodian Way SE Ste 205
Smyrna, GA 30080
Contact: Leigh Sicina COO
Tel: 404-645-7065
Email: lsicina@infiniters.com
Website: www.infiniters.com
Resource management & professional staffing. (Woman, estab 2013, empl 50, sales $2,464,410, cert: WBENC)

9056 Jamison Professional Services, Inc.
2995 E. Point St
East Point, GA 30344
Contact: Tracie Ellis Division Mgr
Tel: 404-684-6008
Email: tellis@jps-online.com
Website: www.jps-online.com
Staffing svcs, mail mgmt, facilities support, help desk etc. (AA, estab 1992, empl 10, sales $4,010,000, cert: NMSDC)

9057 JNX Partners, LLC
2935 Haynes Club Cir
Grayson, GA 30017
Contact: Judy Swanier President
Tel: 770-982-0043
Email: judy.swanier@jnxpartners.com
Website: www.jnxpartners.com
Executive staffing, HR & career transition: sourcing, screening, testing, hiring & retention
practices, coaching & support. (Woman/AA, estab 2005, empl 3, sales , cert: WBENC)

9058 Lorentine Green & Associates, Inc.
12104 Jefferson Creek Dr
Alpharetta, GA 30005
Contact: Lorentine F. Green President
Tel: 770-616-6326
Email: lorentine@lorentinegreen.com
Website: www.lorentinegreen.com
Recruiting & project management, Permanent Placement, Contract & Contract to Permanent. (AA, estab 2013, empl 7, sales $300,000, cert: NMSDC)

9059 Management, Analysis & Utilization, Inc. d.b.a 3Ci
501 Greene St
Augusta, GA 30901
Contact: Harlee Bush Marketing Asst
Tel: 706-823-2337
Email: mausupplier@mau.com
Website: www.mau.com
Strategic temporary staffing, professional recruiting, outsourcing, outplacement and managed services. (Nat Ame, estab 1973, empl 10729, sales $433,592,830, cert: NMSDC)

9060 MarketPro Inc.
53 Perimeter Center E Ste 200
Atlanta, GA 30346
Contact: Cindy Underwood VP
Tel: 404-978-1005
Email: cindy@marketproinc.com
Website: www.marketproinc.com
Contract, contract to hire or direct hire: marketing, advertising & communications. (Woman, estab 1996, empl 20, sales $15,650,000, cert: WBENC)

9061 Olivine LLC
970 Peachtree Industrial Blvd. Ste 100
Suwanee, GA 30024
Contact: Rajeev Maddur Sr Acct Mgr
Tel: 770-596-5155
Email: rajeevm@olivinellc.com
Website: www.olivinellc.com
IT Consulting Services, Contract, Contract to Hire and Direct hire placements. (As-Ind, estab 2006, empl 20, sales , cert: NMSDC)

9062 Pareto Solutions Group, Inc.
8 Piedmont Center Ste 210
Atlanta, GA 30305
Contact: Shaun Harvill CEO
Tel: 770-804-8020
Email: sharvill@paretosg.com
Website: www.paretosg.com
Staffing: temporary, temp-to-hire & direct hire placement of accounting, finance & IT professionals. (Minority, Woman, estab 2006, empl 55, sales , cert: WBENC)

9063 Perimeter Entertainment, Inc.
PO Box 464003
Lawrenceville, GA 30042
Contact: CEO
Tel: 678-866-4066
Email: info@perimeterent.com
Website: www.perimeterent.com
Content Creation & Professional Recruiting Services for Entertainment, Media, Government & Big Brand Companies. (Woman/AA, estab 2010, empl 4, sales , cert: NMSDC, WBENC)

9064 Peritia LLC
4751 Best Rd Ste 179
College Park, GA 30337
Contact: Panseh Tsewole President
Tel: 404-224-9692
Email: ptsewole@peritiafederal.com
Website: www.peritiafederal.com
Program Management, IT Services, Administrative Support Services & Staff Augmentation. (AA, estab 2016, empl 2, sales $123,240, cert: NMSDC)

PROFESSIONAL SERVICES: Staffing Services   9065-9076

9065 PharmaCare Solutions, Inc.
      5555 Glenridge Connector Ste 200
      Atlanta, GA 30342
      Contact: Cassandra Tancil CEO
      Tel: 404-459-2847
      Email: ctancil@pharmacaresolutions.com
      Website: www.pharmacaresolutions.com
Contract & temporary health professional staffing, analytical data reporting, health management initiatives & clinical support services. (Woman/AA, estab 2003, empl 1, sales , cert: NMSDC)

9066 Preferred Personnel Solutions, Inc.
      425 Barrett Pkwy Ste 4045
      Kennesaw, GA 30144
      Contact: Business Devel Specialist
      Tel: 678-662-6471
      Email: cartersville@preferredpersonnel.com
      Website: www.preferredpersonnel.com
Staffing svcs: light industrial, manufacturing, logistics & distribution, office & admin, call center, accounting & finance, executive search. (Woman, estab 2002, empl 500, sales $11,900,000, cert: WBENC)

9067 ProKatchers LLC
      1766 Baxley Pine Trce
      Suwanee, GA 30024
      Contact: Samay Shah CEO
      Tel: 706-254-7008
      Email: samay@prokatchers.com
      Website: www.prokatchers.com/
Traditional staffing & recruiting, direct placement & payroll services, workforce solution programs. (As-Pac, estab 2015, empl , sales $12,000,000, cert: NMSDC, CPUC)

9068 Quality Staffing of America, Inc.
      3525 Piedmont Rd NE
      Atlanta, GA 30305
      Contact: Ken Richards President
      Tel: 404-477-0020
      Email: ken@qualitystaffingamerica.com
      Website: www.QualityStaffingAmerica.com
Temporary/contingent staffing services. (Woman, estab 2013, empl 200, sales $7,400,000, cert: WBENC)

9069 R. Beverly Consulting, LLC dba Silver Fox Staffing
      1140 Newpark View Place
      Mableton, GA 30126
      Contact: Jeannine Lewis Managing Dir
      Tel: 404-512-6441
      Email: info@silverfoxstaffs.com
      Website: www.silverfoxstaffs.com
Staffing, temporary, part-time and seasonal employees for sporting and special events, conferences, corporate and organizational meetings, trade shows. (AA, estab 2011, empl 1, sales $167,000, cert: NMSDC)

9070 Southern Crescent Personnel, Inc.
      7179 Jonesboro Rd Ste 101
      Morrow, GA 30260
      Contact: Krystal Pate President
      Tel: 770-968-4602
      Email:
      Website: www.scp-jobs.com
Temporary, temp-to-hire & perm placement: administrative, medical & dental positions. (Woman, estab 1993, empl 4, sales , cert: WBENC)

9071 Staff Relief Inc
      1190 North Highland Ave
      Atlanta, GA 31106
      Contact: Gabe Pascua CEO
      Tel: 478-974-0075
      Email: gabe@staffreliefinc.com
      Website: www.staffreliefinc.com
Joint Commission Certified staffing agency. (Hisp, estab 1990, empl , sales $4,000,000, cert: NMSDC)

9072 The Experts Bench, Inc.
      1325 Satellite Blvd 615
      Suwanee, GA 30024
      Contact: Ramsey A'Ve Market Practice Lead
      Tel: 770-757-5831
      Email: ramseya@tebww.com
      Website: www.tebww.com/
Professional services, staff marketing & accounting contractors. (Woman, estab 2002, empl 20, sales $1,819,000, cert: WBENC)

9073 The Mom Corps, Inc.
      1205 Johnson Ferry Rd Ste 136-507
      Marietta, GA 30068
      Contact: Allison OKelly CEO
      Tel: 888-438-8122
      Email: allison@momcorps.com
      Website: www.momcorps.com
Temporary staffing. (Woman, estab 2005, empl 15, sales $11,240,405, cert: WBENC)

9074 The Royster Group, Inc.
      934 Glenwood Ave SE Ste 280
      Atlanta, GA 30316
      Contact: Taunton Ken President
      Tel: 770-507-3353
      Email: krtaunton@roystergroup.com
      Website: www.roystergroup.com
Diversity search: healthcare, financial services, consumer products & industrial. (AA, estab 2001, empl 80, sales $18,000,000, cert: NMSDC)

Iowa

9075 CareerPros, LLC dba Sedona Staffing Services
      2065 Holliday Dr
      Dubuque, IA 52002
      Contact: Nikki Kiefer President
      Tel: 563-556-3040
      Email: nikki@careerpros.com
      Website: www.careerpros.com
Staffing services: temporary, temp-to-hire, smart-hire, contract & staff leasing. (Woman, estab 1993, empl 18, sales $11,700,000, cert: WBENC)

9076 Chenhall's Staffing, Inc
      2119 E 12th St
      Davenport, IA 52803
      Contact: Bob Hickman President
      Tel: 563-386-3800
      Email: bhickman@chenhallstaffing.com
      Website: www.chenhallstaffing.com
Staffing augmentation, recruiting & HR, contingent staffing augmentation; temp to perm & transitional probationary staffing recruitment, screening, testing & placement; corporate recruitment, career counseling & outplacement. (Nat Ame, estab 1955, empl 7, sales , cert: NMSDC, 8(a))

PROFESSIONAL SERVICES: Staffing Services

9077 SelectOne Staffing Services LLC
222 Third Ave SE Ste 240-B
Cedar Rapids, IA 52401
Contact: Vincent Clayton President
Tel: 319-373-2325
Email: vclayton@genatek.net
Website: www.genatek.net
Recruiting & staffing: engineering, IT development, telecommunications, technical support. (AA, estab 2003, empl 10, sales , cert: NMSDC)

Illinois

9078 AltaStaff LLC
19 S La Salle Ste 800
Chicago, IL 60603
Contact: Taz Wilson President
Tel: 312-269-9990
Email: kkossack@altastaff.com
Website: www.altastaff.com
Staffing services: temporary, temp-to-hire & direct-hire placements for administrative, creative, financial & sales support. (Woman, estab 2007, empl 5, sales , cert: State)

9079 Anchor Staffing Inc.
9901 S Western Ave, Ste 206
Chicago, IL 60643
Contact: Joyce Johnson CEO
Tel: 773-881-0530
Email: jjohnson@anchorstaffing.com
Website: www.anchorstaffing.com
Temporary & direct hire staffing & employment services. (Minority, estab 2002, empl 350, sales $2,600,000,000, cert: State, City, NMSDC)

9080 Apidel Technologies LLC
13550 U.S. 30, Unit 204 F
Plainfield, IL 60544
Contact: Chris Raut Business Devel Exec
Tel: 847-483-8565
Email: chris@apideltech.com
Website: www.apideltech.com
Temporary Placement, Permanent Placement, Temp to Direct Placement & Payroll, SOW & Call Center. (Woman/As-Ind, estab 2012, empl 770, sales $26,000,000, cert: NMSDC, WBENC)

9081 A-Pro Execs, LLC
208 S Lasalle St Ste 1450
Chicago, IL 60604
Contact: Gladys Jossell Owner
Tel: 312-855-1515
Email: gjossell@aol.com
Website: www.aprotemps.com
Temporary & permanent placement services:administrative/legal office support, accounting, customer service & information technology. (Woman/AA, estab 2004, empl 4, sales $2,700,000, cert: WBENC)

9082 Arlington Resources, Inc.
4902 Tollview Dr
Rolling Meadows, IL 60008
Contact: Patricia Casey President
Tel: 224-232-5900
Email: pcasey@arlingtonresources.com
Website: www.arlingtonresources.com
Temporary staffing services, temp to hire & direct hire placement of Human Resources Professionals. (Woman, estab 1997, empl 25, sales $6,000,000, cert: City)

9083 Arrow Strategies
233 N. Michigan Ave Ste 1960
Chicago, IL 60601
Contact: Mike Colles Division Dir
Tel: 312-561-9202
Email: mikec@arrowstrategies.com
Website: www.arrowstrategies.com
Recruiting: source, profile & present high-end talent. (Nat Ame, estab 2002, empl 250, sales $31,200,000, cert: NMSDC)

9084 Aspen Technical Staffing, Inc.
10123 Mandel Rd
Plainfield, IL 60544
Contact: Amy Negrete VP
Tel: 630-904-8566
Email: amy@atstaffing.net
Website: www.atstaffing.net
Temporary staffing. (Woman, estab 2001, empl 6, sales $2,400,000,000, cert: WBENC)

9085 Assured Healthcare Staffing LLC - Gurnee, IL
495 N Riverside Dr Ste 203
Gurnee, IL 60031
Contact: Leslie Kischer President
Tel: 847-775-7445
Email: leslie.kischer@assuredhealthcare.com
Website: www.assuredhealthcare.com
Healthcare staffing: Registered Nurses, Licensed Practical Nurses, Certified Nurses Aids, Pharmacists, Pharmacy Techs, Medical Assistants, Medical Billers. (Woman, estab 2007, empl 70, sales $2,751,000, cert: WBENC)

9086 Carrington & Carrington
230 W Monroe St Ste 2250
Chicago, IL 60606
Contact: Marian H Carrington Principal
Tel: 312-606-0503
Email: mcarrington@carringtonandcarrington.com
Website: www.carringtonandcarrington.com
Executive search, recruitment & placement of diverse professionals for senior management & executive level positions. (Woman/AA, estab 1979, empl 6, sales , cert: City, WBENC)

9087 Crystal Equation Corporation
1111 Plaza Dr. Ste 480
Schaumburg, IL 60173
Contact: Julie Selders Dir Marketing & Sales
Tel: 847-715-0453
Email: jselders@crystalequation.com
Website: www.crystalequation.com
IT, contract/consulting, direct placement, Software engineers, System Engineers, Testers, Project Management, Database, Administrators, Developers, Network Engineers. (Woman, estab 2006, empl 350, sales $51,000,000, cert: CPUC, WBENC, NWBOC)

9088 Cube Hub Inc.
600 N Commons Dr Ste 109
Aurora, IL 60504
Contact: Sunil Bakhshi Business Devel Mgr
Tel: 630-746-1239
Email: sunil@cube-hub.com
Website: www.cube-hub.com
Technology, Training, Staffing & Professional Services, Staffing/Recruiting services, Software Development, IT, Engineering, Professional, Marketing, Healthcare, Clinical, Scientific, Finance/Audit, Telecommunication, etc. (Minority, Woman, estab 2014, empl 28, sales $3,580,640, cert: NMSDC)

9089 DC McIssac Corp. dba FPC Arlington, Inc.
1400 Renaissance Dr Ste 100
Park Ridge, IL 60068
Contact: Cathy McIsaac President
Tel: 847-228-7205
Email: cathy@fpcarlington.com
Website: www.fpcarlington.com
Executive search & recruiting services. (Woman, estab 1959, empl 7, sales $800,000, cert: WBENC, NWBOC)

9090 Deegit, Inc.
1900 E Golf Rd. Ste 925
Schaumburg, IL 60173
Contact: Jim Dimitriou CEO
Tel: 847-330-1985
Email: jdimitriou@deegit.com
Website: www.deegit.com
Temp and Perm, project-based services(SOW) & Recruitment process outsourcing(RPO). (As-Ind, estab 1993, empl 150, sales $30,000,000, cert: State, NMSDC)

9091 DMD Consulting, LLC
230 S Clark St Ste 113
Chicago, IL 60604
Contact: Darlene Drab CEO
Tel: 312-809-6987
Email: darlene@dmdconsulting.net
Website: www.dmdconsulting.net
Permanent placement, interim resourcing, and co-sourcing, Audit & Compliance, Accounting and Finance, Tax and Information Technology. (Woman/AA, estab 2008, empl 20, sales $408,865, cert: State, City, WBENC)

9092 Elsko, Inc.
3601 Algonquin Rd, Ste 130
Rolling Meadows, IL 60008
Contact: Christina LaSalvia President
Tel: 847-691-2869
Email: clasalvia@elskoinc.com
Website: www.elskoinc.com/home
Executive staffing. (Minority, Woman, estab 1976, empl 8, sales $550,000, cert: WBENC)

9093 Furst Services
2580 Charles St
Rockford, IL 61125
Contact: Darlene Furst President
Tel: 815-997-1426
Email: darlene.furst@furststaff.com
Website: www.furststaff.com
Recruiting services. (Woman, estab 1971, empl 55, sales $25,000,000, cert: WBENC)

9094 Global Staffing Services, Inc.
925 S Main St
Rockford, IL 61101
Contact: Michele Caldwell CEO
Tel: 815-968-5797
Email: mec611@earthlink.net
Website: www.global-staffing.com
Staffing: flexible, contract & permanent placement, employment & background assessment. (Woman/AA, estab 2000, empl 4, sales , cert: NMSDC)

9095 Granthium Corporation
1111 Plaza Dr
Schaumburg, IL 60173
Contact: Salim Mehdi VP Finance & HR
Tel: 224-353-6427
Email: salimmehdi@granthium.com
Website: www.granthium.com
Staffing resources: IT, Project Mgmt, Legacy Modernization, Cloud Migration, Digital Transformation, Telecom, IOT, Retail & Pharmaceutical, Banking & Finance. (As-Ind, estab 2019, empl 3, sales $310,000, cert: NMSDC)

9096 Ignition Network dba Fieldday
400 W Erie
Chicago, IL 60654
Contact: Josh Miller Partner
Tel: 708-223-1191
Email: diversesupplier@fieldaymarketing.com
Website: www.fieldaymarketing.com
Recruit human resources professionals. (Woman, estab , empl 5, sales $753,000, cert: WBENC)

9097 IlinkResources Staffing
24402 W Lockport Rd Ste 226
Plainfield, IL 60544
Contact: VP Sales
Tel: 815-230-5256
Email: info@ilinkresources.com
Website: www.ilinkresources.com
Recruiting & staffing. (Woman, estab 2011, empl 6, sales , cert: WBENC)

9098 Instant Technology LLC
200 W Adams, Ste 1440
Chicago, IL 60606
Contact: Monica Lee Corporate Communications Mgr
Tel: 312-582-2600
Email: mlee@instanttechnology.com
Website: www.instanttechnology.com
Technical professionals, contract, contract-to-hire and permanent placement. (Woman, estab 2001, empl 150, sales $19,787,595, cert: State, City)

9099 JRA Consulting Services, Inc.
10225 W Higgins Rd
Rosemont, IL 60018
Contact: Ross Wolfson Talent Acquisition Mgr
Tel: 847-430-3682
Email: rwolfson@hrcontracting.com
Website: www.hrcontracting.com
Human resources staffing, permanent & contract positions. (Woman, estab 1997, empl 4, sales $2,000,000, cert: NWBOC)

9100 Kyyba, Inc.
900 National Pkwy Ste 155
Schaumburg, IL 60173
Contact: Mike Farrell Branch VP
Tel: 248-813-9665
Email: mikef@kyyba.com
Website: www.kyyba.com
Staffing solutions: IT, Engineering, Professional & Manufacturing. (As-Ind, estab 1998, empl 700, sales $47,979,683, cert: State)

PROFESSIONAL SERVICES: Staffing Services

9101 LBF Recruitment Strategies, LLC
330 N Clinton St Ste 606
Chicago, IL 60661
Contact: Lisa Frank CEO
Tel: 312-725-8544
Email: lisa@lbfstrategies.com
Website: www.LBFStrategies.com
Executive Search & Career Coaching. (Woman, estab 2012, empl 1, sales $112,000, cert: WBENC)

9102 Loftus & O'Meara Staffing Inc.
211 E Ontario Ste 1050
Chicago, IL 60611
Contact: Cindy Loftus Co-Owner
Tel: 312-944-2102
Email: cloftus@loftusomeara.com
Website: www.loftusomeara.com
Staffing: temporary, temp-to-hire & direct hire. (Woman, estab 1978, empl 7, sales $1,804,597, cert: WBENC)

9103 Mutual Target Associates, Inc.
7002 Hamilton Dr
Gurnee, IL 60031
Contact: Chandra Govind CEO
Tel: 847-855-0059
Email: cgovind@mtaincorporated.com
Website: www.mtaincorporated.com
Permanent placements, contract & contract to hire services. (As-Pac, estab 2005, empl 6, sales $750,000, cert: NMSDC)

9104 My Future Consulting, Inc.
15255 S 94th Ave Ste 500
Orland Park, IL 60462
Contact: Anthony Fletcher CEO
Tel: 708-428-6462
Email: anthony.fletcher@myfutureconsulting.com
Website: www.myfutureconsulting.com
Executive search & recruitment. (AA, estab 2012, empl 17, sales $420,000, cert: NMSDC)

9105 Myriad Technical Services
40 Shuman Blvd Ste 210
Naperville, IL 60563
Contact: Mihir Dash President
Tel: 630-369-6369
Email: jobs@myriadcorp.com
Website: www.myriadcorp.com
Staffing recruiting. (As-Pac, estab 1997, empl 40, sales $4,000,000, cert: State)

9106 Premier Systems, Inc
14489 John Humphrey Ste 202 Ste 202
Orland Park, IL 60462
Contact: Tariq Khan Acct Mgr
Tel: 708-349-9200
Email: tkhan@premiersystemsinc.com
Website: www.premiersystemsinc.com
IT consulting & staffing, project mgmt, systems programming & admin: IBM mainframe midrange, client server, PeopleSoft, SAP & Microsoft based systems. (As-Pac, estab 1993, empl 30, sales $2,713,000, cert: City, NMSDC)

9107 PSI Resources, LLC
2001 Butterfield Rd, Ste 1040
Downers Grove, IL 60515
Contact: Scott Fleckenstein Strategic Partnerships
Tel: 602-696-5727
Email: sfleckenstein@psiresources.com
Website: www.psiresources.com
Staffing & recruiting services. (Woman, estab 1993, empl 45, sales $1,411,062, cert: State, City, WBENC)

9108 Remedy Intelligent Staffing
211 53rd St
Moline, IL 61265
Contact: Dir of Sales
Tel: 309-762-7716
Email: kathys@remedystaff.com
Website: www.remedystaff.com
Staffing services: administrative, finance, accounting, customer service, IT, logistics & light industrial. (Woman, estab 1963, empl 8, sales $6,000,000,000, cert: State)

9109 Resource Technology Associates, LLC
10225 W Higgins Rd
Rosemont, IL 60018
Contact: Andrew Konik VP
Tel: 847-430-3667
Email: akonik@rta-inc.com
Website: www.rta-inc.com
Staffing support, outbound recruitment. (Woman, estab 1984, empl 22, sales $2,000,000, cert: NWBOC)

9110 RJSL Group
1956 W Erie St Unit 1E
Chicago, IL 60622
Contact: Richard Lee CEO
Tel: 312-282-4654
Email: richard@rjslgroup.com
Website: www.rjslgroup.com
Staffing and recruiting agency, IT & business resources. (As-Pac, estab 2006, empl 10, sales , cert: State, City, NMSDC)

9111 Shar Enterprises Inc dba HKA Staffing Services
800 Waukegan Rd Ste 200
Glenview, IL 60025
Contact: Kristin Haffner President
Tel: 847-998-9300
Email: khaffner@hkastaffing.com
Website: www.hkastaffing.com
Staffing services. (Woman, estab 1989, empl 45, sales $1,200,000, cert: WBENC)

9112 Smartdept. Inc.
39W581 Bealer Cir
Geneva, IL 60134
Contact: Michelle Pairitz Owner
Tel: 847-579-8202
Email: michelle@thesmartdept.com
Website: www.thesmartdept.com
Creative staffing resources: art directors, graphic designers, presentation specialists, copywriters, project managers, technical writers, etc. (Woman, estab 2001, empl 9, sales $250,000, cert: WBENC)

9113 Special Project Staffing by Salem, Inc.
Two Trans Am Plaza Dr
Oakbrook Terrace, IL 60181
Contact: Don Kraus Managing Dir
Tel: 630-932-7000
Email: dkraus@saleminc.com
Website: www.saleminc.com
Temporary staffing agency for both short term assignments and long term projects. (Woman, estab 1980, empl , sales , cert: WBENC)

9114 Sterling Engineering, Inc.
      Two Westbrook Corporate Center Ste 300
      Westchester, IL 60154
      Contact: Rama Kavaliauskas President
      Tel: 630-993-3433
      Email: rama@sterling-engineering.com
      Website: www.sterling-engineering.com
Engineering & technical staff augmentation solutions. (Woman, estab 1969, empl 75, sales $2,691,294, cert: WBENC)

9115 Superior Staffing
      PO Box 1551
      Melrose Park, IL 60161
      Contact: Heriberto Vale CEO
      Tel: 630-516-3505
      Email: hvale@superior-staffing.com
      Website: www.superior-staffing.com
Staffing: temp light industrial & clerical. (Hisp, estab 2001, empl 600, sales $15,000,000, cert: NMSDC)

9116 Synergy Global Systems Inc
      1580 S Milwaukee Ave, Ste # 425 Ste 425
      Libertyville, IL 60048
      Contact: Renu Suri Dir
      Tel: 630-768-2975
      Email: renusuri@synergygbl.com
      Website: www.synergygbl.com/
Staffing solutions & services, temporary staffing, permanent placement, career transition, talent development, outsourcing. (Woman/As-Ind, estab 2006, empl 1113, sales $434,765,600, cert: NMSDC, WBENC)

9117 The Wellington Group, Inc.
      317 S Third St
      Geneva, IL 60134
      Contact: Ann Anastasio President
      Tel: 630-262-2000
      Email: ann@wellingtongroupinc.com
      Website: www.wellingtongroupinc.com
Staffing services: contract, contract to hire. (Woman, estab 2002, empl 8, sales $10,791,915, cert: WBENC)

9118 Theophany Staffing, Inc.
      1601 Bond St Ste 106
      Naperville, IL 60563
      Contact: Tracy McLean President
      Tel: 630-983-5200
      Email: tracy@theophanystaffing.com
      Website: www.theophanystaffing.com
Staffing services. (Woman, estab 2001, empl 5, sales $1,000,000, cert: WBENC)

9119 US Surgitech Inc.
      551 Kimberly Dr
      Carol Sream, IL 60188
      Contact: Alyssa Cantore
      Tel: 630-456-4114
      Email: alyssa@ussurgitech.com
      Website: www.ussurgitech.com
Temporary & permanent staffing solutions. (As-Ind, estab 2003, empl 7, sales $1,206,246, cert: NMSDC)

Indiana

9120 Alpha Rae Personnel, Inc.
      347 W Berry St, Ste 700
      Fort Wayne, IN 46802
      Contact: Rae Pearson President
      Tel: 260-426-8227
      Email: businessoffice@alpha-rae.com
      Website: www.alpha-rae.com
Contract & temporary staffing, executive search, HR management & HR department outsourcing, employee training, electronics & embedded software contract engineering & manufacturing development. (Woman/AA, estab 1980, empl 400, sales , cert: State, WBENC)

9121 CFA Inc.
      2461 E. Main St.
      Plainfield, IN 46248
      Contact: Teresa Wade President
      Tel: 317-354-1102
      Email: twade@cfastaffing.com
      Website: www.cfastaffing.com
Temporary personnel & mgmt recruiting svcs. (Woman/AA, estab 1999, empl 5179, sales $131,000,000, cert: WBENC)

9122 DaMar Staffing Solutions
      8900 Keystone Crossing, Ste 1060
      Indianapolis, IN 46240
      Contact: Tiffany Thompson President
      Tel: 317-566-8320
      Email: tthompson@damarstaff.com
      Website: www.damarstaffing.com
Staffing: direct hire, temp-to-hire, temporary. (Woman/AA, estab 2003, empl 7, sales $622,423, cert: State, City, 8(a))

9123 Diverse Staffing Services
      6325 Digital Way, Ste #100
      Indianapolis, IN 46278
      Contact: Amber Slaughter Business Devel Mgr
      Tel: 317-813-8000
      Email: aslaughter@diversestaffing.com
      Website: www.diversestaffing.com
Recruiting & staffing solutions: information technology, engineering, life sciences, sales & business operations. (AA, estab 1999, empl 3000, sales , cert: State, NMSDC)

9124 First Call Temporary Services Inc.
      6960 Hillsdale Ct
      Indianapolis, IN 46250
      Contact: John Kulish Sales Mgr
      Tel: 317-596-3280
      Email: jkulish@fcqs.com
      Website: www.firstcallinc.com
Staffing services: temp and temp-hire. (Woman, estab 1991, empl 31, sales $18,000,000, cert: WBENC)

9125 MS Inspection & Logistics, Inc.
      710 E 64th St
      Indianapolis, IN 46220
      Contact: Nicky Benefiel CEO
      Tel: 855-447-3968
      Email: nicky.benefiel@ms-il.com
      Website: www.ms-il.com
Warehousing, contingent labor, staffing, temporary staffing, temporary to full time. (Woman/Hisp, estab 2001, empl 76, sales $45,000,000, cert: NMSDC)

9126 Smart IT Staffing, Inc.
       6500 Technology Center Dr Ste 300
       Indianapolis, IN 46278
       Contact: Bill Ryle Dir of Sales
       Tel: 513-530-0600
       Email: bryle@getsmarterit.com
       Website: www.getsmarterit.com
Information Technology Workforce Solutions. (Woman/AA, estab 2005, empl 480, sales $47,900,000, cert: NMSDC, WBENC)

9127 Specialized Staffing Solutions, LLC
       1001 E Jefferson
       South Bend, IN 46617
       Contact: Jacqueline Barton President
       Tel: 574-234-9944
       Email: jbarton@specializedstaffing.biz
       Website: www.specializedstaffing.biz
Temporary, permanant, technical & professional staffing, employment services, human resource mgmt, managed services. (Minority, Woman, estab 2002, empl 27, sales $17,000,000, cert: State, WBENC)

Kansas

9128 AdamsGabbert
       9200 Indian Creek Pkwy Ste 205
       Overland Park, KS 66210
       Contact: Kristen Winn Support Specialist
       Tel: 913-735-4390
       Email: kwinn@adamsgabbert.com
       Website: www.adamsgabbert.com
Staff Augmentation & Recruiting. (Woman, estab 1999, empl 30, sales $3,900,000, cert: State, City, WBENC)

9129 Choson Resource LLC
       1999 N Amidon, Ste 100B
       Wichita, KS 67203
       Contact: Kim Silcott President
       Tel: 316-729-0312
       Email: kim@chosonresource.com
       Website: www.Chosonresource.com
Aerospace engineering & staffing services for the air, defense & space industries. (Minority, Woman, estab 2010, empl 4, sales $4,254,100, cert: NMSDC)

9130 Staffing Kansas City Inc.
       9930 College Blvd
       Overland Park, KS 66210
       Contact: Michelle Hays Sales Exec
       Tel: 913-663-5627
       Email: michelle@staffingkc.com
       Website: www.staffingkc.com
Temporary & permanent employment placement. (Woman, estab 1998, empl 5, sales $2,283,865, cert: State)

Kentucky

9131 Astute Sourcing, LLC
       10200 Forest Green Blvd Ste 112
       Louisville, KY 40223
       Contact: Dorothy Abernathy Exec Asst
       Tel: 502-499-9440
       Email: info@tktandassociates.com
       Website: www.astutesourcing.com
Staffing services: telecommunications, healthcare, government, financial services, utilities, manufacturing and supply/chain logistics, contingent staffing, direct hire, permanent staffing, rapid deployment. (Woman/AA, estab 2012, empl 7, sales $1,683,311, cert: NMSDC, WBENC)

9132 J.Y. Legner Associates, Inc.
       800 W Market St, Ste 102
       Louisville, KY 40202
       Contact: Josephine Legner CEO
       Tel: 502-585-9000
       Email: jlegner@jyla.com
       Website: www.jyla.com
Staffing & HR mgmt, temporary staffing, long-term employee leasing. (Woman/AA, estab 1999, empl 70, sales $1,000,000, cert: NMSDC)

9133 QP1, Inc. dba Luttrell Staffing Group
       1435 Campbell Ln
       Bowling Green, KY 42104
       Contact: Monica Shuffett VP
       Tel: 270-250-3446
       Email: mshuffett@lstaff.com
       Website: www.lstaff.com
Manufacturing & industrial employment agency, exceptional administrative, call center, technical and professional placement services. (Woman, estab 1977, empl 185, sales $152,475,221, cert: WBENC)

Louisiana

9134 Delta Personnel, Inc.
       2709 L & A Rd
       Metairie, LA 70001
       Contact: Ingrid Delahoussaye Owner
       Tel: 504-833-5200
       Email: tlawrence@deltapersonnel.com
       Website: www.deltapersonnel.com/
Staffing & payroll payroll services. (Minority, Woman, estab 1968, empl 6, sales $3,000,000, cert: State, NMSDC, WBENC)

9135 Frazee Recruiting Consultants, Inc.
       2351 Energy Dr, Ste 1100
       Baton Rouge, LA 70808
       Contact: Chris Bien Business Dev
       Tel: 225-231-7880
       Email: sales@frazeerecruit.com
       Website: www.frazeerecruit.com
Professional staffing, direct hire search, contract/temporary. (Woman, estab 1998, empl 150, sales $6,000,000, cert: WBENC)

9136 Jean Simpson Personnel Services, Inc.
       1318 Shreveport-Barksdale Hwy
       Shreveport, LA 71105
       Contact: Angel Scott Admin Asst
       Tel: 318-869-3494
       Email: ascott@jeansimpson.com
       Website: www.jeansimpson.com
Temporary & full-time staffing: clerical, industrial & professional. (Woman, estab 1974, empl 33, sales , cert: WBENC)

9137 Preferred Standards, LLC
       654 Lobdell Ave
       Baton Rouge, LA 70806
       Contact: Derrick Toussaint CEO
       Tel: 225-924-9552
       Email: dtoussaint@pstandards.net
       Website: www.pstandards.org
Professional staffing, recruiting & payroll services. (AA, estab 2013, empl 5, sales $1,312,529, cert: NMSDC)

PROFESSIONAL SERVICES: Staffing Services

9138 SureTemps LLC
      1631 Elysian Fields Ave
      New Orleans, LA 70117
      Contact: Maxine A. President
      Tel: 504-947-3353
      Email: sunsoundconcerts@yahoo.com
      Website: www.suretemps.biz
Personnel staffing: labors, data entry clerks, custodial services, full food services & supervisors/managers for long or short term basis. (AA, estab 2011, empl 500, sales , cert: City)

9139 Topp Knotch Personnel, Inc.
      401 Whitney Ave Ste 312
      Gretna, LA 70056
      Contact: Diedria Joseph CEO
      Tel: 866-744-2974
      Email: diedria@tkpsi.com
      Website: www.tkpsi.com
Staffing svcs: admin, clerical, customer service, accounting, marketing, computer technology. (Woman/AA, estab , empl , sales $4,055,182, cert: City, WBENC)

9140 Universal Personnel, LLC
      1100 Poydras St Ste 1300
      New Orleans, LA 70163
      Contact: Michele Vignes President
      Tel: 504-561-5627
      Email: michelev@universal-personnel.com
      Website: www.universal-personnel.com
Technical staffing, career & contract job placement: engineering, drafting, architecture & information technology, professional, administrative & clerical. (Woman, estab 1980, empl 650, sales $57,118,011, cert: WBENC)

Massachusetts

9141 Aries Group, Inc.
      500 Cummings Center Ste 1750
      Beverly, MA 01915
      Contact: Frances Dichner President
      Tel: 877-806-7977
      Email: fran@ariesgroupinc.com
      Website: www.ariesgroupinc.com
Contract & permanent placement staffing services. (Woman, estab 2000, empl 10, sales $7,732,415, cert: WBENC)

9142 East Coast Staffing Solutions
      651 Orchard St Ste 307
      New Bedford, MA 02744
      Contact: Randy Silva Business Devel
      Tel: 508-990-7670
      Email: randy@eastcoaststaffingsolutions.com
      Website: www.eastcoaststaffingsolutions.com
Staffing, direct hires, temporary placements & contractual assignments. (AA, estab 2009, empl 5, sales $105,650,836, cert: State)

9143 Griffin Staffing Network, LLC
      1145 Main St Ste 508
      Springfield, MA 01103
      Contact: Michelle O'Meara
      Tel: 413-788-0751
      Email: momeara@griffinstaffingnetwork.com
      Website: www.griffinstaffingnetwork.com
Staffing services. (Woman/AA, estab 2013, empl 2, sales , cert: State)

9144 Hollister Staffing, Inc.
      75 State St, 9th Fl
      Boston, MA 02109
      Contact: Kip Hollister Founder & CEO
      Tel: 617-654-0200
      Email: kip@hollisterstaff.com
      Website: www.hollisterstaff.com
Recruiting services: direct hire, contract & contract-to-hire. (Woman, estab 1988, empl 70, sales $31,100,000, cert: WBENC)

9145 John Leonard Employment Services, Inc.
      75 Federal St, Ste 1120
      Boston, MA 02110
      Contact: Linda Poldoian CEO
      Tel: 617-348-2607
      Email: Info@johnleonard.com
      Website: www.johnleonard.com
Temporary employment: office support personnel. (Woman, estab 1969, empl 18, sales $7,009,497, cert: State, City, WBENC)

9146 KNF&T Staffing Resources
      3 Post Office Square
      Boston, MA 02109
      Contact: Joanna DiTrapano Dir of Marketing
      Tel: 617-574-8200
      Email: jditrapano@knft.com
      Website: www.knft.com
Staffing services: administrative, accounting, finance & healthcare personnel. (Woman, estab 1983, empl , sales $14,000,000, cert: State, WBENC)

9147 S & S Staffing, LLC
      50 Lake Ave
      Worcester, MA 01604
      Contact: Karen DeMichele President
      Tel: 508-799-7171
      Email: karen@savvystaffing.com
      Website: www.savvystaffing.com
Staffing solutions: long or short term, temporary & permanent. (Woman, estab 2006, empl 15, sales $12,000,000, cert: State)

9148 Snelling Staffing Services
      3 Courthouse Lane Ste 2
      Chelmsford, MA 01824
      Contact: Bernice Kaiser Owner/General Mgr
      Tel: 978-970-3434
      Email: bernice@snelling-ma.com
      Website: www.snelling.com/chelmsford
Staffing: engineering, administrative, finance & accounting, sales & marketing, manufacturing direct hire/temp-to-hire/contract labor. (Woman, estab 1988, empl 6, sales $2,000,000, cert: WBENC)

9149 Staffing Solutions, Inc.
      225 Friend St
      Boston, MA 02114
      Contact: Earl Tate CEO
      Tel: 617-248-0048
      Email: earl@staffingww.com
      Website: www.staffingsolutionsworldwide.com
Temporary & permanent staffing service. (Woman/AA, estab 1996, empl 1, sales $4,650,000, cert: WBENC)

PROFESSIONAL SERVICES: Staffing Services

9150 The Resource Connection, Inc.
161 S Main St Ste 300
Middleton, MA 01949
Contact: President
Tel: 978-777-9333
Email: staff@resource-connection.com
Website: www.resource-connection.com
Staffing services: temporary, temp-to-hire, & direct placement of administrative, clerical & light industrial personnel. (Woman, estab 1987, empl 9, sales $8,300,000, cert: State, City, WBENC)

9151 The Vesume Group, LLC
21 High St Ste 210A
North Andover, MA 01845
Contact: Jori Blumsack COO
Tel: 978-687-6000
Email: jori@thevesumegroup.com
Website: www.thevesumegroup.com
Staffing, contract, contract-to-hire & permanent placement of IT, Engineering, Manufacturing, Accounting/Finance & Call Center professionals. (Woman, estab 2009, empl 9, sales $3,663,666, cert: WBENC)

9152 Total Technical Services, Inc.
225 Wyman St
Waltham, MA 02451
Contact: Tim Hovey VP
Tel: 800-776-0562
Email: thovey@total-tech.com
Website: www.total-tech.com
Temporary, contract & permanent staffing svcs, on-site managed vendor program & payroll svcs. (AA, Hisp, estab 1992, empl 300, sales , cert: NMSDC)

9153 United Personnel Services
289 Bridge St
Springfield, MA 01103
Contact: Jennifer Brown VP Business Dev
Tel: 413-314-6073
Email: jbrown@unitedpersonnel.com
Website: www.unitedpersonnel.com
Staffing: temporary, temp-to-hire & full-time placements. (Woman, estab 1984, empl 39, sales $27,000,000, cert: State, WBENC)

Maryland

9154 1st Choice, LLC
8121 Georgia Ave Ste 700
Silver Spring, MD 20910
Contact: Bridgette Cooper
Tel: 301-728-6644
Email: bcooper@1stchoicegov.com
Website: www.1stchoice
Program Management, Consulting & Staff Augmentation. (Woman/AA, estab 2000, empl 250, sales $5,000,000, cert: State, NMSDC, WBENC, SDB)

9155 All-Pro Placement Service, Inc.
116 Old Padonia Rd, Ste D
Cockeysville, MD 21030
Contact: Jennifer Quinn VP
Tel: 410-308-9050
Email: jennifer@allproplacement.com
Website: www.allproplacement.com
Staffing: temp, temp-to-perm & direct hire permanent placements, clerical, executive level, warehousing. (Woman, estab 2002, empl 8, sales $4,364,791, cert: State, City)

9156 Beacon Staffing Alternatives
16-2 S Philadelphia Blvd
Aberdeen, MD 21001
Contact: Sheryl Kohl President
Tel: 410-297-6600
Email: sheryl@beaconstaffing.com
Website: www.Beaconstaffing.com
Staffing services. (Woman, estab 1999, empl 300, sales $4,441,779, cert: State, WBENC)

9157 BizyBee Professional Staffing & Biz'Ness Solutions
8181 Professional Place ste 205
Hyattsville, MD 20785
Contact: Danae Hubbard President
Tel: 301-459-1233
Email: bzbpro@yahoo.com
Website: www.bzbpro.com
Temporary staffing, employment, recruitment, staff augmentation & HR that services. (Woman/AA, estab 2011, empl 5, sales $500,000, cert: State, 8(a))

9158 Contemporaries, Inc.
1010 Wayne Ave, Ste 400
Silver Spring, MD 20910
Contact: Erin Allen President
Tel: 301-775-4392
Email:
Website: www.contemps.com
Administrative temporary & permanent placement services. (Woman, estab 1991, empl 6, sales $1,021,514, cert: WBENC)

9159 Crews Control Inc
11820 West Market Place Ste L
Fulton, MD 20759
Contact: Laura A. Monaco VP Operations
Tel: 301-604-1200
Email: Laura@crewscontrol.com
Website: www.crewscontrol.com
Recruitment, staffing & payroll services. (Woman, estab 1988, empl 12, sales , cert: WBENC)

9160 Crosby Corporation
14405 Laurel Place, Ste 201
Laurel, MD 20707
Contact: Howard Petty President
Tel: 301-585-3105
Email: hpetty@crosbycorp.com
Website: www.crosbycorp.com
Human capital solutions: technical staff augmentation, direct placement services, outsourced projects, educational services & comprehensive workforce management solutions. (AA, estab 2001, empl 100, sales $4,000,000, cert: City, 8(a))

9161 Eigennet LLC
13508 Wisteria Dr
Germantown, MD 20874
Contact: Godfrey Pereira President
Tel: 240-476-5094
Email: gpereira@eigennet.com
Website: www.eigennet.com
IT staffing (Nat Ame, estab 2016, empl 25, sales , cert: State, NMSDC)

PROFESSIONAL SERVICES: Staffing Services

9162 Federal Staffing Resources LLC
2200 Somerville Rd Ste 300
Annapolis, MD 21401
Contact: Tracy Balazs CEO
Tel: 410-990-0795
Email: tbalazs@fsrpeople.com
Website: www.fsrpeople.com
Workforce solutions & integrative business solutions, recruitment & staffing. (Minority, Woman, estab 2004, empl 266, sales $31,325,000, cert: State, NMSDC, WBENC)

9163 Infojini Inc.
10015 Old Columbia Rd Ste B 215
Columbia, MD 21046
Contact: Sandeep Harjani Dir
Tel: 443-257-0086
Email: commercialrfi@infojiniconsulting.com
Website: www.infojiniconsulting.com/
Recruitment, training, assessment, outsourcing & consulting services, temporary & permanent positions. (As-Pac, estab 2006, empl 700, sales $54,000,000, cert: NMSDC)

9164 Innova Project Services LLC
1150 Ripley St, Ste 1616
Silver Spring, MD 20910
Contact: Molly Donaldson CEO
Tel: 301-275-7262
Email: mdonaldson@innovaprojectservices.com
Website: www.innovaprojectservices.com/
Project controls services and staffing. (Woman, estab 2021, empl 5, sales , cert: WBENC)

9165 nTech Solutions, Inc.
9256 Bendix Road Ste 208
Columbia, MD 21045
Contact: Sridhar Kunadi CEO
Tel: 877-689-8448
Email: sridhar@ntechsol.com
Website: www.ntechsol.com
IT staffing/consulting services. (As-Pac, estab 2012, empl 45, sales , cert: State, NMSDC)

9166 PMC Group Inc dba Piper Staffing
8117 Harford Rd, Ste D
Baltimore, MD 21234
Contact: Kimberley West President
Tel: 410-286-1874
Email: kimberley@pmcgrpinc.com
Website: www.piperstaffing.com
Multiple & diverse staffing solutions. (Woman/AA, estab 2010, empl 104, sales $1,669,345, cert: State)

9167 PositivePsyche.Biz Corp.
401 E Pratt St, Ste 2432
Baltimore, MD 21202
Contact: Enrique Ruiz President
Tel: 410-844-5060
Email: enrique@positivepsyche.biz
Website: www.positivepsyche.biz
Staff augmentation services. (Hisp, estab , empl 150, sales $5,400,000, cert: 8(a))

9168 The BOSS Group
4350 East West Hwy, Ste 307
Bethesda, MD 20814
Contact: Truelove, Charisse Owner
Tel: 301-802-3672
Email: linda@thebossgroup.com
Website: www.thebossgroup.com
Human capital solutions, source, evaluate & place exclusive creative, marketing, communications & interactive talent. (Woman, estab 0, empl , sales , cert: WBENC)

9169 The HR Source
8181 Professional Place Ste 120
Landover, MD 20785
Contact: Patricia Hall Jaynes CEO
Tel: 301-459-3133
Email: pathj@thehrsource.com
Website: www.thehrsource.com
Human resources staffing & consulting services, interim/temporary & permanent staffing services, outplacement & payroll services, administrative interim/temporary & permanent staffing services. (Woman/AA, estab 1994, empl 5, sales $2,894,265, cert: State, NMSDC, WBENC)

Michigan

9170 Abacus Service Corporation
25925 Telegraph Rd Ste 206
Southfield, MI 48033
Contact: April Szlaga VP
Tel: 248-522-8005
Email: april@abacusservice.com
Website: www.abacusservice.com
Staff augmentation, contract, temporary & permanent placement services. (Woman/As-Ind, estab 2004, empl 325, sales $65,000,000,000, cert: NMSDC, WBENC)

9171 Accura Services, LLC
51470 Oro Dr
Shelby Township, MI 48315
Contact: Jenifer Cugliari Member
Tel: 586-884-4417
Email: jen@accuraservicesllc.com
Website: www.accuraservicesllc.com
Direct & contract staffing services specializing in Engineering, Technical & Professional areas. (Woman, estab 2015, empl 3, sales , cert: WBENC)

9172 Aegis Group Search Consultants, LLC
1358 Village Dr
Detroit, MI 48207
Contact: John Green President
Tel: 248-344-1450
Email: jgreen@aegis-group.com
Website: www.aegis-group.com
Executive search services. (AA, estab 1991, empl 4, sales $700,000, cert: NMSDC)

9173 Arps International LLC
3003 Silver Spring Dr
Ann Arbor, MI 48103
Contact: Arun Nikore VP
Tel: 734-945-3000
Email: sales@arpsint.com
Website: www.arpsint.com
Executive recruiting services: engineering, information technology, manufacturing & operations, supply chain. (Woman/As-Ind, estab 2002, empl 2, sales $106,127, cert: NMSDC)

PROFESSIONAL SERVICES: Staffing Services

9174 Blake Group LLC
      30986 Stoneridge Dr Ste 14205
      Wixom, MI 48393
      Contact: Jim Blake Sr Exec VP
      Tel: 248-238-5776
      Email: james@blakegroupllc.com
      Website: www.blakegrouptechnicalstaffing.com
Information Technology professional executive staffing. (Woman/AA, estab 2010, empl 7, sales , cert: NMSDC)

9175 Boston Contemporaries, Inc.
      55 Court St Ste 330
      Boston, MI 02108
      Contact: Ron Porter Sr Acct Mgr
      Tel: 617-723-9797
      Email: ron@bostoncontemporaries.com
      Website: www.bostoncontemporaries.com
Staffing temporary and temp to hire Administrative Support, Accounting & Finance, and IT Support professionals. (Woman, estab 1998, empl 20, sales $1,150,000, cert: State)

9176 CIMA Consulting Group
      901 Tower Dr, Ste 420
      Troy, MI 48098
      Contact: Scott Foreman CFO
      Tel: 586-226-2000
      Email: sforeman@cimacg.com
      Website: www.cimacg.com
Talent Management Solutions. (Woman/Hisp, estab 2016, empl 6, sales $260,000, cert: NMSDC, WBENC)

9177 Community Based Staffing
      4369 Seebaldt
      Detroit, MI 48204
      Contact: David Cross President
      Tel: 313-744-5771
      Email: david.cross@cb-staffing.com
      Website: www.cb-staffing.com
Direct hire & staffing: machine operators, production associates, welders, quality inspectors, press operators. (AA, estab 2016, empl 50, sales , cert: NMSDC)

9178 CrossFire Group LLC
      691 N Squirrel Rd Ste 118
      Auburn Hills, MI 48326
      Contact: Deborah Schneider CEO
      Tel: 866-839-2600
      Email: dschneider@xfiregroup.com
      Website: www.xfiregroup.com
Recruiting, Staffing, Business Process Outsourcnig, professional temporary & contract staffing, permanent placement, vendor management &payroll services to large and medium size firms. (Woman, estab 2002, empl 1500, sales $10,000,000, cert: WBENC)

9179 Crystal Employment Services, LLC
      32355 Howard St
      Madison Heights, MI 48071
      Contact: Michael Stanley Partner
      Tel: 248-588-9540
      Email: mstanley@crystaleng.com
      Website: www.crystaleng.com
Staffing services. (Hisp, estab 2004, empl 300, sales , cert: NMSDC)

9180 Entech Staffing Solutions
      1800 Crooks Road
      Troy, MI 48084
      Contact: Colleen Myers Dir of Sales & Recruiting
      Tel: 248-528-1444
      Email: cmyers@teamentech.com
      Website: www.teamentech.com
Temporary staffing: administrative, technical, medical & light industrial positions, short term, long term & permanent employment. (Woman, estab , empl , sales $11,500,000, cert: WBENC)

9181 Galaxy Software Solutions, Inc.
      5820 N Lilley Rd, Ste 8
      Canton, MI 48187
      Contact: Dileep Tiwari VP
      Tel: 734-717-7969
      Email: dileep@galaxy-soft.com
      Website: www.galaxy-soft.com
Staffing highly skilled candidates/consultants on contract and on a full-time basis. (Minority, Woman, estab 2004, empl 251, sales $24,000,000, cert: WBENC)

9182 Gonzalez Production Systems
      1670 Highwood East
      Pontiac, MI 48340
      Contact: Bill Kelly New Business Dev
      Tel: 248-884-0315
      Email: bkelly@gonzales-group.com
      Website: www.gonzalez-group.com
Contract Placement, Contract to Direct, Direct Placement, Managed Services. (Hisp, estab 1975, empl 800, sales $50,000,000, cert: NMSDC)

9183 G-TECH Services, Inc.
      17101 Michigan Ave
      Dearborn, MI 48126
      Contact: Shelby Medina Dir of Business Dev
      Tel: 313-425-3666
      Email: smedina@gogtech.com
      Website: www.gogtech.com
Contract & direct hire staffing solutions, engineering/technical support; information technology; finance/accounting; scientific; administration/clerical; co-employment training & payroll services. (Woman, estab 1986, empl 650, sales $56,000,000, cert: WBENC)

9184 Harvard Resource Group
      210 W Big Beaver Rd Ste 310
      Troy, MI 48084
      Contact: Mark Hicks VP
      Tel: 248-528-1110
      Email: mhicks@hrgus.com
      Website: www.harvardresourcegroup.com
Staffing: permanent, contract, temp to perm, professional & organizational dev, mgmt & leadership dev, wireless dev & deployment svcs. (Nat Ame, estab 2001, empl 6, sales $3,000,000, cert: NMSDC)

9185 Hattrick Professional Staffing
      3228 Norton Lawn
      Rochester Hills, MI 48307
      Contact: Julie Campbell Owner
      Tel: 248-289-6241
      Email: julie.campbell@hattrick-staffing.com
      Website: www.hattrick-staffing.com
Staffing, Direct Hire, Contract or Temp to hire placements: Engineering, Design, Finance/Accounting, IT, Professional, Technical placements & Executive positions. (Woman, estab 2015, empl 1, sales , cert: WBENC)

PROFESSIONAL SERVICES: Staffing Services

9186 Human Capital Staffing LLC
6001 N Adams Rd, Ste 208
Bloomfield Hills, MI 48304
Contact: Mary Adams President
Tel: 248-593-1950
Email: madams@hcsteam.com
Website: www.hcsteam.com
Staffing services. (Woman/Nat-Ame, estab 0, empl 10, sales , cert: NMSDC, WBENC)

9187 Industry Specific Solutions LLC
24901 Northwestern Hwy Ste 400
Southfield, MI 48075
Contact: Earl Newman President
Tel: 248-356-3400
Email: enewman@isscompanies.com
Website: www.isscompanies.com
Full-service staffing in logistics, manufacturing, accounting & finance, education, technology & office administration. (AA, estab 2006, empl 150, sales $122,000, cert: NMSDC)

9188 Inteligente Solutions, Inc.
17199 N Laurel Park Dr Ste 321
Livonia, MI 48152
Contact: Kathy DeCaires VP
Tel: 734-338-8970
Email: kdecaires@igsstaff.com
Website: www.igsstaff.com
Staffing svcs; general labor & light industrial; long term to permanent, clerical & admin support staffing. (Hisp, estab 1993, empl 500, sales , cert: NMSDC)

9189 K&A Staffing, LLC
38700 Van Dyke Rd. Ste 150
Sterling Heights, MI 48312
Contact: Justin Tappero COO
Tel: 586-806-6614
Email: jtappero@knaresourcegroup.com
Website: www.knaresourcegroup.com
Staffing services. (As-Ind, estab 2011, empl 16, sales , cert: NMSDC)

9190 Linked, LLC
6633 18 Mile Rd
Sterling Heights, MI 48314
Contact: Marie Khoury President
Tel: 586-231-1234
Email: marie.khoury@linkedps.com
Website: www.linkedps.com
Staffing, candidate search, recruitment, contract & direct placement services. (Woman, estab 2012, empl 4, sales , cert: WBENC)

9191 MCM Staffing, LLC
415 W 11 Mile Rd
Madison Heights, MI 48076
Contact: Courtney Morales Hofmann President
Tel: 248-436-2616
Email: courtney@mcmstaffing.com
Website: www.mcmstaffing.com
Staffing services. (Minority, Woman, estab 2011, empl 950, sales $19,500,000, cert: NMSDC, WBENC)

9192 Michigan Staffing
29400 Van Dyke Ste 308
Warren, MI 48093
Contact: Frances Lucido VP
Tel: 586-506-7524
Email: francy@michiganstaffing.com
Website: www.michiganstaffing.com
Temporary, contract & direct staffing services: administrative, customer service, light industrial, technical, professional & skilled trades. (Woman, estab 2002, empl 75, sales , cert: WBENC)

9193 Moreno Services LLC
5140 State St #103
Saginaw, MI 48603
Contact: Yvette Serrato CEO
Tel: 989-401-3996
Email: yvette@morenoservices.com
Website: www.morenoservices.com
Professional recruiting, on site services, and indirect and direct placements, temporary staffing. (Hisp, estab 2010, empl 4, sales $12,564,679, cert: NMSDC)

9194 National Career Group
1745 Hamilton Rd
Okemos, MI 48864
Contact: Nadia Sellers CEO
Tel: 517-706-0111
Email: nadia@nationalcareergroup.com
Website: www.nationalcareergroup.com
Permanent staffing & Human Relations Training. (Woman/AA, estab 1997, empl 10, sales $700,000, cert: WBENC)

9195 NexTech Professional Services
25200 Telegraph Rd. Ste 110
Southfield, MI 48033
Contact: Rosanne Davis President
Tel: 248-416-1718
Email: rosanne.davis@nextechps.com
Website: www.nextechps.com
Contract & permanent placement: engineering, technology, finance & executive recruiting. (As-Pac, estab 1994, empl 10, sales $2,600,000, cert: NMSDC)

9196 OpTech, LLC
5440 Corporate Dr
Troy, MI 48098
Contact: Ronia Kruse CEO
Tel: 313-962-9000
Email: info@optechus.com
Website: www.optechus.com
Talent, Business consulting, business strategy, Information Technology, Engineering, Healthcare, Financial, Assessments, Marketing, Training, Technical Services, Business Support, Staffing. (Woman, estab 1999, empl 250, sales $49,032,035, cert: WBENC)

9197 PDS Services, LLC
37633 Pembroke
Livonia, MI 48152
Contact: Derek Dyer President
Tel: 734-953-3300
Email: derek@pdsstaffing.com
Website: www.pdsstaffing.com
Staffing services: contract, contract to hire & permanent placements. (AA, estab 2005, empl 260, sales $9,000,000, cert: NMSDC)

9198 Personnel Unlimited Inc.
      29400 Van Dyke Ave
      Warren, MI 48093
      Contact: Frances Lucido President
      Tel: 586-751-5608
      Email: fllucido@personnel-unlimited.com
      Website: www.personnel-unlimited.com
Temporary & Contract Staffing for Admin, Clerical, Tech/Professional. (Woman, estab 2008, empl 7, sales $2,462,679, cert: WBENC)

9199 Populus Group, LLC
      3001 W Big Beaver Rd Ste 400
      Troy, MI 48084
      Contact: Danielle Hein Sr Proposal Mgr
      Tel: 248-712-7900
      Email: dhein@populusgroup.com
      Website: www.PopulusGroup.com
Temporary staffing services. Professional Payrolling Services, Independent Contractor Engagement Services/1099 Compliance, Immigration Employment Solutions, Managed Services, Strategic Partnerships, Diverse Talent Management Solutions. (Hisp, estab 2002, empl 270, sales $577,322,374, cert: NMSDC)

9200 Premier Automation Contractors
      9015 Davison Rd
      Davison, MI 48423
      Contact: Lisa VanWyk Engineering Accts Dir
      Tel: 248-421-7360
      Email: lisa@premierac.com
      Website: www.premierac.com
Direct & contract hire staffing for skilled trades. (Woman, estab 2008, empl 200, sales $12,000,000, cert: WBENC)

9201 Premier Staff Services
      16250 Northland Dr Ste 224
      Southfield, MI 48075
      Contact: Michael Garcia Acct Mgr
      Tel: 248-809-9675
      Email: michael.garcia.rep@gmail.com
      Website: www.premierstaffservices.net
Contract staffing, temporary help & direct placement of clerical, administrative, financial, janitorial, maintenance, engineering & IT human resources. (AA, estab 2011, empl 24, sales $9,287,194, cert: NMSDC, 8(a))

9202 Reliance One, Inc.
      1700 Harmon Rd Ste One
      Auburn Hills, MI 48326
      Contact: Chad Toms VP Sales
      Tel: 248-922-4500
      Email: ctoms@reliance-one.com
      Website: www.reliance-one.com
Staffing, direct & contract, employment, payroll. (Hisp, estab 1998, empl 700, sales , cert: NMSDC)

9203 Scope Services, Inc.
      2095 Niles Rd
      St. Joseph, MI 49085
      Contact: Trish Melcher President
      Tel: 269-982-2888
      Email: tmmelcher@scope-services.com
      Website: www.scope-services.com
Human capital management, contract &project staffing & managed staffing/consulting, executive search, contingency direct hire placement, career consulting & outplacement services. (Woman, estab 1965, empl 569, sales $58,000,000, cert: WBENC)

9204 Smart Folks, Inc.
      29445 Beck Rd, Ste 202N
      Wixom, MI 48393
      Contact: Lalitha Nandyala President
      Tel: 313-671-5767
      Email: lalitha@smartfolksinc.com
      Website: www.smartfolksinc.com
Provide flexible and permanent staffing solutions. (Woman/As-Ind, estab 2011, empl 50, sales $483,035,949, cert: NMSDC, CPUC, WBENC)

9205 Snelling Personnel Services
      2265 Livernois
      Troy, MI 48083
      Contact: Larry Wright CEO
      Tel: 248-362-5090
      Email: ldwright@snellingmetrodetroit.com
      Website: www.snellingmetrodetroit.com
Temporary, temporary-to-hire & permanent placements: clerical, medical, technical, professional, engineering & information technology. (Woman/AA, estab 1987, empl 25, sales , cert: WBENC)

9206 Staffing Source Personnel dba DriverSource
      15340 Michigan Ave
      Dearborn, MI 48126
      Contact: David J. Olshansky Co-Founder
      Tel: 313-624-9500
      Email: dolshansky@driversource.net
      Website: www.driversource.net
Commercial driver leasing & recruiting services. (Woman, estab 1998, empl 350, sales , cert: WBENC)

9207 The Targa Group
      33228 W 12 Mile Rd Ste 108
      Farmington Hills, MI 48334
      Contact: Rob Ganesan President
      Tel: 248-514-2295
      Email: rganesan@thetargagroup.com
      Website: www.thetargagroup.clom
Staffing, Process Improvement & Information Technology. (As-Pac, estab 2009, empl 6, sales $250,000, cert: NMSDC)

9208 Therapy Staff, LLC
      801 W Ann Arbor Trail, Ste 200
      Pylmouth, MI 48170
      Contact: William Klabo RVP
      Tel: 877-366-2580
      Email: wklabo@therapystaff.com
      Website: www.Therapystaff.com
Therapist recruiting and staffing. (As-Ind, estab 2000, empl 53, sales $15,400,000, cert: NMSDC)

9209 Trialon Corporation
      1477 Walli Strasse Blvd
      Burton, MI 48509
      Contact: Robert Feys Sales Engineer
      Tel: 810-742-8500
      Email: rfeys@trialon.com
      Website: www.trialon.com
Technical Staffing and Engineering & Test Services to the Automotive, Aerospace, Military, Consumer Electronics, Medical, and Telecommunications Industries. (Woman, estab 1982, empl 750, sales $25,050,000, cert: WBENC)

PROFESSIONAL SERVICES: Staffing Services

9210 Trusted Link Staffing Services LLC
12966 Brixham Dr
Warren, MI 48088
Contact: Tochukwu (Tochi) Anyadibe Dir
Tel: 248-403-0689
Email: admin@trustedlinkstaffingservices.com
Website: www.tl-staffing.com
Hospital staffing services, Care facility staffing services, Registered Nurse, Licensed Practical Nurse LPN / LVN Travel contracts, Certified Nurse Assistant CNA Travel contracts. (AA, estab 2022, empl 42, sales , cert: WBENC)

9211 Venator Staffing
888 W Big Beaver Rd, Ste 450
Troy, MI 48084
Contact: Michael Teats Sales Mgr
Tel: 248-269-0000
Email: michael@venatornet.com
Website: www.venatornet.com
Accounting, finance & administrative staffing: temp & permanent placement. (As-Pac, estab 2001, empl 25, sales $2,500,000, cert: NMSDC)

9212 VETBUILT Services, Inc.
1927 Rosa Parks Blvd Ste 125
Detroit, MI 48216
Contact: Hector Malacara CEO
Tel: 989-493-1240
Email: hmalacara@vetbuilt.com
Website: www.vetbuiltservices.com
Staffing services. (Hisp, estab 2013, empl 300, sales $6,853,851, cert: NMSDC)

Minnesota

9213 Avenue Staffing Inc.
7000-57th Ave N Ste 120
Minneapolis, MN 55428
Contact: Chuck Okitikpi President
Tel: 763-537-6104
Email: chuck@avenuestaffing.com
Website: www.Avenuestaffing.com
Temporary & permanent employment. (AA, estab 2006, empl 48, sales $1,200,000, cert: NMSDC)

9214 Billinda Group LLC
4651 Nicols Rd, Ste 106-108
Eagan, MN 55122
Contact: Bill Fitch CEO
Tel: 651-379-5082
Email: bill@techpoweres.com
Website: www.Techpoweres.com
Contract, contract to permanent & direct placement. (Woman, estab 2005, empl 28, sales $3,700,000, cert: WBENC)

9215 Celarity
8120 Penn Ave Ste 220
Minneapolis, MN 55431
Contact: Marlene Phipps President
Tel: 952-941-0022
Email: marlene@celarity.com
Website: www.celarity.com
Contract, temporary recruiting, staffing, full-time direct hires. (Woman, estab 1992, empl 110, sales $7,092,546, cert: WBENC)

9216 Dahl Consulting, Inc.
418 County Rd D East
St. Paul, MN 55117
Contact: Corey Johnson CEO
Tel: 651-772-9225
Email: corey@dahlconsulting.com
Website: www.dahlconsulting.com
Vendor management services, staff augmentation, permanent search. (Woman, estab 1993, empl 808, sales $87,902,216, cert: WBENC)

9217 Doherty Staffing Solutions, Inc.
7645 Metro Blvd
Edina, MN 55439
Contact: David Tuenge Program Mgr
Tel: 952-818-3251
Email: dtuenge@dohertystaffing.com
Website: www.dohertystaffing.com
Contract & temporary staffing. (Woman, estab 1980, empl 151, sales $400,337,900, cert: WBENC)

9218 Finnesse Partners LLC
5000 W 36th St Ste 220
St. Louis Park, MN 55416
Contact: Janie Finn President
Tel: 952-232-6170
Email: janie@finnessepartners.com
Website: www.finnessepartners.com
Recruit for the medical device industry. (Woman, estab 2012, empl 5, sales $804,442, cert: WBENC)

9219 HighCloud Solutions Inc
445 Minnesota St Ste 1552
Saint Paul, MN 55101
Contact: Raghu Chejarla President
Tel: 612-479-3333
Email: raghu@highcloudsolutions.com
Website: www.highcloudsolutions.com/
Staffing, contracting/temp job positions. (Woman/As-Ind, estab 2015, empl 9, sales $774,113, cert: State, City, NMSDC, 8(a))

9220 IG, Inc. dba Indrotec
17 Washington Ave N
Minneapolis, MN 55401
Contact: Kathleen Dolphin CEO
Tel: 612-371-7402
Email: kathydolphin@mydolphingroup.com
Website: www.myindrotec.com
Staffing: light industrial & assembly. (Woman, estab 1968, empl 16, sales $20,000,100, cert: WBENC)

9221 Just In Case, Inc.
6900 Shady Oak Rd, Ste 250
Eden Praire, MN 55344
Contact: Diane Blomberg CEO
Tel: 952-925-3789
Email: diane.blomberg@justincasestaffing.com
Website: www.casestaffingsolutions.com/
Staffing, consulting & integration: packaging, shipping & receiving, taping & assembly, clerical positions, administrative jobs, inbound call center positions, customer support. (Woman, estab 1981, empl 9, sales $5,900,000, cert: WBENC)

PROFESSIONAL SERVICES: Staffing Services

9222 Latitude Technology Group, Inc.
      6800 France Ave South Ste 500
      Edina, MN 55435
      Contact: Dorreen Schmidt CEO
      Tel: 952-767-6802
      Email: dschmidt@latitude-group.com
      Website: www.latitude-group.com
Staffing svcs: contract, contract to hire & permanent placement services. (Woman, estab 2002, empl 45, sales $6,000,000, cert: WBENC)

9223 Nexpro Personnel Services, Inc.
      5353 Gamble Dr, Ste 112
      Minneapolis, MN 55416
      Contact: Julia Zimmer Owner
      Tel: 952-224-9855
      Email: jzimmer@nexprojobs.com
      Website: www.nexprojobs.com
Staffing services: administrative, clerical, temporary, contract, word processors, data entry, customer service reps, accounting & payroll, light industrial, receptionist, executive assistants (Woman, estab 2000, empl 40, sales $5,000,000, cert: WBENC)

9224 Pelican Staffing Solutions
      2323 N 2nd St
      Minneapolis, MN 55411
      Contact: Ebi Itie President
      Tel: 612-545-5330
      Email: ebi@pelicanstaffing.com
      Website: www.pelicanstaffing.com
Contract & temporary staffing, staff & vendor management. (Woman/AA, estab 2011, empl 11, sales , cert: City)

9225 Select Source International
      13911 Ridgedale Dr, Ste 230
      Minnetonka, MN 55305
      Contact: Mandeep Sodhi CEO
      Tel: 952-546-3300
      Email: sales@selectsourceintl.com
      Website: www.SelectSourceIntl.com
Temporary Staffing, Information Technology Staffing, Information Technology Services, Engineering Services, Financial Services, Government Services, Retail Services, Energy & Utility Services, Application Development, Mobile Development. (Nat Ame, estab 2000, empl 771, sales , cert: NMSDC)

9226 Serenity Staffing LLC
      6180 W 143rd St
      Savage, MN 55378
      Contact: Jennifer Sabby President
      Tel: 612-834-6444
      Email: jsabby@serenity-staffing.com
      Website: www.serenity-staffing.com
Place Human Resource professionals. (Woman, estab 2005, empl 5, sales $281,316, cert: WBENC)

9227 Synico Staffing
      3033 Excelsior Blvd Ste 495
      Minneapolis, MN 55416
      Contact: Jerry Marsh VP
      Tel: 612-926-6000
      Email: jmarsh@synico.com
      Website: www.synico.com
Staffing services. (AA, estab 1996, empl 450, sales $13,000,000, cert: NMSDC)

9228 TCG, Inc.
      17 Washington Ave N Ste 500
      Minneapolis, MN 55401
      Contact: Kathleen Dolphin President
      Tel: 612-338-7581
      Email: kathydolphin@mydolphingroup.com
      Website: www.mydolphingroup.com
Workforce management solutions. (Woman, estab 1969, empl 70, sales $52,000,000, cert: WBENC)

9229 Technical Information & Professional Solutions Inc
      15600 35th Ave N Ste 203
      Plymouth, MN 55447
      Contact: Adnan (AJ) Jalil Sales & Marketing Mgr
      Tel: 763-557-7010
      Email: aj@tips2e.com
      Website: www.tips2e.com
Technical staffing: short & long term contract, contract to hire & direct placement staff. (As-Ind, estab 1995, empl 89, sales $9,374,046, cert: NMSDC)

9230 The Advent Group
      7101 York Ave S, Ste 240
      Edina, MN 55435
      Contact: Mary Younggren Owner
      Tel: 952-920-9119
      Email: mary@adventgroupco.com
      Website: www.adventgroupofcompanies.com
Staffing office support positions, administrative & accounting support, call center/customer service, human resources, mortgage/financial areas, manufacturing & logistics. (Woman, estab 2002, empl 12, sales , cert: WBENC)

9231 The Mazzitelli Placement Group
      500 Lake St, Ste 212
      Excelsior, MN 55331
      Contact: Teresa Mazzitelli President
      Tel: 952-476-5449
      Email: tm@mazzsearch.com
      Website: www.mazzsearch.com
Executive search, recruitment & placement services. (Woman, estab 1988, empl 1, sales $110,000, cert: WBENC)

Missouri

9232 Above All Personnel dba S.M. Huber Ent., Inc.
      2228 S Big Bend Blvd
      Saint Louis, MO 63117
      Contact: Susan Huber President
      Tel: 314-781-6008
      Email: team@aboveallpersonnel.com
      Website: www.aboveallpersonnel.com
Temporary, temp-to-hire, direct hire employment svcs: clerical, accounting, customer service, data processing. (Woman, estab 1995, empl 450, sales , cert: State)

9233 American Staffing LLC
      11424A Dorsett Rd
      Maryland Heights, MO 63043
      Contact: Diane Fennel President
      Tel: 314-872-7070
      Email: dfennel@americanstaffingstl.com
      Website: www.americanstaffingstl.com
Staffing: temp, temp to hire & permanent. (Woman, estab 2002, empl 12000, sales $6,777,000, cert: State)

PROFESSIONAL SERVICES: Staffing Services

9234 Applications Engineering Group
12300 Old Tesson Rd, Ste 100-G
St. Louis, MO 63128
Contact: Chris Rakel VP Operations
Tel: 314-842-9110
Email: chris.rakel@aeg-inc.com
Website: www.aeg-inc.com
Provide contract, contract to hire & direct hire IT employment services. (Hisp, estab 1992, empl 35, sales , cert: State)

9235 C & S Business Services, Inc.
1731 Southridge Dr
Jefferson City, MO 65109
Contact: Paula Benne President
Tel: 573-635-9295
Email: paula@cs-business.com
Website: www.cs-business.com
Staffing, temporary, direct hire, contract, employment verification, criminal background checks. (Woman, estab 1977, empl 12, sales $4,000,000, cert: State)

9236 Chief of Staff LLC
601 E 63rd St
Kansas City, MO 64110
Contact: Marny Burke Govt Accounts Mgr
Tel: 816-581-2776
Email: government@chiefofstaffkc.com
Website: www.chiefofstaffkc.com
Temporary administrative staffing services, office management, receptionist, accounting & finance, HR, customer service/call room & data entry/records management positions. (Woman, estab 2011, empl 8, sales $1,190,023, cert: State)

9237 Creatives On Call Inc.
101 S Hanley Road Ste 710
St. Louis, MO 63105
Contact: Corey Zinser Acct Exec
Tel: 513-218-5596
Email: corey.zinser@creativesoncall.com
Website: www.creativesoncall.com
Placement agency, recruit professionals with creative, marketing, communications and/or interactive expertise for permanent, contract & freelance positions. (Woman, estab 1995, empl 12, sales $4,500,000, cert: State, WBENC)

9238 Critique Personnel Service, Inc.
1100 S Jefferson Ave
St. Louis, MO 63104
Contact: Monique Jeans Dir Client Services
Tel: 314-772-5445
Email: mjeans@critiquepersonnel.com
Website: www.critiquepersonnel.com
Temporary & permanent staffing services. (AA, estab 1997, empl 50, sales , cert: State)

9239 EH, Inc. dba HireLevel
415 S 18th St. Ste 205
St. Louis, MO 63103
Contact: Nicole Kline Sr Natl Business Dev
Tel: 314-550-8626
Email: nkline@hirelevel.com
Website: www.hirelevel.com
Staffing services, temporary employment, temporary-to-hire & direct hire. (Woman, estab 1995, empl 60, sales $37,813,000, cert: WBENC)

9240 NextGen Information Services Inc.
906 Olive St Ste 600
Saint Louis, MO 63101
Contact: Christy Herschbach Admin Asst
Tel: 314-588-1212
Email: supplierdiversity@nextgen-is.com
Website: www.nextgen-is.com
IT consulting services: project mgmt, custom application dev, legacy transition svcs & staff augmentation, staff augmentaion. (Minority, Woman, estab 1997, empl 300, sales , cert: State, City, WBENC)

9241 Pangaea, Inc.
1403 Hwy F
Defiance, MO 63341
Contact: Heather Everett President
Tel: 314-925-1783
Email: heverett@pangaea-inc.com
Website: www.Pangaea-inc.com
Supplemental staffing services, contract, direct placement, and contract to hire resources. (Woman, estab 2008, empl 10, sales $750,000, cert: State)

9242 Shelgin Partners
9211 Phoenix Village Pkwy
O'Fallon, MO 63368
Contact: Gerri Lynn Zschetzsche Partner
Tel: 636-625-2333
Email: glz@shelgin.com
Website: www.shelgin.com
Recruiting agency: direct recruitment, advertising, job boards, candidate referrals & partner referrals. (Woman, estab 2005, empl 5, sales $553,000, cert: State)

9243 Supplemental Medical Services, Inc.
10916 Schuetz Road
St. Louis, MO 63146
Contact: Gretchen Curry President
Tel: 314-997-8833
Email: gcurry@stafflinkusa.com
Website: www.stafflinkusa.com
Temporary, contract, travel & direct hire healthcare personnel. (Woman/AA, estab 1987, empl 125, sales $2,643,128, cert: State, NMSDC)

9244 The Herring IMPACT Group
12977 N Outer 40 Dr Ste 300
St. Louis, MO 63141
Contact: Kristy King Exec Asst
Tel: 314-453-9002
Email: diversity1@impactgrouphr.com
Website: www.impactgrouphr.com
Career transitions, relocation support, talent development, and outplacement services. (Woman, estab 1988, empl 121, sales $15,000,000, cert: State, WBENC)

9245 TempStaff Inc.
2282 Lakeland Dr
Flowood, MS 39232
Contact: Jamie Higdon VP Operations
Tel: 601-353-4200
Email: jamie@tempstaff.net
Website: www.tempstaff.net
Temporary & permanent employment. (Woman, estab 1979, empl 24, sales , cert: WBENC)

Montana

9246 Brady Co., Inc
50 West 14th St Ste 300
Helena, MT 59601
Contact: Anna Kazmierowski CEO
Tel: 406-443-7664
Email: anna@a2zmontana.com
Website: www.a2zmontana.com
Workforce solutions, temporary staffing, temporary to permanent placement & direct hire services, employee payroll, scientific & technical staffing, technical & professional recruitment & construction labor. (Woman, estab 2003, empl 7, sales $4,517,215, cert: State, WBENC, SDB)

North Carolina

9247 AccruePartners, Inc.
1000 W Morehead St Ste 200
Charlotte, NC 28208
Contact: Amy Pack Principal Partner
Tel: 704-632-9955
Email: amy@accruepartners.com
Website: www.accruepartners.com
Contract to contract-to-hire, direct hire and executive search, project solutions. (Woman, estab 2002, empl 50, sales $28,000,000, cert: WBENC)

9248 Allied Staff Augmentation Partners, Inc.
7421 Carmel Executive Park Dr Ste 200
Charlotte, NC 28226
Contact: Neal McCraw VP Employment Relations
Tel: 980-288-0082
Email: nealmccraw@asap.us.com
Website: www.asap.us.com
Professional recruiting: engineering; technical including IT; program/project management; facility operations, maintenance & modifications. (AA, estab 2011, empl 100, sales $6,215,297, cert: NMSDC)

9249 Aquest LLC
103 Meadowood Dr
Burlington, NC 27215
Contact: Asia Amin
Tel: 910-463-4700
Email: tanveer@aqueststaffing.com
Website: www.aqueststaffing.com
IT staffing, Accounting, financial, and managerial staffing, Recruitment process outsourcing, Technical and industrial staffing, Offshore requirements. (Woman/As-Pac, estab 2019, empl 25, sales $319,000, cert: NWBOC)

9250 Associate Staffing, LLC
303C Atkinson St
Laurinburg, NC 28352
Contact: Dir
Tel: 980-224-8754
Email: info@astaff.us
Website: www.associatestaffingllc.com
Recruiting & staffing, contract, contract to permanent & direct placement basis. (Woman, estab 2008, empl 450, sales $13,400,000, cert: WBENC)

9251 Aten Solutions, Inc.
5404 Hillsborough St Ste A
Raleigh, NC 27606
Contact: COO
Tel: 919-949-3503
Email: info@a10clinical.com
Website: www.a10clinical.com
Staffing solutions: clinical research, clinical data management, statistical programming & biostatistics space, clinical trial svcs & staffing support. (Woman/AA, estab 2004, empl 64, sales $1,800,000, cert: NMSDC, WBENC)

9252 Best National Services Inc. dba Latin Labor Staffi
4917 South Blvd
Charlotte, NC 28217
Contact: Frank Colunga Sr Acct Mgr
Tel: 704-877-8241
Email: fcolunga@latinlabor.net
Website: www.latinlabor.net
Light Industrial staffing services: General Labor, Logistics, manufacturing, cleaning, events, etc. (Hisp, estab 2005, empl 600, sales $13,000,000, cert: NMSDC)

9253 BPN Concepts
8305 University Executive Park Dr Ste 330
Charlotte, NC 28262
Contact: Brenda Harris Owner
Tel: 980-335-0656
Email: info@bpnconcepts.com
Website: www.bpnconcepts.com
Executive search & staffing services. (Woman/AA, estab 2011, empl 6, sales , cert: State, City)

9254 CEO Inc.
412 Louise Ave
Charlotte, NC 28204
Contact: Deborah Millhouse President
Tel: 704-372-4701
Email: debby@ceohr.com
Website: www.ceohr.com
Temporary staffing, payrolling, HR consulting, executive search & placement. (Woman, estab 1994, empl 15, sales $2,995,605, cert: State)

9255 Concierge Staffing LLC
160 S Main St
Graham, NC 27253
Contact: Denise Brown Owner
Tel: 336-270-3035
Email: denise.brown@concierge-staffing.com
Website: www.concierge-staffing.com
Staffing services and solutions. (Woman/AA, estab 2014, empl 50, sales , cert: State)

9256 Cyber Shield Consulting Inc.
8300 Boone Blvd, Ste 500
Vienna, NC 22182
Contact: Doug Marland Business Devel Mgr
Tel: 571-358-5602
Email: operations@cybershieldincorporated.com
Website: www.cybershieldincorporated.com
Human capital services, temporary & permanent on a nationwide. (AA, estab 2013, empl 25, sales , cert: NMSDC)

PROFESSIONAL SERVICES: Staffing Services

9257 Debbie's Staffing Services, Inc.
4431 N Cherry St
Winston-Salem, NC 27105
Contact: Joanne Altieri Business Devel Mgr
Tel: 704-682-0036
Email: mwoodson@debbiesstaffing.com
Website: www.debbiesstaffing.com
Temporary staffing, distribution, warehouse, data-entry, IT, cashiers. (Woman, estab 1986, empl 105, sales $94,000,000, cert: WBENC)

9258 ER Select
6100 Fairview Road Ste 545
Charlotte, NC 28210
Contact: Jeremy Holland Dir Strategic Accounts
Tel: 407-221-1000
Email: jholland@talentbridge.com
Website: www.talentbridge.com
Recruiting and staffing, short-term, permanent and contract solutions. (Woman, estab 2011, empl 100, sales $83,000,000, cert: WBENC)

9259 Global Pros Staffing Solutions
9635 Southern Pine Blvd Ste 102
Charlotte, NC 28273
Contact: TaWanda Duncan CEO
Tel: 704-648-7355
Email: globalprosstaffingsolutions@gmail.com
Website: www.globalprosstaffingsolutions.com
Staffing: Administrative, Call Center, Healthcare, Human Resources,
Warehouse, Forklift, Landscaping
Janitorial. (AA, estab 2015, empl 50, sales , cert: City)

9260 Greer Group
3109 Charles B. Root Wynd
Raleigh, NC 27612
Contact: Mark Blume Client Devel Mgr
Tel: 919-571-0051
Email: sales@thegreergroup.com
Website: www.thegreergroup.com
Staffing services: temporary staffing, temporary to direct hire staffing, direct hire recruitment, payrolling services & onsite staffing management. (Woman, estab 1986, empl 16, sales $15,802,034, cert: WBENC)

9261 Greytree Partners
121 Greenwich Rd Ste 211
Charlotte, NC 28211
Contact: Clarence Fisher Chief Solutions Architect
Tel: 704-899-4082
Email: clarence.fisher@greytreepartners.com
Website: www.GreytreePartners.com
Identification, recruitment & placement of information technology and engineering services professionals on a contract or permanent basis. (AA, estab 2004, empl 30, sales $2,400,000, cert: State, NMSDC)

9262 In-Flight Crew Connections
338 S Sharon Amity Rd, Ste 311
Charlotte, NC 28211
Contact: Jennifer Guthrie Owner
Tel: 704-236-3647
Email: jennifer.guthrie@inflightcrewconnections.com
Website: www.inflightcrewconnections.com
Temporary Flight Attendants, Pilots & Technicians. (Woman, estab 2002, empl 55, sales $16,000,000, cert: WBENC)

9263 Jennifer Temps, Inc.
1973 JN Pease Pl Ste 201
Charlotte, NC 28262
Contact: Jennifer Singleton President
Tel: 212-964-8367
Email: jsingleton@jennifertemps.com
Website: www.jennifertemps.com
Temporary staffing. (Woman/AA, estab 1992, empl 8, sales $4,500,000, cert: NMSDC)

9264 Omni Source Solutions
13016 Eastfield Rd
Huntersville, NC 28078
Contact: Charisma Smith Managing Member
Tel: 704-412-3031
Email: charisma@omnisourcesolutions.net
Website: www.omnisourcesolutions.net
Offer skilled quality self-performing contractors. (Woman/AA, estab 2012, empl 2, sales , cert: City, NMSDC)

9265 Quality Staffing Solutions, Inc.
120 Towerview Ct
Cary, NC 27513
Contact: Phyllis Eller-Moffett CEO
Tel: 919-481-4114
Email: pmoffett@quality-staffing.com
Website: www.quality-staffing.com
Staffing solutions. (Woman, estab 1995, empl 400, sales $6,526,751, cert: WBENC)

9266 Red Bridge Consulting Group
10700 Sikes Place, Ste 305
Charlotte, NC 28277
Contact: Judith Mackesy Owner
Tel: 704-375-2040
Email: jmackesy@redbridgecg.com
Website: www.redbridgecg.com
Recruiting, Consulting and Staffing Services, permanent placement, project-based consulting, temporary contract, and contract-to-hire services. (Woman, estab 2009, empl 12, sales , cert: WBENC)

9267 Right Choice Solutions, Inc.
316 W Millbrook Rd Ste. 213
Raleigh, NC 27609
Contact: Layce Adams Operations Mgr
Tel: 919-324-3557
Email: layce@thercsolutions.com
Website: www.thercsolutions.com
Staffing: temporary staffing, temp to hire & direct hire quality candidates. (Woman/AA, estab 2005, empl 7, sales , cert: NMSDC)

9268 Talented Fish, Inc.
111 W Lewis St Ste 120
Greensboro, NC 27406
Contact: Tracey Wallace COO
Tel: 336-279-7665
Email: tracey@talentedfish.com
Website: www.talentedfish.com
Executive Search & Placement. (AA, estab 2017, empl 3, sales , cert: NMSDC)

PROFESSIONAL SERVICES: Staffing Services

9269 The KARS Group Ltd LLC
6365 Royal Celadon Way
Charlotte, NC 28269
Contact: Keisha Rivers
Tel: 843-376-1296
Email: admin@karsgroup.com
Website: www.karsgroup.com
Talent optimization consulting; employee engagement consulting; recruitment & retention consulting; pulse surveys; listening sessions; Leadership 360 assessments; Predictive Index Behavioral Assessments (Woman/AA, estab 2005, empl 1, sales $304,000, cert: NMSDC, WBENC)

9270 Two Hawk Employment Services, Inc.
3021 N Roberts Ave
Lumberton, NC 28360
Contact: Harvey Godwin, Jr. Owner
Tel: 910-738-3014
Email: harvey.godwin@twohawk.net
Website: www.twohawk.net
Temporary & permanent employment services: general labor, supervisory & administration positions. (Nat Ame, estab 1999, empl 50, sales $24,000,000, cert: NMSDC)

9271 Xcentri, Inc.
412 Louise Ave
Charlotte, NC 28204
Contact: Debby Millhouse President
Tel: 704-369-3211
Email: deborah.millhouse@xcentri.com
Website: www.xcentri.com
Staffing & recruiting (temp, contract to hire and direct hire); HR Consulting; Background Checks; Drug Screening (Woman, estab 2014, empl 200, sales $9,586,491, cert: WBENC)

New Hampshire

9272 CCSI Inc.
62 Portsmouth Ave
Stratham, NH 03885
Contact: Sarah Latiolais Acct Mgr
Tel: 800-598-0255
Email: sarah@ccsiinc.com
Website: www.ccsiinc.com
Temporary & permanent staffing: IT, accounting, finance, HR, sales, administration, marketing & clinical staff. (Woman, estab 1998, empl 256, sales $16,000,000, cert: WBENC)

9273 The Spencer Thomas Group LLC
One Falkland Place
Portsmouth, NH 03801
Contact: Lori Perkins Acct Mgr
Tel: 603-835-3707
Email: lori.perkins@spencer-thomas.com
Website: www.spencer-thomas.com
Recruiting, staffing, consulting, PeopleSoft, SAP, Oracle, web deveoplers, project management, program managers, outsourced payroll services, employee leasing. (Woman, estab 1998, empl , sales $20,000,000, cert: WBENC)

New Jersey

9274 Accountants For You Inc.
1175 Marlkress Road, Ste 1040
Cherry Hill, NJ 08034
Contact: Marcia Libes President
Tel: 215-988-7200
Email: marcia.libes@accountantsforyou.com
Website: www.accountantsforyou.com
Staffing & recruiting: temporary, temporary to permanent & permanent placement of accounting, finance, human resource & office professionals. (Woman, estab 2006, empl 10, sales $1,376,195, cert: WBENC)

9275 ACCU Staffing Services
911 Kings Hwy N
Cherry Hill, NJ 08034
Contact: Debra Fordyce Operations Mgr
Tel: 856-482-2222
Email: cherryhill@accustaffing.com
Website: www.accustaffing.com
Staffing svcs: human resources, planned staffing, direct placement, corporate outplacement svcs & on-site consulting/mgmt funcations. (Woman, estab 1979, empl 100, sales , cert: WBENC)

9276 AceStack LLC
207 Park Ln
Trenton, NJ 08609
Contact: Ester Gonzalez Dir of Operations
Tel: 609-779-9751
Email: tpatel@ace-stack.com
Website: www.ace-stack.com
Technology consulting & healthcare staffing solutions. (Woman/Hisp, estab 2017, empl 25, sales $1,500,000, cert: WBENC)

9277 APN Consulting Inc.
1100 Cornwall Rd
Monmouth Junction, NJ 08852
Contact: Francis Moser Business Devel Mgr
Tel: 609-924-3400
Email: francis@apnconsultinginc.com
Website: www.apnconsultinginc.com
Contract, contract-to-hire & full time staffing services. (As-Ind, estab 2002, empl 250, sales $20,300,000, cert: NMSDC)

9278 Atlas Consulting Group, LLC
4257 Route 9 N
Freehold, NJ 07728
Contact: Mario Linale President
Tel: 732-637-8063
Email: mlinale@theatlasconsulting.com
Website: www.theatlasconsulting.com
Nationwide staffing services, temporary & consulting placements. (Woman, estab 2009, empl 60, sales $1,300,000, cert: State)

9279 ATRIA Consulting, LLC
1 Aaa Dr Ste 206
Robbinsville, NJ 08691
Contact: Melissa Bordman Managing Member
Tel: 646-722-8702
Email: mbordman@atriaconsutling.com
Website: www.atriaconsulting.com
Staffing & Solutions: Information Technology, Accounting/Finance, Admin/Clerical, HR & Online Media Permanent and Contract Placement services. (Woman, estab 2006, empl 30, sales $1,640,850, cert: WBENC)

PROFESSIONAL SERVICES: Staffing Services

9280 Azzmeiah Vazquez Esq. dba WorkPro
      438 Hamilton Ave
      Trenton, NJ 08609
      Contact: Azzmeiah Vazquez Owner
      Tel: 609-571-1991
      Email: avazquez@workprosolutions.com
      Website: www.workprosolutions.com
Staff augmentation, analytics, operations/logistics, general administrative, training, creative product launch events, staffing & data science. (Woman/Hisp, estab 2003, empl 3, sales $200,000, cert: 8(a))

9281 CNC Consulting
      50 E Palisades Ave Ste 422
      Englewood, NJ 07631
      Contact: Fred Seltzer Business Devel Mgr
      Tel: 201-541-9122
      Email: fseltzer@cncconsult.com
      Website: www.cncconsulting.com
IT professionals for consulting contracts. (AA, estab 1996, empl 25, sales $3,000,000, cert: State)

9282 Datanomics, Inc.
      991 US Hwy 22 West Ste 201
      Bridgewater, NJ 08807
      Contact: Lori Vail CEO
      Tel: 908-707-8200
      Email: vail@datanomics.com
      Website: www.datanomics.com
IT staffing, helpdesk, desktop support, administration, technical writers, validation specialists, business/systems analysts, programmers, mainframe, client/server, & web. (Woman, estab 1982, empl 100, sales , cert: State)

9283 Elite Personnel Group, LLC
      220 Davidson Ave. Ste 102
      Somerset, NJ 08873
      Contact: Junior Recruiter
      Tel: 908-722-1111
      Email: apply@cosmostaff.com
      Website: www.eliteitpersonnel.com
National recruiting and talent acquisition. (As-Pac, estab 2007, empl 40, sales $45,000,000, cert: State)

9284 Fabergent, Inc.
      63 Ramapo Valley Rd, Ste 214
      Mahwah, NJ 07430
      Contact: Ratna Silpa Gorantla President
      Tel: 201-378-0036
      Email: ratna@fabergent.com
      Website: www.fabergent.com
Contract & full-time positions IT staffing in Java, .Net, SharePoint, SAP, Oracle, BI, Analytics, networking & IT security. (Minority, Woman, estab 2005, empl 125, sales , cert: State)

9285 Frink-Hamlett Legal Solutions
      PO Box 2022
      Teaneck, NJ 07666
      Contact: Katherine Frink-Hamlett President
      Tel: 201-357-8975
      Email: katherine@frinkhamlett.com
      Website: www.frinkhamlett.com
Provide legal professionals: attorneys, compliance & paralegals on a temporary and permanent basis. (Woman/AA, estab 2004, empl 3, sales $1,383,371, cert: State, City, NMSDC, WBENC)

9286 Glenmont Group Inc.
      39 S Fullerton Ave Ste 9
      Montclair, NJ 07042
      Contact: President
      Tel: 973-746-0600
      Email: info@glenmontgroup.com
      Website: www.glenmontgroup.com
Recruiting & staffing. (Woman, estab 2001, empl 22, sales $2,404,882, cert: State, WBENC)

9287 Harita Infotech
      601 Crest Stone Circle
      Princeton, NJ 08540
      Contact: Kaushal Sampat President
      Tel: 609-216-1844
      Email: kaushalsampat@haritainfotechinc.com
      Website: www.haritainfotechinc.com
Consulting & Permanent resources in the Business, IT & general fields. (As-Pac, estab 2014, empl 10, sales , cert: State)

9288 Industrial Staffing Services inc.
      25 Kennedy Blvd Ste 200
      East Brunswick, NJ 08816
      Contact: Steve Dern VP
      Tel: 303-323-5179
      Email: SDern@evaluentsolutions.com
      Website: www.industrial-staffing.com
Place contract & permanent workers for all types of staffing needs: staff augmentation, payroll-servicing, &project staffing with qualified & certified pre-screened personnel in all industrial, technical and administrative positions. (Woman, estab 2003, empl 25, sales , cert: State, City, WBENC)

9289 Integrated Resources, Inc.
      4 Ethel Rd, Ste 403B
      Edison, NJ 08817
      Contact: Chris Byram VP
      Tel: 732-549-2030
      Email: chris@irionline.com
      Website: www.irionline.com
Staffing services, Direct Hire, Temporary/Contract and Contract-to-Hire. (Minority, estab 1996, empl 750, sales $53,000,000, cert: State, NMSDC)

9290 IT Staffing, Inc.
      5 Bliss Court Ste 200
      Woodcliff Lake, NJ 07677
      Contact: Jerry G. Myers Dir Business Dev
      Tel: 201-505-0493
      Email: jerry.myers@itstaffinc.com
      Website: www.itstaffinc.com
Strategic contract sourcing, consulting, staff augmentation, managed teams & outsourcing. (Minority, Woman, estab 1998, empl 78, sales $11,500,000, cert: State)

9291 JBK Associates International, Inc.
      607 E Palisade Ave
      Englewood Cliffs, NJ 07632
      Contact: Shari Caloz Exec Admin
      Tel: 201-567-9070
      Email: scaloz@jbkassociates.net
      Website: www.jbkassociates.net
Executive recruitment. (Woman, estab 2003, empl 17, sales $4,642,327, cert: WBENC)

PROFESSIONAL SERVICES: Staffing Services

9292 Jersey Staffing Solutions, LLC
400 Valley Rd Ste 106
Mt. Arlington, NJ 07856
Contact: Kristi Telschow CEO
Tel: 973-810-4495
Email: ktelschow@jerseystaffing.com
Website: www.jerseystaffing.com
Staffing, temporary, temp-to-perm & permanent staffing. (Woman, estab 2010, empl 35, sales $2,160,000, cert: WBENC)

9293 Jomsom Staffing Services
4390 US Hwy One, Ste 203
Princeton, NJ 08540
Contact: Ross Lazio Business Dev Exec
Tel: 973-446-5627
Email: rlazio@jomsomjobs.com
Website: www.jomsomstaffing.com
Staffing solutions, full-time & part-time resources, temporary, temporary to permanent & permanent placement basis. (Woman/As-Ind, estab 2008, empl 55, sales $3,500,000, cert: NMSDC)

9294 Knoodae Staffing, LLC
525 Rt 73N, Ste 104
Marlton, NJ 08053
Contact: Anitra Green Owner
Tel: 856-804-0321
Email: anitra@knoodaestaffing.com
Website: www.knoodaestaffing.com
Professional recruiting and staffing. (AA, estab 2021, empl 70, sales , cert: State)

9295 Madagoni LLC
247 E Front St #109
Trenton, NJ 08611
Contact: Minhaj shaik Scientific officer
Tel: 856-283-2300
Email: minhajs@madagoni-devices.com
Website: www.madagoni.com
Recruiting: Life Sciences, IT, Engineering, Non-IT roles. (As-Pac, estab 2018, empl 25, sales $1,000,000, cert: NMSDC)

9296 MetaSense Inc.
100 Technology Way, Ste 320
Mt. Laurel, NJ 08054
Contact: Jatin V Mehta CEO
Tel: 856-873-9950
Email: jmehta@metasenseusa.com
Website: www.metasenseusa.com
Information system staffing, software development, web design, outsourcing, business process outsourcing, knowledge process outsourcing. (Minority, Woman, estab 1999, empl 5, sales $767,000, cert: State)

9297 Net2Source Inc
270 Davidson Ave, Ste 704 Ste 704
Somerset, NJ 08873
Contact: Ashish Garg Founder & CEO
Tel: 201-340-8700
Email: supplier_registrations@net2source.com
Website: www.net2source.com
Staffing & recruitment services. (Minority, estab 2007, empl 5000, sales $172,000,000, cert: NMSDC)

9298 Next Step Staffing
725 River Road
Edgewater, NJ 07020
Contact: Pratcher CEO
Tel: 646-829-1800
Email: joy@nsstaff.com
Website: www.nsstaff.com
IT solutions, full-time, permanent placement or temporary contract basis. (Woman/AA, Hisp, estab 2012, empl 5, sales $1,804,633, cert: NMSDC, WBENC)

9299 Perry Temps, Inc.
525 Route 73, South Ste 201
Marlton, NJ 08053
Contact: Wendy Brooks Dir Business Dev
Tel: 856-596-9400
Email: wbrooks@perryresources.com
Website: www.perryresources.com
Temporary staffing: administrative, accounting, clerical, customer service call center personnel. (Woman, estab 1986, empl 8, sales $2,174,927, cert: WBENC)

9300 Pride Veteran Staffing
15 Union Ave
Rutherford, NJ 07070
Contact: Beth Firgau CEO
Tel: 732-318-5985
Email: Beth@prideveteran.com
Website: www.prideveteran.com/
Staffing agency. (Woman, estab 2019, empl 21, sales $500,000, cert: WBENC)

9301 Professional Resource Partners
14 Rickland Dr
Randolph, NJ 07869
Contact: Stefanie Wichansky CEO
Tel: 201-259-4739
Email: swichansky@prp-us.com
Website: www.professionalresourcepartners.com
Life Science Consulting & Staffing: contract, contract-to-perm, permanent basis across functional areas. (Woman, estab 2012, empl 20, sales $454,478, cert: WBENC)

9302 Protocall NJ, Inc.
One Mall Dr
Cherry Hill, NJ 08002
Contact: Janis LeBude President
Tel: 856-667-7500
Email: lebude@protocallstaffing.com
Website: www.protocallstaffing.com
General laborers, assemblers, maintenance staff, import/export clerks, bi-Lingual supervisors, warehouse managers/supervisors, quality control inspectors, shipping/receiving clerks, packers, event staff & mail room staff. (Woman, estab 1965, empl 70, sales $23,059,418, cert: WBENC)

9303 RHO, Inc.
507 Omni Dr
Hillsborough, NJ 08844
Contact: Deborah Johnson President
Tel: 908-359-0808
Email: deborah.johnson@rho-inc.com
Website: www.rho-inc.com
Staffing, consulting & training services. (Minority, Woman, estab 1981, empl 120, sales , cert: WBENC)

PROFESSIONAL SERVICES: Staffing Services

9304 Sage Group Technologies Inc
3400 Hwy 35 S Ste 9A
Hazlet, NJ 07730
Contact: Shruthi Reddy Exec VP
Tel: 732-994-6792
Email: sreddy@sagegroupinc.com
Website: www.sagegroupinc.com
Contingent Workforce Services, Contract Staffing, Contract to Hire Staffing, IT & Non-IT Staffing, Clinical & Scientific Staffing. (Minority, estab 2004, empl 120, sales $63,200,000, cert: State, NMSDC)

9305 Software Folks, Inc. dba Saviance Technologies
16 Bridge St
Metuchen, NJ 08840
Contact: Anuj Sakhuja Client Relationship Mgr
Tel: 732-593-8015
Email: anuj.sakhuja@saviance.com
Website: www.saviance.com
Information technology staffing: contract, contract-to-hire & permanent. (As-Pac, estab 1999, empl 60, sales $7,725,180, cert: NMSDC)

9306 Software Galaxy Systems, LLC
4390 US Route 1 N, Ste 210A
Princeton, NJ 08540
Contact: Srini Vengad Sr VP
Tel: 609-919-1133
Email: srini.vengad@sgsconsulting.com
Website: www.sgsconsulting.com
Contingent Workforce Services, integrated suite of services through our global delivery platform. (As-Pac, estab 1997, empl 220, sales $18,000,000, cert: NMSDC)

9307 Synasha LLC
100 Matawan Rd Ste 130
Matawan, NJ 07747
Contact: Geoffrey Crawley VP
Tel: 732-705-3553
Email: geoffrey.crawley@synasha.com
Website: www.synasha.com
Direct Mail, Direct Ship, Retail Display Assembly & Pack Out Drop Ship, Kitting, Multi Branded Displays, Primary Packaging, Promotional Packaging, Rework Repackaging VMI & Sequenced Material Replenishment. (AA, estab 2015, empl 7500, sales $40,000,000, cert: NMSDC)

9308 TNT Staffing
70 Kinderkamack Rd, Ste 202
Emerson, NJ 07630
Contact: Jacqueline Tarnowski Dir of Recruiting
Tel: 201-497-6305
Email: jackie@tntstaffing.com
Website: www.tntstaffing.com
Staff Augmentation & Direct Full Time Placement Services. (Woman/AA, estab 2005, empl 25, sales $4,328,500, cert: State, WBENC)

9309 UserEdge Technical Personnel
1812 Front St.
Scotch Plains, NJ 07076
Contact: Jay Madlangbayan President
Tel: 908-387-7601
Email: jay@useredge.com
Website: www.useredge.com
Direct hire recruitment, short & long-term contract assignments, outsourced staffing. (As-Pac, estab 1995, empl 30, sales $1,750,000, cert: State, NMSDC)

Nevada

9310 My Next Career Path Staffing, LLC
400 S. Fourth St, Ste 500
Las Vegas, NV 89101
Contact: Renee Boyce President
Tel: 844-579-6627
Email: rboyce@mncpstaffing.com
Website: www.mncpstaffing.com
Consulting & staffing: analysts, system/network administrators, project managers, developers, bookkeepers, designers, customer service experts & marketing specialists. (AA, estab 2014, empl 40, sales $1,000,000, cert: State, NMSDC, CPUC, 8(a))

New York

9311 24 Seven Inc.
120 Wooster St, 4th Floor
New York, NY 10012
Contact: Meghan Dewey President
Tel: 212-966-4426
Email: mdewey@24seveninc.com
Website: www.24seveninc.com
Staffing svcs: freelance, freelance to fulltime, fulltime & executive search services. (Woman, estab 2000, empl 93, sales $125,326,911, cert: WBENC)

9312 Admiral Staffing Inc.
18 W 30th St
New York, NY 10001
Contact: Ray Rafeek
Tel: 212-714-3543
Email: irshaad@admiralstaffinginc.com
Website: www.admiralstaffinginc.com
Temporary to permanent staffing services. (As-Pac, estab 2010, empl 25, sales $492,000, cert: City, NMSDC)

9313 Aimssoft Consultants Inc.
13760 45th Ave Ste- 6 -C
Flushing, NY 11355
Contact: Ambreen Imran President
Tel: 718-762-2370
Email: imran@aimssoftconsultant.net
Website: www.aimssoftconsultant.net
Recruiting professional candidates, Interviewing & screening candidates, interviews, hiring paperwork. (As-Pac, estab 2013, empl 45, sales , cert: NMSDC)

9314 Amtex System, Inc
28 Liberty St, 6th Fl
New York, NY 10005
Contact: Rob Collins Sr BDM
Tel: 646-200-7115
Email: rob@amtexsystems.com
Website: www.amtexsystems.com
IT Placement firm. (As-Pac, estab 1997, empl 260, sales $30,000,000, cert: City)

9315 ANR Staffing Solutions, LLC
21702 Jamaica Ave, Ste 2
Queens Village, NY 11428
Contact: Alecia C. Grant CEO
Tel: - -
Email: agrant@anrstaffingsolutions.com
Website: www.anrstaffingsolutions.com
Supplemental staffing of clinical & non-clinical personnel to hospitals, homecare agencies, government agencies & individuals. (AA, estab 2013, empl 40, sales , cert: City)

PROFESSIONAL SERVICES: Staffing Services

9316 Associate Resource Management, Inc.
 2527 Merrick Rd
 Bellmore, NY 11710
 Contact: Kim Robertson Exec Dir
 Tel: 516-785-6211
 Email: kim@armi.bz
 Website: www.armi.bz
Staffing solutions: Front Desk Staff, Receptionist, Centralized Scheduling, Clerical Staff, Human Resources, Customer Service, Office Support Staff, Office Manager, Data Entry Clerks, Accounting, Bookkeepers, Administrative. (Woman, estab 2006, empl 6, sales $1,700,000, cert: WBENC)

9317 Atrium Staffing LLC
 387 Park Ave S 3rd Fl
 New York, NY 10016
 Contact: Kelly Couto VP
 Tel: 732-902-5917
 Email: supplierdiversity@atriumstaff.com
 Website: www.atriumworks.com
Temporary & direct-hire staffing: administration, finance, professional services & science. (Woman, estab 1995, empl 240, sales $293,646,368, cert: WBENC)

9318 Axelon Services Corporation
 44 Wall St Fl 18
 New York, NY 10005
 Contact: Cynthia Lah COO
 Tel: 212-306-0104
 Email: cynthia@axelon.com
 Website: www.axelon.com
Powerful staffing cloud technologies and processes deliver precise talent matches. (Woman, estab 1977, empl 961, sales $89,000,000, cert: City, WBENC, NWBOC)

9319 Broadleaf Results, Inc.
 250 International Dr
 Williamsville, NY 14221
 Contact: Michelle Prue Client Liaison
 Tel: 800-574-5021
 Email: pruem@broadleafresults.com
 Website: www.broadleafresults.com
Staffing svcs: temp, direct hire, payrolling svcs, on-site staffing & web-based vendor mgmt programs. (Woman, estab 1965, empl 500, sales $352,440,788, cert: WBENC)

9320 CompliStaff, Inc.
 381 Lewis St
 West Hempstead, NY 11552
 Contact: April Bernstein VP
 Tel: 646-595-0040
 Email: april.bernstein@complistaff.com
 Website: www.complistaff.com
Staffing & recruitment solutions in legal, compliance, accounting, audit & risk management. (Woman, estab 2010, empl 8, sales $1,270,000, cert: City, WBENC)

9321 Custom Staffing, Inc.
 420 Lexington Ave Ste 550
 New York, NY 10017
 Contact: Managing Dir
 Tel: 212-818-0300
 Email: mrodriguez@customstaffing.com
 Website: www.customgroupofcompanies.com
Staffing, temporary and permanent positions, contract and permanent attorneys and paralegals. (Woman/AA, estab , empl , sales $17,240,885, cert: State)

9322 Dale Workforce Solutions, LLC
 1751 2nd Ave, Ste 103
 New York, NY 10128
 Contact: Lois Dale Holtzman President
 Tel: 212-860-2000
 Email: ldale@daleworkforce.com
 Website: www.daleworkforce.com/
Staff Augmentation, Independent Contractor Compliance, Payroll Services. (Woman, estab 2012, empl 10, sales $1,200,000, cert: WBENC)

9323 Distinctive Personnel
 424 W 33rd St
 New York, NY 10001
 Contact: Gonzalo Vergara Founder/Chairman
 Tel: 917-952-2766
 Email: gus@distinctivepersonnel.com
 Website: www.distinctivepersonnel.com
Staffing services: temporary, permenant, executive search, managed service providers, vendor managed services/, payroll outsourcing. (Hisp, estab , empl , sales $710,000,000, cert: City)

9324 Gainor Temporaries, Inc.
 489 Fifth Ave
 New York, NY 10017
 Contact: Sr Acct Exec
 Tel: 212-697-4145
 Email:
 Website: www.gainor.net
Temporary & permanent administrative personnel placement. (Woman, estab 1984, empl 20, sales $9,064,000, cert: WBENC)

9325 Geneva Consulting Group, Inc.
 14 Vanderventer Ave Ste 250
 Port Washington, NY 11050
 Contact: Gina Santorio Dir Business Dev
 Tel: 516-767-6695
 Email: gsantorio@genevaconsulting.com
 Website: www.genevaconsulting.com
IT consulting & full-time placement services, payrolling services. (Woman, estab 1997, empl 50, sales $8,021,175, cert: WBENC)

9326 HireTalent
 135 W 26th St, Ste 7B
 New York, NY 10001
 Contact: Ashish Kaushal President
 Tel: 646-495-1558
 Email: vms@hiretalent.com
 Website: www.hiretalent.com
Staffing services. (As-Ind, estab 1996, empl 250, sales $29,105,000, cert: NMSDC)

9327 iT Resource Solutions.net, Inc.
 10 Technology Dr, Ste 1
 East Setauket, NY 11733
 Contact: Andrea Dunkle Dir of Diversity Management
 Tel: 631-941-2622
 Email: adunkle@it-rs.net
 Website: www.it-rs.net
Staffing: information technology consultants. (Woman, estab 1995, empl 45, sales , cert: City, WBENC)

PROFESSIONAL SERVICES: Staffing Services

9328 Journee Technology Staffing Inc..
2117Buffalo Rd Ste 275
Rochester, NY 14624
Contact: Dixon President
Tel: 585-210-5314
Email: orville@journeetechnologystaffing.com
Website: www.journeetechnologystaffing.com
Staffing solutions. (Woman/AA, estab 2007, empl 2, sales $310,000, cert: State)

9329 NetPro Resources, Inc.
444 E 75th St, Ste 16e
New York, NY 10021
Contact: Pam Lindheim VP Client Relations
Tel: 212-650-1665
Email: pam@netproresources.com
Website: www.netproresources.com
Accounting, finance, Human Resources, Administrative, Legal and Treasury recruitment and placement of temporary, permanent and consultative professionals (Woman, estab 1999, empl 1, sales $175,000, cert: WBENC)

9330 Noor Associates, Inc.
622 Third Ave, 7th Floor
New York, NY 10017
Contact: Jake Eletto Chief of Staff
Tel: 212-812-3390
Email: jake@noorinc.com
Website: www.noorinc.com
Professional services: staffing, consulting & project based solutions. (As-Ind, estab 2005, empl 100, sales $10,000,000, cert: City, NMSDC)

9331 Noor Staffing Group, LLC
295 Madison Ave 14th Fl
New York, NY 10017
Contact: Frank Cumbo Sr VP
Tel: 212-878-2000
Email: contracts@noorgov.us
Website: www.promptpersonnel.com
Staffing, skills evaluation, reference, background checks & market intelligence. (As-Ind, estab 2005, empl 200, sales $55,000,000, cert: City, NMSDC)

9332 Nueva Solutions Inc
1410 Broadway Ste 1904
New York, NY 10018
Contact: Punit Shetty Business Devel
Tel: 212-937-0056
Email: punit@nuevainc.com
Website: www.nuevainc.com
IT Staffing - contingent & permanent. (Woman/As-Ind, estab 2008, empl 17, sales $3,200,000, cert: State)

9333 Penda Aiken, Inc.
330 Livingston St, 2 Fl
Brooklyn, NY 11217
Contact: Susie Fryer Business Devel Mgr
Tel: 718-643-4880
Email: sfryer@pendaaiken.com
Website: www.pendaaiken.com
Staffing & HR solutions: testing & evaluating, recruiting & retention, quality control, insurance protection, prompt service & guarantee. (Woman/AA, estab 1990, empl 225, sales $6,815,855, cert: State, City, NMSDC)

9334 Pride Technologies LLC
420 Lexington Ave Ste 2220
New York, NY 10170
Contact: David Hellard Major Accounts Mgr
Tel: 614-991-5895
Email: joshua.kaplan@pridetech.com
Website: www.pridetech.com
Project management & staffing services. (Hisp, estab 1983, empl 800, sales $97,000,000, cert: NMSDC)

9335 Procare USA, LLC
845 3rd Ave, Fl 6
New York, NY 10022
Contact: Dominic Sequeira President
Tel: 631-880-6917
Email: dominic@procareus.com
Website: www.procareus.com
Short-term and long-term healthcare staffing solutions. (As-Ind, estab 2011, empl 80, sales $6,200,000, cert: City)

9336 QED National
350 Seventh Ave, 10 Fl
New York, NY 10001
Contact: Colleen Molter President
Tel: 212-481-6868
Email: cmolter@qednational.com
Website: www.qednational.com
IT temporary & permanent staffing. (Woman, estab 1993, empl 40, sales $14,281,567, cert: State)

9337 Russell Tobin & Associates, LLC
420 Lexington Ave, 29th Floor
New York, NY 10170
Contact: Jenny Davis Sr Dir
Tel: 212-235-5300
Email: jennifer.davis@russelltobin.com
Website: www.russelltobin.com
Recruitment and staffing, labor staffing, direct hire recruitment and payroll services. (Hisp, estab , empl 500, sales $80,000,000, cert: NMSDC)

9338 Synergy Staffing & Solutions Inc.
200 Park Ave S Ste 1411
New York, NY 10003
Contact: Ryan Watson President
Tel: 646-553-4458
Email: ryan@sinyc.com
Website: www.sinyc.com
Full-Time Staffing & Freelance Consulting Recruitment. (Minority, estab 2008, empl 50, sales $10,961,383, cert: NMSDC)

9339 Temporary Staffing by Suzanne, Ltd.
370 Lexington Ave, Ste 902
New York, NY 10017
Contact: Suzanne G. Davis President
Tel: 212-856-9500
Email: sdavis@suzannenyc.com
Website: www.suzannenyc.com
Temporary staffing: administrative, secretarial, computer, reception, research, clerical, editorial, project coordinator, events registration & data entry positions. (Woman, estab 1999, empl 6, sales $3,085,963, cert: State, City)

PROFESSIONAL SERVICES: Staffing Services

9340 The Burgess Group - Corporate Recruiters Intl
10 Barclay St Ste 16-C
New York, NY 10007
Contact: William H. Burgess, III CEO
Tel: 212-406-2400
Email: billburgess@theburgessgroup.com
Website: www.theburgessgroup.com
Mid to senior level executive search, diversity recruiting, training & management development consulting. (AA, estab 1997, empl 5, sales , cert: NMSDC)

9341 The May Consulting Group Inc.
174 County Hwy 67
Amsterdam, NY 12010
Contact: Sheila Greco CEO
Tel: 518-843-4611
Email: sgreco@sgatalent.com
Website: www.sgatalent.com
Recruitment research & strategic recruiting solutions. (Woman, estab 1989, empl 20, sales , cert: WBENC)

9342 Tower Legal Solutions
65 Broadway 17th Fl.
New York, NY 10006
Contact: Firtell CEO
Tel: 212-430-6300
Email: rchristenlall@towerls.com
Website: www.towerls.com
Staffing: temporary attorneys, paralegals & project space. (Woman, estab 2007, empl 74, sales $51,956,340, cert: WBENC)

Ohio

9343 A.I.M. Technical Consultants, Inc.
7618 Slate Ridge Blvd
Reynoldsburg, OH 43068
Contact: President
Tel: 614-866-1472
Email:
Website: www.aimtechnical.com
IT and Administrative Staffing (Hisp, estab 2000, empl 10, sales $2,000,000, cert: NMSDC)

9344 Acloche Staffing
1800 Watermark Dr Ste 430
Columbus, OH 43215
Contact: Kimberly Shoemaker CEO
Tel: 614-824-3700
Email: kshoemaker@acloche.com
Website: www.acloche.com
Human capital strategies & workforce resources, recruiting, customized search program. (Woman, estab 1968, empl 40, sales $23,100,000, cert: WBENC, NWBOC)

9345 Career Connections Staffing Services Inc.
26260 Center Ridge Road
Westlake, OH 44145
Contact: Brian DeChant President
Tel: 866-424-1233
Email: bdechant@go2itgroup.com
Website: www.go2itgroup.com
Temporary & permanent information technology & medical support staffing. (Woman, estab 1996, empl 45, sales $3,776,350, cert: WBENC)

9346 CORPTEMPS
7 N Main St
Niles, OH 44446
Contact: Anupama Pulvender
Tel: 248-978-8953
Email: Anupama.pulvender@corptemps.com
Website: www.corptemps.com
Staffing services (Woman/As-Ind, estab 2023, empl 300, sales $9,000,000, cert: NMSDC, WBENC)

9347 Crown Services, Inc.
2800 Corporate Exchange Dr Ste 120
Columbus, OH 43231
Contact: Stacey Diana VP Business Dev
Tel: 614-844-5429
Email: sdiana@crownservices.com
Website: www.crownservices.com
Staffing services. (Woman, estab 1968, empl 245, sales $123,000,000, cert: WBENC)

9348 Eastern Personnel Services, Inc.
619 Central Ave.
Cincinnati, OH 45202
Contact: Angelita Jones VP Smployment Svcs
Tel: 513-421-4666
Email: ajones@easternpersonnelservices.com
Website: www.easternpersonnelservices.com
Staffing: professional, contract, temporary, temp to hire, contract management & on-site supervision. (Woman/AA, estab 1987, empl 7, sales $3,625,356, cert: State, NMSDC, WBENC)

9349 Great Work Employment Services, Inc.
2034 E Market St
Akron, OH 44312
Contact: Bob Frankish Dir Business Dev
Tel: 330-535-3800
Email: bfrankish@greatwork.jobs
Website: www.greatwork.cc
Temporary staffing services. (Woman, estab 1992, empl 16, sales $7,600,000, cert: WBENC)

9350 Howard & O
29525 Chagrin Blvd Ste 100
Cleveland, OH 44122
Contact: Lee Ann Howard
Tel: 216-514-8980
Email: lah@howardobrien.com
Website: www.howardobrien.com
Executive search consulting services. (Woman, estab 2001, empl 4, sales $1,900,000, cert: WBENC)

9351 Hunter International, Inc.
38100 Colorado Ave
Avon, OH 44011
Contact: Gabrielle Christman President
Tel: 440-389-0023
Email: gchristman@hirecruiting.com
Website: www.hirecruiting.com
Project based staffing solutions, contract or temporary, contract to permanent. (Woman, estab 2006, empl 100, sales $15,700,000, cert: WBENC)

PROFESSIONAL SERVICES: Staffing Services

9352 JLS Staffing & Management dba Total Staffing Solutions
11562 Chester Rd
Cincinnati, OH 45246
Contact: Amy Mullett Owner
Tel: 513-771-9675
Email: tmullett@totalstaffsolutions.com
Website: www.totalstaffsolutions.com
Staffing Solutions: temporary positions, temp to hire, as well as direct hire placements. (Woman, estab 2012, empl 10, sales $10,200,000, cert: WBENC)

9353 KNK Recruiting, LLC
6562 Pleasant Valley Court
Loveland, OH 45140
Contact: Matt Baker CEO
Tel: 513-265-5741
Email: mbaker@knkrecruiting.com
Website: www.knkrecruiting.com
Recruitment Process Outsourcing (RPO), recruiting & placement solutions. (AA, estab 2009, empl 1, sales $230,871, cert: State)

9354 Maverick Direct, Inc.
PO Box 1247
Bath, OH 44210
Contact: Cindy Janos President
Tel: 330-668-1800
Email: cjanos@callmaverick.com
Website: www.callmaverick.com
Staffing & search firm capabilities in the IT and IS arena. (Woman, estab 1999, empl 43, sales $5,200,000, cert: NWBOC)

9355 Minority Executive Search
3060 Monticello Blvd.
Cleveland, OH 44118
Contact: Eral Burks CEO
Tel: 216-932-2022
Email: eral@minorityexecsearch.com
Website: www.minorityexecsearch.com
Women & Minority job placements. (AA, estab 1985, empl 10, sales , cert: NMSDC)

9356 Multitec, Inc./Next Step Resources
2731 Sawbury Blvd
Columbus, OH 43235
Contact: Tim Weber
Tel: 614-798-0671
Email: info@nextsr.com
Website: www.nextsr.com
Ppermanent placement, contract staffing, and consulting services (As-Pac, estab 1995, empl 40, sales , cert: NMSDC)

9357 OneSource Services
6700 Beta Dr Ste 110
Mayfield Village, OH 44143
Contact: Tom Puletti Operations
Tel: 440-565-4434
Email: tpuletti@1-sourceservices.com
Website: www.1-sourceservices.com
Temporary, temporary to hire, direct hire & payroll services for technical, professional, and light industrial skill sets. (Woman, estab 2014, empl 25, sales $500,000, cert: NWBOC)

9358 Pearl Interactive Network
1105 Schrock Rd Ste 107
Columbus, OH 43229
Contact: Merry Korn Owner
Tel: 614-258-2943
Email: mkcontracts@pinsourcing.com
Website: www.pinsourcing.com
Provides contact center, and business and staffing services. (Woman, estab 2004, empl 214, sales $11,984,822, cert: WBENC)

9359 Portfolio Creative, LLC
777 Goodale Blvd Ste 300
Columbus, OH 43212
Contact: Shelli Welch Dir Operations
Tel: 614-839-4897
Email: shelli@portfoliocreative.com
Website: www.portfoliocreative.com/
Staffing services: marketing, advertising, design, project management. (Woman, estab 2005, empl 60, sales $6,500,000, cert: WBENC)

9360 Proteam Solutions, Inc.
2750 Airport, Ste 120
Columbus, OH 43219
Contact: Tracy Stearns Dir Client Relations
Tel: 614-454-6488
Email: tstearns@psi92.com
Website: www.psi92.com
Supplemental staffing, direct hire, temp-to-hire, light industrial, administrative & career placement. (AA, estab 1992, empl 16, sales $10,482,357, cert: NMSDC)

9361 Quick Employment LLC
2800 Euclid Ave, Ste 310
Cleveland, OH 44101
Contact: Sherall Hardy President
Tel: 216-361-3030
Email: quickemp@cs.com
Website: www.quickemp.com
Employment services: office services, data entry, receptionist, accounting clerks, file clerks, office administrative, IT, General Labor, shipping & receving, porters, maintenance, drivers, CDL A, CDL B, dental assistants & medical assistants. (Woman/AA, estab 2001, empl 30, sales , cert: State, City)

9362 Reesential Inc.
15804 Terrace Dr
Cleveland, OH 44112
Contact: Charee Fountain President
Tel: 216-451-1820
Email: cfountain@reesential.com
Website: www.reesential.com
Information Technology Staffing: contract, contract to hire & direct hire placement services. (Woman/AA, estab 2014, empl 2, sales , cert: WBENC)

9363 Spherion of Lima Inc.
216 N Elizabeth St
Lima, OH 45801
Contact: Judith Cowan VP
Tel: 419-224-8367
Email: judithc@spherion-schulte.com
Website: www.spherion.com/nwohio
Recruiting and staffing. (Woman, estab 1982, empl 38, sales $26,000,000, cert: WBENC)

PROFESSIONAL SERVICES: Staffing Services

9364 Staffing Solutions Enterprises
5915 Landerbrook Dr Ste 100
Cleveland, OH 44124
Contact: Amy Elder Sales Team Mgr
Tel: 440-684-7218
Email: aelder@staffsol.com
Website: www.staffsol.com
Staffing & workforce management: temporary, temp-to-hire, direct placement, recruiting, managed staffing services, payrolling. (Woman, estab 1974, empl 20, sales $10,434,625, cert: City, WBENC)

9365 Supplemental Staffing
5333 Southwyck Blvd.
Toledo, OH 43614
Contact: Mary Stoneking President
Tel: 419-866-8367
Email: mstoneking@supplemental.com
Website: www.supplemental.com
Employment services. (Woman, estab 1978, empl 3000, sales , cert: WBENC)

9366 The Prout Group, Inc.
1111 Superior Ave, Ste 1120
Cleveland, OH 44114
Contact: Lourdes Bennett Office Mgr
Tel: 216-771-5530
Email: lbennett@proutgroup.com
Website: www.proutgroup.com
Retained executive search consulting services. (Woman/AA, estab 2002, empl 6, sales , cert: NMSDC)

Oregon

9367 BeginRight Employment Services
3708 NE 122nd Ave.
Portland, OR 97220
Contact: Cindy Wilkerson VP Sales & Service
Tel: 503-254-5959
Email: cwilkerson@beginright.com
Website: www.beginright.com/
Temporary, seasonal, contract to hire & direct hire staffing services: clerical, administrative, accounting, technical, engineering & professional placements, payrolling services. (Woman, estab 1985, empl 15, sales $7,200,000, cert: State)

9368 Boly-Welch, Inc.
920 SW 6th Ave, Ste 100
Portland, OR 97204
Contact: Kathleen Everett Dir Client Relations
Tel: 503-242-1300
Email: k.everett@bolywelch.com
Website: www.bolywelch.com
Recruiting/Staffing/Consulting agency. (Woman, estab 1986, empl 46, sales $16,000,000, cert: State, WBENC)

9369 Collaborative Vision LLC
7883 SW Barnard Dr
Beaverton, OR 97007
Contact: Lisa Matar Founder
Tel: 503-941-9444
Email: lisa@cvhires.com
Website: www.cvhires.com
Staffing, Direct Hire, Permanent, Contract, Temp, Contingent Staffing Support. (Woman/As-Ind, estab 2008, empl 19, sales $579,845, cert: State)

9370 OLSA Resources, Inc
3485 NE John Olsen Ave
Hillsboro, OR 97124
Contact: Olsa Martini President
Tel: 503-608-7895
Email: olsamartini@olsaresources.com
Website: www.olsaresources.com
Staffing & recruiting svcs: IT & engineering. (Woman, estab 1996, empl 75, sales $12,000,000, cert: WBENC, SDB)

9371 S. Brooks and Associates Inc.
1130 NE Alberta St
Portland, OR 97211
Contact: Lynn Sanders
Tel: 503-284-7930
Email: lsanders@sbrooks.com
Website: www.sbrooks.com
Staffing: permanent & temporary. (Woman/AA, estab 1981, empl 5, sales $3,000,000, cert: State)

Pennsylvania

9372 Abel Personnel, Inc.
3356 Paxton St
Harrisburg, PA 17111
Contact: Deborah Abel
Tel: 717-561-2222
Email: dabel@abelpersonnel.com
Website: www.abelpersonnel.com
Temp & contract employees, perm placement, business & professional employers. (Woman, estab 1969, empl 12, sales , cert: WBENC)

9373 Advantage Resource Group
1600 Valley View Blvd
Altoona, PA 16602
Contact: Bonnie Williams VP Admin
Tel: 814-944-3571
Email: bonnie.williams@theadvantages.com
Website: www.theadvantages.com
Temporary Staffing, Temporary to hire/contract staffing, Direct Hire, Executive Placement, HR audits, Employee handbooks & Job Descriptions, HR Consulting & training, Resume writing & exit interviews. (Woman, estab 1953, empl 12, sales $3,000,000, cert: State)

9374 American Personnel Managers and Consultants, Inc.
3607 Rosemont Ave, Ste 101
Camp Hill, PA 17011
Contact: Pat Gingrich CEO
Tel: 717-465-5637
Email: patg@apmci.com
Website: www.amerijob.com
Staffing, Human Resource Management, Consulting, Testing & Training, Procurement, Information Technology Staffing, Project Management. (Woman, estab 1998, empl 45, sales $3,000,000, cert: State)

9375 America's Staffing Partner, Inc.
35 E Elizabeth Ave, Ste 41
Bethlehem, PA 18018
Contact: Jorge Cruz CEO
Tel: 610-625-2511
Email: jcruz@americasstaffingpartner.com
Website: www.americasstaffingpartner.com
Provides contracted support personnel: administrative, logistics, healthcare, technical & trades. (Hisp, estab 2006, empl 250, sales $7,040,000, cert: 8(a))

PROFESSIONAL SERVICES: Staffing Services

9376 Assurance Staffing, Inc.
4660 Trindle Rd Ste 100
Camp Hill, PA 17011
Contact: Cinde Holste Mgr
Tel: 717-920-9190
Email: jobs@assurancestaf.com
Website: www.assurancestaf.com
Staffing Services, Temporary, Temp to Hire & Direct Hire placements. (Woman, estab 2003, empl 35, sales $879,179, cert: State, WBENC)

9377 Becker Technical Staffing, Inc.
312 Old Lancaster Rd
Merion Station, PA 19066
Contact: Renee Becker CEO
Tel: 610-667-9155
Email: renee@beckertek.com
Website: www.beckertek.com
Staffing: technical, pharmaceutical/healthcare, marketing sciences & financial/accounting talent acquisition. (Woman, estab 2008, empl 30, sales $2,000,000, cert: State, WBENC)

9378 Blue Plate Minds, Inc.
PO Box 1428
Paoli, PA 19301
Contact: Owner
Tel: 610-240-9001
Email: info@blueplateminds.com
Website: www.blueplateminds.com
Full time & freelance staffing: advertising & marketing, graphic & web designers/directors, editors, writers & proofreaders. (Woman, estab 1999, empl 25, sales $1,893,000, cert: WBENC)

9379 Bradley Temporaries, Inc. dba Bradley Staffing Gro
1400 Liberty Ridge Dr Ste 103
Wayne, PA 19087
Contact: Brad Burns VP
Tel: 610-254-9999
Email: brad@bradleystaffinggroup.com
Website: www.BradleyStaffingGroup.com
Temporary & direct hire placement services. (Woman, estab 1984, empl 6, sales $2,030,000, cert: WBENC)

9380 Choice Counsel, Inc.
535 Smithfield St, Ste 614 Oliver Bldg
Pittsburgh, PA 15222
Contact: Cynthia Scott President
Tel: 412-355-0900
Email: cynthiascott@choicecounsel.com
Website: www.choicecounsel.com
Legal staffing, attorneys & paralegals in temporary and temporary-to-hire positions. (Woman, estab 1998, empl 50, sales $2,400,000, cert: WBENC)

9381 Choice One Staffing Group, Inc.
2009 MacKenzie Way Ste 250
Cranberry Township, PA 16066
Contact: Julie Sacriponte President
Tel: 724-452-5800
Email: julie@choice1staffing.com
Website: www.choice1staffing.com
Temporary, temp to hire & direct hire capacities, custom employee testing, background screens, drug screens, payroll services & skill marketing. (Woman, estab 2003, empl 525, sales $3,300,000, cert: WBENC)

9382 Clutch Group LLC DBA-Clutch
417 N 8th St Ste 500
Philadelphia, PA 19123
Contact: Jewel Schmitz Business Devel
Tel: 215-240-6672
Email: jewel@clutchnow.com
Website: www.clutchnow.com
Flexible staffing solutions: Advertising, Digital, Creative, and Marketing, Freelance/Contract, Temp to Hire, Direct Hire, and Retained Search. (Woman, estab 2018, empl 15, sales $3,500,000, cert: WBENC)

9383 HTSS, Inc.
860 Broad St Ste 111
Emmaus, PA 18049
Contact: Pat Howells President
Tel: 610-432-4161
Email: phowells@htss-inc.com
Website: www.htss-inc.com
Staffing & recruiting services. (Woman, estab 1993, empl 7, sales $4,900,000, cert: State, WBENC)

9384 JH Technical Services, Inc.
3935 Washington Road Unit 1405
Canonsburg, PA 15317
Contact: Cynthia Harrison Henry President
Tel: 412-788-1174
Email: charrison@jhtechnical.com
Website: www.jhtechnical.com
Staffing services. (Woman, estab 1996, empl 20, sales $3,443,126, cert: State, WBENC)

9385 Krown Employment Services, LLC
801 Vinial St, Ste 102
Pittsburgh, PA 15212
Contact: President
Tel: 412-567-7136
Email: jobs@krownempsvc.com
Website: www.krownempsvc.com
Staffing: Administrative, Accounts Payable/Receivable Call Center, Clerical, General Labor, Hospitality, Light Industrial, Janitorial, Maintenance & Warehouse. (Woman, estab 2013, empl 250, sales , cert: WBENC)

9386 London Approach, Inc.
1100 E Hector St Ste 410
Conshohocken, PA 19428
Contact: Courtney Cox
Tel: 610-590-4900
Email: ccox@londonapproach.com
Website: www.londonapproach.com
Results-driven staffing: Temporary Solutions, Direct Hire Recruiting, Diversity Initiatives & Retained Search. (Woman, estab 2018, empl 22, sales $7,000,000, cert: WBENC)

9387 McCallion Temps, Inc.
601A Bethlehem Pike
Montgomeryville, PA 18936
Contact: Lisa McCallion President
Tel: 215-855-8000
Email: lmccallion@mccalliongroup.com
Website: www.mccallionstaffing.com
Staffing, temporary, temp to hire & direct hire personnel. (Woman, estab 1979, empl 12, sales $7,001,821, cert: NWBOC)

PROFESSIONAL SERVICES: Staffing Services

9388   Partner's Consulting, Inc.
       2004 Sproul Road, Ste 206
       Broomall, PA 19008
       Contact: Delivery & Engagement Mgr
       Tel: 215-939-6294
       Email: info@partners-consulting.com
       Website: www.partners-consulting.com
Information technology recruiting for full-time, temp-to-perm & contract positions. (Woman, estab 2006, empl 40, sales $6,000,000, cert: State, WBENC)

9389   RomAnalytics
       1117 Bridge Road, #34 34
       Creamery, PA 19430
       Contact: Kathy Roman President
       Tel: 484-961-8213
       Email: kathy.roman@romanalytics.com
       Website: www.romanalytics.com/
Recruiting & staffing, contract staffing or permanent staff recruiting. (Woman, estab 2013, empl 15, sales $1,900,000, cert: State, WBENC)

9390   Solomon International, LLC
       635 Coles Ct
       Harleysville, PA 19438
       Contact: Paul Solomon President
       Tel: 609-510-9705
       Email: paul.solomon@solomonsint.com
       Website: www.solomonsint.com
Employment services, temporary & direct hire employment & IT consulting services. (Minority, Woman, estab 2004, empl 20, sales $1,018,354, cert: State)

9391   Staffing Pharm, LLC
       PO Box 23
       Cresco, PA 18326
       Contact: Dora Pereda President
       Tel: 610-272-4993
       Email: dora.pereda@staffingpharm.com
       Website: www.staffingpharm.com/
Professional staffing services: pharmaceutical, healthcare, biotechnology & research industries. (Minority, Woman, estab 2012, empl 1, sales , cert: NMSDC)

9392   STAFFusion
       210 W. Pike St Ste 3
       Canonsburg, PA 15317
       Contact: Paula Davey President
       Tel: 724-916-4772
       Email: paula@staffusion.us
       Website: www.staffusion.com
Staffing, recruiting professionals, personnel, office, administrative, (Woman, estab 2003, empl 5, sales $2,800,000, cert: WBENC)

9393   StarsHR, Inc.
       1700 N Highland Rd Ste 200
       Pittsburgh, PA 15241
       Contact: Dir Placement Svcs
       Tel: 412-927-0369
       Email: sales@StarsHR.com
       Website: www.StarsHR.com
Executive placement services. (As-Ind, estab 2007, empl 5, sales $2,700,000, cert: State)

9394   The Carney Group
       1777 Sentry Pkwy West VEVA 14, Ste 301
       Blue Bell, PA 19422
       Contact: Jacquelyn Fowler Client Relationship Mgr
       Tel: 215-646-6200
       Email: jfowler@carneyjobs.com
       Website: www.carneyjobs.com
Staff augmentation or permanent hire. (Woman, estab 1992, empl 20, sales $10,000,000, cert: State, WBENC)

9395   The Drexel Group, Inc
       1832 Market St
       Camp Hill, PA 17011
       Contact: Romayne Johnson President
       Tel: 717-730-9841
       Email: romayne@thedrexelgroup.com
       Website: www.thedrexelgroup.com
Staffing: temporary, permanent, temp to hire, direct hire & contingency. (Woman, estab 1994, empl 200, sales $3,430,086, cert: State, WBENC)

Puerto Rico

9396   Almena Consulting Group, Inc.
       PO Box 1616
       Mayaguez, PR 00681
       Contact: Ana Cuebas President
       Tel: 787-833-7142
       Email: acuebas@almenapr.com
       Website: www.almenapr.com
Employment Agency. Temporary personnel, professional recruiting, seminars. (Hisp, estab 1983, empl 5, sales $1,663,723, cert: NMSDC)

9397   Careers Inc.
       208 Ave Ponce De Leon, Ste 1100 Banco Popular Ctr
       San Juan, PR 00918
       Contact: Blankie Hernandez Curt VP Admin
       Tel: 787-764-2298
       Email: blankieh@careersincpr.com
       Website: www.careersincpr.com
Executive Search & Management Recruiting. (Minority, Woman, estab 1970, empl 21, sales $2,179,173, cert: NMSDC)

9398   Caribbean Temprorary Services, LLC
       PO Box 11873
       San Juan, PR 00910
       Contact: Xiomara Villamil VP Corporate Affairs
       Tel: 787-620-5500
       Email: xiomara.villamil@ctspr.com
       Website: www.ctspr.com
Staffing services. (Minority, Woman, estab 1983, empl 5000, sales , cert: NMSDC)

9399   Job Hunters LLC
       PO Box 56012
       Bayamon, PR 00960
       Contact: John Bruno
       Tel: 787-998-7210
       Email: bruno@jobhunters-pr.com
       Website: www.clasificadosonline.com/PartnersListingJ
Temporary & permanent staffing. (Minority, Woman, estab 2013, empl 50, sales $1,200,000, cert: NMSDC)

PROFESSIONAL SERVICES: Staffing Services

9400 PSS Pathfinders Inc.
      90 carr 165 Ste 310
      Guaynabo, PR 00958
      Contact: Georyanne Rios Alvarez President
      Tel: 787-622-6868
      Email: grios@psspathfinders.com
      Website: www.psspathfinders.com
Staffing solutions: temporary, temporary to hire & executive search. (Minority, Woman, estab 1985, empl 425, sales $8,448,618, cert: WBENC, SDB)

9401 The Cervantes Group
      PO Box 16409
      San Juan, PR 00908
      Contact: Joanna Bauza President
      Tel: 787-729-7597
      Email: joanna@thecervantesgroup.com
      Website: www.thecervantesgroup.com
Staffing solutions, short or long-term requirements. (Minority, Woman, estab 2004, empl 22, sales $2,800,000, cert: WBENC)

9402 Weil Group, Inc.
      Urb. Villa Blanca Calle Aquamarina #78 Ste 1
      Caguas, PR 00725
      Contact: Milagros del R Gonzalez GM
      Tel: 787-633-0025
      Email: clopez@weilgroup.com
      Website: www.weilgroup.com
Temporary staffing, outsourcing IT & automation services: mgmt and/or admin, help desk, servers, WAN, email system, desktop, maintenance, backup & restore. (Hisp, estab 1994, empl 215, sales $12,000,000, cert: NMSDC)

9403 Wisdom Resources, Inc.
      350 Chardon Ave. Ste 119
      San Juan, PR 00918
      Contact: Aissa Betancourt President
      Tel: 787-963-1048
      Email: aissa@snellingpr.com
      Website: www.snellingpr.com
Staffing services: executive, career, temporary, temp-to-hire & contractors, background check & drug testing services. (Woman/Hisp, estab 2008, empl 137, sales $5,200,000, cert: NMSDC, WBENC)

Rhode Island

9404 Silverman McGovern Staffing
      284 W Exchange St
      Providence, RI 02903
      Contact: Faye Silverman Managing Partner
      Tel: 401-632-0580
      Email: Faye@silvermanmcgovern.com
      Website: www.silvermanmcgovern.com
Staffing: Legal, Marketing/Creative, Accounting/Finance, Administrative, Technical. (Woman, estab 2003, empl 7, sales , cert: WBENC)

South Carolina

9405 Augusta Temporaries, Inc. dba Manpower
      101 Broadus Ave
      Greenville, SC 29601
      Contact: Pamelia Davis COO
      Tel: 864-233-4162
      Email: pamelia.davis@manpowersc.com
      Website: www.manpowersc.com
Temporary staffing & customer service. (Woman, estab 1978, empl 300, sales $16,711,520, cert: WBENC)

9406 Eastern Design Services
      25 Woods Lake Rd, Ste 301
      Greenville, SC 29607
      Contact: John Crain Office Mgr
      Tel: 864-271-1228
      Email: jcrain@easterndesign.com
      Website: www.easterndesign.com
Technical & professional staffing: engineers, designers, drafters, office professionals, information technology & administrative personnel. (Woman, estab 1979, empl 5, sales $2,714,000, cert: State)

9407 Express Employment Professionals
      9557 Two Notch Rd Ste N
      Columbia, SC 29223
      Contact: Northan Golden CEO
      Tel: 803-788-8721
      Email: northan.golden@expresspros.com
      Website: www.expresspros.com
Temporary & permanent staffing. (AA, estab 2007, empl 4, sales $450,000, cert: NMSDC)

9408 Godshall and Godshall Personnel Consultants, Inc.
      310 University Ridge
      Greenville, SC 29601
      Contact: Julie Brown President
      Tel: 864-242-3491
      Email: julie.brown@godshallstaffing.com
      Website: www.SCcareerSearch.com
Staffing and recruiting, temporary, contract, temp to direct hire, and direct hire positions. (Woman, estab 1968, empl 18, sales $12,000,005, cert: WBENC)

9409 Marketplace Staffing Services Inc.
      200 Adley Way
      Greenville, SC 29606
      Contact: Jason Mitchell Dir of Sales
      Tel: 864-286-3900
      Email: jmitchell@marketplacestaffing.com
      Website: www.marketplacestaffing.com
Comprehensive staffing & onsite managed contract labor services: manufacturing, warehouse & light industrial staffing solutions. (AA, estab 1996, empl 25, sales $9,000,000, cert: NMSDC)

9410 Onin Staffing
      950 Sunset Blvd.
      Columbia, SC 29169
      Contact: Cierra Belser Dir of Natl Partnersh
      Tel: 334-313-6477
      Email: cbelser@excelsiorstaffing.com
      Website: www.excelsiorstaffing.com
Staffing services: temporary, temporary to permanent, direct placement & VNP. (AA, estab 2008, empl 1000, sales $9,542,011, cert: NMSDC)

9411 Perceptive Recruiting, LLC
      221 Meadow Rose Dr
      Travelers Rest, SC 29690
      Contact: Jill Rose President
      Tel: -   -
      Email: info@perceptiverecruiting.com
      Website: www.perceptiverecruiting.com
Recruiting and staffing services. (Woman, estab 2014, empl 5, sales $3,311,462, cert: WBENC)

PROFESSIONAL SERVICES: Staffing Services

9412   The Whitman Group LLC
       1459 Stuart Engals Blvd Ste 300
       Mt. Pleasant, SC 29464
       Contact: Neil Whitman President
       Tel: 843-375-0031
       Email: ngw@dunhillstaff.com
       Website: www.dunhillsc.com
Full service staffing: temp, temp to hire, and full time positions. (Woman, estab 2001, empl 50, sales $1,885,000, cert: City)

Tennessee

9413   A-One, LLC
       3639 New Getwell Rd., Ste 1 & 2
       Memphis, TN 38118
       Contact: Sterlyn Howell Owner
       Tel: 901-367-5757
       Email: astaffing2@yahoo.com
       Website: www.aonestaffing.com
Temp, temp-to-perm & permanent placement. (Woman/AA, estab 2001, empl 32, sales $2,200,000, cert: City, WBENC)

9414   Atlas Management Corporation
       750 Old Hickory Blvd Bldg Two, Ste 265
       Brentwood, TN 37027
       Contact: Warren Sawyers President
       Tel: 615-620-0977
       Email: wsawyers@atlasmanagement.us
       Website: www.atlasmanagement.us
Recruiting, staffing, call center services, business unit outsourcing. (AA, estab 2003, empl 10, sales $2,600,000, cert: State, SDB)

9415   Gem Quality
       2033 Castaic Lane
       Knoxville, TN 37932
       Contact: Jason Campbell President
       Tel: 865-560-9891
       Email: jcampbell@gem-quality.com
       Website: www.gemcareinc.com
HR services, temporary to hire, direct placement, commercial & professional staffing. (Woman/AA, estab 2005, empl 200, sales $6,428,737, cert: NMSDC, WBENC)

9416   MasterStaff, Inc.
       611 Potomac Pl, Ste 103
       Smyrna, TN 37167
       Contact: Jennifer Sheets CEO
       Tel: 615-223-5627
       Email: jennifer@masterstaffemployment.com
       Website: www.masterstaffemployment.com
Professional recruitment & placement, temporary & temp to hire employees, human resource consulting & contract staffing. (Woman, estab 1999, empl 450, sales $12,789,203, cert: WBENC)

9417   neMarc Professional Services, Inc.
       2500 Mt. Moriah Rd, Ste H231
       Memphis, TN 38115
       Contact: Carmen Bassett President
       Tel: 901-360-1804
       Email: carmenbassett@bellsouth.net
       Website: www.nemarcstaffing.com
Temporary, permanent placement, temp-to-perm staffing svcs: clerical, administrative, distribution, warehouse, IT, accounting & professional placement. (Woman/AA, estab 2002, empl 5, sales $742,000, cert: State, NMSDC)

9418   Omni Staffing Plus, Inc.
       80 N Tillman, Ste 201
       Memphis, TN 38111
       Contact: Dinah Terry
       Tel: 901-843-8433
       Email: dterry@omnistaffingplus.com
       Website: www.omnistaffingplus.com
Temporary/permanent staffing. (Woman/AA, estab 1999, empl 6, sales $1,874,214, cert: NMSDC)

9419   Provide Staffing Services LLC
       6765 E Shelby Dr
       Memphis, TN 38141
       Contact: Pat Morris Mgr
       Tel: 901-505-0005
       Email: pat@provide-staffing.com
       Website: www.pscstaffing.net
Temporary Employees, Clerical positions. (Woman, estab 2013, empl 170, sales , cert: City)

Texas

9420   A3 Solutions, Inc.
       11830 Webb Chapel Ste 1150
       Dallas, TX 75234
       Contact: Ralph Eguilior Branch Mgr
       Tel: 972-247-4100
       Email: admin@a3-inc.com
       Website: www.A3-inc.com
Staff Augmentation, Direct Placemen, Contract, Contract-to-Hire, Turnkey Solutions, Workforce Management Services. (Woman/Hisp, estab 2008, empl 20, sales $2,500,000, cert: State)

9421   ADASTAFF, Inc.
       702 Hunters Row Court
       Mansfield, TX 76063
       Contact: Aaron Flaherty Call Center Solutions Expert
       Tel: 817-469-6234
       Email: aflaherty@adastaff.com
       Website: www.adastaff.com
Temporary, Temporary-to-Hire Staffing, Payroll Administration, Executive Placement, Safety Consulting and Training, Direct Hire and Special Project Outsourcing. Our specialty is in Administrative, Clerical. (Woman, estab 1993, empl 225, sales $7,187,978, cert: WBENC)

9422   Adventus Technologies, Inc.
       6001 Savoy Ste 511
       Houston, TX 77036
       Contact: Vicki Semander
       Tel: 713-995-4446
       Email: vsemander@adventus-tech.com
       Website: www.adventus-tech.com
Professional, para professional & admin personnel: Project Mgt, Finance & Acctg Support, General Consulting Services, Acquisition & Procurement Mgt, Publication, & Logistic Support Svcs. (Woman/AA, estab 2005, empl 8, sales $376,000, cert: State, City, NMSDC, 8(a))

9423   All Temps 1 Personnel
       2606 MLK Jr. Blvd
       Dallas, TX 75215
       Contact: Stacie McGill Sales & Mktg Mgr
       Tel: 214-426-2700
       Email: jjeffrey@alltemps1.com
       Website: www.alltemps1.com
Staffing services. (AA, estab 1994, empl 15, sales $11,800,000, cert: NMSDC)

PROFESSIONAL SERVICES: Staffing Services

9424 Alleare Consulting, LLC
3625 N. Hall St Ste 685
Dallas, TX 75219
Contact: Lana Arnold CFO
Tel: 214-559-9878
Email: larnold@alleareconsulting.com
Website: www.alleareconsulting.com
Recruiting, staffing & consulting services: permanent placement, contract & contract-to-hire. (Woman, estab , empl , sales $816,030, cert: State, WBENC)

9425 All-N-One Services, LLC
12115 English Brook Cir
Humble, TX 77346
Contact: Ann Guliex CEO
Tel: 281-812-3553
Email: annguliex@all-n1.com
Website: www.all-n1.com
Temp to hire, direct-hire, contract & temporary staffing svcs. (Woman/AA, estab 2002, empl 3, sales $583,000, cert: WBENC)

9426 AllTex Staffing & Consulting LLC dba Abba Staffing
2350 Airport Fwy Ste 130
Bedford, TX 76022
Contact: Darla Beggs CEO
Tel: 817-354-2800
Email: darla@abbastaffing.com
Website: www.abbastaffing.com
Direct Placement, Contingent-to-hire-Personnel, Contract personnel, Temporary personnel. (Woman, estab 2001, empl 5, sales $390,000,000, cert: State, WBENC)

9427 AMP Personnel Services, LLC
3700 N 10th St, Ste 302
McAllen, TX 78501
Contact: Marisa Sonnier Admin
Tel: 956-627-0477
Email: amppersonnelservices@gmail.com
Website: www.amppersonnel.com
Staffing services: professional, administrative & commercial job placement. (Minority, Woman, estab 2012, empl 2, sales $100,000, cert: State, 8(a))

9428 ANSERTEAM, LLC
4835 LBJ Freeway Ste 1000
Dallas, TX 75244
Contact: Ann Kramer Dir Strategic Partnerships
Tel: 888-932-6737
Email: akramer@anserteam.com
Website: www.anserteam.com
Specialize in clerical, administrative, customer service, accounting and technical staffing. (Woman, estab 2004, empl 8, sales $47,095,422, cert: WBENC)

9429 Applicantz, Inc.
10235 W Little York Road, Ste 235
Houston, TX 77040
Contact: Nikhil Jain Dir
Tel: 713-834-4909
Email: nikhilj@applicantz.com
Website: www.applicantz.com
IT Contingent Staffing: Contract, Contract-to-hire, and Permanent and Remote Technology Staffing. (Woman/Nat-Ame, estab 2001, empl 125, sales $14,800,000, cert: NMSDC)

9430 ASAP Personnel Inc.
17311 Dallas Pkwy
Dallas, TX 75248
Contact: Evelyn Touchette President
Tel: 972-432-6667
Email: evelyn@asapdo.com
Website: www.asapdo.net
Staffing & Personnel Services. (Woman, estab 2010, empl 22, sales $500,000, cert: State, City)

9431 Aspekt Consultancy Services LLC dba Jubilant Consulting
5008 Mohegan Ln
Frisco, TX 75034
Contact: Manish Bhardwaj
Tel: 214-463-4846
Email: manish.bhardwaj@jubilantconsulting.com
Website: www.jubilantconsulting.com
Technology-led business transformation services, technology implementation & bespoke staffing solutions. (As-Ind, estab 2015, empl 56, sales $1,285,173, cert: NMSDC)

9432 AXIS Staffing
1111 W Mockingbird Ln
Dallas, TX 75247
Contact: Jacob Joseph President
Tel: 214-638-4000
Email: jacob_joseph@axisstaff.com
Website: www.axisstaff.com
Staffing services. (As-Pac, estab 1993, empl 10, sales $4,500,000, cert: State)

9433 Barbara J. Charles dba Perfection Staffing
16502 Brightling Ln
Houston, TX 77090
Contact: Barbara Charles Owner
Tel: 281-781-7587
Email: bcharles@perfectionstaffing.agency
Website: www.perfectionstaffing.agency
Staffing and Recruitment Agency, Direct Hire, Contract/Contract-to-Hire, and Temporary talent for Exempt and Non-Exempt positions.
Our staffing efforts are (Woman/AA, estab 2018, empl 2, sales , cert: City, NMSDC)

9434 BBM Staffing
4242 Medical Dr, Bldg 2200
San Antonio, TX 78229
Contact: Liz Moreno Operations Mgr
Tel: 210-822-0717
Email: lmoreno@bbmstaffing.com
Website: www.bbmstaffing.com
Recruiting, temporary, temp to hire & direct hire solutions. (Minority, Woman, estab 2009, empl 300, sales $11,000,000, cert: State, NMSDC)

9435 Bestica, Inc.
3463 Magic Dr Ste 303
San Antonio, TX 78229
Contact: Harvinder Singh CEO
Tel: 210-614-4198
Email: harvinder@bestica.com
Website: www.bestica.com
IT consulting & staffing firm. (As-Ind, estab 2005, empl 198, sales $7,500,000, cert: NMSDC, 8(a))

PROFESSIONAL SERVICES: Staffing Services

9436 Bresa Tech LLC dba Bresatech LLC
6860 Dallas Pkwy Ste 200
Plano, TX 75024
Contact: Matthew Bomberger
Tel: 866-728-2889
Email: matt.bomberger@bresatech.com
Website: www.bresatech.com
Executive Search, Contract to Hire, Contract. (As-Pac, estab 2017, empl 42, sales $9,500,000, cert: NMSDC)

9437 Brooke Staffing Companies, Inc.
3900 Essex, Ste 555
Houston, TX 77027
Contact: Joe Stephens Treasurer
Tel: 713-337-2222
Email: joes@brookecompanies.com
Website: www.brookecompanies.com
Temporary & full-time placement services. (Woman, estab 1989, empl 213, sales $8,718,523, cert: City, WBENC)

9438 Burnett Specialists
9800 Richmond Ave Ste 800
Houston, TX 77042
Contact: Rick Burnett VP Reg Mgr
Tel: 713-358-1437
Email: rick@burnettspecialists.com
Website: www.burnettspecialists.com
Temporary, contract & direct-hire placement: clerical & administrative, accounting & financial, legal, human resources, information technology, sales, medical, customer service, light industrial & electronics personnel. (Woman, estab 1974, empl 115, sales $66,200,000, cert: WBENC)

9439 Burns Search LLC
1415 Legacy Dr, Ste 310
Frisco, TX 75034
Contact: CEO
Tel: 214-213-4053
Email:
Website: www.burnssearch.com
Staffing, recruiting, consulting: technical, accounting, finance, executive search. (Woman, estab 1999, empl 8, sales $1,394,555, cert: WBENC)

9440 Business Control Systems LP
16415 Addison Rd Ste 150
Addison, TX 75001
Contact: Chevalier Francis Business Devel Mgr
Tel: 972-241-8392
Email: chevalier.francis@bcsmis.com
Website: www.bcsmis.com
Project resources planning, enterprise business architecture, mediation, and outplacement services. (Woman/AA, estab 1981, empl 150, sales $19,127,630, cert: State, WBENC)

9441 C&T Information Technology Consulting, Inc.
201 S Lakeline Ste 803
Cedar Park, TX 78613
Contact: Jennifer Conway Dir Sales/Marketing
Tel: 512-610-0040
Email: sales@candttech.com
Website: www.candttech.com
Entry level, High End & Mid-Level Technical Staffing & Consulting. Project Management, Enterprise Architecture & Technical Solutions Provider Perm Placement, Technical Recruiting. (Woman, estab 2003, empl 34, sales $5,115,202, cert: State)

9442 Cambay Consulting LLC
1838 Snake River Road, Ste A
Katy, TX 77449
Contact: Ashwani Sharma Business Devel Mgr
Tel: 469-393-9501
Email: ashwani.sharma@cambaycs.com
Website: www.cambaycs.com
Temporary & permanent staffing solutions. (Minority, estab 2012, empl 137, sales $19,200,000, cert: NMSDC)

9443 Choice Hire Staffing LLC
3106 Hwy 377 S
Brownwood, TX 76801
Contact: Melissa Mauricio Owner
Tel: 325-643-1416
Email: melissa@choicehirestaffing.com
Website: www.choicehirestaffing.com
Temporary, seasonal, temp to hire & direct placement. (Woman, estab 2013, empl 3, sales , cert: State)

9444 Elise Resources, Inc.
950 Echo Lane Ste 200
Houston, TX 77024
Contact: Nadia Clark CEO
Tel: 281-313-4422
Email: nadia@eliseresources.com
Website: www.eliseresources.com
Call Center: inbound & outbound customer service & sales related calls. (AA, estab 2015, empl 1, sales , cert: State)

9445 Employee Risk Management Co. Inc.
4639 Corona, Ste 99
Corpus Christi, TX 78411
Contact: Laura Escobar President
Tel: 361-808-8367
Email: laura@atrecruiters.com
Website: www.atpersonnelservices.com
Recruiting, direct hire & temporary placement, Background checks, Drug screens, Safety Assured. (Minority, Woman, estab 1994, empl 10, sales $6,000,000, cert: State)

9446 Evins Personnel Consltants
6430 Richmond Ave Ste 415
Houston, TX 77057
Contact: Helen Royston Acct Rep
Tel: 713-977-8555
Email: staffing@hrnetconnection.com
Website: www.HRnetConnection.com
Temporary staffing, direct hire, temp to hire staffing. (Woman, estab 1967, empl 5000, sales $15,000,000, cert: State)

9447 Execusane Inc
2306 Stillwater Dr
Mesquite, TX 75181
Contact: Shiree Alexander President
Tel: 972-277-1176
Email: shayes@execusane.com
Website: www.execusane.com
Direct Placement, Executive Recruiting, HR Consulting, Staffing/Contract Recruiting. (Woman/AA, estab 2012, empl 1, sales , cert: State)

PROFESSIONAL SERVICES: Staffing Services

9448 Foremost Staffing, Inc.
3991 West Vickery
Fort Worth, TX 76107
Contact: Vicki Jordan President
Tel: 817-346-4738
Email: vjordan@foremoststaffing.com
Website: www.foremoststaffing.com
Staffing: temporary, temp to hire, direct placements & payroll services. (Woman, estab 2007, empl 100, sales $2,261,595, cert: State, WBENC)

9449 Fulgent Solutions Inc.
5700 Granite Pkwy Ste 200
Plano, TX 75024
Contact: Shan Adaikalam President
Tel: 972-506-7335
Email: shan.adaikalam@fulgentsol.com
Website: www.fulgentsol.com
Enterprise business consulting & staffing, technology, temporary, temporary-to-hire & permanent placement services. (As-Ind, estab 2013, empl 15, sales $1,500,000, cert: State)

9450 Getcorp Payroll Accounting & Tax dba Get Hire Staffing
8104 Southwest Fwy, Ste C
Houston, TX 77074
Contact: Gloria Towolawi CEO
Tel: 832-680-5225
Email: info@gethirestaffing.com
Website: www.gethirestaffing.com
Employment placement agency that provides pre-screened and qualified candidates- eliminating time and money wasting unproductive job boards. (AA, estab 2019, empl 3, sales , cert: State, City, WBENC)

9451 GS Infovision LLC dba Global Systems LLC
1200 Walnut Hill Lane, Ste 2220
Irving, TX 75038
Contact: Shekhar Gupta VP
Tel: 214-717-4344
Email: account@globalsyst.com
Website: www.globalsyst.com
IT Consulting, Staffing, BPO, IT Consulting, temporary, contract, temp to perm & permanent staffing solutions. (Minority, Woman, estab 2005, empl 110, sales $11,000,000, cert: NMSDC)

9452 Hawkins, Associates, Inc.
909 NE Loop 410, Ste 104
San Antonio, TX 78209
Contact: Elizabeth Hawkins VP
Tel: 210-349-9911
Email: liz@hawkinspersonnel.com
Website: www.hawkinspersonnel.com
Temporary, temp-to-hire, direct hire professional services, payrolling services & on-site management services. (Woman, estab 1977, empl 35, sales $18,000,000, cert: State, City)

9453 HirePower Personnel, Inc.
14100 Southwest Freeway Ste 320
Sugar Land, TX 77478
Contact: Travis Hamblet Global Operations Mgr
Tel: 281-455-6802
Email: travis.hamblet@hppstaffing.com
Website: www.hppstaffing.com
Temp, Temp to Hire & Direct Hire Placements. (Woman, estab 0, empl , sales $4,000,000, cert: State, WBENC)

9454 ICON Information Consultants, LP
100 Waugh Dr Ste 300
Houston, TX 77007
Contact: Pamela O'Rourke Founder & CEO
Tel: 713-438-0919
Email: porourke@iconconsultants.com
Website: www.iconconsultants.com
Recruit information technology, accounting & finance professionals. (Woman, estab 1998, empl 6000, sales $589,013,900, cert: WBENC)

9455 IMCS Group
9901 East Valley Ranch Pkwy Ste 3020
Irving, TX 75063
Contact: Nipun Baldua
Tel: 972-929-6600
Email: presales@imcsgroup.net
Website: www.imcsgroup.net
Customized staffing solutions: Office Administration, Customer Support, Manufacturing, Engineering, Executive Management, Finance. (Woman/As-Ind, estab 2002, empl 1300, sales $64,000,000, cert: NMSDC, WBENC)

9456 Imprimis Group
4835 LBJ Frwy, Ste 1000
Dallas, TX 75244
Contact: Valerie Freeman CEO
Tel: 972-419-1635
Email: vfreeman@imprimis.com
Website: www.imprimis.com
Staffing; temp, temp to hire, direct hire: admin/office, accounting, bilingual, cstnmr svc, legal, mktg, medical, mortgage, etc. (Woman, estab 1982, empl 60, sales $21,000,000, cert: State, WBENC)

9457 InGenesis, Inc.
10231 Kotzebue St
San Antonio, TX 78217
Contact: Dr. Veronica Edwards CEO
Tel: 210-366-0033
Email: commercial@ingenesis.com
Website: www.ingenesis.com
Workforce solutions: direct placement, direct hire, executive search, temporary staffing, contingent staffing, managed vendor, recruitment process outsourcing, managed services programs & locum tenens. (Minority, Woman, estab , empl , sales $174,785,000, cert: NMSDC, WBENC)

9458 International Genesis Professional Solutions, Inc.
PO Box 692205
San Antonio, TX 78269
Contact: Shelah Simmons CEO
Tel: 210-867-4182
Email: simmons@genesisprofsol.com
Website: www.genesisprofsol.com
Human Capital, Business Process Optimization & Project Management, Strategic Executive Recruitment, Human Resources Staffing (Temporary Help Service). (Woman/AA, estab 2006, empl 5, sales $149,100, cert: State)

9459 iSTAFF Solutions, Inc.
PO Box 118440
Carrollton, TX 75011
Contact: Wanda Young Dir
Tel: 972-251-9877
Email: wanda.young@istaffsolutions.org
Website: www.istaffsolutions.org
IT Staffing, Light Warehouse, Admin. (Woman/AA, estab 2010, empl 20, sales , cert: State)

PROFESSIONAL SERVICES: Staffing Services

9460   JK Flenory & Company, LLC
PO Box 5069
Frisco, TX 75035
Contact: Marcellas Flenory Sr. CEO
Tel: 972-480-2667
Email: recruiter@jkfcompany.com
Website: www.JKFCompany.com
Staffing, recruiting, retention & outplacement services. (AA, estab 2012, empl 1, sales , cert: City)

9461   KeyStaff Inc.
2909 Hillcroft St, Ste 620 Ste 620
Houston, TX 77057
Contact: Tammie Jeffers Branch Mgr
Tel: 713-422-2710
Email: tammie.jeffers@keystaffinc.com
Website: www.keystaffinc.com
Staffing: temporary, temp-to-perm & direct-hire placements. (Woman, estab 2004, empl 20, sales $18,989,644, cert: State, City)

9462   King Finders, LLC
6575 West Loop South, Ste 500
Bellaire, TX 77401
Contact: Manny Coronado President
Tel: 713-936-2695
Email: mcoronado@kingfinders.com
Website: www.kingfinders.com
Temp-to-Hire, Contingent and Direct Hire placements for Business & Administrative Professionals, Oil & Gas, Energy, Finance & Accounting, Information Technology and Manufacturing. (Hisp, estab 2018, empl 25, sales , cert: State)

9463   Labor On Demand Inc.
851 Culebra Rd
San Antonio, TX 78201
Contact: Ricardo Tovar Dir of Business Develop
Tel: 210-865-0445
Email: richard.tovar@lodstaffing.com
Website: www.lodstaffing.com
Temporary and Temp-to-Hire, Direct Placement, Payrolling, Recruitment. (Woman/Hisp, estab 2003, empl 24, sales , cert: State, SDB)

9464   Labor On Demand Inc., Dba, LOD Resource Group
851 Culebra Road
San Antonio, TX 78201
Contact: Richard Tovar Business Devel
Tel: 210-865-0445
Email: rtovar@lodresourcegroup.com
Website: www.lodresourcegroup.com/
Temporary & permanent employment services. (Minority, Woman, estab 2003, empl 31, sales $13,475,568, cert: State, 8(a), SDB)

9465   LaneStaffing Inc.
2211 Norfolk, Ste 150
Houston, TX 77098
Contact: Elaine Jackson Sr Recruiter
Tel: 713-522-0000
Email: ejackson@lanestaff.com
Website: www.lanestaff.com
Staffing: light industrial, construction, information technology, administrative/clerical, security, call center, finance, accounting, and engineering/technical support specialists. (Woman/AA, estab 2007, empl 525, sales $20,000,000, cert: City)

9466   LK Jordan & Associates
7550 IH 10 West Ste 105
San Antonio, TX 78229
Contact: Stefanie Chavez Business Devel
Tel: 210-488-9360
Email: stefanie.chavez@lkjordan.com
Website: www.lkjordan.com
Staffing services: temporary, temporary to hire & direct hire employees. (Woman, estab 1990, empl 52, sales $25,000,000, cert: State)

9467   Lotus Staffing Group, LLC
1925 E Beltline Rd Ste 419
Carrollton, TX 75006
Contact: Tyra Roberts Managing Dir
Tel: 972-410-3685
Email: tyra@lotusstaffingagency.com
Website: www.lotusstaffingagency.com
Contingent staffing solutions. (Woman/AA, Hisp, estab 2008, empl 23, sales $3,450,000, cert: State, City)

9468   Magnum Staffing Services, Inc.
2900 Smith St, Ste 250
Houston, TX 77006
Contact: Caroline Brown President
Tel: 713-658-0068
Email: caroline.brown@magnumstaffing.com
Website: www.magnumstaffing.com
Background, drug-screening, SS verification, temporary placement, temp-to-hire, direct hire, industrial, clerical & managerial arenas. (Woman, estab 1996, empl 43, sales $38,000,000, cert: WBENC)

9469   MIT Professionals, Inc.
22611 Duncan Brush Trace
Richmond, TX 77469
Contact: Rebecca Morgan President
Tel: 713-934-9700
Email: rebecca@mitprof.com
Website: www.mitprof.com
Staffing services: information technology, supply chain resources, engineering & professional services. (Woman, estab 1995, empl 50, sales , cert: State)

9470   Mobile Temporary Services
9110 Jones Rd Ste 131
Houston, TX 77065
Contact: Allison Holmes President
Tel: 713-344-4148
Email: allison@mobiletempstaff.com
Website: www.mobiletempstaff.com
Temporary employees, direct hire, temp-to-perm & contract employees, on-site applications, backgrounds checks, drug-screen & on-boarding. (Woman/AA, estab 2016, empl 4, sales , cert: WBENC, SDB)

9471   Nelson Search Group
3001 Lake Oak Dr
Arlington, TX 76017
Contact: D. Gayle Barton Principal
Tel: 817-466-7117
Email: gayle@nelsonsearchgroup.com
Website: www.nelsonsearchgroup.com
Ethical, consultative, confidential, quality-driven direct recruiting & on-boarding (full life-cycle). (Woman, estab 2009, empl 1, sales $150,000, cert: State, WBENC)

PROFESSIONAL SERVICES: Staffing Services

9472 Peyton Resource Group, LP
100 Decker Ct, Ste 140
Irving, TX 75062
Contact: Bryan Mayhew
Tel: 972-717-7701
Email: bmayhew@prg-usa.com
Website: www.prg-usa.com
Staffing services, temp, temp to perm: IT, telecom, engineering, finance, accounting, clerical, admin & customer support. (Hisp, estab 2001, empl 15, sales , cert: State, NMSDC)

9473 Primary Services LP
520 Post Oak Blvd Ste 550
Houston, TX 77027
Contact: MaryKay Foy-Hinton Strategic Accounts Mgr
Tel: 713-850-7010
Email: marykay@primaryservices.com
Website: www.primaryservices.com
Staffing solutions, contract, contract-to-hire & direct hire placement. (Woman, estab 1988, empl 39, sales $44,928,501, cert: WBENC)

9474 Pro Health Medical Staffing
700 Milam St
Houston, TX 77022
Contact: Ginger Delance CEO
Tel: 713-655-1555
Email: ginger@phmstaffing.com
Website: www.phmstaffing.com
Staffing Physicians, Advanced Practitioners, Nursing, Allied Health, Information Technology, and medical administrative professionals. (Hisp, estab 0, empl 200, sales $13,524,000, cert: State)

9475 Pro-Touch Nurses Inc.
1701 Legacy Dr Ste 1100
Frisco, TX 75034
Contact: Harry Holt Dir of Business Develop
Tel: 972-544-6347
Email: harry.holt@protouchstaffing.com
Website: www.protouchstaffing.com
Credentialing services for direct hire & perm staff. (Woman/As-Ind, estab 1989, empl 150, sales $24,000,000, cert: WBENC)

9476 QSTAFF Incorporated
PO Box 580622
Houston, TX 77258
Contact: Richard Green
Tel: 281-218-6574
Email: r.green@qualified-staff.com
Website: www.qualified-staff.com
Staffing svcs: accounting, admin, clerical, chemical plant operators, data entry, engineering, IT, light industrial. (Minority, Woman, estab 1999, empl 75, sales $3,000,000, cert: State, WBENC)

9477 RD Data Solutions
2340 E Trinity Mills Ste 349
Carrollton, TX 75006
Contact: Reuben D'Souza CEO
Tel: 972-899-2334
Email: reuben.dsouza@rddatasolutions.com
Website: www.rddatasolutions.com
Technology staffing: SAP & ERP. (Minority, Woman, estab 2002, empl 26, sales $25,000,000, cert: State, NMSDC)

9478 Recruiting Force, LLC
1464 E. Whitestone Blvd. Ste 1903
Cedar Park, TX 78613
Contact: Rudy Uribe President
Tel: 512-996-0999
Email: rudy.uribe@recruitveterans.com
Website: www.recruitveterans.com
Direct hire professional executive search, permanent placement, information technology, engineering, project management, logisitics, finance, accounting. (Hisp, estab 2003, empl 60, sales $4,437,363, cert: NMSDC, 8(a))

9479 Recruiting Source International
21414 Julie Marie Ln, Ste 2301
Katy, TX 77449
Contact: Bianca Jackson COO
Tel: 281-277-1411
Email: bjackson@recruiting-source.com
Website: www.recruiting-source.com
Executive Search, Staffing & 1099 Management Services. (Woman/AA, estab , empl , sales $1,410,000, cert: State, City, NMSDC, WBENC, SDB)

9480 Resource Personnel Consultants, LLC
14070 Proton Rd
Farmers Branch, TX 75244
Contact: Acct Mgr
Tel: 972-371-2934
Email: hmckinley@rpccompany.com
Website: www.rpccompany.com
Staffing: clerical, administrative & customer service employees, temporary, temporary to permanent or direct hire. (Minority, Woman, estab 2001, empl 8, sales $1,827,499, cert: State)

9481 RG Talent Solutions, LLC
726 Dalworth St Ste 1000
Grand Prairie, TX 75050
Contact: Reginald W Calhoun, Sr. CEO
Tel: 817-405-2838
Email: rcalhoun@rgtalentsolutions.com
Website: www.rgtalentsolutions.com
Business process outsourcing (BPO), talent management, talent acquisition, agency and marketing firm. (AA, estab 2009, empl 14, sales $4,000,000, cert: State, NMSDC)

9482 RightStaff, Inc
6060 N Central Expy Ste 222
Dallas, TX 75206
Contact: Shelley Amason CEO
Tel: 214-615-6015
Email: samason@rightstaffinc.com
Website: www.rightstaffinc.com
Staffing services: permanent, temporary, project staff augmentation, computer software & hardware, computer programing, systems design, technology infrastructure. (Woman, estab 1998, empl 20, sales $2,862,677, cert: State, WBENC)

9483 Riverway Business Services
5213 Spruce St Ste 100
Bellaire, TX 77401
Contact: Margo Costello President
Tel: 713-664-5900
Email: margo.costello@riverway.jobs
Website: www.riverway.jobs
Staffing services: admin/clerical, accounting, human resource, professional & information technology. (Woman, estab 1990, empl 22, sales $2,000,000, cert: WBENC)

PROFESSIONAL SERVICES: Staffing Services

9484 RMPersonnel, Inc.
      4707 Montana Ave
      El Paso, TX 79903
      Contact: Debra Underwood Branch Mgr
      Tel: 915-565-7674
      Email: debras@rmpersonnel.com
      Website: www.rmpersonnel.com
Staffing services: employee leasing, temporaries, temp to hire, executive recruiting & HR consulting services. (Minority, Woman, estab 1990, empl 33, sales $34,000,000, cert: WBENC)

9485 Saba Quaility System
      1456 FM 1960 W
      Houston, TX 77090
      Contact: Patricia Carter Mgr/HR Business Devel
      Tel: 281-537-7676
      Email: qualitysystem.qs@gmail.com
      Website: www.qualitysystemssite.com
IT staffing, sourcing, prescreening, interviewing & placement. (Minority, Woman, estab 2010, empl 14, sales $1,700,000, cert: State)

9486 Search Plus International
      5900 Balcones Dr Ste 242
      Austin, TX 78731
      Contact: Bruce Bagwell Managing Dir
      Tel: 512-459-8200
      Email: bbagwell@searchplustexas.com
      Website: www.searchplustexas.com
Executive mid-management & highly-technical searches. (Woman, estab 1988, empl 9, sales $500,000, cert: WBENC)

9487 Smith & Dean, Inc.
      11511 Katy Freeway Ste 430
      Houston, TX 77079
      Contact: Jennifer Dean President
      Tel: 713-785-7483
      Email: jdean@dpsinc-texas.com
      Website: www.deansprofessionalservices.com
Staffing solutions, recruiting, workshops & seminars, IT consulting. (Woman/AA, estab 1993, empl 2180, sales $10,681,149, cert: State, City, NMSDC, WBENC)

9488 Snelling Employment, LLC
      4055 Valley View Lane Ste 700
      Dallas, TX 75244
      Contact: Bryan Lee
      Tel: 972-776-1309
      Email: bryan.lee@snelling.com
      Website: www.snelling.com
Temporary, temp-to-hire, contract, contract-to-direct hire, direct hire, executive search, and payrolling services. (Woman, estab 1951, empl 2300, sales $144,376,000, cert: WBENC)

9489 SNS Global Corporation
      1000 Heritage Center Circle
      Round Rock, TX 78664
      Contact: Misty Carr HR
      Tel: 512-250-2959
      Email: m.carr@snsglobalstaffing.com
      Website: www.snsglobalstaffing.com
Staffing services. (As-Ind, estab 2003, empl 20, sales , cert: State, NMSDC)

9490 Softel Techsource LLC
      2100 Alamo Rd., Ste T,
      Richardson, TX 75080
      Contact: Mohammed Al-Baki Managing Partner
      Tel: 469-475-2297
      Email: malbaki@softeltechsource.com
      Website: www.softeltechsource.com
Recruiting practices & continuous training. (Woman/As-Ind, estab 2010, empl 10, sales , cert: State)

9491 SOLRAC Corporation
      6 Founders Blvd Ste A
      El Paso, TX 79906
      Contact: Masazumi Aso Exec VP & COO
      Tel: 915-772-3073
      Email: maso@solraccorp.com
      Website: www.solraccorp.com
Assembly, sorting & rework operation, staffing services, warehouse & logistic operation. (Hisp, estab 1989, empl 300, sales , cert: State, NMSDC)

9492 Solution Tech Staffing Inc.
      2825 Wilcrest, Ste 678
      Houston, TX 77042
      Contact: Emon Carroll President
      Tel: 713-988-5325
      Email: emon@ststaff.com
      Website: www.ststaff.com
Staffing: short term temporary, long term temporary, temp-to-hire & direct hire. (Woman/AA, estab 2001, empl 7, sales , cert: State, City)

9493 Southwest Staffing
      12025 Rojas, Ste L
      El Paso, TX 79936
      Contact: James Tidwell Dir
      Tel: 915-857-9719
      Email: info@southweststaffing.com
      Website: www.southweststaffing.com
Temporary employee placement & management, staffing & recruiting solutions in technical & professional placement. (Minority, Woman, estab 1994, empl 23, sales $15,298,011, cert: State)

9494 SV Meditrans, Inc.
      100 S 8th St
      Richmond, TX 77469
      Contact: Rohini Dinesh CEO
      Tel: 832-520-8742
      Email: rohinid@svmtinc.com
      Website: www.svmtinc.com
Staffing services, interviews, screening & training. (Minority, Woman, estab 2002, empl 20, sales $1,650,000, cert: WBENC)

9495 The Burchell Group
      11200 W Broadway, Ste 2348
      Pearland, TX 77584
      Contact: Jamie Burchell President
      Tel: 281-607-5990
      Email: jamie@theburchellgroup.com
      Website: www.theburchellgroup.com
Staffing solutions: engineering, information technology & GIS. (Hisp, estab 2001, empl 45, sales , cert: NMSDC)

9496 The HR Source, Inc.
2307 Oak Ln, Ste 2B-213
Grand Prairie, TX 75051
Contact: Brett Farley Acct Exec
Tel: 972-264-9800
Email: contactus@thehrsource.net
Website: www.thehrsource.net
Temporary, temp to hire & permanent placement: IT, administrative, engineering, clerical & general labor. (Woman/AA, estab 2003, empl 101, sales , cert: WBENC)

9497 The Omega Staff, LLC
14756 Dallas Pkwy, Ste 805
Dallas, TX 75254
Contact: Michelle Deriggs Owner
Tel: 972-948-7754
Email: mderiggs@omegastaff.com
Website: www.omegastaff.com
Professional recruiting & staffing services to automotive, engineering, defense, and manufacturing companies. (Woman/AA, estab 2007, empl 6, sales $130,000, cert: State, City)

9498 The Unbeatable Connection LLC
111 Brand Lane, Ste 3
Stafford, TX 77477
Contact: La Teasha Smith Owner
Tel: 832-363-2566
Email: tuctruckingsales@gmail.com
Website: www.tuctrucking.com/
Staffing services: temp, temp to perm & direct hire positions. (Woman/AA, estab 2010, empl 5, sales $308,826, cert: City)

9499 Three PDS Inc.
13355 Noel Rd Ste 1100
Dallas, TX 75240
Contact: Trisha Kana-Mistry Director
Tel: 214-222-3737
Email: tkana@threepds.com
Website: www.threepds.com
Recruiting, Staffing, Consulting: Accounting/Finance, Supply Chain, IT, Marketing, Administration, Human Resources, Call Center. (As-Ind, estab 2003, empl 50, sales $3,500,000, cert: NMSDC)

9500 TMC Workforce Solutions
2313 W Sam Houston Pkwy N Ste 155
Houston, TX 77043
Contact: James Morris President
Tel: 832-473-3993
Email: james.morris@tmcworkforce.com
Website: www.tmcworkforce.com
Staffing, Recruiting and Procurement Services. (AA, estab 2016, empl 342, sales $12,000,000, cert: NMSDC)

9501 TriQuest Business Services, LLC
13526 George Rd, Ste 201
San Antonio, TX 78230
Contact: Stephanie Balditt President
Tel: 210-598-1539
Email: stephanie@triquestbusiness.com
Website: www.triquestbusiness.com
Temporary & permanent placement services: IT, Accounting, Finance, Administrative & Human Resource placement. (Minority, Woman, estab 2010, empl 6, sales $931,239, cert: State)

9502 Walker Elliott, LP
11200 Westheimer
Houston, TX 77042
Contact: Victor M. Taveras Contract Mgr
Tel: 713-482-3750
Email: belliott@walker-elliott.com
Website: www.walker-elliott.com
Information technology & healthcare direct hire, contract & contract to hire placement firm. (Woman, estab 2006, empl 17, sales , cert: WBENC)

Utah

9503 Premier Employee Solutions LLC
3596 Mountain Vista Pkwy, #2
Provo, UT 84606
Contact: Dan Riley Dir of Natl Sales
Tel: 800-385-0855
Email: driley@thepremierpride.com
Website: www.thepremierpride.com
Staffing & payroll services. (Woman, estab 2005, empl 500, sales $391,331,571, cert: WBENC)

Virginia

9504 22nd Century Solutions Inc
8251 Greensboro Dr Ste 900
McLean, VA 22102
Contact: Avinash Singh President
Tel: 866-537-9191
Email: ravis@22csi.com
Website: www.22csi.com
Staffing services, IT staffing & workforce management services, contract or permanent positions. (Woman/As-Ind, estab 1997, empl 6500, sales $350,000,000, cert: WBENC)

9505 Action Technology, Inc.
3121 E Boundary Ct
Midlothian, VA 23112
Contact: Thomas Hammerstone Reg Mgr
Tel: 804-464-1271
Email: thammerstone@action-tech.com
Website: www.action-tech.com
Staff augmentation: direct hire, contract & temporary. (Woman, estab 1982, empl 200, sales $8,000,000, cert: State, CPUC, WBENC)

9506 Alcove Resources
1900 Campus Commons Dr, Ste 100
Reston, VA 20191
Contact: Quan Woodard CEO
Tel: 703-652-4732
Email: info@alcoveresources.com
Website: www.alcoveresources.com
Recruiting & executive search services, information management consulting. (Woman/AA, estab 2005, empl 5, sales $100,000, cert: State)

9507 Apertus Partners
722 E Market St Ste 102
Leesburg, VA 20176
Contact: Erin Adams Managing Partner
Tel: 703-721-8417
Email: eadams@apertuspartners.com
Website: www.apertuspartners.com
Staffing services. (Woman, estab 2015, empl 25, sales $406,000, cert: SDB)

PROFESSIONAL SERVICES: Staffing Services

9508 ARK Solutions Inc.
1939 Roland Clarke Pll Ste 300
Reston, VA 20191
Contact: Anuj Khurana Managing Dir
Tel: 703-502-6999
Email: anuj@arksolutionsinc.com
Website: www.arksolutionsinc.com
Staffing & consulting, staffing support, Enterprise IT Solutions, Information Assurance Solutions, Business Process Management & Integration Competency. (Minority, Woman, estab 2003, empl 43, sales , cert: State, NMSDC)

9509 Arthur Grand Technologies Inc.
44355 Premier Plaza, Ste 110
Ashburn, VA 20147
Contact: Jeff Prater Sr VP
Tel: 571-251-9509
Email: contracts@arthurgrand.com
Website: www.arthurgrand.com
Staffing and technology consulting services. (Minority, estab 2012, empl 25, sales $1,750,000, cert: NMSDC)

9510 BEST Employment SoluTions, LLC
110 Coliseum Crossing
Hampton, VA 23666
Contact: Kipland Albright Owner
Tel: 757-589-2675
Email: kalbright@thebestllc.com
Website: www.thebestllc.com
Staffing: Light Industrial, Warehousing, Manufacturing, Admin Clerical, Customer Support, & Transportation positions. (AA, estab 2016, empl 20, sales , cert: State, NMSDC)

9511 Cammas & Associates
5870 Trinity Pkwy Ste 170
Centreville, VA 20120
Contact: Diane Cammas Owner/Mgr
Tel: 703-579-1100
Email: diane.cammas@snelling.com
Website: www.Snelling.com/NoVa
Staffing & recruiting services: Administrative & Support, Information Technology, Accounting & Finance, Human Resources, Engineering, Manufacturing & Production, Construction, Pharmaceutical, Sales & Marketing. (Woman, estab 2008, empl 3, sales , cert: WBENC)

9512 Checks and Balances, Inc.
10550 Linden Lake Plaza Ste 200
Manassas, VA 20109
Contact: Lovey Hammel Owner
Tel: 703-361-2220
Email: aharkins@eeihr.com
Website: www.checksbalancesinc.com
Workforce solutions, Employer of Record, Independent Contractor/1099, Corp-to-Corp (SOW). (Woman, estab 1989, empl 46, sales $13,000,000, cert: State, WBENC)

9513 Cynet Systems Inc.
21000 Atlantic Blvd #700
Sterling, VA 20166
Contact: Arpit Paul VP Strategy & Partnerships
Tel: 571-442-1007
Email: arpitp@cynetsystems.com
Website: www.cynetsystems.com
IT & engineering staffing consulting, direct/full time hiring, contract (temp hiring) or contract to hire services. (Minority, estab 2010, empl 1200, sales $65,000,000, cert: NMSDC)

9514 Gillman Services, Inc.
3300 Tyre Neck Rd Ste E
Portsmouth, VA 23703
Contact: Jeremy Andrews Exec Acct Mgr
Tel: 757-439-0800
Email: jandrews@gillmannservices.com
Website: www.gillmannservices.com
Staffing services. (Woman, estab 2008, empl 300, sales $8,850,000, cert: State)

9515 Hire 1 Staffing
PO Box 34337
Richmond, VA 23234
Contact: Sandra Smith Owner
Tel: 804-223-2110
Email: ssmith@hire1staffing.net
Website: www.hire1staffing.net
Temporary staffing: administrative, clerical, call center/customer service representatives & light industrial positions. (Woman/AA, estab 2005, empl 1, sales , cert: State)

9516 Key Personnel, Inc.
5540 Falmouth St, Ste 100
Richmond, VA 23230
Contact: Thomas Bowles President
Tel: 804-716-9450
Email: thomasbowles@keypersonnel.net
Website: www.keypersonnel.net
Staffing: temporary, temporary to hire & direct hire employment services. (AA, estab 1998, empl 40, sales $2,000,000, cert: State)

9517 Leading Edge Systems Richmond
3711-A Westerre Pkwy
Richmond, VA 23233
Contact: Adish Jain Mgr
Tel: 804-673-5100
Email: adishj@leadingedgesys.com
Website: www.leadingedgesys.com
Staffing svcs; information tech, clerical support & professional svcs. (Minority, estab 1997, empl 42, sales $4,500,000, cert: State)

9518 McKinley Marketing Partners, Inc.
201 N. Union St Ste 110
Alexandria, VA 22314
Contact: Susie President
Tel: 703-836-4445
Email: clientservices@mckinleyinc.com
Website: www.mckinleymarketingpartners.com/
Staffing: short-term marketing mgrs. (Woman, estab 1995, empl 15, sales $9,395,256, cert: WBENC)

9519 MillenniumSoft, Inc
8301 Arlington Blvd, Ste 504,
Fairfax, VA 22031
Contact: Swathi Billa
Tel: 703-698-9232
Email: time@millenniumsoft.com
Website: www.millenniumsoft.com
Permanent, long term or short term staffing. (Minority, Woman, estab 2000, empl 45, sales $293,466,000, cert: State, NMSDC)

9520 Outcomes Inc.
4215 Lafayette center Dr Ste 6
Chantilly, VA 20151
Contact: Sonali Kakatkar CEO
Tel: 703-996-8833
Email: sonali@out-comes.com
Website: www.out-comes.com
Staffing, recruiting, payroll services & vendor managed services. (Minority, Woman, estab 2002, empl 8, sales $3,000,000, cert: State, WBENC, SDB)

9521 Preferred Staffing Group/Preferred Temporary Services, Inc.
2001 Jefferson Davis Hwy Ste 303
Arlington, VA 22202
Contact: Barbara Posner President
Tel: 703-415-0182
Email: ejackson@ourpsg.com
Website: www.ourpsg.com
Staffing svcs: administrative, telecommunications fiber optic, IT, legal, light construction, housekeeping. (Woman, estab 1987, empl 150, sales , cert: WBENC)

9522 ProTask Inc.
542 Springvale Road
Great Falls, VA 22066
Contact: Jessie Covington Sr Acct Mgr
Tel: 703-231-4275
Email: jcovington@protaskinc.com
Website: www.protaskinc.com/
Staffing solutions, IT contractors, IT consultants, IT Staff Augmentation, Traditional direct hire talent search (full life cycle), Executive recruitment. (Woman, estab 2010, empl 22, sales $3,300,000, cert: State, WBENC)

9523 Pyramind LLC
1069 W Broad St, Ste 781
Falls Church, VA 22046
Contact: Hope Johnson CEO
Tel: 703-241-2996
Email: hope@pyramindsearch.com
Website: www.pyramindsearch.com
Executive search. (Woman, estab 2001, empl 5, sales $400,000, cert: WBENC)

9524 Seaborn Health Care Inc.
16600 Jefferson St
Amelia Court House, VA 23002
Contact: Jacqueline Amadio President
Tel: 727-398-1710
Email: jacky@seabornhc.com
Website: www.seabornhc.com
Staffing: medical, clerks & administration, IT Tech, legal & accounting (Woman, estab 1995, empl 50, sales $1,000,000, cert: 8(a))

9525 Skill Path Talent, Inc.
8300 Boone Blvd, Ste 500
Vienna, VA 22182
Contact: Sharon Campbell Business Devel Mgr
Tel: 571-358-5602
Email: operatons@skillstalent.com
Website: www.skillstalent.com
Human capital services, temporary & permanent placement. (AA, estab 2013, empl 25, sales , cert: NMSDC)

9526 TeamPeople LLC
180 S Washington St Ste 200
Falls Church, VA 22046
Contact: Kathy Roma Dev Consultant
Tel: 917-751-6088
Email: kroma@teampeople.tv
Website: www.teampeople.tv
Media Staffing & Support Services. (Woman, estab 2004, empl 600, sales $51,714,354, cert: WBENC)

9527 Temporary Solutions, Inc.
10550 Linden Lake Plaza, Ste 200
Manassas, VA 20109
Contact: Lovey Hammel VP Marketing
Tel: 703-361-2220
Email: lhammel@eeihr.com
Website: www.eeihr.com
Staffing services: temporary staffing, temp-to-hire staffing, direct placement, on-site services & single source mgmt solutions. (Woman, estab 1980, empl 921, sales $7,245,894, cert: State, WBENC)

Washington

9528 2rbConsulting, Inc.
19515 North Creek Pkwy Ste 310
Bothell, WA 98011
Contact: Betta Beasley CEO
Tel: 425-406-7644
Email: betta@2rbconsulting.com
Website: www.2rbconsulting.com
Provide contract consultants, permanent staff & managed services at all levels of expertise. (Woman, estab 2007, empl 25, sales $3,200,000, cert: WBENC)

9529 Aditi Staffing LLC
2002 156th Ave NE Ste 200
Bellevue, WA 98004
Contact: Malcolm Cooper Strategic Relations
Tel: 425-305-5091
Email: malcolm@aditistaffing.com
Website: www.aditistaffing.com
Staff Aug/Contingent Labor/SOW. (As-Ind, estab 2007, empl 516, sales $38,691,000, cert: NMSDC)

9530 All StarZ Staffing and Consulting LLC
841 Central Ave N Ste C-208
Kent, WA 98032
Contact: Debra Kerner Mgr
Tel: 253-277-4000
Email: debra@allstarzstaffing.com
Website: www.allstarzstaffing.com
Provide innovative staffing programs for candidate sourcing, screening, selection, retention, and labor cost management. (Woman, estab 2005, empl 150, sales $3,043,715, cert: WBENC)

9531 Allegiance Staffing
400 Industry Dr, Ste 180
Tukwila, WA 98188
Contact: Luis Perez Acct Mgr
Tel: 253-854-7000
Email: lperez@allegiancestaffing.com
Website: www.allegiancestaffing.com
Staffing solutions: temporary, contract employees, executive search & permanent placement. (As-Ind, estab 1994, empl 10, sales $6,500,000, cert: State)

9532   Allovus Design, Inc.
       15822 Peacock Hill Ave NW
       Gig Harbor, WA 98332
       Contact: Hayley Nichols Client Services Dir
       Tel: 253-222-0274
       Email: hayley@allovus.com
       Website: www.allovus.com
Staffing services, direct hire, staff augmentation & studios project teams. (Woman, estab 2009, empl 75, sales $9,000,000, cert: WBENC)

9533   Archer & Associates I, Inc.
       16625 Redmond Way, Ste M8
       Redmond, WA 98052
       Contact: Ann-Marie Archer CEO
       Tel: 425-869-6350
       Email: aarcher@archer-associates.com
       Website: www.archer-associates.com
Executive search & consulting. (Woman, estab 2000, empl 2, sales $852,500, cert: State)

9534   Ci2i Services, Inc.
       410 Bellevue Way SE Ste 205
       Bellevue, WA 98004
       Contact: Raul Ramos CEO
       Tel: 425-279-7992
       Email: raul@ci2iservices.com
       Website: www.Ci2iServices.com
IT Consulting & Staffing services: Program & Project Management, Software development, Business strategy & Marketing resource needs. (As-Ind, estab 1998, empl 40, sales $3,600,000, cert: State, NMSDC)

9535   MB Diversity
       6523 California Ave SW, Ste B-255
       Seattle, WA 98136
       Contact: Anthony Burnett Owner
       Tel: 206-941-2834
       Email: anthony@mbdiversity.com
       Website: www.MBDiversity.com
Staffing recruiting & managed resources. (AA, estab 2014, empl 10, sales $573,315, cert: State, City, NMSDC)

9536   VanderHouwen & Associates, Inc.
       2018 156th Ave NE Ste 220
       Bellevue, WA 98007
       Contact: Jennifer Boyle Client Specialist
       Tel: 425-453-7300
       Email: jennifer@vanderhouwen.com
       Website: www.vanderhouwen.com
Professional Staffing Services: IT, Engineering, Accounting, and Administrative talent. (Woman, estab 1987, empl 410, sales , cert: WBENC)

Wisconsin

9537   Division 10 Personnel Services of Milwaukee, Inc.
       4425 N Port Washington Rd, Ste 401
       Milwaukee, WI 53212
       Contact: Wendy Koppel, CPC President
       Tel: 414-963-8700
       Email: wendy@division10personnel.com
       Website: www.division10personnel.com
Recruiting & staffing: Administrative & Professional level candidates. (Woman, estab 1980, empl 30, sales $1,563,690, cert: State, WBENC)

9538   Hatch Staffing Services
       700 W Virginia St, Ste 400
       Milwaukee, WI 53204
       Contact: Lucas Harvey Branch Mgr
       Tel: 414-272-4544
       Email: lucas@hatch.com
       Website: www.hatch.com
Staffing services: temp, temp to hire & direct hire candidates. (Woman, estab 1983, empl 23, sales $12,269,000, cert: WBENC)

9539   ON-SITE Inc.
       4635 South 108th St
       Milwaukee, WI 53228
       Contact: Crystal Kent President
       Tel: 414-349-8546
       Email: ckent@onsitestaffing.com
       Website: www.onsitestaffing.com
Employee leasing, payrolling, on site mgmt, permanent placement, contract engineering, temporary help. (Minority, Woman, estab 1998, empl 5, sales $531,825, cert: WBENC)

9540   SEEK Careers/Staffing, Inc.
       PO Box 148
       Grafton, WI 53024
       Contact: Debbie Fedel VP Business Dev
       Tel: 262-377-8888
       Email: dfedel@seekcareers.com
       Website: www.seekcareers.com
Staffing services, office/accounting, light industrial & skilled manufacturing positions. (Woman, estab 1971, empl 96, sales $53,824,639, cert: WBENC)

9541   TotalMed Staffing, Inc.
       5517 Waterford Ln
       Appleton, WI 54913
       Contact: Nick Palleria Dir Sales
       Tel: 920-750-7157
       Email: npalleria@totalmed.com
       Website: www.totalmedstaffing.com
Clinical Staffing, Registered Nurses & Allied Health, temporary staffing shortages. (As-Ind, estab , empl , sales $22,000,000, cert: NMSDC)

9542   Victory Personnel Services, Inc.
       735 N Water St Ste 1411
       Milwaukee, WI 53202
       Contact: Mike Farrell VP
       Tel: 414-271-0749
       Email: mfarrell@victoryprofessional.com
       Website: www.victorypersonnel.com
Staffing: temporary, permanent & payroll services. (AA, estab 1991, empl 400, sales $18,510,506, cert: NMSDC)

> **PROFESSIONAL SERVICES: Technical**
> Provide consulting services on a variety of technically oriented topics: technical writing and editing, information systems, record management, educational research, scientific research, program evaluation, nuclear energy consulting, technical manuals. NAICS Code 54

Connecticut

9543 Access Consulting
31 Island Heights Circle
Stamford, CT 06902
Contact: Arun Sinha President
Tel: 203-975-2950
Email: contact@accessc.com
Website: www.accessc.com/
Corporate communications, marketing communications & technical writing services. (As-Ind, estab 2003, empl 2, sales , cert: NMSDC)

Florida

9544 The Med Writers LLC
9314 Forest Hill Blvd, Ste 6
Wellington, FL 33411
Contact: Karen Vieira President
Tel: 561-247-2190
Email: karen@themedwriters.com
Website: www.themedwriters.com
Medical & scientific writing, offsite writing services. (Woman/AA, estab 2007, empl 8, sales , cert: CPUC)

9545 The Solers Reseach Group
1445 Dolgner Place #10
Sanford, FL 32771
Contact: Thomas Wilson Sr Strategy Mgr
Tel: 407-873-1456
Email: twilson@solersrg.com
Website: www.solersrg.com
Cyber awareness interventions, mobile & game-based learning; digital propensity, learning & literacy; examine learning & evidence-based practice in gifted, special education & assistive technology. (Woman, estab 2008, empl 15, sales $1,500,000, cert: 8(a))

Georgia

9546 A-Z Sophisticated Solutions
12850 Hwy 9 N, Ste 600-205
Alpharetta, GA 30004
Contact: Ana Maria Marin Managing Dir
Tel: 404-996-1358
Email: ap@a-zssolutions.com
Website: www.a-zssolutions.com
Engineering, Technical Writing, Technical Instruction & written Translation services. Technical Instruction: plastics seminars & CAE plastics. (Woman/Hisp, estab 2010, empl 1, sales , cert: WBENC)

9547 Continental Technical Services
260 Peachtree St, Ste 2200
Atlanta, GA 30303
Contact: Willie Dunlap CEO
Tel: 404-527-6297
Email: henri@ctsnationally.com
Website: www.ctsnationally.com
Staff augmentation, temp personnel, technical publications, integrated logistics support, validations & verifications, ECPs, technical writing, quality assurance & control, quality inspection. (AA, estab 1992, empl 54, sales $7,400,000, cert: NMSDC)

9548 Eubio, LLC
PO Box 16555
Atlanta, GA 30321
Contact: Alita Anderson Principal
Tel: 404-632-2435
Email: alita@eubiomed.com
Website: www.eubiomed.com
Medical communications, medical writing. (Woman/AA, estab 2012, empl 2, sales $885,503, cert: City, NMSDC, WBENC)

Indiana

9549 Techcom, Inc.
PO Box 39206
Indianapolis, IN 46239
Contact: Ilene Adams President
Tel: 317-865-2530
Email: inadams@techcom.com
Website: www.techcom.com
Technical publications producer including: engineering, research, writing, data management, photography, illustration, CAD drawing, video production, animation, interactive multimedia creation. (Woman, estab 1976, empl 38, sales , cert: WBENC)

Michigan

9550 Good Fortune Trading Co. dba GFT Services
3959 Nash Dr
Troy, MI 48083
Contact: Janice Girling President
Tel: 248-884-4635
Email: janice.girling@gftservices.com
Website: www.gftservices.com
Procurement services, project planning, technical writing. (Woman, estab 2016, empl 1, sales , cert: WBENC)

Minnesota

9551 Shepherd Data Services, Inc.
527 Marquette Ave 400 Rand Tower
Minneapolis, MN 55402
Contact: Dennis Waldrop VP
Tel: 612-659-1234
Email: cchalstrom@shepherddata.com
Website: www.shepherddata.com
Data collection for litigation. (Woman, estab 2002, empl 12, sales $2,283,392, cert: WBENC)

North Carolina

9552 Hurley Write Inc
21835 Advocates Ct
Cornelius, NC 28031
Contact: Pamela Hurley President
Tel: 910-233-7670
Email: info@hurleywrite.com
Website: www.hurleywrite.com
Develop and teach customized onsite technical, business, and scientific writing courses, online writing courses, webinars and series. (Woman, estab 2000, empl 1, sales $388,000, cert: WBENC)

PROFFESIONAL SERVICES: Technical

9553 Whitsell Innovations Inc.
18 Kendall Dr
Chapel Hill, NC 27517
Contact: Robin Whitsell President
Tel: 919-321-9017
Email: robin.whitsell@whitsellinnovations.com
Website: www.whitsellinnovations.com
Medical, scientific & technical writing, GCP, GMP & GLP, clinical regulatory writing, clinical study reports, protocols, investigator brochures, narratives & full submissions of investigational new drug, applications & new drug applications. (Woman, estab 2006, empl 32, sales $5,262,000, cert: WBENC)

Pennsylvania

9554 FMD K&L Inc.
1300 Virginia Dr Ste 408
Fort Washington, PA 19034
Contact: Xin Ke President
Tel: 215-283-6035
Email: xin.ke@klserv.com
Website: www.klserv.com
Data Management, Biostatistics, Statistical Programming, Medical Writing. (As-Pac, estab 1995, empl 200, sales $27,000,000, cert: NMSDC)

9555 KB Comm LLC
985 State Rd
West Grove, PA 19390
Contact: Kathy Breuninger Owner
Tel: 610-357-8625
Email: kathy@kbcommllc.com
Website: www.kbcommllc.com
Scientific & technical writing services, business & marketing communications; instructions & procedures; installation, operation & maintenance manuals; computer documentation; training materials & document templates. (Woman, estab 2006, empl 8, sales $610,154, cert: WBENC)

9556 Provider Resources Inc.
153 E 13th St Ste 1400
Erie, PA 16503
Contact: Nadine Manzi Program Mgr
Tel: 814-480-8732
Email: nmanzi@provider-resources.com
Website: www.provider-resources.com
Policy and Regulatory, Healthcare Quality & Disparities, Program Integrity, and Education. (Woman, estab 2003, empl 130, sales $13,400,000, cert: NWBOC)

Texas

9557 A. Miller Consulting Services, Inc.
4425 Plano Pkwy, Ste 803
Carrollton, TX 75010
Contact: Carie Joyce Team Lead
Tel: 972-580-0812
Email: cjoyce@mcs.biz
Website: www.mcs.biz
Technical documentation: technical writing, project mgmt, technical illustration & graphics creation, web design, web-based training dev, manual dev & consolidation, proposal writing & consulting, process dev & documentation, engineering guides. (Woman, estab 2000, empl 13, sales $2,449,127, cert: WBENC)

9558 Integrity International, Inc.
11767 Katy Frwy, Ste 750
Houston, TX 77079
Contact: Susan Lake Project Mgr
Tel: 877-955-0707
Email: info@tarrenpoint.com
Website: www.tarrenpoint.com
Documentation consulting services, project management, content development (technical documentation), graphic design, technical illustration, desktop publishing, editing & quality assurance, indexing, localization & translation. (Woman, estab 1994, empl 63, sales $6,000,000, cert: State, WBENC)

9559 QA Consulting Inc.
7500 Rialto Blvd Bldg 1, Ste 225
Austin, TX 78735
Contact: Amber Hilfiger Dir of Operations
Tel: 512-328-9404
Email: info@qaconsultinginc.com
Website: www.qaconsultinginc.com
Quality, Microbiology, Regulatory & Auditing consulting services, QMS development, design, risk management, biocompatibility, verification and validation. (Woman, estab 2000, empl 6, sales $1,294,768, cert: State, WBENC)

9560 Shea Writing and Training Solutions, Inc.
5807 Benning Dr
Houston, TX 77096
Contact: Evalyn Shea President
Tel: 713-723-9142
Email: info@sheaws.com
Website: www.sheaws.com
Technical writing & editing, risk assessment & meeting scribing, web content, training materials, proposals, presentations, reports, technical manuals, etc. (Woman, estab 1997, empl 12, sales $861,472, cert: WBENC)

9561 TECHNIKOS Information Development, LLC
PO Box 2693
Stafford, TX 77497
Contact: Ora Gibson CEO
Tel: 281-568-7955
Email: ora@technicallyclear.com
Website: www.technicallyclear.com
Technical writing, editing, formatting, reviewing, proofreading, documentation, manuals, guides, web content, user guides, operations manuals, procedure manuals, processes, procedures, training guides. (Woman/AA, estab 2007, empl 2, sales , cert: State, NMSDC)

Virginia

9562 AccuWrit Inc.
118 Primrose Dr
Blacksburg, VA 24060
Contact: Eileen Y. Ivasauskas President
Tel: 540-961-1611
Email: eileen@accuwrit.com
Website: www.accuwrit.com
Editorial consulting — Editorial specialist in medical, scientific, and technical information and communication materials. Custom writing services and editorial support for the preparation of manuscripts, monographs, abstracts, critiques. (Woman, estab 1984, empl 1, sales , cert: State)

RECORDING & VIDEO PRODUCTION

Produce videos (in studio or remote), TV shows, records, sound recordings, pre and post production services, talent arrangers, video distribution. NAICS Code 51

Arizona

9563 Blade Inc
       3033 N Central Ave Ste 440
       Phoenix, AZ 85012
       Contact: Louise Parker President
       Tel: 602-307-5577
       Email: louise@bladeinc.com
       Website: www.bladeinc.com

Production, Editing, Video Production, Video Editing, Post Production, 3D Animation, Animation, Motion Graphics, VFX, Visual Effects, Visual Design, Motion Design, Illustration. TV Commercials, Web, Training, Corporate. (Woman, estab 2002, empl 65, sales , cert: WBENC)

California

9564 Aahs Entertainment, Inc.
       10707 Camarillo St, Ste 312
       Toluca Lake, CA 91602
       Contact: Gwenn Smith President
       Tel: 818-279-2416
       Email: gwenn@aahsentertainment.com
       Website: www.aahsentertainment.com

Video Production Services, Media Production, Media Services, Advertising, Marketing, Content Creation, Branded Content, Brand Marketing, DVD Extras, DVD Special Features, Marketing, Advertising, EPKs. (Woman/AA, estab 2011, empl 1, sales , cert: WBENC)

9565 Agnew Multilingual
       2625 Townsgate Road Ste 330
       Westlake Village, CA 91361
       Contact: Irene Agnew President
       Tel: 805-494-3999
       Email: i.agnew@agnew.com
       Website: www.agnew.com

Translation, interpretation & audiovisual production. (Woman, estab 1986, empl 7, sales $700,000, cert: CPUC, WBENC, SDB)

9566 Backhand Productions, Inc.
       12400 Wilshire Blvd, Ste 1275
       Los Angeles, CA 90025
       Contact: Jeff Atlas President
       Tel: 626-351-4390
       Email: BackhandProductionsInc@cmcregistrations.com
       Website: www.backhandproductions.com

Full service production company with an experienced staff of industry pros. Our team has executed dozens of successful TV shows and special projects and have overcome almost every type of production challenge imaginable. (AA, estab 2000, empl 1, sales $335,109, cert: NMSDC)

9567 CF Entertainment, Inc.
       1925 Century Park E Ste 1000
       Los Angeles, CA 90067
       Contact: Darren Galatt
       Tel: 310-277-3500
       Email: darren@es.tv
       Website: www.es.tv

Media & advertising, produce, distribute & sell commercials in 25+ first-run programs for TV stations & high definition cable networks. (AA, estab 1993, empl 75, sales $44,987,627, cert: NMSDC)

9568 Fire Starter Studios, LLC
       28348 Constellation Rd Ste 820
       Santa Clarita, CA 91355
       Contact: Rachel Klein CEO
       Tel: 747-201-7400
       Email: bids@firestarterstudios.com
       Website: www.firestarterstudios.com

Media, animation, live-action and VR/AR. (Woman, estab 2012, empl 5, sales , cert: WBENC)

9569 Hybrid Edit, LLC
       5782 W. Jefferson blvd.
       Los Angeles, CA 90016
       Contact: Susan Munro President
       Tel: 310-586-9799
       Email: diversity@hybridcollective.tv
       Website: www.hybridcollective.tv

Commercial, television & motion picture post production & production services: creative editorial offline, online/compositing, color correction, graphic design, motion graphic design, sound design & mixing. (Woman, estab 2009, empl 8, sales $1,400,000, cert: WBENC)

9570 International Communication Network
       901 Lane Ave, Ste 200
       Chula Vista, CA 91914
       Contact: Michelle Diaz COO
       Tel: 619-421-0426
       Email: mdiaz@inctv50.com
       Website: www.lnctv50.com

Television broadcasting, video production, marketing, Hispanic market. (AA, estab 1997, empl 5, sales , cert: NMSDC)

9571 Kaboom Productions
       2169 Folsom St Ste 201M
       San Francisco, CA 94110
       Contact: Denise Militzer Exec Producer
       Tel: 415-434-2666
       Email: denise@jzuntosmedia.com
       Website: www.kaboomproductions.com

TV commercials, corporate videos, branded content, TV shows, feature films. (Woman, estab 1997, empl 3, sales $3,051,256, cert: WBENC)

9572 Panaloma Productions, LLC
       2015 Half South Sherbourne Dr
       Los Angeles, CA 90034
       Contact: Rashaan Dozier-Escalante President
       Tel: 424-298-0966
       Email: rashaan@panalomaproductions.com
       Website: www.PanalomaProductions.com

Develop & produce media, event production, films. (Woman/AA, estab 2012, empl 1, sales $150,000, cert: 8(a))

9573 Showreel International Inc.
      639 S. Glenwood Place, Ste. 200
      Burbank, CA 90038
      Contact: Jessica Ristic CEO
      Tel: 323-464-5111
      Email: jessica@weareshotglass.com
      Website: www.weareshotglass.com
Film & video production. (Woman, estab 1985, empl 7, sales , cert: State)

9574 The Traveling Picture Show Company
      1531 N. Cahuenga Blvd
      Los Angeles, CA 90028
      Contact: Partner
      Tel: 323-769-1115
      Email: info@thetpsc.com
      Website: www.thetpsc.com
Commercial video production services, television commercials, online branded content &visual media. (Woman, estab 2011, empl 9, sales $5,500,000, cert: WBENC)

9575 Total Media Group
      432 N Canal St
      South San Francisco, CA 94080
      Contact: Megan McKenna Acct Exec
      Tel: 650-583-8236
      Email: megan@totalmediagroup.com
      Website: www.totalmediagroup.com
Video production, motion graphics, 3D animation, editorial, event production, web design & mobile apps. (Woman, estab 1971, empl 10, sales $4,900,000, cert: WBENC)

Colorado

9576 PayReel, Inc.
      211 Violet St Unit 100
      Golden, CO 80401
      Contact: Heidi McLean President
      Tel: 303-526-4900
      Email: heidi@payreel.com
      Website: www.payreel.com
Provides outsourcing services for corporate video and media production departments. (Woman, estab 1995, empl 7, sales $15,914,000, cert: WBENC)

Connecticut

9577 Anderson Productions Inc.
      71 Dolphin Rd
      Bristol, CT 06010
      Contact: Tom Stanwicks Sales/Mktg
      Tel: 503-287-3004
      Email: tstanwicks@anderson3.com
      Website: www.andersonprod.com
Video production, post production, graphics, animations, sound design, audio editing, product models, digital signage. (Woman, estab 1994, empl 24, sales $4,500,000, cert: WBENC)

9578 Creative Video Corporation
      9 Mott Ave, Ste 108
      Norwalk, CT 06850
      Contact: Francisca Bogdan Production Specialist
      Tel: 203-866-8700
      Email: francisca.bogdan@creativevideocorp.com
      Website: www.creativevideocorp.com
Corporate communication videos & multi-media products, internal communications, sales & markeitng, event opening video, promotional video, event coverage. (Minority, Woman, estab 1997, empl 4, sales $380,000, cert: NMSDC)

Delaware

9579 DelVideo Productions
      583 Barley Court
      Smyrna, DE 19977
      Contact: Milton Melendez VP
      Tel: 302-223-4049
      Email: info@delvideo.com
      Website: www.delvideo.com
Bilingual video production, Pre-Production, Pre-Planning & vision writing, Location & set assessment, Research, Script writing, Talent arrangement, Recording Services, Video recording, Audio capture & recording, Project management, Directing. (Woman/AA, Hisp, estab 2013, empl 2, sales , cert: State, 8(a))

Florida

9580 Campbell Advertising and Design, LLC
      103 NE 4th St
      Delray Beach, FL 33444
      Contact: Lucia Alvarez Principal
      Tel: 561-562-6119
      Email: info@campbellcreative.com
      Website: www.campbellcreative.com
Photography, art direction, web videos, social content, broadcast commercials, testimonial videos, training videos, animated videos. (Woman/Hisp, estab 2010, empl 6, sales $1,600,000, cert: WBENC)

9581 Coda Sound Inc.
      4819 N Hale Ave
      Tampa, FL 33614
      Contact: Maritza Astorquiza Owner
      Tel: 813-353-8151
      Email: maritza@codasoundusa.com
      Website: www.codasoundusa.com
Event production: sound, lights, stages & audio visual. (Minority, Woman, estab 1998, empl 2, sales $471,000, cert: State, City, NMSDC)

9582 Graphix 360, LLC
      7777 N Wickham Rd Ste 12710
      Melbourne, FL 32940
      Contact: Bobbi Gerardot CEO
      Tel: 321-693-9293
      Email: bobbi@graphix360.com
      Website: www.Graphix360.com
Multimedia design, photo, video, graphic/web design & printing services, multimedia equipment. (Woman, estab 2013, empl 4, sales , cert: City)

9583 Kreative Kontent Co.
3019 Ravenswood Road Ste 110
Fort Lauderdale, FL 33312
Contact: Debbie Margolis-Horwitz Exec Producer
Tel: 954-312-3660
Email: debbie@kreativekontent.com
Website: www.kreativekontent.com
Production specializing in content creation, broadcast, web based, theatrical & marketing fulfillment programs, broadcast commercials, corporate video communications, product placement, branded content, promotional products. (Woman, estab 2010, empl 4, sales $2,000,000, cert: State, WBENC)

Georgia

9584 A-1 Audio Visual, LLC
863 Flat Shoals Rd SE Ste C359
Conyers, GA 30094
Contact: Keith McNeil CEO
Tel: 800-805-7210
Email: kmcneil@a1audiovisual.com
Website: www.a1audiovisual.com
Audio visual, video & lighting. (AA, estab 2003, empl 6, sales $190,000, cert: State, NMSDC)

9585 One Production Place
1945 Colland Dr, NW
Atlanta, GA 30318
Contact: Elisa Gambino President
Tel: 404-452-3500
Email: elisa@oneproductionplace.com
Website: www.oneproductionplace.com
Multi media video production & communications: shooting, lighting, editing, color grading, writing & scoring music. (Woman, estab 2002, empl 2, sales $300,000, cert: WBENC)

9586 Onyx Media Services, Inc.
57 Forsyth St NW Ste 250-G
Atlanta, GA 30303
Contact: Jennifer Rocke VP Finance
Tel: 404-420-0030
Email: info@onyxmsgroup.com
Website: www.onyxmsgroup.com
Production services: audio visual, facility, technical production design, presentation video, graphic design, sound reinforcement, theatrical lighting. (AA, estab 2006, empl 15, sales , cert: NMSDC)

9587 Popoff Enterprises Inc.
3035 Wallace Circle SE
Atlanta, GA 30339
Contact: Dana Popoff President
Tel: 404-307-1979
Email: popoffdana@gmail.com
Website: www.popoffenterprises.com
Video production & still photography services, commercial distribution, web sites, point of purchase, social media, internal corporate communications - training, company meetings & conferences, President's address, legacy knowledge, etc. (Woman, estab 1997, empl 1, sales $138,750, cert: WBENC)

9588 Works of Bawbee Films
704 Brambling Way
Stockbridge, GA 30281
Contact: Brian Ezeike Video Producer
Tel: 478-390-7375
Email: info@wobfilms.com
Website: www.wobfilms.com
Video production/digital content creation, write, shoot & edit a wide variety of video content. (AA, estab 2010, empl 1, sales , cert: NMSDC)

Illinois

9589 Hootenanny LLC
230 E Ohio St Ste 700
Chicago, IL 60611
Contact: Elizabeth Tate President
Tel: 312-266-0777
Email: liz@hootenanny.tv
Website: www.hootenanny.tv
Post-production, creative editorial, finishing, graphic design & visual effects, television, print, web, corporate video & interactive media. (Woman, estab 2008, empl 11, sales $2,100,000, cert: State, WBENC)

Indiana

9590 Multitek Corporate Communications
6531 Greencove Ave
Evansville, IN 47715
Contact: Earl Milligan President
Tel: 812-760-7488
Email: earl.milligan@gmail.com
Website: www.multitekcorporate.com
Corporate safety & training video production services, construction archival videos, 3 d survey mapping, drone aerial photography & videography. (AA, estab 1984, empl 1, sales , cert: State)

Massachusetts

9591 Real Cool Productions, Inc. dba RCP Learning
800 S Main St, Ste 203
Mansfield, MA 02048
Contact: President
Tel: 508-878-8907
Email: info@rcplearning.com
Website: www.rcplearning.com
Integrated communications, technology & production services, internal & external facing content (mixed media, animations and videos), corporate overviews, business documentaries, executive interviews & announcements, testimonials, product videos, training (Woman, estab 2010, empl 10, sales $1,100,000, cert: WBENC)

Michigan

9592 Freshwater Film, Inc.
3061 Myddleton Court
Troy, MI 48084
Contact: Sue Witham CEO
Tel: 248-840-5400
Email: sue@mediumfilm.com
Website: www.mediumfilm.com
Film & digital production, influential storytelling, relevant creative content & serious production expertise. (Woman, estab 1991, empl 1, sales $656,756, cert: WBENC)

RECORDING & VIDEO PRODUCTION

9593 Seventy 7 Productions
      620 Cherry Ave
      Royal Oak, MI 48073
      Contact: Nora Urbanski Producer
      Tel: 313-610-0109
      Email: nora@seventy7productions.com
      Website: www.seventy7productions.com
Full service video production, post production & creative services for broadcast commercials, social media videos, 360 and VR videos, etc. (Hisp, estab 2011, empl 5, sales , cert: NMSDC)

9594 ShawneTV Inc
      29558 English Way
      Novi, MI 48377
      Contact: CEO
      Tel: 248-444-7573
      Email: info@shawnetv.com
      Website: www.shawnetv.com
Promotional & sponsorships, media & networking training, TV production. (Woman, estab 1999, empl 2, sales $150,000, cert: WBENC)

9595 VideoWorks Production Services, Inc.
      4851 Fernlee Ste 100
      Royal Oak, MI 48073
      Contact: Ruben Rodriguez President
      Tel: 248-563-0371
      Email: ruben@videoworksonline.com
      Website: www.videoworksonline.com
Video production: instructional & training videos, corporate, communications, news-style event coverage, multi-camera events & live media tours. (Hisp, estab 1995, empl 2, sales $150,000, cert: NMSDC)

Minnesota

9596 Orange Filmworks Inc.
      3912 Harriet Ave
      Minneapolis, MN 55409
      Contact: Marco Baca Owner
      Tel: 612-868-7875
      Email: marco@orangefilmworks.com
      Website: www.orangefilmworks.com
Broadcast television commercials, videos or commercials for web, long format instructional video, internal & in-store content. (Hisp, estab 2005, empl 1, sales $674,623, cert: NMSDC)

9597 Peterson Productions LLC
      1501 Spring Valley Rd
      Golden Valley, MN 55422
      Contact: Janie Peterson President
      Tel: 763-521-4746
      Email: janie@petersonproductionslive.com
      Website: www.PetersonProductionsLive.com
Video production house for corporate communications. (Woman, estab 2007, empl 2, sales $195,000, cert: State)

9598 Slang Productions, LLC
      3207 E 51st St
      Minneapolis, MN 55417
      Contact: Sue Lang Principal
      Tel: 612-310-4622
      Email: sue@slangproductions.net
      Website: www.slangproductions.net
Production: live events, video, audio & interactive media. (Woman, estab 2003, empl 2, sales $200,560, cert: WBENC)

Missouri

9599 CAC Reps, LLC
      5965 jamieson ave
      St. Louis, MO 63109
      Contact: Charlene Colombini Owner
      Tel: 314-752-0994
      Email: charlenecolo@hotmail.com
      Website: www.cacreps.com
Design, illustration, photography, computer imaging, computer 3D Rendering, video production & post, videography & on set styling. (Woman, estab 2008, empl 1, sales , cert: State, CPUC)

9600 Haller Concepts, Inc.
      4501 Mattis Rd
      St. Louis, MO 63128
      Contact: Mike Haller President
      Tel: 314-913-5626
      Email: mikeh@hallerconcepts.com
      Website: www.hallerconcepts.com
Corporate, event, training, web & TV video production filming. (Woman, estab 1982, empl 2, sales $174,400, cert: State)

New Jersey

9601 Harlan Media LLC
      494 Broad St, Ste 104
      Newark, NJ 07102
      Contact: Harlan Brandon CEO
      Tel: 973-623-6200
      Email: hb@harlanmedia.com
      Website: www.harlanmedia.com
Film & Video Production, Marketing, Advertising, Public Relations, Graphic Design, Independent Artist and Writers, Direct Mail Advertising, Commercial Photography (AA, estab 2008, empl 8, sales , cert: NMSDC)

9602 KVibe Productions, LLC
      591 Summit Ave Ste 101
      Jersey City, NJ 07306
      Contact: Khoa Le CEO
      Tel: 201-936-8033
      Email: khoa.le@kvibe.com
      Website: www.kvibe.com
Video production, product video, corporate video, commercial production, feature films. (As-Pac, estab 2005, empl 2, sales , cert: State)

9603 Modat Productions
      29 Windermere Rd
      Montclair, NJ 07043
      Contact: Shana Scott Founder & Content Creator
      Tel: 201-763-6666
      Email: shana@mOdatVideo.com
      Website: www.mOdatVideo.com
Full service video production, digital and broadcast content for television, businesses, social media and the government with end to end production. (Woman, estab 2010, empl 2, sales $150,000, cert: State, WBENC)

New York

9604 Adrienne Nicole Productions, LLC
14 Dekalb Ave 3rd Fl
Brooklyn, NY 11201
Contact: Adrienne Nicole Exec Producer
Tel: -   -
Email: info@producedbyanp.com
Website: www.producedbyanp.com
Videography, aerial video, drone video photography, drone photography, progress photos, story development, pre-production, post-production, motion graphics and animation, casting, photography, progress photos. (Woman/AA, estab 2011, empl 1, sales $986,000, cert: State, City, NMSDC)

9605 Amber Heavenly USA, Ltd.
250 Lafayette St 4th Fl
New York, NY 10012
Contact: Michelle Curran President
Tel: 212-352-1888
Email: michelle@ambermusic.com
Website: www.ambermusic.com
Commercial music production, composition, music licensing & publishing. (Woman, estab 1997, empl 7, sales $1,400,000, cert: State, WBENC)

9606 Bardin Palomo Ltd.
432 W 19th St Ste 3
New York, NY 10011
Contact: Robert Palomo President
Tel: 212-989-6113
Email: rrpalomo@bardinpalomo.com
Website: www.bardinpalomo.com
Special Events design & production: floral design, lighting design, stage design, prop & furniture rental. (Hisp, estab 1992, empl 5, sales $3,200,000, cert: NMSDC)

9607 Be Real Company
114 W 26th St, Fl 8
New York, NY 10001
Contact: CEO
Tel: 551-574-7006
Email: ola@berealcompany.com
Website: www.berealcompany.com
Integrated creative & production services: Live Action Shoots: commercials, documentaries, social videos, branded content Post-Production: editing, CGI, color correction, animation, music composing and mix, websites. (Woman, estab 2017, empl 5, sales $100,000, cert: WBENC)

9608 Cutter Productions
236 W 27th St Ste 1001
New York, NY 10001
Contact: Hillary Cutter Exec Producer
Tel: 646-588-1133
Email: hillary@cutterproductions.com
Website: www.cutterproductions.com
Full-service production. (Woman, estab 2005, empl 4, sales , cert: WBENC)

9609 Loftin Productions
104 Belmont Pkwy
Hempstead, NY 11550
Contact: Dushka Petkovich Co-Owner
Tel: 917-825-5412
Email: vze26rdi@verizon.net
Website: www.loftinpro.com/
Produce product demonstration & employee training videos. (Woman/AA, estab 1991, empl 2, sales , cert: State)

9610 Media2, Inc. dba M2
72 Madison Ave, Fl 2
New York, NY 10016
Contact: Cathy Humphrey Producer
Tel: 212-213-4004
Email: cathy@m2nyc.tv
Website: www.m2nyc.tv
Creative offline editorial, 2D/3D design & animation, television & live event production, install digital & high definition production studios, monitors, cameras & lighting. (AA, Hisp, estab 1997, empl 10, sales $25,000,000, cert: NMSDC)

9611 Resilient Media
10 E 39th St, 4th Fl
New York, NY 10016
Contact: Emilio Mahomar CEO
Tel: 646-580-9391
Email: emilio@resilient.tv
Website: www.resilient.tv
Production, post production, duplication & language localization (translation, closed captions, subtitles, language dubbing). (Hisp, estab 2010, empl 2, sales $200,000, cert: NMSDC)

9612 The Studio
80- 8th Ave Ste 307
New York, NY 10011
Contact: Mary Nittolo Founder / CCO
Tel: 212-661-1363
Email: mary@studionyc.com
Website: www.studionyc.com
Art & animation studio, 3d/2d animation, motion capture, animatics, pre-vis, storyboards, presentation art, digital art, comps & character design. (Woman, estab 1988, empl 30, sales $3,500,000, cert: WBENC)

9613 TimeLine Video
One Bridge St
Irvington, NY 10533
Contact: Timothy Englert VP Dev
Tel: 914-591-7360
Email: tim@timelinevideo.com
Website: www.timelinevideo.com
Video, production & post-production, graphic design. (Woman, estab 1994, empl 7, sales $1,700,000, cert: WBENC)

9614 Transcendent Enterprise
37 W 26th St, Ste 408
New York, NY 10010
Contact: Chris Alvarez Founder & CEO
Tel: 718-304-6384
Email: chris@t-enter.com
Website: www.transcendententerprise.com
Video production, live stream services, post production, editing & filming, photography. (Hisp, estab 2004, empl 4, sales $230,000, cert: City, NMSDC)

9615 United Sources of America, Inc.
      253 West 35th St 2nd Fl
      New York, NY 10001
      Contact: Kenny Khan CEO
      Tel: 212-398-6400
      Email: kkhan@usastudios.tv
      Website: www.usastudios.tv
Post-production facilities, motion picture or video, TV commercial spot distribution to station services, edit, direct response prep, closed caption, legalize, encode for broadcast verification, format spot for each station and network specs, final qualit (As-Ind, estab 1988, empl 27, sales $2,528,241, cert: NMSDC)

9616 VMIX, LLC.
      163 William St, 3 Fl
      New York, NY 10038
      Contact: Wening Cintron relationship Mgr
      Tel: 800-436-8618
      Email: wening@vmix.tv
      Website: www.vmix.tv
Digital media, audio/visual (A/V) content, music, television & urban entertainment. (AA, estab 2004, empl 2, sales , cert: State)

9617 Wild Child Editorial, Inc.
      44 West 28th St
      New York, NY 10001
      Contact: Scott Spanjich Managing Dir
      Tel: 212-725-5333
      Email: scott@wildchildpost.com
      Website: www.wildchildpost.com
TV commercials, music videos, feature films & emerging media. (Minority, Woman, estab , empl , sales $4,500,000, cert: WBENC)

Ohio

9618 MMG Corporate Communication, Inc.
      515 W Loveland Ave
      Loveland, OH 45140
      Contact: President
      Tel: 513-677-8787
      Email: info@mmgonline.com
      Website: www.mmgonline.com
Multi-media production: in-studio & field video production, multiple non-linear digital post production, CD & DVD-ROM programming, 2D & 3D animation, web site dev, duplication svcs, public relations, marketing & broadcast. (Woman, estab 1993, empl 7, sales $804,000, cert: WBENC)

9619 New Vision Media Inc.
      6804 Caine Rd
      Columbus, OH 43235
      Contact: Jerrud Smith Co-Owner
      Tel: -   -
      Email: jsmith@newvisionmediainc.com
      Website: www.newvisionmediainc.com
Video production services including aerial drone cinematography. (AA, estab 2000, empl 3, sales $350,000, cert: NMSDC)

Pennsylvania

9620 Crossover Ent. LLC
      728 Copeland St
      Pittsburgh, PA 15232
      Contact: Freya Saxon Producer
      Tel: 651-347-3831
      Email: fs@deepcea.com
      Website: www.deepcea.com
Script to screen production, Corporate Videos, Training Videos, Commercials, Film & Documentaries. (AA, estab 2014, empl 14, sales , cert: State)

9621 Karasch & Associates
      1646 W Chester Pike Ste 4
      West Chester, PA 19382
      Contact: Edward Sarkissian Sales Mgr
      Tel: 800-621-5689
      Email: esarkissian@karasch.com
      Website: www.karasch.com
Video production, duplications & captioning services. (Woman, estab 1980, empl 25, sales $4,000,000, cert: State, WBENC)

9622 Panta Rhei Media, Inc.
      565 Beulah Rd
      Turtle Creek, PA 15145
      Contact: Martha O'Grady President
      Tel: 412-824-8858
      Email: info@panta-rhei.com
      Website: www.panta-rhei.com
Video production with a specialty in health care, product demonstration and promotion, web testimonials, employee communications and streaming live events, consultation, concepts, script writing, location and studio video. (Woman, estab 1984, empl , sales , cert: WBENC)

South Carolina

9623 Mad Monkey, Inc.
      1631 Main St
      Columbia, SC 29201
      Contact: Lorie Gardner CEO
      Tel: 803-252-2211
      Email: lorie@gomadmonkey.com
      Website: www.gomadmonkey.com
Creates video stories for television, laptops, mobile devices & social platforms. (Woman, estab 2000, empl 15, sales $1,650,351, cert: State, WBENC)

9624 Red Heritage Media, LLC
      1974 Carolina Place, Ste 200C
      Fort Mill, SC 29708
      Contact: Gerry Martin Exec Producer
      Tel: 803-792-7331
      Email: gerry@redheritagemedia.com
      Website: www.redheritagemedia.com
Content creation, film, documentary, commercial & episodic television production. (Nat-Ame, estab 2015, empl 3, sales , cert: 8(a))

RECORDING & VIDEO PRODUCTION

Texas

9625 1820 Productions, LLC
6301 N Riverside Dr Bldg One, Ste 2C
Irving, TX 75039
Contact: Sara Madsen Miller COO
Tel: 972-869-7777
Email: sara@1820productions.com
Website: www.1820productions.com
Television & film production, creative concept development, producing, directing, editing, graphics & animation. (AA, estab 2001, empl 5, sales $1,012,000, cert: State, NMSDC)

9626 Abernethy Media Professionals, Inc.
10763 Sanden Dr
Dallas, TX 75355
Contact: Sandy Mason Abernethy President
Tel: 214-632-4518
Email: mason@ampcreative.com
Website: www.ampcreative.com
Video production services. (Woman, estab 2002, empl 10, sales $3,634,579, cert: State, WBENC)

9627 Cactex Media
2231 Valdina St, Unit 100
Dallas, TX 75207
Contact: Claire Brooks Head of Business Devel
Tel: 214-346-3456
Email: claire@cactexmedia.com
Website: www.cactexmedia.com
Video & Interactive production, video production, B2B videos, Web video, Webcast/live stream, Sales tools, Explainer videos, Training videos, Executive interviews, Customer testimonials, Case studies. (Woman, estab 2006, empl 14, sales $4,000,000, cert: State, WBENC)

9628 CM Productions, Inc.
4228 North Central Expressway Ste 340
Dallas, TX 75206
Contact: Carrie Martinez President
Tel: 214-528-2700
Email: carrie@cmproductions.tv
Website: www.cmproductions.tv
Video production, employee & marketing communications, documentaries, commercials, scriptwriting, stunning photography & sharp editing, still photography. (Woman, estab , empl , sales $194,628, cert: WBENC)

9629 Julye Newlin Productions, Inc.
129 E 13th St
Houston, TX 77008
Contact: Julye Newlin Owner
Tel: 713-869-3609
Email: julye@julyenewlin.com
Website: www.julyenewlin.com
Video, film & photography services: digital video, digital editing, web, broadcast, print advertising, CD business cards, DVD presentations, etc. (Woman, estab 1993, empl 3, sales , cert: City, WBENC)

9630 Small Pond Video Productions, Inc.
2217 Clarebrooke Dr.
Grand Prairie, TX 75050
Contact: Silvana Rosero President
Tel: 214-686-1092
Email: silvana@lagunamg.com
Website: www.lagunamg.com
Video production & meeting support, marketing, motivational, product introductions, testimonials, training videos & broadcast commercials. (Minority, Woman, estab , empl , sales $178,412, cert: State, NMSDC, WBENC)

9631 Sue Abrams Productions, LLC
2709 Prestonwood Dr
Plano, TX 75093
Contact: Sue Abrams Owner
Tel: 972-418-2034
Email: sue@saproductions.net
Website: www.saproductions.net
Video production: sales pieces, public education videos, corporate overviews, recruiting videos, commercials, training pieces, product launches, event videos & video news releases. (Woman, estab 1999, empl 1, sales $152,620, cert: WBENC)

9632 ZapBoomBang Studios, LLC
3336 Richmond Ave
Houston, TX 77098
Contact: Catherine Lopez Negrete
Tel: 713-877-8777
Email: cathy@zapboombang.com
Website: www.zapboombang.com
Audio, Video Post Production Services. (Woman, estab 0, empl , sales , cert: WBENC)

Washington

9633 Native Ways LLC - Apachewolf Productions
15313 NE 13th Place
Bellevue, WA 98008
Contact: Freddie Begay CEO
Tel: 360-930-9615
Email: chipbegay@gmail.com
Website: www.apachewolf.com
Video productions, video shooting & editing services, develop & create television & radio commercials, video streaming, DVD & CD duplication, Radio/TV broadcast development & marketing. (Minority, estab 2015, empl 1, sales , cert: State, SDB)

TELECOMMUNICATIONS

Manufacture and distribute telecommunications systems and products: CATV, telephones, intercoms, test and control equipment, etc. Includes firms which provide cellular and internet services, phone line installation, service and consulting. NAICS Code 51

Alabama

9634 Palco Telecom Service Inc.
2914 Green Cove Rd
Huntsville, AL 35803
Contact: Phil Terry Vice President
Tel: 256-426-5272
Email: pterry@gotopalco.com
Website: www.gotopalco.com
Telecommunications: logistics, forward & reverse, technical product repair upgrade & remanufacture, warranty fulfillment. (Woman, estab 1986, empl 250, sales $17,193,208, cert: WBENC)

Arizona

9635 Denali Telecom Solutions, Inc.
6524 S McAllister Ave
Tempe, AZ 85283
Contact: Karen Tynan CEO
Tel: 855-239-7776
Email: karen.tynan@denalicorp.com
Website: www.denalicorp.com
Mfr telecommunications products & value added service solutions for Broadband & Network Projects. (Minority, Woman, estab 2013, empl 4, sales $1,000,000, cert: WBENC)

9636 Native Technology Solutions Inc.
7065 W Allison Rd
Chandler, AZ 85226
Contact: Mabel Tsosie
Tel: 480-639-1234
Email: mtsosie@gilarivertel.com
Website: www.native-tech.net
Cabling & computing services, structured cabling, phone, security systems, video conferencing, & technology solutions. (Nat Ame, estab 2007, empl 14, sales $4,000,000, cert: State)

9637 Tower Safety and Instruction
3620 S 40th St
Phoenix, AZ 85040
Contact: Kathy Brand CEO
Tel: 480-313-0678
Email: kathy@towersafety.com
Website: www.towersafety.com
Safety School for the Wireless/Crane Industry, Wireless & Microwave, Construction & Telecommunications-Fiber Optics/Copper Installation & Testing, Project Management, Installation, Telecommunications Maintenance & Testing. (Woman, estab 2013, empl 8, sales , cert: WBENC)

California

9638 49er Communications Inc
361 Railroad Ave
Nevada City, CA 95959
Contact: Logistics & Solutions
Tel: 530-477-2590
Email: bids@49er.cc
Website: www.49ercommunications.com
Single-site dealers of Land Mobile Radio (LMR) Equipment. (Woman, estab 1997, empl 5, sales $2,100,000, cert: State)

9639 Aponi Products and Services
3805 Florin Rd Ste 1228
Sacramento, CA 95823
Contact: Lisa M Davis lacy Owner
Tel: 916-392-6571
Email: lisad@aponitelecommunication.com
Website: www.aponitelecom.com
Telecommunication Equipment, Installation, Voice, Data, Cabling, Maintenance, Repair, Security System, DVR, Security Cameras. (Woman/Nat-Ame, estab 2007, empl 7, sales $360,000, cert: State, 8(a))

9640 Business Communications Solutions
9910 Irvine Center Dr
Irvine, CA 92618
Contact: Afsaneh Rajab CEO
Tel: 949-333-1000
Email: srajab@bcsconsultants.com
Website: www.bcsconsultants.com
Telecommunication & networking: phone systems, internet & telephone services, cabling, networking, & server room design & installation. (Woman, estab 2001, empl 15, sales $3,700,000, cert: State)

9641 Cico Electrical Contractors Inc.
365 Whipporwill Dr
Riverside, CA 92507
Contact: Ron Veloz Office Mgr
Tel: 951-213-2229
Email: ron.veloz@cicoele.com
Website: www.cicoele.com
Electrical, Electrical Subcontractor, New Construction, Remodeling, Renovations, Improvements-Relocations, Maintenance, Switchgear Change out, Critical Power-UPS, Generators, Predictive Maintenance (circuit (Hisp, estab 2004, empl 25, sales $4,464,384, cert: NMSDC)

9642 Coast to Coast Communications
34145 Pacific Coast Hwy 635
Dana Point, CA 92629
Contact: Nikki Clark Natl Acct Exec
Tel: 949-481-6550
Email: nikki@c2ccomm.com
Website: www.c2ccomm.com
Voice, data cabling & phone systems. (Woman, estab 2000, empl 10, sales $5,040,175, cert: WBENC)

9643 Dataoptek Corp
573 E. Fairview Blvd. #43
Inglewood, CA 90302
Contact: Roderick Byrd CEO
Tel: 310-367-2826
Email: rbyrd@dataoptek.com
Website: www.dataoptek.com
Structured cabling, LAN, WAN, VoIP, wireline, wireless network infrastructure installations & maintenance. (AA, estab 1999, empl 10, sales , cert: NMSDC)

TELECOMMUNICATIONS

9644 E-3 Systems
1220 Whipple Rd
Union City, CA 94587
Contact: Kofi Tawiah President
Tel: 510-487-7393
Email: kofi@e3systems.com
Website: www.e3systems.com
Low voltage voice & data structured cabling, electronic security systems & telecom. (AA, estab 1989, empl 58, sales $3,900,000, cert: NMSDC, CPUC)

9645 GovMobile, LLC
120 Vantis, Ste 300
Aliso Viejo, CA 92656
Contact: Lambert Matias President
Tel: 949-505-9600
Email: lmatias@govmobile.com
Website: www.govmobile.com
Mobility, Wireless & Internet of Things (IoT)solutions. (As-Pac, estab , empl 2, sales $1,200,000, cert: 8(a))

9646 JM Fiber Optics, Inc.
13941 Ramona Ave Ste A
Chino, CA 91710
Contact: Marlene Vidana Business Devel Mgr
Tel: 909-628-3445
Email: mvidana@jmfiberoptics.com
Website: www.jmfiberoptics.com
Fiber optic & copper voice, video & data communication systems, transit system passenger information systems & intrusion dectection systems. (Hisp, estab 1992, empl 8, sales $5,701,490, cert: State, City, NMSDC, CPUC, SDB)

9647 Koru Communications, Inc.
19852 MacArthur Blvd, Ste 420
Irvine, CA 92612
Contact: Esther VanKirk Mktg Mgr
Tel: 949-222-2208
Email: evankirk@koruinc.com
Website: www.koruinc.com
Provide voice over IP (VoIP) phone systems, low voltage cabling, and telecommunication services. (Hisp, estab 2010, empl 3, sales $200,000, cert: City)

9648 Pinnacle Telecommunications, Inc. (PTI Solutions)
4242 Forcum Ave, Ste 200
McClellan, CA 95652
Contact: Marketing Program Mgr
Tel: 916-426-1046
Email: ap@pti-s.com
Website: www.pti-s.com
Install communications cabling & equipment, cell tower upgrades, structured wire, WiFi & laser communications. (Woman, estab 1984, empl 140, sales $17,000,000, cert: CPUC, WBENC)

9649 Rincon Technology
810 East Montecito St
Santa Barbara, CA 93103
Contact: Mike Bartling Founder EVP Sales
Tel: 805-319-7830
Email: mbartling@rincontechnology.com
Website: www.rincontechnology.com
Wireless transmission gear T1 to 3DS3 capacity, native Ethernet/IP backhaul, up to 800mbps transmission, wireless SONET backhaul. (Hisp, estab 2003, empl 45, sales $55,000,000, cert: State, NMSDC)

9650 Serene Innovations
14731 Carmenita Rd
Norwalk, CA 90650
Contact: James McGehee Sales Coord
Tel: 562-407-5400
Email: j.mcgehee@sereneinnovations.com
Website: www.sereneinnovations.com/
Amplified Phones, TV Listening Devices, Ringer/Flasher, Alerting Notification System, Telephone Amplifier. (As-Pac, estab 2004, empl 15, sales $3,000,000, cert: NMSDC)

9651 Solutionz Videoconferencing Inc. (Solutionz Conferencing, Inc.)
901 Bringham Ave
Los Angeles, CA 90049
Contact: Paul Mitnick Sales Acct Exec
Tel: 234-303-2300
Email: pmitnick@solutionzinc.com
Website: www.solutionzinc.com
Audio, video, Videoconferencing, Telecommunications retailer. (Hisp, estab 2001, empl 295, sales $140,000,000, cert: NMSDC, CPUC)

9652 Tempest Telecom Solutions, LLC
136 W Canon Perdido Ste 100
Santa Barbara, CA 93101
Contact: Elda Rudd VP Mktg
Tel: 805-879-4800
Email: tempestsupplier@tempesttelecom.com
Website: www.tempesttelecom.com
New & refurbished networking equipment. (Woman, estab 2005, empl 160, sales , cert: CPUC, WBENC)

9653 Towne Communications, Inc.
4640 Duckhorn Dr
Sacramento, CA 95834
Contact: Jeanette Towne CEO
Tel: 916-993-2100
Email: jmtowne@synectic.us
Website: www.synectic.us
Voice, data, VOIP, telecommunication services. (Woman, estab 1995, empl 35, sales $4,200,000, cert: WBENC)

9654 Unified TelData Inc.
425 2nd St
San Francisco, CA 94107
Contact: Eric Clauss GSS
Tel: 415-977-7031
Email: eclauss@utdi.com
Website: www.utdi.com
Communications solutionsL Avaya, Cisco & Nortel hardware & services. (Woman, estab 1981, empl 50, sales $10,000,000, cert: CPUC, 8(a))

9655 Universal Network Development Corp.
2555 Third St Ste 112
Sacramento, CA 95818
Contact: Cinthia Larkin Kazee President
Tel: 916-475-1200
Email: undc@undc.com
Website: www.undc.com
Telecommunication eng, fiber optic & copper splicing, installation & repair, project mgmt, CAD drafting. (Woman/As-Pac, estab 1980, empl 250, sales $21,302,795, cert: CPUC, WBENC)

9656 WP Electric & Communications, Inc.
14198 Albers Way
Chino, CA 91710
Contact: Laura Nesbitt President
Tel: 909-606-3510
Email: roseann@wpelectric.com
Website: www.wpelectric.com
Electrical & network cabling services. (Woman, estab 1975, empl 45, sales $7,800,000, cert: CPUC, WBENC)

Colorado

9657 M.R. Research
8003 S Corona Way
Centennial, CO 80122
Contact: Madeline K. Reilly President
Tel: 303-795-4353
Email: rkreilly@aol.com
Website: www.m-r-research.com
Applied research, electronic design & telecommunications components for satellites, base stations & mobile wireless systems. (Minority, Woman, estab 2010, empl 4, sales $334,900, cert: NMSDC)

9658 Sage Telecommunications Corp.
6700 Race St
Denver, CO 80229
Contact: President
Tel: 303-227-0986
Email:
Website: www.sagecom.net
Engineers, build & maintain fiber optic, cable & other networks. (Woman, estab 1992, empl 90, sales $10,000,000, cert: State)

9659 Tripwireless, Inc.
4941 Allison St Ste 7 & 8
Arvada, CO 80022
Contact: Kimberly Koch Founder
Tel: 720-361-4998
Email: kym@tripwireless.com
Website: www.tripwireless.com
Network infrastructure equipment & services, cell sites, microwave, outside power plant, transmission, routers, data centers, de-commissioning, trenching, fiber, installation & preventative maintenance. (Woman, estab 2005, empl 6, sales , cert: WBENC)

Connecticut

9660 IQ Telcom, LLC dba IQ Telecom
78 Beaver Road
Wethersfield, CT 06109
Contact: Carol Guerra Dir Business Devel
Tel: 860-882-0500
Email: carol.guerra@iqt360.com
Website: www.iqt360.com
Telecommunications expense: voice, data & wireless, audit, optimization, spend base lining, invoice processing, monthly reporting for cost allocation, vendor/carrier mgmt; contract negotiation, network design & optimization. (Woman, estab 2001, empl 35, sales $3,000,000, cert: State, WBENC)

9661 VisionPoint LLC
152 Rockwell Rd
Newington, CT 06111
Contact: Louise Mastroianni Acct Mgr
Tel: 860-436-9673
Email: visionpointct@gmail.com
Website: www.visionpointllc.com
Technology acquisition, integration, design, installation, technical meeting support & service. (Woman, estab 2003, empl 24, sales $7,002,015, cert: WBENC)

District of Columbia

9662 MJS Communications LLC
1343 First St NW
Washington, DC 20001
Contact: Marlon Boykin President
Tel: 888-829-1658
Email: mboykin@mjscommunications.biz
Website: www.mjscommunications.biz
Information technology, telecommunications services, structure cabling system, voice/data cabling, CCTV cabling, POS & wireless, CCTV, digital video recorders, Interior/exterior cameras, monitors, perimeter security. (AA, estab 2009, empl 2, sales $110,000, cert: State, City)

9663 National Fiber and Copper, Inc.
1701 Pennsylvania Ave NW Ste 300
Washington, DC 20006
Contact: Kimberly Valentine President
Tel: 202-729-6339
Email: kimvalentine@nationalfiberandcopper.com
Website: www.nationalfiberandcopper.com
Low-voltage communication installation & services, communications, structured cabling, fiber optics, network installation & management, VOIP, phone systems, security solutions, on-site & support services. (Woman, estab 1999, empl 10, sales $1,350,000, cert: City, WBENC, SDB)

9664 Tecknomic LLC
2322 First St NW
Washington, DC 20001
Contact: Dexter Spencer President
Tel: 202-829-2953
Email: dspencer@tecknomic.com
Website: www.tecknomic.com
Emergency management & services training, information technology, wireless/wireline communications. (AA, estab 2003, empl 12, sales $391,000, cert: State, 8(a))

Florida

9665 Advanced IT Concepts, Inc.
1351 Sundial Point
Winter Springs, FL 32708
Contact: Gabriel Ruiz President
Tel: 407-914-2484
Email: eve.maldonado@aitcinc.com
Website: www.aitcinc.com
Telecommunications & Information Technology services. (Hisp, estab 2006, empl 51, sales $24,860,693, cert: City, 8(a))

TELECOMMUNICATIONS

9666 Cell Antenna
12453 NW 44th St
Coral Springs, FL 33065
Contact: Barbara Melamed Owner
Tel: 954-340-7053
Email: barbara@cellantenna.com
Website: www.cellantenna.com
Signal enhancement using Distributed Antenna Systems for cell phone carriers (AT&T, Verizon, T-Mobile and Sprint) (Woman, estab 2002, empl 21, sales $8,000,000, cert: State)

9667 ClearTone Communications Inc.
840 Edgewood Ave S, Ste 209
Jacksonville, FL 32205
Contact: Jerry Irizarry President
Tel: 904-240-0490
Email: jerry@cleartonejax.com
Website: www.cleartonejax.com
Telecommunications, voice, data & structured cabling. (Hisp, estab 2007, empl 1, sales , cert: State)

9668 Satya Acquisition Management, Inc. dba SAM, Inc.
3300 South OBT Ste 106
Orlando, FL 32839
Contact: Bob Chopra President
Tel: 267-973-4228
Email: bchopra@sam-inc.com
Website: www.sam-inc.com
Telecommunications, new site builds, antenna modifications, generator installations, microwave installations, temporary cell site installations cells & Distributed Antenna Systems. (As-Pac, estab 2006, empl 2, sales $350,000, cert: NMSDC)

9669 SENCOMMUNICATIONS, INC.
9208 FLORIDA PALM Dr
Tampa, FL 33619
Contact: Stacie Miller CEO
Tel: 813-626-4404
Email: rgeneral@sencomm.com
Website: www.sencomm.com
Provides telephone headsets, desksets, teleconferencing units, and other products. (Woman, estab 1989, empl 16, sales $14,528,491, cert: WBENC)

9670 Smith Corona/Comfort Telecommunications
1407 SE 47th Terr
Cape Coral, FL 33904
Contact: Louise Bergen Sales
Tel: 800-399-3224
Email: louise@comfortel.com
Website: www.comfortel.com
Mfr & dist telephone headsets & accessories. (Woman, estab 1985, empl 15, sales $11,000,000, cert: State)

9671 TSG Enterprises, LLC dba RadiusPoint
1211 State Road 436, Ste 295
Casselberry, FL 32707
Contact: CEO
Tel: 407-661-6840
Email: sales@radiuspoint.com
Website: www.radiuspoint.com
Telecommunications & utility invoices auditing, expense management & bill processing. (Woman, estab 1992, empl 42, sales , cert: WBENC)

Georgia

9672 Agile Perspective
27 Edwin Pl
Atlanta, GA 30318
Contact: Rae-Anne Alves
Tel: 917-648-7544
Email: rae-anne.alves@anagileperspective.com
Website: www.anagileperspective.com
Telecommunication sourcing, cost reduction initiatives, strategic management, best practice benchmarking, technology integration. (Woman/AA, Hisp, estab 2012, empl 1, sales , cert: NMSDC, WBENC)

9673 Atlanta Communications Co.
1510 Huber St
Atlanta, GA 30318
Contact: Carrie Davis Exec Asst
Tel: 404-875-9316
Email: cdavis@atlantacomm.com
Website: www.atlantacomm.com
Dist, service, install, rent, site preparation & project management of two-way communications equipment. (Woman/AA, estab 1947, empl 43, sales , cert: WBENC)

9674 Concise, Inc.
191 Peachtree St, Ste 3300
Alanta, GA 30303
Contact: David Johnson CEO
Tel: 404-736-3669
Email: info@conciseinc.com
Website: www.conciseinc.com
Telecommunications svcs: network & telephone cabling, wireless networks, surveillance & security systems. (AA, estab 2003, empl 2, sales $560,000, cert: NMSDC, 8(a))

9675 Digicomm Systems, Inc.
3221 Hill St, Ste 103-B
Duluth, GA 30096
Contact: Undra Patrick VP Operations
Tel: 770-497-8080
Email: management@digicommsystems.com
Website: www.digicommsystems.com
Telecommunication services: data center design & consulting, data network design & consulting, systems integration & installation, internal communications, low-voltage cabling, equipment relocation. (Woman/AA, estab 1988, empl 7, sales , cert: City, NMSDC)

9676 FamTeck, LLC
4484 Covington Hwy, Ste 105
Decatur, GA 30038
Contact: Conrad Meertins CEO
Tel: 404-822-1117
Email: cmeertins@famteck.com
Website: www.famteck.com
New technologies & mobility, Streamline IT Operations. (AA, estab 2006, empl 7, sales , cert: NMSDC)

9677   Litra Manufacturing Inc.
       6733-A Jones Mill Ct
       Norcross, GA 30092
       Contact: Skip York Sales Mgr
       Tel: 800-445-4617
       Email: skipyork@litramfg.com
       Website: www.litramfg.com
Mfr copper & pre-terminated fiber optic cable assemblies: coax, multipair copper cable assemblies, high strand fiber assemblies, single-mode, multi-mode, fiber jumpers, components & accessories. (Woman, estab 1986, empl 25, sales , cert: CPUC)

9678   North Georgia Telecom, Inc.
       4200 Steve Reynolds Blvd., Ste 12
       Norcross, GA 30093
       Contact: Brittany Gold President
       Tel: 678-482-0015
       Email: b.gold@ngtinc.com
       Website: www.ngtinc.com
Install, deinstall, switching sales, asset mgmt. (Woman, estab 1994, empl 20, sales , cert: WBENC)

9679   ProComm Telecommunications, Inc.
       1377 Business Center Dr
       Conyers, GA 30094
       Contact: Josh Franklin Sales
       Tel: 770-760-8660
       Email: jfranklin@ptinc.org
       Website: www.ptinc.org
Installation, engineering & design telecommunications networks: wireless, fiber optics, digital cross connects, switch, multiplexer & channel bank, calibrate & repair test equipment. (Minority, Woman, estab 1989, empl 55, sales $7,000,000, cert: WBENC)

9680   VanRan Communications Services, Inc.
       2939 Pacific Dr
       Norcross, GA 30071
       Contact: Dir Govt & Enterprise Solutions
       Tel: 540-728-1941
       Email: sales@vanran.com
       Website: www.vanran.com
Telecommunications systems: traditional, converged, voice over internet protocol, voice mail & unified messaging, contact ctr solutions, networking services. (Woman, estab 1986, empl 35, sales $9,650,000, cert: WBENC)

9681   Washington Communications Group LLC
       6465 Hwy 85
       Riverdale, GA 30274
       Contact: Stacy Washington President
       Tel: 770-991-3000
       Email: washingtoncommunication@yahoo.com
       Website: www.washingtoncommunication.com
Structured Network Cabling, Fiber Optic Installation, Single mode, Multimode, Fiber Optic Testing & Terminations, Voice/Data Network Installation, Business & VoIP Phone Systems, Patch panel installation & termination. (AA, estab 2013, empl 10, sales , cert: State)

Illinois

9682   Chicago Communications, LLC
       200 W Spangler Ave
       Elmhurst, IL 60126
       Contact: Lisa MacGillivray Mktg Dir
       Tel: 630-832-3311
       Email: sales@chicomm.com
       Website: www.chicomm.com
Dist, install & maintain communication equipment. (Woman, estab 2004, empl 68, sales $10,000,000, cert: State, WBENC)

9683   ClearSounds Communication
       1743 Quincy Ave, Ste 155
       Naperville, IL 60540
       Contact: Michelle Maher Dir of Sales/ops
       Tel: 866-657-2855
       Email: michelle.maher@clearsounds.com
       Website: www.clearsounds.com
Amplified phones, Bluetooth headsets, amplified neckloops, mobile accessories & listening systems for people with hearing loss and those looking for a remarkable listening experience. (Woman, estab 2004, empl 15, sales , cert: WBENC)

9684   Cymbal Communications Corporation
       4N419 Mountain Ash Dr
       Wayne, IL 60184
       Contact: Antoinette Calarco Dir Sales/service
       Tel: 877-296-2666
       Email: antoinette@cymbalcomm.com
       Website: www.cymbalcomm.com
Dist telecommunication products: VXi, GN Netcom, Plantronics, Polycom,ClearOne, Avaya & Nortel Phones. (Minority, Woman, estab 2005, empl 5, sales $930,000, cert: WBENC)

9685   Integrated Installations, inc.
       514 Pratt Ave N
       Schaumburg, IL 60193
       Contact: Kate Novelle Contracts/Sales Dir
       Tel: 847-985-1170
       Email: kate@i3install.com
       Website: www.i3install.com
Telecom installation services, Wireless & Wireline Industries. (Woman, estab 2000, empl 25, sales $2,330,161, cert: State, City, WBENC, NWBOC)

9686   Level-(1) Global Solutions, LLC
       233 S. Wacker Dr 84th Fl
       Chicago, IL 60606
       Contact: CEO
       Tel: 312-202-3300
       Email:
       Website: www.level-1.com
Infrastructure solutions: office technology & data ctr facilities, IDF/telecom infrastructure, UPS power protection, emergency generator power, HVAC enviromental systems, fire protection, security & access control, CATV & LAN/WAN video surveillance. (AA, estab 2001, empl 25, sales $1,800,000, cert: City)

9687 Phoenix Business Solutions LLC
12543 S Laramie Ave
Alsip, IL 60803
Contact: Peggy Hrindak CEO
Tel: 708-388-1330
Email: phrindak@getpbsnow.com
Website: www.getpbsnow.com
Design, install & maintain telecom & data systems. (Woman, estab 2000, empl 35, sales $5,853,538, cert: WBENC)

9688 Pilot Services, Inc.
317 Mustang Dr
Oswego, IL 60543
Contact: Kimberly Warren President
Tel: 630-554-7413
Email: kwarren@pilotservicesinc.com
Website: www.pilotservicesinc.com
Telecommunications, voice & data, cabling, wiring, installation & maintenance for telecommunications equipment. (Woman, estab 1996, empl 10, sales $817,915, cert: WBENC)

9689 Raptor Industries, Inc.
1602 N Park Dr
Mount Prospect, IL 60056
Contact: Anthony Kalama
Tel: 708-417-9190
Email: gkalama@raptorindustriesinc.com
Website: www.raptorindustriesinc.com
Voice, Data, Fiber Optic & CATV Cable Installation and Certification, Copper and Fiber Optic Splicing, Audio/Visual, CCTV, Riser Management, Intercom. (As-Pac, estab 2013, empl 5, sales $162,554, cert: State, City, NMSDC)

9690 SI Tech Inc.
1101 N Raddant Rd
Batavia, IL 60510
Contact: Ramesh Sheth (ramesh@sitech-bitdriver.com) President
Tel: 630-761-3640
Email: admin@sitech-bitdriver.com
Website: www.sitech-bitdriver.com
Mfr & develop fiber optic communications products. (As-Ind, estab 1984, empl 20, sales , cert: NMSDC)

9691 TelePlus, Inc.
724 Racquet Club Dr
Addison, IL 60101
Contact: Mike Warda Sales Mgr
Tel: 630-543-3066
Email: mwarda@telepluscom.com
Website: www.telepluscom.com
Voice/data low voltage cabling systems, electrical, paging systems, CCTV, Nortel BCM and Norstar telephone systems. (Woman, estab 1986, empl 56, sales $6,250,000, cert: City, WBENC)

9692 The Northridge Group, Inc.
9700 W Higgins Rd Ste 600
Rosemont, IL 60018
Contact: Sue Antkowiak Dir of Program Mgmt & Compliance
Tel: 847-692-7002
Email: registrations@northridgegroup.com
Website: www.northridgegroup.com
Telecommunications. (Woman/AA, Hisp, estab 1999, empl 82, sales $10,000,000, cert: City, WBENC)

9693 Viadata1 Communications Inc.
3118 Elder Ln
Franklin Park, IL 60131
Contact: Eddie Villariny President
Tel: 773-593-1346
Email: edvilla@viadata1.net
Website: www.viadata1.net
Low Voltage Cabling, Fiber Optic, CCTV, Card Access, Wireless Access Points, Network Data Center design & Installation, Data & Voice Cabling. Computer equipment installation. (Hisp, estab 2008, empl 4, sales $800,000, cert: NMSDC)

Indiana

9694 C-CAT, Inc.
1726 W. 15th St
Indianapolis, IN 46202
Contact: Kristi Johnson President
Tel: 317-568-2899
Email: kjohnson@c-cat.com
Website: www.c-cat.com
Infrastructure & low-voltage cabling services: video, voice & data, security/safety cabling & Cat 5E, Cat-6 & fiber-optic wiring systems. (Woman, estab 2001, empl 30, sales $5,200,000, cert: WBENC)

9695 Dixon Phone Place, Inc.
5335 N Tacoma Ave, Ste 3
Indianapolis, IN 46220
Contact: Juli Fritsch
Tel: 317-251-3504
Email: dixonphoneplace1@att.net
Website: www.dixonphone.com
Telephone equipment, plantronics telephone & computer headsets, cell phone corded & bluetooth headsets, corded & wireless headsets, telephone parts, line & handset cords, polycom conference equipment, cordless phones, business phones. (Woman, estab 1983, empl 2, sales , cert: State, City)

9696 Summitline Industries, Inc.
7822 Opportunity Dr
Fort Wayne, IN 46825
Contact: Stan Richard President
Tel: 260-490-2213
Email: stan.richard@summitline.com
Website: www.Summitline.com
Telecommunications, supply chain solutions, material mgmt, warehousing & kit fulfillment. (AA, estab 1983, empl 20, sales $15,000,000, cert: NMSDC, CPUC)

9697 Telamon Corporation
1000 E 116th St
Carmel, IN 46032
Contact: John L. Weeks Dir of Sales
Tel: 317-818-6757
Email: john.weeks@telamon.com
Website: www.telamon.com
Mfr & dist voice & data communications products: cables & connectors to cstmrs specs, modular voice & data accessories; engineering & install telecommunication equip. (As-Pac, estab 1984, empl 1100, sales , cert: NMSDC)

9698 Thomas Telecom Inc.
      7106 Lakeview Pkwy West Dr
      Indianapolis, IN 46268
      Contact: Earl Thomas President
      Tel: 317-757-5247
      Email: ethomas@thomastelecominc.com
      Website: www.thomastelecominc.com
Project Management, New installations, Network Infrasrtucture & Design services, Firewalls/VPN, Help Desk support. (AA, estab 1999, empl 20, sales $5,000,000, cert: NMSDC)

Kentucky

9699 Strategic Communications, LLC
      310 Evergreen Rd, Ste 100
      Louisville, KY 40243
      Contact: Kathy Mills CEO
      Tel: 502-493-7234
      Email: info@yourstrategic.com
      Website: www.stratcomllc.com
Voice, data & communications solutions: structured cabling, telecommunications systems, carrier services, security/alarm, data communications products & services. (Minority, Woman, estab 1993, empl 40, sales $4,200,000, cert: NMSDC, WBENC)

Louisiana

9700 Ad-Comm International
      1710 Orleans St
      Mandeville, LA 70448
      Contact: Otto Mehrgut President
      Tel: 985-674-5757
      Email: otto@profit-on-hold.com
      Website: www.profit-on-hold.com
Provide Music & Messages On-Hold, for your Telephone Systems. (Hisp, estab 1991, empl 6, sales $620,000, cert: NMSDC)

9701 TCN
      1016 Harimaw Court E
      Metairie, LA 70001
      Contact: Victor Hess Sales Mgr
      Tel: 504-838-9600
      Email: vhess@executonesystems.com
      Website: www.executonesystems.com
Furnish & install wiring, digital & Voice over IP telephone systems, Overhead Paging, Music, Sound, Masking, School Intercom & Mass Notification Systems. (Woman, estab 1947, empl 28, sales $357,531,124, cert: WBENC)

Massachusetts

9702 C.E. Communication Services, Inc.
      25 Grove St
      Franklin, MA 02038
      Contact: Bruce Baltz
      Tel: 866-966-1555
      Email: bruceb@cecommunication.com
      Website: www.cecommunication.com/
Dist telecommuncations & networking products. (Woman, estab 1998, empl 10, sales , cert: State)

9703 C4Cable, LLC
      257 Scadding St
      Taunton, MA 02780
      Contact: Carole Derringer Principal
      Tel: 508-944-5573
      Email: caroled@c4cable.com
      Website: www.c4cable.com
Dist Telecommunications & Data Networking Products: Bulk Copper & Fiber Optic Cables, Patch Panels, Enclosures, Copper & Fiber Patch Cords, Pre-Terminated MTP/MPO Backplane Fiber Cables & Cassettes, Free Standing Racks. (Woman, estab 2014, empl 2, sales , cert: State, WBENC)

9704 Coastal Telecommunications Inc.
      35 Main St Ste 116C
      Topsfield, MA 01983
      Contact: Angela Gill President
      Tel: 978-744-4900
      Email: angela@gocti.us
      Website: www.gocti.us
Low Voltage Cabling, Voice & Data Structured Cabling, Communication System Design, Installation & Maintenance, Voice & Network Equipment & Service Solutions. (Woman/AA, estab 1990, empl 5, sales $250,000, cert: State, WBENC)

9705 Mallory Headsets
      679 N Main St
      West Bridgewater, MA 02379
      Contact: Kelly Mallory President
      Tel: 508-586-0117
      Email: donna@malloryheadsets.com
      Website: www.malloryheadsets.com
Telecommunications products, audio conferencing products. (Woman/AA, estab 1997, empl 10, sales , cert: State)

Maryland

9706 Crest Telecom, Inc.
      PO Box 410
      Bel Air, MD 21014
      Contact: Tammy Halley Principal
      Tel: 410-420-1044
      Email: tammy.halley@cresttelecom.com
      Website: www.cresttelecom.com
Wireless & wireline telecommunication products: routers, microwave radios, central service units, cross connect panels, fuse alarm panels, racks, fiber management systems, filters, duplexers, cable, channel element cards, etc. (Woman, estab 2007, empl 10, sales , cert: WBENC)

9707 G Tech Contracting, LLC
      8008 Dorado Terr
      Brandywine, MD 20613
      Contact: Agustin Nunez CEO
      Tel: 240-281-1856
      Email: info@gtechcontracting.com
      Website: www.gtechcontracting.com
Integrated security, voice/data communications. (Hisp, estab 2013, empl 5, sales $1,200,000, cert: 8(a))

9708 KSC Consultant Services LLC
18216 Darnell Dr
Olney, MD 20832
Contact: Kimberlie Manns Owner
Tel: 240-389-1882
Email: kmanns@kscconsultants.net
Website: www.kscconsultants.net
Telecommunication consulting & infrastructure wiring, designing & installing voice & data infrastructure/cabling, troubleshoot, repair, testing & installing voice & data lines, rewiring, installing & replacing jacks. (Woman/AA, estab 2004, empl 2, sales , cert: State, SDB)

9709 SRL TotalSource LLC
83 High St Ste B
Waldorf, MD 20602
Contact: John Johnson COO
Tel: 301-885-0097
Email: jjohnson@srltotalsource.com
Website: www.srltotalsource.com/
Wireless Telecommunications Carriers, Data Processing, Hosting, and Related Services. (AA, estab 2011, empl 6, sales $589,253, cert: State, 8(a))

Michigan

9710 Advanced Communication Cabling, Inc.
PO Box 308
Spring Arbor, MI 49283
Contact: Ruth Fritz President
Tel: 517-524-2224
Email: ruthacci@direcway.com
Website: www.acci-mi.com
Voice, data, video, sound reinforcement, networking, copper & fiber optics, feed cable installation, cable repair & removal, testing & inspection, emergency repair, project mgmt, engineering, consulting & surveys. (Woman, estab 1992, empl 22, sales , cert: WBENC)

9711 AMI Strategies, Inc.
17187 N Laurel Park Dr Ste 125
Livonia, MI 48152
Contact: Jane Sydlowski President
Tel: 248-957-4200
Email: jsydlowski@amistrategies.com
Website: www.amistrategies.com
Telecom expense management & professional services. (Woman, estab 1991, empl 80, sales $3,000,000, cert: WBENC)

9712 Cellular Solutions Signal Enhancing Specialists
2737 N Meridian Rd
Sanford, MI 48657
Contact: Devin O'Neil Acct Exec
Tel: 989-687-4023
Email: aimeek@cellularsolutions.com
Website: www.cellularsolutions.com
Cellular signal enhancement throughout homes, vehicles commercial buildings & large facilities. (Woman, estab 2004, empl 13, sales $8,000,000, cert: WBENC)

9713 Communication Brokers, Inc.
437 44th St SW
Grand Rapid, MI 49548
Contact: Mimi Micu CEO
Tel: 616-301-3733
Email: mmicu@cbitelecom.com
Website: www.cbitelecom.com
Telecommunications consulting services, data, local & wireless communications analysis. (Woman, estab 1991, empl 30, sales $5,000,000, cert: WBENC)

9714 Federated Service Solutions, Inc.
41100 Plymouth Rd Ste 165
Plymouth, MI 48170
Contact: Susan Troyer Sales Admin
Tel: 248-539-9000
Email: stroyer@federatedservice.com
Website: www.federatedservice.com
POS, server, kiosks/self-service, low voltage cabling (voice/data/video/audio), security/LP, network devices, and wireless (Woman, estab 2004, empl 70, sales $21,500,000, cert: WBENC)

9715 Prima Communications, Inc.
PO Box 338
Schoolcraft, MI 49087
Contact: Charlotte Hubbard Owner
Tel: 269-679-3800
Email: primaadmin@voyager.net
Website: www.primacommunications.com
Technical communications. (Woman, estab 1991, empl 25, sales , cert: WBENC)

Minnesota

9716 Building Systems Solutions, Inc.
1250 E Moore Lake Dr Ste 230
Fridley, MN 55432
Contact: Megan Beaver CEO
Tel: 763-502-1515
Email: meganb@bssmn.com
Website: www.buildingsystemssolutions.com
Design commercial audio & communications systems: paging, sound masking, music & emergency notification systems. (Woman, estab 2003, empl 2, sales $200,145, cert: State)

9717 Seacom, LLC
160 Birchwood Ave
Saint Paul, MN 55110
Contact: Sandee Ebbott President
Tel: 612-207-7423
Email: sandee@seacomllc.com
Website: www.seacomllc.com
Telecommunication solutions: legacy equipment, VoIP, video conferencing, voice & data cabling, electrical cabling, data networking & security systems. (Woman, estab 2010, empl 10, sales $1,500,000, cert: WBENC)

9718 Technology Management Corporation
4790 Lakeway Terr
Shorewood, MN 55331
Contact: Brendon O'Brien Dir Business Devel
Tel: 952-470-0217
Email: bobrien@tmc-1.com
Website: www.tmc-1.com
Telecommunications consulting: cable design; phone system design; phone, data, & internet network design, data/server room design. telecommunications audit & contract negotiation. (Woman, estab 1988, empl 12, sales $788,715, cert: State, City, WBENC, NWBOC)

9719 TRiCOM Communications
      1301 Corporate Center Dr, Ste 160
      Eagan, MN 55121
      Contact: Diane Evans President
      Tel: 651-686-9000
      Email: diane.evans@tricom1.com
      Website: www.tricom1.com
Design & install structured cabling: copper & fiber optics, Data Centers, Telecom Rooms, Equipment Rooms, Outside Plant Construction, Security Cameras, Card Access Systems, In-Building Wireless Distributed Antenna Systems (DAS). (Woman, estab 1989, empl 20, sales $2,250,000, cert: State, City, WBENC)

Missouri

9720 American Cable Products LLC
      4 Forest Park Circle Dr
      Lake St. Louis, MO 63367
      Contact: Richard Politte Managing Partner
      Tel: 636-265-6602
      Email: rmpolitte@amercp.net
      Website: www.americancableproducts.com
Install voice & data cable, routers, switches, modems, racks, wireless equipment, fiber optic cable & hardware, PA & video systems, arial cable & single mode fiber & buried drop service, trenching, boring, etc. (As-Pac, estab 2002, empl 25, sales $12,000,000, cert: State, City, CPUC, SDB)

9721 eTech Solutons, LLC
      1813 Zumbehl Rd
      Saint Charles, MO 63303
      Contact: Sara Hagemeyer Owner
      Tel: 314-282-8318
      Email: brad@etechstl.com
      Website: www.etechstl.com
Cellphone supplier, Cellphone repair, Tablet repair, Tablet supplier electronic repair - ie micro soldering, laptop repair, Cellphone & tablet data recovery, Chipoff data recovery, jtag data recovery, cellphone forensics. (Woman, estab 2012, empl 2, sales $530,000, cert: WBENC)

9722 TSI Global Companies LLC
      700 Fountain Lakes Blvd
      Saint Charles, MO 63301
      Contact: Christine Robinson Accounting Dept
      Tel: 636-949-8889
      Email: crobinson@tsi-global.com
      Website: www.tsi-global.com
Electrical & Low-voltage systems integrator providing convergent audio and video, networked communications & security system solutions. (Nat Ame, estab 1980, empl 100, sales $43,110,684, cert: State, City, NMSDC)

Montana

9723 Alamon Telco, Inc.
      315 W. Idaho St
      Kalispell, MT 59901
      Contact: Margaret Gebhardt President
      Tel: 800-252-8838
      Email: peg@alamon.com
      Website: www.alamon.com
Communication svcs: outside plant engineering, splicing & inspection; cable installations; CO transmission, engineering, installation, testing, maintenance & support. (Woman, estab 1975, empl 150, sales $14,053,000, cert: WBENC)

North Carolina

9724 Atlantic Communication Products, Inc.
      4324 Barringer Dr Ste. 112
      Charlotte, NC 28217
      Contact: Winn Pray President
      Tel: 704-676-5880
      Email: w.pray@goacp.com
      Website: www.goacp.com
Resell voice & data products, installation & maintenance services of wire & cabling. (Hisp, estab 1997, empl 10, sales $900,000, cert: NMSDC)

9725 Lexair Electronics Sales Corp.
      4807-B Koger Blvd
      Greensboro, NC 27407
      Contact: Paula Edwards Contract Mgr
      Tel: 336-294-5300
      Email: alisawatts@lexairsales.com
      Website: www.lexair.com
Dist communications equipment: headsets, telephones, audio conferencing equipment & peripherals. (Woman, estab 1998, empl 15, sales $6,550,000, cert: WBENC)

9726 Team Telecom, LLC
      220 N. Main St
      Lexington, NC 27292
      Contact: Jennifer Sturgell
      Tel: 888-305-4772
      Email: jsturgell@teamtelecom.net
      Website: www.teamtelecom.net
Dist new, surplus & refurbished telecommunications equipment. (Woman/AA, estab 2005, empl 8, sales $3,050,000, cert: State, NMSDC, WBENC)

9727 TelExpress
      406 Interstate Dr
      Archdale, NC 27263
      Contact: Tabitha Brock Sr Acct Mgr
      Tel: 434-990-2644
      Email: tabitha@telexpressinc.com
      Website: www.telexpressinc.com
Mfr central office, wireless, cable, fiber & DC power equipment. (Woman, estab 1992, empl 35, sales $5,785,800, cert: WBENC)

9728 Walker and Associates, Inc.
      7129 Old Hwy 52
      Welcome, NC 27374
      Contact: Jane Brightwell VP Business Dev
      Tel: 336-731-5236
      Email: governcon@walkerfirst.com
      Website: www.walkerfirst.com
Dist data & telecommunication equip, material mgmt & installation. (Woman, estab 1970, empl 120, sales , cert: CPUC)

New Jersey

9729 D.M. Radio Service Corp.
      45 Perry St
      Chester, NJ 07930
      Contact: Sandy Drysdale President
      Tel: 908-879-2525
      Email: sdrysdale@csiradio.com
      Website: www.csiradio.com
Dist two-way radio communications equipment, design/build service, supply & support for radio systems, Emergency Call Boxes, BDA & DAS systems. (Woman, estab 1968, empl 6, sales $700,000, cert: State, WBENC)

TELECOMMUNICATIONS 9730-9739

9730 e.comm Technologies
11 Melanie Ln
East Hanover, NJ 07936
Contact: Chuck Tarantino global acct Mgr
Tel: 973-503-5814
Email: ctarantino@ecommt.com
Website: www.ecommtechnologies.com
Avayas Radvision video conferencing, contact center, call recording, speech access, predictive dialers, wireless solutions, video conferencing both room to room & desktop to desktop. (Woman, estab 1999, empl 20, sales $6,622,113, cert: State)

9731 Office Solutions Inc.
217 Mount Horeb Rd
Warren, NJ 07059
Contact: Michael Scannelli Div Mgr
Tel: 732-356-0200
Email: mscannelli@osidirect.com
Website: www.osidirect.com
Designs & implement converged voice & data solutions: VoIP, IP telephony telecommunications equipment, telephone maintenance contracts, headsets, media servers & gateways, voice messaging, call centers, contact centers, video conferencing. (Woman, estab 1982, empl 30, sales $6,200,000, cert: WBENC)

9732 Spectrotel
3535 Route 66, Building 7
Neptune, NJ 07753
Contact: Jack Dayan President
Tel: 732-345-7936
Email: sales@spectrotel.com
Website: www.spectrotel.com
Dedicated Voice Services, Business Calling Services (POTs), VoIP Services, Conferencing Services, Managed Services, Network Monitoring, Managed Security, Cyber Security, SD-WAN, Dedicated Network Services, Dedicated Internet Access, Virtual Network Svcs. (Hisp, estab 1997, empl 130, sales $78,000,000, cert: NMSDC)

9733 The Seideman Company
4 Canterbury Ct
Marlton, NJ 08053
Contact: Patricia Seideman Owner
Tel: 856-988-0117
Email: pseideman@aol.com
Website: www.seidemancompany.com
Telecommunications & data networking services. (Woman, estab 1991, empl 2, sales $156,382, cert: WBENC)

9734 TRAK Communications, Inc.
710 Tennant Rd Ste 101
Manalapan, NJ 07726
Contact: President
Tel: 732-786-1355
Email: rsmaldone@trakcommunications.com
Website: www.trakcommunications.com
Telecommunications Billing Audit & Consulting Services, Contract Negotiations, contract compliance audits, wireless audits & optimizations, Bid Management Services, Vendor Management, Telecom Expense Management. (Woman, estab 1999, empl 2, sales $338,371, cert: WBENC)

Nevada

9735 ECF Data LLC
6149 S Rainbow Blvd, Ste 400
Las Vegas, NV 89118
Contact: Joseph Henderson
Tel: 702-664-0075
Email: jhenderson@ecfdata.com
Website: www.ecfdata.com
Polycom telephones & video equipment, Audio Codes, Dialogic, Acme Packet voice gateways, HP, Dell, Lenovo Server Hardware, Cisco, Juniper, HP network switches and Routers, Contact Center, Voice Response Applications. (AA, estab 2010, empl 4, sales $220,000, cert: NMSDC, 8(a))

New York

9736 Annese & Associates, Inc.
4781 Route 5 W
Herkimer, NY 13350
Contact: Yvonne Annese LoRe VP Corp Projects
Tel: 315-849-9194
Email: yannese@annese.com
Website: www.annese.com
Design, install & maintain IP telephony, wireless, voice & data networks, remote monitoring, 24 x 7 maintenance, security. (Woman, estab 1970, empl 94, sales $53,000,010, cert: State)

9737 Coranet Corp
277 Fairfield Road Ste 320A
Fairfield, NY 07004
Contact: Kevin O'Brien Acct Exec
Tel: 212-635-2770
Email: kobrien@coranet.com
Website: www.coranet.com
VoIP convergence solutions, data networking, project mgmt, video networking, structured cabling systems, mobility & wireless solutions, installation & maintenance, IP audits, call center applications, billing audits, e-collaboration. (Woman, estab 1987, empl 85, sales $63,000,000, cert: State, WBENC)

9738 HAVE, Inc.
309 Power Ave
Hudson, NY 12534
Contact: Lowell Stringer Sales
Tel: 518-828-2000
Email: lstringer@haveinc.com
Website: www.haveinc.com
Custom audio/video/data cable assemblies, dist bulk cable, connectors, tools & accessories. (Woman, estab 1977, empl 18, sales $3,120,541, cert: City)

9739 Information Transport Solutions Inc.
3204 Route 22
Patterson, NY 12563
Contact: President
Tel: 855-472-7701
Email: Info@4yourITS.com
Website: www.4yourITS.com
Wireless & structured cabling: wifi, DAS, AV, Access Control & Sound Masking. (Woman, estab 2001, empl 5, sales $2,000,000, cert: WBENC)

9740 Pivotel LLC
       6066 State Hwy 12
       Norwich, NY 13815
       Contact: Ronald Martin Jr Tech Sales Eng
       Tel: 607-334-7400
       Email: ron.martin@pivotelonline.com
       Website: www.pivotelonline.com
Communications & network wiring: AC/DC & fiber optic cabling & terminations. (Woman, estab 2001, empl 30, sales , cert: WBENC)

9741 Reliance Communications, LLC
       555 Wireless Blvd
       Hauppauge, NY 11788
       Contact: Jeanne Healey VP Marketing
       Tel: 631-952-4800
       Email: jeanne.healey@reliance.us
       Website: www.reliance.us
Dist wireless communications handsets & accessories. (As-Ind, estab 2005, empl 290, sales $715,079,538, cert: NMSDC)

9742 Saia Communications, Inc.
       100 Stradtman St
       Buffalo, NY 14206
       Contact: Cheryl Kirchmeyer Sales
       Tel: 716-892-2900
       Email: cheryl.kirchmeyer@saiacomm.com
       Website: www.saiacomm.com
Motorola two-way radio products. (Woman, estab 1980, empl 25, sales $5,000,000, cert: State)

9743 Sintel Satellite Services
       373 Nesconset Hwy Ste 133
       Hauppauge, NY 11788
       Contact: Sanjay Singhal COO
       Tel: 212-202-0678
       Email: sanjay@sintelsat.com
       Website: www.sintelsat.com
Satellite communication & terrestrial telecom solutions, infrastructure rebuilding, IP connectivity, fiber, microwave & satellite, Vsat, broadcasting & IT solutions. (Minority, Woman, estab 1997, empl 30, sales $1,132,000, cert: State, City)

Ohio

9744 Ameridial, Inc.
       4877 Higbee Ave NW, 2nd Fl
       Canton, OH 44718
       Contact: Ganesh Marve SVP
       Tel: 234-401-8104
       Email: ganesh.marve@fusionbposervices.com
       Website: www.ameridial.com
Customer service,Tele-sales,Telephone Answering Services, Debt recovery,Technical support services, Order Taking, Online Order Processing, Collection Services. (As-Pac, estab 1987, empl 663, sales $42,391,472, cert: CPUC)

9745 Ameridial, Inc. dba Fusion BPO Services
       4877 Higbee Ave NW
       Canton, OH 44718
       Contact: Matt McGeorge EVP
       Tel: 330-704-6792
       Email: mmcgeorge@fusionbposervices.com
       Website: www.fusionbposervices.com
Customer service,Tele-sales,Telephone Answering Services, Debt recovery,Technical support services, Order Taking, Online Order Processing, Collection Services. (As-Pac, estab 1987, empl 12000, sales , cert: NMSDC, CPUC)

9746 Cincinnati Cable Technology
       1177 W 8th St, Ste A
       Cincinnati, OH 45203
       Contact: Sheryl Yeager President
       Tel: 513-579-1888
       Email: sherylyeager@ccablet.com
       Website: www.ccablet.com
Structured cabling, fiber optics, coax network infrastructure, wireless networks, security solutions, IP based door entrance, IP security cameras, audio/visual system design. (Woman, estab 2010, empl 7, sales $1,500,000, cert: WBENC)

9747 ClarkTel Communications Corp.
       1661 Copley Rd
       Akron, OH 44320
       Contact: Terence N Clark President
       Tel: 330-869-8657
       Email: tclark@clarktel.net
       Website: www.clarktel.net
Design, installation, warranty & service business telephone systems: NEC, Nortel, Mitel, Toshiba, Panasonic, Comdial, Vodavi Sprint, voice/data cable. (AA, estab 1996, empl 10, sales , cert: NMSDC)

9748 Fine Line Communications Inc.
       PO Box 91
       Aurora, OH 44202
       Contact: Barbara Hoover President
       Tel: 330-562-0731
       Email: bhoover@finelinecomm.com
       Website: www.finelinecomm.com
Design, intall & maintain voice & data network systems. (Woman, estab 1981, empl 25, sales $2,480,000, cert: State, WBENC)

9749 Ohio Cables, LLC
       5288 Dietrich Ave
       Orient, OH 43146
       Contact: Mindy Dimel Owner
       Tel: 614-991-0404
       Email: mindy@ohiocables.com
       Website: www.ohiocables.com
Mfr & dist cables. (Woman, estab 2008, empl 2, sales $950,000, cert: City)

9750 One Source Mobile
       1066 Reading Rd
       Mason, OH 45040
       Contact: Amy Baumhower President
       Tel: 513-870-9300
       Email: abaumhower@onesourcemobile.com
       Website: www.onesourcemobile.com
Telecommunication services: wireless cell phone accessories, bluetooth items, car chargers & holsters etc. (Woman, estab 2005, empl 10, sales $925,000, cert: WBENC)

9751 SpeakSpace, LLC
       600 Superior Ave, Ste 1300
       Cleveland, OH 44114
       Contact: Behan Rebecca Managing Partner
       Tel: 440-263-1919
       Email: beckybehan@speakspace.com
       Website: www.speakspace.com
Teleconferencing services/conference calling, audio, web & video conferencing services. (Woman, estab 1999, empl 5, sales $800,000, cert: WBENC)

9752 The Fishel Company
1366 Dublin Road
Columbus, OH 43215
Contact: Erick Piscopo Dir Marketing & BD
Tel: 614-274-8100
Email: ejpiscopo@teamfishel.com
Website: www.teamfishel.com
Underground & aerial utility construction; inside & outside installation of fiber optic, copper, coaxial cabling; right of way services; structured cabling; network electronic installation; conduit construction & maintenance (Woman, estab 1936, empl 2575, sales $438,251,280, cert: WBENC)

9753 US Communications and Electric
4933 Neo Pkwy
Garfield Heights, OH 44128
Contact: Jim Connole COO
Tel: 216-478-0810
Email: jconnole@uscande.com
Website: www.uscande.com
Technology-based communications cabling systems, design & install outdoor copper systems, horizontal copper cabling solutions. (Woman, estab , empl , sales $17,000,000, cert: State, City, WBENC)

Oklahoma

9754 Ford Audio-Video Systems, LLC
4800 West Interstate 40
Oklahoma City, OK 73128
Contact: Sales Center Mgr
Tel: 405-946-9966
Email: johnj@fordav.com
Website: www.fordav.com
Design, mfr & install audio video communication equip: conference & board rooms, network operation ctrs, war rooms, command & control rooms, emergency response ctrs, video conferencing, media streaming, educational & training facilities. (Woman, estab 1973, empl , sales $200,000,000, cert: WBENC)

Pennsylvania

9755 Clark Resources, Inc.
321 N Front St
Harrisburg, PA 17101
Contact: Christa Anderson
Tel: 717-230-8861
Email: christaanderson@fclarkresources.com
Website: www.fclarkresources.com
Inbound and outbound telephone services. Call Center/Customer Support Center. (AA, estab 2002, empl 180, sales $6,000,000, cert: State, NMSDC)

9756 Enterprise Cable Group, Inc.
805 W Fifth St
Lansdale, PA 19446
Contact: WBE Dir
Tel: 215-361-4114
Email: Sales@EnterpriseCableGroup.com
Website: www.enterprisecablegroup.com
Communication & computer cable systems design & installation. (Woman, estab 2001, empl 20, sales $2,420,839, cert: WBENC)

9757 Fiber Business Solutions Inc.
PO Box 103
Fairview Village, PA 19409
Contact: Cindy Gallo President
Tel: 484-576-0876
Email: cgallo@fbsginc.com
Website: www.fbsginc.com
Fiber Optic Cable Placement & Splicing, Copper Cable Placement & Splicing, Right of Way & Permit Acquisition Services, Engineering & Design Services, CAD & As-Built Services, Project Management Services. (Woman, estab 2004, empl 8, sales $1,300,000, cert: WBENC, 8(a))

9758 IVN Sound & Communication, LLC
3341 w. Hunting Park ave
Philadelphia, PA 19132
Contact: Vincent Lane COO
Tel: 609-381-1106
Email: projects@ivnsound.com
Website: www.ivnsound.com
Data & communication, AV, security systems & network integration. (AA, estab 2011, empl 5, sales $700,000, cert: NMSDC)

9759 MobileStrat, Inc.
642 Cowpath Rd, Ste 390
Lansdale, PA 19446
Contact: Larry Blackshear CEO
Tel: 215-237-3874
Email: lb@mobilestrat.com
Website: www.mobilestrat.com
Wireless, cellular, voice & data, gap analysis, billing management, WiFi site surveys
wire line, WAN design, WiFi security. (AA, estab 2004, empl 18, sales , cert: NMSDC)

9760 Pagoda Electrical
2003 Friedensburg Rd
Reading, PA 19606
Contact: Bernette Wrobel President
Tel: 610-779-3216
Email: bernie@pagoda-electrical.com
Website: www.pagoda-electrical.com
Electrical Contractor, Tele/Data. (Woman, estab 1994, empl 70, sales $24,248,481, cert: WBENC)

9761 Point Breeze Communications, Inc.
1417 State Rt 118
Sweet Valley, PA 18656
Contact: Kimberly Butcofski Co-Owner
Tel: 570-477-3257
Email: pbc@epix.net
Website: www.pointbreezecommunications.com
Dist new & refurbished telecom equipment, superstructure framing, cable rack, bracing, frames, relay racks, antiTerrorism security solutions. (Woman, estab 2005, empl 6, sales $3,000,000, cert: State)

9762 Telecom Electric Supply Inc.
320 Constance Dr, Bldg 5
Warminster, PA 18974
Contact: Theresa Flaherty CEO
Tel: 267-960-2601
Email: theresa@tessupply.com
Website: www.tessupply.com
Dist central office installation supplies, telecommunication & electrical equipment. (Woman, estab 1995, empl 6, sales $1,295,272, cert: WBENC)

9763 Veteran Call Center, LLC
1545 W 38th St
Erie, PA 16508
Contact: Garrye Hepburn President
Tel: 800-335-0776
Email: ghepburn@verancontactcenter.com
Website: www.veterancontactcenter.com
Full Service Contact Center, inbound/outbound IVR, recording, tabulating, presenting marketing & public opinion data, answering telephone calls & relaying messages to clients, operating call centers that initiate or receive communications. (Woman/AA, estab 2009, empl 420, sales $14,000,000, cert: State)

Puerto Rico

9764 B&B Communications Group
220 Plaza Western Auto PMB-370 Ste 101
Trujillo Alto, PR 00976
Contact: Benjamin Bravo Sales
Tel: 787-760-2698
Email: bbravo@bbcorp.net
Website: www.bbcorp.net
Communications, Fiber Optics, UPS, Cabling, Network, Cat-5e, cat-6, cat-6a, telecomm, telecommunications, voice, data, IP phones, power supply, design, site survey, training, service (Minority, Woman, estab 2014, empl 5, sales , cert: State, NMSDC)

South Carolina

9765 Globenet Telecommunications, LLC
210 Titus Ln
Pineville, SC 29468
Contact: Cavid Middleton President
Tel: 828-320-3291
Email: dlmiddleton@charter.net
Website: www.globenetusa.net
Low voltage system integration, install security devices & fiber optic cable. (AA, estab 2007, empl 32, sales $14,500,000, cert: CPUC)

Tennessee

9766 1 Point Procurement Solutions, LLC
406 N Irish St, Ste 206
Greeneville, TN 37745
Contact: Steve Meriweather President
Tel: 423-702-4700
Email: steve.meriweather@1pointps.com
Website: www.1pointps.com
Value-added reseller of wireless products from base station infrastructure, broadband connectivity, critical communications, indoor/outdoor network architecture, remote monitoring and control, and mobile devices. (AA, estab 2012, empl 1, sales $1,063,916, cert: State)

9767 Ashaun
5100 Poplar Ave Ste 726
Memphis, TN 38137
Contact: Anthony Tate CEO
Tel: 901-312-7025
Email: atate@ashaun.com
Website: www.ashaun.com
Call center services. (AA, estab 2000, empl 35, sales , cert: State, NMSDC)

9768 Power & Telephone Supply Co,
2673 Yale Ave
Memphis, TN 38112
Contact: Annmarie Templeton Natl Acct Mgr
Tel: 800-238-7514
Email: annmarie.templeton@ptsupply.com
Website: www.ptsupply.com
Communications products. (Woman, estab 1963, empl 350, sales , cert: State, City, CPUC, WBENC)

9769 Televergence Solutions, Inc.
424 Church St, Ste 2000
Nashville, TN 37219
Contact: Ira Globerson VP Enterprise & Govt Sales
Tel: 213-943-2023
Email: igloberson@televergence.com
Website: www.televergence.com
Toll Free, Long Distance and Cloud Phone System services, high call volume and/or in-house or outsourced Contact Centers. (Woman, estab 1988, empl 19, sales $2,982,863, cert: WBENC)

9770 Tel-XL
5462 McGill
Memphis, TN 38120
Contact: Linda Hawkins President
Tel: 866-848-3595
Email: lhawkins@tel-xl.com
Website: www.tel-xl.com
Dist new & refurb telecom equip, systems, accessories. (Woman, estab , empl , sales , cert: WBENC)

9771 Walker Warren Communications
155 S Mendenhall Rd
Memphis, TN 38117
Contact: Sharlene H. Warren Principal
Tel: 901-337-6326
Email: Sharlene@ww911.net
Website: www.ww911.net
Radio Systems /Infrastructure, 2-way radios, mobile (vehicles), Telephone Systems, GPS, Logger Recorders, Computer Aided Dispatch Systems, Redundancy analysis for critical applications. (Woman/AA, estab 2016, empl 2, sales , cert: City, WBENC)

Texas

9772 Austin Tele-Services Partners, LP dba Genesis ATS
4209 S Industrial Dr Ste 300
Austin, TX 78744
Contact: Patrick Manning VP Business Dev
Tel: 512-437-3041
Email: pmanning@genesis-ats.com
Website: www.genesis-ats.com
IT, Networking, Telecommunications & Computer related equipment & services. (Hisp, estab 2003, empl 45, sales $25,000,000, cert: State, NMSDC)

9773 Can-Am Wireless LLC dba Can-Am IT Solutions
1333 Corporate Dr, Ste 110
Irving, TX 75038
Contact: Johan Rahardjo Dir of Engineering
Tel: 866-976-4177
Email: johan.rahardjo@canamitsolutions.com
Website: www.canamitsolutions.com
Telecommunications and Information Technology Hardware & Software. (As-Pac, estab 2001, empl 7, sales $1,020,000, cert: NMSDC)

9774 Clayborn Inc.
      PO Box 703212
      Dallas, TX 75370
      Contact: Jacquelyn Clayborn CEO
      Tel: -   -
      Email: onc@oncnational.com
      Website: www.oncnational.com
Installation (Cat5 Cat6) Voice, Data, Fiber Optic, Coax (tv), Wireless access point installation, splicing of building entrance and riser cable, cable abatement, abandoned cable removal, sound masking systems, extensions services. (Woman/AA, estab 2016, empl 5, sales $569,399, cert: NMSDC, WBENC)

9775 Clearvue Networks, LLC
      100 E Main St Ste 201
      Round Rock, TX 78664
      Contact: Shanna Schmidt Admin Asst
      Tel: 512-861-5319
      Email: shanna.schmidt@clearvuenetworks.com
      Website: www.clearvuenetworks.com
Business networking solutions, work station installs/configs, server installs/configs, network assessments, wireless installs, telecom services, voice/data/fiber cabling, alarm/surveillance systems, card access security systems. (Hisp, estab 2011, empl 9, sales , cert: State)

9776 Continental Wireless
      10455 VISTA PARK RD
      Dallas, TX 75238
      Contact: Rita Weber President
      Tel: 972-926-7443
      Email: RITA.WEBER@CNTLWIRE.COM
      Website: www.cntlwire.com
Wireless communication, dist & rent two way radios. (Woman, estab 2000, empl 25, sales $15,263,348, cert: WBENC)

9777 Crystal Application Software Services, LLC
      3201 Cherry Ridge Dr Ste B-218
      San Antonio, TX 78230
      Contact: Veronica Vela Acct Mgr
      Tel: 210-698-2410
      Email: veronica.vela@cnetcable.com
      Website: www.cnetcable.com
Design-build telecommunications, low voltage cabling, wireless & access points, voice & data networks, security cameras, audio & visual, fiber optics, phone systems & microwave. (Hisp, estab 2014, empl 10, sales , cert: State)

9778 Diamond P Enterprises, Inc.
      PO Box 483
      Brownwood, TX 76804
      Contact: Erin Toft Operations Mgr
      Tel: 325-643-5629
      Email: admin.assist@diamondpenterprises.com
      Website: www.diamondpenterprises.com
Cable Placing Materials, Closures/Splicing Materials, Copper Cable, Cutting & Distribution, Corrugated Products, Fiber Optic Cable, Cutting & Distribution. (Hisp, estab , empl , sales $60,309,360, cert: NMSDC, CPUC)

9779 DMI Technologies, Inc.
      14900 Grand River Rd, Ste 100
      Fort Worth, TX 76155
      Contact: L Samentha Tiller President
      Tel: 817-355-5385
      Email: stiller@dmitechinc.com
      Website: www.dmitechinc.com
Voice, data, audio, video, CCTV, CATV cabling contractor. (Woman, estab , empl , sales $27,000,000, cert: WBENC)

9780 Dynamic Voice Data
      4403 Greenbriar Dr
      Stafford, TX 77477
      Contact: Tina Greenfield Business Devel Mgr
      Tel: 800-838-5070
      Email: tgreenfield@dvd-inc.com
      Website: www.dvd-inc.com
Mfr custom OEM products using injection mold technology, interconnect products & telephone parts, harnesses & power supplies. (Minority, Woman, estab 1993, empl 15, sales $11,300,000, cert: State, NMSDC)

9781 JG Haney & Associates LLC
      9711 Haven Crossing Court
      Houston, TX 77065
      Contact: Joyce Haney CEO
      Tel: 281-653-2441
      Email: haney@jghaneyassociates.com
      Website: www.jghaneyassociates.com
Telecommunications Services, IT products & services, data acquisition systems, telemetry products, circuit card assemblies, shipping containers, test set cases, special nonmetallic, preformed packing material. (Woman/AA, estab 2011, empl 2, sales $300,000, cert: 8(a))

9782 KMM Telecommunications
      4051 N Hwy 121 Ste 400
      Grapevine, TX 76051
      Contact: Sarah McNab Dir HR & Marketing
      Tel: 844-566-8488
      Email: s.mcnab@kmmcorp.net
      Website: www.kmmcorp.net
Sourcing products & services; contract management; inventory planning & procurement; material management & deployment; material warehousing; material fulfillment, 3PL services; last-mile staging services; reverse logistics. (Woman, estab 1991, empl 130, sales $892,823,959, cert: CPUC, WBENC)

9783 Micro-Design, Inc.
      10210 Monroe Dr
      Dallas, TX 75229
      Contact: Douglas Ramsey VP Operations
      Tel: 972-488-8725
      Email: dramsey@levelcon.com
      Website: www.micro-design.com
Remote telemetry solutions: wireless, WiFi, cellular & satellite, engineering & solutions for CNG pump stations & infrastructure. (Woman, estab 1984, empl 15, sales $2,000,000, cert: State)

9784 Operational Technologies Corporation
      4100 NW Loop 410, Ste 23
      San Antonio, TX 78229
      Contact: Louisa Alaniz Sr Mgr. Client Services
      Tel: 210-731-0000
      Email: louisa.alaniz@otcorp.com
      Website: www.otcorp.com
Fulfillment center kitting, warehousing & distribution, telecommunications & communications engineering & installation, environmental svcs. (Hisp, estab 1986, empl 70, sales $15,192,216, cert: State, NMSDC)

9785 Premier Paging, Inc.
      12220 Murphy Rd Ste F
      Stafford, TX 77477
      Contact: Lea Bogle President
      Tel: 281-575-8500
      Email: lea.bogle@premierwirelesstx.com
      Website: www.premierwirelesstx.com
Wireless equipment, accessories & service, GPS tracking for fleets & assets, electronic forms. (Woman, estab 1993, empl 17, sales $2,500,000, cert: State, WBENC)

9786 Ransor, Inc.
      7055 Pipestone
      Schertz, TX 78154
      Contact: Randy Sorrell VP
      Tel: 210-651-6451
      Email: randy@ransor.com
      Website: www.ransor.com
Install communication equipment & maintains monopoles, guyed & self supporting towers, tower construction, tower modifications & tower maintenance. (Woman, estab 1987, empl 7, sales $984,000, cert: State)

9787 Sky Communications, Inc.
      6101 Long Prairie Rd, Ste 744-162
      Flower Mound, TX 75028
      Contact: Exec VP
      Tel: 214-789-5090
      Email: contact@skycomglobal.com
      Website: www.skycomglobal.com
Telecommunications services, engineering, design, implementation & managed services, unified communications, VOIP, call center & project management. (AA, estab 1995, empl 13, sales $1,735,567, cert: State, NMSDC)

9788 Teltech Communications LLC
      3211 Internet Blvd Ste 300
      Frisco, TX 75034
      Contact: Lisa Hanlon CEO
      Tel: 469-713-3801
      Email: lhanlon@teltech.com
      Website: www.teltech.com
Network infrastructure equipment, wireless, wireline, asset & inventory management services. (Minority, Woman, estab 1999, empl 106, sales $34,827,298, cert: NMSDC, CPUC, WBENC)

9789 The Wilkins Group, Inc.
      1710 Firman Dr, Ste 200
      Richardson, TX 75081
      Contact: ConTrenia McKinzie Cameron VP Admin
      Tel: 972-479-1090
      Email: trenia@wilkins.com
      Website: www.wilkins.com
Telecommunications services, equipment installation, voice, video & data systems. (Woman/AA, estab 1986, empl 30, sales $7,400,000, cert: State, NMSDC)

Utah

9790 Discountcell Inc.
      350 West 500 South
      Provo, UT 84601
      Contact: Janiel Jones Mgr
      Tel: 801-235-9809
      Email: corp@discountcell.com
      Website: www.discountcell.com
Dist cell phone accessories: antennas, boosters, cases, chargers, holsters, screen protectors, batteries, headsets, Bluetooth, data kits, data cables, covers, stylus, neoprene, canvas, heavy duty, leather. (Woman, estab 1998, empl 10, sales $700,000, cert: WBENC)

Viriginia

9791 Opterna-AM Inc.
      44901 Falcon Pl Ste 116
      Sterling, VA 20166
      Contact: Matt Onojafe Dir Govt Contracting
      Tel: 571-294-7652
      Email: matt.onojafe@opterna.com
      Website: www.opterna.com
Fiber optic products & solutions, fiber optic communication solutions. (As-Ind, estab 1994, empl 17, sales $10,000,000, cert: NMSDC)

9792 Secured Network Solutions, Inc.
      929 Ventures Way Ste 113
      Chesapeake, VA 23320
      Contact: Alphonzo Barney President
      Tel: 757-819-7647
      Email: abarney@teamsns.com
      Website: www.teamsns.com
Telecommunications & information technology: cabling, design, install, fiber optics single/multi-strand, fiber fusion & splicing, LAN/WAN/wireless network engineering, drafting & information systems security. (AA, estab 2006, empl 11, sales , cert: State)

9793 Shore Communications, Inc.
      600 N Witchduck Rd, Ste 106
      Virginia Beach, VA 23462
      Contact: Laura Castner President
      Tel: 757-468-0855
      Email: lcastner@shorecomusa.com
      Website: www.shorecomusa.com
Engineering, design, installation & testing structured cabling systems, telephone & paging systems, including adds, moves or changes to existing systems. (Woman, estab 1995, empl 28, sales , cert: State)

9794 TEKCONNX
      608 Westwood Office Park
      Fredericksburg, VA 22401
      Contact: Kevin Wlliams CEO
      Tel: 703-635-4439
      Email: kevinw@tekconnx.com
      Website: www.tekconnx.com
Interactive Audio Visual (IAVT) Solutions & Integration, A/V Telepresence Conferencing (HW & SW), Design/Build Interactive Audio Visual Solutions, Command & Control Centers, Wireless Video/Audio Solutions. (AA, estab 2013, empl 3, sales $850,000, cert: State, NMSDC)

Washington

9795 Roadswest Construction Inc.
      307 N Olympic Ave, Ste 209
      Arlington, WA 98223
      Contact: Kirby Lundberg VP
      Tel: 360-403-8782
      Email: roadswestinc@verizon.net
      Website: www.RoadsWestInc.com
Dist, service & install voice & data wiring & audio/vidio systems. (Nat Ame, estab 1987, empl 30, sales $873,949, cert: State)

Wisconsin

9796 1Prospect Technologies, LLC
      PO Box 1045
      Rhinelander, WI 54501
      Contact: Brad Kowieski Dir of Business Dev
      Tel: 715-369-1119
      Email: info@1prospect.com
      Website: www.oneprospect.com
Design & build flexible cabling infrastructure supporting multiple voice, data, video & multimedia systems. (Nat Ame, estab 2000, empl 33, sales $10,400,000, cert: State)

TEXTILES

Includes thread, trimmings, woven and nonwoven material manfucaturers. NAICS Code 31

California

9797 A & R Tarpaulins Inc.
16246 Valley Blvd
Fontana, CA 92335
Contact: Didi Truong Aerospace Project Mgr
Tel: 909-829-4444
Email: didi@artech2000.com
Website: www.artech2000.com
Multilayer insulation, Acoustic blankets, payload fairing, sound barriers, high temperture insulation & protection, thermal radiational heat control, EMI & RFI shielding, antistatic & security enclosures. (Minority, Woman, estab 1976, empl 49, sales $4,500,000, cert: CPUC)

9798 H & A Enterprise
530 N Baldwin Park Blvd
City of Industry, CA 91746
Contact: Huma Latif Owner
Tel: 909-714-3960
Email: ahuma@hotmail.com
Website: www.hnaenterprise.com
Dist textile goods, socks, towels, bar mops . (Woman/As-Ind, estab 2012, empl 1, sales , cert: NMSDC)

9799 International Textile and Apparel, Inc.
1875 Century Park E Ste 1040
Los Angeles, CA 90067
Contact: Shoaib Kothawala CEO
Tel: 310-556-8088
Email: nbaresabidia@intlinen.com
Website: www.donothaveone.com
Mfr bar mop & shop towels, weaving dye & finish, cut & sew. (As-Pac, estab 1983, empl 15, sales , cert: NMSDC)

9800 Venus Group, Inc.
25861 Wright St
Foothill Ranch, CA 92610
Contact: Ryen Masters Sales Mgr
Tel: 800-421-4595
Email: rmasters@venusgroup.com
Website: www.venusgroup.com
Mfr, cut and sew textiles, towels, sheets and napery. (As-Ind, estab 1972, empl 130, sales $75,000,000, cert: NMSDC)

Georgia

9801 PBR Inc.
335 Athena Dr
Athens, GA 30601
Contact: Palak Patel Exec Business Devel
Tel: 706-354-3700
Email: palak@skaps.com
Website: www.skaps.com
Fabricate Geosynthetic & nonwoven drainage products, produce polypropylene & polyester needle-punched nonwoven geotextiles. (As-Pac, estab 1995, empl 250, sales $390,000,000, cert: NMSDC)

9802 Unitex International Inc.
2222 Northmont Pkwy Ste 100
Duluth, GA 30096
Contact: Anwer Anwer Shakoor Dir
Tel: 770-232-0060
Email: a.shakoor@unitexonline.com
Website: www.unitexonline.com
Textile & fabric finishing. (Minority, estab 1990, empl 29, sales $83,000,000, cert: NMSDC)

Illinois

9803 R&R Textile Mills Inc.
1101 N Lombard Rd
Lombard, IL 60148
Contact: Rajan Barad COO
Tel: 630-424-8000
Email: rbarad@rrtextilemills.com
Website: www.rrtextilemills.com
Mfr & dist textile products. (Minority, estab 1988, empl 40, sales $9,800,000, cert: NMSDC)

9804 Revere Mills International Group, Inc.
2860 S River Rd Ste 250
Des Plaines, IL 60018
Contact: Jeff Gregg President
Tel: 847-759-6800
Email: jgregg@reveremills.com
Website: www.reveremills.com
Mfr, import & dist textile products: beach towels, bath towels, kitchen towels, golf & rally towels. (Woman, estab , empl 22, sales $24,000,000, cert: WBENC)

Massachusetts

9805 Spectro Coating Corp.
101 Scott Dr
Leominster, MA 01453
Contact: Wayne Turcotte VP Sales
Tel: 978-534-1800
Email: ssnyer@spectrocoating.com
Website: www.spectrocoating.com
Mfr fibers: silk, cotton, rayon, Kevlar, Tencel, bamboo, nylon, acrylic, polyester, etc. (As-Pac, estab 1988, empl 70, sales $12,000,000, cert: NMSDC)

Maine

9806 Auburn Manufacturing, Inc.
PO Box 220
Mechanic Falls, ME 04256
Contact: Kathie M Leonard CEO
Tel: 207-345-8771
Email: kleonard@auburnmfg.com
Website: www.auburnmfg.com
Design & mfr heat-resistant textiles for MRO applications. (Minority, Woman, estab 1979, empl 49, sales $10,300,000, cert: WBENC)

Michigan

9807 National Manufacturing, Inc.
25426 Ryan Rd
Warren, MI 48091
Contact: Paul Cano Sales
Tel: 586-755-8983
Email: paul.cano@nationalmanufacturinginc.com
Website: www.nationalmanufacturinginc.com
Leather & vinyl wrapping of steering wheels, pull handles, shift knobs, arm rests, bolsters, sew by hand or machine, emergency kits, jack bags, utility bags, tools bags for the automotive industry. (Woman/Hisp, estab 1964, empl 32, sales , cert: NMSDC, WBENC)

9808 Plastikon Michigan
2300 Pine Lake Rd
West Bloomfield, MI 48324
Contact: Martin Fisher Dir
Tel: 248-798-8292
Email: mfisher@trimsllc.com
Website: www.trimsllc.com
Contract mfr sew leather, vinyl, cloth for automotive interiors, boat seats, office chairs, top of bed for hotel industry. (As-Ind, estab 1980, empl 16, sales , cert: NMSDC)

TEXTILES

Missouri

9809 Phoenix Textile Corporation
21 Commerce Dr
OFallon, MO 63366
Contact: Laura Mahnken Sales Admin
Tel: 314-291-2151
Email: lmahnken@phoenixtextile.com
Website: www.phoenixtextile.com
Reusable institutional textiles & interior products. (Woman, estab , empl , sales , cert: WBENC)

North Carolina

9810 Kilop USA, Inc.
4100 Mendenhall Oaks Pkwy
High Point, NC 27265
Contact: Christine Chen President
Tel: 336-402-5979
Email: cchen@kilopusa.com
Website: www.kilopusa.com
Global nonwoven and textile raw material supply chain services. (Minority, Woman, estab 0, empl , sales , cert: NMSDC, WBENC)

New Jersey

9811 Centryco Inc.
300 W Broad St
Burlington, NJ 08016
Contact: Mary Gordon President
Tel: 609-386-6448
Email: mtg@centryco.com
Website: www.centryco.com
Mfr point of operation barriers for machinery & equipment: bellows, way covers, telescoping covers, flat bellows & screens, spring guards/covers. (Woman, estab 1949, empl 35, sales $3,910,958, cert: WBENC)

9812 Offray Specialty Narrow Fabrics, Inc.
4 Essex Ave Ste 403
Bernardsville, NJ 07924
Contact: Denise A. Offray CEO
Tel: 908-879-3636
Email: doffray@osnf.com
Website: www.osnf.com
Engineer & mfr quality, high performance, innovative narrow fabric textiles, weave specialty branded yarns. (Woman, estab 1921, empl 45, sales $8,674,420, cert: State)

New York

9813 Sigmatex, Inc
551 Fifth Ave, Ste 1110
New York, NY 10176
Contact: Marcia Rodriguez General Mgr
Tel: 212-593-0934
Email: mrodriguez@sigmatexlanier.com
Website: www.sigmatexlanier.com
Mfr institutional textile products: terry towels, sheets & pillowcases, table linens, kitchen linen, aprons, blankets. (Minority, Woman, estab 1976, empl 25, sales $18,155,425, cert: State)

Ohio

9814 Casco Manufacturing Solutions, Inc.
3107 Spring Grove Ave
Cincinnati, OH 45225
Contact: Melissa Mangold President
Tel: 800-843-1339
Email: mmangold@cascosolutions.com
Website: www.cascosolutions.com
Design & mfr fabric or textiles products. (Woman, estab , empl , sales $5,300,000, cert: WBENC)

9815 Niche Consumer Products, LLC
2600 Civic Center Dr
Cincinnati, OH 45231
Contact: Benjamin Moore President
Tel: - -
Email: info@nicheconsumerproducts.com
Website: www.nicheconsumerproducts.com
License, dist & mfr non-woven consumer products. (AA, estab 2007, empl 5, sales $330,000, cert: State, NMSDC)

South Carolina

9816 Calitex International
106 Thousand Oaks Ct
Summerville, SC 29485
Contact: John Sylvester President
Tel: 864-278-2621
Email: john@calitexintl.com
Website: www.calitex.us
Dist Industrial Fabrics 26" to 144", Cotton Canvas, Single fill duck, Numbered Ducks, Army Duck, Twill, 100% cotton and Polycotton Blends, Treated fabric for Tarps, Tents, Tipis, Boat covers. (Minority, Woman, estab 2005, empl 2, sales $1,500,000, cert: NMSDC)

9817 MVP Textiles and Apparel, Inc.
1031 Le Grand Blvd
Charleston, SC 29492
Contact: Mary Propes CEO
Tel: 843-216-8380
Email: marypropes@mvpgroupint.com
Website: www.mvptextiles.com
Mfr textiles. (Woman, estab 2005, empl 15, sales $16,800,000, cert: WBENC)

Texas

9818 Orr Textile Co., Inc.
4777 Blalock
Houston, TX 77041
Contact: Hilary Orr VP Sales
Tel: 713-939-7788
Email: hilary@orrtextile.com
Website: www.orrtextile.com
Dist sheets, towels, blankets, pillows, bath mats, robes, slippers, kitchen towels, bar mops, table linen, napkins, janitorial supplies, mops, buckets and wringers, mattress pads, pillow slips, pool towels, spa linen, chef wear, etc. (Woman, estab 1967, empl 11, sales , cert: WBENC)

Washington

9819 Lancs Industries Holdings, LLC
12704 NE 124th St, Bldg 36
Kirkland, WA 98034
Contact: Raymond Suarez
Tel: 425-823-6634
Email: rsuarez@lancsindustries.com
Website: www.lancsindustries.com
Mfr custom lead wool blankets, glovebags, tents, protective clothing, related shielding & containment products & supplies for nuclear naval shipyards & maintenance facilities; nuclear remediation, decontamination, decommissioning & laboratory sites. (AA, estab 2010, empl 65, sales $6,000,000, cert: State)

TRANSPORTATION SERVICES

Transport office and household furniture and equipment. Commercial freight and general commodities and have ICC rights for other states. Storage, wharehousing and packaging services. Charter bus, limousine service and air couriers. Custom house clearance, export documentation, export packing and crating. NAICS Code 48

Alabama

9820 ARD Logistics, LLC
      10098 Brose Dr
      Vance, AL 35490
      Contact: Courtney Waters Sales & Marketing Rep
      Tel: 205-393-5207
      Email: cwaters@ardlogistics.com
      Website: www.ardlogistics.com
Distribution operations: sequencing, sub-assembly, warehousing, inventory mgmt, shipping & receiving materials handling maintenance, packaging & repackaging, transportation mgmt, transportation svcs. (AA, estab 1998, empl 900, sales $68,717,549, cert: NMSDC)

9821 Universal Logistics Services, Inc.
      5330 Stadium Trace Pkwy, Ste 200
      Birmingham, AL 35244
      Contact: Alan Washburn Operations Mgr
      Tel: 205-682-8505
      Email: awashburn@ufsystems.com
      Website: www.universallogisticsservices.com
Transportation services. (AA, estab 1999, empl 100, sales $3,500,000, cert: NMSDC)

Arkansas

9822 Heartland Supply Company
      1248 Pump Station Rd
      Fayetteville, AR 72702
      Contact: Timothy J McNicholas Key Acct Mgr
      Tel: 773-617-6214
      Email: tmcnicholas@heartlandsupply.com
      Website: www.heartlandsupply.com
Logistic, distribution, supply chain optimization & warehousing services. (Nat Ame, estab 1987, empl 15, sales $100,000,000, cert: NMSDC)

9823 WMJ Enterprises, LLC.
      PO Box 979
      Lowell, AR 72745
      Contact: Justin Winberry VP
      Tel: 888-782-5828
      Email: jwinberry@leon-cannon.com
      Website: www.leon-cannon.com
Asset based transportation & logsitics. (Hisp, estab 1994, empl 38, sales $27,200,000, cert: State)

Arizona

9824 Aerocean Freight Solutions, Inc.
      9414 E. San Salvador Dr Ste 242
      Scottsdale, AZ 85258
      Contact: Yeon-Hee (Jennifer) Hwang President
      Tel: 480-515-1912
      Email: jennifer@aeroceanfreight.com
      Website: www.aeroceanfreight.com
Third party logistical services, road transportation, rail, ocean freight transportation. (Woman/As-Pac, estab 2006, empl 4, sales $5,314,734, cert: WBENC)

9825 Arizona Trailer Specialists Inc dba C&I Equipment
      3841 E 38th St
      Tucson, AZ 85713
      Contact: Mike Mellor GM
      Tel: 520-579-7458
      Email: mm@ciequip.com
      Website: www.ciequip.com
Manufacture custom water trailers & water skids used to transport potable and non-potable water for drinking water, or construction. (As-Pac, estab 1996, empl 4, sales $3,250,000, cert: State, City)

9826 BC Logistics LLC
      4405 E Baseline Rd Ste 114
      Phoenix, AZ 85042
      Contact: Vicki Boisjolie President
      Tel: 480-966-5000
      Email: phx@bclogisticsllc.com
      Website: www.bclogisticsllc.com
Air freight, ground transportation, domestic & international, next flight out, same day, conventions, blank wrap, pad van, flat beds, double flat beds. (Woman, estab , empl , sales $3,061,531, cert: WBENC)

9827 GIT Global Services
      2049 W Hwy Dr
      Tucson, AZ 85705
      Contact: D'Angelo Brenda Dir of Operations
      Tel: 520-269-6372
      Email: info@gitgs.com
      Website: www.gitgs.com
Freight forwarding, worldwide logistics services. (Hisp, estab 2011, empl 10, sales $3,000,000, cert: City, NMSDC)

9828 Mach 1 Global Services, Inc.
      1530 W Broadway Rd
      Tempe, AZ 85282
      Contact: Jamie Fletcher CEO
      Tel: 480-921-3900
      Email: jfletcher@mach1global.com
      Website: www.mach1global.com
Transportation & logistics, domestic heavy weight expedited freight forwarding, international freight forwarding, ocean & air import & export, distribution, warehousing & supply chain management. (Minority, Woman, estab 1988, empl 290, sales $165,000,000, cert: WBENC)

9829 Patriot Movers, LLC
      3060 N Ridgecrest, Unit 128
      Mesa, AZ 85207
      Contact: Christopher Palos COO
      Tel: 877-793-7775
      Email: patriotmovers57@yahoo.com
      Website: www.Patriotmover.us
Moving & Transportation, Local a& nd Long Distance Moving, (intrastate and interstate), Packing, Unpacking, Crating, Specialized Freight, Residential, Commercial, Office, Relocation services. (Minority, Woman, estab 2012, empl 5, sales , cert: City)

TRANSPORTATION SERVICES 9830-9840

9830 QBP Logistics, Inc.
6006 N 83rd Ave Ste 201
Glendale, AZ 85303
Contact: Marlin Banks Operations Mgr
Tel: 602-314-5099
Email: marlin@landstarmail.com
Website: www.qbpfreight.com
Transportation. Truckload transportation, Rail Intermodal service, Heavy Haul Specialized transport, Ocean freight forwarding, Expedited ground transport & Air freight forwarding. (AA, estab 2007, empl 6, sales $560,000, cert: CPUC)

9831 Reflex Logistics, LLC
7114 E Stetson Dr Ste 400
Scottsdale, AZ 85251
Contact: Cory Clapper VP Sales
Tel: 602-859-5969
Email: coryclapper@reflexlogistics.com
Website: www.reflexlogistics.com
Domestic full truckload van, refrigerated & flatbed transportation services. (Woman, estab 2013, empl 8, sales $750,000, cert: WBENC)

9832 The ILS Company
8350 E Old Vail Rd
Tucson, AZ 85747
Contact: Roy Austin Business Dev Dir
Tel: 520-618-4309
Email: roy.austin@ilscompany.com
Website: www.ilscompany.com
International Freight Forwarding & Logistics Services, Door to Door Transportation Management (Air, Ground, Ocean and Rail), Project Cargo Management, Vendor Managed Inventory, Hot Shot, Remote & White Glove. (Hisp, estab 2002, empl 54, sales $24,320,000, cert: NMSDC)

California

9833 Aeronet Logistics Inc.
42 Corporate Park
Irvine, CA 92606
Contact: Andres Aceves President
Tel: 949-474-9292
Email: diversity@aeronet.com
Website: www.aeronet.com
Global integrated logistics svcs: freight & cargo transportation, distribution & supply chain mgmt, air freight, expedited ground freight & urgent shipments, ocean cargo, import & export. (Hisp, estab 1982, empl 125, sales $70,858,000, cert: NMSDC, CPUC)

9834 ASI Computer Technologies, Inc.
48289 Fremont Blvd
Fremont, CA 94538
Contact: Louis Kim Business Devel Mgr
Tel: 510-445-4112
Email: louis.kim@asipartner.com
Website: www.asipartner.com
Freight dispatch capabilities, containers by Sea, air or Ground Trucking, Supply Chain Programs. (Minority, Woman, estab 1987, empl , sales $23,000,000, cert: NMSDC, WBENC)

9835 Bulk or Liquid Transport, LLC
576 Camino Mercado
Arroyo Grande, CA 93420
Contact: Tracy Thomas CEO
Tel: 800-975-2658
Email: tthomas@bolt-transport.com
Website: www.BOLT-Transport.com
Interstate transportation: liquid food-grade products. (Woman, estab 2006, empl 10, sales $2,253,148, cert: WBENC)

9836 Cargo Solutions Express
14587 Valley Blvd
Fontana, CA 92335
Contact: Harsimran Singh Operations Mgr
Tel: 909-350-1644
Email: karan@cargosolutionexpress.com
Website: www.cargosolutionexpress.com/
Transportation: fleet of 1500+ tractors and 2700+ trailers. (As-Pac, estab 2001, empl 550, sales $106,521,000, cert: NMSDC)

9837 Casas International Brokerage, Inc.
9355 Airway Rd, Ste 4 Otay Mesa
San Diego, CA 92154
Contact: Syliva Casas President
Tel: 619-710-4619
Email: s.casas@casasinternational.com
Website: www.casasinternational.com
US Customs broker & freight forwarder, warehouse & distribution. (Minority, Woman, estab 1984, empl 85, sales $6,055,615, cert: NMSDC)

9838 Contractors Cargo Companies
500 S Alameda St
Compton, CA 90221
Contact: Steve Cummins Natl Sales Mgr
Tel: 310-609-1957
Email: scummins@contractorscargo.com
Website: www.contractorscargo.com
Heavy haul transportation company, oversized, overweight or overdimensional cargo, rail logistics, heavy haul transport & shipping, nationally & internationally. (Woman, estab 1929, empl 85, sales $24,000,000, cert: CPUC)

9839 Crown Xpress Transport Inc.
9931 Via de la amistad
San Diego, CA 92154
Contact: Lorena Guillen Business Devel
Tel: 619-671-9611
Email: assistant@crownxt.com
Website: www.crownxt.com
FTL freight services. (Minority, Woman, estab 2003, empl 39, sales $12,434,665, cert: NMSDC, WBENC)

9840 CurDor Group Inc.
2321 Del Amo Blvd
Rancho Dominguez, CA 90220
Contact: Curlee Dorn President
Tel: 310-885-5200
Email: curlee.dorn@360globaltransportation.com
Website: www.360globaltransportation.com
Intermodal, Import / Export, Haz-mat, Over-Weight Containers, Warehousing, Less Than truck Load, Transloading, Dedicated Services, Flatbed, Reefer, Rail Services, Cross-Drocking, Truckload (TL), Outsourcing, Dryvan. (AA, estab 2012, empl 7, sales $400,000, cert: NMSDC)

TRANSPORTATION SERVICES

9841 D.W. Morgan Company, Inc.
      4185 Blackhawk Plaza Circle Ste 260
      Danville, CA 94506
      Contact: Dawn Kim Dir of Business Dev
      Tel: 310-938-9091
      Email: dawn.kim@dwmorgan.com
      Website: www.dwmorgan.com
Supply chain consulting, transportation management, and thrid-party logistics. (As-Pac, estab 1990, empl 750, sales $98,310,000, cert: NMSDC)

9842 EXCEL Moving Services
      30047 Ahern Ave
      Union City, CA 94587
      Contact: Bruce Owashi President
      Tel: 800-392-3596
      Email: bruce@excelmoving.com
      Website: www.excelmoving.com
Moving & storage, employee relocations, storage & distribution, air-ride inside PU/Del transportation, intl shipping/receiving, household goods specialist. (AA, As-Pac, estab 1994, empl 55, sales $4,000,000, cert: State, NMSDC, CPUC)

9843 Exp Global Logistics
      9440 Perrett Rd
      Patterson, CA 95363
      Contact: Richard Ricks CEO
      Tel: 877-777-1817
      Email: rricks@expcouriers.com
      Website: www.expcouriers.com
We provide transportation & logistic solutions. (Woman/AA, estab 2006, empl 6, sales $530,000, cert: NMSDC)

9844 FNS, Inc.
      18301 S Broadwick St
      Rancho Dominguez, CA 90220
      Contact: Josh Taxon Sales/Mktg Mgr
      Tel: 310-747-8530
      Email: joshua.taxon@pantos.com
      Website: www.fnsusa.com
Global third party logistics: ocean transport, air transport, trucking, warehousing & custom house brokerage. (As-Pac, estab 1995, empl 250, sales $12,881,358, cert: NMSDC)

9845 Freight Express Shipping Corp (FESCO)
      15330 Fairfield Ranch Rd., Unit G
      Chino Hills, CA 91709
      Contact: Michael Yu General Mgr
      Tel: 909-586-3000
      Email: service@fescous.com
      Website: www.fescous.com
Import & export freight forwarding services. (Minority, Woman, estab 2012, empl 6, sales $900,000, cert: State)

9846 Global Freight Experts, Inc.
      1950 E Miner Ave
      Stockton, CA 95205
      Contact: Rajinder Singh President
      Tel: 209-547-9210
      Email: raj@gfbontime.com
      Website: www.gfbontime.com
Asset based trucking. (As-Pac, estab 2010, empl 25, sales $3,100,000, cert: NMSDC)

9847 Golden Gate Air Freight Inc.
      1809 Sabre St
      Hayward, CA 94545
      Contact: John Cardenas President
      Tel: 510-785-5720
      Email: jcardenas@ggaf.com
      Website: www.ggaf.com
Domestic & international freight forwarding. (Hisp, estab 1982, empl 22, sales $8,055,928, cert: NMSDC)

9848 Intrade Industries, Inc.
      2559 S East Ave
      Fresno, CA 93706
      Contact: Tracy Farrell logistics/Mktg Mgr
      Tel: 559-256-3291
      Email: tracy.intradeindustries@gmail.com
      Website: www.intradeindustries.com
Transportation services for refrigerated cargo & freight from coast to coast. (Minority, Woman, estab 1997, empl 14, sales $23,000,000, cert: NMSDC)

9849 KLS Air Express, Inc. dba Freight Solution Provide
      2870 Gold Tailings Ct.
      Rancho Cordova, CA 95670
      Contact: Chrissie Cruz Natl Exec Accounts Mgr
      Tel: 513-532-1297
      Email: chrissie_cruz@shipfsp.com
      Website: www.shipfsp.com/about/index.html
Customized frieght transportation, logistics, warehousing & supply chain management solutions. (Minority, Woman, estab 1989, empl 110, sales $42,000,000, cert: NMSDC, WBENC)

9850 KW International, Inc.
      18655 Bishop Ave
      Carson, CA 90746
      Contact: Steve Cho Sr Mgr
      Tel: 310-354-6944
      Email: steve@kwinternational.com
      Website: www.kwinternational.com/default.aspx
Total logistics, transportation, freight forwarding, in-house customs brokerage, warehousing & distribution, reverse logistics, customer call center, field service, drayage, information & technology. (As-Pac, estab 1996, empl 1000, sales , cert: NMSDC)

9851 Mayor Logistics Inc.
      17214 S Figueroa St
      Gardena, CA 90248
      Contact: Henry Mayor
      Tel: 424-221-5225
      Email: hruiz@mayorusa.com
      Website: www.mayorusa.com
Domestic drayage, import/export, truckload, local & over the road, regional carrier. (Hisp, estab 2004, empl 10, sales $5,636,670, cert: NMSDC)

9852 Mosaic Global Transportation
      743 S Winchester Blvd Ste 210
      San Jose, CA 95128
      Contact: Maurice Brewster CEO
      Tel: 800-398-7881
      Email: info@mosaicglobaltransportation.com
      Website: www.mosaicglobaltransportation.com
Transportation & corporate charters. (AA, estab 2001, empl 101, sales $11,100,000, cert: NMSDC)

9853 Music Express Limousine Service
2601 Empire Ave
Burbank, CA 91504
Contact: Gary Dye General Counsel
Tel: 818-260-6630
Email: gdye@musiclimo.com
Website: www.musiclimo.com
National & international limousine svcs. (Woman, estab , empl , sales , cert: WBENC)

9854 National Freight Logistics Inc.
3150 N Weber Ave
Fresno, CA 93722
Contact: Ethan Lee
Tel: 559-827-4092
Email: ethan@nflfreight.com
Website: www.NFLfreight.com
Freight transportation & logistics. (Minority, Woman, estab 2006, empl 4, sales $1,534,690, cert: NMSDC)

9855 Northwest Freightway Inc.
3421 Industrial Dr
Yuba City, CA 95991
Contact: Nicholas Schlaff Dir of Sales
Tel: 539-788-2742
Email: nick@nwfreightway.com
Website: www.nwfreightway.com
Freight transportation services. (AA, estab 2007, empl 26, sales $28,000,000, cert: NMSDC)

9856 Oakley Relocation LLC
13026 Stowe Dr
Poway, CA 92064
Contact: Dir of Business Dev
Tel: 858-602-1010
Email:
Website: www.oakleyrelocation.com
Full-service moving & storage company. (Woman, estab 2008, empl 15, sales $4,250,000, cert: WBENC)

9857 Public Special
3147 Progress Circle
Mira Loma, CA 91752
Contact: Anna Aguiar President
Tel: 951-360-4466
Email: aaguiar@publicspecial.net
Website: www.publicspecial.net
Transportation, US and Canada. (Minority, Woman, estab 1980, empl 4, sales $22,048,000, cert: NMSDC)

9858 Red Rose Transportation, Inc
5705 N West Ave
Fresno, CA 93711
Contact: Mark Rose Operations Mgr
Tel: 559-277-1060
Email: mark@redrosetrans.net
Website: www.redrosetransportation.com
Logistic services, dedicated truckloads, Heavy haul, 53 dry van & reefers, flatbeds & LTL. (Minority, Woman, estab 2007, empl 7, sales $8,300,000, cert: CPUC, WBENC)

9859 Roland International Freight Services, Inc.
5710 W Manchester Ave Ste 104
Los Angeles, CA 90045
Contact: Roland Furtado President
Tel: 310-337-1775
Email: roland@rolandfreight.com
Website: www.rolandfreight.com
International freight forwarder by air & ocean. (As-Ind, estab 1991, empl 4, sales $1,310,617, cert: State, CPUC, 8(a))

9860 Say Cargo Express, Inc.
700 E Debra Lane
Anaheim, CA 92805
Contact: Doug Childers President
Tel: 714-772-7735
Email: dchilders@saycargo.com
Website: www.saycargo.com
Freight; Shipping; Expedited; Cargo; Oversized; Tradeshows; Logistics; LTL; Air Freight; Truckload, domestic freight forwarder that specializes in expedited freight. (Minority, Woman, estab 2000, empl 13, sales $2,700,000, cert: CPUC, WBENC)

9861 Tina Miller, Inc
30025 Alicia Pkwy, Box 172
Laguna Niguel, CA 92677
Contact: Faith Kennedy Acct exec
Tel: 877-211-7767
Email: info@tmisalesinc.com
Website: www.tmisalesinc.com
Customized traffic & freight management. (Woman, estab 2004, empl 14, sales $14,337,571, cert: WBENC)

9862 Trans Global Shipping Alliance, LLC
25255 Cabot Rd, Ste 212
Laguna Hills, CA 92653
Contact: William Cordova President
Tel: 949-699-1491
Email: bill@trustglobal.com
Website: www.trustglobal.com
Global shipping, trucking, ocean, air & special air couriers - standard & charter, full truckloads, flatbeds to LTL. (Woman, estab 2000, empl 5, sales $338,896, cert: State, CPUC)

9863 Transit Air Cargo Inc.
2204 East 4th St
Santa Ana, CA 92705
Contact: Gulnawaz Khodayar President
Tel: 714-915-0657
Email: gkhodayar@transitair.com
Website: www.transitair.com
Global tradeshow logistics: air, ocean & ground. Product freight services international & domestic. (Woman/As-Ind, estab 1989, empl 55, sales $23,933,988, cert: NMSDC, WBENC)

9864 Tricor America, Inc.
PO Box 8100 - SFIA
San Francisco, CA 94128
Contact: Scott Tanaka Major Acct Exec
Tel: 650-877-3650
Email: scott.tanaka@mail.tricor.com
Website: www.tricor.com
National & intl courier services. (As-Pac, estab 1957, empl 500, sales , cert: NMSDC)

Colorado

9865 Corporate GT Denver, Inc.
505 Nucla Way, Unit D
Aurora, CO 80011
Contact: Mary Norby VP
Tel: 303-243-3900
Email: mary@gtdenver.com
Website: www.corporategtdenver.com
Luxury Ground Transportation. Sedan, Vans, SUVs, Limousines. (Woman, estab 1985, empl 31, sales $2,000,000, cert: WBENC)

9866 Craters and Freighters
      331 Corporate Circle, Ste J
      Golden, CO 80401
      Contact: Chad Brockmeyer Natl Sales Mgr
      Tel: 720-287-7805
      Email: chad@cratersandfreighters.com
      Website: www.cratersandfreighters.com
Custom wood crating, plastic hard cases and freight services. (Woman, estab 1990, empl 12, sales $55,000,000, cert: WBENC)

9867 FAK, Inc.
      10885 E 51st Ave
      Denver, CO 80239
      Contact: Ron Harms GM
      Tel: 303-289-5433
      Email: rharms@fakinc.com
      Website: www.fakinc.com
Transportation: refrigerated, dry van, flatbed, specialized & intermodal. US & Canada. (Woman, estab 1983, empl 62, sales $69,359,561, cert: WBENC)

9868 Logistics Innovators Inc. dba Adcom Worldwide
      16600 E 33rd Dr, Unit 26
      Aurora, CO 80011
      Contact: Toni Brock President
      Tel: 303-329-0702
      Email: tbrock@adcomworldwide.com
      Website: www.adcomworldwide.com
Worldwide logistics, customs brokerage, ocean, air ground, warehouse. (Woman, estab 1997, empl 10, sales $2,167,000, cert: WBENC)

Delaware

9869 Bayshore Transportation System, Inc.
      901 Dawson Dr
      Newark, DE 19713
      Contact: M. Folz
      Tel: 651-430-2929
      Email: mfolz@bayshoreteam.com
      Website: www.bayshoreallied.com
Transportation svcs, moving & storage, relocation. (Woman, estab 1973, empl , sales $24,000,000, cert: WBENC)

Florida

9870 Air Marine Forwarding Company
      3409-B NW 72 Ave
      Miami, FL 33122
      Contact: Roger Madan President
      Tel: 305-477-3496
      Email: r.madan@airmarine.com
      Website: www.airmarine.com
Global logistics, intl air & ocean freight forwarding, customs brokerage, NVOCC, warehousing & distribution, bonded facilities & trucks, packing & crating. (Hisp, estab 1968, empl 28, sales $3,108,366, cert: NMSDC)

9871 Avanti Limousine Service, LLC.
      5425 N Dixie Hwy
      Boca Raton, FL 33487
      Contact: Serena Leverrier Affiliate Relations Dir
      Tel: 561-241-9955
      Email: res@avanticar.com
      Website: www.avanticar.com
Global ground transportation. (Woman, estab 1985, empl 12, sales $1,000,000, cert: WBENC)

9872 Clover Systems Inc.
      1910 NW 97th Ave
      Miami, FL 33172
      Contact: Dir Business Dev
      Tel: 305-499-7056
      Email: houston@clovergroup.com
      Website: www.clovergroup.com
Integrated logistics, air & ocean shipping, domestic & intl distribution svcs, warehouse, export packing & trucking. (Hisp, estab 1985, empl 70, sales , cert: NMSDC)

9873 CW Carriers USA Inc.
      509 S Falkenburg Rd
      Tampa, FL 33619
      Contact: Zach Valjarevic Sr Sales Mgr
      Tel: 813-771-0391
      Email: zach@cwcarriersinc.com
      Website: www.cwcarriersinc.com
Asset-based trucking company with a brokerage arm. (Woman, estab 2009, empl 151, sales $96,000,000, cert: WBENC)

9874 Edward Estevez CHB, Inc.
      6910 Main St, Ste 150
      Miami Lakes, FL 33014
      Contact: Edward Estevez President
      Tel: 786-247-1961
      Email: admin@eechb.com
      Website: www.eechb.com
U.S. Customs brokerage & logistics services. (Hisp, estab 2004, empl 1, sales , cert: State)

9875 Faith Transport & Logistics, Inc.
      190 SE 3rd Ave
      Deerfield Beach, FL 33441
      Contact: Aldo Goncalves Jr. President
      Tel: 954-274-0357
      Email: transportwithfaith@faithtlinc.com
      Website: www.transportwithfaith.com
Transportation & logistics, United States & Canada as an Interstate Motor Carrier. (Hisp, estab 2012, empl 3, sales $244,948, cert: NMSDC)

9876 Florida Freight Lines Inc.
      451 Harbor Dr N
      Indian Rocks Beach, FL 33785
      Contact: Marie Mazzara President
      Tel: 727-800-9870
      Email: mmazzara@floridafreightlines.com
      Website: www.FloridaFreightLines.com
LTL (Less Than Truckload), Full Truckload, Dry, Fresh, Frozen. (Woman, estab 2013, empl 2, sales $245,570, cert: WBENC)

9877 Giovanni Transport, LLC
      3066 Shady Dr
      Jacksonville, FL 32257
      Contact: Shatise Johnson President
      Tel: 904-612-5988
      Email: smjohnson@giovannitrans.com
      Website: www.giovannitrans.com
Transportation solutions, ship truckload freight, dedicated dry van transportation. (Woman/AA, estab 2006, empl 4, sales $230,000, cert: State)

9878 GUYDLOGISTICS Corp.
      10200 W State Road 84 Ste. 205
      Davie, FL 33324
      Contact: Tatiana Guydouk President
      Tel: 954-414-0561
      Email: tatiana@globaltransservicecorp.com
      Website: www.globaltransservicecorp.com/
Dry Van, Reefer, Flat Bed, Tracking Shipment, Logistics. (Woman, estab 2014, empl , sales $5,105,052, cert: WBENC)

9879 Harbor Transport, Inc.
      7320 NW 70th St
      Miami, FL 33166
      Contact: Roberto Victorero President
      Tel: 305-592-5357
      Email: roberto@harbor.com
      Website: www.harbor.com
Transportation services. (Minority, Woman, estab 1987, empl 7, sales , cert: NMSDC)

9880 Hermes Global Logistic Services, LLC
      5323 Millenia Lakes Blvd Ste 300
      Orlando, FL 32839
      Contact: Dena Kirschbaum
      Tel: 407-734-4046
      Email: dena.kirschbaum@hglservices.com
      Website: www.hglservices.com
3PL supply chain management solutions, integrating operations, warehousing & transportation services. (Woman/AA, estab 2015, empl 4, sales $500,000, cert: NMSDC)

9881 Iconic Logistics Services LLC
      1421 Thames Ln
      Clearwater, FL 33755
      Contact: Catrecia Walker
      Tel: 727-506-7810
      Email: catrecia@iconic-logistics.com
      Website: www.iconic-logistics.com
Haul general & specialized freight, debris removal. (AA, estab 2022, empl 50, sales , cert: State, City)

9882 Interstate Transport, Inc.
      324 1st Ave North
      St. Petersburg, FL 33701
      Contact: Zach Aufmann COO
      Tel: 727-822-9999
      Email: WBENC@interstatetransport.com
      Website: www.InterstateTransport.com
TL (truckload) & LTL (less than truckload) freight in US & Canada. Specialized freight capabilities (live goods, plants, perishables, lumber) dry, flatbed & refrigerated (reefer/refer) trailers, utilizing single or team drivers. (Woman, estab 2002, empl 40, sales $43,524,625, cert: WBENC)

9883 Magno International LP
      11014 NW 33 St, Ste 100
      Doral, FL 33172
      Contact: Jesus Lovo Exec VP
      Tel: 305-392-4726
      Email: jesus.lovo@magnointl.com
      Website: www.magnointl.com
Multi modal domestic & international transportation, warehouse & distribution, customs. (Hisp, estab 2005, empl 18, sales , cert: NMSDC)

9884 Newco Services, Inc.
      1831 16th St
      Boynton Beach, FL 33435
      Contact: Sales
      Tel: 561-375-9930
      Email: info@newcoservices.com
      Website: www.newcoservices.com
Transportation, warehousing, repair, refurbishment, prevenative maintenance, data reporting & consolidated billing svcs. (Woman, estab 1994, empl 20, sales $4,200,000, cert: WBENC)

9885 North American Transport Services LLC
      160 Ali baba Ave
      Opa-Locka, FL 33054
      Contact: Kasey Cano Business Devel Rep
      Tel: 305-455-1150
      Email: kcano@nalogistics.com
      Website: www.nalogistics.com
Assist customers with inbound & outbound freight, manage pick-up & delivery schedules. (Hisp, estab 2004, empl 45, sales $45,000,000, cert: NMSDC)

9886 Ocean Cargo Logistics Group, LLC
      12161 SW 132 Ct
      Miami, FL 33186
      Contact: Lorenzo Macias Sales
      Tel: 305-471-8442
      Email: lorenzo@oceancargologistics.com
      Website: www.oceancargologistics.com
Freight Forwarding, Air transportation, Domestic Trucking Transportation, Deep Ocean Transportation, Packing and Crating, LCL, FCL, LTL. (Hisp, estab 2008, empl 4, sales $1,200,000, cert: 8(a))

9887 One Horn Transportation Inc.
      8374 Market St #470
      Lakewood Ranch, FL 34202
      Contact: Mary Morra Operations Mgr
      Tel: 973-595-7700
      Email: help@onehorn.com
      Website: www.OneHorn.com
Freight brokerage, flatbed & dry van tractor-trailer services, 48 contiguous states & Canada. (Woman/AA, estab 2005, empl 40, sales $20,000,000, cert: NMSDC, WBENC)

9888 Prime Air Cargo Inc.
      1316 NW 78th Ave
      Doral, FL 33126
      Contact: Omar Zambrano GM
      Tel: 305-592-2044
      Email: ozambrano@primeaircargo.com
      Website: www.primeaircargo.com
Air, land & ocean transport services. (Hisp, estab 2004, empl 15, sales , cert: NMSDC)

9889 Raven Transport Company, Inc.
      6800 Broadway Ave
      Jacksonville, FL 32254
      Contact: Andrew Rhodes VP Sales & Marketing
      Tel: 904-425-5230
      Email: andrew.rhodes@raventrans.com
      Website: www.raventrans.com
Truckload carrier, 48 states authority. (AA, estab 1985, empl 579, sales $85,297,000, cert: NMSDC)

9890 Surge Transportation, Inc.
      7077 Bonneval Rd Ste 550
      Jacksonville, FL 32216
      Contact: Tadina Ross Managing Dir
      Tel: 844-591-6090
      Email: diversity@surgetransportation.com
      Website: www.surgetransportation.com
Builds partnerships between shippers & motor-carriers, utilizing Real-Time pricing & Real-Time load booking. (As-Pac, estab 2016, empl 250, sales $142,479,724, cert: NMSDC)

9891 Time Definite Services Transportation, LLC
      1935 CR525E
      Sumterville, FL 33521
      Contact: Michael Suarez President
      Tel: 800-466-8040
      Email: sales@timedefinite.com
      Website: www.timedefinite.com
Freigth transportation: truckload LTL air freight, hot shots, warehousing, domestic & international. (Hisp, estab 1990, empl 60, sales $45,700,000, cert: NMSDC)

Georgia

9892 AFCLS Logistics Services LLC
      975 Cobb Place Blvd Ste 101
      Kennesaw, GA 30144
      Contact: Brenda Collins Brown VP
      Tel: 770-514-1456
      Email: brenda.collinsbrown@afcls.com
      Website: www.afcls.com
Global freight logistics svcs: motor freight forwarding, freight brokerage, ocean transportation intermediary & non-vessel operating common carrier services & indirect air carriage. (AA, estab 2008, empl 10, sales $1,300,000, cert: NMSDC)

9893 Atlanta Peach Movers, Inc.
      2911 Northeast Pkwy
      Doraville, GA 30360
      Contact: Orlando Lynch Office Mgr
      Tel: 770-447-5121
      Email: olynch@atlpeachmovers.com
      Website: www.atlantapeachmovers.com
Moving & storage, furnishings & equipment. (AA, estab , empl , sales , cert: NMSDC)

9894 Axiom Logistics LLC
      5000 Austell-Powder Springs Rd Ste 189
      Austell, GA 30106
      Contact: Morgan Perry Founder & CEO
      Tel: 770-694-6248
      Email: morgan@axiomtrans.com
      Website: www.axiomtrans.com
Logistics, Dry, frozen & refrigerated truckload, Flatbed, drop deck & double drop, Over-Dimensional, heavy haul & expedited, Power Only, Team & expedited truckload and (LTL) less than truckload services. (Woman/AA, estab 2012, empl 6, sales $1,099,963, cert: NMSDC, WBENC)

9895 Bennett International Group LLC
      1001 Industrial Pkwy
      McDonough, GA 30253
      Contact: Marcia Taylor CEO
      Tel: 770-957-1866
      Email:
      Website: www.bennettig.com
Customs brokerage, freight forwarding air & ocean, project cargo, domestic trucking, oversized & over weight cargo, warehousing, third party logistics. (Woman, estab 1973, empl 650, sales , cert: WBENC)

9896 CorTrans Logistics, LLC
      6465 E Johns Crossing Ste 300
      Johns Creek, GA 30097
      Contact: Gloria Cortez CEO
      Tel: 678-969-9529
      Email: gcortez@cortrans.com
      Website: www.cortrans.com
Transportation svcs: air freight, charters, next day, second day, and deferred delivery, logistics svcs & supply chain mgmt. (Hisp, estab 1999, empl 20, sales $35,290,000, cert: WBENC)

9897 Eagle Transportation Services, Inc.
      731 Queen City Pkwy Ste 101
      Gainesville, GA 30501
      Contact: Lynn Mull President
      Tel: 770-965-1242
      Email: lynn@eagletransportation.com
      Website: www.eagletransportation.com
Third party logistics. (Woman, estab 1988, empl 6, sales , cert: WBENC)

9898 Efficient Courier & Logistics Services LLC
      5475 Tulane Dr
      Atlanta, GA 30336
      Contact: Patrick Chukwudolue Exec Dir
      Tel: 800-590-2155
      Email: partners@ecourierlogistics.com
      Website: www.ecourierlogistics.com
Integrated end to logistics & freight services, customized supply chain, warehousing, logistics & delivery. (AA, estab 2013, empl 5, sales , cert: NMSDC)

9899 Expedited Transportation Services, Inc
      505 Plantation Park Dr
      Atlanta, GA 30052
      Contact: Traci Taylor President
      Tel: 770-413-1700
      Email: expedited@ets-atlanta.com
      Website: www.ets-atlanta.com
Mail & cargo transport, air cargo, local area trucking, marine cargo, rail cargo, regional or natl trucking, vehicle carrier services, air charter transport. (Woman, estab 1982, empl 11, sales , cert: WBENC)

9900 KCH Trucking, LLC
      6695 Peachtree Industrial Blvd Ste 250
      Atlanta, GA 30360
      Contact: Alan Whitten VP Sales
      Tel: 770-962-6829
      Email: awhitten@kchtrans.com
      Website: www.kchtrans.com
National truckload transportation services. (Woman, estab 2006, empl 5, sales $8,000,001, cert: WBENC)

9901 Premier Expediters, Inc.
      598 Red Oak Rd
      Stockbridge, GA 30281
      Contact: Jay Patterson Exec Dir
      Tel: 888-744-7911
      Email: jpatterson@shippei.com
      Website: www.shippei.com
Transportation, Carrier Authority, Freight Forwarding Authority & Brokerage, FTL, LTL, Expedited, Specialized, Air & Ocean Freight services. (Woman, estab 1992, empl 32, sales $13,000,000, cert: WBENC)

TRANSPORTATION SERVICES

9902 R2 Trucking Solutions
1882 Princeton Ave, Ste 1
College Park, GA 30337
Contact: Amari Ruff CEO
Tel: 770-892-3699
Email: aruff@r2truckingsolutions.com
Website: www.r2truckingsolutions.com
Global logistics, air, ocean & ground carriers. (AA, estab 2014, empl 22, sales $1,867,989, cert: NMSDC)

9903 S-2international LLC
395 McDonough Pkwy
McDonough, GA 30253
Contact: Jennifer Mead CEO
Tel: 678-432-9502
Email: jennifer.mead@s-2international.com
Website: www.s-2international.com
Transportation services, expedited/JIT movement, LTL, Airfreight, Charter & Ocean shipments. (Woman, estab 2005, empl 37, sales $17,200,000, cert: WBENC)

9904 Scott Logistics Corp.
375 Technology Pkwy
Rome, GA 30165
Contact: Jayme Gauthreaux Dir of Natl Sales
Tel: 470-419-6209
Email: jayme.gauthreaux@scottlogistics.com
Website: www.scottlogistics.com
Transportation brokerage. (Woman, estab 1995, empl 165, sales $155,000,000, cert: WBENC)

9905 Southeastern Transfer & Storage Co., Inc.
2561 Plant Atkinson Rd
Smyrna, GA 30080
Contact: Debra Wallace Co-Owner
Tel: 404-794-2401
Email: dwallace@setransfer.com
Website: www.setransfer.com
Transportation services: heavy-haul trucking & storage, 48 states authority. (Woman, estab 1929, empl 30, sales $3,000,000, cert: WBENC)

9906 The FSL Group
200 Corporate Center Dr
Stockbridge, GA 30253
Contact: Cheryl Gaita Admin Asst
Tel: 770-506-9100
Email: kcrowley@fslgroup.com
Website: www.fslgroup.com
Consulting & management services, logistics operations, Transportation, Shipment Auditing. (Woman, estab 1996, empl 21, sales $45,241,000, cert: CPUC, WBENC)

9907 Transgroup World Wide Logistics
650 Atlanta S Pkwy, Ste 109
Atlanta, GA 30349
Contact: Tamara Barnes President
Tel: 404-725-3660
Email: tamib.atl@transgroup.com
Website: www.transgroup.cam
Domestic Air: Next flight out, Next Day AM, Second day, 3-5 day service, Air Charters, Express LTL & Full Truckload, Flatbed/Oversize loads, Trade Show Services, Canada/Mexico TransBoarder. (Woman, estab 1986, empl 37, sales $291,000,000, cert: NWBOC)

9908 Tribe Express
2251 Jesse Jewell Pkwy NE
Gaineville, GA 30507
Contact: Fred Schloth Dir New Business Dev
Tel: 904-222-0445
Email: fschloth@tribetrans.com
Website: www.tribeexpress.com
Asset based transportation, Expedited Services, Power Only, Dedicated Services, Logistics Services for Temp Controlled, Deep Frozen & all Dry modes. (Minority, Woman, estab 2005, empl 118, sales $39,000,000, cert: NMSDC)

9909 Tribe Express Inc
PO Box 908300
Gainesville, GA 30501
Contact: Ralph Navarro CFO
Tel: 678-780-3700
Email: accounting@tribetrans.com
Website: www.tribetrans.com
Logistics and transportation. (Nat-Ame, estab 2010, empl 275, sales $130,000,000, cert: NMSDC)

9910 Upward Global Logistics & Distribution
5421 Legacy Trail
Douglasville, GA 30135
Contact: Nick Byers President
Tel: 949-484-5231
Email: nrbyers@uglad.us
Website: www.uglad.us
Transportation solutions to air, ground, rail, expedited, drayage or port logistics. (As-Pac, estab 2010, empl 6, sales $315,000, cert: 8(a))

9911 Vector Global Logistics LLC
887 W Marietta St NW, Ste M201
Atlanta, GA 30318
Contact: Enrique Alvarez Managing Dir
Tel: 404-554-1150
Email: enrique.alvarez@vectorgl.com
Website: www.VectorGL.com
Sea freight, air freight, truck, rail & general logistics. (Hisp, estab 2012, empl 19, sales $9,100,000, cert: NMSDC)

Hawaii

9912 Hawaii Transfer Company, Ltd.
94-1420 Moaniani St
Waipahu, HI 96797
Contact: Financial Analyst
Tel: 770-496-9500
Email: rshumake@lanier.com
Website: www.hawaiitransfer.com
Transportation, warehousing and other services. (As-Pac, estab 1931, empl 180, sales $20,000,000, cert: NMSDC)

Iowa

9913 JMS Transportation Inc.
5650 6th St SW
Cedar Rapids, IA 52404
Contact: Riley Larson GM
Tel: 800-877-1529
Email: rileylarson@jmstransport.com
Website: www.jmstransport.com
Trucking & logistics, asset-based transportation, Midwest regional LTL & FTL dry van freight hauling. (Woman, estab 1990, empl 39, sales $19,048,850, cert: NWBOC)

9914 Johnsrud Transport, Inc.
200 SE 34th St
Des Moines, IA 50317
Contact: Jackie Johnsrud CEO
Tel: 800-237-9795
Email: jjohnsrud@johnsrudtransport.com
Website: www.johnsrudtransport.com
Transport bulk foodgrade liquids. (Woman, estab 1963, empl 170, sales $21,000,000, cert: WBENC)

9915 Legacy Logistics Freight, Inc.
500 College Dr, Ste 127B
Mason City, IA 50401
Contact: President
Tel: 641-423-5187
Email: legacylogisticsandfreight@gmail.com
Website: www.legacylogisticsfreight.com
Freight brokerage, 48 states in the lower continental US. (Woman, estab 2006, empl 8, sales , cert: WBENC)

9916 Weinrich Truck Line, Inc.
27932 C 60
Hinton, IA 51024
Contact: Ranae Allen Operations Mgr
Tel: 800-831-0814
Email: ranaewtl@hotmail.com
Website: www.weinrichtruckline.com
Liquid bulk food grade transportation. (Woman, estab 1960, empl 75, sales $9,284,328, cert: WBENC)

Illinois

9917 AGT Global Logistics
800 Roosevelt Rd, Building C, Ste 300
Glen Ellyn, IL 60137
Contact: Jeff Mock Sales
Tel: 630-953-4366
Email: jeffm@agt3pl.com
Website: www.agt3pl.com
Certified 3rd Party Logistics, air freight carrier, asset based. (Woman, estab 2005, empl 21, sales $1,141,103,297, cert: WBENC, NWBOC)

9918 ALG Diversifed LLC
372 Shenstone Rd
Riverside, IL 60546
Contact: Chris Agne Managing Partner
Tel: 630-380-4410
Email: cagne@algdiversified.com
Website: www.algdiversified.com
Mail transportation & logistics, Print media materials providing postage discounts via drop ship/destination entry, co-mail and co-palletization. (As-Pac, estab 2009, empl 5, sales $1,875,000, cert: NMSDC)

9919 All Girl Transportation & Logistics, Inc
216 S Prater
Northlake, IL 60164
Contact: Angela Mock President
Tel: 877-816-5477
Email: amock@allgirlstrucking.com
Website: www.allgirlstrucking.com
Transportation: ground & ground expedited, air & air-freight package, auditing, transportation management services. (Woman, estab 2005, empl 30, sales $12,000,000, cert: WBENC)

9920 Box Truck Logistics, LLC
1517 Golfview Court
Glendale Heights, IL 60139
Contact: Hayden Lynch President
Tel: 312-602-2639
Email: hlynch@boxtrucklogistics.com
Website: www.boxtrucklogistics.com
Freight brokerage - FTL, LTL shipments, project freight & out of gauge shipments. (AA, estab 2014, empl 2, sales , cert: NMSDC)

9921 Chela Logistics Inc.
1521 Brummel Ave
Elk Grove Village, IL 60007
Contact: President
Tel: 847-290-9040
Email: marcela@chelalogistics.com
Website: www.chelalogistics.com
Local & nationwide transportation. (Woman, estab 2001, empl 11, sales $2,500,000, cert: WBENC)

9922 CTL Global, Inc.
11697 W Grand Ave
Northlake, IL 60164
Contact: Sharon Dalenberg President
Tel: 708-223-1196
Email:
Website: www.ctlglobalsolutions.com
Fulfillment & logistics, transportation & technology services. (Woman, estab 1978, empl 250, sales $53,723,000, cert: WBENC)

9923 DSC Logistics, Inc.
1750 S Wolf Rd
Des Plaines, IL 60018
Contact: Tracy Drake Dir Diversity
Tel: 847-390-6800
Email: tracy.drake@dsc-logistics.com
Website: www.dsclogistics.com
Supply chain mgmt, strategic solutions-based consulting, business process integration, process improvement & management, logistics operations, warehousing, transportation, packaging & fulfillment. (Woman, estab 1960, empl 2200, sales $330,000,000, cert: WBENC)

9924 GTS Express, Inc.
13851 S Janas Pkwy
Homer Glen, IL 60491
Contact: Olivia Metelanski President
Tel: 844-487-9777
Email: olivia@gtsexpressinc.com
Website: www.gtsexpressinc.com
Asset based transportation logistics & 3PL. (Woman, estab 2013, empl 12, sales $550,000, cert: NWBOC)

9925 Hassett Express
17W775 Butterfield Rd. Ste 109
Oakbrook Terrace, IL 60181
Contact: Tim Cunningham Business Devel Mgr
Tel: 630-730-7346
Email: tim.cunningham@teamhassett.com
Website: www.hassettlogistics.com
Transportation, Domestic Air Freight, Domestic Ground Freight, White Glove, Logistics Services, International Air, International Moving. (Woman, estab 1980, empl 133, sales $52,000,000, cert: WBENC)

9926 Integrated Demolition Service LLC
1312 Prospect Ave
Willow Springs, IL 60480
Contact: Jeffrey Griffard
Tel: 708-369-7508
Email: estimating@integrateddemolition.com
Website: www.integrateddemolition.com
Trucking & Scrap Removal. (Woman/Hisp, estab 2017, empl 20, sales $6,000,000, cert: State, City, WBENC)

9927 Mid-West Moving & Storage, Inc.
1255 Tonne Rd
Elk Grove Village, IL 60007
Contact: Luis Toledo President
Tel: 847-593-7201
Email: diversity@midwestmoving.com
Website: www.midwestmoving.com
Office & residential moving, record storage & destruction, ware housing, distribution & local hauling. (Hisp, estab 1983, empl 100, sales $7,306,878, cert: NMSDC, 8(a))

9928 Milano Railcar Services
PO Box 1357
Mount Vernon, IL 62864
Contact: Mary Burgan President
Tel: 618-242-4004
Email: mary@milanorail.com
Website: www.milanorail.com
Logistics, Storage, Pipe Laydown Yard, Trucking, Logistics, Inventory Control, Warehousing, Materials Handling, Transloading, Consulting. (Woman, estab 2009, empl 3, sales $264,085, cert: WBENC)

9929 New Age Transportation, Distribution & Warehousing
1881 Rose Rd
Lake Zurich, IL 60047
Contact: Pam Troy VP Admin
Tel: 847-545-9200
Email: pamt@newagetransportation.com
Website: www.newagetransportation.com
National & international transportation & logistics: dist, warehousing, fulfillment & e-commerce, expedition & rail shipments, freight bill auditing. (Woman, estab 1989, empl 45, sales $28,000,000, cert: WBENC)

9930 Pactrans Air & Sea, Inc.
951-961 W Thorndale Ave
Bensenville, IL 60106
Contact: Kitty Pon President
Tel: 847-766-9988
Email: kittyp@pactrans.com
Website: www.pactrans.com
International freight forwarding: air & sea freight consolidation logistics, world wide charter, warehousing, distribution, trucking & Customs brokerage services. (Minority, Woman, estab 1991, empl 50, sales $30,000,000, cert: City, NMSDC)

9931 Par Logistics, Inc.
1251 N Plum Grove Rd, Ste 120
Schaumburg, IL 60173
Contact: Jim Vasquez President
Tel: 847-519-1990
Email: jvasquez@parlogistics.net
Website: www.parlogsitics.net
Transportation svcs: truckload, domestic air freight, ground expedite, air charter services, int'l air & ocean. (Hisp, estab 2006, empl 8, sales $35,000,000, cert: NMSDC)

9932 Passion Transportation Inc.
145 Sayton Road Ste C
Fox Lake, IL 60020
Contact: Suzanne Thompson WBE Liasion/Customer Relations
Tel: 847-587-2700
Email: quotes@passiontrans.com
Website: www.passiontrans.com
Truckload, less than truckload & partial truckloads, air, ocean, expidited, temperature controlled & flatbed freight. (Woman, estab 2007, empl 6, sales $4,134,507, cert: WBENC)

9933 Pelican Logistics Inc.
101 Frontier way
Bensenville, IL 60106
Contact: Keith Kim Sales Mgr
Tel: 847-337-5255
Email: keith.kim@pelicanloginc.com
Website: www.pelicanti.com
Air freight transportation. (As-Pac, estab 1995, empl 8, sales $10,000,000, cert: WBENC)

9934 Precision Transportation, Inc.
1010 Dixie Hwy Ste 309
Chicago Heights, IL 60411
Contact: Division VP
Tel: 630-352-3311
Email: service@precisiontransportation.net
Website: www.precision-nal.com
Logistics, transportation, warehousing, project management & inventory control. (Woman, estab 1992, empl 10, sales , cert: State, WBENC)

9935 Reilly International Ltd.
1555 N Michael Dr
Wood Dale, IL 60191
Contact: Vickie Reilly President
Tel: 630-238-4900
Email: vickie@reillyinternational.com
Website: www.reillyinternational.com
International freight forwarding, consolidation & brokerage. (Woman, estab 1984, empl 20, sales $8,417,000, cert: WBENC)

9936 Riverbend Logistics Solutions, Inc.
65 E Ferguson Ave
Wood River, IL 62095
Contact: Murdock Moss
Tel: 618-254-2687
Email: mmoss@rls-global.com
Website: www.rls-global.com
Third-party logistics, freight management & shipping. (Woman, estab 1992, empl 8, sales $2,680,000, cert: State, NWBOC)

9937 Select Logistics Network Inc.
PO Box 496
Clinton, IL 61727
Contact: Lisa Edwards President
Tel: 800-353-9113
Email: lisa@selectlogistics.net
Website: www.selectlogistics.net
Freight logistics: rail, intermodal, over the road, in North America. (Woman, estab 1997, empl 6, sales $2,599,924, cert: WBENC)

9938 Servex, Inc.
      1567 Frontenac Rd
      Naperville, IL 60563
      Contact: John Rizek Dir Mktg
      Tel: 630-369-9500
      Email: j.rizek@servex.com
      Website: www.servex.com
Third party warehousing & warehousing services (Woman, estab 1981, empl 35, sales , cert: CPUC)

9939 W.O.L.F. Elite LLC
      5741 W Lawrence Ave Unit 1
      Chicago, IL 60630
      Contact: Sandra Martinez CEO
      Tel: 773-510-8776
      Email: sandra@gowolfelite.com
      Website: www.gowolfelite.com
Truckload (FTL/LTL) Drayage Dedicated service. (Hisp, estab 2019, empl 4, sales $1,000,000, cert: NMSDC)

9940 Williams NationaLease, Ltd.
      404 W Northtown Road Ste B
      Normal, IL 61761
      Contact: Sandy Hotlen President
      Tel: 800-779-8785
      Email: shotlen@wnlgroup.com
      Website: www.wnlgroup.com
Truck leasing & rental: 130 power units & 180 trailers. (Woman, estab 1984, empl 210, sales $36,000,000, cert: State, WBENC)

9941 Worldwide Freight Solutions Inc.
      6518 Marble Lane
      Carpentersville, IL 60110
      Contact: Bob Grady CEO
      Tel: 847-915-1025
      Email: bob@wwfsolutions.com
      Website: www.wwfsolutions.com
Transportation Brokerage Organization. (AA, estab 2019, empl 1, sales , cert: NMSDC)

Indiana

9942 AGI International Inc.
      2525 N. Shadeland Ave Bldg 30, Door 12
      Indianapolis, IN 46219
      Contact: Allen C Gray, SR VP Business Development
      Tel: 317-536-2415
      Email: allengray@agiintl.com
      Website: www.agiintl.com
Freight Forwarding, Managed Transportation, LTL & FTL, Expedited, Intermodal & Drayage, Bulk. (AA, estab 2006, empl 11, sales $3,500,000, cert: NMSDC)

9943 Butler Tillman Express Trucking, Inc.
      PO Box 1017
      Belverly Shores, IN 46301
      Contact: Sue Lundberg Office Mgr
      Tel: 219-764-2100
      Email: info@btexpresstrucking.com
      Website: www.btexpresstrucking.com
Tanker trucking, bulk liquid and dry materials. (Woman/AA, estab 2003, empl 6, sales $388,518, cert: NMSDC)

9944 Chaser, LLC
      415 E 31st St
      Anderson, IN 46016
      Contact: Nammy Eskar CEO
      Tel: 765-640-8620
      Email: neskar@chaserllc.com
      Website: www.chaserllc.com
Transportation & logistics, hauling truckload shipments of general commodities in both interstate & intrastate commerce. (Minority, estab 2011, empl 50, sales , cert: NMSDC)

9945 Global Perspectives, Inc. dba Global Orientations
      690 Pro-Med Ln Ste B
      Carmel, IN 46032
      Contact: John Merriweather President
      Tel: 317-848-2022
      Email: jm@goresourcelink.com
      Website: www.globalorientations.com
Relocation services, personalized tours & orientations, temporary corporate housing & third-party relocation management services. (AA, estab 1998, empl 13, sales $365,113, cert: NMSDC, 8(a))

9946 HeLP Logistics, Inc.
      2130 S Oakwood Dr
      New Palestine, IN 46163
      Contact: Lorri Lord President
      Tel: 866-504-9620
      Email: lorri.lord@helplogistics.com
      Website: www.helplogistics.com
Transportation & logistics. (Woman, estab 2007, empl 12, sales $3,768,517, cert: WBENC)

9947 Langham Logistics Inc.
      5335 W 74th St
      Indianapolis, IN 46268
      Contact: Cathy Langham President
      Tel: 317-471-5120
      Email: cathylangham@elangham.com
      Website: www.elangham.com
Global freight management: FF, expedite, warehousing, distribution, fulfillment. (Woman, estab 1988, empl 150, sales , cert: State, WBENC)

9948 Mid-American Specialized Transport, Inc.
      2827 W State Rd 66
      Rockport, IN 47635
      Contact: Paula Joyner President
      Tel: 812-649-2599
      Email: paula.joyner@mastusa.com
      Website: www.mastusa.com
General freight & hazardous materials, transportation logistics, brokerage, third party logistics & transportation consutling services. (Woman, estab 2008, empl 19, sales $8,000,000, cert: WBENC)

9949 MyWay Logistics LLC
      1300 E 86th St, Ste 14 # 128
      Indianapolis, IN 46240
      Contact: Owner
      Tel: 888-557-4213
      Email: admin@myway-logistics.com
      Website: www.myway-logistics.com
Non-asset based logistics. Licensed & bonded to service all 48 states & Canada. (Woman, estab 2014, empl 3, sales $913,754, cert: WBENC)

9950 Pinnacle Industries LLC
717 Ley RD
Fort Wayne, IN 46825
Contact: Stan Richards President
Tel: 260-267-9199
Email: stan.richard@pinnacleindustriesllc.com
Website: www.pinnacleindustriesllc.com
Material management services, Supply Chain Management, logistical fulfillment operations and warehousing services. (AA, estab 2014, empl 10, sales $15,000,000, cert: NMSDC)

9951 TOC Logistics International, LLC
2601 Fortune Circle East Ste 201B
Indianapolis, IN 46241
Contact: Gary Cardenas CEO
Tel: 317-759-2132
Email: gcardenas@toclogistics.com
Website: www.toclogistics.com
Logistics management organization. (Hisp, estab 2010, empl 20, sales $15,000,000, cert: NMSDC)

9952 Xpress Cargo Inc. (XCIQ)
2330 Enterprise Park Dr
Indianapolis, IN 46218
Contact: Brandon Collingwood
Tel: 317-426-5410
Email: brandon@xpresscargoinc.com
Website: www.xpresscargoinc.com
Freight forwarding. (As-Ind, estab 2005, empl 150, sales $36,000,000, cert: NMSDC)

Kansas

9953 Butler Transport, Inc
347 N James St
Kansas City, KS 66118
Contact: Bill Taylor Controller
Tel: 913-321-0047
Email: billtaylor@butlertransport.com
Website: www.butlertransport.com
Transportation services. (Woman, estab 1991, empl 350, sales $67,000,000, cert: WBENC, NWBOC)

9954 Gold Star Transportation, Inc.
9424 Reeds Rd
Overland Park, KS 66207
Contact: Anthony Janiak
Tel: 913-433-4133
Email: tonyj@goldstartrans.com
Website: www.goldstartransportation.com
Third party transportation logistics. (Woman, estab 1982, empl 29, sales $24,781,811, cert: NWBOC)

9955 Nationwide Transportation & Logistics Services Inc.
PO Box 3190
Shawnee, KS 66203
Contact: Kim Isenhower President
Tel: 913-888-1685
Email: kim@nationwidetransportation.com
Website: www.nationwidetransportation.com
Transportation freight brokerage services. (Woman, estab 1998, empl 18, sales $20,000,000, cert: WBENC)

Kentucky

9956 A. Blair Enterprises Inc.
3801 Springhurst Blvd Ste 106
Louisville, KY 40241
Contact: Steve Orlowski General Mgr
Tel: 502-326-0500
Email: sorlowski@goablair.com
Website: www.goablair.com
Ground Expedite Freight Carrier with a fleet of over 1000 trucks of all sizes, from a cargo van to a tractor trailer at our disposal. (Woman, estab 1984, empl 5, sales $30,000,000, cert: WBENC)

9957 HJI -Vascor Logistics LLC
13200 Complete Court
Louisville, KY 40223
Contact: Brian Palmer Sr Mgr inbound logistics
Tel: 502-638-8021
Email: bpalmer@vascorltd.com
Website: www.vascorlogistics.com
Transportation services. (Woman/AA, estab 2012, empl 500, sales $20,000,000, cert: WBENC)

9958 Liberty Transportation, Inc. dba Team Worldwide
1348 Jamike Dr
Erlanger, KY 41018
Contact: Bobbie Mattis President
Tel: 859-282-0505
Email: bobbie.mattis@teamww.com
Website: www.teamww.com
Freight forwarding & logistics services. (Woman, estab 1989, empl 15, sales $6,000,000, cert: WBENC)

9959 Missouri Sea & Air Services, Inc.
500 Meijer Dr Ste 107
Florence, KY 41042
Contact: Katie Adler GM
Tel: 859-283-1919
Email: katie.adler@msatrans.com
Website: www.msatrans.com
Transportation, Truckload, LTL, Air, Intermodal, counter to counter and ocean. (Woman, estab 1982, empl 17, sales $27,000,000, cert: WBENC)

9960 Stett Transportation Inc.
224 Grandview Dr
Ft. Mitchell, KY 41017
Contact: Chris Jolevski Sales Team Lead
Tel: 859-384-2400
Email: chris@stett.net
Website: www.stett.net
Non-asset based 3PL transporting liquid bulk, both Hazmat & non hazardous products. (Woman, estab 1995, empl 24, sales $11,500,000, cert: WBENC)

Louisiana

9961 Morine Networking, Inc.
PO Box 363
Opelousas, LA 70570
Contact: Rodney Morine VP
Tel: 337-942-1790
Email: rodney@morinetrucking.com
Website: www.morinenetworking.com
Freight brokerage, 3rd party property logistics. (Woman/AA, estab 2007, empl 2, sales , cert: State, NMSDC)

9962 Quality First Construction LLC
      1254 N Columbia St
      Covington, LA 70433
      Contact: Michelle Fortson
      Tel: 985-888-6152
      Email: mfortson@qualityfirstmarine.com
      Website: www.qualityfirstmarine.com
Marine Transportation. (Woman/As-Pac, estab 2005, empl 18, sales $2,632,182, cert: NMSDC, WBENC)

9963 Trucking Innovation, LLC
      5623 N Villere St
      New Orleans, LA 70117
      Contact: Otis Tucker Sr Mgr
      Tel: 504-905-6719
      Email: info@truckinginnovationnola.com
      Website: www.truckinginnovationNola.com
Trucking/hauling & logistics services. (AA, estab 2013, empl 4, sales $2,140,883, cert: 8(a))

Massachusetts

9964 Advantage Global Logistics
      41 Highland Ave
      Randolph, MA 02368
      Contact: Maureen Powers VP Sales
      Tel: 781-986-3832
      Email: maureen.powers@landstarmail.com
      Website: www.landstar.com
Domestic & international, white glove inside delivery, debris removal & scheduled appointment deliveries, exporting & importing, air or ocean, door to door or door to airport/port, clear customs. (Woman, estab 1960, empl 5000, sales , cert: State)

9965 American Moving and Installation, Inc.
      100 Wearguard Dr Unit A
      Hanover, MA 02339
      Contact: CEO
      Tel: 781-878-8000
      Email:
      Website: www.americanmovingandinstall.com
Commercial moving & installation services. (Woman, estab 2009, empl 60, sales $6,080,000, cert: WBENC)

9966 Normandin Transportation Services Inc.
      10 Tandem Way, Ste B
      Hopedale, MA 01747
      Contact: Stephen Normandin VP Strategy
      Tel: 508-278-6579
      Email: steve@normandintrans.com
      Website: www.normandintrans.com
Transportation & logistics, LTL & truckload service. (Woman, estab 2008, empl 56, sales , cert: WBENC)

9967 Performance Trans. Inc.
      70 Benson St
      Fitchburg, MA 01420
      Contact: Julie Taylor President
      Tel: 978-345-5300
      Email: julie@performancetransinc.com
      Website: www.performancetransinc.com
Transportation: haul petroleum products (gas,diesel, heating oil, bio diesel, etc), building materials. (Woman, estab 1985, empl 45, sales $8,000,000, cert: State)

9968 USA Couriers, Inc.
      1320 Centre St, #202
      Newton, MA 02459
      Contact: Kris Wiegman President
      Tel: 800-450-4872
      Email: k.wiegman@usacouriers.com
      Website: www.usacouriers.com
Same day package delivery nationwide by land & air. Routed & on-demand work. (Woman, estab 2003, empl 75, sales $2,913,424, cert: WBENC)

Maryland

9969 1821 Freight, LLC
      9102 Helmsley Dr Ste G
      Clinton, MD 20735
      Contact: Kim Thrower President
      Tel: 301-235-3170
      Email: Freight@1821freight.com
      Website: www.1821freight.com
Carrier Network Management, Freight Booking & Scheduling, Route Optimization, Freight Rate Negotiation. (AA, estab 2022, empl 4, sales $215,000, cert: NMSDC)

9970 Air Freight Plus Inc. dba AFP Global Logistics
      611 N. Hammonds Ferry Rd Ste L-N
      Linthicum, MD 21076
      Contact: Holly Jones VP
      Tel: 410-590-1234
      Email: holly.jones@afplus.com
      Website: www.afplus.com
Full service logistics; air freight, ground freight, international air cargo, warehouse, (Woman, estab 1991, empl 13, sales $3,500,000, cert: State, WBENC)

9971 C J International Inc.
      519 S Ellwood Ave
      Baltimore, MD 21224
      Contact: Samya Murray Compliance Officer
      Tel: 410-563-6020
      Email: sdmurray@cjinternational.com
      Website: www.cjinternational.com
Global Logistics: air/ocean/ground freight transportation, warehousing & Customs brokerage. (Woman, estab 1987, empl 50, sales $3,600,000, cert: WBENC)

9972 Patriot Air Freight, Inc.
      806 Cromwell Park Dr
      Glen Burnie, MD 21061
      Contact: Heidi Gordon Acct Exec
      Tel: 410-766-2422
      Email: hgordon@aitworldwide.com
      Website: www.aitworldwide.com
Domestic Air Freight, Ground Transportation, International Air & Ocean, Custom House Brokerage, Transborder Services. (Woman, estab 1980, empl 16, sales $4,790,000, cert: WBENC)

9973 Samuel Shapiro & Company, Inc.
      1215 E Fort Ave Ste 201
      Baltimore, MD 21230
      Contact: Olga Lyakhovetskaya Mktg Dev
      Tel: 410-539-0540
      Email: web@shapiro.com
      Website: www.shapiro.com
Transport management/freight forwarding, ocean, air, surface, documentation & letters of credit, Automated Export System (AES), classification & binding rulings, export compliance & consulting, public & private export seminars. (Woman, estab , empl 120, sales $12,284,800, cert: WBENC)

9974 Velocity Global Logistics, Inc.
6805 Douglas Legum Dr Ste 201
Elkridge, MD 21075
Contact: Joseph Armstead President
Tel: 888-845-9855
Email: joe.armstead@velocitygloballogistics.com
Website: www.velocitygloballogistics.com
Global transportation. (Woman/AA, estab 2005, empl 2, sales $158,000, cert: NMSDC)

Michigan

9975 Acme Global Logistics, Inc.
31500 W 13 Mile Rd, Ste 219
Farmington Hills, MI 48334
Contact: Corey Dickerson Freight Broker
Tel: 844-260-0463
Email: cdickerson@aglogistics.us
Website: www.aglogistics.us
Freight Brokerage, Logistics Consulting, Specialized Pick-Up & Delivery, Intermodal. (AA, estab 2015, empl 6, sales , cert: NMSDC)

9976 ADED Logistics a Division of Hearn Industrial Services NA, Inc
13500 Huron St
Taylor, MI 48180
Contact: Johanna Leon Dir Business Devel
Tel: 519-990-1207
Email: johanna.leon@hearnindustrial.com
Website: www.hearnindustrial.com
Transportation, Supply Chain and Quality Services to the automotive industry. (AA, estab 2016, empl 75, sales , cert: NMSDC)

9977 Aero Expediting Inc.
37529 Huron Pointe Dr
Harrison Township, MI 48045
Contact: President
Tel: 586-260-2456
Email:
Website: www.aeroexp.com
Logistics & Transportation Services, air freight forwarding services. (Woman, estab 1988, empl , sales $750,000, cert: WBENC)

9978 American Motor Lines, Inc.
36253 Michigan Ave
Wayne, MI 48184
Contact: Christopher Burcham Mgr
Tel: 313-849-3500
Email: cburcham@alcotrans.com
Website: Www.steelpro.us
Steel hauling, heavy haul, transportation, cross dock. (Woman, estab 1978, empl 100, sales , cert: WBENC)

9979 Aristocat Limousine Service Inc.
3410 East 12 Mile Rd Ste B
Warren, MI 48092
Contact: Indu Kumar President
Tel: 586-574-0700
Email: invoices@aristocattransportation.com
Website: www.aristocattransportation.com
Chauffeured ground transportation in a variety of luxury vehicles. (Woman, estab 1987, empl 7, sales $998,000, cert: WBENC)

9980 BLT Logistics LLC
34450 Goddard Rd
Romulus, MI 48174
Contact: Joe Goryl VP Supply Chain
Tel: 586-467-1437
Email: jgoryl@bltship.com
Website: www.bltship.com
Transportation & logistics services in the U.S., Canada, and Mexico, domestic intermodal, drayage, air & ocean forwarding services. (Woman, estab 2014, empl 22, sales $1,500,000, cert: WBENC)

9981 BNM Transportation Services
91 N Saginaw, Ste 100
Pontiac, MI 48342
Contact: Marsha Rutherford Owner
Tel: 888-621-5592
Email: m.rutherford@bnmtrans.com
Website: www.bnmtransportation.com
Third party logistics, warehousing basics, public storage & order fulfillment for manufacturers. (Woman/AA, estab 2008, empl 45, sales $12,000,000, cert: NMSDC, WBENC)

9982 Camryn Logistics LLC
36500 Ford Rd
Westland, MI 48185
Contact: Jimmie Comer Business Dev Mgr
Tel: 866-670-8680
Email: jcomer@camrynlogistics.com
Website: www.camrynlogistics.com
Freight management, warehousing, sequencing, parts assembly, custom packing & transportation. (AA, estab 2008, empl 15, sales $600,000, cert: NMSDC)

9983 Chat of Michigan Inc.
35790 Northline Rd
Romulus, MI 48174
Contact: Greg Katcher President
Tel: 734-941-5004
Email: chatgk@aol.com
Website: www.chatofmichigan.com
Transportation, crating, rigging, plant relocation, freight forwarding. (AA, estab 1995, empl 40, sales $5,758,000, cert: NMSDC)

9984 D & D Logistics, LLC
3130 Glade St, Ste A
Muskegon Heights, MI 49444
Contact: Denise Kanaar CEO
Tel: 231-737-0100
Email: denise.kanaar@d-dlogistics.com
Website: www.d-dlogistics.com
Logistics services. (Woman, estab 2005, empl 12, sales $16,000,000, cert: WBENC)

9985 Detroit Logistics Company
9119 Thaddeus St
Detroit, MI 48209
Contact: Michael O'Neil COO
Tel: 313-843-7281
Email: moneil@detroitlogisticscompany.com
Website: www.detroitlogisticscompany.com
Asset-based logistics, warehousing, distribution, local & international transportation, express/ground carrier shipping, desktop delivery, liftgate delivery, just-in-time delivery & same day delivery. (AA, estab 1981, empl 8, sales $260,000, cert: NMSDC)

9986 E.L. Hollingsworth & Co.
       3039 Airpark Dr N
       Flint, MI 48507
       Contact: Steven Barr President
       Tel: 810-233-7331
       Email: sbarr@hollingsworthgroup.com
       Website: www.elhc.net
Transportation services: truckload & expedite delivery, warehouse & packaging svcs. (Nat Ame, estab 1927, empl 501, sales $45,000,000, cert: NMSDC)

9987 El Camino Transport Logistics & Management, LLC
       PO Box 28
       Union Lake, MI 48387
       Contact: Mary Kilgore President
       Tel: 248-242-0047
       Email: mkilgore@elcaminotransport.com
       Website: www.elcaminotransport.com
Warehousing specializing in pick & pack, kitting, sequencing & building batches. (Woman/Hisp, estab 2007, empl 4, sales , cert: NMSDC)

9988 EPJ Logistics Inc.
       50270 E Russell Schmidt
       Chesterfield Township, MI 48051
       Contact: Pamela Flynn CEO
       Tel: 586-421-1375
       Email: pflynn@epjlogistics.com
       Website: www.epjlogistics.com
Domestic & international transportation svcs, warehouse storage, fulfillment, inventory control, design & layout. (Woman, estab 1998, empl 9, sales $2,200,000, cert: WBENC)

9989 Expedite Express Transportation Inc.
       20411 W 12 Mile Rd Ste 200
       Southfield, MI 48076
       Contact: William Hamblin VP
       Tel: 248-443-1970
       Email: dispatch@expeditexp.com
       Website: www.expeditexp.com
Local & long distance TL & FTL, dedicated, same day & next day services to small & large businesses within the auto industry. (Woman/AA, estab 2005, empl 7, sales $622,635, cert: WBENC)

9990 February 14 Inc.
       4525 - 50th St SE
       Grand Rapids, MI 49512
       Contact: Bridget Carey President
       Tel: 616-656-0267
       Email: bridgetcarey@ffitransportation.com
       Website: www.FFItransportation.com
Transportation logistics. (Woman, estab 1984, empl 75, sales $18,875,000, cert: WBENC)

9991 First Choice of Elkhart
       10888 US Hwy 12
       White Pigeon, MI 49099
       Contact: Misty Campagna President
       Tel: 269-483-2010
       Email: mfirstchoice@gmail.com
       Website: www.firstchoiceautotransport.com
Automotive transportation & logistics. (Woman, estab 1992, empl 2, sales $3,407,867, cert: WBENC)

9992 Foreway Management Services Inc.
       1413 W Randall St
       Coopersville, MI 49404
       Contact: Pam Hassevoort President
       Tel: 616-997-9771
       Email: pamh@foreway.com
       Website: www.foreway.com
Qualcomm equipped 53 dry van units, 48 state coverage specializing in time sensitive and job site deliveries. (Woman, estab 1977, empl 60, sales $33,000,000, cert: WBENC)

9993 Global TEAM Associates, LLC
       11301 Metro Airport Center Dr Ste 170
       Romulus, MI 48174
       Contact: Petra Clark CEO
       Tel: 734-992-3208
       Email: petra.clark@globalteamusa.com
       Website: www.globalteamusa.com
Freight Forwarding & Customs House Brokerage services. (Woman, estab 2013, empl 21, sales , cert: WBENC)

9994 GMT Logistic Inc.
       50706 Varsity Ct
       WIXOM, MI 48393
       Contact: Tim Easley
       Tel: 844-898-2627
       Email: teasley@gmtlogisticinc.com
       Website: www.gmtlogisticinc.com
Logistics & Warehousing. (Woman, estab 2009, empl 80, sales , cert: WBENC)

9995 Go-To Transport
       1320 Washington Ave
       Bay City, MI 48708
       Contact: Allison Short President
       Tel: 989-891-2521
       Email: ashort@gototransport.com
       Website: www.gototransport.com
Truckload carrier: 48 contiguous states & Canada. (Woman, estab 2003, empl 160, sales $38,900,000, cert: WBENC)

9996 Grupo Logico, LLC
       42400 Grand River Ave, Ste 103
       Novi, MI 48375
       Contact: Darin Dittenber Dir Sales/Marketing
       Tel: 248-613-1699
       Email: ddittenber@grupologico.com
       Website: www.grupologico.com
Full service logistics solutions. (Hisp, estab 2004, empl 25, sales , cert: NMSDC)

9997 Gumro and Associates
       69 N Squirrel Ct
       Auburn Hills, MI 48326
       Contact: Ryan Gumro CEO
       Tel: 248-652-6200
       Email: rgumro@gumroandassociates.com
       Website: www.gumroandassociates.com
3PL trucking logistics, heavy haul, curtain sides, double drop, Lift-gate Straight truck & Vans. (Woman, estab 1974, empl 15, sales $20,000,000, cert: WBENC)

9998 HNT Logistics LLC
PO Box 603
New Boston, MI 48164
Contact: Mark Bowers VP Operations
Tel: 866-984-8840
Email: sales@hntlogistics.net
Website: www.hntlogistics.com
3PL logistics, truck freight, bulk freight, ocean freight, air freight, expedited freight & rail freight. (Woman, estab 2005, empl 34, sales $23,000,000, cert: WBENC)

9999 Hollingsworth Logistics Group, L.L.C.
14225 W Warren Ave
Dearborn, MI 48126
Contact: Greg Martinez Jr Dir of Govt Sales
Tel: 313-768-1306
Email: gmartinez@hlgllc.com
Website: www.hlgllc.com
Warehousing, container management, packaging services, kit packaing, fullfillment services, direct ship,d istribution, transportation OTR/LTL. (Nat Ame, estab 1991, empl 1900, sales , cert: NMSDC)

10000 KACE Logistics, LLC
862 Will Carleton Rd
Carleton, MI 48117
Contact: Paul Pavelich VP Business Dev
Tel: 734-946-8600
Email: pavelichp@kcintegrated.com
Website: www.kcintegrated.com
Logistics Management Services, Freight Brokerage & Management. (Hisp, estab 2014, empl 125, sales $27,200,000, cert: NMSDC)

10001 LB Transportation Group & Omni Warehouse
966 Bridgeview S
Saginaw, MI 48604
Contact: Tony Lander CEO
Tel: 989-759-5544
Email: tlander@lb-omni.com
Website: www.lb-omni.com
Transportation: expediting & dedicated svcs, warehousing, inspection, kitting, assembly, repacking. (Hisp, estab 1976, empl 70, sales $9,859,567, cert: NMSDC)

10002 Logos Logistics, Inc.
16490 Warhman Rd
Romulus, MI 48174
Contact: James (Jong-uk) Kim COO & President
Tel: 734-403-1777
Email: jkim@logos3pl.com
Website: www.logos3pl.com
Transportation & logisitics. (Woman/As-Pac, estab 2008, empl 120, sales $15,500,000, cert: NMSDC)

10003 Mexus Transport, Inc.
18600 Northville Rd, Ste 900
Northville, MI 48167
Contact: Alba R. McConell President
Tel: 248-344-8060
Email: alba@mexustransport.com
Website: www.mexustransport.com
Transportation: general freight, machinery & heavy haul, Canada, United States & Mexico. (Minority, Woman, estab 2003, empl 5, sales $300,000, cert: State)

10004 New Dimension Logistics, LLC
12256 Universal Dr
Taylor, MI 48180
Contact: Kurmmell Knox CEO
Tel: 734-865-9960
Email: kwknox@ndlx.us
Website: www.ndlx.us
Integrated supply chain solutions delivering safe, specialized transportation, warehousing and logistics services. (AA, estab 2007, empl 14, sales $3,588,000, cert: NMSDC)

10005 Northfield Trucking Company, Inc.
28800 Nothline Rd
Romulus, MI 48174
Contact: Leigh Ann Frederick President
Tel: 313-624-4900
Email: leighannl@northfieldtruck.com
Website: www.northfieldtruck.com
Transportation, regional, long haul & dry freight long distances operation. (Woman, estab 2002, empl 100, sales $12,000,000, cert: WBENC)

10006 O & I Transport Inc.
PO Box 807
Dearborn, MI 48121
Contact: Mike Schofiled Sales Mgr
Tel: 800-270-0020
Email: mschofield@oitransport.com
Website: www.oitransport.com
Flatbed trucking. (AA, estab 1981, empl 21, sales $25,000,000, cert: NMSDC)

10007 Oneida Solutions Group
10049 Harrison, Ste 500A
Romulus, MI 48174
Contact: Fred Rogers Exec Dir
Tel: 248-252-2260
Email: frogers@oneidasolutions.com
Website: www.oneidasolutions.com
Transportation svcs: intl household & office moving, project mgmt. (Nat Ame, estab 2001, empl 200, sales , cert: WBENC)

10008 Palmer Logistic Services
24660 Dequindre Rd
Warren, MI 48091
Contact: Terri Palmer Burton President
Tel: 313-220-5433
Email: terripb@palmerlogisticsservices.com
Website: www.palmerls.com
Global household relocation, commercial relocation, regional distribution, trade show transportation & store fixture distribution. (Woman, estab 2007, empl 9, sales $42,000,000, cert: WBENC)

10009 Prime Time Delivery
9354 Harrison Rd
Romulus, MI 48174
Contact: Paul Davis CEO
Tel: 800-336-3678
Email: pdavis@ptlogistics.com
Website: www.ptlogistics.com
Nationwide airfreight & ground transportation. (AA, estab 1997, empl 11, sales $3,000,000, cert: NMSDC)

TRANSPORTATION SERVICES

10010 Promesa Logistics, LLC
3068 Highland Dr
Hudsonville, MI 49426
Contact: Lon Agular President
Tel: 800-646-1016
Email:
Website: www.promesalogistics.com
Dedicated route transportation, Local Transportation, Brokerage, Warehouse, Distribution, Consolidation, Expediting, Cargo Van, Straight Truck, Semis. (Hisp, estab 1997, empl 10, sales $2,400,000, cert: NMSDC)

10011 Promesa Transportation
3068 Highland Dr
Hudsonville, MI 49426
Contact: Lon Aguilar President
Tel: 616-748-2340
Email: lonagu@chartermi.net
Website: www.chartermi.net
Transportation services. (Hisp, estab 0, empl , sales , cert: NMSDC)

10012 Rich Davis Enterprises, Inc.
4831 Wyoming Ave
Dearborn, MI 48126
Contact: Melissa Matsos Acct Exec
Tel: 313-584-3334
Email: melmatsos@richdavistrucking.com
Website: www.richdavistrucking.com
Transport auto parts, steel, machinery & general commodity freight. (Woman, estab 1987, empl 17, sales $1,995,074, cert: WBENC)

10013 Rodriguez Expedited Freight Systems, Inc.
9400 Pelham
Taylor, MI 48180
Contact: Dennis Schmidt VP Operations
Tel: 800-718-0066
Email: dschmidt@rodexp.com
Website: www.rodexp.com
Ground & air expedition: cargo van, cube truck, straight truck & semi, 48 state authority, plus Canada. (Minority, Woman, estab 1992, empl 20, sales $5,600,000, cert: NMSDC)

10014 Rose-Allied International
41775 Ecorse Rd Ste 190
Belleville, MI 48111
Contact: Brad Koch Global Business
Tel: 734-957-8000
Email: bkoch@rosemoving.com
Website: www.rosemoving.com
Global Relocation services. (Woman, estab 1964, empl 200, sales $30,020,000, cert: WBENC)

10015 RSP Express Inc.
28169 Van Born Road
Romulus, MI 48174
Contact: Maria Pop President
Tel: 734-578-0799
Email: rspexpress1@yahoo.com
Website: www.rspexpress.com
Brokerage and Transportation Services. (Woman, estab 2006, empl 140, sales $19,896,325, cert: WBENC)

10016 Rush Trucking Corporation
35160 E Michigan Ave
Wayne, MI 48184
Contact: Rob Allgary Dir of Sales
Tel: 800-526-7874
Email: rallgary@rushtrucking.com
Website: www.rushtrucking.com
Truckload transportation, expedited transportation. (Minority, Woman, estab 1984, empl 950, sales $125,000,000, cert: NMSDC, WBENC)

10017 Silence Lines LLC
9276 Marine City Hwy
Casco, MI 48064
Contact: Valerio Cean Operations Mgr
Tel: 586-826-9545
Email: operations@silencelines.com
Website: www.silencelines.com
Transportation services, Door to door, Canada, US, Mexico. (Woman, estab 2009, empl 80, sales $36,000,000, cert: WBENC)

10018 Sterling Services Ltd.
1530 Commor
Hamtramck, MI 48212
Contact: Jason Eddleston VP
Tel: 248-298-2973
Email: jason@sterlingoilchem.com
Website: www.sterlingoilchem.com
Provides high-quality bulk liquid storage, custom blending, warehousing & bulk liquid transport services. (Woman, estab 1985, empl 9, sales $2,036,474, cert: WBENC)

10019 T & M Incorporated
930 Interchange Dr
Holland, MI 49423
Contact: Helen Zeerip President
Tel: 269-751-8050
Email: helen@teddystransport.com
Website: www.teddystransport.com
Transportation svcs, expediting to all 48 states & Ontario/Quebec, Canada, dedicated fleet services, full-truck load services. (Woman, estab 1982, empl 75, sales $7,276,168, cert: WBENC)

10020 Technology Ventures, Inc.
25200 Malvina Ave
Warren, MI 48089
Contact: Constance E. Blair President
Tel: 586-573-6000
Email: cblair@tvihq.com
Website: www.tvihq.com
Logistics, warehousing, light assembly, fulfillment, kitting, distribution & foreign trade zone. (Minority, Woman, estab 1992, empl 30, sales , cert: NMSDC, NWBOC)

10021 The Harmon Group LLC
269 Walker St Ste 201
Detroit, MI 48207
Contact: Tina Harmon CEO
Tel: 313-414-6332
Email: harmont@theharmongroup.com
Website: www.theharmongroup.com
Warehouse storage facilities. (Woman/AA, estab 2000, empl 3, sales $3,000,000, cert: WBENC)

10022 The Outbound Group
9900 Harrison
Romulus, MI 48174
Contact: Karl Randolph President
Tel: 734-947-1333
Email: karlr@outboundgroup.com
Website: www.outboundgroup.com
Interstate & intrastate motor truck transportation service, fright brokerage, air freight forwarding services & warehouseing. (Woman/AA, estab 1982, empl 100, sales $7,200,000, cert: NMSDC)

10023 Three Star Trucking Co.
36860 Van Born Rd
Wayne, MI 48184
Contact: Tedd Rowe Logistics Mgr
Tel: 734-728-5500
Email: operations@threestartrucking.com
Website: www.threestartrucking.com
Transportation svcs; automotive. (Minority, Woman, estab 1979, empl 60, sales , cert: NMSDC, WBENC)

10024 Top Worldwide, LLC
3039 Air Park Dr N
Flint, MI 48507
Contact: B. Hall VP Sales
Tel: - -
Email: bhall@elhc.net
Website: www.topworldwide.com/
Third Party Logistics. (Nat Ame, estab 2007, empl 15, sales $15,000,000, cert: NMSDC)

10025 Trans Overseas Corporation
28000 Goddard Road
Romulus, MI 48174
Contact: Brett Ouellette VP- Sales & Logistics
Tel: 734-946-8750
Email: bouellette@trans-overseas.com
Website: www.trans-overseas.com
US Customs Broker, International Air/Ocean Freight Forwarder, Bonded Warehouse, Foreign Trade Zone, Container Freight Station, Barcode Labeling, Inspections, Repackaging & Distribution. (Woman, estab 1978, empl 65, sales $6,200,000, cert: WBENC)

10026 Transphere Inc.
5800 Commerce Dr
Westland, MI 48185
Contact: Smita Koradia CEO
Tel: 734-727-1307
Email: skoradia@transphereinc.net
Website: www.transphereinc.com
International logistics/transportation, warehousing, cargo by sea, air & land. (Woman/As-Ind, estab 1987, empl 3, sales $980,000, cert: NMSDC)

10027 University Moving & Storage
23305 Commerce Dr
Farmington Hills, MI 48335
Contact: Ben Cross VP
Tel: 248-949-5755
Email: bcross@universitymoving.com
Website: www.universitymoving.com
Transportation, moving & storage. (Woman, estab 1969, empl 150, sales $14,490,725, cert: WBENC)

10028 Warehouse Properties, Inc.
16000 W. Nine Mile Rd. Ste 302
Southfield, MI 48075
Contact: Kathleen Eberle President
Tel: 248-569-6106
Email: keberle@npotransportation.com
Website: www.npotransportation.com
Truckload transportation services: seating companies, kitting & JIT components. (Woman, estab 1984, empl 4, sales $1,641,592, cert: WBENC)

Minnesota

10029 Assure Shipping, LLC
9462 Stevens Ave S
Bloomington, MN 55420
Contact: Jane Mahowald CEO
Tel: 612-270-6889
Email: jane@assureshipping.com
Website: www.assureshipping.com
Logistics: air, truck & rail, import/export. (Minority, Woman, estab 2008, empl 2, sales , cert: NMSDC)

10030 Jade Logistics, Inc.
1333 Northland Dr Ste 210
Mendota Heights, MN 55120
Contact: Ni Suphavong Owner
Tel: 651-405-3141
Email: ni@shipjade.com
Website: www.shipjade.com
Domestic & international freight transportation services. (Minority, Woman, estab 2007, empl 20, sales $13,000,000, cert: State, NMSDC, WBENC)

10031 Malark Logistics
PO Box 438
Maple Grove, MN 55369
Contact: Sr Sales Exec
Tel: 763-428-3564
Email: info@malark.com
Website: www.malark.com
Logistics, transportation, warehousing, trucking, airfreight, expedited, freight auditing, crating, claims filing, distribution, pick and pack, LTL, tradeshow services, 3PL & 4PL. (Woman, estab 1994, empl 60, sales $35,000,000, cert: WBENC)

Missouri

10032 ABC Moving & Storage Co., Inc.
633 Goddard Ave
Chesterfield, MO 63005
Contact: Rebeckah Hoover CEO
Tel: 636-532-1300
Email: beckyh@abcatlas.com
Website: www.abcatlas.com
Move office furniture & equipment, assembling/ disassembling work stations, high value artifacts, etc. (Woman, estab 1972, empl 35, sales $2,306,997, cert: WBENC)

10033 All America Transportation, Inc.
910 S Kirkwood Rd Ste 120
St. Louis, MO 63122
Contact: Lianne Reizer President
Tel: 314-835-9499
Email: lianne@allamericatrans.com
Website: www.allamericatrans.com
Licensed freight broker, truckload shipments throughout US & Canada. (Woman, estab 1996, empl 7, sales $2,579,000, cert: State, CPUC, WBENC)

10034 Crossland Carriers Inc.
421 Cedar Hills Rd
Ozark, MO 65721
Contact: Patricia Schmig President
Tel: 800-217-0898
Email: tschmig@crosslandcarriers.us
Website: www.crosslandcarriers.com
Trucking long haul, short haul, partial truckload, logistics, mobile home, mobile office moves, heavy haul, specialized logistics. (Woman, estab 1999, empl 3, sales $1,750,000, cert: State)

10035 Kings Warehouse Logistics LLC
6008 N Lindbergh Blvd Ste B
Hazelwood, MO 63042
Contact: Eric Wright Dir Sales Operations
Tel: 314-716-3499
Email: ericwright@kingswarehouselogistics.com
Website: www.kingswarehouselogistics.com
Cross Docking, FTL and LTL Trucking, General 3PL Services, General Warehousing & Distribution, Labeling, Light Assembly Outsourcing Services, Logistic Transportation of General Merchandise. (AA, estab 2014, empl , sales , cert: State)

10036 LHP Transportation Services, Inc.
2032 E Kearney St Ste 213
Springfield, MO 65803
Contact: Greg Gloeckner
Tel: 972-812-7370
Email: gloeg@lhptransport.com
Website: www.lhptransport.com
Multimodal transportation svcs: truck, rail, LTL, steamship & air, 48 states, Canada, Mexico & abroad. (Minority, Woman, estab 1993, empl 9, sales $30,000,001, cert: NMSDC)

10037 Marleon International, LLC
5630 NE Lake Dr
Kansas City, MO 64118
Contact: Marquez Cesar CEO
Tel: 816-249-2319
Email: camarquez@mar-leon.com
Website: www.marleoninternational.com
Freight transportation: less than container load, less than truckload, full truckload, flatbed freight, air transportation services, distribution & warehousing services. (Hisp, estab 2005, empl 4, sales $560,000, cert: State, NMSDC)

10038 Shaeffer Logistics
2 Cityplace Dr Ste 200
Saint Louis, MO 63141
Contact: Dene Shaeffer President
Tel: 314-635-9344
Email: partnership@shaefferlogistics.com
Website: www.shaefferlogistics.com
Domestic & international transportation services. (Woman/AA, estab 2019, empl 8, sales $910,000, cert: City, WBENC)

10039 The Thomas Family Business, Inc.
8194 Lackland Rd
Saint Louis, MO 63114
Contact: Rolondo Thomas CEO
Tel: 314-423-6111
Email: rolondo.thomas@ttfbcompanies.com
Website: www.ttfbcompanies.com
Transportation services, local & regional, warehousing, supply chain management & logistics. (AA, estab 2009, empl 7, sales $750,000, cert: City)

10040 ValDivia Enterprises, Inc.
#5C The Pines Court
St. Louis, MO 63141
Contact: steve ellis VP Sales
Tel: 314-275-7941
Email: steve@valdiviaenterprises.net
Website: www.valdiviaenterprises.net
Transportation services serving North America & Mexico. (Minority, Woman, estab 2006, empl 1450, sales , cert: State)

Montana

10041 Bridger Transportation, LLC
132 W. Haley Springs Rd.
Bozeman, MT 59718
Contact: Clayton Rickert VP of Operation
Tel: 406-586-0648
Email: clayton.rickert@bridgertrans.com
Website: www.bridgertrans.com
Logistics services. (Woman, estab 2007, empl 20, sales $22,000,000, cert: WBENC)

10042 Meadow Lark Companies
935 Lake Elmo Dr
Billings, MT 59105
Contact: Chris Verlanic Dir of Freight Management
Tel: 406-657-8645
Email: cverlanic@meadowlarkco.com
Website: www.meadowlarkco.com
Transportation, Freight Management & Logistics: TL, LTL, Vans/Reefers, Flatbed & Heavy Haul. (Woman, estab 1983, empl 160, sales $65,000,000, cert: WBENC)

North Carolina

10043 All-State Express, Inc.
121-I Shields Park Dr
Kernersville, NC 27284
Contact: Sherri Squier President
Tel: 336-992-6880
Email: sherri@all-stateexpress.com
Website: www.all-stateexpress.com
Transportation Services, Expedited Trucking, Air Charter, TruckLoad, Expedite Trucking, Truck Load (TL), Milk Runs, Dedicated Truck Load, Air Freight, Air Charter, Hazmat Carrier 48 States, Canada and Mexico. (Woman, estab 1996, empl 28, sales $23,755,580, cert: WBENC)

10044 Graebel Vanlines Holdings, LLC
2901 Stewart Creek Blvd
Charlotte, NC 28216
Contact: Colin Holden VP Corporate Sales
Tel: 704-281-7129
Email: colin.holden@graebelmoving.com
Website: www.graebelmoving.com
Facility management services, commercial moving services, warehousing services. (Woman, estab 1960, empl 1360, sales $266,000,000, cert: WBENC)

10045 Intermodal Logistics Consulting, Inc.
301 N Main St, Ste 2409B
Winston-Salem, NC 27101
Contact: Senanu Ashiabor President
Tel: 540-257-3830
Email: senanu@imlconsulting.com
Website: www.imlconsulting.com
Moves freight for FedEx CustomCritical. (AA, estab 2013, empl 10, sales $200,000, cert: 8(a))

TRANSPORTATION SERVICES

10046 Logical Logistics Solutions
7508 E Independence Blvd Ste 112
Charlotte, NC 28227
Contact: Noel Sanchez President
Tel: 704-566-4770
Email: nsanchez@llsolutions.com
Website: www.llsolutions.com
Logistics services: freight cost reduction & admin, warehousing, consolidation & distribution & inventory mgmt. (AA, estab 1996, empl 5, sales $3,128,798, cert: City)

10047 PWJ Enterprises dba as Team Worldwide
3400 Yorkmont Rd Ste 700
Charlotte, NC 28208
Contact: Mark Patrick Dir of Business Dev
Tel: 704-357-9857
Email: mark.patrick@teamww.com
Website: www.teamww.com
Freight forwarding: air, ocean, logistics, charter, warehousing, distribution, order fulfillment. (AA, estab 2006, empl 7, sales $6,500,000, cert: NMSDC)

10048 Southeastern Fleet Management, LLC
215 W Plaza Dr, Ste 200
Mooresville, NC 28117
Contact: Patty Bretz Procurement Mgr
Tel: 704-658-1613
Email: patty@sefmgt.com
Website: www.southeasternfleet.com
Transportation solutions, Vehicle Acquisitions Leasing Maintenance Licensing & Registration Remarketing Funding Solutions Personal Fleet Advisor. (Woman, estab 2012, empl 2, sales $2,400,156, cert: State)

10049 Synchrogistics, LLC
900 Ridgefield Dr Ste 350
Raleigh, NC 27609
Contact: Mary MacIsaac Mgr Admin
Tel: 877-879-0668
Email: mary@synchrogistics.com
Website: www.synchrogistics.com
National transportation, domestic truckload and LTL transportation, intermodal, international shipping, warehousing. (Woman, estab 2010, empl 24, sales $18,803,598, cert: WBENC)

North Dakota

10050 S & S Transport, Inc
PO Box 12579
Grand Forks, ND 58208
Contact: Brian Seng Operations Mgr
Tel: 701-746-8484
Email: brian_seng@sstransport.com
Website: www.sstransport.com
Trucking Transportation Services (Woman, estab 1981, empl 120, sales $18,500,000, cert: State)

Nebraska

10051 Kirsch Transportation Services Inc.
1102 Douglas St
Omaha, NE 68102
Contact: Lucas Bird Govt Operations
Tel: 531-213-2153
Email: lucasb@kirschtrans.com
Website: www.kirschtrans.com
Dry Van, Open Deck and Temp Control Over-Dimensional and Heavy Haul Intermodal - Domestic and Cross Border Freight Management. (Woman, estab 2001, empl 60, sales $128,033,344, cert: NWBOC)

10052 Nationwide Auto Transport, Inc.
730 Pier 3
Lincoln, NE 68528
Contact: Julie Delp President
Tel: 402-742-4000
Email: nwat90@tahoo.com
Website: www.nwat.com
Automobile transport services. (Woman, estab 2001, empl 35, sales $3,900,000, cert: WBENC, SDB)

New Jersey

10053 Andrew Vazquez Inc.
24 Tuttle Ave
Bedminster, NJ 07921
Contact: Andrew Vazquez President
Tel: 908-719-2444
Email: avaquez@dlgroup.com
Website: www.aviquality.com
Vehicle Logistics Services. (Hisp, estab 1979, empl 30, sales $4,500,000, cert: NMSDC)

10054 Bett-A-Way Traffic Systems Inc.
110 Sylvania Pl
South Painfield, NJ 07080
Contact: Betty Vaccaro VP
Tel: 908-222-2500
Email: laura.vaccaro@bettaway.com
Website: www.bett-a-way.com
Logistics management, freight nationwide, truck load & LTL, dry & refrigerated. (Woman, estab 1982, empl 107, sales , cert: WBENC)

10055 Blisset Transportation
50 Triangle Blvd.
Carlstadt, NJ 07072
Contact: Roseanne Magliato President
Tel: 201-549-0672
Email: rmagliato@blissetllc.com
Website: www.blissetllc.com
Transportation & logistics services, warehousing, fulfillment & technology solutions. (Minority, Woman, estab 1991, empl 35, sales $10,000,001, cert: NMSDC, WBENC)

10056 Bohren's Moving & Storage/United Van Lines
3 Applegate Dr
Robbinsville, NJ 08691
Contact: Charlene Heath Sales/Mktg Mgr
Tel: 800-326-4736
Email: cheath@bohrensmoving.com
Website: www.bohrensmoving.com
Transportation & storage svcs; brokerage & international divisions. (Woman, estab 1924, empl 90, sales $28,798,613, cert: WBENC)

10057 Business Relocation Services, Inc.
20 Aquarium Dr
Secaucus, NJ 07094
Contact: Jesus Linares President
Tel: 718-399-8000
Email: jesus.linares@brsrelocations.com
Website: www.brsmove.com
Commercial Relocation services, Warehousing, Trucking, Project Management, Furniture Installation & Storage. (Hisp, estab 1987, empl 45, sales $14,133,451, cert: City, NMSDC)

10058 Evergreen Corporate Car & Limousine Service
27 Lewis Ave, Ste 2
Jersey City, NJ 07306
Contact: Paul Lipsey Sales
Tel: 201-217-0070
Email: sales@evergreenlimos.com
Website: www.evergreenlimos.com
Corporate car & limousine services. (AA, estab 1997, empl 100, sales $5,025,000, cert: State)

10059 Gem Limousine Service, Inc.
70 Amboy Ave
Woodbridge, NJ 07095
Contact: Ed Walch VP Client Relations
Tel: 732-596-0900
Email: ewalch@gemlimo.com
Website: www.gemlimo.com
Worldwide ground transportation for individual & groups. (Woman, estab 1976, empl 140, sales $14,485,851, cert: WBENC)

10060 Global Transit Solutions
110 Chestnut Ridge Rd, Ste 188
Montvale, NJ 07645
Contact: Fernando Mateo Co-Owner
Tel: 201-949-8755
Email: FM@gowithgts.com
Website: www.gowithgts.com
Third Party Logistics throughout the nation, transportation services, trucks, and intermodal, full truck loads (FTL), and less than a trailer. (Hisp, estab 2018, empl 2, sales , cert: State)

10061 Ltd Logistics, Inc.
222 Outwater Lane Ste 3
Garfield, NJ 07026
Contact: Tracy Flood Transportation Sales Rep
Tel: 973-340-4428
Email: tracy.flood@ltdnj.com
Website: www.ltdnj.com
Ground & air freight transportation, full truckload & LTL/partials via over the road, intermodal & air freight. (Woman, estab 1995, empl 10, sales $4,922,477, cert: State, City)

10062 ProFreight Inc.
35A Brunswick Ave
Edison, NJ 08817
Contact: Ben Leuenberger President
Tel: 732-429-1600
Email: ben@profreight.us
Website: www.profreight.us
Licensed US customs brokerage, int'l freight forwarding, 3PL supply chain management. (Woman, estab 1989, empl 37, sales $15,000,000, cert: State)

10063 Royal Coachman Worldwide
88 Ford Rd, Unit 26
Denville, NJ 07834
Contact: Amy Birnbaum CEO
Tel: 973-400-3200
Email: amy.birnbaum@royalcoachman.com
Website: www.royalcoachman.com
Corporate limousine & transportation svcs: luxury sedans, stretch limousines, 14 passenger motor coaches. (Woman, estab 1969, empl 150, sales $13,034,000, cert: WBENC)

New Mexico

10064 Loadstone Transportation, LLC
1811 Copper Loop, Ste K
Las Cruces, NM 88007
Contact: Bridgette Snow Marketing Coord
Tel: 575-523-7000
Email: bridgette@loadstonetransportation.com
Website: www.loadstonetransportation.com
Transportation services, multitude of local, state, & federal government contracts. (Woman, estab 2011, empl 6, sales $5,823,500, cert: State, WBENC)

Nevada

10065 Full Tilt Logistics LLC
150 Isidor Court
Sparks, NV 89441
Contact: Customer Management Team
Tel: 702-852-2228
Email: remit@fulltitlogistics.com
Website: www.fulltitlogistics.com
LTL, Partial loads, Full truck load, Rail, Heavy haul. (Woman, estab 2014, empl 11, sales $16,403,958, cert: WBENC)

10066 Railroad Industries Inc.
1575 Delucchi Ln, Ste 210
Reno, NV 89502
Contact: Anastacia Sullivan Dir of Operations
Tel: 775-329-4855
Email: reg@railroadindustries.com
Website: www.railroadindustries.com
Transportation consulting. (Woman/AA, As- Pac, estab 1983, empl 9, sales $775,382, cert: State)

New York

10067 A & Z Trucking, Inc.
115 Corporate Dr
New Windsor, NY 12550
Contact: Maria Zakar Broker
Tel: 845-569-7299
Email: az.trucking01@gmail.com
Website: www.AandZtrucking.com
Transportation solutions, temperature-controlled reefer trucks, dry vans, flatbeds, full truckload (TL), less-than-truckload (LTL), refrigerated freight. (Minority, Woman, estab 2003, empl 15, sales , cert: NMSDC)

10068 AWLI Group, Inc.
147-60 175 St
Jamaica, NY 11434
Contact: Keith Milliner VP
Tel: 718-244-8923
Email: keith@amberworldwide.com
Website: www.amberworldwide.com
International freight forwarding. (Woman, estab 1990, empl 20, sales $12,594,223, cert: State)

10069 Continental Trading & Services, Inc.
167-43 148th Ave
Jamaica, NY 11434
Contact: Gabriel Gorre
Tel: 718-995-9560
Email: ggorre@ctslogi.com
Website: www.ctslogi.com
Domestic & international transportation. (Hisp, estab 1994, empl 10, sales $3,329,233, cert: State, NMSDC)

10070 Deluxe Delivery Systems, Inc.
729 7th Ave 2nd Fl
New York, NY 10019
Contact: Yoindra Ramnarayan President
Tel: 212-376-4500
Email: ryan@deluxedelivery.com
Website: www.deluxedelivery.com
Distribution services, regional & local trucking, moving (internal and external), overnight mail and messenger service. (As-Ind, estab 1985, empl 500, sales $18,000,000, cert: NMSDC)

10071 Eagle Transfer Corporation
23-02 49 Ave
Long Island City, NY 11101
Contact: Marisol Morales Dir Mktg
Tel: 718-663-0400
Email: mmorales@eagletransfer.com
Website: www.eagletransfer.com
Office moving & storage, installation, dissasemble modular furniture & shelving, project mgmt, records storage. (AA, Hisp, estab 1971, empl 74, sales , cert: NMSDC)

10072 Native Trax Logistics LLC
767 Warren Rd
Ithaca, NY 14850
Contact: Ryan Van Alstine GM
Tel: 607-319-5122
Email: ryan@nativetraxlogistics.com
Website: www.nativetraxlogistics.com
Transportation Management, Nationwide service, Asset tracking & reporting, Driver safety screenings, Driver credential checks, Timely proof of delivery, On call 24 hours. (Nat Ame, estab 2014, empl 5, sales $3,500,000, cert: NMSDC)

10073 Spearhead Transportation Services, Inc.
PO Box 1984
Blasdell, NY 14219
Contact: Joe Dotterweich CFO
Tel: 716-823-4942
Email: joed@spearheadlogistics.com
Website: www.spearheadlogistics.com
Transportation & logistics services. (Nat Ame, estab 0, empl , sales $14,000,000, cert: NMSDC)

10074 V G Francis Logistics Inc.
800 Et 180th St
Bronx, NY 10460
Contact: Victor Francis President
Tel: 866-970-8866
Email: vgfrancislogistics@gmail.com
Website: www.vgfrancislogistics.com
Transportation, logistics & related information services: air, rail & sea transportation. (AA, estab 2006, empl 1, sales , cert: City, NMSDC)

10075 Walker SCM, LLC
70 E Sunrise Hwy Ste 611
Valley Stream, NY 11581
Contact: Emmett F. Walker CEO
Tel: 516-568-2080
Email: sales@walkerscm.com
Website: www.walkerscm.com
International transportation, logistics, sub- assembly, sequencing, kitting, warehousing, distribution & customs brokarage. (AA, estab 1989, empl 852, sales $147,000,000, cert: NMSDC, SDB)

10076 Wings Air Helicopters LLC
136 Tower Rd
West Harrison, NY 10604
Contact: Anna Macsai General Mgr
Tel: 914-202-3440
Email: anna@wingsairhelicopters.com
Website: www.wingsair.net
FAA Part 135 helicopter charter: able to transport key personnel, supplies and critical goods quickly into most areas, including remote/confined areas & offshore platforms. (Hisp, estab 2002, empl 12, sales $3,850,000, cert: State)

Ohio

10077 1st Express, Inc.
227 Matzinger Rd
Toledo, OH 43612
Contact: Patrick Southward VP
Tel: 419-476-6881
Email: pat@1stexpressinc.com
Website: www.1stexpressinc.com
Trucking & warehousing. (AA, estab 1984, empl 85, sales $10,000,000, cert: NWBOC)

10078 All AMerican Relocation Inc.
14675 Foltz Pkwy
Strongsville, OH 44149
Contact: Mike McGill SVP, Sales & Customer Service
Tel: 440-846-0722
Email: mikem@allamericarelo.com
Website: www.allamericarelo.com
Full-service moving & storage. (Woman, estab 2003, empl 35, sales $2,000,000, cert: WBENC)

10079 American Shipping and Packing, Inc.
1252 Mina Ave, Ste B
Akron, OH 44321
Contact: President
Tel: 330-670-8100
Email: asapincs@aol.com
Website: www.asapcompany.net
Business Relocation Services, Complete Office & Business Moving Services. (AA, estab 1989, empl 10, sales $1,300,000, cert: State, City)

10080 ASW Global, LLC
3375 Gilchrist Rd
Mogadore, OH 44260
Contact: Pam Harris Dir Mktg & Supplier Diversity
Tel: 330-733-8176
Email: pharris@aswglobal.com
Website: www.aswglobal.com
Third-party logistics, warehousing, order fulfillment, pick pack & ship, pkging/re-packaging, contract logistics retail supply chain support, bulk resin transloading, records retention, file storage, & retrieval services. (AA, estab 1983, empl 120, sales $27,000,000, cert: NMSDC)

10081 BD Transportation, Inc.
9590 Looney Rd
Piqua, OH 45356
Contact: Tom Stirnaman Sales
Tel: 309-531-1370
Email: toms@ptc-inc.net
Website: www.ptc-inc.net
Dry van freight, 62 tractors & 125 dry van trailers. (Woman, estab 2000, empl 95, sales $14,600,000, cert: WBENC)

TRANSPORTATION SERVICES

10082 Black Star Logistics Inc.
2350 Greenvale Rd
Cleveland, OH 44121
Contact: Malike Moore President
Tel: 216-307-0767
Email: mmoore@blackstarlogisticsincorporated.org
Website: www.blackstarlogisticsincorporated.org
Shipping commercial freight and all other courier services. (AA, estab 2017, empl 4, sales , cert: State)

10083 Cam Logistics, LLC
7800 Robinett Way
Canal Winchester, OH 43110
Contact: Patrick Shea VP
Tel: 614-409-1776
Email: patrick@camlogisticsllc.com
Website: www.camlogisticsllc.com
Third party logistics, transportation, truckload & intermodal arrangements. (Woman, estab 2006, empl 9, sales $5,400,000, cert: WBENC)

10084 Cimarron Express Inc.
21611 State Rt 51
Genoa, OH 43430
Contact: Jim Shepperd VP /Admin Asst
Tel: 419-855-7713
Email: jshepperd@cimarronexpress.com
Website: www.cimarronexpress.com
Motor carrier svcs, truckload. (AA, estab 1984, empl 325, sales , cert: NMSDC)

10085 Cordell Transporation Company LLC
2942 Boulder Ave
Dayton, OH 45414
Contact: Lori Van Opstal President
Tel: 937-277-7271
Email: lvanopstal@cordelltransportation.com
Website: www.cordelltransportation.com
Dedicated Truckload Transportation services throughout the US & Canada. (Minority, Woman, estab 1999, empl 225, sales $20,947,709, cert: NMSDC, WBENC)

10086 Debo Enterprises Incorporated
16021 Dunbury Dr Ste 103
Maple Heights, OH 44137
Contact: Tommie Rodgers Operations Dir/Co-Owner
Tel: 404-333-5008
Email: deboenterprise@gmail.com
Website: www.deboenterprises.com
Logistics & transportation services, Short term & long term line haul services, railroad/shipyards, Hauling services for construction worksites. (AA, estab 2001, empl 3, sales $137,000, cert: State)

10087 Grand Aire, Inc.
11777 W. Airport Service Road
Swanton, OH 43558
Contact: Katrina Cheema Business Advisor
Tel: 419-861-6700
Email: diversity@grandaire.com
Website: www.grandaire.com
Air charter transportation: passengers & cargo. (As-Ind, estab 1997, empl , sales $18,894,688, cert: NMSDC, SDB)

10088 H & W Trucking
15 W Locust St
Newark, OH 43055
Contact: Barcy Vidt President
Tel: 800-572-2120
Email: barcy@handwtrucking.com
Website: www.handwtrucking.com
Third party logistics & freight, LTL & rail, US & Canada. (Woman, estab 1979, empl 3, sales $5,300,000, cert: WBENC)

10089 InterChez Global Services, Inc.
600 Alpha Pkwy
Stow, OH 44224
Contact: Ivette Tam Exec VP
Tel: 330-923-5080
Email: itam@interchez.com
Website: www.interchezglobal.com
Logistics engineering, network modeling, logistics execution, freight bill payment, premium freight management, logistics consulting, translation, interpretation. (Minority, Woman, estab 2001, empl 12, sales $18,000,000, cert: State, NMSDC, WBENC)

10090 J Rayl Trasnport Inc.
1016 Triplett Blvd
Akron, OH 44306
Contact: Tara Vance President
Tel: 800-753-5050
Email: tara.rayl@jrayl.com
Website: www.jrayl.com
Asset based transportation firm. (Woman, estab 1987, empl 20, sales $68,000,000, cert: WBENC)

10091 Kingsgate Transportation Services LLC
9100 West Chester Towne Centre
West Chester, OH 45069
Contact: Amy Barnett Managing Partner
Tel: 513-874-7447
Email: abarnett@kingsgatetrans.com
Website: www.kingsgatetrans.com
Freight services: truck, rail, air or ocean. (Woman, estab 1986, empl 21, sales $19,500,000, cert: WBENC)

10092 KLN Logistics dba AIT Worldwide Logistics
6749 Eastland Rd, Ste C
Middleburg Heights, OH 44130
Contact: Kimberly Martinez-Giering Owner
Tel: 440-816-1505
Email: info@klnlogistics.com
Website: www.klnlogistics.com
Air freight, expedited trucking, import, export, logistics. (Minority, Woman, estab 2005, empl 28, sales $427,000,000, cert: State, NMSDC, WBENC)

10093 Marine Services International, Inc.
14508 S Industrial Ave
Cleveland, OH 44137
Contact: Kenton Woodhead President
Tel: 216-587-3500
Email: kenton@marineservicesintl.com
Website: www.marineservicesintl.com
Air, Sea, Land International Freight Transportation (freight forwarder), warehousing, labeling, repackaging, packaging & re-palletizing capabilities. (Minority, Woman, estab 2006, empl 18, sales $5,000,000, cert: State)

TRANSPORTATION SERVICES

10094 Rush Expediting, Inc.
PO Box 2810
Dayton, OH 45401
Contact: Steve Parker President
Tel: 800-989-7874
Email: parkersl@rush-delivery.com
Website: www.rush-delivery.com
Freight transportation services. (Woman, estab 2004, empl 200, sales $36,361,000, cert: WBENC)

10095 T.V. Minority Company, Inc.
30 Lau Pkwy
Clayton, OH 45315
Contact: Sales Mgr
Tel: 313-299-2177
Email: info@tvmtrucking.com
Website: www.tvmtrucking.com
Freight distribution and transportation. (AA, estab 1990, empl 2, sales , cert: NMSDC)

10096 Trio Trucking, Inc.
7750 Reinhold Dr
Cincinnati, OH 45237
Contact: Carvel Simmons President
Tel: 513-679-7100
Email: simmons.ce@onecalldoesall.com
Website: www.trioenterprises.com
Transportation svcs: intermodal & full truckload transportation. (AA, estab 1982, empl 75, sales $18,300,000, cert: State, NMSDC)

Oklahoma

10097 3Li, LLC
470550 East 810 Rd
Stillwell, OK 74960
Contact: Michael Doublehead President
Tel: 918-905-0047
Email: mike@3lillc.com
Website: www.3lillc.com
Transportation svcs: air freight, ocean freight, emergency, next day, 2nd day, deferred. (Nat-Ame, estab 2003, empl 4, sales $7,402,400, cert: NMSDC)

10098 STI Trucking LLC
PO Box 700
Kiefer, OK 74041
Contact: Sam Mookerjee Accountant
Tel: 918-446-6181
Email: twyla.johnson@stonetrucking.com
Website: www.stonetrucking.com
Premier legal flatbed, oversize & heavy haul carrier servicing the US, Canada & Mexico. Hot shot trucks, tankers, pole trucks, slick backs, RGN's. (AA, estab 1945, empl 200, sales , cert: NMSDC)

Oregon

10099 Alliance Trucking Inc.
1209 Stowe Ave
Medford, OR 97501
Contact: Jordan Kell Acct Exec
Tel: 541-734-4844
Email: jkell@alliancetrucking.com
Website: www.alliancetrucking.com
Asset-based trucking, haul truckload & LTL shipments via vans, flatbeds, step decks & multi-axle heavy haul trailers, 48 states, Canada & Mexico. (Woman, estab 1996, empl 20, sales $9,726,975, cert: State)

10100 Lile International Companies
8060 SW Pfaffle St, Ste 200
Tigard, OR 97223
Contact: Diane DeAutremont President
Tel: 503-726-4800
Email: diane.deautremont@lile.com
Website: www.lile.com
National & international transportation svcs, warehousing, distribution & logistics. (Woman, estab 1959, empl 275, sales , cert: WBENC)

10101 Mulino Trading, LLC
16570 SE McLoughlin Blvd
Oak Grove, OR 97267
Contact: Mike Theis Agent
Tel: 503-786-8000
Email: info@mulinotrading.com
Website: www.mulinotrading.com
Freight truck transportation, broker forwarding. (Hisp, estab 2012, empl 6, sales , cert: State)

Pennsylvania

10102 Advanced Shipping Technologies
526 W Ogle St
Ebensburg, PA 15931
Contact: Emily Steberger Business Dev Dir
Tel: 877-692-0570
Email: diversity@astship.com
Website: www.astship.com
Third party logistics: on-line transportation management system. (Woman, estab 2002, empl 25, sales $28,191,650, cert: WBENC)

10103 Allegheny Valley Transfer Co., Inc.
1512 Lebanon Church Rd
Pittsburgh, PA 15236
Contact: Mary Jessup Owner
Tel: 412-653-1200
Email: alleghenyallied@aol.com
Website: www.pghmover.com
Moving, storage & packing of household & office goods. (Woman, estab 1925, empl 45, sales $1,561,882, cert: State, WBENC)

10104 C.B. Transportation Inc
2452 Horseshoe Trail
Chester Springs, PA 19425
Contact: Carole Borden CEO
Tel: 610-416-4058
Email: clborden@cbtransportation.com
Website: www.cbtransportation.com
Provides truckload, distribution and logistics services. (Woman, estab 1995, empl 11, sales $11,200,000, cert: WBENC)

10105 Horwith Trucks, Inc.
1449 Nor-Bath Blvd.
Northampton, PA 18067
Contact: Regina Grim President
Tel: 610-261-2220
Email: info@horwithfreightliner.com
Website: www.horwithfreightliner.com
Transportation of hazardous and non hazardous waste, deicing salt, wall panels, general freight. (Woman, estab 1968, empl 84, sales , cert: WBENC)

10106 Knichel Logistics
   5347 William Flynn Hwy
   Gibsonia, PA 15044
   Contact: Ashley Caloia Marketing Coord
   Tel: 724-449-3300
   Email: acaloia@knichellogistics.com
   Website: www.knichellogistics.com
Intermodal, drayage & truckload services. (Woman, estab 2003, empl 42, sales $73,000,000, cert: WBENC)

10107 Maroadi Transfer & Storage
   1801 Lincoln Hwy
   North Versailles, PA 15137
   Contact: Mary V. Maroadi President
   Tel: 412-824-4420
   Email: mary@maroadi.com
   Website: www.maroadi.com
Local, interstate & international moving services, office & electronics moving, household goods moving, displays & exhibits. (Woman, estab 1967, empl 45, sales $3,800,000, cert: WBENC)

10108 Parks Moving Systems
   1234 Wrights Ln
   West Chester, PA 19380
   Contact: Relocation Consultant
   Tel: 610-429-4125
   Email:
   Website: www.parksmoving.com
Transportation: local, long distance, storage, record storage, trade show moves, etc. (Woman, estab 1992, empl 20, sales $1,300,000, cert: WBENC)

10109 Shepherd Transport, LLC
   296 Cumberland Rd
   Bedford, PA 15522
   Contact: Sandy Jones CEO
   Tel: 814-623-9346
   Email: sandy@shepherdtransport.com
   Website: www.shepherdtransport.com
Third party Logistics (3PL), non-asset based platform to serve a variety of transportation requirements. (Woman, estab 2008, empl 12, sales $7,682,700, cert: WBENC)

10110 Yourway Transport Inc.
   6681 Snowdrift Rd
   Allentown, PA 18106
   Contact: Frank DiStefano Sr VP Global Sales
   Tel: 442-222-4665
   Email: frank.distefano@yourwaytransport.com
   Website: www.yourway.com
Clinical supply chain management, 24x7 door to door transport, cold chain packaging, distribution, bio sample management, IRT, and a proprietary inventory management system. (As-Ind, estab 1997, empl 75, sales $55,000,000, cert: NMSDC)

Puerto Rico

10111 Allied Logistics Corp.
   PO Box 101
   Guaynabo, PR 00970
   Contact: Alberto Cruz VP
   Tel: 787-622-9393
   Email: alberto@alliedpr.com
   Website: www.alliedpr.com
Logistic services. (Hisp, estab 2001, empl 14, sales , cert: NMSDC)

10112 Nestor Reyes, Inc.
   PO Box 9023474
   San Juan, PR 00902
   Contact: Edmundo Rodriguez President
   Tel: 787-289-6465
   Email: e.rodriguez@nreyes.com
   Website: www.nreyes.com
Foreign freight forwarding. (Hisp, estab 1973, empl 35, sales $7,753,580, cert: NMSDC)

10113 PR Global Logistics JP Corporation
   200 Rafael Cordero Ave, Ste 140
   Caguas, PR 00726
   Contact: Ivelisse Baba-Portalatin VP
   Tel: 787-653-5070
   Email: ivelisse@prgloballogistics.com
   Website: www.prgloballogistics.com
Logistics & distribution operations, packaging, quality control, supply chain technology, and organizational excellence. (Minority, Woman, estab 2007, empl 2, sales , cert: NMSDC)

Rhode Island

10114 Trans-Link LLC
   1249 Oaklawn Ave
   Cranston, RI 02920
   Contact: President
   Tel: 401-463-3862
   Email: Info@Translinkllc.com
   Website: www.translinkllc.com
Transportation & trucking: LTL, truckload, rail & flatbeds, refrigerated & dry freight, 48 states & Canada. (Woman, estab 2000, empl 5, sales $5,600,000, cert: State)

South Carolina

10115 Alpha Logistics Solutions, LLC
   8201 Arrowridge Blvd ste 123
   Charlotte, SC 28273
   Contact: Arthur Cottingham COO
   Tel: 877-356-6102
   Email: arthur@alphals-biz.com
   Website: www.alphals-biz.com/
Less Than Truckload (LTL), Truckload (TL), Domestic Air & Ground Expedited Shipping, International, Intermodal. (Woman/AA, estab 2014, empl 5, sales $350,000, cert: NMSDC)

10116 Atlantic-Pacific Express, Inc.
   1350 Browning Rd, Ste B
   Columbia, SC 29210
   Contact: Irene Brotherton President
   Tel: 877-739-1116
   Email: irene@apexpedite.com
   Website: www.apexpedite.com
Asset based & non-asset based ground & air freight. (Woman, estab , empl 13, sales $28,000,000, cert: WBENC)

10117 Key Logistics Solutions, LLC
   4279A Cross Point Dr.
   Ladson, SC 29456
   Contact: Sylvester Hester President
   Tel: 404-597-1652
   Email: shester@keylogistics.com
   Website: www.keylogistics.com
3rd Party Logistics, Sorting, Kitting, Warehousing, Inventory management,Transportation, Sequencing, and Light assembly. (AA, estab 2003, empl 410, sales $218,796,533, cert: NMSDC)

TRANSPORTATION SERVICES

10118 Kontane Inc.
1000 Charleston Regional Pkwy
Charleston, SC 29492
Contact: Rusty Byrd President
Tel: 843-352-0011
Email: rusty@kontanelogistics.com
Website: www.kontanelogistics.com
Logistics, warehousing & distribution, cross-docking, freight consolidation, import material receipt, line sequencing, parts distribution, development of logistics information systems, sub-assembly & foreign trade zones services. (Woman, estab 1975, empl 100, sales $40,000,000, cert: WBENC)

10119 Logisticus Projects Group
20 W North St
Greenville, SC 29601
Contact: Vikash Patel President
Tel: - -
Email: commercial@logisticusgroup.com
Website: www.logisticusgroup.com
Turnkey Transportation, Barge, Rail, Heavy Haul Truck, Crane & Rigging, Port, Distribution Centers, Warehousing, Field Support, Owners Representatives, GPS Tracking. (As-Pac, estab 2012, empl 25, sales $14,000,000, cert: NMSDC)

10120 Premier Logistics Solutions Warehousing, LLC
904 Commerce Circle
Hanahan, SC 29410
Contact: Stewart Bauknight Dir Sales
Tel: 843-554-7529
Email: bauknights@premier3pl.com
Website: www.premier3pl.com
Provide transportation, transportation brokerage, fulfillment, packaging, just in time deliveries, trans loading of bulk products, rail service with CSX, a container freight station, foreign trade zone. (Woman, estab 2003, empl 100, sales $15,000,000, cert: WBENC)

10121 TPS Logistics
PO Box 9493
Columbia, SC 29229
Contact: Al Stokes VP Sales & Mktg
Tel: 803-622-2970
Email: alstokes@tpslogisticsinc.com
Website: www.tpslogisticsinc.com
Transportation services. (Woman, estab 2004, empl 3, sales $20,000,000, cert: NWBOC)

10122 Warehouse Services, Inc.
58 S Burty Rd
Piedmont, SC 29673
Contact: Michelle Dender Mktg Coord
Tel: 864-422-6079
Email: michelledender@wsi-ismi.com
Website: www.wsionline.com
Warehousing, transportation svcs: distribution, client system integration, domestic & international supply chain (SC) enhancement. (Woman, estab 1985, empl 2000, sales $220,000,000, cert: WBENC)

South Dakota

10123 K & J Trucking, Inc.
1800 East 50th St North
Sioux Falls, SD 57104
Contact: John Kemp Marketing Mgr
Tel: 605-332-5531
Email: jkemp@kandjtrucking.com
Website: www.kandjtrucking.com
Long haul & regional refrigerated transportation services. (Woman, estab 1979, empl 45, sales $21,235,776, cert: WBENC)

Tennessee

10124 Ewing Moving Services
4006 Air Park St
Memphis, TN 38118
Contact: Ashleigh Hayes Natl Acct Coordinator
Tel: 901-774-2197
Email: admin@ewingmovingservice.com
Website: www.ewingmovingservice.com
Moving & storage services. (AA, estab 1980, empl 57, sales $3,047,104, cert: NMSDC)

10125 Infinity Logistics Group, LLC
2115 Chapman Rd
Chattanooga, TN 37421
Contact: Dallas Holder Sales Mgr
Tel: 423-373-2600
Email: Dholder@infinitylogisticsgroup.com
Website: www.infinitylogisticsgroup.com
Transportation, warehousing, storage, logistic services. (As-Ind, estab 2019, empl 18, sales $3,131,559, cert: NMSDC)

10126 Lanigan Worldwide Moving & Warehousing, Inc.
1870 Airways Blvd
Memphis, TN 38114
Contact: Lynn L. Lanigan CEO
Tel: 901-744-7070
Email: llanigan@alliedagent.com
Website: www.laniganmoving.com
Transportation svcs: local, intrastate, interstate & international relocations. (Woman, estab 1955, empl 38, sales $3,600,000, cert: WBENC)

10127 Time Logistics, Inc
1406 Nashville Hwy
Columbia, TN 38401
Contact: Laura Shorette Business Devel Exec
Tel: 866-293-8463
Email: lshorette@timelogisticsinc.com
Website: www.timelogisticsinc.com
Transporation provider that specializes in the managment of pre-printed inserts and direct mail promotions. (Woman, estab 2001, empl 50, sales $12,010,000, cert: WBENC)

10128 Total Control Logistics
1519 Union Ave, Ste 177
Memphis, TN 38104
Contact: Terica Lamb President
Tel: 901-830-1864
Email: tlamb@tclogistix.com
Website: www.tclogistix.com
Third party logistics provider (3PL), Warehousing & Distribution. (Woman/AA, estab 2009, empl 1, sales , cert: NMSDC)

10129 Western Express Inc.
7135 Centennial Place
Nashville, TN 37209
Contact: Hannah Sweeney Detention
Tel: 615-369-8208
Email: hyoung@westernexp.com
Website: www.westernexp.com
Full truck load carrier operates 3800 power units 48 states, Canada & Mexico border cities. (Woman, estab 1991, empl 3600, sales $430,250,000, cert: WBENC)

Texas

10130 A-1 Freeman Relocation
4727 Macro
San Antonio, TX 78218
Contact: Jonathan Hightower Corporate Relocation & Logistics Consultant
Tel: 210-661-1404
Email: jhightower@a-1freeman.com
Website: www.a-1freemanrelo.com
Domestic & international household goods moving & transportation services. (Woman, estab 1994, empl 450, sales $10,000,000, cert: WBENC)

10131 Action Transportation Services, Inc.
PO Box 15711
Houston, TX 77220
Contact: Lucy Bowerman Sales
Tel: 713-673-4817
Email: actiontransport@sbcglobal.net
Website: www.actionfrtservices.com
Transportation services: flatbeds, van, stepdecks, hotshots, power only, local & specialized equipment for partial & full loads, US & Canada, 24 hrs a day 7 days a week. (Woman, estab 1998, empl 3, sales $245,878, cert: State, WBENC)

10132 AIM Over-The-Road
PO Box 259
Katy, TX 77492
Contact: Tabitha Becker Public Relations Coord
Tel: 713-489-8911
Email: tbecker@aimgloballogistics.com
Website: www.aimgloballogistics.com
Provide cost-effective, customized transportation solutions & logistical services. (Woman/Hisp, estab 2009, empl 15, sales $5,619,643, cert: State, NMSDC)

10133 Americorp Xpress Carriers
5201 N Veterans Blvd
Pharr, TX 78577
Contact: Frank Flores President
Tel: 956-283-0052
Email: fflores@axcarriers.com
Website: www.axcarriers.com
Transportation services. (Hisp, estab 2010, empl 250, sales , cert: NMSDC)

10134 Amerimex Air Charter LLC
6420 Polaris, Ste 101
Laredo, TX 78041
Contact: Monica Martinez Managing Partner
Tel: 727-213-0723
Email: ops@amerimex.org
Website: www.AmeriMex.org
Air Charters, Bilingual staff 24/7/365, handling every aspect of your shipment via Air Charter in Mexico, USA, Canada and beyond. (Hisp, estab 2005, empl 10, sales $7,650,000, cert: NMSDC)

10135 A-Rocket Moving & Storage, Inc.
3401 Corder St
Houston, TX 77021
Contact: Lewis Grisby TQM
Tel: 713-748-6024
Email: arocket@arocket.com
Website: www.arocket.com
Relocation services: material handling & warehousing, local, long-distance & international. (AA, estab 1959, empl 120, sales $3,700,000, cert: State, City, NMSDC)

10136 Best Logistics and Freight LLC
3516 Chatham Green Ln
Arlington, TX 76014
Contact: Domonique Chantal Donegan Freight Broker
Tel: 682-208-1193
Email: broker@blnfreight.com
Website: www.blnfreight.com
Freight transportation services. (AA, estab 2020, empl 3, sales , cert: State)

10137 Candor Expedite
1404 Gables Court, Ste 202
Plano, TX 75075
Contact: John Kennedy Sr Business Dev
Tel: 469-661-3360
Email: jkennedy@candorexp.com
Website: www.candorexp.com
Expedite transportation and nationwide hotshot services. (Woman, estab 2017, empl 21, sales $6,000,000, cert: WBENC)

10138 Cargo One Logistics, LLC
5802 Val Verde, Ste 165
Houston, TX 77057
Contact: Diego Alexander President
Tel: 713-290-9922
Email: dalexander@cargo1logistics.com
Website: www.cargo1logistics.com
Transportation services, over the road, full truck load, Mexico, US & Canada. (Hisp, estab 2000, empl 7, sales $4,000,000, cert: NMSDC)

10139 DFW LinQ Transport
2300 Valley View Ste 100
Irving, TX 75062
Contact: Sylvia Dayer Dir Brokerage Div
Tel: 972-522-1500
Email: sdayer@linqtransport.com
Website: www.linqtransport.com
Transportation & logistic services. (Hisp, estab 2005, empl 52, sales $39,400,000, cert: NMSDC)

10140 EP Logistics LLC
9601 Pan American Dr
El Paso, TX 79927
Contact: Ingrid Hurtado Marketing Business Dev Mgr
Tel: 915-881-9100
Email: ingridh@eplogistics.com
Website: www.eplogistics.com
Warehousing, customs brokerage, sorting/rework services, transportation. (Hisp, estab 2005, empl 50, sales $1,200,000, cert: State, NMSDC)

TRANSPORTATION SERVICES

10141 Epsilon Brokerage Corporation
12110 Sara Rd
Laredo, TX 78045
Contact: Rick Laurel President
Tel: 956-728-8713
Email: rick.laurel@epsilonbrokerage.com
Website: www.epsilonbrokerage.com
Logistics, customs broker, freight forwarding, warehousing. (Hisp, estab 2011, empl 50, sales $4,000,000, cert: State, NMSDC)

10142 Expedited Specialized Logistics LLC
801 Pellegrino Court
Laredo, TX 78045
Contact: Armando Correa Commercial Dir
Tel: 956-712-8350
Email: acorrea@es-logistics.net
Website: www.es-logistics.net
USA and International Truck Load Transportation Services. Dryvan Trailers Flatbeds Stepdecks double drop open or curtain trailers. RGN Lowboys. (Hisp, estab 2011, empl 30, sales $7,661,250, cert: NMSDC)

10143 Forza Transportation Services, Inc.
16360 US Hwy 83 N
Laredo, TX 78045
Contact: Eduardo Barba Commercial Dir
Tel: 956-267-6441
Email: eduardobarba@forzatrans.com
Website: www.forzatrans.com
Transportation services, cross border. (Hisp, estab 2014, empl 178, sales $178,320,227, cert: State)

10144 Group of Global Suppliers, LLC
279 Shadow Mountain, Ste 200
El Paso, TX 79912
Contact: Roberto Gonzalez President
Tel: 915-727-2811
Email: sales@ggscorporation.com
Website: www.ggscorporation.com
Logistics, warehousing, inspection, sorting, etc. (Minority, estab 2013, empl 5, sales $1,620,000, cert: State, NMSDC)

10145 Hazel's Hot Shot, Inc.
2009 McKenzie Dr Ste 110
Carrollton, TX 75006
Contact: Dustin Marshall CEO
Tel: 972-620-8812
Email: dustin@hazels.com
Website: www.hazels.com
Expedited freight, 48 contiguous states. (Woman, estab , empl , sales $6,000,000, cert: State, WBENC)

10146 InstiCo Freight Management, Inc.
3011 Gateway Dr. Ste 340
Irving, TX 75063
Contact: Cory Allen Business Dev Exec
Tel: 469-293-9549
Email: callen@insticologistics.com
Website: www.insticologistics.com
International Services- Ocean cargo, Air cargo, and Non-Vessel Operating Common Carrier. (Hisp, estab 2011, empl 25, sales , cert: NMSDC)

10147 Intercon Carriers
19810 FM 1472
Laredo, TX 78045
Contact: Enrique Serna Managing Partner
Tel: 956-725-7275
Email: enrique.serna@intercomlogistics.com
Website: www.interconcarriers.com
Transportation & logistics services in the United States, Canada & Mexico. (Hisp, estab 1996, empl 175, sales , cert: State, NMSDC)

10148 J.O. Alvarez, Inc.
1 Andy Ramos Rd
Laredo, TX 78043
Contact: Tanya Alvarez Marketing Dir
Tel: 956-723-5521
Email: tanyaa@joalvarez.com
Website: www.joalvarez.com
Provides expert customs brokerage, distribution, freight forwarding & global logistics services. (Hisp, estab 1957, empl 70, sales $10,000,000, cert: NMSDC)

10149 Kaliber Choice, LLC
12705 S Kirkwood Rd, Ste 213
Stafford, TX 77477
Contact: Valesco Raymond President
Tel: 512-774-5838
Email: vraymond@nxglogistics.com
Website: www.nxglogistics.com
Freight brokerage: LTL (Less-Than-Truckload), Full Truckload (FTL), Airfreight, Ocean Container (20/40ft) Drayage package ecommerce shipping (Fedex, UPS, DHL). (AA, estab 2016, empl 9, sales $997,898, cert: NMSDC)

10150 Logisti-K USA, LLC
13151 S Unitec
Laredo, TX 78045
Contact: Cesar Roberto Flores Dir of Inland Forwarding
Tel: 956-723-7606
Email: cflores@logisti-k.com.mx
Website: www.logisti-k.com.mx
Truckload, Flatbed, Refrigerated & Intermodal services. (Hisp, estab 2005, empl 30, sales $1,225,062, cert: State, NMSDC)

10151 Mac Converting, Inc.
10901 Pellicano Dr
El Paso, TX 79935
Contact: Gerardo Vasquez President
Tel: 915-633-8622
Email: jerry@macconverting.com
Website: www.macconverting.com
Warehousing, Inventory Maintainance & Distribution. (Hisp, estab 0, empl , sales $1,000,000, cert: NMSDC)

10152 MagRabbit, Inc.,
1464 E. Whitestone Blvd Ste 1001
Cedar Park, TX 78613
Contact: Tommy Hodinh President
Tel: 512-993-5730
Email: tommy.hodinh@magrabbit.com
Website: www.magrabbit.com
Global supply chain solutions, air, surface & ocean tranportation. (As-Pac, estab 1990, empl 1001, sales , cert: State, NMSDC)

TRANSPORTATION SERVICES

10153 MagRabbit-Alamo Iron Works, LLC
PO Box 2341
San Antonio, TX 78298
Contact: Wayne Dennis Diversity Coord
Tel: 210-704-8520
Email: wdennis@aiwnet.com
Website: www.magrabbit-aiw.com
Dist industrial supplies, steel service & fabrication, hand & power tools, equipment repair & installation, logistics, transportation & freight forwarding. (As-Pac, estab 2004, empl 150, sales , cert: NMSDC)

10154 Moore Transport of Tulsa LLC
661 N Plano Rd Ste 319
Richardson, TX 75081
Contact: Gary Moore Owner
Tel: 972-578-0606
Email: danchase@mooretransport.com
Website: www.mooretransport.com
Freight transportation. (AA, estab 2005, empl 300, sales $63,000,000, cert: NMSDC)

10155 Multi-Trans, Inc.
606 Grand Central Blvd.
Laredo, TX 78045
Contact: Emilio Villarreal New Projects
Tel: 210-418-4889
Email: evillarreal@multitransinc.com
Website: www.multitransinc.com
Air, Sea & Land Transportation service, LTL, TL & Sea Containers, Flat Beds, Lowboys, Drop Decks & Heavy Equipment Hauling, Air Charters. (Minority, Woman, estab 2000, empl 8, sales $10,000,000, cert: State)

10156 Munoz Trucking, Inc.
12460 Weaver Rd
El Paso, TX 79928
Contact: Marvin Arellano Dir of Sales
Tel: 915-852-7722
Email: marvin@munoztruckinginc.com
Website: www.munoztrucking1@verizon.net
Over the Road Transportation Services, 300 plus dry vans , 5 reefers, 150+ Units, drop trailer, long haul, 48 states. (Hisp, estab 1994, empl 175, sales $25,000,000, cert: NMSDC)

10157 Mustang Express Ltd.
11436 Rojas Dr, Ste B-10
El Paso, TX 79936
Contact: Josh Hernandez Dir Operations
Tel: 915-598-2600
Email: jhernandez@mustangexpress.net
Website: www.mustangexpress.net
Freight transportation. (Minority, estab 2001, empl 15, sales , cert: NMSDC)

10158 MW Logistics, LLC
12770 Coit Road, Ste 1040
Dallas, TX 75251
Contact: Brian Thompson Sr Dir
Tel: 214-393-8211
Email: bthompson@mwlogistics.com
Website: www.mwlogistics.com
Transportation & logistics: over the road, intermodal & bulk. (AA, estab 2001, empl 17, sales $16,800,000, cert: NMSDC)

10159 Navigator Express
14587 Kelmscot Dr
Frisco, TX 75035
Contact: Furqan Khan VP Operations
Tel: 972-330-2340
Email: ops@navex.us
Website: www.navex.us
Authorized motor carrier, interstate transportation of commodities to all 48 contiguous states. (As-Ind, estab 2009, empl 15, sales , cert: State)

10160 Nobis Logistics LLC
1100 E Campbell Rd Ste 247
Richardson, TX 75081
Contact: Bonnie MacEslin Owner
Tel: 214-446-2400
Email: bonnie.maceslin@gonobis.com
Website: www.gonobis.com
Transportation management, manufacturing, distribution, supply chain, executive management & logistics. (Woman, estab , empl , sales $3,000,000, cert: WBENC)

10161 Pan American Express, Inc.
4848 Riverside Dr
Laredo, TX 78041
Contact: Ric Guardado CEO
Tel: 214-762-9912
Email: ric@panamex-zero.com
Website: www.panamex-zero.com
International transportation svcs; 48 states, Mexico & Canada. (Hisp, estab 1988, empl 185, sales $43,000,000, cert: NMSDC)

10162 Perimeter Global Logistics (PGL)
2800 Story Rd W Ste 100
Irving, TX 75038
Contact: Tammy Williams Global Sales Exec
Tel: 214-914-2654
Email: tammy.williams@shippgl.com
Website: www.shippgl.com
Freight forwarding, contract logistics, transportation and distribution management. (Woman, estab 2007, empl 140, sales $120,000,000, cert: WBENC)

10163 Pronto Delivery, Courier, and Logistics, LLC
7420 S Cooper St
Arlington, TX 76001
Contact: Matthew Hince Mgr
Tel: 817-261-0035
Email: matt.hince@pronto-delivery.com
Website: www.pronto-delivery.com
Hot Shot delivery, Route delivery, Scheduled delivery, pick-up truck, cargo van, pipe rack truck, box truck, flatbed, tractor trailer. (Woman, estab 1984, empl 85, sales $13,000,000, cert: WBENC)

10164 Purpose Transportation, LLC
701 Hanover Dr
Grand Prairie, TX 75053
Contact: Greg Crawford VP Sales
Tel: 972-746-4585
Email: chuck@purposetransportation.com
Website: www.purposetransportation.com
Domestic transportation, freight & logistics services. (Woman, estab 2011, empl 10, sales $4,874,185, cert: State, WBENC)

TRANSPORTATION SERVICES

10165 Royal Freight, LP
407 W Sioux Rd
Pharr, TX 78577
Contact: Mike Kelley Sales Mgr
Tel: 956-283-2200
Email: mikek@royalfreight.net
Website: www.royalfreight.net
Direct, Truckload, Asset Based Carrier, serving U.S.(48), Canada, and Mexico, Satelitte equipped (tractors and trailers). (Woman, estab 2001, empl 350, sales , cert: State)

10166 Russell Transport Inc.
12365 Pine Springs
El Paso, TX 79928
Contact: Rosa Marin President
Tel: 915-542-1495
Email: rmarin@russelltransport.com
Website: www.russelltransport.com
Full TL & logistics. (Minority, Woman, estab 1992, empl 300, sales $27,000,000, cert: State, NMSDC)

10167 Shire Express Transportation
6651 Watauga Rd, Ste 48803
Fort Worth, TX 76148
Contact: Brenda Jackson Logistics Coord
Tel: 214-243-5872
Email: brenda.jackson@landstarmail.com
Website: www.shireexpressgov.com/
Transportation & logistic services across the United States and Canada. (AA, estab 2015, empl 7, sales , cert: State)

10168 Siam Logistics
2320 Dean Way Ste 160
Southlake, TX 76092
Contact: Sarah Baldwin Acct Mgr
Tel: 734-619-8576
Email: sarah.baldwin@siam-logistics.com
Website: www.siam-logistics.com
Transportation, oversized loads, specialized equipment & special weight requirements, US, Mexico & Canada. (Minority, Woman, estab 2009, empl 13, sales $1,920,000, cert: NMSDC, WBENC)

10169 Southwest Freight Lines
PO Box 371736
El Paso, TX 79936
Contact: Jesus Lares Operations Mgr
Tel: 915-860-8592
Email: jesus.lares@swflines.com
Website: www.swflines.com
Truckload services, 48 states & Mexico. (Hisp, estab 1988, empl 300, sales $50,000,000, cert: State)

10170 Spirit Truck Lines
200 W Nolana
San Juan, TX 78589
Contact: Steve Garza VP Ops & Sales
Tel: 956-781-7715
Email: sgarza@spirittrucklines.com
Website: www.spirittrucklines.com
Dedicated carrier service, bonded shipmment, expedited loads, cargo tracking. (Hisp, estab 1990, empl 300, sales $30,000,000, cert: NMSDC)

10171 Sun City Group Inc
1009 Myrtle Ave Ste 100 A
El Paso, TX 79901
Contact: Patrick Warrington Dir of Sales
Tel: 915-593-5900
Email: pwarrington@suncitygroup.com
Website: www.suncitygroup.com
Multimodal transportation services, over the road, intermodal, sea & air. (Hisp, estab 2006, empl 21, sales $15,000,000, cert: NMSDC)

10172 Sunrise Delivery Inc.
2020 Lawrence St
Houston, TX 77008
Contact: Lanette Martinez President
Tel: 713-864-2020
Email: lm@sditex.com
Website: www.sunrisedeliveryinc.com
LTL freight, warehousing & logistics. (Minority, Woman, estab 1981, empl 15, sales $799,616, cert: City, NMSDC, CPUC, WBENC)

10173 Swift Logistics, Inc.
1809 Stoney Brook Dr Ste 204
Houston, TX 77063
Contact: Rosemarie Patterson Logistics Consultant
Tel: 713-425-4175
Email: rpatterson@swiftlogisticsinc.com
Website: www.swiftlogisticsinc.com
Freight brokerage. (Woman, estab 2014, empl 4, sales , cert: WBENC)

10174 TBM Carriers
4241 E. Piedras, Ste. 200
San Antonio, TX 78228
Contact: Gerardo Villarreal Natl Accts mgr
Tel: 830-775-8283
Email: gerardo@tbmcarriers.com
Website: www.tbmcarriers.com
Provide competitive and unique logistics solutionS. (Hisp, estab 1999, empl 250, sales $45,000,001, cert: State, NMSDC)

10175 Texas Freight
1207 NE Big Bend Trail, Ste L
Glen Rose, TX 76043
Contact: Preston Shuffield Broker
Tel: 254-898-1117
Email: preston@texasfreight.net
Website: www.texasfreight.net
Commercial motor carrier, brokerage authority serving 48 states, flatbeds, drop decks, RGN's, lowboys, and dry vans. (Woman, estab 2002, empl 8, sales , cert: NWBOC)

10176 Teyrachi Logistics LLC
2717 Commercial Center Blvd Ste E200
Katy, TX 77494
Contact: Tierra Daniels
Tel: 346-205-3995
Email: info@teyrachillc.com
Website: www.teyrachillc.com
General freight services. (AA, estab 2021, empl 4, sales $500,000, cert: City)

10177 Trans-Expedite Inc
7 Founders Blvd Ste 100
El Paso, TX 79906
Contact: Claudia Fuentes CEO
Tel: 915-205-5500
Email: diversity@trans-expedite.com
Website: www.trans-expedite.com
Transportation & logistics: air charters, warehousing, customs brokerage. (Minority, Woman, estab 2001, empl 11, sales $30,000,000, cert: NMSDC, WBENC)

10178 Transmaquila, Inc.
1385 Cheers Blvd
Brownsville, TX 78521
Contact: Alejandra Torres HR Asst
Tel: 956-831-0128
Email: alejandra.torres@transmaquila.com
Website: www.transmaquila.com
Cargo transportation throughout Mexico, the United States and Canada. (Hisp, estab 2002, empl 32, sales , cert: NMSDC)

10179 Tri Star Freight System Inc.
5407 Mesa Dr
Houston, TX 77028
Contact: Shana Whittington Administrative Asst
Tel: 713-631-1095
Email: shanaw@tristarfreightsys.com
Website: www.tristarfreightsys.com
Linehaul, FTL & LTL, airport pick up & delivery, drayage, local & OTR container drayage, warehousing. (Woman, estab 1987, empl 89, sales $32,634,980, cert: NWBOC)

10180 Twenty-Two Global Transport, LP
PO Box 62588
Houston, TX 77205
Contact: Kevin Smoot Reg Mgr
Tel: 901-362-3707
Email: ksmoot@22global.com
Website: www.xxiiglobal.com
International ocean freight forwarding, customs brokerage, hot shot/expedited services, logistics services, global information services. (AA, estab 2007, empl 4, sales $200,000, cert: NMSDC)

10181 Verde Logistics, LLC
9525 Escobar Dr
El Paso, TX 79907
Contact: Holly Webb Business Devel
Tel: 915-791-4034
Email: holly.jones@verdelogistics.com
Website: www.verdelogisticsllc.com/home
Third party transportation, full truck load van, reefer, flat bed & heavy haul. (Minority, Woman, estab 2010, empl 6, sales $20,000,000, cert: NMSDC, WBENC)

Virginia

10182 Accurate Courier Express
1711 Ellen Rd
Richmond, VA 23230
Contact: Dwight Hicks CEO
Tel: 804-354-8880
Email: dhicks@accuratecourierexpress.com
Website: www.accuratecourierexpress.com
Transportation and delivery services. (AA, estab 1990, empl 80, sales $15,000,000, cert: State)

10183 High Plains Logistics Consulting, LLC
PO Box 8
Highland Springs, VA 23057
Contact: Burt Epps VP
Tel: 804-437-0066
Email: HGPSlogistics@gmail.com
Website: www.highplainslogistics.com
Transprotation brokerage & third party logistics. (Nat Ame, estab 2002, empl 3, sales $8,200,000, cert: NMSDC)

10184 Hough Transport Express LLC
PO Box 38411
Richmond, VA 23231
Contact: Timothy Hough President
Tel: 804-241-7026
Email: hought@comcast.net
Website: www.houghtransport.com
Transportation: general freight, dry van & flat bed, dump trucks. (AA, estab 2002, empl 3, sales $155,000, cert: State)

10185 LAS Logistical Services LLC
3031 N Lakebridge Dr
Norfolk, VA 23324
Contact: Sam Kearson CEO
Tel: 855-232-5866
Email: samkearson@laslogistical.com
Website: www.laslogistical.com
Logistic services: land, air & sea. (AA, estab 2012, empl 10, sales , cert: State)

10186 TH Logistics,LLC
2150 Magnolia St
Richmond, VA 23223
Contact: Devon Henry President
Tel: 888-929-7323
Email: dhenry@thlogistics.net
Website: www.thlogistics.net
Third party logistics & supply chain services, value added warehousing distribution, contract packaging, product acquisition, transload & transportation. (AA, estab 2016, empl 200, sales $50,000,000, cert: NMSDC)

Washington

10187 Radiant Logistics Partners, LLC
405 114th Ave SE, 3rd Fl
Bellevue, WA 98004
Contact: Bohn Crain Managing Member
Tel: 425-462-1094
Email: mbe@radiantdelivers.com
Website: www.radiantdelivers.com
Domestic and international transportation and logistics services. (Nat Ame, estab 2006, empl 20, sales $102,000,000, cert: NMSDC)

10188 Red Arrow Logistics
150 120th Ave NE, Ste F110
Bellevue, WA 98005
Contact: Liz Lasater CEO
Tel: 425-747-7914
Email: ashley.moise@redarrowlogistics.com
Website: www.redarrowlogistics.com
Warehousing & distribution services, vendor compliance programs, ground, sea & air transportation. (Woman, estab 2003, empl 8, sales $6,747,398, cert: WBENC)

TRANSPORTATION SERVICES

10189 Vetrans LLC
1420 Meridian E Ste 2
Milton, WA 98354
Contact: Vincent W. Santiago Owner
Tel: 253-833-4688
Email: vince@go-vetrans.com
Website: www.go-VETrans.com
Transportation, railroad transloading, other transportation brokerage services. (Hisp, estab 2006, empl 3, sales $3,967,124, cert: NMSDC)

Wisconsin

10190 Black River Truck Brokers, LLC
N613 Colonial Ave
Pittsville, WI 54466
Contact: Heather Jacobson Owner
Tel: 800-241-2785
Email: heather.brtb@yahoo.com
Website: www.blackrivertruckbroker.com
Transportation & Logistics Services. (Woman, estab 2007, empl 2, sales $4,800,000, cert: State, WBENC)

10191 D & G Express Service, Ltd.
9434 North 107th St
Milwaukee, WI 53224
Contact: Duane Crowley President
Tel: 262-395-4264
Email: duane@dgexpress.net
Website: www.dandgexpress.com
Haul dry goods & refrigerated freight. (Woman/AA, estab 1990, empl 42, sales $5,768,024, cert: State, NMSDC, 8(a))

10192 KM Logistics LLC
4375 S Kansas Ave
Saint Francis, WI 53235
Contact: Muny Chen Sales
Tel: 414-856-0020
Email: mchen@SHIPKML.com
Website: www.shipkml.com
Nationwide direct/exclusive transporation services. (Minority, Woman, estab 2008, empl 15, sales $2,500,000, cert: State)

10193 Merchants Delivery Moving & Storage Co.
1215 State St
Racine, WI 53404
Contact: Jennifer Eastman President
Tel: 262-631-5680
Email: jeastman@merchants-moving.com
Website: www.merchants-moving.com
Moving services. (Woman, estab 1921, empl 84, sales , cert: WBENC)

10194 Trans International, LLC
N93 W16288 Megal Dr
Menomonee Falls, WI 53051
Contact: Denise Lawien CSMO
Tel: 262-253-3500
Email: sales@ticominc.com
Website: www.ticominc.com
Transportation consulting & logistics services: freight pre-audit & payment, post audit, transportation reporting software & tools, freight rating & routing, carrier contract negotiations & general logistics consulting. (Woman, estab 1975, empl 115, sales $5,790,000, cert: State, WBENC)

10195 Veriha Trucking, Inc.
2830 Cleveland Ave
Marinette, WI 54143
Contact: Kyle Cheney Sales Mgr
Tel: 715-330-5921
Email: kcheney@veriha.com
Website: www.veriha.com
Transportation services. (Woman, estab 1978, empl 300, sales $45,000,000, cert: WBENC)

10196 Wisconsin International Services Inc.
5600 S Westridge Dr
New Berlin, WI 53151
Contact: Michael Pflugheoft Dir of Sales
Tel: 262-501-0098
Email: mpflughoeft@wislogistics.com
Website: www.wislogistics.com
Full service logistics solutions. (As-Pac, estab 1996, empl 9, sales $10,000,000, cert: NMSDC)

TRAVEL ARRANGEMENTS
Full service travel agencies with domestic and international capabilities. NAICS Code 48

Arizona

10197 El Sol Travel, Inc.
4500 S. Lakeshore Dr Ste 450
Tempe, AZ 85282
Contact: Christine Davidson VP Business Travel Solutions Strategist
Tel: 480-693-0218
Email: cdavidson@elsoltravel.net
Website: www.elsoltravel.net
Full service travel agency. (Woman, estab 1986, empl 27, sales $213,395,700, cert: WBENC)

California

10198 Incentive Travel Inc.
311 Fourth Ave, Ste 617
San Diego, CA 92101
Contact: Penny Wing President
Tel: 619-515-0880
Email: penny@incentiveinc.com
Website: www.incentiveinc.com
Incentive & meeting planning, consulting, creating, promoting. (Woman, estab 1988, empl 14, sales $5,000,000, cert: WBENC)

10199 Pinnacle Travel Services, LLC
390 N Sepulveda Blvd Ste 3100
El Segundo, CA 90245
Contact: Bob Singh President
Tel: 310-343-4284
Email: ptsbsingh@earthlink.net
Website: www.pinnaclecallsolutions.com
Full service travel agency. (Hisp, estab 1999, empl 150, sales $10,600,000, cert: NMSDC)

Florida

10200 Cruise.Com
255 E Dania Beach Blvd
Dania Beach, FL 33004
Contact: Jessica Speirs Reg Sales Dir
Tel: 954-805-7810
Email: jspeirs@cruise.com
Website: www.cruise.com
Leisure products: cruise, affinity revenue share program. (Woman, estab 2002, empl 200, sales , cert: WBENC)

10201 Landry & Kling, Inc.
1390 S Dixie Hwy
Coral Gables, FL 33146
Contact: Cyndi Murphy VP Corporate Planning
Tel: 305-661-1880
Email: cmurphy@landrykling.com
Website: www.landrykling.com
Full service travel agency. (Woman, estab 1982, empl 24, sales $11,739,216, cert: WBENC)

Georgia

10202 Four Seasons Travel
4060 Johns Creek Pkwy Bldg. D
Suwanee, GA 30024
Contact: Michael Morrison Business Devel
Tel: 770-441-2170
Email: mmorrison@travelleaders.com
Website: www.fscorporatetravel.com
Travel Fulfillment, Consulting & Analytics, and Meetings Management. (Woman, estab 1979, empl 30, sales $35,000,000, cert: WBENC)

10203 Georgia International Travel, Inc.
6285 Barfield Rd Ste 150
Atlanta, GA 30328
Contact: Vela McClam Mitchell CEO
Tel: 404-851-9166
Email: corporatetravel@dt.com
Website: www.gitravel.com
Corporate travel management. (Woman/AA, estab 1984, empl 24, sales $21,000,000, cert: NMSDC)

10204 Teplis Travel Service
244 Perimeter Center Pkwy, Ste 280
Atlanta, GA 30346
Contact: Van Henderson VP Business Dev
Tel: 404-843-7460
Email: van@teplis.com
Website: www.teplis.com
Full service travel agency. (Woman, estab 1972, empl 45, sales $50,000,000, cert: WBENC)

Illinois

10205 Travelex International, Inc.
2500 W. Higgins Road
Hoffman Estates, IL 60169
Contact: Ursula Pearson President
Tel: 847-882-0400
Email: ursulap@travelexonline.com
Website: www.travelexonline.com
Full service travel agency, travel management. (Woman, estab 1992, empl 12, sales $725,435, cert: State, WBENC)

Kansas

10206 WingGate Travel, Inc.
8645 College Blvd, Ste 100
Overland Park, KS 66210
Contact: Young Sexton CEO
Tel: 913-451-9200
Email: young.sexton@winggatetravel.com
Website: www.winggatetravel.com
Full service travel management, online fulfillment, VIP executive travel & leisure travel services. (Minority, Woman, estab 1991, empl 38, sales $4,000,000, cert: NMSDC)

TRAVEL ARRANGEMENTS

Massachusetts

10207 Atlas Travel & Technology Group, Inc.
One Maple St
Milford, MA 01757
Contact: Kerin McKinnon SVP Global
Tel: 508-488-1160
Email: kerin.mckinnon@atlastravel.com
Website: www.atlastravel.com
Full service travel agency. (Woman, estab 1986, empl 138, sales $179,000,000, cert: WBENC)

Michigan

10208 American Center Travel
2451 W Stadium Blvd
Ann Arbor, MI 48103
Contact: Sue Konarska Owner
Tel: 734-827-1030
Email: sue.act@travelleaders.com
Website: www.travelleaders.com
Full service travel agency. (Woman/As-Ind, estab 1986, empl 4, sales , cert: NMSDC)

10209 Boersma Travel Services
3368 Washtenaw Ave
Ann Arbor, MI 48104
Contact: James Kimble President
Tel: 734-971-3148
Email: jkimble@boersmatravel.com
Website: www.boersmatravel.com
Full svc travel agency. (AA, estab 1945, empl 23, sales $24,000,000, cert: NMSDC)

10210 Departure Travel Management
344 N Old Woodward, Ste 100
Birmingham, MI 48011
Contact: Maria Garcia Reg acct exec
Tel: 210-913-8016
Email: maria@dtmdeparture.com
Website: www.dtmdeparture.com
Full service travel agency. (Woman/AA, estab 1999, empl 21, sales $29,000,000, cert: NMSDC, WBENC)

10211 Global Business Travel, LLC
2100 Coe Court Ste A
Auburn Hills, MI 48326
Contact: Nick Ladney Sales Mgr
Tel: 877-227-8770
Email: globaltravel@myway.com
Website: www.gbtah.com
Full service travel agency. (AA, estab 0, empl 1, sales $4,600,000, cert: NMSDC)

10212 Motor City Travel
29566 Northwestern Hwy Ste 400
Southfield, MI 48034
Contact: Tracey Campbell VP Business Dev
Tel: 248-799-0752
Email: tcampbell@motorcitytravel.com
Website: www.motorcitytravel.com
Full service travel agency. (Woman/AA, estab 0, empl , sales $12,095,618, cert: NMSDC)

10213 Sky Bird Travel & Tours Inc.
26500 Northwestern Hwy Ste 260
Southfield, MI 48076
Contact: Arvin Shah President
Tel: 248-727-1697
Email: info@skybirdtravel.com
Website: www.skybirdtravel.com
Full svc travel agency. (As-Ind, estab 1976, empl 52, sales , cert: NMSDC)

10214 The Travel Exchange
755 W Big Beaver Ste 100
Troy, MI 48084
Contact: Pamela Edwartoski President
Tel: 248-269-9721
Email: pam@travelexchangemi.com
Website: www.travelexchangemi.com
Full service travel agency. (Woman, estab 1976, empl 15, sales , cert: WBENC)

Minnesota

10215 Metro Travel
9298 Central Ave NE, Ste 222
Minneapolis, MN 55434
Contact: Diane Cyrus CEO
Tel: 763-784-0560
Email: dianecyrus@metrotravel.biz
Website: www.metrotravel.biz
Full service travel management. (As-Ind, estab 1982, empl 14, sales $890,000, cert: NMSDC)

North Carolina

10216 Aquila Travel & Events
2 Mill Creek Ct
Greensboro, NC 27407
Contact: Yolande Wainwright President
Tel: 336-580-9796
Email: aquila@triad.rr.com
Website: www.eventsbyaquila.com
Corporate event & travel services. (Woman/AA, estab 2008, empl 1, sales , cert: State)

New York

10217 Global Network Tours, Inc.
1 West 34 St Ste 1203
New York, NY 10001
Contact: Farida Garda President
Tel: 212-695-1647
Email: fgarda@air-supply.com
Website: www.air-supply.com/
Corporate travel agency. (Woman/As-Ind, estab 1993, empl 4, sales $2,750,000, cert: WBENC)

TRAVEL ARRANGEMENTS

10218 Van Zile Travel
3540 Winton Place
Rochester, NY 14623
Contact: Rebecca Mineo VP
Tel: 585-244-1100
Email: katie@vanzile.com
Website: www.vanzile.com
Full service travel agency. (Woman, estab , empl 45, sales $35,000,000, cert: WBENC)

Ohio

10219 ATG
7775 Walton Pkwy Ste 100
New Albany, OH 43054
Contact: Paula Aquizap Sr Proposal Admin
Tel: 614-901-4100
Email: paquizap@atg.travel
Website: www.atgtravel.com
Full service travel agency. (Woman, estab 1995, empl 3000, sales $593,580,200, cert: WBENC)

10220 Uniglobe Travel Designers
480 S Third St
Columbus, OH 43215
Contact: Elizabeth Blount McCormick President
Tel: 614-237-4488
Email: elizabethb@uniglobetd.com
Website: www.uniglobetraveldesigners.com
Full service travel agency. (Woman/AA, estab , empl , sales $22,500,000, cert: NMSDC, WBENC)

Tennessee

10221 World Ventures Tours and Travel Inc.
6601 Kingston Pike
Knoxville, TN 37919
Contact: Constantine Christodoulou President
Tel: 865-588-7426
Email: cdc@wvtt.com
Website: www.wvtt.com
Travel and meeting management, airline reservarions, car rental reservations, hotel reservations, travel insurance, domestic travel, international travel. (Woman, estab 1977, empl 20, sales $8,000,000, cert: WBENC)

Texas

10222 The Alamo Travel Group LP
8930 Wurzbach Rd Ste 100
San Antonio, TX 78240
Contact: Patricia Pliego Stout President
Tel: 210-593-0084
Email: pstout@alamotravel.com
Website: www.alamotravel.com
Full service travel agency. (Minority, Woman, estab 1990, empl 11, sales $111,000,000, cert: State, NMSDC, WBENC)

10223 The Travel Group LLC
5930 Royal Lane Ste E277
Dallas, TX 75230
Contact: Greg Corley COO/CFO
Tel: 800-514-9132
Email: info@thetravelgroup.travel
Website: www.thetravelgroup.travel
Full service travel agency. (Minority, Woman, estab 1986, empl 55, sales $15,000,000, cert: WBENC)

10224 Travel Acquisition Group, Ltd.
5700 W Plano Pkwy Ste 1400
Plano, TX 75093
Contact: Exec VP
Tel: 972-422-4000
Email: info@artatravel.com
Website: www.artatravel.com
Corporate travel, management & consulting. (Woman, estab 1980, empl 21, sales $30,500,000, cert: State, WBENC)

Virginia

10225 Omega World Travel
3102 Omega Office Park
Fairfax, VA 22031
Contact: Jackie Olt Marketing & PR Specialist
Tel: 703-359-0200
Email: jolt@owt.net
Website: www.OmegaTravel.com
Full service travel agency. Meeting Planning & Strategic Meetings Management Services. (Minority, Woman, estab 1972, empl 475, sales $1,400,000,000, cert: WBENC)

Wisconsin

10226 JCCOB Smith Gardner Smith/Keystone AMEX Tvl Svs
16735 W Greenfield Ave
New Berlin, WI 53151
Contact: Art Smith President
Tel: 262-782-8750
Email: artkeystone@yahoo.com
Website: www.travelbykeystone.com
Full service travel agency. (AA, estab 1990, empl 12, sales $705,000, cert: NMSDC)

> **WOOD PRODUCTS**
> Produce videos (in studio or remote), TV shows, records, sound recordings, pre and post production services, talent arrangers, video distribution. NAICS Code 51

Alabama

10227 Containers Plus, Inc.
3068 Alabama Hwy 53
Huntsville, AL 35806
Contact: Ajesh Khanijow Business Devel
Tel: 256-746-8002
Email: akhanijow@containersplususa.com
Website: www.containersplususa.com
Wooden crates, pallets, cardboard boxes, heat shrink, milspec packaging, packaging, RFID, UID, Mil-std-129, mil-std-2073, warehousing, logistics, hazmat packaging. (As-Pac, estab 2014, empl 5, sales $180,000, cert: NMSDC)

California

10228 Commercial Lumber & Pallet Company, Inc.
135 Long Ln
City of Industry, CA 91746
Contact: Kathleen Dietrich VP
Tel: 626-968-0631
Email: kathy@clcpallets.com
Website: www.clcpallets.com
Mfr & dist wooden pallets, skids & boxes. (Hisp, estab 1941, empl 100, sales $35,000,000, cert: CPUC)

10229 Cutter Lumber Products
10 Rickenbacker Cir
Livermore, CA 94550
Contact: Todd Samuels General Mgr
Tel: 925-443-5959
Email: todd@cutterlumber.com
Website: www.cutterlumber.com/
Mfr wooden pallets, wooden boxes. (As-Pac, estab 1965, empl 85, sales , cert: NMSDC, CPUC)

10230 Pallet Recovery Service Inc.
PO Box 35
Westley, CA 95387
Contact: Lisa Kilcoyne President
Tel: 209-839-1224
Email: lisa@palletrecoveryservice.com
Website: www.palletrecoveryservice.com
Mfr new pallets, dist repairable pallets, remove unwanted scrap pallets. (Woman, estab 2007, empl 14, sales $596,456, cert: WBENC)

10231 TransPak
520 N. Marburg Way
San Jose, CA 95133
Contact: Sharon Spina Strategic Accounts Mgr
Tel: 408-590-6543
Email: sharon.spina@transpak.com
Website: www.transpak.com
Mfr wood crates & crating systems, custom packaging solutions, logistics, transportation & rigging services. (Woman, estab 1952, empl 800, sales $120,000,000, cert: WBENC)

10232 Winship Stake and Lath
PO Box 909
Riverside, CA 92502
Contact: Lisa Winship Hankin President
Tel: 951-682-8761
Email: lisa@winshipstakeandlath.com
Website: www.winshipstakeandlath.com
Mfr & dist wood stakes & lath used in building, surveying & landscaping. (Woman, estab 1972, empl 8, sales $400,000, cert: CPUC)

Colorado

10233 Pro Pallet, Inc.
920 E Collins
Eaton, CO 80615
Contact: Jean Kyne President
Tel: 970-353-5311
Email: propallet@qwestoffice.net
Website: www.propallet.net
New, recycled & new/recycled pallets, crates & boxes. (Woman, estab 1988, empl 45, sales $8,258,291, cert: WBENC)

Florida

10234 Pallet Consultants Corporation
951 SW 12th Ave
Pompano Beach, FL 33069
Contact: Brian Groene President
Tel: 954-946-2212
Email: brian.groene@palletconsultants.com
Website: www.palletconsultants.com
Recycle wood pallets, mfr new & used pallets. (Hisp, estab 1996, empl 178, sales $45,000,000, cert: NMSDC)

Georgia

10235 A & B Pallets, Inc.
6323 Riverview Rd
Mableton, GA 30126
Contact: Alberto Dominguez President
Tel: 404-691-0567
Email: aandbpalletsinc@yahoo.com
Website: www.aandbpalletsinc.com
Recycled, new & remanufactured pallets. (Hisp, estab 1997, empl 15, sales , cert: NMSDC)

10236 First Nations Pallet Solutions
4237 Garretts Chapel Rd
Chickamauga, GA 30707
Contact: Alison Meyer
Tel: 800-810-7109
Email: ameyer@firstnationspalletsolutions.com
Website: www.firstnationspalletsolutions.com
Pallet management and supply chain agility. (Nat-Ame, estab 2022, empl 4, sales $1,012,000, cert: NMSDC)

10237 Pallet Central Enterprises, Inc.
2B Lenox Pointe
Atlanta, GA 30324
Contact: Jameson Humber Assistant Sales Mgr
Tel: 404-671-3494
Email: jhumber@palletcentralent.com
Website: www.palletcentralent.com
Pallets. (Minority, Woman, estab 2005, empl 25, sales $26,000,000, cert: WBENC)

Illinois

10238 Harvey Pallets Inc.
2200 W 139th St
Blue Island, IL 60406
Contact: Manuel Tavarez President
Tel: 708-293-1831
Email: manuel@harveypallets.com
Website: www.harveypallet.com
Mfr wood pallets, skids, crates & lumber. (Hisp, estab 1997, empl 50, sales $24,000,000, cert: NMSDC)

10239 Perma Treat of Illinois
PO Box 99
Marion, IL 62959
Contact: Sara Bond CEO
Tel: 618-694-2898
Email: sara@permatreatlumber.com
Website: www.permatreatlumber.com
Wood Treated products: Utility Poles, Railroad Ties, Pallets, Wood Quality Control Inspection, Rail Spur on site can ship via rail or truck. (Woman, estab 1982, empl 7, sales $330,866, cert: State, WBENC)

10240 Phoenix Woodworking Corporation
PO Box 459
Woodstock, IL 60098
Contact: Sandra Pierce President
Tel: 815-338-9338
Email: spierce@phoenixwoodworking.com
Website: www.phoenixwoodworking.com
Custom & commercial cabinetry & casework, reception centers, filing cabinets, wooden lockers & millwork, custom desks & wooden store fixtures. (Woman, estab 1996, empl 10, sales , cert: State, WBENC)

Massachusetts

10241 Native Lumber LLC dba Paper City Bat Company
653 Northampton St
Holyoke, MA 01040
Contact: Kipngetich Rutto Owner
Tel: 413-265-0920
Email: Kip@nativelumberllc.com
Website: www.papercitybatco.com
Farm-to-Table Manufacturer of Custom Baseball Bats. Log-to-Bat, we process the Highest Quality Lumber Species: Ash, Birch and Hard Maple- The Best, tested and approved Wood. (AA, estab 2016, empl 2, sales , cert: State)

Maryland

10242 Timber Industries, LLC
PO Box 6879
Towson, MD 21285
Contact: Danielle Sutphen Sales & Mktg Coord
Tel: 410-823-8300
Email: danielle.sutphen@timberindustries.com
Website: www.timberindustries.com
Custom & standard pallets, skids & crates. (Woman, estab 2013, empl 6, sales $2,500,000, cert: State, WBENC)

Michigan

10243 J&G Pallets and Trucking, Inc.
2971 Bellevue
Detroit, MI 48207
Contact: Les Lance Business Mgr
Tel: 313-921-0222
Email: llance@jgpalletsandtrucking.com
Website: www.jgpalletsandtrucking.com
Wood pallets, design custom pallets, recycle/reuse wood pallets & wood pallet materials. (Woman/AA, estab 1992, empl 22, sales $1,625,000, cert: NMSDC)

Minnesota

10244 R and L Woodcraft, Inc
823 Industrial Park Dr SE
Lonsdale, MN 55046
Contact: Randall Rivers Business Devel
Tel: 507-744-2318
Email: randall@randlwoodcraft.com
Website: www.randlwoodcraft.com
Mfr commercial millwork & casework: cabinets, countertops, workstations, service counters, point of service counters, tables, booths, upholstered seating, running trim, trash recepticles, lockers & toilet partitions. (Woman, estab 1986, empl 22, sales $3,600,000, cert: WBENC)

North Carolina

10245 The Pallet Alliance
200 N Greensboro St Ste D-8
Carrboro, NC 27510
Contact: Joe Movic Program Specialist
Tel: 919-442-1400
Email: joe@tpai.com
Website: www.tpai.com
Design & implement national pallet management programs. (Woman, estab 1995, empl 16, sales $50,000,000, cert: WBENC)

New Jersey

10246 Bett-A-Way Pallet Systems
110 Sylvania Pl
South Plainfield, NJ 07080
Contact: Laura Vaccaro VP Business Dev
Tel: 800-795-7255
Email: laura.vaccaro@bettaway.com
Website: www.bettaway.com
Pallet management: sales, repairs, retrievals & inventory management. (Woman, estab 1996, empl 15, sales $20,986,000, cert: WBENC)

New York

10247 Ongweoweh Corp
5 Barr Road
Ithaca, NY 14850
Contact: Brett Bucktooth Supplier Diversity Mgr
Tel: 607-266-7070
Email: supplierdiversity@ongweoweh.com
Website: www.ongweoweh.com
Mfr & dist wooden pallets & specialty containers. (Nat Ame, estab 1978, empl 96, sales $252,000,000, cert: NMSDC)

Ohio

10248 LEFCO Worthington, LLC
18451 Euclid Ave
Cleveland, OH 44112
Contact: Larry Fulton President
Tel: 216-432-4422
Email: larry.fulton@lefcoworthington.com
Website: www.LEFCOWorthington.com
Dist wooden crates, OSB Boxes, custom pallets, sub-assembly & packaging services. (AA, estab 2003, empl 30, sales $3,600,000, cert: State, NMSDC)

10249 Prime WoodCraft
5755 Granger Rd Ste 900
Independence, OH 44131
Contact: Michelle Morere Admin
Tel: 216-588-9053
Email: michelle@primewoodcraft.com
Website: www.primewoodcraft.com
Warehousing, pallets, third party logistics. (As-Ind, estab 1997, empl 300, sales , cert: NMSDC)

10250 The Lima Pallet Company, Inc.
1470 Neubrecht Rd
Lima, OH 45801
Contact: Brian Cunningham VP
Tel: 419-229-5736
Email: bcunningham@limapallet.com
Website: www.limapallet.com
Mfr wood pallets & crates. ISP certified. (Woman, estab 1977, empl 49, sales $3,000,000, cert: WBENC)

10251 Wood Concepts
2401 Train Ave
Cleveland, OH 44113
Contact: Jacquline Even President
Tel: 216-579-0500
Email: jackieeven@att.net
Website: www.woodconceptsinc.com
Mfr & fabricate casework, millwork & cabinetry. (Woman, estab 1983, empl 8, sales $1,025,215, cert: City)

Texas

10252 Apache Products Inc.
PO Box 187
Silsbee, TX 77656
Contact: Brenda Killingsworth President
Tel: 409-385-7021
Email: acmeskid@aol.com
Website: www.pallet-mall.com/apache/
Mfr & dist wooden pallets, skids & crates for shipping & storage. (Woman, estab 1952, empl 90, sales $11,000,000, cert: WBENC)

10253 Austin Lumber Company, Inc.
630 S Washington St
La Grange, TX 78945
Contact: Laura Culin President
Tel: 512-476-5534
Email: info@austinlumbercompany.com
Website: www.austinlumbercompany.com
Construction mill. (Woman, estab 1929, empl 5, sales , cert: State, City)

COMPANY ALPHABETICAL LISTING

1
	INDEX#
1 Industrial Source	2919
1 Point Procurement Solutions, LLC	9766
110 Technology LLC	5908
123GermFree, LLC dba TrackedMobility	2953
17 Machinery, LLC	4193
180 Management Group, LLC	8233
1820 Productions, LLC	9625
1821 Freight, LLC	9969
1Prospect Technologies, LLC	9796
1Source International, LLC	4553
1st Choice Financial Group LLC	5103
1st Choice, LLC	9154
1st Express, Inc.	10077
1st Metropolitan Translation Services, Inc.	1087
1st Needs Medical LLC	6431
1st Team Insurance Agency	6001
1-Stop Translation	1004

2
2 Oceans Promotions, LLC	1550
2 Tier Wholesalers	2030
2.718 Marketing	1088
20/20 Solutions, Inc.	5104
2020 Brand Solutions	1454
21st Century Expo Group, Inc.	1116
22nd Century Solutions Inc	9504
22nd Century Technologies, Inc.	5105
24 Seven Inc.	9311
24/7 Background Checks LLC	7962
24-Hour Medical Staffing Services, LLC	8888
24X7SYSTEMS, Inc.	4554
2iSolutions Inc.	5106
2K Tool LLC	3958, 6822
2nd Spark Consulting LLC	8747
2rbConsulting, Inc.	9528
2V Industries, Inc.	1951

3
3 Birds Marketing, LLC	5061, 8614
3 Bridge Networks LLC	8889
3 Fuerzas Technology Solutions, LLC	4787
3 Points Packaging LLC	7118
314e Corporation	4260
360 IT Professionals, Inc.	4261
360 Virtual Assistance, LLC	8835
365 Machine Inc.	6905
3A Engineering & Validation LLC	3201
3A Press	7257, 7668
3Core Systems, Inc.	4668
3D Leadership Group LLC	8083
3D Machine Company, Inc.	6766
3D Promoplastic, Inc.	1480
3DIF LLC	8283
3i Construction, LLC	2524
3i People, Inc.	4555
3K Technologies LLC	4262
3Li, LLC	10097
3LK Construction, LLC	2393
3rd Degree Screening Inc.	2640
3S Global Business Solutions	4263
3V Signs & Graphics, LLC	7455

4
	INDEX#
4 Banner Inc. (DBA Alchemy Printing)	7597
49er Communications Inc	9638
4Consulting, Inc.	5509
4D Systems	3146
4front Tooling LLC dba 4front Manufacturing	7318
4WardTech Inc.	4264

5
5 Seasons Mechanical	2353
5 Star Consulting Group, LLC.	4843
5 Star Enterprise, Inc.	2123
5th Avenue Digital	7312

6
600 lb Gorillas, Inc.	3629
661 Electric	2926

7
70kft, LLC	8779
71 & Change	8211

8
826 & Co. LLC	2593
82's, LLC	3596
84 Lumber Company	2492
889 Global Solutions	4140, 6476

A
A & A Aero Structures Inc.	6689
A & B Pallets, Inc.	10235
A & M Door, Inc.	2377
A & R Tarpaulins Inc.	9797
A & Z Trucking, Inc.	10067
A Branovan Company, LLC.	1597
A Family Affair Productions, LLC	3642
A M King LLC	3725
A Plus Installs LLC	3801
A&A Custom Automation, Inc.	6806
A&A Industrial Piping	2437
A&A Maintenance Enterprise, Inc.	2207
A&D Quality Construction Company, LLC	2567
A&E Enterprises II	6149
A&L Service Industries, Inc	2265
A&R Janitorial Service, Inc.	2133
A. Ashland Lock Company	1619
A. Blair Enterprises Inc.	9956
A. Bright Idea	1117
A. H. Furnico, Inc.	7357
A. Harold and Associates, LLC	4489
A. Kershaw, PC//Attorneys & Consultants	6187
A. Miller Consulting Services, Inc.	9557
A. Pomerantz & Co. / Pomerantz Acquisition Corp.	3829
A. Reddix & Associates Inc.	8284
A.C. Roman & Associates, Inc.	2671
A.F.C. Industries, Inc.	3810
A.I.M. Technical Consultants, Inc.	9343
A.K. Rose Inc.	1455
A.K.Adams, PLC dba A|Squared Legal Group, PLC	6153
A.M.C. Mechanical, Inc.	2364

COMPANY ALPHABETICAL LISTING

A

Company	INDEX#
A.P.R., Inc. (Alpha Professional Resources)	8890
A.R. Acosta, Ltd. dba Alisa Acosta Business Conslt	5277
A.S.K. Associates, Inc.	8524
A.S.K. Foods Inc.	3697
A+ Letter Service	7598
A-1 Audio Visual, LLC	9584
A1 Cable Solutions, Inc.	2783
A-1 Electric Service Co., Inc.	2927
A-1 Freeman Relocation	10130
A-1 Printing Services	7671
A1 Shredding Inc.	3521
A-1 Supply Company	1971
A-1 Technology Inc.	5286
A-1 Truck and Equipment, Inc.	6577
A1PlusSoft, Inc.	4669
A2 Studios Inc.	1729
A3 Environmental, LLC	3414
A3 Solutions, Inc.	9420
A3B, LLC	7757
A3i, Inc.	8020
AAA Electrical Supply, Inc.	2786
AAA Fire Protection Resources, Inc.	1615
AAA Ventures LLC	1279
AACANN Mechanical, Inc.	5510
AAECON General Contractors, LLC.	2384
Aahs Entertainment, Inc.	1005, 9564
Aarisha Inc.	5672
Aaron's Fabrication, Inc.	6624
Aarthun Enterprises, LLC dba Taste of Scandinavia	3660
AAW Products Inc.	3951
A-B Computer Solutions, Inc.	4802
AB Design, Inc.	1280
Abacus Service Corporation	9170
Abator Information Services, Inc.	5429
Abaxent, LLC	5818
Abba Construction LLC	2446
ABC Cookie Co., Inc.	3691
ABC Eco Solutions LLC	1922
ABC Laser USA, Inc.	6989
ABC Moving & Storage Co., Inc.	10032
ABC Security Service, Inc.	2606
ABCO Products, Inc.	2107
ABE Associates, Inc.	3147
ABEL Building Systems	1640
Abel Personnel, Inc.	9372
Abell Marketing Group, Inc.	1666, 6334
Abercrumbie Group	8721
Abernethy Media Professionals, Inc.	9626
Aberson Narotzky & White	1481
Abform, Inc.	1686
Able Industrial Products, Inc.	4048
Able Sales Company	3705
ABOTTS Consulting Inc.	4265
About Xtreme LLC	4670
ABOUT-Consulting LLC	5430
Above All Personnel dba S.M. Huber Ent., Inc.	9232
Above the Sill	3761
Abraxas Energy Consulting	3049
Absolute Credit LLC	7788
Absolute Employment Solutions, Inc.	8891
Absolute Resource Associates, LLC	3463
Absolute Risk Management Strategies	3109
Absolute Sign, Inc	2928

A

Company	INDEX#
Absolute Supply and Services, LLC	3902
Abtron Associates Corp.	3475
ABZ Creative Partner	8615
AC & DC Power Technologies	2819
AC Flag & Banner, Inc.	1331
AC Gentrol, Inc.	2962
AC Printing LLC	7677
AC4S Technologies	4490
Acadia Lead Management Services Inc.	8722
ACC Construction Corporation	2447
ACC Precision, Inc.	6767
Accede Solutions Inc.	4671
Accel inc.	7235
Accel Lifestyle LLC	6513
Accelerated Business Results an A Fox Corporation	5358
Accelon Inc.	8892
Accendo International, LLC	8242
Accent Group Solutions	1467
Access Consulting	9543
Access Office Products	7081
Access Sciences Corporation	8243
Accolades, Inc.	1363
Accolite Inc.	5511
Accountant In A Minute	7750
Accountants For You Inc.	9274
AccountSight	4266
Accredo Packaging, Inc.	2031
Accretive Technologies, Inc.	4556
Accro-Met, Inc.	6951
AccruePartners, Inc.	9247
ACCU Staffing Services	9275
Accudyn Products Inc.	7427
Accu-Mold, LLC	7369
Accura Analytical Laboratory, Inc.	3408
Accura Services, LLC	9171
Accuracy Machine	4232
Accurate Background	7876
Accurate Box Company	7210
Accurate C&S Services Inc	6019
Accurate Connections Inc.	2773
Accurate Courier Express	10182
Accurate Lubricants & Metalworking Fluids Inc.	1995
Accurate Solutions & Designs, Inc.	3264
AccurReg, Inc.	6371
Accu-Shape Die Cutting, Inc.	6823
AccuSource, Inc.	7877
Accutech Mold & Machine, Inc.	6807, 7358
Accutron Inc.	2737
AccuWrit Inc.	9562
Ace Delivery	5512
Ace Healthy Products LLC	3491
Ace Metal Craft	6596
Ace Technologies, Inc.	4267
Acela Technologies, Inc.	4844
Acento Advertising, Inc.	8329
AceStack LLC	9276
ACF Components & Fasteners, Inc.	3878
A-Check Global	7878
ACHR Incorporated	4152
ACI Solutions Inc.	5673
Acility, LLC	4672
Acloche Staffing	9344
Acme Arts Inc.	8330

COMPANY ALPHABETICAL LISTING

A INDEX#

Company	Index#
ACME Bag Inc Dba The Bulk Bag Company	7096
Acme Global Logistics, Inc.	9975
Acme Press Inc., dba California Lithographers	7456
Acorn Distributors, Inc.	4086
ACP Facilitiy Services	2150
Acquire Med LLC	6531
Acro Service Corporation	4901
ACS Learning Inc.	8212
ACS Solutions	4557
ACT Safe, LLC	3108
Action 9-A, Inc.	4491
Action Bag Company	1381, 7133
Action Calendar & Specialty Co., Inc.	1482
Action Chemical, Inc.	2235
Action Environmental LLC	3341
Action Fire Alarm and Action Automatic Sprinkler	1655
Action Precision Products Inc.	6877
Action Resources	8168
Action Resources, Inc.	3342
Action Service Corporation	2230
Action Staffing Solutions	8964
Action Technology, Inc.	9505
Action Tool & Machine Inc.	6824
Action Transportation Services, Inc.	10131
Active Ergonomics, Inc.	5062
Active Fire Extinguisher Co., Inc.	4130
Active Potential Inc.	6335
ActOne Government Solutions, Inc.	7939
Actualink Designs LLC	1598
Actuan Global LLC	5107
Actuated Medical, Inc.	6491
Acutec Precision Aerospace Inc.	6892
Acutek US	6768
Ad Hoc Communication Resources, LLC	8667
Ad Specs of Delaware,LLC d/b/a Levy Recognition	1340
Ad Specs of Florida, LLC	1341
Adair Visual, Inc.	6514
Adam Graphic Corporation	7541
Adams & Knight, Inc.	8393
Adams Electric Company	2995
AdamsGabbert	9128
Adaptive Manufacturing Solutions	6825
Adaptive Tech Resources Inc.	5108
ADASTAFF, Inc.	9421
ADC LP	6793
Ad-Comm International	9700
Adcotron EMS	2975
Addison Stuart	5513
ADDO, LLC	1187
ADED Logistics a Division of Hearn Industrial Services NA, Inc	9976
Adekoya Business Consulting LLC	7871
Adelfia LLC	7758
Adept Professional Staffing Inc.	8985
Adhesive Systems, Inc.	1952
Adhezion, Inc.	1953
Ad-Image Creative Promotions Co.	1557
Aditi Staffing LLC	9529
AdMed, Inc.	2718
Administrative Controls Management, Inc.	3148
Administrative Resource Options Inc.	8052
Admiral Staffing Inc.	9312
AdNet/AccountNet, Inc.	7777

A INDEX#

Company	Index#
Adonai Spring Water Inc.	3630
Adonius Corp.	5514
Adrea Rubin Marketing Inc.	8671
Adrienne Nicole Productions, LLC	7313, 9604
Adrienne's Classic Creations, LLC	3674
Adroit Resources Inc.	4268
Adroix Corp DBA CodeForce 360	4558
Adsource Media, Inc.	1470
Advaion LLC	8021
Advance Coating Solutions	6557
Advance Energy LLC	1938
Advance Federated Protection	1641
Advance Research Chemicals	2010
Advance Sourcing Concepts, LLC	7949
Advanced Assembly Products, Inc.	1863
Advanced Barcode & Label Technologies, Inc.	7496
Advanced Business Graphics, Inc.	7678
Advanced Business Software Consulting LLC dba NCN	5946
Advanced Cad/Cam Service dba Engineering People	3110
Advanced Communication Cabling, Inc.	9710
Advanced Computer Concepts	5674
Advanced Control Services, Inc.	3013
Advanced Energy Products, Inc.	3050
Advanced Engineering Consultants, Ltd.	3229
Advanced Engineering Design, Inc.	4845
Advanced Engineering Solutions Incorporated	7411
Advanced Environmental Consultants, Inc.	3456
Advanced Environmental Management Group, LLC	3436
Advanced Equipment Co. dba Prime Distributing Co.	2900
Advanced Ergonomic Concepts Inc.	3793
Advanced Food Systems	3675
Advanced Graphic Engraving, LLC	7539
Advanced ImmunoChemical, Inc.	6020
Advanced Indoor Air Quality Care	3464
Advanced Integration Group Inc.	5431
Advanced IT Concepts, Inc.	4492, 9665
Advanced Label Worx	7451
Advanced Manufacturing Technology For Bottles, Inc	6262
Advanced Mechatronics Solutions, Inc.	4049
Advanced Nitriding Solutions, LLC	6558
Advanced Presentation Systems dba CCS	5097
Advanced Resources Group, Inc.	5030
Advanced Safety & Energy (American Safety & Equipment, Inc.)	3149
Advanced Shipping Technologies	10102
Advanced Surgical Technologies, Inc.	6372
Advanced Systems	8075
Advanced Technology Computers, Inc.	5788
Advanced Technology Solutions, Inc.	4663
Advanced Turbine Solutions LLC	6690
Advanced Underground Inspection, LLC	2394
Advanced Window Fashions LLC	3835
Advanced-Cable, LLC	2753
Advancio Inc.	4269
Advans IT Services, Inc.	4807
Advansoft International Inc.	4673
Advanta Pacific International	1281
Advantage Chevrolet	1830
Advantage Environmental Services, Inc.	3394
Advantage Global Logistics	9964
Advantage Mailing, LLC.	7457
Advantage Marketing Inc.	8525

COMPANY ALPHABETICAL LISTING

A

Company	INDEX#
Advantage Research, Inc.	8315
Advantage Resource Group	9373
Advantco International LLC	5063
Advantium Capital, LLC	7743
Advantus Engineers	3248
Advent Creative Group	8577
Advent Global Solutions, Inc	5515
Adventium Marketing & Design	1188
Ad-Venture Promotions	1420
Adventures in Advertising dba Resource Marketing	1049
Adventus Technologies, Inc.	9422
Advertising Audit Services International, LLC	7717
Advertising Resources, Inc. (ARI Packaging)	7134
Advertising Ventures, Inc. dba (add)ventures	8771
Advisory Environmental Technologies, Inc.	3395
Advitam IP, LLC	6129
Advoqt, LLC	4808
AE & Associates, LLC	4270
AEC Group, Inc.	3009
AEE Productions	1069
Aeffect, Inc.	8473
Aegis Electronic Group, Inc.	2784
Aegis Environmental, Inc.	3533
Aegis Fire and Integrated Services, LLC	1609
Aegis Group Search Consultants, LLC	9172
AEi International LLC	8285
Aequor Technologies Inc.	5109
Aero Assemblies, Inc.	2763
Aero Expediting Inc.	9977
Aero Supply USA	2812
Aerobodies Fitness Company, Inc.	8286
Aerocean Freight Solutions, Inc.	9824
Aeroflite Enterprises	2728, 2787
Aerolution Inc.	3286
Aeronet Logistics Inc.	9833
Aerostar Manufacturing	6548, 6826
AespaTech, LLC	5359
Aether NY LLC	1189
Aetypic, Inc.	1730, 3051
Afaf Translations, LLC	8331
AFC International Inc	6312
AFCLS Logistics Services LLC	9892
Affigent, LLC	5675
Affirmative Biosolutions	6066, 6515
Affordable Language Services	8723
AFL Maintenance Group, Inc.	2101
AfterMarket Services	5880
AfterViolet Inc.	8332
AG Commodties, Inc.	3552
AG Group Inc.	3014
AG Manufacturing Inc.	2979
AG Marketing & Consulting Group	8627
Agama Solutions Inc.	4271
Agape Plastics, Inc.	7370
Agape Precision Manufacturing, LLC	6893
AGB Investigative Services, Inc.	2641
AGC Products Inc.	6049
Age Industries, Ltd.	7276
Ageatia Technology Consultancy Services Inc	4674
AGF Enterprise LLC	8145
AGI International Inc.	9942
Agile Global Solutions, Inc	4272
Agile Perspective	9672

A

Company	INDEX#
Agile Sourcing Partners, Inc.	7985
Agile1	8893
Agilea Solutions, Inc.	5278
AgileTalent, Inc.	4273, 8894
Agilify LLC	8081
Agilus Global Services, LLC	4451
A-Global Solution, LLC DBA Environmental Services of North America, Inc	3437
Agnew Multilingual	9565
Agnosco Technologies Inc.	5110
AgreeYa Solutions, Inc.	4274
AGResearch International, LLC	7963
AGT Global Logistics	9917
Aguirre Roden Inc.	3287
AHA Mechanical Contractors	2520
Aha! Leadership LLC	7927
AhaApps LLC	5676
AHI Facility Services, Inc.	2242
AHJ Construction, LLC	2493
Ahlers Designs, Inc.	1549
Ahrens Contracting, Inc.	3450
AHRMDCO International LLC	8244
Ahtna Contractors, LLC	4275
Ahtna Government Services Corporation	2284
AIA New Dimensions in Marketing, Inc.	1503
aiaTranslations LLC	8748
Aikerson Consulting Group, Inc.	8022
AIM Global Trading, LLC	3789
AIM Over-The-Road	10132
AIM Solutions, Inc.	7158
Aimssoft Consultants Inc.	9313
AIOPX Management Consulting	8169
Air Control, Inc.	6593
Air Corps Mechanical	2414
Air Energy Systems & Services	4045
Air Freight Plus Inc. dba AFP Global Logistics	9970
Air Hub, LLC	3513
Air Marine Forwarding Company	9870
Air Mechanix, LLC	2525
Airea	3783
Airecon Manufacturing Corporation	3230
Aireko Construction Management Services, LLC	3265
Aireko Construction, LLC	2505
Airetel Staffing, Inc.	8990
Airfoil Public Relations, Inc.	8563
Airmate Company	1517
Airodyne Industries, Inc.	6625
Airosmith, Inc.	3211
AirQuest Environmental, Inc.	3396
Airtelligence Inc.	3046
AIT Global Inc.	5111
AITA Consulting Services Inc.	5112
AIVI Global Inc.	2701
AJ Images.com	7599
AJ Quality Services, Inc.	3125
AJ Smith Enterprise Inc	2838
AJT Technology Designs Inc	4675
Akisha Networks, Inc.	5516
AKKO Fastener, Inc.	3968
Akorbi Translations, LLC	8780
AKRAYA, Inc.	4276
Akula & Associates, P.C.	6228
AL & CM Broadcasting Network, Inc.	1006

COMPANY ALPHABETICAL LISTING

A — INDEX#

Company	Index#
Alabama Safety Products Inc.	4038
Alamon Telco, Inc.	9723
ALBAH Manufacturing Technologies Corp.	6827
Albar Industries	7371
Albion Healthcare Staffing	8991
Albrecht Events LLC	8749
Albu & Associates, Inc.	2332
ALC Enterprises, Inc.	4676
Alcam Medical Inc.	6336
Alcatex, Inc. Data Center Design & Build	2526
Alcove Resources	9506
Aldez Containers, LLC	7171
Aldis Systems, Inc.	4979
Aldo Design Group	3802
Alea Health dba Kersh Health	6516
Alegna Technologies, Inc.	4559
Alego Health	5360
Alegre, Inc.	8188
Aleias Gluten Free Foods, LLC	3578
Alert IT Solutions Inc.	4677
Alexander and Davis Consulting	8245
Alexander Perry Inc.	1806
Alexa's Catering Inc.	3729
Alexton Incoporated	3318
Alfa Management Solutions LLC	8246
Alfa Scientific Designs	6337
Alfie Logo Gear	1438
ALG Diversifed LLC	9918
Algon Corporation	1914, 6034
Algoriom Inc.	5113
Alianza Services LLC	3811
Alice Ink, Inc. dba Plastec Industries	7332
Alicon Group, Inc.	4277
Align4Profit, Inc.	2720
Aligned Partner Group LLC	4560
Alignment Simple Solutions, LLC	1847
Alin Machining Co, Inc. dba Power Plant Services	3890
Alkat Electrical Contractors, Inc.	3942
All About Events	8781
All About People	8875
All About People, Inc.	8876
All About Presentation, LLC	8836
All About Technology	4902
All America Transportation, Inc.	10033
All American Containers, Inc	7119
All American Lock	2285
All AMerican Relocation Inc.	10078
All American Rentals, Inc.	2286
All American Seasonings, Inc.	3575
All A's Spices	3597
All Business Machines, Inc. dba AttainIt	5517
All Girl Transportation & Logistics, Inc	9919
All Green Recycling Inc.	3457
All Media Supplies, Inc.	5899
All Pro Janitorial Service Inc.	2108
All Service Contracting Corp.	3415
All StarZ Staffing and Consulting LLC	9530
All Steel Fabrication Inc.	6691
All Team Franchise Corp	8992
All Temps 1 Personnel	9423
ALL(n)1 Security Services, Inc.	2630
AllCare, Inc.	6408
Alleare Consulting, LLC	9424
Allegheny Valley Transfer Co., Inc.	10103
Allegiance Staffing	9531
Allegiance Technologies Inc.	4903
Allegiant International LLC	3126
Allen, Maxwell & Silver, Inc.	7807
Allfon LLC	4278
Alliance Fire Protection Services, Inc.	1616
Alliance Group Technologies Company Calumet, Inc.	4767
Alliance Industries LLC	4117
Alliance of Diversity Printers, LLC	7679
Alliance of Professionals & Consultants, Inc.	5064
Alliance Packaging Group, Inc.	7126
Alliance Rubber Company, Inc.	7092
Alliance Sourcing Network Inc	5114
Alliance Supply, Inc.	2208
Alliance Technology Group, LLC	4846
Alliance Trucking Inc.	10099
Alliant Consulting, Inc.	8126
Alliant Event Services	5834
Alliant Global Strategies Inc.	5677
Allied Door Systems	2462
Allied Electrical & Industrial Supply Company Inc.	4113
Allied Fuel LLC	2068
Allied Logistics Corp.	10111
Allied National Services	2177
Allied Shipping and Packaging Supplies	7236
Allied Staff Augmentation Partners, Inc.	9248
Allied Technology Inc.	6549, 6723
All-N-One Services, LLC	9425
AllOut Marketing, Inc.	8578
Allovus Design, Inc.	9532
Alloy Valves and Control	6303
All-Pac Distributng LLC	7094, 7319
Allpoints Security & Detective, Inc.	2642
All-Pro Placement Service, Inc.	9155
ALL-SHRED, Inc.	3431
AllSource Global Management	3047
Allstaff Technical Solutions	4561
All-State Express, Inc.	10043
Allstem Connections, Inc.	8895
Alltech International, Inc.	5678
All-Tex Pipe & Supply, Inc.	4174
AllTex Staffing & Consulting LLC dba Abba Staffing	9426
Ally Solutions Group LLC	8153
Allyon, Inc.	9030
Alma Bell	3522
Almena Consulting Group, Inc.	9396
Almond Consulting Group	4493
Aloha Document Services, Inc.	4678
ALOM Technologies Corporation	7097
Alonso & Carus Iron Works, Inc.	6684
Alorica Inc.	7986
Alpha Athletics Sports LLC	1667
Alpha Circuit Corporation	2742
Alpha Graphics, Inc.	7553
Alpha Identification, Inc.	5886
Alpha Industries Inc. dba Sigma Stretch Film	7211
Alpha Logistics Solutions, LLC	10115
Alpha Medical Distributor, Inc.	6468
Alpha Office Supplies, Inc.	3830, 7056
Alpha Omega Integration LLC	5679
Alpha Omega Solutions, Inc.	4279
Alpha Pack LLC	7262

COMPANY ALPHABETICAL LISTING

A INDEX#

Company	Index#
Alpha Press, Inc.	7484
Alpha Printing & Graphics, Inc.	7458
Alpha Rae Personnel, Inc.	9120
Alpha Source Inc.	6543
Alpha Stone Solutions	3845
Alpha Technologies USA, Inc.	4485
Alpha1 Staffing/Search Firm, LLC.	8993
AlphaVets, Inc.	6499
Alphaworks LLC	5518
Alphi Manufacturing, LLC	6828
Alpine Packaging Inc.	7249
Al-Pros Construction Inc.	2448
Al-Razaq Computing Services	5519
Alta Max, LLC	3898
Alta Packaging, Inc.	7135
AltaFlux Corporation	4904
Altak Inc.	6717, 6960
AltaStaff LLC	9078
ALTECOR Engineering	3288
ALTEK Information Technology, Inc.	4847
Alter Agents	8333
Alternative Office Solutions	3741
Alternatives In Engineering, Inc.	1630
Altimetrik Corp	4905
Altobelli Advantage, Inc.	1456
Altol Enterprises Management Corp.	3510
Altus Technology Solutions	4848
Aluf Plastics div. of API Industries, Inc.	7223
Aluminum Blanking Company, Inc	6829
Aluminum Distributing, Inc. dba ADI Metal	6933
Alvarado Construction, Inc.	2319
Alvarado Tax & Business Advisors LLC	7847
Alvin K. Brown, P.A.	6102
AM Copiers Inc.	6975
AM Manufacturing Company	4209
Amare & Associates LLC dba ABA Tax Accounting	7800
Amaril Uniform Company	1695
Amaxra, Inc.	5789
Amazing Edibles Gourmet Catering, Inc.	3605
Amazon Hose and Rubber Company	3993
Amazon Services Inc.	7485
AMBCO Electronics Corporation	4280
AMBE Engineering, LLC	3150
Amber Heavenly USA, Ltd.	9605
AmberTech Technologies LLC	2025
Ambiance Cosmetics Inc. dba CPR Cleaning Products	2077
Ambient Technologies, Inc.	3397
Amboseli Foods, LLC	3724
AMC Industries, LLC	3919
AMDA dba New England Promotional Marketing	1428
Amec, LLC	3018
Amee Bay LLC	3279
Ameex Technologies Corp.	4679
American Biochemicals	2032
American Business Solutions, Inc.	5361
American Cable Company	2769
American Cable Products LLC	9720
American Carton Company	7277
American Casuals	1304
American Center Travel	10208
American Chemie, Inc.	2033
American Chrome Chicago Company, Inc.	6597
American Clinics for Preventive Medicine	6398

A INDEX#

Company	Index#
American Dawn Inc.	3742
American Demolition & Nuclear Decommissioning, Inc	3476
American Diversity Business Solutions	6993
American Eagle Protective Services Inc.	2607
American Energy Products, Inc.	6617
American Energy Supply Corporation	2015
American Environmental Assessment & Solutions, Inc	3477
American Executive Private Security Inc.	2608
American Fashion Network, LLC	1706
American Fire & Sprinkler LLC	1642
American Fire Control	1636
American Fire Equipment	1603
American Fire Sprinkler Corp.	1622
American General Contractor Inc.	3903
American Global Facility Services, Inc.	2078
American Green Building Services, Inc.	2151
American Guard Services, Inc.	2626
American Healthcare Products, Inc.	6338
American Hydrostatics Distribution Co.	2754
American Industrial Control, Inc.	2788
American Information Technology Corp.	5520
American Installation and Management, LLC	8782
American International Mailing, Inc.	1118
American Kitchen Machinery and Repair Co., Inc.	4222
American Language Services	1007
American LED and Energy, Corp.	2961
American Maintenance Janitorial Services & Supplies Co.	2209
American Marketing Services and Consultants Inc.	7509
American Medicals	6373
American Megatrends Inc.	5965
American Merchandising Services	1996
American Metal Technologies LLC	6923
American Motor Lines, Inc.	9978
American Moving and Installation, Inc.	9965
American Overseas Book Company, Inc.	2713
American Paper Converting Inc.	7086
American Personnel Managers and Consultants, Inc.	7950, 9374
American Plus Printers, Inc.	7600
American Pride Fasteners, LLC	3966
American Product Distributors, Inc.	7026
American Professional Security, Inc.	2609
American Project Management LLC	5279, 8165
American Purchasing Services	6374
American Renewable Energy	2527
American Reprographics Corporation	7497
American Resource Training System, Inc.	8106
American Shipping and Packing, Inc.	10079
American Sign Language Services Corporation	8023
American Software LLC	5115
American Staffing LLC	9233
American Standard Circuits	2743
American Supply	7098
American Systems, Inc. dba Simon Sign Systems	1070
American Tec Electric Company	2996
American Test & Balance	6326
American Textile Systems, Inc. dba American Paper	6976
American Tool and Mold LLC	7333
American Traders Enterprises, Inc.	1342
American Trading International Co, LLC	1343
American Unit, Inc.	5521
Americas Engineers, Inc.	3127
America's Staffing Partner, Inc.	9375

COMPANY ALPHABETICAL LISTING

A

Company	INDEX#
Americhem Sales Corporation	1954
Americlerk, Inc. dba Lumen Legal	6154
AmeriCoat Corporation	6556
Americorp Xpress Carriers	10133
Ameridial, Inc.	9744
Ameridial, Inc. dba Fusion BPO Services	9745
Amerimex Air Charter LLC	10134
Ameri-Pac, Inc.	3190
AmeriPrint Corporation	7510
Amerisearch Background Alliance	7943
Ameritex Guard Services	2692
Amerivet Securities, Inc.	7718
Ames Medical Equipment, Inc.	6339
Ames Research Laboratories, Inc.	2013
AMEX Investments, LLC	2268
AMG Engineering & Machining, Inc.	6808
AMG, Inc.	3231
AMI Imaging Systems, Inc.	4980
AMI Risk Consultants	7744
AMI Strategies, Inc.	9711
Amick Brown LLC	4281
Amigo Mobility International Inc.	4213
Amitron, Inc.	2963
Amity Industries	6894
AMKA Global, LLC	4114
AMKO Trading	4131
Ammex Plastics	7372
AMMKCORP	5116
AmmMm Inc.	4282
Amneal Pharmaceuticals	6452
Amodu Engineering Solutions, LLC	2423
AmorServ LLC	4680
Amp Inc.	4283
AMP Personnel Services, LLC	9427
AmPac Chemical Company Inc.	2034
Ampak Co., Inc.	1990
Ampcus Inc.	5680
Amphenol Tecvox, LLC.	2923
Ampie Enterprises, Inc.	7622
Amplidyne, Inc.	3078
Amplio Marketing, Inc.	8579
Amreli Technology Solutions, LLC	5790
Amsys Innovative Solutions	5522
AMSYSCO, Inc.	4074
Amtec Molded Products, Inc.	7343
Amtech Electrocircuits, Inc.	2980
Amtek Consulting LLC	5523
Amtex System, Inc	9314
Amzur Technologies, Inc.	4494
Ana M Fisher dba A & A Glove & Safety Co.	4218
Anahau Energy, LLC	1894
Analysts International Corporation (AIC)	4562
Analytica LLC	4474
Analytical Food Laboratories, Inc.	3289
Analytical Solutions by Kline	5362
Analytiks International, Inc.	4981
Anblicks	5524
Anchor Point Technology Resources, Inc	4768
Anchor Staffing Inc.	9079
Ancira	1843
Andavo Meetings & Incentives	8831
Andean Consulting Solutions International, LLC	8091
Anderson & Egan, Co.	3416

A

Company	INDEX#
Anderson Advertising dba The Anderson Group	1226
Anderson Burton Construction	2287
Anderson Express, Inc.	6626
Anderson Productions Inc.	9577
Anderson Seal Inc.	4034
Anderson Security Agency, Ltd.	2603
Andinas dba/ Inlingua Utah	8832
Andrew Associates, Inc.	1040
Andrew Vazquez Inc.	10053
Andytown LLC	3553
Anesthesia Equipment Supply, Inc.	6540
Anexa Biomedical, Inc.	6375
Angel Flight Marketing Services, Inc.	1089
Angel Screen Printing, Inc.	7704
Anita Fire Hose Company Etc.	4050
AnITConsultant, LLC	4797
Annese & Associates, Inc.	9736
Anointed Professional Enterpises Inc.	2124
ANOPS Limited	8305
ANR Staffing Solutions, LLC	9315
ANS Inc.	2217
Anselux LLC	5681
ANSERTEAM, LLC	9428
Anthony's Janitorial/Maintenance Service Ltd.	2210
Antina Promotions, LLC	1439
A-One, LLC	9413
Aonsoft International, Inc	4681
AOSS Medical Supply, Inc.	6423
AP42	8334
Apac Chemical Corp.	1895
Apache Products Inc.	10252
APB & Associates, Inc.	8189
APCO Worldwide LLC	1045
Apertus Partners	9507
Apex Beverage Equipment Distribution Group, LLC.	4210
Apex Computer Systems, Inc.	4284
Apex CoVantage	5682
Apex Facility Resources, Inc.	3848
Apex Impact Marketing LLC	8750
Apex Investigative Services Inc.	2610
Apex Office Products, Inc.	6985
Apex Spring & Stamping	6724
Apex Veteran Staffing, Inc.	9031
APG Office Furnishings	3818
Apidel Technologies LLC	9080
APImaging, Inc.	7302, 7486
Apis LLC	6155
APISource, Inc.	1433
A-Plus Meetings and Incentives	8406
Aplusdealz LLC	2813
APN Consulting Inc.	9277
APN Software Services Inc.	4285
Apogee Law Group, P.C.	6070
Apollo Energy Components Inc. t/a Apollo Supply	3943
Apollo Mechanical Contractors	2568
Apollo Professional Solutions, Inc.	5098
Apollos Partners LLC	9032
Apollos Waters LLC	3514
APOMed Systems, Inc.	3052
Aponi Products and Services	1604, 9639
AppleOne Employment Services	8896
Applicantz, Inc.	9429
Applications Alternatives, Inc.	4849

COMPANY ALPHABETICAL LISTING

A

Company	INDEX#
Applications Engineering Group	5031, 9234
Applications Technology Group, Inc.	4563
Applied Computer Solutions	4286
Applied Controls & Contracting Services, Inc.	1620
Applied Development LLC	4850, 8092
Applied Engineering Group & Company, Corp.	3266
Applied Integrity Consulting, LLC	5683
Applied Sales & Installation Services, Inc.	2921
Applied Training Resources Inccorporated	5525
AppliedInfo Partners, Inc.	5117
APR Consulting, Inc.	8897
A-Pro Execs, LLC	9081
Apropos Promotions	1305
Apsis Solutions Inc.	8994
APTIVA Corp.	5118
AptoTek Inc.	5432
Aptude, Inc.	4682
APW Construction, Inc.	2288
Aqual Corp.	2289
AQuate II, LLC	3280
Aquatech International Corporation	3249
Aquent LLC	4809
Aquest LLC	9249
Aquila Travel & Events	10216
Aquinas Consulting, LLC	4452
ARA Food Corporation	3586
ArachnidWorks, Inc.	1119
Aranda Tooling, Inc.	6769
Arayal Consulting, LLC	5065
ARBA Technology, Inc.	4683
Arbelos Partners LLC	5363
Arbill Industries, Inc.	4153
Arbor Electronics Inc.	2901
Arborsys Group	5119
ARC Government Solutions, Inc	5526
Arch Plastics Packaging, LLC	6505
Archaeological Consulting Services, Ltd.	3347
ArchaeoPaleo Resource Management, Inc.	1731
Archer & Associates I, Inc.	9533
Archer Corporate Services	8564
Architechnical, Inc.	1745
Architect for Life - A Professional Corporation	1814, 3523
Architectural Design Collaborative	1746
Architectural Flooring Resources, Inc.	3812
Architectural Mailboxes	6578
Arcons Design Studio Professional Corporation	1781
Arcturis, Inc.	1774
ARD Logistics, LLC	7087, 9820
Ardent Technologies Inc.	5364
ARDETECH Industries, Inc.	5934
Ardian Group, Inc.	7057
AREA51-ESG	2789
AREM Container & Supply Co.	7136
Ares Construction Co, LLC	5032
Arete Technology Solutions, Inc. dba Statement	4564
Argent Associates, Inc.	2528
Argent International	7373
Argent Tape & Label, Inc.	7560
Argo Navis IT	5120
Argos Global Partner Services, LLC	8024
Argus Investors' Counsel, Inc.	7738
Argus Logistics, LLC	4906
Argus Talent, LLC	5527

A

Company	INDEX#
Arias & Associates, Inc.	3290
Ariel Information Technology Corporation	4238
Ariel Investments	7759
Aries Group, Inc.	9141
Arion Systems, Inc.	4565
Arise Solutions Inc.	2774, 3980
Aristocat Limousine Service Inc.	9979
Arita-Poulson General Contracting, LLC	2362
Arizona Trailer Specialists Inc dba C&I Equipment	9825
ARK Solutions Inc.	9508
ARK Temporary Staffing, LLC	9033
Arkren Inc.	2333
Arlington Machine & Tool	6868
Arlington Resources, Inc.	9082
Armacost Lighting LLC	2977
Armedia LLC	4566
Armor Metal Group	6662
Armstrong Archives LLC	5528
Armstrong/Robitaille/Riegle, Inc.	6003
Arna Marketing	7601
Arnev Products, Inc.	3038
Arnold Solutions, LLC	8190
A-Rocket Moving & Storage, Inc.	10135
Arora Systems Group, LLC	1647
Arps International LLC	9173
Arrasmith Promotions LLC	1518
Array of Engineers, LLC	3151
ARRC Enterprises, Inc	4287
Arrow Magnolia International, Inc.	2035
Arrow Motor & Pump Inc.	2848
Arrow Strategies	9083
Arrowhead Global, LLC	3886
Arrowhead Packaging Services	7237
Arrowhead Promotion & Fulfillment Co., Inc.	4982
Arroyo Process Equipment Inc.	4066
ARS Aleut Remediation, LLC	3135
Arseal Technologies, LLC	1749
Art & Negative Graphics, Inc.	7554
Art Cortez Construction, Inc.	2491
Art Partners Group, LLC	8580
Arteaga & Arteaga Advertising	1242
Arteaga Construction, Inc.	2573
Artech L.L.C.	5121
Artesia Springs LLC	3714
Artesian Collaborative	8053
Arthur Grand Technologies Inc.	9509
Artic Air Heating & Cooling	2276
Artifex Technology Consulting, Inc.	5495
Artisan Creative Inc.	1008, 8335
Artisan Management LLC	5066
Artist Touch Design Firm	1558
Artistic Promotions	1332
Artitudes Design Inc	8855
ARTU-USA, Inc.	3920
Arva, LLC	3019
As You Wish Promotions	1542
Asaman, Inc.	6424
ASAP Identification Security, Inc.	5881
ASAP Personnel Inc.	9430
ASAP Solutions Group, LLC	4567
Ascendo Resources, LLC	8995
Ascendum	5365
Ascent Group Medical LLC	6489

COMPANY ALPHABETICAL LISTING

A

Company	INDEX#
Ascent Innovations, LLC	4684
ASD - Automation Systems & Design	4220
Aseptic Haven LLC	8146
Asez Inc.	1656, 2693
ASG Renaissance	8107
Ash Ingredients, Inc.	1978
Ashaun	9767
Ashe Consultants, PLLC	3319
Asher Media, Inc.	1247
Ashlor Management Corporation	7928
Ashton Staffing, Inc	9034
Ashunya Inc	4288
ASI Computer Technologies, Inc.	9834
Asia-Link, Inc.	2839
Asian & Hispanic Trading & Consulting Inc.	7041
Asiana Cusine Enterprises (ACE Sushi)	3554
Asil White Enterprises, Inc.	8039
Ask IT Consulting Inc	5288
ASK Staffing, Inc.	9035
ASM Aerospace Specifications Metals, Inc.	6934
ASM Security Inc.	1637
Asociar, LLC	4019
ASP Industries	6659
Aspect Consulting, Inc.	5433
Aspekt Consultancy Services LLC dba Jubilant Consulting	9431
Aspen Capital Company, Inc.	4435, 7737
Aspen Technical Staffing, Inc.	9084
Aspire HR, Inc.	7964
Aspire Systems	4453
Aspiryon, LLC	5529
Assaycell Technologies LLC	1979
Assent Solutions LLC	5530
Assessment Plus, Inc.	7906
Asset LifeCycle, LLC	7775
Asset Surplus Reallocation LLC (SurgiShop)	6376
Assigned Counsel Inc.	6216
Associate Resource Management, Inc.	9316
Associate Staffing, LLC	9250
Associated Building Maintenance Co., Inc.	2157
Associated Design & Services, Inc.	2395
Associated Renewable	3212
Associated Visual Communications, Inc.	7635
Associates Systems LLC	5531
Assura, Inc.	8287
Assurance Staffing, Inc.	9376
Assure Shipping, LLC	10029
Assured Healthcare Staffing LLC - Gurnee, IL	9085
Aster Industries	6663
Astir IT Solutions	5122
Astra/CFX Holdings, LLC	1851
Astute Sourcing, LLC	9131
Astyra Corporation	5684
ASW Global, LLC	10080
At Work Sales Corporation	1665
ATEC Electrical Contractors	2970
Ateeca Inc.	7808
Aten Solutions, Inc.	9251
ATG	10219
Atier	3152
Atlanta Brand Central LLC	1364
Atlanta Caster & Equipment	6267
Atlanta Communications Co.	9673
Atlanta Life Insurance Company	5992
Atlanta Peach Movers, Inc.	9893
Atlanta Promotional Products	1365
Atlan-Tec, Inc. (Atlantic Technical Sales & Svc)	4161
Atlantic Communication Products, Inc.	9724
Atlantic Hardware Supply	3904
Atlantic Petroleum & Mineral Resources Inc.	2036
Atlantic Precision Products	7374
Atlantic Resource Group, Inc.	5685
Atlantic South Consulting Services	3281
Atlantic Testing Laboratories, Limited	3213
Atlantic-Pacific Express, Inc.	10116
Atlantis Paper & Packaging	7099
Atlas Consulting Group, LLC	9278
Atlas Data Systems DBA Atlas	5123
Atlas Machining & Welding, Inc.	6895
Atlas Management Corporation	9414
Atlas Tool Inc.	6725
Atlas Travel & Technology Group, Inc.	10207
Atmos360, Inc	3232
Ato Apiafi Architects PLLC	1822
Atomized Products Group of Chesapeake, Inc.	3032
ATR International, Inc.	8898
ATRIA Consulting, LLC	9279
Atrium Staffing LLC	9317
ATS Associates LLC	5289
ATS Training and Consulting Co	8191
Attain Med, Inc.	6399
Attunix Corporation	5791
AU & Associates Inc.	2651
Auburn Manufacturing, Inc.	9806
Audio Video Systems, Inc.	1610
Augie Leopold Advertising Specialties, Inc.	1424
Augusta Temporaries, Inc. dba Manpower	9405
Auld Technologies, LLC	1840
Aumtech, Inc.	5124
Aura Innovative Technology	4685
Aureus Tech Systems, LLC	4436
Auritas	4495
Aurora Electric Inc.	2870
Aurora Product Inc.	3579
Aurora Solutions, Inc.	4686
Austin Ad Group	1559
Austin Business Forms Inc.	1471
Austin Foam Plastics, Inc.	7278
Austin Lumber Company, Inc.	10253
Austin Tele-Services Partners, LP dba Genesis ATS	5532, 9772
Austin Texas Mediators LLC	8247
AustinCSI LLC	5533
AutoCell Electronics	2790
Automae	4289
Automation Anywhere, Inc.	4290
Automotive and Industrial Equipment LLC	4124
Automotive Quality & Logistics, Inc.	3153
Avalon Chemicals, Inc.	2037
Avance IT Solutions LLC	4851
Avani Technology Solutions Inc.	5290
Avant Healthcare	8521
Avantgarde Translations	8616
Avanti Limousine Service, LLC	9871
Avantia, Inc.	5366
Avanza Advertising	1050

COMPANY ALPHABETICAL LISTING

A INDEX#

Company	Index#
AVE Solutions	7009
Avenue Event Group LLC	8407
Avenue Staffing Inc.	9213
Avenues International Inc.	5125
Avery Group Inc.	2079
AVI Integrators Inc. dba Security 101	1611
Aviana Global Technologies, Inc.	4291
Avid Promotions	1306
Avinash K. Malhotra Architects (AKM)	1790
Avineon, Inc.	5686
AVM Industries	6321
AWA Lighting Designers Inc.	1791
Awards Unlimited, Inc.	1405
AWICS Security & Investigations, Inc.	2672
AWLI Group, Inc.	10068
Axelerate	5792
Axelliant LLC	4292
Axelon Services Corporation	9318
Axiom Actuarial Consulting	6016
Axiom Consulting LLC	8170
Axiom Global Technologies, Inc.	4293
Axiom Logistics LLC	9894
Axis Employment Services	8877
AXIS Staffing	9432
Axium Plastics LLC	7412
Axtria Inc.	5126
Ayota, LLC	2080
AZ Construction Resources, Inc., dba AZCR Staffing	8878
A-Z Sophisticated Solutions	9546
Azachorok Contract Services LLC	6770
Aztec Facility Management, LP	2243
Aztec Manufacturing Corporation	6830
Aztec Promotional Group, LP	1560
Azul 7, Inc.	8581
Azzmeiah Vazquez Esq. dba WorkPro	9280

B

Company	Index#
B & B Lighting Supply, Inc.	3905
B & B Maintenance, Inc.	2134
B & S Electric Supply Co., Inc	2820
B&B Communications Group	9764
B&B Instruments, Inc.	6311
B&B Socket Products, Inc.	3879
B&H Total Office Solutions	3837
B&M Construction, Inc.	2320
B&N Legal Interpreting, Inc.	6188
B&T Tool & Engineering Inc.	3946
B. Gunther & Company, Inc.	1382
B. King's Audio Visual Services	8440
B.A.G. Corp.	7279
B2B Enterprises Inc. dba Prism Sign Group	1248
B2B Holdings Inc	7006
B2B Strategic Solutions, Inc.	8054
Baanyan Software Services, Inc.	5910
Backbone Consultants	4983
Backhand Productions, Inc.	9566
Baer Reed	6071
BAF Packaging, LLC	7137
BahFed	5420
Bailey Edward Design, Inc.	1753
Bailey Manufacturing Co., LLC	6660, 6745
Bailey Office Equipment, Inc.	6994

B INDEX#

Company	Index#
Bailey's Premier Services LLC	3291
Bain Enterprises, LLC	3929
Bainbridge Environmental Consultants, Inc.	3352
Baker Creative Ltd.	1213, 8724
Balady Promotions, Inc.	1483
Balance Product Development, Inc.	3233
Balance Technology Group, Inc.	5687
Balance Vibration Technologies, Inc.	3292
Baldwin & Obenauf, Inc.	8628
Baldwin Richardson Foods Co.	3606
Ball Office Products, LLC	7082
Bambeck & Vest Associates, Inc.	2463
Bamboo Worldwide Inc.	8474
Banas and Associates PLLC	6156
Banda Group International, LLC	7982
Banerasoft Inc.	5067
Banker's Hill Law Firm, A.P.C.	6072
Banneker Industries, Inc.	7261
Barazzo, LLC	1366, 3854
Barb Clapp Advertising and Marketing, LLC	1120
Barbara J. Charles dba Perfection Staffing	9433
Barbee Tax Consulting, LLC	7760
Barbera & Watkins, LLC	6143
Barcode Industrial Systems, Inc.	5367
Barcode Warehouse	7498
Bardach Awards, Inc.	1406
Bardess Group Ltd.	8154
Bardin Palomo Ltd.	9606
Bare International Inc.	8837
Barnes Business Solutions, Inc.	4984
Baron Sign Manufacturing	1051
Baron Wealth Management	7789
Barquin & Associates Inc.	5484
Barrchin, Inc.	5068
Barrientos Design & Consulting, Inc.	3335
Barrister Global Services Network Inc	4803
Barron Marketing Communications	8405
Basal Solutions LLC	3293
Bascom & Adams Business Solutions, LLC	8725
Baseline Design, Inc	1190
Basha Services, LLC	3409
Bashen Corporation	7965
Basiqa, LLC	1071, 7499
Bastion Technologies, Inc.	3294, 5534
Bates Creative Group, LLC	8548
Battery Consulting	4175
Battle and Battle Distributors, Inc	1855
Bauer Latoza Studio, Ltd.	1754
Bavier Design, LLC	1743
Bay Corrugated Container, Inc.	7172
Bay Electric Co., Inc.	2555
Bay Ridge Security Service, Inc.	2673
Bay Tank and Boiler Works	6771
BayInfotech LLC	4294
BayLab USA	6517
BayOne Solutions	4295
Bayshore Transportation System, Inc.	9869
Bayside Printing Co, Inc	7680
BBG Consulting, LLC	2674
BBM Staffing	9434
BBR Print Inc.	7700
BBW Holdings Inc.	1864
BC Laboratories, Inc.	3353

COMPANY ALPHABETICAL LISTING

B	INDEX#
BC Logistics LLC	9826
BCA Watson Rice LLP	7815
BCforward	4985
BCM Global Technologies Consultants, Inc.	4437
BCM Media	8394
BD Transportation, Inc.	10081
BDJ Ventures, LLC	1543
BDM2	8040
Be Real Company	9607
Beach Construction, Inc.	2529
Beacon Staffing Alternatives	9156
Beacon Systems, Inc.	4496
Beacon Training Services Inc.	8248
Beaman Public Relations, Inc.	8475
Bear Staffing Services Corporation	8996
Beardwood&Co. LLC	8672
Bearings & Industrial Supply	1856, 3996
Beasley Financial Group LLC	7778
Beck Environmental and Remediation, Ltd.	3348
Becker Technical Staffing, Inc.	9377
Beehive Specialty Co.	1561
Beehive Strategic Communication GBC	8127
BeginRight Employment Services	9367
Behind the Scenes	8775
Behmke Reporting & Video Services	6073
Behrnes Pepper Salts	3715
Being Present Inc	7987
Belco Manufacturing Company, Inc.	7434
Bell & Manning, LLC	6252
Bell Imaging Inc.	7623
Bell Janitorial Supplies & Services, Inc.	2244
Bell Marketing, Inc.	3607
Bell Performance	1915
Bella Creative LLC	1138
Bellak Color	7487
Belle Communications	8476
Bellomy Research, Inc.	8617
Bellsoft	4568
Bel-Ray Co.	1980
Ben Hyatt Corporation	6074
Benalytics Consulting Group, LLC	5993
Bench International Search Inc.	8899
Benchmarc360, Inc.	8441
Benchmark Contracting, Inc.	2514
Benchmark Displays LLC	7320
Benchmark Industrial Supply, LLC	4141
Bench-Tek Solutions, LLC	6257
Benefit Advocates, Inc.	7933
Benefits Law Group, PK Keesler, PC	6119
Benefits Plus Consulting Group	6015
Benford Brown & Associates LLC	7761
Bennett International Group LLC	9895
Bennett Law Office, PC	6229
Bennett Packaging of Kansas City, Inc.	7199
Bennett Wholesale Distributors LLC	6500
Benten Technologies	5688
BEPC, Inc.	3295
Berkeley Integration Group dba Fiber.com	2929
Berkhemer Clayton	8900
Berkshire Group Inc.	8192
Berner Construction, Inc.	2494
Berry Industrial Group, Inc.	7224
Berwin, Inc.	3762

B	INDEX#
Beryllium Corporation	5485
Best Bolt & Nut Corp.	3899
Best Datacom, Inc.	5900
Best Ed, LLC	2725
BEST Employment SoluTions, LLC	9510
Best Finishing, Inc.	6554
Best Foam Fabricators, Inc.	7344
Best Logistics and Freight LLC	10136
Best Medical International Inc.	6533
Best National Services Inc. dba Latin Labor Staffing	9252
Best Press Inc.	7681
Best Sheet Metal Solutions	6906
Bestica, Inc.	5535, 9435
Beta Soft Systems Inc.	4296
BETAH Associates, Inc.	8093
Bethrant Industries LLC	3083
Betis Group. Inc.	5689
Betmar Languages, Inc.	1139
Bett-A-Way Pallet Systems	10246
Bett-A-Way Traffic Systems Inc.	10054
Better and Best Corporation	3643
Better Built Construction Services, Inc.	2464
Beyond The Bottom Line, Inc.	7779
Beyond Zebra Inc.	1307
BeyondCurious, Inc.	4297
BFE Construction, Inc.	2556
BFFL Co., LLC	6469
BFW Inc.	2840
BG Technologies of Austin, LLC	2902
BGI Resources International Corporation	3465
BHP Engineering & Construction, LP	2038
Bickley Innovations, LLC	7238
Biens Chocolate Centerpieces Corp	3868
Big Apple Visual Group Inc.	1191
Big Red Print Solutions, LLC	6977
Bigelow Family Holdings LLC	8108
Billinda Group LLC	9214
Bilmor with Advertising Specialties Inc.	1344
BIO PLAS, Inc.	6021
BioMed Resources Inc.	6340
Bionomics, Inc.	3515
Biopeptek Pharmaceuticals LLC	2016
Biopharm Project Solutions	3250
BioRepository Resources, LLC	6050
BioStaff Solutions Inc.	8997
Birch Equipment Rental & Sales	4198
Bird Electric Enterprises, LLC	2530
Birko Corporation	1909
Bishop-Wisecarver Corporation	2930
BiSoft Consultancy Services	5793
Bison Data Systems, Inc.	9036
Biswas Information Technology Solutions Inc.	5690
BIT DIRECT	5861
BITHGROUP Technologies, Inc.	4852
Bitoy's Sweet Treats Inc.	3608
BitWise Inc.	4687
Bixby & Co., LLC	3653
BizyBee Professional Staffing & Biz'Ness Solutions	9157
Bjork Construction Co. Inc.	2290
BKC Industries, Inc.	4125
BKM Resources, Inc. Global Chemicals	1981
Black Classic Press	7555
Black Diamond Manufacturing Company	2729

COMPANY ALPHABETICAL LISTING

B — INDEX#

Company	Index#
Black Dog Inc.	1052
Black Enterprise	2716
Black Knight Medical, LLC	6400
Black River Truck Brokers, LLC	10190
Black Star Logistics Inc.	10082
Blackbird Associates, Inc.	1732
Blackdog Corporation	1930
Blackhawk Management	3021
Blackstone Consulting, Inc.	3053
Blackwell Burke P.A.	6163
Blade Inc	9563
Blair, Church & Flynn	3054
Blake Group LLC	9174
Blank2Branded powered by Axis	1484
Blaylock Van, LLC	7719
Blaze Contracting, Inc.	2396
Blaze Information Systems Inc.	4569
Blazin' Inc.	7979
BLeadersEdge LLC	7983
Bleu Marketing Solutions	8336
Bley Investment Group	7848
BLH Consulting, Inc.	8442
Blink Marketing LLC dba Blink Signs; BlinkSwag	1214
Blisset Transportation	10055
BLOXR Solutions LLC	6453
BLT Logistics LLC	9980
Blu Pharmaceuticals	6421
Blubandoo Inc.	1668
BluCase	1691
Blue Beyond Consulting, Inc	8337
Blue Chip Talent	4907
Blue Crest Creative, LLC	8856
Blue Dove Promotions LLC	1472
Blue Eye Soft Corp.	5498
Blue Fields Digital LLC	5280
Blue Isis LLC	8025
Blue Lake Packaging Inc.	7100
Blue Ocean Ventures LLC	9037
Blue Planet Solutions Inc.	5127
Blue Plate Minds, Inc.	9378
Blue Rose Promotions, LLC	1367
Blue Sky Apparel & Promotions, LLC	1468
Blue Sky Industries	3948
Blue Sky Produce	3654
Blue Sun LLC	1249
Blue Water Dynamics LLC dba Dougherty Manufacturing	6589
Blue Wave Communications, Inc.	1612
BlueAlly Technology Solutions, LLC	5691
Bluebix Solutions Inc	3202
Bluecolt Lighting LLC	2849
Bluedog Design, LLC	1090
BlueFletch LLC	4570
Bluepack	7225
Blueprint Consulting Services, LLC	8306
BlueStreak Learning, LLC	4497
BlueWater Technologies Group Inc.	1126
BMC Solutions, Inc.	4571
BME Ventures LLC	7866
BNG Consulting, Inc.	5128
BNM Transportation Services	9981
BNS Engineering Inc.	2506
Bob Ross Auto Group	1841
Bob Williams Specialty Co.	1473
Bocci Engineering, LLC	3524
BodenPR Inc.	8408
Boersma Travel Services	10209
Boggs, Avellino, Lach & Boggs	6174
Bohren's Moving & Storage/United Van Lines	10056
Bokers Inc.	6742
Bolana Enterprises, Inc.	2158
BoLinds Solutions Services, Inc.	7050
Boly-Welch, Inc.	9368
Boomer Technology Group, Inc.	5129
Boomers Consulting, LLC	9038
Boone DeLeon Communications, Inc.	8783
Booth Publications Ink	7571
Bootie Shoe Cover Inc	1726
Borinquen Container Corp.	7239
Borrowed Time Enterprises, Inc.	5858
Bosha Design Inc.	8751
Boston Baking, Inc.	3631
Boston Contemporaries, Inc.	9175
Bothe Associates Inc.	6924
Bottom-Line Performance, Inc.	4769
Boulevard Machine & Gear	6815
Bourntec Solutions, Inc.	4688
Boutchantharaj Corporation	2694
Bouzounis LLC dba Artina Promotional Products	1519
Box Truck Logistics, LLC	9920
Boxes 4 U, Inc.	7280
Bozell and Jacobs LLC	8626
Bozoian Group Architects, LLC	1775
BPI Communications, LLC	8565
BPK Inc.	4986
BPN Concepts	9253
Bracane Company, Inc.	6518
Bradley Technologies Inc.	2652
Bradley Temporaries, Inc. dba Bradley Staffing Group	9379
Brady Co., Inc	9246
Braille Works International, Inc.	4498
Brand Cool Marketing, Inc.	1192
Brand Spirit Inc.	1368
Brand|Pride	1593
BrandEra, Inc.	8784
BrandGov	8338
BrandRPM, LLC	1474
Brandwidth Solutions, LLC	8752
Bratton & Co., Inc. DBA Hyperdrive Agile	8901
Bravo Technical Resources, Inc.	5536
BRAVO! Building Services, Inc.	2197
Bravo! Promotional Products	1594
Breakthrough Marketing Technology	8629
Bredemus Hardware Co Inc.	3917
BREED Enterprises, Inc.	3101
Brenneman Printing, Inc.	7655
Brenner Design Incorporated	1761
Bresa Tech LLC dba Bresatech LLC	9436
Brewer & Lormand, PLLC	6230
Brewster Procurement Group, Inc.	4099
Briabe Media, Inc.	8339
Bridge Foods, Inc.	3628
Bridge Media, LLC	7636
Bridgeforth Wolf & Associates, Inc.	1383
Bridgeport Resources, LLC	8879
Bridger Transportation, LLC	10041
Brigar XPress Solutions Inc, dba Digital XPress	7624

COMPANY ALPHABETICAL LISTING

B INDEX#

Company	Index#
Bright Future Partners, Inc. dba RED212	1215
Bright Light LED Inc.	2791
Bright Regards LLC	2912
Brighter Days & Nites, Inc.	2897
BrightFields, Inc.	3393
BrightKey, Inc.	8549
Brighton Agency, Inc.	1157, 8605
Brightwork Consulting, Inc.	8307
Briljent, LLC	2707
Brilliant Gifts LLC	1384, 3856
Brillio, LLC	5130
Brinco Mechanical Services, Inc.	2449
Brindley Pieters & Associates, Inc.	3087
Brinkerhoff Environmental Services, Inc.	3466
Brinly-Hardy Company	6809
Brisk/RCR Coffee Company	3587
BriteWorks, Inc.	2081
Brittain-Kalish Group, LLC	8249
Britt's Industries Inc.	7556
Broad Street Capital Markets LLC	7809
BroadAxis Inc.	5537
BroadBased Communications, Inc.	1053
Broadgate Inc.	4908
Broadleaf Results, Inc.	9319
Broadline Medical, Inc.	6341
Brockman Designs LLC	1799
BRODY Professional Development	7951
Bromberg & Associates, LLC	8566
Bromley Printing, Inc.	7572
Brook Architecture	1755
Brook Consultants Inc.	7966
Brooke Staffing Companies, Inc.	9437
Brooksmade Gourmet Foods	3598
Bross Group LLC	4438
Brown Graphics Inc.	1250
Brown Tape Products Company	7159
Brownrigg Companies LTD	6004
Browns Machine	6890
Brune & Richard LLP	6189
BruteForce Solutions Inc	5291
Brylen Technologies	6022, 6304
Bry-Lex Promotional LLC	1544
Bryson Constructors, Inc.	2354
Bryson/Tucker Electric, LLC	3004
Bryton Corporation	6419
BS Cable Company, Inc.	3010
BSA Design Group Inc.	1815
BSC Solutions, Inc.	4909
BTII Institute	8155
BTM Global Consulting LLC	4987
BTR Solutions, LLC	4689
BTS Consulting & Training LLC	8109
Buch Construction Inc.	2390
Budget Office Interiors LLC	3819
Budnick Converting Inc.	1931
Bueno Enterprises	6579
Buick GMC of Moosic Inc.	1842
Building & Earth Sciences, Inc.	3043
Building Maintenance Services, LLC	2131
Building Systems Solutions, Inc.	9716
Built Right Construction, LLC	2515
Buks Tool Company, Inc.	6907
Bulk or Liquid Transport, LLC	9835

B INDEX#

Company	Index#
Bulldog Consulting Services	8076
Bullock's Techology Solutions	4298
Bullseye Database Marketing, LLC	8743
Bullzyeye Equipment & Supply	4162
Bunty, LLC	6899
Burck Oil Co., Inc.	1916
Burgher Gray Jaffe LLP	6190
Burke Consortium, Incorporated	5692
Burly Products, Inc.	6595
Burnett Process, Inc.	3967
Burnett Specialists	9438
Burns Search LLC	9439
Burris Inc.	3737, 6973
Burt Fleet Services, Inc.	1827
Burton-Fuller Managment	8288
Bush Seyferth PLLC	6157
Business Communications Solutions	9640
Business Control Systems LP	9440
Business Environments	3803
Business Information Technology Solutions.Com	4499
Business Integra Technology Solutions, Inc.	4853
Business Interiors	3838
Business Partner Solutions Inc.	4250
Business Processes Redefined, LLC	7810
Business Relocation Services, Inc.	10057
Business Technology Solutions, Inc.	4988
Busy Bee Cleaning Services, LLC	2159
Butler America, LLC	3082
Butler Supply, Inc.	2860
Butler Technologies, Inc.	3011
Butler Tillman Express Trucking, Inc.	9943
Butler Transport, Inc	9953
Butler/Till Media Services, Inc.	1193
Buyer Advertising & Talent Solutions	1109
BuzzBack Market Research dba Buzzback LLC	8673
BUZZRegistration	8630
Buzzword PR Corp.	8674
BXI Consultants, Inc.	5914
Byce & Associates, Inc.	3154
Byrne Software Technologies, Inc.	5033
Bytes of Knowledge, Inc.	8776
Bywater Business Solutions LLC	7573

C

Company	Index#
C & C Janitorial Supplies, Inc.	2102
C & D Electronics	2841
C & D Industrial Tools & Supplies Inc.	3921
C & R Communications Group	3251
C & S Business Services, Inc.	9235
C E McKenzie & Associates, LLC	8234
C H Smith & Associates dba Scale Strategic Solution	8193
C J International Inc.	9971
C Plus Electronics, Inc.	2792
C&B Construction Company Ltd.	2465
C&B Lift Truck Service, Inc.	6285
C&C International Computers and Consultants, Inc.	4500
C&M Medical Supply, Inc.	6477
C&T Information Technology Consulting, Inc.	9441
C. Edward Lewis & Associates	7873
C.A. Spalding, Co.	6896
C.B. Transportation Inc	10104
C.E. Communication Services, Inc.	9702

COMPANY ALPHABETICAL LISTING

C — INDEX#

Company	Index#
C.J. Chemicals, LLC	1955
C.J. Maintenance, Inc.	2160
C.L. King & Associates, Inc.	7816
C.W. Brown Inc.	2450
C.W. Hines and Associates, Inc.	8289
C4Cable, LLC	9703
Cable Harness Resources, Inc.	2752
CableNetwork Associates Inc.	2954
Cabral Roofing & Waterproofing Corp.	2291
Cabrera Capital Markets, LLC	7762
CAC Reps, LLC	9599
Cacique, Inc.	3555
Cactex Media	9627
CAD Concepts, Inc.	3234
CAD Engineering Resources, Inc.	3155
CaDan Technologies	5901
Cadeco Industries, Inc.	3716
Caden Concepts	1308
Cadena Specialty Advertising	1562
Cadena, LLC.	3438
Cadence Keen Innovations d/b/a CKI Solutions	3763
Cadence Leasing, Inc	7720
Cadre Computer Resources Co.	5368
CADworks Solutions, Inc.	4910
CAEI Inc.	4854
CAET Project Management Consultants	7849
CAEtech International, Inc.	4911
Cajam Marketing, Inc.	8631
CAL Inc.	3354
Cal-Am Switch & Relay Co., Inc.	2730
Caldwell Everson PLLC	8250
CalGar Enterprises, LLC	2245
Calico Precision Molding, LLC	7359
Caliente Construction, Inc.	2277
California Creative Solutions, Inc.	4299
California Deposition Reporters	6075
California Electronic Asset Recovery	4300
California Hazardous Services Inc	3355
California Metal & Supply Inc.	6929
Calitex International	9816
Callahan Creek, Inc.	1103
Callier & Garza, L.L.P.	6231
Callor Sales, Inc	2793
Calpak USA, Inc.	2731, 2931
Calpion Inc.	5538
Calumet Brass Foundry, Inc.	6547
Calvada Surveying, Inc.	3055
Calvary Industries, Inc.	1997
Calvine's Coffee LLC	3664
Cam Logistics, LLC	10083
CAMACO, LLC	1865
Cambay Consulting LLC	9442
Cambridge Computer Services, Inc.	4810
Cambridge Marketing, Inc.	6501
Cameron Glass	3245
CamLow, LLC	7435
Cammas & Associates	9511
Campbell Advertising and Design, LLC	9580
Campbell Litigation, P.C.	6092
Camryn Logistics LLC	9982
Can Lines Engineering	6258
Can See Fire Service Co Inc. t/a Fire Solutions	4194
Can-Am Consultants Inc.	7940
Can-Am Wireless LLC dba Can-Am IT Solutions	5539, 9773
Candice Bennett & Associates, Inc.	8838
Candid Services	8156
Candor Expedite	10137
Canela Media	1009
Cannell Graphics	7637
Cannon Industries, Inc.	6746, 6873
Cano Container Corporation	7138
Canon Recruiting Group LLC	8902
Canterbury Pointe LLC	6401
CAO Group, Inc.	6532
Capaccio Environmental Engineering Inc.	3426
Cape Cod Select LLC	3632
Cape Environmental Management Inc.	3410
Capital Brand Group, LLC	2391
Capital Exhibits	1282
Capital Ideas, Inc.	1369
Capital Inventory, Inc.	3102
Capital Legal Solutions dba Capital Novus	5693
Capital Printing Corporation	7602
Capitol Management Consulting Services, Inc.	8290
Capitol Reproductions, Inc.	3156
Capricorn Systems, Inc.	4572
Capsonic Automotive & Aersopace	1866
Capsonic Group, LLC	2964
CAP-STONE & Associates, Inc.	3492
Capstone Facilities Group LLC	2198
Captiva Group	7619
Captura Group	8340
Caraballo Consulting & Associates, LLC	8026
Caracal Products & Services Inc.	7010
Caravan Consulting, LLC	5540
Caravan Facilities Management, LLC	2164
Caravan Technologies, Inc.	2165
Carbide Tool Services, Inc.	3961
Card Quest, Inc.	5862
Cardinal Components, Inc.	6925
Cardinal Environmental Operations Corp.	3451
Cardinal Technology Solutions Inc.	5131
Care Security Systems Inc	1638
Career Center, Inc.	8998
Career Concepts, Inc.	7952
Career Connection, Inc.	7907
Career Connections Staffing Services Inc.	9345
Career Management International, Inc.	8251
Career Solutions International Inc.	8999
Career Uniforms	1716
CareerPros, LLC dba Sedona Staffing Services	9075
Careers Inc.	9397
CareersUSA, Inc.	9000
CareerUnlocked, Inc.	7934
Care-Full Products	6377
Caresoft Inc.	5132
Cargo One Logistics, LLC	10138
Cargo Solutions Express	9836
Caribbean Blue Organic Foods, LLC	3644
Caribbean Temprorary Services, LLC	9398
Carla's Pasta, Inc.	3580
Carlin Solutions, LLC	8171
Carlisle Packaging Company, Inc.	7250
Carlo Lachmansingh Sales, Inc.	2857
Carlos Steffens, Inc.	3556
Carlsmith Ball LLP	6127

COMPANY ALPHABETICAL LISTING

C | INDEX#

Company	Index#
Carmazzi of Florida, Inc.	1010
Carol Nygard & Associates	6076
Carol Philp Inc	1545
Carolina Cartridge Systems, Inc.	5905
Carolina Diagnostic Solutions	6502
Carolina Industrial Products, Inc.	4163
Carolina Industrial Resources, Inc	7204
Carolina IT Professionals, Inc.	5069
Carolina Product Solutions, LLC	2895
Carpet Concepts, Inc.	2218
Carrco Painting Contractors, Inc.	6571
Carriage Works, Inc.	3827
Carrington & Carrington	9086
Carroll Communications Group	1110
Carson Manufacturing Company, Inc.	2971
Carson Solutions, LLC	4855
Cartel Creativo, Inc.	1251
Carter Brothers Security Services LLC	1613
Carter Contracting Co. Corp.	2438
Carter Paper & Packaging, Inc.	7139
Carter Scholer Arnett Hamada & Mockler PLLC	6232
Carter-Health LLC	7745
Cartridge Savers, Inc.	5950
CASADA Industrial	4176
Casalingo LLC	3698
Casas International Brokerage, Inc.	9837
Cascade Management and Consulting	8308
Casco Contractors, Inc.	2292
Casco Manufacturing Solutions, Inc.	9814
Casco Manufacturing, Inc	2744
Case Medical, Inc.	6454
Casemer Tool	6831
Cassel Communications, Inc.	6541
Caster Connection, Inc.	6292
Castillo & Associates	5541
Castle Business Solutions, LLC	1252, 7281
Castle Cop Inc.	1628
CastleOak Securities, L.P.	7817
Catallia Mexican Foods, LLC	3661
Catalpha Advertising & Design	1121
Catalyst Advertizing	1054
Catalyst Learning Co.	8080
causeIMPACTS	7988
Causemedia, Inc.	8536
Cavalier Workforce, Inc	5133
CAVU Securities, LLC.	7818
Cayuse Technologies, LLC	5421
CB Tech	5369
CB Technologies, Inc.	5953
CBA Research Corp.	8675
CBC Sales, Inc.	3609
CBI Consulting Group	5542
CBS Technologies	5134
CCA Distributions	7282
C-CAT, Inc.	9694
CCCS International, LLC	2516
CCG Marketing Services	7603
CCI Environmental, Inc.	3452
CCIntegration, Inc.	5954
CCOM Group, Inc	1055
CCS/PR, Inc.	8341
CCSI Inc.	9272
CD & Associates, Inc.	2495

C | INDEX#

Company	Index#
CD Covenant Distributors International LLC	4039
CDCE Inc.	5835
CDR Assessment Group, Inc.	8209
CDS Architects, Inc.	1733
CE Competitive Edge LLC	1440
CE Supply	2794
CEC Industries Ltd.	2965
Cedar Concepts Corporation	1932
Celarity	9215
CeLeen LLC	4690
Celer Systems, Inc.	4301
Celerit	4246
Celerity Consulting Group, Inc.	7989
Cell Antenna	9666
Cellular Solutions Signal Enhancing Specialists	9712
Cellworx LLC	4573
Celta Chemical, Inc.	1933
Cenmed Enterprises	6455
Centacor, Inc.	5828
Centaur Graphics LLC	7557
Centennial Securities Advisory Services	7790
Centerline Services LLC	3088
Central Carolina Products	7400
Central Computer Systems Inc.	4302
Central Metals, Inc.	6657
Central Wisconsin Flex	4035
Centricity Technology Partners, Inc.	4475
Centryco Inc.	9811
Century Hosiery, Inc.	1698
Century Products LLC	2188
Century Security Services, Inc.	2683
Century Wire & Cable	2932
CEO Inc.	9254
Cerami & Associates, Inc.	5292
Cerna Solutions, LLC	4303
Certes Financial Pros, Inc.	7801
Certified Constructors' Services Inc.	2334
Certified Credit Reporting, Inc.	7879
Certified Independent Adjusters, Inc.	4304
Certified Translations LLC	1056
Certintell, Inc.	4664
Cervantes Distribution Companies, Inc.	1896
CES Network Services, Inc.	5543
Cesar Castillo, Inc.	6496
CESCO, Inc.	5544
Cetan Corp.	5694
CETS LLC	3033
Cetus Digital LLC	4989
CF Entertainment, Inc.	9567
CFA Inc.	9121
CFJ Manufacturing	1563
CG Plastics, Inc.	7375
CGB Tech Solutions Inc	5370
CGN & Associates, Inc.	8055
CGS, Inc.	2027
Chagrin Consulting Services Inc.	5371
Chambers Gasket & Manufacturing Co.	3997
Chameleon Technologies, Inc.	5794
Champion Business Services	7889
Champion Fuel Solutions	2039
Champion Life Safety Solutions	1657
Chapin LLC	3610
Chapman Lean Enterprise	8172

COMPANY ALPHABETICAL LISTING

C

Company	INDEX#
Chapman Manufacturing Company	3950
Char Mason & Associates, LLC, dba Mason Creative	8582
Chard Snyder	7837
Char-Dell Sign Co.	7574
Charles Gojer & Associates, Inc.	3296
Charleston Gourmet Burger Company	3706
Charleston's Rigging and Marine Hardware Inc	4164
Charm Consulting	8726
CharmedBar, LLC	3645
Charter Controls, Inc.	3034
Charter Global Inc.	4574
Charter Solutions, Inc.	4990
Chase Components LLC	2814
Chaser, LLC	9944
Chasm Communications, Inc.	8409
Chat of Michigan Inc.	9983
Chaucer Press, Inc.	7656
Checks and Balances, Inc.	9512
Chef Belinda LLC dba Chef Belinda Spices	3707
Chela Logistics Inc.	9921
Chelsea Partners Inc.	8753
ChemCeed LLC	2072
Chemical Distribution Solutions, LLC	1892
Chemical Systems	1917
Chemico Systems, Inc.	1956
ChemicoMays, LLC	1957
Chemplast, Inc.	7436
Chenango Contracting, Inc.	3478
Chenhall's Staffing, Inc	9076
Chenoa Information Services, Inc.	5135
Cherry	1697
Cherry City Electric	3035
Cheseldine Management Consulting, LLC	8094
Cheshil Consultants, Inc.	5695
Chester Engineers, Inc.	3252
Chica Intelligente LLC	8342
Chicago Communications, LLC	9682
Chicago Green Office Company dba National Office Works, Inc.	6995
Chicago Parts & Sound, LLC	1857
Chico & Nunes, P.C.	6130
Chicopee Industrial Contractors	2386
Chief of Staff LLC	9236
Chippewa Capital LLC	7791
Chippewa Industries, Inc.dba Thaymar Medical	6832
Chippewa Systems, Ltd.	4003
Chocolate Promises, Inc.	3685, 3870
Choctaw-Kaul Distribution Company	4102
Choice Counsel, Inc.	9380
Choice Hire Staffing LLC	9443
Choice One Staffing Group, Inc.	9381
Choice Premiums	1370
Choson Resource LLC	3132, 9129
Christian Brothers Mechanical Services, Inc.	2293
Chrom Tech, Inc.	4007
Chrysalis Coaching & Consulting	8084
Chrysan Industries, Inc.	1958
Chryspac - Quality Custom Solutions	7295
Church Hill Classics	1333
Church Metal Spinning Company	6707, 6760
CI2, Inc.	4575
Ci2i Services, Inc.	9534
Ciber Global, LLC	4912

C

Company	INDEX#
CIC Construction Group, SE	2507
Cici Boiler Rooms Inc.	4212
Cico Electrical Contractors Inc.	9641
CIMA Consulting Group	9176
Cima Solutions Group, Ltd.	5545
Cimarron Express Inc.	10084
Cimarron Graphics	7575
Cimarron Software Services, Inc.	5546
Cimcon Finishing, LLC	6572
CIMCOR Inc.	4770
Cincinnati Cable Technology	9746
Cincinnati Sub-Zero Products, LLC	6478
CIR Law Offices International	6077
Circle City Rebar, LLC	6606, 6941
Circom, Inc.	2745
Circuitronics LLC	2746
Circuitronix, LLC	2739
CIS Cenergy International Services	5547
Citadel NY Inc.	5293
Citation Plastics, LLC	7336
Citra Solv, LLC	2103
Civil Design Inc.	3191
CJ & Associates, Inc.	3850
CJ Industrial Supply Inc.	3930
CK&M Direct Mail Advertising, Inc.	1072
CKS Precision Machining	6833
CKSports and Associates LLC	1371
Clara I. Brown Interiors, Inc. (CIBI)	3820
Clariti Eyewear, Inc.	6342
Clarity Concepts Inc.	8213
Clarity Tek, Inc.	4991
Clark Consulting Group, Inc.	7916
Clark Environmental, Inc.	3398
Clark Media Corp.	1168
Clark Resources, Inc.	9755
Clark-Powell Associates, Inc.	5070
ClarkTel Communications Corp.	9747
Classic Acrylics Inc.	7395
Classic Conferences Inc.	8632
Classic Labels Inc.	7625
Classical Marketing LLC	8477
Clavél	2594
Clay Precision, Ltd.	6908, 7437
Clayborn Inc.	9774
Clayborne, Sabo, and Wagner LLP	6131
CLC Publicidad dba Sherpa Marketing Solutions	8343
Clean Advantage, Inc.	2232
Clean Clean, Inc.	2109
Clean Impressions Corp.	2135
Clean Sweep Group Inc	2082
Clear Image Printing, Inc.	7459
Clear Lake Press, Inc.	7576
CLEAR Solutions, Inc.	3989
ClearPath Management Group, Inc	7880
ClearRES LLC	5548
ClearSounds Communication	9683
ClearTone Communications Inc.	9667
Clearvue Networks, LLC	9775
ClemCorp	5372
Clerysys Incorporated	4691
Cleveland Die & Mfg. Co.	6565, 6878
Clinical Choice LLC	6046
Clinton Gaddy Inc.	5071

COMPANY ALPHABETICAL LISTING

C

Company	INDEX#
Clint's Picante Inc.	3717
Clipper Corporation	1669
Clips & Clamps Industries	6627, 6834
Cloud Track, LLC	1073
Clover Systems Inc.	9872
Clovity Inc.	4305
CLS Technology, Inc.	1658
Cluso Investigation LLC	6233
Clutch Group LLC DBA-Clutch	9382
Clutch Solutions LLC	4251
Clyde Printing Company	7511
CM Productions, Inc.	9628
CMA Architects & Engineers LLC	1812
CMA Enterprise Incorporated	8027
CMMD Enterprises, Inc.	3534
cmnd+m LLC	1140
CMS Sourcing Solutions	2166
CMT Agency	8443
CNC Consulting	5136, 9281
CnC Controls	4913
CNC Products Inc.	6835
Coach for Higher	8110
Coast Sign Inc.	1011
Coast to Coast Communications	9642
Coast to Coast Conferences & Events	8344
Coast to Coast Financial Solutions Inc.	7721
Coastal Machine & Mechanical, LLC	6909
Coastal Steel Inc.	6590
Coastal Telecommunications Inc.	9704
Coating Solutions, Inc.	6563
Coda Sound Inc.	9581
Codale Energy Services & Supply, LLC	2869
Code Creative Services	7309
COEX Coffee International Inc.	3588
Cogent Data Solutions LLC	4692
Cogent Integrated Business Solutions, Inc.	4914
Cognis IT Advisors LLC	5434
Cognitive Technologies, Inc.	5549
Cognixia Inc.	5137
Cold Headed Fasteners & Assemblies, Inc.	3969
Cole Chemical & Distributing, Inc.	2040
Coleman Laboratories	6492
Coles Marketing Communications	8522
Collabera	5138
Collaborative Advantage Marketing	8567
Collaborative Food & Beverage, LLC dba Mayorga Coffee	3646
Collaborative Vision LLC	9369
Colliers Facility Solutions, LLC	2355
Colonial Plastics, Inc	7376
Colonial Press International, Inc.	7488
Color Media Group, LLC	1111, 8537
Colorado Lighting, Inc.	2949
Colorado's Advanced Restoration Experts, LLC	3384
Colour One O One, Inc.	8444
Columbia Data Systems, Inc.	5929
Columbia Enterprises	2326
Columbia Sanitary Products, Inc.	6580
Com Serv LLC	3896
Com2 Computers and Technologies	4693
Combined Computer Resources, Inc.	5139
Combined Metals of Chicago LLC	6598
Combustion Associates, Inc.	4204

C

Company	INDEX#
Comcentia, LLC	5819
COMFORCE	9039
ComGraphics Inc.	7512
Command Marketing Innovations	8633
Commercial Bag Company	7140
Commercial Construction Inc.	2397
Commercial Cutting & Graphics, LLC	1216
Commercial Interiors, Inc.	3795
Commercial Lumber & Pallet Company, Inc.	10228
Commercial Office Environments Inc.	3773
Commercial Site Improvements, Inc.	2294
Commodity Management Services CMS	7638
commonground	1091
Commonwealth Capital Corp	7746
Communication Brokers, Inc.	9713
Communication Experts, Inc.	5140
Communication Management, Inc.	8085
Communications & Electrical Supplies, Inc.	2861
Communications Media, Inc.	1227
Communications Professionals, Inc.	4915
Communitronics Corp.	5034
Community Based Staffing	9177
Community Marketing Concepts, Inc.	8754
COMNet Group, Inc.	5072
Compact Industries	3611
Compact International	3743
Compact Solutions, LLC.	4694
Company 20, Inc.	8676
Company Apparel Safety Items, Inc.	1687
Compas, Inc.	1485
Compass Consulting Services, LLC	8194
Compass Technology Group, LLC	5550
Competent Systems Inc.	4576
Competitive Choice, Inc.	2246
Competitive Edge Media Management	1012
Complemar Partners	8677
Complete Carpet Care Inc.	2146
Complete Discovery Source Inc.	6191
Complete Solutions LLC	7586
CompleteSource Inc.	1441
Complex Network Solutions	4695
CompliStaff, Inc.	9320
CompNova LLC.	5551
Component Design Northwest, Inc.	6325
Composite Technologies LLC	7413
CompQsoft, Inc.	5552
Comprehensive Drug Testing, Inc. (CDT, Inc.)	6023
CompuCycle, Inc.	4239
CompuGain LLC	5696
Compulink Technologies, Inc.	5294
Compunnel Software Group, Inc.	5141
CompuPlus International Inc.	5142
CompuPro Global	5935
CompuSoft Integrated Solutions, Inc.	4916
Computa-Base Machining	6869
Computech Corporation	4917
Computer Enterprises, Inc.	5435
Computer Upgrade King, LLC	5947
ComputerSuppliers.Com	5836
Computize Inc.	5981
Compu-Vision Consulting Inc.	5143
Comrise Technology, Inc.	5144
ComSolutions Inc.	5035

COMPANY ALPHABETICAL LISTING

C   INDEX#

Company	Index#
ComTec Consultants Inc.	4804
Con Rac Construction Group LLC	2451
Concept Industries, Inc.	1867
Concept Software & Services Inc	4577
Concepts & Associates	1300
Concepts Office Furnishings, Inc.	3804
Conch Technologies, Inc.	5505
Concierge Staffing LLC	9255
Concise, Inc.	9674
Concord Information Systems, LLC	5973
Concordant Healthcare Solutions, Inc.	7377
Concours Direct, Inc.	1848
Coneybeare Inc.	8903
Confero, Inc.	8618
Confidential Security Agency, Inc.	2631
Connect Technology Solutions	5295
ConnectedSign, LLC	1228, 5436
Connexions Data Inc.	5145
Conover + Gould Strategic Communications, Inc.	8538
Consolidated Cordage Corp Inc.	3887
Consolidated Energy Design, Inc.	3203
Consolidated Marketing Services, Inc.	8539
Consolidated Printing Company	7513
ConstructAbility, Inc.	2466
Construction & Environmental Services of Virginia	2557
Construction and Service Solutions Corp.	2452
Construction Support Solutions, LLC	2467
Consult Our Sorce, LLC	4306
Consulting Management Inspection Design, Inc.	3128
Consultis	5553
Consumer and Market Insights, LLC (CMI)	8785
Consumer Financial Service Corporation	7722
Containers Plus, Inc.	7088, 10227
Containers Unlimited, Inc.	7120
Contemporaries, Inc.	9158
Contemporary Business Interiors, LLC	3781
Contemporary Motives, Inc	3805
Content Spectrum	8619
Contine Corporation	2770
Continental Building Maintenance	2083
Continental Chemicals, LLC	1972
Continental Manufacturing, LLC	2972
Continental Painting and Decorating	2365
Continental Resources Inc.	4811
Continental Technical Services	9547
Continental Trading & Services, Inc.	10069
Continental Wireless	9776
Continental, Inc.	3129
Continuum Architects + Planners, S.C.	1824
Contract Direct, LLC	2167
Contract Furniture Group, LLC	3778
Contract Source & Assembly Inc.	7173
Contractors Cargo Companies	9838
Contractors Corner, LLC	2247
Control Specialties, Inc.	4069
Controls and Automation Consultants LLC	5296
ConvenePro	8530
Convenience Electronics, Inc.	3039
Convenient Tape & Supplies LLC	5882
Converge Marketing Services, LLC	8678
Conversions Technology	5837
Conviso Inc.	5697
Conway Machine, Inc.	6763

C   INDEX#

Company	Index#
Cook & Schmid, LLC	8345
Cook Paving & Construction Co., Inc.	2468
Cookies by Design	3718
Cool Tactics LLC	6591
Coolant Control, Inc.	1998
Cooling Components Inc.	2862
Cooper Atkins	6322
Cooper Electrical Construction	2997, 6319
Coover-Clark & Associates, Inc.	1742
Cope Plastics Inc.	7345
Copiosity, LLC	3865
Copy King, Inc.	7639
Cor Creative, Inc.	1092
Coradorables,LLC	1682
Coranet Corp	9737
Corbus, LLC	5373
Cordell Transporation Company LLC	10085
Cordova Bolt, Inc.	3880
Cordova Marketing Group	8410
Core Diagnostics	6024
Core Technology Molding Corp.	7401
CORE10 Architecture	1776
CoreLogix Consulting Incorporation	5698
Corley Gasket Company	4020
Cornerstone EHS, LLC	3467
Cornerstone Supply, Inc.	4040
Cornfields, Inc.	3612
Corpnet Consulting LLC	4578
Corporate Advertising & Incentives	1457
Corporate Artworks, Ltd.	3857
Corporate Computer Solutions	5297
Corporate Concepts, Inc.	3770
Corporate Diversity Solutions	7030
Corporate Document Solutions, Inc.	7640
Corporate Environmental Advisors, Inc.	3138, 3427
Corporate Environmental Risk Management	3411
Corporate Environments of GA, Inc.	3766
Corporate Facilities of New Jersey, LLC	3831
Corporate Fitness Works, Inc.	8028
Corporate GT Denver, Inc.	9865
Corporate Identity, Inc.	1385
Corporate Image Maintenance	2084
Corporate Interior System	3738
Corporate Interiors, Inc.	3760
Corporate Leasing Associates, Inc.	7819
Corporate Office Solutions, LLC	7083
Corporate Records Management Inc.	5554
Corporate Reports, Inc.	7751
Corporate Screening Consulting, LLC	7941
Corporate Subscription Management Services, LLC	4501
Corporate Tax Incentives	7723
Corporate Temps, Inc.	9040
Corporate Training Group, Inc.	5146
Corporate Translations, Inc.	8346
Corporate World Public Relations	8531
Corpotel, Inc	4502
CORPTEMPS	9346
CorTech	9041
Cortes Construction Services, LLC	2335
CorTrans Logistics, LLC	9896
CosaTech, Inc.	4696
Cosmic Software Technology, Inc.	5147
Costello Enterprises, LLC	6836

COMPANY ALPHABETICAL LISTING

C — INDEX#

Company	Index#
Costello Machine LLC	6837
Cotapaxi Custom Design & Manufacturing, LLC	1486
Cotter Consulting, Inc.	2366
CottonImages.com, Inc.	1345
CounterTrade Products Inc.	5961
County Draperies, Inc.	3813
Courier Graphics Corporation	7453
Courington Kiefer & Sommers, LLC	6144
Courtney Material Handling, Inc.	4087
Coverall Health Based Cleaning System	2189
Covert Manufacturing, Inc.	6879
Cox Financial Corporation	6013
Coxco, Inc.	7089
Coyanosa Gas Services Corporation	2063
CP Industries, LLC	2060
CP Lab Safety	6025
CPAC Inc.	4307
CPI (USA) Inc.	5977
CPM PR, LLC	2508
CPR Insurance Group LLC	6018
CQ fluency, Inc.	1169
CR Environmental Inc	3428
CR Quality Roofing of PR, Inc.	2509
CR&A Custom, Inc.	1013
CRA Communications LLC	8869
Craftsman Custom Metals, LLC	6794
Craig Enterprises, Inc. dba CommGap	8833
Craig Technical Consulting, Inc.	4503
Craters and Freighters	7109, 9866
Crave InfoTech LLC	5148
Crawford & Associates Services, LLC	3235
Crawford Consulting Services, Inc.	2496
CRB Caribe, LLP	3267
CREA Construction	2367
Creality Promo+Retail, inc.	1458
Creative & Response Research Services, Inc.	8478
Creative CNC LLC	6708
Creative Connections	8583
Creative Corporate Ideas Inc	1372
Creative Enterprise Solutions LLC (dba Beyond20)	4252
Creative Human Resources Concepts LLC	8880
Creative Innovators, Inc.	1373
Creative Juice LLC	8445
Creative Maintenance Solutions, LLC	2064
Creative Menus & Folders, LLC dba Texas Covers	1564, 7682
Creative Merchandise Displays Inc.	1001
Creative Packaging Solutions Corporation	7212
Creative Research Management	3557
Creative Resources Agency	1459
Creative Video Corporation	9578
Creative Zing Promotion Group	8411
Creatives On Call Inc.	9237
Credit Financial Group Inc.	8606
Credit Systems International, Inc.	7850
CREDO Technology Solutions, Inc.	5437
Creekwood Energy Partners, LLC	1999
Crescens Inc.	5149
Crescent Chemical Co., Inc.	1991
Crest Foodservice Equipment Company	4229
Crest Telecom, Inc.	9706
Crew Design Inc.	1041
Crews Control Inc	9159
CRG Global, Inc.	8412

C — INDEX#

Company	Index#
Crimcheck	7944
Crispy Green Inc.	3676
Cristina Foods, Inc.	3613
Critical Start LLC	5555
Critique Personnel Service, Inc.	9238
Cromedy Construction Corporation	6680
Crosby Corporation	9160
Cross Management Services, Inc.	8316
Cross Packaging Supply, Inc.	7141
Cross River Medical LLC dba Proforma Edge	7226
CrossComm, Inc.	5073
Crossfire Consulting	5298
CrossFire Group LLC	9178
Crossing Cultures LLC	2579
Crossland Carriers Inc.	10034
Crossmark Graphics, Inc.	7707
Crossover Ent. LLC	9620
Crossroads USA	7200
Cross-Spectrum Acoustics Inc	6037
CrossUSA Inc.	4992
Crowdstaffing, a Zenith Talent Company	8904
Crown CyberSystems	4993
Crown Marking, Inc.	7021
Crown Services, Inc.	9347
Crown Sign Systems	1194
Crown Trophy Winston-Salem	1475
Crown Xpress Transport Inc.	9839
CRSGroup, Inc.	4697
Cruise.Com	10200
Crutchfield & Associates Inc.	1160
Cruvel Data Analytics	7967
CRW Graphics	7604
CryoPlus, Inc.	3931
Crystal Application Software Services, LLC	9777
Crystal Data LLC	5150
Crystal Employment Services, LLC	9179
Crystal Equation Corporation	9087
Crystal Inc. PMC	2017
Crystal, Inc.	2018
CS Creative	8786
CS Insurance Strategies	5996
CS Solutions, Inc.	4994
CS3W Associates, Inc.	3327
CSA Central, Inc.	3479
CSBO Architecture P.C.	1782
CSCG Inc.	2510
CSG LLC	5496
C-Shore International Inc.	3558
CSI International, Inc.	2225
CSS Building Services Inc	2199
CSS Building Services Inc.	7031
CSS Distribution Group, Inc.	7166
CST2000 dba iCST IT Solutions	4900
CSW Inc.	7542
CT Metal Source	6953
CTI and Associates, Inc.	3157
CTL Engineering, Inc.	3236, 3493
CTL Global, Inc.	9922
CTL Resources (Caribou Thunder)	5820
CTS Services Inc.	4812
Cube Care Company	2110
Cube Hub Inc.	4698, 9088
Cube Intelligence Corporation	4813

COMPANY ALPHABETICAL LISTING

C INDEX#

Company	Index#
Culturati Research & Consulting, Inc.	8347
Culture Coach International	8086
CultureBrokers, LLC	8128
Cummins Facility Services, LLC	2219
CurDor Group Inc.	9840
Curia Document Solutions LLC	4504
Curtin & Associates, LLP	6207
CurtMont Global Services, Inc.	5699
Custom Business Solutions, Inc.	4918
Custom Essence	2586
Custom Machining Corporation	6784
Custom Manufacturing & Engineering, Inc.	6788
Custom Mechanical Systems, Corp.	2378
Custom Millcraft Corp.	3970
Custom Paper Tubes	7240
Custom Results Corporate Consulting LLC	6005
Custom Service Plastics, Inc.	7447
Custom Staffing, Inc.	9321
Customed USA, LLC	6378
Customer Lifecycle, LLC	8479
Customer Relationship Metrics	8839
Cutter Lumber Products	10229
Cutter Productions	9608
Cutting Source Precision, Inc.	6910
CVAL Innovations LLC	4021
CW Carriers USA Inc.	9873
CX Enterprise Inc.	6581
Cyber Clarity Inc.	5700
Cyber Management Systems	4856
Cyber Professionals Inc. dba Encore Software Service	4308
Cyber Research Group	4788
Cyber Security Consulting Ops	5151
Cyber Shield Consulting Inc.	9256
CyberAnalysis, LLC	8446
Cyberbridge Intl. Inc. dba Creospan Inc.	4699
Cybergear, Inc.	5829
Cybern Consulting Group, LLC	4857
Cybersoft Technologies Inc.	5556
cyberThink, Inc.	5152
Cybervation, Inc.	5374
Cygnus Professionals Inc.	5153
Cylinders Inc.	3998
CYMA Systems Inc.	8975
Cymbal Communications Corporation	9684
Cynergies Solutions Group	5375
Cynergy Professional Systems LLC	3056
Cynet Systems Inc.	5701, 9513
CyQuest Business Solutions, Inc.	7908

D

Company	Index#
D & D Logistics, LLC	9984
D & G Express Service, Ltd.	10191
D & J Tool Supply, LLC	3938
D & R Machine Co.	6897
D Exposito & Partners, LLC	8679
D Unique Tools Inc	3949
D&A Building Services, Inc.	2111
D&D Business Inc. dba DDI Printing	7514
D. Gillette Industrial Service, Inc.	4223
D.A.G. Construction Company, Inc.	2469
D.M. Radio Service Corp.	9729
D.Trio Marketing Group	8584

D INDEX#

Company	Index#
D.W. Morgan Company, Inc.	9841
DA/PRO Rubber Inc.	7424
DaBrian Marketing Group	8755
DACK Consulting Solutions	7820
Dacus Fence Co. Inc.	4247
Dahl Consulting, Inc.	9216
Dairyland Electric Co, Inc.	3040
Dakkota Integrated Systems, LLC	3158
Dakota Consulting Inc.	4858
Dakota Print and Premiums LLC	1504, 7626
Dalany Metal Products Inc.	6838
Dale Workforce Solutions, LLC	9322
Dallas Digital Services, LLC	5557
Dallas Fan Fares, Inc.	8787
Dallas Paper & Packaging	7065
Dalton Medical Corp.	6519
DaMar Staffing Solutions	9122
Damasco Design Inc	4505
DAMRON Corporation	3614
Dan Dolan Printing	7577
Dana Graphics, Inc.	7641
Dancor Inc.	7642
Daniel Penn Associates, LLC	8012
Danlee Medical Products, Inc.	6470
Danrick Industries Inc.	3981
Danta Technologies	4309
DAP Construction Management, LLC	2278
Darana Hybrid	6293
Darling Geomatics	3349
Darlyng & Co.	1699
DARRAN Furniture Industries, Inc.	3797
Darwin Securities, LLC	2627
Data Access Inc.	2668
Data Bridge Consultants LLC	5074
Data Concepts	5702
Data Defenders, LLC	4700
Data Destruction LLC	4439
Data Dynamics, Inc.	5036
DATA Inc. USA	5911
Data Integration Consulting, Inc.	4771
Data Ranger Computer Products	5891
Data Research Inc.	8480
Data Video Systems	1646
Databased Solutions Inc.	5154
Data-Clear	5703
DataEdge Consulting, Inc.	5155
Datamatics Consultants Inc.	4579
Datanomics, Inc.	5156, 9282
Dataoptek Corp	9643
DataSavers of Jacksonville, Inc.	4506
Dataservinc	5099
Dataset, Inc.	4580
Datasoft Global LLC	5037
Datasoft Technologies Inc.	5499
Datasyst Engineering & Testing	3336
Daten System Consulting	4240
Datrose	5299
Datum Software Inc.	4581
Dave Scott & Associates, Inc.	3739
Davenport Capital Management	7763
David Carrie LLC	6192
David Mason & Associates, Inc.	3192
Davies Office Refurbishing, Inc.	3814

COMPANY ALPHABETICAL LISTING

D | INDEX#

Company	Index#
Davis & Company, Inc.	8157
Davis & Davis Professional Services Firm LLC	7851
Davis & Green, Inc.	2558
Davis & Stanton, Inc.	1565
Davitz Group	2531
Dawn Incorporated	2470
Dawood Engineering, Inc.	3253
Dawson & Dawson Staffing Inc.	8905
Dawson Mfg Co. - Benton Harbor Division	1868
Daxwell	4177
DayBlink	5704
Daybreak Marketing Services, LLC	1476
Daycoa, Incorporated	2879
Dayton Mailing Services, Inc.	1217
Dazmed, Inc.	6379
DB Commercial Group LLC	4859
DBG Construction, LLC	2488
DBS Marketing & Promotions LLC	1566
Dbsys Inc.	4507
DC Engineering Group, PSC	3268
DC McIssac Corp. dba FPC Arlington, Inc.	9089
DCC Marketing, LLC	8481
DCM Technology Solutions, Inc.	4440
DCR Denmark Court Reporting Agency, LLC	6208
DD Consulting and Management	5075
DD Office Products, Inc	6978
DDM Professional Leasing Services	7895
De Clercq Office Group	3757
DeAmertek	3111
Dean Baldwin Painting, LP	6555
Debbie Lynn, Inc.	1434
Debbie's Staffing Services, Inc.	9257
Debo Enterprises Incorporated	10086
Deborah Wood Associates, Inc.	1100
Debra Gould & Associates, Inc.	7922
Decca Consulting LLC	5558
Decentxposure LLC	8634
Dechen Consulting Group, Inc.	4919
Decision Distribution America, Inc.	2887
Decision Insight Inc.	8607
Decision Tree Technologies	5559
DecisionOne Corporation	5438
DecisivEdge LLC	4486, 8018
Decor Interior Design	3744
Dedicated Tech Services, Inc.	5376
Deegit, Inc.	9090
Deemsys Inc.	5377
Deep Roof Lighting	2871
Deep Well, Inc.	1141
Deerwalk, Inc.	4814
Defense Support Services, Inc.	5560
Definiti Healthcare Management	5986
Deirdre Sanborn & Associates	8252
Del Ray Security	2656
Del Toro & Santana	6225
Delaco Steel Corporation	6726, 6943
Delaire USA, Inc.	2765
Delaney & Delaney LLC	6142
Delaware Resource Group of Oklahoma LLC	5417
Delina Inc.	3589
Dellrone Services LLC	1705
Delta Automation, Inc.	2913
Delta Computer Consulting, Inc.	4310, 8906

D | INDEX#

Company	Index#
Delta Consulting Group, Inc	8238
Delta Leasing LLC	7714
Delta Personnel, Inc.	9134
Delta Risk Capital Group LLC	7821
DeltaTRAK Inc.	3057
Deltronix Technologies Inc.	5300
Deluxe Delivery Systems, Inc.	10070
DelVideo Productions	9579
DeMahy Labrador & Drake PA (DLD Lawyers)	6103
Demand Lighting USA Inc	2903
Demeter's Pantry dba GreenFood Associates LLC	3647
Dempsey Business Systems of Louisiana	5884
Denali Telecom Solutions, Inc.	9635
Denise Meridith Consultants Inc.	8320
Denison Consulting Group LLC	1688
Denysys Corporation	4995
Departure Travel Management	10210
Dependable Facility Cleaning Services, LLC	2152
DePirro/GarroneLLC	1195
Depo International	6164
Deque Systems, Inc.	5705
Derive Technologies	5301
Derrah Morrison Enterprises, LLC	7066
DES Wholesale, LLC	1923
DESA, Inc	8235
Desai Communication	1042
Desert Paper & Envelope Company, Inc.	7036
Desert Star Enterprises, Inc	1253
Design & Promotions Corp.	1346
Design & Source Productions, Inc.	8680
Design Alternatives NY LLC	1701
Design Associates International, Inc	6297
Designer Installation Services, Inc.	3784
Designer Sign Systems	1142
Designs That Compute	5936
Desktop Color Systems	5903
Desktop Service Center, Inc.	5706
DESMAN, Inc. dba DESMAN Associates	3214
Dessert Gallery Bakery & Cafe	3874
Destiny Management Services, LLC	8095
Detail Planners, LLC	8413
Detroit Chassis LLC	1869
Detroit Engineered Products (DEP)	3159
Detroit Logistics Company	9985
Detroit Manufacturing Systems	2755
DevCare Solutions	5378
Development Management & Consulting Group, Inc.	8227
Development One, Inc.	1734
DEVLINHAIR Production Inc.	8681
DevMar Products, LLC	7063
DEW Electric, Inc.	2888
Dew Software, Inc.	4311
DeWhit, Inc.	2233
Dexen Industries, Inc.	3990
deZinnia, Inc.	8585
DFI Technologies, LLC	4312
DFM Solutions (Devon Facility Management LLC)	2168
DFW LinQ Transport	10139
DGH Enterprises, Inc. dba K-O Products Co.	6628, 6727
DGS Create, Inc.	8840
DGX, LLC	1635
DH Security Solutions	1617
Dhaivat Maharaja Enterprises Inc.	4860

COMPANY ALPHABETICAL LISTING

D

Company	INDEX#
Dhake Industries	6560
DHDC Engineering Consulting Services, Inc.	6054
Diagnocine LLC	8635
Diamond Display Group Partners, Inc.	7283
Diamond Graphics Inc.	7657
Diamond P Enterprises, Inc.	9778
Diamond Packaging	7227
Diamond T Services Inc.	3385
Diamond Wipes International	2085
Diamonds Management Group, Inc.	2559
Diaz Foods	3599
Die Cad Group	6728
Die Cut Technologies/Denver Gasket	3992, 7110
Die-Mension Corporation	6747
Dien, Inc.	2041
Dienamic Tool Corporation	6839
Diesel Electrical Equipment, Inc.	2835
Diggs Construction, LLC	2323
Digi-Color, LP	7683
Digicomm Systems, Inc.	9675
Digilent Consulting, LLC	5707
Digital Brand Expressions	8636
Digital Business Solutions, Inc.	8532
Digital Consulting & Software Services, Inc.	5561
Digital Foundation Computer Consulting Services Co	4861
Digital Hands	4508
Digital Intelligence Systems, LLC dba Dexian DISYS	5708
Digital Mania, Inc.	7460
Digital Mountain	4313
Digital Outdoor Advertising	1170
Digital Partners Incorporated	5038
Digital Prospectors Corp.	5100
Digital Services Enterprises	7461
Digital Thrive, LLC	1254
Digital Video Solutions, Inc.	1625
Digitive LLC	4314
Dilan Consulting Group	7990
DINATCO Inc.	7643
Dine Modular Construction, LLC	2275
Dinucci Corporation	6772
Diper Designers LLC	8414
Direct Line To Compliance, Inc.	5562
Direct Mail Depot	7605
Direct Marketing Alliance Inc.	8756
Direct Medical Supplies, LLC	6506
Direct Results Radio, Inc.	1014
Directed Action, Inc.	7991
DirecToHispanic, LLC	8788
Discount Lab Supplies	6026
Discountcell Inc.	9790
Discovery ChemScience LLC	6456
Discreet Check, LLC	7931
Display America	1074
Distinctive Marketing Ideas	1567
Distinctive Marketing, Inc.	8637
Distinctive Personnel	9323
Distributed Technology Associates	4815
DISYS Solutions, Inc.	5709
DIVERSA LLC	7968
Diversant, LLC	4582
Diverse Concepts, Inc.	4862
Diverse Industries, Inc.	3282
Diverse Lynx LLC	5157
Diverse Maintenance Solutions Inc.	2178
Diverse Services USA, Inc.	6309
Diverse Solution and Supplies	7121
Diverse Staffing Services	9123
Diverse Supply Chain Partner, LLC	8195
Diversified Adjustment Service, Inc.	7802
Diversified Business Consultants, Inc.	1546
Diversified Chemical and Supply, Inc.	2042
Diversified Chemical Technologies, Inc.	1959
Diversified Consulting Consortium, LLC	7936
Diversified Diamond Products	4046
Diversified Engineering & Plastics	7378
Diversified Global Systems, LLC.	3254
Diversified Quality Services of Indiana, LLC	6607
Diversified Risk Management	2611
Diversified Staffing & Consulting Group LLC	9042
Diversified Supply, Inc.	2898
Diversified Technical Services, Inc.	5563
Diversified Technology Consultants	3089
Diversitech, Inc.	1870
Diversity Benefits	6017
Diversity Marketing and Communications	8638
Diversity Products	7174
Diversity Resources Group	2532
DiversityInPromotions, Inc.	8253
DivIHN Integration Inc.	4701
Divine Capital Markets	7822
Division 10 Personnel Services of Milwaukee, Inc.	9537
Dixie Graphics	7500
Dixien LLC	6716, 7337
Dixon Phone Place, Inc.	9695
Dixon Services, Inc.	4168
DJDC Inc.	1807
DJG Chemical, Inc.	1924
DK Cleaning Contractors, LLC	2497
DK Consulting, LLC	4863
DLZ Industrial, LLC	3237
DM Connect LLC	8348
DMC Design	1229
DMD Consulting, LLC	9091
DMG Commercial Construction Services, Inc.	2533
DMI Technologies, Inc.	9779
DMN3	1255
DN Plastics	7379
DNK Architects, Inc.	1800
Dnutch Associates, Inc.	4816
Doc Stephens Scientific	2933
doc2e-file,Inc.	5564
Doc-Development, Inc., LLC	6402
Document Imaging Systems of St. Louis	5039
Docunet Corporation	7578
DocuSource of North Carolina	7592
Doddi Information Technologies	5302
Doherty Staffing Solutions, Inc.	9217
Dollar Aisle, LLC	2974
Domar Companies, LLC	8907
Dominion Builders, LLC	2336
Dominus Gray, LLC	4583
Domo Domo IMG	8395
Domus Inc.	1230
Don Jagoda Associates, Inc	1505
Donnelly & Moore Corporation	5303
D'Onofrio Consulting Partners	8254

COMPANY ALPHABETICAL LISTING

D | INDEX#

Company	Index#
Dose Engineering, PLLC	3215
Doshi Associates, Inc.	3160
Dothan Security Inc. dba DSI Security Services	2600
Double T. Signs Inc.	1002
DoubleShot Creative, LLC	8349
Doubletake Studios, Inc.	1057
Dougherty Sprague Environmental, Inc.	3525
Dove Direct	1075
Dover Foods, Inc.	3665
DoverStaffing	9043
Dow-Caide Industrial, Inc.	4178
Dowding Industries	6840
Doyensys, Inc.	5565
DP Distribution & Consulting, LLC	8291
DPN Group, LLC	8096
Dragonfly Group	7684
Drake Incorporated	2327
Drakonx, Inc.	2628
Dramatic Conclusions, LLC	8255
Dream Big Media Solutions dba Alphagraphics 114	7685
Driven to Succeed LLC	8196
Drohan Lee LLP	6193
Drury Design Dynamics, Inc.	8682
DSC Logistics, Inc.	9923
DSI Warehouse Inc	7267
DSSI Group Holding, LLC	4798
DSSI LLC	8111
DT Investments Inc. dba Beacon Printing Inc.	7479
Dtocs LLC	3828
Dual Sales & Associates, Inc.	3655
Duarte Communications, Inc.	8350
Dudak Production, Inc.	1143
Dudas IT Resources & Advisory, Inc.	4454
DuffyGroup, Inc.	8881
Duggal Visual Solutions	7627
Duncan & Duncan Medical, Inc.	6343
Duncan/Day Advertising, LP	1256
Dunkin & Bush, Inc.	2069, 3541, 6574
Duran Industries Inc.	4179, 6067
DuraTech USA, Inc.	5955
Durfold Corporation	3796
Dutch Gold Honey, Inc.	3699
DV Roland Enterprises, Inc.	1885
DW Practice, LLC	4584
DW Training and Development Incorporated	4789
DWG CPA PLLC	7852
DWY Inc.	2795
Dynamic Color Graphics	7686
Dynamic Computer Corporation	5975
Dynamic Computing Services	5566
Dynamic Conveyor Corp	6275
Dynamic Events Inc	8857
Dynamic Language	1290
Dynamic Packaging	7142
Dynamic Voice Data	9780
Dynamix Engineering Ltd.	2471
Dynaric Inc.	7445
DynPro	5076

E

Company	Index#
E James & Co.	7346
E&R Minority Supplier LLC	4033

E | INDEX#

Company	Index#
E&R Pharma and Industrial Consulting Corp.	3269
E&R Sales Inc.	1586
E. L. Goldberg & Associates	7881
E. Lee White Photography, LLC	7314
E. R. Abernathy Industrial Inc.	4202
E. Smith Box, Inc.	7127
E.C. Ortiz & Co., LLP	7764
e.comm Technologies	9730
E.L. Hollingsworth & Co.	9986
E.S. Robbins Corp.	3736, 6972
E2C Group, LLC	4230
E-3 Systems	9644
EAC Consulting, Inc.	3090
Eagle EGC dba Miura Contracting	2279
Eagle Fasteners	7380
Eagle Hill Consulting	8309
Eagle Magnetic Company Inc.	6608
Eagle Promotions	1502
Eagle Steel Products, Inc.	6942
Eagle Transfer Corporation	10071
Eagle Transportation Services, Inc.	9897
EALI Logistics Solutions LLC	1890
EAP Lifestyle Management, LLC	7874
EARL Security, Inc.	1605
Early Bird Power LLC	3139
Earth2Earth LLC	6457
East Bay Manufacturing	6898
East Coast Metallic Tubing & Hardware Supply Corp	2872
East Coast Staffing Solutions	9142
Eastern Bag & Paper Company, Inc.	7114
Eastern Data, Inc.	5871, 5966
Eastern Design Services	9406
Eastern Personnel Services, Inc.	9348
Eastern Power Technologies, Inc.	4016
Eastern States Components, LLC dba ES Components	2842
Eastmed Enterprises, Inc.	6458
Eastside Groups LLC	5795
Easy Verification Inc.	4509
Eat It Read It Placemats	1520
EB ART EB ADS LLC	1521
E-Base Technologies, Inc.	4315
Ebco	7347
Ebinger Manufacturing Company	2850
EBM, Inc (Executive Building Maintenance	2136
Ebonex	3656
Ebony Holding	7062
Ebony Marketing Systems, Inc.	8683
Ebony Office Products, Inc.	7042
Ebsco Spring Company, Inc.	6966
Ebyte Technologies, Inc.	4510
EC Corporation Export	5948
EC London & Associates	9044
EC Purdy & Associates	1756
ECCO Select Corporation	5040
ECF Data LLC	9735
ECHO Consulting Group	8228
Echo Imaging Inc.	5379
ECI Holdings, LLC dba Exam Coordinators Network	6380
ECI Unlimited, Inc.	6276
Eclaro International, Inc.	5304
Eclipse Direct Marketing LLC	8684
Eclipse Marketing Services Inc.	1171
ECM Instructional Systems	8129

COMPANY ALPHABETICAL LISTING

E

Company	INDEX#
Eco Graphics Media	1058
ECO Trend Cases, LLC	1670
ECOM Consulting, Inc.	5567
ECommerce Holdings, Inc.	3745
Econobuild, LLC	6277
Economic Project Solutions, Inc.	3204
Economical Janitorial & Paper Supplies	2149
eConsulting Partners Global, Inc	5568
Ecoprocleaningsolutions Inc.	2220
ecoservices, LLC	2498
EcoTeal, Inc.	6078
ecoThynk	7022
eDataWorld LLC	5569
EDF Company	3091
Edge Electronics Inc.	2873
Edge Solutions, LLC	4585
Edgewood Electrical, LLC	1627
Edgilent Corp.	4702
Edify Technologies, Inc.	4703
EDJ Inc.	7537
Edmik Inc.	6795
EDS Manufacturing Inc.	2727
Edward Estevez CHB, Inc.	9874
Edwards & West, Inc. dba Divspec	3922
Edwards Management Consultants, Inc.	7978
Edwards Supply Company	2899
EE Printing. LLC	7705
Efficient Courier & Logistics Services LLC	9898
Efficient Lighting Technologies	2815
EFK Moen, LLC	3193
EFR Environmental Services Inc.	3356
Egami Group, Inc.	8685
Egg Strategy, Inc.	8389
Egnite LLC	8882
EGS, Inc.	8965
EGSE Holdings, LLC. dba Emergency Response Team	3516
EH, Inc. dba HireLevel	9239
EHS-International, Inc.	3542
Eigennet LLC	9161
Eighth Day Design	1283
EIP Manufacturing, LLC	6594
EIS Office Solutions, Inc.	7067
Eisen Electric Corporation	2981
Eitzen Creative LLC	8757
eiWorkflow Solutions, LLC	5305
eJangar, Inc.	4316
Ekeholm and Associates, LLC	2632
Ekla Corporation	6409
EKS Services Incorporated	3439
El Camino Transport Logistics & Management, LLC	9987
El Mundo Communications	2705
El Mundo, Ltd.	1185
El Paso Industrial Supplies	4022
El Sol Travel, Inc.	10197
ELA Enterprises	6259
Elan Chemical Co., Inc.	1982
ELB Enterprises, Inc.	2137
Elcon Associates, Inc.	3247
eLead Resources, Inc. DBA eLead Promo	1386
ElectraLED, Inc.	2955
Electric Metal Fab, Inc.	6609
Electric Motor Corporation	2824
Electric Motors and Specialties, Inc.	2973
Electrical Builders, Inc.	6648
Electrical Safety Products LLC	3957
Electrical Systems & Construction Supplies	2889
Electrical Testing Solutions	3041
Electritex	2896
Electro Enterprises, Inc.	2885
Electro Mechanical Industries (EMI)	2992
Electro Plate Circuitry, Inc.	2775, 3022
Electro-Kinetics Inc.	2825
Electronic Assembly Services, Inc.	2776
Electronic Knowledge Interchange, Co.	4704
Electronic Responsible Recyclers, LLC	5952
Electronic Supply Co, Inc.	2863
ElectroSystems Engineers Inc.	5570
Electro-Wire Inc.	2826
Element Technologies Corporation	5158
Elementi Designs	1309
Elemento L2, LLC	8482
Elements of Architecture, Inc.	3297
Elevan LLC dba Elevate Systems	3298
Elevate Planning	8351
Elevate USA Inc	8236
Elevated Solutions Team LLC	2534
Elevation Energy Group LLC	2043
Elgia, Inc.	4586
Elgiloy Specialty Metals	6936
Elgin Micro	5956
Elia Erickson, LLC	7992
Elias Events, LLC	8789
Elise Resources, Inc.	9444
Elite Meetings & Events of Washington	8858
Elite Mold & Engineering	7381
Elite Personnel Group, LLC	9283
Elite Technical Services, Inc.	5306
Elite Touch Cleaning Services, Inc.	2190
Elizabeth Coffey Design	8841
Ellco Promotions, Inc.	1429
Elle Waterworks Supply, LLC	3987, 4041
Ellen Freeman Immigration Law Group	6217
Ellen's Silkscreening, Inc.	1310
Ellsworth Healthcare Staffing LLC	9045
Elmark Group, Inc.	7823
E-Logic, Inc.	4476
Elontec	3740
ELP Enterprises, Inc.	5937
ELS ESQ. LLC	6234
Elsko, Inc.	9092
Elsner Human Resources	8883
Elwood Staffing Services, Inc.	2583
ELYON International Inc.	5796
Embedded Logix Inc.	2756, 3161
Emed Medical Company	6444
emedia, LLC	5307
Emerald, Inc.	4199
Emergent Safety Supply	4075
Emergent Systems Corp.	4920
Emeric Facility Services	2138
Emerson Human Capital Consulting, Inc.	7993
EMI Strategic Marketing Inc.	8540
EMI Supply	4121
Eminent Group, Inc	5439
Empire Electric	2851
Empire Electronics Inc.	5978

COMPANY ALPHABETICAL LISTING

E

Company	INDEX#
Empire Safety & Supply	4051
Employee Development Systems, Inc.	7890
Employee Risk Management Co. Inc.	9445
Employee Solve	6006
Employer Management Solutions, Inc.	4511
Employers Choice Online Inc.	7882
Employment Screening Services	2601
EmployVision, Inc.	5159
Empores LLC	5077
Empower Benefits Inc. dba Corestream	7747
EMR, Inc.	3422
EMS Consulting	8056
EMS Safety Services, Inc.	6344
EMSCO Scientific Enterprises, Inc.	2019
EMY Consulting LLC	8292
En Pointe IT Solutions, LLC	4317
En Pointe Technologies Sales, Inc.	4318
Enchanted Acres Farm, Inc.	3700
Enclipse Corp.	4996
Encompass Supply	4195
EncompasUnlimited, Inc.	6381
Encore Events, ltd. dba Encore Design	1172
Encore Fruit Marketing, Inc.	3559
Encore Images	5887
Encore Solutions Inc.	4864
End to End Computing	5710
Endata Corporation	5571
Endure, Inc.	3417
Energy Infrastructure Partners LLC	3216
Energy Utility Group, LLC	2044
Enfusion, Inc.	7748
Engage Integrated Systems Technology	4319
Engaging Solutions, LLC	7770
Engineered Design Services LLC	3092
Engineered Mechanical Systems	6902
Engineered Packaging Systems, Inc.	7201
Engineered Plastic Components Inc.	7342
Engineered Plastic Products	7382
Engineering Design Solutions PLC	3162
Engineering/Remediation Resources Group, Inc.	3058, 3357
Enhance a Colour Corp.	7481
Enhance Performance Consulting, Inc.	8029
Enhanced Due Diligence Advisory, Inc.	7811
Enigma, LLC	1257
Enin Systems, Inc.	5160
EnKon, LLC dba Broadway	6880, 7414
Enovox Technical Group, LLC	5572
ENPULSE Energy Conservation, Inc.	3196
Enrich Inc	4587
Enspire Energy, LLC	2065
Ensunet Consulting Corporation	1897
Entech Staffing Solutions	9180
Entelli Consulting LLC	4705
Entellimetrix LLC	4588
Enterprise Cable Group, Inc.	9756
Enterprise IT Experts LLC dba EITE LLC	5573
Enterprise ITech Corp.	5711
Enterprise Logic, Inc.	5574
Enterprise Project Solutions Group Corporation	9046
Enterprise Resource Services, Inc.	8908
Enterprise Risk Management, Inc.	4512
Enterprise Solutions Inc	4706
Entertainment Retail Enterprises, LLC	1347
Enthusias Media Group	1541
Entrust One Facility Services, Inc.	2248
EnviroBate, Inc.	3449
Environics, Inc.	6308
Environmental and Safety Solutions, Inc.	3494
Environmental Assessment Services, LLC	3543
Environmental Compliance Office Inc.	3440
Environmental Data Validation, Inc.	3500
Environmental Design & Research, DPC	3217, 3480
Environmental Equipment + Supply, LLC	3501
Environmental Health and Safety Solutions, LLC	3432
Environmental Industrial Services Corp. of NJ	3468
Environmental International Corporation	3412
Environmental Process Solutions, PLLC	3458
Environmental Service Systems, LLC	3459
Environmental Strategy Consultants, Inc.	3502
Environmental Systems Design, Inc.	3112
Environmental Testing and Consulting Inc.	3441
Environmental Waste Specialists, Inc.	3535
Environmental, Engineering & Construction, Inc.	3433
Environments Plus, Inc.	3746
EnVision Performance Solutions	8087
Eon Office	6982
EP Logistics LLC	10140
ePATHUSA	4665
Epcon Industrial Systems	4226
Epiphany Insurance Company LLC	5989
Episerve Corp.	5308
Epitec	4921
EPJ Logistics Inc.	9988
Epsilon Brokerage Corporation	10141
Equilibrium Perceptum LLC	8197
Equity Industrial	4076
Equity Staffing Group, Inc.	8966
ER Select	9258
Erb Equipment Co., Inc.	4215
ERB Industries, Inc.	1679
Ergonomic Group, Inc.	5979
eRichards Consulting LLC	4455
Eriksen Translations Inc.	1196
Ernie Green Industries	7415
ERP Analysts, Inc	5380
ERP Logic	5575
ERPMatrix LLC	4865
ESA Investigations & Security, LLC	2633
ESI Ergonomic Solutions, LLC	5830
ESM Group LLC	4922
ESM Products LLC	6410
Esource Resources, LLC	4772
eSpin Technologies, Inc.	4169
Espinosa Architecture + Consulting, PC	1783
Espirit Systems, LLC	5309
Essence Printing	7462
Essential Creations Chicago, Inc.	1387
Essential Water Technologies LLC	1934
Essex Newbury North Contracting Corporation	2387, 3429
EsteemLogic	5712
Estes Thorne Ewing & Payne PLLC	6235
Estime Enterprises, Inc.	2392
Estrella LLC	6226
ETC Group, Inc.	8790
ETCS Inc.	3163
eTeam, Inc.	5161

COMPANY ALPHABETICAL LISTING

E

Company	INDEX#
eTech Solutons, LLC	9721
eTechSecurityPro, LLC	5713
ETELIC Inc.	5714
Etisbew Technology Group Inc.	4799
eTouch Systems	4320
Eubio, LLC	9548
EurekaFacts, LLC	7780
Eurow & O'Reilly Corp.	2086
EUS IT Solutions, LLC	4321
Evans Inc.	8293
Evanston Technology Partners, Inc.	4707
Evco Industries, Inc.	7251
Evco Partners dba Burgoon Company	4180
Eved Services, Inc.	8483
Evelyn's Professional Janitorial Services, Inc.	2249
Event Source Professionals, inc.	8791
EventEssentials, LLC	8447
EventLink International, Inc.	8792
EventPro Strategies, Inc.	8321
Everbrite, LLC	1297
Everest Consultants, Inc.	5422
EvereTech LLC	5715
Everfield Consulting, LLC	1015, 8352
Evergreen Computer Products Inc	5949
Evergreen Corporate Car & Limousine Service	10058
Evergreen Environmental	3423
Evergreen Technologies, LLC	5162
eVerifile.com Inc.	7909
Everyone Loves Buttons Inc.	1302
Evident, Inc.	6534
Evins Personnel Consltants	9446
EVOLUTION Creative Solutions	8727
Evolutyz Corp.	4708
Evolv Solutions, LLC.	4790
Evolve Advisors I, LLC	8214
Evolve Manufacturing Technologies Inc	2934
EVS, Inc.	3183
eWaste Tech Systems, LLC	5716
Ewie Co., Inc.	3906
Ewing Moving Services	10124
Eworld Solutions, Inc.	3036
Exacto, Inc. of South Bend	6810
Exalt Integrated Technologies LLC	4589
Exalt Printing Solutions	7687
Excalibur Exhibits	1258
Excalibur Machine & Sheet Metal	6587, 6785
Excel Construction Services, Inc.	2295
Excel Electrocircuit Inc.	2982
Excel Global Solutions Inc.	5821
Excel Gloves & Safety Supplies, Inc.	4200
EXCEL Moving Services	9842
Excel Screen Printing & Embroidery, Inc.	1388
Excel Staffing Inc.	9047
Excel Technical Services, Inc.	4923
Excelgens, Inc.	5163
Excell Home Fashions Inc.	3798
Excellence Engineering, LLC	3246
Excellian Inc.	7969
Excelsior Consulting Services	4709
Execusane Inc	9447
ExecuSys, Inc.	4513
Executive Coaching Connections	7917
Executive Consultants United, LLC	8057

E

Company	INDEX#
Executive Meeting Management, Inc.	8415
Executive Meetings & Incentives, Inc.	8639
Executive Office Services	7883
Executive Technology Inc.	4254
Exhibit Arts, LLC	8526
Exhibit Concepts Inc.	8728
Exhibit Edge Inc.	8842
Exhibits South	1076
EXIGIS LLC	7824
Exp Global Logistics	9843
Expect Advertising, Inc.	1173
Expedien Inc.	5576
Expedite Express Transportation Inc.	9989
Expedited Specialized Logistics LLC	10142
Expedited Transportation Services, Inc	9899
Expeed Software LLC	5381
Expert Technical Consultants, Inc.	5382
Expinfo, Inc.	5310
ExpoMarketing Group LLC	8353
Exponential Interactive, Inc.	1016
Express Employment Professionals	9407
ExterNetworks Inc.	5164
Extol of Ohio, Inc.	6664
Extreme Molding LLC	7409
Extreme Tooling LLC	3907, 4103
Extron-Knurr USA	7994
Extrovertic Communications, LLC	8686
Exude, LLC	7953
Eyak Technology	5717
EYP, Inc.	4322
E-Z Electric Motor Service, Inc.	2880
Ezbake Technologies	3719
EZKutter Company	3982

F

Company	INDEX#
F&D International, LLC	3079
F&L Construction Inc.	2328
F. Gavina & Sons, Inc.	3560
Fabergent, Inc.	5165, 9284
Fabrication Group LLC	6665
Fabtronics, Inc.	6773
Fabulous Sites, Inc.	4590
Facilities Connection, Inc.	3839
Facility Interiors Inc.	3840
Facility Maintenance & Services Group	2147
Fact Finders Group, Inc.	2643
Fair Measures, Inc.	6093
Fair Oaks Farms, LLC	3733
Fair Pattern Inc.	5311
Fairway Injection Molding Systems, Inc.	7321
Faison Office Products, Inc	6983
Faith Com, Inc.	3059
Faith Transport & Logistics, Inc.	9875
FAK, Inc.	9867
Falcon Manufacturing LLC	3130
Falcon Square Capital, LLC	7804
Falkenberg Construction Company, Inc.	2535
Fallon Trading Co., Inc.	3701
FamTeck, LLC	9676
Fancy That	1389
Farrow-Gillespie & Heath LLP	6236
FASIC Design LLC	3023

COMPANY ALPHABETICAL LISTING

F | INDEX#

Company	Index#
Fasone Construction inc	2296
Fast Dolphin Inc	9001
Fast Lane Interactive	5312
Fastenation, Inc.	3923
FAVOR Design + Communications	8772
Faw Casson	7742
Fayette Janitorial Service LLC	2236
FBC Enterprises, Inc.	7688
FCF Schmidt Public Relations	7954
FDY, Inc.	3666
Feamold, Inc.	3164
February 14 Inc.	9990
Federal Business Products Inc.	7606
Federal Staffing Resources LLC	9162
Federated Service Solutions, Inc.	9714
Fenco Global Industries Corp.	5974
Ferco Color	1898
Ferguson Consulting Inc.	5041
Fermat Software LLC	5577
Ferragon Corporation	6666
Ferreira Construction Co Inc.	2439
Ferrolux Metals Co. of Ohio, LLC	6954
Ferrous Processing & Trading	6944
FFG Strategic Consulting LLC	8256
Fiber Business Solutions Inc.	9757
Fiddler Gonzalez & Rodriguez, PSC	6227
Fidelis Companies, LLC	5578
Fiducia TechneGroup LLC	5383
FilmLOC Inc.	7128
Filters South, Inc.	4017
Financial Statement Services, Inc.	7463
Financial Technologies Inc	5313
Finch Constructors, Inc.	2379
Fine Line Communications Inc.	9748
Fine Line Construction contractors, Inc.	2337
Fineline Printing Group	7526
Finial Showcase, Inc.	3846
Finnesse Partners LLC	9218
Fintech Consulting LLC DBA ApTask	7937
Fire & Flavor Grilling Co.	3600
Fire Boss of Louisiana, Inc.	1623
Fire Fighter Sales & Service Company	1648
Fire Starter Studios, LLC	9568
Fire Tech Systems, Inc.	1624
FireSign Inc. Promotional Products & Print	1374
FireWater CleanUp Crew Corp.	3460
Firmament Solutions	4591
First American Engineered Solutions, LLC	2922
First American Plastics Molding Enterprise	7348
First Assured Quality Systems, LLC	3299
First Call Services, Inc.	5912
First Call Temporary Services Inc.	9124
First Capital Engineering	3255
First Choice Background Screening	7896
First Choice of Elkhart	9991
First Credit Services, Inc.	7812
First Due Gear	1722
First Electric Supply	2836
First Financial Network, Inc.	7844
First Independence Bank	7792
First Nations Pallet Solutions	10236
First Star Safety, LLC	4142
First World Architects Studio, PSC	1766
FirstEye Media Works	8640
FirstIdea, Inc.	7891
FirstPro Inc.	9048
Firstronic LLC	1871
Fishnet, LLC	1587
Fitz Machine Inc.	6816
Fitzhugh & Mariani LLP	6145
Five Star Productions	8586
FlagCenter.com, LLC	1244
Flairsoft, Ltd.	5384
Flamm Pickle & Packing Co., Inc.	3657
Fleet Maintenance, Inc.	1839
Flex Pre-Press, Inc.	7708
Flexaco, Inc.	5875
FlexFit Hose LLC	6820
Flexible Packaging Company, Inc.	7258
Flexo Converters USA, Inc.	7115
Flexon Technologies Inc.	4323
Flexospan Steel Buildings, Inc.	6681
FlexSol Packaging Corp.	7122
Flexstar Packaging, Inc.	7129
Floral Group, Inc.	3853
Florida Freight Lines Inc.	9876
Fluid Line Components, Inc.	4004
Fly My Photo, LLC	1161
Flying Medical USA	6345
Flynn Heath Holt Leadership, LLC	8147
FM Office Express dba FM Resources	7043
FM Solutions, PLLC	8294
FMD K&L Inc.	9554
FNS, Inc.	9844
Foam Design Inc.	7365
Focal PLLC	6250
Focus Latino	8793
Focus Merchandising	1487
Focus USA, Inc	8641
Focused Coaching LLC	8112
Focused HR-Solutions, LLC	4592
Foglamp Research Corp.	8687
Foit-Albert Associates, Architecture, Engineering and Surveying, P.C.	1792, 3218, 3481
Folio, Inc. Design & Illustration	8448
Fondungallah & Kigham, LLC	6165
Fong & Fong Printers and Lithographers	7464
Food Packaging Consultants, Inc.	7143
Foodtopia, Inc.	1983
Foos Fire, Inc.	1639
For The Record, Inc.	6150
Force 1 Global, LLC	5718
Ford Audio-Video Systems, LLC	9754
Fore Dimensions LLC	1728
Foreman Tool & Mold Company	3954
Foremost Staffing, Inc.	9448
Forensic Fluids Laboratories Inc.	6040
Forest City Companies, Inc.	7241
Forest City Erectors, Inc.	6667
Foreway Management Services Inc.	9992
Formers International, Inc.	7284
Forms & Supply, Inc.	3799
Fortes Laboratories	8416
Fortidm Technologies LLC	5166
Fortune Metal Group	3469
Fortune Metal Inc. of RI	3470

COMPANY ALPHABETICAL LISTING

F | INDEX#

Company	Index#
Forty Nine Corp.	4126
Forza Electronics	2796
Forza Transportation Services, Inc.	10143
Four Seasons Travel	10202
Fourth Factor Engineering, LLC	3184
Fourth Technologies Inc.	5167
Fox Converting, Inc.	6544
Fox Scientific, Inc.	6068
Fox Specialties, Inc. dba Encompass Elements	8758
Framework LLC	8013
Frank, Frank, Goldstein & Nager, PC	6194
Fraser/White, Inc.	1017
Frazee Recruiting Consultants, Inc.	9135
Frazier Engineering, Inc.	3093
Fred Weidner & Daughter Printers	7628
Freddie Georges Production Group	8354
Frederick Hart Co. Inc.	2125
Free Spirit Publishing Inc.	2712
Freedom Air Filtration Inc.	4077
Freedom Industries, Inc.	2998
Freedom Solutions LLC	4514
Freestyle Marketing, LLC	1506
Fre-Flo Distribution	7242
Freight Express Shipping Corp (FESCO)	9845
Fresh Comfort, Inc.	1717
Fresh Wata, LLC	8668
Freshwater Film, Inc.	9592
Frey Produce	3615
Fridkin Valo, Inc. dba TPG Live Events	8484
Frieda's Inc.	3561
Friese Legal, LLC	6120
Frink-Hamlett Legal Solutions	9285
Frisson, Inc.	1018
Froehling & Robertson, Inc.	3536
FrontEnd Graphics Inc.	7607
Frontier Bag Company, Inc	7209
Frontier Electronics	2935
Frontier Technologies LLC	4710
Frontier Technologies, Inc.	4487
Frontline Marketing LLC	8843
Frontline Public Strategies, Inc.	8485
FRS Environmental	3358
Fruitridge Printing and Lithograph	7465
FS3, Inc.	2297
FSTI Inc.	2045
FTG, Inc.	4052
FTS Lighting Services, Inc.	2797
Fuel7 Inc.	1568
Fuentes Enterprises, Inc	7501
Fulgent Solutions Inc.	9449
Fulgent Therapeutics LLC	6027
Full Circle Events	8449
Full Circle Recycling	3512
Full Disclosure	7923
Full Tilt Logistics LLC	10065
Full Umbrella Talent LLC	8909
Furniture Installation Solution Inc	3764
Furst Services	9093
Fuse Solutions Inc.	5579
Fusia Communications, Inc.	1197
Fusion Communications, Inc.	8417
Fusion Integrated Solutions LLC	3337
Fusion Plus Solutions Inc.	5827

F | INDEX#

Company	Index#
Fusion Ranch, Inc. dba Fusion Jerky	3562
Futran Solutions Inc.	5168
Futura Marketing, Inc.	8587
Futura Services, Inc.	5440
Future Commodities Int'l Inc.	7101
Future Force Personnel	9002
Future Power Corporation	3359
Future Technologies, Inc.	3165
Futurewave Systems Inc.	9049
FYI Systems Inc.	5169
FYVE STAR, Inc.	2061

G

Company	Index#
G Tech Contracting, LLC	9707
G&A Partners	7970
G&D Coffee Mud LLC	2587
G&I Security Company, LLC.	2688
G&T Trading International	7213
G. ALAN Inc.	1477
G. Stephens Inc.	8198
G.D. Barri & Associates, Inc.	3048
G2 Global Solutions, LLC	5719
G2 Ops Inc.	5720
Gabba LLC	1649
GABS LLC	6692
GACC Video Electronics Inc.	2368
GAI Construction Monitoring Services, Inc. dba CMT Services Group	3256
Gainor Temporaries, Inc.	9324
Gala & Associates Inc.	1772, 3166
Galaxy Electronics Company	2777
Galaxy Forest Products LLC	7175
Galaxy Software Solutions, Inc.	9181
Galica, LLC	8173
Galmont Consulting, LLC	4711
Galosi LLC	7853
Gammon & Associates	8688
Gangi Printing, Inc.	7543
Gap Engineering	3300
GAP Promotions LLC	1430
Garcia & Ortiz Staffing, LLC	9003
Garcia Baldwin Inc.	8794
Garcoa, Inc.	2575
Garic Inc.	5915
Garnier Group and Associates	7724
Garrison & Sisson, Inc.	6098
Garry Struthers Associates, Inc.	3328
Garza Industries	6979
GASmith Enterprises, Inc.	1000
Gasochem International LLC	2046
Gavin Law Offices, PLC	6248
GB Manufacturing Company	6748, 6881
GBG The Corporate Gift Source, Inc.	1334
GC Electrical Solutions, LLC	2821
GC Micro Corporation	5838
GCI Technologies	3024
GCom Software, Inc.	5314
GDI Infotech, Inc.	4924
GDKN Corporation	4515, 9004
GDSTA, LLC	3060
Gear One Enterprise	5839
Gelato Giuliana, LLC	3581
GEM Janitorial LLC	2112

COMPANY ALPHABETICAL LISTING

G — INDEX#

Company	Index#
Gem Limousine Service, Inc.	10059
Gem Quality	9415
Gemini Plastics, Inc.	7383
Genard, inc. dba Lennova	1899
Gene Ptacek & Son Fire Equipment Co, Inc.	1643
General Air Conditioning and Heating Inc.	2388
General Building Maintenance, Inc.	2126
General Carbide Corporation	6682
General Circuit Corporation	2747
General Factory/ WD Supply	3932
General Fire Equipment Company, Inc.	4154
General Microsystems Inc.	5797
General Office Plus	7068
General Sheet Metal Works, Inc.	6679
Generalety, LLC	3167
Genesee Packaging, Inc (The Genesee Group)	7176
Genesis Architects Inc.	1808
Genesis Global Recruiting	9005
Genesis Medical Products, Inc.	6425
Genesis Networks Enterprises, LLC	5580
Genesis Professional Staffing, Inc.	8910
Genesus One Enterprise, Inc.	2453
GENESYS Consulting Services, Inc.	5315
Geneva Consulting Group, Inc.	9325
Genisys Technologies, Inc.	4997
Genius Business Solutions, Inc.	4712
Genoa Employment Solutions, Inc	9006
Genoa International	2047
Genome International Corporation	5822
Gentile and Associates, Inc.	2684
Genzeon Corporation	5441
Geodata IT	5042
Geologics Corporation	5721
Georgia Green Energy Services	2958
Georgia International Travel, Inc.	10203
Georgia Time Recorder Co., Inc.	6310
GeoTest Services, Inc.	3329, 3544
Gerard Design, Inc.	8486
Getcorp Payroll Accounting & Tax dba Get Hire Staffing	9450
Gethmann Construction Company, Inc.	2363
Geyer Fire Protection, LLC	1621
GFIS	3590
GGG Demolition Inc.	3360
Gholkar's, Inc.	5916
Gianco Environmental Services Inc.	3482
Gibraltar Graphics	7466
Gibson Arnold & Associates, Inc.	6094
Giffen & Kaminski, LLC	6209
Gifts by Design, Inc.	1595, 3875
Gilbert International Inc.	2211
Gilbreath Communications, Inc.	1259
Gill Digital Services, LLC	5581
Gill Industries Inc.	6629
Gillespie Associates, Ltd.	8174
Gillman Services, Inc.	9514
Gina Sofola & Associates, Inc.	8210
Giovanni Transport, LLC	9877
Gipson Mechanical Contractors Inc.	2521
GIT Global Services	9827
GJ Chemical	1984
GK Tech, LLC	6550, 6729, 6841
Glazer Design, LLC	1488
Glenmont Group Inc.	9286

G — INDEX#

Company	Index#
Global Amchem Inc.	2048
Global Associates, Inc.	5385
Global Bridge Infotech Inc.	7689
Global Building Services, Inc.	2087
Global Bureau of Security & Investigations	2634
Global Business Travel, LLC	10211
Global Capital, Ltd.	7765
Global Coffee Company	3720
Global Connection Co. of America, Inc.	3925
Global Control Systems, Inc.	4791
Global Enterprises	1872
Global Environmental Products	2000
Global Environmental, Inc.	3453
Global Essence Inc.	1985
Global Exhibit Management	8795
Global Freight Experts, Inc.	9846
Global Gateway Solutions Inc.	4516
Global Geographic Inc.	5722
Global Industrial Components Inc.	6507
Global Information Technology	4517
Global Installation Resources LLC	3806
Global International LLC	6441
Global Investigations Inc.	2635
Global IT Services	4324
Global IT Solutions, Inc.	5170
Global IT, Inc.	5582
Global Language Solutions	1019
Global Link Language Services, Inc.	8541
Global LT, Inc.	8113
Global Manufacturing, Inc.	2924
Global Medical Services LLC	6411
Global Network Tours, Inc.	10217
Global Organization and Planning Services, LLC	8450
Global Packaging Solutions LLC	7228
Global Partner's of Virginia, LLC	1588, 1723
Global Personnel Solutions, Inc.	9050
Global Perspectives, Inc. dba Global Orientations	9945
Global Planners, Inc.	8642
Global PPE Inc.	6535
Global Promotions & Incentives, LLC	1522
Global Pros Staffing Solutions	9259
Global Protective Services, Inc.	7884
Global Resource Manangement, Inc.	4593
Global Software Resources, Inc.	3061
Global Sourcing Connection, Ltd.	1390
Global Sourcing, LLC	6382
Global Staffing Services, Inc.	9094
Global Steel Alliance Corp.	6930
Global Strategic Supply Solutions	7177
Global Supply Innovative Engineering LLC	3168
Global TEAM Associates, LLC	9993
Global Technology Services Group, Inc.	4594
Global Test Equipment Inc.	2827
Global to Local Language Solutions, LLC	7945
Global Traders, Inc.	2212
Global Trading, Inc.	1675
Global Transit Solutions	10060
Global Unit 1	2612
Globalnest LLC	5171
Globalpundits Technology Consultancy Inc.	5500
Globalquest	5316
GlobalVise Inc.	9007
Globe Tech LLC.	6630, 6730

COMPANY ALPHABETICAL LISTING

G | INDEX#

Company	Index#
Globenet Telecommunications, LLC	9765
Glopak Corporation	7214
Glove Ventures LLC	6520
GlowTouch LLC	4800
GM Supply Company, Inc.	4088
GM&T Engineering, Inc.	2757
GMI Group, Inc.	2127
GMR Protection Resources, Inc.	3301
GMT Logistic Inc.	9994
GND Consulting & Supply LLC	2049
Go Fetsch Mechanical LLC	2415
Go Green LED-Alternatives, LLC	2828
GoAhead Solutions LLC.	4325
Goddess Products, Inc.	6974
Godshall and Godshall Personnel Consultants, Inc.	9408
GOJO Industries, Inc.	6668
Gold Star Transportation, Inc.	9954
Goldbelt Specialty Services LLC	2703
Golden Gate Air Freight Inc.	9847
Golden Glow Cookie Co. Inc.	3686
Golden Group International, Ltd.	7229
Golden Leaf Energy, Inc.	1946
Golden Sands General Contractors	2429
Golden Tech Systems Inc.	5078
Goldman, Imani & Goldberg, Inc.	7854
Gong Gong Communications	8729
Gonzales Financial Consulting, LLC	7793
Gonzalez Aerospace	3169
Gonzalez Group LLC/	6903
Gonzalez Production Systems	9182
Gonzalez, Hawkins & Johnson LLC	7781
Good Fortune Trading Co. dba GFT Services	9550
Goodhealth Medical Products	6412
Gordon & Polscer LLC	6215
Gordon Electric Supply Co.	2829
Gorham Paper and Tissue LLC	7029
Gorilla Marketing	1311
Gorilla Paper Inc.	6996
Goss LLC	6007
Gossett Marketing	1348
Got Broccoli, Inc.	3563
Go-To Transport	9995
Gottscho Printing Systems, Inc.	4224
Gourmail Inc.	3702
Government Business Solutions	8030
Government Staffing Associates	8911
Government Systems Technologies, Inc.	5172
GovMobile, LLC	9645
GovSmart, Inc.	5984
GP Supply Company	4122
GPI Enterprises Inc.	8199
GQSI	3285
Graebel Vanlines Holdings, LLC	10044
Graham Trading Company, LLC	1918
Gramieri Design Services	1786
Grand Aire, Inc.	10087
Grand Design, Inc.	8542
Grandmas Garden	3726
Granger Warburton Consulting, LLC	5497, 8232
Granite City Electric Supply	2918
Grant Law, LLC	6132
Granthium Corporation	9095
Granwood Inc	5317
Grapevine Designs, LLC	1418
Graphic Arts Inc.	7629
Graphic Arts, Incorporated	7658
Graphic Designs International LLC	7489
Graphic Label Solutions	7672
Graphic Matter, Inc.	1174
Graphic Resource Group	7561
Graphic Source Group, Inc.	1391
Graphicolor Systems, Inc.	1127
Graphics Solutions	1489
Graphix 2 Go	1442
Graphix 360, LLC	9582
Gratitude Goodies, LLC	3855
Graves Group Promotions	1569
Gray Design Group, Inc.	1777
Gray Systems, Inc.	4326
Graywolf Printing	7562
Great Lakes Finishing, Inc.	6561
Great Lakes Maintenance, Inc.	6566
Great Lakes Metals	6599
Great Pacific Securities	7725
Great Work Employment Services, Inc.	9349
Greater Than One Inc.	8689
Green Cat Dzine, Inc.	8859
Green International Affiliates, Inc.	3140
Green Point Technology Services LLC	6195
Green Rock Lighting, LLC	6749, 6882
Green Silk Associates, LLC	8175
GreenerVolts	2845
GreenPath Energy Solutions	3094
Green's Commercial Cleaning	2191
Greenspeed Energy Solutions, LLC	3103
Greenville Fluid System Technologies	4018
Greenway Solid Waste & Recycling, Inc.	3361
Greenwood, Inc.	2517
Greer Group	9260
Greno Industries Inc.	6874
Gretna Machine Shop, Inc.	6911
Greytree Partners	9261
Griesing Law, LLC	6218
Griffin Staffing Network, LLC	9143
Griffith Rubber Mills	7425
GrimeGuru Janitorial Service	2192
Grimes Oil Co., Inc.	1948
Gripp Inc.	4089
Grosvenor Building Services Iinc.	2113
Groundwork Tech, LLC	8310
Group O, Inc.	8487
Group of Global Suppliers, LLC	10144
Group Ventures Inc.	8588
Grove Technical Resources	4327, 8912
Grow Now, LLC	8451
GRP Services	2020
Grubb Printing & Stamp Co.	7701
Grupo Logico, LLC	9996
GS Infovision LLC dba Global Systems LLC	5583, 9451
GSB Architects & Interiors, Inc.	1750
GSHA Quality Services	8114
GSquared Group, LLC	9051
GST Manufacturing, Ltd.	6693
GT Business Supplies LLC	5917
GT Industrial LLC Co.	3936
G-TECH Services, Inc.	9183

DIR 2025 II-30

COMPANY ALPHABETICAL LISTING

G INDEX#

GTL Supply Solutions, LLC	6521
GTS Express, Inc.	9924
GTS, Inc.	4595
Guardem Security Group Inc.	2660
Guardian Industrial Supply, LLC	4181
Guardian Packaging Industries, LP	7285
Guardmax Corporation	1650
Guidance Law Firm, P.C.	6249
GuideSoft Inc. dba Knowledge Services	4773
Guilford Group LLC	4774
Gulf South Engineering & Testing, Inc.	3136
Gumro and Associates	9997
Guna Enterprises, Inc.	6288
Gupton & Associates, Inc.	5723
Gurman Container & Supply Co.	3419
Gutierrez-Palmenberg, Inc.	3350
Guy Brown, LLC	5930, 7064
GUYDLOGISTICS CORP.	9878
Guzman Manufacturing, Inc.	6912
GyanSys Inc.	4775

H

H & A Enterprise	9798
H & W Trucking	10088
H Benton Capital, LLC	2073
H Rizvi Consulting Inc.	8016
H&H Metal Source	6945
H&H Sorting Services	7144
H&S Supply Co., Inc.	4070
H. Hendy Associates	1735
H. Walker Enterprises, LLC	3601
H. Weiss LLC	2213
H.Derksen & Sons Co., Inc.	7709
H.R. Technologies, Inc.	1873
H2O Engineering, Inc.	3362
Habsco Inc.	2890
Hacha Products Corporation	3891
Hacware, Inc.	5584
Hagerman & Company Inc.	5967
Haig's Quality Printing	7621
Halcyon Solutions, Inc.	5386
Hale Contracting, Inc.	2398
Hall Whitener Investments, Inc.	1835
Haller Concepts, Inc.	9600
Halogen Lighting Products Corp.	2830
Hamburger Woolen Company	1707
Hamilton Contracting	2399
Hamilton-Malone Corp	9008
Hamlin Acquisition, LLC dba Hamlin Steel Products	6750
Hamlin Newco, LLC	6751
Hammerman and Gainer, Inc.	6002
Hanabi Networks Systems, LLC	5442
Hand and Hand Medical	6346
Handling Technologies, Inc.	6272
Hanker Systems, Inc.	9009
Hanlon Brown Design	1225
Hansell Tierney, Inc.	5798
Hansen Thorp Pellinen Olson, Inc.	3185
Hanstine LLC	6694
Hanusoft Inc.	5724
HAP Marketing Services, Inc.	8643
Hapak Enterprises Inc.	6420

H INDEX#

Harbar LLC	3633
Harbin Steel	6631
Harbison Bros., Inc.	4132
Harbor Enterprises, LLC	6592
Harbor Transport, Inc.	9879
Hardware Inc.	3900
Hardy Beverage LLC	3713
Hargrove Inc.	8550
Harita Infotech	9287
Harlan Media LLC	9601
Harmelin Media	1231
Harmon Construction, Inc.	2380
HarmonyTech	5725
Harquin Graphics, Inc.	1198
Harriman Material Handling	6273
Harrington Technology & Associates, Inc dba HTA Technology Security	4713
Harris & Dickey, LLC.	7855
Harris and Ford, LLC	1939
Harris Composites, Inc.	6695
Harris Design & Construction Services	2400
Harris Freeman & Co LP	3677
Harris Group Services, Inc.	7752
Harris Ice Company	3616
Harris Industrial Gases	4053
Harris Marketing Group, Inc.	8568
Harris Packaging Corporation	7286
Hart Employment Services	8913
Hart Precision Products, Inc.	2983
Hartford Technologies, Inc.	1910
Hartford Toner & Cartridge	5857
Harvard Resource Group	9184
Harvard Services Group, Inc.	2114
Harvest Technical Services	8914
Harvey & Daughters, Inc.	1122
Harvey Pallets Inc.	10238
HAS Art Solutions LLC	8418
Hassett Express	9925
Hatch Staffing Services	9538
Hatcher Construction & Development, Inc.	2338
Hatteras Printing, Inc.	7563
Hattrick Professional Staffing	9185
HAVE, Inc.	9738
Havens & Company	5990
Hawaii Transfer Company, Ltd.	9912
Hawkins Point Partners LLC	4817
Hawkins, Associates, Inc.	9452
Hawque Protection Services, LLC.	2636
Hawthorne Direct LLC	1086
Hazel's Hot Shot, Inc.	10145
Hazlow Electronics	2768
Haz-Waste, Inc.	3454
HB Computers, Inc.	4328
HBL Search	8915
HC Constructors, Inc.	2440
HC Services Fire Protection	1632
HDN F&A, Inc. dba F&A Fabricating	6632
Heagney Logan Group, LLC	4596, 9052
Health and Natural Beauty Corp LLC	2588
Health Education Services	2298
Healthcare Resources Staffing Agency	9053
Healthcare Supply Solutions, Inc.	6383
Healthier & Happier, Inc.	6959

COMPANY ALPHABETICAL LISTING

H — INDEX#

Company	Index#
Healthy America, LLC	3662
Healthy Solutions Spice Blends, LLC	3672
Heartland Supply Company	9822
Heat Exchanger Products Corp.	6621
HeatRep, LLC	4071
Heavner Beyers & Mihlar LLC	6133
Heidi's Real Food LLC	3582
Helios HR LLC	7974
HeLP Logistics, Inc.	9946
Hendon Group, Inc.	8058
Henegan Construction Co., Inc.	2454
Henjum Goucher Reporting Services, LP	6237
Henry Consulting LLC	8082
Henry Roberts BBQ Sauce	3591
Henry-Aaron Inc.	1375
Henssgen Hardware Corporation	3926
Henya Direct LLC	1570
HERA Laboratory Planners	6044
Herbert E. Orr Comany, Inc.	6567, 6964
Herco Technology div. of Hernandez Companies	5831
Hercules & Hercules, Inc.	3785, 7011
Heritage Global Solutions, Inc.	4329
Heritage Global, Inc.	2299
Heritage Vision Plans, Inc.	6434
Hermes Global Logistic Services, LLC	9880
Herrmann Advertising|Branding|Technology	1123
HESS Advanced Technology, Inc.	7416
Hexagon Technologies, Inc.	1945
HIC Energy, LLC	1949
Hicks-Carter-Hicks, LLC	7932
HI-Gene	2181
High Country Springs LLC	3667
High End Beauty Inc.	2581
High Five, LLC	1460
High Plains Contactors and Management Group, Inc.	2536
High Plains Logistics Consulting, LLC	10183
High Point Solutions	5913
HighCloud Solutions Inc	9219
Highlight Printing Inc.	7579
HighRoad Press, LLC	7608
High-Tech Machine Mfg, Inc.	6919
Hightowers Petroleum Company	2001
HimalaSalt - Sustainable Sourcing, LLC	3634
Hines Industries, Inc.	6314
Hinsdale Lighting	2831
Hire 1 Staffing	9515
Hired by Matrix, Inc.	5173
HireGenics, Inc.	4597
HirePower Personnel, Inc.	9453
HireTalent	9326
HispaniSpace LLC	8355
Hi-Tech Foam Products, LLC	7360
Hi-Tech Products Inc.	3015
HJD Capital Electric, Inc.	2537
HJI Supply Chain Solutions	1861
HJI -Vascor Logistics LLC	9957
HL Metals, LLC	6937
HLF Distributing, Inc.	4182
HMB Enterprises LLC	8031
HNM Enterprises, LLC	3765
HNM Medical USA	6384
HNT Logistics LLC	9998
HOBI International, Inc.	4714
Hoffmann Murtaugh Advertising, Inc.	1232
Holden Custom Products	1571
Holland Capital Management LLC	7766
Holland Engineering Inspection Services dba HEIS	3095
Hollingsworth Davis, LLC	6166
Hollingsworth Logistics Group, L.L.C.	9999
Hollister Construction Company	2300
Hollister Staffing, Inc.	9144
Hollstadt & Associates, Inc.	8130
Holt Brothers Construction LLC	2430
Holt Motors, Inc.	1837
Holtec International	6658
Home and Travel Solutions, LLC dba BedVoyage	3849
Homefree, LLC	3673
Homeland Industrial Supp	2226
Homrich, Klein & Associates	9054
Hood River Juice Company	3695
Hoosier Equipment Service, Inc.	3420
Hoosier Molded Products	7361
Hootenanny LLC	9589
Hooven-Dayton Corporation	7644
Hop Industries Corp.	4219
Hope Capital LLC	2604
Hope Law PLLC	6167
HOPET Engineering Services LLC	8014
Horizon Group USA	2714
Horizon Leadership, Inc.	8041
Horizon Services Company	2104
Horizon Services Corporation	4241
Horizon Staffing Services	8976
Horizontal Integration, Inc.	4998
Horologiii, Inc.	4330
Horwith Trucks, Inc.	10105
Hospitality Solutions Corporation	8322
Houdal Corporation dba 2M Business Products	7069
Hough Transport Express LLC	10184
Hover Group, LLC	3979
Howard & O	9350
Howe Corporation	4211
Howell Packaging	7230
Howse Solutions LLC	8200
HPC International, Inc.	2708
HR Allen Consulting Services	7885
HR Alternative Consulting, Inc.	7920
HR Anew, Inc.	7924
HR Strong	7893
HR Wise, LLC	7875
HRSS Consulting Group	7897
HRU Technical Resources	4925
HSE USA, Inc.	3747
HST Materials, Inc.	7349
HTC Global Services Inc.	4926
HTSS, Inc.	9383
HUB Corporation	6920
Huber & Associates, Inc.	5904
Hudson & Calleja LLC	6104
Hudson Reporting & Video Inc.	6178
Hudson Valley Press LLC	2717
Hugo Neu Recycling, LLC	5918
Hu-Lift Equipment	6291
Human Capital Consultants, LLC	7975
Human Capital International, LLC dba Integrated Human Capital	7971

COMPANY ALPHABETICAL LISTING

H | INDEX#

Human Capital Staffing LLC	9186
Human Potential Consultants, LLC	8916
Human Touch Translations Ltd.	8690
Humbition Consulting, LLC	8311
Humdinger Enterprises LLC	8551
Hunter Hawk, Inc.	6774
Hunter International, Inc.	9351
Hunter-Blyden, Katherine	8356
Hurley Write Inc	9552
Hurt Electric Inc.	1664
Husco Automotive, LLC	4036
Hutchins & Hutchins, Inc.	2266
Hy Speed Machining, Inc.	6891
Hybrid Design Services	3170
Hybrid Edit, LLC	9569
Hybrid Studios LLC	1284
Hybrid Teams, Inc.	8257
Hydro Dyne Inc.	4143
Hydro-Marine Construction Company, Inc.	2441
Hylie Products, Inc.	6714
Hyper IC Florida Inc.	2740
HyperGen Inc.	5726
Hyun & Associates, Inc.	8176

I

I AM Safety	4183
I Chispa, LLC	1572
I F Metalworks	6633
I Love Promos, Inc.	1349
I*LOGIC, Inc.	3171
I. Studio, Inc.	1020
I.V. House, Inc.	6445
i9 Systems, Inc.	5799
IBC	2625
IBC - Industrial Supply Plus	4064
IBC, Inc. - International Builders & Consultants	2339
iBeta, LLC	4441
IBEX IT Business Experts LLC	4598
IBG Global Consulting	5079
iBizSoft	5585
iBridge LLC	5423
IBS Solutions Corporation	6459
iBusiness Solution, LLC	5443
IC3D	7645
ICDI Inc.	2738, 2952
ICE Safety Solutions Inc.	7995
ICG Software Corporation	5863
ICON Information Consultants, LP	9454
Icon IT Group	4999
Iconic Logistics Services LLC	9881
ICONMA, LLC	4927
ID Discovery, Inc.	5444
Idea Entity Corporation	5800
Idea Planet, LP	7438
Ideal Commercial Interiors LLC	3790
Ideal Contracting, LLC	2401
Ideal Electrical Supply Corporation	2811
Ideal Engineering Solutions, PSC	2511
Ideal Interiors Group, LLC	2455
Ideal Machine Tool Technologies, LLC	3959
Ideal Printers	7580
Ideamart Inc.	1233

I | INDEX#

IDEAON	4331
Ideas to Impress, LLC	1490
Identico Print Services dba Print.Save.Repeat.com	5832
Identification Systems, Inc. dba Identity Systems	7646
IdentiPhoto Company Ltd.	5387
Idexcel, Inc.	5727
IDM Products	2904
IDSC, Inc.	2139
IES Engineers	3257
Ifrah PLLC	6099
IFSI General Contractor, Co.	3205
IG, Inc. dba Indrotec	9220
Igbanugo Partners Int'l Law Firm, PLLC	6168
IGI Detroit dba Villc, LLC	4928
IGIS Technologies Inc.	4332
Ignition Network dba Fielday	9096
iii Technologies Inc.	5174
Iknowvate Technologies, Inc.	4929
Ilana Ashley Events	8357
IlinkResources Staffing	9097
ILLUME Advising, LLC	3338
Illumination Research, Inc.	8730
ILM Professional Services, Inc.	5000
Image Office Environments, LLC	3807
Image Projections West, Inc.	5854
Image Quest Plus, LLC	7467
Image Studios, Inc.	7317
ImageTech Systsems, Inc.	5445
ImageWork USA LLC	5318
Imagination Specialties, Inc.	1554
Imagine 360 Marketing	8691
Imagine Enterprises International	8419
Imani Lee, Inc.	7996
Imax Company Inc.	7564
IMB Development Corporation, LLC	7782
IMC Products, Inc.	4104
IMCS Group	9455
IMK Products, Inc.	3687
Immersion Graphics Inc.	1128
ImmunoReagents Inc.	3197
Impact Absorbents, Inc.	1900, 3363
Impact Consulting, LLC	8177
Impact Dimensions, LLC and Affiliate	1491
Impact Enterprises, Inc.	7044
Impact Label Corp.	7565
Impact Mitigation Consultants LLC.	3386
Impact Printing	7468
Impact Strategies Consultants	8796
Impactivo LLC	8229
Impel Professional Consulting, LLC	4599
Impex International Inc.	3892
IMPEX Technologies, Inc.	4333
Impresiv Health	8032
Impress Marketing Studios, LLC	1425
Imprimis Group	9456
Imprint Source LLC	1492
Improve Consulting & Training Group LLC	8201
IN Food Mktg & Design, Inc.	1144
In Time Tec, LLC	4667
in3corp Inc.	8009
Incentive Travel Inc.	10198
IncentiveAmerica, Inc.	1573
Incite Visual Communications	8731

COMPANY ALPHABETICAL LISTING

I

Company	INDEX#
Incite, Inc.	8088
Inclusion, Inc.	7930
Inconen Corporation	8917
Inconen Temporary Services, Inc.	8918
InConsulting Inc.	5801
Indcon Inc.	4165
Independence Flowers & Gifts	3871
Independent Computer Consulting Group, Inc.	5446
Independent Packing Services, Inc.	7194
Independent Professional Management	5586
Indian Industries LP	4023
Indiana Bridge	6610
Indiana Bridge-Midwest Steel, Inc.	6611
INDOFINE Chemical Company	1986
Indoshell Precision Technologies, LLC	6792
Indotronix International Corporation	5319
INDU LLC dba intiGrow	4600
Indus Solutions LLC	1852
Indusa Technical Corp.	4715
Industrial Container Corporation	7102
Industrial Control Repair - ICR Services	2984
Industrial Control Service, Inc.	2852
Industrial Electronics LLC dba Indel-USA	4097
Industrial Fittings & Valves	6969
Industrial Graphics Inc.	7710
Industrial Hose & Hydraulics, Inc.	3994
Industrial Labeling Systems, Inc.	7609
Industrial Metal Fabrication, Inc.	6618
Industrial Piping Systems, Inc.	4155
Industrial Safety Solutions Corporation	7653
Industrial Solution Company	2250
Industrial Specialties Supply, Inc.	4047
Industrial Specialty Products	4054
Industrial Staffing Services inc.	9288
Industrial Water Services	4184
Industry Junction, Inc.	4024
Industry Products Company	7417
Industry Specific Solutions LLC	9187
Infestus Inc.	5080
Inficare, Inc.	5728
Infinart, Inc.	1431
Infinite Computer Solutions Inc.	4866
Infinite Energy Corp d/b/a Definite Energy Group	1992
Infinite Financial Concepts, LLC	7753
Infinite Resouce Solutions	9055
Infinite Scale Design Group	1277
Infiniti Energy & Environmental, Inc.	1960
Infiniti Energy & Environmental, Inc. dba Infiniti	1961
Infiniti Group International, LLC	3442
Infinity Enterprises, Inc.	7310
Infinity Logistics Group, LLC	10125
Infinity Precision Inc.	6775
Infinity Systems, Inc.	5001
In-Flight Crew Connections	9262
Infobahn Softworld, Inc.	4334
Infobeam Technologies LLC	5587
Infocus Specialties, Inc.	1312
Infojini Inc.	9163
Infolob Solutions, Inc.	5588
InfoLynx Services, Inc.	4456
InfoMart	7910
Infomatics Corporation	5729
Infomatics Inc.	4930
Infopro Learning Inc	2715
InfoQuest Consulting Group Inc.	5175
Inforeem	5176
Information Design Consultants, Inc.	4335
Information Protection Solutions	4867
Information Security Enterprise Consulting, LLC	4868
Information Systems Resources	4931
Information Technology Consulting Company	4601
Information Technology Group	5043
Information Transport Solutions Inc.	9739
Infortal Associates, Inc. dba Infortal Worldwide	2613
InfoSmart Technologies Inc.	4602
Infosoft Inc.	4336
InfoVision Consultants, Inc.	5589
Infoyogi LLC	4337
Ingage, LLC	1350
Ingellicom Corp	5486
Ingels Engineering Inc.	6776
Ingenarius, Inc.	5281
InGenesis, Inc.	9457
Ingenium Research Boutique, Inc.	8420
Ingenuity Consulting Partner, Inc.	5044
Ingleside Machine Company, Inc.	6875
InGroup, Inc.	8644
Ink Link, Incorporated	7469
Inktel Direct	8421
Inland Associates, Inc.	5883
InmartGroup, Ltd.	1443
INNERSOURCE Inc.	1218
InnoSoul, Inc.	5320
Innospire Systems Corporation	5177
Innov8 Solutions USA,LLC	2810
Innova Project Services LLC	9164
Innovate Marketing Group	8358
Innovate Medical, LLC	6508
Innovation Marketing Communications LLC	7659
Innovation Network Technologies Corporation	5590
Innovation Partners LLC	7805
Innovative Business Products & Services, LLC	8215
Innovative Chemical Corporation	2179
Innovative Learning Group, Inc.	8115
Innovative Office Solutions, LLC	7023
Innovative Plastics	7432
Innovative Premiums Inc.	1507
Innovative Printing & Graphics	7490
Innovative Recycling Technologies, Inc.	3483
Innovative Regulatory Risk Advisors LLC	7856
Innovative Software Solution	5864
Innovative Systems Group of Florida, Inc. dba ISGF	9010
Innovative Systems Group, Inc.	4716
Innpack LLC	7203
Inoditech LLC, dba Camino Information Services	5591
Inoventures, LLC/SciMetrika, LLC	5730
inQueue Designs LLC	1508
inRange Solutions II, LLC	3206
Insights Marketing	8452
Insignia Marketing	1574
Inspiration Zone, LLC	4818
Inspired Marketing	8543
Instaknow.com, Inc.	5178
Instant Data Technologies	5592
Instant Technology LLC	9098
InstiCo Freight Management, Inc.	10146

COMPANY ALPHABETICAL LISTING

I

Company	INDEX#
Instramed	6946
Instrumed Services Corp.	6057
Instrumentation Corps, Inc.	6327
Insurers Review Services, Inc.	5997
Integra Electronics, Inc.	2798
Integrated Benefits Group, Inc.	6012
Integrated Business Supplies Inc.	5923
Integrated Circuit Development, Inc.	3062
Integrated Construction Technology Corp.	2369
Integrated Control Corporation	3002
Integrated Control Solutions Inc.	2843
Integrated Demolition Service LLC	9926
Integrated Design Solutions	3834
Integrated Finance and Accounting Solutions, LLC	7867
Integrated Focus	8797
Integrated Installations, inc.	9685
Integrated Management & Controls, Inc.	8230
Integrated Manufacturing and Assembly, LLC	1874
Integrated Packaging Company	7178
Integrated Recycling Industries	3443
Integrated Resources, Inc.	9289
Integrated Science Solutions (ISSI)	3364
Integrated Services for Productivity & Validation	5487
Integrated Solutions and Services	5388
Integrated Spatial Solutions, Inc.	4338
Integrated Supply Chain Solutions LLC	7012
Integrated Support Systems Inc (ISSi)	5731
Integrated Systems Management	5321
Integrated Talent Solutions, Inc. dba Vivo	8919
Integrated Technology & Compliance Services	5488
Integration International Inc.	5179
Integration Technology, Inc.	4819
IntegriPrint, Inc.	7581
Integritas Resources, Inc.	8920
Integrity Development	8202
Integrity International, Inc.	8798, 9558
Integrity Medicolegal Enterprises	6169
Intek, Inc.	6323
Intelecox inc	4339
Inteliblue	4248
Inteligente Solutions, Inc.	9188
Intelimas Corporation	6426
IntellectFaces, Inc.	5732
Intellectual Concepts LLC	4603
Intelligent Decision Systems, Inc.	8295
Intelligent Image Management Inc.	5282
Intelligent Interiors, Inc.	3841
IntelliSource	8967
Intelliswift Software, Inc.	4340
Intellisys Technology, LLC	4717
Intellyk Inc.	5180
Intention Advertising	1313
IntePros Incorporated	4820
Interactive Tactical Group	4821
InterChez Global Services, Inc.	10089
Inter-City Supply Co	4078
Intercon Carriers	10147
Inter-Con Security Systems, Inc.	2614
Intercross Design, Inc.	1145
Interface Consulting Services, LLC	6990
Interior Plus, Inc.	2301
Interior Services Incorporated dba Enriching Spaces	3821
Intermodal Logistics Consulting, Inc.	10045
International Asbestos Removal, Inc.	3484
International Coil, Inc.	2976
International Communication Network	9570
International Computer Systems, Inc.	4869
International Digital Systems	5181
International Diversified Marketing, Inc.	7470
International Filter Manufacturing Corporation	4079
International Genesis Professional Solutions, Inc.	9458
International Institute for Learning, Inc. (IIL)	8178
International Label Mfg.	7527
International Medical & Laboratory Supply, LLC	6509
International Metal Source	6931
International Print & Packaging, Inc.	7287
International Robot Support, Inc.	6634
International Specialty Tube	6635
International Technology Solutions, Inc.	5182
International Textile and Apparel, Inc.	9799
International Word Processing Services, Inc.	4341
Internet Operations Center, Inc.	4932
Interport Trading Corp.	4158
Interprise/Southwest Interior & Space Planning, Inc	1816
Interspec, LLC	3320, 3537
Interstate Packaging Corp.	7268
Interstate Premier Services Corp	2227
Interstate Transport, Inc.	9882
Inter-Strap Packaging Systems	7259
InterWorking Labs, Inc.	6028
Intex Technologies LLC	1875
Intrade Industries, Inc.	9848
Intras LLC	5593
Intrinsyx Technologies	4342
Intrinz Inc.	8077
Intrinzic Marketing & Design	8533
Intstrux LLC	8692
INTU Corporation	8669
Intuity Technologies, LLC	5183
Invero Group	8921
Invision Engineering Corp.	3016
IP Consulting, Inc.	4933
IP International, Inc.	4343
Ipax Cleanogel, Inc.	1962, 2169
IPM Asset Solutions, Inc.	5594
IPROVEIT.COM	7911
IPS Group LLC	4144
IPS Technology Services	4934
IQ Telcom, LLC dba IQ Telecom	9660
iQuanti, Inc.	5184
iQuasar, LLC	5733
Iris Communications LLC	1175, 8645
Iris Software Inc.	5185
IROK Solutions, Inc.	8453
Iron Eagle Enterprises, LLC	3495
Iron Lady Enterprises Inc.	5447
Ironpines Welding Inc.	6649
Irons Metal Processing LLC	6612
ISCG	3786
IsComp Systems Inc.	4344
ISES, Inc	5186
Isringhaus Printing LLC	7587
ISS Action, Inc.	2675
ISSGR, Inc. dba ImageSet	7690
iSTAFF Solutions, Inc.	9459
Istonish	4442

COMPANY ALPHABETICAL LISTING

I — INDEX#

Company	Index#
iSustain Inc.	3517
IT by Design	5187
IT Consulting Services, Inc.	4792
IT Data Consulting LLC	5734
IT Division, Inc.	4604
IT People Corporation	5081
IT Reserves, LLC	5389
iT Resource Solutions.net, Inc.	9327
IT Staffing, Inc.	5188, 9290
IT Trailblazers	5189
ITA, Inc.	4080
iTalent Corporation	4345
ITC Translations USA Inc.	8422
I-Tech Personnel Services, Inc.	9011
iTech Solutions, Inc.	4457
iTech US, Inc.	5787
Iterators LLC	4822
ITG Global, LLC	3096, 4518
Ithaca Promotions	1461
ITM Information & Technology Management	5190
It's A Breeze Specialties, LLC	1589
It's My Affair, LLC	8620
ITTConnect Inc.	4519
Ivan Carlson & Associates	8488
Ivie & Associates, Inc.	8799
IVN Sound & Communication, LLC	9758
IVS Solutions, LLC	2846
Ivy Cohen Corporate Communications, Inc.	8693
Ivy Planning Group, LLC	8097
IVY Services, LLC	7558
IW Group, Inc.	1021
iWorks Corporation	5735
Iyka Enterprises, Inc.	4718

J — INDEX#

Company	Index#
J & B Equipment Company, Inc.	6284
J & K Mechanical	2340
J and B Medical Supply Company Inc.	6435
J Michael Industries	1462
J R Rodriguez International Corporation	7070
J Rayl Trasnport Inc.	10090
J&B Franchise Venture, Inc.	2182
J&G Pallets and Trucking, Inc.	10243
J&J Contractors, Inc.	2389
J&J's Creative Colors, Inc.	1858
J. J. Sosa & Associates, Inc.	3399
J. R. Caskey, Inc.	2560, 3538
J. Selmer Law, P.A.	6170
J.C. Gonzalez, Inc.	6058, 6497
J.C. Schultz Enterprises, Inc./FlagSource	1093
J.I.T. Manufacturing, Inc.	6686, 6900
J.L. Wallace, Inc.	2341
J.O. Agency	1260, 8800
J.O. Alvarez, Inc.	10148
J.P. Investigative Group, Inc.	2662
J.T. Dillard, LLC dba ZayMat Distributors	2221
J.T. Systems, Inc.	4133
J.Y. Legner Associates, Inc.	9132
J2 Medical Supply	6347
J2 Systems and Supply, LLC	1940
JA Quality Assurance Group, LLC	2985
JAC Consulting LLC dba The Champagne Group	6253
JAC Janitorial Services	2193
Jackson & Associates, Inc.	6522
Jackson LMS and Associates Inc.	8019
Jackson Tumble Finish	6562
Jade Logistics, Inc.	10030
JAK Graphic Design, LLC	8489
Jamapchi LLC	1351
James Group International	7179
James River Solutions	2066
Jamison Professional Services, Inc.	9056
Janco & Winnex Inc	1314
Janeice Products Co. Inc	3937
Janel Inc.	2200
Janik Vinnakota LLP	6238
Janitorial Services Inc.	2222
janlitlfeather	1689
Jansen Advertising	1376
JANUS Software, Inc. (d/b/a JANUS Associates)	4458
Jarvis Handling Equipment Co.	6278
Jasper Solutions Inc.	5322
JASStek, Inc.	5390
JAT Energy Services LLC	3302
JAUST Consulting Partners Inc.	4346
Javen Technologies, Inc.	5002
Jayne Agency, LLC	1094
Jays and Fancy Interiors, Inc.	2512
Jazzy Sportswear Promotional Co.	1432
JB Manufacturing	6777
JB Software and Consulting, Inc.	5595
JBE, Inc.	6569
JBK Associates International, Inc.	9291
JBN & Associates, LLC	8884
JC Automation, Corp.	5489
JC Office Consultants,LLC	3808
JCB Enterprises, Inc. dba Reluminate	2858
JCCOB Smith Gardner Smith/Keystone AMEX Tvl Svs	10226
JCD Engineering, Inc.	2513, 3270
JCM Machine, Inc.	1886
JCPG LLC dba Popbar	3602
JCQ Services, Inc	2342
JCW Computer Consulting, LLC	5448
JD2 Environmental, Inc.	3503
JDC Events, LLC	8552
JDH Pacific Inc.	6545
JDR Consulting, LLC	8179
JDV Products, Inc.	3963
JE Components Inc.	5957
Jean Martin Inc.	5323
Jean Simpson Personnel Services, Inc.	9136
Jeannette McClennan LLC	8694
Jeevtek Inc.	5003
Jefferson Cleaning Services, LLC	2187
Jelmar LLC	2140
JEM Engineering, LLC	2978
JEM Tech Group	5892
Jeneil Biotech, Inc.	3734
Jenerxx Inc.	7384
Jenkins Construction, Inc.	2402
Jennifer Brown LLC	8180
Jennifer Temps, Inc.	9263
Jensay Co.	3635
JERO Medical Equipment & Supplies, Inc.	1683, 6413
Jersey Staffing Solutions, LLC	9292

COMPANY ALPHABETICAL LISTING

J | INDEX#

Company	Index#
Jervay Agency, LLC	1162
JFE International Consultants, Inc.	8258
JG Advisory Services LLC	6196
JG Haney & Associates LLC	9781
JH Technical Services, Inc.	9384
JHJ Computer Supplies, Inc.	5938
Jill Hickman Companies	8259
Jim Roberts Enterprises LLC	8116
Jimco Maintenance Inc.	2115
JISI Group, LLC	4105
JIT Energy Services	8131
JIT Manufacturing	6706
JK Enterprise Solutions LLC	3678
JK Flenory & Company, LLC	9460
JKICT, Inc.	6536
JLC Group LLC	6636, 7385
JLGJ Trading, Inc.	6471
JLM Risk Management Group	5994
JLR Invesitgations	2615
JLS Staffing & Management dba Total Staffing Solutions	9352
JLT Promotions Inc.	1315
JM Fiber Optics, Inc.	9646
JMA Chartered	4793
JMC Electrical Contractor, LLC dba JMC Technologies	2986
JML Fabrication, LLC	6650
JMS Transportation Inc.	9913
JN3 Global Enterprises LLC	7857
J-n-K Services, Inc.	1316
JNX Partners, LLC	7912, 9057
Jo Kell, Inc.	2914, 6971
JOA Group	2302
Job Hunters LLC	9399
Job Store, Inc.	8968
JOBMA LLC	5004
JOBPRO Temporary Services, Inc.	8977
Jogue, Inc.	3658
John A. Romeo & Associates, Inc.	2771, 3012
John Davenport Engineering, Inc.	3198
John F. Ruggles, Inc.	1104
John Leonard Employment Services, Inc.	9145
John Michael Associates, Inc.	1335
Johnico LLC	2987
Johnny Rullan & Co.,	7260
Johnson & Associates	6179
Johnson & Pace Inc.	3303
Johnson Blumberg & Associates	6134
Johnson Bryce, Inc.	7269
Johnson Liebman, LLP	6197
Johnson Security Bureau, Inc.	2676
Johnson, Inc.	8844
Johnson-Peltier Electric	2936
Johnsrud Transport, Inc.	9914
Jolico/J-B Tool, Inc.	6842
JoMoCo Studio LLC	7702
Jomsom Staffing Services	9293
Jones Metal Inc.	6651
Jones Worley Design, Inc.	1077
Jorgensen Steel Machining & Fabrication	6637
José A. Batlle & Asociados C.S.P.	3271
Josephine's Professional Staffing, Inc.	8922
Joshen Paper and Packaging	7243
Jouard Wozniak LLC dba JWDesign	1176
Journee Technology Staffing Inc.	9328

J | INDEX#

Company	Index#
Journey Steel, Inc.	6669
Joyce Fabrication LLC dba Custom Plastics and More	7338
JP Simons & Co.	2832
JPA Health Communications	8400
JPG & Associates, Inc.	1146
JPI Technology LLC	5736
JQ Infrastructure, LLC	3304
JR Language Translation Services, Inc.	8181
JR Resources	8359
JRA Consulting Services, Inc.	9099
JRD Systems, Inc.	4935
JRE & Associates Inc.	4719
JRE LLC dba Ascension Roofing and Sheet Metal	6620
JRS Consulting, Inc.	8490
JSCS Group, Inc. dba Market Direct	7647
JSL Computer Services, Inc.	5324
JT Promotions	1352
JTS Manage Services	2569
JUICE Pharma Worldwide	1199
Juice Studios	8454
Jules & Associates, Inc.	7726
Julianna Hynes & Associates	7997
Julye Newlin Productions, Inc.	9629
JumpGarden Consulting, LLC	8491
JumpStart Point of Arrival, LLC	4776
JuneGem Technologies, Inc.	4870
Jung Design, Inc.	1762
Jupiter LLC	4871
JURISolutions, Inc.	6219
Just In Case, Inc.	9221
JustinBradley, Inc.	8986
JVB Electronics dba Multilayer Technology	2778
JVJ Can 22 Corp	8323
JVM Sales Corp.	3679
JWT&A LLC	2472

K

Company	Index#
K & J Trucking, Inc.	10123
K & S Engineers, Inc.	3131
K&A Staffing, LLC	9189
K&M International, Inc.	3872
K&R Holdings, Inc.	2280
K&S Construction Group, Inc.	2381
K. Dixon Architecture, PLLC	1768
K. Fernandez and Associates LLC	8801
K. Neal International Trucks, Inc.	1834
K. Singh & Associates, Inc.	3339, 3545
K.L. Scott & Associates LLC	4605
K.O. Strategies	8492
Kaasm, LLC	5802
Kaboom Productions	9571
KACE Logistics, LLC	10000
KACO Supply Company	4072
Kaddas Enterprises, Inc.	7444
Kadiri Health, LLC	6479
KAE Consultants, Inc.	3113
Kahlig Enterprises, Inc	1844
Kahn Architecture & Design, PC	1793
Kairos Consulting Worldwide	8059
Kaiser Consulting, LLC	7838
Kaizen Technologies Inc.	6870
Kalani Packaging, Inc.	7294

COMPANY ALPHABETICAL LISTING

K

Company	INDEX#
Kaliber Choice, LLC	10149
Kalstar Enterprises, LLC	7252
KamarOE	7013
Kambrian Corporation	5840
Kamco Industries LLC	2203
Kamflex Conveyor Corporation	6269
Kamlesh Shah Designs Inc.	1787
Kampack, Inc	7215
Kamptos Technologies, LLC	5191
Kanu Asset Managment, LLC	7839
KAPAX Solutions LLC	8296
Kaplan Interpreting Services	1022
Karasch & Associates	9621
Karm Corporation	1407
Karnak Corporation	6564
Karp Strategies, LLC	3219
KarSun Enterprises, Inc.	1509
KAS Consulting Group	7972
Kaskell Manufacturing, Inc.	6883
Kat@KMGSolutionsInc.com	2445
Kathcart Open Systems & Consulting, Inc.	5803
Katherine Christensen & Associates, Inc.	8324
Kathy Schaeffer and Associates, Inc.	8493
Katie Schibler & Associates LLC	8773
Kavaliro	8923
Kavayah Solutions Inc.	5192
Kavi Software Inc.	4606
Kaygen, Inc.	4347
KB Comm LLC	9555
KBL, LLP Certified Public Accountants & Advisors	7825
KBS	4720
KCH Trucking, LLC	9900
KCM Technical Inc.	7794
KCS	5005
KDG InterActive, Inc.	8589
KDI Technology Solutions, Inc	5325
Keating Environmental Management, Inc.	3504
KEDAR Integration Services, Inc.	5596
KeeClean Management Inc.	2105
Keen Branding	1047
Keeper of the Brand	1200, 8695
Keiki Enterprises LLC	5865
Kelley Chunn & Associates	8544
Kelley Solution, Inc.	1166
Kelly & Berens, P.A. dba Berens & Miller, P.A.	6171
Kelly Computer Supply	3791
Kelly Mitchell Group, Inc.	5045
Kemron Environmental Services, Inc.	3413
Kenco Group	6296
Kenne Shepherd Interior Design Architecture PLLC	1794
Kennedy Associates/Architects, Inc.	1778
Kennedy Office Supply Inc.	7027
Kenowa Industries	6279
Keramida Environmental, Inc.	3421
Kerrick Williams Photography LLC	7303
Kerricook Construction, Inc.	2473
Ketterer Company	1523
Key Alliance Staffing, LLC	8978
Key Concepts Knowledgebase LLC	5737
Key Lime Interactive	8423
Key Logistics Solutions, LLC	10117
Key Personnel, Inc.	9516
Key Services, Inc.	5906

K

Company	INDEX#
Key Technical Resources, Inc.	9012
KeYAH International Trading, LLC	6670
KeyStaff Inc.	9461
KeyStaff, Inc.	9013
Keystats Inc	5326
Keystone Laboratories, Inc.	2592
KFM International Industries, Inc.	6546, 6778
KGM Consulting Inc.	8182
KickStart Specialists, LLC	8297
Kili Summit Corporation	6348
Kilop USA, Inc.	9810
Kim Gardner, Inc.	2088
Kim Winston LLP	6180
Kimprint, Inc. dba Progressive Printing	7566
King Business Interiors	3822
King Filtration Technologies, Inc.	4118
King Finders, LLC	9462
Kingchem	1987
Kings Aire, Inc.	2538
King's Eco Plastics, LLC	7439
Kings Warehouse Logistics LLC	10035
Kingsgate Transportation Services LLC	10091
Kipany Productions, Ltd.	8696
Kipling Jones & Co., Ltd.	7858
KIRA, Inc.	3080
Kirsch Transportation Services Inc.	10051
Kittredge Equipment Company	3815
KJ International Resources, Ltd.	1147
KJL Industries, Inc.	6843
KLD Engineering PC	3220
Kleenslate Concepts, LP	6980
KLI Inc.	2748, 2966
KLN Logistics dba AIT Worldwide Logistics	10092
KLS Air Express, Inc. dba Freight Solution Provide	9849
KM Logistics LLC	10192
KME Architects LLC	1789
KMM Telecommunications	9782
KN Machine & Tool, Inc.	6789
KNF&T Staffing Resources	9146
Knichel Logistics	10106
KNK Recruiting, LLC	9353
KNOCK, inc.	1148
Knoodae Staffing, LLC	9294
Knowledge Connections, Inc.	5738
Knowledge Information Solutions, Inc.	5739
KnowledgeSources Consulting Inc.	8183
KnowledgeStart, Inc.	8216
Kodiak Finance LLC	7868
Koi Computers Inc.	5968
Kolter Solutions	4520
Komplete Group, Inc.	7288
Konie Cups International, Inc.	6986
Konik and Company, Inc.	1392
Kontane Inc.	10118
K'ontinuous Technologies, Inc.	7998
Kool Breeze Solar Hats, Inc.	1671
Kool Ink/Sir Speedy Printing	7482
Koru Communications, Inc.	9647
KORYAK Consulting, Inc.	5449
K-Pak Consulting, Inc.	2456
KR Wolfe, Inc.	2937
Kramer & Leonard, Inc.	7002
Kramer Laboratories, Inc.	6035, 6385

COMPANY ALPHABETICAL LISTING

K INDEX#

Company	Index#
Kramer Translation	1023
Krasamo Inc.	5597
Kreative Kontent Co.	1059, 9583
Kreative Zeno Systems, Inc.	5598
KRETETEK Industries, LLC	1913
Krick Enterprises, Inc.	7515
KrisDee & Associates, Inc.	6796
Kristine Fallon Associates, Inc.	4721
Krown Employment Services, LLC	9385
Kruger Foods Inc.	3564
Krypton Solutions	3025
Krystal Marketing, Inc.	1444
KS Engineers, P.C.	3207
KSC Consultant Services LLC	9708
KSO Metalfab, Inc.	6600
KTL Communications LLC	8845
Kubin-Nicholson Corporation	7711
Kupcha Marketing Services	8697
Kupferstein Manuel LLP	6079
Kusar Court Reporters & Legal Services, Inc.	6080
Kutir Corporation	4348
KV & Associates, LLC	1317
KVibe Productions, LLC	9602
KVJINC Consulting	1060
KW Construction	2303
KW International, Inc.	9850
Kwame Building Group, Inc.	8139
Kyana Packaging & Industrial Supply, Inc.	7167
Kylie B's Pastry Case LLC	3730
Kyyba, Inc.	9100

L

Company	Index#
L & D Mail Masters Inc.	1101
L and N Promotions, Inc.	1393
L J Ross Associates, Inc.	7795
L Tech network Services, Inc.	1606
L&R Security Services, Inc.	2648
L.A. Rag Maker, LLC	1672
L.W. Reinhold Plastics	7322
L.W. Survey Engineering & Design Company	3186
L3 Agency	8494
La Canada Ventures Inc.	2576
LA Exhibits, Inc.	1129
La Fiesta Label & Packaging Systems	7095
La Med Facility Maintenance	2251
La Roza Construction, Inc.	2304
La Solucion Corp.	1876
Laacke & Joys LLC	3851
LabChemS	3272
Label Systems, Inc.	7691
Labels, Tags & Inserts, Inc.	7593
Labor On Demand Inc.	9463
Labor On Demand Inc., Dba, LOD Resource Group	9464
Laboratory Data Consultants, Inc.	4349
Laboratory Design & Construction, Inc.	2570
Laboratory Disposable Products	6051
Lacay Fabrication and Mfg Inc.	6613, 6720
LACOSTA Facility Support Services, Inc.	2141
Ladd Safety, LLC	2237
Lafayette & Kumagai LLP	6081
Lafayette Steel Erector	2385

L INDEX#

Company	Index#
Lagarda Security	2657
LAI International, Inc.	6652, 6859
Lakefront Capital, LLC	7796
Lakeshore Talent, LLC	8969
Lakeside Project Solutions	2431
Lakeview Industries	7396
Lakeview Precision Machining, Inc.	6797
Lamar's Fabrication, Inc.	6687
Lambent Risk Management Services, Inc.	5998
Lancaster Packaging, Inc.	7169
Lancesoft, Inc.	4521
Lanco Manufacturing Corp.	2023
Lancs Industries Holdings, LLC	9819
Land Development Consultants, Inc.	3330
Landmark Construction Company, Inc.	2518
Landry & Kling, Inc.	10201
LaneStaffing Inc.	9465
Langham Logistics Inc.	9947
Language Bank, Inc.	8698
Language Concepts Consulting LLC	1003
Language Resource Center Inc.	1163
Language Select, LLC.	8360
Language Services Associates	1234
Language Solutions Inc.	1158
Languages Houston	8260
Languages International Inc.	1130
LanguageSpeak, Inc.	1061
Lanier's Fine Candies	3731
Lanigan Worldwide Moving & Warehousing, Inc.	10126
Lanin Technologies	4607
Lapeer Metal Stamping Companies, Inc.	6731
Lapine Group, Inc.	8217
Lapsley Inc.	3774
Laredo Technical Services, Inc.	1659
Largin Construction Services LLC	2539
Las Cruces Machine, Mfg. & Engineering	6872
LAS Logistical Services LLC	10185
Laser Printers Plus	5890
Laser Recharge Inc.	5931
Laser Tone, Inc.	5860
Latin American Industries, LLC	7386
Latin Nation Live LLC	8361
Latinworks	1261
Latitude Prime LLC	1149
Latitude Technology Group, Inc.	9222
Laughing Willow, Inc.	1318
Laurie Sall & Associates	6008
Lavelle Industries, Inc.	2270
Law Enforcement Specialists, Inc.	2605
Law Office of Marian Polovy	6198
LAW Ventures, Ltd.	6135
Lawton Printers, Inc.	7491
Laxmi's Delights	3565
LB Manufacturing	1862
LB Transportation Group & Omni Warehouse	10001
LBF Recruitment Strategies, LLC	9101
LBI LLC	2075
LBJR Consulting LLC	8042
LCF - Farmer Group	2170
LCS Entertainment LLC	4722
Lead Dog, Inc.	8759
Lead IT Corporation	4723
LEADCARE, Inc.	3485

COMPANY ALPHABETICAL LISTING

L	INDEX#
Leader Promotions, Inc.	1524
Leading Edge Systems Richmond	9517
LEAP Leadership	8043
LeapFrog Solutions, Inc.	8846
Learning Designs, Inc.	8117
LebenTech Innovative Solutions Inc.	4522
Lebenthal Holdings, LLC	7826
LECGI Inc.	3133
Ledtronics, Inc.	2938
LedZed International Inc.	2816
Lee Anav Chung White Kim Ruger & Richter LLP	6199
LEE Branding	8590
Lee Office Solutions	7071
Lee, Hong, Degerman, Kang & Waimey, APC	6121
LeeMAH Electronics Inc.	2732
LEFCO Worthington, LLC	7244, 10248
Legacy Building Group	2424
Legacy Construction, LLC	4134
Legacy Information Systems, LLC	7058
Legacy Logistics Freight, Inc.	9915
LegalEase Solutions LLC	6158
Legend Medical Devices Inc.	6349
LEGO Construction Co.	2343
Lehtola & Cannatti PLLC	6239
L-E-M Plastics& Supply Inc.	6952, 7406
LEM Products, Inc.	6967
Lemak, LLC dba Lemak Lubricants	1941
Lemartec Corporation	2344
Lemire LLC	2677
Lenco, Inc. - PMC	7405
Lenserf & Co. Inc.	7894
Leon Cosgrove, LLC	6105
LeRoe Corporate Gifts, Inc.	1493
Leslie Saunders Insurance Agency, Inc.	5991
Lester Lithograph Inc. (dba Castle Press)	7471
Level-(1) Global Solutions, LLC	9686
Levi G. Williams, Jr., P.A.	6106
Lewandowska Architect PLLC	1795
Lewis & Munday	6159
Lewis Unlimited, Inc.	6884
Lexair Electronics Sales Corp.	9725
LexHarbor, LLC	5193
Lexicon & Line LLC	8834
Lexicon Promo	1319
LFL International Inc.	8010
LG Associates Inc. dba Asen Computer Associates	4724
LHP Software, LLC	4777
LHP Transportation Services, Inc.	10036
Lianda Corporation	2002
Liberty Commercial Finance	7727
Liberty Glove, Inc.	4055
Liberty Laser Solutions	5876
Liberty Lithographers, Inc.	8495
Liberty Transportation, Inc. dba Team Worldwide	9958
Liehr Marketing & Communications, Inc.	8362
LifeHealth LLC	6363
Lifeline Medical Services, Inc.	6432
Lifeline Pharmaceuticals LLC	6386
Life's Eyes Media, LLC	1105
Lightbeam Communications Corp	8699
Lightbox Libraries	7300
Lighthouse Management Group Inc.	8924
Lightning Bolt and Supply	3901

L	INDEX#
Lightning Printing dba Wallace Carlson Co.	7582
LightPath OM LLC dba strut AGENCY	8455
Lightwell Inc.	5391
LiivData Inc.	4488
Lile International Companies	10100
LilyGild Ltd.	8700
Lim Service Industries Inc.	2252
Lim, Norris & Associates	5450
Lima Consulting Group, LLC	8218
Limb Design LLC	1262
Limelight Media LLC, Inc.	1024
Limitless Investigative Solutions, L.L.C.	3952
Limitless Office Products	7072
Lincoln Manufacturing USA, LLC	6721
Lincoln Security Services, LLC	2644
Lindsay Law	6240
Line2Line Architectural Design Group, LLP	1736
Lingua Franca Translations, LLC	8424
Linguanational Translations, Inc.	1095
Linguis-Techs, Inc.	8760
Liniform Service	1711
LinJen Promotions, Inc.	1394
Link Tech, LLC	5283
Link to Success dba HARKNESServices	2223
Link2consult, Inc.	5194
Linked, LLC	9190
Linrose Electronics Inc.	2874
Linz and Company	1408
Lions & Tigers	8312
Lipotriad LLC	6387
Lipscomb Plant Services, Inc.	2519
Liquid-Solids Separation Corp.	4011
Listo Translating Services & More LLC	8802
Litigation Management, Inc.	6210
Litra Manufacturing Inc.	9677
LittKare, LLC	7502
Live Marketing	8496
Livesay IP Law, PLLC	6100
LiveWell Insurance Products, Inc.	1263
LiveWire Electrical Systems, Inc.	2370
Livingston Law Firm, A Professional Corporation	6082
LIZard Apparel & Promotions	1525
Lizzie Bullets LLC dba KDC	7660
LJP Lab LLC	6047
LK Jordan & Associates	9466
LKG-CMC, Inc.	7999
LKT Laboratories, Inc.	1967, 6043
Llano River Fence Company, LLC	6696
Lloyd Security Incorporated	1629
LMC Enterprises, dba Chemco Products Company	1901
LMG Technology Services, LLC	5599
LMK Clinical Research Consulting, LLC	8148
LNL Solutions LLC	7728
LNT 3 Group	8803
Loadstone Transportation, LLC	10064
Loan Administration Network Inc.	8925
Local Concept	1025
LocalBizNetwork	4350
Locked on Referrals Protection Inc.	2616
Lockman-Brooks Marketing Services, LLC	8621
Lodestar Solutions, Inc.	4523
Loeffler Construction and Consulting, LLC	2416
Loftin Productions	9609

COMPANY ALPHABETICAL LISTING

L	INDEX#
Loftus & O'Meara Staffing Inc.	9102
Logic Soft, Inc.	5392
Logic Solutions, Inc.	4936
Logical Logistics Solutions	10046
Login Consulting Services	8926
Logistic Solutions Inc.	5195
Logistics Innovators Inc. dba Adcom Worldwide	9868
Logistics Systems Incorporated	4477
Logisticus Projects Group	10119
Logisti-K USA, LLC	10150
Logix Guru LLC	5451
LogixService, Inc.	4351
LogoBranders Inc.	1301
Logos Logistics, Inc.	10002
Logsdon Office Supply	6997
London Approach, Inc.	9386
Lone Star Interpreters LLC	8261
Longhorn Office Products, Inc.	7073
Loop Capital Markets	7767
Lopez Marketing Group, Inc.	1264
Lopez Negrete Communications, Inc.	1265
Lord & Mitchell, Inc.	1435
Lord and Tucker Management Consultants, LLC	8098
Lord Electric company of PR, Inc.	3017
Lorentine Green & Associates, Inc.	9058
Lorentson Manufacturing Co., Inc.	7362
Losey PLLC	6107
Lotus Connect LLC	7032
Lotus International Company	2988
Lotus Staffing Group, LLC	9467
Love and Long, LLP	6181
Loyola Enterprises Inc.	5740
LRE Inc. dba Lee Ryder Lamination	5866
LRSolutions, LLC	5393
LSL Industries, Inc.	7350
LT CNC Machining, Inc.	6779
Ltd Logistics, Inc.	10061
Lu Smith Engineers	3321
Lucerne International	6551, 6732
Lucidia IT	4778
Lucio Family Enterprises, Inc.	4205
Lucky Foods, LLC	3696
Lugo Nutrition Inc.	3688
Luminous Tec LLC	4352
Luth Research	8363
LUZ, Inc.	8000
LWH Enterprises	8118
LXI Components Inc.	2817
Lyerly Agency	8622
Lynnae's Gourmet Pickles LLC	3732
Lynnco Supply Chain Solutions	5418
Lynx Ltd	3526

M

M	INDEX#
M & B Holdings, LLC	6315
M & R Consultants Corporation	4823
M & R Graphics	7516
M Plus Embroidery & Promotions	1463
M&A Technology Inc.	5982
M&G Expresso, Inc	3592
M&K Engineering	6817
M&L Precision Machining	6780
M&R Energy Resources Corporation	1993
M. Davis & Sons, Inc.	2331
M. Gill & Associates, Inc.	8425
M. Nelson and Associates	1409
M.A.N.S. Distributors, Inc.	2253
M.A.P. Consulting Services, Inc.	5452
M.E.P. Consulting Engineers, Inc.	3305
M.E.Z Distributors LLC	6537
M.O.M. Tools, LLC	3971
M.O.R.E. Computer Supplies, LLC	5893
M.R. Nyren Company	1395
M.R. Research	9657
M+M Design Construction Project Management (MPJI)	1737
M3 Associates, Inc.	6970
Mac Converting, Inc.	10151
Mach 1 Global Services, Inc.	9828
Machine Tools of Virginia, Inc.	3944
Machine Works, LLC	3877
Machined Products Co.	6798
Mack Engineering Corporation	6860
Mackenzie Aircraft Parts, Inc.	3881
Mackey Group LLC	8534
Maclean Precision Machine	6867
MACNAK Construction LLC	2571
Macomb Wholesale Supply Corp.	7180
Mac-Par Services, LLC	3539
Macro Industries, Inc	1320
Mad Monkey, Inc.	9623
MAD Studio LLC	1201
Madagoni LLC	9295
Madison Avenue Worldwide LLC	8862
Madison Avenue Worldwide, LLC	1599
Madison Design Group	1106
Madison Floral, Inc.	3864
Maestro LLC	8569
Maestro Technologies, Inc.	5196
Magee Enterprises, LLC dba Event1Source	8646
Magellan Architects	1823
Magenta LLC	7145, 7351
Magic Moments Parties and Events	8804
Magid Glove & Safety Mfg. Co., LLC	4081
Magnetic Products and Services, Inc.	5902
Magni-Fab Southwest Company	6697
Magni-Power Company	6671, 6752, 6885
Magno International LP	9883
Magnolia Insights	8497
Magnum Medical LLC	6333
Magnum Staffing Services, Inc.	9468
Magnuson Products LLC	2939
Magnys Innovative Solutions LLC	3172
MagRabbit, Inc.,	10152
MagRabbit-Alamo Iron Works, LLC	4185, 6698, 10153
Mahar Tool Supply Company, Inc.	4106
Mahin Impressions, Inc. DBA Kirkwood Mahin	7610
Mahogani Collections LLC	3866
MAI Enterprises, Inc.	5741
Mail Call Direct LLC	1285
Mail Centers Plus LLC	1078
Mail Everything, Inc.	1096
Main Street Mobile Billboards	1164
Mainstream IP Solutions, Inc.	1614, 2956
Maintenance Mart	2076

COMPANY ALPHABETICAL LISTING

M

Company	INDEX#
Majestic Solutions, Inc.	6575
Makro Technologies, Inc.	5197
Malark Logistics	10031
MalikCo	4353
Malkoff Promotions	8805
Mall Lobby.com, Inc.	5859
Malleswari Inc.	5823
Mallory Headsets	9705
Mamais Contracting Corp.	2457
Maman Corp.	2371
Mammoth Office Products, LLC	6987
Managed Business Solutions	4443
Managed Care Advisors	7925
Managed Staffing Inc	5600
Management Decisions, Inc. - MDI Group	4608
Management, Analysis & Utilization, Inc. dba 3Ci	9059
Maniilaq Services, LLC	3331
Manna Supply, Inc.	2891
Mantych Metalworking, Inc.	6886
Mantz Automation	6926
Manufacturers Industrial Group, LLC	6688
Manufacturers/Machine Builders Services Co.	4214
Manufacturing & Automation Cost Solutions, LLC	2853
Manufacturing Technical Solutions, Inc.	3044
Manzi Metals, Inc.	6935
Marand Builders, Inc.	2432
Maremar Design, Inc.	8770
Marfield Corporate Stationery	7692
MarFran Cleaning, LLC	2254
Marglen Industries	7339
Maria R Pearson Inc dba Own Your World	8033
Marian Medical, Inc.	6422
Marimba Auto, LLC	1877
Marina Graphic Center, Inc.	7472
Marinar Technology Co LLC dba VantageOne Software	5394
Marine Services International, Inc.	10093
Marissa L. Promotions	1494
Mark One	1631, 2425
Market Hut dba United Graphics	7693
Market Inquiry, Inc.	8732
Market Probe, Inc.	8863
Marketing & Engineering Solutions	5395
Marketing Displays, Inc.	1131
Marketing Innovators International Inc.	8498
Marketing Maven Public Relations, Inc.	8364
Marketing Resource Solutions LLC	5082
Marketplace Staffing Services Inc.	9409
MarketPro Inc.	9060
Marketry Inc.	8318
Marketsmith Inc.	8647
MarketView Research Group, Inc.	8648
MarketZing Inc.	8060
Markitects, Inc.	8761
MarkMaster, Inc.	1062, 6988
Marlabs Inc.	5198
Mar-Len Supply Inc.	2089
Marleon International, LLC	10037
Maroadi Transfer & Storage	10107
Marquee Workforce Solutions, Inc.	8927
Marrero & Wydler	6108
Marrero Couvillon & Associates, LLC	1767
Mars Electric	2881
MARS Industries, LLC	4025
Marshall Sales Inc.	3908
Mar-Tek Industries, Inc.	7480
Martin Litho, Inc.	7492
Martindale Associates, Inc.	4824
Martin's Got You Covered	5424
Martirx Infotech LLC	5804
MARVEL INFOTECH Inc.	5199
Marvin Groves Electric Company, Inc.	2540
Marwol Metals, Ltd.	6947
Mary O'Connor & Company	8499
Maryland Chemical Company, Inc.	1950
MAS Foods International, LLC	3648
MAS Global Consulting, LLC	4524
MASAI Technologies Corporation	4872
MASCOT Workwear	1712
MashPoint, LLC	5200
Maslowski Controls, LLC	3306
Mason's Professional Cleaning Service, LLC	2238
Mastech Digital Technologies, Inc.	5453
Master Gage & Tool Company	3984
Master Manufacturing Co, Inc.	3823, 3972
Master Marketing International	7517
Master Pneumatic Detroit, Inc.	4107
Master Products Corp.	4159
Mastercraft Printed Products & Services	7694
Masterex Technologies, Inc.	5201
Masterpiece Accounting Services LLC	7827
MasterStaff, Inc.	9416
MasterWord Services, Inc.	1266
Mat Holdings Inc	3114
Matel Manufacturing Inc.	1321
Material Handling Inc.	6268
Material Management	3391
Materials Management Services Inc.	3909
Matoaka Enterprises, LLC	7503
Matrex Exhibits	8500
Matrix IV, Inc.	7352
Matrix New World Engineering, Land Surveying and Landscape Architecture	3208, 3471
Maureen Data Systems, Inc.	5327
Maven Communications, LLC	8762
Maven Companies	4444
Mavensoft Technologies	5425
Maverick Direct, Inc.	9354
Maveryck Marketing Group, LLC	8456
Mavich LLC	2905
Max International	7059
MAX Technical Training Inc.	5396
Maya Jig Grinding & Gage Co.	6844
Mayner Business Law, P.S.	6251
Mayor Logistics Inc.	9851
Mays Chemical Company	1942
Maysonet LLC	2442
Mazur/Zachow, Inc.	8864
MB Diversity	9535
MB Five Consulting LLC	5601
MB Research Laboratories	6056
MBE Cleaning LLC	2255
MBI, LLC	3084
MBJ Consultants, Inc.	2474
MC Builders, LLC	2522
McCallion Temps, Inc.	9387
McCarthy, Burgess & Wolff	7840

COMPANY ALPHABETICAL LISTING

M

Company	INDEX#
McClain & Canoy, LLC	6136
McClellan Sales Inc	4115
McConnell & Jones LLP	7859
McCormack Schreiber Legal Solutions Inc.	6137
McCulloch England Associates Architects, Inc.	1784
McDowell Information Group Public Relations LLC.	8457
McElroy Scenic Services LLC	3779
MCEM LLC	1963, 4005
MCFS Enterprises, Inc.	3496
McKallen Medical	8001
McKechnie Vehicle Components	1878
McKinley Marketing Partners, Inc.	9518
McKissack & McKissack of Washington, Inc.	7741
McKlein Company, LLC	1684
McLaren Photographic LLC	7304
MCM Ind. Co., Inc.	6672
MCM Staffing, LLC	9191
McMillon Communications, Inc.	8553
McMurray-Stern Inc.	6260
McNeal Professional Services, Inc.	4609
McNeely Technology Solutions, Inc.	5602
McPherson, Berry & Associates, Inc.	7913
McTech Corp.	2475
MCV Technologies Inc.	2799
MDA Leadership Consulting	8132
MDD Marketing Inc.	6523
Meadow Lark Companies	10042
Meadowlands Consumer Center Global Marketing Research	8649
Meadows Office Supply Co., Inc.	3816
Measurement Controls, Inc.	6320
Mechanical Design Solutions, Inc.	3085
Mechanical Heating Supply, Inc.	4135
Mechanical Rubber Products Company, Inc.	7410
Mechanical Testing, Inc.	3486
MedEdNow, LLC	8701
Medefil, Inc.	6414
Medgluv Inc	6388
Medgyn Products Inc.	6415
Medi Max Tech	6350
Media Advantage, Inc.	1235
Media Bridge, Inc.	1150
Media Global Group, LLC	8426
Media Works, Ltd.	1124
Media2, Inc. dba M2	9610
Mediascript, LLC	5397
Medical Applications Specialists, Inc.	6416
Medical Monofilament Manufacturing	6427
Medical Receivables Solutions, Inc.	6351
Medical Resources	6480
Medical Support International, LLC	6389
MediGreen Medical Supplies & Services, LLC	6481
Medius & Associates, Inc.	1097
Med-Lab Supply Co. Inc	6390
Med-Tech Equipment, Inc.	6368
MedX Diagnostic Solutions, LLC	6403
Meeting Excellence, Inc.	8527
Meeting Logistics, LLC	8650
Meeting Management Associates, Inc.	8702
Meeting Planners Plus	8365
Meetings & Incentives Worldwide, Inc.	8865
Meetings by Design, Inc.	1048
Meijun LLC	4354, 8366

M

Company	INDEX#
Mekky Media Relations	8501
Mel Lanzer Co.	2476
Mellow Enterprises LLC	6391
MelroseMAC, Inc.	5841
Melvin's Photo	7307
Memmert USA, LLC	4233
Menco Pacific, Inc.	2305
Mendoza Enterprises LLC	1445
Mendoza Group Inc.	1236
Mennie's Machine Company	6799
Mentco Inc.	6913
MentorTechnical Group, Corp.	6059, 6328
Mer Wil Industries, Inc.	3910
Mercado Associates	3063
Mercer Machine	6811
Merchandise Partners	1353
Merchants Delivery Moving & Storage Co.	10193
Mercommbe Inc.	5877
Mercury P&F	1446
Mercury Systems, Inc.	5202
Meridian Office Systems, Inc.	5939
Meristem Packaging Company LLC	7130
Merit Laboratories, Inc.	3444
Meritke Electronics Corp.	2800
Merlin Techncial Solutions	4445
Merrimac Energy Group	1902
Merrimak Capital Company LLC	7865
Merriwether & Williams Insurance Services	5987
Merton Partners LLC	2116
Meryman Environmental, Inc.	3400
Mesa Associates Inc.	3045
Meta Dimensions Inc.	5742
Metabyte Inc.	4355
Metal Craft Machine & Engineering, Inc.	6861
Metal Tech Inc.	6702, 6921
Metalbuilt LLC	6733
Metal-Era, Inc.	6709
Metaphrasis Language and Cultural Solutions, LLC	8502
MetaSense Inc.	9296
Metasys Technologies	4610
Metcon Inc.	2433
Method360, Inc	4356
Metro Contract Group	3748
Metro Golf Cars, Inc.	1845
Metro Medical Equipment & Supply, Inc.	6446
Metro Printed Products, Inc.	1410
Metro Travel	10215
Metromarketing Services Inc	1267
Metropolitan Security Inc. dba Walden Security	2689
Metropolitan West, Inc.	7473
Mexican Technologies Co	7440
Mexus Transport, Inc.	10003
Meyer Contracting Inc.	2417
Meyer Material Handling Products Inc.	6274
Meylan Enterprises, Inc.	2196
MF Supply Corp.	3924
MFR Consultants, Inc.	8763
MFS Consulting Engineers & Surveyor, DPC	3209
MG Automation, Inc.	4725
MGE Architects, Inc.	1747
MH Food Group LLC	3593
MH Specialties LLC	1354
MHa Technical Staffing, Inc.	8970

COMPANY ALPHABETICAL LISTING

M	INDEX#
MHJohnson & Associates, Inc.	8503
Michael Resource Group LLC	8262
Michigan Staffing	9192
Mico Industries, Inc.	6734
Mico Promotions, Inc.	8703
Micro Analog Inc.	2733, 2940
Micro Fixtures, Inc.	3960
Micro Wise, Inc.	5894
MicroAutomation, Inc.	5743
Microbial Insights, Inc.	3518
Micro-Design, Inc.	9783
Microexcel Inc.	8158
Microland Electronics Corporation	4357
microMEDIA Imaging Systems, Inc.	5203
Microtech Machine Company, Inc.	6800
MicroTechnologies, LLC	5744
Mid West Fabricating	6965
Mid-American Specialized Transport, Inc.	9948
Midbrook Industrial Washers Inc.	6638
Midco Electric Supply	2833
MIDCOM	8928
Middletown Tube Works, Inc.	6673
Midland Scientific Inc.	6048
MIDpro Fluid Power and Automation	3999
Midtown Personnel, Inc.	8987
Midtown Scientific, Inc.	6055
Midway Industrial Equipment Inc.	6270
Midway Office Supply Inc.	7037
Midwest Background Inc.	7898
Midwest Insert Composite Molding & Assembly Corp.	7353
Midwest Janitorial Service	2132
Midwest Legal and eData Services, Inc.	6254
Midwest Mailing & Shipping Systems Inc.	7146
Midwest Maintenance Services, Inc.	2171
Mid-West Materials, Inc.	6674, 6955
Midwest Molding, Inc.	2749
Mid-West Moving & Storage, Inc.	9927
Midwest Ohio Tool Company, Inc.	3973
Midwest Safety Products of Michigan	4108
Midwest Solution Providers, Inc.	4726
Midwest Steel Company, Inc.	2541
Mighty Lift Inc.	6298
Migu Press Inc.	7661
Mihnovich Consulting LLC	9014
Mikan Corporation	5895
MikaPak Inc.	3749
Mike Nakamura Photography LLC	7316
Milagro Packaging LLC	7263, 7431
Milano Railcar Services	9928
Miles McClellan Construction Co., Inc.	2434
Miles Printing Corporation	7528
Milestone Construction Partners	2458
Milhench Supply Company	2153
Milhouse Engineering and Construction, Inc.	3115
Millennium Franchise Group	4358
Millennium Industrial Equipment, LLC	6286
Millennium Info Tech. Inc.	5204
Millennium Signs & Display, Inc.	1202, 7630
Millennium Software Inc.	4937
MillenniumSoft, Inc	9519
Miller Environmental Group, Inc.	3487
Miller Machine Company	6862
Miller Tanner Associates, LLC	8777

M	INDEX#
Milletech Systems Inc.	4611
Milligan & Company LLC	7845
Milligan Events	8472
Milner & Schooley LLC	5603
Mimar Architects & Engineers, Inc.	1769
Mind The Gap, LLC	8263
Mind Your Business Inc.	7935
Mindlance, Inc.	5205
Mindseeker, Inc.	5745, 8298
Minitab Inc.	5454
Minoria Tech LLC	5919
Minority Alliance Capital, LLC	7797
Minority Business News	2721
Minority Executive Search	9355
Minority Graphics Inc.	7631
Minority Opportunity News, Inc.	2722
Minority Print Media, LLC	2542
Mint Legal Solutions	6109
Mintech LLC	6639
Minuteman Trucks, Inc.	1833
Miracle Security Inc.	2678
Miracle Software Systems	4938
Mirg Corporation	2882
Mirror Show Management	8704
Mirus Consulting Group Corp	5490
Mission Critical Technologies, Inc.	4359
Missouri Office Systems & Supplies, Inc.	7024
Missouri Sea & Air Services, Inc.	9959
MIT Professionals, Inc.	9469
Mitaja Corporation	8099
Mitchell & Titus LLP	7828
Mix On Digital, LLC	1203
Mixed Promotions, LLC	1447
MJ Learning Inc.	8061
Mjach Designs	8554
MJB Plastics, Inc.	7323
MJS Communications LLC	1608, 9662
MKAssociates, Inc.	3322
MKI Group, LLC dba IS3 Solutions	5206
MKSD. LLC	1809
MMG Corporate Communication, Inc.	9618
MMI Inc.	8651
MMP LLC	8733
MMS Holdings Inc.	6436
MNJ Technologies Direct, Inc.	5878
MNP Corporation	6640, 6735
Mobile Cardiac Imaging LLC	6487
Mobile Electrical Distributors, Inc.	2920
Mobile ID Solutions, Inc.	5842
Mobile Temporary Services	9470
Mobilematics, Inc.	4360
MobileStrat, Inc.	9759
Mobius Partners Enterprise Solutions	8806
MOD Worldwide	8764
Modat Productions	9603
ModelPeople Inc	8504
Modern Construction Services, LLC	2435
Modern Graphics	8765
Modern Litho-Print Co.	7588
Modern Maintenance Building Services, Inc.	2271
Modern Manufacturing & Engineering, Inc.	6863
Modern Technique, LLC	1219, 8734
Modo Modo Agency LLC	8458

COMPANY ALPHABETICAL LISTING

M | INDEX#

Company	Index#
Modpak, Inc.	7216
Modular Installation Services, Inc.	3842
Mohawk Ltd.	4136
Mohr Partners, Inc.	8264
Mohr Stamping, Inc.	6753
Mola Group Corporation	5328
Molded Dimensions, Inc.	7448
Molding Concepts, Inc.	7387
Moltron Builders Inc.	2418
Momento USA LLC	5207
Momentum, Inc.	5455
Mona Terrell & Associates LLC	8652
Monarch Litho, Inc.	7474
Mona's Granola and Cookies, Inc.	3576
Monnex Precision Inc.	6801
Monsoon Kitchens, Inc.	3636
Montage Marketing Group, LLC	8847
Montenegro Paper, Ltd.	7147
Monterey Consultants, Inc.	8203
Moody Engineering, LLC	3238
MoonRock Enterprises LLC	1243
Moore Accounting, LLC	7771
Moore Transport of Tulsa LLC	10154
Morales Group, Inc.	7160
Moreno Services LLC	9193
Morine Networking, Inc.	9961
Morris Packaging	7148
Morrison Metalweld Process Corporation	6675
Morrissey & Associates, LLC	8325
Morse Communications Inc.	4779
MorSports & Events, Inc.	8390
Mosaic Global Transportation	9852
Mosaic Solutions, Inc.	5746
Moser Law Co LLC	6122
Moten Tate, Inc.	7899
Motir Services, Inc.	2329
Motivate Design, LLC	5329
Motivate, Inc.	1026
Motivated Security Services, Inc.	2669
Motor City Stamping	6736
Motor City Travel	10212
MOTR GRAFX, LLC	7518
Mountain Consulting, Inc.	3086
Mountain Printing Company Inc.	7611
Mountainside Medical Colorado, LLC	6364, 6786
Moura's Cleaning Service, Inc.	2154
Movad	7662
Moving Ideas, Inc.	1165
Moxi Events, LLC	8608
Mozaic Management, Inc.	8609
MPM Marketing, Inc	2709
MPS Group, Inc.	3173, 3445
Mpulse Healthcare, LLC	6524
MRA Advertising/Production Support Services, Inc.	1220
MRC - Medical Research Consultants	6525
MRP, LLC dba Aquabiliti & AmUSA	6510
Mrs. Paper	7045
MS Inspection & Logistics, Inc.	9125
MS Rubber Company	4120
MSB Analytics, Inc.	7715
MSF Global Solutions, LLC	4805
MSH Construction Co., Inc.	2306
Mshana Group LLC dba AriesPro	5604
MSquare Systems Inc.	5208
MSR Group, Inc.	8807
MSRCOSMOS LLC	4361
MSW (Mahomed Sales & Warehousing, LLC)	7161
MSys Inc.	4478
MT & Associates, LLC	8610
MTech Partners, LLC	5605
MTM LinguaSoft	1237
Mtronics.com, Inc.	2726
Mu Sigma Inc.	4727
Mudrasys Inc.	4362
Mulino Trading, LLC	10101
Muller & Muller Ltd.	1757
Mullins Food Products, Inc.	3617
Multatech	3307
Multi Image Group, Inc.	1063
Multi Media Promotions	1510
Multi-Craft Litho, Inc.	7538
Multi-Cultural Convention Services Network (MCCSN)	8367
Multilingual Connections, LLC	8062
MultiLingual Solutions, Inc.	8555
Multitec, Inc./Next Step Resources	9356
Multitech Industries, Inc.	6802
Multitek Corporate Communications	9590
Multi-Trans, Inc.	10155
Munaco Sealing Solutions, Inc.	4166
Munnlane LLC	8159
Munoz Trucking, Inc.	10156
Munroe Creative Partners	1238
Munson Business Interiors	3777
MurTech Consulting LLC	5398
Murti LLC	3750
Murzan Inc.	3104
Muscle Products Corp.	2021
Muse Communications, Inc.	1027
Muse GME Enterprises LLC	8100
Music Express Limousine Service	9853
Mustang Express Ltd.	10157
Mustardseed Cultural & Environmental Services, LLC	8140
Mutex Systems Inc.	5209
Mutual Target Associates, Inc.	9103
MVC Consulting Inc.	4728
MVP Plastics, Inc.	7418
MVP Textiles and Apparel, Inc.	9817
MW Logistics, LLC	10158
MWH Law Group LLP	6128
MWM Consulting Group Inc.	7768
MX4 Electronics, Inc.	2847
My Brother's Salsa LLC	3550
My Business Matches, Inc.	5606
My Future Consulting, Inc.	9104
MY HR Supplier	8979
My Next Career Path Staffing, LLC	9310
MYCA Material Handling Solutions, Inc.	6289
Myca Multimedia and Training Solutions, LLC	5399
MYCO Medical Supplies, Inc.	6449
Myers Power Products, Inc.	2941
Mynela Staffing LLC	8929
Myriad Technical Services	9105
Myron Zucker, Inc.	2989
MYS LLC	8670
MyThreeSons Gourmet, LLC	3668
MyWay Logistics LLC	9949
MZI Group Inc.	4729

COMPANY ALPHABETICAL LISTING

N | INDEX#

Company	Index#
N2 Services Inc	4525
n8 Solutions	8808
Nadicent Technologies LLC	4459
NAECO, LLC	2822
NAIWBE Natural As I Wanna Be	2582
Nakitare Builders LLC	2345
Nance Carpet & Rug Inc.	3767
Nancy Conner Consulting, LLC	8063
Nanland LLC	3735
Naterra International	2595
Nathan Kimmel Company, LLC	4056
Nation Waste Inc.	3527
National Access Design, LLC	4145
National Alliance Security Agency, Inc.	2679
National Associates, Inc.	8988
National Background Investigations, Inc.	2653
National Beverage Screen Printers, Inc	7669
National Business Advisory Group, Inc.	8459
National Career Group	9194
National Eagle Security, Inc.	2617
National Electric Corporation	1112
National Events LLC	8848
National Fiber and Copper, Inc.	9663
National Freight Logistics Inc.	9854
National Gifts Ltd.	1511
National Industrial Supply Co.	3911
National Integrated Systems	4109
National Manufacturing, Inc.	9807
National Material Co.	6948
National Material Trading, LLC	6938
National Packaging, LLC	7123
National Raisin Company	3566
National Relocation Services, Inc. dba NRS, Inc.	3064
National Systems America, L.P.	5607
National Tek Services, Inc.	4730
Nationwide Auto Transport, Inc.	10052
Nationwide Envelope Specialists, Inc.	7014
Nationwide Investigations & Security, Inc.	1660, 2695
Nationwide Transportation & Logistics Services Inc.	9955
Native American Industrial Solutions L.L.C.	5501
Native American Natural Foods LLC	3712
Native Hawaiin Veterans LLC	8051
Native Lumber LLC dba Paper City Bat Company	10241
Native Technology Solutions Inc.	4255, 9636
Native Trax Logistics LLC	10072
Native Ways LLC - Apachewolf Productions	9633
NatSoft Corporation	5210
Natural Evolution, Inc.	3498
Naughton Energy Corp.	2022
NavasDRSTi, LLC	6442
Navatar Consulting Group Inc.	5330
Navigator Express	10159
Navisource Holdings LLC dba Golden Hill Foods LLC	3618
nbj Architecture	1820
NC & Sons The Nicholson Corporation	2443
NC Moving & Storage Solutions	3567
NCS Technologies, Inc.	5211
NCT Holdings, Inc.	6460
NDR Energy Group, LLC	1973
Need a Part Now, LLC	1879
Neiger Design, Inc.	8505
Neighboring Concepts, PLLC	1785
Neka Creative LLC	8591

N | INDEX#

Company	Index#
Nella Pasta LLC	3637
Nelson Consulting LLC	8133
Nelson Search Group	9471
neMarc Professional Services, Inc.	9417
Nemovi Law Group APC	6083
Neo Tech Solutions, Inc.	5212
NeoChild	6488
Neotecra, Inc.	5213
NES Incorporated	3418
Nesso Strategies	8002
Nest Builders	3116
Nestor Reyes, Inc.	10112
Net Anchor, Inc.	5006
Net2Source Inc	9297
Neta Scientific Inc.	6052
NetCablesPlus Inc.	5928
Netfast Technology Solutions Inc.	5331
NETHOST, Inc.	5747
Netlink Software Group	4939
Netpace Inc.	8368
NetPlus Marketing, Inc.	1239
netPolarity, Inc.	8930
NetPro Resources, Inc.	9329
netRelevance LLC	4446
Netrion Global Solutions, Inc	4731
NetSource, Inc.	8931
NetTarius Technology Solutions, LLC	5214
NetVision Resources	5748
Network Embroidery Inc.	1575
Neutral Posture, Inc.	3843
Never Ending Technology, Inc.	4242
New Age Transportation, Distribution & Warehousing	9929
New Century Advisors, LLC	7783
New Century Packaging Systems, LLC	7289
New Computech, Inc.	5920
New Dimension Logistics, LLC	10004
New Eagle, LLC	3912
New Echelon	7567
New England Die Cutting, Inc.	4101
New England Machinery, Inc.	4207
New England Packaging Co. LLC	7116
New Era Contract Sales Inc.	5805
New Generation Product, Inc.	7028
New Horizons Computer Learning Center Minnesota	5007
New Instruction, LLC	5215
New K-Stone Management, Inc.	2050
New Products Corporation	6552
New Renewable Energy Technologies, LLC dba NERETEC	5608
New Vision Media Inc.	9619
New West LLC	1107, 8535
New York Technology Partners	5332
New York Wiping & Industrial Products, Inc.	4160
NewAgeSys, Inc.	5216
Newco Services, Inc.	9884
NewData Strategies	5609
Newtech 3, Inc.	2758, 2990
Newtype, Inc.	1177
NewVolt Solutions, Inc.	5333
NexAge Technologies USA Inc.	5217
NexEco Energy Conservation, Inc.	2942
NexInfo Solutions, Inc.	4363
Nexlevel Consulting Services, LLC	8017

DIR 2025   II- 46

COMPANY ALPHABETICAL LISTING

N INDEX#

Company	Index#
Nexo Services LLC	2269
Nexpro Personnel Services, Inc.	9223
Next Generation Fuel, LLC	2003
Next Generation Technology Inc.	5610
Next Generation, Inc.	4732
Next Level Business Services Inc.	4612
NEXT Medical Products Company, LLC	6461
Next Step Staffing	9298
NexTech Professional Services	9195
NextGen Information Services Inc.	5046, 9240
NexThreat	5749
Nexus Direct, LLC	8849
Nexus Pharmaceuticals, Inc.	6417
Nexus Staffing Solutions Corp.	8971
NFD, Inc.	1770
Niche Assurance LLC	8265
Niche Consumer Products, LLC	9815
Niche Waste Reduction and Recycling Systems, Inc	3505
Nicholas Earth Printing, LLC	7695
Nicholson Printing Inc.	7529
Nicor Inc.	7441
Nieman Printing	7696
Nifty Concept	4137
Night Eyes Protective Services Inc.	2696
Nightowl Document Management Services, Inc.	6172
NIKSUN Inc.	5218
Nina Hale Inc.	8592
Nineteen Eleven Solutions Inc.	4613
Ninyo & Moore	3365
Nirav Dye & Chemicals Inc.	3669
Nirvana International Inc.	5750
NiuSource Inc.	3568
NM1, LLC	1828, 1853
NMS Management Inc.	2090
NMS Security Services, LLC	2599
No Other Impressions, Inc.	7632
Nobis Logistics LLC	10160
Noble Plastics Inc.	7366
Noble Technologies Corp. (DBA NobleTek)	3239
Nobles Research, Inc.	8427
Noetic Strategies, Inc.	4243
Noise Consulting Group, Inc.	4526
nomADic genius, LLC	1245
Nonpareil Ventures LLC	1028
Noor Associates, Inc.	9330
Noor Staffing Group, LLC	9331
Norfleet Distributors LLC	4146
Normandin Transportation Services Inc.	9966
North American Assemblies, LLC	2772
North American Commercial Construction, LP	2543
North American D.F., Inc.	7633
North American Transport Services LLC	9885
North Georgia Telecom, Inc.	9678
North Shore Components Inc.	2875
North Star Marketing, Inc.	8774
North Star Stamping & Tool, Inc.	6718
North States Steel Corp.	6939
Northbound LLC	4364
Northcott Banners, Inc.	1151
Northeast Construction Contractors, Inc.	2499
Northern Industrial Products Corp.	3913
Northern Technical Group LLC	5980
Northern U & S, Inc. dba Quali-Mac, Inc.	6864

N INDEX#

Company	Index#
Northfield Trucking Company, Inc.	10005
Northstar Contracting, Inc	2477
Northstar Environmental Remediation	3366
Northstar Imaging Services, Inc.	7583
NorthStar Print, LLC	1377, 7504
NorthStar Strategies, Inc.	1098
Northwest Freightway Inc.	9855
Norwood Paper	6998
Nostrum, Inc.	8369
NOVA Electronic Materials LLC	2906
Novatek Communications, Inc.	8705
N-ovation Technology Group	5400
Novel Geo-Environmental, LLC	3506
NOVO Consulting Group LLC	3273
NPD Global Inc.	5219
NPTS, Inc.	3488
NSM Inc.	3308
NTE Legacy, LLC	2596
nTech Solutions, Inc.	9165
N-Touch Strategies, LLC	8015
Nu Tek Steel, LLC	6956
NuAngel Inc.	6331
NucoreVision, Inc	4873
Nueva Solutions Inc	9332
Number 3 Inc.	7301
Numeridex, Inc.	7149
Nu-Pulse Technologies, Inc.	4874
Nurses And Medical Staffing Agency LLC	9015
Nutech Systems Inc.	4614
Nvelup Consulting	5806
Nvision Media Group, LLC	1286
Nwaneri Law Firm, PLLC	6173
NXTevent, Inc.	8545
NY Plumbing Wholesale & Supply, Inc.	3927
Nygala Corp.	1495
NYX Inc.	1880

O

Company	Index#
O & I Transport Inc.	10006
O&S Associates, Inc.	1788
O.G.I.H. Enterprises, Inc.	1680
O.T. Trans Inc.	4067
O2 Marketing & Design, Inc.	1322
Oakley Relocation LLC	9856
OakTree Software, Inc.	7652
OAS Computer Supplies	5940
Oatridge Security Group Inc.	2704
Object Information Services, Inc.	5611
ObjectWin Technology, Inc.	5612
Obsidian Technical Communications, Ltd.	8266
OCAA Solutions LLC	5284
Occasions Staffing Solutions, LLC	8932
Ocean (Caribbean) Distributors, Inc.	6392
Ocean Cargo Logistics Group, LLC	9886
Ocean Inc. dba Omega Systems	4940
Oceandrum LLC dba Zydeco Design	1152
Ocher Technology Group	4615
OCS Inc.	6437
OCS Process Systems	4221
Oculus Inc.	1779
Office and Business Resources LLC	3775
Office Design Concepts, LLC	2544

COMPANY ALPHABETICAL LISTING

O

Company	INDEX#
Office Design Group	3751
Office Partners, LLC	7051
Office Solutions Inc.	9731
Officemate International Corporation	7033
Offices Unlimited Inc.	7025
OfficeWorks Services LLC	7003
Offray Specialty Narrow Fabrics, Inc.	9812
Offset House Printing, Inc.	7530
OG Energy Solutions LLC	4026
OGC Construction, LLC	3546
OHC Environmental Engineering	3401
Ohio Cables, LLC	9749
Ohio Services-CLE, LLC dba Jani-King of Cleveland	2224
Ohio Transitional Machine & Tool Inc.	6887
Ohm Systems, Inc.	5456
Oil Field Development Engineering	3309
Ojibway, Inc.	4941
Old Dominion Electrical Supply Co Inc	2915
Olivine LLC	4616, 9061
OLSA Resources, Inc	9370
Omega Business Systems	5613
Omega Micro Services	4875
Omega Natchiq, Inc.	3137
Omega World Travel	8850, 10225
OMNEX	8119
Omni Machine Works, Inc.	6791
Omni Packaging Corporation	4151
Omni Source Solutions	9264
Omni Sourcing, Inc.	5060
Omni Staffing Plus, Inc.	9418
Omni2max, Inc.	4365
Omnikron Systems Inc.	4366
OmniSource Marketing Group, Inc.	1411
Omni-Tech Sales, Inc.	6316
OmniTek Consulting, Inc.	8299
On Line Design, Inc.	3240
ON Point Next Level Leadership	8134
On Track Consulting	4825
on3 Promotional Partners, LLC	1600
One 2 One Marketing Inc.	8593
One Accord, LLC	7872
One Corps, Inc	1651, 2687
One Horn Transportation Inc.	9887
One Nation Energy Solutions, LLC	2051
One Production Place	9585
One Pytchblack, LLC DBA PytchBlack	1268
One Source Mobile	9750
One Stop Environmental, LLC	3343
One Way Safety, LLC	4082
One-E-Way, Inc.	2943
Oneida Solutions Group	10007
Onesource Distributors, Inc.	2801
OneSource Services	9357
OneSource Supply Solutions (OSS)	8003
Ongweoweh Corp	7231, 10247
Onin Staffing	9410
Online Computer Prodcuts, Inc.	4826
Online Training Solutions, Inc.	5807
OnPoint, LLC	4027
OnShore Technology Group, Inc.	4733
ON-SITE Inc.	9539
On-Site LaserMedic Corp.	5843
Onyx Media Services, Inc.	9586
Onyx Power and Gas LLC	3310
Onyx Spectrum Technology, Inc. dba Shearwater EM	4827
OP4 Security Solutions	7900
Open Channels Group, LLC	8809
Open Systems Inc.	4617
Open Systems Technologies DE, LLC	4942, 5896
Open Technology Group	4876
OpenLogix Corporation	4943
Operational Technologies Corporation	9784
Operations Service Systems	8166
OpTech, LLC	9196
Opterna-AM Inc.	9791
Optical Interconnect	2779
Optima Global Solutions, Inc.	5220
Optimal Computer Aided Engineering, Inc.	3174
Optimal Leasing LLC	7798
OPTiMO Information Technology LLC	5457
Optimum Contracting Solutions	2403
Optimum Financial Corporation	7716
Optimus Technologies, LLC	4479
Optitek, Inc.	6175
Orange Coast Analytical, Inc.	3367, 6029
Orange Filmworks Inc.	9596
Orange Legal Inc.	6110
OrangePeople	4367
Orchem Corporation	2004
Orgro	4480
ORI	8851
Orion Offset	7519
Orlando Conference Management Group, Inc.	8428
O'Rourke Wrecking Co.	2478
Orpine Inc.	4618
Orr Textile Co., Inc.	9818
Orri Corporation	2759, 2991
Orrs Environmental, LLC	3344
Ortiz & Lopez, LLC	6186
O'Ryan Group	7673
Osceola Consulting llc	8004
Osceola Supply, Inc.	1919
Ospro Systems, LLC	4527
Ossanna Corporation	7918
OST Trucks and Cranes, Inc.	2307, 3368
OTB Container, LLC	7270
Otis Construction Company	2372
Ottsie, LLC	2834
Outcomes Inc.	9520
Outreach Promotional Solutions	1526
Outreach Strategists LLC	8810
OutSecure Inc.	4460
Outsource Consultants, Inc.	3221
Outsource Events, Inc.	8460
Outward Media, Inc.	8370
Oveana	5614
OverNite Software Inc.	5615
Overture, LLC	1396
Owens Hervey PLLC	6241
Oxyde Chemicals, Inc.	2052
Ozanne Construction Co., Inc.	2479

P

Company	INDEX#
P.D. Morrison Enterprises, Inc.	7074
P.S. Let's Eat Inc.	3569

COMPANY ALPHABETICAL LISTING

P	INDEX#
P/EK Press	7612
P/Strada, LLC	8141
P2 Solutions Group LLC	5808
P3 Protective Packaging Products	7168
Pa Na Solutions Inc.	4877
PABULUM Consulting, LLC	8267
Pac Basic	7296
Pace Solutions, Inc.	5047
Pace Systems, Inc	4734
Pacific HVAC Depot Corporation	6582
Pacific Protection Services, Inc.	2618
Pacific Rim Capital, Inc.	7729
PACIV Inc.	5491
Packaging Integration, LLC	7181
Packaging Specialties Inc.	7297
Packed with Purpose	3858
Packrite, LLC	7205
PACO Communications, Inc. dba PACO Collective	8506
Pactrans Air & Sea, Inc.	9930
Page Security Inc.	2645
Pagoda Electrical	9760
Palco Telecom Service Inc.	9634
Pallet Central Enterprises, Inc.	10237
Pallet Consultants Corporation	10234
Pallet Recovery Service Inc.	10230
Palmer Logistic Services	10008
Palmer Promotions	1527
Palmetto Industries International, Inc.	7131
PALS International	1132
PamTen Inc.	5221
Pan American Express, Inc.	10161
Pan Asia Resources Pte Ltd.	5751
Panaloma Productions, LLC	9572
PanAmerica Supply, Inc.	3026
Panga Eco-Friendly Dental Supply	6490
Pangaea, Inc.	9241
Panta Rhei Media, Inc.	9622
Pantheon Inc.	5752
Panther Graphics Inc.	7634
Panther Solutions, LLC	5334
PAP Technologies, Inc.	7663
Paperworks, Inc.	7015
Par Logistics, Inc.	9931
Paradigm General Contractors	2308
Paragon Events, Inc.	8429
Paragon Language Services, Inc.	1029
Paragon Management Group	7980
Paragon Productions Inc.	8653
Paramount Safety Supply	4057
Paramount Software Solutions, Inc	4619
Paramount Software Solutions, Inc.	4620
Paramount Technology Solutions LLC	5101
Para-Plus Translations, Inc.	1178
Pareto Solutions Group, Inc.	9062
Pari & Gershon Inc.	3065, 3369
Paris Laser Printer Repair	5844
Park Enterprises	6876
Park Place Services	1528
Parker Battery, Inc.	4196
Parker Business Forms, Inc.	7697
Parker Law Group, Inc.	6084
Parks Moving Systems	10108
Parle Enterprises, Inc.	8371

P	INDEX#
Parmetech, Inc.	5927
Parms & Company, LLC	7841
Parra & Co., LLC	3311
Parrish Law Offices	6220
Parson Adhesives Inc.	1964
Partner Engineering and Science, Inc.	4368
Partner's Consulting, Inc.	5458, 9388
Partners In Diversity, Inc.	8933
Partners In Planning One Inc.	8735
PAS Technologies, Inc.	6329
Paskon, Inc.	4944
Passion Transportation Inc.	9932
Pat Taylor and Associates, Inc.	8989
PAT USA, Inc.	2404, 3175
Patel International	6601
Patricia J. Mayer & Associates, LLC	8934
Patrick Law Group, LLC	6123
Patriot Air Freight, Inc.	9972
Patriot Group, Ltd.	5941
Patriot Movers, LLC	9829
Patriot Packaging Solutions and Consulting	7182
Paul Carlson Associates, Inc.	3499
Paula P. White and Associates, Inc dba DataMasters	5083
Paulette Carter Design, Inc. (PCD Group)	8744
Paxton Consultants Limited Liability Company	5222
PayReel, Inc.	9576
PayTech, Inc.	7892
PBR Inc.	9801
PC Pitstop LLC	4666
PCC Technology Group	4461
PCH Communications	8507
PChange LLC	2654
PCNet, Inc.	5963
PDS Services, LLC	9197
Peach State Packaging Solutions	7183
Peachtree Supplies, Inc.	6991
Peacock Press LLC	7698
Peak Electric, Inc.	2883
Peak Security Inc.	2685
Peak Technology Solutions, Inc.	4481
Pearl Interactive Network	9358
Pearle, Inc.	7075
Pearl's Girl Sweet Treats	3859
Peas of Mind LLC	3570
Peck Training Group LLC	8268
Pecos Construction	2545
Pediatric Medical Solutions	6503
Peer Solutions Group, Inc.	4945
Peerless Performance, LLC	8044
Peerless Wall and Window Coverings, Inc.	3832
Peggy Lauritsen Design Group, Inc.	1153
Peistrup Paper Products, Inc.	2183
Pelican Logistics Inc.	9933
Pelican Staffing Solutions	9224
PenCo Industrial Supply, Inc.	4147
Penda Aiken, Inc.	9333
Pendulum Studio LLC	1780
Penmar Industries, Inc.	7117
Pensari, LLC	8556
People Places and Spaces, LLC	3758
People Primary LLC	7942
PEOPLE3, Inc.	8239
PeopleNTech LLC	5753

COMPANY ALPHABETICAL LISTING

P INDEX#

Company	Index#
PeoplePlus software Inc.	4946
Peoples Choice Staffing, Inc.	8935
PeopleTech Group	5809
Peoria Contract Services, LLC	3194
Pep Promotions	8204
Peralta Illustration & Design LLC	8396
Perau Power Technology, Inc.	3027
Perceptive Recruiting, LLC	9411
Percepture	8706
Perez & Morris LLC	6211
Perfect Output, LLC	4794
Perfect Parts Corporation	2802
Perfection Commercial Services, Inc.	2172
Performance Clean LLC	2272
Performance Consulting Group, Inc.	8240
Performance Designed Products	5845, 5958
Performance Development Corporation	8101
Performance Trans. Inc.	9967
Performix	5008
Peri Software Solutions	5223
Perimeter Entertainment, Inc.	9063
Perimeter Global Logistics (PGL)	10162
Peritia LLC	9064
Perkins & Associates, LLC	8594
Perlinski & Company	4369
Perma Treat of Illinois	10239
Permac Industries, Inc.	6865
Permatron	4083
Permian Machinery Movers Inc.	6299
Perpetual Solutions LLC	5335
Perry Temps, Inc.	9299
Perryman Building and Construction Services, Inc.	2500
Personal Mail International, Inc.	1179
Personal Touch Marketing & Manufacturing, Inc.	1464
Personnel Unlimited Inc.	9198
Peterson Productions LLC	9597
PetroCard, Inc.	2070
Petrochem Insulation, Inc.	2309
Petrochem, Inc.	1935
Petroleum Accessories, Inc.	4028
Petruj Chemical Corporation	1920
Peyak Solutions, Inc.	4878
Peyton Resource Group, LP	9472
PFA Recycling, Inc.	5897
PFITECH	8936
PGI Pacific Graphics International	7475
PGS Incorporated	6845
Phamatech, Inc.	6030
Pharma Consulting Corp.	6060
PharmaBioServ US, Inc. (PBSV)	5492
PharmaCare Solutions, Inc.	9065
Pharmaceutical Processes Systems, Inc.	4015
PharmaPress, Inc.	7594
Pharos Financial Services LP	7860
Phase 3 Marketing and Communications	8461
Phelco Technologies, Inc.	4780
Phelps Industrial Products	4002
Phelps Security Inc.	2690
Philatron Wire and Cable	2944
Phipps Reporting, Inc.	6111
Phoenix Business Solutions LLC	9687
Phoenix Textile Corporation	9809
Phoenix Translations	8269

P INDEX#

Company	Index#
Phoenix Woodworking Corporation	3771, 10240
Photomation	7476
Phronetik	8270
PHT International Inc.	1974
Phymet	2005
PIA International LLC	1478
PIE Technology Consulting	4621
Pierson Computing Connection, Inc.	5459
Pierson Grant Public Relations	8430
Pilot Services, Inc.	9688
Pinkney-Perry Insurance Agency, Inc.	6014
Pinnacle Consulting Solutions	5009
Pinnacle Environmental Management Support, Inc.	3402
Pinnacle Industries LLC	9950
Pinnacle Mailing Products, LLC	4781
Pinnacle Petroleum, Inc.	1903
Pinnacle Security & Investigation Inc.	2649
Pinnacle Services Group, Inc.	2356
Pinnacle Technical Resources, Inc.	5616
Pinnacle Tek LLC	5084
Pinnacle Telecommunications, Inc. (PTI Solutions)	9648
Pinnacle Travel Services, LLC	10199
Pino Gelato, LLC	3708
Pinpoint Resource Group, LLC	4370
Pioneer Air Systems, Inc.	2028
Pioneer Business Systems	5921
Pioneer Construction, Inc.	2357
Pioneer Data Systems, Inc.	5224
Pioneer Logistics Group, Inc.	3134
Pioneer Machine & Tech	6846
Pioneer Service Inc. - Addison, IL	3955, 6803
Piper Environmental Group, Inc.	3370
Piping Technology and Product Inc.	4029
Piston Automotive	1881
Pitt Plastics, Inc. dba IBS Solutions	7165
Pittleman & Associates	6200
Pittsburgh Plastics Manufacturing	7428
Pivot Manufacturing	6764
Pivotal Practices Consulting	3142
Pivotal Search Partners	8937
Pivotel LLC	9740
Pivox Corporation	3066, 3371
Pixie Stuff LLC	8611
PKG Packaging	7103
PKP Industries, Inc.	1708
PL Medical Co., LLC	6367
Planet Canit, LLC	3860
Planet Popcorn, Inc.	3571
Planned Packaging of Illinois Corp.	7150
Planned Systems International, Inc.	4879
Planning Professionals, Ltd.	8811
Plantlife Natural Body Care	2577
PlaqueMakerPlus, Inc.	1412
Plastec USA Inc.	7334
Plastek Cards, Inc.	7324
Plastikon Industries, Inc.	7325
Plastikon Michigan	9808
Platys Group	5225
Playtime Edventures LLC	6450
Pleasant Consulting, LLC	5010
Plego Technologies	4735
PLP Enterprises, Inc.	4227
Plumlogix LLC	5460

DIR 2025

COMPANY ALPHABETICAL LISTING

P	INDEX#
Plus One Lab Works Inc.	6352
PM Business Holdings LLC	4371, 8938
PM Group, Inc.	8319
PM Publicidad	1079
PMA Consultants of Illinois LLC	3117
PMB Precision Medical Billing Inc.	7861
PMC Group Inc dba Piper Staffing	9166
PMC SMART Solutions LLC	7419
PMC-Polymer Products Company, Inc.	7429
PMG, Inc.	1240
PMP Products Inc.	1323
Pn Automation	4880
PNH Technology, Inc.	5846
POGO Inc.	8939
Point Breeze Communications, Inc.	9761
Point View Displays, LLC	1043
Pointe International	6999
Polaris Direct	1167
Polaris Engineering, Inc.	3507
Polstar Commercial Cleaning Services	2173
Polybest, Inc.	7195
Polyfab Display Company	7446
Polymer Technologies	7420
Polyneer, Inc.	7367
Poly-Pak and Ship, Inc.	7151
PolySi Technologies, Inc.	1975, 7206
Popoff Enterprises Inc.	9587
Populus Group, LLC	9199
Port Electronics Corporation	2844
Portable Power Systems Inc.	2907
Portage Marketing	1154
Porter Scientific Inc.	3461
Porter-Walker LLC	4170
Portfolio Creative, LLC	9359
POSHnFIT	1692
Posi Lock Puller, Inc.	3962
Positive Publications LLC	7613
PositivePsyche.Biz Corp.	9167
Possible Missions, Inc.	8271
Potenza Promotions, LLC	1576
Powell Photography, Inc.	7305
Powell Tool Supply Co., Inc.	3893, 4090
Power & Telephone Supply Co,	9768
Power Assemblies LLC	2767
Power Lube Industrial LLC	2074
Power Of Two Productions, LLC	1577
Power Presentations, Inc.	8736
Power Tool & Supply Co., Inc.	3933
Power Tool Service Co., Inc.	3939
Powerlink Electrical	2405
PowerLogics, Inc.	2957
PowerOne and Associates, LLC	3940
Powers & Sons Construction Co, Inc.	2382
PowerVolt Inc. (DBA Ensign Corporation)	2967
Powin Energy Corporation	3008
Powr-Guardian, Inc.	3941
PPE Catalog LLC	6467
PR Global Logistics JP Corporation	10113
Prairie Engineers	3118
Prairie Quest Consulting	8078
Prairie States Enterprises, Inc.	5999
Pramac Engineering LLC	4881
Precedent Technologies LLC	4622

P	INDEX#
Precise Infotech Inc.	5401
Precise Products Inc.	6804
Precision Air & Liquid Solutions, LLC	4100
Precision Cadcam, Inc.	6812
Precision Components Manufacturing, LLC	6553, 6847
Precision Engineering & Contracting, Inc.	2480
Precision Gage & Tool Co.	6324
Precision Graphics Inc.	7452
Precision Graphics, Inc.	2766
Precision Medical Devices, Inc.	6462
Precision Metal Products, Inc.	6787
Precision Metrology, Inc.	6330
Precision Mold & Tool Group	7442
Precision Molding Inc.	7433
Precision Task Group, Inc.	5617
Precision Tool and Mold, Inc.	7335
Precision Transportation, Inc.	9934
Precision Wire Assemblies, Inc.	2750
Preferred Data Systems, LLC	4947
Preferred Personnel Solutions, Inc.	9066
Preferred Promotions, LLC	1336
Preferred Staffing Group/Preferred Temporary Services, Inc.	9521
Preferred Standards, LLC	9137
Preferred Translations, Inc.	1269
PremaTech Advanced Ceramics	6818
Premier Advisors Staffing and Sales, LLC	9016
Premier Automation Contractors	9200
Premier Benefit Consultants, Inc.	5995
Premier Business Solutions	7162
Premier Commercial Interiors, Inc.	3755
Premier Consultants International, Inc.	8401
Premier Employee Solutions LLC	9503
Premier Expediters, Inc.	9901
Premier Group Services, Inc	7784
Premier Logistics Solutions Warehousing, LLC	10120
Premier Manufactuirng and Supply Chain Services	2736, 2950
Premier Manufacturing	6922
Premier Manufacturing Corporation	6602
Premier Packaging/Assembly div of Haringa Inc.	7104
Premier Paging, Inc.	9785
Premier Plastic Resins, Inc.	7388
Premier Polymers LLC	2053, 7443
Premier Remodeling Services, Inc.	8034
Premier Reprographics, Inc.	7703
Premier Software Solutions	4623
Premier Staff Services	9201
Premier Staffing, Inc	8940
Premier Supplies	2214
Premier Systems, Inc	4736, 9106
Premiere Building Maintenance Corporation	2239
Premiere Solutions, LLC	1825
Premio, Inc.	5959
Premium Contractor Solution LLC	6482
Premium Resource	1324
Premium Surge Promotions, L.L.C.	1397
Premium Technologies, Inc.	4372
Presafe Technologies, LLC	5226
Presence Inc.	1421
Present Energi LLC	3105
Prestige Ameritech LTD	6526
Prestige Auto Specialists	8431
Prestige Construction Group, Inc.	2561

P

Company	INDEX#
Prestige Environmental, Inc.	3472
Prestige Maintenance USA Ltd.	2256
Prestige Mold	7326
Prestige Staffing, Inc.	8972
Pretek Corporation	5754
PriceSenz LLC	5618
Pride Healthcare, LLC	5336
Pride Technologies LLC	9334
Pride Veteran Staffing	9300
Prim Construction LLC	2546
Prima Communications, Inc.	9715
Primary Colors Graphics Inc.	7614
Primary Resources Inc.	7152
Primary Services LP	9473
Prime Air Cargo Inc.	9888
Prime Power Services	3106
Prime Time Delivery	10009
Prime Wheel Corp.	1849
Prime WoodCraft	10249
Primera Engineers	3119
Primera Plastics	7389
Primesource Staffing	8973
Primitive Logic Inc.	4373
Primus Software Corporation	4624
Prince Technology Solutions, Inc.	4948
Princeton Medical Group, Inc.	6511
Princeton Web Systems Inc.	5227
Principle Information Technology	5619
Print & Mail Partners, Inc.	1512
Print & More Associates	7544
Print Solutions Inc.	7670
PrintabiliTees, LLC	1674
PrintCOR Solutions	7589
PrinTech Label Corporation	7505
PrintFlex Graphics	7590
Printing and Marketing Services, Inc.	7506
Printing Inc of Louisville Kentucky	7531
Printing Systems, LLC	8462
PrintSync, Inc.	7654
Private Eyes, Inc	7886
PRMS Inc.	3003
Pro AV Systems, Inc.	5888
Pro Biz Products LLC	1398
Pro Circuit, Inc.	2426
PRO Consulting Services, Inc.	7862
Pro Health Medical Staffing	9474
Pro Pack Inc.	7217
Pro Pallet, Inc.	10233
PRO Scientific Inc.	6033
ProActive Solutions Inc.	5972
Pro-Am Team Sports	1413
Probitas Technology Inc.	5461
Procare USA, LLC	9335
Procellis Technology Inc.	5011
Process Control & Engineering Inc.	3176
Process Excellence & Engineering Consultants Inc	8231
Prochimie International, Inc.	1911
ProComm Telecommunications, Inc.	9679
Procura Select	6483
Production & Event Services, Inc.	8812
Production Distribution Companies	4084
Production Partners Company LLC	8508
Production Services Management, Inc.	3914

Company	INDEX#
Productive Automoated Systems Corp. (PASCO)	4216
Products 2 Brand, LLC	1436
Products Distribution, Inc.	7218
Products Unlimited, Inc.	6069, 6527
ProExhibits	8372
Professional CAD Services, Inc. dba PCSI Design	3332
Professional Choice Fire & Security Systems	4030
Professional Healthcare Services LLC	6062
Professional Information Systems	5970
Professional Materials Management	4528
Professional Police Services Inc	2663
Professional Power Engineering Company, LLC	3042
Professional Resource Partners	9301
Professional Retail Services	2459
Professional Technology Integration, Inc.	4625
Professional Translating Services, Inc.	4529
Proficient Learning LLC	8149
Profitmaster Displays Inc.	1080
Proforma Albrecht & Co.	1529
Proforma Joe Thomas Group	1530
Proformance Manufacturing, Inc.	6712
ProFreight Inc.	10062
Proftech LLC	7046
Program Evaluation Services Inc.	8035
Programmer Resources International Inc.	5048
Progressive Business Solutions, Inc.	7595
Progressive Engineering & Construction, Inc.	3403
Progressive Machinery Inc.	6871
Progressive Packaging	7264
Progressive Promotions Inc.	1496
Progressive Technology Solutions	4374
ProjDel Corporation	2481
Proje Inc.	8272
Project Controls Group, Inc.	8142
Project Management and Consulting LLC	8300
ProKatchers LLC	9067
PROLIM Global Corporation	4949
Pro-Lite	2945
Promacsolution Inc.	5620
Promark Custom Solutions LLC	5402
Promesa Logistics, LLC	10010
Promesa Transportation	10011
Promo Depot Inc.	1419
Promo Print Solutions Inc.	7712
Promo Victory, Inc.	1339
PromoHits! Ltd.	1531
Promolux Inc.	1601
PROMOQUEST Inc.	1479
Promotion Concepts Inc.	1448
Promotion Management Center, Inc.	7196
Promotion Support Services, Inc.	7508
Pro-Motion Technology Group	4950
Promotional Solutions LLC	1449
Promotions Etc., LLC	1532
Promotions Unlimited, LLC	1551
Pronto Delivery, Courier, and Logistics, LLC	10163
Proos Manufacturing, Inc.	6737
Pro-Pak Products, Ltd.	7184
Propane Studio	4375
Property Doctors Inc.	3387
Prospance Inc	4376
Pro-Staffing Agency	9017
Prosum, Inc.	4377

COMPANY ALPHABETICAL LISTING

P — INDEX#

Company	Index#
Prosys Information Systems	4626
ProTask Inc.	9522
Proteam Solutions, Inc.	9360
Protech Excellens Inc.	5426
ProTech Restoration, LLC	2562
Protege LLC	5755
Proto Edge Inc.	7397
Protocall NJ, Inc.	9302
Pro-Touch Nurses Inc.	9475
ProTrials Research, Inc.	6353
Proven Solutions Inc	8941
Provide Staffing Services LLC	9419
Providence Staffing LLC	8870
Provider Resources Inc.	9556
Prowess Consulting, LLC	5810
ProWest Engineering, Inc.	2310
PRR, Inc.	8860
Prudent Technologies and Consulting Inc.	5621
PRWT Services, Inc.	5462
PryCor Technologies, LLC	8143
Prystup Packaging Products	7090
PS Energy Group, Inc.	1925
PSI Resources, LLC	9107
PSJ Engineering, Inc.	3340
PSR Associates, Inc.	4627
PSRI TecHnologies LLC	5049
PSS Pathfinders Inc.	9400
PT Coupling Co.	4014
PTM Corporation	6738
PTMW, Inc.	6619
PTS Advance Life Sciences	8942
PTS Consulting Services LLC	4737, 8064
Pub Construction, Inc.	2311
Public Communications Inc.	8509
Public Special	9857
Pueri Elmental LLC dba Bonk Fit	1552
Puerto Rico Alarm Systems, Inc.	1652
Puffy Stuff	7271
Pure Advertising, LLC	1125
Pure Air Control Services, Inc.	3404
Pure Business Solutions, LLC	5622
Pure Lab Solutions, Inc.	6031
Purple Consulting	4738
Purpose & Action, LLC	8167
Purpose Generation LLC	8373
Purpose Transportation, LLC	10164
Pursley Friese Torgrimson, LLP	6124
Pursuit of Excellence Inc.	7973
Putnam Industries Inc.	7772
PVSR Corporation	3274
PWJ Enterprises dba as Team Worldwide	10047
Pynergy, LLC	1904
Pyramid Consulting, Inc.	4628
Pyramid Printing and Advertising Inc	7545
Pyramid Quality Solutions & Innovations, Inc.	8120
Pyramind LLC	9523
Pyratech Security Systems, Inc.	2658

Q

Company	Index#
Q&A Entertainment Inc.	8463
Q1 Technologies, Inc.	4739
QA Consulting Inc.	9559
Qassurance Technology Inc.	5756
QBP Logistics, Inc.	9830
QCentric Consultants, LLC	5085
QCM Technologies, Inc.	4256
QED National	9336
QMF Metal & Electronic Solutions, Inc.	6655
QMF Steel, Inc.	6914
QMP Inc.	6781
QP1, Inc. dba Luttrell Staffing Group	9133
QPS, LLC	6369
QSACK & Associates, Inc.	5757
Qsolv Inc.	4378
QSTAFF Incorporated	9476
Quacoapit LLC	8219
Quad Chemical Corporation	2067
Quadco Printing & Signs	7493
QualComp Consulting Services LLC	8160
Qualese, LLC	9018
Qualex Consulting Services, Inc.	4530
Qualfon Solutions, Inc,	7185
Qualitask, Inc.	6782
Quality Adhesives LLC	2029
Quality Assured Plastics, Inc.	7390
Quality Biological, Inc.	6038
Quality Building Services	2215
Quality Building Supplies For Industry, Inc.	4148
Quality CCTV Systems, Inc.	1662
Quality Concepts Manufacturing Inc.	2951
Quality Design Services, Inc.	6280
Quality Driver Solutions, Inc.	8943
Quality Fabrication & Design	6699
Quality First Construction LLC	9962
Quality High-Tech Services, Inc.	5623
Quality Material Handling	6261
Quality Packaging Specialists International, LLC	7219
Quality Ribbons and Supplies Co.	7052
Quality Solutions Now, Inc.	8220
Quality Staffing of America, Inc.	9068
Quality Staffing Solutions, Inc.	9265
Quality Standby Services, LLC	2823
Quality Tools & Abrasives	3120
Quality Touch Janitorial Service, Inc.	2234
QualityWorks Consulting Group, LLC	4379
Qualmar Technology Group, LLC	5874
Quanteq, Inc.	5050
Quantilus Inc.	5337
Quantronic Corporation	2764
Quantum Associates Inc.	7919
Quantum Installation Group	2358
Quaternary Resource Investigations, LLC	3425
Queensgate Hardware & Security, Inc.	3934
Quest Corporation of America	8432
Quest Project Controls, Inc.	3067
Quest Safety Products, Inc.	3894
Questions & Solutions Engineering	3187
Quez Media Marketing	8737
Quezada Architecture, Inc.	1738
Quick Employment LLC	9361
Quicksilver Associates, Inc.	8510
Quigley-Simpson & Heppelwhite, Inc.	1030
Quiltcraft Industries	3844
Quimex, Inc.	1936
Quinn Engineering & Employment Network LLC	1801

COMPANY ALPHABETICAL LISTING

Q INDEX#

Quinnox Inc. 4740
Quintairos, Prieto, Wood, and Boyer 6112
Quintana Associates, Inc. 4123
Quintec Integration, Inc. 4234
Quintech Security Consultants, Inc. 1654
Quirch Foods Co. 3594
QuisLex, Inc. 6201
Quixerve Corporation 7186
Qumulus Solutions LLC 5971

R

R & G Clean Room Laboratory, Inc. 6061
R & M Government Services 6466
R & T Architects, Inc. 1817
R and L Woodcraft, Inc 3792, 10244
R Engineering Team, LLC 3241
R L Burns Inc. 2346
R L Hill Management, Inc. 2482
R Square Desserts LLC 3638
R&D Systems Group, Inc. 5867
R&R Textile Mills Inc. 9803
R. Beverly Consulting, LLC dba Silver Fox Staffing 9069
R. Scheinert & Sons, Inc. 2892
R.A.W. Consulting, LLC 6968
R.B. Construction Company 2406
R.Dorsey & Company, Inc. 5403
R.J. Roberts, Inc. 3068
R.J. Runge Company, Inc. 2483
R.J. Safety Supply Company Inc. 4058
R.J. Zeman Tool & Mfg. Co., Inc. 3985, 6927
R.W. Chavez, Inc. 7620
R.W. Gonzalez Office Products, Inc. 7076
R/P Marketing Public Relations 8738
R2 Trucking Solutions 9902
R2T, Inc. 3107
Raare Solutions LLC 8654
Rabin Research Company 8511
RAC Enterprises, Inc. 3511, 6685
Race Ahead 1533
RADgov Inc. 4531
Radia Enterprises Inc. 1578, 1718
Radian Compliance LLC 4741
Radiant Infotech 4882
Radiant Logistics Partners, LLC 10187
Rafael A Colon Voices Internacional 8313
Ragha Systems, LLC 4951
RagsWarehouse & Cleaning Supplies 2117
Rahman LLC 6151
Railroad Industries Inc. 10066
Rainbow Technology Corporation 4042
Raise Tech Solutions, LLC 5463
Raisman Corporation 3953
RAK Technologies LLC 2803
Raleigh-Durham Rubber & Gasket Co., Inc. 4009, 7402
Ram Tool & Supply Co., Inc. 3876
Ramos Oil Company, Inc. 1905
Ramsoft Systems, Inc.. 4952
Ramtec Controls Corporation 1607
Rang Technologies Inc. 5228
Rangam Consultants Inc. 5229
Ranger Distributing, Inc dba Ranger Label 7591
Ransor, Inc. 9786

R INDEX#

Rapid External Solutions, Inc. 5427
Rapid Global Business Solutions, Inc. 4953
Rapid IT, Inc. 4629
Rapid Response Computer Service Inc. 5230
Rapid Staffing, Inc. 9019
Rapport International, LLC 1113
Raptor Industries, Inc. 9689
Raul V. Bravo + Associates, Inc. 3323
Raven Transport Company, Inc. 9889
RaviG Inc. dba Salient Global Technologies 4380
Ray Machine Inc. 6821
Raycom Data Technologies, Inc. 4381
Raymond Young & Associates, LLC 8079
Razor Consulting Solutions, Inc. 5096
RB Tool & Mfg Co. 3974
RBB Public Relations LLC 8433
RBG Marketing, Inc. dba Crescendo 1031
RC & JT Inc. dba Computer Masters 5847
RCI Associates 2619
RCI Technologies 5231
RCI Technologies, Inc. 1906
RCR Technology Corporation 4782
RD Data Solutions 5624, 9477
RD Plastics 7272
RDAF Energy Solutions 3199
RDB Enterprises II LLC 6447
RDS Environmental, Inc. 3388
Reach Media Inc. 1270
Real Cool Productions, Inc. dba RCP Learning 9591
Real Physics, Inc. 5493
Real Property Tax Advisors 7754
Real Soft Inc. 5232
Real Time Resolutions, Inc. 7863
Real World Technologies Inc. 4954
Realistic Computing, Inc. 4883
Rearden Logic Inc. 4447
Reardon Scanlon LLP 6096
Rebel Green LLC 2273
Receivables Solutions, Inc. 7730
ReCredit 7814
Recruiting Force, LLC 9478
Recruiting Source International 9479
RecruitSource, Inc. 8871
RECS, Inc. 4228
Rector Communications, Inc. 8766
Recycle Technologies, Inc. 2859
Red Arrow Logistics 10188
Red Bridge Consulting Group 9266
Red Cloud LLC 1325
Red Coats, Inc. 2161
RED Company 8374
Red Heritage Media, LLC 9624
Red Iron Brand Solutions, LLC 1553
Red Kite Business Advisors LLC 8375
Red Oak Label, LLC 7713
Red Rose Transportation, Inc 9858
Red Star Oil Company 1976
Red Stone Construction Services, LLC 2489
Redapt, Inc. 5811
RedKnot Resource Group, LLC 4244
Redlee/SCS, Inc. 2257
RedSalsa Technologies, Inc. 5233
Reed Global Networks, Inc. 5625

COMPANY ALPHABETICAL LISTING

R

Company	INDEX#
Reese Enterprises	4059
Reesential Inc.	9362
Reeves & Brightwell LLP	6242
Reflex Logistics, LLC	9831
Refractory Service Corp.	6614
Refulgent Technologies Inc.	5086
Regali Inc.	8813
Regency Construction Services Inc.	2484
Reggie Mckenzie Industrial Materials, Inc.	3915
Reggios' Pizza, Inc.	3619
Regulatory and Quality Solutions LLC	6493
RehabWest, Inc. (RWI)	7887
Reidy Medical Supply, Inc.	6484
Reilly Connect	8512
Reilly International Ltd.	9935
Related Technologies, Inc.	4382
Relevante, Inc	7846
Reliable Building Solutions, Inc.	2240
Reliable Government Solutions Inc.	4884
Reliable Investments LLC	3037
Reliable Machine Company	6719
Reliable Pharmaceutical Returns, LLC	3519
Reliable Solutions Construction, LLC dba Reliable Restorations	3462
Reliance Communications, LLC	9741
Reliance Distributing	1859
Reliance One, Inc.	9202
Reliant Business Products, Inc	7077
Reliant Medical Supply	6538
Reliant Protective Services LLC	2620
Reliant Tech., Inc.	5234
Relius Medical LLC	6365
Remar Inc	7273
Remco Storage Systems, Inc.	3787, 7016
ReMedi Health Solutions LLC	5626
Remedy Intelligent Staffing	9108
Remedy Technological Services, L.P.	5627
Remnant Management Group Inc.	8241
Renaissance Capital Alliance	7799
Renaissance S & S Inc.	3177
Rene Garza and Associates, Inc.	2621
RennickBarrett Recruiting, Inc.	8944
Renovo Data, Inc.	4630
Republica, LLC	8434
RER Solutions Inc.	7869
Rescon Inc.	4885
Research Analysis and Maintenance, Inc.	5628
Research Explorers, Inc	8513
ResiliEnt Business Solutions, LLC	4631
Resilient Media	9611
Resolve Tech Solutions	5629
Resource Employment Solutions	9020
Resource International	3242
Resource Management 1, LLC	7901
Resource One	3772
Resource Partners, LLC	5502
Resource Personnel Consultants, LLC	9480
Resource Regeneration LLC dba S3 Asset Management	5506
Resource Technology Associates, LLC	9109
ResourceSoft, Inc.	4828
Resourcesys Inc.	4886
Resurgens Risk Management, Inc.	7755

R

Company	INDEX#
Retail Solution Center	1064
Revel Global Events	8514
Revelation, LLC	1298, 8866
Revere Mills International Group, Inc.	9804
ReviewWorks	6009
Revision Technologies Inc.	5235
RevOne Design, Inc.	8376
Reyes Kurson, Ltd.	6138
Reynolds Lighting Supply Co.	2916
RFE Engineering, Inc.	3069
Rfs Group	4091
RG Apparel Co.	1579, 1719
RG Talent Solutions, LLC	9481
RGG Services Inc.	2697
RGMA	8065
RHD Enterprises, Inc.	2572
RHF, Inc.	6305
Rhino Medical Supply	6504
Rhinotrax Construction, Inc.	2321
RHO, Inc.	9303
Rhodes+Brito Architects	1748
Rhonda Crowder & Associates LLC	8739
Rhudy & Co. Communications and Marketing, Inc.	8852
Rich Davis Enterprises, Inc.	10012
Richalin Digue, LLC	8121
Richards Graphic Communications, Inc.	7520
Richardson and Associates, LLC	7842
Rickinson Marketing Inc.	7926
Rickman Enterprise Group, LLC	2407
Ricochet Fuel Distributors, Inc.	2054
RICOM	5960
Ridgway LLC dba The Price Erecting Co.	6710
Riegel Printing Inc.	7615
Rig-Chem Inc.	1947
Right Choice Computers & Networks, LLC	4887
Right Choice Solutions, Inc.	9267
Right Tek Enterprises	2091
RightStaff, Inc	9482
RIK Data Solutions Inc.	4532
Rika Group Corporation	1644
Rimco Marketing Products, Inc.	1355
Rincon Technology	9649
Rio Motor	1846
Risk & Insurance Management Services, Inc.	6000
Risk & Re-Insurance Solutions Corporation	7749
Risk Management Consulting Services, LLC.	8135
Risk Mitigation Worldwide	8273
Risque Inc.	7706
Rite Quality Office Supplies, Inc.	7004
Rivanna Natural Designs, Inc.	1590
River City Building Solutions, LLC	3935
River City Furniture, LLC	3824
River City Metrology LLC	6317
River Development Corporation	5464
Rivera & Associates, Inc.	8867
Riverbend Logistics Solutions, Inc.	9936
RiverCity Workwear LLC	1685
Riverside Manufacturing, Inc.	6866
RiverStone Associates, LLC	7756
Riverway Business Services	9483
Rivet Consulting LLC	8314
RiVi Consulting Group LLC	4632
RJ Graphics, Inc.	7616

COMPANY ALPHABETICAL LISTING

R	INDEX#
RJ Manray - Promotional Products	1534, 1713
RJC Contracting, Inc.	2281
RJSL Group	9110
RJT Compuquest	4383
RK Management Consultants, Inc.	4742
RKA Petroleum Company, Inc.	1965
RKG Technologies Inc	4384
RKL Resources	7976
RKS Plastics Inc.	7220
RL Canning Inc.	4743
RL Enterprise & Associates, LLC	7960
RLB Procurement	5932
RLJ Enterprises Inc. dba Genesis VII, Inc.	3097
RLR Associates, Inc.	1102
RLS Interests, Inc.	5942
RM International Resource Group. Ltd.	7017
RMC Consultants, Inc.	3389
RMD Group Inc.	8377
RMI International	2622
RMK Consulting, Inc.	5338
RMPersonnel, Inc.	9484
RMR Technology Group LLC	3324
RMS Computer Corp.	5339
RMT Construction & Development Group, Inc.	2563
RNDI Companies, Inc.	3528
RNDT, Inc.	3258
Roadswest Construction Inc.	9795
Robert Ganter Contractors, Inc.	2501
Robert P Madison International, Inc	1802
Robinson Industries, Inc.	6848
Robotic Research, LLC	3143
Rochester Tube Products, Ltd.	6641
Rock Industries Inc.	2312
Rock Solid Janitorial, Inc.	2267
Rockford Specialties Company	6603
Rockwell Labs Ltd.	2184
Rocky Mountain Pioneer, LLC	7111
Rodriguez Consulting LLC	3259
Rodriguez Expedited Freight Systems, Inc.	10013
Roeming Industries, Inc.	4037
Rohtek Automation LLC	4201
ROI Communication Inc.	8005
Roig Lawyers	6113
Roland International Freight Services, Inc.	9859
Romaguera Law Group, PA	6114
Roman Industries, Inc.	3028
RomAnalytics	9389
Romar Supply	4186
Rona M. Lum, P.C., dba Law Offices of Rona M. Lum	6160
RORE, Inc.	3372
Rose International, Inc.	5051
Rose-A-Lee Technologies, Inc	6642, 6739
Rose-Allied International	10014
Rosenberg & Associates	6182
Roses Southwest Paper, Inc.	7038
Roth-Williams Industries Inc. dba Lunar Industries	6740
Rotolo Chevrolet, Inc.	1826
ROUGE 24, Inc.	8435
Rowland Design, Inc.	1763
Roxbury Technology Corp	5889
Roy Smith Company	1966
Royal Automation Supplies	7047
Royal Coachman Worldwide	10063

R	INDEX#
Royal Freight, LP	10165
Royal Recognition, Inc.	1602
Royalty Investments, LLC	6615, 6813
Royberg Inc.	6700
Roytec Industries LLC	2741, 2959
Rozario & Associates, P.C.	6202
RP & Associates, Inc.	1032
RPI Color Service, Inc.	7648
RPM Engineers, Inc.	4385
RPT Toner LLC	5879
RRMAE Engineering LLC	3141
RSI Solutions Inc.	5630
RSP Express Inc.	10015
RST Solutions Inc.	5465
RSVP Premier Group, LLC	8570
RTH Solutions LLC	4888
RTI Laboratories, Inc.	3446, 6041
RTX Technology Partners, LLC	4633
Rubber Stamps Unlimited, Inc.	7018
RubberMill, Inc.	7403
Rudolph's Office & Computer Supply, Inc.	7007
Rudram Engineering, Inc.	4533
Ruiz Protective Service, Inc.	2698
Ruiz Strategies	8006
Rumba Solutions, LLC	4955
Runnymede Capital Management, Inc.	7813
Rush Expediting, Inc.	10094
Rush Trucking Corporation	10016
Russell Tobin & Associates, LLC	9337
Russell Transport Inc.	10166
Rutabaga Rags, Inc.	1465
Rutherford & Christie LLP	6125
Rutherford Enterprises, Inc.	8814
RVM Enterprises, Inc.	6183
RWG Consulting, Inc.	8274
Ryan Consulting Group, Inc.	4783
Ryan Industries, Inc.	7187

S	
S & B Computer & Office Products Inc.	7048
S & F Software Solutions Inc.	4744
S & H Uniform Corp.	1709
S & S International,Inc.	6940
S & S Staffing, LLC	9147
S & S Transport, Inc	10050
S & V Industries, Inc.	3005
S and Y Industries, Inc.	2751
S&G Corrugated Packaging	7253
S. Brooks and Associates Inc.	9371
S-2international LLC	9903
S3Global Consulting Services, LLC	5812
SA Technologies Inc.	4386
Saba Quaility System	9485
Sabella Gabino Inc. dba Bella Marketing Inc.	1497
Sabir, Richardson & Weisberg Engineers PLLC	3222
Sachs Chemical Inc.	2024
SAF Technologies, Inc.	1633
Safe & Secure Worldwide Protection Group	2664
Safe Choice LLC	2680
Safe T Professionals LLC	8885
Safeguard Security Solutions LLC	2637
Safety Controls Technology Inc.	6212

COMPANY ALPHABETICAL LISTING

S — INDEX#

Company	Index#
Safety Management Systems, Inc.	4462
Safety Plus, LLC	6063
Safety Research Corporation of America, LLC	4245
Safety Services, Inc.	4110
Safety Signs	4116
Safety Supply, Inc.	4187
Safetyvibe	4060
SafetyWeb Product Sales, LLC	4061
Safeway Sling USA, Inc.	6711
Sage Advertising LLC	8707
Sage Energy Trading, LLC	2011
Sage Group Technologies Inc	9304
Sage Telecommunications Corp.	9658
Saia Communications, Inc.	9742
Saigan Technologies Inc.	5052
Saisystems International	4463
Saitech Inc.	5848
Sajiton LLC	5087
Sales Trac Coaching & Mgmt Development	8275
Salomon Roofing & Construction	2347
Salsa-The Designer Solution LLC.	1710
Samantha Smith Productions LLC	8378
Samaripa Oilfield Services, LLC	2547
Sambatek	3188
Samiti Technologies, Inc.	5236
Samson Electrical Supply Co Inc	2867
Samuel A. Ramirez & Company, Inc.	7829
Samuel Engineering, Inc.	3081
Samuel Shapiro & Company, Inc.	9973
San Benito Textile Inc.	2258
Sanchez Daniels & Hoffman, LLP	6139
Sanchez, Tennis & Associates, LLC	8011
Sanchez-Medina, Gonzalez, Quesada, et al.	6115
Sanders Wingo Advertising, Inc.	8815
SandHurst-AEC	1821
Sandstorm Design	8066
Sandtx International Corp.	5631
Sandy Valley Fasteners, LLC	3897
Santanna Tool &Design LLC	6643
Santex	1720
Saponi Industries, Inc.	5088
Sapphire Printing Group, Inc.	7454
Saratoga Software Solutions, Inc.	5632
Sarchem Laboratories, Inc.	6053
Saris and Things Inc.	6418
Sassafras Marketing, Inc.	8528
Satnam Data Systems, Inc.	5237
Satori Seal, Inc.	3882
Saturn Electronics Corporation	2760
Satya Acquisition Management, Inc. dba SAM, Inc.	9668
Sauerbach Associates	1513
Savaspice LLC	3727
Savi Solutions, Inc.	5758, 8301
Savin Products Co., Inc.	2155
Sawyer Services Inc.	2854
Sax Productions Inc.	8379
Say Cargo Express, Inc.	9860
Sayers Technology	4745, 5969
Sayre Enterprises Inc.	1724
SB & Company, LLC.	7785
SBM Management Services	2092
SCA Environmental, Inc.	3373
Scadea Solutions Inc	5238
Scalable Systems Inc.	5239
Scalar Solutions, LLC.	5240
SCANVenger Hunt LLC	8740
Scarritt Group	8326
SCG Capital Leasing, LLC	7739
Schaaf Floral	3867
Schaffer Partners, Inc.	1535
Schisla Design, LLC dba Enrich	1159
Schmidt Printing, Inc.	7546
Schoeman Updike Kaufman & Gerber LLP	6203
Schwartz Hannum PC	6146
Schweiger Construction Company	2427
Scientific Sales, Inc.	6064
Scintel Technologies Inc.	4634
Scion Steel	6949
Scitics Inc.	4829
SCMSP (dba) of Spotswood Consulting	8007
Scope IT Consulting	4635
Scope Services, Inc.	9203
Scott Business Group, LLC	8886
Scott Circle Communications, Inc.	8402
Scott Engineering, Inc.	6583
Scott Logistics Corp.	9904
Scout Exchange LLC	4830
Scout Sourcing, Inc.	7153
ScreenThem Background Investigations	7977
ScrumPoint	5813
SD Shredding, Inc.	4387
SDA Consulting, Inc.	4746
SDI International Corp	4534
SDI Presence LLC	4747
SDI Systems Division, Inc.	2093
SDK Software Inc aka Sudhko Inc.	5012
SDQ, Ltd.	2180
Sea Consulting Group	3540
Seaborn Health Care Inc.	9524
SeaChange Print Innovations	7197, 7584
Seacom, LLC	9717
SeaGate Office Products, Inc.	7053
SEAL Consulting Inc.	5241
SealingLife Technology	4000
SeaMax Corporation	3312
Search Plus International	9486
Search Wizards, Inc.	9021
SearchPros	8945
Searle Petroleum Co.	1929
Seating, Inc.	7049
SeaYu Enterprises Inc.	2094
Seba International	1326
Secondary Solutions, Inc.	6901
Securance LLC	4535
Securatex Ltd.	2646
Secure Applications, LLC	7254
Secure Traces LLC	4636
Secured Network Solutions, Inc.	5759, 9792
Security 1 Solutions LLC	2655
Security Professionals of Illinois, Inc.	2647
Security Walls LLC	2691
Sedulus Group LLC	4448
Seeds of Nature, LLC	3603
SEEK Careers/Staffing, Inc.	9540
Seilevel Partners, LP	8276
Sejasmi Industries, Inc.	7391

COMPANY ALPHABETICAL LISTING

S

Company	INDEX#
Select Industries Corp	6754
Select Logistics Network Inc.	9937
Select Power Systems, LLC	3283
Select Source International	5013, 9225
SelectOne Staffing Services LLC	9077
Seliger-Braun Inc. dba Keylingo Translations	1180
Seminarios Imagen, Inc.	2719
SENCOMMUNICATIONS, INC.	9669
Seniors Medical Supply, Inc.	6451
Sensis Inc.	1033
Sentec Promotions, Inc	1514
Sentinel Fence and Contracting LLC	2282
Separation Systems Consultants, Inc.	3529
Sequoia Financial Services	7731
Sequoia Tool	6741, 6849
Serendipity Electronics, Inc.	2876
Serene Innovations	9650
Serenity Infotech, Inc.	4637
Serenity Staffing LLC	9226
ServeKool Technologies LLC	5053
Servex, Inc.	9938
Servexo Protective Services	2623
Service Manufacturing & Supply Co.	4006
Service Packaging Design, Inc.	7154
Set Enterprises, Inc.	6850
Seven Seven Softwares, Inc.	5242
Seventy 7 Productions	9593
SEW, Inc.	8403
SF&B, LLC	5962
SFM Services, Inc.	2118
SFR&R Inc.	3689
SGF US Inc.	4536
SGM Contracting Inc.	6485
SGS Technologies	4537
Shaeffer Logistics	10038
Shafiis' Inc.	7547
Shah Industrial Sales Inc.	4156
Shaheen & Associates, Inc.	8184
Shakthy Information Systems, Inc.	4889
Shames Construction Company, Ltd	2313
Shani International Corporation	1702
Shar Enterprises Inc dba HKA Staffing Services	9111
Shared Vision LLC	1081
Sharp Business Consulting Services LLC	8237
Sharp Decisions, Inc.	5340
Shaw-Lundquist Associates, Inc.	2419
Shawnee Construction and Engineering	2383
ShawneTV Inc	9594
ShazTEK LLP	5466
Shea Writing and Training Solutions, Inc.	9560
Shea Yeleen Health and Beauty, LLC	2580
Sheila Lee & Associates, LLC - Learning Everywhere	8102
Shelby Welded Tube	6676
Shelgin Partners	9242
Shell Plastics LLC	7449
Shelton Communications Group, Inc.	8778
Shema Global, LLC	2591
Shen Wei USA Inc.	6354
Shepherd Data Services, Inc.	9551
Shepherd Transport, LLC	10109
Sheroy Printing	7617
Shickel Corporation	6703
SHIFT Employment Law Training, LLC	7938
Shiloh Event Management	8380
Shimento Inc.	4388
Shinemound Enterprise Inc.	6428
Shingle Belting	6295
Shingler Lewis LLC	6126
Shingobee Builders, Inc.	2420
Shire Express Transportation	10167
Shirley Hollywood & Associates, Inc.	5633
Shirley K's Storage Trays LLC	7421
Shirubaa Inc	4389
Shivan Technologies, Inc.	5760
ShockTheory Interactive, Inc.	2128
Shore Communications, Inc.	9793
Shore Manufacturing LLC	2201
Showcraft, Inc.	8595
Showreel International Inc.	9573
Shred King Corporation	4831
Shree Ganesha, Inc.	7521
SHWorldwide	8861
SI Engineering, P.C.	3223
SI Tech Inc.	9690
SIA Solutions, LLC	3530
Siam Logistics	10168
Sibley Laboratories LLC	7188
Siboney Contracting Co.	2119
Sidebench Studios	4390
Sideman & Bancroft LLP	6085
Sidewinder Holdings, Inc.	5922
Sidra Medical Supply Inc	6472
Sieler Construction	2408
Sienna Environmental Technologies, LLC	3489
Sierra Forensic Group	7769
Sierra Proto Express, Inc.	2734
Sigma Associates, Inc.	3178
Sigma Extruding Corp. DBA Sigma Stretch Film	7407
Sigma International	1882
Sigma Resources LLC	5467
Sigma Supply North America	7093
Sigma Systems, Inc.	4832
Sigmatex, Inc	9813
Sigmaways, Inc	4391
Sign Acquisition LLC dba American and Interstate Signcrafters	3098
Sign Up Inc.	1181
Signature Breads, Inc.	3639
Signature Building Maintenance, Inc.	2095
Signature Media Group Talk	8515
Signature Promotions	1547
Signcraft Screenprint, Inc.	7522
Signet, Inc.	1555
Significant Printz	1498
Signs & Decal Corp.	1204
Silarx Pharmaceuticals, Inc.	6473
Silence Lines LLC	10017
SilenX Corporation	2804
Silicon Alley Group, Inc.	5243
Silk Screen Express, Inc.	1399
SilTek, Inc.	5761
Silver Wings Aerospace	4068
Silveredge Business Systems, Ltd.	4748
Silverman McGovern Staffing	9404
Silverman Shin & Byrne PLLC	6204
Simcol Group, LLC	1926

COMPANY ALPHABETICAL LISTING

S | INDEX#

Company	Index#
SimmCo Distribution	6448
Simon Marketing Group, LLC	4111
Simple Truth Communication Partners Inc	8516
SimpleQuE, Inc.	8205
Simplified Technologies, LLC	4538
Simplistek, LLC	5634
Simply Displays	1034
Sims Petroleum Company, LLC	2026
Sinclair Industries, Inc.	6654
Sino Brite (USA), Inc.	1883
Sintel Satellite Services	9743
Sir Aubrey's Tea Company, Ltd	3551
Siris Pharmaceutical Services	6463
Sirius Solutions, LLLP	8277
Sirrah Construction & Co, LLC	2574
Sissy Siero Voiceover & Media LLC	8816
Sisterville Tank Works, Inc.	4236
Site Resources, Inc.	3144
Site Solutions Worldwide	8708
Sivad PPE, LLC	6370
Siwel Consulting, Inc.	5341
Six Consulting, Inc.	4638
Six Twenty Six, LLC.	1303
SJB Bagel Makers of Boston	3640
SJB Enterprises, Inc. dba Sandra Network	4833
SK Services, LLC	8872
SK&T Integration Inc.	5855
Skansoft Inc.	4956
Skill Path Talent, Inc.	9525
Skutchi Designs Inc.	3836
Sky Bird Travel & Tours Inc.	10213
Sky Communications, Inc.	9787
Sky Leap LLC	7404
Skye Suh, PLC.	6161
Skylightsys, LLC	8980
Skyline Container Corporation	7155
Skyline Exhibits of Central Ohio, LLC	1221
Skyline Exhibits West Michigan	8571
Slade Land Use, Environmental & Transportation Planning LLC	3345
Slang Productions, LLC	9598
SlateBelt Safety	6494
Slice Communications, LLC	8767
Slice, Inc dba SliceWorks	8557
SLM Waste & Recycling Services Inc.	3508
Slow Life Games, LLC	8666
SLR Designs, LLC	7207
SM Engineering Co.	3189
Small Beginnings, Inc.	6355
Small Pond Video Productions, Inc.	9630
Smalls Senibaldi Services LLC	2204
Smart Cleaning Solutions LLC	2205
Smart Folks, Inc.	9204
Smart Information Management Systems Inc	5244
Smart IT Frame LLC	5245
Smart IT Pros, Inc.	5635
Smart IT Staffing, Inc.	9126
Smart Option Search	7959
SMART Resources, Inc.	5762
Smart Source Technologies, Inc.	5246
SmartBase Solutions LLC	8596
Smartbridge	5636
Smartdept. Inc.	9112

S | INDEX#

Company	Index#
Smartecute LLC	4639
SMC Consulting, LLC d/b/a/ Studio SMC	1810
SMC Ltd.	7450
SMG Services, LLC	3964
Smiling Cross Inc.	1414
Smith & Dean, Inc.	9487
Smith Corona/Comfort Telecommunications	9670
Smith Design Associates Inc.	8655
Smith Seal of NC	4010
Smith-Dahmer Associates, LLC	8572
SMTAutomation LLC	7568
Snap Creative Marketing	8656
Snap Office Supplies, LLC	7084
Snappy Solutions	2216
Snelling Employment, LLC	9488
Snelling Personnel Services	9205
Snelling Staffing Services	9148
SNS Global Corporation	9489
SNtial Technologies, Inc.	4749
SOAL Technologies, LLC	5637
Sobriety On the Sea / Danette Arthur MD PA	7902
Sociologie Wines Vintage LLC	3721
SodexoMagic (Magic Food Provision, LLC)	3434, 3649
SoFine Food	3650
Soft Stuff Distributors, Inc.	3651
Softal Technologies LLC	4750
SoftCorp International, Inc.	4957
Softech Int'l Resources, Inc.	4640
Softel Techsource LLC	9490
Softlinx, Inc.	4834
SoftNice Inc.	5468
Softpath System, LLC	4641
Softpath Systems Inc.	5342
SoftPath Technologies LLC	4958
SoftSages, LLC	5469
Software Folks, Inc. dba Saviance Technologies	9305
Software Galaxy Systems, LLC	9306
Software Guidance & Assistance, Inc.	5343
Software People Inc.	5344
Software Professional Solutions, Inc.	5247
Software Professionals, Inc.	5638
Software Synergy, Inc.	5248
Software Technology, Inc.	5249
Softway Solutions, Inc.	5639
Sohum Inc	4392
Sojo, Inc.	8464
Sol Davis Printing, Inc.	7494
Solace Risk Management	7773
Solar Spring & Wire Forms	6961
Solares Electrical Services, Inc.	5868
Solartech Power, Inc.	2946, 3070
Solid Surface Care, Inc.	2194
Solidus Technical Solutions, LLC	4835
Solomon International, LLC	9390
SOLRAC Corporation	9491
Soltrix Technology Solutions Inc.	4836
Solugenix Corporation	4393
Solution Packaging LLC	7265
Solution Tech Staffing Inc.	9492
Solutions For You Inc.	5404
Solutions3 LLC	5250
solutions4networks, Inc.	5470
Solutionz Videoconferencing Inc.	9651

COMPANY ALPHABETICAL LISTING

S | INDEX#

Company	Index#
SolvChem, Inc.	2055
Solved Engineering	3121
Solvitur Systems LLC	5763
Somax Inc.	3572
Sondhi Solutions LLC	4784
Sonoi Solutions LLC	4539
Sontesa Technologies Inc.	5640
Sorella Group, Inc.	4095
Soul Sisters Foods, Inc.	3680
Soule Medical	7124
SoundSense, LLC	3224
SoundTech Inc.	3179
Soundview Capital Solutions	7740
Source Diversified, Inc.	4394
Source Graphics	5849
Source Group Professionals	8887
Source IT Technologies, LLC	4464
Source Of Future Technology (SOFT), Inc.	5345
Source One Technical Solutions, LLC	5251
Source West	1739
South Atlantic Marine Services	3928
South City Construction Inc.	2314
South Coast Paper LLC	6992
Southeast Exhibits and Events	8465
Southeastern Aerospace Services, LLC	3099
Southeastern Conveyor Services, Inc.	6255
Southeastern Fleet Management, LLC	10048
Southeastern Transfer & Storage Co., Inc.	9905
Southern California Leasing Inc.	7732
Southern California Metals, Inc.	6932
Southern Chinese Daily News LLC	2723
Southern Crescent Personnel, Inc.	9070
Southern Energy Solution Group, LLC	3100
Southern Film Extruders, Inc.	7208
Southern Global Safety Services, Inc.	3531
Southern Precision Machining, LLC	6904
Southern Print & Imaging, Inc.	7596
Southern States, LLC	2960
Southland Technology Inc.	5850
Southtown Electronics Inc.	2877
Southwest Country	3752
Southwest Freight Lines	10169
Southwest Office Systems, Inc.	5943
Southwest Packaging Solutions, LLC	7290
Southwest Staffing	9493
Southwest Synergistic Solutions, LLC	3029
Sovereign	3210, 3473
Sovereign Employee Benefits, Inc.	5988
Sowell Law Partners PLLC	6162
SOYAC Industrial	2259
SPA Digital Images, Ltd.	7315
SpaceBound, Inc.	5924
SpaceCraft International	1751
Spafford Leasing Associates, Inc.	7776
Spalding Automotive, Inc.	6758
SPAR Information Systems	5641
SPAR Solutions, LLC	8466
Sparkle Janitorial Service	2174
Spartan Promotional Group, Inc.	1466
Spartanburg Meat Processing Co., Inc.	3709
Spaulding Decon, LLC	3405
SpeakSpace, LLC	9751
Spearhead Protection Inc.	2624
Spearhead Transportation Services, Inc.	10073
Special Carbide Tools	3947
Special D Events, Inc.	8573
Special Project Staffing by Salem, Inc.	9113
Special Respiratory Care, Inc.	6356
Specialized Marketing Services, Inc.	8381
Specialized Services, LLC	2202
Specialized Staffing Solutions, LLC	9127
Specialty Optical Systems, Inc.	2908
Specialty Steel Supply Co., Inc.	6683
Specific Waste Industries	3424
Spec-Metal Inc.	6783
Spectraforce Technologies, Inc.	5089
Spectro Coating Corp.	9805
Spectrotel	9732
Spectrum Broadcasting Corporation	1114
Spellman Brady & Company	3794
Spencer Cole, LLC	3313
SpendCheQ, Inc.	4540
SPHERE Technology Solutions	5252
Spherion Corporation	9022
Spherion of Lima Inc.	9363
Sphynx Software Solutions LLC	5346
SpikeDDB, LLC	1205
Spiral Design Studio, LLC	8709
Spirit Distribution and Logistics, Inc.	2785
Spirit Truck Lines	10170
Spit Shine LLC	2206
SPK and Associates, LLC	4395
Spotlight Graphics, Inc.	7548
Spring International	6915
Spring Rivers Ecological Sciences LLC	3374
Springboard Benefits, LLC	7914
SpringboardPC	1356
Springer Equipment Co., Inc.	6256
Springfield Spring	6722, 6963
Spruce Technology, Inc.	5253
SPRYTE Communications	8768
SPS Medical Supply Corp.	6474
Spurgetech, LLC	5764
SQS, Inc. (Successful Quality Systems)	3275
Square Shooting	7311
SquarePac LTD	7132
Squeaky	1206
SRB Communications, LLC	1046
Sritech Global Inc.	8206
SRL TotalSource LLC	9709
SRM & Associates, LLC	8207
SRS Consulting Inc.	4396
SRS, Inc.	2523
SSKJ Enterprises Inc. dba Vital Signs	1241
St. Julien Communications Group, LLC	1271
Stackable Sensations	1499
Staco Electric Construction Co	2994
Staff Relief Inc	9071
Staffing By Choice LLC	9023
Staffing Kansas City Inc.	9130
Staffing Pharm, LLC	9391
Staffing Solutions Enterprises	9364
Staffing Solutions, Inc.	9149
Staffing Source Personnel dba DriverSource	9206
STAFFusion	9392
Staffwear 2	1681

COMPANY ALPHABETICAL LISTING

S | INDEX#

Company	Index#
Stag Enterprise, Inc.	4073
Stage 3 Productions	7308
Stage 4 Solutions, Inc.	8382
Stainless Integrity	4119
Stakeholder Insights, LLC	8612
Stallings Industries Inc.	3889
Stand Energy Corporation	2006
STANDA, Inc.	2667
Standard Bag Manufacturing Company	7247
Standard Industrial Products Company	6916
Standard Modern Company, Inc.	7549
Standard Scale & Supply Co.	6318
Standberry Enterprises, Inc.	7864
Standing Partnership	8144
Standridge Color Corp.	7340
Stanek Lemon Crouse + Meeks, PA	6177
Stanek Tool Corporation	6928
Stanton Secure Technologies, LLC	5765
Star Building Services, Inc.	2106
Star Poly Bag Inc.	7232
Star Textile, Inc.	3788
Starburst Printing & Graphics	7550
STARDUST Spill Products, LLC	1907
Starpak Ltd.	7291
Starr and Associates LLC	8103
Stars Clothing Manufacturing Company	1693
StarsHR, Inc.	9393
StarSource Management Services, Inc.	1694, 2175
StarTech Consulting, Inc.	5405
State Tax Group, LLC	6243
State Technology & Manufacturing	6765
STATProg Inc.	5090
Stay Online Corp.	5907
Stay Visible, LLC	1337
STB Electrical Test Equipment, Inc.	6306
Steadfast Engineered Products, LLC	6851
Steam Turbine Alternative Resources	3975
Steel Digital Studios, Inc.	8817
Steelbridge Solutions, Inc	7915
Steelcote, Inc.	6568
Stelfast Inc.	3976
Stellar Consulting Solutions, LLC	4642
Stellar Corporation	4837
Stemac Inc	4838
Stenco Construction Company, LLC	2409
Stenzel Sealing Solutions, LLC	3988
Steren Electronics International, LLC	2947
Steri-Tech Inc.	6498
Sterling Engineering, Inc.	3122, 9114
Sterling Services Ltd.	10018
Stern Brothers & Co.	7803
Stern Ingredients, Inc.	3620
Stett Transportation Inc.	9960
Steven C. Fraser, P.A.	6116
Steven Engineering, Inc.	2805
Stevenson Crane Service, Inc.	6271
Stevenson Oil & Chemical Corp.	2007
STEWART Industries, LLC	7189
Stewart Marketing Group, LLC	8745
STI Trucking LLC	10098
Stillwell Hansen, Inc.	4127
Stitch Me LLC	1400
STLogics	4785
STOA International Architects, Inc.	1818
Stokes Creative Group, Inc.	8657
Stone Environmental Services	1921, 3406
STONE Resource, LLC	4643
Stonelaurel Consulting, Inc.	5091
Storage Assessments LLC	5642
Storage Systems Unlimited	4171
Stragistics Technology	5507
Straight-Up, Inc.	1727
STRATCO, Inc.	4203
Strategar LLC	8818
Strategic Benefit Solutions	7955
Strategic Business Communications	8383
Strategic Communications, LLC	9699
Strategic Defense Solutions, LLC	8036
Strategic Environmental	3430
Strategic Market Research Group, Inc.	8574
Strategic Marketing & Promotions, Inc.	8710
Strategic Marketing, Inc.	8517
Strategic Partners Consultants	7733
Strategic Performance Systems, LLC	7946
Strategic Procurement Group	4138
Strategic Research I	8658
Strategic Staffing Solutions	5054
Strategic Systems & Technology Corporation	4644
Strategic Systems, Inc.	5406
Stratice, LLC	4249
Stratitude	4397
Stratium Consulting Group, Inc.	5643
Stratos Legal Services	6244
Stratoserve LLC	4465, 8981
Strickland Security & Safety Solutions	1618
Stride Inc.	7039
Stride, Inc.	7040
Strike Group LLC	2855
Strive Well-Being, Inc.	6357
Strother Enterprises Inc.	3260
Strouse	7559
Structural Steel of Carolina, LLC	6656
Structural Testing Laboratory	6042
Structure Designs, Inc.	3123
Stryker Green, LLC	7947
STS Marketing Services, LLC	1133
Stuart Page Company, Inc.	3800
Studio 3 Design, Inc.	1764
Studio AH LLC dba HPZS	1758
Studio B Dallas, LLC	8819
Studio Hive Inc.	1773
Studio J Designworks LLC	8820
StudioLabs LLC.	5347
Stutton Corporation	1891
STX, Inc. DBA Alta Industries	3883
Styer & Associates, Inc.	1811
Stylerite Label Corporation	7569
Su International Group, Inc.	1988
Subco Foods	3621
Suburban Auto Seat Co., Inc.	1887
Suburban Bolt and Supply Co.	3916
Sud Associates PA	3200
Sue Abrams Productions, LLC	9631
Sue-Ann's Office Supply, Inc.	7008
Sugar Associates, LLC	1771
Sullivan-Brough, Inc. dba SafetyWear	4092

COMPANY ALPHABETICAL LISTING

S — INDEX#

Company	Index#
Sulpice Better Bites	3622
Sumac Inc.	1759, 2373
Summit Container Corporation	7112
Summit Court Reporting, Inc.	6221
Summit Graphics Inc.	7477
Summit Imaging	6542
Summit Information Solutions, Inc.	5766
Summit Press Inc.	7551
Summitline Industries, Inc.	9696
Summus Industries, Inc.	7078
Sun Builders Co.	2548
Sun City Group Inc	10171
Sun Coast Merchandise Corporation	1327
Sun Coast Resources, Inc.	2056
Sun MicroSolutions Inc.	4398
Sun State International Trucks, LLC	1829
Sun Technologies, Inc.	4645
Suncoast Compliance Services, LLC	7903
Suncraft Technologies, Inc.	1099
Sundial Marketing Research, Inc.	8384
SunFlex Packagers Inc.	7221
Sunkiko	7961
Sunland Group	3314
Sunlure, Inc.	1065
Sunny City Enterprises, Inc.	4399
Sunrise Credit Services, Inc.	7830
Sunrise Delivery Inc.	10172
Sunrise Global Solutions, Inc.	4400
Sunrise Hitek Service, Inc.	7523
Sunrise Systems, Inc.	5254
Sunset Printing and Engraving Corp	1182
SunSoft Technologies Inc.	4959
Sunstates Security, LLC	2665
Supa Tech Inc.	2909
Super Bakery	3692
Super Stores Service	2886
Superbag USA Corp.	7292
SuperbTech, Inc.	8946
Supergreen Inc.	4208
Superior Environmental Corp.	3497
Superior Industrial Supply & Services Inc.	4149
Superior Industrial Supply Co.	4172
Superior Maintenance Co.	2148
Superior Security	2681
Superior Staffing	9115
SuperLatina Inc.	1272
Supplemental Medical Services, Inc.	9243
Supplemental Staffing	9365
SupplierGATEWAY LLC	4401
Supplies Express LLC	7005
Supply Innovations Co, LLC	4188
Supply Sanitation Systems	2260
Supply Solutions	2096
SUPRA Office Solutions, Inc.	7060
Supreme Discount Uniforms, LLC	1676
Supreme Oil Company	1943
Supreme Resources, Inc.	1927
Supreme Safety Inc.	4157
Sure Solutions LLC	6852
SureTemps LLC	9138
Surface Art Engineering Inc	2735
SurfBigData LLC	4541
Sur-Flo Plastics & Engineering, Inc.	7392
Surge Transportation, Inc.	9890
Surgimed Corporation	6393
Sur-Seal, Inc.	4012
Survey Launch Co.	8397
Sustainable Solutions Corporation	8221
Sutherland Global Services	5348
Sutter Design, Inc. dba The Sutter Group	8558
Sutton Ford, Inc.	1831
Suzanne's Specialties, Inc.	3681
Suzy Q Cleaning Services	2144
Suzy's Swirl	3623
SV Meditrans, Inc.	9494
SVAM International Inc.	5349
SVI. Inc.	1838
Svitla Systems, Inc.	4402
SW Safety Solutions Inc.	3071
SWAG247 Branded Solutions	1580
Swan Packaging Inc.	7202
Swath Design, LLC	1222
Sweet Additions, Inc.	3595
Sweet Bottom Cookies	3710
Sweet Harvest Foods Management Company	3663
Sweet Street Desserts	3703
Swift Computer Supply, Inc.	7019
Swift Logistics, Inc.	10173
Swift Office Solutions	5833
Swift Pace Solutions, Inc	5644
Swimmer Printing dba Alphagraphics	7649
SwitchLane Inc.	5471
SWITZER Architecture, P.C.	1796
Swoon Group	4751
SWS Capital Management, LLC (formerly Williams Capital Management, LLC	7831
Sybis LLC	1663
Sycomp a Technology Company., Inc.	4403
Sygma Technology Solutions, Inc.	5350
Sygna Technologies Inc	5767
Sylver Rain Consulting	4482
Symbioun Technologies, Inc.	4646
Symphony Enterprises LLC	5472
Sympora Technologies	4890
Symposit LLC	5768
Syna Medical	6394
Synapse Business Systems	5769
Synaptein Solutions Inc.	5770
Synasha LLC	9307
Synchrogistics, LLC	10049
Synchronous Solutions, Inc.	4752
Syncreon.US Inc.	8122
Synectics Inc.	4753
Synergem, Inc.	5255
Synergy America, Inc.	4647
Synergy Bodycare LLC.	2597
Synergy Computer Solutions, Inc,	4960
Synergy Development Partners, LLC	2359
Synergy EnterPrize, LLC	5473
Synergy Global Systems Inc	9116
Synergy Project Consultants, Inc.	2549
Synergy Staffing & Solutions Inc.	9338
Synergy Technologies, LLC	4542
Synesis International, Inc.	5503
Synico Staffing	9227
Synop LLC	3722

COMPANY ALPHABETICAL LISTING

S INDEX#

Company	Index#
Synova Inc.	4961
Syntel Inc.	4962
Synterex, Inc.	8089
SysIntelli, Inc.	4404
Sysmind LLC	3965, 7408
Systec101	5856
System Soft Technologies, Inc	4543
System Solutions, Inc.	4754
Systemart, LLC	5256
SystemGuru,Inc.	5257
SYSTEMIAN LLC	5407
Systems Design, Inc.	1744
Systems Integration Solutions, Inc.	4405
Systems Integration, Inc.	3315, 6917
Systems Service Enterprises, Inc.	5055
Systems Source Inc.	3753
Systems Staffing Group Inc.	5474
Systems Technology Group, Inc. (STG)	4963
Systems Technology International, Inc.	4964
Systemware Professional Services, Inc.	5645
Systrand Manufacturing Corporation	6853

T

Company	Index#
T & M Incorporated	10019
T G Inc.	4173
T Wynne Art & Design Inc.	1066
T&G Corporation	2348
T. Frank McCall's, Inc.	2228
T. K. Davis Construction, Inc.	2564
T. Mak's International, Inc.	8436
T.V. Minority Company, Inc.	10095
T3	8821
T3 Design Corporation	3325
Tabb Packaging Solutions	7190
Table Decor International Inc.	3768
Table Thyme Designs	1415
Tactegra	8150
Tactical Response Security Consulting Inc.	2686
Tag Tool Services, Inc.	3956
TaiParker Consulting LLC	1645
TAJ Technologies, Inc.	5014
Talencio, LLC	8136
Talent Logic Inc.(formerly Sai People Solutions, Inc.)	5646
Talent Tool & Die, Inc.	3977
TalentBurst, Inc	4839
TalentCode Management Group	8523
Talented Fish, Inc.	9268
Talson Solutions, LLC	8222
Talteam,Inc	5771
Talus Partners, LLC	8982
Tam Partners Consulting, LLC	5814
Tamazari Inc	3333
Tampa T-Shirts	1357, 1677
Tampon Tribe	6358
Tan Check Consolidated, Inc.	5475
Tandem Axle Inc. dba Mixed Media Creations	8822
Tandem By Design LLC	1287
Tanen Directed Advertising	1044
Tanfel	6584, 6713
Tanisha Systems Inc.	4840
Tanson Corp.	5015
Tap3Solutions	4406

T INDEX#

Company	Index#
Tape Central, Inc.	5925
Tape Services, Inc.	5909
TAPEANDMEDIA.com, LLC	5944
Tarlton Corporation	2428
Tartan Marketing, Inc.	8597
Taurus Market Research	8659
Tavarez Sporting Goods	1678
Tax Roof, LLC dba JT Project Management Office	7984
TayganPoint Consulting Group	8223
Taylor & Hill, Inc.	3316
Taylor & Ryan, LLC	6152
Taylor and Associates, Inc.	6176
Taylor Distribution Group, LLC	6528
Taylor Made Business Solutions LLC	7000
Taylor Scientific	6045
Taylor Smith Consulting, LLC	8278
TBK Promotions, Inc.	1401
TBM Carriers	10174
TCA Consulting Group, Inc.	4466
TCG Events	8623
TCG, Inc.	9228
TCN	9701
tCognition, Inc.	4841
TCP Universal	7293
TDEFERIAMEDIA, Inc.	1082, 8467
TDMC Enterprises Inc.	1928
TDR Consulting Inc	4257
TDW+Co	1291
Team 1 Texas LLC	2550
Team Askin Technologies, Inc	5772
Team Clean, Inc.	2229
Team Cruiser Supply LLC	4093
Team One Printing, Inc.	7585
Team Telecom, LLC	9726
TeamPeople LLC	9526
TEC Electric, LLC	2999
TEC, Inc.	3072
Tech Army, LLC	4544
Tech Providers, Inc.	8873
TechBios, Inc.	4648
TechCircle, Inc.	4755
Techcom, Inc.	9549
TechGuard Security LLC	5056
TechLink Systems, Inc.	4407
Tech-Matic Industries, Inc.	6755
Technalink, Inc.	5773
TechNet Resources	4649
Technical Communication Concepts Inc.	4650
Technical Conveyor Group, Inc.	6281
Technical Industries, Inc.	7331
Technical Information & Professional Solutions Inc	9229
Technical Maintenance, Inc.	6302
Technical Source, Inc.	4756
Technical Welding Fabricators LLC	6661
TECHNIKOS Information Development, LLC	9561
TechniSource Services Group	7298
Technology Asset LLC	5647
Technology Assurance Group, Inc.	5774
Technology Concepts & Design, Inc.	5092
Technology Concepts Group International, LLC	5258
Technology for Education	5648
Technology Group Solutions, LLC	4795
Technology Management Corporation	9718

COMPANY ALPHABETICAL LISTING

T

Company	INDEX#
Technology Media Group	7699
Technology Solutions Group LLC	5016
Technology Solutions Inc.	5504
Technology Ventures	7870
Technology Ventures, Inc.	10020
TechnoSmarts, Inc.	5057
Technosoft Corporation	4965
TechnoSphere, Inc.	5259
Technossus LLC	4408
Technosteps LLC	4467
Techno-Transfers of Florida, Inc.	4545, 9024
Technovision, Inc.	5260
Techolution LLC	5351
TechSoft Systems, Inc.	5408
Techstyle Group LLC	1273
TechTrans International, Inc.	5649
Techwave Consulting Inc.	5476
Techway Services	5650
Tecknomic LLC	9664
Tec-Link	4546
Teco Diagnostics Inc.	6359
Tec-Print, LLC	7674
Teddy Bear Fresh Produce, LLC	3652
Tedia Company, Inc.	2008
Tejas Office Products, Inc.	7079
Tejas Premier Building Contractor, Inc.	2551
Tek Leaders, Inc	5651
TEKCONNX	9794
Teklink International Inc.	4757
Teknia Networks & Logistics, Inc.	6264
Tekshapers Inc.	4966
teksoft ventures, inc.	4758
TEKtalent Inc.	8947
TELA Technologies, Inc.	5652
Telamco, Inc.	2993
Telamon Corporation	9697
telCade.Com	2806
Telco Intercontinental Corporation	3030
Telecom Electric Supply Company	2910
Telecom Electric Supply Inc.	9762
Telecom Resources of America, Inc.	5869
TelePlus, Inc.	9691
Televergence Solutions, Inc.	9769
TelExpress	9727
Tellus Solutions, Inc	4409
TelNet Technologies, LLC	3006
Telrose Corporation	3833, 7061
Teltech Communications LLC	9788
Tel-XL	9770
Tembua Inc (fka Precision Language Services)	1155
Tempco Electric Heater Corp.	2968
Tempest Telecom Solutions, LLC	9652
Temporaries Plus, Inc.	8874
Temporary Solutions, Inc.	9527
Temporary Staffing by Suzanne, Ltd.	9339
TempStaff Inc.	9245
Ten 10 Design LLC	1536, 7650
Teneo Linguistics Company, LLC	8823
Teplis Travel Service	10204
TERRA Solutions & Services, LLC	3375
Terralogic Integrated Systems Analysts, Inc.	5775
TerraNext	3390
Terrell & Associates, LLC	7981
TerryWorldWide, LLC	6438
TESCRA	4410
TesTex, Inc.	3261
Texas Finishing Company	6573, 6701
Texas Freight	10175
Texas Mgt Associates, Inc	3031
Texas Microfiber Incorporated	2261
Texas Seal Supply Co, Inc.	4031
Texas Storage Systems	6300
Texcel, Inc.	5409
Texican Natural Gas Company	1977
Teya Technologies, LLC	2274
Teyrachi Logistics LLC	10176
TGE Resources, Inc.	3532
TH Logistics,LLC	10186
Thacker Martinsek LPA	6213
Thayer Distribution, Inc.	7034
The ACT 1 Group, Inc.	8948
The Advent Group	9230
The Advertising Specialist, L.C.	1591
The AG Group, Inc. dba AG PrintPromo Solutions	1537
The Ajamu Group, LLC.	1134
The Alamo Travel Group LP	10222
The Alden Group	3659
The American Cleaning Services Inc	2120
The Andwin Corp.	6032, 6360
The 'Apps' Consultants Inc.	4449
The Asaba Group	8090
The Ashvins Group, Inc.	4547
The Aspen Group, Inc.	4891
The Axelrod Firm, PC	6222
The Backshop, Inc. DBA Mercury Mambo	8824
The Barr Group, Inc.	1556
The Bernd Group Inc.	2818, 6265
The Best Direct Marketing Group LLC	1067
The Bites Company	3583
The Black Moon Group dba BMG Medical Supply	6439
The BOSS Group	9168
The Bradley Company, Inc.	1450
The Bradley Partnerships, Inc.	7956
The Burchell Group	9495
The Burgess Group - Corporate Recruiters Intl	9340
The Burks Companies, Inc.	2129
The Busha Group LLC	3670
The CADD Department, Inc.	8208
The Cadence Group, Inc.	8045
The CAD-Scan Connection	3073
The CALER Group, Inc.	9025
The Callard Company	1538
The Capre Group	8468
The Carney Group	9394
The Castle Group, Inc.	8546
The Caswood Group, Inc.	8185
The Cedalius Group LLC	2638
The CementBloc	8711
The Certif-a-gift Company Inc.	1402
The Cervantes Group	9401
The Chester Group, Inc.	2360
The Claiborne Consulting Group, Inc.	8224
The Computer Company, Inc.	4468
The Computer Group, Inc.	5898
The Computer Support People, LLC	4469
The Coniglio Co.	2485

COMPANY ALPHABETICAL LISTING

T | INDEX#

Company	Index#
The Conxsis Group, Inc.	8279
The Corporate Gift Service, Inc.	1328, 3852
The Corporate Shop, Inc.	1378
The Crafton Group, Inc.	8469
The Creative Touch, Inc.	1426
The CREW Corporation	6313
The CTS Group, LLC	7786
The Danby Group, LLP	4651
The Dearborn Agency	6010
The Design Factory, LLC	1186
The Dessert Ladies	3682, 3869
The Dieringer Research Group, Inc.	8868
The Dominion Group Marketing Research & Consulting	8853
The Donna Bender Company	1581
The Drexel Group, Inc	9395
The Edlong Corporation	3624
The ELOCEN Group	2330, 4483
The Entermedia Group, LLC	2262
The Event Concierge	8327
The Experts Bench, Inc.	9072
The Falmer Associates, Inc.	6559
The Fehlig Group, LLC	8104
The Fishel Company	9752
The Fisher Group	7035
The Forefront Group	8161
The Fountain Group, LLC	9026
The FSL Group	9906
The Future Procurement Group, LLC	8151
The G Crew	2315
The Garrigan Lyman Group	1292
The Geo Group	1299
The Gilson Group, LLC	7734
The Goal Inc.	4548
The Good Search, LLC	8983
The Green Chemical Store, Inc.	2057
The Green Garmento, LLC	1673
The Green Glider Company LLC	2121
The Green Way Environmental Group, LLC.	3351
The Guardian Protective Services, LLC	2639
The Hamilton Group	1338, 6984
The Hannon Group, LLC	8559
The Harmon Group LLC	10021
The Herring IMPACT Group	9244
The Horrocks Company LLC dba Volu-Sol	2062
The HR Source	9169
The HR Source, Inc.	9496
The I4 Group Consulting, LLC	8280
The Ian Thomas Group, LLC	4652
The ID Development Group	8825
The Ideal Group	2410, 6644
The ILS Company	9832
The Improve Group	8137
The InnovateHers	8854
The Intuition Consulting Firm, LLC.	8046
The Jay Group	1548
The John K. Howe Company, Inc.	1539
The JPI Group LLC	7957
The KARS Group Ltd LLC	9269
The Kiesel Company	1968, 3455
The Kingfisher Group, LLC	8746
The Landmark Group Companies LLC	2374
The Lane Group LLC	8660
The Language Shop	1207

T | INDEX#

Company	Index#
The Law Office of Kathryn N Karam	6245
The Lazers Edge LLC	5885
The Lexinet Corporation	8529
The Lima Pallet Company, Inc.	10250
The Logo Warehouse	1422
The LSC Group, Inc.	4411
The M.K. Morse Company	3978
The MACRO GROUP, Inc.	5017
The Madison Consulting Group, Inc.	8186
The Management Edge, Inc.	7904
The MardonGroup LLC	7570
The Maris Group	8974
The Mark USA, Inc.	8385
The Marker Group, Inc.	6246
The Matlet Group	7552
The Maxcel Company	8826
The May Consulting Group Inc.	9341
The Mazzitelli Placement Group	9231
The Med Writers LLC	9544
The Medcom Group, Ltd.	6366
The Media Pro	8624
The Melior Group, Inc.	8769
The Mice Groups, Inc.	8949
The Millcraft Paper Company	7054
The Mixx	8712
The Mom Corps, Inc.	9073
The Mt. Olivet Group, LLC	2917
The Muffin Mam, Inc.	3711
The Mundial Group, Inc.	8713
The net.America Corporation	4892
The Northridge Group, Inc.	9692
The Olab Group, LLC	1358
The Olympic Glove & Safety Co. Inc.	4128
The Omega Staff, LLC	9497
The O'Riordan Bethel Law Firm, LLP	6101
The Orsus Group, Inc.	7929
The Outbound Group	10022
The Pallet Alliance	10245
The Part Works Inc.	3945
The Pension & Retirement Group LLC	7843
The Perspectives Group	8302
The Phillips Company, Inc.	6616
The Premier Group	6065, 6512
The Printing People, Inc.	7507
The Prout Group, Inc.	9366
The R.E.M. Engineering Co., Inc.	3074
The Real Advice Plus LLC	8187
The REIA Corporation	4653
The Research Edge LLC	8598
The Resource Connection, Inc.	9150
The Right Method, LLC	7905
The Ross Group Construction Corporation	2490
The Royster Group, Inc.	9074
The S3 Agency	1183
The Safety Source, LLC	4112
The Sartell Group, Inc.	5018
The Security Group Corp.	1653
The Seideman Company	9733
The Servants, Inc.	7163
The Silicon Blackgroup, LLC	4759
The Skinner Company	4167
The Social Lights, LLC	8599
The Solers Reseach Group	9545

COMPANY ALPHABETICAL LISTING

T   INDEX#

Company	Index#
The Sourcium Group	5261
The Special Event Company	8625
The Spencer Thomas Group LLC	9273
The Squires Group	4893
The Standard Group	7233
The Stroud Group	8105
The Studio	9612
The Switzer Group	1797
The Symmetry Group, LLC	1083
The Tagos Group, LLC	8281
The Targa Group	9207
The Ternio Group LLC	5653
The Thomas Collective LLC	8714
The Thomas Family Business, Inc.	10039
The Thrower Group, LLC.	8152
The Training Associates Corporation	2710
The Translation Team	8328
The Travel Exchange	10214
The Travel Group LLC	10223
The Traveling Picture Show Company	9574
The Trevino Group, Inc.	2552
The Trinity Design Group, LLC	7091
The Unbeatable Connection LLC	9498
The Uniform Store, LLC	1725
The Valve Agency Inc.	4032
The Vandiver Group, Inc.	8613
The Vesume Group, LLC	9151
The Wagner Law Group	6147
The Wellington Group, Inc.	9117
The Wellspring Group, Inc.	4470
The Westmark Group	3474
The Whitman Group LLC	9412
The Widget Development & Trading Company, LLC	3549
The Wilkins Group, Inc.	9789
The Wynning Experience	8518
The Zamzow Group, Inc.	7735
Themesoft Inc.	5654
Theodore Williams Construction Company, LLC	2460
Theonics Inc.	6762
Theophany Staffing, Inc.	9118
TheraEx Rehab Services, Inc.	8950
Therapy Staff, LLC	9208
Thermal Control Products	3000
Thermal-Tech Systems, Inc.	7354
Thermotech, Inc.	7398
Thiel Tool & Engineering Co., Inc.	6744
Thieman Quality Metal Fab, Inc.	6677
Think Development Systems	4654
Think Ink	1035
Think Tank Studio	1359
Thinking Cap Communications & Design	1293
Third Law Enterprises, LLC	5093
Third Term Inc.	5655
THISAI LLC	2807, 6585
THM Creative, Inc. dba Advanced Imaging Inc.	7524
Thomas & Reed, LLC	7774
Thomas Direct Sales, Inc.	1500
Thomas E. Slade, Inc.	1416, 7532
Thomas Gallaway Corporation	4412
Thomas Imports LLC	3625
Thomas Land Clearing Company	3376
Thomas Protective Service, Inc.	2699
Thomas Sign and Awning Company, Inc.	1068
Thomas Telecom Inc.	9698
Thomco Enterprises Inc.	2349
Thompson Distribution Company	3895
Thompson Hospitality Services, LLC	3728
Thompson Marketing, LLC	6645
Thornton Construction Company, Inc.	2350
Thoro Packaging	7105
Thors, LLC	3243
Thoughtpowers LLC	4413
Three Leaf Productions, Inc.	7651
Three PDS Inc.	9499
Three Point Graphics, Inc.	1246
Three Squares International Inc.	3377
Three Star Trucking Co.	10023
THT Electronics Company, Inc.	2780
Thunder Island Coffee Roasters, L.L.C.	3690
Tiagha & Associates, Ltd.	6223
Tier One Marketing	1451
Tier One Property Services	2185
Tiffany Stuart Solutions, Inc.	8951
Tiger Controls Inc.	2865
Tiger Natural Gas, Inc.	2012
Tiger Studio Co.	1135
Tigerman McCurry Architects	1760
Tigress Financial Partners LLC	7832
Timber Industries, LLC	10242
Time Definite Services Transportation, LLC	9891
Time Logistics, Inc	10127
Time Out Systems, Inc.	2361
TimeLine Video	9613
Tina Miller, Inc	9861
Tioga Environmental Consultants, Inc.	3520
TIPS Consultants LLC	4258
Titan Associates, Inc. dba A.G. Maas Company	2145
Titan Data Group Inc.	5019
TITANIUM Worldwide LLC	1208, 8715
TJ's Packaging Inc	7198
TKC Enterprises Inc. dba Batteries Plus	4189
TLB Holdings, Inc.	1696
TLC Adcentives LLC	1582
TLC Investments, LLC	3020
TLS by Design, LLC	3776
TMC Workforce Solutions	9500
TMCS, LLC	4894
TMH Solutions LLC	5410
TMI Coatings, Inc.	7399
TMMPROMOS.COM dba The Artifactori	7664
TMNcorp	8560
TMS Consulting LLC	8303
TMW Enterprises, Inc.	8661
TNT Staffing	9308
TOC Logistics International, LLC	9951
Today's Business Solutions	7080
Toddy, LLC	3577
Toll International LLC	3225
Tom Smith Industries, Inc.	7422
Tomken Plastic Technologies, Inc.	7363
Toole Design Group, LLC	3145
Tooles Contracting Group LLC	2411
Top Guard, Inc.	2702
Top Tool Company	6743
Top Worldwide, LLC	10024
Topeka Capital Markets Inc.	7833

COMPANY ALPHABETICAL LISTING

T

Company	INDEX#
Topp Knotch Personnel, Inc.	9139
Top-Shelf Fixtures	6958
Torch Steel Sales LLC	6950
Torix General Contractors a Tepa Company	2322
Torres Architects, Inc.	1740
Torres Llompart, Sanchez Ruiz LLP	7834
Torricella Law, PLLC	6117
Tortillas Inc.	3684
Total Building Maintenance, Inc.	2263
Total Construction and Equipment, Inc.	2421
Total Control Logistics	10128
Total Event Resources	8519
Total Glow Enterprise	2578
Total Media Group	9575
Total Packaging Solutions LLC	7191
Total Print Solutions, Inc.	7536
Total Resources International	6361
Total Response Technology, LLC	4760
Total System Services US, Inc.	5776
Total Technical Services, Inc.	9152
TotalCom Management Inc	1661
TotalMed Staffing, Inc.	9541
Totalpack, Inc.	7125
Tottser Tool and Manufacturing	6759
Touch Enterprises LLC	4096
Touch Of Magic Inc.	8600
Touch World, Inc.	4967
Touchpoint Inc.	5870
Touchpoint Integrated Communications, LLC	8398
Tower Legal Solutions	9342
Tower Safety and Instruction	9637
Town & Country Printing	7533
Towne Communications, Inc.	9653
TPE Solutions, Inc.	7368
TPS Logistics	10121
TPSi, LLC	5411
Trabus	4414
Tracepoint, LLC	2650
Track Trading Co./ dba Exaco USA	4190
Tracy Becker Construction, Inc.	2502
Trademark Plastics, Inc.	6362, 7327
Trademarks Promotional Products	1583
Tradex International Inc.	4150
TrainSmart, Inc.	8067
TRAK Communications, Inc.	9734
Tra-Lin Corp.	1994
Trans Global Shipping Alliance, LLC	9862
Trans International, LLC	10194
Trans Overseas Corporation	10025
Transcend Business Solutions, LLC	4471
Transcendent Enterprise	9614
TransChemical, Inc.	1969
Transcomp Inc. DBA: Evolve Systems	5020
Trans-Expedite Inc	10177
Transgroup World Wide Logistics	9907
TransHire	9027
Transient Identiti, Inc.	8561
Transit Air Cargo Inc.	9863
Translating Services, Inc.	7888
Translation Excellence	8391
Translation Solutions Corp.	1294
Translation Station, Inc.	8047
Trans-Link LLC	10114
Transmaquila, Inc.	10178
TransPak	7106, 10231
Transphere Inc.	10026
Trans-Plants Inc.	3862
Transportation Safety Apparel	1700
TransTech, LLC	4761
Transtek Magnetics Inc.	2925
TransWorld Plastic Films, Inc.	7156, 7355
Transworld Printing Services, Inc.	7478
Transworld Supply Network, LLC	6486
Tranzact Technologies, Inc.	4762
Trascent Management Consulting LLC	8162
Travel Acquisition Group, Ltd.	10224
Travelex International, Inc.	10205
Traveling Coaches Inc.	5656
Tray-Tec, Inc.	8282
Tre Weekly Magazine	2724
Treasure Enterprise, Inc.	2122
Treat and Company, LLC	8601
TREC Group, Inc.	3262
Treco Stainless Solutions, LLC	4001
TreCom Systems Group	5477
Tree Naturals Inc.	2598
Trendsetter Electronics	2781
Trent Design LLC	1136
Trester Hoist Equipment, Inc.	4235
Tri County Cleaning Supply, Inc.	2176
Tri Star Freight System Inc.	10179
Triad Technology Group	5428
Trialon Corporation	9209
Triangle Press Inc.	7665
Tribal Capital Markets, LLC	7835
Tribe Express	9908
Tribe Express Inc	9909
Tribes-A-Dozen, LLC	3584
Tri-Chem Specialty Chemicals, LLC	2058
Tricia Browning Design Group	8048
Trickey Jennus, Inc.	8437
TRiCOM Communications	9719
TRI-CON Construction Managers, LLC	2324
Tricon Security Group, LLC	2659
Tricor America, Inc.	9864
TriCor Employment Screening	7948
Trident Consulting	4415
Trident Fluid Power, LLC	4013
TriFactor Solutions, LLC	6266
Tri-force Consulting Services Inc.	5478
Trillium Teamologies Inc.	4968
TriLogic Corporation	5479
Trilogy Circuits, Inc.	2782
Trilogy Consulting Group, Inc.	8068
Trilogy LLC	8827
Trimensions Inc.	8662
TriMetro Security Services LLC	2666
Trinal, Inc.	8069
Trinidad Construction, LLC	2375
Trinity Enterprise Group LLC	1584
Trinity Graphic & Packaging Solutions, LLC	7157
Trinity Sterile, Inc.	6039
Trinus Corporation	4416
Trio Northwest Business Solutions, Inc.	1295
Trio Trucking, Inc.	10096
Triple Diamond Plastics, Inc.	7423

COMPANY ALPHABETICAL LISTING

T | INDEX#

Company	Index#
TripleNet Technologies, Inc.	5815
Tripwireless, Inc.	9659
TriQuest Business Services, LLC	9501
Tristana R Harvey Career Planning & Consulting Series LLC	8070
TriStar Fulfillment Services, Inc.	1184
Tri-Starr Services of Pennsylvania, Inc.	7958
Triton Light Medical, LLC	6539
Triveni Group LLP	5262
Trivision Group Inc.	5352
Tronex International Inc	1703
Troon Inc.	2283
Tropic Fasteners LLC	3888
Tropical Nut & Fruit Co	3671
Tropical Surveillance & Investigations, Inc.	4549
TruBlu Cleaning Pros, LLC	2162
Truck City of Gary, Inc.	1832
Trucking Innovation, LLC	9963
True Champions	2316
TrueChoicePack Corp.	7245
TruEvents LLC	8399
Trusted Link Staffing Services LLC	9210
Trusted Translations, Inc.	1288
Trustee Capital LLC	8037
Truth Technology Inc.	1626
Trutron Corporation	6854
Tryon Clear View Group, LLC	7806
TSA Sales Associates, LLC	4217
TSAO Design Group	1741
TSC Enterprise	7787
TSG Direct LLC	1329
TSG Enterprises, LLC dba RadiusPoint	9671
TSG Server and Storage	5021
TSI Global Companies LLC	9722
TSK Products, Inc.	6464
TSM Design, Inc.	1115
TSRC, Inc.	7085
TSS Industrial Packaging, LLC	7274
TSS Redmond	5816
TTi Global	4969
TTI of USA	5353
Tuknik Government Services, LLC	4237
Tunabear, Inc.	5657
Tunheim	8602
Turbo Air, Inc.	4206
Turbo America Technology, LLC	6588
TurnGroup Technologies, LLC	5058
Turnstone Inc. dba Alphagraphics	7483
Turtle & Hughes, Inc.	4129
Turtle Wings Inc.	3435
Tuson Corporation	6805
Twang Partners, Ltd.	3723
Twenty-Two Global Transport, LP	10180
Twin Cities Solutions, Inc.	5022
Twin City Security, Inc.	2661
Twin River LLC	7299
Twintron Data Systems Inc.	5263
Twirling Tiger Press Inc.	8547
Two Hawk Employment Services, Inc.	9270
Two Roads Professional Resources, Inc.	8952
Two Shea Consulting, Inc.	4417
Two Way Direct, Inc.	4418
TWT Distributing Inc.	2585

T | INDEX#

Company	Index#
Tycho Services, Inc.	3378
Tychon, Inc.	6790
Tylie Jones & Associates, Inc.	1036
Tylok International, Inc.	6678
Tyndale Company	1715
Type A Events, LLC	8603

U

Company	Index#
U.S Construction Group Inc.	2503
U.S. Chemicals, LLC	1912
U.S. Facilities, Inc. PRWT Services Company	2504
U.S. Imaging, Inc.	6404
U.S. Translation Company	1278
Ubiquitous Design, Ltd.	1803
UCS Group LLC	2553
UFC Technology, Inc.	4763
Ulmer Pharmacal	6443
Ultimate Maintenance Services, Inc.	2097
Ultimate Ventures	8828
Ultimation Industries LLC	6282
UltraViolet Devices, Inc.	3379
UMF Medical	6495
UN Communications Group, Inc.	7534
Unatek, Inc.	4895
Undercover Chocolate Company LLC	3683
Underground Graphics Inc.	1360
Undisclosed Location, Inc	8386
Unic Pro Inc.	2156
Unical Aviation Inc.	2808
Unicom Government, Inc.	5777
UNICON International, Inc.	5412
Unicorn Technologies, LLC	4655
Unicorp, Inc.	2948
Unified Business Technologies Inc.	4970
Unified Industries Inc.	3326
Unified TelData Inc.	9654
Uniglobe Travel Designers	10220
Union Packaging, LLC	7255
UNIPRO Architects Engineers LLP	1813, 3276
Uniq Seal, LLC	7107
Unique Experience Custom Embroidery & Screen-Print	1596
Unique Expressions, LLC	1452
Unique Image, Inc.	1037
Uniquely Lisa Designs dba Our Favorite Things Boutique	3873
UNISERVE Facilities Services	2098
Unistar-Sparco Computers, Inc.	5933
Unitec Distribution Systems	1690
Unitech Consulting, LLC dba Chameleon	5059
United American Supply, LLC	4098
United Building Maintenance, Inc.	2142
United Data Technologies	5964
United Geo Technologies LLC	3317
United Global Technologies	5094
United Manufacturing Network Inc.	6855
United Medical Supplies Inc.	6465
United Personnel Services	9153
United Print Group, Inc.	1515
United Scrap Metal	6957
United Seal & Rubber Co. Inc.	7341
United Software Group Inc.	5413
United Sources of America, Inc.	9615
United Unlimited Construction, Inc.	2565

COMPANY ALPHABETICAL LISTING

U INDEX#

Company	Index#
Unitex International Inc.	9802
Unity Printing Co., Inc.	7666
Universal Business Solutions, LLC	4656
Universal Cleaning Concept LLC	2231
Universal Die & Stampings	6761
Universal Display & Fixtures	1274
Universal Environmental Consulting, Inc.	3490
Universal Graphics, Inc.	1379
Universal Logistics Services, Inc.	9821
Universal Medical Associates, Inc.	6433
Universal Network Development Corp.	9655
Universal Packaging Corp	7113
Universal Packaging Systems	7234
Universal Personnel, LLC	9140
Universal Printing Company LLC	7667
Universal Products	2584
Universal Sanitizers and Supplies, Inc.	2241
Universal Software Corporation	5102
Universal Tool Equipment & Controls, Inc.	3180
Universal. Innovative. Intelligent, Inc.	8071
University Moving & Storage	10027
Uniworld Group Inc.	1209
Uniworld Omniport	3754
Unlimited Recycling, Inc.	3447
Unyter Enterprises	6405
UpNet Technologies, Inc.	5023
Upward Global Logistics & Distribution	9910
Urban E Consulting, Inc.	3407
Urban Food Concepts LLC	3693
Urban Harvest Partnership, LLC	5480
Urban Strategies US LLC DBA SMCG	8317
URimagination, Inc.	5354
Urooj LLC	5264
Urrabazo Law, P.C.	6086
US Communications and Electric	9753
US Electronics Inc.	2864
US Medical International LLC	6395
US Metro Group, Inc.	2099
US Organic Group Corp.	2589
US Surgitech Inc.	9119
US Tech Solutions, Inc.	5265
US&S, Inc.	3284
US21, Inc.	5985
USA Couriers, Inc.	9968
UserEdge Technical Personnel	9309
USM Business Systems, Inc.	5778
USS Rhino	4225
Utilicon Services, Inc.	1752
Utility Reduction Analysts, Inc.	8123
UV Solutions, LLC	2837
UX Design Collective LLC	8716

V

Company	Index#
V & L Research and Consulting, Inc.	8470
V G Francis Logistics Inc.	10074
V Group Inc.	5266
V&V Supremo Foods Inc.	3626
V2Soft Inc.	4971
V3Gate, LLC	4450
Vac Pac, Inc.	7170
VAI Architects Inc.	1819
Valbrea Technologies, Inc.	5658

V INDEX#

Company	Index#
Valdes Architecture and Engineering	3124
ValDivia Enterprises, Inc.	10040
Valencia, Perez & Echeveste	8387
Valenko Incorporated	2893
Valentine Austriaco & Bueschel, P.C.	6140
Valicom Corp	5824
Validus Construction Services LLC	2351
Valley Grinding & Mfg. / Mario Cotta America	3986
Valley Industrial Piping, Inc.	6704
Valley Lahvosh Baking Co.	3573
Valley Screen Process Company, Inc.	7535
Valmec Inc.	6283
ValorPoint, LLC	6396
ValSource, Inc.	3263
Vampire Tools, Inc.	3884
Van Ness Law Firm, PLC	6118
Van Tech Industries	4065
Van Zile Travel	10218
Vanadams Sports Group LLC	8663
VanderHouwen & Associates, Inc.	9536
Vangel Inc.	4896
Vanguard Computers, Inc.	5825, 5951
Vanguard Electrical Services, LLC	2554
Vanguard Instruments Company, Inc.	6307
Vanguard Safety Company LLC	6406
Vani Quality Quest, Inc.	8124
Vanir Construction Management, Inc.	2317
VanRan Communications Services, Inc.	9680
Vantage Agora	6888
VaOpto, LLC	3001
Vari-Form, Inc.	6646
Various Views Research, Inc.	8741
VARITE, Inc.	4419
Varitek, Inc.	5851
Varunes & Assocaites, P.C.	6097
VAS Consulting Services	8125
Vassallo International	7430
Vast Industries	6814, 6962
Vaswani Inc	3809
Vaughn Management LLC	8072
VCM Technologies, Inc.	5659
VDart Inc.	4657
VDC Technologies	5095
VDP Safety & Uniforms Ltd.	1714
Veatic dba of Proxy Management Group	2352
Vector Global Logistics LLC	9911
Vedicsoft Solutions Inc.	5267
Vega Construction Company, Inc.	2436
Vega Consulting Solutions, Inc.	5268
Vehicle Maintenance Program, Inc.	1854
Velocity Global Logistics, Inc.	9974
Velocity Works, LLC	5481
VELOX Integration Services, LLC	6332
Venator Staffing	9211
Venchurs, Inc.	7192
Venpalia LLC	7736
Vensiti Inc	5660
Ventura Manufacturing	1884
Ventures Unlimited Inc.	5269
Venus Group, Inc.	9800
Venus Power-Com Supply, LLC	2878
Veracity Consulting, Inc.	4796
Verde Logistics, LLC	10181

COMPANY ALPHABETICAL LISTING

V

Company	INDEX#
Verge Information Technologies, Inc.	5661
Veridian Environmental, Inc.	3380
Veriha Trucking, Inc.	10195
Veris Associates, Inc. dba VerisVisalign	8225
Vermont Precision Tools, Inc.	6705
Vernalis Group Inc	5355
Vernance, LLC	4842
Versa Shore Inc.	4420
Versatech, LLC	3983
Vertex Computer Systems, Inc	5414
Vertisystem Inc.	4421, 8953
Vest Marketing Design, LLC	1108
Vesta Ingredients, Inc.	7164
VETBUILT Services, Inc.	9212
Veteran Call Center, LLC	9763
Veteran Medical Products, Inc.	6440
VetMeds, Inc.	6036, 6397
Vetrans LLC	10189
VetWorks LLC	8049
Via Technology	5983
Viadata1 Communications Inc.	9693
VIAIR CorporatioN	1850, 3991
Vic Salazar Enterprises, LLC	8388
Vichara Technologies Inc.	5270
Vicksburg Chrysler Dodge Jeep	1836
Vics Welding Company, LLC	6576
Victoria & Associates Career Services, Inc.	9028
Victoria Legal + Corporate Services	6141
Victory Global Solutions, Inc.	4897
Victory Personnel Services, Inc.	9542
Victory Productions, Inc.	2711
Vidal Plastics, LLC	7364
Video & Security Specialists	1634, 2866
VideoWorks Production Services, Inc.	9595
Vidhwan Inc dba E-Solutions, Inc.	4422, 8954
View Finders Market Research	8717
ViewSonic Corporation	5852
ViewTech Group, LLC	5662
Vigilant Technologies	4972
Vigintis LLC	5779
Viking Chemicals, Inc.	2163
Village Tea Company Distribution Inc.	3585
Vinali LLC	9029
VINFORMATIX L.L.C.	4806
Virpie Inc	4472
Virtelligence, Inc	5024
Virtual Computing Technology	4423
Virtual Matrix Corporation (dba 1 Source, Inc.)	5025
Virtue Group	4658
Virtuo Group Corporation	5663
Visibility Marketing, Inc.	8742
Vision Global Technology, Inc.	4043
Vision Information Technologies, Inc.	4973
Vision Specialties, Inc.	4062
Visional Technology LLC	3277
Visionary Integration Professionals, LLC	4424
VisionOnline, Inc.	5780
VisionPoint LLC	4473, 9661
Visions, Inc.	8604
Visions2000 Inc.	8304
VisionSoft International, Inc.	4659
Vista Color Corporation	7495
Vista Industrial Packaging, Inc.	7246

V

Company	INDEX#
Vista Latinos LLC	8575
Vistam, Inc.	3075
Vistara Construction Services, Inc.	2376
Vistra Communications, LLC	8438
Visual Citi Inc.	1210
Visual Consultants, Inc.	5026
Viswam Bala Enterprises	1084
Vitalizing Business Solutions	8073
Vitaver and Associates, Inc.	4550
Vitesse Recruiting & Staffing, Inc.	8955
Vitiello Communications Group	8163
Vitusa Products Inc.	1989
VIVA USA Inc.	4764
Vivek Systems, Inc.	4974
VJN Associates. LLC	7836
VKNetworks IT Solutions	5664
Vladimir Jones	8392
VLJ Inc. dba Smith Tool & Mfg.	6918
VM Cardio Vascular Inc.	6529
VM Graphic Packaging & Safety Products LLC	4191
VMEK Group LLC	4231
VMIX, LLC.	9616
VMX International, LLC	3448
VNB Consulting Services, Inc.	5271
Vobecky Enterprises, Inc.	8956
Vocalink, Inc.	1223
Vocon Partners, LLC	3825
Voigt & Associates, Inc.	8957
Volante Enterprise Consulting	4425
Von Pok & Chang	1516
Von Technologies, LLC	4765
VonCreations, Inc.	8471
Vorce & Associates	1540
Vosges, Ltd.	3861
Votum Enterprises, LLC	3847
VQV Services LLC	5356
VRD Contracting, Inc.	2461
VS Research LLC	8664
V-Soft Consulting Group Inc.	4801
VSR Enterprise, LLC	3641
vTech Solution Inc	4484
VTI Contracting, Inc.	1944
Vuelta Management Group, LLC	8138
Vulcan Industrial Contractors Co., LLC	3346
VVL Systems & Consulting, LLC	4898
VXI Global Solutions, LLC	4426
VYD and Associates, LLC	8050

W

Company	INDEX#
W. Allen Engineering PLLC	3226
W. K. Merriman, Inc.	3509
W. M. Martin Advertising	1585
W.E.B. Production & Fabricating, Inc.	6604
W.O.L.F. Elite LLC	9939
W.S Molnar Company dba SlipNOT Metal Safety Flooring	6647
W-3 Construction Company	2412
WA, Inc. (dba WA Architects, Inc.)	1804
Wabash Transformer (PowerVolt and Ensign Corp)	4085
Waisun Corporation	2809
Waldner's Business Environments, Inc.	3817
Walker & Jocke Co., LPA	6214
Walker and Associates, Inc.	9728

COMPANY ALPHABETICAL LISTING

W

Company	INDEX#
Walker Elliott, LP	9502
Walker Flags, Inc.	1423
Walker Nell Partners Inc.	6224
Walker SCM, LLC	10075
Walker Warren Communications	9771
Wall & Tong, LLP	6184
Wall Street Greetings, LLC	3863
Walla Walla Environmental	2071
Wallace & Associates Protective Services, LLC	2682
Walle Corporation	7540
Wallis Oil Company	1970
Walt Medina & Associates, LLC	8984
Waltons Welding & Fabrication, Inc.	6623
Wang & Chang	6087
Wanix Architects, LLC	1805
Ward Creative Communications, Inc.	8829
Warehouse One Inc.	6287
Warehouse Properties, Inc.	10028
Warehouse Services, Inc.	10122
Warm Springs Composite Products	7426
WarmlyYours.com Inc.	2969
Warner Specialty Products, Inc.	6263
WARP Services, LLC	6290
Warwick Communications, Inc.	5415
Washington Communications Group LLC	9681
Washington Liftruck	6301
Washington Office Interiors	3782
Washingtonian Custom Media	8404
Water Technology Resources	4008
Water Treatment Specialists, Inc.	3278
Watkins Lighting & Sign Mtc, Inc.	3007
Wats International Inc.	4139
Watts Engineering & Architecture, P.C.	3227
Wave Technologies	5665
Wavicle Data Solutions	4766
Wayfinder, LLC	4551
WCES, Inc.	6715
WCS Maintenance Services, Inc.	2130
WDi Architecture, Inc.	1765
WDS, Inc.	7266
We Muv U, LLC	6247
We See You limited liability	2670
Wearable Imaging, Inc.	1330
Web Traits, Inc.	4899
Webb Engineering Services, Inc.	3195
Webbege, Inc.	4427
Web-Hed Technologies, Inc. dba Webhead	1275
WebRunners, Inc. dba W3R Consulting	4975
Websignia	8665
Wedgeworth Business Communications	8520
Weiatech, LLC	5781
Weil Group, Inc.	5494, 9402
Weinman Schnee Morais, Inc.	8718
Weinrib & Connor Associates, Inc.	1211
Weinrich Truck Line, Inc.	9916
Weissco Power Limited Liability Company	2868
Weldex Sales Corporation	4197
Weldon Enterprise Global IT, LLC	4976
Weldon Works, Inc.	1038, 7328
Wellard, Inc.	1453
Welling Inc.	2486
Wells Technology, Inc.	3918
Wells, Anderson & Race, LLC	6095

W

Company	INDEX#
WellSol Medical Inc.	6407
Welsco, Inc.	1893, 4044
Welsh Construction, LLC	2422
Wendt Productions Inc.	1361
Wensco of Michigan Corporation	1137
Wentworth Consulting Group, LLC	8008
West Cary Group	1289
West Coast Environmental Solutions	3381
West Coast Form Grinding	6586
West Fuels Inc.	1937
West Hill Technology Counsel, Inc.	6148
West Michigan Flocking	6856
West Pack Industries, LLC.	7222
West Reach Construction Company, Inc.	2325
WestCarb Enterprises, Inc.	6429
Western Diversified Plastics LLC	7393
Western Express Inc.	10129
Western Indoor Environmental Services	2100
Western Reserve Technology	5416
Western States Distributing	1908
Westmoreland Protection Agency, Inc.	2629
Westnet Inc.	6430
Westwind Computer Products	5276
Wet Cement, Inc.	8164
Wexco Industries	1888
Wexford Labs, Inc.	2186
Wexler Packaging Products, Inc.	7256
WFQ, Inc.	3181
What Works Studio LLC	8562
What's the Big Idea?	1276
Wheal-Grace Corporation	7618
Wheatley Electric Service Co.	2884
White Glove Environmental	3547
White Glove Group, Inc.	3548
White Glove Janitorial Services & Supply, Inc.	2143
Whitehall, Inc.	3694
White-Tucker Company	4192
Whitham Group Executive Search	8958
Whitsell Innovations Inc.	9553
Whitty IT Solutions LLC	4660
WHM Equipment Co.	6294
Wholesale Distribution	3780
Wholesale Electric Caribe Inc.	2894
Wholesale Electric Supply of Houston	2911
Wholesale T-shirts Depot, Inc.	1721
WHPacific, Inc.	3334
Widescope Consulting And Contracting Services LLC	4552
Widespread Industrial Supplies, Inc.	3885, 4063
Wightman & Associates LLC	8038
Wild Child Editorial, Inc.	9617
Wildscape Restoration, Inc.	3382
Wilkin Enterprises, Inc.	1427
Williams Engineering LLC	3244
Williams Interior Designs, Inc	3826
Williams NationaLease, Ltd.	9940
Williams Solutions Group, LLC	1437
Williams, West & Witt's Product Co.	3627
Williamston Products, Inc.	7394
Willie Horton Inc.	3182
Wilson Emergency Medical Training, LLC	2706
Wilson Turner Kosmo LLP	6088
Wilson-Taylor Associates, Inc.	8576
Windjammer Environmental	3392

COMPANY ALPHABETICAL LISTING

W | INDEX#

Windy City Silkscreening, Inc. 1403
Wingard Quality Supply, LLC 1889
Wingard Wheel Works, LLC 1860
WingGate Travel, Inc. 10206
Wings Air Helicopters LLC 10076
Winkler Public Relations 8830
Winship Stake and Lath 10232
WINTEC Software Corporation 4428
Wisco Promo Uniform, INC. 1501, 1704
Wisconsin International Services Inc. 10196
Wisdom Resources, Inc. 9403
Wise Construction Management, Inc. 2487
Wise Men Consultants Inc 5666
WisEngineering, LLC 5272
Wissen Infotech Inc 5826
WIT Inc. 4977
Witco Inc. 6857
WKG Global Enterprises, Inc. 1592
WM Group Services, LLC 3228
WMB Financial Solutions 2318
WMBE Payrolling, dba TargetCW 4429
WMG, LLC 5926
WMJ Enterprises, LLC. 9823
Wolf Run Marketing 1417
Wolverine Assemblies, LLC 2761
Women Impact Tech, LLC 4786
Women in Printing, LLC 7675
Womenkind, LLC 1212
Wong Fleming 6185
Wood Concepts 10251
Word Tech Secretarial Service Inc. 5027
Workable Solutions Investigative & Protective
   Services, LLC 2602
Work-Comp Management Services 7921
Workforce Solutions Group 8959
Working Hands, Inc. 7001
Workplace Elements LLC 3756
Workplace Integrators 7020
Works of Bawbee Films 9588
Workspace Consulting Group, LLC 3759
WorkSquare West 8960
Worksters 4430
Worktank Enterprises, LLC 1296
World Centric 7108
World Corrugated Container 7193
World of Colors - Break The Cycle LLC 1380
World Of Promotions 1404
World Pac Paper, LLC 7055
World Ventures Tours and Travel Inc. 10221
Worldcom Exchange Inc. 5976
Worldgate, LLC 5782
Worldwide Audio Visual Services Inc 5872
Worldwide Filters, LLC 4094
Worldwide Freight Solutions Inc. 9941
Worldwide Label & Packaging LLC 7275, 7676
Wotko LLC 2762
WP Electric & Communications, Inc. 9656
Wragg & Casas Public Relations, Inc. 8439
Wrap City Graphics 1156
Wrena, LLC dba Angstrom-USA, LLC 6756, 6889
Wright Engineered Plastics, Inc. 7329
Wrobel Engineering Co., Inc. 6622, 6819

W | INDEX#

WRW Engineering 3076
Wu & Associates, Inc. 2444
Wunna Contracting Corporation 2566
Wyka LLC d/b/a Edison Graphics 7525
Wyoming Machine, Inc. 6653

X

Xavient Information Systems, Inc. 4431
XBI Tech Corporation 5667
XCELLAS, LLC 8226
Xcentri, Inc. 9271
XD Ventures, LLC 2059, 2264
Xela Group, LLC dba Grupo Xela 1224
Xenna Corporation 2590
XentIT, LLC 4661, 5873
XGen Pharmaceuticals DJB, Inc. 6475
Xinnovit Inc. 4432
XIOSS, Inc. 5285
XL Impex Inc DBA Atika Technologies 5273
XL Technology Group, LLC 4259
Xpediant Solutions 5668
Xperteks Computer Consultancy, Inc. 5357
Xpress Cargo Inc. (XCIQ) 9952
XTGlobal, Inc. 5669
Xtra Pair of Hands 8961
Xtreme Solutions, Inc. 4662
Xyant Technology, Inc. 5419
Xybion Corporation & Subsidiaries 5274
Xylo Technologies Inc. 5028

Y

Y&W Technologies LLC 6570
Yadari Enterprises 4433
Yamada Enterprises Inc. 7330
Yang Professional Law Corporation 6089
YASME Soft Inc. 5670
Yates Enterprises 7306
Yee & Associates LLC 6011
Yellobee Studio 1085
YFI Technologies 5029
YIKES, Inc. 5482
Y-Not Design & Mfg. Inc. 1362
YOLO Colorhouse LLC 2014
York Electric Motors, Inc. 2856
Yorkson Legal, Inc. 6205
Yorkville Marketing Consulting LLC 8719
Yoshida Foods International 7248
Young G's Barbecue Sauce, LLC 3604
Young Technology Inc. 6605, 7356
Youngsoft Inc. 4978
Younkins & Schecter LLP 6206
Yourway Transport Inc. 10110
Yu Ken Cut It Inc. 2195

Z

Z Venture Capital Frontiers, Inc. 6981
Z&A Infotek Corporation 5275
Zabatt Engine Service, Inc. 3995
Zana Cakes, Inc. 3704
ZapBoomBang Studios, LLC 9632

COMPANY ALPHABETICAL LISTING

Company	INDEX#
ebing Solutions LLC	2413
ebra Marketing Corporation	1469
Zebra Strategies	8720
Zebra-net Incorporated	4434
Zeesman Communications, Inc.	1039
Zego LLC	3574
Zeitgeist Expressions, Inc.	6530
ZELJKA ONE Management LLC dba: Green Way Pavement	1798
Zelos Consulting, LLC	3077
Zempleo, Inc.	8962
Zenex Partners Inc	8963
Zephyr Solutions, LLC.	2009
Zepol Productions, Inc.	5945
Zepol Productions, Inc. dba KiloTech	5671
Zero Waste Solutions Inc.	3383
Zetta Pros - Total IT Solutions	5853
Zeva Inc	5783
Zig Zag Inc.	3769
Zillion Technologies, Inc.	5784
Zip Tool & Die Inc.	6757
Zirtex Systems Corporation	5785
Z-MAS International	2700
Zoatex	6858
Zodiac Solutions Inc.	5483
ZOI Incorporated	8074
Zolon Tech Solutions, Inc.	5786
Zones, LLC	5817
Zuber Lawler & Del Duca LLP	6090
Zumizi Corp, dba iDepo Reporters	6091
Zycron, Inc.	5508